Red Pennant
Holiday In

C000202663

Outstanding Continental holiday protection

For more than 45 years Red Pennant Overseas Holiday Insurance has protected Club members touring abroad. Specially tailored for caravanners, motorhomers and trailer tenters, it covers your whole holiday, from car hire to hotel costs and much more.

Red Pennant cover includes:

- **24/7 multi-lingual helpline** manned by Club trained staff
- **Breakdown roadside assistance**
- **Vehicle and passenger repatriation**
- **Continuation of holiday travel** and/or accommodation
- **Cancellation cover**
- **Medical cover**

> **To all members going abroad, PLEASE use Red Pennant. You will, like us, find them invaluable**
>
> *Mrs Smith, Gwent*

Get peace of mind, get your quote today

01342 336 633
www.caravanclub.co.uk/redpennant

Lines are open Monday to Friday 8.45am - 5.30pm. (calls may be recorded)

THE
CARAVAN
CLUB

Explanation of a Campsite Entry
Caravan Europe 2013/2014

The town under which the campsite is listed, as shown on the relevant Sites Location Map at the end of each country's site entry pages

Distance and direction of the site from the centre of the town the site is listed under in kilometres (or metres), together with site's aspect

Site Location Map grid reference

Site open all year

GPS co-ordinates – latitude and longitude

Campsite name

Telephone and fax numbers including national code where applicable

Campsite address, including post code

Contact email address and website address

Directions to the campsite

Description of the campsite and its facilities

Comments and opinions of caravanners who have visited the site

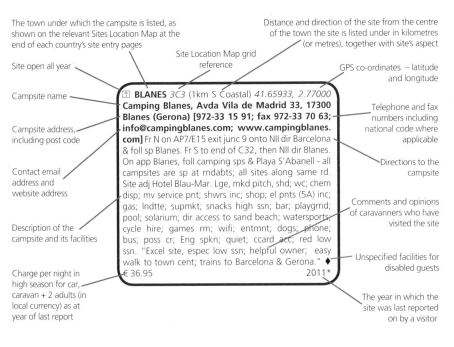

⊞ **BLANES** *3C3* (1km S Coastal) *41.65933, 2.77000*
Camping Blanes, Avda Vila de Madrid 33, 17300 Blanes (Gerona) [972-33 15 91; fax 972-33 70 63; info@campingblanes.com; www.campingblanes. com] Fr N on AP7/E15 exit junc 9 onto NII dir Barcelona & foll sp Blanes. Fr S to end of C32, then NII dir Blanes. On app Blanes, foll camping sps & Playa S'Abanell - all campsites are sp at rndabts; all sites along same rd. Site adj Hotel Blau-Mar. Lge, mkd pitch, shd; wc; chem disp; mv service pnt; shwrs inc; shop; el pnts (5A) inc; gas; Indtte; supmkt; snacks high ssn; bar; playgrnd; pool; solarium; dir access to sand beach; watersports; cycle hire; games rm; wifi; entmnt; dogs; phone; bus; poss cr; Eng spkn; quiet; ccard acc; red low ssn. "Excel site, espec low ssn; helpful owner; easy walk to town cent; trains to Barcelona & Gerona." ♦
€ 36.95   2011*

Charge per night in high season for car, caravan + 2 adults (in local currency) as at year of last report

Unspecified facilities for disabled guests

The year in which the site was last reported on by a visitor

Popular Abbreviations
(for a full list of abbreviations please see page 14).

Site Description

hdg: hedged
mkd: marked
sm: max 50 pitches

hdstg: some hard standing or gravel pitches
pt shd: part shaded   **sl**: sloping site
terr: terraced site   **unshd**: no shade

lge: 151-500 pitches   **med**: 51–150 pitches
pt sl: sloping in parts   **shd**: plenty of shade
v lge: 501+ pitches

Popular Abbreviations for Site Facilities

Adv bkg: advanced booking accepted
CCI or CCS: Camping Card International or Camping Card Scandinavia accepted
chem disp: dedicated chemical toilet disposal facilities
chem disp (wc): no dedicated point; disposal via wc only
CL-type: very small, privately-owned, informal and usually basic, farm or country site
El pnts: mains electric hook-ups
Eng spkn: English spoken
entmnt: entertainment (facilities or organised)
Indtte: washing machine(s) with or without tumble dryers

NH: suitable as a night halt;
quiet: peaceful, tranquil site
rest: restaurant
shwrs: hot showers available at a fee
shwrs inc: cost included in site fee quoted
tradsmn: tradesman call at the site, e.g. baker
sbs: Site Booking Service – Ref No. for a site included in the Caravan Club's network i.e. bookable through the Club
ssn: season
□ open all year

Popular Generic Abbreviations

Adj: adjacent, nearby; **app**: approach, on approaching; **arr**: arrival, arriving **bef**: before **bet**: between **c'van**: caravan; **ccard acc**: Credit and/or debit cards accepted; **CChq acc**: Camping Cheques accepted **clsd**: closed **E**: East; **ent**: entrance/ entry to **excel**: excellent; **facs**: facilities; **fr**: from; **gd**: good; **inc**: included/inclusive; **L**: left; **m'van**: motorhome/ motor caravan; **narr**: narrow **N**: North; **o'fits**: outfits; **R**: right; **rec**: recommend/ed ; **red**: reduced/reduction; **rte**: route **S**: South; **sh**: short; **sp**: sign post/signposted; **strt**: straight, straight ahead **sw**: swimming **vg**: very good; **W**: West

Caravan Europe
France

© The Caravan Club Limited 2014
Published by The Caravan Club Limited
East Grinstead House, East Grinstead
West Sussex RH19 1UA

General Enquiries: 01342 326944
Brochure Requests: 01342 327410
Travel Service Reservations: 01342 316101
Red Pennant Overseas Holiday Insurance:
01342 336633
Website: www.caravanclub.co.uk
Email: enquiries@caravanclub.co.uk

Editor: Kate Walters
Email: kate.walters@caravanclub.co.uk

Printed by Stephens and George Ltd
Merthyr Tydfil

ISBN 978-0-9569510-3-8

Maps and distance charts generated from Collins Bartholomew
Digital Database. Maps © Collins Bartholomew Ltd 2013,
reproduced by permission of HarperCollins Publishers.

Contents

Exceptional Caravan Insurance tailored to tourers' needs

Protect your caravan with The Club's 40 years of know-how

Caravan Club Comprehensive Caravan Cover includes:

- **New for old cover** for up to 5 years for Standard cover and up to 15 years for Super
- **Comprehensive cover on or off the road** including cover for accidental damage, fire, theft, vandalism, storm and flood
- **NEW** **Protected No Claims Discount** available
- **Cover for contents and equipment**
- **Cover for storm and flood damage to awnings**
- **Personal accident cover** £20,000 cover on Standard policies and £50,000 cover on Super policies.

> **"I found the staff very helpful – they sorted everything out and explained it clearly to me. Thank you"**
>
> *Mr Eccles, Member, Lancashire*

Get peace of mind, get your quote today

01342 336 610

www.caravanclub.co.uk/caravaninsure

defaqto
2013
★★★★★
CARAVAN INSURANCE
Independently rated
5 star insurance

THE CARAVAN CLUB

Welcome
to Caravan Europe 2014

For over 50 years, Caravan Europe guides have been helping independent tourers get the very best out of their continental adventures. As well as containing information on thousands of sites, the books are full of country-by-country advice on everything from medical issues to speed limits.

In this guide to France you will find information on planning your trip, which documents to pack, what to expect from foreign sites, customs regulations, ferries and Channel Tunnel crossings, money, insurance, driving regulations and much more.

The sites listings themselves are designed to be concise and easy to read. Uniquely, the entries are based on reports from Caravan Club members and each one is accompanied by GPS co-ordinates, contact information, travel directions and prices. We rely on your feedback to produce the Caravan Europe books, so if you visit a continental site in 2014, please let us know what you thought of it. You can find report forms at the back of this book – alternatively visit www.caravanclub.co.uk/europereport to give us your views online.

When you're planning your overseas trip, remember that The Caravan Club can help you out with ferry bookings, Overseas Holiday Insurance and a wealth of other products and services.

We hope that this edition of Caravan Europe helps you to plan and enjoy the trip of a lifetime. Happy touring!

Kate Walters

Kate Walters, Editor

Read on to discover thousands of sites, recommended by members.

www.caravanclub.co.uk/caravaneurope

THE
CARAVAN
CLUB

How to use this guide
Introduction

The information contained within Caravan Europe is presented in the following categories:

The Handbook

This includes general information about touring in Europe, such as legal requirements, advice and regulations. The Handbook chapters are at the front of the guide under the section headings:

Planning and Travelling

During Your Stay

These two sections are divided into chapters in alphabetical order, not necessarily the order of priority. Cross-references are given where additional information is provided in another chapter.

Country Introduction

Following on from the Handbook chapters you will find the *Country Introduction* chapter containing information, regulations and advice specific to each country. You should read the Country Introduction carefully in conjunction with the Handbook chapters before you set off on your holiday. Cross-references to other chapters are provided where appropriate.

Campsite Entries

After the Country Introduction you will find the campsite entries listed alphabetically under their nearest town or village. Where several campsites are shown in and around the same town they will be listed in clockwise order from the north.

To find a campsite all you need to do is look for the town or village of where you would like to stay in or nearby. If a campsite is not shown under the name of the particular town or village that you are searching for, then a cross-reference may indicate an alternative village or town under which it may be found in the guide. For example, for Domme (France) the cross-reference will direct you to the campsites listed under Sarlat-la-Canéda.

To maintain consistency we have used local versions of town or city names.

In order to facilitate such a large number of campsites within Caravan Europe we have used abbreviations in the site entries.

For a full and detailed list of these abbreviations please refer to the chapter **Explanation of a Campsite Entry**.

We have also included some of the most regularly used abbreviations, as well as an explanation of a campsite entry, on the tear-out bookmark page for your convenience. Simply pull out the bookmark page at the front of Caravan Europe and you can then always have it to hand whenever you need to check a site entry in the guide.

Campsite Fees

Campsite entries show high season fees per night in Euros for a car, caravan, plus two adults, as at the year of the last report. In addition a deposit or booking fee may be charged, which might not be refundable. Prices given do not necessarily include electricity or showers, unless indicated, or local taxes. Outside of the main holiday season many sites offer discounts on the prices shown and some sites may also offer a reduction for longer stays.

Campsite fees may vary to the prices stated in the site entries. You are advised to always check fees when booking, or at least before pitching, as those shown in site entries should be used as a guide only.

Sites Location Maps

Each town and village listed alphabetically in the site entry pages has a map grid reference number, e.g. 3B4. The map grid reference number is shown on each site entry. The maps can be found at the end of each country's site entry pages. The reference number will show you where each town or village is located. Place names are shown on the maps in two colours:

Red where we list a site which is open all year (or for at least approximately eleven months of the year)

Black where we only list seasonal sites which close in winter.

Please note: these maps are for general campsite location purposes only; a detailed road map or atlas is essential for route planning and touring.

Town names in capital letters (**RED**, **BLACK** or in *ITALICS*) correspond with towns listed on the Distance Chart.

The scale used for the Sites Location Maps means that it is not possible to pinpoint every town or village where a campsite exists. Where we cannot show an individual town or village on a Sites Location Map for reasons of space, we list it under another nearby town which then acts as a central point for campsites within that particular local area. With some exceptions sites are listed under towns up to approximately 15 kilometres away. The place names used as a central point are usually, but not always, the largest towns in each region; some may be only small villages.

Satellite Navigation

Most campsite entries in this guide now show a GPS (sat nav) reference. It is in the format 48.85661 (latitude north) and 2.35222 (longitude east), i.e. decimal degrees. Readings shown as -1.23456 indicate that the longitude position in question is west of the 0 degrees Greenwich meridian. This is important to bear in mind when inputting co-ordinates into your sat nav device for campsites in western France, most of Spain and Portugal. Readings given in other formats such as degrees + minutes + seconds or degrees + decimal minutes can be converted using www.cosports.com then click on GPS Lat/ Long Conversion, or simply use Google maps (http://maps. google.co.uk) and input a GPS reference in any format to locate a town, village or campsite.

Please be aware if you are using a sat nav device some routes may take you on roads that are narrow and/or are not suitable for caravans or large outfits.

The GPS co-ordinates given in this guide are derived from a number of reliable sources but it has not been possible to check them all individually. The Caravan Club cannot accept responsibility for any inaccuracies, errors or omissions or for their effects.

Site Report Forms

With the exception of campsites in The Club's Overseas Site Booking Service (SBS) network, The Caravan Club does not inspect sites listed in this guide. Virtually all of the site reports in Caravan Europe are submitted voluntarily by both members and non-members of The Caravan Club during the course of their own holidays.

We rely on you, the users of this guide, to tell us about campsites you have visited

Sites which are not reported on for five to six years may be deleted from the guide. We therefore rely very much on you, the users of this guide, to tell us about campsites you have visited – old favourites as well as new discoveries.

You will find some site report forms towards the back of this guide which we hope you will complete and return to us by freepost. An abbreviated site report form is provided if you are reporting no changes (or only minor changes) to a site entry. Additional site report forms are available online and on request.

You can complete both the full and abbreviated versions of the site report forms on our website. Simply go to www.caravanclub.co.uk/europereport and either complete the form online or download blank forms to fill in later and post to The Caravan Club.

Complete site report forms online – www.caravanclub.co.uk/europereport

For an explanation of the abbreviations that are used in the site entries, please refer to the chapter *Explanation of a Campsite Entry* or use the tear-out bookmark

page at the front of the guide which shows some of the most popular abbreviations used.

Please submit reports as soon as possible. Information received by **mid August 2014** will be used wherever possible in the next edition of Caravan Europe. Reports received after that date are still very welcome and will be retained for entry in a subsequent edition. The editor is unable to respond individually to site reports submitted due to the large quantity that we receive.

Tips for Completing Site Reports

- If possible it is best to fill in a site report form while you are at the campsite or shortly after your stay. Once back at home it can be difficult to remember details of individual sites, especially if you visited several during your trip.

- When giving directions to a site, remember to include the direction of travel, e.g. 'from north on D137, turn left onto D794 signposted Combourg' or 'on N83 from Poligny turn right at petrol station in village'. Wherever possible give road numbers, together with junction numbers and/or kilometre post numbers, where you exit from motorways or main roads. It is also helpful to mention useful landmarks such as bridges, roundabouts, traffic lights or prominent buildings, and to advise whether the site is signposted. If there are any roads that are difficult to access or narrow please also mention this in the report.

- When noting the compass direction of a site **this must be in the direction FROM THE TOWN the site is listed under TO THE SITE, and not the direction from the site to the town.** Distances are measured in a straight line and may differ significantly from the distance by road.

- If you are only amending a few details about a site there is no need to use the longer version form. You may prefer to use the abbreviated version but, in any event, do remember to give the campsite name and the town or village under which it is listed in the guide. Alternatively, use the online version of the form – www.caravanclub.co.uk/europereport
- If possible, give precise opening and closing dates, e.g. 1 April to 30 September. This information is particularly important for early and late season travellers.

We very much appreciates the time and trouble you take submitting reports on campsites that you have visited; without your valuable contributions it would be impossible to update this guide.

Win a Sat Nav

If you submit site reports to the editor during 2014 – whether by post, email or online – you will have your name entered into a prize draw to win the Snooper Ventura Caravan Club Edition Sat Nav (terms and conditions apply). Four runners up will also receive the latest editions of Caravan Europe.

The Snooper Ventura Caravan Club Edition Sat Nav will already have the GPS co-ordinates programmed in for the majority of campsites within the current edition of Caravan Europe as well as Club sites throughout the UK, allowing you to find sites around your present or future location at the touch of a button. It has been specifically designed for caravanners and will calculate routes that avoid obstacles such as narrow roads and low bridges, based on the size of your vehicle. The

perfect equipment for anyone with a caravan or large motorhome!

Acknowledgements

The Caravan Club's thanks go to the AIT/FIA Information Centre (OTA), the Alliance Internationale de Tourisme (AIT), the Fédération International de Camping et de Caravaning (FICC) and to the national clubs and tourist offices of those countries who have assisted with this publication.

How to use this guide
Explanation of a Campsite Entry

The town under which the campsite is listed, as shown on the relevant Sites Location Map at the end of each country's site entry pages

Site Location Map grid reference

Distance and direction of the site from the centre of the town the site is listed under in kilometres (or metres), together with site's aspect

Site open all year

GPS co-ordinates – latitude and longitude

Campsite name

⊞ **BLANES** *3C3* (1km S Coastal) *41.65933, 2.77000*
Camping Blanes, Avda Vila de Madrid 33, 17300 Blanes (Gerona) [972-33 15 91; fax 972-33 70 63; info@campingblanes.com; www.campingblanes.com] Fr N on AP7/E15 exit junc 9 onto NII dir Barcelona & foll sp Blanes. Fr S to end of C32, then NII dir Blanes. On app Blanes, foll camping sps & Playa S'Abanell - all campsites are sp at rndabts; all sites along same rd. Site adj Hotel Blau-Mar. Lge, mkd pitch, shd; wc; chem disp; mv service pnt; shwrs inc; shop; el pnts (5A) inc; gas; Indtte; supmkt; snacks high ssn; bar; playgrnd; pool; solarium; dir access to sand beach; watersports; cycle hire; games rm; wifi; entmnt; dogs; phone; bus; poss cr; Eng spkn; quiet; ccard acc; red low ssn. "Excel site, espec low ssn; helpful owner; easy walk to town cent; trains to Barcelona & Gerona." ♦
€ 36.95   2011*

Campsite address, including post code

Telephone and fax numbers including national code where applicable

Contact email address and website address

Directions to the campsite

Description of the campsite and its facilities

Comments and opinions of caravanners who have visited the site

Charge per night in high season for car, caravan + 2 adults (in local currency) as at year of last report

Unspecified facilities for disabled guests

The year in which the site was last reported on by a visitor

NOJA *1A4* (700m N Coastal) *43.49011, -3.53636*
Camping Playa Joyel, Playa del Ris, 39180 Noja (Cantabria) [942-63 00 81; fax 942-63 12 94; playajoyel@telefonica.net; www.playajoyel.com] Fr Santander or Bilbao foll sp A8/E70 (toll-free). Approx 15km E of Solares exit m'way junc 185 at Beranga onto CA147 N twd Noja & coast. On o'skirts of Noja turn L sp Playa del Ris, (sm brown sp) foll rd approx 1.5km to rndabt, site sp to L, 500m fr rndabt. Fr Santander take S10 for approx 8km, then join A8/E70. V lge, mkd pitch, pt sl, pt shd; wc; chem disp; mv service pnt; baby facs; shwrs inc; el pnts (6A) inc; gas; Indtte (inc dryer); supmkt; tradsmn; rest; snacks; bar; BBQ (gas/charcoal); playgrnd; pool; paddling pool; jacuzzi; direct access to sand beach adj; windsurfing; sailing; tennis; hairdresser; car wash; cash dispenser; wifi; entmnt; games/TV rm; 15% statics; no dogs; no c'vans/m'vans over 8m high ssn; phone; recep 0800-2200; poss v cr w/end & high ssn; Eng spkn; adv bkg; ccard acc; quiet at night; red low ssn/snr citizens; CCI. "Well-organised site on sheltered bay; v busy high ssn; pleasant staff; gd, clean facs; superb pool & beach; some narr site rds with kerbs; midnight silence enforced; Wed mkt outside site, highly rec." ♦
15 Apr-1 Oct. € 47.40 SBS - E05   2011*

Reference number for a site included in The Caravan Club's Site Booking Service network i.e. bookable through the Club

Opening dates

Site Description Abbreviations

Each site entry assumes the following unless stated otherwise:

Level ground, open grass pitches, drinking water on site, clean wc unless otherwise stated (own sanitation required if wc not listed), site is suitable for any length of stay within the dates shown.

aspect

urban – within a city or town, or on its outskirts
rural – within or on edge of a village or in open countryside
coastal – within one kilometre of the coast

size of site

sm – max 50 pitches
med – 51 to 150 pitches
lge – 151 to 500 pitches
v lge – 501+ pitches

pitches

hdg pitch – hedged pitches
mkd pitch – marked or numbered pitches
hdstg – some hard standing or gravel

levels

sl – sloping site
pt sl – sloping in parts
terr – terraced site

shade

shd – plenty of shade
pt shd – part shaded
unshd – no shade

Site Facilities Abbreviations

adv bkg

Advance booking accepted;
adv bkg rec – advance booking recommended

baby facs

Nursing room/bathroom for babies/children

beach

Beach for swimming nearby;
1km – distance to beach
sand beach – sandy beach
shgl beach – shingle beach

bus/metro/tram

Public transport within an easy walk of the site

chem disp

Dedicated chemical toilet disposal facilities;
chem disp (wc) – no dedicated point; disposal via wc only

CKE/CCI

Camping Key Europe and/or Camping Card International accepted

CL-type

Very small, privately-owned, informal and usually basic, farm or country site similar to those in the Caravan Club's network of Certificated Locations

dogs

Dogs allowed on site with appropriate certification (a daily fee may be quoted and conditions may apply)

el pnts

Mains electric hook-ups available for a fee;
inc – cost included in site fee quoted
10A – amperage provided
conn fee – one-off charge for connection to metered electricity supply
rev pol – reversed polarity may be present

(see *Electricity and Gas* in the section *DURING YOUR STAY*)

Eng spkn

English spoken by campsite reception staff

entmnt

Entertainment facilities or organised entertainment for adults and/or children

fam bthrm

Bathroom for use by families with small children

gas

Supplies of bottled gas available on site or nearby

internet

Internet point for use by visitors to site;
wifi – wireless local area network available

lndtte

Washing machine(s) with or without tumble dryers, sometimes other equipment available, eg ironing boards;
lndtte (inc dryer) – washing machine(s) and tumble dryer(s)
lndry rm – laundry room with only basic clothes-washing facilities

Mairie

Town hall (France); will usually make municipal campsite reservations

mv service pnt

Special low level waste discharge point for motor caravans; fresh water tap and rinse facilities should also be available

NH
>   Suitable as a night halt

noisy
>   Noisy site with reasons given;
>   **quiet** – peaceful, tranquil site

open 1 Apr-15 Oct
>   Where no specific dates are given, opening
>   dates are assumed to be inclusive, ie Apr-Oct –
>   beginning April to end October **(NB: opening
>   dates may vary from those shown; check
>   in advance before making a long journey,
>   particularly when travelling out of the
>   main holiday season)**

phone
>   Public payphone on or adjacent to site

playgrnd
>   Children's playground

pool
>   Swimming pool (may be open high season
>   only);
>   **htd** – heated pool
>   **covrd** – indoor pool or one with retractable
>   cover

poss cr
>   During high season site may be crowded or
>   overcrowded and pitches cramped

red CCI/CCS
>   Reduction in fees on production of a
>   Camping Card International or Camping Card
>   Scandinavia

rest
>   Restaurant;
>   **bar** – bar
>   **BBQ** – barbecues allowed (may be restricted to
>   a separate, designated area)
>   **cooking facs** – communal kitchen area
>   **snacks** – snack bar, cafeteria or takeaway

SBS
>   Site Booking Service (pitch reservation can
>   be made through the Caravan Club's Travel
>   Service)

serviced pitch
>   Electric hook-ups and mains water inlet and
>   grey water waste outlet to pitch;
>   **all** – to all pitches
>   **50%** – percentage of pitches

shop(s)
>   Shop on site;
>   **adj** – shops next to site
>   **500m** – nearest shops
>   **supmkt** – supermarket
>   **hypmkt** – hypermarket
>   **tradsmn** – tradesmen call at the site, eg baker

shwrs
>   Hot showers available for a fee;
>   **inc** – cost included in site fee quoted

ssn
>   Season;
>   **high ssn** – peak holiday season
>   **low ssn** – out of peak season

50% statics
>   Percentage of static caravans/mobile homes/
>   chalets/fixed tents/cabins or long term
>   seasonal pitches on site, including those run
>   by tour operators

sw
>   Swimming nearby;
>   **1km** – nearest swimming
>   **lake** – in lake
>   **rv** – in river

TV
>   TV available for viewing by visitors (often in
>   the bar);
>   **TV rm** – separate TV room (often also a games
>   room)
>   **cab/sat** – cable or satellite connections to
>   pitches

wc
>   Clean flushing toilets on site;
>   **(cont)** – continental type with floor-level hole
>   **htd** – sanitary block centrally heated in winter
>   **own san** – use of own sanitation facilities
>   recommended

Other Abbreviations

AIT	Alliance Internationale de Tourisme
a'bahn	Autobahn
a'pista	Autopista
a'route	Autoroute
a'strada	Autostrada
adj	Adjacent, nearby
alt	Alternative
app	Approach, on approaching
arr	Arrival, arriving
avail	Available
Ave	Avenue
bdge	Bridge
bef	Before
bet	Between
Blvd	Boulevard
C	Century, eg 16thC
c'van	Caravan
CC	Caravan Club
ccard acc	Credit and/or debit cards accepted (check with site for specific details)
CChq acc	Camping Cheques accepted

cent	Centre or central	o'look(ing)	Overlook(ing)
clsd	Closed	o'night	Overnight
conn	Connection	o'skts	Outskirts
cont	Continue or continental (wc)	PO	Post office
conv	Convenient	poss	Possible, possibly
covrd	Covered	pt	Part
dep	Departure	R	Right
diff	Difficult, with difficulty	rd	Road or street
dir	Direction	rec	Recommend/ed
dist	Distance	recep	Reception
dual c'way	Dual carriageway	red	Reduced, reduction (for)
E	East	reg	Regular
ent	Entrance/entry to	req	Required
espec	Especially	RH	Right-hand
ess	Essential	rlwy	Railway line
excel	Excellent	rm	Room
facs	Facilities	rndabt	Roundabout
FIA	Fédération Internationale de l'Automobile	rte	Route
FICC	Fédération Internationale de Camping & de Caravaning	RV	Recreational vehicle, ie large motor caravan
FFCC	Fédération Française de Camping et de Caravaning	rv/rvside	River/riverside
		S	South
FKK/FNF	Naturist federation, ie naturist site	san facs	Sanitary facilities ie wc, showers, etc
foll	Follow	snr citizens	Senior citizens
fr	From	sep	Separate
g'ge	Garage	sh	Short
gd	Good	sp	Sign post, signposted
grnd(s)	Ground(s)	sq	Square
hr(s)	Hour(s)	ssn	Season
immac	Immaculate	stn	Station
immed	Immediate(ly)	strt	Straight, straight ahead
inc	Included/inclusive	sw	Swimming
indus est	Industrial estate	thro	Through
INF	Naturist federation, ie naturist site	TO	Tourist Office
int'l	International	tour ops	Tour operators
irreg	Irregular	traff lts	Traffic lights
junc	Junction	twd	Toward(s)
km	Kilometre	unrel	Unreliable
L	Left	vg	Very good
LH	Left-hand	vill	Village
LS	Low season	W	West
ltd	Limited	w/end	Weekend
mkd	Marked	x-ing	Crossing
mkt	Market	x-rds	Cross roads
mob	Mobile (phone)		
m'van	Motor caravan		
m'way	Motorway		
N	North		
narr	Narrow		
nr, nrby	Near, nearby		
opp	Opposite		
o'fits	Outfits		

Symbols Used

◆ Unspecified facilities for disabled guests check before arrival

⊞ Open all year

* Last year site report received (see Campsite Entries in Introduction)

Most Campéole campsites enjoy a great location close to water, first-class infrastructures and are designed where possible to sit harmoniously within their environments. They are popular with families with children of all ages, as well as couples and small groups.

Campsites

1. Saint Grégoire
2. Les Monts Colleux
3. Penn Mar
4. La Grande Côte
5. Les Sirènes
6. Plage des tonnelles - Dornier
7. La Redoute
8. Le Platin
9. Les Amis de la Plage
10. Clairefontaine
11. Médoc Plage
12. Le Lac de Sanguinet
13. Le Vivier
14. Plage Sud
15. Navarrosse
16. Les Tourterelles
17. Ondres
18. Le Coiroux
19. Les Reflets du Quercy
20. La Boissière
21. Le Domaine de Combelles
22. Millau plage
23. La Côte des Roses
24. Île des Papes
25. Les Mûriers
26. Eurosurf
27. Le Dramont
28. La Croix du Sud
29. La Plage
30. L'Avena
31. Le Clos du Lac
32. Camping du Lac
33. Le Courounba
34. Les Vaudois
35. La Nublière
36. La Pinède
37. Le Lac des Sapins
38. Le Brabois
39. Le Giessen
40. Le Val de Coise
41. Castell Mar
42. Castell Montgri
43. Neptuno
44. Interpals
45. Valldaro
46. Montblanc park
47. Torre del Sol
48. La Masia
49. Ca' Savio
50. Club del Sole Spina
51. Adriano
52. Il capannino
53. Free Time
54. Orbetello

Campéole

In Their Own Words...

We will listen to you and advise you

Our helpful booking office is there to listen to you and to advise you accordingly. We can recommend a campsite suited to your needs and making a reservation is only a simple phone call away.

We will offer you a variety of holiday options

With over 50 destinations in France and elsewhere, around ten different types of accommodation, several possible lengths of stay and two arrival days per week, Campéole aims to provide maximum choice and flexibility.

We will ensure that our holidays are affordable for everyone

A range of services is available to make life easier for you during your holiday. We also guarantee the quality and comfort of our accommodation and therefore offer several solutions at different price levels.

We will all be committed to making a success of your holiday

The Campéole teams are professionals set on providing a holiday to remember. Each team member has your holiday at heart and will take it on themselves to make your stay as pleasant as possible.

We will cater for young children and teenagers

Campéole welcomes children and has created special amenities for them in its campsite villages: like Campitoo, popular with the little ones, or activity clubs for each age bracket and a dedicated Teen Space for teenagers.

We will create a friendly and festive atmosphere

On Campéole campsites you can take your pick from a range of sporting activities and join in the evening entertainments. Each site has a specific entertainment programme for all ages.

We will respect nature

Do your bit for the environment by opting for the unique Campéole holiday experience in unspoilt natural surroundings. Come and join us – we look forward to welcoming you!

www.campeole.co.uk

Planning and Travelling
Caravanning and Touring Abroad – Practical Advice

You may be new to caravanning abroad, or perhaps it has been a while since you last toured in Europe. If so then this section of the handbook will offer you practical and useful advice, giving you the knowledge and confidence that you need to make the most of your trip and enjoy your holiday.

Travelling through Europe can be a daunting prospect. That's why the practical advice offered in this chapter has been put together, providing you with a summary of the comprehensive information contained elsewhere within the guide. Please be aware that laws, customs, regulations and advice differ in each country so you are advised to make sure you are familiar with these for each country that you are planning to visit.

Before You Travel

Choosing Your Campsite

The great thing about touring is the freedom that it offers you. However, if you are new to travelling in Europe we would suggest that it might be wise not to be overly ambitious and to plan your trip carefully.

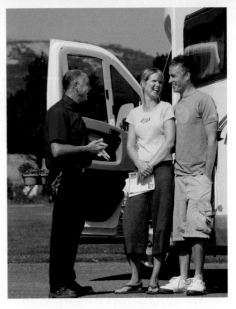

> **The great thing about touring is the freedom that it offers you**

The wide range of campsites available across Europe offer a choice of different facilities and amenities, but we would recommend that you stay in a campsite close to port on your first night of arrival. This will give you a little time to get used to driving on the right hand side of the road and you can then make a fresh start to your journey the next day, or spend a couple of days (or indeed your whole holiday) enjoying the campsite and surrounding area.

When choosing your campsite (or campsites) there are some important factors that you need to keep in mind. Firstly, the location, do you want to be by the sea or near to a city, or perhaps you have a specific interest such as museums or hiking?

You need to consider what facilities and amenities are available as well, both on the campsite and in the nearby area. If you have children then you may want to make sure there is a playground and entertainment on site, or maybe you would like a good restaurant within

easy walking distance. These are all important factors to consider before you decide on where to stay during your holiday in order to avoid disappointment.

You should also take into account the time of year you are planning on travelling. If you are going in low season then many facilities and amenities may be closed. If you are going in high season or during public holidays it is likely there will be a high volume of traffic and tourists, therefore advanced booking is really recommended.

For further information to help you choose the right campsite for your holiday, please refer to the chapter *Continental Campsites*. This chapter includes useful information on campsites in Europe and also has a site booking letter, and translations of the letter into relevant languages, for you to use when making a reservation.

Overseas Site Booking Service

For peace of mind you may prefer to use The Caravan Club's Overseas Site Booking Service which offers Club members pitch bookings on over 200 campsites throughout Europe. This gives you freedom and flexibility of travel while eliminating language problems, international deposit payments or waiting for replies by letter or email. Furthermore, you will have the reassurance of a confirmed pitch reservation and pitch fees paid in advance.

The Club's Continental Caravanning brochure (available from November every year) gives full details of the Overseas Site Booking Service and of the sites available, as well as information on the Club's range of package tours and excursions for caravanners. These sites may be booked via the Club's website, www.caravanclub.co.uk/overseas

All the sites in the Club's Overseas Site Booking Service are listed in this guide and are marked 'SBS' in their site entries. The Caravan Club cannot make advance reservations for any other campsites listed in this guide.

Choosing Your Ferry Crossing

There is a wide choice of ferry operators and routes available. The use of ferry crossings, or the Channel Tunnel, is a matter of personal preference and convenience. The Channel Tunnel and crossings from Dover to Calais are quickest, but if you have a long drive from home to your departure port, you may prefer a longer crossing giving you the chance to relax for a few hours and enjoy a meal onboard. The chapter *Ferries and the Channel Tunnel* contains a list of ferry routes and additional information.

Make sure you know the overall length, as well as the height, of your vehicle(s), as vehicle decks on some ferries have areas where height is restricted, and this should be checked when making your booking.

The Club's website has a direct link through to a number of the most popular ferry operators' reservations systems and Club members can make their own reservations while still taking advantage of the Club's negotiated offers as well as the ferry companies' own early booking offers.
See www.caravanclub.co.uk/overseas

Insurance

UK motor vehicle policies will usually give you the legal minimum of insurance for EU countries, however it is very important to check whether your comprehensive cover becomes third-party-only when you leave the UK. It may be necessary to pay an additional premium for comprehensive cover abroad.

Having insurance for your vehicles does not cover any other risks that may arise when you are on holiday, for example, emergency medical and hospital expenses, or loss or theft of personal belongings. The Caravan Club's Red Pennant Overseas Holiday Insurance gives you maximum protection against a variety of mishaps which might otherwise ruin your holiday and is tailor-made for

the caravanner and motorhome tourer. This is backed by the Club's own helpline with multi-lingual staff available 24 hours a day, 365 days a year.

If you are going to leave your home unoccupied for any length of time, check your house and contents insurance policies regarding any limitations or regulations.

You will find further details, information and advice in the *Insurance* chapter or see www.caravanclub.co.uk/redpennant and www.caravanclub.co.uk/insurance

Documents

All members of your party must have a valid passport, including babies and children. The chapter **Documents** sets out the requirements and explains how to apply for a passport.

In some countries a passport must be carried at all times as a form of photographic identification. You should also keep a separate photocopy of your passport details and leave a copy of the personal details page with a relative or friend.

You are best to carry a full valid photocard driving licence with paper counterpart. If you have an all green license issued before 1991, which does not conform to EU standards or have a pictorial representation of what you are allowed to drive/tow, we would strongly recommend that you change this for a photo-card license or carry an International Driving Permit (IDP). Police overseas may have problems understanding the all green license, and subsequently you may be delayed on your journey if they have to wait for help in translating it. International Driving Permits (IDP's) can be obtained from selected Post Offices, The AA and the RAC.

Carry your vehicle's Vehicle Registration Certificate (V5C), insurance certificate and MOT road worthiness certificate, if applicable. If you have a CRIS document (proof of ownership) in respect of your caravan, also carry this with you.

For hired or leased vehicles (including company cars) you will not normally have the V5C and therefore will need to get a VE103 Vehicle on Hire Certificate from the vehicle owner instead.

See the *Documents chapter* in the section *PLANNING AND TRAVELLING* for full details.

Vehicles and Equipment

Ensure your car and caravan or motorhome are properly serviced and ready for the journey, paying particular attention to tyres and tyre pressures.
Make sure caravan tyres are suited to the maximum weight of the caravan and the maximum permitted speed when travelling abroad - see the chapter *Motoring - Equipment* and, if you're a member of The Caravan Club, the Technical Information chapter of the Club's UK Sites Directory & Handbook.

Take a well-equipped spares and tool kit. Spare bulbs, a warning triangle (two are required in some countries), a reflective jacket/vest, fire extinguisher and a first-aid kit as these are legal requirements in many European countries. Nearside and offside extending mirrors are essential to give the best possible vision, together with a spare tyre/wheel for both car and caravan.

In many countries drivers who leave their vehicle when it is stationary on the carriageway must by law wear a reflective jacket or waistcoat, but it is sensible to do so in any country. A second jacket is a common-sense requirement for any passenger who also gets out of your vehicle to assist. Keep the jackets readily to hand inside your vehicle, not in the boot.

If headlights are likely to dazzle other road users, they must be adjusted to deflect to the right instead of the left using suitable beam deflectors or (in some cases) a built-in adjustment system.

Even if you are not planning to drive at night, you will need to switch your headlights on in tunnels or if visibility is poor. Some countries require dipped headlights to be used during daylight hours.

Bulbs are more likely to fail with constant use and therefore it is always recommended to carry spares, whether it is a legal requirement or not.

For a checklist of equipment please see page 22.

Towing

Before you tow make sure you know your car well and have the correct mirrors suitable for your car and caravan. Plan carefully to avoid roads that are too narrow or may have low bridges, and never stop where it is unsafe to do so, i.e. on bends, narrow roads, etc.

Pull over safely to allow any build up of traffic behind you to pass wherever it is possible to do so and always keep a safe stopping distance between you and the vehicle in front. If you are overtaking or pulling across a main road allow yourself plenty of time to do this safely.

If you are new to towing, or if you would like to gain some valuable experience and knowledge, The Caravan Club runs 'Practical and Caravan Manoeuvring' courses, as well as 'Motorhome Manoeuvring' courses. These courses are open to both members and non-members of The Caravan Club and are designed to help you enjoy caravanning and touring more confidently.

For more information please visit www.caravanclub.co.uk/courses

Money

It is a good idea to carry a small amount of foreign currency, including loose change, for countries you are travelling through in case of emergencies, or when shopping. Many credit/debit cards issued in the UK will allow you to obtain cash from cash dispensers but it is best to check with your bank before you leave. Look for the same symbol on the machine as on your debit or credit card. Cash dispensers are often found in supermarkets as well as outside banks. The rate of exchange is often as good as anywhere else but there may be a charge.

Travellers' cheques are not widely accepted in some countries and credit cards issued by British banks may not be universally accepted, therefore it is wise to check before incurring expenditure. In some countries you may be asked to produce your passport for photographic identification purposes when paying by credit card.

*See the chapter **Money** and the **Country Introduction** for further information.*

On the Journey

Ferries and Eurotunnel

Report to the check-in desk at the ferry port or Eurotunnel terminal allowing plenty of time before the scheduled boarding time. As you approach the boarding area after passport control and Customs, staff will direct you to the waiting area or the boarding lane for your departure. As you are driving a 'high vehicle' you may be required to board first, or last. While waiting to board stay with your vehicle so that you can board immediately when instructed to do so. Virtually all ferries operate a 'drive on – drive off' system and you will not normally be required to perform any complicated manoeuvres, such as reversing.

While waiting, turn off the 12V electricity supply to your fridge to prevent your battery going flat. Most fridges will stay adequately cool for several hours, as long as they are not opened. If necessary, place an ice pack or two (as used in cool boxes) in the fridge. You may be required to show that your gas supply has been turned off correctly.

Neither the ferry companies nor Eurotunnel permit you to carry spare petrol cans, empty or full, and Eurotunnel will not accept vehicles powered by LPG or dual-fuel vehicles. However Eurotunnel will accept vehicles fitted with LPG tanks for the purposes of heating, lighting, cooking or refrigeration, subject to certain conditions.

If your vehicle has been converted and is powered by LPG, some ferry companies require a certificate showing that the conversion has been carried out to the manufacturer's specification.

You will be instructed when to drive onto the ferry and, once on board, will be directed to the appropriate position. Treat ferry access ramps with caution, as they may be steep and/or uneven. Drive slowly as there may be a risk of grounding of any low point on the tow bar or caravan hitch. If your ground clearance is low, consider whether removing your stabiliser and/or jockey wheel would help.

Once boarded apply your car and caravan brakes. Vehicles are often parked close together and many passengers leaving their vehicles will be carrying bags for the crossing. It may, therefore, be wise to remove extended rear view mirrors as they may get knocked out of adjustment or damaged.

Make sure your car and caravan are secure and that, wherever possible, belongings are out of sight. Ensure that items on roof racks or cycle carriers are difficult to remove – a long cable lock may be useful.

Note the number of the deck you are parked on and the number of the staircase you use. You will not usually be permitted access to your vehicle during the crossing so take everything you require with you, including passports and boarding cards.

On ferry routes where you are permitted to transport pets, animals are usually required to remain in their owners' vehicles or in kennels on the car deck. On longer ferry crossings you can make arrangements at the onboard information desk for permission to visit your pet at suitable intervals.

*See also **Pet Travel Scheme** under **Documents** in the section **PLANNING AND TRAVELLING**.*

If you have booked cabins or seats go to the information desk immediately after boarding to claim them. Many ferries have a selection of restaurants and cafés, a shop, a children's play area, even a cinema, disco or casino to while away the time during the crossing. If you wish to use the main restaurant it may be advisable to make a reservation.

Listen carefully to onboard announcements, one of which will be important safety information at the time of departure. A further announcement will be made when it is time to return to your vehicle. Allow plenty of time to get down to the car deck. Don't start your engine until vehicles immediately in front of you start to move. Once off the ferry you may want to pull over into a parking area to allow the queue of traffic leaving the ferry to clear.

If you have made an advance booking on the Eurotunnel proceed to the signposted self check-in lanes. You will need to present the credit or debit card used when you made your booking. Having checked in you may, if you wish, visit the terminal to make any last minute purchases, etc, and then follow signs to passport control and customs. Your gas cylinder valves will be closed and sealed as a safety precaution and you will be asked to open the roof vents.

You will then join the waiting area allocated for your departure and will be directed onto the single-deck wagons of the train and told to park in gear with your brake on. You then stay in or around your vehicle for the 35 minute journey but will not be allowed to use your caravan until arrival. Useful information and music are supplied via the on-board radio station. On arrival, close the roof vent and release the caravan brake. When directed by the crew, drive off, remembering to drive on the right hand side of the road!

Motoring on the Continent

For comprehensive advice please see the chapters **Motoring Advice** and **Motoring Equipment** and the **Country Introduction** chapter. The following additional points may be helpful if you are feeling nervous about driving abroad.

Many roads are not as busy as those in the UK, but try to avoid rush hours in larger towns. There are fewer lorries on the roads at weekends and generally you will find that roads are quieter between 12pm and 2pm.

Don't attempt long distances in a single stint. Share the driving, if possible, and plan to break your journey overnight at a suitable campsite. There are thousands of sites listed in this guide, many of which are located near to motorways and main roads.

You are most likely to forget to drive on the right when pulling away from a parked position. It may be helpful to make yourself a sign and attach it to the dashboard to remind you to drive on the right. This can be removed before driving and replaced each time you stop. Alternatively, make a member of your party responsible for reminding the driver every time you start the car. Pay particular attention when turning left or when leaving a rest area, service station or campsite, and after passing through a one-way system.

Make sure the road ahead is clear before overtaking. Stay well behind the vehicle in front and, if possible, have someone with good judgement in the left-hand seat to give you the 'all clear'.

You will be charged tolls to use many European motorways. Credit cards are widely accepted as payment but not always. The **Country Introduction** chapters contain more details. Motorways provide convenient service stations and areas for a rest and a picnic en-route but, for your own safety, find an established campsite for an overnight stop.

Beware of STOP signs. You will encounter more of them than you find in the UK. Coming to a complete halt is compulsory in many European countries and failure to do so may result in a fine.

The maximum legal level of alcohol in the blood in most European countries is lower than that permitted in the UK. It is better not to drink at all when driving as penalties are severe.

If you are unfortunate enough to be involved in a road accident, take some photographs to back up the written description on your claim form.

During Your Stay

Arriving at the Campsite

Go to the campsite reception and fill in any registration forms required. A Camping Card International/ Camping Card Scandinavia is recommended and usually accepted in lieu of handing over your passport.

If you have not booked in advance it is perfectly acceptable to ask to have a look around the campsite before deciding whether to stay or accept a particular pitch.

Pitches are usually available when the site re-opens after the lunch break and not normally before this time. Aim to arrive before 7pm or you may find the campsite reception closed; if this is the case you will probably find a member of staff on duty in the bar. It is essential to arrive before 10pm as the gates or barriers on most sites are closed for the night at this time. If you are delayed, remember to let the site know so that they keep your pitch. When leaving, you will usually need to vacate your pitch by midday at the latest.

Many campsites offer various sporting activities, such as tennis, fishing, watersports, horseriding and bicycle hire, as well as entertainment programmes for children and/ or adults in high season. Many also have a snack bar, restaurant and bar. Restrictions may apply to the use of barbecues because of the risk of fire; always check with site staff before lighting up.

Dogs are welcome on many campsites but some sites will not allow them during the high season (or at all), or will require them to be on a lead at all times. Check in advance. In popular tourist areas local regulations may ban dogs from beaches during the summer months.

If you have any complaints, make site staff aware of them there and then. Staff on site may be able to rectify the problem for the remainder of your stay, whereas complaining after the event is unlikely to have any effect.

Food and Water

Currently there are no restrictions on the movement of food (for personal use) between all EU countries (including Switzerland) however, all food products must be produced and/or packaged within the EU.

Be reasonable with the amount of food that you take with you and stick to basic items and/or children's special favourites. On occasion it may be difficult to obtain supplies of fresh milk, bread and cereals at campsite shops, particularly outside the summer season, so stock up before your arrival on site. It's often helpful to take your own supply of carrier bags and a cool box in hot weather.

Drinking water is normally clean and safe in the countries included in Caravan Europe, but you may find the taste different from your own local mains supply and prefer to drink bottled water.

Electricity and Gas

Calor Gas is not normally available on the continent. Campingaz is widely available but you will need an adaptor to connect to a standard regulator. Alternatively carry sufficient gas for your stay, subject to the cross-Channel operator's regulations which may restrict the amount of gas you can carry - often the restriction is three cylinders, but always check when making your booking.

Voltage on most sites is usually 220V or 230V nominal but may be lower. Most UK mains appliances are rated at 220V to 240V and usually work satisfactorily. Many

sites have the European standard EN60309-2 connectors (formerly known as CEE17), into which you can plug your UK 3-pin connector and mains lead. However, on some sites you may need a continental 2-pin adaptor available from UK caravan accessory shops.

You may encounter the problem known as reverse polarity. This is where the site's 'live' line connects to the caravan's 'neutral' and vice versa and is due to different standards of plug and socket wiring that exist in other countries. The Club recommends checking the polarity immediately on connection, using a polarity tester, obtainable from a caravan accessory shop before you leave home.

The caravan mains electrical installation should not be used while a reversed polarity situation exists. Ask the site manager if you can use an alternative socket or bollard, as the problem may be restricted to that particular socket only. Frequent travellers to Europe who are electrically competent often modify an adaptor to reverse the live and neutral connections. This can be tried in place of the standard connector, to see if the electricity supply then reverts to 'normal'. It is important that you are electrically competent or use an electrician to carry out the modification.

*See the chapter **Electricity and Gas** and **Country Introduction** for further information.*

Medical Matters

Before leaving home obtain a European Health Insurance Card (EHIC) which entitles you to emergency health care in the EU and some other countries. An EHIC is required for each individual family member, so allow enough time before your departure to obtain them. You can apply online on www.ehic.org.uk or by phoning 0845 6062030, or you can get an application form from a post office. The EHIC is free, but be aware that there are some non-official websites which charge you to make an application on your behalf. Always make sure you use the official website or telephone number above to apply for your EHIC.

Specific advice on obtaining emergency medical treatment in the countries included in this guide is summarised in the relevant country chapters and is also covered on the NHS website www.nhs.uk/healthcareabroad. Alternatively you can contact the Department of Health on 020 7210 4850.

Check with your GP for the generic name of any prescription medicines you are taking. If you need more, or lose your supply, this will help a doctor or pharmacist to identify them. Keep receipts for any medication or treatment purchased abroad, plus the labels from the medicines, as these will be required if you make a claim on your travel insurance on returning home.

*For further advice and information see the chapter **Medical Matters**.*

Safety and Security

Safety is largely your own responsibility – taking sensible precautions and being aware of possible hazards won't spoil your holiday, but neglecting your safety and ignoring possible risks might.

The chapter entitled **Safety and Security** covers aspects of your own and your family's personal safety whilst on holiday. You are strongly advised to read this section carefully and follow the advice contained.

Other Information

Tourist Boards

Many European countries maintain tourist offices in the UK and they will supply you with information on their respective countries on request. In addition, a great deal of information can be obtained from the tourist board websites. Contact details of relevant tourist boards are given in the **Country Introduction** chapters.

Route Planning

It is wise to plan your route beforehand wherever possible. We have a **Route Planning Map** chapter under the **Planning and Travelling** section for your reference.

Both the AA and RAC have useful websites offering a European route planning service: www.theaa.com and www.rac.co.uk. Please be aware that some routes may not be suitable for caravans or large vehicles.

Satellite Navigation

GPS co-ordinates are given for most site entries in this guide. Your sat nav is a valuable aid in finding a campsite, but remember that such systems are not perfect and they may take you on routes that are not suitable for caravans or large vehicles. It is wise, therefore, to use your sat nav in conjunction with an up to date map or atlas or use a sat nav that has been

designed specifically for caravanners and motorhome owners such as the Snooper Ventura Caravan Club Edition.

*For further advice see the chapter **Motoring – Equipment**.*

Technical Leaflets

The Caravan Club publishes technical leaflets for its members (some available to non-members) on a wide range of topics, many of which are relevant to caravanning abroad.

You are advised to request copies or see www.caravanclub.co.uk/expert-advice

Checklist

You'll know what domestic and personal items are necessary for trips away and of the checks to be made to vehicles before setting off. The Caravan Club's Technical Office can supply a copy of a leaflet 'Things to Take' to Club members on request, or you can download it from www.caravanclub.co.uk

This checklist is intended as a reminder only and covers some of the necessary items:

Car

Extending mirrors

Fire extinguisher

First aid kit

Fuses

Headlight converters/deflectors

Jack and wheelbrace

Mobile phone charger

Nationality stickers – GB or IRL (car and caravan) if not included within number plate

Puncture kit (sealant)

Radiator hose

Reflective safety jacket(s)/vest(s)

Satellite navigation device

Snow chains (if possibility of using snow covered roads)

Spare bulbs

Spare key

Spare parts, e.g. fan belt

Spare wheel/tyre

Stabiliser

Tool kit

Tow ball cover

Tow rope

Warning triangle/s

Caravan

- Awning and groundsheet
- Bucket
- Chemical toilet and fluid/sachets
- Corner steady tool and pads
- Electrical extension lead and adaptor(s)
- Extra long motorhome water hose pipe
- Fire extinguisher
- Gas cylinders
- Gas regulator (Campingaz) if planning to use Campingaz, or as a back-up in case other gas is not available
- Gas adaptor and hoses (where regulator is fitted to the caravan) to suit 'local' gas cylinders
- Hitch and/or wheel lock
- Levelling blocks
- Mains polarity tester
- Nose weight gauge
- Peg mallet
- Spare bulbs, fuses and lengths of wire
- Spare key
- Spare 7-pin plug (12S plug is especially vulnerable to damage)
- Spare water pump (submersible types are vulnerable to failure)
- Spare wheel/tyre
- Spirit level
- Step and doormat
- Water containers - waste/fresh
- Water hoses – waste/fresh

Documents and Papers

- Address book, contact telephone numbers
- Camping Card International/Camping Card Scandinavia
- Car/caravan/motorhome insurance certificates
- Campsite booking confirmation(s)
- Caravan Club membership card
- Caravan Europe guide book/s
- Copy of your CRIS document
- Credit/debit cards, contact numbers in the event of loss
- Valid driving licence (not provisional)
- European Health Insurance Card (EHIC)
- European Accident Statement
- Ferry booking confirmation and timetable
- Foreign currency
- Holiday travel insurance documents (Red Pennant)
- International Driving Permit (if applicable)
- Letter of authorisation from vehicle owner (if applicable)
- Maps and guides
- MOT roadworthiness certificate (if applicable)
- NHS medical card
- Passport (plus photocopy of details page) and visas (if applicable)
- Pet's passport and addresses of vets abroad
- Phrase books
- Telephone card
- Travellers' cheques and/or travel money card
- Vehicle Registration Certificate V5C or Vehicle on Hire Certificate VE103

Introduction

There are thousands of excellent campsites throughout Europe belonging to local municipalities, families, companies or camping, touring and automobile clubs. Most sites are open to everyone but a few are reserved for their own members.

Compared with Caravan Club sites in the UK, pitches may be small and 80 square metres is not uncommon. Pitches may also be very close together, particularly in Germany and Italy where it is not uncommon to put your hand out of your caravan window and touch the caravan on the next pitch. This may present problems for large outfits and/or outfits with awnings. In the summer season it may also be difficult to put up awnings because of hard ground conditions in hot climates.

Generally the approaches and entrances to campsites are well signposted, but often only with a tent or caravan symbol or with the word 'Camping', rather than the site's full name.

There are usually sinks for washing up and laundry rooms containing washing machines and dryers. Many sites have a shop in high season, even if only for basic groceries, however some shops stock a wide variety of items. Often there is a restaurant or snack bar, Wi-Fi access, swimming pool and playground. Occasionally there may be a car wash, sauna, solarium, bureau de change, tourist information office and other facilities on site.

In the high season all campsite facilities are usually open and some sites offer organised entertainment for children and adults as well as local excursions. However, bear in mind that in the months of July and August, toilet and shower facilities and pitch areas will be under the greatest pressure.

Booking a Campsite

It is advisable to pre-book pitches during the high season. If you are planning a long stay then contact campsites early in the year. Some sites impose a minimum length of stay in order to guarantee their business. Usually there are one or two unreserved pitches available for overnight tourers.

Often it is possible to book directly via a campsite's website using a credit or debit card to pay a deposit if required. Otherwise you can write (enclosing a reply envelope or letters may be ignored) or email the campsite. A word of warning: **some campsites regard the deposit as a booking or admin fee and will not deduct the amount from your final bill.**

Site booking letters in English, German and Italian are provided at the end of this chapter. Detachable response letters are also provided which should encourage site operators to reply. It is worth remembering that a site will very rarely reserve a special place for you. The acceptance of a reservation merely means you will be guaranteed a pitch; the best being allocated first or for repeat visitors. Not all campsites accept advance bookings.

If you don't book ahead you should plan to arrive no later than 4pm (even earlier at popular resorts) in order to secure a pitch, after that time sites fill up quickly. You also need to allow time to find another campsite if your first choice is fully booked.

Caravan Club Overseas Site Booking Service

The Caravan Club's Travel Service offers Club members an Overseas Site Booking Service (to which terms and conditions apply) to over 200 campsites throughout Europe. This service gives freedom and flexibility of travel but with the reassurance of a confirmed pitch reservation and pitch fees paid in sterling in advance. Full details of this service, plus information on special offers with ferry operators, tours & excursions programmes (some specifically aimed at motorhomes) and details of Red Pennant Overseas Holiday Insurance appear in the Club's Continental Caravanning brochure – telephone 01342 327410 to request a copy, or visit www.caravanclub.co.uk/overseas

Booking a site through The Caravan Club gives you a price guarantee and no matter what happens to exchange rates, there will be no surcharges.

All Overseas Site Booking Service sites are listed in this guide and are marked 'SBS' in their site entries. Many of them can be booked via the Club's website, www.caravanclub.co.uk. **The Caravan Club cannot make advance reservations for any other campsites listed in this guide.**

Except in the case of those campsites bookable via the Club's Overseas Site Booking Service, The Caravan Club has no contractual arrangements with any of the sites featured in this guide. Even in the case of these Sites Booking Service sites with whom we work, we have no control over day-to-day operations or administration. Only those sites marked SBS have been inspected by Caravan Club staff.

It is assumed by The Caravan Club Ltd, but not checked (except in the case of sites marked SBS), that all campsites fall under some form of local licensing, which may or may not take account of matters of safety and hygiene. Caravanners are responsible for checking such matters to their own satisfaction.

Sites Direct

In addition to the sites in the Site Booking Service network, Club members now have a greater choice of campsites available to book direct through the Club's website. The Club has implemented a link to enable direct reservations within, for example, a particular

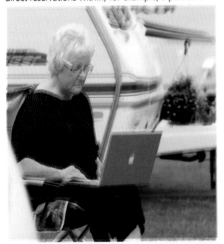

region, or on sites with specific facilities. These sites (approximately 500) have not been inspected by Caravan Club representatives and all the information about them has been input by site owners themselves. Payment is direct to the site and any booking made through this channel is subject to the individual site's terms and conditions. For more information see www.caravanclub.co.uk/sitesdirect

Camping Cheques

The Caravan Club operates a low season scheme in association with Camping Cheques offering Club members flexible touring holidays. The scheme covers approximately 635 sites in 29 countries.

Camping Cheques are supplied through The Caravan Club as part of a package which includes return ferry fare and a minimum of seven Camping Cheques. Each Camping Cheque is valid for one night's low season stay for two people, including car and caravan/motorhome/trailer tent, electricity and one pet. Full details are contained in the Club's Continental Caravanning brochure.

Those sites which feature in the Camping Cheques scheme and which are listed in this guide are marked 'CChq' in their site entries.

Caravan Storage Abroad

The advantages of storing your caravan on a campsite in Europe are obvious, not least being the avoidance of the long tow to your destination, and a saving in ferry and fuel costs. Some campsites advertise a long-term storage facility or you may negotiate with a site which appeals to you.

However, there are pitfalls and understandably insurers in the UK are reluctant to insure a caravan which will be out of the country most of the time. There is also the question of invalidity of the manufacturer's warranty for caravans less than three years old if the supplying dealer does not carry out annual servicing.

See also *Insurance* in the section *PLANNING AND TRAVELLING*.

Electricity Supply

For your own safety you are strongly advised to read the chapter *Electricity and Gas* in the section *DURING YOUR STAY*.

Many campsites now include electricity and/or shower facilities in their 'per night' price and where possible this has been included in site entries. Where these are not included, a generous allowance should be made in your budget. It is not unknown for sites to charge up to the equivalent of £4 per night or more for electric hook-ups and £2 per shower. In winter sports areas, charges for electricity are generally higher in winter – the prices given in this guide are usually those charged during the summer months.

Facilities and Site Description

Campsite descriptions, facilities, directions, prices and other information are reported to the editor by users of this guide. The comments (in inverted commas) within each site entry are from people who have visited the site and naturally people's tastes, opinions, priorities and expectations can differ greatly. Please also bear in mind that campsites change hands, opening dates and prices change and standards may rise or fall, depending on the season.

Facilities Out of Season

During the low season (this can be any time except July and early August) campsites may operate with limited facilities. Shops, swimming pools, bars and restaurants may be closed. A municipal site warden may visit in the morning and/or evening only to collect fees, which may be lower during the low season.

Sanitary Facilities

Facilities normally include toilet and shower blocks with shower cubicles, wash basins and razor sockets. Toilets are not always fitted with seats and do not always have toilet paper. The abbreviation 'wc' indicates the normal, pedestal type of toilet found in the UK. Some sites have footplate 'squatter' toilets and, where this is known, it is indicated by the abbreviation 'cont', i.e. continental.

It is recommended that you take your own universal flat plug (to fit all basin sizes) and toilet paper. During the low season it is not uncommon for only a few toilet and shower cubicles to be in use on a 'unisex' basis and they may not be cleaned as frequently as they are during the site's busy season. Hot water, other than for showers, may not be generally available.

In recent years many campsites have upgraded their sanitary facilities in line with visitors' expectations, but you may find that some are still unheated and may not offer items such as pegs on which to hang clothes/towels, or shelves for soap and shampoo. Rarely, there may be no shower curtains or shower cubicle doors and hence little or no privacy.

Waste Disposal

Site entries in this guide indicate (when known) where a campsite has a chemical disposal facility and/or a motorhome service point, which is assumed to include a waste (grey) water dump station and toilet cassette-emptying point.

Continental caravanners in general tend to prefer to use a site's toilet and shower facilities, together with its dishwashing and vegetable preparation areas, more than their British counterparts who prefer to use their own facilities in their caravan. Caravanners used to the level of facilities for the disposal of waste water on Caravan Club sites may well find that facilities on Continental campsites are not always of the same standard.

Chemical disposal points are occasionally difficult to locate and may be fixed at a high level requiring some strenuous lifting of cassettes in order to empty them. Disposal may simply be down a toilet – continental or otherwise. Wastemaster-style emptying points are not very common in Europe.

Formaldehyde chemical cleaning products are banned in many countries. It is recommended to always use formaldehyde free cleaning products that are kinder to the environment and the overwhelming proportion of current products are now formaldehyde free. In Germany the 'Blue Angel' (Blaue Engel) Standard, and in the Netherlands the 'Milieukeur' Standard, indicates that the product has particularly good 'green' credentials.

Rubbish bins are normally provided and at many campsites you will also find recycling bins. At some campsites, notably in Switzerland and Germany, you may have to purchase special plastic bags for the disposal of rubbish or pay a daily rubbish or environmental charge.

Finding a Campsite

Directions are given for all campsites listed in this guide and most listings also include GPS co-ordinates. Where known full street addresses are also given. The directions have been supplied by users of this guide and The Caravan Club is unable to check each one in detail for accuracy.

*See the chapter **Motoring – Equipment** in the section **PLANNING AND TRAVELLING** for more information on satellite navigation.*

Lunch Breaks

Some campsites close for a long lunch break, sometimes up to three hours, and occasionally there is no access for vehicles during this period. The time during which a site's entrance gate or barrier is closed may be reduced or extended according to the time of year. This may also apply to the overnight closure of gates and barriers. In addition, use of vehicles within the site may be restricted during certain hours to ensure a period of quiet. Check with individual campsites for their regulations.

Motorhomes – Overnight Stops

Towns and villages across Europe may provide dedicated overnight or short stay areas specifically for motorhomes, many of which have good security, electricity, water and waste facilities. These are known as 'Aires de Services', 'Stellplatz' or 'Aree di Sosta' and are usually well signposted with a motorhome pictogram.

Likewise, to cater for this growing market, many campsites in popular tourist areas have separate overnight areas of hardstanding with appropriate facilities often just outside the main campsite area. Fees are generally very reasonable.

A number of organisations publish guides listing thousands of these sites. Alternatively see www.campercontact.nl for details of thousands of sites for motorhomes in many countries in Europe.

For reasons of security The Caravan Club strongly advises against spending the night on petrol station service areas, ferry terminal car parks or isolated 'aires de repos' or 'aires de services' along motorways. *See the chapter Safety and Security in the section DURING YOUR STAY.*

Where known, information on the availability of public transport within easy reach of a campsite, as reported by caravanners, is given in the site entries in this guide.

Municipal Campsites

Municipal sites are found in towns and villages all over Europe, in particular in France, and in recent years many municipalities have improved standards on their sites while continuing to offer good value for money. However, on some municipal sites you may still find that sanitary facilities are basic and old-fashioned, even though they may be clean. Bookings for a municipal site can usually be made during office hours through the local town hall or, increasingly, the local tourist office.

Outside the high season you may find significant numbers of seasonal workers, market traders and itinerants resident on sites – sometimes in a separate, designated area. In most cases their presence does not cause other visitors any problem (other than possible early morning traffic noise as they leave for work) but where they are not welcome some sites refuse entry to caravans with twin-axles ('deux essieux' in French) or restrict entry by caravan height, weight or length, or charge a hefty additional fee. Check if any such restrictions apply if booking in advance.

Recent visitors report that bona fide caravanners with twin-axle or over-height/weight/length caravans may be allowed entry, and/or may not be charged the higher published tariff, but this is negotiable with site staff at the time of arrival.

When approaching a town you may find that municipal sites are not always named and signposts may simply state 'Camping' or show a tent or caravan symbol.

Naturist Campsites

Details of a number of naturist sites are included in this guide and are shown with the word 'naturist' after their site name. Some, shown as 'part naturist' have separate areas for naturists. Visitors to naturist sites aged 16 and over usually (but not always) require an INF card or Naturist Licence and this is covered by membership of British Naturism (tel 01604 620361 or www.british-naturism.org.uk). Alternatively, holiday membership is available on arrival at any recognised naturist site (a passport-size photograph is required). When looking for a site you will find that naturist campsites generally display the initials FNF, INF or FKK on their signs.

Opening Dates

Opening dates (where known) are given for campsites in this guide, many of which are open all year. Sometimes sites may close without notice for refurbishment work, because of a change of ownership or simply because of a lack of visitors or a period of bad weather.

Outside the high season it is always best to contact campsites in advance as some owners have a tendency to shut campsites when business is slack. Otherwise you may arrive to find the gates of an 'all year' campsite very firmly closed. In particular, municipal campsites' published opening dates cannot always be relied on at the start and end of the season. It is advisable to phone ahead or arrive early enough to be able to find an alternative site if your first choice is closed.

Pets on Campsites

See also **Pet Travel Scheme** under **Documents** and **Holiday Insurance for Pets** under **Insurance** in the section **PLANNING AND TRAVELLING**.

Dogs are welcome on many campsites provided they conform to legislation and vaccination requirements, and are kept under control. Be prepared to present documentary evidence of vaccinations on arrival at a campsite.

Please be aware however that some countries authorities do not permit entry to certain breeds of dogs and some breeds will need to be muzzled and kept on a lead at all times. You are advised to contact the appropriate authorities of the countries that you plan to visit via their embassies in London before making travel arrangements for your dog. A list of banned breeds and breeds with restrictions can be found at www.caravanclub.co.uk/pets.

Campsites usually have a daily charge for dogs. There may be limits on the number of dogs allowed, often one per pitch, or the type or breed accepted. Some campsites will not allow dogs at all or will require them to be on a lead at all times. Some campsites may also not allow dogs during the peak holiday season or will forbid you to leave your dog unattended in your caravan/motorhome, which can make going out for an evening meal or a day trip difficult. Dog owners must conform to site regulations concerning keeping dogs on a lead, dog-walking areas and fouling, and may find restricted areas within a site where dogs are not permitted.

In popular tourist areas local regulations may ban dogs from beaches during the summer.

Think very carefully before taking your pet abroad. Dogs used to the UK's temperate climate may find it difficult to cope with prolonged periods of hot weather. In addition, there are diseases transmitted by ticks, caterpillars, mosquitoes or sandflies, particularly in southern Europe, to which dogs from the UK have no natural resistance. Consult your vet about preventative treatment well in advance of your holiday. You need to be sure that your dog is healthy enough to travel and, if in any doubt, it may be in its best interests to leave it at home.

Visitors to southern Spain and Portugal, parts of central France and northern Italy, from mid-winter to late spring should be aware of the danger to dogs of pine processionary caterpillars. Dogs should be kept away from pine trees if possible or fitted with a muzzle that prevents the nose and mouth from touching the ground. This will also protect against poisoned bait sometimes used by farmers and hunters.

In the event that your pet is taken ill abroad a campsite will usually have information about local vets. Failing that, most countries have a telephone directory similar to the Yellow Pages, together with online versions such as www.pagesjaunes.fr.

Most European countries require dogs to wear a collar at all times identifying their owners. If your dog goes missing, report the matter to the local police and the local branch of that country's animal welfare organisation.

Prices

Campsite prices per night (for a car, caravan and two adults) are shown in local currencies. In EU member states where euros is not the official currency they are usually accepted for payment of campsite fees and other goods and services.

Payment of campsite fees should be made at least two hours before departure. Remember that if you stay on site after midday you may be charged for an extra day. Many campsites shown in this guide as accepting credit card payments may not do so for an overnight or short stay because of high transaction charges. Alternatively, a site will impose a minimum amount or will accept credit cards only in peak season. It is always advisable to check the form of payment required when you check in.

On arrival at a campsite which has an automatic barrier at the entrance you may be asked for a deposit, returnable on departure, for the use of a swipe card to operate the barrier. The amount will vary from site to site with the average cost usually being between €10 and €30.

Campsites may impose extra charges for the use of swimming pools and other leisure facilities, showers and laundrette facilities. Sites may also charge extra for dogs, Wi-Fi, tents and extra cars.

Registering on Arrival

On arrival at a campsite it is usual to have to register in accordance with local authority requirements, and to produce an identity document which the campsite office may retain during your stay. Most campsites now accept the Camping Key Europe (CKE) or Camping Card International (CCI) instead of a passport and, where known, their site entries are marked CKE/CCI. CKE are available for Caravan Club members to purchase at a cost of £7.50 (2013 price) by calling 01342 336633 or are free to members if you take out the 'motoring' level of cover from the Club's Red Pennant Overseas Holiday Insurance.

Alternatively, a photocopy of your passport may be acceptable and it is a good idea to carry a few copies with you to avoid depositing your passport and to speed up the check-in process.

Sites' Contact Details

Telephone numbers are given for most campsites listed in this guide together with fax numbers, website and email addresses where known.

The telephone numbers assume you are in the country concerned and the initial zero should be dialled, where applicable. If you are telephoning from outside the country concerned you should dial the international country code and omit the initial zero. For more details see the chapter *Keeping in Touch* and the *Country Introduction* chapter.

General Advice

Most campsites close from 10pm until 7am or 8am, however, late night arrival areas are sometimes provided for late travellers. Motorhomes in particular should check the gate/barrier closing time before going out for the evening in their vehicle. Check out time is usually between 10am and 12pm. Advise reception

staff if you need to leave very early, for example, to catch a ferry.

If possible inspect the site and facilities before booking in. If your pitch is allocated at check-in ask to see it first to check the condition and access, as marked or hedged pitches can sometimes be difficult for large outfits. Riverside pitches can be delightful but keep an eye on the water level; in periods of heavy rain this may rise rapidly and the ground becomes boggy.

If the weather has been bad early in the season you may find that site staff have not been able, for example, to cut grass or hedges and prepare the site fully for visitors. At the end of the season grass pitches may be well worn and could be muddy or slippery after rain.

Often campsites have a daily discounted charge for children, however it is not unknown for site owners to charge the full adult daily rate for children from as young as three years old.

A tourist tax may be imposed by local authorities in some European countries. VAT may also be payable on top of your campsite fees. These charges are not usually included in the prices listed in this guide.

Speed limits on campsites are usually restricted to 10 km/h (6 mph). You may be asked to park your car in a separate area away from your caravan, particularly in the high season.

Some campsites ban the wearing of boxer shorts-style swimming trunks in pools on the grounds of hygiene. This rule may be strictly enforced.

The use of the term 'statics' in the campsite reports in this guide in many instances refers to long-term seasonal pitches, chalets, cottages, tour operators' fixed tents and cabins, as well as mobile homes.

Complaints

If you have a complaint take it up with site staff or owners at the time so that it can be dealt with promptly. It is much better to make staff aware of a problem at the time, while something could be done to rectify the situation for the rest of your stay, than to complain after the event. In France, if your complaint cannot be settled directly with the campsite, and if you are sure you are within your rights, you may take the matter up with the Préfecture of the local authority in question.

The Caravan Club has no control or influence over day to day campsite operations or administration of the sites listed in this guide. Therefore we aren't able to intervene in any dispute you should have with a campsite, unless the booking has been made through our Site Booking Service - see listings marked 'SBS' for sites we are able to book for you.

Site Booking Letter – English

Date: .... Address (block caps)..

....

....

Tel No: (0044) ....

Fax No: (0044) ....

Email ....

Dear Sir/Madam

I wish to make a reservation as follows:

Arriving (date and month)................. **Departing** (date and month)................. (........nights)

Adults .... **Children (+ ages)** ....

| **Car** | o | **Caravan** | o | **Motor Caravan** | o | **Trailertent** | o |
| **Electrical Hook-up** | o | **Awning** | o | **Extra tent** | o | | |

I look forward to an early reply and enclose an addressed envelope. When replying please advise all charges and deposit required. I look forward to meeting you and visiting your site.

Yours faithfully,

[Name in block capitals after signature]

Caravan Club Membership No........................

" --

Reply

Date: .... Address..

....

....

Dear Mr/Mrs/Ms ....

Thank you for your reservation from .... to .... (........ nights).

- **YES, OK** – I am pleased to confirm your reservation (with/without electrical hook-up) and look forward to welcoming you.
- **NO, SORRY** – I regret that the site is fully booked for the dates you request.

Yours sincerely

....

Großbuchstaben)..

....

....

Telefonnummer.: (0044)...

Faxnummer: (0044)...

Email ....

Sehr geehrter Herr/sehr geehrte Dame

Ich möchte wie folgt reservieren:

Site Booking Letter – French

Date: Adresse (lettres majuscules)..

....

....

Tél   : (0044)...

Fax   : (0044)..

Email..

Monsieur/Madame

J'aimerais désire effectuer la réservation suivante :

Arrivée (jour et mois) .... **Départ** (jour et mois)...................... (.........nuits)

Adultes .... **Enfants (+ âges)** ....

Voiture ☐ **Caravane** ☐ **Camping car** ☐ **Tente-remorque** ☐

Branchement électrique ☐ **Auvent** ☐ **Tente supplémentaire** ☐

Ci-joint une enveloppe avec mon adresse. En vous remerciant par avance pour votre réponse je vous demanderais de bien vouloir me communiquer vos tarifs complets ainsi que le montant des arrhes à verser.

En attendant le plaisir de faire votre connaissance et de séjourner sur votre terrain, je vous prie de croire, Monsieur/Madame, à l'assurance de mes sentiments les meilleurs.

(Nom en lettres majuscules après la signature)

No. d'adhérent du Caravan Club ....

✂---

Réponse

Date: Adresse ....

....

....

Monsieur/Madame/Mademoiselle

J'accuse réception de votre bulletin de réservation pour la période

du...................... au ....(.........nuits).

* **OUI** – Je confirme votre réservation (avec/sans branchement électrique) en attendant le plaisir de faire votre connaissance.
* **NON** – Je suis au regret de vous informer que le terrain est complet pendant la période de votre choix.

Veuillez croire, Monsieur/Madame/Mademoiselle, à l'assurance de mes sentiments les meilleurs.

....

Campsites on a human scale

The Flower philosophy is to avoid the style of so-called 'factory campsites'; to ignore anonymous standardisation but celebrate individuality and personality. Campsites in this group are all modestly sized: high quality facilities, for sure, but all on a very personable level and with a distinct personal touch.

Campsites

By the sea

Les Vertes Feuilles
Les Aubépines
Le Domaine du Rompval
La Chênaie
Utah Beach
Le Haut Dick
Camping du Golf
Camping Longchamp
Camping des Vallées
Camping Le Mât
Le Domaine de Mesqueau
Camping de la Baie de Douarnenez
Les Genêts
Aux 2 Chênes
Le Cabellou-Plage
Le Kergariou
Camping de l'Océan
Le Bois d'Amour
Le Kernest
Camping Le Lac
Le Conleau
Domaine de Pont-Mahé
Les Paludiers
Camping du Bord de Mer
La Guichardière
Les Brillas
Plein Sud
La Bretonnière
Le Beauchêne
Le Clos Cottet
Le Grand'R
Les Ilates
Le Bel Air
La Cailletière
Les Côtes de Saintonge
Camping Walmone
Le Lac de Saujon
Camping Des Pins
La Canadienne
Camping Harrobia
La Ferme Erromardie
La Garenne
Le Soleil Bleu
Domaine de la Palme
Le Soleil d'Oc
L'Etoile de Mer
Le Neptune
Robinson
Domaine de Gajan
Le Mas de Mourgues
Le Marius
Camping de Ceyreste
Le Mas de la Plage
Le Romarin

In the mountains

La Sténiole
Verte Vallée
Le Belvédère
Soleil du Pibeste
La Pène Blanche
L'Eden de la Vanoise
Les Lanchettes

Flower Campings

In Their Own Words...

Campsites on a human scale

On a Flower campsite you are not a number;
you are not lost in the crowd. It's a sociable
place, and camping is all about enjoying the
company of others so the staff like to say hello
and chat. We often remark on the warm and
friendly 'micro climate' among residents on
our campsites.

Quality campsites

On all our campsites, neither too big nor too
small, quality is uppermost. We like small scale
but we insist on high quality. We run campsites,
we often live on campsites and we enjoy
campsite life – we want you to enjoy it too.
We have developed our ideal: camping on
a human scale where you get to become part of
the 'family', great facilities, wonderful locations.
We hope this is your ideal too.

Discover the locality

The best advice we can give you is to get out
of the campsite to explore our various regions.
Each adds a real flavour to life: meet the local
people, attend the local festivals and markets,
and enjoy the local produce and the local
traditions.

www.flowercampings.com

Planning and Travelling
Customs Regulations

Travelling to the UK from the European Union

On entry into the UK no tax or duty is payable on goods bought tax-paid in other EU countries which are for your own use and which have been transported by you. VAT and duty are included in the price of goods purchased and travellers can no longer buy duty-free or tax-free goods on journeys within the EU.

The following are guidance levels for the import of alcohol and tobacco into the UK but Customs do not enforce any absolute limits. However, if you bring in more than the following quantities Customs may suspect that they are for a commercial purpose and may ask questions and make checks. If you break the rules Customs may seize the goods – and the vehicle(s) used to transport them – and may not return them to you.

800 cigarettes

400 cigarillos

200 cigars

1kg tobacco

10 litres of spirits

20 litres of fortified wine (e.g. port or sherry)

90 litres of wine

110 litres of beer

No one under 17 years of age is entitled to the tobacco or alcohol allowances.

When entering the UK from another member state of the EU without having travelled to or through a non-EU country, you should use the blue Customs channel or exit reserved for EU travellers, provided your purchases are within the limits for imports from that country and you are not importing any restricted or prohibited goods, details of which are given later in this chapter.

Travelling to/from Non-EU Countries to/from the UK

Customs allowances for countries outside the EU apply to the following countries: Andorra, Croatia, Gibraltar, Norway and Switzerland.

You may purchase goods free of duty if travelling from the UK direct to a country outside the EU. Duty-free allowances for travellers returning to the UK (or entering any other EU country) from a non-EU country are generally as follows:

200 cigarettes, or 100 cigarillos, or 50 cigars, or 250gms tobacco

1 litre of spirits or strong liqueurs over 22 per cent volume, or 2 litres of fortified wine, sparkling wine or any other alcoholic drink that's less than 22 per cent volume

4 litres of still wine

16 litres of beer

£390 worth of all other goods including perfume, gifts and souvenirs without having to pay tax and/or duty (or £270 if you arrive by private plane or private boat for pleasure purposes)

To bring in alcohol or tobacco (or to be entitled to the above allowances) you must be aged 17 or over.

When entering the UK from a non-EU country, or having travelled to or through a non-EU country, you should go through the red Customs channel or use the telephone at the Red Point if you have exceeded your Customs allowances, or if you are carrying any prohibited, restricted or commercial goods. Use the green Customs channel if you have 'nothing to declare'.

All dutiable items must be declared to Customs on entering the UK; failure to do so may mean that you forfeit them and your vehicle(s). Customs officers are legally entitled to examine your baggage and your vehicles and you are responsible for packing and unpacking. Whichever Customs channel you use, you may be stopped by a Customs officer and you and your vehicles may be searched.

If you are caught with goods that are prohibited or restricted, or goods in excess of your Customs allowances, you risk a heavy fine and possibly a prison sentence.

For further information contact HM Revenue & Customs National Advice Service on 0845 010 9000 (+44 2920 501 261 from outside the UK).

Travelling Within the European Union

While there are no limits on what travellers can buy and take with them when travelling between EU countries (provided the goods are for personal use and not for re-sale), the guidance levels are below:

800 cigarettes or 400 cigarillos or 200 cigars or 1kg tobacco

10 litres spirits over 22 per cent volume or 20 litres fortified wine not over 22 per cent volume

90 litres wine

110 litres beer

Boats

Virtually all boats of any size taken abroad must carry registration documents when leaving UK waters. Contact the Maritime and Coastguard Agency on 02380 329100 or www.mcga.gov.uk for details. The Royal Yachting Association recommends that all boats have marine insurance and can provide details of the rules and regulations for taking a boat to countries bordering the Atlantic Ocean and the Baltic, Mediterranean and Black Seas – tel 023 8060 4100, www.rya.org.uk. Some countries require owners of certain types of vessels to have an International Certificate of Competence and information is contained in RYA publications.

If planning to take a boat abroad check with the appropriate tourist office before departure as rules and regulations for boat use vary from country to country. Third party insurance is compulsory in most European countries and is advisable elsewhere.

Currency

Any person entering or leaving the EU will have to declare the money that they are carrying if this amounts to €10,000 (or equivalent in other currencies) or more. This includes cheques, travellers' cheques, bankers' drafts and any cash - notes and coins. This ruling does not apply to anyone travelling within the EU.

For further information contact HMRC Excise & Customs Helpline on 0845 010 9000.

Food and Plants

Travellers from within the EU may bring into the UK any fruit, vegetable or plant products without restriction as long as they are grown in the EU, are free from pests or disease and are for your own consumption. For food products Andorra, the Channel Islands, the Isle of Man, San Marino and Switzerland are treated as part of the EU.

From most countries outside the EU you are not allowed to bring into the UK any meat or dairy products. Other animal products may be severely restricted or banned and it is important that you declare any such products on entering the UK.

HM Revenue & Customs publish leaflets broadly setting out the rules, entitled 'Bringing Food Products into the UK' and 'Bringing Fruit, Vegetable and Plant Products into the UK'. These can be downloaded from their website or telephone the National Advice Service on 0845 010 9000.

Rules regarding food and plants can change at any time without notice. For up to date information please contact the Food and Environment Research Agency (Fera) on 0844 248 0071. If you are unsure about any item you are bringing in, or are simply unsure of the rules, you must go to the red Customs channel or use the phone provided at the Red Point to speak to a Customs officer.

In the light of animal health concerns in recent years in the UK, authorities abroad will understandably take a cautious approach to the import of foodstuffs. There is no guarantee that such products, if found, will not be confiscated by Customs officers.

Medicines

There is no limit to the amount of medicines you can take abroad if they are obtained without prescription (i.e. over the counter medicines), but medicines prescribed by your doctor may contain controlled drugs (i.e. subject to control under the Misuse of Drugs legislation). You must obtain a licence if you are leaving the UK for 3 months or more with medication containing a controlled drug. Visit www.gov.uk/travelling-controlled-drugs or tel. 020 7035 0771 for a list of controlled drugs and information on how to apply for a licence.

You don't need a licence if you carry supplies for less than 3 months or if your medication doesn't contain controlled drugs, but you should carry a letter from your doctor stating your name, a list of your prescribed drugs and dosages for each drug. You may have to show this letter when going through customs.

You should also check the regulations for controlled drugs with each country you are travelling to by contacting their embassy in the UK.

Motor Vehicles and Caravans

Travellers between member states of the EU are entitled to import temporarily a motor vehicle, caravan or trailer into other member states without any Customs formalities.

Motor vehicles and caravans may be temporarily imported into non-EU countries generally for a maximum of six months in any twelve month period, provided they are not hired, sold or otherwise disposed of in that country.

Temporarily imported vehicles should not be left behind after the importer has left, should not be used by residents of the country visited and should not be left longer than the permitted period.

If you intend to stay longer than six months, take up employment or residence, or dispose of a vehicle you should seek advice well before your departure from the UK, for example from one of the motoring organisations.

Anyone temporarily importing a vehicle into another country which does not belong to them (either borrowed or hired) should carry a letter of authority from the vehicle owner and/or a VE103 Vehicle on Hire Certificate from the vehicle owner (this includes company cars).

*See the chapter **Documents** in the section **PLANNING AND TRAVELLING** for further details.*

Use of Caravan by Persons other than the Owner

Many caravan owners reduce the cost of a holiday by sharing their caravan with friends or relatives. Either

the caravan is left on the Continent on a campsite or it is handed over at the port. In making these arrangements it is important to consider the following:

- The total time the vehicle spends abroad must not exceed the permitted period for temporary importation.

- The owner of the caravan must provide the other person with a letter of authority. It is not permitted to accept a hire fee or reward.

- The number plate on the caravan must match the number plate on the tow car used.

- Both drivers' motor insurers must be informed if a caravan is being towed and any additional premium must be paid. If travelling to a country where an International Motor Insurance Certificate (Green Card) is required, both drivers' Certificates must be annotated to show that a caravan is being towed.

- If using The Caravan Club's Red Pennant Overseas Holiday Insurance, both drivers must be members of The Caravan Club and both must take out a Red Pennant policy.

*See the chapter **Insurance** in the section **PLANNING AND TRAVELLING**.*

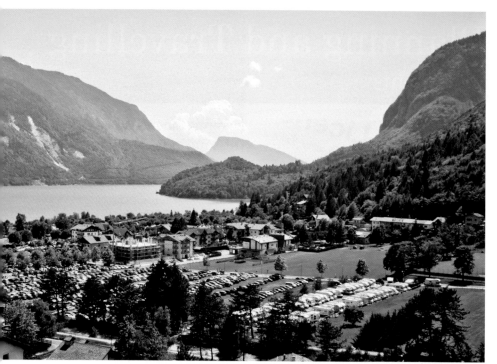

Personal Possessions

Generally speaking, visitors to countries within the EU are free to carry reasonable quantities of any personal articles, including valuable items such as jewellery, cameras, laptops, etc, required for the duration of their stay. It is sensible to carry sales receipts for new items, particularly of a foreign manufacture, in case you need to prove that tax has already been paid.

Visitors to non-EU countries may temporarily import personal items on condition that the articles are the personal property of the visitor and that they are not left behind when the importer leaves the country.

Prohibited and Restricted Goods

Just because something is on sale in another country does not mean it can be freely brought back to the UK. Regardless of where you are travelling from, the importation into the UK of some goods is restricted or banned, mainly to protect health and the environment.

These include:

- Endangered animals or plants including live animals, birds and plants, ivory, skins, coral, hides, shells and goods made from them such as jewellery, shoes, bags and belts even though these items were openly on sale in the countries where you bought them.

- Controlled, unlicensed or dangerous drugs e.g. heroin, cocaine, cannabis, LSD, morphine, etc.

- Counterfeit or pirated goods such as watches, CDs and sports shirts; goods bearing a false indication of their place of manufacture or in breach of UK copyright.

- Offensive weapons such as firearms, flick knives, knuckledusters, push daggers or knives disguised as everyday objects.

- Pornographic material depicting extreme violence or featuring children such as DVDs, magazines, videos, books and software.

This list is by no means exhaustive; if in doubt contact HM Revenue & Customs National Advice Service on 0845 010 9000 or +44 2920 501 261 from outside the UK for more information or, when returning to the UK, go through the red Customs channel or use the telephone at the Red Point and ask a Customs officer.

It is your responsibility to make sure that you are not breaking the law. Never attempt to mislead or hide anything from Customs officers; penalties are severe.

Planning and Travelling
Documents

Camping Key Europe (CKE) and Camping Card International (CCI)

The Camping Key Europe (CKE) is a useful companion for touring in Europe. Not only does it serve as a valid ID at campsites, meaning that you don't have to leave you passport with the site reception, it also entitles you to discounts at over 2200 sites.

In addition, the CKE offers you Third Party Liability Insurance for up to 6 people travelling in one party, and Personal Accident Cover while on site. Full Terms and Conditions and details of the levels of cover of this insurance are provided with the card.

The CKE is available to purchase from The Caravan Club by calling 01342 336633, or is provided free for all members taking out the 'Motoring' level of cover of The Club's Red Pennant Overseas Holiday Insurance.

The CKE has also replaced the old Camping Card Scandinavia, which ceased to exist in 2012.

An alternative, similar scheme is the Camping Card International (CCI) The CCI offers similar benefits as the CKE.

If you are using a CKE or CCI card as a method of ID at a site, make sure that you retrieve your card on leaving the site. Also check that you have been given your own card instead of someone else's

*See the **Country Introduction** for more information and www.campingkey.com or www.campingcardinternational.com*

Driving Licence & International Driving Permit (IDP)

Driving Licence

A full, valid driving licence should be carried at all times when driving abroad as you must produce it when asked to do so by the police and other authorities. Failure to do so may result in an immediate fine. If your driving licence is due to expire while you are away it can normally be renewed up to three months before the expiry date. If you need to renew your licence more than three months ahead of the expiry date contact the DVLA and they will advise you.

All European Union countries should recognise the pink EU-format paper driving licence introduced in the UK in 1990, subject to the minimum age requirements of the country concerned (normally 18 years in all the countries covered in this guide for a vehicle with a maximum weight of 3,500 kg and carrying not more than 8 people). However, there are exceptions in some European Countries and the Country Introductions in the relevant volumes of Caravan Europe contain details. It is strongly recommended that you upgrade your license to the current photocard license, which conforms to European Union standards.

Holders of an old-style green UK paper licence or a licence issued in Northern Ireland prior to 1991, which is not to EU format, should update it to a photocard licence before travelling in order to avoid any local difficulties with the authorities. Alternatively, obtain an International Driving Permit to accompany your UK licence. A photocard driving licence is also useful as a means of identification in.other situations, e.g. when using a credit card, when the display of photographic identification may be required. Application forms are available from most post offices or apply online at www.gov.uk.

If you have a photocard driving licence, remember to carry both the plastic card and its paper counterpart.

Allow enough time for your application to be processed and do not apply if you plan to hire a car in the very near future. Selected post offices and DVLA local offices offer a premium checking service for photocard applications but the service is not available for online applications.

Driving licence – carry both the photocard and its paper counterpart

International Driving Permit (IDP)

If you hold a British photocard driving licence, no other form of photographic identification is required within the EU. If you plan to travel outside of the EU then an IDP may still be required and you can obtain one over the counter at selected post offices (search on www.postoffice.co.uk or call 08457 223344) and from motoring organisations, namely the AA or the RAC, whether or not you are a member. An IDP costs £5.50 and is valid for a period of 12 months from the date of issue but may be post-dated up to three months.

To apply for an IDP you will need to be resident in Great Britain, have passed a driving test and be over 18 years of age. When driving abroad you should always carry your full national driving licence with you as well as your IDP.

European Health Insurance Card – Emergency Medical Benefits

For information on how to apply for a European Health Insurance Card (EHIC) and the medical care to which it entitles you, see the chapter *Medical Matters* in the section *DURING YOUR STAY*.

MOT Certificate

You are advised to carry your vehicle's MOT certificate of road worthiness (if applicable) when driving on the Continent as it may be required by the authorities if your vehicle is involved in an accident, or in the event of random vehicle checks. If your MOT certificate is due to expire while you are away you should have the vehicle tested before you leave home.

Passport

Many countries require you to carry your passport at all times and immigration authorities may, of course, check your passport on return to the UK. While abroad, it will help gain access to assistance from British Consular services and to banking services. Enter next-of-kin details in the back of your passport, keep a separate record of your passport details and leave a copy of it with a relative or friend at home.

The following information applies only to British citizens holding, or entitled to hold, a passport bearing the inscription 'United Kingdom of Great Britain and Northern Ireland'.

Applying for a Passport

Each person (including babies) must hold a valid passport. It is not now possible to add or include children on a parent's British passport. A standard British passport is valid for ten years, but if issued to children under 16 years of age it is valid for five years.

All new UK passports are now biometric passports, also known as ePassports, which feature additional security features including a microchip with the holder's unique biometric facial features. Existing passports will remain valid until their expiry date and holders will not be required to exchange them for biometric passports before then.

Full information and application forms are available from main post offices or from the Identity & Passport Service's website, www.gov.uk where you can complete an online application. Allow at least six weeks for first-time passport applications, for which you will probably need to attend an interview at your nearest Identity and Passport Service (IPS) regional office once you have submitted your application – telephone the IPS helpline on 0300 222 0000 to arrange one. Allow three weeks for a renewal application and at least one week for the replacement of a lost, stolen or damaged passport.

Main post offices offer a 'Check & Send' service for passport applications costing £8.17. To find your nearest 'Check & Send' post office call 0845 611 2970 or see www.postoffice.co.uk

Passport Validity

Most countries covered in this guide merely require you to carry a passport valid for the duration of your stay. However, in the event that your return home is delayed for any reason, and in order to avoid any local difficulties with immigration authorities, it is advisable to ensure that your passport is valid for at least six months after your planned return travel date. You can renew your passport up to nine months before expiry, without losing the validity of the current one.

Schengen Agreement

All the countries covered in all three volumes of Caravan Europe – except Andorra and Croatia – are party to the Schengen Agreement, which allows people and vehicles to pass freely without border checks from country to country within the Schengen area. Where there are no longer any border checks you should still not attempt to cross land borders without a full, valid passport. It is likely that random identity checks will continue to be made for the foreseeable future in areas surrounding land borders.

The United Kingdom and Republic of Ireland do not fully participate in the Schengen Agreement.

Do remember that your passport is a valuable document and it can be expensive, time-consuming and inconvenient to replace. Its loss or theft can lead to serious complications if your identity is later used fraudulently.

Pet Travel Scheme (PETS)

The Pet Travel Scheme (PETS) allows owners of dogs, cats and a number of other animals from qualifying European countries, to bring their pets into the UK (up to a limit of five per person) without quarantine, providing the animal has an EU pet passport, is microchipped and has been vaccinated against rabies. Dogs must also have been treated for tapeworm. It also allows pets to travel from the UK to other EU qualifying countries. All of the countries covered in this guide are qualifying countries. However, the procedures to obtain the passport are lengthy and the regulations, out of necessity, are strict.

Be aware that some countries may not allow entry to certain types or breeds of dogs and may have rules relating to matters such as muzzling and transporting dogs in cars. You are advised to contact the appropriate authorities of the countries you plan to visit via their embassies in London before making travel arrangements for your dog. You should also check with your vet for the latest available information or call the PETS Helpline on 0870 2411710, email: pettravel@ahvla.gsi.gov.uk or more information is available at www.gov.uk/take-pet-abroad. You can find out more about the restrictions and which breeds are affected at www.caravanclub.co.uk/pets.

The PETS scheme operates on a number of ferry routes between the Continent and the UK as well as on Eurotunnel services and Eurostar passenger trains from Calais to Folkestone. Some routes may only operate at certain times of the year; routes may change and new ones may be added – check with the PETS Helpline for the latest information.

Pets normally resident in the Channel Islands, Isle of Man and the Republic of Ireland can also enter the UK under the PETS scheme if they comply with the rules. Pets resident anywhere in the British Isles (including the Republic of Ireland) will continue to be able to travel freely within the British Isles and will not be subject to PETS rules. Owners of pets entering the Channel Islands or the Republic of Ireland from outside the British Isles should contact the appropriate authorities in those countries for advice on approved routes and other requirements.

It is against the law in the UK to possess certain types of dogs (unless an exemption certificate is held) and the introduction of PETS does not affect this ban.

For a list of vets near Continental ports, look in the local equivalent of the Yellow Pages telephone directory. Campsite owners or tourist offices located near Channel ports will be familiar with the requirements of British visitors and will probably be able to recommend a vet. Alternatively, the local British Consulate or the ferry company transporting your pet may be able to help.

Adequate travel insurance for your pet is essential

Last but by no means least, adequate travel insurance for your pet is essential in the event of an accident abroad requiring veterinary treatment, emergency repatriation or long-term care if treatment lasts longer than your holiday. Travel insurance should also include liability cover in the event that your pet injures another animal or person or damages property whilst abroad. Contact The Caravan Club on 0800 0151396 or visit www.caravanclub.co.uk/petins for details of the Pet Insurance scheme, specially negotiated to take into account Club members' requirements both at home and abroad.

*See **Holiday Insurance for Pets** under **Insurance** in the section **PLANNING AND TRAVELLING**.*

Travelling with Children

Some countries require documentary evidence of parental responsibility from single parents travelling alone with children before allowing them to enter the country or, in some cases, before permitting children to leave the country. The authorities may want to see a birth certificate, a letter of consent from the other parent and some evidence as to your responsibility for the child.

If you are travelling with a minor under the age of 18 who is not your own, you must carry a letter of authorisation, naming the adult in charge of the child, from the child's parent or legal guardian.

For further information on exactly what will be required at immigration contact the Embassy or Consulate of the countries you intend to visit before your visit.

Vehicle Excise Licence

While driving abroad it is necessary to display a current UK vehicle excise licence (tax disc). If your vehicle's tax disc is due to expire while you are abroad you may apply to re-license the vehicle at a post office, by post, or in person at a DVLA local office, up to two months

in advance. If you give a despatch address abroad the licence can be sent to you there.

Vehicle Registration Certificate (V5C)

You must always carry your Vehicle Registration Certificate (V5C) when taking your vehicle abroad. If you do not have one you should apply to a DVLA local office on form V62. If you need to travel abroad during this time you will need to apply for a Temporary Registration Certificate if you are not already recorded as the vehicle keeper.

Telephone DVLA Customer Enquiries on 0300 790 6802 for more information.

Caravan – Proof of Ownership (CRIS)

In Britain and Ireland, unlike most other European countries, caravans are not formally registered in the same way as cars. This may not be fully understood by police and other authorities on the Continent. You are strongly advised, therefore, to carry a copy of your Caravan Registration Identification Scheme (CRIS) document.

Hired or Borrowed Vehicles

If using a borrowed vehicle you must obtain a letter of authority to use the vehicle from the registered owner. You should also carry the Vehicle Registration Certificate (V5C).

In the case of hired or leased vehicles, including company cars, when the user does not normally possess the V5C, ask the company which owns the vehicle to supply a Vehicle On Hire Certificate, form VE103, which is the only legal substitute for a V5C. See www.bvrla.co.uk or call them on 01494 434747 for more information.

If you are caught driving a hired vehicle abroad without this certificate you may be fined and/or the vehicle impounded.

Visas

British citizens holding a full UK passport do not require a visa for entry into any countries covered by this guide. EU countries may require a permit for stays of more than three months and you should contact the relevant country's UK embassy before you travel for information.

British subjects, British overseas citizens, British dependent territories citizens and citizens of other countries may need visas that are not required by British citizens. Again check with the authorities of the country you are due to visit at their UK embassy or consulate. Citizens of other countries should apply to their own embassy, consulate or High Commission for information.

Planning and Travelling
Ferries and the Channel Tunnel

Planning Your Trip

If travelling in July or August, or over peak weekends during school holidays, such as Easter and half-term, it is advisable to make a reservation as early as possible. Space for caravans on ferries is usually limited, especially during peak holiday periods. Off-peak crossings, which may offer savings, are usually filled very quickly.

When booking any ferry crossing, account must be taken of boats, bicycles, skylights and roof boxes in the overall height/length of your car and caravan or motorhome. Ferry operators require you to declare total dimensions. It is important, therefore, to report the dimensions of your outfit accurately when making a ferry booking, as vehicles which have been under-declared may be turned away at boarding.

Individual ferry companies may impose vehicle length or height restrictions according to the type of vessel in operation on that particular sailing or route. Always check when making your booking.

> **Report the dimensions of your outfit accurately when making a ferry booking**

Advise your booking agent at the time of making your ferry reservation of any disabled passengers. Ferry companies can then make the appropriate arrangements for anyone requiring assistance at ports or on board ships.

For residents of both Northern Ireland and the Republic of Ireland travelling to the Continent via the British mainland, Brittany Ferries, Irish Ferries and P & O Irish Sea offer special 'Landbridge' or 'Ferrylink' through-fares for combined crossings on the Irish Sea and the English Channel or North Sea.

The table on the following page shows current ferry routes from the UK to the Continent and Ireland. Some ferry routes may not be operational all year, and during peak holiday periods the transportation of caravans or motorhomes may be restricted. Current ferry timetables and tariffs can be obtained from The Caravan Club's Travel Service, from a travel agent or from ferry operators' websites.

Booking Your Ferry

The Caravan Club is an agent for most major ferry companies operating services to the Continent, Scandinavia, Ireland and the Isle of Wight, and each year provides thousands of Club members with a speedy and efficient booking service. Our Continental Caravanning brochure (available from November) and Winter Escapes brochure (available from June) feature a range of special offers with ferry operators – some of them exclusive to The Caravan Club. The brochure also includes full information on the Site Booking Service for campsites on the Continent, the Tours & Excursions programme, and Red Pennant Overseas Holiday Insurance. Telephone 01342 327410 to request a brochure or see www.caravanclub.co.uk/overseas

During the course of the year, new special offers and promotions are negotiated and these are featured on the Travel Service News page of The Caravan Club Magazine and on The Club's website.

The Club's website has a direct link to a number of ferry operators' reservations systems allowing Club members to make their own reservations and still take advantage of the Club's negotiated offers and the ferry companies' own early booking offers. A credit card deposit is taken and the balance collected ten weeks before departure date. Reservations may be made by telephoning The Caravan Club's Travel Service on 01342 316101 or at www.caravanclub.co.uk/overseas

Route	Operator	Approximate Crossing Time	Maximum Frequency
Belgium			
Hull – Zeebrugge	P & O Ferries	12½ hrs	1 daily
Denmark			
Harwich – Esbjerg	DFDS Seaways	18¼ hrs	3 per week
France			
Dover – Calais	P & O Ferries	1½ hrs	22 daily
Dover – Dunkerque	DFDS Seaways	2 hrs	12 daily
Folkestone – Calais	Eurotunnel	35 mins	3 per hour
Newhaven – Dieppe	Transmanche Ferries	4 hrs	2 daily
Plymouth – Roscoff	Brittany Ferries	6 hrs	2 daily
Poole – Cherbourg	Brittany Ferries	4½ hrs	1 daily
Poole – St Malo (via Channel Islands)	Condor Ferries	5 hrs	1 daily (May to Sep)
Portsmouth – Caen	Brittany Ferries	3¾ / 7½ hrs	4 daily
Portsmouth – Cherbourg	Brittany Ferries	3 / 4½ hrs	3 daily
Portsmouth – Cherbourg	Condor Ferries	5½ hrs	1 weekly (May to Sep)
Portsmouth – Le Havre	LD Lines	3¼ / 8 hrs	2 daily
Portsmouth – St Malo	Brittany Ferries	9 hrs	1 daily
Weymouth – St Malo (via Channel Islands)	Condor Ferries	9½ hrs	1 daily
Ireland – Northern			
Cairnryan/Troon – Larne	P & O Irish Sea	1 / 2 hrs	11 daily
Liverpool (Birkenhead) – Belfast	Stena Line	8 hrs	2 daily
Cairnryan – Belfast	Stena Line	2 / 3 hrs	7 daily
Ireland – Republic			
Cork – Roscoff†	Brittany Ferries	14 hrs	1 per week
Fishguard – Rosslare	Stena Line	2 / 3½ hrs	3 daily
Holyhead – Dublin	Irish Ferries	1¾ / 3¼ hrs	4 daily
Holyhead – Dublin	Stena Line	3¼ hrs	4 daily
Holyhead – Dun Loaghaire	Stena Line	2 hrs	2 daily
Liverpool – Dublin	P & O Irish Sea	8 hrs	2 daily
Liverpool (Birkenhead) – Dublin	Stena Line	7 hrs	2 daily
Pembroke – Rosslare	Irish Ferries	4 hrs	2 daily
Rosslare – Cherbourg†	Irish Ferries	19½ hrs	3 per week
Rosslare – Cherbourg†	Celtic Link Ferries	17 hrs	3 per week
Rosslare – Roscoff†	Irish Ferries	19½ hrs	4 per week
Netherlands			
Harwich – Hook of Holland	Stena Line	6½ hrs	2 daily
Hull – Rotterdam	P & O Ferries	10¼ hrs	1 daily
Newcastle – Ijmuiden (Amsterdam)	DFDS Seaways	15½ hrs	1 daily
Spain			
Portsmouth – Bilbao	Brittany Ferries	24 hrs	2 per week
Portsmouth or Plymouth – Santander	Brittany Ferries	24 / 20 hrs	4 per week

† Not bookable through the Club's Travel Service.
Note: Services and routes correct at time of publication but subject to change.

Channel Tunnel

The Channel Tunnel operator, Eurotunnel, accepts cars, caravans and motorhomes (except those running on LPG) on their service between Folkestone and Calais. While they accept traffic on a 'turn up and go' basis, they also offer a full reservation service for all departures with exact timings confirmed on booking.

Note: information correct at the time of publication and may be subject to change.

Gas - Safety Precautions and Regulations on Ferries and in the Channel Tunnel

UK based cross Channel ferry companies usually allow up to three gas cylinders per caravan, including the cylinder currently in use. However some may restrict this to a maximum of two cylinders, which have to be securely fitted into your caravan. Some operators may request that you hand your gas cylinders to a member of the crew for safe storage during sailing. It is always advisable to check with the ferry company before setting out as regulations may change.

Cylinder valves should be fully closed and covered with a cap, if provided, and should remain closed during the crossing. Cylinders should be fixed securely in or on the caravan in the manner intended and in the position designated by your caravan's manufacturer. Ensure gas cookers and fridges are fully turned off. Gas cylinders must be declared at check-in and ships' crew may wish to inspect each cylinder for leakage before shipment. They will reject leaking or inadequately secured cylinders.

Eurotunnel will allow vehicles fitted with LPG tanks for the purposes of heating, lighting, cooking or refrigeration to use their service, but regulations stipulate that a total of no more than 47 kg of gas can be carried through the Channel Tunnel. Tanks must be switched off before boarding and must be less than 80% full; you will be asked to demonstrate this before you travel. **Vehicles powered by LPG cannot be carried through the Channel Tunnel.**

Most ferry companies, however, are willing to accept LPG-powered vehicles provided they are advised at the time of booking. During the crossing the tank must be no more than 75% full and it must be turned off. In the case of vehicles converted to use LPG, some ferry companies also require a certificate showing that the conversion has been carried out to the manufacturer's specification.

The carriage of spare petrol cans, whether full or empty, is not permitted on ferries or through the Channel Tunnel.

It is your responsibility to check current safety precautions and regulations on ferries and channel tunnels before you travel.

Pets on Ferries and Eurotunnel

It is possible to transport your pet on a number of ferry routes to the Continent and Ireland, as well as on Eurotunnel services from Folkestone to Calais. At the time this guide was compiled the cost of return travel for a pet was between £30 and £50, depending on the route used. Advance booking is essential as restrictions apply to the number of animals allowed on any one departure. Make sure you understand the carrier's terms and conditions for transporting pets.

> **It's important to ensure that ferry staff know that your vehicle contains an animal**

On arrival at the port ensure that ferry staff know that your vehicle contains an animal. Once on board pets are normally required to remain in their owner's vehicle or in kennels on the car deck and, for safety reasons, access by pet owners to the vehicle decks while the ferry is at sea may be restricted. On longer ferry crossings you should make arrangements at the on-board information desk for permission to visit your pet at suitable intervals in order to check its well-being.

Information and advice on the welfare of animals before and during a journey is available on the website of the Department for Environment, Food and Rural Affairs (Defra), www.defra.gov.uk

See also **Pet Travel Scheme** *under* **Documents** *and* **Holiday Insurance for Pets** *under* **Insurance** *in the section* **PLANNING AND TRAVELLING.**

Caravan Club Sites Near Ports

Once you have chosen your ferry crossing and worked out your route to the port of departure you may like to consider an overnight stop at one of The Caravan Club sites listed in the table on the opposite page, especially if your journey to or from home involves a long drive.

Book online using the Club's UK Advance Booking Service at www.caravanclub.co.uk or call 01342 327490. Otherwise when sites are open, contact them direct.

Advance booking is recommended, particularly if you are planning to stay during July and August or over Bank Holidays.

Port	Nearest Club Site and Town	Tel No.
Cairnryan, Stranraer	New England Bay, Drummore	01776 860275
Dover, Folkestone, Channel Tunnel	Bearsted, Maidstone	01622 730018
	Black Horse Farm*, Folkestone	01303 892665
	Daleacres, Hythe	01303 267679
	Fairlight Wood, Hastings	01424 812333
Fishguard, Pembroke	Freshwater East, Pembroke	01646 672341
Harwich	Cambridge Cherry Hinton*, Cambridge	01223 244088
	Commons Wood*, Welwyn Garden City	01707 260786
	Mildenhall (formerly Round Plantaton)	01638 713089
Holyhead	Penrhos, Benllech, Anglesey	01248 852617
Hull	York Beechwood Grange, York	01904 424637
	York Rowntree Park, York	01904 658997
Newcastle upon Tyne	Old Hartley, Whitley Bay	0191 237 0256
Newhaven	Brighton* (formerly Sheepcote Valley)	01273 626546
Plymouth	Plymouth Sound, Plymouth	01752 862325
Poole	Hunter's Moon*, Wareham	01929 556605
Portsmouth	Rookesbury Park, Fareham	01329 834085
Rosslare	River Valley, Wicklow	00353 (0)404 41647
Weymouth	Crossways, Dorchester	01305 852032

* Site open all year

When seasonal Club sites near the ports are closed, the sites listed below may be useful overnight stops for early and late season travellers using cross-Channel or Irish Sea ports. Although they may not be 'on the doorstep' of the ports in question they are open all year or most of the year. All 'open all year' sites offer a limited supply of hardstanding pitches.

Port	Nearest Club Site and Town	Tel No.
Dover, Folkstone, Channel Tunnel	Abbey Wood, London	020 8311 7708
	Alderstead Heath, Redhill	01737 644629
	Gatwick (formerly Amberley Fields), Crawley	01293 524834
	Crystal Palace, London	020 8778 7155
Fishguard, Pembroke, Swansea	Pembrey Country Park, Llanelli	01554 834369
Portsmouth	Abbey Wood, London	20 8311 7708
	Alderstead Heath, Redhill	01737 644629
	Amberley Fields, Crawley	01293 524834
	Crystal Palace, London	020 8778 7155

Alternatively, consider an overnight stay at a CL (Certificated Location) site within striking distance of your port of departure. Many CLs are open all year.

Full details of all these sites can be found in the latest edition of The Caravan Club's Sites Directory & Handbook and on the Club's website, www.caravanclub.co.uk

Please note that Commons Wood, Daleacres, Fairlight Wood, Hunter's Moon, Mildenhall, Old Hartley and Rookesbury Park are open to Caravan Club members only.

Non-members are welcome at all the other Caravan Club sites listed above.

Planning and Travelling
Insurance

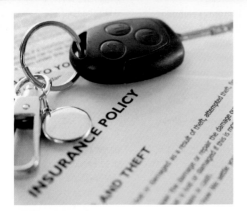

Car, Motorhome and Caravan Insurance

Insurance cover for your car, caravan, motorhome or trailer tent whilst travelling abroad is of the utmost importance. In addition, travel insurance, such as The Caravan Club's Red Pennant Overseas Holiday Insurance (available only to Club members), not only minimises duplication of cover offered by your motor and caravan insurance, but also covers other contingencies such as despatch of spare parts, medical and hospital fees, vehicle hire, vehicle recovery, etc.

See **Holiday Insurance** later in this section.

In order to be covered for a period abroad please remember:

- **Caravan** – Inform your caravan insurer/broker of the dates of your holiday and pay any additional premium required. The Caravan Club's 5Cs Caravan Insurance gives free foreign use cover for up to 182 days.

- **Car or Motorhome** – If your journey is outside the EU or EU Associated Countries (listed on the next page) inform your motor insurer/broker of the dates of your holiday, together with details of all the countries you will be visiting, and pay any additional premium. Also inform them if you are towing a caravan and ask them to include it on your Green Card if you need to carry one.

The Caravan Club's Car Insurance and Motorhome

Insurance schemes extend to provide full policy cover for European Union or Associated Countries free of charge, provided the total period of foreign travel in any one annual period of insurance does not exceed 180 days for car insurance and 270 days for motorhome insurance. It may be possible to extend this period, although a charge will apply. The cover provided is the same as what a Club member enjoys in the UK, rather than just the minimum legal liability cover required by law in the countries that you are visiting.

Should you be delayed beyond the limits of your insurance you must, without fail, instruct your insurer or broker to maintain cover.

For full details of The Caravan Club's Caravan Insurance telephone 01342 336610 or for car and motorhome insurance products, telephone 0800 0284809 or visit our website, www.caravanclub.co.uk/insurance

Taking Your Car or Motorhome Abroad – Evidence of Insurance Cover (Green Card)

All countries require visiting motorists to have motor insurance cover for their legal liability to third parties. An International Motor Insurance Certificate, commonly known as a Green Card, is evidence of compliance with this requirement. However, motorists with a UK Motor Insurance Certificate visiting EU and Associated Countries do not need a Green Card as, under EU legislation, it is now accepted in all such countries as evidence that the obligatory motor insurance cover is in force.

> **A UK Motor Insurance Certificate is now accepted in EU countries as evidence that motor insurance cover is in force**

Those travelling outside of the EU and Associated Countries will need to obtain a Green Card document, for which insurers usually make a charge. If a Green Card is issued, your motor insurers should be asked to include reference on it to any caravan or trailer that you may be towing. If you do not have evidence of the obligatory insurance cover, you may have to pay for temporary insurance at a country's border.

Irrespective of whether a Green Card is required, it is

advisable to notify your insurer/broker of your intention to travel outside of the UK and obtain confirmation that your policy has been extended to include use of the insured vehicle abroad, as your motor insurer may not automatically provide you with full policy cover when abroad. You should ensure that your vehicle and motorhome policies provide adequate cover for your purposes, rather than the minimum cover that the country you are visiting obliges you to have.

European Accident Statement

You should also check with your motor insurer/broker to see if they provide a European Accident Statement to record details of any accident you may be involved in with your motor vehicle. Travelling with your Vehicle Registration Certificate, (V5C) or vehicle on hire certificate (VE103), MOT certificate (if applicable), certificate of motor insurance, copy of your CRIS document, European Accident Statement and valid UK pink EU-format paper driving licence or photocard driving licence should be sufficient in the event that you are stopped for a routine police check or following an accident whilst travelling within the EU or an Associated Country. These documents should never be left in your vehicle when it is unattended.

European Union and Associated Countries

European Union: Austria, Belgium, Bulgaria, Cyprus, Czech Republic, Denmark, Estonia, Finland, France, Germany, Greece, Hungary, Ireland, Italy, Latvia, Lithuania, Luxembourg, Malta, Netherlands, Poland, Portugal, Romania, Slovakia, Slovenia, Spain, Sweden and the United Kingdom.

Associated EU Countries (i.e. non-EU signatories to the motor insurance Multilateral Guarantee Agreement): Andorra, Croatia, Iceland, Norway, Switzerland and Liechtenstein.

Although EU Countries, you may still wish to obtain a Green Card if visiting Bulgaria or Romania in order to avoid local difficulties which can sometimes arise in these countries. If you do not take a Green Card you should carry your certificate of motor insurance. If you plan to visit countries outside the EU and Associated Countries, and in particular central and eastern European countries, you should check that your motor insurer will provide the necessary extension of cover.

Caravans Stored Abroad

Caravan insurers will not normally insure caravans left on campsites or in storage abroad.

In these circumstances specialist policies are available from Towergate Bakers on 0800 4961516, www.tower gatebakers.co.uk, email bakers@towergate.co.uk or K Drewe Insurance, tel 0845 4085929,

www.lookinsurance services.co.uk, email support@lookcaravans.co.uk.

> **Insurers will not normally insure caravans left on campsite or in storage abroad**

Legal Costs Abroad

A driver who is taken to court following a road traffic accident in a European country runs the risk of being held liable for legal costs, even if cleared of any blame.

Motor insurance policies in the UK normally include cover for legal costs and expenses incurred (with insurer's consent) which arise from any incident that is covered under the terms and conditions of the policy. The Caravan Club's Car Insurance and Motorhome Insurance schemes incorporate such cover, together with optional additional legal expenses cover for recovering any other losses that are not included in your motor insurance policy. Similar optional legal expenses insurance is also offered as an addition to the Club's 5Cs Caravan Insurance scheme.

Holiday Travel Insurance

Having insured your vehicles, there are other risks to consider and it is essential to take out adequate travel insurance. The Caravan Club's Red Pennant Overseas Holiday Insurance is designed to provide as full a cover as possible at a reasonable fee. The Club's scheme is tailor-made for people with caravans, motorhomes or trailer tents and includes cover against the following:

Recovery of vehicles and passengers

Chauffeured recovery

Towing charges

Emergency labour costs

Spare parts location and despatch

Storage fees

Continuation of holiday travel, i.e. car hire, etc

Continuation of holiday accommodation, i.e. hotels, etc

Emergency medical and hospital expenses

Personal accident benefits

Legal expenses

Loss of deposits/cancellation cover

Emergency cash transfers

Personal effects and baggage insurance

Loss of cash or documents

Cost of telephone calls

If you are proposing to participate in dangerous sporting activities such as skiing, hang-gliding or mountaineering, check that your personal holiday insurance includes cover for such sports and that it also covers the cost of emergency mountain and helicopter rescue.

Look carefully at the exemptions to your insurance policy, including those relating to pre-existing medical conditions or the use of alcohol. Be sure to declare any pre-existing medical conditions to your insurer.

Club members can obtain increased cover by taking out Red Pennant **Plus** cover. The Club also offers a range of annual multi-trip and long stay holiday insurance schemes for Continental and worldwide travel. For more details and policy limits refer to the Continental Caravanning brochure from the Caravan Club. Alternatively see www.caravanclub.co.uk/redpennant for details or telephone 01342 336633.

Holiday Insurance for Pets

The Club's Red Pennant Overseas Holiday Insurance can be extended to cover extra expenses in respect of your pet that may arise as part of a claim for an incident normally covered under the Red Pennant policy, such as pet repatriation expenses. It does not, however, cover costs arising from an injury to, or the illness of your pet, or provide any legal liability cover to you as a pet owner.

For this you will require separate pet insurance, such as that offered by The Caravan Club, which covers treatment abroad, quarantine costs, emergency expenses, including boarding fees, as well as holiday

cancellation costs. It also covers legal liability in the event of injury or damage caused by your pet.

Contact The Caravan Club on 0800 0151396 or see www.caravanclub.co.uk/petins for details of the Club's Pet Insurance scheme, specially negotiated to take into account Club members' requirements both at home and abroad.

> **See, www.caravanclub.co.uk/ petins for details of our Pet Insurance scheme**

Marine Insurance

Car Ferries

Vehicles driven by their owner are normally conveyed in accordance with the terms of the carrying companies' published by-laws or conditions, and if damage is sustained during loading, unloading or shipment, this must be reported at the time to the carrier's representative. Any claim arising from such damage must be notified in writing to the carrier concerned within three days of the incident. Nonetheless it is unwise to rely upon the carrier accepting liability for your claim so it is advisable to have separate transit insurance.

The majority of motor policies provide transit insurance cover for vehicles during short sea crossings up to 65 hours normal duration – check with your insurer/broker.

The Caravan Club's 5Cs Caravan Insurance policy automatically covers you for crossings of any length within the area covered by Red Pennant Overseas Holiday Insurance.

Boats

The Royal Yachting Association recommends that all boats have marine insurance. Third party insurance is compulsory for many countries, together with a translation of the insurance certificate into the appropriate language(s). Check with your insurer/broker before taking your boat abroad.

Medical Insurance

It is important to make sure your travel insurance also covers medical emergency expenses. Regardless of whether you have an European Health Insurance Card (EHIC), medical expenses can still be incurred so make sure your travel insurance policy will cover you.

The Caravan Club's Red Pennant cover is available to members. Please visit www.caravanclub.co.uk/redpennant for further information or telephone 01342 336633.

*See the chapter **Medical Matters** in the section **DURING YOUR STAY** for further information.*

Home Insurance

Most home insurers require advance notification if you are leaving your home unoccupied for 30 days or more. They often require that mains services (except electricity) are turned off, water drained down and that somebody visits the home once a week. Check your policy documents or speak to your insurer/broker.

> **Most home insurers require advance notice if your home is unoccupied for 30 days or more**

The Caravan Club's Home Insurance policy provides full cover for up to 90 days when you are away from home (for instance when touring) and requires only common sense precautions for longer periods of unoccupancy.

Contact 0800 0284815 or see www.caravanclub. co.uk/homeins for details of our Home Insurance scheme, specially negotiated to suit the majority of Club members' requirements.

Personal Belongings

The majority of travellers are able to cover their valuables such as jewellery, watches, cameras, laptops, bicycles and, in some instances, small boats, under the All Risks section of their Householders' Comprehensive Policy. This includes The Caravan Club's Home Insurance scheme.

Vehicles Left Behind Abroad

If you are involved in an accident or breakdown whilst abroad which prevents you taking your vehicle home, you must ensure that your normal insurance cover is maintained to cover the period that the vehicle remains abroad, and that you are covered for the cost of recovering it to your home address.

You should remove all items of baggage and personal belongings from your vehicles before leaving them unattended. If this is not possible you should check with your insurer/broker to establish whether extended cover can be provided. In all circumstances, you must remove any valuables and items which might attract Customs duty, including wine, beer, spirits and cigarettes.

Planning and Travelling
International Holidays 2014 and 2015

International Holidays, Important Dates & UK Bank Holidays

2014				2015	
January	1	Wednesday	New Year's Day	1	Thursday
	6	Monday	Epiphany	6	Tuesday
March	1	Saturday	St David's Day	1	Sunday
	5	Wednesday	Ash Wednesday	18 Feb	Wednesday
	17	Monday	St Patrick's Day	17	Tuesday
	30	Sunday	Mother's Day	15	Sunday
	30	Sunday	British Summer Time Begins	29	Sunday
April	13	Sunday	Palm Sunday	29 Mar	Sunday
	18	Friday	Good Friday	3	Friday
	20	Sunday	Easter Day	5	Sunday
	21	Monday	Easter Monday	6	Monday
	23	Wednesday	St George's Day	23	Thursday
May	5	Monday	May Bank Holiday	4	Monday
	27	Monday	Spring Bank Holiday UK	25	Monday
	29	Thursday	Ascension Day	14	Thursday
June	15	Sunday	Father's Day	21	Sunday
	8	Sunday	Whit Sunday	24 May	Sunday
	19	Thursday	Corpus Christi	4	Thursday
	29	Sunday	1st Day of Ramadan*	18	Thursday
July	29	Tuesday	Ramadan Ends (Eid-al-Fitr)*	18	Saturday
August	15	Friday	Assumption	15	Saturday
	25	Monday	Bank Holiday UK	31	Monday
September	25	Thursday	Jewish New Year (Rosh Hashanah)	14	Monday
October	4	Saturday	Jewish Day of Atonement (Yom Kippur)	23 Sept	Wednesday
	25	Saturday	Islamic New Year (Al Hijra)	15	Thursday
	26	Sunday	British Summer Time ends	25	Sunday
	31	Friday	Halloween	31	Saturday
November	1	Saturday	All Saints' Day	1	Sunday
	9	Sunday	Remembrance Sunday	8	Sunday
	30	Sunday	St Andrew's Day	30	Monday
December	25	Thursday	Christmas Day	25	Friday
	26	Friday	St Stephen's Day; Boxing Day UK	26	Saturday

* Subject to the lunar calendar

NOTES   1) Outside the UK when a holiday falls on a Sunday it will not necessarily be observed the following day.

2) Public holidays in individual countries are listed in the relevant Country Introductions.

3) Dates listed here and in the Country Introduction Chapters are believed to be correct at time of publication, however please note some dates may not have officially been confirmed and may be subject to change.

Planning and Travelling
Money

Take your holiday money in a mixture of cash, credit and debit cards and/or pre-paid travel cards and keep them separately. Do not rely exclusively on only one method of payment.

See **Customs** in the section **DURING YOUR STAY** for information about declaring the amount of cash you carry when entering or leaving the EU.

Local Currency

It is not necessary to carry a large amount of cash but it is a good idea to take sufficient foreign currency for your immediate needs on arrival, including loose change if possible. Even if you intend to use credit and debit cards for most of your holiday spending, it makes sense to take some cash to tide you over until you are able to find a cash machine (ATM), and you may need change for parking meters or the use of supermarket trolleys.

You can change money at ports and on ferries but the rates offered do not generally represent the best value. The Post Office, many High Street banks, exchange offices and travel agents offer commission free foreign exchange, some will charge a flat fee and some offer a 'buy back' service. Most stock the more common currencies such as Euros, but it is wise to order in advance in case demand is heavy, or if you require an unusual currency.

> **Shop around and compare commission and exchange rates to make sure you get the best deal**

Currency can also be ordered by telephone or online for delivery to your home address on payment of a handling charge. Online providers such as the Post Office, Moneycorp and Travelex, and most of the High Street banks offer their customers an online ordering service which usually represents the best value. It can pay to shop around and compare commission and exchange rates, together with minimum charges.

If you pay for your currency with a credit or debit card the card issuer may charge a cash advance fee in addition to the commission and/or handling charge.

Banks and money exchanges in central and eastern Europe are not willing to accept Scottish and Northern Irish bank notes and may be reluctant to change any sterling which has been written on, is creased or worn, or is not in virtually mint condition.

Exchange rates are given in the Country Introductions in this guide. Up to date currency conversion rates can be obtained from your bank or national newspapers. Alternatively, www.oanda.com updates currency rates around the world daily and allows you to download a currency converter to your mobile phone.

Foreign Currency Bank Accounts

Frequent travellers or those who spend long periods abroad may find a euro bank account useful. Most such accounts impose no currency conversion charges for debit or credit card use and allow fee-free cash withdrawls at ATMs. Some banks may also allow you to spread your account across different currencies, depending on your circumstances. Your bank will advise you.

Travellers' Cheques

Recent visitors report difficulties in finding a bank that will cash Travellers Cheques for non-account holders, and where they are accepted high commission charges may be incurred. Travellers Cheques may still be useful if you are travelling off the beaten track or in far-flung locations, but bear in mind that small bank branches may not offer foreign exchange services.

Commission is usually payable when you buy the cheques and/or when you cash them in. See the Country Introduction for more information.

Travel Money Cards

Travel money cards are issued by the Post Office, Travelex, Lloyds Bank and American Express amongst many others. For a comparison table see www.which-prepaid-card.co.uk.

They are an increasingly popular and practical alternative to Travellers Cheques, as a pre-paid PIN protected travel money card offers the security of Travellers Cheques, with the convenience of plastic. Load the card with the amount you need before leaving home, and then simply use cash machines to make withdrawals and/or present the card to pay for goods and services in shops and restaurants as you would a credit or debit card. You can obtain a second card so that another user can access the funds and you can also top the card up over the telephone or online while you are abroad.

These cards can be cheaper to use than credit or debit cards for both cash withdrawals and purchases as there are usually no loading or transaction fees to pay. In addition, because they are separate from your bank account, if the card is lost or stolen there is less risk of identity theft.

The Caravan Club have partnered with Moneycorp to offer the Explorer prepaid card to members. The card has no application fee and you can load as many as 14 currencies onto it. There are no fees for withdrawing from ATMs, loading money or transactions, so can work out much more cost effective than using a credit or debit card abroad. For more infomation visit www.caravanclub.co.uk/travelmoney.

Credit and Debit Cards

Credit and debit cards offer a convenient way of spending abroad. You can use a card to pay for goods and services wherever your card logo is displayed and also to obtain cash from ATMs using your PIN. ATMs usually offer an English language option once you insert your card.

For the use of cards abroad most banks impose a foreign currency conversion charge (typically 2.75% per transaction) which is usually the same for both credit and debit cards. If you use your credit card to withdraw cash there will be a further commission charge of up to 3% and you will be charged interest (possibly at a higher rate than normal) as soon as you withdraw the money.

In line with market practice, Barclaycard, which issues The Caravan Club's credit card, charges a 2.75% fee for all card transactions outside the UK. Cash withdrawals abroad are subject to a further 2% handling charge as in the UK. A £2 minimum fee applies with a maximum charge of £50 (information correct at time of publication).

Contact your credit card issuer before you leave home to let them know you will be travelling abroad

Check the expiry date of your cards before you leave and memorise the PIN for each one. If you have several cards, take at least two in case you come across gaps in acceptance of certain cards, e.g. shops which accept only MasterCard or only VISA.

If you are planning an extended journey arrange for your credit or charge card account to be cleared each month by variable direct debit, ensuring that bills are paid on time and no interest is charged.

Credit and debit 'chip and PIN' cards issued by UK banks may not be universally accepted abroad and it is wise to check before incurring expenditure.

Contact your credit or debit card issuer before you leave home to let them know that you will be travelling abroad. In the battle against card fraud, card issuers are frequently likely to query transactions which they regard as unusual or suspicious. This may result in a cash withdrawal from an ATM being declined, or a retailer at the point of sale having to telephone for authorisation and/or confirmation of your details. Difficulties can occur if there is a language barrier or if the retailer is unwilling to bother with further checks. Your card may be declined or, worse still, temporarily stopped. In this instance you should insist that the retailer contacts the local authorisation centre but, in any event, it is a good idea to carry your card issuer's helpline number with you. You will also need this number should you need to report the loss or theft of your card.

Dynamic Currency Conversion

When you pay with a credit or debit card, retailers may offer you the choice of currency for payment, e.g. a euro amount will be converted into sterling and then charged to your card account. You may be asked to sign an agreement to accept the conversion rate used and final amount charged and, having done so, there is no opportunity to change your mind or obtain a refund. This is known as a 'dynamic currency conversion' but the exchange rate used is unlikely to be as favourable as that used by your card issuer. You may also find retailers claiming that a sterling bill will automatically be generated when a UK-issued credit card is tendered and processed. If this is the case then you may prefer to pay by cash.

Some ATMs may give you the option to convert your withdrawal into sterling when you withdraw euros. It is often best to decline and opt to pay in the national currency.

Emergency Cash

If an emergency or robbery means that you need cash in a hurry, then friends or relatives at home can use the MoneyGram instant money transfer service available at post offices and branches of Thomas Cook.

This service, which does not necessarily require the sender to use a bank account or credit card, enables the transfer of money to over 233,000 money transfer agents around the world. Transfers take approximately ten minutes and charges are levied on a sliding scale.

> **As a last resort, contact the nearest British Embassy or Consulate for help**

Western Union operates a similar secure, worldwide service and has offices located in banks, post offices, travel agents, stations and shops. You can also transfer funds instantly by telephone on 0800 833833 or online at www.westernunion.co.uk.

As a last resort, contact the nearest British Embassy or Consulate for help. The Foreign & Commonwealth Office in London can arrange for a relative or friend to deposit funds which will be authorised for payment by embassy staff. See the country introduction for embassy and consulate addresses abroad.

Most travel insurance policies, including the Club's Red Pennant Overseas Holiday Insurance, will cover you for only a limited amount of lost or stolen cash (usually between £250 and £500) and you will probably have to wait until you return home for reimbursement.

The Euro

The Euro is the currency in use in many countries in Europe. Each country's versions of banknotes and coins are valid in all the countries of the single currency euro zone.

Police have issued warnings that counterfeit euro notes are in circulation on the Continent. You should be aware and take all precautions to ensure that €10, €20 and €50 notes and €2 coins that you receive from sources other than banks and legitimate bureaux de change (for example any money received as change) are genuine.

Holiday Money Security

Treat your cards as carefully as you would cash. Use a money belt, if possible, to conceal cards and valuables and do not keep all your cash and cards in the same place. Split cash between members of your party. Memorise your PINs and never keep them with your credit/debit cards.

If you keep a wallet in your pocket, place a rubber band around it, as it is then more difficult for a pickpocket to slide the wallet out without your noticing.

To avoid credit or debit card 'cloning' or 'skimming' never let your card out of your sight. In restaurants follow the waiter to the till or insist that the card machine is brought to your table. If you do allow your card to be taken and it is gone for more than a minute, become suspicious.

If you suspect your card has been fraudulently used, or if your card is lost or stolen, or if a cash machine retains it, call the issuing bank immediately. All the major card companies and banks operate a 24-hour emergency helpline.

If you are unlucky enough to become a victim of fraud your bank should refund the money stolen, provided you have not been negligent or careless.

Keep your card's magnetic strip away from other cards and objects, especially if they are also magnetic. If the card is damaged in any way electronic terminals may not accept your transaction.

If you use Travellers' Cheques keep a separate note of their serial numbers in case of loss, and a record of where and when you cash them. If they are lost or stolen, contact the appropriate refund service immediately.

Carry your credit card issuer/ bank's 24 hour UK helpline number with you in the event of loss or theft

Carry your credit card issuer/bank's 24-hour UK helpline number with you. You might also want to consider joining a card protection plan so that in the event of loss or theft, one telephone call will cancel all your cards and arrange replacements.

Take care when using cash machines. If the machine is obstructed or poorly lit, avoid it. If someone near the machine is behaving suspiciously or makes you feel uneasy, find another one. If there is something unusual about the cash machine do not use it and report the matter to the bank or owner of the premises. Do not accept help from strangers and do not allow yourself to be distracted.

Always log off from internet banking upon completion of your session

Be aware of your surroundings and if someone is watching you closely do not proceed with the transaction. Shield the screen and keyboard so that anyone waiting to use the machine cannot see you enter your PIN or transaction amount. Put your cash, card and receipt away immediately. Count your cash later and always keep your receipt to compare with your monthly statement.

If you bank over the internet and are using a computer in a public place such as a library or internet café, do not leave the PC unattended and ensure that no-one is watching what you type. Always log off from internet banking upon completion of your session to prevent the viewing of previous pages of your online session.

The cost of credit and debit card fraud is largely borne by banks and ultimately its customers, but the direct cost to cardholders should not be under-estimated in terms of inconvenience and frustration, not to mention the time taken for incidents to be investigated and fraudently withdrawn funds to be returned to your account. There is the additional danger of identity theft.

Learn more about card fraud and preventative measures to combat it on www.cardwatch.org.uk.

See also *Security and Safety* in the section *DURING YOUR STAY.*

Planning and Travelling
General Motoring Advice - Europe

Preparing For Your Journey

Adequate and careful preparation of your vehicles should be your first priority to ensure a safe and trouble free journey. Make sure your car and caravan, or motorhome, are properly serviced before you depart and take a well equipped spares kit and a spare wheel and tyre for your caravan to avoid any unnecessary disruptions to your holiday.

If you are a member of The Caravan Club re-read the Technical Information section of your UK Sites Directory & Handbook as it contains a wealth of information which is relevant to caravanning anywhere in the world.

Whether you are newcomers to caravanning or old hands, The Caravan Club offers a free advice service to Club members on technical and general caravanning matters, and also publishes information leaflets on a wide range of topics, all of which members can download from the Club's website. Alternatively, write to the Club's Technical Department or telephone for more details. For advice on issues specific to countries other than the UK, Club members should contact the Travel Service Information Officer, email: travelserviceinfo@caravanclub.co.uk.

Documentation

Along with your driving licence always carry your Vehicle Registration Certificate (V5C) or the Vehicle on Hire Certificate (VE103), insurance certificate and MOT certificate (if applicable) when taking your vehicle abroad. You are also strongly advised to carry a copy of your Caravan Registration Identification Scheme (CRIS) document. You may be asked to show these documents when entering some countries.

If you are driving a hired or borrowed vehicle you must be in possession of a letter of authorisation from the owner, or a hire agreement.

*See **Documents** in the section **PLANNING AND TRAVELLING***

Weight Limits

From both a legal and a safety point of view, it is essential not to exceed vehicle weight limits. European authorities are alert to the danger of over-weight vehicles and drivers are advised to carry with them documentation confirming their vehicle's maximum permitted laden weight. If your Vehicle Registration Certificate (V5C) does not clearly state this, you will need to produce alternative certification, e.g. from a weighbridge.

If your vehicle(s) are pulled over by the police and you cannot produce this documentation you may have to accompany police to a weighbridge. Subsequently if your vehicle(s) are found to be overweight you will be liable to a fine and may have to jettison items. The Caravan Club, therefore, recommends a trip to a local weighbridge with your vehicle(s) fully laden before embarking on your holiday.

Some Final Checks

Experienced caravanners will be familiar with the checks necessary before setting off and the following list is a reminder:

- All car and caravan lights are working and sets of spare bulbs are packed
- The coupling is correctly seated on the towball and the breakaway cable is attached
- All windows, vents, hatches and doors are shut
- All on-board water systems are drained
- All mirrors are adjusted for maximum visibility
- Corner steadies are fully wound up and the brace is handy for your arrival on site
- Any fires or flames are extinguished and the gas cylinder tap is turned off. Fire extinguishers are fully charged and close at hand
- The over-run brake is working correctly
- The jockey wheel is raised and secured, the handbrake is released.

Driving On The Continent

Probably the main disincentive to driving abroad, particularly for caravanners, is the need to keep to the right-hand side of the road. However, for most people this proves to be no problem at all after the first hour or so. There are a few basic, but important, points to remember:

- Buy a good road map or atlas and plan ahead to use roads suitable for towing. See *Route Planning and GPS* in the chapter *Motoring – Equipment.*

- In your eagerness to reach your destination, don't attempt vast distances in a single stint. Share the driving, if possible, and plan to break your journey overnight at a suitable campsite. There are many sites listed in this guide and a lot of them are well situated near to motorways and main roads.

- Adjust all your mirrors for maximum rear-view observation. The vast majority of towed caravans – whatever the type of towing vehicle – will require extension mirrors to comply with legal requirements for an adequate rearwards view.

- Make sure the road ahead is clear before overtaking. Stay well behind the vehicle in front and, if possible, have someone with good judgement in the left-hand seat to give you the 'all clear'.

- If traffic builds up behind you, pull over safely and let it pass.

- Pay particular attention when turning left, when leaving a rest area/petrol station/campsite, or after passing through a one-way system, to ensure that you continue to drive on the right-hand side of the road.

- If your headlights are likely to dazzle other road users, adjust them to deflect to the right instead of the left, using suitable beam deflectors or (in some cases) a built-in adjustment system. Some lights can have the deflective part of the lens obscured with tape or a pre-cut adhesive mask, but check in your car's handbook if this is permitted or not. Some lights run too hot to be partially obscured in this way.

- When travelling, particularly in the height of the summer, it is wise to stop at least every two hours to stretch your legs and take a break.

- In case of a breakdown or accident, use hazard warning lights and warning triangle(s). Remember to wear a reflective jacket or waistcoat if you leave your vehicle.

Another disincentive for caravanners to travel abroad is the worry about roads and gradients in mountainous countries. However, Britain has steeper gradients on many of its main roads than many other European countries and traffic density is higher.

The chapter *Mountain Passes and Tunnels* under *PLANNING AND TRAVELLING* gives detailed advice on using mountain passes.

Another worry involves vehicle breakdown and language difficulties. The Caravan Club's comprehensive and competitively priced Red Pennant Overseas Holiday Insurance is geared to handle all these contingencies with multi-lingual staff available at the Club's headquarters 24 hours a day throughout the year – see www.caravanclub.co.uk/redpennant.

Driving Offences

You are obliged to comply with the traffic rules and regulations of the countries you visit. Research shows that non-resident drivers are more likely to take risks and break the law due to their feeling of impunity.

However, a number of bi-lateral agreements exist between European countries which means that there is no escaping penalty notices and demands for payment for motoring offences.

Make sure you are familiar with traffic laws in the countries you plan to visit, including speed limits and equipment you are legally required to carry. See the *Speed Limits* and *Essential Equipment* tables later in this guide and the additional information contained in the Country Introduction chapters.

Some foreign police officers can look rather intimidating to British visitors used to unarmed police. Needless to say, they expect you to be polite and show respect and, in return, they are generally helpful and may well be lenient to a visiting motorist. Never consider offering a bribe!

The authorities in many countries are hard on parking and speeding offenders. Visiting motorists should not be influenced by the speed at which locals drive; they often know where the speed traps are and can slow down in time to avoid being caught! In general, it is no use protesting if caught, as anyone who refuses to pay may have their vehicle impounded.

Be particularly careful if you have penalty points on your driving licence. If you commit an offence on the Continent which attracts penalty points, local police may well do checks on your licence to establish whether the addition of those points renders you liable to disqualification. If so you would then have to find other means to get yourself and your vehicle(s) home.

Many police forces are authorised to carry out random breath tests

Drink-Driving

The maximum legal level of alcohol in the blood in most Continental countries is lower than that in the UK (in some it is zero), and many police forces are authorised to carry out random breath tests. It is wise to adopt the 'no drink when driving' rule at all times; offenders are heavily fined all over Europe and penalties can include confiscation of driving licence, vehicle(s) and even imprisonment. For more detailed information see the Country Introduction chapter.

It has been a legal requirement to carry an NF approved breathalyzer in France since the 1st July 2012. For more information see the Essential Equipment chapter of this guide.

On-the-Spot Fines

Many countries allow their police officers to issue fines which must be paid immediately, up to certain limits. The fine may be a deposit for a larger fine which will be issued to your home address. In most countries credit cards are not accepted in payment of on-the-spot fines and you may find yourself accompanied to the nearest cash machine. Always obtain a receipt for money handed over.

Fuel

During ferry crossings make sure your petrol tank is not over-full. Don't be tempted to carry spare petrol in cans; the ferry companies and Eurotunnel forbid this practice and even the carriage of empty cans is prohibited.

Grades of petrol sold on the Continent are comparable to those sold in the UK with the same familiar brands; 95 octane is frequently known as 'Essence' and 98 octane as 'Super'. Diesel is sometimes called 'Gasoil' and is normally available in all the countries covered in the Caravan Europe guides. The fuel prices given in the table at the end of this chapter were correct according to the latest information available at the time of publication. Members of The Caravan Club can also check current fuel prices by visiting www.caravanclub.co.uk/overseasadvice.

In sparsely populated regions it is a sensible precaution to travel with a full petrol tank and to keep it topped up. Similarly in remote rural areas in any country you may have difficulty finding a manned petrol station at night or on Sundays. Petrol stations offering a 24-hour service may involve an automated process which occasionally work only with locally issued credit cards.

*See the **Fuel Price Guide Table** at the end of this chapter.*

Automotive Liquified Petroleum Gas (LPG)

The increasing popularity of LPG – known as 'autogas' or GPL – and use of dual-fuelled vehicles means that the availability of automotive LPG has become an important issue for some drivers, and the Country Introductions provide more information.

There are different tank-filling openings in use in different countries. Pending the adoption of a common European filling system, UKLPG, the trade association for the LPG industry in the UK, and the major fuel suppliers recommend the use of either of the two types of Dutch bayonet fitting. UKLPG also recommends that vehicle-filling connections requiring the use of adaptors in order to fill with the Dutch bayonet filling gun should not be used. However, The Club recognises that in some circumstances it may be necessary to use an adaptor and these are available from Autogas 2000 Ltd on 01845 523213, www.autogas.co.uk.

E10 Petrol

E10 Petrol (containing 10% Ethanol) is available in some European countries (notably France, Germany and Finland) and is likely to become more common in coming years For more details about E10 fuel, see www.lowcvp.org.uk/e10

Most modern cars are E10 compatible, but some are not and could be damaged by using it. Check whether your vehicle is compatible in your vehicle handbook or online at www.acea.be/news/news_detail/vehicle_compatibility_with_new_fuel_standard/

Lead Replacement Petrol

Leaded petrol has been withdrawn from sale in many countries in Europe and, in general, is only available from petrol stations in the form of a bottled additive. Where lead replacement petrol is still available at the pump it is generally from the same pumps previously used for leaded petrol, i.e. red or black pumps, and may be labelled 'Super Plus', 'Super 98' or 'Super MLV', but it is advisable to check before filling up if this is not clear from information at the pump.

Low Emission Zones

Many cities in countries around Europe have introduced 'Low Emission Zones' (LEZ) in order to regulate vehicle pollution levels. Some schemes require you to buy a windscreen sticker, pay a fee or register your vehicle before entering the zone and you may need to show proof that your vehicle meets the required standard.

Before you travel visit the website www.lowemissionzones.eu for maps showing the locations of LEZs. See the Country Introductions for country specific information on LEZs.

Motorhomes Towing Cars

A motorhome towing a small car using an A-frame or towing dolly is illegal in most European countries, although such units are sometimes encountered. Motorhome users wishing to tow a small car abroad should transport it on a braked trailer so that all four of the car's wheels are off the road.

Motorway Tolls

For British drivers who may never, or rarely, have encountered a toll booth, there are a couple of points to bear in mind. First of all, you will be on the 'wrong' side of the car for the collection of toll tickets at the start of the motorway section and payment of tolls at the end. If you are travelling without a front seat passenger, this can mean a big stretch or a walk round to the other side of the car. Most toll booths are solidly built and you should be careful of any high concrete kerbs when pulling up to them.

On entering a stretch of motorway you will usually have to stop at a barrier and take a ticket from a machine to allow the barrier to rise. Avoid the lanes dedicated to vehicles displaying electronic season tickets. You may encounter toll booths without automatic barriers where it is still necessary to take a ticket and, if you pass through without doing so, you may be fined. On some stretches of motorway there are no ticket machines as you enter and you simply pay a fixed sum when you exit.

Your toll ticket will indicate the time you entered the motorway. Be warned that in some countries electronic tills at exit booths calculate the distance a vehicle has travelled and the journey time. The police are automatically informed if speeding has taken place and fines are imposed.

Payment can be made by credit cards in most, but not all countries.

See the Country Introduction chapters for specific information.

Parking

Make sure you check local parking regulations, as fines may be imposed and unattended vehicles clamped or towed away. Look out for road markings and for short-term parking zones. It might be helpful to make a note of the words for the days of the week in the local language and the words for 'height', 'length', 'over' for example.

Ensure you are in possession of parking discs in towns where they are required. As a general rule, park on the right-hand side of the road in the direction of traffic flow, avoiding cycle and bus lanes and tram tracks. Vehicles should not cause an obstruction and should be adequately lit when parked at night.

The following are some signs that you may encounter.

No parking on Monday, Wednesday Friday or Sunday   No parking on Tuesday, Thursday or Saturday   Fortnightly parking on alternative sides

No parking from the 1st-15th of the month   No parking from the 16th-end of the month

In parts of central Europe car theft may be a problem and you are advised to park only in officially designated, guarded car parks whenever possible.

Parking Facilities for the Disabled

The Blue Badge is recognised in most European countries and it allows disabled motorists to use the same parking concessions enjoyed by the citizens of the country you are visiting. Concessions differ from country to country, however, and it is important to know when and where you can and, more importantly, cannot park. If you are in any doubt about your rights, do not park.

The FIA have a website which offers a guide to the concessions availble to Blue Badge holders in countries inside and outside of the EU.
See www.fiadisabledtravellers.com.

Priority and Roundabouts

When driving on the Continent it is essential to be aware of other vehicles which may have priority over you, particularly when they join from the right into the road you are using. Road signs indicate priority or loss of priority and motorists must be sure that they understand the signs.

> ### Never rely on being given right of way, even if you have priority

Care should be taken at intersections and you should never rely on being given right of way, even if you have priority, especially in small towns and villages where local, often slow-moving, traffic will take right of way. Always give way to public service and military vehicles and to buses, trams and coaches.

In some countries in Europe priority at roundabouts is given to vehicles entering the roundabout (i.e. on the right) unless signposted on the contrary. This is a reversal of the UK rule and care is needed.

See the Country Introduction Chapter for more information.

Public Transport

In general in built-up areas be prepared to stop to allow a bus to pull out from a bus stop when the driver is signalling his intention to do so. Take particular care when school buses have stopped and passengers are getting on and off.

Overtaking trams in motion is normally only permitted on the right, unless on a one way street where you can overtake on the left if there is not enough space on the right. Do not overtake a tram near a tram stop. These may be in the centre of the road. When a tram or bus stops to allow passengers on and off, you should stop to allow them to cross to the pavement. Give way to trams which are turning across your carriageway.

Do not park so as to obstruct tram lines or force other drivers to do so; trams cannot steer round obstructions! Take care when crossing tram tracks, especially if the rails are wet, and be particularly careful when crossing them at shallow angles, on bends and at junctions.

Road Signs and Markings

Many road signs have the same general design in most countries in Europe making them fairly easily recognisable. Blue and green direction and marker signs are used to identify motorways and main roads but their use may be the opposite of that in the UK, i.e. motorways marked by green signs and main roads

by blue. This can be particularly confusing, for example when crossing from France where motorway signs are blue, into Switzerland or Italy where they are green.

Where text descriptions rather than symbols are used on information signs it can be helpful to make a note of a few basic words for flood, diversion, by-pass, etc. The country introduction lists a few such basic words and phrases in the local language for your reference.

You will often encounter STOP signs in situations which, in the UK, would probably be covered by a Give Way sign. Be particularly careful – coming to a complete halt is usually compulsory, even if local drivers seem unconcerned by it, and failure to do so may result in a fine. Be careful too in areas where maintenance of roads may be irregular and where white lines have been worn away.

A solid single or double white line in the middle of the carriageway always means no overtaking.

Direction signs in general may be confusing, giving only the name of a town on the way to a larger city, or simply the road number and no place name. They may be smaller than you expect and not particularly easy to spot.

Across the EU you will find that major routes have not only an individual road number, such as A6, but also a number beginning with an 'E' displayed on green and white signs. Routes running from east to west have even 'E' numbers, whereas routes running from north to south have odd 'E' numbers. This can be helpful when planning long-distance routes across international frontiers.

In some countries, particularly in Scandinavia and Belgium, through routes or motorways may only show the 'E' road numbers, so it would be advisable to make a note of them when planning your route. The E road system is not recognised in the UK and there are no such road signs.

Pedestrian Crossings

Stopping to allow pedestrians to cross at zebra crossings is not nearly as common a practice on the Continent as it is in the UK. Pedestrians often do not expect to cross until the road is clear and may be surprised if you stop to allow them to do so. Check your mirrors carefully when braking as other drivers behind you, not expecting to stop, may be taken by surprise. The result may be a rear-end shunt or, worse still, vehicles overtaking you at the crossing and putting pedestrians at risk.

Speed Limits

Remember speed limit signs are in kilometres per hour, not miles per hour. General speed limits are given in the table at the end of this chapter. Refer to the Country Introduction for detailed information.

Radar-detection devices, whether in use or not, are illegal in many countries on the Continent and should not be carried at all. If you have one in your vehicle remove it before leaving home.

Speed cameras are becoming more widespread throughout Europe but you should not expect them to be highly visible as they are in the UK. In many instances, for example on the German motorway network, they may be hidden or deliberately inconspicuous. The use of unmarked police cars using speed detection equipment is common.

See the item *Radar/Speed Camera Detectors* in the chapter *Motoring – Equipment.*

Traffic Lights

Traffic lights may not be placed as conspicuously as they are in the UK, for instance they may be smaller, differently shaped or suspended across the road, with a smaller set on a post at the roadside. You may find that lights change directly from red to green, by-passing amber completely. Flashing amber lights generally indicate that you may proceed with caution if it is safe to do so but must give way to pedestrians and other vehicles.

> **Be cautious when approaching a green light, especially in fast-moving traffic**

A green filter light should be treated with caution as you may still have to give way to pedestrians who have a green light to cross the road.

You may find that drivers are not particularly well-disciplined about stopping as they approach a light as it turns red and if they are behind you in this situation, they will expect you to accelerate through the lights rather than brake hard to stop. Therefore be cautious when approaching a green light, especially if you are in a relatively fast-moving stream of traffic.

Similarly, be careful when pulling away from a green light and check left and right just in case a driver on the road crossing yours has jumped a red light.

Winter Driving

If you regularly caravan in wintry conditions a four-wheel drive car or all-terrain vehicle may be a good investment. An ABS braking system offers significant advantages as do other comforts such as heated seats and steering wheels.

Winter driving abroad requires extra preparation and caution, especially if you are heading for mountainous areas or to northern Europe. Major mountain passes are kept open in winter except in particularly extreme conditions. Otherwise keep to main roads wherever possible as they are more likely to be clear of snow and ice, and adjust your speed and driving technique to the road conditions. Scenic diversions are probably not a good idea in the depths of winter.

The law in some countries requires the fitting of winter tyres and/or the use of snow chains – see *Winter Tyres and Snow Chains* in the chapter *Motoring – Equipment.*

You can also visit www.caravanclub.co.uk/overseasadvice to access and download the Winter Equipment Requirements leaflet.

Fuel Price Guide
Prices per litre as at August 2013

Country	Unleaded		Diesel	
	Unleaded	Translation of Unleaded	Diesel	Translation of Diesel
Andorra (EUR)	1.29 (95) 1.36 (98)	Sans plomb or sin plomo	1.16	Gazole or gasóleo
Austria (EUR)	1.41 (95) 1.54 (98)	Bleifrei	1.35	Diesel
Belgium (EUR)	1.68 (95) 1.73 (98)	Sans plomb or loodvrije	1.47	
Croatia (HRK)	10.69 (95) 10.95 (98)	Eurosuper or bez olova	9.89	Dizel
Czech Republic (CZK)	36.30 (95)	Natural or bez olova	35.80	Nafta
Denmark (DKK)	13.19 (95) 13.62 (98)	Blyfri	11.68	
Finland (EUR)	1.64 (95) 1.70 (98)	Lyijyton polttoaine	1.49	
France (EUR)	1.54 (95) 1.61 (98)	Essence sans plomb	1.35	Gazole
Germany (EUR)	1.60 (95) 1.64 (98)	Bleifrei	1.40	Diesel
Greece (EUR)	1.75 (95) 1.92 (98)	Amoliwdi wensina	1.48	Petreleo
Hungary (HUF)	414 (95)	Olommentes uzemanyag	422	Dizel or gázolaj
Italy (EUR)	1.78 (95) 1.93 (98)	Sensa piombo	1.66	Gasolio
Luxembourg (EUR)	1.35 (95) 1.40 (98)	Sans plomb	1.21	Gazole
Netherlands (EUR)	1.83 (95) 1.90 (98)	Loodvrije	1.48	Diesel or gasolie
Norway (NOK)	15.56 (95) 16.31 (98)	Blyfri bensin	14.15	Diesel
Poland (PLN)	5.50 (95) or 5.78 (98)	Bezolowiu	5.49	
Portugal (EUR)	1.60 (95) 1.68 (98)	Sem chumbo	1.38	Gasóleo or diesel
Slovakia (EUR)	1.48 (95) 1.66 (98)	Natural or olovnatych prisad	1.35	Nafta
Slovenia (EUR)	1.49 (95) 1.51 (98)	Brez svinca	1.36	
Spain (EUR)	1.46 (95) 1.57 (98)	Sin plomo	1.38	Gasóleo A or Gas-oil
Sweden (SEK)	14.78 (95) 15.28 (98)	Blyfri normal, premium	14.58	Diesel
Switzerland (CHF)	1.83 (95) 1.89 (98)	Bleifrei or sans plomb or sensa piomba	1.90	Diesel or gazole or gasolio
UK (GBP)	1.37 (95) 1.45 (98)		1.42	

Fuel prices courtesy of the AIT/FIA Information Centre (OTA) (August 2013)

Prices shown are in local currency, price per litre. The contents are belived to be correct at the date of publication but should be used for guideline purposes only. Differences in prices actually paid may be due to currency and oil price fluctuations as well as regional variations within countries.

Please note that fuel prices can change significantly in a short space of time. For the most recent fuel prices please visit www.caravanclub.co.uk/overseasadvice where the fuel price guide is updated on a monthly basis.

Speed Limits

Kilometres per hour (see Conversion Table below for equivalent miles per hour)

Country	Open Road			Motorways		
	Solo*	Towing	Motorhome (3,500-7,500kg)	Solo*	Towing	Motorhome (3,500-7,500kg)
Andorra	60-90	60-90	60-90	n/a	n/a	n/a
Austria	100	80***	70	100-130	100***	80
Belgium	90	90	90	120	120	90
Croatia	90-110	80	80	110-130	90	90
Czech Republic	80-90	80	80	130	80	80
Denmark	80-90	70	70	110-130	80	70
Finland	80-100	70-80	80	100-120 (100 for motorhome under 3,500kg)	80	80
France**	90-110	80-110**	80-100	110-130	90-130**	90-110
Germany	100	80	80	130	80	100
Greece	90-110 (80 for motorhome under 3,500kg)	80	80	130 (90 for motorhome under 3,500kg)	80	80
Hungary	90-110	70	70	130	80	80
Italy	90-110	70	80	130	80	100
Luxembourg	90	75	90	130	90	130
Netherlands	80-90	80-90***	80	120	90***	80
Norway	80	80	80	90-100	80	80
Poland	90-120	70-80	70-80	140	80	80
Portugal	90-100	70-80	70-90	120	100	100
Slovakia	90	90	80	130	90	80
Slovenia	90-100	80	80	130	80	80
Spain	90-100 (80-90 for motorhome under 3,500kg)	70-80	80	120 (100 for motorhome under 3,500kg)	80	90
Sweden ****	70-100	70-80	70-100	90-120	80	90-120
Switzerland	80-100	60-80	80	100-120	80	80

Converting Kilometres to Miles

km/h	20	30	40	50	60	70	80	90	100	110	120	130
mph	13	18	25	31	37	44	50	56	62	68	74	81

* Also including motorhomes under 3,500kg unless otherwise stated.
** Speed limits when towing a caravan/trailer in France is based on the gross train mass of your car/vehicle combination. If the gross train mass of the car/vehicle is over 3,500kg the speed limit is 90kph on motorways and 80-90kph on open roads. If the gross train mass of car/ vehicle is under 3,500kg the speed limit is 130kph on motorways and 90-110kph on open roads. To work out the gross train mass of your car/vehicle you need to add the fully laden weight of your car to your cars towing limit. For further information and for an example please visit www.caravanclub.co.uk/overseastravel. Please note that for vehicles permitted to drive at the maximum speed limits (130kph and 90 - 110kph), these reduce to 110kph and 80-100kph in adverse weather conditions.
*** If the combined weight of your car and caravan is over 3,500kg then the speed limit is the same as a motorhome over 3,500kg.
**** Speed limits vary greatly in Sweden and are dependent on the quality and safety of the road.

NOTES: 1) See Country Introductions in the relevant guides for further details, including special speed limits, where applicable.
2) Speed limits in built-up areas are generally much lower, and in some countries speed limits in residential areas may be as low as 20kph.
3) All information on this page is believed to be correct at the time of publication but may be subject to change. Speed limits often vary and some countries may trial new speed limits on certain roads and motorways. Check before you travel and always look for signs advising of speed limits on the journey. Please visit www.caravanclub.co.uk/overseasadvice to check the latest speed limits before you travel and for more detailed information and advice.

Distances are shown in kilometres and are calculated from town/city centres along the most practical roads, although not necessarily taking the shortest route.

1km = 0.62 miles

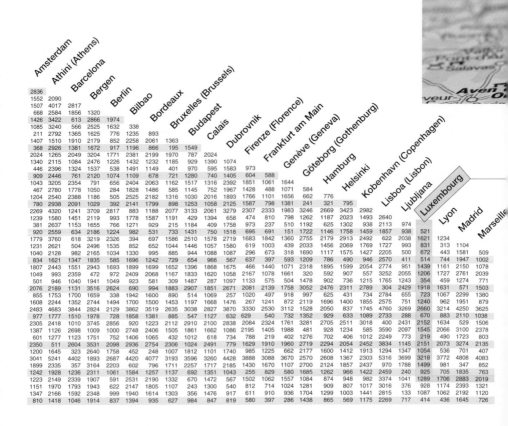

City column headers (diagonal labels):
1. Amsterdam
2. Athini (Athens)
3. Barcelona
4. Bergen
5. Berlin
6. Bilbao
7. Bordeaux
8. Bruxelles (Brussels)
9. Budapest
10. Calais
11. Dubrovnik
12. Firenze (Florence)
13. Frankfurt am Main
14. Genève (Geneva)
15. Göteborg (Gothenburg)
16. Hamburg
17. Helsinki
18. Kobenhavn (Copenhagen)
19. Lisboa (Lisbon)
20. Ljubljana
21. Luxembourg
22. Lyon
23. Madrid
24. Marseille

Amsterdam	Athini	Barcelona	Bergen	Berlin	Bilbao	Bordeaux	Bruxelles	Budapest	Calais	Dubrovnik	Firenze	Frankfurt	Genève	Göteborg	Hamburg	Helsinki	Kobenhavn	Lisboa	Ljubljana	Luxembourg	Lyon	Madrid	Marseille
2836																							
1552	2090																						
1507	4017	2817																					
668	2584	1856	1320																				
1426	3422	613	2866	1974																			
1085	3240	566	2525	1632	338																		
211	2792	1365	1625	776	1235	893																	
1407	1510	1910	2179	852	2258	2061	1363																
368	2926	1381	1672	917	1196	866	195	1549															
2024	1265	2049	3204	1771	2381	2199	1970	787	2024														
1340	2115	1084	2476	1226	1432	1232	1185	929	1390	1074													
446	2396	1324	1537	538	1491	1149	401	970	595	1583	973												
909	2446	761	2120	1074	1109	678	721	1280	740	1405	604	588											
1043	3205	2354	791	656	2404	2063	1162	1517	1316	2392	1851	1061	1644										
467	2780	1778	1050	284	1828	1486	585	1145	752	1967	1428	488	1071	584									
1204	2540	2388	1186	505	2525	2182	1316	1030	2016	1893	1766	1101	1656	662	776								
780	2938	2091	1029	392	2141	1799	898	1253	1058	2125	1587	798	1381	241	321	795							
2269	4320	1241	3709	2817	883	1188	2077	3133	2061	3279	2307	1983	3246	2669	3423	2982							
1239	1580	1451	2119	993	1778	1587	1191	429	1394	658	474	810	798	1262	1187	2023	1493	2640					
381	2637	1153	1655	766	1271	929	215	1184	409	1758	973	237	510	1192	625	1302	938	2113	974				
920	2559	634	2186	1224	982	531	733	1431	750	1518	695	691	151	1722	1146	1758	1459	1857	938	521			
1779	3760	618	3219	2326	394	697	1586	2510	1578	2719	1683	1842	1360	2755	2179	2913	2492	622	2038	1621	1234		
1231	2621	504	2496	1535	852	652	1044	1446	1057	1580	619	1003	439	2033	1456	2069	1769	1727	993	831	313	1104	
1040	2128	982	2165	1034	1330	995	885	944	1088	1087	296	673	318	1690	1117	1575	1427	2205	500	672	443	1581	509
834	1621	1347	1835	585	1696	1242	729	654	966	567	637	397	593	1209	786	490	946	2570	411	514	744	1947	1002
1807	2443	1551	2943	1693	1899	1699	1652	1396	1868	1675	466	1440	1071	2318	1895	1599	2054	2774	951	1439	1161	2150	1078
1049	993	2359	472	972	2409	2068	1167	1833	1620	2167	1078	1661	320	592	907	557	3252	2055	1206	1727	2761	2039	
501	946	1040	1941	1049	923	581	309	1487	287	1097	1133	575	504	1478	902	736	1215	1765	1243	354	459	1274	771
2076	2189	1131	3516	2624	690	994	1883	2907	1851	2671	2081	2139	1758	3052	2476	2311	2789	304	2429	1918	1631	571	1503
855	1753	1700	1659	338	1942	1600	890	514	1069	257	1020	497	918	997	625	431	734	2784	655	723	1067	2299	1380
1608	2244	1352	2744	1494	1700	1500	1453	1197	1668	1476	267	1241	872	2119	1696	1400	1855	2575	751	1240	962	1951	879
2483	4683	3844	2824	2129	3862	3519	2635	3038	2827	3870	3330	2530	3112	1528	2050	837	1745	4760	3269	2660	3214	4250	3625
977	1777	1510	1978	728	1858	1381	885	547	1127	632	629	540	732	1352	929	633	1089	2733	288	670	883	2110	1038
2305	2418	1010	3745	2856	920	1223	2112	2910	2100	2838	2084	2324	1761	3281	2705	2511	3018	400	2431	2152	1634	529	1506
1387	1126	2698	1009	1000	2748	2406	1505	1861	1662	1086	2195	1405	1988	481	928	1234	585	3590	2097	1545	2066	3100	2378
601	1277	1123	1751	752	1406	1065	432	1012	618	734	788	219	402	1276	702	406	1012	2249	773	219	490	1723	803
2350	511	2604	3531	2098	2936	2754	2306	1024	2491	779	1629	1910	1960	2719	2294	2054	2452	3834	1145	2151	2073	3274	2135
1200	1645	323	2640	1758	452	248	1007	1812	1101	1740	985	1225	662	2177	1600	1412	1913	1294	1347	1054	536	701	407
3041	5241	4402	1893	2687	4420	4077	3193	3596	3260	4428	3888	3088	3670	2570	2608	1367	2303	5316	3699	3218	3772	4808	4083
1899	2335	357	3164	2203	602	796	1711	2257	1717	2185	1430	1670	1107	2700	2124	1857	2437	970	1788	1499	981	347	852
1242	1928	1236	2311	1061	1584	1257	1137	692	1351	1043	255	829	580	1685	1262	966	1422	2459	240	925	705	1835	763
1223	2149	2339	1907	591	2531	2190	1332	670	1472	567	1502	1062	1557	1084	874	948	982	3374	1041	1289	1706	2883	2019
1151	1970	1793	1943	622	2147	1805	1107	243	1300	540	812	714	1024	1281	909	807	1017	3016	376	928	1174	2393	1321
1347	2166	1592	2348	999	1940	1614	1303	356	1476	917	611	910	936	1704	1299	1003	1441	2815	133	1087	1062	2192	1120
810	1418	1046	1914	837	1394	935	627	984	847	819	580	397	286	1438	865	569	1175	2269	717	414	436	1645	726

Luxembourg - Warszawa (Warsaw) = 1289 km

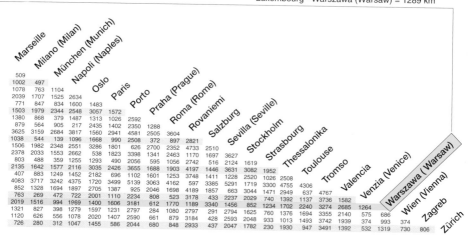

Distance chart (km). Column headers in order: Marseille, Milano (Milan), München (Munich), Napoli (Naples), Oslo, Paris, Porto, Praha (Prague), Roma (Rome), Rovaniemi, Salzburg, Sevilla (Seville), Stockholm, Strasbourg, Thessalonika, Toulouse, Tromso, Valencia, Venzia (Venice), Warszawa (Warsaw), Wien (Vienna), Zagreb, Zürich

	Marseille	Milano	München	Napoli	Oslo	Paris	Porto	Praha	Roma	Rovaniemi	Salzburg	Sevilla	Stockholm	Strasbourg	Thessalonika	Toulouse	Tromso	Valencia	Venzia	Warszawa	Wien	Zagreb
Milano (Milan)	509																					
München (Munich)	1002	497																				
Napoli (Naples)	1078	763	1104																			
Oslo	2039	1707	1525	2634																		
Paris	771	847	834	1600	1483																	
Porto	1503	1979	2344	2548	3057	1572																
Praha (Prague)	1380	868	379	1487	1313	1026	2592															
Roma (Rome)	879	564	905	217	2435	1402	2350	1288														
Rovaniemi	3625	3159	2684	3817	1560	2941	4581	2505	3604													
Salzburg	1038	544	139	1096	1668	990	2508	372	897	2821												
Sevilla (Seville)	1506	1982	2348	2551	3286	1801	626	2700	2352	4733	2510											
Stockholm	2378	2033	1553	2662	538	1823	3398	1341	2463	1170	1697	3627										
Strasbourg	803	488	359	1255	1293	490	2056	595	1056	2742	516	2124	1619									
Thessalonika	2135	1642	1577	2116	3035	2426	3655	1688	1903	4197	1446	3631	3082	1952								
Toulouse	407	883	1249	1452	2182	696	1102	1601	1253	3748	1411	1228	2520	1026	2508							
Tromso	4083	3717	3242	4375	1720	3499	5139	3063	4162	597	3385	5291	1719	3300	4755	4306						
Valencia	852	1328	1694	1897	2705	1387	925	2046	1698	4189	1857	663	3044	1471	2949	637	4767					
Venzia (Venice)	763	269	472	722	2001	1110	2234	808	523	3178	433	2237	2029	740	1392	1137	3736	1582				
Warszawa (Warsaw)	2019	1516	994	1969	1400	1606	3181	612	1770	1189	3340	1456	852	1234	1702	2240	3274	2685	1264			
Wien (Vienna)	1321	827	398	1279	1597	1231	2797	284	1080	2797	291	2794	1625	760	1376	1694	3355	2140	575	686		
Zagreb	1120	626	556	1078	2020	1407	2590	661	879	3184	428	2593	2048	933	1013	1493	3742	1939	374	993	374	
Zürich	726	280	312	1047	1455	586	2044	680	848	2933	437	2047	1782	230	1930	947	3491	1392	532	1319	730	806

Route Planning

Planning and Travelling
Motoring - Equipment

Please note equipment requirements and regulations change frequently. To keep up to date with the latest equipment information please visit www.caravanclub.co.uk/overseasadvice

Bicycle and Motorbike Transportation

Regulations vary from country to country but as a general rule separate registration and insurance documents are required for a motorbike or scooter and these vehicles, as well as bicycles, must be carried on an approved carrier in such a way that they do not obscure rear windows, lights, reflectors or number plates. Vehicles should not be overloaded, i.e. exceed the maximum loaded weight recommended by your vehicle manufacturer.

Car Telephones

It is illegal to use a hand-held car phone or mobile phone while driving. Hands-free equipment should be fitted in your vehicle if you must use the phone while driving.

First Aid Kit

A first aid kit, in a strong dust-proof box, should be carried in case of an emergency. This is a legal requirement in several countries in Europe and is a must have item regardless.

See *Essential Equipment Table* at the end of this chapter and the chapter *Medical Matters*.

Fire Extinguisher

As a recommended safety precaution, an approved fire extinguisher should be carried in all vehicles. This is a legal requirement in several countries in Europe.

See *Essential Equipment Table* at the end of this chapter.

Glasses

In some countries it is a legal requirement for residents to carry a spare pair of glasses if they are needed for driving, and it is recommended that visitors also comply. Elsewhere, if you do not have a spare pair, you may find it helpful to carry a copy of your prescription.

Lights

When driving on the Continent headlights need to be adjusted to deflect to the right if they are likely to dazzle other road users. This can be by means of suitable beam deflectors or (in some cases) a built-in adjustment system. Do not leave headlight conversion to the last minute as, in the case of some modern high-density discharge (HID), xenon or halogen-type lights, a dealer may need to make the necessary adjustment. Remember also to adjust headlights according to the load being carried and to compensate for the weight of the caravan on the back of your car.

Even if you do not intend to drive at night, it is important to ensure that your headlights will not dazzle others as you may need to use them in heavy rain or fog and in tunnels. If using tape or a pre-cut adhesive mask remember to remove it on your return home.

Dipped headlights should be used in poor weather conditions and in a tunnel even if it is well lit. You may find police waiting at the end of a tunnel to check vehicles. In some countries the use of dipped headlights is compulsory at all times, day and night, and in others they must be used in built-up areas, on motorways or at certain times of the year.

Take a full set of spare light bulbs. This is a legal requirement in several countries.

See *Essential Equipment Table* at the end of this chapter.

Headlight-Flashing

On the Continent headlight-flashing is used as a warning of approach or as an overtaking signal at night, and not, as is commonly the case in the UK, an indication that you are giving way, so use with great care in case it is misunderstood. When another driver flashes you, make sure of his intention before moving.

Hazard Warning Lights

Generally hazard warning lights should not be used in place of a warning triangle, but they may be used in addition to it.

Nationality Plate (GB/IRL)

A nationality plate of an authorised design must be fixed to the rear of both your car and caravan on a vertical or near-vertical surface. Checks are made and a fine may be imposed for failure to display a nationality plate correctly. These are provided free to members taking out the Caravan Club's Red Pennant Overseas Holiday Insurance. See www.caravanclub.co.uk/redpennant.

Regulations allow the optional display on number plates of the Euro-Symbol which is a circle of stars on a blue background with an EU Member State's national identification letter(s) below – e.g. GB or IRL. On UK-registered vehicles whose number plates incorporate the Euro-Symbol, the display of an additional GB sticker on a vehicle is unnecessary when driving within the EU and Switzerland. However, it is still required when driving outside the EU even when number plates incorporate the Euro-Symbol, and it is still required for all vehicles without Euro-Symbol plates.

GB is the only permissible national identification code for cars registered in the UK. Registration plates displaying the GB Euro-Symbol must comply with the appropriate British Standard.

Radar/Speed Camera Detectors

The possession or use of a radar-detection device, whether in use or not, is illegal in many countries on the Continent and you should not carry one in your vehicle. Penalties include fines, vehicle confiscation or a driving ban. Some countries also ban the use of GPS satellite navigation devices which pinpoint the position of fixed speed cameras and you must, therefore, deactivate the relevant Points of Interest (PoI) function. Alternatively some sat nav manufacturers offer acceptable alternative services, such as TomTom's 'Danger Zone' service in France, which highlights accident blackspots and the general area in which speed cameras are in operation.

Rear View External Mirrors

In order to comply with local regulations and avoid the attention of local police forces, ensure that your vehicle's external mirrors are adjusted correctly to allow you to view both sides of your caravan or trailer – over its entire length – from behind the steering wheel. Some countries stipulate that mirrors should extend beyond the width of the caravan but should be removed or folded in when travelling solo, and this is common-sense advice for all countries.

Reflective Jackets/Waistcoats

Legislation has been introduced in many countries in Europe (see individual Country Introductions in relevant guides) requiring drivers to wear a reflective jacket or waistcoat if leaving a vehicle which is immobilised on the carriageway outside a built-up area. A second jacket is also recommended for a passenger who may need to assist in an emergency repair. Carry the jackets in the passenger compartment of your vehicle, rather than in the boot. The jackets should conform to at least European Standard EN471, Class 2 and are available from motor accessory shops and from the Club's shop – see www.caravanclub.co.uk/shop.

Route Planning

An organisation called Keep Moving www.keepmoving.co.uk provides information on UK roads, tel 09003 401100 or 401100 from a mobile phone. The Highway Agency has information for roads in England, including channel port access, visit www.trafficengland.com. Both the AA and RAC have useful websites offering a route planning service: www.theaa.com and www.rac.co.uk. Other websites offering a European routes service and traffic information include www.viamichelin.com and www.mappy.com which also provides city centre maps for major towns across Europe.

Detailed, large-scale maps or atlases of the countries you are visiting are essential. Navigating your way around other countries can be confusing and the more care you take planning your route, the more enjoyable your journey will be.

If you propose travelling across mountain passes check whether the suggested route supplied by the route-planning website takes account of passes or tunnels where caravans are not permitted or recommended.

See the chapter *Mountain Passes and Tunnels*.

Satellite Navigation/GPS

Continental postcodes do not, on the whole, pinpoint a particular street or part of a street in the same way as the system in use in the UK. A French five-digit postcode, for example, can cover a very large area.

GPS co-ordinates are given for most site entries in this guide and wherever possible full street addresses are given, enabling you to programme your sat nav as accurately as possible.

It is important to remember that sat nav devices rarely allow for towing a caravan or driving a large motorhome and may try to send you down unsuitable roads. Always use your common sense, and if a road looks unsuitable find an alternative route.

You should always use your Sat nav in conjunction with the written directions provided in this guide, provided by members who have actually visited, and an up to date atlas or map. It may be best to programme your sat nav to a nearby village or road junction which is mentioned in the site directions and then follow the directions from that point rather than following sat nav. Please note the directions given in site entries have not been checked by The Caravan Club.

Update your sat nav device regularly and remember that, in spite of detailed directions and the use of a sat nav, local conditions such as road closures and roadworks may on occasion make finding your destination difficult.

See the chapter Introduction in the section HOW TO USE THIS GUIDE for more information on satellite navigation.

Seat Belts

The wearing of seat belts is compulsory in all the countries featured in this guide. On-the-spot fines will be incurred for failure to wear them and, in the event of an accident and insurance claim, compensation for injury may be reduced if seat belts are not worn.

As in the UK, legislation in many countries in Europe, requires all children up to a certain age or height to use a child restraint appropriate for their weight or size and, in addition, some countries' laws prohibit them from sitting in the front of a car.

Rear-facing baby seats must never be used in a seat protected by a frontal airbag unless the airbag has been deactivated.

Spares

Caravan Spares

On the Continent it is generally much more difficult to obtain spares for caravans than for cars and it will usually be necessary to obtain spares from a UK manufacturer or dealer before you travel.

Car Spares Kits

Some car manufacturers can supply spares kits; contact your dealer for details. The choice of spares will depend on the vehicle, how long you are likely to be away and your own level of competence in car maintenance, but the following is a list of basic items which should cover the most common causes of breakdown:

• Radiator top hose

• Fan belt

• Fuses and bulbs

• Windscreen wiper blade

• Length of 12V electrical cable

• Tools, torch and WD40 or equivalent water repellent/dispersant spray

Spare Wheel

Your local caravan dealer should be able to supply an appropriate spare wheel. If you have any difficulty in obtaining one, The Caravan Club's Technical Department will provide Club members with a list of suppliers' addresses on request.

Tyre legislation across Europe is more or less consistent and, while the Club has no specific knowledge of laws on the Continent regarding the use of space-saver spare wheels, there should be no problems in using such a wheel provided its use is strictly in accordance with the manufacturer's instructions.

Towing Bracket

The vast majority of cars registered after 1 August 1998 are legally required to have a European Type approved towing bracket (complying with European Directive 94/20) carrying a plate giving its approval number and various technical details, including the maximum noseweight. The approval process includes strength testing to a higher value than provided in the previous British Standard, and confirmation of fitting to all the car manufacturer's approved mounting points. Your car dealer or specialist towing bracket fitter will be able to give further advice. Checks may be made by foreign police. From 29 April 2011 for brand new motorhome designs (launched on or after that date) and 29 April 2012 for existing designs (those already being built before 29 April 2011), all new motorhomes will need some form of type approval before they can be registered in the UK and as such can only be fitted with a type approved towing bracket. Note also that some manufacturers are type approving their vehicles ahead of these required dates, so check carefully with any vehicle built from 2009 onwards. This change will not affect older vehicles, which can continue to be fitted with non-approved towing brackets.

Tyres

Safe driving and handling when towing a caravan or trailer are very important and one major factor, which is frequently overlooked, is tyre condition. Your caravan tyres must be suitable for the highest speed at which you can legally tow, not for any lower speed at which you may choose to travel. Some older British caravans (usually over ten years old) may not meet this requirement and, if you are subject to a police check, this could result in an on-the-spot fine for each tyre, including the spare. Check your tyre specification before you leave and, if necessary, upgrade your tyres. The Caravan Club's technical advice leaflet 'Caravan Tyres and Wheels', available to members on the Club's website or by post, explains how to check if your tyres are suitable.

Most countries require a minimum tread depth of 1.6 mm over the central part of the whole tyre, but motoring organisations recommend at least 3 mm across the whole tyre. If you plan an extended trip and your tyres are likely to be more worn than this before you return home, replace them before you leave.

Tyre Pressure

Tyre pressure should be checked and adjusted when the tyres are cold; checking warm tyres will result in a higher pressure reading. The correct pressures will be found in your car handbook, but unless it states otherwise it is wise to add an extra four to six pounds per square inch to the rear tyres of a car when towing to improve handling and to carry the extra load on the hitch.

Make sure you know what pressure your caravan tyres should be. Some require a pressure much higher than that normally used for cars. Check your caravan handbook for details.

Tyre Sizes

It is worth noting that some sizes of radial tyre to fit the 13" wheels commonly used on older UK caravans are virtually impossible to find in stock at retailers abroad, e.g. 175R13C.

After a Puncture

The Caravan Club does not recommend the general use of liquid sealants for puncture repair. Such products should not be considered to achieve a permanent repair, and may indeed render the tyre irreparable. If sealant is used to allow the vehicle to be removed from a position of danger to one of safety, the damaged tyre should be removed from the vehicle, repaired and replaced as soon as practically possible.

Following a caravan tyre puncture, especially on a single-axle caravan, it is advisable to have the opposite side (non-punctured) tyre removed from its wheel and checked inside and out for signs of damage resulting from overloading during the deflation of the punctured tyre. Failure to take this precaution may result in an increased risk of a second tyre deflation within a very short space of time.

Winter Tyres and Snow Chains

Winter tyres should be used in those countries with a severe winter climate and in some it is a legal requirement. Winter tyres are designed to minimise the hardening effect of low temperatures which in turn leads to less traction on the road, and to provide extra grip on snow and ice and in wet conditions. If you intend to make an extended winter trip or to travel regularly to where there may be snow or ice on the roads, it would be advisable to buy a set of winter tyres. Your local tyre dealer will be able to advise you.

Snow chains may be necessary on some roads in winter. They are compulsory in some countries during the winter where indicated by the appropriate road sign, when they must be fitted on at least two drive-wheels. They are not difficult to fit and it's a good idea to carry sturdy gloves to protect your hands when handling the chains in freezing conditions. For further information see the Country Introduction.

Polar Automotive Ltd sells and hires out snow chains (10% discount for Caravan Club members), tel 01892 519933 www.snowchains.com, email: polar@snowchains.com

Warning Triangles

In almost all European countries it is a legal requirement to use a warning triangle in the event of a breakdown or accident; some countries require two. It is strongly recommended that approved red warning triangles be carried as a matter of course.

A warning triangle should be placed on the road approximately 30 metres (100 metres on motorways) behind the broken down vehicle on the same side of the road. Always assemble the triangle before leaving your vehicle and walk with it so that the red, reflective surface is facing oncoming traffic. If a breakdown occurs round a blind corner, place the triangle in advance of the corner. Hazard warning lights may be used in conjunction with the triangle but they do not replace it.

See **Essential Equipment Table** at the end of this chapter.

Technical information compiled with the assistance of the Automobile Association.

Planning and Travelling
Essential Equipment in Europe

See also the information contained in the Handbook chapter and in the Country Introductions within the relevant Caravan Europe Volumes. For up to date information on essential equipment requirements for countries in Europe please visit www.caravanclub.co.uk/overseasadvice

Country	Warning Triangle	Spare Bulbs	First Aid Kit	Reflective Jacket	Additional Equipment to be Carried/Used
Andorra	Yes (2)	Yes	Rec	Yes	Dipped headlights in poor daytime visibility. Winter tyres recommended; snow chains when road conditions or signs dictate.
Austria	Yes	Rec	Yes	Yes	Winter tyres from 1 Nov to 15 April.*
Belgium	Yes	Rec	Rec	Yes	Dipped headlights in poor daytime visibility.
Croatia	Yes (2 for vehicle with trailer)	Yes	Yes	Yes	Dipped headlights at all times from last Sunday in Oct - last Sunday in Mar. Spare bulbs compulsory if lights are xenon, neon or LED. Snow chains compulsory in winter in certain regions.*
Czech Rep	Yes	Yes	Yes	Yes	Dipped headlights at all times. Replacement fuses. Winter tyres or snow chains from 1 Nov - 31st March.*
Denmark	Yes	Rec	Rec	Rec	Dipped headlights at all times. On motorways use hazard warning lights when queues or danger ahead.
Finland	Yes	Rec	Rec	Rec	Dipped headlights at all times. Winter tyres Dec - Feb.*
France	Yes	Rec	Rec	Yes	Dipped headlights recommended at all times. Legal requirement to carry a breathalyser, but no penalty for non-compliance.
Germany	Rec	Rec	Rec	Rec	Dipped headlights recommended at all times. Winter tyres to be used in winter weather conditions.*
Greece	Yes	Rec	Yes	Rec	Fire extinguisher compulsory. Dipped headlights in towns at night and in poor daytime visibility.
Hungary	Yes	Rec	Yes	Yes	Dipped headlights at all times outside built-up areas and in built-up areas at night. Snow chains compulsory on some roads in winter conditions.*
Italy	Yes	Rec	Rec	Yes	Dipped headlights at all times outside built-up areas and in poor visibility. Snow chains from 15 Oct - 15 April.*
Luxembourg	Yes	Rec	Rec	Yes	Dipped headlights at night and in daytime in bad weather.
Netherlands	Yes	Rec	Rec	Rec	Dipped headlights at night and in bad weather and recommended during the day.
Norway	Yes	Rec	Rec	Rec	Dipped headlights at all times. Winter tyres compulsory when snow or ice on the roads.*
Poland	Yes	Rec	Rec	Rec	Dipped headlights at all times. Fire extinguisher compulsory.
Portugal	Yes	Rec	Rec	Rec	Dipped headlights in poor daytime visibility, in tunnels and in lanes where traffic flow is reversible.
Slovakia	Yes	Rec	Yes	Yes	Dipped headlights at all times. Winter tyres compulsory when compact snow or ice on the road.*
Slovenia	Yes (2 for vehicle with trailer)	Yes	Rec	Yes	Dipped headlights at all times. Hazard warning lights when reversing. Use winter tyres or carry snow chains 15 Nov - 15 Mar.
Spain	Yes (2 Rec)	Rec	Rec	Yes	Dipped headlights at night, in tunnels and on 'special' roads (roadworks).
Sweden	Yes	Rec	Rec	Rec	Dipped headlights at all times. Winter tyres 1 Dec to 31 March.
Switzerland (inc Liechtenstein)	Yes	Rec	Rec	Rec	Dipped headlights recommended at all times, compulsory in tunnels. Snow chains where indicated by signs.

NOTES:
1) All countries: seat belts (if fitted) must be worn by all passengers.
2) Rec: not compulsory for foreign-registered vehicles, but very strongly recommended
3) Headlamp converters, spare bulbs, fire extinguisher, first aid kit and reflective waistcoat are strongly recommended for all countries.
4) In some countries drivers who wear prescription glasses must carry a spare pair.
5) Please check information for any country before you travel as rules and regulations change. This information is to be used as a guide only and it is your responsibility to make sure you have the correct equipment.
* For information and regulations on winter driving in these countries, please see the Country Introduction chapters in the relevant Caravan Europe guide.

Conversion Tables

Length & Distance

Centimetres/Metres	Inches/Feet/Yards	Inches/Feet/Yards	Centimetres/Metres
1 cm	0.4 in	1 in	2.5 cm
10 cm	4 in	1 ft	30 cm
25 cm	10 in	3 ft/1 yd	90 cm
1 m	3 ft 3 in	10 yds	9 m
100 m	110 yds	100 yds	91 m
Kilometres	**Miles**	**Miles**	**Kilometres**
1	0.6	1	1.6
10	6.2	10	16.1
25	15.5	25	40.2
50	31.1	50	80.5
100	62.2	100	160.9

Kilometres to Miles

km/h	20	30	40	50	60	70	80	90	100	110	120	130
mph	13	18	25	31	37	44	50	56	62	68	74	81

Weight

Grams/Kilograms	Ounces/Pounds	Ounces/Pounds	GramsKilograms
10 gm	0.3 oz	1 oz	28 gm
100 gm	3.5 oz	8 oz	226 gm
1 kg	2 lb 3 oz	1 lb	453 gm
10 kg	22 lb	10 lb	4.54 kg
25 kg	55 lb	50 lb	22.65 kg

Capacity

Millilitres/Litres	Fluid Ounces/Pints/Gallon	Fluid Ounces/Pints/Gallon	Millilitres/Litres
10 ml	0.3 fl oz	1 fl oz	28 ml
100 ml	3.5 fl oz	20 fl oz/1 pint	560 ml
1 litre	1.8 pints	1 gallon	4.5 litres
10 litres	2.2 gallons	5 gallons	22.7 litres
50 litres	11 gallons	10 gallons	45.5 litres

Area

Hectares	Acres	Acres	Hectares
1	2.5	1	0.4
5	12.4	5	2
10	24.7	10	4
50	123.5	50	20.2

Map Scales

Scale	Equivalent Distance	
1:100 000	1 cm = 1 km	1 in = 1¾ miles
1: 200 000	1 cm = 2 km	1 in = 3¼ miles
1: 400 000	1 cm = 4 km	1 in = 6¼ miles
1: 500 000	1 cm = 5 km	1 in = 8 miles
1: 750 000	1 cm = 7.5 km	1 in = 12 miles
1:1 000 000	1 cm = 10 km	1 in = 16 miles
1:1 250 000	1 cm = 12.5 km	1 in = 20 miles
1: 2 000 000	1 cm = 20 km	1 in = 32 miles

Tyre Pressures

Bar	PSI (lb/sq.in)	Bar	PSI (lb/sq.in)
1.00	15	3.05	44
1.50	22	3.50	51
2.00	29	4.15	60
2.50	36	4.75	69

Planning and Travelling
Mountain Passes and Tunnels

The mountain passes, rail and road tunnels listed in the tables are shown on the following maps. Numbers and letters against each pass or tunnel in the tables, correspond with the numbers and letters on the maps.

Please read the following advice carefully.

Advice for Drivers

Mountain Passes

The conditions and comments in the following tables assume an outfit with good power/weight ratio. Even those mountain passes and tunnels which do not carry a 'not recommended' or 'not permitted' warning may be challenging for any vehicle, more so for car and caravan outfits.

If in any doubt whatsoever, it is probably best to restrict yourself to those mountain passes which can be crossed by motorway. In any event, mountain passes should only be attempted by experienced drivers in cars with ample power and in good driving conditions; they should otherwise be avoided.

In the following table, where the entry states that caravans are not permitted or not recommended to use a pass, this generally – but not always – refers to towed caravans, and is based on advice originally supplied by the AA and/or local motoring organisations, but not checked by The Caravan Club. Motorhomes are seldom prohibited by such restrictions, but those which are relatively low powered or very large should find an alternative route. Always obey road signs at the foot

of a pass, especially those referring to heavy vehicles, which may apply to some large motorhomes.

Do not attempt to cross passes at night or in bad weather. Before crossing, seek local advice if touring during periods when the weather is changeable or unreliable. Warning notices are usually posted at the foot of a pass if it is closed, or if chains or winter tyres must be used.

Caravanners are obviously particularly sensitive to gradients and traffic/road conditions on passes. Take great care when negotiating blind hairpins. The maximum gradient is usually on the inside of bends but exercise caution if it is necessary to pull out. Always engage a lower gear before taking a hairpin bend and give priority to vehicles ascending. Give priority to postal service vehicles – signposts usually show their routes. Do not go down hills in neutral gear.

Keep to the extreme right of the road and be prepared to reverse to give way to descending/ascending traffic.

On mountain roads it is not the gradient which taxes your car but the duration of the climb and the loss of power at high altitudes: approximately 10% at 915 metres (3,000 feet) and even more as you get higher. Turbo power restores much of the lost capacity.

To minimise the risk of the engine overheating, take high passes in the cool of the day, don't climb any faster than necessary and keep the engine pulling steadily. To prevent a radiator boiling, pull off the road safely, turn the heater and blower full on and switch off airconditioning. Keep an eye on water and oil levels. Never put cold water into a boiling radiator or it may crack. Check that the radiator is not obstructed by debris sucked up during the journey.

A long descent may result in overheating brakes; select the correct gear for the gradient and avoid excessive use of brakes. Note that even if using engine braking to control the outfit's speed, caravan brakes may activate due to the action of the overrun mechanism, causing them to overheat. Use lay-bys and lookout points to stop and allow brakes to cool.

In alpine areas snow prevents road repairs during the winter, resulting in road works during the summer, which may cause traffic delays. At times one-way traffic only may be permitted on some routes. Information will be posted at each end of the road.

Main roads crossing major passes are rarely totally unguarded; but minor passes may be unguarded or simply have stone pillars placed at close intervals. If you do not have a good head for heights consider a different route.

Leave the blade valve of your portable toilet open a fraction when travelling at altitude. This avoids pressure build-up in the holding tank. Similarly, a slightly open tap will avoid pressure build up in water pipes and fittings.

Tunnels

British drivers do not often encounter road tunnels but they are a common feature in Europe, for example, through mountain ranges. Tolls are usually charged for the use of major tunnels.

Ensure you have enough fuel before entering a tunnel. Emergency situations often involve vehicles stranded because of a lack of fuel.

When approaching a tunnel in bright sunshine, slow down to allow your eyes to adjust and look out for poorly-lit vehicles in front of you and for cyclists. Take sunglasses off before entering a tunnel and take care again when emerging into sunshine at the other end.

Signposts usually indicate a tunnel ahead and its length. Once inside, maintain a safe distance from the vehicle in front in case the driver brakes sharply. Minimum/maximum speed limits usually apply. Dipped headlights are usually required by law even in well-lit tunnels, so switch them on before you enter. Some tunnels may be poorly or totally unlit.

Snow chains, if used, must be removed before entering a tunnel in lay-bys provided for this purpose.

'No overtaking' signs must be strictly observed. Never cross central single or double lines. If overtaking is permitted in twin-tube tunnels, bear in mind that it is very easy to under-estimate distances and speed once inside. Watch out for puddles caused by dripping or infiltrating water.

In order to minimise the effects of exhaust fumes close all car windows and set the ventilator to circulate air, or operate the air conditioning system coupled with the recycled air option. If there is a traffic jam, switch your hazard warning lights on and stop a safe distance from the vehicle in front. Sound the horn only in a real emergency. Never change direction unless instructed to do so by tunnel staff or a police officer.

If you break down, try to reach the next lay-by and call for help from an emergency phone. If you cannot reach a lay-by, place your warning triangle at least 100 metres behind your vehicle. Passengers should leave the vehicle through doors on the right-hand side only. Modern tunnels have video surveillance systems to ensure prompt assistance in an emergency.

Mountain Pass Information

The dates of opening and closing given in the following tables are approximate and inclusive. Before attempting late afternoon or early morning journeys across borders, check their opening times as some borders close at night.

Gradients listed are the maximum which may be encountered on the pass and may be steeper at the inside of curves, particularly on older roads.

Gravel surfaces (such as dirt and stone chips) vary considerably; they can be dusty when dry and slippery when wet. Where known to exist, this type of surface has been noted.

In fine weather winter tyres or snow chains will only be required on very high passes, or for short periods in early or late summer. In winter conditions you will probably need to use them at altitudes exceeding 600 metres (approximately 2,000 feet).

Abbreviations

MHV	Maximum height of vehicle
MLV	Maximum length of vehicle
MWV	Maximum width of vehicle
MWR	Minimum width of road
OC	Occasionally closed between dates stated
UC	Usually closed between dates stated
UO	Usually open between dates stated, although a fall of snow may obstruct the road for 24-48 hours.

Mountain Passes and Tunnels Report Form

The Caravan Club welcomes up-to-date information on mountain passes and tunnels from caravanners who use them during the course of their holidays. Please use the Mountain Passes and Tunnels report forms at the back of the book and complete and return them as soon as possible after your journey.

Converting Gradients

20% = 1 in 5	11% = 1 in 9
16% = 1 in 6	10% = 1 in 10
14% = 1 in 7	8% = 1 in 12
12% = 1 in 8	6% = 1 in 16

Much of the information contained in the following tables was originally supplied by The Automobile Association and other motoring and tourist organisations. Additional updates and amendments have been supplied by caravanners who have themselves used the passes and tunnels. The Caravan Club has not checked the information contained in these tables and cannot accept responsibility for their accuracy, or for errors, omissions or their effects.

Major Alpine Mountain Passes - France

Before using any of these passes, PLEASE READ CAREFULLY THE ADVICE AT THE BEGINNING OF THIS CHAPTER

	Pass Height In Metres (Feet)	From To	Max Gradient	Conditions and Comments
1	**Allos** (France) 2250 (7382)	Colmars *Barcelonette*	10%	UC early Nov-early Jun. MWR 4m (13'1") Very winding, narrow, mostly unguarded pass on D908 but not difficult otherwise; passing bays on southern slope; poor surface, MWV 1.8m (5'11"). **Not recommended for caravans.**
2	**Aravis** (France) 1498 (4915)	La Clusaz *Flumet*	9%	OC Dec-Mar. MWR 4m (13'1"). Fine scenery; D909, fairly easy road. Poor surface in parts on Chamonix side. Some single-line traffic.
3	**Ballon d'Alsace** (France) 1178 (3865)	Giromagny *St Maurice-sur-Moselle*	11%	OC Dec-Mar. MWR 4m (13'1") Fairly straightforward ascent/descent; narrow in places; numerous bends. On road D465.
4	**Bayard** (France) 1248 (4094)	Chauffayer *Gap*	14%	UO. MWR 6m (19'8") Part of the Route Napoléon N85. Fairly easy, steepest on the S side with several hairpin bends. Negotiable by caravans from N-to-S via D1075 (N75) and Col-de-la-Croix Haute, avoiding Gap.
5	**Brouis** (France) 1279 (4196)	Nice *Col-de-Tende*	12.50%	UO. MWR 6m (19'8") Good surface but many hairpins on D6204 (N204)/S20. Steep gradients on approaches. Height of tunnel at Col-de-Tende at the Italian border is 3.8m (12'4) **Not recommended for caravans.**
6	**Bussang** (France) 721 (2365)	Thann *St Maurice-sur-Moselle*	7%	UO. MWR 4m (13'1") A very easy road (N66) over the Vosges; beautiful scenery.
7	**Cabre** (France) 1180 (3871)	Luc-en-Diois *Aspres-sur-Buëch*	9%	UO. MWR 5.5m (18') An easy pleasant road (D93/D993), winding at Col-de-Cabre.
8	**Cayolle** (France) 2326 (7631)	Barcelonnette *Guillaumes*	10%	UC early Nov-early Jun. MWR 4m (13'1") Narrow, winding road (D902) with hairpin bends; poor surface, broken edges with steep drops. Long stretches of single-track road with passing places. **Caravans prohibited.**
9	**Croix Haute** (France) 1179 (3868)	Monestier-de-Clermont *Aspres-sur-Buëch*	7%	UO on N75. MWR 5.5m (18') Well-engineered road (D1075/N75); several hairpin bends on N side.
10	**Faucille** (France) 1323 (4341)	Gex *Morez*	10%	UO. MWR 5m (16'5") Fairly wide, winding road (N5) across the Jura mountains; negotiable by caravans but probably better to follow route via La Cure-St Cergue-Nyon.

Before using any of these passes, PLEASE READ CAREFULLY THE ADVICE AT THE BEGINNING OF THIS CHAPTER

Pass Height In Metres (Feet)	From To	Max Gradient	Conditions and Comments
⑪ **Forclaz** (Switzerland – France) 1527 (5010)	Martigny *Argentière*	8.50%	UO Forclaz; OC Montets Dec-early Apr. MWR 5m (16'5") MWV 2.5m (8'2") Good road over the pass and to the French border; long, hard climb out of Martigny; narrow and rough over Col-des-Montets on D1506 (N506).
⑫ **Galibier** (France) 2645 (8678)	La Grave *St Michel-de-Maurienne*	12.50%	UC Oct-Jun. MWR 3m (9'10") Mainly wide, well-surfaced road (D902) but unprotected and narrow over summit. From Col-du-Lautaret it rises over the Col-du-Telegraphe then 11 more hairpin bends. Ten hairpin bends on descent then 5km (3.1 miles) narrow and rough; easier in N to S direction. Limited parking at summit. **Not recommended for caravans.** (There is a single-track tunnel under the Galibier summit, controlled by traffic lights; caravans are not permitted.)
⑬ **Gorges-du-Verdon** (France) 1032 (3386)	Castellane *Moustiers-Ste Marie*	9%	UO. MWR probably 5m (16'5") On road D952 over Col-d'Ayen and Col-d'Olivier. Moderate gradients but slow, narrow and winding. Poss heavy traffic.
⑭ **Iseran** (France) 2770 (9088)	Bourg-St Maurice *Lanslebourg*	11%	UC mid Oct-late Jun. MWR 4m (13'1") Second highest pass in the Alps on road D902. Well-graded with reasonable bends, average surface. Several unlit tunnels on N approach. **Not recommended for caravans.**
⑮ **Izoard** (France) 2360 (7743)	Guillestre *Briançon*	12.50%	UC late Oct-mid Jun. MWR 5m (16'5") Fine scenery. Winding, sometimes narrow road (D902) with many hairpin bends; care required at several unlit tunnels near Guillestre. **Not recommended for caravans.**
⑯ **Larche (della Maddalena)** (France – Italy) 1994 (6542)	La Condamine-Châtelard *Vinadio*	8.50%	OC Dec-Mar. MWR 3.5m (11'6") An easy, well-graded road (D900); long, steady ascent on French side, many hairpins on Italian side (S21). Fine scenery; ample parking at summit.
⑰ **Lautaret** (France) 2058 (6752)	Le Bourg-d'Oisans *Briançon*	12.50%	OC Dec-Mar. MWR 4m (13'1") Modern, evenly graded but winding road (D1091), and unguarded in places; very fine scenery; suitable for caravans but with care through narrow tunnels.
⑱ **Leques** (France) 1146 (3760)	Barrême *Castellane*	8%	UO. MWR 4m (13'1") On Route Napoléon (D4085). Light traffic; excellent surface; narrow in places on N ascent. S ascent has many hairpins.
⑲ **Mont Cenis** (France – Italy) 2083 (6834)	Lanslebourg *Susa*	12.50%	UC Nov-May. MWR 5m (16'5") Approach by industrial valley. An easy highway (D1006/S25) with mostly good surface; spectacular scenery; long descent into Italy with few stopping places. Alternative Fréjus road tunnel available. See **Road Tunnels** in this section.
⑳ **Montgenèvre** (France – Italy) 1850 (6070)	Briançon *Cesana-Torinese*	9%	UO. MWR 5m (16'5") An easy, modern road (N94/S24) with some tight hairpin bends on French side; road widened & tunnels improved on Italian side. Much used by lorries; may be necessary to travel at their speed and give way to oncoming large vehicles on hairpins.
Montets (See Forclaz)			

Pass Height In Metres (Feet)	From To	Max Gradient	Conditions and Comments
(21) **Morgins** (France – Switzerland) 1369 (4491)	Abondance Monthey	14%	UO. MWR 4m (13'1"). A lesser used route (D22) through pleasant, forested countryside crossing French/Swiss border. **Not recommended for caravans.**
(22) **Petit St Bernard** (France – Italy) 2188 (7178)	Bourg-St Maurice Pré–St Didier	8.50%	UC mid Oct-Jun. MWR 5m (16'5"). Outstanding scenery, but poor surface and unguarded broken edges near summit. Easiest from France (D1090); sharp hairpins on climb from Italy (S26). **Closed to vehicles towing another vehicle.**
(23) **Restefond (La Bonette)** (France) 2802 (9193)	Barcelonnette St Etienne-de-Tinée	16%	UC Oct-Jun. MWR 3m (9'10"). The highest pass in the Alps. Rebuilt, resurfaced road (D64) with rest area at summit – top loop narrow and unguarded. Winding with hairpin bends. **Not recommended for caravans.**
(24) **Schlucht** (France) 1139 (3737)	Gérardmer Munster	7%	UO. MWR 5m (16'5") An extremely picturesque route (D417) crossing the Vosges mountains, with easy, wide bends on the descent. Good surface.
(25) **Tenda (Tende)** Italy – France 1321 (4334)	Borgo-San Dalmazzo Tende	9%	UO. MWR 6m (19'8") Well-guarded, modern road (S20/ND6204) with several hairpin bends; road tunnel (height 3.8m) at summit narrow with poor road surface. Less steep on Italian side. **Caravans prohibited during winter.**
(26) **Vars** (France) 2109 (6919)	St Paul-sur-Ubaye Guillestre	9%	OC Dec-Mar. MWR 5m (16'5") Easy winding ascent and descent on D902 with 14 hairpin bends; good surface.

Technical information by courtesy of the Automobile Association. Additional update and amendments supplied by caravnners and tourers who have themselves used the passes and tunnels. The Caravan Club has not checked the information contained in these tables and cannot accept responsibility for their accuracy, or for any errors, omissions, or their effects.

The Alpine maps only show the major Alpine mountain passes for France. For other countries please refer to Caravan Europe Guide to Sites and Touring in Austria, Benelux, Central Europe, Germany, Greece, Italy, Scandinavia and Switzerland.

Major Alpine Road Tunnels - France

Before using any of these tunnels, PLEASE READ CAREFULLY THE ADVICE AT THE BEGINNING OF THIS CHAPTER

Tunnel	Route and Height above Sea Level	General Information and Comments
(A) **Frejus** (France – Italy) 12.8 km (8 miles)	**Modane to Bardonecchia** 1220m (4000')	MWR 9m (29'6"), tunnel height 4.3m (14'). Min/max speed 60/70 km/h (37/44 mph). Return tickets valid until midnight on 7th day after day of issue. Season tickets are available. Approach via A43 and D1006; heavy use by freight vehicles. Good surface on approach roads. **Tolls charged.** www.sftrf.fr
(B) **Mont Blanc** (France – Italy) 11.6 km (7.2 miles)	**Chamonix to Courmayeur** 1381m (4530')	MHV 4.7m (15'5"), MWV 6m (19'6") On N205 France, S26 (Italy). Max speed in tunnel 70 km/h (44 mph) – lower limits when exiting; min speed 50 km/h. Leave 150m between vehicles; ensure enough fuel for 30km. Return tickets valid until midnight on 7th day after issue. Season tickets are available. **Tolls charged.** www.tunnelmb.net
-	**Ste Marie-aux-Mines (France)** 6.8 km (4.25 miles)	**St Dié to Ste-Marie-aux Mines** 772m (2533')	At 7km, this is the longest road tunnel situated entirely in France. Also known as Maurice Lemaire Tunnel, through the Vosges in north-east France from Lusse on N159 to N59. **Tolls charged.** Alternate route via Col-de-Ste Marie on D459.

NOTES: Dipped headlights should be used (unless stated otherwise) when travelling through road tunnels, even when the road appears to be well lit. In some countries police make spot checks and impose on-the-spot fines.

During the winter wheel chains may be required on the approaches to some tunnels. These must not be used in tunnels and lay-bys are available for the removal and refitting of wheel chains.

For information on motorway vignettes, see the relevant Country Introductions.

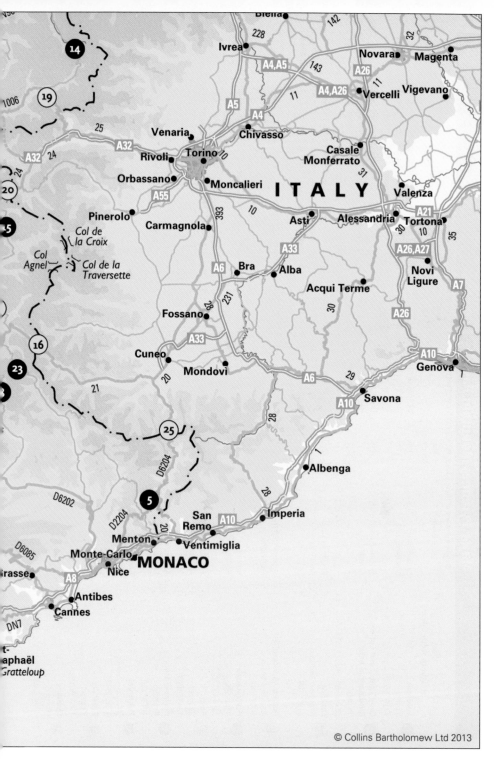

© Collins Bartholomew Ltd 2013

Major Pyrenees Mountain Passes – France and Andorra

Before using any of these passes, PLEASE READ CAREFULLY THE ADVICE AT THE BEGINNING OF THIS CHAPTER

	Pass / Height In Metres (Feet)	From / To	Max Gradient	Conditions and Comments
27	Aubisque (France) 1710 (5610)	Eaux Bonnes / Argelés-Gazost	10%	UC mid Oct-Jun. MWR 3.5m (11'6") Very winding; continuous on D918 but easy ascent; descent including Col-d'Aubisque 1709m (5607 feet) and Col-du-Soulor 1450m (4757 feet); 8km (5 miles) of very narrow, rough, unguarded road with steep drop. Not recommended for caravans.
28	Col-d'Haltza and Col-de-Burdincurrutcheta (France) 782 (2565) and 1135 (3724)	St Jean-Pied-de-Port / Larrau	11%	UO. A narrow road (D18/D19) leading to Iraty skiing area. Narrow with some tight hairpin bends; rarely has central white line and stretches are unguarded. Not for the faint-hearted. Not recommended for caravans.
29	Envalira (France – Andorra) 2407 (7897)	Pas-de-la-Casa / Andorra	12.5%	OC Nov-Apr. MWR 6m (19'8") Good road (N22/CG2) with wide bends on ascent and descent; fine views. MHV 3.5m (11'6") on N approach near l'Hospitalet. Early start rec in summer to avoid border delays. Envalira Tunnel (toll) reduces congestion and avoids highest part of pass. See *Pyrenean Road Tunnels* in this section.
30	Ibañeta (Roncevalles) (France – Spain) 1057 (3468)	St Jean-Pied-de-Port / Pamplona	10%	UO. MWR 4m (13'1") Slow and winding, scenic route on N135.
31	Peyresourde (France) 1563 (5128)	Arreau / Bagnères-de-Luchon	10%	UO. MWR 4m (13'1") D618 somewhat narrow with several hairpin bends, though not difficult. Not recommended for caravans.
32	Port (France) 1249 (4098)	Tarascon-sur-Ariège / Massat	10%	OC Nov-Mar. MWR 4m (13'1") A fairly easy, scenic road (D618), but narrow on some bends.
33	Portet-d'Aspet (France) 1069 (3507)	Audressein / Fronsac	14%	UO. MWR 3.5m (11'6") Approached from W by the easy Col-des-Ares and Col-de-Buret; well-engineered but narrow road (D618); care needed on hairpin bends. Not recommended for caravans.
34	Pourtalet (France – Spain) 1792 (5879)	Laruns / Biescas	10%	UC late Oct-early Jun. MWR 3.5m (11'6") A fairly easy, unguarded road, but narrow in places. Easier from Spain (A136), steeper in France (D934). Not recommended for caravans.
35	Puymorens (France) 1915 (6283)	Ax-les-Thermes / Bourg-Madame	10%	OC Nov-Apr. MWR 5.5m (18') MHV 3.5m (11'6") A generally easy, modern tarmac road (N20). Parallel toll road tunnel available. See *Pyrenean Road Tunnels* in this section.
36	Quillane (France) 1714 (5623)	Axat / Mont-Louis	8.5%	OC Nov-Mar. MWR 5m (16'5") An easy, straightforward ascent and descent on D118.

	Pass Height In Metres (Feet)	From To	Max Gradient	Conditions and Comments
③⑦	**Somport** (France – Spain) 1632 (5354)	Accous *Jaca*	10%	U.O. MWR 3.5m (11'6") A favoured, old-established route; not particularly easy and narrow in places with many unguarded bends on French side (N134); excellent road on Spanish side (N330). Use of road tunnel advised – see *Pyrenean Road Tunnels* in this section. NB Visitors advise re-fuelling no later than Sabiñánigo when travelling south to north.
❸❽	**Tourmalet** (France) 2114 (6936)	Ste Marie-de-Campan *Luz-St Sauveur*	12.5%	UC Oct-mid Jun. MWR 4m (13'1") The highest French Pyrenean route (D918); approaches good, though winding, narrow in places and exacting over summit; sufficiently guarded. Rough surface & uneven edges on west side. Not recommended for caravans.

Major Pyrenean Road Tunnels France and Andorra

	Tunnel	Route and Height Above Sea Level	General Information and Comments
Ⓐ	**Bielsa** (France – Spain) 3.2 km (2 miles)	**Aragnouet to Bielsa** 1830m (6000')	Open 24 hours but possibly closed October-Easter. On French side (D173) generally good road surface but narrow with steep hairpin bends and steep gradients near summit. Often no middle white line. Spanish side (A138) has good width and is less steep and winding. Used by heavy vehicles. No tolls. Please note the tunnel may be undergoing repair works and as a result may be closed at certain times and on certain days.
Ⓑ	**Envalira** (France – Spain via Andorra) 2.8 km (1.75 miles)	**Pas de la Casa to El Grau Roig** 2000m (6562')	Tunnel width 8.25m. On N22/CG2 France to Andorra. **Tolls charged.**
Ⓒ	**Puymorens** (France –Spain) 4.8 km (2.9 miles)	**Ax-les-Thermes to Puigcerda** 1515m (4970')	MHV 3.5m (11'6"). Part of Puymorens pass on N20/E9. **Tolls charged.**
Ⓓ	**Somport** (France – Spain) 8.6 km (5.3 miles)	**Urdos to Canfranc** 1116m (3661')	Tunnel height 4.55m (14'9"), width 10.5m (34'). Max speed 90 km/h (56 mph); leave 100m between vehicles. On N134 (France), N330 (Spain). No tolls.

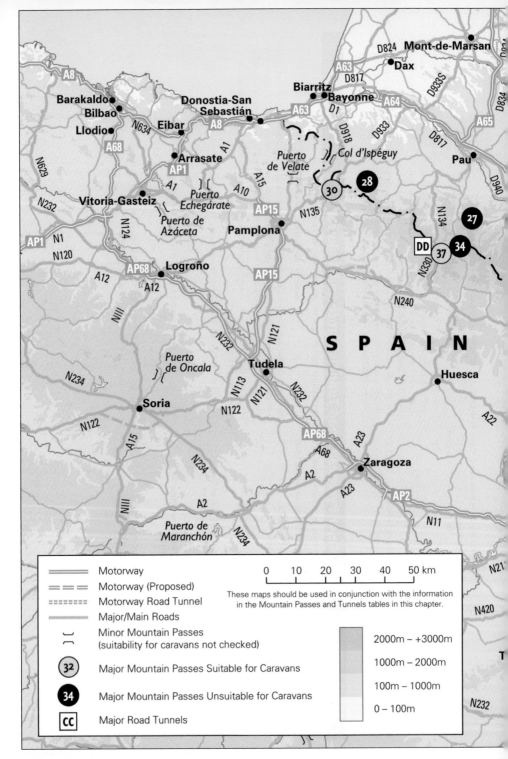

Motorway

Motorway (Proposed)

Motorway Road Tunnel

Major/Main Roads

Minor Mountain Passes
(suitability for caravans not checked)

32 Major Mountain Passes Suitable for Caravans

34 Major Mountain Passes Unsuitable for Caravans

CC Major Road Tunnels

0   10   20   30   40   50 km

These maps should be used in conjunction with the information
in the Mountain Passes and Tunnels tables in this chapter.

2000m – +3000m

1000m – 2000m

100m – 1000m

0 – 100m

THE MOST BEAUTIFUL DESTINATIONS FOR A SUCCESSFUL HOLIDAY

La Côte de Nacre
★★★★★

Camping International
Maisons-Laffitte
★★★★

Soulac Plage
★★★★

Le Plein Air des Chênes
★★★★

Les Vagues
★★★★

Résidence du Campeur
★★★★

SPAIN

Cypsela Resort
★★★★★

TENT LODGES - CABINS

(+33) 04 11 32 90 00

During Your Stay
Electricity and Gas in Europe

Electricity – General Advice

The nominal voltage for mains electricity has been 230V across the European Union for more than ten years, but varying degrees of 'acceptable tolerance' have resulted in significant variations in the actual voltage found. Harmonisation of voltage standards remains an on-going project. Most appliances sold in the UK are rated at 220-240V and usually work satisfactorily. However, some high-powered equipment, such as microwave ovens, may not function well and you are advised to consult the manufacturer's literature for further information.

Appliances which are 'CE' marked should work acceptably, as this marking indicates that the product has been designed to meet the requirements of relevant European directives.

The site entries in this guide contain information on minimum amperage supplied on campsites and the Country Introduction contains additional information (where known). Frequently you will be offered a choice of amperage and the following table gives an approximate idea of which appliances can be used (erring on the side of caution). You can work it out more accurately by noting the wattage of each appliance in your caravan. The kettle given is the caravan type, not a household kettle which usually has at least a 2000W element. Note that each caravan circuit also has a maximum amp rating which should not be exceeded.

Electrical Connections – EN60309-2 (CEE17)

Whilst there is a European Standard for connectors, namely EN60309-2 (formerly known as CEE17), this does not apply retrospectively and you may find some Continental campsites where your UK 3-pin connector, which is to European Standard, will not fit. Accurate information is not easy to come by, but based on The Caravan Club's overseas sites booking service, approximately 80% of campsites in Europe do have some, or all, UK 3-pin hook-ups, leaving approximately 20% of campsites with only 2-pin hook ups. Therefore it is a good idea to carry a 2-pin adapter. See the relevant Country Introductions for more information.

Different types of connector may be found within one campsite, as well as within one country. If you find your CEE17 connector does not fit, ask campsite staff to borrow or hire an adaptor.

Even with a European Standard connection, a poor electrical supply is possible. The existence of the EN60309-2 (CEE17) standard should not be taken as an automatic sign of a modern system.

Amps	Wattage (Approx)	Fridge	Battery Charger	Air Conditioning	Colour TV	Water Heater	Kettle (750W)	Heater (1kW)
2	400	✓	✓					
4	800	✓	✓		✓	✓		
6	1200	✓	✓	*	✓	✓	✓	
8	1600	✓	✓	✓**	✓	✓	✓	✓**
10	2000	✓	✓	✓**	✓	✓	✓	✓**
16	3000	✓	✓	✓	✓	✓	✓	✓**

*   *Possible, depending on wattage of appliance in question*
**   *Not to be used at the same time as other high-wattage equipment*

Other Connections

French – 2-pin, plus earth socket. Adaptors available from UK caravan accessory shops.

German – 2-pin, plus 2 earth strips, found in Norway and Sweden and possibly still Germany.

Switzerland - 3-pin (but not the same shape as UK 3-pin). Adapters available to purchase in Switzerland. Most campsites using the Swiss 3-pin will have adaptors available for hire or to borrow.

If the campsite does not have a modern EN60309-2 (CEE17) supply, ask to see the electrical protection for the socket outlet. If there is a device marked with IDn = 30mA, then the risk is minimised.

Hooking Up to the Mains

Connection

Connection should always be made in the following order:

- Check your caravan isolating switch is at 'off'.
- Uncoil the connecting cable from the drum. **A coiled cable with current flowing through it may overheat.** Take your cable and insert the connector (female end) into the caravan inlet.
- Insert the plug (male end) into the site outlet socket.
- Switch caravan isolating switch to 'on'.
- Preferably insert a polarity tester into one of the 13A sockets in the caravan to check all connections are correctly wired. **Never leave it in the socket.** Some caravans have these devices built in as standard.

It is recommended that the supply is not used if the polarity is incorrect *(see Reversed Polarity overleaf).*

WARNING

In case of doubt or, if after carrying out the above procedures the supply does not become available, or if the supply fails, consult the campsite operator or a qualified electrician.

From time to time, you may come across mains supplies which differ in various ways from the common standards on most sites and your test equipment may not be able to confirm that such systems are satisfactory and safe to use. While it is likely that such systems will operate your electrical equipment adequately in most circumstances, it is possible that the protective measures in your equipment may not work effectively in the event of a fault.

If your test equipment is not built into your caravan it should be readily available for everyday use.

Site Hooking Up Adaptor

(MAINS CONTINENTAL)
EXTENSION LEAD TO CARAVAN
Câble de rallonge à la caravane
Verlãengerungskabel zum wohnwagen

ADAPTATEUR DE PRISE AU SITE (SECTEUR)   CAMPINGPLATZ-ANSCHLUSS (NETZ)

SITE OUTLET
Prise du site
Campingplatz-Steckdose

MAINS ADAPTOR
Adaptateur Secteur
Netzanschlußstacker

16A 230V AC

To ensure your safety, the Club recommends that unless the system can be confirmed as safe, it should not be used.

Disconnection

- Switch your caravan isolating switch to 'off'.
- At the site supply socket withdraw the plug.
- Disconnect the cable from the caravan.
- Motorhomes – if leaving your pitch during the day, do not leave your mains cable plugged into the site supply, as this creates a hazard if the exposed live connections in the plug are touched or if the cable is not seen during grass-cutting.

Reversed Polarity

Even when the site connector is to European Standard EN60309-2 (CEE17), British caravanners are still likely to encounter the problem known as reversed polarity. This is where the site supply's 'live' line connects to the caravan's 'neutral' and vice versa. The Club strongly recommends that you always check the polarity immediately on connection, using a polarity tester available from caravan accessory shops.

The caravan mains electrical installation **should not be used** while reversed polarity exists. Try using another nearby socket instead, which may cure the problem. Frequent travellers to the Continent who are electrically competent often make up an adaptor themselves, clearly marked 'reversed polarity', with the live and neutral wires reversed. (The 'German' plug can simply be turned upside down, so no further adaptor is required.) If these steps do not rectify the reversed polarity, the site supply may be quite different from that used in the UK and we recommend, for your own safety, that you disconnect from the mains and **do not use the electrical supply.**

> ### Always check the polarity immediately on connection

Using a reversed polarity socket will probably not affect how an electrical appliance works BUT your protection in the event of a fault is greatly reduced. For example, a lamp socket may still be live as you touch it while replacing a blown bulb, even if the light switch is turned off.

Even when polarity is correct, it is always a wise precaution to check that a proper earth connection exists. A good indication of this can be achieved using a proprietary tester such as that shown on the previous page. However, there are earth faults that these simple devices are unable to identify and if there is any doubt about the integrity of the earth system, **do not use the electricity supply.**

Shaver Sockets

Most campsites provide shaver sockets on which the voltage is generally marked as either 220V or 110V. Using an incorrect voltage may cause the shaver to become hot or to fail. The 2-pin adaptor obtainable in the UK is sometimes too wide for Continental sockets. It is advisable to buy 2-pin adaptors on the Continent, where they are readily available. Many shavers will operate on a range of voltages and these are most suitable when travelling abroad.

Gas – General Advice

The rate of gas consumption is difficult to predict as it depends on many factors, including how many appliances you use in your outfit, whether you use a mains electric hook-up when available, how much you eat out and, of course, what the temperature is! As a rough guide plan to allow 0.45kg of gas a day for normal summer usage.

With the exception of Campingaz, LPG cylinders normally available in the UK, e.g. Calor gas (both butane and propane), cannot be exchanged abroad. If possible, take sufficient gas with you for your holiday and bring back the empty cylinder(s). If additional capacity is required beyond what you would normally carry, check with cylinder suppliers to see if you can swap to a larger one (if there is room in your gas locker to carry it) or check if it is economic to carry a second cylinder. Note that ferry and tunnel operators may restrict the number of cylinders you are permitted to carry.

The wide availability of Campingaz means it is worth considering it as a fall-back if you run out of your 'normal' gas. However, prices vary widely from country to country, and maximum cylinder sizes are quite limited (2.75kg of gas in a 907 cylinder), making it less practical for routine use in larger vehicles with several gas appliances. A Campingaz adapter is relatively inexpensive, though, and is widely available in the UK. It can be a prudent purchase prior to travelling, especially if taking a long holiday. It is also wise to hold a spare Calor gas cylinder in reserve in case you experience difficulty in finding a Campingaz supplier locally. With 130,000 stockists in 100 countries, however, these occasions should be rare, but prices may vary considerably from country to country. Alternatively, adaptors are available from Campingaz/Calor stockists to enable use of the normal Calor 4.5kg regulator with a Campingaz cylinder.

If you are touring in winter or wherever cold weather conditions may be encountered, it is advisable to use propane gas instead of butane. BP Gaslight (propane) cylinders, which have been gaining in popularity in the UK, are available in several European countries. However, you cannot exchange cylinders bought in other European countries, nor bring ones back to other European countries for exchange. For news of further developments check the BP Gaslight website, www. bpgaslight.com

Take sufficient gas with you for your holiday

Many other brands of gas are available in different countries and, subject to the availability of suitable regulators, adapters and connecting hoses, as long as the cylinders fit in your gas locker these local brands can also be used with your outfit. If you regularly visit a country, it may well be worth buying a 'local' cylinder, as you can then exchange it in that country when necessary. If you are travelling across several countries this may not be a viable option.

The use of 30mbar has been standardised for both butane and propane within the EU, replacing several different pressures previously used. On later model UK-specification caravans and motorhomes (2004 models and later) a 30mbar regulator suited to both propane and butane use is fitted to the bulkhead of the gas locker. This is connected to the cylinder by means of a connecting hose (and sometimes an adaptor) to suit different brands or types of gas. Older outfits and some foreign-built ones may use a cylinder-mounted regulator, which may need to be changed to suit different brands or types of gas.

Hoses and adapters to suit the most common brands and types of gas are available in the UK from suppliers such as Gaslow (0845 4000 600 or www.gaslow.co.uk) or from good dealerships, and it may be easier to buy these before travelling, rather than rely on local availability when you are abroad.

WARNING

Refilling your own UK standard cylinder is prohibited by law in most countries, unless it is carried out at certain designated filling plants. Since these plants are few and far between, are generally highly mechanised and geared for cylinders of a particular size and shape, the process is usually not practical. Nevertheless, it is realised that many local dealers and site operators will fill your cylinders regardless of the prohibition. The Caravan Club does not recommend the user-refilling of gas cylinders **which have not been specifically designed for this purpose**; there is real danger if cylinders are incorrectly filled.

- Cylinders must never be over-filled under any circumstances.

- Regular servicing of gas appliances is important. A badly adjusted appliance can emit carbon monoxide, which could prove fatal. Check your vehicle or appliance handbook for service recommendations.

- Never use a hob or oven as a space heater.

For information about the carriage of gas cylinders on ferries and in the Channel Tunnel, including safety precautions and regulations, see the chapter **Ferries and the Channel Tunnel** in the section **PLANNING AND TRAVELLING.**

The Caravan Club publishes a range of technical leaflets for its members (some available to non-members) including detailed advice on the use of electricity and gas. You are advised to request copies or see www.caravanclub.co.uk/practical-advice.

During Your Stay
Keeping in Touch

Emails and the Internet

Wi-Fi hotspots are increasingly available on lots of campsites in Europe and many (but not all) offer Wi-Fi to their guests free of charge.

A Wi-Fi enabled laptop, tablet (such as an iPad) or a mobile 'smartphone' should enable the sending and receiving of emails, photos and video clips, together with website browsing, plus numerous other internet functions.

Alternatively there are internet cafés all over the world where you can log on to the internet and collect and send emails. You will be charged for the time you are logged on, however some public libraries in many countries offer free internet access.

WARNING:

Wi-Fi internet surfing abroad by means of a dongle (which uses a mobile phone network) is still prohibitively expensive, as is data roaming on internet enabled mobile phones.

Text Messages (SMS)

Using a mobile phone to send text messages is a cost-effective way of keeping in touch. There is a charge for sending texts but receiving them abroad is free.

A number of websites offer a free SMS text message service to mobile phones, e.g. www.cbfsms.com or www.sendsmsnow.com

International Direct Dial Calls

International access codes are given in the relevant Country Introduction chapters. To make an IDD call, first dial the international access code from the country

you are in, followed by the local number you wish to reach including its area code (if applicable), e.g. from the UK to France, dial 0033 – the international access code for France.

Most, but not all countries include an initial 0 in the area code. With the exception of Italy, where the 0 must be dialled, you should omit the initial 0 when calling from outside the country in question. Some countries' telephone numbers do not have area codes at all (e.g. Denmark, Luxembourg, Norway). If this is the case simply dial the international access code and the number in full. The international access code to dial the UK from anywhere in the world is 0044.

International calls can be made from telephone boxes in most countries using coins or, more commonly, phonecards or credit cards, and often instructions are given in English.

Ring Tones

Ring tones vary from country to country and the UK's double ring is not necessarily used in other countries.

Global Telephone Cards

Rechargeable global telephone cards offer rates for international calls which are normally cheaper than credit card or local phonecard rates. Payment methods vary, but are usually by monthly direct debit from your credit card or bank account. Also widely available are pre-paid international phonecards available on-line or locally from post offices, newsagents, kiosks or shops. There are many websites selling international phonecards for use all over the world such as www.planetphonecards.com and www.thephonecardsite.com

Making Calls from your Laptop

If you download Skype to your laptop you can make free calls to other Skype users anywhere in the world using a Wi-Fi broadband connection. Rates for calls to non-Skype users (landline or mobile phone) are also very competitively-priced. You will need a computer with a microphone and speakers, and a webcam is handy too. It is also possible to download Skype to an internet-enabled mobile phone to take advantage of the same low-cost calls – see www.skype.com.

Radio and Television

Radio and Television Broadcasts

The BBC World Service broadcasts radio programmes 24 hours a day worldwide from a network of FM/AM/SW transmitters and you can listen on a number of platforms: online, via satellite or cable, DRM digital radio, internet radio or mobile phone. In addition, many local radio stations broadcast BBC World Service programmes in English on FM frequencies. You can find detailed information and programme schedules at www.bbc.co.uk/worldservice.

Listeners in northern France can currently listen to BBC Radio 5 Live on either 693 or 909 kHz medium wave or BBC Radio 4 on 198 kHz long wave. Whereas analogue television signals were switched off in the UK during 2012, no date has yet been fixed for the switch off of analogue radio signals.

BBC News Online is available on internet-enabled mobile phones, tablets and other wireless handheld devices – text 81010 from your mobile phone or type www.bbc.co.uk/mobile into your browser for set-up information. Mobile phone network providers also have links to the BBC or Sky News from their own portals for breaking news and headlines. Be aware that roaming charges for mobile phones in mainland Europe (especially in non-EU countries such as Switzerland) can be extremely expensive for large data downloads.

Digital Terrestrial Television

As in the UK, television transmissions in most of Europe have been converted to digital. The UK's high definition transmission technology may be more advanced than any currently implemented or planned in Europe. This means that digital televisions intended for use in the UK might not be able to receive HD terrestrial signals in some countries.

Satellite Television

For English-language TV programmes the only realistic option is satellite, and satellite dishes are a common sight on campsites all over Europe. A satellite dish mounted on the caravan roof or clamped to a pole fixed to the drawbar, or one mounted on a foldable free-standing tripod, will provide good reception and minimal interference. Remember however that obstructions to the south east (such as tall trees or even mountains) or heavy rain, can interrupt the signals. A specialist dealer will be able to advise you on the best way of mounting your dish. You will also need a satellite receiver and ideally a satellite-finding meter. Many satellite channels are transmitted clear, or 'free-to-air', which means they can be received by any make of receiver, but others are encrypted and require the use of a Sky viewing card and digibox.

For the free-to-air channels, there is a choice of receivers including Sky, Freesat and generic makes. There is nothing to stop you taking a Sky digibox from home unless your Sky contract says you have to keep your it connected to your phone line, in which case charges may apply. Alternatively you can take a Freesat receiver or a generic free-to-air receiver. There is also a camping kit which comprises a receiver, dish and stand, and 10m of cable all enclosed in a convenient plastic carrying case. They are available from caravan accessory shops and a variety of other outlets.

Freesat boxes are widely available on the high street, or you can buy a non-subscription Sky digibox from a number of online suppliers. To watch any encrypted channels, there is no option other than to use a Sky digibox, equipped with a viewing card. However, although it is not illegal to use a Sky viewing card outside the UK, it is against Sky's terms and conditions and it will be within their rights to cancel the card. The digibox itself is your own personal property and can be taken abroad without restriction. It will provide access to most free-to-air channels without having a viewing card in it. However, do note that if you intend to take a Sky+ box with you, it will not perform any of the record or playback functions without its designated Sky card. A Freesat+ recorder on the other hand has no such restrictions and can be used freely across Europe.

There are hundreds of English-language TV channels and national radio stations that can be received anywhere in the UK and, in some cases, large parts of Europe. The main entertainment channels such as BBC1, ITV1 and Channel 4 have for a number of years been more difficult to pick up in mainland Europe than others such as the Sky channels. Unfortunately that situation has intensified and will continue to do so in 2014 as the older satelliteds are replaces by new narrow-beam satellites. Channel 5 which used to be relatively easy to pick up has already belcome much more difficult and other main broadcasters will follow suit. A 60cm dish will still suffice for most of France, Belgium and the Netherlands but as you travel further afield, you'll need a progressively larger dish to pick up the traditional entertainment channels. Even in the South of France, bordering the mediterranean coast and the Pyrenees, you might need up to a 1 meter diameter dish.

Many news channels such as Sky News and France 24 will probably remain accessible across most of Europe, though BBC News (which uses the same narrow-beam transmitters as the rest of the BBC output) will not.

In total there will be three new satellites transmitting the UK channels, but as Caravan Europe went to press only one was in service. It carries the Channel 5 family and it is already apparent that reception in Southern Europe wil be much mroe difficult or impossible. With the next satellite carrying the remaining main free broadcasters, the BBC ITV and Channel 4, the situation will worsen. See the website www.satelliteforcaravans.co.uk (created and operated by a Caravan Club member) for the latest changes and developments, and for information on how to set up your equipment.

Television via a Laptop

With a modern laptop this is straightforward. In order to process the incoming signal the laptop must, as a minimum, be fitted with a TV tuner and a TV-in connector – basically an aerial socket. Some laptops have them built in, but if not you can obtain a plug-in USB adaptor. An alternative connection is the HDMI socket (High Definition Multimedia Interface) which is fitted to most modern laptops, for which you will need an HD digital receiver. For more information see www.radioandtelly.co.uk.

Currently television programmes via BBC iPlayer are only available to users to download or stream in the UK . This is due to rights agreements, however the BBC

are aware that there is a demand for an international version. Most radio programmes are available outside of the UK via BBC iPlayer as well as highlights from many BBC News programmes and BBC Sport video content. Check for updates before you travel www.bbc.co.uk/iplayer.

Using Mobile Phones Abroad

Mobile phones have an international calling option called 'roaming,' which will automatically search for a local network when you switch your phone on, wherever you are in Europe. You should contact your service provider to obtain advice on the charges involved as these are partly set by the foreign networks you use and fluctuate with exchange rates. Most network providers offer added extras or 'bolt-ons' to your tariff to make the cost of calling to/from abroad cheaper.

When you arrive at your destination, your mobile will automatically select a network with the best service. You should also be able to access most of the features you use in the UK, including voicemail and pay-as-you-go top-up.

When calling UK landline or mobile phone numbers prefix the number with +44 and drop the initial 0 of the area code. Storing telephone numbers in your phone's contact list in this format will mean that your contacts will automatically work abroad as well as in the UK.

Because mobile phones will only work within range of a base station, reception in some remote rural areas may be patchy, but coverage is usually excellent in main towns and near main roads and motorways. Approximate coverage maps can be obtained from many dealers.

If you are making calls to numbers within the country you are visiting, you only need to use the standard dialling code without the international code, rather like using your phone in the UK. To make a call to a country other than the UK from abroad, simply replace the +44 country code with the applicable country code.

You should note that if you receive an incoming call while abroad, the international leg of the call will be charged to your mobile phone account because the caller has no way of knowing that they are making an international call. It is possible to bar or divert incoming calls when abroad and your service provider will supply a full list of options.

Mobile service providers have responded to pressure from the EU to reduce roaming charges but while mobile phone charges are coming down, sending and receiving video messages is still expensive – check with your network provider.

Global SIM Cards

As an alternative to paying your mobile service provider's roaming charges it is possible to buy a global SIM card which will enable your mobile phone to operate on a foreign mobile network more cheaply.

When you go abroad you simply replace the SIM card in your phone with the new card, remembering to leave a voicemail message on the old card telling callers that you have temporarily changed number. This service is offered by a number of network providers as well as companies such as www.roameo.co.uk, www.truphone.com and www.0044.co.uk.

You may, however, find it simpler to buy a SIM card abroad but before doing this, check with your UK service provider to find out whether it has locked your phone against the use of a different SIM card and what, if anything, it will charge to unlock it. The website www.0044.co.uk has instructions on how to unlock mobile phones. If you plan to use a mobile phone a lot while abroad, e.g. to book campsites, restaurants, etc, then give some thought to buying a cheap 'pay-as-you-go' phone in the country you are visiting.

Hands-Free

Legislation in Europe forbids the use of mobile or car phones while driving except when using hands-free equipment. **If you are involved in an accident whilst driving and, at the same time, you were using a hand-held mobile phone, your insurance company may refuse to honour the claim.**

Internet & Wi-Fi-Enabled Phones

As technology advances VoIP (voice-over internet protocol) permits you to be contacted on and make calls from your usual mobile phone number while abroad. Part of your call is routed over the internet – see www.truphone.com for information about the latest mobile apps. You will need a Wi-Fi or 3G internet-enabled phone.

Mobile Internet Costs - Data Roaming

Please be aware that accessing the internet overseas via your mobile can be very expensive. It is recommended that you disable your internet access by switching 'data roaming' to off, in order to avoid a large mobile phone bill on your return. If you need to go online or check your email, find a free Wi-Fi hotspot. These are now often available on some campsites or in some cafes, bars and restaurants.

Finally...

Make a note of your mobile phone's serial number, your own telephone number and the number of your provider's customer services and keep them in a safe place separate from your mobile phone.

Remember to pack your charger and travel adaptor. Charging packs, available from major mobile phone and other retailers, provide a power source to recharge your phone if you do not have access to a mains supply. Whichever network you use, check that you have the instructions for use abroad.

During Your Stay
Medical Matters

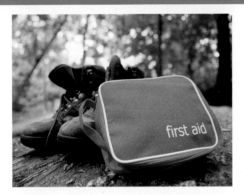

This chapter offers advice and information on what to do before you travel, how to avoid the need for healthcare when you are away from home and what to do when you return.

Specific advice on obtaining emergency medical treatment in European countries is comprehensively covered country-by-country in the Healthcare Abroad section of the NHS Choices website, www.nhs.uk. Alternatively obtain a copy of the Department of Health's leaflet, T7.1 Health Advice for Travellers which is downloadable from www.dh.gov.uk, or call 020 7210 4850.

Very few countries offer such easy access to medical facilities as Britain. Obtaining medical treatment abroad may seem complicated to UK residents who are used to the NHS. Also in most countries around the world you will have to pay, often large amounts, for relatively minor treatment.

Before You Travel

If you have any pre-existing medical conditions it is wise to check with your GP that you are fit to travel. If your medical condition is complex then ask your doctor for a written summary of your medical problems and a list of medications currently used, together with other treatment details, and have it translated into the language of the country, or countries, that you are visiting. This is particularly important for travellers whose medical conditions require them to use controlled drugs or hypodermic syringes, in order to avoid any local difficulties with Customs.

See *Customs Regulations* in the section *PLANNING AND TRAVELLING*.

Check the health requirements for your destination; these may depend not only on the countries you are visiting, but which parts, at what time of the year and for how long. If you are travelling to an unusual destination, heading well off the beaten track, or if you simply want to be sure of receiving the most up-to-date advice, your first step should be to get a MASTA Travel Health Brief. This is designed to meet your specific travel health needs, helping you understand the travel health risks you may face together with any relevant vaccination, antimalarial and other protective advice. To obtain a MASTA Travel Health Brief free of charge simply log on to www.masta-travel-health.com.

Always check that you have enough of your regular medications to last the duration of your holiday and carry a card giving your blood group and details of any allergies or dietary restrictions (a translation of these may be useful when visiting restaurants). Your doctor can normally prescribe only a limited quantity of medicines under the NHS so if you think you will run out of prescribed medicines whilst abroad, ask your doctor for the generic name of any drugs you use, as brand names may be different abroad. If you don't already know it, find out your blood group. In an emergency this may well ensure prompt treatment.

If you have any doubts about your teeth or plan to be away a long time, have a dental check-up before departure. An emergency dental kit is available from High Street chemists which will allow you temporarily to restore a crown, bridge or filling or to dress a broken tooth until you can get to a dentist.

A good website to check before you travel is www.nathnac.org/travel. This website gives general health and safety advice and reports of disease outbreaks, as well as highlighting potential health risks by country.

European Heath Insurance Card (EHIC)

Before leaving home apply for a European Health Insurance Card (EHIC). British residents who are temporarily visiting another EU member state, as well as Iceland, Liechtenstein, Norway or Switzerland, are entitled to receive state-provided emergency treatment during their stay on the same terms as residents of those countries. As well as treatment in the event of an emergency, this includes on-going medical care for a chronic disease or pre-existing illness, i.e. medication, blood tests and injections. The card shows name and date of birth and a personal identification number. It holds no electronic or clinical data.

Apply online for your EHIC on www.ehic.org.uk or by telephoning 0845 6062030 or by obtaining an application form from a post office. An EHIC is required by each individual family member, so allow enough time before your departure for applications to be processed. A child under 16 must be included in a parent or guardian's application as a dependant, and will receive his/her own card.

The EHIC is free of charge, is valid for up to five years and can be renewed up to six months before its expiry date. Before you travel remember to check that your EHIC is still valid.

Before you travel remember to check that your EHIC is still valid and allow enough time to apply

Private treatment is generally not covered by your EHIC, and state-provided treatment may not cover everything that you would expect to receive free of charge from the NHS. If charges are made, these cannot be refunded by the British authorities but may be refundable under the terms of your holiday travel insurance policy.

An EHIC is not a substitute for travel insurance and **it is strongly recommended that you arrange full travel insurance before leaving home (see below) regardless of the cover provided by your EHIC.** Some insurance companies require you to have an EHIC and some will waive the policy excess if an EHIC has been used.

An EHIC issued in the UK is valid provided the holder remains ordinarily resident in the UK and eligible for NHS services. Restrictions may apply to nationals of other countries resident in the UK. For enquiries about applications see www.ehic.org.uk or call EHIC Enquiries on 0845 6062030. For other enquiries call 0845 6050707. If your EHIC is stolen or lost while you are abroad contact 0044 191 2127500 for help.

Residents of the Republic of Ireland, the Isle of Man and Channel Islands, should check with their own health authorities about reciprocal arrangements with other countries.

Holiday Travel Insurance

Despite the fact that you have an EHIC you may incur thousands of pounds of medical costs if you fall ill or have an accident, even in countries with which Britain has reciprocal health care arrangements. The cost of bringing a person back to the UK, in the event of illness or death, is never covered by reciprocal arrangements. Therefore, separate additional travel insurance adequate for your destination is essential, such as The Caravan Club's Red Pennant Overseas Holiday Insurance, available to Club members – see www.caravanclub.co.uk/redpennant.

First Aid

A first aid kit containing at least the basic requirements is an essential item, and in some countries it is compulsory to carry one in your vehicle (see the *Essential Equipment Table* in the chapter *Motoring – Equipment*). Kits should contain items such as sterile pads, assorted dressings, bandages and plasters, hypo-allergenic tape, antiseptic wipes or cream, painkillers, gauze, cotton wool, scissors, finger stall, eye bath and tweezers. Add to that travel sickness remedies, a triangular bandage, medicated hand cleaner or wipes, a pair of light rubber gloves and a pocket mask in case you ever find yourself in a situation where you need to give mouth-to-mouth resuscitation. Also make sure you carry something for the treatment of upset stomachs, which often spoil more holidays than anything else.

It is always wise to carry a good first aid manual containing useful advice and instructions. The British Red Cross publishes a comprehensive First Aid Manual in conjunction with St John Ambulance and St Andrew's Ambulance Association, which is widely available. First aid essentials are also covered in a number of readily-available compact guide books.

Emergency Multilingual Phrasebook

The British Red Cross, with the advice of the Department of Health, produces an Emergency Multilingual Phrasebook covering the most common medical questions and terms. It is aimed primarily at health professionals but the document can be downloaded as separate pages in a number of European languages from the Department of Health's website. See www.dh.gov.uk/publications and use the search facility.

Vaccinations

The Department of Health advises long stay visitors to some eastern European countries to consider vaccination against hepatitis A. See the Country Introductions in the relevant edition of Caravan Europe for further information. Polio and tetanus booster injections are no longer routinely administered unless you are at particular risk – see www.nhs.uk.

Tick-Borne Encephalitis (TBE) and Lyme Disease

Hikers and outdoor sports enthusiasts planning trips to forested, rural areas in some parts of central and eastern Europe, including many countries popular with tourists, such as (amongst others) Austria and Croatia, should seek medical advice well ahead of their planned departure date about preventative measures and immunisation against tick-borne encephalitis which is transmitted by the bite of an infected tick. TBE is a potentially serious and debilitating viral disease of the central nervous system, with the risk highest between spring and autumn when ticks are active in long grass, bushes and hedgerows in forested areas and in scrubland and areas where animals wander, including in and around campsites and at rural motorway rest areas. It is endemic in many countries in mainland Europe.

There is no vaccine against Lyme disease, an equally serious tick-borne infection, which, if left untreated, can attack the nervous system and joints. Early treatment with antibiotics will normally halt the progress of the disease, but you should be vigilant about checking yourself and your family for ticks and be aware of signs and symptoms of the disease.

If you think you might be at risk use an insect repellent containing DEET, wear long sleeves and long trousers, inspect the body for ticks after outdoor activity and remove with tweezers. Avoid unpasteurised dairy products in risk areas. See www.tickalert.org or telephone 01943 468010.

During Your Stay

Take your NHS medical card with you if visiting a non-EU country as you may be asked for it when seeking medical assistance. Some UK Primary Care Trusts will only issue medical cards on request.

If you require treatment in an EU country but do not have an EHIC, or are experiencing difficulties in getting your EHIC accepted, telephone the Department for Work & Pensions for assistance on the overseas healthcare team line 0044 (0)191 218 1999. The office is open from 8am to 5pm Monday to Friday and they will fax documents if necessary.

Claiming Refunds

If you are entitled to a refund from the authorities of the country in which you received treatment you should make a claim in that country either in person or by post before you return home. You must submit the original bills, prescriptions and receipts (keep photocopies for your records). The booklet T7.1 contains details of how to claim refunds, as does NHS Choices on www.nhs.uk/nhsengland/Healthcareabroad. If you

cannot claim until your return home you should contact the Department for Work & Pensions on 0191 218 1999. The DWP will liaise with overseas authorities on your behalf to obtain a refund, which may take some time.

Accidents and Emergencies

If you are unfortunate enough to be involved in, or witness a road accident, or become involved in an emergency situation, firstly summon help early by any means available, giving the exact location of the accident or emergency and the number of casualties. Notify the police; most police officers have first aid training.

If you witnessed an accident the police may question you about it. Before leaving the scene, make a brief note and a rough sketch to indicate details of the time you arrived and left, the position of the vehicles and the injured, the surface of the road, camber, potholes, etc, the weather at the time of the accident, skid marks and their approximate length – in fact anything you feel might be relevant – then date it and sign it. Take photographs if possible. You may never be called on to use these notes, but if you are you have a written record made at the time, which could be of great value.

Calling the Emergency Services

The telephone numbers for police, fire brigade and ambulance services are given in each Country Introduction within each of the relevant Caravan Europe Guides. In all EU member states the number 112 can be used from landlines or mobile phones to call any of the emergency services. In most instances operators speak English.

In all EU member states dial 112 to call any of the emergency services

Insect Bites

Most of the temperate parts of Europe have their fair share of nuisance insects such as mosquitoes and midges, particularly near lakes, and it is wise to use an insect repellant. A number of products are available including impregnated wrist and ankle bands and insect repellant sprays and coils. Covering exposed skin with long trousers and long-sleeved shirts is recommended after dark. Also see information earlier in this chapter about tick-borne encephalitis and Lyme disease.

Rabies

Rabies incidence across Europe has reduced in recent years, in large part due to EU-sponsored vaccination programmes. Apart from isolated incidents, rabies is now confined to a few member states in the east of the

EU, principally Romania and Latvia.

Despite this, **do not** bring any animals into the UK without first complying with the legal requirements.

Always seek medical attention immediately if you get bitten by an animal. Rabies is an acute viral infection and can be fatal.

Swimming

Pollution of sea water at some Continental coastal resorts, including the Mediterranean, may still present a health hazard. Where the water quality may present risks, e.g. in rivers and lakes, as well as at the coast, or where it is simply unsafe to bathe, signs are usually erected, often accompanied by warning flags, which forbid bathing:

French: Défense de se baigner or Il est défendu de se baigner

Italian: Vietato bagnarsi or Evietato bagnarsi

Spanish: Prohibido bañarse or Se prohibe bañarse

Warning flags should always be taken very seriously – red is for danger, when you should not enter the water; usually yellow or orange means you may paddle at the water's edge, but may not swim.
A green flag normally indicates that it is ok to swim. A chequered flag generally means that the lifeguard is temporarily absent. You should never go swimming alone and you should always make sure you know what each flag means and be aware of any risks before you decide to enter the water.

See *Safety and Security* in the next chapter for further information.

Sun Protection

Never under-estimate how ill careless exposure to the sun may make you. If you are not used to the heat it is very easy to fall victim to heat exhaustion or heat stroke. The symptoms include headache, tiredness, weakness and thirst, leading to confusion, disorientation and, in very extreme cases, coma and death. Anyone showing signs of serious over-exposure to the sun should be placed indoors or in the shade, encouraged to sip water and kept cool by fanning or sponging down with cool water. Call a doctor if the patient becomes unconscious or delirious

Take sensible precautions: avoid sitting in the sun between 11am and 3pm; use a good quality sun-cream with high sun protection factor (SPF) and re-apply frequently; wear a sun hat and cover up with a cotton T-shirt when swimming; wear good quality sunglasses which filter UV rays, and finally take extra care at high altitude, especially in the snow and in windy conditions.

Children need extra protection as they burn easily, tend to stay out in the sun longer and are unaware of the dangers of over-exposure. Keep babies out of the sun at all times.

Water and Food

Water from mains supplies throughout Europe is generally good but the level of chemical treatment may make it unpalatable and you may prefer to use bottled water.

Food poisoning is a potential risk anywhere in the world, but in extremely hot conditions a common-sense approach is called for. Avoid food that has been kept warm for prolonged periods or left unrefrigerated for more than two to four hours.

If the source is uncertain, do not eat unpasteurised dairy products, ice-cream, under-cooked meat, fish or shellfish, salads, raw vegetables or dishes containing mayonnaise.

Returning Home

If you become ill on your return home do not forget to tell your doctor that you have been abroad and which countries you have visited. Even if you have received medical treatment in another country, always consult your doctor if you have been bitten or scratched by an animal while on holiday.

If you were given any medicines in another country, it may not be legal to bring them back into the UK. If in doubt, declare them at Customs when you return.

If you develop an upset stomach while away or shortly afterwards and your work involves handling food, tell your employer immediately. If after returning home you develop flu-like symptoms, a fever or rash, contact your GP or NHS Direct.

Claim on your travel insurance as soon as possible for the cost of any medical treatment. Holders of an EHIC who have not been able to claim while abroad should put in a claim for a refund as soon as possible – see *Claiming Refunds* earlier in this chapter.

During Your Stay
Safety and Security

The European Union has strong and effective safety legislations. Nevertheless, safety is largely your own responsibility. Taking sensible precautions and being aware of possible hazards won't spoil your holiday, but a careless attitude might. The following advice will help you and your family have a safer and hopefully trouble-free holiday.

Overnight Stops

The Caravan Club strongly recommends that overnight stops should always be at campsites and not at motorway service areas, ferry terminal car parks, petrol station forecourts or isolated 'aires de services' or 'aires de repos' on motorways where robberies, muggings and encounters with illegal immigrants are occasionally reported. If you ignore this advice and decide to use these areas for a rest during the day or overnight, then you are advised to take appropriate precautions, for example, shutting all windows, securing locks and making a thorough external check of your vehicle(s) before departing. Safeguard your property, e.g. handbags, while out of the caravan and beware of approaches by strangers.

Having said that, there is a wide network of 'Stellplätze', 'Aires de Services', 'Aree di Sosta' and 'Áreas de Servicio' in cities, towns and villages across Europe, many specifically for motorhomes, and many with good security and overnight facilities. It is rare that you will be the only vehicle staying on such areas, but avoid any that are isolated, take sensible precautions and trust your instincts. For example, if the area appears run down and there are groups of people hanging around

who seem intimidating, then you are probably wise to move on.

Around the Campsite

The Caravan Club gives safety a high priority at its UK sites but visitors to the Continent sometimes find that campsites do not always come up to Club standards on electrical safety, hygiene and fire precautions.

Take a few minutes when you arrive on site to ensure that everyone, from the youngest upwards, understands where safety equipment is, how things work and where care is needed to avoid an accident. Once you've settled in, take a walk around the site to familiarise yourself with its layout and ensure that your children are familiar with it and know where their caravan is. Even if you have visited the site before, layout and facilities may have changed.

Locate the nearest fire-fighting equipment and the nearest telephone box and emergency numbers.

Natural disasters are rare, but always think about what could happen. A combination of heavy rain and a riverside pitch could lead to flash flooding, for instance, so make yourself aware of site evacuation procedures.

Be aware of sources of electricity and cabling on and around your pitch. Advice about electrical hook-ups is given in detail in the chapter *Electricity and Gas* in the section *DURING YOUR STAY* – read it carefully.

A Club member has advised that, on occasion, site owners and/or farmers on whose land a site is situated, use poison to control rodents. Warning notices are not always posted and you are strongly advised to check if staying on a rural site and accompanied by your dog.

Common sense should tell you that you need to be careful if the site is close to a main road or alongside a river. Remind your children about the Green Cross Code and encourage them to use it. Adults and children alike need to remember that traffic is on the 'wrong' side of the road.

Incidents of theft from visitors to campsites are rare but when leaving your caravan unattended make sure you lock all doors and shut windows. Conceal valuables from sight and lock bicycles to a tree or to your caravan.

Children

If staying at a farm site, remember that the animals are not pets. Do not approach any animal without the farmer's permission and keep children supervised. Make sure they wash their hands after touching any farm animal. Do not approach or touch any animal which is behaving oddly or any wild animal which appears to be tame.

Watch out for children as you drive around the site and observe the speed limit (walking pace).

Children riding bikes should be made aware that there may be patches of sand or gravel around the site and these should be negotiated at a sensible speed. Bikes should not be ridden between or around tents or caravans.

Children's play areas are generally unsupervised. Check which installations are suitable for your children's ages and abilities and agree with them which ones they may use. Read and respect the displayed rules. Remember it is your responsibility to know where your children are at all times.

Be aware of any campsite rules concerning ball games or use of play equipment, such as roller blades and skateboards. Check the condition of bicycles which you intend to hire.

When your children attend organised activities, arrange when and where to meet afterwards.

Make sure that children are aware of any places where they should not go.

Never leave children alone inside a caravan.

Fire

Fires can be a dangerous hazard and it is important to follow a few basic safety rules. Any fire that starts will spread quickly if not properly dealt with. Follow these rules at all times:

- Never use portable paraffin or gas heaters inside your caravan. Gas heaters should only be fitted when air is taken from outside the caravan.
- Never search for a gas leak with a naked flame or change your gas cylinder inside the caravan. If you smell gas (or in the event of a fire starting), turn off the cylinder immediately, extinguish all naked flames and seek professional help.
- Never place clothing, tea towels or any other items over your cooker or heater to dry.
- Never leave a chip pan or saucepan unattended.
- Keep heaters and cookers clean and correctly adjusted.

- Know where the fire points and telephones are on site and know the site fire drill. Establish a family fire drill. Make sure everyone knows how to call the emergency services.
- Where regulations permit the use of barbecues, take the following precautions to prevent fire:
  Never locate a barbecue near trees or hedges. Have a bucket of water to hand in case of sparks. Only use recommended fire-lighting materials. Do not leave a barbecue unattended when lit and dispose of hot ash safely. Do not let children play near a lit or recently extinguished barbecue.

Swimming Pools

Make the first visit to the pool area a 'family exploration' - not only to find out what is available, but also to identify features and check information which could be vital to your family's safety. Even if you have visited the site before, the layout may have changed, so check the following:

- Pool layout – identify shallow and deep ends and note the position of safety equipment. Check that poolside depth markings are accurate and whether there are any sudden changes of depth in the pool. The bottom of the pool should be clearly visible.
- Are there restrictions about diving and jumping into the pool? Are some surfaces slippery when wet? Ensure when diving into a pool that it is deep enough to do so safely.
- Check opening and closing times. For pools with a supervisor or lifeguard, note any times or dates when the pool is not supervised, e.g. lunch breaks or in low season. Read safety notices and rules posted around the pool. Check the location of any rescue equipment.
- Establish your own rules about parental supervision. Age and swimming ability are important considerations and at least one responsible adult who can swim should accompany and supervise children at the pool at all times. Remember that even a shallow paddling pool can present a danger to young children. Even if a lifeguard is present, you are responsible for your children and must watch them closely.
- Do not swim just after a meal, nor after drinking alcohol.

Water Slides

Take some time to watch other people using the slides so that you can see their speed and direction when entering the water. Find out the depth of water in the landing area. Ensure that your children understand the need to keep clear of the landing area.

Consider and agree with your children which slides they may use. Age or height restrictions may apply.

Check the supervision arrangements and hours of use; they may be different from the main pool times.

Check and follow any specific instructions on the proper use of each slide. The safest riding position is usually feet first, sitting down. Never allow your children to stand or climb on the slide.

Do not wear jewellery when using slides.

Beaches, Lakes and Rivers

Check for any warning signs or flags before you swim and ensure that you know what they mean. Check the depth of water before diving and avoid diving or jumping into murky water as submerged swimmers or objects may not be visible. Familiarise yourself with the location of safety apparatus and/or lifeguards.

Children can drown in a very short time and in relatively small amounts of water. Supervise them at all times when they are in the water and ensure that they know where to find you on the beach.

Use only the designated areas for swimming, windsurfing, kayaking, jetskiing, etc. Always use life jackets where appropriate. Swim only in supervised areas whenever possible.

Familiarise yourself with tides, undertows, currents and wind strength and direction before you or your children swim in the sea. This applies in particular when using inflatables, windsurfing equipment, body boards, kayaks or sailing boats. Sudden changes of wave and weather conditions combined with fast tides and currents are particularly dangerous.

Establish whether there are submerged rocks or a steeply shelving shore which can take non-swimmers or weak swimmers by surprise. Be alert to the activities of windsurfers or jetskiers who may not be aware of the presence of swimmers.

On the Road

Do not leave valuable items on car seats or on view near windows in caravans, even if they are locked. Ensure that items on roof racks or cycle carriers are locked securely.

Beware of a 'snatch' through open car windows at traffic lights, filling stations, in traffic jams or at 'fake' traffic accidents. When driving through towns and cities keep your doors locked. Keep handbags, valuables and documents out of sight at all times.

In view of recent problems with stowaways in vehicles on cross-Channel ferries and trains, check that your outfit is free from unexpected guests at the last practical opportunity before boarding.

If flagged down by another motorist for whatever reason, take care that your own car is locked and windows closed while you check outside, even if someone is left inside. Be particularly careful on long, empty stretches of motorway and when you stop for fuel. Even if the people flagging you down appear to be officials (e.g. wearing yellow reflective jackets or dark, 'uniform-type' clothing) show presence of mind and lock yourselves in immediately. They may appear to be friendly and helpful, but may be opportunistic thieves prepared to resort to violence. Have a mobile phone to

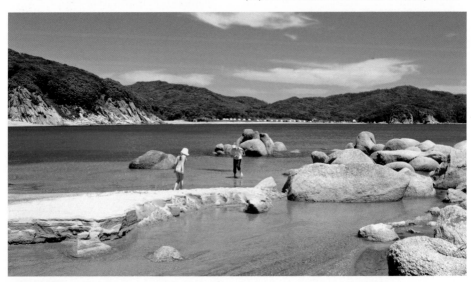

hand and, if necessary, be seen to use it.

Road accidents are a significant risk in some countries where traffic laws may be inadequately enforced, roads may be poorly maintained, road signs and lighting inadequate, and driving standards poor. The traffic mix may be more complex with animal-drawn vehicles, pedestrians, bicycles, cars, lorries, and perhaps loose animals, all sharing the same space. In addition you will be driving on the 'wrong' side of the road and should, therefore, be especially vigilant at all times. Avoid driving at night on unlit roads.

Pursuing an insurance claim abroad can be difficult and it is essential if you are involved in an accident, to take all the other driver's details and complete a European Accident Statement supplied by your motor vehicle insurer.

It's a good idea to keep a fully-charged mobile phone with you in your car with the number of your breakdown organisation saved into it.

Personal Security

There is always the risk of being the victim of petty crime wherever you are in the world. As an obvious tourist you may be more vulnerable, but the number of incidents is very small and the fear of crime should not deter you from holidaying abroad.

The Foreign & Commonwealth Office produces a range of material to advise and inform British citizens travelling abroad about issues affecting their safety, including political unrest, lawlessness, violence, natural disasters, epidemics, anti-British demonstrations and aircraft safety. See the FCO's travel advice for all the countries covered by the Caravan Europe guides on www.fco.gov.uk.

Specific advice on personal security in countries covered in Caravan Europe are given in the Country Introduction chapters. The following points are a few general precautions to help ensure you have a safe and problem-free holiday:

- Leave valuables and jewellery at home. If you do take them, fit a small safe in your caravan and keep them in the safe or locked in the boot of your car. Do not leave money or documents, such as passports, in a car glovebox, or leave handbags and valuables on view. Do not leave bags in full view when sitting outside at cafés or restaurants. Do not leave valuables unattended on the beach.

- When walking be security-conscious. Avoid unlit streets at night, walk well away from the kerb and carry handbags or shoulder bags on the side away from the kerb. The less of a tourist you appear, the less of a target you are.

Never read a map openly in the street or carry a camera over your shoulder.

- Carry only the minimum amount of cash. Distribute cash, credit cards and passports amongst your party; do not rely on one person to carry everything. Never carry a wallet in your back pocket. A tuck-away canvas wallet, moneybelt or 'bumbag' can be useful and waterproof versions are available. It is normally advisable not to resist violent theft.

- Do not use street money-changers; in some countries it is illegal.

- Keep a separate note of bank account and credit/debit card numbers. Join a card protection plan so that in the event of loss or theft, one telephone call will cancel all your cards and arrange replacements. Carry your credit card issuer/bank's 24-hour UK contact number with you.

- Keep a separate note of your holiday insurance reference number and emergency telephone number.

- Your passport is a valuable document; it is expensive and time-consuming to replace and its loss or theft can lead to serious complications if your identity is later used fraudulently. Keep a separate record of your passport details, preferably in the form of a certified copy of the details pages. Fill in the next-of-kin details in your passport. A photocopy of your birth certificate may also be useful.

- Many large cities have a drug problem with some addicts mugging and pickpocketing to fund their habit. Pickpockets often operate in groups, including children. Stay alert, especially in crowds, on trains, undergrounds and stations, near banks and foreign exchange offices, and when visiting well-known historical and tourist sites.

- Beware of bogus plain-clothes policemen who may ask to see your foreign currency or credit cards and passport. If approached, decline to show your money or to hand over your passport but ask for credentials and offer instead to go to the nearest police station.

- Laws vary from country to country and so does the treatment of offenders; find out something about local laws and customs and respect them. Behave and dress appropriately, particularly when visiting religious sites, markets and rural communities. Be aware of local attitudes to alcohol consumption. Do not get involved with drugs.

- Do respect Customs regulations. Smuggling is a serious offence and can carry heavy penalties. Do not carry parcels or luggage through Customs for other people and do not cross borders with people you do not know in your vehicle, such as hitchhikers. If you are in someone else's vehicle do not cross the border in it – get out and walk across; you do not know what might be in the vehicle. Do not drive vehicles across borders for other people.

- Hobbies such as birdwatching and train, plane and ship-spotting, combined with the use of cameras or binoculars, may be misunderstood (particularly near military installations) and you may risk arrest. If in doubt, don't.

- In the event of a natural disaster or if trouble flares up, contact family and friends to let them know that you are safe, even if you are nowhere near the problem area. Family and friends may not know exactly where you are and may worry if they think you are in danger.

The Risk of Terrorism

There is a global underlying risk of indiscriminate terrorist attacks, including in places frequented by foreign travellers, but it is important to remember that the overall risk of being involved in a terrorist incident is very low. Injury and death are far more likely through road accidents, swimming, alcohol-related occurrences or health problems.

Most precautions are simple common sense. Make sure you are aware of the political situation in the country you are visiting and keep an eye on the news. Report anything you think is suspicious to the local police. The FCO Travel Advice for each country within the Caravan Europe guides is summarised in the Country Introduction chapters, but situations can change so make a point of reading the FCO's advice before you travel and register for its email alerts, www.fco.gov.uk.

British Consular Services Abroad

British Embassy and Consular staff offer practical advice, assistance and support to British travellers abroad. They can, for example, issue replacement passports, help Britons who have been the victims of crime, contact relatives and friends in the event of an accident, illness or death, provide information about transferring funds and provide details of local lawyers, doctors and interpreters. But there are limits to their powers and a British Consul cannot, for example, give legal advice, intervene in court proceedings, put up bail, pay for legal or medical bills, or for funerals or the repatriation of bodies, or undertake work more properly done by banks, motoring organisations and travel insurers.

Most British consulates operate an answerphone service outside office hours giving opening hours and arrangements for handling emergencies. If you require consular help outside office hours you may be charged a fee for calling out a Consular Officer. In countries outside the European Union where there are no British Consulates, you can get help from the embassies and consulates of other EU member states.

If you have anything stolen, e.g. money or passport, report it first to the local police and insist on a statement about the loss. You will need this in order to make a claim on your travel insurance. In the event of a fatal accident or death from whatever cause, get in touch with the nearest consulate at once.

If you commit a criminal offence you must expect to face the consequences. If you are charged with a serious offence, insist on the British Consul being informed. You will be contacted as soon as possible by a Consular Officer who can advise on local procedures, provide access to lawyers and insist that you are treated as well as nationals of the country which is holding you. However, they cannot get you released as a matter of course.

If you need help because something has happened to a friend or relative abroad contact the Consular Assistance Service on 020 7008 1500 (24 hours).

BRITISH AND IRISH EMBASSY AND CONSULAR CONTACT DETAILS can be found in the Country Introduction chapters of the relevant Caravan Europe Guides.

France (with Andorra)
Country Introduction

Paris, France

Population France (approx): 63 million

Capital: Paris (population approx 12 million)

Area: 543,965 sq km

Bordered by: Andorra, Belgium, Germany, Italy, Luxembourg, Monaco, Spain, Switzerland

Terrain: Mostly flat plains or gently rolling hills in north and west; mountain ranges in south and east

Climate: Temperate climate with regional variations; generally warm summers and cool winters; harsh winters in mountainous areas; hot summers in central and Mediterranean areas

Coastline: 3,427km

Highest Point: Mont Blanc 4,807m

Language: French

Local Time: GMT or BST + 1, i.e. 1 hour ahead of the UK all year

Currency: Euros divided into 100 cents; £1 = €1.18, €1 = £0.85 (September 2013)

Telephoning: From the UK dial 0033 for France and omit the initial 0 of the 10-digit number you are calling. Mobile phone numbers start 06.
The international dialling code for Andorra is 00376 plus the 6-digit number. For Monaco the code is 00377. To call the UK from France dial 0044 omitting the initial zero of the area code

Emergency Numbers: Police 112; Fire brigade 112; Ambulance 112. In Andorra dial 110 for police, 118 for fire brigade and ambulance, or 112 for general emergencies and mountain rescue

Public Holidays 2014

France: Jan 1; Apr 21; May 1, 8 (VE Day), 29; Jun 9; Jul 14 (Bastille Day); Aug 15; Nov 1, 11 (Armistice Day); Dec 25.

Andorra: Jan 1, 6; Mar 14 (Constitution Day); Apr 18; May 1, 29; Jun 9; Nov 1; Dec 8, 25.

Tourist Offices

FRENCH GOVERNMENT TOURIST BOARD
MAISON DE LA FRANCE
LINCOLN HOUSE
300 HIGH HOLBORN
LONDON WC1V 7JH
Tel: 09068 244123
Personal visits/written
requests preferred
www.franceguide.com
info.uk@franceguide.com

EMBASSY OF THE PRINCIPALITY OF ANDORRA
63 WESTOVER ROAD
LONDON SW18 2RF
Tel: 020 8874 4806
www.andorra.com
info@andorra.com
(Visits by appointment only)

107

The following introduction to France should be read in conjunction with the important information contained in the Handbook chapters at the front of this guide.

Camping and Caravanning

General Information

There are approximately 10,400 campsites throughout France classified from 1 to 5 stars, including many small farm sites. The 5 star classification was introduced in 2010 and is awarded to top of the range campsites, often with a wider range of facilities available. All classified sites must display their classification, current charges, capacity and site regulations at the site entrance. Some sites have an inclusive price per pitch, whereas others charge per person + vehicle(s) + pitch + electric. It is worth remembering that if you stay on site after midday you may be charged for an extra day.

In terms of site tariffs, high season dates and the qualifying age for charging for children varies from site to site. It is quite common for site owners to charge the full adult daily rate for children from seven years and sometimes from as young as three years of age.

Credit cards are widely accepted at campsites, but you may well find payment by this method refused for overnight or short stays because of high transaction charges.

Visitors are usually required to pay a tourism tax (taxe de séjour) that is imposed by local authorities and which can be over €1 per person per day, according to the quality and standard of accommodation. Children under 4 years of age are usually exempt and children under 10 may be charged a reduced rate. This tax is collected by campsite owners and will be included in your bill.

Casual/wild camping is prohibited in many state forests, national parks and nature reserves. It is also prohibited in all public or private forests in the départements of Landes and Gironde, along the Mediterranean coast including the Camargue, parts of the Atlantic and Brittany coasts, Versailles and Paris, and along areas of coast that are covered by spring tides.

A Camping Card International (CCI) is recommended and accepted by most sites in lieu of a passport. Holders of a CCI may also enjoy discounted fees at some campsites.

The Camping Club de France owns a number of sites in France (some of which are listed in this guide and marked CC de F in their site entries) and has partnership agreements with others including the Campéole, Camping du Midi and Huttopia chains.

Members of the CC de F qualify for a reduction when presenting a CCI at these sites. Caravanners wishing to join the CC de F pay an annual fee of €50 per family (2013). Email the CC de F secretariat@campingclub.asso.fr or visit their website www.campingclub.asso.fr. In addition there are sites operating in association with the Fédération Française de Camping & de Caravaning (marked FFCC in their site entries) which also give a discount to holders of a CCI.

July and August are the busiest holiday months and campsites in popular tourist areas, such as the Atlantic Coast, Brittany or the south of France, may be crowded. To be certain of a pitch, make an early booking yourself or use The Caravan Club's Overseas Site Booking Service. For details see the Club's Continental Caravanning brochure or visit www.caravanclub.co.uk/overseas. Campsites included in the Site Booking Service network are marked SBS in their site entries in this guide. **The Caravan Club cannot make advance reservations for any other campsites listed in this guide.**

Many French campsites ban the wearing of boxer-style shorts in swimming pools on grounds of hygiene. This rule may be strictly enforced by inspectors who have the power to close a site's swimming pool. As a result site owners have the right to insist on the wearing of conventional (brief-style) swimming trunks. Many sites also require swimmers to wear swimming caps.

During the low season it is not uncommon for only a few toilet and shower cubicles to be in use on a 'unisex' basis, and they may not be cleaned as frequently as they are during the site's busy season. Hot water, other than for showers, may not be available.

If the weather has been bad early in the season you may find that site staff have not been able, for example, to cut grass or hedges and prepare the site fully for visitors. At the end of the season grass pitches may be well worn and could be muddy or slippery after rain.

Many sites are increasing their proportion of statics – bungalows, tents, chalets and mobile homes – and these are often situated in premium positions thus reducing the choice of pitches for touring caravanners. However, in many instances these statics are only occupied during the main French holiday season.

Following incidents in recent years some authorities in southern France have introduced tighter regulations concerning sites that are potentially liable to flooding. It is understood that many have been advised to limit their opening dates from mid-April/early May until end August/mid-September.

Certain areas of southern France experience severe water shortages in summer months with a consequent increased fire risk. This may result in some local authorities imposing restrictions at short notice on the use of barbecues. When they are used, you should be vigilant in ensuring that they do not pose a fire risk.

Motorhomes – Overnight Stops

There are two types of "Aires" in France, those that can be found on motorways and those that can be found in towns, villages and coastal areas. For safety reasons we do not advise using the motorway Aires for overnight stops, however Aires in towns and villages are usually safer but you should always take sensible precautions and avoid any that are isolated. Aires vary from region to region and you will find that some are free of charge, some charge a small fee, some will have electrics available as well as other facilities, whilst others will just be a basic parking area.

See **Safety and Security** later in this chapter and in the section **DURING YOUR STAY.**

In addition many campsites in popular tourist resorts have separate overnight areas of hardstanding with appropriate facilities, often adjacent to, or just outside, the main campsite area. Fees are generally very reasonable. Look for the 'Stop Accueil Camping-Car' sign.

The Fédération Française de Camping et de Caravaning (FFCC) publishes a 'Guide Officiel Aires de Services Camping-Car', listing 'aires' and stopping places specifically set aside for motorhomes in France and in a number of other countries. Vicarious books publish an English guide to the Aires including directions, GPS co-ordinates and photographs. Please contact 0131 208 333 or visit their website www.vicariousbooks.co.uk.

Motorhomes are also welcome to park overnight free of charge at approximately 1,500 vineyards and farms throughout France through an organisation called France Passion. Your motorhome must be completely self-contained and you must have your own sanitation. In addition you must arrive and depart in daylight hours. Membership is open to motorhomes only and to become a member you need to purchase an invitation card and stopover guide which cost €29 a year (2013) from France Passion, BP 57, 84202 Carpentras. Alternatively join online at www.france-passion.com, or email info@france-passion.com

It is illegal to spend the night in a caravan or motorhome at the roadside.

Municipal Campsites

Municipal campsites are found in most towns and many villages in France. They can usually be booked in advance through the local town hall ('Mairie') or tourist office during office hours. Their published opening dates cannot always be relied on at the start and end of the season and it is advisable to phone ahead or arrive at a site early enough to be able to find an alternative if your first choice is closed.

When approaching a town you may find that municipal sites are not always named. Signposts may simply state 'Camping' or show a tent or caravan symbol. Most municipal sites are clean, well-run and very reasonably priced but security may be rudimentary – at best there may be a barrier at the main entrance which is lowered at night. Occasionally a warden lives on site or nearby, but more often they will only call for an hour or so each morning and evening to clean and collect fees. When selecting a municipal site, therefore, try to take account of the character of the area in which it is situated – evident 'problem' urban areas are probably best avoided, as are isolated sites where yours is the only caravan.

In recent years, in order to deter 'itinerants' from staying on municipal sites, some local authorities have restricted entrance by caravan height or length. Some sites refuse to accept caravans with twin-axles ('deux essieux'), or they make a large additional charge for them, possibly as high as €45 a night. It is advisable to check for restrictions when booking in advance and/or on arrival. You are, however, more likely to encounter groups of market traders or seasonal workers, e.g. grape pickers. In general their presence does not cause other visitors any problems. Recent visitors report that bona fide caravanners with twin-axle caravans or over-height/weight/length caravans may be allowed entry and/or may not be charged the higher published tariff, but this is negotiable with site staff at the time of arrival.

Naturism

The French Government Tourist Board has links to naturist centres approved by the French Federation of Naturism, or visit www.naturisme.fr and www.france4naturisme.com for details of naturist centres throughout the country.

Visitors aged 15 and over are recommended to have a Naturist Licence, although this is no longer compulsory at many naturist centres. A licence can be obtained in advance from British Naturism (tel 01604 620361, www.british-naturism.org.uk, email headoffice@british-naturism.org.uk) or on arrival at any recognised naturist campsite (passport-size photo required).

For further details contact the French Federation of Naturism, email contact@ffn-naturisme.com, www.ffn-naturisme.com.

FRANCE

Sites in Andorra, Corsica, Ile d'Oléron and Ile de Ré

Please note that campsites for these areas are listed separately at the end of the French site entry pages.

Country Information

Caravan Storage in France

You can download a list of some of the sites offering caravan storage facilities in France from www.caravanclub.co.uk, or you may find that many other commercial campsites also offer a long-term storage facility. See the Handbook chapters *Continental Campsites* and *Insurance* for more information.

Cycling

See *Local Travel* at the end of this chapter for information on cycle paths and routes.

It is compulsory for cyclists to use front and rear lights and wear a reflective jacket when riding at night outside built-up areas and in poor daytime visibility. The wearing of safety helmets is not yet officially compulsory, but is highly recommended.

Transportation of Bicycles

Transportation on a support fixed to the rear of a vehicle is permitted provided the rear lights and number plate of the carrying vehicle are not obscured.

Electricity and Gas

Current on campsites is usually between 6 and 20 amps, but on some sites may be as low as 3 amps. Plugs have two round pins. Most campsites now have CEE socket connections. Visitors from the UK should be aware of the problem of reversed polarity which may be found on sites in France. If embarking on a tour of several campsites it may be useful to take two differently wired electric adaptors, one wired normally and one wired for reversed polarity.

The full range of Campingaz cylinders is widely available from large supermarkets and hypermarkets, although recent visitors report that at the end of the holiday season stocks may be low or shops may have run out altogether. Other popular brands of gas which visitors have found to be economical and easy to use are Primagaz, Butagaz, Totalgaz and Le Cube. A loan deposit is required and if you are buying a cylinder for the first time you may also need to buy the appropriate regulator or adaptor hose, as cylinder connections vary considerably. Compare prices carefully between the different brands and check that cylinders fit into your gas cylinder locker.

French and Spanish butane and propane gas cylinders

are understood to be widely available in Andorra. See *Electricity and Gas* in the section **DURING YOUR STAY.**

Entry Formalities

A visitor remaining more than 90 days has to apply for a sojourn permit, however this does not apply to visitors from EEA countries or Switzerland.

On arrival at a hotel visitors are usually asked to complete a form for identification purposes. At campsites visitors presenting a Camping Card International do not have to complete such a form.

Regulations for Pets

See *Pet Travel Scheme* under *Documents* in the section **PLANNING AND TRAVELLING.**

Some campsites in France do not accept dogs at all and some have restrictions on the number and breed of dogs allowed. Further information can be found on www.caravanclub.co.uk/overseasadvice.

In popular tourist areas local regulations may ban dogs from beaches during the summer months.

In preparation for your return home with your dog you can find the names and addresses of vets in France in 'Pages Jaunes' (the equivalent of the Yellow Pages) on www.pagesjaunes.fr. Alternatively you can ask the campsite staff to recommend a local vet.

Medical Services

British nationals requiring emergency treatment can take advantage of the French health service on production of a European Health Insurance Card (EHIC). This will allow you to claim reimbursement of around 70% of standard doctors' and dentists' fees, and between 35% and 65% of the cost of most prescribed medicines.

For the address of a doctor 'conventionné', i.e. working within the French state healthcare system, ask at a pharmacy. After treatment make sure you are given a signed statement of treatment ('feuille de soins') showing the amount paid as you will need this for a refund.

Pharmacies dispense prescriptions and first aid. Your prescription will be returned to you and you should attach this, together with the stickers (vignettes) attached to the packaging of any medication or drugs, to the 'feuille de soins' in order to obtain a refund.

If you are admitted to hospital make sure you present your EHIC on admission. This will save you from paying any refundable costs up front and ensure that you only pay the patient contribution. You may have to pay a co-payment towards your treatment and if you are an inpatient you will have to pay a daily hospital charge. These charges are not refundable in

France but you may be able to seek reimbursement when you are back in the UK.

Applications for refunds should be sent to a local sickness insurance office (Caisse Primaire d'Assurance-Maladie) and you should receive payment at your home address within about two months.

All visitors should take out comprehensive travel and medical insurance to cover all eventualities, such as the Caravan Club's Red Pennant Overseas Holiday Insurance – see www.caravanclub.co.uk/redpennant.

For sports activities such as skiing and mountaineering, travel insurance must include provision for covering the cost of mountain and helicopter rescue. Visitors to the Savoie and Haute-Savoie areas should be aware that an accident or illness may result in a transfer to Switzerland for hospital treatment. There is a reciprocal healthcare agreement for British citizens visiting Switzerland but you will be required to pay the full costs of treatment and afterwards apply for a refund.

Andorra

Andorra is not a member of the EU and, therefore, the EHIC is not accepted and there are no reciprocal emergency health care arrangements with Britain. You will be required to pay the full cost of medical treatment and are strongly advised to obtain comprehensive travel and medical insurance which includes cover for travel to non-EU countries, such as the Club's Red Pennant Overseas Holiday Insurance – see www.caravanclub.co.uk/redpennant.

See **Medical Matters** in the section **DURING YOUR STAY**.

Opening Hours

Banks – Mon-Fri 9am-noon & 2pm-4pm/5pm/6pm; in Paris Mon-Fri 10am-5pm; some open Sat & close on Mon. Early closing the day before a public holiday.

Museums – Daily 10am-5pm; closed Mon or Tues, check locally. In Paris many are open late once a week.

Post Offices – Mon-Fri 8am/9am-6pm/7pm; Sat 8am/9am-noon.

Shops: Food shops - Tues-Sat 7am/9am-6.30pm/7.30pm; some food shops i.e. bakers, grocers, etc, are open sun morning. Other shops - Tues-Sat 9am/10am-7.30pm. Shops generally close all or half day on Mon; in small towns shops close for lunch from noon to 2pm. Major Shops - Mon-Sat 9am/10am-7pm. Supermarkets may stay open until 9pm/10pm. Shops in tourist areas may open on Sunday.

Clothing

In April 2011 a new law was introduced in France prohibiting the wearing of a garment or clothing which hides the face i.e. burka, nikab, balaclava, in public places. This also applies to visitors.

Safety and Security

See **Safety and Security** in the section **DURING YOUR STAY**.

In and around Calais and Dunkerque, British owned cars have been targetted by thieves, both while parked and on the move, e.g. by thieves flagging drivers down for a lift or indicating that a vehicle has a flat tyre. In some cases tyres have been punctured at service stations forcing drivers to stop soon afterwards. If you stop in such circumstances be extremely wary of anyone offering help, ensure that car keys are not left in the ignition and that vehicle doors are locked while you investigate.

Pedestrians should beware of bag-snatchers operating on foot and from motorbikes. Avoid carrying passports, credit cards and money together in handbags or pockets. Do not leave bags in full view when sitting outside at cafés or restaurants. Do not leave valuables unattended on the beach. Valuables, including tobacco and alcohol, should not be left unattended in a parked car and should be kept out of sight at all times.

Thieves and pickpockets operate on the Paris metro and RER (regional suburban rail network), especially RER line B, and you should be extra vigilant. Be particularly careful in and around shopping centres and car parks. Avoid illegal street vendors, many of whom employ persistent and often intimidating techniques to sell their wares, and who are now to be found at many tourist sites and attractions in Paris.

Visitors to Commonwealth War Graves Commission cemeteries in northern France, many of which are in isolated areas, are advised not to leave handbags or other valuables in parked cars as they can be a target for thieves.

France shares with the rest of Europe a general threat from terrorism. Attacks could be indiscriminate and against civilian targets, including tourist attractions.

Overnight Motorway Stops

The Caravan Club strongly recommends that overnight stops should always be at recognised campsites and not at motorway service areas, ferry terminal car parks or 'aires de services' or 'aires de repos' along motorways, where robberies and muggings are occasionally reported. This advice applies to all motorways but particularly to isolated rest areas (those without petrol stations or caféterias), especially those on the A10 between Paris and Bordeaux, the A16 between Calais and Dunkerque and the A25 between Dunkerque and Lille.

If you do decide to use these motorway areas for a

rest during the day or overnight, then you are advised to take appropriate precautions. Avoid parking in isolated or dark areas, shut all windows, secure locks and make a thorough external check of your vehicle(s) before departing. Consider fitting an alarm to your caravan.

The South of France and Corsica

Always keep car doors locked and windows closed when driving in populated areas of the south of France, especially in the Marseille to Menton area. It is common for bags to be snatched from a front passenger seat, usually by individuals on motorbikes, often when the vehicle is stationary at traffic lights. Conceal bags and purses when driving and never leave valuables in a vehicle even for a short period of time.

In recent years there has been a number of bomb and other attacks on public buildings by the Corsican nationalist group, the FLNC. All the buildings were closed at the time of the attacks. While there is no specific threat to British tourists, visitors should take care, particularly in town centres and near public buildings, and be wary of unattended packages.

Fires can be a regular occurrence in forested areas, especially along the Mediterranean coast and in Corsica during summer months. They are generally extinguished quickly and efficiently but short term evacuations are sometimes necessary. If visiting forested areas familiarise yourself with local emergency procedures in the event of fire.

Avoid leaving your vehicle(s) unattended by the roadside, especially on beach roads, as thefts are frequent.

Visitors to Corsica are warned that most road accidents occur during the tourist season. Many roads in Corsica are mountainous and narrow with numerous bends. Drivers should be extra vigilant and beware of wandering farm animals.

Andorra

Street crime is not common but take the usual common sense precautions to safeguard your passports and money.

If you are planning a skiing holiday you should contact the Andorran Embassy in London (tel 020 8874 4806) for advice on safety and weather conditions before travelling. All safety instructions should be followed meticulously given the dangers of avalanches in some areas. See www.ski.andorra.com or www.avalanches.org for more information.

British Embassy in France
35 RUE DU FAUBOURG ST HONORE
75363 PARIS CEDEX 08 PARIS
Tel: 01 44 51 31 00
www.ukinfrance.fco.gov.uk/en/

There are also Consulates in Bordeaux, Lille, Lyon and Marseilles.

Irish Embassy in France
12 AVENUE FOCH, 75116 PARIS
Tel: 01 44 17 67 00
www.embassyofireland.fr

There are also Irish Consulates-General/Consulates in Cannes, Cherbourg, Lyon and Monaco.

For Consular help while in Andorra contact the British Consulate-General in Barcelona:
AVDA DIAGNOL 477-13, 08036 BARCELONA
Tel: 00 34 902 109 356
www.ukinspain.fco.gov.uk/en/

Customs Regulations

Alcohol and Tobacco

For general import allowances for alcohol and tobacco products see *Customs Regulations* in the section *PLANNING AND TRAVELLING.*

Duty-Free Imports from Andorra

Duty-free shopping is permitted in Andorra, which is not a member of the EU, but there are strict limits on the amount of goods which can be exported from there into France and Spain, and Customs checks are frequently made. Each person aged 17 years or over is permitted to export the following items from Andorra free of duty or tax:

1.5 litre of spirits over 22 degrees or 3 litres spirits or apertifs under 22 degrees or sparkling wine

5 litres of table wine

300 cigarettes or 150 cigarillos or 75 cigars or 400 gm of tobacco

75g of perfumes + 375 ml of eau de cologne

Other items (industrial products) up to the value of €900

There are no Customs formalities when entering Andorra from France or Spain. There are no identity checks at the borders with other EU countries or with Switzerland but you may encounter Customs checks when entering or leaving Switzerland as well as when leaving Andorra.

Caravans and Motorhomes

A caravan, motorhome or trailer tent imported into France from an EU country may remain indefinitely. The importer must be in possession of the purchase invoice showing that tax (VAT) has been paid in the country of purchase. The temporary importation of a caravan by persons other than the owner requires written authorisation from the owner.

Although a permit is not required for vehicles being imported on a permenant basis, they must be covered by a certificate of conformity to EU standards issued by the manufacturer or his representative in France or by the "Direction Régionale de l'Environnement, de l'Aménagement et du Logement" (DREAL). Any vehicles that do not conform to these standards, and vehicles over 4 years old, must be presented to the DREAL for an inspection.

Caravans, motorhomes and trailer tents must not exceed the maximum authorised laden weight displayed on the vehicle's registration certificate.

Some border crossings in the Alps to Italy and in the Pyrénées to Spain close in winter. Border crossing posts with Germany are normally open continuously, except for those on ferries crossing the Rhine.

Documents

Driving Licence

Carry your driving licence at all times when driving.

Passport

Everyone, whatever their nationality, must carry identity papers, e.g. a passport, as the police are empowered to check a person's identity at any time. This is also a requirement in Andorra.

Vehicle(s)

Carry your original vehicle registration document (V5C), insurance certificate and MOT certificate (if applicable). If the vehicle is not registered in your name carry a letter of authorisation from the owner. A copy of your Caravan Registration Certificate (CRIS) document is also advisable. This advice applies to both France and Andorra. However, don't forget to check that your insurance policy covers you for your trip.

Green Card

As an EU country, British residents do not need an International Motor Insurance Certificate (Green Card) for France. Andorra is now an Associated Country of the European Union and, therefore, a Green Card is also no longer required.

Money

*See **Money** in the section **PLANNING AND TRAVELLING**.*

French banks generally do not cash travellers' cheques for non-account holders, therefore the use of travellers cheques is not recommended as a means of obtaining cash. You may be able to cash them at some post offices but handling charges and rates of commission for exchanging both travellers' cheques and bank notes may vary considerably and you should check all charges before the transaction goes through. An

alternative to travellers' cheques is a pre-paid currency card - see www.caravanclub.co.uk/travelmoney for details of the Moneycorp Explorer prepaid card.

Frequent visitors may wish to consider opening a euro bank account in France in order to obtain a French credit/debit card. This will then avoid the problem of using credit cards at automated petrol stations (which may occasionally reject cards issued by foreign banks) and means that you will not have to pay any foreign exchange fees or commission charges to withdraw euros from cash machines or when you use the card in shops, restaurants, campsites, etc. Britline, a branch of Crédit Agricole is one bank which provides an English-speaking French banking service to residents of the UK and Ireland, tel 0033 231 55 67 89 or see www.britline.com.

Major credit cards are widely accepted and cash dispensers are widespread and usually allow users to choose instructions in English. VISA cards are displayed as 'Carte Bleue' or 'CB'.

When shopping in supermarkets near the Channel ports and paying with a credit or debit card you will be offered the choice of paying in euros or sterling. You are recommended always to pay in euros as the exchange rate used is likely to be less favourable than that used by your card issuer.

Carry your credit card issuers'/banks' 24-hour UK contact numbers in case of loss or theft of your cards.

Motoring

Accidents

A driver involved in an accident or one who has committed a traffic offence may be required to take a saliva or urine drugs test as well as a breathalyser test. In the event of an accident where people are injured or if emergency assistance is required, dial 17 (police) or 112 from any phone. A European Accident Statement form should be completed and signed by all persons involved in an accident – see the chapter *Insurance* in the section *PLANNING AND TRAVELLING*.

Alcohol

In both France and Andorra the maximum legal level of alcohol is 50 milligrams in 100 millilitres of blood, i.e. less than permitted in the UK (80 milligrams). It is advisable to adopt the 'no drink and drive' rule at all times. The police carry out random breath tests and penalties are severe.

There is a legal requirement to carry a breathalyser, however there is currently no punishment for non-compliance. Check www.caravanclub.co.uk/overseasadvice for the most up-to-date advice before you travel.

Breakdown Service

Breakdown and accident assistance on motorways and on motorway service and rest areas can only be obtained by contacting the police direct. They can be called from one of the orange emergency telephones placed every 2km along motorways. If you are in a service area, ask service station staff to contact the police for you, or dial 17 or 112 from a public phone and the police will be able to pinpoint your exact whereabouts. The police will arrange breakdown and towing assistance. No breakdown vehicle will enter a motorway without police authority.

Charges for motorway assistance are fixed by the government and vary according to category/weight of vehicle, time of day and whether the breakdown occurred over a weekend or public holiday. The basic cost (2013) of repairing a vehicle up to 1,800 kg in weight, on the spot, between Monday and Friday, from 0800 to 1800, is €119.75 or €148.00 for vehicles over 1800kg. Higher charges apply at night and over weekends and public holidays.

If you have taken out breakdown insurance (e.g. The Caravan Club's Red Pennant Overseas Holiday Insurance) you should contact your insurance provider once the breakdown service has arrived in order to establish a means of payment. Your insurance provider cannot summon the police on your behalf if you breakdown on a motorway. There are a number of expressways (N roads) where the same rules apply.

Essential Equipment

See **Motoring – Equipment** in the section **PLANNING AND TRAVELLING.**

Lights

The use of dipped headlights is recommended at all times, day and night. Headlights must be adjusted for driving on the right if they are likely to dazzle other road users.

Bulbs are more likely to fail with constant use and, if practical, it is a good idea to carry spares. Drivers able to replace a faulty bulb when requested to do so by the police may not avoid a fine, but may avoid the expense of calling out a garage.

If a driver flashes his headlights in France he is generally indicating that he has priority and you should give way, contrary to standard practice in the UK.

Reflective Jacket/Waistcoat

It is a legal requirement for all vehicle occupants (driver and passengers) to wear a reflective jacket when getting out of a vehicle which is stationary on the carriageway or on the side of the road at any time of the day or night, regardless of visibility. Keep the jacket(s) to hand in your vehicle, not in the boot.

Child Restraint System

In France children under 10 years of age are not permitted to travel on front seats of vehicles, unless there are no rear seats in the vehicle, or the rear seats are already occupied with other children who are also under 10 years old, or there are no seat belts in the rear. In these situations a child must not be placed in the front seats in a rear-facing child seat, unless any airbag is deactivated. Children up to 10 must travel in an approved child seat or restarint system, adapted to their size. A baby up to 13kg in weight must be carried in a rear facing baby seat. A child between 9kg and 18kg in weight must be seated in a child seat. A child from 15kg in weight up to the age of 10 can use a booster seat with a seat belt or harness.

In Andorra children under 10 years of age and under 1.5m in height must always use a restaraint system that has been approved by the EU and has been adapted to their size. Children must not travel in the front of a vehicle if there are rear seats available. If they travel in the front the airbag must be deactivated and again they must use an EU approved restaraint system adapted to their size.

Warning Triangles

It is compulsory to carry a warning triangle which, in the event of vehicle breakdown or accident, must be placed (providing it is safe to do so) on the carriageway at least 30 metres from the vehicle. In some instances it is not compulsory to use the triangle but only when this action would endanger the driver. The French Tourist Board recommends carrying two triangles, as do the authorities in Andorra.

Winter Driving

Snow chains must be fitted to vehicles using snow-covered roads in compliance with the relevant road signs. Fines may be imposed for non-compliance. Vehicles fitted with chains must not exceed 50 km/h (31mph).

Snow chains can be hired or purchased from Polar Automotive Ltd, tel 01892 519933, www.snowchains.com, email: polar@snowchains.com (10% discount for Caravan Club members).

In Andorra winter tyres are recommended. Snow chains must be used when road conditions necessitate their use and/or when road signs indicate.

Fuel

Unleaded petrol pumps are marked 'Essence Sans Plomb'. Diesel pumps are marked Gas Oil or Gazole.

Petrol stations may close on Sundays and those at supermarkets, where petrol is generally cheaper, may close for lunch. At supermarkets it is advisable to check the height and width clearance before towing past the pumps. Credit cards are generally accepted. Some automatic pumps at unmanned petrol stations are operated by credit cards and increasingly these accept cards issued outside France and have instructions in English, but you should not rely on this being the case.

To find the cheapest fuel in any area log on to www.zagaz.com and simply click on the map of France to find the locations of petrol stations, together with prices charged. Alternatively view the French government website, www.prix-carburants.gouv.fr which gives fuel prices all over the country.

LPG and Biofuel

LPG (also called Gepel or GPL) is available in petrol stations across France, especially on motorways. Maps showing their company's outlets are issued free by most LPG suppliers, e.g. Shell, Elf, etc. A list of their locations is available online on http://stations.gpl.online.fr. LPG is not available in Andorra.

Recent visitors report that a number of service stations have stopped selling LPG. The advice is to fill up at the first opportunity once your tank gets low. It is understood the BP garages can generally be relied on to sell LPG.

Fuel containing 10% bioethanol has been on sale at many petrol stations in France since 2009 alongside the regular Euro 95 unleaded fuel, which it will eventually replace. Pumps are labelled SP95-E10. This fuel can be used in most modern vehicles manufactured since 2000 but if you are in any doubt about using it then regular Euro 95 or 98 Super Plus unleaded fuel is still available at most petrol stations. For a list of vehicles which can safely use SP95-E10 see www.carburante10.fr (in French only) or check with your vehicle manufacturer.

See also **Fuel Price Guide** *under* **Motoring – Advice** *in the section* **PLANNING AND TRAVELLING.**

Mountain Passes and Tunnels

See the chapter **Mountain Passes and Tunnels** *in the section* **PLANNING AND TRAVELLING.**

In recent years safety features in both the Mont Blanc and Fréjus tunnels have been significantly overhauled and improved. Both tunnels are heavily used by freight vehicles and traffic is subject to a number of restrictions including minimum and maximum speed limits. All drivers should listen to the tunnels' radio stations and if your vehicle runs on LPG you should tell the toll operator before entering the tunnel. See www.tunnelmb.net and www.sftrf.fr

Overtaking and Passing

Overtaking where it means crossing a solid single or double centre line is heavily penalised.

Outside built-up areas, outfits weighing more than 3,500 kg, or more than 7m in length, are required by law to leave at least 50m between themselves and the vehicle in front. They are only permitted to use the two right-hand lanes on roads with three or more lanes and, where overtaking is difficult, should slow down or stop to allow other smaller vehicles to pass.

There are tram systems in a number of French towns and cities. Overtaking stationary trams is prohibited when passengers are boarding or alighting.

Parking

As a general rule, all prohibitions are indicated by road signs or by yellow road markings. Stopping or parking on the left-hand side of the road is prohibited except in one-way streets.

In most French cities parking meters have largely been replaced by 'pay and display' machines which take coins and credit or debit cards. Where parking signs show 'Horodateur' or 'Stationnement Payant' you must obtain a ticket from a nearby machine.

In Paris two red routes ('axe rouge') have been created on which stopping and parking are absolutely prohibited. Elsewhere, drivers must observe parking restrictions indicated by signs. It is prohibited to leave a parked vehicle in the same place on a public road in Paris for more than 24 consecutive hours. This provision also applies to the following départements which surround Paris: Haut-de-Seine (92), Seine-St Denis (93) and Val-de-Marne (95). Needless to say, car parks are expensive and the best advice is to use public transport which is cheap and efficient.

In many cities and towns there are blue zones (indicated by blue street markings) where you can sometimes park for free, usually for one hour between 9am and 12pm, and between 2pm and 7pm, from Monday to Saturday. There is normally no limit outside these hours or on Sunday and public holidays but always check to make sure. You must display a parking disc ('disque de contrôle/ stationnement') in your windscreen; these are available free, or for a small fee, from garages, travel agencies, motoring organisations, tourist offices, police stations, tobacconists and some shops.

Illegally parked vehicles, even if registered abroad, may be towed away, impounded or immobilised by wheel clamps.

If you need to stop on the open road ensure that your vehicle(s) are driven completely off the road. Overnight parking in a layby is not permitted anywhere in France.

See also **Parking Facilities for the Disabled** *under* **Motoring – Advice** *in the section* **PLANNING AND TRAVELLING.**

Priority

It is always advisable to be watchful at major junctions and roundabouts. In built up areas, give way to traffic coming from the right, unless otherwise indicated. Outside built-up areas traffic on all main roads of any importance has right of way, indicated by the following signs:

Priority road

End of priority road

Priority road

On entering towns, the same sign will often have a line through it, warning that vehicles may pull out from a side road on the right and will have priority.

On steep gradients, vehicles travelling downhill must give way to vehicles travelling uphill.

Roundabouts

At roundabouts drivers must give way to traffic already on the roundabout, i.e. on the left, if indicated by a red-bordered triangular sign showing a roundabout symbol with the words 'Vous n'avez pas la priorité' or 'Cédez le passage' underneath.

Traffic on the roundabout has priority

If no such sign exists the traffic entering the roundabout has priority, however it is always very important to be watchful and to take extra care at roundabouts and junctions to avoid accidents.

See *Priority and Roundabouts* under *Motoring – Advice* in the section *PLANNING AND TRAVELLING*.

Roads

France has a very extensive network of good quality roads falling into three categories: autoroutes (A) i.e. motorways; national (N) roads; and departmental (D) roads. There are over 10,500 kilometres of motorways, most of which tolls are levied. British motorists will find French roads relatively uncongested. Lorries are not allowed on the road for a 24-hour period from 11pm on Saturdays and the eve of public holidays.

Re-Numbering of French Roads

The French government has transferred the administration of approximately 18,000 kilometres of national N roads to local authorities, resulting in the significant re-classification and re-numbering of roads.

For example, the N21 has become the D821 and a part of the N20 is now the D820. The process started in 2006 and has taken several years to complete as each local authority chooses its own re-numbering system and changes road signs.

Where known at the time this guide was compiled, such road number changes have been incorporated into the directions contained in the campsite entries.

Andorra

Travellers to Andorra from France should be aware that conditions on the road from Toulouse to Andorra, the N20/E9, can quickly become difficult in severe winter weather and you should be prepared for delays.

It is advisable to stick to main roads in Andorra when towing and not to attempt the many unsurfaced roads.

Road Signs and Markings

Directional signposting on major roads is generally good. Signs may be placed on walls pointing across the road they indicate and this may be confusing at first until you get the feel for them. Generally a sign on the right pointing left means that you go straight ahead. The same sign on the right pointing right means 'turn right' at the first opportunity.

The words 'tout droit' have nothing to do with turning right, instead they mean 'go straight ahead' or 'straight on'.

Although roads are clearly numbered, it is not advisable to plan your route solely by road numbers. Road signs on approach to roundabouts and at junctions usually do not show road numbers, merely the destination, with numbers being displayed once you are on the road itself. Make sure you know the names of places along your proposed route, and not just the road numbers. Once you have seen your destination town signposted continue along the road until directed otherwise. Intermediate junctions or roundabouts where you do not have to turn usually omit the destination name if the route to it is straight on.

Lines on the carriageway are generally white. A yellow zigzag line indicates a bus stop, blue markings indicate that parking is restricted and yellow lines on the edge of the roadway also indicate that stopping and/or parking is prohibited. A solid single or double white line in the centre of the road indicates that overtaking is not permitted.

STOP signs mean stop. Your wheels must stop rolling; creeping slowly in a low gear is not acceptable, even if local drivers do so. You must come to a complete halt otherwise you may be liable to a fine if caught.

Whilst road signs conform to international standards, some other commonly used signs you may see include:

- Allumez vos feux – *Switch on headlights*
- Attention – *Caution*
- Bouchon – *Traffic jam*
- Chausée deformée – *Uneven road*
- Chemin sans issue – *No through road*
- Col – *Mountain pass*
- Créneau de dépassement – *2-lane passing zone, dual carriageway*
- Déviation – *Diversion*
- Fin d'interdiction de stationner – *End of parking restrictions*
- Gravillons – *Loose chippings*
- Interdit aux piétons – *No pedestrians*
- Itineraire bis – *Alternative route*
- Nids de poules – *Potholes*
- Péage – *Toll*
- Poids lourds – *Lorries*
- Ralentissez – *Slow down*
- Rappel – *Continued restriction (eg no overtaking or speed limit)*
- Rétrécissement – *Narrow lane*
- Route barrée – *Road closed*
- Sens interdit – *No entry*
- Sens unique – *One-way street*
- Serrez à gauche/droite – *Keep left/right*
- Sortie d'usine – *Factory exit*
- Stationnement interdit – *No parking*
- Tout droit – *Straight on*
- Toutes directions – *All directions*
- Travaux – *Road works*
- Virages – *Bends*
- Voie unique – *Single-lane road*
- Voitures – *Cars*

Andorra

Main roads are prefixed 'CG' (Carretera General) and side roads are prefixed 'CS' (Carretera Secundaria). CG road signs are white on red and CS signs are white on green.

Speed Limits

*See **Speed Limits Table** under **Motoring – Advice** in the section **PLANNING AND TRAVELLING**.*

Speed limits on motorways (in dry weather) are higher than in the UK – although they are lower on ordinary roads – and the accident rate is greater. If you are undertaking a long journey in or through France, plan carefully and take sufficient breaks; a minimum of 15 minutes every two hours is recommended.

Fixed speed cameras are common on both motorways and major roads and they used to be prominently signposted well ahead of the actual camera position. However, the signposts indicating the prescence of a fixed radar are being removed and the map that showed the position of radars is no longer available to the pubklic.

The use of mobile speed cameras and radar traps is frequent, even on remote country roads, and may be operated from parked vans or motor bikes, or they may be hand-held. They may also be in use on exit slip roads from motorways or major roads where there is a posted speed limit. Oncoming drivers may flash warnings but headlight-flashing for this purpose is itself illegal, so do not be tempted to do it yourself.

Radar Detectors

Motorists should be aware that non-GPS radar detectors, laser detectors or speed camera jammers are illegal in France, whether in use in your vehicle or not. If caught carrying one – even if it is not in use – you are liable to both a fine of up to €1,500 and confiscation of the device, and possibly confiscation of your vehicle if unable to pay the fine. Such devices should be removed from your vehicle before travelling to France. GPS devices which pinpoint the position of fixed speed cameras are legal but be warned that local law enforcement officers may not be aware of the difference between legal and illegal devices.

Inside Built-up Areas

The general speed limit is 50 km/h (31 mph) which may be raised to 70 km/h (44 mph) on important through roads, indicated by the appropriate sign. The beginning of a built-up area is marked by a road sign giving the name of the town or village in blue or black letters on a light background with a red border. The end of the built-up area is indicated by the same sign with a red diagonal line through it – see below. Signs showing the name of a locality in white letters on a blue background do not indicate a built-up area for the purpose of this regulation.

Therefore, when you enter a town or village, even if there is no actual speed limit warning sign, the place name sign itself indicates that you are entering a 50 km/h zone. This is one of the points at which you may encounter the flash of a hidden speed camera, even as you attempt to slow down. The end of the 50 km/h zone is indicated by the place name sign crossed out. The word 'rappel' on a speed limit sign is a reminder of that limit.

The speed limit on stretches of motorway in built-up areas is 110 km/h (68 mph), except on the Paris ring road where the limit is 80 km/h (50 mph).

Outside Built-up Areas

General speed limits are as follows:

- On single carriageway roads 90 km/h (56 mph)
- On dual-carriageways separated by a central reservation 110 km/h (68 mph)
- On motorways 130 km/h (81 mph)

In long road tunnels there are lower maximum speed limits; in addition minimum speeds are enforced.

These general speed limits also apply to private cars towing a trailer tent or caravan, provided the gross train mass (fully laden weight of the car, plus the cars towing limit) of the vehicle does not exceed 3,500 kg. If the gross train mass of the towing vehicle is over 3,500 kg the speed limits are 90 km/h (56 mph) on motorways, 80-90 km/h (50 mph) on dual carriageways and 80 km/h (50 mph) on single carriageway roads.

Large motorhomes over 3,500 kg have a speed limit of 110 km/h (68 mph) on motorways, 100 km/h (62 mph) on dual carriageways and 80 km/h (50 mph) on single carriageway roads.

For full details of speed regulations visit the Club's website, www.caravanclub.co.uk/overseasadvice. To request a hard copy email the Club's Travel Service Information Officer (Club members only) on travelserviceinfo@caravanclub.co.uk

Speed Limit Stickers

The Club has received confirmation from the French authorities that, despite these new regulations, cars towing caravans and trailers are not required to display speed stickers although drivers are, of course, required to observe the speed limits.

However, from a safety point of view you may like to consider attaching a speed sticker in order to alert drivers behind you that your vehicles are subject to a lower speed limit. Stickers are obtainable from www.speedstickers.co.uk, telephone 0800 988 7329.

Recently-Qualified Drivers

The minimum age to drive in France is 18 years and this also applies to foreign drivers. Driving without professionally qualified supervision/instruction on a

provisional licence is not allowed. Visiting motorists who have held a full driving licence for less than two years must comply at all times with the adverse weather speed limits shown below. New drivers exceeding these speed limits are liable to be fined.

Rumble Strips and Sleeping Policemen

Such means of slowing vehicles are becoming more prevalent particularly, it is reported, in the Massif Central. They are much more offensive than the British versions and should be shown the greatest respect. The advance warning sign shows 'Ralentissez' (slow down).

Adverse Weather Conditions

In case of rain or adverse weather conditions, general speed limits are lowered as follows:

- On motorways 110 km/h (68 mph)
- On urban motorways and dual carriageways 100 km/h (62 mph)
- Outside built-up areas 80 km/h (50 mph)

A speed limit of 50 km/h (31 mph) applies on all roads (including motorways) in foggy conditions when visibility is less than 50 metres.

Traffic Jams

The A6/A7 (the Autoroute du Soleil) from Paris via Lyon to the south are busy motorways prone to traffic jams. Travelling from the north, bottlenecks are often encountered at Auxerre, Chalon-sur-Saône, Lyon, Valence and Orange. An alternative route to the south is the A20, which is largely toll-free, or the toll-free A75 via Clermont-Ferrand.

During periods of severe congestion on the A6, A7 and A10 Paris-Bordeaux motorways, traffic police close off junctions and divert holiday traffic onto alternative routes or 'Itinéraires Bis' which run parallel to main roads. Yellow and black signs indicate these routes. For a summer traffic calendar, indicating when certain areas are most prone to traffic jams, together with a real-time congestion map and regional telephone numbers to call for traffic and travel information, see www.bison-fute.equipement.gouv.fr.

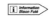

Alternative holiday routes

Information centre for holiday route

Realtime traffic information on traffic conditions on motorways can be found on www.autoroutes.fr. In addition, travel information may be obtained from orange emergency telephone boxes located every 4 km on main roads and every 2 km on motorways. Calls are free.

In general, Friday afternoons and Saturday mornings are busiest on roads leading to the south, and on Saturday and Sunday afternoons roads leading north may well be congested. It is still generally true that many French people drop everything for lunch and, therefore, between noon and 2pm roads are quieter and good progress can often be made.

At the start of the school holidays in early July, at the end of July and during the first and last few days of August, roads are particularly busy. Avoid the changeover weekend at the end of July/beginning of August when traffic both north and south bound can be virtually at a standstill. Traffic can also be very heavy around the Christmas/New Year period and on the weekend of any public holiday.

Andorra

There is heavy traffic in Andorra-la-Vella town centre on most days of the year. During the peak summer holiday period you are likely to encounter queues of traffic on the Envalira pass from France on the N22. Traffic is at its worst in the morning from France and in the afternoon and evening from Andorra and you are recommended to use the Envalira Tunnel to avoid some of the congestion and reduce travel time.

*See **Mountain Passes – Pyrenees** and **Major Pyrenean Road Tunnels** in the section **PLANNING AND TRAVELLING***

Traffic Lights

There is no amber light after the red light in the traffic light sequence.

A flashing amber light indicates caution, slow down, proceed but give way to vehicles coming from the right. A flashing red light indicates no entry; it may also be used to mark level crossings, obstacles, etc.

A yellow arrow at the same time as a red light indicates that drivers may turn in the direction of the arrow, traffic permitting, and providing they give way to pedestrians.

Watch out for traffic lights which may be mounted high above the road and hard to spot.

Violation of Traffic Regulations

Severe fines and penalties are in force for motoring offences and the police are authorised to impose and collect fines on the spot. Violations include minor infringements such as not wearing a seat belt, not carrying a set of spare bulbs or not respecting a STOP sign. More serious infringements such as dangerous overtaking, crossing a continuous central white line and driving at very high speeds, can result in confiscation of your driving licence.

If the offence committed is serious and likely to entail a heavy fine and the suspension of your driving licence or a

prison sentence, a motorist who is not resident in France and has no employment there must deposit a guarantee. The police may hold a vehicle until payment is made.

In some cases instead of, or in addition to, a fine or prison sentence, a vehicle may be confiscated. Although this measure is not often taken, the main offences for which it may be applied are hit and run, refusal to stop when requested or driving under the influence of alcohol or drugs. In such a case the vehicle becomes the property of the French government.

Drivers who are deemed to have deliberately put the lives of others in danger face a maximum fine of €15,000 and a jail sentence. Failure to pay may result in your car being impounded. Your driving licence may also be suspended for up to five years.

Police are particularly strict about speeding (see Speed Limits earlier in this chapter) and many automatic speed controls and speed cameras have been introduced and more are planned. Motorists caught doing more than 40 km/h (25 mph) over the speed limit face immediate confiscation of their driving licence. No distinction is made between French and foreign drivers. British motorists without a co-driver could be left stranded and face heavy costs to get their vehicle(s) home, which would not be covered by insurance.

Computerised tills at motorway toll booths tell the cashier not only how much a driver needs to pay, but also whether they have been speeding. By calculating the distance a vehicle has travelled and the journey time, the computer will indicate whether the speed limit has been exceeded, prompting the cashier to call the police who will impose an immediate fine.

By paying fines on the spot (request a receipt) or within three days, motorists can avoid court action and even reduce the fine. Standard fines can now be paid electronically in post offices and newsagents equipped with a dedicated terminal or by visiting www.amendes.gouv.fr.

The authorities are concerned at the serious overloading of many British-registered vehicles touring in France. Drivers of overloaded vehicles may be prosecuted and held responsible for any accident in which they are involved.

Motorways

France has over 11,400 kilometres of excellent motorways and more are under construction or planned. Tolls are payable on most routes according to distance travelled and category of vehicle(s) and, because motorways are privately financed, prices per kilometre vary in different parts of the country.

Emergency telephones connected to the police are located every 2 km.

Motorway Service Areas

Stopping is allowed for a few hours at the service areas of motorways, called 'aires', and some have sections specially laid out for caravans. All have toilet facilities and a water supply but at 'aires' with only basic facilities, water may not be suitable for drinking, indicated by a sign 'eau non potable'. In addition there are 'aires de repos' which have picnic and play areas, whereas 'aires de services' resemble UK motorway service areas with fuel, shop, restaurant and parking facilities for all types of vehicle. It should be noted that toll (péage) tickets are only valid for 24 or 48 hours depending on the particular autoroute used – check your ticket for details.

'Aires' along motorways are not campsites and should not be confused with 'aires de services' in towns and villages, specifically provided for motorhomes. For reasons of security, The Caravan Club recommends that when seeking an overnight stop you leave the motorway system and find a suitable campsite.

See *Safety and Security* earlier in this chapter.

Motorway Tolls

Motorways tolls are charged extensively throughout France by a number of different operating companies, although there are numerous stretches, particularly around large cities, where no tolls are levied. Vehicles are classified as follows:

Category 1: (Light Vehicles) Vehicle with overall height under 2m and gross vehicle weight not exceeding 3,500kg. Train with overall height under 2m and gross vehicle weight of towing vehicle not exceeding 3,500kg.

Category 2: (Intermediate Vehicles) Vehicle with overall height from 2m to 3m and gross vehicle weight up to 3,500kg. Train with overall height from 2m to 3m and gross vehicle weight up to 3,500kg.

Category 3: (HGV or bus with two axles) Vehicle with overall height of 3m or more. Vehicle with gross vehicle weight of more than 3,500kg. On the A14 all twin-axle buses are in category 4.

Category 4: (HGV or bus with three or more axles) Vehicle with more than two axles and height of 3m or more, or gross vehicle weight of more than 3,500kg. Train with overall height of 3m or more. Train with towing vehicle having gross vehicle weight of more than 3,500kg.

Motorists driving Category 2 vehicles adapted for the transport of disabled persons pay the toll specified for Category 1 vehicles. Holding a disabled person's Blue Badge does not automatically entitle foreign motorists to pay Category 1 charges, and the decision whether to downgrade from Category 2 to 1 will be made by the person at the toll booth, based on experience of similar vehicles registered in France.

To calculate the tolls payable on your planned route see www.viamichelin.com and tick the box marked 'Caravan' (ticking this box will also give the toll for a motorhome) and select the 'Michelin recommended' route. For more detailed information, consult the websites of the individual motorway operating companies, a list of which can be found on www.autoroutes.fr/en/asfa/french-motorway-companies (English option). Alternatively calculate tolls payable on your chosen route on www.autoroutes.fr.

Payment

Payments may be made in cash or by credit card, but be aware that when paying with a credit card you may not be asked for a signature or required to key in a PIN. Pre-paid credit cards, Maestro and Electron are not accepted.

Pay booths marked as accepting credit cards only are usually geared to Category 1 vehicles and may have a height restriction which does not permit the passage of caravans.

On less frequently-used motorways, toll collection is increasingly by automatic machines equipped with 'magic-eye' height detectors. It is probably simplest to pay with a credit card but there should be a cash/change machine adjacent. There are lanes at nearly all toll plazas specifically for drivers who have a Liber-t toll tag which allows them to pay for tolls directly from their bank account. Details and costs of the Liber-t toll tag can be found at www.sanefttolling.co.uk.

Travelling for long distances on French motorways can prove expensive. For example, a vehicle or vehicle combination in Category 2 (car + caravan or motorhome) will pay €28 to travel the 282km from Calais to Paris and €57.20 for the 493km from Paris to Strasbourg (2013 prices).

Toll -Bridges

Tolls are charged across the Pont de Tancarville on the River Seine estuary near Le Havre (A15) and the Pont de Normandie near Honfleur. Current charges (2013) are €3.10 and €6.30 respectively for car/caravan outfits and motorhomes.

The Pont de l'Ile-d'Oléron and Pont de la Seudre (linking La Tremblade with Marennes) south-west of Rochefort are toll-free, but a return charge is made on the Pont de l'Ile-de-Ré from La Rochelle of €27 for a car + caravan and €16.50 for a motorhome (2013).

The 2.5 km long Millau Viaduct spans the Tarn Valley

on the A75 autoroute between Clermont-Ferrand and Béziers. The charge (2013) in summer is €13.30 for a car + caravan, or a motorhome under 3500kg; a lower charge applies outside of July and August, for a full list of current charges see www.leviaducdemillau.com.

Touring in France

France is divided administratively into 'régions', each of which consists of several 'départements'. There are 96 départements in total including Corsica, and these are approximately equivalent to our counties, although with more autonomy.

Paris, the capital and hub of the region known as the Ile-de-France, remains the political, economic, artistic, cultural and tourist centre of France. Visit www.parisinfo.com for a wealth of information on what to see and do in the city. A Paris Pass, valid for 2 to 6 days, entitles you to free entrance (ahead of the queues) to over 60 Paris attractions and free unlimited public transport plus a range of discounts and free offers – see www.parispass.com

Visitors under the age of 26 are admitted free to permanent collections in national museums; show your passport as proof of age. National museums, including the Louvre, are closed on Tuesday, with the exception of Versailles and the Musée d'Orsay which are closed on Monday. Entrance to national museums, including the Louvre, is free on the first Sunday of every month. Municipal museums are usually closed on Monday and most museums close on public holidays.

Sunday lunch is an important occasion for French families; if you have found a restaurant that appeals to you it is advisable to book in advance. Many restaurants do not open on Sunday evening. Restaurants must display priced menus outside and most offer a set menu 'plat du jour' or 'table d'hôte' which usually represents good value. A service charge of 15% is included in restaurant bills but if you have received good service an additional tip may be left. Smoking is not allowed in bars and restaurants.

Information on shopping in Calais, including tips on where best to buy wine, beer, cigarettes, etc, and DIY supplies, as well as opening hours and price comparisons, can be found on www.day-tripper.net.

When planning a holiday to the south of France bear in mind the fact that the Mistral wind can blow down the Rhône and Durance valleys to the Mediterranean coast for several days at a time in spring and early autumn. It is a strong, cold, usually dry wind, which can reach speeds of up to 90 km/h (56 mph), but is usually accompanied by clear blue skies.

France has a large network of well-marked, long-distance footpaths and hiking trails – Les Sentiers de Grande Randonnée – which generally follow ancient tracks formerly used by pilgrims, merchants and soldiers. In addition to these 'GR' paths there are also 'PR' paths (Chemins de Petite Randonnée) which are most suited for local hiking. For a list of GR routes see www.gr-infos.com or contact the French Tourist Board or local tourist offices in France for more information.

For personalised itineraries based on your interests and recommended places to visit during your break visit www.france-voyage.com.

Channel Islands

Ferry services operate for cars and passengers between Poole and Portsmouth and St Malo via Jersey and Guernsey. Caravans and motorhomes are permitted to enter Jersey, subject to certain conditions, including pre-booking direct with a registered campsite and the acquisition of a permit. For further information and details of the campsites on Jersey where caravans are permitted, see www.jersey.com or contact The Club's Travel Service Information Officer, email: travelserviceinfo@caravanclub.co.uk

There are three campsites on Guernsey but, for the moment, the authorities in Guernsey do not permit entry to trailer caravans. Motorhomes can only be taken onto the island if they are stored under cover and not used for human habitation. Trailer tents can be taken onto the island without restrictions.

Local Travel

Several large cities in addition to Paris have metro or tram systems and all have a comprehensive bus network. The Paris metro network comprises 16 lines and around 300 stations, and has many connections to the RER (regional suburban rail network) and the SNCF national railway system. Tickets for the metro – also valid on RATP buses – can be bought singly from vending machines at the turnstiles or from ticket offices, but a 'carnet' of 10 tickets is a more economical option. Your ticket is valid for an hour and a half from the time it is validated at the machines, on buses or at metro stations.

For tourists Paris Visite travel passes are available allowing unlimited travel for one to five days across some or all of the travel zones and a range of discounts at attractions. For further information see www.ratp.fr.

Senior citizens aged 60 and over are entitled to a discount of up to 25% when using French railways. Show your passport as proof of age.

Much of France remains undiscovered because visitors lack the time, inclination or courage to deviate from the prescribed checklist of what-to-see. Often it's just a question of taking D roads instead of autoroutes and N roads. Many of the country's most appealing treasures, whether man-made or natural features, are sometimes within easy reach of more familiar sights. Ask at local tourist information offices (Syndicats d'Initiative) for leaflets about routes connecting points of interest and discover some of those 'off the beaten track' places.

Ferries

Car ferry services operate all year across the Gironde estuary between Royan and Le Verdon eliminating a 155km detour. Approximate 2013 prices are €40.60 single journey for car, caravan under 3m and 2 adults or €53.20 for car, caravan over 3m and 2 adults or €47 for motorhome and 2 adults. Between Blaye and Lamarque north of Bordeaux approximate 2013 prices are €28.80 single journey for car, caravan under 3m and 2 adults or for a motorhome and 2 adults, or €34.20 for car, caravan over 3m – see www.bernezac.com for more details.

Ferry services operate from Marseille, Nice and Toulon to Corsica. For information contact:

SOUTHERN FERRIES
30 CHURTON STREET
LONDON SW1V 2LP
Tel: 0844 8157785
www.southernferries.co.uk
mail@southernferries.com

Cycling

A number of French towns are actively promoting the use of bicycles. Initiatives include increasing the number of cycle paths, providing parking space for bicycles and constructing shelters and cycle hire points in car parks. You may hire bicycles at many local tourist offices and from some railway stations.

Recent initiatives have included the improvement of cycle tracks along rivers and canals and many former gravel tracks have been replaced with tarmac along the Rivers Rhône, Loire and Yonne/Canal de Nivernais. It is understood that similar improvements will take place along the Canal de Bourgogne.

In and around Paris there are 370 kilometres of cycle lanes, and bicycles, known as 'Les Vélibs', are available for hire at very reasonable rates at more than 1,600 self-service stations – roughly one every 300 metres.

The French Tourist Board has information on cycle routes and tours throughout France.

Place names used in the Site Entry listings which follow can be found in Michelin's France Atlas, scale 1:200,000 (1 cm = 2 km).

ABBEVILLE *3B3* (14km SE Rural) *50.03416, 1.98383* **Camp Municipal La Peupleraie, 80510 Long [03 22 31 84 27 or 03 22 31 80 21; fax 03 22 31 82 39; bacquet.lionel@free. fr; www.long.fr]** Exit A16 at junc 21 for D1001 N then turn L at Ailly-le-Haut Clocher onto D32 for Long & foll sp. Med, mkd pitch, pt shd; wc (some cont); chem disp; shwrs inc; el pnts (6A) inc (caution - poss rev pol & poss other elec concerns) (long lead req); lndry rm; tradsmn; shop, rest, snacks, bar in vill; BBQ; playgrnd; fishing adj; 90% seasonal statics; dogs; phone adj; poss cr; adv bkg; ccard not acc; red long stay; CKE/CCI. "Pretty, busy site beside Rv Somme; gd san facs; gd walking/cycling by rv; site busy 1st week Sep - flea mkt in town; interesting area; old power station museum; warden lives on site; conv en route Calais; san facs very clean; Quiet peaceful site; Highly rec" 15 Mar-15 Nov. € 9.00   2013*

"There aren't many sites open at this time of year"

If you're travelling outside peak season remember to call ahead to check site opening dates – even if the entry says 'open all year'.

ABBEVILLE *3B3* (5km S Urban) *50.07826, 1.82378* **Camp Municipal du Marais-Talsac/Le Marais Communal, 62 Rue du Marais-Talsac, 80132 Mareuil-Caubert [03 22 31 62 37 or 03 22 24 11 46 (Mairie); fax 03 22 31 34 28; mairie. mareuilcaubert@wanadoo.fr]** Leave A28 at junc 3; at T-junc turn L onto D928; foll camping sp; in 4km turn sharp R onto D3 into Mareuil-Caubert; in 1km turn L thro housing est to site by stadium. Well sp. Med, mkd pitch, hdstg, pt shd; wc; chem disp; mv service pnt; shwrs inc; el pnts (6A) €2.90 (poss rev pol); shop & 5km; rest 5km; playgrnd; 25% statics; quiet; CKE/CCI. "Well-kept, friendly site; sm pitches; helpful staff; clean dated facs, poss tired low ssn; no twin-axles or o'fits over 8m; hdstgs stony/loose gravel; gates clsd 2000-0800; interesting area; poss itinerants low ssn (2010); vg NH Calais." 1 Apr-30 Sep. € 11.60   2011*

ABBEVILLE *3B3* (10km SW Rural) *50.08586, 1.71519* **Camping Le Clos Cacheleux, Rue des Sources, Route de Bouillancourt, 80132 Miannay [03 22 19 17 47; fax 03 22 31 35 33; raphael@ camping-lecloscacheleux.fr; www.camping-lecloscacheleux. fr]** Fr A28 exit junc 2 onto D925 sp Cambron. In 5km at Miannay turn S onto D86 sp Bouillancourt. Site thro vill of R opp sister site Camping Le Val de Trie which is sp fr A28. Med, hdg/mkd pitch, pt sl pt shd; wc; chem disp; baby facs; fam bthrm; shwrs inc; el pnts (10A) inc (poss long lead req); gas; lndtte (inc dryer); shop; tradsmn; rest & 1km; snacks; bar; BBQ (charcoal/gas); playgrnd; htd, covrd pool adj; paddling pool adj; jacuzzi; sand beach 20km; fishing pond; tennis 3km; games area; games rm; farm animals; wifi; entmnt; TV rm; dogs €2.10; no c'vans/m'vans over 18m; some Eng spkn; adv bkg; quiet; ccard acc; red low ssn; CKE/CCI. "Pleasant, peaceful, wooded site; lge pitches; charming, helpful owner; excel facs; all services (inc shop, rest & pool) are on sister site 'Le Val de Trie' on opp side of rd, accessed via steep track 50m fr site ent; gd walking, cycling; gd for dogs." ◆ 15 Mar-15 Oct. € 25.90 SBS - P12   2013*

ABBEVILLE *3B3* (10km SW Rural) *50.08570, 1.71480* **Camping Le Val de Trie, 1 Rue des Sources, Bouillancourt -sous-Miannay, 80870 Moyenneville [03 22 31 48 88; fax 03 22 31 35 33; raphael@camping-levaldetrie.fr; www.camping-levaldetrie.fr]** Fr A28 exit junc 2 onto D925 sp Cambron. In 5km at Miannay turn S onto D86 sp Bouillancourt. Site thro vill on L. Site sp fr A28. NB Last part of app narr with bends. Med, hdg/mkd pitch, hdstg, pt sl, shd; htd wc; chem disp; mv service pnt; baby facs; shwrs inc; el pnts (6A) €4.40; gas; lndtte (inc dryer); shop; tradsmn; rest, snacks; bar; BBQ; playgrnd; htd, covrd pool; paddling pool; lake fishing; games rm; wifi; entmnt; TV rm; 1% statics; dogs €2; phone; Eng spkn; adv bkg; quiet but poss noise nr generator for bouncy castle; ccard acc; red long stay/low ssn; CKE/CCI. "Beautiful, well-run site; well- shaded; welcoming, helpful, conscientious owner; excel clean san facs, ltd low ssn; gd family site; woodland walks; interesting area; conv Calais." ◆ 1 Apr-15 Oct. € 21.40 (CChq acc)   2011*

See advertisement

ABBEVILLE *3B3* (7km NW Rural) *50.14166, 1.76237* **Camping Le Château des Tilleuls, Rue de la Baie, 80132 Port-le-Grand [03 22 24 07 75; fax 03 22 24 23 80; contact@chateaudestilleuls.com; www.chateaudestilleuls.com]** Fr N on an A16 join A28 dir Rouen. At junc 1 take D40 dir St Valery-sur-Somme, site on R in approx 3km. Med, hdg/mkd pitch, hdstg, sl, terr, pt shd; wc; chem disp; mv service pnt; shwrs inc; el pnts (16A) €4; lndtte; shop & 5km; snacks; BBQ; playgrnd; htd pool; sand beach 7km; tennis; cycle hire; games rm; wifi; TV rm; dogs free; adv bkg; quiet; ccard acc; red long stay; CKE/CCI. "Pleasant site; improvements in progress (2011); lge, v sloping pitches; find suitable pitch bef booking in; long uphill walk fr recep; unisex san facs; new pitches far from ent; Site being updated" ♦ 1 Mar-31 Dec. € 30.50   2013*

ABJAT SUR BANDIAT see Nontron *7B3*

ABREST see Vichy *9A1*

ABRETS, LES *9B3* (2km E Rural) *45.54065, 5.60834* **Kawan Village Le Coin Tranquille, 6 Chemin des Vignes, 38490 Les Abrets [04 76 32 13 48; fax 04 76 37 40 67; contact@coin-tranquille.com; www.coin-tranquille.com]** Fr N exit A43 at junc 10 Les Abrets & foll D592 to town cent. At rndbt at monument take D1006 twd Chambéry/Campings; cont for 500m then turn L sp Le Coin Tranquille; cross level x-ing & cont for 500m to site. Fr S on A48 exit junc 10 at Voiron onto D1075 to Les Abrets; turn R at rndabt onto D1006 twd Le Pont-de-Beauvoisin, then as above. Lge, hdg/mkd pitch, pt shd; wc (some cont); chem disp; mv service pnt; baby facs; shwrs inc; el pnts (6A) inc (poss rev pol & long lead poss req); gas; lndtte (inc dryer); shop; tradsmn; rest, snacks; bar; BBQ; playgrnd; pool; paddling pool; cycle hire; archery; horseriding & fishing 7km; golf 15km; games area; games rm; wifi; entmnt; TV rm; dogs €1.50; Eng spkn; no c'vans/m'vans over 8m unless bkd in adv; adv bkg ess high ssn; noisy high ssn; ccard acc; red low ssn; CKE/CCI. "Well-kept, well-run site in gd location; lge narr pitches; busy/noisy site, but some quiet pitches avail; helpful & friendly staff; well-kept, clean san facs, ltd low ssn; lovely pool; vg activities for children; poss flooding in wet weather; excel." ♦ 1 Apr-1 Nov. € 33.50 (CChq acc) SBS - M05   2012*

ABRETS, LES *9B3* (3km S Rural) *45.47079, 5.54688* **Camping Le Calatrin (formerly Municipal), 799 Rue de la Morgerie, 38850 Paladru [04 76 32 37 48; fax 04 76 32 42 02; le.calatrin@gmail.com; www.camping-paladru.fr]** S fr Les Abrets on D1075; turn R onto D50 to Paladru; site 1km beyond vill on L, on brow of hill. Or exit A48 junc 9 & foll sp 'Lac de Paladru'; 3km after rndabt junc of D50 & D17, site on R (by another rndabt). Med, hdg/mkd pitch, terr, shd; wc (some cont); chem disp; mv service pnt; baby facs; shwrs inc; el pnts (10A) €4 (long lead poss req); gas; lndtte; shop & 500m; tradsmn; snacks; bar; BBQ; playgrnd; lake sw & shgl beach adj; fishing; watersports; cycle hire; tennis 500m; games area; games rm; entmnt; wifi; TV; 30% statics; dogs €3.50; bus 200m; Eng spkn; adv bkg; quiet; no twin-axles; red low ssn/long stay; CKE/CCI. "Attractive site; direct access to lake; lge pitches; welcoming & helpful owners; gd recreational facs; nice walks; excel." ♦; 1 Apr-30 Sep. € 17.00   2013*

ABRETS, LES *9B3* (8km S Rural) *45.46736, 5.55857* **Camping International Le Lac, La Veronnière, 38620 Montferrat [04 76 32 31 67; fax 04 76 32 38 15; infos@camping-interdulac]** D1075 5km S of Les Abrets turn R onto D50 dir Paladru. Turn L sp La Veronnière, site on R on lakeside. Lge, mkd pitch, pt shd; wc; chem disp; shwrs inc (6A) inc; lndtte; tradsmn; rest, snacks; bar; BBQ; playgrnd; lake sw & shgl beach; fishing; sailing; wifi; 25% statics; dogs €1.30; phone; Eng spkn; adv bkg; quiet; ccard acc; CKE/CCI. "Lovely lake; plenty of activities; gd touring base & conv NH; shwrs need refurb (2010)." ♦ 30 Apr-30 Sep. € 18.20   2010*

ABRETS, LES *9B3* (11km SW Rural) *45.44621, 5.53183* **Camp Municipal le Bord du Lac, 687 route du Bord du Lac, 38850 Bilieu [04 76 06 67 00 or 04 76 06 62 41 (Mairie); fax 04 76 06 67 15; www.camping-bilieu.com]** S on D1075 fr Les Abrets. Turn R onto D50. Just bef Paladru, turn L to Charavines. site on R on ent Bilieu, by lakeside. Med, mkd pitch, pt sl, terr, pt shd; htd wc; chem disp; shwrs inc; el pnts (10A) €3; lndtte; tradsmn; playgrnd; wifi; 10% statics; poss cr; quiet; ccard acc; CKE/CCI. "Nice site by lake; san facs v gd; staff helpful; no sw in lake fr site, only boat launch; pitch access poss diff; gd." 1 Apr-30 Sep. € 23.30   2013*

ABZAC see Coutras *7C2*

⊞ **ACY EN MULTIEN** *3D3* (700m SE Rural) *49.09842, 2.96144* **Caravaning L'Ancien Moulin (CC de F), 60620 Acy-en-Multien [tel/fax 03 44 87 21 28; ccdf_acy@cegetel.net; www.campingclub.asso.fr]** Exit N2 at Lévignen onto D332 S dir Betz; cont thro Betz to Acy-en-Multien; cont thro Acy on D332 dir Rosoy-en-Multien; site on R as leaving Acy. Med, mkd pitch, pt shd; htd wc; chem disp; shwrs inc; el pnts (6A) inc; lndtte; shops, rest, snacks, bar, playgrnd 1km; fishing; games area; games rm; entmnt; TV rm; 90% statics; dogs €2.20; adv bkg; quiet but poss aircraft noise; CKE/CCI. "Touring pitches by mill pool; helpful, friendly staff; clean, adequate san facs; recep 1400-1700; site tired & has seen better days (2011); mainly tired statics, many unoccupied (2011); 30km fr Disneyland Paris & conv other theme parks." ♦ € 24.00   2011*

ADRETS DE L'ESTEREL, LES see Napoule, La *10F4*

AGAY See also site listed under St Raphaël.

AGAY *10F4* (4km E Coastal) *43.43740, 6.89165* **Camping Azur Rivage, Blvd Eugène Brieux, 83530 Anthéor [04 94 44 83 12; fax 04 94 44 84 39; info@camping-azur-rivage.com; www.camping-azur-rivage.com]** On D559 heading NE dir Cannes pass Agay. Opp sandy cove at Anthéor, turn L under viaduct. Med, shd; wc (mainly cont); chem disp; mv service pnt; shwrs; el pnts (6A) €5; gas; lndtte (inc dryer); shop; rest, snacks; bar; cooking facs; BBQ; playgrnd; pool; paddling pool; dir access to sand beach across rd; fishing; wifi; some statics; dogs €2; poss cr; adv bkg; some rlwy noise; red low ssn. "Virtually under rlwy viaduct but excel, v clean site; pitches sm." ♦ 1 Apr-30 Sep. € 40.00 (4 persons)   2009*

FRANCE

AGAY *10F4* (1.5km S Coastal) *43.41995, 6.85696* **Royal Camping, Plage de Camp-Long, 83530 Agay [tel/fax 04 94 82 00 20; contact@royalcamping.net; www. royalcamping.net]** On D559 twd St Raphaël. Turn at sp Tiki Plage & site. Stop in ent rd at recep bef ent site. Sm, mkd pitch, hdstg, pt shd; wc; chem disp; shwrs inc; el pnts (6A) €3.50; gas; lndtte; shops; tradsmn; rest, snacks, bar 300m; sand beach adj; wifi; some statics; dogs; phone; bus 200m; poss cr; Eng spkn; adv bkg; quiet but some rd/rlwy noise; CKE/CCI. "Gd walks; some pitches adj to beach in sep area; vg." ◆ ltd 7 Feb-10 Nov. € 29.00   2009*

AGAY *10F4* (2km W Coastal) *43.41787, 6.84828* **Campéole Camping Le Dramont, 986 Blvd de la 36ème Division du Texas, 83530 Agay [04 94 82 07 68; fax 04 94 82 75 30; dramont@campeole.com; www.camping-mer.com or www.campeole.com]** W fr Agay on D559 (D1098) dir St Raphaël; site on L in 1.8km. Or E fr St Raphaël on D559; site on R in 7km. Lge, mkd pitch, hdstg, pt sl, pt shd; wc; chem disp; mv service pnt; baby facs; shwrs inc; el pnts €4.10; gas adj; lndtte (inc dryer); shop; rest, snacks & bar adj; playgrnd; shgl beach adj; scuba diving adj; games area; games rm; wifi; entmnt; 50% statics; dogs €3.90; phone; bus adj; poss cr; Eng spkn; ccard acc; red low ssn. "Walking fr site; great discovery on crowded coast; gd." ◆ 20 Mar-10 Oct. € 38.90   2009*

See advertisement on pages 14 & 15

AGAY *10F4* (600m NW Coastal) *43.43376, 6.85245* **Camping des Rives de l'Agay, Ave de Gratadis, 83530 Agay [04 94 82 02 74; fax 04 94 82 74 14; reception@ lesrivesdelagay.fr; www.lesrivesdelagay.fr]** Fr Agay take D100 dir Valescure, site in 400m on L. NB Dangerous bend & steep ent. Med, hdg/mkd pitch, shd; htd wc; chem disp; baby facs; shwrs inc; el pnts (6A) €3.60; gas; lndtte; shop; rest, snacks; bar; htd pool; paddling pool; sand beach 500m; entmnt; some statics; dogs €3; poss cr; Eng spkn; adv bkg; poss noisy; CKE/CCI. "San facs & pool v clean; gd pool with shade; excel site." ◆ 11 Mar-2 Nov. € 28.00 (3 persons)   2013*

AGAY *10F4* (5km NW Rural) *43.45408, 6.83254* **Esterel Caravaning, Ave des Golfs, 83530 Agay/St Raphaël [04 94 82 03 28; fax 04 94 82 87 37; contact@esterel-caravaning.fr; www.esterel-caravaning.fr]** Fr A8 foll sps for St Raphaël & immed foll sp 'Agay (par l'interieur)/Valescure' into D100/Ave des Golfs, approx 6km long. Pass golf courses & at end of rd turn L at rndabt twds Agay. Site ent immed after a L hand bend. Lge, hdg/mkd pitch, hdstg, terr, pt sl, pt shd; htd wc; chem disp; mv service pnt; shwrs inc; baby facs; indiv san facs to some pitches (extra charge); el pnts (10A) inc (poss rev pol); gas; lndtte; shop; rest, snacks; bar; no BBQ; playgrnd; htd, covrd pools inc padding pool; waterslide; sand beach 3km; lake sw 20km; 8 local golf clubs; tennis; squash; cycle hire; archery; games rm; entmnt; underground disco; wifi; TV rm; 50% statics; dogs €4; twin-axles acc (rec check in adv); poss cr; Eng spkn; adv bkg; ccard acc; red low ssn/long stay; CKE/CCI. "Superbly situated, busy site adj Esterel forest; friendly, helpful staff; gd san facs; gd for families - excel leisure activities; excel rest & shop; now classified as a 5 star site; conv Gorges du Verdon, Massif de l'Estérel, Monaco, Cannes & St Tropez; min stay 1 week high ssn (Sun to Sun); various pitch prices; ltd lge pitches avail; some pitches v sl & poss diff; ltd facs low ssn; mkt Wed; excel." ◆ 31 Mar-29 Sep. € 49.00 SBS - C21   2011*

See advertisement on next page

⊞ **AGDE** *10F1* (2km NE Rural) **Camping Les Chalets du Rec de Rieu, Ave de Pomérols, 34510 Florensac [04 67 77 94 64; ortiz.freddy@wanadoo.fr; http://freddy. ortiz.pagesperso-orange.fr/]** Leave Florensac on D18 dir Pomérols & Montpellier; site on L in 2km. Sm, mkd pitch, pt shd; htd wc; chem disp; shwrs; el pnts (5A) inc; lndtte; shop; tradsmn; snacks; bar; BBQ; sm above-grnd pool; adv bkg; quiet; CKE/CCI. "Welcoming owner; vg." ◆ ltd € 15.00   2009*

AGDE *10F1* (1.5km E Coastal) *43.31091, 3.51158* **Camping Le Cap Agathois, Route de Sète, 34300 Agde [tel/fax 04 67 94 02 21; info@campingcapagathois.com; www. campingcapagathois.com]** Exit A9 junc 35; foll sp Agde & Sète onto D612; just bef Vias turn L onto D912 & cont thro Agde town dir Sète; 1km after supmkt complex site sp on L. Med, pt shd; wc; baby facs; shwrs inc; el pnts (6A) inc; lndtte; tradsmn; snacks; bar; BBQ (sep area); playgrnd; pool; waterpark; sand beach 3km; games area; 40% statics (sep area); dogs €2; phone; Eng spkn; some rlwy noise; red low ssn. "Newish site (2008) & expanding; excel pool; gd." ◆ ltd May-Sep. € 23.00   2008*

"That's changed – Should I let The Club know?"

If you find something on site that's different from the site entry, fill in a report and let us know. See www.caravanclub.co.uk/europereport.

AGDE *10F1* (3km SE Coastal) *43.27949, 3.48114* **Camping Le Rochelongue, Chemin des Ronciers, Route de Rochelongue, 34300 Le Cap d'Agde [04 67 21 25 51; fax 04 67 94 04 23; le.rochelongue@wanadoo.fr; www. camping-le-rochelongue.fr]** Exit A9 junc 34 sp Agde. Foll D612 to Le Cap d'Agde then thro Rochelongue. Site on L just bef rndabt. Med, mkd pitch, hdstg, pt shd; wc (cont); chem disp (wc); mv service pnt; baby facs; shwrs inc; el pnts (6A) inc; gas; lndtte; shop; rest; takeaway; snacks; bar; BBQ; playgrnd; htd pool; conv store; table tennis; sand beach 500m; cycle hire; golf 1.5km; internet; entmnt; 50% statics; dogs €4; phone; poss cr; Eng spkn; adv bkg; poss noisy high ssn; CKE/CCI. "Friendly, well-kept site; sh walk to vill & beach." ◆ 29 Mar- 28 Oct. € 47.00   2013*

AGDE *10F1* (5km SE Coastal) *43.29645, 3.52255* **Centre Hélio-Marin René Oltra (Naturist), 1 Rue des Néréïdes, 34307 Le Cap-d'Agde [04 67 01 06 36 or 04 67 01 06 37; fax 04 67 01 22 38; infos@chm-reneoltra.fr; www.chm-reneoltra.fr]** S fr m'way A9 Agde-Pézenas junc on N312/D612 for 14km to Cap d'Agde turn-off; foll Camping Naturist sp to site on E side of Le Cap-d'Agde. V lge, hdg/mkd pitch, pt shd; all serviced pitches; wc (some cont); mv service pnt; chem disp; shwrs inc; el pnts (5A) inc; gas inc; lndtte; shop; tradsmn; rest; bar; pool; sand beach adj; bus adj; 50% statics; dogs €3.40; poss cr high ssn; Eng spkn; adv bkg rec; quiet; ccard acc; red low ssn; INF card. "Naturist area in Cap-d'Agde has all facs; lovely beach; gd size pitches; friendly atmosphere; modern san facs; gd family facs; excel." ◆ 15 Mar-14 Oct. € 41.00   2013*

ESTEREL
CARAVANING
SAINT-RAPHAËL . FRENCH-RIVIERA

**The first 5 Star Campsite
in the French Riviera !**

Between Cannes and Saint-Tropez, in the heart of the Esterel mountains yet only 3 km from the sandy beaches at Agay.

5 swimming pools, indoor heated childrens'pool, sports activities, beauty center, baby club...

New mobile homes for 2 to 8 persons, pitches with all comfort and private Jacuzzi !

www.esterel-caravaning.fr

Avenue des Golfs - 83530 Agay/Saint-Raphaël FRANCE
Tel : +33 4 94 82 03 28 - Fax : +33 4 94 82 87 37

Camping-Caravaning ★★★★
AU DE CAP D'AGDE

Route de Rochelongue - 34300 Agde
Tel: 0033 467 94 23 42 - Fax: 0033 467 94 87 81
contact@campingleschampsblancs.com - www.campingleschampsblancs.com

AGDE *10F1* (1km S Rural) *43.29657, 3.47714* **Kawan Village Les Champs Blancs, Route de Rochelongue, 34300 Agde [04 67 94 23 42; fax 04 67 94 87 81; champs-blancs@wanadoo.fr; www.champs-blancs.fr]** Exit fr A9 & foll sps to Agde (not Le Cap d'Agde). Thro cent of Agde foll sps to campsite & Rochelongue. Site on R after bdge over dual c'way. V lge, hdg pitch, shd; wc; chem disp; mv service pnt; private san facs some pitches (extra charge); shwrs inc; el pnts (10A) inc (poss rev pol); gas; lndtte (inc dryer); shop, rest, snacks, bar adj; playgrnd; 2 htd pools; waterslide; sand beach 2km; tennis; games area; golf 2km; wifi; 10% statics; dogs €2; adv bkg; quiet; CKE/CCI. "Friendly site; excel san facs; hot water to shwrs only; vg." ♦ 4 Apr-29 Sep. € 43.00 (CChq acc) 2010*

See advertisement above

AGDE *10F1* (4km S Coastal) *43.28856, 3.44266* **Camping de la Tamarissière, 4 Rue du Commandant Malet, 34300 Agde [04 67 94 79 46; fax 04 67 94 78 23; contact@camping-tamarissiere.com; www.camping-tamarissiere.com]** At Agde bdge take D32E on R bank of Rv Hérault to La Tamarissière; sp. V lge, mkd pitch, pt sl, shd; wc; shwrs; el pnts (6A) €4.20; lndtte; shop; rest, snacks; bar; playgrnd; sand beach adj; games area; cycle hire; entmnt; harbour nr for boat owners; 5% statics; dogs €3.20; poss cr; adv bkg; quiet; ccard acc; red long stay/low ssn; CKE/CCI. "Sandy site under pines; ferry across rv; ltd facs on site & in vill; lge areas flood after heavy rain; gate shut 2200-0700." ♦ 15 Apr-15 Sep. € 22.50 2009*

AGDE *10F1* (2km SW Coastal) *43.29343, 3.45295* **Camping La Pepinière, 3 Route du Grau, 34300 Agde [04 67 94 10 94; lapepiniere@free.fr; www.campinglapepiniere.com]** S fr Agde on D32 dir Le Grau d'Agde; Blvd de St Christ is part of D32; 500m after passing under D612, D32 becomes Route du Grau. Site sp on L. Med, mkd pitch, pt shd; wc; chem disp; mv service pnt; shwrs inc; el pnts (6A) €4.50; lndtte; shop; tradsmn; snacks; bar; BBQ; playgrnd; htd pool; games area; entmnt; wifi; TV; 30% statics; dogs €3.50; phone; poss cr; ccard acc; quiet; red low ssn; CKE/CCI. "Friendly staff; vg cycle paths; attractive area; vg." 1 Apr-15 Oct. € 19.50 2011*

AGDE *10F1* (2km SW Rural) *43.29806, 3.45639* **Camping Le Neptune, 46 Boulevard du St Christ, 34300 Agde [04 67 94 23 94; fax 04 67 94 48 77; info@campingleneptune.com; www.campingleneptune.com]** Fr A9 exit junc 34 onto N312, then E on D612. Foll sp Grau d'Agde after x-ing bdge. Site on D32E on E bank of Rv Hérault on 1-way system. Lge, hdg/mkd pitch, pt shd; wc (some cont); chem disp; baby facs; fam bthrm; shwrs inc; el pnts (6-10A) inc; gas; lndtte; shop & bar in ssn; hypmkt 3km; rest 2km; bar; BBQ; playgrnd; htd pool; paddling pool; sand beach 2km; tennis; games area; wifi; entmnt; TV; 40% statics; dogs €3 (no Pitbulls or Rottweillers); phone; bus 2km; poss cr; Eng spkn; adv bkg rec; quiet; ccard acc; red low ssn; CKE/CCI. "Peaceful, pleasant, clean site; helpful owners; modern facs, ltd low ssn; liable to flood after heavy rain; easy rvside walk/cycle to vill; gd cycleways; rv cruises; boat launch/slipway 500m." ♦ 1 Apr-30 Sep. € 27.20 (CChq acc) 2009*

See advertisement on pages 32 & 33

AGEN *8E3* (12km SE Rural) *44.10456, 0.75061* **Camping au Lié, Aulié, 47220 Caudecoste [05 53 87 42 93 or 01473 832388 (UK); td.s@btinternet.com; www.aulie.co.uk]** Easy access fr A62 bet junc's 7 or 8 (ideal to/fr Spain); Fr N113 dir Toulouse, turn off sp Layrac approx 8km E of Agen. Fr A62 exit junc 7 & turn R at 1st rndabt turn, R at 2nd rndabt sp Layrac. Drive thro vill & turn L at 2nd traff lts (sharp turn) sp Caudecoste, cross bdge over Rv Gers & Caudecoste sp 1st R (silver horse at junc). In Caudecoste take D290 sp Miradoux, cross m'way in approx 1km, on L is farmhouse, turn L just after this onto sm rd with grass growing in middle. At T-junc turn R, site on R. Sm, pt shd, wc; chem disp; shwrs inc; el pnts (6A) inc; lndtte (inc dryer); shops, bar in vill; BBQ; pool; wifi; dogs €1; c'van storage avail; quiet; red long stay. "CL-type site in owners' garden; sm & lge pitches; welcoming British owners; san facs v clean but need update; excel meals avail at farm house, inc coeliac & vegetarian; peaceful countryside; gd cycling & walking area; always phone ahead." ♦ ltd 15 Mar-1 Nov. € 20.00 2011*

FRANCE

AGEN *8E3* (8km NW Rural) *44.24368, 0.54290* **Camping Le Moulin de Mellet, Route de Prayssas, 47450 St Hilaire-de-Lusignan [05 53 87 50 89; fax 05 53 47 13 41; moulin.mellet@wanadoo.fr; www.camping-moulin-mellet.com]** NW fr Agen on N113 twd Bordeaux for 5km. At traff lts just bef Colayrac-St Cirq take D107 N twd Prayssas for 3km. Site on R. Sm, mkd pitch, shd; wc; chem disp; baby facs; shwrs inc; el pnts (10A) €3.80 (poss rev pol); gas; lndtte (inc dryer); shop 3km; tradsmn high ssn; rest, snacks; BBQ; playgrnd; 2 pools; games rm; dogs €2.55; phone; adv bkg; quiet; Eng spkn; adv bkg; quiet, but some rd noise & poss croaking fr frogs at night; red low ssn; CKE/CCI. "Delightful, well-run site; helpful, friendly owners; small children's farm; RVs & twin-axles phone ahead; excel." ♦ 1 Apr-30 Sep. € 21.20   2011*

AGNAC see Eymet *7D2*

AGON COUTAINVILLE *1D4* (300m NE Urban/Coastal) *49.05163, -1.59136* **Camp Municipal Le Marais, Blvd Lebel-Jéhenne, 50230 Agon-Coutainville [02 33 47 05 20; martinetmarais@wanadoo.fr; http://campings.martinetmarais.pagesperso-orange.fr/]** Fr Coutances take D44 to Agon-Coutainville. Site sp adj Hippodrome. Lge, unshd; wc; chem disp; shwrs inc; el pnts (5A) €3.10; lndtte; shops adj; tradsmn; playgrnd; sand beach 600m; sailing; fishing; dogs €3.10; adv bkg; quiet. ♦ 1 Jul-31 Aug. € 11.00   2010*

AGON COUTAINVILLE *1D4* (300m NE Urban/Coastal) *49.05105, -1.59112* **Camp Municipal Le Martinet, Blvd Lebel-Jéhenne, 50230 Agon-Coutainville [02 33 47 05 20; martinetmarais@wanadoo.fr; www.agoncoutainville.fr or www.coutainville.com]** Fr Coutances take D44 to Agon-Coutainville; site sp nr Hippodrome. Med, hdg/mkd pitch, pt shd; wc; mv service pnt; shwrs inc; el pnts (5A) €3.10; lndtte (inc dryer); shop 250m; tradsmn; BBQ; playgrnd; sand beach 600m; 55% statics; dogs €3.20; bus; poss cr; Eng spkn; adv bkg; ccard acc; CKE/CCI. "V pleasant site; ltd facs low ssn; horse racecourse adj; vg." ♦ 1 Apr-30 Oct. € 11.00   2010*

AGON COUTAINVILLE *1D4* (6km SE Rural) *48.99275, -1.52881* **Camp Municipal Les Gravelets, 3 Rue du Rey, 50590 Montmartin-sur-Mer [tel/fax 02 33 47 70 20; campgrav@chez.com; www.chez.com/campgrav]** Fr Coutances take D971 S twd Granville. Turn W at Hyenville to Montmartin-sur-Mer, site sp in vill. Med, mkd pitch, pt sl, terr, pt shd; wc; shwrs inc; el pnts (6A) €2; lndry rm; shop 300m; tradsmn; playgrnd; sand beach, fishing & sailing 2km; tennis adj; dogs €0.80; some statics; adv bkg; quiet; CKE/CCI. "Gd." ♦ 1 Apr-31 Oct. € 9.30   2010*

AGUESSAC see Millau *10E1*

AIGLE, L' *4E2* (12km NW Rural) *48.78841, 0.46533* **Camp Municipal des Saints-Pères, 61550 St Evroult-Notre-Dame-du-Bois [06 78 33 04 94 (mob) or 02 33 34 93 12 (Mairie); catherine-matte@orange.fr]** Fr L'Aigle on D13, on ent vill site on L by lake. Sm, hdstg, terr, pt shd; wc; chem disp; mv service pnt; shwrs inc; el pnts (4-10A) €1.50-2.50; shop, rest, snacks, bar 500m; playgrnd; lake sw adj; watersports; fishing; dogs €0.20; no adv bkg; poss noisy; CKE/CCI. "Pleasant lakeside vill; facs clean, ltd low ssn." ♦ 1 Apr-30 Sep. € 7.00   2009*

⊞ **AIGNAN** *8E2* (600m S Rural) *43.69290, 0.07528* **Camping Le Domaine du Castex, 32290 Aignan [05 62 09 25 13; fax 05 62 09 24 79; info@gers-vacances.com; www.gers-vacances.com]** Fr N on D924/N124 turn S on D20 thro Aignan onto D48; in 500m garage on R, immed after turn L; site sp. Fr S on D935 turn E at Monplaisir onto D3/D48 to Aignan; site on R bef vill. Sm, hdg/mkd pitch, hdstg, pt shd; wc; chem disp; mv service pnt; shwrs inc; el pnts (10A) €3; lndtte; shop 500m; tradsmn; rest, snacks; bar; BBQ; playgrnd; pool; lake sw 4km; tennis & squash adj; games area; TV rm; 4% statics; dogs €4; phone; poss cr; Eng spkn; adv bkg; quiet; red low ssn; ccard acc; CKE/CCI. "Lovely site in grnds of medieval farmhouse; helpful Dutch owners; modern san facs; excel pool & rest; gd touring cent for Bastide vills; mkt Mon; phone ahead low ssn; vg." ♦ ltd € 16.00   2009*

AIGREFEUILLE D'AUNIS *7A1* (2km N Rural) *46.14621, -0.94571* **Camp Municipal de la Garenne, Route de la Mazurie, 17220 St Christophe [05 46 35 51 79 or 05 46 35 16 15 (LS); fax 05 46 35 64 29; saintchristophe@mairie17.com]** Fr Aigrefeuille-d'Aunis take D112 2.5km N to vill of St Christophe, site sp. Sm, hdg, mkd pitch, pt shd; wc; chem disp; mv service pnt; shwrs inc; el pnts (4A) €2.50; lndry rm; shop 250m; playgrnd; lake fishing 3km; tennis; horseriding; dogs €0.85; quiet; CKE/CCI. "V clean site in sm vill; unrel opening dates, phone ahead low ssn." ♦ 15 Mar-15 Oct. € 23.00   2012*

AIGUES MORTES See also sites listed under La Grande Motte and Le Grau-du-Roi.

AIGUES MORTES *10F2* (5km N Rural) *43.61130, 4.21010* **Camping Fleur de Camargue, 30220 St Laurent-d'Aigouze [04 66 88 15 42; fax 04 66 88 10 21; contact@fleur-de-camargue.com; www.fleur-de-camargue.com]** Exit A9 junc 26 onto D6313/D979 dir Aigues-Mortes; turn L into St Laurent d'Aigouze; cont thro St Laurent onto D46; site on R in 2.5km. Or N fr Aigues-Mortes at junc with D58 over high-level bdge onto D46, site 2.5km on L on D46. NB Do not go thro St Laurent-d'Aigouze cent, v narr & one-way. Med, mkd pitch, pt shd; wc; chem disp; mv service pnt; shwrs inc; el pnts (10A) €4; gas; lndtte; shops 2km; rest, snacks & bar; playgrnd; htd pool; paddling pool; sand beach 11km; rv & fishing 3km; wifi; entmnt; TV rm; 40% statics; dogs €4; phone; adv bkg; quiet; ccard acc; red low ssn; CKE/CCI. "Peaceful, relaxing site; lge pitches; pleasant owners; gd clean san facs; gd pool; site floods easily; gd." ♦ 9 Apr-25 Sep. € 26.00   2010*

AIGUES MORTES *10F2* (4km E Rural) **Camping à la Ferme (Loup), Le Mas de Plaisance, 30220 Aigues-Mortes [04 66 53 92 84 or 06 22 20 92 37 (mob); info@ot-aiguesmortes.fr; www.ot-aiguesmortes.fr]** Site sp in Aigues-Mortes or foll D58 E dir Stes Maries-de-la-Mer, then R along farm road (v narr & potholed) at end of rv bdge. NB Fr town narr rd with much traff calming & sharp bends. Either way for v sm o'fits only. Sm, pt shd; wc; chem disp; mv service pnt; shwrs inc; el pnts inc; lndry rm; tradsmn; BBQ; quiet; CKE/CCI. "Excel CL-type site; superb san facs; helpful owners; rec not to use water at m'van service point as off irrigation system - other water points avail; video security at gate." 1 Apr-30 Sep. € 22.00   2013*

AIGUES MORTES *10F2* (3.5km W Rural) *43.56300, 4.15910* Yelloh! Village La Petite Camargue, 30220 Aigues-Mortes [04 66 53 98 98; fax 04 66 53 98 80; info@yellohvillage-petite-camargue.fr; www.yellohvillage-petite-camargue.com or www.yellohvillage.co.uk] Heading S on N979 turn L onto D62 bef Aigues-Mortes & go over canal bdge twd Montpellier; site on R in 3km; sp. V lge, mkd pitch, pt shd; wc; chem disp; mv service pnt; some serviced pitch; baby facs; jaccuzi; shwrs inc; el pnts (10A) inc; lndtte (inc dryer); shop, rest, snacks; bar; BBQ (charcoal/gas); playgrnd; pool; paddling pool; sand beach 3km; horseriding; cycle hire; tennis; games area; games rm; wifi; entmnt; TV; 50% statics; dogs €4; no c'vans/m'vans over 7m; bus to beach high ssn; Eng spkn; adv bkg; ccard acc; red low ssn; CKE/CCI. "Lively, busy, well-run, youth-oriented commercial site with many sports facs; clean san facs, poss stretched high ssn; excel pool complex; some sm pitches; take care o'head branches; gd cycling; mkt Wed & Sun." ♦ 20 Apr-16 Sep. € 44.00 SBS - C04   2011*

See advertisement on inside front cover

AIGUEZE see Pont St Esprit *9D2*

AIGUILLES *9D4* (1km NE Rural) *44.78783, 6.88849* Camp Municipal Le Gouret, 05470 Aiguilles-en-Queyras [04 92 46 74 61 or 04 92 46 70 34; fax 04 92 46 79 05; www.aiguilles.com] Fr Aiguilles on D947 dir Abriès, sp to site on R across rv bdge. Lge, shd; wc; chem disp; mv service pnt; baby facs; shwrs inc; el pnts (3-10A) €2.20-3.20; lndtte; shop, rest, snacks, bar 700m; BBQ; playgrnd; games area; some statics; dogs €1; phone; bus 100m; quiet. "Site on bank of Rv Guil; random pitching in lge area of larch forest; excel cent for Queyras National Park; vg." 1 Jun-15 Sep. € 11.80   2013*

AIGUILLON *7D2* (E Rural) *44.30467, 0.34491* Camp Municipal du Vieux Moulin, Route de Villeneuve, 47190 Aiguillon [05 53 79 61 43; fax 05 53 79 82 01; mairie@ville-aiguillon.fr; www.ville-aiguillon.eu] On ent town on D813, turn E onto D666 to site on bank of Rv Lot. Clearly sp. Or exit A62 junc 6 at Damazan onto D8 to Aiguillon. Med, mkd pitch, shd; wc (some cont); own san rec; chem disp (wc); shwrs; el pnts (10A) inc; tradsmn; supmkt, rest & bar 1km; playgrnd; rd noise. "Gd site adj old mill house by rv; gd san facs; conv A62; NH only." 1 Jul-31 Aug. € 9.60   2010*

AIGUILLON SUR MER, L' *7A1* (S Coastal) *46.32942, -1.29846* Camp Municipal de la Baie, Blvd du Communal, 85460 L'Aiguillon-sur-Mer [02 51 56 40 70; fax 02 51 97 11 57; camping.delabaie@aiguillonsurmer.fr; www.laiguillonsurmer.fr] On D46 fr La Tranche, cross bdge into Aiguillon-sur-Mer onto D746a. Foll rd to R; after it turns L site on R in 100m. Lge, mkd pitch, pt shd; wc; shwrs inc; el pnts (6A) inc; lndtte (inc dryer); shop; lge supmkt 500m; rest nr; snacks; bar; BBQ; playgrnd; pool; waterslide; lake sw & sand beach 600m; entmnt; TV; 50% statics; dogs; phone; bus adj; poss cr; Eng spkn; adv bkg (rec peak ssn); quiet; red long stay/low ssn. "Gd beaches in area; vg sailing, walking & cycling; gd birdwatching." 1 Apr-30 Sep. € 16.00   2008*

AIGUILLON SUR MER, L' *7A1* (1km W Coastal) *46.33218, -1.31764* Camp Municipal La Côte de Lumière, Place du Dr Pacaud, 85460 La Faute-sur-Mer [02 51 97 06 16; fax 02 51 27 12 21; camping.municipal.lafautesurmer@orange.fr; www.lafautesurmer.com] On D46 E of La Tranche, thro town. Site bef bdge over rv. Lge, shd; wc (some cont); shwrs inc; el pnts (6A) inc; lndtte; shop; snacks; playgrnd; sand beach 600m; tennis; dogs; quiet; ccard acc; CKE/CCI. "Naturist beach adj; bird sanctuary, oyster/mussel beds adj; poss problem with insects; facs poss ltd & run down low ssn." ♦ 1 Apr-15 Oct. € 18.00   2009*

AIGUILLON SUR MER, L' *7A1* (1km W Coastal) *46.34349, -1.32006* Camping Le Bel Air, 2, Route de Bel Air, 85460 L'Aiguillon-sur-Mer [02 51 56 44 05 or 02 54 77 33 08 (LS); fax 02 51 97 15 58; camping.belair@wanadoo.fr; www.camping-belair.com] Fr La Roche-sur-Yon take D747 to La Tranche-sur-Mer via coast rd D46 to La Faute-sur-Mer. Cross bdge to L'Aiguillon-sur-Mer. Site 1km W of town on D44. Sp fr all dir. Lge, pt shd; wc; baby facs; shwrs; el pnts (3A) €3.50; lndtte; shop; rest, snacks; bar; BBQ; playgrnd; pool; waterslide; sand beach 800m; entmnt; cycle hire; pony trekking; archery; some statics; dogs €3.50; adv bkg; red low ssn. "Excel, clean, friendly site." 1 Apr-30 Sep. € 25.00   2010*

See advertisement below

AILLON LE JEUNE see Châtelard, Le *9B3*

AINHOA *8F1* (NW) *43.30873, -1.50173* **Aire Naturelle Harazpy (Zaldua), 64250 Ainhoa [tel/fax 05 59 29 89 38 or 05 59 29 90 26 (LS)]** Take D918 E fr St Jean-de-Luz sp Espelette: in approx 20km turn R on D20 sp Ainhoa. App church in Ainhoa turn R thro open car park to rd at rear; site on R in 250m. Site sp. Sm, mkd pitch, terr, pt sl, pt shd; wc; chem disp; mv service pnt; shwrs; el pnts (10A) inc; lndtte; sm shop; tradsmn; lake sw 10km; dogs; phone; adv bkg; quiet; ccard not acc; CKE/CCI. "Beautiful location; conv Spanish border; helpful staff; excel walking area." ♦ 1 Apr-30 Sep. € 13.50   2009*

AIRE SUR LA LYS *3A3* (2km NE Urban) *50.64390, 2.40630* **Camp Municipal de la Lys, Bassin des Quatre Faces, Rue de Fort Gassion, 62120 Aire-sur-la-Lys [03 21 95 40 40; fax 03 21 95 40 41; camping@ville-airesurlalys.fr; www.ville-airesurlalys.fr]** Fr town cent, find main sq & exit to R of town hall. Thro traff lts turn R into narr lane just bef rv bdge dir of Hazebrouck. Site poorly sp. Sm, hdg/mkd pitch, hdstg, pt shd; htd wc; chem disp (wc); shwrs inc; some el pnts (6A) €2.10; quiet; 95% statics. "Ltd touring pitches; ltd but clean san facs; not suitable lge o'fits; rec for NH only" 1 Apr-31 Oct. € 10.50   2013*

> ## "I like to fill in the reports as I travel from site to site"
> You'll find report forms at the back of this guide, or you can fill them in online at www.caravaclub.co.uk/europereport.

AIRE SUR L'ADOUR *8E2* (E Urban) *43.70283, -0.25738* **Camping Les Ombrages de l'Adour, Rue des Graviers, 40800 Aire-sur-l'Adour [tel/fax 05 58 71 75 10; hetapsarl@yahoo.fr; www.camping-adour-landes.com]** Turn E on S side of bdge over Rv Adour in town. Site close to bdge & sp, past La Arena off rd to Bourdeaux. Med, pt shd; wc; chem disp; mv service pnt; shwrs inc; el pnts (10A) €3; lndtte; sm shop; snacks; BBQ; playgrnd; pool 500m; sports area; canoeing, fishing, tennis 500m; wifi; dogs €1.80; poss cr; red low ssn. "Vg." 6 Apr-24 Oct. € 13.50   2009*

⊞ **AIRE SUR L'ADOUR** *8E2* (9km E Rural) *43.69699, -0.13803* **Camping Le Lahount, Hameau de Lahount, 32400 Lelin-Lapujolle [tel/fax 05 62 69 64 09 or 06 81 52 39 15 (mob); camping.de.lahount@wanadoo.fr; www.campingdelahount.fr]** SE fr Aire-sur-l'Adour on D935, turn L in St Germé dir Lelin-Lapujolle. In 1.5km turn L, site on R, sp. Med, mkd pitch, terr, pt shd; wc; mv service pnt; baby facs; shwrs inc; el pnts (10A) inc; lndtte; shop; rest, snacks; bar; BBQ; playgrnd; pool; paddling pool; lake fishing; games area; cycle hire; entmnt; 60% statics; dogs €1; phone; adv bkg; ccard acc; CKE/CCI. "Ltd facs low ssn; pitches soft when wet; barrier at ent awkward for long o'fits; suitable sm o'fits only; poss contract workers & site unkempt low ssn." € 16.00   2010*

AIRES, LES see Lamalou les Bains *10F1*

AIRVAULT *4H1* (1km N Rural) *46.83200, -0.14690* **Camping de Courte Vallée, 8 Rue de Courte Vallée, 79600 Airvault [tel/fax 05 49 64 70 65; camping@caravanningfrance.com; www.caravanningfrance.com]** Fr N, S or W leave D938 sp Parthenay to Thouars rd at La Maucarrière twd Airvault & foll lge sp to site. Site on D121 twd Availles-Thouarsais. NB If app fr NE or E c'vans not permitted thro Airvault - watch carefully for sp R at Gendarmerie. Well sp fr all dirs. Sm, hdg/mkd pitch, some hdstg, pt sl, pt shd; wc; chem disp; mv service pnt; shwrs inc; el pnts (8A) inc (poss long lead req); gas; lndtte (inc dryer); shop; tradsmn; rest, snacks; bar; BBQ; playgrnd; htd pool; fishing; cycle hire; c'van storage; wifi; games/TV rm; 8% statics; dogs €1.50; twin-axles acc (rec check in adv); adv bkg; quiet; ccard acc; red low ssn/long stay; CKE/CCI. "Peaceful, popular, well-kept site; pleasant, helpful British owners; excel, clean facs, poss stretched high ssn; conv Futuroscope & Puy du Fou theme park; mkt Sat." ♦ 24 Mar-27 Oct. € 33.00 SBS - L14   2012*

AIX EN PROVENCE *10F3* (9km E Rural) *43.51771, 5.54128* **FFCC Camping Ste Victoire, Quartier La Paradou, 13100 Beaurecueil [04 42 66 91 31; fax 04 42 66 96 43; campingvictoire@orange.fr; www.campingsaintevictoire.com]** Exit A8/E80 junc 32 onto D7n dir Aix, then R onto D58 & foll sp for 3km. Sm, hdg/mkd pitch, hdstg, shd; htd wc (some cont); chem disp; mv service pnt; baby facs; shwrs inc; el pnts (6A) €3.40 (some rev pol & poss no neutral); lndtte; shop 3km; tradsmn; playgrnd; pool 9km; rv 1km; archery; cycle hire; wifi; TV; dogs €1.10; phone; bus; adv bkg; quiet; some rd noise; red low ssn/long stay; no ccard acc; CKE/CCI. "Well-run site in attractive hilly, wooded area; friendly, helpful owners; clean, basic, dated san facs, ltd low ssn; various pitch sizes; lge o'fits poss diff manoeuvring; some pitches too soft for lge o'fits when wet; no twin axles; no lighting at night; gd walking & climbing." ♦ 1 Feb-15 Nov. € 29.10   2013*

AIX EN PROVENCE *10F3* (2.5km SE Urban) *43.51250, 5.47196* **Camping L'Arc-en-Ciel, 45 Ave Henri Malacrida, Pont des 3 Sautets, 13100 Aix-en-Provence [04 42 26 14 28; camping-arcenciel@neuf.fr; www.campingarcenciel.com]** Fr E or W exit A8 at junc 31 onto D7n dir Aix; (turn N for 300m to 1st rndabt where turn R; in 200m at 2nd rndabt turn R again onto D7n dir SE); pass under m'way; site ent immed on R; sp. Take care at ent. NB Access easier if go past site for 1km to rndabt, turn round & app fr S. Sm, hdg/mkd pitch, terr, shd; htd wc; chem disp; shwrs inc; el pnts (6A) €3.60 (poss rev pol); gas; lndtte; shops nr; tradsmn; rest, snacks, bar 100m; BBQ; playgrnd; lge pool; fishing; canoeing; games area; golf 1km; TV; dogs; phone; bus adj; Eng library; poss cr; Eng spkn; adv bkg; m'way noise not too intrusive; ccard not acc; CKE/CCI. "Delightful, well-kept, well-run site; friendly, helpful owner; some pitches sm; some steep site rds, tow avail; gd clean facs; superb pool; if recep clsd use intercom in door; gd dog walk adj; bus to Marseille; conv NH nr a'route; highly rec." 1 Apr-30 Sep. € 24.00   2013*

⊞ **AIX EN PROVENCE** *10F3* (3km SE Urban) *43.51556, 5.47431* **Airotel Camping Chantecler, Val-St André, 13100 Aix-en-Provence [04 42 26 12 98; fax 04 42 27 33 53; info@ campingchantecler.com; www.campingchantecler.com]** Fr town inner ring rd foll sps Nice-Toulon, after 1km look for sp Chantecler to L of dual c'way. Foll camp sp past blocks of flats. Well sp in Val-St André. If on A8 exit at junc 31 sp Val-St André; R at rndabt; R at Rndabt; L at 2nd traff lts onto Ave Andre Magnan; R ar rndabt; site sp. If app fr SE on D7n turn R immed after passing under A8. Lge, hdg pitch, hdstg, sl, pt terr, pt shd; htd wc; chem disp; mv service pnt; shwrs inc; el pnts (5A) €4.10 (long lead poss req); gas; lndtte; shop; tradsmn; rest in ssn; snacks; bar; BBQ (gas/elec); playgrnd; pool; entmnt; TV; dogs €3.60; bus; poss cr; adv bkg; some rd noise; ccard acc; site clsd 1 & 2 Jan; red long stay/low ssn; CKE/ CCI. "Lovely, well-kept, wooded site; facs ltd low ssn & in need of refurb (2010); some site rds steep - gd power/weight ratio rec; access poss diff some pitches; rec request low level pitch & walk to pitch bef driving to it; ent narr; recep clsd 12.30-13.30; gd pool; conv city; vg touring base; Acces diff to some pitches, some taps not working" ◆ € 20.60   2012*

AIX LES BAINS *9B3* (10km N Urban) *45.78484, 5.94262* **FFCC Camping Beauséjour, La Rippe, 73410 Albens [04 79 54 15 20 or 06 43 33 01 93 (mob); www. campingbeausejour-albens.com]** N fr Aix-les-Bains on D1201 dir Annecy to Albens; in Albens turn L at traff lts in town cent; site in 600m on left, over sm bdge. Site sp at traff lts. Med, pt sl, pt shd; htd wc (some cont); chem disp; mv service pnt; shwrs inc; el pnts (6-10A) €3-3.80; gas; lndtte; ice; shops & rest 500m; BBQ; playgrnd; games area; dogs €1; phone adj; bus 500m; adv bkg; quiet, some rd & rlwy noise; ccard acc; red low ssn; CKE/CCI. "Friendly, pleasant site; rarely full; no twin-axles; vg." 15 Jun-15 Sep. € 8.40   2010*

AIX LES BAINS *9B3* (7km SW Rural) *45.65511, 5.86142* **Camp Municipal L'Ile aux Cygnes, La Croix Verte, 501 Blvd Ernest Coudurier, 73370 Le Bourget-du-Lac [04 79 25 01 76; fax 04 79 25 32 94; camping@ lebourgetdulac.fr; www.lebourgetdulac.fr]** Fr N foll Bourget-du-Lac & Lac sp soon after Tunnel Le Chat. Fr Chambéry take D1504 dir Aix-les-Bains; foll sp to Le Bourget-du-Lac & Le Lac, bear R at Camping/Plage sp to site at end of rd. Lge, shd; wc; mv service pnt; baby facs; shwrs inc; el pnts (6A) inc; gas; lndtte (inc dryer); tradsmn; rest; snacks; bar; playgrnd; private lake beach & sw; waterslide; boating; watersports; entmnt; wifi; TV; some statics; dogs €1.50; phone; bus; adv bkg; quiet; red low ssn; CKE/CCI. "On beautiful lake; mountain scenery; ground stoney." ◆ 28 Apr-30 Sep. € 22.60   2013*

AIX LES BAINS *9B3* (3km W Rural) *45.70005, 5.88666* **Camp Municipal International du Sierroz, Blvd Robert Barrier, Route du Lac, 73100 Aix-les-Bains [tel/fax 04 79 61 21 43; campingsierroz@aixlesbains.com; www.aixlesbains.com/ campingsierroz]** Fr Annecy S on D1201, thro Aix-les-Bains, turn R at site sp. Keep to lakeside rd, site on R. Nr Grand Port. Lge, hdg/mkd pitch, shd; htd wc; chem disp; mv service pnt; baby facs; shwrs inc; el pnts (6A) inc; gas; lndtte; shop; tradsmn; rest, snacks; bar; playgrnd; pool 1km; games area; golf 4km; TV; 5% statics; dogs €1.60; bus (ask at recep for free pass); poss cr; adv bkg; quiet; ccard acc; red low ssn; CKE/CCI. "Pleasant location; lake adj for watersports; lge pitches; poss itinerants & v unclean facs low ssn (June 2010)." ◆ 15 Mar-15 Nov. € 18.90   2010*

AIXE SUR VIENNE *7B3* (N Rural) *45.79887, 1.13928* **Camp Municipal Les Grèves, Ave des Grèves, 87700 Aixe-sur-Vienne [06 73 67 23 48; fax 05 55 70 43 00; mairie-aixesurvienne.fr; www.mairie-aixesurvienne.fr]** SW fr Limoges for approx 13km, on N21 twds Périgueux, cross bdge over Rv Vienne & in about 600m turn to R (site sp) by rv. Steep down hill app & U-turn into site - take care gate posts! Med, shd; wc (some cont); chem disp; mv service pnt; shwrs inc; el pnts (10A) €2.50 (poss rev pol); lndtte; tradsmn; shops, rest, snacks & bar 300m; playgrnd; pool adj; fishing; quiet; poss cr; adv bkg; dogs free; red long stay. "Pleasant, clean site by rv; spacious pitches; helpful, friendly warden; gd san facs, but ltd low ssn; conv Limoges area & Vienne valley; several chateaux in easy reach; no twin-axles; vg." ◆ 1 Jun-30 Sep. € 19.00   2013*

AIZELLES *3C4* (500m N Rural) *49.49076, 3.80817* **Camping du Moulin (Merlo), 16 Rue du Moulin, 02820 Aizelles [03 23 22 41 18 or 06 14 20 47 43 (mob); magali.merlo@ orange.fr; www.camping-du-moulin.fr]** Fr Laon take D1044 dir Reims; in 13km turn L on D88 to Aizelles; site sp in vill 'Camping à la Ferme'. Fr Reims on A26 exit junc 14 onto D925 then D1044 N. Turn R to Aizelles on D889 past Corbeny. Turn onto Rue du Moulin & site on R in 250m. Camping sp at church says 100m but allow 300m to see ent. NB Lge o'fits take care sharp R turn at ent to site. Sm, pt sl, pt shd; wc (cont); chem disp; shwrs €1; el pnts (6A) €3.60 inc (poss rev pol, poss long lead req); shop 2km; tradsmn; playgrnd; fishing 800m; 70% statics (not visible); poss cr; little Eng spkn; quiet but poss noisy w/end; ccard acc; red low ssn; CKE/CCI. "Attractive, well-kept CL-type farm site; friendly, helpful owners; basic san facs need update; gates clsd 2200-0700; lovely quiet vill; conv Calais 3 hrs." 15 Apr-15 Oct. € 15.00   2013*

AIZENAY *2H4* (1.5km SE Rural) *46.73410, -1.58950* **FFCC Camping La Forêt, 1 Rue de la Clairière, 85190 Aizenay [tel/fax 02 51 34 78 12; info@camping-laforet.com; www. camping-laforet.com]** Exit Aizenay on D948 twd La Roche-sur-Yon. Site 1.5km on L. Med, hdg/mkd pitch, pt shd; wc; chem disp; mv service pnt; shwrs inc; el pnts (6A) €2.70; gas; lndtte; shop; tradsmn; rest 1.5km; snacks; bar; BBQ; playgrnd; htd pool; lake beach & sw 1km; tennis; cycle hire; 10% statics; dogs €1.30; phone; adv bkg; quiet; ccard acc; red low ssn/CKE/CCI. ◆ ltd Easter-30 Sep. € 16.00   2009*

AIZENAY *2H4* (6km NW Rural) *46.75282, -1.68645* **Camping Val de Vie, Rue du Stade, 85190 Maché [tel/ fax 02 51 60 21 02; campingvaldevie@bbox.fr; www. campingvaldevie.fr]** Fr Aizenay on D948 dir Challans. After 5km turn L onto D40 to Maché. Fr vill cent cont twd Apremont. Sm, blue site sp 100m on L. Med, hdg/mkd pitch, pt sl, pt shd; wc; chem disp; 10% serviced pitches; baby facs; fam bthrm; shwrs inc; el pnts (6-10A) €3.30-4.10; gas; lndtte; shops 200m; BBQ; playgrnd; htd pool; sand beach 20km; tennis adj; lake 300m; fishing; boat hire; cycle hire; 10% statics; dogs €2.80; phone in vill; Eng spkn; adv bkg; quiet; red low ssn/long stay; CKE/CCI. "Lovely, peaceful, well-run site in pretty vill; new young owners upgrading facs & rds (2011); warm welcome; clean san facs; steel pegs useful; gd touring base; gd cycling; excel." WiFi; ♦ 1Apr-30 Sep. € 20.10   2013*

ALBAN *8E4* (Rural) *43.89386, 2.45416* **Camp Municipal La Franquèze, 81250 Alban [05 63 55 91 87 or 05 63 55 82 09 (Mairie); fax 05 63 55 01 97; mairie.alban@ wanadoo.fr]** W of Albi on D999 turn L at ent to Alban. Site 300m on R, sp. Sm, hdg pitch, terr, pt sl, pt shd; wc; mv service pnt; shwrs; el pnts (6A) €2.10; lndtte; playgrnd; rv fishing; adv bkg; quiet; CKE/CCI. "Beautiful area, conv Tarn Valley; vg." 1 Jun-30 Sep. € 7.20   2008*

ALBEPIERRE BREDONS see Murat *7C4*

ALBERT *3B3* (500m N Urban) *50.01136, 2.65556* **Camp Municipal du Vélodrome, Ave Henri Dunant, 80300 Albert [03 64 62 22 53; fax 03 22 74 38 30; campingalbert@ laposte.net; www.ville-albert.fr]** Fr town cent take Rue Godin E adjacent to Basilica & foll sp for site. Easiest access fr Bapaume (N) towards Albert; turn R at camping sp on edge of town. Med, mkd pitch, unshd; wc; chem disp; mv service pnt; shwrs €1.50 tokens; el pnts (4-10A) €2.20-3.60 (rev pol); shop 1km open 7 days; fishing adj; 40% statics; dogs; poss cr in high ssn; Eng spkn; poss rwly noise; adv bkg; red long stay; CKE/CCI. "Pleasant, well-run, clean site; friendly, helpful warden; poss security probs; conv for Lille, Arras & Amien by train & for WW1 battlefields etc; facs basic but rates reasonable; well maintained clean site" ♦ 1 Apr-15 Oct. € 21.40   2013*

ALBERT *3B3* (5km NE Rural) *50.04141, 2.66868* **International Camping Bellevue, 25 Rue d'Albert, 80300 Authuille [03 22 74 59 29 / 06 71 96 88 78 (mob); fax 03 22 74 05 14; camping.bellevue0767@orange.fr; www.visit-somme.com]** Take D929 Albert to Bapaume rd; in 3km turn L at La Boiselle, foll sp to Aveluy cont to Authuille. Site on R in vill cent. Med, hdg pitch, pt sl, pt shd; wc; chem disp; shwrs; el pnts (5A) inc (rev pol); shop 7km; tradsmn; rest; playgrnd; rv fishing 500m; 80% statics; dogs €1; adv bkg; quiet; poss noisy at w/end; CKE/CCI. "Helpful owner; basic site - poss run down (5/2010); useful touring Somme WW1 battlefields; walking dist of Thiepval Ridge; gd NH; lovely site; excel rest in village" 15 Mar-31 Oct. € 14.00   2013*

ALBERT *3B3* (10km SE Rural) *49.92943, 2.74891* **Camp Municipal Les Charnilles, Les Près Bana, 80340 Cappy [03 22 76 14 50, 06 45 19 60 63 (mob) or 03 22 76 02 13 (Mairie); fax 03 22 76 62 74; mariedecappy@ wandoo.fr; http://picardietourisme.com]** Fr Albert S on D329 to Bray-sur-Somme; turn L in Bray onto D1; 100m after vill sp Cappy, turn R (opp D197 to Lille). Site in 500m at end of lane. Med, hdg/mkd pitch, hdstg, pt shd; wc; chem disp; shwrs €1.50; el pnts (6A) inc; lndry rm; shops 1km; tradsmn; dogs €0.10; Eng spkn; quiet; ccard not acc; CKE/CCI. "Lovely, clean, well-laid out site; friendly, helpful warden; immac san facs; ltd touring pitches; pretty vill on Rv Somme; conv A1." ♦ 1 Apr-31 Oct. € 15.50   2011*

"I need an on-site restaurant"

We do our best to make sure site information is correct, but it is always best to check any must-have facilities are still available or will be open during your visit.

ALBERT *3B3* (10km SW Rural) *49.91930, 2.57985* **FFCC Camping Les Puits Tournants, 6 Rue du Marais, 80800 Sailly-le-Sec [tel/fax 03 22 76 65 56; camping.puitstournant@ wanadoo.fr; www.camping-les-puits-tournants.com]** Fr N exit A1 junc 14 onto D929 dir Amiens, at Albert take D42 S to Sailly-Laurette then turn R onto D233 to Sailly-le-Sec & foll sp. Or fr S exit junc 13 twd Albert onto D1029. At Lamotte-Warfusée R onto D42 to Sailly-Laurette, turn L to Sailly-le-Sec. Med, some hdg pitch, some hdstg, pt shd; htd wc; chem disp; mv service pnt; shwrs inc; el pnts (4A) €3; gas; lndtte; shop & 7km; tradsmn; rest 2km; BBQ; playgrnd; htd pool; paddling pool; lake sw; fishing; sports area; canoe & cycle hire; tennis 2km; horseriding 5km; TV rm; 60% statics; dogs; adv bkg; quiet; ccard acc. "Lovely family-run site; amiable staff; gd clean san facs; grass pitches muddy when wet; tight ent, lge o'fits poss diff; gd pool; walks by rv; excel." ♦ 1 Apr-31 Oct. € 18.00 (3 persons) (CChq acc)   2011*

⊞ **ALBERTVILLE** *9B3* (2km SE Urban) *45.66501, 6.42232* **Camping La Maladière, 2263 Route de Tours, 73200 Albertville [tel/fax 04 79 37 80 44; camping@camping-lamaldiere.com; www.camping-lamaldiere.com]** SE fr cent Albertville take N90 twds Moûtiers. After approx 4km turn off sp La Bâthie & Tours-en-Savoie. Turn L under D90 & left onto D990 thro Tours-en-Savoie. Site 300m after exit sp on R. Sm, pt shd; htd wc; shwrs inc; el pnts (5-10A) €3-4.50; playgrnd; wifi; mostly statics; dogs €1.20; poss cr; adv bkg; quiet. "Well-kept site; friendly; gd clean san facs; conv Fréjus tunnel; gd NH." ♦ € 11.00   2010*

ALBERTVILLE *9B3* (6km SE Urban) *45.62527, 6.45074* **Camping Le Joli Mont, Rue Victor Hugo, 73540 La Bâthie [04 79 89 61 13 or 04 89 65 59 (LS); camping.joli.mont@ wanadoo.fr]** Fr Albertville on N90 exit junc 33 sp La Bâthie; turn L under N90; then turn 1st R, then 1st L; site on L. Sm, pt shd; wc; chem disp (wc); shwrs inc; el pnts (10A) €2.50; lndry rm; playgrnd; 50% statics; dogs; adv bkg; quiet; CKE/CCI. "Mountain views; helpful, friendly staff; san facs dated but clean; gd." 1 Jun-1 Oct. € 10.45   2008*

ALBERTVILLE *9B3* (W Urban) *45.67922, 6.39636* **Camp Municipal Les Adoubes, Ave du Camping, 73200 Albertville [04 79 32 06 62 or 04 79 32 04 02; fax 04 79 32 87 09; tourisme@albertville.com; www.albertville.com]** Site is 200m fr town cent; over bdge on banks of Rv Arly. Med, pt shd; wc (some cont); own san rec top of site; chem disp (wc); shwrs inc; el pnts (6A) €2.95; gas; lndtte; shop 200m; tradsmn; rest, bar 200m; playgrnd; pool 1km; entmnt; games rm; TV rm; dogs €0.90; phone; poss cr; Eng spkn; adv bkg; some rd noise; red CKE/CCI. "Excel site in excel location; plenty of room, even high ssn; helpful warden; site yourself if recep clsd." 14 Jun-13 Sep. € 10.25   2008*

ALBI *8E4* (1.5km E Urban) *43.93485, 2.16213* **Albirondack Park, Camping Lodge & Spa (formerly Camping Caussels), 1 Allée de la Piscine, 81000 Albi [05 63 60 37 06 or 06 84 04 23 13 (mob); fax 05 31 60 51 86; albirondack@ orange.fr; www.albirondack.fr]** Fr Albi ring rd/bypass exit sp Lacause/St Juéry (do not turn twd Millau). Strt over & foll sp Géant-Casino hypmkt & 'Centre Ville', then foll camping/ piscine sp. Med, mkd pitch, pt sl, pt shd; htd wc; chem disp; mv service pnt; shwrs inc; el pnts (10A) €5.70; lndtte; supmkts adj; rest, snacks; BBQ; playgrnd; pool; spa; some statics & chalets; dogs €5; bus; adv bkg; quiet; red low ssn/CKE/CCI. "Vg site in conv position; pitches unlevelled - soft in wet & some poss diff lge o'fits due trees (2009); san facs need upgrade (2011); gd walk by rv to town cent; Albi Cathedral; Toulouse Lautrec exhibitions; spa & pool inc; excel rest" ♦ ltd 1 Apr-15 Oct. € 28.00   2013*

ALBIES see Cabannes, Les *8G3*

ALBINE *8F4* (1km SW Rural) *43.45406, 2.52706* **Camping L'Estap Albine, Le Suc, 81240 Albine [05 63 98 34 74; campinglestap@orange.fr; www.campinglestap.com]** Fr Mazamet on D612 dir Béziers for approx 12km; turn R onto D88 sp Albine. On app to vill turn R at sp 'Camping du Lac'. Site in 1km. Sm, hdg/mkd pitch, hdstg, terr, pt shd; wc; chem disp; baby facs; shwrs inc; el pnts (6A) €4.; lge; lndtte; shop 1km; tradsmn; snacks; bar; BBQ (gas) playgrnd; pool; fishing; games area; dogs €2; poss cr; Eng spkn; adv bkg; quiet; ccard acc; CKE/CCI. "Well-kept, clean site; superb views; facs adequate; excel touring base; poss diff lge o'fits due sm pitches & steep access; vg; new friendly French owners" ♦ 30 Mar-31 Nov. € 32.40   2013*

ALBOUSSIERE *9C2* (300m N Rural) *44.95000, 4.73000* **Camp Municipal La Duzonne, 07440 Alboussière [04 75 58 20 91; camping-la-duzonne@camping-la-duzonne.com; www. camping-la-duzonne.com]** App fr Valence on D533 (Valence-Lamastre) turn L on ent vill of Alboussière onto D219 sp Vernoux. (Do not take D14 which is 1st Vernoux turn). Site well sp. Med, pt shd; wc; shwrs inc; el pnts (10A) €3; lndry rm; shops 1.2km; playgrnd; tennis; rv fishing; lake sw adj; dogs; adv bkg; quiet; red low ssn; excel." 1 Apr-13 Oct. € 9.50   2008*

ALENCON *4E1* (1km SW Rural) *48.42566, 0.07321* **Camp Municipal de Guéramé, 65 Rue de Guéramé, 61000 Alençon [tel/fax 02 33 26 34 95; camping.guerame@ orange.fr; www.ville-alencon.fr]** Located nr town cent. Fr N on D38 take N12 W (Carrefour sp). In 5km take D1 L sp Condé-sur-Sarthe. At rndabt turn L sp Alençon then R immed after Carrefour supmkt, foll site sp. Site is sp fr D112 inner ring rd. Med, hdg pitches, hdstg, pt shd; htd wc (some cont); chem disp; mv service pnt; baby facs; shwrs inc; el pnts (5A) €3.10 (check el pnts carefully) (poss long lead req); lndtte (inc dryer); shop, snacks, bar adj; BBQ; playgrnd; pool complex 700m; tennis; rv fishing; canoeing; cycle hire; horseriding; wifi; entmnt; TV rm; dogs €1.90; poss cr; Eng spkn; adv bkg; quiet but w/end disco noise; no ccard acc; CKE/CCI. "Helpful warden; clean san facs; o'night area for m'vans; barrier/recep clsd 1800 low ssn; low ssn phone ahead to check site open; some pitches poss flood in heavy rain; rvside walk to town thro arboretum." ♦ 1 Apr-30 Sep. € 18.30   2013*

ALES *10E1* (13km SE Rural) *44.04705, 4.23024* **Camping Les Vistes, 30360 St Jean-de-Ceyrargues [04 66 83 29 56 or 04 66 83 28 09; info@lesvistes.com; www.lesvistes.com]** Fr Alès take D981 sp Uzès. After 12km take D7 S sp Brignon. At St Jean-de-Ceyrargues foll sp. Site S of vill on D7. Med, hdg/mkd pitch, pt sl, pt shd; wc; chem disp; baby facs; fam bthrm; shwrs inc; el pnts (4A) €3; lndtte; shops, rest, bar 2km; tradsmn; playgrnd; pool; TV rm; dogs free; quiet; CKE/ CCI. "Excel views; excel pools; conv for Pont du Gard, Uzès; diff access some pitches; ltd facs low ssn." ♦ 1 Apr-30 Sep. € 16.50   2008*

ALES *10E1* (6km S Rural) *44.07912, 4.09700* **Camping Mas Cauvy (Maurin-Daumet), Chemin du Mas Cauvy, 30380 St Christol-lès-Alès [tel/fax 04 66 60 78 24; maurin.helene @wanadoo.fr; http://fermemascauvy.free.fr]** Fr Alès S on N110/D6110 S sp Montpellier. At S end of Christol-lès-Alès (shortly after stone needle) take 2nd L into Rue de Mas Rouge; foll sp to site in 1.5km. NB Sps fr main rd diff to see. Sm, pt terr, pt shd; wc; chem disp (wc); shwrs inc; el pnts (6A) €3; gas 1.5km; lndtte; shop 1.5km; tradsmn; rest & snacks; 1.5km; BBQ; playgrnd; pool; tennis 3km; bus (1km); dogs €2; poss cr; adv bkg; quiet; red low ssn/CKE/CCI. "Attractive, CL-type site with lovely views; friendly, helpful owner; book early for shd pitch; excel." 1 Apr-30 Sep. € 15.00   2010*

⊞ **ALET LES BAINS** *8G4* (S Rural) *42.99490, 2.25525* **Camping Val d'Aleth, Ave Nicolas Pavillon, 11580 Alet-les-Bains [04 68 69 90 40; fax 04 68 69 94 60; info@ valdaleth.com; www.valdaleth.com]** Fr Limoux S on D118 twd Quillan; in approx 8km ignore 1st L turn over Aude bdge into vill but take alt rte for heavy vehicles. Immed after x-ing rv, turn L in front of casino & ent town fr S; site sp on L. Sm, hdg/ mkd pitch, hdstg, pt sl, shd; htd wc; chem disp; mv service pnt; baby facs; shwrs inc; el pnts (4-10A) €2.75-4; gas; lndtte (inc dryer); shop; rest nrby; BBQ (gas only); playgrnd; pool 1km; adj (no sw); cycle hire; wifi; 25% statics; dogs €1.55; phone; poss cr; adv bkg; Eng spkn; rd & train noise, church bells daytime; ccard acc; red low ssn/long stay; CKE/CCI. "Rvside site in attractive, medieval vill; sm pitches (lge o'fits need to book); friendly British owner; gd clean san facs; v few facs in vill; poss unkempt early ssn; conv Carcassonne & Cathar country - scenic." ♦ € 21.50   2013*

ALEX see Annecy *9B3*

FRANCE

ALLAS LES MINES see Sarlat la Canéda *7C3*

ALLEGRE *9C1* (300m NE Rural) *45.20834, 3.71873* **Camp Municipal La Pinède, Le Chier, 43270 Allègre [04 71 00 76 79 or 04 71 00 71 21 (Mairie); mairie.allegre@wanadoo.fr; www.mairie-allegre.com]** N on D13 fr Allègre, then take D21; site visible on N edge of Allègre adj football pitch, sp. Sm, pt shd; wc (some cont); chem disp (wc); shwrs inc; el pnts (3-6A) €1.90-2.70; gas; lndtte; shop, rest, bar in vill; playgrnd; no statics; dogs €0.95; bus 300m; quiet; red long stay. "Attractive pine-shaded site; gd cent for S Auvergne & Le Puy; gd NH & longer." ♦ ltd 15 Jun-15 Sep. € 9.80   2010*

ALLEGRE LES FUMADES *10E2* (2km NE Rural) *44.2089, 4.25665* **Camping Le Château de Boisson, 30500 Allègre-les-Fumades [04 66 24 85 61 or 04 66 24 82 21; fax 04 66 24 80 14; reception@chateaudeboisson.com; www. chateaudeboisson.com or www.les-castels.com]** Fr Alès NE on D904, turn R after Les Mages onto D132, then L onto D16 for Boisson. Fr A7 take exit 19 Pont l'Esprit, turn S on N86 to Bagnols-sur-Cèze & then D6 W. Before Vallérargues turn R onto D979 Lussan, then D37 & D16 to Boisson. Lge, hdg/mkd pitch, pt sl, shd; wc; chem disp; mv service pnt; baby facs; shwrs inc; el pnts (6A) inc; gas; lndtte (inc dryer); shop; tradsmn; rest, snacks, bar; BBQ (gas & elec); playgrnd; 2 pools (1 htd & covrd); paddling pool; tennis; cycle hire; games rm; wifi; entmnt; 80% statics; dogs €5 (no dogs 9 Jul-20 Aug); phone; no c'vans/m'vans over 7m high ssn; poss cr; Eng spkn; adv bkg; quiet; ccard acc; red low ssn/long stay. "Vg, well-run, peaceful site; gd sized pitches, poss some v sm; helpful staff; excel san facs; excel rest & facs; superb pool complex." ♦ 9 Apr-24 Sep. € 39.00 SBS - C34   2011*

See advertisement on inside back cover

ALLEGRE LES FUMADES *10E2* (2km S Rural) *44.18538, 4.22918* **Camping Le Domaine des Fumades, 30500 Allègre-les-Fumades [04 66 24 80 78; fax 04 66 24 82 42; domaine.des.fumades@wanadoo.fr; www.domaine-des-fumades.com or www.campings-franceloc.fr]** Take Bollène exit fr A7 m'way, foll sps to Bagnols-sur-Cèze, take D6 twd Alès; 10km bef Alès turn R sp Allègre-les-Fumades on D7 to site in 5km. Easy to find fr Alès ring rd. Med, mkd pitch, pt shd; wc; chem disp; baby facs; shwrs inc; el pnts (6A) €4; gas; lndtte (inc dryer); shop; tradsmn; rest, snacks, bar; playgrnd; 2 pools (1 htd, covrd); paddling pool; waterslide; tennis; games rm; golf & watersports nr; wifi; entmnt; some statics; dogs €5; adv bkg. "Pleasant location; friendly staff; beautiful, well-run site." ♦ 10 Apr-19 Sep. € 28.00   2010*

ALLEMANS DU DROPT see Miramont de Guyenne *7D2*

ALLEMONT/ALLEMOND see Bourg d'Oisans, Le *9C3*

ALLES SUR DORDOGNE see Bugue, Le *7C3*

ALLEVARD *9B3* (11km S Rural) *45.31869, 6.08430* **Camp Municipal Neige & Nature, Chemin de Montarmand, 38580 La Ferrière-d'Allevard [tel/fax 04 76 45 19 84; contact@neige-nature.fr; www.neige-nature.fr]** Fr Allevard take D525A S to La Ferrière; foll sp Collet & Le Pleynet. Sm, hdg/mkd pitch, pt sl, terr, pt shd; htd wc; chem disp; baby facs; shwrs; el pnts (10A) €3.90; gas 200m; lndtte; shop 200m; snacks; bar; playgrnd; rv & lake fishing; games area; entmnt; TV; dogs free; Eng spkn; adv bkg; quiet; ccard not acc; red long stay. "Excel, scenic site; helpful owners; many mkd walks." ♦ ltd 15 May-15 Sep. € 16.80   2010*

ALLIAT see Tarascon sur Ariege *8G3*

ALLONNES see Saumur *4G1*

⊞ **ALTKIRCH** *6F3* (1km SE Rural) *47.61275, 7.23336* **Camp Municipal Les Acacias, Route de Hirtzbach, 68130 Altkirch [03 89 40 69 40 or 03 89 40 00 04 (Mairie); camping.les. acacias@gmail.com; www.sundgau-sudalsace.com]** Sp on D419 on app to town fr W. Sp in town. Sm, mkd pitch, shd; htd wc (some cont); chem disp; baby facs; shwrs inc; el pnts (10A) €3; shop in ssn & 1km; rest, snacks; bar; playgrnd; pool 1km; 20% statics; dogs; Eng spkn; adv bkg rec high ssn; CKE/ CCI. "Lovely quiet site; gd, clean facs; office clsd until 1700 - site yourself & pay later; gd NH." € 13.50   2013*

ALTKIRCH *6F3* (12.5km SW Rural) *47.53919, 7.18005* **Village Center Les Lupins, 1 Rue de la Gare, 68580 Seppois-le-Bas [03 89 25 65 37 or 04 99 57 21 21; fax 03 89 25 54 92; contact@village-center.com; www.village-center.com]** SW fr Altkirch on D432, after 3km turn R to Hirtzbach on D17, foll sp to Seppois-le-Bas. Site sp in vill. Med, mkd pitch, pt shd; htd wc; chem disp; shwrs inc; baby facs; el pnts (6A) inc; lndtte; shop 500m; supmkt nrby; tradsmn; rest, snacks, bar 100m; BBQ; playgrnd; pool; paddling pool; fishing; golf 5km; games area; wifi; TV; 60% statics; dogs €3; phone; adv bkg; quiet midwk; noisy w/end; ccard acc; red low ssn/CKE/CCI. "Excel modern facs; Belfort worth visit; stork sanctuary adj; 1 hour Germany; 30 mins Switzerland; lge groups w/end." ♦ 30 Apr-13 Sep. € 20.00   2008*

AMBERT *9B1* (1km S Urban) *45.53951, 3.72867* **Camping Les Trois Chênes, Rue de la Chaise-Dieu, 63600 Ambert [04 73 82 34 68 or 04 73 82 23 95 (LS); fax 04 73 82 44 00; tourisme@ville-ambert.fr; www.camping-ambert.com]** On main rd D906 S twd Le Puy on L bet Leisure Park & Aquacentre. Med, hdg/mkd pitch, pt shd, serviced pitch; wc (some cont); chem disp; shwrs inc; el pnts (10A) €3.25; gas 400m; lndtte; supmkt adj; tradsmn; snacks; rest nrby; playgrnd; htd pool adj; waterslide; many statics; dogs €1; poss cr; adv bkg; quiet but some traff noise; ccard not acc; CKE/CCI. "Excel, well-kept site; gd, clean san facs; rvside walk to town; rec arrive bef noon peak ssn; recep & barrier clsd 1900 low ssn; steam museum & working paper mill nr; steam train 1.5km; vg." ♦ 8 May-30 Sep. € 20.00   2012*

FRANCE

AMBERT 9B1 (10km W Rural) 45.57449, 3.63393 **Camp Municipal Saviloisirs, 63890 St Amant-Roche-Savine [tel/fax 04 73 95 73 60 or 04 73 95 70 22 (Mairie); saviloisirs@wanadoo.fr; www.saviloisirs.com]** W fr Ambert on D996 to St Amant, turn R onto D37 into vill. In vill cent turn R & foll site sp. Bear L at lge building facing site on L. Sm, hdg/mkd pitch, pt shd; wc; shwrs inc; el pnts (16A) inc (rev pol); lndtte; shops adj; playgrnd; TV; dogs €0.30; quiet; CKE/CCI. "Tranquil vill site in wooded area; clean, modern facs; pleasant staff; easy walk to vill." 1 May-30 Oct. € 11.00   2009*

AMBIALET 8E4 (500m SE Rural) 43.94181, 2.38686 **Camping La Mise à l'Eau, Fédusse, 81430 Ambialet [05 63 79 58 29; fax 05 63 79 58 09; contact@camping-ambialet.com; www.camping-ambialet.com]** Fr Albi E on D999; in 15km, after Villefranche-d'Albigeois, turn L onto D74 to Ambialet; turn R at junc; in 100m bear L; site on L. NB Sharp turn, turning pnt avail down rd. Sm, mkd pitch, pt shd; wc; shwrs; el pnts (6-10A) €2.15; lndtte; shops, rest & bar 500m; snacks; dogs €1.50; playgrnd; pool; kayaking; poss cr; adv bkg; some rd noise; ccard not acc; CKE/CCI. "Easy walk to pretty vill; clean facs; excel." ♦ ltd; pretty riverside site." 15 Jun-30 Sep. € 12.00   2011*

AMBLETEUSE see Wimereux 3A2

AMBOISE 4G2 (4km N Rural) 47.43113, 0.95430 **Camp Municipal des Patis, 37530 Nazelles-Négron [02 47 57 71 07 or 02 47 23 71 71; mairie.nazelles-negron@wanadoo.fr; www.ville-amboise.fr]** Fr Amboise, take D952 on N bank of rv twd Tours & turn R (N) onto D5 to Nazelles-Négron. Foll sp to vill. Site N of bdge over Rv Cisse, on R immed after x-ing bdge. Sm, mkd pitch, pt shd; wc (some cont); chem disp; shwrs inc; el pnts (3-5A) inc (long lead poss req); lndry rm; shops 100m; playgrnd; dogs €0.90; poss cr; quiet; CKE/CCI. "Peaceful, clean, well-kept site; some lge pitches; excel san facs; no lge c'vans or twin-axles; boggy in wet weather; excel." 12 Apr-15 Sep. € 10.90   2010*

AMBOISE 4G2 (1km NE Rural) 47.41763, 0.98717 **Camp Municipal L'Ile d'Or, 37400 Amboise [02 47 57 23 37 or 02 47 23 47 38 (Mairie); fax 02 47 23 19 80; camping@ville-amboise.fr; www.camping-amboise.com]** Fr N exit A10 exit junc 18 onto D31/D431 to Amboise; at rndabt by rv turn R onto D751 dir Blois & get in L lane to cross bdge on D431; site a turning L off bdge, on lge wooded island in Rv Loire. Fr S exit A85 junc 11 onto D31 dir Amboise; at lge rndabt (where main rd swings R) foll Centre Ville sp to rv on D431; get in L/H lane to cross bdge (dir Nazelles); turn R off bdge to site on island. Lge, mkd pitch, pt shd; wc; chem disp; mv service pnt; baby facs; shwrs inc; el pnts (6A) €2.35 (poss rev pol); lndtte (inc dryer); shop 1km; rest, snacks; bar; playgrnd nrby; htd pool & waterslide 500m (high ssn); fishing; tennis; games area; entmnt; wifi; TV; no statics; dogs €1.15; phone; poss cr; Eng spkn; adv bkg; quiet, but rd noise if pitched nr rd; ccard acc; red low ssn/long stay; CKE/CCI. "Lovely, spacious, secure site in gd location adj Rv Loire & park; well-kept; lge pitches; gd clean san facs; nice rest & bar; easy walk to interesting old town; vg dog walking; conv Parc Léonardo Da Vinci (last place he lived) & Château d'Amboise; midsummer week music festival in adj park - check date; no twin-axles; m'van o'night area open all year, excel stop out of ssn; gd value; vg." ♦ 1 Apr-30 Sep. € 10.75   2012*

⊞ **AMBOISE** 4G2 (6km NE Rural) 47.44580, 1.04669 **Camping Le Jardin Botanique, 9 bis, Rue de la Rivière, 37530 Limeray [02 47 30 13 50; fax 02 47 30 17 32; info@camping-jardinbotanique.com; www.camping-jardinbotanique.com]** NE fr Amboise on D952 on N side of Rv Loire dir Blois; in approx 6km turn L for Limeray & then immed turn L onto Rue de la Rivière; site on L in 500m. NB Rec not to app fr Limeray, narr rds & diff for lge o'fits. Med, hdg/mkd pitch, hdstg, pt shd; htd wc; chem disp; mv service pnt; baby facs; fam bthrm; shwrs inc; el pnts (10A) €5 (poss rev pol); gas; lndtte; shop 2km; tradsmn; rest, snacks; bar; BBQ; playgrnd; pool; sand beach 15km; tennis; games area; cycle hire; TV; 20% statics; dogs €1.50; Eng spkn; adv bkg; rd & rlwy noise; red long stay/CKE/CCI. "Gd for Loire chateaux; 500m fr rv; friendly & helpful owner; gd for children; gd gourmet rest adj; poss muddy when wet; gd cycle rtes." ♦ € 17.00   2011*

See advertisement above

AMBOISE *4G2* (5km E Rural) *47.43491, 1.02818* **Camp Municipal Le Verdeau, Rue de Verdeau, 37530 Chargé [02 47 57 04 22 or 02 47 57 04 01 (Mairie); fax 02 47 57 41 52; mairiedecharge@wanadoo.fr; www.amboise-valdeloire.com]** Fr Amboise take D751 twd Blois, site sp on L. Med, pt shd; wc; chem disp; mv service pnt; shwrs inc; el pnts (5A) €2.50; lndtte; tradsmn; playgrnd; rv fishing & boating; adjacent sports cent adj; dogs €1; no twin-axle c'vans; adv bkg rec high ssn; quiet; CKE/CCI. "Gd cent for Loire Valley; gd san facs." ♦ 30 Jun-2 Sep. € 7.50   2008*

AMBON PLAGES see Muzillac *2G3*

AMBRIERES LES VALLEES *4E1* (2km SW Rural) *48.39121, -0.61680* **Camping Le Parc de Vaux, 35 Rue des Colverts, 53300 Ambrières-les-Vallées [02 43 04 90 25; parcdevaux@camp-in-ouest.com; www.parcdevaux.com]** Fr S on D23 turn R at sp 'Parc de Loisirs de Vaux'. Site in approx 100m on bank Rv Varenne. Check in at Office de Tourisme bef site recep. Med, hdg/mkd pitch, some hdstg, terr, pt shd; wc; shwrs inc; el pnts (10A) €3.20 (poss long lead req) (poss rev pol); lndtte (inc dryer); shops 500m; tradsmn; rest; bar; BBQ; playgrnd; htd pool; waterslide; lake adj; canoe hire; fishing; tennis; cycle hire; games area; wifi; entmnt; TV rm; 40% statics; dogs €1.80; Eng spkn; adv bkg; quiet; red long stay/low ssn/CKE/CCI. "Excel site in beautiful surroundings; helpful recep; poss unkempt early ssn." ♦ 9 Apr-30 Oct. € 14.00 (CChq acc)   2011*

AMELIE LES BAINS PALALDA see Ceret *8H4*

AMIENS *3C3* (800mtrs N Rural) *49.97240, 2.30150* **FFCC Camping du Château, Rue du Château, 80260 Bertangles [tel/fax 09 51 66 32 60; camping@chateaubertangles.com; www.chateaubertangles.com]** Foll N25 N of Amiens; after 8km turn W on D97 to Bertangles. Well sp in vill. Sm, hdg pitch, pt shd; wc; chem disp; shwrs inc; el pnts (5A) €3.70 (poss rev pol); tradsmn; tabac/bar in vill; bus; poss cr; quiet but slight rd noise; ccard notacc; red long stay; CKE/CCI. "Pleasant, peaceful, well-kept site by chateau wall; busy high ssn - early arr rec (bef 1600); pleasant welcome; clean san facs; ltd recep hrs, pitch yourself; grnd soft when wet; Amiens attractive city; gd walks; conv a'routes & NH; excel" ♦ 19 Apr-9 Sep. € 25.20   2013*

AMIENS *3C3* (8km NW Urban) *49.92091, 2.25883* **Camping Parc des Cygnes, 111 Ave des Cygnes, 80080 Amiens-Longpré [03 22 43 29 28; fax 03 22 43 59 42; alban@parcdescygnes.com; www.parcdescygnes.com]** Exit A16 junc 20 or fr ring rd Rocade Nord exit junc 40. At 1st rndabt foll sp Amiens, Longpré D412; foll sp Parc de Loisirs & site. Med, mkd pitches, ltd shd; htd wc; chem disp; mv service pnt; baby facs; shwrs inc; el pnts (10A) inc on most pitches (poss long lead req); gas; lndtte (inc dryer); sm shop; snacks; bar; BBQ; playgrnd; fishing nrby; kayaking; cycle hire; games rm; wifi; TV; dogs €1.87; no c'vans/m'vans over 11m high ssn; bus to city adj; adv bkg rec; quiet; ccard acc; red low ssn. "Peaceful, well-kept, secure site in parkland; leisure park adj; lge pitches; helpful, welcoming staff; gd, clean san facs, ltd low ssn; ring bell by recep if office clsd; access to grass pitches off hard areas - m'vans can keep driving wheels on in wet weather; gd canal-side cycling/walk to city; Amiens cathedral worth visit; longer leads required for some pitches; conv Somme battlefields; excel." ♦ 1 Apr-15 Oct. € 36.20 SBS - P11   2013*

AMPILLY LE SEC see Châtillon sur Seine *6F1*

ANCENIS *2G4* (12km E Rural) *47.36702, -1.01275* **Camping de l'Ile Batailleuse, St Florent-le-Vieil, 44370 Varades [02 40 83 45 01; serge.rabec@aliceadsl.fr; http://campingilebatailleuse.com.chez-alice.fr]** On Ancenis-Angers rd D723 turn S in Varades onto D752 to St Florent-le-Vieil. After x-ing 1st bdge over Rv Loire site on L on island immed bef 2nd bdge. Med, pt shd; wc; chem disp; shwrs inc; el pnts (10A) €2; shops 1km; rest 20m; playgrnd; pool 1km; tennis 1km; cycle hire; games area; dogs €1; poss cr; Eng spkn; quiet but poss road noise; CKE/CCI. "Basic, clean site; main shwr facs up stone staircase; panoramic views of Rv Loire in town; gd cycle rtes along rv." ♦ 28 Apr-15 Nov. € 11.00   2009*

ANCENIS *2G4* (5km SW Rural) *47.34400, -1.20693* **Camp Municipal Beauregret, 49530 Drain [02 40 98 20 30 or 02 40 98 20 16 (Mairie); fax 02 40 98 23 29; mairie-sg.drain@wanadoo.fr]** Fr Ancenis take D763 S for 2km, turn R onto D751 & cont for 3km. Site on R bef vill of Drain on L. Sm, hdg pitch, pt shd; wc; chem disp; mv service pnt; shwrs inc; el pnts (6A) inc (poss rev pol); lndtte; shop nr; tradsmn; BBQ; playgrnd; lake nrby; games area; entmnt; TV rm; adv bkg; quiet. "Secluded, tranquil site; immac san facs up steps - ltd number; poss not suitable lge o'fits; warden calls am & pm; gd fishing; Nice quiet site" ♦ 1 May-30 Sep. € 11.55   2013*

ANCENIS *2G4* (1km W Rural) *47.36201, -1.18721* **FFCC Camping de l'Ile Mouchet, La Davrays, 44150 Ancenis [02 40 83 08 43 or 06 83 52 73 44 (mob); fax 02 40 83 16 19; efberthelot@wanadoo.fr; www.camping-estivance.com]** Fr S, exit N249 at Vallet onto D763 to Ancenis; turn L immed after x-ing Rv Loire & foll sp; site on banks of rv. Or fr N, exit A11 junc 20 onto D923 to Ancenis; cont on D923 over rndabt; foll D923 along rv; in 400m, at next rndabt, do not cross rv but cont strt on onto D23; site sp to left in 700m. Med, mkd pitch, pt shd; htd wc; chem disp; mv service pnt; shwrs inc; el pnts (6-10A) €3.30; lndtte; gas; shops adj; rest, snacks, bar high ssn; playgrnd; pool; waterslide; tennis 50m; games rm; TV; 12% statics; dogs; Eng spkn; adv bkg; quiet; ccard acc; red low ssn/CKE/CCI. "Excel touring base; ltd facs low ssn; some steps; rvside walks." 2 Apr-23 Oct. € 14.00   2011*

ANCTEVILLE see Coutances *1D4*

ANDELOT BLANCHEVILLE *6F1* (1km W Rural) *48.25220, 5.29901* **Camping du Moulin, 5 Rue du Moulin, 52700 Andelot-Blancheville [03 25 32 61 28 or 03 25 01 33 31 (Mairie); fax 03 25 03 77 54; mairie.andelot@wanadoo.fr; www.camping-andelot.com]** Fr N on D974 site sp on ent Andelot-Blancheville. Foll sp & turn L onto D147. Site on R in 1km. Med, hdg/mkd pitch, hdstg, shd; htd wc; chem disp; shwrs inc; el pnts (9A) €2 (poss rev pol); lndtte; shop 1km; tradsmn; snacks; bar; playgrnd; lake/rv fishing; games rm; wifi; TV rm; 10% statics; dogs free; phone; Eng spkn; quiet; red low ssn; CKE/CCI. "Peaceful, quiet site by rv; gd NH on journey S." ♦ 15 Jun-15 Sep. € 16.50   2009*

L'Ile des Trois Rois

The park Ile des Trois Rois is situated in the most beautiful bend of the Seine nearby Castle Gaillard in Normandy and is a haven of peace. Paris is situated of less than than an hour and Rouen is half an hour driving from the camp site. Facilities: two heated swimming pools, ping pong, camper service, bar and restaurant (high season) and play area

1, Rue Gilles Nicole - F-27700 Les Andelys - France - Tel. 0033 (0) 2 32 54 23 79
Fax 0033 (0) 2 32 51 14 54 - Email campingtroisrois@aol.com - www.camping-troisrois.com

FRANCE

ANDELYS, LES 3D2 (1km S Rural) 49.23582, 1.40016 **FFCC** Camping de L'Ile des Trois Rois, 1 rue Gilles Nicolle, 27700 Les Andelys [02 32 54 23 79; fax 02 32 51 14 54; campingtroisrois@aol.com; www.camping-troisrois. com] Fr Rouen S on A13, exit junc 18 onto D135 & foll sp Les Andelys. Cross bdge over Rv Seine & turn immed R at rndabt, site on R on rvside. Site sp fr town cent. Lge, hdg/mkd pitch, some hdstg, pt shd; htd wc (some cont); chem disp; mv service pnt; shwrs inc; el pnts (10A) inc; gas; lndtte (inc dryer); snacks; bar; BBQ; playgrnd; htd pool; paddling pool; fishing; bowling alley; cycle hire; games rm; wifi; entmnt; TV rm; 50% statics; dogs €2; phone; poss cr; Eng spkn; quiet but some rd noise; ccard acc; red long stay/CKE/CCI. "Well-kept site on Rv Seine; extra lge pitches avail; friendly, helpful staff; clean san facs, but ltd number; gd security; conv Rouen, Evreux, Giverny; view ruins of Château Gaillard; nice place, nice people" ♦ 15 Mar-15 Nov. € 37.00   2013*

See advertisement

ANDERNOS LES BAINS 7D1 (3km NE Rural) 44.75777, -1.07194 Camping Les Arbousiers, 134 Ave de Bordeaux, 33510 Andernos-les-Bains [05 56 82 12 46; fax 05 56 26 15 21; lesarbousiers@yahoo.fr; www.camping-les-arbousiers.fr] E of Arès fr Bordeaux on D106 for approx 7km, take D215 sp Andernos. Site on L in 2km, ent rd to airport. Lge, hdg/mkd pitch, pt shd; htd wc; chem disp; baby facs; shwrs inc; el pnts (6A) inc (poss rev pol); lndtte (inc dryer); shop 2km; snacks; bar; BBQ; pool; sand beach 3km; wifi; 50% statics; dogs €1; Eng spkn; quiet; ccard acc. "Friendly staff; pleasantly situated site." 1 Apr-30 Sep. € 21.00   2009*

ANDERNOS LES BAINS 7D1 (2.5km SE Coastal) 44.72568, -1.08083 Camping Fontaine Vieille, 4 Blvd du Colonel Wurtz, 33510 Andernos-les-Bains [05 56 82 01 67; fax 05 56 82 09 81; contact@fontaine-vieille.com; www. fontaine-vieille.com] Take D106 fr Bordeaux then D215 on L after 40km sp Andernos. Well sp. Site situated 600m off D3. V lge, hdg/mkd pitch, pt shd; wc (some cont); chem disp; mv service pnt; baby facs; shwrs inc; el pnts (5A) inc; gas; lndtte; shop & 3km; tradsmn; rest, snacks; bar; BBQ; pool/waterpark; sand beach adj; watersports; windsurfing; tennis; games area; wifi; entmnt; TV; dogs €3; adv bkg rec high ssn; quiet; ccard acc; red long stay/low ssn. "Nice site; some pitches sea view (extra charge); excel for families & beach holiday; organised bus trips & sports." ♦ 1 Apr-30 Sep. € 29.00   2011*

⊞ **ANDERNOS LES BAINS** 7D1 (5km SE Coastal) 44.70435, -1.04856 Camping Domaine du Roumingue, 60 Ave de la Libération, 33138 Lanton [05 56 82 97 48; fax 05 56 82 96 09; info@roumingue.fr; www.roumingue.fr] Approx 7km SE of Andernos-les-Bains on D3 bet Cassy & Lanton. Lge, hdg/mkd pitch, pt shd; htd wc (some cont); mv service pnt; chem disp; serviced pitches; shwrs inc; el pnts (6A) €3.50; gas; lndtte; shop; tradsmn; rest, snacks; bar; playgrnd; pool; guarded private sand beach adj; lake sw; fishing; windsurfing; tennis; archery; games/sports area; cycle hire; entmnt; sat TV; 30% statics; dogs €2; phone; site clsd Jan; Eng spkn; adv bkg; ccard acc; red low ssn/long stay; CKE/CCI. "Excel family site; many facs/activities; lge pitches avail; helpful, friendly staff; vg." ♦ € 22.00   2009*

ANDERNOS LES BAINS 7D1 (6km W Coastal) 44.73443, -1.1960 Airotel Camping Les Viviers, Ave Léon Lesca, Claouey, 33950 Lège-Cap-Ferret [05 56 60 70 04 or 01 76 76 70 10; fax 05 57 70 37 77; reception@lesviviers. com; www.airotel-les-viviers.com] Fr N exit A10/A630 W of Bordeaux onto D106 sp Cap-Ferret. Foll D106 thro Arès & vill of Claouey on W side of Bassin d'Arcachon, site on L after LH bend (approx 1.5km after Claouey). V lge, hdg/mkd pitch, pt shd; htd wc; mv service pnt; chem disp; baby facs; sauna; shwrs inc; el pnts (10A) €9; gas; lndtte (inc dryer); supmkt; rest, snacks; bar; BBQ (gas/elec); playgrnd; htd, covrd pool; paddling pool; waterslide; sea water lagoon with private sand beach adj; fishing; sailing; windsurfing; tennis; cycle hire; games area; games rm; cinema; wifi; entmnt; TV rm; 27% statics; dogs €5; bus; Eng spkn; adv bkg ess; quiet; ccard acc; red long stay/low ssn/CKE/CCI. "Sand pitches, various positions & prices; clean san facs; vg leisure facs; free night bus along peninsular; vg site." ♦ 27 Mar-30 Sep. € 50.00   2010*

ANDERNOS LES BAINS 7D1 (6km W Coastal) 44.75234, -1.18474 Camping Les Embruns, Ave Edouard Branly, Claouey, 33950 Lège-Cap-Ferret [05 56 60 70 76; fax 05 56 60 49 79; lesembruns4@wanadoo.fr; www.camping-lesembruns.fr] Foll D106 Bordeaux to Cap-Ferret. On ent Claouey turn R at rndabt. Site sp. V lge, mkd pitch, pt sl, terr, shd; wc; chem disp; shwrs inc; el pnts (16A) €3; lndtte; shops adj; pizzeria; bar; playgrnd; htd pool; sand beach 700m; entmnt; some statics; dogs €1.50; quiet. "Well laid-out & organised; 20km cycle path adj; gd." ♦ 1 Apr-30 Sep. € 17.00   2008*

ANDERNOS LES BAINS *7D1* (5km NW Coastal) *44.77108, -1.14306* **Camping Domaine des Abberts, 17 Rue des Abberts, 33740 Arès [tel/fax 05 56 60 26 80; campinglesabberts@wanadoo.fr; www.lesabberts.com]** Fr town sq in Arès, take D106 twd Cap Ferrat, turn 1st L to site in 100m. Med, hdg/mkd pitch, pt shd; wc; chem disp; shwrs inc; el pnts (6A) €5; gas; lndtte; snacks; shops 400m; tradsmn; snacks; bar; BBQ; playgrnd; pool; sand beach 600m; cycle hire; 25% statics; dogs €2; poss cr; adv bkg; quiet; CKE/CCI. "Nr cycle paths to Arès; mkt Tues; gd." ♦ 1 Jun-15 Sep. € 24.00   2010*

ANDERNOS LES BAINS *7D1* (5km NW Coastal) *44.75799, -1.11931* **Camping Les Goëlands, Ave de la Libération, 33740 Arès [05 56 82 55 64; fax 05 56 82 07 51; campingles.goelands@wanadoo.fr; www.goelands.com]** Fr Bordeaux m'way by-pass take D106 for Cap-Ferret. At Arès take D3 SE twd Andernos. Site on R 200m after end of Arès town sp. Site sp. Lge, mkd pitch, shd; wc; chem disp; shwrs inc; el pnts (10A) inc; gas; lndtte (inc dryer); shop; tradsmn; snacks; bar; playgrnd; htd pool; sand beach 200m; seawater lake 200m; games rm; wifi; TV; 90% statics; dogs; phone; poss cr; adv bkg; poss noisy; ccard acc; red low ssn; CKE/CCI. "Many gd beaches." ♦ 1 Mar-31 Oct. € 27.45   2010*

ANDERNOS LES BAINS *7D1* (5km NW Coastal) *44.77792, -1.14280* **FLOWER Camping La Canadienne, 82 Rue du Général de Gaulle, 33740 Arès [05 56 60 24 91; fax 05 57 70 40 85; info@lacanadienne.com; www.lacanadienne.com or www.flowercampings.com]** N fr town sq at Arès on D3 (Rue du Général de Gaulle) dir Cap Ferret. Site on R after 1km. Med, shd; wc; baby facs; shwrs inc; el pnts (15A) inc; gas; lndtte; shop; rest, snacks; bar; sand beach 2km; playgrnd; pool; paddling pool; cycle & canoe hire; fishing, sailing & windsurfing 1km; tennis; archery; entmnt; games/TV rm; dogs €2.50; adv bkg rec high ssn; quiet, but some rd noise; red low ssn. ♦ 1 Feb-30 Nov. € 30.90   2012*

See advertisement on pages 32 & 33

ANDERNOS LES BAINS *7D1* (7.5km NW Rural) *44.80288, -1.13362* **Camping La Prairie, 93 Ave de Médoc, 33950 Lège-Cap-Ferret [tel/fax 05 56 60 09 75; camping-laprairie@wanadoo.fr; www.campinglaprairie.com]** Site 1km N of Lège-Cap-Ferret on D3 dir Porge. Med, pt shd; htd wc; chem disp; shwrs inc; el pnts (10A) €3.10; lndtte; shop; snacks; BBQ; playgrnd; pool; sand beach 5km; games area; games rm; entmnt; some statics; dogs €1.50; Eng spkn; adv bkg; quiet; CKE/CCI. "Poss run down & unclean low ssn; friendly owner; long distance cycle paths; gd baker nrby." 1 Mar-1 Nov. € 14.70   2009*

ANDERNOS LES BAINS *7D1* (8km NW Rural) *44.80330, -1.13264* **FFCC Camping Mer et Forêt, 101 Ave du Médoc, 33950 Lège-Cap-Ferret [05 56 60 18 36 or 05 56 60 16 99; fax 05 56 60 39 47]** Fr Bordeaux take D106 W dir Arès. Fr cent Arès take D3 N sp Lège-Cap-Ferret. Site on L in 5km adj 'Camping Prairie'. Med, mkd pitch, shd; wc; chem disp; mv service pnt; shwrs €1; el pnts (3-6A) €1.25-2.50; shop 2km; tradsmn; sand beach 6km; dogs; phone; quiet; CKE/CCI. "Lovely site; generous pitches; warm welcome, friendly owner; excel, clean san facs; vg." ♦ ltd 1 Jun-30 Sep. € 9.50   2009*

ANDORRA Campsites in Andorra are listed together at the end of the French site entry pages.

ANDOUILLE see Laval *2F4*

ANDRYES see Clamecy *4G4*

ANDUZE *10E1* (5km E Rural) *44.03585, 4.02390* **Kawan Village Domaine de Gaujac, 2406 Chemin de la Madeleine, 30140 Boisset-et-Gaujac [04 66 61 67 57; fax 04 66 60 53 90; contact@domaine-de-gaujac.com; www.domaine-de-gaujac.com]** S fr Alès on D6110 & turn R onto D910A dir Anduze. At Bagard (3km bef Anduze) turn L at mini rndabt onto D246 dir Boisset-et-Gaujac. At next rndbt turn R, then immed L. Foll vill & camping sp. Lge, some hdstg, pt terr, shd; htd wc (some cont); chem disp; mv service pnt; some serviced pitches; shwrs inc; baby facs; el pnts (4-6A) €4-4.50; gas; lndtte (inc dryer); shop; rest, snacks; bar; BBQ; playgrnd; 1 htd pool; paddling pool; rv adj; fishing; tennis; cycle hire; games area; games rm; wifi; entmnt; TV; 30% statics; dogs €2.50; Eng spkn; adv bkg rec high ssn; quiet, but noisy until late in café area high ssn; red low ssn. "Tranquil site; friendly, helpful family owners; clean san facs; pitches poss unkempt; Trabuc caves, Tarn gorges nrby. ♦ 1 Apr-20 Sep. € 21.00 (CChq acc)   2009*

ANDUZE *10E1* (1.5km SE Rural) *44.03824, 3.99454* **Camping Le Bel Eté, 1870 Route de Nîmes, 30140 Anduze [tel/fax 04 66 61 76 04; contact@camping-bel-ete.com; www.camping-bel-ete.com]** S fr Alès on D6110; W on D910A to Anduze. In Anduze take D907 SE twds Nîmes. Site on L, 200m after rlwy bdge. Med, mkd pitch, pt shd; wc; chem disp; serviced pitches; shwrs inc; el pnts (6A) €4.50; gas; lndtte; shop 1.5km; tradsmn; rest; playgrnd; pool; rv adj; 10% statics; dogs €1.50; phone; adv bkg ess; quiet but some rd noise; ccard acc; CKE/CCI. "Delightful, well-kept site in superb location; vg facs but ltd low ssn; helpful owner; gd base for Cévennes area; Thurs mkt." ♦ 8 May-17 Sep. € 33.50   2012*

ANDUZE *10E1* (5km SW Rural) *44.02733, 4.02736* **Camping Le Fief, 195 Chemin du Plan d'Eau, 30140 Massillargues-Attuech [04 66 61 81 71; fax 04 66 61 87 80; lefief@wanadoo.fr; www.campinglefiefdanduze.com]** Leave Anduze S on D982 dir Nîmes; site on L on leaving Attuech; sp. Med, mkd pitch, some hdstg, shd; wc; chem disp; baby facs; sauna; shwrs inc; el pnts (6A) €3 (poss no earth); lndtte; shops; tradsmn; rest, snacks; bar; playgrnd; pool; paddling pool; spa; rv sw adj, shgl beach; wifi; 10% statics; dogs €2.10; phone; poss cr; adv bkg; quiet; ccard acc; CKE/CCI. "Clean facs; gd for cycling." 1 Apr-30 Sep. € 19.00   2010*

ANDUZE *10E1* (10km W) **Camping La Pommeraie, Route de Lassalle, 30140 Thoiras [04 66 85 20 52; fax 04 66 85 20 53; info@la-pommeraie.fr; www.la-pommeraie.fr]** Fr Alès take D6110, & D910A to Anduze, over bdge, R onto D907. In 6km L under rlwy onto D57, site on L 2.5km bef Lasalle. Med, shd; wc; baby facs; shwrs; el pnts (6A) €4.50; gas; lndtte; shop; rest, snacks; bar; cooking facs; playgrnd; 2 pools; rv & beach adj; tennis; games area; entmnt; TV rm; some statics; dogs €3; adv bkg; quiet; red low ssn. 13 Apr-29 Sep. € 38.55   2013*

ANDUZE *10E1* (1.4km NW Rural) *44.06430, 3.97694*
**Camping Castel Rose, 30140 Anduze [04 66 61 80 15;
contact@castelrose.com; www.castelrose.com]** Fr Alès S
on D6110 & W on N910A to Anduze. Foll sp Camping L'Arche.
Lge, shd; wc; shwrs inc; el pnts (6-10A) €3.20-4; gas; lndtte;
shop; rest, snacks; bar; pool; fishing; boating; wifi; entmnt; TV;
dogs €2; poss cr; Eng spkn; adv bkg rec high ssn. "Excel site
by rv; friendly, helpful owners; attractive countryside; gd cent
touring Cévennes." 1 Apr-30 Sep. € 12.00   2009*

ANDUZE *10E1* (2km NW Rural) *44.06785, 3.97336*
**Camping L'Arche, Quartier de Labahou, 30140 Anduze
[04 66 61 74 08; fax 04 66 61 88 94; contact@camping-
arche.fr; www.camping-arche.fr]** Fr Alès S on D6110/D910A
to Anduze. On D907, sp on R. Access poss dff lge o'fits/m'vans.
Lge, mkd pitch, shd; htd wc; chem disp; mv service pnt; baby
facs; shwrs inc; el pnts (10A) €2; gas; lndtte; shop; tradsmn; rest,
snacks; bar; BBQ; playgrnd; pool; waterslide; wifi; entmnt; TV;
some statics; dogs €3.80; Eng spkn; adv bkg; quiet; red long stay;
CKE/CCI. "Well-run site; gd san facs; beautiful area; bamboo
gardens worth visit; 24hr security patrols." ♦ 1 Apr-30 Sep.
€ 28.50   2009*

ANDUZE *10E1* (4km NW Rural) *44.07814, 3.96533* **Camping
Cévennes-Provence, Corbès-Thoiras, 30140 Anduze
[04 66 61 73 10; fax 04 66 61 60 74; marais@camping-
cevennes-provence.fr; www.camping-cevennes-
provence.fr]** Fr Anduze D907 & D284 along rvside after
bdge, site sp. Diff ent espec for lge o'fits. Lge, mkd pitch,
terr, shd; htd wc (some cont); chem disp; some serviced
pitches; mv service pnt; baby facs; shwrs inc; el pnts (3-15A)
inc; gas; lndtte (inc dryer); shop; tradsmn; rest, snacks; bar;
BBQ; playgrnd; discovery park; shgl beach & rv sw adj; fishing;
tennis; games area; games rm; wifi; entmnt; TV; some statics;
dogs €2.90; Eng spkn; adv bkg; quiet; red low ssn; CKE/CCI.
"Variable pitch sizes; direct access to private rv beach; helpful
recep; gd walking; dog walks & dog shwrs; gd touring base;
vg site." ♦ 20 Mar-2 Oct. € 26.90   2010*

See advertisement below

ANET *3D2* (500m N Urban) *48.86183, 1.44166* **Camp
Municipal Les Eaux Vives, 1 Route des Cordeliers,
28260 Anet [02 37 41 42 67 or 06 09 74 16 90 (mob); fax
02 37 62 20 99; martine.desrues@cegetel.net; www.
camping-anet.fr]** Take D928 NE fr Dreux; in Anet thro town
& take 1st L after chateau; turn L on rd to Ezy & Ivry (camp sp
on corner), site in 150m N of rv. Lge, pt shd; htd wc; chem
disp (wc); mv service pnt; 75% serviced pitches; shwrs €1.10;
el pnts (10A) €3; lndry rm; supmkt 1km; playgrnd; rv adj; lake
sw & fishing 2km; tennis; 95% statics; dogs €1.10; poss cr;
Eng spkn; ccard not acc; red low ssn; CKE/CCI. "Rvside pitches;
helpful warden; clean, v basic san facs, poss stretched high
ssn; ground soft in wet - site poss clsd early; gd walks in forest;
chateau in vill; easy drive to Paris; untidy statics (2010); conv
NH." 1 Mar-31 Oct. € 14.20   2013*

"Satellite navigation makes touring much easier"

Remember most sat navs don't know if
you're towing or in a larger vehicle – always
use yours alongside maps and site directions.

ANET *3D2* (1km N Urban) *48.86278, 1.41552* **Camp Municipal
Les Trillots, Chemin des Trillots, 27530 Ezy-sur-Eure
[02 37 64 73 21 or 02 37 64 73 48 (Mairie)]** N fr Dreux on
D928/D143. Site on N side of Rv Eure. Med, pt shd; htd wc;
shwrs inc; el pnts (4A) inc; lndtte; supmkt nr; rest, snacks &
bar 1km; BBQ; 95% statics; dogs; quiet. "Quiet site adj rvside
walks; gd san facs; helpful warden; poss not suited to tourers;
not rec" 1 Mar-15 Nov. € 13.40   2012*

⊞ **ANGERS** *4G1* (10km SE Rural) *47.44332, -0.40881*
**Camping du Port Caroline, Rue du Pont Caroline, 49800
Brain-sur-l'Authion [02 41 80 42 18; info@camping
duportcaroline.fr; www.campingduportcaroline.fr]**
E fr Angers on D347 turn onto D113, site sp at ent to vill. Med,
hdg/mkd pitch, hdstg, pt shd; htd wc; chem disp; shwrs inc;
el pnts (10A) inc; lndtte; shop 300m; snacks; BBQ; playgrnd;
htd pool; paddling pool; tennis; fishing nrby; games area adj;
games rm; skateboarding; entmnt; TV rm; 5% statics; dogs
€3; site clsd Feb; adv bkg; some rd & rlwy noise (& owls,
woodpeckers); ccard acc. "Gd touring base; lge pitches." ♦
€ 15.00 (CChq acc)   2010*

FRANCE

ANGERS *4G1* (5km S Urban) *47.42442, -0.52701* **Camping Hortus L'Ile du Château, Ave de la Boire Salée, 49130 Les Ponts-de-Cé [02 41 44 62 05; info@camping-hortus.com; www.camping-hortus.com]** Fr Angers take D160 (sp Cholet) to Les Ponts-de-Cé. Foll sp 'Centre Ville' & turn R at rndabt in town opp Hôtel de Ville, & site on R in 200m on banks of Rv Loire. Med, hdg pitch, pt shd; wc; chem disp; mv service pnt; child/baby facs; shwrs inc; el pnts (10A) inc (poss rev pol); lndtte (inc dryer); shop; tradsmn; rest, snacks; BBQ; playgrnd; htd pool, waterslide adj; sand beach 500m; tennis; games area; games rm; golf 5km; internet; TV; 4% statics; dogs €2; phone; poss cr; Eng spkn; quiet; ccard acc; red low ssn; CKE/CCI. "Well-kept, scenic site; excel pool adj; gd touring base for chateaux, vineyards; gd dog walking; highly rec." ♦ 1 Apr-31 Oct. € 23.00   2012*

> ## "There aren't many sites open at this time of year"
>
> If you're travelling outside peak season remember to call ahead to check site opening dates – even if the entry says 'open all year'.

⊞ **ANGERS** *4G1* (6km SW Urban) *47.41878, -0.61160* **Camping Aire d'Accueil de Camping Cars, 25 Rue Chevrière, 49080 Bouchemaine [02 41 77 11 04 or 02 41 22 20 00 (Mairie); adm.generale@ville-bouchemaine. fr; www.ville-bouchemaine.fr]** Fr Angers take D160 S, at intersection with D112 W sp Bouchemaine. Cross Rv Maine via suspension bdge. At rndabt on W bank turn L, site on L in 100m dir La Pointe adj rv. Fr Château-Gontier take N162, then D106, then D102E. Bouchemaine well sp. Sm, hdstg, pt shd; wc; chem disp; mv service pnt; shwrs inc; el pnts (16A) €2.55 (poss rev pol); lndtte; shops 1km; tradsmn; rest 500m; pool 500m; games area; dogs; bus; phone; poss cr; adv bkg quiet; CKE/CCI. "M'vans & tents only; warden calls am & pm; free Oct-Apr but no el pnts; san facs upstairs; poss flooding nr rv; vg NH; automated access; excel cycling, track into Angers" € 7.50   2013*

ANGERS *4G1* (5km W Urban) *47.45387, -0.59463* **Camping du Lac de Maine, Ave du Lac de Maine, 49000 Angers [02 41 73 05 03; fax 02 41 73 02 20; camping@lacdemaine. fr; www.camping-angers.fr]** W fr Angers on D723, exit at 'Quartier du Lac de Maine' then foll sp to site & Bouchemaine. After 4 rndabts site on L; sp W of Rv Maine. Fr S on D160 or A87, turn onto D4 at Les Ponts-de-Cé. In 6km, cross Rv Maine to Bouchemaine & turn R to Pruniers dir Angers. Site on R at Pruniers town exit sp. Med, hdg/mkd pitch, hdstg, pt shd; htd wc; chem disp; mv service pnt; serviced pitches; baby facs; shwrs inc; el pnts (10A) €4.20 (rev pol); gas; lndtte (inc dryer); shop 1.5km; tradsmn; hypmkt 2km; rest, snacks & bar high ssn; BBQ; playgrnd; htd pool; paddling pool; jacuzzi; lake sw, sand beach 800m; fishing; boating; windsurfing 500m; tennis 800m; games area; cycle hire; wifi; TV rm; 10% statics; dogs €2.30; bus adj; phone; Eng spkn; adv bkg rec high ssn; quiet; ccard acc; twin-axles extra; red low ssn/long stay/CKE/CCI. "Excel, well-run site in leisure park; pitches narr, some suitable v l'ge o'fits; height barrier at ent 3.20m; conv Loire chateaux; Pay 6 nights, stay 7" ♦ 25 Mar-10 Oct. € 29.70 (CChq acc) 2013*

ANGOULEME *7B2* (15km N Rural) *45.78194, 0.11915* **FFCC Camp Municipal Les Platanes, 16330 Montignac-Charente [05 45 39 89 16 or 05 45 39 70 09 (Mairie); fax 05 45 22 26 71; www.campings-poitou-charentes.com]** Fr N, on N10, turn W on D11 then N on D737 thro vill onto D15. Narr rds on app, site on R by Rv Charente. Med, pt shd; wc (some cont); chem disp; shwrs inc; el pnts (10A) €4.40 (poss rev pol); gas 2km; lndry rm; shop 800m; rest, snacks in vill; bar; rv & fishing adj; canoeing; direct access to rv; dogs; poss cr; quiet; 25% red 16 days; ccard not acc; CKE/CCI. "Pleasant, basic, grassy, under-used site in gd position; friendly staff; warden calls am & pm; excel clean facs; many trees; no twin-axles; poss itinerants; site open to public at one end; pleasant vill." ♦ 1 Jun-30 Aug. € 9.75   2011*

ANGOULEME *7B2* (11km SW Rural) *45.60773, 0.02365* **Camping Le Nizour, 2 Route de la Charente, 16440 Sireuil [05 45 90 56 27 or 06 87 54 64 05 (mob); fax 05 45 90 92 67; contact@campingdunizour.com; www. campingdunizour.com]** SW fr Angouleme on N10; in 11km exit N10 at junc with D7 sp Sireuil; cont on D7 for 3km; site on R just after x-ing rv. Site 1.5km bef Sireuil & sp in town. Sm, pt shd; wc; chem disp; shwrs inc; el pnts €3.20; lndtte; shop 1.5km; rest, snacks; bar; playgrnd; pool; 5% statics, sep area; dogs € 1.30; poss cr; quiet. "Pleasant, well-run site nr Rv Charente; conv NH fr N10 & longer stay." 15 Apr-Sep. € 15.25   2009*

ANGOULEME *7B2* (5.5km NW Rural) *45.68573, 0.14994* **Camping du Plan d'Eau de la Grande Prairie, Impasse des Rouyères, 16710 St Yrieix-sur-Charante [tel/fax 05 45 92 14 64 or 05 45 95 16 84; info@angouleme-tourisme.com; www.angouleme-tourisme.com]** Fr N or S on N10/E606 turn NW & foll sp St Yrieix-sur-Charante, 'Plan d'Eau' & 'Nautilis - Centre Nautique'. Site sp. Med, hdg/mkd pitch, pt shd; htd wc; chem disp; mv service pnt; shwrs inc; el pnts €3.50; gas; lndtte; shop; tradsmn; rest, snacks; bar; BBQ; playgrnd; pool; lake sw & beach 500m; watersports; games area; wifi; TV rm; 10% statics; dogs; Eng spkn; adv bkg; quiet; ccard acc. "Superb location; excel." ♦ 1 Apr-31 Oct. € 18.00   2009*

ANGOULEME *7B2* (10km NW Rural) *45.79761, 0.06284* **Camping Marco de Bignac (formerly Les Sablons), Chemin de la Résistance, 16170 Bignac [05 45 21 78 41; fax 05 45 21 52 37; info@marcodebignac.com; www. marcodebignac.com]** Fr N10 approx 14km N Angouleme take exit La Touche & foll D11 W thro Vars; at Basse turn R onto D117 & foll sp in Bignac. Med, mkd pitch, pt shd; htd wc; chem disp; shwrs inc; child/baby facs; fam bthrm; el pnts (3-6A) €2-3; lndtte; shop or 10km; tradsmn; rest, snacks; bar; BBQ; playgrnd; pool high ssn; lake adj; fishing; watersports; tennis; pets corner; tennis; games area; games rm; wifi; few statics; dogs free; phone; bus adj; Eng spkn; adv bkg; quiet; ccard acc; red low ssn/long stay; CKE/CCI. "Attractive, peaceful, tidy, lakeside site; worth long drive; scenic area; lge pitches; welcoming, helpful British owners; clean san facs; gd rest; pleasant walk round lake; ideal for Angoulême Circuit des Remparts; vg" ♦ ltd 1 Apr-31 Oct. € 34.10   2013*

ANGOULINS SUR MER see Rochelle, La *7A1*

ANIANE *10E1* (1.5km SW Rural) *43.67550, 3.56542* **Camping La Source St Pierre (Naturist), 1 Route de Gignac, 34150 Aniane [tel/fax 04 67 57 76 95; campingstpierre@hotmail. com; www.campingstpierre.com]** Exit A750 at Gignac onto D32 dir Aniane; site on L in 2.5km (bef Aniane). Med, pt shd; wc (some cont); chem disp; shwrs inc; el pnts (5-10A) €3.30-3.90; gas; lndtte; tradsmn; rest, snacks; bar; BBQ (sep area); playgrnd; rv adj; canoe & kayak hire; wifi; dogs € 2.50; phone; Eng spkn; quiet; ccard acc; red low ssn; CKE/CCI. "Friendly site - many regs; vg rv bathing & rv sports; excel." ♦ ltd 1 May-30 Sep. € 19.50   2009*

ANNECY *9B3* **For more sites near Lake Annecy see also Doussard and Faverges.**

ANNECY *9B3* (8km SE Rural) *45.88990, 6.22367* **Camping La Ferme de Ferrières, 74290 Alex [04 50 02 87 09; fax 04 50 02 80 54; campingfermedesferrieres@voila.fr; www. camping-des-ferrieres.com]** Take D909 on E side of lake out of Annecy twds Thônes; look out for sp on L after turn off to Château de Menthon. Site off D909 approx 1km W of Alex. Med, pt sl, terr, pt shd; wc (cont); chem disp; baby facs; shwrs inc; el pnts (5A) €2.80; lndtte; shop & 2km; tradsmn; snacks; playgrnd; lake sw 4km; dogs €1; poss cr; quiet; phone; adv bkg; CKE/CCI. "Spectacular views; peaceful, clean site away fr crowds; friendly & accommodating owner; high standard san facs; pitches muddy when wet." ♦ ltd 1 Jun-30 Sep. € 12.00   2011*

ANNECY *9B3* (8km SE Rural) *45.86305, 6.19690* **Camping Le Clos Don Jean, Route du Clos Don Jean, 74290 Menthon-St-Bernard [tel/fax 04 50 60 18 66; donjean74@wanadoo. fr; www.clos-don-jean.com]** Fr N site clearly sp fr vill of Menthon. L uphill for 400m. Med, mkd pitch, pt sl, pt shd; wc (some cont); chem disp; mv service pnt; shwrs inc; el pnts (3-6A) €2.60-3.00; gas; lndtte; shop; playgrnd; lake sw 900m; dogs €1; poss cr; Eng spkn; quiet; CKE/CCI; "Excel site in orchard; clean san facs, ltd low ssn; fine views chateau & lake; walk to lake." ♦ ltd 1 Jun-15 Sep. € 21.50   2012*

ANNECY *9B3* (9km SE Urban) *45.82902, 6.18861* **Camp Municipal Les Champs Fleuris, 631 Voie Romaine, Les Perris, 74410 Duingt [04 50 68 57 31, 06 78 99 20 74 (mob) or 04 50 68 67 07 (Mairie); fax 04 50 77 03 17; camping@ duingt.fr; www.camping-duingt.com]** Fr Annecy take D1508 sp Albertville. Site on R bef Duingt vill (2km after St Jorioz). Foll sp Camping Le Familial, over cycle path & turn L. Med, mkd pitch, pt sl, terr, pt shd; htd wc; chem disp; mv service pnt; shwrs inc; el pnts (3-10A) €2.50-5.25; gas 1km; lndtte; shops 1km; tradsmn; rest, snacks; bar; BBQ; playgrnd; lake sw 750m; wifi; 3% statics; dogs €1.85; phone; bus 200m; poss cr; Eng spkn; adv bkg; quiet; CKE/CCI. "Pleasant site with mountain scenery; busy high ssn; gd sized pitches; friendly, helpful warden; facs basic but clear; vg lakeside beach; gd walking & cycling; cycle track fr site along old rlwy into Annecy; v cr if Tour de France in area; poss muddy after heavy rain; gd." ♦ 23 Apr-17 Sep. € 15.50   2011*

ANNECY *9B3* (10km SE Rural) *45.82423, 6.18523* **Camping Le Familial, 400 Route de Magnonnet, 74410 Duingt [tel/ fax 04 50 68 69 91; contact@annecy-camping-familial.com; www.annecy-camping-familial.com]** Fr Annecy on D1508 twd Albertville. 5km after St Jorioz turn R at site sp Entrevernes onto D8, foll sp past Camping Champs Fleuris. Sm, mkd pitch, some hdstg, pt sl, pt shd; wc; shwrs inc; el pnts (6A) €3.40; lndtte; tradsmn; playgrnd; lake & shgl beach 500m; TV rm; dogs €1.70; some Eng spkn; adv bkg rec Jul/Aug; quiet but rd noise; CKE/CCI. "Gd site in scenic area; gd atmosphere; generous pitches; friendly owner; communal meals & fondu evenings; conv lakeside cycle track." ♦ ltd 1 Apr-30 Sep. € 14.00   2010*

ANNECY *9B3* (10km SE Rural) *45.84070, 6.16450* **Camping Le Solitaire du Lac, 615 Route de Sales, 74410 St Jorioz [04 50 68 59 30 or 06 88 58 94 24 (mob); fax 04 50 68 59 30; contact@campinglesolitaire.com; www. campinglesolitaire.com]** Exit Annecy on D1508 twd Albertville. Site sp on N o'skts of St Jorioz. Med, mkd pitch, pt shd; wc; chem disp; mv service pnt; shwrs inc; el pnts (5A) €3.50; water to MH's charge €0.20 per 60l; gas; lndtte; supmkt 2km; tradsmn; pizza; snacks; bar & 2km; BBQ; playgrnd; lake sw; boat-launching; cycle hire; games area; cycle track; wifi; TV rm; 10% statics; dogs €2.60; poss v cr high ssn; some Eng spkn; adv bkg; v quiet; ccard acc; red low ssn/long stay; CKE/ CCI. "Nice, well-run site in excel location; popular but quiet; sm pitches; clean, modern san facs; direct access to Lake Annecy; sh walk to public beach & water bus; cycle path nr; gd touring base; no twin-axles; excel." 6 Apr-21 Sep. € 23.50   2013*

ANNECY *9B3* (12km SE Rural) *45.80153, 6.15166* **Aire Naturelle Le Combarut (Cottard), Chef-Lieu Le Verger, 74410 St Eustache [04 50 32 00 20]** Take D1508 S fr Annecy to Sévrier, turn R onto D912, site on farm just bef St Eustache. Sm, shd; wc (cont); mv service pnt; shwrs €1.20; el pnts (4A) €2.20; shop; lake sw; pool 15km; dogs €1; quiet. "Basic facs but clean; gd mountain views; tortuous access on winding rds, but not diff with care." 15 Jun-15 Sep. € 12.00   2010*

ANNECY *9B3* (1.5km S Rural) *45.89100, 6.13236* **Camp Municipal Le Belvédère, 8 Route du Semnoz, 74000 Annecy [04 50 45 48 30; fax 04 50 51 81 62; camping@ ville-annecy.fr; www.annecy.fr]** Exit A41 junc 16; initially foll sp 'Albertville' into town; then foll sp 'Le Lac' and 'Le Semnoz'; site is on R off Route du Semnoz (Route du Semnoz is A41). 'Le Semnoz is a mountain running S fr Annecy. Lge, mkd pitch, pt sl, terr, pt shd; htd wc; chem disp; shwrs inc; el pnts (16A) €3.20 (poss rev pol); gas; lndtte; shop; tradsmn; rest, snacks; playgrnd; cycle hire; sailing; fishing; forest walks; excursions; wifi; TV; sep statics area; dogs free; phone; poss cr; Eng spkn; adv bkg; poss noisy; ccard acc; CKE/CCI. "Lovely, tidy site in beautiful setting; well lit at night; sm pitches; staff helpful; san facs OK; steep footpath to old town; excel; v friendly helpful staff, rec adv bkg" ♦ 29 Mar-13 Oct. € 30.60   2013*

ANNECY *9B3* (5km S Urban) *45.85482, 6.14395* **Camping au Coeur du Lac, Les Choseaux, 74320 Sévrier [04 50 52 46 45; fax 04 50 19 01 45; info@aucoeurdulac. com; www.campingaucoeurdulac.com]** S fr Annecy on D1508 sp Albertville. Pass thro Sévrier cent. Site on L at lakeside 1km S of Sévrier. 300m after McDonald's. Med, mkd pitch, terr, pt sl, pt shd, some hdstg; wc (some cont); chem disp; mv service pnt; shwrs inc; el pnts (4A) €3.60, long cable rec; lndtte; shop; supmkt 2km; snacks; playgrnd; lake sw; grass & shgl beach; cycle/boat hire; entmnt; dogs free low ssn (not acc high ssn); bus nrby; poss cr; some Eng spkn; adv bkg ess high ssn; quiet; ccard acc; red low ssn; CKE/CCI. "Busy site in lovely location; gd views of lake fr upper terr; tight for lge o'fits - sm, sl pitches; gd san facs; gd access to lake beach & cycle path; excel, espec low ssn." ♦ 28 Mar-30 Sep. € 36.60 2013*

ANNECY *9B3* (6km S Rural) *45.84333, 6.14175* **Camping Le Panoramic, 22 Chemin des Bernets, Route de Cessenaz, 74320 Sévrier [04 50 52 43 09; info@camping-le-panoramic.com; www.camping-le-panoramic.com]** Exit A41 junc 16 Annecy Sud onto D1508 sp Albertville. Thro Sévrier to rndabt at Cessenaz (ignore all prior sp to site) & take 1st R onto D10. In 200m turn R up hill to site in 2km. Lge, mkd pitch, pt sl, terr, pt shd; htd wc; chem disp; shwrs inc; el pnts (4-6A) €3.20-4.20 (some rev pol); lndtte; shop; supmkt 2km; tradsmn; rest, snacks; bar; playgrnd; pool; beach 2km; lake sw; games rm; wifi; TV; dogs €1.60; poss cr; Eng spkn; quiet; ccard acc; red low ssn; CKE/CCI. "Gd views; blocks/wedges ess for sl pitches; excel pool; rec for families; New san facs (2012) excel views of lake, v friendly staff, high rec" ♦ ltd 26 Apr-30 Sep. € 27.80 2012*

ANNECY *9B3* (6.5km S Urban) *45.84412, 6.15354* **Camping de l'Aloua, 492 Route de Piron, 74320 Sévrier [04 50 52 60 06 or 04 50 52 64 54 (LS); fax 04 50 52 64 54; camping. aloua@wanadoo.fr; www.campingaloua.free.fr]** Foll sp for Albertville D1508 S fr Annecy. Site on E side, approx 1.4km S of Sevrier vill. Turn L at Champion supmkt rndabt & foll sp twd lake. Lge, pt hdg/mkd pitch, shd; wc (some cont); chem disp; mv service pnt; shwrs inc; el pnts (2-10A) €2.50-4.80; gas 400m; lndtte; shop; supmkt 400m; tradsmn; rest, snacks; bar; playgrnd; shgl beach 300m; lake sw, fishing, boating & watersports adj; archery; entmnt; TV; dog €2; phone; poss cr; quiet, but rd noise; Eng spkn; adv bkg; red low ssn; CKE/CCI. "Gd base for lake (no dir access fr site); cycle track around lake; night security; poss noisy at night with youths & some rd noise; basic san facs; pleasant owners; vg." ♦ 4 May-20 Sep. € 29.70 2013*

ANNECY *9B3* (6.5km S Rural) *45.84806, 6.15129* **FFCC Camping Les Rives du Lac, 331 Chemin du Communaux, 74320 Sévrier [04 50 52 40 14; lesrivesdulac-annecy@ffcc. fr; www.lesrivesdulac-annecy.com]** Take D1508 S fr Annecy sp Albertville, thro Sévrier sp FFCC. Turn L 100m past (S) Lidl supmkt, cross cycle path & turn R & foll sp FFCC keeping parallel with cycle path. Site on L in 400m. Med, mkd pitch, pt shd; wc (some cont); chem disp; mv service pnt; baby facs; shwrs inc; el pnts (10A) €4; lndtte; shops 500m; BBQ; playgrnd; private shgl beach; lake sw; sailing; fishing; walking; wifi; entmnt; dogs €1.20; bus nr; poss cr; Eng spkn; adv bkg; quiet; red CC members (not Jul/Aug)/long stay/low ssn/ CKE/CCI. "Beautiful situation; generous pitches; helpful staff; san facs ltd low ssn & inadequate if site full; water bus to Annecy nr; gd touring base; gd walking, sailing & cycling; cycle rte adj." ♦ 01 Apr-30 Sep. € 21.60 (CChq acc) 2011*

ANNECY *9B3* (9km S Rural) *45.49484, 6.1055* **Camping International du Lac d'Annecy, 1184 Route d'Albertville, 74410 St Jorioz [tel/fax 04 50 68 67 93; contact@camping-lac-annecy.com; www.camping-lac-annecy.com]** Fr Annecy take D1508 sp Albertville. Site on R just after St Jorioz. Med, hdg/mkd pitch, some hdstg, pt shd; wc; chem disp; mv service pnt; baby facs; fam bthrm; shwrs inc; el pnts (6-10A) €4-5.60; gas; lndtte; shop & 2km; tradsmn; rest, snacks; bar; BBQ (gas/elec); playgrnd; htd pool; lake sw 2km, shgl beach; cycle hire; games area; TV rm; 30% statics; dogs €2.50; bus 500m; phone; poss cr; Eng spkn; adv bkg; quiet; ccard acc; red low ssn; CKE/CCI. "Lovely site; gd san facs; excel for touring lake area; site ent tight for med/lge o'fits (2009); vg cycling; gd rest nrby." 8 May-18 Sep. € 36.00 2012*

ANNECY *9B3* (7km SW Rural) *45.86131, 6.05214* **Aire Naturelle La Vidome (Lyonnaz), 74600 Montagny-les-Lanches [tel/fax 04 50 46 61 31; j.lyonnaz@wanadoo.fr; www.lavidome.fr]** Exit Annecy on D1201 sp Aix-les-Bains/Chambéry; after 6km at Le Treige turn R sp Montagny-les-Lanches. In 1km turn R in Avulliens; site on R in 100m. Sm, pt sl, pt shd; wc; chem disp; shwrs; el pnts (3-10A) €2.10-4; lndtte; hypermkt 3km; meals avail; playgrnd; pool 3km; beach & mini-golf 10km; fishing 1km; horseriding 1km; dogs €0.80; quiet but some rd noise; adv bkg; gd views; CKE/CCI. "Excel site; friendly owners; vg san facs; access poss tight for lge o'fits; gd touring base." 1 May-30 Sep. € 11.60 2008*

ANNECY *9B3* (9km SW Rural) *45.86183, 6.09029* **Aire Naturelle Le Pré Ombragé (Metral), Chef-Lieu, 74600 Montagny-les-Lanches [04 50 46 71 31; fax 04 50 57 20 04; lepreombrage@wanadoo.fr]** Exit Annecy on D1201 sp Aix-les-Bains/Chambéry, after 8km at Le Treige turn R sp Montagny-les-Lanches; site sp in vill. Sm, pt sl, pt shd; wc; shwrs inc; el pnts (6A) inc; shops 2.5km; BBQ; playgrnd; pool; dogs €0.50; adv bkg; quiet; CKE/CCI. "Friendly, family-run, basic site in orchard; excel views." 15 Jun-30 Sep. € 12.00 2010*

ANNECY *9B3* (8km NW Rural) *45.97811, 6.03564* **Camping La Caille, 18 Chemin de la Caille, 74330 La Balme-de-Sillingy [04 50 68 85 21; fax 04 50 68 74 56; contact@aubergedelacaille.com; www.aubergedelacaille.com]** Fr Annecy take D1508 dir Bellgarde-sur-Valserine. Strt on at rndabt at end of La Balme-de-Sillingy, foll sp. At mini-rndabt strt on, site on R in 1km. Sm, hdg/mkd pitch, pt sl, shd; wc; chem disp; el pnts (4-12A) €3-5; lndtte; shop 750m; tradsmn; rest, snacks; bar; playgrnd; pool; 25% statics; dogs €4; adv bkg; quiet; CKE/CCI. "Gd, well-kept site." ♦ 1 May-30 Sep. € 21.00 2010*

ANNET SUR MARNE see Meaux *3D3*

ANNONAY *9C2* (1km N Urban) *45.25799, 4.67426* **Camp Municipal de Vaure, Rue Mathieu Duret, 07100 Annonay [04 75 33 73 73 or 04 75 33 46 54; fax 04 75 34 62 36; www.mairie-annonay.fr]** Sp fr o'skts of town & foll sp St Etienne. Fr St Etienne & NW on D1082 & D820 twd Annonay. For R onto D206 S & foll camping/piscine sp to site. Sm, hdg/mkd pitch, pt shd; wc (some cont); shwrs inc; el pnts (6-10A) €2.50-3.50; lndtte; snacks; bar; supmkt adj; htd, covrd pool; paddling pool; tennis; games area; few statics; dogs €1.50; poss cr; quiet. "Helpful staff; gd." 1 Apr-31 Oct. € 10.00 2009*

FRANCE

ANNOT *10E4* (1km N Rural) *43.97195, 6.65777* **Camping La Ribière, Route de Fugeret, 04240 Annot [04 92 83 21 44; info@la-ribiere.com; www.la-ribiere.com]** On N202 exit at Les Scaffarels to Annot on D908. Site 1km beyond vill on L bank of rv. Med, mkd pitch, some hdstg, pt shd; htd wc (some cont); chem disp; shwrs €0.80; el pnts (10A) €3.40; lndtte; shops 1km; rest, snacks; bar; playgrnd; fishing; games rm; wifi; 30% statics; dogs €1; adv bkg; quiet. "Interesting medieval vills & gorges." 27 Feb-24 Oct. € 13.00   2010*

ANNOVILLE *1D4* (1km SW Coastal) *48.95521, -1.54911* **Camp Municipal Les Peupliers, 177 Rue de la Libération, 50660 Annoville [02 33 47 67 73 or 02 33 47 67 (LS); campinglespeupliers@orange.fr]** N fr Granville on D971 to Bréhal then take D20 for approx 6km dir Annonville, turn L at Hameau Hébert, site sp on R. Med, mkd pitch, pt sl, unshd; wc; chem disp; baby facs; shwrs inc; el pnts €3; supmkt in Bréhal; snacks; playgrnd; sand beach 500m; 10% statics; dogs €1.20; Eng spkn; adv bkg; quiet; CKE/CCI. "Gd walking, birdwatching; gd site." 12 Jun-5 Sep. € 8.00   2010*

ANOULD see Corcieux *6F3*

ANSE see Villefranche sur Saône *9B2*

ANTIBES *10E4* (2km N Urban/Coastal) *43.60536, 7.11255* **Camping Caravaning Le Rossignol, Ave Jean Michard-Pelissier, Juan-les-Pins, 06600 Antibes [04 93 33 56 98; fax 04 92 91 98 99; campingrossignol@wanadoo.fr; www.campingrossignol.com]** Turn W off N7 Antibes-Nice at sp to Hospitalier de la Fontonne then bear L along Chemin des Quatres past hospital & traff lts junc. In 400m turn R at rndabt into Ave Jean Michard Pelissier, site 200m on R. NB Narr ent off busy rd. Med, hdg/mkd pitch, hdstg, terr, shd; wc; chem disp; mv service pnt; baby facs; shwrs inc; el pnts (10A) €5; gas; lndtte; shop 400m; tradsmn ndte ssn; bar; BBQ (gas/elec); playgrnd; htd pool; paddling pool; shgl beach 1.2km; tennis 2km; games area; games rm; wifi; entmnt; TV rm; dogs €3.50; Eng spkn; adv bkg; quiet; ccard acc; red long stay/CKE/CCI. "Conv Antibes & surrounding area; peaceful site; sm pitches." ♦ 1 Apr-30 Sep. € 22.40   2008*

ANTIBES *10E4* (3km N Coastal) *43.61009, 7.12473* **Camping le Logis de la Brague, 1221 Route de Nice, 06600 Antinbes [04 93 33 54 72; contact@camping-logisbrague.com; www.camping-logisbrague.com]** N fr Antibes on D6007 Route de Nice; site on L in 2km, just after sm rv brdge. Med, pt shd; wc; chem disp; mv service pnt; shwrs inc; el pnts (6A) €4.50 (poss rev pol); shops 3km; rest; bar; BBQ; pebble beach 250m; dogs €2; bus & train 250m; poss cr; rd & rlwy noise; ccard not acc; red low ssn. "Basic site; access to beach across busy main rd & under rlwy; helpful owner; gd." 2 May-30 Sep. € 22.00   2011*

ANTIBES *10E4* (3.5km N Coastal) *43.61101, 7.11675* **Camping Antipolis, Ave du Pylone, La Brague, 06600 Antibes [04 93 33 93 99; fax 04 92 91 02 00; contact@ camping-antipolis.com; www.camping-antipolis.com]** Exit A8 at Biot dir Marineland. In 800m turn R & foll site sp. Lge, mkd pitch, hdstg, unshd; wc (some cont); chem disp; shwrs; el pnts (10A) inc; gas; lndtte (inc dryer); shop; tradsmn; rest, snacks; bar; BBQ; playgrnd; 2 pools (1 htd); paddling pool; shgl beach 800m; tennis; cycle hire; games area; wifi; entmnt; 30% statics; no dogs; phone; train 1km; no c'vans over 6m; adv bkg; quiet; ccard acc; CKE/CCI. "Situated beside m'way, but pitches away fr rd; sm pitches bet statics; walk to beach along busy rds & across dual c'way; excel pool complex & activities; some pitches private san facs; knocking in pegs diff due lge sized gravel; unshd due severe pruning (2010)." ♦ 2 Apr-26 Sep. € 29.00 (CChq acc)   2010*

"That's changed — Should I let The Club know?"

If you find something on site that's different from the site entry, fill in a report and let us know. See www.caravanclub.co.uk/europereport.

ANTIBES *10E4* (3.5km N Coastal) *43.61270, 7.12522* **Camping Les Embruns, 63 Route de Biot, Quartier de la Brague, 06600 Antibes [04 93 33 33 35; fax 04 93 74 46 70; contact@campingembruns-antibes.com; www.campingembruns-antibes.com]** Fr Antibes take D6007 sp Nice, after 3.5km at rndabt with palm trees turn inland into Route de Biot; site sp on L. Sm, pt shd; wc; baby facs; shwrs inc; el pnts (5) €3; lndtte; snacks; bar; shop; shgl beach adj; fishing & watersports adj; cycle hire; tennis; TV; dogs €3; bus & metro adj; adv bkg; poss noise fr adj rd & rlwy, aslo fr adj amusement park; ccard acc; red low ssn. "Lovely, well-run site; helpful owner; walking dist beach, bus & metro; sm pitches; no turning space - not suitable lge o'fits; some pitches waterlogged in wet weather; gd." 11 Apr-31 Oct. € 24.00   2011*

ANTONNE ET TRIGONANT see Périgueux *7C3*

APREMONT *2H4* (2km N Rural) *46.77848, -1.73394* **Camping Les Charmes, Route de la Roussière, 85220 Apremont [02 51 54 48 08 or 06 86 03 96 93 (mob); fax 02 51 55 98 85; contact@campinglescharmes.com; www.campinglescharmes.com]** Fr D948 Challans to Aizenay turn W onto D94 sp Commequiers; after 2km L, sp Les Charmes. Med, mkd pitch, pt shd; wc (some cont); chem disp; fam bthrm; shwrs inc; el pnts (6-10A) €3.30-4 (poss rev pol); gas; lndtte; shop; tradsmn; playgrnd; pool; lake sw with beach 3km; sand beach 18km; TV rm; 60% statics; dogs €2.80; poss cr; Eng spkn; adv bkg; quiet; ccard acc; red low ssn/long stay; CKE/CCI. "Beautiful, well-kept site; generous pitches but soft when wet; welcoming, helpful owners; excel, clean san facs; a great find; friendly reception" ♦ 1 Apr-12 Sep. € 19.30   2013*

FRANCE

APT *10E3* (9km N Rural) *43.92050, 5.34120* **Camping Les Chênes Blancs, Route de Gargas, 84490 St Saturnin-lès-Apt [04 90 74 09 20 or 06 12 72 47 87 (mob); contact@ leschenesblancs.com; www.les-chenes-blancs.com]** Fr W on D900 twd Apt, at NW o'skts of Apt turn N on D101, cont approx 2km turn R on D83 into Gargas; thro Gargas & in 4km turn L at camp sp; site on R in 300m. Narr rd. Lge, hdg pitch, shd; wc; mv service pnt; shwrs inc; el pnts (6A) inc; lndtte; shop; tradsmn; rest, snacks; bar; BBQ; playgrnd; htd pool; paddling pool; lake fishing 5km; games area; entmnt; TV rm; dogs €4; poss cr; Eng spkn; adv bkg rec; quiet; red low ssn; ccard acc. "Well-run, popular site in gd location; pitches amongst oaks poss diff lge outfits; steel pegs req due stony ground; friendly staff; vg, modern san facs; nice pool; excel touring base." ♦ 2 Apr-29 Oct. € 30.00 (CChq acc) 2011*

APT *10E3* (500m NE Urban) *43.87753, 5.40302* **Camp Municipal Les Cèdres, 63 Impasse de la Fantaisie, 84400 Apt [tel/fax 04 90 74 14 61 / 04 90 74 14 61 (mob); lucie. bouillet@yahoo.fr; www.camping-les-cedres.fr]** In town turn N off D900 onto D22 twd Rustrel, site sp. Site on R in 200m immed after going under old rlwy bdge. Med, mkd pitch, pt shd; htd wc (some cont); chem disp; mv service pnt; shwrs inc; el pnts (6-10A) €3.50; gas; lndtte; shop & snacks (high ssn); cooking facs; playgrnd; entmnt; wifi; dogs €1; poss cr; adv bkg; ccard acc; CKE/CCI. "Excel site in lovely location; sm pitches; pitching poss haphazard low ssn; friendly staff; clean san facs; some pitches muddy when wet; cycle tracks; conv Luberon vills & ochre mines; phone ahead to check open low ssn; v lge mkt Sat; gd NH; site in 2 parts" ♦ 15 Feb-15 Nov. € 17.85 2013*

APT *10E3* (2km SE Rural) *43.86636, 5.41275* **Camping Le Luberon, Route de Saignon, 84400 Apt [04 90 04 85 40; fax 04 90 74 12 19; leluberon@wanadoo.fr; www. camping-le-luberon.com]** Exit Apt by D48 sp Saignon & site on R in 2km. Sharp turn into site. Med, mkd pitch, pt sl, pt shd; wc; chem disp; baby facs; shwrs inc; el pnts (6A) €4.50; gas; lndtte; shops 2km; tradsmn; rest, snacks; bar; BBQ; playgrnd; pool; fishing, sailing 3km; TV; 20% statics; dogs €3.50; phone; poss cr; Eng spkn; adv bkg; quiet; ccard acc; red low ssn; CKE/ CCI. "Pitches well laid-out in woodland; well-run, clean site; helpful owners; poss not suitable teenagers; gd." ♦ ltd 3 Apr-25 Sep. € 20.45 2009*

ARAMITS *8F1* (1km SW Rural) *43.12135, -0.73215* **Camping Barétous-Pyrénées, Quartier Ripaude, 64570 Aramits [05 59 34 12 21; atso64@hotmail.com; www.camping-pyrenees.com]** SW fr Oloron-Ste Marie take D919 sp Aramits, Arette. Fr Aramits cont on D919 sp Lanne; site on R; well sp. Sm, mkd pitch, pt shd; wc; chem disp; mv service pnt; serviced pitches; shwrs inc; el pnts (10A) €4.90; lndtte (inc dryer); supmkt 500m; tradsmn; rest; snacks; bar high ssn; playgrnd; htd pool; paddling pool; cycle hire; games rm; TV; 50% statics; dogs €2.80; poss cr; Eng spkn; adv bkg; CKE/CCI. "Friendly, helpful owner; well-kept, clean site but muddy when wet; ltd facs low ssn; twin-axles extra; gd base for Pyrenees; poss unrel opening dates - phone ahead low ssn." ♦ ltd 12 Feb-29 Oct. € 21.30 (CChq acc) 2011*

ARBOIS *6H2* (1.5km E Urban) *46.90331, 5.78691* **Camp Municipal Les Vignes, 5 Rue de la Piscine, 39600 Arbois [03 84 66 14 12 or 03 84 25 26 19; fax 03 84 25 14 12; reservation@rsl39.com or campinglesvignes@hotmail.fr; www.relaisoleiljura.com]** Fr N or S, ent town & at rndabt in cent foll camp sp on D107 dir Mesnay. Site adj stadium & pool. NB Steep slopes to terr & narr ent unsuitable lge o'fits. Med, some hdg pitch/mkd pitch, some hdstg, pt sl, terr, pt shd; wc; chem disp; mv service pnt; shwrs inc; el pnts (10A) inc; gas; lndtte; shop & 1km; rest, snacks; bar; playgrnd; htd pool adj; tennis; fishing 1km; entmnt; wifi; TV; dogs €2.50; twin-axles €45; poss cr; Eng spkn; adv bkg; quiet; ccard acc; red low ssn; CKE/CCI. "Beautiful setting; clean san facs but poss stretched high ssn; site clsd 2200-0800 low ssn; ltd facs low ssn; pitches on lower tier mostly sloping; pleasant sm town, home of Louis Pasteur; Roman salt works, grottoes nr; lge fair 1st w/end in Sep; excel." ♦ 16 Apr-2 Oct. € 20.00 2013*

ARC EN BARROIS *6F1* (500m W Urban) *47.95052, 5.00523* **Camp Municipal Le Vieux Moulin, 52210 Arc-en-Barrois [03 25 02 51 33 (Mairie); fax 03 25 03 82 89; mairie.arc. en.barrois@wanadoo.fr]** Exit A5 junc 24 onto D10 S to Arc-en-Barrois; turn R onto D3 thro vill; site on L on o'skirts. Or fr D65 turn L onto D6 about 4km S of Châteauvillain; site on R on D3 at ent to vill, adj rv. Med, pt shd; htd wc; chem disp; mv service pnt; shwrs inc; el pnts (6A) inc; gas in vill; shops 500m; BBQ; sm playgrnd; tennis adj; TV; dogs €2.18; wifi; phone in vill; quiet; ccard not acc; CKE/CCI. "Attractive, peaceful, well-kept site by sm rv; adj vill sports field; basic, clean san facs but need update - excel hot shwrs; warden calls early eve; gd wildlife; beautiful vill; conv NH fr A5 or longer; Weekends poss noisy due to on-site funfair" 1 May - 30 Sep. € 17.00 2013*

ARCACHON *7D1* (10km E Coastal) *44.64400, -1.11167* **Camping de Verdalle, 2 Allée de l'Infante, La Hume, 33470 Gujan-Mestras [tel/fax 05 56 66 12 62; camping.verdalle@ wanadoo.fr; www.camping-bassin-arcachon.fr]** Fr A63 take A660 twd Arcachon. Turn R at rndabt junc with D652 sp La Hume. In vill at junc with D650 turn L, then R at rndabt; then 3rd turning on R after rlwy line. Med, hdg pitch, pt shd; wc; chem disp; mv service pnt; shwrs inc; el pnts (10A) inc; lndtte; shops nrby; snacks; BBQ (sep area); playgrnd nrby; sand beach adj; wifi; dogs €1.50; bus adj; phone; poss cr; Eng spkn; adv bkg; ccard acc; red low ssn; CKE/CCI. "Lovely, well-kept site in excel position; friendly, helpful owner; pitches uncomfortable in wet - dirty sand (2011); cycling/walking; conv local attractions; vg." ♦ 1 Apr-3 Oct. € 26.00 2013*

⊞ **ARCACHON** *7D1* (2km S Coastal) *44.65089, -1.17381* **Camping Club d'Arcachon, 5 Allée de la Galaxie, 33312 Arcachon [05 56 83 24 15; fax 05 57 52 28 51; info@ camping-arcachon.com; www.camping-arcachon.com]** Exit A63 ont A660 dir Arcachon. Foll sp 'Hôpital Jean Hameau' & site sp. Lge, hdg/mkd pitch, some hdstg, terr, pt shd; htd wc; chem disp; mv service pnt; baby facs; private san facs avail; shwrs inc; el pnts (10A) €4; gas; lndtte (inc dryer); shop; tradsmn; rest, snacks; bar; BBQ; playgrnd; pool; sand beach 1.5km; lake sw 10km; cycle hire; wifi; entmnt; TV rm; 40% statics; dogs €4; site clsd mid-Nov to mid-Dec; adv bkg; Eng spkn; quiet; ccard acc; red low ssn; CKE/CCI. "Vg site in pine trees; excel touring base; gd facs; access rds narr - poss diff manoeuvring into pitches; gd network cycle tracks." ♦ € 32.00 (CChq acc) 2010*

ARCHIAC 7B2 (400m W Urban) 45.52322, -0.30452
Camp Municipal, Rue des Voituriers, 17520 Archiac
[05 46 49 10 46 or 05 46 49 10 82 (Mairie); fax
05 46 49 84 09; archiacmairie@free.fr] Site sp fr D731
100m past sw pool. Sm, mkd pitch, terr, pt sl, pt shd; wc; mv
service pnt; shwrs inc; el pnts (5A) €3.50; lndtte; tradsmn;
shops 400m; 2 pools adj; tennis; games rm; dogs €0.85;
quiet. "Spacious site; gates locked when warden absent but
access details displayed; vg pool adj; rec." 15 Jun-15 Sep.
€ 6.80   2010*

ARCIS SUR AUBE 4E4 (300m N Urban) 48.53907, 4.14270
Camping de l'Ile Cherlieu, Rue de Châlons, 10700 Arcis-
sur-Aube [03 25 37 98 79; fax 03 25 37 91 29; camping-
arcis@hermans.cx] Fr A26 junc 21 foll sp to Arcis. Fr town
cent take D677 dir Châlons-en-Champagne. Turn R after rv
bdge, site sp. Med, mkd pitch, shd, wc (some cont); chem disp;
shwrs inc; el pnts (10A) €3.50 (poss rev pol); lndtte (inc dryer);
shop, rest, bar 500m; BBQ; playgrnd; rv adj; fishing; wifi; dogs
€1.60; Eng spkn; poss cr w/end & noisy; no ccard acc; CKE/CCI.
"Pleasant, well-kept site on island surrounded by rv; friendly,
helpful Dutch owners; gd, clean san facs; popular NH, rec arr
early." ♦ ltd 15 Apr-1 Oct. € 27.50   2013*

⊞ **ARCIS SUR AUBE** 4E4 (8km S Rural) 48.46696, 4.12633
FFCC Camping La Barbuise, 10700 St Remy-sous-Barbuise
[03 25 37 50 95 or 03 25 37 41 11; www.camping-ffcc.
com] Fr Arcis-sur-Aube, take D677 twd Voué; site on L bef
vill of Voué, sp. Fr S exit A26 junc 21 onto D441 W; then
onto D677 S twd Voué & as bef. Sm, pt sl, pt shd; wc; chem
disp; mv service pnt; shwrs inc; el pnts (4A) inc (poss rev pol);
tradsmn; shops 8km; sm bar (high ssn); BBQ; pool 8km; dogs
(if on lead); phone; adv bkg; rd noise; red facs low ssn; ccard
not acc; CKE/CCI. "Lovely, peaceful, spacious CL-type site; early
arr rec; site yourself, owner calls eves (cash only); easy access
& pitching for lge o'fits; charming owners; san facs basic but
clean; elec poss unrel (2010); elec heaters not allowed; conv
NH off A26 or sh stay." ♦ ltd € 13.50   2013*

ARDRES 3A3 (500m N Urban) 50.85726, 1.97551 **Camping**
Ardresien, 64 Rue Basse, 62610 Ardres [03 21 82 82 32]
Fr St Omer on D943 to Ardres, strt on at lights in town onto
D231; site 500m on R - easy to o'shoot; v narr ent, not suitable
twin-axles. Sm, hdg pitch, pt shd; wc; shwrs; el pnts (16A) inc;
95% statics; dogs free; poss cr; CKE/CCI. "Basic site; friendly
staff; walk to lakes at rear of site; ltd touring pitches; conv
Calais & local vet; NH only." 1 May-30 Sep. € 11.00   2011*

ARDRES 3A3 (9km NE Rural) 50.88147, 2.08618 **Camp**
Municipal Les Pyramides, Rue Nord Boutillier, 62370
Audruicq [03 21 35 59 17 or 03 21 46 06 60 (Mairie)]
Fr Calais take A16 dir Dunkerque, after 8km exit S at junc 21
onto D219 to Audruicq; foll camp sp. Fr Ardres NE on D224 to
Audruicq. Site on NE side of Audruicq nr canal. Med, hdg pitch,
unshd; wc; chem disp; shwrs inc; el pnts (6A); gas; lndtte;
tradsmn; playgrnd; 80% statics; dogs; no ccard acc; quiet;
CKE/CCI. "Conv Calais; few sm pitches for tourers; rec phone
ahead." ♦ ltd 1 Apr-30 Sep.   2013*

ARDRES 3A3 (8km SE Rural) 50.80867, 2.05569 **Hôtel Bal**
Caravaning, 500 Rue du Vieux Château, 62890 Tournehem-
sur-la-Hem [03 21 35 65 90; fax 03 21 35 18 57; hotelbal@
yahoo.fr; www.hotel-bal.com] Fr S on A26 leave at exit 2;
turn R onto D217 then R onto D943 dir St Omer. Turn R in
Nordausques onto D218 (approx 1km), pass under A26, site
is 1km on L - ent thro Bal Parc Hotel gates. Fr N or S on D943,
turn R or L in Nordausques, then as above. Med, hdg/mkd
pitch, hdstg, pt sl, pt shd; htd wc (in hotel in winter); chem
disp; shwrs inc; el pnts (10A) inc (poss rev pol); gas; tradsmn;
rest, snacks & bar in adj hotel; playgrnd; sports ground &
leisure cent adj; tennis; entmnt; 80% statics; poss cr; Eng spkn;
adv bkg; quiet; ccard acc; red low ssn/CKE/CCI. "New owners
(2010); tidy area for tourers, but few touring pitches; gd rest &
bar; san facs refurbed (2010); 25km Cité Europe mall; gd NH"
♦ 1 Apr-31 Oct. € 20.30   2013*

ARDRES 3A3 (9km SE Rural) 50.82193, 2.07577 **Camping Le**
Relax, 318 Route de Gravelines, 62890 Nordausques [tel/
fax 03 21 35 63 77; camping.le.relax@cegetel.net] Fr N on
D943 in vill 25km S of Calais at beginning of vill, turn L at sp.
Site 200m on R. Or fr S on A26, leave at junc 2 & take D943 S
for 1km into Nordausques, then as above. NB Ent diff, beware
low o'hanging roof on recep. Med, hdg pitch, pt shd; wc;
chem disp; shwrs €1.50; el pnts (6A) €2.20 (poss rev pol); lndry
rm; shop 200m; tradsmn; snacks; playgrnd; 90% statics; poss
cr; adv bkg ess; quiet, but rd noise; CKE/CCI. "Obliging owner;
sm pitches & sharp access, not suitable lge o'fits; basic san facs,
poss tired high ssn; conv A26, Calais & war sites; NH only."
1 Apr-30 Sep. € 11.20   2011*

ARDRES 3A3 (2km S Rural) 50.83865, 1.97612
Camping St Louis, 223 Rue Leulène, 62610 Autingues
[03 21 35 46 83; fax 03 21 00 19 78; campingstlouis@sfr.
fr; www.campingstlouis.com] Fr Calais S on D943 to Ardres;
fr Ardres take D224 S twd Licques, after 2km turn L on D227;
site well sp in 100m. Or fr junc 2 off A26 onto D943 dir Ardres.
Turn L just after Total g'ge on R on app to Ardres. Well sp. If app
fr S via Boulogne avoid Nabringhen & Licques as narr, steep hill
with bends. NB Mkt Thurs am - avoid R turn when leaving site.
Med, hdg/mkd pitch, pt shd; wc; chem disp; mv service pnt;
baby facs; shwrs inc; el pnts (6A) inc (long lead poss req; poss
rev pol); gas; lndtte; sm shop & 1km; supmkt 3km; tradsmn;
rest, snacks; bar; BBQ; playgrnd; lake 1km; games rm; wifi;
entmnt; 70% statics; dogs free; phone; poss cr; Eng spkn; adv
bkg ess high ssn; quiet, but some rwly noise & poss music w/end
fr bar; ccard acc; CKE/CCI. "Peaceful, well-kept, well-run, busy
site; conv Dunkerque, Calais ferries; some gd sized pitches; gd
welcome & friendly; clean san facs poss stretched high ssn; ltd
touring pitches - phone ahead to check avail high ssn; early dep/
late arr area; automatic exit barrier; barrier opens 0600 high ssn;
gd rest; vg vet in Ardres; gd, conv NH; shwrs very hot, no temp
control; lovely clean site" ♦ 20 Mar-20 Oct. € 26.00   2013*

ARECHES see Beaufort 9B3

ARES see Andernos les Bains 7D1

ARFEUILLES see Châtel Montagne 9A1

FRANCE

ARGELES GAZOST 8G2 (500m N Rural) 43.01218, -0.09709
Camping Sunêlia Les Trois Vallées, Ave des Pyrénées, 65400 Argelès-Gazost [05 62 90 35 47; fax 05 62 90 35 48; 3-vallees@wanadoo.fr; www.l3v.fr] S fr Lourdes on D821, turn R at rndabt sp Argelès-Gazost on D821A. Site off next rndabt on R. Lge, mkd pitch, pt shd; htd wc; chem disp; sauna; shwrs inc; el pnts (6A) inc (poss rev pol); lndtte; supmkt opp; tradsmn; bar; playgrnd; htd pool; waterslide; games rm; cycle hire; games area; golf 11km; wifi; entmnt; TV rm; 30% statics; dogs €2; poss cr; adv bkg ess high ssn; some rd noise nr site ent; ccard acc; red low ssn. "Excel touring base; views of Pyrenees; conv Lourdes; interesting area; red facs low ssn." ◆ 11 Mar-2 Nov. € 34.00   2010*

ARGELES GAZOST 8G2 (1km N Rural) 43.01725, -0.09670
Camping La Bergerie, 54 Ave des Pyrénées, 65400 Ayzac-Ost [tel/fax 05 62 97 59 99; info@camping-labergerie.com; www.camping-labergerie.com] Sp off D821. Sm, pt shd; wc; shwrs inc; el pnts (2-6A) €1.80-5.40; lndtte; rest, bar 100m; BBQ; playgrnd; htd pool; games area; entmnt; some statics; dogs €1; Eng spkn; adv bkg; quiet; ccard acc; red low ssn. "Clean, friendly site." ◆ 1 May-30 Sep. € 16.50   2009*

ARGELES GAZOST 8G2 (2km N Rural) 43.01885, -0.09167
Camping Aire Naturelle Bellevue (Hourcastagnou), 24 Chemin de la Plaine, 65400 Ayzac-Ost [tel/fax 05 62 97 58 81; camping.bellevue65@wanadoo.fr] Fr Lourdes S on D821, foll sp for Ayzac-Ost then sp for 'Camping La Bergerie' but cont past ent for 200m. Site on R behind farm buildings. Sm, pt shd; wc; chem disp; mv service pnt; shwrs inc; el pnts (6A) inc; lndtte; shop, rest, snacks, bar 1km; tradsmn; playgrnd; fishing 300m; 2% statics; dogs €1; phone; quiet; CKE/CCI. "Surrounded by fields; gd san facs block; site poss muddy; gd." ◆ 1 Jun-30 Sep. € 12.36   2011*

ARGELES GAZOST 8G2 (4km N Rural) 43.03560, -0.07086 **Camping Soleil du Pibeste, 65400 Agos-Vidalos [05 62 97 53 23; fax 05 61 06 67 73; info@campingpibeste.com; www.campingpibeste.com]** On D821, S of Lourdes. Exit at rndabt sp Agos-Vidalos, site on R on ent vill. Med, terr, pt shd; htd wc; chem disp; mv service pnt; shwrs inc; el pnts (6-10A) €4-6; gas; lndtte; shops adj; lndtte; tradsmn; rest, snacks; bar; playgrnd; sm pool; rv 500m; entmnt; TV; 10% statics; dogs €8; bus; Eng spkn; adv bkg rec high ssn; some rd noise; CKE/CCI. "Open outlook with views; beautiful area; warm welcome; guided mountain walks; excel, family-run site." ◆ ltd 1 Apr-15 Oct. € 26.00   2009*

See advertisement on pages 32 & 33

ARGELES GAZOST 8G2 (5km N Rural) 42.98120, -0.06535
Camping Le Viscos, 16 Route de Préchac, 65400 Beaucens [05 62 97 05 45; domaineviscos@orange.fr] Fr Lourdes S twd Argelès-Gasost on D821. Cont twd Luz & Gavarnie to L of Argelès town, & turn L within 500m, sp Beaucens. Turn R to D13, site 2.5km on L. Med, pt sl, shd; wc; chem disp; shwrs inc; el pnts (2-10A) €2-4.50 (rev pol); gas; lndtte; shops 5km; tradsmn high ssn; snacks; BBQ; playgrnd; pool 4km; lake fishing 500m; dogs €1; quiet; adv bkg ess Jul-Aug; red long stay; ccard not acc; CKE/CCI. "Delightful site; landscaped grnds; clean san facs; gd rests in area." 15 May-30 Sep. € 10.90   2008*

ARGELES GAZOST 8G2 (1km S Rural) 42.98670, -0.08854
Camping Les Frênes, 46 Route des Vallées, 65400 Lau-Balagnas [05 62 97 25 12; fax 05 62 97 01 41; campinglesfrenes.fr] Site on R of D821 twd S. Med, pt terr, pt shd; htd wc; chem disp; baby facs; shwrs inc; el pnts (10A); gas; lndtte; shop 100m; BBQ; playgrnd; pool; rv & fishing 1km; entmnt; TV; some statics; adv bkg rec; quiet; red long stay. ◆ 15 Dec-15 Oct. € 18.25   2009*

⊞ **ARGELES GAZOST** 8G2 (2km S Rural) 42.98826, -0.08923
Kawan Village Le Lavedan, 44 Route des Vallées, 65400 Lau-Balagnas [05 62 97 18 84; fax 05 62 97 55 56; contact@lavedan.com; www.lavedan.com] Fr Lourdes S on D821 dir Argelès-Gazost/Cauterets; 2km after Argelès on D921 site on R after vill of Lau-Balagnas. Med, mkd pitch, shd; htd wc; chem disp; baby facs; shwrs inc; el pnts (3A) €3 (poss rev pol; extra for 10A); gas; lndtte (inc dryer); shops 2km; rest, snacks; bar; BBQ; playgrnd; htd, covrd pool; paddling pool; wifi; entmnt; games/TV rm; many statics; dogs €2.50; phone; poss cr; Eng spkn; adv bkg; rd noise if pitched adj to rd & poss noise fr entmnt in café; ccard acc; red low ssn; CKE/CCI. "In beautiful valley; friendly, relaxed staff; clean modern san facs; excel cycle rte to Lourdes; vg." ◆ ltd € 24.00 (CChq acc)   2010*

ARGELES GAZOST 8G2 (2.5km S Rural) 42.9871, 0.1061
Camping du Lac, 29 Chemin d'Azun, 65400 Arcizans-Avant [tel/fax 05 62 97 01 88; campinglac@campinglac65.fr; www.campinglac65.fr] Fr Lourdes S thro Argelès-Gazost on D821 & D921. At 3rd rndabt take exit for St Savin/Arcizans-Avant. Cont thro St Savin vill & foll camp sp; site on L just thro Arcizans-Avant vill. NB: Dir rte to Arcizans-Avant prohibited to c'vans. Med, hdg/mkd pitch, pt sl, pt shd; wc; chem disp; baby facs; shwrs inc; el pnts (5-10A) €4.30-5; gas; lndtte; shop; tradsmn; rest 500m; snacks; playgrnd; htd pool; games rm; cycle hire; TV rm; dogs €2.50; Eng spkn; adv bkg; quiet; red low ssn; CKE/CCI. "Excel, peaceful, scenic site; gd size pitches; clean san facs; gd for touring." ◆ 15 May-30 Sep. € 24.50   2009*

ARGELES GAZOST 8G2 (5km S Rural) 42.98493, -0.10506
Camping Les Châtaigniers, 65400 Arcizans-Avant [05 62 97 94 77 or 06 30 58 11 00 (mob); contact@camping-les-chataigniers.com; www.camping-les-chataigniers.com] At rndabt on S side of Argelès-Gazost take D921 S dir Pierrefitte-Nestalas & foll sps to Arcizans-Avant & Les Châtaigniers. Med, hdg/mkd pitch, pt sl, pt shd; wc; chem disp; baby facs; el pnts (2-6A) €2-4; lndtte; tradsmn; playgrnd; pool; TV; some statics; dogs €1.20; no twin-axles; phone; poss cr; adv bkg; red low ssn; exce. "Immac site & facs; friendly, helpful owners; excel walking & cycling in mountains; excel." ◆ 15 May-15 Sep. € 13.50   2008*

ARGELES GAZOST 8G2 (2km SW Rural) 42.99502, -0.12076
Camping L'Idéal, Route de Val d'Azun, 65400 Arras-en-Lavedan [05 62 97 03 13 or 05 62 97 02 12; info@camping-ideal-pyrenees.com; www.camping-ideal-pyrenees.com] Leave Argelès Gazost SW on D918. Site on N side of rd on E o'skts of Arras-en-Lavedan. Ent on bend. Med, terr, pt shd; wc; chem disp; shwrs inc; el pnts (3-10A) €2.85-€9.50; sm shop; playgrnd; pool high ssn; tennis 1km; dogs free; adv bkg; quiet; CKE/CCI. "Vg, clean, scenic site; gd sized pitches; friendly owner; gd clean facs, v ltd low ssn; steel awning pegs rec; cooler than in valley." ◆ 1 Jun-15 Sep. € 12.00   2008*

ARGELES GAZOST *8G2* (10km SW Rural) *42.94139, -0.17714*
**Camping Pyrénées Natura, Route du Lac, 65400 Estaing
[05 62 97 45 44; fax 05 62 97 45 81; info@camping-
pyrenees-natura.com; www.camping-pyrenees-natura.com]**
Fr Lourdes take D821 to Argelès Gazost; fr Argelès foll sp Col
d'Aubisque & Val d'Azun onto D918; after approx 7.5km turn
L onto D13 to Bun; after Bun cross rv & turn R onto D103 twd
Estaing; site in 3km - rd narr. NB Rd fr Col d'Aubisque steep,
narr & not suitable c'vans or lge m'vans. Med, hdg/mkd pitch,
terr, pt shd; htd wc; chem disp; mv service pnt; baby facs;
sauna; shwrs inc; el pnts (3-10A) €2-5 (poss rev pol); gas; lndtte
(inc dryer); basics shop; tradsmn; snacks; bar; BBQ with legs
(gas/elec/charcoal); no playgrnd (2010); pool 4km; solarium;
games area; internet; games/TV rm; 20% statics; dogs €3; no
c'vans/m'vans over 7.50m high ssn; Eng spkn; adv bkg; quiet;
ccard acc; red low ssn; CKE/CCI. "Superb, peaceful, well-kept,
scenic site; friendly, helpful owners; clean unisex san facs; vg
takeaway; gd for young families; no plastic ground-sheets
allowed; adj National Park; birdwatching area; excel; home
cooked food at bar; vg site, one of the best ever visited" ♦
1 Apr-30 Oct. € 38.40 SBS - D22   2013*

ARGELES SUR MER *10G1* (1km N Coastal) *42.55726,
3.02893* **Camping de Pujol, Ave de la Retirada, Route du
Tamariguer, 66700 Argelès-sur-Mer [04 68 81 00 25; fax
04 68 81 21 21; www.campingdepujol.com]** Fr Perpignan
on D914 exit junc 10 dir Argelès. L off slip rd foll sp Pujol,
site on R - wide entrance. Lge, mkd pitch, pt shd; wc (some
cont); chem disp; mv service pnt; baby facs; shwrs inc; el pnts
(3-6A) €4; gas 2km; lndtte (inc dryer); shop; rest, snacks; bar;
playgrnd; pool; paddling pool; sand beach 1km; car wash;
entmnt; 30% statics; dogs free; phone; poss cr; Eng spkn; adv
bkg rec high ssn; quiet but poss noisy disco; CKE/CCI. "Vg san
facs but poss cold water shwrs only low ssn; pool poss cr high
ssn; excel cycling." ♦ ltd 1 Jun-30 Sep. € 25.00   2011*

"I like to fill in the reports as I travel from site to site"
You'll find report forms at the back of
this guide, or you can fill them in online
at www.caravaclub.co.uk/europereport.

ARGELES SUR MER *10G1* (1km N Rural) *42.57158, 3.02607*
**Camping Les Galets, Route de Taxo-à la Mer, Plage Nord,
66701 Argelès-sur-Mer [04 68 81 08 12; fax 04 68 81 68 76;
lesgalets@campinglesgalets.fr; www.campmed.com]**
Fr Perpignan take D914 dir Elne, Argelès, 4km after Elne pass
Municipal Camping on L, sp listing many camp sites. Lge, pt
shd; wc; mv service pnt; baby facs; shwrs inc; el pnts (10A)
inc; gas; lndtte; shop; rest, snacks; bar; playgrnd; htd pool;
paddling pool; sand beach 1.5km; fishing, sailing & windsurfing
1.5km; rv sw 3km; equestrian cent nr; games area; wifi;
entmnt; TV rm; 90% statics; dogs €4; poss cr; adv bkg rec all
year; quiet; red low ssn. "Ltd touring pitches; gd for families."
♦ 1 Apr-30 Sep. € 37.50   2010*

ARGELES SUR MER *10G1* (1km N Coastal) *42.56320, 3.03498*
**Camping Les Marsouins, Ave de la Retirada, 66702
Argelès-sur-Mer [04 68 81 14 81; fax 04 68 95 93 58;
marsouin@campmed.com; www.campmed.com]**
Fr Perpignan take exit 10 fr D914 & foll sp for Argelès
until Shell petrol stn on R. Take next L just bef rv into Allée
Ferdinand Buisson to T-junc, turn L at next rndabt dir Plage-
Nord. Take 2nd R at next rndabt, site on L opp Spanish war
memorial. V lge, hdg/mkd pitch, shd; wc; chem disp; mv service
pnt; shwrs inc; el pnts (5A) inc; gas; lndtte (inc dryer); shops;
lge supmkt 3km; rest, snacks; bar; BBQ (gas/elec); playgrnd; htd
pool; sand beach 800m; sailing & windsurfing 1km; cycle hire;
games area; games rm; entmnt; internet; 20% statics; dogs
€3; poss cr; Eng spkn; adv bkg; ccard acc; red low ssn. "Lovely,
well-kept, well-run site; clean san facs; busy rd to beach, but
worth it; many sm coves; gd area for cycling; tourist office on
site; excel. ♦ 16 Apr-24 Sep. € 43.00   2012*

ARGELES SUR MER *10G1* (2km N Rural) *42.5724, 3.02171*
**Camping Le Dauphin, Route de Taxo à la Mer, 66701
Argelès-sur-Mer [04 68 81 17 54; fax 04 68 95 82 60; info@
campingledauphin.com; www.campingledauphin.com]**
Fr Perpignan take D914 sp Elne & Argelès-sur-Mer. 4km after
Elne, sp on L to Taxo d'Avall, turn L, site 2km on R. Lge, hdg/
mkd pitch, pt shd; wc; chem disp; private bthrms avail some
pitches - extra charge; baby facs; shwrs inc; el pnts (10A) inc;
gas; lndtte; shop; rest, snacks; bar; BBQ (gas/elec); playgrnd;
2 pools; paddling pool; waterslides; sand beach 3km; fishing;
sailing; windsurfing; tennis; games area; games rm; internet;
entmnt; TV rm; 80% statics; dogs €4; Eng spkn; adv bkg; ccard
acc; red low ssn. "Gd for families; superb pool area; helpful
staff; excel facs; free transport to beach high ssn; vg site." ♦
14 May-17 Sep. € 43.00   2011*

ARGELES SUR MER *10G1* (2km N Coastal) *42.55775, 3.03140*
**Camping Paris Roussillon, Ave de la Retirada 1939,
Quartier Pujol, 66700 Argelès-sur-Mer [04 68 81 19 71;
fax 04 68 81 68 77; contact@parisroussillon.com; www.
parisroussillon.com or www.campings-franceloc.fr]**
Fr Perpignan, take D914, junc 10 twds Pujol. Site 2km on
R. Lge, mkd pitch, shd; wc; chem disp; shwrs inc; baby facs;
el pnts (6A) inc; lndtte; shop 1km; rest, snacks; bar; BBQ;
playgrnd; pool; waterslide; paddling pool; beach 1.5km;
tennis; games area; wifi; some statics; dogs €2.50; Eng spkn;
quiet; red low ssn. "Satisfactory site." ♦ 3 Apr-26 Sep.
€ 29.90   2010*

ARGELES SUR MER *10G1* (2km NE Coastal) *42.54819,
3.03617* **Camping du Stade, 8 Ave du 8 Mai 1945, 66702
Argelès-sur-Mer [04 68 81 04 40; info@campingdustade.
com; www.campingdustade.com]** S on D914 thro traff lts at
Argelès; turn L after 400m at clearly mkd turn sp 'A la Plage'.
Site 800m on L. Lge, shd; wc; baby facs; shwrs inc; el pnts (6A)
inc; lndtte; supmkt 500m; rest, snacks; bar; playgrnd; sand
beach 800m; sports complex adj; entmnt; TV rm; some statics;
dogs €2; poss cr; adv bkg rec high ssn; quiet; red low ssn. "Lge
pitches; gd walking area; mountain views; friendly owners."
1 Apr-30 Sep. € 24.50   2010*

FRANCE

ARGELES SUR MER *10G1* (2km NE Coastal) *42.57245, 3.04115* **Camping La Marende, Chemin de la Salanque, 66702 Argelès-sur-Mer [tel/fax 04 68 81 03 88; info@ marende.com; www.marende.com]** Fr Perpignan S on D914 exit junc 10 Argelès-sur-Mer; foll sp Plage Nord; after 2km at rndabt turn L sp St Cyprian; at next rndabt turn R sp Plages Nord & Sud; site on L in 800m. L onto unmade rd. V lge, hdg/mkd pitch, shd; wc; chem disp; some serviced pitches; mv service pnt; baby facs; shwrs inc; el pnts (6-10A) inc; gas; lndtte; shop; rest & snacks (high ssn); bar; BBQ (el/gas); playgrnd; pool & paddling pool; jacuzzi; games area; sand beach adj; aquarobics, scuba-diving lessons Jul & Aug; internet; TV; 12% statics; dogs €2.50; phone; poss cr; Eng spkn; quiet; adv bkg; ccard acc; CKE/CCI. "Beautiful site; lge pitches; friendly, helpful family owners; 1st class facs; excel pool; many static tents high ssn; gd area for cycling & walking; v quiet Sept." ♦ 26 Apr-27 Sep. € 26.00   2012*

ARGELES SUR MER *10G1* (2km NE Rural) *42.56940, 3.02713* **Camping La Sirène, Route de Taxo, 66701 Argelès-sur-Mer [04 68 81 04 61; fax 04 68 81 69 74; contact@ camping-lasirene.fr; www.camping-lasirene.fr]** Take D914 fr Perpignan twd Argelès. Cross Rv Tech & take 1st L twd Taxo d'Avall, site 1 of many about 2.5km on R. V lge, mkd pitch, shd; wc; baby facs; shwrs inc; el pnts (12A) €3; gas; lndtte; shop; rest, snacks; bar; BBQ; cooking facs; playgrnd; pool; waterslide; sand beach 1.5km; fishing, sailing & windsurfing 1km; tennis; horseriding; archery; cycle hire; games area; dogs €4; adv bkg; quiet; red low ssn. "Well-appointed site; gd pool complex." ♦ 18 Apr-28 Sep. € 43.00   2008*

ARGELES SUR MER *10G1* (2km NE Coastal) *42.56728, 3.04425* **Camping Le Roussillonnais, Blvd de la Mer, 66700 Argelès-sur-Mer [04 68 81 10 42; fax 04 68 95 96 11; contact@ le-roussillonnais.com; www.le-roussillonnais.com]** S fr Perpignan on D914 thro Elne to Argelès-sur-Mer, turn L in Argelès-sur-Mer foll coast rd & site on R in 1.5km. V lge, hdg/ mkd pitch, pt shd; wc (some cont); chem disp; mv service pnt; baby facs; shwrs inc; el pnts (6A) €3.80; gas; lndtte; shop; rest, snacks; bar; playgrnd; sand beach 500m; boating; watersports; tennis; games area; entmnt; some statics; dogs €1.50; shuttle bus to beach; poss cr; Eng spkn; adv bkg; quiet; ccard acc; CKE/CCI. "Site open all yr for m'vans; ltd facs low ssn." 20 Apr-27 Sep. € 22.50   2009*

ARGELES SUR MER *10G1* (3km NE Coastal) *42.55682, 3.04082* **Camping Beauséjour, Ave de Tech, Argelès-Plage, 66700 Argelès-sur-Mer [04 68 81 10 63; fax 04 68 95 75 08; contact@camping-lebeausejour.com; www.camping-lebeausejour.com]** Fr Perpignan, foll D914 to Argelès-sur-Mer. Turn L after Champion supmkt & Shell g'ge; foll sp to Plage Nord. At coast rd turn R to Argelès-Plage cent. Site on R shortly after supmkt. Lge, mkd pitch, shd; wc; chem disp; baby facs; shwrs inc; el pnts (6A) inc; lndtte; shop adj; rest, snacks; playgrnd; 2 pools (1 htd, covrd); paddling pool; waterslide; jacuzzi; sand beach 300m; wifi; entmnt; 50% statics; dogs €3 (not acc Jul-Aug); phone; poss cr; Eng spkn; adv bkg rec; CKE/ CCI. ♦ ltd 1 May-30 Sep. € 38.00 (3 persons)   2010*

ARGELES SUR MER *10G1* (3.5km NE Coastal) *42.57543, 3.0431* **Camping Le Soleil, Route du Littoral, Plage-Nord, 66700 Argelès-sur-Mer [04 68 81 14 48 or 04 68 95 94 62 (LS); fax 04 68 81 44 34; camping.lesoleil@wanadoo.fr; www. campmed.com]** Exit D914 junc 10 & foll sp Argelès Plage-Nord. Turn L onto D81 to site. Site sp among others. V lge, mkd pitch, pt shd; wc (some cont); chem disp; mv service pnt; baby facs; shwrs inc; el pnts (6A) €3.70; gas; lndtte; shop; tradsmn; rest, snacks; bar; no BBQ; playgrnd; pool; paddling pool; sand beach adj; rv fishing adj; tennis; cycle hire; horseriding; games area; wifi; entmnt; TV; 50% statics; no dogs; phone; Eng spkn; adv bkg (ess Aug); noisy nr disco; ccard acc; red low ssn. "Lovely views; excel site for partially-sighted & handicapped; rec visit to Collioure; vg." ♦ 16 May-30 Sep. € 32.50   2009*

ARGELES SUR MER *10G1* (500m E Coastal) *42.55072, 3.03120* **Camping La Massane, 25 Ave Molière (Zone Pujol), 66700 Argelès-sur-Mer [04 68 81 06 85; fax 04 68 81 59 18; info@camping-massane.com; www. camping-massane.com]** Fr D914 exit junc 10, at traff island take 2nd exit, site sp further down rd. Site just bef municipal stadium on L. Lge, hdg/mkd pitch, pt shd; wc (some cont); chem disp; baby facs; shwrs inc; el pnts (6A) inc; gas; lndtte; shop & 500m; snacks; bar; BBQ (gas/elec only); playgrnd; htd pool; paddling pool; sand beach 1km; tennis adj; entmnt; dogs €2; poss cr; Eng spkn; adv bkg rec high ssn; red long stay/low ssn; quiet; ccard acc; CKE/CCI. "Vg site; friendly welcome; steel pegs req." ♦ 1 Apr-30 Sep. € 25.50   2008*

ARGELES SUR MER *10G1* (1km E Coastal) *42.54993, 3.04183* **Camping Europe, Ave du Général de Gaulle, 66700 Argelès-sur-Mer [04 68 81 08 10; fax 04 68 95 71 84; camping.europe@wanadoo.fr; www.camping-europe. net]** Fr Perpignan take D914 to Argelès-sur-Mer. Exit junc 12 to Argelès. At rndabt take last exit L to Argelès Ville. At next rndabt turn R, site on L after Dyneff g'ge 50m fr 'Tropical Golf'. Med, mkd pitch, shd; wc (some cont); chem disp; baby facs; shwrs inc; el pnts (10A) €4.10; gas; lndtte; shop; tradsmn; rest, snacks; bar; BBQ; playgrnd; pool 800m; sand beach 300m; wifi; 10% statics; dogs €2.15; phone; bus adj; poss cr; Eng spkn; adv bkg; quiet; red low ssn; CKE/CCI. "Friendly, secure, family-run site; shady pitches; helpful staff; clean, modern, unisex san facs; cycling nrby." 3 Apr-25 Sep. € 20.30   2010*

ARGELES SUR MER *10G1* (2km E Urban/Coastal) *42.55317, 3.04375* **Camping La Chapelle, Ave du Tech, 66702 Argelès-sur-Mer [04 68 28 14; fax 04 68 95 83 82; contact@camping-la-chapelle.com; www.camping-la-chapelle.com]** Fr A9 exit junc 42 onto D900/D914 to Argelès-sur-Mer. At junc 10 cont thro Argelès vill & foll sp Argelès-Plage. In 2.5km turn L at rndabt, bear L at Office de Tourisme, site immed L. Lge, hdg/mkd pitch, shd; wc (mainly cont); baby facs; shwrs inc; el pnts (6A) €6.50; lndtte; shop; rest, snacks, bar 100m; playgrnd; pool 2km; beach 200m; tennis 200m; wifi; entmnt; 30% statics; dogs €4; poss cr; Eng spkn; adv bkg; quiet; red low ssn; CKE/CCI. "Narr site rds poss diff lge o'fits; ltd facs low ssn; gd." ♦ 17 Apr-25 Sep. € 30.00   2010*

ARGELES SUR MER *10G1* (4km SE Coastal) *42.53413, 3.06826* **Camping Les Criques de Porteils, Corniche de Collioure, 66701 Argelès-sur-Mer [04 68 81 12 73; fax 04 68 95 85 76; info@lescriques.fr; www.lescriques.com or www.les-castels.com]** Fr N on A9/E15 take exit junc 42 onto D914 Argelès-sur-Mer. Fr S exit junc 43 onto D914. At exit 13 leave D914 sp Collioure & foll site sp. Site by Hôtel du Golfe 1.5km fr Collioure. Lge, hdg/mkd pitch, pt sl, terr, pt shd; htd wc (some cont); chem disp; mv service pnt; baby facs; shwrs inc; el pnts (5A) €6; gas; lndtte (inc dryer); shop; rest, snacks; bar; playgrnd; htd pool; sand/shgl beach adj; fishing; watersports; scuba-diving; tennis; games rm; games area; wifi; TV rm; 15% statics; dogs €4; phone; Eng spkn; adv bkg; quiet; red low ssn/CKE/CCI. "Excel, well-run site; variable size pitches - not all suitable for lge o'fits; gd views fr many terr pitches; steps to beach; clean, modern san facs; exposed, poss windy." ♦ 3 Apr-23 Oct. € 38.00   2010*

See advertisement on inside back cover

ARGELES SUR MER *10G1* (4.5km SE Coastal) *42.53147, 3.07167* **Camping Les Amandiers, Route des Campings, 66190 Collioure [04 68 81 14 69; fax 04 68 81 09 95; contact@camping-les-amandiers.com; www.camping-les-amandiers.com]** On D914 SE fr Perpignan, leave at junc 13 sp Collioure. After rndabt foll rd to Collioure. Climb coastal rd; site on L, steep descent, not rec lge o'fits. Med, mkd pitch, pt sl, terr, shd; htd wc (some cont); chem disp; mv service pnt; shwrs inc; el pnts (10A) inc; lndtte; gas; sm shop; tradsmn; sm rest, bar high ssn; sm playgrnd; shgl beach 200m; 10% statics; dogs €3; poss cr; Eng spkn; adv bkg; (rec high ssn); some rlwy noise; ccard not acc; CKE/CCI. "Site access v diff, espec for lge/med o'fits, manhandling prob req - rec investigation bef ent; sm pitches; facs stretched high ssn; many trees - dusty site; steep site rds; friendly, helpful owners; Collioure historic port; gd." ♦ 1 Apr-30 Sep. € 45.40 (CChq acc)   2013*

ARGELES SUR MER *10G1* (2.5km SW Rural) *42.53999, 2.99515* **Camping Le Romarin, Route de Sorède, Chemin des Vignes,66702 Argelès-sur-Mer [04 68 81 02 63; fax 04 68 81 57 43; contact@camping-romarin.com; www.camping-romarin.com]** S fr Perpignan on D914; at rndabt junc with D618 foll sp St André on minor rd; in 500m L & immed L & foll sp to site. Or fr A9 exit junc 43; foll D618 to rndabt junc with D914; then as above. Med, pt sl, shd; wc (some cont); shwrs inc; el pnts (6A) €2-3.50; gas; lndtte; shop; rest, snacks; bar; playgrnd; pool; waterslide; beach 4km; sports activities; entmnt; some statics; dogs €3 (not acc Jul/Aug); train 2km; Eng spkn; adv bkg; quiet; red low ssn. "Pleasant site; conv Spanish border." 15 May-30 Sep. € 32.50 2009*

See advertisement on pages 32 & 33

ARGELES SUR MER *10G1* (8km W Urban) *42.52667, 2.93515* **Camp Municipal Le Vivier, 31 Rue du Stade, 66740 Laroque-des-Albères [04 68 89 00 93 or 04 68 95 49 97; fax 04 68 95 42 58; tourisme@laroque-des-alberes.fr; www.laroque-des-alberes.fr]** D2 fr Argelès-sur-Mer to Laroque-des-Albères; foll sp in cent of vill. Site on rvside. Lge, mkd pitch, pt sl, pt shd; wc; chem disp; shwrs inc; el pnts (6A) €4; lndtte; shop 300m; BBQ; playgrnd; 5% statics; dogs €4; bus 300m; adv bkg; quiet; CKE/CCI. "Peaceful, simple site on edge Pyrenees, pleasant vill; vg." ♦ 15 Jun-15 Sep. € 24.00   2009*

> ## "We must tell The Club about that great site we found"
> Get your site reports in by mid-August and we'll do our best to get your updates into the next edition of Caravan Europe.

ARGELES SUR MER *10G1* (8km W Rural) *42.52366, 2.94446* **Camping Les Albères, 66740 Laroque-des-Albères [04 68 89 23 64; fax 04 68 89 14 30; contact@camping-des-alberes.com; www.camping-des-alberes.com]** Fr A9 exit junc 43 onto D618 dir Argelès-sur-Mer/Port Vendres. Turn R onto D50 to Laroque-des-Albères. In vill at T-junc turn L, then turn R at rndabt & foll sp to site on D11. Lge, mkd pitch, terr, pt shd; wc; chem disp; mv service pnt; baby facs; shwrs inc; el pnts (6A) €5; lndtte; shop; rest, snacks; bar; BBQ (gas only); playgrnd; pool (high ssn); sand beach 8km; tennis; entmnt; wifi; TV rm; 5% statics; dogs €3.50; phone; quiet; poss cr; red low ssn; CKE/CCI. "Attractive, peaceful site under slopes of Pyrenees; friendly owners; gd san facs; gd walking area; excel." ♦ ltd 2 Apr-15 Oct. € 24.00   2011*

ARGELES SUR MER *10G1* (8km W Rural) *42.52547, 2.91412* **Camping-Caravaning Las Planes, 117 Ave du Vallespir, 66740 Laroque-des-Albères [04 68 89 21 36 or 06 24 49 06 46 (mob); fax 04 68 89 01 42; info@lasplanes.com; www.lasplanes.com]** Exit A9 junc 43 onto D618 dir Argelès. In 8.5km take D2 S dir Laroque. In vill turn W onto D11, site on L in 2km - steep ent. Med, mkd pitch, pt sl, shd; wc; chem disp; shwrs inc; el pnts (4-6A) €4; gas; lndtte; shop; snacks; bar; BBQ (el/gas); playgrnd; 2 pools; sand beach 8km; cycle hire; dogs €2.50; poss cr; adv bkg rec high ssn; quiet; CKE/CCI. "Friendly owners & staff; gd security; pitches tight due o'hanging trees." 15 Jun-31 Aug. € 20.00   2008*

ARGELES SUR MER *10G1* (3km NW Rural) *42.57018, 3.01239* **Camping Etoile D'Or, Chemin de la Gabarre, Route de Taxo à la Mer, 66701 Argelès-sur-Mer [04 68 81 04 34; fax 04 68 81 57 05; info@aletoiledor.com; www.aletoiledor.com]** Fr D914 exit junc 10 dir Taxo-Plage. Site in 1km on R. Lge, hdg/mkd pitch, pt shd; wc; chem disp; baby facs; shwrs inc; el pnts (6A) inc; gas; lndtte (inc dryer); shop; tradsmn; rest, snacks; bar; BBQ (elec/gas); playgrnd; pool complex; paddling pool; waterslide; sand beach 2.5km; tennis; fitness rm; games area; games rm; wifi; entmnt; TV rm; 45% statics; dogs €3; Eng spkn; adv bkg; quiet; ccard acc; red long stay. "Welcoming site; gd for families; bus to beach fr site." ♦ 15 May-15 Sep. € 35.00   2011*

*Sidebar:* FRANCE

FRANCE

ARGENTAN *4E1* (500m SE Urban) *48.73991, -0.01668* **Camp Municipal du Parc de la Noé, 34 Rue de la Noé, 61200 Argentan [02 33 36 05 69; fax 02 33 39 96 61; camping@argentan.info; www.argentan.fr]** S fr Caen on D958 foll camping sp fr by-pass. (Rue de la Noé becomes Rue de l'Abbaye S of site). Not v well sp, poss not easy to find - ent through ornamental wrought iron gates shared by park. Sm, shd; htd wc; chem disp; mv service pnt; shwrs; el pnts (6A) €2.60; lndtte (inc dryer); shop 1km; playgrnd; pool 1km; rv & pond; games area; wifi; TV; few statics; poss cr; adv bkg ess high ssn; quiet. "Superb, clean, tidy site adj town park; helpful warden; excel, clean san facs; gd touring base; lovely town; immac site run by efficient warden" ◆ 1 Apr-30 Sep. € 9.10   2013*

"I need an on-site restaurant"

We do our best to make sure site information is correct, but it is always best to check any must-have facilities are still available or will be open during your visit.

⊞ **ARGENTAN** *4E1* (2km S Rural) *48.71841, -0.01077* **FFCC Aire Naturelle du Val de Baize (Huet des Aunay), 18 Rue de Mauvaisville, 61200 Argentan [02 33 67 27 11; fax 02 33 35 39 16; www.normandiealaferme.com]** Take D958 fr Argentan twd Sées & Alençon; site clealy sp on D958 - turn R just bef leaving Argentan boundary. Site adj T-junc N of farm buildings. Sm, some hdstg, pt shd; wc; chem disp; mv service pnt; shwrs inc; el pnts (3-6A) €2.50-4.60; shops 1.5km; snacks; playgrnd; pool 2.5km; B&B; 10% statics; dogs; Eng spkn; adv bkg; quiet; ccard not acc; CKE/CCI. "Charming, well-kept site; lge pitches in orchard; clean but dated facs, ltd low ssn; friendly welcome; NH only." € 15.10   2013*

ARGENTAT *7C4* (10km N Rural) *45.16601, 1.97861* **Camp Municipal La Croix de Brunal, Route de Freygnac, 19320 St Martin-la-Méanne [05 55 29 11 91 or 05 55 29 12 75 (Mairie); fax 05 55 29 28 48]** Fr Argentat take D18 to St Martin-la-Méanne. Site well sp on ent to vill. Sm, hdg/mkd pitch, pt shd; wc; shwrs inc; el pnts (5A); gas; lndtte; shop, rest, snacks, bar 1km; BBQ; htd pool 1km; sand beach 15km; rv sw 8km; tennis 1km; games area; some statics; dogs; phone; quiet. "Simple site; warden calls am & pm; gd walking; fishing, horseriding, watersports within 15km." ◆ ltd 1 Jul-31 Aug.   2009*

ARGENTAT *7C4* (1km NE Urban) *45.10205, 1.94390* **Camp Municipal Le Longour, Route d'Egletons, 19400 Argentat [05 55 28 13 84; fax 05 55 28 81 26; camping@argentat.fr; www.argentat.fr]** Fr cent of Argentat head N dir Egletons on D18. Med, pt shd; wc; chem disp; shwrs inc; el pnts (10A) €3.20; lndtte; shops 1km; tradsmn; playgrnd; htd pool & sports complex adj; tennis; fishing; dogs €1.30; phone; poss cr; quiet; red low ssn. "Efficiently run, clean site; pleasant rvside walk to old quay & cafés; gd touring base; excel." 1 Jun-3 Sep. € 14.00   2011*

ARGENTAT *7C4* (4km NE Rural) *45.11151, 1.95908* **Camping Château de Gibanel, 19400 Argentat (Correza) [05 55 28 10 11; fax 05 55 28 81 62; contact@camping-gibanel.com; www.camping-gibanel.com]** Exit Argentat on D18 twd Egletons & fork R on lakeside past hydro-electric dam. Sp fr all dir. Site in grounds of sm castle on N bank of Rv Dordogne. App rd narr but satisfactory. Lge, mkd pitch, pt sl, pt shd; wc (some cont); chem disp; child/baby facs; fam bthrm; shwrs inc; el pnts (10A) €3.70; gas; lndtte; shop; tradsmn; rest, snacks; bar; BBQ; playgrnd; pool; paddling pool; lake sw; boating; fishing; games area; games rm; entmnt; TV; 15% statics; dogs €22 (free low ssn); Eng spkn; adv bkg; quiet; red low ssn; ccard acc; CKE/CCI. "Excel, well-managed site in idyllic location; helpful owner; gd san facs; various pitch sizes; lovely sm town; excel." ◆ ltd 31 May-7 Sep. € 24.00 2013*

ARGENTAT *7C4* (3km SW Rural) *45.07686, 1.92945* **Camping Europe, Le Chambon, 19400 Monceaux-sur-Dordogne [05 55 28 07 70; fax 05 55 28 19 60; camping-europe@wanadoo.fr; www.camping-europe.fr]** Fr Argentat take D12 twd Beaulieu-sur-Dordogne. Site 2km fr D1120. Ent on L by awkward RH bend in Le Chambon. Med, hdg/mkd pitch, pt sl, pt shd; wc; chem disp; mv service pnt; shwrs inc; el pnts (5A) €3.10; gas; lndtte; shops 1km; tradsmn; rest 500m; snacks 1km; playgrnd; pool; paddling pool; rv sw & sand beach; canoeing; fishing; tennis; games area; wifi; entmnt; some statics; dogs €1.60; phone; poss cr; quiet. "Lovely rvside site; interesting town." 5 Apr-8 Nov. € 17.40   2010*

ARGENTAT *7C4* (4km SW Rural) *45.07531, 1.91689* **Camping Sunêlia au Soleil d'Oc, 19400 Monceaux-sur-Dordogne [05 55 28 84 84 or 05 55 28 05 97 (LS); fax 05 55 28 12 12; info@dordogne-soleil.com; www.dordogne-soleil.com]** Fr N exit A20 junc 46a dir Tulle, then D1120 to Argentat. Fr Argentat take D12 sp Beaulieu. In 4km in Laygues turn L over bdge x-ing Rv Dordogne, site in 300m. Med, hdg/mkd pitch, terr, pt shd; wc (some cont); chem disp; mv service pnt; baby facs; shwrs inc; el pnts (6A) €4.10; gas; lndtte (inc dryer); shop; rest, snacks; bar; BBQ; playgrnd; pool & paddling pool; rv & shgl beach; canoeing; games area; games rm; cycle hire; archery; wifi; entmnt; TV; some statics; dogs €3 (free low ssn); phone; Eng spkn; adv bkg; quiet; ccard acc; red low ssn/long stay/CKE/CCI. "Ideal family site high ssn & peaceful low ssn; some pitches on rv bank; ltd water points; gd walking & other activities; many beautiful vills in area; tours arranged." ◆ 16 Apr-30 Oct. € 20.70 (CChq acc)   2008*

ARGENTAT *7C4* (9km SW Rural) *45.04583, 1.88388* **Camping Le Vaurette, 19400 Monceaux-sur-Dordogne [05 55 28 09 67; fax 05 55 28 81 14; info@vaurette.com; www.vaurette.com]** SW fr Tulle on D1120; fr Argentat SW on D12 sp Beaulieu; site sp on banks of Rv Dordogne. Med, mkd pitch, pt shd; wc; chem disp; mv service pnt; baby facs; shwrs inc; el pnts (6A) €3.30; gas; lndtte; shop; snacks; bar; BBQ; playgrnd; htd pool; shgl beach & rv sw adj; tennis; badminton; fishing; canoe expeditions; games area; games rm; wifi; TV rm; statics; dogs €3.50; Eng spkn; adv bkg; quiet; ccard acc; red low ssn; CKE/CCI. "Lovely setting; helpful, friendly owners; many sports avail." ◆ 1 May 21 Sep. € 23.50   2009*

FRANCE

ARGENTIERE LA BESSEE, L' *9C3* (2.5km S Rural) *44.77775, 6.55798* **Camp Municipal Les Ecrins, 05120 L'Argentière-la-Bessée [04 92 23 03 38; fax 04 92 23 09 89; contact@ camping-les-ecrins.com; www.camping-les-ecrins.com]** Fr L'Argentière on N94, turn R onto D104, site sp. Med, some mkd pitch, pt shd, htd wc (some cont); shwrs inc; el pnts (10A) €2.40; lndtte; shop; snacks; playgrnd; pool, tennis 300m; games area; dogs €2.10; phone; adv bkg; rd/rlwy noise. "Mountain scenery." ♦ 20 Apr-15 Sep. € 14.20   2013*

⊞ **ARGENTIERE LA BESSEE, L'** *9C3* (5km S Rural) *44.75765, 6.57995* **FFCC Camping Le Verger, 05310 La Roche-de-Rame [tel/fax 04 92 20 92 23; info@campingleverger.com; www.campingleverger.com]** S fr Briançon on N94; site 500m L of road bef vill; sp. Sm, hdg pitch, terr, shd; wc; chem disp; mv service pnt; shwrs inc; el pnts (3-10A) €2.10-3.60; lndtte; shop 5km; rest, snacks, bar 1km; lake sw 1km; TV; 25% statics; dogs free; phone; bus 5km; Eng spkn; adv bkg; quiet; red low ssn. "Grass pitches in orchard; excel, well-maintained facs; excel." € 15.50   2010*

ARGENTIERE LA BESSEE, L' *9C3* (4km NW Rural) *44.82455, 6.52575* **Campéole Camping Le Courounba, Le Village, 05120 Les Vigneaux [04 92 23 02 09; fax 04 92 23 04 69; courounba@campeole.com or campeolelesvigneaux@ orange.fr; www.camping-courounba.com or www. campeole.com]** Take N94 S fr Briançon to L'Argentiere-la-Bessée, turn R onto D994E dir Vallouise. Site on L over rv bdge. Lge, hdstg, pt shd; htd wc; chem disp; mv service pnt; baby facs; shwrs inc; el pnts (6A) €4.10 (poss long lead req); lndtte (inc dryer); shop 500m; tradsmn; rest, snacks; bar; BBQ; playgrnd; htd pool; paddling pool; waterslide; fishing; tennis; cycle hire; horseriding nr; wifi; entmnt; TV; 20% statics; dogs; phone; Eng spkn; adv bkg; quiet; ccard acc; red low ssn; CKE/CCI. "Gd site, beautifully situated in woods by rv in mountains; gd clean san facs; no site lighting." ♦ 16 May-23 Sep. € 39.60   2013*

See advertisement on pages 14 & 15

ARGENTIERE LA BESSEE, L' *9C3* (8km NW Rural) *44.84354, 6.48989* **Camping Les Chambonnettes, 05290 Vallouise [tel/fax 04 92 23 30 26 or 06 82 23 65 09 (mob); campingvallouise@hotmail.fr; http:// campingchambonnettesvallouise.chez-alice.fr]** Take N94 Briançon-Gap, on N o'skts of L'Argentière-la-Bessée take D994 W dir Vallouise. In cent of Vallouise turn L over bdge & immed L, site in 200m on rvside. Lge, mkd pitch, pt sl, pt shd; htd wc (some cont); chem disp; mv service pnt; shwrs inc; el pnts (3-6A) €3.30; gas 1.5km; lndtte; shops 200m; tradsmn, rest, snacks, bar 500m; playgrnd; pool 3km; tennis; TV; 50% statics; dogs €1.80; phone; poss cr; Eng spkn; adv bkg; quiet; red low ssn "Mountain scenery; basic facs; gd cent for walking, skiing, canoeing; white-water rafting at nrby rv; interesting vill; fair." 20 Dec-24 Oct. € 13.50   2009*

ARGENTON LES VALLEES *4H1* (500m N Rural) *46.9877, -0.4504* **Camp Municipal du Lac d'Hautibus, Rue de la Sablière, 79150 Argenton-les-Vallées [05 49 65 95 08 or 05 49 65 70 22 (Mairie); fax 05 49 65 70 84; mairie-argenton-chateau@cegetel.net; www.campings-poitou-charentes.com]** Fr E or W on D759, site well sp in town, on lakeside. Med, hdg pitch, pt sl, terr; wc (some cont); chem disp; mv service pnt; shwrs inc; el pnts (6A) €2.50; lndtte; shops in town; playgrnd; pool 100m; lake sw 500m; tennis 100m; games rm; some statics; Eng spkn; quiet; CKE/CCI. "Beautifully-situated, well-kept site; interesting, quiet town; excel." ♦ 1 Apr-30 Sep. € 8.80   2011*

ARGENTON SUR CREUSE *7A3* (12km SE Rural) *46.50709, 1.58355* **La Chaumerette Camping Club à Tou Vert, 36190 Gargilesse-Dampierre [02 54 47 73 44; campinglachaumerette@wanadoo.fr]** Fr A20 take exit 17 for D48 to Badecon-le-Pin then R onto D40. Turn R sp Barsize then foll sp to site. Sm, shd; wc; chem disp; baby facs; shwrs inc; el pnts (6A) inc; tradsmn; snacks; bar; playgrnd; fishing; adv bkg; quiet; CKE/CCI. "Superb location in wooded valley adj rv; v isolated & poor security; gd san facs; additional o'flow area when site full." 1 May-31 Oct. € 12.00   2011*

ARGENTON SUR CREUSE *7A3* (12km SW Rural) *46.54192, 1.40328* **Camping La Petite Brenne (Naturist), La Grande Metairie, 36800 Luzeret [02 54 25 05 78; fax 02 54 25 05 97; la.petite.brenne@wanadoo.fr; www.lapetitebrenne.com]** Fr A20 exit junc 18 sp Luzeret/Prissac; foll D55 to Luzeret vill. After bdge in vill turn L, then next L to site. Lge, pt sl, unshd; wc; chem disp; sauna; shwrs inc; el pnts (10A) €5 (long leads poss req); lndtte; shop 12km; tradsmn; rest; bar; playgrnd; 2 pools (1 htd); horseriding; wifi; no dogs; Eng spkn; adv bkg rec high ssn; quiet; ccard acc; red long stay/low ssn. "Excel family site; friendly Dutch owners; lge pitches; excel san facs; ideal for children; pools excel; gd rest; gd walking in National Park." 26 Apr-30 Sep. € 24.00   2013*

ARGENTON SUR CREUSE *7A3* (2km NW Rural) *46.59636, 1.50619* **Camp Municipal Les Chambons, 37 Rue des Chambons, 36200 Argenton-sur-Creuse [02 54 24 15 26; camping-les-chambons@orange.fr; www.entreprisefrery. com]** Fr A20 exit junc 17 onto D937 dir Argenton; turn R at rndabt, then L at mini rndabt nr supmkt sp St Marcel; foll rd downhill over rlwy bdge; then 1st R in 100m. But best app fr N on D927 to avoid traff calming rd humps; at town sp cross rlwy bdge & turn R immed past LH turn for Roman archaeological museum; foll camping sp on narr, busy app rd. Med, mkd pitch, some hdstg, pt sl, shd; wc; chem disp; shwrs inc; el pnts (5A) €3.60 (poss long lead req); gas; shop 1.5km; tradsmn; bar; rest 1km; playgrnd; wifi; quiet but some rd noise. "Beautiful, peaceful, well-kept site by rv; helpful warden; v muddy after heavy rain & poss uneven pitches by rv; rvside walk into interesting old town; no need to unhitch so useful for early start; quiet in day, busy in evening as popular NH high ssn; excel." 1 May-30 Sep. € 23.45   2013*

ARGENTON SUR CREUSE *7A3* (6km NW Rural) *46.62965, 1.47882* **Camp Municipal Les Rives de la Bouzanne, 36800 Le Pont Chrétien-Chabenet [02 54 25 80 53 or 02 54 25 81 40 (Mairie); fax 02 54 25 87 59; commune. pontchretien@wanadoo.fr]** Exit A20 junc 17 onto D927; site well sp over rv bdge. Or fr St Gaultier on D927 dir Argenton-sur-Creuse; turn R in Le Pont Chrétien-Chabenet, bef rv bdge, site 50m on L. Med, pt shd; wc (some cont); chem disp (wc); shwrs inc; el pnts inc; lndtte; shop & bar adj; supmkt 3km; BBQ; playgrnd; rv adj; dogs €0.50; phone; Eng spkn; adv bkg rec; quiet; CKE/CCI. "Picturesque, quiet site; site yourself, warden calls; gd, drained pitches; immac san facs; conv A20; excel NH." 15 Jun-10 Sep. € 11.50   2011*

ARLANC *9C1* (1km W Rural) *45.41344, 3.71866* **Camp Municipal Le Metz, Loumas, 63220 Arlanc [04 73 95 15 62; fax 04 73 95 78 31; jardin-terre.arlanc@wanadoo.fr; www.arlanc.fr]** Fr Ambert on D906 to Arlanc, turn R (W) onto D300 dir St Germain-l'Herm. Site on R in 800m, sp. Med, some hdg pitch, pt shd; wc (some cont); chem disp (wc); shwrs inc; el pnts (6A) inc (long lead poss req); lndtte (inc dryer); shop 800m; rest, snacks & bar 150m; playgrnd; pool 100m; games area; 10% statics; dogs; phone; adv bkg; quiet. "Lace-making museum in Arlanc." ♦ 15 Jun-30 Sep. € 11.40   2009*

ARLES *10E2* (8km NE Rural) *43.72336, 4.71861* **Camp Municipal des Pins, Rue Michelet, 13990 Fontvieille [04 90 54 78 69; fax 04 90 54 81 25; campingmunicipal. lespins@wanadoo.fr; www.fontvieille-provence.com]** Take D570 fr Arles to Avignon; in 2km turn R on D17 to Fontvieille; at far end of vill turn R & foll sp. Med, pt sl, shd; wc; chem disp; shwrs inc; el pnts (6A) €3; gas fr Shell g'ge in vill; lndtte; shops 1km; playgrnd; pool 500m high ssn; tennis in vill; TV rm; dogs €1.50; bus; poss cr; Eng spkn; adv bkg; red long stay: CKE/CCI. "Delightful, quiet site in pines; friendly staff; vg facs; 15-20 mins walk to lively vill; quiet forest walks; tight access/exit long o'fits; site closes last Sunday in Sep; mosquitoes!" Easter-30 Sep. € 13.00   2011*

"Satellite navigation makes touring much easier"

Remember most sat navs don't know if you're towing or in a larger vehicle – always use yours alongside maps and site directions.

⊞ **ARLES** *10E2* (7km E Rural) *43.64799, 4.70625* **Camping La Bienheureuse, 13280 Raphèle-les-Arles [04 90 98 48 06; fax 04 90 98 37 62; contact@labienheureuse.com; www. labienheureuse.com]** Fr Arles E on D453, site on L 5km after Pont-de-Crau. W fr Salon-de-Provence on A54/N113; exit N113 junc 12 onto N1435 to St Martin-de-Crau; cont past St Martin-de-Crau on N1435; in 2km rd becomes D435 to Raphèle-les-Arles; site on R 900m after Raphèle-les-Arles. Med, hdg pitch, pt shd; wc; chem disp; shwrs inc; el pnts (10A) €3.50; lndtte; tradsmn; snacks; bar; playgrnd; pool; paddling pool; tennis; horseriding nr; entmnt; some statics; dogs €2.50; phone; bus adj; Eng spkn; adv bkg; quiet; CKE/CCI. "Pleasant site; obliging British owners; 700m to shops/bar in vill; gd facs." ♦ € 17.00   2011*

ARLES *10E2* (2km SE Urban) *43.66981, 4.64422* **Camping Le City, 67 Route de la Crau, 13200 Arles [04 90 93 08 86 / 06 13 46 28 22 (mob); contact@camping-city.com; www.camping-city.com]** Fr town cent foll rd to Pont-de-Crau. Site well sp on L in 2km. Or exit N113 at junc 7 sp Arles & Pont de Crau; at rndabt go L alongside arches; site on R in 350m; well sp. Med, mkd pitch, pt shd; wc (some cont); chem disp; mv service pnt; baby facs; shwrs inc; el pnts (5A) €4; gas 1km; lndtte; shop; supmkt 1km; tradsmn; rest, snacks; bar; playgrnd; pool; paddling pool; sand beach 25km; tennis; cycle hire; entmnt; TV; many statics; dogs €2; bus; some Eng spkn; quiet; CKE/CCI. "Vg site; modern, clean san facs - low ssn ltd & poss upstairs; walk to town cent; Roman Amphitheatre well worth seeing." ♦ 1 Mar-30 Sep. € 20.00   2013*

ARLES *10E2* (4km SE Urban) *43.65942, 4.65416* **Camping Les Rosiers, 145 Draille Marseillaise, Pont-de-Crau, 13200 Arles [04 90 96 02 12; fax 04 90 93 36 72; lesrosiers.arles@ wanadoo.fr; www.arles-camping-club.com]** Exit Arles E by D453 sp Pont-de-Crau or junc 7 fr N113 dir Raphèle-les-Arles; 200m after exit vill take 1st exit at rndabt then R at Flor Hotel sp on D83E. Site in 50m on R adj hotel. Med, pt shd; htd wc (some cont); mv service pnt; shwrs inc; chem disp; el pnts (6A) €4; lndtte; shop 500m; rest; bar; playgrnd; pool; games area; entmnt; TV; many statics; dogs €1.50; bus fr rndabt; no c'vans/m'vans over 5.50m allowed (but poss not enforced); poss cr; Eng spkn; some rd & rlwy noise; red low ssn. "Many mosquitoes; red facs low ssn; v muddy after rain; visit Les Baux citadel early morning bef coach parties arr; gd birdwatching; poss no site lighting low ssn; conv Arles." 3 Apr-31 Oct. € 17.00   2010*

ARLES *10E2* (14km W Rural) *43.66200, 4.47380* **Camping Caravaning Crin-Blanc, Hameau de Saliers, 13123 Albaron [04 66 87 48 78; fax 04 66 87 18 66; camping-crin.blanc@ wanadoo.fr; www.camping-crin-blanc.com]** E fr St Gilles on D572 twd Arles; in 3km turn R onto D37 sp Saliers; site sp. Lge, pt shd; wc (some cont); chem disp; mv service pnt; baby facs; shwrs; el pnts (10A) inc; gas; lndtte (inc dryer); shop; tradsmn; rest, snacks; bar; BBQ; playgrnd; htd pool; paddling pool; tennis; horseriding; wifi; 70% statics; dogs €2.50; Eng spkn; adv bkg; quiet; red low ssn; ccard acc; CKE/CCI. "Poss muddy; mosquitoes; bird reserve." ♦ 1 Apr-30 Sep. € 24.00   2010*

ARLES SUR TECH *8H4* (2km NE Rural) *42.46646, 2.65150* **Camping Le Vallespir, Route d'Amélie-les-Bains, 66150 Arles-sur-Tech [04 68 39 90 00; fax 04 68 39 90 09; info@ campingvallespir.com; www.campingvallespir.com]** Site on D115 mid-way between Amélie-les-Bains & Arles-sur-Tech. Clearly sp on RH side of rd. Avoids narr vill. Med, some hdg pitch, pt shd; wc; chem disp; mv service pnt; baby facs; shwrs inc; el pnts (6-10A) €3.20-4.95; lndtte; tradsmn; rest, snacks; bar; playgrnd; pool; paddling pool; tennis; entmnt; golf 2km; TV rm; 50% statics; dogs €2.20; phone; poss cr; poss noisy by rd. "Pleasant, quiet site; well-organised & maintained; lovely area for hiking & cycling; ltd facs low ssn." ♦ 1 Apr-31 Oct. € 17.60   2008*

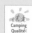
FRANCE

ARLES SUR TECH *8H4* (500m W Urban) *42.45783, 2.62563* **Camping du RiuFerrer, 66150 Arles-sur-Tech [04 68 39 11 06; fax 04 68 39 12 09; pascal.larreur@ campingduriuferrer; www.campingduriuferrer.fr]** Take D115 fr Le Boulou thro Arles-sur-Tech (v narr but poss). Twd town exit just bef rv bdge, turn R. Foll sp 500m to site. Ent across narr footbdge. O'fits width across axle over 2.19m ask for guidance to rear ent. Med, mkd pitch, hdstg, pt sl, shd; wc (some cont); chem disp; shwrs inc; el pnts (10A) €3; gas; lndtte; snacks, bar in ssn; shops 500m; tradsmn; playgrnd; pool, tennis, games area adj; poss cr; adv bkg; 20% statics; dogs €1; quiet; ccard not acc; red low ssn/long stay; Eng spkn; red CKE/ CCI. "Helpful owner; some sm pitches diff for manoeuvring; beautiful area; vg." ♦ 1 Mar-15 Oct. € 14.00   2010*

⊞ **ARMENTIERES** *3A3* (3km E Rural) *50.68774, 2.93279* **Camping L'Image, 140 Rue Brune, 59116 Houplines [03 20 35 69 42 or 06 81 61 56 82 (mob); fax 03 20 87 21 53; campimage@wanadoo.fr; www.campingimage.com]** Exit A25 junc 8 sp Armentieres, onto D945 N twd Houplines; pass on R Chemin du Pilori in 1.8km; then pass on R Hameau de L'Hépinette in 2.2km; turn R into Rue Brune in 3km; site in 1km on R. Ent not v clearly sp. Med, hdg pitch, shd; htd wc; chem disp; mv service pnt; serviced pitches; shwrs inc; el pnts (6-10A) inc (take care electrics, poss prob 2011); lndtte; shop high ssn & 4km; snacks; playgrnd; tennis; games area; wifi; entmnt; 90% statics; poss cr; adv bkg; quiet; CKE/CCI. "Mainly statics, adv bkg rec; friendly, helpful staff; dated san facs, poss unclean & unkempt (2011); pitches exposed & poss v windy; gd NH prior to ferry." € 19.00   2013*

ARNAY LE DUC *6H1* (1km E Rural) *47.13388, 4.49835* **Camping L'Etang de Fouché, Rue du 8 Mai 1945, 21230 Arnay-le-Duc [03 80 90 02 23; fax 03 80 90 11 91; info@ campingfouche.com; www.campingfouche.com]** App by D906 to Arnay (site sp); turn E onto D17, site on R in 2km. Lge, hdg/mkd pitch, hdstg, pt shd; htd wc; chem disp; baby facs; shwrs inc; el pnts (6A) €4; lndtte; shop; tradsmn; rest, snacks; bar; BBQ; playgrnd; htd pool; paddling pool; waterslide; lake sw & beach adj; fishing; tennis; cycle hire; games rm; wifi; entmnt; sat TV/TV rm; dogs €2; Eng spkn; adv bkg; quiet; ccard acc; red low ssn; CKE/CCI. "Excel lakeside site with pleasant views; lge pitches; friendly staff; gd san facs; attractive sm town; gd touring base S Burgundy; gd for young families." ♦ 15 Apr-15 Oct. € 21.90   2011*

ARRADON see Vannes *2F3*

ARRAS *3B3* (12km SE Rural) *50.27347, 2.94852* **Camping La Paille Haute, 145 Rue de Seilly, 62156 Boiry-Notre-Dame [03 21 48 15 40; fax 03 21 22 07 24; lapaillehaute@ wanadoo.fr; www.la-paille-haute.com]** Fr Calais take A26/ A1 twd Paris, exit junc 15 onto D939 twd Cambrai; in 3km take D34 NE to Boiry-Notre-Dame & foll camp sp. Fr D950 Douai-Arras rd, at Fresnes turn S onto D43, foll sp to Boiry in 7km, site well sp in vill. Med, pt hdg pitch, hdstg, terr, pt shd; wc; chem disp; mv service pnt; baby facs; shwrs inc; el pnts (6A) €4. (poss rev pol); lndtte (inc dryer); rest & snacks high ssn; bar; BBQ; playgrnd; htd pool; paddling pool; lake fishing; tennis; games rm; wifi; entmnt; 60% statics in sep area; dogs; site open w/ ends in winter; poss cr; Eng spkn; quiet; red long stay/low ssn; ccard acc; CKE/CCI. "Popular NH; useful & reliable; pretty site with views; rec arr early; lge pitches; friendly, helpful owner; gd for children; facs poss stretched high ssn but clean and adquate; Calais over 1hr; conv WW1 sites." ♦ 01 Apr -31 Oct. € 31.00   2013*

See advertisement above

⊞ **ARREAU** *8G2* (7km N Rural) *42.97176, 0.37710* **Camp Municipal d'Esplantats, 65410 Sarrancolin [05 62 98 79 20 or 06 78 12 40 10 (mob); camping.esplantats.sarrancolin@ wanadoo.fr; www.camping-esplantats.com]** Site on E side of D929 at N end of vill; ent by Total petrol stn, sp. Med, mkd pitch, pt shd; htd wc; mv service pnt; shwrs inc; el pnts (2-8A) €2.50-5.60 (long lead poss req); lndtte; shops, rest in vill; pool; some statics; dogs €2; quiet. "Site on rv bank; warden calls am & pm; clean san facs." ♦ € 10.40   2009*

ARREAU *8G2* (12km SE Rural) *42.79631, 0.40674* **FLOWER Camping Pène Blanche, 65510 Loudenvielle [05 62 55 68 85; fax 05 62 99 98 20; info@peneblanche.com; www. peneblanche.com or www.flowercampings.com]** S fr Arreau on D618 in dir of Avajan. Take D25 thro Genos. Site on W of D25 just bef turn over bdge to Loudenvielle. Avoid app fr E over Col de Peyresourde. Med, some mkd pitch, terr, pt shd; htd wc; chem disp; shwrs inc; el pnts (5-10A) €3.15-7; lndtte; shop 500m; rest, snacks; bar; BBQ; playgrnd; htd pool opp; lake 1km; 20% statics; dogs €1.90; clsd Nov; adv bkg; ccard acc. "Lge sports complex opp; quiet low ssn." ♦ 3 Apr-4 Nov. € 21.50   2010*

See advertisement on pages 32 & 33

FRANCE

⊞ **ARREAU** *8G2* (500m SW Urban) *42.90098, 0.35478* **Camp Municipal Beuse Debat, 8 Rue de la Courbère, 65240 Arreau [05 62 98 65 56 (Mairie); fax 05 62 98 68 78]** Foll sp fr D929 across bdge (D618 sp Luchon) immed turn R on D19 & foll sp to site on banks of Rv Neste. Med, terr, pt sl, pt shd; htd wc; chem disp; baby facs; shwrs; el pnts (4-10A) €3-5.90 (rev pol); lndtte; shops 1km; rest, snacks; playgrnd; rv fishing adj; tennis; entmnt; TV rm; some statics; dogs €1; site poss clsd Oct; poss cr; adv bkg; quiet. "Gd facs." € 11.50   2008*

ARRENS MARSOUS *8G2* (800m E Rural) *42.9613, -0.2034* **Camping La Hèche, 54 Route d'Azun, 65400 Arrens-Marsous [05 62 97 02 64; laheche@free.fr; www. campinglaheche.com]** Fr Argelès-Gazost foll D918. Site on L immed bef Arrens. If towing c'van do not app fr Col d'Aubisque. Lge, mkd pitch, pt shd; htd wc; baby facs; shwrs inc; el pnts (3A) €2.70; gas; lndtte (inc dryer); shop; tradsmn; playgrnd; pool in vill high ssn; waterslide; tennis; games area; TV; 10% statics; dogs €0.50; phone; no adv bkg; quiet; CKE/ CCI. "Beautiful location; gd san facs." ♦ 1 Jun-30 Sep. € 12.50-17.65   2013*

ARROMANCHES LES BAINS *3D1* (3km E Coastal) *49.33963, -0.58188* **Camp Municipal Quintefeuille, Ave Maurice Schumann, 14960 Asnelles [02 31 22 35 50; fax 02 31 21 99 45; campingquintefeuille@wanadoo.fr]** Site sp on D514, but visible fr vill sq in Asnelles. Med, mkd pitch, unshd; wc; chem disp; shwrs; el pnts; lndtte; shops adj; rest, snacks, bar 300m; playgrnd; sand beach 300m; fishing; tennis; games area; quiet. ♦ 1 Apr-30 Sep.   2008*

ARROMANCHES LES BAINS *3D1* (W Urban/Coastal) *49.33793, -0.62647* **Camp Municipal, Ave de Verdun, 14117 Arromanches-les-Bains [02 31 22 36 78; fax 02 31 21 80 22; campingarromanches@wanadoo.fr]** App fr Bayeux on D516. Turn R on onto D65 on app to Arromanches to site on L. Med, pt sl, terr, pt shd; wc; shwrs inc; el pnts (10A) inc; gas; sand beach 500m; poss cr. "Conv Mulberry Harbour exhibition & invasion beaches; friendly warden; gd san facs; levelling blocks req most pitches; ground soft when wet; sh stay pitches stony; water access diff for m'vans (2010); gd." 1 Apr-2 Nov. € 16.00   2012*

ARROU *4F2* (NW Rural) *48.10189, 1.11556* **Camp Municipal du Pont de Pierre, 28290 Arrou [02 37 97 02 13 (Mairie); fax 02 37 97 10 28; mairie.arrou@wanadoo.fr; http:// www.loirevalleytourism.com]** Take D15 fr Cloyes. Site sp in vill of Arrou. Med, hdg/mkd pitch, pt sl, unshd; wc; chem disp; mv service pnt; shwrs inc; el pnts (6-10A) €2-3; lndry rm; supmkt nr; rest, bar, snacks in vill; BBQ; playgrnd; htd pool & paddling pool adj; lake fishing & sand beach adj; tennis; horseriding; cycle hire; 10% statics; phone; adv bkg; quiet; CKE/CCI. "Lovely, peaceful, well-kept site in park-like setting; lge pitches; excel san facs; gd security; phone warden (or call at house) if office & barrier clsd; gd rvside walks/cycle rides; excel value." ♦ 1 May-30 Sep. € 4.60   2013*

ARS SUR FORMANS see Villefranche sur Saône *9B2*

ARTAIX see Marcigny *9A1*

ARTEMARE see Virieu le Grand *9B3*

⊞ **ARTIGAT** *8F3* (Edge of Town) *43.13776, 1.44407* **Camping Les Eychecadous, 09130 Artigat, [(033) 05 61 68 98 24; campingartigat@hotmail.fr; http://www.camping-artigat. com]** Fr Toulouse take A64 S, take exit 28 twrds Capens. Marquefave, St. Sulpice. Turn L onto D10, at rndabt take 2nd exit onto D622, turn L sp Av. Antonin Triqué, cont twrds Lombardi on D622, go thro 1 rndabt, turn R sp Rue de la République/ D622 cont on D622, to Av. Des Pyrénées/D4 cont onto D919 cont thro 3 rndabts then L onto Chemin du Comté then L twrds Les Eychecadous, then R, then L to site. Sm, mkd pitch, pt shd; wc; chem disp; mv service pnt; child/baby facs; shwrs; el pnts (10A); tradsmn; rest, snacks, bar; BBQ; playgrnd; pool; entmnt; tv rm; wifi; ccard not acc; CKE/CCI; dogs; few statics; twin axles; adv bkg; " v gd site on edge of Lèze; warm welcome; fishing, boating, & horse riding." ♦ € 12.00 2012*

ARZAL *2G3* (4.5km W Rural) *47.5143, -2.4343* **Camping de Kernéjeune, 56190 Arzal [02 97 45 01 60 or 06 18 79 65 10 (mob); fax 02 97 45 05 42; contact@ camping-de-kernejeune.com; www.camping-de-kernejeune.com]** Fr E on N165 exit onto D139 sp Arzal. Opp town hall turn L sp Billiers & foll sp to site. Site on rd on R after vill of Bourgerelle. Med, mkd pitch, pt shd; htd wc; shwrs; el pnts (6-10A) €3.05; lndtte; shop; tradsmn; BBQ; playgrnd; htd pool high ssn; fishing; games area; entmnt; TV; 30% statics; dogs €1.50; phone; red low ssn; quiet. "Gd base for interesting area; helpful, friendly owners; rec." ♦ 1 Apr-1 Nov. € 13.80   2009*

ARZON *2G3* (800m NE Coastal) *47.55303, -28.8294* **Camp Municipal Le Tindio, Kerners, 56640 Arzon [02 97 41 25 59; fax 02 97 53 91 23; letindio@arzon.fr; www.arzon.eu]** Fr Vannes or Muzillac on D780 turn R at rndabt on o'skts of Arzon. Site clearly sp. Lge, pt sl, pt shd; wc; chem disp; mv service pnt; shwrs; el pnts (6A) €2.50; lndtte; playgrnd; sand beach 1km; golf nr; dogs €1.20; poss cr; adv bkg; red low ssn. "Site o'looks Gulf of Morbihan; direct access to sea; excel san facs." ♦ 1 Apr-3 Nov. € 14.20   2010*

ASCAIN see St Jean de Luz *8F1*

ASCOU see Ax les Thermes *8G4*

ASNIERES SUR OISE *3D3* (1km NE Rural) *49.14083, 2.38861* **Camping Domaine Les Princes, Route des Princes, 95270 Asnières-sur-Oise [tel/fax 01 30 34 49 92; lesprinces@ clubinternet.fr; www.lesprinces.fr]** Site sp fr D909, nr Abbaye de Royaumont. Med, hdg/mkd pitch, pt shd; htd wc; shwrs inc; el pnts (3A) €3.50; lndtte; shop, rest 1km; playgrnd; fishing 500m; games area; golf, horseriding nr; BBQ; 90% statics; dogs €2.50; adv bkg; quiet; red long stay. "Pleasant, attractive, secure site; conv Parc Astérix & Paris." 1 Mar-30 Nov. € 13.00   2008*

ASPET *8G3* (S Rural) *43.00969, 0.79665* **Camp Municipal Le Cagire, 31160 Aspet [05 61 88 51 55; fax 05 61 88 44 03; camping.aspet@wanadoo.fr]** Exit A64 at junc 18 St Gaudens & take D5 S. In 14km, site sp on R in vill of Aspet. Sp 'Camping, Stade.' Sm, mkd pitch, shd; wc; chem disp (wc); shwrs; el pnts (6A) €2.50; lndtte; shop, rest, snacks, bar 500m; pool, tennis 300m; games area; 30% statics; dogs €0.50; quiet; adv bkg; CKE/CCI. "Pleasant, well kept site nr lively, sm town; rec arr bef 1800 hrs high ssn; basic facs; some pitches muddy when wet." 1 Apr-30 Sep. € 8.30   2009*

ASPRES SUR BUECH 9D3 (1km S Rural) 44.51497, 5.74347
Camping L'Adrech, Route de Sisteron, 05140 Aspres-sur-
Buëch [04 92 58 60 45; ladrech.camping@wanadoo.fr;
http://camping.ladrech.pagesperso-orange.fr/] Site on L
of D1075 fr Aspres. Med, hdg pitch, hdstg, pt sl, pt shd; wc;
chem disp; shwrs; el pnts (6-10A) €4-6.50; gas; lndtte; shop
& 1km; tradsmn; snacks; BBQ; playgrnd; fishing; rv/lake 5km;
entmnt; 50% statics; dogs €1; phone; poss cr; Eng spkn; adv
bkg; quiet; ccard acc; CKE/CCI. "Wooded site; lovely views; lge
pitches; helpful owner; ltd facs low ssn; useful NH." ◆
1 Apr-1 Nov. € 10.00   2010*

ASPRES SUR BUECH 9D3 (8km NW Rural) 44.53048,
5.68371 FFCC Aire Naturelle La Source (Pardoe), 05140
St Pierre-d'Argençon [tel/fax 04 92 58 67 81; info@
lasource-hautesalpes.com; www.lasource-hautesalpes.
com] Fr D1075 at Aspres-sur-Buëch turn onto D993 dir Valence
to St Pierre-d'Argençon; site sp. Or fr N on D93, cont onto D993
over Col de Cabre; site sp on L bef St Pierre-d'Argençon. Sm,
mkd pitch, pt sl, pt shd; wc; chem disp; mv service pnt; shwrs
inc; el pnts (10A) €2.80; lndtte; tradsmn; rest, bar 5km; BBQ;
playgrnd; wifi; dogs €1; adv bkg; quiet; ccard acc; red long stay;
CKE/CCI. "Peaceful, well-kept CL-type site in woodland/open
field; friendly, helpful British owners; clean san facs; chambre
d'hôte on site; highly rec." 15 Apr-15 Oct. € 13.50   2012*

ASSERAC 2G3 (5km NW Coastal) 47.44533, -2.44766
Camping Le Moulin de l'Eclis, Pont Mahé, 44410 Assérac
[02 40 01 76 69; fax 02 40 01 77 75; info@camping-moulin-
de-leclis.fr; www.camping-moulin-de-leclis.fr] Fr D774 turn
N onto D83 to Assérac. Take D82 two coast to Pont Mahé,
site sp. Lge, hdg/mkd pitch, pt shd; wc; chem disp; mv service
pnt; baby facs; shwrs inc; el pnts (6-10A) €3.60-4; lndtte (inc
dryer); shop high ssn & 5km; rest 100m; snacks; bar; BBQ (gas/
elec); playgrnd; htd, covrd pool; paddling pool; waterslide; dir
access to sand beach adj; watersports; sailing school; games
area; cycle hire; wifi; entmnt; TV rm; 60% statics; dogs €3;
phone; adv bkg; Eng spkn; quiet; ccard ac; red low ssn. "Excel
family site; conv Guérande; vg touring base." ◆ 1 Apr-14 Nov.
€ 24.80   2010*

ASTON see Cabannes, Les 8G3

ATTICHY 3C4 (500m SW Rural) 49.40664, 3.05295 Camping
De l'Aigrette (Formaly Camp municipal Fleury), 22
Rue Fontaine-Aubier, 60350 Attichy [03 44 42 15 97 or
06 62 83 79 35 (mob); contact@campingdelaigrette.com;
www.campingdelaigrette.com] Fr Compiègne E on N31.
After 16km turn L at traff lts sp Attichy & site. Over iron bdge
& turn R to site on lakeside. Med, hdg pitch, pt shd; htd wc;
chem disp; mv service pnt; shwrs inc; el pnts (10A) €2; shop
1km; tradsmn; rests in town; BBQ; playgrnd; pool; fishing;
80% statics; dogs €0.50; wifi; poss cr; quiet; ccard not acc;
site clsd 25 Dec - 31 Jan; CKE/CCI. "Attractive, clean site in
pleasant vill; many w/end statics, few touring pitches; helpful
wardens live on site; modern san facs, stretched high ssn;
gd security; excel NH low ssn; excel site" ◆ 1 Feb-24 Dec.
€ 19.50   2013*

ATTIGNY see Rethel 5C1

ATUR see Périgueux 7C3

AUBAS see Montignac 7C3

AUBAZINES 7C3 (4km E Rural) 45.18620, 1.70730
Campéole Camping Le Coiroux, Parc Touristique
du Coiroux, 19190 Aubazines [05 55 27 21 96; fax
05 55 27 19 16; coiroux@campeole.com; www.camping-
coiroux.com or www.campeole.com] Fr Brive-La-Gaillarde
take N89 NE twd Tulle. At Cornil turn R onto D48 & foll sp.
Site in 8km - long, fairly steep climb. Med, pt hdg/mkd pitch,
pt shd; wc; chem disp; mv service pnt; baby facs; shwrs inc;
el pnts (5A); gas; lndtte; shop; rest, snacks; bar; playgrnd; htd
pool; paddling pool; lake sw & sand beach; fishing; boating;
tennis; golf; cycle hire; entmnt; TV rm; 50% statics; dogs; poss
cr; Eng spkn; adv bkg; quiet; red low ssn; CKE/CCI. "Excel,
wooded site." ◆ 15 Mar-15 Oct. € 25.00   2011*

See advertisement on pages 14 & 15

AUBENAS 9D2 (3km N Rural) 44.64268, 4.37925 Camping
Domaine de Gil, Route de Vals-les-Bains, 07200 Ucel
[04 75 94 63 63; fax 04 75 94 01 95; info@domaine-de-gil.
com; www.domaine-de-gil.com] Fr Aubenas NE on D104
to St Privat. Cross bdge over Rv Ardèche 1km. At Pont d'Ucel,
turn L along D578 twds Ucel; site 3km on L. Med, hdg/mkd
pitch, pt shd; wc; chem disp; mv service pnt; serviced pitch;
baby facs; shwrs inc; el pnts (10A) €5 (poss rev pol); lndtte;
shop; tradsmn; rest, snacks; bar; BBQ (gas/elec); playgrnd; htd
pool; tennis; canoeing; wifi; entmnt; TV; 75% statics; dogs €3;
phone; adv bkg ess in Aug; quiet; ccard acc; red low ssn; CKE/
CCI. "Neat, clean site in scenic area; lge pitches; excel, family
site; efficient, helpful staff; gd, clean san facs; vg." ◆ 18 Apr-
20 Sep. € 31.00   2009*

AUBENAS 9D2 (7km N Urban) 44.66920, 4.36343 Camping
au Fil de la Volane, Quartier du Stade, 07600 Vals-
les-Bains [04 75 37 46 85; camping.aufildelavolane@
wanadoo.fr; www.campingaufildelavolane.com]
Fr Aubenas NW on N102 dir Le Puy-en-Velay; in 3.5km take
D578 to Vals-les-Bains. Clearly sp at N end of town by sports
complex. Med, mkd pitch, terr, shd; wc (cont); chem disp (wc);
mv service pnt; fam bthrm; shwrs inc; el pnts (10A) inc; lndtte
(inc dryer); shops 500m; snacks; bar; BBQ; playgrnd; pool;
entmnt; rv fishing & sw adj; few statics; dogs €1; phone; quiet;
red low ssn. "Lovely, peaceful site; helpful owners; rv walk to
spa town; vg." 1 Apr-30 Sep. € 17.60   2009*

AUBENAS 9D2 (2km E Rural) 44.61885, 4.43220 Camping
Le Plan d'Eau, Route de Lussas, 07200 St Privat [tel/
fax 04 75 35 44 98; info@campingleplandeau.fr; www.
campingleplandeau.fr] Exit A7 at Montélimar dir Aubenas.
Bef Aubenas turn R at rndabt onto D104 dir St Privat. In approx
1km turn R twd Lussas & foll site sp. Site on R on rvside.
Med, mkd pitch, pt shd; wc; chem disp; baby facs; shwrs inc;
el pnts (8A) €4.20; lndtte (inc dryer); shop adj; (rest, snacks;
bar; clsd low ssn); BBQ (gas only); cooking facs; playgrnd;
htd pool; games rm; wifi; entmnt; TV rm; 25% statics; dogs
€2.70; phone; Eng spkn; adv bkg; quiet; red long stay/CKE/
CCI. "Vg, peaceful site; gd san & sports facs." 26 Apr-13 Sep.
€ 43.00   2012*

FRANCE

AUBENAS *9D2* (7km E Rural) *44.60495, 4.47126*
Ludocamping, Route de Lavilledieu, 07170 Lussas
[04 75 94 21 22; fax 04 75 88 60 60; info@ludocamping.
com; www.ludocamping.com] SE fr Aubenas on N102 twd
Montélimar. Turn L after 10km in vill Lavilledieu onto D224 sp
Lussas. Site sp on R in 4km. Med, mkd pitch, terr, pt shd; wc;
chem disp; shwrs inc; el pnts (6A) €3 (poss rev pol); gas; lndtte;
shop; rest in vill 600m; bar; playgrnd; htd pool; paddling pool;
dogs €1.50; poss cr; Eng spkn; adv bkg; quiet. "Gd walking
country; peaceful; facs poss stretched in high ssn; Dutch
owned; excel." ♦ 1 Apr-15 Oct. € 27.00   2010*

AUBENAS *9D2* (7km SE Rural) *44.56401, 4.46119* **Camping**
Les Rives d'Auzon, Route de St Germain, 07170 Lavilledieu
[tel/fax 04 75 94 70 64; contact@camping-rivesdauzon.fr;
www.camping-rivesdauzon.fr] Fr Aubenas on N102 turn R
immed after Lavilledieu, sp St Germain (D103) site on L. Sm,
pt shd; wc (some cont); mv service pnt; shwrs; el pnts (6A)
€3.50; lndry rm; shop; rest, snacks; bar; playgrnd; pool; TV rm;
entmnt; dogs €2; Eng spkn; adv bkg; some rd noise. "Friendly
owner; beautiful location; poss diff for lge o'fits due trees."
6 Apr-30 Sep. € 17.00   2009*

AUBENAS *9D2* (8km SE Rural) *44.55315, 4.44855* **Camping**
à la Ferme Le Bardou (Boule), 07170 St Germain [tel/fax
04 75 37 71 91; info@lebardou.com; www.lebardou.com]
On N102 Aubenas-Montélimar turn S at Lavilledieu on D103,
site on L in 2km. Site ent fairly narr bet stone houses in
St Germain. Sm, pt shd; wc (some cont); chem disp; shwrs inc;
el pnts (6A) €3.50; shops 150m; pool; fishing adj; some statics;
dogs; adv bkg; red low ssn; quiet. "Lovely views; pleasant site
low ssn; helpful owners; clean, basic facs but poss inadequate
high ssn; gd." 1 Apr-31 Oct. € 16.00   2011*

AUBENAS *9D2* (3km S Urban) *44.59671, 4.37644* **Camping Les**
Acacias, 07200 St Etienne-de-Fontbellon [04 75 93 67 87;
fax 04 75 93 71 77; camping-les-acacias@wanadoo.fr;
www.camping-les-acacias.fr] Fr Aubenas travel thro cent of
St Etienne. Turn 2nd R at rndabt S of Leclerc hypmkt & foll
sps. Fr S turn off D104 N of Lachapelle to St Etienne. At next
rndabt turn L & foll sp. NB Do not tow thro vill. Sm, mkd pitch,
pt shd; wc (cont); chem disp; mv service pnt; baby facs; shwrs
inc; el pnts (6A) €2.70 (poss rev pol); lndtte; shops 1.5km; rest,
snacks, bar high ssn; BBQ; playgrnd; pool; entmnt; dogs €0.70;
Eng spkn; adv bkg; quiet; no ccard acc; red low ssn; CKE/
CCI. "Pleasant site; mover needed most pitches; irreg office
hrs, pitch & call in when open; gd touring cent." 3 Apr-3 Oct.
€ 11.00   2010*

AUBENAS *9D2* (8km S Rural) *44.54113, 4.41495* **Camping**
Les Roches, 07200 Vogüé [tel/fax 04 75 37 70 45; hm07@
free.fr; www.campinglesroches.fr] Fr Aubenas take D104
S. Then L onto D579 to Vogüé. Site on L 1.5km past Vogüé -
do not turn twd Vogüé. Med, pt
sl, shd; wc (most cont); mv service pnt; baby facs; shwrs inc;
el pnts (6-10A) inc; lndtte (inc dryer); shop; rest, snacks; bar;
playgrnd; pool; tennis; games area; entmnt; TV; some statics;
dogs free; adv bkg; quiet. "Pleasant site; pitch yourself, warden
calls." ♦ 8 May-31 Aug. € 27.80   2010*

AUBENAS *9D2* (10km S Rural) *44.53693, 4.41039* **Camping**
Les Peupliers, 07200 Vogüé [04 75 37 71 47; fax
04 75 37 70 83; girard.jean-jacques@club-internet.fr;
www.campingpeupliers.com] Fr Aubenas take D104 S twd
Alès. In 2km, turn L onto D579 dir Vogüé/Vallon Pont d'Arc.
In 9km, pass L turn to Vogüé. Immed after crossing rv, turn R
at rndabt. Site on R in 300m, (2nd site of 3 on rd). Lge, mkd
pitch, pt shd; wc (some cont); chem disp; mv service pnt; baby
facs; shwrs inc; el pnts (6A) €4.10; gas; lndtte; shop; rest,
snacks; bar; BBQ; playgrnd; pool; rv & shgl beach adj; entmnt;
some statics; dogs €2.30; phone; poss cr; adv bkg; quiet; ccard
acc; CKE/CCI. "Gd touring base; access to rv for canoeing &
fishing; basic site well worn facs but clean." 5 Apr-30 Sep.
€ 24.15   2011*

AUBENAS *9D2* (10km S Rural) *44.53416, 4.40690* **Domaine du**
Cros d'Auzon, 07200 St Maurice-d'Ardèche [04 75 37 75 86;
fax 04 75 37 01 02; camping.auzon@wanadoo.fr; www.
camping-cros-auzon.com] Take D104 S fr Aubenas for 2km;
at island turn L onto D579. After 9km, pass L turn to Vogüé vill,
cross rv & turn R immed. Site 600m on R, 1km fr Vogüé stn.
Lge, hdg/mkd pitch, pt shd; htd wc; chem disp; mv service pnt;
serviced pitch; child/baby facs; shwrs inc; el pnts (6A) inc; gas;
lndtte; shop 1km; tradsmn; rest, snacks; bar; playgrnd; pool;
waterslide; fishing; cycle hire; tennis; entmnt; games/TV rm;
cinema; 70% statics; dogs €3; Eng spkn; adv bkg; quiet; red
low ssn/long stay; ccard acc; CKE/CCI. "Gd touring base; poss
long walk to shwrs; excel." ♦ 3 Apr-18 Sep. € 29.50   2010*

AUBENAS *9D2* (7km NW Rural) *44.65157, 4.32384* **Camp**
Municipal le Pont des Issoux, Allée de Vals, 07380 Lalevade-
d'Ardèche [04 75 94 14 09 (Mairie) or 04 75 94 01 92 (LS);
fax 04 75 94 01 92; contact@campingdesissoux.com; www.
campingdesissoux.com/livredor.php] Fr Aubenas, N102 sp
Mende & Le Puy-en-Velay; Lalevade in 10km; R in vill; well sp.
Med, mkd pitch, pt shd; wc (mostly cont); chem disp (wc);
shwrs inc; el pnts (10A) €3.10 (poss rev pol); gas; lndtte;
supmkt adj; rest, snacks & bar 250m, playgrnd; lake sw & shgl
beach adj; tennis & children's park nrby; wifi; dogs €1.20; bus
250m; poss cr; Eng spkn; adv bkg; quiet; CKE/CCI. "Pleasant,
shady site beside Rv Ardèche; friendly, helpful warden; san facs
dated but clean, poss scruffy low ssn; no twin-axles; close to
vill; conv touring base; vg." ♦ 1 Apr-15 Oct. € 11.50 2013*

AUBENCHEUL AU BAC *3B4* (500m E Rural) *50.25576, 3.16264*
FFCC Camping Les Colombes, 2 Rue des Colombes, 59265
Aubencheul-au-Bac [03 27 89 25 90; fax 03 27 94 58 11;
campinglescolombes@club-internet.fr; http://camping.
lescolombes.ifrance.com] Fr S on D643 dir Douai, on ent vill
of Aubencheul-au-Bac, turn R at camp sp onto D71, site on
L down lane. Site app thro housing estate. Med, hdg pitch,
pt shd; wc; chem disp; shwrs inc; el pnts (4-6A) €2-€4; shops
1km; tradsmn; BBQ; playgrnd; lake fishing; 90% statics; dogs;
poss cr; adv bkg; quiet; CKE/CCI. "Pretty, clean, tidy site;
friendly, helpful staff; excel facs, poss stretched high ssn; ltd
touring pitches; poss aircraft noise; gate locked 2200-0700." ♦
1 Apr-31 Oct. € 11.00   2008*

AUBENCHEUL AU BAC *3B4* (2km W Rural) *50.26134, 3.14042* **Camping aux Roubaisiens, Rue de l'Abbeye, 62860 Oisy-le-Verger [03 21 59 51 54; lagep@hotmail.fr]** Fr Cambrai take D643 NW twd Douai. In 10km immed turn L (W) twd Oisy-le-Verger, site sp in vill Sm, pt shd; wc; own san rec; chem disp; shwrs; el pnts (6A) €2; lndtte (inc dryer); shop; playgrnd; fishing; 95% statics; quiet. "Fine as NH/sh stay; helpful owner; gd shop." 1 Apr-15 Oct. € 8.40   2010*

> ## "There aren't many sites open at this time of year"
>
> If you're travelling outside peak season remember to call ahead to check site opening dates – even if the entry says 'open all year'.

AUBERIVE *6F1* (SE Rural) *47.78445, 5.06488* **Camp Municipal Les Charbonnières, 52160 Auberive [tel/fax 03 25 86 21 13 (Mairie); mairie.auberive@wanadoo.fr]** Leave A31 at junc 6 W twds Châtilion-sur-Seine on D428 for 12km, site on L bef vill. Site sp. Sm, mkd pitch, sl, pt shd; htd wc (some cont); chem disp (wc); shwrs inc; el pnts (6A) €1.60; lndry rm; shops in vill; rest in vill; playgrnd; phone; quiet; CKE/CCI. "Pleasant, clean, well-maintained site in wooded area; site yourself, friendly warden calls; ltd el pnts; attractive vill adj; music festival in abbey early Jul; gd." 15 Apr-1 Oct. € 7.40   2009*

AUBERIVES SUR VAREZE *9B2* (8km E Rural) *45.42830, 4.92823* **Kawan Village Camping Le Bontemps, 5 Impasse du Bontemps, 38150 Vernioz [04 74 57 83 52; fax 04 74 57 83 70; info@campinglebontemps.com; www.camping-lebontemps.com]** Take N7 S fr Vienne. At Le Clos turn L onto D37 thro Cheyssieu & Vernioz, site approx 9km E of Vernioz. Fr S, on N7 N of vill of Auberives R onto D37, site on R in 8km. Tight ent - rec swing wide. NB Also sp Hotel de Plein Air. Lge, mkd pitch; terr, pt shd; wc; mv service pnt; baby facs; shwrs inc; el pnts (6A) inc (poss long lead req); lndtte (inc dryer); shop; rest, snacks; bar; BBQ; playgrnd; pool; paddling pool; fishing lake; wildlife sanctuary; tennis; games area; games rm; wifi; entmnt; TV; 30% statics; dogs €3; no c'vans/m'vans over 10m high ssn; adv bkg; ccard acc; CKE/CCI. "Attractive, well-kept site; popular NH high ssn; helpful staff; excel sports facs; vg NH." ♦ 1 Apr-30 Sep. € 41.00 (CChq acc) SBS - M10   2013*

AUBERIVES SUR VAREZE *9B2* (1km S Rural) *45.41284, 4.81358* **Camping des Nations, 38550 Clonas-sur-Varèze [04 74 84 95 13 or 04 74 84 97 17; fax 04 74 79 93 75]** Fr Vienne S on N7; site sp on R in 12km. Or fr S exit A7 junc 12 onto N7 dir Vienne; do not go into Clonas vill; site on L adj Hotel des Nations. Med, hdg/mkd pitch, shd; htd wc; chem disp; shwrs inc; el pnts (6A) inc; tradsmn; rest nr; snacks; pool; dogs €1; adv bkg (ess high ssn); quiet; ccard not acc; Eng spkn; rd noise fr N71; CKE/CCI. "Pleasant, well-kept, well-laid out site; gd sized pitches; gd, clean san facs; site muddy when wet; poss under-used; ltd facs low ssn; poss irreg cleaning end of ssn; useful NH/touring base for Spain & the Med." ♦ 23 Mar-20 Oct. € 17.00   2010*

AUBETERRE SUR DRONNE *7C2* (200m E Rural) *45.26975, 0.17566* **Camp Municipal, Route de Ribérac, 16390 Aubeterre-sur-Dronne [05 45 98 60 17 or 06 87 29 18 36 (mob); camping.aubeterre-sur-dronne@orange.fr; www.camping-aubeterre.fr]** On D2 fr Chalais, take D17 around S end of town. Turn R over rv & site on R adj sports ground. Med, pt shd; wc (cont); chem disp (wc); mv service pnt; shwrs inc; el pnts (10A) €2.50; shop 250m; rest in town; snacks; bar; playgrnd; beach & rv adj; fishing & boating adj; tennis adj; cycle hire; wifi; some statics; dogs €1; poss cr; Eng spkn; quiet. "Excel site; gd for children; friendly staff; picturesque town; conv touring Périgord." 1 May-30 Sep. € 17.85   2013*

AUBIGNAN see Carpentras *10E2*

AUBIGNY SUR NERE *4G3* (1.5km E Rural) *47.48435, 2.45703* **FLOWER Camping des Etangs, Route de Sancerre, 18700 Aubigny-sur-Nère [02 48 58 02 37; camping.aubigny@orange.fr; www.camping-aubigny.com or www.flowercampings.com]** D940 fr Gien, turn E in vill of Aubigny onto D923, foll sp fr vill; site 1km on R by lake, after Camp des Sports & just bef end of vill sp. Avoid town cent due congestion. Med, mkd pitch, some hdstg, pt shd; htd wc; chem disp; shwrs inc; el pnts (6-10A) inc; lndtte; shop, rest & bar nr; tradsmn; snacks; BBQ; playgrnd; htd, covrd pool; paddling pool; fishing; cycle hire; games rm; wifi; TV; 10% statics; dogs €2; phone; poss cr; Eng spkn; adv bkg; quiet; red low ssn/CKE/CCI. "Vg site with lake views; pretty vill; mkt Sat; 2nd w/e July Scottish Son & Lumière event adj site!" ♦ 1 Apr-30 Oct. € 29.70   2013*

See advertisement on pages 32 & 33

⊞ **AUBUSSON** *7B4* (10km N Rural) *46.02133, 2.17052* **Camping La Perle, Fourneaux, 23200 St Médard-la-Rochette [05 55 83 00 72; fax 05 55 83 34 18; info@camping-laperle.nl; www.camping-laperle.nl]** On D942 N fr Aubusson dir Guéret; site on R bef Fourneaux. Sm, hdg/mkd pitch, some hdstg, terr, pt shd; wc; shwrs inc; el pnts (10A) poss rev pol €3.50; lndtte; shops 10km; tradsmn; rest; bar; BBQ; playgrnd; htd pool; cycle hire; wifi; TV rm; some statics; dogs; Eng spkn; adv bkg; quiet; red low ssn; CKE/CCI. "Site ever improving (2011); various sized pitches; Dutch owners; tapestry museum in Aubusson & other historical attractions; vg site." € 18.50   2013*

AUBUSSON *7B4* (1.5km S Urban) *45.94652, 2.17608* **Camp Municipal La Croix Blanche, Route de Felletin, 23200 Aubusson [05 55 66 18 00]** Site on D982 on banks of Rv Creuse; sp fr all dir. NB Do not drive thro town cent to site - narr main street with iron pillars. Med, shd; wc (some cont); shwrs inc; el pnts (6A) €2.20; lndry rm; tradsmn; snacks; playgrnd; pool 1km; wifi; phone; adv bkg; quiet but some rd noise; CKE/CCI. "Vg site in pleasant location by rv; excel shwrs; park on site rds if pitches waterlogged; conv tapestry factories." 1 Apr-30 Sep. € 10.20   2010*

FRANCE

AUBUSSON *7B4* (5km S Rural) *45.91939, 2.17044* **Camping des Combes, Les Combes, 23500 Felletin [05 55 66 77 29 or 07799 138014 (UK); info@campingdescombes-creuse-france. co.uk; www.campingdescombes-creuse-france.co.uk]** Fr Aubusson on D982 to Felletin, when in Felletin & immed bef rlwy line, turn R at cemetery. Foll camping sp approx 4km. Sm, hdg/mkd pitch, pt shd; wc; chem disp; mv service pnt; shwrs inc; el pnts (10A) €2 (long lead poss req); lndtte; shop & 6km; tradsmn; rest, snacks, bar 6km; playgrnd; fishing; boating; no statics; no dogs; phone; adv bkg; quiet. "Peaceful, British-owned site on edge Lake Combes; ideal touring base; vg; spotless" ♦ 1 Mar-30 Sep. € 20.00   2013*

AUCH *8F3* (8km N Rural) *43.7128, 0.5646* **Kawan Village Le Talouch, Au Cassou, 32810 Roquelaure [05 62 65 52 43; fax 05 62 65 53 68; info@camping-talouch.com; www. camping-talouch.com]** Head W on N124 fr Auch, then N on D148 for 7km to site. Med, mkd pitch, pt shd; wc; chem disp; mv service pnt; baby facs; steam rm; sauna; shwrs; el pnts (6A) inc; gas; lndtte (inc dryer); shop; rest, snacks; bar; BBQ; playgrnd; 2 pools (1 htd, covrd pool); paddling pool; tennis; golf driving range; games area; wifi; entmnt; TV rm; 15% statics; dogs €2.40; Eng spkn; adv bkg; quiet; red low ssn; CKE/CCI. "Well-kept site; set in lovely countryside with lge grassed pitches, maintained to high standard; friendly Dutch owners who spk excel Eng; recreational facs superb for all age groups; gd walking & nature trails; poss liable to flooding." ♦ 1 Apr-30 Sep. € 33.40   2012*

AUCH *8F3* (1.5km SW Rural) *43.63664, 0.58858* **Camp Municipal d'Ile St Martin, Rue de Mouzon, Parc des Sports, 32000 Auch [05 62 05 00 22; frederic.estave@ mairie-auch.fr]** Fr S on N21 approx 750m after business area, turn R at traff lts into Rue Général de Gaulle which runs into Rue du Mouzon, site in 500m adj rv. NB There is also a Parc des Sports on N side of Auch. Med, hdg pitch, hdstg, unshd; wc; shwrs inc; el pnts (6A) inc; shops 300m; pool 250m; few statics; poss cr; quiet but some rd noise. "Basic site with no shade; sm pitches; san facs dated but clean; facs up stairs; rec arr bef 1700; lovely walk along rv to town." 15 Apr-15 Oct. € 9.70   2010*

AUCUN *8F2* **Camping Azun Nature, 1 Route des Poueyes, 65400 [05 62 97 45 05; azun.nature@wanadoo.fr; www. camping-azun-nature.com]** Fr Toulouse- A64 exit Tarbes west. Fr Bordeaux or Bayonne- A64 Exit Soumoulou. Fr Lourdes-drive twd Argeles-Gazost, take exit Aubisque col-Val d'Azun; Fr town cent of Argeles-Gazost go twd Aubisque col, Soulor col; Cross Arras-en-Lavedan, go on twd Aucun vill, turn left sp Las Poueyes, site ent 100m on r right bet barns. Sm, mkd pitch, pt shd; wc; chem disp; child/baby facs; shwrs inc; el pnts (3-6A) €2.50-3.50; lndtte; shop; tradsmn; BBQ; playgrnd; pool 3km; games area; games rm; wifi; tv rm; 50% statics; dogs free; adv bkg; CKE/CCI; "Stunning setting; ideal walking & cycling area; gd for exploring the Pyrenees, visits to Lourdes; well maintained; friendly, helpful owner." ♦ 01 May-30 Sep. € 15.00   2013*

AUDENGE *7D1* (1km E Rural) *44.68410, -1.00433* **Camping Le Braou, Route de Bordeaux, 33980 Audenge [tel/fax 05 56 26 90 03; info@camping-audenge.com; www. camping-audenge.com]** SW fr Bordeaux turn R off D1250 twd Andernos onto D3; at traff lts in Audenge turn R; site 750m on R. Lge, mkd pitch, pt shd; wc; mv service pnt; shwrs inc; el pnts (3A) €3.50; lndtte (inc dryer); shops 1km; tradsmn; snacks; BBQ; pool; beach 1.5km; tennis; cycle hire; games area; internet; entmnt; some statics; dogs €3.50; bus 1km; quiet; CKE/CCI. ♦ ltd 27 Mar-2 Oct. € 19.50   2010*

AUDENGE *7D1* (10km SE Urban) *44.60486, -0.94225* **Camp Municipal de l'Eyre, Allée de la Plage, 33380 Mios [05 56 26 42 04; fax 05 56 26 41 69]** Fr N or S on A63, join A660 sp Arcachon; leave at junc 1 to Mios. After vill turn L after traff lts (sm sp) bet tourist & post offices. Site adj Rv Eyre. Med, mkd pitch, pt shd; htd wc; shwrs inc; el pnts (10A) inc; lndtte; shop 500m; sports hall adj; dogs €1.50; CKE/CCI. "Excel touring base; helpful warden; ltd facs low ssn; park outside site to book in; san facs poss stretched if site full; poss noisy at night." ♦ 15 Jun-15 Sep. € 18.50   2010*

AUDENGE *7D1* (5km S Urban) *44.65076, -0.97914* **Camping Le Marache Vacances, 25 Rue Gambetta, 33380 Biganos [05 57 70 61 19; fax 05 56 82 62 60; contact@ marachevacances.com; www.marachevacances.com]** Exit A660 junc 2 sp Facture; take D3 dir Audenge, site clearly sp. NB Height restriction 2.6m in Facture, use ring rd. Med, mkd pitch, pt shd; wc; mv service pnt; baby facs; shwrs inc; el pnts (6A) €4.50; lndtte (inc dryer); shops 1km; tradsmn; rest, snacks; bar; BBQ; playgrnd; htd pool; rv & fishing 1km; tennis 1km; games rm; wifi; entmnt; TV; dogs €3.80; adv bkg; quiet; ccard acc. "Pleasant staff; basic facs, ltd low ssn; NH only." ♦ 1 Mar-31 Oct. € 24.50   2010*

AUDIERNE *2F1* (4.5km NE Rural) *48.04924, -4.48235* **Camp Municipal de Langros, 29790 Pont-Croix [tel/ fax 02 98 70 40 38; otsi.pontcroix@wanadoo.fr; www. pont-croix.info]** Site sp at ent to Pont-Croix on D765; also sp fr town cent. Med, pt shd; wc; chem disp (wc); shwrs inc; el pnts €2.20; gas 700m (in Super U); lndtte; shop; rest, snacks; bar; BBQ; playgrnd; beach 4km; 6% statics; dogs; bus; phone (card only); adv bkg; quiet; CKE/CCI. "Beautiful site with some magnificent trees; pretty sm town; gd." ♦ ltd 15 Jun-15 Sep. € 9.20 2008*

AUDIERNE *2F1* (700m SE Coastal/Rural) *48.02458, -4.52863* **Camping Le Loquéran, Bois de Loquéran, 29770 Audierne [02 98 74 95 06; fax 02 98 74 91 14; pointe.raz@free.fr; http://pointe.raz.free.fr]** Fr Quimper on D784 thro Plozévet & Plouhinec dir Audierne. Look out for sm, yellow/purple camping sp on R, site 500m on L. Sm, mkd pitch, terr, pt shd; wc; chem disp; shwrs inc; el pnts (6A) €2; lndtte; shop & 600m; playgrnd; beach 1km; dogs €1; ccard acc; quiet; CKE/CCI. "Gd san facs; peaceful site." 15 May-30 Sep. € 9.00   2010*

AUDIERNE *2F1* (3km SE Coastal) *48.00723, -4.50799*
Camping de Kersiny-Plage, 1 Rue Nominoé, 29780
Plouhinec [02 98 70 82 44; info@kersinyplage.com; www.
kersinyplage.com] Fr Audierne on D784 turn R at 2nd traff
lts in Plouhinec, cont for 1km; turn L into Rue Nominoé (sp diff
to see) for 100m. Or fr Quimper on D784 to Plouhinec, turn L
at 1st traff lts & as bef. Med, hdg pitch, terr, pt shd; wc; chem
disp; baby facs; shwrs inc; el pnts (8A) €3; lndry rm; tradsmn
high ssn; BBQ (gas); playgrnd; direct access to sand beach; wifi;
dogs €2; Eng spkn; quiet; barrier clsd 2300-0730; red low ssn;
CKE/CCI. "Quiet, peaceful site; beautiful location & beach;
most pitches superb sea views; welcoming, friendly owner;
clean san facs; not much in area for children except beach; gd
coastal walks; vg, rec." 14 May-17 Sep. € 14.80   2011*

AUDIERNE *2F1* (8km W Coastal) *48.02527, -4.61830*
Camp Municipal de Kermalero, 29770 Primelin [tel/fax
02 98 74 84 75 or 02 98 74 81 19 (LS); campingkermalero@
wanadoo.fr] Exit D784 Audierne-Pointe-du-Raz for Primelin;
in Primelin turn R dir Ecomarché supmkt; site on L in 500m; site
sp. Med, hdg pitch, terr, pt shd; wc; chem disp; mv service pnt;
shwrs inc; el pnts (6A) €2.50; lndtte; supmkt 1km; tradsmn;
playgrnd; games area; sand beach 1km; tennis; TV; 5% statics;
quiet. "Pleasant site; gd outlook/views; helpful warden; clean
facs; gd." ♦ 1 Mar-22 Oct. € 12.00   2010*

> # "That's changed – Should I let The Club know?"
> If you find something on site that's different from the site entry, fill in a report and let us know. See www.caravanclub.co.uk/europereport.

AUDIERNE *2F1* (1.5km NW Urban) *48.02859, -4.55675* **FFCC**
Camping de Kerivoas, Route de la Pointe du Raz, 29770
Audierne [02 98 70 26 86 or 02 98 70 27 75 (LS); camping.
kerivoas@wanadoo.fr] W fr Audierne on D784 sp Pointe du
Raz; site on L at top of hill opp Leclerc supmkt. Sm, pt sl, pt
shd; wc; chem disp (wc); shwrs inc; lndry rm; el pnts (6-10A)
€2.60- 3.20 (poss long lead req); lndry rm; shops & rests nrby;
beach 1.5km; dogs €1.20; bus; no twin-axles; adv bkg; some
rd noise; red long stay; CKE/CCI. "Sm pitches poss diff long
o'fits." 1 Apr-31 Oct. € 11.10   2009*

AUDRUICQ see Ardres *3A3*

AUGIGNAC see Nontron *7B3*

AUGIREIN *8G3* (S Rural) *42.93151, 0.91917* **Camping La Vie
en Vert**, 09800 Augirein [05 61 96 82 66; fax 05 61 04 73 00;
daffis@lavieenvert.com; www.lavieenvert.com] Fr St Girons
on D618 twd Castillon. On app Castillon turn R foll sp to
Luchon. 1km after vill Orgibet turn L into vill of Augirein. Site
on L over bdge. Sm, hdg/mkd pitch, pt shd; wc; baby facs;
shwrs inc; el pnts (3-10A) €3-5; lndtte; shop; tradsmn; rest in
vill; BBQ; playgrnd; dogs €1; Eng spkn; adv bkg; quiet; red long
stay; CKE/CCI. "Charming owners who own bar/café in vill;
excel little site." ♦ 15 May-15 Sep. € 15.00   2009*

⊞ **AULUS LES BAINS** *8G3* (500m NW Rural) *42.79402,
1.33197* **Camp Municipal Le Coulédous**, 09140 Aulus-les-
Bains [05 61 66 43 56; campinglecouledous@orange.fr;
www.couledous.com] Take D618 fr St Girons. After 13km
cross rv; turn R onto D3 sp Aulus-les-Bains. On app to Oust
turn L onto D32, site approx 17km on R at ent to vill on rvside.
Med, mkd pitch, hdstg, sl, pt shd; htd wc; chem disp; mv
service pnt; shwrs inc; el pnts (6-10A) €4.50-6.50; lndtte; shop
500m; bar 300m, playgrnd; some statics; dogs €1; site clsd
mid-Nov to mid-Dec; poss cr; Eng spkn; adv bkg; quiet; CKE/
CCI. "Gd walking & skiing (16km); sm spa in vill; excel." ♦
€ 14.50   2010*

AUMALE *3C3* (500m W Rural) *49.76618, 1.74618* **Camp
Municipal Le Grand Mail**, Chemin du Grand Mail, 76390
Aumale [02 35 93 40 50 (Mairie); fax 02 35 93 86 79;
communeaumale@wanadoo.fr; www.aumale.com] Clearly
sp in town; long steep climb to ent. Med, pt shd; wc; mv
service pnt; shwrs €1.80; el pnts (6A) €2.40; lndtte; shops 1km;
playgrnd; pool 1km; cycle hire €1; fishing 1km; dogs €2; noise
fr rd. "Gd site; clean, modern san facs; conv Channel ports;
steep slope fr town to site." ♦ Easter-30 Sep. € 9.60   2009*

AUNAC see Mansle *7B2*

AUNAY SUR ODON *3D1* (500m NE Urban) *49.02530,
-0.62515* **Camp Municipal La Closerie**, Rue de Caen, 14260
Aunay-sur-Odon [02 31 77 32 46 or 07850 511893; fax
02 31 77 70 07; mairieaunaysurodon@orange.fr; www.
aunaysurodon.fr] Exit A84 junc 43 sp Villers-Bocage/Aunay
& take D6 twd Aunay. In approx 3km bef Aunay town sp, turn
L sp 'Zone Industrielle', in 200m turn R at rndabt. Site on R
in 100m nr sports stadium. Sm, mkd pitch, pt sl, pt shd; wc;
chem disp; mv service pnt; shwrs inc; el pnts €2.80; gas, shops
200m; games area; dogs €1.55; Eng spkn; quiet; CKE/CCI.
"Delightful, attractive vill; Sat mkt; vet avail; conv NH for Caen
ferry & gd touring base; helpful, welcoming warden" ♦ ltd
6 Jul - 31 Aug. € 7.50   2013*

⊞ **AUPS** *10E3* (300m SE Rural) *43.62525, 6.23103*
Camping Les Prés, 181 Route de Tourtour, 83630 Aups
[04 94 70 00 93; fax 04 94 70 14 41; lespres.camping@
wanadoo.fr; www.campinglespres.com] Fr cent of Aups
on rd to Tourtour, site on R. Rough rd. Med, hdg/mkd pitch,
pt shd; htd wc; baby facs; fam bthrm; shwrs inc; el pnts (4-6A)
€3.70; gas; lndtte; shop 300m; tradsmn; rest, snacks; bar;
playgrnd; pool; entmnt; TV rm; some statics; adv bkg; quiet.
"Peaceful, friendly site; Recep clsd 12:00 to 15:00; Ent not rec
for lge o'fits" € 15.50   2012*

AUPS *10E3* (500m W Rural) *43.62455, 6.21760*
International Camping, Route de Fox-Amphoux,
83630 Aups [04 94 70 06 80; fax 04 94 70 10 51;
info@internationalcamping-aups.com; www.
internationalcamping-aups.com] Site on L on D60 nr vill
cent. Lge, hdg/mkd pitch, pt shd; wc; chem disp; shwrs inc;
el pnts (16A) €5.30; lndtte; shop; tradsmn; snacks & rest high
ssn; bar; pool; tennis; games rm; entmnt; many statics (sep
area); dogs €1; Eng spkn; rec adv bkg high ssn; quiet; ccard
acc; red low ssn. "Vg site in beautiful area; lge pitches; gd
rest." 1 Apr-30 Sep. € 19.10   2009*

FRANCE

AUPS *10E3* (1km NW Rural) *43.63631, 6.20793* **Camping St Lazare, Route de Moissac, 83630 Aups [04 94 70 12 86; fax 04 94 70 01 55; camping.caravaning.st-lazare@orange. fr]** NW fr Aups twd Régusse on D9, site sp. Med, hdg/mkd pitch, pt sl, pt shd; wc (some cont); chem disp; baby facs; shwrs inc; el pnts (10A) €4; gas; lndtte; shop 1.5km; snacks; playgrnd; pool; paddling pool; games area; cycle hire; entmnt; 25% statics; dogs €1; phone; TV; 10% statics; adv bkg rec; CKE/CCI. "Excel touring base; poss unkempt low ssn; vg, quiet site." 1 Apr-30 Sep. € 16.10   2009*

AURAY *2F3* (5km SE Coastal) *47.64909, -2.92540* **Camp Municipal Kergouguec, Route de Bequerel, 56400 Plougoumelen [02 97 57 88 74; marie.plougoumelen@ wanadoo.fr; www.plougoumelen.fr]** Site is S of N165, 13km W of Vannes; sp fr vill sq 500m S on R, nr stadium. Med, pt sl, pt shd; wc (some cont); chem disp; shwrs; el pnts (6A) €3.16; playgrnd; beach & windsurfing 300m; tennis; dogs €1.58; adv bkg; quiet; CKE/CCI. "Well-run, under-used site; report (2011) site may close due to lack of visitors, phone ahead; gd touring base." ♦ 1 Jul-28 Aug. € 9.52   2011*

AURAY *2F3* (7km SE Rural) *47.64320, -2.89890* **Aire Naturelle La Fontaine du Hallate (Le Gloanic), 8 Chemin du Poul Fétan, La Hallate, 56400 Plougoumelen [09 64 04 90 16 or 06 16 30 08 33 (mob); clegloanic@orange.fr; www. camping-hallate.fr]** Fr N165 Vannes-Lorient, turn S onto D101E to Plougoumelen; watch for sp after Plougoumelen, site in La Hallate. Narr, bumpy app rd. Sm, hdg/mkd pitch, pt sl, pt shd; shwrs inc; el pnts (6A) €3.40 (poss rev pol); lndtte; shops 2km; playgrnd; golf/tennis adj; 2% statics; dogs €2.88; phone; adv bkg ess Jul/Aug; CKE/CCI. "Gd alternative to lge/noisier sites; gd coast paths; conv local boat trips & Ste Anne-d'Auray; vg." 29 Mar-24 Oct. € 15.95   2013*

AURAY *2F3* (5km S Rural) *47.64402, -2.93774* **FFCC Camping du Parc-Lann, 52 Rue Thiers, Le Varquez, 56400 Le Bono [02 97 57 93 93; campingduparclann@wanadoo.fr; www. lebono.fr]** S fr Auray on D101 sp Le Bono. Site well sp in Le Bono. Med, hdg/mkd pitch, pt shd; wc; chem disp; mv service pnt; baby facs; shwrs inc; el pnts (6A) €2.30; lndtte; ice; shop 2km; tradsm; rest, snacks; bar; BBQ; playgrnd; pool 5km; sand beach 9km; games area; dogs €0.70; bus; phone; red low ssn; CKE/CCI. "Lovely quiet site in pretty area; gd, clean san facs poss stretched high ssn & ltd low ssn; warden on site 1800-1900 only low ssn; gd walking." ♦ ltd 1 May-30 Sep. € 13.20   2009*

⊞ **AURAY** *2F3* (8km W Rural) *47.66406, -3.09985* **FFCC Camp Municipal Le St Laurent, Kergonvo, 56400 Ploemel [tel/fax 02 97 56 85 90; info@campingdesaintlaurent.com; www.campingdesaintlaurent.com]** Fr Auray on D22 twd Belz/Etel; after 8km turn L on D186 to Ploemel & site on L in 200m. Med, some hdstg, shd; htd wc; chem disp; mv service pnt; baby facs; shwrs inc; el pnts (10A) €4; lndtte; shop & 3km; rest; bar; BBQ; playgrnd; htd pool; paddling pool; sand beach 6km; games area; some statics; dogs €1.40; adv bkg; quiet. "Peaceful site; friendly staff; red facs low ssn." ♦ € 13.90   2010*

AUREILHAN see Mimizan *7D1*

AURIBEAU SUR SIAGNE see Grasse *10E4*

AURILLAC *7C4* (2km NE Urban) *44.93551, 2.45596* **Camp Municipal de l'Ombrade, Chemin du Gué Bouliaga, 15000 Aurillac [tel/fax 04 71 48 28 87]** Take D17 N fr Aurillac twd Puy-Mary; site on banks of Rv Jordanne. Well sp fr town. Lge, mkd pitch, pt sl, shd; wc; shwrs inc; el pnts (10A) €2.10; lndtte; shops adj; BBQ; entmnt; TV & games rm; dogs; quiet. "Well-managed, spacious site; lge pitches; old san facs, but clean; poss not well-kept low ssn; interesting, lge mkt town; vg." ♦ ltd 15 Jun-15 Sep. € 10.50   2010*

AURILLAC *7C4* (2km S Urban) *44.89858, 2.46265* **Camp Municipal de la Cère, Rue Félix Ramond, 15130 Arpajon-sur-Cère [tel/fax 04 71 64 55 07; sebastienpradel@yahoo. fr]** Fr Rodez take D920 twd Aurillac. Site sp 2km bef Aurillac on S side of Arpajon. Med, hdg pitch, pt shd; wc; shwrs inc; el pnts (10A) inc; gas; lndtte; shops adj; pool; rv fishing adj; beach 20km; sports facs adj; golf 5km; tennis; statics; dogs; adv bkg; some rd noise; ccard acc; CKE/CCI. "Pleasant site in pretty area; public access to site - not secure; generous pitches." ♦ ltd 1 Jun-30 Sep. € 14.10   2010*

AUSSOIS see Modane *9C4*

⊞ **AUTERIVE** *8F3* (1km S Rural) *43.34228, 1.48084* **Camp Municipal du Ramier, Allée Ramier, 31190 Auterive [05 61 50 65 73 or 05 61 08 33 98]** Turn E off D820 onto D622; cross rv bdge & immed turn R into no-thro-rd. Site at end. Sm, pt shd; htd wc; shwrs; el pnts (6A) €3.50; shop 1km; pool adj; tennis; rv fishing; many statics; quiet but poss noise fr disco. "Space found even when 'Complet' sign up but rec arr by 1730; fair NH." € 6.30   2008*

⊞ **AUTERIVE** *8F3* (7km NW Rural) *43.43109, 1.43504* **Camp Municipal Le Ramier, 31810 Vernet [05 61 08 33 98 or 05 61 08 50 47 (Mairie)]** Site at S exit of Vernet, sp fr D820 Toulouse-Pamiers rd. Med, shd; wc (some cont); chem disp; shwrs; el pnts (5A); shops adj; quiet. "Conv NH for Andorra; gd location by rv."   2008*

AUTHUILLE see Albert *3B3*

AUTRANS *9C3* (E Rural) *45.17520, 5.54770* **Kawan Village au Joyeux Réveil, Le Château, 38880 Autrans [04 76 95 33 44; fax 04 76 95 72 98; camping-au-joyeux-reveil@wanadoo. fr; www.camping-au-joyeux-reveil.fr]** Fr Villard-de-Lans take D531 to Lans-en-Vercors & turn L onto D106 to Autrans. On E side of vill site sp at 1st rndabt. NB App on D531 fr W fr Pont-en-Royans not rec - v narr rd & low tunnels. Med, mkd pitch, pt sl, pt shd; htd wc; chem disp; mv service pnt; baby facs; shwrs inc; el pnts (2-10A) €2-8; gas; lndtte (inc dryer); shop 300m; tradsmn; rest 300m; snacks; bar; BBQ; playgrnd; htd pool; paddling pool; waterslide; rv fishing; tennis 300m; cycle hire; golf 20km; games area; wifi; TV rm; cab TV to pitches; 60% statics; dogs; bus 300m; phone; quiet; adv bkg; Eng spkn; red low ssn; ccard acc; CKE/CCI. "Site in Vercors National Park with excel views; winter sport facs, 1050m altitude; modern san facs; excel." ♦ ltd 1 Dec-31 Mar & 1 May-30 Sep. € 30.00   2009*

AUTUN *6H1* (1km N Rural) *46.96478, 4.29381* **Camp Municipal de la Porte d'Arroux, Les Chaumottes, 71400 Autun [03 85 52 10 82; fax 03 86 37 79 20; camping. autun@orange.fr; www.camping-autun.com]** Foll sp fr town on D980 dir Saulieu & site on L; only site in Autun. Med, some hdg pitch, some hdstg, pt shd; wc (some cont); mv service pnt; baby facs; shwrs inc; el pnts (10A) €3.05; (poss rev pol); gas high ssn; lndry rm; shop; rest high ssn; snacks; playgrnd; rv sw & fishing; canoe & cycle hire; wifi; dogs €1.35; phone; Eng spkn; adv bkg; rd noise some pitches; ccard acc; red low ssn; CKE/CCI. "Lovely, quiet, clean site; busy NH high ssn; sm pitches, views fr some; friendly, helpful staff; gd san facs, poss stretched high ssn; no twin-axles; v muddy when wet (tow avail); vg, lively rest; medieval architecture & Roman walls around town; m'van Aire de Service nr lake in town; mkt Wed/ Fri." ♦ 1 Apr-31 Oct. € 16.00 (CChq acc) 2013*

AUVERS SUR OISE see Pontoise *3D3*

AUXERRE *4F4* (3km SE Urban) *47.78678, 3.58721* **Camp Municipal, 8 Rue de Vaux, 89000 Auxerre [03 86 52 11 15 or 03 86 72 43 00 (Mairie); fax 03 86 51 17 54; camping. mairie@auxerre.com; www.auxerre.com]** Exit A6 at Auxerre; at junc N6 ring rd foll sp Vaux & 'Stade'; site sp by Rv Yonne. Or fr N6 (N) take ring rd, site/stadium sp. Site also well sp fr town cent as 'L'Arbre Sec'. Lge, mkd pitch, pt shd; wc; chem disp; mv service pnt; shwrs inc; el pnts (6A) inc (long lead poss req); lndtte; shop; supmkt 400m; bar/café; playgrnd; pool 250m; fishing 300m; TV; 10% statics; dogs; adv bkg; quiet; ccard acc; CKE/CCI. "Lovely, peaceful, well-kept site; lge pitches; friendly staff; gd clean san facs; poss cr & noisy during football ssn; site poss flooded stormy weather; no c'vans/ m'vans over 5m; ltd el pnts for site size; no vehicles 2200-0700; pretty town; popular NH." 15 Apr-30 Sep. € 12.80 2011*

AUXERRE *4F4* (10km S Rural) *47.70704, 3.63563* **FFCC Camping Les Ceriselles, Route de Vincelottes, 89290 Vincelles [03 86 42 50 47; fax 03 86 42 39 39; camping@ cc-payscoulangeois.fr; www.campingceriselles.com]** Leave A6 at Auxerre Sud. Fr Auxerre, take D606 S twd Avallon. 10km fr Auxerre turn L into Vincelles. In 400m immed after 'Maxi Marche', turn L into site access rd, sp as Camping Les Ceriselles. Site is approx 16km fr a'route exit. Med, mkd pitch, some hdstg, pt shd; htd wc; chem disp; mv service pnt; baby facs; shwrs inc; el pnts (10A) inc (poss rev pol); gas adj; lndtte (inc dryer); sm supmkt adj; tradsmn; rests 500m; snacks; bar; BBQ; playgrnd; sm pool; rv adj; cycle hire; wifi; TV rm; 10% statics; dogs free (2nd €1.50); phone; no twin-axles; poss v cr; some Eng spkn; adv bkg; quiet but rd noise; ccard acc; high ssn overflow area; red long stay/low ssn; CKE/CCI. "Excel, busy site by canal, poss full late Jun; sm pitches, tight lge o'fits; friendly, helpful owner; gd san facs, poss insufficient high ssn & ltd low ssn; lovely walks to vill & along canal; cycle track to Auxerre & Clamecy; highly rec." ♦ 1 Apr-30 Sep. € 22.00 (CChq acc) 2013*

AUXI LE CHATEAU *3B3* (500m NW Rural) *50.2341, 2.1058* **Camp Municipal des Peupliers, 22 Rue du Cheval, 62390 Auxi-le-Château [03 21 41 10 79; fax 03 21 04 10 22; www. ternois-tourisme.com / www.ville-auxilechateau.fr]** Fr S on D925, turn N onto D933 at Bernaville to Auxi-le-Château; turn W onto D941; then turn R in 300m into Rue du Cheval; site sp on R in 500m by football stadium. Or take D928 S fr Hesdin; in 11km take D119 to Auxi-le-Château. Med, hdg pitch; unshd; wc; chem disp; shwrs inc; el pnts (3-6A) €1.85; lndtte; shops, rest, snacks & bar 500m; playgrnd; fishing; sailing; dir access to rv; 80% statics; poss cr; adv bkg; quiet; ccard acc; "Easy walk into town" 1 Apr-30 Sep. € 8.90 2013*

⊞ **AUXONNE** *6G1* (500m NW Rural) *47.19838, 5.38120* **Camping L'Arquebuse, Route d'Athée, 21130 Auxonne [03 80 31 06 89; fax 03 80 31 13 62; camping.arquebuse@ wanadoo.fr; www.campingarquebuse.com]** On D905 Dijon-Geneva, site sp on L bef bdge at ent to Auxonne. Med, pt shd; htd wc (some cont); chem disp; mv service pnt; shwrs inc; el pnts (10A) €3.70 (poss rev pol); gas; lndry rm; shop 500m; rest, snacks; bar; BBQ; playgrnd; htd pool adj; fishing; sailing; windsurfing; waterskiing; wifi; entmnt; TV rm; 20% statics; dogs €1.80; adv bkg; quiet; clsd 2200-0700; CKE/ CCI. "Pleasant rvside site; friendly staff; san facs poss tatty; poss busy w/ends as NH; interesting town; Child friendly site" € 26.30 2013*

AVAILLES LIMOUZINE see Pressac *7A3*

AVAILLES LIMOUZINE *7A3* (7km E Rural) *46.12342, 0.65975* **FFCC Camp Municipal Le Parc, 86460 Availles-Limouzine [05 49 48 51 22; fax 05 49 48 66 76; camping.leparc@ wanadoo.fr; www.campingleparc.monsite-orange.fr]** Fr Confolens N on D948 & turn R on D34 to Availles-Limouzine. Site on Rv Vienne by town bdge. Med, pt shd; wc; chem disp; mv service pnt; shwrs inc; el pnts (10A) inc; gas; shops 750m; playgrnd; lge paddling pool; dogs €2.65; poss cr; Eng spkn; adv bkg; quiet; CKE/CCI. "Attractive, well-run site in beautiful position; rv views; vg playgrnd; barrier clsd 2200-0800; poss scruffy low ssn; vg value; permanent warden." ♦ 1 May-30 Sep. € 17.40 2013*

AVALLON *4G4* (2km SE Rural) *47.48030, 3.91246* **Camp Municipal Sous Roches, Rue Sous Roche; 89200 Avallon [tel/fax 03 86 34 10 39; campingsousroche@ville-avallon.fr; www6.campingsousroche.com]** App town fr a'route or fr SE on N6. Turn sharp L at 2nd traff lts in town cent, L in 2km at sp Vallée du Cousin (bef bdge), site 250m on L. If app fr S care needed when turning R after bdge. Med, some hdstg pitches, terr, pt shd; wc; mv service pnt; shwrs inc; el pnts (6A) €3.50; lndtte; shop; tradsmn; snacks 1km; rest 2km; BBQ; playgrnd; pool 1km; rv & fishing adj; wifi; dogs free; phone adj; CKE/ CCI. "Popular, well-kept site in lovely location nr rv; friendly, helpful staff; excel immac san facs; conv Morvan National Park; poss flood warning after heavy rain; no twin-axles or o'fits over 2,500kg; attractive town; excel." ♦ 1 Apr-15 Oct. € 19.50 2013*

AVANTON see Poitiers *7A2*

AVIGNON *10E2* (2km N Rural) *43.97063, 4.79928* **Camp Municipal de la Laune, Chemin St Honoré, 30400 Villeneuve-lès-Avignon [tel/fax 04 90 25 76 06 or 04 90 25 61 33; campingdelalaune@wanadoo.fr; www. camping-villeneuvelezavignon.com]** Fr Avignon, take N100 twd Nîmes over rv bdge. At W end of 2nd part of rv bdge, turn R onto N980 Sp Villeneuve-lès-Avignon. Site is 3km on R just past town battlements on L. Adj sports complex. Med, hdg/mkd pitch, hdstg, shd; wc; chem disp; mv service pnt; shwrs inc; el pnts (6A) €3.10 (poss rev pol); lndtte; shop; snacks; bar; pool & sports complex adj (free to campers); wifi in vill sq; dogs €1.50; phone; bus; Eng spkn; quiet; ccard acc; red low ssn; CKE/CCI. "Lovely, peaceful well-run site; gd, clean facs; helpful staff; excel security; sports facs adj; gd walks/cycle rides; in walking dist of Villeneuve-lès-Avignon with fort & abbey; gd bus to Avignon; vg local mkt." ♦ ltd 1 Apr-15 Oct. € 28.30   2013*

AVIGNON *10E2* (4km NE Rural) *43.97651, 4.88475* **Camping du Grand Bois, 1340 Chemin du Grand Bois, Quartier La Tapy, 84130 Le Pontet [04 90 31 37 44; fax 04 90 31 46 53; campinglegrandbois@orange.fr; www. campinglegrandbois.webeasysite.fr]** Exit A7/E714 at junc 23 onto D53 S, Chemin du Pont Blanc. At rndabt turn onto Chemin du Grand Bois, site on R, sp. Med, hdg pitch, pt shd; wc; chem disp; shwrs inc; el pnts (5A) €3; lndtte; shop; hypmkt 3km; tradsmn; rest, snacks; playgrnd; cycle hire; wifi; TV; dogs €2; phone; Eng spkn; adv bkg; quiet; ccard acc; CKE/CCI. "Superb location; plenty of rm; family-run alt to main Avignon sites; ltd facs; helpful staff; insects poss a problem." ♦ 15 May-15 Sep. € 26.00   2009*

AVIGNON *10E2* (8km S Urban) *43.88361, 4.87010* **Camping de la Roquette, 746 Ave Jean Mermoz, 13160 Châteaurenard [04 90 94 46 81; fax 09 72 14 01 53; contact@camping-la-roquette.com; www.camping-la-roquette.com]** Exit A7/D907 Avignon S to Noves; take D28 to Châteaurenard 4km; foll sp to site & Piscine Olympic/Complex Sportiv. Med, hdg/mkd pitch, pt shd; wc; chem disp; some serviced pitches; mv service pnt; baby facs; shwrs inc; el pnts (10A) €4; lndtte; shops 1.5km; tradsmn; rest, snacks; bar; playgrnd; pool; paddling pool; tennis; wif; dogs €2; phone; TV; Eng spkn; adv bkg rec; quiet but rd noise; ccard acc; red low ssn; CKE/CCI. "Gd touring cent; sm pitches; owners friendly, helpful; clean facs; gd walks." ♦ ltd 1 Apr-31 Oct. € 37.00   2013*

AVIGNON *10E2* (12km W Rural) *43.95155, 4.66451* **Camping Le Bois des Ecureuils, 947 Chemin De La Beaume, 30390 Domazan [tel/fax 04 66 57 10 03; infos@boisdesecureuils.com; www.boisdesecureuils.com]** Exit A9/E15 at Remoulins junc 23 twd Avignon on N100. Site on R in 6km. Fr S on N7 foll sp for Nîmes onto N100. Go over 2 lge rndabts, site about 6km on L at rndabt. Sm, mkd pitch, all hdstg, shd; wc (some cont); chem disp (wc); baby facs; shwrs inc; el pnts (6A) inc; gas; lndtte; shop; rest adj; snacks; bar high ssn; BBQ; playgrnd; htd pool; entmnt; TV; 5% statics; dogs €1.70; phone; poss cr; Eng spkn; adv bkg (rec high ssn); quiet but some rd noise; red low ssn CKE/CCI. "Ideal for touring Avignon & Pont du Gard; friendly owners; clean facs; steel awning pegs ess; many long-stay residents low ssn." € 20.00   2013*

AVIGNON *10E2* (500m NW Urban) *43.95216, 4.79946* **FFCC Camping Bagatelle, Ile de la Barthelasse, 84000 Avignon [04 90 86 30 39; fax 04 90 27 16 23; camping. bagatelle@wanadoo.fr; www.campingbagatelle.com]** Exit D907 at Avignon Nord. After passing end of old bdge bear L, then onto new Daladier bdge & take immed R turn over bdge foll sp to Barthelasse & Villeneuve-lès-Avignon. Caution - do not foll Nîmes sp at more southerly bdge (Pont d'Europe). Lge, mkd pitch, pt shd; htd wc; mv service pnt; baby facs; shwrs inc; el pnts (6-10A) €3.50-4.50; gas; lndtte; shop; rest; pool 100m; playgrnd; boating; fishing; tennis 2km; games area; entmnt; dogs €2.40; some traffic noise at night; ccard acc; red low ssn/CKE/CCI. "Busy site on rv bank; sm pitches; helpful staff; facs dated but clean; ltd low ssn & poss stretched high ssn; narr site rds, suggest find pitch bef driving in; if recep unmanned, go to bar or supmkt to check in; free ferry to town; site low lying & poss damp; highly rec." ♦ € 35.05   2013*

AVIGNON *10E2* (5km NW Rural) *43.99573, 4.81843* **Campéole Camping L'Ile des Papes, Quartier l'Islon, 30400 Villeneuve-lès-Avignon [04 90 15 15 90; fax 04 90 15 15 91; ile-des-papes@campeole.com; www. avignon-camping.com or www.campeole.com]** Fr A9 exit sp Roquemaure; head S on D980. Site adj to rv 2km NW of city. Fr D907 (A7) exit Avignon Nord, twds Avignon cent & cross bdge twds Villeneuve. Turn off after x-ing rv before x-ing canal. Site bet rv & canal. Lge, pt shd; wc; shwrs; el pnts (6A) €4; lndtte; cooking facs; rest; supmkt; playgrnd; pool; archery; lake fishing adj; hiking; entmnt; TV; statics 35%; dogs €3.50; adv bkg; quiet but some rlwy noise; Eng spkn; red low ssn; ccard acc; red low ssn/CKE/CCI. "Lovely area; well-run site; pleasant staff; lge pitches; gd site rest." ♦ 27 Mar-6 Nov. € 25.10 (CChq acc)   2012*

See advertisement on pages 14 & 15

AVRANCHES *2E4* (6km S Rural) *48.62092, -1.36556* **FFCC Camping Rural Avallonn (Martinet), La Caufetière, 50220 Céaux [02 33 68 39 47]** Fr Avranches on N175 exit La Buvette & W onto D43. Site in approx 2km. Sm, pt shd; wc; shwrs inc; el pnts (5A) €3.50; rest, snacks; playgrnd; pool; sand beach 20km; dogs; Eng spkn; adv bkg; quiet. "In apple orchard; friendly, helpful owners; clean, rustic san facs; goats & horses in pens on site; many activities, museums nrby; 10km fr Mont-St Michel; uneven grnd, steep & narr ent but gd NH." ♦ 15 Apr-30 Sep. € 14.10   2009*

AVRANCHES *2E4* (10km W Rural) *48.69663, -1.47434* **FFCC Camping La Pérame, 50530 Genêts [02 33 70 82 49; www. wix.com/campinglaperame/home]** Fr Avranches on N175; in 1km turn L on D911 thro Genêts. Turn R onto D35 immed after passing thro Genêts, site on R in 1km. Sm, pt shd; wc; shwrs inc; el pnts (10A) €3 (rev pol); tradsmn; farm produce; playgrnd; 60% statics; dogs €0.90; phone; poss cr; red low ssn; quiet; CKE/CCI. "CL-type site in apple orchard nr sm vill; pleasant owner; gd views of Mont-St Michel fr vill; poss ltd & unkempt low ssn; poss boggy after heavy rain; guided walks to Mont St Michel; rec." 1 May-30 Sep. € 12.50   2011*

AVRILLE 7A1 (500m N Rural) 46.47641, -1.49373
**Camping Le Domaine des Forges, Rue des Forges,
85440 Avrillé [02 51 22 38 85; fax 02 51 90 98 70;
contact@campingdomainedesforges.com; www.
campingdomainedesforges.com or www.les-castels.com]**
Fr N on D747 turn R at Moutiers-les-Mauxfaits onto D19 to
Avrillé. In town cent cont strt & after sm rndabt foll yellow/
white site sp. Turn R into Rue des Forges, site on R in 600m.
Med, mkd pitch, pt shd; wc; chem disp; mv service pnt; baby
facs; shwrs; el pnts (16A) inc; gas; lndtte (inc dryer); sm shop;
snacks; bar; BBQ; playgrnd; 2 pools, 1 htd, covrd; paddling
pool; lake fishing; sand beach 10km; tennis; cycle hire; fitness
rm; games area; games rm; wifi; entmnt; TV; dogs €4; no
c'vans/m'vans over 10m Apr-Oct; Eng spkn; adv bkg; ccard acc;
red low ssn. "Attractive site in lovely location; spacious, well-
kept pitches; helpful, friendly owner; gd, clean, modern san
facs; lots of fish in lake; highly rec." ♦ 30 Mar-29 Sep. € 43.40
SBS - A43   2013*

AVRILLE 7A1 (1km E Rural) 46.47005, -1.48691 **Camping
Le Beauchêne, Ave de Lattre de Tassigny, 85440 Avrillé
[02 51 22 30 49; fax 02 51 22 37 60; campinglebeauchene@
club-internet.fr; www.lebeauchene.com]** On E o'skts of
Avrillé, on D949, visible fr rd. Med, mkd pitch, unshd, wc;
chem disp; baby facs; shwrs inc; el pnts (6A) €3; lndtte; shops
500m; tradsmn; snacks; rest adj; BBQ; playgrnd; htd pool;
sand beach 9km; games area; entmnt; TV rm; 40% statics;
dogs €3; poss cr; Eng spkn; adv bkg; rd noise; CKE/CCI. "On
o'skts of Avrillé; friendly, helpful owners; pitches well packed
in; gd facs; fair." ♦ 1 May-6 Sep. € 14.00   2008*

See advertisement on pages 32 & 33

AVRILLE 7A1 (1km S Rural) 46.45578, -1.48365 **Camping
Les Mancellières, Route de Longeville-sur-Mer, 85440
Avrillé [02 51 90 35 97; fax 02 51 90 39 31; camping.
mancellieres@wanadoo.fr; www.lesmancellieres.com]**
Fr Avrillé take D105 S twd Longeville-sur-Mer. Site on L in
1.5km. Med, hdg/mkd pitch, pt sl; wc (some cont); chem disp;
baby facs; shwrs inc; el pnts (6A) €3.90; gas; lndtte; shop;
snacks; BBQ (charcoal/gas); playgrnd; htd pool; paddling pool;
waterslide; beach 5km; fishing 2km; tennis 800m; cycle hire;
horseriding 3km; games rm; entmnt; 30% statics; dogs €2;
some Eng spkn; adv bkg; quiet; 30% red low ssn; ccard not
acc. "Friendly owners; peaceful; ent gates set on angle & poss
diff lge o'fits." ♦ 1 May-15 Sep. € 17.00   2009*

⊞ **AX LES THERMES** 8G4 (2km NE Rural) 42.73308,
1.85386 **FFCC Camp Municipal La Prade, 09110 Sorgeat
[05 61 64 36 34 or 05 61 64 21 93; fax 05 61 64 63 38;
camping@sorgeat.com; www.sorgeat.com]** In cent of
Ax-les-Thermes turn E off N20 onto D613. In 5km in Sorgeat
turn R & foll sp thro vill to site, 800m on R. V steep, winding,
narr app with hairpins - not rec lge car/c'van o'fits. Sm, hdg/
mkd pitch, terr, pt shd; htd wc (some cont); chem disp; shwrs
inc; el pnts (5-10A) €2.80-5.40; lndtte; shop 1km; rest 5km;
snacks; playgrnd; pool 5km; 15% statics; dogs €0.60; phone;
poss cr; adv bkg; quiet; ccard not acc; CKE/CCI. "Clean site
1150m high o'looking Ariège valley; ski lifts at Ax; gd walks;
not suitable lge o'fits." € 10.00   2008*

⊞ **AX LES THERMES** 8G4 (7km E Rural) 42.72421,
1.89311 **FFCC Camping Ascou La Forge, 09110 Ascou
[05 61 64 60 03; fax 05 61 64 60 06; mountain.sports@
wanadoo.fr; www.mountain-sports.net]** On N20 S turn L
at rndabt by church in Ax sp Ascou. In 4km turn R sp Ascou-
Pailhères. Foll site sp to site on R in 3km after lake & hamlet
Goulours. Rd narr & mountainous, not rec med/lge o'fits. Sm,
mkd pitch, pt sl, pt shd; wc; chem disp; shwrs inc; el pnts
(4-10A) €3-5; lndtte; shop & 7km; tradsmn; bar; playgrnd;
fishing; entmnt; dogs €1.50; adv bkg; red low ssn; CKE/CCI.
"Mountain scenery; simple, immac facs; gd walking; charming,
helpful Dutch owners." ♦ € 15.00   2008*

⊞ **AX LES THERMES** 8G4 (4km SE Rural) 42.70245, 1.88345
**Camp Municipal Les Ioules, 09110 Orlu [05 61 64 21 70;
fax 05 61 64 64 23; camping.orlu@orange.fr]** On N20 S foll
sp for Spain thro town cent. On exit town turn L immed bef
bdge sp Orlu. Site on R in 3km. Med, mkd pitch, pt shd; htd
wc; mv service pnt; shwrs inc; el pnts (6A) €3.95; gas; lndtte;
shop 3km; rest, snacks, bar 500m; playgrnd; pool high ssn; rv
adj; fishing; games area; entmnt; 30% statics; dogs €2; phone;
poss cr; adv bkg; quiet; CKE/CCI. "Gd, friendly, scenic site; poss
floods in bad weather; excel walks; conv Andorra or Spain." ♦
€ 13.30   2010*

⊞ **AX LES THERMES** 8G4 (1km NW Rural) 42.72870,
1.82541 **Camping Sunêlia Le Malazéou, 09110 Ax-les-
Thermes [05 61 64 69 14; fax 05 61 64 65 00; camping.
malazeou@wanadoo.fr; www.campingmalazeou.com]**
Sp on N20 to Foix. Lge, hdg pitch, pt sl, shd; htd wc (some cont);
chem disp; mv service pnt; baby facs; shwrs inc; el pnts (6A) inc;
gas; lndry rm; shop & 1km; tradsmn; playgrnd; 70% statics; dogs
€3; train 500m; site poss clsd Nov; Eng spkn; adv bkg; quiet but
some rd noise; red low ssn; CKE/CCI. "Pleasant site by rv; lovely
scenery; gd fishing; gd heated san facs; rvside walk to town; gd."
♦ ltd € 37.00   2013*

⊞ **AX LES THERMES** 8G4 (8km NW Rural) 42.75880,
1.76319 **Camp Municipal Le Castella, 09250 Luzenac
[05 61 64 47 53; fax 05 61 64 40 59; campinglecastella@
orange.fr; www.campingcastella.com]** Site on W of N20
bet Ax-les-Thermes & Foix. Med, mkd pitch, terr, pt shd;
htd wc; shwrs inc; el pnts (4-10A) €3-5.95; lndtte; shop, bar
300m; playgrnd; pool in ssn; fishing; tennis; archery; entmnt;
70% statics; quiet; ccard acc; red low ssn. "Mountain views;
gd walking; prehistoric caves at Niaux; barrier locked until 0900
when office opens." ♦ € 13.20   2010*

AXAT 8G4 (2km E Rural) 42.80775, 2.25408 **Camping de
la Crémade, 11140 Axat [tel/fax 04 68 20 50 64; www.
lacremade.com]** S fr Quillan on D117, cont 1km beyond junc
with D118 twd Perpignan. Turn R into site, sp, narr access. Med,
hdg pitch, pt sl; wc; chem disp; shwrs inc; el pnts (6A)
€2.50; lndtte; shop & 3km; BBQ; playgrnd; games rm; 5% statics;
dogs €1; Eng spkn; adv bkg; quiet; CKE/CCI. "Pleasant, well-
maintained site in beautiful location; few level pitches." ♦
1 May-24 Sep. € 12.50   2010*

AYDAT *9B1* (2km NE Rural) *45.66777, 2.98943* **Camping du Lac d'Aydat, Forêt du Lot, 63970 Aydat [04 73 79 38 09; fax 04 73 79 34 12; info@camping-lac-aydat.com; www. camping-lac-aydat.com]** Exit A75 S fr Clermont-Ferrand at junc 5 onto D13 W. Foll sp Lake Aydat. At x-rds at end of Rouillas-Bas, turn L at rndabt & foll site sp. Med, mkd pitch, some hdstg, terr, shd; wc (some cont); chem disp; mv service pnt; serviced pitches; shwrs inc; el pnts (10A) €4; lndtte; shop 1km; tradsmn high ssn; rest 500m; snacks; bar 500m; playgrnd; lake sw 500m; fishing; entmnt; 30% statics; dogs €1.50; phone; poss cr; adv bkg; quiet; red low ssn; CKE/CCI. "On shore of Lake Aydat; gd for m'vans; Charming woodland pitches, facs tired." ♦ 1 Apr-30 Sep. € 24.00   2012*

AYDAT *9B1* (3km W Rural) *45.66195, 2.94857* **Camping Les Volcans, La Garandie, 63970 Aydat [tel/fax 04 73 79 33 90; campinglesvolcans@akeonet.com; www. campinglesvolcans.com]** Fr N exit A75 junc 2 onto D2089 dir Bourboule; in 18km turn S onto D213 to Verneuge; in 1km fork R onto D5 dir Murol; in 1.5km turn R onto D788 sp La Grandie; turn R into vill; turn R again & site on L in 100m. Fr S exit A73 junc 5 onto D213 W; in 16km turn S in Verneuge onto D5; after 1.5km turn W onto D788 sp La Garandie; in vill turn R just after phone box, site on L in 100m. Sm, mkd pitch, pt sl, pt shd; wc; chem disp; mv service pnt; shwrs inc; el pnts (6A) €5; lndtte; sm shop; tradsmn; rest 4km; snacks; bar; playgrnd; htd pool; lake sw, sand beach & water sports 3km; horseriding 3km; games area; wifi; 2% statics; dogs €2; phone adj; Eng spkn; adv bkg; quiet; red low ssn. "Relaxing site; friendly, helpul new owners improving (2011); lge pitches; no twin-axles; excel walking & cycle rtes nr; beautiful area; gd touring base; excel." 1 May-30 Sep. € 18.00   2011*

⊞ **AZAY LE FERRON** *4H2* (8km N Rural) *46.91949, 1.03679* **Camping Le Cormier, Route de St Flovier, 36290 Obterre [02 54 39 27 95 or 0844 232 7271 (UK); mike@ loireholidays.biz; www.loireholidays.biz]** Fr Azay-le-Ferron N on D14, site on R just N of Obterre. Or fr Loches S on D943 for 3.5km, turn onto D41 to St Flovier then turn L onto D21 sp Obterre. In 1km turn R onto D14, site on L in 4km. Sm, hdg/ mkd pitch, hdstg, pt shd; htd wc; chem disp; shwrs inc; el pnts (8A) €4; lndry rm; ice; tradsmn; rest, snacks & bar 5km; BBQ; pool; games area; games rm; wifi; TV; dogs free; Eng spkn; adv bkg; twin axle acc; quiet; red low ssn. "Friendly, helpful British owners (CC members); spacious pitches; gd san facs; excel touring/walking base; nr Brenne National Park; excel birdwatching; vg." € 19.00   2013*

AZAY LE FERRON *4H2* (E Rural) *46.85086, 1.07306* **Camp Municipal Le Camp du Château, Rue Hersent-Luzarche, 36290 Azay-le-Ferron [02 54 39 21 91 (Mairie); mairieazayleferron@mcom.fr]** On D975 Châtillon-sur-Indre to Le Bland, turn R in vill onto D925, site on R in 100m. Sm, pt shd; wc (some cont); shwrs inc; el pnts (10A) inc; shops 100m; rest; playgrnd; fishing; tennis; quiet. "Warden calls pm." 15 Apr-15 Oct. € 10.00   2008*

AZAY LE RIDEAU *4G1* (300m E Urban) *47.25919, 0.46992* **FFCC Camp Municipal Le Sabot, Rue du Stade, 37190 Azay-le-Rideau [02 47 45 42 72 or 02 47 45 42 11 (Mairie); fax 02 47 45 49 11; camping.lesabot@wanadoo.fr; www. azaylerideau.fr]** Best app is fr D751 by-pass to avoid narr town - ignore Azay-le-Rideau sps until Carrefour rndabt. Strt ahead for 1km, site visible at 2nd rndabt. Lge, mkd pitch, pt shd; wc (some cont); chem disp; mv service pnt; shwrs inc; el pnts (10A) €4.50 (poss rev pol); gas 1km; shop, snacks, rest in town; BBQ; htd pool adj; playgrnd; fishing; wifi; TV; phone; dogs; poss cr fr Son et Lumière in high ssn; Eng spkn; adv bkg rec; quiet; ccard acc; red low ssn/long stay; CKE/CCI. "Pleasant, spacious, scenic site by rv & chateau; friendly, helpful recep; poss long dist to san facs fr some pitches - central facs have steps; san facs stretched high ssn, ltd low ssn; site prone to flooding; recep open 0800-1200 & 1400-1700; when site clsd m'vans can stay on car park by rv o'night - no facs but well lit (enq at tourist office); gd loc nr to town and rests." ♦ 1 Apr-31 Oct. € 18.50   2012*

AZAY SUR THOUET see Parthenay *4H1*

AZUR see Soustons *8E1*

BACCARAT *6E2* (1km SE Rural) *48.44360, 6.74360* **Camp Municipal Pré de Hon, 54120 Baccarat [03 83 76 35 35 or 03 83 75 13 37 (LS); fax 03 83 75 36 76; info-baccarat@ orange.fr; www.ot-baccarat.fr]** Fr Baccarat cent opp town hall take D158 S past church twd Lachapelle. Site in 500m down lane on L. Sm, pt shd, wc; chem disp; shwrs; el pnts (10A) €4; shop 200m; pool nr; bus 400m; poss cr; adv bkg; quiet, some rd noise; CKE/CCI. "Pleasant, quiet rvside site; pleasant, helpful warden, if absent site yourself; vg san facs; rvside walk to interesting town; gd NH." ♦ ltd 30 Apr-10 Oct. € 9.40   2013*

BADEN *2F3* (500m SW Rural) *47.61410, -2.92540* **Camping Mané Guernehué, 52 Rue Mané er Groëz, 56870 Baden [02 97 57 02 06; fax 02 97 57 15 43; info@camping-baden. com; www.camping-baden.com]** Exit N165 sp Arradon/L'Ile aux Moines onto D101 to Baden (10km); in Baden vill turn R at camp sp immed after sharp L-hand bend; in 200m bear R at junc; site on R. Sp at both ends of vill. Lge, hdg/mkd pitch, terr, pt shd; htd wc; chem disp; mv service pnt; sauna; baby facs; some serviced pitches; shwrs inc; el pnts (10A) €4.70; gas 1km; lndtte (inc dryer); sm shop; rest/snacks; bar; BBQ; playgrnd; lge htd pool complex (covrd & outdoor); paddling pool; waterslide; jacuzzi; sand beach 3km; fishing; tennis 600m; fitness rm; games area; games rm; cycle hire; golf 1.5km; wifi; entmnt; TV rm; 35% statics; dogs €3.90; phone; Eng spkn; quiet; ccard acc; red low ssn/long stay. "Mature, pleasant site; gd views; excel san facs; some narr site rds; excel." ♦ 9 Apr-31 Oct. € 39.00 (CChq acc)   2011*

BAERENTHAL *5D3* (500m N Rural) *48.98170, 7.51230* **Camp Municipal Ramstein-Plage, Rue de Ramstein, 57230 Baerenthal [tel/fax 03 87 06 50 73; camping.ramstein@ wanadoo.fr; www.baerenthal.eu]** Fr N62 turn onto D36 sp Baerenthal, site sp on lakeside. Lge, hdg/mkd pitch, pt sl, pt shd; htd wc; chem disp; mv service pnt; baby facs; shwrs inc; el pnts (12A) €3.50; lndtte; shop 1km; rest, snacks; bar; playgrnd; htd pool; lake sw, sand beach adj; tennis; games area; entmnt; 80% statics (sep area); dogs €1.90; m'van o'night area; poss cr; Eng spkn; adv bkg; quiet. "Attractive location in important ecological area; generous pitches; modern san facs; gd walks; birdwatching; conv Maginot Line; excel." ♦ ltd 1 Apr-30 Sep. € 28.15   2013*

BAGNEAUX SUR LOING see Nemours *4F3*

BAGNERES DE BIGORRE *8F2* (9km NE Rural) *43.11196, 0.04931* **Aire Naturelle Le Cerf Volant (Dhom), 7 Cami de la Géline, 65380 Orincles [tel/fax 05 62 42 99 32; lecerfvolant1@yahoo.fr]** Fr Bagnères-de-Bigorre on D935; turn L onto D937 dir Lourdes; site on L opp D407. Single track app rd for 150m. Sm, pt shd; wc; chem disp; shwrs inc; el pnts (15A) €2.30; lndtte; tradsmn; playgrnd; no statics; dogs free; poss cr; no ccard acc; CKE/CCI. "Farm site - produce sold Jul-Aug; conv Lourdes & touring Pyrenees; gd, clean site." ♦ 15 May-15 Oct. € 7.70   2010*

BAGNERES DE BIGORRE *8F2* (1km E Urban) *43.07158, 0.15692* **Camping Les Fruitiers, 9 Rue de Toulouse, 65200 Bagnères-de-Bigorre [tel/fax 05 62 95 25 97; daniellevillemur@wanadoo.fr; www.camping-les-fruitiers.com]** NE fr town cent on D938 dir Toulouse; in 500m turn L at traff lits at x-rds onto D8; site on R in 50m. Site well sp on app; take care on final app to ent. Med, mkd pitch, pt sl, pt shd; htd wc; chem disp; baby facs; shwrs inc; el pnts (4-6A) €3.40-5; lndtte; shops 200m; rest 300m; snacks 200m; playgrnd; pool 200m; tennis; dogs €1; phone; bus; poss cr; adv bkg; quiet/some traff noise; ccard acc; CKE/CCI. "Lovely, well-kept site; helpful staff; excel facs; sharp bends on site rds & o'hanging trees poss diff lge o'fits; attractive town with thermal baths; gd touring base; vg mkt; vg." ♦ Apr-Oct. € 12.60   2011*

BAGNERES DE BIGORRE *8F2* (3km E Rural) *43.08180, 0.15139* **Camping Le Monlôo, 6 Route de la Plaine, 65200 Bagnères-de-Bigorre [tel/fax 05 62 95 19 65; campingmonloo@yahoo.com; www.lemonloo.com]** Fr A64 exit junc 14 onto D20/D938 to Bagnères-de-Bigorre. At traff lts on ent turn R onto D8, site on R in 1km, sp at ent. Fr Tarbes (N) on D935 turn L at 1st rndabt, L again over old rlwy line, site in R. Med, sl, pt shd; wc; chem disp; mv service pnt; shwrs inc; el pnts (10A) €5.20; lndtte; shop 1km; playgrnd; pool (high ssn); waterslide; tennis; entmnt; wifi; TV; 30% statics; phone; dogs €1.50; Eng spkn; adv bkg; quiet; ccard acc; red low ssn; CKE/CCI. "Pleasant, peaceful, scenic site; spacious & well-kept site; friendly, welcoming, helpful owners; ltd water points; gd facs, poss stretched high ssn; pleasant town; conv Pyrenean mountain passes; nice views of Pyrenees" ♦ 1 Jan-19 Oct, 10 Nov-31 Dec. € 30.75 (3 persons)   2013*

⊞ **BAGNERES DE BIGORRE** *8F2* (2km SE Rural) *43.05566, 0.16510* **Camping La Pommeraie, 2 Ave Philadelphe, 65200 Gerde [05 62 91 32 24; fax 05 62 95 16 42]** App fr E, exit A64 junc 14 (Tournay) onto D20/D938 to Bagnères-de-Bigorre; on ent town turn L at traff lts & foll sp to site. App fr W, exit A64 junc 12 (Tarbes); leave ring rd at junc with D935 & cont to Bagnères-de-Bigorre; foll site sps fr town. Sm, mkd pitch, some hdstg, pt sl, pt shd; wc; chem disp; shwrs inc; el pnts (6A) inc; gas 2km; lndry area; shop 2km; BBQ; sm playgrnd; htd, covrd pool 2km; cycle hire in Bagnères; some statics; dogs; phone; Eng spkn; adv bkg; quiet; CKE/CCI. "Mountain views; friendly owners; excel walking, mountain biking & touring base; vg." € 16.80   2008*

BAGNERES DE BIGORRE *8F2* (6km S Rural) *43.01777, 0.17567* **Camping FFCC Le Layris, Quartier Bourg, 65710 Campan [05 62 91 75 34; lelayris@campan-pyrenees.com; www.campan-pyrenees.com]** Exit A64 junc 14 S on D20/ D938 to Bagnères. Fr Bagnères, take D935 S, site on R after ent to Campan, sp. Sm, mkd pitch, pt shd; htd wc (cont); chem disp; shwrs inc; el pnts (8A) €7.50; lndtte; shops adj; playgrnd; pool 5km; fishing; tennis adj; wintersports 12km; dogs; poss cr; adv bkg; quiet; CKE/CCI. "Gd site for walkers. " 1 Jan-1 Oct. € 12.10   2008*

BAGNOLES DE L'ORNE *4E1* (1.3km SW Urban) *48.54783, -0.41995* **Camp Municipal de la Vée, Avenue du President Coty, 61140 Bagnoles-de-l'Orne [02 33 37 87 45; fax 02 33 30 14 32; info@campingbagnolesdelorne.com; www.campingbagnolesdelorne.com]** Access fr D335 in vill of Bagnoles-Château. Or fr La Ferté-Macé on D916 for 6km sp Couterne. Well sp fr all dirs. Lge, hdg/mkd pitch, pt sl, pt shd; htd wc (some cont); chem disp; mv service pnt; baby facs; shwrs inc; el pnts (10A) €3.50 (poss rev pol); gas; lndtte; shop 1km; tradsmn; rest, snacks; bar; BBQ; playgrnd; htd pool 1.5km; rv & lake nrby; golf, archery, tennis & mini-golf nrby; wifi; TV; dogs €1.55; phone; free bus to town cent at site ent; poss cr; Eng spkn; no adv bkg; quiet; ccard acc; red low ssn; CKE/CCI. "Excel, well-kept, well-run site in vg location; vg, spotless facs; easy walk to beautiful thermal spa town & lake; forest walks; gd for dogs." ♦ 10 Mar-27 Oct. € 13.25 2012*

See advertisement opposite

BAGNOLS SUR CEZE *10E2* (1.5km N Rural) *44.17585, 4.63540* **Camping La Coquille, Route de Carmignan, 30200 Bagnols-sur-Cèze [04 66 89 03 05; fax 04 66 89 59 86; jose. gimeno@free.fr; www.campinglacoquille.com]** Head N fr Bagnols-sur-Cèze over rv bdge turn R at Total stn, site 2km on RH side. Sm, pt shd; wc (cont); chem disp; shwrs inc; el pnts (4-6A) €4-4.50; gas in town; lndtte; rest; shop 2.5km; pool; canoe hire; fishing; dogs; adv bkg rec high ssn; CKE/CCI;ccard acc; "Site under military aircraft flightpath, otherwise gd, friendly, family-run site" 24 Apr-19 Sep. € 33.50   2013*

BAGNOLS SUR CEZE *10E2* (2km NE Rural) *44.17358, 4.63694* **Camping Les Genêts d'Or, Chemin de Carmigan, 30200 Bagnols-sur-Cèze [tel/fax 04 66 89 58 67; info@camping. genets-dor.com; www.camping-genets-dor.com]** N fr Bagnols on N86 over rv bdge, turn R into D360 immed after Total stn. Foll sp to site on rv. Med, mkd pitch, some hdstg, pt sl, pt shd; htd wc; chem disp; baby facs; shwrs inc; el pnts (6A) €5 (poss rev pol); gas; lndtte (inc dryer); shop; tradsmn; rest; snacks; bar; playgrnd; htd pool; paddling pool; canoeing, fishing 2km; games area; games rm; wifi; entmnt; some statics; no dogs Jul/Aug; poss cr; Eng spkn; adv bkg ess; quiet; ccard acc. "Excel, clean site; welcoming Dutch owners; gd pool; wildlife in rv; gd rest; highly rec." ♦ 20 Apr-20 Sep. € 25.00   2013*

⊞ **BAGNOLS SUR CEZE** *10E2* (7km S Rural) *44.08434, 4.59177* **Camping Le Vieux Verger, Ave des Platanes, 30330 Connaux [04 66 82 91 62; fax 04 66 82 60 02; www. campinglevieuxverger.com]** Fr S on D6086 turn L into vill fr bypass to x-rds in 200m & then L into Ave des Platanes. Site on R. S fr Bagnols-sur-Cèze on D6086 to Connaux. Look for green site sp 1km after turn. Site sp. Sm, hdg/mkd pitch, pt sl, terr, pt shd; wc; chem disp; shwrs; el pnts (10A) €3; lndtte; shop; snacks; bar; playgrnd; 2 htd pools; games area; 25% statics; dogs €1.90; poss cr; Eng spkn; adv bkg; quiet; ccard acc; red low ssn; CKE/CCI. "Well-maintained steep, sloping site; excel san facs; not suitable v lge o'fits; no twin-axles; excel." ♦ € 14.90 (CChq acc)   2008*

BAGNOLS SUR CEZE *10E2* (8km NW Rural) *44.18865, 4.52448* **Camping Les Cascades, Route de Donnat, 30200 La Roque-sur-Cèze [04 66 82 72 97; fax 04 66 82 68 51; infos@campinglescascades.com; www. campinglescascades.com]** Fr Bagnols take D6 W twd Alès. After 4km turn N on D143 & foll sp to La Roque-sur-Cèze. Site on R in 7km. App fr N not rec. Long narr bdge (2.3m). Med, pt sl, pt shd; htd wc (cont); chem disp; mv service pnt; baby facs; shwrs inc; el pnts (6-10A) €4.10-4.30; gas; lndtte (inc dryer); shop; tradsmn; supmkt 6km; rest, snacks; bar; BBQ; playgrnd; htd pool; shgl beach & rv adj; tennis; fishing; boating; wifi; entmnt; TV; dogs €1.85; poss cr; adv bkg; quiet. "Tranquil site; modern san facs." 19 Apr-13 Oct. € 44.00 (CChq acc)   2013*

BAGUER PICAN see Dol de Bretagne *2E4*

BAIGNES STE RADEGONDE *7B2* (500m SW Rural) *45.38187, -0.23862* **FFCC Camp Municipal, Le Plein, 16360 Baignes-Ste-Radegonde [05 45 78 79 96 or 05 45 78 40 04 (Mairie); fax 05 45 78 47 41; point.i@live.fr; www.baignes-sainte-radegonde.fr]** Fr N10 turn W onto D2 to Baignes; site well sp on rvside. Sm, pt shd; wc; baby facs; shwrs inc; chem disp in vill; el pnts (5A) €2; lndtte; shops 100m; pool & tennis nrby; adv bkg; quiet; ccard acc; red CKE/CCI. "Warden calls pm; gd san facs; attractive sm town; gd." 1 May-19 Sep. € 10.00   2010*

> ## "I like to fill in the reports as I travel from site to site"
>
> You'll find report forms at the back of this guide, or you can fill them in online at www.caravaclub.co.uk/europereport.

BAILLEUL *3A3* (3km N Rural) *50.76160, 2.74956* **Camping Les Saules (Notteau), 453 Route du Mont Noir, 59270 Bailleul [03 28 49 13 75]** N fr Lille on A25 exit junc 10 & head N into Bailleul cent; in town at traff lts turn R onto D23/N375; in 2km just bef Belgian border turn L onto D223. Site on L in 300m. Sm, hdstg, pt shd; wc; chem disp; shwrs inc; el pnts (6A) €2.84; farm shop; BBQ; playgrnd; 90% statics; dogs; Eng spkn; quiet but some rd noise; CKE/CCI. "Farm site; friendly owner; clean san facs; conv Calais, Dunkerque & WW1 sites; excel site, highly rec." 1 Apr-31 Oct. € 10.00   2013*

BAILLEUL *3A3* (4km N Rural) *50.77909, 2.73692* **Camping Domaine de la Sablière, Mont-Noir, 59270 St Jans-Cappel [03 28 49 46 34; fax 03 28 42 62 90]** Fr A25 exit junc 10, on D10 thro Bailleul to St Jans-Cappel. Thro vill turn R at x-rds onto D318 to Mont-Noir. Site on R at top of hill. Med, hdg/mkd pitch, terr, shd; wc; chem disp; some serviced pitches; shwrs inc; el pnts (6A) inc; lndtte; shop, rest & bar 3km; bar; playgrnd; fishing 2km; tennis; mini-golf 100m; 80% statics; phone. "Well-kept site; new owners (2009); clean san facs; pitch access poss diff lge o'fits due steep gradients & tight turns; conv WW1 battlefields, Dunkerque & Calais; gd." 15 Mar-15 Oct. € 18.00   2009*

BAILLEUL *3A3* (8km NE Rural) *50.79397, 2.67311* **Camping Les 5 Chemins Verts, 689 Rue des 5 Chemins Verts, 59299 Boeschepe [tel/fax 03 28 49 42 37; camping5cheminsverts@orange.fr; www.camping-5-chemins-verts.fr]** Fr N exit A25 junc 13 onto D948 W; in 5km turn R onto D10 to Boeschepe; turn R in vill. Or fr S exit A25 at Bailleul; N onto D10 to Boeschepe; turn L in vill. Site sp. V narr app rds, not suitable lge o'fits. Med, pt sl, pt shd; wc (some cont); chem disp; fam bthrm; shwrs inc; gas; el pnts (5A) inc; gas; lndtte; tradsmn; rest, snacks; bar; BBQ; playgrnd; games area; games rm; wifi; entmnt; 98% statics; dogs; phone; some Eng spkn; adv bkg; ccard acc; CKE/CCI. "Pleasant site with well-kept gardens; just a few touring pitches; clean, roomy modern san facs up steps; gd rest; poss diff access to pitches due sl & overhanging branches, not suitable lge o'fits; lots of activities, a child-oriented site; fishing in pond with ducks; gd rests around Mont des Cats; conv WWI sites & Calais; gd." ♦ ltd 15 Mar-31 Oct. € 12.00   2011*

BAIN DE BRETAGNE *2F4* (500m SE Rural) *47.83000, -1.67083* **Camping du Lac, Route de Launay, 35470 Bain-de-Bretagne [02 99 43 85 67; info@campinglac.fr; www.campinglac.fr]** Fr Bain-de-Bretagne take N772 SE dir Châteaubriant, foll sp. Up hill & turn R into narr lane & foll site sp; narr ent. Not rec to tow thro Bain-de-Bretagne. Med, hdg/mkd pitch, pt shd; wc; chem disp; mv service pnt; sauna; shwrs inc; el pnts (10A) €2.50; shop 1km; tradsmn; rest, snacks; bar; playgrnd; htd, covrd pool 500m; lake sw, sailing school nr; some statics; dogs €1.50; no twin-axles; phone; poss cr; Eng spkn; quiet; red low ssn; CKE/CCI. "Pretty site with lake views; new owners (2010) - much improved site; attractive sm town; many leisure facs in walking dist; conv NH." ◆ 15 Mar-15 Oct. € 12.00   2010*

See advertisement on pages 32 & 33

BAIN DE BRETAGNE *2F4* (11km W Rural) *47.8200, -1.8299* **Camp Municipal Le Port, Rue de Camping, 35480 Guipry [02 99 34 72 90 (Mairie) or 02 99 34 28 26; fax 02 99 34 28 06]** W fr Bain-de-Bretagne on D772, cross rv at Messac; cont on D772 sharp L at Leader supmkt into Ave du Port; site sp bef ent Guipry. NB Do not app after dark as rv is at end of app rd. Med, hdg/mkd pitch, pt shd; wc; mv service pnt; shwrs; el pnts (6A) €2.65 (poss long lead req); shop & rest nrby; playgrnd; pool nrby; rv fishing; train noise; CKE/CCI. "Excel site; friendly; warden on duty am & late pm; barrier 1.90m locked at times but phone for help or go to pitch 30; delightful rv walks & cycle paths; cruising & hire boats avail; nr classic cars museum." ◆ ltd Easter-15 Oct. € 9.80   2013*

BAIX *9D2* (2km W Rural) *44.70527, 4.73794* **Camping Le Merle Roux, 07210 Baix [04 75 85 84 14; fax 04 75 85 83 07; www.lemerleroux.com]** Fr A7/E15 exit junc 16. Foll sp Le Pouzin, x-ing Rv Rhône. Turn L onto D86 (S), go thro Le Pouzin, in 2km immed bef rlwy x-ing, turn R twd Privas; in 500m turn L at sp & foll rd approx 2km. Single track rd to site, not rec low powered car + lge c'van. Med, pt sl, terr, pt shd; wc; chem disp; shwrs inc; el pnts (6A) inc; lndtte; shop; tradsmn; rest, snacks; bar; no BBQ; playgrnd; pool; 15% statics; dogs €2.50; adv bkg; quiet; red low ssn; CKE/CCI. "Scenic site; welcoming Dutch owners; excel facs & pitches; poss diff to reverse onto pitch; excel." 1 Apr-31 Oct. € 31.10   2010*

BALARUC LES BAINS *10F1* (300m NE Coastal) *43.44084, 3.68320* **Camp Municipal du Pech d'Ay, Ave de la Gare, 34540 Balaruc-les-Bains [04 67 48 50 34; pechday@mairie-balaruc-les-bains.fr; www.herault-tourisme.com]** Exit N113 to Balaruc-les-Bains; foll sp Centre Commercial & then head for prom. Site on prom. Lge, mkd pitch, pt sl, pt shd; htd wc; chem disp; mv service pnt; shwrs; el pnts (10A) €3.40; lndtte in town; shops, rest & bar adj; playgrnd; shgle beaches nrby; bus; poss cr; Eng spkn; adv bkg rec (even low ssn); poss noisy; CKE/CCI. "Delightful holiday resort; busy site all ssn, rec arr early; vg, clean san facs poss stretched peak times; many gd rests adj; thermal baths in vill; bus to Sète" ◆ 20 Apr-14 Dec. € 15.94   2013*

BALARUC LES BAINS *10F1* (500m NE Coastal) *43.45344, 3.68802* **Camping Les Vignes, 34540 Balaruc-les-Bains [04 67 48 04 93; fax 04 67 18 74 32; camping.lesvignes@free.fr; www.camping-lesvignes.com]** Fr N113 take D2 sp Sète, turn W sp Balaruc-les-Bains, after 2nd rndabt turn R, well sp in 100m on R. Med, hdg/mkd pitch, pt shd; wc (some cont); chem disp; mv service pnt; shwrs inc; el pnts (6-10A) €3-3.50; lndtte; shops 1km; snacks; bar; playgrnd; pool; shgl beach 1km; sand beach 7km; fishing, horseriding & tennis nr; 30% statics; dogs €2.50; poss cr; adv bkg rec high ssn; quiet; ccard acc; CKE/CCI. "Gd touring base; narr site rds tight for long o'fits; Sète worth a visit." ◆ ltd 1 Apr-31 Oct. € 18.50   2009*

BALAZUC *9D2* (1km NE Rural) *44.51199, 4.38667* **FFCC Camping La Falaise, Hameau Les Salles, 07120 Balazuc [tel/fax 04 75 37 74 27; /www.camping-balazuc.com]** Sp on D579 on rvside. Sm, hdg pitch, pt sl, shd; wc; chem disp; baby facs; shwrs inc; el pnts (6A) €3.80; gas; lndtte; shop; tradsmn; snacks; bar; playgrnd; rv beach; canoe hire; dogs €1.50; phone; poss cr; Eng spkn; adv bkg; CKE/CCI. "Site beside Rv Ardèche; helpful and friendly owners; vg." ◆ 1 Apr-30 Sep. € 21.00   2013*

BALAZUC *9D2* (2km E Rural) *44.50778, 4.40333* **Camping Le Chamadou, Mas de Chaussy, 07120 Balazuc [04 75 37 00 56; fax 04 75 37 70 61; infos@camping-le-chamadou.com; www.camping-le-chamadou.com]** Fr Ruoms foll D579 dir Aubenas. After approx 9km turn R under viaduct, site sp. Keep R up narr rd to site. App recep on foot fr car pk. Med, hdg pitch, hdstg, pt sl, pt shd; htd wc; chem disp; baby facs; fam bthrm; shwrs inc; el pnts (10A) €4.20 (some rev pol); lndtte; shop & 3km; tradsmn; snacks; bar; BBQ (elec); playgrnd; pool; paddling pool; waterslide; rv & beach 1.5km; canoe & kayak hire; wifi; entmnt; TV rm; some statics; dogs €2.60; phone; poss cr; Eng spkn; adv bkg rec; v quiet; ccard acc; CKE/CCI. "Excel, well-run, family site; panoramic views; most pitches spacious." 1 Apr-31 Oct. € 24.00   2010*

BALBIGNY *9B1* (3km NW Rural) *45.82558, 4.16196* **Camping La Route Bleue, Route D56 du Lac de Villerest, Pralery, 42510 Balbigny [tel/fax 04 77 27 24 97 or 06 85 52 98 66 (mob); camping.balbigny@wanadoo.fr; www.camping-de-la-route-bleue.fr]** Fr N on D1082, take 1st R after a'route (A89/72) junc N of Balbigny onto D56. Fr S on D1082, turn L at RH bend on N o'skirts of Balbigny, D56, sp Lac de Villerest & St Georges-de-Baroille. Well sp. Med, hdg/mkd pitch, pt sl, pt shd; chem disp; mv service pnt; wc; shwrs inc; el pnts (6-10A) inc (poss long lead req); lndtte; shops 1.5km; tradsmn; rest, snacks; bar; playgrnd; pool & paddling pool; rv adj; fishing; games rm; sports complex adj; adv bkg; quiet; ccard acc; red low ssn/long stay; CKE/CCI. "Nice site on rv bank; views over rv some pitches; helpful & welcoming staff; san facs need update (2010); ltd el pnts (2010); extra for twin-axles; conv A72; excel; lovely area." ◆ ltd 15 Mar-31 Oct. € 16.20   2013*

BALLEROY *1D4* (5km SW Rural) *49.15677, -0.92287* Camping Domaine de Litteau, Le Perron, 14490 Litteau [02 31 22 22 08 or 05 56 07 90 17; domainedelitteau@ siblu.fr; www.siblu.fr/litteau] Fr St Lô, take D972 to Bayeux. After 14km, at La Malbreche, turn R onto D209 to Litteau. Site on L in approx 500m. Med, some hdg/mkd pitch, pt sl, unshd; wc; chem disp; baby facs; shwrs inc; el pnts (6A) inc; lndtte; shop & 4km; snacks; bar; playgrnd; htd covrd pool; lake fishing adj; sand beach 25km; horseriding; child entmnt; TV; 90% statics; dogs; phone; poss cr; Eng spkn; adv bkg; ccard acc; CKE/CCI. "Busy high ssn; forest adj; conv D-Day beaches, museums, Bayeux tapestry." 9 Apr-1 Nov. € 40.00 2009*

BAN DE SAPT see Raon l'Etape *6E3*

BANDOL *10F3* (3km NW Rural) *43.15980, 5.72905* Camping Le Clos Ste Thérèse, Route de Bandol, 83270 St Cyr-sur-Mer [04 94 32 12 21; fax 04 94 32 29 62; camping@clos-therese.com; www.clos-therese.com] Fr Bandol take D559 twd St Cyr & Marseilles. Site on R after 3km. Caution - site ent sharp U turn fr rd. Site service rds steep & narr; not suitable lge vans. Med, terr, shd; htd wc; chem disp; shwrs; el pnts (6-10A) €4-5.20; gas; lndtte; supmkt 1km; rest, snacks; bar; playgrnd; 2 pools (1 htd); paddling pool; sand beach 4km; golf, tennis, horseriding nr; entmnt; TV rm; 30% statics; dogs €2.30; adv bkg rec; some daytime rd noise. "Many beaches & beauty spots in area; tractor will site c'vans." ♦ 5 Apr-30 Sep. € 22.50 2013*

BANDOL *10F3* (6km NW Coastal) *43.17236, 5.69641* Camping Les Baumelles, 1 Roiute de la Madrague, 83270 St Cyr-sur-Mer [04 94 26 21 27; fax 04 94 88 76 13; baumellesloisirs@ aol.com; www.campinglesbaumelles.com] Fr Bandol take coast rd D559 NW to St Cyr. Turn L by statue on rd to La Madrague. Foll this coast rd 1.5km. Site on L at junc of coast rd. V lge, some mkd pitch; pt sl, shd; wc; baby facs; shwrs inc; el pnts (10A) €3.50; gas adj; lndtte; shop; rest, snacks; bar; playgrnd; sand beach adj; golf 2km; entmnt; TV; 60% statics; dogs €2; poss cr; Eng spkn; quiet; ccard not acc. "Great location, even if site below average." ♦ 1 Apr-30 Oct. € 27.00 2011*

BANNALEC see Pont Aven *2F2*

BANNES see Langres *6F1*

BANON *10E3* (1.5km S Rural) *44.02607, 5.63088* Camping L'Epi Bleu, Les Gravières, 04150 Banon [04 92 73 30 30 or 06 15 61 68 63 (mob); campingepibleu@aol.com; www. campingepibleu.com] Fr D4100 8km S of Forcalquier turn R onto D5 N thro St Michel-L'Observatoire & Revest twd Banon (approx 25km). Turn L on D51 twds Simiane-la-Rotunde. Site on R in 500m immed bef town, sp at junc. Med, shd; wc; mv service pnt; baby facs; shwrs inc; el pnts (10A) €5; lndtte; shop; rest, snacks; bar; BBQ; playgrnd; htd pool; paddling pool; games area; entmnt; TV; some statics; dogs €3; adv bkg; quiet; red low ssn; CKE/CCI. "Vg, wooded site; pleasant owners; gd walking & cycling tours." ♦ 15 Apr-15 Oct. € 13.50 (CChq acc) 2010*

BANYULS SUR MER *10H1* (700m S Rural) *42.47665, 3.11904* Camp Municipal La Pinède, Ave Guy Malé, 66650 Banyuls-sur-Mer [04 68 88 32 13; fax 04 68 88 32 48; camp. banyuls@banyuls-sur-mer.com; www.camping-banyuls-sur-mer.com] On D914 foll sp to Banyuls-sur-Mer; turn R at camping sp at cent of sea-front by town hall; foll sp to site. Lge, hdg/mkd pitch, pt sl, pt terr; pt shd; wc; chem disp; mv service pnt; shwrs; el pnts (4-13A) €2-3; lndtte; snacks; supmkt 100m; playgrnd; shgl beach 1km; dogs; Eng spkn; quiet; ccard acc; red low ssn; CKE/CCI. "Busy, friendly site; spacious pitches, some with sea view; narr site rds; vg, clean facs." ♦ 26 Mar-15 Nov. € 13.10 2011*

BAR LE DUC *6E1* (1km E Urban) *48.77433, 5.17415* FFCC Camp Municipal du Château de Marbeaumont, Rue du Stade, off Rue de St Mihiel, 55000 Bar-le-Duc [03 29 79 17 33 (TO) or 03 29 79 11 13 (LS)); fax 03 29 79 21 95; barleduc.tourisme@wanadoo.fr; www. tourisme-barleduc.com] Fr town cent foll Camping sps. Rue de St Mihiel is part of D1916 dir Verdun. Fr NW on D994/ D694 or fr SE on N1135, at rndabt turn E onto D1916 sp Metz, Verdun & St Mihiel. In 200m turn L into Rue du Stade sp Camping. Site on L in 100m. Sm, pt shd; wc; chem disp; shwrs inc; el pnts (6A) €3 (poss long lead req); lndtte (inc dryer); shops adj; no twin-axles; Eng spkn; some rd noise. Barrier clsd 11:00 - 15:00 "Delightful site in grounds of chateau; friendly & helpful warden; clean, modern san facs; check gate opening times; lovely walk into historic town; gd NH" 1 May-15 Oct. € 11.60 2013*

BAR SUR LOUP, LE see Grasse *10E4*

BARBATRE see Noirmoutier en l'Ile *2H3*

BARBIERES *9C2* (1km NE Rural) *44.97942, 5.16357* Camping Combe d'Oyans, 26300 Rochefort-Samson [04 75 47 33 23; fax 04 75 82 90 57; combe-doyans@orange.fr; www. combedoyans.fr] Exit A49 junc 7 onto D149 to Chatuzange; cont on D149 for 5.5km to rndabt just bef Barbières; turn L onto D125 to Rochfort-Samson; cont thro vill; in 600m cont over x-rds; site on R in 500m. Sm, hdg/mkd pitch, terr, pt shd; wc; chem disp (wc); shwrs inc; el pnts €3; shops 3km; tradsmn; snacks; playgrnd; htd pool; 15% statics; dogs €1; phone adj; adv bkg; ccard not acc; red low ssn; CKE/CCI. "Conv Vercors Massif; gd walking, cycling, rockclimbing; children's activity camping adj; vg." ♦ 6 May-29 Sep. € 17.00 2009*

BARBIERES *9C2* (1km SE Rural) *44.94470, 5.15100* Camping Le Gallo-Romain, 1090 Route de Col de Tourniol, 26300 Barbières [tel/fax 04 75 47 44 07; info@legalloromain. net; www.legalloromain.net] Exit A49 junc 7 onto D149 dir Marches & Barbières. Go thro vill & ascend Rte du Col de Tourniol for 2km, site on R, well sp. Med, mkd pitch, pt sl, terr, pt shd; wc; chem disp; baby facs; shwrs inc; el pnts (6A) €3.75; lndtte; shop & 1km; rest, snacks; bar; BBQ; playgrnd; pool; entmnt; internet; TV; 15% statics; dogs €5.50; phone; poss cr; Eng spkn; adv bkg; quiet; no ccard acc; red low ssn; CKE/CCI. "Mountain setting; welcoming, friendly, helpful Dutch owners; ltd facs low ssn; gd; nice location" ♦ 22 Apr-30 Sep. € 45.70 2013*

See advertisement on pages 32 & 33

You can now fill in site reports online

66420 Le Barcarès - Tel: 0033 468 86 12 60
Internet: www.precatalan.com - Email: info@precatalan.com

Set between the Leucate salt lake and the Mediterranean sea.
Le Pré Catalan Yelloh! Village is located in Le Barcarès
in the Pays Catalan region

FRANCE

BARBOTAN LES THERMES *8E2* (1km S Rural) *43.94027,
-0.04557* **Camping Le Lac de l'Uby, Cazaubon, 32150
Barbotan-les-Thermes [05 62 09 53 91; fax 05 62 09 56 97;
balia-vacances@wanadoo.fr; www.camping-uby.com]**
Fr Eauze take D626/N524 sp Cazaubon, immed bef Cazaubon
turn R sp Barbotan. Site on R in 2km. Lge, mkd pitch, some
hdstg, pt shd; htd wc; chem disp; el pnts (5-10A) €6; lndtte;
shop & 2km; cooking facs; playgrnd; pool; lake sw & beach
300m; fishing; sailing; windsurfing; tennis; games area; cycle
hire; entmnt; some statics; dogs €1.80; adv bkg rec; ccard acc;
red low ssn; CKE/CCI. "Gd, well-kept, well-run site; interesting
Bastide towns nrby." ♦ 15 Mar-30 Nov. € 16.00   2009*

BARCARES, LE *10G1* (1.5km S Coastal) *42.77607,
3.02435* **Camping L'Oasis, Route de St Laurent, 66423 Le Barcarès
[04 68 86 12 43; fax 04 68 86 46 83; info@camping-oasis.
com; www.camping-oasis.com]** Fr N exit A9/E15 junc 40
Leucate onto D627 & D83 twd Le Barcarès. Exit junc 9 onto
D81 dir Canet-Plage. Take 1st exit then turn L onto D90 sp
Le Barcarès, site sp on L in approx 800m. Lge, shd; wc (some
cont); chem disp; baby facs; shwrs; el pnts (10A) inc; lndtte
(inc dryer); supmkt; rest, snacks; bar; BBQ; playgrnd; 3 pools;
waterslide; sand beach 1km; tennis; games area; wifi; entmnt;
TV; dogs €4.50; red low ssn; CKE/CCI. "Ltd facs low ssn." ♦
24 Apr-18 Sep. € 35.00 (CChq acc)   2010*

BARCARES, LE *10G1* (2km S Coastal) *42.77570, 3.02300*
**Camping California, Route de St Laurent, 66420 Le
Barcarès [tel/fax 04 68 86 16 08; camping-california@
orange.fr; www.camping-california.fr]** Exit A9 junc 41 onto
D627 sp Leucate. Ignore sp Le Barcarès & Port Barcarès; exit junc 9
sp Canet onto D81; then at D90 intersection turn R dir St Laurent-
de-la-Salangue & go under D81; site on L (after Les Tamaris). Lge,
hdg/mkd pitch, shd; wc; chem disp; baby facs; shwrs inc; el pnts
(10A) inc (poos rev pol); lndtte (inc dryer); supmkt 1km; shop; rest,
snacks; bar; BBQ (gas/elec only); playgrnd; htd pool; waterslide;
paddling pool; sand beach 1.5km; watersports 1km; tennis;
games area; wifi; entmnt; games/TV rm; 20% statics; dogs €5;
Eng spkn; adv bkg; poss v busy/noisy high ssn; ccard acc; red low
ssn/long stay; CKE/CCI. "Vg reception; various pitch sizes, some
poss diff; friendly, helpful owners; excel, modern san facs, ltd low
ssn; mosquito repellant useful; busy rd thro site; highly rec." ♦
7 Apr-16 Sep. € 36.00 SBS - C02   2011*

⊞ **BARCARES, LE** *10G1* (1km SW Coastal) *42.77462, 3.02207*
**Camping L'Europe, Route de St Laurent, 66420 Le Barcarès
[04 68 86 15 36; fax 04 68 86 47 88; reception@europe-
camping.com; www.europe-camping.com]** Exit A9 at
Perpignan N & take D83 sp Le Barcarès. After 9km turn R on
D81 sp Canet Plage, L on D90 sp Le Barcarès. Site on R. Lge,
hdg/mkd pitch, shd; wc; shwrs inc; el pnts (16A) €4.50; gas;
lndtte; shop & 2km; rest, snacks; bar; playgrnd; 2 pools high
ssn; waterslides; rv & beach 500m; tennis; archery; entmnt;
disco; 50% statics; dogs €8; Eng spkn; adv bkg; poss noisy;
red long stay/low ssn; CKE/CCI. "Gd location; tidy pitches,
all have individual san facs (tired early ssn 2010); ltd facs low
ssn; gd cycle rte to beach & shops; gd winter NH." ♦ ltd
€ 43.00   2010*

BARCARES, LE *10G1* (1km SW Coastal) *42.78094, 3.02267*
**Yelloh! Village Le Pré Catalan, Route de St Laurent,
66420 Le Barcarès [04 68 86 12 60; fax 04 68 86 40 17;
info@precatalan.com; www.precatalan.com or www.
yellohvillage.co.uk]** Exit A9 junc 41 onto D83; app Le
Barcarès turn R onto D81, then L onto D90 to Le Barcarès, site
sp. Lge, shd; wc; shwrs inc; el pnts (6A) €4; gas; shop; rest,
snacks; bar; playgrnd; htd pool; paddling pool; sand beach
1km; tennis; games area; games rm; wifi; entmnt; TV; dogs €3;
phone; quiet; adv bkg. 14 May-17 Sep. € 32.00   2012*

See advertisement above

BARCELONNETTE *9D4* (8km NE Urban) *44.42027, 6.73639*
**Camping Le Planet, Place d'Arnaudville, 04850 Jausiers
[04 92 81 06 57; info@jausiers.com; www.jausiers.com]**
N fr Barcelonnette on D900; at N end of Jausiers on E side of
D900, just bef turn to Col de la Bonette. Sm, pt shd; wc (some
cont); chem disp (wc); shwrs €0.90; el pnts €3; shop, rest & bar
200m; snacks; dogs €1; quiet. "Simple, CL-type site nr all facs;
gd cent for mountain walking/cycling; fair." 15 Jun-19 Sep.
€ 8.50   2008*

BARCELONNETTE *9D4* (2km SE Rural) *44.38166, 6.67603*
**Camping La Chaup, Route du Sauze, 04400 Enchastrayes
[04 92 81 02 82]** Fr D900 at W end of Barcelonnette turn R
twds La Sauze & Enchastrayes; site sp. Sm, mkd pitch, sl, unshd;
htd wc (some cont); shwrs €1.50; el pnts (6A) €3.90; lndtte;
shop & snacks nrby; BBQ; playgrnd; rv & lake 2km; dogs €1; poss
cr; adv bkg; quiet; CKE/CCI. "Relaxing site with mountain views;
friendly owners." 1 Jun-15 Sep. € 9.70   2010*

FRANCE

⊞ **BARCELONNETTE** *9D4* (1km S Urban) *44.38294, 6.63470*
**Camping Le Tampico, 70 Ave Emile Aubert, 04400
Barcelonnette [tel/fax 04 92 81 02 55; le-tampico@
wanadoo.fr; www.letampico.fr]** Exit Barcelonnette onto
D902 sp Col d'Allos & Col de la Cayolle; site on R in 1.3km. NB
Do not app fr Col d'Allos or Col de la Cayolle. Med, mkd pitch,
pt shd; htd wc; chem disp; baby facs; fam bthrm; shwrs inc;
el pnts (6A) €3.50-6.00; gas; lndtte; ice; tradsmn; rest, snacks;
bar; BBQ (gas, charcoal); playgrnd; white water canoeing/rafting;
htd pool 2km; games area; TV; 10% statics; dogs €1.50; phone;
wifi; bus; poss cr; Eng spkn; adv bkg; quiet; ccard acc; red long
stay. "Lovely wooded site; mountain views; friendly owner;
walk to town by rv; vg walking & outdoor activities; vg." ♦ ltd
€ 15.90   2011*

BARCELONNETTE *9D4* (500m W Rural) *44.38393,
6.64281* **Camping du Plan, 52 Ave Emile Aubert, 04400
Barcelonnette [tel/fax 04 92 81 08 11; legaudissart@
orange.fr; www.campingduplan.fr]** Exit town on D902
sp Col d'Allos & Col de la Cayolle. Site on R. Sm, mkd pitch,
pt shd; wc; shwrs inc; el pnts (3-10A) €2.95-4.25 gas; lndtte;
shop; tradsmn; rest; dogs €1; adv bkg; quiet. "Garden site;
helpful owners; unisex san facs; lovely views & walks; pleasant
vill; excel." 25 May-30 Sep. € 13.15   2013*

BARCELONNETTE *9D4* (6km W Rural) *44.39229, 6.57340*
**Camping Le Fontarache, 04580 Les Thuiles [tel/fax
04 92 81 90 42; reception@camping-fontarache.fr; www.
camping-fontarache.fr]** Site sp fr D900 on ent Les Thuiles
fr Barcelonnette. Lge, mkd pitch, some hdstg, pt shd; wc (some
cont); chem disp; mv service pnt; shwrs inc; el pnts (6A) €3.20;
lndtte; shop 100m; tradsmn; snacks; BBQ; playgrnd; htd pool;
paddling pool; fishing; kayaking; tennis; games area; wifi;
entmnt; TV; some statics; dogs €3; poss cr; Eng spkn; adv bkg;
quiet. "Pleasant, scenic site." ♦ 1 Jun-5 Sep. € 19.00   2010*

BARCELONNETTE *9D4* (6km W Rural) *44.39686, 6.54605*
**Domaine Loisirs de l'Ubaye, Vallée de l'Ubaye, 04340
Barcelonnette [04 92 81 01 96; fax 04 92 81 92 53; info@
loisirsubaye.com; www.loisirsubaye.com]** Site on S side
of D900. Lge, mkd pitch, terr, shd; wc; shwrs inc; el pnts
(6A) €3.50; lndry rm; gas; shop; rest, snacks; bar; playgrnd;
htd pool; rv adj; watersports; cycle hire; entmnt; TV rm;
statics; dogs €3.50; phone; red low ssn/long stay; CKE/CCI.
"Magnificent scenery." ♦ 1 Apr-30 Oct. € 21.00   2009*

BAREGES see Luz St Sauveur *8G2*

BARFLEUR *1C4* (500m NW Urban/Coastal) *49.67564,
-1.26645* **Camp Municipal La Blanche Nef, 12 Chemin de
la Masse, 50760 Gatteville-le-Phare [02 33 23 15 40; fax
02 33 23 95 14; lablanchenef@wanadoo.fr]** Foll main rd to
harbour; half-way on L side of harbour & turn L at mkd gap in
car pk; cross sm side-street & foll site sp on sea wall; site visible
on L in 300m. Site accessible only fr S (Barfleur). Med, pt sl,
unshd; wc; chem disp; mv service pnt; shwrs inc; el pnts
(6-10A); lndtte; shops 1km; tradsmn; snacks; bar; playgrnd; sand
beach adj; internet; 45% statics; dogs €1.30; Eng spkn; quiet;
adv bkg; ccard acc; red low ssn; CKE/CCI. "Gd sized pitches; vg
facs; sea views; gd beach; gd birdwatching, walking, cycling;
m'vans all year." ♦ Mid Feb-Mid Nov. € 15.00   2010*

⊞ **BARFLEUR** *1C4* (1km NW Coastal) *49.67971, -1.27364*
**Camping La Ferme du Bord de Mer, 50760 Gatteville-le-
Phare [02 33 54 01 77; fax 02 33 54 78 99; fdbm@caramail.
com]** On D901 fr Cherbourg, on o'skts of Barfleur turn L onto
D116 for Gatteville-Phare. Site on R in 1km. Sm, hdg/mkd
pitch, pt sl, pt shd; wc; chem disp; shwrs inc; lndry rm; some
serviced pitches; el pnts (3-10A) €2.60-4.40; gas; lndry rm;
shop 1.5km; rest, snacks & bar high ssn or 1.5km; playgrnd; sm
sand beach adj; internet; games rm; 25% statics; dogs €1.45;
phone; poss cr; quiet; red low ssn. "CL-type site; sheltered
beach; coastal path to vill & lighthouse; conv ferries (30 mins);
Sep 2002 member reported high-strength poison against
rodents in field adj site - no warning notices displayed, beware
children or dogs; gd." ♦ ltd € 10.85   2009*

BARJAC (GARD) *9D2* (3km S Rural) *44.26685, 4.35170*
**Domaine de la Sablière (Naturist), 30430 St Privat-de-
Champclos [04 66 24 51 16; fax 04 66 24 58 69; contact@
villagesabliere.com; www.villagesabliere.com]** Exit A7
junc 19 onto D994/N86 to Pont-St Esprit; then take D6086
N; in 2km turn L onto D901 dir Barjac; 3km before Barjac, nr
St Privat-de-Champclos, turn L onto D266; in 2km turn L onto
unclassified rd & foll site sp. NB Steep ent. Lge, hdg/mkd pitch,
some hdstg, pt sl, shd; wc; chem disp; mv service pnt; sauna;
baby facs; shwrs; el pnts (10A) €5.20; gas; lndtte (inc dryer);
shop; rest, snacks; bar; BBQ; playgrnd; 2 pools (1 htd, covrd);
paddling pool; rv & beach; fishing; canoeing; tennis; games
area; games rm; beauty treatment cent; wifi; entmnt; TV rm;
40% statics; dogs €2.70; bus; red low ssn; Eng spkn; adv bkg;
quiet; ccard acc; red low ssn. "Helpful owners; excel facs; steep
rds, narr bends & sm pitches - poss diff access lge o'fits; site
shop gd value; risk of flooding after heavy rain; gd shopping
& excel local mkt; many naturist trails in forest." 1 Apr-2 Oct.
€ 34.80 (CChq acc)   2011*

BARJAC (GARD) *9D2* (9km S Rural) *44.26738, 4.37041*
**Naturissimo La Génèse (Naturist), Route de la Génèse,
30430 Méjannes-le-Clap [04 66 24 51 73 or 04 66 24 51 82;
fax 04 66 24 50 38; info@lagenese.com; www.lagenese.
com]** Fr A7 exit junc 19, take dir Bagnols-sur-Cèze (D994 &
N86) then in Bagnols head twd Alès on D6. Exit twd Lusanne
onto D979 & foll sp for Méjannes-le-Clap. Site on banks of
Rv Cèze. Lge, hdg/mkd pitch, pt sl, shd; wc; chem disp; shwrs
inc; el pnts (6A) inc; gas; lndtte; shop & 5km; rest, snacks; bar;
playgrnd; htd pool; fishing; sailing; canoe & cycle hire; tennis;
archery; entmnt; TV rm; 10% statics; dogs €4; phone; adv bkg;
quiet; ccard acc; red low ssn; INF card. "Excel site; gd rest &
shop." 1 Apr-30 Sep. € 25.55 (CChq acc)   2010*

BARJAC (LOZERE) see Mende *9D1*

BARNEVILLE CARTERET *1C4* (6km N Coastal) *49.42963,
1.80472* **Camping Bel Sito, Le Caumont de la Rue, 50270
Baubigny [02 33 04 32 74 or 06 75 80 72 80 (mob);
camping@bel-sito.com; www.camping-normandie-belsito.
com]** Fr Cherbourg take D950 twd Coutances thro Les Pieux
& on twd Carteret. 10km S of Les Pieux turn R onto D131 sp
Baubigny to site 1km on L. Med, pt sl, pt shd; wc; shwrs inc;
el pnts (6A) €3.50; gas; lndtte; shop; tradsmn; sand beach
900m; wifi; some statics; dogs €3; quiet. 15 Apr-13 Sep.
€ 22.00   2008*

BARNEVILLE CARTERET *1C4* (3km SE Coastal/Rural)
49.36211, -1.74644 **Camping Les Mimosas, 1 Chemin de Coutances, 50210 St Jean-de-la-Rivière [02 33 04 78 90; fax 02 33 04 06 62; contact@les-mimosas-normandie.com; www.les-mimosas-normandie.com]** Take D650 fr Cherbourg to Barneville-Carteret, site sp. Med, mkd pitch, pt shd; wc; mv service pnt; baby facs; shwrs inc; el pnts (6A) €4.20; lndtte; shop; snacks; bar; BBQ; playgrnd; htd pool; sand beach 500m; solarium; tennis; games area; games rm; wifi; entmnt; TV; 60% statics; dogs €3; adv bkg; quiet. "Pleasant site; roomy pitches; vg touring base." ♦ 1 Apr-30 Sep. € 22.60   2008*

BARNEVILLE CARTERET *1C4* (2.5km S Coastal) *49.36383, -1.75386* **Yelloh! Village Les Vikings, 50270 St Jean-de-la-Rivière [02 33 53 84 13; contact@camping-lesvikings.com; www.camping-lesvikings.com or www.yellohvillage.co.uk]** Fr D650 foll sp dir St Jean-de-la-Rivière. Site well sp. Lge, mkd pitch, pt shd; wc; chem disp; baby facs; shwrs inc; el pnts (4A) inc (poss rev pol); lndtte (inc dryer); shop; rest, snacks; bar; BBQ; playgrnd; 2 htd pool (1 covrd); paddling pool; waterslide; sand beach 500m; games rm; games area; golf, tennis nr; wifi; entmnt high ssn; TV; 50% statics; dogs; Eng spkn; adv bkg; quiet; red low ssn; ccard acc; CKE/CCI. "Gd site; helpful owner; vg touring base; gd walking." ♦ 1 Apr-2 Oct. € 39.65   2010*

See advertisement on inside front cover

BARNEVILLE CARTERET *1C4* (2.5km SW Coastal) *49.36758, -1.75773* **Camping Les Bosquets, Rue du Capitaine Quenault, 50270 Barneville-Plage [02 33 04 73 62; fax 02 33 04 35 82; lesbosquets@orange.fr; www.camping-lesbosquets.com]** Fr D650 at Barneville-Carteret turn S dir Barneville-Plage, site sp. Lge, terr, pt shd; wc; chem disp; shwrs inc; el pnts (10A) €3.80; lndtte; shop; bar; playgrnd; htd pool; paddling pool; sand beach 400m; horseriding nrby; games rm; TV; 50% statics; dogs €1.80; bus; poss cr; adv bkg; quiet; CKE/CCI. "Pleasant site; beach ideal for children." ♦ 1 Apr-15 Sep. € 17.40   2009*

BARNEVILLE CARTERET *1C4* (10km SW Coastal) *49.30323, 1.68825* **Camping L'Espérance, 36 Rue de la Gamburie, 50580 Denneville-Plage [02 33 07 12 71; fax 02 33 07 58 32; camping.esperance@wanadoo.fr; www.camping-esperance.fr]** S fr Cherbourg on D950 thro Barneville-Carteret; in 7km fork R & cont on D650 & then R onto D137 sp Denneville-Plage & camping. Med, hdg/mkd pitch, pt shd; wc; chem disp; shwrs inc; el pnts (4-6A) €2.90-3.80; gas; lndtte; shop; snacks; bar; playgrnd; htd pool; sand beach 300m; tennis; cycle hire; games rm; entmnt; 50% statics; dogs €2; phone; poss cr; Eng spkn; adv bkg; quiet; ccard acc; CKE/CCI. "Helpful owners." 1 Apr-30 Sep. € 21.00   2009*

BARNEVILLE CARTERET *1C4* (2.5km W Urban/Coastal) *49.38081, -1.78614* **FFCC Camping du Bocage, Rue du Bocage, Carteret, 50270 Barneville-Carteret [02 33 53 86 91; fax 02 33 04 35 98; www.barneville-carteret.fr]** Fr Cherbourg take D650 to Carteret, turn R onto D902, site by disused rlwy stn & nr tourist office. Med, hdg pitch, shd; wc (some cont); chem disp; baby facs; shwrs inc; el pnts (3-6A) €2.50-3; lndtte; shops adj; rest 200m; snacks; playgrnd; sand beach 500m; 40% statics; poss cr; adv bkg; quiet; red low ssn; CKE/CCI. "Pleasant seaside resort with excel beaches; well-kept site; pitches soft in wet weather." 1 Apr-30 Sep. € 21.80   2011*

BARREME *10E3* (S Urban) *43.95225, 6.37316* **Camping Napoléon, Le Bas Paraire, 04330 Barrême [tel/fax 04 92 34 22 70 or 06 72 90 42 74 (mob); campingnapoleon@hotmail.com; www.camping-napoleon.com]** Fr Digne-les-Bains on N85; strt ahead at rndabt on ent Barrême; site on L over bdge, site sp. Med, mkd pitch, shd; wc; chem disp; mv service pnt; baby facs; shwrs inc; el pnts (10A) inc; gas; lndtte; shop & rest 300m; snacks; bar; playgrnd; pool; rv fishing & sw adj; entmnt; TV; some statics; dogs €1.50; bus; phone; Eng spkn; adv bkg; quiet; red low ssn; CKE/CCI. "Nice position; helpful owners; OK facs; narr gauge rlwy adj site so some noise; vg." ♦ ltd 11 Apr-29 Sep. € 20.00   2008*

BARROU *4H2* (Rural) *46.86500, 0.77100* **FFCC Camping Les Rioms, Les Rioms, 37350 Barrou [02 47 94 53 07; campinglesrioms@orange.fr; www.lesrioms.com]** Fr D750 Descartes to La Roche-Posay rd turn R at sp Camping at ent to Barrou vill. Site sp. NB Site has barriers, phone if clsd. Sm, hdg/mkd pitch, pt shd; wc; chem disp (wc); shwrs inc; el pnts (16A) €4; lndry rm; tradsmn; shop, rest & snacks nr; BBQ; playgrnd; htd pool; sand rv beach 2km; 35% statics; dogs free; Eng spkn; adv bkg; quiet; red low ssn; CKE/CCI. "Pleasant, peaceful site on bank of Rv Creuse; clean san facs; friendly owners; gd pool; excel." ♦ 30 Mar- 26 Oct. € 10.50   2013*

"We must tell The Club about that great site we found"
Get your site reports in by mid-August and we'll do our best to get your updates into the next edition of Caravan Europe.

BASSOUES *8F2* (600m NE Rural) *43.57972, 0.25560* **Camp Municipal St Fris, 32320 Bassoues [05 62 70 90 47 (Mairie); www.bassoues.net]** W fr Montesquiou on D943; site on L 200m after junc with D35 (immed after rugby stadium & bef ent to Bassoues). Sm, mkd pitch, pt sl, pt shd; wc; shwrs inc; el pnts €2.20; shop, rest & bar 1km; BBQ; games area; dogs; no twin-axles; adv bkg; quiet, but some traff noise; CKE/CCI. "Site next to delightful sm lake; various pitch sizes; warm welcome; barrier closes access, warden visits 0830-1000 & 1700-2000; Bassoues an interesting Bastide town; excel." ♦ ltd 1 Jun-30 Sep. € 11.50   2011*

BASTIDE DE SEROU, LA *8G3* (1km S Rural) *43.00150, 1.44472* **Camping L'Arize, Route de Nescus, 09240 La Bastide-de-Sérou [05 61 65 81 51; fax 05 61 65 83 34; mail@camping-arize.com; www.camping-arize.com]** Fr Foix on D117 on ent La Bastide-de-Sérou turn L at Tourist Office/Gendarmerie on D15 sp Nescus, site 1km on R. Med, hdg/mkd pitch, pt shd; wc; chem disp; mv service pnt; baby facs; serviced pitch; shwrs inc; el pnts (6A) inc (poss rev pol); gas; lndtte (inc dryer); shop & 2km; tradsmn; rest 5km; snacks; playgrnd; pool; lake sw 5km; fishing; cycle hire; golf 5km; horseriding adj; golf nr; wifi; entmnt; 10% statics; dogs €2; poss cr; Eng spkn; adv bkg; ccard acc; CKE/CCI. "Pleasant, scenic site on bank Rv Arize; modern facs; gd mkd walking/cycle rtes." ♦ ltd 8 Mar-12 Nov. € 35.20   2013*

See advertisement on pages 32 & 33

BATHIE, LA see Albertville *9B3*

BATZ SUR MER see Croisic, Le *2G3*

BAUBIGNY see Barneville Carteret *1C4*

BAUD *2F3* (3.5km S Rural) *47.84613, -3.01354* **Camp Municipal du Petit Bois, Route de Lambel-Camors, 56330 Camors [02 97 39 18 36 or 02 97 39 22 06; fax 02 97 39 28 99; commune.de.camors@wanadoo.fr]** S fr Baud on D768 to Camors. Sp in vill on D768. Sm, mkd pitch, pt sl, terr, unshd; wc; chem disp; mv service pnt; shwrs inc; el pnts (10A) €2.50; lndtte; playgrnd; horseriding adj; dogs; adv bkg; quiet; CKE/CCI. "Pleasant surroundings; vg facs; well-managed site." ♦ 1 Jul-31 Aug. € 9.60   2010*

BAUD *2F3* (7km W Rural) *47.88239, 3.10818* **Camp Municipal de Pont Augan, Pont Augan, 56150 Baud [02 97 51 04 74 or 02 97 65 19 19; accueil@languidic.fr]** Fr N24 exit onto D172 & foll sp Bubry & Quistinic; fr S on D768 to Baud, turn W onto D3, foll sp Bubry & Quistinic. Sm, hdg/mkd pitch, pt shd; htd wc; chem disp (wc); mv service pnt; baby facs; shwrs inc; el pnts (10A); lndtte (inc dryer); rest, snacks, bar 200m; playgrnd; pool; fishing, canoeing in lake on site or in Rv Blavet adj; dogs; adv bkg; quiet; no ccard acc; CKE/CCI. "Peaceful site; barrier & office ltd opening hrs but parking area avail." ♦ ltd 1 Jun-30 Sep.   2008*

BAUDREIX see Nay *8F2*

BAUGE *4G1* (1km E Rural) *47.53889, -0.09637* **Camp Municipal du Pont des Fées, Chemin du Pont des Fées, 49150 Baugé [02 41 89 14 79 or 02 41 89 18 07 (Mairie); fax 02 41 84 12 19; camping@ville-bauge.fr; www.ville-bauge.fr]** Fr Saumur traveling N D347/D938 turn 1st R in Baugé onto D766. Foll camping sp to site by sm rv; ent bef rv bdge. Sm, hdg/mkd pitch, pt shd; wc; chem disp; mv service pnt; shwrs inc; el pnts (4A) €2.70; lndtte; shops 1km; BBQ; pools & tennis 150m; fishing; no twin-axles; phone; adv bkg; quiet; ccard acc. "Excel countryside; pleasant, well-kept site; obliging wardens." 15 May-15 Sep. € 9.40   2010*

BAULE, LA *2G3* (2km NE Rural) *47.29833, -2.35722* **Airotel Camping La Roseraie, 20 Ave Jean Sohier, Route du Golf, 44500 La Baule-Escoublac [02 40 60 46 66; fax 02 40 60 11 84; camping@laroseraie.com; www.laroseraie.com]** Take N171 fr St Nazaire to La Baule. In La Baule-Escoublac turn R at x-rds by church, site in 300m on R; sp fr La Baule cent. Lge, mkd pitch, some hdstg, pt shd; wc (some cont); chem disp; mv service pnt; baby facs; fam bthrm; shwrs inc; el pnts (6-10A) €5.50-€7.50; gas; lndtte (inc dryer); shop 400m; tradsmn; rest, snacks; bar; BBQ; playgrnd; htd, covrd pool; paddling pool; waterslide; sand beach 2km; fishing; watersports; tennis; games area; games rm; fitness rm; wifi; entmnt; TV rm; 80% statics; dogs €5; phone; Eng spkn; adv bkg; quiet but rd noise; ccard acc; red long stay/low ssn; CKE/CCI. "Gd site & facs; sm pitches; clean unisex san facs; ltd facs low ssn; easy walk into La Baule-Escoublac; excel beach nrby; vg." ♦ 1 Apr-25 Sep. € 40.00 (CChq acc)   2012*

BAULE, LA *2G3* (1km E Coastal) *47.28864, -2.37236* **Camping Le Bois d'Amour, Allée de Diane, 44500 La Baule [02 40 60 17 40 or 04 73 77 05 05 (LS); fax 04 73 73 05 06; contact@lesbalconsverts.com; www.lesbalconsverts.com]** Fr Ave du Bois d'Amour bear L & immed under rlwy bdge, turn R at traff lts. Ent to site on R. Lge, mkd pitch, shd; wc; chem disp; shwrs inc; el pnts (6A) inc; gas; lndtte; shop; rest; playgrnd; sand beach 800m; wifi; 50% statics; dogs €2; phone; bus & railway adj; no dogs high ssn; poss cr; Eng spkn; adv bkg; quiet, but some rd/rlwy noise at site perimeter; red low snn; CKE/CCI. "Useful NH, some pitches v sm; sm area for tourers." ♦ 1 Apr-3 Oct. € 25.00 (CChq acc)   2009*

BAULE, LA *2G3* (1km W Rural) *47.29372, -2.37916* **Camping Les Ajoncs d'Or, Chemin du Rocher, 44500 La Baule [02 40 60 33 29; fax 02 40 24 44 37; contact@ajoncs.com; www.ajoncs.com]** Fr D13 foll sp for La Baule cent & turn L at rndabt nr Champion supmkt, site sp. Lge, mkd pitch, pt shd; wc; chem disp; baby facs; shwrs; el pnts (6A) inc; lndtte; shop; supmkt 1km; rest, snacks; bar; playgrnd; sand beach 1.5km; games area; entmnt; TV; 25% statics; dogs €1; adv bkg; quiet; red low ssn. "Peaceful, well-run site; vg." ♦ 1 Apr-30 Sep. € 21.00   2010*

BAUME LES DAMES *6G2* (500m S Rural) *47.34050, 6.35752* **Comping du Complex Touristique (Domaine d'Aucroix), Quai du Canal, 25110 Baume-les-Dames [03 81 84 38 89; fax 03 81 80 29 53; www.domainedaucroix.fr]** Fr D683 in Baume-les-Dames turn S onto D50, cross canal & turn W. Site sp. Sm, some hdstg, pt shd; wc; chem disp; shwrs; el pnts (16A) inc; lndtte; some cabins; dogs €3; quiet; red low ssn. "Peaceful site; gd nh/long stay, very conv from m/way" 1 May-30 Sep. € 17.00   2013*

BAUME LES DAMES *6G2* (5km S Rural) *47.32506, 6.36127* **Camping L'Ile, 1 Rue de Pontarlier, 25110 Pont-les-Moulins [03 81 84 15 23; info@campingdelile.fr; www.campingdelile.fr]** S fr Baume-les-Dames on D50, site on L on ent Pont-les-Moulins. Sm, pt shd; wc (some cont); chem disp; mv service pnt; shwrs inc; el pnts (6A) €2.50; gas; lndtte; shops 5km; bread 100m; rest & bar 500m; playgrnd; pool 6km; 10% statics; dogs free; Eng spkn; adv bkg; rd noise; red long stay; CKE/CCI. "Tidy, basic site in pleasant setting by Rv Cusancin; helpful, friendly owner; clean, basic facs; gd." 1 May-7 Sep. € 11.50   2009*

BAUME LES MESSIEURS see Lons le Saunier *6H2*

BAYAS see Coutras *7C2*

⊞ **BAYAS** *45.08273, -02.0702* **Camping Le Chene du Lac, 3 lieu-dit "Chateauneuf" 33230, Bayas (Gironde) [05 57 69 13 78 06 10 64 94 98 (mob); lechenedulac@ orange.fr; www.camping-lechenedulac.com]** Fr N10 Bordeaux - Angouleme exit Laruscade/Guitres. Site sp fr D247 N of Guitres Sm, shd; wc; shwrs; el pnts €4.30; lndtte; shop; tradsmn; snacks; dog €2; "excel site" € 12.10   2013*

BAYEUX *3D1* (500m N Urban) *49.28392, -0.69760* **Camp Municipal des Bords de L'Aure, Blvd d'Eindhoven, 14400 Bayeux [tel/fax 02 31 92 08 43; campingmunicipal@ mairie-bayeux.fr; www.mairie-bayeux.fr]** Site sp off Périphérique d'Eindhoven (Bayeux by-pass, D613). Fr W (Cherbourg) exit N13 junc 38, turn L over N13, then R onto D613 thro Vaucelles. At rndabt cont on D613 (3rd exit) Blvd d'Eindhoven. Site on R immed after traff lts, almost opp Briconaute DIY store. Fr E (Caen) on N13 exit junc 36 onto D613 N; foll ring rd across 2 rndabts, 4 traff lts, site on L opp Bayeux town sp. Lge, pt shd, some hdg pitch, some hdstg; wc (some cont); chem disp; mv service pnt; shwrs inc; el pnts (5A) €3.60 (poss rev pol); gas; lndtte; shop (Jul/Aug); playgrnd; indoor pool adj; sand beach 10km; dogs; phone; some; adv bkg ess high ssn; rd noise; 10% red 5+ days; CKE/CCI. "Gd, well-kept site; clean, basic san facs; avoid perimeter pitches (narr hdstgs & rd noise); no twin-axles;Office open ls; gd footpath to town along stream; Bayeux festival 1st w/end July; conv ferries; lge mkt Sat." ♦ 15 Apr-31Oct. € 24.25   2013*

BAYEUX *3D1* (7km SE Rural) *49.24840, -0.60245* **Camping Le Château de Martragny, 52 Hameau Saint-Léger, 14740 Martragny [02 31 80 21 40; fax 02 31 08 14 91; chateau. martragny@wanadoo.fr; www.chateau-martragny.com / www.chateau-martragny.fr]** Fr Caen going NW on N13 dir Bayeux/Cherbourg, leave at Martragny/Carcagny exit. Strt on & take 2nd R (past turn for Martragny/Creully) into site & chateau grounds. Fr Bayeux after leaving N13 (Martragny/Carcagny), go L over bdge to end of rd, turn L then take 2nd R into Chateau grounds. Lge, some mkd pitch, pt sl, pt shd; wc; chem disp; mv service pnt; baby facs; shwrs inc; el pnts (15A) €4.80 (long lead poss req, poss rev pol); gas; lndtte (inc dryer); shop; tradsmn; snacks; bar; BBQ; playgrnd; htd pool; paddling pool; sand beach 12km; fishing; tennis; horseriding 500m; wifi; entmnt; games/TV rm; dogs free; no c'vans/m'vans over 8m; poss cr; Eng spkn; adv bkg; quiet; ccard acc; red low ssn; CKE/CCI. "Popular, attractive site on lawns of chateau; attractive area; relaxed atmosphere; friendly, helpful staff; poss long trek to san facs & poss stretched high ssn; gd rest; poss muddy when wet; conv cemetaries; D-Day beaches 15km; Sat mkt in Bayeux; conv Caen ferry; excel." ♦ 12 May-12 Sep. € 48.30 (CChq acc) SBS - N06   2013*

See advertisement on inside back cover

⊞ **BAYEUX** *3D1* (8km SE Rural) *49.25041, -0.59251* **Camping Le Manoir de l'Abbaye (Godfroy), 15 Rue de Creully, 14740 Martragny [tel/fax 02 31 80 25 95; yvette.godfroy@ libertysurf.fr; http://godfroy.pagesperso-orange.fr]** Take N13 Bayeux, Caen dual c'way for 7km, fork R sp Martagny. Over dual c'way L at T-junc, then 1st R sp D82 Martragny & Creully site on R 500m. Sharp L steep turn into site. Sm, pt shd; wc unisex; chem disp; shwrs inc; el pnts (15A) €4.(poss rev pol); lndtte; tradsmn; dogs €2.30; Eng spkn; adv bkg; red low ssn; CKE/CCI. "Peaceful, relaxing, well-kept site; lovely grounds; helpful, welcoming owners; steps to san facs; meals & wine avail on request; winter storage; conv Ouistreham ferries; highly rec; wc, shwr, kitchen fac's in same room" ♦ ltd € 16.00   2013*

BAYEUX *3D1* (15km SE) **Camping Caravaning Escapade, Rue de l'église, 14490 CAHAGNOLLES [02 31 21 63 59; www.campinglescapade.net]** Fr Saint Paul du Varnay take D99 Cahagnolles on the L; foll rd for aprrox 2.5km; turn L & aft church campsite on R. Med, mkd pitch, pt shd; wc; chem disp; shwrs inc; el pnts (10A) €3.90; lndtte; bar/bistro; BBQ; pool (htd); lake; recep rm for events; dogs €2.70; adv bkg; ccard acc. "Lovely site; well looked after & cared for; clean san facs; friendly owners & staff." 1 Apr-31 Oct. € 18.30 (CChq acc)   2011*

See advertisement on pages 32 & 33

BAYEUX *3D1* (9km NW Rural) *49.33120, -0.80240* **Camping Reine Mathilde, 14400 Etréham [02 31 21 76 55; fax 02 31 22 18 33; camping.reine.mathilde@wanadoo.fr; www.campingreinemathilde.com]** NW fr Bayeux on D6 turn L to Etréham (D100); site 3km (sp). Or W fr Bayeux on N13 for 8km, exist junc 38. At x-rds 1.5km after vill of Tour-en-Bessin turn R on D206 to Etréham & bear L at church. Med, hdg/mkd pitch, pt shd; htd wc; chem disp; mv service pnt adj; baby facs; shwrs inc; el pnts (6A) €4.70; lndtte; sm shop & 4km; tradsmn; rest, snacks & pizza van (high ssn); bar; playgrnd; htd pool; paddling pool; sand beach 5km; cycle hire; fishing 1km; wifi; entmnt; TV; 15% statics; dogs €2.50; phone; Eng spkn; adv bkg; quiet; ccard not acc; red low ssn; CKE/CCI. "Well-kept site; lge pitches; app rds quite narr; friendly, helpful warden; gd, clean san facs; conv D-Day beaches etc; excel." ♦ 1 Mar-30 Sep. € 19.10   2011*

BAYON *6E2* (500m NW Rural) *48.47898, 6.30645* **Camp Municipal du Passetemps, Rue de la Moselle, 54290 Bayon [tel/fax 03 83 72 45 60 or 03 83 72 51 52 (Mairie)]** Fr N57 N fr Charmes or S fr Nancy; turn onto D9 sp Bayon; in 2.5km strt on at x-rds & over bridge; site on L in 500m by Rv Moselle. Med, pt shd; wc (some cont); chem disp; shwrs €0.90; el pnts (8A) inc; rest 500m; playgrnd; rv & sports facs adj; 50% statics; quiet. "Rv adj liable to dry out & also flood - care in wet weather; barrier clsd 2200-0700." 15 Apr-15 Oct. € 12.00   2009*

BAYONNE *8F1* (8km NE Rural) *43.54858, -1.40381* **Aire Naturelle L'Arrayade (Barret), 280 Chemin Pradillan, 40390 St Martin-de-Seignanx [05 59 56 10 60; www. seignanx-tourisme.com]** On D26 midway bet D810 & D817, 3km W of St Martin. (Opp tall crenellated building). Sm, pt sl, pt shd; wc (some cont); shwrs; el pnts €2.50 (long lead rec); lndry rm; BBQ; playgrnd; dogs; quiet. "Delightful little site; warm welcome; helpful owner; simple facs poss stretched high ssn; gd base for exploring Basque country" 1 Jun-30 Sep. € 12.00   2013*

⊞ **BAYONNE** *8F1* (10km NE Rural) *43.55588, -1.36115* **FFCC Camping Le Ruisseau, 40390 St André-de-Seignanx [05 59 56 71 92; campingle@aol.com; www. campingleruisseau.fr]** Fr Bayonne, take D817 dir Orthez. Turn L after 10km at traff lts in St Martin & foll sp for 5km to site. Sp fr all dir. Take care on ent - by rd junc. Med, hdg/mkd pitch, terr, pt shd; wc; chem disp; 15% serviced pitches; shwrs inc; el pnts (6A) €4; lndtte; shop; tradsmn; rest, snacks & bar 1km; playgrnd; pool; sand beach 10km; TV; 20% statics; dogs €2.50; adv bkg; quiet; red long stay/low ssn; CKE/CCI ess. "Away fr busy coastal area; helpful owner; not suitable lge o'fits." € 24.50 (3 persons)   2009*

BAYONNE *8F1* (11km NE Rural) *43.52820, -1.39157* **Camping Lou P'tit Poun, 110 Ave du Quartier Neuf, 40390 St Martin-de-Seignanx [05 59 56 55 79; fax 05 59 56 53 71; contact@louptitpoun.com; www.louptitpoun.com]** Fr Bordeaux exit A63 junc 6 dir Bayonne Nord; then take D817 dir Pau & St Martin-de-Seignanx; site sp on R in 7km. Lge, hdg/mkd pitch, terr, pt shd; wc; chem disp; mv service pnt; serviced pitch; baby facs; shwrs inc; el pnts (10A) inc; gas; lndtte (inc dryer); shop & 4km; tradsmn; rest (high ssn); snacks; bar; BBQ (el/gas); playgrnd; pool; paddling pool; sand beach 10km; tennis; games area; entmnt; games/TV rm; 17% statics; dogs €5; phone; Eng spkn; adv bkg; quiet; rd noise some pitches; ccard acc; red low ssn/long stay; CKE/CCI. "Charming, spacious, family-run site; gd sized pitches; friendly staff; gd clean san facs; ltd facs low ssn; conv Biarritz, St Jean-de-Luz & a'route; excel." ♦ ltd 1 Jun-15 Sep. € 34.30 SBS - A39   2011*

See advertisement below

BAZINVAL see Blangy sur Bresle *3C2*

BEAUCENS see Argelès Gazost *8G2*

BEAUFORT *9B3* (300m NW Rural) *45.72160, 6.56418* **Camp Municipal Le Domelin, Domelin, 73270 Beaufort [tel/fax 04 79 38 33 88 or 04 79 38 33 15 (LS)]** Fr Albertville take D925 dir Beaufort & Bourg-St Maurice; site on L just bef ent Beaufort 100m up side rd (after passing D218B); clearly sp. Med, mkd pitch, pt sl, pt shd; htd wc (some cont); chem disp; baby facs; shwrs inc; el pnts (10A) €2.65; lndtte; shops, rest, snacks & bar 1km; playgrnd; htd pool 1km; dogs; phone; bus 1km; poss cr; adv bkg; ccard acc; CKE/CCI. "Quiet, pleasant site; vg walking; attractive town; gd touring base." 1 Jun-30 Sep. € 11.84   2009*

BEAUGENCY *4F2* (500m E Rural) *47.77628, 1.64294* **Camp Municipal du Val de Flux, Route de Lailly-en-Val, 45190 Beaugency [02 38 44 50 39 or 02 38 44 83 12; fax 02 38 46 49 10; camping@ville-beaugency.fr; www. beaugency.fr]** Exit A10 junc 15 onto N152. In Beaugency turn L at traff lts nr water tower onto D925 & again over rd bdge. Site sp on S bank of Rv Loire. Med, mkd pitch, pt shd; htd wc; chem disp; mv service pnt; shwrs inc; el pnts (10A) €3.60 incl; lndry rm; sm shop & 500m; rest 1km; snacks; bar; playgrnd; sand beach; fishing; watersports; entmnt; 10% statics; dogs €1.10; poss cr w/end in ssn; quiet; Eng spkn; ccard acc; red long stay; CKE/CCI. "Beautiful, well-kept site; views over Loire; helpful staff; free 1 night site for m'vans over rv on other side of town; poss unrel opening dates low ssn, rec phone ahead; vg location close to town." ♦ 12 Apr-1 Sep. € 18.15   2013*

⊞ **BEAUGENCY** *4F2* (8km S Rural) *47.68679, 1.55802* **Camp Municipal L'Amitié, 17 Rue du Camping, Nouan-sur-Loire, 41220 St Laurent-Nouan [02 54 87 01 52; fax 02 54 87 09 93; camping@stlaurentnouan.fr; http://www. campingdelamitie.fr]** On D951 SW fr Orléans cont past power stn into Nouan-sur-Loire. Site on R sp. Med, hdg/mkd pitch, pt shd; htd wc; mv service pnt; shwrs; el pnts (10A) €2.80; lndtte (inc dryer); shop, rest 500m; pools & sports activities nr; direct access to rv; 50% statics; dogs €1; site clsd Xmas & New Year; adv bkg; quiet; 10% red CKE/CCI. "Interesting area; view of Rv Loire; workers poss resident on site; friendly staff; well-maintained site; clean san facs in Portacabins; phone ahead low ssn to check open; well maintained site, being redeveloped" € 7.50   2013*

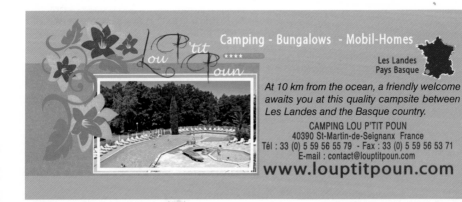

BEAULIEU SUR DORDOGNE *7C4* (3km N Rural) *45.00911, 1.85059* Aire Naturelle La Berge Ombragée (Lissajoux), Valeyran, 19120 Brivezac [05 55 91 01 17 or 06 08 40 78 69 (mob); contact@berge-ombragee.com; / www.berge-ombragee.com] N fr Beauliew-sur-Dordogne on D940; in 500m turn R onto D12; site on R in 2km. Office down on rv bank. NB Front wheel drive tow cars may find diff on gravel hill leading up from office. Sm, pt sl, pt shd; wc; chem disp; mv service pnt; shws inc; el pnts (6A) €3; sm shop; snacks; BBQ area; playgrnd; rv sw adj; canoeing; wifi; dogs €0.30; CKE/CCI. "CL-type site; friendly; canoeing fr site; gd." 15 Apr-15 Oct. € 16.90   2012*

"I need an on-site restaurant"

We do our best to make sure site information is correct, but it is always best to check any must-have facilities are still available or will be open during your visit.

BEAULIEU SUR DORDOGNE *7C4* (250m E Urban) *44.97950, 1.84040* FLOWER Camping des Iles, Blvd Rodolphe-de-Turenne, 19120 Beaulieu-sur-Dordogne [05 55 91 02 65; fax 05 55 91 05 19; info@campingdesiles.fr; www.campingdesiles.fr or www.flowercampings.com] Exit A20 junc 52 ont D158/D38 dir Collonges-la-Rouge; cont on D38 & turn R onto D940 to Beaulieu-sur-Dordogne; site sp fr o'skts of town. Or on D940 N fr Bretenoux, turn R in Beaulieu town sq, site around 200m on island in Rv Dordogne. NB 3m height limit at ent. Med, mkd pitch, shd; htd wc; chem disp; baby facs; fam bthrm; shws inc; el pnts (10A) inc (poss long lead req); lndtte; shops 500m; rest, snacks; bar; BBQ (gas); playgrnd; pool; rv & fishing; canoeing; cycle hire; games area; games rm; wifi; entmnt; 15% statics; dogs €1.60; poss cr; Eng spkn; adv bkg rec; quiet; red long stay/low ssn. "Delightful, wooded site; pitches by rv excel (extra charge); plenty shade; friendly owners; gd clean san facs; ltd low ssn; attractive medieval town; gd value; highly rec." 23 Apr-24 Sep. € 23.90   2011*

See advertisement on pages 32 & 33

BEAULIEU SUR LOIRE *4G3* (300m E Rural) *47.54407, 2.82167* FFCC Camp Municipal du Canal, Route de Bonny, 45630 Beaulieu-sur-Loire [02 38 35 89 56 or 02 38 35 32 16 (LS); fax 02 38 35 86 57; renault.campingbeaulieu@orange.fr; www.beaulieu-sur-loire.fr] Exit A77 junc 21 Bonny-sur-Loire, cross rv to Beaulieu-sur-Loire on D296. On E o'skirts of vill on D926, nr canal. Sm, hdg/mkd pitch, hdstg, pt shd; wc; chem disp; mv service pnt; shws inc; el pnts (10A) €3.10; shop 2km; rest/takeaway & bar 500m; poss cr; Eng spkn; adv bkg; some rd noise; CKE/CCI. "Well-kept site in pleasant area; direct access to canal; some sm pitches diff lge o'fits; site yourself; warden calls 0800-0900 & 1830-1930; no security; clean modern san facs; gd walking along canal & Rv Loire; boat trips; poss workers' statics low ssn; mkt Wed." ♦ Easter-1 Nov. € 6.60   2011*

BEAUMES DE VENISE see Carpentras *10E2*

BEAUMONT DE LOMAGNE *8E3* (800m E Urban) *43.88406, 0.99800* Village de Loisirs Le Lomagnol (formerly Municipal Le Lac), Ave du Lac, 82500 Beaumont-de-Lomagne [05 63 26 12 00; fax 05 63 65 60 22; villagedeloisirslelomagnol@wanadoo.fr; www.villagelelomagnol.fr] On SE of D928 at E end of vill. Sp 'Centre de Loisirs, Plan d'Eau'. Med, mkd pitch, pt shd; wc; chem disp; baby facs; sauna; shwrs inc; el pnts (10A) inc (poss long lead req); lndtte; shop; rest, snacks; bar; playgrnd; pool; waterslide; jacuzzi; lake sw; fishing; canoe & cycle hire; tennis; golf; 25% statics; dogs €2; poss cr; quiet; red low ssn. "Gd quality, modern site; interesting old town; mkt Sat." ♦ 1 Apr-30 Oct. € 16.90   2010*

BEAUMONT DU PERIGORD *7D3* (6km W Rural) *44.75603, 0.70216* Centre Naturiste de Vacances Le Couderc (Naturist), 24440 Naussannes [05 53 22 40 40; fax 05 53 23 90 98; info@lecouderc.com; www.lecouderc.com] Fr D660 at D25 W thro Naussannes & hamlet of Leydou. Just beyond Leydou turn R into site, well sp. Lge, mkd pitch, pt sl, pt shd; wc; chem disp; sauna; shwrs inc; el pnts (5A) €4.50; shop; rest, snacks; bar; playgrnd; htd pool; paddling pool; jacuzzi; sm lake; cycle hire; wifi; entmnt; some statics; dogs €4.65; adv bkg, ess high ssn; quiet; ccard acc; red long stay/low ssn. "Beautiful site with relaxed atmosphere; friendly, helpful Dutch owners; gd san facs; superb pool; naturist walks on site; gd walking/cycling area; Bastide towns nrby." ♦ 1 Apr-1 Oct. € 27.90   2009*

BEAUMONT HAGUE *1C4* (5km N Rural/Coastal) *49.70442, -1.84116* Camp Municipal du Hable, 50440 Omonville-la-Rogue [tel/fax 02 33 52 86 15 or 02 33 01 86 00] W fr Cherbourg on D901 to Beaumont-Hague; turn N onto D45 dir Omonville-la-Rogue. Med, hdg/mkd pitch, pt shd; wc; chem disp; mv service pnt; shwrs €1; el pnts (5-10A) €2.95-4.80; lndtte; shop, gas adj; rest; bar; playgrnd; beach 100m; dogs €0.95; quiet; CKE/CCI. "In pretty vill with gd harbour; 30 mins fr Cherbourg; gd NH." 1 Apr-30 Sep. € 8.50   2009*

"Satellite navigation makes touring much easier"

Remember most sat navs don't know if you're towing or in a larger vehicle – always use yours alongside maps and site directions.

BEAUMONT SUR OISE *3D3* (8km SW Rural) *49.12805, 2.18318* Parc de Séjour de l'Etang, 10 Chemin des Belles Vues, 95690 Nesles-la-Vallée [01 34 70 62 89; campinparis@gmail.com; www.campinparis.com] Fr D927 Méru-Pontoise rd, turn L onto D64 at sp L'Isle Adam. After passing thro Nesles-la-Vallée camp sp on L. Med, hdg pitch, pt shd; htd wc (cont); chem disp; serviced pitches (extra charge); shwrs inc; el pnts (3A) inc (rev pol); lndtte; shops 1km; playgrnd; lake fishing adj; dogs €2; Eng spkn; quiet; red CKE/CCI. "Lovely, peaceful, out-of-the-way setting; spacious pitches; friendly, helpful staff; gd facs; conv day trips to Paris & Versailles; excel." 1 Apr-30 Sep. € 18.50   2010*

BEAUMONT SUR SARTHE *4F1* (500m E Rural) *48.22382, 0.13651* FFCC Camp Municipal du Val de Sarthe, Rue de l'Abreuvoir, 72170 Beaumont-sur-Sarthe [02 43 97 01 93; camping-beaumontssarthe@orange.fr; www.ville-beaumont-sur-sarthe.fr] Fr D338 Alençon-Le Mans, turn L at traff lts in cent of Beaumont & foll site sp twd E of town. Fr Le Mans on A28 exit 21 onto D6, R onto D338 & R at traff lts & foll sp. NB Narr, sloping app thro town rds with blind corners. Narr site access. Med, hdg/mkd pitch, pt shd; wc; chem disp; mv service pnt; shwrs inc; el pnts (6A) €3.20; (long cable poss req & poss rev pol); lndtte; shops & rest 500m; playgrnd; pool 500m; rv boating & fishing adj; dogs €0.50; poss cr w/end; adv bkg rec high ssn; ccard acc; CKE/CCI. "Beautiful, peaceful, well-run rvside site; lge pitches, some by rv; no twin-axles & poss no c'vans over 2,000 kg; barrier clsd 2200; easy walk to interesting, pretty town; mkt Tues; rec; nice clean site, pleasant & friendly; well maintained site" ♦ 1 May-30 Sep. € 14.25   2013*

BEAUMONT SUR SARTHE *4F1* (9.5km S Rural) *48.14267, 0.18428* FFCC Camp Municipal Le Pont d'Orne, 72380 Montbizot [02 43 27 60 44 or 02 43 27 62 16 (LS); mairie. montbizot@wanadoo.fr] Exit A28 junc 21 onto D47 to Montbizot; cont on D47, site 300m S of vill on L. Sm, hdg/mkd pitch, shd; wc; mv service pnt; shwrs inc; el pnts inc; snacks; bar; playgrnd. "Busy but quiet site with access to rv; excel facs; warden calls am/pm." 15 May-27 Sep. € 9.50   2011*

"There aren't many sites open at this time of year"

If you're travelling outside peak season remember to call ahead to check site opening dates – even if the entry says 'open all year'.

BEAUNE *6H1* (800m NE Urban) *47.03304, 4.83911* Camp Municipal Les Cent Vignes, 10 Rue Auguste Dubois, 21200 Beaune [03 80 22 03 91; fax 03 80 20 15 51; campinglescentvignes@mairie-beaune.fr; www.beaune.fr] Fr N on A31 & fr S on A6 at junc with m'ways A6/A31 take A6 sp Auxerre-Paris; after 1km leave at junc 24 to join D974 twd Beaune; after approx 1.5km, turn R at 2nd traff lts fr a'route to site (sp) in 200m. If app fr S on D974 site well sp fr inner ring rd & foll sp to Dijon (not a'route sps). Also sp fr Mersault/ L'Hôpital x-rds. Med, hdg/mkd pitch, some hdstg, pt shd; htd wc; chem disp; mv service pnt; shwrs inc; el pnts (6A) €3.80 (some rev pol); gas; lndtte (inc dryer); shop; hypmkt 2km; rest, snacks; bar; BBQ; playgrnd; pool 800m; tennis; cycle hire; games area; wifi; TV rm; dogs; phone; some Eng spkn; adv bkg in writing only bef 30 May; red low ssn; ccard acc; CKE/CCI. "Popular, well-run site; rec arr early even low ssn; gd modern san facs; vg rest; most pitches gd size but narr site rds makes access some pitches diff, a mover useful; tight turns & low trees poss diff lge o'fits; twin-axles; in walking dist of Beaune; v conv site." ♦ 15 Mar-31 Oct. € 24.10   2013*

⊞ **BEAUNE** *6H1* (3.5km NE Rural) *47.02458, 4.88711* Camping Les Bouleaux, 11 Rue Jaune, 21200 Vignoles [tel/fax 03 80 22 26 88] Exit A6 at junc 24.1; 500m after toll turn R at rndabt, in 1.5km turn R sp Dole rndabt. Immed after x-ing m'way turn L sp Vignoles. L again at next junc then R & foll camping sp. Site in approx 1.5km in cent Chevignerot; fr town cent take D973 (E) sp Dole. In 2km cross a'route & 1st L (N) sp Vignoles. Med, sm, hdg/mkd pitch, pt shd; htd wc; chem disp; shwrs inc; el pnts (6A) inc (rev pol altered on request); shop; tradsmn; supmkt 2km; dogs; adv bkg rec; quiet but some rd noise; CKE/CCI. "Attractive, well-kept, busy site; rec arr early high ssn; some gd sized pitches, most sm; helpful & friendly owners; superb clean san facs, poss stretched high ssn & ltd low ssn; poss muddy after rain - park on rdways; conv NH fr a'route; muddy, basic site, owner not very helpful; vg san facs; long lead maybe req'd; excel site; excel walking in area" ♦ € 22.60   2013*

"That's changed – Should I let The Club know?"

If you find something on site that's different from the site entry, fill in a report and let us know. See www.caravanclub.co.uk/europereport.

BEAUNE *6H1* (8km SW Rural) *46.98573, 4.76855* La Grappe d'Or (formally Kawan Village), 2 Route de Volnay, 21190 Meursault [03 80 21 22 48; fax 03 80 21 65 74; info@ camping-meursault.com; www.camping-meursault.com] Fr N-S, Exit A6 Junc 24.1 SP Beaune Centre Hospices, at rndabt foll sp to Chalon sur Saône RN 74, after 7km foll sp to Meursault, turn r, foll sp for site. Med, mkd pitch, terr, pt shd; htd wc; chem disp; mv service pnt; baby facs; shwrs inc; el pnts (15A) €4; gas; lndtte (inc dryer); shop; rest, snacks; bar; playgrnd;sw; paddling pool; waterslide; tennis; rambling;games court; cycle hire; wifi; phone; dogs €1.40; poss cr; Eng spkn; adv bkg ess in ssn; some rd noise; red low ssn; CKE/CCI. "Lovely family site; busy high ssn - arr early; all pitches views over vineyards; friendly, helpful owners; basic facs stretched; ltd water pnts & poss steep climb fr lower pitches; some pitches uneven, sm or obstructed by trees - poss diff access lge o'fits; poss muddy when wet; barrier clsd 2200-0730; sh walk to lovely vill; gd cycle paths; vg; popular site; well run" ♦ 30 Mar-15 Oct. € 18.00 (CChq acc)   2013*

BEAUNE *6H1* (5km NW Rural) *47.06861, 4.80292* FFCC Camping Les Premiers Prés, Route de Bouilland, 21420 Savigny-lès-Beaune [tel/fax 03 80 26 15 06 or 06 83 23 93 37 (mob); contact.camping@x-treme-bar.fr; www.camping-savigny-les-beaune.fr] Fr Beaune ring rd turn N on D974 sp Dijon; in 200m turn L sp Savigny; in 100m ignore camping sp & bear R to Savigny (3km); site 1km thro vill on L. Med, mkd pitch, pt sl, pt shd; wc; chem disp; mv service pnt; shwrs inc; el pnts (6A) €3.50 (some rev pol); dogs 1km; supmkt 3km; tradsmn; snacks; BBQ; playgrnd; cycle hire; internet; dogs €1.20; adv bkg; quiet; CKE/CCI. "Pleasant, busy NH in beautiful area; pleasant staff; modern basic san facs; no twin-axles; gd touring base; conv A6, A31, A36 & Beaune; easy walk to vill; excel quiet site" ♦ ltd 15 Mar-15 Oct. € 15.00   2013*

⊞ **BEAURAINVILLE** *3B3* (750m SE Rural) *50.41971, 1.91243*
Camp Municipal La Source, Rue des Etangs, 62990
Beaurainville [03 21 81 40 71 or 06 80 32 17 25 (mob); fax
03 21 90 02 88; campingbeaurainville@orange.fr; www.
commune.beaurainville.fr www.beaurainville.fr/tourisme/
camping] Fr Hesdin take D349 NW to Beaurainville. Site on R
bef cent of town, sp. Med, mkd pitch, pt shd; htd wc; shwrs
inc; el pnts (10A) €2.70 (poss rev pol); lndtte; shop 1km; bar;
playgrnd; fishing; boating; games area; horseriding; wifi;
90% statics; dogs free; red long stay; CKE/CCI. "Ltd touring
pitches; site poss clsd in winter - phone ahead; pleasant area
with plenty wildlife; gd NH." ♦ € 12.00   2011*

BEAURECUEIL see Aix en Provence *10F3*

BEAUREPAIRE *9C2* (S Urban) *45.33825, 5.06101*
Camp Intercommunal, Ave Charles de Gaulle, 38270
Beaurepaire [04 74 84 64 89 or 04 74 84 67 29; fax
04 74 79 24 14; camping.beaurepaire@orange.fr; www.
territoire-de-beaurepaire.fr] Sp in town on L of Beaurepaire-
Romans rd, adj pool & stadium. Med, shd; wc (some cont);
shwrs inc; el pnts (10A) €2.50; shops 250m; 2 supmkts nr; pool
& tennis nrby; rv fishing; games rm; wifi; dogs €0.50; quiet;
mkt Wed am. 15 Apr-15 Oct. € 8.00   2010*

BEAUREPAIRE *9C2* (10km S Rural) *45.25332, 5.02803*
Camping du Château, Route de Romans, 26390
Hauterives [04 75 68 80 19; fax 04 75 68 90 94; contact@
camping-hauterives.com; www.camping-hauterives.com]
Take D538 S to Hauterives, site sp in vill adj Rv Galaure. Med,
mkd pitch, pt shd; wc; mv service pnt; shwrs; el pnts (6-10A)
€2.50-3; lndtte; snacks; sm supmkt adj; playgrnd; htd pool;
paddling pool; rv & fishing adj; tennis; games area; some
statics; dogs €2.20; adv bkg; quiet. "Gd NH; friendly; gd pool;
Do not use SatNav, inaccurate" ♦ 1 Apr-30 Sep. € 26.50
2012*

See advertisement on pages 32 & 33

BEAUREPAIRE *9C2* (9km SW Rural) *45.28250, 4.97833*
**Camping Château de la Pérouze, Le Meyerie,
26210 St Sorlin-en-Valloire [04 75 31 70 21 or
06 70 00 04 74 (mob); fax 04 75 31 75 75; contact@
campingfrance.info]** Exit Beaurepaire on D130/D139 sp
Manthes for approx 1km; bef St Sorlin turn L at site sp in
1.5km. Narr site ent. Med, mkd pitch, pt shd; shwrs; htd wc;
chem disp; baby facs; sauna; jacuzzi; shwrs inc; el pnts (6-10A)
€2.30-4.20; gas; lndtte; shop 2km; tradsmn; rest; bar; pool;
fishing; tennis; 30% statics; no dogs; quiet; adv bkg; CKE/CCI.
"Friendly, helpful warden; in 14thC chateau grounds; sep, shd
car park; gates clsd 2100-0900; access to pitches poss diff;
winter c'van storage." 15 Jun-15 Sep. € 18.90   2008*

⊞ **BEAUVAIS** *3C3* (10km E Rural) **Camping de la Trye,
Rue de Trye, 60510 Bresles [03 44 07 80 95 or
06 10 40 30 29 (mob); www.camping-de-la-trye.com]**
Exit N31 (Beauvais to Clermont) at Bresles; foll site sp. Med,
hdg/mkd pitch, pt sl; wc; chem disp; mv service pnt; shwrs
inc; el pnts (6A) inc; lndtte (inc dryer); tradsmn; playgrnd;
pony rides; cycle hire; trampoline; entmnt; wifi; dogs; ccard
acc; CKE/CCI. "New Dutch owners, improving site (2011);
cycle & walking rtes; theme parks nrby; fair NH/sh stay."
€ 17.00   2011*

BEAUVILLE *7D3* (500m SE Rural) *44.27210, 0.88850*
**Camping Les Deux Lacs, 47470 Beauville [tel/fax
05 53 95 45 41; camping-les-2-lacs@wanadoo.fr; www.
les2lacs.info]** Fr D656 S to Beauville, site sp on D122. NB Steep
descent to site - owners help when leaving if necessary. Med,
hdg/mkd pitch, terr, shd; wc; chem disp; mv service pnt; shwrs
inc; el pnts (6A) €2.45; lndtte; rest, snacks; bar; shop 600m;
playgrnd; lake sw adj; games area; fishing; watersports; wifi;
10% statics; dogs €2.15; Eng spkn; adv bkg; quiet; ccard acc;
red long stay/low ssn; CKE/CCI. "Peaceful; gd fishing; pleasant
walk to vill; vg." ♦ 1 Apr-31 Oct. € 14.90   2012*

BEAUVOIR see Mont St Michel, Le *2E4*

BEAUVOIR EN ROYANS see St Marcellin *9C2*

> ## "I like to fill in the reports
> ## as I travel from site to site"
> You'll find report forms at the back of
> this guide, or you can fill them in online
> at www.caravaclub.co.uk/europereport.

BEAUVOIR SUR MER *2H3* (4km E Rural) *46.89984, -1.98840*
**Camp Municipal, 85230 St Gervais [02 51 68 73 14 (Mairie);
fax 02 51 68 48 11]** On D948, 1km E of St Gervais on R. Sm,
mkd pitch, pt shd; wc; chem disp; shwrs; el pnts (10A) €2.50;
gas; lndry rm; shop; BBQ; quiet; CKE/CCI. "Facs basic but
clean." ♦ 1 Apr-15 Sep. € 8.50   2009*

BEAUVOIR SUR MER *2H3* (4km E Rural) *46.92298,
-1.99036* **Camping Le Fief d'Angibaud, 85230 St Gervais
[02 51 68 43 08; camping.fief.angibaud@orange.fr; www.
campinglefiefangibaud.com]** Fr Beauvoir-sur-Mer E on D948
to St Gervais turn L after PO/Mairie onto D59 twd Bouin (narr
ent easy to miss); in 2km pass sm chapel; take 2nd rd on L;
site on R after 500m. Sm, unshd; wc; chem disp; shwrs inc;
el pnts (6-13A) €4.-7.; gas 4km; basic lndry rm; shops 2km;
tradsmn; sand beach 5km; fishing/golf nrby; no statics; dogs
€1.50; wifi; adv bkg rec high ssn; quiet; red long stay/CKE/
CCI. "Excel, simple site adj farm; lge pitches; pleasant, helpful
British owners; clean san facs but need update (2010); conv Ile
de Noirmoutier; ferry to Ile d'Yeu, coastal resorts; free parking
close to beach (blue flag); gd cycling area; vg value; gd for
rallies." ♦ 1 Mar-31 Oct. € 17.50   2013*

BEC HELLOUIN, LE see Brionne *3D2*

BEDARIEUX *10F1* (8km N Rural) *43.67313, 3.17265* **FFCC**
**Camping La Sieste, 34260 La Tour-sur-Orb [04 67 23 72 96;
fax 04 67 23 75 38; campinglasieste@orange.fr; http://
campinglasieste.pagesperso-orange.fr]** Fr Bédarieux, take
D35 N twd Lodève; site 3km N of La Tour-sur-Orbe at sm vill
of Vereilles. Med, pt shd; wc; chem disp; shwrs inc; el pnts
(4-10A) €2.40-5.20; lndtte; shop; tradsmn; rest; bar; BBQ; pool
open June; dogs €3; phone; adv bkg; Eng spkn; quiet; poss v
cr; ccard acc; red low ssn/CKE/CCI. "Well-kept site; charming
owners; immac pool; unspoilt countryside; excel." ♦
1 May-31 Aug. € 16.00   2011*

⊞ **BEDENAC** *7C2* (1km E Rural) *45.16944, -0.28777* **Camping Louvrignac, 17210 Bedenac [05 46 70 31 88; lyn.carpenter@ hotmail.co.uk or ken.carpenter@live.co.uk]** Fr N10 exit sp Bedenac onto D145. Thro Bedenac vill take D158 sp Montguyon & in 500m take 1st L sp Bernadeau. Site on L in 100m - narr rd. Sm, pt shd; own san; el pnts (10A) inc; shop 1km; supmkt, shops, rest, snacks, bar 10km; pool; no dogs; adv bkg; quiet. "CL-type site with 5 pitches; ground firm; friendly British owners; rec phone in advance." € 14.00   2010*

BEDOIN *10E2* (1.5km NE Rural) *44.13363, 5.18738* **Camping Domaine de Bélézy (Naturist), 84410 Bédoin [04 90 65 60 18; fax 04 90 65 94 45; info@belezy.com; www.belezy.com]** Fr Carpentras D974 to Bédoin. Go thro vill & turn R at rndabt sp Mont Ventoux. In 300m turn L & foll sp to site. Lge, pt sl, shd; htd wc (some cont); chem disp; mv service pnt; sauna; steam rm; baby facs; shwrs inc; el pnts (12A) €5.60; gas; lndtte; shop; rest, snacks; bar; cooking facs; playgrnd; 2 htd pools; paddling pool; tennis; games area; horseriding 2km; golf 20km; wifi; entmnt; TV rm; 20% statics; phone; sep car park high ssn; poss cr; Eng spkn; adv bkg; quiet; ccard acc; red long stay/ low ssn; INF card. "Delightful, peaceful, well-kept site in lovely location; warm welcome, helpful staff; extensive facs; many acitivies; some sm & awkward pitches; gd base for Mt Ventoux, Côtes du Rhône; excel; No pets; Pitches very close together" ♦ 2 Apr-2 Oct. € 41.00 (3 persons)   2013*

> ## "We must tell The Club about that great site we found"
> Get your site reports in by mid-August and we'll do our best to get your updates into the next edition of Caravan Europe.

BEDOIN *10E2* (1km W Rural) *44.12468, 5.17249* **Camp Municipal de la Pinède, Chemin des Sablières, 84410 Bédoin [04 90 65 61 03; fax 04 90 65 95 22; la-pinede. camping.municipal@wanadoo.fr]** Take D938 S fr Malaucène for 3km, L onto D19 for 9km to Bédoin. Site adj to vill & sp. Med, sl, terr, shd; htd wc; mv service pnt; shwrs inc; el pnts (10A) inc; lndtte; shops in vill; snacks; playgrnd; pool (high ssn); dogs €1; quiet; ccard not acc; CKE/CCI. "Pool clsd Mon; 5 min walk to vill; mkt Mon." 15 Mar-31 Oct. € 14.70   2010*

BEDUER see Figeac *7D4*

BEGARD *2E2* (2km S Rural) *48.61666, -3.28227* **Camping du Donant, Gwenezhan, 22140 Bégard [02 96 45 46 46; fax 02 96 45 46 48; camping.begard@wanadoo.fr; www. camping-donant-bretagne.com]** Fr N12 at Guingamp take D767 dir Lannion, Perros-Guirec. S of Bégard foll sp Armoripark, site sp. Med, hdg/mkd pitch, hdstg, terr, pt shd; wc; chem disp; mv service pnt; baby facs; shwrs inc; el pnts (12A) €2.80; gas 1km; lndtte (inc dryer); shop & bar adj; BBQ; playgrnd; htd pool & leisure facs; tennis adj; TV rm; statics; dogs €1.35; Eng spkn; adv bkg; quiet; ccard acc. "Pleasant countryside; friendly, helpful staff; san facs poss not well-maintained low ssn & stretched high ssn; conv coast; gd touring base." ♦ Easter-15 Sep. € 12.60   2008*

⊞ **BELCAIRE** *8G4* (4km SW Rural) *42.79207, 1.92477* **Camping Les Sapins, Ternairols, 11340 Camurac [04 68 20 38 11; info@lessapins-camurac.com; www. lessapins-camurac.com]** Easiest app fr N - at Bélesta on D117 turn S onto D16/D29/D613 to Belcaire then cont to Camurac, site 1km SE of vill. Or take D613 fr Ax-les-Thermes (1st 10km over Col de Chioula diff climb - gd power/weight ratio). Site sp in vill of Camurac & visible fr rd. App rd fairly steep for sh distance. Med, mkd pitch; pt sl, pt shd; htd wc; chem disp; shwrs inc; el pnts (10A) €3; lndtte (inc dryer); shop 5km; tradsmn; rest & adj; snacks; bar; BBQ (gas, elec); playgrnd; pool; paddling pool; horseriding; mountain biking; winter sports; games area; wifi; entmnt; TV; 33% statics; dogs €2; poss cr; Eng spkn; adv bkg; quiet; ccard acc; red low ssn; site clsd 1 Nov-15 Dec; CKE/CCI. "Lovely, peaceful site in beautiful surroundings; welcoming Dutch owners; excel walking; in Cathar region; vg." ♦ ltd € 20.00   2011*

BELCAIRE *8G4* (300m W Rural) *42.81598, 1.95098* **Camp Municipal La Mousquière/Le Lac, 4 Chemin Lac, 11340 Belcaire [04 68 20 39 47 or 04 68 20 31 23 (Mairie); fax 04 68 20 39 48; mairie.belcaire@wanadoo.fr]** Site on D613 bet Ax-les-Thermes & Quillan. Sm, mkd pitch, pt sl, shd; wc; chem disp; shwrs inc; el pnts (10A) €2; gas 1km; lndtte; lake sw adj; tennis & horseriding nrby; dogs; phone; quiet; ccard not acc; CKE/CCI. "Site by lake; site yourself, warden calls; gd cent for walking; historic vill of Montaillou nr; excel." ♦ ltd 1 Jun-30 Sep. € 11.00   2010*

BELFORT *6G3* (1.5km N Urban) *47.65335, 6.86445* **FFCC Camping de l'Etang des Forges, 11 Rue du Général Béthouart, 90000 Belfort [03 84 22 54 92; fax 03 84 22 76 55; contact@camping-belfort.com; www.camping-belfort.com]** Exit A36 junc 13; go thro cent of Belfort; then foll sp Offemont on D13, then site sp. Or fr W on N19 site well sp. Med, hdg/ mkd pitch, pt shd; htd wc (some cont); chem disp; mv service pnt; baby facs; shwrs inc; el pnts (6A) €3.50; lndtte (inc dryer); shop 500m; tradsmn; rest & adj; snacks, bar high ssn; BBQ; playgrnd; pool; fishing & watersports adj; archery; wifi; entmnt; TV rm; 5% statics; dogs €2; bus; extra for twin-axles; Eng spkn; adv bkg; quiet; ccard acc; red low ssn/long stay; CKE/CCI. "Pleasant,well-kept, basic site; some lovely pitches; friendly; modern, unisex san facs; lovely walk around lake fr site ent; cycle paths; conv for Corbusier's chapel at Ronchamp." ♦ 7 Apr-30 Sep. € 16.00 (CChq acc)   2011*

BELGENTIER see Cuers *10F3*

⊞ **BELLAC** *7A3* (700m N Urban) *46.12744, 1.05052* **Camp Municipal Les Rochettes, Rue des Rochettes, 87300 Bellac [05 55 68 13 27; camping.bellac@wanadoo.fr; www. camping-limousin.com]** On N147 ent Bellac fr Poitiers take sharp L at 1st traff lts onto D675. Cont to rndabt & turn L. Foll sp, site on L in 400m adj football pitch. Fr Limoges on N147 take R at 3rd traff lts after ent Bellac onto D675 then foll sp as above. NB Sl ent to site. Med, mkd pitch, pt sl, pt shd, terr; htd wc; own san; mv service pnt; shwrs inc; el pnts (10A) €2.50 (long lead poss req); gas; shops 500m; supmkt 1km; bar 500m; playgrnd; pool & waterslide 1km; games area; dogs €1.10; quiet; ccard not acc; red long stay/low ssn. "Spacious site but poss diff if wet; coded barrier clsd 2000-0800; san facs run down/dirty (June 2010); phone ahead to check open low ssn; NH only with own san." € 10.30   2010*

⊞ **BELLAC** 7A3 (9km SE Rural) 46.05718, 0.97766 **Camping Fonclaire, 87300 Blond [tel/fax 05 55 60 88 26; fontclair@ neuf.fr; www.limousin-gites.com]** Fr Bellac take D675 S dir St Junien. Site on L in approx 7km, 2km bef Mortemart. Sm, some hdstg, pt shd, wc; chem disp; shwrs inc; (own san facs Nov-Mar) el pnts (6A) €3 (poss long lead req); gas 1km; lndtte; shop 4km; rest & bar 2km; sm htd pool; lake sw; fishing; golf 2km; horseriding 3km; no statics; dogs; phone 2km; Eng spkn; adv bkg; quiet; ccard not acc; CKE/CCI. "Peaceful, spacious CL-type site in lovely location; welcoming, helpful British owners; gd facs; gd hdstg in wet; nr Oradour-sur-Glane martyr vill; conv Futuroscope; gd cycling; gd; very quiet rural location." ◆ ltd € 14.00   2013*

BELLEME 4E2 (SW Urban) 48.37420, 0.55370 **Camp Municipal Le Val, Route de Mamers, 61130 Bellême [02 33 85 31 00 (Mairie) 06 07 11 27 39 (After 19h00); fax 02 33 83 58 85; mairie.bellame@wanadoo.fr; www. lepaysbellemois.com]** Fr Mortagne, take D938 S to Bellême; turn R ent town on D955 Alençon rd; site sp on L half-way down hill. Sm, hdg pitch, pt sl, pt shd; wc; chem disp (wc); shwrs inc; el pnts (8A) €2.65 (poss long lead req); shops 1km by footpath; supmkt 1km; playgrnd, pool, fishing; tennis adj; dogs €0.50; adv bkg rec high ssn. "Pretty, well-kept site; some pitches v sl; warden visits twice daily; gd san facs; poss long water hoses req; pitches poss soft when wet; steep walk to town." 15 Apr-15 Oct. € 9.30   2013*

BELLENTRE 9B4 (2km E Rural) 45.57576, 6.73553 **Camping L'Eden, 73210 Landry [04 79 07 61 81; fax 04 79 07 62 17; info@camping-eden.net; www.camping-eden.net]** Fr N90 Moûtiers to Bourg-St Maurice at 20km turn R sp Landry; site on L after 500m adj Rv Isère. Med, hdg/mkd pitch, hdstg, pt shd; htd wc; chem disp; shwrs inc; el pnts (10A) €4-6; gas; lndtte (inc dryer); shop; tradsmn; snacks; bar; playgrnd; htd pool; games rm; TV; dogs €1.50; phone; ski bus; poss cr; Eng spkn; adv bkg; quiet; ccard acc. "Gd cent mountain sports; helpful, friendly owner; red facs low ssn; ltd site lighting; poss unkempt end of ssn." 15 Dec-5 May & 25 May-15 Sep. € 21.40   2010*

See advertisement on pages 32 & 33

⊞ **BELLENTRE** 9B4 (3km SE Rural) 45.56057, 6.73956 **Camping de Montchavin, 73210 Bellentre [04 79 07 83 23; fax 04 79 07 80 18; info@montchavin-lescoches.com; www.montchavin-lescoches.com]** On N90 fr Moûtiers to Bourg-St Maurice (ignore site sps on N90); at 20km turn R onto D87E sp Landry & Montchavin-les-Coches; in 1km turn R onto D220, in 500m turn L onto D225; site in 7km on L at Montchavin. Med, mkd pitch, terr, pt shd; htd wc; mv service pnt; shwrs inc; el pnts (4-10A) €3.80-€7.60; gas; lndtte; shops 500m; pool in vill; games area; chairlift 200m; 60% statics; site clsd Oct; adv bkg (ess Jul/Aug & winter); quiet; ccard acc. "Site at 1200m; steep hill to shops; walking in summer, skiing in winter; magnificent setting." € 13.20   2009*

BELLEY 9B3 (8km E Rural) 45.76860, 5.76985 **Camping Du Lac du Lit du Roi, La Tuilière, 01300 Massignieu-de-Rives [04 79 42 12 03; fax 04 79 42 19 94; info@camping-savoie. com; www.camping-savoie.com]** Fr D1504 turn E onto D992 to Massignieu-de-Rives, site sp. Site on NE of lake nr Les Mures. Med, hdg/mkd pitch, terr, pt shd; htd wc; chem disp; mv service pnt; shwrs inc; el pnts (10A) inc (long lead req); gas; lndtte (inc dryer); shop 8km; tradsmn; rest, snacks; bar; BBQ; playgrnd; pool; lake sw & beach; boating; tennis; cycle hire; wifi; TV rm; 20% statics; dogs €4; phone; Eng spkn; adv bkg (fee); ccard acc; red long stay/low ssn; CKE/ CCI. "Superb location; many pitches on lake with lovely views; some lge pitches, others v sm; lack of site maintenance (2010); few water pnts (2009); very friendly site, idyllic location" ◆ 10 Apr-3 Oct. € 30.00 (CChq acc)   2013*

"I need an on-site restaurant"

We do our best to make sure site information is correct, but it is always best to check any must-have facilities are still available or will be open during your visit.

BELMONT SUR RANCE 8E4 (500m W Rural) 43.81777, 2.75108 Camping Val Fleuri du Rance, Route de Lacaune, 12370 Belmont-sur-Rance [05 65 99 04 76 or 06 88 42 28 78 (mob); marjandejong@wanadoo.fr; www.campinglevalfleuri.com] On D32 on ent vill fr SW; on L side of rd on sh unmade service rd. NB diff ent/exit to/fr S. Sm, hdg/mkd pitch, pt shd; wc; chem disp; shwrs inc; el pnts (6A) €3.50; gas; lndry rm; shop 500m; rest; pool 500m; rv fishing; tennis; wifi; some statics; dogs €1.50; Eng spkn; adv bkg; quiet; red low ssn; CKE/CCI. "Attractive valley setting; helpful Dutch owners; attractive sm town." ◆ ltd 1 Apr-30 Sep. € 14.00   2011*

BELUS see Peyrehorade 8F1

BELVES 7D3 (4km N Rural) 44.82560, 0.98902 **Camping du Port, 24170 Siorac-en-Périgord [05 53 28 63 81 or 06 18 12 64 75 (mob); contact@campingduport.net; www.campingduport.net]** On D25 in vill turn down beside Carrefour supmkt. Site ent strt ahead. Med, hdg/mkd pitch, shd; wc; shwrs; el pnts (10A) €3; lndtte; shops 1km; snacks; bar; playgrnd; beach, sw & fishing; Eng spkn; adv bkg rec; quiet; red low ssn. "Friendly owners; pleasant site; low trees - poss fruit drop onto vehicles." ◆ 15 May-30 Sep. € 12.00   2010*

BELVES 7D3 (7km SE Rural) 44.74150, 1.04518 **Camping Les Hauts de Ratebout, 24170 Ste Foy-de-Belvès [05 53 29 02 10; fax 05 53 29 08 28; ratebout@franceloc.fr; www.camping-hauts-ratebout.fr or www.campings-franceloc.fr]** Turn E fr D710 onto D54 2km S of Belvès & foll camp sp. NB Do not ent Belvès. Lge, pt sl, terr, pt shd; htd wc; chem disp; shwrs inc; el pnts inc (6-10A); gas; lndtte; shop; rest, snacks; bar; playgrnd; covr'd pool & paddling pool; waterslide; fishing; tennis; cycle hire; games area; golf 7km; horseriding; entmnt; adv bkg Jul/Aug; Eng spkn; ccard acc; red low ssn; CKE/CCI. "Excel hilltop site; lge pitches; gd cent for touring." ◆ 12 May-9 Sep. € 34.00   2008*

BELVES 7D3 (2km S Rural) 44.76192, 1.01457 **RCN Le Moulin de la Pique, 24170 Belvès [05 53 29 01 15; fax 05 53 28 29 09; info@rcn-lemoulindelapique.fr; www. rcn-campings.fr]** Site sp S of Belvès on L. Med, shd; htd wc; chem disp; baby facs; shwrs inc; el pnts (6A) inc; lndtte (inc dryer); shop; rest, snacks; bar; BBQ; playgrnd; 3 pools (1 htd); paddling pool; waterslides; boating; fishing; tennis; games area; wifi; entmnt; TV; some statics; dogs €6; Eng spkn; adv bkg; red low ssn. "Well-kept, well-run site in great location; friendly, helpful Dutch owners; vg for children; poss soft in wet weather; rd to to town 2.5km uphill; gd Sat mkt." ♦ 9 Apr-1 Oct. € 43.90 (CChq acc)   2011*

See advertisement above

BELVES 7D3 (4km SW Rural) 44.75258, 0.98330 **FLOWER Caming Les Nauves, Le Bos-Rouge, 24170 Belvès [05 53 29 12 64; campinglesnauves@hotmail.com; www. lesnauves.com or www.flowercampings.com]** On D53 fr Belvès. Site on L just after junc to Larzac. Avoid Belves cent - use lorry rte dir Monpazier. Med, hdg pitch, pt sl, pt shd; wc; chem disp; mv service pnt; baby facs; shwrs inc; el pnts (6A) inc; lndtte; shop adj; rest, snacks; bar; BBQ; playgrnd; pool; paddling pool; games rm; horseriding; cycle hire; games rm; internet; entmnt; TV; some statics; dogs €2.30; adv bkg; quiet. "Excel site; gd views fr some pitches." ♦ 23 Apr-25 Sep. € 19.50   2012*

See advertisement on pages 32 & 33

BELVES 7D3 (8km SW Rural) 44.75813, 0.90222 **Camping Terme d'Astor (Naturist), St Avit-Rivière, 24480 Bouillac [05 53 63 24 52; fax 05 53 63 25 43; termdastor@ wanadoo.fr; www.termedastor.com]** Leave D710 at Belvès onto D53; in 4km turn R onto D26 to Bouillac; pass thro vill; then turn 2nd L. Well sp. Med, mkd pitch, pt sl, shd; wc (some cont); chem disp; shwrs inc; el pnts (6A) €5.20; gas; lndtte; shop; tradsmn; rest, snacks; bar; BBQ; playgrnd; pool; paddling pool; jacuzzi; excursions; rafting; archery; tennis; horserding & canoeing nrby; games rm; internet; entmnt; TV; 10% statics; dogs free; phone; Eng spkn; adv bkg; quiet; ccard acc; red low ssn; INF. "Gd cent for Dordogne rv & chateaux; vg." ♦ ltd 23 Apr-25 Sep. € 28.00   2012*

BELZ 2F3 (W Coastal) 47.68288, -3.18869 **Camping St Cado, Port de St Cado, 56550 Belz [02 97 55 31 98; fax 02 97 55 27 52; info@camping-saintcado.com; www. camping-saintcado.com]** W fr Auray on D22 then D16. Well sp fr Belz. Med, hdg pitch, pt shd; wc; el pnts (3-6A) €2.60-3.60; lndtte; tradsmn; shop, rest 300m; playgrnd; fishing; boat hire 300m; tennis; volleyball; boules; games area; games rm; some statics; dogs €1.60; Eng spkn; adv bkg; quiet. "Popular site in beautiful location; seas views fr some pitches; helpful owner; rec phone ahead high ssn; vg; rec." 1 Apr-30 Sep. € 14.90   2013*

FRANCE

BENODET *2F2* (1.5km E Coastal) *47.86670, -4.09080* **Camping Du Letty, Rue du Canvez, 29950 Bénodet [02 98 57 04 69; fax 02 98 66 22 56; reception@campingduletty.com; www.campingduletty.com]** Fr N ent town on D34, foll sp Fouesnant D44. Le Letty sp R at rndabt. Fr E on N165 take D44 sp Fouesnant & foll rd to outskirts Bénodet. After town sp, site is sp. Lge, hdg/mkd pitch, hdstg, pt sl, pt shd; wc (some cont); chem disp; mv service pnt; baby facs; sauna; shwrs €0.60; el pnts (10A) €4; gas; lndtte; shop; snacks; bar; BBQ (gas); playgrnd; htd, covrd pool; paddling pool; waterslides & aquapark (new in 2011); sand beach adj; kayak hire; tennis; squash; games area; games rm; gym; golf & horseriding nr; library; wifi; entmnt; TV rm; dogs €2.30; phone; poss cr; Eng spkn; adv bkg; quiet; ccard acc; red low ssn; CKE/CCI. "Excel, well-run, beautifully laid-out site; clean & well-equipped; lovely beach adj; excel playgrnd; many activities; friendly, helpful staff; highly rec." ♦ 11 Jun-5 Sep. € 33.20   2011*

See advertisement opposite

BENODET *2F2* (500m SE Coastal) *47.86780, -4.09750* **Camping du Poulquer, 23 rue du Poulquer, 29950 Bénodet [02 98 57 04 19; fax 02 98 66 20 30; contact@ campingdupoulquer.com; www.campingdupoulquer. com]** Fr N ent town on D34. At rndabt after junc with D44 strt onto Rue Penfoul. At next rndabt (tourist info office on R after rndabt) go strt dir La Plage until reach seafront; turn L at seafront then L at end of prom at camping sp; site in 100m on R. Fr E on N165 take D44 sp Fouesnant & foll rd to outskirts Bénodet. After town sp, site is sp. Lge, hdg/mkd pitch, pt sl, pt shd; wc; chem disp; baby facs; shwrs inc; jaccuzi; el pnts (6-10A) inc (long lead poss req, poss rev pol); lndtte (inc dryer); shop; rest 600m; snacks; bar; BBQ; playgrnd; htd pool; covrd pool planned (2011); paddling pool; waterslide; aqua park; sand beach adj; tennis; golf & boat trips nr; cycle hire 1km; entmnt; wifi; games/TV rm; dogs €2; no c'vans/m'vans over 7.50m high ssn; Eng spkn; adv bkg; quiet; ccard not acc; red low ssn; CKE/CCI. "Lovely, well-kept, family-run site; friendly, helpful owner; gd, clean san facs, poss tired end of ssn; quiet site low ssn; mkt Mon; rec." ♦ 1 May-30 Sep. € 35.05 SBS - B16   2013*

> ## "Satellite navigation makes touring much easier"
>
> Remember most sat navs don't know if you're towing or in a larger vehicle – always use yours alongside maps and site directions.

BENODET *2F2* (7km W Coastal) *47.86903, -4.12848* **Camping Le Helles, 55 Rue du Petit-Bourg, 29120 Combrit-Ste Marine [tel/fax 02 98 56 31 46; contact@le-helles.com; www.le-helles.com]** Exit D44 S dir Ste Marine, site sp. Med, mkd pitch, pt sl, pt shd; htd wc; chem disp; baby facs; fam bthrm; shwrs inc; el pnts (6-10A) €3.50-4.40; lndtte; shop; tradsmn; snacks; BBQ; playgrnd; htd pool; paddling pool; sand beach 300m; some statics; dogs €2.60; Eng spkn; adv bkg; quiet; ccard acc; red low ssn; CKE/CCI. "Vg site with lge pitches; gd, clean san facs; friendly, helpful staff; excel beach. " ♦ 10 May-15 Sep. € 21.50   2011*

BENODET *2F2* (1km NW Rural) *47.88237, -4.10334* **Yelloh! Village Port de Plaisance, Route de Quimper, Clohars-Fouesnant, 29950 Bénodet [tel/fax 02 98 57 02 38; info@ campingbenodet.fr; www.campingbenodet.fr or www. yellohvillage.co.uk]** Fr Bénodet take D34 twd Quimper, site on R 200m bef rndabt at ent to town. Lge, hdg pitch, pt sl, pt shd; wc; chem disp; mv service pnt; shwrs inc; baby facs; el pnts (6A) inc; lndtte; shop; tradsmn; rest, snacks; bar; playgrnd; htd pool; sand/shgl beach 1.5km; tennis; games area; cycle hire; internet; entmnt; 80% statics; dogs €4; phone; poss cr; Eng spkn; poss noisy (disco); adv bkg; ccard acc; red low ssn; CKE/CCI. "Many tour ops on site; some pitches poss diff lge o'fits; excel." ♦ ltd 8 Apr-18 Sep. € 39.00   2009*

See advertisement on inside front cover

BENON see Courçon *7A2*

BENOUVILLE see Ouistreham *3D1*

BERAUT see Condom *8E2*

BERCK *3B2* (4km E Rural) *50.41861, 1.60556* **Camping L'Orée du Bois, 251 Chemin Blanc, 62180 Rang-du-Fliers [03 21 84 28 51; fax 03 21 84 28 56; oree.du.bois@ wanadoo.fr; www.oreedubois.fr]** Exit A6 junc 25 onto D140 & D917. Thro Rang-du-Fliers, turn R bef pharmacy into Chemin Blanc, site sp. V lge, hdg/mkd pitch, pt shd; wc (some cont); chem disp; mv service pnt; serviced pitches; shwrs inc; el pnts (6A) inc; gas; lndtte (inc dryer); shop adj; tradsmn; rest, snacks; bar; playgrnd; 2 pools (1 htd, covrd); paddling pool; tropical water park; sand beach 4km; tennis; games area; fishing lake; cycle hire; internet; entmnt; 80% statics; dogs €4; phone; Eng spkn; adv bkg; quiet; ccard acc; red low ssn/long stay/CKE/CCI. "Conv Le Touquet, Boulogne, Montreuil & Calais; peaceful site in woodland; ltd space for tourers; vg pools; pleasant, helpful owners; m'van pitches cramped" ♦ 30 Mar-31 Oct. € 47.00   2013*

BERGERAC *7C3* (500m S Urban) *44.84902, 0.47635* **Camp Municipal La Pelouse, 8 bis Rue Jean-Jacques Rousseau, 24100 Bergerac [tel/fax 05 53 57 06 67; population@ mairie-bergerac.fr; www.ville-bergerac.com]** On S bank of Rv Dordogne 300m W of old bdge opp town cent. Do not ent town, foll camping sp fr bdge, ent on R after L turn opp block of flats. Well sp, on Rv Dordogne. Med, mkd pitch, pt sl, pt shd; htd wc; chem disp; mv service pnt; shwrs inc; el pnts (6A) €3.20-4.50; gas; lndtte; shop in town; playgrnd; rv fishing adj; dogs €1.25; poss cr; adv bkg; Eng spkn; quiet; CKE/CCI. "Peaceful, spacious site on rv bank; friendly warden; san facs need update & ltd low ssn; easy walk by rv into attractive old town; no twin-axles & c'vans over 6m; site poss clsd earlier if weather bad; pitches poss muddy when wet; rec arr bef 1400 high ssn site has lots of trees so not all pitches in sun; Facs updated 2012" ♦ 1 Apr-31 Oct. € 17.20   2012*

BERGERAC *7C3* (8km W Rural) *44.83849, 0.33052* **FFCC Camping Parc Servois, 11 Rue du Bac, 24680 Gardonne [06 84 38 24 33; mfounaud24@orange.fr; www.bergerac-tourisme.com]** Fr D936 Bergerac to Bordeaux, in vill of Gardonne turn R into sm rd 100m after traff lts; site at end of rd by rv. Well sp in vill. Sm, pt shd; wc; chem disp; mv service pnt; shwrs inc; el pnts (10A) €2.60 (poss rev pol); shops 200m; rest 300m; dogs €0.70; phone 200m; Eng spkn; quiet; CKE/CCI. "Pretty, CL-type site on bank of Rv Dordogne; lge pitches; helpful warden; facs immac but dated & poss stretched when site full; gates clsd 2200-0800 with pedestrian access; sm mkt Wed & Sun; excel, well run site" 1 Jun-30 Sep. € 9.20   2013*

> ## "There aren't many sites open at this time of year"
>
> If you're travelling outside peak season remember to call ahead to check site opening dates – even if the entry says 'open all year'.

BERGUES *3A3* (7km N Rural) *50.96500, 2.43300* **Aire de Camping-Car Municipal, 59380 Bergues** Exit A25 junc 16 twd Bergues (N) on D916 then R onto D110. When town ramparts appear on L turn L twd town ent arch. Turn R bef drawbridge, site in 200m. NB m'vans only. Med, all hdstg, unshd; no facs; own san; shop, rest, snacks, bar in town; BBQ; dogs; bus adj; quiet. "Only avail when all-weather, winter sports pitch adj not in use; no charge; gd views of town; clean & tidy; pleasant walks."   2009*

BERGUES *3A3* (500m NE Urban) *50.97248, 2.43420* **Camping Le Vauban, Blvd Vauban, 59380 Bergues [03 28 68 65 25; fax 03 28 63 52 60; cassiopee.tourisme@wanadoo.fr; http://campingvauban.free.fr]** Exit A16 junc 60 twd Bergues on D916. In 2km turn L onto D2 dir Coudekerque vill. In 2km turn R at rndabt onto D72 to Bergues, turn R immed bef canal, site strt on at foot of town ramparts. Med, hdg/mkd pitch, terr, pt shd; wc (cont); chem disp; mv service pnt; baby facs; fam bthrm; shwrs €1.30; el pnts (6A) inc (poss rev pol); lndtte; tradsmn; shop, rest, snacks & bar in town; playgrnd; pool nr; 60% statics; no twin-axles; dogs €1.05; poss cr; adv bkg; quiet; no ccard acc; red low ssn; CKE/CCI. "Pleasant site; sm pitches poss diff lge o'fits; ltd manoeuvring in site rds; friendly & helpful; basic, dated san facs, but improvements in hand (2011); gates clsd 2130-0700 & poss clsd 1230-1730; lovely fortified town; conv Dunkerque & Calais; NH only." ◆ ltd 1 Apr-31 Oct. € 16.00   2011*

⊞ **BERGUES** *3A3* (4km NE Rural) *50.97720, 2.50447* **FFCC Parc Les Résidences La Becque, 791 Rue de l'Est, 59380 Warhem [03 28 62 00 40; fax 03 28 62 05 65; www.residences-la-becque.com]** Exit A25 at junc 16 sp Bergues. At top of slip rd turn L D916 then turn R at rndabt onto D110; L in 4km to Warhem. Site well sp in vill. Med, hdg/mkd pitch, hdstg, pt shd, wc (cont); own san; shwrs €1.55; el pnts (6A) €2.50; gas; lndry rm; shop 1km; supmkt in Hoymille; playgrnd; rv fishing 2km; tennis; 99% statics; dogs €1.55; quiet. "Only 2 pitches for tourers; low ssn ltd office opening (clsd Mon & Fri) & access/exit diff (Jun 08) - not rec to arr on these days; otherwise last resort NH; clean facs." ◆ € 17.00   2009*

BERNAY *3D2* (1km S Urban) *49.08020, 0.58703* **Camp Municipal, Rue des Canadiens, 27300 Bernay [02 32 43 30 47; camping@bernay27.fr; www.ville-bernay27.fr]** Site sp fr S'most (Alençon) rndabt off Bernay by-pass D438; twd France Parc Exposition then 1st L & on R. Well sp. Sm, hdg/mkd pitch, pt shd; wc; chem disp; mv service pnt; shwrs inc; el pnts (10A) €3.65 (poss rev pol); lndry rm; shop 500m; tradsmn; rest, bar 1km; playgrnd; pool 300m; wifi; TV rm; dogs; phone; adv bkg; quiet; no ccard acc; CKE/CCI. "Well-kept site; well set-out pitches, diff sizes; helpful & friendly staff; gd clean facs; barrier clsd 2200-0700; conv NH A28; excel, lovely site" ◆ 1 May-30 Sep. € 15.60   2013*

BERNERIE EN RETZ, LA see Pornic *2G3*

BERNEVAL LE GRAND *3B2* (500m N Coastal) *49.96158, 1.1933* **FFCC Camp Municipal Le Val Boisé, 56 Ave Capitaine Porthéous, 76340 Berneval-le-Grand [02 35 85 29 18; camping-berneval@wanadoo.fr; http://bernevallegrand.fr/camping]** Fr Dieppe take D925 for 6km, turn L at Graincourt onto D54 past Silo on R. Site sp. Sm, mkd pitch, hdstg, terr, pt shd; wc; chem disp; mv service pnt; shwrs; el pnts (16A) €2.70; shop 2km; playgrnd; shgl beach 700m; entmnt; some statics; dogs €0.80; Eng spkn; adv bkg rec; quiet, but rd noise some pitches; CKE/CCI. "Lovely quiet spot; v hilly area, poss diff lge o'fits; gd." 1 Apr-1 Nov. € 9.40   2009*

⊞ **BERNY RIVIERE** *3C4* (1.5km S Rural) *49.40603, 3.12860* **Camping La Croix du Vieux Pont, Rue de la Fabrique, 02290 Berny-Rivière [03 23 55 50 02; fax 03 23 55 05 13; info@la-croix-du-vieux-pont.com; www.la-croix-du-vieux-pont.com]** On N31 bet Soissons & Compiègne. At site sp turn onto D13, then at Vic-sur-Aisne take next R, R again then L onto D91. Foll sp to site on o'skts of Berny. V lge, hdg pitch, hdstg, pt shd; htd wc; chem disp; mv service pnt; some serviced pitch; baby facs; shwrs inc; el pnts (6A) €2.50 (poss rev pol, no earth & ltd supply); gas; lndtte (inc dryer); supmkt; tradsmn; rest, snacks; bar; playgrnd; 4 htd pools (2 covrd); waterslide; lake beach & sw; fishing; boating; tennis; games rm; horseriding; archery; golf; cycle hire; beauty cent; gym; wifi; entmnt; TV rm; many tour op statics high ssn; dogs; poss cr; Eng spkn; adv bkg rec; quiet; ccard acc; CKE/CCI. "Pleasant, well-run, clean site; busy low ssn; lge pitches, some rvside; excel for families or older couples; friendly, helpful staff; vg san facs; ltd low ssn; some sh stay pitches up steep bank; some pitches worn/uneven end of ssn (2010); some pitches liable to flood; site open all yr but no services Nov-Mar; excel." ◆ € 22.50   2010*

⊞ **BERNY RIVIERE** *3C4* (2km W Rural) *49.39280, 3.15161* **Camping La Halte de Mainville, 18 Chemin du Routy, 02290 Ressons-le-Long [03 23 74 26 69; fax 03 23 74 03 60; lahaltedemainville@wanadoo.fr; www.lahaltedemainville.com]** Fr Soissons W on N31 dir Compiègne, in approx 8km look for site sp on L. Clearly sp. Lge, hdg/mkd pitch, pt shd; htd wc; chem disp; shwrs inc; el pnts (6A) €3 (poss rev pol); lndtte; shop 4km; tradsmn; playgrnd; htd pool; paddling pool; fishing; tennis; 60% statics; dogs; phone; Eng spkn; adv bkg rec; quiet but poss some rd noise; no ccard acc; red CKE/CCI. "Pleasant, clean, conv NH; friendly staff; 1 hr fr Disneyland; vg." € 16.00   2010*

BERT see Donjon, Le *9A1*

BERTANGLES see Amiens *3C3*

BESANCON *6G2* (5km NE Rural) *47.26472, 6.07255* **Camping de Besancon - La Plage, 12 Route de Belfort, 25220 Chalezeule [03 81 88 04 26; fax 03 81 50 54 62; contact@campingdebesancon.com; www.campingdebesancon.com]** Exit A36 junc 4 S; foll sp Montbéliard & Roulons onto D683; site in 1.5km on R, 200m after rlwy bdge; well sp fr D683. Fr Belfort 2.65m height restriction; foll sp to Chalezeule & 300m after supmkt turn L to rejoin D683, site in 200m on rvside. Med, mkd pitch, terr, pt shd; htd wc; chem disp; mv service pnt; baby facs; shwrs inc; el pnts (6A) €3.95 (poss rev pol); lndtte (inc dryer); supmkt 1km; rest 500m; snacks; BBQ; playgrnd; htd pool adj; rv adj; kayaking; 50% statics; dogs €1.35; bus to city; poss cr; Eng spkn; quiet but some rd & rlwy noise; ccard acc; red low ssn; CKE/CCI. "Helpful staff; dated but well-kept san facs adequate; twin-axles extra." ♦ 1 Apr-30 Sep. € 26.90   2013*

BESANCON *6G2* (11km NW Rural) *47.32933, 5.97165* **Camping Les Peupliers, 25870 Geneuille [03 81 57 72 04]** Fr Besançon take N57 towards Vesoul then take L into D1 & fork R to Geneuille. Site sp thro vill. Sm, mkd pitch, pt shd; wc (some cont); chem disp (wc); el pnts (10A) inc; shops 1km, rest, snacks, bar 500m; rv; 10% statics; quiet. "Fairly run down, old fashioned but peaceful site nr rv; friendly welcome; some refurbed san facs; access to facs by stairs; poss mosquitoes." 23 Jun-15 Sep. € 10.90   2008*

BESSE SUR BRAYE *4F2* (S Rural) *47.83114, 0.75394* **Camping Le Val de Braye, 25 Rue du Val de Braye, 72310 Bessé-sur-Braye [02 43 35 31 13; fax 02 43 35 58 86; camping.bessesurbraye@orange.fr]** Fr D357 at St Calais take D303 to Bessé-sur-Braye; ignore Centre Ville sp & cont on by-pass. Site on L 300m beyond traff lts by sw pool. NB Avoid town cent. Med, pt shd; htd wc; chem disp; mv service pnt; shwrs inc; el pnts (13A) €2 (some rev pol); lndtte; shop adj; BBQ; playgrnd; htd, covrd pool adj; walking; fishing; TV; adv bkg; quiet; red long stay; CKE/CCI; "Helpful resident warden; pitch area ltd low ssn; well-kept, excel site." ♦ 15 Apr-15 Sep. € 8.00   2008*

BESSEGES see St Ambroix *9D2*

⊞ **BESSINES SUR GARTEMPE** *7A3* (4km N Rural) *46.14777, 1.36505* **Camp Municipal, 87250 Morterolles-sur-Semme [05 55 76 05 09 (Mairie) or 05 55 76 09 28 (LS) or; fax 05 55 76 68 45; ot.bessines@wanadoo.fr]** S on A20 take exit 23.1 sp Châteauponsac. Take 1st turn R, site on L in vill of Morterolles by stadium. N on A20 take exit 24.2 sp Bessines, turn under a'route & take 1st R sp Châteauponsac to Morterolles in 3km. Sm, mkd pitch, pt shd; htd wc; shwrs inc; el pnts (10A) inc (poss rev pol); lndry rm; playgrnd; covrd pool 200m; cycle hire; dogs; poss cr; Eng spkn; quiet; CKE/CCI. "Delightful farm site nr Limoges; gd san facs; helpful warden; poss itinerants; conv A20, excel NH; excel in all respects" ♦ ltd € 10.00   2013*

BESSINES SUR GARTEMPE *7A3* (1.5km SW Urban) *46.10013, 1.35423* **Camp Municipal Lac de Sagnat, Route de St Pardoux, 87250 Bessines-sur-Gartempe [05 55 76 17 69 or 05 55 76 05 09 (Mairie); fax 05 55 76 11 24; ot.bessines@wanadoo.fr; www.tourisme-bessines87.fr]** Exit A20 junc 24 sp Bessines-sur-Gartempe onto D220; then D27 sp lake. Foll sp to Bellevue Restaurant. At rest, turn R foll site sp. Well sp fr junc 24. Med, hdg/mkd pitch, pt sl, terr, pt shd; wc; chem disp (wc); shwrs inc; el pnts (6A) inc; lndtte; shops 1km; tradsmn high ssn; rest 500m; snacks high ssn; playgrnd adj; sand beach & lake sw adj; TV rm; Eng spkn; poss cr; quiet. "Pretty site with lake views; peaceful location; friendly staff; gd, clean san facs; poss unkempt low ssn (Jun 2009); hotel for meals nrby; conv NH A20." ♦ 15 Jun-15 Sep. € 18.70   2012*

BEUZEC CAP SIZUN see Douarnenez *2E2*

BEYNAC ET CAZENAC see Sarlat la Canéda *7C3*

BEZ, LE see Brassac *8F4*

BEZIERS *10F1* (8km NE Rural) *43.36254, 3.31924* **FFCC Aire Naturelle Domaine de Clairac (Philippon), Route de Bessan, 34500 Béziers [04 67 76 78 97 or 06 11 19 98 13 (mob); fax 04 67 76 78 98; camping.clairac@free.fr; www.campingclairac.com]** Exit A9 junc 35 Béziers Est; after toll take dir 'Centre Ville'; at 1st & 2nd rndabts foll sp Pézenas onto fr, in 5km turn R to Domaine de Clairac. Sm, pt shd; wc; chem disp; shwrs inc; el pnts (6A) €3; lndtte; tradsmn; snacks; bar; BBQ; playgrnd; htd pool; dogs; Eng spkn; quiet. "Friendly, helpful Swedish owner; gd." ♦ 1 Apr-30 Sep. € 15.00   2009*

BEZIERS *10F1* (10km NE Rural) *43.39849, 3.37338* **Camping Le Rebau, 34290 Montblanc [04 67 98 50 78; fax 04 67 98 68 63; gilbert@camping-lerebau.fr; www.camping-lerebau.fr]** NE on N9 fr Béziers-Montpellier, turn R onto D18. Site sp, narr ent 2.50m. Lge, hdg/mkd pitch, hdstg, pt shd; wc; chem disp; baby facs; shwrs inc; el pnts (5A) €4.50; gas 2km; lndtte; shop in vill; snacks & bar high ssn; playgrnd; pool; wifi; entmnt; TV; 10% statics; dogs €2.80; phone; bus 1km; poss cr; Eng spkn; adv bkg; quiet; red low ssn; CKE/CCI. "Gd site; tight ent & manoeuvring onto pitches; some facs old, but modern shwrs; ltd facs low ssn, but clean; helpful owner; gd pool; gd touring base; low ssn phone ahead to check open." 1 May-31 Aug. € 19.50   2012*

BEZIERS *10F1* (6km SE Urban) *43.3169, 3.2842* **Camping Les Berges du Canal, Promenade des Vernets, 34420 Villeneuve-les-Béziers [04 67 39 36 09; fax 04 67 39 82 07; contact@lesbergesducanal.com; www.lesbergesducanal.com]** Fr A9 exit junc 35 & foll sp for Agde. Exit 1st rndabt for D612 dir Béziers then 1st L onto D37 sp Villneuve-les-Béziers. Foll site sp to site adj canal. Med, hdg/mkd pitch, shd; wc; chem disp; mv service pnt; baby facs; shwrs inc; el pnts (16a) €2.50 (poss rev pol); lndtte; shop; rest, snacks; playgrnd; htd pool; beach 10km; cycle hire; 45% statics; dogs €3; poss cr; Eng spkn; adv bkg; CKE/CCI. "Pleasant site; facs clean but poss stretched in ssn; some pitches tight lge o'fits." 09 Mar-19 Oct. € 22.00 (CChq acc)   2013*

⊞ **BEZIERS** *10F1* (7km SW Rural) *43.31864, 3.14276* **Camping Les Peupliers, 7 Promenade de l'Ancien Stade, 34440 Colombiers [tel/fax 04 67 37 05 26; contact@camping-colombiers.com; www.camping-colombiers.com]** SW fr Béziers on D609 (N9) turn R on D162E & foll sp to site using heavy vehicle rte. Cross canal bdge & fork R; turn R & site on L. Easier ent fr D11 (Béziers-Capestang) avoiding narr vill rds, turn L at rndabt at end of dual c'way sp Colombiers; in 1km at rlwy bdge, go strt on; in 100m turn L (bef canal bdge) where rd turns sharp R. Med, mkd pitch, pt shd; wc; chem disp; mv service pnt; fam bthrm; shwrs inc; el pnts (10A) €3.50 (inc in high ssn) (poss rev pol); gas; lndtte (inc dryer); shop, rest 1km; snacks; bar; BBQ; playgrnd; pool; sand beach 15km; wifi; 25% statics; dogs €3; adv bkg; some rlwy noise; red low ssn/long stay; CKE/CCI. "Nr Canal du Midi away fr busy beach sites; modern san facs; no twin-axles; excel walking & cycling; pleasant sm vill, conv ofr NH" ♦ € 32.80   2013*

BIARRITZ *8F1* (3.5km E Rural) *43.46416, -1.53222* **Camping Le Parme, 2 Allée Etchécopar, 64600 Anglet [05 59 23 03 00; fax 05 59 41 29 55; campingdeparme@ wanadoo.fr; www.campingdeparme.com]** On D810 fr St Jean-de-Luz to Bayonne. Site sp on R bef Biarritz aerodrome, 500m down tarmac app rd. Lge, pt sl, terr, shd; htd wc (some cont); shwrs inc; el pnts (6-10A) €4-4.50; gas; lndtte; shops 3km; rest, snacks; bar; playgrnd; pool; paddling pool; sand beach 3km; tennis; golf 2km; wifi; entmnt; TV; dogs €3; ccard acc. "Diff exit up steep slope & by blind corner - owner will advise alt R-turn rte; pleasant site." ♦ 4 Apr-7 Nov. € 28.00   2009*

"That's changed – Should I let The Club know?"

If you find something on site that's different from the site entry, fill in a report and let us know. See www.caravanclub.co.uk/europereport.

BIARRITZ *8F1* (3km S Coastal) *43.43838, -1.58184* **Village Camping Sunêlia Berrua, Rue Berrua, 64210 Bidart [05 59 54 96 66; fax 05 59 54 78 30; contact@berrua.com; www.berrua.com]** Exit A63 junc 4 dir Bidart, fr Bidart on D810 sp St Jean de Luz, L at 1st traff lts, site sp. Lge, pt sl, pt shd; wc; chem disp; mv service pnt; steam rm; shwrs inc; baby facs; el pnts (6A) €5.70; (poss long lead req); gas; lndtte (inc dryer); shop; tradsmn; rest, snacks; bar; BBQ; playgrnd; htd pool & paddling pool; waterslides; beach 1km; tennis; cycle hire; archery; golf 2km; wifi; TV; 50% statics; dogs €4; phone; bus 1km; poss cr; Eng spkn; adv bkg; some rd & rlwy noise; ccard acc; red low ssn; CKE/CCI. "Busy, well-kept site in attractive location; excel, clean facs; pitches tight lge o'fits; site rds narr, low trees, some high kerbs; muddy after rain; gd rest; sh walk to vill; gd." ♦ 2 Apr-25 Sep. € 35.30 (CChq acc)   2012*

BIARRITZ *8F1* (3km S Coastal) *43.45305, -1.57277* **Yelloh! Village Ilbarritz, Ave de Biarritz, 64210 Bidart [05 59 23 00 29; fax 05 59 41 24 59; contact@camping-ilbarritz.com; www.camping-ilbarritz.co.uk or www. yellohvillage.com]** S fr Bayonne on D810, by-pass Biarritz. 1km after A63 junc turn R at rndabt immed after Intermarché on R; sp to Pavillon Royal. Site 1km on R sp. Lge, mkd pitch, pt sl, terr, shd; wc; chem disp; shwrs inc; baby facs; el pnts (10A) inc; gas; lndtte; shop; tradsmn; rest & snacks high ssn; bar; playgrnd; htd pool; sand beach 600m; tennis; games area; cycle hire; golf nr; horseriding; internet; TV; many statics & tour ops; dogs €4; phone; poss cr; Eng spkn; adv bkg over 15 days & high ssn; ccard acc; red low ssn; CKE/CCI. "Attractive, mature site; lge pitches; narr access rds poss diff long o'fits; excel pool; gd beaches nrby; gd." ♦ 8 Apr-25 Sep. € 39.00   2009*

See advertisement on inside front cover

BIARRITZ *8F1* (5km S Rural) *43.43678, -1.56780* **Camping Le Ruisseau des Pyrénées, Route d'Arbonne, 64210 Bidart [05 59 41 94 50; fax 05 59 41 95 73; francoise. dumont3@wanadoo.fr; www.camping-le-ruisseau.fr or www.les-castels.com]** Exit D810 at Bidart take rd sp Arbonne, site sp. Rds twisty & narr. Lge, some hdg pitch, pt sl, terr, pt shd; wc; chem disp (wc); mv service pnt; shwrs inc; el pnts (6A) inc; gas; lndtte; shop; rest, snacks; bar; playgrnd; 3 pools (1 covrd) & paddling pool; waterslide; lake fishing; boating; sand beach 2.5km; tennis; games area; cycling; 90% statics; dogs €1.50; poss cr; adv bkg ess high ssn; poss noisy; red low ssn; golf nr; CKE/CCI. "Steep slope/short run to barrier poss diff; best pitches by lake; site muddy after rain; excel for children & teenagers." 24 Apr-14 Sep. € 37.00   2008*

See advertisement on inside back cover

BIARRITZ *8F1* (5km S Coastal) *43.43371, -1.59040* **Camping Ur-Onéa, Rue de la Chapelle, 64210 Bidart [05 59 26 53 61; fax 05 59 26 53 94; contact@uronea.com; www.uronea.com]** Exit A63 junc 4 dir Bidart, fr Bidart on D810 sp St Jean de Luz, L at traff lts in town where site sp, then 2nd R, L at motel, site is 300m on L. Access fr main rd a bit tricky, 2nd access further S is easier. Lge, mkd pitch, hdstg, pt terr, pt shd; wc (some cont); chem disp; some serviced pitches; baby facs; fam bthrm; shwrs inc; el pnts (10A) inc; gas; lndtte (inc dryer); shop high ssn; tradsmn; rest, snacks; bar, BBQ; playgrnd; htd pool; paddling pool; sand beach 600m; lake sw 12km; wifi; entmnt; TV; 20% statics; dogs €2.50; phone; Eng spkn; adv bkg; quiet; ccard acc; red low ssn; CKE/CCI. "Well-kept site 600m fr Bidart; various pitch sizes, most not terr; suitable for o'fits up to 8m; staff friendly & helpful; excel, clean san facs; conv Pays Basque vills." ♦ 9 Apr-17 Sep. € 32.50   2011*

See advertisement opposite

BIARRITZ *8F1* (2km SW Coastal) *43.4625, -1.5672* **Camping Biarritz, 28 Rue Harcet, 64200 Biarritz [05 59 23 00 12; fax 05 59 43 74 67; info@biarritz-camping.fr; www.biarritz-camping.fr]** S fr Bayonne on D810, by-pass Biarritz & cont to junc of D810 coast rd sp Bidart & Biarritz; double back on this rd, take 1st exit at next rndabt, 1st L dir Biarritz Cent, foll sp to site in 2km. Lge, mkd pitch, pt sl, terr, pt shd; wc; chem disp; shwrs inc; el pnts (10A) €4; gas; lndtte; shop; tradsmn; rest, snacks; bar; playgrnd; htd pool; padddling pool; sand beach 1km; tennis 4km; entmnt; 10% statics; no dogs; bus at gate; poss cr; adv bkg; ccard acc; noisy in high ssn; red low ssn/ CKE/CCI. "One of better sites in area, espec low ssn." ♦ ltd 12 May-14 Sep. € 24.00 2010*

BIARRITZ *8F1* (3.5km SW Coastal) *43.45525, -1.58119* **Camping Pavillon Royal, Ave du Prince de Galles, 64210 Bidart [05 59 23 00 54; fax 05 59 23 44 47; info@pavillon-royal.com; www.pavillon-royal.com]** Exit A63/E4 junc 4; then take D810 S dir Bidart. At rndabt after Intermarché supmkt turn R (sp Biarritz). After 600m turn left at site sp. Lge, hdg/mkd pitch, pt sl, pt shd, wc (some cont); chem disp; mv service pnt; serviced pitch; baby facs; shwrs inc; el pnts (10A) inc (long lead poss req); gas; lndtte (inc dryer); shop; tradsmn; rest, snacks; bar; BBQ; playgrnd; htd pool; paddling pool; sand beach adj; tennis nr; fitness rm; games rm; golf 500m; horseriding 2km; wifi; entmnt; games rm/TV; no statics; no dogs; no c'vans/m'vans over 8m; poss cr; Eng spkn; adv bkg (ess Jul/Aug); ccard acc; red low ssn. "Lovely, well-kept, friendly, busy site in beautiful location beside beautiful beach; various pitch sizes, some with sea views, some sm & diff lge o'fits; direct access via steps to excel beach; san facs poss irreg cleaning low ssn; mkt Sat; excel." ♦ 15 May-30 Sep. € 80.10 SBS - A06 2013*

BIARRITZ *8F1* (5km SW Coastal) *43.43584, -1.58295* **Camping Oyam, Chemin Oyamburua, 64210 Bidart [05 59 54 91 61; fax 05 59 54 76 87; accueil@camping-oyam.com; www.camping-oyam.com]** Leave A63 at junc 4 onto D810; 150m after Bidart boundary sp turn L at traff lts sp Arbonne. In 600m at brow of hill turn R & then immed L. Med, mkd pitch, pt sl, terr, pt shd; wc; chem disp; baby facs; shwrs inc; el pnts (3A) €4.50; lndtte; shop; rest, snacks; bar; BBQ; playgrnd; pool; paddling pool; sand beach 1.2km; games area; entmnt; TV; 90% statics; dogs €2.50; free bus to vill; Eng spkn; adv bkg; some rd & rlwy noise; CKE/CCI. "Well-managed site in lovely surroundings; clean, modern san facs; pitches sm & awkward." ♦ 1 Jun-30 Sep. € 26.00 2008*

BIDART see Biarritz *8F1*

BIESHEIM see Neuf Brisach *6F3*

BIGANOS see Audenge *7D1*

BIGNAC see Angoulême *7B2*

BILIEU see Abrets, Les *9B3*

BINIC *2E3* (1km S Coastal) *48.59216, -2.8238* **Camping Le Panoramic, Rue Gasselin, 22520 Binic [02 96 73 60 43; fax 02 96 69 27 66; camping.le.panoramic@wanadoo.fr; www.lepanoramic.net]** D786 St Brieuc-Paimpol. 1st slip rd for Binic & 1st R up hill 100m, site sp. Med, mkd pitch, pt sl, terr, pt shd; htd wc; chem disp; shwrs; el pnts (10A) €5 (poss rev pol); gas; lndtte; shop; snacks; bar; BBQ; htd pool; paddling pool; sand beach 500m; golf adj; wifi; entmnt; 75% statics; dogs €2.50; quiet; red low ssn. "Pleasant site; clean facs; coastal path nr; excel facs, easy walk to beach" 1 Apr-30 Sep. € 18.70 2012*

BINIC *2E3* (2.5km S Coastal) *48.58269, -2.80477* **Camping Les Madières, Rue du Vau Madec, 22590 Pordic [02 96 79 02 48; fax 02 96 79 46 67; campinglesmadieres@wanadoo.fr; www.campinglesmadieres.com]** Site at E end of Pordic vill, sp. Med, pt sl,pt shd; htd wc (mainly cont); shwrs inc; el pnts (10A) €4; gas; lndtte; sm shop; rest, snacks; bar; htd pool; shgl beach 800m; sand beach & watersports 3km; entmnt; 10% statics; dogs €2.50; adv bkg; quiet; red low ssn/CKE/CCI. "Pleasant, clean, child-friendly site; helpful, friendly owners; immac facs; poss diff access to shgl beach, Binic beach OK; highly rec; quiet site" ♦ 30 Mar-2 Nov. € 32.00 2013*

BINIC *2E3* (4km S Coastal) *48.57875, -2.78498* **Camping Le Roc de l'Hervieu, 19 Rue d'Estienne d'Orves, 22590 Pordic [tel/fax 02 96 79 30 12; le.roc.de.lhervieu@wanadoo.fr; www.campinglerocdelhervieu.fr]** Site on E side of vill off N786, Binic-St Brieuc rd. Turn E in cent of vill, sp to Les Madières then sp Le Roc de l'Hervieu. Med, hdg pitch, pt shd; wc (some cont); chem disp; mv service pnt; shwrs inc; el pnts (10A) €3.60; lndtte; shop; bar; BBQ; playgrnd; sand beach 600m; fishing; some statics; quiet. "Gd walking; pleasant site." ♦ 1 May-30 Sep. € 16.20 2009*

BINIC *2E3* (8km SW Rural) *48.55622, -2.94635* **Camping à la Ferme La Corderie (Hello), Le Courtil Rault, 22170 Plélo [02 96 74 21 21 or 06 71 05 12 49 (mob); hello.odile@22. wanadoo.fr]** Fr Binic take D4 dir Châtelaudren, site on R at La Corderie. Sm, pt shd; wc; chem disp; shwrs inc; el pnts (10A); lndtte; playgrnd; sand beach 8km; TV; 20% statics; no dogs; quiet. "CL-type site." May-Sep. 2010*

> ## "I like to fill in the reports as I travel from site to site"
> You'll find report forms at the back of this guide, or you can fill them in online at www.caravaclub.co.uk/europereport.

BINIC *2E3* (1.2km W Rural) *48.60539, -2.84124* **Camping des Palmiers, Ker Viarc'h, 22520 Binic [tel/fax 02 96 73 72 59 or 06 67 32 78 66 (mob); campingpalmiers.chantal@laposte. net; www.campingpalmiers.com]** N fr St Brieuc on D786 dir Pordic/Paimpol on coast rd. Foll sp to site on o'skts on Binic. Sm, mkd pitch, hdstg, terr, pt shd; htd wc; chem disp; mv service pnt; baby facs; shwrs inc; el pnts (10A) €6; lndtte; gas; shop; supmkt 1km; tradsmn; rest 1.5km; snacks; bar; BBQ; playgrnd; htd, covrd pool; paddling pool; sand beach 1.5km; tennis 1km; games rm; wifi; entmnt; TV; 6% statics; dogs €2; Eng spkn; adv bkg; quiet; red low ssn/CKE/CCI. "Warm welcome; excel site in gd situation." ♦ 1 Jun-30 Sep. € 21.00 2009*

BINIC *2E3* (6km W Rural) *48.60640, -2.86160* **FFCC Camping Les Etangs, Pont de la Motte, Route de Châtelaudren, 22410 Lantic [02 96 71 95 47; contact@campinglesetangs. com; www.campinglesetangs.com]** D786 fr Binic twd Paimpol; turn L approx 1km on D4 sp Châtelaudren & Lantic; in 3km at x-rds turn L foll camping sp; site in 50m on R. Fr N12 Guingamp-St Brieuc take D4 at Châtelaudren. Med, hdg/mkd pitch, pt sl, terr, pt shd; wc (cont); chem disp; mv service pnt; shwrs inc; el pnts (6A) €3.40; gas; lndtte (inc dryer); sm shop; tradsmn; snacks; BBQ; playgrnd; htd pool; paddling pool; beach 3km; wifi; TV; 2% statics; dogs €1.30; phone; poss v cr; Eng spkn; adv bkg; quiet; ccard acc; CKE/CCI. "Gd base slightly away fr cr coast sites; helpful, friendly owners; gd pool; excel." ♦ 1 Apr-30 Sep. € 13.80 2010*

BIRON *7D3* (4km S Rural) *44.60035, 0.87111* **Camping Le Moulinal, 24540 Biron [05 53 40 84 60; fax 05 53 40 81 49; lemoulinal@franceloc.fr; www.lemoulinal.com or www. campings-franceloc.fr]** Fr Bergerac S dir Agen, then E Issigeac & Villeréal; fr Villeréal dir Lacapelle-Biron, site sp. Fr Monpazier take D104 twd Villeréal; in 4km S on D53 thro Biron & onto Lacapelle-Biron. Head W twd Villeréal for 2km to site. Lge, mkd pitch, terr, pt shd; htd wc (some cont); baby facs; shwrs; el pnts (10A) inc; gas; lndtte; shop; rest, snacks; bar; BBQ; playgrnd; htd pool; sand beach for lake sw; boating; tennis; games area; games rm; wifi; entmnt; many statics; dogs €5; poss cr; Eng spkn; adv bkg; quiet; ccard acc; red low ssn; CKE/CCI. "Lovely site; extra for lakeside & 'super' pitches; access to some pitches diff due trees." ♦ 3 Apr-19 Sep. € 37.00 2008*

BIRON *7D3* (4km SW Rural) *44.61394, 0.83535* **Camping Laborde (Naturist), 47150 Paulhiac [05 53 63 14 88; fax 05 53 61 60 23; domainelaborde@wanadoo.fr; www.domainelaborde.com]** Leave Montpazier on D2 sp Monflanquin/Villeréal; in 5.6km at Source de la Brame turn L onto D2E sp Monflanquin. Turn R onto D255 at sp Laborde FFN dir Lacapelle-Born. Med, pt sl, pt shd; wc; chem disp; sauna; shwrs inc; el pnts (3-10A) €3.50-4.50 (poss long lead req); gas; lndtte; ltd shop; tradsmn; supmkt 14km; rest, snacks; bar; playgrnd; 2 tropical indoor pools & outdoor pool; lake sw adj; tennis; games rm; dogs €3; Eng spkn; adv bkg; quiet; ccard acc; red low ssn; INF card not req. ♦ 31 Mar-1 Oct. € 23.00 2008*

BIRON *7D3* (W Rural) *44.6305, 0.8733* **Aire Communale, Route de Vergt de Biron, 24540 Biron [05 53 63 15 23; fax 05 53 24 28 12]** Fr Villeréal or Monpazier on D104/D2 turn onto D53 to Biron, foll sp for Information. M'vans only. Sm, unshd; own san; chem disp; mv service pnt; water €2; el pnts €2; shop 8km; rest, snacks & bar 100m; dogs; poss cr; quiet. "Extensive views fr site; gd NH." 1 Apr-31 Oct. € 2.00 2009*

BISCARROSSE *7D1* **See also sites listed under Gastes, Sanguinet and Parentis-en-Born.**

BISCARROSSE *7D1* (3km N Coastal) *44.42955, -1.16792* **Campéole Camping Navarrosse, 712 Chemin de Navarrosse, 40600 Biscarrosse [05 58 09 84 32; fax 05 58 09 86 22; navarrosse@campeole.com; www. camping-navarrosse.com or www.campeole.com]** Fr Biscarrosse N on D652 dir Sanguinet; 1km beyond turning to L to Biscarrosse-Plage, turn L onto D305 & foll sp to Navarrosse. V lge, mkd pitch, pt shd; htd wc; baby facs; mv service pnt; baby facs; shwrs inc; el pnts (10A) inc (poss rev pol); lndtte (inc dryer); tradsmn; supmkt adj; rest 200m; snacks; bar; BBQ; playgrnd; sand beach & lake sw adj; fishing; sailing; tennis; cycle hire; games area; games rm; wifi; entmnt; TV; 40% statics; dogs; late arr area; Eng spkn; quiet; ccard acc; red low ssn/CKE/CCI. "Pleasant site; vg for children; helpful staff; gd walking; sailing lessons; cycle rtes; gd value." ♦ 30 Apr-12 Sep. € 32.80 2012*

See advertisement on pages 14 & 15

BISCARROSSE *7D1* (5km N Rural) *44.43996, -1.14068* **Aire Naturelle Le Frézat (Dubourg), 2583 Chemin de Mayotte, 40600 Biscarrosse [06 22 65 57 37]** Fr Biscarrosse on D652 dir Sanguinet; after 5km turn L at water tower onto D333; site 2nd on R in 1km. Med, shd; wc (some cont); chem disp (wc); shwrs €1.20; el pnts (6A) inc; shops 4km; tradsmn; BBQ; playgrnd; lake & sand beach 3km; dogs; Eng spkn; adv bkg; quiet; CKE/CCI. "Lovely site; friendly owners; clean facs; cycle paths." 15 Apr-15 Oct. € 14.00 2009*

BISCARROSSE *7D1* (5km N Rural) *44.43535, -1.15496*
Camping Village Mayotte Vacances, 368 Chemin des Roseaux, 40600 Biscarrosse [05 58 78 00 00; fax 05 58 78 83 91; camping@mayottevacances.com; www. mayottevacances.com] Twd NE fr Biscarrosse on D652 L sp Navarrosse & at 1st fork R to Mayotte, foll camping sp. V lge, mkd pitch, pt shd; wc; chem disp; mv service pnt; shwrs inc; el pnts (10A) inc (poss rev pol); snacks; gas; lndtte; shop; rest, snacks; bar; BBQ; playgrnd; pool complex; waterslide; jacuzzi; lake sw adj; sailing school; sand beach 9km; tennis; cycle hire; games rm; entmnt; TV; 95% statics; dogs €5; Eng spkn; adv bkg (ess Jul/Aug); quiet; ccard acc; red low ssn/CKE/CCI. "Excel leisure facs; vg for families; suitable o'fits up to 8m; rec." ♦ 3 Apr-3 Oct. € 43.00   2010*

See advertisement above

BISCARROSSE *7D1* (3km NE Rural) *44.43374, -1.13064*
Aire Naturelle Camping Les Bruyères, 3725 Route de Bordeaux, 40600 Biscarrosse [05 58 78 79 23] N fr Biscarrosse on D652 twd Arcachon; site on L visible fr rd, just bef sm concrete water tower. Sm, shd; wc; chem disp (wc); shwrs €1.10; baby facs; el pnts (3-10A) inc (poss rev pol); shop adj; BBQ; cooking facs; sand beach 10km; lake sw & watersports 3km; adv bkg; quiet. "Helpful owners; CL-type site; beach 10km excel for surfing; rec Latécoère seaplane museum." 1 Apr-30 Sep.   2008*

BISCARROSSE *7D1* (8km NE Rural) *44.46230, -1.12900*
Camping de la Rive, Route de Bordeaux, 40600 Biscarrosse [05 58 78 12 33; fax 05 58 78 12 92; info@ larive.fr; www.larive.fr] Fr Bordeaux on A63 dir Bayonne/ San Sebastian; at junc 22 turn off onto A660; cont until 1st junc where turn L onto D216; cont for 17km to Sanguinet; cont on A652 for 3km; site sp on R nr Lake Cazaux. V lge, hdg/ mkd pitch, pt shd; htd wc; chem disp; mv service pnt; baby facs; shwrs inc; el pnts (6A) inc; gas; lndtte (inc dryer); shop; rest, snacks; bar; BBQ zone (gas); playgrnd; 7 pools (1 htd covrd) inc paddling pool; waterslide; jacuzzi; lake sw & private, sand beach adj; watersports; tennis; cycle hire; games area; games rm; wifi; entmnt; games/TV rm; 30% statics; dogs €8.20; no c'van/m'van over 9m; poss cr; phone; Eng spkn; adv bkg; some noise fr entmnt high ssn; ccard acc; red low ssn; CKE/CCI. "On banks of Lake Cazaux-Sanguinet in delightful area; bustling, noisy site high ssn; many acitivies for all ages; some pitches diff lge o'fits due trees; gd beaches; gd cycling; lovely rest, pleasant staff" ♦ 6 Apr-8 Sep. € 68.20 (CChq acc) SBS - A38   2013*

See advertisement on next page

BISCARROSSE *7D1* (1.5km S Rural) *44.38869, -1.18170*
**Camping Latécoère, 265 Rue Louis Bréguet, 40600
Biscarrosse [05 58 78 13 01; fax 05 58 78 16 26; latecoere.
biscarrosse@wanadoo.fr]** S on D652 Sanguinet-Biscarrosse rd
to cent of town. Strt in front of church by mkt sq; site in 1.5km
adj lake. Lge, mkd pitch, pt shd; wc; shwrs inc; el pnts (10A)
inc; lndtte; shop; snacks; bar; BBQ; playgrnd adj; pool; lake sw
& sand beach adj; watersports; 40% statics; dogs €2; quiet.
"Yacht club adj; museums opp; seaplanes." 1 May-30 Sep.
€ 25.00   2009*

BISCARROSSE *7D1* (8km NW Coastal) *44.45804, -1.23968*
**Campéole Camping Le Vivier, 681 Rue du Tit, 40600
Biscarrosse-Plage [05 58 78 25 76; fax 05 58 78 35 23;
vivier@campeole.com; www.camping-biscarrosse.info
or www.campeole.com]** Fr Arcachon & Pyla-sur-Mer, take
D218, D83 to Biscarrosse Plage. Town o'skts site sp to R. Foll
sps. Lge, pt shd; wc; chem disp; baby facs; shwrs; el pnts
(10A) inc (poss rev pol); lndtte (inc dryer); shop; rest, snacks;
bar; playgrnd; htd pool; paddling pool; sand beach 800m;
boating; fishing; tennis; games rm; horseriding nr; cycle hire;
wifi; entmnt; some statics; dogs €3.50; quiet; ccard acc; red
low ssn. "Sandy site in pine forest; access to beach via path
thro dunes." 1 May-19 Sep. € 31.70   2010*

See advertisement on pages 14 & 15

BISCARROSSE *7D1* (9km NW Coastal) *44.44133,
-1.24558* **Campéole Camping Plage Sud, 230 Rue des
Bécasses, 40600 Biscarrosse-Plage [05 58 78 21 24; fax
05 58 78 34 23; plage-sud@campeole.com; www.landes-
camping.net or www.campeole.com]** Clearly sp on D146
on ent to Biscarrosse-Plage in pine forest. V lge, mkd pitch,
pt sl, pt shd; wc; chem disp; baby facs; shwrs inc; el pnts (6A)
inc; lndtte (inc dryer); shop adj; tradsmn; snacks; bar; BBQ;
playgrnd; htd pool; paddling pool; sand beach 800m; cycle
hire; wifi; entmnt; 50% statics; dogs €3.50; Eng spkn; adv
bkg (rec high ssn); ccard acc; red low ssn; CKE/CCI. "Gd site,
lively high ssn; helpful staff; facs stretched high ssn; gd beach,
inc surfing; some pitches on soft sand; sm, modern town, lots
of rests; New entmnt, pool and san facs (2013); excel for sh or
long stay" 27 Apr-15 Sep. € 54.45   2013*

See advertisement on pages 14 & 15

BIZANET see Narbonne *10F1*

BIZE MINERVOIS *8F4* (300m SW Urban) *43.31584, 2.87070*
**Camping La Cesse, Esplanade Champs de Foire, 11120 Bize-
Minervois [tel/fax 04 68 46 14 40; marieange.lurqui@gmail.
com; www.audetourisme.com]** Exit N fr D5/D11 Béziers-
Carcassonne rd onto D26 to Bize-Minervois (D26 is 800m to E of
D607); site in 1.8km on L, just bef rv bdge in S of vill. Sm, mkd
pitch, pt shd; wc; chem disp (wc); shwrs inc; el pnts (5A) €2.30;
lndtte; shops, rest & snacks nrby; BBQ; rv 400m; dogs €1.20;
phone; poss cr; adv bkg; quiet; red low ssn; CKE/CCI. "Peaceful,
relaxing site; in need of TLC but some maintenance works in
progress (2011)." 1 May-30 Sep. € 11.40   2011*

BLACERET see Villefranche sur Saône *9B2*

BLAIN *2G4* (1km S Rural) *47.46782, -1.76787* **Camp Municipal Le Château, Route de St Nazaire, 44130 Blain [02 40 79 11 00; otsi.blain@free.fr; www.ville-blain.fr]** Fr N on N137 turn W onto N171; fr S on N137 turn W onto D164 to Blain. On app town, take L at rndabt on N171 dir St Nazaire/ Bouvron. Immed after x-ing Brest-Nantes canal bdge, site on L adj to chateau. Sm, mkd pitch, pt shd; wc; shwrs inc; chem disp; mv service pnt; el pnts (10A) €2.40; lndry rm; shops 500m; tradsmn; rest, bar 500m; playgrnd; pool 1km; fishing; boating; dogs €1; phone adj; adv bkg; quiet but some rd noise; CKE/CCI. "Super, well-managed site; gd pitch size; helpful staff; immac san facs; chateau museum adj; no twin-axles; no access for vehicles after 2000 high ssn." ♦ 1 May-30 Sep. € 7.50   2010*

BLAMONT *6E3* (1km E Rural) *48.58890, 6.85051* **Camp Municipal de la Vezouze, Route de Cirey, 54450 Blâmont [03 83 76 28 28 (Mairie) or 06 07 70 27 39 (mob); fax 03 83 76 28 32; www.tourisme-meurtheetmoselle.fr]** Fr Sarrebourg on N4 dir Blâmont; foll sps Town Cent, then turn L onto D74/ D993 dir Cirey-sous-Vezouze & foll sp for site. Sm, pt shd; wc; shwrs inc; el pnts (16A) €2; shop, rest, snacks, bar 300m; playgrnd; sports area; sw, fishing adj; dogs €1; quiet. "Gd rvside site; gd walking, cycling." 15 May-15 Sep. € 12.00   2011*

BLANC, LE *4H2* (2km E Rural) *46.63202, 1.09389* **Camping L'Ile d'Avant, Route de Châteauroux, 36300 Le Blanc [02 54 37 88 22; fax 02 54 36 35 42; info@tourisme-leblanc.fr; www.tourisme-leblanc.fr]** Fr town cent take D951 twd St Gaultier/Argenton; site on R 1km after supmkt. Med, hdg/mkd pitch, pt shd; wc; mv service pnt; shwrs inc; el pnts (6A) inc; lndtte; shops 1km; rest, snacks, bar 2km; BBQ; playgrnd; htd pool adj inc; fishing; tennis adj; adv bkg; quiet but some rd noise. "Gd pitches; adj sports field & club house; open Apr with adv bkg only, otherwise May." 1 Apr-30 Sep. € 14.00   2012*

BLANGY LE CHATEAU *3D1* (500m N Rural) *49.24670, 0.27370* **Camping Le Domaine du Lac, 14130 Blangy-le-Château [02 31 64 62 00; fax 02 31 65 03 46; info@domaine-du-lac.fr; www.domaine-du-lac.fr]** Fr Pont-l'Evêque & A13 S on D579 twd Lisieux. In 5km turn L onto D51 to Blangy where at fountain (rndabt) turn L, taking care. In 200m at end of vill turn L onto D140 Rte de Mesnil & site 200m on R. Site is 5km SE of Pont-l'Evêque. Med, mkd pitch, pt sl, pt shd; wc; chem disp; baby facs; shwrs inc; el pnts (6A) inc (long lead poss req); gas; lndtte; shop & 1km; rest, snacks; bar; BBQ; beach 22km; lake fishing; tennis; games rm; wifi; 70% statics; dogs; adv bkg; some rd noise; ccard acc; CKE/CCI. "Peaceful NH in lovely area; friendly British owner; poss uneven pitches; tired, access to pitches diff when wet; pretty vill; gd walks; conv Honfleur; 1hr to Le Havre ferry; NH only; mainly statics" 1 Apr-31 Oct. € 24.30   2013*

BLANGY LE CHATEAU *3D1* (3km SE Rural) *49.22525, 0.30438* **Camping Le Brévedent, 14130 Le Brévedent [02 31 64 72 88 or 02 31 64 21 50 (LS); contact@campinglebrevedent.com; www.campinglebrevedent.com or www.les-castels.com]** Fr Pont l'Evêque & A13 go S on D579 twd Lisieux; after 5km turn L onto D51 twd Blangy-le-Château. In Blangy bear R at rndabt to stay on D51 & foll sp to Le Brévedent & Moyaux; site on L in 3km. Med, mkd pitch, pt sl, pt shd; htd wc; chem disp; mv service pnt; baby facs; shwrs inc; el pnts (10A) (poss long leads req, poss rev pol); lndtte (inc dryer); sm shop & 3km; tradsmn; rest, snacks; bar; BBQ; playgrnd; htd pool; paddling pool; sand beach 22km; lake fishing; tennis; games area; games rm; cycle hire; horseriding 2km; golf 11km; wifi; entmnt; TV; 10% statics in sep area; no dogs; no c'vans/ m'vans over 8m; phone; poss cr; Eng spkn; adv bkg; quiet; ccard acc; red low ssn; CKE/CCI. "Pleasant, busy site with all amenities, around lake in grnds of chateau; welcoming, helpful staff; some modern san facs; ltd low ssn; gd pool; rallies welcome; excel." ♦ 3 May-13 Sep. € 42.60 SBS - N01   2013*

See advertisement on inside back cover

BLANGY SUR BRESLE *3C2* (2.5km E Rural) *49.92378, 1.65693* **Camping Aux Cygnes d'Opale (Formerly Municipal), Zone de Loisirs, 76340 Blangy-sur-Bresle [02 35 94 55 65 / 09 72 32 88 40; fax 09 72 32 88 41; contact@auxcygnesdopale.fr; www.auxcygnesdopale.fr]** Leave A28 at junc 5, R at T-junc onto D49, site on L in 800m. Med, mkd pitch, unshd; wc unisex; chem disp; shwrs inc (clsd 1130-1400 & 2100-0700); el pnts (5-10A) €3 (poss rev pol); lndry rm; supmkt 1km; rest, snacks, bar 2km; BBQ; playgrnd; tennis & mini-golf nrby; wifi; ccard not acc; adv bkg rec; CKE/CCI. "Attractive, well-kept site adj lakes; conv Calais, A28 & D928; gd san facs; adv bkg rec lge o'fits high ssn; no twin-axles; pleasant & helpful warden; rec wait for warden for pitching; poss waterlogged in wet (& entry refused); avoid during Int'l Petanque Competition 3rd w/e June on adj leisure cent; excel NH; New owners (2013), many improvements" ♦ 1 Apr-30 Oct. € 16.50   2013*

BLAUVAC see Carpentras *10E2*

BLAVOZY see Puy en Velay, Le *9C1*

BLAYE *7C2* (5km NE Rural) *45.16708, -0.61666* **Aire Naturelle Les Tilleuls (Paille), Domaine Les Alberts, 33390 Mazion [05 57 42 18 13; fax 05 57 42 13 01; chateau-alberts@hotmail.com]** Fr Blaye on D937 N, sp to site on L. Sm, pt sl, pt shd; own san; el pnts (3-10A) €2.50; BBQ; dogs; some Eng spkn; rd noise; CKE/CCI. "Lovely, family-run site in vineyards; charming owners; clean basic san facs; wine-tasting; easy cycling nrby, cycle track to Blaye." 1 May-15 Oct. € 12.50   2013*

FRANCE

BLAYE *7C2* (W Urban) *45.12936, -0.66621* **Camp Municipal La Citadelle, 33390 Blaye [05 57 42 00 20 or 05 57 42 16 79 (LS); info@tourisme-blaye.com; www. tourisme-blaye.com]** Fr N ent town, over x-rds, sp in town; ent thro narr gateways in fortifications; access by narr track, single in places. Fr S on D669 cont thro town passing citadel on L; turn L at mini rndabt, go over bdge & take 1st L; sp strt on thro arches - recep to R of barrier. NB Site access unsuitable m'vans higher than 2.7m due to narr, curved arches. Sm, terr, pt shd; wc (mostly cont); serviced pitches; shwrs inc; el pnts (10-15A) €2.60; shops 500m; tradsmn high ssn; no BBQ; pool 250m; tennis; phone adj; poss cr; quiet; no ccard acc. "Lovely site within ancient monument, partly o'lookng rv; spacious pitches; clean but basic san facs; vineyards nr." 1 May-30 Sep. € 9.90   2011*

> ## "We must tell The Club about that great site we found"
>
> Get your site reports in by mid-August and we'll do our best to get your updates into the next edition of Caravan Europe.

BLENEAU *4G3* (600m N Rural) *47.70473, 2.94891* **Camp Municipal La Pépinière, Rue du Lieutenant Travers, 89220 Bléneau [03 86 74 93 73 or 03 86 74 91 61 (Mairie); fax 03 86 74 86 74; mairiedebleneau@wanadoo.fr; www. bleneau.fr]** At junc of D47/D22 & D90 in Bléneau take D64 twd Champcevrais & site. Sp in Bléneau. Sm, hdg pitch, shd; wc (cont); chem disp; shwrs inc; el pnts (10A); shops, rest, snacks, bar 600m; pool adj; paddling pool; tennis; games rm; fishing adj; poss cr; adv bkg; quiet; CKE/CCI. "Set in orchard; gd." 1 Apr-30 Sep.   2009*

⊞ **BLENEAU** *4G3* (12km NE Rural) *47.75833, 3.09960* **Camping Le Bois Guillaume, 89350 Villeneuve-les-Genêts [03 86 45 45 41; fax 03 86 45 49 20; camping@bois-guillaume.com; www.bois-guillaume.com]** Fr W on D965 dir St Fargeau. At Mézilles take D7 thro Tannerre-en-Puisaye; stay on D7 & after 3.5km foll sp for site. Or fr A6 exit junc 18 onto D16 thro Charny, then turn L onto D119 to Champignelles; take D7 dir Tannere for approx 2km; turn R & foll sp to site. Med, hdg/mkd pitch, some hdstg, shd; htd wc; chem disp; mv service pnt; shwrs inc; el pnts (5-10A) €3.10-4.60; gas; rest; bar; playgrnd; htd pools; games area; cycle hire; tennis; wifi; dogs €1.40; poss cr; Eng spkn; CKE/CCI. "Friendly staff; clean, tidy site; facs ltd low ssn; vg rest." € 14.30 2011*

BLENEAU *4G3* (7km NW Urban) *47.74321, 2.88508* **Camp Municipal Les Lancières, Rue André Henriat, 89220 Rogny-Les-Sept-Ecluses [03 86 74 57 50 or 06 74 43 43 04 (mob); fax 03 86 74 56 91; campingleslancieres@orange.fr; www.campingdeslancieres.fr]** Site sp fr D90 on S edge of vill on rvside. Sm, pt shd; wc; mv service pnt; shwrs inc; el pnts €2.10; lndtte; shop, rest, snacks, bar in vill; playgrnd; games area; fishing; tennis nr; some statics; quiet. "Pretty site." 1 May-30 Sep. € 5.50   2010*

BLERE *4G2* (500m NE Urban) *47.32791, 0.99685* **Camping La Plage Bléré Gâtine (Formaly Municipal La Gâtine), Rue de Cdt Le Maître, 37150 Bléré [tel/fax 02 47 57 92 60; info@campingblereplage.com; www.campingblereplage.com]** Exit A10 S of Tours onto A85 E. Exit A85 junc 11 dir Bléré. Site in 5km adj sports cent on S side of Rv Cher. Lge, mkd pitch, pt shd; wc; chem disp; mv service pnt; shwrs inc; el pnts (10A) €3.80 (poss rev pol & long lead poss req); lndtte (inc dryer); shops 300m; supmkt 400m; htd pool adj high ssn; rv fishing adj; wifi; dogs €1.10; no adv bkg; quiet; ccard acc; CKE/CCI. "Excel, well-kept site; sm pitches; wardens are enthusiastic & helpful; clean san facs, some dated & stretched when site full; some dated el pnts poss unrel in wet; gd security; cycle rte to Chenonceau; gd cent for wine rtes & chateaux; unrel opening dates low ssn; rec" ♦ 1 Apr-15 Oct. € 15.60   2013*

BLESLE see Massiac *9C1*

BLIGNY SUR OUCHE *6H1* (500m NW Rural) *47.10858, 4.66000* **Camping des Isles, 2 Allée de la Gare, 21360 Bligny-sur-Ouche [03 80 20 00 64 or 06 62 97 19 28 (mob)]** On D17/D970 fr Arnay-le-Duc, site on L on ent vill. Med, pt shd; wc (mainly cont); shwrs inc; el pnts (15A) €2.35; shop 500m; café/rest 300m; playgrnd; quiet; red long stay. "Peaceful, clean & tidy; helpful owner; in reach of Côte d'Or wine areas; steam rlwy 100m; noise fr cornmill at harvest time; poss flooding in adverse weather; gd." 1 May-30 Sep. € 11.75   2009*

BLOIS *4G2* (12km NE Rural) *47.68666, 1.48583* **Camping Le Château de la Grenouillère, 41500 Suèvres [02 54 87 80 37; fax 02 54 87 84 21; la.grenouillere@wanadoo.fr; www.camping-loire.com or www.les-castels.com]** Exit A10 junc 16 sp Chambord, Mer; take rd to Mer; go thro Mer on D2152 dir Blois; site in 5km, 2km NE of Suèvres. Lge, mkd pitch, pt shd; wc; chem disp; mv service pnt; sauna; baby facs; shwrs inc; el pnts (10A) inc; gas; lndtte (inc dryer); shop; rest; pizzeria; snacks; bar; BBQ (gas/charcoal); playgrnd; 2 pools (1 covrd); paddling pool; waterslide; boating; fishing; tennis; cycle hire; gym; wifi; entmnt; games/TV; statics (tour ops); dogs €4; no c'vans/m'vans over 15m; Eng spkn; adv bkg (min 3 nts); some pitches some rd & rlwy noise; ccard acc; red low ssn; CKE/CCI. "Ideal for Loire area; clean modern san facs, poss ltd low ssn; some superb leisure facs; mkt Wed & Sat Blois." ♦ 15 Apr-15 Sep. € 46.00 SBS - L04   2013*

See advertisement on inside back cover

BLOIS *4G2* (10km E Rural) *47.59149, 1.45894* **Camping de Chatillon (Formerly Aire Naturelle), 6 Rue de Châtillon, 41350 Huisseau-sur-Cosson [02 54 20 35 26]** Fr Blois cross Rv Loire on D765 dir Vineuil. 1km S turn L onto D33. Site at E end of vill of Huisseau on R. Sm, hdg/mkd pitch, pt sl, pt shd; wc; chem disp; mv service pnt; shwrs inc; el pnts (10A) €4.20 (poss rev pol); gas; shops 400m, supmkt 4km; dogs €1.50; poss cr; adv bkg; ccard acc; red low ssn; CKE/CCI. "Pretty, peaceful, garden site; lovely, even low ssn; beautiful area; friendly owner; gd clean san facs, but ltd; conv Loire Valley chateaux; cycle rte thro Chambord forest; Son et Lumière show in town; rec." ♦ ltd 1 May-20 Sep. € 17.90   2012*

BLOIS *4G2* (8km S Rural) *47.52539, 1.38675* **Camp Municipal, Rue du Conon, 41120 Cellettes [02 54 70 48 41 or 02 54 70 47 54 (Mairie)]** On D956, Blois to Châteauroux rd, pass almost thro Cellettes, site 120m fr D956 down 1st L after rv bdge, site on L in 100m, well sp. NB Turn-in narr fr v busy main rd. Med, pt shd; wc; chem disp; shwrs inc; el pnts (5A)€2.80; snacks; shops, pool, playgrnd & tennis adj; fishing; games area; poss cr; phone; quiet, some daytime rd noise; ccard acc; CKE/CCI. "Lovely, peaceful site in pleasant rvside location; lge pitches; friendly, helpful warden; gd san facs; don't checkout late without telling warden - she locks el pnts boxes; poss boggy after rain; excel for Loire châteaux; rec."
♦ ltd 1 Jun-30 Sep. € 9.45   2013*

BLOIS *4G2* (6km SW Rural) *47.54379, 1.31114* **FFCC Camping Le Cosson, 1 Rue de la Forêt, 41120 Chailles [02 54 79 46 49]** Fr Blois foll sp dir Montrichard (D751); after x-ing rv bdge at rndabt take 1st exit sp Montrichard/Chailles (D751); after x-ing sm rv bdge in Chailles take 1st L onto Rue de la Forêt; site in 50m; sm sp easily missed. Sm, hdg pitch, pt shd; wc (cont); chem disp (wkr); shwrs inc; baby facs; el pnts (6A) €3.50; shops 1km; baker 500m; games area; playgrnd; dogs; phone; poss cr; adv bkg; rd noise; CKE/CCI. "Well-maintained, quiet site nr chateaux; pleasant, helpful owners; walks & cycle paths in local forest; poss tired pitches & facs end of ssn." 15 Jun-10 Sep. € 11.35   2009*

BLOIS *4G2* (15km W) *47.54427, 1.15712* **Ferme de Prunay, 41150 SEILLAC [2 54 70 02 01; fax 2 08 42 17 56; contact@ prunay.com; www.prunay.fr]** Take exit Blois on the A10; foll dir for Angers Chateau Renault until Molineuf, then Chambon sur Cisse and Seillac, rd D131. Med, mkd pitch, pt shd; wc; chem disp; baby facs; shwrs inc; el pnts €3.70; lndtte (inc dryer); shop; rest, snacks; bar; BBQ; playgrnd; pool; paddling pool; lake; fishing; cycle hire; games area; entmnt; internet; TV; statics; dogs; Eng spkn; ccard acc. "In the heart of the Loire Valley; spacious pitches; v nice site." 31 Mar-7 Oct.
€ 22.90   2011*

BOIRY NOTRE DAME see Arras *3B3*

BOISSE PENCHOT see Decazeville *7D4*

BOISSIERE DU MONTAIGU, LA see Montaigu *2H4*

⊞ **BOLLENE** *9D2* (2.5km N Rural) **Camping Le Barry, Quartier St Pierre de Sénos, 84500 Bollène [04 90 30 13 20; fax 04 90 40 48 64; info@campinglebarry. com; www.campinglebarry.com]** Exit A7 junc 19 at Bollène onto D26 twd Pierrelatte. Foll sp 'Site Troglodytique'. Sm, shd; own san; chem disp; mv service pnt; el pnts (10A) inc; gas; rest; bar; BBQ (gas/elec); playgrnd; pool; games area; games rm; internet; many statics; Eng spkn; quiet; ccard acc; CKE/CCI. "Mainly superior park homes; ltd facs low ssn; access to pool up steep slope; NH or sh stay only." € 17.00   2010*

⊞ **BOLLENE** *9D2* (5.5km E Rural) *44.29811, 4.78645* **FFCC Camping et Centre Equestre La Simioune, Quartier Guffiage, 84500 Bollène [04 90 30 44 62; fax 04 90 30 44 77; la-simioune@wanadoo.fr; www.la-simioune.fr]** Exit A7 junc 19 onto D994/D8 dir Carpentras (Ave Salvatore Allende D8). At 3rd x-rd turn L into Ave Alphonse Daudet dir Lambique & foll rd 3km to sp for camping on L, then site 1km. Sm, pt sl, shd; wc; chem disp; baby facs; shwrs €1; el pnts (6A) €3; lndtte; shops & supmkt 4km; tradsmn; rest; bar; BBQ; playgrnd; pool; paddling pool; horseriding; entmnt; 10% statics; dogs €2; adv bkg rec high ssn; quiet; redCKE/CCI. "In pine forest; facs ltd in winter; pony club for children & adults; NH only."
€ 14.00   2011*

BOLLENE *9D2* (7km E Rural) *44.29124, 4.83837* **FFCC Camping Le Pont du Lez, Suze-la-Rousse, Côtes du Rhône, 26790 Suze-la-Rousse [tel/fax 04 75 98 82 83; camping-lepontdulez@wanadoo.fr; www.campinglepontdulez.fr]** E fr Bollène on D94 to Suze-la-Rousse; L in vill sq; R immed bef rv bdge. Sm, pt shd; wc; shwrs inc; el pnts (6-10A) €3.40 (long lead poss req); lndtte; shop 300m; supmkt 7km; snacks; bar; playgrnd; fishing; games area; TV; dogs €1.40; no twin-axles; red low ssn; CKE/CCI. "Lovely but decrepit (2009); basic, clean facs - hot water to shwrs only; lovely area." 1 Apr-30 Sep.
€ 12.80   2009*

BOLLENE *9D2* (6km SW Rural) *44.24335, 4.72931* **FFCC Camping La Pinède en Provence, Quartier des Massanes, 84430 Mondragon [04 90 40 82 98; fax 09 59 92 16 56; contact@camping-pinede-provence.com; www.camping-pinede-provence.com]** Exit A7 junc 19 dir Bollène & take D26 S, site 1.5km N of Mondragon. Steep access. Med, mkd pitch, pt sl, terr, pt shd; htd wc; chem disp; mv service pnt; baby facs; shwrs inc; el pnts (8-13A) €4.40-4.85; lndtte; shop; BBQ; playgrnd; pool; some statics; dogs €2; adv bkg; quiet; red low ssn; CKE/CCI. "Gd, clean site; gd touring base; conv Ardèche Gorge." 14 Feb-14 Nov. € 20.00   2013*

"I need an on-site restaurant"

We do our best to make sure site information is correct, but it is always best to check any must-have facilities are still available or will be open during your visit.

BONLIEU *6H2* (1km E Rural) *46.59689, 5.87163* **Camping L'Abbaye, 2 Route du Lac, 39130 Bonlieu [03 84 25 57 04; fax 03 84 25 50 82; camping.abbaye@wanadoo.fr; www. camping-abbaye.com]** Fr W on D678 thro Bonlieu twd St Laurent-en-Grandvaux. In 1km turn R at sp for Lac de Bonlieu & site. Site 1km bef lake. Steep ent. Med, hdg/mkd pitch, pt sl, terr, pt shd; wc; chem disp; baby facs; shwrs inc; el pnts (6A) €3.80 (poss rev pol); lndtte (inc dryer); shop & 4km; tradsmn; rest, snacks; bar; BBQ; playgrnd; games area; no statics; dogs €1; adv bkg; quiet, some rd noise w/end; ccard acc; CKE/CCI. "Pleasant, peaceful site in attractive area; lge pitches, blocks req for most; modern san facs; access to disabled facs fr upper terr; bar/rest open low ssn; gd walks; gd dog walks." ♦ 1 May-30 Sep. € 14.50   2011*

BONNAC LA COTE *7B3* (1km S Rural) *45.93238, 1.28977*
Camping Le Château de Leychoisier, 1 Route de
Leychoisier, 87270 Bonnac-la-Côte [tel/fax 05 55 39 93 43;
contact@leychoisier.com; www.leychoisier.com or www.
les-castels.com] Fr S on A20 exit junc 27 & L at T-junc onto
D220. At rndabt take 3rd exit then 1st L onto D97. At mini-
rndabt in Bonnac take 2nd exit, site on L in 1km. Fr N exit
A20 junc 27, turn R at T-junc onto D97, then as above. Med,
mkd pitch, pt sl, shd; wc; chem disp; mv service pnt; baby
facs; shwrs inc; el pnts (10A) inc; lndtte (inc dryer); ltd shop;
rest, snacks; bar; BBQ (gas/charcoal); playgrnd; pool; tennis;
fishing; wifi; games rm/TV; dogs €3; no c'vans/m'vans over
20m; Eng spkn; adv bkg; ccard not acc; red low ssn; CKE/CCI.
"Peaceful site in grnds of chateau; lge pitches; welcoming,
friendly & helpful staff; clean san facs; excel rest; extra for
m'vans; blocks req some pitches; rallies welcome; conv NH nr
m'way; excel; ccard not acc for 1 night stay" ♦
15 Apr-20 Sep. € 30.00 SBS - L11   2012*

See advertisement above

BONNAL *6G2* (3.5km N Rural) *47.50777, 6.35583* **Camping
Le Val de Bonnal, 1 Chemin du Moulin, 25680 Bonnal
[03 81 86 90 87; fax 03 81 86 03 92; val-de-bonnal@
wanadoo.fr; www.camping-valdebonnal.fr or www.
les-castels.com]** Fr N on D9 fr Vesoul or Villersexel to Esprels,
turn S onto D49 sp 'Val de Bonnal'. Fr S exit A36 junc 5 &
turn N onto D50 sp Rougemont, site sp to N of Rougemont.
Lge, mkd pitch, pt shd; wc; chem disp; mv service pnt; baby
facs; shwrs inc; el pnts (5-10A) inc (poss rev pol); gas; lndtte
(inc dryer); sm shop; rest, snacks; bar; BBQ; playgrnd; pool;
waterslide; paddling pool; lake sw & sand beach adj; fishing;
watersports; canoe, cycle hire; gym; golf 6km; wifi; entmnt;
games/TV rm; 40% statics; dogs €2; twin-axles acc (rec check
in adv); poss cr; Eng spkn; adv bkg; quiet; ccard acc; red low
ssn; CKE/CCI. "Attractive, busy site; lge accessible pitches;
excel welcome; modern, clean san facs; gd child activities; ltd
facs low ssn; tour ops." ♦ 6 May-7 Sep. € 48.40
SBS - J01   2011*

See advertisement on inside back cover

BONNARD see Joigny *4F4*

BONNES see Chauvigny *7A3*

BONNEUIL MATOURS *4H2* (1km S Rural) *46.67600, 0.57640*
Camp Municipal du Parc de Crémault, 8 Allée du Stade,
86210 Bonneuil-Matours [tel/fax 05 49 85 20 47] Fr D910
20km N of Poitiers take D82 E to Bonneuil-Matours. Site sp in
vill next to stadium & Rv Vienne but site ent not well sp. Med,
mkd pitch, shd; htd wc; chem disp; mv service pnt; shwrs €1;
el pnts €2.70; lndry rm; shops 1km; tradsmn; rest, snacks; bar;
BBQ; playgrnd; rv & fishing adj; tennis; archery; entmnt; TV;
quiet, but some traff noise fr across rv. "Nature reserve adj;
clean facs; lovely site." Mid Apr-Mid Sep. € 9.15   2008*

BONNEVAL *4F2* (1km SE Rural) *48.17080, 1.38640* **Camping
Le Bois Chièvre, Route de Vouvray, St Maurice, 28800
Bonneval [02 37 47 54 01; fax 02 37 96 26 79; camping-
bonneval-28@orange.fr; www.camping-bonneval-28.
monsite-orange.fr]** Rec app fr N (Chartres), or SE (D27
fr Patay/Orléans) as app fr S thro town is narr & diff. Fr Chartres
take N10 into Bonneval & foll camp sp (mainly to L). Med, hdg/
mkd pitch, hdstg, pt sl, shd; htd wc; chem disp; mv service pnt;
shwrs inc; el pnts (6A) inc (rev pol); lndtte; shop 1km; tradsmn;
rest, snacks; bar; BBQ; playgrnd; htd pool adj inc; some statics;
dogs €1.20; Eng spkn; adv bkg; quiet; CKE/CCI. "Well-run,
well-kept site in woodland; gd, lge pitches; friendly, helpful
staff; vg facs but poss stretched in ssn; vg NH for Le Havre or
Dieppe." ♦ 29 Mar-20 Oct. € 20.95   2013*

BONNEVILLE *9A3* (500m NE Rural) *46.08206, 6.41288* **Camp
Municipal Le Bois des Tours, 314 Rue des Bairiers, 74130
Bonneville [04 50 97 04 31 or 04 50 25 22 00 (Mairie)]**
Fr A40 junc 16 take D1203, or fr Cluses take D1205 to
Bonneville. Cross rv bdge into town cent; site sp. Med, pt
shd; wc (some cont); chem disp; shwrs; el pnts (5A) €2.50;
shops 500m; BBQ; playgrnd; poss cr peak ssn; adv bkg; quiet.
"Well-maintained, immac site; gd san facs." 1 Jul-6 Sep.
€ 8.00   2012*

⊞ **BONNIERES SUR SEINE** *3D2* (2km N Rural) *49.05804,
1.61224* **Camping Le Criquet, 42 Rue du Criquet, 78840
Freneuse [tel/fax 01 30 93 07 95; www.camping-le-
criquet.fr]** Fr D915 at Bonnières to Freneuse on D37. Thro
vill, site sp at end of vill past cematery. Lge, pt shd; wc; chem
disp; shwrs €3; el pnts (10A) €3; BBQ; playgrnd; games area;
mainly statics; adv bkg; quiet. "V run down - san facs unclean
& need refurb, pitches unkempt; Monet's garden 12km"
€ 12.30   2011*

BONNIERES SUR SEINE *3D2* (5km E Rural) *49.04646, 1.66256* **Camping Loisirs des Groux, Chemin de Vétheuil, 78270 Mousseaux-sur-Seine [01 34 79 33 86; campingloisirsdesgroux@wanadoo.fr; www. campingdesgroux.com]** Fr W exit A13 junc 15 onto D113 dir Bonnières. Cont thro Bonnières, turn L onto D37 Mousseaux/ Base de Loisirs. Cont strt on D37/D124/D125 & then turn R & foll site sp. Fr E exit A13 junc 14 sp Bonnières & foll sp Zone Industrielle. At rndabt take D113 Bonnières, then as above. Med, hdg/mkd pitch, pt shd; wc (some cont); chem disp (wc); mv service pnt; shwrs inc; el pnts (10A) €2; lndtte; BBQ; leisure cent inc pool 500m; lake sw & beach 500m; games area; wifi; 90% statics; dogs; Eng spkn; adv bkg rec high ssn; quiet; ccard acc; CKE/CCI. "Conv Paris (65km), Versailles, Rouen, Giverny; lge pitches; friendly, helpful staff; basic, dated san facs; excel walks or cycling along Rv Seine; poss clsd earlier than published dates - phone ahead to check in low ssn." ♦ 1 Apr-30 Nov. € 16.00   2012*

See advertisement below

"Satellite navigation makes touring much easier"

Remember most sat navs don't know if you're towing or in a larger vehicle – always use yours alongside maps and site directions.

BONNIEUX *10E2* (1km W Rural) *43.81893, 5.31170* **Camp Municipal du Vallon, Route de Ménerbes, 84480 Bonnieu [tel/fax 04 90 75 86 14 / 06 48 08 46 79 (mob); campingvallon@wanadoo.fr]** Fr Bonnieux take D3 twd Ménerbes, site sp on L on leaving vill. Med, mkd pitch, terr, pt shd; wc (some cont); chem dsip; shwrs inc; el pnts (10A) €3.80; lndtte; shop; tradsmn; snacks; bar; playgrnd; wifi; dogs €2; some Eng spkn; quiet; red low ssn; CKE/CCI. "Beautiful, quaint, 'olde worlde' site in wooded area; friendly warden; basic facs but clean; gd walking & mountain biking; attractive hilltop vill; gd touring base; gd rest in walking distance, facs basic but clean" 15 Mar-15 Oct. € 19.00   2013*

BONO, LE see Auray *2F3*

⊞ **BORDEAUX** *7C2* (7km N Rural) *44.89701, -0.58317* **Camping Le Village du Lac Bordeaux, Blvd Jacques Chaban Delmas, 33520 Bordeaux-Bruges [05 57 87 70 60; fax 05 57 87 70 61; contact@village-du-lac.com; www. camping-bordeaux.com]** On ring rd A630 take exit 5 twd lake; site sp on N side of lake, 500m N of Parc des Expositions. Lge, mkd pitch, some hdstg, pt shd; htd wc; chem disp; mv service pnt; baby facs; shwrs inc; elec pnts (6A) inc; lndtte (inc dryer); shop; tradsmn; rest, snacks; bar; BBQ; playgrnd; pool; paddling pool; lake sw & fishing adj; cycle hire; games rm; wifi; TV; 50% statics; dogs €5; bus/tram to city; Eng spkn; adv bkg; quiet; ccard acc; red low ssn; CKE/CCI. "Busy, well laid out, modern site; friendly staff; san facs poss streched high ssn; plenty elec & water pnts; excel rest; conv Bordeaux; easy access fr ring rd; pitches poss soft and muddy after rain" ♦ € 45.80   2013*

"There aren't many sites open at this time of year"

If you're travelling outside peak season remember to call ahead to check site opening dates – even if the entry says 'open all year'.

⊞ **BORDEAUX** *7C2* (4km S Urban) *44.75529, -0.62772* **Camping Beau Soleil, 371 Cours du Général de Gaulle, 33170 Gradignan [tel/fax 05 56 89 17 66; campingbeausoleil@wanadoo.fr; www.camping-gradignan.com]** Fr N take exit 16 fr Bordeaux ring rd onto D1010 sp Gradignan. Fr S exit A63 junc 24 onto D211 to Jauge then D1010 to Gradignan. Site S of Gradignan on R after Beau Soleil complex, sp. Sm, hdg/mkd pitch, hdstg, pt sl, pt shd; htd wc; chem disp; shwrs inc; el pnts (6-10A) €1.50 -3. (poss rev pol); lndtte (inc dryer); shop 3km; rest, snacks, bar 1km; gas/elec BBQ; htd pool & waterslides 5km; rv/lake sw 2km; wifi; 70% statics; dogs €1; bus/tram 250m; poss cr; Eng spkn; adv bkg rec; quiet; red low ssn; CKE/CCI. "Pleasant, family-run site; helpful owners; vg, modern, clean san facs; ltd touring pitches; sm pitches not suitable lge o'fits; adv bkg rec; excel" ♦ € 23.00   2013*

BORMES LES MIMOSAS see Lavandou, Le *10F3*

Loisirs des Groux Camping Caravaning

1 Chemin de L'île, 78270 Mousseaux-sur-Seine
Tél: 0033 1 34 79 33 86
Email: campingloisirsdesgroux@wanadoo.fr

15 minutes from Monet's Garden

FRANCE

BORT LES ORGUES *7C4* (4km N Rural) *45.43213, 2.50461*
**Camping Les Ch'tis de la Siauve, Rue du Camping, 15270
Lanobre [04 71 40 31 85; canoubgdeschtisdelasiauve@
orange.fr; www.camping-chtis-15.com]** On D992 Clermont-
Ferrand to Bort-les-Orgues, site on R 3km S of Lanobre. Site
sp. Lge, hdg/mkd pitch, terr, pt shd; wc; chem disp; mv service
pnt; baby facs; shwrs inc; el pnts (6A) €3; lndtte (inc dryer);
shop 3km; tradsmn; rest, snacks; bar; BBQ; playgrnd; htd
pool; paddling pool; lake sw adj; fishing; tennis nr; games
area; cycle hire; wifi; entmnt; TV rm; dogs €2; phone; Eng
spkn; adv bkg; noisy high ssn; ccard acc; red low ssn; CKE/CCI.
"Scenic, family-run site; friendly & helpful; gd clean san facs;
high hedges make some pitches dark; footpaths (steep) to lake;
gd sw, boating etc; excel touring base; interesting area." ♦
1 Apr-15 Oct. € 16.00   2011*

BORT LES ORGUES *7C4* (6km S Rural) *45.33671,
2.47379* **Camp Municipal de Bellevue, 15240 Saignes
[04 71 40 68 40 or 04 71 40 62 80 (Mairie); saignes-mairie@
wanadoo.fr; www.saignes-mairie.fr]** Fr Bort-les-Orgues take
D922 S twd Mauriac. In 5km, turn L onto D22. Site sp on R after
ent vill. Foll sp 'Piscine/Stade'. Sm, hdg/mkd pitch, pt shd; wc
(some cont); chem disp; shwrs inc; el pnts (6-10A) €2.25; lndtte;
shops, rest 500m; snacks; bar; BBQ; playgrnd; 3 pools adj; 2
tennis courts adj; dogs; Eng spkn; adv bkg; quiet; no ccard acc;
CKE/CCI. "Pleasant situation with views; roomy pitches; vill in
walking dist; gd touring base." 1 Jul-31 Aug. € 6.35   2010*

BORT LES ORGUES *7C4* (7km SW Rural) *45.33249,
2.48713* **Camping à la Ferme (Chanet), Domaine de
la Vigne, 15240 Saignes [tel/fax 04 71 40 61 02 or
06 83 12 39 32 (mob); chanetcollete@wanadoo.fr]**
Take D922 S fr Bort-les-Orgues sp Mauriac. After 5.5km at
junc with D15 take sharp L sp Saignes; then turn R onto D22.
In cent of Saignes turn L at T-junc onto D30. After 200m
turn L onto C14 sp La Vigne & Camping. Farmhouse on L
after 400m, site on R. Sm, pt sl, pt shd; wc; cold shwrs inc; el
pnts (6A) €2.30 (rev pol); shops 800m; sm pool; poss cr; adv
bkg; quiet. "Beautiful, peaceful setting; CL-type site; friendly
owners; ltd facs; san facs poss neglected low ssn." Mar-Nov.
€ 10.50   2009*

BOUCHEMAINE see Angers *4G1*

BOUGE CHAMBALUD see St Rambert d'Albon *9C2*

BOULANCOURT see Malesherbes *4E3*

BOULOGNE SUR GESSE *8F3* (6km NE Rural) *43.33135,
0.68046* **Camping Le Canard Fou, Laron, 31350 Lunax
[05 61 88 26 06]** Fr Boulogne-sur-Gesse N on D632 sp
Toulouse. In 6km turn L sp Lunax, foll site sp for 1km. Turn
L at x-rds, site 300m on R. Sm, pt sl, pt shd; wc; chem disp
(wc); shwrs inc; el pnts (9A) inc; gas; lndtte; shop 6km; BBQ;
pool 6km; reservoir adj; some statics; phone 800m; Eng spkn;
adv bkg; quiet. "Peaceful CL-type site; friendly owners; san
facs clean but open to elements; breakfast & eve meals avail;
perfect site for walking, cycling; rec phone ahead as ltd touring
pitches." ♦ 15 Mar-15 Dec. € 11.00 (4 persons)   2009*

BOULOGNE SUR GESSE *8F3* (1.3km SE Rural) *43.28323,
0.65544* **Camp Municipal du Lac, Ave du Lac, 31350
Boulogne-sur-Gesse [05 61 88 20 54; fax 05 61 88 62 16;
villagevacancesboulogne@wanadoo.fr; www.ville-
boulogne-sur-gesse.fr]** Fr Boulogne-sur-Gesse, take D633 for
1km. Foll sp, turn L to site. Lake (watersports cent) adj ent. Lge,
mkd pitch, pt sl, pt shd; wc (some cont); chem disp; shwrs inc;
el pnts (10A) €3.70; gas; shops 1km; rest; bar; playgrnd; htd
pool 300m; boating; fishing; tennis; golf; entmnt; 90% statics;
dogs €1; phone; Eng spkn; quiet. "High kerbs poss diff lge
o'fits; clean facs; phone ahead to check open early ssn." ♦
1 Apr-30 Sep. € 10.30   2009*

⊞ **BOULOGNE SUR MER** *3A2* (6km E Rural) *50.75133,
1.72013* **Camping Manoir de Senlecques, 45 Rue de la
Fontaine, 62126 Pernes lez Boulogne [03 21 30 09 85 or
06 16 76 75 22 (mob); isabelleansel@orange.fr; www.
lemanoirdesenlecques.com]** Exit A16 junc 33 sp Wimille;
at rndabt turn under m'way onto D233 (pt of rd is narr) to
Pernes in 7km & site is on L 1km past vill. Alt rte for longer
o'fits (rds wider): exit A16 onto N42 dir St Omer. Turn R for
La Capelle, then L on D233E for Pernes; turn R at junc in vill.
NB Foll sp 'Manoir de Senlecques' if no 'Camping' sp. Long
o'fits take care at ent. Sm, some hdstg, pt shd; wc; chem disp;
mv service pnt; shwrs; el pnts (6A) inc(some rev pol); lndtte;
shop, supmkt 5km; rest in walking dist; BBQ; sand beach 6km;
fishing; 10% statics; dogs; some Eng spkn; adv bkg; quiet; red
CKE/CCI. "Beautiful area; site in manor house grounds; gite
avail; conv NH; vet within 3km; conv Calais, Channel Tunnel &
Nausica Seaworld." € 12.00   2013*

BOULOGNE SUR MER *3A2* (8km E Rural) *50.73111, 1.71582*
**Camp Municipal Les Sapins, Route de Crémarest, 62360
La Capelle-lès-Boulogne [03 21 83 16 61]** Exit A16 junc
31 E onto N42 to La Capelle vill; cont to next rndabt & take
sp Crémarest; site on R. Sm, pt shd; wc; shwrs inc; el pnts
(4-6A) €2.35-4.60 (poss rev pol); lndtte; hypmkt, rest, snacks
& bar 2km; BBQ; playgrnd; sand beach 4km; bus 1km; poss
cr; adv bkg; poss rd noise & fr adj horseriding school; no ccard
acc; CKE/CCI. "Helpful warden; gd modern san facs; office
0800-0900 & 1600-1700; gd NH for Calais." 15 Apr-15 Sep.
€ 10.15   2011*

⊞ **BOULOGNE SUR MER** *3A2* (16km E Rural) *50.73400,
1.82400* **Camping à la Ferme Le Bois Groult (Leclercq),
120 impasse du Bois Groult, 62142 Henneveux Le Plouy
[03 21 33 32 16; leclercq.gilbert0643@orange.fr; www.
leboisgroult.fr]** Take N42 fr Boulogne twd St Omer, take
exit S dir Desvres (D127). Immed at rndabt foll sp Colembert.
On ent Le Plouy turn R at the calvary & foll sp to site in 1km.
Sm, hdstg, pt sl, pt shd; wc; shwrs; el pnts (6-10A) €5. (poss
long lead req); shops 6km; dogs €1; adv bkg; quiet; ccard not
acc. "Charming, well-kept, peaceful CL-type site; pleasant
owner; no barrier; WWI places of interest; easy access fr N42;
ideal NH to/from ferry/tunnel; excel; new shwrs (2012)" ♦
€ 9.00   2013*

BOULOGNE SUR MER *3A2* (6km S Coastal) *50.67128, 1.57079* **FFCC Camp Municipal La Falaise, Rue Charles Cazin, 62224 Equihen-Plage [03 21 31 22 61; fax 03 21 80 54 01; camping.equihen.plage@orange.fr; www.camping-equihen-plage.fr]** Exit A16 junc 28 onto D901 dir Boulogne, then D940 S. Turn R to Condette then foll sp Equihen-Plage, site sp in vill. Access fr D901 via narr rds. Med, hdg pitch, sl, terr, pt shd; wc; chem disp; mv service pnt; shwrs inc; el pnts (10-16A) €4.90-5.40 (poss rev pol); lndtte; playgrnd; sand beach 200m; watersports; games rm; 85% statics (sep area); dogs €2.40; phone; adv bkg; ccard acc; red low ssn; CKE/CCI. "Pleasant, well-run site in excel location, but poss windy; excel clean facs; sl pitches poss diff long o'fits; steep rd to beach." 28 Mar - 12 Nov. € 19.00   2013*

BOULOGNE SUR MER *3A2* (7km S Urban) *50.67752, 1.64335* **Camping Les Cytises, Chemin Georges Ducrocq, 62360 Isques [tel/fax 03 21 31 11 10 / 06 62 91 72 71 (ls); campcytises@orange.fr; www.lescytises.fr]** S fr Boulogne on D901 to Isques; site 150m fr D901. Or on A16 exit junc 28 & foll sp Isques & camp sp. Med, hdg pitch, hdstg, terr, pt shd; htd wc; chem disp; mv service pnt; baby facs; shwrs inc; el pnts (6A) inc (poss rev pol); gas; lndtte; shop 400m; snacks; playgrnd; pool & sand beach 4km; rv adj; games area; games rm; 50% statics; dogs €1; Eng spkn; adv bkg; some rlwy noise; ccard acc; red low ssn; CKE/CCI. "Pleasant site; poss sm pitches; friendly staff; clean, modern san facs, ltd low ssn; barrier clsd 2300-0700; conv Channel Tunnel & 5 mins fr Nausicaá; poss unkempt low ssn; conv NH nr m'way; gd" ♦ 20 Mar-31 Oct. € 23.90   2013*

BOULOU, LE *8G4* (2km N Rural) *42.54157, 2.83431* **Camping Le Mas Llinas, 66165 Le Boulou [04 68 83 25 46; info@camping-mas-llinas.com; www.camping-mas-llinas.com]** Fr Perpignan, take D900 S; 1km N of Le Boulou turn R at Intermarché supmkt 100m to mini rndabt, turn L & foll sp to Mas-Llinas to site in 2km. Or fr A9 exit 43 & foll sp Perpignan thro Le Boulou. L at rndabt adj Leclerc supmkt, site well sp. Med, terr, pt shd; htd wc; shwrs inc; chem disp; el pnts (5-10A) €4.10-5.20; gas; lndtte; shops adj; tradsmn; snacks; BBQ; playgrnd; pool; paddling pool; cycle hire; games area; games rm; TV rm; some statics; dogs €2.20; phone; adv bkg; Eng spkn; quiet; red low ssn; CKE/CCI. "Friendly, welcoming owners; peaceful, scenic site; beware poss high winds on high pitches; ltd water points at top levels; ltd facs low ssn; facs clean; gd sized pitches; golden orioles on site." ♦ ltd 1 Feb-30 Nov. € 19.40   2013*

⊞ **BOULOU, LE** *8G4* (1km SE Rural) *42.52088, 2.84509* **Camping Les Oliviers, Route d'Argelès-sur-Mer, 66160 Le Boulou [04 68 83 12 86 or 06 15 43 99 89; fax 04 68 87 60 08; infos@lesoliviers.com; www.lesoliviers.com]** Exit A9 junc 43 at Le Boulou. Foll sp onto D618 twds Argelès-sur-Mer. Site on R in 1km, well sp fr D618. Med, mkd pitch, pt shd; htd wc; chem disp; mv service pnt; shwrs inc; el pnts (6-10A) €3.50; gas 1km; lndtte; shop 1km; tradsmn; bar; playgrnd; shgl beach 12km; 40% statics; dogs €1.50; site clsd mid-Dec to mid-Jan; poss cr; adv bkg; quiet; red low ssn; CKE/CCI. "Helpful, friendly owner; san facs basic but adequate, poss stretched peak ssn; dog-friendly; conv juncs of A9 & N9; popular NH en rte Spain." ♦ ltd € 18.00   2009*

BOULOU, LE *8G4* (S Urban) *42.50964, 2.82680* **Camping L'Olivette, Route du Perthus, 66160 Le Boulou [04 68 83 48 08; fax 04 68 87 46 00; info@camping-olivette.fr; www.camping-olivette.fr]** D900 twd Spanish border, site on R - v busy rd. Med, hdg/mkd pitch; pt sl, pt shd; wc; baby facs; shwrs inc; el pnts (10A) €2.50; lndtte; shops; snacks; bar; many statics; dogs €1.60; poss cr; Eng spkn; some rd noise. "Conv for Salvador Dali Museum & ruins at Empurias; security gate; poss tired pitches; clean san facs; helpful owners; gd NH." 15 Mar-31 Oct. € 14.50   2009*

"That's changed – Should I let The Club know?"

If you find something on site that's different from the site entry, fill in a report and let us know. See www.caravanclub.co.uk/europereport.

BOULOU, LE *8G4* (5km S Rural) *42.49083, 2.79777* **Camping Les Pins/Le Congo, Route de Céret, 66480 Maureillas-las-Illas [04 68 83 23 21; fax 04 68 83 45 64; lespinslecongo@hotmail.fr; www.camping-lespinslecongo.com]** Fr Le Boulou take D900 S, fork R after 2km onto D618 dir Céret. Site on L 500m after Maureillas. Med, hdg pitch, shd; htd wc (cont); chem disp (wc); shwrs inc; el pnts (10A) €3.50; gas; lndtte; shop 500m; tradsmn; rest, snacks; BBQ; playgrnd; pool; sand beach 20km; 10% statics; dogs; phone; adv bkg; Eng spkn; ccard acc. "Shabby and expensive, shwrs OK" (2010) ♦ 1 Feb-30 Nov. € 23.00   2012*

BOULOU, LE *8G4* (4km SW Rural) *42.50664, 2.79502* **Camping de la Vallée/Les Deux Rivières, Route de Maureillas, 66490 St Jean-Pla-de-Corts [04 68 83 23 20; fax 04 68 83 07 94; campingdelavallee@yahoo.fr; www.campingdelavallee.com]** Exit A9 at Le Boulou. Turn W on D115. Turn L after 3km at rndabt, into St Jean-Pla-de-Corts, thro vill, over bdge, site on L. Med, mkd pitch, pt shd, htd wc; chem disp; mv service pnt; baby facs; shwrs inc; el pnts (5A) €4; gas 800m; lndtte; shop 800m; tradsmn; rest, snacks; bar; playgrnd; pool; sand beach 20km; lake sw & fishing 1km; archery; internet; entmnt; TV; 50% statics (sep area); dogs €2.50; phone; bus adj; poss cr; Eng spkn; adv bkg; quiet; ccard acc; red long stay/low ssn; CKE/CCI. "Lovely well-kept site; easy access lge pitches; friendly, helpful owners with gd local info; excel san facs; conv NH fr A9 or longer; highly rec." ♦ 1 Apr-31 Oct. € 17.20   2011*

BOULOU, LE *8G4* (5km SW Rural) *42.47853, 2.80399* **Camping La Clapère (Naturist), Route de Las Illas, 66400 Maureillas-las-Illas [04 68 83 36 04; fax 04 68 83 34 44; clapere@nordnet.fr; www.clapere.com]** Exit Le Boulou S on D900 twd Le Perthus; after 3km take N618 twd Maureillas, D13 for 2km twd Las Illas. Lge, terr, pt shd; wc; chem disp; sauna; shwrs inc; el pnts (6-10A) €5-8; lndtte; shop; rest, snacks; bar; playgrnd; pool; paddling pool; rv adj; fishing; tennis; archery; cycle hire; games area; entmnt; TV; dogs €3; poss cr; Eng spkn; adv bkg; quiet. "Excel with easy access for c'vans; INF card req or may be purchased; vg for children; friendly recep." ♦ 1 May-30 Sep. € 25.00   2010*

FRANCE

FRANCE

⊞ **BOULOU, LE** *8G4* (4km W Rural) *42.50908, 2.78429*
**FFCC Camping Les Casteillets, 66490 St Jean Pla-de-Corts
[04 68 83 26 83; fax 04 68 83 39 67; jc@campinglescasteillets.
com; www.campinglescasteillets.com]** Exit A9 at Le Boulou;
turn W on D115; after 3km turn L immed after St Jean-Pla-
de-Corts; site sp on R in 400m. NB Narr app last 200m. Med,
mkd pitch, pt shd; wc; chem disp; some serviced pitches; shwrs
inc; el pnts (6A) €3.30 (poss rev pol); gas; lndtte; shop; rest,
snacks; bar; playgrnd; pool; tennis; sand beach 20km; games
area; internet; entmnt; TV; 10% statics; poss cr; Eng spkn; adv
bkg ess high ssn; quiet; red low ssn/long stay. "Lovely, friendly,
scenic site; lge pitches; conv for touring & en rte NE Spain." ♦
€ 18.00   2009*

BOURBON LANCY *4H4* (300m Urban) *46.62098, 3.76557*
**Camping St Prix, Rue de St Prix, 71140 Bourbon-Lancy
[tel/fax 03 85 89 20 98 or 03 86 37 95 83; aquadis1@
wanadoo.fr; www.aquadis-loisirs.com]** Fr N turn L fr D979
on D973 & foll into Bourbon-Lancy. Turn R at traff lts after
Attac Sup'mkt, keep L, site on R after mini-rndabt. Med, hdg
pitch, hdstg, terr, pt sl, shd; htd wc (some cont); chem disp;
shwrs inc; el pnts (10A) €2; lndry rm; shop; snacks; playgrnd;
htd pool; lake sw/fishing; 25% statics; dogs €3.10; Eng spkn;
quiet; CKE/CCI. "Tidy, well-run site; helpful staff; new san
facs; lovely old town 10 min uphill walk; rec." ♦ Easter-1 Nov.
€ 14.50   2012*

BOURBON LANCY *9A1* (1km S Rural) **Camping Le Plan
d'Eau du Breuil, 71140 Bourbon Lancy [03 86 37 95 83; fax
03 86 37 79 20; aquadis1@orange.fr; www.aquadis-loisirs.
com]** Site sp fr town, on lakeside. Sm, pt sl, pt shd; wc; chem
disp; shwrs inc; el pnts (6A); snacks; tradsmn; lake adj; poss
cr; quiet; adv bkg; excel; CKE/CCI; WiFi; Tv rm; lndtte (inc
dryer); BBQ; dogs; pool; paddling pool 1 Jun-15 Sep. € 15.90
(CChq acc)   2013*

BOURBON L'ARCHAMBAULT *9A1* (10km NE Rural)
46.66050, 3.09490 **Camping Domaine Naturiste Les
Fourneaux (Naturist), Route Limoise, 03160 Couzon [tel/
fax 04 70 66 23 18; lesfourneaux@wanadoo.fr; www.
lesfourneaux.org]** Fr Bourbon NE on D139 to Couzon, then
L onto D13, site in 2.5km on L. Med, pt sl, pt shd; wc; chem
disp; shwrs el pnts (4-6A) €4; tradsmn; bar; playgrnd; pool;
cycle hire; no dogs; phone; Eng spkn; quiet; red long stay; INF
card req. "V lge pitches; helpful Dutch owners; site not suitable
children; conv touring base; many pitches o'grown/unkempt
(2009)." ♦ ltd 1 Jun-30 Aug. € 22.25   2009*

BOURBON L'ARCHAMBAULT *9A1* (1km W Rural) *46.58058,
3.04804* **Camp Municipal de Bignon, 03160 Bourbon-
l'Archambault [04 70 67 08 83; fax 04 70 67 35 35;
mairie-bourbon-archambault@wanadoo.fr]** Exit D953 at
Bourbon-l'Archambault onto D1 northwards; in 400m turn L
into Boulevard Jean Bignon. Site sp. Lge, sl, pt shd; wc (some
cont); shwrs inc; el pnts (6-10A) €2-2.20; lndtte; shops 1km; htd
pool & waterslide 300m; tennis nr; wifi; 75% statics (sep area);
poss cr; quiet. "Beautifully laid-out in park surroundings; gd
pitches; excel san facs; charming town; excel." 1 Mar-12 Nov.
€ 6.40   2011*

BOURBONNE LES BAINS *6F2* (500m NW Urban) *47.95723,
5.74011* **Camping Le Montmorency, Rue du Stade, 52400
Bourbonne-les-Bains [03 25 90 08 64; fax 03 25 84 23 74;
c.montmorency@wanadoo.fr; www.camping-
montmorency.com]** Sp on ent town either way on D417.
After exit D417, sp at 1st turn L at telephone box. Site adj to
pool & stadium. Med, hdg/mkd pitch, pt sl, unshd; wc; mv
service pnt; shwrs inc; el pnts (6-10A) €3.10-3.60; gas; lndry
rm; shops 500m; snacks; playgrnd; pool adj; tennis; wifi; dogs
€1.50; adv bkg; quiet; red low ssn. "Pleasant site; helpful
warden; popular with visitors to spa cent; OK NH."
26 Mar-31 Oct. € 12.80   2011*

BOURBOULE, LA *7B4* (1km N Rural) *45.59680, 2.75130*
**FFCC Camping Le Panoramique, Le Pessy, 63150 Murat-
le-Quaire [04 73 81 18 79; fax 04 73 65 57 34; info@
campingpanoramique.fr; www.campingpanoramique.fr]**
Exit A89 junc 25; cont strt until junc with D922; turn R; in
3km turn R onto D219 dir Mont-Dore; in 5km pass thro
Murat-le-Quaire; in 1km turn L in Le Pessy; site on L in 300m.
Site well sp fr D922. Med, mkd pitch, terr, pt shd; htd wc;
chem disp; mv service pnt; baby facs; shwrs inc; el pnts (6-10A)
€4.30-5.60; gas; lndtte; shop & snacks 2km; tradsmn; rest
1km; bar; playgrnd; pool; games rm; 30% statics; dogs €1.70;
phone; adv bkg; quiet; CKE/CCI. "Site well set-out; mountain
views; friendly, helpful recep; clean facs; vg." 15 May-30 Sep.
€ 24.00   2012*

BOURBOULE, LA *7B4* (1km E Rural) *45.58980, 2.75257*
**Camp Municipal des Vernières, Ave de Lattre de
Tassigny, 63150 La Bourboule [04 73 81 10 20 or
04 73 81 31 00 (Mairie); fax 04 73 65 54 98]** Fr N on N89
or S on D922 turn E onto D130 dir Le Mont-Dore, site sp. Lge,
some hdg pitch; pt terr, pt shd; htd wc (some cont); chem disp;
shwrs inc; el pnts (10A) €3.50; lndtte; supmkt nr; playgrnd;
pool nr; fishing nr; dogs €1; poss cr; no adv bkg; some rd noise
daytime. "Lovely setting in mountains; gd clean facs; short
walk to fine spa town; gd family site; rec." ♦ Easter-30 Sep.
€ 10.10   2012*

BOURBOULE, LA *7B4* (4km E Rural) *45.59456, 2.76347*
**Camping Les Clarines, 1424 Ave Maréchal Leclerc, 63150
La Bourboule [04 73 81 02 30; fax 04 73 81 09 34; clarines.
les@wanadoo.fr; www.camping-les-clarines.com]** Fr La
Bourboule take D996/D88 on N bank of rv (old rd sp Piscine &
Gare); fork L at exit fr town. Site sp on R, nr junc with D219.
Lge, terr, pt shd; htd wc (some cont); baby facs; shwrs inc; el
pnts (6-10A) €3.50-€5.80; gas; lndtte (inc dryer); shop & adj;
bar; BBQ; htd pool; paddling pool; playgrnd; games area; wifi;
entmnt; TV rm; dogs €2; poss cr; adv bkg rec; quiet; 15% red
low ssn. "Gd winter sports cent; excel htd facs." ♦
19 Dec-17 Oct. € 16.00   2012*

BOURDEAUX *9D2* (3km E Rural) *44.59572, 5.16203*
**Aire Naturelle Le Moulin (Arnaud), 26460 Bézaudun-
sur-Bine [tel/fax 04 75 53 37 21 or 04 75 53 30 73;
arnocamping26@orange.fr; www.camping-moulin-
drome.fr]** Exit A7 junc 16; D104 to Crest then D538 to
Bourdeaux; just bef bdge L to Bézaudun-sur-Bine. Site on R in
3km. Sm, pt sl, pt shd; wc; chem disp (wc); shwrs €1; el pnts
(6A) €2.50; lndtte; shop 3km; tradsmn; snacks; bar; pool; no
statics; dogs €1.50; quiet; CKE/CCI. "Lovely area; wonderful
views; pretty vills; gd walking; vg." ♦ ltd 15 Apr-30 Sep.
€ 12.00   2008*

BOURDEAUX *9D2* (1km SE Rural) *44.57854, 5.12791*
Camping Les Bois du Châtelas, Route de Dieulefit, 26460 Bourdeaux [04 75 00 60 80; fax 04 75 00 60 81; contact@chatelas.com; www.chatelas.com] Fr N exit A7 m'way junc 16 onto D104, head twd Crest. Shortly bef Crest turn R onto D538 S thro Bourdeaux & cont dir Dienlefit (still on D538), site in 1km on L, well sp. Med, mkd pitch, terr, pt shd; htd wc; chem disp; mv service pnt; baby facs; sauna; shwrs inc; el pnts (10A) inc; gas; lndtte; shop; tradsmn; rest, snacks; bar; BBQ (gas/elec); cooking facs; playgrnd; 2 pools (1 htd covrd); paddling pool; waterslide; rv & horseriding 5km; games area; fitness rm; games rm; cycle hire; wifi; entmnt; TV rm; 30% statics; dogs €5; no c'vans/m'vans over 8m high ssn; phone; Eng spkn; adv bkg ess high ssn; ccard acc; red low ssn; CKE/CCI. "In lovely, scenic area; site on steep slope; gd walking." ♦ 6 Apr-16 Sep. € 34.70 SBS - M11   2011*

BOURDEAUX *9D2* (300m S Rural) *44.58389, 5.13615* FFCC
Camp Municipal Le Gap des Tortelles, 26460 Bourdeaux [tel/fax 04 75 53 30 45; info@campingdebourdeaux.com; www.campingdebourdeaux.com] Foll camping/piscine sp in vill. Gd app fr S via D94 & D70 fr Nyons. Sm, terr, pt shd; wc; mv service pnt; shwrs inc; el pnts (6A) €2.80; lndtte; shop, 600m; rest; bar; playgrnd; sw rv; tennis adj; few statics; dogs €2; adv bkg; quiet. "Attractive area away fr tourist scene; helpful warden; sh path into vill." ♦ 1 Apr-30 Sep. € 11.00   2009*

BOURDEAUX *9D2* (4km NW Rural) *44.59583, 5.11127*
Kawan Village Le Couspeau, Quartier Bellevue, 26460 Le Poët-Célard [04 75 53 30 14; fax 04 75 53 37 23; info@couspeau.com; www.couspeau.com] Fr D538 Crest-Bourdeaux; pass thro Saou & after several kms turn R over bdge to Le Poët-Célard, site sp in vill. Med, terr, mkd pitch, sl, pt shd; wc; chem disp; serviced pitches; baby facs; shwrs inc; el pnts (6A) €3 (poss rev pol); gas; lndtte; sm shop; tradsmn; rest, snacks, bar high ssn; playgrnd; 2 htd pools (1 covrd); paddling pool; rv & fishing; canoeing; tennis; cycle hire; horseriding 4km; wifi; TV rm; 20% statics; dogs €2; Eng spkn; adv bkg; quiet; ccard acc; min 6 days high ssn; red low ssn; CKE/CCI. "On steep hillside; gd views; site rds steep; tractor assistance avail on arr/dep; excel." ♦ 15 Apr-14 Sep. € 32.00   2010*

BOURG see Langres *6F1*

BOURG ACHARD *3D2* (1km W Rural) *49.35330, 0.80814*
Camping Le Clos Normand, 235 Route de Pont Audemer, 27310 Bourg-Achard [02 32 56 34 84 or 06 03 60 36 26 (mob); eric.tannay@wanadoo.fr; www.leclosnormand.eu] 1km W of vill of Bourg-Achard, D675 Rouen-Pont Audemer or exit A13 at Bourg-Achard junc. Med, hdg/mkd pitch, pt sl, pt shd; wc; shwrs inc; el pnts (6A) €3.40 (poss rev pol & poss long lead req); gas; shop; supmkt nr; playgrnd; pool; paddling pool; 10% statics; dogs free; poss cr; adv bkg; some rd noise; ccard acc; red low ssn; CKE/CCI. "Vg, clean san facs; plenty hot water; many pitches uneven; gd." ♦ 1 Apr-30 Sep. € 16.10   2011*

BOURG ACHARD *3D2* (10km NW Rural) *49.44783, 0.81400*
Camping Les Cerisiers, Quai Edouard Salmon Marie, 76940 Heurteauville [02 35 37 41 37 or 06 13 56 05 06; alain.planes405@orange.fr; http://pagesperso-orange.fr/aire-les-cerisiers] Exit A13 junc 25 onto D313/D490 N dir La Mailleraye-sur-Seine; then turn R onto D65 to Heurteauville. Site on bank of Seine nr ferry. Sm, mkd pitch, hdstg, pt shd; own san; chem disp; mv service pnt; no shwrs; el pnts €2; shops 5km; dogs; no twin-axles; adv bkg; CKE/CCI. "Sm CL-type site (12 pitches) aimed at m'vans; sm c'vans accepted; gd location by Rv Seine; friendly owner; vg." 1 Apr-31 Oct. € 8.00   2008*

⊞ **BOURG ARGENTAL** *9C2* (S Rural) *45.29910, 4.58183*
Camping Domaine de l'Astrée, L'Allier, 42220 Bourg-Argental [tel/fax 04 77 39 72 97 or 04 77 39 63 49 (OT); prl@bourgargental.fr] S fr St Etienne on D1082 to Bourg-Argental, thro town, site well sp on R soon after rndabt & opp filling stn. Fr Annonay or Andance site on L of D1082 at start of Bourg-Argental, adj rv. Sm, mkd pitch, some hdstg, pt shd; wc; chem disp (wc); shwrs inc; el pnts (4-6A) inc (long cable poss req); gas; lndtte; shop 250m; snacks; BBQ; playgrnd; htd pool 600m; paddling pool; waterslide; fishing; tennis; games rm; cycle hire; 60% statics; dogs €1.60; phone; poss cr; some rd noise; red low ssn; ccard acc; red low ssn; CKE/CCI. "Pleasant site with modern facs; vg." ♦ € 20.00   2013*

BOURG DES COMPTES *2F4* (500m W Rural) *47.92741, -1.75354* Camp Municipal La Courbe, 11 Rue du Camping, 35580 Bourg-des-Comptes [06 77 04 37 47 (mob) or 02 99 05 62 62 (Mairie); fax 02 99 05 62 69; bourg-des-comptes@wanadoo.fr] Fr Rennes take N137 S dir Nantes. At Crévin take rd W dir Guichen. Site sp on L bef bdge over Rv Vilaine. Sm, mkd pitch, pt shd; wc; chem disp; shwrs €0.91; el pnts (10A); shops 800m; rest 1km; bar 200m; playgrnd; lake & rv 100m; fishing; some long-stay statics; dogs; adv bkg; quiet. "Rough field." 1 Apr-31 Oct.   2008*

BOURG D'OISANS, LE *9C3* (1.5km NE Rural) *45.06557, 6.03980* Camping à la Rencontre du Soleil, Route de l'Alpe-d'Huez, La Sarenne, 38520 Le Bourg-d'Oisans [04 76 79 12 22; fax 04 76 80 26 37; rencontre.soleil@wanadoo.fr; www.alarencontredusoleil.com] Fr D1091 approx 800m E of town turn N onto D211, sp 'Alpe d'Huez'. In approx 500m cross sm bdge over Rv Sarennes, then turn immed L to site. (Take care not to overshoot ent, as poss diff to turn back.) Med, hdg/mkd pitch, pt shd; htd wc (some cont); chem disp; mv service pnt; baby facs; shwrs inc; el pnts (10A) inc; lndtte; supmkt 300m; tradsmn; rest, snacks; bar; BBQ; playgrnd; htd pool; fishing; tennis; games area; horseriding 1.5km; wifi; entmnt; TV/games rm; 45% statics; dogs €1; no c'vans/m'vans over 7m high ssn; adv bkg ess; rd noise; ccard acc; red low ssn; CKE/CCI. "Busy site with lovely views; various pitch sizes/shapes; excel, spotless san facs, some unisex; helpful owner; excel rest; La Marmotte cycle race (early Jul) & Tour de France usually pass thro area & access poss restricted; pitches poss flooded after heavy rain, but staff excel at responding; mkt Sat; highly rec." 1 May-30 Sep. € 37.90   2012*

FRANCE

BOURG D'OISANS, LE *9C3* (1.5km NE Rural) *45.06401, 6.03895* **Camping La Cascade, Route de l'Alpe d'Huez, 38520 Le Bourg-d'Oisans [04 76 80 02 42; fax 04 76 80 22 63; lacascade@wanadoo.fr; www. lacascadesarenne.com]** Fr W drive thro Le Bourg-d'Oisans & cross bdge over Rv Romanche. Approx 800m E of town turn onto D211, sp Alpe-d'Huez. Site on R in 600m. Med, mkd pitch, pt shd; htd wc; chem disp; baby facs; shwrs; el pnts (16A) €4.30; lndtte; supmkt 1km; snacks; bar high ssn; playgrnd; htd pool high ssn; some statics; dogs free; poss cr; Eng spkn; adv bkg; quiet; ccard acc; CKE/CCI. "Friendly site; discounts for ski passes fr recep." 1Jan-30 Sep / 12 Dec-31 Dec. € 45.80   2013*

⊞ **BOURG D'OISANS, LE** *9C3* (1.5km NE Rural) *45.06357, 6.03772* **Camping La Piscine, Route de l'Alpe d'Huez, 38520 Le Bourg-d'Oisans [04 76 80 02 41; fax 04 76 11 01 26; infos@camping-piscine.com; www. camping-piscine.com]** Fr D1091 approx 800m E of town, take D211 sp Alpe d'Huez. After 1km turn L into site. Fountains at ent. Med, mkd pitch, pt shd; htd wc (some cont); chem disp; shwrs inc; el pnts (16A) inc; lndtte; shops 1.5km; tradsmn; snacks; bar; BBQ; playgrnd; htd pool (summer); paddling pool; rv adj; tennis 2km; entmnt; wifi; TV; 10% statics; dogs €1; phone; poss cr; Eng spkn; adv bkg; quiet but wth some rd noise; red long stay/low ssn; ccard acc; CKE/CCI. "Excel site; excel lge pool; facs stretched high ssn & when La Marmotte cycle race (early Jul) & Tour de France in area; ski slopes 10-18km." ◆ € 30.00   2011*

BOURG D'OISANS, LE *9C3* (500m SE Rural) *45.05258, 6.03561* **Camping Le Colporteur, Le Mas du Plan, 38520 Le Bourg-d'Oisans [04 76 79 11 44 or 06 85 73 29 19 (mob); fax 04 76 79 11 49; info@camping-colporteur.com; www. camping-colporteur.com]** W fr Briançon on D1019 to Le Bourg-d'Oisans. Ent town, pass Casino supmkt, site sp on L; 150m to sw pool - 2nd site sp, site 50m - sp on side of house. Fr Grenoble on A480 exit 8 onto N85, cont on D1019 to Le Bourg-d'Oisans. Foll sp R in cent of town. Med, hdg/mkd pitch, hdstg, pt shd; wc; chem disp; baby facs; shwrs inc; el pnts (6-15A) €4.50; lndtte; shops 500m; tradsmn; rest, snacks; bar; BBQ; playgrnd; htd pool opp; waterslide; lake sw 10km; fishing; tennis; squash; mountain bikes; rockclimbing; horseriding; cycle hire 200m; entmnt; games rm; wifi; TV; 10% statics; dogs €2; Eng spkn; adv bkg; quiet; ccard acc; red low ssn; CKE/CCI. "Well-organised, high standard site; lge pitches; gd security; mountain scenery; many activities; conv National Park des Ecrins." ◆ 14 May-18 Sep. € 26.00   2011*

BOURG D'OISANS, LE *9C3* (13km SE Rural) *44.98611, 6.12027* **Camping Le Champ du Moulin, Bourg d'Arud, 38520 Vénosc [04 76 80 07 38; fax 04 76 80 24 44; info@ champ-du-moulin.com; www.champ-du-moulin.com]** On D1091 SE fr Le Bourg-d'Oisans sp Briançon for about 6km; turn R onto D530 twd La Bérarde & after 8km site sp. Turn R to site 350m after cable car stn beside Rv Vénéon. NB Site sp bef vill; do not cross rv on D530. Med, mkd pitch, pt shd; wc; chem disp; mv service pnt; baby facs; shwrs inc; sauna; el pnts (6-10A) €4.60-5.60 (extra charge in winter; poss rev pol); gas; lndtte (inc dryer); sm shop; tradsmn; rest, snacks; bar; BBQ; playgrnd; htd pool adj; fishing, tennis, rafting & horseriding nr; wifi; games/TV rm; 20% statics; dogs €1.70; no c'vans/m'vans over 10m; poss cr; Eng spkn; adv bkg ess; quiet; ccard acc; red long stay/low ssn; CKE/CCI. "Lovely, well-run site by alpine torrent (unguarded); friendly, helpful owners; ltd facs low ssn; access to pitches poss diff lge o'fits; ideal for walking, climbing & relaxing; cable car to Les Deux Alpes adj (closes end Aug); mkt Tue Vénosc (high ssn); highly rec." ◆ 1 Jan-30 Apr, 1Jun-15 Sep, 15 Dec-31 Dec. € 39.70 SBS - M03   2013*

BOURG D'OISANS, LE *9C3* (4km NW Rural) *45.09000, 6.00750* **Camping Ferme Noémie, Chemin Pierre Polycarpe, Les Sables, 38520 Le Bourg-d'Oisans [tel/fax 04 76 11 06 14 or 06 87 45 08 75 (mob); ferme.noemie@ orange.fr; www.fermenoemie.com]** On D1091 Grenoble to Briançon; Les Sables is 4km bef Le Bourg-d'Oisans; turn L next to church, site in 400m. Sm, mkd pitch, unshd; htd wc; chem disp; mv service pnt; shwrs inc; el pnts (16A) €2.50; lndtte; tradsmn; shop, rest, snacks & bar 3km; BBQ (gas); playgrnd; pool 3km; fishing; skiing; cycling; walking; games area; internet; 25% statics; dogs free; phone; bus 500m; poss cr; adv bkg; quiet; red long stay; ccard acc; CKE/CCI. "Simple site in superb location with excel facs; helpful British owners; lots of sports; gd touring base lakes & Ecrins National Park." ◆ May-Oct. € 28.50   2012*

BOURG D'OISANS, LE *9C3* (7km NW Rural) *45.11595, 6.00591* **Camping Le Château de Rochetaillée, Chemin de Bouthéon, 38520 Rochetaillée [04 76 11 04 40; fax 04 76 80 21 23; jcp@camping-le-chateau.com; www. camping-le-chateau.com or www.les-castels.com]** On D1091 fr Grenoble turn 7km bef Le Bourg-d'Oisans onto D526 sp Allemont. Site is 50m on L. Med, pt shd; wc; chem disp; baby facs; shwrs inc; el pnts (6A) €4.10; lndtte; shop; rest, snacks; bar; BBQ; playgrnd; pool; spa; games area; games rm; gym; entmnt; dogs €1; 5% statics; quiet; red low ssn; CKE/CCI. "Vg site with mountain views; helpful staff; san facs clean & modern." ◆ 13 May-14 Sep. € 31.00   2010*

See advertisement on inside back cover

BOURG D'OISANS, LE *9C3* (7km NW Rural) *45.12075, 6.01326* **Camping Les Bouleaux, La Pernière Basse, 38114 Allemont/ Allemond [04 76 80 71 23 or 06 87 56 17 48 (mob); campinglesbouleaux@wanadoo.fr]** Take D1091 fr Bourg-d'Oisans, then turn onto D526 dir Allemont/Allemond. After x-ing 1st bdge, turn immed L at x-rds over another bdge, site on R, well sp. Recep up narr lane beside stream. Sm, pt shd; wc; chem disp; shwrs inc; el pnts inc; tradsmn; pool 2km; dogs; poss cr; Eng spkn; quiet; red 7+ days & low ssn; CKE/CCI. "Vg sheltered, peaceful, much improved, delightful farm site; helpful owners." ◆ ltd 15 Jun-15 Sep.   2008*

FRANCE

BOURG D'OISANS, LE 9C3 (7km NW Rural) 45.11388,
6.00785 **RCN Camping Belledonne, Rochetaillée, 38520
Le Bourg-d'Oisans [04 76 80 07 18; fax 04 76 79 12 95;
belledonne@rcn.fr; www.rcn-campings.fr]** Fr S of Grenoble
take N85 to Vizille then D1091 twd Le Bourg-d'Oisans; in
approx 25km in Rochetaillée turn L onto D526 sp Allemont.
Site 100m on R. Med, hdg pitch, shd; wc (some cont); chem
disp; mv service pnt; sauna; baby facs; sauna; shwrs inc;
el pnts (6A) inc; lndtte (inc dryer); shop; rest, snacks; bar;
BBQ; playgrnd; 2 htd pools & paddling pool; fishing 500m;
windsurfing; tennis; horseriding; games area; wifi; entmnt;
games/TV rm; dogs €7; no twin-axles; no c'vans/m'vans over
7.50m high ssn; Eng spkn; quiet; ccard acc; red low ssn; CKE/
CCI. "Beautiful, well-run site in lovely location; friendly Dutch
owners; access to many pitches tight; no twin-axles; gd for
teenagers; excel pool with views; many walks; gd touring base;
La Marmotte cycle race (early Jun) & Tour de France usually
pass thro area & access poss restricted; mkt Sat; excel San Facs,
gd restaurant, V helpful staff" ♦ 21 Apr-22 Sep. € 51.85
SBS - M02   2013*

BOURG D'OISANS, LE 9C3 (8km NW Rural) 45.12914,
6.04130 **Camp Municipal Le Plan, 38114 Allemont/
Allemond [04 76 80 76 88 or 04 76 80 70 30 (Mairie);
fax 04 76 79 80 28; info@camping-leplan-allemont.com;
www.camping-leplan-allemont.com]** At Rochetaillée on
D1091 fr Grenoble turn N 7km bef Le Bourg-d'Oisans on D526
sp Allemont site on R at N end of vill below dam. Med, mkd
pitch, hdstg; pt shd; htd wc; chem disp; shwrs inc; el pnts
(16A) €2.50; lndtte; snacks; shops in vill; pool adj high ssn
only; no statics; dogs €0.50; adv bkg; quiet; some rd noise;
ccard acc high ssn; CKE/CCI. "In quiet vill with lovely mountain
scenery; excel, clean facs; helpful staff." ♦ 1 May-30 Sep.
€ 9.70   2010*

BOURG DUN, LE see Veules les Roses 3C2

BOURG EN BRESSE 9A2 (1km NE Urban) 46.20943, 5.24013
**FFCC Camp Municipal de Challes, 5 Alleée du Centre
Nautique, 01000 Bourg-en-Bresse [04 74 45 37 21 or
04 74 22 92 20 (LS); fax 04 74 45 59 95; camping-municipal-
bourgenbresse@wanadoo.fr; www.bourgenbresse.fr]** Fr N
or S ON N83 foll sp Camping/Piscine/Stade. Site opp stadium.
Med, hdstg, shd; wc (most cont); chem disp; shwrs inc; el pnts
(6-16A) €2.50 (poss rev pol); lndry rm; hypermkt nr; snacks;
rest; BBQ; htd, covrd pool & sports ground adj; lake sw 2km;
wifi; 10% statics; bus adj; poss cr; adv bkg; some rd noise;
ccard acc; long stay/CKE/CCI. "Vg site; site poss full by 1800;
suitable lge o'fits; gd shwr block; gd touring base; daytime
noise fr stadium; poss workers staying on site (no problem);
mkt Wed." 1 Apr-15 Oct. € 19.80   2013*

BOURG EN BRESSE 9A2 (11km NE Rural) 46.29078,
5.29078 **Camp Municipal du Sevron, Chemin du
Moulin, 01370 St Etienne-du-Bois [04 74 30 50 65 or
04 74 30 50 36 (Mairie); fax 04 74 25 85 72; mairie@st-
etienne-du-bois.fr; www.st-etienne-du-bois.fr]**
On D1083 at S end of vill of St Etienne-du-Bois on E side of
rd. Sm, hdg pitch, shd; wc; chem disp; shwrs inc; el pnts (10A)
€2.05; shops 300m; tennis; rv fishing; dogs €1.06; Eng spkn;
ccard not acc. "Gd NH; clean facs; friendly; sm pitches; late arr
get v sm pitches; poss rd & rlwy noise; gd shwrs & plenty hot
water." 1 Mar-25 Oct. € 9.90   2008*

BOURG EN BRESSE 9A2 (13km SE Rural) 46.14705, 5.33159
**Camp Municipal de Journans, Rue de Boisserolles/
Montée de Lachat, 01250 Journans [04 74 42 64 71 or
04 74 51 64 45; fax 04 74 42 64 83; mairiejournans@
wandaoo.fr]** Exit A40 junc 7, turn L onto D1075, then L onto
D64 dir Tossiat & Journans. Or SE fr Bourg-en-Bresse on D1075
for 9.5km E onto D64 to Journans. Site sp on D52 Sm, mkd
pitch, sl terr, pt shd; wc (some cont); shwrs inc; el pnts (5-10A)
€2.60; shops 1km (Tossiat); dog €1; poss cr; quiet; CKE/CCI.
"Pleasant setting, gd views; helpful warden calls pm; some
pitches diff for c'vans; v quiet low ssn; poss mkt traders; excel
value." 1 May-15 Sep. € 7.90   2010*

BOURG EN BRESSE 9A2 (20km SE Rural) 46.12775, 5.4282
**Camping de l'Ile Chambod, Route du Port, 01250
Hautecourt-Romanèche [04 74 37 25 41; fax 04 74 37 28 28;
camping.chambod@free.fr; www.campingilechambod.com]**
Fr S exit A42 junc 9 onto D1075 dir Geneva. In 1km turn L onto
N84 dir Nantua. At Poncin turn L at traff lts dir Ile Chambod &
site. Fr N turn S off D979 in Hautecourt at x-rds (site sp). Site sp
in 4km off D59. At rvside cont for 500m. Med, mkd pitch; pt
shd; wc; mv service pnt; baby facs; shwrs inc; el pnts (5-10A)
€2.90-3.90 (poss rev pol); gas; lndtte; shop; rest, snacks; BBQ;
playgrnd; pool; lake 100m; fishing/boat hire 400m; cycle hire;
games area; games rm; internet; entmnt; 10% statics; dogs
€1.20; poss cr; Eng spkn; adv bkg; quiet; ccard acc; red low
ssn. "Lovely, picturesque, remote site opp lake & adj rv; superb
san facs; helpful manager; rest ltd menu; gd for families; gd
cycling; 2 nights min w/end; conv Geneva; highly rec." ♦
22 Apr-25 Sep. € 16.20   2011*

⊞ **BOURG ET COMIN** 3D4 (500m NE Rural) 49.39871,
3.66072 **Camping de la Pointe, 5 Rue de Moulins, 02160
Bourg-et-Comin [03 23 25 87 52; fax 03 23 25 06 02; michel.
pennec@9online.fr; www.tourisme-paysdelaon.com]**
Leave A26/E17 at junc 14 & turn W along D925 dir Soissons
for 15km. Site on R on ent vill. Sm, hdg pitch, pt shd; htd
wc; chem disp; mv service pnt; shwrs inc; el pnts (6A) €3.20;
lndtte; baker 500m; tradsmn; crêperie adj; rest; bar 500m;
BBQ; playgrnd; htd, covrd pool; internet; dogs €2; phone; bus
500m; adv bkg; quiet; CKE/CCI. "CL-type site in orchard; narr
ent & access to pitches poss diff lge o'fits; most pitches sm &
not suitable lge o'fits; el pnts poss not working (2010); gd rest;
gd walking area; 10 mins fr Parc Nautique de l'Ailette with
watersports; conv Aisne Valley." € 12.60   2011*

⊞ **BOURG MADAME** 8H4 (200m N Urban) 42.43531,
1.94469 **Camping Le Sègre, 8 Ave du Puymorens, 66760
Bourg-Madame [04 68 04 65 87; fax 04 68 04 91 82;
camping.lesegre@free.fr]** N on N20 site on R immed under
rlwy bdge. Med, pt shd; wc; shwrs inc; el pnts (3-6A); lndtte;
shops adj; playgrnd; pool & sports cent 3km; site clsd Oct;
some statics; dogs; poss cr; some rd & rlwy noise. "Ltd touring
pitches in winter, rec arr early." ♦   2009*

⊞ **BOURG MADAME** 8H4 (1km N Rural) 42.43878, 1.94391
**Camping Mas Piques, Rue du Train Jaune, 66760 Bourg-
Madame [04 68 04 62 11; fax 04 68 04 68 36; campiques@
wanadoo.fr]** Last camp site in France bef Spain & Cadí Tunnel.
App via N20 or N116. Med, pt shd; htd wc; chem disp; baby
facs; shwrs inc; el pnts (6A) inc; shop 500m; lndtte; playgrnd;
95% statics; dogs €1.50; poss v cr; adv bkg ess high ssn. "Vg;
popular with w/end skiers; can walk to Puigcerda in Spain; gd
san facs & el pnts." ♦ ltd € 18.90   2008*

FRANCE

⊞ **BOURG MADAME** 8H4 (5km NE Rural) 42.46902, 1.99870 **Camping L'Enclave, 66800 Estavar [04 68 04 72 27; fax 04 68 04 07 15; contact@camping-lenclave.com; www. camping.lenclave.com]** Leave Saillagouse on D33 sp Estavar vill. Lge, pt sl, terr, pt shd; htd wc; chem disp; mv service pnt; baby facs; shwrs inc; el pnts (3A) inc; gas; lndtte; shop, rest adj; snacks; bar; playgrnd; htd, covrd pool; tennis; cycle hire; entmnt; dogs €1.52; site clsd Oct; adv bkg; quiet; red low ssn; CKE/CCI. "Nr ski resorts & Spanish border, friendly." ♦ € 26.00   2008*

⊞ **BOURG MADAME** 8H4 (6km NW Rural) 42.45979, 1.91075 **Camping Le Robinson, 25 Ave Gare Internationale, 66760 Enveitg [tel/fax 04 68 04 80 38 or 06 11 81 25 46 (mob); lerobinson-cerdagne@wanadoo.fr; www.robinson-cerdagne.com]** Fr Bourg-Madame, take N20 N twd Foix. Thro vill of Enveitg & turn L down Chemin de la Gare & L at camping sp. Lge, mkd pitch, pt sl, shd; wc; chem disp; baby facs; shwrs inc; el pnts (4-13A) €3-9; gas; lndtte; shops adj; tradsmn; rest adj; snacks; BBQ; playgrnd; pool; games rm; entmnt; TV rm; some statics; dogs €1.50; phone; adv bkg; quiet. "Beautiful setting; winter sports cent; conv Barcelona, Andorra; conv scenic rte train (Train Jaune); New management; new shower block (excel)" ♦ € 18.50   2013*

BOURG ST ANDEOL 9D2 (1.5km N Rural) 44.38131, 4.64840 **Camping Le Lion, Chemin du Chenevrier, 07700 Bourg-St Andéol [tel/fax 04 75 54 53 20; contact@campingdulion; www.campingdulion.com]** Exit A7 at junc 18 or 19 onto N7. At Pierrelatte turn W on D59 to Bourg-St Andéol. Site sp fr cent town dir Viviers. Med, mkd pitch, shd; wc; shwrs inc; el pnts (6A) €3; lndtte; shop; snacks; bar; playgrnd; pool; games area; games rm; dir access to rv; wifi; some statics; dogs €1.70; poss cr; adv bkg; quiet; red low ssn. "Peaceful site in woodland setting; some modern san facs, some need update; muddy when wet; highly rec." 1 Apr-15 Sep. € 21.00   2011*

⊞ **BOURG ST MAURICE** 9B4 (2km NE Rural) 45.62578, 6.79386 **FFCC Camp Municipal Le Reclus, Pont du Reclus, 73700 Séez [04 79 41 01 05; fax 04 79 40 18 54; contact@ campinglereclus.com; www.campinglereclus.com]** Site on R of D1090 bet Bourg-St Maurice & St Bernard Pass, bef vill of Séez. Med, terr, pt sl, shd; htd wc; chem disp; shwrs inc; el pnts (4-10A) €4-4.70; lndtte; shops 300m; tradsmn; BBQ; playgrnd; pool 350m; wifi; dogs €1; quiet; CKE/CCI. "Busy site high ssn; rec arr bef midday; helpful warden; diff exit fr site due slope up to rd & bend." ♦ € 12.40   2008*

BOURG ST MAURICE 9B4 (1km E Rural) 45.62241, 6.78503 **Camping Le Versoyen, Route des Arcs, 73700 Bourg-St Maurice [04 79 07 03 45; fax 04 79 07 25 41; leversoyen@ wanadoo.fr; www.leversoyen.com]** Fr SW on N90 thro town turn R to Les Arcs. Site on R in 1km. Do not app fr any other dir. Lge, hdstg, pt shd; wc; chem disp; mv service pnt; sauna; shwrs inc; el pnts (4-10A) €4.60-5.20; lndtte; shops 200m; playgrnd; 2 pools adj; tennis adj; games area; entmnt; fishing, canoeing; dogs €1; Eng spkn; quiet; red low ssn; red CKE/CCI. "Excel for winter sports; mountain views; mkd walks fr site; rvside walk to town; well-organised site; dated but clean facs." ♦ 1 Jan-24 Apr, 25 May-3 Nov, 14 Dec-31 Dec. € 31.60   2013*

BOURG ST MAURICE 9B4 (8km S Rural) 45.53100, 6.77530 **Camping Les Lanchettes, Route de Boverêche-Nancroix, 73210 Peisey-Nancroix [04 79 07 93 07; fax 04 79 07 88 33; lanchettes@free.fr; www.camping-lanchettes.com]** Fr Moûtiers foll N90 NE twds Bourg-St Maurice. In 20km turn R sp Landry & Peisey-Nancroix. Up v steep rd with hairpin bends for 6km. Site 1km beyond Nancroix. Long steep ascent with many hairpin bends. Med, pt sl, terr, pt shd; htd wc; chem disp; mv service pnt; shwrs inc; el pnts (3-10A) €3.40-8.40; gas adj; lndtte (inc dryer); shop 200m (summer); tradsmn; rest, snacks; bar; playgrnd; rv fishing; tennis 100m; games area; ski cent in winter; wifi; TV rm; some statics; dogs €2; adv bkg; CKE/CCI. "Lovely setting in National Park; excel for outdoor pursuits, walking." ♦ 10 Dec-29 Apr & 4 Jun-25 Sep. € 14.10   2010*

See advertisement on pages 32 & 33

BOURG SUR GIRONDE 7C2 (S Urban) 45.03880, -0.56065 **Camp Municipal La Citadelle, 33710 Bourg-sur-Gironde [05 56 68 40 04; fax 05 57 68 39 84; commune-de-bourg@ wanadoo.fr]** Take D669 fr St André-de-Cubzac (off A10) to Bourg. Foll sp Halte Nautique & Le Port into Rue Franklin on L twd town cent & foll sp to site. Or fr Blaye, foll Camping sp on app Bourg, cont round by-pass to other end of town to Rue Franklin. NB Do not attempt to take c'van thro town. Sm, mkd pitch, pt shd; wc; chem disp; mv service pnt; shwrs inc; el pnts (3-10A) €3-6 (poss long lead req); shops in town; BBQ; pool, playgrnd adj; dogs; no statics; adv bkg; quiet; CKE/CCI. "Scenic, CL-type rvside site; well-maintained but basic facs; poss variable opening dates; excel." ♦ ltd 15 May-30 Sep. € 13.00   2013*

BOURGANEUF 7B4 (5km E Rural) 45.94684, 1.81331 **Aire Naturelle Les Quatre Saisons, Chignat, 23250 Soubrebost [05 55 64 23 35; les4saisons0314@orange.fr; www.les-4-saisons.com]** Fr Bourganeuf take D8 sp Lac de Vassivière; in 3.5km turn L (on bend) onto D37 thro Chignat & foll sp to site. White gates at site ent. Well sp. NB Ent fr narr lane, turn sharp R up incline to site. Lge o'fits may req assistance from owners, check in adv. Sm, pt sl, terr, pt shd; wc; shwrs; chem disp in Bourgneuf; el pnts (3A) €4; lndtte (inc dryer); tradsmn; rest; BBQ; games rm; wifi; 2 statics; dogs €2; poss cr; Eng spkn; adv bkg; quiet; CKE/CCI. "Lovely, peaceful, wooded site; friendly, helpful British owners; B&B, meals & produce avail; gd walking; vg." ♦ 1 Apr-1 Oct. € 13.00   2011*

★★★★ Grand Confort — *Le Château de Poinsouze*

CASTELS — La Clef Verte · Camping Qualité · Ecolabel

FR/026/024

FRANCE

B.P. 12 Route de la Châtre
F-23600 BOUSSAC-BOURG
Tel.: 05 55 65 02 21 · Fax: 05 55 65 86 49
info.camping-de.poinsouze@orange.fr
www.camping-de-poinsouze.com

· Nature · Peace · Lake
· Heated swimming pool from 15/6 · Water slide
· Restaurant · Take away
· Bar · Animation 4-12 years
· Internet access
· Online reservation

Opening dates: from 15/05 to 16/09

[Map showing: Paris, Vierzon, Chateauroux, La Châtre, St. Amand, Boussac, Poinsouze, Montluçon, La Rochelle, Gouzon, Moulins, Limoges, Clt Ferrand]

BOURGES *4H3* (1km S Urban) *47.07228, 2.39497* **Camp Municipal Robinson, 26 Blvd de l'Industrie, 18000 Bourges [02 48 20 16 85; fax 02 48 50 32 39; camping@ ville-bourges.fr]** junc 7, foll sp Bourges Centre & bear R at 'Autres Directions' sp; foll site sp; site at traff lts on N side of S section of inner ring rd half-way bet junc with D2144 & D2076. NB: site access is via a loop - no L turn at traff lts, but rndabt just past site if turning missed. If on outer ring rd D400, app city on D2144 & then as above. Sp on app rds to site gd. Med, hdg/mkd pitch, hdstg, pt shd; htd wc; chem disp; some serviced pitches; shwrs; el pnts (6-16A) €3.40-8.00 (poss rev pol); gas 3km; lndtte; rest, snacks & bar 1km; BBQ (gas/elec); playgrnd; pool 300m inc; dogs €2.15; bus adj; poss cr; Eng spkn; quiet; extra for twin-axles; ccard acc; red long stay; CKE/CCI. "Attractive, well-kept, busy, rvside site in gd location; friendly staff; excel, immac san facs; some v lge pitches, some sm & poss diff entry; most pitches hdstg; excel NH or longer." ♦ 15 Mar-15 Nov. € 24.10   2013*

BOURGET DU LAC, LE see Aix Les Bains *9B3*

BOURGUEIL *4G1* (700m S Rural) *47.26991, 0.16873* **Camp Municipal Parc Capitaine, 37140 Bourgueil [02 47 97 85 62 or 02 47 97 25 00 LS; www.bourgueil.fr]** Exit A85, junc 5 of A85, site 1km on R. Fr W (Longue) via D10 & by-pass, S at rndabt on D749 to site on L in 200m. Do not app fr N via D749 thro town cent. Med, hdg/mkd pitch, pt shd; wc; chem disp; mv service pnt; shwrs inc; el pnts (10A) €2.15 (poss long lead req); gas; lndtte; shops 1km; supmkt nrby; playgrnd; sw lake; dogs €1.25; quiet; ccard acc; CKE/CCI. "Gd san facs; ideal cent Loire châteaux; 2 sites - one on R for tourers; excel." ♦ ltd 15 May-15 Sep. € 13.40   2012*

BOURNEL see Villereal *7D3*

BOURNEZEAU *2H4* (500m N Rural) **Camp Municipal Les Humeaux, Rue de la Gare, 85480 Bournezeau [02 51 40 01 31 or 02 51 40 71 29 (Mairie); fax 02 51 40 79 30; mairie@bournezeau.fr; www.bournezeau.fr]** Exit A83 junc 6 to Bournezeau cent. Take D7 sp St Martin-des-Noyers. Site on R in 500m, well sp. Sm, mkd pitch, pt shd; wc; chem disp; mv service pnt; shwrs; el pnts (6A) €2.90; lndtte; shop, rest, snacks, bar 500m; playgrnd; dogs €1; adv bkg; quiet. "Vg, conv NH; gd facs; easy walk to town." 1 Jun-15 Sep. € 8.60   2008*

BOUSSAC *7A4* (2km NE Rural) *46.37192, 2.20036* **Camping du Château de Poinsouze, Route de la Châtre, 23600 Boussac-Bourg [05 55 65 02 21; fax 05 55 65 86 49; info. camping-de.poinsouze@orange.fr; www.camping-de-poinsouze.com or www.les-castels.com]** Fr junc 10 on A71/E11 by-pass Montluçon via N145 dir Guéret; in 22km turn L onto D917 to Boussac; cont on D917 dir La Châtre; site 3km on L. Or fr Guéret on N145, exit Gouzon, at rndabt take D997 to Boussac, then as above. Med, mkd pitch, pt sl, unshd; wc; chem disp; mv service pnt; serviced pitch; baby facs; shwrs inc; el pnts (10A) inc (poss rev pol); lndtte (inc dryer); shop & 3km; tradsmn; rest, snacks; bar; BBQ; playgrnd; pool; paddling pool; waterslide; lake fishing; horseriding 5km; golf 20km; cycle hire; games area; wifi; entmnt; games/ TV rm; 10% statics; dogs €3 (not acc mid-July to mid Aug; no c'vans/m'vans over 15m; Eng spkn; adv bkg ess high ssn; quiet; ccard acc; red low ssn; CKE/CCI. "Peaceful, relaxed site by lake in chateau grnds; well-kept & well-run; lge pitches, some sl; welcoming, helpful owners; superb san facs; excel rest & snacks; gd for young children; gd walking." ♦ 1 Jun-1 Sep. € 41.00 SBS - L16   2013*

See advertisement

BOUSSAC *7A4* (2km W Rural) *46.34938, 2.18662* **Camping Creuse-Nature (Naturist), Route de Bétête, 23600 Boussac [05 55 65 18 01; fax 05 55 65 81 40; creuse-nature@ wanadoo.fr; www.creuse-nature.com]** Fr Boussac take D917 N twd La Châtre. In 500m turn L (W) on D15 sp Bétête. Site on R in 2.5km, clearly sp. Med, hdg/mkd pitch, pt sl, pt shd; wc; shwrs; el pnts (10A) €4.50 (poss long lead req); lndtte; sm shop; rest, snacks; bar; playgrnd; 2 htd pools (1 covrd); paddling pool; fishing; games area; entmnt; some statics; dogs €5.50; Eng spkn; adv bkg; v quiet; ccard acc; red low ssn. "Excel site in lovely area; great pitches; charming & helpful owners; clean facs; easy walk to town & interesting château." ♦ 1 Apr-31 Oct. € 26.00   2011*

BOUZIGUES see Meze *10F1*

BOUZONVILLE AUX BOIS see Pithiviers *4F3*

FRANCE

BRACIEUX *4G2* (500m N Urban) *47.55060, 1.53743* **Indigo les Châteaux, 11 Rue Roger Brun, 41250 Bracieux [02 54 46 41 84; fax 02 54 46 41 21; chateaux@camping-indigo.com; www.camping-indigo.com/]** Fr S take D102 to Bracieux fr Cour-Cheverny. Fr N exit Blois on D765 dir Romorantin; after 5km take D923 to Bracieux & site on R on N o'skts of town opp church, sp. Lge, pt hdg/mkd pitch, hdstg, pt shd; wc (some cont); chem disp; shwrs inc; el pnts (10A) €2.75 (poss long lead req); gas 300m; lndtte; shop 300m; supmkt 1km; tradsmn high ssn; rest, snacks 300m; playgrnd; htd pool high ssn adj; tennis; cycle hire & tracks; games rm; TV; 10% statics; dogs €2.80; Eng spkn; adv bkg; quiet; ccard acc; red long stay/low ssn; CKE/CCI. "Peaceful spot; attractive forest area; busy high ssn; gd security; gd touring base; excel; well run site; all san blocks replaced (2013); superb" ♦ 28 Mar-4 Nov. € 38.30   2013*

BRAIN SUR L'AUTHION see Angers *4G1*

BRAIZE see Urcay *4H3*

BRAMANS LE VERNEY see Modane *9C4*

BRANTOME *7C3* (1km E Rural) *45.36074, 0.66035* **Camping Brantôme Peyrelevade, Ave André Maurois, 24310 Brantôme [05 53 05 75 24; fax 05 53 05 87 30; info@camping-dordogne.net; www.camping-dordogne.net]** Fr N on D675 foll sp Centre Ville; ent vill & turn L onto D78 Thiviers rd, site sp at turn; in 1km on R past stadium opp g'ge. Fr S D939 foll sp 'Centre Ville' fr rndabt N of town. Then L onto D78 Thiviers rd & foll sp. Do not foll 'Centre Ville' sp fr rndabt S of town, use by-pass. Football stadium best ref point for ent. Lge, hdg/mkd pitch, pt shd; htd wc; chem disp; mv service pnt; baby facs; shwrs inc; el pnts (10A) €4; lndtte (inc dryer); shop 1km; supmkt 2km; tradsmn (bread baked on site); snacks, bar high ssn; BBQ; playgrnd; pool; paddling pool; rv sw & sand beach adj; tennis nr; games area adj; wifi; entmnt; 7% statics; dogs €2; Eng spkn; adv bkg; quiet; ccard acc; red low ssn/CKE/CCI. "Spacious, well-kept rvside site; attractive courtyard layout; friendly, helpful owners; excel modern san facs; gd facs; grnd poss soft after heavy rain; 10 min walk to lovely town (the Venice of Périgord); beautiful countryside; gd walking & cycling; excel." ♦ ltd 1 May-30 Sep. € 20.00   2013*

BRANTOME *7C3* (4km SW Rural) *45.32931, 0.63690* **Camping du Bas Meygnaud, 24310 Valeuil [05 53 05 58 44; camping-du-bas-meygnaud@wanadoo.fr; www.basmeygnaud.fr]** Fr Brantôme, take D939 S twd Périgueux; in 4.5km turn R at sp La Serre. In 1km turn L to in 500m, well sp. Winding, narr app thro lanes; poss diff lge o'fits. Sm, pt sl, pt shd; wc; chem disp; shwrs inc; el pnts (6A) €3.50; gas 4km; lndtte; shop; tradsmn; rest 4km; snacks; bar; BBQ; playgrnd; pool; entmnt; wifi; dogs €2.50; phone; Eng spkn; quiet; CKE/CCI. "Most pitches shaded by pine trees; helpful & friendly owner; dated san facs; unspoilt countryside." 1 Apr-30 Sep. € 15.50   2013*

BRASSAC *8F4* (11km SE Rural) *43.59700, 2.60732* **Camping Le Rouquié, Lac de la Ravièze, 81260 Lamontélarie [05 63 70 98 06; fax 05 63 50 49 58; camping.rouquie@wanadoo.fr; www.campingrouquie.fr]** Fr Brassac take D62 to N side of Lac de la Ravièze; site on lakeside. Med, mkd pitch; terr, pt shd; wc; baby facs; shwrs; el pnts (3-6A) €4; lndtte; shop; tradsmn; snacks; bar; playgrnd; lake sw; fishing; sailing & watersports adj; games area; cycle hire; entmnt; TV; poss cr; quiet; CKE/CCI. "Ltd facs low ssn; gd lake views; Site needs TLC" 15 Apr-31 Oct. € 25.00   2012*

BRASSAC *8F4* (5km S Rural) *43.60835, 2.47148* **FFCC Camping Le Plô, Le Bourg, 81260 Le Bez [tel/fax 05 63 74 00 82; info@leplo.com; www.leplo.com]** Fr Castres on D622 to Brassac; then D53 S to Le Bez, site sp W of Le Bez. Med, mkd pitch,terr, pt shd; wc; chem disp; fam bthrm; shwrs inc; el pnts (6A) €3; lndtte; shop 5km; snacks; BBQ; playgrnd; sm freestanding pool; cycle hire; games area; games rm; wifi; dogs €1.50; Eng spkn; adv bkg; quiet; red low ssn; CKE/CCI. "Lovely location; well-equipped site; excel, clean san facs; friendly, helpful Dutch owners; beautiful, historical area with National Park; much wildlife; cafés & gd rest nrby; vg" ♦ 1 May-30 Sep. € 25.50   2013*

⊞ **BRAUCOURT** *6E1* (9km W Rural) *48.55754, 4.70629* **Camping Le Clos du Vieux Moulin, 33 Rue du Lac, 51290 Châtillon-sur-Broué [tel/fax 03 26 41 30 43; leclosduvieuxmoulin@wanadoo.fr; www.leclosduvieuxmoulin.fr]** Fr N take D13 fr Vitry-le-François. Turn R at sp for Châtillion-sur-Broué; site 100m on R. Fr S 2nd L fr Giffaumont (1km); site 100m on R. Med, hdg/mkd pitch, hdstg, pt sl, pt shd; htd wc; chem disp; baby facs; shwrs inc; el pnts (5A) €3.70; gas; lndtte; shops; rest 400m; snacks; bar; playgrnd; pool; lake 400m; watersports; birdwatching; 80% statics; dogs; phone; poss cr; quiet; ccard acc; red low ssn; CKE/CCI. "Busy high ssn; san facs need refurb (2010) & ltd low ssn; site poss unkempt (2010); grnd soft after rain." ♦ € 17.00   2013*

BRAUCOURT *6E1* (3km NW Rural) *48.55425, 4.79235* **FLOWER Camping Presqu'île de Champaubert, Lac du Der, 52290 Braucourt [03 25 04 13 20; fax 03 25 94 33 51; camping-de-braucourt@wanadoo.fr; www.lacduder.com or www.flowercampings.com]** Fr St Dizier take D384 SW twd Montier-en-Der & Troyes. In Braucourt R onto D153 sp Presq'ile de Champaubert, site on L in 2km. Site situated on Lac du Der-Chantecoq. Lge, hdg/mkd pitch, shd; wc (some cont); chem disp; mv service pnt; serviced pitch; shwrs inc; el pnts (10A) €4 (rev pol); gas; lndtte; basic shop; tradsmn; rest, snacks; bar; playgrnd; htd pool; lake sw & sand beach nrby; watersports; boating, fishing, birdwatching; TV; dogs €1; poss cr; quiet; 60% statics; dogs; phone; quiet; ccard acc; red low ssn; CKE/CCI. "Beautiful lge beach; lge pitches; improved san facs; gates clsd 2230." ♦ 3 Apr-11 Sep. € 22.00   2009*

BRAY DUNES see Dunkerque *3A3*

BRAY SUR SEINE *4E4* (200m E Rural) *48.41425, 3.24623*
Camping La Peupleraie, Rue des Pâtures, 77480 Bray-sur-Seine [01 60 67 12 24; camping.lapeupleraie@wanadoo.fr; www.lapeupleraie.com] Exit A5 at junc 18 onto D41, in 20km turn N to Bray. Turn L bef bdge, foll rd down under bdge, cont on rvside to site. Foll 'complex sportif' & camping sp. Lge, hdg/mkd pitch, pt shd; wc (cont); shwrs inc; el pnts (6A); lndtte; supmkt adj; snacks; playgrnd; pool adj; boating; tennis; 80% statics; dogs; adv bkg; quiet. "Diff to exit bef 0900 when office opens; clean site; helpful warden; site adapted for handicapped." ♦ 1 Apr-31 Oct. € 14.40   2009*

BRECEY *2E4* (1km S Rural) *48.72110, -1.15199* **Camp Municipal Le Pont Roulland, 50370 Brécey [02 33 48 60 60; fax 02 33 89 21 09; mairie-brecey@wanadoo.fr]** Fr Villedieu-les-Poêles S on D999. In Brécey cent L by church on D911; after 1km turn S on D79 sp Les Cresnays. Site in 50m on L thro car park. Med, terr, pt sl, pt shd; wc; chem disp; shwrs; el pnts (16A) €2.50; (rev pol); shops 1km; tradsmn; lndtte; tennis; playgrnd; htd pool adj; dogs €0.50; adv bkg; quiet but noisy tractors at harvest time, inc at night; CKE/CCI. "Lovely, well-kept orchard site; excel, clean san facs; friendly staff; nr fishing lake; grnd soft after prolonged rain." 1 Jun-30 Sep. € 8.00   2008*

BREHAL *1D4* (4km N Coastal) *48.90863, -1.56473* **FFCC Camp Intercommunal de la Vanlée, 50290 Bréhal [02 33 61 63 80; fax 02 33 61 87 18; contact@camping-vanlee.com; www.camping-vanlee.com]** Turn W off D971 onto D20 thro Bréhal to coast, then N. Site sp, nr 'route submersible'. Lge, mkd pitch, pt sl, unshd; wc; chem disp; mv service pnt; baby facs; shwrs inc; el pnts (6A) €3.80; lndtte; shop high ssn; supmkt nr; rest, snacks; bar; playgrnd; pool; paddling pool; sand beach adj; games area; entmnt; TV rm; dogs €2.60; poss cr; Eng spkn; ccard acc; quiet; CKE/CCI. "Beware soft sand when pitching." ♦ 1 May-30 Sep. € 13.90   2009*

BREIL SUR ROYA *10E4* (500m N Urban) *43.94026, 7.51634* **Camp Municipal Azur et Merveilles, 06540 Breil-sur-Roya [04 93 62 47 04 or 04 93 04 99 76 (LS); fax 04 93 04 99 80; contact@camping-azur-merveilles.com; www.camping-azur-merveilles.com]** On D6204, 500m N of Breil-sur-Roya. Sp fr town & fr N. Med, hdg/mkd pitch, hdstg, pt shd; wc; chem disp; shwrs inc; el pnts €3; lndtte; shop & rest 500m; BBQ; pool adj; kayaking; canoeing; 15% statics; dogs €2; train 300m (to Nice); ccard acc; CKE/CCI. "Site beside Rv Roya; gd canoeing etc; gd." 1 May-14 Sep. € 16.00   2008*

BRENGUES *7D4* (1.5km N Rural) *44.58683, 1.83738* **Camping Le Moulin Vieux, Route de Figeac, 46320 Brengues [05 65 40 00 41; fax 05 65 40 05 65; contact@camping-lemoulinvieux.com; www.brengues.com]** Fr Figeac on D13, in 6km L onto D41. In approx 17km site well sp on L bef Brengues vill. Med, shd; wc; chem disp; shwrs inc; el pnts (10A) €2.60; lndtte; shop; snacks; bar; playgrnd; pool; entmnt; some statics; adv bkg; some rd noise; ccard acc; red low ssn; CKE/CCI. "Beautiful site; helpful owners; facs stretched high ssn; poss scruffy/unkempt early ssn (2009); excel." ♦ 1 Jul-30 Sep. € 13.00   2009*

BRENGUES *7D4* (S Rural) *44.57550, 1.83334* **Camp Municipal de Brengues, 46320 Brengues [tel/fax 05 65 40 06 82 or 05 65 40 05 71 (Mairie)]** W fr Figeac on D13. After 6km turn L onto D41. After 17km, turn L at x-rds with D38, site ent 100m on R bef bdge over Rv Célé. Sm, mkd pitch, pt shd; wc; shwrs €2; el pnts (10A) inc (rev pol); lndtte; shop 300m; rest; bar; playgrnd; tennis; CKE/CCI. "Warden visits." 1 Jun-30 Sep. € 11.25   2009*

BRENGUES *7D4* (8km SW Rural) *44.55571, 1.77079* **Camp Municipal Le Pré de Monsieur, 46160 Marcilhac-sur-Célé [tel/fax 05 65 40 77 88; lepredemonsieur@gmail.com; www.camping-marcilhac.com]** W fr Figeac on D802; L onto D41; site on L on ent Marcilhac. App fr E, site on R at far end of vill. Med, pt shd; wc; baby facs; fam bthrm; shwrs inc; el pnts €2.35; lndtte; shop 200m; rest, snacks; bar; BBQ; playgrnd; sm play pool; rv adj; fishing; canoeing; tennis; cycle hire; games area; games rm; wifi; TV; 2% statics; dogs €0.95; phone; Eng spkn; adv bkg; quiet; CKE/CCI. "Vg." ♦ ltd 1 Apr-30 Sep. € 10.05   2008*

⊞ **BRESSE, LA** *6F3* (3.2km E Rural) *47.99878, 6.91831* **FFCC Camp Municipal Le Haut des Bluches, 5 Route des Planches, 88250 La Bresse [03 29 25 64 80; fax 03 29 25 78 03; hautdesbluches@labresse.fr; www. domainehautdesbluches.labresse.fr]** Leave La Bresse on D34 Rte de la Schlucht. Site on R in 3km. Med, mkd pitch, terr, pt shd; htd wc; chem disp; mv service pnt; child/baby facs; shwrs inc; el pnts (4-13A) €2-4.80; lndtte; shop; tradsmn; rest, snacks; bar; BBQ; playgrnd; pool in vill; games area; games rm; internet; TV; 10% statics; dogs free; NH area for m'vans; site clsd early Nov-mid Dec; Eng spkn; adv bkg; red low ssn; ccard acc; red low ssn/CKE/CCI. "Excel site in attractive setting; excel san facs; gd walks fr site; conv winter sports." ♦ € 12.80   2009*

BRESSUIRE *4H1* (1km S Rural) *46.82981, -0.50326* **Camping Le Puy Rond, Allee du Puy Rond, Cornet, 79300 Bressuire [05 49 72 43 22 or 06 85 60 37 26 (mob); puyrondcamping@gmail.com; www.puyrondcamping.com]** Fr N149 foll site sp on rte 'Poids Lourds' to site on D38. Fr 'Centre Ville' foll sp for Fontenay-Le-Comte; turn R 100m after overhead bdge & go across junc to site. Well sp. Sm, mkd pitch, pt sl, pt terr, pt shd; htd wc; chem disp (wc); mv service pnt; baby facs; shwrs inc; el pnts (10A) €3.50; gas 1.50m; lndtte; shop & 1.5km; tradsmn; snacks; rest, bar 1.5km; BBQ; playgrnd; pool; fishing 1km; 15% statics; dogs €1.50; bus 2km; adv bkg; quiet; red low ssn/long stay; ccard acc; CKE/CCI. "Gd touring base, poss tired early ssn; friendly British owners; basic, clean san facs; adv bkg ess for twin-axles; winter storage avail" ♦ 1 Apr-30 Oct. € 36.00   2013*

⊞ **BREST** *2E2* (6km W Coastal) *48.36544, -4.54163* **Camping du Goulet, Ste Anne-du-Porzic, 29200 Brest [tel/fax 02 98 45 86 84; campingdugoulet@wanadoo.fr; www. campingdugoulet.com]** On D789 turn L at site sp. Approx 4km fr Brest after R bend at T junc, turn L & L again at site sp; down hill to site. Med, pt sl, terr, unshd; htd wc; chem disp; baby facs; shwrs inc; el pnts (6-10A) €3-3.50; lndtte; shop high ssn; snacks; playgrnd; pool complex; waterslides; sand beach 1km; games area; games rm; 15% statics; dogs €1.50; adv bkg; quiet; CKE/CCI. ♦ € 23.00   2010*

BRETENOUX *7C4* (N Urban) *44.91650, 1.83816* **Camping La Bourgnatelle, 46130 Bretenoux [05 65 10 89 04; fax 05 65 10 89 18; contact@dordogne_vacances.fr; www. dordogne-vacances.fr]** In town 100m fr D940. Lge, pt shd; wc; mv service pnt; shwrs inc; el pnts (5-10A) €3; lndtte; shops adj; rest, snacks; playgrnd; pool; rv & fishing; canoe hire; entmnt; dogs €1.50; adv bkg; quiet; red low ssn. "On banks of Rv Cère; clean site; gd fishing; lovely town MD Tues." 1 Apr-31 Dec. € 18.00   2012*

BRETENOUX *7C4* (4km W Rural) *44.91937, 1.80262* **Camping Les Chalets sur La Dordogne, Pont de Puybrun, 46130 Girac [05 65 10 93 33; contact@camping-leschalets. com; www.camping-leschalets.com]** Fr Bretenoux on D803 dir Puybrun. Site on L on rvside - sp on rd barrier easily missed. Sm, mkd pitch, shd; wc; chem disp; shwrs inc; el pnts (6A) inc; lndtte; shop; tradsmn; rest, snacks; bar; playgrnd; pool; rv & shgl beach adj; canoeing; TV rm; 20% statics; dogs €1.50; Eng spkn; quiet; ccard acc. "Gd, clean family site; helpful owners." ♦ 10 Apr-30 Sep. € 18.30   2009*

BRETIGNOLLES SUR MER *2H3* (2km N Coastal) *46.63024, -1.86048* **Camping Les Vagues, 85470 Bretignolles-sur-Mer [02 51 90 19 48 or 02 40 02 46 10; fax 02 40 02 49 88; lesvagues@free.fr; www.campinglesvagues.fr]** Well sp on D38. Lge, hdg pitch, pt shd; wc; chem disp; sauna; baby facs; shwrs; el pnts (6A) €4; lndtte (inc dryer); rest, snacks; bar; BBQ; playgrnd; 2 pools (1 htd, covrd); paddling pool; waterslide; sand beach 900m; games area; games rm; entmnt; TV; 50% statics; dogs €2.50; adv bkg; red low ssn; CKE/CCI. "Gd sized pool; close to town cent with shops & rests." ♦ 1 Apr-30 Sep. € 25.00   2009*

BRETIGNOLLES SUR MER *2H3* (1km E Coastal) **Camping La Haute Rivoire, Route des Rivoires, 85470 Bretignolles-sur-Mer [02 51 33 80 34 or 0207 193 6613 (UK); hauterivoire@ gmail.com]** Fr St Gilles Croix-de-Vie take D38 S twd Les Sables. Cross bdge over Rv Jaunay. Turn L on D12 sp Chaize-Giraud. Site 2nd turning on R sp Chambres. Site in 400m. Take ent after barns. Sm, unshd; wc; chem disp; shwrs inc; el pnts (6A) €4.50 (poss rev pol); snacks; supmkt; shop 2km; pool; sand beach 2km; fishing, watersports, golf, horseriding nr; no dogs; sep car park adj; adv bkg req; red low ssn. "British-owned, adults-only, peaceful CL-type farm site; san facs v clean; twin-axles extra; phone bef arr to check open; payment on arr."   2010*

BRETIGNOLLES SUR MER *2H3* (1km E Urban) *46.63583, -1.85861* **Chadotel Camping La Trévillière, Route de Bellevue, 85470 Bretignolles-sur-Mer [02 51 90 09 65 or 02 51 33 05 05; fax 02 51 33 94 04; info@chadotel.com; www.chadotel.com]** S along D38 fr St Gilles Croix-de-Vie twd Olonne-sur-Mer, site is sp to L in Bretignolles-sur-Mer. Site 1km fr town cent nr football stadium. Sp from town cent. Lge, hdg/mkd pitch, pt shd; wc; chem disp; mv service pnt; 50% serviced pitches; baby facs; shwrs inc; el pnts (6A) inc; gas; lndtte (inc dryer); shop; tradsmn; snacks; bar; BBQ (gas); playgrnd; htd, covrd pool; waterslide; paddling pool; sand beach 1.5km; fishing; watersports 3km; horseriding 5km; cycle hire; wifi; entmnt; games/TV rm; 70% statics; dogs €3.20; phone; no c'van/m'van over 8m high ssn; Eng spkn; adv bkg; ccard acc; red long stay/low ssn; CKE/CCI. "Friendly, family site; lge pitches; quiet low ssn; nice cycling area; salt marshes worth a visit; mkt Thu & Sun." ♦ 7 Apr-22 Sep. € 30.50 SBS - A26   2012*

BRETIGNOLLES SUR MER *2H3* (5km E Rural) *46.64817, -1.83334* **Camping Les Alouettes, Route de St Gilles, 85220 La Chaize-Giraud [02 51 22 96 21; fax 02 51 22 92 68; contact@lesalouettes.com; www.lesalouettes.com]** Take D38 N fr Bretignolles; in 2.5km take D12 to La Chaize-Giraud. Site on L in 5km. Med, pt sl, pt shd; wc (some cont); chem disp; shwrs inc; el pnts (6A) inc; gas; lndtte; shop; tradsmn; snacks; playgrnd; htd pool; sand beach 5km; lake sw 14km; games area; 75% statics; dogs €2.20; adv bkg; quiet; ccard acc; CKE/CCI. "Few touring pitches; gd san facs." ♦ ltd 1 Apr-31 Oct. € 23.00   2008*

> **"That's changed – Should I let The Club know?"**
>
> If you find something on site that's different from the site entry, fill in a report and let us know. See www.caravanclub.co.uk/europereport.

BRETIGNOLLES SUR MER *2H3* (5km E Rural) *46.63502, -1.79735* **Camping L'Evasion, Route des Sables, 85220 Landevieille [tel/fax 02 51 22 90 14; contact@camping-levasion.fr; www.camping-levasion.fr]** Site sp in Landevieille. Med, hdg/mkd pitch, pt shd; wc (some cont); chem disp; baby facs; shwrs inc; el pnts (10A) inc; gas; lndtte (inc dryer); shop; supmkt 750m; rest, snacks; bar; BBQ; playgrnd; 3 htd pools; waterslides; jacuzzi; beach 5km; fishing lake; games area; wifi; entmnt; 75% statics; dogs; dog exercise area; phone; some Eng spkn; quiet except for bar/disco high ssn; ccard acc; CKE/CCI. "Vg." 1 Apr-15 Oct. € 25.10   2010*

BRETIGNOLLES SUR MER *2H3* (5km E Rural) *46.64021,
-1.80708* **Camping L'Oree de l'Océan, Rue Capitaine
de Mazenod, 85220 Landevieille [02 51 22 96 36; fax
02 51 22 29 09; info@camping-oreedelocean; www.
camping-oreedelocean.com]** Take D12 fr La Mothe-Achard
to St Julien-des-Landes & cont to x-rds bef La Chaize-Giraud.
Turn L onto D32, take 1st R in Landevieille to site on L in 50m.
Adj Mairie. Med, hdg/mkd pitch, pt sl, pt shd; wc; chem disp;
shwrs inc; el pnts (10A) €4; lndtte; shops 500m; bar; playgrnd;
htd pool; tennis; sand beach 5km; TV rm; phone; 40% statics;
dogs €3; phone; poss cr; quiet; adv bkg; Eng spkn; 15%
red 7+ days; ccard acc; CKE/CCI. "Gd, friendly, family site;
many gd beaches & mkd cycle tracks nr." ♦ 1 Apr-30 Sep.
€ 23.00   2008*

BRETIGNOLLES SUR MER *2H3* (5km E Urban) *46.64220,
-1.79950* **Camping Pong, Rue du Stade, 85220 Landevieille
[02 51 22 92 63; fax 02 51 22 99 25; info@lepong.com;
www.lepong.com]** Fr Challans S on D32. Pass Landevieille
church on L, then rd bends R; turn L immed after sm bdge into
Rue de la Stade; foll rd, site on L. Fr Vaire N on D32, soon after
ent Landevieille & immed bef sm bdge turn R into Rue de la
Stade, then as above. Lge, pt sl, pt shd; wc (some cont); chem
disp; serviced pitches; baby facs; shwrs inc; el pnts (10A) inc;
gas; lndtte (inc dryer); shop; rest, snacks; bar; BBQ (charcoal/
gas); playgrnd; htd pool; paddling pool; waterslide; sand beach
5km; lake 2.5km; fishing; tennis; cycle hire; wifi; entmnt; games/
TV rm; some statics; dogs €3.50; c'vans/m'vans over 8m high
ssn by request; adv bkg; quiet; ccard acc; red low ssn. "Beautiful
site with great facs; extra charge for lger pitches; friendly owners
& pleasant, helpful staff; Lac d'Apremont with 16thC chateau
13.5km; vineyards in area." ♦ 1 Apr-15 Sep. € 29.90   2011*

BRETIGNOLLES SUR MER *2H3* (W Coastal) *46.62708,
-1.86488* **Camping La Motine, 4 Rue des Morinières, 85470
Bretignolles-sur-Mer [02 51 90 04 02; fax 02 51 33 80 52;
campinglamotine@wanadoo.fr; www.lamotine.com]**
Foll sp fr D38 in Bretignolles-sur-Mer dir Plage de la Parée along
Ave de la Plage, then turn R into Rue des Morinières. Med,
hdg pitch, pt sl, pt shd; wc; chem disp; mv service pnt; serviced
pitches; baby facs; shwrs inc; el pnts (6A) inc; lndtte; rest; bar;
playgrnd; htd, covrd pool; sand beach 600m; 60% statics; dogs
€3; adv bkg; quiet; ccard acc; CKE/CCI. "Unisex san facs low
ssn; vg site." ♦ 1 Apr-30 Sep. € 27.00   2009*

BRETTEVILLE see Cherbourg *1C4*

BREUILLET *7B1* (1.5km S Rural) *45.67839, -1.05166* **Camping
Transhumance, Chemin des Métairies, Route de Royan,
17920 Breuillet [05 46 22 72 15; fax 05 46 22 66 47; contact@
transhumance.com; www.transhumance.com]** Fr Saujon
take D14 NW dir St Sulphice-de-Royan & La Tremblade. After
approx 8km turn L at junc with D140 sp Breuillet & Camping
Transhumance; site well sp on L. Or Fr Rochefort S on D733;
turn R onto D14 to Breuillet & as above. Lge, hdg pitch, unshd;
wc; chem disp; baby facs; shwrs inc; el pnts (10A) €4.50; gas;
lndtte; shop; rest, snacks; bar; BBQ; playgrnd; 2 pools; paddling
pool; waterslide; beach 3.5km; watersports 6km; fishing; tennis;
games rm; cycle hire; archery; horseriding 4km; golf 7km;
entmnt; statics; dogs €3; adv bkg; quiet; ccard acc; CKE/CCI.
"Facs poss stretched high ssn." ♦ Easter-9 Sep. € 18.00 2008*

BREUILLET *7B1* (1.5km NW Rural) *45.69998, -1.06576*
**Camping à la Belle Etoile, 27 Route des Renouleaux,
17920 Breuillet [tel/fax 05 46 02 14 07; contact@alabelle-
etoile.com; www.alabelle-etoile.com]** Fr Saujon on D14 W
dir La Tremblade, turn L onto D242 dir St Augustin then 1st R
after 800m. Site sp. Med, mkd pitch, pt shd; wc (cont); chem
disp; mv service pnt; shwrs inc; el pnts (10A) €4.30; gas; lndtte;
shop 1.5km; tradsmn; rest 500m; snacks; bar 1.5km; playgrnd;
pool; sand beach 10km; wifi; 60% statics; dogs €2; adv bkg;
quiet; ccard acc; red low ssn/CKE/CCI. "Gd cycle rtes nr; conv
Royan, Ile d'Oléron, La Rochelle; insufficient facs for size of
site." ♦ ltd 4 Apr-27 Sep. € 17.20   2008*

BREVEDENT, LE see Blangy le Château *3D1*

BREVILLE SUR MER see Granville *1D4*

⊞ **BRIANCON** *9C4* (3km NE Rural) *44.91731, 6.67517*
**Camping Les Gentianes, La Vachette, 05100 Val-des-Prés
[02 92 21 21 41; fax 04 92 21 24 12; campinglesgentianes@
wanadoo.fr; www.campinglesgentianes.com]** Fr Briançon
take N94 dir Montgenèvre. At La Vachette site sp in vill.
Med, pt sl, pt shd; htd wc; chem disp; mv service pnt; shwrs
inc; el pnts (6-10A) €5-7; lndtte; shops, rest in vill; snacks;
bar; playgrnd; pool; canoeing; fishing; x-country skiing; wifi;
40% statics; dogs €1; adv bkg; quiet; CKE/CCI. "Suitable
winter sports users; mountain stream runs thro site; needs
renovation; NH only." € 14.10   2008*

BRIANCON *9C4* (5km NE Rural) *44.93905, 6.68323* **Camp
Municipal l'Iscle du Rosier, Le Rosier, 05100 Val-des-Prés
[04 92 21 06 01; fax 04 92 21 46 46]** Fr Briançon on N94
E & take 3rd L after leaving Briançon (5km) sp Le Rosier. Foll
rd thro until Le Rosier, site on L after bdge. Med, pt shd; wc
(some cont); chem disp; shwrs inc; el pnts (5-10A) €3.50-5.20;
gas; lndtte; shop; snacks; bar; BBQ; playgrnd; 5% statics; dogs
€1.70; phone; bus adj; Eng spkn; quiet. "Nice, well-kept site
by rv; friendy, helpful staff; superb walking, cycling & climbing
nrby; conv Col de Montgenèvre rd; gd bus service." ♦
15 Jun-15 Sep. € 10.10   2011*

⊞ **BRIANCON** *9C4* (6km NE Rural) *44.93034, 6.68169* **Camp
Municipal du Bois des Alberts, 05100 Montgenèvre
[04 92 21 16 11 or 04 92 21 52 52; fax 04 92 21 98 15;
www.montgenevre.com]** Take N94 fr Briançon sp Italie. In
4km turn L onto D994, site 200m past Les Alberts vill on L. Lge,
hdstg, shd; htd wc (some cont); chem disp; mv service pnt;
baby facs; shwrs inc; el pnts (6-10A) €4.25 (rev pol); lndtte;
shop; tradsmn; rest, snacks, bar high ssn; playgrnd; fishing;
kayak tuition; tennis; games area; cycle & walking paths;
fishing; x-country skiing; 30% statics; adv bkg; quiet; ccard
acc; CKE/CCI. "Pleasant, friendly site in pine trees; random
pitching; facs dated but clean, ltd low ssn; lge pine cones can
fall fr trees - park away fr tall ones; gd touring base; nice site;"
♦ € 13.00   2013*

BRIANCON *9C4* (2km S Rural) **Camping Les Cinq Vallées, St Blaise, 05100 Briançon [04 92 21 06 27; fax 04 92 20 41 69; infos@camping5vallees.com; www. camping5vallees.com]** S of Briançon by N94 to vill St Blaise. Ent on L. Med, pt sl, pt shd; wc; chem disp; mv service pnt; baby facs, shwrs inc; el pnts (10A) inc; lndtte; rest; shop; snacks; bar; playgrnd; htd pool; games rm; TV rm; many statics; some noise fr by-pass. "VG site, free bus pass fr office" ♦ 1 Jun-30 Sep. € 21.20   2012*

BRIARE *4G3* (7km S Rural) *47.59713, 2.76617* **Camping L'ecluse des Combles, Chemin de Loire, 45360 Châtillon-sur-Loire [tel/fax 02 38 36 25 32; campingchatillonsurloire@recrea.fr; www. campingdescombles.fr]** SE fr Briare on N7, in 4km turn SW onto D50. Site immed bef rv bdge on R. Care needed over bdge after ent. Med, terr, pt shd; htd wc; chem disp; mv service pnt; shwrs inc; el pnts (6A) inc ; gas; lndtte; shops 1km & 4km; tradsmn; rest, snacks & bar adj; BBQ; playgrnd; fishing; games rm; dogs €1.20; no twin-axles; Eng spkn; quiet; red low ssn; CKE/CCI. "Lovely, peaceful site by Rv Loire & historic canal; pleasant staff; right of way along rv bank passes thro site; mkt 2nd Thurs of month; vg" ♦ 1 Apr-31 Oct. € 17.00   2013*

BRIARE *4G3* (500m W Rural) *47.64137, 2.72560* **Camping Le Martinet, Quai Tchékof, 45250 Briare [02 38 31 24 50 or 02 38 31 24 51; fax 02 38 31 39 10; campingbriare@ recrea.fr; www.campinglemartinet.fr]** Exit N7 into Briare. Fr N immed R after canal bdge; fr S L bef 2nd canal bdge; sp. Lge, mkd pitch, unshd; wc (some cont); shwrs inc; el pnts (10A) €3.60; lndry rm; shops 500m; rest, snacks, bar 500m; fishing adj; dogs €1; poss cr; adv bkg; quiet; red low ssn. "Gd views some pitches; pretty bars & rests along canal; gd walking & cycling; interesting town; gates close 2200; slightly neglected (2009), OK sh stay." ♦ 1 Apr-30 Sep. € 16.70   2012*

"I need an on-site restaurant"

We do our best to make sure site information is correct, but it is always best to check any must-have facilities are still available or will be open during your visit.

⊞ **BRIENNE LE CHATEAU** *6E1* (6km S Rural) *48.34835, 4.53265* **Camping Le Colombier, 8 Ave Jean-Lanez, 10500 Dienville [tel/fax 03 25 92 23 47; lecolombier10500@ wanadoo.fr; http://lecolombier10500.e-monsite.com]** On D443 S fr Brienne; in Dienville town cent turn L immed after church & bef bdge, site on R thro archway. Sm, hdg pitch, pt shd; htd wc; chem disp; mv service pnt; shwrs inc; el pnts (6A) €4; gas; lndry rm; shop 400m; rest; snacks (high ssn); bar; playgrnd; rv adj; lake 500m; watersports; dogs €2.50; Eng spkn; adv bkg; quiet. "Pretty rvside site - pitches away fr bdge quieter; rv view extra; some sm pitches; facs poss stretched high ssn & ltd low ssn; less pitch/site care low ssn; access poss diff lge o'fits if site busy; church clock strikes 24 hrs." ♦ ltd € 17.00   2010*

BRIENNE LE CHATEAU *6E1* (6km S Rural) *48.34800, 4.5270* Camping Le Tertre, Route de Radonvilliers, 10500 Dienville [tel/fax 03 25 92 26 50; campingdutertre@wanadoo.fr; www.campingdutertre.fr]** On D443 S fr Brienne-le-Château; at Dienville turn R at rndabt onto D11; site on R in 200m, sp. NB Site opp Lake Amance harbour, foll sp 'Le Port'. Med, hdg/ mkd pitch, hdstg, pt shd; wc; chem disp; mv service pnt; 50% serviced pitches; baby facs; shwrs inc; el pnts (6-10A) €4 (poss long lead req); gas; lndtte (inc dryer); shop; tradsmn; rest, snacks; bar; BBQ; playgrnd; htd pool; paddling pool; sand rv beach 200m; man-made lake with sailing, fishing; gym; games area; games rm; entmnt; internet; TV rm; 10% statics; dogs €1; phone; bus 500m; poss cr; Eng spkn; adv bkg; quiet; ccard acc; red low ssn/CKE/CCI. "Pleasant site 2 mins fr vill; excel site for all watersports & other activities; cycle tracks; vg." ♦ 1 Apr-15 Oct. € 23.60   2012*

BRIEY *5D2* (1km NW Rural) *49.25153, 5.92992* **Camping Intercommunal Plan d'Eau de la Sangsue, 54150 Briey [03 82 20 96 22; fax 03 82 46 19 47; maisondutourisme@ ccpb54.fr; www.cc-paysdebriey.fr]** Exit A4 junc 33 to Briey, site sp. Access rd v steep & narr with bends & rough surface. Exit also diff due steep rd. Sm, hdstg, terr; wc; chem disp; shwrs inc; el pnts (16A) €1.50; snacks; playgrnd; dogs €0.50; CKE/CCI. "Gd site adj lake; gd walks; suitable m'vans only due steep access." 1 May-31 Oct. € 7.00   2010*

BRIGNOGAN PLAGES *1D2* (1km NW Coastal) *48.67278, -4.32916* **Camping de la Côte des Légendes, Keravezan, 29890 Brignogan-Plages [02 98 83 41 65; fax 02 98 83 59 94; contact@campingcotedeslegendes.com; www.campingcotedeslegendes.com]** Fr Roscoff on D10, fr Brest on D788/770 or fr N12 exit dir Lesneven. In Brignogan foll sp Brignogan-Plages & 'Centre Nautique'. Lge, hdg/mkd pitch, some hdstg, pt shd; wc; chem disp; mv service pnt; baby facs; shwrs inc; el pnts (5-10A) €2.60-3.60 (poss rev pol); lndtte; shop; tradsmn; snacks; bar; BBQ; playgrnd; dir access to sand beach adj; sailing & watersports; entmnt; TV rm; site guarded 24 hrs; 30% statics; dogs €1.30; phone; Eng spkn; adv bkg; quiet; ccard acc; red long stay/low ssn/CKE/CCI. "On beautiful sandy cove; friendly, helpful staff; ltd facs low ssn; vg touring base in interesting area; vg." ♦ 1 Apr-3 Nov. € 14.20   2011*

BRIGNOGAN PLAGES *1D2* (2km NW Coastal) *48.67535, -4.34534* **Camping du Phare, Plage du Phare, 29890 Brignogan-Plages [02 98 83 45 06; fax 02 98 83 52 19; camping.du.phare@orange.fr; www.camping-du-phare. com]** Take D770 N fr Lesneven to Brignogan-Plages; take L fork in town cent & foll site sp dir Kerverven. Med, some hdg pitch, some hdstg, pt shd; wc; chem disp; mv service pnt; shwrs €1; el pnts (6A) €3; gas; lndtte; shop 1km; tradsmn; snacks; playgrnd; sand beach adj; wifi; 10% statics; dogs €2; poss cr; Eng spkn; adv bkg; quiet; CKE/CCI. "Next to pretty bay & gd beach; helpful owner; vg site nr walking rte GR34." 1 Apr-30 Sep. € 12.10   2011*

BRIGNOLES *10F3* (1km E Rural) *43.40573, 6.07885* **Camp Municipal, 786 Route du Lac, 83170 Brignoles [tel/fax 04 94 69 20 10; campingbrignoles@aol.com]** Exit A8 junc 35 onto D554/D N7 E dir Le Luc/Nice/Fréjus; turn R at rndabt by Intermarché supmkt dir Centre Ville; site on R in 300m. Or fr E on D N7, at edge of town at Intermarché rndabt cont strt on dir Centre Ville; site on R in 300m. Med, hdg pitch, pt shd; wc; chem disp; shwrs inc; el pnts (10A) €3; gas; lndtte; Aldi supmkt opp; snacks; playgrnd; municipal pool 500m; 10% statics; phone; dogs €1.50; Eng spkn; some rd noise; adv bkg; ccard acc; red low ssn; CKE/CCI. "Well-run site by friendly family; some sm pitches; san facs clean but need update; site tired end ssn (2010); NH." 27 Mar-15 Oct. € 12.80   2010*

BRIGNOLES *10F3* (9km SE Rural) *43.33919, 6.12579* **Camping La Vidaresse, 83136 Ste Anastasie-sur-Issole [04 94 72 21 75; fax 04 98 05 01 21; www. campinglavidaresse.com; www.campinglavidaresse.com]** On DN7 2km W of Brignoles at rndabt take D43 dir Toulon. In about 10km turn L at rndabt to D15. Do not ent vill, go strt & site is approx 250m on R. Med, hdg/mkd pitch, terr, pt shd; wc (some cont); chem disp; mv service pnt; shwrs inc; el pnts (10A) €5 (poss rev pol); gas; lndtte; shop in vill 1km & 5km; rest high ssn; snacks & bar (all ssn); BBQ (gas/elec only); playgrnd; htd, covrd pool; paddling pool; sand beach 40km; tennis; games area; fishing 200m; wifi; 40% statics; dogs €3; poss cr; adv bkg; ccard acc; red low ssn; CKE/CCI. "Well-managed, family site in lovely area; peaceful; friendly & helpful; facs adequate; excel pool; gd touring base Haute Provence, Gorges du Verdon & Riviera; vineyard adj; gd." ♦ 20 Mar-30 Sep. € 25.00 2011*

BRILLANE, LA *10E3* (2km E Rural) *43.92282, 5.92369* **Chemin St Sauveur, 04700 Oraison, Chemin St Sauveur, 04700 Oraison [tel/fax 04 92 78 20 00; camping-oraison@wanadoo.fr; www.camping-oraison.com]** Exit A51 junc 19; take rd E to Oraison in 2km; site sp in vill. Med, mkd pitch, pt sl, pt terr, pt shd; wc; chem disp; mv service pnt; baby facs; fam bthrm; shwrs inc; el pnts (16A) €3.80; gas; lndtte; tradsmn (in ssn); shops, snacks & bar (in ssn) or 500m; playgrnd; pool; cycle hire; games area; games rm; TV rm; 10% statics; dogs €2.50; Eng spkn; adv bkg; quiet; ccard acc; CKE/CCI. "Pleasant, family-run site among olive trees; friendly, helpful owners; walks fr site; conv Verdon gorge; adj elec sub-station, elec cables run over site; gd." 15 Apr-30 Sep. € 16.00   2008*

BRILLANE, LA *10E3* (3km W Rural) *43.93305, 5.86777* **Camping Le Moulin de Ventre, 04300 Niozelles [04 92 78 63 31 or 06 63 51 53 55 (mob); fax 04 92 79 86 92; moulindeventre@aol.com; www.moulin-de-ventre.com]** Exit A51 junc 19 at La Brillane; turn R onto D4096, then L onto D4100 sp Niozelles & Forcalquier. Site in 3km on L just after bdge, adj Rv Lauzon. Med, hdg/mkd pitch, pt sl, pt shd; htd wc; chem disp; mv service pnt; serviced pitches; baby facs; shwrs inc; el pnts (10A) inc; gas; lndtte (inc dryer); sm shop & 2km; tradsmn; rest, snacks; bar; BBQ (gas); playgrnd; pool; paddling pool; rv beach, fishing, boat hire adj; wifi; entmnt; games/TV rm; 10% statics; dogs €3; twin-axles acc (rec check in adv); phone; Eng spkn; adv bkg; quiet; ccard acc; red low ssn/long stay; CKE/CCI. "Pleasant, peaceful, wooded site by lake & rv; well-run; rvside pitches have drop to rv; excel touring base; lavendar fields in flower Jun/Jul." ♦ 7 Apr-30 Sep. € 34.00 SBS - M09   2013*

BRIONNE *3D2* (500m N Urban) *49.20256, 0.71554* **Camp Municipal La Vallée, Rue Marcel Nogrette, 27800 Brionne [02 32 44 80 35; fax 02 32 46 25 61; www.ville-brionne.fr]** Fr D438 N or S on by-pass, turn N at D46 junc, pass Carrefour supmkt on L & take 1st R, site on L. Sm, hdg pitch, pt shd; wc; chem disp; mv service pnt; shwrs inc; el pnts (8A) inc; gas; lndtte; shop, rest etc only; BBQ; playgrnd; some statics; dogs; poss cr; quiet; CKE/CCI. "Excel site in lovely vill; gd san facs, poss ltd low ssn; No arr 10:00 to 16:00 barrier clsd; short walk to supmkt" 30 Apr-30 Sep. € 12.00   2013*

BRIONNE *3D2* (5km N Rural) *49.23648, 0.72265* **FFCC Camp St Nicolas (Formaly Municipal), 15 Rue St Nicolas, 27800 Le Bec-Hellouin [tel/fax 02 32 44 83 55 or 02 32 44 86 40 (Mairie); campingstnicolas@orange.fr; www.lebechellouin.fr]** Exit A28 junc 13 onto D438 then take D581 to Malleville-sur-le-Bec; site on R 1km aft Malleville. Well sp. Med, pt shd; htd wc; chem disp; mv service pnt ; shwrs inc; el pnts (10A) €3.50; lndtte; tradsmn (excel bakeries); rest, snacks, bar in vill; BBQ; playgrnd; tennis, horseriding nr; some statics; dog €1.50; poss cr; quiet; CKE/CCI. "Attractive, peaceful, well-kept site in pleasant location; spacious pitches; friendly, helpful warden; vg, clean san facs; gate clsd 2200-0700; gd dog walks; vg cycling; attractive countryside; conv NH nr Calais; rec." ♦ ltd 15 Mar-15 Oct. € 24.30 (CChq acc)   2013*

⊞ **BRIONNE** *3D2* (6km N Rural) *49.24174, 0.70339* **Camp Municipal Les Marronniers, Rue Louise Givon, 27290 Pont-Authou [02 32 42 75 06 or 06 27 25 21 45 (mob); fax 02 32 56 34 51; lesmarronniers27@orange.fr / campingmunicipaldesmarronniers@orange.fr; www.normandie-accueil.fr]** Heading S on D438 take D130 just bef Brionne sp Pont-Audemer (care req at bdge & rndabts). Site on L in approx 5km, well sp on o'skts of Pont-Authou; foll sp in vill. Med, mkd pitch, ltd hdstg, pt shd; htd wc; chem disp; mv service pnt; shwrs; el pnts (10A) €3.40 (poss rev pol); lndtte (inc dryer); shops 500m; tradsmn; rest & bar in vill; BBQ; playgrnd; fishing; cycle hire; 50% statics; dogs €1.35; adv bkg; quiet but rd noise; CKE/CCI. "Useful, clean stop nr Rouen & m'way; friendly recep; clean san facs; best pitches far side of lake; few hdstg; adv bkg rec; some statics unsightly; stream runs thro site; beautiful valley with many historic towns & vills; excel walking; gd NH." € 9.30   2013*

BRIOUDE *9C1* (2km S Rural) *45.2813, 3.4045* **Camping La Bageasse, Ave de la Bageasse, 43100 Brioude [04 71 50 07 70; fax 04 73 34 70 94; aquadis1@wanadoo. fr; www.aquadis-loisirs.com]** Turn off N102 & foll sp for Brioude town centre; then foll site sp. Narr app rd. Site on Rv Allier. Med, mkd pitch, terr, pt shd; wc (some cont); chem disp; baby facs; shwrs inc; el pnts (6A) €2 (some rev pol); lndtte (inc dryer); sm shop; tradsmn; snacks; bar; BBQ; playgrnd; pool 2km; fishing & boating adj; canoe hire; 8% statics; dogs €1.50; phone; Eng spkn; adv bkg; quiet; ccard acc; red long stay; CKE/CCI. "Well-kept site; lge pitches; helpful warden; gd, clean san facs; phone ahead to check open low ssn; interesting basilica." ♦ Easter-15 Oct. € 14.00 (CChq acc)   2013*

BRIOUX SUR BOUTONNE see Melle *7A2*

BRISSAC see Ganges *10E1*

BRISSAC QUINCE *4G1* (2km NE Rural) *47.35944, -0.43388* Camping de l'Etang, Route de St Mathurin, 49320 Brissac-Quincé [02 41 91 70 61; fax 02 41 91 72 65; info@campingetang.com; www.campingetang.com] Fr N on A11, exit junc 14 onto N260 passing E of Angers, following sp for Cholet/Poitiers. After x-ing Rv Loire, foll sp to Brissac-Quincé on D748. Foll sp for St Mathurin/Domaine de l'Etang on D55 to site. Med, hdg/mkd pitch, hdstg, pt shd; htd wc; mv service pnt; chem disp; baby facs; some serviced pitches (€3 extra charge); shwrs incl; el pnts (10A) inc; gas; lndtte (inc dryer); shop; tradsmn; rest, snacks; bar; BBQ (charcoal/gas); playgrnd; 2 pools (1 htd, covrd); paddling pool; waterslide; lake fishing; cycle hire; golf 8km; wifi; entmnt; games/TV rm; dogs €2.10-9.10; twin-axles acc (rec check in adv); Eng spkn; adv bkg; quiet; ccard acc; red long stay/low ssn; CKE/CCI. "Excel, well-cared for site amongst vineyards; lge pitches; staff pleasant & helpful; clean, modern facs; leisure facs gd for children; pleasant 15 min rvside walk to Brissac-Quincé; wine tasting; gd touring base Loire valley; mkt Thu." ♦ 27 Apr-15 Sep. € 33.00 SBS - L15 2011*

BRISSAC QUINCE *4G1* (1km S Rural) *47.33317, -0.43664* Camping à la Ferme Domaine de la Belle Etoile, La Belle Etoile, 49320 Brissac-Quincé [06 62 32 99 40 (mob); www.domaine-belle-etoile.fr] Take D748 S fr Angers dir Poitiers. At D761 rndabt cont on D748 sp N-D-d'Allençon. Site sp at 2nd turn on L in 500m. Sm, pt shd; wc; chem disp; shwrs €1; el pnts (5A) €3; lndtte; BBQ; playgrnd; quiet. "Vg CL-type site in vineyard with wine-tasting & farm produce; clean, modern facs; troglodyte caves, mushroom farms & château nrby." 1 Apr-1 Nov. € 7.90 2011*

BRIVE LA GAILLARDE *7C3* (8km S Rural) *45.10049, 1.52423* FFCC Camping à la Ferme (Delmas), Malfarges, 19600 Noailles [tel/fax 05 55 85 81 33] Fr A20/E9 take exit 52 sp Noailles, immed after tunnel; in vill take 1st R across yellow paving at vill café/shop (to avoid steep dangerous hill); turn R at T-junc, site on L. Sp fr m'way. NB All vill rds have a 3,500kg limit. Sm, mkd pitch, terr, shd; wc; chem disp; mv service pnt; shwrs inc; el pnts (5A) €2.70-5.30 (poss rev pol); shop 500m; farm meals & produce; fishing 200m; dogs €2.60; few statics; adv bkg; quiet; CKE/CCI. "Conv NH/sh stay adj A20; friendly, helpful farmer; if owner not around choose a pitch; basic san facs; parking on terr poss awkward; fly problem in hot weather; strict silence after 2200; excel." € 9.00 2010*

BRIVE LA GAILLARDE *7C3* (6km SW Rural) *45.09975, 1.45115* Camping Nautica, 19600 Lissac-sur-Couze [05 55 85 37 97; fax 05 55 85 37 11; lecausse.correzien@wanadoo.fr; www.caussecorrezien.fr] A20 exit 51; D1089 to Larche; L onto D19 sp Lissac; take 1st L after St Cernin-de-Larche onto D59 round N side of Lac de Causse, sharp R down hill then bear L over dam; R to site in 2km. Site sp as 'Camping Nautica'. Med, mkd pitch, hdstg, terr, pt shd; wc; serviced pitches; shwrs inc; el pnts (16A) €2; gas 4km; lndtte; shop; snacks; bar; playgrnd; pool; lake sw; boating; windsurfing; 5% statics; dogs €3; quiet; Eng spkn; adv bkg; no ccard acc; red low ssn; CKE/CCI. "Beautiful site in idyllic setting o'looking lake; friendly recep; clean san facs; recep poss clsd Tues & Sun - site inaccessible when recep clsd, phone ahead rec; many outdoor activities." ♦ € 18.00 2012*

BRIVE LA GAILLARDE *7C3* (10km SW Rural) *45.06942, 1.43060* Camping La Magaudie, La Magaudie Ouest, 19600 Chartrier-Ferrière [tel/fax 05 55 85 26 06; camping@lamagaudie.com; www.lamagaudie.com] Exit A20 junc 53 onto D920/D19 dir Chasteaux. After rlwy bdge take 2nd L to Chartrier & foll blue sps to site. NB Diff app climbing up narr lane with no passing paces for 1km. Sm, mkd pitch, sl, pt shd; htd wc; chem disp; shwrs inc; el pnts (10A) €2.75; lndtte; shop 2km; tradsmn; rest, snacks; bar; gas BBQ; playgrnd; pool; lake sw 3km; 5% statics; dogs €1.25; Eng spkn; adv bkg; quiet; red low ssn; CKE/CCI. "Dutch owners; vg site & facs but v ltd low ssn; rec arr early high ssn." ♦ € 14.00 2008*

BRIVEZAC see Beaulieu sur Dordogne *7C4*

BROGLIE *3D2* (200m S Rural) Aire de Camping-Car Broglie, Route de la Barre-en-Ouche, 27270 Broglie [02 32 44 60 58; mairie-broglie@wanadoo.fr] Exit A28 junc 15 onto D49 E dir Broglie. Turn R in vill onto D6138 Rue des Canadiens, then L into Rue de la Victoire over rv, site on R in former rlwy yard, nr municipal library. Sm, mkd pitch, hdstg, pt shd; chem disp; mv service pnt; lndtte 200m; supmkt 800m; rest 200m; rest 400m; quiet. "M'vans only; gate secured at night; ideal NH." € 5.00 2013*

BROU *4F2* (1km W Rural) *48.20787, 1.14637* Parc de Loisirs de Brou, Route des Moulins, 28160 Brou [02 37 47 02 17; fax 02 37 47 86 77; contact@parc-loisirs-brou.fr; www.parc-loisirs-brou.fr] Sp in town on D13. Lge, hdg/mkd pitch, shd; wc; chem disp; shwrs inc; el pnts (10A) €6; lndtte; shops 2km; rest; playgrnd; htd pool; waterslide; lake adj; fishing; golf; many statics; quiet; red low ssn; CKE/CCI. "Ent to site by card, so no ent when office clsd (winter office clsd Mon & Wed); vg san facs." ♦ 16 Feb-14 Dec. € 11.00 2008*

BRUERE ALLICHAMPS see St Amand Montrond *4H3*

BRUGHEAS see Vichy *9A1*

BRULON *4F1* (500m SE Rural) *47.96275, -0.22773* Camping Le Septentrion, Le Bord du Lac, 72350 Brûlon [02 43 95 68 96; fax 02 43 92 60 36; le.septentrion@wanadoo.fr; www.campingleseptentrion.com] Exit A81 junc 1; foll D4 S to Brûlon; site sp on ent to town to L; turn on L down narr rd (Rue de Buet); then turn R in 300m. Site well sp. Sm, pt sl, shd; htd wc; mv service pnt; baby facs; shwrs inc; el pnts (6A) €3; lndtte; shop 600m; tradsmn; rest, snacks; bar; BBQ; playgrnd; htd pool (high ssn); lake sw; boating; fishing; cycle hire; games/TV rm; wifi; 50% statics; dogs €1.20; phone; adv bkg; quiet, but poss noise fr teepee centre adj; red long stay/low ssn. "Attractive, well-kept site; spacious pitches; welcoming staff; gd, clean san facs - unisex low ssn; poss a bit unkempt early ssn; gd cycling & walking area; excel." ♦ 3 Apr-30 Oct. € 13.50 2013*

BRUYERES 6E2 (6km SE Rural) 48.18987, 6.77508 **Camping Les Pinasses, La Chapelle-devant-Bruyères, 88600 Bruyères [03 29 58 51 10; fax 03 29 58 54 21; info@camping-les-pinasses.com; www.camping-les-pinasses.com]** Fr Bruyères, take D423 twd Gérardmer. In 3km turn L on D60 sp Corcieux, Site on R in 3km at La-Chapelle-devant-Bruyères. Med, hdg/mkd pitch, pt shd; wc (some cont); chem disp; shwrs inc; el pnts (4-6A) €3.70-4.70; gas; lndtte; shop; tradsmn; rest, snacks; bar; BBQ; playgrnd; htd pool; paddling pool; tennis; TV rm; 30% statics; dogs €1.30; adv bkg; some rlwy noise; CKE/CCI. "Beautiful area." Apr-15 Sep. € 18.10 (CChq acc)   2008*

BRUYERES 6E2 (6km S Rural) 48.17870, 6.74309 **Camping Domaine des Messires, 1 La Feigne, 88600 Herpelmont [03 29 58 56 29 or 0031 321 331456 (N'lands); fax 03 29 51 62 86; mail@domainedesmessires.com; www.domainedesmessires.com]** SE fr Bruyères at Laveline turn R sp Herpelmont & foll site sp. Site 1.5km N of Herpelmont. Med, pt shd; wc; mv service pnt; chem disp; serviced pitches; baby facs; shwrs inc; el pnts (6A) inc; gas; lndtte (inc dryer); shop; tradsmn; rest, snacks; bar; BBQ; playgrnd; lake sw; fishing; boating; games rm; wifi; child entmnt; TV; dogs €4; Eng spkn; adv bkg; quiet; ccard acc; red low ssn/long stay; CKE/CCI. "Attractive, peaceful, lakeside site; gd touring base Alsace & Vosges; friendly, helpful staff." ♦ 23 Apr-18 Sep. € 25.50   2010*

BUGEAT 7B4 (3km NW Rural) 45.60608, 1.88446 **Camp Municipal Puy de Veix, 19170 Viam [05 55 95 52 05 (Mairie); fax 05 55 95 21 86; viam.mairie@wanadoo.fr; www.viam.correze.net]** Fr Bugeat NW on D979; in 4km L onto D160; foll sp to Viam. Sm, mkd pitch, pt sl, terr, pt shd; wc; chem disp; mv service pnt; el pnts (6-10A) €2.60; lndtte (inc dryer); shop 4km; tradsmn; rest 500m; BBQ; playgrnd; lake sw & sand beach adj; fishing; games area; dogs €0.50; phone; poss cr; Eng spkn; adv bkg; quiet; CKE/CCI. "On lakeside; beautiful views; peaceful; mainly sm pitches; vg." ♦ 1 Jun-30 Sep. € 7.40   2011*

BUGUE, LE 7C3 (4km NE Rural) 44.93436, 0.93571 **Camping La Linotte, Route de Rouffignac, 24260 Le Bugue [05 53 07 17 61; fax 05 53 54 16 96; infos@campinglalinotte.com; www.campinglalinotte.com]** E off D710 onto D32E after passing thro town heading N twd Périgueux on rd to Rouffignac. Site sp fr D710. Med, hdg pitch, pt sl, terr, pt shd; wc; chem disp; baby facs; fam bthrm; shwrs inc; el pnts (6A) €3.30; lndtte; shop; rest, snacks; playgrnd; htd pool; waterslide; entmnt; quiet; adv bkg; CKE/CCI. "Splendid views; lovely site; gd mkt Tues." 5 Apr-13 Sep. € 22.15 2008*

BUGUE, LE 7C3 (1km SE Urban) 44.90980, 0.93160 **FFCC Camping Les Trois Caupain, Le Port, 24260 Le Bugue Dordogne [05 53 07 24 60 or 06 85 48 44 25 (mob); fax 05 53 08 72 66; info@camping-bugue.com; www.camping-des-trois-caupain.com]** Exit Le Bugue town cent on D703 twd Campagne. Turn R at sp after 400m to site in 600m on rvside. Med, mkd pitch, pt shd; wc; chem disp; mv service pnt; baby facs; shwrs inc; el pnts (6-16A) €3.60-4 (rev pol); gas; shops 1km; rest & snacks (high & low ssn); bar; playgrnd; htd covrd pool; rv & games area adj; wifi; 25% statics, sep area; dogs €2; adv bkg; quiet; red low ssn. "Beautiful site; pleasant, helpful owners; cycle along rv to pretty town; excel; lovely site; new pool; market in Le Bugue well worth a visit; Ideal centre for touring the Dordogne region" 1 Apr-30 Oct. € 30.40   2013*

BUGUE, LE 7C3 (3km SE Rural) 44.90663, 0.97412 **Camping Le Val de la Marquise, 24260 Campagne [05 53 54 74 10 or 06 89 29 04 92 (mob); fax 05 53 54 00 70; contact@levaldelamarquise.com; www.levaldelamarquise.com]** Fr D703 bet Le Bugue & Les Eyzies take D35 at Campagne dir St Cyprien, site sp. Med, mkd pitch, terr, pt shd; wc; chem disp; mv service pnt; baby facs; shwrs inc; el pnts (15A) €4; lndtte; shops 4km; tradsmn, rest high ssn; snacks; bar; BBQ; playgrnd; pool; paddling pool; fishing lake; games aea; 5% statics; dogs €2; phone; Eng spkn; adv bkg; quiet; CKE/CCI. "Peaceful, attractive site; poss diff access to pitches for lge c'vans due narr site rds & low terrs; clean san facs; beautiful pool; Michelin starred rest nrby." 1 Apr-30 Sep. € 17.80   2008*

BUGUE, LE 7C3 (7km SE Rural) 44.86199, 0.98150 **Camping Le Clou, Meynard, 24220 Coux-et-Bigaroque [05 53 31 63 32; fax 05 53 31 69 33; info@camping-le-clou.com; www.camping-le-clou.com]** S fr Le Bugue on D703 twd Belvès; site 8km on R. Med, mkd pitch, pt sl, pt shd; htd wc; chem disp; mv service pnt; serviced pitches; baby facs; fam bthrm; shwrs inc; el pnts (4-6A) €3.80; gas; lndtte; tradsmn; rest, snacks; bar; BBQ; playgrnd; 2 pools & paddling pool; waterslide; fishing; canoeing; horseriding; entmnt; games rm; TV; phone; 10% statics; dogs €2.50; Eng spkn; adv bkg; quiet; ccard acc; red long stay/low ssn/CKE/CCI. "Pleasant owners; ideal base for Dordogne; lovely wooded site with much wildlife." ♦ 17 Apr-3 Apr. € 23.70   2009*

FRANCE

Camping Brin d'Amour***

WITH A ROMANTIC HISTORY, THE SITE'S NAME TRANSLATES AS "A PIECE OF LOVE"
Wonderful views across the undulating hills. Small site where you can relax in a friendly,
family atmosphere. Near SARLAT, ideal place from witch to explore the prehistorical sites.
90 pitches, few Chalets and mobile-homes for rent. Covered and heated pool, tennis.

WWW.BRINDAMOURCAMPING.COM ▪ TEL: 00 33 5 53 07 23 73 ▪ CAMPINGBRINDAMOUR@ORANGE.FR

BUGUE, LE *7C3* (8km S Rural) *44.85416, 0.91208* **Camping Le Pont de Vicq, 24480 Le Buisson-de-Cadouin [05 53 22 01 73; fax 05 53 22 06 70; le.pont.de.vicq@wanadoo.fr; www. campinglepontdevicq.com]** Fr Le Bugue foll sp to Le Buisson. Site immed S of bdge over Rv Dordogne on rd D51E. Sp fr all dir in Le Buisson. Med, hdg/mkd pitch, pt shd; wc; baby facs; shwrs inc; el pnts (6A) €3.50 (poss rev pol); lndtte; shops 1.5km; rest adj; snacks in ssn; playgrnd; shgl beach & rv; games area; games rm; entmnt; TV; 60% statics; dogs €1.10; phone adj; poss cr; adv bkg; quiet; CKE/CCI. "Pleasant site on rv; poss mosquitoes." 27 Mar-30 Oct. € 20.40   2009*

BUGUE, LE *7C3* (5km SW Rural) *44.89323, 0.87955* **Camping La Ferme des Poutiroux, 24510 Limeuil [05 53 63 31 62; fax 05 53 58 30 84; infos@poutiroux.com; www. poutiroux.com]** W fr Le Bugue on D703 twd Bergerac; in 2km take D31 S for 4km; bef bdge take R fork twd Trémolat/Lalinde; in 300m fork R (sp), site well sp. Sm, mkd pitch, pt sl, terr, pt shd; wc; chem disp; mv service pnt; baby facs; shwrs; el pnts (6A) €4; lndtte; shop; tradsmn; snacks; playgrnd; htd pool; paddling pool; canoes & rv sw nrby; wifi; 50% statics; dogs €1; phone; Eng spkn; adv bkg; quiet; ccard not acc; red low ssn; CKE/CCI. "Peaceful, well-kept, well-positioned, family-run site; friendly, helpful farmer; facs clean; vg value low ssn; highly rec." ♦ 1 Apr-2 Oct. € 17.40   2013*

BUGUE, LE *7C3* (6km SW Rural) *44.87990, 0.88576* **Camping du Port de Limeuil, 24480 Alles-sur-Dordogne [05 53 63 29 76; fax 05 53 63 04 19; didierbonvallet@aol. com; www.leportdelimeuil.com]** Exit Le Bugue on D31 sp Le Buisson; in 4km turn R on D51 sp Limeuil; at 2km turn L over rv bdge; site on R after bdge. Med, hdg/mkd pitch, pt sl, pt shd; wc; chem disp; 50% serviced pitches; shwrs inc; el pnts (5A) €3.50; gas; lndtte; shop & 1km; bar; snacks; BBQ; playgrnd; htd pool; shgl beach & rv adj; games rm; canoe & cycle hire; 40% statics (tour ops); dogs €2; poss cr; Eng spkn; adv bkg; quiet; red low ssn; CKE/CCI. "Superb location & site for all ages; lge pitches; clean san facs; ltd low ssn; tour ops." ♦ ltd 1 May-30 Sep. € 24.90   2012*

BUGUE, LE *7C3* (7km SW Rural) *44.87390, 0.85840* **Camping La Pénétie, Route de Trémolat, 24510 Paunat [05 53 22 80 53; fax 05 53 74 17 88; ferme-la-penetie@orange.fr; www. penetie.fr]** Fr Le Bugue take D31 S dir Le Buisson. After 5km turn R to Limeuil then D31 sp Trémolat. Site on L 5km out of Limeuil. Sm, hdg pitch, terr, pt shd; wc; chem disp (wc); baby facs; shwrs inc; el pnts €3; lndtte; shop, rest 2km; bar; playgrnd; games; wifi; dogs €0.80; adv bkg; red low ssn; CKE/CCI. "Gd views fr pitches on S side of site; friendly, helpful staff; gd touring base Dordogne; excel." 1 Apr-30 Sep. € 13.00   2010*

BUGUE, LE *7C3* (9km SW Rural) *44.87909, 0.82751* **Camping de Trémolat, Centre Nautique, Route de Mauzac, 24510 Trémolat [05 53 22 81 18 or 05 53 05 65 65 (res); fax 05 53 06 30 94; semitour@perigord.tm.fr]** Fr Le Bugue, take D703 W twd Pezuls. In vill, turn L onto D30 twd Trémolat. Site 700m N of Trémolat, well sp fr all dir. Med, hdg pitch, pt shd; wc; chem disp; shwrs inc; el pnts (10A) inc; lndtte; shops 700m; rest, snacks; BBQ; pool; rv adj; fishing; canoeing; 20% statics; dogs; phone; poss cr; Eng spkn; adv bkg; quiet; CKE/CCI. "Peaceful site; most touring pitches have rv frontage; excel for fishing & canoeing; facs poss stretched high ssn." ♦ ltd 1 May-30 Sep. € 21.40   2009*

BUGUE, LE *7C3* (10km W Rural) *44.91527, 0.82083* **Camping La Forêt, Ste Alvère, 24510 Pezuls [05 53 22 71 69; camping.laforet@wanadoo.fr; www.camping-la-foret.com]** Off D703 fr Le Bugue to Lalinde rd, sp on L 1.5km bef Pezuls. In Le Bugue do not foll sp to Lalinde but cont thro town on D703, turn R, L & R, passing fire stn. Med, pt sl, pt shd; wc; chem disp; baby facs; shwrs inc; el pnts (10A) inc; gas; lndtte; sm shop; bar; BBQ (gas/charcoal only); playgrnd; pool; tennis; games area; games/TV rm; entmnt; dogs free; no c'vans/m'vans over 5.50m high ssn; poss cr; adv bkg; quiet; ccard not acc; red low ssn; CKE/CCI. "Simple, peaceful site set amongst sm oak trees; nature lovers' paradise; friendly, helpful Dutch owner; gd san facs, ltd low ssn; manoeuvring poss diff lge o'fits due trees; under-used low ssn; gd touring base; excel." ♦ 1 Apr-1 Oct. € 21.50   2010*

FRANCE

BUGUE, LE *7C3* (5km NW Rural) *44.95130, 0.85070*
**Camping St Avit Loisirs, 24260 St Avit-de-Vialard
[05 53 02 64 00; fax 05 53 02 64 39; contact@saint-
avit-loisirs.com; www.saint-avit-loisirs.com or www.
les-castels.com]** Leave N89/E70 SE of Périgueux & turn S onto
D710 for approx 32km; about 3km N of Le Bugue turn R sp
St Avit-de-Vialard. Turn R in vill & conf for approx 1.5km, site
on R. NB Narr, twisting app rd. Lge, hdg pitch, pt sl, pt shd; wc;
chem disp; mv service pnt; baby facs; shwrs inc; el pnts (6A) inc;
gas; lndtte (inc dryer); shop; rest, snacks; bar; BBQ; playgrnd;
2 pools (1 htd, covrd); waterslide; paddling pool; tennis; golf,
watersports, archery & horseriding nr; cycle hire; games area;
wifi; entmnt; games/TV rm; many static tents/vans; dogs €2-
5.10; no c'vans/m'vans over 7m; poss cr; adv bkg; quiet; ccard
acc; red low ssn; CKE/CCI. "Excel, well-kept, well-run, busy
site; gd sized pitches; friendly welcome; gd, clean san facs; gd
touring base; conv for Lascaux." ♦ 31 Mar-15 Sep. € 42.70
SBS - D10   2011*

See advertisement on inside back cover

BUIS LES BARONNIES *9D2* (300m N Urban) *44.27558,
5.27830* **Camp Municipal, Quartier du Jalinier, 26170 Buis-
les-Baronnies [04 75 28 04 96 or 06 60 80 40 53 (mob)]**
Fr Vaison-la-Romaine S on D938; turn L onto D54/D13/D5 to
Buis-les-Baronnies; cont N onto D546; at bend turn R over rv
bdge; turn L along rv, then 1st R. Site split into 2 either side of
sw pool; recep in upper site. Med, hdg/mkd pitch, pt sl, pt shd;
wc; chem disp; shwrs inc; el pnts (6A) €3; lndry rm; pool nrby;
5% statics; dogs €1.20; phone; bus 300m; poss cr; quiet, but
poss noise fr pool; CKE/CCI. "Lovely views; san facs dated but
clean; not suitable lge o'fits but lger, more accessible pitches
on lower level; attractive town; gd mkt Wed & Sat; fair."
1 Mar-11 Nov. € 11.20   2008*

BUIS LES BARONNIES *9D2* (3km N Rural) *44.30364, 5.27250*
**Camping Le Romegas (Naturist), 26170 Buis-les-Baronnies
[tel/fax 04 75 28 10 78; leromegas@free.fr; http://
leromegas.free.fr/]** S fr Nyons on D938, E on D46/D4/D5
to Buis-les-Baronnies. On D546 turn N on D108 sp St Jalle.
Site on L bef summit of Col d'Ey. Rd access gd although high
altitude. Med, terr, pt shd; wc (some cont); shwrs; el pnts (6A)
€3.50; lndtte; shop; rest; playgrnd; pool; paddling pool; TV;
some statics; dogs €3; quiet; red low ssn; CKE/CCI. "Beautiful
situation; gd walking; friendly staff; access round site diff due
tight bends & steep hillside."
1 Apr-30 Sep. € 20.00 (3 persons)   2008*

BUIS LES BARONNIES *9D2* (7km E Rural) *44.26325, 5.37744*
**Camping/Gîte du Lièvre (Taponnier), 26170 La Roche-sur-
les-Buis [04 75 28 11 49; fax 04 75 28 19 26; gitedulievre@
wanadoo.fr; www.gitedulievre.com]** In Buis-les-Baronnies
travel N on D546; at edge of town after x-ing rv turn R onto
D159; foll for 10km to Poët-en-Percip; site sp on L; 3km down
unmade rd. Sm, mkd pitch, hdstg, terr, pt shd; wc (some
cont); chem disp (wc); shwrs inc; el pnts (3A) €2.50 (poss
long lead req); tradsmn; rest, snacks; bar; playgrnd; pool;
mountain bike trails; horseriding; some statics; adv bkg; quiet;
no ccard acc; CKE/CCI. "Site on farm; scenic but v isolated at
3,000 feet; views of Mt Ventoux; walks; climbing." May-Oct.
€ 16.60   2010*

BUIS LES BARONNIES *9D2* (4km SW Rural) *44.25190,
5.24370* **Camping La Gautière, La Penne-sur-l'Ouvèze,
26170 Buis-les-Baronnies [04 75 28 02 68; fax
04 75 28 24 11; accueil@camping-lagautiere.com; www.
camping-lagautiere.com]** On D5 Vaison-la-Romaine to Buis-
les-Baronnies rd, on L. Sm, mkd pitch, pt shd; htd wc; shwrs
inc; el pnts (3-10A) €3-4.60; gas; lndtte; shop & 4km; snacks;
bar; BBQ; playgrnd; pool; climbing at Rocher St Julien & Gorges
d'Ubrieux; horseriding & fishing nr; games area; games rm;
5% statics; dogs €2.50; phone; bus adj; Eng spkn; adv bkg;
quiet; ccard acc; CKE/CCI. "Beautiful situation; haphazard pitch
size; diff for o'fits over 6m; helpful owners." 1 Apr-16 Nov.
€ 17.50   2013*

BUISSON DE CADOUIN, LE see Bugue, Le *7C3*

BUJALEUF see St Léonard de Noblat *7B3*

"Satellite navigation makes touring much easier"

Remember most sat navs don't know if
you're towing or in a larger vehicle – always
use yours alongside maps and site directions.

BULGNEVILLE *6F2* (750m SE Rural) *48.19828, 5.84554*
**Camping Porte des Voges, La Grande Tranchée, Route
de Contrexéville, 88140 Bulgnéville [03 29 09 12 00; fax
03 29 09 15 71; camping.portedesvosges@wanadoo.fr;
www.camping-portedesvosges.com]** Exit A31 junc 9; at
1st rndabt foll sp Bulgnéville onto D164; in 2km turn R onto
D14; site on L in 200m. Site sp. NB Foll site sp, ignore m'van sp.
Med, pt hdstg, pt sl, pt shd; wc; chem disp; baby facs; shwrs
inc; el pnts (10A) €3; lndry rm; shop 2km; tradsmn; takeaway;
playgrnd; games area; wifi; dogs €2; phone; Eng spkn; quiet;
ccard acc. "Lge pitches; clean san facs; conv NH fr A31; poss
closes 22 Sept, phone ahead; excel NH; rec." ♦ 14 Apr-30 Sep.
€ 16.00   2011*

BURNHAUPT LE HAUT see Cernay *6F3*

BURTONCOURT *5D2* (1km W Rural) *49.22485, 6.39929* **FFCC
Camping La Croix du Bois Sacker, 57220 Burtoncourt [tel/
fax 03 87 35 74 08; camping.croixsacker@wanadoo.fr;
www.campingcroixsacker.com]** Exit A4 junc 37 sp Argancy;
at rndabt foll sp Malroy; at 2nd rndabt foll sp Chieuilles & cont
to Vany; then take D3 for 12km dir Bouzonville; turn R onto
D53A to Burtoncourt. Lge, hdg/mkd pitch, some hdstg, terr,
pt shd; wc (mainly cont); mv service pnt; shwrs €1; el pnts
(6A) inc; gas; lndtte; shop; tradsmn; rest, snacks 1km; bar;
playgrnd; games area; fishing; tennis; wifi; entmnt; TV; some
statics; dogs €1.70; phone; bus 300m; Eng spkn; adv bkg;
quiet; CKE/CCI. "Lovely, wooded site in beautiful location; lge
pitches; pleasant, friendly owners; clean san facs; forest walks;
gd security; gd NH or sh stay en rte Alsace/Germany; conv
Maginot Line; excel." ♦ 1 Apr-20 Oct. € 16.00   2010*

BUSSANG see St Maurice sur Moselle *6F3*

BUSSEROLLES see St Mathieu *7B3*

⊞ **BUSSIERE POITEVINE** *7A3* (S Urban) *46.23282, 0.90242*
Camp Municipal La Croix de L'Hozanne, 87320 Bussière-
Poitevine [05 55 60 08 17; fax 05 55 68 40 72] NW fr Bellac
on N147, 8km after St Bonnet-de-Bellac turn R onto D4 sp
Bussière-Poitevine. Site 500m on R opp water tower. Sm, hdg
pitch, pt shd; htd wc (some cont); shwrs inc; el pnts (10-15A)
€1.90-2.80; shops, rest & bar 500m; snacks; playgrnd; CKE/
CCI. "Pleasant site in attractive town; old but clean facs; grass
pitches poss water-logged in winter but can pitch in rd; ltd facs
low ssn; gd NH/sh stay." € 6.00   2009*

BUYSSCHEURE see St Omer *3A3*

BUZANCAIS *4H2* (500m N Urban) *46.89309, 1.41801*
Camp Municipal La Tête Noire, Allée des Sports, 36500
Buzançais [02 54 84 17 27 or 06 15 85 53 04 (mob);
fax 02 54 02 13 45; buzancais@wanadoo.fr] D943
fr Châteauroux thro town cent, cross rv, immed turn R into
sports complex. Lge, some hdstg, pt shd; wc (some cont); mv
service pnt; shwrs inc; el pnts (16A) inc; lndtte; shop, rest,
snacks, bar 500m; playgrnd; pool 500m; entmnt; some statics;
dog €1.50; adv bkg; quiet; red low ssn/long stay; CKE/CCI.
"Pleasant, peaceful, well-kept site on rv; clean facs; no access
when office clsd but ample parking; no twin-axles; gd fishing."
♦ 1 May-30 Sep. € 15.00 (CChq acc)   2013*

BUZANCY *5C1* (1.5km SW Rural) *49.42647, 4.93891*
Camping La Samaritaine, 08240 [03 24 30 08 88; fax
03 24 30 29 39; info@campinglasamaritaine.com; www.
campinglasamaritaine.com] Fr Sedan take D977 dir Vouziers
for 23km. Turn L onto D12, cont to end & turn L onto D947
for Buzancy. On ent Buzancy in 100m turn 2nd R immed after
g'ge on R sp Camping Stade. Foll sp to site on L past football
pitches. Med, hdg/mkd pitch, some hdstg, pt shd; wc; chem
disp (wc); mv service pnt; 45% serviced pitches; mv service
pnt; baby facs; shwrs inc; el pnts (10A) inc; lndtte; sm shop;
tradsmn; rest 1.6km; snacks, bar high ssn; BBQ (gas/charcoal);
playgrnd; lake sw & sand beach adj; fishing; horseriding nrby;
tennis; library; games/TV rm; 10% statics; dogs €2.20; phone;
Eng spkn; adv bkg; quiet; ccard not acc; red low ssn; CKE/CCI.
"Beautiful area for walking/cycling; helpful, pleasant staff; excel
facs, ltd low ssn." ♦ 29 Apr-20 Sep. € 18.50   2011*

BUZY see Louvie Juzon *8F2*

⊞ **CABANNES, LES** *8G3* (2km SE Rural) *42.77444, 1.70328*
Camp Municipal La Coume, 09310 Albiès [tel/fax
05 61 64 98 99; camping.albies@wanadoo.fr] Site sp fr N20
in vill. Med, hdg pitch, pt sl, terr, pt shd; htd wc; chem disp
(wc); shwrs inc; el pnts (5-10A) €1.75-2.70; lndtte; shop, rest
in vill; BBQ; Rv Ariège 100m; fishing; games area; some statics;
quiet. "Gd san facs." ♦ € 7.80   2009*

CABANNES, LES *8G3* (2km SW Rural) FFCC Camping Le
Pas de l'Ours, Les Gesquis, 09310 Aston [05 61 64 90 33;
fax 05 61 64 90 32; contact@lepasdelours.fr; www.
campingariege.fr] S on N20, after Tarascon-sur-Ariège turn
R sp Plateau de Beille/Les Cabannes. Pass thro Aulos, site well
sp. Sm, hdg/mkd pitch, pt sl, pt shd; htd wc; chem disp; baby
facs; shwrs inc; el pnts (6A) €4; lndtte (inc dryer); shop, rest
2km; snacks; bar; BBQ; playgrnd; pool adj; tennis; cycle hire;
games area; wifi; entmnt; TV rm; 50% statics; dogs €2; phone;
Eng spkn; adv bkg; quiet; ccard acc; red low ssn; CKE/CCI.
"Attractive site surrounded by mountains; v clean san facs; not
suitable lge o'fits; helpful owners; gd touring base; access poss
diff for lge o'fits" ♦ ltd 26 May-15 Sep. € 32.00   2013*

CABOURG *3D1* (1km E Coastal) *49.28618, -0.09024*
Camp Municipal Les Tilleuls, Route de Lisieux, 14160
Dives-sur-Mer [02 31 91 25 21; fax 02 31 91 72 13;
campinglestilleuls@wanadoo.fr; www.dives-sur-mer.com]
Fr Cabourg cross bdge to Dives-sur-Mer, turn R at traff lts (Rue
Gaston Manneville) & foll camping sp past church at bottom of
hill up to D45. Turn L, site on R in 300m. Or fr A13 take D400
sp Cabourg, pass Super U & Intermarché supmkts & turn R sp
Camping Touristique, site on R in 1.2km. Lge, pt sl, pt shd; htd
wc (mainly cont); shwrs inc; el pnts (6A) inc; lndry rm; shops
500m; playgrnd; sand beach 3km; horseriding; dogs; quiet.
Easter-15 Sep. € 16.00   2008*

CABOURG *3D1* (8km SW Rural) *49.25210, -0.18823* Camping
Le Clos Tranquille, 17 Route de Troarn, 14810 Gonneville-
en-Auge [02 31 24 21 36; fax 02 31 24 28 80; le.clos.
tranquille@wanadoo.fr; www.campingleclostranquille.fr]
Fr Cabourg, take D513 twd Caen. 2km after Varaville turn R to
Gonneville-en-Auge (by garden cent) D95A. Foll sp to vill, site
ent on R after LH bend. Med, pt shd; wc; chem disp; el pnts
(6-10A) €3.50-€5 (poss rev pol & long lead req); shwrs inc; gas;
lndtte; tradsmn; snacks; shop; playgrnd; cycle hire; sand beach
5km; 12% statics; dogs €2; poss cr; Eng spkn; adv bkg; quiet;
ccard acc; CKE/CCI. "Excel, quiet site, no bar and nothing
within walking dist" 2 Apr-1 Oct. € 27.00   2013*

CABOURG *3D1* (1km W Coastal) *49.28166, -0.13795*
Camping La Pommeraie, Le Bas Cabourg, 14390 Cabourg
[02 31 91 54 58 or 06 07 15 84 67; fax 02 31 91 66 57]
Take D513 fr Cabourg twd Caen. Site on L 1km after Bas-
Cabourg sp. Med, pt shd; wc; shwrs €1; el pnts (5A) €4; gas;
lndtte; shop; sand beach 800m; 90% statics; dogs; adv bkg;
ccard acc. "Few touring pitches; mkt Sat." 1 Apr-30 Sep.
€ 18.00   2009*

CABOURG *3D1* (2km W Coastal) *49.28326, -0.17053*
Camping Les Peupliers, Allée des Pins, 14810 Merville-
Franceville-Plage [tel/fax 02 31 24 05 07; contact@
camping-peupliers.com; www.camping-peupliers.com]
Exit A13 to Cabourg onto D400, take D513 W, turn R sp Le
Hôme, site sp, 2km E of Merville-Franceville. Med, pt sl, unshd;
htd wc; chem disp; baby facs; shwrs inc; el pnts (10A) €5.50;
lndtte; shop 2km; tradsmn; rest high ssn; snacks; bar; BBQ;
playgrnd; htd pool; sand beach 300m; games area; tennis
2km; entmnt; TV; 50% statics; dogs €3.10; phone; poss cr;
Eng spkn; adv bkg; ccard acc; red low ssn; CKE/CCI. "Pleasant,
friendly, well-run, busy site; some lge pitches; clean, modern
san facs; vg facs for children; conv ferries." ♦ 1 Apr-31 Oct.
€ 21.30   2009*

CABOURG *3D1* (6km W Coastal) *49.28319, -0.19098*
**Camping Le Point du Jour, Route de Cabourg, 14810
Merville-Franceville-Plage [02 31 24 23 34; fax
02 31 24 15 54; contact@camping-lepointdujour.com;
www.camping-lepointdujour.com]** Fr Ouistreham on D514
turn E at Bénouville onto D224, cross bdge onto D514, site on
L dir Cabourg. Or fr A13/D675 exit Dozulé dir Cabourg, then
D514 to site. Med, hdg pitch, pt shd; htd wc; chem disp; mv
service pnt; baby facs; shwrs inc; el pnts (10A) €5 (poss rev
pol); gas; lndtte (inc dryer); shop; tradsmn; rest, snacks; bar;
BBQ; playgrnd; htd, covrd pool; sand beach adj; games rm;
wifi; entmnt; TV rm; 10% statics; dogs €3; bus; poss cr; adv
bkg; quiet; ccard acc; red low ssn/long stay/CKE/CCI. "Excel
site with sea views; direct access to Sword Beach (D-Day) &
sand dunes; conv Pegasus Bridge." ♦ 4 Apr-5 Nov. € 29.40
SBS - N03   2012*

CABOURG *3D1* (6km W Coastal) *49.28296, -0.19072*
**Camping Village Ariane, 100 Route de Cabourg,
14810 Merville-Franceville-Plage [02 31 24 52 52; fax
02 31 24 52 41; info@loisirs-ariane.com; www.camping-
ariane.com]** Fr Ouistreham on D514 turn E at Bénouville onto
D224, cross bdge onto D514 to site dir Cabourg. Or fr A13/
D675 exit Dozulé dir Cabourg, then D514 to site. Lge, mkd
pitch, pt shd; htd wc; chem disp; baby facs; fam bthrm; shwrs
inc; el pnts (6-10A) €4; gas; lndtte; shop 500m; tradsmn;
snacks; playgrnd; sand beach 300m; watersports & tennis nr;
games area; games rm; wifi; entmnt; TV rm; 10% statics; dogs
€3; Eng spkn; adv bkg; quiet; red long stay/low ssn; CKE/CCI.
♦ 1 Apr-5 Nov. € 19.20   2009*

CABRERETS *7D3* (1km NE Rural) *44.50771, 1.66234*
**Camping Cantal, 46330 Cabrerets [05 65 31 26 61; fax
05 65 31 20 47]** Fr Cahors take D653 E for approx 15km bef
turning R onto D662 E thro Vers & St Géry. Turn L onto D41
to Cabrerets. Site 1km after vill on R. Sm, pt sl, pt shd; wc;
chem disp (wc); 50% serviced pitch; shwrs inc; el pnts €2.50;
rv canoeing nrby; quiet; CKE/CCI. "Superb situation; peaceful
site; warden calls; ground slightly bumpy; excel san facs; not
suitable lge o'fits; conv Pech Merle; excel." 1 Apr-15 Oct.
€ 9.10   2010*

CABRERETS *7D3* (7km NE Rural) *44.52609, 1.71944*
**Camping Mas de Nadal (Naturist), 46330 Sauliac-sur-Célé
[05 65 31 20 51; fax 05 65 31 20 57; info@masdenadal.
com; www.masdenadal.com]** Fr Cahors take D653 E. After
35km turn R onto D40 S, sp Blars. Fr Blars cont S for 2km to
site ent on R. Sm, mkd pitch, pt sl, pt shd; wc; shwrs inc; el
pnts (3-9A) €4; lndtte; shops 2km; tradsmn; rest; bar; playgrnd;
pool; canoe hire; games area; phone; dogs €4.50; poss cr; Eng
spkn; adv bkg; quiet; CKE/CCI/INF card req. "Secluded wooded
hillside; ltd rough pitches not suitable lge o'fits; rec phone
ahead to check avail; suitable for m'vans." 1 Apr-30 Sep.
€ 21.00   2009*

CABRIERES D'AIGUES see Pertuis *10E3*

CADENET *10E3* (10km NE Rural) *43.76871, 5.44970*
**Camping Lou Badareu, La Rasparine, 84160 Cucuron
[04 90 77 21 46; fax 04 90 77 27 68; contact@loubadareu.
com; www.loubadareu.com]** In Cadenet foll sp for church
(église) onto D45 dir Cucuron; S of Cucuron turn onto D27 (do
not go into town); site is E 1km. Well sp fr D27. Sm, mkd pitch,
pt sl, pt shd; ltd wc (own san rec); chem disp; shwrs inc; el pnts
(10A) €4.50 (long lead poss req); lndtte; shop & 1km; tradsmn;
playgrnd; pool; few statics; dogs €1.80; phone; quiet; CKE/CCI.
"Pretty farm site in cherry orchard; friendly, helpful owner; sep
access for high vans." ♦ 1 Apr-15 Oct. € 11.10   2011*

CADENET *10E3* (10km NE Rural) *43.75667, 5.44448* **FFCC**
**Camping Le Moulin à Vent, Chemin de Gastoule, 84160
Cucuron [04 90 77 25 77; fax 04 90 77 28 12; camping_
bressier@yahoo.fr; www.le-moulin-a-vent.com]** Fr A51
exit junc 15 to Pertuis. N on D56 fr Pertuis to Cucuron. Site sp
S fr Cucuron vill dir Villelaure. Med, hdg/mkd pitch, pt sl, terr,
shd; wc (cont); chem disp; mv service pnt; baby facs; shwrs
inc; spa; el pnts inc (6-10A) €3-4; lndry rm; shop; tradsmn; rest,
snacks & bar 2km; playgrnd; htd pool 4km; wifi; 10% statics;
dogs €2.70; poss cr; Eng spkn; adv bkg; quiet; CKE/CCI.
"Spacious pitches, but access poss diff; friendly, helpful staff;
no twin-axles; vg." ♦ ltd 1 Apr-15 Oct. € 14.50   2011*

CADENET *10E3* (2km SW Rural) *43.71968, 5.35479*
**Camping Val de Durance, Les Routes, 84160 Cadenet
[04 90 68 37 75 or 04 42 20 47 25 (LS); fax 04 90 68 16 34;
info@homair.com; www.homair.com]** Exit A7 at Cavaillon
onto D973 dir Cadenet. In Cadenet take D59, site sp. Lge,
hdg pitch, pt shd; wc; chem disp; shwrs inc; el pnts (4-10A)
inc (long lead req); gas; lndtte; shop & 2km; rest, snacks; bar;
BBQ; playgrnd; pool; paddling pool; rv sw & beach; archery;
canoeing; cycling; games area; wifi; entmnt; TV; 70% statics;
dogs €5; adv bkg; red low ssn; ccard acc; CKE/CCI. "Dir access
to lake; adj Luberon Park; noisy entmnt till late most evenings
high ssn." ♦ 06 Apr - 29 Sep. € 32.00   2013*

CAEN *3D1* (14km N Coastal) *49.32551, -0.39010* **Yelloh!
Village Côte de Nacre, 17 Rue du Général Moulton, 14750
St Aubin-sur-Mer [02 31 97 14 45; fax 02 31 97 22 11;
camping-cote-de-nacre@wanadoo.fr; www.camping-cote-
de-nacre.com or www.yellohvillage.co.uk]** Fr Caen on D7
dir Douvres-la-Délivrande, Langrune-sur-Mer & St Aubin. Site
in St Aubin-sur-Mer on S side of D514; clearly sp on o'skts.
Lge, hdg/mkd pitch, hdstg, unshd; htd wc; chem disp; mv
service pnt; baby facs; sauna; shwrs inc; el pnts (10A) inc;
lndtte (inc dryer); shop high ssn; tradsmn; rest, snacks; bar;
BBQ; playgrnd; htd pools (1 covrd); paddling pool; waterslide;
sand beach 500m; tennis 200m; cycle hire; games rm; wifi;
entmnt; TV; 15% statics; dogs €4; quiet; phone; poss cr; Eng
spkn; adv bkg rec; ccard acc; CKE/CCI. "Ideal for families; lge
pitches; conv Caen ferry, Normandy beaches, WW2 sites;
helpful staff; excel modern san facs; poss waterlogging; gd
cycle tracks along sea front low ssn; easy walk into quiet vill;
vg; payment on arr, no refund for early dep" ♦
29 Mar-22 Sep. € 58.20   2013*

See advertisement on inside front cover

CAGNES SUR MER *10E4* (2km N Rural) *43.67855, 7.12593* **Camping Caravaning St Paul, 637 Chemin du Malvan, 06570 St Paul [04 93 32 93 71; fax 04 93 32 01 97; booking@caravaningsaintpaul.fr; www.caravaningsaintpaul.fr]** Fr W exit A8 junc 47 dir Vence; fr E exit junc 48; in cent of Cagnes take D36 sp St Paul. At 3rd rndabt in 2km turn R & in 100m L to site in further 1km. Site sp. Med, hdg/mkd pitch, shd; wc; chem disp; mv service pnt; baby facs; shwrs inc; el pnts (6-10A) €3-4; gas; lndtte; shop 500m; tradsmn; rest, snacks; bar; playgrnd; pool; shgl beach 4.5km; cycle hire; entmnt; dogs €1.50; poss cr; Eng spkn; adv bkg; quiet; CKE/CCI. "Attractive, family-run site; well-kept & clean; conv Côte d'Azur." ♦ 1 Apr-30 Sep. € 24.00   2008*

CAGNES SUR MER *10E4* (3km N Rural) *43.68944, 7.15666* **Camping Green Park, 159 Vallon-des-Vaux, 06800 Cagnes-sur-Mer [04 93 07 09 96 or 06 80 48 25 74 (mob); fax 04 93 14 36 55; info@greenpark.fr; www.greenpark.fr]** Exit A8 junc 47 onto D6007 sp Villeneuve-Loubet, Cagnes-sur-Mer & Nice; at Cagnes at 1st traff lts (do not foll sp Centre Ville) - racecourse on R; go strt for 1.5km (8 sets of traff lts); then turn L onto Chemin du Val Fleuri; cont strt for 4km. Fr Nice take D6098 coast rd dir Cannes. Shortly after Cagnes turn R opp Le Port & foll sp Camping. Turn R then L at traff lts, site 3rd on L in 3km opp Camping Le Todos (same owner). Med, mkd pitch, pt shd; wc; chem disp; mv service pnt; baby facs; shwrs inc; el pnts (16A) inc; gas; lndtte; sm shop; rest, snacks; bar; BBQ (gas/elec); playgrnd; 2 htd pools; shgl beach 4.3km; fishing 4.5km; horseriding 12km; tennis 400m; sports area; cycle hire; disco; wifi; entmnt; games/TV rm; mainly statics; dogs €2.50-3.60; adv bkg rec; quiet; red low ssn; CKE/CCI. "Friendly; well-run; gd pool; excel; v ltd touring pitches." ♦ 31 Mar-18 Oct. € 57.90 (4 persons)   2008*

CAGNES SUR MER *10E4* (3km N Rural) *43.69018, 7.15643* **Camping Le Todos, 159 Vallon-des-Vaux, 06800 Cagnes-sur-Mer [04 93 31 20 05; fax 04 92 12 81 66; info@letodos.fr; www.letodos.fr]** Fr Aix on A8 exit junc 47 & foll dir Cagnes-sur-Mer/Nice on D6007 (do not foll sp 'Centre Ville'). After 1st traff lts beside racecourse strt on for 2km, then turn L dir Val Fleuri, site in 3km. Fr Nice take D6098 coast rd dir Cannes. Shortly after Cagnes turn R opp Le Port & foll sp Camping. Turn R then L at traff lts, site on L in 3km opp Camping Green Park. Med, mkd pitch, some terr, pt shd; wc; chem disp; mv service pnt; shwrs inc; el pnts (6-10A) €4.10-5.70; lndtte; tradsmn; shop; rest, snacks, bar at adj Camping Green Park; BBQ (gas/elec); playgrnd; pool & use of htd pool at Green Park; sand beach 4.5km; tennis 400m; cycle hire; games area; internet; TV; mainly statics; dogs €5; poss cr; adv bkg; quiet; red low ssn. "Owners also own Camping Green Park - some facs shared; v ltd touring pitches." ♦ ltd 22 Mar-12 Oct. € 36.00   2009*

CAGNES SUR MER *10E4* (3.5km N Rural) *43.69468, 7.14323* **Camping La Rivière, 168 Chemin des Salles, 06800 Cagnes-sur-Mer [tel/fax 04 93 20 62 27; www.campinglariviere06.fr]** Fr D6007 N on D18 sp Val de Cagne. Site on rvside. Med, hdg/mkd pitch, pt shd; wc; shwrs inc; el pnts (4-6A) €2.90-€3.30; gas; lndtte; shop; rest; bar; playgrnd; pool; sand beach 4.5km; entmnt; 10% statics; dogs €1.50; poss cr; quiet; adv bkg; ccard acc. ♦ 1 Mar-31 Oct. € 20.50   2008*

CAGNES SUR MER *10E4* (3.5km N Rural) *43.68717, 7.15589* **Camping Le Val Fleuri, 139 Vallon-des-Vaux, 06800 Cagnes-sur-Mer [tel/fax 04 93 31 21 74; valfleur2@wanadoo.fr; www.campingvalfleuri.fr]** Fr Nice take D6007 W twd Cannes. On app Cagnes turn R & foll sp Camping; site on R after 3km, well sp. NB 3.3m height restriction on this rte. Sm, terr, pt shd; wc (some cont); shwrs; el pnts (3-10A) €4 shop 3km; tradsmn; rest; shgl beach 4km; playgrnd; htd pool; wifi; entmnt; dogs €1.50; poss cr; Eng spkn; adv bkg; red low ssn. "Gd, improving site, divided by rd (not busy); some sm pitches; helpful, friendly owners; gd." 14 Feb-3 Mar & 1 Apr-31 Oct. € 26.50   2012*

CAGNES SUR MER *10E4* (8km NE Rural) *43.71466, 7.17775* **Camping Magali, 1814 Route de la Baronne, 06700 St Laurent-du-Var [04 93 31 57 00; fax 04 92 12 01 33; info@camping-magali.com; www.camping-magali.com]** Exit A8 junc 49 to St Laurent-du-Var. Site sp fr town cent. Or fr Digne S on D6202 bis, turn R onto D2210 at Pont-de-la-Manda; foll sp to St Laurent-du-Var for approx 7km, site on L. Med, mkd, pitch pt shd; htd wc (mainly cont); chem disp; shwrs inc; baby facs; el pnts (2-4A) €2.70-3.50; gas; lndtte; shop; rest, snacks; bar; pool; shgl beach 6km; sailing; fishing; tennis; horseriding; some statics; dogs €2; bus nrby; poss cr; adv bkg; quiet; ccard acc; red low ssn. "Conv Nice ferry (25 mins to port), Nice carnival/Menton Lemon Fair; sm pitches." ♦ 1 Feb-31 Oct. € 22.30   2008*

CAGNES SUR MER *10E4* (2km S Coastal) *43.63128, 7.12993* **Camping Parc des Maurettes, 730 Ave du Docteur Lefebvre, 06270 Villeneuve-Loubet [04 93 20 91 91; fax 04 93 73 77 20; info@parcdesmaurettes.com; www.parcdesmaurettes.com]** Fr Nice exit A8 junc 47, turn L onto D6007 dir Antibes; foll sp Intermarché, then R into Rue des Maurettes; site in 250m. N fr Cannes on A8 exit Villeneuve-Loubet-Plage junc 46; foll D241 over D6007 & rwly line, U-turn back over rwly line, then R onto D6007 dir Antibes as above. NB Site on steep cliff with narr winding rds packed with trees; diff ent. Med, mkd pitch, terr, pt shd; htd wc; chem disp; mv service pnt; some serviced pitches; shwrs inc; el pnts (3-10A) €5.30; gas; lndtte; shops adj; snacks; playgrnd; htd, covrd pool; shgl beach 500m; wifi; sat TV; dogs €4; train Nice 400m; poss cr; Eng spkn; adv bkg; quiet; ccard acc; red long stay; CKE/CCI. "Well-kept site; variable pitch size/price." ♦ 10 Jan-15 Nov. € 29.50   2009*

⊞ **CAGNES SUR MER** *10E4* (7km S Rural) *43.62027, 7.12583* **Camping La Vieille Ferme, 296 Blvd des Groules, 06270 Villeneuve-Loubet-Plage [04 93 33 41 44; fax 04 93 33 37 28; info@vieilleferme.com; www.vieilleferme.com]** Fr W (Cannes) take Antibes exit 44 fr A8, foll D35 dir Antibes 'Centre Ville'. At lge junc turn onto D6007, Ave de Nice, twd Biot & Villeneuve-Loubet sp Nice (rlwy line on R). Just after Marineland turn L onto Blvd des Groules. Fr E (Nice) leave A8 at junc 47 to join D6007 twd Antibes, take 3rd turning after Intermarché supmkt; site well sp fr D6007. Med, hdg/mkd pitch, pt terr, pt sl, pt shd; htd wc; chem disp; mv service pnt; serviced pitches; baby facs; shwrs inc; el pnts (2A-10A) €3 - €7; gas; lndtte (inc dryer); tradsmn; supmkt 800m; snacks; BBQ (gas/elec); playgrnd; htd covrd pool; paddling pool; shgl beach 1km (across busy rd & rlwy); games rm; wifi; games/TV rm; 40% statics; dogs €2.50; no c'vans/m'vans over 8m; bus, train nrby; Eng spkn; adv bkg; some aircraft & rd noise; ccard acc; red long stay/low ssn. "Peaceful, well-kept family-run site; well-drained pitches, some lge; san facs need refurb (2010); beach not suitable children & non-swimmers; excel pool; gd walking, cycling & dog walking as lge park adj; vg value low ssn; excel." ♦ € 28.00 SBS - C22   2013*

Tell us about the sites you visit

FRANCE

CAGNES SUR MER *10E4* (4km SW Rural) *43.66001, 7.1000*
**Parc Saint James Le Sourire, Route de Grasse, 06270
Villeneuve-Loubet [04 93 20 96 11; fax 04 93 22 07 52;
lesourire@camping-parcsaintjames.com; www.
camping-parcsaintjames.com]** Exit A8 at junc 47; take D2 to
Villeneuve; at rndbt take D2085 sp Grasse. Site on L in 2km. Sp
Le Sourire. Med, hdg pitch, hdstg, pt shd; htd wc; shwrs inc;
el pnts (6A) inc; lndtte; tradsmn; rest; bar; playgrnd; htd pools;
shgl beach 5km; tennis, golf & horseriding nr; games area;
entmnt; 70% statics; dogs €5; Eng spkn; adv bkg; ccard acc;
red long stay/low ssn. "Vg site; park in visitors' car park bef
registering; lovely location conv Nice, Cannes & beaches." ♦
7 Apr-29 Sep. € 31.00   2011*

CAGNES SUR MER *10E4* (1km NW Urban) *43.67159, 7.13845*
**Camping Le Colombier, 35 Chemin de Ste Colombe,
06800 Cagnes-sur-Mer [tel/fax 04 93 73 12 77;
campinglecolombier06@wanadoo.fr; www.
campinglecolombier.com]** N fr Cagnes cent foll 1-way system
dir Vence. Half way up hill turn R at rndabt dir Cagnes-sur-Mer
& R at next island. Site on L 300m, sp fr town cent. Sm, hdg/
mkd pitch, pt shd; htd wc; chem disp; mv service pnt; shwrs
inc; el pnts (2-16A) €2-8; lndry rm; shop 400m; rest 800m;
snacks; bar; no BBQ; playgrnd, sm pool adj; TV; beach 2.5km;
cycle hire; some statics; no dogs Jul/Aug; phone; Eng spkn;
quiet; red long stay/low ssn/CKE/CCI. "Friendly, family-run
site." 30 Apr-1 Sep. € 22.20   2013*

CAGNES SUR MER *10E4* (4km NW Rural) *43.68449, 7.07297*
**Camping Le Vallon Rouge, Route de Gréolières, 06480 La
Colle-sur-Loup [04 93 32 86 12 or 06 82 90 93 05 (mob);
fax 04 93 32 80 09; info@auvallonrouge.com; www.
auvallonrouge.com]** Exit A8 junc 47 onto D6007 dir Nice
then D2 to Villeneuve-Loubet. Foll sp Villeneuve-Loubet over rv
& thro sh tunnel to rndabt. Turn L at rndabt & foll sps for D6
La Colle-sur-Loup; after La Colle-sur-Loup site on R in 2.5km.
NB Lge o'fits park in lay-by & ask at recep bef tackling steep,
winding downhill ent driveway. NB Ask recep for code for rear
gate on leaving. Med, mkd pitch, hdstg, shd; wc; chem disp;
mv service pnt; baby facs; shwrs inc; solarium; el pnts (10A)
inc; lndtte (inc dryer); sm shop; tradsmn; rest, snacks; bar; BBQ
(gas/elec); playgrnd; pool; paddling pool; sand/shgl beach 9km;
fishing; cycle hire; games area; wifi; entmnt; games/TV rm;
40% statics; dogs €3.50; adv bkg; ccard acc; red low ssn; CKE/
CCI. "On banks of Rv Loup; conv Nice, Cannes, St Paul-de-
Vence & Grasse; steep drop fr pitches down to shallow rv; Sat
mkt; vg site." ♦ 3 Apr-26 Sep. € 35.50   2010*

CAGNES SUR MER *10E4* (4km NW Rural) *43.68272, 7.08391*
**Camping Les Pinèdes, Route de Pont de Pierre, 06480 La
Colle-sur-Loup [04 93 32 98 94; fax 04 93 32 50 20; info@
lespinedes.com; www.lespinedes.com]** Exit A8 junc 47;
take D6007 dir Nice, then D2 sp Villeneuve-Loubet; turn R
at rndabt sp Villeneuve-Loubet & cross rv bdge; go thro sh
tunnel, other side is Cagnes-sur-Mer & rndabt; turn L onto D6
to Colle-sur-Loup; site on R sh dist after Colle-sur-Loup. NB
Take 2nd turning into site (1st leads to restaurant). Lge, hdg/
mkd pitch, hdstg, pt sl, terr, pt shd; wc; chem disp; mv service
pnt; serviced pitches; shwrs inc; el pnts (6-10A) €4.60-5.90
(poss rev pol); lndtte; shop (high ssn) & 1.5km; tradsmn; rest,
snacks; bar; BBQ (gas/elec); playgrnd; htd pool; paddling
pool; solarium; sand beach 13km; rv fishing & sw adj; tennis,
horseriding adj; archery; games area; wifi; entmnt; games/
TV rm; 20% statics; dogs €3.60; no c'vans over 6m (excluding
towbar) & m'vans over 8m high ssn; no twin axle c'vans; Eng
spkn; adv bkg; quiet; ccard acc over €50; red long stay/low
ssn/CKE/CCI. "Excel, family-run site set in pine & oak trees;
helpful & friendly; spacious pitches; steep access to pitches
- poss diff lge o'fits, help avail; luxurious san facs; gd rest at
site ent; highly rec; vg site has everything you need; spacious
pitches." ♦ 15 Mar-30 Sep. € 50.60 SBS - C30   2013*

See advertisement

CAHORS *7D3* (8km N Rural) *44.52585, 1.46048* **Camping Les
Graves, 46090 St Pierre-Lafeuille [tel/fax 05 65 36 83 12;
infos@camping-lesgraves.com; www.camping-lesgraves.
com]** Leave A20 at junc 57 Cahors Nord onto D820. Foll sp
St Pierre-Lafeuille; at N end of vill, site is opp L'Atrium wine
cave. Med, hdg pitch, sl, pt shd; wc; chem disp; mv service pnt;
shwrs inc; el pnts (6-10A) €2.50-3.50 (poss rev pol); lndtte;
shop 10km; tradsmn; rest, snacks; bar; playgrnd; pool; cycle
hire; 5% statics; dogs €1.50; Eng spkn; adv bkg rec high ssn; rd
noise; ccard acc; red low ssn/CKE/CCI. "Clean, scenic site; lge
pitches; poss clsd during/after wet weather due boggy ground;
disabled facs over stony rd & grass; ltd facs low ssn; conv A20."
♦ 1 Apr-31 Oct. € 17.20   2013*

CAHORS *7D3* (8km N Rural) *44.53136, 1.45926* **Quercy-Vacances, Mas de la Combe, 46000 St Pierre-Lafeuille [05 65 36 87 15; fax 05 65 36 02 39; quercyvacances@wanadoo.fr; www.quercy-vacances.com]** Heading N on D820, turn L at N end of St Pierre-Lafeuille turn W at site sp N of vill, site in 700m down lane; new site opened adj so care needed to spot correct sp. Fr A20 exit junc 57 & foll sp N20. Med, pt sl, pt shd; wc; chem disp; baby facs; shwrs inc; el pnts (6-10A) €3.30-5.30; gas; lndtte; shops 10km; tradsmn; rest, snacks; bar; playgrnd; pool; tennis; games area; TV; some statics; dogs €1.50; phone; Eng spkn; adv bkg; quiet; ltd facs low ssn; ccard acc; red low ssn; CKE/CCI. "Pretty site; most pitches slightly sloping; clean, modern san facs; poss unkempt low ssn; helpful owner; vg." ♦ 1 Apr-31 Oct. € 18.80   2008*

CAHORS *7D3* (1.5km E Urban) *44.46318, 1.44226* **Camping Rivière de Cabessut, Rue de la Rivière, 46000 Cahors [05 65 30 06 30; fax 05 65 22 99 46; contact@cabessut.com; www.cabessut.com]** Fr N or S on D820, at S end Cahors by-pass take D911 sp Rodez. At traff lts by bdge do not cross rv but bear R on D911. In 1km at site sp turn L. Site on E bank of Rv Lot, well sp fr town. 1.8km to site fr bdge (Pont Cabessut). Med, hdg/mkd pitch, pt shd; wc; chem disp; mv service pnt; some serviced pitches; baby facs; shwrs inc; el pnts (10A) €2 (poss rev pol); gas; lndtte; shop; hypmkt 1.5km; tradsmn; snacks; bar; BBQ (gas only); playgrnd; pool; rv adj; wifi; 5% statics; dogs €2; phone; bus to Cahors 600m; poss cr; adv bkg rec - ess high ssn; quiet; CKE/CCI. "Lovely, well-run site by rv; beautiful area; pleasant, helpful owners; mostly lge pitches, sm pitches diff access when site full; gd for children; walk to town by rv 1.8km; food mkt Wed, full mkt Sat; excel new san facs (2012); well maintained site, helpful owners" ♦ 1 Apr-30 Sep. € 26.50   2013*

CAJARC *7D4* (300m SW Urban) *44.48374, 1.83928* **Camp Municipal Le Terriol, Rue Le Terriol, 46160 Cajarc [05 65 40 72 74 or 05 65 40 65 20 (Mairie); fax 05 65 40 39 05; mairie.cajarc@wanadoo.fr; www.cajarc.fr]** Fr Cahors dir Cajarc on D662 on L foll sp to site. Sm, hdg/mkd pitch, some hdstg, pt shd; wc (cont); chem disp; baby facs; fam bthrm; shwrs inc; el pnts (10A) inc (poss rev pol); lndtte; shop, rest, bar in vill; BBQ; playgrnd; pool & tennis 500m; dogs; phone; no twin-axles; Eng spkn; adv bkg; some rd noise; CKE/CCI. "Gd sized pitches; clean, basic facs; lovely sm town on Rv Lot." 1 May-30 Sep. € 14.50   2013*

CAJARC *7D4* (6km SW Rural) *44.46630, 1.75077* **Camp Municipal Le Grand Pré, 46330 Cénevières [05 65 30 22 65 or 05 65 31 28 16 (Marie); fax 05 65 31 37 00; mairie.cenevieres@wanadoo.fr]** Fr Villefranche on D911 twd Cahors turn R onto D24 at Limogne for Cénevières. Foll sp. Fr St Cirq-Lapopie on D24 thro vill & over rlwy. Sm, hdg/mkd pitch, pt shd; wc; chem disp (wc); mv service pnt; shwrs inc; el pnts (10A) inc; lndtte; shop, rest, snacks, bar 1km; BBQ; rv sw; dogs; bus; phone; quiet. "Peaceful site by rv; wonderful views of cliffs; vg san facs; site self & warden calls pm; excel highly rec." 1 Jun-30 Sep. € 12.40   2012*

CAJARC *7D4* (6km W Rural) *44.4735, 1.7835* **Camping Ruisseau de Treil, 46160 Larnagol [05 65 31 23 39; fax 05 65 31 23 27; lotcamping@wanadoo.fr; www.lotcamping.com]** Exit A20 junc 57 onto D49 sp St Michel; in 4km turn R onto D653; after 5.5km in Vers at mini-rndabt turn L onto D662; site on L immed after leaving Larnagol. Or fr Figeac foll D19 thro Cajarc. At top of hill leaving Cajarc turn R onto D662 sp Cahors & Larnagol. Site sp on R 300m bef Larnagol on blind bend. Sm, mkd pitch, pt sl, pt shd; wc; chem disp; baby facs; shwrs inc; el pnts (6A) €3.60; lndtte; tradsmn; rest, snacks; bar; BBQ; playgrnd; 2 pools; rv sw, fishing, canoeing adj; horseriding; cycle hire; library; TV rm; 4% statics; dogs €3.90; poss cr; adv bkg; quiet; red low ssn/snr citizen; CKE/CCI. "Beautiful, spacious, peaceful site site in lovely area; well-run; friendly, helpful British owners; clean san facs but ltd when site full; lge pitches poss uneven; many long-stay/returning campers; guided walks; vg touring base; excel." ♦ ltd 14 May-10 Sep. € 20.90   2011*

CALAIS *3A3* (8km E Rural) *50.98020, 2.01393* **Camping Les Petits Moulins, 1634 Rue des Petits Moulins, 62215 Oye-Plage [03 21 85 12 94]** Fr A16 junc 21 proceed to Oye-Plage. Strt thro traff lts & take 2nd L to site past derelict windmill. Sm, unshd; wc (own facs low ssn); chem disp (wc); shwrs inc; el pnts (10A) inc; shops 2km; sw beach 2km; 90% statics; dogs; poss cr; quiet. "Busy, well-kept CL-type site at end of statics site; open view; friendly, helpful owner; gd, basic san facs; ltd el pnts; poss run down low ssn; find pitch, book in house adj; ltd touring pitches; phone ahead; conv ferries; NH only." 15 Apr-30 Sep. € 12.00   2009*

⊞ **CALAIS** *3A3* (12km E Coastal) *50.99657, 2.05062* **Camping Clairette, 525 Route des Dunes, 62215 Oye-Plage [03 21 35 83 51 / 06 14 22 92 71 (mob); fax 03 21 35 83 51; camping.clairette.sarl@cegetel.net; www.camping.clairette.ifrance.com]** Exit A16 junc 50 & foll sp Oye-Plage. At traff lts at end strt. At junc with D119 turn R then L, site on L in 2km. Foll sp 'Réserve Naturelle'. Med, hdg/mkd pitch, pt sl, unshd; htd wc; chem disp (wc); mv service pnt; shwrs inc; el pnts (10A) €4; gas 5km; lndtte; shops 5km; tradsmn; BBQ; sm playgrnd; htd, covrd pool 5km; beach 500m; 95% statics; dogs €1.40; clsd 16 Dec-14 Jan; poss cr; Eng spkn; adv bkg; quiet; ccard acc; CKE/CCI. "Ltd touring pitches, rec phone/email in adv; warm welcome; helpful owners; security barrier; nature reserve nrby; conv ferries; fair; san facs ok (2013)" € 14.80   2013*

⊞ **CALAIS** *3A3* (12km E Rural) *50.96613, 2.05270* **Camping Le Pont d'Oye, 308 Rue de la Rivière, 62215 Oye-Plage [06 21 85 65 25; ch.lavallee@laposte.net; www.campingdupontdoye.fr]** Exit A16 at junc 50 onto D219 to Oye-Plage; cross rv & immed turn R sp camping; foll rv; site on L. Sm, unshd hdg pitch; wc; chem disp (wc); child/baby facs; shwrs €1; el pnts (6A) €2.50; Snacks; Bar; BBQ; gas; lndtte; shop 2km; tradsmn; playgrnd; sandy beach 5km; dogs; wifi; 85% statics, Eng spkn, adv bkg; CKE/CCI; "Basic CL-type site; few touring pitches; grassed field for c'vans; friendly, helpful owners; san facs adj statics park - v dated but clean; conv ferries; NH only; new owner (2012); site improved." ♦ € 13.10   2013*

FRANCE

⊞ **CALAIS** *3A3* (1km SW Coastal) *50.96603, 1.84370*
Aire Communale, Plage de Calais, Ave Raymond
Poincaré, 62100 Calais [03 21 97 89 79, 03 21 46 66 41 or
06 79 62 93 22 (mob); camping@marie-calais.fr] A16 exit
junc 43 dir Blériot-Plage/Calais cent & foll sp for beach (plage).
Site nr harbour wall & Fort Risban. Well sp fr town cent. Med;
wc (Jun-Sep); water; shop, rest nrby; obtain token/pass fr Camp
Municipal adj; wc part-time (charge); warden calls to collect
fee pm or pay at Camp Municipal; noise fr ferries; m'vans only.
"Well-kept, busy site; gd NH to/fr ferries." € 7.00   2010*

> # "There aren't many sites open at this time of year"
>
> If you're travelling outside peak season
> remember to call ahead to check site opening
> dates – even if the entry says 'open all year'.

CALAIS *3A3* (4km SW Coastal) *50.95677, 1.81101* **Camp du
Fort Lapin, Route Provincial 940, 62231 Sangatte-Blériot
Plage [tel/fax 03 21 97 67 77; campingdufortlapin@
orange.fr; www.ville-sangatte.fr]** Fr E exit junc 43 fr A16
Calais cent, dir beach (Blériot-Plage). Turn L along coast onto
D940 dir Sangatte; site on R in dunes shortly after water
tower, opp sports cent; site sp fr D940. Fr S exit A16 junc 41
to Sangatte; at T-junc turn R onto D940; site on L just bef
water tower. Med, mkd pitch, pt sl, unshd; wc (some cont);
chem disp; baby facs; shwrs inc (poss clsd 2130); el pnts (10A)
inc (poss rev pol); lndtte; shop 1km; rest, snacks; bar; BBQ;
playgrnd; sand beach adj; 50% statics; dogs; phone; bus; poss
cr; adv bkg; quiet; CKE/CCI. "Conv ferry; warden lives on site;
rec arr bef 1700 high ssn; gates clsd 2300-0700; recep 0900-
1200 & 1500-2000; ltd parking outside espec w/end - phone
ahead for access code; poss cr; gd bus service; basic, clean,
adequate san facs (shwrs and lndry clsd after 21:00); conv
Auchan & Cité Europe shops; poss youth groups high ssn; conv
NH; Clean tidy site; quite crowded holiday site; lots of statics;
adequate facs; ground very well drained; easy cycle into Calais
or walk along the promenade to the harbour ent" ♦ 1 Apr-
31 Oct. € 15.95   2013*

CALAIS *3A3* (8km SW Rural) *50.91160, 1.75127* **Camping
Les Epinettes, Impasse de Mont Pinet, 62231 Peuplingues
[03 21 85 21 39; fax 03 21 85 26 95; lesepinettes@aol.com;
www.lesepinettes.fr]** A16 fr Calais to Boulogne, exit junc 40
W on D243 sp Peuplingues, go thro vill & foll sp; site on L in
3km. Med, hdg pitch, pt sl, pt shd; wc; chem disp; shwrs €1;
el pnts (4-6A) €2.70-3.60; lndtte; sm shop & 3km; hypmkt
5km; tradsmn; rest 1.5km; playgrnd; sand beach 3km;
80% statics; dogs €1.50; phone; wifi; Library; poss cr; adv
bkg; quiet; ccard acc; CKE/CCI. "Pleasant, easy-going site;
conv NH for ferries & tunnel; some pitches sm; san facs clean
but insufficient for site size; when bureau clsd, site yourself -
warden calls eve or call at cottage to pay; if arr late, park on
grass verge outside main gate - use facs excl elec, pay half
price; few touring pitches." 1 Apr-31 Oct. € 14.00   2013*

CALAIS *3A3* (5km W Coastal) *50.94610, 1.75798* **Camping
des Noires Mottes (formerly Cassiopée), Rue Pierre
Dupuy, 62231 Sangatte [tel/fax 03 21 82 04 75;
campingdesnoiresmottes@orange.fr; www.ville-sangatte.fr]**
Fr A16 exit junc 41 sp Sangatte onto D243, at T-junc in vill turn
R then R again bef monument. Lge, hdg/mkd pitch, pt sl, pt
shd; wc (some cont); chem disp; mv service pnt; shwrs inc (clsd
2130-0800); el pnts (10A) €4.10; lndtte; shop 200m; tradsmn;
playgrnd; sand beach 500m; 90% statics; dogs €1.30; bus
500m; poss cr; some Eng spkn; adv bkg rec high ssn; ccard not
acc; CKE/CCI. "Conv ferries & Eurotunnel; lge pitches; san facs
clean but need update (2010); barrier - no arr bef office opens
1500 (1600 low ssn); san facs clsd o'night & poss 1200-1600;
some pitches boggy when wet; windy spot; OK NH." ♦ ltd
01 Apr-31 Oct. € 15.95   2013*

CALVIAC EN PERIGORD see Sarlat la Canéda *7C3*

CAMARET SUR MER *2E1* (2km NE Coastal) *48.28070,
-4.56490* **Camping Le Grand Large, Lambézen, 29570
Camaret-sur-Mer [02 98 27 91 41; fax 02 98 27 93 72;
contact@campinglegrandlarge.com; www.
campinglegrandlarge.com]** On D8 bet Crozon & Camaret,
turn R at ent to Camaret onto D355, sp Roscanvel. Foll sps to
site in 3km. Med, hdg/mkd pitch, pt sl, pt shd; wc; chem disp;
mv service pnt; baby facs; shwrs inc; el pnts (10A) inc; gas;
lndtte (inc dryer); shop; tradsmn; snacks; bar; BBQ; playgrnd;
htd pool; paddling pool; sandy & shgl beach 500m; boating;
tennis; wifi; TV; dogs €1.50; adv bkg; quiet; ccard acc; red low
ssn. "Coastal views fr some pitches, lovely beach; pleasant,
helpful owners; cliff top walk to town; excel." ♦
1 Apr-30 Sep. € 26.50 (CChq acc)   2011*

CAMARET SUR MER *2E1* (3.5km NE Coastal) *48.28788,
-4.56540* **Camping Plage de Trez-Rouz, Route de
Camaret à Roscanvel, 29160 Crozon [02 98 27 93 96; fax
02 98 27 84 54; contact@trezrouz.com; www.trezrouz.com]**
Foll D8 to Camaret-sur-Mer & at rndabt turn N sp Roscanvel/
D355. Site on R in 3km. Med, hdg/mkd pitch, pt sl, pt shd; wc;
chem disp; mv service pnt; baby facs; shwrs inc; el pnts (16A)
€3.50; lndtte (inc dryer); shop; tradsmn; rest, snacks; playgrnd;
sand beach; tennis 500m; horseriding 2km; wifi; 10% statics;
dogs €1.50; poss cr; adv bkg; poss cr; quiet; CKE/CCI. "Great
position opp beach; conv for Presqu'île de Crozon; gd facs but
stretched high ssn; site scruffy low ssn; friendly owner." ♦
15 Mar-15 Oct. € 16.50   2010*

⊞ **CAMARET SUR MER** *2E1* (500m W Urban) *48.27698,
-4.60430* **Camp Municipal du Lannic, Rue du Grouanoc'h,
29570 Camaret-sur-Mer [02 98 27 91 31 or 02 98 27 94 22;
camaret@wanadoo.fr; www.camaret-sur-mer.com]**
On ent town foll sp to Port, on quayside to L turn sp Camping-
Golf Miniature/m'van parking. Foll sp to site in 500m behind
sports cent. Lge, pt sl, pt shd; wc; chem disp; mv service pnt;
baby facs; shwrs inc; el pnts €3; lndtte (inc dryer); shops 500m;
playgrnd; sand beach 500m; some statics; dogs €1.10; poss cr;
quiet. "Gd site bet town & beach; sections for vans & tents."
€ 12.00   2010*

CAMBIAC see Caraman *8F4*

FRANCE

CAMBO LES BAINS *8F1* (1.3km SW Rural) *43.35526, -1.41484* **Camping Bixta-Eder, Route de St Jean-de-Luz, 64250 Cambo-les-Bains [05 59 29 94 23; fax 05 59 29 23 70; contact@camping-bixtaeder.com; www.camping-bixtaeder.com]** Fr Bayonne on D932 (ignore 1st sp Cambo-les-Bains) exit at junc with D918 L twd Cambo. Site on L nr top of hill (Intermarché supmkt at by-pass junc). Med, mkd pitch, pt sl, pt shd; wc; baby facs; shwrs inc; el pnts (6-10A) €3.55-4; lndtte; shops 500m; rest, bar 100m; sand beach 20km; playgrnd; pool; tennis 400m; wifi; TV; dogs €1.50; poss cr; adv bkg; ccard acc; red low ssn/long stay. "Gd, well-run site; clean san facs; muddy when wet." ♦ 4 Apr-25 Oct. € 23.00   2011*

⊞ **CAMBO LES BAINS** *8F1* (3km SW Rural) *43.33863, -1.40129* **Camping L'Hiriberria, 64250 Itxassou [05 59 29 98 09; fax 05 59 29 20 88; hiriberria@wanadoo.fr; www.hiriberria.com]** Fr Cambo-les-Bains on D932 to Itxassou. Site on L 200m fr D918. Lge, hdg/mkd pitch, hdstg, pt sl, pt shd; htd wc (some cont); chem disp; mv service pnt; shwrs inc; baby facs; el pnts (5A) €3.25; gas; lndtte; shops 2km; tradsmn; rest, bar 1km; snacks 3km; BBQ; playgrnd; htd, covrd pool; rv 2km; games area; wifi; TV rm; 20% statics; dogs €1; Eng spkn; phone; quiet; 10% red 21+ days; CKE/CCI. "Popular site, phone ahead rec; gd views Pyrenees; pretty vill in 1km; some rd noise; vg walks; friendly owners." ♦ € 35.00   2013*

CAMBO LES BAINS *8F1* (5km W Rural) *43.33969, -1.47000* **Camping Alegera, 64250 Souraïde [05 59 93 91 80 / 06 13 76 66 87 (mob); www.camping-alegera.com]** Fr St Jean-de-Luz take D918 to Souraïde, site sp on L on rvside. Lge, hdg/mkd pitch, pt shd; wc (cont); chem disp; mv service pnt; baby facs; shwrs inc; el pnts (4-10A) €3.40-4 (poss rev pol); gas; lndtte; ice, shop (high ssn) & 150m; snacks; BBQ (gas/elec); playgrnd; pool; fishing 4km; games rm; tennis; golf; 10% statics; dogs €1.30; poss cr; adv bkg; quiet. "Excel for coast & Pyrenees; spacious pitches; red facs low ssn; pretty vill; v quiet, clean, lovely site" ♦ 1 Apr-31 Oct. € 17.80   2013*

CAMBRAI *3B4* (1km W Urban) *50.17533, 3.21534* **FFCC Camp Municipal Les Trois Clochers, 77 Rue Jean Goudé, 59400 Cambrai [03 27 70 91 64; camping@mairie-cambrai.fr; www.villedecambrai.com/decouverte.html]** Exit A2 junc 14; at rndabt after slip rd (with 6 exits) take D630 dir Cambrai; in 1km (by Buffalo Grill) turn L onto D630; in 200m turn L onto D939; in 100m turn L into Rue Jean Goudé. Or fr Cambrai W on D939; after x-ing rv bdge cont on D939 until traff lts in 300m; go strt over traff lts, then in 100m turn L into Rue Jean Goudé. Site sp fr all dirs on ent town. Sm, hdg pitch, unshd; htd wc; chem disp; mv service pnt; baby facs; shwrs inc; el pnts (5-8A) €2.50; shop, rest adj; Eng spkn; noise fr busy rd adj & early cockerel. "Beautiful, well-kept site; gd, spacious pitches; conv Calais; early arr rec high ssn; helpful, friendly manager; vg san facs but ltd & stretched when site full; interesting town; excel." ♦ 1 Apr-15 Oct. € 12.00   2013*

CAMIERS see Touquet Paris Plage, Le *3B2*

CAMON see Mirepoix (Ariege) *8F4*

CAMPAN see Bagnères de Bigorre *8F2*

CAMPOURIEZ see Entraygues sur Truyère *7D4*

CAMURAC see Belcaire *8G4*

CANCALE *2E4* (3km N Coastal) *48.70369, -1.84829* **Camp Municipal La Pointe du Grouin, 35260 Cancale [02 99 89 63 79 or 02 99 89 60 15; fax 02 99 89 54 25; campingcancale@orange.fr; www.ville-cancale.fr]** Take D76 twd Cancale & cont on D201 sp Pointe de Grouin; site on R in 3km on cliffs above sea, on N side of Cancale (diff to see, on RH bend mkd with chevrons); sp 'Camp Municipal'. Care req at ent. Med, pt sl, terr; wc (mainly cont); mv service pnt; shwrs inc; el pnts (8-13A) €3.30-4.30 (poss long lead req); lndtte; shop; rest in town; BBQ; playgrnd; rocky beach adj; watersports; fishing; dogs €1.65, Eng spkn; poss cr; quiet; ccard acc; red low ssn. "Lovely, well-kept site in gd location; sea views; some pitches uneven; excel san facs; gates clsd 2300-0700; conv Dinan, Mont-St Michel, St Malo; gd walking." 9 Mar-25 Oct. € 14.75   2013*

CANCALE *2E4* (6km S Coastal) *48.61893, -1.84946* **Camp Municipal des Ondes, Rue Bord de la Mer, 35114 St Benoît-des-Ondes [02 99 58 65 21]** In vill cent on D155. Med, unshd; wc; chem disp (wc); mv service pnt; shwrs inc; el pnts (6A) €2.55; lndtte; shop, rest, snacks adj; playgrnd; sand/shgl beach adj; dogs; phone; rd noise; CKE/CCI. "Site adj main rd; gd san facs; gd walking & cycling." 1 Jun-30 Sep. € 12.75   2009*

CANCALE *2E4* (6km S Coastal) *48.61592, -1.85151* **Camping de l'Ile Verte, 42 Rue de l'Ile Verte, 35114 St Benoît-des-Ondes [02 99 58 62 55; camping-ile-verte@sfr.fr; www.campingdelileverte.com]** Site on S side of vill. Fr Cancale, take D76 SW for approx 4km, then turn L onto D155 into St Benoît. Foll site sp. Sm, hdg pitch, pt shd; htd wc (cont); chem disp; mv service pnt; shwrs inc; el pnts (6A) €4 (poss rev pol); gas; lndtte; shop; rest, bar adj; playgrnd; sand beach adj; dog €2.50; 3% statics; phone; adv bkg; quiet; red low ssn; CKE/CCI; "Well-kept site on edge of vill; facs poss stretched high ssn." 30 Mar-2 Nov. € 30.15   2013*

CANCALE *2E4* (7km NW Coastal) *48.68861, -1.86833* **Camping Le Bois Pastel, 13 Rue de la Corgnais, 35260 Cancale [02 99 89 66 10; fax 02 99 89 60 11; camping.bois-pastel@wanadoo.fr; www.campingboispastel.fr]** Fr Cancale take D201 dir Pointe du Grouin & St Malo by Rte Touristique. Site sp on L 2.5km after Pointe du Grouin. Med, mkd pitch, pt shd; wc; shwrs inc; chem disp; mv service pnt; shwrs inc; el pnts (6A) €4; lndtte (inc dryer); shop; tradsmn; snacks; bar; BBQ; playgrnd; htd, covrd pool; paddling pool; sand beach 800m; fishing; games area; games rm; 25% statics; dogs €2.50; adv bkg; quiet; red long stay/low ssn. "Conv Mont-St Michel, St Malo; gd touring base." 1 Apr-30 Sep. € 22.00   2012*

FRANCE

CANCALE 2E4 (2km W Rural) 48.68823, -1.86061 **Camping La Ville ès Poulain, 35260 Cancale [02 99 89 87 47; www. ville-cancale.fr]** Turn of D201 coast rd on o'skts of town onto D355 at traff lts. Turn R at rndabt by bar & foll sp; site in 1km. Sm, hdg pitch, pt shd; wc; chem disp; shwrs; el pnts (10A) €2.60; lndry rm; supmkt 1.5km; sand beach 2km; dog €1; quiet; no ccard acc; CKE/CCI. "CL-type site; lge pitches; gd base but no views - entire site surrounded by high hdg; conv St-Malo ferry & Mont St Michel." 15 Apr-30 Sep. € 13.50   2010*

CANCON 7D3 (5km N Rural) 44.57728, 0.62128 **Camp Municipal de St Chavit, 47290 Lougratte [05 53 01 68 25; fax 05 53 41 18 04; mairie.lougratte@wanadoo.fr; www. lougratte.com]** N on N21 fr Cancon, site at lake, L turn 50m bef church, site seen fr rd 500m fr turn. Med, pt hdg pitch, pt shd; wc; chem disp (wc); shwrs; el pnts (10A) €2.70; lndtte; shop 500m; bar; BBQ; playgrnd; games rm; sand beach; boating; fishing; tennis nr; phone; v quiet. "Nice position; spacious; clean san facs high ssn; warden calls eves; gd touring base; highly rec." ♦ 15 Jun-15 Sep. € 8.60   2010*

CANCON 7D3 (2km E Rural) 44.52358, 0.63987 **Camp Municipal Le Lac, 47290 Cancon [05 53 36 54 30 or 05 53 01 60 24 (Mairie); fax 05 53 01 64 70; mairie. cancon@wanadoo.fr; www.cancon.fr/cancon_cadre.htm]** Sp fr N21 on both sides of Cancon & in town. Med, mkd pitch, pt sl, shd; wc; shwrs inc; el pnts (10A) €3.30; lndtte; shop 2km; rest, snacks; bar; playgrnd; pool; fishing; games area; dogs €1; no twin-axles; CKE/CCI. "Peaceful site in woodland & lake setting; opening dates poss unrel." 15 Jun-15 Sep. € 8.45   2008*

⊞ **CANCON** 7D3 (8km W Rural) 44.53461, 0.50555 **Camping Le Moulin, Lassalle, 47290 Monbahus [05 53 01 68 87; info@lemoulin-monbahus.com; www.lemoulin-monbahus.com]** Fr N21 turn W at Cancon on D124 sp Miramont. In 7.5km at Monbahus pass thro vill cent take L turn, still on D124 sp Tombeboeuf. In 3km lge grain silos on L, site next on R. Sm, mkd pitch, hdstg, pt shd; wc; chem disp; shwrs inc; fam bthrm; el pnts (5-10A) €3 (most pitches 5A only avail); lndtte; tradsmn; shop 3km; bistro; snacks; BBQ; playgrnd; htd pool; lake 5km; cycle hire; wifi; entmnt; dogs; poss cr; Eng spkn; adv bkg; some rd noise; ccard not acc; CKE/ CCI. "CL-type site in garden; friendly British owners; clean, basic san facs; vg pool; B & B avail; extra for twin-axles over 5m; excel." € 13.00   2010*

CANCON 7D3 (12km NW Rural) 44.61653, 0.51841 **Camping La Vallée de Gardeleau, 47410 Sérignac-Péboudou [tel/ fax 05 53 36 96 96; valleegardeleau@wanadoo.fr; http:// camping.valleegardeleau.fr.pagesperso-orange.fr]** Fr Cancon take N21 N; turn L twds Montauriol & Sérignac-Péboudou; foll camping sp. Sm, hdg pitch, pt sl, shd; wc; chem disp; shwrs inc; el pnts (5A) €3.15 (poss rev pol); gas 5km; lndtte; shop & 5km; tradsmn; rest, snacks; bar; playgrnd; pool; lake fishing 2km; entmnt; 8% statics; dogs €2.50; phone; poss cr; Eng spkn; adv bkg; quiet; ccard acc; red low ssn; CKE/CCI. "Calm & peaceful atmosphere; v shady; sm pitches; friendly, helpful owners; grnd soft after heavy rain; nr Bastide towns." ♦ 22 Mar-31 Oct. € 14.05   2008*

CANDE SUR BEUVRON 4G2 (500m S Rural) 47.48952, 1.25834 **Kawan Village La Grande Tortue, 3 Route de Pontlevoy, 41120 Candé-sur-Beuvron [02 54 44 15 20; fax 02 54 44 19 45; contact@la-grande-tortue.com; www. la-grande-tortue.com]** Exit A10 junc 17 (Blois); at rbdabt after toll foll 'Toutes Directions' to cross Rv Loire on D951 sp Chaumant & Amboise; at rndabt on S side of Rv Loire turn R onto D751 sp Chaumant & Amboise; cont on D751 to Candé-sur-Beuvron (ignore D173, R fork); immed after x-ing Rv Beuvron at Candé fork R (keeping on D751); site on L in 400m. Lge, hdg/mkd pitch, some hdstg, pt sl, pt shd; htd wc (some cont); chem disp; mv service pnt; baby facs; shwrs inc; el pnts (10A) €3.50; gas; lndtte (inc dryer); shop; tradsmn; rest, snacks; bar; BBQ; playgrnd; htd, covrd pool; paddling pool; cycle hire; horseriding; games area; wifi; entmnt; TV rm; 25% statics; dogs €3.70; Eng spkn; adv bkg; quiet; ccard acc; red low ssn; CKE/CCI. "Excel, rustic site amongst trees; poss diff access due trees; helpful staff; vg, clean san facs; gd pool; gd for children; gd cycling; gourmet rest by rv bdge in village; conv Loire chateaux." ♦ 1 Apr-25 Sep. € 29.00 (CChq acc) 2011*

See advertisement

CANET DE SALARS see Pont de Salars 7D4

CANET EN ROUSSILLON see Canet Plage 10G1

CANET PLAGE *10G1* (3km N Coastal) *42.70808, 3.03332*
Camping Le Brasilia, 2 Ave des Anneux du Roussillon,
66140 Canet-en-Roussillon [04 68 80 23 82; fax
04 68 73 32 97; contact@brasilia.fr; www.brasilia.fr or
www.yellohvillage.co.uk] Exit A9 junc 41 sp Perpignan Nord
& Rivesaltes onto D83 dir Le Barcarès & Canet for 10km; then
take D81 dir Canet for 10km until lge rndabt which goes under
D617 (do not foll sp to Canet to R) - cont round rndabt & foll sp
Ste Marie-le-Mer (to go back the way you came). Then take 1st
R sp Le Brasilia. V lge, hdg/mkd pitch, pt shd, wc (some cont);
chem disp; all serviced pitch; mv service pnt; baby facs; shwrs
inc; el pnts (10A) inc; gas; lndtte (inc dryer); supmkt; tradsmn;
rest, snacks; bar; BBQ (gas/elec); playgrnd; htd pool high ssn;
paddling pool; direct access to sand beach 150m; fishing; tennis;
cycle hire; archery; wifi; entmnt; games/TV rm; 35% statics; dogs
€4; twin-axles acc (rec check in adv); bus to Canet; Eng spkn;
quiet but poss noisy entmnt; ccard acc; red low ssn; CKE/CCI.
"Excel, well-run, well laid-out site; gd sized pitches; friendly staff;
immac san facs; excel facs, espec for families/children/teenagers;
in Jul & Aug identity card for pool - passport size photo needed;
rvside walk adj; conv day trips to Andorra; daily mkt in Canet
except Mon." ♦ 21 Apr-29 Sep. € 53.67 SBS - C01   2011*

CANET PLAGE *10G1* (4km N Coastal) *42.73897, 3.03355*
Camp Municipal de la Plage, Ave de Las-Illas, 66470
Ste Marie-Plage [04 68 80 68 59; fax 04 68 73 14 70;
contact@camping-municipal-de-la-plage.com; www.
camping-municipal-de-la-plage.com] Exit A9 junc 41 onto
D83, then D81 to Ste Marie-Plage. Look for sm red sp, site
adj Camping La Palais de la Mer. Lge, hdg pitch, pt shd; wc;
chem disp; mv service pnt; baby facs; shwrs; el pnts (6A) inc;
lndtte; shop; rest, snacks; bar; BBQ; playgrnd; pool; paddling
pool; sand beach adj; games area; games rm; cycle hire; TV;
30% statics; dogs €2.40; poss cr; Eng spkn; adv bkg; quiet;
CKE/CCI. "Direct access to beach; v busy high ssn." ♦ ltd
1 Mar-31 Oct. € 32.00   2010*

CANET PLAGE *10G1* (4km N) Camping La Pergola, 66140
Ste Marie la Mer [02 51 20 41 94; contact@camp-
atlantique.com; www.campinglapergola.com]
S fr Narbonne, exit N9 at Salses & foll D11 to St Marie-sur-
Mer. St Marie-Plage beach for St Marie-sur-Mer. Site not sp
but on D12 to coast. Lge, pt shd; wc (cont); shwrs inc; gas;
shops; el pnts; sand beach 500m; adv bkg; quiet. Apr-Sep.
€ 12.35   2012*

See advertisement above

CANET PLAGE *10G1* (500m S Coastal) *42.67540, 3.03120*
Camping Club Mar Estang, Route de St Cyprien, 66140
Canet-Plage [04 68 80 55 53; fax 04 68 73 32 94; contact@
marestang.com; www.marestang.com] Exit A9 junc 41
Perpignan Nord dir Canet, then foll sp St Cyprien, site sp. Site
on D81A bet Canet-Plage & St Cyprien-Plage. V lge, mkd pitch,
hdstg, pt shd; wc; chem disp; mv service pnt; baby facs; shwrs
inc; el pnts (6A) €7; gas; lndtte; shop; tradsmn; rest, snacks;
bar; playgrnd; htd pool; paddling pool; waterslide; private sand
beach adj; tennis; cycle hire; fitness rm; TV rm; 50% statics;
dogs €4; Eng spkn; adv bkg; quiet; ccard acc; red low ssn/
long stay/CKE/CCI. "Conv Spanish border & Pyrenees; gd
birdwatching." ♦ 23 Apr-17 Sep. € 37.00   2011*

CANET PLAGE *10G1* (4km W Rural) *42.68914, 2.99877*
FFCC Camping Les Fontaines, Route de St Nazaire,
66140 Canet-en-Roussillon [tel/fax 04 68 80 22 57 or
06 77 90 14 91 (mob); campinglesfontaines@wanadoo.fr;
www.camping-les-fontaines.com] Take D11 fr Canet dir
St Nazaire; site sp on L in 1.5km. Easy access. Lge, hdg/mkd
pitch, unshd; wc; chem disp; mv service pnt; baby facs; fam
bathrm; shwrs inc; el pnts (10A) €3.50; gas 2km; lndtte (inc
dryer); shop & 1km; tradsmn; snacks; bar; BBQ (gas/elec);
playgrnd; pool; paddling pool; sand beach 2.5km; games area;
wifi; entmnt; 30% statics; dogs €3.50; bus; phone; Eng spkn;
adv bkg; quiet. "Pitches lge; conv Etang de Canet et St Nazaire
nature reserve with flamingos; excel; relaxed atmosphere;
friendly staff" 1 May-30 Sep. € 30.00   2013*

FRANCE

CANET PLAGE *10G1* (4km W Urban) *42.70114, 2.99850*
Kawan Village Ma Prairie, 1 Ave des Coteaux, 66140 Canet-en-Roussillon [04 68 73 26 17; fax 04 68 73 28 82; ma.prairie@wanadoo.fr; www.maprairie.com] Leave A9/E15 at junc 41, sp Perpignan Centre/Canet-en-Roussillon. Take D83, then D81 until Canet-en-Roussillon. At rndabt, take D617 dir Perpignan & in about 500m leave at exit 5. Take D11 dir St Nazaire, pass under bdge & at rndabt turn R. Site on L. Lge, hdg pitch, shd; wc; chem disp; mv service pnt; baby facs; serviced pitches; shwrs inc; el pnts (10A) inc; gas; lndtte (inc dryer); supmkt adj; tradsmn; rest, snacks; bar; BBQ (gas/elec); playgrnd; pool; paddling pool; waterslide; sand beach 3km; waterskiing; sailing; canoeing; wifi; entmnt; games/TV rm; 20% statics; dogs €3; c'vans/m'vans 7.50m & over by request; bus to town nr; poss cr; Eng spkn; adv bkg ess Aug; quiet; rd noise some pitches; ccard acc; red low ssn; CKE/CCI. "Peaceful, popular site; friendly, helpful owners; reg bus to beach (Jul/Aug); daily mkt Perpignan; gd." ♦
5 May-25 Sep. € 43.00 (CChq acc) SBS - C05   2011*

See advertisement below

CANNES *10F4* (3km NE Urban) *43.55610, 6.96060* **Camping Parc Bellevue, 67 Ave Maurice Chevalier, 06150 Cannes [04 93 47 28 97; fax 04 93 48 66 25; contact@parcbellevue.com; www.parcbellevue.com]** A8 exit junc 41 twd Cannes. Foll N7 & at junc controlled by traff lts, get in L lane. Turn L & in 100m turn L across dual c'way, foll sp for site. Site in 400m on L after sports complex - steep ramp at ent. Lge, mkd pitch, pt shd; wc; chem disp; baby facs; shwrs; el pnts (6A) €4; gas; lndtte; shops; rest, snacks; bar; htd pool; sandy beach 1.5km; wifi; entmnt; sat TV; many statics; dogs; phone; bus/train nr; poss cr; Eng spkn; adv bkg; rd noise; red low ssn; CKE/CCI. "Site on 2 levels; gd security; gd san facs; some pitches long way fr facs; many steps to gd pool; helpful; conv beaches & A8; green oasis in busy area; gd bus to prom; no m'van facs; rec use sat nav; not rec in wet weather; no hdstg; outfits have to be towed off pitches in bad weather." ♦ ltd 1 Apr-30 Sep. € 17.50 (CChq acc)   2013*

CANNES *10F4* (4km NW Urban) *43.56469, 6.97765* **Ranch Camping, L'Aubarède, Chemin de St Joseph, 06110 Le Cannet [04 93 46 00 11; fax 04 93 46 44 30; www.leranchcamping.fr]** Exit A8 at junc 42 Le Cannet. Foll sp L'Aubarède & then La Bocca. Site well sp via D9. Med, hdg pitch, pt sl, terr, pt shd; htd wc (some cont); baby facs; shwrs inc; el pnts (6A) inc; lndtte (inc dryer); shop; tradsmn; playgrnd; htd, covrd pool; sand beach 2km; games area; wifi; 10% statics; dogs €1; bus; adv bkg summer ssn ess by March; some rd noise; quiet. "Conv location; pitches at cent or top of site quieter; vg, modern san facs; gd." ♦ 1 Apr-30 Oct. € 25.00   2009*

CANNES *10F4* (9km NW) *43.59005, 6.92376* **FFCC Caravaning Les Mimosas, Quartier Cabrol, 06580 Pégomas [04 93 42 36 11; fax 04 93 60 92 74]** Site on L of D109 Mandelieu to Grasse. Exit A8 junc 41 at Mandelieu turn R & foll sp to Pégomas on D9. Turn L immed bef rv bdge app Pégomas. Med, hdg/mkd pitch, shd; wc; chem disp; mv service pnt; baby facs; shwrs inc; el pnts (5A) inc; lndtte; shop; rest, bar 1km; snacks; playgrnd; pool; sand beach 8km; fishing in rv adj; games area; entmnt; 40% statics; dogs €1.60; adv bkg; quiet; ccard acc; CKE/CCI. "Pleasant site; conv for Cannes, Côte d'Azur & mountain vills; poor san facs; dogs roaming site; night security guard in ssn; barrier clsd 2300-0600." ♦ ltd Easter-31 Oct. € 20.00   2008*

CANOURGUE, LA *9D1* (2km E Rural) *44.40789, 3.24178* **Camping Le Val d'Urugne, Route des Gorges-du-Tarn, 48500 La Canourgue [04 66 32 84 00; fax 04 66 32 88 14; lozereleisure@wanadoo.fr; www.lozereleisure.com]** Exit A75 junc 40 dir La Canourgue; thro vill dir Gorges-du-Tarn. In 2km site on R 600m after golf clubhouse. Sm, hdg pitch, pt sl, pt shd; wc; chem disp; mv service pnt; shwrs inc; el pnts (6A) €3.50; lndtte; shop (high ssn) & 2km; tradsmn; rest, snacks, bar at golf club; TV rm; some chalets adj; dogs €2; Eng spkn; adv bkg; quiet; ccard acc; red low ssn; CKE/CCI. "Vg site; golf adj; conv A75 & Gorges-du-Tarn; low ssn stop at golf club for key to site; site poss tired end of ssn." ♦ ltd 1 May-30 Sep. € 14.50   2009*

CANOURGUE, LA 9D1 (1km SE Rural) 44.44238, 3.19646
Camping La Mothe, 75 Route d'Espagne, 48500 Banassac
[04 66 32 88 11 or 04 66 32 97 37; fax 04 66 32 97 37]
Leave A75 at junc 40, foll sp D998 La Canourgue. Take
2nd exit at each of 2 rndabts sp St Geniez-d'Olt N9 twds La
Mothe. Site on L in 300m immed over Rv Lot. Med, shd; wc
(some cont); chem disp (wc); shwrs inc; el pnts (6A) €3; lndtte;
supmkt 1.5km; rest 2km; snacks; bar; BBQ; playgrnd; rv sw &
fishing 1.5km; dogs €1; some rd noise; CKE/CCI. "Basic site by
Rv Lot; gd for birdwatching & fishing; interesting area; phone
ahead to check opening dates; no warden on site end ssn." ♦
1 Apr-30 Oct. € 11.00   2008*

⊞ **CANY BARVILLE** 3C2 (3km N Rural) 49.80375, 0.64960
Camping Maupassant, 12 Route de la Folie, 76450
Vittefleur [tel/fax 02 35 97 97 14; campingmaupassant@
orange.fr; www.camping-maupassant.com] S fr St Valery-
en-Caux on D925 dir Cany-Barville; site sp turning to R 700m
bef Cany-Barville. Med, hdg/mkd pitch, hdstg, pt shd; htd wc;
chem disp; mv service pnt; baby facs; shwrs €1.70; el pnts (6A)
€3.30; gas; lndtte (inc dryer); shop, rest, snacks & bar 6km;
BBQ (charcoal); some statics; dogs; phone; adv bkg; quiet; CKE/
CCI. "Friendly staff; gd NH" 9 Mar-14 Dec. € 16.60   2013*

CANY BARVILLE 3C2 (500m S Urban) 49.78335, 0.64214
Camp Municipal, Route de Barville, 76450 Cany-Barville
[02 35 97 70 37; fax 02 35 97 72 32; camping@cany-barville.fr;
www.cany-barville.fr] Sp fr town cent, off D268 to S of
town, adj stadium. Med, hdg/mkd pitch, hdstg, pt shd; htd wc;
chem disp; mv service pnt; shwrs inc; el pnts (10A) €3.25 (poss
rev pol); lndtte; shop 500m; playgrnd; pool 1km; lake 1.5km;
25% statics; dogs €1.25; adv bkg; poss noisy at w/ends & late
evenings; ccard acc; red long stay; CKE/CCI. "Vg facs but poss
stretched at high ssn; poss no check-in on Sun; within reach of
Dieppe & Fécamp chateau; gd cycling; poss market traders on
site." ♦ 1 Apr-30 Sep. € 11.30   2010*

CAPELLE LES BOULOGNE, LA see Boulogne sur Mer 3A2

CAPESTANG 10F1 (500m W Urban) 43.32759, 3.03865 **Camp**
Municipal de Tounel, 1 Rue Georges Brassens, Ave de
la République, 34310 Capestang [04 67 93 34 23 (TO) or
06 07 97 52 09 (mob); oacinfocapestang@orange.fr; www.
ville-capestang.fr] Fr Béziers on D11, turn R twd vill of
Capestang, approx 1km after passing supermarket. Site on L
in leisure park opp Gendamarie. Med, hdg pitch, pt shd; wc
(cont); chem disp; shwrs; el pnts (6A) €3; lndtte; shops, rest
500m; playgrnd; fishing; tennis; cycle hire; internet; dogs free;
rd noise. "300m fr Canal du Midi; excel walks or cycle rides;
lovely rest in vill; low ssn site yourself, fees collected; facs poss
tired low ssn; poss diff access to pitches for long o'fits; ltd
el pnts; poss resident workers; NH only." ♦ 1 May-30 Sep.
€ 12.00   2011*

CAPVERN see Lannemezan 8F2

CARAMAN 8F4 (5km SE Rural) 43.48123, 1.79511 **FFCC**
Camping La Ferme du Tuillié, 31460 Cambiac [05 61 83 30 95
or 06 88 16 27 14 (mob); fax 05 62 18 52 48; www.couleur-
lauragais.fr/camping-tuillie] Fr Toulouse E onto D826; in 30km
turn R onto D11 to Caraman; cont thro vill onto D25; in 4km
turn L onto D18; site on L in 500m. Sm, hdg/mkd pitch, hdstg,
unshd; wc; chem disp; mv service pnt; shwrs inc; el pnts (6A)
inc; lndry rm; tradsmn; BBQ; playgrnd; cycle hire; fishing; TV;
5 statics; phone adj; adv bkg; quiet; no ccard acc. "Beautiful,
remote site by lake; friendly owners; excel." ♦ 1 Apr-30 Oct.
€ 13.00   2008*

CARANTEC see St Pol de Léon 1D2

CARCANS 7C1 (8km W Rural) 45.06657, -1.13903 **Camping**
Le Maubuisson, 81 Ave de Maubuisson, 33121 Carcans
[05 56 03 30 12; fax 05 56 03 47 93; camping.maubuisson@
orange.fr; www.camping-maubuisson.com] Fr D1215 at
Castelnau-de-Médoc turn W onto D207 to Carcans & onto
Maubuisson, in vill camp ent on L, sp. V lge, mkd pitch, pt sl,
shd; wc; baby facs; shwrs inc; el pnts (5A) €3.50; gas; lndtte;
shop; rest, snacks; bar; playgrnd; sand beach 3km; lake sw
100m; fishing; watersports; windsurfing; tennis; some statics;
dogs €1.60; poss cr; adv bkg; quiet. "Site in wooded park;
conv Médoc wine region & many sandy beaches." ♦
1 Mar-30 Nov. € 19.60   2009*

CARCASSONNE 8F4 (5km N Rural) 43.25999, 2.36509 **FFCC**
Camping Das Pinhiers, Chemin du Pont Neuf, 11620
Villemoustaussou [04 68 47 81 90; fax 04 68 71 43 39;
campingdaspinhiers@wanadoo.fr; www.camping-
carcassonne.net] Exit A6 junc 23 Carcassonne Ouest & foll
sp Mazamet on D118; R at rndabt with filling stn; turn R &
foll camping sp. Med, hdg pitch, pt sl, shd; wc; chem disp; mv
service pnt; shwrs inc; el pnts (10A) inc; shop (high ssn) & 1km;
rest, snacks; bar; playgrnd; pool; 10% statics; no twin-axles;
dogs €3; bus 1 km; Eng spkn; adv bkg; quiet; ccard acc; red
low ssn; CKE/CCI. "Diiff to pitch lge vans due hdg pitches &
sl; san facs basic & stretched high ssn; general area rather run
down (2009); Office clsd noon-2pm" ♦ ltd 1 Mar-31 Oct.
€ 23.90   2013*

CARCASSONNE 8F4 (10km NE Rural) 43.28305, 2.44166
Camping Le Moulin de Ste Anne, Chemin de Ste Anne,
11600 Villegly-en-Minervois [04 68 72 20 80; fax
04 68 72 27 15; campingstanne@wanadoo.fr; www.
moulindesainteanne.com] Leave A61 junc 23 Carcassonne
Ouest dir Mazamet; after approx 14km onto D620 to Villegly,
site sp at ent to vill. NB Turning R off D620 hidden by trees,
then over narr bdge; long o'fits need wide swing in. Med,
hdg/mkd pitch, pt sl, terr, unshd; htd wc; chem disp (wc); mv
service pnt; baby facs; shwrs inc; el pnts (10A) inc; lndtte; shop
300m; tradsmn; snacks; bar; BBQ; playgrnd; htd pool; sand
beach 60km; games area; wifi; 25% statics; dogs €3.50; poss
cr; adv bkg; Eng spkn; quiet; ccard acc; min 3 nights high ssn;
red long stay/low ssn; CKE/CCI. "Pretty, clean site; lge pitches;
friendly, helpful owner; ltd san facs; pitches poss diff/muddy
in wet; gd touring base; poss local youths congregate on
motorbikes nrby in eve; vg." ♦ 1 Mar-29 Oct. € 23.00   2010*

CARCASSONNE *8F4* (6km E Rural) *43.20700, 2.44258* **FFCC**
**Camping à l'Ombre des Micocouliers, Chemin de la Lande,
11800 Trèbes [04 68 78 61 75 or 04 68 78 88 77 (LS); fax
04 68 78 88 77; infos@campingmicocouliers.com; www.
campingmicocouliers.com]** Fr Carcassonne, take D6113 E for
6km to Trèbes; go under rlway bdge; fork L onto D610; turn R
immed bef rv bdge; site on L in 200m. Site sp. Med, mkd pitch,
shd; wc; chem disp; mv service pnt; shwrs (up steps); el pnts
(6A) €3; lndtte; shop in ssn; rest in ssn; snacks; BBQ; htd, covrd
pool nr,entmnt; rv fishing; TV; no statics; dogs €1.50; phone;
poss cr; some Eng spkn; red low ssn; CKE/CCI. "Pleasant, sandy
site by rv; well shaded; friendly staff, gd san facs, 1 block up 15
steps; ltd el pnts; Trèbes in walking dist; vg cycling, 13 km cycle
to Carcassonne along canal; gd base Canal du Midi; can be
noisy from local youths on mbikes; walk into town needs care
with busy rd" ♦ 1 Apr-30 Sep. € 32.30   2013*

CARCASSONNE *8F4* (10km E Rural) *43.21498, 2.47031*
**Camping La Commanderie, 6 Chemin Eglise,11800
Rustiques [04 68 78 67 63 or 06 25 28 35 80 (m);
contact@campinglacommanderie.com; www.
campinglacommanderie.com]** Fr Carcassonne take D6113/
D610 E to Trèbes (approx 8km); at Trèbes take D610 &
after 2km L onto D906, then L onto D206; site on R; foll sp
'Rustiques'. Or fr A61 ext junc 24 onto D6113 to Trèbes & then
as bef. Sm, mkd pitch, pt sl, pt shd, htd wc; chem disp; shwrs
inc; el pnts (6A) inc; lndtte; shop 1km; tradsmn; rest, snacks;
bar; playgrnd; pool; wifi; 10% statics; dogs €2; phone; quiet;
adv bkg; Eng spkn; quiet; ccard acc; red low ssn; CKE/CCI.
"Pleasant, helpful owner & staff; modern san facs; patron sells
own wines; gd cycling along canal fr Trèbes; conv A61; gd NH
en rte Spain; excel." 1 Apr-15 Oct. € 22.00   2013*

CARCASSONNE *8F4* (2km SE Rural) *43.19994, 2.35271*
**Camping d la Cité, Route de St Hilaire, 11000 Carcassonne
[04 68 10 01 00; fax 04 68 47 33 13; campingdelacite@
carcassonne.fr; www.camping-delacite-carcassonne.com]**
Fr N & W exit Carcassonne by D6113 twd Narbonne; cross rv
& turn S onto D104; foll sp. Fr S (D118) take D104 to E & foll sp.
Fr E (D6113) take D342 S to D104; foll sp. Or exit A61 junc 23;
at rndabt in 900m turn R onto D6161 sp Limoux; at traff lts in
1km turn L onto D118 sp La Cité; at rndabt in 700m turn R over
rv for D104; in 600m turn L at rndabt onto D104 sp Camping
La Cité; site on L in 1.4km. Or exit A61 junc 24 to D6113 sp
Carcassonne; stay on rd until sp La Cité; cont to sp Camping
La Cité. NB Site (La Cité) well sp fr all dirs & easy access fr A61
junc 23. Lge, hdg/mkd pitch, pt shd; wc (some cont); chem disp;
mv service pnt; shwrs inc; el pnts (10A) inc (poss rev pol); lndry
rm; shops 1.5km; tradsmn; rest, snacks; bar; playgrnd; pool
(high ssn); tennis; wifi; entmnt; some statics; dogs €3.50; Eng
spkn; adv bkg (rec high ssn - min 7 days); quiet with some rd
noise; ccard acc; red low ssn; CKE/CCI. "Delightful, well-kept
site in gd location adj woods; popular - bkg arr bef 1600; mixed
pitch sizes & types; friendly, helpful staff; san facs need refurb &
stretched high ssn, poss irreg cleaning low ssn (2009); ltd water
& waste water pnts; many leisure facs; parking area for waiting
if office clsd, 1200-1400 low ssn; pleasant, well-lit walk along rv
to La Cité; muddy after rain; no twin-axles; high ssn o'spill area
without el pnts; excel site for visiting Carcassonne " ♦
02 Apr-13 Oct. € 44.90   2013*

⊞ **CARCASSONNE** *8F4* (5km S Rural) *43.17938, 2.37024*
**Camping à l'Ombre des Oliviers, Ave du Stade, 11570
Cazilhac [tel/fax 04 68 79 65 08 or 06 81 54 96 00 (mob);
florian.romo@wanadoo.fr; www.alombredesoliviers.com]**
Fr N & W exit Carcassonne by D6113 dir Narbonne. Cross rv
& turn S onto D104, then D142/D56 to Cazilhac, site sp. Sm,
pt shd; wc; baby facs; shwrs inc; el pnts (6-10A) €3 (poss rev
pol); lndry rm; supmkt in vill; bar; BBQ; playgrnd; pool; tennis;
games area; TV; 10% statics; dogs €2; site clsd 1st week
Jan; poss v cr; adv bkg; quiet; red low ssn. "Site in pleasant
position; if office clsd phone owner on mobile, or site yourself;
helpful owners; v ltd facs low ssn; insufficient san facs when
site full & ltd other facs; few water pnts; pitches poss muddy/
soft when wet; bus to old city nrby." € 22.00   2013*

"I like to fill in the reports as I travel from site to site"

You'll find report forms at the back of
this guide, or you can fill them in online
at www.caravaclub.co.uk/europereport.

CARCASSONNE *8F4* (7km S Rural) *43.1588, 2.2930* **Airotel**
**Camping Grand Sud, Route de Limoux, 11250 Preixan
[04 68 26 88 18; fax 04 68 26 85 07; sudfrance@wanadoo.fr;
www.camping-grandsud.com]** A61 exit junc 23 at
Carcassonne Ouest onto D118 dir Limoux. Site visible fr rd on
lakeside at end of dual-carriageway section. Lge, hdg/mkd
pitch, hdstg, pt shd; wc; chem disp; mv service pnt; baby facs;
shwrs inc; el pnts (6A) inc (poss rev pol); lndtte (inc dryer);
shop; tradsmn; rest, snacks; bar; BBQ; playgrnd; htd pool;
waterslide; private access to rv; fishing; boating; horseriding;
tennis; games area; games rm; wifi; entmnt; TV; 50% statics;
dogs €4; adv bkg; quiet; ccard acc; red low ssn; CKE/CCI.
"Pleasant, attractive site by lake; easy access A61; friendly,
helpful owners; gd rest; wild fowl reserve; conv Carcassonne;
gd walking; excel." 1 Apr-15 Sep. € 30.00   2010*

CARCASSONNE *8F4* (12km SW Rural) *43.12410, 2.26080*
**Yelloh! Village Domaine d'Arnauteille, 11250 Montclar
[04 68 26 84 53; fax 04 68 26 91 10; info@arnauteille.com;
www.arnauteille.com or www.yellohvillage.co.uk]**
Fr Carcassonne take D118 S twd Limoux. Turn R bef end of
sm section dual c'way (not 1st section) & foll sp to Montclar.
Site approx 2.5km on L. NB Site app along single track - site
ent steep & narr & sp v insignificant on gatepost & driveway
appears to be to private house. V lge, hdg/mkd pitch, pt sl,
terr, pt shd; htd wc; chem disp; mv service pnt; some serviced
pitches; baby facs; fam bthrm; shwrs inc; el pnts (6-10A) inc;
gas; lndtte; shop; tradsmn; rest, snacks; bar; playgrnd; pool;
waterpark; horseriding; fishing 2km; golf 14km; games rm;
games area; entmnt; internet; TV rm; 70% statics; dogs €4;
Eng spkn; adv bkg; v quiet; ccard acc; red low ssn; CKE/CCI.
"Vg site but huge & impersonal; wonderful views; helpful
staff; superb pool complex & facs; excel rest; steep site rds;
siting poss diff in wet weather; site muddy after rain." ♦
9 Apr-25 Sep. € 39.00   2010*

See advertisement on inside front cover

FRANCE

CARCASSONNE *8F4* (15km NW Rural) *43.29861, 2.22277*
Camping de Montoliu, L'Olivier, 11170 Montoliu
[04 68 76 95 01 or 06 31 90 31 92 (mob); nicole@camping-
de-montolieu.com; www.camping-de-montolieu.com]
Fr D6113 4km W Carcassonne, take D629 twd Montoliu; site
on R in 2.5km after Moussoulens. Sp fr D6113, approx 5km
dist. App thro Montoliu not rec. Sm, hdg/mkd pitch, pt shd;
wc; chem disp; shwrs inc; el pnts (5A) inc; gas; lndtte; shops
1.5km; tradsmn; rest, snacks, bar 100m; BBQ; pool 100m;
games area; games rm; wifi; few statics; dogs €2; phone;
adv bkg; some rd noise; red low ssn; CKE/CCI. "Well-run
site in lovely countryside; manoeuvring tight; excel facs; conv
Carcassonne; highly rec." ♦ 1 Mar-31 Oct. € 15.00   2010*

CARCES *10F3* (500m SE Urban) *43.47350, 6.18826* **Camping
Les Fouguières, Quartier Les Fouguières, 83570 Carcès**
[34 94 59 96 28 or 06 74 29 69 02 (mob); fax 34 94 59 96 28;
info@camping-les-fouguieres.com; www.camping-les-
fouguieres.com] Exit A8 junc 35 at Brignoles onto D554 to Le
Val; then take D562 to Carcès. Site sp off D13. Med, pt shd;
wc; mv service pnt; shwrs inc; el pnts (14A) €3; gas; lndtte;
snacks; playgrnd; pool; Rv Caramy runs thro site; rv sw, fishing
& canoeing nrby; wifi; TV; many statics; dogs €2; phone; bus;
Eng spkn; quiet; red low ssn. "Pleasant, clean, well-shaded
site; friendly, helpful owner; interesting, medieval town; Lake
Carcès 2km; don't miss Entrecasteaux chateau; mkt Sat; excel."
♦ 6 Feb-26 Nov. € 19.00   2010*

CARENNAC *7C4* (1km SE Rural) *44.90985, 1.74070*
Camping L'Eau Vive, Route de St Céré, 46100 Carennac
[05 65 10 97 39; fax 05 55 28 12 12; info@dordogne-soleil.
com; www.dordogne-soleil.com] Exit A20 junc 53 or 54
onto D803/D840 to Martel; then D803 to Bétaille in 10km; turn
R onto D20 dir Carennac; in 3km cross rv; in 300m turn L onto
D30; site on L in 400m. Med, hdg/mkd pitch, pt shd; wc (cont);
chem disp; mv service pnt; baby facs; shwrs inc; el pnts (6A)
€3.20; gas; lndtte (inc dryer); sm shop & 1km; tradsmn; snacks;
bar; BBQ; playgrnd; pool; paddling pool; rv sw, shgl beach
adj; white water rafting; canoeing; fishing; horseriding nrby;
tennis; cycle hire (cycle rtes fr site); games area; games rm; wifi;
entmnt; TV; 20% statics; dogs €2.20; phone; Eng spkn; adv
bkg; quiet; ccard not acc; red low ssn; CKE/CCI. "Direct access
to rv; friendly, helpful staff; ideal for rallies; vg." ♦
30 Apr-15 Oct. € 19.80   2011*

CARENTAN *1D4* (600m NE Urban) *49.30988, -1.2388*
Camping Le Haut Dick, 30 Chemin du Grand-Bas Pays,
50500 Carentan [tel/fax 02 33 42 16 89; contact@
camping-lehautdick.com; www.camping-lehautdick.com]
Exit N13 at Carentan; clearly sp in town cent, nr pool, on L
bank of canal, close to marina.Foll sp to Port de Plaisance.
Med, hdg/mkd pitch, pt shd; wc; chem disp; mv service pnt;
shwrs inc; el pnts (6A) €4 (rev pol); gas; shop 500m; tradsmn;
snacks; rest & bar 500m; BBQ; playgrnd; htd pool adj; crazy
golf; sand beach 10km; cycle hire; games rm; 5% statics;
dogs €1.50; phone; poss cr; adv bkg; quiet; ccard not acc;
red low ssn; CKE/CCI. "Some pitches poss tight for lge o'fits;
gd security; eve meals avail; gates locked 2200-0700; conv
Cherbourg ferry & D-Day beaches; gd birdwatching & cycling;
mkt Mon." ♦ 1 Apr-30 Sep. € 25.50   2012*

See advertisement on page 32 & 33

CARENTAN *1D4* (6km SE Rural) *49.27849, -1.16945* **FFCC
Camping à la Ferme Le Clos Fleuri (Duval), 50620
Montmartin-en-Graignes [02 33 56 84 87]** On N13 by-pass
Carantan going S; join N174; site on L in 4km. Sm, unshd;
wc; shwrs inc; chem disp; el pnts inc; playgrnd; adv bkg;
quiet. "Charming CL-type site, also B&B; pleasant owner; 1 hr
fr Cherbourg." 15 Jun-15 Sep.   2010*

CARHAIX PLOUGUER *2E2* (1.5km W Rural) *48.27763,
-3.60183* **Camp Municipal La Vallée de l'Hyères, Rue de
Kerniguez, 29270 Carhaix-Plouguer [02 98 99 10 58; fax
02 98 99 15 92; tourismecarhaux@wanadoo.fr; www.
ville-carhaix.com]** SE fr Huelgoat on D794 for 17km; sm site
sps on all apps to Carhaix. Med, pt shd; wc (some cont); chem
disp (wc); shwrs inc; el pnts (6A) €2.20; lndtte; shop 1.5km;
tradsmn, snacks; bar; playrnd nr; pool 1.5km; canoe/kayak hire;
5% statics; adv bkg; quiet; CKE/CCI. "Pleasantly situated in
parkland; resident warden; muddy after rain; poss waterlogged
due adj rv; forest trail nrby." ♦ ltd
1 May-15 Sep. € 7.45   2010*

CARLEPONT see Noyon *3C3*

Le Moulin de Kermaux **** Route de kerlescan 56340 Carnac.
Tel: 02 97 52 15 90 • www.camping-moulinkermaux.com• moulin-de-kermaux@wanadoo.fr

FRANCE

GPS long 47°35' 45,528 " lat 3° 3' 41,22"

Campsite is located in the heart of the megalithic site of Carnac, very peaceful, in a wooded park of 3.5 hectares. Near the beach and seaside resort of Carnac. Ideal for family holidays, successful holidays.

CARLUCET 7D3 (1.5km NW Rural) 44.72880, 1.59692
Camping Château de Lacomté Country Club, 46500 Carlucet [05 65 38 75 46; fax 05 65 33 17 68; lacomte2@wanadoo.fr; www.campingchateaulacomte.com] Exit A20 junc 56 onto D802. In 2km take D807 & then turn L onto D32 to Carlucet. In approx 1.6km turn L & foll site sp for 4.8km. App rd narr with no passing places. Or fr Gramat SW on D677/D807. After approx 14km turn R onto D32 sp Carlucet, foll site sp. NB Take care sat nav directions (2011). Med, hdg pitch, some hdstg, pt sl, terr, pt shd; wc; chem disp; all serviced pitches; shwrs; el pnts (10A) inc; gas 7km; lndtte; sm shop & 12km; rest, snacks; bar; BBQ; pool; tennis; table tennis; golf 9km; boat trips; wifi; entmnt; 5% statics; dogs €4; c'vans/m'vans over 8.50m by request high ssn; poss cr; adv bkg; quiet; ccard acc; red low ssn/CKE/CCI. "British-owned site in attractive area; adults-only; some pitches gd size, others sm & diff long o'fits; some pitches too sm for car, c'van & awning; levelling blocks req some pitches; 'freedom' pitches for m'vanners inc use of sm car, bookable daily; conv Rocamadour & Lot, & A20; excl walking in area." ♦ 15 May-15 Sep. € 35.00   2011*

CARLUX see Sarlat la Canéda 7C3

CARNAC 2G3 (1km N Rural) 47.59683, -3.06035
Camping La Grande Métairie, Route des Alignements de Kermario, 56342 Carnac [02 97 52 24 01; fax 02 97 52 83 58; info@lagrandemetairie.com; www.lagrandemetairie.com or www.les-castels.com] Fr Auray take N768 twd Quiberon. In 8km turn L onto D119 twd Carnac. La Métairie site sp 1km bef Carnac (at traff lts) turn L onto D196 to site on R in 1km. V lge, hdg/mkd pitch, pt shd; htd wc; chem disp; mv service pnt; baby facs; shwrs inc; el pnts (6A) €3; gas; lndtte (inc dryer); shop; tradsmn; rest, snacks; bar; BBQ; playgrnd; 2 pools (1 htd, covrd); paddling pool; waterslide; sand beach 2.5km; watersports, sailing 2.5km; tennis; games rm; wifi; entmnt; TV; 80% statics; dogs €4; Eng spkn; adv bkg; quiet; ccard acc; red low ssn. "Excel facs; vg pool complex; friendly, helpful staff; rec." ♦ 2 Apr-10 Sep. € 42.00   2011*

See advertisement opposite

CARNAC 2G3 (1km N Rural) 47.5964, -3.0617 Camping Le Moulin de Kermaux, Route de Kerlescan, 56340 Carnac [02 97 52 15 90; fax 02 97 52 83 85; moulin-de-kermaux@wanadoo.fr; www.camping-moulinkermaux.com] Fr Auray take D768 S sp Carnac, Quiberon. In 8km turn L onto D119 twds Carnac. 1km bef Carnac take D196 (Rte de Kerlescan) L to site in approx 500m opp round, stone observation tower for alignments. Med, hdg/mkd pitch, pt shd; htd wc; chem disp; mv service pnt; baby facs; sauna; shwrs inc; el pnts (6A) €4 (poss rev pol); gas; lndtte (inc dryer); shop; tradsmn; snacks; bar; BBQ; playgrnd; htd, covrd pool; paddling pool; waterslide; jacuzzi; sand beach 3km; games area; wifi; entmnt; TV; 50% statics; dogs €2.50; phone; bus adj; Eng spkn; adv bkg; quiet; ccard acc; red low ssn; CKE/CCI. "Well-kept, friendly, attractive site nr standing stones; peaceful & comfortable low ssn; many repeat visitors; excel." ♦ 1 May-10 Sep. € 26.90   2011*

See advertisement above

CARNAC 2G3 (1km N Rural) 47.60225, -3.07869
Camping Les Ombrages, Kerlann, 56340 Carnac [02 97 52 16 52 (Jul & Aug) or 02 97 52 14 06] Exit Auray SW on D768; in 9.5km turn L onto D119; in 3km turn R at carwash, sp Kerlann; site 600m on R. Sp fr D119. Med, hdg/mkd pitch, shd; wc; shwrs; el pnts (6A) €2.70; lndtte; shops 1km; playgrnd; sand beach 3km; tennis; dogs €1; some statics; poss cr; quiet. "Well-kept site in wooded area; san facs old but clean." 15 Jun-15 Sep. € 15.20   2010*

CARNAC 2G3 (3km N Rural) 47.60801, -3.09049 Camping Les Bruyères, Kerogile, 56340 Plouharnel [02 97 52 30 57; camping.les.bryeres@wanadoo.fr; www.camping-lesbruyeres.com] Fr Vannes W on E60/N165, at Auray take D768 dir Quiberon. At rndabt approx 2km fr Plouharnel turn L into Rte du Hahon, site in 500m, sp. Med, hdg/mkd pitch, hdstg, pt shd; htd wc; chem disp; mv service pnt; baby facs; shwrs inc; el pnts (6A) €3.70; lndtte (inc dryer); shop; rest, snacks; bar; BBQ; playgrnd; sand beach 3km; tennis; bicycles; games area; wifi; child entmnt; TV rm; library; pony rides; 30% statics; dogs €2; Eng spkn; adv bkg; quiet; ccard acc; red low ssn; CKE/CCI. "V pleasant, well-run, peaceful site; vg." ♦ 29 Mar- 30 Sep. € 22.20   2013*

CARNAC *2G3* (2km NE Rural) *47.60820, -3.06605* **Kawan Village Le Moustoir, 71 Route du Moustoir, 56340 Carnac [02 97 52 16 18; fax 02 97 52 88 37; info@lemoustoir.com; www.lemoustoir.com]** Fr N165 take D768 at Auray dir Carnac & Quiberon. In 5km take D119 dir Carnac, site on L at ent to Carnac. Lge, hdg/mkd pitch, pt sl, pt shd; wc; chem disp; mv service pnt; baby facs; shwrs inc; el pnts (6A) €4.80; lndtte (inc dryer); shop; tradsmn; rest, snacks; bar; BBQ; playgrnd; 2 htd pools (1 covrd); paddling pool; waterslide; sand beach 4km; tennis; games area; cycle hire; wifi; TV rm; 30% statics; dogs free; phone; poss cr & noisy; Eng spkn; adv bkg; red low ssn; ccard acc; CKE/CCI. "Attractive, friendly, well-run site; facs clean but stretched; megaliths nrby; Sun mkt." ◆ 13 Apr-22 Sep. € 45.90 (4 persons) (CChq acc) 2012*

CARNAC *2G3* (3.5km NE Rural) *47.60198, -3.03672* **Camping de Kervilor, Route du Latz, 56470 La Trinité-sur-Mer [02 97 55 76 75; fax 02 97 55 87 26; camping.kervilor@wanadoo.fr; www.camping-kervilor.com]** Sp fr island in cent of Trinité-sur-Mer. Lge, hdg/mkd pitch, hdstg, pt shd; wc; chem disp; mv service pnt; baby facs; shwrs inc; el pnts (6-10A) €3.85-4.35; gas; lndtte; shop; snacks; bar; BBQ; playgrnd; htd, covrd pool; paddling pool; waterslides; solarium; sand beach 4km; tennis; games area; cycle hire; internet; entmnt; 5% statics; dogs €2.90; poss cr; Eng spkn; adv bkg; ccard acc; red low ssn; CKE/CCI. "Busy, well-kept family site; lge pitches; clean dated unisex san facs; 20 min walk into La Trinité-sur-Mer (1.5km); gd cycling to Carnac & megaliths; gd." ◆ 1 Apr-18 Sep. € 29.25 2010*

CARNAC *2G3* (8km NE Rural) *47.61538, -2.98965* **Camping Le Fort Espagnol, Route de Fort Espagnol, 56950 Crac'h [02 97 55 14 88; fax 02 97 30 01 04; fort-espagnol@wanadoo.fr; www.fort-espagnol.com]** Fr Auray take D28 S; in Crac'h turn L at rndabt; site sp in 1km on R. Lge, pt shd; htd wc (some cont); chem disp; baby facs; shwrs inc; el pnts (10A) €4; gas; lndtte; shops 1km; tradsmn; snacks; bar; playgrnd; pool; waterslide; sand beach 5km; tennis; games area; entmnt; 30% statics; dogs €3.50; poss cr; adv bkg rec high ssn; quiet; ccard acc; CKE/CCI. "Helpful, pleasant management; popular with British; some lge pitches." 1 May-12 Sep. € 28.00 2009*

CARNAC *2G3* (2km E Rural/Coastal) *47.5810, -3.0576* **Camping Les Druides, 55 Chemin de Beaumer, 56340 Carnac [02 97 52 08 18; fax 02 97 52 96 13; contact@camping-les-druides.com; www.camping-les-druides.com]** Go E on seafront Carnac Plage to end; turn N onto Ave d'Orient; at junc with Rte de la Trinité-sur-Mer, turn L, then 1st R; site 1st on L in 300m. Med, hdg pitch, pt sl, pt shd; wc; chem disp; mv service pnt; baby facs; shwrs inc; el pnts (6A) €3.70; lndtte; shop 1km; rest adj; playgrnd; htd pool; sand beach 500m; entmnt; games/TV rm; 5% statics; dogs €2.30; phone adj; Eng spkn; adv bkg; quiet; ccard acc; CKE/CCI. "Friendly welcome." ◆ ltd 24 May-13 Sep. € 29.00 2008*

CARNAC *2G3* (3km E Rural) *47.61122, -3.02908* **Camping du Lac, 56340 Carnac [02 97 55 78 78 or 02 97 55 82 60; fax 02 97 55 86 03; camping.dulac@wanadoo.fr; www.camping-carnac.com]** Fr Auray (by-pass) take D768 sp Carnac; in 4km turn L on D186; after 4km look for C105 on L & foll sp to site. Fr E end of quay-side in La Trinité-sur-Mer take main Carnac rd & in 100m turn R onto D186; in 2km R on C105, R on C131; sp. Med, hdg pitch, pt sl, pt shd; wc; chem disp; mv service pnt; serviced pitches; baby facs; shwrs inc; el pnts (6A) €3.60; gas; lndtte; shop; tradsmn; rest 3km; BBQ; playgrnd; htd pool; sand beach 3km; cycle hire; multi-sport court; fitness rm; TV rm; entmnt; 50% statics; dogs €2; phone; poss cr; Eng spkn; adv bkg; quiet; ccard acc; red low ssn; CKE/CCI. "Excel woodland site o'looking tidal lake; helpful owner; clean, well-cared for; superb pool; gd cycling & walking; vg." 1 Apr-20 Sep. € 19.40 2008*

See advertisement on pages 32 & 33

CARNAC *2G3* (1.5km SE Coastal) *47.58116, -3.05804* **Camping Le Dolmen, Chemin de Beaumer, 56340 Carnac [02 97 52 12 35; fax 02 97 52 63 91; contact@campingledolmen.com; www.campingledolmen.com]** Fr N on D768 twd Quiberon; turn L onto D781 twd La Trinité-sur-Mer. At Montauban turn R at rndabt dir Kerfraval & Beaumer, site in 700m, sp. Med, hdg/mkd pitch, hdstg, pt sl, pt shd; htd wc (some cont); chem disp; mv service pnt; baby facs; shwrs €2; el pnts (10A) €4.70; lndtte; shop 800m; tradsmn; rest, snacks; BBQ; playgrnd; htd pool; paddling pool; sand beach 500m; games area; games rm; wifi; entmnt; 2% statics; dogs €3; Eng spkn; adv bkg; quiet; ccard acc; red low ssn/CKE/CCI. "Excel, pleasant site." ◆ 1 Apr-20 Sep. € 28.00 2011*

"We must tell The Club about that great site we found"

Get your site reports in by mid-August and we'll do our best to get your updates into the next edition of Caravan Europe.

CARNAC *2G3* (2km SE Coastal) *47.5810, -3.0572* **Camping Le Men Dû, Chemin de Beaumer, 56340 Carnac [tel/fax 02 97 52 04 23; contact@camping-mendu.com; www.camping-mendu.fr]** Go E on seafront (Carnac Plage) to end; N on Ave d'Orient; at junc with Rte de la Trinité-sur-Mer turn L & 1st R; 2nd site on R. Med, hdg/mkd pitch, pt sl, pt shd; wc; chem disp; shwrs inc; el pnts (6-10A) €3-4; gas; lndtte; shop 500m; rest, snacks, bar high ssn; sand beach 150m; 50% statics; dogs €2; bus 100m; poss cr; adv bkg; poss noisy; CKE/CCI. "Friendly staff; mkd pitches not rec for manoeuvring twin-axles; manhandling req for long or heavy vans; narr rds on site; yachting (inc school)." ◆ ltd Easter-30 Sep. € 22.00 2008*

CARNAC *2G3* (3km SE Coastal) *47.57566, -3.02900* **Camping de la Plage, Plage de Kervilen, 56470 La Trinité-sur-Mer [02 97 55 73 28; fax 02 76 01 33 05; info@camping-plage. com; www.camping-plage.com]** Fr Auray on D28 & D781 dir La Trinite. Foll sp Kervilen-Plage to S. Lge, hdg pitch, pt shd; wc; chem disp; mv service pnt; chem disp; serviced pitches; baby facs; shwrs inc; el pnts (6-10A) €3.50-4.30; lndtte (inc dryer); shop 200m; rest, snacks; bar; BBQ; playgrnd; htd pool; paddling pool; waterslide; jacuzzi; sand beach adj; fishing; tennis adj; cycle hire; wifi; 80% statics; dogs €1.30; poss cr; Eng spkn; adv bkg; quiet; red long stay/low ssn; ccard acc; CKE/CCI. "Pleasant site; friendly staff; tight ent; variable pitch sizes." ♦ 7 May-19 Sep. € 36.50   2010*

CARNAC *2G3* (4km SE Coastal) *47.57396, -3.02653* **Camping La Baie, Plage de Kervillen, 56470 La Trinité-sur-Mer [02 97 55 73 42; fax 02 97 55 88 81; contact@ campingdelabaie.fr; www.campingdelabaie.fr]** Fr Carnac take D186. Turn R after causeway, keep R, past Camping de la Plage site, & site on L. Fr E app vill along seafront sp Carnac, cont strt thro traff lts, after 2nd traff lts take 1st L & foll rd for 1km. Site ent on L. Lge, hdg/mkd pitch, hdstg, pt shd; wc; chem disp; mv service pnt; baby facs; serviced pitches; shwrs inc; el pnts (6-10A) €3.50-5; lndtte; shops, snacks, rest, bar 500m; playgrnd; entmnt; htd pool; sand beach 50m; fishing; boat hire, mini-golf & tennis 250m; TV rm; 30% statics; dogs €1.30; phone; poss cr; Eng spkn; adv bkg; quiet; red low ssn; ccard acc. "Excel, well-kept site in superb location; vg recep; excel san facs; sm pitches; some narr site rds - pitching poss diff lge o'fits inc lge m'vans; vg family beach across rd; v sm pool; highly rec." ♦ 8 May-12 Sep. € 42.20   2010*

CARNAC *2G3* (9km SW Coastal) *47.57169, -3.12638* **Camp Municipal Les Sables Blancs, Route de Quiberon, 56340 Plouharnel [02 97 52 37 15 or 02 97 52 30 90 (Mairie); fax 02 97 52 48 49; mairie@plouharnel.fr]** Fr Auray take by-pass to Quiberon (clearly mkd), cont thro Plouharnel (D768) twd Quiberon - site clearly mkd after Plouharnel. Lge, mkd pitch, unshd; wc; shwrs inc; el pnts (4-13A) €2.45-3.45; gas; lndtte; shops, rest, snacks, bar in ssn; sand beach; 30% statics; dogs €1.05; Eng spkn; quiet. "Situated on a sand spit, care needed over soft sand." 1 Apr-30 Sep. € 12.00   2008*

CARNAC *2G3* (1.5km NW Rural) *47.59468, -3.09659* **Camping Les Goélands, Kerbachic, 56340 Plouharnel [02 97 52 31 92; angelina.oliviero@wanadoo.fr]** Take D768 fr Auray twd Quiberon. In Plouharnel turn L at rndabt by supmkt onto D781 to Carnac. Site sp to L in 500m. Med, pt shd; wc (some cont); chem disp; shwrs inc; el pnts (3-5A) €2-3; gas; lndtte; shops 1km; playgrnd; sand beach 3km; dogs €1; poss cr; adv bkg. "Friendly owners; excel facs; gd-sized pitches; gate clsd at 2200; nr beaches with bathing & gd yachting; bells fr adj abbey not too intrusive; conv for megalithic sites; high standard site; Pleasant quiet site; facs basic; clean and tidy" 1 Jun-15 Sep. € 15.00   2012*

CARNAC *2G3* (8km NW Rural) *47.63282, -3.14743* **Camping Kerzerho, Route de Plouharnel, 56410 Erdeven [tel/ fax 02 97 55 63 17; info@camping-kerzerho.com; www. camping-kerzerho.com]** N fr Carnac on D781, site sp 400m S of Erdeven. Med, hdg/mkd pitch, pt shd; wc; baby facs; sauna; baby facs; shwrs; el pnts (10A) €5.30; lndtte (inc dryer); shop; tradsmn; rest, snacks; bar; playgrnd; htd, covrd pool; paddling pool; waterslide; beach 2km; cycle hire; excursions; entmnt; some statics; dogs €3.20; adv bkg; quiet; red low ssn. "Busy site; some sm pitches diff lge o'fits." 1 Jun-3 Sep. € 24.10   2010*

CARNAC *2G3* (8km NW Coastal) *47.62165, -3.16462* **Idéal Camping, Route de la Plage de Kerhilio, Lisveur, 56410 Erdeven [02 97 55 67 66; contact@camping-l-ideal.com; www.camping-l-ideal.com]** Fr Carnac take D781 to Erdeven, turn L at rndabt. Site 2km on R at hotel/cafe. Sm, hdg pitch, pt shd; wc; chem disp (wc); baby facs; shwrs inc; el pnts (6A) €5; gas; lndtte; rest; shops 500m; tradsmn; rest, snacks; bar; BBQ; playgrnd; htd, covrd pool; paddling pool; sand beach 800m; sailing; fishing; tennis nr; games rm; TV; 90% statics; dogs €4; sep parking area for cars; Eng spkn; no adv bkg; quiet; ccard acc; red low ssn; CKE/CCI. "Peaceful site nr excel beach & cent of mkt town; not rec twin-axles or lge o'fits due narr site rds." ♦ 1 Apr-30 Oct. € 23.00 (3 persons)   2009*

"I need an on-site restaurant"

We do our best to make sure site information is correct, but it is always best to check any must-have facilities are still available or will be open during your visit.

CARNAC *2G3* (12.5km NW) *47.65500, -3.17194* **Camping Les Sept Saints, 56410 Erdeven [02 97 55 52 65; fax 02 97 55 22 67; info@septsaints.com; www.septsaints.com]** Fr Erdeven on D781 going NW dir Lorient; site on L in 2km. Lge, hdg/mkd pitch, pt sl, pt shd; wc; chem disp; baby facs; shwrs inc; el pnts (10A) inc; gas; lndtte; shop; snacks; bar; BBQ (charcoal/gas); playgrnd; htd pool; paddling pool; waterslide; sand beach 4km; watersports 1.5km; cycle hire; internet; entmnt; games/TV rm; many statics; dogs €5; c'vans over 8m not acc high ssn; adv bkg; quiet; ccard acc; red low ssn; CKE/ CCI. "V pleasant site; gd lge pitches; superb unspoilt beaches nrby; excel cycling rtes; Etel 3km worth visit; vg." ♦ 1 May-15 Sep. € 37.50   2009*

CAROMB see Malaucène *10E2*

FRANCE

CARPENTRAS *10E2* (5km N Rural) *44.09723, 5.03682* Camping Le Brégoux, Chemin du Vas, 84810 Aubignan [04 90 62 62 50 or 04 90 67 10 13 (LS); camping-lebregoux@wanadoo.fr; www.camping-lebregoux.fr] Exit Carpentras on D7 sp Bollène. In Aubignan turn R immed after x-ing bdge, 1st R again in approx 250m at Club de Badminton & foll site sp at fork. Lge, hdg/mkd pitch, hdstg, pt shd; wc; chem disp; mv service pnt; baby facs; shwrs inc; el pnts (6-10A) inc (poss long lead req); lndtte; shops, rest, bars etc 1km; BBQ; sm playgrnd; pool 5km in ssn; tennis; go-karting, golf nrby; entmnt; games rm; wifi; TV; 2% statics; dogs €1.60; phone; poss v cr; Eng spkn; adv bkg; poss noisy high ssn; ccard acc; CKE/CCI. "Popular site in beautiful area; lge pitches & gd access; helpful, friendly staff; new san facs planned (for 2012); gates clsd 2200-0700; poss flooding in heavy rain; excel walking & cycling nrby; gd value; gd." ♦ ltd 1 Mar-31 Oct. € 14.54   2011*

See advertisement above

CARPENTRAS *10E2* (7km N Rural) *44.12246, 5.03437* Camp Municipal de Roquefiguier, 84190 Beaumes-de-Venise [04 90 62 95 07 or 04 90 62 94 34 (Mairie); camping.roquefiguier@orange.fr; www.beaumes-de-venise.fr] Leave A7 exit 22, take N7 S then L onto D950 sp Carpentras. At rndabt after Sarrians sp turn L onto D21 to Beaumes-de-Venise. Cross Beaumes & foll site sp. Turn L bef Crédit Agricole to site on R. Med, hdg/mkd pitch, pt sl, terr, pt shd; wc (some cont); chem disp; mv service pnt; baby facs; shwrs inc; el pnts (6A) €3.00; lndtte; BBQ; pool in vill; playgrnd,mini golf; wifi; dogs €1.45; phone; no adv bkg; quiet; ccard acc; CKE/CCI. "Gd site; gd views; facs clean; steel pegs req for pitches; poss diff access lge o'fits; steep access some pitches; gate clsd 1900-0830; 5 mins walk to Beaumes-de-Venise; wine caves adj; mkd walks & cycle ways; conv for Mt Ventoux, Orange & Avignon. MD Tues, excel hot shwrs" ♦ 1 Mar-31 Oct. € 13.65   2013*

CARPENTRAS *10E2* (7km E Rural) *44.08057, 5.11385* Camping Le Ventoux, 1348 Chemin La Combe, 84380 Mazan [tel/fax 04 90 69 70 94; info@camping-le-ventoux.com; www.camping-le-ventoux.com] Take D974 twd Bédoin; after 7km turn R at x-rds on D70 sp Mazan. Site on R in 300m. Sm, mkd pitch, pt shd; wc; chem disp; mv service pnt; baby facs; shwrs inc; el pnts (6A) €3.50 (poss rev pol); gas; lndtte (inc dryer); shop (high ssn) & 3km; tradsmn; rest, snacks; bar; BBQ; playgrnd; pool; lake fishing 4km; entmnt; 25% statics; dogs €2.50; phone; poss cr; Eng spkn; adv bkg (ess high ssn); quiet; ccard acc; red low ssn; CKE/CCI. "Busy site, even low ssn - bkg rec; friendly, helpful Dutch owners; excel rest; wine-tasting area; excel." ♦ ltd 1 Mar-1 Nov. € 19.00   2011*

CARPENTRAS *10E2* (12km E Rural) *44.02904, 5.19974* Camp Municipal Aéria, Le Portail, 84570 Blauvac [tel/fax 04 90 61 81 41 (Mairie)] E fr Carpentras on D942; E of Mazan fork onto D150. Site 100m N of Blauvac vill cent. Sm, mkd pitch, pt shd; wc (some cont); shwrs; el pnts (10A) €2; shop; rest, snacks; bar; playgrnd. "Superb, quiet site on hilltop with view; basic facs; warden calls am & pm; may be exposed in bad weather." 15 Mar-15 Oct. € 8.00   2009*

CARPENTRAS *10E2* (10km SE Rural) *44.01428, 5.17098* Camping Font Neuve, Rte de Méthamis, 84570 Malemort-du-Comtat [04 90 69 90 00 or 04 90 69 74 86; fax 04 90 69 91 77; camping.font-neuve@libertysurf.fr; http://camping.font.neuve.free.fr] Fr Malemort take Méthanis rd D5; as rd starts to rise look for sp on L to site. NB Take care narr app rds. Med, hdg pitch, terr, pt shd; wc (some cont); chem disp; serviced pitches; baby facs; shwrs inc; el pnts (10A) €4.50; lndtte; tradsmn; rest, snacks; bar; playgrnd; pool; tennis; entmnt; TV; some statics; dogs €1.70; adv bkg req high ssn; quiet. "Friendly, family-run site; gd rest; immac san facs." ♦ 1 May-30 Sep. € 16.50   2011*

CARPENTRAS *10E2* (500m S Urban) *44.04379, 5.05363*
FLOWER Camp Lou Comtadou, 881 Ave Pierre de
Coubertin, Route de St Didier, 84200 Carpentras
[04 90 67 03 16 or 06 09 36 67 56 (mob); fax
04 90 46 01 81; info@campingloucomtadou.com; www.
campingloucomtadou.com or www.flowercampings.
com] Exit A7 junc 22 or 23 to Carpentras; foll sp dir St Didier
thro one-way system onto D4; in 200m turn L into Ave Pierre
de Coubertin. Site sp in 500m. Med, hdg/mkd pitch, hdstg,
shd; htd wc; chem disp; baby facs; shwrs inc; el pnts (6A) €3;
lndtte; ice; shop; tradsmn; rest, snacks; BBQ; playgrnd; pool;
wifi; dogs €3; phone; bus adj; Eng spkn; quiet; ccard acc; red
low ssn; CKE/CCI. "Well-kept, clean site; lge pitches; attractive
walled town; excel. " ♦ 1 Apr-30 Sep. € 19.60   2010*

See advertisement on pages 32 & 33

CARPENTRAS *10E2* (6km S Urban) *43.99917, 5.06591* Camp
Municipal Coucourelle, Ave René Char, 84210 Pernes-les-
Fontaines [04 90 66 45 55 or 04 90 61 31 67 (Mairie); fax
04 90 61 32 46; www.perneslesfontaines.fr]
Take D938 fr Carpentras to Pernes-les-Fontaines; then take
D28 dir St Didier (Ave René Char pt of D28). Site sp (some sps
easily missed). Foll sp sports complex, site at rear of sw pool.
Sm, hdg/mkd pitch, shd; wc; chem disp; mv service pnt; shwrs
inc; el pnts (10A) €3.50 gas 1km; lndtte; shops & rests 1km;
BBQ; playgrnd; pool, sw & fishing 2.5km; tennis adj; dogs
€0.50; poss cr; adv bkg; quiet; ccard acc; CKE/CCI. "Pleasant,
well-run site; views of Mont Ventoux; most pitches lge but
some sm & narr; gd, clean facs; m'vans can park adj to mv
point free when site clsd; gates close 1930; no twin-axles; free
use of adj pool; attractive old town, easy parking; adv bkg rec
low ssn; vg. " ♦ 1 Apr-30 Sep. € 12.00   2011*

"There aren't many sites open at this time of year"

If you're travelling outside peak season
remember to call ahead to check site opening
dates – even if the entry says 'open all year'.

CARPENTRAS *10E2* (6km S Rural) *44.00611, 5.03861*
Camping Les Fontaines, 125 Chemin de la Chapelette,
Route de la Sudre, 84210 Pernes-les-Fontaines
[04 90 46 82 55; fax 04 90 63 42 91; campinglesfontaine@
gmail.com; www.campingfontaines.fr] Take D938 S
fr Carpentras to Pernes-les-Fontaines. On o'skts of Pernes
turn L into Route de la Sudre, site sp in 1km on R, well sp.
Med, hdg/mkd pitch, pt shd; wc; chem disp; mv service pnt;
baby facs; shwrs inc; el pnts (6A) €4.50; lndtte; shop & 1km;
tradsmn; supmkt nr; rest, snacks; bar; BBQ; playgrnd; pool
complex; games area; wifi; entmnt; TV rm; 30% statics; dogs
€3; Eng spkn; adv bkg; quiet; red low ssn; CKE/CCI. "Vg,
newly developed site; clean, modern san facs; friendly, helpful
owners; view of Mt Ventoux. " ♦ 1 Apr-31 Oct. € 24.00
(CChq acc)   2010*

CARPENTRAS *10E2* (4km SW Rural) *44.0398, 5.0009* Camp
Municipal de Bellerive, 54 Chemin de la Ribière, 84170
Monteux [04 90 66 81 88 or 04 90 66 97 52 (TO); camping.
bellerive@orange.fr; www.provenceguide.com] Site on
N edge of Monteux cent, sp off ring rd Monteux N, immed
after rlwy x-ing. Sm, hdg/mkd pitch, some hdstg, pt shd; some
serviced pitches; wc; chem disp; shwrs inc; el pnts (6-10A)
€2.50; lndtte; shops 500m; rest, snacks, bar 500m; playgrnd;
pool 4km; some statics; dogs €1; phone; bus; poss cr; quiet,
but poss noise fr park adj (music); red long stay; CKE/CCI. "Gd,
busy site; rec arr early high ssn; helpful, friendly warden lives
adj; gd security; vg, clean, modern san facs; trees a problem for
sat TV - choose pitch carefully; park adj gd for children; 5 min
walk to vill; poss muddy when wet; poss some workers' statics
low ssn; Mistral blows early & late ssn; gd touring base. " ♦
1 Apr-15 Oct. € 13.40   2013*

"That's changed – Should I let The Club know?"

If you find something on site that's different from
the site entry, fill in a report and let us know. See
www.caravanclub.co.uk/europereport.

CARPENTRAS *10E2* (7km NW Urban) *44.07981, 4.97693*
Camp Muncipal de la Sainte Croix, Quartier Ste Croix,
84260 Sarrians [tel/fax 04 90 65 43 72; campingdestecroix@
orange.fr; www.camping-sainte-croix.com] Fr Carpentras
on D950 dir Orange; in 7km turn L at rndabt on o'skts of
Sarrians onto D221; site in 200m on R. Sm, hdg/mkd pitch,
some hdstg, pt shd; wc; chem disp; shwrs inc; el pnts €3.50;
lndtte; shop 500m; snacks; bar; BBQ; playgrnd; pool; rv sw
5km; tennis; 20% statics; dogs €2; phone; poss cr; adv bkg;
red low ssn; CKE/CCI. "Pleasant site; helpful warden; clean
facs; gd touring base." ♦ ltd 30 Mar-31 Oct. € 17.50 2009*

CARPENTRAS *10E2* (11km NW Rural) *44.14269, 4.98646*
Camp Municipal Les Queyrades, Route de Vaison, 84190
Vacqueyras [04 90 12 39 02 (TO); fax 04 90 65 83 28;
tourisme.vacqueyras@wanadoo.fr; www.vacqueyras.tm.fr]
Site on W of D7 at N end of Vacqueyras, clearly sp. Sm, hdg
pitch, pt shd; wc; shwrs inc; el pnts (6-10A) €3; shops 1km;
playgrnd; rv sw 3km; tennis adj; Eng spkn; adv bkg; quiet, but
some rd noise; CKE/CCI. "Clean, popular site; wine caves opp;
D7 v fast & busy." Easter-Sep. € 9.40   2008*

CARQUEIRANNE see Hyères *10F3*

⊞ **CARRY LE ROUET** *10F2* (750m W Coastal) *43.33024,
5.13747* Camping Lou Souleï, 68-72 Avenue Draïo de la Mar,
13620 Carry-le-Rouet [04 42 44 75 75; fax 04 42 44 57 24;
lousoulei@wanadoo.fr; www.lousoulei.com] Fr Martigues
take A55 & exit dir Carry-le-Rouet. Site on beach rd. V lge, hdg/
mkd pitch, hdstg, pt shd; htd wc; chem disp; serviced pitch;
shwrs inc; el pnts (6A) inc; lndtte; shop adj; rest, snacks; bar;
playgrnd; htd pool; beach adj; games rm; games area; entmnt;
TV rm; 60% statics; dogs; phone; poss cr; Eng spkn; adv bkg;
red low ssn. "Gd base for Marseille, Camargue, Aix, etc; red
facs low ssn." € 51.00 (4 persons)   2010*

CARSAC AILLAC see Sarlat la Canéda *7C3*

CASSAGNABERE TOURNAS *8F3* (S Rural) *43.22583, 0.78920* **Camping Pré Fixe, 31420 Cassagnabère-Tournas [05 61 98 71 00 or 06 48 23 46 79 (mob); camping@instudio4.com; www.instudio4.com/pre-fixe]** Exit A64 at junc 21 onto D635 dir Aurignac. Cont thro vill on D635 sp Cassagnabère for 8km, sp in vill. Sm, hdg/mkd pitch, terr, pt shd; wc (some cont); chem disp; mv service pnt; baby facs; shwrs inc; el pnts (6-10A) €4; gas; lndtte; shop 500m; tradsmn, rest, snacks; bar; BBQ; playgrnd; pool; entmnt; TV rm; 10% statics; no dogs; phone; Eng spkn; adv bkg; quiet; CKE/CCI. "Friendly owners; beautiful landscape; gd touring base; excel." ♦ 15 Apr-30 Sep. € 18.00   2009*

CASSEL *3A3* (3km SW Rural) *50.79288, 2.43113* **Camping Le Val de Cassel, 1035 Route des Trois Rois, 59670 Zuytpeene [03 28 48 45 82; charley.chris@hotmail.fr; www.levaldecassel.skyrock.com]** S fr Cassel on D933, turn R onto D138 to Zuytpeene. Site adj church in vill. Sm, hdg pitch, pt shd; wc; chem disp; shwrs inc€1.50; el pnts (4A) €2-2.20; lndry rm; BBQ; playgrnd; tennis; games area; 90% statics; dogs €1; Eng spkn; adv bkg; quiet; CKE/CCI. "Site is single, narr lane cul-de-sac & only suitable sm o'fits; v few touring pitches; Cassel is unsuitable c'vans as main street is cobbled, twisting & uneven for 1km; fair NH." 1 Apr-31 Oct. € 14.00   2011*

CASSIS *10F3* (1.5km N Coastal) *43.22417, 5.54126* **Camping Les Cigales, Ave de la Marne, 13260 Cassis [04 42 01 07 34; fax 04 42 01 34 18; www.campingcassis.com]** App Cassis on D41E, then at 2nd rndabt exit D559 sp Cassis, then turn 1st R sp Les Calanques into Ave de la Marne, site immed on R. Avoid town cent as rds narr. Lge, hdg/mkd pitch, hdstg, pt sl, pt shd; wc (some cont); chem disp; mv service pnt; shwrs inc; el pnts (3A) €2.60 (poss long lead req); gas; lndtte; shop; tradsmn; rest, snacks; bar; playgrnd; shgl beach 1.5km; 30% statics; dogs €1.10; phone; rd noise some pitches; Eng spkn; ccard acc; CKE/CCI. "Gd base for Calanques; v busy w/ends; attractive resort, but steep walk to camp site; poss tired san facs end ssn; poss diff lge o'fits due trees; v strong pegs req to penetrate hardcore." 15 Mar-15 Nov. € 16.50   2009*

CASTELFRANC *7D3* (9km N Rural) *44.57710, 1.19283* **Camping La Pinède, Le Bourg, 46250 Goujounac [05 65 36 61 84; camping-goujounac@orange.fr; http://camping-de-goujounac.monsite-orange.fr/]** Fr Gourdon take D673 SW. At Frayssinet-le-Gelet turn L onto D660 for 2.5km. Site on L at ent to vill. Sm, mkd pitch, terr, pt shd; wc; chem disp; shwrs inc; el pnts (20A) €2; lndtte; shop 1km; bar; pool; tennis; quiet. "Attractive vill & site in pine wood; gd rest 1km." 15 Jun-15 Sep. € 12.00   2008*

CASTELFRANC *7D3* (6km SE Rural) *44.48095, 1.28160* **Camp Municipal L'Eau Berge de Caix, 46140 Luzech [05 65 30 72 32 (Mairie); fax 05 65 76 80; commune.luzech@wanadoo.fr; www.ville-luzech.fr]** Fr Cahors take D811 NW, turn L onto D8 foll sp to Luzech; cross both bdges in Luzech; site on R in 1km on D8; do not foll camp sp on D88 to Sauzac. Sm, pt shd; wc (cont); sauna; shwrs inc; el pnts (6-10A) (rev pol); shops 1km; bar; playgrnd; dogs; some rd noise; red low ssn. "Peaceful site on Rv Lot; rv not suitable for sw; sluice gates of dam upstream liable to be opened, causing rv to rise sharply; warden visits am & pm - arrange for barrier to be open; peaceful site." 1 May-30 Sep.   2009*

CASTELFRANC *7D3* (2km SW Rural) *44.47636, 1.19942* **Camping Base Nautique Floiras, 46140 Anglars-Juillac [05 65 36 27 39; fax 05 65 21 41 00; info@campingfloiras.com; www.campingfloiras.com]** Fr Castelfranc head S on D45; cross rv, then turn R onto D8 to Anglars-Juillac; in vill turn R just after rest on L; site at end of lane; site sp. Or fr W on D811 turn R at main sq Prayssac sp Mont Cuq. In 2km cross rv at Pont Juillac, turn 1st R & foll sp to site. Sm, mkd pitch, pt shd; htd wc; chem disp; mv service pnt; shwrs inc; el pnts (10A) €3.50 (rev pol); gas; lndtte (inc dryer); sm shop; tradsmn; rest adj; snacks; sm bar; BBQ; pool 2km; cycle & canoe hire; dogs €1.30; phone adj; poss cr; Eng spkn; adv bkg ess high ssn; quiet but poss youth groups; ccard acc; CKE/CCI. "Well-kept site on Rv Lot set in vineyards; lge pitches; vg, clean san facs; helpful Dutch owner; nr mkts & rests; super site." ♦ 1 Apr-15 Oct. € 16.40   2008*

CASTELJALOUX *7D2* (500m N Urban) *44.31472, 0.09153* **Camp Municipal de la Piscine, Rue du Souvenir Français, Route de Marmande, 47700 Casteljaloux [05 53 93 54 68; fax 05 53 89 48 07; www.casteljaloux.com]** On N side of town on D933 visible fr rd. Sm, pt shd; wc; shwrs inc; el pnts (10A) €2.15; shops 750m; rest; bar; pool adj inc; rv & lake sw; fishing; rd noise. "Gd, old-fashioned site; sm park nr; helpful warden; gd san facs; conv for town; useful NH; extra charge c'vans over 4m." ♦ 1 Apr-15 Nov. € 7.35   2009*

CASTELJALOUX *7D2* (8km SE Rural) *44.27262, 0.18969* **Camping Moulin de Campech, 47160 Villefranche-du-Queyran [05 53 88 72 43; fax 05 53 88 06 52; camping@moulindecampech.co.uk; www.moulindecampech.co.uk]** Fr A62 exit junc 6 (sp Damazan & Aiguillon). Fr toll booth take D8 SW sp Mont-de-Marsan. In 3km turn R in Cap-du-Bosc onto D11 twd Casteljaloux. Site on R in 4km. Or fr Casteljaloux S on D655 then SW on D11 after 1.5km. Site on L after 9.5km. Sm, hdg/mkd pitch, pt shd; wc (some cont); chem disp; shwrs inc; el pnts (6A) €4; lndtte (inc dryer); sm shop; tradsmn; rest, snacks; bar; BBQ; htd pool; lake fishing; golf nr; games rm; entmnt; wifi; dogs €2.40; no c'vans/m'vans over 8.20m; phone; poss cr; adv bkg; quiet; ccard acc; red low ssn; CKE/CCI. "Superb, peaceful rvside site in wooded valley; well-run; lge pitches; friendly, helpful British owners; clean, dated san facs, poss tired early ssn (2011); gd pool; excel, gd value rest; BBQ suppers; gd cycling; interesting area ideal for nature lovers; excel site; friendly helpful staff" ♦ 1 Apr-7 Oct. € 39.20 SBS - D16   2013*

CASTELLANE *10E3* (1.5km N Rural) *43.85598, 6.49563* **Camping Le Provençal, Route de Digne, 04120 Castellane [tel/fax 04 92 83 65 50; accueil@camping-provencal.com; www.camping-provencal.com]** Fr N on D4085 at foot of Col de Lècques site on R on LH bend. Fr Castellane site on D4085 in 1km on L. Med, mkd pitch, pt sl, pt shd; wc; chem disp; baby facs; shwrs inc; el pnts (6A) inc; lndtte; shop; supmkt 500m; tradsmn; snacks; bar; pool; tennis 1.5km; dogs €2; some rd noise; red low ssn. "Gd, clean site; fine scenery; friendly owners; conv Gorges du Verdon." 1 May-15 Sep. € 18.00   2009*

CASTELLANE *10E3* (8km N Rural) *43.88354, 6.51455*
Camping Castillon de Provence (Naturist), La Grande Terre, La Baume, 04120 Castellane [04 92 83 64 24; fax 04 92 83 68 79; info@castillondeprovence.com; www. castillondeprovence.com] Fr Castellane take D955 at Casino supmkt & after 5km turn L on D402 (up narr mountain rd) site in 7km. NB up access for car & vans only after 1400, down before 1300. Med, pt sl, pt shd; wc (some cont); chem disp (wc); shwrs inc; el pnts (2-6A) €3.50-4.50; gas; lndtte; shop; tradsmn; rest, snacks; bar; playgrnd; htd pool; paddling pool; lake sw, fishing, watersports 2km; TV rm; 20% statics; dogs €2; phone; poss cr; Eng spkn; adv bkg; quiet; ccard not acc; INF card. "Site 1000m high & cold at night; mountain views o'looking Lac de Castillon; friendly, family owners; v lge pitches." ♦ 14 Apr-4 Oct. € 24.00   2008*

CASTELLANE *10E3* (2km SE Rural) *43.83833, 6.54194*
Camping La Ferme de Castellane, Quartier La Lagne, 04120 Castellane [04 92 83 67 66 or 06 82 82 02 91; accueil@camping-la-ferme.com; www.camping-la-ferme.com] Fr Castellane take D6085 dir Grasse. In 1km turn R then site in 1km, sp. Narr app rd with passing places. Sm, mkd pitch, terr, pt shd; wc; chem disp; mv service pnt; baby facs; shwrs inc; el pnts €3.50; lndtte (inc dryer); tradsmn; shop, rest, snacks, bar 2km; sm playgrnd; pool 2km; games rm; wifi; TV rm; 25% statics; dogs €1; bus 2km; Eng spkn; adv bkg; quiet; ccard acc; red low ssn; CKE/CCI. "Vg, clean, friendly site; gd touring base." ♦ 27 Mar-20 Sep. € 17.00   2010*

CASTELLANE *10E3* (5km SE Rural) *43.81631, 6.57296* **RCN Camping Les Collines de Castellane, Route de Grasse, 04120 La Garde [04 92 83 68 96; fax 04 92 83 75 40; info@rcn-lescollinesdecastellane.fr; www.rcn-campings.fr]** Fr Castellane, take D4085 for 5km to La Garde, go thro will & foll sp. Site on R in 1km. Lge, terr, pt shd; wc; mv service pnt; baby facs; shwrs inc; el pnts (10A) inc; gas; lndtte; shop; rest, snacks; bar; playgrnd; pool; lake sw 5km; games area; organised activites inc watersports, rock climbing, paragliding, hiking; entmnt; TV; dogs €6; Eng spkn; adv bkg; red low ssn. "Friendly owners; peaceful site on steep hillside with views; main site rd v steep." ♦ 17 Apr-25 Sep. € 39.50   2009*

CASTELLANE *10E3* (300m SW Urban) *43.84623, 6.50995*
Camping Frédéric Mistral, 12 Ave Frédéric Mistral, 04120 Castellane [04 92 83 62 27; contact@camping-fredericmistral.com; www.camping-fredericmistral.com] In town turn onto D952 sp Gorges-du-Verdon, site on L in 100m. Med, mkd pitch, pt shd; htd wc; chem disp; some serviced pitches; shwrs inc; el pnts (6A) €3 (poss rev pol); gas 200m; shops adj; supmkt nr; rest; bar; snacks; pool 200m; 2% statics; poss cr; adv bkg; quiet; red low ssn; CKE/CCI. "Friendly owners; gd san facs but poss stretched in ssn; poss music fr adj community cent till late w/end; gd base for gorges etc; gd." ♦ 1 Mar-11 Nov. € 14.00   2010*

CASTELLANE *10E3* (500m SW Rural) *43.84570, 6.50447*
Camping Notre Dame, Route des Gorges du Verdon, 04120 Castellane [tel/fax 04 92 83 63 02; camping-notredame@wanadoo.fr; www.camping-notredame.com] N fr Grasse on D6085, turn L in Castellane at sq onto D952 to site on R in 500m. Sm, pt shd; wc; chem disp; mv service pnt; shwrs inc; el pnts (6A) €3.50; gas; lndtte; sm shop; rest 600m; playgrnd; 20% statics; dogs free; phone; poss cr; Eng spkn; adv bkg; some rd noise; red low ssn; CKE/CCI. "Ideal touring base; helpful owners; poss a bit unkempt early ssn; excel." ♦ ltd 1 Apr-15 Oct. € 16.00   2009*

CASTELLANE *10E3* (1.5km SW Rural) *43.83921, 6.49370*
Camping Domaine du Verdon, 04120 Castellane [04 92 83 61 29; fax 04 92 83 69 37; contact@camp-du-verdon.com; www.camp-du-verdon.com or www.les-castels.com] Fr Castellane take D952 SW twd Grand Canyon du Verdon & Moustiers-Ste Marie. After 1.5km turn L into site. NB To avoid Col de Lèques with hairpins use N202 & D955 fr Barrême instead of D6085. V lge, hdg/mkd pitch; pt shd; wc (some cont); chem disp; mv service pnt; ltd baby facs; shwrs inc; el pnts (6A) inc; gas; lndtte (inc dryer); shop; rest, snacks; bar; BBQ (gas/elec); playgrnd; htd pool; waterslides; paddling pool; rv fishing adj; canoeing; horseriding nrby; archery; games area; wifi; entmnt; games/TV rm; dogs €3; no c'vans/m'vans over 8m; poss cr; Eng spkn; poss noisy; ccard acc; red low ssn; CKE/CCI. "Excel site by rv; gd sized pitches; gd, clean san facs, modern & dated blocks; quiet, rural walk to town; mkt Wed & Sat." ♦ 15 May-15 Sep. € 34.00 (3 persons)   2011*

See advertisement on inside back cover

CASTELLANE *10E3* (8.5km SW Rural) *43.82842, 6.42743*
FFCC Domaine de Chasteuil-Provence, Route de Moustiers, Chasteuil, 04120 Castellane [04 92 83 61 21; fax 04 92 83 75 62; contact@chasteuil-provence.com; www.chasteuil-provence.com] Take D952 W fr Castellane; site by rv on L. Lge, mkd pitch, pt terr, shd; wc; chem disp; shwrs inc; el pnts (6-10A) €3.30-5.40; gas; lndtte; shop; tradsmn; rest, snacks; bar; playgrnd; htd pool; paddling pool; rv beach; boating; fishing; games area; entmnt high ssn; 10% statics; dogs free; poss cr; adv bkg; quiet; red low ssn; ccard acc; CKE/CCI. "Lovely location by rv; dated facs & poss not clean; excel touring & walking base; access OK for lge o'fits." 1 May-15 Sep. € 22.80 (3 persons)   2008*

CASTELLANE *10E3* (12km SW Rural) *43.79596, 6.43733*
Camp Municipal de Carajuan, 04120 Rougon [04 92 83 70 94; fax 04 92 83 66 49; campingverdon.carajuan@gmail.com; www.rougon.fr] Fr N on D4085 turn R on D952 & foll sps for 16km to rv bank of Gorges du Verdon nr Carajuan bdge; site on L. Fr E on D952 ignore turning to Rougon; site sp in 5km. Med, mkd pitch, pt shd; wc; chem disp (wc); shwrs inc; el pnts (6A) €2.70; lndtte; shop 10km; tradsmn; snacks; playgrnd; 10% statics; dogs €1.20; phone; bus Jul/Aug; poss cr; quiet; Eng spkn; adv bkg; quiet; red long stay; CKE/CCI. "Natural, unspoilt site nr rvside with shingle beach (no sw); friendly staff; basic, dated facs, poss unclean low ssn; gd walking; fair." 21 Mar-30 Sep. € 11.40   2008*

CASTELLANE 10E3 (9km W Rural) 43.82276, 6.43143 **Camp des Gorges du Verdon, Clos d'Aremus, 04120 Castellane [04 92 83 63 64; fax 04 92 83 74 72; aremus@camping-gorgesduverdon.com; www.camping-gorgesduverdon.com]** On D6085 fr Grasse turn L on D952 in Castellane. Camp in 9km on L. Look for sp Chasteuil on R of rd; site in 500m. Lge, mkd pitch, shd; wc; chem disp; mv service pnt; shwrs inc; el pnts (6A) inc; gas; lndtte; sm shop; rest, snacks; bar; playgrnd; htd pool; fishing; boating; canoeing; games area; games rm; wifi; entmnt; TV; 10% statics; dogs free; poss cr; Eng spkn; adv bkg ess; red low ssn; CKE/CCI. "Some sm pitches; rd along Gorges du Verdon poss diff for lge o'fits." ♦ 26 Apr-15 Sep. € 28.50 (3 persons)   2008*

CASTELLANE 10E3 (2km NW Rural) 43.85861, 6.49795 **Kawan Village Camping International, Route Napoléon, La Palud, 04120 Castellane [04 92 83 66 67; fax 04 92 83 77 67; info@camping-international.fr; www.camping-international.fr]** Site sp fr D4085 & D602. Lge, hdg pitch, pt sl, pt shd; htd wc; chem disp; mv service pnt; serviced pitches; baby facs; shwrs inc; el pnts (6A) €4.50; gas; lndtte (inc dryer); sm supmkt; tradsmn; rest, snacks; bar; playgrnd; pool; lake sw & sand beach 5km; games area; golf; horseriding; wifi; entmnt; TV rm; 50% statics; dogs €2; adv bkg; Eng spkn; ccard acc; red low ssn; CKE/CCI. "Busy site; friendly, helpful owners; main san facs vg, some dated, but clean; most pitches on gentle slope; conv Gorges de Verdon; gd walking; gd." ♦ 31 Mar-1 Oct. € 22.45 (CChq acc)   2013*

CASTELNAU MAGNOAC 8F2 (2km SE Rural) 43.26610, 0.52140 **Camping L'Eglantière (Naturist), 65230 Aries-Espénan [05 62 99 83 64 or 05 62 39 88 00; fax 05 62 39 81 44; infos@leglantiere.com; www.leglantiere.com]** Fr Castelnau-Magnoac take D929 S sp Monléon; in 2.5km L on D9 sp Monléon; in 1km L on unclass rd for 500m; L at T-junc & foll L'Eglantiere sp to site; app fr D632 not rec. Lge, hdg/mkd pitch, some hdstg, pt sl, pt shd; wc; chem disp; mv service pnt; serviced pitch; sauna; shwrs inc; el pnts (16A) €5.20 (rev pol); gas; lndtte (inc dryer); shop; tradsmn; rest, snacks; bar; BBQ; playgrnd; htd pool; paddling pool; fishing; canoeing; archery; cycle hire; golf nrby; wifi; 15% statics; dogs €4.20; adv bkg; Eng spkn; quiet; various pitch prices; ccard acc; red low ssn; CKE/CCI. "Beautiful, relaxing site on rv; helpful staff; pitches poss soft after rain; plenty naturist walks; conv Pyrenees." ♦ 1 Apr-25 Sep. € 34.00 (CChq acc)   2009*

CASTELNAUD LA CHAPELLE see Sarlat la Canéda 7C3

CASTELNAUDARY 8F4 (4km E Rural) 43.31723, 2.01582 **FFCC Camping à la Ferme Domaine de la Capelle (Sabatte), St Papoul, 11400 St Martin-Lalande [04 68 94 91 90; lacapelle2@orange.fr; http://www.wmaker.net/lacapelle/]** Fr D6113 Castelnaudary/Carcassonne, take D103 E & foll sp to St Papoul & site in 2km. Well sp. NB Ent poss awkward lge o'fits. Sm, hdg/mkd pitch, pt sl, pt shd; htd wc; chem disp (wc); shwrs inc; el pnts (4A) €2.50; lndtte (inc dryer); shop 2km; tradsmn; BBQ; no statics; dogs €1; phone; Eng spkn; quiet; CKE/CCI. "Delightful, peaceful, spacious CL-type site; friendly, helpful owner; vg san facs, poss stretched when site full; ltd el pnts; gd walking; nr St Papoul Cathar vill with abbey; ideal NH for Spain; excl; Close to ind site, noisy, gd cycling" 1 Apr-30 Sep. € 14.50   2012*

CASTETS 8E1 (800m E Urban) 43.88069, -1.13768 **Camp Municipal Le Galan, 73 Rue du Stade, 40260 Castets [05 58 89 43 52 or 05 58 89 40 09; fax 05 58 55 00 07; contact@camping-legalan.com; www.camping-legalan.com]** Exit N10 junc 12 onto D947; foll sp Castets centre; turn R onto D42; in 500m (after passing over rndabt) turn R onto Rue de Galan; in 200m turn R into Rue du State. Site on L at end of wide cul-de-sac. Site sp in Castets. Lge, pt sl, shd; wc; hot water & shwrs inc; el pnts (10A) inc; gas; lndtte; shop high ssn & 1km; tradsmn; rest 100m; playgrnd; paddling pool; tennis; few statics; dogs €1.70; bus to Dax; adv bkg; quiet but some rd noise; twin-axles extra; red low ssn; CKE/CCI. "Peaceful, clean site in pleasant vill; NH area poss cr; rv walks; excel." ♦ 1 Feb-30 Nov. € 14.45   2011*

CASTIES LABRANDE 8F3 (1.5km W Rural) 43.32502, 0.99046 **Camping Le Casties, Le Bas de Lebrande, 31430 Casties-Labrande [05 61 90 81 11; fax 05 61 90 81 10; lecasties@wanadoo.fr; www.camping-lecasties.com]** S fr Toulouse, exit A64 junc 26 onto D626; after Pouy-de-Touges turn L onto & foll camping sp. Med, hdg pitch, pt shd; wc; chem disp; shwrs inc; el pnts (5A) €1; lndtte; tradsmn; snacks; bar; BBQ; playgrnd; pool; paddling pool; fishing; tennis; 10% statics; dogs free; phone; Eng spkn; adv bkg; quiet; ccard acc; CKE/CCI. "In the middle of nowhere!; lge pitches; staff friendly & helpful; lovely pool; excel; new vg san facs (2013)" ♦ ltd 1 May-30 Sep. € 10.20   2013*

CASTILLON LA BATAILLE 7C2 (E Urban) 44.85350, -0.03550 **Camp Municipal La Pelouse, Chemin de Halage, 33350 Castillon-la-Bataille [05 57 40 04 22 or 05 56 40 00 06 (Mairie)]** Site in town on N bank of Rv Dordogne. After x-ing rv on D17 fr S to N, take 1st avail rd on R to rv. Sm, shd; wc; shwrs inc; el pnts (15A) inc; shop; poss cr; adv bkg; quiet; CKE/CCI. "Peaceful site by rv; busy high ssn; pitches poss rough & muddy when wet; helpful warden; facs dated but clean; conv St Emillion & wine area; gd NH." 1 May-15 Oct. € 15.50   2011*

CASTILLONNES 7D3 (300m N Urban) 44.65566, 0.59111 **Camp Municipal La Ferrette, Route de Bergerac, 47330 Castillonnès [05 53 36 94 68 or 05 58 36 80 49 (Mairie); fax 05 53 36 88 77; mairie.castillonnes@wanadoo.fr]** On N21, 27km S of Bergerac, on N side of Castillonnès. Easily seen fr main rd. Med, mkd pitch, pt sl, pt shd; wc (cont); mv service pnt; shwrs inc; el pnts (6A) €2; lndtte; shops 300m; pool 100m; playgrnd; tennis adj; some statics; quiet. "Beautiful situation; interesting town; gd san facs." ♦ 15 Jun-15 Sep. € 9.50   2010*

⊞ **CASTILLONNES** 7D3 (5km NW Rural) **Camping Le Bost, Le Bost, 24560 Plaisance [05 53 22 84 98 or 06 75 54 18 44 (mob); camping@lebost.com]** S fr Bergerac on N21 to Plaisance in 16km; cont thro vill, going up hill, to lane in 500m sp Le Bost; site set back off rd just after sp. Sm, hdstg, pt sl, pt shd; wc; chem disp; shwrs; el pnts (10A) €3.50; shop 5km; rest, snacks, bar 2km; BBQ; wifi; dogs €1; red long stay. "CL-type site; ideal base for Bergerac wine area; friendly, helpful British owners; gd NH en rte Spain." € 12.00   2008*

FRANCE

CASTRES *8F4* (2km NE Urban) *43.62054, 2.25401* **Camping Gourjade, Ave de Roquecourbe, 81100 Castres [tel/ fax 05 63 59 33 51; contact@campingdegourjade.net; / www.campingdegourjade.net]** Leave Castres NE on D89 sp Rocquecourbe; site on R in 2km. Well sp. Ave de Roquecourbe is part of D89. Med, hdg pitch, pt terr, pt shd; wc unisex; chem disp; mv service pnt; shwrs; el pnts (6-10A) inc (poss rev pol); gas; lndtte; shop in ssn; rest adj; snacks; bar; BBQ; playgrnd; pool; 9 hole golf course adj; cycling; boat fr site to town; 5% statics; dogs €2; bus; quiet; ccard acc; red low ssn; CKE/ CCI. "Lovely site in beautiful park on Rv Agout; lge pitches; helpful staff; gd, tired clean san facs; some lower pitches sl & poss soft; extra charge twin-axles; gd security; poss groups workers low ssn; leisure cent adj; vg cycling; highly rec" ♦ 1 Apr-3 Oct. € 16.50   2012*

⊞ **CASTRIES** *10E1* (1.5km NE Rural) *43.69406, 3.99585* **Camping Domaine de Fondespierre, 277 Route de Fontmarie, 34160 Castries [04 67 91 20 03; fax 04 67 16 41 48; accueil@campingfondespierre.com; www. campingfondespierre.com or www.flowercampings.com]** Fr A9 exit junc 28 dir Castries onto N110; site 1.5km after vill on L. Not well sp. Med, hdg/mkd pitch, hdstg, terr, ptshd; htd wc; chem disp; mv service pnt; baby facs; shwrs inc; el pnts (10A) inc (poss long lead req); gas 5km; lndtte; shops 1.5km; tradsmn; rest, snacks 1.5km; bar; BBQ (sep area); playgrnd; pool; lake sw 5km; tennis adj; golf 2.5km; cycle hire; 40% statics; dogs €3; phone; poss cr; Eng spkn; ccard acc; red CKE/CCI. "Gd walking area; poss itinerants & site poss unkempt low ssn; site rds narr with sharp, tree-lined bends - poss diff access to pitches for lge o'fits; NH." € 24.00   2008*

CAUDEBEC EN CAUX *3C2* (6km S Urban) *49.48373, 0.77247* **Camp Municipal du Parc, Rue Victor Hugo, 76940 La Mailleraye-sur-Seine [02 35 37 12 04; mairie-sg. lamaillerayesurseine@wanadoo.fr]** Fr N on D131/D490 turn E onto D65. Or fr S on D913. Site sp in cent of town close to rv bank. Sm, hdg pitch, pt sl, pt shd; wc; chem disp; shwrs; el pnts (6A) inc; shop, rest, bar 200m; playgrnd; poss cr; quiet. "Pleasant, tidy site; site yourself, warden calls; adequate, clean san facs; gd walking area; vg NH." 1 Apr-30 Sep. € 12.50   2011*

CAUDEBEC EN CAUX *3C2* (1.5km W Rural) *49.52303, 0.70606* **FFCC Camping Barre-y-Va, Route de Villequier, 76490 Caudebec-en-Caux [02 35 96 26 38 or 02 35 95 90 10 (Mairie); campingbarreyva@orange.fr; www.camping-barre-y-va.com]** Fr Caudebec take D81 W twd Villequier & site on R in 1.5km next to Rv Seine. Med, some hdstg, pt shd; wc (some cont); chem disp; shwrs inc; el pnts (10A) €4.30 (poss rev pol); lndtte (inc dryer); shop & 1.5km; tradsmn; rest, snacks; bar; playgrnd; pool 300m; rv fishing & boating adj; cycle hire; games area; games rm; wifi; TV; some statics; dogs €2.60; no twin-axles; phone; Eng spkn; noise fr rd, rv & nrby disco; red low ssn/CKE/CCI. "Popular, well-kept site in interesting area; basic, clean unisex san facs; san block ltd; ent awkward long o'fits; barrier clsd 2200-0700." ♦ 2 Apr-24 Oct. € 17.45   2010*

CAUDECOSTE see Agen *8E3*

CAUNES MINERVOIS *8F4* (1km S Rural) *43.32380, 2.52592* **Camp Municipal Les Courtals, Ave du Stade, 11160 Caunes-Minervois [04 68 78 46 58; mairie.de.caunes@ wanadoo.fr; www.caunesminervois.com]** Sp fr D620 at stadium & adj rv. Sm, pt shd; wc; mv service pnt; shwrs; el pnts (4A) inc; shops adj; tradsmn; playgrnd; pool 6km; games area; rv adj; phone; quiet. "Pleasantly situated site; office opens 1800; gate locked 2100; site self, warden calls; interesting town." 15 Jun-15 Sep. € 12.10   2011*

CAUREL see Mûr de Bretagne *2E3*

CAUSSADE *8E3* (750m NE Urban) *44.16582, 1.54446* **Camp Municipal de la Piboulette, Rue de la Piboulette, 82300 Caussade [05 63 93 09 07; secretariat@mairie-caussade.com; www.mairie-caussade.fr]** S on D820 fr Cahors (40km), turn L off D820 on ent Caussade onto D17 (Rte de Puylaroque). About 750m turn L (sp), site on R in 100m; lge grass stadium. Med, mkd pitch, pt shd; wc (some cont); chem disp; serviced pitches; shwrs inc; el pnts (6A) €1.90; lndtte; shop 500m; tradsmn; playgrnd; sports cent adj; pool on far side of stadium; dogs €1.25; adv bkg; quiet; CKE/CCI. "Pleasant site adj lake; spacious, mostly shaded pitches; pleasant warden; excel, clean san facs, poss tired low ssn; gates locked 2100 low ssn; easy 15 min walk to town; gd walks; gd cycling round lake; conv A20 & Gorges de l'Aveyron; vg mkt Mon; excel value; vg." ♦ 1 May-30 Sep. € 9.10   2012*

CAUSSADE *8E3* (7km NE Rural) *44.18273, 1.60305* **Camping de Bois Redon, 10 Chemin de Bonnet, 82240 Septfonds [05 63 64 92 49 / 06 78 35 79 97 (Mob); info@ campingdeboisredon.com; www.campingdeboisredon.com]** Exit A20 junc 59 to Caussade, then onto D926 to Septfonds (narrow roads); after rndabt turn 3rd L; site sp. Site in 2km. One-way system when leaving site. Sm, mkd pitch, pt sl, pt shd; wc; chem disp; baby facs; shwrs inc; el pnts (10A) €3.50; lndtte; shop; tradsmn; snacks; bar; playgrnd; pool; cycle hire; 10% statics; dogs €2; Eng spkn; adv bkg (dep); quiet; red low ssn; CKE/CCI. "Well-shaded, spacious site in ancient oak forest with walks; charming Dutch owners; immac facs; Septfonds nr with all facs." ♦ ltd 26 Mar-30 Oct. € 18.50   2013*

CAUSSADE *8E3* (10km NE Rural) *44.21700, 1.61297* **Camping Le Clos de la Lère, Clergue, Route de Septfonds, 82240 Cayriech [05 63 31 20 41; contact@camping-leclosdelalere.com; www.camping-leclosdelalere.com]** Take D17 fr Caussade. Turn R at junc with D103 (sp Cayriech/ Septfonds). In Cayriech vill turn R at T-junc by church, site on R in 200m. Foll sp only for Camping Le Clos de la Lère. Fr Septfonds turn N off D926, site in 5.3km on L just bef Cayriech sp. Sm, hdg/mkd pitch, hdstg, pt shd; htd wc; chem disp; mv service pnt; baby facs; shwrs; el pnts (6A) inc; gas; lndtte; shop & 4km; tradsmn; snacks; no BBQ; playgrnd; pool; few statics; dogs €2; adv bkg; quiet; ccard acc; red low ssn/ long stay; CKE/CCI. "Attractive tidy site; site being sold (2011), phone ahead for new opening dates; helpful staff; clean san facs; ltd low ssn; excel games facs; rec arr bef dark; excel NH." ♦ 1 Mar-15 Nov. € 19.50   2011*

CAUSSADE *8E3* (10km NW Rural) *44.24323, 1.47735*
Camping Le Faillal, 46 Blvd Pasteur, 82270 Montpezat-de-Quercy [05 63 02 07 08; fax 04 73 93 71 00; contact@revea-vacances.com; www.revea-vacances.fr/campings] N on D820, turn L onto D20, site clearly sp on R in 2km. (Do not take D38 bef D20 fr S). Med, hdg pitch, pt sl, terr, pt shd; wc; chem disp; shwrs inc; el pnts (4-6A) €3.50; lndtte; shops 200m; playgrnd; pool; tennis adj; games area; few statics; dogs €1.50; phone; adv bkg; quiet; red low ssn/CKE/CCI. "Pretty, well-kept site; friendly, helpful staff; gd, clean san facs, poss ltd; super pool; many pitches unavail after heavy rain; old town a 'must'; rec pay night bef dep; excel." ♦ 31 Mar-28 Oct. € 17.04 (CChq acc)   2012*

⊞ **CAUTERETS** *8G2* (500m N Urban) *42.89402, -0.11255*
Camping Les Glères, 19 Route de Pierrefitte, 65110 Cauterets [05 62 92 55 34; fax 05 62 92 03 53; camping-les-gleres@wanadoo.fr; www.gleres.com] Fr N on D920 ent town; site on R with sharp turn but sp. Narr ent (take care long o'fits). Med, hdg/mkd pitch, hdstg, pt shd; htd wc; chem disp; mv service pnt nr; some serviced pitches; shwrs inc; el pnts (6A) inc; gas; lndtte; rest, snacks, bar, shop, pool 500m; playgrnd; 10% statics; dogs €1.10; phone; site clsd 21 Oct-30 Nov; Eng spkn; quiet; red low ssn; CKE/CCI. "Conv town cent; gd walking area with cable car 500m; superb san facs; friendly & helpful; tight access to pitches; municipal m'van site adj; excel." € 21.10   2010*

CAUTERETS *8G2* (1km N Rural) *42.90254, -0.10605* **Camping Le Péguère, Route de Pierrefitte, 65110 Cauterets [tel/fax 05 62 92 52 91 or 06 28 27 37 24 (mob); campingpeguere@wanadoo.fr; www.campingpeguere.com]** Fr Lourdes on N21 foll sp for Cauterets. On app Cauterets site on R immed after rv bdge. Med, pt sl, pt shd; wc; mv service pnt; shwrs inc; el pnts (6A) inc; lndtte; tradsmn; snacks; playgrnd; rv fishing adj; entmnt; TV rm; some statics; dogs €0.85; adv bkg; quiet; ccard acc; red low ssn; CKE/CCI. "Spacious rvside site in beautiful setting; clean facs; stunning views; ideal base for walking in Pyrenees; rec." ♦ 30 Apr-30 Sep. € 13.50   2010*

CAUTERETS *8G2* (2.5km NE Rural) *42.91092, -0.09934*
Camping GR10, Route de Pierrefitte, 65110 Cauterets [06 70 72 05 02 or 06 20 30 25 85 (LS); contact@gr10camping.com; www.gr10camping.com] N fr Cauterets on D920; site in 2.5km on R. Med, mkd pitch, terr, shd; htd wc; chem disp; shwrs inc; el pnts €4; lndtte; supmkt nrby; playgrnd; htd pool; tennis; canyoning (guide on site); games area; games rm; TV; 25% statics; dogs €1.30; poss cr; Eng spkn; quiet. "Pretty site; excel." 25 Jun- 1 Sep. € 20.00 2012*

CAVAILLON *10E2* (8km E Rural) *43.84220, 5.13284* **Camp Municipal Les Royères du Prieuré, La Combe-St Pierre, 84660 Maubec [04 90 76 50 34; fax 04 32 52 91 57; camping.maubec.provence@wanadoo.fr; www. campingmaubec-luberon.com]** Heading E fr Cavaillon on D2, thro vill of Robion, in 400m at end vill sp turn R to Maubec. Site on R in 1km bef old vill. (Avoid any other rte with c'van). Diff access at ent, steep slope. Sm, terr, pt shd; wc (mainly cont); shwrs inc; shops 1.4km; el pnts (6-10A) €3-4; lndtte; playgrnd; 30% statics; dogs €2; poss cr; quiet; CKE/CCI. "Awkward site for lge o'fits - otherwise vg; san facs stretched high ssn; conv A7." 1 Apr-15 Oct. € 10.00   2009*

CAVAILLON *10E2* (10km E Rural) *43.85568, 5.16803*
Camping Les Boudougnes (Guiraud), Les Chênes, Petit-Coustellet, 84580 Oppède [tel/fax 04 90 76 96 10] Fr N180 in Coustellet, take D2 dir Cavaillon. After 1km turn L onto D3 sp Ménerbes. Turn L at x-rds, site on L in approx 2km just after hamlet of Petit-Coustellet. Take care, hump at ent to lane leading to site, danger of grounding. Sm, pt shd; wc; chem disp (wc); shwrs inc; el pnts (6A) €1; shop 700m; snacks; playgrnd; pool; dogs free; adv bkg; CKE/CCI. "Pleasant, peaceful farm site on edge Luberon National Park; parking among oak trees; levelling blocks req; old facs but clean; nr lavender museum; Oppède-le-Vieux worth visit; rec." 10 Apr-1 Oct. € 9.60   2011*

CAVAILLON *10E2* (1km S Rural) *43.82107, 5.03723* **Camp Municipal de la Durance, 495 Ave Boscodomini, 84300 Cavaillon [04 90 71 11 78; fax 04 90 71 98 77; contact@camping-durance.com; www.camping-durance.com]** S of Cavaillon, nr Rv Durance. Fr A7 junc 25 foll sp to town cent. In 200m R immed after x-ing rv. Site sp (Municipal Camping) on L. Lge, pt shd; htd wc; chem disp; baby facs; shwrs; el pnts (4A-10A) €2.50- 6.50; shops 1.5km; snacks; pool adj; paddling pool; fishing; tennis; games area; TV; 30% statics; dogs €1.50; poss cr; adv bkg; some noise during early am. "Site OK; NH only." 1 Apr-30 Sep. € 13.70   2011*

CAVAILLON *10E2* (8km S Rural) *43.78182, 5.04040*
Camping de la Vallée Heureuse, Quartier Lavau, 13660 Orgon [04 90 44 17 13; fax 04 90 55 16 49; information@camping-lavalleheureuse.com; www.camping-lavalleeheureuse.com] Sp in Organ town cent. Lge, mkd pitch, terr, shd; wc; chem disp; mv service pnt; baby facs; shwrs inc; el pnts €3.50; gas 1km; lndtte; rest & snacks 1km; bar; BBQ; supmkt 10k; playgrnd; pool; lake sw 500m; wifi; TV; dogs €1.70; poss cr; Eng spkn; adv bkg; v quiet; red low ssn; CKE/CCI. "Site in old quarry in beautiful position; friendly, helpful staff; superb san facs; gd pool; gd walking; interesting area; conv m'way; isolated site, vill 1.5km" 15 Mar-15 Oct. € 19.00 (CChq acc)   2012*

> ## "I like to fill in the reports as I travel from site to site"
> You'll find report forms at the back of this guide, or you can fill them in online at www.caravaclub.co.uk/europereport.

CAVAILLON *10E2* (12km SW Rural) *43.76058, 4.95154* **FFCC Camping Les Oliviers, Ave Jean Jaurès, 13810 Eygalières [04 90 95 91 86; fax 04 90 95 91 86; campinglesoliviers13@gmail.com; www.camping-les-oliviers.com]** Exit A7 junc 25; D99 dir St Rémy-de-Provence; in 8km camping sp on L; in vill well sp. Sm, hdg pitch, pt shd; htd wc; el pnts (6A) inc; shop, rest, snacks, bar 250m; BBQ; playgrnd; dogs €1; bus 3km; adv bkg; quiet. "Lovely, friendly site in olive grove nr scenic vill; quiet site; facs rustic but v clean" 30 Mar-15 Oct. € 17.00   2013*

⊞ **CAVAILLON** *10E2* (7km W Rural) *43.83331, 4.94650*
Camp Municipal St Andiol, 13670 St Andiol [tel/fax
04 90 95 01 13] Exit Avignon on N7 & D7n to St Andiol, site on
R of D7n past vill. Sm, hdg pitch, pt shd; wc; shwrs inc; el pnts
(6-10A) €3-4; gas; lndtte; snacks; shop in vill; bar; BBQ; pool;
tennis 1km; golf 15km; entmnt; dogs €1; some rd noise; CKE/
CCI. "Facs adequate; NH only." € 16.50   2010*

CAVALAIRE SUR MER *10F4* (Urban/Coastal) *43.16956,
6.53005* Camping La Baie, Blvd Pasteur, 83240 Cavalaire-
sur-Mer [04 94 64 08 15 or 04 94 64 08 10; contact@
camping-baie.com; www.camping-baie.com] Exit A8 sp
Ste Maxime/St Tropez & foll D25 & D559 to Cavalaire. Site sp
fr seafront. Lge, mkd pitch, pt sl, pt shd; htd wc; baby facs;
shwrs inc; el pnts (10A) €5; lndtte; shop; rest, snacks; bar; BBQ;
playgrnd; htd pool; paddling pool; jacuzzi; sand beach 400m;
sailing; watersports; diving 500m; games area; games rm;
internet; 10% statics; dogs €4; bus to St Tropez & Toulon! poss
cr; Eng spkn; adv bkg; quiet; ccard acc; red low ssn. "Well-run,
busy site; pleasant staff; excel pool & facs; nr shops, beach,
marina & cafes; cycle paths." ♦ 15 Mar-15 Nov.
€ 45.60 (3 persons)   2010*

CAVALAIRE SUR MER *10F4* (1.5km NE Rural) *43.18220,
6.51610* Kawan Village Cros de Mouton, Chemin de Cros
de Mouton, 83240 Cavalaire-sur-Mer [04 94 64 10 87 or
04 94 05 46 38; fax 04 94 64 63 12; campingcrosdemouton@
wanadoo.fr; www.crosdemouton.com] Exit A8 junc 36
dir Ste Maxime on D125/D25, foll sp on D559 to Cavalaire-
sur-Mer. Site sp on coast app fr Grimaud/St Tropez & Le
Lavandou; diff access. Lge, mkd pitch, terr, mainly shd; wc;
chem disp; mv service pnt; serviced pitches; baby facs; shwrs
inc; el pnts (10A) €4.50; gas; lndtte; shop; rest, snacks; bar;
playgrnd; htd pool; paddling pool; sand beach 1.8km; cycle
hire; wifi; TV rm; some statics; dogs €2; phone; Eng spkn; adv
bkg (ess Jul/Aug book by Jan); quiet; ccard acc; red low ssn;
CKE/CCI. "Attractive, well-run, popular site in hills behind
town - rec adv bkg even low ssn; lge pitches avail; poss diff
access to pitches due steep site rds - help avail; pleasant,
welcoming site; gd san facs; gd pool; vg rest & bar; excel." ♦
15 Mar-3 Nov. € 29.60   2013*

See advertisement

CAVALAIRE SUR MER *10F4* (3km NE Coastal) *43.19450,
6.55495* Sélection Camping, 12 Blvd de la Mer, 83420 La
Croix-Valmer [04 94 55 10 30; fax 04 94 55 10 39; camping-
selection@wanadoo.fr; www.selectioncamping.com]
Off N559 bet Cavalaire & La Croix-Valmer, 2km past La Croix
at rndabt turn R sp Barbigoua, site in 200m. Lge, hdg/mkd
pitch, terr, shd; htd wc; chem disp; mv service pnt; baby facs;
private bthrms avail; shwrs inc; el pnts (10A) €5; gas; lndtte
(inc dryer); shop; tradsmn; rest, snacks; bar; playgrnd; htd pool;
paddling pool; sand beach 400m; games area; wifi; entmnt; TV
rm; 20% statics; dogs (not acc Jul/Aug) €4; phone; bus; poss
cr; Eng spkn; adv bkg ess high ssn; quiet. "Excel location; sm
pitches; vg san facs; excel pool; excel site" ♦ 15 Mar-15 Oct.
€ 35.00 (3 persons)   2012*

CAVALAIRE SUR MER *10F4* (1km W Coastal) *43.16681,
6.51910* Camping Bonporteau, 83240 Cavalaire-sur-Mer
[04 94 64 03 24; fax 04 94 64 18 62; contact@bonporteau.
fr; www.camping-bonporteau.com] Sp on S side of N559
Cavalaire-Toulon rd, approx 100m on R after rndabt. Lge, sl,
terr, shd; htd wc; shwrs inc; el pnts (10A) €5; gas; lndtte; shop;
supmkt 500m; rest, snacks; bar; playgrnd; htd pool; jacuzzi;
sand beach 200m; cycle hire; TV; some statics; dogs €4.50; min
1 week's stay Jul/Aug; adv bkg; red low ssn; quiet. "Gd cycle
rte to town, beach & port." 15 Mar-15 Oct.
€ 41.50 (3 persons)   2009*

CAYEUX SUR MER *3B2* (2km NE Coastal) *50.19765,
1.51675* Camping Le Bois de Pins, Rue Guillaume-le-
Conquérant, Brighton, 80410 Cayeux-sur-Mer [tel/fax
03 22 26 71 04; info@campingleboisdepins.com; www.
campingleboisdepins.com] Take D940 out of St Valery to
Cayeux, then D102 NE for 2km & foll sp. Lge, mkd pitch, terr, pt
shd; htd wc; shwrs; chem disp; mv service pnt; el pnts (6-10A)
inc; lndtte; shop; tradsmn; BBQ; playgrnd; beach 500m; sailing &
fishing adj; cycle hire; horseriding; games rm; 50% statics; dogs
€2; adv bkg; quiet; red low ssn/CKE/CCI. "Friendly, clean, busy
site; attractive sm town; gd cycling & birdwatching area; gd." ♦
1 Apr-1 Nov. € 28.50 (3 persons)   2011*

CAYEUX SUR MER *3B2* (3km NE Coastal) *50.20291, 1.52641* **Camping Les Galets de la Mollière, Rue Faidherbe, 80410 La Mollière-d'Aval [03 22 26 61 85; fax 03 22 26 65 68; info@campinglesgaletsdelamolliere.com; www. campinglesgaletsdelamolliere.com]** Fr Cayeux-sur-Mer take D102 N along coast for 3km. Site on R. Lge, mkd pitch, pt shd; wc; chem disp; mv service pnt; baby facs; shwrs inc; el pnts (6A) inc; gas; lndtte (inc dryer); shop; snacks; bar; BBQ; playgrnd; htd pool; paddling pool; sand beach 500m; games area; games rm; wifi; 25% statics; dogs €3; phone adj; quiet; red low ssn; CKE/CCI. "Spacious, much improved, wooded site with lge pitches; barrier clsd 2300-0700; pleasant staff." 1 Apr-1 Nov. € 31.00 (3 persons)   2011*

CAYLAR, LE *10E1* (4km SW Rural) *43.83629, 3.29045* **Aire Naturelle Mas de Messier, St Félix-de-l'Héras, 34520 Le Caylar [tel/fax 04 67 44 52 63; info@masdemessier.com; www.masdemessier.com]** Fr N exit A75 junc 49 onto D9 thro Le Caylar. Turn R sp St Félix & foll sp St Félix-de-l'Héras; at x-rds in St Félix turn R, site in 1km on L. Fr S exit A75 junc 50; foll sp to St Félix-de-l'Héras; at x-rds turn R & as bef. Sm, hdg pitch, pt sl, pt shd; wc; chem disp; mv service pnt; shwrs; el pnts (6A) €3; lndtte; shop 4km; tradsmn; playgrnd; pool; wifi; dogs free; adv bkg, ess high ssn; quiet; Eng spkn; red low ssn; CKE/CCI. "Excel views fr some pitches; friendly, helpful Dutch owner; facs fair; access unsuitable lge o'fits; meals avail some eves; gd walking." ♦ ltd 11 Apr-15 Oct. € 15.00   2010*

CAYLUS *8E4* (500m E Rural) *44.23368, 1.77636* **FFCC Camping de la Bonnette, 672 route de la Bonnette, 82160 Caylus [tel/ fax 05 63 65 70 20; info@campingbonnette.com; www.campingbonnette.com]** Fr A20 exit junc 59 dir Caylus; thro Caylus to g'ge on L. Turn R in 1km over next crossroads & foll site sps to site on right in 1km; med, hdg/mkd pitch, pt shd; wc; chem disp; mv service pnt; baby facs; shwrs inc; el pnts (10A) €3.50; lndtte (inc dryer); shop 1km; tradsmn; bar & rest; BBQ; playgrnd; pool; games area; wifi; entmnt; some statics; dogs €1.50; Eng spkn; adv bkg (rec high ssn); quiet; red 7 days. "Nice, tidy, scenic site on edge of medieval vill - worth a visit; pitches in groups of 4, not v pvt" ♦ 29 Mar-5 Oct. € 32.00   2013*

CAYRIECH see Caussade *8E3*

CAZALS *7D3* (Rural) *44.64186, 1.22179* **Camp Municipal du Plan d'Eau, La Cayré, 46250 Cazals [05 65 22 84 45 or 05 65 22 82 84 (Mairie); fax 05 65 22 87 15; mairiecazals@ wanadoo.fr]** Fr Frayssinet-le-Gélat N on D673 dir Gourdon; site on L immed after ent Cazals. Ent just past red/white 'No Entry' sp. Med, mkd pitch, pt shd; wc; mv service pnt; shwrs; el pnts; lndtte; shops 500m; rest; bar; playgrnd; lake sw; entmnt; some statics; poss cr; quiet. "Basic, clean facs; friendly warden; tractor/machinery museum nrby." 1 May-30 Sep. € 9.80   2009*

CAZOULES see Souillac *7C3*

CEAUCE *4E1* (1km N Rural) *48.49812, -0.62481* **Camp Municipal de la Veillotière, Chemin de la Veillotière, 61330 Ceaucé [02 33 38 31 19; mairie-ceauce@wanadoo.fr]** S fr Domfront on D962 dir Mayenne, at rndabt in Ceaucé turn L. Site in 200m on R adj sm lake. Sm, hdg pitch, pt sl, pt shd; wc; chem disp; mv service pnt; shwrs inc; el pnts (5A) inc; shop; rest; bar 200m; playgrnd; fishing adj; quiet. "Well-kept site on edge vill; gd." ♦ ltd 1 May-30 Sep. € 10.00   2010*

CELLES SUR BELLE see Melle *7A2*

CELLES SUR PLAINE see Raon l'Etape *6E3*

CELLETTES see Blois *4G2*

CENAC ET ST JULIEN see Sarlat la Canéda *7C3*

CENDRAS see Alès *10E1*

CENEVIERES see Cajarc *7D4*

CERCY LA TOUR *4H4* (Urban) *46.86680, 3.64328* **Camp Municipal Le Port, 58360 Cercy-la-Tour [03 86 50 55 27 or 03 86 50 07 11 (Mairie)]** At Decize take D981 E; in 12 km L onto D37, then L onto D10 to Cercy-la-Tour; site sp in vill. Adj municipal pool, Rv Aron & canal. Med, hdstg, pt shd; wc; chem disp; shwrs inc; el pnts inc; pool nrby; dogs; phone; quiet; CKE/ CCI. "Clean & tidy site; immac san facs; gd cycling/walking along canal; great value; excel." 15 May-15 Sep. € 8.95 2012*

CERESTE *10E3* (2.5km SW Rural) *43.84564, 5.56394* **Camping Bois de Sibourg (Vial-Ménard), 04280 Céreste [04 92 79 02 22 or (mobs) 06 30 88 63 29 or 06 70 64 62 01; campingsibourg@orange.fr; www.sibourg.com]** W fr Céreste on D900/D4100; turn L in 2km (site sp); site on L in 1km. Sm, pt shd; wc (cont); shwrs inc; el pnts (6A) €2.80; dogs free; phone; Eng spkn; CKE/CCI. "Delightful 'green' farm site; St Michel l'Observatoire 15km; gd NH or longer; excel." 15 Apr-15 Oct. € 8.70   2009*

CERESTE *10E3* (6km W Rural) *43.84361, 5.49666* **Camping à la Ferme (Bouscarle), Les Monguets, 84400 Castellet-en-Luberon [04 90 75 28 62]** Fr W on D900 (Apt) ignore Camping à la Ferme sp to R nr St Martin-de-Castillon (v narr rd). Cont 2km to La Bègude & turn R onto D233 dir Le Boisset. Site 3km on R, well sp. Sm, pt sl, shd; wc; chem disp (wc); shwrs inc; el pnts (4A) €3 (long lead req); shop 6km; no statics; dogs €1; poss cr; some Eng spkn; adv bkg; CKE/CCI. "Excel, scenic CL-type site on fruit farm; friendly owners; excel walking, cycling." Easter-1 Nov. € 13.00   2009*

CERET *8H4* (7km N Rural) *42.54833, 2.75361* **Camp Municipal Al Comu, Route de Fourques, 66300 Llauro [04 68 39 42 08; alcomu@wanadoo.fr]** Fr N on A9 exit junc 43. Take D115 dir Céret. Bef bdge R onto D615 to Llauro. Site on L after vill. Sm, mkd pitch, hdstg, terr, pt shd; wc; chem disp; baby facs; fam bthrm; shwrs inc; el pnts (16A) €2.75; lndtte; shop in vill; tradsmn; BBQ; playgrnd; pool 10km; lake sw 6km; dogs; Eng spkn; quiet; red low ssn; CKE/CCI. "Attractive setting in lower Pyrenees; gd views; friendly, helpful owners live on site; vg." ♦ ltd 1 Apr-31 Oct. € 13.50   2010*

CERET *8H4* (500m E Urban) *42.48421, 2.75871* **Camp Municipal Bosquet de Nogarède, Ave d'Espagne, 66400 Céret [04 68 87 26 72; www.tourisme-pyreneesorientales. com]** Exit A9 junc 43 onto D115 twd Céret, then foll sp Maureillas D618. Site clearly sp 500m fr cent Céret. Med, mkd pitch, terr, shd; wc; chem disp; shwrs inc; el pnts (6A) inc; gas 1km; lndtte; shop 1km; rest, snacks; bar 1km; BBQ; playgrnd; htd, covrd pool; tennis 400m; 10% statics; dogs; phone; poss cr; some rd noise; CKE/CCI. "Attractive town with modern art museum; san facs fair; gd NH." ♦ ltd 1 Apr-31 Oct. € 15.00   2011*

⊞ **CERET** *8H4* (1km E Rural) *42.48981, 2.76305* **Camping Les Cerisiers, Mas de la Toure, 66400 Céret [04 68 87 00 08 or 06 83 22 64 57 (mob); camping.lescerisiers@club-internet. fr; www.campingcerisiers.com]** Exit A9 junc 43 onto D115, turn off for cent of Céret. Site is on D618 approx 800m E of Céret twd Maureillas, sp. Tight ascent for lge o'fits. Med, mkd pitch, shd; wc; chem disp; baby facs; fam bthrm; shwrs inc; el pnts (4A); gas; lndtte; shop, rest, snacks, bar 1km; playgrnd; pool 600m; lake sw 2km; sand beach 28km; entmnt; TV; 60% statics; dogs; phone; site clsd Jan; quiet; CKE/CCI. "Site in cherry orchard; gd size pitches; facs dated & ltd low ssn; footpath to attractive vill with modern art gallery; conv Andorra, Perpignan, Collioure." ♦   2009*

CERET *8H4* (8km SW Rural) *42.47879, 2.67418* **Camp Municipal Can Day, Rue des Lledoners, Ave Beausoleil, 66112 Amélie-les-Bains-Palalda [04 68 39 22 37; fax 04 68 39 06 46; www.amelie-les-bains.com]** S fr Céret on D115, site sp on N edge of vill. Med, hdg/mkd pitch, pt shd; htd wc; mv service pnt; shwrs; el pnts inc; playgrnd; fishing nr; dogs €1; quiet. ♦ 1 Feb-1 Dec. € 10.30   2010*

CERILLY *4H3* (8km N Rural) *46.68210, 2.78630* **Camping des Ecossais, La Salle, 03360 Isle-et-Bardais [04 70 66 62 57 or 04 70 67 55 89 (LS); fax 04 70 66 63 99; ecossais@ campingstroncais.com; www.campingstroncais.com]** Fr Lurcy-Lévis take D978A SW, turn R onto D111 N twd Isle-et-Bardais & foll camp sp. Ent tight. Med,hdg, pt sl, pt shd; wc; Chem disp; mv service pnt; child/baby facs; shwrs inc; el pnts (10A) inc; lndtte; shop, tradsmn, snack, bar, BBQ, playgrnd; rest nr; lake sw; fishing; dogs €1.50; games area/room, wifi, 10% statics, twin axle acc, adv bkg; quiet; red low ssn; CKE/CCI. "Excel; V busy high ssn; Ltd facs low ssn; gd cycling; site in oak forest; rec;" 1 Apr-30 Sep. € 11.55   2013*

CERILLY *4H3* (11km NW Rural) *46.65683, 2.68837* **FFCC Camping de Champ Fossé, 03360 St Bonnet-Tronçais [04 70 06 11 30; fax 04 70 06 15 01; champfosse@ campingstroncais.com; www.campingstroncais.com]** Fr D2144 turn E on D978A sp Forêt de Tronçais; after 8km foll sp to vill of St Bonnet-Tronçais. Med, some hdstg, sl, pt shd; wc (some cont); mv service pnt; shwrs inc; el pnts (10A) inc; lndtte; shops 1km; snacks; bar; playgrnd; sand beach; bathing; boat hire; fishing; walking; dogs €0.80; quiet; adv bkg. "Poor supervision; sl, so blocks req; lovely location; excel walks; sh walk to vill." 1 Apr-31 Oct. € 10.30   2008*

CERNAY *6F3* (5km N Rural) *47.8324, 7.16833* **Camping Les Sources, Route des Crêtes, 68700 Wattwiller [03 89 75 44 94; fax 03 89 75 71 98; www.camping-les-sources.com; www.camping-les-sources.com]** Fr Cernay take D5 NE to Soultz; thro Uffholtz & turn L foll sp to Wattwiller; turn L immed after vill sp & foll camp sp. Park outside bef check-in. Some site rds steep. Lge, mkd pitch, hdstg, terr, pt shd; wc (v steep app to facs - 25% gradient); chem disp; mv service pnt; serviced pitches; baby facs; shwrs inc; el pnts (5A) €3.50 (poss rev pol); gas; lndtte; shop; tradsmn; rest; BBQ (gas/charcoal); playgrnd; htd, covrd pool; tennis; games rm; games area; horseriding adj; entmnt; internet; 25% statics; dogs €2; Eng spkn; adv bkg ess high ssn; quiet; ccard acc; CKE/CCI. "Steep wooded app to site; diff getting on & off some pitches; tractor avail; not suitable lge o'fits; on 'wine rte'; barrier clsd 2200; mkt Tue & Fri Cernay." ♦ 3 Apr-10 Oct. € 28.50   2008*

CERNAY *6F3* (500m S Urban) *47.80448, 7.16999* **Camping Les Acacias, 16 Rue René Guibert, 68700 Cernay [03 89 75 56 97; fax 03 89 39 72 29; www.camping-les-acacias.com]** Fr N on D83 by-pass, exit Cernay Est. Turn R into town at traff lts, immed L bef rv bdge, site sp on L; well sp. Lge, mkd pitch, pt shd; wc; chem disp; mv service pnt; shwrs inc; el pnts (5A) €3.50 (poss rev pol); lndtte; shop, rest, bar & pool (high ssn); entmnt; 25% statics; dogs €1.20; poss cr; quiet; red long stay; 10% red CKE/CCI (pitch only). "Friendly staff; clean, tidy site; storks nesting over some pitches; sh walk to town." ♦ 1 Apr-1 Oct. € 12.00   2010*

CERNAY *6F3* (6km S Rural) *47.74684, 7.12423* **Camping Les Castors, 4 Route de Guewenheim, 68520 Burnhaupt-le-Haut [03 89 48 78 58; fax 03 89 62 74 66; camping.les. castors@wanadoo.fr; www.camping-les-castors.fr]** Exit A36 junc 15 sp Burnhaupt-le-Haut onto D83, then D466 sp Masevaux. Site on R. Med, mkd pitch, pt shd; htd wc; chem disp; baby facs; shwrs inc; el pnts (5-10A) €4-5; gas; lndtte; shop 2km; tradsmn; rest, snacks; bar; BBQ; playgrnd; games rm; wifi; 40% statics; dogs €15; phone; poss cr; Eng spkn; adv bkg; quiet; CKE/CCI. "Conv German & Swiss borders, Black Forest; wine route; Mulhouse motor museum; gd san facs; vg; excel site, nice area. Friendly owner. Gd cycle path" ♦ 1 Apr-31 Oct. € 12.80 (CChq acc)   2013*

CESSERAS see Olonzac *8F4*

CEYRAT see Clermont Ferrand *9B1*

CHABEUIL see Valence *9C2*

CHABLIS *4F4* (600m W Rural) *47.81376, 3.80563* **Camp Municipal Le Serein, Quai Paul Louis Courier, 89800 Chablis [03 86 42 44 39 or 03 86 42 80 80 (Mairie); fax 03 86 42 49 71; mairie-chablis@chablis.net; www.chablis. net]** W fr Tonnere on D965; in approx 16km exit D965 for Chablis; in 300m, just bef x-ing Rv Serein, turn L at camping sp onto Quai Paul Louis Courier; site in 300m on R. Med, hdg/mkd pitch, shd; wc (some cont); shwrs inc; el pnts (5A) €2; gas 1km; lndtte; shops, rest & snacks 1km; tradsmn; playgrnd; rv adj; no dogs; poss cr; Eng spkn; adv bkg; quiet; CKE/CCI. "Attractive site; facs poss stretched high ssn; site untidy (2011) warden calls 0800-1200 & 1600-2000; easy walk to attractive town; vineyards & wine cellars nrby; excel Sun mkt." ♦ ltd 2 Jun-15 Sep. € 11.00   2011*

CHAGNY *6H1* (W) *46.91187, 4.74567* **FFCC Camp Municipal du Pâquier Fané, 20 Rue du Pâquier Fané, 71150 Chagny [03 85 87 21 42 or 06 18 27 21 99 (mob); camping-chagny@orange.fr; www.chagny-bourgogne-tourisme.com]** Clearly sp in town. Med, hdg/mkd pitch, pt shd; wc; chem disp; mv service pnt; shwrs inc; el pnts (6A) €3.50 (rev pol); gas; lndtte; shop, rest, snacks & bar 500m; playgrnd; htd pool adj; fishing; tennis adj; dogs €1; Eng spkn; adv bkg (ess Jul/Aug); quiet except rlwy noise adj; red low ssn; CKE/CCI. "Well laid-out, well-lit site; friendly, helpful resident wardens; clean san facs; many pitches sm & diff med/lge o'fits; on wine rte; gd cycling nrby (voie verte)." ♦ 1 Apr-31 Oct. € 18.00   2011*

⊞ **CHAILLAC** *7A3* (SW Rural) *46.43260, 1.29602* **Camp Municipal Les Vieux Chênes, 36310 Chaillac [02 54 25 61 39 or 02 54 25 74 26 (Mairie); fax 02 54 25 65 41; chaillac-mairie@wanadoo.fr]** Exit N20 S of Argenton-sur-Creuse at junc 20 onto D36 to Chaillac. Thro vill, site 1st L after sq by 'Mairie', adj Lac du Rochegaudon. Sm, hdg/mkd pitch, pt sl, pt shd; htd wc (some cont); chem disp; shwrs inc; el pnts (16A) inc (poss rev pol); lndry rm; shop, rest, bar 200m; BBQ; playgrnd; lake sw & fishing adj; waterslide; tennis adj; 35% statics; dogs; phone adj; poss cr; adv bkg; quiet; CKE/CCI. "excel site, beautiful location, friendly wardens, well kept san facs, gd local supermarket 2mins walk. " ♦ € 9.60   2013*

CHAILLES see Blois *4G2*

CHAISE DIEU, LA *9C1* (2km NE Rural) *45.33526, 3.70388* **Camp Municipal Les Prades, 43160 La Chaise-Dieu [04 71 00 07 88; fax 04 71 00 03 43; andre.brivadis@orange.fr]** Site well sp fr D906. Med, pt sl, shd; wc (some cont); chem disp; baby facs; shwrs inc; el pnts (10A) inc (long lead poss req); lndtte; shops 2km; tradsmn; BBQ; playgrnd; lake sw 300m; 10% statics; quiet. "Fair sh stay/NH; tourist info office in vill; 14thC church; vg for mushrooms in ssn." 1 Jun-30 Sep. € 12.20   2010*

CHAIZE GIRAUD, LA see Bretignolles sur Mer *2H3*

CHALANDRAY *4H1* (750m N Rural) *46.66728, -0.00214* **Camping du Bois de St Hilaire, Rue de la Gare, 86190 Chalandray [tel/fax 05 49 60 20 84 or 01246 852823 (UK); acceuil@camping-st-hilaire.com; www.camping-st-hilaire.com]** Foll N149 bet Parthenay & Vouille; at xrds in vill, turn N into Rue de la Gare (D24); site 750m on R over rlwy line. Sm, mkd pitch, pt shd; wc; chem disp; shwrs inc; el pnts (10A) €3.95; lndtte; shop; rest, snacks, bar in vill; BBQ; playgrnd; pool; tennis; games rm; TV rm; dogs free; bus 750m; c'van storage; adv bkg; ccard acc; quiet; CKE/CCI. "Friendly, helpful British owners; situated in mature forest area, sh walk fr vill; 20 mins fr Futuroscope; lge pitches; excel, clean site & pool; poss muddy in wet weather." ♦ 1 May-30 Sep. € 23.25   2013*

> **"We must tell The Club about that great site we found"**
> Get your site reports in by mid-August and we'll do our best to get your updates into the next edition of Caravan Europe

CHALARD, LE see St Yrieix la Perche *7B3*

⊞ **CHALLANS** *2H4* (10km S) *46.81522, -1.77472* **Camping Domaine de Bellevue, Bellevue Du Ligneron, 85670 Saint Christophe du Ligneron [02 51 93 30 66 / 06 21 55 54 29 (mob); campingdebellevue85@orange.fr; www.vendee-camping-bellevue.com]** From S: On Route National D948 exit Saint Christophe du Lingeron; turn W in dir Saint Gilles Croix de Vie/Commequiers; at rndbt continue straight on; take 2nd R at Bellevue du Ligneron. Med, hdg pitch; wc; baby facs; shwrs (inc); el pnts (16) €4.00; lndtte; bar; take away; BBQ; pool (htd); fishing; cycle hire; games rm; wifi; 50% statics; dogs €3; adv bkg; Eng spkn; ccard acc; CKE/CCI. "Gd value for money; in lovely Vendee region; gd fishing on site; new site with friendly owners" ♦ € 17.00   2013*

See advertisement

CHALLES LES EAUX see Chambéry *9B3*

CHALON SUR SAONE *6H1* (1km E Rural) *46.78411, 4.87136* **Camping du Pont de Bourgogne, Rue Julien Leneveu, 71380 St Marcel [03 85 48 26 86 or 03 85 94 16 90 (LS); fax 03 85 48 50 63 or 03 85 94 16 97 (LS); campingchalon71@ wanadoo.fr; www.camping-chalon.com]** Fr A6 exit junc 26 (sp Chalon Sud) onto N80 E; foll sp Chalon-sur-Saône; at 1st rndabt go strt over (sp Louhans & St Marcel) & over flyover; take 4th exit on 2nd rndbt; immed after this rndabt fork R thro Les Chavannes (still on N80). Turn R at traff lts bef bdge. (DO NOT CROSS BRIDGE). Site in 500m. Med, hdg/mkd pitch, hdstg, terr, pt shd; htd wc; chem disp; mv service pnt; shwrs inc; el pnts (6A) inc; gas; lndtte (inc dryer); sm shop; hypmkt nr; tradsmn; rest, snacks; bar; BBQ; playgrnd; pool 500m; rv fishing; canoeing nrby; cycle hire; wifi; games/TV rm; dogs €2.60; no c'vans/ m'vans over 12m; Eng spkn; some noise fr rd & rv pathway; ccard acc; red low ssn; CKE/CCI. "Peaceful, well-run rvside site; lge pitches, some by rv; helpful, friendly staff; excel clean san facs, poss stretched high ssn; vg rest/bar; rvside walks; lovely town; conv NH fr A6; vg; Gd cycling" ♦ 1 Apr-30 Sep. € 38.30 (CChq acc) SBS - L17   2013*

CHALON SUR SAONE *6H1* (12km SE Rural) *46.69813, 4.92751* **Mini-Camping Les Tantes, 29 Route de Grigny, 71240 Marnay [03 85 44 23 88 or 06 19 22 09 73 (mob)]** On D978 SE fr Chalon-sur-Saône, turn R in vill of Ouroux-sur-Saône onto D6 twd Marnay. Over bdge, foll site sp. Sm, hdg pitch, pt shd; wc; chem disp; shwrs inc; el pnts (5-10A) €2.90-4.20; lndry rm; tradsmn; snacks; BBQ; sm playgrnd; pool; games area; 30% statics; dogs; phone; no twin-axles; o'night area; quiet. "Gd." ♦ 1 Apr-30 Sept. € 8.90   2012*

CHALONNES SUR LOIRE *2G4* (1km E Rural) *47.35013, -0.74951* **Camping Le Candais, Route de Rochefort, 49290 Chalonnes-sur-Loire [02 41 78 02 27 or 02 41 78 26 21 (OT); fax 02 41 74 10 80; camping@ chalonnes-sur-loire.fr]** Turn E in Chalonnes to D751. Site on L in 1km on S bank of Loire. Med, mkd pitch, hdstg, pt shd; wc; shwrs inc; chem disp (wc); el pnts (5A) €2.50; gas 1km; ice; lndtte; shop adj; tradsmn; BBQ; playgrnd; pool 200m; fishing; cycle hire; games area; entmnt; TV rm; 2% statics; dogs €1.50; Eng spkn; adv bkg; quiet but some rd noise; CKE/ CCI. "Peaceful rvside site in beautiful location; lge pitches; gd cycling along rv; gd touring base; liable to flooding; gd." ♦ 21 May-11 Sep. € 9.50   2013*

CHALONNES SUR LOIRE *2G4* (8km SE Rural) *47.32285, -0.71428* **Camp Municipal Les Patisseaux, Route de Chalonnes, 49290 Chaudefonds-sur-Layon [02 41 78 04 10 (Mairie); fax 02 41 78 66 89; mairie. chaudefondsurlayon@wanadoo.fr]** Fr Chalonnes on D961 S dir Cholet. Turn L onto D125. At narr rlwy bdge after 3km, foll sp to site on Rv Layon. Sm, hdg/mkd pitch, pt shd; wc; mv service pnt; shwrs; el pnts; shop, bar 500m; quiet. "V basic, clean site nr rv; lots of interest in area." ♦ 1 May-31 Aug. € 5.60   2010*

CHALONNES SUR LOIRE *2G4* (9km SE Urban) *47.32803, -0.67134* **Camp Municipal du Layon, Rue Jean de Pontoise, 49190 St Aubin-de-Luigné [02 41 78 33 28 (Mairie); fax 02 41 78 68 55; mairie-sg.staubin@wanadoo.fr]** Exit N160 Angers-Chemillé at sp St Aubin or turn S off D751 at sp St Aubin. Site sp in vill. Sm, hdg/mkd pitch, pt shd; wc; mv service pnt in adj car pk with access to facs; shwrs inc; el pnts €4.90; shop 150m; playgrnd; rv adj; boat hire; quiet. "Pleasant, historic vill; warden calls 0800-0945 or pay at Mairie nrby; unsuitable lge o'fits due diff manoeuvring; san facs adequate; public footpath thro site; gd walking/cycling." ♦ 1 May-30 Sep. € 7.00   2009*

CHALONNES SUR LOIRE *2G4* (9km NW) *47.39211, -0.87082* **Camping La Promenade, Quai des Mariniers, 49570 Montjean-sur-Loire [02 41 39 02 68 or 06 26 32 60 28 (mob); contact@campinglapromenade.com; www.campinglapromenade.com]** Exit Angers on N23 twd Nantes. Exit 1km beyond St Germain-des-Prés dir Montjean-sur-Loire. Cross rv then R on D210 to site in 500m. Med, pt shd; wc (some cont); shwrs inc; el pnts (6-9A) €2.60; lndtte; shops adj; rest, snacks; BBQ; playgrnd; pool; sand beach 600m; entmnt; TV; 30% statics; dogs €1.05; Eng spkn; adv bkg; quiet; CKE/CCI. "Friendly, young owners; interesting sculptures in vill & at Ecomusée." 1 Apr-7 Oct. € 11.40   2012*

See advertisement on pages 32 & 33

CHALONS EN CHAMPAGNE *5D1* (2km S Urban) *48.93579, 4.38299* **Camping de Châlons en Champagne, 11-15 Rue de Plaisance, 51000 Châlons-en-Champagne [tel/ fax 03 26 68 38 00; camping.chalons@orange.fr; www. aquadis-loisirs.com]** Fr N on A26 exit junc 17 take D3 to Châlons, site sp. Fr S exit junc 18 onto D977, then D5 over rv & canal nr town cent; then foll site sp to R. Fr N44 S of Châlons sp St Memmie; foll site sp. D977 fr N into Châlons, cont on main rd to traff lts at 6 x-rds & turn R, site well sp. Or exit A4 junc 27 onto N44; turn R at St Memmie; site sp. NB some sps in area still show old town name 'Châlons-sur-Marne'. Med, hdg/mkd pitch, hdstg, pt shd; htd wc; chem disp; mv service pnt; shwrs inc; el pnts (10A) €3.60 (poss long lead req & rev pol); lndtte (inc dryer); sm shop 100m; hypmkt 1km; tradsmn; snacks; BBQ; playgrnd; pool 2km; sm lake; tennis; wifi; TV rm; dogs €1.50; bus; poss cr; Eng spkn; adv bkg; quiet but poss noisy high ssn - pop concerts in adj area; ccard acc; red long stay; CKE/ CCI; "Popular site adj park; generous pitches, inc hdstg; rec arr early or phone ahead; check barrier arrangements if need early dep; gates shut 2130 low ssn & 2300 high ssn; friendly staff; ltd bus service; flat walk to lovely, interesting town; conv touring base & NH; San facs dated; Site tired, but everything works; Friendly helpful Eng spking recep" ♦ 15 Mar-15 Nov. € 28.85 (CChq acc)   2013*

CHALUS *7B3* (12km S Rural) *45.54711, 0.95487* **FFCC Camping Le Périgord Vert, Fardoux, 24450 La Coquille [05 53 52 85 77; fax 05 53 55 14 25; leperigordvert@aol.com]** On N21 Périgueux/Châlus rd bet Thiviers & Châlus, turn L in vill of La Coquille at traff lts foll sps for Mialet. In 1.5km turn R, site 500m on L; sp. Sm, pt shd, pt sl; wc; chem disp; mv service pnt; shwrs inc; el pnts (6A) inc; gas; lndtte; shops 2km; tradsmn; rest, snacks, bar high ssn; playgrnd; pool high ssn; free fishing; tennis; 5% statics; dogs; phone; poss cr; Eng spkn; adv bkg; quiet; red low ssn; CKE/CCI. "Pleasant site; helpful staff; choice of meadow or woodland pitch; poor facs, ltd low ssn." ♦ 15 Apr-30 Oct. € 13.30   2010*

⊞ **CHALUS** *7B3* (9km NW Rural) *45.71540, 0.91956* **Camping Parc Verger, Le Halte, 87150 Champagnac-la-Rivière, Limousin [05 55 01 22 83 or 06 04 09 05 20 (mob); pvbureau@parcverger.com; www.parcverger.com]** N fr Châlus on D901; in 9km turn L onto D75 sp Champagnac-la-Rivière; site on L in 150m. Sm, some mkd pitch, hdstg, unshd; htd wc; chem disp; mv service pnt; shwrs inc; el pnts (16A) inc; gas 1km; lndtte (inc dryer); shop 1km; tradsmn; rest, snacks & bar 1km; BBQ; no playgrnd (2009); sm pool; lake sw & sand beach 10km; wifi; dogs; bus 150m; Eng spkn; adv bkg; v quiet; ccard acc; red grass pitch; red long stay; CKE/CCI. "Lovely site; welcoming, friendly, helpful British owners; lge pitches suitable for RVs; gd clean san facs, poss stretched high ssn; gd mkd walks nrby; 15km-long walk/cycle path adj (old rwly track); excel local vet; excel area for walking" ♦ € 22.00   2013*

CHAMBERY *9B3* (5km E Rural) *45.55151, 5.98416* **Camp Municipal Le Savoy, Parc des Loisirs, Chemin des Fleurs, 73190 Challes-les-Eaux [tel/fax 04 79 72 97 31; camping73challes-les-eaux&wanadoo.fr; www.ville-challesleseaux.com]** On o'skts of town app fr Chambéry on D1006. Pass airfield, lake & tennis courts on L, L at traff lts just before cent of Challes-les Eaux sp Parc de Loisirs, at Hôtel Les Neiges de France foll camp sp to site in 100m. Fr A41 exit junc 20, foll sp Challes-les-Eaux, then 'Centre Ville', then D1006 N. Med, mkd pitch, hdstg, shd; wc; chem disp; serviced pitches; shwrs; el pnts (6-10A) €2.90; gas; lndtte; shop, rest adj; snacks in ssn; lake sw, fishing, tennis adj; dogs €1; bus; adv bkg; quiet but some rd noise; ccard acc; red long stay. "Well-designed, well-run, clean site in beautiful setting; diff sized pitches; level (suitable wheelchairs); friendly, helpful staff; excel modern san facs; excel walking; Well run site, rec hotel school rest in term time" ♦ 1 May-30 Sep. € 15.60   2013*

CHAMBERY *9B3* (10km SW Rural) *45.53804, 5.79973* **Camping Les Peupliers, Lac d'Aiguebelette, 73610 Lépin-le-Lac [04 79 36 00 48 / 06 66 10 09 99 (mob); fax 04 79 44 12 48; info@camping-lespeupliers.net; www.camping-lespeupliers.net]** Exit A43 junc 12 & foll sp Lac d'Aiguebelette (D921). Turn L at rndabt & foll rd on L of lake. Site on R after sm vill. Lge, hdg/mkd pitch, pt shd; wc; chem disp; shwrs inc; el pnts (6A) €3.20; lndtte; shop 3km; tradsmn; rest 3km; snacks; bar; playgrnd; lake sw adj; fishing; wifi; dogs €1.10 (NO SW); poss cr; quiet; ccard acc; red low ssn; CKE/CCI. "Pleasant site in beautiful setting, espec lakeside pitches; friendly, helpful owner; busy weekends" 1 Apr-30 Oct. € 22.45   2013*

CHAMBERY *9B3* (11km SW Rural) *45.53990, 5.77940* **Camping Le Curtelet, 73610 Lépin-le-Lac [tel/fax 04 79 44 11 22; lecurtelet@wanadoo.fr; www.camping-le-curtelet.com]** Fr A43 E to Chambéry exit junc 12 onto D921 bef Tunnel L'Epine sp Lac d'Aiguebelette. Foll rd round lake, turn L on D921D to Lépin-le-Lac. Site sp after stn on L over level x-ing. Med, mkd pitch, pt sl, pt shd; wc; chem disp; baby facs; shwrs inc; el pnts (2-6A) €2.30-3; lndtte; shop 1km; tradsmn; bar; BBQ; playgrnd; lake sw; sand beach adj; dogs €1.40; Eng spkn; adv bkg; some rlwy noise at top of site; red low ssn; CKE/CCI. "Beautiful scenery; well-maintained site; no twin-axles due terrain; public beach adj poss scruffy low ssn; highly rec." 15 May-30 Sep. € 15.00   2009*

CHAMBERY *9B3* (12km W Rural) *45.55582, 5.79095* **Camping Le Sougey, Lac Rive Ouest, 73610 St Alban-de-Montbel [04 79 36 01 44; fax 04 79 44 19 01; info@camping-sougey.com; www.camping-sougey.com]** Fr A43 E to Chambéry take D921 sp Lac d'Aiguebelette. On W side of lake 3km to site on L. Med, hdg/mkd pitch, some hdstg, pt sl, pt shd; wc; chem disp; 30% serviced pitches; baby facs; shwrs inc; el pnts (6A) inc; gas; lndtte (inc dryer); shop; rest, snacks; bar; playgrnd; lake sw & fishing adj; tennis; horseriding; cycle hire; archery; entmnt; TV; 20% statics; dogs €1.80; Eng spkn; adv bkg rec high ssn; quiet; red low ssn; ccard acc. "Attractive area; spacious site; helpful staff." ♦ 1 May-11 Sep. € 20.70   2010*

⊞ **CHAMBON LA FORET** *4F3* (800m N Rural) *48.06381, 2.28192* **Camping Domaine La Rive du Bois, Route de la Forêt, 45340 Chambon-la-Forêt [02 38 32 29 73/ 06 79 95 26 53 (mob); rive.bois@wanadoo.fr; www.larivedubois.com]** Fr Pithiviers take D921 S. Immed after x-ing over A19 turn L onto D30 sp Chambon-la-Forêt, Sully-sur-Loire. At La Rive-du-Bois traff lts foll sp to site on R. Sm, pt shd; htd wc; chem disp; shwrs inc; el pnts (10A) inc; lndtte; BBQ; playgrnd; pool; fishing; tennis; games area; cycle hire; 70% statics; dogs free; Eng spkn; adv bkg; quiet; CKE/CCI. "Helpful, friendly manger; gd walking & cycling fr site; deer & red squirrels in woods around; gd; Lovely woodland setting" ♦ € 15.00   2013*

CHAMONIX MONT BLANC *9B4* (2km NE Rural) *45.9378, 6.8925* **Camping La Mer de Glace, 200 Chemin de la Bagna, Praz de Chamonix, 74400 Chamonix [04 50 53 44 03; fax 04 50 53 60 83; info@chamonix-camping.com; www.chamonix-camping.com]** Foll sp on D1506 thro Chamonix dir Argentière & Swiss Frontier; site well sp on R in 3km but ent under bdge 2.4m. Rec, to avoid low bdge cont to 1st rndabt in Praz-de-Chamonix & foll sp to site (R at rndabt). Med, hdg/mkd pitch, hdstg, pt sl, pt shd; htd wc (some cont); chem disp; mv service pnt; baby facs; shwrs inc; el pnts (10A) €3; gas 500m; lndtte (inc dryer); shop, rest & bar 500m; tradsmn; snacks; BBQ; playgrnd; htd pool 2km; sports cent nr; wifi; dogs free; phone adj; bus & train 500m; poss cr; Eng spkn; no adv bkg; arr early high ssn; quiet but helicopter noise; ccard not acc; red low ssn; CKE/CCI. "Well-run, wooded site with superb views; sm pitches; helpful staff; vg facs; v conv trains/buses; close to Flégère lift; path to town via woods & rv; excel." ♦ 29 Apr-2 Oct. € 36.20   2013*

CHAMONIX MONT BLANC 9B4 (7km NE Rural) 45.97552, 6.92224 Camping Le Glacier d'Argentière, 161 Chemin des Chosalets, 74400 Argentière [04 50 54 17 36; fax 04 50 54 03 73; info@campingchamonix.com; www. campingchamonix.com] On Chamonix-Argentière D1506 rd bef Argentière take R fork twd Argentière cable car stn. Site immed on R. Med, pt sl, pt shd; wc; chem disp; shwrs inc; el pnts (2-10A) €2.60+.03 per extra amp; lndtte; shops 1km; tradsmn; BBQ; dogs €0.50; phone adj; poss cr; adv bkg; Eng spkn; quiet; CKE/CCI. "Alpine excursions; cable cars adj; mountain views; friendly, helpful owners; Gd friendly site; Alpine views" ◆ 15 May-30 Sep. € 16.50   2013*

"Satellite navigation makes touring much easier"

Remember most sat navs don't know if you're towing or in a larger vehicle – always use yours alongside maps and site directions.

CHAMONIX MONT BLANC 9B4 (1km SW Rural) 45.91466, 6.86138 Camping Iles des Barrats, 185 Chemin de l'Ile des Barrats, 74400 Chamonix [tel/fax 04 50 53 51 44; www. campingdesbarrats.com] Fr Mont Blanc tunnel take 1st L on app Chamonix, foll sp to hospital, site opp hospital. Do not go into town. Sm, mkd pitch, pt sl, unshd; wc; chem disp; mv service pnt; shwrs inc; el pnts (5-10A) €3.30-4.30; gas; lndtte; shops 1km; tradsmn; sw 250m; dogs €1; poss cr; Eng spkn; adv bkg; quiet; CKE/CCI. "Great little site; superb mountain views; friendly family owners; immac facs; 10 mins level walk to town; 10 mins cable car Mont Blanc; excel." 15 May-20 Sep. € 28.30   2012*

CHAMONIX MONT BLANC 9B4 (3km SW Rural) 45.90578, 6.83673 Camping Les Ecureuils, Rue Chemin des Doux, Les Bossons, 74400 Chamonix [tel/fax 04 50 53 83 11; contact@campingsecureuils.fr; www. campingdesecureuils.fr] Fr St Gervais on D1205 twd Chamonix. L fork to vill. L at x-rd. Under rlwy, sharp R. Site at end of rd. NB Not suitable twin-axles due narr app thro v sm tunnel under rlwy. Sm, mkd pitch, hdstg, pt shd; wc; shwrs inc; el pnts (6A) €3.30; lndtte; shop 3km tradsmn; internet; some statics; poss v cr; adv bkg; quiet; ccard acc; CKE/CCI. "Warm welcome; helpful owners; v sm pitches - not suitable lge o'fits; vg." 15 Apr-30 Sep. € 12.90   2011*

CHAMONIX MONT BLANC 9B4 (3.5km SW Rural) 45.90233, 6.83672 Camping Les Cimes, 28 Route des Tissières, Les Bossons, 74400 Chamonix [04 50 53 19 00 or 04 50 53 58 93; info@campinglescimesmontblanc.com; www.campinglescimesmontblanc.com] Exit Mont Blanc tunnel foll sps Geneva turn L on D1506 (Chamonix-Geneva rd), in 2km turn R for Les Bossons & L under bdge. Fr Sallanches foll sps Chamonix & Mont Blanc tunnel. On dual c/way turn R at sp `Les Bossons' & site after Novotel adj to Les Deux Glaciers site. Med, pt sl, pt shd; wc (cont); shwrs inc; el pnts (3A) €2.80; lndtte; shop 4km; tradsmn; rest 500m; snacks; BBQ; playgrnd; dogs; poss cr; adv bkg; rd noise; CKE/CCI. "Fair site; poss diff lge o'fits." 1 Jun-30 Sep. € 14.80   2008*

⊞ CHAMONIX MONT BLANC 9B4 (3.5km SW Rural) 45.90203, 6.83716 Camping Les Deux Glaciers, 80 Route des Tissières, Les Bossons, 74400 Chamonix [04 50 53 15 84; fax 04 50 55 90 81; info@les2glaciers.com; www.les2glaciers.com] Exit Mont Blanc tunnel foll sps Geneva turn L on D1506 (Chamonix-Geneva rd), in 2km turn R for Les Bossons & L under bdge. Fr W foll sps Chamonix & Mont Blanc tunnel. On dual c/way turn R at sp `Les Bossons' & site after Mercure Hotel; adj Les Cimes site; site clearly sp from D1205. Med, sl, pt shd; htd wc; chem disp; shwrs inc; baby facs; el pnts (6-10A) €2.50-7; lndtte (inc dryer); shop; tradsmn; rest, snacks; bar; playgrnd; pool & skating rink 4km; games rm; table tennis; wifi; dogs free; bus; Eng spkn; CKE/CCI. "Pleasant, well-kept site in wonderful location just under Mont Blanc; roomy pitches; clean facs; poss diff site for lge o'fits over 6m; if recep clsd pitch & wait until 1730; ideal for walking; funicular adj to Glacier des Bossons; rec arr early high ssn; highly rec." ◆ 1 Jan- 15 Nov, 15 Dec- 31 Dec. € 26.30   2013*

CHAMPAGNAC LA RIVIERE see Chalus 7B3

CHAMPAGNAT (SAONE ET LOIRE) see Cuiseaux 9A2

CHAMPAGNE SUR LOUE see Quingey 6H2

CHAMPAGNOLE 6H2 (1km NW Urban) 46.74680, 5.89919 Camp Municipal de Boyse, 20 Rue Georges Vallerey, 39300 Champagnole [03 84 52 00 32; fax 03 84 52 01 16; camping.boyse@wanadoo.fr; www.camping. champagnole.com] Turn W onto D5, N of town off D5 to Dijon. Look for sp. Site adj to sw pool. Lge, mkd pitch, pt sl, pt shd; wc; chem disp; mv service pnt; baby facs; shwrs inc; el pnts (5A) €3.20; lndtte; shops & supmkt 1km; tradsmn; rest, snacks; bar; htd sw pools adj; dogs €2; phone; adv bkg; no admissions 1200-1400; quiet; ccard acc; red low ssn; CKE/CCI. "Spacious, well-kept site; friendly warden; gd san facs, inc dog washing area; vg rest; direct access to Rv Ain; pleasant town; gd touring base." ◆ 1 Jun-15 Sep. € 14.40   2010*

CHAMPIGNY SUR MARNE see Paris 3D3

CHAMPS ROMAIN see Nontron 7B3

CHANAC 9D1 (500m S Urban) 44.46519, 3.34670 Camp Municipal La Vignogue, Rue de Plaisance, 48230 Chanac [04 66 48 24 09 or 06 82 93 60 68 (mob); gites-camping-chanac@orange.fr; www.chanac.fr] Exit A75 junc 39.1 onto N88 to Chanac; site well sp in vill. Sm, mkd pitch, pt sl, pt shd; htd wc (some cont); chem disp; shwrs inc; el pnts (6A) inc; lndtte; shops, rest, bar 500m; BBQ; pool adj; wifi; some statics; dogs €1; Eng spkn; adv bkg; quiet. "Excel; rec arr early (bef 1800)." ◆ ltd 15 Apr-30 Sep. € 10.50   2011*

CHANAS see St Rambert d'Albon 9C2

CHANTEMERLE LES BLES see Tain l'Hermitage 9C2

⊞ **CHANTILLY** *3D3* (5km W Rural) *49.21225, 2.40270*
Camping L'Abbatiale, 39 Rue Salvador Allendé,
60340 St Leu-d'Esserent [tel/fax 03 44 56 38 76;
contact@camping-abbatiale.com; www.wix.com/
campingabbatiale/campingabbatiale] S twds Paris on A1
exit Senlis; cont W fr Senlis on D924/D44 thro Chantilly x-ing
Rv Oise to St Leu-d'Esserent; cont on D44, x-ing D603 which
becomes Rue Salvador Allendé in 700m; foll site sps; avoid rv
x-ing on D17 fr SW; v narr bdge. Lge, pt shd; htd wc; shwrs
€1; el pnts (3A) €2; lndtte; shop; playgrnd; some statics; dogs
€0.50; red long stay. "Chantilly & chateau interesting; site
mainly statics." € 10.00   2008*

CHANTILLY *3D3* (5km NW Rural) *49.22571, 2.42862*
Camping Campix, 60360 St Leu d'Esserent [03 44 56 08 48;
fax 03 44 56 28 75; campix@orange.fr; www.
campingcampix.com] Exit A1 junc 8 to Senlis; cont W fr Senlis
on D924 thro Chantilly, x-ing Rv Oise to St Leu-d'Esserent;
leave town on D12 NW twd Cramoisy thro housing est; foll
site sp for 1km, winding app. Med, mkd pitch, hdstg, terr, shd;
htd wc; chem disp; mv service pnt; baby facs; shwrs inc; el pnts
(6-10A) €3.50 (min 25m cable poss req); gas; lndtte (inc dryer);
shop; tradsmn; rest, snacks; pizza delivery; BBQ; playgrnd; pool
complex; sand beach & lake sw 1km; fishing; games rm; wifi;
no statics; dogs €2; phone; Eng spkn; adv bkg; quiet; red long
stay/low ssn; ccard acc; CKE/CCI. "Beautiful, peaceful site in
former quarry - poss unguarded, vertical drops; helpful owner
& friendly staff; gd quality san facs; wide variety of pitches -
narr, steep access & o'hanging trees on some; conv Paris Parc
Astérix & Disneyland (Astérix tickets fr recep); sh walk to vill;
rec." ♦ 7 Mar-30 Nov. € 16.50 (CChq acc)   2011*

⊞ **CHANTONNAY** *2H4* (12km NE Rural) *46.75168, -0.94568*
Camping La Baudonnière, Route des Salinières, 85110
Monsireigne [02 51 66 43 79; bannigan.tom@orange.fr;
www.labaudonniere.com] Fr Chantonnay take D960B
NE dir St Prouant & Pouzauges. In St Prouant take D23 to
Monsireigne. Foll rd downhill, cross sm rv & as rd starts to climb
take 2nd L sp Reaumur; in 400m L onto Rue des Salinières.
Site on L in 800m. Sm, pt sl, pt shd; wc; chem disp; shwrs
inc; el pnts (10A) €4; lndtte (inc dryer); shops, rest, snacks,
bar 3km; BBQ; playgrnd; pool; tennis 2km; lake 5km; games
rm; no statics; dogs; Eng spkn; adv bkg; quiet. "V relaxing,
peaceful, pretty CL-type site; welcoming, friendly, helpful Irish
owners; excel san facs; conv Puy de Fou theme park; vg." ♦
€ 16.50   2011*

CHANTONNAY *2H4* (7km NW Rural) *46.74516, -1.11817*
Camp Municipal La Rivière, 25 Rue du Stade, 85110
Ste Cécile [02 51 40 24 07; fax 02 51 40 25 59;
mairiestececile85@wanadoo.fr; www.saintececile85.fr]
Fr Chantonnay NW on D137; in St Vincent-Sterlanges turn
onto D39 to Ste Cécile (2.5km); site sp clearly fr main rd. Sm,
hdg/mkd pitch, pt shd; wc; shwrs inc; el pnts (10A); lndtte;
playgrnd; pool; paddling pool; rv fishing adj; tennis; statics;
adv bkg rec high ssn; quiet. "Part of larger complex of holiday
bungalows; some facs dated & poor." 1 Jun-30 Sep.   2010*

CHAPELLE AUX FILTZMEENS, LA see Combourg *2E4*

CHAPELLE D'ANGILLON, LA *4G3* (1km SE Rural)
47.36044, 2.44261 Camp Municipal Les Murailles,
Route d'Henrichemont, 18380 La Chapelle-d'Angillon
[02 48 73 40 12 (Mairie); fax 02 48 73 48 67] Fr Bourges or
Aubigny-sur-Nère on D940, turn E onto D926; turn onto D12
in vill, site on R, sp. Sm, pt sl, pt shd; wc (some cont); chem
disp (wc); shwrs inc; el pnts (6A) €3.20; gas, shop, rest, & bar
1km; BBQ; playgrnd; lake fishing adj; some statics; dogs; ccard
acc; CKE/CCI. "Lake adj with castle o'looking; v quiet; facs
dated but adequate; site yourself, warden calls; vg." ♦ ltd
1 Jun-15 Sep. € 7.15   2009*

CHAPELLE EN VERCORS, LA *9C3* (N Urban) *44.9695,
5.4156* Camp Municipal Les Bruyères, Ave des Bruyères,
26420 La Chapelle-en-Vercors [04 75 48 21 46;
campinglesbruyeres@wanadoo.fr; http://lesbruyeres.
camping.pagesperso-orange.fr] Take D518 N fr Die over
Col de Rousset. Fr N on A49 exit 8 to N532 St Nazaire-en-
Royans, then D76 thro St Thomas-en-Royans, then D216 to
St Laurent-en-Royans. Take D2 round E flank of Combe Laval
(2 short 2-lane tunnels). Fr Col de la Machine foll D76 S 1km,
then D199 E over Col de Carri to La Chapelle. (D531 fr Villard
de Lons, D76 over Combe Laval & D518 Grandes Goulet not
suitable for c'vans & diff lge m'vans due narr rds & tunnels &
5km of o'hanging ledges.) Med, pt sl, pt shd; htd wc; chem
disp; mv service pnt; shwrs inc; el pnts €3.50; lndtte; shops adj;
rest, snacks, bar 200m; playgrnd; pool 2km; fishing; climbing;
horseriding; cycling; TV; some statics; dogs €1; adv bkg; quiet;
CKE/CCI. "Excel base for beautiful Vercors plateau." ♦
1 May-1 Oct. € 12.00   2008*

CHAPELLE EN VERCORS, LA *9C3* (6.5km N Rural) *45.02534,
5.44370* Camping La Porte St Martin, 26420 St Martin-en-
Vercors [04 75 45 51 10; infos@camping-laportestmartin.
com; www.camping-laportestmartin.com] Sp 200m N of
vill on D103. (D531 fr Villard-de-Lans W not rec for c'vans.)
Med, mkd pitch, pt terr, pt shd; wc; shwrs inc; el pnts (10A)
€2.80; lndtte; tradsmn; shops, rest, snacks & bar 500m; pool;
paddling pool; wifi; some statics; dogs €2; phone; Eng spkn;
quiet; red low ssn; CKE/CCI. "Superb mountain views fr most
pitches; excel walking." ♦ 1 May-30 Sep. € 14.00   2010*

CHAPELLE EN VERCORS, LA *9C3* (2km E Rural) *44.96808,
5.43048* Camping Les Myrtilles, Les Chaberts, 26420 La
Chapelle-en-Vercors [tel/fax 04 75 48 20 89; camping.
des.myrtilles@wanadoo.fr; http://camping.des.myrtilles.
pagesperso-orange.fr] Fr A49/E713 exit 8 to N532
St Nazaire-en-Royans, then D76 thro St Thomas-en-Royans,
then D216 to St Laurent-en-Royans. Take D2 around E flank
of Combe Laval (2 short 2-lane tunnels). Fr Col de la Machine
foll D76 S 1km, then D199 E over Col de Carri to La Chapelle.
Fr S fr Die, foll D518 over Col de Rousset. (D76 over Combe
Laval, D531 fr Villard-de-Lans & D518 fr Pont-en-Royans over
Grandes Goulet not suitable for c'vans.) Med, pt sl, pt shd; wc;
chem disp; shwrs inc; el pnts (4-6A) €2.45-3; lndtte; shop 1km;
snacks; bar; playgrnd; htd pool; rv fishing 2km; 20% statics;
dogs €1.50; adv bkg; v quiet; red low ssn; CKE/CCI. "Beautiful
setting; excel walking, caves & gorges; gates locked 2200-
0700." ♦ 1 May-15 Sep. € 14.45   2010*

CHAPELLE HERMIER, LA *2H4* (4km SW Rural) *46.66652, -1.75543* **Camping Le Pin Parasol, Châteaulong, 85220 La Chapelle-Hermier [02 51 34 64 72; fax 02 51 34 64 62; contact@campingpinparasol.fr; www.campingpinparasol. fr]** Exit A83 junc 4 onto D763/D937 dir La Roche-sur-Yon; turn R onto D948; at Aizenay turn R onto D6 twd St Gilles Croix-de-Vie; after 10km at x-rds turn L onto D21; in La Chapelle-Hermier foll D42 twds L'Aiguillon-sur-Vie; site sp in 4km. Lge, hdg/mkd pitch, pt sl, terr, unshd; wc; chem disp; mv service pnt; baby facs; shwrs inc; el pnts (16A) €4.50; gas; lndtte (inc dryer); sm shop; tradsmn; rest 500m nr lake; snacks; bar; BBQ; playgrnd & adventure zone; 2 pools (1 htd); paddling pool; waterslide; sand beach 12km; lake sw, boating, fishing, canoeing 200m; cycle hire; archery; fitness rm; tennis; games area; excursions; wifi; entmnt; games/TV rm; 70% statics; dogs €4.20; no c'vans/m'vans over 11m; poss v cr; Eng spkn; adv bkg; quiet; ccard acc (Visa only); red low ssn; CKE/CCI. "On banks of Lake Jaunay; access to lake down sm path; lge pitches; friendly staff; excel facs; lovely pools; away fr crowds but close to beaches; pleasant walks & cycle tracks around lake; Beautiful site, very well kept" ♦ 19 Apr-25 Sep. € 43.80 SBS - A36 2013*

"There aren't many sites open at this time of year"

If you're travelling outside peak season remember to call ahead to check site opening dates – even if the entry says 'open all year'.

CHAPELLE TAILLEFERT, LA see Guéret *7A4*

CHARCHIGNE see Lassay les Châteaux *4E1*

CHARITE SUR LOIRE, LA *4G4* (500m W Urban) *47.17683, 3.01058* **FFCC Camp Municipal La Saulaie, Quai de la Saulaie, 58400 La Charité-sur-Loire [tel/ fax 03 86 70 00 83 / 03 86 70 15 06 (ls); contact@ lacharitesurloire-tourisme.com; www.lacharitesurloire-tourisme.com / www.nievre-tourisme.com]** Exit A77 junc 30 & foll sp 'Centre Ville'. Turn L over Rv Loire sp Bourges; take 2nd R bef next bdge. Fr Bourges on N151, turn L immed after x-ing 1st bridge over Rv Loire. Foll sp. NB Take care when turn R over narr rv bdge when leaving site - v high kerb. Med, mkd pitch, pt shd; wc; chem disp; shwrs inc; el pnts (10A) €3.10; lndtte; shop 500m; tradsmn; snacks; playgrnd & htd pool, paddling pool adj inc (pool opens 1 Jul); rv beach & sw adj; dogs €2; no twin-axles; quiet; ccard not acc; red long stay; CKE/CCI. "Lovely, well-kept site on rv island; warm welcome, helpful staff; san facs in need of refurb (2011) & ltd low ssn; gd security; poss school groups high ssn; low ssn phone to check open; beautiful town; welcoming staff, site scruffy and in need of maintenance" ♦ 28 Apr-23 Sep. € 6.10 2013*

CHARLEVAL see Cadenet *10E3*

CHARLEVILLE MEZIERES *5C1* (500m N Urban) *49.77813, 4.72245* **Camp Municipal Mont Olympe, Rue des Pâquis, 08000 Charleville-Mézières [03 24 33 23 60 or 03 24 32 44 80; fax 03 24 33 37 76; camping-charlevillemezieres@ wandadoo.fr]** Fr N43/E44 head for Hôtel de Ville, with Hôtel de Ville on R, cont N along Ave des Arches, turn R at 'Gare' sp & cross rv bdge. At 'Gare' turn sharp L immed along Rue des Pâquis, site on L in 500m, visible fr rd. Well sp from town cent. Med, hdg/mkd pitch, some hdstg, pt shd; htd wc (some cont); chem disp; mv service pnt; all serviced pitches; baby facs; fam bthrm; shwrs inc; el pnts (10A) €3.95; gas; lndtte; shops 500m; tradsmn; rest 300m; bar; BBQ; playgrnd; htd covrd pool adj; fishing & boating; wifi; TV/games rm; some statics; dogs €1.60; poss cr; Eng spkn; quiet; ccard acc; CKE/CCI. "Lovely, spacious, well-kept site on Rv Meuse; lge pitches; v lge pitches extra; helpful staff; superb san facs; useful snack bar; easy walk to charming town; excel; NH for m'van's" 16 Apr-30 Sep. € 23.15 2013*

CHARLEVILLE MEZIERES *5C1* (12km N Urban) *49.87757, 4.74187* **Camp Municipal au Port à Diseur, Rue André Compain, 08800 Monthermé [03 24 53 01 21 / 03 24 53 00 09; fax 03 24 53 01 15]** Fr D988 at Revin turn E onto D1 TO Monthermé. Site is on D1 S of town. Site on R, 100m past supmkt on L. Med, hdg/ mkd pitch, pt sl, pt shd; wc (some cont); chem disp (wc); shwrs inc; el pnts (4-10A) inc; gas 100m; lndtte; shop 100m; rest, snacks, bar 1km; few statics; dogs; phone; poss cr; quiet but some rd noise; CKE/CCI. "Pleasant, rvside site in conv location; lge pitches; excel, clean san facs, poss stretched if site full; gd rvside walks; 20 min easy walk to Monthermé; gd cycling & walking; popular with fishermen & canoeists; excel site" ♦ 13 Apr-30 Sep. € 20.30 2013*

⊞ **CHARLEVILLE MEZIERES** *5C1* (12km NE Rural) *49.85655, 4.79235* **Camping Departemental d'Haulmé, Pont Semoy, 08800 Haulmé [03 24 32 81 61; fax 03 24 32 37 66]** Fr Charleville, take N43 & turn R at sp to Nouzonville. Turn onto D988, D989 to Monthermé. In town turn R over bdge onto D31. In 5km turn R sp Haulmé, site in 1.5km on rvside. Lge, mkd pitch, pt shd; wc (cont); mv service pnt; shwrs inc; el pnts (6-10A) €2.65-4.60; gas; shop 5km; tradsmn; rest, bar 500m; fishing; tennis; cycle hire; dogs €0.90; poss cr; adv bkg; fairly quiet; ccard acc. "Vg; excel for fishing; top end of site noisy due to semi-perm tents; rec pitch mid-site as lower site adj public park; v wet pitches in rain; gd san facs; sh walk to town cent." ♦ € 11.30 2008*

CHARLIEU *9A1* (E Urban) *46.15851, 4.18088* **FFCC Camp Municipal de la Douze, Rue Riottier, 42190 Charlieu [04 77 69 01 70 or 06 65 34 77 39 (mob); fax 04 77 69 07 28; camp-charlieu@voila.fr]** N fr Roanne on D482 to Pouilly-sous-Charlieu, then E on D487 to Charlieu town cent, site sp in town, by rv pool. NB Do not confuse with Camp Municipal Pouilly-sous-Charlieu which is sp fr main rd. Med, hdg/mkd pitch, pt shd; wc; chem disp; mv service pnt; shwrs inc; el pnts (6A) inc; lndtte; shops 1km; snacks; bar; playgrnd; pool adj; sports area; fishing, boating adj; entmnt; 40% statics; poss cr; Eng spkn; adv bkg; CKE/CCI. "Gd clean san facs; facs poss stretched high ssn, excel low ssn; vg value." ♦ 1 Apr-30 Sep. € 11.00 2009*

FRANCE

CHARLIEU 9A1 (4km W Rural) 46.15003, 4.11204 **FFCC Camp Municipal Les Ilots, Rue de Marcigny, 42720 Pouilly-sous-Charlieu [04 77 60 80 67; fax 04 77 60 79 44; mairie.pouilly-sous-charlieu42@wanadoo.fr]** N fr Roanne on D482 sp Pouilly-sous-Charlieu. Site sp on ring rd 1km N of town, turn E into stadium. Med, mkd pitch, pt shd; htd wc (cont); mv service pnt; shwrs inc; el pnts (6A) €3; gas; lndtte; shops 1km; rest, bar 500m; playgrnd; pool; fishing; games area; poss cr; Eng spkn; quiet; ccard not acc; red CKE/CCI. "Lge pitches grouped in circles." 15 May-15 Sep. € 7.00   2009*

CHARLY SUR MARNE 3D4 (500m S Urban) 48.97363, 3.28210 **Camp Municipal Les Illettes, Route de Pavant, 02310 Charly-sur-Marne [03 23 82 12 11 or 03 23 82 00 32 (Mairie); fax 03 23 82 13 99; mairie.charly@wanadoo.fr; www.charly-sur-marne.fr]** Exit A4 junc 18 onto D603 dir La Ferté; then take D402/D969 NE to Charly. Site sp in town. Sm, hdg pitch, pt shd; wc; chem disp; shwrs; el pnts (5-10A) €2-3; lndry rm; supmkt adj; dogs €2.50; quiet, but poss noise eves fr sports complex adj; no twin-axles; red long stay/low ssn. "Lovely, well-kept site; pleasant warden; 10 min walk to rv & rvside walks; conv for touring Champagne route; rec arr early to secure pitch during grape harvest; excel." ♦ 1 Apr-30 Sep. € 14.50   2012*

CHARMES 6E2 (500m NE Rural) 48.37706, 6.28974 **Camp Municipal Les Iles, 20 Rue de l'Ecluse, 88130 Charmes [tel/fax 03 29 38 87 71 or 03 29 38 85 85; andre.michel63@wanadoo.fr; www.ville-charmes.fr]** Exit N57 for Charmes, site well sp on Rv Moselle. Do not confuse with sp for 'Camping Cars'. Med, mkd pitch, pt shd; wc; chem disp; mv service pnt; shwrs inc; el pnts (10A) €3.55; gas; lndtte; shop 300m; tradsmn; rest, snacks; bar; BBQ; playgrnd; fishing; kayak hire; wifi; dogs; phone; Eng spkn; adv bkg; quiet; red long stay; CKE/CCI. "Lovely site bet rv & canal; lge pitches; friendly staff; footpath to town; m'van o'night area in town; vg value; gd; V lge pitches" ♦ 1 Apr-30 Sep. € 19.30   2013*

CHARMES SUR L'HERBASSE see St Donat sur l'Herbasse 9C2

CHARNY 4F3 (500m N Rural) 47.89078, 3.09419 **FFCC Camping des Platanes, 41 Route de la Mothe, 89120 Charny [tel/fax 03 86 91 83 60; campingdesplatanes@wanadoo.fr; www.campingdesplatanes.com]** Exit A6 junc 18 onto D943 to Montargis. Turn S onto D950 to Charny, site on R as ent vill; sp. Med, hdg/mkd pitch, pt shd; htd wc; chem disp; mv service pnt; serviced pitch; shwrs inc; el pnts (10A) inc; gas; lndtte (inc dryer); shop 500m; tradsmn; snacks; BBQ; playgrnd; pool; rv fishing 150m; tennis 500m; cycle hire; wifi; TV rm; 60% statics; dogs €3; Eng spkn; adv bkg; quiet; red low ssn/long stay; CKE/CCI. "Pleasant, peaceful site; gd sized pitches; friendly, helpful owners; excel, clean san facs; short walk to vill; gd walking; gd touring base." ♦ 1 Apr-30 Oct. € 20.50   2013*

See advertisement on pages 32 & 33

CHARNY-SUR-MEUSE see Verdun 5D1

CHAROLLES 9A2 (500m E Rural) 46.43972, 4.28208 **FFCC Camp Municipal, Route de Viry, 71120 Charolles [03 85 24 04 90; fax 03 85 24 08 20; camping.charolles@orange.fr]** Exit N79 at E end of by-pass sp Vendenesse-lès-Charolles; at rndabt foll camping sp; then sharp R bottom hill bef town; site on L, next to Municipal pool. Med, hdg/mkd pitch, hdstg, pt sl, pt shd; htd wc; chem disp; mv service pnt (outside ent); shwrs inc; el pnts (6A) €2; lndtte; shops 300m; rest, snacks; bar; playgrnd; pool adj high ssn (proper sw trunks req); wifi; TV; dogs €1; adv bkg rec; quiet, but faint rd noise; ccard acc; CKE/CCI. "Well-kept site; sm pitches; friendly, helpful warden; gd, modern san facs; m'van area outside site; negligible security." ♦ 1 Apr-5 Oct. € 9.00   2010*

CHARRIN see Decize 4H4

CHARTRE SUR LE LOIR, LA 4F2 (500m W Rural) 47.73220, 0.57451 **Camping Le Vieux Moulin, Chemin des Bergivaux, 72340 La Chartre-sur-le Loir [02 43 44 41 18; camping@lachartre.com; www.le-vieux-moulin.fr]** Sp fr D305 in town. Fr S exit A28 junc 27 onto D766 dir Beaumont-la-Ronce; then take D29 to La Chartre-sur-le Loir; go over rv, turn L immed after bdge. Med, hdg/mkd pitch, pt shd; htd wc (some cont); chem disp; mv service pnt; baby facs; fam bthrm; shwrs inc; el pnts (5-10A) 4A-5 (poss rev pol); gas 500m; lndtte; sm shop & 500m; tradsmn; snacks; bar; BBQ; playgrnd; htd pool; rv fishing, canoeing adj; cycle hire; wifi; entmnt; TV; 20% statics; dogs €1.50; poss cr; Eng spkn; adv bkg rec high ssn; quiet; 15% red CC members; red low ssn; CKE/CCI. "Beautiful, well-kept rvside site; helpful, friendly staff; excel pool; gd for dogs; v lge m'vans acc; gd base for chateaux, forest & Loir Valley; excel." ♦ 1 May-15 Sep. € 13.20   2010*

CHARTRES 4E2 (1.5km SE Urban) 48.43433, 1.49914 **Camping Les Bords de l'Eure, 9 Rue de Launay, 28000 Chartres [tel/fax 02 37 28 79 43; camping-roussel-chartres@wanadoo.fr; www.camping-de-chartres.com]** Exit N123 ring rd at D935, R at T-junc dir Chartres; then R at 2nd traff lts dir Chartres immed after rlwy bdge; site on L in 400m; inside of ring rd. Also sp fr town cent on N154 fr N, foll sp town cent under 2 rlwy bdges, L at traff lts sp Orléans, after 1km site sp. Fr SE on N154 cross ring rd, foll site sp & turn L at 2nd traff lts; site on R. Med,some hdg/mkd pitch, pt shd; htd wc (mostly cont); chem disp; mv service pnt; baby facs; shwrs inc; el pnts (6A) €3.40 (poss rev pol); lndry rm; shop; tradsmn; BBQ; shop in ssn; supmkt 1km; playgrnd; fishing; wifi; some statics; dogs €1.08; poss cr; Eng spkn; adv bkg; quiet, some rlwy noise; ccard acc; red low ssn; CKE/CCI; Wifi. "Popular, spacious, well laid-out, well-kept site; direct access to rv; friendly, helpful staff; unisex san facs clean but need update (2010) & insufficient when site busy; some pitches diff lge o'fits; gates clsd 2200-0700; poor security (2011); poss itinerants & long-stay workers; poss unkempt early ssn; when wet ground soft in places; walk along rv to Chartres; rec Son et Lumière; ideal NH & longer; vg; Attractive site, bottom of hill, next rv; some awkward pitches and can be very wet after rain" ♦ 1 Mar-15 Nov. € 19.80   2013*

Tell us about the sites you visit

CHARTRES *4E2* (9km S Rural) 48.40100, 1.48918 **Camp Municipal de Morancez, Rue de Chartres, 28630 Morancez [02 37 30 02 80, 07 86 40 65 49 (mob) or 02 37 28 49 71 (Mairie); fax 02 37 33 05 25; mairie. morancez@wanadoo.fr; www.morancez.fr]** S on Chartres by-pass (N123) take exit D935; L at T-junc twd Morancez; R on D114/Base de Loisirs at S end of vill (abrupt turn); cross bdge; after 200m turn R onto track, site at end of lake 300m. Travelling N on N10/D910 turn R onto D114 sp Morancez; strt over at x-rds at La Varenne; cont on narr rd for 1.5km; cross rv bdge, site on L. Sm, hdg/mkd pitch, shd; wc (some cont); chem disp (wc); shwrs inc; el pnts (6A) €2.90 (poss rev pol); shops & supmkt 2km; playgrnd adj; fishing adj; 20% statics; adv bkg; quiet but some rd noise; CKE/CCI. "Pleasant, peaceful site; surrounded by woods, lakes & rvs; friendly, helpful warden; san facs could be improved (2009); site locked 2200-0700; unrel opening dates; bus fr vill to Chartres every hr (high ssn); excel NH." 17 May-31 Aug. € 14.50 (3 persons) 2013*

CHASSENEUIL DU POITOU see Jaunay Clan *4H1*

⊞ **CHASSENEUIL SUR BONNIEURE** *7B3* (9km E Rural) 45.83283, 0.55811 **Camping Le Paradis, Mazières, 16270 Mazières [tel/fax 05 45 84 92 06 / 078 66 49 67 41 (mob); info@le-paradis-camping.com; www.le-paradis-camping. com]** Fr Limoges W on N141 twd Angoulême, turn L at 1st traff lts in Roumazières-Loubert D161. Site sp in 2km at t-junc. Sm, hdg/mkd pitch, hdstg, pt shd; wc; chem disp; mv service pnt; fam bthrm; shwrs inc; el pnts (10-16A) €5.50-8.50; gas 3km; lndtte; shop; tradsmn; rest, snacks & bar 1km; BBQ; playgrnd; lake sw & watersports 5km; fishing nrby; tennis nr; games area; 20% statics; dogs free; phone; bus 1km; adv bkg rec; quiet; CKE/CCI. "Clean, tranquil site; gd sized pitches; vg, immac san facs; welcoming British owners, helpful & friendly; gd touring base; adv bkg rec lge o'fits; excel." ♦ ltd € 17.50 2013*

CHASSENEUIL SUR BONNIEURE *7B3* (W Urban) 45.82389, 0.44415 **Camp Municipal Les Charmilles, Rue des Ecoles, 16260 Chasseneuil-sur-Bonnieure [05 45 39 55 36; jctelemaque@free.fr]** On N141 Angoulême-Limoges leave by-pass sp Chasseneuil. In town turn L onto D27 sp Mémorial de la Résistance. Turn R at camping sp, site ahead. Med, hdg/ mkd pitch, pt shd; wc; chem disp; shwrs inc; el pnts (10A) inc; lndtte; gas 200m; shop; supmkt 100m; rest, snacks, bar 50m; playgrnd; htd, covrd pool adj; dogs; quiet. "Warden calls pm or key fr Mairie; diff to ent/leave site without key to bollard; gd san facs; vg value." ♦ ltd Easter-30 Sep. € 9.00 2009*

⊞ **CHATAIGNERAIE, LA** *2H4* (8km N Rural) 46.7325, -0.7425 **Camping Le Grand Fraigneau, Le Grand Fraigneau, 85700 Menomblet Vendée [02 51 51 68 21 / 06 42 68 48 12 (mob); info@ legrandfraigneau.com; www.legrandfraigneau.com]** NE fr La Châtaigneraie on D938T to St Pierre-du-Chemin; turn L onto D49 to Menomblet; in 500m turn L to Le Grand Fraigneau. Site sp. Sm, pt shd; wc; fam bathrm; shwrs; el pnts (10A) €3; BBQ; pool (above grnd); lake sw & boating 9km; wifi; dogs free; Eng spkn; adv bkg; twin-axles acc; quiet; "CL-type site; friendly, helpful British owners; fenced pond; walks in lovely countryside; excel." ♦ ltd € 9.00 2013*

CHATAIGNERAIE, LA *2H4* (5km E Rural) **Camping La Viollière, 85120 Breuil-Barret [02 51 87 44 82; vendeevacances@gmail.com; http://vendeevacances. googlepages.com/]** Take D949 E dir Poitiers thro La Châtaigneraie. Cont thro Breuil-Barret & site 2nd R after passing under rlwy bdge. Sm, pt sl, pt shd; wc; chem disp; shwrs inc; el pnts (6A) inc (poss long lead req); shop 2km; supmkt 6km; rest, bar 2km; tradsmn; htd, covrd pool 8km; dogs €1; adv bkg; quiet. "Peaceful, relaxing CL-type site; 6 spacious pitches & 5 el pnts only; helpful British owners." Apr-Oct. € 14.00 2008*

CHATEAU ARNOUX *10E3* (3km NE Rural) 44.10611, 6.01556 **Camping Sunélia L'Hippocampe, Route Napoléon, 04290 Volonne [04 92 33 50 00; fax 04 92 33 50 49; camping@l-hippocampe.com; www.l-hippocampe.com]** Exit A51 junc 21 onto D4085 12km S of Sisteron twd Volonne will over rv. Turn R on D4 on ent vill & foll camp sp 1km. Lge, hdg/mkd pitch, some hdstg, pt shd; wc; chem disp; mv service pnt; baby facs; serviced pitches; shwrs inc; el pnts (10A) inc (poss rev pol); lndtte (inc dryer); shop; tradsmn; rest; bar; BBQ (elec/ gas); playgrnd; 2 pools (1 htd); paddling pool; waterslide; rv sw & beach 150km; fishing; canoeing; rafting; tennis; cycle hire; games area; games rm; wifi; entmnt; TV rm; some statics; dogs €2; Eng spkn; adv bkg; quiet; ccard acc; red low ssn/ long stay; CKE/CCI. "Pleasant, busy, well-run site; spacious, well-screened pitches; various pitch sizes/prices, some by lake; some pitches poss diff due trees; excel." ♦ Easter-30 Sep. € 40.00 (CChq acc) 2009*

See advertisement

CHATEAU CHINON *4H4* (1km S Urban) *47.05513, 3.92626* **Camp Municipal du Gargouillat, Rue de Pertuy d'Oiseau, 58120 Château-Chinon [03 86 85 08 17; fax 03 86 85 01 00]** Sp fr D978 rndabt at E end town. Med, hdg/mkd pitch, sl, pt shd; wc (some cont); shwrs inc; el pnts (10A) €2.50; shops, rest, bar 1km; tradsmn; dogs free; poss cr; quiet. "Gd location; some pitches diff; san facs need refurb & ltd low ssn; poss itinerants; conv Morvan National Park; levelling blocks rec; gd NH." 1 May-30 Sep. € 7.50   2008*

CHATEAU CHINON *4H4* (6km S Rural) *47.00587, 3.90548* **FFCC Camping L'Etang de la Fougeraie, Hameau de Champs, 58120 St Léger-de-Fougeret [03 86 85 11 85; fax 03 86 79 45 72; campingfougeraie@orange.fr; www. campingfougeraie.com]** Fr Château-Chinon S on D27; in approx 3km turn R onto D157 to St Léger-de-Fougeret; in vill foll sps S dir Onlay to site in 2.5km. Med, hdg/mkd pitch, terr, pt shd; wc; chem disp; baby facs; shwrs inc; el pnts (6A) €3.20; lndtte; shop; tradsmn; rest, snacks; bar; BBQ; playgrnd; cycle hire; lake sw & fishing; donkey rides; games area; games rm; TV; dogs €1.70; Eng spkn; quiet; red low ssn; CKE/CCI. "Beautiful, tranquil situation; most pitches lge & face lake; welcoming, efficient owners; facs at top of terr - poss stretched high ssn & ltd low ssn; gd rest; poss diff lge o'fits; pitches muddy when wet; excel." 3 Apr-2 Oct. € 13.50   2010*

CHATEAU D'OLONNE see Sables d'Olonne, Les *7A1*

CHATEAU DU LOIR *4G1* (6km E Rural) *47.71250, 0.49930* **Camping du Lac des Varennes, Route de Port Gauthier, 72340 Marçon [02 43 44 13 72; fax 02 43 44 54 31; lacdesvarennes@camp-in-ouest.com; www.camp-in-ouest.com or www.lacdesvarennes.com]** Fr N on D338 fr Château-du-Loir dir Vendôme for 3km. Turn L onto D305 sp Marçon. In vill turn L onto D61 over bdge. Site on R by lake. Lge, hdg/mkd pitch, hdstg, pt shd; htd wc; chem disp; mv service pnt; baby facs; shwrs inc; el pnts (10A) €3.20 (poss rev pol, poss long lead req); lndtte (inc dryer); shop high ssn; tradsmn; rest, snacks; bar; BBQ; playgrnd; lake sw & sand beach adj; boat hire; watersports; tennis; cycle hire; horseriding; cycle hire; wifi; entmnt; 11% statics; dogs €1.80; Eng spkn; adv bkg rec; quiet; ccard acc; red long stay/low ssn; CKE/CCI. Low ssn office clsd 12:00-16:00. "Pretty site in lovely situation bet lake & rv; friendly, helpful staff; gd security; gd walks & cycling." ♦ 12 Apr-27 Oct. € 18.60 2013*

See advertisement on pages 32 & 33

⊞ **CHATEAU GONTIER** *4F1* (1km N Urban) *47.83851, -0.69965* **Camping Le Parc, 15 Route de Laval, 53200 Château-Gontier [02 43 07 35 60; fax 02 43 70 38 94; camping.parc@cc-chateau-gontier.fr; www.sudmayenne. com]** App Château-Gontier fr N on N162, at 1st rndabt on bypass take 1st exit. Site on R in 250m. Sm, mkd pitch, sl, pt shd; htd wc; chem disp; mv service pnt; shwrs inc; el pnts (10A) inc (rev pol); lndtte; shops 1km; bar; playgrnd; pool 800m; fishing; tennis; entmnt; games rm; TV; 20% statics; dogs; quiet; ccard acc; red low ssn; CKE/CCI. "V pleasant site; most pitches sloping, some o'look rv; superb clean unisex san facs; rvside path to attractive town; mkt Thurs; Excel site, gd pitches; superb clean san facs; helpful staff" ♦ € 12.00   2013*

⊞ **CHATEAU GONTIER** *4F1* (11km N Rural) *47.92109, -0.68334* **Camping Village Vacances et Pêche, Rue des Haies, 53170 Villiers-Charlemagne [02 43 07 71 68; fax 02 43 07 72 77; vvp.villiers.charlemagne@wanadoo.fr; www.villiers-charlemagne.mairie53.fr]** N fr Château-Gontier on N162; turn R onto D20 to Villiers-Charlemagne; site on R. Sm, pt shd; wc; chem disp; shwrs inc; el pnts (6A) inc; lndtte; BBQ; cooking facs; playgrnd; cycle hire; lake 200m; fishing; tennis; games rm; entmnt; dogs; wifi; 10% statics; twin axle acc; Eng spkn; CKE/CCI; red low ssn; "Small wooded site in rural surroundings; each pitch has own san facs & kitchenette; site is amazing; helpful, friendly staff; v peaceful; well maintained" € 16.90   2013*

CHATEAU LA VALLIERE *4G1* (500m W Rural) *47.54565, 0.31354* **FFCC Camp Municipal du Val Joyeux, 37330 Château-la-Vallière [02 47 24 00 21 or 02 47 24 04 93; fax 02 47 24 06 13; info@chateaulavalliere.com; www. chateaulavalliere.com]** Turn L off D959, in vill 1km S on D749. Site on R after x-ing bdge with lake on L. Med, hdg/mkd pitch, pt shd; wc; chem disp; mv service pnt; serviced pitch; shwrs inc; el pnts (5A) €2.50; shops 1km; tradsmn; playgrnd; lake beach & fishing adj; dogs €0.80; Eng spkn; adv bkg rec high ssn; quiet; CKE/CCI. "Friendly welcome; modern san facs; mkd walks; conv Loire chateaux; v soft ground after heavy rain; site untidy & irreg cleaning of facs (2010) due being run by students; unrel opening dates." ♦ 27 Apr-17 Sep. € 10.50   2010*

CHÂTEAU LARCHER see Vivonne *7A2*

CHATEAU RENAULT *4G2* (6km S Urban) *47.54471, 0.88786* **Camp Municipal du Moulin, Rue du Lavoir, 37110 Villedômer [02 47 55 05 50 or 02 47 55 00 04 (Mairie); fax 02 47 55 07 26; mairie.villedomer@wanadoo.fr]** Fr A10 exit junc 18 onto D31 dir Château-Renault. Turn W onto D73 sp to Auzouer & Villedômer. Fr Château-Renault S on D910, site sp dir Villedômer. Sm, hdg pitch, shd; wc (male cont); chem disp; shwrs inc; el pnts (10A) €3; shops, rest, bar adj; rv fishing; lake & fishing 2km; dogs €1; adv bkg. "Gd, clean facs but old-fashioned; pitch yourself if warden not present." 15 Jun-15 Sep. € 6.70   2009*

CHATEAU RENAULT *4G2* (500m W Urban) *47.59283, 0.90687* **Camp Municipal du Parc de Vauchevrier, Rue Paul-Louis-Courier, 37110 Château-Renault [02 47 29 54 43 or 02 47 29 85 50 (LS); fax 02 47 56 87 50]** At Château-Renault foll sp to site 800m fr D910. If app fr a'route turn L on ent town & site on R of main rd adj Rv Brenne. Med, mkd pitch, pt shd; wc; chem disp; mv service pnt; shwrs inc; el pnts (6A) €2.20 (long lead poss req); shops 800m; rest 600m; bar 300m; playgrnd; htd pool; fishing; tennis; some rd noise; ccard not acc; CKE/CCI. "Pleasant site by rv in park; lge pitches; friendly, helpful warden; clean san facs, ltd low ssn; gd NH nr D910." ♦ 1 May-15 Sep. € 8.90   2009*

CHATEAUBRIANT *2F4* (1.5km S Urban) *47.70305, -1.37789*
Camp Municipal Les Briotais, Rue de Tugny, 44110
Châteaubriant [02 40 81 14 38 or 02 40 81 02 32; mairie.
chateaubriant@wanadoo.fr] App fr Nantes (D178) site sp
on S end of town. Or fr Angers on D963/D163 foll sp at 1st
rndabt; fr town cent, foll sps thro town. Sm, hdg pitch, pt shd;
wc; mv service pnt; shwrs; el pnts €2.70; shops, rest, snacks,
bar 1km; pool in town; games area; dogs; €0.35; quiet. "11thC
chateau in town; site locked o'night; site on municipal playing
field; gd NH." ♦ 2 May-30 Sep. € 6.00   2009*

CHATEAUDUN *4F2* (1km N Urban) *48.08008, 1.33141*
Camp Municipal Le Moulin à Tan, Rue de Chollet, 28200
Châteaudun [02 37 45 05 34 or 02 37 45 22 46 (LS);
fax 02 37 45 54 46; tourisme-chateaudun@wanadoo.fr]
App Châteaudun fr N on N10; turn R onto D3955 at 2nd
rndabt (coming fr town on L); L at next rndabt onto
D955; in 800m turn L into Rue de Chollet. App Châateaudun
fr S on N10, turn L onto D3955 & then as bef. Site adj Rv Loir
& well sp fr D955. Med, mkd pitch, pt shd; wc (some cont);
chem disp; mv service pnt; shwrs inc; el pnts (5A) inc; lndtte;
tradsmn; shops, rest & snacks 2km; playgrnd; htd, covrd pool
2km; fishing; canoeing; games area; TV; 5% statics; CKE/CCI.
"Gd touring base; quiet/under-used low ssn; helpful warden;
some night flying fr nrby military airfield; security gate 2.10m
height; no twin-axles; gd." 1 Apr-30 Sep. € 8.90   2011*

CHATEAULIN *2E2* (1.5km S Rural) *48.18754, -4.08515*
Camping La Pointe, Route de St Coulitz, 29150 Châteaulin
[tel/fax 02 98 86 51 53; lapointecamping@aol.com; www.
lapointesuperbecamping.com] Exit N165 onto D887 to
Châteaulin; in town cent, cross bdge & turn L along rv on
D770; after approx 750m, turn L at sp for St Coulitz; in 100m
turn R into site. NB if app fr S to Châteaulin on D770, do not
attempt to turn R at sp for St Coulitz (tight turn); go into town
& turn round. Med, hdg/mkd pitch, some hdstg, pt sl, pt shd;
wc; chem disp; mv service pnt; baby facs; shwrs inc; el pnts
(10A) €3 (poss rev pol); lndtte (inc dryer); shop; supmkt 1.5km;
tradsmn; rest, snacks & bar 1km; BBQ; playgrnd; covrd pool
1km; sand beach 15km; rv fishing nr; cycle hire; games rm;
wifi; dogs €1; phone; bus 1.5km; Eng spkn; adv bkg; quiet but
some rd noise; no ccard acc; red low ssn; CKE/CCI. "Charming,
peaceful, spacious site in wooded setting; well-run; helpful &
friendly British owners; immac san facs; rvside path to town; gd
cycling, walking & fishing; gd touring base; gd." ♦ 12 Mar-
15 Oct. € 17.00 (CChq acc)   2013*

CHATEAULIN *2E2* (500m SW Urban) *48.19099, -4.08597*
Camping de Rodaven (formerly Municipal), Rocade
de Prat Bihan 29150 Châteaulin [02 98 86 32 93; fax
02 98 86 31 03; contact@campingderodaven.fr; www.
campingderodaven.fr] Fr canal/rv bdge in town cent take
Quai Moulin (SE side of rv) for about 350m; site down track on
R opp sw pool. Med, pt shd; wc; chem disp; mv service pnt;
shwrs inc; el pnts (10A) €2.90; shops 200m; snacks; playgrnd;
htd, covrd pool 300m; direct rv access; fishing; sand beach 5km;
wifi; entmnt; dogs free, 2nd dog €1.00; phone; poss cr; Eng
spkn; adv bkg; quiet; CKE/CCI. "Well-kept site; pleasant, helpful
owner; vg clean facs; walk along rv bank to town; gd touring
base; Locronan vill worth the visit" ♦ ltd 7 Apr-30 Sep.
€ 18.60   2013*

CHATEAUMEILLANT *7A4* (500m NW Rural) *46.56807,*
2.18823 **Camp Municipal L'Etang Merlin, 18370**
Châteaumeillant [02 48 61 31 38; fax 02 48 61 39 89;
ot.chateaumeillant@wanadoo.fr; http://chalets.etang.
merlin.monsite-orange.fr/] Rec app fr W to avoid narr
town rds. Site sp fr rndabt at W end of town on D80 N of
Châteaumeillant on lakeside. Fr Culan by pass town on D943,
then as above. Sm, hdg/mkd pitch, pt shd; wc; serviced pitches;
chem disp; shwrs inc ; el pnts (5A) inc; lndry rm; shop 3km;
playgrnd; pool; lake adj (no sw); fishing; tennis & basketball
at sports complex adj; dogs €1; Eng spkn; adv bkg; quiet;
no ccard acc; CKE/CCI. "Superb, well-kept site; lge pitches;
friendly & helpful staff; rec arr early high ssn to secure pitch;
easy walk to town." ♦ 1 May-30 Sep. € 11.45   2012*

CHATEAUNEUF D'ILLE ET VILAINE *2E4* (1.5km NE Rural)
48.57589, -1.91941 **Camping Le Bel Event, 35430 St Père**
[02 99 58 83 79; fax 02 99 58 82 24; contact@camping-bel-
event.com; www.camping-bel-event.com] Fr terminal at
St Malo, at 1st rndabt foll sp Toutes Directions; at 2nd traff lts
turn R & cont foll dir Toutes Directions, then sp Rennes; cont
twd Rennes on D137 for approx 10km & take exit for Dinan/
Châteauneuf; take immed L twds Cancale; past an old rlwy stn
on R & take 1st little rd on L (500m fr stn) opp rest; site 100m
further on L. Fr S on D137 at Châteauneuf junc turn R onto
D74 sp Cancale, then as above. Med, mkd pitch, pt sl, pt shd;
wc; chem disp; shwrs inc; el pnts (10A) €4.20 (rev pol poss);
lndtte; tradsmn; sm shop; snacks; bar; htd pool (high ssn);
playgrnd; lake sw, fishing & watersports adj; sand beach 5km;
cycle hire; tennis; TV; 75% statics (sep area); dogs €2.10; quiet;
some rd noise; adv bkg; red low ssn . "Excel NH for St Malo
& ferry; clean & tidy site; immac san facs, ltd low ssn; some
sm pitches - 4 per enclave; gd touring base." 9 Apr-25 Sep.
€ 18.60   2011*

"That's changed – Should I let The Club know?"

If you find something on site that's different from
the site entry, fill in a report and let us know. See
www.caravanclub.co.uk/europereport.

CHATEAUNEUF DU FAOU *2E2* (4km SE Rural) *48.16853,*
-3.77578 **Camp Municipal du Goaker, Moulin du Pré,**
29520 St Goazec [02 98 26 84 23; fax 02 98 26 86 48]
D36 fr Châteauneuf-du-Faou, turn L sp St Goazec & foll sps
to site 800m N of vill nr rv. Sm, pt shd; wc (cont); shwrs inc;
el pnts €1.50; shops 750m; playgrnd; rest & bar 1km; quiet.
"Pleasantly situated on Rv Aulne adj Goaker lock on Nantes-
Brest canal; clean san facs." 15 Jun-15 Sep. € 7.00   2008*

CHÂTEAUNEUF DU PAPE see Sorgues

CHATEAUNEUF LES BAINS see St Gervais d'Auvergne *7A4*

CHATEAUNEUF SUR ISERE see Valence *9C2*

FRANCE

CHATEAUNEUF SUR LOIRE *4F3* (500m S Rural) *47.85643, 2.22426* **FFCC Camping de la Maltournée, Sigloy, 45110 Châteauneuf-sur-Loire [02 38 58 42 46 or 06 32 11 41 13 (mob); contact@ camping-chateauneufsurloire.fr; www.camping-chateauneufsurloire.fr]** S fr Chateauneuf cent, cross rv on D11; take 1st L, site in 300m on S bank of Rv Loire. Lge, pt shd; htd wc; chem disp; mv service pnt; shwrs inc; el pnts (10A) €3.90; lndtte; shops 1.5km; tradsmn; snacks; playgrnd; pool 2km; canoeing; wifi; 75% statics in sep area; dogs free; security barrier; poss cr; adv bkg; quiet; CKE/CCI. "Well-kept, busy site; helpful, pleasant staff; clean, modern san facs; chem disp v basic; m'van pitches beside rv; conv Orléans." ♦ 1 Apr-31 Oct. € 12.80   2013*

CHATEAUNEUF SUR LOIRE *4F3* (7km W Urban) *47.86884, 2.11597* **Camping de l'Isle aux Moulins, Rue du 44ème Régiment d'Infanterie, 45150 Jargeau [tel/fax 02 38 59 70 04 or 02 54 22 26 61 (LS); camping.jargeau@ orange.fr; www.jargeau.fr]** Exit Châteauneuf W on D960 dir Orléans; at St Denis-de-l'Hôtel turn sharp L onto D921 to Jargeau over Loire bdge; immed after x-ing bdge turn R into Blvd Jeanne d'Arc sp Camping; in 200m cont strt on into Rue du 44ème Régiment d'Infanterie; site on R in 300m. Site clearly visible on R of bdge on W bank of rv. NB App rd & turning to site is v narr; do not arr 1200-1330 (lunch time) as parking diff. Lge, mkd pitch, pt sl, pt shd; htd wc (mainly cont); chem disp; mv service pnt; baby facs; shwrs inc; el pnts (5A) €3.50; lndtte; tradsmn; shop, rest, bar 500m; BBQ; playgrnd; pool adj; rv fishing adj; cycle hire; games area; entmnt; wifi; twin axle; 2% statics; dogs €1.20; bus 500m; poss cr; Eng spkn; adv bkg; quiet; ccard acc; red long stay/low ssn/CKE/CCI. "Pleasant rvside site; lge pitches amongst trees; friendly farming family; modern san facs; poss muddy when wet; sh walk to sm town" ♦ 1 Apr-31 Oct. € 22.40   2013*

> "I like to fill in the reports as I travel from site to site"
>
> You'll find report forms at the back of this guide, or you can fill them in online at www.caravaclub.co.uk/europereport.

CHATEAUNEUF SUR SARTHE *4G1* (E Rural) *47.67745, -0.48673* **Camp Municipal du Port, Rue de la Gare, 49330 Châteauneuf-sur-Sarthe [02 41 69 82 02 or 02 41 96 15 20; fax 02 41 96 15 29; tourismechateauneufsursarthe@ wanadoo.fr; www.chateauneufsursarthe.fr]** Site clearly sp in vill, 18km E of Le Lion-d'Angers. Access to site fr bdge. Sm, pt shd; wc; chem disp; shwrs inc; el pnts (10A) €2.70 (long lead poss req); lndtte; shops & rest in vill; playgrnd; rv adj; fishing; sailing; v quiet but some rd noise; CKE/CCI. "Attractive area; lge pitches; clean facs but poss stretched high ssn; warden on site am & pm; very few elctric points" 1 May-30 Sep. € 7.15   2013*

⊞ **CHATEAUPONSAC** *7A3* (200m SW Rural) *46.13163, 1.27083* **Camp Municipal La Gartempe - Le Ventenat, Ave de Ventenat, 87290 Châteauponsac [05 55 76 55 33 or 05 55 76 31 55 (Mairie); fax 05 55 76 98 05; chateauponsac.tourisme@wanadoo.fr; www. holidayschateauponsac.com]** Fr N exit A20 junc 23.1 sp Châteauponsac; go thro vill, well sp on L on rvside. Fr S exit A20 junc 24 sp Châteauponsac & then as above. Sm, hdg/mkd pitch, terr, pt shd; htd wc; chem disp; shwrs inc; el pnts (6A) €3 (poss rev pol); lndtte; supmkt 500m; rest, snacks, bar (Jul-Aug); playgrnd; pool; kayaking; lake 10km; archery; children's activites; adj to holiday bungalows/gites; dogs €1; poss cr; Eng spkn; poss noise fr parties in rest; adv bkg; red low ssn; CKE/ CCI. "Pleasant site; helpful staff; gd san facs; pitches muddy in wet; not suitable lge m'vans; activities down steep hill; low ssn warden visits eves only." € 15.00   2009*

CHATEAURENARD see Avignon *10E2*

CHATEAUROUX *4H2* (1km N Rural) *46.82368, 1.69496* **Camp Municipal Le Rochat-Belle Isle, Rue du Rochat, 36000 Châteauroux [02 54 34 26 56 or 02 54 22 26 61; camping-le-rochat@orange.fr; www.aquadis-loisirs.com]** Exit A20 junc 13 onto D943/N143 S; foll sp Châteauroux; site sp bef town. Site on banks of Rv Indre, just S of Lac de Belle-Isle. Sp in town. Med, pt shd; wc (some cont); chem disp; mv service pnt; baby facs; shwrs inc; el pnts (5-10A) inc; gas; lndtte; shops 300m; rest, snacks, bar 100m; playgrnd; wifi; dogs €1.50; Eng spkn; poss noise fr low-flying aircraft. "Leisure park adj with pool & windsurfing on lake; friendly welcome & helpful; modern, clean san facs; poss music till late w/end high ssn; poss itinerants; pleasant walk into town along rv; lge brocante mkt 1st Sun of month; vg." ♦ 2 Apr-16 Oct. € 19.10 (CChq acc)   2012*

CHATEAUROUX *4H2* (9km SW Rural) *46.74214, 1.61983* **Camping Les Grands Pins, Les Maisons-Neuves, 36330 Velles [02 54 36 61 93; contact@les-grands-pins.fr; www. les-grands-pins.fr]** Fr N exit A20 junc 14 dir Châteauroux; in 500m turn R onto D920 parallel with m'way. Foll sp Maisons-Neuves & site. Fr S exit A20 junc 15, turn R then L onto D920, site on R. Med, pt sl, pt shd; wc; chem disp; some serviced pitches; shwrs inc; el pnts (10A) €4.50 (poss rev pol; long lead req if in open field); shop 8km; tradsmn; rest high ssn; bar; playgrnd; pool; tennis; wifi; entmnt; dogs €1.50; site clsd w/ end 1 Nov-14 Dec; Eng spkn; adv bkg; quiet; ccard acc; CKE/ CCI. "Gd, tidy site in pine forest; clean facs; gd rest; low ssn recep in rest; max weight m'van 3,500kg Oct-Apr - heavier acc in summer; vet in Châteauroux; excel NH nr m'way, some noise; nice site, pitches in the woods; san facs need attention; pleasant helpful staff; popular NH" ♦ 30 Mar-31 Oct. € 27.80   2013*

See advertisement opposite

CHATEL *9A4* (1.5km SW Rural) *46.25768, 6.83023* **Camping Caravaneige L'Oustalet, 1428 Route des Freinets, 74390 Châtel [04 50 73 21 97; fax 04 50 73 37 46; oustalet@valdabondance.com; www.oustalet.com]** Fr Thonon-les-Bains, take D902 & D22 to Châtel. Site sp fr church in cent. Med, hdg/mkd pitch, unshd; htd wc; mv service pnt; sauna; shwrs inc; el pnts (3-10A) €4-7.50; gas; lndtte; shop, rest, bar 100m; playgrnd; htd, covrd pool high ssn; tennis; games rm; wifi; entmnt; some statics; dogs €2.10; adv bkg rec winter; quiet; red low ssn. "Excel, well-kept site; excel clean facs; vg indoor pool; gd mountain walks; conv for ski lifts; ski bus stop adj." ♦ 19 Jun-5 Sep & 19 Dec-25 Apr. € 25.00   2010*

CHATEL CENSOIR see Coulanges sur Yonne *4G4*

CHATEL DE NEUVRE *9A1* (N Rural) *46.4131, 3.31884* **Camping Deneuvre, Route De Moulins, 03500 Châtel-de-Neuvre [04 70 42 04 51; fax 09 72 25 62 63; campingdeneuvre@wanadoo.fr; www.deneuvre.com]** S fr Moulins on D2009; sp N of vill on E side of D2009. Med, mkd pitch, hdstg, pt shd; wc; chem disp; mv service pnt; baby facs; shwrs inc; el pnts (4A) inc; gas; lndtte; tradsmn; rest, snacks; bar; playgrnd; canoe hire; wifi; dogs €1; adv bkg; Eng spkn; quiet; ccard not acc; CKE/CCI. "Site by Rv Allier in nature reserve; clean but not smart; useful NH without unhitching; Dutch management; friendly welcome; excel clean san facs; ltd facs low ssn; meals avail; splendid place for walking, fishing, cycling & birdwatching; diff ent/exit for lge o'fits; no twin-axles." ♦ 1 Apr-30 Sep. € 28.00   2013*

⊞ **CHATEL DE NEUVRE** *9A1* (400m W Rural) *46.40320, 3.31350* **FFCC Canoë Camping de la Courtine, 7 Rue de St Laurant, 03500 Châtel-de-Neuvre [04 70 42 06 21; fax 04 70 42 82 89; campinglacourtine@gmail.com; www.camping-lacourtine.com]** Fr N on D2009 to cent of vill, turn L at x-rds onto D32; site in 500m. Sm, mkd pitch, hdstg, pt shd; htd wc; chem disp; mv service pnt; baby facs; shwrs inc; el pnts (6-10A) €3-5 (poss rev pol); lndtte (inc dryer); shop 400m; tradsmn; rest 400m; snacks; bar; playgrnd; wifi; TV; dogs €1; poss cr; Eng spkn; adv bkg; quiet; red low ssn; CKE/CCI. "Friendly welcome; untidy ent masks very nice site; German family-owned site; access to Rv Allier for canoeing, fishing; walking in nature reserve; liable to flood & poss clsd low ssn; phone ahead to check; conv low ssn NH." ♦ € 12.50   2012*

CHATEL GUYON see Riom *9B1*

CHATEL MONTAGNE *9A1* (10km NE Rural) *46.15938, 3.73506* **Camp Municipal La Boulère, 03120 Arfeuilles [04 70 55 50 11 (Mairie); fax 04 70 55 53 28]** Site off D207 at NE exit to Arfeuilles 50m fr town name sp. 8km fr N7. Sm, pt sl, pt shd; wc (some cont); chem disp; shwrs inc; el pnts (6A) inc; lndry rm; shops, rest, snacks, bar 500m; sm playgrnd; tennis; dogs; quiet; CKE/CCI. "Lovely, peaceful, under-used site set in beautiful countryside; local fishing; gd walking; excel." ♦ 1 May-1 Oct. € 11.45   2010*

CHATEL MONTAGNE *9A1* (1km NW Rural) *46.11526, 3.67700* **FFCC Camping La Croix Cognat, 03250 Châtel-Montagne [tel/fax 04 70 59 31 38 or 06 65 53 91 93 (mob); campinglacroixcognat@wanadoo.fr; http://campinglacroixcognat.monsite-orange.fr/]** SW fr Lapalisse on D7; in 15km L on D25 to Châtel-Montagne in 5km & foll sp; site on L bef vill. 'Sleeping policemen' at ent. Sm, mkd pitch, terr, sl, pt shd; wc (some cont); chem disp; mv service pnt; baby facs; shwrs inc; el pnts (6A) €3; gas; lndtte; supkmt 6km; rest, snacks; playgrnd; pool (high ssn); paddling pool; fishing; tennis 100m; mountain bike hire; horseriding & windsurfing adj; entmnt; 5% statics; dogs €0.50; adv bkg; quiet; CKE/CCI. "Sm pitches poss diff o'fits over 6m." 1 May-30 Sep. € 11.00   2010*

CHATELAILLON PLAGE *7A1* (2km N Urban) *46.08632, -1.09489* **Camping L'Océan, Ave d'Angoulins, 17340 Châtelaillon-Plage [05 46 56 87 97; www.campingocean17.com]** Fr La Rochelle take D602 to Châtelaillon-Plage, site sp on L in 300m (after passing g'ge & L'Abbaye camp site). Med, hdg/mkd pitch, san fan; wc (some cont); chem disp (wc); baby facs; shwrs inc; el pnts (10A) €5.00; lndry rm; tradsmn; ice; shops, rest, snacks & bar 1km; BBQ; pool complex; waterslide; sand beach 500m; dogs €2; bus; park & ride 400m; phone; poss cr; some Eng spkn; occasional noise fr rlwy & clay pigeon range; ccard acc; red low ssn. "Very nice site, no statics and gd cycle routes" ♦ 18 May- 23 Sep. € 25.50   2013*

CHATELAILLON PLAGE *7A1* (2.5km SE Coastal) *46.05491, -1.08331* **Camping Port Punay, Les Boucholeurs, Allée Bernard Moreau, 17340 Châtelaillon-Plage [05 46 56 01 53; fax 05 46 56 86 44; contact@camping-port-punay.com; www.camping-port-punay.com]** Fr N exit D137 La Rochell-Rochefort rd onto D109; strt on at 1st rndabt, L at 2nd rndabt; then cont for 2.8km to end (harbour); turn L, keep R along narr one-way st; at next junc to L, site sp. Fr S exit D137 onto D203 sp Les Boucholeurs; at rndabt in 1km foll site sp to edge of Châtelaillon & turn R, foll sp. Site in 500m. Lge, pt shd; wc; baby facs; shwrs inc; el pnts (10A) €5; gas; Indtte; Indry rm; shops adj; rest, snacks; bar; playgrnd; pool; sand beach 500m; games area; cycle hire; wifi; entmnt; TV; 25% statics; dogs €2.50; poss cr; Eng spkn; adv bkg; quiet; red low ssn. "Busy but quiet site; Immac san facs; friendly, energetic, helpful owners; steel pegs req; sm pitches; excel." 22 Apr-25 Sep. € 24.50 (3 persons) 2011*

See advertisement

⊞ **CHATELARD, LE** *9B3* (8km SW Rural) *45.61020, 6.09658* **Camping Les Aillons, La Chapelle, 73340 Aillon-le-Jeune [04 79 54 60 32; fax 04 79 54 62 88; ggay@icor.fr]** Fr town hall/TO take rd to Aillon stn (winter sports development); site on L after bdge in 3km. Sm, pt shd; wc; shwrs inc; basic shop/bar/hotel in vill in summer, in winter at Aillon station; 30% statics; dogs; no twin-axles; CKE/CCI. "Mountain scenery; sm, basic site; conv orchid walk (May/Jun) & winter sports; local ski lift (winter & Jul/Aug); prize-winning cheese factory in old vill." € 9.80 2008*

CHATELARD, LE *9B3* (500m NW Rural) *45.68783, 6.13078* **Camping Les Cyclamens, 73630 Le Châtelard [04 79 54 80 19 or 07 86 86 03 58 (mob); contact@camping-cyclamens.com; www.camping-cyclamens.com]** Exit A41 junc 14 at Grésy-sur-Aix onto D911 E to Le Châtelard; turn R at rndabt at ent to Le Châtelard onto Route du Champet; in 600m turn R to site. Or S fr Annecy on D508/D1508; in 3km fork R onto D912/D911 to Le Châtelard; then as bef. Site well sp. Sm, pt sl, pt shd; wc; chem disp; mv service pnt; baby facs; shwrs inc; el pnts (2-10A) €2.40-3.10; gas; Indtte; supmkt 400m; tradsmn; BBQ; rv sw 1km, lake sw 5km; fishing; kayaking; rock-climbing; paragliding; canyoning; horseriding; games rm; wifi; dogs; €0.80; bus 600m; Eng spkn; adv bkg; quiet; red low ssn/long stay; CKE/CCI. "Attractive site with stunning views; lge pitches; friendly staff; clean san facs; easy access to walks; excel." ♦ 22 Apr-30 Sep. € 11.80 2011*

CHATELLERAULT *4H1* (1km N Rural) *46.83850, 0.53443* **FFCC Le Relais du Miel, Route d'Antran, 86100 Châtellerault [05 49 02 06 27 or 06 07 52 04 74; camping@lerelaisdumiel.com; www.lerelaisdumiel.com]** On A10 exit junc 26 at Châtellerault-Nord. Foll sp twd Antran; site on R fr rndabt, well sp (easy to find). Med, hdstg, terr, shd; wc; chem disp; mv service pnt; serviced pitches; shwrs inc; el pnts (10A) inc; Indtte; shop 400m; tradsmn; bar; BBQ; playgrnd; pool; tennis; wifi; dogs €5; Eng spkn; adv bkg; some rd & rlwy noise; ccard acc; red long stay; CKE/CCI. "Beautifully situated rvside site in Château de Valette park; friendly owners; clean san facs - ltd low ssn & need updating; extra charge over 5m; conv Futuroscope, Chinon, Loches; conv A10." ♦ 15 May-30 Sep. € 26.00 (2 nights) 2010*

CHATILLON COLIGNY *4F3* (500m S Rural) *47.81717, 2.84447* **Camp Municipal La Lancière, Rue de la Lancière, 45230 Châtillon-Coligny [02 38 92 54 73 or 06 16 09 30 26 (mob); lalanciere@wanadoo.fr]** N fr Briare twd Montargis on N7; E fr Les Bézards on D56 twd Châtillon-Coligny; site sp on ent town on R immed bef canal bdge. Fr town cross Canal de Briare on D93 twd Bléneau; immed turn S along canal rd sp Camping & Marina. Med, mkd pitch, pt shd; wc (some cont); chem disp (wc); shwrs inc; el pnts (3-6A) €2.-3.10 (poss long lead req & rev pol); Indtte; shops, rest, bar in town; playgrnd; pool high ssn; rv fishing; games area; quiet;dogs; 25% statics; no ccard acc; CKE/CCI. "Attractive, peaceful, tidy site; many lge pitches; clean, dated facs; site yourself, warden calls; gd walking/cycling along canal & historic vill; Superb site for simple caravaning, excel value" 1 Apr-30 Sep. € 10.00 2013*

CHATILLON EN DIOIS *9D3* (E Urban) *44.69450, 5.48817* **Camp Municipal Les Chaussières, 26410 Châtillon-en-Diois [04 75 21 10 30 or 04 75 21 14 44 (Mairie); fax 04 75 21 18 78; camping.chatillonendiois@wanadoo.fr; www.camping-chatillonendiois.com]** Fr Die take D93 S for 6km then L on D539 to Châtillon (8km) site sp on R on ent to town. Med, mkd pitch, pt shd; wc (some cont) chem disp; mv service pnt; shwrs inc; el pnts (10A) €3.60; ice; shop 200m; snacks & bar 200m; BBQ; playgrnd; pool adj; canoeing; fishing; tennis; horseriding; cycling; entmnt; 30% statics; dogs €2.10; phone; poss cr; Eng spkn; adv bkg; quiet; ccard acc; red low ssn; CKE/CCI. "Wardens off site 11:30pm- 4:30am. Pleasant sweet site, wardens friendly and helpful." 1 Apr-30 Oct. € 15.70 2013*

CHATILLON EN VENDELAIS see Vitre *2F4*

FRANCE

CHATILLON SUR CHALARONNE *9A2* (500m SE Urban)
46.11622, 4.96172 **FFCC Camp Municipal du Vieux
Moulin, Ave Jean Jaurès, 01400 Châtillon-sur-Chalaronne
[04 74 55 04 79; fax 04 74 55 13 11; campingvieuxmoulin@
orange.fr; www.camping-vieuxmoulin.com]** Exit A6 junc
30 to Châtillon-sur-Chalaronne; pick up D7 on S site of vill;
site on R in 400m. Ave Jean Jaurès is part of D7. Site sp in
town. Med, hdg pitch, hdstg, shd; wc (some cont); chem
disp; baby facs; shwrs inc; el pnts (10A) €4 (long lead req on
some pitches); lndtte (inc dryer); supmkt 200m; rest & bar
adj; snacks; playgrnd; pool adj inc; fishing; leisure cent adj;
50% statics; dogs €2; phone; adv bkg; quiet, noisy eves high
ssn; ccard acc; red CKE/CCI. "Lovely site in picturesque area;
helpful warden; immac facs, ltd low ssn; check office opening
hrs for early dep; if office clsd ring bell, warden will open
barrier; lovely medieval town cent; excel model railway; mkt
Sat; excel." ♦ 1 May-30 Sep. € 15.70   2010*

CHATILLON SUR INDRE *4H2* (500m N Rural) *46.99116,
1.17382* **Camp Municipal Les Rives de L'Indre (formerly
Camp Municipal de la Ménétrie), Rue de Moulin de la
Grange, 36700 Châtillon-sur-Indre [06 78 27 16 39 or
02 54 38 75 44 (Mairie); fmadjointdgs@orange.fr; www.
chatillon-sur-indre.fr]** Site well sp in vill. N twd Loches then
foll sp. Med, some hdg/mkd pitch, pt shd; wc; shwrs inc; el pnts
(6A) €3; gas, shop & rest 400m; BBQ; playgrnd adj; htd pool
400mtrs (proper sw trunks only); dogs; no twin-axles; no adv
bkg; quiet; CKE/CCI. "Lovely, relaxed, well-kept site; friendly,
helpful warden; gd, clean san facs; conv Loire chateaux; gd
birdwatching area; interesting old town; lge mkt Fri; excel
value." ♦ 15 May-15 Sep. € 8.00   2013*

CHATILLON SUR LOIRE see Briare *4G3*

"We must tell The Club about that great site we found"

Get your site reports in by mid-August
and we'll do our best to get your updates
into the next edition of Caravan Europe.

CHATILLON SUR SEINE *6F1* (500m E Urban) *47.85955,
4.57975* **Camp Municipal Louis Rigoly, Esplanade Saint
Vorles, 21400 Châtillon-sur-Seine [03 80 91 03 05 or
03 80 91 13 19 (LS); fax 03 80 91 21 46; camping-chatillon-
sur-seine@orange.fr; www.mairie-chatillon-sur-seine.fr]**
Fr N, cross rv bdge (Seine); cont approx 400m twd town cent;
at lge fountain forming rndabt turn L into street with Bureau
de Tourisme on corner; foll sp to site. Fr S ignore all camping
sp & cont into town cent to fountain, turn R & cont as above.
Med, hdg/mkd pitch, pt sl, pt shd; wc; chem disp; mv service
pnt; shwrs inc; el pnts (4-6A) €2.30-4.65; gas; lndtte; shops
500m; snacks adj municipal pool; playgrnd; htd pool adj,j
acuzzi,Wifi,fishing,tennis,riding; dogs; Eng spkn; adv bkg;
quiet; CKE/CCI. "Pretty site adj park; clean, tidy, well-spaced
pitches; helpful, welcoming warden; excel, clean san facs; easy
walk to old town; no twin-axles; vg." ♦ ltd 1 Apr-30 Sep.
€ 18.20   2013*

CHATILLON SUR SEINE *6F1* (6km S Rural) *47.81390, 4.53896*
Camping de la Forge, La Forge, 21400 Ampilly-le-Sec [tel/
fax 03 80 91 46 53; campingdelaforge@gmail.com; www.
campinglaforge.com]** S fr Châtillon-sur-Seine on D971, on
leaving Buncey take 1st turn R immed after layby (narr rd); site
on R in 1km, on bend immed bef rv bdge, sp. Or app fr S on
D971, after passing Chamesson, Ampilly-le-Sec & site sp - note
sharp R turn in Ampilly. Sm, pt shd; wc; chem disp; shwrs
inc; el pnts (6-16A) €3 (poss long lead req); lndtte; shop 2km;
tradsmn; rest 2.5km; BBQ; rv sw adj; fishing; dogs; phone;
Eng spkn; adv bkg rec high ssn; ltd facs winter - phone ahead
Dec to Feb to check open; quiet; red long stay; CKE/CCI.
"Beautiful, secluded, CL-type site in woodland by rv; helpful,
friendly British owners; clean, basic san facs; area for lge
m'vans across rd; access diff lge o'fits; levelling blocks poss req;
phone ahead rec; NH only; facs V basic" ♦ ltd 1 May-30 Sep.
€ 19.00   2012*

CHATRE, LA *7A4* (3km N Rural) *46.60131, 1.97808* **Camp
Municipal Solange-Sand, Rue du Pont, 36400 Montgivray
[02 54 06 10 34 or 02 54 06 10 36; fax 02 54 06 10 39;
mairie.montgivray@wanadoo.fr]** Fr La Châtre take rd to
Montgivray, foll camping sp. Fr Châteauroux on D943 SE
twd La Châtre turn R 2km S of Nohant on D72. Site behind
church. Med, mkd pitch, pt shd; wc; chem disp; shwrs inc; el
pnts (6A) inc (poss rev pol); lndry rm; BBQ; dogs; quiet; CKE/
CCI. "Pleasant site in chateau grounds; new san facs planned
(2010); gd access; warden calls am & pm; gd rest adj; gd
walks." ♦ 15 Mar-15 Oct. € 10.80   2010*

CHATRE, LA *7A4* (2km SE Rural) *46.56862, 1.99921* **Camping
Intercommunal Le Val Vert, Route de Briantes, 36400 La
Châtre [02 54 48 32 42; fax 02 54 48 32 87]** Fr La Châtre
take D943 dir Montluçon. On o'skts La Châtre turn R to
Briantes, site sp at this junc. Or fr Montluçon on D943, turn
L just bef La Châtre; site sp. Sm, hdg pitch, terr, pt shd; wc;
chem disp; mv service pnt; shwrs inc; el pnts (10A) €2.50; lndry
rm; shop 1km; tradsmn; BBQ; playgrnd; htd pool 5km; some
statics; adv bkg; quiet; ccard not acc; CKE/CCI. "Spacious,
pleasant site; excel grounds; dated san facs; walk/cycle to
shops; poss itinerants." ♦ 1 Jun-12 Sep. € 8.50   2009*

CHATRES SUR CHER see Villefranche sur Cher *4G3*

CHAUDEFONDS SUR LAYON see Chalonnes sur Loire *2G4*

CHAUDES AIGUES *9C1* (3km SW Rural) *44.84583, 3.00039*
Camp Municipal Le Château du Couffour, 15110 Chaudes-
Aigues [tel/fax 04 71 23 57 08 or 04 71 23 52 47 (Mairie);
www.chaudesaigues.com]** Sp on L of D921 N dir Laguiole.
Lge, pt shd; wc; shwrs inc; el pnts (6A) €2.50; lndtte; shops,
rest, snacks, bar 2.5km; BBQ; playgrnd; pool 3km; sports
area; tennis; fishing 1km; golf 2km; TV; quiet. "Scenic area;
attractive, family-run site with fine views; gd walking; 1000m
altitude; thermal spa in town; excel." ♦ 1 May-20 Oct.
€ 8.00   2009*

CHAUFFAILLES see Clayette, La *9A2*

FRANCE

CHAUMARD *4H4* (W Rural) *47.14428, 3.90658* **Camp Municipal Les Iles, 58120 Chaumard [03 86 78 03 00; fax 03 86 78 05 83]** Fr Château-Chinon take D944 dir Pannecière-Chaumard; in 500m turn R onto D37 to Corancy; then D12 to Chaumard; foll camping sp, then turn L into site 100m after cemetary. Sm, hdg pitch, hdstg, pt shd; wc (some cont); chem disp (wc); shwrs; el pnts; lake sw adj; fishing; bus 250m. "Access poss diff lge o'fits." 2009*

"I need an on-site restaurant"

We do our best to make sure site information is correct, but it is always best to check any must-have facilities are still available or will be open during your visit.

CHAUMONT *6F1* (800m NW Urban) *48.11790, 5.13334* **Camp Municipal Parc Ste Marie, Rue des Tanneries, 52000 Chaumont [03 25 32 11 98 or 03 25 30 60 27 (Mairie); fax 03 25 30 59 50; sports@ville-chaumont.fr]** Site on Chaumont W by-pass joining N19 Troyes rd to N67 St Dizier rd. Do not try to app fr town cent. Exit A5 at exit 24, foll sp to town cntr, befr town foll sp to site. Sm, hdg/mkd pitch, pt sl, pt shd; wc (cont); chem disp; shwrs inc; el pnts (10A) inc (poss long lead req); shops 1km; tradsmn; snacks; playgrnd; 20% statics; dogs €1.50; poss cr; some traff noise; CKE/CCI. "Rec arr early; care needed with steep access to some sl pitches; friendly warden; ent barrier under warden control at all times; gd NH." 2 May-30 Sep. € 14.25 2012*

CHAUMONT SUR LOIRE *4G2* (500m NE Rural) *47.48444, 1.19417* **Camp Municipal Grosse Grève, Ave des Trouillas, 41150 Chaumont-sur-Loire [02 54 20 95 22 or 02 54 20 98 41 (Mairie); fax 02 54 20 99 61; mairie. chaumontsloire @ wanadoo.fr; www.camping-chaumont-sur-loire.com]** Fr N side of rv on D952 cross bdge to Chaumont on D1, turn R immed & R under bdge. Site sp in vill on D751. Med, pt shd; htd wc; chem disp; shwrs inc; el pnts (6-16A) €2-3.50 (poss long lead req); lndry rm; rest & bar 1km; BBQ; playgrnd; fishing; horseriding; canoeing; tennis; cycle hire; quiet, but some rd/rlwy noise; no ccard acc; CKE/CCI. "Pleasant site by rv; gd, clean san facs; no twin-axles; interesting chateau; cycle track along Loire; gd value; excel." ♦ 1 May-30 Sep. € 9.00 2013*

CHAUVIGNY *7A3* (1km E Urban) *46.57072, 0.65326* **Camp Municipal de la Fontaine, Rue de la Fontaine, 86300 Chauvigny [tel/fax 05 49 46 31 94; camping-chauvigny@ cg86.fr; www.chauvigny.fr]** N151 fr Poitiers to Chauvigny. Turn L in cent Chauvigny just before gate.Site well sp fr Chauvigny. Med, pt shd; htd wc (some cont); chem disp; mv service pnt; baby facs; shwrs; el pnts (15A) inc; lndtte; shop 500m; tradsmn; BBQ; playgrnd; pool & tennis 1km; rv 1km; cycle hire; wifi; dogs €1.15; adv bkg; red low ssn; CKE/CCI. "Popular, well-kept, well-run site adj park & lake; views of castle; lge pitches; helpful, friendly staff; immac san facs; o'night area for m'vans; delightful walk to cent; mkts Tue, Thur & Sat; a real find; Excel facs; gd value; old style electric plug/socket adaptor needed, poss rev pol; rec" ♦ 6 Apr-6 Oct. € 15.90 2013*

CHAUVIGNY *7A3* (7km NW Rural) *46.60189, 0.59838* **Camp Municipal, 13 Rue de la Varenne, 86300 Bonnes [05 49 56 44 34 or 05 49 56 40 17 (Mairie); fax 05 49 56 48 51; camping_bonnes86@hotmail.com]** Sp fr D951 & D749. Sp to site easily missed in vill. Site on rvside. Med, hdg pitch, pt shd; wc; chem disp; mv service pnt; shwrs inc; el pnts (15A) €2.70; lndtte; shop adj in vill; tradsmn; rest & bar 500m; pool adj; waterslide; playgrnd; rv & sand beach adj; tennis; dogs €1.05; poss cr; adv bkg; quiet; Eng spkn; dogs; CKE/CCI. "Friendly, helpful staff; clean & welcoming; vg pool; poss itinerants." 15 May-15 Sep. € 9.70 2010*

CHAVANNES SUR SURAN *9A2* (500m E Rural) *46.26601, 5.42819* **Camp Municipal, Le Village, 01250 Chavannes-sur-Suran [04 74 51 70 52; fax 04 74 51 71 83; mairiechavannessuran@wanadoo.fr]** Turn E off N83 at St Etienne-du-Bois onto D3, cross D52 bef Treffort (v narr rds). Then steep climb & bends & after 6km turn N onto D936 sp Chavannes. Turn E at town hall (Mairie), site sp. Fr Bourg-en-Bresse turn E onto D936 sp Jasseron about 1km after joining N83 in Bourg. Foll D936 for approx 18km to Chavannes. Sm, hdg/mkd pitch, pt shd; wc; chem disp (wc); shwrs inc; el pnts (5A) inc (poss rev pol & poss long lead req); shop 500m; BBQ; quiet. "Pretty rvside site in beautiful area; lge pitches; site self, warden calls; clean san facs; excel cycling, fishing, walking; attractive vill; Cize-Bolozon viaduct worth visit; highly rec." ♦ ltd 1 May-30 Sep. € 11.50 2010*

CHAZELLES SUR LYON *9B2* (3km E Rural) *45.63454, 4.42789* **Camping d'Hurongues, 69590 Pomeys [04 78 48 44 29; campinghurongues@orange.fr; www.camping-hurongues.com]** Fr N on D389/D1089 turn S onto D103, thro Chazelles-sur-Lyon, exit on D2, twd St Symphorien-sur-Coise. Site on L 3km fr Chazelles. Med, pt sl, terr, pt shd; htd wc (some cont); chem disp; mv service pnt; baby facs; shwrs; el pnts (13A) €3; lndtte (inc dryer); shop; tradsmn; rest 3km; snacks; BBQ; htd, covrd pool adj; tennis; cycle hire; games area; some statics; dogs €3; phone; sep car park high ssn; adv bkg; quiet. ♦ 16 Apr-16 Oct. € 17.00 (CChq acc) 2010*

⊞ **CHEF BOUTONNE** *7A2* (2km W Rural) *46.10767, -0.09342* **Camping Le Moulin, 1 Route de Niort, 79110 Chef-Boutonne [05 49 29 73 46; campinglemoulin. chef@aliceadsl.fr; www.campingchef.com]** Fr D950 to or fr Poitiers, turn E onto D740 to Chef-Boutonne, site on R. Fr N10 turn onto D948 to Sauzé-Vaussais then L onto D1 to Chef-Boutonne; then take D740 dir Brioux-sur-Boutonne; site on L. Sm, hdg/mkd pitch, ltd hdstg, pt shd; htd wc; chem disp; mv service pnt 1km; shwrs inc; el pnts (10A) €4; lndtte; ice; shop 2km; tradsmn; rest, snacks; bar; BBQ; playgrnd; pool; wifi; entmnt; dogs €1.20; bus 2km; poss cr; Eng spkn; adv bkg; quiet; ccard acc; red long stay/low ssn; CKE/CCI. "Well-kept site; lge pitches; friendly, helpful British owners; gd rest; ltd facs in winter; much bird life; conv Futuroscope & La Rochelle; vg; san facs dated but very clean" ♦ € 18.80 2013*

CHEMERY see Contres *4G2*

CHEMILLE *2G4* (1km SW Rural) *47.20182, -0.73486*
**FFCC Camping Coulvée, Route de Cholet, 49120
Chemillé [02 41 30 42 42 or 02 41 30 39 97 (Mairie); fax
02 41 30 39 00; camping-chemille-49@wanadoo.fr; www.
camping-coulvee-chemille.com]** Fr Chemillé dir Cholet on
D160, turn R in 1km. Sm, hdg pitch, terr, pt shd; wc; chem
disp; mv service pnt; shwrs inc; el pnts (10A) €3.60; lndtte;
tradsmn; bar; BBQ; playgrnd; sm sand beach; lake sw; pedalos;
dogs €1.70; some Eng spkn; adv bkg; quiet; ccard not acc; red
long stay; CKE/CCI. "Clean facs; helpful staff; gd pitches; poss
unrel opening dates; mkt Thurs." ♦ 1 May-15 Sep. € 23.60
(CChq acc)   2012*

CHENAC ST SEURIN D'UZET see Cozes *7B1*

CHENERAILLES *7A4* (2km SW Rural) *46.10337, 2.16059*
**Camp Municpal La Forêt, 23130 Chénérailles
[05 55 62 38 26 or 05 55 62 37 22; fax 05 55 62 95 55;
mairie.chenerailles@wanadoo.fr]** SW fr Chénérailles on
D55; site in 2km on R. Sm, mkd pitch, pt sl, pt shd; wc (some
cont); chem disp (wc); shwrs inc; el pnts (10A) €2.30; lndtte;
shop, rest, bar 2km; BBQ; playgrnd; lake sw adj; dogs €0.60;
Eng spkn; adv bkg; CKE/CCI. "Sand beach on lake adj; warden
on site am & pm." ♦ ltd 15 Jun-15 Sep. € 7.35   2010*

CHENONCEAUX *4G2* (1.5km E Rural) *47.32905, 1.08816*
**Camping de l'Ecluse, Route de la Plage, 37150 Chisseaux
[02 47 23 87 10 or 06 15 83 21 20 (mob);
campingdelecluse-37.fr; www.campingdelecluse-37.fr]**
E fr Chenonceaux on D176; cross bdge; immed hard R & foll
rv bank; site in 300m. Med, mkd pitch, pt shd; wc; chem disp;
mv waste; shwrs inc; el pnts (16A) €3.90 (rev pol); lndtte; shop
1km; supmkt 6km; tradsmn; snacks; bar; playgrnd; fishing;
canoeing; watersports; dogs €1.50; phone; poss cr; Eng
spkn; adv bkg; quiet tho some rd/rlwy noise; ccard acc; CKE/
CCI. "Rv trips; fishing; gd walking; gd." ♦ 1 Mar-31 Oct.
€ 11.55   2009*

"Satellite navigation makes touring much easier"

Remember most sat navs don't know if
you're towing or in a larger vehicle – always
use yours alongside maps and site directions.

CHENONCEAUX *4G2* (S Rural) *47.33033, 1.06947* **Camp
Municipal, Fontaine des Prés, 37150 Chenonceaux
[02 47 23 90 13 (Mairie); fax 02 47 23 94 46; www.
chenonceaux-blere-tourisme.com]** In town cent foll sp
Château de Chenonceaux & site. Ent as if visiting chateau &
attendants will direct you. Site ent narr & twisting, poss not
suitable long o'fits. Sm, pt sl, pt shd; wc (some cont); chem
disp; mv service pnt; shwrs inc; el pnts (6A) €2.65; shop, rest,
bar 500m; BBQ; sm playgrnd; dogs €1; phone; bus adj; poss cr;
no adv bkg; some rlwy noise; CKE/CCI. "Simple site conv for
chateau; v nr rlwy." ♦ 1 Jun-15 Sep. € 8.55   2011*

CHENONCEAUX *4G2* (1.5km S Rural) *47.32765,
1.08936* **Camping Le Moulin Fort, Pont de Chisseaux,
37150 Francueil [02 47 23 86 22; fax 02 47 23 90 83;
lemoulinfort@wanadoo.fr; www.lemoulinfort.com]**
Exit A85 junc 11 N, then take D976 E dir Montrichard; site on S
bank of Rv Cher just off D976. Fr Tours take D976 sp Vierzon;
keep on D976 by-passing Bléré until sm rndabt (5km) where
site sp to L twd rv. Take sm rd on R to site, bef actually x-ing
bdge. Site well sp. Med, hdg/mkd pitch, pt shd; wc; chem disp;
baby facs; shwrs inc; el pnts (6A) €4. (long lead poss req); gas;
lndtte (inc dryer); shop; tradsmn; rest, snacks; bar; BBQ (gas/
charcoal); playgrnd; pool; paddling pool; fishing; cycle hire;
wifi; entmnt; games/TV rm; dogs €3; no c'vans/m'vans over
8m high ssn; lge o'fits check in adv; Eng spkn; adv bkg rec
for Jul & Aug; min 3 nights preferred; rd noise & a little rlwy
noise; ccard acc; red low ssn; CKE/CCI. "Lovely, well-kept site
on rv bank; beautiful area; friendly, helpful British owners; gd
san facs; easy access most pitches; many sm & v shady pitches;
some pitches suitable for large o'fits; footpath by rv with view
of chateau; gd cycle rtes; poss security probs due access to site
fr rv bank; Fri mkt Montrichard & Sun mkt Amboise; excel." ♦
24 May -27 Sep. € 23.00 SBS - L08   2013*

CHENS SUR LEMAN see Douvaine *9A3*

CHERBOURG *1C4* (5km NE Urban/Coastal) *49.65405,
-1.56675* **Camp Municipal Espace Loisirs de Collignon,
Plage Collignon, 50110 Tourlaville [02 33 54 80 68; fax
02 33 20 53 03; camping-collignon@wanadoo.fr; www.
mairie-tourlaville.fr]** Foll sp fr ferry terminal for Espace
Loisirs Collignon or Tourlaville-Plage; site on D116; turn L at
lge rndabt beyond Tourlaville boundary. Med, mkd pitch,
unshd; wc; chem disp; shwrs inc; el pnts (10A) €3.75; gas;
lndtte; shops 500m; rest 2km; bar 500m; covrd pool adj; sand
beach adj; fishing, sw & watersports adj; games rm; entmnt;
TV; 30% statics; dogs; poss cr; adv bkg (rec high ssn); poss
noisy high ssn (youth groups); some rd noise; ccard acc; CKE/
CCI. "Lge landscaped complex; generous pitches; poss poor
security; conv ferries." ♦ 1 May-30 Sep. € 15.90   2009*

CHERBOURG *1C4* (12km NE Coastal) *49.6928, -1.4387*
**Camping La Plage, 2 Village de Fréval, 50840 Fermanville
[02 33 54 38 84; fax 02 33 54 74 30; contact@camping-
femanville.com; www.camping-fermanville.com]**
Fr Cherbourg on D116 dir Barfleur, site in 12km on L. Med,
some hdg pitch, unshd; wc; chem disp; shwrs inc; el pnts (5A)
€2.50; snacks; bar; playgrnd; beach 300m; 70% statics; dogs
€2; poss cr; adv bkg ess summer, rec winter; quiet. "Friendly
owner; conv for ferry & D-Day landing beaches; poss unrel
opening dates." 1 Mar-30 Nov. € 13.00   2008*

⊞ **CHERBOURG** *1C4* (10km E Coastal) *49.65703, -1.52645*
**Camp Municipal Le Fort, 47 Route du Fort, 50110
Bretteville [02 33 22 27 60 or 02 33 88 78 20 (Mairie);
mairie.brettevilleensaire@orange.fr; www.
brettevilleensaire.fr]** Immed exit car ferries in Cherbourg,
turn L on D116. On leaving Bretteville turn sharp L at junc of
D116 & D611, 1st turn R. App poss diff lge o'fits. Med, pt
sl, unshd; wc; chem disp; shwrs; el pnts (10A) €2.50; shops
4km; BBQ; playgrnd; shgl beach adj; 90% statics; quiet. "Sep
area tourers, sm pitches; some pitches view of coast; locked
2200-0700; poss diff in wet; some pitches diff lge o'fits; sh stay
only." € 11.70   2010*

FRANCE

CHERBOURG 1C4 (10km E Coastal) 49.66720, -1.48772 **Camping L'Anse du Brick, 18 L'Anse du Brick, 50330 Maupertus-sur-Mer [02 33 54 33 57; fax 02 33 54 49 66; welcome@anse-du-brick.com; www.anse-du-brick.com or www.les-castels.com]** At rndabt at port take 2nd exit sp Caen, Rennes & Mont St Michel; at 2nd rndabt take 3rd exit sp Caen & Mont St Michel (N13); at 3rd rndabt take 2nd exit onto dual c'way sp St Lô, Caen (N13), Bretteville-sur-Mer; exit on D116 & foll sp thro Bretteville-en-Saire (take care lge speed hump in Le Becquet); turn R for site just after R-hand blind bend & turning for Maupertus; up v steep incline. Med, hdg/mkd pitch, terr, sl, shd; wc; chem disp; mv service pnt; baby facs; serviced pitches; shwrs inc; el pnts (10A) inc (poss rev pol); gas; lndtte (inc dryer); shop 3km; tradsmn; rest, snacks; bar; BBQ; playgrnd; htd pool; paddling pool; waterslide; sand beach adj (via bdge over coastal rd); tennis; cycle hire; archery; wifi; games/TV rm; dogs €6; no c'vans/m'vans over 8m; poss cr; adv bkg; quiet; ccard acc; red low ssn; CKE/CCI. "Attractive, well-kept site in beautiful setting; conv ferry; gd clean san facs; some pitches for lge o'fits; conv Landing Beaches, Barfleur, coastal nature reserve." ♦ 1 Apr-30 Sep. € 52.50 SBS - N14   2013*

See advertisement on inside back cover

⊞ **CHERBOURG** 1C4 (6km S Rural) 49.58951, -1.59433 **Camping Le Village Vert, 50470 Tollevast [02 33 43 00 78; fax 02 33 43 03 38; le-village-vert@wanadoo.fr; www.le-village-vert.com]** S'bound take N13 sp Caen out of town. Cont on N13 fr Auchan rndabt for approx 5km to D56 slip rd sp Delasse. Turn L at x-rds over N13 onto N13 sp Cherbourg. Site on R approx 3.5km, sp nr Auchan hypmkt. N'bound exit sp Tollevast & site. Lge, some hdstg, pt sl, pt shd; wc; chem disp; mv service pnt; shwrs inc; baby facs; el pnts (10A) €1.50 (check rev pol); gas; sm shop & 1km; tradsmn; rest 200m; playgrnd; tennis; golf & horseriding 2km; 95% statics (sep); dogs €2; Eng spkn; adv bkg; quiet but poss rd noise at front of site; ccard acc; red CKE/CCI. "Conv NH for ferries in woodland setting; ltd space for tourers but spacious pitches; friendly & efficient; poss waterlogged pitches in wet weather; poss itinerants; office closes 1930, night arr area." ♦ € 13.00   2009*

⊞ **CHERBOURG** 1C4 (3km NW Urban/Coastal) 49.65576, -1.65257 **Camp Municipal de la Saline, Rue Jean Bart, 50120 Equeurdreville-Hainneville [02 33 93 88 33 or 02 33 53 96 00 (Mairie); fax 02 33 93 12 70; mairie-equeurdreville@dialoleane.com; www.equeurdreville.com]** Fr ferry terminal foll D901 & sp Beaumont-Hague. On dual c'way beside sea look out for site sp to L at traff lts. Med, hdg/mkd pitch, hdstg, pt sl, terr, pt shd; htd wc; chem disp; mv service pnt in 100m; shwrs inc; el pnts (10A) €4.56 lndry rm; shop, rest, snacks & bar 500m; sand beach adj; fishing; 50% statics; dogs €0.50; phone; rd noise; adv bkg; CKE/CCI. "Sea views; boules & skateboard park adj; aquatic cent 500m; cycle path to town; secured at night; gd NH." ♦ ltd € 9.12   2010*

CHERRUEIX see Dol de Bretagne 2E4

CHESNE, LE 5C1 (2km NE Rural) 49.53166, 4.77430 **Camp Departmental du Lac de Bairon, 08390 Le Chesne [tel/fax 03 24 30 11 66; campinglacdebairon@cg08.fr]** Leave A203 exit Sedan, W on D764, in 500m L on D977 sp Vouziers. 2km bef Le Chesne R on D12, in 500m L on D312. Site 2km on L. Lge, mkd pitch, some hdstg, pt shd; htd wc; chem disp; mv service pnt; shwrs inc; el pnts (6-10A) €3-5; lndtte (inc dryer); shop 2km; tradsmn; snacks; bar; BBQ; playgrnd; tennis; cycle hire; watersports; entmnt; lake sw, sand beach, fishing, boat & canoe hire; TV rm; entmnt; 20% statics; dogs €1.20; phone; CKE/CCI. "Pleasant, quiet site; gd, clean san facs, but air of neglect (Sep 2010); poss diff site ent with lge o'fits; forest walks." ♦ 16 Mar-4 Nov. € 11.00   2010*

CHEVENON see Nevers 4H4

CHEVERNY 4G2 (2km S Rural) 47.47798, 1.45070 **Camping Les Saules, 102 Route de Contres, 41700 Cheverny [02 54 79 90 01; fax 02 54 79 28 34; contact@camping-cheverny.com; www.camping-cheverny.com]** Exit A10 junc 17 dir Blois Sud onto D765 to Romorantin. At Cour-Cheverny foll sp Cheverny & chateau. Fr S on D956 turn R onto D102 just N of Contres, site on L just bef Cheverny. Well sp fr all dirs. Lge, mkd pitch, shd; htd wc; chem disp; mv service pnt; baby facs; shwrs inc; el pnts (10A) €3.50 (poss long lead req); gas; lndtte; shop; tradsmn; rest, snacks; bar; BBQ; playgrnd; htd pool; paddling pool; fishing; tennis; golf nr; excursions; games rm; cycle hire; wifi; 2% statics; TV; dogs €2; Eng spkn; adv bkg rec high ssn; quiet but some rd noise; ccard acc; red long stay/low ssn; CKE/CCI. "Beautiful, well-run site; friendly, welcoming, helpful owners; excel san facs; excel pool; all pitches under trees; muddy after heavy rain; many excel cycle & walking rtes nr; Cheverny chateau worth visit; little train & boat rides." ♦ 30 Mar-23 Sep. € 27.00 SBS - L01   2012*

CHEYLARD, LE 9C2 (1km E Rural) 44.90721, 4.43198 **Camping La Chèze, Route de St Christol, 07160 Le Cheylard [tel/fax 04 75 29 09 53 or 06 89 38 21 32 (mob); mosslercat@wanadoo.fr; www.camping-lecheylard.fr]** Fr Le Cheylard take D264 SE & foll camping sp. App up steep hill & sharp bend into final app. Less steep app fr Valence on N86 & D120. Site 25km fr St Agrève by rd. NB If overshoot acute L-hand bend proceed thro Le Cheylard & turn in car park. Med, mkd pitch, terr, pt shd; wc (some cont); chem disp (wc); shwrs inc; el pnts (10A) €2.50; lndtte; shops 1.2km; tradsmn; rest; playgrnd; rv sw 2km; some statics; dogs €0.50; phone; security barrier; poss cr; Eng spkn; adv bkg; v quiet; 10% red CKE/CCI. "In grounds of château; views over attractive town & mountains; gd walks nrby." ♦ Easter-1 Nov. € 10.50   2008*

⊞ **CHEZERY FORENS** 9A3 (500m S Rural) 46.21770, 5.86378 **Camp Municipal Le Valserine, Route de Confort, 01410 Chézery-Forens [tel/fax 04 50 56 20 88 or 06 77 94 04 56 (mob); camping.valserine@orange.fr; www.chezery.fr]** Site off D991 on app to vill. Sm, pt shd; wc; chem disp; shwrs inc; el pnts (5-10A) €3-3.50; lndtte; shops adj; rv adj; dogs €1; quiet. "Gd walks." € 12.00   2008*

CHILLY LE VIGNOBLE see Lons le Saunier 6H2

FRANCE

CHINON *4G1* (500m SW Rural) *47.16397, 0.23377* FFCC Camping de L'Ile Auger, Quai Danton, 37500 Chinon [02 47 93 08 35; fax 02 47 98 47 92; camping-ile-auger@ hotmail.fr; www.ville-chinon.com] On S side of rv at bdge. Fr S foll sp Chinon St Jacques; when app 2nd bdge on 1-way 'loop', avoid R lane indicated for x-ing bdge & cont strt past S end of main bdge to site on R. Fr N foll sp 'Centre Ville' round castle, cross bdge, site on R. Well sp in town & opp castle. Lge, hdg/mkd pitch, pt shd; wc (some cont); chem disp (wc); mv service pnt; baby facs; shwrs inc; el pnts (8-12A)inc (poss rev pol); lndtte; shop 200m; snacks adj; playgrnd; canoe hire; htd pool 300m; wifi sat TV; dogs €1.20; phone; quiet; ccard acc; red long stay/CKE/CCI. "Excel, well-kept site in gd location; clean, dated san facs, poss stretched if site busy; twin-axles discretionary; poss midge prob; poss itinerants; gd cycle rtes; gd views of chateau; rec; Automatic ent barrier" ◆ 1 Apr-30 Oct. € 14.00   2013*

See advertisement above

CHINON *4G1* (14km NW Rural) *47.20693, 0.08127* Camping Belle Rive, 2 Route de Chinon, 37500 Candes-St Martin [02 47 95 98 11; fax 02 47 95 80 95; contact@ campingcandes37.com; www.cdc-rivegauchevienne.com] Fr Chinon take D751. Site on R bef junc with D7, on S bank of Rv Vienne. Med, mkd pitch, pt shd; wc; shwrs; el pnts (16A) €3.10; lndtte (inc dryer); shops 1km; tradsmn; rvside café; bar; rv sw 1km; playgrnd; fishing adj; dogs €1.30; adv bkg; quiet; CKE/CCI. "Pleasant rvside site; san facs, on 2 floors, need update & poss stretched if site busy; conv Saumur & chateaux." ◆ 15 Apr-30 Sep. € 13.40   2012*

CHOLET *2H4* (5km SE Rural) *47.03699, -0.84171* Camping Village Vacances Le Lac de Ribou, Allée Léon Mandin, 49300 Cholet [02 41 49 74 30; fax 02 41 58 21 22; info@ lacderibou.com; www.lacderibou.com] Fr Cholet ring rd foll sp Parc des Loisirs de Ribou. Sp fr Cholet. Lge, hdg/mkd pitch, hdstg, terr, pt shd; htd wc; chem disp; mv service pnt; serviced pitches; shwrs inc; el pnts (10A) €3.85 (long lead req); lndtte; tradsmn; shop; hypmkt 1.5km; rest, snacks, bar; BBQ; playgrnd; 2 htd pools; waterslides; lake sw & sand beach 500m; fishing; boating; windsurfing; skating; tennis; archery; golf nr; entmnt; TV rm; dogs €2.10; extra for twin-axles; poss cr; Eng spkn; adv bkg ess; quiet; ccard acc; 5% red CKE/CCI. "Excel touring area; excel site." ◆ 1 Apr-30 Sep. € 18.90   2009*

CHOLET *2H4* (8km SE Rural) *47.01915, -0.82976* Camping du Verdon, Le Bois Neuf, Route du Verdon, 49280 La Tessoualle [02 41 49 74 61; fax 02 41 58 21 22; lacduverdon@cholet-sport-loisirs.fr; www.cholet-sports-loisirs.com] Exit Cholet ring rd S onto D258 sp L Tessoualle; turn L bef La Tessoualle sp Barrage du Verdon dam. Site adj dam. Poss diff to app fr other rds. Sm, hdg pitch, pt shd; wc; chem disp; shwrs; el pnts (3-5A) €2.10-3.05 (long lead req some pitches, poss rev pol); shop; rest, snacks, bar adj; lake sw & beach; dogs €1; Eng spkn; adv bkg; quiet; CKE/CCI. "Peaceful location, lovely pitches; facs dated but clean; site yourself, warden calls; windsurfing on Lac du Verdon; excel walking, cycling." 1 Jul-31 Aug. € 9.85   2010*

CHORGES *9D3* (9km NE Rural) *44.56169, 6.34642* Campéole Camping Le Clos du Lac, Route des Lacs, 05160 St Apollinaire [04 92 44 27 43; fax 04 92 43 46 93; clos-du-lac@campeole.com; www.camping-closdulac.com or www.campeole.com] N94 to Chorges, then take D9 to St Apollinaire. Take D509 to NW of vill, site in 2.2km, sp. Med, terr, pt shd; htd wc; chem disp; baby facs; shwrs inc; el pnts (7A) €4.10; lndtte; shop; tradsmn; playgrnd; lake sw & beach adj; fishing; watersports; games area; some statics; dogs €1.80; Eng spkn; adv bkg; quiet; ccard acc; red low ssn. "Pleasant, peaceful, well-kept site in lovely location; gd facs." ◆ 22 May-25 Sep. € 14.20   2009*

See advertisement on pages 14 & 15

CHORGES *9D3* (2.5km E Rural) *44.53515, 6.30231* Camping Le Rio Claret, Les Chabes, 05230 Chorges [tel/fax 04 92 50 62 16; rio-claret@wanadoo.fr; www.camping-lerioclaret.com] Fr Gap foll N94 E dir Embrun; take main rd by-passing Chorges & 4km past traff lts look for sp to site. Turn L at junc (narr lane), turn R & R again to site. Sm, mkd pitch, pt shd; wc (some cont); chem disp; mv service pnt; shwrs inc; el pnts (4-10A) €2.80-4.20; lndry rm; tradsmn; shop 2.4km; rest, snacks; bar; playgrnd; pool; lake sw & beach 2km; TV; 10% statics; dogs €2.20; phone; adv bkg; some rd noise at lower level. "Conv touring base; spectacular views; helpful, pleasant owners; gd san facs; nice pool; conv Lac de Serre-Ponçon; boat excursions; day trip to Italy via Briançon." ◆ 1 Jun-30 Sep. € 16.00   2010*

CHORGES 9D3 (5km E Rural) 44.52289, 6.34125 **Camping Club Le Roustou, 05230 Prunières [04 92 50 62 63; fax 04 92 50 90 48; info@campingleroustou.com; www. campingleroustou.com]** E fr Gap on N94. Site on side of Lac de Serre-Ponçon. Do not attempt to go to Prunières vill, always stay on N94. Lge, mkd pitch, hdstg, terr, pt shd; wc; chem disp; mv service pnt; baby facs; shwrs inc; el pnts (4A) inc; lndtte; shops 10km; tradsmn; snacks; bar; playgrnd; pool (no shorts); beach & lake sw adj; canoe hire; tennis; cycle hire; games area; wifi; TV; dogs €2; poss cr; Eng spkn; quiet; red low ssn; ccard acc; CKE/CCI. "Beautiful views; excel scenery; relaxing area; always park on E side in case of poss problem with wind; excel." 1 May-30 Sep. € 19.90   2010*

CHORGES 9D3 (6km E Rural) 44.52701, 6.35876 **Camping Le Nautic, Lac de Serre-Ponçon, 05230 Prunières [04 92 50 62 49; fax 04 92 53 58 42; campinglenautic@ wanadoo.fr; www.campinglenautic.fr]** Fr Gap or Embrun take N94, site sp bet Savines & Chorges. Med, terr, shd; wc; chem disp; mv service pnt; shwrs; el pnts (6A) €3; gas; lndtte; shop; tradsmn; snacks; bar; playgrnd; pool; shgl beach & lake sw; boating; wifi; dogs €2; adv bkg; quiet. "Beautiful location; lake sw excel in sheltered bay; vg san facs." ♦ 15 May-15 Sep. € 20.35   2010*

CHORGES 9D3 (10km SW Rural) 44.47581, 6.26330 **Camping La Viste, Le Belvédère de Serre-Ponçon, 05190 Rousset [04 92 54 43 39; fax 04 92 54 42 45; camping@laviste.fr; www.laviste.fr]** N on A51 or D1085 twds Gap; take D942 sp Barcelonnette; after Espinasses turn L onto D3 to Barrage de Serre-Ponçon; then L onto D103. Site on L. NB D3 long, v steep climb, hairpin bends. Med, hdg/mkd pitch, pt sl, pt shd; wc; chem disp; mv service pnt; shwrs inc; el pnts (5A) €3.30; gas; lndtte; shop & 4km; tradsmn; rest, snacks; bar; BBQ; playgrnd; pool; lake sw 2km; some statics; dogs €2.40; phone; adv bkg; quiet; ccard acc; CKE/CCI. "Ltd facs low ssn; site o'looks Lac de Serre-Poncon (amenity area); site rds narr; access diff lge o'fits; gd walking." ♦ ltd 15 May-15 Sep. € 18.20   2009*

CIOTAT, LA 10F3 (4km NE Coastal) 43.18733, 5.65810 **Camping Les Oliviers, Chemin des Plaines Baronnes, 13600 La Ciotat [04 42 83 15 04; fax 04 42 83 94 43; www. camping-lesoliviers.com or www.homair.com]** Fr La Ciotat, foll D559 coast rd sp Bandol & Toulon. Site in 4km, look for lge sp on L. Caution x-ing dual c'way. V lge, pt sl, terr, shd; wc; chem disp; mv service pnt; shwrs inc; el pnts (6A) (poss rev pol); gas; lndtte; shops 300m; rest, snacks, bar 300m; playgrnd; pool; sand/shgle beach 800m; tennis; 5% statics; dogs; bus 300m; poss v cr; Eng spkn; adv bkg; quiet but some noise fr main rd & rlwy adj; ccard acc; CKE/CCI. "Sea views many pitches; friendly staff; gd touring base." ♦ 3 Apr-3 Oct.   2010*

⊞ **CIOTAT, LA** 10F3 (3km E Coastal) 43.18938, 5.64605 **Camping Santa Gusta, Domaine de Fontsainte, 13600 La Ciotat [04 42 83 14 17; santagusta@wanadoo.fr; www. santagusta.com]** Foll D559 coast rd fr La Ciotat twd Les Lecques to Total filling stn on R. Site down by filling stn. Lge, pt sl, pt shd; wc (cont); chem disp (wc); shwrs inc; el pnts (5A) €2.90; lndtte; shop; rest, snacks, bar high ssn; playgrnd; rocky beach adj; boat-launching facs; wifi; entmnt; 95% statics; dogs; poss cr; quiet; CKE/CCI. "San facs open 0730-2000; adj beach not suitable for bathing; ltd facs low ssn; smart card access; NH only." € 19.50   2009*

CIVRAY 7A2 (1km NE Urban) 46.15835, 0.30169 **Camping Les Aulnes, Les Coteaux de Roche, 86400 Civray [05 49 87 17 24 / 06 32 95 00 77 (mob); fax 05 49 87 17 24; campingaulnes@yahoo.fr; www.camping-les-aulnes.com]** Civray 9km E of N10 halfway bet Poitiers & Angoulême. Site outside town SE of junc of D1 & D148. Sp on D148 & on S by-pass. Avoid town cent narr rds. Med, pt sl, pt shd; wc (cont); chem disp (wc); shwrs; el pnts (6-10A) €3 (poss long lead req); lndtte; shop 500m; rest, snacks; bar; BBQ; playgrnd; htd pool 1km; rv sw & fishing adj; cycle hire; golf; few statics; dogs €1; Eng spkn; quiet; ccard acc; CKE/CCI. "Pleasant rvside site; old, but clean san facs, poss irreg cleaning low ssn; pitches soft when wet; vg rest; conv town cent; mkt Wed; vg." 1 Apr-15 Oct. € 7.50   2013*

CLAIRVAUX LES LACS 6H2 (1.2km SE Rural) 46.56431, 5.7562 **Yelloh! Village Le Fayolan, Chemin de Langard, 39130 Clairvaux-les-Lacs [03 84 25 26 19 or 08 20 00 55 93; reservation@rsl39.com; www. relaisoleiljura.com or www.yellohvillage.co.uk]** Fr town foll campsite sp, last site along lane adj to lake. V lge, hdg/ mkd pitch, terr, pt shd; wc; serviced pitches; chem disp; sauna; some serviced pitches; shwrs inc; el pnts (6A) inc (poss rev pol); gas; lndtte; shop; rest, snacks; bar; playgrnd; htd pools (1 covrd); waterslide; sand lake beach adj; games rm; tennis 1km; cycle hire; entmnt; TV; 16% statics; dogs €4; extra for twin axles; Eng spkn; adv bkg rec; quiet; ccard acc; red low ssn; CKE/CCI. "Excel, clean site; extra for lakeside pitches high ssn; pleasant sm town in easy walking dist; lovely area." ♦ 6 May-4 Sep. € 38.00   2011*

See advertisement on inside front cover

CLAIRVAUX LES LACS 6H2 (1km S Rural) 46.56761, 5.75480 **Camping La Grisière et Europe Vacances, Chemin Langard, 39130 Clairvaux-les-Lacs [03 84 25 80 48; fax 03 84 25 22 34; bailly@la-grisiere.com; www.la-grisiere.com]** Turn S off D678 in Clairvaux opp church onto D118; fork R in 500m & foll site sps to lake. Sp in vill. Camping La Grisière ent after Camping Les Lacs. V lge, mkd pitch, pt sl, pt shd; htd wc (some cont); chem disp; mv service pnt; baby facs; shwrs inc; el pnts (6-10A) €2.60; lndry rm; shop; tradsmn; snacks; bar; BBQ; playgrnd; lake sw & beach adj; rv sw 5km; fishing; watersports; cycle & canoe hire; tennis 1km; wifi; TV; 5% statics; dogs €1; phone; bus 700m; Eng spkn; no adv bkg; quiet; ccard acc; red low ssn; CKE/CCI. "Lovely views in beautiful area; lge pitches; excel site." ♦ 1 May-30 Sep. € 17.30   2009*

CLAIRVAUX LES LACS 6H2 (1km S Rural) 46.56822, 5.75513 **Camping Le Grand Lac, Chemin du Langard, 39130 Clairvaux-les-Lacs [03 84 25 22 14 or 03 84 25 26 19; reservation@rsl39.com; www.relaisoleiljura.com]** SE on D678 fr Lons-le-Saunier; in Clairvaux vill turn R opp church on L, 1st R then fork R, foll sp. Ent 2.7m wide. Lge, hdg/mkd pitch, terr, pt shd; wc; mv service pnt; baby facs; shwrs inc; el pnts (6A) inc; lndtte; shop; tradsmn; snacks; bar; BBQ; sand beach; fishing; boating; 30% statics; dogs €2; Eng spkn; ccard acc. "Lovely country nr Jura mountains; gd site." ♦ 31 May-5 Sep. € 19.00   2008*

See advertisement on pages 32 & 33

CLAIRVAUX LES LACS 6H2 (10km SW Rural) 46.52311, 5.67350 Camping de Surchauffant, Pont de la Pyle, 39270 La Tour-du-Meix [03 84 25 41 08; fax 03 84 35 56 88; info@camping-surchauffant.fr; www.camping-surchauffant.fr] Fr Clairvaux S on D27 or D49 to D470. Foll sp Lac de Vouglans, site sp. Med, mkd pitch, pt sl, pt shd; wc; chem disp; mv service pnt; shwrs inc; el pnts (6A) €3; lndtte; shops adj; rest, snacks; bar; BBQ; playgrnd; pool; paddling pool; dir access to lake 120m; sailing; watersports; entmnt; TV rm; some statics; dogs €1.60; Eng spkn; adv bkg; quiet; ccard acc; red low ssn. "Vg facs; lovely location; hiking trails." ♦ 22 Apr-19 Sep. € 19.00   2010*

CLAIRVAUX LES LACS 6H2 (4km W Rural) 46.58625, 5.70194 Camping Le Moulin, 39130 Patornay [03 84 48 31 21; fax 03 84 44 71 21; contact@camping-moulin.com; www.camping-moulin.com] Exit A39 junc 8 to Lons-le-Saunier, then take D52/D678 SE to Pont-de-Poitte. After x-ing bdge over Rv Ain, ent to site on L. Lge, hdg/mkd pitch, hdstg, pt terr, shd; wc; chem disp; mv service pnt; baby facs; shwrs inc; el pnts (6A) inc; gas; lndtte; shop; tradsmn; snacks; bar; BBQ; playgrnd; htd pool; waterslide; rv sw & sand beach 5km; fishing; games area; games rm; wifi; entmnt; TV; dogs €2; phone; poss cr; Eng spkn; adv bkg; ccard acc; red low ssn; CKE/CCI. "Site clsd 1200-1400, do not arr during this time as narr app rd poss blocked with queuing traff; excel cent for touring Jura; vg site." ♦ 25 Apr-13 Sep. € 28.00   2008*

CLAIRVAUX LES LACS 6H2 (7km W Rural) 46.59976, 5.68824 Camping Beauregard, 2 Grande Rue, 39130 Mesnois [tel/fax 03 84 48 32 51; reception@juracamping beauregard.com; www.juracampingbeauregard.com] S fr Lons-le-Saunier on D52/D678, about 1km bef Pont-de-Poitte turn L on D151. Site 1km on L opp rd junc to Pont-de-Poitte. Lge, hdg/mkd pitch, hdstg, pt sl, terr, pt shd; htd wc (some cont); chem disp; baby facs; shwrs inc; el pnts (6A) €4 (poss long lead req); gas; lndtte; shop 1km; tradsmn; rest; playgrnd; htd pool high ssn; sand beach 800m; kayaking nr; tennis; cycle hire; games rm; 10% statics; dogs €2.20; poss cr; Eng spkn; adv bkg; quiet. "Super site, clean & well-run; different sized pitches; excel san facs, ltd low ssn; excel rest; poss muddy when wet; New indoor pool with jacuzzi and sauna (2012), extremely gd quality. ♦ 1 Apr-30 Sep. € 25.50 2012*

See advertisement below

CLAMECY 4G4 (5km NE Rural) 47.51665, 3.48001 Camping Le Bois Joli, 2 Route de Villeprenoy, 89480 Andryes [tel/fax 03 86 81 70 48; info@campingauboisjoli.com; www.campingauboisjoli.com] S on N151 fr Auxerre to Coulanges-sur-Yonne; W on D39 to Andryes. Foll sps `Camping Andryes'; site in 500m after vill. Med, mkd pitch, terr, shd; htd wc; chem disp; baby facs; baby facs; fam bthrm; shwrs inc; el pnts (10A) €4.80 (poss rev pol); gas; lndry rm; shop; tradsmn; BBQ; playgrnd; pool inc; rv sw, fishing & boat hire 2km; tennis; cycle hire; wifi; TV; 10% statics; dogs €3.50; phone; Eng spkn; quiet; ccard acc; red low ssn; CKE/CCI; "Dutch owners; beautiful countryside; gd pitches; muddy in rain; excel facs; excel; Nice site in wooded area" ♦ 1 Apr-31Oct. € 22.85   2013*

"There aren't many sites open at this time of year"

If you're travelling outside peak season remember to call ahead to check site opening dates – even if the entry says 'open all year'.

CLAMECY 4G4 (8km SE Rural) 47.41390, 3.60828 Camp Municipal Les Fontaines, 58530 Brèves [tel/fax 03 86 24 25 26; www.vaux-yonne.com] On D985 (Clamecy-Corbigny) at Brèves. Both app clearly sp. Med, pt sl, unshd; wc; chem disp (wc); shwrs inc; el pnts (6A) €2; lndtte; tradsmn; shop; BBQ; playgrnd; 4% statics; dogs; phone. CKE/CCI. "Quiet site in pretty area nr Rv Yonne & canal; friendly staff; grnd soft after heavy rain; vg." ♦ 1 Jun-30 Sep. € 8.60   2009*

CLAMECY 4G4 (S Urban) 47.45231, 3.52772 Camp Municipal du Pont-Picot, Rue de Chevroche, 58500 Clamecy [03 86 27 05 97; clamecycamping@orange.fr; www.clamecy.fr] On N151 fr S, exit N151 at rndabt 3km SW of town cent, cross level x-ing then R at rndabt on D23, take 1st L, site sp in 2.4km. Narr app rd. App fr N or E thro town not rec. Med, pt sl, pt shd; wc; chem disp; shwrs inc; el pnts (6A) inc; lndry rm; shops 1km; tradsmn; playgrnd; sw; no twin-axles; poss cr; Eng spkn; quiet: red low ssn; CKE/CCI. "Pleasant, peaceful site bet rv & canal in beautiful location; friendly, helpful staff; facs poss inadequate when busy; town 10 min walk on towpath; gd cycling; gd NH; narr bridge just before ent" ♦ 25 Mar-30 Sep. € 14.50   2013*

Camping Beauregard
Jura ★★★★

www.juracampingbeauregard.com

Tél. / Fax : +33 (0)3 84 48 32 51
reception@juracampingbeauregard.com

CLAYETTE, LA 9A2 (8km NE Rural) 46.33667, 4.38185
Camping Château de Montrouant, 71800 Gibles
[03 85 84 51 13; campingdemontrouant@wanadoo.fr;
www.chateau-de-montrouant.com] Fr N79 at Trivy take
D41 to Dompierre-les-Ormes & Montmelard, then Gibles. Site
sp fr Gibles. Sm, hdg/mkd pitch, pt sl, pt shd; htd wc; chem
disp; baby facs; shwrs inc; el pnts (6A) €5; lndtte (inc dryer);
basic shop & 2km; rest 1.5km; snacks; bar; BBQ; playgrnd;
htd pool; paddling pool; fishing lake; tennis; wifi; entmnt; TV;
dogs €3; phone; Eng spkn; adv bkg; v quiet. "Pretty location;
charming owners; unsuitable lge o'fits/m'vans due steep rds;
some pitches sm & tight access; gd." ♦ ltd 1 Jun-11 Sep.
€ 26.00 (CChq acc)   2008*

CLAYETTE, LA 9A2 (500m E Urban) 46.29159, 4.32020
Camping des Bruyères, 9 Route de Gibles, 71800 La
Clayette [03 85 28 09 15 or 03 86 37 95 83 (LS); http://
campingbruyeres.com/] Site on D79, 100m fr D987 & lake.
Med, hdg/mkd pitch, hdstg, pt sl, shd; htd wc; chem disp;
mv service pnt; shwrs inc; el pnts (6A) inc; gas; lndtte; shops
adj; tradsmn; snacks, bar 500m; BBQ; playgrnd; htd pool adj
Jun-Aug inc; boating; tennis; games area; entmnt; 10% statics;
dogs €1.60; phone; poss cr; adv bkg; quiet; CKE/CCI. "Pleasant,
well-kept site o'looking lake & chateau; friendly, helpful staff;
gd-sized pitches, mostly sloping; excel." ♦ 1 Apr-31 Oct.
€ 18.30   2012*

CLAYETTE, LA 9A2 (13km S Rural) 46.2011, 4.3391 FFCC
Camping Les Feuilles, 18 Rue de Châtillon, 71170
Chauffailles [03 85 26 48 12; fax 03 85 26 55 02;
campingchauffailles@gmail.com / chalets@chalets-
decouverte.com; www.chauffailles.fr / www.
chalets-decouverte.com] S fr La Clayette on D985 (dir Les
Echarmeaux), turn R at camp sp down hill & cross Rv Botoret
to site. Med, mkd pitch, hdstg, pt shd; htd wc; chem disp;
mv service pnt; shwrs; el pnts (5A) inc; lndtte; supmkt 500m;
playgrnd; pool adj; fishing; tennis; games rm; wifi; TV; Eng
spkn; adv bkg ess; quiet; red CKE/CCI. "Attractive site; poss
rallies May/June & Sep (poss noisy); gd san facs but hot
water to shwrs & dishwashing only; easy walk to interesting
town; sep m'van Aire de Service adj rear ent." 1 May-30 Sep.
€ 18.80   2013*

See advertisement below

CLECY 3D1 (E Rural) 48.91366, -0.47399 FFCC Camping Les
Rochers des Parcs, La Cour, 14570 Clécy [02 31 69 70 36;
camping.normandie@gmail.com; www.camping-
normandie-clecy.fr] Fr Condé take D562 dir Caen; turn R
onto D133a sp Clécy & Le Vey; do not take turning to Clécy
cent but cont downhill, past museum on L & then over bdge;
turn R in 150m at campsite sp; site on R. Med, mkd pitch,
some hdstg, pt sl, pt shd; htd wc; mv service pnt; baby facs;
shwrs inc; el pnts (6A) €3.50; lndtte (inc dryer); shop 1km;
tradsmn; rest 1km; snacks; bar; BBQ; playgrnd; rv fishing;
cycle hire; games area; wifi; some statics; dogs €1; phone;
poss cr; Eng spkn; quiet; red long stay low ssn. "Lovely rvside
situation; friendly, helpful owner; facs poss stretched high
ssn & ltd low ssn; excel cent for walking." ♦ 1 Apr-30 Sep.
€ 17.50 (CChq acc)   2013*

See advertisement opposite

CLEFMONT 6F2 (500m E Rural) Camp Municipal du Mont
Clair, 52240 Clefmont [03 25 31 31 63] Well sp on D74, site
behind sm school. Sm, hdg pitch, pt shd; wc; chem disp; mv
service pnt; shwrs inc; el pnts (6A) €1.50; tradsmn; BBQ; no
statics; dogs; quiet; CKE/CCI. "Lovely, neat site with modern
facs; vg." ♦ 15 Apr-15 Oct. € 8.00   2009*

CLELLES 9C3 (4km N Rural) 44.85118, 5.62478 FFCC Camp
Municipal de la Chabannerie, 38930 St Martin-de-Clelles
[tel/fax 04 76 34 00 38; camping.chabannerie@yahoo.fr;
www.camping-isere.fr] D1075 fr Grenoble, after St Michel-
les-Portes look for rest on R. Turn L after 300m to St Martin-
de-Clelles, site sp. Site well sp fr N & S. Sm, mkd pitch, hdstg,
terr, shd; wc; chem disp; baby facs; shwrs inc; el pnts (10A)
€3.50; gas 5km; lndtte; shop 5km; rest, snacks; bar; no BBQs;
playgrnd; pool; games area; TV rm; 4% statics; dogs €1;
phone; Eng spkn; adv bkg; quiet, rd noise some pitches; ccard
acc; red low ssn/long stay/CKE/CCI. "Pitches in pine trees; conv
Vercours National Park & mountains; pleasant staff; some san
facs dated; low ssn san facs poss unclean (2011); beautiful
pool; sm pitches & steep site rds, access diff lge o'fits; gd
walking; tranquil site with 38 species of orchids in ssn." ♦
1 May-30 Sep. € 15.50   2011*

FRANCE

CLEON D'ANDRAN *9D2* (200m SE Urban) *44.60985, 4.93715* Camp Municipal Les Cigales, Rue de Piscine, 26450 Cléon-d'Andran [06 87 90 40 80 (mob) or 04 75 90 12 73 (Mairie); mairie.cleon.andran@wanadoo.fr] Fr A7 leave at junc 16 sp Privas/Crest. S fr Crest on D538. In 5km take D6. In 11km at Cléon-d'Andran turn L in vill, in 100m turn R. Sm, shd; wc (cont); shwrs inc; el pnts €2.50; lndtte; shop 500m; playgrnd; pool; dogs €1; quiet; CKE/CCI. 1 Jul-31 Aug. € 11.00   2010*

CLERE SUR LAYON see Vihiers *4G1*

CLEREY see Troyes *4E4*

CLERGOUX *7C4* (300m E Rural) *45.27871, 1.96566* FFCC Camping La Petite Rivière, 19320 Clergoux [05 55 27 68 50; jcbakker@xs4all.nl; www.compumess. nl/lapetiteriviere] Exit A89 junc 21 onto D1089. Go E until next rndabt, turn R & after approx 5km turn L onto D978 to Clergoux. Site on R just bef W end of vill. Or fr Tulle on D978 site in approx 20km, sp. Sm, mkd pitch, pt sl, pt shd; wc; chem disp; mv service pnt; baby facs; shwrs inc; el pnts (6A) €2.25; lndtte; tradsmn; lake sw & sand beach 1.5km; 20% statics; dogs €1.30; Eng spkn; adv bkg; quiet; red low ssn; CKE/CCI. "Helpful Dutch owner; 25 mkd walks in area; excel." 1 Apr-15 Sep. € 10.20   2009*

⊞ **CLERMONT FERRAND** *9B1* (7km SE Rural) *45.70018, 3.16902* Camping Le Clos Auroy, Rue de la Narse, 63670 Orcet [tel/fax 04 73 84 26 97; aanvraag@camping-le-clos-auroy.com; www.camping-le-clos-auroy.com] S on A75 take exit 5 sp Orcet; foll D213 to Orcet for 2km, at rndabt onto D52, take 1st L, site on R, sp. Med, hdg/mkd pitch, hdstg, terr, pt shd; htd wc; chem disp; mv service pnt; shwrs inc; el pnts (10A) €5 (poss rev pol); gas; lndtte; sm shop 500m; supmkt 4km; tradsmn; snacks; bar; playgrnd; htd pool; paddling pool; rv fishing 500m; tennis; wifi; entmnt; 5-10% statics; dogs €2.25; site poss open all year; phone; Eng spkn; adv bkg; quiet; ccard acc; red low ssn/long stay/senior citizens; CKE/CCI. "Excel, well-kept; easy access; lge pitches, poss v high hedges; superb htd san facs; pitches by rv poss liable to flood; extra charge for sh stay m'vans; ltd fresh water points & diff to use for refill; vg winter site; interesting town; gd dog walks adj; Snack & bar only open high ssn; Vg value, helpful staff" ♦ 3 Jan-31 Oct. € 39.70   2013*

CLERMONT FERRAND *9B1* (9km SE Urban) *45.74015, 3.22247* Camp Municipal Le Pré des Laveuses, Rue des Laveuses, 63800 Cournon-d'Auvergne [04 73 84 81 30; fax 04 73 84 90 65; camping@cournon-auvergne.fr; www. cournon-auvergne.fr] Fr S o'skts Clermont-Ferrand take D212 E to Cournon & foll sp in town; by Rv Allier, 1km E of Cournon. Lge, mkd pitch, pt shd; wc (some cont); chem disp; baby facs; shwrs inc; el pnts (5-10A) €3.30; lndtte; shop; supmkt nrby; snacks; bar; playgrnd; htd pool; slide paddling pool; rv sw/lake adj; fishing & boating; 40% statics; dogs €2.10; poss cr; Eng spkn; quiet low ssn; red low ssn; ccard acc; CKE/CCI. "Well-kept site - even low ssn; lge pitches; helpful manager; sports grnd adj; excel." ♦ 4 Apr-31 Oct. € 17.60   2012*

"That's changed – Should I let The Club know?"

If you find something on site that's different from the site entry, fill in a report and let us know. See www.caravanclub.co.uk/europereport

⊞ **CLERMONT FERRAND** *9B1* (6km SW Urban) *45.73866, 3.06168* Camp Municipal Le Chanset, Ave Jean-Baptiste Marrou, 63122 Ceyrat [tel/fax 04 73 61 30 73; camping. lechanset@wanadoo.fr; www.campingdeceyrat63.com] Exit A75 junc 2 onto D2089 dir Aubière/Beaumont. Foll sp Beaumont then in approx 7km at rndabt junc foll sp Ceyrat. Uphill into Ceyrat; curve R to traff lts; cross main rd & take L fork up hill. Site at top on R - turn poss diff so cont 50m for U-turn back to site. Lge, hdg/mkd pitch, terr, pt sl, pt shd; htd wc (some cont); chem disp; mv service pnt; baby facs; shwrs inc; el pnts (10A) €4.50 (poss rev pol); gas; lndtte; shop; rest, snacks; bar; BBQ; playgrnd; htd pool high ssn; games & TV rm; 25% statics; dogs €1.80; bus; phone; security barrier; poss cr; some Eng spkn; adv bkg; poss noisy when cr; ccard acc; red low ssn/long stay; CKE/CCI. "Gd base for Clermont Ferrand - gd bus service; friendly, helpful staff; shops & supmkt in Vill; late arr can park nr reception." ♦ € 16.70   2013*

CLERMONT FERRAND *9B1* (5km W Rural) *45.75845, 3.05453* Camping Indigo Royat, Route de Gravenoire, Quartier de l'Oclède, 63130 Royat [04 73 35 97 05; fax 04 73 35 67 69; royat@camping-indigo.com; www.camping-indigo.com] Site diff to find fr Clermont-Ferrand cent. Fr N, leave A71 at Clermont-Ferrand. Foll sp Chamalières/Royat, then sp Royat. Go under rlwy bdge & pass thermal park on L. At mini-rndabt go L & up hill. At statue, turn L & go up long hill. Look for site sp & turn R. Site on R. NB Do not go down steep rd with traff calming. NB Sat nav directs up v narr rds & steep hills. Lge, mkd/hdstg pitch, terr, pt shd; htd wc; chem disp; mv service pnt; some serviced pitches; baby facs; shwrs inc; el pnts (10A) €5.20; gas; lndtte (inc dryer); sm shop; tradsmn; rest, snacks high ssn; bar; BBQ; playgrnd; htd pool; paddling pool; tennis; cycle hire; internet; entmnt; TV rm; some statics; dogs €4; phone; Eng spkn; adv bkg; quiet; ccard acc; red low ssn; CKE/ CCI. "Excel, clean, spacious site; set on hillside in trees; views at top levels over Clermont; clean san facs; facs ltd in low ssn; conv touring base." ♦ 17 Apr-02 Nov. € 22.50 (CChq acc) SBS - L18   2013*

⊞ **CLERMONT L'HERAULT** *10F1* (5km NW Rural) *43.64491, 3.38982* Camp Municipal du Lac du Salagou, 34800 Clermont-l'Hérault [04 67 96 13 13; fax 04 67 96 32 12; contact@le-salagou.fr; www.le-salagou.fr] Fr N9 S take D909 to Clermont-l'Hérault, foll sp to Lac du Salagou 1.5km after town sp. Fr by-pass foll sp Bédarieux. Well sp. Lge, mkd pitch, pt sl, pt shd; htd wc (winter poss all cont); chem disp; mv service pnt; shwrs inc; el pnts (5-10A) €2.90-3.40; lndtte; shops 4km; tradsmn; rest, snacks; BBQ; playgrnd; shgl beach & lake 300m; fishing; watersports; entmnt; TV; many statics; dogs €1.70; phone; poss cr; adv bkg; noise fr disco some nights; red low ssn; CKE/CCI;Eng spkn; "Unique location; poss muddy low ssn & poss windy; facs dated; gd undeveloped beaches around lake; beautiful scenery" ♦ € 16.00   2013*

CLERY SUR SOMME see Péronne *3C3*

CLISSON *2H4* (S Urban) *47.09582, -1.28216* Camp Municipal du Vieux Moulin, Rue de la Fontaine Câlin, Route de Nantes, 44190 Clisson [02 40 54 44 48 or 02 40 54 02 95 (LS); camping@valleedeclisson.fr; www. mairie-clisson.com] 1km NW of Clisson cent on main rd to Nantes, at rndabt. Look for old windmill nr ent on L of rd. Leclerc hypmkt on opp side of rd; site sp fr town cent. Narr ent. Sm, hdg pitch, pt sl, pt shd; wc; chem disp; shwrs inc; el pnts inc; hypmkt, rest, snacks & bar 500m; tradsmn; fishing, tennis, horseriding adj; boating; dogs €1.12; phone (card only); Eng spkn; adv bkg; quiet but some rd noise. "Gd municipal site; lge pitches; gd clean san facs; if office clsd pitch self, book in later; picturesque town 15 min walk; mkd walks; interesting old town with castle ruins; next to retail park" ♦ 6 Jul-13 Oct. € 17.00   2013*

CLOHARS CARNOËT see Pouldu, Le *2F2*

CLOYES SUR LE LOIR *4F2* (1km N Rural) *48.00240, 1.23304* Parc de Loisirs Le Val Fleuri, Route de Montigny, 28220 Cloyes-sur-le-Loir [02 37 98 50 53; fax 02 37 98 33 84; info@parc-de-loisirs.com; www.val-fleuri.fr] Located on L bank of Rv Loir off N10; site sp. Med, hdg pitch, pt shd; wc (some cont); chem disp; shwrs inc; el pnts (5A) inc; shop; rest, snacks; bar; playgrnd; pool; waterslide; cycle hire; 50% statics; dogs €1.80; adv bkg; quiet. "Facs gd for children but ltd low ssn; well-run, pleasant site in wooded valley; site fees inc use of sm leisure park, pedalos & rowing boats on Rv Loir." 15 Mar-15 Nov. € 24.60   2009*

> ## "I like to fill in the reports as I travel from site to site"
> You'll find report forms at the back of this guide, or you can fill them in online at www.caravaclub.co.uk/europereport.

CLOYES SUR LE LOIR *4F2* (2km S Rural) *47.97326, 1.23292* FFCC Aire Naturelle Camping Les Fouquets (Fetter), 41160 St Jean-Froidmentel [02 54 82 66 97; lesfouquets@aol.com] Off N10 twd Vendôme. Sp Les Fouquets 200m SE of N10. Sm, shd; wc; shwrs inc; el pnts (15A) €3; lndry rm; shop, rest 2km; pool; fishing, tennis & sailing 2km; dogs €1; quiet; CKE/CCI. "Lovely, family-run site in woodland; friendly, welcoming owner; gd pool." ♦ 1 Apr-30 Sep. € 9.00   2011*

CLUNY *9A2* (500m E Urban) *46.43086, 4.66756* Camp Municipal St Vital, 30 Rue de Griottons, 71250 Cluny [tel/ fax 03 85 59 08 34; camping.st.vital@orange.fr; www. camping-cluny.blogspot.com] E fr Cluny on D15 (sp Azé & Camping) across narr rv bdge; in 200m turn R into Rue de Griottonste; site on L in 100m. Site adj sw pool. Lge, mkd pitch, some hdstg, sl, pt shd; htd wc (some cont); chem disp; shwrs inc; el pnts (6A) €4.50 (poss rev pol); gas; lndtte (inc dryer); sm shop open weekends & 500m; tradsmn; BBQ; playgrnd; htd pool adj inc; tennis; fishing; horseriding nrby; cycle hire; games rm; wifi; dogs; poss cr; adv bkg rec high ssn; frequent rlwy noise daytime; ccard acc; twin-axles extra. "Well-run, tidy site; helpful staff; gd clean san facs; cycle & walking rte adj (Voie Verte); interesting town; excel, reliable site; well organised and pleasant; busy site" ♦ 23 Apr-10 Oct. € 24.55   2013*

CLUNY *9A2* (10km S Rural) *46.81195, 6.30285* Camping du Lac de St Point-Lamartine, 8 Rue du Port, 71520 St Point [03 85 50 52 31; reservation@campingsaintpoint.com; www.campingsaintpoint.com] Turn S off N79, Mâcon/ Paray-le-Monial rd, turn L bef Ste Cécile on D22; site sp at junc; site 100m on R after St Point vill. Med, hdg/mkd pitch, pt terr, pt sl, pt shd; htd wc; chem disp; mv service pnt; shwrs inc; el pnts (16A) inc; gas 800m; lndtte (inc dryer); shop 800m; rest, snacks; bar; BBQ; playgrnd; TV; lake sw adj; fishing; boat hire; tennis 4km; wifi; 30% statics; dogs €1; phone; adv bkg; quiet; CKE/CCI. "Cluny attractive town & abbey; lovely scenery & pleasant lake; on edge of Beaujolais; sp walks fr site." 1 Apr-31 Oct. € 16.00 (4 persons)   2010*

CLUNY *9A2* (11km NW Rural) *46.51775, 4.59865* **FFCC Camp Municipal de la Clochette, Place de la Clochette, 71250 Salornay-sur-Guye [03 85 59 90 11; fax 03 85 59 47 52; mairie.salornay@wanadoo.fr; www.cluny-tourisme.com]** Sp fr N or S on D980; turn E on D14 sp Cormatin & Taizé. Ent in 300m. Well sp in vill & fr D980. Med, mkd pitch, pt shd; wc; shwrs €1; chem disp; mv service pnt; el pnts (8-10A) €2-3; lndry rm; shop & bar 200m; BBQ; playgrnd; rv adj; fishing; adv bkg; quiet; CKE/CCI. "Pleasant, tidy site on sm rv & mill pond; site yourself, warden comes 0930-1030 & 1900-2000; clean, dated san facs; poss long walk to chem disp & rubbish disposal (2011); rvside pitches poss subject to flooding; well sp walks around vill; vill shops poss clsd Mon." 21 May-4 Sep. € 8.00   2011*

CLUSAZ, LA *9B3* (6km N Rural) *45.93972, 6.42777* **Camping L'Escale, Route de la Patinoire, 74450 Le Grand-Bornand [04 50 02 20 69; fax 04 50 02 36 04; contact@ campinglescale.com; www.campinglescale.com]** Exit A41 junc 17 onto D16/D909 E dir La Clusaz. At St Jean-de-Sixt turn L at rndabt sp Le Grand Bornand. After 1.5km foll camping sp on main rd & at junc turn R sp for site & 'Vallée du Bouchet'. Site is 1st exit R at end of this rd. D4 S fr Cluses not rec while towing as v steep & winding. Med, mkd pitch, pt sl, terr, pt shd; htd wc; chem disp; mv service pnt; serviced pitch in summer; baby facs; shwrs inc; el pnts (10A) inc poss rev pol); gas; lndry (inc dryer); shop 250m; tradsmn; rest, snacks; bar; BBQ; playgrnd; 2 pools (1 htd, covrd); paddling pool; fishing; wintersports; cycle hire 250m; tennis; archery; wifi; games/ TV rm; 20% statics; dogs €2.30; no c'vans over 8.50m or m'vans over 8m high ssn, Feb & wk of New Year; skibus; poss cr; adv bkg ess; ccard acc; red low ssn; CKE/CCI. "Family-run site in scenic area; gd san facs; vg rest; sh walk to attractive vill; free use htd ski/boot rm in winter; boggy in wet weather; vg mkt Wed" ♦ 25 May-26 Sep & 14 Dec-15 Apr. € 29.80 SBS - M07   2013*

CLUSAZ, LA *9B3* (12km NE) *46.00449, 6.39449* **Camp Municipal Les Marronniers, 74130 Le Petit-Bornand-Les-Glieres [04 50 03 54 74; maptbo@mairie-petit-bornand. fr; www.mairie-petit-bornand.fr]** E fr Annecy on D909 for 28km to St Jean-de-Sixt. N on D4 for 1km, turn W on D12 for 11km to Le Petit Bornand. Site thro vill on L. Sm, pt sl, pt shd; wc; chem disp; shwrs €0.70; el pnts (3A) €2.50; lndtte; fishing; tennis nr; dogs €1; adv bkg; quiet; CKE/CCI. "Vg site in National Park; shop 500m walk uphill." 1 Jun-15 Sep. € 9.20   2008*

CLUSAZ, LA *9B3* (2km E Rural) *45.90921, 6.45208* **Camping Le Plan du Fernuy, 1800 Route des Confins, 74220 La Clusaz [04 50 02 44 75; fax 04 50 32 67 02; fernuy@ franceloc.fr; www.plandufernuy.com or www.campings-franceloc.fr]** Fr Annecy take D909 to La Clusaz (32km). Turn L for Les Confins & site on R in 2km. Med, mkd pitch, pt sl, unshd; wc; chem disp; shwrs inc; baby rm; el pnts (4-13A) €4-8; gas; lndtte (inc dryer); shop; snacks; bar; playgrnd; htd, covrd pool; paddling pool; wifi; TV; some statics; dogs €5; free ski bus; poss cr; quiet. "Site at 1200m alt; excel site & facs; poss diff lge o'fits." ♦ 12 Jun-5 Sep & 2 Jan-24 Apr. € 25.00   2010*

CLUSES *9A3* (1km N Urban) *46.06896, 6.57390* **Camping La Corbaz, Ave des Glières, 74300 Cluses [04 50 98 44 03; fax 04 50 96 02 15; camping.lacorbaz@wanadoo.fr; www. camping-lacorbaz.com]** Take D1205 W fr Chamonix or fr Annecy D1203 NE to Bonneville & D1205 E to Cluses; take D902 N dir Taninges; after x-ing rlwy turn L onto D19 beside rlwy; site on R in 500m. Med, pt shd; htd wc; chem disp; mv service pnt; shwrs; el pnts (4-10A) €2.50; shop; rest; bar; playgrnd; pool; lake sw 2km; TV; 70% statics; dogs €1.50; adv bkg; quiet but some rd & rlwy noise. "Excel touring base; pleasant park setting; lge pitches; helpful staff; facs dated but clean; conv A40." 1 Apr-15 Oct. € 14.50   2008*

COEX *2H4* (2.5km W Rural) *46.67679, -1.76899* **RCN Camping La Ferme du Latois, 85220 Coëx [02 51 54 67 30; fax 02 51 60 02 14; info@rcn-lafermedulatois.fr; www. rcn-campings.fr]** Exit D948 at Aizenay onto D6 dir St Gilles-Croix-de-Vie; at Coëx take D40 SW sp Brétignolles; site in 1.5km on L. Lgd, pt shd; htd wc; chem disp; shwrs inc; el pnts inc (poss rev pol); lndry rm; shop; tradsmn; rest, snacks; bar; BBQ (gas); playgrnd; pool; lake fishing; cycle hire; games area; games rm; wifi; 20% statics; dogs €5; phone; Eng spkn; adv bkg; quiet; red low ssn. "Spacious pitches; cycle rtes adj; conv Lac du Jaunay & Lac du Gué-Gorand; excel." ♦ 11 Apr-10 Oct. € 43.50   2008*

See advertisement

COGNAC *7B2* (200m N Urban) **Aire Communautaire, Place de la Levade, Quartier St Jaques, 16700 Cognac [05 45 36 64 30; contact@cc-cognac.fr]** M'vans only. N fr Cognac, cross rv bdge & foll m'van sp on L. Opp Hennessy Cognac House. Chem disp, mv service pnt, el pnts; lndtte; shop; rest. "Free NH adj rv." 1 Jun-15 Sep.   2010*

COGNAC 7B2 (2.5km NE Rural) 45.70920, -0.31284
**Camping de Cognac, Blvd de Châtenay, 16100 Cognac
[05 45 32 13 32 or 05 45 36 64 30 (LS); fax 05 45 32 15 82;
info@campingdecognac.com; www.campingdecognac.com]**
Fr N141 foll 'Camping' sp to town cent. Turn R at 'Speedy'
g'ge, site immed on R in 2km after x-ing rv. - foll sp 'Base de
Plein Air'. Take care ent barrier. Med, hdg/mkd pitch, some
hdstg, pt shd; wc (some cont); chem disp; mv service pnt;
shwrs inc; el pnts (6A) inc (poss long leads req & poss rev pol);
lndtte; shop high ssn & 2km; tradsmn; rest, snacks high ssn;
bar; BBQ; playgrnd; pool; rv boating & fishing; games area;
entmnt; 5% statics; dogs €1.50; bus; phone; poss cr; Eng spkn;
adv bkg; rd noise; ccard acc; red long stay/low ssn; CKE/CCI.
"Excel lge park with many facs; helpful staff; clean modern san
facs; gates clsd 2200-0700 (1800 low ssn); night watchman
high ssn; no twin axles; footpath to town; conv Cognac
distilleries (vouchers fr site recep); cycle rte to town cent." ♦
25 Apr-30 Sep. € 20.00   2011*

COGNAC 7B2 (10km E Rural) 45.67160, -0.22218 **Camping
du Port, 16200 Bourg-Charente [06 03 98 60 19 (mob)]**
Exit N141 onto D158 dir Bourg-Charente; turn L in 800m &
site on R. Site sp fr D158. Chicane-type ent gates. Sm, pt sl, pt
shd; wc (some cont); chem disp; mv service pnt; shwrs; el pnts
(6A) €2.50; rest & shop 500m; fishing; tennis; dogs; ccard acc;
red long stay; "Delightful site on banks of Rv Charente; friendly
staff; facs basic but clean, poss stretched high ssn; site on 2
levels, lower one sl; gd walks & cycle path to Jarnac & Cognac;
gd." 1 May-15 Sep. € 17.80   2013*

COGNAC 7B2 (14km E Urban) 45.67606, -0.17349 **FFCC
Camping de l'Ile Madame, 16200 Jarnac [05 45 81 18 54
or 05 45 81 68 02; fax 05 45 81 24 98; camping.jarnac@
wanadoo.fr; www.camping-jarnac.com]** Turn E at S end of
rv bdge at S end of town. Fr Angoulême on N141, exit junc sp
'Jarnac Est'; foll sp Jarnac thro 1 rndabt into Jarnac; at traff lts
(LH lane) turn L sp Tourist Info/Camping; cross rv brge & immed
turn L to site. Lge, pt shd; wc; shwrs inc; el pnts (6-10A) €2.80
(rev pol); lndtte; shops & rest adj; playgrnd; pool inc; games
area; golf, canoe & cycle hire nrby; entmnt; TV; dogs €0.50;
poss cr; adv bkg; poss noise fr adj sports ground & disco; red
long stay; CKE/CCI. "Pleasant, well-run site; gd sized pitches;
san facs clean but update needed; no twin-axles; easy walk into
Jarnac with shops & rests; gd walks along rv; nr Courvoisier
bottling plant." 1 Apr-30 Sep. € 13.60   2010*

⊞ **COGNAC** 7B2 (8km S Rural) 45.60148, -0.36067
**Camping Le Chiron (Chainier), 16130 Salles-d'Angles
[05 45 83 72 79; fax 05 45 83 64 80; mchainier@voila.fr]**
Fr Cognac D731 Barbezieux to Salles-d'Angles, R at bottom hill
onto D48; then in 3km turn L onto D151; site on L in 500m
(foll Chambres d'Hôtes sps). Sm, pt sl, pt shd; htd wc (1 cont);
chem disp; shwrs inc; el pnts (10A) inc (rev pol); shop 3km; no
dogs; Eng spkn; quiet; ccard not acc. "Vg; meals avail at farm."
€ 12.00   2012*

COGNAC LA FORET 7B3 (1.5km W Rural) 45.82494, 0.99674
**Camping des Alouettes, Les Alouettes, 87310 Cognac-la-
Forêt [05 55 03 26 93; info@camping-des-alouttes.com;
www.camping-des-alouettes.com]** Fr Aixe-sur-Vienne on
D10, site W of Cognac-la-Forêt on D10, sp to L. Med, hdg
pitch;pt sl; pt shd; wc; chem disp; shwrs inc; el pnts (10A) €3;
lndtte; shop 1km; tradsmn; rest, snacks; bar; BBQ; playgrnd;
pool & paddling pool; lake sw & sand beach 1km; tennis 700m;
wifi; 10% statics; dogs €1; Eng spkn; adv bkg; quiet; red low
ssn; CKE/CCI. "Beautiful location; friendly owners; conv war
vill Oradour-sur-Glane & Richard Lion Heart sites; vg site & facs;
excel site" ♦ 1 Apr-30 Sep. € 22.80   2013*

COGNIN LES GORGES 9C3 (E Rural) 45.17183, 5.41503 **Aire
Naturelle La Chatonnière (Boucher), Route de Malleval,
38470 Cognin-les-Gorges [04 76 38 18 76; info@la-chato.
com; www.la-chato.com]** Exit A49 junc 10 S onto N532,
turn 1st L after Cognin-les-Gorges sp at service stn. Fr vill cent,
take 1st R past church. In 50m turn L at stop sp, site 100m on
L. Sm, pt shd; wc; chem disp; mv service pnt; baby facs; shwrs
inc; el pnts (10A) €3 (rev pol); shop 500m; tradsmn; pool 6km;
no statics; dogs; bus; phone 100m; Eng spkn; adv bkg; quiet;
red long stay; CKE/CCI. "Welcoming, helpful owners; bread
baked on site; meals avail; picturesque mountain setting; conv
Grenoble & Vercours." Jun-Sep. € 15.00   2008*

COLLE SUR LOUP, LA see Cagnes sur Mer 10E4

COLLET DE DEZE, LE 9D1 (7km W Rural) 44.23016, 3.86326
**Domaine Naturiste La Combe Ferrière (Naturist), 48160
St Michel-de-Dèze [04 66 45 52 43; info@la-combe.com;
www.la-combe.com]** Fr Alès N on N106 twd Florac. Just after
Le Collet-de-Dèze take D13 L for 10km to Col de Pendédis,
then keep R & in 20m turn R bet 2 houses. Site on L in 2km.
Do not app fr St Michel-de-Dèze as rd unsuitable. Sm, pt sl, pt
shd; wc; baby facs; sauna; shwrs inc; el pnts (6A) €3.05; lndtte;
tradsmn; rest; bar; BBQ; playgrnd; pool; games area; cycle
hire; no statics; dogs free; poss cr; Eng spkn; adv bkg; quiet;
INF card. "Ltd pitches for m'vans - rec phone ahead; site rds
narr & winding but passable with care; friendly Dutch owners;
recep on opp side of public rd to site (must dress to cross); gd."
15 May-15 Sep. € 18.25   2010*

COLLIAS see Remoulins 10E2

COLLIOURE see Argeles sur Mer 10G1

COLMAR 6F3 (2km E Urban) 48.07942, 7.38665 **Camping
de l'Ill, 1 Allée du Camping, 68180 Horbourg-Wihr [tel/
fax 03 89 41 15 94; camping@agglo-colmar.fr; www.
campingdelill.com]** Exit A35 junc 25 onto D415, foll
Freibourg sp. At 2nd rndabt turn L to Colmar cent, site on
rvside on L bef bdge. Lge, hdg/mkd pitch, hdstg, pt sl, terr,
shd; htd wc; chem disp; mv service pnt; shwrs; el pnts (10A)
€4.80 (poss rev pol); lndtte (inc dryer); shop & tradsmn (high
ssn); supmkt nr; rest, snacks; bar; playgrnd; cycle hire; wifi;
entmnt; TV; 10% statics; dogs €4.; bus/train to city cent; poss
cr; some Eng spkn; adv bkg; much noise fr a'route; ccard acc
(over €20); CKE/CCI. "Lovely, clean, rvside site; excel san facs;
gd rest; some pitches req steel pegs; gd for town; sep area for
NH." ♦ ltd 21 Mar-31 Dec. € 22.50   2013*

COLMAR 6F3 (7km S Rural) 48.01613, 7.34983 **Camping Clair Vacances, Route de Herrlisheim, 68127 Ste Croix-en-Plaine [03 89 49 27 28; fax 03 89 49 31 37; clairvacances@ wanadoo.fr; www.clairvacances.com]** Exit D83 at sp Herrlisheim onto D1 bis. Take 2nd rd to vill sp camping, foll site sp thro vill. NB Rd thru vill narr with traff calming bollards. Fr A35 turn off at junc 27 sp Herrlisheim/Ste Croix-en-Plaine onto D1 dir Herrlisheim to site in 1km. Med, hdg/mkd pitch, some hdstg, pt shd; htd wc; chem disp; mv service pnt; baby facs; shwrs inc; el pnts (16A) €4 (long lead poss req); gas; service wash; shop 2km; tradsmn; snacks high ssn; BBQ (gas); playgrnd; htd pool; paddling pool; tennis 3km; cycle hire; child entmnt; no dogs; phone; poss cr; Eng spkn; adv bkg; quiet; ccard acc; red low ssn; CKE/CCI. "Beautiful site; well-kept & supervised; can be busy, adv bkg rec; helpful, friendly owners; gd size pitches; excel, clean san facs; gd touring base Alsace wine rte; excel." ♦ 15 Apr-17 Oct. € 29.00   2012*

COLMAR 6F3 (7km SW Rural) 48.04238, 7.29935 **Camping des Trois Châteaux, 10 Rue du Bassin, 68420 Eguisheim [03 89 23 19 39; fax 03 89 24 10 19; camping.eguisheim@ orange.fr; www.camping-eguisheim.fr]** Foll D83 S (Colmar by-pass) R at sp Eguisheim. R into vill to site at top of vill, foll camp sp. Med, mkd pitch, pt sl, terr, pt shd; wc; chem disp; mv service pnt; shwrs inc; el pnts (8-10A) €3-5 (poss rev pol); gas; lndtte; shops, rest & bars in vill 300m; hypmkt 5km; playgrnd; dogs €3; phone adj; poss cr; adv bkg (tel 2 days bef arr); poss noisy; ccard acc; red low ssn; CKE/CCI. "Populer, well-run, busy site; no c'vans over 7m (inc draw bar); mv pitches flat but some c'van pitches sl & poss diff; gd touring base; weekly wine-tasting events; stork park adj; rec arr early; excel; Cycle route to centre of Colmar" ♦ ltd 23 Mar-27 Oct, 29 Nov-22 Dec. € 21.00   2013*

COLMAR 6F3 (7km W Urban) 48.08517, 7.27253 **FFCC Camp Municipal Les Cigognes, Quai de la Gare, 68230 Turckheim [03 89 27 02 00; fax 03 89 80 86 93; municipc@ calixo.net; www.camping-turckheim.com]** On ent vill, turn Turckheim turn W onto D11 to Turckheim. On ent vill, turn immed L down 1-way rd after x-ing rlwy lines. Do not cross rv bdge. Site on L bef bdge, adj stadium. Med, hdg pitch, pt shd; wc; chem disp; mv service pnt; baby facs; shwrs inc; el pnts (5-10A) €3.60-5.70; lndtte (inc dryer); shop 500m; hypmkt nrby; BBQ; playgrnd; wifi; entmnt; TV; 50% statics; dogs €1.60; bus adj; train 250m; poss cr; quiet; ccard acc; red low ssn; CKE/CCI. "Lovely site with spacious pitches; dated san facs, ltd low ssn; cycle rtes nr; resident storks; short walk to interesting, beautiful old vill with rests; gd touring base; Site being refurbished (2012)" ♦ ltd 15 Mar-31 Oct. € 11.90   2012*

COLMARS 9D4 (400m S Rural) 44.17733, 6.62151 **Aire Naturelle Les Pommiers, Chemin des Mélèzes, 04370 Colmars-les-Alpes [04 92 83 41 56; fax 04 92 83 40 86; contact@camping-pommier.com; www.camping-pommier.com]** Fr N on D908 on ent Colmars take 1st R over rd bdge & foll site sp. Sm, pt terr, pt shd; wc (some cont); chem disp; mv service pnt; shwrs inc; el pnts (10A) €2; lndtte; shop 400m; tradsmn; rest, snacks, bar 400m; BBQ; htd pool 800m; dogs €1; phone; adv bkg; CKE/CCI. "Beautifully-situated, well-maintained CL-type site nr medieval town; friendly owner; gd walking." ♦ ltd 1 May-1 Oct. € 12.00   2008*

COLMARS 9D4 (1km S Rural) 44.17472, 6.61629 **Camping Le Bois Joly, Chemin des Buissières, 04370 Colmars-les-Alpes [04 92 83 40 40; fax 04 92 83 50 60; camping-le-bois-joly@ sfr.fr; www.colmars-les-alpes.fr]** Fr S on D955 & D908 twds Colmars, go thro Beauvezer & Villars-Colmars. Ignore two other sites en rte. Site sp. Sm, mkd, hdstg, shd; wc (some cont); chem disp (wc); mv service pnt; shwrs inc; el pnts (6A) €2.43; gas; lndtte; rest, snacks, bar & shop 1km; BBQ; tradsmn high ssn; rv fishing adj; no dogs; phone; adv bkg; quiet; CKE/CCI. "Well-kept, wooded site with gd atmosphere; gd facs; ideal base for walking in Haute Provence; friendly owners." 1 May-1 Oct. € 11.10   2008*

COMBOURG 2E4 (8km NE Rural) 48.45304, -1.65031 **Camping Le Bois Coudrais (Ybert), 35270 Cuguen [02 99 73 27 45; fax 02 99 73 13 08; info@ vacancebretagne.com; www.vacancebretagne.com]** Fr Combourg take D796 twd Pleine-Fougères, 5km out of Combourg turn L on D83 to Cuguen; 500m past Cuguen, turn L, site sp. Or fr Dol-de-Bretagne, take D795 then turn L onto D9 to Cuguen. Sm, hdg/mkd pitch, pt shd; wc; chem disp; shwrs inc; el pnts (10A) €3; shop 500m; snacks; bar; BBQ; playgrnd; pool; fishing, watersports, golf, zoo, adventure park nr; cycle hire; wifi; dogs €1; Eng spkn; adv bkg; v quiet; red long stay; no ccard acc; red CKE/CCI. "CL-type site, friendly British owners; gd clean facs, great for young children, sm animal-petting area, gd touring base" ♦ 27 Apr-30 Sep. € 18.50   2013*

"We must tell The Club about that great site we found"

Get your site reports in by mid-August and we'll do our best to get your updates into the next edition of Caravan Europe.

COMBOURG 2E4 (1.5km SE Rural) 48.40449, -1.74271 **Camp Municipal Le Vieux Châtel, Route de Lanrigan, Ave de Waldmünchen, 35270 Combourg [02 99 73 13 93; campingcombourg@gmail.com; www.camping-combourg.com]** Fr W, N & E foll sp for D795 dir Rennes, Hede. Take 1st L after lake twd Lanrigan. Fr S on D795, turn R at lake. Site on L in approx 500m. Med, hdg/mkd pitch, pt shd; wc; chem disp; shwrs inc; el pnts (5A) €2.35; lndtte; shop, rest, snacks, bar 500m; BBQ; playgrnd; htd, covrd pool 1km; lake fishing nrby; tennis; games area; games rm; entmnt; dogs €1.50; phone; Eng spkn; adv bkg; quiet; ccard acc; CKE/CCI. "Forests, chateaux & churches nrby; 20 mins to Emerald Coast; castle in Combourg." ♦ 28 May-18 Sep. € 10.87   2010*

FRANCE

35190 LA CHAPELLE AUX FILTZMEENS (Ille et Vilaine)
Tél.: 02 99 45 25 45
E-mail: domainedulogis@wanadoo.fr
www.domainedulogis.com

COMBOURG *2E4* (6km SW Rural) *48.38090, -1.83290*
FFCC Camping Domaine du Logis, 35190 La Chapelle-aux-Filtzméens,Ille-et-Vilaine [02 99 45 25 45 or 06 85 78 69 71 (mob); fax 02 99 45 30 40; domainedulogis@wanadoo.fr; www.domainedulogis.com] Fr N176 at junc for Dol-de-Bretagne branch R onto D155 sp Dol & take D795 S to Combourg. Then take D13 twd St Domineuc, go thro La Chapelle-aux-Filtzméens & site on R in 1km. Lge, hdg/mkd pitch, pt shd; wc; chem disp; mv service pnt; shwrs inc; el pnts (10A) inc; gas; lndtte (inc dryer); shop 5km; tradsmn; rest, snacks; bar; BBQ; playgrnd; htd pool; paddling pool; sand beach 20km; fitness rm; canoes 800m; fishing nr; cycle hire; gym; games area; games rm; wifi; entmnt; TV rm; 10% statics; dogs €2; no c'vans/m'vans over 12m; phone; Eng spkn; adv bkg; quiet; ccard acc; red low ssn/long stay/CKE/CCI. "set in chateau grnds; lge grassy pitches; helpful staff; gd san facs; gd touring base, conv St Malo, Mont St Michel, Dinan & Channel Islands; mkt Mon; excel" ♦ 1 Apr-5 Nov. € 15.00 (CChq acc) SBS - B02   2013*

See advertisement

"I need an on-site restaurant"

We do our best to make sure site information is correct, but it is always best to check any must-have facilities are still available or will be open during your visit.

COMBRIT STE MARINE see Bénodet *2F2*

COMPEYRE see Millau *10E1*

COMPREIGNAC *7B3* (2.5km N Rural) *46.01402, 1.27814*
Camp Municipal de Montimbert, 87140 Compreignac [05 55 71 04 49 or 05 55 71 00 23 (Mairie)] S on A20 to Limoges, turn W at exit 26 Le Crouzill. Foll D5 W to Compreignac, turn N by church onto D60, fork L, foll sp 'Montimbert' for site. Sm, pt sl, pt shd; wc; chem disp; shwrs inc; el pnts (5A) (poss rev pol); shop in vill; playgrnd; lake sw; fishing & boating 1km; CKE/CCI. "Facs ltd; unrel opening dates." 1 Jun-15 Sep.   2008*

COMPREIGNAC *7B3* (6km N Rural) *46.03282, 1.29559* **Camping Santrop, Lac de St-Pardoux, 87640 Razès [05 55 71 08 08 or 05 55 71 04 40 (LS); fax 05 55 71 23 93; lacsaintpardoux@wanadoo.fr; www.lac-saint-pardoux.com]** N fr Limoges on A20, exit junc 25 Razès, sp Lac de St Pardoux; foll sp 4km to site. Lge, hdg pitch, pt sl, shd; wc; baby facs; shwrs inc; el pnts (16A) €3.80; lndtte (inc dryer); shop; rest; bar; playgrnd; pool; waterslide; lake adj; watersports; games area; entmnt; TV rm; dogs €1.10; poss cr; Eng spkn; poss noisy. "Popular, busy site on lake beach; random pitching under trees in woodland; gd rest on lakeside; poss late night noise fr revellers on beach; pitches unkempt & site tired end ssn (2009)." 1 May-20 Sep. € 16.40   2009*

COMPS SUR ARTUBY *10E3* (1km NW Rural) *43.71543, 6.49862* **Camp Municipal du Pontet, 83840 Comps-sur-Artuby [04 94 76 91 40; mairie-comps-sur-artuby@wanadoo.fr]** Fr Comps-sur-Artuby take D71 sp Grand Canyon du Verdon. Site sp on R in 1km. Med, mkd pitch, terr, pt shd; wc; chem disp (wc); shwrs inc; el pnts (6A) €3; shop; rest; bar; dogs; phone; quiet; CKE/CCI. "Vg, well-laid out, wooded site; conv Gorges du Verdon; easy access." 16 May-31 Oct. € 7.50   2010*

CONCARNEAU *2F2* (2km S Coastal) *47.85628, -3.89999* **Camping Le Cabellou Plage, Ave de Cabellou, Kersaux, 29185 Concarneau [02 98 97 37 41; fax 02 98 60 78 57; info@le-cabellou-plage.com; www.le-cabellou-plage.com]** Fr N165 turn onto D70 dir Concarneau. At 5th rndabt (Leclerc supmkt) foll dir Tregunc. After Moros bdge take 2nd exit a next rndabt dir Le Cabellou-Plage. Site sp on L. Lge, mkd/hdg pitch, hdstg, pt shd; wc (cont); chem disp; baby facs; shwrs; el pnts (10A) inc; lndtte; tradsmn; snacks; bar; playgrnd; htd pool; paddling pool; sand beach adj; watersports; cycle hire; games area; games rm; wifi; TV; 16% statics; dogs €2; bus at site ent; Eng spkn; adv bkg; quiet; ccard acc; red low ssn. "Pleasant seaside site; vg san facs; gd walking fr site." ♦ 25 May-18 Sep. € 27.00   2009*

See advertisement on pages 32 & 33

CONCARNEAU *2F2* (3km W Coastal) *47.88910, -3.94070*
Camping Les Prés Verts, Kernous-Plage, 29186 Concarneau
[02 98 97 09 74; info@presverts.com; www.presverts.com]
Exit N165 onto D70 dir Concarneau. At rndabt by Leclerc
supmkt foll sp 'Centre Ville' (Town Centre) with Leclerc on
L. At x-rds with traff lts go strt over, then fork R into Rue de
Kerneach & down slope. Bear L at 1st rndabt & R at next.
Keep R to join coast rd & foll sp La Forêt-Fouesnant; pass Hôtel
Océans; site 3rd rd on L in 1.5km. Med, hdg/mkd pitch, pt sl,
pt shd; wc; chem disp; mv service pnt; serviced pitch; shwrs
inc; el pnts (6A-10A) inc (poss rev pol & long lead req); gas
2km; lndtte; rest 3km; BBQ (charcoal/gas); playgrnd; htd pool;
paddling pool; dir access to sand beach 300m; sailing 1km;
horseriding 1km; games rm; wifi; TV; 10% statics; dogs €2; no
c'vans/m'vans over 8m; poss cr; adv bkg; quiet; ccard acc; red
low ssn. "Peaceful, scenic, busy site; path to sandy cove below;
gd sized pitches; lge pitches extra; family-run, friendly staff;
basic san facs, ltd low ssn; poss unkempt low ssn; gd touring
base; walk along coastal path to Concarneau; mkt Mon & Fri."
1 Jun-31 Aug. € 19.50 SBS - B24   2011*

CONCARNEAU *2F2* (1.5km NW Urban/Coastal) *47.8807,
-3.9311* **Camping Les Sables Blancs, Ave du Dorlett, 29900
Concarneau** [tel/fax 02 98 97 16 44; contact@camping-
lessablesblancs.com; www.camping-lessablesblancs.com]
Exit N165 to Concarneau dir 'Centre Ville'. Then foll sp 'La
Côte' 300m after traff lts. Site on R, sp. Med, hdg/mkd pitch,
hdstg, pt sl, terr, pt shd; htd wc; chem disp; mv service pnt;
baby facs; fam bthrm; shwrs inc; el pnts (10A) €4; lndtte; shop
1.5km; tradsmn; rest, snacks; bar; BBQ; playgrnd; htd pool;
paddling pool; sand beach 300m; games area; games rm; wifi;
entmnt; TV rm; 3% statics; dogs €2; phone; bus 300m; poss cr;
Eng spkn; adv bkg; quiet; ccard acc; red low ssn/long stay; CKE/
CCI. "Nice, clean, family site in woodland; many sm pitches;
friendly staff; excel san facs; superb pool; gd rest; pleasant walk
to town; mkt Fri; vg." ♦ 3 Apr-31 Oct. € 23.00   2011*

CONCHES EN OUCHE *3D2* (8km NE Urban) *49.00228, 1.03462*
**Camping Les Sapins, 2 La Mare Hue, 27190 La Bonneville-
sur-Iton** [02 32 37 11 03 or 06 29 98 15 17 (mob); arlette.
mercier@wanadoo.fr; www.labonnevillesuriton.fr]
Fr Evreux W on D830 dir Conches-en-Ouche; site on R in 6km;
sp. Sm, pt shd; wc; no chem disp; shwrs; el pnts (6A) €4.50;
lndtte; shop; snacks; playgrnd; fishing; poss cr; quiet. "NH only;
rv 900m, lake 1km." 14 Feb-14 Nov. € 14.00   2009*

CONDE SUR NOIREAU *3D1* (10km E Rural) *48.87142,
-0.41104* **Camp Municipal, Rue du Stade René Vallée,
14690 Pont-d'Ouilly** [02 31 69 80 20 or 02 31 69 46 12]
Fr Cherbourg take N13 to Vire, D512 for Condé-sur-Noireau
& D562/D1 twd Falaise to site in 11km on W side of vill. On
ent Pont-d'Ouilly turn R, site bef bdge over rv. Well sp in vill.
Med, hdg/mkd pitch, pt sl, pt shd; wc (some cont); own san
rec; chem disp; shwrs inc; el pnts (7A) €2.50; shops, rest,
snacks, bar in vill; BBQ; playgrnd; tennis; canoeing & leisure
cent adj; phone; poss cr; adv bkg; quiet; CKE/CCI. "Gd
walking; conv WW2 battle areas; facs poss stretched high ssn."
Easter-15 Sep. € 8.00   2008*

CONDE SUR NOIREAU *3D1* (500m W Urban) *48.85146,
-0.55703* **Camp Municipal du Stade, Rue de Vire, 14110
Condé-sur-Noireau** [02 31 69 02 93; fax 02 31 59 15 51;
www.conde-sur-noireau.com] On D562 (Flers to Caen rd). In
town, turn W on D512 twd Vire. After Zone Industrielle, sports
complex on L, no L turn. Go 1 block further & foll lge white sp
'Espace Aquatique' to site. Site 500m on R in grounds of sports
cent. Sm, pt shd; wc; chem disp; shwrs inc; el pnts (6-10A)
inc; lndry rm; shops, rest, snacks, bar 300m; playgrnd; htd
pool adj; tennis; dogs; quiet; CKE/CCI. "Well-kept clean site
in grounds of leisure cent; gd size pitches; gd clean san facs;
staff friendly & helpful; pleasant town; gd NH." 2 May-30 Sep.
€ 8.30   2013*

CONDETTE see Hardelot Plage *3A2*

CONDOM *8E2* (4km NE Rural) *43.97491, 0.42038*
Camping à la Ferme (Rogalle), Guinland, 32100 Condom
[05 62 28 17 85; rogalle.guinland@wanadoo.fr; http://
campingdeguinland.monsite-orange.fr/] NE fr Condom
on D931, turn R onto D41. Pass water tower on R, site ent on
L at bottom of hill just bef sm lake on R. Sm, shd; wc; chem
disp; shwrs inc; el pnts (6-10A) €2.50; shop, rest etc 4km; BBQ;
playgrnd; tennis & canoe hire nrby; 10% statics; dogs; quiet.
"Vg CL-type site in pine grove; gd views; friendly owner; clean
facs." 1 Apr-30 Oct. € 12.00   2011*

⊞ **CONDOM** *8E2* (5km SE Rural) **Camping à la Ferme
(Vignaux), Bordeneuve, 32100 Béraut** [05 62 28 08 41]
E fr Condom on D7 to Caussens; far end of vill turn R on D204,
sp St Orens; in 1.2km turn R sp Béraut, bear R at fork, site on
L in 400m. Also sp fr D654. Sm, pt sl, pt shd; wc; chem disp;
shwrs inc; el pnts (12A) €2.50 (long lead poss req); lndtte;
shops 2.5km; adv bkg; quiet. "Peaceful & secluded CL-type
site; friendly owners; basic san facs; waymkd trails nr; phone
ahead to check open low ssn - poss not open until Apr."
€ 12.00   2012*

CONDOM *8E2* (1.5km SW Rural) *43.94813, 0.36435* **Camp
Municipal de l'Argenté, Chemin de l'Argenté, Gauge,
32100 Condom** [tel/fax 05 62 28 17 32; camping.
municipal@condom.org; http://www.condom.org/index.
php/camping-municipal] Fr Condom, take D931 twd Eauze;
site ent on L opp municipal sports grnd. Med, mkd pitch, pt
shd, wc; chem disp; baby facs; shwrs inc; el pnts (6A) €3.60;
shop 500m; tradsmn; rest & bar adj; playgrnd; pool 200m;
fishing; tennis adj; dogs €1.30; phone; red low ssn. "Pleasant,
spacious, well-kept site adj rv; lge pitches; well shaded; friendly
staff; excel san facs but ltd low ssn; levelling blocks useful; no
twin-axles; lots for older children to do; interesting, unspoilt
town nr pilgrim rte; rec visit Armagnac distilleries; excel."
1 Apr-30 Sep. € 20.10   2013*

CONDOM *8E2* (2km SW Rural) *43.93638, 0.35711* **Camping
La Ferme de Laillon (Danto), Route d'Eauze, 32100
Condom** [tel/fax 05 62 28 19 71 or 06 07 69 14 19 (mob);
dominique.danto1@free.fr; http://calaf32.free.fr/laillon]
Site sp fr D931 dir Vopillon. Bumpy lane to site. Sm, pt sl, shd;
wc; chem disp; shwrs inc; el pnts inc; lndtte; farm produce;
playgrnd; some statics; dogs; Eng spkn; quiet. "Delightful,
wooded site; helpful owner; pleasant area." 21 Mar-19 Dec.
€ 9.20   2010*

FRANCE

CONDRIEU *9B2* (4km N Rural) *45.50949, 4.77330* **Camping Domaine du Grand Bois (Naturist), Tupin et Semons, 69420 Condrieu [04 74 87 89 00 or 04 74 87 04 29; fax 04 74 87 88 48; domainedugrandbois@free.fr; www. domainedugrandbois.fr]** Fr Vienne take D502 dir Rive-de-Gier; site well sp after x-ing Rv Rhône. NB Do not app fr Condrieu - v steep with hairpins. Lge, sl, pt shd; wc (most cont); chem disp (wc); shwrs inc; el pnts (6A) €4.50; shop 6km; snacks; bar; playgrnd; pool; TV; 75% statics; phone; poss cr; adv bkg; quiet; INF card. "Spectacular views, v basic san facs." ♦ ltd 15 Apr-15 Oct. € 17.56   2013*

CONDRIEU *9B2* (750m E Rural) *45.46021, 4.77701* **Camping Belle Rive, Chemin de la Plaine, 69420 Condrieu [tel/fax 04 74 59 51 08]** Heading S on D386 fr Vienne after ent vill turn L immed bef Elf g'ge on R. Site in 600m. NB Headroom under rlwy 2.60m. Alt rte avoiding bdge after vill. Lge, mkd pitch, unshd; wc; shwrs; el pnts (3-6A) €2-4; gas; lndtte; shop; rest adj; snacks; bar; BBQ; playgrnd; pool; paddling pool; waterslide; lake fishing 2km; tennis; cycle hire; games area; 60% statics; dogs €1.20; poss cr; some rlwy noise. "C'vans over 6.50m poss need manhandling." 1 Apr-30 Sep. € 14.40   2008*

CONDRIEU *9B2* (2km SE Rural) *45.42413, 4.78251* **Camping Le Daxia, Route du Péage, 38370 St Clair-du-Rhône [04 74 56 39 20; fax 04 74 56 45 57; info@campingledaxia. com; www.campingledaxia.com]** S fr Vienne on D386; turn L in Condieu sp D28 Les Roches-de-Condrieu & Le Péage-de-Roussillon; foll sp A7 Valance & 'Camping' onto D4. Site on L well sp fron Condrieu. Med, hdg/mkd pitch, pt shd; wc; chem disp; mv service pnt; baby facs; shwrs inc; el pnts (5-6A) €2.40-2.85; lndtte; shop 1km; sm rest, snacks; bar; BBQ; playgrnd; pool; paddling pool; games rm, wifi; dogs €1.85; adv bkg; quiet; CKE/CCI; "Vg site; on edge of sm rv with beach." ♦ ltd 1 Apr-30 Sep. € 18.95   2013*

CONFOLENS *7A3* (500m N Rural) *46.01905, 0.67531* **Camp Municipal des Ribières, Ave de St Germain, 16500 Confolens [05 45 85 35 27 or 05 45 84 01 97 (Mairie); fax 05 45 85 34 10; contact@mairieconfolens.com; www. mairieconfolens.com]** Fr N foll D951 dir Confolens turn L sp St Germain-de-Confolens, site on R in 7km at edge of town bet rd & rv. NB Diff app fr S thro vill. Med, mkd pitch, pt shd; wc (most cont); shwrs inc; gas; el pnts (16A) €2; lndry rm; shop 700m; tradsmn; BBQ; pool 200m; rv sw adj; fishing & boating; no statics; dogs; phone; m'van o'night area outside site; adv bkg (post only 2010); some rd noise; ccard & CKE/CCI not acc. "Interesting, pretty town; facs neglected & ltd low ssn; warden calls am & pm." ♦ 15 May-15 Sep. € 7.00   2009*

CONFOLENS *7A3* (7km S Rural) *45.96605, 0.70888* **Camp Municipal Moulin de la Cour, 16500 St Maurice-des-Lions [05 45 85 55 99; fax 05 45 85 52 89]** Fr Confolens take D948 S. In 6.5km turn L thro vill, site 700m, well sp. Sm, hdg/mkd pitch, terr, pt shd; wc (some cont); chem disp (wc); shwrs inc; el pnts (6A) €2; shop, rest, bar 500m; BBQ; adv bkg; quiet. "Pleasant site in quiet location; pitch yourself, warden calls pm; old, inadequate facs; height limitations when site clsd (see sp at ent to sports cent & site); ent thro stone pillars; site used by Boules Club & football; nr pretty vill with 12thC church & old houses; Confolens folk festival mid-Aug." 1 Jun-30 Sep. € 6.00   2009*

CONNERRE *4F1* (8km SE Urban) *48.03945, 0.59302* **Camp Municipal La Piscine, 36 Rue du Parc, 72390 Dollon [02 43 93 42 23; fax 02 43 71 53 88; mairie.dollon@ wanadoo.fr; www.tourisme-en-sarthe.com]** Fr Connerré take D302 sp Vibraye & Thorigné-sur-Dué. In Dollon foll 'La Piscine' sp to sports complex at E end of vill. Sm, hdstg, pt shd; wc; chem disp; shwrs; el pnts (10A) inc; gas; shops 300m; playgrnd; pool; tennis; fishing; adv bkg rec; quiet. "Popular site; part of sports complex; rec arr early high ssn." 15 May-15 Sep. € 10.00   2011*

CONQUES *7D4* (8km E Rural) *44.55948, 2.46184* **Camping L'Etang du Camp, 12320 Sénergues [05 65 46 01 95; info@ etangducamp.fr; www.etangducamp.fr]** Fr S on D901 dir Conques; at St Cyprien turn R onto D46 sp Sénergues; foll sp Sénergues up hill for 6km; 2nd L at the top; foll Camping sp. Med, hdg/mkd pitch, pt shd; wc; chem disp; mv service pnt; baby facs; fam bthrm; shwrs inc; el pnts (6A) €3.50; lndtte; ice; sm shop; supmkt 3km; rest, bar 6km; tradsmn; BBQ (charcoal); playgrnd; htd pool 6km; fishing in private lake; cycle hire; canoeing nrby; cycle hire; games area; games rm; wifi; dogs €1.50; some statics; Eng spkn; adv bkg; quiet; red low ssn; 10% red CKE/CCI . "Well-situated, well-kept site; quiet & relaxing; warm welcome, British owners; modern, clean san facs; gd base for touring, walking & cycling; conv Conques; highly rec; excel." ♦ 1 Apr-30 Sep. € 25.50   2013*

CONQUES *7D4* (1km W Rural) *44.60041, 2.39461* **Camping Beau Rivage, 12320 Conques [05 65 69 82 23 or 05 65 72 89 29 (LS); fax 05 67 72 89 29; camping. conques@wanadoo.fr; www.campingconques.com]** Site on D901 Rodez-Aurillac rd on Rv Dourdou. Med, mkd pitch, pt sl, pt shd; wc (some cont); mv service pnt; shwrs inc; el pnts (6-10A) €3.50; gas; lndry rm; shop; tradsmn; rest, snacks; bar; playgrnd; pool; fishing; rv adj; some statics; dogs €1.50; adv bkg; quiet; red low ssn; CKE/CCI. "Gd position by rv bank; sm pitches; some modern san facs, others dated; tight for lge o'fits due trees & narr pathways; poss run down low ssn; gd." ♦ 1 Apr-30 Sep. € 17.50   2010*

CONQUES *7D4* (5km NW Rural) *44.62222, 2.36101* **Camping Du Moulin, Les Passes, 12320 Grand-Vabre [tel/fax 05 65 72 87 28 or 06 82 88 53 33 (mob); campingdumoulin12@orange.fr; www.grand-vabre.fr]** N fr Conques on D901, site sp on banks Rv Dourdou. Sm, mkd pitch, terr, shd; wc; mv service pnt; shwrs; el pnts (10A) €2; tradsmn; snacks; bar; playgrnd; htd pool; tennis 1km; games area; TV rm; mainly statics; poss cr; quiet. "Pleasant rvside site; gd, modern san facs; gd." 1 Apr-31 Oct. € 16.00   2012*

CONQUET, LE *2E1* (2km N Coastal) *48.36748, -4.75990* **Camping Les Blancs Sablons, 29217 Le Conquet [tel/fax 02 98 89 06 90]** Exit Brest on D789 to Le Conquet. Turn R after 22km (1.8km bef Le Conquet) on D67 twd St Renan, turn L after 700m on D28 twd Ploumoguer. After 2km, turn L at x-rds twd Plage des Blancs Sablons, site on L in 1km. Lge, mkd pitch, pt sl, unshd; wc; chem disp (wc); shwrs inc; el pnts (16A) €3 (long lead poss req); lndtte; shop in ssn & 1km; rest, snacks 1km; bar 500m; playgrnd; htd pool; sand beach 100m; adv bkg; ccard acc; CKE/CCI. "Gd views fr some pitches; some soft pitches; ltd facs low ssn; site badly run down & office hardly ever open (2010); lovely old fishing town." ♦ 1 Apr-31 Oct. € 16.40   2010*

⊞ **CONQUET, LE** *2E1* (7km SE Coastal) *48.34154, -4.70749*
Camping Les Terrasses de Bertheaume, Rue de Perzel, 29217 Plougonvelin [tel/fax 02 98 48 32 37; camping-lesterrassesdebertheaume@wanadoo.fr; www.camping-brest.com] Sp nr town. Sm, mkd pitch, pt sl, terr, unshd; wc (some cont); chem disp (wc); shwrs €1; el pnts €2.50; lndtte; shop 1km; snacks; bar; BBQ; playgrnd; htd pool; sand beach adj (steps); TV rm; 80% statics; dogs €1; poss cr; CKE/CCI. "Some sea views; Le Fort de Bertheaume 500m interesting; cliff walk; steep access poss diff lge o'fits." ♦ ltd € 17.00   2010*

CONTIS PLAGE *8E1* (500m E Coastal) *44.08895, -1.31678*
Yelloh! Village Lous Seurrots, 40170 Contis-Plage [05 58 42 85 82; fax 05 58 42 49 11; info@lous-seurrots.com; www.lous-seurrots.com or www.yellohvillage.co.uk] S fr Mimizan take D652; 14km turn R onto D41 sp Contis-Plage; site on L. Or fr N10/E5/E70 exit junc 14 onto D38/D41 to Contis. V lge, hdg pitch, shd; htd wc; chem disp; baby facs; fam bthrm; shwrs inc; el pnts (6A) €4; gas; lndtte (inc dryer); shop; tradsmn; rest, snacks; bar; BBQ; playgrnd; pool; paddling pool; sand beach 400m; tennis; cycle hire; games area; wifi; entmnt; TV; 30% statics; dogs €4; adv bkg; quiet; Eng spkn; ccard acc; red low ssn. "Pitches vary in size, some req levelling blocks; excel." ♦ 9 Apr-27 Sep.
€ 36.00   2010*

See advertisement on inside front cover

CONTRES *4G2* (6km SW Rural) *47.38261, 1.36251* Camping à la Ferme La Presle (Boucher), 41700 Oisly [02 54 79 52 69 or 06 15 70 74 02; fax 02 54 79 80 44; lapresle@lapost.net; www.gites-centre-loire.com] Fr Contres take D675 SW for 3km D21 to just past Oisly. Well sp. Sm, pt sl, pt shd; wc; el pnts (4A) €2.20 (poss no earth); shops 1.5km; lake fishing; v quiet. "Excel CL-type site; owner helpful." Easter-1 Nov. € 12.00   2011*

CONTREXEVILLE *6F2* (1km SW Rural) *48.18005, 5.88519*
Camp Municipal du Tir aux Pigeons, Rue du 11 Septembre, 88140 Contrexéville [03 29 08 15 06; secretariat@ville.contrexeville.fr; www.ville-contrexeville.fr] Off D164. App town fr NW on D164 turn R onto D13 & foll sp. 200m W of level x-ing, adj to stadium. Med, mkd pitch, pt shd; wc; chem disp; shwrs inc; el pnts (5A) €2.50; lndtte; shops 1km; tradsmn; paddling pool; lake fishing 2km; tennis adj; games area; games rm; poss cr; some rd noise. "Popular NH." ♦ 1 Apr-31 Oct.
€ 13.00   2008*

COQUILLE, LA see Chalus *7B3*

CORBIGNY *4G4* (3.5km W Rural) *47.25858, 3.64131* **Camp Intercommunal L'Ardan, Route de Germeney, 58800 Chaumot** [03 86 20 07 70; campingdelardan@wanadoo.fr; www.camping-bourgogne.com] D977 fr Corbigny to Chaumot. Turn on D130 sp Germenay. Site on R after 50m. Med, shd; wc (some cont); chem disp; shwrs inc; el pnts €3; shop 3.5km; rest; bar; playgrnd; lake adj; fishing; boat hire; some statics; dogs €1; Eng spkn; adv bkg; quiet. 1 Apr-1 Oct.
€ 12.00   2009*

CORCIEUX *6F3* (8km NE Urban) *48.18436, 6.95784* **Camping Les Acacias, 191 Rue Léonard de Vinci, 88650 Anould** [03 29 57 11 06; contact@acaciascamp.com; www.acaciascamp.com] Site in vill of Anould sp fr all dir; just off main rd. (Annexe Camping Nature Les Acacias 800m fr this site open 15 Jun-15 Sep, terr in woods.) Med, pt shd; wc (some cont); chem disp; mv service pnt; baby facs; shwrs inc; el pnts (6-10A) €3.50-6; gas; lndtte (inc dryer); shops 500m; supmkt 2km; rest, snacks; sm bar; playgrnd; sm, htd pool; rv fishing nrby; games rm; tennis & karting 2km; cycle trails; 10% statics; dogs €1; poss cr; Eng spkn; adv bkg; quiet; CKE/CCI. "Gd standard site; helpful owners; gd, clean san facs; excel." ♦ 5 Dec-5 Oct. € 11.00   2011*

CORCIEUX *6F3* (600m E Rural) *48.16826, 6.89006* **Camping Le Clos de la Chaume, 21 Rue d'Alsace, 88430 Corcieux** [tel/fax 03 29 50 76 76 or 06 85 19 62 55 (mob); info@camping-closdelachaume.com; www.camping-closdelachaume.com] Take D145 fr St Dié, then D8 thro Anould & bear R onto D60. Site in 3km on R at ent to vill. Med, hdg/mkd pitch, hdstg, pt shd; wc; chem disp; mv service pnt; some serviced pitches; fam bthrm; baby facs; shwrs inc; el pnts (8-10A) €3.50 ; gas; lndtte (inc dryer); shop, rest, snacks & bar 600m; BBQ; playgrnd; pool; sand beach & lake sw 12km; fishing; cycle hire 800m; games area; games rm; wifi €5; TV; 15% statics; dogs €1.70; twin-axles acc (rec check in adv); phone; Eng spkn; adv bkg; quiet; ccard acc; red low ssn/long stay/CKE/CCI. "Lovely, peaceful site in beautiful area; stream runs thro; friendly & helpful owners; san facs poss stetched high ssn; conv Gérardmer & Alsace wine rte; excel; acess rd vg; highly rec" ♦ 27 Apr-16 Sep. € 31.10 SBS - J08   2013*

See advertisement above

CORCIEUX *6F3* (1km E Rural) *48.16631, 6.89366* **Camping au Mica, 8 Route de Gérardmer, 88430 Corcieux [tel/fax 03 29 50 70 07; info@campingaumica.com; www.campingaumica.com]** S fr fr St Dié on D415 to Arnould; at rndabt turn right onto D8; in 3km (at La Plafond) turn R onto D60 sp Corcieux; site on L in 3km. Med, hdg/mkd pitch,pt shd; wc (some cont); chem disp; mv service pnt; baby facs; serviced pitches; shwrs inc; el pnts (6A) €3.50; gas; lndtte (inc dryer); shop; tradsmn; BBQ; playgrnd; pool 150m; rv fishing adj; games area; games rm; wifi; TV; some statics; dogs €1; phone; bus; poss cr; Eng spkn; adv bkg; quiet; red low ssn/long stay; ccard acc; CKE/CCI. "Peaceful site on edge of vill; nice scenery; generous pitches; friendly Dutch owners; gd clean san facs; walking rtes in beautiful National Park; a very pleasant stay; excel." ♦ ltd 24 Apr-15 Sep. € 13.00   2011*

CORCIEUX *6F3* (S Rural) *48.1690, 6.88023* **Yelloh! Village Le Domaine des Bans, La Rochotte, 88430 Corcieux [03 29 51 64 67; fax 03 29 51 64 65; info@domaine-des-bans.com; www.domaine-des-bans.com or www.yellohvillage.co.uk]** Fr St Dié by-pass join D415 S to Anould. After approx 10km turn R on D8 & in 5km R on D60 to Corcieux. Or fr S take D8 N fr Gérardmer thro Gerbépal. In 2km turn L onto D60 twd Corcieux, site on L. V lge, hdg/mkd pitch, terr, pt shd; wc; chem disp; baby facs; shwrs inc; el pnts (6A) inc; gas; lndtte; sm shop, rest, snacks, bar high ssn; BBQ; playgrnd; pool high ssn; sm lake; tennis; games rm; horseriding; entmnt; 75% tour ops static tents/vans; dogs €3; poss cr; Eng spkn; adv bkg ess high ssn (min 7 days); poss noisy; ccard acc; CKE/CCI. "Pitches by lake quieter than nr vill; gd site with gd facs; poss stretched high ssn; care needed on narr site rds with speed control ditches; mkt Mon." ♦ 30 Apr-3 Sep. € 39.00   2008*

See advertisement on inside front cover

CORDELLE see Roanne *9A1*

CORDES SUR CIEL *8E4* (5km SE Rural) *44.04158, 2.01722* **Camping Redon, Livers-Cazelles, 81170 Cordes-sur-Ciel [tel/fax 05 63 56 14 64; info@campredon.com; www.campredon.com]** Off D600 Albi to Cordes rd. Exit on D107 to E. Site sp. Sm, hdg pitch, pt sl, pt shd; wc; chem disp; mv service pnt; baby facs; shwrs inc; el pnts (6-16A) €4.25; gas; lndtte; shops 5km; tradsmn; ltd shop; rest, snacks; bar; sm playgrnd; pool; wifi; TV rm; dogs €2.25; phone; bus 1km; poss cr; Eng spkn; adv bkg; quiet; red long stay/low ssn/CKE/CCI. "Well-kept, well-run site; views fr some pitches; friendly, helpful Dutch owner; excel facs, poss stretched high ssn; ecological septic tank - environmentally friendly liquid sold on site; conv Bastides in area; highly rec." ♦ 1 Apr-1 Nov. € 29.00   2012*

CORDES SUR CIEL *8E4* (2km W Rural) *44.06681, 1.92408* **Camping Le Garissou, Les Cabannes, 81170 Cordes-sur-Ciel [05 63 56 27 14; fax 05 63 56 26 95; aquadis1@orange.fr; www.aquadis-loisirs.com/domaine-du-garissou]** Take D600 fr Cordes thro Les Cabanes; site sp on L at bottom of hill, 1.5km after Les Cabanes. Med, mkd pitch, terr, pt shd; wc; shwrs inc; el pnts (6A) inc; lndtte; sm shop; playgrnd; pool complex adj; dogs €1.50; quiet; red low ssn. "Hilltop site; excel views; clean facs." 11 Mar-10 Nov. € 13.90 (CChq acc) 2013*

CORMAC see St Sulpice les Feuilles *7A3*

CORMATIN *9A2* (500m N Rural) *46.54841, 4.68351* **Camping Le Hameau des Champs, Route de Chalon, 71460 Cormatin [03 85 50 76 71; fax 03 85 50 76 98; camping.cormatin@wanadoo.fr; www.le-hameau-des-champs.com]** Fr Cluny N on D981 dir Cormatin for approx 14km, site N of town sp on L, 300m after chateau. Look for line of European flags. Sm, hdg/mkd pitch, pt sl, unshd; htd wc; chem disp; mv service pnt; shwrs inc; el pnts (13A) €3.25 (long lead poss req); gas 500m; lndtte; shop 500m; tradsmn; rest, snacks; bar; BBQ (gas/elec); cooking facs; playgrnd; rv sw 1km; shgle beach 7km; cycle hire; TV rm; 10% statics; dogs €1; phone; wifi; Eng spkn; adv bkg; quiet; ccard acc; red low ssn; CKE/CCI. "Well-kept, secure site in lovely countryside; welcoming, friendly owner; lge pitches; ltd el pnts, adv bkg rec; gd facs, poss stretched high ssn; rest open low ssn; muddy when wet; Voie Verte cycling rte adj; excel municipal site" ♦ 1 Apr-30 Sep. € 21.55   2013*

CORMATIN *9A2* (6km NW Rural) *46.57139, 4.66245* **Camping du Gué, Messeugne, 71460 Savigny-sur-Grosne [03 85 92 56 86; camping.messeugne@orange.fr; www.camping-messeugne.monsite-orange.fr]** Fr Cluny N on D981, 2km N of Cormatin fork L sp Malay. Site 3km on R bef rv bdge. Med, mkd pitch, shd; htd; chem disp; shwrs €1.20; el pnts €3; tradsmn; bar; BBQ; playgrnd; games area; dir access to rv; fishing; 80 - 90% statics; dogs €1.20; CKE/CCI. "Pleasant, friendly site; nr St Genoux-le-National (national monument), Cluny & Taizé; on Burgundy wine rte; fairly boggy when wet; caravans parked on concrete bases" ♦ 29 Mar-27 Oct. € 10.70   2013*

CORMEILLES *3D1* (4km E Rural) *49.24623, 0.44954* **Camping Les Pommiers (Desbois), La Febvrerie, 27260 St Sylvestre-de-Cormeilles [02 32 42 29 69; cmaraisc@aol.com; www.campinglespommiers.com]** Exit A13 junc 28 Beuzeville onto N175 then D27 S sp Epaignes & Bernay twds Lieurey. Cont on D27 for approx 15km & at rndabt with D139 at Epaignes strt on for 5.6km, turn R down narr lane D706 sp St Sylvestre, Camping. Site on R in 1.5km. Fr S on D27 turn L onto D810 at Lieurey & in approx 2km turn R to St Sylvestre. Sm, hdg pitch, pt shd; wc; chem disp (wc); shwrs inc; el pnts inc (6A) €2.50 (poss rev pol); lndry rm; shops 4km, rest, snacks, bar; BBQ; playgrnd; some statics; dogs free; phone; poss cr; Eng spkn; adv bkg; quiet. "Pleasant, secluded, family-run site in orchard; friendly; san facs need refurb (2010)." 1 Apr-31 Oct. € 9.10   2010*

CORMORANCHE SUR SAONE see Macon *9A2*

CORNY SUR MOSELLE 5D2 (Rural) 49.03768, 6.05736 Camping Le Pâquis, rue de la Moselle, 57680 Corny-sur-Moselle [03 87 52 03 59 or 03 87 60 68 67; fax 03 87 52 05 78; campinglepaquis@orange.fr; http://campinglepaquis.free.fr] SW fr Metz on D657; site sp on ent to vill. Or S on A31 take junc 29 Féy & turn R onto D66 into Corny-sur-Moselle; at rndabt in vill turn R & foll sp. Site 300m on L. Lge, pt shd; htd wc; chem disp; shwrs inc; el pnts (6A) inc (long cable poss req); lndtte; shops 1km; tradsmn; snacks; bar; playgrnd; sm lake; rv sw adj; games rm; entmnt; TV; dogs €1.30; poss cr; adv bkg; poss rlwy noise; ccard acc; opening dates vary according to public holidays; CKE/CCI. "Gd, well-run site on Rv Moselle; friendly, helpful owners; rec early for quieter pitch at far end site; many pitches long, drive-thro so no need unhitch; pleasant" 1 May-30 Sep. € 20.10   2013*

CORPS 9C3 Camping Municipal Les Aires, Route du Sautet, 38970 Corps [04 76 30 03 85; fax 04 76 81 12 28; www.isere-tourisme.com] Fr N85, Route de Napoleon, Grenoble to Gap. Vill of Corps turn R on D537, site on L in 400m. Sm, mkd pitch, pt shd; wc; chem disp; shwrs; el pnts (6A) inc; lndry rm; games room; 30% statics; dog; "quiet site; san facs old but clean; in pretty villon the Route de Napoleon" 06 Apr-30 Sep. € 13.40   2013*

CORREZE 7C4 (400m E Urban) 45.37249, 1.88076 Camp Municipal La Chapelle, 19800 Corrèze [05 55 21 29 30 or 05 55 21 25 21 (Mairie); mairie.correze@wanadoo.fr] N fr Tulle on D1089 dir Egletons, turn L at La Gare de Corrèze onto D26 sp to Corrèze. Site 400m fr town cent on D143. Med, mkd pitch, pl sl, terr, pt shd; wc; chem disp; shwrs inc; el pnts (5A) €2.08; gas; lndtte; shop, rest, shops; snacks; playgrnd; htd pool 500m; canoeing & rv fishing; phone; Eng spkn; quiet; CKE/CCI. "Lovely area; old vill; areas for c'vans on opp side of rv fr recep." ♦ ltd 15 Jun-15 Sep. € 8.65   2008*

CORSICA Campsites in towns in Corsica are listed together at the end of the French site entry pages.

COSNE COURS SUR LOIRE 4G3 (SW Rural) 47.40923, 2.91792 Camping de l'Ile, Ile de Cosne, 18300 Bannay [03 86 28 27 92; fax 03 86 28 18 10; contact@restaurantcamping.com; www.restaurantcamping.com] Fr Cosne take Bourges rd, D955, over 1st half of bdge, ent immed on L, 500m strt. On rv island. Lge, shd; htd wc; chem disp; shwrs inc; el pnts (10A) €4; lndtte; ltd shop; rest, snacks; bar; BBQ; playgrnd; paddling pool; entmnt; cycle hire; TV; some statics; dogs €0.90; quiet; ccard acc; CKE/CCI. "Helpful staff; views of Rv Loire; gd san facs; gd NH." ♦ 1 Apr-30 Oct. € 14.00   2009*

"There aren't many sites open at this time of year"

If you're travelling outside peak season remember to call ahead to check site opening dates – even if the entry says 'open all year'.

COUBON see Puy en Velay, Le 9C1

COUCHES see Nolay 6H1

COUCOURDE, LA see Montélimar 9D2

COUHE 7A2 (1km N Rural) 46.31254, 0.18216 Camping Les Peupliers, 86700 Couhé [05 49 59 21 16; fax 05 49 37 92 09; info@lespeupliers.fr; www.lespeupliers.fr] Site 35km S of Poitiers on N10 his (old rd off by-pass); ent by bdge over Rv Dive. Fr N or S on N10 take N exit for Couhé. Site on R in 800m. Lge, hdg/mkd pitch, pt shd; wc; 30% serviced pitch; chem disp; mv service pnt; shwrs inc; el pnts (10A) €4.50; gas; lndtte (inc dryer); sm shop & 1.5km; tradsmn; rest, snacks; bar; BBQ; playgrnd; 2 htd pools & paddling pool high ssn; waterslides; jacuzzi; fishing; games area; games rm; wifi; entmnt; TV rm; some statics; dogs free; Eng spkn; adv bkg; quiet, poss some rd noise; ccard acc; red low ssn/long stay/CKE/CCI. "Beautiful, well-run & well-kept site; friendly, helpful staff; immac san facs; easy access fr N10; conv Futuroscope; excel." ♦ 2 May-30 Sep. € 26.50   2011*

See advertisement above

⊞ **COUHE** *7A2* (8.5km SW Rural) *46.25652, 0.08892* **Camping La Grande Vigne, 11 Rue du Paradis, 79120 Messé [05 49 29 39 93 or 0800 073 8385; grande.vigne@ orange.fr; www.grande-vigne.com]** Fr N10 exit at Chaunay onto D35/D55 sp Lezay, thro Vanzay & in approx 1.5km turn R onto C11. Site sp. Sm, pt shd; htd wc; chem disp (wc); shwrs inc; el pnts (10A) €3.50; lndtte (inc dryer); shop, rest 8km; tradsmn; bar 5km; BBQ; htd pool; cycle hire; games area; 2 gîtes to rent; wifi; dogs €0.75 (by prior agreement); twin axle acc; adv bkg; quiet; CKE/CCI. "Gd walking, cycling; gd birdwatching; British owners; friendly welcome; excel" ♦ ltd € 18.50   2013*

COULANGES SUR YONNE *4G4* (9km E Rural) *47.53610, 3.63326* **Camp Municipal Le Petit Port, 89660 Châtel-Censoir [03 86 81 01 98 (Mairie) or 06 80 32 59 50 (mob); campinglepetitport@orange.fr / mairie-de-chatel-censoir@wanadoo.fr; www.chatel-censoir.com]** Fr Auxerre or Clamecy on N151 at Coulanges turn E onto D21, S side of rv & canal to Châtel-Censoir; site sp. Med, pt shd; wc (some cont); chem disp; shwrs inc; el pnts (6A) €2 (poss rev pol); lndry rm; basic shop 400m; snacks; bar; BBQ; playgrnd; rv sw & fishing adj; wifi; some statics; dogs €0.50; twin-axles extra; phone; Eng spkn; some rlwy noise; CKE/CCI. "Attractive, peaceful site bet rv & canal; friendly, busy resident warden; OK san facs; some pitches muddy when wet; beautiful area with gd cycling; concerts at w/ends" 27 Apr-30 Sep. € 8.50 2013*

COULANGES SUR YONNE *4G4* (S Rural) *47.52269, 3.53817* **Camping des Berges de l'Yonne, 89480 Coulanges-sur-Yonne [03 86 81 76 87]** On N151 dir Nevers. Med, pt shd; wc; chem disp; shwrs; el pnts (10A) €2.80; shop; snacks; playgrnd; pool; fishing; tennis. "V pleasant site in beautiful area; dated facs but adequate & clean; superb pool." 1 May-30 Sep. € 14.40   2012*

COULLONS *4G3* (1km W Rural) *47.62319, 2.48444* **Camp Municipal Plancherotte, Route de la Brosse, 45720 Coullons [02 38 29 20 42 or 06 86 73 94 94 (mob); coullons.mairie@wanadoo.fr; www.coullons.fr]** Fr cent of Coullons foll sp twd Cerdon (D51). Bef leaving vill & after passing lake, take 1st rd on L. Site in 500m on L side of lake. Med, pt shd, hdg/mkd pitch; wc (cont); chem disp; some serviced pitches; shwrs; el pnts (15A) inc; gas 1km; shop 1km; playgrnd; tennis; 30% statics; phone; adv bkg; CKE/CCI. "Excel, well-kept site; pleasant mkd walks nrby." ♦ 1 May-31 Oct. € 9.85   2010*

COULON *7A2* (500m N Rural) *46.32739, -0.58437* **Camp Municipal La Niquière, Route de Benet, 79510 Coulon [05 49 35 81 19 or 05 49 35 90 26 (Mairie); fax 05 49 35 82 75; tourisme.coulon79@orange.fr; www. ville-coulon.fr]** Fr N148 at Benet take D1 to Coulon to site on L at ent to Coulon. Sm, pt shd; wc (some cont); chem disp (wc); shwrs inc; el pnts (10A) €3.10; gas; shops 1km; sports facs adj; boats for hire; dogs €0.50; poss cr. "Well-kept site; dated but clean san facs; ent only with barrier card - collect fr Mairie when site office clsd; 10 min walk to vill; gd NH." 1 Apr-30 Sep. € 7.80   2010*

COULON *7A2* (2km W Rural) *46.31444, -0.60888* **Camping La Venise Verte, 178 Route des Bords de Sèvre, 79510 Coulon [05 49 35 90 36; fax 05 49 35 04 69; accueil@camping-laveniseverte.fr; www.camping-la-venise-verte.com]** Exit A83 junc 9 onto D148 to Benet. Turn R at rndabt onto D25E sp Benet cent & foll sp for Coulon thro Benet. In Coulon turn R at traff lts onto D123 sp Le Vanneau-Irleau & Arcais. Cont for approx 3km with canal on L to site R bef canal bdge. Site sp. Med, mkd pitch, pt shd; wc; chem disp; mv service pnt; baby facs; shwrs inc; el pnts (10A) inc (poss rev pol); lndtte (inc dryer); tradsmn; rest, snacks, bar (high ssn); BBQ (charcoal/gas); playgrnd; pool; paddling pool; boating; fishing; canoe/cycle hire; games rm; wifi; entmnt; 25% statics; dogs €2; twin-axles acc (rec check in adv); phone; poss cr; adv bkg; poss noisy high ssn; ccard acc; red low ssn; ACSI; CKE/CCI. "Superb, peaceful site in park-like setting; helpful, friendly owner; excel facs; gd rest; gd sized pitches, but some sm & diff due trees & posts; excel touring base for nature lovers; gd walking & cycle paths beside waterways; pretty town; lovely area; much revisited site; well placed pitches; gd facs; very friendly owner; beautiful, tranquil location; highly rec" ♦ 1 Apr-30 Oct. € 39.60 SBS - A37   2013*

COULON *7A2* (6km W Rural) *46.33020, -0.67524* **Camping Le Relais du Pêcheur, 85420 Le Mazeau [02 51 52 93 23 or 02 51 52 91 14 (Mairie); fax 02 51 52 97 58]** Fr Fontenay-le-Comte take N148 SE. At Benet turn R onto D25 thro vill to Le Mazeau. Turn L in vill then R over canal bdge. Site on L in 500m. Med, hdg pitch, pt shd; wc (most cont); chem disp; shwrs inc; el pnts (16A) €2.85; lndtte; shop 500m; supmkt 5km; playgrnd; paddling pool; boat hire nrby; adv bkg; quiet; CKE/CCI. "Pleasant, clean site in delightful location; gd cyling & walks; facs need updating" ♦ ltd 1 Apr-30 Sep. € 11.10   2013*

COULONGES SUR L'AUTIZE *7A2* (500m S Rural) *46.4794, -0.5990* **Camp Municipal Le Parc, Rue du Calvaire, 79160 Coulonges-sur-l'Autize [05 49 06 27 56; fax 05 49 06 13 26; mairie-coulanges-sur-lautize@wanadoo.fr; www.ville-coulanges-sur-lautize.fr]** Fr Fontenay take D745 sp Parthenay/St Hilaire E to Coulonges, site sp nr 'piscine' on D1. Fr Niort take D744 N to Coulonges. Sm, hdg/mkd pitch, pt shd; wc; chem disp (wc); shwrs inc; el pnts €1.80; lndry rm; shop adj; tradsmn; playgrnd; pool nr; rv sw & fishing 4km; cycle hire; 80% statics; dogs; phone; quiet; CKE/CCI. "Site yourself; warden calls." ♦ May-Oct. € 7.40   2008*

⊞ **COURBIAC** *7D3* (S Rural) *44.37818, 1.01807* **FFCC Le Pouchou, 47370 Courbiac [tel/fax 05 53 40 72 68 or 06 80 25 15 13 (mob); le.pouchou@wanadoo.fr; www. camping-le-pouchou.com]** S fr Fumel on D102 thro Tournon-d'Agenais; Courbiac sp to L on S side of town; site on R in 2.5km (1.5km bef Courbiac). Sm, pt sl, pt shd; wc; chem disp; mv service pnt; baby facs; shwrs inc; el pnts (10A) €3.50 (poss rev pol); lndry rm; shop; snacks; bar; playgrnd; pool & paddling pool; cycle hire; fishing; horseriding; archery; wifi; sat TV; some statics; dogs €1.80; site clsd 21 Dec-9 Jan; Eng spkn; adv bkg ess high ssn; quiet; red low ssn; CKE/CCI. "Vg site in lovely setting; lge pitches each with picnic table; many sl pitches poss diff; gd, clean facs; gd views; friendly, hospitable owners; gd cycling." ♦ € 16.00   2011*

COURCON 7A2 (6km N Rural) 46.30089, -0.80782 **Camping du Port (Naturist), Rue du Port, 17170 La Ronde** [05 46 41 65 58 or 06 26 06 72 37 (mob); camping. naturisteduport@orange.fr; www.camping-naturiste-du-port.com] Fr Marans E on D114, bef Courçon head N on D116 dir Maillezais. Site on R after leaving vill of La Ronde. Sm, hdg/mkd pitch, hdstg, pt shd; wc; chem disp; shwrs inc; el pnts (6-10A) €3.50; gas; lndtte; shops adj; BBQ; playgrnd; pool high ssn; sand beach 30km; few statics; dogs €2; poss cr; adv bkg; quiet. "Excel, well looked-after site; helpful owner; facs clean; site poss open outside dates shown." ♦ 1 May-30 Sep. € 17.00   2009*

"That's changed – Should I let The Club know?"

If you find something on site that's different from the site entry, fill in a report and let us know. See www.caravanclub.co.uk/europereport.

COURCON 7A2 (500m SE Rural) 46.24060, -0.80635 **Camp Municipal La Garenne, 12 Rue du Collège, 17170 Courçon** [05 46 01 60 19 or 05 46 01 60 50 (Mairie); fax 05 46 01 63 59; mairie.courcon@mairie17.com] Fr E on N11 turn N at La Laigne on D114 to Courçon. Site on L on app to vill. Fr W turn N onto D116 to Courçon. Sm, pt shd; wc; mv service pnt; shwrs; el pnts (3A) €3.50; lndtte; shops 500m; htd pool adj; rv sw 5km; fishing 5km; dogs €1.50; adv bkg rec high ssn; quiet. 1 Jul-31 Aug. € 8.80   2009*

COURCON 7A2 (5km S Urban) 46.20365, -0.81619 **Camp Municipal du Château, 17170 Benon** [06 66 90 35 59 (mob) or 05 46 01 61 48 (Mairie); fax 05 46 01 01 19; mairie-benon@smic17.fr; www.tourisme-aunisverte.com] Fr N11 turn S to Benon onto D116. On S side of Benon turn E onto D206 twd St Georges-du-Bois, site immed on R thro tall, narr, metal gateway; take wide sweep on ent (or use easier access at rear - foll wall round to L). Site also sp in Benon. Sm, pt sl, mainly shd; wc; chem disp; mv service pnt; shwrs inc; el pnts (10A) €2.50; lndtte; tradsmn; playgrnd; pool 6km; tennis; dogs €1; quiet; adv bkg; ccard acc; CKE/CCI. "Attractive site adj Mairie; immac & tidy; no lighting; oyster beds at Châtelaillon; gd cycling area; 20 mins La Rochelle; poss itinerants." 15 May-30 Sep. € 9.40   2011*

COURNON D'AVERGNE see Clermont Ferrand 9B1

COURPIERE 9B1 (5km NE Rural) 45.79199, 3.60583 **Camping Le Grün du Chignore, Les Plaines, 63120 Vollore-Ville** [tel/fax 04 73 53 73 37; camping-du-chignore@hotmail.fr; www.campingauvergne.fr] D906 S fr Thiers; at Courpière turn L onto D7 to Vollore-Ville; cont on D7 past vill; site on R in 500m. Sm, hdg/mkd pitch, pt shd; wc (some cont); chem disp (wc); mv service pnt; shwrs inc; el pnts (10A) €4.: lndtte; shop 500m; tradsmn; rest, snacks; bar; BBQ (gas area); playgrnd; pool; games area; some statics; wifi; dogs €1.50; some Eng spkn; adv bkg; quiet; ccard acc; "Situated above fishing lake; rolling hills; helpful & welcoming owners; facs poss stretched high ssn; poss clsd on Weds in April; gd walks; chateau in Vollore-Ville; bar part of vill life; highly rec; excel; vg, new deep pool" ♦ 1 Apr-31 Oct. € 11.00   2013*

COURSEULLES SUR MER 3D1 (500m NE Coastal) 49.33417, -0.44433 **Camping Le Champ de Course, Ave de la Libération, 14470 Courseulles-sur-Mer** [02 31 37 99 26 (Mairie); fax 02 31 37 96 37; camping. courseulles@wanadoo.fr; www.courseulles-sur-mer.com] Fr N814 by-pass thro Caen, take exit 5 onto D7 & D404 dir Courseulles-sur-Mer. On ent to town, foll sp 'Campings' at 1st rndabt Site on D514 on R. Gd sp's for site. Lge, hdg/mkd pitch, unshd; wc; chem disp; mv service pnt; baby facs; shwrs inc; el pnts (10A) €4.50; lndtte; tradsmn; rest, snacks, bar adj; BBQ; playgrnd; pool adj; sand beach; games area; boat hire; tennis, mini-golf & horseriding nr; TV rm; 15% statics; dogs €1.90; phone; wifi; poss cr; Eng spkn; adv bkg; quiet; ccard acc; CKE/CCI. "Nice site adj beach; friendly staff; facs clean; early dep for ferry catered for; conv D-Day landing beach; gd dog walks; oyster beds & daily fish mkt; vg; excel san facs" ♦ 1 Apr-30 Sep. € 25.00   2013*

COURSEULLES SUR MER 3D1 (2km E Coastal) 49.33225, -0.42820 **Camping Le Havre de Bernières, Chemin de Quintefeuille, 14990 Bernières-sur-Mer** [02 31 96 67 09; fax 02 31 97 31 06; info@camping-normandie.com; www. camping-normandie.com] W fr Ouistreham on D514 for 20km. Site well sp. Lge, mkd pitch, pt sl, pt shd; wc; chem disp; 50% serviced pitches; shwrs inc; el pnts (20A) €6; lndtte; shop; rest, snacks; bar; playgrnd; pool; sand beach adj; tennis; games area; entmnt; many statics; dogs €4.20; poss v cr; Eng spkn; adv bkg; poss noisy; red low ssn; CKE/CCI. "Gd beaches & watersports; conv Ouistreham ferries; busy site, poss untidy; inadequate san facs high ssn & poss unclean; pool unclean (8/09); when site cr c'vans poss need manhandling." ♦ 28 Mar-31 Oct. € 27.50   2009*

COURSEULLES SUR MER 3D1 (8km SW Rural) 49.28949, -0.52970 **Camp Municipal des Trois Rivières, Route de Tierceville, 14480 Creully** [tel/fax 02 31 80 12 00 or 02 31 80 90 17; camping.creully@orange.fr; www. campingdes3rivieres.fr] Fr Caen ring rd, exit junc 8 onto N13 dir Bayeux; in 15km turn R onto D82 to Creully; site on R 500m past cent of Creully. Med, hdg pitch, pt sl, pt shd; htd wc; chem disp (wc); shwrs inc; chem disp; el pnts (10A) €4.10 (long leads req, poss rev pol); lndtte; tradsmn; shops, rest, snacks, bar 1km; BBQ; playgrnd; pool 5km; games area; games rm; sand beach 5km; dogs €1.20; Eng spkn; adv bkg; quiet; ccard acc; CKE/CCI. "Well-kept, clean site; gd pitches; friendly, helpful warden; excel facs, stretched high ssn; conv D-Day beaches, Bayeux; barrier clsd 1500-1700; gd cycling; excel." ♦ 1 Apr-30 Sep. € 11.00   2011*

COURTILS see Mont St Michel, Le 2E4

COURVILLE SUR EURE 4E2 (S Urban) 48.44629, 1.24157 **Camp Municipal Les Bords de l'Eure, Ave Thiers, 28190 Courville-sur-Eure** [02 37 23 76 38 or 02 37 18 07 90 (Mairie); fax 02 37 18 07 99; secretaria-mairie@courville-sur-eure.fr; www.courville-sur-eure.fr] Turn N off D923 19km W of Chartres. Site on bank of rv. Foll sp. Med, hdg pitch, pt shd; htd wc (some cont); chem disp; mv service pnt (outside ent); shwrs; el pnts (6A) €3.30; lndtte; supmkt 1km; rest in town; pool 200m; dogs; poss cr; quiet. "Lovely, peaceful rvside site; spacious pitches; friendly warden; san facs clean but need update & poss stetched high ssn; poss no twin-axles; conv Chartres; mkt Thurs; easy walk into town" 1 May - 22 Sep. € 11.95   2013*

CAMPING ★ ★ ★ ★
Parc de Montsabert
Space is our luxury
Between Angers and Saumur

Our Luxury is the space. Our campsite is ideally located to discover the castles of the Loire. But you can also relax, while your kids enjoy our animation and swimming pools.

150 route de Montsabert
49320 Coutures
Tel: 0033 (0)241 57 91 63
camping@parcdemontsabert.com
www.parcdemontsabert.com

yelloh! VILLAGE   La Tzigane

⊞ **COUTANCES** *1D4* (1km W Urban) *49.05172, -1.45927*
FFCC Camp Municipal Les Vignettes, 27 Rue de St Malo, 50200 Coutances [02 33 45 43 13; fax 02 33 45 74 98]
Fr N on D971 or D2 turn R onto Coutances by-pass, sp St Malo & Avranches. At rndabt turn L. Site 200m on R after Cositel ent. Fr S foll sp for Valognes or Cherbourg. Site in Coutances on L immed after Logis sp. Med, hdg/mkd pitch, pt sl, pt shd; wc (some cont); chem disp; mv service pnt; shwrs inc; ltd el pnts (6A) inc; shops 500m; snacks; bar; BBQ; playgrnd; htd pool adj; sports stadium adj; few statics; dogs €1.05; poss cr; some rd noise; CKE/CCI. "Pretty site; gd, clean san facs; friendly warden; access poss diff to some pitches; muddy when wet; gd NH for Cherbourg." € 12.40   2011*

⊞ **COUTANCES** *1D4* (6.5km NW Rural) *49.00951, -1.48421*
Camping La Renaudière Féret, 50200 Ancteville [02 33 45 57 53; service.clients@renaudiere-feret.com; www.renaudiere-feret.com] N fr Coutances on D2; in 6.5km take 1st R after R turn for Servigny; site on R in 200m. App fr N on D2, take 1st L turn after L turn for Ancteville (site on rd bet turnings for Ancteville & Servigny). Sm, unshd; wc; chem disp; mv service pnt; fam bthrm; shwrs inc; el pnts (10-16A) inc; shops nrby; BBQ area; wifi; dogs; adv bkg; quiet; red long stay. CKE/CCI. "Tranquil, scenic farm site; British owners; conv NH or longer; vg. ◆ ltd € 15.00   2009*

COUTRAS *7C2* (3km SW Rural) *45.01335, -0.10856*
Camping Résidential de Loisir Le Paradis, 8 Champ des Ardouins, Port-du-Mas, 33230 Abzac [05 57 49 05 10; fax 05 57 49 18 88; campingleparadis@free.fr; http://campingleparadis.free.fr/] Fr Coutras on S on D17 to Abzac, site well sp. Sm, pt shd; htd wc; mv service pnt; baby facs; shwrs inc; el pnts (6A) €3; gas; lndtte; shop; tradsmn; rest, snacks; BBQ; playgrnd; pool; lake sw, sand beach; fishing; games rm; entmnt;TV rm; 90% statics; dogs €1.50; ccard acc; m'vans only; CKE/CCI. "Excel site; san facs need refurb; gd for vineyards." 1 May-15 Sep. € 15.20   2009*

⊞ **COUTRAS** *7C2* (7.5km NW Rural) *45.07944, -0.20622*
Camping Le Chêne du Lac, 3 Lieu-dit Chateauneuf, 33230 Bayas [05 57 69 13 78 or 06 07 98 92 65 (mob); lechenedulac@orange.fr; www.camping-lechenedulac.com] Fr Coutras W on D10 to Guitres; N fr Guitres on D247 to Bayas; site 2km N of Bayas, sp. Sm, mkd ptch, pt shd; wc (some cont); chem disp; shwrs inc; el pnts (10A) €4.30-5; gas; lndry rm; shop; tradsmn; snacks; bar; BBQ sep area; playgrnd; internet; 25% statics; no twin-axles; dogs €2; adv bkg; Eng spkn; quiet; CKE/CCI. "Helpful owner; pedalos & canoes adj; vg; red facs in winter; great site; friendly, helpful new owners; v relaxed atmosphere" ◆ ltd € 24.00   2013*

COUTURES *4G1* (1km NE Rural) *47.37440, -0.34690*
Camping Parc de Montsabert, 49320 Coutures [02 41 57 91 63; fax 02 41 57 90 02; camping@parcdemontsabert.com; www.parcdemontsabert.com] Easy access on R side of Rv Loire bet Angers & Saumur. Take D751 to Coutures & fr town cent foll sp for site. First R after 'Tabac' & foll rd to site (first on R bef chateau). Med, hdg/mkd pitch, hdstg, pt sl, pt shd; htd wc; chem disp; 50% serviced pitches; child/baby facs; shwrs inc; el pnts (5-10A) inc; lndtte; shop 1.5km; tradsmn; rest, snacks; bar; playgrnd; htd, covrd pool; paddling pool with slide; tennis; games area; games rm; cycle hire; gym; entmnt; TV; 15% statics; dogs €4; phone; bus 1km; Eng spkn; adv bkg; quiet; ccard acc; CKE/CCI. "Ideal for chateaux & wine cellars; lge pitches." ◆ 12 Apr - 8 Sep. € 29.00   2010*

See advertisement

COUX see Montendre *7C2*

COUX ET BIGAROQUE see Bugue, Le *7C3*

COUZON see Bourbon L'Archambault *9A1*

FRANCE

COZES 7B1 (9km S Rural) 45.50148, -0.83518 **Camp Municipal St Seurin-d'Uzet, 12 Quai Esturgeon, 17120 Chenac-St Seurin-d'Uzet [05 46 90 45 31 or 05 46 90 44 03 (Mairie); fax 05 46 90 40 02; chenac-saint-seurin.duzet@mairie17.com]** SE fr Royan take D25/D145 thro St Georges-de-Didonne, Meschers-sur-Gironde & Talmont to St Seurin-d'Uzet. Site sp in vill. Med, hdg/mkd pitch, pt shd; wc; chem disp (wc); shwrs inc; el pnts (5A) €1.55 (poss rev pol & poss long lead req); lndtte; shop 100m; playgrnd; rv sw & sand beach adj; dogs €0.80; adv bkg rec high ssn; quiet. "Rec; pretty, well-maintained site beside creek; lge pitches; gd views & walks; pleasant staff; poss mosquito prob; gd vill shop." ◆ 1 May-30 Sep. € 7.10   2008*

COZES 7B1 (4km SW Rural) 45.54536, -0.88901 **Camping Fleur des Champs, Le Coudinier, 17120 Arces-sur-Gironde [05 46 90 40 11; fax 05 46 97 64 45; contact@campingfdc. com; www.campingfdc.com]** Site on D114 on R 1km fr Arces to Talmont. Sm, mkd pitch, pt sl, pt shd; wc; shwrs inc; el pnts (6A) €3.30; gas; tradsmn; lndtte; shop 1km; tradsmn; playgrnd; pool 4km; lake sw & beach; cycle hire; entmnt; wifi; 80% statics; dogs €1.70; quiet. "Pleasant, basic site; ideal for seaside holiday away fr typical coastal sites; clean, dated san facs, ltd if site full; NH/sh stay only." 1 Jun-15 Sep. € 9.50   2011*

COZES 7B1 (W Urban) 45.58650, -0.83568 **Camp Municipal Le Sorlut, Rue de Stade, 17120 Cozes [05 46 90 75 99 or 05 46 90 90 97 (Mairie); fax 05 46 90 75 12]** Clearly sp in Cozes, 150m fr D730. Turn into app rd on R of Champion supmkt. Med, mkd pitch, pt shd; wc; chem disp; shwrs inc; el pnts (5A) €2.50; lndry rm; shops adj; supmkt 500m; playgrnd; pool; sand beach 6km; tennis; poss cr; quiet; CKE/CCI. "Pleasant site close to Royan; friendly, helpful warden; gd, clean san facs; poss unkempt low ssn; no twin-axles; popular with long stay British." 15 Apr-14 Oct. € 10.50   2010*

CRAC'H see Carnac 2G3

"I like to fill in the reports as I travel from site to site"

You'll find report forms at the back of this guide, or you can fill them in online at www.caravaclub.co.uk/europereport.

CRAON 2F4 (E Urban) 47.84819, -0.94409 **Camp Municipal du Mûrier, Rue Alain Gerbault, 53400 Craon [02 43 06 96 33 or 02 43 06 13 09 (Mairie); fax 02 43 06 39 20; contact@ville-craon53.fr; www.ville-craon53.fr]** Fr Laval take D771 S to Craon. Site sp fr town cent. Sm, hdg pitch, pt shd; wc; shwrs inc; el pnts (6A) €2.10; lndtte; snacks; playgrnd; pool 200m; tennis; wifi; entmnt; no twin-axles; adv bkg; quiet; red long stay. "Lge pitches; san facs poss stretched when site full; easy walk to town; office clsd Tues & Sun low ssn, when barrier key req (2010); local chateau gardens." 1 May-21 Sep. € 10.00   2010*

CRAYSSAC 7D3 (500m SW Rural) 44.50694, 1.32416 **Campéole Camping Les Reflets du Quercy, Mas de Bastide, 46150 Crayssac [05 65 30 00 27; fax 05 17 47 50 80; reflets-du-quercy@campeole.com; www. camping-lot.info or www.campeole.com]** Take D911 W fr Cahors; 1km after steep winding climb foll camp sp on L sp Luzech for 1km. NB: D9 to Crayssac not rec. Med, hdg pitch, hdstg, pt sl, pt shd; htd wc; chem disp; mv service pnt; baby facs; shwrs inc; el pnts (10A) €4.10; gas; lndtte (inc dryer); shop; tradsmn; rest; bar; BBQ; playgrnd; pool; paddling pool; fishing, canoeing nr; tennis; horseriding nr; games area; wifi; entmnt; games/TV rm; 60% statics; dogs €2.60; Eng spkn; adv bkg; quiet; ccard acc; red low ssn; CKE/CCI. "Beautiful touring & walking area; pleasant, helpful staff." ◆ 3 Apr-19 Sep. € 20.00   2009*

See advertisement on pages 14 & 15

CREISSAN 10F1 (Urban) 43.37550, 3.00909 **Camp Municipal Les Oliviers, 34370 Creissan [04 67 93 81 85 or 04 67 93 75 41 (Mairie); fax 04 67 93 85 28; mairie@ creissan.com; www.creissan.com]** Fr D612 foll sp Creissan & site. Sm, mkd pitch, pt shd; shwrs inc; el pnts €3; lndtte; shop, rest, bar in vill; BBQ; playgrnd; pool adj; tennis; entmnt; adv bkg; quiet. "Pleasant site located in housing estate (30 pitches); helpful & friendly; key req to immac san facs - warden's hrs ltd (2009); excel." 1 Apr-30 Sep. € 10.25   2009*

⊞ **CREMIEU** 9B2 (5km NW Rural) 45.74829, 5.22486 **Camping à la Ferme des Epinettes, 11 Rue de l'Eglise, 38460 St Romain-de-Jalionas [tel/fax 04 74 90 94 90 or 06 19 31 03 50 (mob); info@camping-cremieu.com; www. camping-cremieu.com or www.isere-tourisme.com]** N fr Crémieu on D517; in 3km site sp on R, immed bef rndabt on edge of St Romain-de-Jalionas. 200m after turning R off D517 (into Rue de l'Eglise), turn L into Rue des Epinettes & site ent. Site on R in 100m. Sm, mkd pitch, pt shd; htd wc; chem disp (wc); shwrs inc; el pnts (10A) €3; lndry rm; shops etc 5km; jacuzzi; 20% statics; dogs €1; no twin-axles; quiet; red low ssn. "Gd NH for interesting & historic town of Lyon and Crémieu; helpful owners; ltd facs low ssn; gd touring base; Pérouges worth visit; trams/metro fr Meyzieu to Lyon; rec; lovely, peaceful site." ◆ ltd € 12.40   2013*

⊞ **CREON** 7D2 (3km NW Rural) 44.78372, -0.37108 **FFCC Camping Caravaning Bel Air, 33670 Créon [05 56 23 01 90; fax 05 56 23 08 38; info@camping-bel-air.com; www. camping-bel-air.com]** Fr A10/E70 at junc 24 take D936 E fr Bordeaux sp Bergerac. Approx 15km E turn SE onto D671 sp Créon & cont for 5km. Site on L, 1.5km after Lorient. Med, hdg/mkd pitch, hdstg, pt shd; htd wc (some cont); chem disp; mv service pnt; shwrs inc; el (10A) €3.60 ; gas; lndtte (inc dryer); shop high ssn; tradsmn; rest, snacks; bar; playgrnd; pool; wifi; 50% statics; dogs €2.50; clsd to vehicles 2200-0800; Eng spkn; adv bkg; quiet; ccard acc; red long stay; CKE/CCI. "Helpful owners; immac, modern san facs; rest sm & ltd; facs v ltd low ssn; no twin-axles; phone ahead to check open low ssn; gd NH." ◆ ltd € 15.70   2011*

CRESPIAN *10E1* (S Rural) *43.87850, 4.09590* **Kawan Village Le Mas de Reilhe, 30260 Crespian [04 66 77 82 12; fax 04 66 80 26 50; info@camping-mas-de-reilhe.fr; www. camping-mas-de-reilhe.fr]** Exit A9 at Nîmes Ouest N onto N106 dir Alès for 5km. Fork R, then L over bdge onto D999 dir Le Vigan. Foll rd for 24km, R at x-rds onto D6110 to site on R just on ent Crespian. Take care - ent on a bend on busy rd. Med, mkd pitch, pt sl, terr, pt shd; htd wc; chem disp; mv service pnt; baby facs; shwrs inc; el pnts (10A) inc; lndtte (inc dryer); sm shop; rest, snacks; bar; BBQ (gas/elec); playgrnd; htd pool; paddling pool; tennis; fishing & horseriding 10km; games area; games rm; wifi; entmnt; TV; dogs €3; no c'vans/m'vans over 7.50m; poss cr; Eng spkn; quiet but poss some rd noise; ccard acc; red low ssn/long stay; CKE/CCI. "Quiet & relaxing site; friendly staff; clean, modern san facs; wine-tasting adj; conv Nîmes, Uzès & Cévennes National Park; excel." ◆ 14 Apr-16 Sep. € 30.00 (CChq acc) SBS - C10   2011*

CREST *9D2* (5km E Rural) *44.71095, 5.08960* **Gervanne Camping, Quartier Bellevue, 26400 Mirabel-et-Blacons [04 75 40 00 20; fax 04 75 40 03 97; info@gervanne-camping. com; www.gervanne-camping.com]** Exit A7 junc 16 Loriol onto D104/D164, turn off onto D93. Site E of Mirabel-et-Blacons on both sides or rd. Recep by shop. Lge, hdg/mkd pitch, pt shd; htd wc; chem disp; mv service pnt; shwrs inc; baby facs; el pnts (6A) €4; gas; lndtte (inc dryer); shop; tradsmn; rest, snacks; bar; BBQ (gas/elec); playgrnd; htd pool; rv sw & beach adj; canoeing; kayaking; canyoning; cycle hire; games area; games rm; wifi; TV; 12% statics; dogs €3; poss cr; Eng spkn; adv bkg (ess high ssn); quiet; ccard acc; red low ssn; CKE/CCI. "Excel, family-run site in beautiful area by Rv Drôme; gd sized pitches; vg pool complex; vg rest; poss soft after rain - no hdstg." ◆ 2 Apr-30 Sep. € 23.00   2011*

CREST *9D2* (500m S Urban) *44.72410, 5.02755* **Camping Les Clorinthes, Quai Soubeyran, 26400 Crest [04 75 25 05 28; fax 04 75 76 75 09; clorinthes@wanadoo.fr; www. lesclorinthes.com]** S fr Crest twd Nyons on D538, cross bdge cont to rndabt,take last exit foll sp to site. Lge, hdg/mkd pitch, some hdstg, pt sl, pt shd; wc; chem disp; baby facs; shwrs; el pnts (6A) €3.90; gas; lndtte (inc dryer); shop & 500m; tradsmn; snacks; bar; pool; paddling pool; rv sw adj; sports complex 500m; wifi; entmnt; TV; 20% statics; dogs €2.80; phone; adv bkg; poss cr; quiet, some train noise; red low ssn; CKE/CCI. "Well-maintained site in beautiful situation; dir access rv; gd, modern san facs; easy walk or cycle to vill" ◆ ltd 10 Apr-19 Sep. € 21.00   2012*

CREST *9D2* (8km W Rural) *44.72717, 4.92664* **Camping Les Quatre Saisons, Route de Roche-sur-Grâne, 26400 Grane [04 75 62 64 17; fax 04 75 62 69 06; contact@camping-4-saisons.com; www.camping-4saisons.com]** Exit A7 at junc for Loriol or Crest, take D104 E for 18km. Turn R thro vill twd Roche-sur-Grane, site well sp. If a lge unit, access thro 4th junc to Grane. Site well sp fr Crest. Med, pt sl, terr, pt shd; wc; chem disp; mv service pnt; baby facs; shwrs inc; el pnts (6A) €4; lndtte; shop; tradsmn; rest 800m; snacks; bar; BBQ; htd pool; paddling pool; tennis; cycle hire; games area; wifi; TV; some statics; dogs; phone; poss cr; adv bkg; Eng spkn; quiet; ccard acc; red long stay/low ssn; CKE/CCI. "Beautiful views; well-run site; pleasant, helpful owner; sm & lge pitches; excel san facs; gd pool; Grane (supmkt, rest etc) in walking dist; Some pitches far from el pnts and san facs up steep hill; paths a bit uneven - need attention; pleasant stay " ◆ 1 May-15 Sep. € 27.00 (CChq acc)   2013*

See advertisement on pages 32 & 33

CREULLY see Courseulles sur Mer *3D1*

CREVECOEUR EN BRIE see Fontenay Trésigny *4E3*

⊞ **CREVECOEUR LE GRAND** *3C3* (7km SE Rural) **Camping à la Ferme (Fontana), 8 Hameau de la Neuve Rue, 60480 Ourcel-Maison [03 44 46 81 55]** NE fr Beauvais on D1001 to Froissy; turn W at traff lts onto D151. Avoid 1st sp to Francastel but cont to x-rds & turn into vill on D11. Francastel adjoins Ourcel-Maison & site at far end. Or fr A16 exit junc 16 W onto D930 & foll sp. Sm, pt shd; wc (some cont); chem disp; shwrs inc; el pnts (5A) inc (rev pol); shop 6km; tradsmn; rest; BBQ; playgrnd; quiet; ccard not acc. "Farm produce & occasional eve meals avail; no hdstg & poss muddy/diff in wet; gd NH." € 8.00   2008*

CREVECOEUR LE GRAND *3C3* (10km SW Rural) *49.57569, 1.93899* **Camping du Vieux Moulin, 9 Rue Larris Boissy, 60690 Roy-Boissy [03 44 46 33 06]** Fr Marseille-en-Beauvasis SW onto D930 dir Gournay-en-Bray; in 1.5km site sp to R at Roy-Boissy. Sm, pt shd; wc; chem disp; shwrs inc; el pnts inc (poss rev pol); playgrnd; 90% statics; phone; v quiet. "Farm site in area with few sites; beautiful countryside; pitch yourself, owner calls eves; excel." ◆ 1 Apr-31 Oct. € 8.00   2009*

CREYSSE see Martel *7C3*

⊞ **CRIEL SUR MER** *3B2* (2km N Coastal) *50.02568, 1.30855* **FFCC Camp Municipal Le Mont Joli Bois, 29 Rue de la Plage, 76910 Criel-sur-Mer [02 35 50 81 19 or 06 08 80 67 35 (mob); fax 02 35 50 22 37; contact@ camping-montjolibois.fr; http://www.camping-montjolibois.fr]** Fr D925 take D222 into Criel cent. Turn R opp church into D126 for 1.6km to beach. Turn L then immed R & foll beach rd to site in 1.5km. Med, hdg/mkd pitch, pt sl, terr, pt shd; wc; chem disp; mv service pnt; shwrs inc; el pnts (4-6A) €3-4.60; lndtte; tradsmn; shops, rest, snacks, bar 2km; playgrnd; shgl beach 500m; TV rm; 50% statics; dogs €1.60; bus; poss cr; quiet; CKE/CCI. "Fair" ◆ ltd € 13.30   2013*

CRIEL SUR MER *3B2* (1.5km NW Coastal) *50.03048, 1.30815* **Camping Les Mouettes, Rue de la Plage, 76910 Criel-sur-Mer [tel/fax 02 35 86 70 73; contact@camping-lesmouettes.fr; www.camping-lesmouettes.fr]** Fr D925 take D222 thro Criel to coast, site sp. Care needed with narr, steep access. Sm, mkd pitch, terr, unshd; wc; chem disp; shwrs; el pnts (6A) €3.70; lndtte; shop; supmkt 5km; snacks; bar; BBQ; games area; games rm; TV; some statics; dogs €2; Eng spkn; adv bkg; quiet; red low ssn. "Pleasant, well-kept site; friendly, helpful owner; gd san facs; sea views." 1 Apr-1 Nov. € 14.80   2013*

CRIQUETOT L'ESNEVAL see Etretat *3C1*

CROISIC, LE *2G3* (3.5km SE Coastal) *47.27888, -2.49138*
Flower Camping Les Paludiers, Rue Nicolas Appert,
44740 Batz-sur-Mer [02 40 23 85 84; fax 02 40 23 75 55;
paludiers@flowercampings.com; www.camping-
paludiers.com] Fr Guérande take D774/D245 to Batz-sur-
Mer. Thro Batz sp Le Croisic, site is opp windmill. Lge, hdg/
mkd pitch, unshd; wc; mv service pnt; baby facs; shwrs;
el pnts inc; lndtte (inc dryer); tradsmn; rest, snacks; bar;
BBQ; playgrnd; htd pool; paddling pool; sand beach 100m;
watersports; cycle hire; games area; games rm; wifi; TV rm;
50% statics; dogs €2.50-3.20; Eng spkn; adv bkg; quiet; ccard
acc; red low ssn; CKE/CCI. "Vg, family site; helpful, friendly
staff." ♦ 1 Apr-30 Sep. € 26.60   2009*

See advertisement on pages 32 & 33

CROISIC, LE *2G3* (2km S Coastal) *47.29272, -2.52850*
Camping La Pierre Longue, Rue Henri Dunant,
44490 Le Croisic [02 40 23 13 44; fax 02 40 23 23 13;
contact@campinglapierrelongue.com; www.
campinglapierrelongue.com] Turn L off Le Pouliguen-Le
Croisic rd at g'ge at Le Croisic sp; foll camp sps. Lge, hdg/mkd
pitch, pt shd; htd wc; chem disp; mv service pnt; baby facs;
shwrs inc; el pnts (6-10A) inc; gas; lndtte; shop; rest, snacks;
bar; BBQ; playgrnd; htd pool; sand beach 500m; entmnt; TV;
60% statics; phone; dogs; Eng spkn; adv bkg; quiet; ccard acc;
red low ssn; CKE/CCI. "Lge pitches; warm welcome, helpful
staff; excel, clean facs, unisex low ssn; excel beaches." ♦
1 Mar-30 Nov. € 23.70   2011*

CROISIC, LE *2G3* (1km W Coastal) *47.29558, -2.53605*
Camping de l'Océan, 15 Route de la Maison Rouge,
44490 Le Croisic [02 40 23 07 69; fax 02 40 15 70 63;
info@camping-ocean.com; www.camping-ocean.com]
Foll N171/D213 to Guérande. At junc take D774 to La Baule,
Batz-sur-Mer, then D245 to Le Croisic. At rndabt foll site sp.
Lge, hdg/mkd pitch, pt shd; wc; chem disp; mv service pnt;
serviced pitches; baby facs; shwrs inc; el pnts (6A) €4-6; gas;
lndtte; shop; rest, snacks; bar; BBQ; playgrnd; 2 htd pools,
(1 covrd); waterslide; jacuzzi; shgl beach 150m; tennis; games
area; fitness rm; wifi; entmnt; 30% statics; dogs €6.50; adv
bkg; Eng spkn; quiet; red low ssn; ccard acc; red low ssn/CKE/
CCI. "Interesting coast line nr La Baule; salt flats at ent to Le
Croisic; pleasant walk to Guérande adj; excel pool complex."
♦ 3 Apr-30 Sep. € 40.00   2009*

See advertisement on inside back cover

CROISIC, LE *2G3* (2km W Coastal) *47.29415, -2.53846*
Camping Le Paradis, Chemin Turballo, 44490 Le Croisic
[02 40 23 07 89; www.camping-paradis.com] Fr La Baule
take D245 to Le Croisic; on ent Le Croisic cont on D245 (R
fork), which then becomes D45 coast rd; cont on coast rd anti-
clockwise for approx 4km until site sp on L. Med, hdg/mkd pitch,
pt shd; wc; chem disp; shwrs inc; el pnts (3-6A) €2.90-€3.60;
gas; lndtte (inc dryer); shop 2km; tradsmn; rest, snacks; bar;
BBQ; playgrnd; sand/shgl beach 500m; horseriding; golf adj; TV;
10% statics; dogs €2; phone; poss cr; adv bkg; quiet; red low
ssn/long stay; CKE/CCI. "Beaches sm bet rocks; gd cycling; gd
mkt; vg." ♦ ltd 1 May-30 Sep. € 16.00   2010*

CROMARY see Rioz *6G2*

CROTOY, LE *3B2* (Urban/Coastal) *50.22226, 1.61804*
Camping La Prairie, 2 Rue de Mayocq, 80550 Le Crotoy
[tel/fax 03 22 27 02 65; info@camping-laprairie.fr; www.
camping-laprairie.fr] Fr S exit A16 at Abbeville onto D86/
D940 to Le Crotoy to rndabt at ent to town. Cont strt for
1.5km then 2nd L, site on L in 500m. Fr N exit A16 for Rue
onto D32, then D940, then as above. Lge, hdg pitch, pt
shd; wc (some cont); chem disp (wc); shwrs; el pnts (3A) inc;
tradsmn; playgrnd; sand beach 400m; 90% statics; dogs €1;
phone; poss cr; quiet. "Busy site; ltd pitches for tourers; conv
beach & town; gd san facs; gd cycle paths." ♦ 1 Apr-30 Sep.
€ 19.20   2010*

CROTOY, LE *3B2* (1.5km N Rural) *50.22968, 1.64140*
Camping La Ferme de Tarteron, Route de Rue, 80550
Le Crotoy [03 22 27 06 75; fax 03 22 27 02 49; contact@
letarteron.fr; www.letarteron.fr] Fr A16 exit junc 24
onto D32, then D940 around Rue twd Le Crotoy. Pass D4 dir
St Firmin site on L. Med, hdg/mkd pitch, pt shd; wc; chem disp;
shwrs inc; el pnts (4-10A) €3.50-8; gas; shop; tradsmn; snacks;
bar; playgrnd; htd pool; sand beach 1.5km; many statics; quiet.
"Conv Marquenterre bird park & steam train fr Le Crotoy."
1 Apr-31 Oct. € 21.20   2011*

"We must tell The Club about that great site we found"

Get your site reports in by mid-August
and we'll do our best to get your updates
into the next edition of Caravan Europe.

CROTOY, LE *3B2* (3km N Rural/Coastal) *50.23905, 1.63182*
Kawan Club Camping Le Ridin, Mayocq, 80550 Le
Crotoy [03 22 27 03 22; fax 03 22 27 70 76; leridin@
baiedesommepleinair.com; www.campingleridin.com]
Fr N exit A16 junc 24 dir Rue & Le Crotoy; at rndabt on D940
on app to Le Crotoy take D4 (due W) sp St Firmin; take 2nd
rd to L, site sp. Or fr S exit A16 junc 23 onto D40/D940 to
Le Crotoy; at rndabt cont strt over onto D4; in 800m turn R;
site on R in 1km. NB Do not ent Le Crotoy town with c'van
Lge, hdg/mkd pitch, hdstg, unshd; htd wc; chem disp; mv
service pnt; baby facs; fam bthrm; shwrs inc; el pnts (4-10A)
€3-5.50; gas; lndtte (inc dryer); shop; supmkt 1km; tradsmn;
rest, snacks; bar; playgrnd; htd pool; paddling pool; sand
beach 1km; tennis 4km; cycle hire; fitness rm; games rm; golf
10km; wifi; entmnt; TV rm; 60% statics; dogs €2; poss cr;
Eng spkn; adv bkg; quiet except noise fr adj gravel pit/lorries;
ccard acc; red long stay/CKE/CCI. "Some sm, tight pitches bet
statics; narr site rds not suitable lge o'fits; helpful staff; clean
san facs, unisex low ssn; bird sanctuary at Marquenterre; Le
Crotoy interesting town; vg site." ♦ 31 Mar-6 Nov. € 30.00
(CChq acc)   2012*

See advertisement on next page

CROTOY, LE *3B2* (4km N Coastal) *50.24941, 1.61145* Camping Les Aubépines, 800 Rue de la Maye, St Firmin, 80550 Le Crotoy [03 22 27 01 34; fax 03 22 27 13 66; lesaubepines@baiedesommepleinair.com; www.baiede sommepleinair.com] Exit A16 junc 23 to Le Crotoy via D40 & D940; then foll sp St Firmin; site sp. Or exit A16 junc 24 onto D32 dir Rue; by-pass Rue but take D4 to St Firmin; after church look for site sp. Site on rd to beach on W of D4. Med, hdg/mkd pitch, pt shd; htd wc; chem disp; baby facs; shwrs inc; el pnts (3-10A) €3-8 (poss long lead req); gas; lndtte (inc dryer); sm shop & 4km; tradsmn; BBQ; playgrnd; htd pool; paddling pool; sand beach 1km; horseriding; cycle hire; games rm; internet; entmnt; 40% statics; dogs €2; phone; poss cr; Eng spkn; adv bkg; quiet; ccard acc; red low ssn; CKE/CCI. "Peaceful, popular, well-run site; tourers sited with statics; lovely pool; gd cycling & walking; check office opening hrs for early dep; Marquenterre ornithological park 3km; steam train 3km; excel." ♦ 1 Apr-6 Nov. € 21.50   2011*

See advertisement above

"I need an on-site restaurant"

We do our best to make sure site information is correct, but it is always best to check any must-have facilities are still available or will be open during your visit.

CROTOY, LE *3B2* (4km N Coastal) *50.24959, 1.61207* **Les 3 Sablières, 1850, Rue de la Maye, 80550 St. Firmin les Crotoy** [03 22 27 01 33; fax 03 22 27 10 06; contact@ camping-les-trois-sablieres.com; www.camping-les-trois-sablieres.com]** Fr Calais foll sp for RUE & then St Firmin Crotoy. Med, mkd pitch, hdstg; wc; chem disp; mv service pnt; baby facs; shwrs inc; el pnts (6A) €4.50; lndtte (inc dryer); shop; bar; BBQ; playgrnd; htd pool; fitness rm; sauna & solarium; games rm; TV; statics; dogs €2.10; ccard acc. "V nice site with clean facs; lovely atmosphere in gd location; cycle tracks start from campsite; would rec." € 24.00   2011*

See advertisement below

CROUY SUR COSSON see Muides sur Loire *4G2*

CROZANT *7A3* (S Rural) *46.38890, 1.61893* Camp Municipal Fontbonne, Le Bourg, 23160 Crozant [05 55 89 80 12; fax 05 55 89 83 80; mairie-crozant@wanadoo.fr] Fr A20 exit junc 20 onto D36 to Eguzon-Chantôme; turn R on D913 & after 11km turn L on D30 to Crozant. Site sp. Sm, mkd pitch, some hdstg, pt sl, pt shd; wc; shwrs inc; el pnts (6A) inc; lndry rm; shops, rest, snacks, bar 500m; BBQ; playgrnd; lake sw 7km; dogs €0.50; adv bkg; quiet; ccard not acc. "Attractive vill on Lake Chambon; rvside walk." 1 May-30 Sep. € 9.20   2010*

CROZON *2E2* (5km E Coastal) *48.24204, -4.42932* **Camping L'Aber, Tal-ar-Groas,50 Route de la Plage de l'Aber, 29160 Crozon [02 98 27 02 96 or 06 75 62 39 07 (mob); contact@ camping-aber.com; www.camping-aber.com]** On D887 turn S in Tal-ar-Groas foll camp sp to site in 1km on R. Med, mkd pitch, pt sl, terr, pt shd; wc; shwrs inc; el pnts (5A) €3.40; gas; lndtte; snacks; bar; htd pool; sand beach 1km; sailing; fishing; windsurfing; dogs €1.50; 50% statics; adv bkg; quiet.
♦ 1 Apr-1 Oct. € 24.15   2013*

CROZON *2E2* (3km SW Rural) *48.22138, -4.52285* **Camping Les Bruyères, Le Bouis, 29160 Crozon-Morgat [tel/fax 02 98 26 14 87; info@camping-bruyeres-crozon.com; www.camping-bruyeres-crozon.com]** Take D887 then D255 SW fr Crozon (sp Cap de la Chèvre). In 1.5km turn R & site on R in 700m. Lge, mkd pitch, pt shd; wc (mainly cont); baby facs; shwrs inc; el pnts (5A) €3; gas; lndtte; shop in ssn; playgrnd; sand beach 1.8km; dogs €1.50; Eng spkn; adv bkg; quiet.
"Conv beaches & mkt town." 1 Jun-15 Sep. € 16.80   2010*

CUBJAC *7C3* (1.5km S Rural) *45.2167, 0.9333* **Camping L'Ilot, 24640 Cubjac [05 53 05 39 79; fax 05 53 05 37 82; musitelli@wanadoo.fr; http://www.domainelafaurie. com/campingdelilot/]** Take D5 E fr Périgueux to Cubjac (21km). Fork R off D5 into vill. At x-rds in vill turn S & site on R in 1.5km. Sm, mkd pitch, pt shd; wc (some cont); baby facs; shwrs inc; el pnts (5A) €3; lndtte; shop adj; rest, snacks; bar; BBQ; playgrnd; pool 4km; fishing; canoes; tennis adj; games area; wifi; entmnt; dogs free; adv bkg. ♦ 1 Apr-30 Sep.
€ 12.00   2008*

CUCURON see Cadenet *10E3*

CUERS *10F3* (6km W Rural) *43.23243, 6.00645* **Camping Les Tomasses, 83210 Belgentier [04 94 48 92 70; fax 04 94 48 94 73; camping.tomasses@wanadoo.fr; www. camping-tomasses.fr]** First rte rec for small o'fits only: Exit A8 junc 34 St Maximin onto N7; after Tourves take D205 then D5/ D554 sp Solliès-Pont; after Belgentier in 1.5km turn R at yellow sp, site in 200m on L. Or exit A57 at junc 7 onto D554 dir Belgentier; approx 1.5km bef vill; sp on L. Med, hdg/mkd pitch, pt shd; wc (mainly cont); chem disp (wc); shwrs inc; el pnts (6A) €4; gas; lndtte; shop; rest, snacks; bar; BBQ; playgrnd; pool; tennis; entmnt; 10% statics; dogs €2.20; phone; bus 300m; adv bkg; quiet; red low ssn; CKE/CCI. "Pretty CL-type site; friendly management; twin-axles welcome; acces poss diff lge o'fits" ♦ ltd 1 Apr-15 Sep. € 20.00   2011*

CUISEAUX *9A2* (5km W Rural) *46.49570, 5.32662* **Camping Le Domaine de Louvarel, 71480 Champagnat [03 85 76 62 71; info@louvarel.com; www.louvarel.com]** Exit A39 junc 9 dir Cuiseaux; foll sp 'Base de Loisirs de Louvarel'. Or fr D1083 exit Champagnat & foll sp to site on lakeside. Med, hdg/mkd, terr, pt shd; htd wc; chem disp; mv service pnt; baby facs; fam bthrm; shwrs inc; el pnts (10A) incl; lndtte (inc dryer); tradsmn; rest, snacks; bar; BBQ; playgrnd; htd pool; paddling pool; lake sw adj, sand beach; fishing; boating; games area; cycle hire; wifi; 7% statics; dogs €2; phone; o'night area for m'vans; Eng spkn; adv bkg; quiet; red low ssn; CKE/CCI. "Excel, clean site; helpful manager; excel, immac san facs; nice rest & bar; gd walking; free use of canoes." ♦ 1 Apr-30 Sep. € 26.20   2013*

CULOZ see Ruffieux *9B3*

CUVILLY *3C3* (1.5km N Rural) *49.56750, 2.70790* **Camping de Sorel, 24 Rue St Claude, 60490 Orvillers-Sorel [03 44 85 02 74; fax 03 44 42 11 65; contact@aestiva.fr; www.camping-sorel.com]** Exit A1/E15 at junc 12 (Roye) S'bound or 11 (Ressons) N'bound. Site on E of D1017. Med, mkd pitch, pt shd; wc; chem disp; mv service pnt; baby facs; shwrs inc; el pnts (10A) €3; lndtte; shop; tradsmn; rest, snacks; bar; BBQ; playgrnd; rv fishing 10km; games area; wifi; TV rm; 50% statics; poss cr; quiet; red low ssn. "Pleasant situation; conv NH A1 & Calais; friendly staff; gd facs; rec early arr in ssn; busy at w/end; 30 mins Parc Astérix." ♦
2 Feb-15 Dec. € 15.00 (CChq acc)   2011*

DAGLAN *7D3* (3km Rural) *44.76762, 1.17590* **Camping Le Moulin de Paulhiac, 24250 Daglan [05 53 28 20 88; fax 05 53 29 33 45; info@moulin-de-paulhiac.com; www. moulin-de-paulhiac.com]** D57 SW fr Sarlat, across rv into St Cybranet & site in 2km. Fr Souillac W on D703 alongside Rv Dordogne; x-ing rv onto D46 (nr Domme) & D50, to site. Med, hdg/mkd pitch, shd; wc (some cont); chem disp; mv service pnt; shwrs; el pnts (6-10A) €3.70-4.40; gas; lndtte; shop; rest, snacks; bar; playgrnd; 4 htd pools; waterslide; TV rm; entmnt; shgl beach/rv adj with canoeing/fishing; 20% statics; dogs €1.90; poss cr; Eng spkn; adv bkg; quiet with some rd noise; red low ssn; ccard acc; CKE/CCI. "Pretty site; friendly, helpful staff; vg fruit/veg mkt Sun in vill; highly rec." ♦ ltd
15 May-16 Sep. € 25.10   2011*

DALLET see Pont du château

DAMBACH *5D3* (500m E Rural) *48.32271, 7.44320* **Aire Naturelle Municipal du Hohenfels, Rue du Stade, 67110 Dambach [03 88 09 24 08 or 03 88 09 26 68; fax 03 88 09 21 81]** Fr N on D35 turn S onto D853, site sp. Med, pt sl, terr, pt shd; wc; chem disp; shwrs inc; el pnts (6A) €3; quiet. "Delightfully peaceful setting; lovely area; warden calls 0900-0930, site yourself; access poss diff lge o'fits; walk fr site to Maginot Line relics." 1 Apr-31 Oct. € 10.30   2008*

DAMBACH LA VILLE see Sélestat *6E3*

DAMGAN see Muzillac *2G3*

DAMPIERRE SUR BOUTONNE *7A2* (Rural) *46.06642, -0.41459* **Camp Municipal, 17470 Dampierre-sur-Boutonne [05 46 24 02 36 (Mairie); fax 05 46 33 95 49; dampierre-sur-boutonne@mairie17.com; www.aulnaytourisme.com]** S fr Niort on D150 twds St Jean-d'Angély; in vill of Tout-y-Faut turn E on D115 sp Dampierre; turn N in vill on D127 twds Rv Boutonne, site behind vill hall; well sp. Sm, hdg pitch, shd; wc (some cont); shwrs inc; el pnts (6A) €2; shop, rest, snacks, bar 500m; rv fishing; dogs €0.80; quiet. "Clean site; san facs outside camp boundary & wc's open to public; poss noisy, local youths congregate nrby; rec sh stay/NH only." 30 Apr-30 Sep.
€ 7.90   2009*

DAMVIX see Maillezais *7A2*

DANGE ST ROMAIN *4H2* (3km N Rural) *46.96944, 0.60399*
**Camp Municipal, 8 Rue des Buxières, 86220 Les Ormes
[05 49 85 61 30 (Mairie); fax 05 49 85 66 17; les-ormes@
cg86.fr; www.tourisme-vienne.com]** Turn W off D910 in
cent Les Ormes onto D1a sp Vellèches & Marigny-Marmande,
foll site sp to site on rv. Sm, mkd pitch, pt sl, pt shd; wc; chem
disp (wc); shwrs inc; el pnts (6A) inc; lndtte; shop; rest & bar
800m; playgrnd; tennis 100m; a few statics; dogs €1.20; quiet,
but some rlwy noise; adv bkg; dogs; CKE/CCI. "Lovely, quiet
setting on rv bank; helpful warden; clean basic modern san
facs; poss itinerants; quiet vill; chateau in walking dist; gd NH."
1 Apr-30 Sep. € 12.00   2011*

DAON see Château Gontier *4F1*

DARBRES *9D2* (10km NE) *44.63370, 4.50740* **Camping
Les Charmilles, Le Clapas, 07170 Darbres, Ardèche [tel/
fax 04 75 88 56 27; info@campinglescharmilles.fr; www.
campinglescharmilles.fr]** E fr Aubenas on D259; turn L on
D224 at Lussas; fork R after Darbres & site in 2km on L sp.
Steep app. Med, terr, pt shd; wc; chem disp; shwrs inc; el pnts
(5-10A) inc; rest, snacks; shop; 2 pools; dog €2; adv bkg; few
statics; Eng spkn; some noise to 2300; "free tow if in trouble
on app" ♦ 27 Aprr-30 Sep. € 44.50   2013*

DARDILLY see Lyon *9B2*

⊞ **DAX** *8E1* (3.5km NE Urban) *43.74707, -0.99539*
**Camping Les Jardins de l'Adour, 848 Rue de Pouy,
40990 St Vincent-de-Paul [tel/fax 05 58 89 99 60 or
06 03 03 09 77 (mob); info@camping-jardinsdeladour.fr;
www.camping-jardinsdeladour.fr]** NE on D824 fr Dax twd
Mont-de-Marsan on dual c'way, take exit to St Vincent-de-Paul
at rndabt; site in 200m on L, sp. Med, hdg/mkd pitch, shd;
wc; chem disp; mv service pnt; shwrs inc; el pnts (6A) €3; gas;
lndtte; shop 1km & 5km; rest, snacks; pool; sand beach 30km;
50% statics; dogs €1.50; phone; barrier clsd 2230-0730; Eng
spkn; adv bkg; CKE/CCI. "Pretty, well-kept site; friendly, helpful
owners; clean san facs; excel." ♦ € 14.00   2008*

DAX *8E1* (1.5km W Rural) *43.71189, -1.07304* **Camping
Les Chênes, Allée du Bois de Boulogne, 40100 Dax
[05 58 90 05 53; fax 05 58 90 42 43; camping-chenes@
orange.fr; www.camping-les-chenes.fr]** Fr D824 to Dax, foll
sp Bois de Boulogne, cross rlwy bdge & rv bdge & foll camp sp
on rv bank. Well sp. Lge, mkd pitch, shd; htd wc (cont); chem
disp; mv service pnt; some serviced pitches; shwrs inc; el pnts
(5A) inc; gas; lndtte (inc dryer); shop; tradsmn; rest adj; snacks;
bar; playgrnd; pool; beach 20km; wifi; TV rm; cycle hire; many
statics; dogs €1.50; poss cr; Eng spkn; adv bkg; ccard acc; red
low ssn; CKE/CCI. "Excel position; gd, clean san facs; easy walk
along rv into town; poss noise fr school adj; conv thermal baths
at Dax." ♦ 20 Mar-6 Nov. € 18.10   2010*

DAX *8E1* (6km W Rural) *43.72680, -1.12302* **Camping
L'Etang d'Ardy, Route de Bayonne, 40990 St Paul-lès-Dax
[05 58 97 57 74; info@etangardy.com; www.etangardy.
com]** Fr E on D824 dir Dax; turn R onto D16 dir Magescq; then
L sp Ardy; foll camping sp. Fr W leave D824 sp La Pince/Dax/
Magescq; at rndabt U-turn onto D824 going E; take 1st exit
& foll site sp. Med, hdg pitch, shd; wc; chem disp; serviced
pitches; shwrs inc; el pnts (5A) inc; lndtte (inc dryer); shops;
tradsmn; BBQ; playgrnd; pool; paddling pool; lake fishing;
wifi; 30% statics; dogs €1.60; adv bkg; quiet; red long stay.
"Friendly site." ♦ 3 Apr-22 Oct. € 20.50   2010*

DAX *8E1* (9km W Rural) *43.68206, -1.14974* **Camping Lou
Bascou, 40180 Rivière-Saas-et-Gourby [05 58 97 57 29;
fax 05 58 97 59 52; loubascou@orange.fr; www.
campingloubascou.fr]** Leave N10 at junc 9 for D824 twd
Dax. In 3.5km turn R onto D13 sp Rivière-Saas-et-Gourby. Well
sp fr D824. Beware speed humps in Rivière vill. Med, hdg/mkd
pitch, pt shd; htd wc; chem disp; mv service pnt; shwrs inc; el
pnts (6-10A) €3-5; lndtte; shop 300m; tradsmn; snacks; bar;
BBQ; playgrnd; pool 9km; sand beach 25km; tennis; entmnt;
50% statics in sep area; dogs €1.50; Eng spkn; adv bkg; red long
stay/low ssn. "Quiet, friendly site; excel, clean facs; thermal facs
in Dax; nrby wetlands wildlife inc storks worth seeing; vg NH." ♦
1 Apr-31 Oct. € 16.00   2009*

⊞ **DAX** *8E1* (11km W Rural) *43.68706, -1.14687* **FFCC
Camping à la Ferme Bertranborde (Lafitte), 975 Route des
Clarions, 40180 Rivière-Saas-et-Gourby [05 58 97 58 39;
bertranborde@orange.fr]** Turn S off D824 5km W of Dax
onto D113, sp Angoumé; at x-rd in 2km turn R (by water
tower); then immed L; site on R in 100m, well sp. Or fr N10/
A63, exit junc 9 onto D824 dir Dax; in 5km turn R onto D113,
then as bef. Sm, pt shd, pt sl; wc (own san); chem disp; mv
service pnt; shwrs inc; el pnts (4-10A) €2.50-4; lndtte; ice;
shops 3km; BBQ; playgrnd; rv sw 7km; dogs €0.50; poss cr;
Eng spkn; quiet; adv bkg; CKE/CCI. "Peaceful CL-type site;
beautiful garden; friendly, helpful owners; meals on request;
min 2 nights high ssn; poss itinerants festival time; excel."
€ 9.50   2009*

DAX *8E1* (3km NW Rural) *43.72020, -1.09365* **FFCC Camping
Les Pins du Soleil, Route des Minières, La Pince, 40990
St Paul-les-Dax [05 58 91 37 91; fax 05 58 91 00 24; info@
pinsoleil.com; www.pinsoleil.com]** Exit N10 junc 11 sp Dax
onto D16. Cross D824 & turn R onto D459 S. Cross rndabt &
cont on D459, Route des Minières. Site sp in pine forest. Med,
hdg/mkd pitch, pt sl, pt shd; htd wc, chem disp; mv service
pnt; serviced pitches; baby facs; shwrs inc; el pnts (5A) €2; gas;
lndtte (inc dryer); shop; tradsmn; rest 1km; snacks; bar; BBQ;
playgrnd; pool; paddling pool; tennis 2km; cycle hire; games
area; wifi; entmnt; TV rm; 25% statics; dogs €2; phone; Eng
spkn; some rd noise; red long stay/low ssn; ccard acc. "Nice,
quiet site (low ssn); various pitch sizes, some spacious; soft,
sandy soil poss problem when wet; helpful, friendly staff; excel
pool; spa 2km; conv Pyrenees & Biarritz; vg." ♦ 1 Apr-6 Nov.
€ 24.00 (CChq acc)   2010*

DAX *8E1* (12km NW Rural) *43.82364, -1.15103* **FFCC**
Camping Aire Naturelle Le Toy (Fabas), 1284 Chemin de Carroués, 40990 Herm [05 58 91 55 16; www.camping-du-toy.com] Exit N10 junc 11 at Magescq; foll sps for cent vill & then Herm on D150; at Herm x-rds by church turn L onto rd to Castets. Site 1km on R. Sm, hdg/mkd pitch, shd; wc; shwrs inc; el pnts (4-10A) €3-5; shops 1km; lndtte; playgrnd; sand beach 20 mins; games area; trampolines; dogs €1.50; Eng spkn; quiet. "Pleasant woodland site." Easter-31 Oct. € 12.00   2011*

"Satellite navigation makes touring much easier"

Remember most sat navs don't know if you're towing or in a larger vehicle – always use yours alongside maps and site directions.

DEAUVILLE *3D1* (2km NE Rural) *49.34946, 0.11172*
Camping des Haras, Chemin du Calvaire, 14800 Touques [02 31 88 44 84; fax 02 31 88 97 08; contact@camping-des-haras.com; www.camping-des-haras.com] N on D677 Pont l'Evêque-Deauville rd, ignore 1st slip rd sp Touques (too narr, vans prohibited); stay on by-pass & turn R at traff lts by g'ge sp Trouville. Turn R again at next rndabt sp Touques then L on D62; fork L to site after church. Also sp fr D513 Deauville-Caen rd. Lge, hdg/mkd pitch, pt sl, pt shd; wc; own san; chem disp; shwrs; el pnts (10A) €4.12; gas; lndtte; shop; rest, snacks; bar; playgrnd; pool 2km; sand beach 2km; entmnt; 60% statics; dogs €1.55; poss cr; adv bkg; red low ssn. "Conv Honfleur & WW2 sites; some pitches poss diff lge o'fits; low ssn phone ahead; office clsd fr 1830 low ssn & Sun; c'vans sited nr playgrnd." ♦ 1 Mar-30 Nov. € 16.35   2008*

DEAUVILLE *3D1* (3km S Urban) *49.32903, 0.08593* **Camping La Vallée de Deauville, Ave de la Vallée, 14800 St Arnoult [02 31 88 58 17; fax 02 31 88 11 57; www.camping-deauville.com]** Fr Deauville take D27 dir Caen, turn R onto D278 to St Arnoult, foll site sp. Lge, hdg/mkd pitch, hdstg, pt shd; htd wc (some cont); baby facs; shwrs inc; el pnts (10A) €4; gas; lndtte; shop; tradsmn; rest, snacks; bar; playgrnd; htd pool; waterslide; sand beach 4km; fishing lake; games rm; wifi; entmnt; 80% statics; dogs €4; phone; Eng spkn; some rlwy noise; red low ssn; ccard acc; CKE/CCI. "Easy access to beaches & resorts; conv Le Havre using Pont de Normandie; lake walks & activities on site; excel san facs." ♦ 1 Apr-2 Nov. € 30.00   2011*

DECAZEVILLE *7D4* (9km NE Rural) *44.62920, 2.32030* **Camping La Plaine, Le Bourg, 12300 St Parthem [tel/fax 05 65 64 05 24 or 05 65 43 03 99; infos@camping-laplaine.fr; www.camping-laplaine.fr]** N fr Decazeville on D963; in 6km turn R onto D42 to St Parthem. Site 1km past vill on R. Med, hdg/mkd pitch, pt shd; wc; chem disp; shwrs inc; el pnts (6A) inc; lndtte; tradsmn; rest, snacks; bar; BBQ; playgrnd; pool; tennis; 5% statics; dogs €1; phone; poss cr; Eng spkn; adv bkg; quiet; CKE/CCI. "Idyllic setting on banks of Rv Lot; friendly Dutch owners; excel walking; vg." ♦ Mid Apr-30 Sep. € 12.50   2008*

⊞ **DECAZEVILLE** *7D4* (3km NW Rural) *44.58819, 2.22145* **FFCC Camping Le Roquelongue, 12300 Boisse-Penchot [tel/fax 05 65 63 39 67; info@camping-roquelongue.com; www.camping-roquelongue.com]** Fr D963 N fr Decazeville turn W onto D140 & D42 to Boisse-Penchot. Rte via D21 not rec (steep hill & acute turn). Site mid-way bet Boisse-Penchot & Livinhac-le-Haut on D42. Med, hdg/mkd pitch, pt shd; wc; chem disp; shwrs inc; el pnts (6-10A) 3.60-4.30; gas; lndtte; shop; tradsmn; supmkt 5km; snacks; bar; playgrnd; htd pool; fishing; canoeing; tennis; cycle hire; entmnt; internet; 10% statics; dogs free; phone; adv bkg; quiet; CKE/CCI. "Direct access Rv Lot; pitches gd size; san facs clean; no twin-axles; excel base for Lot Valley." ♦ ltd € 15.80   2009*

DECIZE *4H4* (500m NE Urban) *46.83487, 3.45552*
Camping des Halles, Allée Marcel Merle, 58300 Decize [03 86 25 14 05 or 03 86 25 03 23 (Mairie); fax 03 86 77 11 48; aquadis1@wanadoo.fr; www.des-vacances-vertes.com or www.aquadis-loisirs.com] Fr Nevers take D981 to Decize, look for sp for 'Stade Nautique Camping'. Lge, mkd pitch, pt shd; wc (some cont); snacks; shwrs inc; el pnts (6A) €2.30 (poss rev pol); gas; shop; rv & sand beach adj; sat TV; dogs €1.60; poss cr; some Eng spkn; quiet; ccard acc; CKE/CCI. "Site on banks of Rv Loire; lge pitches, some by rv; helpful staff; san facs clean but need update; no twin-axles; poss diff access pitches due trees; shady, flat walk into town; mkt Fri; town very interesting ,15 min walk" ♦ 1 May-15 Oct. € 17.70   2013*

DELLE *6G3* (5km N Rural) *47.53220, 7.01719* **Camp Municipal du Pâquis, Rue des Chênes, 90100 Joncherey [03 84 56 32 63; fax 03 84 56 27 66; www.joncherey.fr]** Exit A75 junc 11 Sevenans onto N1019 S dir Delle. Turn L onto D3 N dir Boron, site on R in approx 3km. Med, sl, pt shd; wc; chem disp; shwrs inc; el pnts (6A) €3.50; playgrnd; lake fishing adj; 45% statics; dogs €1.25; quiet; CKE/CCI. "Pleasant, spacious site; basic san facs." 1 Apr-31 Oct. € 10.50   2008*

DENNEVILLE PLAGE see Barneville Carteret *1C4*

DESCARTES *4H2* (S Urban) *46.97152, 0.69586* **Camp Municipal La Grosse Motte, Allée Léo Lagrange, 37160 Descartes [02 47 59 85 90 or 02 47 92 42 20; fax 02 47 59 72 20; www.ville-descartes.fr]** Fr S on D750 turn L just bef Descartes sp, cross rlwy line & in 500m turn L into site. Fr N turn R after Descartes sp. V narr turn into site due stone house walls. Sm, hdg pitch, pt sl, shd; wc (some cont); baby facs; shwrs inc; shops in town; el pnts (10A) €2.10 (poss rev pol); pool adj; playgrnd; tennis, mini-golf nr; boating on rv; dogs €1; adv bkg; quiet; ccard not acc; CKE/CCI. "Beautiful site; public gardens adj; spacious pitches; friendly staff; clean facs; popular with school parties; gd NH." 1 Jun-30 Sep. € 6.75   2009*

DEUX CHAISES see Montmarault *9A1*

DEVILLAC see Villéreal *7D3*

⊞ **DEYME** *8F3* (500m NE Rural) *43.48672, 1.5322*
**Camping Les Violettes, Porte de Toulouse, 31450 Deyme
[05 61 81 72 07; fax 05 61 27 17 31; campinglesviolettes@
wanadoo.fr]** SE fr Toulouse to Carcassonne on N113, sp
on L, 12km fr Toulouse (after passing Deyme sp). Med, mkd
pitch, hdstg, pt shd; htd wc; mv service pnt; shwrs inc; el pnts
(6A) €4; lndtte; shop; rest, snacks; bar; BBQ; playgrnd; TV;
60% statics; dogs €0.70; poss cr; quiet but rd noise; CKE/CCI.
"Helpful, friendly staff; facs run down (Jun 2009); poss muddy
when wet; 800m fr Canal du Midi & 10km fr Space City; Park
& Ride 2.5km & metro to Toulouse." € 13.00   2012*

DIE *9D2* (N Urban) *44.75123, 5.36604* **Camp Municipal Le
Justin (formally de la Piscine), Rue de Chabestar, 26150
Die [tel/fax 04 75 22 14 77 or 04 75 22 06 19 (Mairie);
camping-municipal-die@wanadoo.fr]** Ent town fr W on
D93, fork R D751, sp Gap & 'rugby stade' (not football); foll sps
for Camp Municipal & piscine; site on S of rlwy line bef sw pool
'piscine'. Poss diff bdge for long o'fits. Med, pt sl, pt shd; wc
(some cont); chem disp; mv service pnt; shwrs inc; el pnts (10A)
€2.90; lndtte; shops, rest 500m; tradsmn; snacks; playgrnd; rv
sw adj; entmnt; dogs €1.50; Eng spkn; adv bkg; ccard acc; red
low ssn; CKE/CCI. "Site in beautiful setting in Drôme valley;
gd facs; poor security - vehicles use track thro site as short
cut; easy walk to Die - interesting town." 15 May-30 Sep.
€ 12.00   2008*

DIE *9D2* (300m N Rural) *44.75444, 5.37778* **FFCC Camping
La Riou-Merle, Route de Romeyer, 26150 Die [tel/fax
04 75 22 21 31; lerioumerle@gmail.com; www.camping-
lerioumerle.com]** Fr Gap on D93 heading twd Valence. Cont
on D93 twd town cent; R on D742 to Romeyer. Site on L in
200m. On D93 fr Crest foll sp round town cent onto D742.
Med, pt sl, pt shd; wc (some cont); chem disp; mv service pnt;
shwrs inc; el pnts (10A) €4.20; lndtte; shops in town; rest;
playgrnd; pool; fishing; wifi; 30% statics; dogs €2; Eng spkn;
quiet; red low ssn. "Clean site; friendly, helpful staff; gd san
facs; attractive town." 1 Apr-15 Oct. € 17.00   2011*

DIE *9D2* (2km NW Rural) *44.76250, 5.34674* **Camping
de Chamarges, Route de Crest, 26150 Die [tel/fax
04 75 22 14 13 or 04 75 22 06 77; campingchamarges@
orange.fr]** Foll D93 twd Valence, site on L by Rv Drôme. Med,
mkd pitch, pt shd; wc (some cont); chem disp; shwrs inc; el
pnts (3-6A) €2.90-3.60; gas; shop 1km; rest, snacks; bar; BBQ
(gas); playgrnd; pool; rv sw, fishing & canoeing adj; entmnt; TV;
wifi; dogs €1.60; phone; Eng spkn; rec adv bkg high ssn; quiet;
ccard acc; CKE/CCI. "Beautiful mountainous area; vg; friendly
owners" ♦ 1 Apr-13 Sep. € 12.10   2012*

⊞ **DIENNE** *7A3* (800m NE Rural) *46.44613, 0.56023* **Camping
Domaine de Dienné, 86410 Dienné [05 49 45 87 63;
fax 05 49 54 17 96; info@domaine-de-dienne.fr; www.
domaine-de-dienne.fr]** Fr Poitiers on N147/E62 S thro Fleuré
& in 2.5km turn R to Dienné. Foll site sp. Med, pt shd; wc;
sauna; shwrs; el pnts inc; lndtte; rest, snacks; playgrnd; 2 pools
(1 htd, covrd); fishing; horseriding; games area; statics; site clsd
1-17 Jan; adv bkg; quiet. € 43.00   2009*

DIENVILLE see Brienne Le Château *6E1*

DIEPPE *3C2* (4km S Urban) *49.90040, 1.07472* **Camping
Vitamin, 865 Chemin des Vertus, 76550 St Aubin-sur-Scie
[02 35 82 11 11; camping-vitamin@wanadoo.fr; www.
camping-vitamin.com]** Foll dir to Formule 1 & Hotel B&B.
Lge, hdg pitch, unshd; wc; chem disp; mv service pnt; shwrs
inc; el pnts (10A) inc; lndtte; shops 1km; bar; playgrnd; pool;
shgl beach 2km; adv bkg; many statics; dogs €1.50; quiet; red
low ssn; CKE/CCI. "Lovely, well-kept site; san facs immac; poss
boggy in wet; conv ferries; excel; auto barrier for early dep"
1 Apr-15 Oct. € 23.40   2012*

"There aren't many sites open at this time of year"

If you're travelling outside peak season
remember to call ahead to check site opening
dates – even if the entry says 'open all year'.

DIEPPE *3C2* (5km S Rural) *49.87063, 1.14426* **Camping
des 2 Rivières, 76880 Martigny [02 35 85 60 82; fax
02 35 85 95 16; www.camping-2-rivieres.com]** Martigny
vill on D154 S fr Dieppe. If appr fr Dieppe, ent is on L befr vill
sp. Med, pt shd; wc; el pnts €3.05; lndtte; shop; playgrnd;
covrd pool, watersports, mountain biking, horseriding &
Arques forest nrby; dogs €1.70; tax .55c pppn adv bkg; quiet.
"Attractive, spacious site by lge lake; access poss diff long o'fits
due parked vehicles; cycle paths; highly rec." 26 Mar-10 Oct.
€ 19.50   2013*

DIEPPE *3C2* (4km SW Rural) *49.89820, 1.05705* **Camping
La Source, 63 Rue des Tisserands, Petit-Appeville, 76550
Hautot-sur-Mer [02 35 84 27 04; fax 02 35 82 25 02;
info@camping-la-source.fr; www.camping-la-source.fr]**
Fr Dieppe ferry terminal foll sp Paris, take D925 W dir Fécamp.
In 2km at Petit Appeville turn L, site in 800m on rvside. NB 4m
bdge bef ent & narr rd to site - not suitable v lge o'fits. Med,
mkd pitch, pt shd; wc (some cont); chem disp; mv service pnt;
shwrs inc; el pnts (10A) €4.20; lndtte (inc dryer); shop 3km;
tradsmn; bar; playgrnd; htd pool; sand beach 3km; rv sw,
fishing & boating adj; games area; games rm; cycle hire; golf
4km; wifi; entmnt; TV rm; few statics; dogs €2.20; Eng spkn;
some rlwy & rd noise; adv bkg; quiet; ccard acc; red low ssn;
CKE/CCI. "Lovely, well-kept site in attractive setting; some lge
pitches; pleasant, helpful staff; vg, clean san facs; footpath to
Le Plessis vill; gd cycling; excel NH for ferry." ♦ 15 Mar-15 Oct.
€ 36.90 (CChq acc)   2013*

DIEPPE *3C2* (4km SW Rural) *49.90886, 1.04069* **Camping
Marqueval, 1210 Rue de la Mer, 76550 Pourville-sur-Mer
[02 35 82 66 46; fax 02 34 00 02 82; contact@camping
lemarqueval.com; www.campinglemarqueval.com]** Site
well sp fr D75. Lge, hdg/mkd pitch, pt shd; htd wc; chem disp;
mv service pnt; baby facs; shwrs; el pnts (6A) €2.50; lndtte
(inc dryer); shop; rest, snacks; bar; BBQ; playgrnd; htd pool;
paddling pool; spa; lake fishing; sand beach 1.2km; games
rm; wifi; entmnt; TV; some statics; dogs €2; Eng spkn; adv
bkg; quiet; ccard acc; red CKE/CCI. "Attractive, well-kept site;
gd facs; vg family site." ♦ 21 Mar-15 Oct. € 21.50   2012*

See advertisement opposite

280   ⊞Site open all year   Tell us about the sites you visit

FRANCE

CAMPING LE MARQUEVAL***

CAMPING LE MARQUEVAL*** – 1210 RUE DE LA MER – 76550 POURVILLE SUR MER
TEL: 0033 235 82 66 46 – FAX: 0033 235 84 55 03
CONTACT@CAMPINGLEMARQUEVAL.COM – WWW.CAMPINGLEMARQUEVAL.COM

DIEPPE *3C2* (6km SW Urban) *49.87297, 1.04497* **Camp Municipal du Colombier, 453 Rue Loucheur, 76550 Offranville [02 35 85 21 14; fax 02 35 04 52 67]** W fr Dieppe on D925, take L turn on D55 to Offranville, site clearly sp in vill to Parc du Colombier. NB Part of site cul-de-sac, explore on foot bef towing in. Med, hdg/mkd pitch, pt shd; wc; chem disp; shwrs inc; el pnts (10A) €2.20 (poss rev pol); gas; lndtte; shop & supmkt 500m; rest; shgl beach 5km; many statics; ltd Eng spkn; CKE/CCI. "Pleasant setting in ornamental gardens; vg clean site & facs; helpful staff; gates clsd 2200-0700; ask warden how to operate in his absence; conv ferries; easy walk to town; rec." ♦ 1 Apr-15 Oct. € 22.20   2013*

DIGNE LES BAINS *10E3* (1km NE Rural) *44.10011, 6.24915* **Camping Notre Dame du Bourg, Route de Barcelonnette, 04000 Digne-les-Bains [04 92 31 04 87; contact@campingdubourg-alpes-provence.com; www.campingdubourg-alpes-provence.com]** Fr rndabt by rv bdge take main st (Boulevard Gassendi) thro cent town, sp D900 La Javie, Barcelonnette. Camp sp on R. Med, unshd; wc; shwrs inc; el pnts (4A) inc; lndrtte; shops 1.5km; playgrnd; pool 1.5km; tennis; games area; entmnt; TV; 40% statics; dogs €1.50; quiet. "Views fr terr areas but poss diff access lge o'fits; recep manned ltd hrs; pleasant town; thermal baths; beautiful, fascinating area." ♦ 1 Apr-31 Oct. € 16.50   2009*

DIGNE LES BAINS *10E3* (1.5km SE Rural) *44.08646, 6.25028* **Camping Les Eaux Chaudes, 32 Ave des Thermes, 04000 Digne-les-Bains [04 92 32 31 04; fax 04 92 34 59 80; info@campingleseauxchaudes.com; www.campingleseauxchaudes.com]** Fr S foll N85 sp 'Centre Ville' over bdge keeping L to rndabt, turn 1st R sp Les Thermes (D20). Past Intermarché, site on R 1.6km after leaving town. Med, mkd pitch, pt shd; htd wc; chem disp; shwrs inc; el pnts (4-10A) €2-3.50 (poss rev pol); gas; lndtte; shops 1.5km; snacks; pool; lake sw 3km; games area; wifi; 50% statics; dogs €1.50; poss cr; adv bkg; quiet; red low ssn; CKE/CCI. "Pleasant site with plenty shd; vg san facs; gd pool; gd touring base; 500m fr thermal baths; National Geological Reserve in town cent; phone ahead low ssn to check open." ♦ ltd 1 Apr-31 Oct. € 31.50   2013*

DIGOIN *9A1* (500m W Urban) *46.47985, 3.96780* **Camping de la Chevrette, 41 Rue de la Chevrette, 71160 Digoin [03 85 53 11 49; fax 03 85 88 59 70; info@lachevrette.com; www.lachevrette.com]** Fr S exit N79/E62 at junc 24 sp Digoin-la-Grève D994, then on D979 cross bdge over Rv Loire. Take 1st L, sp campng/piscine. Sm, some hdg pitch, hdstg, pt sl, terr for tents, pt shd; htd wc (some cont); chem disp; mv service pnt; shwrs inc; el pnts (10A) inc; tradsmn; lndtte (inc dryer); shops 500m; sm rest & 500m; snacks high ssn; playgrnd; htd pool adj; fishing; wifi; dogs €1; poss cr w/ends; Eng spkn; adv bkg; red low ssn; CKE/CCI. "Pleasant, well-run site by rv; diff sized pitches, some lge; friendly, helpful owner; ltd facs low ssn; barrier clsd 2200-0700; pleasant walk by rv to town; lovely cycle rides along canals; gd dog walking along the river" ♦ 16 Mar-12Oct. € 24.70   2013*

See advertisement on pages 32 & 33

"That's changed – Should I let The Club know?"

If you find something on site that's different from the site entry, fill in a report and let us know. See www.caravanclub.co.uk/europereport.

DIJON *6G1* (2km W Urban) *47.32127, 5.01108* **Camping du Lac Kir, 3 Blvd du Chanoine Kir, 21000 Dijon [tel/fax 03 80 30 54 01; campingdijon@wanadoo.fr / reservation@camping-du-lac-dijon.com; www.camping-du-lac-dijon.com]** Site situated nr N5, Lac Kir. Fr Dijon ring rd take N5 exit (W) sp A38 twd Paris. At traff lts L sp A31, site immed on R under 3m high bdge. Do not tow thro town cent. Med, mkd pitch, pt hdstg, pt shd; wc; chem disp; shwrs inc; el pnts (10A) inc; (poss rev pol, poss long lead req); gas; supmkt nr; tradsmn; sw lake 1km; fishing, sw & boating; dogs €2.vaccinated on lead; bus adj; poss cr; Eng spkn; quiet but some rd noise; ccard acc; red low ssn; CKE/CCI. "Site a bit unkempt (2012/13); rvside path to town; gd security; poss flooding." 30 Mar-13 Oct. € 22.30   2013*

DINAN *2E3* (3km N Rural) *48.48903, -2.00855*
**Camping Beauséjour (formaly municipal), La Hisse,
22100 St Samson-sur-Rance [02 96 39 53 27 or
02 96 39 16 05 (Mairie); fax 02 96 87 94 12; beausejour-
stsamson@orange.fr; www.beausejour-camping.com]**
Fr Dinan take N176/D766 N twd Dinard. In 3km turn R onto
D12 dir Taden then foll sp thro Plouer-sur-Rance to La Hisse;
site sp. Fr N exit N176/E401 dir Plouer-sur-Rance, then foll sp
La Hisse. Med, hdg/mkd pitch, pt sl, pt shd; wc; chem disp; mv
service pnt; baby facs; shwrs inc; el pnts (10A) €3.45 (poss rev
pol); lndtte; sm shop; supmkt 5km; tradsmn; rest, snacks; bar;
playgrnd; htd pool; tennis; games area; sailing; wifi; 40% statics;
dogs €2.05; phone; poss cr; Eng spkn; adv bkg; quiet; red
low ssn/long stay; CC acc; CKE/CCI. "Pleasant, well-kept site;
helpful, friendly staff; gd pool; quiet & spacious Jun & Sep; no
twin-axles; excel rv walks; excel well maintained site; footpath
down to Rance and riverside walks"   ♦ ltd 1 Jun-30 Sep.
€ 14.50   2013*

> "I like to fill in the reports
> as I travel from site to site"
> You'll find report forms at the back of
> this guide, or you can fill them in online
> at www.caravaclub.co.uk/europereport.

DINAN *2E3* (3km NE Rural) *48.47138, -2.02277* **Camp
International de la Hallerais, 4 rue de la Robardais,
22100 Taden [02 96 39 15 93 or 02 96 87 63 50 (Mairie);
fax 02 96 39 94 64; camping.la.hallerais@wanadoo.fr;
www.camping-lahallerais.com]** Fr Dinan take N176/D766 N
twd Dinard. In 3km turn R onto D12 to Taden. Foll La Hallerais
& Taden sp to site. Fr N176 take exit onto D166 dir Taden; turn
onto D766 dir Taden, then L onto D12A sp Taden & Camping.
At rndabt on ent Taden take 1st exit onto D12 sp Dinan; site rd is
500m on L. Do not ent Dinan. Site adj Rv Rance. Lge, mkd pitch,
terr, pt shd; wc; chem disp; mv service pnt; serviced pitches; shwrs
inc; el pnts (6A) inc (rev pol); gas; lndtte; shop adj; tradsmn; snacks
(high ssn); rest & bar adj; BBQ; playgrnd; htd pool; paddling pool;
shgl beach 10km; tennis; fishing; horseriding 500m; wifi; games/
TV rm; many statics (sep area); dogs free; no c'vans/m'vans over
9m (check in adv rec); storage facs; Eng spkn; adv bkg; quiet;
ccard acc; red low ssn. "Lovely site; excel, excel, clean san facs;
vg pool; phone ahead if arr late at night low ssn; ltd office hours
low ssn - report to bar; sh walk to Taden; rvside walk to Dinan
medieval town; rv trips; gd walking, cycling; mkt Thur am, Fri eve;
rec"   ♦ 15 Mar-11 Nov. € 27.05 SBS - B01   2013*

DINAN *2E3* (10km NE Coastal) *48.52466, -1.96617* **Camping
Ville Ger, 22690 Pleudihen-sur-Rance [02 96 83 33 88;
reservation@campingdelavilleger.fr; www.
campingdelavilleger.fr]** Fr Dinan take D675/D676 in dir Dol
de Bretagne; turn L on D29 after 6km; site sp after 4km on L.
Sm, mkd pitch; pt shd; wc (cont); rec own san high ssn; shwrs
€1; el pnts (3-10A) €2.30-4.80; lndtte; shops 1.5km; rest; bar;
playgrnd; dogs €1; poss cr; adv bkg ess high ssn; quiet; CKE/CCI.
"Lovely area; close to rv; gd for dog-walking." 1 Apr-15 Oct.
€ 9.30   2011*

DINAN *2E3* (200m S Urban) *48.44743, -2.04631* **Camp
Municipal Châteaubriand, 103 Rue Châteaubriand,
22100 Dinan [02 96 39 11 96 or 02 96 39 22 43 (LS); fax
02 96 87 08 40; campingmunicipaldinan@wanadoo.fr;
http://www.brittanytourism.com/accommodation/
campsites/camping-municipal-chateaubriand]** Fr N176 (E
or W) take slip rd for Dinan cent; at lge rndbt in cent take 2nd
R; down hill to site on L (500m). Sm, mkd pitch, pt sl, pt shd;
wc; chem disp; mv service pnt; shwrs inc; el pnts (6A) €2.70;
gas 500m; lndry rm; shop, rest, snacks 500m; bar adj; BBQ;
sand beach 18km; games area; dogs €1.50; phone; poss cr;
Eng spkn; adv bkg; daytime rd noise; ccard not acc; CKE/CCI.
"Pleasant, helpful staff; high kerb onto pitches; poss market
traders; opening dates vary each year; check time when barrier
locked, espec low ssn; gd cent for Rance valley, St Malo &
coast." 01 Jun- 30 Sep. € 11.35   2013*

DINARD *2E3* (1.5m W Coastal) *48.6309, -2.08413*
**Camping La Touesse, 171 Rue de la Ville Gehan,
La Fourberie, 35800 St Lunaire [02 99 46 61 13; fax
02 99 16 02 58; camping.la.touesse@wanadoo.fr; www.
campinglatouesse.com]** Exit Dinard on St Lunaire coast rd
D786, site sp. Med, mkd pitch, pt shd; wc; mv service pnt;
baby facs; shwrs inc; el pnts (5-10A) €3.30-3.70; lndtte;
shop; snacks; bar; playgrnd; sand beach 300m; tennis 1.5km;
golf 2km; entmnt; TV rm; dog €1.50; adv bkg (dep); quiet,
some late night noise; red low ssn; CKE/CCI. "Vg well-kept
site; gd beach & rocks nr; friendly recep."   ♦ 1 Apr-30 Sep.
€ 21.80   2011*

DINARD *2E3* (1km W Coastal) *48.63486, -2.07928* **Camping
Le Port Blanc, Rue de Sergent Boulanger, 35800 Dinard
[02 99 46 10 74; fax 02 99 16 90 91; info@camping-port-
blanc.com; www.camping-port-blanc.com]** Fr Dinard foll sp
to St Lunaire on D786 for 1.5km. Turn R at traff lts by football
ground to site. Lge, mkd pitch, pt sl, terr, pt shd; wc (some
cont); chem disp; child/baby facs; shwrs inc; el pnts (10A)
€3.95; lndtte; sm shop; supmkt 800m; rest 500m; snacks;
bar; playgrnd; sand beach adj; 40% statics; dogs €1.90;
phone; bus; poss cr; adv bkg; quiet at night; ccard acc; CKE/
CCI. "Overlooks sand beach; gd san facs."   ♦ 1 Apr-30 Sep.
€ 19.00   2009*

DINARD *2E3* (4km W Coastal) *48.63406, -2.12039*
**Camping Longchamp, Blvd de St Cast, 35800 St Lunaire
[02 99 46 33 98; fax 02 99 46 02 71; contact@camping-
longchamp.com; www.camping-longchamp.com]**
Fr St Malo on D168 turn R sp St Lunaire, in 1km turn R at g'ge
into St Lunaire, site sp to W of vill on D786 dir St Briac. Lge,
hdg/mkd pitch, pt shd; wc; chem disp; mv service pnt; baby
facs; shwrs inc; el pnts (4-10A) €3.40-4.20; gas; lndtte; shop;
tradsmn; rest, snacks; bar; BBQ; playgrnd; sand beach 300m;
30% statics; dogs €2; phone adj; bus 500m; Eng spkn; adv
bkg rec; quiet; red low ssn. "Excel, well-run site; clean facs;
friendly, helpful staff; clean beach 300m; conv Brittany Ferries
at St Malo; Site under new ownership, much improved (2013);
heated pool; friendly quiet site nr beautiful seaside town"
♦ ltd 1Apr-30 Sep. € 34.70   2013*

See advertisement opposite

DIOU see Dompierre sur Besbre *9A1*

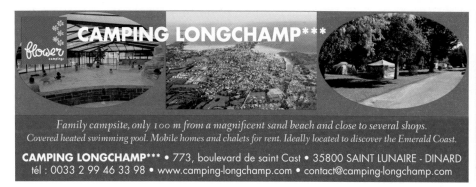

FRANCE

DISNEYLAND PARIS see Meaux _3D3_

DISSAY see Jaunay Clan _4H1_

DIVONNE LES BAINS _9A3_ (3km N Rural) _46.37487, 6.12143_
Camping Le Fleutron, Quartier Villard, 01220 Divonne-les-Bains [04 50 20 01 95 or 04 42 20 47 25 (LS); fax 04 50 20 00 35; info@homair.com; www.homair.com] Exit E62 dir Divonne-les-Bains approx 12km N of Geneva. Fr town on D984, foll sp to site. Lge, hdg/mkd pitch, sl, terr, shd; htd wc; shwrs inc; chem disp; el pnts (4A) €5; gas; lndtte; shop, snacks & rest in ssn; bar; supmkts 3km; lake sw 3km; htd pool; paddling pool; lake sw 3km; tennis; games area; entmnt in ssn; TV rm; 50% statics; dogs €5; Eng spkn; adv bkg; quiet; ccard acc; red low ssn; CKE/CCI. "Helpful owner; levellers req; Lake Geneva 8km." 4 Apr-18 Oct. € 26.00   2009*

DOL DE BRETAGNE _2E4_ (6km N Coastal) _48.60290, -1.77241_
Camp Municipal L'Abri des Flots, 35960 Le Vivier-sur-Mer [02 99 48 91 57; fax 02 99 48 98 43; campinglabridesflots@orange.fr; www.pays-de-dol.com] Site ent off D155/D797 (coast rd) in Le Vivier-sur-Mer. On sea front at E end of town, ent almost opp Mairie, sp. Med, mkd pitch, pt shd; wc; mv service pnt; shwrs; el pnts (6A) inc (long lead poss req); lndtte; sm shop & in vill; tradsmn; dogs €1; poss cr; no adv bkg; noise fr adj port; Eng spkn; CKE/CCI. "Clean site in vill cent & on sea front; resident warden; friendly; muddy beach not suitable for sw; gd NH to see mussel/oyster beds; tours fr museum nrby." 1 Apr-15 Oct. € 15.60   2010*

DOL DE BRETAGNE _2E4_ (7km NE Coastal) _48.60052, -1.71182_ **Camping de l'Aumône, 35120 Cherrueix [02 99 48 84 82 or 06 48 64 60 16 (mob); laumone@orange.fr; www.camping-de-laumone.fr]** Exit D797 Pontorson-Cancale rd S onto D82, opp rd leading into vill of Cherrueix. Site in 100m. Med, unshd; wc; chem disp; mv service pnt; baby facs; shwrs inc; el pnts (10A) €3.50; gas; lndtte (inc dryer); shops 300m; snacks; bar; BBQ; playgrnd; muddy beach 1km (not suitable for sw); sand yachting nrby; cycle hire; internet; 5% statics; dogs free; Eng spkn; adv bkg rec high ssn; noise fr adj rd daytime; red low ssn/CKE/CCI. "Friendly; sm chateau; gd sized pitches; modern san facs; vg; pleasant friendly owners" 22 Apr-14 Nov. € 13.00   2013*

DOL DE BRETAGNE _2E4_ (4km E Rural) _48.54941, -1.68386_ **FFCC Camping du Vieux Chêne, Le Motais, 35120 Baguer-Pican [02 99 48 09 55; vieux.chene@wanadoo.fr; www.camping-vieuxchene.fr]** Leave N176 E of Dol on slip rd sp Baguer-Pican. At traff lts turn L thro vill, site on R of D576 at far end vill adj lake. Lge, hdg/mkd pitch, pt sl, pt shd; wc; chem disp; mv service pnt; baby facs; shwrs inc; el pnts (10A) inc (poss rev pol & poss long cable req); gas; lndtte (inc dryer); shop; supmkt nr; rest, snacks; bar; BBQ (charcoal & gas); playgrnd; 2 htd pools; paddling pool; lake fishing; horseriding; tennis; games area; games rm; wifi; entmnt; TV rm; dogs €3; no c'vans/m'vans over 7.50m high ssn; phone; Eng spkn; adv bkg; quiet; ccard acc; red low ssn/long stay; CKE/CCI. "Well-kept site in grnds of former farm; 3 sm unfenced lakes; plenty rm for pitch access; various pitch sizes, some sm & some with fruit trees; friendly & helpful; gd san facs; shop & rest ltd low ssn; mkt in Dol Sat; gd." ♦ 12 May-23 Sep. € 29.00   2011*

DOL DE BRETAGNE _2E4_ (7km SE Rural) _48.49150, -1.72990_ **Camping Le Domaine des Ormes, 35120 Epiniac [02 99 73 53 60 or 02 99 73 53 01; fax 02 99 73 53 55; info@lesormes.com; www.lesormes.com or www.les-castels.com]** Exit N176/E401 at W end of Dol-de-Bretagne; then S fr Dol on D795 twd Combourg & Rennes, in 7km site on L of rd, clearly sp. V lge, hdg/mkd pitch, pt sl, pt shd; wc; chem disp; baby facs; shwrs inc; el pnts (6A) inc (poss long lead req); gas; lndtte (inc dryer); shop; tradsmn; rest, snacks; bar; BBQ (charcoal/gas); playgrnd; htd pool complex; waterslide; covrd aquacentre; paddling pool; lake fishing, canoeing; pedalos; sand beach 25km; tennis; cycle hire; horseriding; archery; golf course adj (discount to campers); cricket; cycle hire; wifi; entmnt; games/TV rm; 80% statics; dogs €2; c'vans/m'vans 8m & over by request only; poss cr; adv bkg; Eng spkn; poss noisy (disco); ccard acc; red low ssn; CKE/CCI. "Busy site set in well-kept chateau grnds; helpful staff; clean san facs; suitable RVs; conv Mont St Michel, St Malo & Dinan; disco at night; mkt Sat; excel all round." ♦ 28 Apr-23 Sep. € 44.60 SBS - B08   2011*

See advertisement on next page

DOLE *6H2* (6km NE Rural) *47.12557, 5.58825* **Camping Les Marronniers, Rue Chaux, 39700 Rochefort-sur-Nenon [03 84 70 50 37; fax 03 84 70 55 05; www.camping-les-marronniers.com]** NE fr Dole on D673 twds Besançon. Turn R on D76 & pass thro vill of Rochefort-sur-Nenon. Site in 2km, well sp. Med, hdg pitch, pt shd; wc; mv service pnt; serviced pitches; shwrs inc; el pnts (6A) €2.50; lndtte; tradsmn; snacks; bar; playgrnd; pool; cycle hire; entmnt; 10% statics; dogs €1; Eng spkn; adv bkg; poss noisy; red low ssn; CKE/CCI. ◆ 1 Apr-31 Oct. € 18.50   2008*

DOLE *6H2* (300m E Rural) *47.08937, 5.50339* **FFCC Camping Le Pasquier, 18 Chemin Victor et Georges Thévenot, 39100 Dole [03 84 72 02 61; fax 03 84 79 23 44; camping-pasquier@wanadoo.fr / lola@camping-le-pasquier.com; www.camping-le-pasquier.com]** Fr A39 foll sp dir Dole & Le Pasquier. Fr all dir foll sp 'Centre ville' then foll site name sp & 'Stade Camping' in town; well sp. Site on rvside private rd. Narr app. Lge, hdg/mkd pitch, pt shd; htd wc; chem disp; mv service pnt; shwrs inc; el pnts (10A) inc (rev pol); lndry rm; shop & 1km; tradsmn; snacks; bar; playgrnd; pool; aqua park 2km; dir access rv 500m; fishing; entmnt; wifi; 10% statics; dogs €1.50; extra for twin-axle c'vans; poss cr; Eng spkn; quiet; ccard acc; red long stay/low ssn; CKE/CCI. "Generous pitches; friendly recep; gd clean san facs; pleasant pool; walk along rv (otters!) into Dole; poss mosquito problem; mkt Tues, Thur, Sat; gd NH." 15 Mar-25 Oct. € 17.00   2013*

DOLE *6H2* (8km SE Rural) *47.01660, 5.48160* **FFCC Camping Les Bords de Loue, 39100 Parcey [03 84 71 03 82; fax 03 84 71 03 42; contact@jura-camping.fr; www.jura-camping.fr]** Leave A39 at junc 6 onto D905 dir Chalon-sur-Saône. Turn L (SE) at rndabt after going under A39 & in 6km turn R into vill of Parcey at 'Camping' sp. Lge, pt shd; wc; chem disp; 10% serviced pitches; shwrs inc; el pnts (6A) inc; lndtte; tradsmn; rest, snacks; bar; BBQ; playgrnd; paddling pool; beach adj; pool; fishing; boating; shops 7km; 20% statics; dogs €2, must keep on lead; phone; wi-fi; poss cr; Eng spkn; adv bkg; poss some noise when busy; ccard acc; red low ssn; CKE/CCI. "Pleasant site." ◆ 14 May-15 Sep. € 28.00   2013*

DOLLON see Connerré *4F1*

DOMAZAN see Avignon *10E2*

DOMFRONT *4E1* (500m S Urban) *48.58808, -0.65045* **Camp Municipal Champ Passais, 4 Rue du Champ Passais, 61700 Domfront [02 33 37 37 66 or 02 33 38 92 24 (LS); fax 02 33 30 60 67; mairie-de-domfront@wanadoo.fr; www.domfront.com]** Fr N on D962 foll Laval sps into Domfront; then take D976 W dir Mont-St-Michel; site turning in 400m on L; well sp bet old quarter & town cent. Fr S on D962 well sp fr edge of town. Sm, hdg/mkd pitch, hdstg, terr, pt shd; wc; chem disp; shwrs inc; el pnts (10A) €4; lndtte; shops, rest, snacks, bar 1km; playgrnd; rv fishing nr; TV rm; dogs €0.80; phone; Eng spkn; some rd noise; red low ssn; CKE/CCI. "Pleasant, well-kept terr site with views; helpful, charming staff; few shady pitches; gd security; sh, steep walk to medieval town; no twin-axles; vg; site still excel value, but showing signs of wear." ◆ 1 Apr-30 Sep. € 12.35   2013*

DOMME see Sarlat la Canéda *7C3*

DOMPIERRE LES ORMES *9A2* (500m NW Rural) *46.36369, 4.47460* **Camp Municipal Le Village des Meuniers, 71520 Dompierre-les-Ormes [03 85 50 36 60; fax 03 85 50 36 61; contact@villagedesmeuniers.com; www.villagedesmeuniers.com]** Fr A6 exit Mâcon Sud onto N79 dir Charolles. After approx 35km take slip rd onto D41 for Dompierre-les-Ormes. Well sp nr village. Med, hdg/mkd pitch, terr, pt shd; wc; chem disp; mv service pnt; 50% serviced pitch; shwrs inc; el pnts (16A) €4.50; gas; lndtte; shops 2km; tradsmn; rest, snacks; bar; playgrnd; htd pools; waterslide; cycle hire; tennis; wifi; entmnt; dogs €2; adv bkg (ess high ssn); quiet; ccard acc; red low ssn; CKE/CCI. "Excel, clean site with views; v lge pitches; o'flow field with full facs high ssn; facs stretched high ssn; excel for children; gd sp walks in area; pools, rest, bar etc used by public; free m'van hdstg outside site ent." ◆ 15 Mar-1 Nov. € 23.00   2010*

DOMPIERRE SUR BESBRE *9A1* (E Urban) *46.51378, 3.68276* **Camp Municipal, La Madeleine, Parc des Sports, 03290 Dompierre-sur-Besbre [04 70 34 55 57 or 04 70 48 11 39 (Mairie); camping@mairie-dsb.fr; www.dompierre-sur-besbre.fr]** At E end of town nr rv behind stadium; sp. Med, hdg pitch, shd, pt sl; htd wc; chem disp; mv service pnt; baby facs; shwrs inc; el pnts (10A) €2.20; lndtte; shop 500m; BBQ; full sports facs adj; dogs; phone; poss cr; Eng spkn; adv bkg; quiet; CKE/CCI. "Smart, well-run, busy site; clean san facs, but poss stretched high ssn; excel sports complex; gd for Loire Valley, vineyards & chateaux; highly rec low ssn; excel." ◆ 15 May-15 Sep. € 6.80   2011*

DOMPIERRE SUR BESBRE *9A1* (5km E Rural) *46.53546, 3.74388* **Camping du Gué de Loire, 03290 Diou [03 85 53 97 79 (Mairie); info@campingguedeloire.com; www.campingguedeloire.com]** Sp in cent of vill in both dirs on rvside, off N79. Sm, hdg/mkd pitch, pt sl, shd; wc; chem disp; mv service pnt; shwrs inc; el pnts €2.50; lndry rm; shop 800m; rest, bar 500m; cycle hire; dogs €1; rd noise; no ccard acc; CKE/CCI. "Simple site; vg, modern san facs; gd touring base." ♦ 15 Jun-31 Aug. € 9.50   2010*

DONJON, LE *9A1* (500m N Urban) *46.35317, 3.79188* **Camp Municipal, 4 Chemin Denys Bournatot, 03130 Le Donjon [04 70 99 56 35 or 04 70 99 50 25 (Mairie); fax 04 74 99 58 02; mairie-le-donjon@wanadoo.fr; www. allier-tourisme.com]** Fr Lapalisse N on D994. Site sp fr town cent on D166 dir Monétay-sur-Loire. Sm, pt sl, pt shd; wc (some cont); mv service pnt; shwrs inc; el pnts (10A) €2.50; shop 500m; rest & bar 400m; playgrnd; fishing, sailing & windsurfing 900m; dogs; quiet; CKE/CCI. ♦ 1 May-31 Oct. € 7.00   2009*

DONZENAC *7C3* (1.5km S Rural) *45.21978, 1.51784* **FFCC Camping La Rivière, Route d'Ussac, 19270 Donzenac [tel/ fax 05 55 85 63 95; info@campingdonzenac.com; www. campingdonzenac.com]** Fr N exit A20 at junc 47 (do not use junc 48); take exit at rndabt dir Donzenac D920. In 3km on ent Donzenac keep on D920 & go down hill to rndabt. Take 2nd exit D170 on D920, site on R in 500m. NB Avoid app thro Donzenac as narr & diff for lge o'fits. Fr S exit junc 49 to Ussac. Med, mkd pitch, pt shd; wc; chem disp; mv service pnt; shwrs inc; el pnts (10A) €3.10; gas; lndtte (inc dryer); sm shop & 1km; snacks; bar; playgrnd; htd pool Jul/Aug; rv adj; fishing 5km; cycle hire; tennis; games area; games rm; wifi; TV rm; dogs €1.10; adv bkg rec high ssn; red low ssn. "Excel facs." ♦ 1 Apr-15 Sep. € 16.10   2010*

DORAT, LE *7A3* (600m S Urban) *46.21161, 1.08237* **Camp Municipal, Route de la Planche des Dames, 87210 Le Dorat [05 55 60 72 20 (Mairie) or 05 55 60 76 81 (TO); fax 05 55 68 27 87]** Site sp fr D675 & in town cent. Sm, hdg/mkd pitch, pt shd; wc; shwrs inc; el pnts (16A) €3.10; shop, rest, bar 600m; quiet; Eng spkn; CKE/CCI. "Excel, basic site; permanent barrier, code fr tourist office; clean facs, but ltd & own san rec high ssn; warden calls eves; public uses footpath as short-cut; very clean, quiet site, must book in tourist office in town square; friendly & helpful" 1 May-30 Sep. € 5.95   2013*

⊞ **DORCEAU** *4E2* (2km N Rural) *48.43717, 0.82742* **Camping Forest View, L'Espérance, 61110 Dorceau [tel/ fax 02 33 83 78 55; peter@forestviewfrance.com; www. forestviewleisurebreaks.co.uk]** Fr D920 (ring rd) in Rémalard take D38 sp Bretoncelles; site in 4km on corner on L. Sm, pt sl, pt shd; wc; chem disp; shwrs inc; el pnts (10A) inc; lake fishing; painting workshops; wifi; dogs €1.40; some statics; adv bkg; quiet; red low ssn; CKE/CCI. "Simple, well-kept site in beautiful countryside; helpful, friendly British owners; gd touring base or NH; excel; evening meal avail with hosts, reasonable price" € 10.20   2013*

DORMANS *3D4* (7km NE Rural) *49.10638, 3.73380* **Camping Rural (Nowack), 10 Rue de Bailly, 51700 Vandières [03 26 58 02 69 or 03 26 58 08 79; fax 03 26 58 39 62; champagne@nowack.fr; www.champagne-nowack.com]** Fr N3, turn N at Port Binson, over Rv Marne, then turn W onto D1 for 3km, then N into Vandières. Site on R about 50m fr start of Rue Bailly, sp 'Champagne Nowack' or 'Camping Nowack.' Sm, pt sl, pt shd; wc; shwrs inc; el pnts (6A) inc; lndtte; tradsmn; BBQ; playgrnd; pool 8km; fishing 1km; rv sw & boating 6km; tennis 2km; TV; adv bkg; ccard acc; CKE/CCI. "Charming, peaceful, CL-type site in orchard; friendly owners; lovely, well-kept modern san facs; fresh water tap beside chem disp (2011); site poss muddy when wet; poss grape pickers on site Sep; site part of vineyard, champagne can be bought on site; excel value." 1 Apr-1 Nov. € 15.00   2013*

DORMANS *3D4* (1km W Urban) *49.07830, 3.63530* **Camping Sous Le Clocher, Route de Vincelles, 51700 Dormans [03 26 58 21 79 or 03 26 58 21 45; fax 03 26 57 29 62; roussel.b@resopharma.fr; www.champagne-ardenne- tourism.co.uk]** On D1003 E fr Château-Thierry; in Dormans foll sp, over Rv Marne; camp site 50m fr end of bdge. Med, hdg pitch, pt shd; wc (some cont); shwrs; el pnts (6A) €3 (rev pol); shop 200m; rest, bar 1km; playgrnd; htd pool adj high ssn; games area; TV; some statics; dogs €2; poss cr; rlwy noise & noisy at w/end; ccard acc. "Ideal for Champagne area; sm pitches; basic facs; poss stretched high ssn; unrel opening low ssn, phone ahead." 2 Apr-15 Sep. € 8.00   2008*

DORTAN *9A3* (3km N Rural) *46.34129, 5.63028* **Camp Municipal Les Cyclamens, La Presqu'île, 01590 Chancia [tel/fax 04 74 75 82 14 or 04 74 77 71 37 (Mairie); infos@ camping-chancia.com; www.camping-chancia.com]** Fr N on D436 to Dortan; R at traff lts sp Bourg-en-Bresse; in 1.5km R (furniture shop) onto D60 sp Chancia; foll sp. NB go past Camping du Lac. Lge, mkd pitch, pt shd; wc; chem disp; mv service pnt; shwrs inc; el pnts (6A) €2.10; gas; lndtte; shop 6km; tradsmn; rest, bar 1km; playgrnd; lake sw & shgl beach 100m; fishing, tennis, walking & watersports nr; 50% statics; dogs €1.40; phone; poss cr; adv bkg; quiet; CKE/CCI. "Beautiful area; clean site; friendly; few tourists; excel." 1 May-30 Sep. € 7.80   2008*

DOSCHES see Troyes *4E4*

DOUAI *3B4* (10km S Rural) *50.27374, 3.10565* **Camp Municipal Les Biselles, Chemin des Bisselles, 59151 Arleux [03 27 89 52 36 or 03 27 93 10 00; fax 03 27 94 37 38; office.tourisme@arleux.com]** Exit A2 junc 14 at Cambrai & take D643 twd Douai, after 5km turn W at Bugnicourt to Arleux. Site sp in vill adj canal La Sensée. Lge, hdg/mkd pitch, shd; wc (some cont); shwrs inc; el pnts €6.85; playgrnd; pool; rv fishing; tennis 200m; games area; 96% statics; dogs; phone; poss cr; adv bkg; quiet. "Very few touring pitches; basic san facs; gd cycling along canal." ♦ 1 Apr-31 Oct. € 13.95 2010*

DOUAI *3B4* (10km S Rural) *50.29004, 3.04945* **FFCC Camp Municipal de la Sablière, Rue du 8 Mai 1945, 62490 Tortequesne [03 21 24 14 94; fax 03 21 07 46 07; camping@tortequesne.fr; www.tortequesne.fr]** Fr D643 Douai-Cambrai rd; turn S onto D956 to Tortequesne where site sp. Sm, hdg/mkd pitch, hdstg; pt shd; wc (some cont); shwrs inc; el pnts (6A) €3; supmkt 5 mins; playgrnd; walking in La Valée de la Sensée; tennis; games area; 80% statics; dogs €0.50; CKE/CCI. "Gd site; san facs clean but need update; park & fishing adj; late night arr area." 1 Apr-30 Sep. € 11.20   2008*

DOUARNENEZ *2E2* (2km W Rural) *48.09270, -4.35220* **Camping de Trézulien, Route de Trézulien, 29100 Douarnenez [02 98 74 12 30 or 06 80 01 17 98 (mob); fax 09 70 06 31 74; contact@camping-trezulien.com; www.camping-trezulien.com]** Ent Douarnenez fr E on D7; foll sp 'Centre Ville'; turn L at traff lts sp to Tréboul. Cross rv bdge into Ave de la Gare, at post office turn L, then 1st L. Turn R at island, foll site sp. Lge, pt terr, pt shd; wc; baby facs; shwrs inc; el pnts (10A) €3.50; gas; lndtte; shops 1km; playgrnd; sand beach 1.5km; dogs €2; quiet. "Pleasant site; steep hill fr ent to recep; 1km by foot to Les Sables Blancs; conv Pointe du Raz." 1 Apr-30 Sep. € 14.10   2013*

DOUARNENEZ *2E2* (6km W Rural) *48.08166, -4.40722* **Camping de la Baie de Douarnenez, Route de Douarnenez, 29100 Poullan-sur-Mer [02 98 74 26 39; fax 02 98 74 55 97; info@pil-koad.com; www.camping-douarnenez.com or www.flowercampings.com]** Fr E take circular rd around Douarnenez on D7/D765 dir Audierne & Poullan-sur-Mer, Tréboul & Pointe-du-Van. Site on L off D7 1km fr Poullan-sur-Mer vill, shortly after church spire becomes visible. Med, hdg/mkd pitch, pt shd; htd wc; chem disp; mv service pnt; baby facs; shwrs inc; el pnts (10A) inc; gas; lndtte; shop; rest, snacks; bar; BBQ (charcoal/gas); playgrnd; htd, covrd; paddling pool; sand beach 5km; watersports 4km; lake fishing; tennis; cycle hire; games area; wifi; entmnt; games/ TV rm; statics (tour ops); dogs €4; no c'vans/m'vans over 10m high ssn; Eng spkn; adv bkg; quiet; ccard acc; red low ssn; CKE/CCI. "Tranquil site in woodland; gd sized pitches; staff friendly; ltd facs low ssn; enmnt well away fr most pitches; gd for families; mkd walks, guided high ssn; mkt Mon & Fri; pools & water slides great fun" ♦ 27 Apr-15 Sep. € 35.85 SBS - B04   2013*

See advertisement below

DOUARNENEZ *2E2* (11km W Coastal) *48.08416, -4.48194* **Camping Pors Péron, 29790 Beuzec-Cap-Sizun [02 98 70 40 24; fax 02 98 70 54 46; info@ campingporsperon.com; www.campingporsperon.com]** W fr Douarnenez take D7 sp Poullan-sur-Mer. Thro Poullan & in approx 4km turn R sp Pors-Piron, foll site & beach sp. Site bef Beuzec-Cap-Sizun vill. Med, hdg/mkd pitch, pt sl, pt shd; wc (some cont); chem disp; mv service pnt; baby facs; shwrs inc; el pnts (10A) inc (long lead req); gas; lndtte (inc dryer); shop & 3km; snacks; BBQ; playgrnd; sand beach 200m; games area; cycle hire; wifi; 5% statics; dogs €1.60; phone 200m; poss cr; adv bkg; quiet; red low ssn; CKE/CCI. "Pleasant site nr beautiful sandy cove; friendly, helpful British owners; gd san facs, poss insufficient high ssn & long way fr some pitches; poss ltd privacy in ladies' facs; site rds poss diff lge o'fit; gd." ♦ ltd 1 Apr-30 Sep. € 24.65   2013*

DOUCIER *6H2* (3km N Rural) *46.67755, 5.78080* **Camping La Pergola, 1 Rue des Vernois, Lac de Chalain, 39130 Marigny [03 84 25 70 03; fax 03 84 25 75 96; contact@lapergola.com; www.lapergola.com or www.les-castels.com]** Fr D471 Lons-le-Saunier to Champagnole rd, turn S on D27 twd Marigny, site on L in 6km on N shore of Lac de Chalain. Lge, hdg/mkd pitch, pt sl, terr, pt shd; wc; chem disp; baby facs; some serviced pitches; shwrs inc; baby facs; el pnts (12A) inc; gas; lndtte (inc dryer); shop; rest, snacks; bar; BBQ; playgrnd; htd pool; paddling pool; lake sand beach adj; fishing; games rm; games area; wifi; entmnt; TV; 50% statics; dogs €4; phone; poss cr; Eng spkn; adv bkg; red long stay; ccard acc; CKE/CCI. "Popular, busy site; beautiful gorges nrby; superb san facs; naturist beach on lake 500m; some sm pitches." ♦ 28 Apri--9 Sep. € 38.00 (CChq acc)   2011*

See advertisement on inside back cover

DOUCIER *6H2* (6km N Rural) *46.71221, 5.79709* **Camping du Gît, Monnet-le-Bourg, 39300 Montigny-sur-l'Ain [03 84 51 21 17 or 03 84 37 87 58 (LS); christian.olivier22@ wanadoo.fr; www.campingdugit.com]** W fr Champagnole on D471 foll sp Monnet-la-Ville, foll camp sp thro vill, turn L at x-rds to church; site immed afterwards on R behind church in Monnet-la-Ville (also known as Monnet-le-Bourg). Med, mkd pitch, pt sl, pt shd; wc; chem disp; shwrs inc; el pnts (5A) €2.50; lndtte; supmkt 800m; rest, snacks; bar; playgrnd; lake sw 4km; sports area; fishing, kayaking 1.5km; dogs €1.50; adv bkg; quiet; CKE/CCI. "Peaceful site; beautiful views; lge pitches; gd san facs. "♦ 1 Jun-31 Aug. € 12.00   2012*

FRANCE

DOUCIER *6H2* (8km N Rural) *46.72383, 5.78463* **Camping Le Bivouac, Route du Lac de Chalain, 39300 Pont-du-Navoy [03 84 51 26 95; fax 03 84 51 29 70; campinglebivouac-jura@orange.fr; www.bivouac-jura.com]** D471 to Pont-du-Navoy, S over bdge & immed fork R onto D27; 2nd site on R. Med, mkd pitch, pt shd; htd wc; chem disp; shwrs inc; el pnts (16A) €2.80 (poss rev pol/no earth); lndtte; shops 1km; tradsmn; rest, snacks; bar; playgrnd; rv adj; lake sw 6km; TV; 20% statics; dogs €0.50; adv bkg; quiet; ccard acc; CKE/CCI. "In beautiful countryside; new owner (2011); ltd san facs." 1 Mar-5 Oct. € 12.20   2011*

"We must tell The Club about that great site we found"

Get your site reports in by mid-August and we'll do our best to get your updates into the next edition of Caravan Europe.

DOUCIER *6H2* (3km NE Rural) *46.66361, 5.81333* **Camping Domaine de Chalain, 39130 Doucier [03 84 25 78 78; chalain@chalain.com; www.chalain.com]** Fr Lons-le-Saunier take D39 E. In Doucier, site sp to L. Fr Champagnole take D471 for 11km, L onto D27 at Pont-du-Navoy to Doucier & foll sp to site. V lge, pt shd; wc (some cont); mv service pnt; chem disp; sauna; shwrs inc; el pnts (7A) €3; gas; lndtte; shops; rest, snacks; bar; htd, covrd pools; waterslide & aquatic cent; lake sw adj; boating; fishing; games area; entmnt; internet; statics; dogs €2; poss cr; adv bkg ess. "Extra for lakeside pitches; famous caves Grottes des Beaume adj; vg site." 29 Apr-21 Sep. € 33.00 (3 persons)   2009*

DOUCIER *6H2* (6km SE Rural) *46.61429, 5.84780* **Camping Le Relais de l'Eventail, Route de la Vallée du Hérisson, 39130 Menétrux-en-Joux [03 84 25 71 59; fax 03 84 25 76 66; relais-de-leventail@club-internet.fr]** Fr Doucier take D326 E (site not accessable fr D39). Adj tourist office. Med, mkd pitch, pt shd; wc; chem disp; mv service pnt; shwrs inc; el pnts (6A) €2.70 lndtte; rest; bar; tradsmn; pool; dogs €1.50; quiet. "Lovely, peaceful site; helpful staff; site in limestone gorge nr dramatic waterfall 'Herisson Cascades'; gd walks." 26 Jun-31 Aug. € 14.30   2008*

DOUCIER *6H2* (1.5km S Rural) *46.65260, 5.72119* **Kawan Village Domaine de l'Epinette, 15 Rue de l'Epinette, 39130 Châtillon-sur-Ain [03 84 25 71 44; fax 03 84 25 71 25; contact@domaine-epinette.com; www.domaine-epinette.com]** Exit A39 junc 7 to Poligny, then N5 to Champagnole & D471 W. Turn S onto D27 to Lac de Chalain then D39 to Châtillon. Med, mkd pitch, mainly sl, terr, pt shd; wc (some cont); chem disp; shwrs inc; el pnts (12A) inc; lndtte (inc dryer); shop; tradsmn; rest 1km; snacks; bar; BBQ; playgrnd; htd pool; paddling pool; rv sw & fishing; canoeing, kayaking & horseriding 3km; games rm; wifi; TV; 30% statics; dogs €2; phone; adv bkg; quiet. "Gd base for Jura; vg." ◆ 2 Jun-11 Sep. € 27.00 (CChq acc)   2011*

DOUE LA FONTAINE *4G1* (1km N Rural) *47.20338, -0.28165* **Camp Municipal Le Douet, Rue des Blanchisseries, 49700 Doué-la-Fontaine [02 41 59 14 47 or 06 22 71 25 53 (mob); camping.doue@orange.fr / contact@camping-lesrivesdudouet.fr-camping-lesrivesdudouet.fr; www. camping-lesrivesdudouet.fr]** Fr Doué N on D761 twd Angers; site in sports ground on o'skts of town; sp. Med, mkd pitch, pt shd; htd wc; chem disp; shwrs inc; el pnts (6A) inc; lndtte; shop 2km; rests nr; htd pool high ssn adj; tennis; wifi; few statics; poss cr; quiet but some factory noise at E end; no ccard acc; CKE/CCI. "Clean, well-run site; gd, flat pitches; helpful warden; gd san facs; lovely park & museum; conv zoo, rose gardens & Cadre Noir Equestrian Cent; poss itinerant workers low ssn." ◆ ltd 1 Apr-15 Oct. € 14.60   2013*

DOUE LA FONTAINE *4G1* (2km SW Rural) *47.17390, -0.34750* **Camping La Vallée des Vignes, 49700 Concourson-sur-Layon [02 41 59 86 35; fax 02 41 59 09 83; campingvdv@wanadoo.fr; www.campingvdv.com]** D960 fr Doué-la-Fontaine (dir Cholet) to Concourson-sur-Layon; site 1st R 250m after bdge on leaving Concourson-sur-Layon. Or fr Angers foll sp dir Cholet & Poitiers; then foll sp Doué-la-Fontaine. Med, mkd pitch, pt shd; htd wc; chem disp; serviced pitches; baby facs & fam bthrm; shwrs inc; el pnts (10A) €4; gas; lndtte; shop; tradsmn; rest, snacks; bar; BBQ; playgrnd; htd pool; paddling pool; lake sw 10km; cycle hire; entmnt; TV rm; 5% statics; dogs €3; bus; poss cr; Eng spkn; adv bkg; quiet, some rd noise; ccard acc; red long stay low ssn; ccard acc; CKE/CCI. "Peaceful site poss open all yr weather permitting - phone to check; friendly, helpful British owners; vg, clean, well-maintained facs; pool open & htd early ssn; some pitches diff lge o'fits due o'hanging trees; conv for Loire chateaux & Futuroscope." ◆ 1 Apr-30 Sep. € 23.00   2009*

DOUE LA FONTAINE *4G1* (8km W Rural) *47.19355, -0.37075* **Camping Les Grésillons, Chemin des Grésillons, 49700 St Georges-sur-Layon [02 41 50 02 32; fax 02 41 50 03 16; camping.gresillon@wanadoo.fr; www.camping-gresillons.com]** Fr Doué-la-Fontaine on D84, site sp. Sm, hdg pitch, hdstg, terr, pt shd; htd wc; chem disp; baby facs; shwrs inc; el pnts (6-10A) €2.90-3.50; lndtte; shop & 500m; rest; snacks, bar 500m; playgrnd; htd pool; rv fishing 200m; games area; entmnt; 28% statics; dogs free; Eng spkn; adv bkg; quiet; ccard acc; red long stay/CKE/CCI. "Delightful site in area of vineyards; friendly, helpful owner." ◆ 1 Apr-30 Sep. € 11.00   2009*

DOUE LA FONTAINE *4G1* (15km W Rural) **Camping KathyDave, Les Beauliers, 49540 La Fosse de Tigné [02 41 67 92 10 or 06 14 60 81 63 (mob); bookings@camping-kathydave.co.uk; www.camping-kathydave.co.uk]** Fr Doué-la-Fontaine on D84 to Tigne, turn S thro La Fosse-de-Tigné. Pass chateau, site sp on R. NB Tight turn in, access poss diff lge o'fits. Sm, mkd pitch, pt shd; htd wc; chem disp; shwrs inc; el pnts (8A) €3 (poss rev pol); lndtte; tradsmn; rest nr; BBQ (gas); wifi; dogs free; adv bkg; quiet; CKE/CCI. "Tranquil orchard site in picturesque area; welcoming, helpful British owners; gd san facs; some pitches restricted by trees; gd touring base; adults only preferred; phone ahead rec; excel; small cl type site in an old orchard" 1 May-31 Oct. € 11.50   2013*

DOUHET, LE *7B2* (2km S Rural) *45.81080, -0.55288*
Camping La Roulerie, 17100 Le Douhet [05 46 96 40 07 or 06 75 24 91 96 (mob); www.camping-laroulerie.fr] Fr Niort to Saintes, site on W side of D150 in vill of La Roulerie. Sm, some hdg/mkd pitch, some hdstdg, pt shd; wc; chem disp; mv service pnt; shwrs inc; el pnts (16A) €3.50; lndtte; shop; supmkt 9km; playgrnd; pool; games area; dog €1; some statics; Eng spkn; adv bkg; quiet but some rd noise; ccard not acc; CKE/CCI. "Sm pitches; full by early eve; friendly, helpful owner; gd san facs; vg value; gd NH." 1 May-15 Oct. € 9.00   2013*

DOURDAN *4E3* (700m NE Urban) *48.52572, 2.02878*
Camping Les Petits Prés, 11 Rue Pierre Mendès France, 91410 Dourdan [01 64 59 64 83 or 01 60 81 14 17; fax 01 60 81 14 29; camping@mairie-dourdan.fr; www. mairie-dourdan.fr] Exit A10 junc 10 dir Dourdan; foll by-pass sp Arpajon; after 5th rndabt site 200m on L. Med, mkd pitch, pt sl, unshd; htd wc; shwrs; el pnts (4A) €3.40; gas & supmkt 500m; rest 1km; playgrnd; pool 500m; poss cr; 75% statics; Eng spkn; adv bkg; poss noisy. "Gd NH; friendly welcome; clean dated san facs, ltd low ssn; town worth visit." 1 Apr-30 Sep. € 13.95 (3 persons)   2012*

DOUSSARD *9B3* (1.5km N Rural) *45.79120, 6.21599*
Camping International de Lac Bleu, Route de la Plage, 74210 Doussard [04 50 44 30 18 or 04 50 44 38 47; fax 04 50 44 84 35; contact@camping-lac-bleu.com; www. camping-lac-bleu.com] S fr Annecy on D1508 twd Albertville. Site on L in 20km just past Bout-du-Lac & bef Camp La Nublière. Lge, hdg/mkd pitch, pt sl, pt shd; wc; chem disp; mv service pnt; some serviced pitches; shwrs inc; el pnts (8A) €3.90; gas adj; lndtte; shop; hypmkt 4km; rest & snacks in high ssn; bar; playgrnd; pool; lake beach adj; watersports; wifi; dogs €4; phone; bus adj; poss cr; Eng spkn; adv bkg; rd noise some pitches; red low ssn/long stay; ccard acc; CKE/CCI. "Excel lakeside location; some lge pitches; gd watersports; cycle path to Annecy; ltd facs low ssn." ♦ 4 Apr-26 Sep. € 28.90 2009*

DOUSSARD *9B3* (2.5km N Rural) *45.79534, 6.20589*
Camping L'Idéal, 715 Route de Chaparon, 74210 Lathuile [04 50 44 32 97; fax 04 50 44 36 59; info@camping-ideal. com; www.camping-ideal.com] Take Annecy Sud exit fr A41, foll Albertville sp on D1508 on W side of lake. In vill of Brédannaz R at traff lts, immed L on narr rd for 100m; site on R after 2km. Lge, mkd pitch, pt sl, pt shd; wc; chem disp; shwrs inc; el pnts (6A) €3.90; gas; lndtte; shop; rest, snacks; bar; BBQ: playgrnd; htd, covrd pool; waterslide; lake sw 800m; games area; entmnt; TV; 15% statics; dogs €3.20; phone; poss cr high ssn; adv bkg; quiet; red long stay; CKE/CCI. "Pleasant, family-run site; less cr than lakeside sites; views of mountains & lake." 1 May-23 Sep. € 23.00   2009*

DOUSSARD *9B3* (3km N Rural) *45.80256, 6.20960* Camping La Ravoire, Route de la Ravoire, Bout-du-Lac, 74210 Doussard [04 50 44 37 80; fax 04 50 32 90 60; info@ camping-la-ravoire.fr; www.camping-la-ravoire.fr] On D1508 S fr Annecy twd Doussard, keep lake to your L; at Bredannaz cont past traff lts & turn R after vill opp rest & boat landing stage (site sp); turn R again immed after cycle track; site on R in 300m. Med, hdg/mkd pitch, pt sl, pt shd; htd wc; chem disp; mv service pnt (poss diff access); serviced pitches; baby facs; shwrs inc; el pnts (5A) inc (poss rev pol); gas; lndtte (inc dryer); sm shop; tradsmn; supmkt 5km; rest 800m; snacks; bar; playgrnd; htd pool; paddling pool; waterslide; lake sw 800m; fishing, golf, horseriding, sailing & windsurfing adj; cycle hire; games area; TV rm; some statics; dogs; phone; poss cr; Eng spkn; adv bkg rec Jul/Aug; quiet; ccard acc; red low ssn; CKE/CCI. "Excel, well-kept, busy site with mountain views; friendly staff & atmosphere; immac facs; lake ferry fr Doussard; cycle paths adj." ♦ 15 May-7 Sep. € 30.60 (CChq acc)   2011*

See advertisement above

FRANCE

DOUSSARD 9B3 (3km N Rural) 45.80302, 6.20608 **Camping Le Taillefer, 1530 Route de Chaparon, 74210 Doussard [tel/fax 04 50 44 30 30; info@campingletaillefer.com; www.campingletaillefer.com]** Fr Annecy take D1508 twd Faverges & Albertville. At traff lts in Bredannaz turn R, then immed L for 1.5km; site immed on L by vill sp 'Chaparon'. Do NOT turn into ent by Bureau but stop on rd & ask for instructions as to access to pitches fr Bureau ent. Or, to avoid Annecy, fr Faverges, along D1508, turn L (sp Lathuile) after Complex Sportif at Bout-du-Lac. Turn R at rndabt (sp Chaparon), site is on R after 2.5km. Sm, mkd pitch, pt sl, terr, pt shd; wc; chem disp; mv service pnt; shwrs inc; el pnts (6A) inc (check rev pol); lndtte (inc dryer); sm shop & 3km; tradsmn; snacks & bar (high ssn); BBQ (gas/charcoal only); playgrnd; lake sw 1km; shgl beach 3km; tennis 100m; watersports 2km; sailing; rafting; canyoning; climbing; cycle hire; games/TV rm; dogs €2; no c'vans/m'vans over 8m high ssn; Eng spkn; adv bkg; quiet, some rd noise; ccard not acc; red low ssn/long stay. "Peaceful, simple, family-run site nr Lake Annecy; fantastic mountain views; access some pitches poss diff due steep terraces; friendly, helpful owners; dated, clean san facs; vg rest in easy walking dist; mkt Mon; worth another visit." ♦ 1 May-30 Sep. € 21.00 SBS - M06 2011*

DOUSSARD 9B3 (500m NW Rural) 45.79115, 6.21298 **Camping Le Polé, 1430 Route du Bout du Lac, 74210 Lathuile [04 50 44 32 13 or 06 88 04 68 70 (mob); contact@camping-le-pole.fr; www.camping-le-pole.fr]** S fr Annecy on D1508 dir Albertville; in 14km at Bout-du-Lac turn R dir Lathuile; site on L in 70m, just after cylce track. Or N fr Faverges on D1508; in 8km turn sharp L after passing Camping International du Lac Bleu; site on L. Med, hdg/mkd pitch, pt shd; wc; chem disp; baby facs; shwrs inc; el pnts (2-6A) €3.50-7; lndry rm; ice; shops 3km; tradsmn rest 2km; snacks 500m; bar 200m; BBQ; playgrnd; pool; paddling pool; lake sw adj; games area; games rm; TV; 50% statics; dogs €2.50; phone; Eng spkn; adv bkg; quiet. "Quiet, scenic site in busy area high ssn; helpful manager; gd pool; cycle path adj; gd walks; vg." ♦ 1 Jun-30 Sep. € 15.50 2009*

DOUVAINE 9A3 (8km NE Rural) 46.36812, 6.32809 **Camping Mathieu Le Léman 1, 74140 Yvoire [04 50 72 84 31; fax 04 50 72 96 33; www.campingsmathieu.com]** Exit D1005 at Sciez (bet Geneve & Thonon) onto D25 sp Yvoire; site in 10km; at Yvoire foll camping sp. NB Narr ent to site. Med, mkd pitch, pt sl, pt shd; wc (mainly cont); chem disp; mv service pnt; shwrs inc; el pnts (6A) €2.50; lndtte; tradsmn; shop, snacks & bar 500m; BBQ; playgrnd; lake sw 500m; 75% statics; dogs €1; Eng spkn; adv bkg; quiet; red low ssn; ccard not acc; CKE/CCI. "Excel site above beautiful medieval vill; friendly owner; lge pitches, some sloping; clean san facs; gd lake sw; adj site Mathieu Le Léman 2 open Jul-Aug only - same ownership, sep recep & facs; conv Geneva & Thonon-les-Bains." 1 Apr-28 Oct. € 14.50 2010*

DOUVAINE 9A3 (4km NW Rural) 46.32441, 6.26101 **Camping Lémania II, Plage de Tougues, 74140 Chens-sur-Léman [04 50 94 22 43 or 06 16 42 90 25 (mob); contact@camping-nautique.com; www.camping-nautique.com]** Fr Geneva dir Thonon on D1005 turn L onto D20 dir Tougues at Douvaine. Site sp. Med, pt shd; wc (some cont); chem disp; shwrs inc; el pnts (5A); lndtte; shop 300m; rest, snacks 200m; shgl beach on lake 200m; some statics; dogs; red low ssn. "Gd lake sw nr; gd NH." 1 May-30 Sep. € 15.00 2010*

DOUVILLE 7C3 (2km S Rural) 44.99271, 0.59853 **Camping Lestaubière, Pont-St Mamet, 24140 Douville [05 53 82 98 15; fax 05 53 82 90 17; lestaubiere@cs.com; www.lestaubiere.com]** Foll sp for 'Pont St Mamet' fr N21; then watch for camping sp. Med, pt sl, pt shd; wc; chem disp; baby facs; fam bthrm; shwrs inc; el pnts (6-10A) €4-5; gas; lndtte; shop in ssn; tradsmn; rest & snacks (high ssn); bar; BBQ; playgrnd; pool; paddling pool; lake sw, sm sand beach; fishing lake; tennis 5km; games area; games rm; child entmnt (high ssn); wifi; TV; dogs €3.50; phone; twin-axles (high ssn only); Eng spkn; adv bkg; quiet but some rd noise; ccard acc; red low ssn; CKE/CCI. "Spacious, park-like site with beautiful views; v lge pitches; owned by friendly, helpful Dutch couple; vg modern san facs; superb out of ssn; excel." ♦ 29 Apr-15 Sep. € 26.50 2011*

DOUZE, LA 7C3 (3km E Rural) 45.06493, 0.88817 **Camping Laulurie en Périgord (Naturist), 24330 La Douze [05 53 06 74 00; fax 05 53 06 77 55; toutain@laulurie.com; www.laulurie.com]** Fr Périgueux S on N221; in 8km turn S on D710 twd Le Bugue. Or exit A89 onto D710 S. On ent La Douze turn L & foll arrow signs. Sm, hdg/mkd pitch, pt sl, pt shd; wc (some cont); chem disp; shwrs inc; el pnts (3-10A); gas; shop; rest, snacks; bar; playgrnd; pool; dogs €3.00; sep car park; adv bkg; quiet; red low ssn; ccard acc. "Excel site; friendly owners; gd touring base for Dordogne & Périgueux; INF card req." ♦ ltd 15 May-15 Sep. € 34.50 2013*

DOUZE, LA 7C3 (6km SE Rural) 45.00765, 0.93039 **FFCC Camping Roc de Lavandre, Le Bourychou, 24620 St Félix-de-Reillac-et-Mortemart [tel/fax 05 53 03 23 47 or 06 81 12 52 71 (mob); contact@camping-roc-lavandre.com; www.camping-roc-lavandre.com]** Fr Les Eyzies-de-Tayac N on D47 dir Périgueux; site on R just bef St Félix-de-Reillac. Med, hdg/mkd pitch, pt shd; wc (some cont); chem disp; shwrs inc; el pnts (6A) €2.50; lndry rm; shops over 5km; tradsmn; rest, snacks; bar; playgrnd; lake sw; fishing; cycle hire; entmnt; 15% statics; dogs €1; Eng spkn; adv bkg; quiet, some rd noise; red low ssn; CKE/CCI. "Friendly, helpful owners; excel food in rest." 22 Mar-28 Oct. € 12.00 2008*

DOUZY see Sedan 5C1

DRAGUIGNAN 10F3 (2km S Rural) 43.51796, 6.47836 **Camping La Foux, Quartier La Foux, 83300 Draguignan [tel/fax 04 94 68 18 27; www.camping-lafoux.com]** Fr A8, take Le Muy intersection onto N555 N to Draguignan. Site ent on R at ent to town sp Sport Centre Foux. Fr Draguignan, take N555 S; just after 'End of Draguignan' sp, double back at rndabt & turn R. Lge, pt sl, unshd; wc; shwrs inc; el pnts (4-10A) €3.50-5; lndtte; shop; rest; bar; playgrnd; sand beach 20km; rv adj; fishing; entmnt; TV rm; dogs €3.90; poss cr; quiet. "Friendly staff; clean, dated san facs; care needed long vehicles on ent site; unshaded, but many trees planted (2011); poss flooding when wet; easy access to Riviera coast." 20 Jun-30 Sep. € 15.90 2011*

FRANCE

⊞ **DREUX** *4E2* (6km NW Rural) *48.76149, 1.29041* **Camping Etangs de Marsalin, 3 Place du Général de Gaulle, 28500 Vert-en-Drouais [02 37 82 92 23; camping.etangs. de.marsalin@wanadoo.fr; www.campingdemarsalin.fr]** Fr W on N12 dir Dreux, cross dual c'way bef petrol stn onto D152 to Vert-en-Drouais; on ent turn R to church, site on L. Well sp. Med, hdg/mkd pitch, some hdstg, pt sl, pt shd; htd wc (some cont); chem disp; shwrs inc; el pnts (6-10A), €4.60 (poss rev pol, long leads poss req, avail at recep); lndtte (inc dryer); shop; tradsmn; rest 4km; snacks; bar 100m; lake fishing 2km; wifi; 80% statics; dogs; phone adj; poss cr; Eng spkn; quiet; CKE/CCI. "Peaceful location; working families on site; statics area untidy/scruffy; friendly, helpful staff; basic, clean san facs; touring pitches at far end far fr facs; muddy when wet; lovely vill; conv Versailles; NH only." ♦ ltd € 11.40   2011*

DUCEY see Pontaubault *2E4*

DUN LE PALESTEL *7A3* (1.5km N Rural) *46.31698, 1.66545* **Camp Municipal de la Forêt, Route d'Argenton, 23800 Dun-le-Palestel [05 55 89 01 30; mairie-dunlepalestel@ orange.fr; www.mairie-dunlepalestel.fr]** Exit N145 N midway bet La Souterraine & Guéret onto D5 to Dun-le-Palestel; turn L onto D951; in 200m to R onto D913; site sp to R in1.5km. Site sp in town. Sm, mkd pitch, pt sl, pt shd; wc; shwrs inc; el pnts €2.30; shop 1 km; BBQ; rest, snacks & bar 800m; playgrnd; dogs; phone; quiet. "Pretty site with lovely views; gates kept locked; phone numbers listed at gate or call at Mairie 08.30-1200 & 1330-1630 (-1800 Tues & Thur); worth the trouble; vg." ♦ 15 Jun-15 Sep. € 5.60   2011*

> ## "Satellite navigation makes touring much easier"
>
> Remember most sat navs don't know if you're towing or in a larger vehicle – always use yours alongside maps and site directions.

DUN SUR MEUSE *5C1* (10km SE Rural) *49.32071, 5.26589* **Camping Le Brouzel, 55110 Sivry-sur-Meuse [03 29 85 86 45]** On D964 11km S of Dun twd Verdun, site sp in vill of Sivry. Sm, some hdstg, unshd; wc (cont); chem disp; shwrs inc; gas; el pnts (6A) €3.15; shop adj; rest, snacks; bar; playgrnd; games area; dir access to rv; fishing; sailing 2km; 80% statics; dogs; Eng spkn; quiet. "Clean site; friendly owner; gd san facs." 1 Apr-1 Oct. € 10.40   2009*

DUN SUR MEUSE *5C1* (10km S Rural) *49.32112, 5.08136* **Camping La Gabrielle, Ferme de la Gabrielle, 55110 Romagne-sous-Montfaucon [03 29 85 11 79; info@ lagabrielle.nl; http://www.lagabrielle.nl]** Site is on D998, 800m beyond end of Romagne. Well sp. Sm, pt sl, pt shd; wc; chem disp (wc); shwrs inc; el pnts (6A) €2 (rev pol); playgrnd; TV; 10% statics; dogs €1; Eng spkn; adv bkg; quiet; CKE/CCI. "Restful site in pretty setting; friendly Dutch owners; meals by arrangement; nr WW1 monuments; gd." ♦ 1 Apr-1 Nov. € 12.00   2011*

DUNKERQUE *3A3* (3km NE Coastal) *51.05171, 2.42025* **Camp Municipal La Licorne, 1005 Blvd de l'Europe, 59240 Dunkerque [03 28 69 26 68; fax 03 28 69 56 21; campinglalicorne@ville-dunkerque.fr; www. campingdelalicorne.com]** Exot A16 junc 62 sp 'Malo'; at end of slip rd traff lts turn L sp Malo-les-Bains; in 2km (at 5th traff lts) turn R at camping sp; at 2nd traff lts past BP g'ge turn L. Site on L (cont strt to rndabt & return on opp side of dual c'way to ent). Lge, mkd pitch, pt sl, unshd; htd wc; chem disp; mv service pnt; shwrs; el pnts (10A) €4.25 (poss long lead); gas; lndtte; sm shop; supmkt 500m; rest, snacks; bar; playgrnd; pool in high ssn; sand beach adj; 50% statics; dogs €0.90; bus fr site ent; clsd 2200-0700; poss cr; Eng spkn; adv bkg; quiet; red low ssn; CKE/CCI. "Gd, secure NH for ferries - obtain gate code for early depart; pitches uneven; many site rd humps; promenade along sea front to town cent; poss windy; m'van o'night area." ♦ ltd 1 Apr-30 Nov. € 17.10   2011*

DUNKERQUE *3A3* (12km NE Coastal) *51.07600, 2.55524* **Camping Perroquet Plage, 59123 Bray-Dunes [03 28 58 37 37; fax 03 28 58 37 01; www.camping-perroquet.com]** On Dunkerque-Ostend D601, about 100m fr Belgian frontier, thro vill on D947; cont 1km to traff lts, R on D60 thro vill, past rlwy stn to site on L. NB Take care some speed humps. V lge, hdg pitch, hdstg, pt shd; htd wc; chem disp; sauna; shwrs €1; el pnts (4A) €4.50; lndtte (inc dryer); shop; rest, snacks; bar; playgrnd; sand beach adj; watersports; tennis; gym; wifi; enmnt; 85% statics; dogs €0.50; poss cr; adv bkg (ess high ssn); Eng spkn; CKE/CCI. "Busy, well-kept site; lge pitches; if parked nr site ent, v long walk to beach; lge bar & rest nr beach (long walk fr ent); gd san facs, poss far; many local attractions; conv NH for ferries; gd." ♦ 1 Apr-1 Oct. € 15.20   2012*

⊞ **DUNKERQUE** *3A3* (6km S Urban) *51.00340, 2.40670* **Camping Les Bois des Forts, 59380 Coudekerque [03 28 61 04 41 or 06 73 83 28 81 (mob); www.campings-nord.com]** Exit A16 junc 60 onto D916, in 2km turn L onto D2 dir Coudekerque. In 2km at rndabt turn L, site on R. Med, hdg pitch, unshd; wc; shwrs €1.50; el pnts (10A) inc; lndtte; bar; playgrnd; games area; 95% statics; quiet. "gd NH close to ferry, basic san facs" € 13.00   2013*

⊞ **DURAS** *7D2* (500m N Rural) *44.68293, 0.18602* **Camping Le Cabri, Malherbe, Route de Savignac, 47120 Duras [05 53 83 81 03; fax 05 53 83 08 91; holidays@lecabri.eu.com; www.lecabri.eu.com]** Fr N on D708, turn R on ent Duras onto D203 at mini-rndabt by tourist info shop; site in 800m. Sm, hdg pitch, hdstg, terr, unshd; htd wc; chem disp; baby facs; shwrs inc; el pnts (4-10A) €3-5; gas 500m; lndtte (inc dryer); shop 500m; rest, snacks; bar; BBQ; playgrnd; sm pool; tennis 1km; games area; games rm; entmnt; wifi; 30% statics; dogs €2; bus 500m; Eng spkn; adv bkg; quiet; ccard acc; red low ssn; CKE/CCI. "Spacious site with wide views; lge pitches; British owners (CC members); san facs poss tired high ssn (2011); vg rest; Duras an attractive town; excel." ♦ € 17.00   2012*

DURAVEL see Puy l'Evêque *7D3*

FRANCE

⊞ **DURFORT** *8F3* (1km S Rural) *43.19206, 1.45685* **FFCC Camping Le Bourdieu, 09130 Durfort [05 61 67 30 17; fax 05 61 67 29 00; contact@lebourdieu.net; www. lebourdieu.com]** Exit Pamiers NW on D119; in 6km turn R onto D626 to St Martin-d'Oydes in 6km; cont on D626 for another 4km; turn R onto D14; in 200m turn R onto sm rd sp Durfort; almost immed turn R again; site in 200m. Sm, some hdstg, pt shd; htd wc; baby facs; fam bthrm; shwrs inc; el pnts (6A) inc; lndtte (inc dryer); shop; tradsmn; snacks; bar; BBQ; playgrnd; pool; games area; wifi; entmnt; TV; dogs €1; adv bkg; red low ssn. € 21.00 (CChq acc)   2010*

DURTAL *4G1* (200m W Urban) *47.67115, -0.23798* **Camping Les Portes de l'Anjou, 9 Rue du Camping, 49430 Durtal [02 41 76 31 80; lesportesdelanjou@camp-in-ouest.com; www.lesportesdelanjou.com]** Exit A11 junc 11 dir La Flèche, by-passing Durtal. At D323 turn R for Durtal, site on L at ent to town. Sps not readily visible, look out for 'Motor Caravan Parking'. Med, hdg/mkd pitch, pt shd; htd wc; own facs adv high ssn; chem disp; baby facs; shwrs inc; el pnts (6A) €3.40; gas; lndtte (inc dryer); shops 500m; tradsmn; snacks; bar; playgrnd; htd pool; paddling pool; fishing; canoeing; games rm; wifi; entmnt; TV rm; 12% statics; dogs €2.50; Eng spkn; office clsd 12.30-3.30; adv bkg; quiet; ccard acc; red long stay/low ssn/CKE/CCI. "Site in need of TLC, in pleasant position on Rv Loir; helpful staff; interesting vill" ♦ 12 Apr-27 Oct. € 22.60 (CChq acc)   2013*

EAUX BONNES see Laruns *8G2*

⊞ **EAUX PUISEAUX** *4F4* (1km S Rural) *48.11587, 3.88508* **Camping à la Ferme des Haut Frênes (Lambert), 6 Voie de Puiseaux, 10130 Eaux-Puiseaux [03 25 42 15 04; fax 03 25 42 02 95; les.hauts.frenes@wanadoo.fr; www. les-hauts-frenes.com]** N fr St Florentin or S fr Troyes on N77. Ignore D374 but take next turning D111 in NW dir. Site in 2km; well sp. Long o'fits take care at ent gate. Med, hdg/mkd pitch, hdstg, pt shd; htd wc; own facs adv high ssn; chem disp; shwrs inc; el pnts (6-12A) €2-3 (poss some rev pol); gas; lndtte; shop 2km; tradsmn; rest 3km; snacks; BBQ; playgrnd; tennis 3km; TV & games rm; wifi; dogs €2; poss cr; Eng spkn; adv bkg; quiet; red long stay; CKE/CCI. "Well-kept, tidy farm site in beautiful setting; lge, level pitches; helpful, friendly owners; gd san facs; meals on request; loyalty card; cider museum in vill; conv m'way; excel NH en rte S" ♦ € 14.00   2013*

EAUZE *8E2* (Urban) *43.87043, 0.10671* **Camp Municipal Le Moulin du Pouy, 32800 Eauze [05 62 09 86 00; fax 05 62 09 79 20; camplinglemoulin@tiscali.fr]** On D931 on N o'skts, sp. Site in 2 parts, connected by bdge. Sm, well shd; wc (cont); shwrs inc; el pnts (6-10A) inc; rest, snacks; bar; supmkt 500m; pool; library; TV rm; quiet; red low ssn/CKE/CCI. "Friendly staff; facs basic but clean; gd rest & pool; noise fr pool during day; gd." 15 May-30 Sep. € 18.50   2008*

EBREUIL see Gannat *9A1*

ECHELLES, LES *9B3* (6km NE Rural) *45.45679, 5.81327* **Camping La Bruyère, Hameau Côte Barrier, 73160 St Jean-de-Couz Chartreuse [04 79 65 79 11/ 04 79 65 74 27 (ls) / 06 29 47 27 43 (mob); camping-labruyere@orange.fr; www.campingsavoie.com]** Heading S on D1006 Chambéry-Lyon rd, after x-ing Col de Coux 15km S of Chambéry take D45 to St Jean-de-Couz; site sp. Med, hdg pitch, pt sl, pt shd; wc (most cont); chem disp; shwrs inc; el pnts (4-10A) €2.90-5.90; gas; shop; lndtte; tradsmn; rest, snacks high ssn; bar; BBQ; playgrnd;volleyball; football; video games; TV rm; 3% statics; dogs €1; adv bkg; quiet. "Peaceful site; magnificent scenery; friendly, helpful owner; vg, clean facs; gd walking area; Chartreuse caves open to public adj; vg base for touring Chartreuse mountains; waymarked walks from site; site well looked after" 15 May-30 Sep. € 10.80   2013*

ECHELLES, LES *9B3* (200m SE Urban) *45.43462, 5.75615* **Camping L'Arc-en-Ciel, Chemin des Berges, 38380 Entre-Deux-Guiers [04 76 66 06 97; info@camping-arc-en-ciel. com; www.camping-arc-en-ciel.com]** Fr D520 turn W sp Entre-Deux-Guiers. On ent will turn R into Ave de Montcelet dir Les Echelles & R again in 100m. Site sp fr D520. Med, some hdg/mkd pitch, pt sl, pt shd; wc (some cont); chem disp; shwrs inc; el pnts (2-4A) €2.50-4.30; gas; lndtte; shops, rest, snacks & bar nrby; 40% statics; dogs €1.10; poss cr; red low ssn; CKE/CCI. "Conv La Chartreuse area with spectacular limestone gorges; gd." ♦ ltd 1 Mar-15 Oct. € 15.10   2009*

See advertisement on inside front cover

ECLASSAN see St Vallier *9C2*

ECOMMOY *4F1* (400m NE Urban) *47.83367, 0.27985* **Camp Municipal Les Vaugeons, Rue de la Charité, 72220 Ecommoy [02 43 42 14 14 or 02 43 42 10 14 (Mairie); fax 02 43 42 62 80; mairie.ecommoy@wanadoo.fr]** Heading S on D338 foll sp. Turn E at 2nd traff lts in vill; sp Stade & Camping. Also just off A28. Med, pt sl, pt shd; well mkd; wc (some cont); chem disp; shwrs €1.30; el pnts (6A) €2.35; lndtte; shops 1km; playgrnd; tennis; poss cr; Eng spkn; adv bkg; quiet; ccard not acc; red low ssn; CKE/CCI. "Site full during Le Mans week (nr circuit); immaculate san facs; new arr no access when recep clsd. Hours 09:00 -11:30 & 15:00 -20:30; coarse sand/grass surface." ♦ ltd 1 May-30 Sep. € 8.50   2012*

ECOMMOY *4F1* (4km SE Rural) *47.81564, 0.33358*
Camp Municipal Le Chesnaie, 72220 Marigné-Laillé
[02 43 42 12 12 (Mairie); fax 02 43 42 61 23; mairie.
marigne-laille@wanadoo.fr / mairie.marigne-laille.
catherine@wanadoo.fr; www.tourisme-en-sarthe.com]
S on D338 Le Mans-Tours, turn E 3km after Ecommoy twds
Marigné-Laillé. Site in 1.5km. Sm, pt shd, hdstg, mkd pitch; wc;
shwrs; el pnts (10A) inc; shops 300m; playgrnd; pool 5km; lake
& fishing adj; tennis; poss cr; v quiet; CKE/CCI. "Lovely site;
clean, adequate san facs; pleasant warden; if height barrier
down, use phone at ent; easy access A28; Very warm welcome;
basic site, but clean; pretty site, Great NH" 1 May-30 Sep.
€ 8.00   2013*

ECOMMOY *4F1* (8km S Rural) *47.75641, 0.28780*
Camp Municipal Plan d'Eau du Fort des Salles, 72360
Mayet [02 43 46 68 72, 06 89 93 76 05 (mob) or
02 43 46 60 11 (Mairie); fax 02 43 46 07 61] On D338 Le
Mans-Tours rd turn W at St Hubert onto D13 to Mayet &
site. Sp 'Camping Plan d'Eau'. Or exit A28 sp Ecommoy &
then as above. Med, mkd pitch, pt shd; wc, chem disp; mv
service pnt; shwrs inc; el pnts (10A); gas; lndtte; shops 500m;
playgrnd; pool nrby; lake fishing; cycle hire; statics; quiet; CKE/
CCI. "Well-maintained, clean site; mkd walks nrby; recep
open 0830-1130 & 1600-1900; arr only bet these times as no
waiting area." ♦ ltd 1 Apr-15 Sep.   2009*

ECRILLE *4H2* (SE Rural) *46.50973, 5.62042*
Camping La Faz, 4 Pont de Vaux 39270 Ecrille
[03 08 25 40 27 06 22 48 10 63 (mob); camping.la.faz@sft.fr;
www.jura-camping-lafaz.com] Fr Stye at the rndabt (the
only rndabt onmain rd through Stye) take dir Geneva, then 50
meters down on R is Ecrille. Site is 1.5km from Stye. el pnts
€3.10; dog €1.40; "excel" 27 Apr-30 Sep. € 16.45   2013*

ECUEILLE *4H2* (1km SE Urban) *47.08238, 1.35257* **Camp**
Municipal de la Potinière, Ave de la Gare, 36240 Ecueillé
[02 54 40 21 10; fax 02 54 40 27 51; mairie.ecueille@
wanadoo.fr] Well sp fr town cent in Ave de la Gare - 1st part of
D8 SE fr Ecueillé. Site adj lake. Sm, hdg/mkd pitch, pt sl, pt shd;
wc (some cont); chem disp; mv service pnt; shwrs inc; el pnts (6A)
€2; gas 1km; dogs; no twin-axles; some Eng spkn; quiet; CKE/CCI.
"Immac site in lovely setting; do not arr after 1700, no site office;
park in lake car park & tel Mairie to open height barrier; lake
fishing Wed & w/end; excel." ♦ ltd 1 Jun-30 Sep. € 6.00 2008*

⊞ **EGLETONS** *7C4* (2km NE Rural) *45.41852, 2.06431*
Camping du Lac, 10 Le Pont, 19300 Egletons [tel/fax
05 55 93 14 75; campingegletons@orange.fr; www.
camping-egletons.com] Fr Egletons on D1089 for approx
2km, site 300m past Hôtel Ibis on opp site of rd. Med, mkd
pitch, terr, pt shd; wc; chem disp; baby facs; fam bthrm;
shwrs inc; el pnts (4-8A) €2.90-3.80; gas; lndtte; shops 2km;
tradsmn; rest, snacks; bar; lake sw, fishing & watersports
300m; playgrnd; entmnt; TV; 30% statics; dogs €1.30; phone;
Eng spkn; quiet; red low ssn; CKE/CCI. "Lovely, wooded
site in attractive area; lge pitches; friendly owners; vg."
€ 12.00   2011*

EGUISHEIM see Colmar *6F3*

EGUZON CHANTOME *7A3* (300m N Urban) *46.44562,*
1.58331 **Camping La Garenne, 1 Rue Yves Choplin,**
36270 Éguzon-Chantôme [02 54 47 44 85; info@
campinglagarenne.eu; www.campinglagarenne.eu]
Exit A20 junc 20 onto D36 to Eguzon; on ent vill sq cont strt on,
foll sp; site on L in 300m. Med, hdg pitch, pt sl, pt shd; wc; chem
disp; mv service pnt; baby facs; shwrs inc; el pnts (6A) €3.20;
gas 300m; lndtte (inc dryer); shop 300m; rest, snacks; bar; BBQ;
playgrnd; htd pool; cycling; lake sw & water sports 4km; entmtn;
wifi; TV rm; 20% statics; dogs €1.50; phone; site clsd 16 Dec-
14 Jan; poss cr; Eng spkn; adv bkg; poss open all year, phone
ahead; quiet; red low ssn; CKE/CCI. "All you need on site or in
vill; excel" ♦ ltd 11 Mar-18 Oct. € 31.60   2013*

> # "There aren't many sites open at this time of year"
>
> If you're travelling outside peak season remember to call ahead to check site opening dates – even if the entry says 'open all year'.

⊞ **EGUZON CHANTOME** *7A3* (3km SE Rural) *46.43372,*
1.60399 **Camp Municipal du Lac Les Nugiras, Route de**
Messant, 36270 Eguzon-Chantôme [02 54 47 45 22;
fax 02 54 47 47 22; nugiras@orange.fr; www.
eguzonlaccreuse.com] Fr A20 exit junc 20, E on D36 to
Eguzon; in vill turn R & foll site sp. Lge, hdg/mkd pitch, pt sl,
terr, pt shd; htd wc; shwrs inc; el pnts (10A) €3 (rev pol); lndtte;
shop; tradsmn; rest, snacks; bar; playgrnd; sand beach 300m;
watersports; waterski school; entmnt; games rm; some statics;
security barrier; quiet but poss noise fr statics or entmnt; red
low ssn; CKE/CCI. "Scenic site & region; ample, clean facs but
v ltd low ssn; site yourself on arr; warden avail early eves; gd
winter site; muddy after heavy rain." ♦ € 8.00   2009*

ELNE *10G1* (1.8km NE Rural) *42.60701, 2.99021* **Camp**
Municipal Al Mouly, Blvd d'Archimède, 66200 Elne
[04 68 22 08 46; fax 04 68 37 95 05; cpg.elmoli@orange.fr]
Exit A9 at Perpignan Sud dir Argelès. Site well sp fr Elne cent
in dir St Cyprien on D40. Lge, pt shd; wc; chem disp; baby
facs; shwrs inc; el pnts (10A) €3; lndtte; shop; rest & snacks
high ssn; playgrnd; pool; sand beach 5km; tennis; horseriding;
games area; entmnt; TV; poss cr; quiet; adv bkg; CKE/CCI. ♦
1 Jun-30 Sep. € 19.90   2008*

ELNE *10G1* (1km E Coastal) *42.60695, 2.99098*
Camping Le Florida, Route Latour-Bas-Elne, 66200
Elne [04 68 37 80 88; fax 04 68 37 80 76; info@
campingleflorida.com; www.campingleflorida.com]
Exit A9 junc 42 Perpignan-Sud onto D914 dir Argelès-sur-
Mer. Exit D914 junc 7 onto D11 dir Elne Centre, then D40 sp
St Cyprien to Latour-Bas-Elne, site sp. Lge, mkd pitch, pt shd;
wc; chem disp; mv service pnt; baby facs; shwrs inc; el pnts
(5A) €4; lndtte (inc dryer); shop adj; rest 400m; snacks; bar;
BBQ; playgrnd; pool; paddling pool; sand beach 4km; tennis;
games area; games rm; wifi; entmnt; TV; 70% statics; dogs;
phone; Eng spkn; adv bkg; quiet; ccard acc; red low ssn; CKE/
CCI. "Excel site; bus to beach high ssn." ♦ 4 Apr-8 Nov.
€ 28.00   2010*

FRANCE

ELNE *10G1* (4km S Rural) *42.57570, 2.96514* **Kawan Village Le Haras, Domaine St Galdric, 66900 Palau-del-Vidre [04 68 22 14 50; fax 04 68 37 98 93; haras8@wanadoo.fr; www.camping-le-haras.com]** Exit A9 junc 42 sp Perpignan S dir Argelès-sur-Mer on D900 (N9) & then D914; then exit D914 junc 9 onto D11 to Palau-del-Vidre. Site on L at ent to vill immed after low & narr rlwy bdge. Med, shd; wc; chem disp; mv service pnt; baby facs; shwrs inc; el pnts (10A) €5.; lndtte (inc dryer); supmkt 6km; tradsmn; rest, snacks & bar high ssn; BBQ (gas/elec only); playgrnd; pool; paddling pool; sand beach 6km; fishing 50m; tennis 1km; archery; wifi; entmnt; games/TV rm; some statics; dogs €4; no c'vans/m'vans over 7m high ssn; poss cr; Eng spkn; adv bkg; some rlwy noise; ccard acc; red low ssn; CKE/CCI. "Peaceful, well-kept, family-owned site in wooded parkland; helpful, friendly warden; san facs poss red low ssn; gd rest & pool; 5 mins walk to delightful vill; rds around site poss liable to flood in winter; many walks in area; Collioure worth visit; conv Spanish border; excel." ♦ 1 Apr-30 Sep. € 31.50 (CChq acc) SBS - C26 2013*

EMBRUN *9D3* (6km N Rural) *44.60290, 6.52150* **FFCC Camping Les Cariamas, Fontmolines, 05380 Châteauroux-les-Alpes [04 92 43 22 63 or 06 30 11 30 57 (mob); p.tim@free.fr; http://les.cariamas.free.fr]** Fr Embrun on N94; in 6km slip rd R to Châteauroux & foll sp to site. Site in 1km down narr but easy lane. Med, mkd pitch, pt sl, terr, pt shd; wc; chem disp; mv service pnt; baby facs; shwrs inc; el pnts (6A) €3.15; lndtte; shop 1km; tradsmn; rest, snacks; bar; BBQ; playgrnd; htd pool; lake sw adj; fishing; watersports; tennis 500m; cycle hire; wifi; 20% statics; dogs €2.50; phone; Eng spkn; adv bkg; some rd noise; red low ssn; CKE/CCI. "Excel for watersports & walking; mountain views; National Park 3km." 1 Apr-30 Oct. € 21.50 2012*

EMBRUN *9D3* (1km SE Urban) *44.55440, 6.48610* **Camping La Vieille Ferme, La Clapière, 05200 Embrun [04 92 43 04 08; fax 04 92 43 05 18; info@campingembrun.com; www.campingembrun.com]** On N94 fr Gap, cross Rv Durance just bef Embrun town, take 1st R sp La Vieille Ferme. Med, mkd pitch, pt shd; wc; chem disp; mv service pnt; shwrs inc; el pnts (6-10A) €3-5; lndtte; supmkt nr; rest, snacks; bar; playgrnd; rv 200m, lake 400m; watersports; rafting; canyonning; entmnt; some statics; dogs €2; Eng spkn; adv bkg; red long stay; quiet. "Friendly, family-run site; gd facs; pretty town." ♦ 1 May-30 Sep. € 27.00 2010*

EMBRUN *9D3* (4km S Rural) *44.54808, 6.49638* **Camping Les Grillons, Route de la Madeleine, 05200 Embrun [tel/fax 04 92 43 32 75; info@lesgrillons.com; www.lesgrillons.com]** Fr Embrun take N94 twds Gap; over bdge; L at rndabt onto D40. Turn L at 1st sharp bend; site on L in 400m. Med, mkd/hdg pitch, pt sl, pt shd; wc; chem disp; shwrs inc; el pnts (3-10A) €3.20-4; lndtte; tradsmn; snacks high ssn; BBQ; playgrnd; htd pool; paddling pool; lake sw & fishing 2km; tennis; games area; 5% statics; dogs €2; phone; Eng spkn; adv bkg; red low ssn; CKE/CCI. "Helpful, pleasant owners." 15 May-10 Sep. € 14.90 2010*

⊞ **EMBRY** *3B3* (200m NW Rural) *50.49365, 1.96463* **Aire de Service Camping-Cars d'Embryère, 62990 Embry [03 21 86 77 61]** N fr Embry site is just off D108 dir Hucqueliers & Desvres. Sm, hdstg; wc; shwrs; el pnts; mv service pnt; el pnts £2; lndry sinks; picnic area & gardens; BBQ; m'vans only. "Modern, well-kept site; jetons fr credit card-operated dispenser for services; conv Boulogne & Calais." ♦ ltd € 6.00 2009*

ENTRAIGUES *9C3* (500m W Rural) *44.90064, 5.94606* **Camp Municipal Les Vigneaux, 38740 Entraigues [04 76 30 17 05 or 06 43 76 22 66 (mob); camping.murielbillard@orange.fr]** S on D1085 (N85) fr La Mure, turn L on D114, fork R on D26 to Valbonnais. This rd becomes D526. Site on L on ent Entraigues, 4km beyond Lake Valbonnais. Ent on bend in rd, more diff if ent fr Bourg-d'Oisans. Sm, mkd pitch, pt shd; wc; mv service pnt; shwrs inc; el pnts (5A) €2 (poss rev pol); lndtte; shops 100m; rv 100m; lake 4km; fishing; 15% statics; dogs €1; adv bkg; quiet; red long stay; CKE/CCI. "Clean facs; National Park adj; warden visits am & pm." ♦ 1 May-30 Sep. € 12.00 2010*

ENTRAINS SUR NOHAIN *4G4* (200m N Rural) *47.46574, 3.25870* **Camping Salixcamp, 12 Route d'Etais, 58410 Entrains-sur-Nohain [tel/fax 03 45 50 20 45 or 06 34 44 71 46 (mob); salixcamp@camping58.com; www.camping58.com]** On D1 fr Entrains-sur-Nohain, sp on R. Sm, hdg pitch, pt shd; wc (some cont); chem disp; mv service pnt; shwrs inc; el pnts (10A) inc (poss rev pol); lndry rm; shop, rest, bar 300m; BBQ; htd pool 500m; entmnt; 1% statics; dogs €1.50; phone 300m; quiet, but church bells & cockerel (2011); CKE/CCI. "Basic site; friendly warden; san facs clean but v ltd; poss unkempt early ssn; NH only." ♦ ltd 1 Jun-30 Sep. € 13.20 2011*

ENTRAUNES *9D4* (500m E Rural) *44.18896, 6.75011* **Camping Le Tellier, Route des Grandes Alpes, 06470 Entraunes [04 93 05 51 83; campingletellier@yahoo.fr]** 15km N of Guillaumes on D2202; sp fr top end of vill. Sm, mkd pitch, pt sl, terr, pt shd; wc (some cont); chem disp (wc); shwrs inc; el pnts €3.50; shops etc 500m; quiet. "Beautiful mountain setting at foot of Col de la Cayolle; gd walking base; vg." 1 Jun-30 Sep. € 13.00 2008*

ENTRAYGUES SUR TRUYERE *7D4* (4km NE Rural) *44.67777, 2.58279* **Camping Le Lauradiol (Formaly Municipal), Banhars, 12460 Campouriez [05 65 44 53 95; fax 05 65 44 81 37; info@camping-lelauradiol.com; www.camping-lelauradiol.com]** On D34, sp on rvside. Sm, hdg/mkd pitch, pt shd; wc; el pnts (6A) inc; lndtte; shop 5km; htd pool; paddling pool; rv adj; tennis; some statics; dogs €2; quiet; CKE/CCI. "Beautiful setting & walks; excel; Power mover needed for large o'fits to access pitches; beautiful site; very friendly helpful staff; a real gem" ♦ 1 Jul-31 Aug. € 17.50 2013*

FRANCE

ENTRAYGUES SUR TRUYERE 7D4 (1.6km S Rural) 44.64218, 2.56406 **Camping Le Val de Saures (formerly Municipal),** 12140 Entraygues-sur-Truyère [05 65 44 56 92; fax 05 65 44 27 21; info@camping-valdesaures.com; www.camping-valdesaures.com] Fr town cent take D920 & in 200m turn R over narr bdge onto D904, foll site sp. Med, mkd pitch, pt shd; wc; shwrs; el pnts (6A) €3.50; lndtte; shops in town; playgrnd; pool adj; entmnt; some statics; dogs €1.50; Eng spkn; quiet; red low ssn. "Pleasant, friendly site; footbdge to town over rv; vg, well-kept san facs; recep clsd Sun & pm Mon low ssn; gd touring base." ♦ 7 Apr-30 Sep. € 18.50   2011*

ENTRECHAUX see Vaison la Romaine 9D2

"That's changed – Should I let The Club know?"

If you find something on site that's different from the site entry, fill in a report and let us know. See www.caravanclub.co.uk/europereport.

ENTREVAUX 10E4 (1.5km NW Rural) 43.96163, 6.79830 **Camping Le Brec, 04320 Entrevaux** [tel/fax 04 93 05 42 45; info@camping-dubrec.com; www.camping-dubrec.com] Site sp on R just after bdge 2km W of Entrevaux on N202. Rd (2km) to site narr with poor surface, passing places & occasional lge lorries. Med, mkd pitch, pt sl, pt shd; htd wc; chem disp; mv service pnt; baby facs; shwrs inc; el pnts (10A) €3 (poss long lead req); lndtte; tradsmn; snacks; BBQ; watersports cent, rv sw, fishing, boating/canoeing adj; wifi; TV; 10% statics; dogs €1; phone; train 2km; poss cr; Eng spkn; adv bkg; quiet; ccard acc; red CKE/CCI. "In beautiful area lake on site; friendly family owners; popular with canoeists; easy rv walk to town; beautiful area; gd" ♦ ltd 15 Mar-15 Oct. € 17.00   2013*

ENVEITG see Bourg Madame 8H4

EPERLECQUES see St Omer 3A3

EPERNAY 3D4 (1km NW Urban) 49.05734, 3.95042 **Camp Municipal d'Epernay, Allées de Cumières, 51200 Epernay** [03 26 55 32 14; fax 03 26 52 36 09; camping.epernay@ free.fr; www.epernay.fr] Fr Reims take D951 twd Epernay, cross rv & turn R at rndabt onto D301 sp Cumières (look for sp 'Stade Paul Chandon'), site sp. Site adj Stadium. Avoid town at early evening rush hour. Med, hdg/mkd pitch, pt shd; htd wc; chem disp; mv service pnt; shwrs inc; el pnts (5A) inc (poss long lead req); lndtte (inc dryer); tradsmn; supmkt 500m; snacks; bar; BBQ; playgrnd; htd, covrd pool & waterslide 2km; fishing; canoeing; tennis; cycle hire; games area; wifi; dogs €1.80; phone; poss cr; Eng spkn; adv bkg; quiet but noisy tannoy; ccard acc; red long stay/low ssn/CKE/CCI. "Attractive, well-run site on Rv Marne in lovely location; generous pitches; friendly, helpful staff; gd spacious san facs; barrier open 0800-2100 & 0700-2200 high ssn; parking outside; rec arr bef 1600; footpaths along rv into town; Mercier train tour with wine-tasting; used by grape pickers; no twin-axles or c'vans over 6m acc; gd value; vg; excel" ♦ 30 Apr-2 Oct. € 21.90   2013*

See advertisement

EPESSES, LES 2H4 (500m N Rural) 46.88920, -0.89950 **FFCC Camping La Bretèche, La Haute Bretèche, 85590 Les Epesses** [02 51 57 33 34; fax 02 51 57 41 98; contact@ campinglabretache.com; www.camping-la-bretache.com] Fr Les Herbiers foll D11 to Les Epesses. Turn N on D752, site sp on R by lake - sp fr cent Les Epesses. Med, hdg/mkd pitch, pt shd; wc, chem disp; mv service pnt; baby facs; shwrs inc; el pnts (10A) €3 (poss rev pol); lndtte (inc dryer); shop 1km; tradsmn, rest, snacks; bar; playgrnd; htd pool adj inc; fishing; tennis; horseriding; entmnt; TV; 30% statics; dogs €1.85; poss cr; Eng spkn; adv bkg; ccard acc; red low ssn; CKE/CCI. "Well-kept, well-run site; busy high ssn; helpful staff; plenty of attractions nr; events staged in park by lake high ssn; conv Puy du Fou; vg; No waste or water on site, long leads req." ♦ 1 Apr-30 Sep. € 22.10   2012*

EPINAC 6H1 (500m SW Rural) 46.98577, 4.50617 **Camp Municipal du Pont Vert, Rue de la Piscine, 71360 Epinac** [03 85 82 00 26; fax 03 85 82 13 67; info@ campingdupontvert.com; www.campingdupontvert.com] On D973 Autun dir Beaune for 16km. Turn L on D43 to Epinac, site nr public sports facs, sp in town. Med, pt shd; wc; chem disp; shwrs inc; el pnts (10A) €3.70; lndtte; shops in vill; snacks; cycle hire; wifi; some statics; dogs €1.05; extra charge for twin axles (€44 in 2009); quiet. 1 Apr-1 Nov. € 11.65   2009*

EPINAL 6F2 (1km E Urban) 48.17930, 6.46780 **Camping Parc du Château, 37 Rue du Petit Chaperon Rouge, 88000 Epinal [03 29 34 43 65 or 03 29 82 49 41 (LS); fax 03 29 31 05 12; parcduchateau@orange.fr]** Sp fr town cent. Or fr N57 by-pass take exit sp Razimont, site sp in 1km. Med, hdg/mkd pitch, some hdstg, terr, pt shd; htd wc (some cont); chem disp; mv service pnt; shwrs inc; el pnts (6-10A) €5-6; gas; lndtte; shop; snacks; BBQ; playgrnd; pool; lake sw 8km; tennis; TV; 20% statics; dogs €3; Eng spkn; adv bkg; quiet but stadium adj; ccard acc; red low ssn/long stay; CKE/CCI. "Lge pitches; ltd facs low ssn;walk through park to town; helpful new owners who have improved site " ♦ 1 Apr-30 Sep. € 18.00   2013*

⊞ **EPINAL** 6F2 (8km W Rural) 48.16701, 6.35975 **Kawan Village Club Lac de Bouzey, 19 Rue du Lac, 88390 Sanchey [03 29 82 49 41; fax 03 29 64 28 03; lacdebouzey@orange.fr; www.lacdebouzey.com]** Fr Epinal take D460 sp Darney. In vill of Bouzey turn L at camp sp. Site in few metres, by reservoir. Lge, hdg/mkd pitch, some hdstg, pt sl, terr, pt shd; htd wc (some cont); chem disp; mv service pnt; baby facs; shwrs inc; el pnts (10A) €7; gas; lndtte (inc dryer); shop; tradsmn; rest, snacks; bar; BBQ; playgrnd; htd pool; paddling pool; sand beach & lake adj; fishing; games area; cycle hire; horseriding; wifi; entmnt; TV rm; 15% statics; dogs €4; phone; adv bkg; Eng spkn; quiet; ccard acc; red low ssn/long stay; CKE/CCI. "gd site, sloping slightly but pitches fairly level. ACSI discount in LS" ♦ € 27.00 (CChq acc)   2013*

EPINIAC see Dol de Bretagne 2E4

ERDEVEN see Carnac 2G3

ERQUY 2E3 (1km N Coastal) 48.63838, -2.45561 **Yelloh! Village Les Pins, Le Guen, Route des Hôpitaux, 22430 Erquy [02 96 72 31 12; fax 02 96 63 67 94; camping.des. pins@wanadoo.fr; www.camping-les-pins-erquy.com or www.yellohvillage.co.uk]** Site sp on all app rds to Erquy. Lge, hdg/mkd pitch, pt sl, pt shd; wc (some cont); chem disp; sauna; baby facs; shwrs inc; el pnts (6A) inc; lndtte (inc dryer); shop; tradsmn; rest, snacks; bar; BBQ; playgrnd; htd, covrd pool; paddling pool; waterslide; sand beach 600m; tennis; fitness rm; jacuzzi; games area; games rm; internet; entmnt & TV rm; 40% statics; dogs €4; Eng spkn; adv bkg; quiet; ccard acc; red low ssn; CKE/CCI. "Gd family holiday site; excel facs." ♦ 29 Apr-17 Sep. € 36.00   2011*

See advertisement on inside front cover

ERQUY 2E3 (3km NE Coastal) 48.64201, -2.42456 **Camping Les Hautes Grées, Rue St Michel, Les Hôpitaux, 22430 Erquy [02 96 72 34 78; fax 02 96 72 30 15; hautesgrees@ wanadoo.fr; www.camping-hautes-grees.com]** Fr Erquy NE D786 dir Cap Fréhel & Les Hôpitaux sp to site. Med, hdg/ mkd pitch, hdstg, pt shd; htd wc (some cont); chem disp; mv service pnt; sauna; shwrs inc; el pnts (10A) €4.70 (rec long lead); gas; lndtte; shop; tradsmn; rest & snacks or 2km; bar; BBQ; playgrnd; htd pool; sand beach 400m; fishing; tennis; horseriding; gym; child entmnt; TV rm; some statics; dogs €1.70; adv bkg; ccard acc; red low ssn; CKE/CCI. "Lovely, well-run site; well-kept pitches, extra charge lge ones; helpful staff; clean, modern facs." ♦ 10 Apr-2 Oct. € 21.20   2010*

ERQUY 2E3 (1km E Coastal) 48.63828, -2.44233 **Camping Le Vieux Moulin, 14 Rue des Moulins, 22430 Erquy [02 96 72 34 23 or 06 42 22 20 36 (mob); fax 02 96 72 36 63; www.camping-vieux-moulin.com]** Sp fr all dirs on D786. Lge, mkd pitch, sl, pt shd; wc; mv service pnt; shwrs inc; el pnts (6-10A) €5-5.50; gas; lndtte (inc dryer); shop; tradsmn; rest, snacks; bar; 2 htd pools (1 covrd); paddling pool; waterslide; sand beach 900m; games rm; wifi; entmnt; TV; statics; dogs €4; poss cr; quiet; red low ssn. "Site set in pine woods; plenty of beaches in 20 mins drive; ideal for family holiday; poss diff access lge o'fits; lower pitches subject to flooding." ♦ 25 Apr-5 Sep. € 41.10   2010*

ERQUY 2E3 (5km S Rural) 48.59410, -2.48530 **Camping Bellevue, Route de Pléneuf-Val-André, La Couture, 22430 Erquy [02 96 72 33 04; fax 02 96 72 48 03; campingbellevue@yahoo.fr; www.campingbellevue.fr]** Fr Erquy, take D786 twd Le Val-André, site sp. Med, hdg/ mkd pitch, hdstg, pt shd; wc; chem disp; mv service pnt; baby facs; shwrs inc; el pnts (6-10A) €3.30-4.80; gas; lndtte; shop; tradsmn; snacks; bar; BBQ; 3 playgrnds; htd, covrd pool; paddling pool; sand beach 2km; watersports; tennis 2km; games area; games rm; entmnt; child entmnt high ssn; TV rm; 40% statics; dogs €1.70; phone; Eng spkn; adv bkg; quiet; red low ssn/long stay; ccard acc; CKE/CCI. "Excel for families; rec." ♦ 12 Apr-15 Sep. € 19.50   2009*

See advertisement below

FRANCE

⊞ **ERQUY** *2E3* (700m SW Coastal) *48.61821, -2.47638*
Aire Communale Erquy, Ave de Caroual, 22430 Erquy
[02 96 63 64 64] Take D786 fr Erquy dir Pleneuf-Val-André.
Site on R at Plage de Caroual, sp. Med, chem disp; mv
service pnt; el pnts €2; water fill €2 for 100 litres; rest; beach
100m; poss cr; m'vans only. "Rec arr early as full by 1700."
€ 3.00   2008*

"I like to fill in the reports as I travel from site to site"

You'll find report forms at the back of this guide, or you can fill them in online at www.caravaclub.co.uk/europereport.

ERQUY *2E3* (4km SW Rural/Coastal) *48.60695, -2.49723*
Camping de la Plage de St Pabu, 22430 Erquy
**[02 96 72 24 65; fax 02 96 72 87 17; camping@saintpabu.
com; www.saintpabu.com]** Sp on D786 bet Erquy & Le
Val-André at St Pabu. Narr rd, restricted passing places. Lge,
hdg/mkd pitch, hdstg, terr, pt shd; wc; chem disp; mv service
pnt; baby facs; shwrs inc; el pnts (10A) €4.80; gas; lndtte (inc
dryer); shop; tradsmn; snacks; bar; BBQ; playgrnd; sand beach
adj; wind surfing; cycle hire; games/TV rm; wifi; entmnt; some
statics; dogs €1.60; Eng spkn; adv bkg; quiet; ccard acc; red
long stay/low ssn; CKE/CCI. "In beautiful location; vg beach
adj; lge pitches; upper terrs poss diff lge o'fits; friendly; san facs
gd; vg touring base; conv St Malo, Dinan, Granit Rose coast;
excel." ♦ 1 Apr-10 Oct. € 19.90   2010*

ERR see Bourg Madame *8H4*

ESCALLES see Wissant *3A2*

ESNANDES see Rochelle, La *7A1*

ESPALION *7D4* (300m E Urban) *44.52176, 2.77098* **Camping
Roc de l'Arche, 12500 Espalion [tel/fax 05 65 44 06 79;
info@rocdelarche.com; http://www.rocdelarche.com/]**
Sp in town off D920 & D921. Site on S banks of Rv Lot 300m
fr bdge in town. Med, hdg/mkd pitch, pt shd; wc; mv service
pnt; baby facs; shwrs inc; el pnts (6-10A); lndtte; shops 250m;
snacks; BBQ; playgrnd; pool adj inc; tennis; fishing; canoeing;
dogs €0.50; poss cr; adv bkg; quiet; red low ssn. "Well-kept
site; gd sized pitches, water pnts to each; service rds narr;
friendly, helpful warden; clean, modern san facs; excel."
16 May - 10 Sept. € 32.00 (CChq acc)   2012*

ESPALION *7D4* (4km E Rural) *44.51376, 2.81849* **Camping Belle
Rive, Rue de Terral, 12500 St Côme-d'Olt [05 65 44 05 85;
bellerive12@voila.fr; http://bellerive.site.voila.fr]** Fr Espalion
take D987 E to St Côme-d'Olt; in 6km, just bef vill, turn R onto
D6. Site on N bank of Rv Lot, site sp. NB Avoid vill cent, v narr
rds. Med, pt shd; wc; mv service pnt; shwrs inc;
el pnts (6-10A) inc (poss rev pol & long lead may be req); lndtte;
shop, rest in vill; 10% statics; dogs €0.70; poss cr; Eng spkn;
quiet. "Pleasant rvside site; friendly, helpful owner; delightful
medieval vill; excel." 1 May-30 Sep. € 13.30   2010*

ESSARTS, LES *2H4* (800m W Urban) *46.77285, -1.23558*
**Camp Municipal Le Pâtis, Rue de la Piscine, 85140 Les
Essarts [02 51 62 95 83 / 06 30 02 37 09 (mob); camping.
lepatis@wanadoo.fr; www.ville-les-essarts85.fr]** Exit A83
junc 5 onto D160. On ent Les Essarts, foll sp to site. Site on
L just off rd fr Les Essarts to Chauché. Med, mkd pitch, pt
shd; htd wc; baby facs; shwrs inc; el pnts (6A) €2.80; lndtte;
supmkt, rests in town; tradsmn; snacks; BBQ (gas/charcoal);
playgrnd; 2 pools (1 Olympic size), paddling pool, tennis &
sports cent adj; 40% statics; dogs €1.60; some statics; v quiet;
ccard not acc; CKE/CCI. "Excel NH off A83; gd, clean san facs;
warden resident." ♦ 15 Apr-15 Sep. € 18.70   2013*

ESSAY *4E1* (S Rural) *48.53799, 0.24649* **FFCC Camp Municipal
Les Charmilles, Route de Neuilly, 61500 Essay [02 33 28 40 52;
fax 02 33 28 59 43; si-paysdessay@orange.fr]** Exit A28 junc 18
(Alençon Nord) onto D31 to Essay (sp L'Aigle); turn R in vill dir
Neuilly-le-Bisson; site on R in 200m. Sm, mkd pitch, pt shd; wc;
shwrs €1.60; el pnts (6A) €1.60; lndry rm; playgrnd; adv bkg;
quiet. "Lge pitches, some diff to access; park, then find TO in
vill to pay; historical vill; fair NH." 1 Apr-30 Sep. € 5.80   2009*

ESTAGEL *8G4* (3km W Rural) *42.76566, 2.66583* **Camping La
Tourèze, Route d'Estagel, 66720 Latour-de-France [tel/fax
04 68 29 16 10; camping.latoureze@wanadoo.fr;
http://campinglatoureze.monsite-orange.fr/]** Fr D117
at Estagel turn S onto D612 then R onto D17 to Latour. Site
on R on ent to vill. Med, mkd pitch, shd; wc; chem disp; mv
service pnt; baby facs; shwrs inc; el pnts (10A) €3.50; lndtte;
tradsmn; shop, rest, bar 500m; playgrnd; htd pool 3km; rv sw
adj; 13% statics; dogs €1.80; phone; Eng spkn; adv bkg; quiet;
ccard acc; red low ssn/long stay. "Pretty vill & wine 'cave' in
walking dist; rec visit Rv Agly barrage nrby; helpful staff; excel."
3 Apr-16 Oct. € 14.00   2010*

ESTAING (AVEYRON) *7D4* (2km N Rural) *44.56211,
2.67826* **Camp Municipal La Chantellerie, 12190 Estaing
[05 65 44 72 77 or 05 65 44 70 20; fax 05 65 44 03 20;
mairie-estaing@wanadoo.fr; www.estaingdouze.fr]**
Fr D920 in Estaing nr rv bdge take D167; fork R onto D97; site
on L. Well sp fr Estaing cent adj stadium. Med, hdg/mkd pitch;
pt shd; wc (some cont); mv service pnt; shwrs inc; el pnts €2;
shop 2km; rest, snacks & bar 2km; pool 2km; rv sw 2km; phone;
quiet; CKE/CCI. "Gd walking country; vg rest in Logis Hotel
in Estaing; warden calls am & pm; NH only." 22 May-30 Sep.
€ 9.10   2008*

ESTAING (HAUTES PYRENEES) see Argelès Gazost *8G2*

ESTANG *8E2* (500m E Rural) *43.86493, -0.10321*
**Camping Les Lacs de Courtès, 32240
Estang [05 62 09 61 98; fax 05 62 09 63 13; contact@
lacsdecourtes.com; www.lacsdecourtes.com]**
W fr Eauze site sp fr D30. Fr Mont-de-Marsan D932 take D1 to
Villeneuve-de-Marsan, then D1/D30 to Estang. Med, mkd pitch,
pt shd; wc; chem disp; mv service pnt; el pnts (6A) €3; lndtte (inc
dryer); tradsmn; shop 300m; supmkt 5km; rest 300m; snacks;
bar; playgrnd; htd pool; paddling pool; lake fishing; tennis;
games area; internet; entmnt; TV rm; some statics; dogs €3;
area for m'vans open all yr; adv bkg; quiet. "Gd family site." ♦
1 Apr-31 Oct. € 24.50 (CChq acc)   2011*

See advertisement on pages 32 & 33

ESTAVAR see Bourg Madame *8H4*

ETABLES SUR MER *2E3* (1km S Coastal) *48.63555, -2.83526* **Camping L'Abri Côtier, Rue de la Ville-ès-Rouxel, 22680 Etables-sur-Mer [02 96 70 61 57 or 06 07 36 01 91 (mob LS); fax 02 96 70 65 23; camping.abricotier@wanadoo.fr; www.camping-abricotier.fr]** Fr N12 round St Brieuc take D786 N thro Binic & 500m after Super U supmkt turn L to Etables. Go thro vill for approx 3 km & turn L into Rue de la Ville-es-Rouxel just after R turn for Plage-du-Moulin. Site ent just after sm x-rds. NB Long c'vans & big m'vans (to avoid going thro vill): cont on D786, past Chapel, down hill & turn L at boatyard dir Etables; take 2nd turn on R. To avoid manoeuvring, park on rd & go to recep on foot. Med, mkd pitch, pt sl, pt shd; htd wc; chem disp; mv service pnt; 15% serviced pitch; baby facs; shwrs inc; el pnts (10A) inc; gas; lndtte (inc dryer); shop; tradsmn; snacks; bar; BBQ; playgrnd; htd pool; paddling pool; jacuzzi; sand beach 500m; watersports 2km; tennis in vill; golf 4km; games rm; wifi; entmnt; TV; 10% statics; dogs €2; adv bkg; quiet; ccard acc; red low ssn; CKE/CCI. "Popular, immac site; excel beach (poss strong currents); entry narr & steep, narr corners on site rds poss diff lge o'fits; mkt Tues & Sun; vg." ♦ 03 May-16 Sep. € 31.00 SBS - B09 2013*

⊞ **ETAMPES** *4E3* (3km S Rural) *48.41015, 2.14413* **FFCC Caravaning Le Vauvert, Route de Saclas, 91150 Ormoy-la-Rivière [01 64 94 21 39; fax 01 69 92 72 59]** Fr Etampes S on N20 take D49 sp Saclas. Site on L in approx 1.5km. NB acess on a loop to cross rd. Lge, hdg/mkd pitch, shd; htd wc (cont); chem disp; mv service pnt; shwrs inc; el pnts (10A) €4; gas; shop & hypmkt 3km; rest & 3km; snacks; bar; htd, covrd pool 2km; tennis; fishing; rv adj; games area; 90% statics; quiet; site clsd 16 Dec-14 Jan; red long stay; ccard acc; CKE/CCI. "If travelling in winter phone to check site open; few touring pitches; san facs in touring area clean, ltd low ssn & clsd winter; conv train to Paris; gd NH only." € 17.00 2010*

⊞ **ETANG SUR ARROUX** *4H4* (S Rural) *46.86170, 4.19230* **FFCC Camping des 2 Rives, 26-28 Route de Toulon, 71190 Etang-sur-Arroux [03 85 82 39 73; fax 03 85 82 32 97; camping@des2rives.com; www.des2rives.com]** Fr Autun on N81 SW for 11km; turn L onto D994 to Etang-sur-Arroux; site on R after passing thro main part of town. Med, shd; wc; chem disp; mv service pnt; shwrs inc; el pnts (6-10A) €3.60; lndtte; shop 1km; rest, snacks & bar high ssn or 1km; playgrnd; pool 500m; rv sw adj; canoeing; kayaking; 20% statics; dogs €2.40; phone; Eng spkn; adv bkg; wifi; CKE/CCI. "Well-kept site bet two rvs; Dutch owners; dated but adequate san facs; gd rv sports; ltd opening Jan & Feb; nice site; helpful owners" ♦ € 27.30 2013*

ETAPLES *3B2* (2km N Rural) *50.53238, 1.6257* **Camp Municipal La Pinède, Rue de Boulogne, 62630 Etaples [tel/fax 03 21 94 34 51; www.etaples-tourisme.com]** Take D940 S fr Boulogne-sur-Mer for 25km, site on R after war cemetary & bef Atac supmkt. Or N fr Etaples for 2km on D940. Med, hdg pitch, terr, pt sl, pt shd; wc; mv service pnt; shwrs €0.70; el pnts (6A) €6; gas 500m; lndtte; rest, snacks & bar high ssn; shop high ssn 500m & 1km; playgrnd; beach 4km; rv 500m; some statics; dogs €2.80; phone; poss cr; adv bkg; some rd/rlwy noise; CKE/CCI. "No twin-axles; helpful warden; dated, tired san facs; ltd low ssn; war cemetery 200m; conv Calais; gd NH." ♦ 15 Feb-15 Nov. € 15.92 2012*

ETREAUPONT see Vervins *3C4*

ETREHAM see Bayeux *3D1*

ETRETAT *3C1* (5km E Rural) *49.69880, 0.27580* **FFCC Camping de l'Aiguille Creuse, 24 Rue de l'Aiguille, 76790 Les Loges [02 35 29 52 10; fax 02 35 10 86 64; camping@aiguillecreuse.com; www.campingaiguillecreuse.com]** On S side of D940 in Les Loges; sp. Med, unshd; wc (some cont); chem disp; mv service pnt; shwrs inc; el pnts (10A) inc; lndtte (inc dryer); shops 500m; rest 3km; snacks; bar; BBQ; playgrnd; pool; beach 3km; tennis; games rm; wifi; TV; dogs €2.50; adv bkg; quiet. "Facs ltd low ssn." ♦ 1 Apr-30 Sep. € 21.80 (CChq acc) 2010*

ETRETAT *3C1* (1km SE Urban/Coastal) *49.70053, 0.21428* **Camp Municipal, 69 Rue Guy de Maupassant, 76790 Éetretat [tel/fax 02 35 27 07 67]** Fr Fécamp SW on D940 thro town cent of Etretat & site on L. Or fr Le Havre R at 2nd traff lts; site on L in 1km on D39. Med, mkd pitch, some hdstg, pt sl, pt shd; htd wc (some cont); chem disp; mv service pnt; shwrs inc; el pnts (6A) €6 (poss rev pol); gas; lndtte (inc dryer); shop 1km; BBQ; playgrnd; shgl beach 1km; no statics; phone; poss cr; no adv bkg; quiet; ccard acc; CKE/CCI. "Busy, well-kept site; lge pitches; conv Le Havre ferry; friendly staff; clean san facs; level walk to pleasant seaside resort, attractive beach nr; gd cliff top walks nr; m'van o'night area adj (no el pnts) open all yr; early arr high ssn rec; excel; Lovely site." ♦ 1 Apr-15 Oct. € 23.60 2013*

ETRETAT *3C1* (3km S Rural) *49.68302, 0.21319* **Camping Les Tilleuls, Hameau de Grosse Mare, Impasse Dom-Filastre, 76790 Le Tilleul [tel/fax 02 35 27 11 61]** Fr Le Havre N on D940 18km to vill of Le Tilleul. Turn R after filling stn, site sp. Med, shd; wc (some cont); chem disp; shwrs €1.30; el pnts (4A) inc; lndtte; shop; snacks; BBQ; playgrnd; beach 3km; adv bkg; quiet. "Pleasant site; vg." 1 Apr-30 Sep. € 10.50 2010*

"We must tell The Club about that great site we found"

Get your site reports in by mid-August and we'll do our best to get your updates into the next edition of Caravan Europe.

ETRETAT *3C1* (10km SW Rural) *49.62271, 0.24904* **Camping Le Beau Soleil, 41 Route de Turretot, 76280 Criquetot-l'Esneval [02 35 20 24 22; fax 02 35 20 82 09; le.beau.soleil@wanadoo.fr; www.campinglebeausoleil.com]** S fr Etretat on D39 to Criquetot-l'Esneval on D79 twd Turretot. Med, pt shd; wc; chem disp; mv service pnt; shwrs €1.10; el pnts (2-10A) €1.20-6; lndtte (inc dryer); bar; playgrnd; beach 8km; 70% statics; dogs €0.70; Eng spkn; CKE/CCI. "Pleasant site, friendly owners; conv Le Havre ferry." 1 Apr-30 Sep. € 8.50 2010*

ETRIGNY see Tournus *9A2*

EU *3B2* (300m W Rural) *50.05065, 1.40996* **Camp Municipal des Fontaines, Le Parc du Château, 76260 Eu [02 35 86 20 04; camping-du-chateau@ville-eu.fr; www.ville-eu.fr]** App fr Blangy on D1015 turn L at junc with D925 & foll camp sp to site in grounds of Hôtel de Ville (chateau). Fr Abbeville on D925 fork R at 1st rndabt in town S of rlwy then immed strt on over cobbled rd to chateau walls. Turn R at chateau walls into long, narr app rd thro trees. Med, some hdg pitch, hdstg, mainly terr, pt shd; wc; chem disp; shwrs inc; el pnts (6A) €5 (poss rev pol); gas; lndtte (inc dryer); shops 250m; shgl beach 3km; 10% statics; poss cr. "Louis-Philippe museum in chateau; clean san facs; easy uphill walk to town thro forest behind chateau; Eu worth visit, an alternative to seaside towns nrby; vg Fri mkt." 1 Apr-31 Oct. € 9.20   2011*

"I need an on-site restaurant"

We do our best to make sure site information is correct, but it is always best to check any must-have facilities are still available or will be open during your visit.

EVAUX LES BAINS *7A4* (400m NE Rural) *46.17841, 2.49009* **Camp Municipal Ouche-de-Budelle, Bois du Chez, 23110 Evaux-les-Bains [05 55 65 55 82 or 05 55 65 50 20 (Mairie)]** Fr N on D993/D996 sp 'International'. Also site sp fr other dirs. Sm, hdg/mkd pitch, pt sl, pt shd; wc (some cont); chem disp (wc); shwrs inc; el pnts (10A) €3.20; lndtte; shops 400m; playgrnd; pool, tennis 200m; 10% statics; dogs €0.70; quiet. "Well-kept, well-run site; friendly; gd facs; site rds a bit narr & manoeuvring poss diff due hedges; Evaux attractive, interesting health spa; gd." ♦ ltd Mar-Oct. € 6.60   2011*

EVAUX LES BAINS *7A4* (5km W Rural) *46.18597, 2.43391* **Camp Municipal La Pouge, Rue du Stade, 23170 Chambon-sur-Voueize [05 55 82 13 21; fax 05 55 82 19 11; www.ville-chambonsurvoueize.fr]** Take D915 fr Evaux-les-Bains; at ent to Chambon-sur-Voueize turn R bef x-ing rv. Site adj municipal stadium. Sm, mkd pitch, pt shd; wc; chem disp; mv service pnt; shwrs inc; el pnts (10A) €1.30; lndtte; shops, rest & bar 150m; BBQ; tennis; games rm; 10% statics; dogs €0.50; phone; bus 1.5km; adv bkg; quiet; no ccard acc; CKE/CCI. "Pleasant rural area; sm pitches; gd walking & cycling; golf at Gouzon; vg." 1 Apr-31 Oct. € 6.20   2008*

EVIAN LES BAINS *9A3* (4km E Rural) *46.40033, 6.64546* **Camping de Vieille Eglise, Route des Prés Parrau, 74500 Lugrin [04 50 76 01 95; campingvieilleeglise@wanadoo.fr; www.camping-vieille-eglise.com]** D21 fr Evian via Maxilly, or turn S off D1005 at Tourronde, sp. Med, hdg/mkd pitch, pt terr, pt sl, pt shd; wc; chem disp; mv service pnt; baby facs; private san facs avail; shwrs inc; el pnts (4-10A) €3.25-4.50; gas; lndtte (inc dryer); shop; supmkt 300m; rest 2km; BBQ; playgrnd; htd pool; paddling pool; shgl beach & lake fishing 1km; games area; wifi; entmnt; 50% statics; dogs €2; adv bkg; quiet; ccard acc; red long stay; CKE/CCI. "View of Lac Léman." ♦ 10 Apr-14 Oct. € 19.50 (CChq acc)   2011*

EVIAN LES BAINS *9A3* (6km W Rural) *46.39388, 6.52805* **FFCC Camping Les Huttins, 350 Rue de la Plaine, Amphion-les-Bains, 74500 Publier [tel/fax 04 50 70 03 09; campingleshuttins@gmail.com; www.camping-leshuttins. com]** Fr Thonon on D1005 twds Evian, at start of Amphion turn L onto Rte du Plaine sp; ent 200m on R after rndabt. Fr Evian on D1005 twds Thonon, at end of Amphion turn R & foll sp. Med, mkd pitch, wc (some cont); chem disp; mv service pnt; shwrs inc; el pnts €3; gas; lndtte; shop; hypermkt 300m; rest, bar 400m; BBQ; playgrnd; pool & sports complex 200m; lake sw 400m; tennis adj; TV; 5% statics; dogs €1; Eng spkn; adv bkg; quiet; red low ssn. "Spacious, simple, relaxed site in beautiful area; enthusiastic, helpful owners; basic, clean san facs; gd base for Lake Léman; poss unrel opening dates - phone ahead; excel." 10 Apr-30 Sep. € 17.00   2013*

EVRON *4F1* (7km SE Rural) *48.09423, -0.35642* **Camp Municipal La Croix Couverte, 10 Rue de la Croix Couverte, 53270 Ste Suzanne [02 43 01 41 61 or 02 43 01 40 10 (Mairie); fax 02 43 01 44 09]** Take D7 SW fr Evron sp Ste Suzanne. Site 800m S (downhill) after this sm fortified town. Sm, some hdg/mkd pitch, hdstg, pt shd; wc; shwrs inc; el pnts (3-5A) inc; shops 800m; playgrnd; htd pool adj; walking & horseriding adj; some statics; quiet; CKE/CCI. "Simple, clean site in lovely area; sm pitches; site open to public for cycling & walking; pool v busy high ssn; unspoilt town & castle with historic Eng connections; excel NH - open all yr for m'vans." ♦ 1 May-30 Sep. € 10.00   2011*

⊞ **EVRON** *4F1* (300m W Urban) *48.15077, -0.41223* **Camp Municipal de la Zone Verte, Blvd du Maréchal Juin, 53600 Evron [02 43 01 65 36; fax 02 43 37 46 20; camping@evron.fr; www.camping.evron.fr]** Site on ring rd 200 yards from Super-U supmkt; clearly sp fr all rds into town. Med, some hdg pitch, pt shd; htd wc (some cont); chem disp; mv service pnt; shwrs inc; el pnts (6-10A) €1.60-2.45; lndtte; shops 1km; playgrnd; htd pool & sports complex adj; 50% statics; dogs €0.80; no twin-axles; adv bkg; quiet; red long stay. "Attractive, peaceful, comfortable, well-kept site with many flowers; gd, clean san facs; restricted recep hrs in winter - warden on site lunchtime & early eve only; poss maintenance issues early ssn (2011); no twin-axles; some worker's c'vans; highly rec for sh or long stay; excel; gd value" ♦ ltd € 12.45   2013*

EXCENEVEX see Thonon les Bains *9A3*

EYMET *7D2* (5km SW Rural) *44.63211, 0.39977* **Camping Le Moulin Brûlé, 47800 Agnac [tel/fax 05 53 83 07 56; thebeales@wanadoo.fr; www.campingswfrance.co.uk]** Fr S on D933 at Miramont-de-Guyenne (6km S of Eymet) turn E onto D1; in 4km turn L onto C501 dir Eymet; site on L in 2km. Or fr N approx 1km after Eymet turn L onto C1 sp Chateau Pèchalbet. In 1.5km at x-rds turn L sp Bourgougnague, site on R in 2km. NB Narr lanes & bends on app. Sm, mkd pitch, hdstg, sl, unshd; wc; shwrs; chem disp (wc); shwrs inc; el pnts (10-16A) €3; lndtte; shops, rest, snacks & bar 6km; BBQ (charcoal); playgrnd; pool; games area; 1% statics; no twin axles; adv bkg. "Lovely, peaceful, well-kept site in pleasant surroundings; friendly British owners; excel san facs; gd cycling & walking; excel." Apr-Oct. € 12.00   2011*

Tell us about the sites you visit

EYMET 7D2 (500m W Urban) 44.66923, 0.39615 Camping du Château (formerly Municipal), Rue de la Sole, 24500 Eymet [05 53 23 80 28 / 06 98 16 97 93 (mob); fax 05 53 22 22 19; eymetcamping@aol.com; www. eymetcamping.fr] Thro Miramont onto D933 to Eymet. Turn opp Casino supmkt & foll sp to site. Sp on ent to Eymet fr all dirs. Sm, hdg/mkd pitch, pt shd, wc; chem disp; mv service pnt; shwrs inc; el pnts (10A) €3 (poss rev pol); gas 300m; lndtte; shops, rest, snacks & bar 300m; playgrnd; pool 1.5km; lake & rv sw nrby; boat & cycle hire; wifi; dogs; poss cr; Eng spkn; adv bkg; no twin-axles; quiet; red long stay; CKE/CCI. "Lovely, well-kept site by rv behind medieval chateau; friendly, helpful owner; immac san facs; wine tasting on site; Thur mkt; excel; Peaceful site nr lovely Bastide town" ♦ 1 Apr-30 Sep. € 10.50   2013*

EYMOUTHIERS see Montbron 7B3

EYMOUTIERS 7B4 45.75069, 1.69194 Domaine des Monts de Bussy (Naturist), Bussy-Varache, 87120 Eymoutiers [05 55 69 68 20; montsdebussy@wanadoo.fr; www. montsdebussy.net] Exit A20 junc 35 onto D979 dir Eymoutiers; in approx 40km, just bef Eymoutiers, turn L onto D129A sp Bussy; pass thro Bussy, in 2km; then 300m after vill turn R onto sm rd leading to site. Sm, pt sl, unshd; wc; chem disp; shwrs inc; el pnts €4; lndtte; sm bar; htd pool; dogs €3.50; Eng spkn; quiet; ccard not acc; red low ssn; CKE/CCI. "Lovely quiet site with views; lge pitches; friendly owners; v clean san facs; lovely pool; in Millevaches en Limousin national park; excel." 21 May-31 Oct. € 23.00   2011*

EYMOUTIERS 7B4 (8km N Rural) 45.80560, 1.84342 Camp Municipal Les Peyrades, Auphelle, Lac de Vassivière, 87470 Peyrat-le-Château [06 11 22 07 06 (mob) or 05 55 69 48 75 (Mairie); peyrat-tourisme@wanadoo.fr; www.peyrat-tourisme.com] Fr Peyrat E on D13, at 5km sharp R onto D222 & foll sp for Lac de Vassivière. At wide junc turn L, site on R. Med, pt sl, pt shd; wc cont; shwrs inc; el pnts (5A) €2.50; lndtte; shop, rest, snacks, bar adj; BBQ; lake sw adj; sand beach adj; dogs; phone; poss v cr; adv bkg; quiet. "Helpful warden; some pitches o'look lake." 1 May-30 Sep. € 8.70   2009*

EYMOUTIERS 7B4 (8km N Rural) 45.82584, 1.76599 Camp Municipal Moulin de l'Eau, 87470 Peyrat-le-Château [05 55 69 41 01 or 05 55 69 48 75; peyrat-tourisme@ wanadoo.fr] 1.5km N of Peyrat on D940 to Bourganeuf, site on L immed bef bdge. Med, pt sl, pt terr, pt shd; wc; shwrs; el pnts (6A); shops 2km; fishing; dogs; no adv bkg; quiet; CKE/CCI. "Pleasant site; beautiful area; pay at Mairie in town." 15 Jun-15 Sep.   2009*

EYMOUTIERS 7B4 (1km S Rural) 45.73061, 1.75249 Camp Municipal, St Pierre-Château, 87120 Eymoutiers [05 55 69 10 21; fax 05 55 69 27 19; mairie-eymoutiers@ wanadoo.fr; www.mairie-eymoutiers.fr] On E of D940 S fr Eymoutiers site sp on R. Diff sharp bend bef ent. Sm, pt sl, terr, pt shd; wc; shwrs; el pnts (6A) €2 (long lead poss req); shops 2km; adv bkg; quiet. "Gd views; clean site; site yourself; warden calls; attractive town & area; excel value; v gd san facs; rec." 1 Jun-30 Sep. € 8.90   2012*

EYMOUTIERS 7B4 (10km W Rural) 45.71633, 1.60127 FFCC Camping Le Cheyenne, Ave Michel Sinibaldi, 87130 Châteauneuf-la-Forêt [05 55 69 39 29; contact@camping-le-cheyenne.com; www.camping-le-cheyenne.com] Fr Limoges E on D979 for approx 33km. Turn R at Lattée onto D15 & in 4km foll sp to site. Med, hdg/mkd pitch, pt shd; htd wc; chem disp; mv service pnt; shwrs inc; el pnts (6A) €3; lndtte; tradsmn; rest, snacks; bar; playgrnd; lake sw & fishing adj; tennis; wifi; some statics; dogs €1; phone; Eng spkn. "Lovely position by lake & woods but also nr town; gd size pitches; reasonable facs; poss unkempt/untidy low ssn (2006); factory on 24hr shift gives cont background hum, but not obtrusive; gd walks; gd." 1 Apr-31 Oct. € 12.00   2011*

EYZIES DE TAYAC, LES 7C3 (4km N Rural) 44.98070, 1.04457 Camping Bouyssou, Lespinasse, 24620 Tursac [05 53 06 98 08; campingbouyssou@wanadoo.fr; http:// campingbouyssou24.pagesperso-orange.fr] N fr Les Eyzies on D707, turn L across rv bdge sp La Madelaine. Take R fork, site sp on L. Sm, hdg pitch, pt shd; wc; chem disp; shwrs inc; el pts (10A) €2; shop, rest 1km; playgrnd; pool; paddling pool; rv fishing 200m; some statics; poss cr; adv bkg; quiet. "Pleasant site with views; friendly, helpful owner; vg modern, unisex san facs; excel touring base." 2 Jun-29 Sep. € 10.00   2010*

EYZIES DE TAYAC, LES 7C3 (4km NE Rural) 44.95633, 1.04410 Camping La Ferme du Pelou, 24620 Tursac [05 53 06 98 17; www.lafermedupelou.com] Fr Les Eyzies-de-Tayac take D706 dir Tursac. In 3km turn R, site sp. 1km up hill on L. Ent poss diff for lge o'fits. Med, hdg pitch, pt shd; wc; chem disp; mv service pnt; shwrs inc; el pnts (6A) €2.80 (long lead poss req); lndtte; shop, rest & bar 4km; BBQ; playgrnd; htd pool; mainly statics; dogs free; phone; adv bkg; quiet low ssn; CKE/CCI. "Well-kept, clean site; views fr part of site without el pnts; friendly, helpful owners; gd san facs, poss too few high ssn; vg pool; gd walking; many dogs, inc owner's; site too sm for v lge o'fits; highly rec." ♦ 15 Mar-15 Nov. € 10.50   2009*

EYZIES DE TAYAC, LES 7C3 (5km NE Rural) 44.96935, 1.04623 Camping Le Pigeonnier, Le Bourg, 24620 Tursac [tel/fax 05 53 06 96 90; campinglepigeonnier@orange.fr; www.campinglepigeonnier.fr/] NE fr Les Eyzies for 5km on D706 to Tursac; site is 200m fr Mairie in vill cent; ent tight. Sm, hdg/mkd pitch, pt sl, terr, shd; wc; chem disp in vill; shwrs inc; el pnts (10A) €3; gas; lndtte; tradsmn; shop 5km; snacks; bar; playgrnd; sm pool; shgl beach, rv sw, fishing & canoeing 1km; horseriding; cycle hire; dogs €1; adv bkg; quiet; no ccard acc; CKE/CCI. "Freshwater pool (v cold); spacious, grass pitches; facs poss stretched high ssn; v quiet hideaway site in busy area; close to prehistoric sites; Friendly Brit owners" 1 Jun-30 Sep. € 20.50   2012*

⊞ EYZIES DE TAYAC, LES 7C3 (6km NE Rural) 44.95277, 1.08820 FFCC Camping Auberge (Veyret), Bardenat, 24620 Marquay [05 53 29 68 44 / 05 53 31 58 00 ls; fax 05 53 31 58 28; contact@auberge-veyret.com; www. auberge-veyret.com] Leave Les Eyzies dir Sarlat on D47; in 4km go L onto D48 (dir Tamniès); in 3.5km turn L & foll sp for Auberge Veyret. Sm, sl, pt shd; wc; chem disp (wc); shwrs inc; el pnts (16A) €3; tradsmn; rest, snacks; playgrnd; pool; adv bkg low ssn ess; quiet; CKE/CCI. "Excel rest; simple CL-type site with sl grass pitches & views; very quiet and lovely site, lovely views; helpful owner" € 12.00   2013*

FRANCE

FRANCE

EYZIES DE TAYAC, LES *7C3* (2km S Rural) *44.92370, 1.02910*
Camping Le Pech Charmant, 24620 Les Eyzies-de-Tayac
[05 53 35 97 08; fax 05 53 35 97 09; info@lepech.com;
www.lepech.com] Fr Sarlat take D47 to Les Eyzies then take
D706 dir Le Bugue. Turn L immed after g'ge & foll sm site sps
round 1-way system. Med, mkd pitch, terr, pt shd; wc; chem
disp; mv service pnt; shwrs; el pnts (10A) €3; gas; lndtte (inc
dryer); shop; tradsmn; snacks; bar; BBQ (gas); playgrnd; pool;
paddling pool; rv sw 2km; horseriding; children's farm; games
area; games rm; wifi; entmnt; 10% statics; dogs €1; phone;
Eng spkn; adv bkg; quiet; ccard acc; CKE/CCI. ♦ 1 Apr-1 Oct.
€ 21.00   2009*

EYZIES DE TAYAC, LES *7C3* (2km SW Rural) *44.92361,
1.00327* Camping Le Queylou, 24620 Les Eyzies-de-Tayac
[05 53 06 94 71; josette.garrigue@orange.fr; www.
vacances24queylou.com] Take D706 fr Les Eyzies dir Le
Bugue; after 2km turn L (after sharp L hand bend) up hill
on narr rd to Le Queylou in 1km sp on app. Sm, pt sl, pt
shd; wc; shwrs inc; el pnts (16A); shops 3km; BBQ; some
statics; dogs; poss cr; Eng spkn; adv bkg; quiet; red long stay/
CKE/CCI. "Pleasant CL-type site; helpful owner; woodland
walks."   2008*

EYZIES DE TAYAC, LES *7C3* (1km NW Rural) *44.93695,
1.00563* Camping La Rivière, 3 Route du Sorcier, 24620
Les Eyzies-de-Tayac [05 53 06 97 14; fax 05 53 35 20 85;
la-riviere@wanadoo.fr; www.lariviereleseyzies.com]
Site off D47 Rte de Périgueux. Lge o'fits use 2nd ent by sw
pool & walk to recep. Med, hdg/mkd pitch, pt shd; wc; chem
disp; mv service pnt; shwrs; el pnts (6-10A) €3.60-4; lndtte;
shop; rest, snacks; bar; playgrnd; pool; paddling pool; canoe
hire 500m; tennis; internet; TV rm; 5% statics; dogs €1; phone;
Eng spkn; adv bkg; quiet; ccard acc; red low ssn; CKE/CCI.
"Pleasant site; sm pitches; gd clean facs; walking dist many
prehistoric caves." ♦ 4 Apr-1 Nov. € 19.10   2009*

FALAISE *3D1* (500m W Urban) *48.89545, -0.20476* FFCC
Camp Municipal du Château, 3 Rue du Val d'Ante, 14700
Falaise [02 31 90 16 55 or 02 31 90 30 90 (Mairie); fax
02 31 90 53 38; camping@falaise.fr; www.falaise.fr/
tourisme/le-camping] Fr N on N158, at rndabt on o'skirts of
town, turn L into vill; at next rndabt by Super U go strt on; at
2nd mini-rndabt turn R; then sp on L after housing estate. Or
fr S on D958, at 1st rndabt foll sp town cent & site. Cont down
hill thro town then up hill to 1st rndabt, site sp, then sp on L
after housing est. Med, hdg/mkd pitch, pt sl, terr, pt shd; wc
(some cont); chem disp; mv service pnt; shwrs inc; el pnts (6-
10A) €4.20; gas 500m; lndry rm; tradsmn; shops, rest, snacks,
bar 500m; BBQ; playgrnd; htd pool in town; tennis; wifi; TV rm;
sat TV some pitches; dogs €2.20; poss cr; some Eng spkn; adv
bkg; quiet; ccard acc; red low ssn/long stay/CKE/CCI. "Lovely,
peaceful, well-kept site in pleasant surroundings; pitches poss
diff lge o'fits; clean san facs (lots of hot water) poss ltd low ssn
& stretched high ssn & clsd 2200-0800; pitch self & pay later;
uphill walk to town, birthplace of William the Conqueror; vet
in Falaise; mkt Sat am; excel; clean well kept facs; easy walking
dist to town" ♦ ltd 1 May-30 Sep. € 23.80   2013*

FANJEAUX *8F4* (2.5km S Rural) *43.18070, 2.03301* FFCC
Camping à la Ferme Les Brugues (Vialaret), 11270
Fanjeaux [04 68 24 77 37; fax 04 68 24 60 21; lesbrugues@
free.fr; http://lesbrugues.free.fr] Exit A61 junc 22 onto D4/
D119 (dir Mirepoix) to Fanjeaux; cont on D119 dir Mirepoix; at
top of hill turn L onto D102 sp La Courtète (past rest La Table
Cathare & fuel station) & in 100m turn R to site in 2.5km. Site
well sp fr Fanjeaux. Sm, hdg/mkd pitch, pt sl, terr, shd; wc;
chem disp; shwrs inc; el pnts (10A) inc (rev pol); lndtte (inc
dryer); shop 2km; tradsmn; rest, bar 2.5km; playgrnd; games
rm; wifi; few statics; dogs; Eng spkn; adv bkg; quiet; CKE/CCI.
"Delightful, peaceful, 'off the beaten track' site adj sm lake;
care req sm children; well-kept; v lge pitches, some o'looking
lake; friendly, helpful owners; gd clean san facs; many walks;
beautful countryside; excel touring base; rec." ♦ 1 Jun-30 Sep.
€ 14.30   2013*

FAOUET, LE *2F2* (2km SE Rural) *48.01826, -3.47142* Camp
Municipal Beg er Roch, Route de Lorient, 56320 Le
Faouët [02 97 23 15 11 or 06 89 33 75 70 (mob); fax
02 97 23 11 66; camping.lefaouet@wanadoo.fr] SE fr Le
Faouët on D769 site sp on L. Med, hdg/mkd pitch, pt shd;
wc; mv service pnt; chem disp; shwrs inc; el pnts (10A) €3;
gas 2km; lndtte; shops, tradsmn; rest, bar 2km; playgrnd; htd
pool; lake sw 2km; fishing; tennis; games area; golf; games/
TV rm; 25% statics; dogs €1.05; Eng spkn; adv bkg; ccard acc;
red long stay/CKE/CCI. "Pleasant, well-kept, quiet rvside site;
helpful warden; kingfishers on rv; many mkd walks; lovely,
historic area." ♦ 10 Mar-30 Sep. € 16.50   2010*

FAUTE SUR MER, LA see Aiguillon sur Mer, L' *7A1*

FAVERGES *9B3* (2km N Rural) *45.76676, 6.30941*
Camp Municipal Les Pins, 90 Rue Pré de Foire, 74210
St Ferréol [04 50 32 47 71 or 04 50 44 56 36 (Mairie); fax
04 50 44 49 76; st.ferreol@wanadoo.fr; www.pays-de-
faverges.com] Fr D1508 nr Faverges go N on D12 for 2km
to site on rvside. Med, mkd pitch, pt sl, pt shd; wc (some
cont); chem disp; shwrs; el pnts (10A) €2.25; gas; lndtte;
shop 2km; tradsmn; rest, snacks; bar; playgrnd; dogs €1.15;
phone; poss cr; Eng spkn; adv bkg; quiet; ccard not acc; CKE/
CCI. "Well-equipped site; gd walking; no twin-axles or 4x4s;
poss boggy in heavy rain; barrier - low ssn may need to contact
Mairie." ♦ 15 Jun-15 Sep. € 10.45   2008*

FAVERGES *9B3* (2km N Rural) *45.79090, 6.21630* Campéole
Camping La Nublière, 30 Allée de la Nublière, 74210
Doussard [04 50 44 33 44; fax 04 50 44 31 78; nubliere@
campeole.com; www.camping-nubliere.com or www.
campeole.com] Fr Annecy take D1508 twd Albertville, site
on L in 20km, 300m after Camp du Lac Bleu. Fr Faverges NW
on D1508. Lge, mkd pitch, pt shd, wc (some cont); chem
disp; mv service pnt; shwrs inc; el pnts (6A) €4.10; gas; lndtte
(inc dryer); shop; rest, snacks; bar; BBQ; playgrnd; lake sw
adj; boating; golf; cycle hire; games area; wifi; entmnt; dogs
€3.50; poss cr; adv bkg; poss noisy; ccard acc; red low ssn.
"Helpful staff; gd san facs." ♦ 30 Apr-19 Sep. € 22.50
2010*

See advertisement on pages 14 & 15

FAVEROLLES *9C1* (S Rural) *44.93932, 3.14759* **Camp Municipal, 15320 Faverolles [04 71 23 49 91 or 04 71 23 40 48 (Mairie); fax 04 71 23 49 65; faverolles. mairie@wanadoo.fr]** Fr A75 exit junc 30 & take D909 S, turn L onto D13 at Viaduct de Garabit & foll sp for Faverolles for 5km, then sp to site dir St Chély-d'Apcher. Sm, mkd pitch, pt sl, pt shd; htd wc (some); chem disp; shwrs inc; el pnts (6A) inc (rev pol); shops 500m; lndtte; playgrnd; some statics; phone; ccard not acc; quiet. "Nr pretty lake; excel, clean san facs; vg rest in vill." ♦ 1 Jun-15 Oct. € 11.40   2009*

FAVEROLLES SUR CHER see Montrichard *4G2*

FAYENCE *10E4* (3km E Rural) *43.60659, 6.74855* **Camping Les Prairies, Chemin des Maures, 83440 Callian [04 94 76 48 36; fax 04 94 85 72 21; info@ campingdesprairies.com; http://campingdesprairies.com]** Site on D562 3km W fr junc with D37. Site next to Renault g'ge. Fr A8 exit junc 39 onto D37 to D562 (gd rd) & as above. Med, mkd pitch, pt sl, pt shd; wc; chem disp; shwrs inc; el pnts (10A) €4; lndtte; shops 400m; supmkt 800m; playgrnd; pool; fishing, sailing 5km; wifi; 70% statics; dogs €2; poss noisy; Eng spkn; adv bkg; CKE/CCI. "Modern san facs." Nice ♦ 1 Apr-31 Oct. € 21.00   2009*

⊞ **FAYENCE** *10E4* (5km E Rural) *43.60139, 6.77278* **FFCC Camp de Loisirs du Lac, Domaine de la Chesnaie, 83440 Montauroux [04 94 76 46 26; fax 04 94 47 66 16; contact@ campingdulac.fr; www.campingdulac.fr]** Fr A8 exit junc 39 onto D37; turn L onto D562 sp Draguignan; site on L in 1km soon after rndabt. Lge, hdg/mkd pitch, shd; wc (some cont); chem disp; shwrs inc; el pnts (2-10A) €1.50; gas; lndtte; shop 500m; snacks; bar; BBQ (gas/elec); playgrnd; pool; mainly statics; dogs €3-4; bus; phone; Eng spkn; adv bkg; quiet; ccard acc; CKE/CCI. "Friendly, helpful staff; poss diff access due trees/shrubs; ltd facs & poss unkempt low ssn (2006)." € 18.50   2008*

FAYENCE *10E4* (10km S Rural) *43.58449, 6.69016* **Camping Le Parc, Quartier Trestaure, 83440 St Paul-en-Forêt [04 94 76 15 35; fax 04 94 84 71 84; campingleparc@ wanadoo.fr; www.campingleparc.fr]** Fr D562 midway bet Draguinan & Grasse turn S onto D4. Site sp on L. Exit A8 junc 39, N on D37 for 11km, at junc with D562 turn L for 10km; L onto D4 for 900m; sm sp, L into sm lane, site on bend. Med, mkd pitch, shd; htd wc; chem disp; mv service pnt; shwrs inc; el pnts (10A) €5; gas; lndtte; shop; tradsmn; rest; snacks; bar high ssn; playgrnd; pool; lake 6km; beach 25km; tennis; fishing; wifi; entmnt; 10% statics; dogs €4.10; poss cr; adv bkg; quiet; red low ssn; CKE/CCI; "Conv hill vills of Provence; gd rests in St Paul; vg." 6 Apr-30 Sep. € 36.00   2013*

FAYENCE *10E4* (6km W Rural) *43.3500, 6.39590* **Camping La Tuquette (Naturist), The High Suanes 83440 Fayence [04 94 76 19 40; fax 04 94 76 23 95; robert@tuquette.com; www.tuquette.com]** Fr Fayence take N562. At km 64.2 sp turn R, site ent 100m. Sm, mkd pitch, terr, pt shd; wc; chem disp; shwrs ind; el pnts (6A) €4.60; lndtte; shop 64km; tradsmn; snacks; bar; BBQ; playgrnd; 2 htd pools; wifi; some statics; dogs €2; poss cr; Eng spkn; adv bkg; quiet; INF card. "Vg, clean site; friendly owners." ♦ 10 Apr-26 Sep. € 36.40   2013*

FECAMP *3C1* (6km SE Rural) *49.74041, 0.41660* **Camp Municipal Le Canada, 76400 Toussaint [02 35 29 78 34 or 02 35 27 56 77 (Mairie); fax 02 35 27 48 82; mairie. toussaint@wanadoo.fr; http://commune-de-toussaint.fr]** On D926 N of Toussaint (sharp turn at side of golf course). Med, hdg pitch, pt sl, shd; htd wc (some cont); shwrs inc; el pnts (4-10A) inc; lndtte; shop; BBQ; playgrnd; games area; 70% statics; dogs; quiet; CKE/CCI. "Lovely quiet site; helpful warden; clean san facs; gd." ♦ 15 Mar-15 Oct. € 12.12   2011*

FECAMP *3C1* (500m SW Coastal) *49.75712, 0.36200* **Camping Le Domaine de Renéville, Chemin de Nesmond, 76400 Fécamp [02 35 28 20 97 or 02 35 10 60 00; fax 02 35 29 57 68; reneville@aliceadsl.fr; www. campingdereneville.com]** Site off Etretat rd (D940) on o'skts of Fécamp; sp. NB Steep cliff site, access poss diff lge o'fits; narr bends. NB Lge o'fits best app fr dir Etretat & not Fécamp town. Lge, hdg/mkd pitch, terr, pt sl, shd; htd wc; chem disp; mv service pnt; shwrs inc; el pnts (6A) inc (poss long cable req; poss rev pol); lndtte (inc dryer); shop; tradsmn; snacks; rest & bar in town; playgrnd; pool adj; shgl beach 500m; 15% statics; phone; Eng spkn; adv bkg fr 1000 same day only - rec peak ssn; CKE/CCI. "Vg site with sea views; gd san facs - poss steep walk to reach; interesting town; sep m'van o'night area on harbour adj TO; highly rec." ♦ 1 Apr-15 Nov. € 18.50 2011*

FEINS *2E4* (2km N Rural) *48.33923, -1.63816* **Camp Municipal L'Etang de Boulet/La Bijouterie, La Bijouterie, 35440 Feins [02 99 69 63 23 or 02 99 69 70 52 (Mairie); fax 02 99 69 70 52; feins@wanadoo.fr; www.feins.fr]** N fr Feins on D91; site on L in 1.5km. Sp fr Feins & fr Marcillé-Raoul. Sm, hdg/mkd pitch, pt shd; wc; chem disp (wc); shwrs inc; el pnts €3; lndtte; shops, rest & snacks nrby; playgrnd; lake & beach adj; sailing & canoe hire; 40% statics; dogs; quiet; CKE/CCI. "Vg site; cycle track." ♦ ltd May-30 Sep. € 11.10   2009*

FELLETIN see Aubusson *7B4*

FENOUILLER, LE see St Gilles Croix de Vie *2H3*

FERE, LA *3C4* (400m N Urban) *49.66554, 3.36205* **Camp Municipal du Marais de la Fontaine, Rue Vauban, 02800 La Fère [03 23 56 82 94; fax 03 23 56 40 04]** S on D1044 (St Quentin to Laon); R onto D338; turn E at rndabt; ignore 1st camping sp; turn N at next rndabt; site sp. Or Exit A26 junc 12 onto D1032 SW; in 2km turn R onto D35; in 4km pass under D1044; in 400m turn R; in 800m turn R at traff lts; foll over bdge to sports complex. Sm, hdg/mkd pitch, pt shd; wc; chem disp (wc); shwrs inc; el pnts (15A) €3; shop; tradsmn; rest, snacks & bar 1km; BBQ; htd, covrd pool adj; dogs €1.20; adv bkg rec; rd & rlwy noise; red long stay; CKE/CCI. "Well-kept site adj leisure cent; conv Calais, 2hrs 30mins; clean san facs; pitching awkward due sm pitches & narr site rds; warden lives adj site - on arr open double gates & ring doorbell to register; gates shut 2200-0700 - no vehicle/person access; avoid 1st w/ end June as Wine & Food Festival held on site; conv A26; gd NH." ♦ ltd 1 Apr-30 Sep. € 14.00   2013*

FERMANVILLE see Cherbourg *1C4*

FERRIERE D'ALLEVARD, LA see Allevard *9B3*

FERRIERES EN GATINAIS *4F3* (300m N Rural) *48.09198,
2.78482* **Camp Municipal Le Perray/Les Ferrières, Rue du
Perray, 45210 Ferrières-en-Gâtinais [06 71 43 25 95 (mob)
or 02 38 87 15 44 (Mairie); fax 02 38 96 62 76; ferrieres.
mairie@wanadoo.fr or cyril.martin@ferrieresengatinais.fr;
www.metiers-art-gatinais.com]** N fr Mantargis on N7; R
onto D96/D32 sp Ferrières & foll camp sp. Med, mkd pitch, pt
shd; wc; chem disp; mv service pnt; shwrs inc; el pnts (10A)
€4.10; lndtte; shops, supmkt & rests 300m; playgrnd; pool &
sports facs adj; tennis; rv fishing adj; entmnt; 5% statics; quiet.
"Vg site; direct access to sm rv; gd facs & security; 2 gd rests
nrby." 1 Apr-30 Oct. € 10.80   2013*

FERRIERES SUR SICHON *9B1* (300m SE Rural) *46.02246,
3.65326* **Camp Municipal, 03250 Ferrières-sur-Sichon
[04 70 41 10 10; fax 04 70 41 15 22]** Well sp in Ferrières-sur-
Sichon. At x-rds of D995 & D122. Sm, pt sl, pt shd; htd wc;
shwrs inc; el pnts €2.20; shop 500m; playgrnd; dogs; quiet.
"CL-type site; friendly warden visits 1930; gd san facs; excel
NH." 1 Jun-30 Sep. € 7.70   2008*

FERTE GAUCHER, LA *4E4* (700m E Rural) *48.77928,
3.31072* **FLOWER Camping La Ferté-Gaucher, Rue de
Coutran, 77320 La Ferté-Gaucher [01 64 20 20 40;
info@flowercampings-la-ferte-gaucher.com; www.
flowercampings.com]** On D634 bet Coulommiers & Sézanne;
site opp leisure cent. Lge, hdg/mkd pitch, pt shd; htd wc (some
cont); chem disp (wc); shwrs inc; el pnts (10A) inc; gas; lndry
rm; shop, rest, snacks, bar 700m; playgrnd; htd pool 100m;
30% statics; dogs; bus 500m; phone; adv bkg; quiet; ccard
acc; red CKE/CCI. "Attractive parkland site by leisure cent;
san facs dated but clean; gd touring base." ♦ 1 Mar-30 Nov.
€ 26.00   2010*

FERTE MACE, LA *4E1* (500m N Urban) *48.59869, -0.36143*
**Camp Municipal La Saulaie, Blvd André Hamonic, 61600
La Ferté-Macé [06 76 86 67 20 (mob)]** Fr town cent foll
D18 to Flers & turn R onto dual c'way in 500m. Site on L adj
stadium. Sp. Sm, pt shd; htd wc; shwrs inc; el pnts (10A) €1.75;
shops 1km; BBQ (gas); playgrnd; rv 2km; dogs; phone; quiet
but little rd noise. "Excel site; call at house adj when recep
clsd." ♦ 15 Apr-1 Oct. € 4.90   2008*

FERTE ST AUBIN, LA *4F3* (1km N Urban) *47.72553, 1.93565*
**Camp Municipal Le Cosson, Ave Löwendal, 45240 La Ferté-
St Aubin [02 38 76 55 90; campingducosson@recrea.fr;
www.campingducosson.fr]** S fr Orléans on D2020; ent on R
on N o'skts twd Municipal pool. Turning onto Sm, pt shd; wc;
chem disp (wc); shwrs inc; el pnts (6A) inc (poss rev pol); shops
1km; tradsmn; rest 100m; htd pool; fishing adj; wifi; dogs €2;
phone; Eng spkn; train noise; ccard not acc; red low ssn; CKE/
CCI. "Agreeable, spacious site; friendly, helpful recep; clean,
ltd facs; easy walk to delightful town & gd rests; nr park &
chateau; poss itinerants low ssn; conv A71; gd NH."
1 May-30 Sep. € 16.00   2011*

FEUILLERES *3C3* (W Rural) *49.94777, 2.84416* **Camping
du Château et de l'Oseraie, 12 Rue du Château, 80200
Feuillères [03 22 83 17 59 or 06 16 97 93 42 (mob) (LS); fax
03 22 83 04 14; jsg-bred@wanadoo.fr; www.camping-
chateau-oseraie.com]** Fr A1/E15 exit 13.1 Maurepas onto D938
dir Albert & then L onto D146; R at staggered x-rds in Feuillères
(by church) & site on R in 500m. Med, hdg/mkd pitch, hdstg, pt
shd; wc; chem disp; mv service pnt; shwrs inc; el pnts (6A) inc
(poss rev pol); gas; lndtte; tradsmn; supmkt 10km; snacks; bar;
BBQ; playgrnd; htd pool; fishing; tennis; games area; games rm;
wifi; entmnt high ssn; 10% statics; dogs €1.20; no twin-axles; Eng
spkn; slight rlwy noise; adv bkg rec high ssn; ccard acc; red long
stay; CKE/CCI. "Excel, well-kept, well-run site; gd sized pitches;
friendly staff; clean san facs; conv A1 a'route, WW1 battlefields &
Disneyland Paris." ♦ 29 Mar-31 Oct. € 19.20   2013*

FEURS *9B2* (1km N Urban) *45.75457, 4.22595* **Camp
Municipal Le Palais, Route de Civens, 42110 Feurs [tel/fax
04 77 26 43 41; www.camping-rhonealpes.com]**
Site sp fr D1082 on N o'skts of town. Lge, pt shd; htd wc;
chem disp (wc); mv service pnt; shwrs inc; el pnts (6A) €3.05;
gas; sm shop; tradsmn; snacks; playgrnd; pool adj; mostly
statics; dogs €0.61; phone; quiet; CKE/CCI. "Pleasant,
spacious, beautifully-kept site; busy, espec w/ends; clean san
facs." ♦ 1 Apr-31 Oct. € 14.90   2013*

FIGEAC *7D4* (1.5km E Rural) *44.60989, 2.05015* **Camping
Caravanning Domaine Du Surgie, Domaine du Surgié,
46100 Figeac [05 61 64 88 54; fax 05 61 64 89 17; contact@
marc-montmija.com; www.domainedusurgie.com]**
Fr Figeac foll sp Rodez (on D840 S) to site by Rv Célé adj
leisure complex. Foll sps 'Base Loisirs de Surgie'. Narr ent,
light controlled. Or appr fr E on D840, immed after passing
under rlwy arch a v sharp R turn into narr rd (keep R thro traff
lts); site on L in 700m. NB Recep at beginning of rd to leisure
cent & camping. Med, hdg/mkd pitch, pt shd, wc; chem disp;
mv service pnt; shwrs inc; el pnts (10A) inc; gas 1km; lndtte;
shop; rest, snacks; bar; playgrnd; htd pool & waterslide adj;
boating; tennis; cycle hire; entmnt; 30% statics; dogs €2.50;
Eng spkn; adv bkg; quiet; red low ssn/long stay. Ent clsd 12:00
-16:00 low ssn. "Excel pool complex at leisure cent adj (free to
campers); peaceful low ssn; pleasant walk to beautiful town
2km; adj rv unfenced; mkt Sat; vg." ♦ 1 Apr-30 Sept. € 34.60
(CChq acc)   2013*

FIGEAC *7D4* (7km SE Urban) *44.57328, 2.07296* **Camp
Municipal Les Rives d'Olt, Blvd Paul-Ramadier, 12700
Capdenac-Gare [05 65 80 88 87 or 05 65 80 22 22 (Mairie);
camping.capdenac@wanadoo.fr]** Fr Figeac on D840 dir
Rodez; at Capdenac turn R onto D994 over rv bdge; immed
after x-ing rv bdge turn R onto D86. Site in 200m on R by rv.
Med, hdg/mkd pitch, shd; wc; chem disp; mv service pnt; shwrs
inc; el pnts (9A) €2.90; gas adj; lndtte; shop, rest, snacks, bar
adj; playgrnd; pool 1km; tennis adj; TV rm; 5% statics; dogs;
quiet, a little rd noise; CKE/CCI. "Site beside Rv Lot; ent clsd
1200-1600 low ssn; gd fishing, walking & cycling." ♦
10 Apr-30 Sep. € 10.90   2010*

FIGEAC 7D4 (7km SW Rural) 44.57833, 1.93750 **FFCC Camping de Pech-Ibert, Route de Cajarc, 46100 Béduer** [05 65 40 05 85; fax 05 65 40 08 33; contact@camping-pech-ibert.com; www.camping-pech-ibert.com] SW fr Figeac on D662/D19 twds Cajarc. Site well sp on R after Béduer. Sm, pt shd; htd wc; chem disp; mv service pnt; baby facs; shwrs inc; el pnts (16A) €3.40 (poss rev pol); snacks high ssn; BBQ; playgrnd; pool; fishing & sw 1km; tennis; cycle hire; a few statics; dogs €2; Eng spkn; adv bkg ess high ssn; quiet; red low ssn; CKE/CCI. "Peaceful, relaxing site on pilgrimage rte; pleasant, helpful owners; gd clean san facs; gd walking fr site (mkd trails); Sat mkt Figeac; excel; rock pegs required"
♦ 15 Mar-15 Nov. € 11.10   2013*

FIQUEFLEUR EQUAINVILLE see Honfleur 3C1

"Satellite navigation makes touring much easier"

Remember most sat navs don't know if you're towing or in a larger vehicle – always use yours alongside maps and site directions.

FISMES 3D4 (800m W Urban) 49.30944, 3.67138 **Camp Municipal de Fismes, Allée des Missions, 51170 Fismes** [03 26 48 10 26; fax 03 26 48 82 25; contact@fismes.fr; www.fismes.fr] Fr Reims NW on N31. At Fismes do not ent town, but stay on N31 dir Soissons. Site down little lane at end of sports stadium wall. Or exit A4 junc 22 sp Soissons & Fismes & as bef. Sm, hdstg, unshd; wc; chem disp; baby facs; shwrs; el pnts (12A) €3.50 (poss rev pol); shop 250m; supmkt 250m; BBQ (gas & el); games area; horseriding 5km; dogs; train; no twin-axles; adv bkg; noisy due to busy rd; ccard not acc; CKE/CCI. "Vg site; gd, clean san facs; warden on site ltd hrs; gates locked 2200-0700; train to Reims nr; conv Laon, Epernay, Reims; mkt Sat am; gd NH; Site clean and tidy; some rd noise;" 1 May-15 Sep. € 10.60   2013*

FITOU see Leucate Plage 10G1

FLECHE, LA 4G1 (10km E Rural) 47.70230, 0.07330 **Camp Municipal La Chabotière, Place des Tilleuls, 72800 Luché-Pringé** [02 43 45 10 00; fax 02 43 45 10 00; contact@lachabotiere.com; www.lachabotiere.com or www.loir-valley.com] SW fr Le Mans on D323 twd La Flèche. At Clermont-Créans turn L on D13 to Luché-Pringé. Site sp. Med, hdg/mkd pitch, pt sl, pt shd; wc (some cont); chem disp; mv service pnt; baby facs; shwrs; el pnts (10A) inc (poss rev pol); lndtte; shops 100m; playgrnd; pool adj high ssn; cycle hire; TV; 10% statics; dogs €1.50; phone; sep car park high ssn; poss cr; Eng spkn; adv bkg; quiet; red low ssn; CKE/CCI. "Lovely, well-kept site by Rv Loir; helpful, friendly warden; clean, modern facs; gd site for children; many cycle rtes; conv chateaux; nice vill nrby; avoid Le Mans motor bike week - poss many bikers on site; excel." ♦ 1 Apr-15 Oct. € 14.70   2011*

FLECHE, LA 4G1 (500m S Urban) 47.69514, -0.07936 **Camping de la Route d'Or, Allée du Camping, 72200 La Flèche** [tel/fax 02 43 94 55 90; info@camping-laroutedor.com; www.camping-laroutedor.com or www.loir-valley.com] Fr NW dir Laval D306, keep to W of town, leave S on D306 twd Bauge; site on L after x-ing rv; sp. Fr S take dir for A11 & Laval, site clearly sp on R on rvside. Lge, hdg/mkd pitch, some hdstg, pt shd; htd wc; chem disp; mv service pnt; shwrs inc; el pnts (10A) €3.80 (poss long lead req); gas; lndtte (inc dryer); shop 500m; supmkt nr; tradsmn; rest & bar nr; BBQ; playgrnd; htd pool; sand lake beach 2km; canoeing, fishing nr; tennis; games area; wifi; child entmnt; dogs €1; phone; Eng spkn; ccard acc; red low ssn; CKE/CCI. "Lovely, busy site in beautiful location by rv; well-kept & well-run; lge pitches; welcoming, helpful staff; facs ltd low ssn; ring for entry code if office clsd; no twin-axles; attractive, easy walk across rv to town; conv ferries; mkt Wed; rec; old san block being replaced (2012); well maitained and run site; Short walk to attractive town, market Sun & Wed; defibrillator on site" ♦ 1 Mar-30 Oct. € 20.90   2013*

⊞ **FLEURAT** 7A4 (500m E Rural) 46.24027, 1.68666 **Camping Les Boueix, Les Boueix, 23320 Fleurat** [09 63 61 23 80; info@campinglesboueix.com; www.campinglesboueix.com] Fr N145 N onto D5 to Fleurat. Foll sp La Boueix & site. Sm, pt hdg/mkd pitch, sl, pt shd; wc; chem disp; shwrs inc; el pnts (13A) €3.50 (€5 winter); shops, rest, snacks & bar 6km; BBQ; fishing; dogs €1.50; Eng spkn; adv bkg; quiet; no ccard acc; CKE/CCI. "Beautiful, quiet & relaxing CL-type site; lge pitches with views; welcoming, helpful British owners; vg san facs; sl poss diff m'vans; well-stocked fishing lake nrby; lovely walks; ideal for beautiful Creuse Valley; rallies welcome; conv A20; highly rec." € 12.50   2013*

"There aren't many sites open at this time of year"

If you're travelling outside peak season remember to call ahead to check site opening dates – even if the entry says 'open all year'.

FLEURIE 9A2 (500m SE Rural) 46.18758, 4.69895 **Camp Municipal La Grappe Fleurie, La Verne, 69820 Fleurie** [04 74 69 80 07; fax 04 74 59 85 18; camping@fleurie.org; www.camping-beaujolais.fr] S dir Lyon on D306 turn R (W) at S end of Romanèche onto D32; 4km to vill of Fleurie (beware sharp turn in vill & narr rds) & foll site sp. Med, hdg/mkd pitch, terr, pt shd; wc; chem disp; mv service pnt; serviced pitches; shwrs inc; baby facs; el pnts (10A) inc; gas; lndtte; tradsmn; shop, rest, snacks, bar 500m; playgrnd; pool; tennis; dog €3.10; wifi; entmnt; some statics; poss cr; Eng spkn; adv bkg rec Jul/Aug; ccard acc; red low ssn/CKE/CCI. "Clean, well-run, busy site; friendly staff; excel san facs; lovely pool; gates & wash rms clsd 2200-0700; path to town thro vineyards (uphill); wine tasting; sm mkt Sat; excel." ♦ 21 Mar-22 Oct. € 29.40   2013*

FLEURY D'AUDE see Narbonne 10F1

FLORAC *9D1* (1km N Rural) *44.33569, 3.59002* **FFCC Camp Municipal Le Pont du Tarn, Route de Pont de Montvert, 48400 Florac [04 66 45 18 26 or 04 66 45 17 96 (LS); fax 04 66 45 26 43; contact@camping-florac.com; www. camping-florac.com]** Exit Florac N on N106 & turn R in 500m by by-pass on D998; site on L in 300m. Lge, pt shd, mkd hdg pitch; htd wc (some cont); chem disp; mv service pnt; shwrs inc; el pnts (10A) €4.20; lndtte; supmkt 2km; tradsmn; rest, snacks, bar 2km; BBQ (no gas); playgrnd; pool; rv fishing & sw adj; wifi; 60% statics; dogs €2; phone; poss v cr; some Eng spkn; adv bkg rec; quiet; red low ssn; CKE/CCI. "Nice, well-kept, well-run site in beautiful area; clean san facs, but insufficient (2011); no twin-axles; 20 min walk to town; gd touring base; lge mkt Thurs; vg value; excel site on rv" ♦ 1 Apr-1 Nov. € 29.10   2012*

FLORAC *9D1* (2.5km NE Rural) *44.34528, 3.61008* **FFCC Camping Chantemerle, La Pontèze, 48400 Bédouès [04 66 45 19 66 or 06 73 86 53 16 (mob); www.camping-chantemerle.com]** Exit Florac N on N106; in 500m turn R onto D998; in 2.5km site on L, past Bédouès vill cent. Med, mkd pitch, pt sl, pt shd; wc; chem disp (wc); shwrs inc; el pnts (6A) €2.80; lndry rm; sm shop; tradsmn; snacks; playgrnd; rv sw adj; games rm; wifi; 10% statics; dogs €1.50; poss cr; Eng spkn; quiet; red low ssn; CKE/CCI. "Lovely location; helpful owner; gd walking; conv Gorges du Tarn, Cévennes National Park; vg; water and el pnts now avail on lower pitches" 15 Apr-15 Sep. € 14.40   2012*

FLORAC *9D1* (4km NE Rural) *44.34433, 3.60533* **Camping Chon du Tarn, 48400 Bédouès [04 66 45 09 14; fax 04 66 45 22 91; info@camping-chondutarn.com; www. camping-chondutarn.com]** Exit Florac N on N106, turn R in 500m onto D998 (sp Pont de Monvert), site on L in 3km in vill. Med, mkd pitch, pt sl, terr, pt shd; wc; chem disp; mv service pnt; shwrs inc; el pnts (6A) €2 (poss rev pol); gas; lndtte; shop & 4km; rest & bar adj; playgrnd; rv sw & sand beach; games area; dogs €1; adv bkg; quiet; ccard not acc; red low ssn; CKE/CCI. "Beautiful rvside site with views; helpful staff; clean dated san facs, ltd low ssn; conv Tarn Gorges, Causses & Cévennes National Park; excel." ♦ 1 Apr-15 Oct. € 10.80   2010*

FLORAC *9D1* (500m S Urban) *44.31760, 3.59968* **FFCC Camping Velay, Le Pont Neuf, 48400 Florac [04 66 45 12 19, 04 66 45 19 23 (LS) or 06 33 44 72 61 (mob); www.mescevennes.com]** Site on Rv Tarn adj to bdge connecting D907 & N106; ent fr N106. At S end of bypass; do not go thro town. Sm, pt sl, pt shd; wc; shwrs inc; el pnts (8A) €2.20; gas; lndtte; shop 300m; tradsmn; rests nr; rv sw & shgl beach adj; dogs €1; some rd noise. "Friendly recep; gd walks; conv Gorges du Tarn & Cévennes National Park; sh walk to town cent." 1 Jul-30 Sep. € 9.20   2008*

FLORENSAC see Agde *10F1*

FLOTTE EN RE, LA see St Martin de Ré *7A1*

⊞ **FLUMET** *9B3* (1.5km NE Rural) *45.82216, 6.53512* **Camping Le Vieux Moulin, 73590 Flumet [tel/fax 04 79 31 70 06; amrey@hotmail.fr]** Fr Albertville go N on D1212 & cont past Flumet for 1km. Turn R, watch for sp. Med, mkd pitch, hdstg, pt shd; htd wc; chem disp; mv service pnt; shwrs inc; el pnts (3-10A) €5.05-10; lndtte; tradsmn; rest nr; playgrnd; ski lifts 200m; 20% statics; dogs €1.20; phone; poss cr; Eng spkn; some rd noise; CKE/CCI. "Gd touring base by sm rv; friendly staff; superb san block but ltd; ltd facs low ssn outside ski ssn; gd boot & drying rm; highly rec." ♦ € 13.50   2010*

⊞ **FOIX** *8G3* (2km N Rural) *42.98911, 1.61565* **Camping du Lac, Quartier Labarre, 09000 Foix [05 61 65 11 58; fax 05 61 05 32 62; camping-du-lac@wanadoo.fr; www. campingdulac.com]** Fr N on N20 foll sp for 'Centre Ville', site on R in 2km. Fr S on N20 thro tunnel & take 1st exit N of Foix & foll sp 'Centre Ville', then as above. Site opp Chausson building materials store. Lge, mkd pitch, pt shd; wc; chem disp; mv service pnt; baby facs; shwrs inc; baby facs; el pnts (6A) inc; lndtte; supmkt adj; tradsmn; rest, snacks; bar; BBQ; playgrnd; pool; paddling pool; lake fishing adj; boating; windsurfing; tennis; wifi; entmnt; TV; 30% statics; dogs €1.50; bus to Foix adj (not Sun); Eng spkn; poss cr; adv bkg rec high ssn; quiet but some rd (N20) noise; ccard acc; red low ssn; CKE/CCI. "Busy site w/end; quiet, spacious pitches on L of camp; modern san facs, poss stretched high ssn; site & facs poss uncared for early ssn (2011); gates clsd 2300-0700; pleasant town; NH only low ssn." ♦ € 24.00 (CChq acc)   2011*

FOIX *8G3* (4km S Urban) *42.93081, 1.63883* **FFCC Camping Roucateille, 15 Rue du Pradal, 09330 Montgaillard [tel/ fax 05 61 64 05 92; info@camping-roucateille.com; www. camping-roucateille.com]** Fr N exit N20 junc 11, fr S exit N20 junc 12; foll sp Montgaillard; site sp fr main rd thro vill. NB Swing wide at ent - sharp turn. Med, hdg/mkd pitch, shd; wc; chem disp; mv service pnt; shwrs inc; el pnts (4-10A) €2.50-4.90; lndtte; shops & hypmkt 2km; rest, snacks & bar 3km; BBQ; playgrnd; pool 3km; wifi; 25% statics in sep area; dogs free; poss cr; some Eng spkn; adv bkg; quiet; ccard acc; red low ssn/long stay; CKE/CCI. "Lovely, picturesque, informal site; clean & well cared for; charming, helpful young owners; excel facs; care needed to avoid trees; garden produce in ssn; gd touring base; gd cycling; Forges de Pyène eco-museum worth visit; excel." ♦ ltd 1 May-30 Sep. € 14.00   2011*

⊞ **FOIX** *8G3* (5km NW Rural) *42.97151, 1.57243* **Camp Municipal de Rieutort, 09000 Cos [05 61 65 39 79 or 06 71 18 10 38 (mob); bernard.blazy09@orange.fr; http:// camping-municipal-cos09.fr]** Fr Foix take D117 dir Tarbes. Foll sp Cos onto D617, site on L in 3km. NB Narr app rds. Sm, pt sl, pt shd; wc (some cont); chem disp; 25% serviced pitches; baby facs; fam bthrm; shwrs inc; el pnts (5A) €1.80; lndtte; shop 5km; rest, snacks, bar 5km; playgrnd; pool; tennis; dogs; quiet; CKE/CCI. "Pleasant site amongst trees with gd views; friendly, helpful warden; gd san facs, ltd low ssn; sm step into disabled facs; no c'vans over 6m." ♦ € 10.00   2011*

FONTAINE DE VAUCLUSE see Isle sur la Sorgue, L' *10E2*

⊞ **FONTAINE SIMON** *4E2* (800m N Rural) *48.51314, 1.01941*
Camping du Perche, 3 Rue de la Ferrière, 28240 Fontaine-Simon [02 37 81 88 11 or 06 23 82 90 28 (mob); info@ campingduperche.com; www.campingduperche.com]
Fr La Loupe on D929 take D25 N to Fontaine-Simon, site sp. Med, hdg pitch, pt sl, pt shd; htd wc (some cont); chem disp; shwrs inc; el pnts €3.60; lndtte (inc dryer); shop; tradsmn; BBQ; playgrnd; htd, covrd pool adj; lake sw adj; fishing; wifi; few statics; dogs €3; adv bkg; quiet; CKE/CCI. "Undulating, lakeside site; gd." ♦ € 15.00   2012*

FONTAINEBLEAU *4E3* (5km NE Rural) *48.42215, 2.74872*
Camp Municipal Grange aux Dîmes, Rue de l'Abreuvoir/ Rue de l'Eglise, 77210 Samoreau [01 64 23 72 25; fax 01 64 23 98 31; mairie-de-samoreau@wanadoo.fr; www. samoreau.fr] Fr cent of Fontainebleau take D210 (dir Provins); in approx 4km at rndabt cross bdge over Rv Seine; take R at rndabt; site sp at end of rd thro Samoreau vill; site twd rv. Med, hdg/mkd pitch, pt sl, pt shd; htd wc; chem disp; mv service pnt; shwrs inc; el pnts (10A) inc (poss rev pol); lndtte; shop 250m; snacks & bar 100m; rest 500m; phone; bus; poss v cr; adv bkg; rlwy & barge noise; CKE/CCI. "Peaceful site in attractive location by Rv Seine; gd sized pitches; helpful staff; gd, immac san facs; adj vill hall poss noisy w/end; jazz festival late Jun; conv palace, Paris (by train) & Disneyland; clsd 2200-0700; excel." ♦ ltd 1 Mar-31 Oct. € 22.06   2012*

FONTAINEBLEAU *4E3* (10km S Rural) *48.33362, 2.75386*
Camping Le Parc du Gué, Route de Montigny, La Genevraye, 77690 Montigny-sur-Loing [01 64 45 87 79; fax 01 64 78 31 46; contact@camping-parcdugue.com; www.camping-parcdugue.com] On D607 foll sp S to Montigny-sur-Loing, site sp. Lge, hdg/mkd pitch, pt shd; htd wc (some cont); chem disp; shwrs inc; el pnts (6A) €3.50; lndtte; tradsmn; BBQ; playgrnd; rv sw adj; watersports; kayaks; fishing; wifi; 10% statics; dogs €3.50; mkt Sat 2km; Eng spkn; adv bkg; quiet; ccard acc; red low ssn/CKE/CCI. "Beautiful, wooded country; excel walking & cycling." ♦ 15 Mar-30 Nov. € 16.00   2011*

FONTAINEBLEAU *4E3* (10km S Rural) *48.31740, 2.69650*
Camping Les Prés, Chemin des Prés, 77880 Grez-sur-Loing [tel/fax 01 64 45 72 75; camping-grez@wanadoo.fr; www. camping-grez-fontainebleau.info] Fr Fontainebleau on D607 twd Nemours (S) for 8km; look for camping sps. At traff island turn L onto D40D, in 1km immed after x-ing bdge turn R; site on L. Do not tow wide veh dir Grez-sur-Loing. Med, pt shd; wc; chem disp; shwrs inc; el pnts (5A) €3; gas; lndtte; shop; rest, bar 200m; snacks; playgrnd; htd, covrd pool 10km; fishing; canoe hire; cycle hire; wifi; mostly statics; dogs; phone; poss cr; Eng spkn; adv bkg; quiet but half touring pitches nr busy rd; ccard acc; red long stay; CKE/CCI. "In attractive area; helpful British owner; mainly statics; site poss unkempt/scruffy end of ssn; adequate NH (2010)." ♦ 20 Mar-11 Nov. € 10.60   2010*

FONTENAY LE COMTE *7A2* (7km NE Rural) *46.52140, -0.76906* **FFCC Camping La Joletière, 85200 Mervent [02 51 00 26 87 or 06 14 23 71 31 (mob LS); fax 02 51 00 27 55; contact@campinglajoletiere.fr; www. campinglajoletiere.fr]** Fr Fontenay-le-Comte N on D938; after 6.5km, turn R onto D99; in 3km enter vill of Mervent; site on R. Or fr A83 exit junc 8 & take bypass to W of Fontenay-le-Comte. Med, hdg/mkd pitch, some hdstg, pt sl, pt shd; wc; mv service pnt; shwrs inc; el pnts (10A) €4.10 (rev pol); gas; lndtte; shop 1km; rest, snacks; bar; playgrnd; htd pool high ssn; sw 2km; fishing; boating/windsurfing 2km; forest walks 500m; 25% statics; dogs €1.70; poss cr; adv bkg; ccard acc. "Quiet & pleasant site; gd lge pitches; friendly owners; poss ltd facs low ssn; san facs old & unclean." ♦ 30 Mar - 26 Oct. € 15.00   2011*

FONTENAY LE COMTE *7A2* (7km NE Rural) *46.52454, -0.76983* **FFCC Camping Le Chêne Tord, 34 Chemin du Chêne Tord, 85200 Mervent [02 51 00 20 63 or 06 43 17 73 70 (mob); fax 02 51 00 27 94; contact@ camping-mervent.fr; www.camping-mervent.fr]** Exit A83 junc 8 & foll D938 N fr Fontenay-Le-Comte twd La Châtaigneraie for 6km to vill of Fourchaud. Turn E to Mervent on D99 & foll camp sps, sharp L turn immed bef vill at stone cross. Site is 500m W of Mervent. Sm, mkd pitch, pt sl, pt shd; htd wc; chem disp; shwrs inc; el pnts (6A) €3; gas; lndtte (inc dryer); 1km; rest, snacks, bar 1km; BBQ (gas only); rv/lake sw & fishing 2km; games area; 90% statics; dogs €1; phone; Eng spkn; adv bkg rec high ssn; v quiet; red low ssn; CKE/CCI. "Nice area; third of site forest adventure park - poss noisy high ssn; poss scruffy low ssn; welcoming & friendly; mainly statics; gd NH." 27 Mar-26 Nov. € 14.00   2009*

FONTENAY TRESIGNY *4E3* (6km NE Rural) *48.75050, 2.89728* **Camping des Quatre Vents, 77610 Crèvecoeur-en-Brie [01 64 07 41 11; fax 01 64 07 45 07; contact@ caravaning-4vents.fr; www.caravaning-4vents.fr]** At Calais take A26/E15 dir Arras; at Arras take A1/E15 dir Paris; next take A104 dir A4 Metz/Nancy/Marne-la-Vallée, then A4 dir Metz/Nancy, exit junc 13 onto D231 dir Provins; after rndabt with lge monument turn R dir Crèvecoeur-en-Brie & foll site sp. Site in 13km. Lge, hdg/mkd pitch, pt shd; htd wc; chem disp; mv service pnt; baby facs; serviced pitches; shwrs inc; el pnts (6A) inc; lndtte (inc dryer); shops 2km; tradsmn; snacks; BBQ; playgrnd; pool; horseriding; games area; games rm; wifi; TV; 50% statics sep area; dogs €3; no c'vans/m'vans over 10m high ssn; phone; poss cr; Eng spkn; adv bkg ess in ssn; quiet but some aircraft noise; ccard acc; CKE/CCI. "Friendly, well-run site; lge, well-kept pitches; welcoming, helpful staff; san facs spacious & clean; pleasant pool; conv Disneyland & Paris; poss muddy when wet; vg." ♦ 15 Mar-1 Nov. € 28.00 SBS - P09   2011*

FONTENOY LE CHATEAU *6F2* (2km S Rural) *47.95637, 6.21157* **Camping Le Fontenoy, Route de la Vierge, 88240 Fontenoy-le-Château [03 29 36 34 74 or 06 84 48 51 48 (mob); marliesfontenoy@hotmail.com; www.campingfontenoy.com]** SE fr Bains-les-Bains on D434 to Fontenoy-le-Château (6km). In cent of vill turn L onto D40 for 2km to site. Med, mkd pitch, pt shd; wc; chem disp; shwrs inc, el pnts (4A) €2.25; lndtte; tradsmn; rest, snacks; bar; playgrnd; pool 5km; 10% statics; dogs €0.60; poss cr; Eng spkn; adv bkg; quiet, ccard not acc; red long stay; CKE/CCI. "Attractive site; lovely area." 15 Apr-30 Sep. € 11.55   2009*

FRANCE

FONTES *10F1* (800m N Rural) *43.54734, 3.37999* **FFCC Camping L'Evasion, Route de Cabrières, 34320 Fontès [04 67 25 32 00; fax 04 67 25 31 96; campingevasion34@ yahoo.fr; http://camping.evasion.free.fr]** Fr A75 exit junc 59 (Pézenas). At rndabt take D124 to Lézignan-la-Cèbe then fork L, cont on D124 to Fontès. In vill foll sp to site. Sm, hdg/ mkd pitch, pt sl, pt shd; wc; chem disp; mv service pnt; baby facs; showrs inc; el pnts (6A) €3; lndtte; rest, snacks; bar; BBQ; playgrnd; pool; beach 30km; wifi; 75% statics; dogs €2.80; phone; adv bkg; quiet; CKE/CCI. "Excel san facs; touring pitches amongst statics (long-term residents)." ♦ ltd 1 Apr-30 Oct. € 12.00 2010*

FONTVIEILLE see Arles *10E2*

FORCALQUIER *10E3* (500m E Urban) *43.96206, 5.78718* **Camping Indigo Forcalquier, Route de Sigonce, 04300 Forcalquier [04 92 75 27 94; fax 04 92 75 18 10; forcalquier@ camping-indigo.com; www.camping-indigo.com]** Fr A51 exit junc 19 La Brillane onto D4100 to Forcalquier. Site sp. Med, mkd pitch, pt sl, pt shd; wc (some cont); chem disp; mv service pnt; baby facs; some serviced pitches; shwrs inc; el pnts (10A) €5.20 (long lead poss req); lndtte (inc dryer); shop 500m; tradsmn; rest, snacks; bar; playgrnd; htd pool; paddling pool; games area; internet; TV rm; some statics; dogs €4; phone; Eng spkn; adv bkg; quiet; red low ssn; CKE/CCI. "Pleasant site in lovely location; excel m'van facs; access for lge o'fits & m'vans poss diff due v narr site rds & awkward corners." ♦ ltd 22 Apr-16 Oct. € 21.90 2011*

⊞ **FORCALQUIER** *10E3* (8km SE Rural) *43.89752, 5.80609* **FLOWER Camping La Rivière, Lieu-Dit 'Les Côtes', 04300 St Maime [04 92 79 54 66; info@camping-lariviere.com; www.camping-lariviere.com or www.flowercampings. com]** S fr Sisteron on D4085, then D4096. Then R at Voix onto D13, site on R in about 5km. Med, hdg/mkd pitch, pt shd; wc; chem disp; shwrs; el pnts (10A) inc; lndry rm; sm shop & 8km; tradsmn; rest, snacks; bar; BBQ; playgrnd; pool; lake fishing adj; games area; games rm; internet; entmnt; TV rm; 50% statics; dogs €2.50; poss cr; adv bkg; some rd noise; ccard acc; CKE/CCI. "Vg, relaxing, friendly site; gd touring base for hilltop towns." ♦ € 23.00 2010*

See advertisement on pages 32 & 33

FORCALQUIER *10E3* (6km S Urban) *43.91096, 5.78210* **FFCC Camping l'Eau Vive, 04300 Dauphin [tel/fax 04 92 79 51 91; info@leauvive.fr; www.leauvive.fr]** S fr Forcalquier on D4100 dir Apt; in 2.5km turn L onto D13 (at Mane); site on R in 3km. Or fr D4096, turn onto D13 at Volx; site on L in 6km (800m past Dauphin). Med, mkd pitch, shd; htd wc; chem disp; shwrs inc; el pnts (3-6A) €3.50-4.50; lndtte; shop; supmkt 6km; snacks; BBQ (gas, sep area); playgrnd; 2 pools; paddling pool; tennis; cycle hire; games area; games rm; child entmnt; TV; dogs €3.50; bus 800m; Eng spkn; adv bkg; quiet; ccard not acc; red low ssn. "Well-run site; helpful owners; vg pools; vg for children; excel. 1 Apr-31 Oct. € 21.00 2009*

FORCALQUIER *10E3* (4km NW Rural) *43.97235, 5.73800* **Camping Le Domaine des Lauzons (Naturist), 04300 Limans [04 92 73 00 60; fax 04 92 73 04 31; leslauzons@ wanadoo.fr; www.camping-lauzons.com]** Exit A51 junc 19 onto N100 dir Avignon; in Forcalquier at rndabt turn L onto D950/D313 sp Banon; site on R in approx 6km. Lge site sp. Diff app. Med, mkd pitch, pt sl, terr, pt shd; wc; chem disp; baby facs; sauna; shwrs inc; el pnts (6A) €4.50; gas; lndtte (inc dryer); ice; sm shop; supmkt 6km; tradsmn; rest, snacks; bar; BBQ (gas or charcoal sep area); playgrnd; 2 htd pools; waterslides; pony rides; archery; games area; games rm; many activities; wifi; entmnt; TV; 25% statics; dogs €4; phone; poss cr; some Eng spkn; adv bkg; quiet; ccard acc; INF req. "Pleasant site in wooded valley; wonderful scenery; excel family site; helpful, friendly staff; most san facs modern, ltd low ssn; excel pool area; walks fr site; Forcalquier lovely town; excel touring base; access diff lge o'fits, tractor help avail." ♦ ltd 1 Apr-30 Sep. € 30.00 2010*

FOREST MONTIERS see Rue

FORET FOUESNANT, LA *2F2* (2.5km SE Coastal) *47.89936, -3.95493* **Camping de Kéranterec, Route de Port la Forêt, Kerleven, 29940 La Forêt-Fouesnant [02 98 56 98 11; fax 02 98 56 81 73; info@camping-keranterec.com; www. camping-keranterec.com]** Fr Quimper take D783 SE. Turn R onto D44 twds La Forêt-Fouesnant; in vill cent foll sp for Beg Menez for 200m, then take 1st R twds Kerleven; turn L at Kerleven seafront rndabt, cont for 500m & at next rndabt foll site sp. (NB: Kéranterec shares same ent with Camping St Laurent.) Lge, hdg/mkd pitch, terr, pt shd; wc; serviced pitches; chem disp; baby facs; shwrs inc; el pnts (6A) €4; gas; lndtte; shop; tradsmn; snacks; bar; playgrnd; htd pool; waterslide; sand beach 400m; tennis; games area; fishing & watersports adj; entmnt; TV; 30% statics; dogs €3; adv bkg (ess high ssn); Eng spkn; ccard acc; red low ssn/CKE/CCI. "Lovely views fr most pitches, many lge; clean, modern san facs; tight turn into sm hdg pitches on steep terr poss diff lge o'fits." ♦ 5 Apr-15 Sep. € 30.00 2008*

FORET FOUESNANT, LA *2F2* (2.5km SE Coastal) *47.89611, -3.95446* **Camping Domaine du St Laurent, Kerleven, 29940 La Forêt-Fouesnant [02 98 56 97 65; fax 02 98 56 92 51; saintlaurent@franceloc.fr; www. campings-franceloc.fr]** Fr Quimper take D783 SE. Turn R onto D44 to La Forêt-Fouesnant; in vill cent foll sp for Plage de Kerleven; turn L at Kerleven seafront rndabt, cont for 500m & at next rndabt foll site sp. (NB: Camping St Laurent shares same ent with Kéranterec.) Lge, hdg/mkd pitch, pt shd; wc; mv service pnt; chem disp; shwrs inc; el pnts (6A) inc (long lead req); gas; lndtte; shop; tradsmn; snacks; bar; playgrnd; htd pool; paddling pool; waterslide; jacuzzi; sauna; sand beach adj; tennis; gym; entmnt; TV; 50% statics; dogs €4.50; poss cr; adv bkg; phone; Eng spkn; ccard acc; red low ssn; CKE/CCI. "Well-run, friendly site; beautiful coast, sea views; lge pitches; excel facs; many excel, quiet beaches within 10km; highly rec. " ♦ End Apr-end Sep. € 37.00 2008*

FRANCE

⊞ **FORGES LES EAUX** *3C2* (500m S Urban) *49.60597, 1.54262* **Aire de Service (M'vans only), Blvd Nicolas Thiessé, 76440 Forges-les-Eaux [02 35 90 52 10; officeforgeslesleaux@wanadoo.fr; www.forgeslesleaux-tourisme.fr]** Fr Forges-les-Eaux cent, take D921 S sp Lyons-la-Forêt. In 500m turn R foll sp, camp on L in 250m opp municipal site. Med, mkd pitch, hdstg, unshd; mv service pnt; water points; el pnts (poss rev pol). "No power, water etc Nov to Mar; max 2 nights; warden visits or pay at Municipal site opp; town cent easy walk; views of open countryside; excel."
€ 5.75   2011*

FORGES LES EAUX *3C2* (1km S Urban) *49.60603, 1.54302* **Camp Municipal La Minière, 3 Blvd Nicolas Thiese, 76440 Forges-les-Eaux [02 35 90 53 91; http://forgeslesleaux-tourisme.fr]** Fr Forges-les-Eaux cent, take D921 S sp Lyons-la-Forêt. In 750m turn R foll sp, camp on R in 150m. NB 3,500kg limit in town all directions. Med, hdg/mkd pitch, pt sl, pt shd; wc (some cont); mv service pnt opp; shwrs inc; el pnts (6A) €2.75 (rev pol); lndry rm; shops nr; htd pool in town; 85% statics (sep area); poss cr; quiet; CKE/CCI. "Well-presented site; lge pitches; friendly warden, warm welcome; basic, clean san facs; poss diff access some pitches; m'van o'night area opp; pleasant town with excel WWII Resistance Museum; gd local vet; useful NH." ♦ 15 Mar-15 Oct.
€ 8.00   2011*

FORT MAHON PLAGE *3B2* (1km E Rural) *50.33230, 1.57990* **Airotel Camping Le Royon, 1271 Route de Quend, 80120 Fort-Mahon Plage [03 22 23 40 30; fax 03 22 23 65 15; info@campingleroyon.com; www.campingleroyon.com]** Exit A16 at junc 24 Forest-Montiers onto D32 to Rue, then dir Quend & Fort-Mahon-Plage, site sp. Lge, hdg/mkd pitch, pt shd; wc (some cont); mv service pnt; chem disp; baby facs; shwrs inc; el pnts (6A) inc; gas; lndtte (inc dryer); shop; tradsmn; snacks; bar; playgrnd; htd, covrd pool; paddling pool; sand beach 2km; games area; sailing, fishing, golf nr; cycle hire; wifi; entmnt; 90% statics; dogs €3; phone; poss cr; Eng spkn; adv bkg; ccard acc; red low ssn/long stay/CKE/CCI. "Modern san facs; med sized pitches, but access poss diff due parked cars; conv Mercanterre nature reserve." ♦ 12 Mar-1 Nov. € 31.00 (3 persons)   2011*

FORT MAHON PLAGE *3B2* (8km S Rural) *50.31950, 1.60583* **FLOWER Camping Les Vertes Feuilles, 25 Route de la Plage, Monchaux, 80120 Quend Plage-les-Pins [03 22 23 55 12; fax 03 22 19 07 52; lesvertesfeuilles@baiedesommepleinair.com; www.baiedesommepleinair.com or www.flowercampings.com]** Exit A16 junc 24 onto D32/D940 N. Turn W dir Quend onto D32, site sp. Med, hdg/mkd pitch, hdstg, pt shd; htd wc; chem disp; baby facs; shwrs inc; el pnts (4-10A) €3.50-6.50; gas; lndtte (inc dryer); shop; tradsmn; snacks; BBQ; playgrnd; htd, covrd pool; paddling pool; sand beach 4km; tennis 6km; cycle hire; games area; games rm; wifi; entmnt; TV rm; 40% statics; dogs €2; poss cr; Eng spkn; adv bkg; quiet; ccard acc; red low ssn. "Pleasant, family site." ♦ 1 Apr-7 Nov. € 24.50   2010*

See advertisement on pages 32 & 33

FORT MOVILLE see Pont Audemer *3D2*

FOUESNANT *2F2* (5km SE Coastal) *47.85938, -3.98650* **Camping Kerolland, Chemin de Kerolland, Route des Dunes, Beg Meil, 29170 Fouesnant [02 98 94 91 00; camping.kerolland@orange.fr; www.camping-kerolland.com]** S fr Quimper on D34/D45; 400m bef Beg Meil, turn R after church into Chemin de Kerolland. Site sp. Route des Dunes is part of D45. Lge, mkd pitch, pt shd; wc (cont); mv service pnt; shwrs inc; el pnts €2.50; lndtte (inc dryer); shops 200m; playgrnd; sand beach 500m; wifi; 60% statics; dogs €1.10; bus 1km; Eng spkn; adv bkg; quiet; red low ssn. "Nr lovely beaches & coastal walks; helpful staff; san facs clean but tired; in walking dist of beaches or vill; gd touring base. 1 May-30 Sep.
€ 14.80   2011*

"That's changed – Should I let The Club know?"

If you find something on site that's different from the site entry, fill in a report and let us know. See www.caravanclub.co.uk/europereport.

FOUESNANT *2F2* (3km S Rural) *47.88202, -4.01863* **Camping Les Hortensias, La Grande Allée, 29170 Fouesnant [02 98 56 52 95 or 06 20 45 73 74 (mob); information@campingleshortensias.com; www.campingleshortensias.com]** Fr Quimper on D34 dir Fouesnant, then S twds Mousterlin, site sp. Med, hdg pitch, pt shd; htd wc; chem disp; mv service pnt; baby facs; shwrs inc; el pnts (6A) €3; gas; lndtte (inc dryer); tradsmn; snacks; BBQ; playgrnd; beach 3km; games area; games rm; wifi; entmnt; TV; dogs €2; phone; adv bkg; quiet. "Guided walks & cycle rides." Easter-30 Sep. € 15.00   2010*

FOUESNANT *2F2* (4km S Coastal) *47.85992, -3.98850* **Camping Le Kervastard, Hent-Kervastard, Beg-Meil, 29170 Fouesnant [02 98 94 91 52; fax 02 98 94 99 83; camping.le.kervastard@wanadoo.fr; www.campingkervastard.com]** Foll rd fr Quimper thro Beg-Meil. Site sp on R immed after rd bends sharply to L. Med, hdg/mkd pitch, pt shd; wc; chem disp; mv service pnt; baby facs; serviced pitches; shwrs; el pnts (6-10A) €3.60-3.90; gas; lndtte; shops adj; playgrnd; htd pool; paddling pool; sand beach 300m; sailing, watersports nr; entmnt; TV; 30% statics; dogs €2.20; phone; adv bkg (fee); Eng spkn; quiet; ccard acc; red low ssn/CKE/CCI. "Quiet part of Brittany with several sheltered coves; excel site." ♦ 23 May-9 Sep.
€ 23.50   2008*

FOUESNANT *2F2* (3.5km SW Rural) *47.86667, -4.01556* **Camping La Piscine, 51 Hent Kerleya, 29170 Fouesnant [02 98 56 56 06; fax 02 98 56 57 64; contact@campingdelapiscine.com; www.campingdelapiscine.com]** Turn R off D45 on exit Fouesnant onto D145 sp Mousterlin; in 1km L at site sp. Lge, mkd pitch, some hdstg, pt shd; wc; chem disp; mv service pnt; baby facs; sauna; shwrs inc; el pnts (6-10A) €4-4.60; gas; lndtte; shop; tradsmn; rest 2km; snacks; BBQ; playgrnd; htd pool; paddling pool; waterslide; sand beach 1.5km; lake adj; golf, tennis nr; golf 7km; games rm; wifi; entmnt; 30% statics; dogs €2.20; Eng spkn; adv bkg; quiet; ccard acc; red low ssn; CKE/CCI. "Highly rec, family-run site; gd walking, cycling." ♦ 13 May-12 Sep. € 26.00   2009*

FOUESNANT

FOUESNANT *2F2* (4.5km SW Coastal) *47.85851, -4.02009* Camping Sunêlia L'Atlantique, Hent Poul an Corre, 29170 Fouesnant [02 98 56 14 44; fax 02 98 56 18 67; sunelia@latlantique.fr; www.camping-bretagne-atlantique.com] Exit Quimper on D34 sp Fouesnant, take D45 L to Fouesnant & after lge intersection with D44 look for next R to Mousterlin, site sp. Lge, hdg/mkd pitch, pt shd; htd wc; chem disp; mv service pnt; baby facs; sauna; shwrs inc; el pnts (6-10A) inc; gas; lndtte (inc dryer); shop; rest, snacks; bar; BBQ; playgrnd; htd pools (1 covrd); paddling pool; waterslide; sand beach 400m; watersports; spa, fitness rm & beauty treatments; lake fishing 200m; tennis; cycle hire; games rm; games area; golf 12km; wifi; entmnt; TV rm; 70% statics; no dogs; phone; poss cr; adv bkg rec; ccard acc; red long stay/low ssn; CKE/CCI. "Excel leisure facs; helpful, friendly staff; ideal for families." ♦ 23 Apr-10 Sep. € 41.00 (CChq acc)   2011*

FOUESNANT *2F2* (5km SW Coastal) *47.85055, -4.03444* Camping Kost-Ar-Moor, Route du Grande Large, 29170 Mousterlin [02 98 56 04 16; fax 02 98 56 65 02; contact@camping-fouesnant.com; www.camping-fouesnant.com] S fr Fouesnant on D145, site sp. Lge, hdg/mkd pitch, pt shd; htd wc; chem disp; baby facs; fam bthrm; shwrs inc; el pnts (10A) €3.50; gas; lndtte; shop; tradsmn; snacks; bar; playgrnd; pools; waterpark; sand beach 400m; lake adj; cycle hire; games area; golf, horseriding nr; wifi; entmnt; TV rm; 10% statics; dog €2.50; phone; Eng spkn; adv bkg; quiet; ccard acc; CKE/CCI. "Vg clean site; helpful owner; gd for beach holiday & walking, cycling." ♦ 24 Apr-11 Sep. € 21.00   2009*

FOUGERES *2E4* (1.5km E Urban) *48.3544, -1.1795* **Camp Municipal de Paron**, Route de la Chapelle-Janson, 35300 Fougères [02 99 99 40 81; fax 02 99 99 70 83; campingmunicipal35@orange.fr; www.ot-fougeres.fr] Fr A84/E3 take junc 30 then ring rd E twd N12. Turn L at N12 & foll sp. Site on D17 sp R after Carrefour. Well sp on ring rd. Med, hdg pitch, hdstg, pt sl, pt shd; wc; serviced pitches; chem disp; shwrs inc; el pnts (5-10A) €3.60-4.10 (poss rev pol); lndtte; shops 1.5km; hypmkt 800m; tradsmn high ssn; rest 600m; playgrnd; pool 1km; tennis; horseriding adj; internet; dogs; adv bkg; quiet; ccard acc; red low ssn; CKE/CCI. "Well-kept site in pleasant parkland setting; lge pitches, poss soggy when wet; popular NH; helpful warden; gd clean facs; gates clsd 2200-0900 card pass avail; tours of 12thC castle; old town worth visit; Sat mkt; excel; excel new (2013) san facs" Apr 25- 30 Sep. € 14.85   2013*

⊞ **FOURAS** *7A1* (500m NE Coastal) *45.99264, -1.08680* Camp Municipal du Cadoret, Blvd de Chaterny, 17450 Fouras [05 46 82 19 19; fax 05 46 84 51 59; www.campings-fouras.com] Fr Rochefort take N137, L onto D937 at Fouras, fork R at sp to site in 1km. At next rndabt take 3rd exit into Ave du Cadoret, then 1st R at next rndabt. Lge, hdg/mkd pitch, pt sl, pt shd; wc (some cont); chem disp; baby facs; shwrs inc; el pnts (6-10A) €3-4.70 (poss long lead req); gas; lndtte; shop 800m; rest; bar; htd pool; paddling pool; sand beach adj; pool; fishing; boating; tennis 1km; golf 5km; games area; wifi; entmnt; 50% statics (sep area); dogs €2.40; bus to La Rochelle, Rochefort, ferry to Ile d'Aix; poss cr; adv bkg; red low ssn; CKE/CCI. "Popular, well-kept site; vg location; well shaded; lge pitches, clean san facs, unisex low ssn; coastal footpath; pleasant town; a favourite; highly rec; gd conv site; Eng spkn" ♦ € 37.50   2013*

⊞ **FOURAS** *7A1* (1km E Rural) *45.99023, -1.05184* Camping Domaine Les Charmilles, Route de l'OcÃcan, 17450 Fouras [05 46 84 00 05; fax 05 46 84 02 84; info@domainedescharmilles.com; www.domainedescharmilles.com] N fr Rochefort on N137, after 2km L onto D937. Site on L in 2km bef ent Fouras. Lge, hdg/mkd pitch, pt shd; htd wc; chem disp; mv service pnt; shwrs inc; el pnts (6A) €4; gas; lndtte; shop & 1km; tradsmn; snacks; bar; BBQ area; playgrnd; 3 pools (1 htd covrd); paddling pool; waterslides; sand beach 3km; cycle hire; games rm; wifi; entmnt; 20% statics; no dogs; bus to beach high ssn; poss cr; adv bkg; ccard acc; red long stay/low ssn; CKE/CCI. "Gd site; Friendly staff; unisex facs" ♦ € 37.50   2013*

FOURCHAMBAULT see Nevers *4H4*

FOURMIES see Hirson *3C4*

FRAISSE SUR AGOUT see Salvetat sur Agout, La *8F4*

"I like to fill in the reports as I travel from site to site"
You'll find report forms at the back of this guide, or you can fill them in online at www.caravaclub.co.uk/europereport.

FRANGY *9A3* (4km E Rural) *46.01060, 5.97610* Camping Le Chamaloup, 74270 Contamine-Sarzin [04 50 77 88 28 or 06 72 80 09 84 (mob); fax 04 50 77 99 79; camping@chamaloup.com; www.chamaloup.com] Exit A40 junc 11 onto D1508 dir Annecy, thro Frangy. Site sp on L in 10km. Med, hdg/mkd pitch, pt shd; htd wc; chem disp; serviced pitches; mv service pnt; baby facs; shwrs inc; el pnts (16A) €4; gas; lndtte; shop; tradsmn; snacks; bar; BBQ; htd pool; games rm; wifi; entmnt; 20% statics; dogs €2; poss cr; Eng spkn; rd noise; some noise fr bar music; adv bkg; ccard acc; CKE/CCI. "Friendly owners; rv & fish pond (fenced-off) on site." ♦ 1 May-15 Sep. € 22.00   2010*

FREJUS *10F4* (2.5km N Urban) *43.46290, 6.7257* Camping Les Pins Parasols, 3360 Rue des Combattants d'Afrique du Nord, 83600 Fréjus [04 94 40 88 43; fax 04 94 40 81 99; lespinsparasols@wanadoo.fr; www.lespinsparasols.com] Fr A8 exit junc 38 sp Fréjus cent. Fr E'bound dir foll Bagnols sp at 2 rndabts & Fréjus cent/Cais at 3rd. Fr W'bound dir foll Bagnols at 3 rndabts & Fréjus cent/Cais at 4th. Site on L in 500m. Lge, hdg/mkd pitch, terr, pt sl, pt shd, htd wc; chem disp; san facs on individual pitches; baby facs; shwrs inc; el pnts (6A) inc; gas; lndtte; shop; tradsmn; rest, snacks; bar; playgrnd; pool; paddling pool; waterslide; sand beach 6km; tennis; wifi; entmnt; TV rm; 30% statics; dogs €2.90; phone; adv bkg; Eng spkn; quiet; red low ssn; CKE/CCI. "Pleasant, family-run site; clean san facs; tractor to terr pitches; some lge pitches; excel." ♦ 2 Apr-24 Sep. € 28.90   2011*

See advertisement opposite

FRANCE

308 ⊞ Site open all year

Send in your site reports by mid August 2014

LES PINS PARASOLS CAMPING CARAVANNING ★★★★

**3360 Rue des Combattants d'Afrique du Nord
ROUTE DE BAGNOLS - F-83600 FRÉJUS
Tel.: 0033 494.40.88.43**

HEATED SWIMMINGPOOL
Supermarket - Snackbar - Individual washing cabins and hot water in all sanitary facilities - Seperated pitches (800-l00m²) all with electricity. Pitches with individual sanitary facilities (shower, washbasin, sink with hot water, WC) - Children's playground and solarium - Caravan pitches - Water points - Mini-tennis **SUN AND SHADE** near the beaches

**Fax : 0033 494.40.81.99
Email : lespinsparasols@wanadoo.fr
Internet : www.lespinsparasols.com**

FREJUS *10F4* (5km SW Rural) *43.39890, 6.67531*
Camping Domaine de la Bergerie, Vallée-du-Fournel, Route du Col-du-Bougnon, 83520 Roquebrune-sur-Argens [04 98 11 45 45; fax 04 98 11 45 46; info@domainelabergerie.com; www.domainelabergerie.com] On DN7 twd Fréjus, turn R onto D7 sp St Aygulf & Roquebrune-sur-Argens; after passing Roquebrune, site sp in approx 6km on R. V lge, hdg/mkd pitch, terr, pt shd; wc; chem disp; sauna; some serviced pitches; baby facs; shwrs inc; el pnts (6A) inc (extra for 10A); gas; Indtte (inc dryer); supmkt; rest, snacks; bar; playgrnd; 2 pools (1 htd, covrd); paddling pool; waterslide; jacuzzi; lake fishing; sand beach 7km; tennis; games area; mini-farm; archery; wifi; entmnt; 70% statics in sep area; dogs €3.10-5.10; Eng spkn; adv bkg; quiet; ccard acc; red low ssn/long stay. "Well-organised site; entmnt/activities for all ages; early bkg ess for summer; excel." ♦ 28 Apr-30 Sep. € 38.50   2011*

See advertisement on next page

"We must tell The Club about that great site we found"

Get your site reports in by mid-August and we'll do our best to get your updates into the next edition of Caravan Europe.

FREJUS *10F4* (8km W Rural) *43.44535, 6.65790* Camping Le Moulin des Iscles, Chemin du Moulin des Iscles, 83520 Roquebrune-sur-Argens [04 94 45 70 74; fax 04 94 45 46 09; moulin.iscles@wanadoo.fr; www.campingdesiscles.com] Twd Fréjus on DN7, turn R onto D7 to St Aygulf sp Roquebrune. Site on L after passing thro Roquebrune vill. Med, mkd pitch, shd; htd wc (some cont); chem disp; baby facs; shwrs inc; el pnts (6A) €2.70; Indtte (inc dryer); shop; tradsmn; rest, snacks; bar; BBQ; playgrnd; rv fishing; canoeing; water skiing nrby; sand beach 12km; games rm; wifi; entmnt; TV rm; 10% statics; dogs €1.30; adv bkg; quiet; red low ssn/long stay; ccard acc. "Excel well-kept, well-run site by rv; helpful owners; gd security." ♦ 1 Apr-30 Sep.€ 24.50 (3 persons) (CChq acc)   2010*

FREJUS *10F4* (8km W Rural) *43.47866, 6.63991* Camping Leï Suves, Quartier du Blavet, 83520 Roquebrune-sur-Argens [04 94 45 43 95; fax 04 94 81 63 13; camping.lei.suves@wanadoo.fr; www.lei-suves.com] Exit A8 junc 36 at Le Muy, thro Le Muy twd Fréjus on DN7. After 5km turn L (under a'route, not into Roquebrune-sur-Argens) at sp. Foll sp to camp 4km N of Roquebrune. Lge, mkd pitch, terr, pt shd; wc; chem disp; baby facs; shwrs inc; el pnts (6A) €4.50; gas; Indtte (inc dryer); shop; tradsmn; rest, snacks; bar; BBQ (gas only); playgrnd; htd pool; paddling pool; sand beach 14km; lake sw & fishing 3km; tennis; games rm; entmnt; excursions; wifi; 45% statics; dogs €3.50; phone; Eng spkn; adv bkg; quiet; ccard acc; red low ssn; CKE/CCI. "V pleasant location in pine forest; well-maintained, family-run site; facs clean; excel pool; some sm pitches; conv Côte d'Azur." ♦ 2 Apr-15 Oct. € 42.00   2011*

See advertisement below

Quartier du Blavet
83520 Roquebrune sur Argens
+33 (0)4 94 45 43 95
camping.lei.suves@wanadoo.fr
GPS 43° 28' 40" N - 06° 38' 20" E

lei-suves.com

Rental of Mobile Homes from 1 March till 15th of November. Camping pitches from 27.04 to 30.09. Between Frejus and Saint Tropez, just 10 minutes from the sea. Set amongst 60 hectares of oak and pine trees and framed by quintessential mimosa flowers, the campsite boasts 4 swimming pools (water park of 1400m², heated indoor pool and one heated outside pool) five tennis courts and a spa centre with a fitness gym. There's also a Jacuzzi and a hammam Turkish bath experience. For the kids, the campsite provides children's entertainment and clubs.

Route du Col du Bougnon - 83520 Roquebrune sur Argens - FRANCE
Tél : 00 33 (0)4 98 11 45 45 - Fax : 00 33 (0)4 98 11 45 46
www.domainelabergerie.com

FREJUS *10F4* (10km W Rural) *43.45070, 6.63320*
Village camping Les Pêcheurs, Quartier Verseil, 83520 Roquebrune-sur-Argens [04 94 45 71 25; fax 04 94 81 65 13; info@camping-les-pecheurs.com; www.camping-les-pecheurs.com] Exit A8 junc 36 dir Le Muy, onto DN7 then D7 sp Roquebrune; camp 800m on L (bef bdge over Rv Argens) at ent to vill. Lge, hdg/mkd pitch, hdstg, pt shd; htd wc; chem disp; mv service pnt; baby facs; sauna; spa; jacuzzi; shwrs inc; el pnts (10A) €5.50; gas; lndtte (inc dryer); shop; tradsmn; rest, snacks; bar; BBQ (gas/elec); playgrnd; htd pool; paddling pool; sand beach 11km; lake sw, fishing, canoeing adj; spa & jacuzzi; tennis 2km; horseriding; cycle hire 1km; wifi; entmnt; TV rm; 25% statics; dogs €3.20; phone; Eng spkn; adv bkg; quiet; ccard acc; red low ssn/CKE/CCI. "Lovely site; popular with families; helpful staff; some pitches v shady; some site rds/pitch access tight for lge outfits, OK with mover; gd walking, cycling." ♦ 5 Apr-30 Sep. € 42.00 SBS - C08   2013*

See advertisement opposite

FREJUS *10F4* (3km NW Rural) *43.46335, 6.7247* **Camping Le Fréjus, 3401, rue des Combattants, d'Afrique du Nord, 83600 FREJUS** [04 94 19 94 60; fax 04 94 19 94 69; contact@lefrejus.com; www.lefrejus.com] Exit A8 junc 38, at 1st rndabt turn L, then L at 2nd rndabt & L again at 3rd rndabt, Site on R in 200m. Lge, mkd pitch, pt sl, pt terr, pt shd; htd wc (some cont); chem disp; mv service pnt; baby facs; shwrs inc; el pnts (10A) inc; gas high ssn; lndtte; shop high ssn & 500m; tradsmn, rest & snacks high ssn; bar; playgrnd; htd pool; waterslide; sand beach 6km; tennis; games rm; entmnt; internet; wifi; 80% statics; dogs(leashed) €4; Eng spkn; adv bkg; quiet; ccard acc; red low ssn; CKE/CCI. "Ideal position for coast bet Cannes & St Tropez; lge pitches; pleasant, friendly staff; gd san facs; muddy after rain; quiet low ssn; v gd site; basin cold water at each pitch" ♦ 15 Jan-15 Dec. € 37.00   2013*

"I need an on-site restaurant"

We do our best to make sure site information is correct, but it is always best to check any must-have facilities are still available or will be open during your visit.

FREJUS *10F4* (4km NW) *43.46616, 6.72203* **Camping La Baume - La Palmeraie, Route de Bagnoles, Rue des Combattants d'Afrique du Nord, 83600 Fréjus [04 94 19 88 88; fax 04 94 19 83 50; reception@labaume-lapalmeraie.com; www.labaume-lapalmeraie.com]** Fr A8 exit junc 38 sp Fréjus cent. Fr E'bound dir foll Bagnols sp at 2 rndabts & Fréjus cent/Cais at 3rd. Fr W'bound dir foll Bagnols at 3 rndabts & Fréjus cent/Cais at 4th. Site on L in 300m. V lge, pt sl, pt shd; htd wc; shwrs; el pnts (6A) inc; gas; lndtte; shop; rest, snacks; bar; playgrnd; 5 pools (1 htd, 2 covrd); sand beach 5km; waterslide; tennis; horseriding; entmnt; many tour ops statics; dogs €4; adv bkg ess Jul/Aug; quiet, except N part of site adj to m'way; 15% red low ssn." ♦ 1 Apr-30 Sep. € 51.00 (3 persons)   2012*

See advertisement on next page

FREJUS *10F4* (4km NW Coastal) *43.44545, 6.72683* **Yelloh! Village Domaine du Colombier, 1052 Rue des Combattants d'Afrique du Nord, 83600 Fréjus [04 94 51 56 01 or 04 94 51 52 38 (LS); fax 04 94 51 55 57; info@clubcolombier.com; www.clubcolombier.com or www.yellohvillage.co.uk]** Fr E (Nice) on A8 exit junc 38 sp Fréjus. Go strt over 3 rndabts, turn R at 4th rndabt, then R again at next rndabt, site on R. Fr W (Aix-en-Provence) exit A8 junc 38 & turn R at 1st rndabt, then L at intersection. Site on L. Lge, hdg/mkd pitch, hdstg, terr, pt shd; htd wc (some cont); chem disp; mv service pnt; 30% serviced pitches; baby facs; shwrs inc; el pnts (16A) inc; gas; lndtte; supmkt; tradsmn; rest, snacks; bar; BBQ (elec) playgrnd; htd pool & waterslides; sand beach 4km; tennis; sports area; games rm; excursions; wifi; entmnt; TV rm; 85% statics/tour ops; dogs €4; poss cr; Eng spkn; adv bkg; quiet but poss noise fr disco; ccard acc; red low ssn; CKE/CCI. "Well-organised, clean site in pine forest with exotic trees; excel." ♦ 9 Apr-10 Oct. € 49.00 (3 persons) 2009*

See advertisement on inside front cover

FREJUS *10F4* (6km NW Rural) *43.46944, 6.67805* **Camping La Bastiane, 1056 Chemin des Suvières, 83480 Puget-sur-Argens [04 94 55 55 94; fax 04 94 55 55 93; info@labastiane.com; www.labastiane.com]** Exit A8 at junc 37 Puget/Fréjus. At DN7 turn R dir Le Muy & in 1km turn R immed after 2nd bdge. Foll sp to site. Fr DN7 turn L at traff lts in Puget, site is 2km N of Puget. Lge, hdg/mkd pitch, pt sl, shd; wc; chem disp; baby facs; fam bthrm; shwrs inc; el pnts (6A) inc; lndtte; shop; tradsmn; rest, snacks; bar; BBQ (elec); playgrnd; htd pool; paddling pool; sand beach 7km; watersports; tennis; cycle hire; games area; games rm; cinema; wifi; entmnt; TV; car wash area; 40% statics; dogs €4; phone; poss cr; Eng spkn; adv bkg; quiet; ccard acc; red long stay/low ssn/CKE/CCI. "Excel, family-run, friendly site; conv m'way (no m'way noise)." ♦ 3 Apr-22 Oct. € 39.90   2010*

"Satellite navigation makes touring much easier"

Remember most sat navs don't know if you're towing or in a larger vehicle – always use yours alongside maps and site directions.

FREJUS *10F4* (7km NW Rural) *43.4835, 6.7190* **Camping La Pierre Verte, Route de Bagnols-en-Forêt, 83600 Fréjus [04 94 40 88 30; fax 04 94 40 75 41; info@campinglapierreverte.com; www.campinglapierreverte.com]** Exit A8 junc 38 onto D4 dir Bagnols-en-Forêt. Site N of military camp. Lge, mkd pitch, hdstg, pt sl, terr, pt shd; wc; chem disp; baby facs; fam bthrm; shwrs inc; el pnts (6A) €4; gas; lndtte; shop; tradsmn; rest; bar; snacks; no BBQ; htd pool; waterslide; sand beach 8km; tennis; games area; cycle hire; games rm; entmnt; internet; TV rm; 50% statics; dogs €4; phone; adv bkg; quiet; Eng spkn; ccard acc; red long stay/low ssn; CKE/CCI. "Well-situated for local attractions; vg." ♦ 4 Apr-27 Sep. € 28.00   2008*

FRELAND see Kaysersberg *6F3*

FRENEUSE see Bonnières sur Seine *3D2*

FRESNAY SUR SARTHE *4E1* (200m NW Rural) *48.28297,
0.0158* Camp Municipal Le Sans Souci, Rue du Haut
Ary, Ave Victor Hugo, 72130 Fresnay-sur-Sarthe
[02 43 97 32 87; fax 02 43 33 75 72; regisseur@camping-
fresnaysursarthe.fr; www.camping-fresnaysursarthe.fr]
Fr Alençon S on D338; in 14km at La Hutte turn R on D310 to
Fresnay; sp in town on traff lts bef bdge; bear R imm after x-ing
bdge, then sharp R, sp diff to see, if missed V diff for c'vans
to turn fr opp dir. Fr Beaumont-sur-Sarthe NW on D39 to
Fresnay. Med, hdg/mkd pitch, pt sl, terr, pt shd; wc; chem disp;
shwrs inc; el pnts (6A) €3.20 (poss rev pol); lndtte (inc dryer);
shops high ssn & 500m; htd pool adj inc; rv adj; fishing; canoe
hire; cycle hire; wifi; entmnt; dogs €1.20; Eng spkn; adv bkg;
quiet; CKE/CCI. "Pleasant, clean site adj Rv Sarthe; gd rvside
pitches; 3 pitches for lge o'fits, mover rec; facs poss stretched
high ssn; gd cycling; vg." ♦ 1 Apr-30 Sep. € 16.55   2013*

FRETEVAL see Morée *4F2*

FRONCLES BUXIERES *6E1* (500m N Urban) *48.3004,
5.1476* Camp Municipal Les Deux Ponts, Rue des
Ponts, 52320 Froncles-Buxières [03 25 02 38 35 or
03 25 02 31 21 (Mairie); fax 03 25 02 09 80; mairie.
froncles@wanadoo.fr; www.tourisme-champagne-
ardenne.com] Fr Chaumont take N67 twd Joinville, ignore
sp to Vouécourt but take R turn E on D253 sp Froncles. Site sp
fr main rd. Sm, hdg pitch, pt shd; wc (some cont); chem disp
(wc); shwrs; el pnts (6A) inc; shops in vill; rv fishing; dogs €1.05;
adv bkg; quiet. "Pleasant situation; friendly; warden calls pm;
san facs clean; gd." 15 Mar-15 Oct. € 11.30   2011*

FRONTIGNAN *10F1* (5km NE Urban) *43.49173, 3.77932*
Camping L'Europe, 31 Route de Frontignan, 34110 Vic-
la-Gardiole [08 25 00 20 30 or 04 67 18 02 61 (LS); resa@
village-center.com; www.village-center.com] Exit A9
junc 32 & foll sp D612 dir Sète; in 10km turn L onto D14 to
Vic-la-Gardiole. Lge, pt shd; wc; baby facs; shwrs inc; el pnts
(6A) inc; lndtte; shop; rest, snacks; bar; BBQ (charcoal); snacks;
bar; playgrnd; 2 pools; paddling pool; waterslide; aqua gym;
beach 5km (free shuttle); archery; games area; games rm; wifi;
entmnt; some statics; dogs; adv bkg; red low ssn. 1 May-5 Sep.
€ 34.00   2010*

⊞ FRONTIGNAN *10F1* (6km NE Rural) *43.50038, 3.78683*
Camping Le Clos Fleuri, Route de la Mer, 34110 Vic-la-
Gardiole [04 67 78 15 68; fax 04 67 78 77 62; reception@
camping-clos-fleuri.fr; www.camping-clos-fleuri.fr] Fr A9
dir Montpellier exit junc 33 for D600 twd Sète. At Sète take
D612 for 13km then R into D114 sp Vic-la-Gardiole. Ignore
1st turn & go round vill & foll sp. Med, hdg/mkd pitch, shd;
wc; chem disp; mv service pnt; shwrs inc; el pnts (3-6A)
€3-3.80; lndtte; shops in ssn or 1km; rest, snacks; bar; htd
pool; shgl beach 2km; cycle hire; 30% statics; dogs €2.80;
phone adj; poss cr; adv bkg; quiet but noise fr bar; CKE/
CCI. "Friendly but not suitable for sm children or lge o'fits;
san facs tired but clean; chem disp facs poor; sheltered
fr Mistral." € 17.50 (3 persons)   2008*

FRONTIGNAN *10F1* (1km S Coastal) *43.42998, 3.75968*
Camping Méditerranée, 11 Ave des Vacances,
Quartier L'Entrée, 34110 Frontignan-Plage
[04 99 04 92 32 / 06 49 39 03 79 l/s; camping-mediterranee@
orange.fr; www.camping-mediterranee34.com] 3km fr Sète
on D612 to Montpellier, turn R at rlwy bdge, in approx 1km L
at x-rds to site. Or on D129 fr Frontignan fr Frontignan-Plage
site on R 100m past reclamation area. Med, pt shd; wc; shwrs
inc; el pnts (6A) €3.50; lndtte; shop adj; tradsmn; rest, snacks;
bar; playgrnd; sand beach 100m; tennis; lake 500m; games
area; entmnt; dogs €1.50; bus adj; adv bkg rec high ssn; quiet
but some rlwy & rd noise; red low ssn" 30 Mar-29 Sep.
€ 17.00 (3 persons)   2013*

FRONTIGNAN *10F1* (6km S Coastal) *43.44970, 3.80540*
Camping Les Tamaris, 140 Ave d'Ingril, 34110
Frontignan-Plage [04 67 43 44 77 or 04 78 04 67 92 (LS);
fax 04 67 18 97 90; les-tamaris@wanadoo.fr; www.les-
tamaris.fr] Fr A9/E15 exit junc 32 St Jean-de-Védas & foll sp
Sète. At next rndbt foll sp Sète N112. After approx 8km turn L
sp Vic-la-Gardiole onto D114. Cross rlwy & Canal du Rhône. Pass
Les Aresquiers-Plages & turn L in 500m, site sp on L in 500m.
Fr N on D613, take N300 to Sète; then N112 to Frontignan-
Plage. Lge, hdg/mkd pitch, hdstg, pt shd; htd wc; chem disp;
mv service pnt; baby facs; shwrs inc; el pnts (10A) inc (poss rev
pol); lndtte (inc dryer); shop; tradsmn; rest, snacks; bar; BBQ;
playgrnd; pool; paddling pool; sand beach adj; watersports; lake
fishing; cycle hire; horseriding nrby; archery; weights rm; wifi;
entmnt; games/TV rm; many statics; dogs €3; phone; poss cr;
adv bkg rec; quiet; ccard acc; red long stay/low ssn; CKE/CCI.
"Popular, family-run site; direct access to beach; sm pitches;
friendly, helpful staff; gd clean san facs; vg for families; excel
pool; late arr area; gd rest; lovely town; mkt Thu & Sat am;
excel." ♦ 24 Apr-25 Sep. € 48.00   2011*

FUILLA see Vernet les Bains *8G4*

FUMEL *7D3* (2km E Rural) *44.48929, 0.99704* Camping
de Condat/Les Catalpas, Route de Cahors, 47500 Fumel
[05 53 71 11 99 or 06 30 24 20 04; fax 05 53 71 36 69; les-
catalpas@wanadoo.fr; www.les-catalpas.com]
Take D811 fr Fumel E twd Cahors. Clearly sp after Condat.
Med, mkd pitch, hdstg, pt sl, pt shd; htd wc; chem disp (wc);
mv service pnt; shwrs inc; el pnts (10A) €3; lndtte; shops
1km; rest in vill; snacks; BBQ; playgrnd; pool; fishing adj; wifi;
entmnt; 15% statics; dogs; Eng spkn; adv bkg; red low ssn;
CKE/CCI. "New owners, friendly helpful, improvements to site,
sec barrier, by rv" ♦ ltd 1 Apr-31 Oct. € 21.00   2012*

⊞ FUMEL *7D3* (4km E Rural) *44.48925, 1.02048*
Aire Naturelle Le Valenty (Baillargues), Rue de
Chantegrue 46700 Soturac, Lot [05 65 36 59 50 or
06 72 57 69 80 (mob); campingdevalenty@gmail.com]
Fr Fumel take D911/811 dir Cahors. Thro Soturac, site immed
on L outside vill. Sm, terr, pt shd; wc; shwrs inc; el pnts (4-10A)
€2.50; gas 3km; lndtte; shops, snacks, bar 2.5km; tradsmn;
rest 1km; playgrnd; pool; minigolf; pony rides; games rm;
20% statics; dogs €1; bus 200m; Eng spkn; adv bkg; quiet;
CKE/CCI. "Delightful CL-type site; helpful owners; tranquil
but secure; organic produce for sale; poss not open low ssn -
phone ahead." € 13.00   2013*

FUMEL *7D3* (8km E Rural) *44.49810, 1.06670* **Camping Le Ch'Timi, La Roque, 46700 Touzac [05 65 36 52 36; fax 05 65 36 53 23; info@campinglechtimi.com; www.campinglechtimi.com]** Exit N20-E9 junc 57 onto D820 dir Cahors; turn R at rndabt onto D811 sp Villeneuve-sur-Lot; in Duravel take 3rd exit at rndabt onto D58, sp Vire-sur-Lot; in 2.5km cross bdge & turn R at rndabt onto D8, sp Touzac; site on R on rvside, on hill, in about 1.5km. Well sp. NB D8 not suitable lge c'vans or m'vans. Med, mkd pitch, pt sl, pt shd; wc; baby facs; shwrs inc, chem disp; el pnts (6A) inc; gas; lndtte; shop & 700m; tradsmn; rest, snacks; bar; BBQ (charcoal/gas); playgrnd; pool; paddling pool; canoeing & fishing 100m; cycle hire; tennis; archery; games area; wifi; entmnt; games/TV rm; 20% statics; dogs €1.75; no c'vans/m'vans over 7m high ssn; poss cr; Eng spkn; adv bkg; quiet; ccard acc; red low ssn; CKE/CCI. "Site in gd position; friendly, helpful Dutch owners; clean facs, ltd low ssn; rv nr site, down steep steps; access some pitches poss diff lge o'fits; gd local rests; wine-tasting tours; mkt Puy l'Evêque Tue; Wonderful stay, everyone friendly; rec. " ♦ 1 Apr-30 Sep. € 22.80 SBS - D05 2012*

FUMEL *7D3* (10km E Rural) *44.48023, 1.05204* **Camping Le Clos Bouyssac, 46700 Touzac [05 65 36 52 21; fax 05 65 24 68 51; camping.leclosbouyssac@wanadoo.fr; www.campingbytheriver.eu]** Fr Fumel on D911/D811, turn R to Touzac. Cross bdge over Rv Lot, turn R in vill to site in 2km on rvside. Site sp. Med, mkd pitch, terr, shd; wc; chem disp; mv service pnt; baby facs; shwrs inc; el pnts (10A) €3.50; gas; lndtte; shop 8km; snacks; bar; BBQ; playgrnd; pool; paddling pool; fishing; canoe hire; games area; games rm; wifi; entmnt; TV rm; 15% statics; dogs €1.75; phone; poss cr; Eng spkn; adv bkg; quiet; ccard acc; red low ssn/CKE/CCI. "Pleasant, tranquil site on S bank of Rv Lot; friendly, welcoming British/Dutch owners; recent refurbs; gd, clean facs, plenty of activities high ssn, inc wine-tasting; vg cycling; guided walks; vg wine area; gd." 1 Apr-30 Sep. € 17.00 2011*

GABARRET *8E2* (E Rural) *43.98250, 0.01562* **Camp Municipal La Chêneraie, 454 Ave de la Chêneraie, 40310 Gabarret [05 58 44 92 62; fax 05 58 44 35 38; la-cheneraie@orange.fr]** Fr cent of vill take D656 dir Mézin & Nérac. After 300m turn R onto D35, site in 300m on R. Sm, hdg pitch, pt sl, pt shd; htd wc; chem disp; shwrs inc; el pnts (10A) inc; lndtte; shops, rest, bar 500m; playgrnd; htd pool; adv bkg ess Jul/Aug; quiet; CKE/CCI. ♦ 1 Mar-31 Oct. € 9.15 2010*

GACE *4E1* (200m E Urban) *48.79475, 0.29926* **Camp Municipal Le Pressoir, Ave de Tahiti, 61230 Gacé [02 33 35 50 24 or 02 33 35 50 18; fax 02 33 35 92 82; ville.gace@wanadoo.fr]** Exit A28 junc 16 onto D932/D438; in 2km turn R off D438 opp Intermarché onto D724; site immed on L. Foll sp. NB Take care corners on app if o'fit v long. Sm, hdg/mkd pitch, sl, pt shd; wc; chem disp (wc); mv service pnt in vill; shwrs inc; el pnts (6A) €2.50 (poss long lead req); lndry rm; supmkt & rest 100m; playgrnd; rv 500m; poss cr; no ccard acc; quiet, but church bells 7 am - midnight. "Clean, well-run site; rec early arr; san facs dated but clean; most pitches gd size, sm pitches poss diff for lge o'fits; pitches rather sl for m'van; twin-axles extra charge; warden calls am & pm; conv NH fr A28; Nice site, well kept" 1 Jun-8 Sep. € 11.30 2013*

GACILLY, LA *2F3* (200m E Rural) *47.76325, -2.12544* **Camping de l'Aff, Le Bout du Pont, 35550 Sixt-sur-Aff [02 99 08 10 59, 06 58 04 16 62 (mob); fax 02 99 08 25 38; lepage.roselyne@orange.fr; www.paysdelagacilly.com]** On ent La Gacilly exit rv bdge onto D777 dir Sixt-sur-Aff. Site on L outside town sp. Well sp fr town cent. Sm, mkd pitch, pt shd; wc; mv service pnt; shwrs inc; el pnts (6A) €2.50; shops 500m; tradsmn; rests 200m; playgrnd; rv adj; boat hire; cycle hire; dogs €0.50; Eng spkn; quiet; CKE/CCI. "Rvside site; new owners (2011); gd san facs; easy walk to pretty vill; vg." ♦ ltd 20 Jun-19 Sep. € 13.00 2011*

GAILLAC *8E4* (8km N Rural) *43.98373, 1.91432* **Camp Municipal au Village, Route de Cordes, 81140 Cahuzac-sur-Vère [05 63 33 91 94 or 05 63 33 90 18 (Mairie); fax 05 63 33 94 03; mairie.cahuzacsurvere@wandoo.fr]** Fr Gaillac, take D922 N twd Cordes. Site on L of rd, clearly sp thro vill of Cahuzac. Sm, pt sl, pt shd; wc; shwrs; el pnts (3A) inc (rev pol); shops, rest, snacks, bar nr; playgrnd; pool; tennis; games area; cycle hire; phone; adv bkg; quiet. "Gd, clean site; call warden on arr; barrier at entry - poss to remove post to ease entry." 1 Jul-31 Aug. € 11.05 2010*

GAILLAC *8E4* (2km W Urban) *43.89674, 1.88522* **FFCC Camping des Sources, 9 Ave Guynemer, 81600 Gaillac [05 63 57 18 30; fax 05 49 52 28 58; camping-gaillac@orange.fr; www.camping-gaillac.fr]** Exit A68 junc 9 onto D999 then in 3.5km at rndabt turn onto D968 dir Gaillac. In 100m turn R immed past Leclerc petrol stn, then L by Aldi. Site 200m on R, well sp fr town cent. Med, hdg/mkd pitch, hdstg, terr, pt shd; htd wc; chem disp; mv service pnt; chem disp (wc); baby facs; shwrs inc; el pnts (10A) €2.50; lndtte (inc dryer); shop 500m; tradsmn; snacks; bar; playgrnd; pool; entmnt; TV; 10% statics; dogs €1.50; quiet; ccard acc (over €15); CKE/CCI. "Peaceful, clean & tidy site; friendly, helpful staff; gd, modern san facs; steep walk to recep & bar but san facs at pitch level; purpose-made dog-walk area; gd touring base Tarn & Albi region & circular tour Bastides; cent of wine area; not suitable lge o'fits; gd." ♦ ltd 1 Apr-31 Oct. € 13.00 2011*

GALLARGUES LE MONTUEUX see Lunel *10E2*

GAMACHES *3B2* (1km NW Rural) *49.99397, 1.54366* **Camping Domaine Les Marguerites, Rue Antonin Gombert, 80220 Gamaches [tel/fax 03 22 30 89 51; domainelesmarguerites@orange.fr]** A28 exit 5 onto D1015 dir Eu & Le Treport to Gamaches in 8km. Site sp fr town, 200m fr stadium, Lge, mkd pitch, hdstg, pt shd; wc (cont); chem disp; shwrs inc; el pnts (6-10A) inc; lndtte; tradsmn; rest, snacks; bar; BBQ; playgrnd; pool; paddling pool; rv adj; games area; 75% statics; dogs; poss cr; quiet; adv bkg; red long stay/CKE/CCI. "Nr forest of Eu & Somme coast; gd fishing, riding." ♦ ltd 21 Mar-15 Sep. € 19.50 2010*

⊞ **GANGES** *10E1* (7km E Rural) *43.92630, 3.78951* **Camp Municipal Le Grillon, Place de l'Eglise, 34190 Montoulieu [04 67 73 30 75; camping@montoulieu.fr; http://camping.montoulieu.fr/]** Fr Ganges take D999 E. At La Cadière-et-Cambo turn R onto D195 (site sp). Site on R in 3km. Sm, some hdg pitch, some hdstg, pt sl, pt shd; wc; mv service pnt; baby facs; shwrs inc; el pnts (6A) inc; lndtte (inc dryer); shop 6km; rest; bar; playgrnd; pool; 40% statics; dogs; quiet. "Gd cent for outdoor activities; gd, modern facs; useful winter NH; fairly isolated." ♦ ltd € 14.00 2009*

Send in your site reports by mid August 2014

GANGES *10E1* (2km S Rural) *43.84685, 3.70488* **Camping Le Val d'Hérault, 34190 Brissac [04 67 73 72 29; fax 04 67 73 30 81; info@camping-levaldherault.com; www. camping-levaldherault.com]** Fr D999 at Ganges take D4 S to Brissac; on D4 by rv. Med, hdg/mkd pitch, pt sl, shd; wc; chem disp; shwrs inc; el pnts (6A) €4.10; gas; lndtte; tradsmn; rest, snacks; bar; playgrnd; htd pool; rv beach 250m; canoeing; games area; wifi; 60% statics; dogs €2.20; poss cr; quiet; red low ssn; CKE/CCI. "Conv Hérault Gorge; steps to san facs; vg." 15 Mar-31 Oct. € 19.90   2008*

GANNAT *9A1* (7km N Rural) *46.16588, 3.18975* **Camp Municipal Champ de la Sioule, Route de Chantelle, 03800 Jenzat [04 70 56 86 35 or 04 70 56 81 77 (Mairie); fax 04 70 56 85 38; mairie-jenzat@pays-allier.com]** D2009 N fr Gannat for 4.5km, turn L onto D42, site in 3km in Jenzat on R, just after rv bdge. Med, pt shd; wc; shwrs inc; el pnts (6-10) €1.90-2.95; lndtte; shops 250m; el pnts (6-10); Eng spkn; clean facs; quiet; CKE/CCI. "Pleasant site on rv bank; helpful warden; clean facs, poss stretched high ssn; muddy after heavy rain; pitches nr river, some mosquitos" ♦ ltd 19 Apr-21 Sep. € 16.00   2013*

> ## "There aren't many sites open at this time of year"
>
> If you're travelling outside peak season remember to call ahead to check site opening dates – even if the entry says 'open all year'.

GANNAT *9A1* (1km SW Rural) *46.09106, 3.19385* **Camp Municipal Le Mont Libre, 10 Route de la Bâtisse, 03800 Gannat [tel/fax 04 70 90 12 16 or 06 73 86 04 95 (mob); camping.gannat@wanadoo.fr; www.camping-gannat.fr]** App Gannat fr S on D2009; at rndabt just after town name sp, turn L for 150m; turn R (stadium on R) for 700m; turn L uphill for 200m, turn R to site. Site sp. Or S fr Gannat on D2009; in 600m to R into Route de la Bâtisse; then R, sp site. Med, hdstg, pt sl, terr, pt shd; wc; chem disp; mv service pnt; el pnts (10A) €2.60 (poss rev pol); lndtte; shop & 500m, supmkt 1km; tradsmn; playgrnd; sm pool; rv 5km; games area; games/TV rm; some statics; dogs free; poss cr; adv bkg; quiet; ccard acc. "Pretty, well-kept site; gd sized pitches; helpful warden; clean facs, but poss tired end of ssn; grnd soft after heavy rain; no twin-axles; pleasant town; popular, busy NH." ♦ 1 Apr-31 Oct. € 10.40   2011*

GANNAT *9A1* (10km W Rural) *46.11077, 3.08082* **Camp Municipal Les Nières, Rue des Nières, 03450 Ebreuil [04 70 90 70 60 or 04 70 90 71 33 (Mairie); fax 04 70 90 74 90; mairie-ebreuil@wanadoo.fr; www. valdesioule.com]** Site 1km SW of Ebreuil, sp fr D915. Sm, shd; wc (cont); chem disp; shwrs; el pnts (4-8A) €1.95-2.80; lndtte; shops 1km; snacks; playgrnd; fishing; access to rv; quiet. "Nice setting on Rv Sioule; san facs dated but clean, poss stretched high ssn; warden present 1700-2000 only low ssn; sh walk into vill." ♦ 1 Jun-30 Sep. € 8.10   2012*

GANNAT *9A1* (10km W Rural) *46.10838, 3.07347* **Camping La Filature de la Sioule, Route de Chouvigny, 03450 Ebreuil [04 70 90 72 01; camping.filature@gmail.com; www.campingfilature.com]** Fr A71 exit 12 (avoid 12.1); foll sp to Ebreuil N 500m, then W for 5km thro vill. Turn W onto D915 dir Chouvigny, site in 1km. Med, hdg/mkd pitch; wc (some cont); chem disp; mv service pnt 800m; baby facs; shwrs inc; el pnts (6A) €3.50; gas; lndtte; shop; tradsmn; snacks; bar; BBQ; playgrnd; canoeing; trout-fishing; tennis 800m; cycle hire; horseriding; TV rm; wifi; some statics; dogs free; Eng spkn; adv bkg; v quiet; ccard acc; red long stay/low ssn; CKE/CCI. "Peaceful, pleasant site in orchard; lge pitches; helpful British owners; clean facs, ltd low ssn; vg value food high ssn (gd home cooking); vg walking area; conv A71; No hdstg, very soft ground" ♦ 31 Mar-1 Oct. € 20.00   2013*

GAP *9D3* (1.5km N Rural) *44.58030, 6.08270* **Camping Alpes-Dauphiné, Route Napoléon, 05000 Gap [04 92 51 29 95; fax 04 92 53 58 42; info@alpesdauphine. com; www.alpesdauphine.com]** On N85, sp. Med, mkd pitch, some hdstg, pt sl, terr, pt shd; htd wc; chem disp; mv service pnt; baby facs; shwrs inc; el pnts (6A) €3; gas; lndtte (inc dryer); shop; tradsmn; rest, snacks; bar; playgrnd; htd pool; paddling pool; games area; wifi; TV; 20% statics; dogs €2.10; phone; poss cr; Eng spkn; adv bkg rec high ssn; quiet; ccard acc; red low ssn; CKE/CCI. "Pleasant site with views; modern san facs; m'vans need levellers; gd touring base; lack of maintenance early ssn (2011); conv NH." ♦ 15 Apr-15 Oct. € 19.80   2011*

GAP *9D3* (10km S Rural) *44.45708, 6.04785* **Camp Municipal Le Chêne, Route de Marseille, 05130 Tallard [04 92 54 13 31 or 04 92 54 10 14 (Mairie); fax 04 92 54 00 81; mairie.tallard@wanadoo.fr]** Fr S take N85 twds Gap; turn R at traff lts onto D942; site on R after 3km. Fr Gap take N85 S; turn L at traff lts, D942; site on R 3km. Med, mkd pitch, hdstg, sl, terr, pt shd; wc (some cont); shwrs inc; el pnts (6A) inc; lndtte; shop 2km; rest; bar; playgrnd; htd pool; tennis; BBQ; entmnt; phone; dogs; adv bkg; CKE/CCI. "Poss unsuitable for lgs o'fits, sm pitches." 15 Jun-31 Aug. € 15.20   2011*

GAP *9D3* (8km SW Rural) *44.49914, 6.02901* **Camping Les Bonnets, Le Haut-du-Village, 05000 Neffes [04 92 57 93 89 or 06 88 73 13 59; camping.les.bonnets@wanadoo.fr; www.camping-les-bonnets.com]** N85 SW fr Gap, turn R onto D46, site sp 1km fr vill. Med, mkd pitch, pt shd; htd wc; baby facs; shwrs; el pnts (6-10A) €3.30-4.20; lndtte; shop; supmkt 5km; rest; bar 1km; playgrnd; pool; fishing 3km; games area; entmnt; wifi; TV rm; some statics; dogs €1.50; quiet; red low ssn. "Well-kept farm site in beautiful area; friendly owner; excel pool; v ltd facs & rather run-down early ssn (2011)." 1 Apr-30 Sep. € 13.50   2011*

GARDE FREINET, LA see Grimaud *10F4*

GARDONNE see Bergerac *7C3*

GARIN see Luchon *8G3*

GASSIN see St Tropez *10F4*

GASTES

FRANCE

GASTES 7D1 (3km SW Rural) *44.31331, -1.16856* **Camping La Réserve, 1229 Ave Félix Ducourneau, 40160 Gastes [05 58 09 74 79 or 05 58 09 79 23; fax 05 58 09 78 71; lareserve@siblu.fr; www.siblu.com/lareserve]** At traff lts in cent Parentis-en-Born, turn L sp Pontenx & Gastes on D652. After 3km turn R dir Gastes, Ste Eulalie & Mimizan-Plage. Cont onto rndabt & take 2nd exit D652, then turn immed R sp La Réserve. Site sp. V lge, pt shd; wc; chem disp; shwrs inc; el pnts (6A) inc; gas; lndtte; rest, snacks; bar; shop; BBQ (gas only); playgrnd; pools (1 htd, covrd); waterslide; lake sw & private sandy beach adj; watersports high ssn; sailing school; windsurfing; cycle hire; tennis; games area; archery; wifi; entmnt; mostly statics; no dogs; Eng spkn; adv bkg ess high ssn; ccard acc; red low ssn; CKE/CCI. "Lakeside site by pine forest; lge pitches; mostly statics, but gd facs for tourers; children's club inc in site fee; highly rec." ♦ 9 Apr-16 Sep. € 67.00   2011*

GAUDONVILLE see St Clar 8E3

GAUGEAC see Monpazier 7D3

GAVARNIE 8G2 (2km N Rural) *42.75896, 0.00069* **Camping Le Pain de Sucre, quartier Couret, 65120 Gavarnie [tel/ fax 05 62 92 47 55 or 06 75 30 64 22 (mob); camping-gavarnie@wanadoo.fr or info@camping-gavarnie.com; www.camping-gavarnie.com]** N of Gavarnie, across rv by sm bdge; clearly visible & sp fr rd. Med, pt shd; wc; mv service pnt; shwrs inc; el pnts (2-10A) €2.30-6.50 (long lead poss req); lndtte; shops, rest, snacks, bar 3km; BBQ; playgrnd; dogs €2.15; quiet; ccard acc. "Gd base for walking; gd facs; access to national park; vg; gd clean san facs; fantastic view of Cirque" ♦ 1 Jun-30 Sep & 15 Dec-15 Apr. € 24.40   2013*

GAVARNIE 8G2 (500m S Rural) *42.72802, -0.00744* **Camping La Bergerie (Rivière Sacaze), Chemin du Cirque , 65120 Gavarnie [05 62 92 48 41 or 06 85 12 68 47 (mob); www. camping-gavarnie-labergerie.com]** Site at S end of Gavarnie on road to Cirque de Gavarnie in Pyrenees National Park. Sm, pt sl, unshd; wc; chem disp (wc); baby facs; shwrs €2; no el pnts; lndtte (inc dryer); shop & rest 500m; snacks; bar; dogs; Eng spkn; quiet; CKE/CCI. "V sm site by rv with views; no el pnts; gd san facs; 1hr walk to Cirque de Gavarnie." 20 Jun-20 Sep. € 14.60   2011*

GEMOZAC 7B2 (400m W Urban) *45.56825, -0.68086* **Camp Municipal, 26 Rue Carnot, 17260 Gémozac [05 46 94 50 16; fax 05 46 94 16 25; gemozac@mairie17.com]** Exit A10 junc 36 (or turn W off off D137) onto D732 sp Gémozac. In 7km foll site sp. Turn L immed after Renault g'ge at end of vill. Sm, mkd pitch, pt shd; wc; chem disp; mv service pnt adj; baby facs; shwrs inc; el pnts (10A) inc (poss rev pol); lndtte; shop, pizzeria & snacks 500m; tradsmn; rest & bar 100m; BBQ; htd pool adj; dogs; Eng spkn; adv bkg; ccard not acc; quiet; CKE/ CCI. "Excel site; pleasant sm town; no twin-axles." 15 Jun-31 Aug.   2009*

GENETS see Avranches 2E4

GENNES 4G1 (Rural) *47.34239, -0.22966* **Camping Au Bord de Loire, Ave des Cadets-de-Saumur, 49350 Gennes [02 41 38 04 67 or 02 41 38 07 30; fax 02 41 38 07 12; auborddeloire@free.fr; www.camping-auborddeloire.com]** At Rv Loire bdge cross S to Gennes on D751B. Site 200m on L. Ent to site thro bus terminus/car park on ent to Gennes. Med, pt sl, pt shd; wc; chem disp; shwrs inc; el pnts (10A) €3; lndtte; shop in vill; snacks; bar; BBQ; shop in vill; tradsmn; snacks; playgrnd; htd pool in vill; entmnt; 2% statics; dogs €1; quiet, but some rd noise; red long stay; CKE/CCI. "Delightful, relaxing, well-kept site by Rv Loire, spacious pitches, main san facs block up steps, vg." 1 May-30 Sep. € 17.00   2013*

GERARDMER See also sites listed under Corcieux, Granges-sur-Vologne, La Bresse and Le Tholy.

⊞ **GERARDMER** 6F3 (3km E Rural) *48.07826, 6.94261* **Camp Municipal du Domaine de Longemer, 121 Route de la Plage, 88400 Xonrupt-Longemer [03 29 63 07 30; fax 03 29 63 27 10; camping.dudomaine@wanadoo.fr]** Fr W thro Gérardmer on D417. immed after sp Xonrupt-Longemer turn R & cont thro vill. Site 1st one; turn L over bdge. App fr E (Colmar), turn L opp hotel Auberge du Lac. Site on both sides of rd. V lge, pt shd; htd wc; mv service pnt; shwrs inc; el pnts (6A) €3; shop; rest, snacks; bar; playgrnd; lake sw; fishing; x-country skiing; 10% statics; phone; poss cr; quiet; red long stay; CKE/CCI. "Attractive, clean lakeside site; gd walking." € 10.80   2009*

GERARDMER 6F3 (6km E Rural) *48.06755, 6.94830* **FFCC Camping Les Jonquilles, Route du Lac, 88400 Xonrupt-Longemer [03 29 63 34 01; fax 03 29 60 09 28; info@ camping-jonquilles.com; www.camping-jonquilles.com]** Sp off D417 SE of Xonrupt-Longemer. Fr W thro Gérardmer on D417 (sp Colmar) in approx 1km over bdge & turn R at T-junc (still on D417). After 3km turn R opp hotel Auberge du Lac & almost immed R round W end of lake for 500m to T-junc, turn L, site on S bank 1km. Lge, mkd pitch, pt sl, unshd; wc (some cont); chem disp; mv service pnt; baby facs; shwrs inc; el pnts (6-10A) €3.30-5.20; gas; lndtte; shop; rest, snacks; bar; playgrnd; lake beach & sw adj; fishing; sailing; TV;wifi; few statics; dogs €1.50; phone; bus 1km; Eng spkn; adv bkg; quiet but some noise fr entmnt at night; ccard acc; red low ssn; CKE/CCI. "Friendly, well-maintained, family-run site; gd views; poss uneven pitches; excel for Haute Vosges region." ♦ 20 Apr-6 Oct. € 22.85   2013*

GERARDMER 6F3 (1.5km SW) *48.06472, 6.85388* **Camping de Ramberchamp, 21 Chemin du Tour du Lac, 88400 Gérardmer [03 29 63 03 82; fax 03 29 63 26 09; info@ camping-de-ramberchamp.com; www.camping-de-ramberchamp.com]** S bank of Lake Gérardmer. Fr W turn R off D417, 1km bef Gérardmer. Fr E thro cent of town foll sps to La Bresse, fork R onto D69, sp Vagney. Foll lakeside rd & camping sps. Lge, pt hdg/mkd pitch, pt shd; htd wc; chem disp; shwrs inc;baby facs; el pnts (4A) €3.50; lndtte; shop 1km; tradsmn; rest, snacks; BBQ; playgrnd; lake sw; fishing; TV; dogs €1; poss cr; Eng spkn; quiet; ccard acc; CKE/CCI. "Comfortable site in excel location; friendly staff; some sm pitches; easy-going walks; walk along lake to town; excel; games for children, giant chessboard, mini golf; excel, stunning area" 6 Apr-30 Sep. € 16.00   2013*

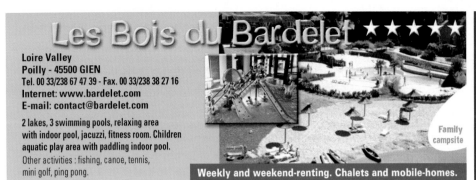

Les Bois du Bardelet ★★★★★

Loire Valley
Poilly - 45500 GIEN
Tel. 00 33/238 67 47 39 - Fax. 00 33/238 38 27 16
Internet: www.bardelet.com
E-mail: contact@bardelet.com

2 lakes, 3 swimming pools, relaxing area
with indoor pool, jacuzzi, fitness room. Children
aquatic play area with paddling indoor pool.
Other activities : fishing, canoe, tennis,
mini golf, ping pong.

Family campsite

Weekly and weekend-renting. Chalets and mobile-homes.

FRANCE

GERARDMER 6F3 (1.5km SW Rural) 48.0636, 6.8561 **Camping Les Sapins, 18 Chemin de Sapois, 88400 Gérardmer [tel/ fax 03 29 63 15 01 or 06 37 35 36 20 (mob); les.sapins@ camping-gerardmer.com; www.camping-gerardmer.com]** On S side of lake 150m up C17 rd sp Col de Sapois. Med, pt shd; wc; mv service pnt; shwrs inc; el pnts (4-6A) €3-4.70; sm shop; rest, snacks; bar; BBQ; playgrnd; lake with beach 200m; fishing & watersports adj; games area; TV rm; 10% statics; dogs €1.20; adv bkg rec; quiet; red low ssn. "Well-kept site in lovely area; lge pitches but o'looked by sports stadium; no lake views; walk along lake into pretty town." 1 Apr-10 Oct. € 13.50   2009*

⊞ GERAUDOT 6E1 (1km E Rural) 48.30268, 4.33752 **Camping Les Rives du Lac/L'Epine aux Moines, 10220 Géraudot [tel/ fax 03 25 41 24 36; camping.lepineauxmoines@orange.fr; www.campinglesrivesdulac.com]** Exit A26 at junc 23 onto D619 to Lusigny-sur-Barse; foll sp Parc de la Forêt d'Orient. Turn N along lake to site. Or fr Troyes D960 E. At Rouilly head S on D43 sp Géraudot. Site 1km E of vill. Lge, hdg/mkd pitch, pt sl, pt shd; htd wc (mainly cont); chem disp; mv service pnt; shwrs inc; el pnts (6A) inc (poss rev pol & long lead req); lndtte; shop 8km; tradsmn; rest & snacks adj; bar; playgrnd; lake sw adj; boat hire; dogs €2; poss cr; adv bkg; quiet; red low ssn/ CKE/CCI. "Nice, well-kept site in attractive area; clean san facs; poss mosquitoes; gd walking & cycle paths; nr bird observatory; lovely vill; conv NH." 1 Mar-31 Dec. € 24.00   2013*

GEX 9A3 (500m E Urban) 46.33410, 6.06744 **Camping Les Genêts, 400 Ave des Alpes, 01170 Gex [04 50 42 84 57 or 06 79 17 13 69 (mob)]** Fr all dir head for 'Centre Ville'; at rndabt take D984 twd Divonne/Lausanne. Site sp to R (tight turn) after rlwy sheds (poor sp in town) & Musée Sapeurs Pompiers. Med, hdg pitch, hdstg, pt sl, pt shd; wc (some cont); chem disp; shwrs inc; el pnts (16A) €2.90; gas 500m; lndtte; shops 500m; tradsmn; snacks; bar; playgrnd; games area; TV rm; dogs €1; phone; gates clsd 2200-0800; Eng spkn; adv bkg; quiet; ccard acc; CKE/CCI. "Excel site; excel games facs/playgrnd; friendly, helpful staff; clean san facs; quiet with lots of privacy; conv Geneva; wifi in recp" ◆ 25 May-30 Sep. € 12.50   2012*

GIBLES see Clayette, La 9A2

GICQ, LE see Matha 7B2

GIEN 4G3 (1km SW Rural) 47.68233, 2.62289 **Camping Touristique de Gien, Rue des Iris, 45500 Poilly-lez-Gien [02 38 67 12 50; fax 02 38 67 12 18; camping-gien@ wanadoo.fr; www.camping-gien.com]** Off D952 Orléans-Nevers rd; turn R over old rv bdge in Gien & then R again onto D951; site on R on Rv Loire.Alt dir fr D940 (Argent-sur-Sauldre - Gien) at rndbt take rd sp Gien. Take L at traff lts before old bdge; site on R, 1km S of rv. Lge, hdg/mkd pitch, hdstg, pt sl, pt shd; htd wc; chem disp; mv service pnt; baby facs; shwrs inc; el pnts (10A) €3.50-5; gas adj; lndtte (inc dryer); shop; rest, snacks; bar adj; BBQ; playgrnd; covrd pool; paddling pool; lake sw 3km; canoeing; tennis; cycle hire; games rm; wifi; entmnt; TV rm; 20% statics; dogs €2; phone; adv bkg; Eng spkn; quiet; ccard acc; red long stay/CKE/CCI. "Lovely rvside site; views of old bdge & town some pitches; excel staff; gd san facs; vg facs; no sw allowed in rv; easy walk to town across bdge; porcelain factory 'seconds'; vg value; gd rest; San facs unisex; Excel site, highly rec; nice situation" ◆ 2 Mar-10 Nov. € 30.00   2013*

GIEN 4G3 (5km SW Rural) 47.64152, 2.61528 **Kawan Village Les Bois du Bardelet, Route de Bourges,Poilly 45500 Gien [02 38 67 47 39; fax 02 38 38 27 16; contact@ bardelet.com; www.bardelet.com]** Fr Gien take D940 dir Bourges; turn R onto D53, then R again onto unclassified rd to go back across D940; foll sp to site on L side of this rd. Site well sp fr D940. Lge, hdg/mkd pitch, some hdstg, pt shd; htd wc; chem disp; mv service pnt; baby facs; shwrs inc; el pnts (10-16A) inc (some rev pol); gas; lndtte (inc dryer); shop; rest, snacks; bar; BBQ; playgrnd; 2 htd pools (1 covrd); paddling pool; jacuzzi; lake fishing & canoeing; horseriding 5km; tennis; games area; games rm; fitness rm; cycle hire; archery; wifi; entmnt; TV; 17% statics; dogs €4; twin-axles acc (rec check in adv); phone; adv bkg; quiet; ccard acc; red couples/low ssn/ long stay; CKE/CCI. "Pleasant, well-kept, well-run site; friendly welcome; modern facs, poss stretched high ssn; some pitches poss diff access; beautiful o'door pool; gd for young children; guided walks." ◆ 19 Apr-30 Sep. € 34.20 (CChq acc) SBS - L05   2013*

See advertisement

GIGNAC *10F1* (1km NE Rural) *43.66192, 3.55887* **Camp Municipal La Meuse, Route d'Aniane, 34150 Gignac** [04 67 57 92 97; contact@campingdelameuse.com; www. campinglameuse.fr] Exit A75 onto A750 sp Montpellier & Gignac. Exit sp Gignac Cent at rndabt & foll D32 sp Aniane. Site sp to L 600m past Aldi supmkt. Med, hdg/mkd pitch, pt shd; wc; mv service pnt; shwrs inc; el pnts (16A) €2.50; gas 1km; lndtte; shop 1km; bar; tennis; ltd wifi; dogs €1.70; Eng spkn; adv bkg; quiet; ccard acc; red long stay; CKE/CCI. "Pleasant, clean site; easy access; lge pitches; warden connects/disconnects el pnts; poss flooding on some pitches in heavy rain; gd cycling; unrel opening low ssn; rec." ♦ ltd 1 Jun-30 Sep. € 13.40   2010*

GIGNAC *10F1* (1.5km W Rural) *43.65395, 3.54056* **Camping du Pont, 730 Blvd du Moulin, 34150 Gignac** [tel/fax 04 67 57 52 40; conto34@free.fr; www.campingdupont. com] Foll sp fr town cent. Sm, pt shd; wc (some cont); chem disp; shwrs inc; el pnts (6A) €2.70; lndtte; shop; tradsmn; rest, snacks; BBQ; playgrnd; pool; fishing; tennis adj; games rm; entmnt; 20% statics; dogs €2; adv bkg; quiet; red low ssn. "Friendly welcome." ♦ 1 Apr-30 Sep. € 22.00   2010*

GIGNAC *10F1* (5km W Rural) *43.64056, 3.49521* **Camping Le Septimanien, Route de Cambous, 34725 St André-de-Sangonis** [04 67 57 84 23; fax 04 67 57 54 78; info@camping-leseptimanien.com; www.camping-leseptimanien.com] Exit A75 junc 57. At rndabt on E side of a'route take D128 to Brignac. In Brignac turn L at T-junc, then fork R on D4 twd St André-de-Sangonis. Site on R in 3km. Med, hdg pitch, pt shd; wc; chem disp; shwrs inc; el pnts (5A) inc; gas; lndtte; shop & 1km; tradsmn; rest, snacks; bar; playgrnd; pool; paddling pool; entmnt; 15% statics; dogs €2.15; phone; adv bkg; quiet; ccard acc; CKE/CCI. "Well-organised site; vg sh stay/NH." ♦ ltd 29 Apr-25 Sep. € 22.50   2009*

GIGNY SUR SAONE see Sennecey le Grand *6H1*

GIROUSSENS *8F4* (2km SE Rural) *43.75478, 1.80461* **FFCC Aire Naturelle La Rigaudié (Gaben/Noual), 81500 Giroussens** [05 63 41 67 20; bernard.gaben@wanadoo. fr or marienoual@live.fr; www.larigaudie.com] Exit A68 junc 7 onto D12 to Giroussens; pass vill & cont on D831 sp Lavaur; in 3km turn L; site in 500m. Sm, pt shd; wc; chem disp; shwrs inc; el pnts (6A) €2.50; lndtte; shop 3km; tradsmn; BBQ; playgrnd; sm pool; games area; dogs free; adv bkg; quiet. "Delightful aire naturelle - attractive & spacious; part grassy field, part woodland; many places of interest; a real find; excel." 1 May-30 Sep. € 9.60   2011*

⊞ **GISAY LA COUDRE** *3D2* (500m S Rural) **Aire Communale La Villette - deleted, 27330 Gisay-la-Coudre** [02 32 44 38 86 or 06 70 29 19 48 (mob); mairie. gisaylacoudre@wanadoo.fr] Turn S of N138 at Bernay onto D833 to La Barre-en-Ouche. In town turn R onto D49 dir Broglie & in 200m turn L onto D35, site on R in 3km, sp. M'vans only. Sm, hdstg, unshd; own san; chem disp; mv service pnt; el pnts €2 for 2 hrs; water €2 for 100 litres; shop, rest, snacks, bar 200m; quiet. "Payment for services with jeton obtainable fr Bar-Rest La Tortue 500m further on fr site; car/c'vans probably acc; vg NH."   2010*

⊞ **GIVET** *5B1* (500m N Urban) *50.14345, 4.82614* **Caravaning Municipal La Ballastière, 16 Rue Berthelot, 08600 Givet** [03 24 42 30 20; fax 03 24 42 02 44; sa.mairiegivet@wanadoo.fr; www.tourisme-champagne-ardenne.com] Site at N end of town on lake. Foll 'Caravaning' sp fr W end of rv bdge or Dinant rd. Med, some hdg pitch, mkd pitch; hdstg, pt shd; htd wc; chem disp; shwrs; el pnts (10A) inc; lndry rm; supmkt, rest, snacks, bar 1km; BBQ; playgrnd; pool adj; 70% statics (sep area); dogs €0.85; quiet; CKE/CCI. "Nr Rv Meuse; adj sports & watersports complex; picturesque town; walking dist to shops & rest; v clean fac; helpful warden; v gd; Conv for River Meuse cycleway" € 8.60   2013*

GIVET *5B1* (2km SW Rural) *50.12993, 4.80721* **Camping Le Sanglier, 63 Rue des Grands Jardins, 08600 Rancennes** [03 24 42 72 61] Off D949 Givet to Beauraing. Immed after x-ing rv bdge turn R. Turn R again foll sp to site at end narr access rd on rvside. Sm, pt sl, terr, pt shd; wc; chem disp; shwrs; el pnts (4A); shop 2km; snacks; fishing; watersports; 60% statics; phone; Eng spkn; adv bkg; quiet; CKE/CCI. "Gd touring base; clean, basic facs; gd NH." 1 May-30 Sep.   2008*

GIVORS *9B2* (7km NW Urban) *45.61498, 4.67068* **Camp Municipal de la Trillonnière, Monts du Lyonnais, Rue de la Loire, 69440 Mornant** [04 78 44 16 47 or 04 78 44 00 46 (Mairie); fax 04 78 44 91 70; mairiemornant@wanadoo.fr; www.ville-mornant.fr] Exit A7 at Givors & foll sp for St Etienne via D488, thro Givors onto D2 till sp seen for Mornant via D34, cont on D34 up hill for 7km, cross D342 & cont 1km to o'skts of Mornant, L at junc island & site on L. Med, pt sl, pt shd; wc; chem disp; shwrs; el pnts (10A) inc; shops, rest, snacks bar 500m; pool 250m; dogs €1; adv bkg; quiet; some rd noise; access for vans 0815-1015 & 1700-2200. 1 May-30 Sep. € 14.00   2009*

GIVRAND see St Gilles Croix de Vie *2H3*

⊞ **GIVRE, LE** *7A1* (1.5km S Rural) *46.44472, -1.39832* **Camping La Grisse, 85540 Le Givre** [02 51 30 83 03; info@campinglagrisse.com; www.campinglagrisse.com] Fr Luçon take D949 & turn L at junc with D747 (La Tranche rd). Turn L in 3km & foll sps. Sm, pt shd; wc; chem disp; shwrs inc; el pnts (16A) €4; lndtte; playgrnd; htd, covrd pool 10km; sand beach 10km; games area; some statics; dogs €2; Eng spkn; adv bkg; ccard not acc; CKE/CCI. "Peaceful, friendly, farm site; lge pitches; clean, modern facs; beautiful area/beach; gd for dogs." ♦ ltd € 21.00   2011*

GIVRY EN ARGONNE *5D1* (200m S Rural) *48.94835, 4.88545* **Camp Municipal du Val d'Ante, Rue du Pont, 51330 Givry-en-Argonne** [03 26 60 04 15 or 03 26 60 01 59 (Mairie); fax 03 26 60 18 22; mairie.givryenargonne@wanadoo.fr; www.mairie-givry-en-argonne.fr] Exit A4 junc 29 at Ste Menéhould; S on D382 to Givry-en-Argonne; site sp on R on lakeside. Sm, pt sl, pt shd; wc (some cont); chem disp; shwrs inc; el pnts (6A) €2.10; shops 200m; playgrnd; shgl lake beach sw; boats for hire adj; dogs €1.20; poss cr; quiet; no ccard acc. "Attractive, basic site; clean san facs; warden calls am & pm; gd birdwatching." 1 May-31 Aug. € 12.40   2013*

GLUIRAS see Ollières sur Eyrieux, Les *9D2*

GONDREXANGE see Héming 6E3

GONDRIN 8E2 (E Rural) 43.88214, 0.23895 **FFCC Camping Domaine Le Pardaillan, Rue du Pardaillon, 32330 Gondrin-en-Armagnac [05 62 29 16 69; camplepardaillan@wanadoo.fr; www.camping-le-pardaillan.com]** Fr Condom take D931 S for 12km to Gondrin. Site clearly sp. Med, hdg/mkd pitch, hdstg, pt shd; htd wc; chem disp; mv service pnt; baby facs; shwrs inc; el pnts (6-10A) inc; gas; lndtte (inc dryer); shop; tradsmn; rest, snacks; bar; playgrnd; paddling pool; lake sw adj; games rm; wifi; entmnt; TV rm; many statics; dogs €3.50; phone; poss cr; Eng spkn; adv bkg; CKE/CCI. "Excel site; lovely region; red facs & NH only low ssn; highly rec." ♦ 1 Apr-15 Oct. € 22.00   2010*

GONDRIN 8E2 (2km S Rural) 43.86936, 0.25844 **Camping La Brouquère, Betbézé, 32330 Gondrin [05 62 29 19 44; camping@brouquere.com; www.brouquere.com]** Fr Condom S on D931; pass thro Gondrin & turn S onto D113 dir Courrensan; site sp in 2km. Sm, mkd pitch, pt sl, sp shd; wc; chem disp; fam bthrm; shwrs inc; el pnts (10A) €2.50; lndtte; tradsmn; bar; BBQ; playgrnd; pool 2km; cycle hire; wifi; TV; dogs €1; Eng spkn; adv bkg; quiet; red low ssn. "V quiet, CL-type site; friendly Dutch owners; immac san facs; wine-tasting; local produce, inc Armagnac; excel." 30 Apr-1 Oct. € 15.30   2011*

GORDES 10E2 (2km N Rural) 43.92689, 5.20207 **Camping Les Sources, Route de Murs, 84220 Gordes [04 90 71 12 48; fax 04 90 72 09 43; campingdessources@wanadoo.fr; www.campingdessources.com]** Fr A7 junc 24, E on D973; then D22; then D900 twds Apt. After 18km at Coustellet turn N onto D2 then L on D15 twds Murs; site on L in 2km beyond Gordes. Med, mkd pitch, hdstg, terr, pt shd; wc (some cont); chem disp; mv service pnt; baby facs; shwrs inc; el pnts (6A) €4.40 (long lead poss req); lndtte; shop & 2km; rest, snacks; bar; playgrnd; pool; cycle hire; games area; games rm; entmnt; 25% statics; dogs €5; Eng spkn; adv bkg; quiet; red low ssn/long stay; ccard acc; CKE/CCI. "Lovely location & views; friendly staff; modern, clean san facs; gd pool; access rds narr; sm pitches v diff lge o'fits; ask for easy pitch & inspect on foot; some steep rds to pitches as site on hillside; 24 hr security barriers; gd walking; mkt Tues." 2 Apr-23 Sep. € 22.60 2011*

GORDES 10E2 (10km NE Rural) 43.94069, 5.22925 **Camp Municipal Les Chalottes, 84220 Murs [04 90 72 60 84 or 04 90 72 60 00 (Mairie); fax 04 90 72 61 73; contact@communedemurs-vaucluse.fr; www.communedemurs-vaucluse.fr]** W on D900 fr Avignon, L onto D2 at Coustellet. Do not turn L sp Gordes but cont 3.5km & turn L D102 sp Joucas/Mura. Or fr Apt twd Avignon on D900, R to D4 after 4km site sp to Murs. Do not app site thro Gordes. NB 2.5t weight restriction on S app. Sm, mkd pitch, pt sl, pt shd; wc (some cont); chem disp; shwrs inc; el pnts (6A) €2; tradsmn; playgrnd; dogs; phone; quiet; CKE/CCI. "Peaceful, pretty site among pines; gd walks; vill 1.8km." Easter-15 Sep. € 10.00   2009*

GOUAREC 2E3 (SW Rural) 48.22555, -3.18307 **Camping Tost Aven, Au Bout du Pont, 22570 Gouarec [tel/fax 02 96 24 87 86; bertrand.cocherel@orange.fr; www.brittanycamping.com]** Sp fr town cent bet rv & canal. Med, mkd pitch, pt shd; wc (some cont); chem disp; shwrs inc; el pnts (10A) €2.40; gas adj; lndry rm; shops adj; supmkt nr; rest, snacks, bar 500m; BBQ; sm playgrnd; sw adj (rv & canal); cycle, canoe hire; entmnt; dogs; bus 200m; Eng spkn; adv bkg; quiet. "Clean, tidy site bet Nantes-Brest canal & rv on edge of vill; towpath for cycling; great!" ♦ ltd 1 May-15 Sep. € 10.15   2013*

GOUDARGUES 10E2 (1km NE Rural) 44.22056, 4.47884 **Camping Les Amarines, La Vérune Cornillon, 30630 Goudargues [04 66 82 24 92; fax 04 66 82 38 64; contact@campinglesamarines.com; www.campinglesamarines.com]** Fr D928 foll sp onto D23 & site between Cornillon & Goudargues. Med, hdg/mkd pitch, shd; htd wc; baby facs; shwrs inc; el pnts (6A) €3.50; lndtte; tradsmn; snacks; bar; playgrnd; htd pool; rv fishing; entmnt; statics; dogs €2.20; adv bkg; quiet; red low ssn. "Lge pitches; site liable to flood after heavy rain; excel." ♦ 1 Apr-10 Oct. € 19.70   2010*

GOUDELIN 2E3 (3km NE Rural) 48.61433, -2.99288 **Camping à la Ferme Kérogel (Le Faucheur), 22290 Goudelin [tel/fax 02 96 70 03 15; kerogel@wanadoo.fr; www.kerogel.com]** NE fr Guingamp on D9 to Goudelin. Fr cent of vill take rd dir Lanvollon, site sp on R. Sm, pt sl, pt shd; wc; chem disp (wc); shwrs inc; el pnts (6A) inc; lndry rm; tradsmn; rest, snacks, bar 3km; BBQ; playgrnd; games rm; dogs €0.50; Eng spkn; adv bkg; quiet; CKE/CCI. "Well-kept farm site; lge pitches; clean facs; helpful owner; gd touring base away fr cr coastal sites." ♦ 1 Apr-30 Sep. € 13.85   2011*

GOUEX see Lussac Les Châteaux 7A3

GOURDON 7D3 (4km E Rural) 44.77304, 1.44097 **Camping Le Rêve, 46300 Le Vigan [05 65 41 25 20; fax 05 65 41 68 52; info@campinglereve.com; www.campinglereve.com]** On D820, 3km S of Payrac. R onto D673, sp Le Vigan & Gourdon. After 2km turn R onto sm lane, foll camp sp for 2.5km. Med, pt shd; wc; chem disp; baby facs; shwrs inc; el pnts (6A) €2.90; gas; lndtte; sm shop & 4km; bar; playgrnd; htd pool & paddling pool; games area; cycle hire; entmnt; TV rm; dogs €0.90; Eng spkn; adv bkg ess Jun-mid Aug; v quiet; red long stay/low ssn; ccard not acc; CKE/CCI. "Welcoming, helpful Dutch owners; poss variable voltage (2010); gd walking; excel." ♦ 1 May-21 Sep. € 18.10 2011*

GOURDON 7D3 (11km S Rural) 44.64954, 1.43508 **Camp Municipal Le Moulin Vieux, 46310 St Germain-du-Bel-Air [05 65 31 00 71 or 05 65 31 02 12; contact@camping-moulin-vieux-lot.com; www.camping-moulin-vieux-lot.com]** W fr D820 Cahors-Souillac rd on D23 sp St Germain-du-Bel Air. On ent vill turn R at camping sp. After 150m turn R & foll narr rd, over sm bdge then immed turn L for site. Lge, shd; wc; chem disp; shwrs; el pnts (6-16A) €3-5; gas; lndtte; rest; shops 1km; pool adj; playgrnd; lake sw & fishing; entmnt; some statics; dogs €2; quiet. "Excel, clean site; friendly recep & helpful warden; vg walks in valley; highly rec." 1 Apr-15 Sep. € 13.00   2009*

GOURDON *7D3* (2km SW Rural) *44.72214, 1.37381* **Aire Naturelle Le Paradis (Jardin), La Peyrugue, 46300 Gourdon [tel/fax 05 65 41 65 01 / 06 72 76 32 60 (mob); contact@ campingleparadis.com; www.campingleparadis.com]** S on D673 Gourdon/Fumel rd, after Intermarché supmkt on L, turn L onto track sp site. Track shares ent to supmkt. Sm, pt sl, terr, pt shd; wc; shwrs inc; el pnts (6A) €2; lndtte; supmkt adj; rest; some statics; dogs €2; quiet; adv bkg; red low ssn. "Gd welcome; facs poss stretched if full; farm produce; delightful site; no entmnt; excel san facs" 1 May-31 Aug. € 13.00   2013*

GOURDON *7D3* (5km W Rural) *44.73507, 1.29533* **Camping Le Marcassin de St Aubin (Naturist), Les Grèzes, 24250 St Aubin-de-Nabirat [tel/fax 05 53 28 57 30; campinglemarcassin@gmail.com; www.lemarcassin.fr]** Fr Gourdon foll sp for hospital. At hospital take R fork sp Nabirat (D1) & in about 8km turn L at Renault tractor g'ge & foll sp for site in 1.5km. Site on R immed past speed limit sp. Sm, hdg pitch, pt shd; wc; shwrs inc; el pnts (6A) €3; lndtte; tradsmn; BBQ; pool; TV rm; some statics; Eng spkn; adv bkg; no ccard acc; INF card. "Beautiful area; helpful, friendly Dutch owners." ♦ ltd 12 Apr-18 Oct. € 25.00   2008*

GOURDON *7D3* (1.5km NW Rural) *44.74637, 1.37700* **Camping Domaine La Quercy, Ecoute S'il Pleut, 46300 Gourdon [05 65 41 06 19; fax 05 65 41 31 62; domainequercy@orange.fr; www.domainequercy.com]** Fr N site on R of D704 1.5km bef Gourdon. Sp fr Gourdon. Med, mkd pitch, some hdstg, terr, pt sl, pt shd; wc; chem disp; mv service pnt; baby facs; fam bthrm; shwrs inc; el pnts (6A) €3.50; lndtte (inc dryer); shop & 4km; tradsmn; rest, snacks; bar; BBQ; entmnt; cooking facs; playgrnd; pool; waterslides; paddling pool; bowling; volleyball; badminton; football; lake beach adj; fishing; sailing; watersports 200m; tennis; games area; games rm; wifi; TV; 30% statics; dogs €2.50; ACSI; phone; no twin-axles; poss cr; Eng spkn; adv bkg rec high ssn; quiet; ccard acc; red low ssn. "Gd leisure facs - gd for families; gd san facs; Gourdon attractive town; vg." ♦ 17 Apr-25 Sep. € 24.45   2013*

GOUZON *7A4* (300m SW Urban) *46.18785, 2.23913* **Camp Municipal de la Voueize, 1 Ave de la Marche, 23230 Gouzon [tel/fax 05 55 81 73 22; camping-gouzon@ orange.fr; www.camping-lavoueize.fr]** On E62/N145 Guéret/Montluçon exit at sp for Gouzon. In cent of vill bear R past church & site is sp on edge of Rv Voueize. Sm, pt shd; wc; chem disp; shwrs inc; el pnts (10A) inc (poss rev pol); gas adj; lndry rm; shop, rest, bar in vill; playgrnd; fishing; cycle hire; golf 2km; birdwatching on lake 8km; dogs €0.50; adv bkg; quiet. "Lovely aspect; friendly recep; clean site; facs poss tired high ssn; gd walking & cycling rtes; gd NH; Snacks/bar Jul & Aug only; big trees; adj rv" 1 May-16 Oct. € 11.90   2013*

GRACAY see Vatan *4H3*

⊞ **GRAMAT** *7D4* (7km SE Rural) *44.74767, 1.79954* **Camping Le Teulière, L'Hôpital Beaulieu, 46500 Issendolus [05 65 40 86 71; fax 05 65 33 40 89; laparro. mcv@free.fr; http://laparro.mcv.free.fr]** Site on R on D840 at L'Hôpital, clearly sp. Access fr ent narr & tight corners, not for underpowered. Sm, pt sl, pt shd; wc; shwrs inc; el pnts (20A) €2.65 (poss rev pol); lndtte; shop; rest, snacks; bar; BBQ; playgrnd; pool; tennis; fishing; TV; some statics; poss cr; adv bkg; quiet. "Conv Rocamadour; basic san facs; ltd facs low ssn; site rds unmade, steep & narr - gd traction req; pitches muddy when wet." € 8.00   2009*

GRAND BORNAND, LE see Clusaz, La *9B3*

GRAND FORT PHILIPPE see Gravelines *3A3*

GRAND PRESSIGNY, LE *4H2* (300m S Rural) *46.91723, 0.80600* **Camp Municipal Croix Marron, Rue St Martin, 37350 Le Grand-Pressigny [02 47 94 90 37 (Mairie); fax 02 47 91 04 77]** Fr Descartes take D750 S for 3km, L onto D42 to Le Grand-Plessigny. Site at SE end of vill by rv. Sm, mkd pitch, pt shd; wc; chem disp; mv service pnt; shwrs €0.50; el pnts €2.35; shop, rest, bar in vill; playgrnd; pool adj; quiet. "Pleasant location; prehistoric sites nr." 9 Apr-30 Sep. € 6.55   2010*

> "That's changed – Should I let The Club know?"
>
> If you find something on site that's different from the site entry, fill in a report and let us know. See www.caravanclub.co.uk/europereport.

GRANDCAMP MAISY *1C4* (500m W Coastal) *49.38814, -1.05204* **Camping Le Joncal, Le Petit Nice, 14450 Grandcamp-Maisy [02 31 22 61 44; fax 02 31 22 73 99; campingdujoncal@hotmail.fr; www.campingdujoncal.com]** Ent on Grandcamp port dock area; visible fr vill. Fr N13 take D199 sp Grandcamp-Maisy & foll Le Port & Camping sps. Lge, hdg/mkd pitch, pt shd; mv service pnt; wc; shops, rest adj; gas; el pnts (6A) €5; lndtte; shop; BBQ; sand beach adj; 80% statics; dogs €1; bus; no adv bkg; quiet. "Conv for D Day beaches; some pitches at water's adge; excel morning fish market close by; gd NH" ♦ 1 Apr-30 Sep. € 31.80   2013*

GRANDE MOTTE, LA *10F1* (Coastal) *43.56440, 4.07528* **FFCC Camping La Petite Motte à La Grande-Motte, 195 Allée des Peupliers, 34280 La Grande-Motte [04 67 56 54 75; fax 04 67 29 92 58; camping.lagrandemotte@ffcc.fr; www. camping-lapetitemotte.com]** Exit A9 for Lunel or Montpellier Est to La Grande Motte, site sp on D59 & D62 coast rd. Lge, shd, wc; shwrs; mv service pnt; el pnts (4A) €4.50; lndtte (no dryer); shop; rest, snacks; bar; playgrnd; sand beach 700m; tennis; horseriding; golf & water sports nrby; games area; entmnt; 10% statics; twin-axles extra; dogs €4; poss cr; adv bkg; m'van o'night area; red low ssn/long stay/CKE/CCI. "Walk to beach thro ave of trees & footbdge over rds; helpful staff; clean modern san facs; cycle rtes nrby; vg." 1 Apr-30 Sep. € 17.50 (CChq acc)   2010*

FRANCE

GRANDE MOTTE, LA *10F1* (700m W Coastal/Urban) *43.56334, 4.07275* **Camping Le Garden, Ave de la Petite Motte, 34280 La Grande-Motte [04 67 56 50 09; fax 04 67 56 25 69; jc.mandel@wanadoo.fr; www.legarden.fr]** Fr La Grande Motte W on D59, site sp. Lge, hdg/mkd pitch, hdstg, pt shd; htd wc; chem disp; mv service pnt; baby facs; fam bthrm; shwrs inc; el pnts (10A) inc; gas; lndtte; shop, rest, snacks; bar; BBQ (gas); pool; paddling pool; sand beach 300m; entmnt; 30% statics; dogs €2; phone; bus; poss cr; Eng spkn; adv bkg; ccard acc; red low ssn (30-40%); CKE/CCI. "Easy access to beach, town & bus; some soft sand on pitches; highly rec." 1 Apr-15 Oct. € 39.50 (3 persons)   2009*

GRANDE MOTTE, LA *10F1* (2km W Coastal) *43.56703, 4.07576* **Camp Intercommunal Les Cigales, Allée des Pins, 34280 La Grande-Motte [tel/fax 04 67 56 50 85; camping. lescigales@wanadoo.fr; www.sivom-etang-or.fr]** Ent La Grande-Motte fr D62. Turn R at 1st traff lts; 1st on R to site. Lge, mkd pitch, pt shd; htd wc (cont); shwrs inc; el pnts (10A) inc; lndtte; shop 200m; snacks; bar; playgrnd; sand beach 900m; quiet; red low ssn. "Spacious, well-organised site; quiet low ssn & ltd facs; pleasant seaside town." 3 Apr-3 Oct. € 20.00   2010*

GRANDE PAROISSE, LA see Montereau Fault Yonne *4E3*

GRAND'LANDES see Legé *2H4*

GRANDPRE *5D1* (300m S Rural) *49.33924, 4.87314* **FFCC Camp Municipal, Rue André Bastide, 08250 Grandpré [03 24 30 50 71 or 03 24 30 52 18 (Mairie); mairiegrandpre@wanadoo.fr; www.sud-ardennes-tourisme.com]** Fr D946 in Grandpré turn S onto D6 at vill sq by church twd rv, site in 300m on rvside. Med, mkd pitch, pt shd; wc; mv service pnt; shwrs €0.60; el pnts (6-10A) €2.60-3.50; lndtte (inc dryer); shops, rest, bar 300m; playgrnd; fishing; dogs €0.70; poss cr; quiet. "Pleasant site; two ents to site: 1st to newer part with new facs, 2nd to office & older part." 1 Apr-30 Sep. € 7.20   2011*

GRANE see Crest *9D2*

GRANGES SUR VOLOGNE *6F3* (5km S Rural) *48.12123, 6.82857* **Camping La Sténiole, 1 Le Haut Rain, 88640 Granges-sur-Vologne [03 29 51 43 75; steniole@ wanadoo.fr; www.steniole.com]** D423 fr Gérardmer NW to Granges-sur-Vologne & foll sp. Well sp. Med, hdg pitch, terr, pt shd; wc (some cont); chem disp; shwrs inc; el pnts (4-10A) €3-5; gas; lndtte; shop; supmkt 3km; tradsmn; rest, snacks; bar; BBQ; playgrnd; lake sw & shgl beach adj; fishing; tennis; walking rte; horseriding 4km; games rm; TV rm; 10% statics; dogs €1; Eng spkn; adv bkg rec high ssn; quiet; CKE/CCI. "Pleasant, wooded, relaxing site; vg rest." 15 Apr-30 Oct. € 11.00   2009*

See advertisement on pages 32 & 33

GRANVILLE *1D4* (6km NE Coastal) *48.86976, -1.56380* **Kawan Village La Route Blanche, 6 La Route Blanche, 50290 Bréville-sur-Mer [02 33 50 23 31; fax 02 33 50 26 47; larouteblanche@camping-breville.com; www.camping-breville.com]** Exit A84 junc 37 onto D924 dir Granville. Bef Granville turn L onto D971, then L onto D114 which joins D971e. Site on R bef golf club. Nr Bréville sm airfield. Lge, hdg/ mkd pitch, hdstg, pt shd; htd wc (some male cont); chem disp; mv service pnt; baby facs; serviced pitches; shwrs inc; el pnts (6-10A) €4-5; gas; lndtte (inc dryer); shop; tradsmn; snacks; bar; BBQ; playgrnd; htd pools; paddling pool; waterpark; waterslide; sand beach 500m; sailing school; golf & tennis nr; games area; wifi; entmnt; TV rm; 40% statics; dogs €3; phone; poss cr; Eng spkn; adv bkg; quiet; ccard acc; red long stay/low ssn/CKE/CCI. "Pleasant, busy site with vg clean facs; staff friendly & helpful; disabled seatlift in pool; gd walking, cycling & beach; pleasant old walled town & harbour; vg." ♦ 1 Apr-1 Oct. € 36.00 (CChq acc)   2012*

GRANVILLE *1D4* (2.5km SE Coastal) *48.8227, -1.5700* **Camping La Vague, 126 Route Vaudroulin, 50400 Granville [02 33 50 29 97; contact@camping-la-vague.com; www.camping-la-vague.com]** On D911 coast rd S fr Granville, or on D973 dir Avranches, site sp. Med, hdg/mkd pitch, pt shd; wc; chem disp; mv service pnt; shwrs inc; el pnts (4A) €4.30; gas; lndtte; shop 1km; tradsmn; rest, bar 1km; snacks; playgrnd; covrd pool; sand beach adj; fishing; TV; dogs €1.90; poss cr; adv bkg; quiet; CKE/CCI. ♦ 1 May-30 Sep. € 21.40   2008*

GRANVILLE *1D4* (3km SE Rural) *48.80033, -1.5517* **Camping de l'Ecutot, Route de l'Ecutot, 50380 St Pair-sur-Mer [02 33 50 26 29; fax 02 33 50 64 94; camping.ecutot@ wanadoo.fr; www.ecutot.com]** Fr Avranches NW on D973 twds Granville. 5km S of Granville turn onto D309 sp St Pair-sur-Mer; site on R (wide rear ent). Lge, hdg pitch, indiv san facs some pitches; wc; chem disp; shwrs inc; el pnts (2-10A) €1.60-4; lndtte; sm shop; snacks; bar; playgrnd; htd pool; beach 1.2km; games area; entmnt; TV rm; 80% statics; dogs €1.20; Eng spkn; adv bkg; quiet; ccard acc. "Soft ground early ssn; san facs OK; chem disp facs poor; conv ferry to Channel Is, Bayeux Tapestry, Mont St Michel." 1 Jun-15 Sep. € 23.00   2008*

GRANVILLE *1D4* (3.5km SE Rural) *48.79054, -1.52598* **Camping Angomesnil, 50380 St Pair-sur-Mer [02 33 51 64 33; info@angomesnil.com; http:// angomesnil.pagesperso-orange.fr/]** Take D973 SE fr Granville twd Avranches. At D154 exit to R sp Kairon-Bourg & site in 1km. Sm, hdg/mkd pitch, pt sl, pt shd; wc; chem disp; mv service pnt; shwrs inc; el pnts (6A) €3.10; lndtte; shops 3km; tradsmn; playgrnd; sand beach 3.5km; tennis; games room; TV; no dogs; adv bkg; quiet. "Nice, quiet little site; roomy pitches; friendly, helpful owners; clean san facs; popular with Dutch." ♦ 20 Jun-10 Sep. € 13.70   2010*

FRANCE

GRANVILLE *1D4* (6km SE Rural) *48.79790, -1.5244*
Camping Le Château de Lez-Eaux, 50380 St Pair-sur-Mer
[02 33 51 66 09; fax 02 33 51 92 02; bonjour@lez-eaux.
com; www.lez-eaux.com or www.les-castels.com]
App site on D973 Granville to Avranches rd (not via St Pair).
Fr rndabt at Intermarché cont for 2km, site sp on R. Lge, mkd
pitch, pt sl, pt shd; htd wc; chem disp; mv service pnt; serviced
pitches; baby facs; shwrs inc; el pnts (10-16A) inc; lndtte (inc
dryer); shop & 4km; snacks; bar; BBQ; playgrnd; 2 pools (1 htd
covrd); paddling pool; waterslide; children's indoor aqua park;
sand beach 4km; lake fishing; tennis; cycle hire; boat hire 7km;
horseriding 4km; games area; wifi; games/TV rm; 80% statics;
dogs free; twin-axles acc (rec check in adv); poss cr; quiet; ccard
acc; red low ssn; CKE/CCI. "Superb site in grnds of chateau;
easy access; spacious pitches, various prices; helpful & friendly
staff; clean, modern san facs; excel pool complex; gd for
children; great for dogs; gd cycling & gd cycle rte to beach; gd
touring base; conv Mont St Michel, Dol & landing beaches; mkt
Thu St Pair; highly rec." ♦ 21 Apr-21 Sep. €49.00
SBS - N02   2013*

See advertisement

GRANVILLE *1D4* (5km S Coastal) *48.78130, -1.56720* **Camping
La Chaussée**, 1 Ave de la Libération, 50610 Jullouville
[02 33 61 80 18; fax 02 33 61 45 26; contact@camping-
lachaussee.com; www.camping-lachaussee.com] On coast
rd D911 fr Granville to Jullouville. Site on L heading S, sp. Lge,
mkd pitch, hdstg, pt shd; wc (some cont); chem disp; mv service
pnt; baby facs; fam bthrm; shwrs inc; el pnts (6-10A) €3.80-5;
gas; lndtte; shop; tradsmn; snacks; bar; BBQ; playgrnd; htd pool;
sand beach 100m; tennis 500m; games area; games rm 400m;
archery; games rm; TV rm; dogs €1.50; phone; bus adj; Eng
spkn; adv bkg; quiet; ccard acc; red low ssn; CKE/CCI. "Pleasant
site on attractive coast; lge pitches; lovely pool; promenade walk;
conv Mont St Michel." 10 Apr-26 Sep. €25.50   2008*

GRANVILLE *1D4* (7km S Urban) *48.77783, -1.56618* **Camp
Municipal du Docteur Lemonnier**, Ave du Dr Lemonnier,
50610 Jullouville [02 33 51 42 60; mairiejullou@wanadoo.fr;
www.jullouville.com] S on D911 Granville-Avranches coast
rd. On on ent Jullouville turn L in mkt sq. Ent in far L corner.
Med, unshd; wc; mv service pnt; shwrs €0.80; el pnts (6A) inc;
gas; lndtte; shop 200m; snacks; BBQ; playgrnd; sand beach
100m; 10% statics; dogs; poss cr high ssn; adv bkg; CKE/CCI.
"Nice, clean, basic site." 8 Apr-30 Sep. €17.70   2011*

GRASSE *10E4* (8km NE Rural) *43.70230, 6.99515* **FFCC**
Camping des Gorges du Loup, Chemin des Vergers, 06620
Le Bar-sur-Loup [04 93 42 45 06; info@lesgorgesduloup.com;
www.lesgorgesduloup.com] E fr Gasse on D2085 sp
Chateauneuf-Grasse; in 4km turn L onto D2210 to Le Bar-
sur-Loup. Site well sp. Med, mkd pitch, some hdstg, terr, pt
shd; wc (some cont); chem disp; shwrs inc; el pnts (6-10A)
€3.50-5.50 (poss rev pol); gas; lndtte; ice: shop; tradsmn;
playgrnd; pool; shgl beach; table tennis,bowls, basket ball;TV
rm; 20% statics; dogs €3; phone; bus 1km; Eng spkn; adv bkg;
quiet; ccard not acc; red low ssn; CKE/CCI. "Peaceful, well-kept
site with superb views; helpful, pleasant owners; clean san facs;
steep access rds; owner will site c'van; gd hilly cycling; highly
rec" 6 Apr-21 Sep. €27.00   2013*

GRASSE *10E4* (S Urban) *43.63507, 6.94859* **Camping
Caravaning La Paoute**, 160 Route de Cannes, 06130
Grasse [04 93 09 11 42; fax 04 93 40 06 40; camppaoute@
hotmail.com; www.campinglapaoute.com] Sp fr Grasse
town cent on Route de Cannes (secondary rd to Cannes, NOT
D6185), a 10 min drive. Med, hdg/mkd pitch, sl, terr, pt shd;
wc; chem disp; mv service pnt; shwrs inc; el pnts (10A) €4;
lndtte (inc dryer); tradsmn; supmkt nr; snacks; bar; playgrnd;
htd pool; games rm; wifi; 15% statics; dogs; bus 500m; poss
cr; red low ssn/ long stay; CKE/CCI. "Gd site; m'vans acc out of
ssn but adv bkg req." 1 Apr-30 Sep. €21.00   2010*

GRASSE *10E4* (8km S Rural) *43.60650, 6.90216* **Camping
Le Parc des Monges**, 635 Chemin du Gabre, 06810
Auribeau-sur-Siagne [tel/fax 04 93 60 91 71; contact@
parcdesmonges.fr; www.parcdesmonges.com] Exit A8 junc
40 or 41 onto D6007 dir Grasse; then onto D109 becoming
D9; foll sp to Auribeau-sur-Siagne; site on rd to Le Gabre. Med,
hdg pitch, shd; htd wc (some cont); chem disp; mv service pnt;
baby facs; fam bthrm; shwrs inc; el pnts (4-10A) €3.50-5.50;
gas 2km; lndtte (inc dryer); ice; shop 600m; tradsmn; rest,
snacks & bar 2km; playgrnd; htd pool; rv sw adj; fishing nrby;
activities & entmnt; 7% statics; dogs €2.50; phone; bus adj;
poss cr; Eng spkn; adv bkg; quiet; ccard acc; red low ssn; CKE/
CCI. "Vg site by Rv Siagne; rv not accessible fr site. Watch
out for branches when manoeurvering" ♦ 4 Apr-26 Sep.
€23.00   2012*

⊞ **GRASSE** *10E4* (8km NW Rural) *43.69088, 6.86450*
**Camping Parc des Arboins, 755 Route Napoléon, 06460
St Vallier-de-Thiey [04 93 42 63 89; fax 04 93 09 61 54;
contact@parc-des-arboins.com]** N fr Cannes on D6085 foll
sp thro Grasse for Digne; approx 1.5km bef vill of St Vallier-
de-Thiey, site located on R of rd. Med, mkd pitch, hdstg, shd;
htd wc; mv service pnt; shwrs; el pnts (3-15A) €3-4; gas; lndtte
(inc dryer); shop; supmkt 1.5km; rest, snacks; bar; playgrnd;
htd pool; paddling pool; sand beach 30km; tennis 1.5km; golf
10km; games area; entmnt; TV rm; 95% statics; dogs €1.20;
adv bkg; quiet but poss rd noise; CKE/CCI. "Lovely position on
hillside; ltd touring pitches; ltd space to manoeuvre; 'quaint'
san facs (own san rec); vg rest adj." € 20.50   2010*

GRAU DU ROI, LE *10F2* (1km N Coastal) *43.55450, 4.10720*
**Camping Le Boucanet, Route de Carnon, 30240 Le Grau-
du-Roi [04 66 51 41 48; fax 04 66 51 41 87; contact@
campingboucanet.fr; www.campingboucanet.fr or www.
campings-franceloc.fr]** Fr A9 fr N exit junc 26, fr S exit junc
29 Montpellier Airport dir Aigues-Mortes. Fr Aigues-Mortes take
D62/D62A to Le Grau-du-Roi, twd La Grande-Motte. Site clearly
sp off rndabt after area called Le Boucanet (on L). Lge, hdg/mkd
pitch, some hdstg, pt shd; wc (some cont); chem disp; mv service
pnt; shwrs inc; el pnts (6A) inc; gas; lndtte; shop; tradsmn; rest,
snacks; bar; no BBQs; playgrnd; htd pool & paddling pool; dir
access to sand beach adj; surf school; tennis; horseriding; golf
2km; creche; entmnt; 50% statics; no dogs; Eng spkn; adv bkg;
quiet; ccard acc; red low ssn/ long stay; CKE/CCI. "Excel, popular
site; some sm pitches poss diff lge o'fits; some pitches sandy;
m'van parking on rd opp site; no waiting area outside site." ♦
10 Apr-3 Oct. € 40.00   2010*

GRAU DU ROI, LE *10F2* (1km S Coastal) *43.52186, 4.14979*
**Camping Les Jardins de Tivoli, Route de l'Espiguette,
30240 Le Grau du Roi [04 66 53 97 00; fax 04 66 51 09 81;
contact@lesjardinsdetivoli.com; www.lesjardinsdetivoli.
com]** Fr A9 take exit 26 to Aigues-Mortes. Then foll D979 twds
Le Grau-du-Roi, Port Camargue & Espiguette. Site sp. Lge,
hdg/mkd pitch, shd; wc; shwrs inc; individ san facs all pitches;
el pnts (6-10A) inc; gas; lndtte; shop; rest, snacks; bar; gas;
BBQ (gas); playgrnd; 3 pools; paddling pool; waterslides; sand
beach 600m; tennis; sports activities; cycle hire; entmnt; TV;
20% statics; dogs €8; phone; adv bkg; ccard acc; red low ssn;
CKE/CCI. "Excel site; superb individ san facs; lge pitches." ♦
1 Apr-30 Sep. € 57.00 (4 persons)   2010*

GRAU DU ROI, LE *10F2* (4km SW Coastal) *43.50609,
4.12975* **Camping L'Espiguette, Route de l'Espiguette,
30240 Le Grau-du-Roi [04 66 51 43 92; fax
04 66 53 25 71; reception@campingespiguette.fr; www.
campingespiguette.fr]** Fr A9 exit junc 26 onto D979 S to
Aigues-Mortes & La Grande-Motte. Foll sps to Port Camargue
& L'Espiguette & site sp on R fr rndabt; access via L bank of Le
Grau-du-Roi; 3km fr Port Camargue & lighthouse. NB Caution
on app due to height barrier. V lge, mkd pitch, pt shd; wc; mv
service pnt; baby facs; shwrs inc; el pnts (5A) inc; gas; lndtte (inc
dryer); shops; rest, snacks; bar; playgrnd; water park/play pool;
waterslides into shallow sea water; sand beach adj & access to
naturist beach 3km; cycle hire; games area; gym; wifi; entmnt;
10% statics; dogs €3.50; adv bkg; quiet; ccard acc; red long
stay/low ssn; CKE/CCI. "Vg family site; beautiful beach adj; some
pitches on sand; many facs high ssn; helpful staff; clean san facs;
gd security." ♦ 27 Mar-3 Nov. € 36.00   2011*

GRAVE, LA *9C3* (1km E Rural) *45.04508, 6.31052* **Camping
de la Meije, 05320 La Grave [tel/fax 04 76 79 93 34 or
06 08 54 30 84 (mob); nathalie-romagne@wanadoo.fr;
www.camping-delameije.com]** On D1091 travelling fr W
site ent end of vill immed after last building. Site sp easily
missed, by stream below vill. Fr E awkward app fr Briançon
(sharp L-hand turn) cont & turn in parking area 150m. NB Rec
app fr W. Sm, hdg/mkd pitch, pt sl, pt shd; wc (cont); chem
disp (wc); baby facs; fam bthrm; shwrs inc; el pnts (4A) €3;
lndtte; shop; tradsmn; rest, snacks; bar; BBQ; playgrnd; htd
pool high ssn; tennis; games area; dogs €1; bus; poss cr; Eng
spkn; adv bkg; quiet; red 5 days+; CKE/CCI. "Well-kept site in
superb setting; mountain views; poss cr early & mid-July due
La Marmotte cycle race & Tour de France." ♦ 15 May-20 Sep.
€ 13.40   2010*

GRAVE, LA *9C3* (1km W Rural) *45.04355, 6.29665* **Camping
Le Gravelotte, La Meije, 05320 La Grave [04 76 79 93 14;
fax 04 76 79 92 39; info@camping-le-gravelotte.com;
www.camping-le-gravelotte.com]** On D1091, sp. Med,
mkd pitch, pt sl, pt shd; wc; chem disp; shwrs inc; el pnts (5A)
€2.50; gas; lndtte; shop; tradsmn; bar; htd pool; rv rafting/sw;
games area; dogs €1; phone; poss cr; quiet; CKE/CCI. "Friendly
welcome; spacious & open situation." ♦ ltd 15 Jun-15 Sep.
€ 12.10   2008*

GRAVELINES *3A3* (3km N Coastal) *51.00777, 2.11777*
**Camping des Dunes, Rue Victor-Hugo, Plage de Petit-
Fort-Philippe, 59820 Gravelines [03 28 23 09 80; fax
03 28 65 35 99; campingdesdunes@campingvpa.fr; www.
camping-des-dunes.com]** E fr Calais on D940 foll sp to
Gravelines. Heading W fr Dunkerque exit D601 E of Gravelines;
turn R into Blvd de L'Europe & foll sp for Petit-Fort-Philippe &
site. Site on both sides of rd. Lge, hdg/mkd pitch, hdstg, pt
shd; htd wc; chem disp; shwrs inc; el pnts (10A) €4.05; lndtte
(inc dryer); shop (high ssn); shop, rest, snacks & bar 1km;
playgrnd; direct access to sand beach adj; entmnt; games rm;
wifi; entmnt; TV; 10% statics; dogs €2.10; phone; bus; Eng
spkn; adv bkg; ccard acc; red low ssn/CKE/CCI. "Site in 2 parts,
various prices; gd site rds; helpful, friendly staff; poss uneven
pitches & raised manhole covers; conv Dunkerque ferries
(15km); adv bkg ess bank holidays; vg." ♦ 1 Apr-31 Oct.
€ 17.75   2012*

GRAVELINES *3A3* (3km W Coastal) *51.00250, 2.09694*
**Camping de la Plage, 115 Rue du Maréchal-Foch, 59153
Grand-Fort-Philippe [03 28 65 31 95 or 03 28 23 09 80; fax
03 28 65 35 99; campingdelaplage@campingvpa.fr; www.
camping-de-la-plage.info]** Exit A16 junc 51 dir Grand-Fort-
Philippe; at o'skts of town turn R sp Camping ***; cont into
town cent; foll rd along quayside; foll rd to L past lge crucifix;
turn R at next x-rds; site on R. Med, hdg pitch, hdstg, terr,
pt shd; htd wc; chem disp; mv service pnt; shwrs inc (clsed
fr 10pm-8am); el pnts (10A) €3.70 (poss long lead req); lndtte;
shop 3km; tradsmn; playgrnd; pool 3km; sand beach 500m;
wifi; entmnt; 5% statics; dogs €2; Eng spkn; adv bkg rec; quiet;
ccard acc; red low ssn/CKE/CCI. "Various pitch sizes; ltd el pnts;
pleasant walk to sea front; night security guard; conv ferries;
new chalets on site means red of pitches so rec adv bkg." ♦
1 Apr-31 Oct. € 15.60   2013*

GRAVESON *10E2* (1km SE Rural) *43.84408, 4.78080*
**Camping Les Micocouliers, 445 Route de Cassoulen,
13690 Graveson [04 90 95 81 49; micocou@free.fr; www.
camping-les-micocouliers-provence.fr]** Leave A7 junc 25
onto D99 St Rémy-de-Provence then D5 N past Maillane, site
on R. Med, hdg/mkd pitch, unshd; wc; chem disp; mv service
pnt; shwrs inc; el pnts (4-13A) €4.40-7.; lndtte; shop 1km;
tradsmn; rest, bar 1km; BBQ; pool; tennis 1km; cycle hire;
games area; wifi; 8% statics; dogs €2; phone; Eng spkn; adv
bkg rec; red low ssn/CKE/CCI. "Peaceful but busy site; pretty
& well-kept; friendly, helpful owners; excel, immac san facs;
lovely sm pool; vg cycling; attractive, interesting area; excel." ♦
15 Mar-15 Oct. € 36.90   2013*

GRAVIERS see Vans, Les *9D1*

GRAY *6G2* (1km E Rural) *47.45207, 5.59999* **Camp
Municipal Longue Rive, Rue de la Plage, 70100 Gray
[03 84 64 90 44; fax 03 84 65 46 26; tourisme-gray@
wanadoo.fr; www.ville-gray.fr]** S on D67 to Gray. cross rv
bdge, L at rndabt, after 300m sp La Plage. Well sp fr all rtes.
Med, hdg/mkd pitch, pt shd; wc (mainly cont); mv service
pnt; shwrs inc; el pnts (10A) €2.45; gas; lndtte; shop 1.5km;
rest, bar, & pool opp; playgrnd; boating & fishing; tennis;
dogs €0.85; poss cr; Eng spkn; poss noisy; ccard not acc; CKE/
CCI. "Lovely setting on Rv Saône; friendly recep; basic facs,
poss stretched high ssn; twin-axles extra charge; many pitches
waterlogged early ssn; several Bastide vills within cycling dist;
NH only." 15 Apr-30 Sep. € 12.05   2011*

GRAYAN ET L'HOPITAL see Soulac sur Mer *7B1*

GRENOBLE *9C3* (12km SE Rural) *45.15431, 5.83758* **Camping
de Luiset, Allée de l'Eglise, 38410 St Martin-d'Uriage
[04 76 89 77 98; fax 04 76 59 70 91; camping@leluiset.com]**
Take D524 SE fr Grenoble to Uriage-les-Bains; turn L on D280
to St Martin-d'Uriage; site behind church in vill; steep climb
fr Uriage-les-Bains. Med, mkd pitch, pt terr, pt shd; wc (cont);
shwrs; el pnts (2-6A); lndtte; shop, rest 200m; BBQ; playgrnd;
rv fishing 100m; games area; quiet. "Beautiful setting; basic
facs." ♦ 1 May-30 Sep.   2008*

GRENOBLE *9C3* (10km S Rural) *45.08553, 5.69872*
**Camping à la Ferme Le Moulin de Tulette (Gaudin),
Route du Moulin de Tulette, 38760 Varces-Allières-
et-Risset [04 76 72 55 98; tulette@wanadoo.fr; http://
moulindetulette.pagesperso-orange.fr/]** Fr A51, exit junc
12 to join D1075 N, Varces in approx 2km. Turn R at traff lts &
foll sp to site, (approx 2km fr D1075). If driving thro Grenoble
look for sp Gap - D1075 diff to find; on ent Varce foll site sp.
Sm, mkd pitch, pt sl, pt shd; wc; chem disp; baby facs; shwrs
inc; el pnts (5-10A) €2.50; shop 1km; tradsmn; sm pool; dogs
€1; poss cr; Eng spkn; adv bkg; quiet; CKE/CCI. "Peaceful,
picturesque, well-kept site with views; friendly, helpful owners;
facs ltd but clean - stretched high ssn; gd base for touring/x-ing
Alps." ♦ 1 May-30 Sep. € 15.00   2011*

⊞ **GRENOBLE** *9C3* (7km SW Urban) *45.16687, 5.69897*
**Camping Caravaning Les 3 Pucelles, 58 Rue des
Allobroges, 38180 Seyssins [04 76 96 45 73; fax
04 38 12 87 51; contact@camping-trois-pucelles.com
/ amico.francoise @ gmail.com; www.camping-trois-
pucelles.com]** On A480 in dir of rocade (by-pass) S exit 5B,
on R after supmkt then foll sp to R then L. Clearly sp. Well sp
fr m'way. Sm, hdg pitch, hdstg, pt shd; htd wc (some cont);
chem disp; shwrs inc; el pnts (16A) meter; lndtte; ice shop;
tradsmn; rest, snacks; bar; playgrnd; pool; 70% statics; phone;
bus nr; poss cr; noise fr indus area; CKE/CCI. "Site part of hotel
campus run by friendly family; sm pitches; san facs need refurb;
conv Grenoble by bus/tram; NH only." € 20.00   2013*

GREOUX LES BAINS *10E3* (600m S Rural) *43.75262,
5.89588* **Yelloh! Village Verdon Parc, Domaine de la
Paludette, 04800 Gréoux-les-Bains [04 92 78 08 08;
fax 04 92 77 00 17; info@yellohvillage-verdon-parc.
com; www.yellohvillage-verdon-parc.com or www.
yellohvillage.co.uk]** On D952 to Gréoux, turn S onto D8 dir
St Pierre. Cross bdge over Rv Verdon (v narr) turn L immed.
Site in 500m. Lge, mkd pitch, hdstg, terr, pt shd; wc; chem
disp; baby facs; fam bthrm; shwrs inc; el pnts (10A) €4; gas
1km; lndtte; shop & 1km; rest, snacks; bar; playgrnd; pool;
paddling pool; lake sw & fishing 3km; tennis; games area;
entmnt; internet; TV rm; 60% statics; dogs €2 (acc low ssn
only); phone; bus 1km; Eng spkn; adv bkg; quiet; CKE/CCI.
"Helpful manager; clean facs; all gravel standings; barrier clsd
2230-0700; pleasant (hilly) spa town; excel." ♦ 1 Apr-27 Oct.
€ 33.00   2008*

See advertisement on inside front cover

GREOUX LES BAINS *10E3* (1.2km S Rural) *43.75158, 5.88185*
**Camping Le Verseau, Route de St Pierre, 04800 Gréoux-
les-Bains [04 92 77 67 10 or 06 22 72 93 25 (mob); info@
camping-le-verseau.com; www.camping-le-verseau.com]**
Fr W on D952 to Gréoux. Go under bdge then bear L just bef
petrol stn. Cross rv (narr bdge), site on R in 500m. Med, hdg
pitch, pt sl, pt shd; wc; chem disp; mv service pnt; baby facs;
shwrs inc; el pnts (10A) €3.50; lndtte; shop 1km; tradsmn; rest,
snacks; bar; BBQ (gas/elec); playgrnd; pool; tennis 1km; wifi;
entmnt; dogs €2; phone; adv bkg; quiet; CKE/CCI. "Friendly
owners; interesting spa town; great views." 1 Mar-31 Oct.
€ 17.50   2010*

GREOUX LES BAINS *10E3* (8km SW Rural) *43.72899, 5.81277*
**Camp Municipal du Verdon, 83560 Vinon-sur-Verdon
[04 92 78 81 51; camping@vinon-sur-verdon.fr; www.
campingduverdon.com]** Exit A51 junc 17 onto D952 N to
Vinon-sur-Verdon (dir Gréoux-Les-Bains); cross rv bdge in vill;
site on R in 100m. Sm, shd; wc (some cont); mv service pnt;
shwrs inc; el pnts (5A) €2.60; lndtte; shop 500m; playgrnd; rv
fishing & sw adj; kayaking; games area; dogs €0.80; phone;
quiet. ♦ 15 May-30 Sep. € 9.70   2010*

GREZ SUR LOING see Fontainebleau *4E3*

GRIGNAN see Valréas *9D2*

GRIMAUD *10F4* (2km E Rural) *43.27924, 6.56409* **Aire Naturelle (Lyons), Les Cagnignons, 83310 Grimaud [04 94 56 34 51; fax 04 94 56 51 26; lyons.cagnignons@ wanadoo.fr]** Leave A8 at junc 36 onto D125/D25 at Le Muy sp Ste Maxime then onto D559 dir St Tropez. Take R onto D14 sp Grimaud & 3rd rd on R to site. Sm, terr, shd; wc; chem disp; shwrs inc; el pnts (3-6A) €3-3.50; lndtte; basic playgrnd; pool adj, tennis 500m; sand beach 2km; horseriding 2km; phone; 30% statics; dogs €1.60; adv bkg; quiet; no ccard acc; CKE/CCI. "Clean site; away fr bustle of St Tropez; not rec teenagers; some pitches ltd for long o'fits." ♦ Easter-30 Sep. € 18.00   2009*

GRIMAUD *10F4* (3km E Coastal) *43.28527, 6.57972* **Domaine des Naïades ACF, St Pons-les-Mûres, 83310 Grimaud [04 94 55 67 80; fax 04 94 55 67 81; info@lesnaiades.com; www.lesnaiades.com]** Exit A8 junc 36 (for Le Muy) onto D125/D25 dir St Maxime; join D559 W dir St Tropez & Grimaud. After 5km at rndabt opp Camping Prairies de la Mer turn R sp St Pons-les-Mûres; site sp & ent 500m on L. Lge, terr, shd, mkd pitch; wc (some cont); chem disp; mv service pnt; baby facs; shwrs inc; el pnts (10A) inc (poss rev pol); lndtte (inc dryer); shops; rest, snacks; bar; BBQ (elec); playgrnd; Olympic-sized htd pool; paddling pool; waterslides; sand beach 900m; watersports; cycle hire; games area; wifi; entmnt; games/TV rm; many statics; dogs €6; no c'vans/m'vans over 6m high ssn; min 7 nights Jul/Aug; poss cr; adv bkg ess; quiet except noisy disco & dog kennels adj; ccard acc; red low ssn/long stay; CKE/CCI. "Gd views; gd recep; mixed reports on san facs (2009); chem disp up many steps (2010); pitch access poss diff lge o'fits due steep hills & tight bends; gd for families; 24hr security." ♦ 31 Nov-21 Oct. € 55.00 (3 persons)   2011*

GRIMAUD *10F4* (3.5km E Coastal) *43.27630, 6.56000* **Camping La Pinède, 83310 Grimaud [04 94 56 04 36; fax 04 94 56 30 86; pinede-grimaud@sfr.fr; www. lapinede-camping.com]** Exit Grimaud E on D14; after junc with D61 cont on D14 for 1km; site on R. Lge, pt shd; wc; chem disp; mv service pnt; baby facs; shwrs; el pnts (10A) inc; lndtte (inc dryer); tradsmn; rest, snacks; bar; playgrnd; htd covrd pool; paddling pool; games rm; wifi; entmnt; some statics; dogs €4; red low ssn. 1 Apr-31 Oct. € 34.00 (CChq acc)   2010*

GRIMAUD *10F4* (4km E Coastal) *43.27080, 6.57320* **Camping Club Holiday Marina, Le Ginestel, 83310 Grimaud [04 94 56 08 43; fax 04 94 56 23 88; info@holiday-marina.com; www.holiday-marina.com]** Exit A8 junc 36 onto D125/D25 dir Ste Maxime; turn R onto D559 dir St Tropez (sea on your L); in approx 6km pass under sm flyover at Port Grimaud. Site on R in approx 500m past flyover just after Villa Verde garden cent. Lge, hdg/mkd pitch, pt shd; htd wc; chem disp; serviced pitches; pitches have private bthrms; shwrs inc; el pnts (16A) inc; lndtte; sm shop; tradsmn; rest, snacks; bar; BBQ (elec); playgrnd; htd pool; paddling pool; jacuzzi; sand beach 950m; fishing; boating; cycle hire; games rm; wifi; entmnt; sat TV; 70% statics; dogs €3; no c'vans/m'vans over 12m; deposit for barrier card & bathrm; sep car park; British owners; poss cr; adv bkg ess high ssn; rd noise; ccard acc; min 3 nights; red low ssn/ long stay; lge pitches extra charge; CKE/CCI. "Lovely pool area; excel sports facs; helpful staff; some pitches poss tight - pitches avail for lge m'vans; recep clsd 1230-1400; conv all Côte d'Azur." ♦ 1 Mar-3 Jan. € 55.00   2011*

GRIMAUD *10F4* (4km E Coastal) *43.28375, 6.59165* **Camping Les Mûres, St Pons-les-Mûres, 83310 Grimaud [04 94 56 16 17; fax 04 94 56 37 91; info@camping-des-mures.com; www.camping-des-mures.com]** Exit Ste Maxime on D559 twd St Tropez, site in 5km visible on both sides of rd midway bet Ste Maxime & Grimaud. V lge, mkd pitch, pt sl, pt shd; wc (some cont); chem disp; shwrs inc; el pnts (6A) inc (poss rev pol); gas; lndtte; shop; rest, snacks; bar; playgrnd; sand beach adj; boat hire; water-skiing; games area; entmnt; some statics; dogs €2; poss cr; quiet but rd noise & disco (high ssn); adv bkg; red low ssn; CKE/CCI. "Well-run, clean site; site has own beach, beach pitches with views avail; v ltd facs low ssn." 4 Apr-3 Oct. € 35.00   2009*

GRIMAUD *10F4* (4km E Coastal) *43.28083, 6.58250* **Camping Les Prairies de la Mer, St Pons-les-Mûres, 83360 Grimaud [04 94 79 09 09; fax 04 94 79 09 10; prairies@riviera-villages. com; www.riviera-villages.com]** Leave A8/E80 at Ste Maxime/ Draguignan exit. Take DD125/D25 twd Ste Maxime. Site on L of D559 heading SW, 400m bef St Pons-les-Mûres with rndabt at ent. Site opp Marina Village. V lge, mkd pitch, hdstg, pt shd; wc; chem disp; mv service pnt; shwrs inc; el pnts (6-10A) inc; gas; lndtte; shop; supmkt; rest, snacks; bar; playgrnd; sand beach adj; fishing; watersports; entmnt; 85% statics; dogs; phone; bus; poss cr; adv bkg ess high ssn; some rd noise; ccard acc; red low ssn; CKE/CCI. "Popular, well-run beach site; gd recep; pitches tight for med to lge o'fits & poss dusty high ssn; gd san facs; Port Grimaud sh walk; gd entmnt; gd." ♦ 23 Mar-13 Oct. € 55.00   2013*

GRIMAUD *10F4* (4.5km E Coastal) *43.28205, 6.58614* **Camping de la Plage, 98 Route National, St Pons-les-Mûres, 83310 Grimaud [04 94 56 31 15; fax 04 94 56 49 61; campingplagegrimaud@wanadoo.fr; www.camping-de-la-plage.fr]** Fr St Maxime turn onto D559 sp to St Tropez; site 3km on L on both sides of rd (subway links both parts). Lge, pt shd; wc; chem disp; mv service pnt; shwrs inc; el pnts (4-16A) €4.70-14.; gas; lndtte; shop; rest, snacks; bar; playgrnd; sand beach on site; tennis; wifi; entmnt; dogs €2.20; poss cr; some rd noise; adv bkg ess high ssn (rec bkg in Jan - non-rtnable bkg fee); ccard acc; red low ssn; CKE/CCI. "Pitches adj beach or in shd woodland - some sm; site tired but lovely situation & views compensate (2011); clean facs but need refurb; cycle tracks; site poss flooded after heavy rain; used every yr for 44 yrs by one CC member (2011); Conv for ferry to St Tropez, rec as beautiful, helpful friendly efficient staff" ♦ 16 Apr-10 Oct. € 34.00   2013*

⊞ GRIMAUD *10F4* (2km SE Rural) *43.26414, 6.53365* **FFCC Camping Domaine du Golfe de St Tropez, Chemin des Vignaux, 83310 Grimaud [04 94 43 26 95; fax 04 94 43 21 06; info@golfe-st-tropez.com; www. golfe-st-tropez.com]** Sp down lane, Carraire de St Pierre, nr junc of D14 & D61 or off D558. Med, hdg/mkd pitch, pt shd; wc; chem disp; shwrs inc; el pnts (6-10A) €4-5; rest, snacks; playgrnd; pool; beach 3.5km; 40% statics; dogs €3; phone; ccard acc. "Conv for Port Grimaud & beaches." € 20.00   2009*

FRANCE

GRIMAUD *10F4 (4.5km NW Rural) 43.29180, 6.49210*
Camping de Berard, 83680 La Garde-Freinet [tel/fax 04 94 43 21 23; camping.berard@wanadoo.fr; http://camping.berard.pagesperso-orange.fr] Exit A8 junc 13 onto D558 to La Garde-Freinet; pass thro vill on D558; site on L in 5km. Sp fr N & S. Site midway bet La Garde-Freinet & Grimaud. Med, terr, pt shd; wc; chem disp; baby facs; shwrs; el pnts (6A) inc; lndtte; shop; tradsmn; rest; take-away; bar; BBQ; playgrnd; pool; paddling pool; sandy beach 8km; games area; games rm; entmnt; wifi; 60% statics; dogs; phone; Eng spkn; adv bkg; quiet, a little rd noise; CKE/CCI. "Friendly, family-run site in hills; well-spaced; san facs dated but clean & plentiful; some pitches v shady; La Garde-Freinet has all shops & excel rests; highly rec if want site close to coast without noise/crowds; vg."
♦ 1 Mar-31 Oct. € 20.00   2011*

GROLEJAC see Sarlat la Canéda *7C3*

⊞ **GROS THEIL, LE** *3D2 (3km SW Rural) 49.21207, 0.81533*
Camp de Salverte, Route de Brionne, 27370 Le Gros-Theil [02 32 35 51 34; fax 02 32 35 92 79; david.farah@wanadoo.fr; www.camping-salverte.com] Fr Brionne take D26 E twd Le Gros-Theil. After 10km turn R at Salverte, site sp. Lge, hdg pitch, terr, pt shd; htd wc; chem dist; baby facs; shwrs inc; el pnts (4A) inc (poss rev pol); el pnts (6A) inc; gas; lndry rm; shop; tradsmn; rest, snacks; bar; BBQ; playgrnd; covrd pool; tennis; games rm; entmnt; 90% statics; dogs; phone; adv bkg; quiet; ccard acc; CKE/CCI. "Conv NH Le Havre/Caen ferries; attractive site but v ltd facs low ssn; lge pitches; sm area for tourers diff when wet; excel." € 17.90   2011*

GRUISSAN *10F1 (5km NE Coastal) 43.1358, 3.1424*
Camping Les Ayguades, Ave de la Jonque, 11430 Gruissan [04 68 49 81 59; fax 04 68 49 05 64; loisirs-vacances-languedoc@wanadoo.fr; www.loisirs-vacances-languedoc.com] Exit A9 junc 37 onto D168/D32 sp Gruissan. In 10km turn L at island sp Les Ayguades, foll site sp. Lge, hdg/mkd pitch, unshd; htd wc; chem disp; mv service pnt; baby facs; shwrs inc; el pnts (6A) inc; lndtte; shop; rest; bar; playgrnd; sand beach adj; entmnt; TV; 75% statics; dogs €2.50; Eng spkn; adv bkg; quiet; ccard acc; CKE/CCI. "Pleasant site; extensive cycle network, 6 night min stay high ssn" ♦ 1 Apr-4 Nov. € 31.00   2012*

GUDAS *8G3 (2km S Rural) 42.99269, 1.67830* **Camping Mille Fleurs (Naturist), Le Tuillier, 09120 Gudas [tel/fax 05 61 60 77 56; info@camping-millefleurs.com; www.camping-millefleurs.com]** App Foix on the N20 fr Toulouse foll sp Foix-Tarbes. Pass Camping du lac on R, cont approx 2.2km, at traff lghts turn L sp D1 Laroque d'Olmes, Lieurac, l'Herm). Foll D1 for 6.5km until junc D13 (Care req, sharp bend). Turn L sp Col de Py, Mirepoix, cont past quarry, L fork (sp Gudas, Varhilles). After 2km sp Millefleurs, le Tuilier, turn L over bdge. Site in approx 2km bef Gudas. Sm, hdg/mkd pitch, terr, pt sl, pt shd; wc; chem disp; shwrs inc; child/baby facs; fam bthrm; sauna; el pnts (6-10A) €3.75; gas 10km; shop 8km; tradsmn; rest; bar; BBQ; pool; games rm; wifi; some statics; dogs €2.25; phone; Eng spkn; adv bkg rec high ssn; quiet; red low ssn; INF card req. "Excel, scenic site; lovely owners; gd pitches; clean facs; gd base Andorra, Toulouse & Carcassonne." ♦ 1 Apr-1 Nov. € 24.00   2012*

GUEGON see Josselin *2F3*

GUEMENE PENFAO *2G4 (1km SE Rural) 47.62575, -1.81857* **Camping L'Hermitage, 36 Ave du Paradis, 44290 Guémené-Penfao [02 40 79 23 48; fax 02 40 51 11 87; camping.hermitage@wanadoo.fr; www.campinglhermitage.com]** On D775 fr cent of Guémené-Penfao, dir Châteaubriant for 500m, turn R, site sp. Med, mkd pitch, hdstg, pt shd; wc; chem disp; mv service pnt; baby facs; shwrs inc; el pnts (6A) €3.50; gas; lndtte; shop 1.5km; tradsmn; rest, snacks; bar; BBQ; playgrnd; htd, covrd pool adj; paddling pool; waterslide; jacuzzi; rv sw & fishing 300m; canoeing; tennis; games area; games rm; cycle hire; entmnt; TV; 20% statics; dogs €2; phone; some Eng spkn; adv bkg; quiet; red low ssn; CKE/CCI. "Gd walking in area; excel site." ♦ 1 Apr-31 Oct. € 18.00   2013*

See advertisement on pages 32 & 33

GUENROUET *2G3 (E Rural) 47.52215, -1.95008* **Camp Municipal St Clair, Route de Plessé, 44530 Guenrouet [tel/fax 02 40 87 61 52 or 06 98 86 89 90; chabliny@wanadoo.fr; www.campingsaintclair.com]** S fr Redon take D164 dir Blain, turn R onto D2 to Guenrouet, over bdge & site directly on L after bdge. Med, hdg/mkd pitch, pt sl, pt shd; wc; chem disp; mv service pnt; 50% serviced pitches; shwrs inc; el pnts (10A) €3; gas; shop & 1km; tradsmn; rest 100m; playgrnd; htd pool adj; waterslide; fishing; canoe hire; dogs €1.50; Eng spkn; quiet; CKE/CCI. "On banks of canal; special area for late arr; excel." ♦ 1 May-27 Sep. € 18.20   2009*

GUERANDE *2G3 (2km N Rural) 47.34954, -2.43170* **Camping La Fontaine, Kersavary, Route de St-Molf, 44350 Guérande [02 40 24 96 19 or 06 08 12 80 96 (mob); lafontaine.guerande@orange.fr; www.camping-lafontaine.com]** Fr Guérande take N774 N sp La Roche-Bernard; in 1 km, opp windmill, fork L onto D233 sp St-Molf; site on L in 500m. Med, mkd pitch, hdstg, pt shd; wc; chem disp; shwrs inc; el pnts (6A) €4; lndtte; snacks; shop, rest & bar 4km; playgrnd; sand beach 4km; statics sep; dogs €2; phone; adv bkg rec high ssn; quiet; red low ssn/CKE/CCI. "Pleasant, peaceful site; lge pitches; helpful staff; san facs dated but clean; gd." ♦ ltd 15 Mar-15 Nov. € 18.00   2011*

GUERANDE *2G3 (2km E Rural) 47.33352, -2.39060* **Camping Le Domaine de Léveno, Route de Sandun, 44350 Guérande [02 40 24 79 30; fax 02 40 62 01 23; contact@camping-leveno.com; www.camping-leveno.com]** Fr Guérande foll sps to L'Etang de Sandun. Lge, pt shd; wc; serviced pitches; shwrs; el pnts (6A) inc; gas; lndtte; shop; rest; snacks, bar; BBQ; playgrnd; htd, covrd pool; paddling pool; waterslide; sand beach 5km; tennis; games area; entmnt; TV rm; 90% statics; dogs €5; adv bkg; quiet; red low ssn. "Conv La Baule; site in lovely park; few touring pitches; pitches shabby (2010)." 3 Apr-30 Sep. € 35.00   2010*

Send in your site reports by mid August 2014

⊞ **GUERANDE** 2G3 (7km E Rural) 47.34621, -2.34613
FFCC Camping de l'Etang en Kerjacob, 47 Rue des Chênes, Sandun, 44350 Guérande [02 40 61 93 51; camping-etang@wanadoo.fr; www.camping-etang.com] Fr Guérande take D51 NE for approx 5km, turn R onto D48 for 3km. Turn L to site on lakeside. Sp fr each junc on Guérande by-pass. Med, hdg/mkd pitch, pt shd; wc; chem disp; baby facs; shwrs inc; el pnts (10A) €3.60; lndtte; shop, rest, snacks, bar high ssn; BBQ; playgrnd; htd pool & paddling pool; sand beach 9km; watersports 9km; lake fishing; cycle hire; games rm; wifi; many statics; dogs €2.50; poss cr; Eng spkn; adv bkg; ccard acc; red low ssn; CKE/CCI. "Pleasant, peaceful site; friendly staff; dated, clean san facs, ltd low ssn; plenty of shade; poss resident workers; mkt Wed & Sat." ◆ € 19.50 2008*

GUERANDE 2G3 (3km S Urban/Rural) 47.29797, -2.39988
Camping Trémondec, 48 Rue du Château Careil, 44350 Guérande [02 40 60 00 07; fax 02 40 60 91 10; camping. tremondec@wanadoo.fr; www.camping-tremondec.com] Fr Nantes on N165/N171/D213 dir La Baule. Take D192 dir La Baule cent, turn W in 800m dir Brenave, Careil. Site sp. Med, hdg/mkd pitch, hdstg, pt sl, pt shd; wc; chem disp; mv service pnt; baby facs; shwrs inc; el pnts (16A) inc; lndtte (inc dryer); sm shop; tradsmn; supmkt 900m; rest, snacks, bar high ssn; BBQ; playgrnd; htd pool; sand beach 1.5km; cycle hire; games area; games rm; wifi; entmnt; TV rm; 50% statics; dogs €3; Eng spkn; adv bkg; quiet; ccard acc; red low ssn/long stay/ CKE/CCI. "V pleasant site; lovely beaches & coast; interesting walks thro salt marshes; cycle rtes; excel." ◆ 1 Apr-Nov. € 25.50 2010*

GUERANDE 2G3 (7km W Coastal) 47.32856, -2.49907 **Camp Municipal Les Chardons Bleus, Blvd de la Grande Falaise, 44420 La Turballe [02 40 62 80 60; fax 02 40 62 85 40; campingleschardonsbleus@mairielaturballe.fr; www. camping-laturballe.fr]** Foll D99 to La Turballe. Site well sp fr town cent along D92. Lge, hdg/mkd pitch, unshd; wc; chem disp; mv service pnt; adj; shwrs inc; el pnts (6-10A) €3.35-4.50; (poss rev pol, long lead poss req); gas; lndtte; shop; tradsmn; rest, snacks; bar; playgrnd; htd pool; sand beach adj (pt naturist) & 2km; entmnt; dogs €2.55; wifi; phone; Eng spkn; ccard acc; red low ssn; CKE/CCI. "Well-run, well-kept site in great location; warm welcome; gd, clean san facs, poss stretched high ssn; ltd el pnts when full; variable opening dates - phone ahead to check early ssn; nature reserve adj with bird life; superb beach adj, walk along beach to pretty fishing port of La Turballe with rests" ◆ 30 Mar-29 Sep. € 18.00 2013*

GUERANDE 2G3 (7km NW Rural) 47.34252, -2.47159 **Camping Le Parc Ste Brigitte, Manoir de Bréhet, 44420 La Turballe [02 40 24 88 91; fax 02 40 15 65 72; saintebrigette@ wanadoo.fr; www.campingsaintebrigitte.com]** Take D99 NW fr Guérande twd La Turballe thro vill of Clis. Sp on R in 900m. Lge, mkd pitch, shd; wc; chem disp; mv service pnt; serviced pitch; shwrs inc; baby facs; el pnts (6-10A) inc; gas; lndtte; shop; rest, snacks; bar; playgrnd; htd, covrd pool; sand beach 2km; fishing; cycle hire; entmnt; TV rm; some statics; dogs €1.50; phone; poss cr; adv bkg; poss noisy; ccard not acc; CKE/CCI. "V peaceful; excel rest & bar; some sm pitches; poss unkempt, untidy & poss poor pitch maintenance low ssn; gd." ◆ 1 Apr-1 Oct. € 30.20 2011*

GUERANDE 2G3 (7km NW Coastal) 47.35388, -2.51722
Camping-Caravaning La Falaise, 1 Blvd de Belmont, 44220 La Turballe [02 40 23 32 53; fax 02 40 62 87 07; info@ camping-de-la-falaise.com; www.camping-de-la-falaise. com] Fr Guérand exit on D99 sp La Turballe/Piriac-sur-Mer; pass La Turballe; site easily seen on L 200m after Intermarché. Med, hdg/mkd pitch, pt shd; htd wc (some cont); chem disp; some serviced pitches; shwrs inc; el pnts (10A) inc; lndtte; shop 200m; tradsmn; rest 100m; bar; BBQ; playgrnd; sand beach adj; watersports; naturist beach 2km; horseriding & mini-golf 3km; entmnt; TV; 5% statics; dogs €2.25; Eng spkn; adv bkg; quiet (some rd noise); CKE/CCI. "V pleasant site." ◆ 25 Mar-31 Oct. € 28.30 (3 persons) 2008*

> "I like to fill in the reports as I travel from site to site"
>
> You'll find report forms at the back of this guide, or you can fill them in online at www.caravaclub.co.uk/europereport.

GUERANDE 2G3 (8km NW Coastal) 47.36045, -2.51473
Camping Le Refuge, 56 Rue de Brandu, 44420 La Turballe [02 40 23 37 17; fax 02 40 11 85 10; info@tourisme-laturballe.fr; www.tourisme-laturballe.fr] On D99 thro La Turballe twd Piriac. Ikm after SuperU supmkt turn R into Rue de Brandu. Site on R in 800m, sp. Lge, hdg pitch, shd; wc; chem disp (wc); mv service pnt; shwrs inc; el pnts (6A) €3.50; lndtte; shop 1km; tradsmn; BBQ (gas); playgrnd; sand beach 300m; fishing; sailing; tennis; no dogs; adv bkg; quiet; CKE/CCI. "Excel, well-kept site; lge grassy pitches pt shd; easy access to gd beach & town; gd cycling area; excel site with large pitches; friendly staff; Eng spkn; easy access to gd beach; town & shops 15 min walk; excel cycling area" ◆ 1 Jun-30 Sep. € 19.20 2013*

⊞ **GUERCHE DE BRETAGNE, LA** 2F4 (6km E Rural) 47.94383, -1.17233 **Camp Municipal, 35130 La Selle-Guerchaise [02 99 96 46 72]** Fr N on D178 Vitré to Châteaubriant rd 3km N of of La Guerche-de-Bretagne; turn L onto D106 to Availles-sur-Seiche, then foll sp La Selle-Guerchaise; site behind Mairie in vill. Sm, hdg/mkd pitch, pt sl, pt shd; htd wc; chem disp (wc); shwrs inc; el pnts (4A); (rev pol, poss long cable req); lndtte; playgrnd, multisports area; fishing adj; 50% statics; dogs; poss noisy; CKE/CCI. "Welcoming; gd san facs; fair NH." ◆ 2009*

GUERCHE SUR L'AUBOIS, LA 4H3 (2km SE Rural) 46.94029, 2.95852 **Camp Municipal Robinson, 2 Rue de Couvache, 18150 La Guerche-sur-l'Aubois [02 48 74 18 86 or 02 48 77 53 53; fax 02 48 77 53 59; camping-laguerche@ orange.fr; www.mairie-la-guerche-sur-laubois.com]** Site sp fr D976 opp church in vill cent. Sm, hdg/mkd pitch, pt shd; wc; shwrs inc; el pnts (10A) €3; lndry rm; shop; tradsmn; rest, bar 300m; playgrnd; lake sw adj; fishing; boating; entmnt; dogs; phone; poss cr; quiet, some rlwy noise; CKE/CCI. "Pleasantly situated; v welcoming; clean san facs; gd cycling area; excel; ideal for visits to Parc Floral gardens at Apremont" ◆ ltd 1 May-30 Sep. € 8.50 2013*

GUERET *7A4* (8km S Rural) *46.10257, 1.83528* **Camp Municipal Le Gué Levard, 5 Rue Gué Levard, 23000 La Chapelle-Taillefert [05 55 51 09 20 or 05 55 52 36 17 (Mairie); www.ot-gueret.fr]** Take junc 48 from N145 sp Tulle/Bourganeuf (D33 thro Guéret); S on D940 fr Guéret, turn off at site sp. Foll sp thro vill, well sp. Sm, hdstg, sl, terr, pt shd; wc; mv service pnt; shwrs inc; el pnts (16A) €2.50; lndtte (inc dryer); shop; rest, snacks & bar 500m; BBQ (sep area); playgrnd; fishing in Rv Gartempe; sports facs nr; 20% statics; dogs; quiet; adv bkg; ccard not acc; CKE/CCI. "Attractive, peaceful, well-kept site hidden away; vg san facs; site yourself, warden calls 1900; all pitches sl so m'van levelling diff; trout stream runs thro site; gd auberge in vill; gd walking; phone ahead to check open low ssn; excel little site." ♦ ltd 1 Apr-1 Nov. € 10.90   2012*

GUERET *7A4* (3km W Rural) *46.16387, 1.85882* **Camp du Plan d'Eau de Courtille (Formerly Municipal), Rue Georges Aullon, 23000 Guéret [05 55 81 92 24]** Fr W on N145 take D942 to town cent; then take D914 W; take L turn bef lake sp; site in 1.5km along lakeside rd with speed humps. Site sp. Med, hdg/mkd pitch, pt sl, pt shd; wc (some cont); chem disp; mv service pnt; baby facs; shwrs inc; el pnts (10A) inc; shops 2km; rest, bar 500m; BBQ; playgrnd; pool 1.5km; sand beach & lake sw; watersports; dogs; phone; poss cr; no adv bkg; quiet; CKE/CCI; "Pleasant scenery; well-managed site; narr ent to pitches; mkd walks nrby; poss noisy w/end." ♦ 1 Apr-5 Nov. € 18.00   2012*

GUERNO, LE see Muzillac *2G3*

GUIDEL see Pouldu, Le *2F2*

GUIERCHE, LA *4F1* (500m W Rural) *48.10863, 0.19244* **Camping Les Platanes, Les Boucheries, 72380 La Guierche [02 43 27 36 29]** N fr Le Mans on D338 turn R onto D149 at Trois Couleurs, thro Souillé. Turn R bef rlwy line, site on R in 300m. Sm, hdg pitch, pt shd; wc; shwrs inc; el pnts (6A) inc; lndtte; shop 500m; tradsmn; BBQ; playgrnd; dogs; train 500m; quiet; ccard not acc; CKE/CCI. "Pretty site; accommodating owners; basic facs; gd NH within easy reach Le Mans." Easter-30 Sep. € 20.00   2010*

GUIGNICOURT *3C4* (500m SE Urban) *49.43209, 3.97035* **Camping au Bord de l'Aisne (Formaly Municipal), 14b Rue des Godins, 02190 Guignicourt [tel/fax 03 23 79 74 58; campingguignicourt@orange.fr; www.camping-aisne-picardie.fr]** Exit A26 junc 14 onto D925 to Guignicourt; after passing under rlway bdge cont on D925 for 800m; then turn R at Peugeot g'ge down narr rd to site (12% descent at ent & ramp). Site sp in vill on rv bank. Med, hdg/mkd pitch, pt shd; htd wc (some cont); chem disp; mv service pnt; shwrs; el pnts (6-10A) €3-5 (poss rev pol, poss long cable req); sm supmkt & shops in vill; tradsmn; rest 600m; pizzeria; snacks; bar; BBQ; playgrnd; htd covrd pool; fishing; wifi; 20% statics; dogs €1.60; phone; train 500m; poss cr; some Eng spkn; adv bkg; quiet; ccard acc; red long stay; CKE/CCI. "Pretty, well-kept site in beautiful setting on banks of rv; popular NH, conv A26; well-guarded; friendly, helpful staff; poss muddy when wet; pleasant town; excel touring base Reims, Epernay; easy access despite gradient; excel; v clean updated facs" ♦ 1 Apr-31 Oct. € 29.90 SBS - P02   2013*

GUILLESTRE *9D4* (800m SW Rural) *44.65854, 6.63836* **Camping La Rochette (formerly Municipal), 05600 Guillestre [tel/fax 04 92 45 02 15; guillestre@aol.com; www.campingguillestre.com]** Exit N94 onto D902A to Guillestre. In 1km fork R on side rd at camp sps. Site on L in 1km. Lge, mkd pitch, pt shd; wc (some cont); shwrs inc; el pnts (6-10A) €2.80-3.40; gas; lndtte; shop; snacks; BBQ; playgrnd; pool, tennis adj; fishing; dir access to rv; sports area; entmnt; dogs free; phone; poss cr; adv bkg; quiet; red low ssn. "Spectacular views; lge pitches; Dutch-owned site; helpful staff; superb san facs; conv Queyras National Park." ♦ 15 May-30 Sep. € 15.20   2012*

GUILVINEC *2F2* (2.5km W Coastal) *47.80388, -4.31222* **Yelloh! Village la Plage, Chemin des Allemands, Penmarc'h, 29730 Guilvinec [02 98 58 61 90; fax 02 98 58 89 06; info@yellohvillage-la-plage.com; www.villagelaplage.com or www.yellohvillage.co.uk]** Fr Quimper, Pont l'Abbé on D785 SW to Plomeur; turn S onto D57 sp Guilvinec. Bear R on app to town & v soon after turn R sp Chapelle de Tremor. Foll site to site in 1.5km. Lge, pt shd; wc; chem disp; mv service pnt; baby facs; sauna; shwrs inc; el pnts (5A) inc; gas; lndtte (inc dryer); shop; rest, snacks; bar; BBQ; playgrnd; 2 htd pools (1 covrd); paddling pool; waterslide; direct accesss sand beach adj; tennis; archery; games rm; fitness rm; cycle hire; wifi; entmnt; 70% statics; dogs €4; no c'vans/m'vans over 8m high ssn; poss cr; adv bkg; quiet; ccard acc; red low ssn. "Ideal for families; spacious pitches; site rds poss diff lge o'fits; excel touring base; mkt Tue & Sun." ♦ 1 Apr-15 Sep. € 43.00 SBS - B15   2011*

See advertisement on inside front cover

GUILVINEC *2F2* (3.5km NW Coastal) *47.81819, -4.30942* **Camping Les Genêts, Rue Gouesnac'h Nevez, 29760 Penmarc'h [02 98 58 66 93 or 06 83 15 85 92 (mob); campinglesgenets29@orange.fr; www.camping-lesgenets.com]** S fr Pont-l'Abbé on D785 to Plomeur; cont on D785 for another 4km, then turn L onto D53 sp Guilvinec; in 300m turn L into Rue Gouesnac'h Nevez to site. Med, hdg/mkd pitch, pt shd; htd wc; chem disp; baby facs; shwrs inc; el pnts (10A) €3.40; gas; lndtte; ice; tradsmn; rest, snacks; bar; BBQ; playgrnd; htd pool; covrd pool & waterslide planned (2010); sand beach 1.5km; cycle hire nrby; horseriding 800m; games area; games rm; wifi; entmnt; TV rm; 25% statics; dogs €2; bus; phone; poss cr; Eng spkn; adv bkg; red low ssn/long stay; CKE/CCI. "Peaceful, well-kept site in beautiful, unspoilt area; family-run; friendly atmosphere; welcoming, helpful owners; easy access to spacious pitches; excel, clean, modern san facs; gd value; excel." ♦ 1 Apr-30 Sep. € 22.00 (CChq acc)   2013*

See advertisement on pages 32 & 33

GUINES *3A3* **La p'tite source, 3438 Route de Guînes, 62340 Hames-Boucres, Pas de Calais [06 18 53 02 69 or 06 24 40 58 40 (mob); contact@laptitesource.com; www.laptitesource.com]** Fr Calais take the national CD127 and the CD247. At the rndabt turn L and you are at the site. Med, hdg pitch numbered, pt shd; chem disp; mv service pnt; shwr inc; el pnts (16A) €2.50; gas; lndtte; rest, bar; BBQ; picnic area; bowling; pool table; karaoke; dances; fishing €12 pp per day; playgrnd; dogs; quiet 1 Apr-30 Oct. € 19.00   2013*

GUINES *3A3* (2km W Rural) *50.86611, 1.85694* **Camping De La Bien Assise, Route D231 62340 Guînes [03 21 35 20 77; fax 03 21 36 79 20; castels@bien-assise.com; www. camping-bien-assise.fr or www.les-castels.com]** Exit A16 at junc 40 dir Fréthun Gare TGV; turn L onto D215 dir Fréthun Gare TGV & foll sp Guînes thro St Tricat & Hamas-Boucres (NB 30km/h zone & must give way on R) to rndabt at site ent. Fr S exit A26 junc 2; foll sp to Ardres then take D231 thro Guînes to rndabt to site. Phone ahead if early or late arr anticipated. Lge, hdg/mkd pitch, pt sl, pt shd; htd wc (some cont); chem disp; mv service pnt; baby facs; shwrs inc; el pnts (6A) €5. (poss rev pol); gas; lndtte (inc dryer); shop; supmkt 3km; tradsmn; rest, snacks; bar; BBQ (charcoal/gas); playgrnd; 2 pools (1 htd, covrd); paddling pool; waterslide; beach 12km; tennis; cycle hire; horseriding 3km; golf nrby; wifi; entmnt; TV/ games rm; 20% statics (tour ops); dogs €3; twin-axles acc (rec check in adv); v cr high ssn; Eng spkn; adv bkg, rec all times; rd & rlwy noise; some pitches; ccard acc; red long stay/low ssn; CKE/CCI. "Pleasant, busy site in grnds of chateau; well-kept & well-run; gd sized pitches with easy access; conv ferries - late arr area; pleasant, cheerful staff; clean san facs, stretched when site full; excel rest; vg pool complex; grass pitches, some soft low ssn & boggy when wet; vet in Ardres (9km), site will book for you; even if notice says 'Complete' check availability for sh stay; mkt Fri; excel; vg site; helpful staff; Shwrs falling below standard; excel rest; ACSI acc" ♦ 05 Apr-28 Sep. € 41.00 SBS - P05 2013*

See advertisement on inside back cover

GUINES *3A3* (1km NW Urban) *50.88562, 1.87080* **Camping La Belle Pêche, Route de Guînes, 62340 Hames-Boucres [03 21 35 21 07 or 06 18 53 02 69 (mob); fax 03 21 82 51 50; camping-belle-peche@wanadoo.fr; www. camping-belle-peche.com]** Fr Guînes foll sp Calais on D127; site on L in 1km. Med, hdg pitch, hdstg, pt shd; wc; chem disp; shwrs €1; el pnts (6A) €2.30; shop 500m, rest; bar; playgrnd; rv fishing; tennis; entmnt; 80% statics; Eng spkn; quiet; no cc. "Conv ferries; Eurotunnel 15 mins; some pitches flood in wet weather; NH only." 1 May-30 Oct. € 16.30 2011*

GUIPRY see Bain de Bretagne *2F4*

GUISE *3C4* (500m SE Urban) *49.89488, 3.63372* **FFCC Camping de la Vallée de l'Oise, 33 Rue du Camping, 02120 Guise [03 23 61 14 86; fax 03 23 61 21 07]** Foll Vervin sp in town & camp clearly sp fr all dirs in town. Lge, pt shd; wc (some cont); shwrs inc; el pnts (3-6A) €3-5 (rev pol); lndry rm; shops 500m; tradsmn; playgrnd; rv fishing & canoe hire adj; cycle hire; games rm; TV; entmnt; 50% statics; dogs; some Eng spkn; adv bkg; v quiet; red low ssn; CKE/CCI. "Spacious, beautifully kept, friendly site; busy w/ends; gd san facs; barrier always open, warden not always on site; if arr late, pitch & pay next morning; interesting old town; gd value" 15 Apr-15 Oct. € 13.00 2013*

GUISE *3C4* (6km NW Rural) *49.92709, 3.57768* **Camp Muncipal de Bovalon, 02120 Vadencourt [tel/fax 03 23 61 07 03 (Mairie); www.vadencourt.com]** Exit Guise NW on D960 dir Bohain-en-Vermandois; in 6km turn R onto D69; site on R in 1km just bef Vadencourt. Or exit D66 S at Vadencourt onto D69; site on L in 150m, just after rv bdg. Site sp in Vadencourt off D66. Sm, hdg pitch, pt shd; wc (some cont); chem disp (wc); shwrs inc; el pnts (6A) €5; shops & bar 250m; dogs €0.45; quiet, but some rd noise daytime; CKE/CCI. "Site by Rv Oise in pleasant area; height barrier, but call mobile number on noticeboard or contact Café du Centre; gd; can't rec due to crowding by travellers (2012) ♦ ltd 1 May-30 Sep. € 9.50 2012*

GUISSENY see Plouguerneau *2E2*

GUJAN MESTRAS see Arcachon *7D1*

HAGETMAU *8E2* (200m S Urban) *43.65020, -0.59190* **Camp Muncipal de la Cité Verte, Chemin des Loussets, 40700 Hagetmau [tel/fax 05 58 79 79 79]** On D933 S fr Mont-de-Marsan, go thro St Sever & cont on D933 to Hagetmau. Take ring rd & ent town fr S, sp 'Cité Verte'. Heading N fr Orthez on D933, also foll sp 'Cité Verte'. Sm, hdg pitch, pt shd; wc; chem disp (wc); mv service pnt; serviced pitch; fam bthrm; sauna; shwrs inc; el pnts (16A) inc; shops 500m; rest, snacks, bar 1km; BBQ; playgrnd; htd, covrd pool; jacuzzi; gym; dogs; phone; adv bkg ess; quiet. "Unique site with sports cent inc Olympic-sized pool; 24 pitches with personal facs; gd base for touring area; attractive town; excel." 1 Jun-30 Sep. € 22.00 2009*

HAGUENAU *5D3* (2km S Urban) *48.80289, 7.76911* **Camp Municipal Les Pins, Route de Strasbourg, 67500 Haguenau [03 88 73 91 43 or 03 88 93 70 00; fax 03 88 93 69 89; tourisme@ville-haguenau.fr; www.ville-haguenau.fr]** Fr S on D263, after passing Haguenau town sp turn L at 2nd set of traff lts (opp Peugeot garage). Site sp fr D263. Med, mkd pitch, terr, pt shd; htd wc; chem disp; shwrs inc; el pnts (6A) inc; gas; lndtte; shop, rest, snack & bar 2km; BBQ; playgrnd; pool 1km inc; dogs €0.90; phone; bus 500m; Eng spkn; adv bkg; quiet; CKE/CCI. "Lge pitches; helpful staff; clean, modern san facs; meals avail fr warden; grnd firm even after heavy rain; excel." ♦ 1 May-30 Sep. € 13.00 2010*

⊞ **HAMBYE** *1D4* (1.5km N Rural) *48.9600, -1.2600* **Camping aux Champs, 1 Rue de la Ripaudière, 50450 Hambye [02 33 90 06 98; michael.coles@wanadoo.fr; www. campingauxchamps.com]** Exit A84 junc 38 onto D999 to Percy; then turn L at town cent rndabt onto D58 to Hambye; at mkt sq proceed to junc, strt sp Le Guislain, past Mairie; site on R in 1.5 km on D51. Sm, some hdstg, unshd; htd wc; chem disp; fam bthrm; shwrs inc; el pnts (10A) €3; lndtte; shop, rest, snacks, bar 2km; adv bkg; red long stay; quiet; red long stay; adv bkg req low ssn (Nov-Mar) for full facs; CKE/CCI. "Peaceful, CL-type site; friendly, helpful British owners; adults only; excel, clean san facs; Hambye Abbey nrby; bell foundry at Villedieu-les-Poêls worth visit; conv ferry ports." € 12.00 2011*

FRANCE

HARDELOT PLAGE *3A2* (3km NE Urban) *50.64661, 1.62539* Caravaning du Château d'Hardelot, 21 Rue Nouvelle, 62360 Condette [tel/fax 03 21 87 59 59; contact@camping-caravaning-du-chateau.com; www.camping-caravaning-du-chateau.com] Take D901 S fr Boulogne, R turn onto D940 dir Le Touquet; then R at rndabt on D113 to Condette; take 2nd turning to Château Camping, R at next rndabt & site 400m on R. Fr S leave A16 at exit 27 to Neufchâtel-Hardelot, take D940 twd Condette & turn L at 1st rndabt onto D113, then as above. Not well sp last 3km. Tight turn into site ent. Med, hdg/mkd pitch, pt sl, pt shd; wc; chem disp; mv service pnt; baby facs; shwrs inc; el pnts (10A) €4.70 (poss rev pol); lndtte; shop 500m; playgrnd; sand beach 3km; tennis 500m; sm multi-gym; horseriding; golf; games rm; child entmnt; wifi; 30% statics; dogs free; poss v cr; some Eng spkn; adv bkg (rec high ssn); some rd noise; no ccard acc; red low ssn; CKE/CCI. "Lovely, well-run, wooded site; busy high ssn; vg low ssn; sm pitches; helpful, friendly owners; clean, modern san facs; tight access some pitches; conv Calais (site barrier opens 0800)." ♦ ltd 1 Apr-31 Oct. € 21.30   2011*

HARDINGHEN *3A3* (500m SE Rural) *50.79462, 1.81369* Camping à la Ferme Les Piloteries, Rue de l'Eglise, 62132 Hardinghen [03 21 85 01 85; lespiloteries@free.fr; http://lespiloteries.free.fr] Fr N exit A16 junc 36 at Marquise onto D191 to Hardinghen; turn R onto D127 (where D191 turns sharp L); site in 1km (concealed ent). Sm, pt sl, pt shd; wc; chem disp (wc); shwrs €1; el pnts (6A) €2; BBQ; playgrnd; quiet. "Vg CL-type site; friendly owner." 16 Apr-2 Oct. € 7.40   2011*

HAULME see Charleville Mézières *5C1*

HAUTECOURT ROMANECHE see Bourg en Bresse *9A2*

HAUTEFORT *7C3* (3km NE Rural) *45.28081, 1.15917* Camping La Grenouille, Brégérac, 24390 Hautefort [tel/fax 05 53 50 11 71; info@lagrenouillevacances.com; www.lagrenouillevacances.com] Fr N on D704 at Cherveil-Cubas take D77 dir Boisseuilh/Teillots. In 4km turn R & in 800m turn L to site. Fr S on D704 at St Agnan take D62 sp Hautefort/Badefols d'Ans. Pass 'Vival' (sm shop on L) in Hautefort & turn L dir Boisseuilh. After 1st bdge turn L to La Besse & site in 2km. Sm, pt sl, pt shd; wc; chem disp; shwrs inc; el pnts (8A) €3.50; lndtte (inc dryer); ice; shop & 3km; tradsmn; rest; bar 3km; BBQ; playgrnd; pool; wifi; dogs free; Eng spkn; adv bkg; v quiet; ccard not acc; red low ssn; CKE/CCI. "Tranquil, scenic, well-kept site; friendly, helpful, Dutch owners; vg san facs; meals avail; goats, guinea pigs, chickens in pens on site; gd walking; highly rec." 22 Apr-15 Oct. € 17.00   2010*

HAUTEFORT *7C3* (8km W Rural) *45.28032, 1.04845* Camping Les Tourterelles, 24390 Tourtoirac [05 53 51 11 17; les-tourterelles@orange.fr; www.les-tourterelles.com] Fr N or S on D704 turn W at Hautefort on D62/D5 to Tourtoirac. In Tourtoirac turn R over rv then L. Site in 1km. Med, hdg/mkd pitch, terr, pt shd; wc; chem disp; mv service pnt; baby facs; shwrs; el pnts (6A) inc; gas; lndtte; shop 2km; rest, snacks; bar; playgrnd; pool; tennis; horseriding; TV rm; 20% statics; dogs €4; bus 1km; phone; poss cr; Eng spkn; adv bkg; quiet; low ssn/snr citizens red; ccard acc; CKE/CCI. "Beautiful Auvézère valley; rallies welcome; owners helpful; equestrian cent; gd walks." ♦ 25 Apr-27 Sep. € 29.00   2008*

HAUTERIVES see Beaurepaire *9C2*

⊞ **HAUTEVILLE LOMPNES** *9B3* (500m SW Rural) *45.97266, 5.59543* Camp Municipal Les Aberreaux, 125 Chemin des Lésines, 01110 Hauteville-Lompnes [tel/fax 04 74 35 36 73; mairie.hauteville.01@wanadoo.fr] Site sp fr only rndabt in Hauteville-Lompnes; adj casino. Access via lane L fr Chemin des Lésines immed after lge terracotta-coloured building. Sm, hdg/mkd pitch, pt shd; wc; chem disp (wc); shwrs inc; el pnts €1.80; gas 1km; lndry rm; shop, rest, snacks & bar 1km; htd covrd pool adj; 30% statics; CKE/CCI. "Clean, pleasant, basic site adj sports complex; lge pitches; vg touring base; winter sports vill; vg." € 6.30   2008*

HAUTOT SUR MER see Dieppe *3C2*

HAYE DU PUITS, LA *1D4* (1km N Rural) *49.29980, -1.54495* Camping L'Etang des Haizes, 43 Rue Cauticotte, 50250 St Symphorien-le-Valois [02 33 46 01 16; fax 02 33 47 23 80; info@campingetangdeshaizes.com; www.campingetangdeshaizes.com] Heading N fr La Haye-du-Puits on D900 under rlwy bdge & site 3rd on L, well sp. Med, hdg pitch, some hdstg, pt sl, pt shd; wc; chem disp; mv service pnt; baby facs; shwrs inc; el pnts (10A) €2-6; gas; lndtte; supmkt 1km; shop; tradsmn; rest, snacks; bar; playgrnd; htd pool; paddling pool; waterslide; fishing; cycle hire; games area; wifi; entmnt; TV rm; 50% statics (sep area); dogs €2; bus; phone; poss cr; Eng spkn; adv bkg rec; quiet; red low ssn; CKE/CCI. "Pretty, well-kept, well-run site in nature park; helpful, pleasant owners; ltd facs low ssn; barrier clsd 2300-0700; conv Cherbourg ferry (1hr)." ♦ 1 Apr-9 Oct. € 27.00 (CChq acc)   2009*

HAYE DU PUITS, LA *1D4* (6km N Urban) *49.38725, -1.52755* FFCC Camp Municipal du Vieux Château, Ave de la Division-Leclerc, 50390 St Sauveur-le-Vicomte [02 33 41 72 04 or 02 33 21 50 44; fax 02 33 95 88 85; ot.ssv@wanadoo.fr; www.ville-saint-sauveur-le-vicomte.fr] Fr Cherbourg on N13/D2 site on R after x-ing bdge at St Sauveur-le-Vicomte, sp. Med, mkd pitch, pt sl, pt shd; wc; chem disp; shwrs inc; el pnts (6A) €2.40 (poss rev pol); lndtte; shop 500m; tradsmn; rest adj; BBQ; playgrnd adj; pool; tennis 1km; games area; games rm; TV; dogs €1.15; phone; adv bkg; quiet; ccard acc; CKE/CCI. "Excel site in chateau grounds; friendly warden; gd clean facs; ideal 1st stop fr Cherbourg; office open until 2200 for late arr; barrier clsd 2200-0800; vg auberge opp; helpful warden; Eng not spkn; friendly town" 1 Jun-15 Sep. € 9.40   2013*

HAYE DU PUITS, LA *1D4* (2km SW Rural) *49.27292, -1.55896* Camping La Bucaille, 50250 Montgardon [02 33 07 46 38; fax 09 62 15 99 39; info@labucaille.com; www.labucaille.com] Fr Cherbourg S on N13 & D2 twd St Sauveur-le-Vicomte, then D900 to La Haye-du-Puits. Fr cent of La Haye turn onto D136 Rte de Bretteville-sur-Ay for approx 2km, site sp at L turn, site on L. Sm, pt sl, pt shd; wc; chem disp; shwrs inc; el pnts (16A) €5; shop, rest, snacks & bar 2km; BBQ; sand beach 4km; wifi; no statics; dogs free; adv bkg; quiet; width restriction 3 meters; "Pleasant quiet, 'hide-way' CL-type site; lge grassy pitches; friendly British owners; ideal for walking; excel." ♦ ltd 1 Apr-30 Sep. € 12.00   2013*

HEIMSBRUNN see Mulhouse *6F3*

HEMING 6E3 (5km SW Rural) 48.69130, 6.92769
**Camping Les Mouettes, 4 Rue de Diane Capelle, 57142
Gondrexange [03 87 25 06 01; www.otsi-gondrexange.
pagesperso-orange.fr]** Exit Héming on N4 Strasbourg-Nancy.
Foll sp Gondrexange & site sp. App fr W on D955 turn to site
sp on L about 1km bef Héming. Lge, mkd pitch, pt sl, unshd;
htd wc; chem disp; mv service pnt; shwrs inc; el pnts (10A) inc
(rev pol); lndtte; shop, rest, snacks, bar 200m; playgrnd; lake
beach, sw, fishing & sailing adj; tennis; cycle hire; dog €1.50;
60% statics; phone; poss cr; quiet; CKE/CCI. "Pleasant site by
lake; poss noisy w/end; basic facs but clean." 1 Apr-30 Sep.
€ 18.40   2013*

HENDAYE 8F1 (2km W Urban/Coastal) 43.37335, -1.75608
**Camping Ametza, Blvd de l'Empereur, 64700 Hendaye-
Plage [05 59 20 07 05; fax 05 59 20 32 16; contact@
camping-ametza.com; www.camping-ametza.com]**
Exit A63 junc 2 St Jean-de-Luz S onto D192. Foll sp to site.
Turn L on hill down to seafront, cross rlwy, site immed on L.
Lge, sl, shd; wc; chem disp; baby facs; shwrs inc; el pnts (6A)
€5 (poss rev pol); lndry rm; shop; snacks; bar; playgrnd; pool;
sand beach 900m; games area; wifi; entmnt; 30% statics; dogs
€2; poss cr; Eng spkn; quiet but rd & rlwy noise; red low ssn;
CKE/CCI. "Lovely relaxed site; some gd sized pitches, some sm;
excel facs; Hendaye pleasant resort; excel beach in walking dist;
excel." 1 May-30 Sep. € 24.50   2009*

HENNEBONT see Lorient 2F2

HENNEVEUX see Boulogne sur Mer 3A2

HENRIDORFF see Phalsbourg 5D3

HENVIC see St Pol de Léon 1D2

HERBIGNAC 2G3 (300m E Rural) 47.44802, -2.31073 **Camp
Municipal Le Ranrouet, Rue René Guy Cadou, 44410
Herbignac [02 40 88 96 23]** Site at intersection D774 & D33
on E edge of vill. Med, mkd pitch, pt shd; wc; chem disp; mv
service pnt; shwrs; el pnts (6A); lndtte; supmkt, bar adj; rest
1km; playgrnd; beach 10km; entmnt; TV; CKE/CCI. "Immac san
facs; gd cent for Guérande." Easter-30 Oct.   2008*

⊞ **HERIC** 2G4 (2km W Rural) 47.41329, -1.67050 **Camping
La Pindière, La Denais, Route de la Fay-de-Bretagne,
44810 Héric [tel/fax 02 40 57 65 41; contact@camping-la-
pindiere.com; www.camping-la-pindiere.com]**
Exit N137 twd Héric at traff lts in town, leave town & turn W
onto D16 (sp Camping). Site on L after rndabt supmkt, turn at
sp Notre Dames-des-Landes. Med, hdg pitch, hdstg, pt shd;
wc; chem disp; mv service pnt; baby facs; shwrs inc; el pnts
(6-10A) €3.20-4.80; gas; lndtte; shop or 1.5km; tradsmn; rest;
bar; playgrnd; htd pool; paddling pool; sports facs; tennis;
horseriding 200m; TV; 80% statics; dogs €1.40; phone; Eng
spkn; adv bkg rec, site poss clsd w/end low ssn; some noise
fr rd on N side; red low ssn; CKE/CCI. "Pleasant site; lge, grass
pitches, soft in wet weather; warm welcome; gd clean san facs;
gd NH." ♦ € 14.00   2010*

HERISSON 7A4 (500m NW Rural) 46.51055, 2.70576
**Camp Municipal de l'Aumance, Rue de Crochepot,
03190 Hérisson [04 70 06 88 22 , 04 70 06 80 45 or
06 63 46 21 49 (mob); www.allier-tourisme.com]** Exit A71
junc 9 onto D2144 N; turn R onto D11 dir Hérisson; immed
bef T-junc with D3 turn L at blue sp (high on L) into Rue de
Crochepot; site on R down hill. Med, mkd pitch, pt shd; wc;
shwrs inc; el pnts (5A) €2.60; playgrnd; games area; rv adj;
phone. "Delightful rvside site; idyllic setting; gd san facs;
warden calls eves; rec; peaceful and picturesque; easy walk to
vill" 1 Apr-31 Oct. € 7.65   2012*

HERMENT 7B4 (N Rural) 45.75481, 2.56683 **Camp Municipal
de Herment, Rue de la Chapelle, 63470 Herment
[04 73 22 11 98]** Fr main rd thro vill, foll sp upwards thro older
part of town. No name on rd to site. Sm, hdg/mkd pitch, pt
shd; wc; el pnts (6A) €0.76; shops 500m; quiet. "Pitches poss
diff access lge o'fits; el pnts hidden behind bushes on pitch."
♦ ltd € 5.50   2009*

HERPELMONT see Bruyères 6E2

HESDIN 3B3 (6km SE Rural) 50.35979, 2.07116 **Camping
Rural St Ladre, 66 Rue Principale, 62770 St Georges
[03 21 04 83 34; fax 03 21 30 04 81; bd-martin@wanadoo.fr;
http://martinbernard.monsite-orange.fr]** Fr Hesdin SE on
D340 for 5.5km. Site on L after St Georges, next narr lane next
cottage on bend. Fr W on D939 or D349 foll sp Frévent, then
St Georges. Sp to site poor. Sm, hdg/mkd pitch, pt shd; wc;
chem disp; shwrs inc; el pnts (5A) €2.40; no statics; adv bkg;
quiet; ccard not acc; CKE/CCI. "Pleasant, peaceful, CL-type site
in orchard; basic facs but clean; welcoming, pleasant owner;
conv Channel ports, Agincourt & Crécy; usual agricultural
noises; gd rests in Hesdin." 1 May-30 Sep. € 8.50   2013*

HEUDICOURT SOUS LES COTES 5D2 (1km NE Rural)
48.94111, 5.71704 **Camp Municipal Heudicourt, Les
Passons Madine 2, 55210 Heudicourt-sous-les-Côtes
[03 29 89 36 08; fax 03 29 89 35 60; contact@lacmadine.
com; www.lacmadine.com]** Fr St Mihiel, take D901 NE to
Chaillon. Turn R on D133 to Heudicourt. Bear L out of vill, still
on D133 & after 1km turn R to Nonsard. Site on R in 1.5km
at N end of Lake Madine. Lge, mkd pitch, pt sl, pt shd; wc
(mainly cont); shwrs inc; el pnts £4; lndtte; shop; rest; lake sw
adj; watersports; fishing; many statics; dogs €1; CKE/CCI. "Gd
location by Lake Madine." 1 Apr-31 Oct. € 15.00   2011*

HEURTEAUVILLE see Bourg Achard 3D2

HILLION see St Brieuc 2E3

HIRSON 3C4 (10km N Rural) 50.00585, 4.06195 **FFCC
Camping Les Etangs des Moines, 59610 Fourmies
[03 27 60 04 32; atouvert.fourmies@wanadoo.fr; www.
atouvert.com]** Fr D1043 Hirson by-pass head N on D963 to
Anor. Turn L onto D156 dir Fourmies, site sp on R on ent town.
Site also well sp off D42 & thro Fourmies. Med, hdg pitch,
hdstg, pt shd; wc; chem disp; mv service pnt; baby facs; shwrs
€1; el pnts (10A) €3.30; lndtte (inc dryer); shop 1km; tradsmn;
snacks; bar; BBQ: playgrnd; htd pool; 80% statics; dogs €1;
no twin-axles; poss cr; Eng spkn; some rlwy noise; CKE/CCI.
"Textile & eco museum in town; shwrs run down, other facs
gd; vg." 1 Apr-31 Oct. € 17.10   2012*

HONFLEUR *3C1* (5km S Rural) *49.40083, 0.30638* **Camping Domaine Catinière, Route d' Honfleur, 27210 Fiquefleur-Equainville [02 32 57 63 51; fax 02 32 42 12 57; info@camping-catiniere.com; www.camping-catiniere.com]** Fr A29/Pont de Normandie (toll) bdge exit junc 3 sp Le Mans, pass under m'way onto D580/D180. In 3km go strt on at rndabt & in 100m bear R onto D22 dir Beuzeville; site sp on R in 500m. Sm, hdg/mkd pitch, pt shd; wc (some cont); chem disp; shwrs inc; baby facs; el pnts (4A) inc (long lead poss req)(poss rev pol), extra charge for (8-13A) €1.-1.50; lndtte; sm shop; supmkt; tradsmn; snacks; bar; BBQ; playgrnd; htd pool; waterslide; rv fishing; games rm; wifi; entmnt; TV rm; 15% statics; dogs €2; no c'vans/m'vans over 8.50m; phone; poss cr; Eng spkn; adv bkg rec high ssn & w/end; ccard acc only over €70; CKE/CCI. "Attractive, well-kept site; pleasant young owners; clean unisex san facs, stretched high ssn & ltd low ssn; some pitches quite sm; unfenced stream on far boundary; poss school groups; gd touring base; gd walks; easy parking for m'vans nr town; 20 mins to Le Havre ferry via Normandy bdge; conv A13; highly rec; nice site well kept and clean; friendly staff; gd NH" ♦ 6 Apr-18 Sep. € 30.00 SBS - N16   2013*

See advertisement

HONFLEUR *3C1* (2.5km SW Rural) *49.39777, 0.20861* **Camping La Briquerie, 14600 Equemauville [02 31 89 28 32; fax 02 31 89 08 52; info@campinglabriquerie.com; www.campinglabriquerie.com]** Fr E ent town cent keeping harbour on R. Turn L onto D279 then in 2km turn R at rndabt at Intermarché. Site on R, N of water tower, E of Equemauville. Site well sp fr town cent. Fr S take D579 dir Honfleur Centre. At water tower on R turn L at Intermarché rndabt, site on R in 300m. Lge, hdg pitch, pt shd; wc; chem disp; mv service pnt; baby facs; fam bthrm; shwrs inc; el pnts (5-10A) €4-5 (poss rev pol); gas; lndtte; supmkt adj; rest, snacks & bar (high ssn); BBQ; playgrnd; 3 htd pools; waterslide; sand beach 2.5km; tennis, horseriding 500m; games rm; fitness rm; wifi; TV rm; entmnt; 50% statics; dogs €3; bus nr; poss cr; Eng spkn; adv bkg (fee for Jul/Aug); poss late noise high ssn; red low ssn; CKE/CCI. "Lge pitches; staff helpful; gd clean san facs; late/early ferry arr; local vets geared up for dog inspections, etc; gd; cash only" ♦ 1 Apr-30 Sep. € 46.80   2013*

HONFLEUR *3C1* (800m NW Coastal) *49.42445, 0.22753* **Camping du Phare, Blvd Charles V, 14600 Honfleur [02 31 89 10 26 / 02 13 24 22 12 (Cen Res); fax 02 31 93 06 05; vival-cabourg@wanadoo.fr / contact@campings-plage.fr; www.campings-plage.fr]** Fr N fr Pont de Normandie on D929 take D144; at ent to Honfleur keep harbour in R; turn R onto D513 sp Trouville-sur-Mer & Deauville (avoid town cent); fork L past old lighthouse to site entry thro parking area. Or fr E on D180; foll sp 'Centre Ville' then Vieux Bassin dir Trouville; at rectangular rndabt with fountain turn R sp Deauville & Trouville, then as above. Med, hdg pitch, pt shd; wc; chem disp; mv service pnt; shwrs €1.20; el pnts (2-10A) €4.10-5.90; gas; lndtte; shop 800m; tradsmn; rest 1km; snacks; bar; BBQ; playgrnd; htd, covrd pool nr; sand beach 100m; fishing; 10% statics; dogs €3; phone; poss v cr; Eng spkn; rd noise; no ccard acc; red low ssn; CKE/CCI. "Gd clean site in excel location; conv NH Le Havre ferry; busy high ssn, rec arr early; friendly owners; san facs dated but clean, ltd low ssn; barrier clsd 2200-0700; m'van pitches narr & adj busy rd; some soft, sandy pitches; easy walk to town/harbour; sep m'van Aire de Service nr harbour." 1 Apr-30 Sep. € 24.00   2013*

HONNECOURT SUR ESCAUT *3B4* (200m E Urban) *50.03834, 3.19940* **FFCC Camping de l'Escaut, 12 Rue de L'Eglise, 59266 Honnecourt-sur-l'Escaut [tel/fax 03 27 74 32 22; camping.de.lescaut@orange.fr; www.campingdelescaut.fr]** Fr Cambrai S on D644 S twd St Quentin; turn R onto D16 to Honnecourt-sur-Escaut; after x-ing canal at ent to vill turn L in 150m; site behind church. Well sp. Or fr D644 exit junc 9 onto D917 E dir Crèvecoeur-sur-l'Escaut; in 1.5km tur R onto D644 & then as bef. Med, hdg/mkd pitch, pt shd; wc; chem disp; shwrs €1.50; mv service pnt; el pnts (6A) €3 (poss rev pol); lndtte; snacks; bar; BBQ; playgrnd; fishing; 80% statics; dogs; adv bkg; red low ssn; CKE/CCI. "Lovely, peaceful site by canal; lge pitches; clean san facs, but need update (2011); resident warden; muddy when wet; gd NH; v welcoming" 30 Mar-28 Sep. € 13.50   2013*

HOSPITALET, L' *8G4* (600m N Rural) *42.59121, 1.80333* **Camp Municipal, 09390 L'Hospitalet-près-l'Andorre [05 61 05 21 10; fax 05 61 05 23 08; mairie.lhospitalet-pres-landorre@wanadoo.fr]** Site clearly sp on N20 fr Ax-les-Thermes to Andorra. Med, terr, unshd; wc; mv service pnt; shwrs inc; el pnts (5A) €2.30; lndtte; shops 200m; dogs; adv bkg; quiet but some rd noise. "Mainly tents, ltd space for tourers; vg walking; immac facs; conv day trips to Andorra & Spain; friendly warden; excel views." 1 Jun-31 Oct. € 9.80   2008*

FRANCE

HOSSEGOR *8E1* (6km N Coastal) *43.69490, -1.42953* **Village Camping Océliances, Ave des Tucs, 40510 Seignosse [05 58 43 30 30; fax 05 58 41 64 21; oceliances@wanadoo. fr; www.oceliances.com]** Take D79 N fr Hossegor. After 6km turn L at rndabt. Site sp. Lge, mkd pitch, pt sl, pt shd; htd wc; chem disp; baby facs; shwrs inc; el pnts (6A) inc; gas; lndtte (inc dryer); shop, rest, snacks; bar; BBQ; playgrnd; pool; paddling pool; sand beach 600m; windsurfing; lake 2km; games area; games rm; cycle hire; wifi; entmnt; 65% statics; dogs €3.40; Eng spkn; adv bkg; quiet; ccard acc; red long stay/low ssn. "Pleasant site in pine forest." ♦ Easter-30 Sep. € 30.50   2010*

HOSSEGOR *8E1* (1.5km NE Urban) *43.67212, -1.42035* **Camping Le Lac, 580 Routes des Lacs, 40150 Hossegor [05 58 43 53 14; fax 05 58 43 55 83; info@camping-du-lac. com; www.camping-du-lac.com]** Exit A63 junc 8 or N10 onto D28 sp Hossegor/Capbreton & foll sp for town cent. Site well sp at Soorts-Hossegor. Lge, hdg/mkd pitch, pt shd; wc (some cont); chem disp (wc); mv service pnt; shwrs inc; el pnts (6A) inc; gas; lndtte (inc dryer); shop; tradsmn; rest, snacks; bar; playgrnd; pool; paddling pool; sand beach 2km; lake 300m; games area; cycle hire; wifi; 80% statics; dogs €4; poss cr; Eng spkn; adv bkg; some rd noise; ccard acc; CKE/CCI. "Ltd space for tourers." ♦ ltd 1 Apr-30 Sep. € 34.00   2009*

> ## "We must tell The Club about that great site we found"
> Get your site reports in by mid-August and we'll do our best to get your updates into the next edition of Caravan Europe.

HOSSEGOR *8E1* (2km S Coastal) *43.62947, -1.43270* **Camping La Civelle, Rue des Biches, 40130 Capbreton [05 58 72 15 11; campinglacivelle@orange.fr; www. campinglacivelle.fr]** Fr N on A63, take exit 8 & foll sps to Capbreton; cont twds cent. At 1st rndabt, turn L past Intermarché. Strt on at 2nd rndabtat. At 3rd rndabt take 3rd exit & foll sp for site. Lge, mkd pitch, shd; wc (some cont); chem disp; 10% serviced pitches; el pnts €3.80; gas; lndtte; shop 1.5km; rest, snacks; BBQ; pool; sand beach 1km; games area; games rm; 40% statics; dogs €2.20; phone; ccard acc; CKE/CCI. "Busy site; no arr bef 1500; some sandy pitches; conv for area; cycle rte dir to beach." 22 Mar-5 Oct. € 21.50   2010*

⊞ **HOSSEGOR** *8E1* (3km S Coastal) *43.65168, -1.42998* **Camp Municipal Bel Air, Ave de Bourret, 40130 Capbreton [05 58 72 12 04; www.capbreton-tourisme.com]** Fr N10 or A63, take D28 to Capbreton; turn R onto D152; turn L at 4th rndabt, site on L in 200m. Diff access long o'fits. Med, hdg pitch, pt sl, pt shd; wc; chem disp; shwrs; el pnts (10A) inc; gas; lndtte; shops 500m; tradsmn; playgrnd; sand beach 1km; cycle hire adj; dogs €2.05; site clsd New Year; quiet; 10% red low ssn; CKE/CCI. "No arr bef 1500; card-op barrier, rec phone ahead to arrange access; arr bef 2000 unless late arr agreed in adv; vg winter NH/sh stay but phone ahead to check open; marina nrby, gd fishing; network of cycle paths; excel surfing; walking dist to Cap Breton & Hossegor; conv Biarritz." ♦ € 24.40   2011*

HOULGATE *3D1* (3.5km NE Coastal) *49.30699, -0.04382* **Camping Les Falaises, Route de la Corniche, 14510 Gonneville-sur-Mer [02 31 24 81 09; fax 02 31 28 04 11; camping.lesfalaises@voila.fr; www.lesfalaises.com]** Fr D513 take D163; site clearly sp close to Auberville. Lge, pt sl, pt shd, wc; chem disp (wc); shwrs inc; el pnts (4-6A) €3.90-4.60 (poss v long lead req); snacks; shop; gas; htd pool; playgrnd; 30% statics; dogs €2.50; poss cr. "Nice site, different areas sep by trees; most pitches sl & poss uneven; pleasant, helpful staff; gd, clean facs, red low ssn." ♦ 1 Apr-15 Oct. € 18.15   2009*

HOULGATE *3D1* (1km E Urban) *49.29223, -0.07428* **Camp Municipal des Chevaliers, Chemin des Chevaliers, 14510 Houlgate [02 31 24 37 93; camping-chevaliers.houlgate@ orange.fr; www.ville-houlgate.fr]** Fr Deauville take D513 SW twds Houlgate; 500m after 'Houlgate' town sp, turn L & foll camping sps to site, 250m after Camping de la Vallée. Lge, mkd pitch, pt sl, pt terr, unshd; wc (some cont); shwrs inc; el pnts (6-10A) €3-5; tradsmn; sand beach, fishing & boating 800m; 70% statics; dogs €0.80; Eng spkn; adv bkg (rec high ssn); v quiet. "Well-kept site; pleasant warden; facs simple but adequate & clean; sep area for tourers nr ent; attractive town; excel." ♦ 1 Apr-30 Sep. € 9.80   2010*

HOULGATE *3D1* (1km E Coastal) *49.29390, -0.06820* **Camping La Vallée, 88 Rue de la Vallée, 14510 Houlgate [02 31 24 40 69; fax 02 31 24 42 42; camping.lavallee@ wanadoo.fr; www.campinglavallee.com]** Exit junc 29 or 29a fr A13 onto D45 to Houlgate. Or fr Deauville take D513 W. Before Houlgate sp, turn L & foll sp to site. Lge, hdg/mkd pitch, pt sl, terr, pt shd; htd wc; chem disp; mv service pnt; some serviced pitches; shwrs inc; el pnts (6A) inc; gas; lndtte (inc dryer); supmkt; tradsmn; rest, snacks; bar; playgrnd; 2 pools (1 htd, covrd); paddling pool; waterslide; sand beach 900m; lake fishing 2km; tennis; cycle hire; golf 1km; games rm; wifi; entmnt; TV rm; 30% statics; dogs €5; Eng spkn; adv bkg (fee); ccard acc; red low ssn; CKE/CCI. "Superb, busy site; friendly recep; clean san facs; some pitches poss sm for lge o'fits; sep area m'vans." ♦ ltd 1 Apr-15 Oct. € 44.80   2013*

See advertisement on next page

HOUMEAU, L' see Rochelle, La *7A1*

HOUPLINES see Armentières *3A3*

HOURTIN *7C1* **Aire Naturelle de Camping l'Acacia, Route de Carcans, 33990 (Gironde) [05 56 73 80 80 06 72 94 12 67 (mob); camping.lacacia@ orange.fr; www.campinglacacia.com]** Fr Carcans on main rd to Hourtin, sp for site about 5km. Turn off rd on left and travel for 1.5km. Sm, v lge pitches, pt shd; wc; shwrs; el pnts inc; tradsmn; snacks; bar; cooking facs; playgrnd; lakes with beaches 5km; beach 16km; games area; games room; bicycles; twin axles acc; adv bkg; red low ssn; "Site well maintained; immac san facs; owner very helpful, ltd Eng; volleyball; table tennis; v lge field; quiet peaceful site; great for families and couples; excel" Apr-Sep. € 20.20   2013*

CAMPING YELLOH!VILLAGE LA VALLEE****

Yelloh!Village La Vallée offers you camping and caravanning pitches, comfortable rental accommodations and various activities for the whole family. 10 minutes from the Normandy Landing Beaches.

88 route de la Vallée, 14510 HOULGATE, Calvados - Normandie
www.campinglavallee.co.uk - camping.lavallee@wanadoo.fr - Tel: 0033 2 31 24 40 69

HOURTIN *7C1* (1.5km W Rural) *45.17919, -1.07502*
Camping Les Ourmes, 90 Ave du Lac, 33990 Hourtin Port [05 56 09 12 76; fax 05 56 09 23 90; info@lesourmes.com; **www.lesourmes.com**] Fr vill of Hourtin (35km NW Bordeaux), foll sp Houtin Port. In 1.5km, L at sp to site. Lge, mkd pitch, pt shd; wc; chem disp; mv service pnt; baby facs; shwrs inc; el pnts (6A) inc; gas; lndtte; shops 1.5km; tradsmn; rest, snacks, bar 1.5km; BBQ; playgrnd; pool; lake sw 1km; sand beach (sea) 10km; watersports; fishing; horseriding; games rm; entmnt; TV; 50% statics; dogs €2; phone; bus; poss cr in ssn; Eng spkn; adv bkg; quiet; CKE/CCI. "Excel for family holiday; Lake Hourtin shallow & vg for bathing, sailing etc; vg beaches nrby; nr Les Landes & Médoc vineyards." 27 Apr-22 Sep.
€ 41.10   2013*

"I need an on-site restaurant"
We do our best to make sure site information is correct, but it is always best to check any must-have facilities are still available or will be open during your visit.

HOURTIN *7C1* (10km W Coastal) *45.22296, -1.16472*
Camping La Côte d'Argent, Rue de la Côte d'Argent, 33990 Hourtin-Plage [05 56 09 10 25; fax 05 56 09 24 96; info@camping-cote-dargent.com; www.camping-cote-dargent.com] On D1215 at Lesparre-Médoc take D3 Hourtin, D101 to Hourtin-Plage, site sp. V lge, mkd pitch, pt sl, some terr, shd; wc; chem disp; mv service pnt; baby facs; fam bthrm; shwrs inc; el pnts (10A) inc; lndtte (inc dryer); ice; shop; rest, snacks; bar; BBQ; playgrnd; 3 htd, pools (1 covrd); waterslide; jacuzzi; huge sand beach 300m; watersports; lake sw & fishing 4km; horseriding; cycle hire; games area; games rm; wifi; entmnt; 30% statics; dogs €5.50; phone; Eng spkn; adv bkg; quiet; ccard acc; red low ssn/long stay; CKE/CCI. "Pleasant, peaceful site in pine trees & dunes; poss steel pegs req; conv Médoc region chateaux & vineyards; ideal for surfers & beach lovers." ♦ 14 May-18 Sep.
€ 53.00 (CChq acc)   2011*

See advertisement opposite

HOURTIN PLAGE see Hourtin *7C1*

HUANNE MONTMARTIN see Baume les Dames *6G2*

FRANCE

HUELGOAT *2E2* (3km E Rural) *48.36275, -3.71532*
**FFCC Camping La Rivière d'Argent, La Coudraie,
29690 Huelgoat [02 98 99 72 50; fax 02 98 99 90 61;
campriviere@orange.fr; www.larivieredargent.com]**
Sp fr town cent on D769A sp Poullaouen & Carhaix. Med,
some hdg/mkd pitch, shd; wc; chem disp; mv service pnt; shwrs
inc; el pnts (6-10A) €3.60-4.30; lndtte; shops 3km; rest, snacks,
playgrnd, pool, tennis & entmnt high ssn; dogs €1.60; adv bkg;
quiet; red long stay/low ssn. "Lovely wooded site on rv bank;
some rvside pitches; helpful owner; ltd facs low ssn; gd walks
with maps provided; Shwrs and cabinas locked overnight;
water not V hot, san facs well maintained" 10 Apr-12 Oct.
€ 15.50   2012*

HUELGOAT *2E2* (800m W Rural) *48.36388, -3.76361* **Camp
Municipal du Lac, Le Faô, 29690 Huelgoat [02 98 99 78 80;
fax 02 98 99 75 72; mairie.huelgoat@wanadoo.fr]** Fr cent
of Huelgoat foll unnumbered rd W sp La Feuillée/Brest; foll
site sp. Med, pt hdstg pitch, pt shd; wc; chem disp; shwrs inc;
el pnts (3-10A) €2.10; lndry rm; shops 600m; rest, bar 500m;
playgrnd; htd pool adj; dogs €1.20; no adv bkg; quiet; no ccard
acc; CKE/CCI. "Peaceful site at end of lake (no sw); gd size
pitches; gd san facs; gd walking." Jul-Aug. € 11.40   2009*

HUISSEAU SUR COSSON see Blois *4G2*

HUMES JORQUENAY see Langres *6F1*

HYERES *10F3* (4km E Coastal) *43.12050, 6.18464* **Camping
Port Pothuau, 101 Chemin des Ourlèdes, 83400 Hyères
[04 94 66 41 17; fax 04 94 66 33 09; pothuau@free.fr;
www.campingportpothuau.com]** Fr Hyères E twds Nice on
D98, turn R on D12 sp Salins d'Hyère. Site 2nd on R. Lge, mkd
pitch, shd; wc; some serviced pitches; shwrs; el pnts (6-10A)
inc (check rev pol/earth & poss long lead req); gas; lndtte;
shop; rest, snacks; bar; playgrnd; pool; paddling pool; sand
beach 1km; tennis; games area; cycle hire; TV; 90% statics;
dogs €3; red low ssn. "Nr interesting town of Hyères;
excursions to peninsula of Giens; basic facs; vg." 3 Apr-17 Oct.
€ 36.00   2010*

HYERES *10F3* (8km E Rural) *43.13017, 6.21650* **Camping
De La Pascalinette, 1800 Ancien Chemin de Heyeres, BP
19, 83250 La Londe-les-Maures [04 94 66 82 72; resa@
lapscalinette.fr; www.lapscalinette.fr or www.var-
camping.eu]** Site sp on D98 E of Hyères. Lge, mkd pitch, shd;
wc; baby facs; shwrs inc; el pnts (10A) inc; gas; lndtte; shop;
rest, snacks; BBQ; playgrnd; htd pool; paddling pool; sand/
shgl beach 3km; games rm; entmnt; wifi; TV; statics; dogs €4
adv bkg; CKE/CCI. "V gd site in a great location; gd pool." ♦
1 Apr-30 Sep. € 39.00   2011*

FRANCE

HYERES *10F3* (8km E Coastal) *43.12240, 6.23542* **Camping Les Moulières, 15, chemin de la Garenne, 83250 La Londe-les-Maures [04 94 01 53 21; fax 04 94 01 53 22; camping.les. moulieres@wanadoo.fr; www.campinglesmoulieres.com]** On D98, in cent La Londe-les-Maures turn S at traff lts. After 1km turn R over white bdge & foll rd for 1km. Camping sp on R. Lge, pt shd; wc; baby facs; shwrs inc; el pnts (6A) €5; lndtte; shop; rest, snacks; bar; playgrnd; sand beach 800m; wifi; entmnt; TV; dogs €3.50; poss cr; adv bkg rec high ssn; quiet. "Pleasant, shd pitches; gd." ♦ 14 Jun-6 Sep. € 24.50   2008*

HYERES *10F3* (8km E Coastal) *43.1186, 6.24693* **Miramar Camping, 1026 Blvd Louis Bernard, 83250 La Londes-les-Maures [04 94 66 80 58 or 04 94 66 83 14; fax 04 94 66 80 98; camping.miramar.lalonde@wanadoo.fr; www.provence-campings.com/azur/miramar]** On D98 in cent of La Londes-les-Maures, turn S at traff lts; in 1km turn R over white bdge & foll rd for 1.5km dir Port Miramar; site on R 150m bef port. Lge, hdg/mkd pitch, shd; wc; chem disp; shwrs inc; el pnts (4-10A) €4.50-6.50; lndtte; v sm shop & 2km; rest, snacks; bar; sand beach 200m; games rm; 25% statics; no dogs; phone; bus 2km; poss cr; Eng spkn; quiet; ccard acc; CKE/CCI. "Vg shade; beach, port, rests & shops 200m, but food shops 2km; vg marina; excel site out of ssn; vg" ♦ ltd 1 May-30 Sep. € 22.00   2013*

HYERES *10F3* (4km SE Coastal) *43.05611, 6.14750* **Campéole Camping Eurosurf, Plage de la Capte, 83400 Hyères [04 94 58 00 20; fax 04 94 58 03 18; eurosurf@ campeole.com; www.camping-hyeres.com or www. campeole.com]** Fr A8 take A57 as far as Hyères, foll sps to Giens & Les Iles, site is just outside La Capte vill on L on D97. V lge, mkd pitch, pt sl, pt shd; wc; chem disp; mv service pnt; baby facs; shwrs inc; el pnts (10A) inc; gas; lndtte; shop; tradsmn; rest, snacks; bar; no BBQ; playgrnd; sand beach adj; watersports; diving cent; 50% statics; dogs €3.90; phone; poss cr; no adv bkg; some rd noise; ccard acc; red low ssn. "Some areas of soft sand where pitches not mkd; excel for watersports; gd location." ♦ ltd 13 Mar-3 Nov. € 43.00   2010*

See advertisement on pages 14 & 15

HYERES *10F3* (5km SE Coastal) *43.10103, 6.16955* **Camping Domaine du Ceinturon III, Rue du Ceinturon, L'Ayguade, 83400 Hyères [04 94 66 32 65; fax 04 94 66 48 43; contact@ceinturon3.fr; www.ceinturon3.fr]** Fr Hyères take L'Ayguade rd sp airport. At T-junc in L'Ayguade turn R. Site 400m twd Hyères harbour & adj airport on D42. Fr NE on D42 drive thro L'Ayguade, turn R at traff lts just after end of vill sp. Lge, hdg/mkd pitch, shd; htd wc (some cont); chem disp; serviced pitch; shwrs inc; el pnts (6-10A) €3-4; gas; lndtte (inc dryer); shop high ssn; tradsmn; rest, snacks; bar; playgrnd; htd pool; paddling pol; beach adj, tennis; wifi; TV rm; 15% statics; dogs €3.85; phone; bus; poss cr; Eng spkn; adv bkg ess Jul/Aug; quiet but some daytime noise fr adj airport; no ccard acc; CKE/ CCI. "Excel, popular, busy site; sm pitches; helpful owners; excel cycle paths in area. ♦ 27 Mar-30 Sep. € 23.10   2010*

HYERES *10F3* (8km S Coastal) *43.04100, 6.14340* **Camping La Presqu'île de Giens, 153 Route de la Madrague, Giens, 83400 Hyères [04 94 58 22 86; fax 04 94 58 11 63; info@ camping-giens.com; www.camping-giens.com]** Fr Toulon A570 dir Hyères. Thro palm-lined main street in Hyères dir Giens-les-Iles & foll sp to La Capte & Giens past airport on L, thro La Capte, turn R at rndabt to site on L, sp. Lge, pt sl, terr, pt shd; htd wc; mv service pnt; baby facs; shwrs inc; el pnts (15A) €5; gas; lndtte (inc dryer); shop; tradsmn; snacks; playgrnd; sand beach 600m; fishing & boat excursions; cycle hire; games area; games rm; wifi; entmnt; TV; 75% statics; dogs €3; poss cr; adv bkg; quiet; red low ssn. "Sm pitches, layout cramped; access to pitches awkward/steep lge o'fits; sister site La Tour Fondue has easier access; ltd water pnts; gd clean san facs; pleasant, helpful staff." ♦ 2 Apr-9 Oct. € 23.90 (CChq acc)   2011*

HYERES *10F3* (9km S Coastal) *43.02980, 6.15490* **Camping La Tour Fondue, Ave des Arbanais, 83400 Giens [04 94 58 22 86; fax 04 94 58 11 63; info@camping-latourfondue.com; www.camping-latourfondue.com]** D97 fr Hyères, site sp. Med, hdg pitch, pt sl, pt terr, pt shd; wc; chem disp; mv service pnt; shwrs inc; el pnts (6A) €4.70; lndtte; rest, snacks; bar; beach adj; games area; entmnt; some statics; dogs €2.90 (not allowed on beach); no adv bkg; ccard acc. "Pleasant, sister site of Camping Presqu'île de Giens with easier access." 28 Mar-1 Nov. € 20.90   2008*

HYERES *10F3* (13km S Coastal) *43.04156, 6.12799* **Camping International, 1737 Route de la Madrague, Presqu'ile de Giens, 83400 Hyères [04 94 58 90 16; fax 04 94 58 90 50; thierry.coulomb@wanadoo.fr; www.international-giens. com]** S fr Hyères on D97 dir Giens, once past La Capte foll sp La Bergerie & La Madrague, site sp. Lge, mkd pitch, hdstg, terr, pt shd; wc; chem disp; mv service pnt; baby facs; shwrs inc; el pnts (6A) €5; gas; lndtte (inc dryer); shop; tradsmn; rest, snacks; bar; no BBQ; playgrnd; htd pool; paddling pool; adj; sand beach 400m; tennis adj; watersports; windsurfing tuition; ski-diving; horseriding; solarium; wifi; entmnt; 60% statics; no dogs; Eng spkn; adv bkg; quiet; CKE/CCI. "Excel family site; many activities for all ages; gd beach; gd walking." 26 Mar-5 Nov. € 38.50   2010*

HYERES *10F3* (6km W Rural) *43.11442, 6.05609* **FLOWER Camping Le Beau Vezé, Route de la Moutonne, 83320 Carqueiranne [tel/fax 04 94 57 65 30; info@camping-beauveze.com; www.camping-beauveze.com or www.flowercampings.com]** Fr Toulon take D559 E dir Carqueiranne. Approx 2km after Le Pradet turn L onto D76 twd La Moutonne. Site on R in 1.5km. Med, mkd pitch terr, pt shd; htd wc (some cont); chem disp; baby facs; shwrs inc; el pnts (4A) €4; gas; lndtte; shop; rest, snacks; bar; BBQ (gas only); playgrnd; 2 pools; paddling pool; waterslide; beach 4km; tennis; cycle hire; wifi; entmnt; few statics; dogs €2.50; poss cr; adv bkg; quiet but some rd noise; red low ssn; ccard not acc. "Poss diff access some pitches for lge o'fits; no twin-axle c'vans; mkt Thu." ♦ 1 May-15 Sep. € 29.00 (CChq acc)   2010*

IGOVILLE see Pont de l'Arche *3D2*

ILE BOUCHARD, L' *4H1* (500m N Urban) *47.12166, 0.42857* **Camping Les Bords de Vienne, 4 Allée du Camping, 37220 L'Ile-Bouchard [02 47 95 23 59; fax 02 47 98 45 29; info@campingbordsdevienne.com; www. campingbordsdevienne.com]** On N bank of Rv Vienne 100m E of rd bdge nr junc of D757 & D760. Med, mkd pitch, pt sl, pt shd; wc; chem disp; shwrs inc; el pnts (6-16A) €3.50; gas; lndtte; supmkt adj; snacks; playgrnd; pool & tennis 500m; rv sw adj; wifi; some statics; dogs €1.50; phone adj; Eng spkn; adv bkg; quiet; ccard acc; red low ssn/long stay; CKE/CCI. "Lovely, clean rvside site; attractive location; poss itinerants; conv Loire chateaux." 1 Apr-30 Oct. € 24.50   2013*

ILE DE RE Campsites in towns on the Ile de Ré are listed together at the end of the French site entry pages.

ILE D'OLERON Campsites in towns on the Ile d'Oléron are listed together at the end of the French site entry pages.

ILLIERS COMBRAY *4E2* (2km SW Rural) *48.28667, 1.22697* **FLOWER Camping Le Bois Fleuri, Route de Brou, 28120 Illiers-Combray [02 37 24 03 04; infos@camping-chartres.com; www.camping-chartres.com or www. flowercampings.com]** S on D921 fr Illiers for 2km twd Brou. Site on L. Med, hdg pitch, some hdstg, pt shd; htd wc; chem disp; some serviced pitches; shwrs inc; el pnts (6A) €3.50; gas; lndtte; shop 2km; rest 2km; snacks; bar; htd pool 200m; paddling pool; fishing adj;games area; entmnt; 30% statics; dogs €1.50; poss cr; adv bkg; quiet; some rd noise; red low ssn; CKE/CCI. "Many pitches wooded & with flowers; popular NH; excel san facs, poss insufficient cleaning (2010); ltd water/ el pnts; uneven grnd makes access diff; gd security; excel cycle path to vill." 2 Apr-29 Oct. € 17.00 (CChq acc)   2011*

See advertisement on pages 32 & 33

INGRANDES *4H2* (1km N Rural) *46.88700, 0.58800* **Camping Le Petit Trianon de St Ustre, 1 Rue du Moulin de St Ustre, 86220 Ingrandes-sur-Vienne [05 49 02 61 47; fax 05 49 02 68 81; petit-trianon@camp-in-ouest.com; www.petit-trianon.com or www.les-castels.com]** Leave A10/E5 at Châtellerault Nord exit 26 & foll sp Tours. Cross rv heading N on D910 twd Tours & Dangé-St Romain. At 2nd traff lts in Ingrandes (by church), turn R. Cross rlwy line & turn L at site sp in 300m. After 1.5km turn R at site sp, site at top of hill. NB Site ent narr, poss diff lge o'fits. Med, mkd pitch, pt sl, pt shd; wc; chem disp; mv service pnt; baby facs; shwrs inc; el pnts (10A) inc; gas; lndtte (inc dryer); shop; tradsmn; rest; snacks; bar; BBQ; playgrnd; htd pool; paddling pool; games area; cycle hire; tennis 1.5km; rv fishing 3km; horseriding 1km; wifi; entmnt; games/TV rm; dogs €2.10; quiet; some rlwy noise at night; Eng spkn; adv bkg; ccard acc; red low ssn; CKE/CCI. "Lovely site in chateau grnds; charming old buildings; gd sized pitches; friendly, helpful staff; excel facs." 9 Apr-30 Sep. € 30.30 SBS - L07   2010*

See advertisement on inside back cover

ISIGNY SUR MER *1D4* (500m NW Rural) *49.31872, -1.10825* **Camping Le Fanal, Rue du Fanal, 14230 Isigny-sur-Mer [02 31 21 33 20; fax 02 31 22 12 00; info@camping-lefanal. com; www.30]** Fr N13 exit into Isigny, site immed N of town. Foll sp to 'Stade' in town, (just after sq & church on narr street just bef R turn). Med, hdg/mkd pitch, pt shd; wc; chem disp; mv service pnt; shwrs inc; el pnts (16A) inc (long cable poss req); lndtte; shop; snacks; bar; playgrnd; pool; aquapark; sand beach 10km; lake fishing adj; horseriding; tennis; games area; games rm; entmnt; TV; 50% statics; dogs €4; phone; adv bkg; quiet; ccard acc; red low ssn; CKE/CCI. "Friendly staff; poss boggy in wet weather; vg site." 1 Apr-30 Sep. € 30.50   2012*

ISLE ET BARDAIS see Cérilly *4H3*

ISLE JOURDAIN, L' *7A3* (500m N Rural) *46.24065, 0.68502* **Camp Municipal du Lac de Chardes, Rue de Chardes, 86150 L'Isle-Jourdain [05 49 48 72 46 or 05 49 48 70 54 (Mairie); fax 05 49 48 84 19; isle-jourdain. mairie@wanadoo.fr]** Fr N147 in Lussac take D11 S to L'Isle-Jourdain. Site sp on R. Sm, mkd pitch, terr, pt shd; wc (some cont); shwrs inc; el pnts inc; lndtte; shops, rest, snacks, bar 700m; tradsmn; htd pool adj; sand beach & fishing 100m; tennis; dogs; adv bkg; quiet. "Lovely peaceful site nr rv; excel san facs; sh walk to Rv Vienne; site yourself, warden calls am & pm." 1 May-31 Aug. € 9.20   2009*

ISLE SUR LA SORGUE L' *10E2* (2km E Rural) *43.91451, 5.07181* **Camping Airotel La Sorguette, 871 Route d'Apt, 84800 L'Isle-sur-la-Sorgue [04 90 38 05 71; fax 04 90 20 84 61; info@camping-sorguette.com; www. camping-sorguette.com]** Fr L'Isle-sur-la-Sorgue take D901 twd Apt, on L site in 1.5km, sp. Med, hdg/mkd pitch; wc; chem disp; mv service pnt; shwrs inc; el pnts (10A) €4.70; gas; lndtte; shop; tradsmn; rest nr; BBQ; playgrnd; beach adj; trout-fishing adj; canoeing (not for faint-hearted!); tennis; games area; wifi; 10% statics; dogs €3.50; adv bkg; poss cr; Eng spkn; quiet; ccard acc; red low ssn; CKE/CCI. "Lovely, well-run site; useful & busy; friendly, helpful staff; beware low trees; dated but clean san facs; rvside walk to attractive town; Sun mkt (shuttle fr site); highly rec." ltd 15 Mar-15 Oct. € 22.80   2013*

ISLE SUR LA SORGUE L' *10E2* (4km E Rural) *43.90345, 5.09083* **Aire Naturelle de Sorgiack, Route de Lagnes, 84800 L'Isle-sur-la-Sorgue [04 90 38 13 95; http:// sorgiack.e-monsite.com/]** 2.5km SE of L'Isle-sur-la-Sorgue on D901; take D99 twd Lagnes; site sp. Sm, mkd pitch, hdstg, pt shd; htd wc; chem disp; shwrs inc; el pnts (10A) inc; lndtte; shop, rest, snacks, bar 2.5km; BBQ; htd, covrd pool 4km; paddling pool; sw 3km; rv & fishing 300m; games rm; dogs free; phone; adv bkg; quiet; ccard not acc; CKE/CCI. "Delightful site in cherry orchard; take care drainage channel at ent; friendly hosts; excel facs; gd mkts in area, esp antiques; vg touring base." 15 Mar-15 Oct. € 16.50   2010*

FRANCE

⊞ **ISLE SUR LA SORGUE L'** *10E2* (5km E Rural) *43.91931, 5.11683* **Aire Communale Vergnes, Ave Robert Garcin, 84800 Fontaine-de-Vaucluse [04 90 20 31 79]** D25 fr L'Isle-sur-la-Sorgue; site on R after vill boundary; or on D24 fr Cavaillon then join D25. Sm, hdstg, unshd; wc; own san; chem disp; shops, rest, snacks & bar 500m; dogs; poss cr; ccard acc. "Pleasant location next to rv; mainly for m'vans but spaces for c'vans; gd NH." € 3.00 2008*

ISLE SUR LA SORGUE L' *10E2* (5km NW Rural) *43.92980, 4.98320* **Camping Domaine du Jantou, 535 Chemin des Coudelières, 84250 Le Thor [04 90 33 90 07; fax 04 90 33 79 84; jantou@franceloc.fr; www.campings-franceloc.fr]** Exit A7 at Avignon Nord onto D942 sp Carpentras. Turn S onto D6; in 8km join D901 E sp Le Thor. Site sp bef vill. App fr E fork R at sharp bend, thro town gate take L turn after passing church & L. Med, hdg/mkd pitch, pt shd; wc; chem disp; mv service pnt; baby facs; shwrs inc; el pnts (16A) €4; lndtte (inc dryer); shop; snacks; playgrnd; 2 htd, covrd pools; paddling pools; waterslide; cycle hire; games area; games rm; wifi; wifi; entmnt; TV rm; 60% statics; dogs €5; phone; Eng spkn; adv bkg; quiet; ccard acc; CKE/CCI. "Vg, attractive site by Rv Sorgue; sm pitches, ltd access; conv Avignon, Camargue." ◆ ltd 3 Apr-26 Sep. € 26.50 2010*

ISLE SUR LA SORGUE, L' *10E2* (5km E Rural) *43.91087, 5.10665* **Camping La Coutelière, Route de Fontaine-de-Vaucluse, 84800 Lagnes [04 90 20 33 97; fax 04 90 20 27 22; info@camping-lacouteliere.com; www.camping-lacouteliere.com]** Leave L'Isle-sur-la-Sorgue by D900 dir Apt, fork L after 2km sp Fontaine-de-Vaucluse. Site on L on D24 bef ent Fontaine. Med, hdg pitch, shd; wc; shwrs inc; el pnts (10A) €4.40; lndtte; rest, snacks; bar; playgrnd; pool; canoeing nr; tennis, entmnt; 40% statics; dogs €3.50; phone; Eng spkn; adv bkg; quiet; red low ssn; CKE/CCI. "Attractive, busy site by rv; walking/cycling on canal towpath; 2km easy cycle ride to Fontaine; ltd san facs low ssn; poss unkempt low ssn; lovely area; gd." ◆ 1 Apr-15 Oct. € 20.90 2010*

ISLE SUR LE DOUBS, L' *6G2* (400m N Rural) *47.45288, 6.58338* **Camping Les Lûmes, 10 Rue des Lûmes, 25250 L'Isle-sur-le-Doubs [tel/fax 03 81 92 73 05; contact@les-lumes.com; www.les-lumes.com]** Well sp fr town edge on D683 bef rv bdge. Med, pt shd; wc; chem disp; shwrs; el pnts (10A) €3.30 (long lead req & poss rev pol); shop; tradsmn; playgrnd; rv sw; 20% statics; dogs €1.20; poss cr; Eng spkn; adv bkg; CKE/CCI. "Busy site; san facs need upgrade & up steps; gd." 1 May-30 Sep. € 11.70 2009*

ISLE SUR SEREIN, L' *4G4* (Rural) *47.58011, 4.00561* **Camp Municipal Le Parc de Château, 89440 L'Isle-sur-Serein [03 86 33 93 50 or 03 86 33 80 74 (Mairie); fax 03 86 33 91 81; mairie-isle-sur-serein@wanadoo.fr; www.isle-sur-serein.com]** Exit A6 junc 21 or 22 & foll sp Noyers or Montréal & L'Isle-sur-Serein on D117. Or fr Avallon, take D957 twd Sauvigny-le-Bois; then D86 to L'Isle-sur-Serein; site on L on ent to vill. Sm, hdg/mkd pitch, some hdstg, shd; wc; chem disp; shwrs inc; el pnts (6A) 2.60; lndtte; shop 1km; rest; bar; BBQ; playgrnd; tennis & boating adj; games area; some statics; dogs; adv bkg; quiet, some rd noise; CKE/CCI. "Basic, well-kept site in attractive area; helpful warden; dated facs; site poss poorly maintained end of ssn (2010); vg." 15 Apr-30 Sep. € 8.20 2010*

⊞ **ISOLA** *9D4* (1km NW Rural) *44.18881, 7.03957* **Camping Lac des Neiges, Quartier Lazisola, 06420 Isola [04 93 02 18 16; fax 04 93 02 19 40]** SE fr St Etienne-de-Tinée on D2205. site on R after approx 13km, site sp. Med, hdg/mkd pitch, hdstg, pt shd; htd wc; chem disp; mv service pnt; shwrs inc; el pnts (3-6A) inc; lndtte; shops 1km; tradsmn; playgrnd; sw pool 1km; lake adj; fishing; kayaking; tennis; ski stn nr; TV rm; 25% statics; dogs €1; phone; Eng spkn; adv bkg; quiet; ccard not acc; CKE/CCI. ◆ € 20.20 2008*

"Satellite navigation makes touring much easier"

Remember most sat navs don't know if you're towing or in a larger vehicle – always use yours alongside maps and site directions.

ISPAGNAC *9D1* (1km W Rural) *44.37232, 3.53035* **FFCC Camp Municipal Le Pré Morjal, 48320 Ispagnac [04 66 44 23 77 or 04 66 44 20 50 (Mairie); fax 04 66 44 23 84; contact@ lepremorjal.fr; www.lepremorjal.fr]** On D907B 500m W of town, turn L off D907B & then 200m on R, sp. Med, hdg pitch, pt shd; htd wc; chem disp; mv service pnt; baby facs; shwrs inc; el pnts (10-16A) €3; lndtte; shops 200m; rest, snacks; BBQ area; playgrnd; pool 50m inc; paddling pool; rv sw 200m; games area; games rm; wifi; TV; dogs €1.20; quiet; red low ssn. "Lovely family site; gd sized pitches on rocky base, poss muddy when wet; friendly staff; gd rvside walks; vg base for Tarn & Joute Gorges; early ssn poss unkempt & irreg cleaning of san facs (2010)." ◆ 1 Apr-31 Oct. € 16.00 2010*

ISQUES see Boulogne sur Mer *3A2*

ISSAMBRES, LES see St Aygulf *10F4*

ISSENDOLUS see Gramat *7D4*

ISSOIRE *9B1* (2.5km E Rural) *45.55113, 3.27423* **FFCC Camp Municipal du Mas, Ave du Dr Bienfait, 63500 Issoire [04 73 89 03 59 or 04 73 89 03 54 (LS); fax 04 73 89 41 05; camping-mas@wanadoo.fr; www.camping-issoire.com]** Fr Clermont-Ferrand S on A75/E11 take exit 12 sp Issoire; turn L over a'route sp Orbeil; at rndabt, take 1st exit & foll site sp. Med, unshd; htd wc (mostly cont); chem disp; mv service pnt; baby facs; shwrs inc; el pnts (10-13A) €3.35 (long lead poss req); gas; lndtte; supmkt 500m; shops 2km; tradsmn; snacks; playgrnd; fishing in adj lake; tennis 500m; wifi; TV rm; 5% statics; dogs €0.50; phone; poss cr; some Eng spkn; adv bkg (rec high ssn); quiet but some rd noise; ccard acc; red long stay/low ssn; CKE/CCI. "Lovely, well-kept, basic site in park-like location; lge pitches; helpful warden; new, modern san facs; site poss boggy after rain; conv A75; excel touring base or NH." ◆ 1 Apr-3 Nov. € 21.30 2013*

FRANCE

ISSOIRE *9B1* (6km SE Rural) *45.50908, 3.2848* **FFCC Camping Château La Grange Fort, 63500 Les Pradeaux [04 73 71 05 93 or 04 73 71 02 43; fax 04 73 71 07 69; chateau@lagrangefort.com; www.lagrangefort.com]** S fr Clermont Ferrand on A75, exit junc 13 onto D996 sp Parentignat. At 1st rndabt take D999 sp St Rémy-Chargnat (new rd); at next rndabt take 1st exit onto D34 & foll sp to site on hill-top. Narr app rd & narr uphill ent. Med, hdg/mkd pitch, shd; htd wc; chem disp; mv service pnt; baby facs; sauna; shwrs inc; el pnts (6A) €3.50; lndtte; gas; shop in vill; tradsmn; rest in chateau; snacks; bar; playgrnd; 2 pools (1 htd, covrd; paddling pool; rv fishing; tennis; canoe & mountain bike facs; internet; TV rm; some statics; dogs €3; phone; Eng spkn; adv bkg (fee); quiet; ccard acc; red low ssn; CKE/CCI. "Pleasant, peaceful Dutch-run site in chateau grounds with views; excel san facs but long walk fr some pitches & ltd low ssn; some sm pitches; most pitches damp & gloomy under lge trees & muddy after rain; mosquito problem on shadiest pitches; ltd parking at recep; conv A75; gd." 1 Apr-30 Oct. € 26.75   2010*

ISSOIRE *9B1* (11km S Rural) *45.47373, 3.27161* **Camping Les Loges, 63340 Nonette [04 73 71 65 82; fax 04 73 71 67 23; les.loges.nonette@wanadoo.fr; www.lesloges.com]** Exit 17 fr A75 onto D214 sp Le Breuil, dir Nonette. Turn L in 2km, cross rv & turn L to site. Site perched on conical hill. Steep app. Med, hdg/mkd pitch, pt shd; wc; chem disp; child/baby facs; shwrs inc; el pnts (10A) €3.50; gas; lndtte; shop; tradsmn; rest, snacks; bar; htd pool; rv sw & fishing adj; entmnt; TV; 30% statics; dogs €1.80; quiet; red low ssn; CKE/CCI. "Friendly site; conv Massif Central & A75; gd NH" Easter-10 Sep. € 20.90   2012*

ISTRES *10F2* (6km S Coastal) *43.46958, 5.02420* **Camping Félix de la Bastide, Allée Plage d'Arthur, 13920 St Mitre-les-Remparts [04 42 80 99 35; fax 04 42 49 96 85; info@campingfelix.com; www.campingfelix.com]** S fr Istres on D5 to end of built up area. At 2nd rndabt turn L (foll sp); approx 2km on L. Med, hdg/mkd pitch, pt shd; wc; chem disp; shwrs inc; el pnts (6A) €3 (poss rev pol); gas 2km; lndry service; shop; tradsmn; rest; bar; BBQ; playgrnd; pool; paddling pool; shgl beach & lake adj; watersports; games area; wifi; dogs €1.50; phone; poss cr; Eng spkn; adv bkg; poss noise fr dogs barking & club nrby; red long stay. "Spacious pitches; poss strong winds; friendly Dutch owners; san facs poss stretched high ssn; beautiful scenery." 1 Apr-1 Nov. € 17.50   2009*

JABLINES see Meaux *3D3*

JARD SUR MER *7A1* (Urban/Coastal) *46.42098, -1.56997* **Chadotel Camping L'Océano d'Or, Rue Georges Clémenceau, 85520 Jard-sur-Mer [02 51 33 65 08 or 02 51 33 05 05 (LS); fax 02 51 33 94 04; chadotel@wanadoo.fr; www.chadotel.com]** D21 & D19 to Jard-sur-Mer. Site sp. Lge, hdg/mkd pitch, pt shd; htd wc; chem disp; baby facs; shwrs inc; el pnts (6A) inc; gas; lndtte; shop; snacks; bar; playgrnd; htd pool; waterslide; sand beach 900m; tennis; cycle hire; entmnt; dogs €3; adv bkg; quiet; red long stay/low ssn; CKE/CCI. "Vg; gd walking." ♦ 7 Apr-22 Sep. € 31.00   2011*

JARD SUR MER *7A1* (2km NE Rural) *46.42624, -1.56564* **Camping La Mouette Cendrée, Les Malécots, 85520 St Vincent-sur-Jard [02 51 33 59 04; fax 02 51 20 31 39; camping.mc@orange.fr; www.mouettecendree.com]** Fr Les Sables-d'Olonne take D949 SE to Talmont-St-Hilaire; then take D21 to Jard-sur-Mer; at rndabt stay on D21 (taking 2nd exit dir La Tranche-sur-Mer & Maison-de- Clemanceau); in 500m turn L onto D19 sp St Hilaire-la-Forêt & foll site sps. Site on L in 700m. Med, hdg/mkd pitch, pt shd; wc (some cont); chem disp; shwrs inc; el pnts (10A) inc; lndtte; supmkt nr; tradsmn; BBQ (gas/elec); playgrnd; pool; waterslide; paddling pool; sand beach 2km; fishing; windsurfing 2km; horseriding 500m; golf 10km; cycle hire; games rm; wifi; entmnt; 30% statics; dogs €3; no c'vans/m'vans over 7.50m high ssn; Eng spkn; adv bkg; ccard acc; red low ssn; CKE/CCI. "Busy site high ssn; gd pitches; welcoming, helpful owners; san facs poss stretched when site full; vg pool; gd woodland walks & cycle routes nr; mkt Mon." ♦ 1 Apr-31 Oct. € 27.50 SBS - A20   2011*

JARD SUR MER *7A1* (1km E Coastal) *46.41433, -1.55181* **Camp Municipal du Pied Girard, 9 Rue de la Forêt, 85520 St Vincent-sur-Jard [tel/fax 02 51 33 65 11; camping.pg@wanadoo.fr]** Fr Talmont-St Hilaire take D21 S to Jard-sur-Mer & on to St Vincent-sur-Jard. Site sp fr edge of vill. Med, mkd pitch, sl, pt shd; wc; chem disp (wc); shwrs inc; el pnts (10A) inc; lndtte; shop & rest 1km; snacks & bar 500m; playgrnd; sand beach 500m; dogs; poss cr; adv bkg; ccard acc. "Vg site in pine wood; uneven pitches; gd clean san facs." 15 Apr-15 Sep. € 14.00   2009*

"There aren't many sites open at this time of year"

If you're travelling outside peak season remember to call ahead to check site opening dates – even if the entry says 'open all year'.

JARD SUR MER *7A1* (SE Coastal) *46.41088, -1.57269* **Chadotel Camping La Pomme de Pin, Rue Vincent Auriol, 85520 Jard-sur-Mer [02 51 33 43 85 or 02 51 33 05 05 (LS); fax 02 51 33 94 04; chadotel@wanadoo.fr; www.chadotel.com]** Foll sp fr town. Lge, hdg/mkd pitch, shd; htd wc; serviced pitches; baby facs; shwrs inc; el pnts (6A) inc; gas; lndtte; shop; snacks; bar; BBQ (gas); playgrnd; pool; waterslide; sand beach 150m; games rm; entmnt; TV rm; mainly statics; dogs €3; Eng spkn; adv bkg; quiet; ccard acc; CKE/CCI. "Well-maintained site; early arr rec; ltd facs low ssn; vg." ♦ 7 Apr-22 Sep. € 32.50   2011*

FRANCE

JARD SUR MER 7A1 (2km SE Coastal) 46.41980, -1.52580
Chadotel Camping La Bolée d'Air, Route du Bouil, Route de Longeville, 85520 St Vincent-sur-Jard [02 51 90 36 05 or 02 51 33 05 05; fax 02 51 33 94 04; info@chadotel.com; www.chadotel.com] Fr A11 junc 14 dir Angers. Take N160 to La Roche-sur-Yon & then D747 dir La Tranche-sur-Mer to Moutier-les-Mauxfaits. At Moutiers take D19 to St Hilaire-la-Forêt & then L to St Vincent-sur-Jard. In St Vincent turn L by church sp Longeville-sur-Mer, site on R in 1km. Lge, hdg/mkd pitch, pt shd; htd wc; chem disp (wc); serviced pitches; baby facs; sauna; jaccuzi; shwrs inc; el pnts (6A) inc; gas; lndtte; shop; snacks; bar; BBQ (charcoal/gas); playgrnd; 2 pools (1 htd covrd); paddling pool; waterslide; whirlpool; sand beach 900m; tennis; cycle hire; wifi; entmnt; games/TV rm; 25% statics; dogs €3.20; no c'vans/m'vans over 8m high ssn; Eng spkn; adv bkg; rd noise & poss fr late night entmnt; ccard acc; red long stay/low ssn; mkt Sun; CKE/CCI. "Popular, v busy site high ssn; access some pitches poss diff lge o'fits; excel." ♦
7 Apr-22 Sep. € 30.00 SBS - A31   2011*

See advertisement above

"That's changed – Should I let The Club know?"

If you find something on site that's different from the site entry, fill in a report and let us know. See www.caravanclub.co.uk/europereport.

JARD SUR MER 7A1 (S Coastal) 46.41184, -1.58355
Camping La Ventouse, Rue Pierre Curie, 85520 Jard-sur-Mer [02 51 33 58 65 or 02 51 33 40 17 (Mairie); fax 02 51 33 91 00; info@campings-parfums-ete.com; www.campings-parfums-ete.com] Fr Talmont St-Hilaire take D21 to Jard turn R on app & foll sps. Look for blue sp Port de Plaisance; pass Camping Les Ecureuils, site shortly after. Lge, pt sl, pt shd; wc; baby facs; shwrs inc; el pnts (10A) €3.60 (poss rev pol & poss long lead req); gas; lndtte; shops, rest, snacks, bar 500m; playgrnd; htd pool; paddling pool; sand beach 500m; some statics; dogs €1.90; poss cr; quiet. "Gd site with plenty of pine trees; adj vill & harbour." 1 May-30 Sep.
€ 15.60   2008*

JARD SUR MER 7A1 (S Coastal) 46.41169, -1.57932
Camping Le Bosquet, Rue de l'Océan, 85520 Jard-sur-Mer [02 51 33 56 57 or 02 51 33 06 72; fax 02 51 33 03 69; info@campings-parfums-ete.com; www.campings-parfums-ete.com] Exit D949 at Talmont St Hilaire onto D21 to Jard-sur-Mer. In town look for sp Port de Plaisance, pass Camping Les Ecureuils & La Ventouse on L & take 2nd rd, Rue de l'Ocean, to R. Sm, pt sl, shd; wc; baby facs; shwrs inc; el pnts (10A) €3; lndry rm; shops adj; playgrnd; pool 1.5km; sand beach; tennis adj; entmnt; 30% statics; dogs €1.50; Eng spkn; adv bkg; quiet. "Gd location nr harbour; picturesque boating cent with man-made harbour; few touring pitches." 1 Apr-30 Sep.
€ 14.00   2009*

JARD SUR MER 7A1 (1km SW Coastal) 46.41130, -1.58960
Camping Les Ecureuils, Route des Goffineaux, 85520 Jard-sur-Mer [02 51 33 42 74; fax 02 51 33 91 14; ecureuils@franceloc.fr; www.camping-ecureuils.com] Fr Talmont St Hilaire take D21 to Jard-sur-Mer. Turn R app vill, site sp. Lge, mkd pitch, shd; wc; chem disp; serviced pitches; baby facs; shwrs inc; el pnts (10A) inc (rev pol); gas; lndtte; sm shop & 1km; snacks; bar; BBQ (gas); playgrnd; htd indoor pool, outdoor pool; rocky beach 400m, sand beach 1km; tennis adj; TV rm; 33% statics; no dogs; poss cr; Eng spkn; adv bkg; quiet; ccard acc; red low ssn; CKE/CCI. "Gd site with helpful staff; gd rds & lighting; gd, clean san facs; night security guard; boating cent & man-made tidal harbour 1km." ♦ 9 Apr-25 Sep.
€ 29.80   2008*

JARGEAU see Châteauneuf sur Loire 4F3

JARNAC see Cognac 7B2

JAULNY 5D2 (500m S Rural) 48.96578, 5.88524 Camping La Pelouse, 54470 Jaulny [tel/fax 03 83 81 91 67; info@campingdelapelouse.com; www.campingdelapelouse.com] SW fr Metz on D657, cross rv at Corny-sur-Moselle onto D6/D1; in 1.5km turn R onto D952 dir Waville & Thiaucourt-Regniéville; in 6km turn L onto D28 dir Thiaucourt-Regniéville; cont on D28 to Jaulny; site sp to L in Jaulny. Med, sl, pt shd; wc; chem disp; shwrs inc; el pnts (6A) €4; lndtte; tradsmn; rest; bar; BBQ; playgrnd; htd pool; rv sw 100m; fishing; many statics; dogs €2; rlwy noise, TGV trains pass nrby; CKE/CCI. "Vg site; friendly owner and staff; basic san facs, poss stretched high ssn; no fresh or waste water facs for m'vans; conv NH." 1 Apr-30 Sep. € 20.60   2012*

JAUNAY CLAN *4H1* (1km N Rural) *46.68302, 0.35851*
Camping La Croix du Sud, Route de Neuville, 86130 Jaunay-Clan [05 49 62 58 14 or 05 49 62 57 20; fax 05 49 62 57 20; camping@la-croix-du-sud.fr; www.la-croix-du-sud.fr] On A10 fr N or S, take Futuroscope exit. Take last exit at rndabt sp Neuville & after 1.5km turn L onto D20/D62. Site on L immed after x-ing m'way. Also clearly sp fr D910 at traff lts in Jaunay-Clan. Lge, hdg/mkd pitch, pt shd, 20% serviced pitches; wc; chem disp; mv service pnt; shwrs inc; el pnts (10A) €3; gas; lndtte; shop & hypmkt 1km; tradsmn; rest, snacks; bar; playgrnd; pool; entmnt; 15% statics; dogs; Eng spkn; adv bkg; some rd noise & dogs barking; ccard acc; red low ssn/CKE/CCI. "Conv position & NH; clean, tidy site; 3km to Futuroscope - mini-bus fr site high ssn; 10km to Poitiers; san facs poss unclean; poss itinerants." ♦ 1 Feb-11 Nov. € 10.70   2009*

JAUNAY CLAN *4H1* (6km NE Rural) *46.69807, 0.42619*
Camp Municipal du Parc, Rue du Parc 86130 Dissay [05 49 62 84 29 or 05 49 52 34 56 (Mairie); fax 05 49 62 58 72; accueil@dissay.fr; www.dissay.fr] N on D910 Poitiers dir Châtellerault. At rndabt turn R on D15 sp Dissay. Turn R ent Dissay & site on R 50m. Sm, mkd pitch, shd; wc; chem disp; shwrs inc; el pnts (10A) €2.65 (poss rev pol); lndry rm; shop 100m; tradsmn; playgrnd; dogs; Eng spkn; quiet; CKE/CCI. "Friendly warden; clean modern facs; conv Futuroscope; 15thC chateau adj; gate locked 2200 but can request key; gd." ♦ 19 Jun-29 Aug. € 10.10   2013*

JAUNAY CLAN *4H1* (7km NE Rural) *46.72015, 0.45982*
FLOWER Camping Lac de St Cyr, 86130 St Cyr [05 49 62 57 22; fax 05 49 52 28 58; contact@camping lacdesaintcyr.com; www.campinglacdesaintcyr.com or www.flowercampings.com] Fr A10 take Châtellerault Sud exit & take D910 dir Poitiers; at Beaumont turn L at traff lts for St Cyr; foll camp sp in leisure complex (Parc Loisirs) by lakeside - R turn for camping. Or fr S take Futuroscope exit to D910. Lge, hdg/mkd pitch, pt sl, pt shd; wc; chem disp; mv service pnt; serviced pitches; shwrs inc; el pnts (10A) inc (poss rev pol); gas; lndtte (inc dryer); shop; rest, snacks; bar; BBQ; playgrnd; sand beach & lake sw; watersports; canoeing; sailing; fishing; tennis; boat & cycle hire; fitness rm; games rm; games area; golf course adj; wifi; entmnt; TV rm; 15% statics; dogs €3; no c'vans/m'vans over 8m; poss cr; some Eng spkn; adv bkg; quiet, some rlwy sound; ccard acc; red low ssn/long stay; CKE/CCI. "Excel, well-kept site in leisure complex; lovely setting by lake; gd sized pitches; helpful recep; gd, clean san facs, poss stretched high ssn; gd rest; some pitches poss diff lge o'fits; rec long o'fits unhitch at barrier due R-angle turn; public access to site fr lakeside beach; Futuroscope approx 13km; highly rec; excel site; gd size pitches; friendly helpful staff" ♦ 1 Apr-30 Sep. € 24.00 SBS - L09   2013*

See advertisement on pages 32 & 33

JAUNAY CLAN *4H1* (2km SE Urban) *46.66401, 0.39466*
Kawan Village Le Futuriste, Rue du Château, 86130 St Georges-les-Baillargeaux [05 49 52 47 52; fax 05 49 37 23 33; camping-le-futuriste@wanadoo.fr; www.camping-le-futuriste.fr] On A10 fr N or S, take Futuroscope exit 28; fr toll booth at 1st rndabt take 2nd exit. Thro tech park twd St Georges. At rndabt under D910 take slip rd N onto D910. After 150m exit D910 onto D20, foll sp. At 1st rndabt bear R, over rlwy, cross sm rv & up hill, site on R. Med, hdg/mkd pitch, pt shd; htd wc; chem disp; mv service pnt; some serviced pitches; shwrs inc; el pnts (6A) €4.40 (check earth & poss rev pol); gas; lndtte (inc dryer); shop; hypmkt 2km; tradsmn; rest, snacks high ssn or 500m; bar; BBQ; playgrnd; 2 htd pools (1 covrd); waterslide; lake fishing; games area; games rm; entmnt; wifi; TV rm; some statics; dogs €2.50; poss cr; Eng spkn; adv bkg; quiet; ccard acc; red low ssn; CKE/CCI. "Lovely, busy, secure site; well-kept; friendly, helpful family owners; vg clean facs, ltd low ssn - facs block clsd 2200-0700; vg pool; vg for families; ideal touring base for Poitiers & Futuroscope (tickets fr recep); vg value, especially in winter; conv a'route; excel" ♦ € 35.50 (3 persons) (CChq acc)   2013*

See advertisement on next page

JAUNAY CLAN *4H1* (4km SE Rural) *46.65464, 0.37786* **Camp Municipal Parc des Ecluzelles, Rue Leclanché, 86360 Chasseneuil-du-Poitou [05 49 62 58 85 / 05 49 52 77 19 (Ls); maire@mairie-chasseneuildupoitou.fr; www.ville-chasseneuil-du-poitou.fr]** Fr A10 or D910 N or Poitiers take Futuroscope exit 28/18. Take Chasseneuil rd, sp in town to site. Sm, mkd pitch, some hdstg, pt shd; wc; chem disp; mv service pnt; shwrs inc; el pnts (8A) inc; shop 1km; tradsmn; BBQ; playgrnd; htd pool adj inc; dogs; poss cr; no adv bkg; quiet; red low ssn. "Vg, clean site; lge pitches; conv Futuroscope; immac; v simple site with the v gd san facs, helpful staff; gd bus service into the city" ♦ 4 Apr-26 Sep. € 18.75   2013*

JAUSIERS see Barcelonnette *9D4*

JAVRON LES CHAPELLES *4E1* (1km SW Rural) **Camp Municipal, Route de Bagnoles, 53250 Javron-les-Chapelles [02 43 03 40 67; fax 02 43 03 43 43; col360@live.co.uk]** Foll sp fr town cent on N12 twds Mayenne. sm, pt terr, unshd; wc; chem disp; shwrs inc; el pnts (10A) €5; shops 1km; rest 3km; snacks 3km; bar 3km; BBQ charcoal & gas; pool 10km; Eng spkn; "v gd site" Apr-Sep. € 15.00   2013*

JOIGNY *4F4* (1.5km N Rural) *47.98143, 3.37439* **FFCC Camp Municipal, 68 Quai d'Epizy, 89300 Joigny [03 86 62 07 55; fax 03 86 62 08 03; villedejoigny3@wanadoo.fr; www.joigny.com]** Fr A6 exit junc 18 or 19 to Joigny cent. Fr cent, over brdg, turn L onto D959; turn L in filter lane at traff lts. Foll sp to site. Sm, hdg pitch, hdstg, pt shd; wc; chem disp; mv service pnt; shwrs; el pnts (10A) €2.07; shops 500m; rest, bar 3km; pool 4km; sw 3km; fishing adj; tennis; horseriding; many statics; poss cr; quiet; CKE/CCI. "V busy site; liable to flood in wet weather; helpful warden; interesting town." 1 Apr-31 Oct. € 5.11   2008*

CAMPING LE FUTURISTE ★★★★

F-86130 St. Georges les Baillargeaux. Tel: 05 49 52 47 52
Fax: 05 49 37 23 33 • www.camping-le-futuriste.fr
Reservations recommended from June till August. 2 km from
FUTUROSCOPE. At the river CLAIN, beautiful panorama on the park
and the CLAIN-valley. Heated sanitary installations. 2 heated
swimming pools with free
waterslide. Quiet site with ample
entertainment and excursions
programme. Fishing on site.
Motorway A10, exit FUTUROSCOPE,
follow signs to park entrance,
then follow St. Georges.

JOIGNY *4F4* (8km E Urban) *47.95646, 3.50657* **Camping Les Confluents, Allée Léo Lagrange, 89400 Migennes [tel/fax 03 86 80 94 55; planethome2003@yahoo.fr; www.les-confluents.com]** A6 exit at junc 19 Auxerre Nord onto N6 & foll sp to Migennes & site, well sp. Med, hdg/mkd pitch, hdstg, pt shd; htd wc (some cont); chem disp; mv service pnt; baby facs; fam bthrm; shwrs inc; el pnts (6-10A) €3.50-4.90; gas; lndtte; shop; rest, snacks; bar; BBQ; playgrnd; pool; watersports 300m; lake sand beach; canoe, cycle hire; games area; entmnt; TV rm; 8% statics; dogs €0.90; phone; bus 10 mins; quiet; red long stay; ccard acc; CKE/CCI. "Friendly, family-run, clean site nr canal & indust area; no twin-axles; medieval castle, wine cellars, potteries nrby; walking dist to Migennes; mkt Thurs; excel." ♦ ltd 1 Apr-1 Nov. € 24.00   2012*

JOIGNY *4F4* (12km SE Rural) *47.92802, 3.51932* **Camp Municipal Le Patis, 28 Rue du Porte des Fontaines, 89400 Bonnard [03 86 73 26 25 or 03 86 73 26 91 (Mairie); mairie.bonnard@wanadoo.fr; www.tourisme-yonne.com]** Exit A6 junc 19; N on N6 dir Joigny; in 8.5km at Bassou turn R & foll sp Bonnard. Site on L immed after rv bdge. Sm, mkd pitch, shd; wc; chem disp; shwrs inc; el pnts (10A) €2.20; lndtte; shop 1km; rest 500m; playgrnd; rv sw, fishing, boating, tennis adj; dogs; phone; poss cr; adv bkg; quiet. "Super little site on banks of Rv Yonne; well-kept; friendly, helpful warden; immac san facs; gd security; vg fishing." ♦ ltd 15 May-30 Sep. € 7.80   2013*

JOIGNY *4F4* (3.5km NW Rural) *47.99550, 3.34468* **Camp Municipal L'Ile de L'Entonnoir, Route de St Aubin-sur-Yonne, 89410 Cézy [03 86 63 17 87 or 03 86 63 12 58 (LS); fax 03 86 63 02 84; info@camping-cezy.com]** Site sp off N6 N & S-bound (Joigny by-pass). Thro St Aubin vill, cross bdge over Rv Yonne. Site on L bank of rv. Or exit N6 Joigny by-pass at N of rndabt onto N2006 twd St Aubin. After St Aubin turn R to Cézy & site in 1km. Rec app via St Aubin - narr bdge 3.5t weight restriction. Alt route for lge outfits, N6 onto N2006 to St Aubin, sp in vill. Sm, mkd pitch, pt shd; wc; shwrs inc; chem disp; mv service pnt; el pnts (6-10A) inc; lndtte; shop 1km; rest, snacks, bar, BBQ; playgrnd; rv sw & beach 100m; dogs €1; Eng spkn; adv bkg; quiet; CKE/CCI. "V pleasant, quiet site; helpful staff; conv Chablis area; barrier clsd 2200." 1 May-31 Oct. € 15.40   2012*

JOINVILLE *6E1* (6km E Rural) *48.43018, 5.23077* **Camp Municipal La Petite Suisse, Rue de Mélaire, 52230 Poissons [03 23 94 55 75 or 03 25 94 51 78 (Mairie); www.tourisme-hautemarne.com]** Fr N67 to Joinville 'Centre Ville'; then onto D60 dir Thonnance; after supmkt turn R onto D427 to Poissons; site on L as exit vill. Site sp in vill. Sm, pt sl, pt shd; htd wc (cont); own san; chem disp (wc); shwrs inc; el pnts (6A) inc; shop 1km; rest 6km, snacks, bar 1km; BBQ; 20% statics; dogs; quiet; CKE/CCI. "Delightful, peaceful, basic CL-type site in great location; warden calls eves or call at No 7 in same rd to pay; dated but immac san facs; easy to find." 1 May-15 Sep.   2012*

JONQUIERES see Orange *10E2*

JONZAC *7B2* (Urban) *45.44366, -0.43358* **Camp Municipal des Mégisseries, Parc des Expositions, 17500 Jonzac [05 46 48 49 29; fax 05 46 48 51 07; tourisme.Jonzac@wanadoo.fr; www.jonzac.fr]** Fr A10/N137 to Bordeaux exit D699 to Jonzac, site well sp in all dirs in town past school & sports complex, adj Rv Seugne - foll sp to football stadium. Sm, mkd pitch, all hdstg, pt shd; wc; own san; mv service pnt; shwrs; el pnts (6-16A) €3.45-5.15; lndtte; shop 2km; tradsmn; pool adj; dogs €1.10; lake fishing 1km; poss cr - pitches close; adv bkg. "Excel situation; pleasant warden; facs clean but basic; pitches well-drained in wet at end ssn but site liable to sudden flooding; public footpath thro site; leisure complex nr." ♦ 1 Apr-30 Oct. € 8.50   2008*

JONZAC *7B2* (2km SW Rural) *45.42916, -0.44833* **FFCC Camping Les Castors, 8 Rue Clavelaud, St Simon de Bordes, 17500 Jonzac [05 46 48 25 65; fax 05 46 04 56 76; camping-les-castors@wanadoo.fr; www.campingcastors.com]** Fr Jonzac take D19 S twds Montendre, after approx 2km, immed after ring rd rndabt, turn R into minor rd. Site ent adj. Med, hdg pitch, hdstg, pt shd; wc; chem disp; mv service pnt; shwrs inc; el pnts (6-10A) €4.20-4.90; lndtte; tradsmn; snacks; bar; playgrnd; covrd pool; rv sw 2km; entmnt; TV; 50% statics; dogs €1.60; no twin-axles; quiet; red low ssn; CKE/CCI. "Peaceful, friendly, well-maintained site; gd facs; excel pool; gd." ♦ 15 Mar-30 Oct. € 13.40   2008*

JOSSELIN 2F3 (1.5km W Rural) 47.95230, -2.57338 **FFCC Camp Municipal du Bas de la Lande, 56120 Guégon [02 97 22 22 20 or 06 24 59 48 26 (mob); campingbasdelalande@wanadoo.fr; www.guegon.fr]** Exit N24 by-pass W of town sp Guégon; foll sp 1km; do not attempt to cross Josselin cent fr E to W. Site on D724 just S of Rv Oust (canal). Med, hdg pitch, terr, pt shd; wc; chem disp; mv service pnt; baby facs; shwrs inc; el pnts (6A) €3.20; lndtte; shops 2km; bar high ssn; playgrnd; dogs €0.50; Eng spkn; quiet but rd noise; ccard not acc; red low ssn/CKE/CCI. "Vg, clean san facs; site rds steep; pleasant walks; walk to Josselin, chateau & old houses; gd cycling." ♦ 1 Apr-31 Oct. € 11.40 2011*

JUGON LES LACS 2E3 (S Rural) 48.40166, -2.31678 **Camping au Bocage du Lac, 22270 Jugon-les-Lacs [02 96 31 60 16; fax 02 96 31 75 04; contact@campingjugon.com; www. campingjugon.com]** Bet Dinan & Lamballe by N176. Foll `Camping Jeux' sp on D52 fr Jugon-les-Lacs. Situated by lakes, sp fr cent of Jugon. Lge, pt sl, pt shd; wc; mv service pnt; baby facs; shwrs inc; el pnts (5A) €3.10; lndtte; shops adj; tradsmn; bar; playgrnd; htd pool; paddling pool; waterslide; fishing & watersports in lake/rv adj; games area; games rm; entmnt; TV; some statics; dogs €2.50; adv bkg; red low ssn. "Well-situated nr pretty vill; many sports & activities; vg, modern san facs; vg, attractive site." 5 Apr-27 Sep. € 19.80 2008*

JULLOUVILLE see Granville 1D4

"I like to fill in the reports as I travel from site to site"

You'll find report forms at the back of this guide, or you can fill them in online at www.caravaclub.co.uk/europereport.

JUMIEGES 3C2 (3km S Rural) 49.41164, 0.84624 **Camping Boucles de la Seine-Normande, Base de Plein Air du Parc de Brotonne, 76480 Jumièges [02 35 37 31 72; fax 02 35 37 99 97; jumieges@ucpa.asso.fr]** E fr Le Havre on N15; foll D131 S fr Yvetot by-pass twd Pont de Brotonne (toll). Bef bdge turn SE on D982, thro Le Trait. Turn S on D143 at Yainville for Jumièges. Cont thro Jumièges on D65, site well sp on R on lake in 3km. Fr S fr Bourg-Achard take D313 twd Pont de Brotonne; turn off after bdge on D982 as above. Med, hdg pitch, pt sl, shd; wc; chem disp; mv service pnt; shwrs inc; el pnts (6A) (check pol); lndtte; shops 3km; tradsmn; rest, snacks, bar 3km; playgrnd; lake sw adj; watersports; tennis; games area; archery; golf, 30% statics; dogs €1.05; barrier clsd 2200-0800; poss cr; adv bkg; quiet; red long stay; CKE/CCI. "Lovely area; helpful warden; lge pitches; poss itinerants low ssn; san facs stretched high ssn; gd." ♦ ltd 1 Apr-31 Oct. 2009*

JUMIÈGES 3C2 (1km E Rural) 49.43490, 0.82970 **Camping de la Forêt, Rue Mainberte, 76480 Jumièges [02 31 87 05 21 or 02 35 37 93 43; fax 02 31 87 09 67 or 02 35 37 76 48; info@campinglaforet.com; www.campinglaforet.com]** Exit A13 junc 25 onto D313/D490 N to Pont de Brotonne. Cross Pont de Brotonne & immed turn R onto D982 sp Le Trait. In Le Trait turn R onto D143 sp Yainville & Jumièges. In Jumièges turn L at x-rds after cemetary & church, site on R in 1km. NB M'vans under 3.5t & 3m height can take ferry fr Port Jumièges - if towing do not use sat nav directions. Med, hdg/mkd pitch, pt shd; htd wc; chem disp; mv service pnt; baby facs; shwrs inc; el pnts (10A) €4.50 (poss rev pol); gas; lndtte (inc dryer); sm shop; tradsmn; snacks; rest & bar nr; BBQ (charcoal/gas/elec); playgrnd; htd pool; paddling pool; lake beach 2.5km; watersports; fishing; tennis; cycle hire; games area; wifi; games/TV rm; 30% statics; dogs free; no c'vans/m'vans over 7m high ssn; phone; bus to Rouen; poss cr; adv bkg; quiet; ccard accp red low ssn. "Nice site, well-situated in National Park; busy; some sm pitches; gd, clean san facs but poss stretched high ssn; interesting vill; conv Paris & Giverny; gd walking, cycling; ferries across Rv Seine; gd for dogs; children loved it" ♦ 1 Apr-30 Oct. € 22.00 (CChq acc) SBS - N15 2013*

KAYSERSBERG 6F3 (Urban) 48.13580, 7.26233 **Aire Communale Erlenbad, Rue Rocade, 68240 Kaysersberg [03 89 78 11 12 (Mairie)]** On D415 foll sp P1, site clearly visible. Med, hdstg, unshd; wc; chem disp; mv service pnt; shop, rest, snacks, bar 300m; poss cr; some rd noise. "Gd NH; m'vans only; pay at machine." 15 Mar-31 Dec. € 6.00 2008*

KAYSERSBERG 6F3 (1km NW Rural) 48.14899, 7.25405 **Camp Municipal, Rue des Acacias, 68240 Kaysersberg [tel/ fax 03 89 47 14 47 or 03 89 78 11 11 (Mairie); camping@ ville-kaysersberg.fr; www.camping-kaysersberg.com]** Fr A35/N83 exit junc 23 onto D4 sp Sigolsheim & Kaysersberg; bear L onto N415 bypass dir St Dié; site sp 100m past junc with D28. Or fr St Dié on N415 over Col du Bonhomme; turn L into Rue des Acacias just bef junc with D28. Med, hdg/ mkd pitch, pt shd; wc; chem disp; shwrs inc; baby facs; el pnts (8-13A) inc (may need cable); gas; lndtte; shops 150m; supmkt 700m; bread del; pool 1km; playgrnd; fishing & tennis adj; wifi; TV; dogs €2 (no dogs Jul/Aug); quiet. "Excel, well-kept, busy site; rec arr early high ssn; many gd sized pitches; friendly staff; clean san facs; rv walk to lovely town, birth place Albert Schweitzer; many mkd walks/cycle rts; Le Linge WWI battle grnd nr Orbey; Excel site" 1 Apr-30 Sep. € 23.15 2013*

KAYSERSBERG 6F3 (7km NW Rural) 48.18148, 7.18449 **Camping Les Verts Bois, 3 Rue de la Fonderie, 68240 Fréland [03 89 47 57 25 or 06 81 71 89 38 (mob); douault. gildas@orange.fr; www.camping-lesvertsbois.com]** Sp off N415 Colmar/St Dié rd bet Lapoutroie & Kaysersberg. Site approx 5km after turn fr main rd on D11 at far end of vill. Turn L into rd to site when D11 doubles back on itself. Sm, pt sl, terr, pt shd; htd wc; chem disp; shwrs inc; el pnts (6-10A) €2.70-3.20; gas; lndtte (inc dryer); shop & bank in vill; tradsmn; rest (open to non-campers); snacks, bar; BBQ; dogs €0.70; poss cr; Eng spkn; poss cr; adv bkg; quiet; ccard acc; red low ssn; CKE/CCI. "Lovely site in beautiful, peaceful setting adj rv; friendly welcome; excel." 1 Apr-31 Oct. € 10.50 2011*

KESKASTEL

Between the Forest, the dunes and the ocean

Yelloh! village SYLVAMAR ★★★★★ - Avenue de l'Océan - 40530 Labenne Océan
Tel. :+33 (0)5 59 45 75 16 - Fax :+33 (0)5 59 45 46 39 - E-mail : camping@sylvamar.fr - Web : www.sylvamar.fr

KESKASTEL 5D3 (700m NE Rural) 48.97684, 7.05354 **Camp Municipal Les Sapins, Centre des Loisirs, 67260 Keskastel [03 88 00 19 25 (Mairie); fax 03 88 00 34 66; camping. keskastel@orange.fr; www.keskastel.fr/camping-municpal-les-sapins]** Exit A4 junc 42 fr N or junc 43 fr S dir Sarralbe/Keskastel. In Keskastel cent turn onto D338 twds Herbitzheim. Cont for approx 1km; turn R for approx 400m; site on L, well sp on lakeside. Med, hdg/mkd pitch, pt shd; htd wc (some cont); chem disp; shwrs inc; el pnts (10A) €4.30 (poss rev pol); lndtte; shop 1km; tradsmn; rest, snacks; bar; BBQ; playgrnd; sand beach adj; lake sw & fishing; tennis nr; 60% statics; dogs; phone; poss cr; some Eng spkn; quiet; adv bkg; ccard acc; CKE/CCI. "Relaxing location; conv m'way; spacious pitches; helpful warden lives above recep, ring bell if office clsd; basic san facs, ltd low ssn; office poss clsd Sun morn; barrier clsd 2300; vg;" ♦ 1 Jan-21 Feb, 8 Mar-23 Oct, 8 Nov-18 Dec. € 15.45   2013*

LABENNE 8E1 (4km S Coastal) 43.56950, -1.46033 **Airotel Camping Lou Pignada, 741 Rue de la Plage, 40440 Ondres [05 59 45 30 65; fax 05 59 45 25 79; info@camping-loupignada.com; www.camping-loupignada.com]** Turn R off N10 at N end of Ondres vill, sp Ondres-Plage, site immed after rlwy level x-ing on L. Med, shd; wc; baby facs; shwrs; el pnts (6-8A) €5; gas; lndtte; shop; rest, snacks; bar; BBQ; playgrnd; pool; paddling pools; waterslide; spa/jacuzzi; sand beach 1.7km; games area; tennis; cycle hire; horseriding; golf nrby; entmnt; TV; 50% statics; dogs €5; adv bkg; red low ssn; v quiet; ccard acc. "Tight manoeuvring amongst trees." 21 Mar-30 Sep. € 27.00   2008*

⊞ **LABENNE** 8E1 (4km S Rural) 43.56470, -1.45240 **Camping du Lac, 518 Rue de Janin, 40440 Ondres [05 59 45 28 45 or 06 80 26 91 51 (mob); fax 05 59 45 29 45; contact@camping-du-lac.fr; www.camping-du-lac.fr]** Fr N exit A63 junc 8 onto N10 S. Turn R just N of Ondres sp Ondres-Plage, at rndabt turn L & foll site sp. Fr S exit A63 junc 7 onto N10 to Ondres. Cont thro town cent & turn L at town boundary, then as above; tight turns thro housing est. Med, hdg/mkd pitch, terr, pt shd; htd wc; chem disp; baby facs; shwrs inc; el pnts (10A) €4; gas; lndtte; shop 500m; rest in ssn; snacks; bar; playgrnd; pool in ssn; sand beach 4km; fishing; boating; games area; entmnt; cycle hire; 60% statics; dogs €5; phone; twin-axles acc low ssn only; Eng spkn; adv bkg (dep); quiet; red long stay/low ssn; CKE/CCI. "Peaceful, charming lakeside site by lake; gd welcome; helpful staff; ltd facs low ssn; vg pool; excel." ♦ € 30.00   2011*

LABENNE 8E1 (3km SW Coastal) 43.59533, -1.45651 **Camping Village Le Sylvamar, Ave de l'Océan, 40530 Labenne [05 59 45 75 16; fax 05 59 45 46 39; camping@sylvamar.fr; www.sylvamar.fr or www.yellohvillage.co.uk]** Exit A63 junc 7 onto D85; then take N10 N to Labenne; turn L onto D126; site sp. Lge, hdg/mkd pitch, pt shd; wc; chem disp; serviced pitches; sauna; spa; baby facs; shwrs inc; el pnts (10A) inc; lndtte (inc dryer); shop adj; tradsmn; rest, snacks; bar; BBQ; pool complex; paddling pool; waterslide; playgrnd; creche; sand beach 800m; fitness rm; beauty cent; wifi; entmnt; 50% statics; adv bkg; appt; Eng spkn; red low ssn; ccard acc; CKE/CCI. "Site amongst pine trees; sandy pitches; gd location; v gd facs." ♦ 9 Apr-25 Sep. € 43.00   2011*

See advertisement above

LABENNE 8E1 (2km W Coastal) 43.59547, -1.45695 **Camping La Côte d'Argent, 60 Ave de l'Océan, 40530 Labenne-Océan [05 59 45 42 02; fax 05 59 45 73 31; info@camping-cotedargent.com; www.camping-cotedargent.com]** Fr N10 take D126 W fr Labenne to Labenne-Plage & site. Lge, hdg/mkd pitch, shd; htd wc; 10% serviced pitches; mv service pnt; chem disp; baby facs; shwrs inc; el pnts (6A) €3.95; gas 300m; lndtte (inc dryer); shop 200m; tradsmn, rest, snacks, bar high ssn; BBQ; playgrnd; 2 pools (1 htd, covrd); paddling pool; sand beach 900m; fishing 300m; cycle hire; games area; games rm; archery; tennis 500m; wifi; entmnt; TV rm; 50% statics; dogs €2.50; poss cr; Eng spkn; adv bkg rec; quiet; ccard acc; CKE/ CCI. "Nice pool area; children's park; gd cycle tracks; ltd facs low ssn; conv Biarritz; excel for family hols." ♦ ltd 1 Apr-31 Oct. € 25.75 (CChq acc)   2010*

LABLACHERE 9D2 (4km NW Rural) 44.47955, 4.17096 **Camping Le Ch'ti Franoi, Route de Planzolles, 07230 Lablachère [04 75 36 64 09; info@campinglechti.com; www.campinglechti.com]** Exit D104 to Lablachère; cont thro vill onto D4 dir Planzolles; site on L in 4km, just bef Cédat. Sm, pt sl, pt shd; wc; chem disp (wc); shwrs inc; el pnts (3A) inc (10-16A extra); lndry rm; shop; tradsmn; rest, snacks; bar; BBQ; playgrnd; pool; entmnt; TV rm; 75% statics; dogs €4; adv bkg. "Welcoming, friendly, helpful British owners." 1 Apr-31 Oct. € 24.00   2009*

344 ⊞Site open all year   Send in your site reports by mid August 2014

LAC D'ISSARLES, LE 9C1 (2km E Rural) 44.81805, 4.05352
Camping La Plaine de la Loire, Pont-de-Laborie, 07470 Le
Lac-d'Issarlès [04 66 46 25 77 or 06 24 49 22 79 (mob); fax
04 66 46 21 55; campinglaplainedelaloire@ifrance.com;
http://campinglaplainedelaloire.ifrance.com] Fr S on N102
take D16 sp Le Lac-d'Issarles. After Coucouron (5km) site on R
after Pont-de-Laborie. Med, mkd pitch, pt shd; wc (cont); chem
disp; shwrs inc; el pnts (6A) €4; gas; lndtte; shop; tradsmn;
snacks; playgrnd; rv sw adj; games area; 5% statics; dogs
€0.80; adv bkg; quiet; CKE/CCI. "Lovely, tranquil site; long
uphill walk to lake; m'van 'aire' adj lake." ♦ 5 Jun-15 Oct.
€ 10.00   2010*

LACANAU 7C1 Camping Les Fougères, Ave de
l'Océan, 33680 Talaris [05 56 03 56 76; contact@
campinglesfougereslacanau.com; www.
campinglesfougereslacanau.com] A630 bypass exit at junc
8 sp Lacanau - Le Verdon. Med, pt shd; wc; chem disp; mv
service pnt; shwrs; el (4A) inc; tradsmn; BBQ; playgrnd; sw
2km; games area; wifi; 10% statics; dogs €2.10; twin axles;
Eng spkn; adv bkg acc; CKE/CCI; "Excel site; watersports
1.5km; tennis 9km" ♦ 1 Jun-30 Sep. € 32.85   2013*

**"We must tell The Club about
that great site we found"**
Get your site reports in by mid-August
and we'll do our best to get your updates
into the next edition of Caravan Europe.

LACANAU OCEAN 7C1 (1km N Coastal) 45.00823, -1.19322
Airotel Camping de l'Océan, 24 Rue du Repos, 33680
Lacanau-Océan [05 56 03 24 45; fax 05 57 70 01 87;
airotel.lacanau@wanadoo.fr; www.airotel-ocean.com]
On ent town at end of sq in front of bus stn turn R, fork R &
foll sp to site (next to Camping Grand Pins). Lge, pt sl, pt shd;
wc; chem disp; shwrs inc; el pnts (15A) inc; gas; lndtte; shop;
rest, snacks; bar; pool; sand beach 600m; tennis; entmnt;
fishing; watersports; cycle hire; TV; statics; dogs €4; poss cr;
adv bkg; quiet; red low ssn. "Attractive site/holiday vill in pine
woods behind sand dunes; surf school nrby; care in choosing
pitch due soft sand; gd, modern san facs; some pitches tight
access." Easter-27 Sep. € 33.00   2008*

LACANAU OCEAN 7C1 (1km N Coastal) 45.01166, -1.19305
Yelloh! Village Les Grands Pins, Plage Nord, Ave des
Grands Pins, 33680 Lacanau-Océan [05 56 03 20 77; fax
05 57 70 03 89; reception@lesgrandspins.com; www.
lesgrandspins.com or www.yellohvillage.co.uk] Fr E on
D6, on ent Lacanau-Océan, at 2nd rndabt fork R (2nd exit)
onto Voie Pénétrante Nord; foll sp 'Plage Nord' & 'Les Grands
Pins'. Site a turning to R in 1km. V lge, hdg/mkd pitch, terr,
pt shd; htd wc; serviced pitches; chem disp; mv service pnt;
baby facs; shwrs inc; el pnts (10A) inc; gas; lndtte; shop; rest,
snacks; bar; playgrnd; htd pool; sand beach 500m; cycle hire;
internet; entmnt; TV; 20% statics; dogs €4; poss cr; adv bkg
red high ssn; quiet; red low ssn; 7 nights min 13 Jul-25 Aug.
"Excel, well organised site; lge pitches; doesn't feel overcr -
even when full." 14 Apr-22 Sep. € 49.00   2011*

See advertisement on inside front cover

LACANAU OCEAN 7C1 (7km E Rural) 45.00808, -1.11230
Camping Talaris Vacances, Route de L'Océan, 33680
Lacanau [05 56 03 04 15; fax 05 56 26 21 56; www.
talaris-vacances.fr] Fr Lacanau-Océan towards Lake Lacanau,
site on R. Lge, mkd pitch, hdstg, shd; wc (some cont); chem
disp; mv service pnt; baby facs; shwrs inc; el pnts (6A) €3.90;
gas; lndtte; shop; rest, snacks; bar; BBQ area; playgrnd; pool;
waterslide; lake sw 2km; tennis; 50% statics; dogs €4; bus adj;
Eng spkn; adv bkg; some rd noise; red low ssn; CKE/CCI. "Nr
Lake Lacanau, sw & watersports; excel network cycle tracks."
♦ 4 Apr-26 Sep. € 32.00   2009*

LACAPELLE VIESCAMP 7C4 (1.6km SW Rural) 44.91272,
2.24853 Camping La Presqu'île du Puech des Ouilhes,
15150 Lacapelle-Viescamp [04 71 46 42 38 or
06 80 37 15 61 (mob); contact@cantal-camping.fr; www.
camping-lac-auvergne.com] W fr Aurillac on D120; at St Paul-
des-Landes turn S onto D53 then D18 to Lacapelle-Viescamp.
Foll sp Base de Loisirs, Plage-du-Puech des Ouilhes & Camping.
Site beside Lake St Etienne-Cantalès. Med, hdg/mkd pitch,
hdstg, pt shd; wc; chem disp; baby facs; shwrs inc; el pnts (16A)
€3; lndtte; shop 200m; rest, snacks; bar; playgrnd; pool; sand
beach adj; lake sw adj; watersports; canoeing; fishing; tennis;
games rm; some statics; dogs €2; Eng spkn; quiet; red low ssn/
long stay. "Friendly, helpful young owners; excel." ♦
15 May-15 Sep. € 16.00 (CChq acc)   2008*

FRANCE

LACAUNE *8E4* (5km E Rural) *43.69280, 2.73790* **Camping Domaine Le Clôt, Les Vidals, 81230 Lacaune [tel/ fax 05 63 37 03 59; campingleclot@orange.fr; www. pageloisirs.com/le-clot]** Fr Castres to Lacaune on D622. Cont on D622 past Lacaune then turn R onto unclassified rd to Les Vidals. Site sp 500m on L after Les Vidals. Sm, terr, pt shd; htd wc; chem disp; shwrs inc; el pnts (6-10A) €3.25-4; lndtte; shop 5km; rest, snacks; playgrnd; lake sw, fishing, sailing, windsurfing 12km; dogs €1.50; Eng spkn; quiet; CKE/ CCI. "Excel site; modern, immac san facs; gd views; gd walking in Monts de Lacaune; friendly Dutch owner; site road steep & narr; vg rest." ♦ 16 Feb-14 Dec. € 21.40   2013*

LADIGNAC LE LONG see St Yrieix la Perche *7B3*

LAFFREY see Vizille *9C3*

LAGRASSE *8F4* (1km NE Rural) *43.09516, 2.61893* **Camp Municipal de Boucocers, Route de Ribaute, 11220 Lagrasse [04 68 43 10 05 or 04 68 43 15 18; fax 04 68 43 10 41; mairielagrasse@wanadoo.fr; www. audetourisme.com]** 1km on D212 fr Lagrasse to Fabrezan (N). Sm, hdstg, pt sl, pt shd; wc; chem disp; mv service pnt; shwrs inc; el pnts (15A) €2.80; shops, rest 500m; rv sw 1km; dogs €2.10; phone; adv bkg; CKE/CCI. "At cent of 'off-the-beaten-track' beautiful touring area; helpful warden; simple but gd san facs; gd walking; o'looks superb medieval town; rec arr early." ♦ ltd 15 Mar-15 Oct. € 15.00   2012*

LAGUENNE see Tulle *7C4*

LAGUEPIE *8E4* (1km E Rural) *44.14780, 1.97892* **Camp Municipal Les Tilleuls, 82250 Laguépie [05 63 30 22 32 or 05 63 30 20 81 (Mairie); mairie.laguepie@info82.com; www.camping-les-tilleuls.com]** Exit Cordes on D922 N to Laguépie; turn R at bdge, still on D922 sp Villefranche; site sp to R in 500m; tight turn into narr lane. NB App thro Laguépie poss diff lge o'fits. Med, pt terr, pt shd; wc (some cont); shwrs inc; el pnts (10A) €2.70; shops 1km; bar/café adj; playgrnd; rv sw; canoe hire; fishing; tennis; games area; TV; 44% statics; dogs; phone; adv bkg; quiet. "Attractive setting on Rv Viaur; friendly welcome; excel playgrnd; gd touring base; conv Aveyron gorges." ♦ May-Oct. € 10.20   2012*

LAGUIOLE *7D4* (500m NE Rural) *44.68158, 2.85440* **Camp Municipal Les Monts D'Aubrac, 12210 Laguiole [05 65 44 39 72 or 05 65 51 26 30 (LS); fax 05 65 51 26 31; http://campinglesmontsdaubraclaguiole.jimdo.com]** E of Laguiole on D15 at top of hill. Fr S on D921 turn R at rndabt bef ent to town. Site sp. Med, hdg/mkd pitch, pt sl, pt shd; wc; chem disp; mv service pnt; shwrs inc; el pnts (16A) inc; lndtte; shops, rest, snacks & bar 500m; dogs; phone; quiet; CKE/CCI. "Clean & well cared for site; pleasant vill." 15 May-15 Sep. € 9.50   2011*

⊞ **LAIGNES** *6F1* (500m N Rural) **Aire Communale, Le Moulin Neuf, 21330 Laignes [03 80 81 43 03; mairie@ laignes.fr]** Fr E or W to Laignes on D965; in town foll sp 'Camping pour Camping Cars', N on D953. Sm (10 m'vans), pt shd; own san; chem disp; mv service pnt; water points; el pnts; picnic tables; shops & rest 15 min walk; m'vans only. "Free of charge; delightful site by mill-pond." 2009*

LAISSAC *7D4* (500m N Urban) *44.38500, 2.82100* **Camping Aire de Service Camping Car, 12310 Laissac [05 65 69 60 45; fax 05 65 70 75 14; mairie-de-laissac@ wanadoo.fr]** Exit N88 sp Laissac. Foll sp to site. Site adj livestock mkt. Sm, mkd pitch, hdstg, unshd; wc (some cont); chem disp; mv service pnt; lndtte; shop, bar 200m; rest, snacks 500m; phone 500m; rd noise. "Gd NH only; room for 6 m'vans only." ♦ ltd 1 Mar-30 Nov.   2008*

LAISSAC *7D4* (3km SE Rural) *44.36525, 2.85090* **FLOWER Camping La Grange de Monteillac, Chemin de Monteillac, 12310 Sévérac-l'Eglise [05 65 70 21 00 or 06 87 46 90 83 (mob); fax 05 65 70 21 01; info@ le-grange-de-monteillac.com; www.la-grange-de-monteillac.com or www.flowercampings.com]** Fr A75, at junc 42, go W on N88 twds Rodez; after approx 22km; bef Laissac; turn L twds Sévérac-l'Eglise; site sp. Med, hdg/ mkd pitch, pt sl, terr, unshd; wc; chem disp (wc); mv service pnt; shwrs inc; el pnts (6A) inc (long lead poss req); lndtte (inc dryer); rest, bar & shops high ssn; playgrnd; pool; paddling pool; tennis; horseriding; cycle hire; wifi; entmnt; TV; some statics; dogs €1.50; phone; Eng spkn; adv bkg rec high ssn; quiet; CKE/CCI. "Beautiful site." ♦ 1 May-15 Sep. € 26.90   2010*

See advertisement on pages 32 & 33

LAIVES see Sennecey le Grand *6H1*

LALINDE *7C3* (1.5km E) *44.83956, 0.76298* **Camping Moulin de la Guillou, Route de Sauveboeuf, 24150 Lalinde [05 53 57 81 60; la-guillou@wanadoo.fr; www.pays-de-bergerac.com]** Take D703 E fr Lalinde (Rv Dordogne on R) & keep strt where rd turns L over canal bdge. Site in 300m; sp. Med, shd; wc; shwrs inc; el pnts (5A) €2.60; shops 1km; tradsmn; pool; playgrnd; rv sw & fishing adj; entmnt; tennis adj; dogs €2; adv bkg. "Charming, peaceful site on bank of Rv Dordogne; lovely views; clean san facs, in need of upgrade; poss itinerants; vg." 1 May-30 Sep. € 15.00   2012*

LALINDE *7C3* (8.5km SE Rural) *44.7944, 0.8336* **Camping La Grande Veyière, Route de Cadouin, 24480 Molières [05 53 63 25 84; la-grande-veyiere@wanadoo.fr; www. lagrandeveyiere.com]** Fr Bergerac take D660 E for 19km to Port-de-Couze. Turn SW still on D660 sp Beaumont. In 6km turn L on D27. Site sp fr here. In approx 6km, ent on R. Med, hdg/mkd pitch, pt sl, terr, pt shd; wc; chem disp; baby facs; shwrs inc; el pnts (6A) €3; gas; lndtte; shop; rest, snacks; bar; BBQ (charcoal); playgrnd; pool; games area; games/TV rm; some statics; dogs €1; Eng spkn; adv bkg (rec Jul/Aug); phone; red low ssn; ccard acc; CKE/CCI. "Wooded site off beaten track, worth finding; warm welcome, owners friendly & helpful; excel facs; tractor tow avail in wet weather; excel; rec." ♦ 15 Jun-15 Sep. € 16.10   2011*

LALINDE *7C3* (4km W Urban) *44.82639, 0.70468* **Camping des Moulins, Route de Cahors, 24150 Couze-St Front [05 53 61 18 36; fax 05 53 24 99 72; camping-des-moulins@wanadoo.fr; www.campingdesmoulins.com]** Fr Lalinde take D703 dir Bergerac. In 2km turn L on D660 sp Port-de-Couze; over bdge (Dordogne Rv) into Couze. Turn R on D37 sp Lanquais, turn immed L, site sp. (NB Do not take D37E.) Sm, hdg pitch, pt sl, pt shd; wc; chem disp; mv service pnt; shwrs inc; el pnts (10A) €4.50; gas; lndtte; snacks; bar; BBQ; playgrnd; 3 pools; lake sw 3km; games area; games rm; 40% statics; dogs €2; phone adj; poss cr; Eng spkn; adv bkg; quiet; ccard acc; CKE/CCI. "Generous pitches; friendly, helpful owner; ltd facs low ssn & poss unclean; gd pools; conv Bergerac; excel." 18 Mar-5 Nov. € 29.00 (4 persons) 2011*

LALLEY *9D3* (300m S Rural) *44.75490, 5.67940* **Camping Belle Roche, Chemin de Combe Morée, 38930 Lalley [04 76 34 75 33 or 06 86 36 71 48 (mob); fax 04 76 34 75 33; camping.belleroche@gmail.com / contact@camping-belleroche.com; www.campingbelleroche.com]** Off D1075 at D66 for Mens; down long hill into Lalley. Site on R thro vill. Med, some hdg pitch, hdstg, pt sl, pt shd; wc; chem disp; mv service pnt; baby facs; shwrs inc; el pnts (10A) €4 (poss rev pol, poss long lead req); gas; lndtte; shop 500m; tradsmn; rest, snacks; bar; BBQ; playgrnd; htd pool; tennis 500m; games area; entmnt; wifi; TV rm; some statics; dogs €1.50; poss cr; adv bkg; quiet; ccard acc over €20; red low ssn; CKE/CCI. "Well-kept, scenic site; spacious pitches but little shade; friendly, welcoming owners; clean, vg modern san facs; poss stretched high ssn; pleasant pool area; nr Vercors National Park; vg walking/cycling; don't miss The Little Train of La Mure; conv NH; highly rec; Very nice site; welcoming owners" ♦ 26 Mar-15 Oct. € 29.80 2013*

LAMALOU LES BAINS *10F1* (400m NE Rural) *43.60074, 3.08314* **Camp Municipal Le Verdale, Blvd de Mourcairol, 34240 Lamalou-les-Bains [04 67 95 86 89 or 04 67 95 27 37 (LS); fax 04 67 95 64 52; camping@mairielamalou.fr; www.ot-lamaloulesbains.fr]** S fr Bédarieux on D908 twds Lamalou. Turn N off D908 at traff lts into Lamalou. At 2nd rndbt turn E foll sp to site on NE side of town. Med, mkd pitch, pt shd; htd wc; mv service pnt; shwrs; el pnts (6A) €2.30; supmkt, shop, pool, tennis & golf in town; games area; 30% statics; dogs; phone; poss cr; adv bkg rec. "Well-kept, popular site; bkg rec even low ssn; sm pitches; friendly, helpful warden; clean san facs; site popular with visitors to thermal baths nrby; easy walk to town & shops." ♦ 1 Mar-31 Oct. € 14.30 2011*

LAMALOU LES BAINS *10F1* (2km SE Rural) *43.57631, 3.06842* **Camping Domaine de Gatinié, Route de Gatinié, 34600 Les Aires [04 67 95 71 95 or 04 67 28 41 69 (LS); fax 04 67 95 65 73; gatinie@wanadoo.fr; www.domainegatinie.com]** Fr D908 fr Lamalou-les-Bains or Hérépian dir Poujol-sur-Orb, site sp. Fr D160 cross rv to D908 then as above. Med, hdg/mkd pitch, pt sl, pt shd; wc (some cont); chem disp; baby facs; shwrs inc; el pnts (6A) inc; lndtte; tradsmn; rest, snacks; bar; BBQ; playgrnd; pool; paddling pool; rv sw 100m; canoeing; fishing; games area; golf, horseriding, tennis 2km; entmnt; some statics; dogs €2; Eng spkn; adv bkg; quiet; red low ssn/long stay/CKE/CCI. "Beautiful, peaceful situation; many leisure activities; vg." ♦ 1 Apr-31 Oct. € 19.00 2009*

LAMASTRE *9C2* (5km NE Rural) *45.01053, 4.62366* **Camping Les Roches, 07270 Le Crestet [04 75 06 20 20; fax 04 75 06 26 23; camproches@nordnet.fr; www.campinglesroches.com]** Take D534 fr Tournon-sur-Rhône dir Lamastre. Turn R at Le Crestet & foll sp for site, 3km fr vill. Sm, mkd pitch, hdstg, terr, pt shd; wc (some cont); chem disp; mv service pnt; baby facs; shwrs inc; el pnts (6A) €5.; lndtte; shop; tradsmn; rest, snacks; bar; BBQ; playgrnd; htd pool; rv sw adj; fishing; tennis 3km; games area; TV rm; 30% statics; dogs €4.50; bus 1km; adv bkg; quiet; ccard acc; 5% red CKE/CCI. "Family-run site; clean facs; lovely views; gd base for touring medieval vills; gd walking; Eng spkn, friendly, Site rd steep" ♦ 1 May-30 Sep. € 32.20 2013*

LAMBALLE *2E3* (700m NE Urban) *48.47576, -2.50472* **Camp Municipal, Rue St Sauveur, 22400 Lamballe [02 96 34 74 33 or 02 96 50 13 50 (LS)]** NE side of town beyond church; nr water tower. Clearly sp. Sm, mkd pitch, terr, pt shd; wc; shwrs inc; el pnts (5A) €3.20; shops 700m; htd pool 700m; dogs free; quiet. "Interesting town, historic 17thC church." 1 Jul-2 Sep. € 9.00 2009*

LAMONTELARIE see Brassac *8F4*

LAMPAUL PLOUDALMESEAU *2E1* (500m NW Coastal) *48.56780, -4.65674* **Camp Municipal Les Dunes, Le Vourc'h, 29830 Lampaul-Ploudalmézon [02 98 48 14 29 or 02 98 48 11 28; fax 02 98 48 19 32; lampaul-ploudalmezeau.mairie@wanadoo.fr; www.vacanceseniroise.com]** Exit Ploudalmézeau E on D28 dir St Pabu & Lannilis; in 500m turn L at campsite sp onto C1 Route du Bourg (opp picnic site on R); foll rd & sp to site on beach. Med, pt sl, pt shd; wc; mv service pnt; shwrs inc; el pnts €2.40; lndry rm; shops 5km; tradsmn; snacks & bar 1km; playgrnd; sand beach adj; games area; dogs; phone; bus adj; quiet. "Spacious site nr amazing sandy beach used for many non-motorised water sports; san facs dated but clean; vg." ♦ ltd 15 Jun-15 Sep. € 10.20 2011*

LANDEBIA see Plancoët *2E3*

LANDEDA *2E1* (2km NW Coastal) *48.59333, -4.60333* **Camping des Abers, 51 Toull Tréaz, Plage de Ste Marguerite, 29870 Landéda [02 98 04 93 35; fax 02 98 04 35 35; info@camping-des-abers.com; www.camping-des-abers.com]** Exit N12/E50 at junc with D788 & take D13 to Lannilis. Then take D128A to Landéda & foll green site sp. Lge, some hdg/mkd pitch, terr, pt shd; wc; chem disp; mv service pnt; baby facs; fam bthrm; shwrs €0.80; el pnts (10A) €3 (long lead poss req); gas; lndtte (inc dryer); shop & snacks in ssn; rest & bar 200m; BBQ; playgrnd; sand beach adj; fishing; cycle hire; wifi; entmnt; games/TV rm; 10% statics; dogs €2.20; Eng spkn; no c'vans/m'vans over 8m high ssn; adv bkg (rec high ssn); quiet; ccard acc; red low ssn/long stay; CKE/CCI. "Attractive, landscaped site on wild coast; views fr high pitches; friendly, helpful manager; san facs clean, some new, others old; some pitches muddy when wet; access to many pitches by grass tracks, some sloping; gd walks, cycling; excel." ♦ 27 Apr-30 Sep. € 24.15 SBS - B30 2013*

LANDEDA

LANDEDA *2E1* (3km NW Coastal) *48.60310, -4.59882* **Camp Municipal de Penn-Enez, 29870 Landéda [02 98 04 99 82; info@camping-penn-enez.com; www.camping-penn-enez.com]** Proceed NW thro Landéda, turn R in 1km sp Penn-Enez then L in 600m. Site sp. Med, pt hdg pitch, pt sl, unshd; wc; chem disp (wc); shwrs €1; el pnts (16A) €2.80; playgrnd; sand beach 500m; 2% statics; dogs €1.45; Eng spkn; quiet. "Site on grassy headland; beach views fr some pitches; site self if warden absent; friendly, helpful staff; vg clean san facs; gd walks; excel." ♦ ltd 25 Apr-30 Sep. € 10.85 2010*

LANDERNEAU *2E2* (SW Urban) *48.44575, -4.25854* **Camp Municipal Les Berges de l'Elorn, Route de Calvaire, 29800 Landerneau [02 98 85 44 94 or 02 98 85 00 66 (Mairie); fax 02 98 85 43 35; ti-ker-landerne@mairie-landerneau.fr; www.ville-landerneau.fr]** Site S of rv. Foll sps to pool, sports stadium & site. Sm, hdg pitch, hdstg, pt shd; wc; chem disp; mv service pnt; shwrs €0.50; el pnts (7A) €3.35; shops, rest, snacks bar 250m; BBQ; playgrnd adj; pool 500m; tennis; dogs €1.15; phone adj; Eng spkn; adv bkg; quiet, some rd noise; CKE/CCI. "Historic, pretty town on tidal rv; conv touring base. Note: An Aire de Service for m'vans 100m E of site on same rd." ♦ Apr-Oct. € 9.60 2008*

LANDEVIEILLE see Bretignolles sur Mer *2H3*

LANDIVISIAU *2E2* (7km NE) *48.57724, -4.03006* **Camp Municipal Lanorgant, 29420 Plouvorn [02 98 61 32 40 (Mairie); fax 02 98 61 38 87; commune-de-plouvorn@wanadoo.fr; www.plouvorn.com]** Fr Landivisiau, take D69 N twd Roscoff. In 8km turn R onto D19 twd Morlaix. Site sp, in 700m turn R. NB Care req entry/exit, poss diff lge o'fits. Sm, hdg/mkd pitch, terr, pt shd; wc (cont for men); mv service pnt; shwrs; el pnts (10A) €2; lndtte; shops, snacks, bar 500m; rest 1km; BBQ; playgrnd; sand beach; lake sw; sailboards & canoes for hire; fishing; tennis; adv bkg; quiet. "Ideal NH for ferries; lge pitches; nr lake." 26 Jun-15 Sep. € 10.00 2009*

LANDRELLEC see Trégastel *1D2*

LANDUDEC *2F2* (2km SW Rural) *47.99190, -4.35353* **Camping Domaine de Bel-Air, Keridreuff, 29710 Landudec [02 98 91 50 27; fax 02 98 91 55 82; camping-dubelair@wanadoo.fr; www.belaircamping.com]** Fr N165 exit dir Quimper Cent. On ring rd foll sp Douarnenez & Audierne & exit ring rd onto D765 immed after Carrefour supmkt sp Douarnenez. Turn L at rndabt onto D784 dir Audierne/Landudec. Strt on at traff lts in Landudec, site on L in 750m. Lge, hdg/mkd pitch, terr, pt shd; wc; chem disp; shwrs inc; el pnts (10A) inc; gas; lndtte; shop; tradsmn; rest, snacks; playgrnd; htd pool; paddling pool; beach 10km; lake adj; waterslide; watersports; tennis; games rm; entmnt; TV; dogs €2; poss cr; Eng spkn; adv bkg; quiet; ccard acc; red low ssn; CKE/CCI. "Well-situated, family site; excel." ♦ 1 May-30 Sep. € 24.00 2009*

LANGEAC *9C1* (1km N Rural) *45.10251, 3.49980* **Camp Municipal du Pradeau/Des Gorges de l'Allier, 43300 Langeac [04 71 77 05 01; fax 04 71 77 27 34; infos@campinglangeac.com; www.campinglangeac.com]** Exit N102 onto D56 sp Langeac; in 7km join D585 into Langeac; pass under rlwy; at 2nd rndabt in 1km turn L to site, just bef junc with D590. Fr S on D950 to Langeac, take 1st R after rv bdge; then 1st exit at rndabt in 100m. Lge, pt shd; wc (some cont); chem disp; mv service pnt; shwrs inc; el pnts (10A) €2.60 (poss long lead req); gas 500m; lndtte; shop 1km; tradsmn; rest 500m; snacks; playgrnd; pool (high ssn); rv sw, fishing, canoeing & walking rtes adj; cycle hire; entmnt; TV rm; some statics; dogs €1.05; phone; bus 1km; poss cr; Eng spkn; quiet; red low ssn; CKE/CCI. "Beautiful location on Rv Allier; tourist train thro Gorges d'Allier fr Langeac; gd san facs; gd local mkt; excel NH." ♦ 1 Apr-31 Oct. € 13.00 2013*

"I need an on-site restaurant"
We do our best to make sure site information is correct, but it is always best to check any must-have facilities are still available or will be open during your visit.

LANGEAIS *4G1* (1km E Urban) *47.32968, 0.41848* **Camp Municipal du Lac, rue Carnot, 37130 Langeais [02 47 96 85 80; fax 02 47 96 69 23; patrimoine@langeais.fr; www.langeais.fr]** Exit A85 junc 7 onto D952 dir Langeais & foll 'Camping Municipal' sp. Med, mkd pitch, pt shd; wc; chem disp; shwrs inc; el pnts (6A) €3.50; shop 1km; rest 1km; snacks; bar1km; playgrnd; htd pool; fishing nr; 5% statics; dogs; rlwy noise; ccard acc; CKE/CCI. "Busy site high ssn; easy walk to town; dated san facs, inadequate when busy; nr Rv Loire cycle path; lovely chateau; gd; poss road/railway noise" 1 Jun-15 Sep. € 18.95 2013*

LANGOGNE *9D1* (1km S Rural) *44.72781, 3.86466* **Camp Municipal de l'Allier, 9 Route de St Alban-en-Montagne, 48300 Langogne [04 66 69 28 98 or 04 66 69 10 33 (Mairie)]** Fr Le Puy take N88 dir Mende. At Langogne over rv bdge & 1st L. Foll sp, site in 1km. Med, mkd pitch, pt sl, pt shd; wc (some cont); chem disp (wc); shwrs inc; el pnts (6A) €2.50; lndtte; shops 500m; rest, snacks; bar; pool 500m; phone; poss cr; quiet; adv bkg; CKE/CCI. "Gd walking area; lake for sailing 2km; 2 san facs blocks - 1 modern; close to walking routes." ♦ 15 May-15 Sep. € 6.65 2010*

LANGOGNE *9D1* (2km W Rural) *44.73180, 3.83995* **Camping Les Terrasses du Lac, 48300 Naussac [04 66 69 29 62; fax 04 66 69 24 78; info@naussac.com; www.naussac.com]** S fr Le Puy-en-Velay on N88. At Langogne take D26 to lakeside, site sp. Lge, terr, pt shd; wc; chem disp; mv service pnt; baby facs; shwrs; el pnts (6A) €2.50; lndtte (inc dryer); shop 2km; rest, snacks; bar; BBQ; playgrnd; pool; paddling pool; lake sw & sand beach adj; watersports adj; sailing school; games area; cycle hire; golf 1km; horseriding 3km; wifi; entmnt; TV rm; 10% statics; dogs €2.50; phone; Eng spkn; adv bkg; quiet; red low ssn; CKE/CCI. "Vg views; steep hill bet recep & pitches; vg cycling & walking." ♦ 15 Apr-30 Sep. € 16.50 2011*

LANGRES *6F1* (6km NE Rural) *47.89505, 5.39510* **Camping Hautoreille, 6 Rue du Boutonnier, 52360 Bannes [tel/fax 03 25 84 83 40; campinghautoreille@orange.fr; www.campinghautoreille.com]** N fr Dijon on D974/D674 to Langres; foll rd around Langres to E; onto D74 NE to Bannes; site on R on ent vill. Or exit A31 junc 7 Langres Nord onto D619, then D74 NE to Bannes. Med, mkd pitch, some hdstg, pt sl, pt shd; htd wc; chem disp; mv service pnt; shwrs inc; el pnts (10A) €4; lndtte; shop & 5km; tradsmn; rest (summer only); snacks; bar; playgrnd; lake sw 2.5km; horseriding & tennis 5km; cycle hire; wifi; some statics; dogs €1; phone; poss cr; Eng spkn; adv bkg; quiet; ccard not acc; CKE/CCI. "Peaceful, clean, tidy site; basic facs, ltd low ssn & poss inadequate high ssn; pleasant owner; gd rest; site muddy when wet - parking on hdstg or owner will use tractor; on Sundays site yourself - recep opens 1700; gd NH." ♦ 2 Jan-30 Nov. € 24.40   2013*

LANGRES *6F1* (5km E Rural) *47.87190, 5.38120* **Kawan Village Le Lac de la Liez, Rue des Voiliers, 52200 Peigney [03 25 90 27 79; fax 03 25 90 66 79; campingliez@gmail.com; www.campingliez.com]** Exit A31 at junc 7 (Langres Nord) onto DN19; at Langres turn L at traff lts onto D74 sp Vesoul, Mulhouse, Le Lac de la Liez; at rndabt go strt on sp Epinal, Nancy; after Champigny-lès-Langres cross over rlwy bdge & canal turning R onto D52 sp Peigney, Lac de la Liez; in 3km bear R onto D284 sp Langres Sud & Lac de la Liez; site on R in 800m. Well sp fr N & S. Lge, hdg/mkd pitch, some hdstg, terr, pt shd; htd wc; chem disp; mv service pnt; sauna; baby facs; shwrs inc; el pnts (10A) €5.50; lndtte (inc dryer); shop; tradsmn; rest, snacks; bar; BBQ; playgrnd; 2 pools (1 htd covrd); paddling pool; spa; lake sw & sand beach adj; fishing; watersports; tennis; boat & cycle hire; horseriding; golf 10km; wifi; entmnt; games/TV rm; 15% statics; dogs €3; no c'vans/m'vans over 10m; phone; poss v cr; Eng spkn; ccard acc; red low ssn; CKE/CCI. "Popular, well-run, secure site; lake views fr some pitches; various sized pitches; helpful, friendly staff; gd, clean san facs, poss ltd low ssn; blocks poss req some pitches; some sm pitches & narr access rds diff manoeuvre lge o'fits; vg rest; rec arr bef 1600 high ssn; gd walks by picturesque lake; interesting town; vg NH; excel." ♦ 1 Apr- 30 Sep. € 28.50 (CChq acc) SBS - J05   2013*

LANGRES *6F1* (5km S Rural) *47.81210, 5.32080* **Camping de la Croix d'Arles, 52200 Bourg [tel/fax 03 25 88 24 02; croix.arles@yahoo.fr; www.croixdarles.fr]** Site is 4km S of Langres on W side of D674 (1km S of junc of D674 with D428). Site opp junc of D51 with D974. Fr Dijon poss no L turn off D974 - can pull into indust est N of site & return to site, but memb reported that L turn now poss (2011). Med, hdg/mkd pitch, ltd hdstg, pt sl, pt shd; wc; chem disp; mv service pnt; shwrs inc; el pnts (10A) €4 (poss rev pol) (long cable req); lndtte; shop; tradsmn; rest, snacks; bar; playgrnd; pool; statics; dogs free; phone; poss cr; Eng spkn; ccard acc; red low ssn; CKE/CCI. "Popular site, fills up quickly after 1600; friendly staff; some lovely secluded pitches in woodland; gd san facs; access poss diff lge o'fits; muddy after rain; unkempt low ssn; poss haphazard pitching when full; conv NH Langres historic town." ♦ 15 Mar-31 Oct. € 17.00   2013*

LANGRES *6F1* (500m SW Urban) *47.86038, 5.32894* **Camp Municipal Navarre, 9 Blvd Maréchal de Lattre de Tassigny, 52200 Langres [03 25 87 37 92 or 06 10 74 10 16; fax 03 25 87 37 92; campingnavarre@free.fr; www. camping-navarre-langres.fr]** App fr N or S on D619/D674, cont on main rd until lge rndabt at top of hill & go thro town arched gateway; site well sp fr there. NB Diff access for lge o'fits thro walled town but easy access fr D619. Med, pt sl, pt shd; htd wc; chem disp; shwrs inc; el pnts (10A) €3 (long lead req & poss rev pol); lndtte (inc dryer); Spar supmkt 500m; BBQ; playgrnd nr; wifi; dogs free; phone; poss cr w/end; Eng spkn; some rd noise; ccard not acc; red low ssn; CKE/CCI. "Well-situated, busy NH, conv on arr site self & see warden; rec arr bef 1630 (every man for himself until warden arrives at 17.30!); helpful staff; excel, modern unisex san facs; part of site muddy after rain; lovely walk round citadel ramparts; delightful town; vg site, views and location" ♦ ltd 9 Mar-2 Nov. € 19.60   2013*

LANGRES *6F1* (4km NW Rural) *47.90213, 5.30238* **Camp Municipal La Mouche, Rue de la Mouche, 52200 Humes-Jorquenay [03 25 87 50 65 (Mairie)]** Exit A31 at junc 7, foll N19 S for 4km; site on W of N19 over rv bdg; sp in vill cent. Or S fr Chaumont on N19, into vill of Humes. Sm, unshd; wc; shwrs inc; el pnts (8A) €2 (poss long cable rec); tradsmn; rest 2km; snacks; playgrnd; poss cr; quiet. "Pretty site; basic but busy; early arr rec; no staff on site, fees collected each pm; no apparent security; interesting area; gd NH." 15 Apr-30 Sep. € 9.00   2008*

LANILDUT *2E1* (1km N Coastal) *48.48012, -4.75184* **Camping du Tromeur, 11 Route du Camping, 29840 Lanildut [02 98 04 31 13; tromeur@vive-les-vacances.com; www. vive-les-vacances.com/tromeur]** Site well sp on app rds to vill. Med; wc; chem disp (wc); shwrs inc; el pnts €2 (poss long lead req & poss rev pol); lndry rm; tradsmn; shop, bar, crêperie & gd rest in vill; BBQ; dogs €1; phone; quiet. "Clean, sheltered site; san facs gd; harbour & sm beach; low ssn warden am & pm only - site yourself." 1 May-30 Sep. € 9.00   2008*

LANLOUP *2E3* (W Rural) *48.71369, -2.96711* **FFCC Camping Le Neptune, 22580 Lanloup [02 96 22 33 35; fax 02 96 22 68 45; contact@leneptune.com; www.leneptune.com]** Take D786 fr St Brieuc or Paimpol to Lanloup, site sp. NB Take care sat nav directions (2011). Med, hdg/mkd pitch, pt shd; wc (some cont); chem disp; mv service pnt; baby facs; shwrs inc; el pnts (10A) €4 (long lead poss req); gas; lndtte (inc dryer); shop (high ssn) or 500m; tradsmn; rest 2km; snacks, bar (high ssn) or 500m; BBQ; playgrnd; htd, covrd pool; sand beach 2km; tennis 300m; horseriding 4km; cycle hire; wifi; TV rm; 15% statics; dogs €3; phone; poss cr; Eng spkn; adv bkg; quiet, rd noise some pitches; red low ssn; CKE/CCI. "Excel, well-maintained site nr beautiful coast; various pitch sizes; clean san facs; friendly, helpful owner; highly rec." ♦ 3 Apr-17 Oct. € 21.00 (CChq acc)   2011*

LANNE 8F2 (1km NW Rural) 43.17067, 0.00186 **Camping La Bergerie, 79 Rue des Chênes, 65380 Lanne [tel/fax 05 62 45 40 05; camping-la-bergerie@orange.com; www.camping-la-bergerie.com]** Fr Lourdes take N21 N dir Tarbes; turn R onto D16 (Rue des Chênes) dir Lanne; site on R in 200m. Med, mkd pitch, shd; htd wc; shwrs; el pnts (10A) €3 (poss rev pol); gas; shop; snacks & bar (high ssn); playgrnd; pool high ssn; tennis; dogs €1.20; bus 200m; Eng spkn; adv bkg; quiet but some rd noise & aircraft noise at night; red low ssn; CKE/CCI. "Well-run site; friendly owners; gd san facs; poss unkempt low ssn; poss flooding wet weather." ♦ 15 Mar-15 Oct. € 15.60   2011*

"Satellite navigation makes touring much easier"

Remember most sat navs don't know if you're towing or in a larger vehicle – always use yours alongside maps and site directions.

LANNEMEZAN 8F2 (6km W Rural) 43.10544, 0.32333 **FFCC Camping Les Craouès, Rue du 8 Mai 1945, 65130 Capvern [05 62 39 02 54; camping-les-craoues@orange.fr; www.camping-les-craoues.net]** Exit A64 junc 15. At rndabt at ent to Capvern foll sp Capvern Village. Site also sp fr Lannemezan on D817. Med, mkd pitch, some hdstg, pt sl, shd; wc (some cont); mv service pnt; baby facs; shwrs inc; el pnts (6-8A) €4-5; gas; lndtte (inc dryer); shops 500m; BBQ; playgrnd; pool; paddling pool; games area; games rm; dogs €1; poss cr; adv bkg; red low ssn. "Basic site; scruffy overall (low ssn report); NH only." ♦ 1 May-15 Oct. € 13.40   2010*

⊞ **LANNION** 1D2 (2km SE) 48.72300, -3.44600 **Camp Municipal Les Deux Rives, Rue du Moulin du Duc, 22300 Lannion [02 96 46 31 40 or 02 96 46 64 22; fax 02 96 46 53 35; infos@ville.lannion.fr; www.ville-lannion.fr]** SW fr Perros-Guirec on D788 to Lannion; fr Lannion town cent foll dir Guincamp on D767; site well sp, approx 1.5km, turn R at Leclerc supmkt (do not confuse with hypmkt). Fr S on D767 sp at rndabts; turn L at Leclerc supmkt. Med, mkd pitch, unshd; wc; chem disp; shwrs inc; el pnts (6A) €2.50; lndtte; shop high ssn & 1km; bar high ssn; playgrnd; security barrier; dogs €1.10; adv bkg; red low ssn; CKE/CCI. "Rvside walk to old town; vg, clean san facs; phone ahead low ssn to check open; warden lives on site but poss no arr acc Sun." ♦ € 13.90   2011*

LANNION 1D2 (4km NW Rural) 48.75143, -3.50693 **Kawan Village Les Alizés, Route de Trébeurden, 22300 Lannion [tel/fax 02 96 47 28 58; info@camping-lesalizes.fr; www.camping-lesalizes.fr]** D65 fr Lannion twd Trébeurden; site sp on L. Med, pt shd; wc; baby facs; shwrs; el pnts (10A) inc; lndtte (inc dryer); shop 2km; tradsmn; rest 3km; snacks; bar; BBQ; playgrnd; 2 pools (1 htd, covrd); paddling pool; waterslide; sand beach 3.5km; games area; games rm; wifi; entmnt; 60% statics; dogs €2; adv bkg; quiet; red low ssn. "Vg touring base." ♦ 1 Apr-1 Oct. € 24.00 (CChq acc)   2010*

LANNION 1D2 (8km NW Coastal) 48.73833, 3.54500 **FFCC Camping Les Plages de Beg-Léguer, Route de la Côte, 22300 Lannion [02 96 47 25 00; fax 02 96 47 27 77; info@campingdesplages.com; www.campingdesplages.com]** Fr Lannion take rd out of town twd Trébeurden then twd Servel on D65, then head SW off that rd twd Beg Léguer (sp). Lge, hdg/mkd pitch, pt shd; wc (some cont); chem disp; mv service pnt; baby facs; shwrs inc; el pnts (6A) €3.50 (poss long lead req); gas; lndtte; sm shop & 5km; tradsmn; rest, snacks; bar; playgrnd; htd, covrd pool; paddling pool; sand beach 500m; fishing; sailing; windsurfing; tennis; wifi; TV; 20% statics; dogs €1; phone; bus 400m; Eng spkn; adv bkg; quiet; red long stay/low ssn; ccard acc; red CKE/CCI. "Pleasant, peaceful, family-run site; lge pitches; immac, modern san facs." ♦ 1 Apr-1 Nov. € 26.00   2010*

LANOBRE see Bort les Orgues 7C4

LANSLEBOURG MONT CENIS 9C4 (W Rural) 45.28417, 6.87380 **Camp Municipal Les Balmasses, Chemin du Pavon, 73480 Lanslebourg-Mont-Cenis [tel/fax 04 79 20 52 77 / 06 19 46 28 18 (mob); info@camping-les-balmasses.com; www.camping-les-balmasses.com]** Fr Modane, site on R on rv on ent to town. Med, mkd pitch, pt shd; wc (some cont); shwrs inc; el pnts (6-10A) €4.30-5.40; lndtte; shop 500m; BBQ; playgrnd; dogs; phone; Eng spkn; CKE/CCI. "Pleasant, quiet site by rv; mountain views; clean facs; conv NH bef/after Col du Mont-Cenis." ♦ ltd 1 Jun-20 Sep. € 12.80   2013*

LANTON see Andernos les Bains 7D1

LANVEOC 2E2 (1km N Coastal) 48.29176, -4.46072 **Camp Municipal La Cale, Route de la Grève, 29160 Lanvéoc [02 98 27 58 91]** N fr Crozon dir Roscanvel. After approx 5.5km turn R onto D55 for Lanvéoc. Site sp. Med, mkd pitch, terr, unshd; shwrs inc; el pnts (10A) €2.90; lndtte; rest, snacks; bar; dir access to coast; fishing; no statics; dogs €1; quiet; CKE/CCI. "Sea views; low ssn unisex san facs; site rd steep with sharp bends to upper levels." 1 Jun-15 Sep. € 8.00   2009*

LAON 3C4 (2.5km W Rural) 49.56190, 3.59583 **Camp Municipal La Chênaie, Allée de la Chênaie, 02000 Laon [03 23 20 25 56/ 03 23 22 85 81 (ls); fax 03 23 22 85 85 (ls); aaussel@ville-laon.fr; www.ville-laon.fr]** Exit A26 junc 13 onto N2 sp Laon; in 10km at junc with D1044 (4th rndabt) turn sp Semilly/Laon, then L at next rndabt into site rd. Site well sp. Med, hdg/mkd pitch, pt shd; htd wc; chem disp; mv service pnt; baby facs; shwrs inc; el pnts (10A) €3.40 (poss rev pol); lndry rm; v ltd shop & 1km; tradsmn; BBQ; playgrnd; fishing lake 50m (no sw); dogs €2; phone; poss cr; Eng spkn; adv bkg; quiet with some rd noise; ccard not acc; red long stay; CKE/CCI. "Peaceful, pleasant site in gd location; popular NH; well-mkd pitches - lgest at end of site; helpful staff; poss unkempt low ssn; no twin-axles; if travelling Sept phone to check site open; m'van parking nr cathedral; vg; tired san facs but clean; woodland glades; gd NH" ♦ 1May-30 Sep. € 20.65   2013*

FRANCE

LAPALISSE 9A1 (250m S Urban) 46.24322, 3.63950 **Camping de la Route Bleue, Rue des Vignes, 03120 Lapalisse [04 70 99 26 31, 04 70 99 76 29 or 04 70 99 08 39 (LS); office.tourisme@cc-paysdelapalisse.fr; www.cc-paysdelapalisse.fr]** S fr Moulins on N7; at rndabt junc with D907 just bef Lapalisse, take 3rd exit onto Ave due Huit Mai 1945 (to town cent); in 1.5km at rndabt turn R onto D707 (Route de St Prix/Rue des Vignes); site on R in 500m. Med, mkd pitch, pt shd; htd wc (some cont); mv service pnt; shwrs inc; el pnts (6-9A) €2.40; lndtte; shops 300m; tradsman; playgrnd; dogs €1; quiet; Eng spkn; CKE/CCI. "Popular NH in pleasant parkland setting; gd clean san facs; pleasant walk thro adj park to town; no twin-axles; poss flooding after heavy rain; adequate sans but need upgrade" ♦ 1 Apr-30 Sep. € 14.50   2012*

LAPEYROUSE 7A4 (2km SE Rural) 46.22159, 2.88339 **Camp Municipal Les Marins, La Loge, 63700 Lapeyrouse [04 73 52 02 73 or 04 73 52 00 79 (Mairie); fax 04 73 52 03 89; mairie-lapeyrouse63@wanadoo.fr; http://63lapeyrouse.free.fr]** Fr Montluçon S on D2144 sp Montaigut. In 24km turn L on D13 sp Lapeyrouse. In 7km turn R onto D998, site on R at end of vill, well sp. Med, hdg/mkd pitch, pt shd; wc; chem disp; baby facs; shwrs inc; el pnts (10-16A) inc; lndtte; bar nr; playgrnd; lake sw adj; windsurfing; fishing; tennis; games area; cycle hire; TV; adv bkg; quiet; CKE/CCI. "Delightful countryside; gd." 15 Jun-1 Sep. € 15.00 (3 persons) (CChq acc)   2010*

LARGENTIERE 9D2 (4km SE Rural) 44.50347, 4.29430 **Camping Les Châtaigniers, Le Mas-de-Peyrot, 07110 Laurac-en-Vivarais [04 75 36 86 26; chataigniers@hotmail.com; www.chataigniers-laurac.com]** Fr Aubenas S on D104 dir Alès; site sp fr D104. Site on one of minor rds leading to Laurac-en-Vivarais. Med, mkd pitch, pt sl, pt shd; wc; chem disp; baby facs; shwrs; el pnts (10A) €3; lndtte; BBQ (gas); playgrnd; pool & sun area; 15% statics; dogs €2; poss cr; adv bkg; quiet, but rd noise on lower terr; red low ssn. "Attractive site; some pitches deep shade; gd pool; sh uphill walk to vill shops & auberge; vg." ♦ 1 Apr-30 Sep. € 17.00   2011*

LARGENTIERE 9D2 (1.6km NW Rural) 44.56120, 4.28615 **Kawan Village Les Ranchisses, Route de Rocher, Chassiers, 07110 Largentière [04 75 88 31 97; fax 04 75 88 32 73; reception@lesranchisses.fr; www.lesranchisses.fr]** Fr Aubenas S on D104 sp Alès. 1km after vill of Uzer turn R onto D5 to Largentière. Go thro Largentière on D5 in dir Rocher/Valgorge; site on L in 1.5km. DO NOT use D103 bet Lachapelle-Aubenas & Largentière - too steep & narr for lge vehicles & c'vans. NB Not rec to use sat nav dirs to this site. Lge, mkd pitch, pt shd; wc; chem disp; mv service pnt; baby facs; shwrs inc; el pnts (10A) inc; lndtte (inc dryer); shop; rest, snacks; bar; BBQ (gas/elec only) playgrnd; 3 htd pools (1 covrd); paddling pool; rv sw, fishing; canoeing; wellness centre; tennis; cycle hire; games area; games rm; wifi; entmnt; TV; 30% statics; dogs €3.60; c'vans/m'vans over 7m by request; poss cr; adv bkg ess; ccard acc; red low ssn. "Lovely, well-run, busy site adj vineyard; gd sized pitches; friendly, helpful staff; gd, immac san facs; excel rest & takeaway; lovely pools; gd choice of sporting activities; poss muddy when wet; noisy rd adj to S end of site; mkt Tues am; first class." ♦ 14 Apr-23 Sep. € 45.00 (CChq acc) SBS - C32   2011*

LARGENTIERE 9D2 (8km NW Rural) 44.56631, 4.22888 **FFCC Camping La Marette, Les Marches du Tanargues, Route de Valgorge, 07110 Joannas [04 75 88 38 88; fax 04 75 88 36 33; reception@lamaratte.com; www.lamarette.com]** Fr Aubenas D104 SW to Largentière. Foll D5 3km N of Largentière then W on D24 to Valgorge. Site 3km past vill of Joannas. Med, mkd pitch; pt sl, terr, pt shd; wc; chem disp; mv service pnt; shwrs; el pnts (10A) €3.70; lndtte; shop; tradsmn; snacks; bar; playgrnd; pool; 5% statics; dogs €2; quiet; adv bkg; Eng spkn; CKE/CCI. "Friendly, family-run site; excel for children; organised tours, canoe hire, walking; gd san facs; not rec for lge trailer o'fits." ♦ Easter-30 Sep. € 22.30   2008*

LARNAGOL see Cajarc 7D4

"There aren't many sites open at this time of year"

If you're travelling outside peak season remember to call ahead to check site opening dates – even if the entry says 'open all year'.

LARNAS 9D2 (2.5km SW Rural) 44.43674, 4.57728 **Camping Le Domaine d'Imbours, 07220 Larnas [04 75 54 39 50; fax 04 75 54 39 20; info@domaine-imbours.com; www.domaine-imbours.com or www.campings-franceloc.fr]** Fr Bourg-St Andéol on D86 take D4 to St Remèze. Do not exit on D462 which has sp for tourists for Imbours site. In St Remèze turn R on D362 to Mas-du-Gras & D262 twd Larnas & site. Do not attempt app to site via D262 thro St Montant. Lge, mkd pitch, some hdstg, pt sl, pt shd; wc; shwrs inc; el pnts inc; lndtte; shop; rest, snacks; bar; playgrnd; htd, pool complex; waterslide; tennis; cycle hire; entmnt; some statics; dogs €4.30; poss cr; adv bkg (ess Jul/Aug); quiet. "Many sports activities; beautiful area." ♦ 1 Jul-26 Aug. € 30.00 (3 persons) 2010*

LAROQUE DES ALBERES see Argelès sur Mer 10G1

⊞ **LARUNS** 8G2 (6km N Rural) 43.02085, -0.42043 **FFCC Camp Municipal de Monplaisir, Quartier Monplaisir, 64260 Gère-Bélesten [05 59 82 61 18]** Site sp on E side of D934 S of Gère-Bélesten. Med, mkd pitch, pt shd, htd wc; shwrs inc; el pnts (6A) €3.90; tradsmn; shops 4km; bar 100m; htd pool 4km; fishing; TV; 75% statics; Eng spkn; adv bkg; quiet; red low ssn. "Helpful warden calls am & pm." € 9.80   2010*

LARUNS 8G2 (2km E Rural) 42.97991, -0.41430 **Camping du Valentin, Quartier Pon, 64440 Laruns [05 59 05 39 33; fax 05 59 05 65 84; campingduvalentin@wanadoo.fr; www.ossau-camping-valentin.com]** Fr Laruns take D934 dir Col de Pourtalet. Site well sp on L Med, hdg/mkd pitch, terr, pt shd; wc; shwrs inc; el pnts (3-6A) €2.50-3.20; lndtte; shop; tradsmn; rest, snacks high ssn; bar; playgrnd; pool 3km; 20% statics; dogs €1.10; adv bkg; quiet at night but some rd noise; red low ssn/ long stay; CKE/CCI. "Pleasant, well-managed site; some pitches cramped for awning; facs ltd low ssn; conv Spanish border, cable car & mountain train; gd sh stay/NH." ♦ 17 Apr-11 Nov. € 14.55   2008*

LARUNS *8G2* (6km SE Rural) *42.96972, -0.38220*
**Camping d'Iscoo, 64440 Eaux-Bonnes [05 59 05 36 81
or 06 98 23 54 93 (mob); camping.iscoo@live.fr; http://
iscoo.free.fr]** Site is on R 1.4km fr Eaux-Bonnes on climb to
Col d'Aubisque (site sp says Camping * * *, no name). Site ent in
middle of S-bend so advise cont 500m & turn on open ground
on L. Sm, mkd pitch, pt sl, pt shd; wc (some cont); shwrs; el pnts
(2-5A) €2.50; shops 1.5km; playgrnd; pool 3km; dogs; quiet;
ccard not acc; CKE/CCI. "V pleasant location; friendly owner."
1 Jun-30 Sep. € 12.00   2008*

⊞ **LARUNS** *8G2* (800m S Rural) *42.98241, -0.41591*
**Camping Les Gaves, Quartier Pon, 64440 Laruns
[05 59 05 32 37; fax 05 59 05 47 14; campingdesgaves@
wanadoo.fr; www.campingdesgaves.com]** Site on S edge
of town, N of Hôtel Le Lorry & bdge. Fr town sq cont on Rte
d'Espagne (narr exit fr sq) to end of 1-way system. After Elf &
Total stns turn L at site sp immed bef bdge (high fir tree each
side of bdge ent). Ignore 1st site on L. At v constricted T-junc at
ent to quartier 'Pon', turn R & foll rd into site. App no suitable
lge o'fits. Med, mkd pitch, pt shd; htd wc; chem disp; serviced
pitch; shwrs inc; el pnts (3-10A) €2.60-4.50; lndtte; shops
800km; tradsmn; bar; playgrnd; htd, covrd pool 800m; fishing;
rv fishing adj; games area; games rm; TV; 75% statics; dogs €3;
quiet; CKE/CCI. "Beautiful site; excel facs; level walk to vill."
€ 18.80   2009*

LARUSCADE *7C2* (4km SW Rural) *45.09274, -0.36742* **Aire
Naturelle Le Lac Vert (Saumon), 33620 Laruscade [tel/fax
05 57 68 64 43]** N on N10 fr Bordeaux for 28km, about 1km S
of Cavignac, sp off to R. Access over narr bdge. Sm, pt shd; wc;
chem disp; shwrs inc; ltd el pnts €2.70 (long cable req); shops
1km; rest, snacks; bar; lake sw; playgrnd; dogs; Eng spkn; quiet
but some rlwy noise; CKE/CCI. "Pretty site nr lake; Auberge
rest on site; fair NH." 1 May-30 Sep. € 8.10   2009*

⊞ **LASSAY LES CHATEAUX** *4E1* (2km N Rural) *48.45478,
-0.47458* **Camping La Cloue, La Cloue, 53110 Ste Marie-
du-Bois [02 43 00 10 80; cheryl_carter@hotmail.co.uk;
www.lovecamping.co.uk/campsites/europe]** Fr D976 turn
S onto D34. In 8km turn R at top of hill bef sm church & in
1km turn R bef junc to site. Sm, pt sl, pt shd; own san req; mv
service pnt in vill car park; shop, rest, bar 2km; no statics; dogs
€1; quiet; ccard not acc; CKE/CCI. "Fair, basic CL-type area
for self-contained o'fits; British owners; conv Caen ferries."
€ 5.00   2009*

LATHUILE see Doussard *9B3*

LATTES see Montpellier *10F1*

⊞ **LAUBERT** *9D1* (300m W Rural) *44.58262, 3.63552* **Camp
Municipal La Pontière, 48170 Laubert [04 66 47 71 37; fax
04 66 47 73 08; pms.laubert@wanadoo.fr]** Site on N side of
N88 in hamlet of Laubert. 7% hill descent fr Laubert to Mende.
Sm, sl, pt shd; wc; shwrs inc; el pnts inc; lndtte; snacks; bar;
playgrnd; quiet. "Peaceful; site at 1000m - can be chilly." ♦
€ 10.50   2010*

⊞ **LAURENS** *10F1* (1km S Rural) *43.53620, 3.18583*
**Camping L'Oliveraie, Chemin de Bédarieux, 34480
Laurens [04 67 90 24 36; fax 04 67 90 11 20; oliveraie@
free.fr; www.oliveraie.com]** Clearly sp on D909 Béziers to
Bédarieux rd. Sp reads Loisirs de L'Oliveraie. Med, mkd pitch,
hdstg, terr, pt shd; htd wc; chem disp; baby facs; sauna high
ssn; shwrs inc; el pnts (10A) €3.20-4.60 (poss rev pol); lndtte;
shop high ssn; tradsmn; rest & bar high ssn; snacks; playgrnd;
pool high ssn; games rm; beach 30km; TV rm; 30% statics;
dogs free, €2 (high ssn); phone; adv bkg; quiet; red low ssn;
ccard acc; site clsd 15 Dec-15 Jan; CKE/CCI. "Helpful staff;
gd, clean san facs (2011); site becoming tatty (2011); in wine-
producing area; gd winter NH." ♦ € 23.60   2011*

LAVAL *2F4* (10km N Rural) *48.17467, -0.78785*
**Camp Municipal Le Pont, 53240 Andouillé
[02 43 69 72 72 (Mairie); fax 02 43 68 77 77]** Fr Laval N on
D31 dir Ernée. In 8km turn R onto D115 to Andouillé. Site on L
bef hill to vill cent. Sm, hdg pitch, pt shd; wc; chem disp; shwrs
inc; el pnts (3A) inc; lndtte; shops 300m; playgrnd; pool 10km;
rv adj; poss cr; quiet; no ccard acc. "Pretty, busy, basic site; vg,
clean san facs; warden on site am & pm; site liable to flood."
1 Apr-31 Oct. € 5.50   2009*

LAVAL *2F4* (4km W Rural) *48.06428, -0.83140* **Camp
Municipal Le Moulin de Coupeau, 53940 St Berthevin
[02 43 68 30 70; fax 02 43 69 20 88; office.tourisme@
mairie-laval.fr; www.ville.saint-berthevin.fr]** Fr Laval W
on D57 twd Rennes. Site sp at St Berthevin. Sm, hdg/mkd
pitch, terr, pt shd; wc; shwrs inc; el pnts (10A) €1.60; shops
2km; rest in ssn; bar adj; BBQ; htd pool adj; paddling pool;
50% statics; dogs €1; bus; adv bkg; quiet; no ccard acc; CKE/
CCI. "Attractive, well-kept site on hillside by rv; helpful staff;
grnd v soft after heavy rain; poss itinerant workers; poss diff
access lge o'fits." 25 Apr-27 Sep. € 9.70   2009*

LAVANDOU, LE *10F3* (2km E Coastal) *43.14471, 6.38084*
**Caravaning St Clair, Ave André Gide, 83980 Le Lavandou
[04 94 01 30 20; fax 04 94 71 43 64; patrick.martini@
wanadoo.fr / lesmandariniers@orange.fr; www.
caravaningsaintclair.com]** N559 thro Le Lavandou twd
St Raphaël; after 2km at sp St Clair turn R immed after bend 50m
after blue 'caravaning' sp (easy to overshoot). Med, mkd pitch,
shd; htd wc (cont); mv service pnt; shwrs inc; el pnts (16A) €4.10
(rev pol); lndtte; shops 100m; rest, bar nrby; playgrnd; sand beach
adj; fishing; boat hire; wifi; TV rm; dogs €2; no tents; poss cr;
adv bkg ess Jul-Aug; some noise fr rd; no ccard acc; red low ssn.
"Popular with British; pitch & ent screened by trees; conv beach &
rests; quiet site" ♦ Apr-Oct. € 29.90 (3 persons)   2013*

LAVANDOU, LE *10F3* (5km E Coastal) *43.15645, 6.44821*
**Parc-Camping de Prasmousquier, Ave du Capitaine
Ducourneau, Pramousquier, 83980 Le Lavandou
[04 94 05 83 95; fax 04 94 05 75 04; camping-lavandou@
wanadoo.fr]** Take D559 E fr Le Lavandou. At Pramousquier
site sp on main rd; awkward bend. Lge, terr on steep hillside,
pt shd; wc; shwrs inc; el pnts (3-6A) €3.304; gas; lndtte; shop;
snacks; bar; playgrnd; sand beach 400m; dogs €2.10; poss
cr; Eng spkn; red low ssn. "Pleasant, relaxing, clean site; site
lighting poor; gd cycle track to Le Lavandou; excel."
26 Apr-30 Sep. € 21.70   2008*

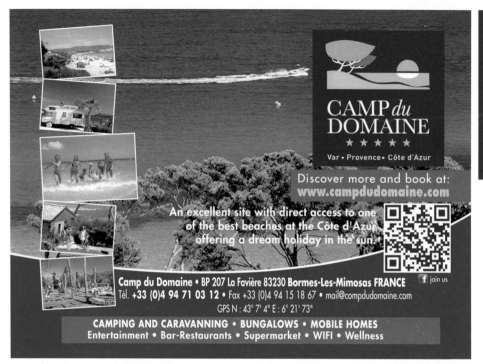
LAVANDOU, LE *10F3* (2km S Coastal) *43.11800, 6.35210*
Camping du Domaine, La Favière, 2581 Route de Bénat, 83230 Bormes-les-Mimosas [04 94 71 03 12; fax 04 94 15 18 67; mail@campdudomaine.com; www.campdudomaine.com] App Le Lavandou fr Hyères on D98 & turn R on o'skts of town clearly sp La Favière. Site on L in 2.3km about 200m after ent to Domaine La Favière (wine sales) - ignore 1st lge winery. If app fr E do not go thro Le Levandou, but stay on D559 until sp to La Favière. V lge, mkd pitch, terr, pt shd, 75% serviced pitch; wc; chem disp; mv service pnt; baby facs; shwrs inc; el pnts (10A) inc (long lead poss req); gas; lndtte (inc dryer); shop; supmkt; tradsmn; rest, snacks; bar; BBQ (gas); playgrnd; sand beach adj; tennis; games rm; wifi; entmnt; TV rm; 10% statics; dogs (not acc Jul/Aug); phone; poss cr; Eng spkn; adv bkg ess high ssn; quiet; ccard acc; red low ssn; CKE/CCI. "Lge pitches, some with many trees & some adj beach (direct access); well-organised site with excel facs; gd walking & attractions in area." ♦ ltd 30 Mar-31 Oct. € 48.00   2013*

See advertisement

LAVANDOU, LE *10F3* (1.5km SW Coastal) *43.13386, 6.35224* **Camping Beau Séjour, Quartier St Pons, 83980 Le Lavandou [04 94 71 25 30; beausejourvar@orange.fr]** Take Cap Bénat rd on W o'skts of Le Lavandou. Site on L in approx 500m. Med, mkd pitch, pt shd; wc; shwrs inc; el pnts (3A) €4; supmkts 400m; rest, snacks & bar adj; beach 900m; poss cr; no adv bkg; rd noise on W side. "Well-kept, clean site; gd sized pitches." ♦ Mid Apr-30 Sep. € 17.60   2010*

LAVANDOU, LE *10F3* (W Urban/Coastal) *43.13630, 6.35439* Camping St Pons, Ave Maréchal Juin, 83960 Le Lavandou [04 94 71 03 93; info@campingsaintpons.com; www.campingstpons.com] App fr W on D98 via La Londe. At Bormes keep R onto D559. At 1st rndabt turn R sp La Favière, at 2nd rndabt turn R, then 1st L. Site on L in 200m. Med, mkd pitch, shd; wc (some cont); chem disp; shwrs inc; el pnts (6A) inc; lndtte; shop adj; rest, snacks, bar high ssn; sand beach 800m; playgrnd; entmnt; 10% statics; dogs €3.90; phone; poss cr; Eng spkn; some rd noise; red low ssn; CKE/CCI. "Much improved site; helpful owner." 25 Apr-3 Oct. € 26.20   2009*

⊞ **LAVANDOU, LE** *10F3* (9km W Rural) *43.16262, 6.32152* Camping Manjastre, 150 Chemin des Girolles, 83230 Bormes-les-Mimosas [04 94 71 03 28; fax 04 94 71 63 62; manjastre@infonie.fr; www.campingmanjastre.com] App fr W on D98 about 3km NE of where N559 branches off SE to Le Lavandou. Fr E site is 2km beyond Bormes/Collobrières x-rds; sp. Lge, hdg/mkd pitch, v sl, terr, pt shd; htd wc; chem disp; mv service pnt; baby facs; shwrs inc; el pnts (10A) €4.70; lndtte (inc dryer); shop; rest, snacks; bar; BBQ; playgrnd; pool; paddling pool; sand beach 8km; wifi; TV; 10% statics; dogs €1.50 (not acc Jul/Aug); poss cr; Eng spkn; adv bkg; quiet; red low ssn; CKE/CCI. "Lovely site in vineyard on steep hillside (but one san facs block at bottom of hill); c'vans taken in & out by tractor; facs poss stretched in ssn; winter storage avail." ♦ € 27.00 (3 persons) (CChq acc)   2010*

LAVELANET

LAVELANET 8G4 (1km SW Urban) 42.92340, 1.84477
Camping Le Pré Cathare, Rue Jacquard, 09300 Lavelanet
[tel/fax 05 61 01 55 54; leprecathare@orange.fr /; www.
campinglavelanet.com] Fr Lavelanet, take D117 twd Foix &
foll sp. Adj 'piscine'. Med, hdg/mkd pitch, pt shd; htd wc; chem
disp; shwrs; el pnts (10A) €3; lndtte; shops 1km; tradsmn;
snacks; BBQ; playgrnd; pool adj; tennis 800m; games area; rv
4km; entmnt; TV rm; some statics; dogs €1; adv bkg; quiet;
CKE/CCI. "Gd sized pitches, some with mountain views; excel
san facs; poss open in winter with adv bkg; gates locked 2200;
quiet town; vg." ♦ 1 April-31 Oct. € 26.60   2013*

LAVIT 8E3 (500m NE Urban) 43.96212, 0.92409 Camp
Municipal Le Bertranon, Route d'Asques, 82120 Lavit
[05 63 94 05 54; fax 05 63 94 11 10; mairie-lavit-de-
lomagne@info82.com; www.tourisme-en-lomagne.com]
Fr N, exit A62 junc 8 onto D953 S; in 5km turn L onto D3 sp
Lavit; on ent town turn L onto D15; Rte d'Asques is 3rd turning
on L. Site adj stadium. Well sp on o'skts. Sm, hdg pitch, pt shd;
wc; chem disp (wc); shwrs inc; el pnts (6A) €2.30; shops, rest
& snacks nrby; playgrnd; 5% statics; dogs €1; bus 500m; no
twin-axles; quiet. "Under-used site - quiet even high ssn; lge
pitches; pay at Mairie (not open w/end); clean, dated san facs;
gd." ♦ 15 Jun-30 Sep. € 8.00   2010*

LAVOUTE SUR LOIRE see Puy en Velay, Le 9C1

LECTOURE 8E3 (2.5km SE Rural) 43.91260, 0.64500
Yelloh! Village Le Lac des Trois Vallées, 32700
Lectoure [05 62 68 82 33; fax 05 62 68 88 82; contact@
lacdes3vallees.fr; www.lacdes3vallees.fr or www.
yellohvillage.co.uk] Site sp fr N21, on lake bet Lectour &
Fleurance. App fr N, look for & foll sps to L after leaving Lectoure;
take this rd for 2.4km & site on L. NB Narr app rd with steep
gradient. Lge, hdg/mkd pitch, pt sl, pt shd; wc; chem disp; mv
service pnt; baby facs; shwrs inc; el pnts (10A) inc; lndtte (inc
dryer); shop; bar; rest, snacks; bar; BBQ (gas/charcoal only);
playgrnd; htd pool; paddling pool; waterslides; lake sw; fishing;
watersports; canoeing; horseriding 6km; tennis; skateboard
course; games area; fitness rm; wifi; entmnt; games/TV rm;
60% statics; dogs €4; no c'vans/m'vans over 7m high ssn;
poss cr; adv bkg; quiet (some disco noise); ccard acc; red low
ssn. "Excel lake pool; busy site - ideal for teenagers; generous
pitch size but some poss diff lge o'fits due terr; modern san
facs; excursions to Pau, Lourdes, Andorra; conv A62; mkt Tue
Fleurance." ♦ 1 Jun-11 Sep. € 47.00   2010*

See advertisement

LEGE 2H4 (7km S Rural) 46.82899, -1.59368 Camp
Municipal de la Petite Boulogne, 12 Rue du Stade, 85670
St Etienne-du-Bois [02 51 34 52 11 or 02 51 34 54 51; fax
02 51 34 54 10; la.petite.boulogne@wanadoo.fr] S fr Legé
on D978 dir Aizenay. Turn E onto D94 twd St Etienne-du-Bois.
Foll sp to site. Sm, mkd pitch, pt sl, terr, pt shd; wc; chem disp
(wc); shwrs inc; el pnts (10A) €2.70; gas 7km; lndtte; shops
500m; bar in vill; pool; sand beach 30km; TV rm; dogs €2.10;
Eng spkn; adv bkg; quiet; CKE/CCI. "Pleasant, clean site;
helpful warden; san facs would be stretched if site full." ♦
1 Apr-30 Sep. € 12.50   2008*

⊞ **LEGE** 2H4 (8km SW Rural) 46.82121, -1.64844 Camp
Municipal Les Blés d'Or, 10 rue de la Piscine, 85670
Grand'Landes [02 51 98 51 86; fax 02 51 98 53 24;
mairiegrandlandes@wanadoo.fr; www.vendee-tourisme.
com] Fr Legé S on D81 & foll sp. Fr S on D978, turn W sp Grand-Landes.
3km N of Palluau. Sm, pt sl; pt shd; wc; chem disp; shwrs
inc; el pnts (16A) €2.30; gas; shop, rest & bar adj; playgrnd
adj; 30% statics; Eng spkn; adv bkg; quiet; ccard not acc. "V
pleasant site; ent barrier clsd 2000 (poss earlier); height barrier
only, cars 24hr access; rec arr early; immac facs; pay at Mairie
adj." € 10.10   2013*

LEGE CAP FERRET see Andernos les Bains 7D1

LELIN LAPUJOLLE see Aire sur l'Adour 8E2

LEMPDES SUR ALLAGNON 9C1 (N Rural) 45.38699, 3.26598
Camping Le Pont d'Allagnon (formerly CM au Delà de
l'Eau), Rue René Filiol, off Route de Chambezon, 43410
Lempdes-sur-Allagnon [04 71 76 53 69; centre.auvergne.
camping@orange.fr; www.campingenauvergne.com]
Going S on A75 exit junc 19 (ltd access) onto D909; turn R on
D654 bef vill, site sp at junc. Or fr junc 20 going N; foll sp. Site
just outside vill. Med, hdg pitch, pt shd; wc (some cont); chem
disp; mv service pnt; shwrs inc; baby facs; el pnts (16A) €3;
lndtte; shops 500m; bar; playgrnd; pool 100m; rv fishing; tennis;
games area; games rm; phone; adv bkg; quiet; ccard acc; red
low ssn. "Pleasant site in beautiful area; conv NH A75; gd." ♦
1 May-30 Sep. € 13.50   2010*

An exceptional site in the valleys of the Gers ! A spacious place for nature-lovers.
An unique water park : 3 lakes, a new aquatic park of more than 3000m²
...a paradise for the whole family.

Lac des 3 Vallées
Camping Caravaning
★ ★ ★ ★ ★
Lectoure Gers en Gascogne

(yelloh!) **Village Lac des 3 Vallées Camping-Village**
32700 LECTOURE
Tel : 0033.5.62.68.82.33 - Fax : 00.33.5.62.68.88.82
Email : contact@lacdes3vallees.fr - www.lacdes3vallees.fr

FRANCE

354   ⊞ Site open all year   You can now fill in site reports online

LEON *8E1* (4km N Rural) *43.90260, -1.31030* **Camping Sunêlia Le Col Vert, Lac de Léon, 40560 Vielle-St Girons [08 90 71 00 01; fax 05 58 42 91 88; contact@colvert.com; www.colvert.com]** Exit N10 junc 12; at Castets-des-Landes turn R onto D42 to Vielle-St Girons. In vill turn L onto D652 twd Léon sp Soustons. In 4km, bef Vielle, take 2nd of 2 RH turns twd Lac de Léon. Site on R at end of rd in 1.5km. V lge, shd; wc; chem disp; mv service pnt; baby facs; serviced pitches; shwrs inc; el pnts (3A) inc; gas; lndtte (inc dryer); shop; tradsmn; rest, snacks; bar; BBQ (gas/elec); playgrnd; 2 pools (1 htd, covrd); wellness centre; paddling pool; sand beach 6km; lake sw, fishing, sailing, canoeing, windsurfing nrby; tennis; fitness rm; wellness cent; archery; horseriding; cycle hire; wifi; entmnt; games/TV rm; 60% statics; dogs €4.70; no c'van/m'van over 6.50m; poss cr; adv bkg; poss noisy (nightclub); ccard acc; red low ssn/long stay; CKE/CCI. "Lakeside site in pine forest; some pitches 800m fr facs; ideal for children & teenagers; daily mkt in Léon in ssn; Excel location" ♦ 1 Apr-23 Sep. € 57.40 SBS - A08 2013*

See advertisement

LEON *8E1* (5km NE Rural) *43.89967, -1.27069* **Camping Aire Naturelle Le Cayre (Capdupuy), 751 Route de Chevreuils, 40550 St Michel-Escalus [05 58 49 23 85]** Fr N10 exit Castets & St Girons onto D42 sp St Girons/Linxe. In Linxe turn L onto D374 sp Escalus & camping. In 1km R sp Léon, site on L in 1km. Sm, pt shd; wc; shwrs inc; el pnts €2.60; gas; lndtte; shops 4km; playgrnd; pool 5km; sand beach 10km; some statics; dogs €1; poss cr; ccard acc. "In pine forest; friendly, helpful owner; ltd facs low ssn." ♦ 15 Apr-15 Sep. € 12.20 2008*

LEON *8E1* (1.5km NW Rural) *43.88528, -1.31510* **Camping Lou Puntaou, 1315 Route du Lac, 40550 Léon [05 58 48 74 30; fax 05 58 48 70 42; reception@ loupuntaou.com; www.loupuntaou.com]** Site sp fr D142 on Etang de Léon. V lge, mkd pitch, pt shd; wc; chem disp; mv service pnt; shwrs inc; el pnts (15A) inc; lndtte; supmkt; rest 100m; snacks; bar; playgrnd; 2 pools (1 htd, covrd); paddling pool; waterslide; jacuzzi; lake sw 100m; sand beach 5km; tennis; watersports; games area; cycle hire; fitness rm; cash machine; entmnt; 20% statics; dogs €4; adv bkg; quiet. "Excel sports facs; lovely location." ♦ 3 Apr-4 Oct. € 35.00 (CChq acc) 2009*

LEON *8E1* (9km NW Coastal) *43.90830, -1.36380* **Domaine Naturiste Arna (Naturist), Arnaoutchot, 5006 Route de Pichelèbe, 40560 Vielle-St Girons [05 58 49 11 11; fax 05 58 48 57 12; contact@arna.com; www.arna.com]** Fr St Girons turn R onto D328 at Vielle sp Pichelèbe. Site in 5km on R. Lge, pt sl, shd; wc (some cont); chem disp; mv service pnt; baby facs; shwrs inc; Arna Forme Spa; el pnts (3-6A) €4.50-6.10 inc; gas; lndtte (inc dryer); shop; rest, snacks; bar; BBQ (gas/elec); playgrnd; 2 pools (1 htd covrd); spa centre; paddling pool; waterslide; sand beach adj; lake adj; watersports 5km; tennis; cycle hire; golf nr; archery; games area; wifi; entmnt; games/TV rm; many statics (sep area); dogs €3.50; no c'vans/m'vans over 6.50m; Eng spkn; adv bkg; quiet; ccard acc; red long stay/low ssn. "Excel site in pine forest; some pitches soft sand; clean san facs, ltd low ssn; excel long stay site; access lge o'fits poss diff due trees; vg beach; daily mkt in Léon in ssn." ♦ 9 Apr-25 Sep. € 39.95 (CChq acc) 2011*

LERAN *8G4* (2km E Rural) *42.98368, 1.93516* **Camping La Régate, Route du Lac, 09600 Léran [tel/fax 05 61 01 92 69]** Fr Lavelanet go N on D625, turn R onto D28 & cont to Léran. Site sp fr vill. Ent easily missed - rd past it is dead end. Med, hdg/mkd pitch, terr, shd; wc; chem disp; baby facs; shwrs; el pnts (8A) €3.70; lndtte; shop 2km; tradsmn; rest adj; bar; BBQ; playgrnd; pool adj; lake adj; watersports; leisure cent nr; cycle hire & pony trekking nrby; entmnt; 10% statics; dogs €1; phone; quiet; adv bkg; ccard acc. "Conv Montségur chateau; clean san facs; gd location." 1 Apr-30 Oct. € 14.00 2008*

LESCAR see Pau *8F2*

LESCHERAINES *9B3* (2.5km SE Rural) *45.70279, 6.11158* **Camp Municipal de l'Ile, Base de Loisirs, Les Iles du Chéran, 73340 Lescheraines [tel/fax 04 79 63 80 00; contact@iles-du-cheran.com; www.iles-du-cheran.com]** Fr Lescheraines foll sp for Base de Loisirs. Lge, mkd pitch, pt shd; wc; chem disp; mv service pnt; baby facs; shwrs inc; el pnts (6-10A) €2.10-3; gas 1km; lndtte; shop; rest 500m; snacks; bar; BBQ; playgrnd; lake sw; canoe & boat hire; fishing; wifi; entmnt; 5% statics; dogs €1.50; phone; Eng spkn; quiet; red low ssn; CKE/CCI. "Beautiful, scenic, lakeside setting; gd walks." ♦ 17 Apr-26 Sep. € 14.00 2010*

LESCONIL see Pont l'Abbé *2F2*

FRANCE

LESCUN *8G2* (1.5km SW Rural) *42.92805, -0.64147*
**Camp Municipal Le Lauzart, 64490 Lescun [tel/fax
05 59 34 51 77; campinglauzart@wanadoo.fr; www.
tourisme-aquitaine.fr]** Turn L (W) off N134 8km N of Urdos
on D339 sp Lescun & foll camping sp for 5km - rd gd but steep
with hairpins; foll Camping sp to fork L - do not ent Lescun vill,
v narr & steep, unsuitable for c'vans. Sm, mkd pitch, terr, pt
shd; htd wc; chem disp; mv service pnt; shwrs inc; el pnts (10A)
€2.80; gas; lndtte; shop; rest & bar nr; dogs €0.80; adv bkg;
quiet. "Mountain views; basic san facs, poss stretched high ssn;
gd walks; vg." ♦ 1 May-30 Sep. € 12.30   2010*

LESPERON *8E1* (4km SW Rural) *43.96657, -1.12940* **FFCC
Parc de Couchoy, Route de Linxe, 40260 Lesperon [tel/
fax 05 58 89 60 15; info@parcdecouchoy.com; www.
parcdecouchoy.com]** Exit N10 junc 13 to D41 sp Lesperon;
in 1km turn L, thro vill of Lesperon; L at junc onto D331;
bottom of hill turn R & immed L; site on R in 3km dir Linxe.
Med, mkd pitch, pt shd; wc; chem disp; child/baby facs;
shwrs inc; el pnts (6A) €3; gas; lndtte; shops 3km; tradsmn;
snacks; bar; playgrnd; pool; sand beach 8km; lake sw 5km;
10% statics; dogs €1; phone; poss cr; adv bkg; quiet; ccard
acc high ssn; 10% red long stay; CKE/CCI. "Lovely but isolated
site on edge of wine country; gd facs on lakes for sailing,
windsurfing; British owners; clean san facs; vg." 1 Jun-15 Sep.
€ 22.00   2009*

LESSAY *1D4* (6km SW Coastal) *49.19753, -1.60427* **Camp
Municipal des Dunes, 832 Blvd de la Mer, 50710 Créances
[02 33 46 31 86 or 02 22 17 25 61; fax 02 33 07 40 42;
www.ville-creances.fr]** Turn W onto D72/D652 in Lessay,
after 3km turn L on D650 at T-junc. After 1.5km turn R at
rndabt on D394 sp 'Créances Plage' & site office opp seafront
car pk. Med, mkd pitch, pt shd; wc; shwrs inc; el pnts (10A)
€4; gas; lndtte; shop 3km; rest, snacks; bar; playgrnd;
paddling pool; sand beach adj; games area; games rm; dogs
€1.50; poss cr; adv bkg; quiet; CKE/CCI. ♦ ltd 27 Jun-6 Sep.
€ 12.50   2011*

"That's changed – Should I let The Club know?"

If you find something on site that's different from
the site entry, fill in a report and let us know. See
www.caravanclub.co.uk/europereport.

LEUCATE PLAGE *10G1* (200m S Coastal) *42.90316, 3.05178*
**Camp Municipal du Cap Leucate, Chemín de Mouret,
11370 Leucate-Plage [04 68 40 01 37; fax 04 68 40 18 34;
cap.leucate@wanadoo.fr; www.mairie-leucate.fr/
capleucate]** Exit A9 junc 40 onto D627 thro Leucate vill to
Leucate-Plage approx 9km. Site sp. Lge, hdg pitch, shd; wc
(some cont); chem disp; mv service pnt; baby facs; fam bthrm;
shwrs inc; el pnts (6A) €2.10 long read required; lndtte; shop
200m; tradsmn; rest, snacks, bar 300m; BBQ; playgrnd; htd
pool 100m; sand beach 100m; games area; entmnt; TV;
60% statics; dogs €2; phone; adv bkg; quiet; red low ssn;
CKE/CCI. "Nice, spacious, sandy site in gd position; popular
with surfers; m'van area outside; gd NH; Immac new san facs
(2012)" 1 Feb-30 Nov. € 18.50   2013*

LEUCATE PLAGE *10G1* (6km W Coastal) *42.91405, 2.99796*
**Camping Le Fun, Domaine des Bergeries, 11510 Fitou
[04 68 45 71 97; contact@lefun-camping.com; www.
camping-lefun.com]** Exit A9 junc 40 dir Perpignan, site sp.
Med, mkd/mkd pitch, pt shd; htd wc; chem disp; shwrs inc;
el pnts (6A) €4; lndry rm; ltd shop; tradsmn; sm bar; BBQ
(communal only); playgrnd; pool; paddling pool; windsurfing;
tennis; games area; horseriding; wifi; 20% statics; dogs
€4; Eng spkn; adv bkg; quiet; ccard acc; red low ssn; CKE/
CCI. "Site in windy, rather isolated position & popular with
windsurfers; clean, adequate san facs; gd." ♦ 1 Apr-13 Nov.
€ 20.00   2011*

LEVIER *6H2* (1km NE Rural) *46.95974, 6.13289* **FFCC
Camping La Forêt, Route de Septfontaine, 25270 Levier
[tel/fax 03 81 89 53 46; camping@camping-dela-foret.
com; www.camping-dela-foret.com]** Fr D72 turn L at rndabt
by supmkt onto D41, site on L in 700m. Med, mkd pitch, pt
sl, terr, shd; wc; mv service pnt; baby facs; shwrs inc; el pnts
(6A) €3.50; gas; lndtte; supmkt 500m; snacks; playgrnd; htd
pool; dogs €0.50; poss cr; adv bkg; quiet. ♦ 11 Apr-20 Sep.
€ 16.50   2008*

LEVIGNAC DE GUYENNE see Miramont de Guyenne *7D2*

LEZIGNAN CORBIERES *8F4* (10km S Rural) *43.11727, 2.73609*
**Camping Le Pinada, Rue des Rousillous, 11200 Villerouge-
la-Crémade [04 68 43 32 29; contact@camping-le-pinada.
com; www.camping-le-pinada.com]** Fr Lézignan-Corbières
on D611 S, pass airfield & fork L thro Ferrals-les-Corbières (steep,
narr) on D106. Site sp & on L after 4km. Alt rte to avoid narr
rd thro Ferrals: exit A61 junc 25 & foll D611 thro Fabrezan. At
T-junc turn L onto D613 & after 2km turn L onto D106. Site
on R after Villerouge-la-Crémade. Med, hdg/mkd pitch, pt sl,
terr, shd; wc; chem disp (wc); baby facs; shwrs inc; el pnts (6A)
€5; lndtte; shop; tradsmn; snacks; bar; playgrnd; pool; rv sw &
fishing 3km; tennis; games area; entmnt; TV rm; 25% statics;
dogs €2; poss cr; Eng spkn; adv bkg, bkg fee; quiet; ccard not
acc; CKE/CCI. "Friendly owners; gd base for Carcassonne & Med
coast; well-run site; dated san facs; excel." ♦ 1 Mar-30 Oct.
€ 18.50   2012*

LEZIGNAN CORBIERES *8F4* (500m NW Urban) *43.20475,
2.75255* **Camp Municipal de la Pinède, Ave Gaston
Bonheur, 11200 Lézignan-Corbières [tel/fax
04 68 27 05 08; reception@campinglapinede.fr; www.
campinglapinede.fr]** On D6113 fr Carcassonne to Narbonne
on N of rd; foll 'Piscine' & 'Restaurant Le Patio' sp. Med, all
hdg/hdstg pitch, pt sl, terr, pt shd; wc; chem disp; mv service
pnt; shwrs inc; el pnts (6A) inc; gas; lndtte; shop 1km; rest,
snacks; bar; BBQ (gas only); htd pool adj; tennis; 5% statics;
dogs €2; adv bkg; quiet; ccard not acc; red low ssn/CKE/
CCI. "Well-run, clean, popular site; helpful, friendly staff; gd
san facs; gd m'van facs; some pitches diff due high kerb; no
c'vans/m'vans over 5m; superb pool; mkt Wed; gd touring base
or NH." ♦ 1 Mar-30 Oct. € 16.70   2009*

FRANCE

LEZINNES *6G1 47.79955, 4.08957* **La Graviere du Moulin, 7 route de Frangey, 89160 Lezinnes [tel/fax 03 86 75 68 67 / 02 29 59 27 (mob); lagravieredumoulin@lezinnes.fr; www.gravieredumoulin.lezinnes.fr]** Fr N on Route Nationale D905 turn L onto D200, foll rd round to the R onto Route de Frangey to site. Sm, wc; shwrs inc; el pnts €2.70; lndtte; playgrnd; canoeing; football; basketball; handball; tennis; "Gated strictly run, great café in Village" 29 Mar-7Oct. € 7.20   2013*

LICQUES *3A3* (1km E Rural) *50.77974, 1.94766* **Camping Les Pommiers des Trois Pays, 273 Rue du Breuil, 62850 Licques [tel/fax 03 21 35 02 02; contact@pommiers-3pays.com; www.pommiers-3pays.com]** Fr Calais to Guînes on D127 then on D215 to Licques; take D191 fr vill & foll sp; site on L in 1km. Or exit A26 junc 2 onto D217 to Licques; turn L onto D215; cont strt on & site on L on far side of vill. NB sloping ent, long o'fits beware grounding. Med, hdg/mkd pitch, sl, pt shd; wc; chem disp; mv service pnt; baby facs; shwrs inc; el pnts (16A) €4.80; lndtte; shops 1km; rest, snacks; bar; BBQ; playgrnd; htd, covrd pool; sand beach, golf, sailing 25km; fishing 2km; games area; games rm; wifi; entmnt; TV rm; 65% statics; dogs €1; adv bkg; ccard acc; red long stay/low ssn. "Site v full early Jun, adv bkg rec; lge pitches; friendly, helpful owners; gd quality facs, ltd low ssn; gd beaches nr; gd walking; conv Calais/Dunkerque ferries; gd" ♦ 1 Apr-1 Nov. € 32.10   2013*

LICQUES *3A3* (2.5km E Rural) *50.77905, 1.95567* **Camping-Caravaning Le Canchy, Rue de Canchy, 62850 Licques [tel/fax 03 21 82 63 41; camping.lecanchy@wanadoo.fr; www.camping-lecanchy.com]** Fr Calais D127 to Guînes, then D215 sp Licques; site sp in vill on D191; site on L in 1km with narr app rd. Or fr Ardres take D224 to Liques then as above. Or A26 fr Calais exit junc 2 onto D217 dir Zouafques/Tournehem/Licques. Foll sp site in vill. Med, hdg/mkd pitch, pt shd; wc (some cont); chem disp; shwrs €0.50; el pnts (6A) €3.70; lndtte; shops 2km; snacks; bar; BBQ; playgrnd; fishing nrby; entmnt; 50% statics; Eng spkn; adv bkg; quiet; ccard acc; red CKE/CCI. "Busy site; friendly, helpful owners; dated san facs, ltd low ssn; gd walking/cycling; conv Calais & ferries; vg." 15 Mar-31 Oct. € 17.70   2012*

LIEPVRE see Seléstat *6E3*

LIGNY EN BARROIS *6E1* (500m W Rural) *48.68615, 5.31666* **Camp Municipal Chartel, Rue des Etats-Unis, 55500 Ligny-en-Barrois [03 29 77 09 36 or 03 29 78 02 22 (Mairie)]** If app fr E, leave N4 at Ligny-en-Barrois N exit, turn S twd town; in approx 500m turn R at junc (before rd narr); foll site sp 500m on L. If app fr W, leave N4 at exit W of town onto N135 (Rue des Etats-Unis); site sp on R. Sm, hdstg, terr, pt shd; wc (some cont); own san facs; chem disp (wc); shwrs; el pnts inc; shop 500m; playgrnd; pool 1km; rv sw & fishing 500m; dogs; rd noise; Eng spkn; CKE/CCI. "Poss diff lge o'fits; modern san facs; further modernisation planned (2010); gd NH; Great site and location" 1 Jun-30 Sep. € 10.65   2012*

LIGNY LE CHATEL *4F4* (500m SW Rural) *47.89542, 3.75288* **Camp Municipal La Noue Marrou, 89144 Ligny-le-Châtel [03 86 47 56 99 or 03 86 47 41 20 (Mairie); fax 03 86 47 44 02; camping.lignylechatel@orange.fr; www.mairie-ligny-le-chatel-89.fr]** Exit A6 at junc 20 Auxerre S onto D965 to Chablis. In Chablis cross rv & turn L onto D91 dir Ligny. On ent Ligny turn L onto D8 at junc after Maximart. Cross sm rv, foll sp to site on L in 200m. Sm, mkd pitch, pt shd; wc; chem disp (wc); mv service pnt; shwrs inc; el pnts (10A) inc (poss rev pol, poss long lead req); lndtte; shop; rest, snacks; bar; wifi; playgrnd; rv sw adj; tennis; dogs; phone; bus 200m; quiet; red low ssn; CKE/CCI. "Well-run site; lge pitches; no twin-axles; friendly warden lives on site; san facs dated but clean; pleasant vill with gd rests; popular NH; excel." ♦ 1 May-30 Sep. € 12.00   2012*

> "I like to fill in the reports as I travel from site to site" You'll find report forms at the back of this guide, or you can fill them in online at www.caravaclub.co.uk/europereport.

⊞ **LIGUEIL** *4H2* (2km N Rural) *47.05469, 0.84615* **Camping de la Touche, Ferme de la Touche, 37240 Ligueil [02 47 59 54 94; booklatouche@hotmail.co.uk; www.theloirevalley.com]** Fr Loches SW on D31; turn L at x-rds with white cross on R 2km after Ciran; in 500m turn R, site on R bef hotel. Fr A10 exit junc 25 Ste Maure-de-Touraine & foll sp to Ligueil; then take D31 dir Loches; turn L at white cross. Sm, mkd ptch, hdstg, pt shd; wc; chem disp (wc); shwrs inc; el pnts (10A) €5; lndtte (inc dryer); sm shop; snacks; playgrnd; pool; cycle hire; fishing; wifi; dogs free; adv bkg; ccard acc; quiet; CKE/CCI. "Well-maintained, relaxed CL-type site; lge pitches; welcoming, helpful British owners; c'van storage; excel san facs; gd walking & touring base; much wild life; conv m'way; gd." € 14.00   2011*

⊞ **LILLEBONNE** *3C2* (4km W Rural) *49.53024, 0.49763* **Camping Hameau des Forges, 76170 St Antoine-la-Forêt [02 35 39 80 28 or 02 35 91 48 30]** Fr Le Havre take rd twds Tancarville bdge, D982 into Lillebonne, D81 W to site on R in 4km, sp (part winding rd). Fr S over Tancarville bdge onto D910 sp Bolbec. At 2nd rndabt turn R onto D81, site 5km on L. NB Concealed ent by phone box. Med, pt shd; wc; chem disp; shwrs €1.20; el pnts (5A) inc; tradsmn; 90% statics; dogs; poss cr; adv bkg; quiet; no ccard acc; CKE/CCI. "Basic, clean site; staff welcoming & helpful; poss statics only low ssn & facs ltd; site muddy when wet; conv NH for Le Havre ferries late arr & early dep; Roman amphitheatre in town worth visit." € 10.40   2010*

LIMERAY see Amboise *4G2*

LIMEUIL see Bugue, Le *7C3*

LIMOGES 7B3 (10km N Rural) 45.52142, 1.16326 **Camping Uzurat Sarl Generation Activities, 40 Ave d'Uzurat, 87280 Limoges [tel/fax 05 55 38 49 43; contact@ campinglimoges.fr; www.campinglimoges.fr]** Fr N twd Limoges on A20 take exit 30 sp Limoges Nord Zone Industrielle, Lac d'Uzurat; foll sp to Lac d'Uzarat & site. Fr S twd Limoges on A20 exit junc 31 & foll sp as above. Well sp fr A20. Lge, hdstg, pt shd; htd wc (some cont); chem disp; mv service pnt; serviced pitches; baby facs; shwrs inc; el pnts (10A) €3.60; lndtte; hypmkt 500m; playgrnd adj; lake fishing; wifi; some statics; dogs €1.50; bus; phone; m'van o'night area; Eng spkn; quiet but some rd noise; ccard acc; red low ssn/long stay; CKE/CCI. "Lovely site by lake; gd sized pitches; friendly & helpful staff; clean modern san facs; pitch on chippings - awnings diff; poss red opening dates - phone ahead low ssn; poss mkt traders; conv martyr vill Oradour-sur-Glane; gd touring base; conv m'way; popular NH" ♦ 15 Mar-31 Oct. € 25.00   2013*

LIMOGNE EN QUERCY 7D4 (600m W Rural) 44.39571, 1.76396 **Camp Municipal Bel-Air, 46260 Limogne-en-Quercy [05 65 24 32 75; fax 05 65 24 73 59; camping. bel-air@orange.fr]** E fr Cahors on D911 just bef Limogne vill. W fr Villefranche on D911 just past vill; 3 ents about 50m apart. Sm, mkd pitch, sl, shd; wc; shwrs inc; el pnts (6A) inc; lndtte; shops & bar 600m; pool; quiet; adv bkg rec high ssn. "Friendly welcome; if warden absent, site yourself; pleasant vill." 1 Apr-1 Oct. € 14.30   2009*

LIMOGNE EN QUERCY 7D4 (6km NW Rural) 44.42344, 1.69609 **Camping Lalbrade (Naturist), Lalbrade, 46260 Lugagnac [05 65 31 52 35 or 06 20 05 98 57 (mob); fax 05 65 24 36 21; lalbrade@orange.fr; http://lalbrade. free.fr/]** Fr D911 Cahors to Villefranche-de-Rouergue rd; at Limogne-en-Quercy take D40 sp Lugagnac (narr rd); site sp after Lugagnac; 2km of single-track ent rd. Diff to find. Sm, pt shd; wc (some cont); shwrs inc; el pnts (6-10A) €3-4; pool; dogs €3; Eng spkn; quiet. "In interesting area; gd walking within site boundaries." ♦ 3 Apr-26 Sep. € 24.00   2010*

LIMOUX 8G4 (200m SE Urban) 43.04734, 2.22280 **Camp Municipal du Breilh, Ave Salvador Allende, 11300 Limoux [04 68 31 13 63; fax 04 68 31 18 43; limoux@limoux.fr]** Fr D118 cross bdge to E side of Rv Aude, then S on D129 Ave de Corbières & foll site sp. Not well sp on ent town fr N. Sm, pt sl; wc; shwrs; el pnts (6A) €2.90; shops adj; pool; tennis adj; fishing; boating; quiet but some rd noise. "Basic rvside site; pleasant town; suitable sh stay." 1 Jun-30 Sep. € 11.30   2013*

LINDOIS, LE see Montbron 7B3

LINXE 8E1 (1km N Rural) 43.93203, -1.25770 **Camp Municipal Le Grandjean, 190 Route de Mixe, 40260 Linxe [05 58 42 90 00; fax 05 58 42 94 67; camping.grandjean@ wanadoo.fr]** Exit N10 junc 12 dir Castets; take D42 to Linxe; turn R & R into site. Site well sp at N of Linxe cent. Med, mkd pitch, pt shd; wc, chem disp; baby facs; shwrs inc; el pnts (10A) inc; lndtte; supmkt 5km; rest, snacks, bar 1km; playgrnd; cycle hire, tennis 1km; dogs; Eng spkn; adv bkg; quiet. "Gd, quiet site; friendly warden; immac facs." End Jun-mid Sep. € 18.45   2010*

LION D'ANGERS, LE 2G4 (500m N Rural) 47.63068, -0.71190 **Camp Municipal Les Frênes, Route de Château-Gontier, 49220 Le Lion-d'Angers [02 41 95 31 56; fax 02 41 95 34 87; mairie.lelionangers@wanadoo.fr; www.leliondangers.fr]** On N162 Laval-Angers rd, site on R bef bdge over Rv Oudon app Le Lion-d'Angers, easily missed. Med, mkd pitch, pt shd; wc; chem disp; shwrs inc; el pnts (10A) €2.75 ; lndry rm; shops adj; rest; BBQ; playgrnd; rv fishing adj; phone; no twin-axle vans; poss cr; Eng spkn; adv bkg; quiet but some rd noise; CKE/CCI. "Excel site; friendly staff; gd location; wc block up 2 flights steps; no m'vans; unrel opening dates - phone ahead." ♦ 18 May-1 Sep. € 6.40   2013*

LISIEUX 3D1 (2km N Rural) 49.16515, 0.22054 **Camp Municipal de La Vallée, 9 Rue de la Vallée, 14100 Lisieux [02 31 62 00 40 or 02 31 48 18 10 (LS); fax 02 31 48 18 11; tourisme@cclisieuxpaysdauge.fr; www.lisieux-tourisme. com]** N on D579 fr Lisieux twd Pont l'Evêque. Approx 500m N of Lisieux take L to Coquainvilliers onto D48 & foll sp for Camping (turn L back in Lisieux dir). Site on D48 parallel to main rd. Med, hdstg, pt shd; wc (some cont); chemp disp; shwrs inc; el pnts (6A) €2.50-4.50; gas; shop 1km; rest, snacks, bar 2km; htd pool, waterslide nrby; 20% statics; bus fr ent; poss cr; ccard not acc; rd noise; CKE/CCI. "Interesting town, childhood home of St Thérèse; helpful warden; v clean san facs; gd." 1 Apr-30 Sep. € 12.00   2010*

LISIEUX 3D1 (10km NE Rural) 49.18009, 0.33238 **Aire Naturalle Le Mont Criquet (Bernard), Clos du Mont Criquet, 14590 Ouilly-du-Houley [02 31 62 98 98 or 06 08 93 19 63 (mob); bernard.ocjh@orange.fr; http:// rmc14.pagesperso-orange.fr/]** Fr D613 turn N onto D137 to Ouilly-du-Houley; foll D137 after x-rds in vill by church; site sp. NB App narr single track rd - owner assists, just phone. Sm, pt sl, pt shd; wc; shwrs inc; el pnts (2-6A) €2.40; lndtte; tradsmn; BBQ; playgrnd; games area; 60% statics; dogs; poss cr; Eng spkn; adv bkg; quiet; CKE/CCI. "Beautiful site in orchard; helpful, knowledgeable owner; gd modern facs; m'vans not acc in periods wet weather" 30 Apr-14 Sep. € 9.00   2009*

LIT ET MIXE 8E1 (8km W Coastal) 44.03861, -1.33477 **Camp Municipal de la Plage du Cap de l'Homy, Ave de l'Océan, 40170 Lit-et-Mixe [05 58 42 83 47; fax 05 58 42 49 79; contact@camping-cap.com; www.camping-cap.com]** S fr Mimizan on D652. In Lit-et-Mixe R on D88 to Cap de l'Homy Plage. Site on R when rd becomes 1-way. Lge, hdg/mkd pitch, pt sl, shd; wc (some cont); chem disp; mv service pnt; shwrs inc; el pnts (10A) €6.90 (poss rev pol); lndtte; shop, rest high ssn; playgrnd; beach 300m; surfing; wifi; dogs €2.80; poss cr; quiet. "Popular site, adv bkg rec high ssn; site in pine woods on sandy soil; gd for beach holiday; gd walks; interesting flora & fauna; Aire de Service for m'vans at ent; vg." 1 May-30 Sep. € 18.70   2011*

LITTEAU see Balleroy 1D4

LIVERDUN see Nancy 6E2

LLAURO see Ceret 8H4

LOCHES *4H2* (500m S Urban) *47.12255, 1.00175* **Kawan Village La Citadelle, Ave Aristide Briand, 37600 Loches [02 47 59 05 91 or 06 21 37 93 06 (mob); fax 02 47 59 00 35; camping@lacitadelle.com; www. lacitadelle.com]** Fr any dir take by-pass to S end of town & leave at Leclerc rndabt for city cent; site well sp on R in 800m. Lge, hdg/mkd pitch, pt shd; htd wc (some cont); chem disp; mv service pnt; shwrs inc; el pnts (10A) €4.30 (poss rev pol) (poss long lead req); gas; lndtte (inc dryer); shop & 2km; tradsmn, rests, snacks; bar; BBQ; playgrnd; htd pool on site & 2 htd pools adj; fishing; boating; tennis nr; games area; cycle hire; golf 9km; wifi; entmnt; sat TV rm; 30% statics; dogs €3; poss cr; Eng spkn; adv bkg rec; poss night noise fr entmnt; ccard acc; red long stay/low ssn; CKE/CCI. "Attractive, well-kept, busy site nr beautiful old town; views of citadel; gd sized pitches, poss uneven; helpful staff; facs poss stretched; barrier clsd 2200-0800; poss no night security (2010); rvside walk into town; poss mosquitoes; site muddy after heavy rain; mkt Wed & Sat am; Excel site; lge serviced pitches; short walk to a beautiful mediaeval town" ♦ 18 Mar - 29 Sep. € 39.10   2013*

LOCMARIAQUER *2G3* (800m N Rural) *47.57339, -2.95774* **Camping La Ferme Fleurie, Kerlogonan, 56740 Locmariaquer [tel/fax 02 97 57 34 06; www. campinglafermefleurie.com]** Sp off D781. Sm, mkd pitch, pt shd; wc; shwrs inc; el pnts (10A) €2.50; shop; lndtte; playgrnd; beach 1km; fishing; sailing; entmnt; some statics; dogs €1; adv bkg ess high ssn; quiet. "Lovely, well-kept CL-type site in great position; coastal path nr; attractive area; friendly; excel, clean facs but poss stretched when site full;; midge repellent rec; unrel opening dates - phone ahead low ssn; conv megalith sites." 15 Mar-20 Oct. € 13.80   2010*

LOCMARIAQUER *2G3* (2km S Coastal) *47.55598, -2.93939* **Camp Municipal de la Falaise, Route de Kerpenhir, 56740 Locmariaquer [tel/fax 02 97 57 31 59 or 02 97 57 32 32 (LS); campinglafalaise@wanadoo.fr; www.ot-locmariaquer. com www.campingmunicipallafalaise.com]** Site sp fr Locmariaquer. On ent vill, site sp R avoiding narr cent (also sp fr vill cent). Lge, mkd pitch, pt sl; wc (some cont); shwrs; chem disp; mv service pnt; el pnts (6A) inc; gas; lndtte; shop 1km tradsmn; rest & 500m; playgrnd; sand beach adj; entmnt (high ssn); dogs €2.101; poss cr; ccard acc. "Gd, quiet site in pleasant countryside; clean san facs, some modern & some dated; archaeological remains; gd fishing, boating, cycling & coastal walking; rest simple but superb food" ♦ 15 Mar-15 Oct. € 16.60   2013*

LOCRONAN *2E2* (E Urban) *48.09657, -4.19774* **Camping de Locronan, Rue de la Troménie, 29180 Locronan [02 98 91 87 76 / 06 28 80 44 74; contact@camping-locronan.fr; www.camping-locronan.fr]** Fr Quimper/ Douarnenez foll sp D7 Châteaulin; ignore town sp, take 1st R after 3rd rndabt. Fr Châteaulin, turn L at 1st town sp & foll site sp at sharp L turn. NB Foll sp around town, do not ent Locronan. Med, hdg pitch, steeply terr, pt shd; wc; chem disp; baby facs; fam bathrm; shwrs; el pnts (10A) €4.30; lndtte (inc dryer); shops 1.5km; tradsmn; rest & bar 400m; playgrnd; htd covrd pool; paddling pool; games area; wifi; dogs €2.20; phone; Eng spkn; adv bkg (rec indicate o'fit size when bkg); quiet; ccard acc; CKE/ CCI. "Gd touring cent with gd views; gd walks; historic town; excel; Ltd san facs low ssn" ♦ 13 Apr-10 Nov. € 32.30   2013*

LOCRONAN *2E2* (5km S Rural) *48.09868, -4.18302* **Camping Ar Voden, La Motte, 29136 Plogonnec [tel/fax 02 98 51 80 02; contact@camping-ar-voden.fr; www. camping-ar-voden.fr]** Fr Locronan take D7 twd Châteaulin. By side of church, foll sp. La Motte at top of hill by La Chapelle Ar-Zonj. Med, hdg/mkd pitch, pt sl; terr, pt shd; wc; chem disp; shwrs inc; el pnts (6A) €3; shop 3km; tradsmn; rest 1km; BBQ; playgrnd; htd covrd pool 800m; sand beach 5km; horseriding 500m; mountain bike tracks; dogs €1.10; Eng spkn; poss cr; adv bkg; quiet; CKE/CCI. "Rallies accepted; mkt Sat." 28 Jun-31 Aug. € 12.80   2008*

LOCUNOLE see Quimperle *2F2*

LODEVE *10E1* (5km NE Rural) *43.76110, 3.36000* **Camping des Sources, Chemin d'Aubaygues, 34700 Soubès [tel/fax 04 67 44 32 02 or 06 86 38 91 31 (mob); camping-sources@ orange.fr; www.camping-sources.com]** Exit A75 junc 52 to Soubès; then 1st R dir Fozières; foll sp. Sm, terr, pt shd; wc; chem disp; shwrs inc; el pnts (6A) inc; lndtte; tradsmn; shop 1km; snacks; playgrnd; children pool; rv sw, sailing & fishing adj; dogs €3; adv bkg rec high ssn; quiet; ccard acc; red low ssn; CKE/CCI. "Peaceful site with relaxed atmosphere; helpful, pleasant owner; immac facs; not suitable lge o'fits as app rd v narr & some pitches sm; lovely bar/rest; excel." ♦ 29 Mar-11 Nov. € 20.00   2009*

⊞ **LODEVE** *10E1* (6km SE Rural) *43.69198, 3.35030* **Camping Les Peupliers, Les Casseaux, 34700 Le Bosc [tel/fax 04 67 44 38 08; contact@camping-les-peupliers-salagou.com; www.camping-les-peupliers-salagou.com]** Take exit 54 on A75; sp Le Bosc. Med, mkd pitch, pt sl, terr, pt shd; wc; shwrs inc; el pnts (5A) €2; gas; shop 4km; tradsmn Jul-Aug; snacks; bar; playgrnd; pool; sand beach 40km; lake 5km; 90% statics; dogs €1; Eng spkn; adv bkg; some rd noise; CKE/ CCI. "Friendly staff; ltd facs low ssn; recep clsd low ssn, phone ahead; windsurfing Lac du Salagou; easy access fr m'way; conv winter NH." ♦ ltd € 20.00   2011*

"We must tell The Club about that great site we found"

Get your site reports in by mid-August and we'll do our best to get your updates into the next edition of Caravan Europe.

LODEVE *10E1* (9km S Rural) *43.67182, 3.35429* **Camp Municipal Les Vailhés, Le Puech, Lac du Salagou, 34702 Lodève [04 67 44 25 98 or 04 67 44 86 00 (LS); fax 04 67 45 65 97; camping@lodevoisetlarzac.fr]** Fr N exit A75 junc 54 onto D148 dir Octon & Lac du Salagou. Foll site sp. Fr S exit A75 junc 55. Lge, hdg/mkd pitch, terr, pt shd; wc; chem disp; shwrs inc; el pnts (16A) inc; lndtte; tradsmn; BBQ; playgrnd; lake sw & beach; fishing; watersports; 20% statics; dogs; poss cr; Eng spkn; quiet; CKE/CCI. "Peaceful, remote site by lake; pleasant staff; no facs nrby; excel walks; gd." ♦ 1 Apr-30 Sep. € 17.50   2010*

LODEVE *10E1* (5km W Rural) *43.73631, 3.26443* **Camping Domaine de Lambeyran (Naturist), Lambeyran, 34700 Lodève [04 67 44 13 99; fax 04 67 44 09 91; lambeyran@ wanadoo.fr; www.lambeyran.com]** Fr N or S on N9 take sliprd to Lodève. Leave town on D35 W twd Bédarieux. In 2km take 2nd R, sp L'Ambeyran & St Martin. Foll sp 3.7km up winding hill to site. Lge, hdg/mkd pitch, terr, pt sl, pt shd; wc; chem disp; shwrs inc; el pnts (6A) €4.20; gas; lndtte; shop & supmkt 4km, rest, snacks, bar high ssn; BBQ; playgrnd; pool; sailing, windsurfing 10km; 5% statics; dogs; phone; Eng spkn; adv bkg; quiet; ccard acc; red low ssn/long stay; CKE/CCI. "Superb location with views; lge pitches; gd walking, inc on site; gates clsd 2000; Lac du Salagou with sports facs 12km." 15 May-15 Sep. € 24.40   2010*

LODS see Ornans *6G2*

LONDES LES MAURES, LA see Hyeres *10F3*

LONG see Abbeville *3B3*

LONGCHAUMOIS see Morez *9A3*

LONGEVILLE SUR MER *7A1* (2km S Coastal) *46.40402, -1.50673* **Camp Le Petit Rocher, 1250 Ave du Dr Mathevet, 85560 Longeville-sur-Mer [02 51 90 31 57; fax 02 51 96 17 93; info@campinglepetitrocher.com; www. campinglepetitrocher.com]** Fr La Tranche-sur-Mer take D105 N. In 8km site clearly sp 'Le Rocher' at 3rd exit fr rndabt (Ave du Dr Mathevet). Site on R in 1km at beginning of beach rd. Lge, hdg/mkd pitch, pt sl, shd; wc; chem disp; shwrs inc; el pnts (6A) inc; gas; shops adj; rest & snacks nrby; playgrnd; sand beach 150m; games area; games rm; cycle hire; entmnt; some statics; dogs €3; adv bkg; quiet; CKE/CCI. "Gd beach holiday; gd facs." 1 May-20 Sep. € 23.00   2008*

See advertisement

LONGEVILLE SUR MER *7A1* (2km S Coastal) *46.39499, -1.48736* **Camping Le Sous-Bois, La Haute Saligotière, 85560 Longeville-sur-Mer [02 51 33 32 73 / 02 51 33 36 90 / 06 71 63 39 62 (mob)]** Sp fr D105 fr La Tranche-sur-Mer. Med, hdg pitch, shd; wc; chem disp; shwrs inc; el pnts (10A) €4. (poss rev pol); lndtte; shop; tradsmn; playgrnd; sand beach 1km; tennis; TV; 15% statics; dogs €1.60; phone; quiet; ccard not acc; CKE/CCI. "Nice, well-managed, family site; pleasant 1km woodland walk to beach; gd walks; cycle tracks; excel; great for cycling; Lovely sandy beach" ♦ 1 Jun-30 Sep. € 19.00   2013*

LONGEVILLE SUR MER *7A1* (3km S Coastal) *46.38830, -1.48777* **Camping Les Clos des Pins, Les Conches, 85560 Longeville-sur-Mer [02 51 90 31 69; fax 02 51 90 30 68; info@campingclosdespins.com; www. campingclosdespins.com]** Fr La Tranche-sur-Mer take D105 coast rd N, turn L in Les Conches into Ave de la Plage, site on R in 1km. Med, mkd pitch, pt sl, shd; wc; chem disp; baby facs; shwrs inc; el pnts (6A) €4; gas; lndtte; shop; tradsmn; rest, snacks; bar; BBQ (gas/elec); playgrnd; htd pool; paddling pool; waterslide; sand beach 200m; watersports; cycle hire; games area; many activities; wifi; entmnt; 60% statics; dogs €3.30; phone; bus; Eng spkn; adv bkg; quiet; red low ssn/CKE/CCI. "Set among pine trees; some pitches in soft sand - adv bkg rec to ensure a suitable pitch; friendly, helpful staff; excel leisure facs; vg." ♦ 3 Apr-26 Sep. € 25.00   2009*

LONGEVILLE SUR MER *7A1* (3km SW Coastal) *46.41310, -1.52280* **Camping Les Brunelles, Rue de la Parée, Le Bouil, 85560 Longeville-sur-Mer [02 51 33 50 75; fax 02 51 33 98 21; camping@les-brunelles.com; www. les-brunelles.com]** Site bet Longeville-sur-Mer & Jard-sur-Mer; foll D21. Lge, mkd pitch, pt sl, shd; wc; mv service pnt; baby facs; sauna; shwrs inc; el pnts (6A) inc; lndtte (inc dryer); shop; tradsmn; rest 500m; snacks; bar; playgrnd; 2 htd pools (1 covrd); paddling pool; waterslides; sand beach 800m; watersports; tennis; cycle hire; games area; gym; horseriding 2km; golf 15km; wifi; entmnt; TV rm; 75% statics; dogs €5; adv bkg; ccard acc. "Gd san facs." ♦ 2 Apr-24 Sep. € 25.00 (CChq acc) SBS - A02   2008*

⊞ **LONGNY AU PERCHE** *4E2* (1km SW Rural) *48.51749, 0.74177* **FFCC Camping Monaco Parc, Route de Monceaux, 61290 Longny-au-Perche [02 33 73 59 59; fax 02 33 25 77 56; info@campingmonacoparc.com; www. campingmonacoparc.com]** Fr N on N12 take D918 to Longny, then D111 S to site, sp. Med, mkd pitch, some hdstg, pt shd; htd wc; chem disp; mv service pnt; baby facs; sauna; shwrs; el pnts; lndtte (inc dryer); shop; tradsmn; supmkt 2km; rest, snacks; bar; BBQ; playgrnd; htd, covrd pool; lake fishing; games area; fitness rm; entmnt; TV; 80% statics; adv bkg; quiet. "Conv NH to/fr Paris; ltd touring pitches." ♦ 2009*

LONS LE SAUNIER *6H2* (1km NE Rural) *46.68437, 5.56843* **Camping La Marjorie, 640 Blvd de l'Europe, 39000 Lons-le-Saunier [03 84 24 26 94; fax 03 84 24 08 40; info@ camping-marjorie.com; www.camping-marjorie.com]** Site clearly sp in town on D1083 twd Besançon. Fr N bear R dir 'Piscine', cross under D1083 to site. Lge, hdg pitch, some hdstg, pt sl, pt shd; wc; baby facs; chem disp; shwrs inc; el pnts (10A) inc (poss rev pol); gas; lndtte; shop; tradsmn; rest; bar; playgrnd; 2 htd pools (1 covrd) & aquatic cent adj; games area; golf 8km; wifi; entmnt; dogs €2.50; phone; Eng spkn; rd noise; ccard accs; red low ssn; twin-axles extra; CKE/CCI. "Lovely site in beautiful area; conv location; lge pitches; welcoming; friendly owners; excel, spotless san facs; 20 mins walk to interesting old town; ideal touring base; rec; Excel" ♦ 1 Apr-15 Oct. €32.80 2013*

LONS LE SAUNIER *6H2* (8km NE Rural) *46.71213, 5.64034* **Camp Municipal de la Toupe, 39210 Baume-les-Messieurs [03 84 44 63 16; fax 03 84 44 95 40; baumelesmessieurs@ wandoo.fr]** On D471 Lons-le-Saunier to Champagnole rd, take L onto D4 then D70 to Baume-les-Messieurs. Site 500m thro vill on D70 - narr, steep app rd not suitable lge o'fits. Or, fr D1083 turn E onto D120 at St Germain-lès-Arlay to Voiteur then onto D70. Sm, pt shd; wc (some cont); shwrs inc; el pnts (6A) €2.80; playgrnd; rv adj; dogs €1; quiet. "Beautiful location nr lovely vill; some outdated facs." 1 Apr-30 Sep. €7.50 2008*

LONS LE SAUNIER *6H2* (8km SW Rural) *46.65854, 5.49934* **Camp Municipal, Grande Rue, 39570 Chilly-le-Vignoble [03 84 43 09 34 or 03 84 43 09 32 (Mairie); fax 03 84 47 34 09; mairie.chillylevignoble@wanadoo.fr; www.ville-lons-le-saunier.fr]** Fr A39 exit junc 8 onto D678. After approx 5km turn R to Courlans & Chilly-le-Vignoble. Site sp 2km. Med, pt shd; wc (most cont); shwrs inc; el pnts (6A) inc; supmkt 3km; tradsmn; rest, snacks; playgrnd; games rm; golf nrby; quiet; CKE/CCI. "V pleasant site in quiet vill; warm welcome, friendly staff; ent for c'vans fr 1530 only; gd." 1 Jun-15 Sep. €13.60 2010*

⊞ **LORIENT** *2F2* (6km N Rural) *47.82041, -3.40689* **Camping Ty Nénez, Route de Lorient, 56620 Pont-Scorff [02 97 32 51 16; fax 02 97 32 43 77; contact@camping-tynenez.com; www.lorient-camping.com]** N fr N165 on D6, look for sp Quéven in approx 5km on R. If missed, cont for 1km & turn around at rndabt. Site sp fr Pont-Scorff. Med, hdg pitch, pt shd; htd wc; chem disp; mv service pnt; baby facs; shwrs inc; el pnts (16A) €3; lndtte; supmkt 1km; bar; games area; some statics; dogs €1; adv bkg; quiet; red low ssn. "Site barrier locked 2200-0800; excel low ssn; peaceful NH." ♦ €10.00 2010*

LORIENT *2F2* (10km NE Rural) *47.80582, -3.28347* **Camp Municipal St Caradec, Quai St Caradec, 56700 Hennebont [02 97 36 21 73; camping.municipal.stcaradec@wanadoo.fr]** Fr S on D781 to Hennebont. In town cent turn L & cross bdge, then sharp R along Rv Blavet for 1km. On R on rv bank. Med, mkd pitch, pt shd; wc; chem disp; shwrs inc; el pnts inc; lndtte; shop 2km; playgrnd; sand beach 12km; some statics; adv bkg; quiet; CKE/CCI. "Pretty site." 15 Jun-15 Sep. 2009*

⊞ **LORIENT** *2F2* (4km SW Coastal) *47.70955, -3.39228* **Camping La Fontaine, Rue de Quéhello, Kerderff, 56260 Larmor-Plage [02 97 33 71 28 or 02 97 65 11 11; fax 02 97 33 70 32; contact@campingdelafontaine.com; www. camping-la-fontaine.com]** At Larmor-Plage 300m fr D152. Well sp. Med, hdg pitch, pt sl, pt shd; htd wc; mv service pnt; chem disp; baby facs; shwrs inc; el pnts (10A) €2.45 (rev pol); lndtte; shop adj; snacks; bar; playgrnd; beach 800m; tennis adj; horseriding; sailing; sports; dogs €1.55; Eng spkn. "Excel site; gd facs." ♦ € 15.00 2009*

LOUDEAC *2E3* (2km E Rural) *48.17827, -2.73010* **Camp Municipal Pont es Bigots, 22600 Loudéac [02 96 28 14 92 or 02 96 66 85 00 (Mairie); fax 02 96 66 08 93; mairie. loudeac@wanadoo.fr; www.ville-loudeac.fr]** Fr Loudéac, take N164 twd Rennes, site on L by lake in 1km, sp. Height barrier into site 1.8m. Med, hdg pitch, pt shd; wc; shwrs; el pnts €2; shops 1km; playgrnd; entmnt; lake sw; fishing; horseriding; quiet. "V pleasant; site clsd 1100-1700." 15 Jun-15 Sep. €6.35 2009*

LOUDENVIELLE see Arreau *8G2*

LOUDUN *4H1* (1km W Rural) *47.00379, 0.06337* **Camp Municipal de Beausoleil, Chemin de l'Etang, 86200 Loudun [05 49 98 14 22 / 05 49 98 15 38; fax 05 49 98 12 88; mairie@ville-loudun.fr; www.ville-loudun.fr]** On main rte fr Poitiers to Saumur/Le Mans; N on D347 around Loudun, foll sp; turn L just N of level x-ing, then on R approx 250m. Sm, hdg/mkd pitch, terr, pt shd; wc, chem disp; shwrs inc; el pnts (10A) €3.15; shop 1km; playgrnd; lake adj for fishing; bus adj; Eng spkn; quiet; CKE/CCI. "Beautiful, well-kept site; lge pitches; low ssn site yourself, warden calls am & pm; friendly & helpful; excel; long way from the town" ♦ 15 May-31 Aug. € 10.40 2013*

LOUE *4F1* (Urban) *47.99606, -0.14777* **Camping Village Loisirs (Au Fil de l'Eau), Place Hector Vincent, 72540 Loué [02 43 88 65 65; fax 02 43 88 59 46; village.dhotes@ orange.fr; www.villageloisirs.com]** Exit A81 junc 1 to Loué. Site in cent of town adj sw pool. Sm, unshd; htd wc; chem disp; shwrs inc; el pnts (6A) €4; lndtte (inc dryer); rest; bar; playgrnd; htd pool; waterslide; paddling pool; cycle hire & fishing adj; games rm; TV; 50% statics; dogs €1; phone; bus; Eng spkn; adv bkg; quiet; CKE/CCI. "Friendly staff; conv Le Mans (rec adv bkg race w/ends); vg." ♦ 1 Apr-31 Oct. € 12.00 2008*

FRANCE

LOUHANS 6H1 (2km W Urban) 46.62286, 5.21733 **Camp Municipal de Louhans, 10, Chemin de la Chapellerie, 71500 Louhans [03 85 75 19 02 or 03 85 76 75 10 (Mairie); fax 03 85 76 75 11; mairiedelouhanschateaurenaud@yahoo.fr]** In Louhans foll sp for Romenay on D971. Go under rlwy & over rv. Site on L just after stadium. Med, hdg/mkd pitch, hdstg, shd; wc (some cont); chem disp; mv service pnt 700mtrs; shwrs inc; el pnts €3.60; lndtte; snacks; playgrnd; pool & tennis courts adj; sw rv adj; poss cr; adv bkg; some rlwy noise; CKE/CCI. "Rv location; clean & well-appointed; sports complex adj; lovely cycling area; lge town mkt Mon am; poss itinerants; vg." ♦ ltd 1 Apr-30 Sep. € 7.40 2012*

LOUPIAC see Payrac 7D3

LOURDES 8F2 (1km N Urban) 43.11425, -0.03661 **Caravaning Plein-Soleil, Route de Tarbes, 65100 Lourdes [05 62 94 40 93; fax 05 62 94 51 20; camping.plein.soleil@wanadoo.fr; www.camping-pleinsoleil.com]** Fr N site sp on N21. Turn R imm opp aquarium sp. Sm, terr, pt shd; htd wc; chem disp; shwrs inc; el pnts (4A) inc; lndtte; snacks; playgrnd; pool; dogs; poss cr; Eng spkn; adv bkg; poss noise fr adj builders' yard; red low ssn; CKE/CCI. "Pleasant site; helpful staff; gd san facs; gd security; ltd access lge o'fits; muddy when wet; conv hypmkt." Easter-10 Oct. € 19.00 2011*

LOURDES 8F2 (2km N Urban) 43.11569, -0.03225 **FFCC Camping Le Moulin du Monge, 28 Ave Jean Moulin, 65100 Lourdes [05 62 94 28 15; fax 05 62 94 20 54; camping.moulin.monge@wanadoo.fr; www.camping-lourdes.com]** Fr N on N21 fr Tarbes, past airport & on app to Lourdes turn L sp 'Zone Indust du Monge'. Site on L of rd in 100m immed bef rlwy bdge. Med, pt shd; htd wc; mv service pnt; sauna; shwrs inc; el pnts (4A) inc; lndtte (inc dryer); shop & farm produce; playgrnd; htd, covrd pool; some statics; some rd & rlwy noise. "Pleasant site." 1 Apr-10 Oct. € 18.30 2010*

LOURDES 8F2 (1km NE Urban) 43.10247, -0.02789 **Camping de Sarsan, 4 Ave Jean Moulin, 65100 Lourdes [tel/fax 05 62 94 43 09; camping.sarsan@wanadoo.fr; www.lourdes-camping.com]** Fr N on N21 past airport, on app to Lourdes turn L sp 'Zone Indust du Monge'. Pass Cmp Le Moulin du Monge & foll site sp for approx 2km. Site on L immed after x-rds. Med, pt sl, pt shd; wc; chem disp; mv service pnt; shwrs inc; el pnts (4-10A) poss rev pol. €2.50-4.60; lndtte; sm shop; supmkt nr; pool; games area; games rm; TV; wifi; some statics; dogs free; adv bkg; quiet; ccard not acc. "Easy 25min walk to town cent." 15 Apr-15 Oct. € 13.20 2012*

LOURDES 8F2 (2.1km E Rural) 43.09316, -0.02091 **Camping du Ruisseau Blanc, Route de Bagnères-Anclades, 65100 Lourdes [05 62 42 94 83 or 05 62 42 98 19 (LS); fax 05 62 42 94 62; www.camping-lourdes-ruisseau-blanc.com]** Exit Lourdes on D937 twd Bagnères & foll sp. Site has 2 ents. C'vans ignore 1st sp for site on R & cont on D937 foll next sp. Med, mkd pitch, some hdstg, pt shd; wc (mainly cont); chem disp; mv service pnt; shwrs; el pnts (6A) €2; lndtte (inc dryer); shop; playgrnd; games area; TV rm; dogs €0.50; "Gd views; beautiful site but facs poss stretched high ssn." 20 Mar-10 Oct. € 8.20 2010*

LOURDES 8F2 (2.5km W Urban) 43.09773, -0.06986 **Camp du Loup, Route de la Forêt, 65100 Lourdes [tel/fax 05 62 94 23 60; www.camping-du-loup-lourdes.com]** Fr N on N21 exit onto D914 to Lourdes; on ent Lourdes turn L off D914 under rlwy brdge dir Centre Ville & hospital; in 100m turn R onto Rue de Pau sp St Pé & Bétharram; in 1km turn L over rv brdge; site on R in 300m. Site sp. Sm, pt shd; wc; chem disp; mv service pnt; shwrs €1; el pnts (6A) €3; lndtte (inc dryer); shop 1km; tradsmn; playgrnd; rv 300m; dogs €1; poss cr; adv bkg ess; quiet; CKE/CCI. "Excel CL-type site; basic facs; friendly, helpful host; gd atmosphere; gd security; adv bkg rec high ssn; rvside walk to shrine." ♦ 1 May-10 Oct. € 12.00 2011*

LOURDES 8F2 (3km W Rural) 43.09561, -0.07463 **Camping La Forêt, Route de la Forêt, 65100 Lourdes [05 62 94 04 38; fax 05 62 42 14 86; campingdelaforet65@orange.fr; http://www.campingdelaforet.fr/]** Fr N on N21 exit onto D914 to Lourdes; on ent Lourdes turn L off D914 under rlwy brdge dir Centre Ville & hospital; in 100m turn R onto Rue de Pau sp St Pé & Bétharram; in 1km turn L over rv brdge; site in 1km. Med, mkd pitch, pt shd; wc; mv service pnt; shwrs €1; el pnts (3-10A) €2.60-7.60; gas; lndtte (inc dryer); shop; rest, snacks; bar; playgrnd; few statics; dogs €1.30; poss cr; adv bkg; quiet; ccard acc; CKE/CCI. "Lovely site; helpful owners; conv town cent & grotto (1km); poss to stay bef official opening date by arrangement; ideal site to visit Lourdes." 1 Apr-31 Oct. € 12.20 2012*

LOURDES 8F2 (4km W Rural) 43.10461, -0.06782 **Camping d'Arrouach, 9 Rue des Trois Archanges, Biscaye, 65100 Lourdes [05 62 42 11 43; fax 05 62 42 05 27; camping.arrouach@wanadoo.fr; www.camping-arrouach.com]** Fr Lourdes take D940 twd Pau. As you leave Lourdes take L fork D937 (sp) Bétharram. Site on R 200m. Med, hdg/mkd pitch, hdstg, pt sl, pt shd; wc; chem disp; mv service pnt; shwrs inc; el pnts (3-6A) €2.50-5; gas; lndtte; shop 2km; tradsmn; bar; BBQ; playgrnd; wifi; 10% statics; dogs; phone; poss cr; adv bkg; quiet; red long stay;CKE/CCI. "Pleasant, elevated site with views; poss flooding in v wet weather; clean san facs; easy access parking for Lourdes via Rte de Pau." ♦ 15 Mar-31 Dec. € 12.40 2010*

LOURDES 8F2 (6km W Rural) 43.10133, -0.12888 **FFCC Camping Le Prat Dou Rey, 31 Route de Pau, 65270 Peyrouse [05 62 41 81 54; fax 05 62 41 89 76; lepradourey@orange.fr; www.camping-lepratdourey.com]** Take D940 fr Lourdes then in 2km take D937 E sp Bétharram. Cont thro Peyrouse vill & site on L in 500m. Med, pt shd; wc; mv service pnt; shwrs inc; el pnts (6-10A) €3.20-4.20 inc; lndtte; shop in ssn & 6km; snacks; BBQ; playgrnd; pool; rv 100m; fishing; 10% statics; dogs €0.95; CKE/CCI. "Various sports activities; san facs poss unclean." 15 Mar-15 Oct. € 12.40 2008*

LOURDES 8F2 (2km NW Rural) 43.10972, -0.06242 **Camping Theil, 23 Chemin de St Pauly, 65100 Lourdes [tel/fax 05 62 94 24 59 or 06 86 65 80 24 (mob)]** Sp at junc D940 and D937, site 500m fr junc, nr stadium. Sm, pt shd; wc; chem disp; shwrs inc; el pnts €1; shop 1km; pool 1.5km; some statics; dogs €1; adv bkg; quiet. "Gd site but san facs in poor condition; 30 min walk to grotto or easy drive." 15 Mar-31 Oct. € 12.00 2011*

LOURES BAROUSSE see Montréjeau 8F3

Send in your site reports by mid August 2014

LOUROUX, LE *4G2* (N Rural) *47.16270, 0.78697* **Camping à la Ferme La Chaumine (Baudoin), 37240 Le Louroux [tel/fax 02 47 92 82 09 or 06 85 45 68 10 (mob); bruno. baudoin@free.fr]** Fr Tours, take D50 S for 30km. Site immed on R bef Le Louroux. Sm, hdg pitch, shd; wc; chem disp; shwrs inc; el pnts (10A) inc; BBQ; playgrnd; dogs; bus 200m; Eng spkn; adv bkg; quiet. "Superb CL-type site nr quaint vill; helpful owners; gd, clean san facs; gd walks fr site." 1 May-15 Oct. € 11.50   2013*

⊞ **LOUVIE JUZON** *8F2* (1km E Rural) *43.08940, -0.41019* **FFCC Camping Le Rey, Quartier Listo, Route de Lourdes, 64260 Louvie-Juzon [05 59 05 78 52; fax 05 59 05 78 97; nadia@camping-pyrenees-ossau.com; www.camping-pyrenees-ossau.com]** Site on L at top of hill E fr Louvie; v steep app. Sm, mkd pitch, pt sl, pt shd; htd wc; chem disp; shwrs inc; el pnts (6A) €3.30; lndtte; shops 1km; tradsmn; rest 1km; snacks; bar; playgrnd; sm pool; watersports, fishing nr; games area; entmnt; 50% statics; dogs €2; phone; site clsd last 2 weeks Nov & last 2 weeks Jan; adv bkg; quiet; CKE/CCI. "Fascinating area; chateau nr." ◆ € 13.25   2009*

LOUVIE JUZON *8F2* (500m S Rural) *43.08277, -0.42050* **Camp Municipal de la Vallée d'Ossau, Route d'Ossau, 64260 Izeste [05 59 05 68 67; fax 05 59 05 73 82; mairie. izeste@9business.fr]** Site 300m fr rv bdge in Louvie-Juzon, on L heading S on D934. Sm, mkd pitch, shd; wc; shwrs inc; el pnts (6A) inc; shops, rest 300m; no statics; quiet; adv bkg; CKE/CCI. "Vg, attractive site adj fast-flowing rv & weir; ideal for access to Vallée d'Ossau; some rd & water noise." 1 Jun-15 Sep. € 14.60   2010*

LOUVIE JUZON *8F2* (3km S Rural) *43.06324, -0.42411* **FFCC Camping L'Ayguelade, 64260 Bielle [05 59 82 66 50 or 06 31 23 06 48 (mob); camping-ayguelade@orange.fr; http://ayguelade.pagesperso-orange.fr/]** S fr Louvie-Juzon on D934, site clearly sp on L. Med, mkd pitch, pt shd; wc; mv service pnt; shwrs inc; el pnts (3-9A) €2.50-4.50; lndtte; shop 4km; tradsmn; rest adj; snacks; bar; playgrnd; entmnt; TV; 75% statics; dogs €1.80; Eng spkn; adv bkg; quiet; CKE/CCI. "Rv runs thro site, pleasant setting." ◆ ltd 1 Mar-1 Nov. € 12.50   2008*

⊞ **LOUVIE JUZON** *8F2* (6km NW Rural) *43.15180, -0.44499* **FFCC Aire Naturelle Les Jardins d'Ossau (Dunan), 2 Chemin de Départ, 64250 Buzy [05 59 21 05 71; dunan. pascal@wanadoo.fr]** S fr Pau on N134; approx 12 km past Gan sp Camping; after restaurant at Belair turn L onto D34 sp Buzy; in 2km turn L after going under 1st rlwy bdge. Site on R, sp. Sm, pt shd; wc; chem disp (wc); shwrs inc; el pnts (6A) €2.10 (long lead poss req); lndtte; games area; games rm; dogs €0.50; Eng spkn; adv bkg; quiet; no ccard acc; CKE/CCI. "Peaceful site on fruit farm with views; san facs basic but clean; easy access; helpful owners; NH only to/fr Spain." ◆ ltd € 11.40   2009*

LOUVIERS *3D2* (2km W Rural) *49.21490, 1.13279* **Camping Le Bel Air, Route de la Haye-Malherbe, Hameau de St-Lubin, 27400 Louviers [tel/fax 02 32 40 10 77; contact@ camping-lebelair.fr; www.camping-lebelair.fr]** Site well sp in Louviers. Fr cent foll D81 W for 2.5km dir La Haye-Malherbe; twisting rd uphill; site on R. Or if travelling S leave A13 at junc 19 to Louviers & as bef. NB In town cent look for sm green sp after Ecole Communale (on L) & bef Jardin Public - a narr rd (1-way) & easy to miss. Med, hdg/mkd/hdstg pitch, shd; wc; chem disp; mv service pnt; shwrs inc; el pnts (6A) €4.90; gas; lndtte (with dryer); supmkt 2km; tradsmn; playgrnd; htd pool; bowling; wifi; 30% statics; dogs €2.50; poss cr; Eng spkn; adv bkg; quiet; ccard acc; red low ssn/CKE/CCI. "Access to pitches diff long o'fits, poss mover req; check barrier opening times; poss NH only (2013); gd site and dog walks on site." 15 Mar-15 Oct. € 23.20   2013*

LOYAT see Ploërmel *2F3*

LUBERSAC *7B3* (300m E Rural) *45.44244, 1.40899* **Camp Municipal La Vézénie, 19210 Lubersac [05 55 73 50 14 (Mairie); fax 05 55 73 67 99; mairie@ ville-lubersac.fr; www.chalets-decouverte.com]** Fr A20 N of Uzerche exit junc 44 & turn W onto D902 to Lubersac. At far end of mkt sq take rd L of Hôtel de Commerce; turn immed L; then 1st L; at T-junc turn R; then L at mini-rndabt onto site. Sm, mkd pitch, pt sl, terr, pt shd; htd wc (some cont); shwrs inc; el pnts (5A) €2.30; lndtte; shop adj; rest, snacks; playgrnd; htd pool; paddling pool; sand beach & lake sw, fishing 400m; tennis; horseriding; poss cr; quiet. "Modern, clean site overlkg lake." 1 Jun-15 Sep. € 9.10   2008*

LUC EN DIOIS *9D3* (Rural) *44.61565, 5.44618* **Camp Municipal Les Foulons, Rue de la Piscine, 26310 Luc-en-Diois [04 75 21 36 14 or 04 75 21 31 01 (Mairie); fax 04 75 21 35 70; contact@camping-luc-en-diois.com; www. camping-luc-en-diois.com/foulons]** Sp in vill off D93. Med, pt shd; wc; shwrs; el pnts (10-16A) €3-4.50; lndtte; shops & rest 500m; playgrnd; pool; rv adj; games area adj; tennis; dog €2; Eng spkn; adv bkg; quiet; red low ssn; CKE/CCI. "Excel site in scenic area; modern & well-maintained; attractive sm town; gd walking/cycling; canoeing, horseriding, hang-gliding avail in area; mkt Fri." ◆ 15 Apr-15 Oct. € 13.00   2008*

LUC EN DIOIS *9D3* (6km N Rural) *44.68144, 5.44720* **Kawan Village L'Hirondelle, Bois de St Ferréol, 26410 Menglon [tel/fax 04 75 21 82 08; contact@campinghirondelle.com; www.campinghirondelle.com]** Foll D93 S twd Luc-en-Diois, in 6km at Pont-de-Quart turn L on D539 sp Châtillon, in 5km turn R on D140 sp Menglon, Recoubeau, site on R in 150m over rv. Med, shd; wc (some cont); baby facs; shwrs inc; el pnts (3-6A) €3.35-4.40 (long lead poss req); lndtte (inc dryer); shop; rest, snacks; bar; BBQ; playgrnd; htd pool complex; waterslide; rv fishing; archery; games area; wifi; entmnt; TV rm; 10% statics; dogs €3.20; Eng spkn; adv bkg; quiet. "Well-run, clean site; most pitches in woodland - some diff access; lovely area." ◆ 23 Apr-10 Sep. € 27.60 (CChq acc)   2010*

LUC EN DIOIS

LUC EN DIOIS *9D3* (5km NW Rural) *44.65910, 5.40970* Camping Le Couriou, 26310 Recoubeau-Jansac [04 75 21 33 23; fax 04 75 21 38 42; camping.lecouriou@ wanadoo.fr; www.campinglecouriou.com] Fr Die on D93 twds Luc-en-Diois for 13 km. Turn R at D140 & foll sp. Med, mkd pitch, some hdstg, terr, pt sd; wc; chem disp; baby facs; shwrs inc; el pnts (6A) €4.20; gas; lndtte; shop high ssn; rest, snacks; bar; playgrnd; htd pool; 5% statics; dogs €2; phone; poss cr; adv bkg ess high ssn; quiet; CKE/CCI. "Mountain views." ♦ ltd 1 May-31 Aug. € 23.50   2008*

LUC SUR MER see Ouistreham *3D1*

LUC, LE *10F3* (4km SE Rural) *43.35838, 6.32778* Camping Les Bruyères, Route de Mayons, 83340 Le Luc [04 94 73 47 07; fax 04 94 60 99 26; Yvonraboin@aol.com] Fr D97 at sports stadium in Le Luc turn L on D33. Site in 3.5km. Med, mkd pitch, hdstg, pt shd; htd wc; shwrs inc; el pnts (6A) inc; gas; lndtte; shop 4km; snacks; bar; playgrnd; pool; games area; TV; some statics; dogs free; quiet; poss some noise fr nrby race circuit. "Friendly owner; fair NH." 1 Mar-15 Nov. € 16.50   2008*

LUÇAY LE MALE *4H2* (4km SW Rural) *47.11066, 1.40504* Camp Municipal La Foulquetière, 36360 Luçay-le-Mâle [02 54 40 52 88 or 02 54 40 43 31 (Mairie); fax 02 54 40 42 47; mairie@ville-lucaylemale.fr] SW fr Valençay & thro Luçay, on D960, then fork L onto D13, site on R in 1km. Sm, hdg/mkd pitch, pt sl, pt shd; htd wc; chem disp; mv service pnt; shwrs inc; el pnts (6A) €1.50; lndtte; shop 3km; rest, snacks; bar; playgrnd; watersports; canoeing; fishing; tennis; games area; no dogs; Eng spkn; adv bkg; v quiet; CKE/CCI. "Excel lakeside site but isolated; gd sized pitches; basic facs; gd walking country; if recep unmanned, pay at Mairie or at rest." 1 Apr-15 Oct. € 6.50   2008*

LUCENAY L'EVEQUE *6H1* (S Rural) *47.07668, 4.24675* Camp Municipal du Ternin, 71540 Lucenay-l'Evêque [03 85 82 61 86; mairie.lucenay.l.eveque@wanadoo.fr; www.lucenay71.fr] On D980 Autun to Saulieu rd, 300m S of Lucenay site ent immed bef vill sp. Ent narr; easier when warden opens 2nd gate. Sm, hdg/mkd pitch, pt shd; wc (some cont); shwrs inc; el pnts €3; playgrnd; shops 300m; dogs €1.50; tennis; quiet; ccard acc; CKE/CCI. "Neat site with brook running thro; gd walking country; quiet low ssn; warden visits am & pm - site yourself; narr ent to pitches with el pnts." 1 May-1 Sep. € 10.00   2010*

LUCHE PRINGE see Flèche, La *4G1*

LUCHON *8G3* (2km N Rural) *42.80806, 0.59667* Camping Pradelongue, 31110 Moustajon [05 61 79 86 44; fax 05 61 79 18 64; camping-pradelongue@wanadoo.fr; www.camping-pradelongue.com] Site is on D125c on W of D125 main rd fr Luchon. Ent at Moustajon/Antignac going S. Site adj Intermarché; sp. Lge, hdg/mkd pitch, pt shd; wc; chem disp; mv service pnt; baby facs; shwrs inc; el pnts (2-10A) €2-4; lndtte; shop 100m; BBQ; playgrnd; htd pool; games area; wifi; 10% statics; dogs €2; Eng spkn; adv bkg; quiet; ccard acc; red low ssn; CKE/CCI. "Excel, well-run site; mountain views; gd sized pitches; friendly, helpful owners; rec." ♦ 1 Apr-30 Sep. € 18.00   2010*

LUCHON *8G3* (1km NE Rural) *42.79472, 0.60826* Camping La Lanette/Arome Vanille, 31110 Montauban-de-Luchon [05 61 79 00 38; info@camping-aromevanille.com; www.camping-aromevanille.com] Exit A64 junc 17 at Montréjeau onto D825/N125/D33/D125; at end of new section of D125 turn L at rndabt sp Luzet-de-Luchon; turn R in vill; site on R in 1km. Lge, hdg/mkd pitch, pt shd; htd wc; baby facs; shwrs inc; el pnts (6-10A) €4-5; gas; lndtte; rest, snacks; bar; playgrnd; games area; child entmnt; 30% statics; dogs €3; poss cr; adv bkg; quiet; ccard acc; red low ssn; CKE/CCI. "Vg site; high level hiking rtes 20-30 mins by car." 1 Apr-30 Oct. € 15.00   2009*

LUCHON *8G3* (7km W Rural) *42.80902, 0.51978* Camping Les Frênes, 31110 Garin [05 61 79 88 44] Fr Bagnères-de-Luchon take D618 W dir Arreau. Turn R in vill of Garin to site. Sm, terr, pt shd; wc; chem disp (wc); shwrs inc; el pnts (3A) inc; shop nr; rest 1km; playgrnd; 30% statics; dogs €1; quiet. "Basic site; conv for Lac d'Oô & mountain walking." 1 Apr-30 Nov. € 16.00   2010*

LUCON *7A1* (11km E Rural) *46.46745, -1.02792* Camp Municipal Le Vieux Chêne, Rue du Port, 85370 Nalliers [02 51 30 91 98 or 02 51 30 90 71; fax 02 51 30 94 06; nalliers.mairie@wanadoo.fr] Fr Luçon E on D949 dir Fontenay-le-Comte; 500m after ent Nalliers turn R onto D10 (Rue de Brantome); after level x-ing cont strt on for 50m (leaving D10); then Rue du Port on L. Site sp on D949 but easy to miss. Sm, hdg/mkd pitch, pt shd; wc; chem disp; shwrs inc; el pnts (4-13A) €3.90; shop 500m; tradsmn; playgrnd; adv bkg; quiet; site yourself on lge pitch; CKE/CCI. "Excel, clean site; in low ssn contact Mairie for ent to site; vg NH; conv for rd to Bordeaux" 15 May-15 Sep. € 11.60   2013*

LUCON *7A1* (10km SW Rural) *46.41170, -1.26527* Camping La Fraignaye, Rue de Beau Laurier, 85580 St Denis-du-Payré [tel/fax 02 51 27 21 36; camping.fraignaye@ wanadoo.fr; www.camping-lafraignaye.com] Fr A8 exit junc 7 onto D137 dir La Rochelle. Turn L after Ste Gemme onto D949 to Luçon, then take D746 to Triaize. Take D25 to St Denis-du-Payré, in vill turn L bef church & foll sp. Sm, mkd pitch, pt shd; wc; chem disp; shwrs inc; el pnts (6A) €3; gas; lndtte; shop & 7km; rest, snacks; bar; playgrnd; sand beach 12km; games rm; cycle hire; TV; 20% statics; dogs €1.50; phone; poss cr; Eng spkn; adv bkg; quiet; ccard acc; red long stay/low ssn. "Pleasant owner; nr nature reserve; site liable to flooding." ♦ 1 Apr-30 Sep. € 15.00   2010*

LUDE, LE *4G1* (1km NE Rural) *47.65094, 0.16221* Camp Municipal au Bord du Loir, Route du Mans, 72800 Le Lude [02 43 94 67 70; fax 02 43 94 93 82; contact@camping-aubordduloir.fr; www.ville-lelude.fr or www.loir-valley.com] Fr town cent take D305 (E); in 1km take D307 (N) sp 'Le Mans'; site immed on L. Well sp. Fr E on D305, avoid cent of Vaas, use HGV route. Med, hdg/mkd pitch, pt shd; wc; chem disp; mv service pnt; shwrs inc; el pnts (5A) €3; lndtte; shops 300m; tradsmn; rests 100m; snacks adj (high ssn); BBQ (gas only); playgrnd; tennis; beach 6km; pool; canoeing; fishing; cycling; entmnt; TV; dog; 10% statics; phone; poss cr; Eng spkn; adv bkg; poss traff noise far end of site; ccard acc; CKE/CCI. "Well-kept, well-run site; warm welcome, helpful staff; modern san facs; vg walk to town; Château du Lude & excel rest nrby; highly rec." ♦ 1 Apr-30 Sep. € 20.05   2013*

LUGAGNAC see Limogne en Quercy *7D4*

FRANCE

LUGNY see Pont de Vaux *9A2*

LUGRIN see Evian les Bains *9A3*

LUNEL *10E2* (2km NE Rural) *43.69000, 4.14800*
FFCC Camping du Pont de Lunel, Chemin du Mas de Viala, 34400 Lunel [04 67 71 10 22; contact@ campingdupontdelunel.com; www.camping-du-pontdelunel.com] Fr N on N113, cross Rv Vidourle & turn R at rndbt onto D34. Site on R in 400m. Sm, hdg/mkd pitch, shd; wc; mv service pnt; shwrs; el pnts (5A) inc; lndtte; shops adj; rest, snacks; bar; BBQ; playgrnd; pool 4km; sand beach 12km; games area; entmnt; dogs €1.50; adv bkg. "Pleasant, family-run site." 15 Mar-15 Sep. € 17.00   2009*

LUNEL *10E2* (5km NE Rural) *43.71675, 4.16704* **Camping Les Amandiers, Clos de Manset, 30660 Gallargues-le-Montueux [04 66 35 28 02; fax 04 66 51 48 57; camping-lesamandiers@ orange.fr; www.camping-lesamandiers.com]** Exit A9 at junc 26 Gallargues/Les Plages. Turn R after toll, site in 2km. Med, mkd pitch, pt shd; wc; chem disp; mv service pnt; baby facs; shwrs inc; el pnts (16A) €4; gas; lndtte; shops adj; snacks; bar; playgrnd; pool; sand beach 15km; fishing 800m; tennis; games area; entmnt; TV; 20% statics; dogs €2.50; adv bkg; quiet; ccard acc; CKE/CCI. "Conv NH en rte to Spain; gd touring area." 30 Apr-1 Sep. € 18.00   2009*

LUNEL *10E2* (2km S Rural) *43.65666, 4.14111* **Camping Le Bon Port, 383 Chemin de Mas St Angé, 34400 Lunel [04 67 71 15 65; fax 04 67 83 60 27; contact@ campingbonport.com; www.campingbonport.com]** Exit A9 junc 27 S dir La Grande Motte, D61. Site sp on L. Lge, hdg/mkd pitch, pt shd; wc; baby facs; shwrs inc; el pnts (5A) €4; lndtte; shop; tradsmn; rest, snacks; bar; BBQ (gas); playgrnd; pool; paddling pool; waterslide; games area; wifi; entmnt; TV rm; 30% statics; dogs €3.50; adv bkg; quiet. ♦ 1 Apr-30 Sep. € 26.00 (CChq acc)   2010*

LUNEL *10E2* (6km SW) *43.65180, 4.06611* **FFCC Camping Le Fou du Roi, Chemin des Codoniers, 34130 Lansargues [04 67 86 78 08; fax 04 67 86 78 06; reservation@ campinglefouduroi.com; www.campinglefouduroi.fr]** SW fr Lunel on D24 to Lansargues, 100m past vill turn N. Site 50m on R. Med, hdg pitch, pt shd; wc; chem disp; mv service pnt; shwrs inc; el pnts (10A) €4; lndtte; shop; supmkt 4km; snacks; bar; playgrnd; pool; tennis; horseriding; wifi; 75% statics; dogs €4; poss cr; adv bkg rec high ssn; quiet; red low ssn; CKE/CCI. ♦ 15 Mar-15 Oct. € 18.60   2008*

LUNEVILLE *6E2* (1km NE Urban) *48.59650, 6.49871*
Camping Les Bosquets, 63 Quai des petit , 54300 Lunéville [03 83 74 05 00; fax 03 83 74 16 27; camping@ cc-lunevillois.fr; www.cc-lunevillois.fr] Exit N333 Lunéville by-pass sp `Lunéville-Château' & foll sp to Lunéville. Fr traff lts in sq in front of chateau, take rd to L at chateau (Quai des Bosquets). At sm rndabt do not ent site on R but cont round rndabt to L to yard opp warden's house. Warden will open barrier. Sm, mkd pitch, terr, pt shd; wc; chem disp; shwrs inc; el pnts (10-15A) €2.55; lndtte; shops 500m; tradsmn; pool 200m; playgrnd nrby; internet; dogs; rd noise; CKE/ CCI. "Friendly staff; rec visit adj chateau gardens; rd noise on bottom pitches; vg." ♦ 1 Apr-31 Oct. € 9.25   2013*

LUREUIL *4H2* (3km N Rural) **Camping La Maloterie, 36220 Lureuil [02 54 37 41 25; domainedelamaloterie@tele2.fr]** N fr Le Blanc on D975; take 2nd L after vill sp La Maloterie; foll lane for 1km, farm on R. Sm, pt sl; own san; chem disp; tradsmn; BBQ; dogs €1; adv bkg; CKE/CCI. "Lovely, quiet CL-type site in National Park; lge pitches; British owner; vg." 1 Apr-31 Oct. € 8.50   2008*

LUS LA CROIS HAUTE see St Julien en Beauchêne *9D3*

LUSIGNAN *7A2* (500m NE Rural) *46.43712, 0.12369* **Camp Municipal de Vauchiron, Chemin de la Plage, 86600 Lusignan [05 49 43 30 08 or 05 49 43 31 48 (Mairie); fax 05 49 42 61 19; lusignan@cg86.fr; www.lusignan.fr]** Site sp fr D611, 22km SW of Poitiers; foll camp sp in Lusignan to rvside. Med, pt shd; wc; chem disp; baby facs; shwrs inc; el pnts (15A) €2.40 (poss rev pol); lndtte; shops 2km; tradsmn; snacks high ssn; bar 1km; BBQ; playgrnd; rv sw adj; fishing; boat hire; entmnt; wifi; dogs free; phone; no twin-axles; adv bkg; quiet; ccard acc; CKE/CCI. "Beautiful, peaceful site in spacious park; lge pitches; forest & rv walks adj; friendly, helpful resident warden; excel clean san facs; steep walk to historic town; highly rec." ♦ 15 Apr-30 Sep. € 16.35   2013*

LUSSAC LES CHATEAUX *7A3* (6km SW Rural) *46.36912, 0.69330* **Camp Municipal du Moulin Beau, 86320 Gouex [05 49 48 46 14; fax 05 48 84 50 01; www.tourisme-vienne.com]** Fr Lussac on N147/E62 dir Poitiers, cross rv bdge sp Poitiers & immed turn L on D25; foll sp to Gouex; site on L in 4km at swimming pool/camping sp. Sm, pt shd; wc (some cont); chem disp; shwrs inc; el pnts (15A) €1.60 (check pol); bakery 500m in vill; pool 300m; v quiet; no ccard acc; CKE/CCI. "Excel site on bank Rv Vienne; facs clean but ltd; bollards at site ent, care needed if van over 7m or twin-axle; highly rec." 15 Jun-15 Sep. € 4.20   2012*

LUSSAC LES CHATEAUX *7A3* (11km SW Rural) *46.32231, 0.67384* **Camp Municipal du Renard, 86150 Queaux [05 49 48 48 32 or 05 49 48 48 08 (Mairie); fax 05 49 48 30 70; contact@queaux.fr; www.queaux.fr]** Fr Lussac cross rv bdge sp Poitiers & immed turn L. Foll sp to Gouex & Queaux. Site on D25 S of vill. Med, mkd pitch, pt sl, pt shd; wc; mv service pnt; shwrs inc; el pnts (6A) €2.50; tradsmn; shops 500m; bar; playgrnd; paddling pool; pool nr. "Lovely rvside site nr pleasant vill; manned high ssn or apply to Mairie." 15 Jun-15 Sep. € 5.50   2009*

LUSSAC LES CHATEAUX *7A3* (3km W Rural) *46.39636, 0.70531* **Camp Municipal Mauvillant, 86320 Lussac-les-Châteaux [tel/ fax 05 49 48 03 32; www.tourisme-vienne.com]** W fr Lussac on N147/E62 dir Poitiers; in 1km (shortly bef bdge) turn L at Municipal sp & foll to site 800m on L. Site parallel to Rv Vienne. Exit L turn onto N147 can be diff for lge o'fits Med, hdg/mkd pitch, hdstg, pt shd; wc (mainly cont); chem disp; baby facs; shwrs inc; el pnts (10A) inc; lndtte; BBQ; playgrnd; pool nr; rv 200m; dogs; Eng spkn; adv bkg; quiet; CKE/CCI. "Site nr rv; if office clsd site yourself & register later; height barrier - o'fits above 2m can't ent if office clsd; gd; NH only." 1 Jun-15 Oct. € 11.95   2011*

LUSSAC LES EGLISES *7A3* (300m E Rural) *46.34372, 1.17942* **Camp Municipal Les Forges, Ave François de Bourdelle, 87360 Lussac-les-Eglises [05 55 68 29 44 or 06 43 20 01 19 (mob)]** Exit A20 junc 22 onto D912 W sp St Sulpice-les-Feuilles. Cont on D912 dir Lussac-les-Eglises, site on R just bef vill. Sm, hdg pitch, pt shd; wc; chem disp; mv service pnt; shwrs inc; el pnts (10A) €1.60; shop, rest, bar 300m; BBQ; fishing adj; dogs; quiet. "Excel, CL-type site; basic, clean facs; warden calls evening." 1 Apr-30 Sep. € 6.50   2010*

LUXEUIL LES BAINS *6F2* (500m N Rural) *47.82315, 6.38200* **FFCC Camping du Domaine de Chatigny, 14 Rue Grammont, 70300 Luxeuil-les-Bains [03 84 93 97 97; fax 03 84 93 61 01; camping.ot-luxeuil@wanadoo.fr; www. camping.luxeuil.fr]** N fr Vesoul on N57; turn L at rndabt into Luxeuil-les-Bains; foll Camping sp. Vehicular access fr Rue Ste Anne. Med, hdg/mkd pitch, hdstg, terr, pt shd; htd wc; chem disp; mv service pnt; baby facs; shwrs inc; el pnts (16A) €3.50-4.50; gas; lndtte; shop; supmkt 100m; tradsmn; rest, snacks; bar; BBQ; playgrnd; pool; indoor tennis court; TV rm; 20% statics; dogs €1.70; bus 300m; no twin-axles; Eng spkn; adv bkg; quiet; ccard acc; red low ssn/long stay; CKE/CCI. "New (2009), high standard site." 28 Mar-7 Nov. € 16.50   2009*

LUYNES see Tours *4G2*

LUZ ST SAUVEUR *8G2* (1km N Rural) *42.88140, -0.01258* **Airotel Camping Pyrénées, 46 Ave du Barège, La Ferme Theil, 65120 Esquièze-Sère [05 62 92 89 18; fax 05 62 92 96 50; contact@airotel-pyrenees.com; www. airotel-pyrenees.com]** On main rd fr Lourdes to Luz on L past International Campsite. L U-turn into ent archway needs care - use full width of rd & forecourt. Med, mkd pitch, pt sl, pt shd; htd wc (some cont); mv service pnt; chem disp (wc); sauna; shwrs inc; fam bthrm; el pnts (3-10A) €3.50-6.50 (rev pol); gas; lndtte; shop; supmkt 800m; tradsmn, rest & snacks in high ssn; bar; playgrnd; 2 pools (1 covrd); ski in winter; fishing; walking; horseriding; wifi; entmnt; TV; dogs €1.50; 30% statics; poss cr; quiet but some rd noise; Eng spkn; adv bkg; site clsd Oct & Nov; ccard acc; CKE/CCI. "Beautiful area; facs poss stretched high ssn; excel walking & wildlife; lovely vill." ♦ ltd 1 Dec-30 Sep. € 26.00   2008*

LUZ ST SAUVEUR *8G2* (1.5km N Rural) *42.88285, -0.01354* **Camping International, 50 Ave de Barège, 65120 Esquièze-Sère [05 62 92 82 02; fax 05 62 92 96 87; camping.international.luz@wanadoo.fr; www. international-camping.fr]** On E side of D921, clearly sp. Ave de Barège is part of D921. Lge, hdg/mkd pitch, pt sl, pt shd; htd wc; chem disp; mv service pnt; baby facs; shwrs inc; el pnts (2-6A) €2-5; lndtte (inc dryer); shop; supmkt 800m; tradsmn; rest 1km; snacks; bar; playgrnd; htd pool; paddling pool; waterslide; tennis; horseriding; skiing; games area; games rm; wifi; entmnt; TV; 10% statics; dogs free; phone; poss cr; Eng spkn; adv bkg; quiet, some rd noise; red low ssn; CKE/ CCI. "Beautiful views fr site; friendly, helpful owners; vg clean san facs, ltd low ssn; gd walking; gd base for cycling inc Col du Tourmalet; mkt Mon; vg; Excel modern san facs" ♦ 20 May-30 Sep. € 41.00   2013*

LUZ ST SAUVEUR *8G2* (500m E Rural) *42.87362, 0.00293* **Camping Le Bergons, Route de Barèges, 65120 Esterre [05 62 92 90 77; info@camping-bergons.com; www. camping-bergons.com]** On D918 to Col du Tourmalet, site on R. Med, mkd pitch, pt sl, terr, pt shd; htd wc; shwrs inc; chem disp; el pnts (2-6A) €2.10-5; gas; lndtte; shops adj; tradsmn; BBQ; playgrnd; pool 500m; 10% statics; dogs €0.80; phone; rd noise; red long stay/low ssn; CKE/CCI. "Well-kept site; friendly, helpful owner; gd san facs; levelling blocks poss req; v tight ent for lge o'fits; excel walking; Donjon des Aigles at Beaucens worth visit; mkt Mon; vg." ♦ 1 Jan-21 Apr, 6 May-20 Oct, 6 Dec-31 Dec. € 20.35   2013*

"I need an on-site restaurant"

We do our best to make sure site information is correct, but it is always best to check any must-have facilities are still available or will be open during your visit.

⊞ **LUZ ST SAUVEUR** *8G2* (8km E Rural) *42.89451, 0.05741* **Camping La Ribère, Route de Labatsus, 65120 Barèges [tel/fax 05 62 92 69 01 or 06 80 01 29 51 (mob); contact@ laribere.com; www.laribere.com]** On N side of rd D918 on edge of Barèges, site sp as `Camping Caraveneige'. Phone kiosk at ent. Sm, pt sl, pt shd; htd wc ltd; chem disp; shwrs inc; el pnts (2-6A) €2-6; lndtte (inc dryer); shop; tradsmn; rest adj; wifi; some statics; dogs €0.95; site clsd end Oct-mid Dec; poss cr; quiet. "Conv, attractive site; gd facs; magnificent views." ♦ 1 Jan-24 Oct, 1 Dec-31 Dec. € 23.10   2013*

⊞ **LUZ ST SAUVEUR** *8G2* (2km NW Rural) *42.88218, -0.02270* **FFCC Camping Le Pyrénévasion, Route de Luz-Andiden 65120 Sazos [05 62 92 91 54; fax 05 62 92 98 34; camping-pyrenevasion@wanadoo.fr; www.campingpyrenevasion.com]** Fr Lourdes S on D921 twd Gavarnie. Shortly bef Luz-St Sauveur after petrol stn & campsites sp, take R fork onto D12 sp Sazos. Cont thro vill & turn R sp Luz-Andiden, then immed R again sp Sazos (D12) & Luz-Andiden. Cont uphill, site on R just after Sazon sp. Med, hdg/mkd pitch, pt shd; htd wc; chem disp; baby facs; shwrs inc; el pnts (3A) inc; gas; lndtte; shop 200m; rest; tradsmn; snacks; bar; BBQ (gas/elec/charcoal); playgrnd; pool; paddling pool; fishing; games rm; wifi; 60% statics; dogs €2.50; no c'vans/m'vans over 7.50m high ssn; poss cr; Eng spkn; quiet; site clsd 20 Oct-19 Nov; red low ssn. "Fair site in mountains; long, steep trek to/fr shops." ♦ € 25.50   2011*

LUZECH see Castelfranc *7D3*

LUZENAC see Ax les Thermes *8G4*

LUZERET see Argenton sur Creuse *7A3*

FRANCE

LUZY *4H4* (1km NE Rural) *46.79622, 3.97685* **Camping La Bédure**, Route d'Autun, 58170 Luzy [03 86 30 68 27; info@ campinglabedure.com; www.campinglabedure.com] Foll sps on D981 to site. Med, mkd pitch, pt sl, pt shd; wc (some cont); baby facs; shwrs inc; shops 1km; el pnts (6A) €3 (poss rev pol); tradsmn; playgrnd; pool adj; dogs 1.50; quiet. "Pleasant site; gd walking; gd touring base." May-Sep. € 10.00   2010*

LUZY *4H4* (7km NE Rural) *46.81680, 4.05650* **Camping Domaine de la Gagère (Naturist)**, 58170 Luzy [03 86 30 48 11; fax 03 86 30 45 57; info@la-gagere.com; www.la-gagere.com] Fr Luzy take D981 dir Autun; in 6.5km over rlwy, turn R onto unclassified rd sp 'La Gagère'. Site at end of rd in 3.5km on L; this rd narr in places. Med, mkd pitch, hdstg, pt sl, terr, pt shd; wc; chem disp; mv service pnt; child/ baby facs; fam bthrm; sauna; shwrs inc; el pnts (6A) €4.50; gas 10km; lndtte; sm shop & shops 10km; tradsmn; rest, snacks; bar; BBQ; playgrnd; 2 htd pools; lake, shgle beach 12km; wifi; entmnt; TV rm; 20% statics; dogs €4; bus 10km; phone; poss cr; Eng spkn; adv bkg; quiet; ccard acc; red low ssn; INF card req. ACSI acc; "Excel, wooded, scenic site in beautiful area; gd views; friendly, helpful owners; superb san facs; gd touring base." ♦ 1 Apr-30 Sep. € 35.50   2012*

LUZY *4H4* (2km SW Rural) *46.75790, 3.94472* **Camping Château de Chigy**, 58170 Tazilly [03 86 30 10 80; fax 03 86 30 09 22; reception@chateaudechigy.com.fr; www. chateaudechigy.com.fr] Fr Luzy take D973 S twd Bourbon-Lancy, in 4km turn L on minor rd sp Chigy, site sp. Fr S turn R onto rd to Chigy. Site is E of D973 - do not take sp rd to Tazilly vill. V lge, pt sl, pt terr, pt shd; wc; chem disp; baby facs; shwrs inc; private san facs cent pitches; el pnts (6A) €4; gas; lndtte; rest, snacks (high ssn); bar; playgrnd; htd covrd pool; paddling pool; fishing; games area; entmnt; TV; some statics; dogs €2; adv bkg; quiet; red low ssn/long stay/snr citizens; CKE/CCI. "Lovely site in grnds of château; lge pitches; gd." ♦ 26 Apr-30 Sep. € 22.00   2009*

LYON *9B2* (12km E Rural) *45.79082, 4.99223* **Camping Le Grand Large**, 81 Rue Victor Hugo, 69330 Meyzieu [04 78 31 42 16; fax 04 72 45 91 78; camping.grand.large@ wanadoo.fr] Exit N346 junc 6, E onto D6 dir Jonage. In approx 2 km turn L twd Le Grand Large (lake), site in 1km. Lge, pt shd; htd wc (mainly cont); chem disp; mv service pnt; shwrs inc; el pnts (5A) inc; gas; lndtte; shop 2km; snacks; pool 2km; lake sw & beach adj; boating, fishing in lake; games area; entmnt; TV; 90% statics; dogs €1; bus 1km; train 2km; poss cr; quiet; adv bkg; ccard acc; CKE/CCI. "Pleasant location; san facs scruffy & unclean (2011); stn 2km for trains to Lyon; mainly statics and chalets; NH only high ssn" 1 Apr-31 Oct. € 28.00 (3 persons)   2013*

⊞ **LYON** *9B2* (7km SW Urban) *45.68702, 4.78636* **Camping des Barolles**, 88 Ave Foch, 69230 St Genis-Laval [04 78 56 05 56; fax 04 72 67 95 01; contact@ campingdesbarolles.fr; www.campingdesbarolles.fr] Exit A7 at Pierre-Bénite cent onto A450 & exit at Basses-Barolles; foll sp. Or fr D342 to St Genis-Laval cent main sq (Place Joffre) then take Ave Foch SW to site.. Sm, hdstg, terr, pt shd; wc; mv service pnt; shwrs; el pnts (6-16A) €4.20-9.50; gas; lndtte; shop, snacks, bar 200m; playgrnd; wifi; some statics; dogs €2.50; site clsd Nov; quiet; twin-axles extra. "Excel site conv Lyon; friendly recep; gd san facs; NH only." € 15.00   2011*

⊞ **LYON** *9B2* (8km NW Urban) *45.81948, 4.76168* **Camping Indigo Lyon**, Ave de la Porte de Lyon, 69570 Dardilly [04 78 35 64 55; fax 04 72 17 04 26; lyon@camping-indigo. com; www.camping-indigo.com] Fr D306 Paris rd, take Limonest-Dardilly-Porte de Lyon exit at Auchan supmkt. Fr A6 exit junc 33 Porte de Lyon. Site on W side of A6 adj m'way & close to junc, foll sp (poss obscured by trees) for 'Complexe Touristique'. Fr E take N ring rd dir Roanne, Paris, then as above. Lge, hdg/mkd pitch, hdstg, pt shd; htd wc; chem disp; mv service pnt; serviced pitches; mv service pnt; baby facs; shwrs inc; el pnts (6-10A) €4.70-7.50; gas 100m; lndtte (inc dryer); hypmkt 200m; sm rest; rest & bar 100m; playgrnd; pool; games rm; internet; TV rm; some statics; dogs €4; phone; bus/train to city nr; extra for twin-axle c'vans; Eng spkn; adv bkg; rd noise; ccard acc; red low ssn; CKE/CCI. "Well-run, secure site; Lyon easy by bus & metro; gd touring base for interesting area; helpful recep; gd, clean san facs" ♦ € 20.25 (CChq acc)   2013*

LYONS LA FORET *3D2* (500m NE Rural) *49.40334, 1.47954* **FFCC Camp Municipal St Paul**, 27480 Lyons-la-Forêt [02 32 49 42 02; camping-saint-paul@orange.fr; www. camping-saint-paul.fr] Fr Rouen E on N31/E46 for 33km; at La Feuillie, S on D921/321 for 8km; site on L at bottom of hill at ent to town adj Rv Lieure. Med, hdg/mkd pitch, pt shd; htd wc (cont); chem disp; shwrs inc; el pnts (6A) inc (poss rev pol); lndtte; shops 1km; tradsmn; rest, snacks, bar 1km; playgrnd; pool adj inc; fishing; tennis; horseriding; poss cr; 50% statics; dogs €1; adv bkg; quiet; no ccard acc; red low ssn/CKE/CCI. "Pleasant, well-kept site; helpful staff; Lyons-la-Forêt lovely town, conv Dieppe ferry; walking & cycling in forests; liable to flood after heavy rain; rec." 1 Apr-31 Oct. € 20.30   2010*

MACHE see Aizenay *2H4*

⊞ **"Satellite navigation makes touring much easier"**
Remember most sat navs don't know if you're towing or in a larger vehicle – always use yours alongside maps and site directions.

MACHECOUL *2H4* (500m SE Urban) *46.98987, -1.81562* **Camp Municipal La Rabine**, Allée de la Rabine, 44270 Machecoul [tel/fax 02 40 02 30 48 / 06 08 49 22 88; camprabine@wanadoo.fr; www.camping-la-rabine. pagesperso-orange.fr] Sp fr most dirs. Look out for prominent twin-spired church in cent; take sm one-way street that leads away fr spire end; site on R in 400m. Med, pt shd; wc; chem disp; shwrs €1; el pnts (4-13A) €2-3.20; lndtte; shops 500m; tradsmn; BBQ (gas only) playgrnd; pool adj; sand beach 14km; entmnt; dogs €0.90; wifi; adv bkg; quiet. "Pleasant site with lge pitches & gd facs; excel base for birdwatching & cycling over marshes; pleasant town; mkt Wed & Sat; Lovely friendly well managed site, generous size pitches, excel facs" 1 Apr-30 Sep. € 10.80   2013*

MACHECOUL

www.caravanclub.co.uk/europereport   *Last year of report **367**

MACON 9A2 (3km N Urban) 46.33023, 4.84491 **Camp Municipal Les Varennes, 1 Route des Grandes Varennes, Sancé, 71000 Mâcon [03 85 38 16 22 or 03 85 38 54 08; fax 03 85 39 39 18; camping@ville-macon.fr; www.macon.fr]** Fr both N & S exit A6 junc 28 & cont S on N6 twd Mâcon; site on L in approx 3km, sp. (Fr S, leaving A6 at junc 28 avoids long trip thro town). Lge, mkd pitch, pt sl, pt shd; htd wc (some cont); chem disp; mv service pnt; baby facs; shwrs inc; el pnts (5-10A) inc (poss rev pol); gas; lndtte; shop; supmkt nr; hypmkt 1km; rest, snacks; bar; playgrnd; 2 pools; tennis 1km; golf 6km; wifi; TV; dogs €1.40; phone; bus; poss cr; Eng spkn; adv bkg; quiet but some rd & rlwy noise; ccard acc; red low ssn/long stay; CKE/CCI. "Well-kept, busy NH nr A6; rec arr early as poss full after 1800; friendly staff; vg, immac san facs; excel rest; gates clsd 2200-0630; poss flooding bottom end of site; twin-axles extra; long level walk to town; excel." ♦ 15 Mar-31 Oct. € 24.60   2013*

MACON 9A2 (8km S Rural) 46.25167, 4.82610 **Base de loisirs du lac de Cormoranche, Les Luizant, 01290 Cormoranche-sur-Saône [03 85 23 97 10; fax 03 85 23 97 11; contact@lac-cormoranche.com; www. lac-cormoranche.com]** Exit A26 junc 29 sp Mâcon Sud onto N6 S to Crêches-sur-Saône. Turn L in town at traff lts onto D31 sp Cormoranche, then D51A. Cross rv, site sp on L. Alt rte: exit N6 in Mâcon & turn E onto D1079 dir St Laurent-sur-Saône then take D933 S to Pont-de-Veyle. Cont on D933 & foll sp to Cormoranche. Med, hdg/mkd pitch, pt shd; htd wc; chem disp; mv service pnt; shwrs inc; el pnts inc; lndtte (inc dryer); shop; tradsmn; rest, snacks; bar; playgrnd; lake sw & sand beach adj; fishing; cycle hire; entmnt; TV rm; 25% statics; dogs €2.20; poss cr; Eng spkn; adv bkg; quiet; ccard acc; CKE/CCI. "Spacious pitches, some with narr access; vg." ♦ 1 May-30 Sep. € 25.60   2013*

MACON 9A2 (8km S Rural) 46.24106, 4.80643 **Camp Municipal du Port d'Arciat, Route du Port d'Arciat, 71680 Crêches-sur-Saône [03 85 37 11 83 or 03 85 37 48 32 (LS); fax 03 85 36 51 57; campingduportdarciat@wanadoo. fr; http://campingduportdarciat.pagesperso-orange.fr]** S fr Mâcon on N6 to Crêches-sur-Saône. Site sp (1 sm sp) at 3rd set of traff lts in cent vill on N6, turn E, cross m'way bdge; site on R by rv, sp on rndabt. Lge, mkd pitch, pt sl, pt shd; wc (some cont); chem disp; mv service pnt; shwrs inc; el pnts (6A) €4; gas; lndtte; shop; supmkt 1km; rest, snacks; bar; playgrnd; pool 1km; fishing & boating; entmnt; dogs €1.40; gates clsd 2200-0700; some Eng spkn; adv bkg; ccard acc; red low ssn; CKE/CCI. "Gd touring base; gd facs; gate to lake/beach clsd bef 1900; twin-axles extra; poss flooding in heavy rain; conv a'route; ideal NH, espec low ssn; vg." ♦ 15 May-15 Sep. € 22.20   2013*

MADIRAN 8F2 (Urban) 43.54955, -0.05712 **FFCC Camp Municipal Le Madiran, Route de Vignoble, 65700 Madiran [tel/fax 05 62 31 92 83 or 06 84 67 26 13 (mob); madiran@ wanadoo.fr; http://madiran.monsite-orange.fr/]** S fr Riscle on D935 after approx 12km turn R onto D58 to Madiran. Site in middle of town. Sm, mkd pitch, pt sl, unshd; wc; chem disp; shwrs inc; el pnts €2.50; gas, shop, snacks, bar 50m; playgrnd; pool; dogs; Eng spkn; quiet; ccard acc; CKE/CCI. "Excel site." ♦ 15 Jun-15 Oct. € 10.00   2008*

MAGNAC BOURG 7B3 (Urban) 45.61965, 1.42864 **FFCC Camp Municipal Les Ecureuils, 87380 Magnac-Bourg [05 55 00 80 28 (Mairie); fax 05 55 00 49 09; mairie.magnac-bourg@wanadoo.fr; www.tourismelimousin.com]** Leave A20 at junc 41 sp Magnac-Bourg; foll sps to site in vill. Site behind town hall. Sm, pt sl, some hdg pitch, pt shd; wc; mv service pnt; shwrs inc; el pnts (16A) €3.10; supmkt, petrol & rest nr; playgrnd; fishing 2km; dogs; CKE/CCI. "Quiet, peaceful site; old but clean san facs; site yourself, warden calls at 1600 or see when avail on door of Mairie; mkt Sat am; gd NH." 15 May-15 Sep. € 10.20   2011*

⊞ **MAICHE** 6G3 (1km S Rural) 47.24705, 6.79952 **Camp Municipal St Michel, 23 Rue St Michel, 25120 Maîche [03 81 64 12 56 or 03 81 64 03 01 (Mairie); fax 03 81 64 12 56; contact@mairie-maiche.fr; www.mairie-maiche.fr]** Fr S turn R off D437 onto D442. App on D464 L on o'skts of town. Sm, pt sl, terr, pt shd; htd wc; chem disp; shwrs inc; el pnts (5A) €4.46; lndtte; shops 1km; playgrnd; pool adj; games area; games rm; a few statics; dogs; phone; site clsd 3rd week Nov & Dec; adv bkg; rd noise. "Attractive, neat, well-run site with views; clean facs; phone ahead low ssn to check open; gd walks in woods." ♦ € 15.62   2013*

MAICHE 6G3 (10km SW Rural) 47.16304, 6.72469 **Camp Municipal Les Sorbiers, Rue Foch, 25210 Le Russey [03 81 43 72 35]** On D437 Maîche-Morteau, 1st R after vill church, site sp on L in 250m. Med, hdstg, pt shd; htd wc (men cont); chem disp; shwrs; el pnts (10A); gas; lndtte; shop 1km; rest, snacks, bar 500m; playgrnd; tennis; games rm; 20% statics; adv bkg; quiet; ccard not acc. "Excel, scenic cent; high altitude, poss cold nights." 15 Jun-15 Sep.   2009*

MAILLE see Maillezais 7A2

MAILLERAYE SUR SEINE, LA see Caudebec en Caux 3C2

MAILLEZAIS 7A2 (S Rural) 46.36912, -0.74027 **Camp Municipal de l'Autize, Rue du Champ de Foire, 85420 Maillezais [02 51 00 70 79 or 06 31 43 21 33 (mob); fax 02 51 00 70 79; camping.lautize@orange.fr; www. maillezais.fr]** Fr Fontenay take D148 twd Niort; after 9km, turn R onto D15 to Maillezais; at church in vill on L, site on R after 200m. Or fr A83, exit junc 9 onto D148, then D15 (do not use v minor rds, as poss directed by sat nav). Sm, hdg/mkd pitch, pt shd; wc; chem disp; shwrs inc; el pnts (4-13A) €3-5; lndtte; shops 200m; playgrnd; games area; games rm; TV; adv bkg; quiet; ccard not acc; red low ssn; CKE/CCI. "Lovely, clean site; spacious pitches, gd views fr some; friendly, helpful warden; excel, immac san facs; warden calls am & pm; some low branches (2010); twin-axles extra; excel mkd cycle paths; conv Marais Poitevin area & Venise Verte; nrby abbey worth a visit; vg NH fr A83; excel." ♦ 1 Apr-30 Sep. € 9.00   2013*

MAILLEZAIS 7A2 (6km S Rural) 46.31308, -0.73342 **FFCC Camping Les Conches, Route du Grand Port, 85420 Damvix [tel/fax 02 51 87 17 06; campingdesconches@ orange.fr; http://campingdesconches.free.fr]** Fr Fontenay-le-Comte exit D148 at Benet then W on D25 thro Le Mazeau to sp on L for Damvix. Or exit A83 junc 8 then S on D938 & E on D25 dir Benet. Site 1km thro vill on R over bdge (sp). Med, mkd, shd; wc; chem disp; mv service pnt; shwrs; el pnts (6-10A) €3; lndtte; shops adj; rest adj; playgrnd; pool; tennis; golf; horseriding; rv fishing & boating adj; dogs €1; adv bkg rec; quiet but some noise fr disco opp high ssn; CKE/CCI. "Gd rest; friendly staff; gd cycling." 1 May-15 Oct. € 11.50   2010*

MAILLEZAIS 7A2 (5km SW Rural) 46.34037, -0.79640 **Camp Municipal La Petite Cabane, 85420 Maillé [02 51 87 07 52; contact@lesasterides.com]** Site is 500m W of Maillé, clearly sp. Sm, pt shd; wc; shwrs inc; el pnts (10) inc (poss rev pol); gas 500m; lndry rm; shops 500m; playgrnd; paddling pool; boat & canoe hire; adv bkg; quiet; CKE/CCI. "Site by canal in cent of Marais Poitevin National Park; diff access lge o'fits; gd cycle rtes." 1 Apr-30 Sep. € 11.50   2011*

"There aren't many sites open at this time of year"

If you're travelling outside peak season remember to call ahead to check site opening dates – even if the entry says 'open all year'.

MAILLY LE CHATEAU 4G4 (S Rural) 47.58906, 3.65332 **Camp Municipal Le Pré du Roi, Pertuis des Bouchets, 89660 Mailly-le-Château [03 86 81 44 85 or 03 86 81 40 37 (Mairie); fax 03 86 81 40 37; mairie-maillylechateau@wanadoo.fr]** NW on N6 fr Avallon twd Auxerre, turn W in Voutenay-sur-Cure on D950 to Mailly-la-Ville. Cross bdge twd Mailly-le-Château, site sp. Heading S fr Auxerre, turn R off N6 SE of Vincelles on D100 to Bazarnes & Mailly-le-Château. Med, mkd pitch, pt shd; wc; shwrs; el pnts (20A) €3; shops 2km; fishing; dogs; quiet. "Pleasant, peaceful situation by Rv Yonne; helpful warden; gd san facs; some pitches uneven & soft when wet." 1 Jun-3 Sep. € 10.90   2010*

⊞ **MAINTENON** 4E2 (4km NW Rural) 48.60890, 1.54760 **Camping Les Ilots de St Val, Le Haut Bourray, 28130 Villiers-le-Morhier [02 37 82 71 30; fax 02 37 82 77 67; lesilots@campinglesilotsdestval.com; www. campinglesilotsdestval.com]** Take D983 N fr Maintenon twd Nogent-le-Roi, in 5km 2nd L onto D101 sp Néron/ Vacheresses-les-Basses/Camping to site in 1km on L at top of hill. NB App fr N on D929 not rec as rds in Nogent-le-Roi narr. Lge, some hdg/mkd pitch, hdstg, pt shd; htd wc; chem disp; mv service pnt; shwrs inc; el pnts (6-10A) €4-6.60; gas; lndtte; shops 4km; tradsmn; BBQ; playgrnd; pool 4km; rv fishing 1km; tennis; games rm; wifi; 50% statics; dogs €2; train 4km; little Eng spkn; adv bkg; quiet but some aircraft noise; red long stay/CKE/CCI. "Pleasant, peaceful site in open countryside; lge private pitches; some vg, modern san facs; helpful staff; conv Chartres, Versailles, Maintenon Château, train to Paris. Dog walking from the site is gd." HCAP] 01 Mar-31 Dec. € 16.20   2013*

See advertisement

MAISONS LAFFITTE see Paris 3D3

MALARCE SUR LA THINES see Vans, Les 9D1

MALAUCENE 10E2 (4km N Rural) 44.20101, 5.12535 **FFCC Camping Aire Naturelle La Saousse (Letilleul), La Madelaine, 84340 Malaucène [04 90 65 14 02]** Fr Malaucène take D938 N dir Vaison-la-Romaine & after 3km turn R onto D13 dir Entrechaux where site sp. After 1km turn R, site 1st on R. Sm, hdg pitch, terr, shd; wc; chem disp; shwrs inc; el pnts (5A) €2.50; lndry rm; tradsmn high ssn; shop, rest, snacks, bar, pool 4km; no statics; dogs; adv bkg rec; quiet; ccard not acc; red low ssn; CKE/CCI. "CL-type site o'looking vineyards with views to Mt Ventoux; some pitches in woods with steep incline - rec pitch on lower level for easy access; friendly, helpful owners; basic, clean facs; v peaceful,excel." 1 Apr-30 Sep. € 14.00   2012*

MALAUCENE *10E2* (8km S Rural) *44.12383, 5.10968*
Camping Le Bouquier, Route de Malaucène, 84330
Caromb [tel/fax 04 90 62 30 13; lebouquier@wanadoo.
fr; www.lebouquier.com] Fr Malaucène S on D938 for
8km; turn L D13 sp Caromb; site 800m on L just bef vill. Or
NE fr Carpentras on D974 then D13; site on R 1.5km after
Caromb cent. NB App fr N (D939/D13) avoids lge speed humps
in Caromb. Med, hdg/mkd pitch, hdstg, terr, pt shd, htd wc;
chem disp; shwrs inc; el pnts (10A) €3; lndtte; shops 1.5km;
tradsmn; snacks; bar; BBQ (gas/elec); playgrnd; htd pool; lake
sw 1km; gd walking/cycling; wifi; 5% statics; dogs €1.60;
phone; poss cr; Eng spkn; adv bkg; quiet but some rd noise;
ccard not acc; red low ss; CKE/CCI. "Well-kept site; attractive
scenery; helpful staff; excel san facs; steps to disabled facs;
steel pegs req; gd touring base; no twin-axles; vg." ♦ ltd
3 Apr-1 Oct. € 15.00   2011*

MALAUCENE *10E2* (400m NW Rural) *44.17789, 5.12533*
Camping Le Bosquet, Route de Suzette, 84340 Malaucène
[04 90 65 24 89 or 04 90 65 29 09; fax 04 90 65 12 52;
camping.lebosquet@wanadoo.fr; www.provence.
guideweb.com/camping/bosquet/] Fr S on D938 dir Vaison-
la-Romaine turn L onto D90 at Malaucène dir Suzette. Site on R
in 300m. Do not tow thro Malaucène. Sm, hdg pitch, all hdstg,
terr, pt shd; htd wc; chem disp; baby facs; shwrs inc; el pnts
(6A) €3.20 (poss rev pol); gas; lndtte; shop 600m; tradsmn;
snacks; bar; playgrnd; pool; 2% statics; dogs €1; phone; adv
bkg; quiet; ccard not acc; red low ssn; CKE/CCI. "Clean san
facs; friendly owner; gd touring base Mt Ventoux; mkt Wed;
Easy walk to the town" ♦ 5Apr-14 Oct. € 16.20   2013*

MALBUISSON *6H2* (S Urban) *46.79223, 6.29377* Camping
Les Fuvettes, 24 Route de la Plage et des Perrières, 25160
Malbuisson [03 81 69 31 50; fax 03 81 69 70 46; les-
fuvettes@wanadoo.fr; www.camping-fuvettes.com]
Site 19km S of Pontarlier on N57 & D437 to Malbuisson, thro
town, R down rd to Plage. Lge, pt sl, pt shd; htd wc (some
cont); shwrs inc; el pnts (4-6A) €3.60-4; gas; lndtte (inc dryer);
shop; rest, snacks; bar; playgrnd; shgl beach for lake sw;
fishing; boating; games rm; 30% statics; dogs €1,50; poss cr;
quiet; CKE/CCI. "Popular, lakeside, family site; mkd walks/cycle
paths in adj woods; petting zoo (llamas etc) nrby."
1 Apr-30 Sep. € 21.00   2008*

MALBUISSON *6H2* (2km S Rural) *46.77449, 6.27370*
Camping du Lac, 10 Rue du Lac, 25160 Labergement-Ste
Marie [03 81 69 31 24; camping.lac.remoray@wanadoo.fr;
www.camping-lac-remoray.com] Exit N57/E23 junc 2 onto
D437 thro Malbuisson to Labergement. Site sp to R of D437
after x-ing Rv Doubs. Med, mkd pitch, pt shd; wc; chem disp;
mv service pnt; baby facs; shwrs inc; el pnts (6A) €3.50; gas;
lndtte; tradsmn; rest, snacks; bar; playgrnd; lake beach adj;
fishing; walking; cycling; sports area; tennis nrby; internet;
TV; 5% statics in sep area; dogs €1.50; phone; Eng spkn; adv
bkg; quiet; ccard acc; red low ssn; CKE/CCI. "Roomy site by
Lake Remoray with forest views; kind & helpful owner; clean
san facs; vill 500m with gd shops; excel." ♦ 1 May-30 Sep.
€ 14.50   2010*

MALEMORT DU COMTAT see Carpentras *10E2*

MALENE, LA *9D1* (200m W Rural) *44.30120, 3.31923*
FFCC Camp Municipal Le Pradet, 48210 La Malène
[04 66 48 58 55 or 04 66 48 51 16 (LS); fax 04 66 48 58 51;
la.malene.mairie@wanadoo.fr] W fr La Malène on D907B
dir Les Vignes. Site on L in 200m. Well sp. Sm, mkd pitch, some
hdstg, pt sl, pt shd; wc (some cont); chem disp; mv service pnt;
shwrs inc; el pnts (10A) €2.50; lndtte; shops, rest, snacks & bar
200m; BBQ; playgrnd; rv sw & fishing; dogs €0.30; phone; poss
cr; adv bkg; quiet; ccard acc; red low ssn; CKE/CCI. "Kayak
hire; boat trips fr vill; helpful warden; excel." 1 Apr-30 Sep.
€ 11.60   2009*

⊞ **MALESHERBES** *4E3* (5km S Rural) *48.25659, 2.43574*
FFCC Camping Ile de Boulancourt, 6 Allée des
Marronniers, 77760 Boulancourt [01 64 24 13 38; fax
01 64 24 10 43; info@camping-iledeboulancourt.com;
www.camping-iledeboulancourt.com] Exit A6 at junc 14
Ury & Fontainebleau. SW on D152 to Malesherbes; S on D410
for 5km into Boulancourt. Site sp fr D410 & in vill. Med, pt shd;
htd wc (many cont); chem disp; mv service pnt; shwrs inc;
el pnts (3-6A) €2.10; lndtte; shop 3km; rest; BBQ; playgrnd;
pool nr; tennis; rv; fishing 3km; watersle 5km;
90% statics; dogs €1; sep field for tourers; Eng spkn; quiet; red
low ssn; CKE/CCI. "Attractive rv thro site; well-maintained facs,
ltd low ssn; friendly, helpful staff; golf course in vill; chateau nr;
excel." € 13.60   2009*

MALESTROIT *2F3* (500m E Urban) *47.80865, -2.37922* Camp
Municipal de la Daufresne, Chemin des Tanneurs, 56140
Malestroit [02 97 75 13 33 or 02 97 75 11 75 (Mairie);
fax 02 97 73 71 13; tourisme@malestroit.com; www.
malestroit.com] S fr Ploërmel on N166 dir Vannes for 9km.
Turn L onto D764 to Malestroit; site sp just off Blvd du Pont
Neuf on E bank of Rv Oust, not well sp. Sm, some hdg pitch,
pt shd; wc; chem disp; mv service pnt; shwrs inc; el pnts (10A)
€2.70 (poss long lead req); lndtte; shop, rest, snacks, bar
300m; playgrnd; tennis; adj BBQ; rv & fishing adj; canoeing
nr; dogs free; poss cr; ccard not acc; CKE/CCI. "Pleasant
site in excel location; narr site rds, some pitches poss diff
to manoeuvre; no twin-axles; clean san facs poss stretched
high ssn; canal towpath adj; gd cycle rtes; Museum of Breton
Resistance in St Marcel; v nice site, highly rec" ♦ ltd 1 May-
15 Sep. € 10.35   2012*

MALICORNE SUR SARTHE *4F1* (N Urban) *47.81736, -0.08791*
Camp Municipal Porte Ste Marie, Route de Noyen, 72270
Malicorne-sur-Sarthe [02 43 94 80 14; fax 02 43 94 57 26;
camping.malicorne@wanadoo.fr; www.ville-malicorne.fr]
Fr A11/E501 take D306 exit twds La Flèche. Turn E onto D23
twds Malicorne. Site across rv on W of town adj stadium. Med,
pt shd; wc; chem disp; mv service pnt; baby facs; shwrs inc;
el pnts (4-13A) €1.60-2.65; lndtte; shops, rest, bar 500m; BBQ;
playgrnd; pool; tennis adj; dogs €0.65; poss cr; quiet; red low
ssn; "Quiet position by rv; gd san facs; no access when recep
clsd 1230-1430 & after 1930; poss noise (church bell); no
waiting area; diff turning; gd." 1 Apr-30 Sep. € 9.20   2010*

MALLEMORT see Salon de Provence *10E2*

MAMERS *4E1* (500m N Rural) *48.35778, 0.37181* **Camp Municipal du Saosnois, Route de Contilly, 72600 Mamers [02 43 97 68 30; fax 02 43 97 38 65; camping.mamers@ free.fr; www.mairie-mamers.fr]** Fr W on D311, at rndabt at top of hill on circular rd, turn R (sp); then easy L (sp). Fr E on D311, strt thro rndabt (at Super U), ignore 1st camping sp, turn R at traff its & 2nd camping sp; at mini-rndabt turn L, sp Contilly; see lake & site. Sm, hdg pitch, hdstg, pt sl, terr, pt shd; htd wc; mv service pnt; shwrs inc; el pnts (10A) €3-4.20 (long lead poss req); lndtte; shop & 500m; snacks; pool 200m; lakeside beach; games area; TV rm; 30% statics; dogs €0.50; poss cr; adv bkg; quiet; CKE/CCI. "Well-kept, secure site; admittance low ssn 1700-1900 only; Mamers pretty; poss itinerants." ♦ 3 Mar-3 Nov. € 12.00   2013*

MANDEURE *6G3* (500m NW Urban) *47.45633, 6.80575* **Camping Les Grands Ansanges, Rue de l'Eglise, 25350 Mandeure [03 81 35 23 79; fax 03 81 30 09 26; mairie. mandeure@ville-mandeure.com; www.ville-mandeure.com]** Exit A36 sp Exincourt, site sp fr cent Mandeure, adj Rv Doubs. Med, mkd pitch, pt shd; wc; chem disp; shwrs inc; el pnts (4-10A) €4; lndry rm; sm shop; supmkt 1.4km; tradsmn; rest; bar; playgrnd; games rm; archery & golf nrby; 10% statics; poss cr; CKE/CCI. "Beautifully laid-out site facing open farmland; helpful staff; basic san facs (disabled up steps)." ♦ ltd 1 May-30 Sep. € 10.90   2008*

MANDRES AUX QUATRE TOURS *5D2* (2km S Rural) *48.82739, 5.78936* **Camp Municipal Orée de la Forêt de la Reine, Route Forêt de la Reine, 54470 Mandres-aux-Quatre-Tours [03 83 23 17 31; mandres.54470@ wandoo.fr]** On D958 Commercy to Pont-à-Mousson, sp as Camping Mandres. Turn R at sp in Beaumont & foll sp to vill Mandres-aux-Quatre-Tours. Sm, pt mkd/hdg pitch, pt shd; wc; chem disp (wc); shwrs inc; el pnts (10A) €2.20 (poss long lead req); tradsmn; playgrnd; tennis; watersports; sailing 500m; horseriding adj; some statics; dogs; quiet; red long stay; CKE/CCI. "Gd, peaceful site; site yourself; basic san facs; site poss muddy when wet; gd birdwatching, walking, cycling; popular NH." 1 Apr-31 Oct. € 11.00   2011*

MANOSQUE *10E3* (4km E Rural) *43.82352, 5.85424* **Camping Oxygene, 04210 Valensole [tel/fax 04 92 72 41 77; info@ camping-oxygene.com; www.camping-oxygene.com]** Exit A51 junc 18 onto D907 E dir Vinon-sur-Verdon; in 1km turn L at rndabt onto D4 N dir Oraison; site in 2.5km on L, at Les Chabrands, just bef Villedieu. Med, hdg/mkd pitch, pt shd; wc; chem disp; mv service pnt; baby facs; shwrs inc; el pnts (6-10A) €3.50-4.20; lndtte (inc dryer); tradsmn; snacks; bar; BBQ (gas/elec); pool; horseriding, angling, canyoning, rafting & paragliding nrby; games area; gym; dogs €2.50; no twin-axles; quiet; ccard not acc; red low ssn. "Peaceful, well-kept site with hill views; vg pool; many places of interest nrby, inc Gorges du Verdon." ♦ 20 Apr-17 Sep. € 20.00   2011*

MANOSQUE *10E3* (1.5km W Rural) *43.82986, 5.76384* **FFCC Camping Les Ubacs, 1138 Ave de la Repasse, 04100 Manosque [04 92 72 28 08; fax 04 92 87 75 29; lesubacs.manosque@ffcc.fr]** Exit A51 junc 18 onto D907 dir Manosque; then D907 dir Apt; site sp at last rndabt on W side of Manosque. NB easy to overshoot. Med, hdg/mkd pitch,pt sl, pt shd; wc (cont); mv service pnt; shwrs inc; el pnts (3-9A) €3.34-4.20; lndtte; shop; rest, snacks (high ssn); bar; playgrnd; pool (high ssn); tennis; lake sw 5km; entmnt; dogs €1; ccard acc; red long stay/low ssn/CKE/CCI. "Conv Gorges du Verdon; helpful." 1 Apr-30 Sep. € 15.40   2013*

MANS, LE *4F1* (8km N Rural) *48.07179, 0.18934* **FFCC Camping Le Vieux Moulin, 72190 Neuville-sur-Sarthe [02 43 25 31 82; fax 02 43 25 38 11; info@lemanscamping.net; www.lemanscamping.net]** Leave D338 6km N of Le Mans at St Saturnin; turn E onto D197 to Neuville & foll sp for 3km to site nr Rv Sarthe. Med, pt shd, hdg/mkd pitch, serviced pitch; wc (some cont); chem disp; mv service pnt; baby facs; shwrs inc; el pnts (10A) €3 (poss rev pol); gas; lndtte; sm shop (high ssn) & 500m; tradsmn; rest adj; playgrnd; sm htd pool; tennis; 5% statics; dogs €1; Eng spkn; adv bkg; quiet; ccard acc; red low ssn/CKE/CCI. "Open for Le Mans 24 hours race ssn only - phone to confirm opening dates; lge, grassy pitches; friendly, helpful owner; clean san facs; sm lake & watermill/ rest adj; peaceful setting; gates clsd 2200-0730; highly rec." € 13.00   2009*

MANS, LE *4F1* (6km NE Rural) *48.01904, 0.27996* **Camping Le Pont Romain, Allée des Ormeaux, Lieu-dit La Châtaigneraie, 72530 Yvré-l'Evêque [02 43 82 25 39; info@lepontromain.com; www.lepontromain.com]** Fr Le Mans take D314 to Yvré-l'Evêque - but do not ent town; just after rv bdge take 1st L into Allée des Ormeaux; site on L in 800m. Or exit A28 junc 23 onto D314 dir 'Le Mans Centre'; site on R just bef Yvré-l'Evêque. Med, hdg/mkd pitch, hdstg, pt shd; htd wc; chem disp; mv service pnt; baby facs; shwrs inc; el pnts (16A) inc; lndtte (inc dryer); shop; rest, snacks; playgrnd; htd pool; games rm; wifi; TV rm; 10% statics; dogs €1; phone; bus to Le Mans 500m; sep car park; no twin-axles; poss cr; Eng spkn; adv bkg; red low ssn; CKE/CCI. "New site (2009); gd san facs; conv Le Mans & m'way; vg." ♦ ltd 1 Mar-1 Nov. € 21.75   2013*

MANSIGNE *4F1* (500m N Rural) *47.75188, 0.13153* **Camping A Tou Vert La Plage, Route du Plessis, 72510 Mansigné [02 43 46 14 17; camping-mansigne@orange.fr; www. atouvert.com]** N fr Le Lude on D307 to Pontvallain. Take D13 E for 5km to Mansigné, thro vill & foll site sp. Lge, pt shd; wc; chem disp; shwrs inc; el pnts (10A) €3.70; lndtte (inc dryer); shop 200m; rest, snacks; bar; BBQ; htd pool; sand beach & lake sw adj; watersports; tennis; some statics; dogs €1.10; adv bkg; quiet; red long stay/low ssn; CKE/CCI. "Pleasant lakeside position; conv for Loir Valley & Le Mans 24-hour race; ltd facs & office hrs low ssn." ♦ 1 Apr-31 Oct. € 11.50   2010*

FRANCE

MANSLE *7B2* (NE Urban) *45.87841, 0.18175* **Camp Municipal Le Champion, Rue de Watlington, 16230 Mansle [05 45 20 31 41 or 05 45 22 20 43; fax 05 45 22 86 30; mairie.mansle@wanadoo.fr; www.mansle.fr]** N on N10 fr Angoulême, foll sp Mansle Ville. Leave N10 at exit to N of town, site rd on L, well sp. Rec ent/leave fr N as rte thro town diff due to parked cars. Site beside Rv Charente. Med, hdg pitch, pt shd; wc; chem disp; mv service pnt; shwrs inc; el pnts (16A) €2.80 (poss long lead req); gas in town; lndtte; shops 200m; rest; snacks, bar adj; BBQ; playgrnd; rv sw & boating adj; fishing; entmnt; 5% statics; phone; poss cr; quiet but some rd noise; adv bkg; phone 1km; Eng spkn; ccard not acc; CKE/ CCI. "Popular, peaceful, well-kept NH nr N10; lge pitches, choose own; helpful warden; immac san facs; grnd poss boggy after heavy rain; mkt Tues, Fri am; vg." ♦ 15 May-16 Sep. € 18.80   2013*

MANSLE *7B2* (8km NE Rural) *45.90904, 0.25247* **Camp Municipal Le Magnerit, Les Maisons Rouges, 16460 Aunac [05 45 22 24 38; fax 05 45 22 23 17; mairie.aunac@ wanadoo.fr]** N on N10 fr Mansle, exit onto D27 to Bayers & Aunac. Site 1km SE vill, well sp. Sm, pt shd; wc; chem disp; shwrs; el pnts (8A) €2.50; shop 1km; playgrnd; rv sw adj; fishing; Eng spkn; quiet; CKE/CCI. "Peaceful, simple, CL-type site beside Rv Charente; ltd, dated facs but clean; warden visits; vg NH." 15 Jun-15 Sep. € 7.30   2010*

⊞ **MANSLE** *7B2* (10km SE Rural) *45.84137, 0.27319* **Camping Devezeau, 16230 St Angeau [tel/fax 05 45 39 21 29; bookings@campingdevezeau.com; www. campingdevezeau.com]** N or S on N10 exit Mansle; in cent vill at traff lts foll sp twd La Rochefoucauld (D6); past Champion supmkt; over bdge; 1st R onto D6. In approx 9km at T-junc turn R, site sp. App down narr rd. Sm, some hdstg, pt sl, pt shd; wc; chem disp; shwrs; el pnts (10A) €2; gas; lndtte; shop 1.5km; tradsmn; supmkt in Mansle; rest 5km; snacks & bar; BBQ; playgrnd; pool; cycling; walking; canoeing; fishing; horseriding; 10% statics; dogs; phone 1km; Eng spkn; adv bkg; quiet; red low ssn; CKE/CCI. "Nice CL-type site; friendly British owners; dated san facs; traction diff in wet (4x4 avail); gd cycling country; phone ahead in winter." ♦ ltd € 18.00   2010*

MANTENAY MONTLIN *9A2* (400m W Rural) *46.42218, 5.09208* **Camp Municipal du Coq, 01560 Mantenay-Montlin [04 74 52 66 91 or 04 74 52 61 72 (Mairie); cdec. sainttriverdecourtes@wanadoo.fr]** Exit A40 junc 5 Bourg-en-Bresse Nord onto D975 to Mantenay-Montlin; site sp in vill on D46. Or exit A39 junc 10 to St Trivier-de-Courtes, then S to Mantenay. Sm, hdg/mkd pitch, pt shd; wc (cont); chem disp; shwrs; el pnts (6A) €1.70; shop, rest & bar 400m; playgrnd; tennis; dogs €1.50; bus 400m; quiet; red long stay; ccard acc. "Vg rvside site in pretty area; lge pitches; san facs old but clean; warden calls pm; poss v soft after rain; conv NH just off D975." 1 Jun-15 Sep. € 11.50   2010*

MARANS *7A1* (2km N Rural) *46.31682, -0.99158* **Camp Municipal Le Bois Dinot, Route de Nantes, 17230 Marans [05 46 01 10 51; fax 05 46 01 01 72; campingboisdinot. marans@wanadoo.fr; www.ville-marans.fr]** Heading S, site on L of D137 bef ent Marans. Heading N, site is well sp on R 300m after supmkt on L. Lge, shd; wc; shwrs inc; el pnts (10A) €4; shops adj; rest, snacks, bar 200m; pool adj; fishing; boat hire; wifi; dogs €1.10; Eng spkn; poss cr; some rd noise; red long stay/low ssn; CKE/CCI. "Well-kept, wooded site; helpful warden; quieter pitches at back of site; vg pool adj; poss mosquitoes; gd cycling; mkt Tues & Sat; excel." 1 Apr-30 Sep. € 12.50   2011*

"That's changed – Should I let The Club know?"

If you find something on site that's different from the site entry, fill in a report and let us know. See www.caravanclub.co.uk/europereport.

⊞ **MARANS** *7A1* (10km NE Rural) *46.38196, -0.97186* **Camping à la Ferme Le Pont Grenouilles (Berjonneau), 24 Rue du Port d'Aisne, 85450 Vouillé-les-Marais [02 51 52 53 96]** SW fr Fontenay-le-Comte on D938, turn R on D25 to Vouillé-les-Marais. In Vouillé turn L into Rue du Port d'Aisne, site sp. Sm, pt shd; wc; chem disp; mv service pnt; shwrs inc; el pnts (3-10A) €3; lndtte; playgrnd; quiet. "Friendly, helpful owners; peaceful site." € 9.20   2009*

MARCENAY *6F1* (1km N Rural) *47.87070, 4.40560* **Camping Les Grèbes du Lac de Marcenay, 5 Route du Lac, 21330 Marcenay [03 80 81 61 72; fax 03 25 81 02 64; info@ campingmarcenaylac.com; www.campingmarcenaylac. com]** On D965 bet Laignes & Châtillon-sur-Seine. Fr Châtillon sp on R 8km after vill of Cérilly. Foll sp to lake & camp. Med, hdg/mkd pitch, hdstg, shd; htd wc; chem disp; mv service pnt; baby facs; shwrs inc; el pnts (10A) €3; gas; lndtte (inc dryer); shop; tradsmn; rest adj; snacks; bar adj; BBQ; playgrnd; pool; lake sw adj; fishing; watersports; boat, canoe & cycle hire; golf; horseriding; games rm; games area; wifi; TV rm; 5% statics; dogs €1; phone; Eng spkn; adv bkg rec; quiet; ccard acc; red low ssn; CKE/CCI. "Lovely, peaceful, well-run site by lake; beautiful area; friendly, helpful Dutch owners; excel san facs; pitches poss soft after rain; gd touring base; gd walking & cycling; Châtillon museum & Abbey de Fontenay worth visit." ♦ 1 May-30 Sep. € 29.70   2013*

MARCHAINVILLE *4E2* (N Rural) *48.58617, 0.81360* **Camp Municipal Les Fosses, 61290 Marchainville [tel/fax 02 33 83 68 14 or 02 33 73 65 80 (Mairie); mairiemarchainville@wanadoo.fr]** Fr Verneuil-sur-Avre take D941 S to La Ferté-Vidame & at start of town turn R onto D4/ D11 SW to Marchainville; site sp at x-rds in vill on D243. Sm, hdg/mkd pitch, pt sl, pt shd; wc; shwrs; el pnts (10A) €2.30; shop, rest, snacks, bar 8km; tennis; no statics; phone; adv bkg; quiet; CKE/CCI. "Clean, basic site; warden visits." ♦ ltd 1 Apr-30 Oct. € 5.60   2010*

MARCIAC *8F2* (1.5km NW Rural) *43.53228, 0.16633*
FFCC Camping du Lac, Bezines, 32230 Marciac [tel/fax
05 62 08 21 19; camping.marciac@wanadoo.fr; www.
camping-marciac.com] E fr Maubourguet take D943 to
Marciac. Take D3 to lake dir Plaisance. At lake turn R & R again
at sp. Site on L in 200m. Fr N exit A62 at junc 3 & foll D932
sp Pau to Aire-sur-Adour then E on D935 & D3 & foll sp. Med,
mkd pitch, some hdstg, pt sl, pt shd; wc chem disp; mv service
pnt; baby facs; shwrs inc; el pnts (6A) inc; gas; lndtte; shop &
800m; tradsmn; rest 300m; snacks; bar; BBQ; playgrnd; pool;
lake adj; wifi; 8% statics; dogs €1.50; phone; adv bkg; red
long stay/low ssn; ccard acc; CKE/CCI. "Friendly British owners;
peaceful site; lge pitches with easy access; interesting old town;
jazz festival 1st 2 weeks Aug (extra charge); Wed mkt." ♦
20 Mar-17 Oct. € 25.00   2013*

"I like to fill in the reports as I travel from site to site"
You'll find report forms at the back of
this guide, or you can fill them in online
at www.caravanclub.co.uk/europereport.

MARCIGNY *9A1* (7km W Rural) *46.26489, 3.95756* **Camping
La Motte aux Merles, 71110 Artaix [03 85 25 37 67]**
Leave D982 (Digoin-Roanne) at Marcigny by-pass. Take D989
twd Lapalisse. In 2km at Chambilly cont on D990, site sp in
5km on L, 200m down side rd. Sm, pt sl, pt shd; wc; shwrs inc;
el pnts (8A) €2.40; lndry rm; snacks; playgrnd; pool (high ssn);
fishing; tennis; golf nrby; dogs €1; quiet. "Friendly owners; gd
sightseeing in peaceful area; site diff in wet; excel." ♦
1 Apr-15 Oct. € 9.80   2012*

MARCILLAC LA CROISSILLE *7C4* (2km SW Rural) *45.26896,
2.00838* **Camp Municipal Le Lac, 28 Route du Viaduc,
19320 Marcillac-la-Croissille [tel/fax 05 55 27 81 38 or
05 55 27 82 05 (Mairie); campingdulac19@wanadoo.fr;
www.campingdulac19.com]** S fr Egletons on D16 & D18.
Site sp at S end of vill at intersection with D978. Lge, pt sl,
shd, wc; shwrs; el pnts (6A) €2.80; lndtte; shops 2km; snacks;
playgrnd; lake & sand beach adj; tennis adj; entmnt; TV; some
statics; dogs €0.90; adv bkg; quiet; red low ssn. "Spacious park
like setting" 1 Jun-1 Oct. € 11.50   2012*

MARCILLAC ST QUENTIN see Sarlat la Canéda *7C3*

MARCILLAC VALLON *7D4* (300m NW Urban) *44.47721,
2.45575* **Camp Municipal Le Cambou, 24 Ave Gustave
Bessières, 12330 Marcillac-Vallon [05 65 71 74 96 or
06 62 39 19 37 (mob); mairie-marcillacvallon@wanadoo.fr;
www.tourisme-aveyron.com]** App Marcillac-Vallon fr N on
D901; on ent town, site on L immed after x-ing rv bdge. Sm, hdg/
mkd pitch, pt sl, pt shd; htd wc; chem disp; shwrs inc; el pnts (6A)
€2.30; shops nrby; tennis nrby; dogs; some statics; quiet. "Otters
in sm rv; NH only." 1 Jul-31 Aug. € 9.10   2011*

MARCILLY LE HAYER *4E4* (300m W Rural) *48.34754, 3.62709*
**Camp Municipal, Rue des Dolmens, 10292 Marcilly-le-
Hayer [03 25 21 74 34 or 03 25 21 70 36 (Mairie)]** Fr N on
D619 turn S at Romilly-sur-Seine onto D440 to Marcilly-le-
Hayer. Fr S on D660 turn N onto D374 to Marcilly. Site sp on
rvside. Sm, hdg/mkd pitch, pt shd; htd wc; chem disp; shwrs
inc; el pnts (5-10A) €2-3; shop, rest, bar in vill; playgrnd;
fishing; quiet. "Height barrier with phone no at office for entry;
gd site." ♦ 1 Apr-31 Oct.   2010*

MARCON see Château du Loir *4G1*

MARENNES *7B1* (5km SE Rural) *45.81083, -1.06027*
**Camping Séquoia Parc, La Josephtrie, 17320 St Just-
Luzac [05 46 85 55 55; fax 05 46 85 55 56; info@
sequoiaparc.com; www.sequoiaparc.com or www.les-
castels.com]** Fr A10/E05 m'way exit at Saintes, foll sp Royan
(N150) turning off onto D728 twd Marennes & Ile d'Oléron;
site sp to R off D728, just after leaving St Just-Luzac. Or
fr Rochefort take D733 & D123 S; just bef Marennes turn L on
D241 st St Just-Luzac. Best ent to site fr D728, well sp fr each
dir. Lge, hdg/mkd pitch, sl, unshd; wc; chem disp; mv service
pnt; baby facs; shwrs inc; el pnts (6A) inc (poss rev pol);
gas; lndtte (inc dryer); shop; rest, snacks; bar; BBQ; playgrnd;
aquapark: 3 pools (2 htd), paddling pool; waterslides,
waterjets & whirlpool; sand beach 6km; fishing 1.5km;
watersports 3km; horseriding; tennis; cycle hire; games area;
games rm; cash machine; wifi; entmnt; TV rm; 50% statics
(tour ops); dogs €5; no c'vans/m'vans over 9m; barrier clsd
2230-0700; adv bkg; ccard acc; red long stay/low ssn; CKE/
CCI. "High standard site; lge pitches; clean san facs; superb
pools; excel free club for children." ♦ 12 May-9 Sep. € 48.00
2012*

See advertisement

FRANCE

MARENNES *7B1* (10.5km SE Rural) *45.77324, -0.96301*
Camping Le Valerick, La Petite Mauvinière, 17600 St Sornin
[tel/fax 05 46 85 15 95; camplevalerick@aol.com;
www.marennes.fr] Fr Marennes take D728 sp Saintes for
10km; L to St Sornin; site sp in vill. Fr Saintes D728 W for
26km; take 2nd R turn R in vill on L sp La Gripperie.
Sm, mkd pitch, pt sl, pt shd; wc; chem disp (wc); shwrs inc;
el pnts (4-6A) €3-€3.80 (poss rev pol); lndtte; shop; rest,
snacks; bar; BBQ; playgrnd; sand beach 18km; entmnt; dogs
€1.40; adv bkg; CKE/CCI. "Nice, friendly site; gd san facs;
plenty of bird life - herons, storks etc; poss mosquito problem."
1 Apr-30 Sep. € 14.00   2010*

MARENNES *7B1* (2km SW Coastal) *45.82668, -1.13411*
Camping La Ferme de la Prée, 17320 Marennes
[05 46 85 03 61] Fr Saintes on D123 & Marennes N by-pass,
foll sps for Ile d'Oléron to concrete water tower. In 150m turn
L on C15 (sp Marennes-Plage 2km). Site on L in 1km. Sm, mkd
pitch, pt shd; wc (some cont); shwrs €0.80; el pnts (6A) inc; gas;
lndry rm; shops 2.5km, supmkt 4km; tradsmn; BBQ; sand beach
500m; few statics; adv bkg; quiet; CKE/CCI. "Gd farm site;
friendly & helpful owners." 15 Jun-15 Sep. € 6.70   2008*

MARENNES *7B1* (2km NW Coastal) *45.83139, -1.15092*
**Camp Municipal La Giroflée, 17560 Bourcefranc-le-
Chapus** [05 46 85 06 43 or 05 46 85 02 02 (Mairie)] fax
05 46 85 48 58; campinglagiroflee@orange.fr; www.
bourcefranc-le-chapus.fr] Fr Saintes on D728/D26 to
Boucefranc, turn L at traff lts. Site on L after 1km (after sailing
school) opp beach. Med, pt shd; wc (few cont); shwrs €0.80;
el pnts (8A) €3; lndry rm; shops 2km; snacks; playgrnd; beach
adj; poss cr; quiet. 1 May-30 Sep. € 7.65   2011*

MAREUIL *7B2* (5km N Rural) *45.49504, 0.44860* FFCC
Camping Les Graulges, Le Bourg, 24340 Les Graulges
[tel/fax 05 53 60 74 73; info@lesgraulges.com; www.
lesgraulges.com] Fr D939 at Mareuil turn L onto D708 & foll
sp to Les Graulges in 5km. Sm, mkd pitch, pt sl, terr, pt shd;
wc; chem disp (wc); baby facs; shwrs inc; el pnts (6A) €3.50;
lndtte; tradsmn; rest, snacks; bar; BBQ; playgrnd; pool; lake
fishing; some statics; dogs €2; phone 300m; poss cr; Eng
spkn; adv bkg; quiet; red 7+ days. "Tranquil site in forested
area; ideal touring base; friendly Dutch owners; excel rest; Not
suitable for elderly; pool dirty; lge dog lives on site (2012)" ◆
1 Apr-15 Sep. € 20.50   2012*

MAREUIL *7B2* (4km SE Rural) *45.44481, 0.50474* **Camping
L'Etang Bleu, 24340 Vieux-Mareuil** [05 53 60 92 70; fax
05 53 56 66 66; marc@letangbleu.com; www.letangbleu.
com] On D939 Angoulême-Périgueux rd, after 5km turn L cent
of Vieux-Mareuil onto D93, foll camping sp to site in 2km.
Narr app thro vill. Lge, hdg/mkd pitch, pt shd; wc; chem disp;
mv service pnt; baby facs; fam bthrm; shwrs inc; el pnts (10A)
€4.75 (poss rev pol); gas; lndtte; shop; tradsmn; rest, snacks;
bar; BBQ; playgrnd; pool; paddling pool; lake fishing 500m; TV;
entmnt; 10% statics; dogs €3; adv bkg; ccard acc; red low ssn;
CKE/CCI. "Pleasant site in unspoilt countryside; lge pitches, but
narr site rds; access diff lge o'fits without mover; friendly British
owners; gd san facs; ltd low ssn; gd walking/cycling area;
excel." ◆ 01 Apr-20 Oct. € 30.50   2013*

MAREUIL *7B2* (6km SE Rural) *45.42465, 0.53012* **Camping
La Charrue, Les Chambarrières, 24340 Vieux-Mareuil**
[tel/fax 05 53 56 65 59; info@la-charruefrance.com;
www.la-charruefrance.com] SE fr Angoulême on D939 sp
Périgueux to Mareuil. Fr Mareuil stay on D939 twds Brantôme,
thro Vieux-Mareuil then in 2km site immed on L after passing
a lge lay-by on R with white stone chippings. Awkward turn.
Sm, mkd pitch, pt shd; wc; chem disp; shwrs inc; el pnts (4A)
€3; gas 3km; lndtte; shop 2km; tradsmn; rest & bar 500m;
snacks; BBQ; playgrnd; pool; sand beach, lakes & watersports
nr; fishing 3km; cycle hire; golf nr; dogs (low ssn only); adv bkg
(full payment req); some rd noise; red long stay/low ssn; CKE/
CCI. "CL-type site in Regional Park; friendly, helpful British
owners; immac facs; gd touring base for beautiful area; B&B &
gites avail; excel." 1 May-31 Oct. € 13.00   2009*

MAREUIL *7B2* (500m SW Rural) *45.44680, 0.45153* **Camp
Municipal Vieux Moulin, Rue des Martyrs/Rue Arnaud
de Mareuil; 24340 Mareuil** [05 53 60 91 20 (Mairie)
or 05 53 60 99 80; fax 05 53 60 51 72; mariemareuil@
wanadoo.fr] Fr town cent take D708 (sp Ribérac); after 300m
turn L on D99 (sp 'La Tour Blanche'); after 100m turn L opp lge
school, site 100m ahead. Well sp all dirs. Sm, mkd pitch, shd;
wc; shwrs; el pnts (6A) €1.70; shop 500m; rest, snacks, bar
400m; playgrnd; rv 1km; dogs €0.50; adv bkg; quiet. "Clean, tidy
site; friendly warden; ltd, well-kept facs; lovely walk by stream
to vill; interesting chateau; vg, immac site" ◆ 1 Jun-30 Sep.
€ 8.00   2012*

MARIGNY see Doucier *6H2*

MARNAY (HAUTE SAONE) *6G2* (500m SE Urban) *47.28975,
5.77628* **Camp Municipal Vert Lagon, Route de Besançon,
70150 Marnay** [03 84 31 71 41 or 03 84 31 73 16;
sidmarnay@wanadoo.fr; www.camping-vertlagon.com]
Fr N stay on D67 Marnay by-pass; ignore old camping sp into
town. Proceed to S of town on by-pass then turn L at junc. Bef
bdge in 1km take gravel rd on S side, round under bdge to site
(app thro town fr N v narr). Med, some hdg/mkd pitch, pt shd;
wc; chem disp; mv service pnt; baby facs; shwrs inc; el pnts
(10A) €4; lndtte; shops & rest 500m; snacks (high ssn); BBQ;
playgrnd; fishing; canoeing; 40% statics; dogs €1; poss cr; adv
bkg; quiet; ccard acc; red low ssn; CKE/CCI. "Pleasant, popular,
family site by Rv Ognon; gd san facs; lake adj; tree-top walks;
gd." 1 May-30 Sep. € 13.40 (CChq acc)   2009*

MARNAY (SAONE ET LOIRE) see Chalon sur Saône *6H1*

MARNE LA VALLEE see Meaux *3D3*

MARQUAY see Eyzies de Tayac, Les *7C3*

MARQUION *3B4* (2km N Rural) *50.22280, 3.10863* **FFCC Camping de l'Epinette, 7 Rue du Calvaire, 62860 Sauchy-Lestrée [03 21 59 50 13; epinette62@wanadoo.com; www.lepinette62.com]** Fr A26 exit junc 8 onto D939 to Marquion. On ent Marquion turn R at x-rds to Sauchy-Lestrée; on ent vill turn R at 1st T-junc & site on L in 100m. Fr Cambrai take D939 twd Arras, then as above. Sm, pt sl, pt shd; wc (own san rec); chem disp; shwrs €2; el pnts (6A) €3 (poss rev pol); gas; lndtte; shops 3km; playgrnd; games area; many statics; dogs free; adv bkg; quiet but some military aircraft noise; ccard not acc; CKE/CCI. "Charming, well-kept site in tranquil spot; sm CL-type area for tourers; helpful owner; clean simple but adequate facs, ltd low ssn; levelling blocks ess for m'vans; conv Calais/Dunkerque; WW1 cemetary nr; gd value; popular NH." 1 Apr-31 Oct. € 17.00   2013*

MARQUISE *3A3* (4km S Rural) *50.78316, 1.67035* **FFCC Camping L'Escale, 15 Route Nationale, 62250 Wacquinghen [tel/fax 03 21 32 00 69; camp-escale@ wanadoo.fr; www.escale-camping.com]** Fr A16 S fr Calais exit junc 34. Fr A16 N fr Boulogne exit junc 33. Foll sp. Lge, pt shd; wc (cont); chem disp; mv service pnt; shwrs inc; el pnts (4A) €3.50 (poss rev pol); gas; lndtte; shop; supmkt 3km; rest, snacks; bar; playgrnd; entmnt; wifi; 90% statics; dogs; poss cr; quiet; ccard acc. "Pleasant site; open 24 hrs; conv NH nr ferries, Channel tunnel & WW2 coastal defences; o'fits staying 1 night pitch on meadow at front of site for ease of exit (but some noise fr m'way); m'van 'aire' open all yr; vg." ♦ 1 Apr-15 Oct. € 18.00   2011*

MARS see St Agrève *9C2*

MARSAC EN LIVRADOIS see Ambert *9B1*

MARSANNE *9D2* (2.5km NE Rural) *44.64870, 4.87930* **Camping Les Bastets, Quartier Les Bastets, 26740 Marsanne [04 75 90 35 03; fax 04 75 90 35 05; contact@ campinglesbastets.com; www.campinglesbastets.com]** Exit A7 junc 17 onto N7; pass thro Les Tourettes & La Coucourde to Marsanne. In La Coucourde turn L onto D74 & in 6km L onto D105 thro Marsanne. Site sp fr D105. App fr N on D57 not rec. Med, hdg/mkd pitch, sl, terr, pt shd; htd wc; chem disp; mv service pnt; baby facs; fam bthrm; shwrs inc; el pnts (10A) €4; lndtte (inc dryer); shop; tradsmn; rest, snacks; bar; BBQ; playgrnd; pool; archery; cycle hire; games area; games rm; golf 10km; wifi; entmnt; TV rm; 10% statics; dogs €4; Eng spkn; adv bkg; quiet; red low ssn. "Tractor tow to pitches - not rec to attempt under own steam; pleasant site with gd views; beautiful area; vg." ♦ ltd 1 Apr-15 Oct. € 22.00 (CChq acc)   2009*

⊞ **MARSEILLAN PLAGE** *10F1* (1km NE Coastal) *43.32158, 3.55932* **Camping Le Paradou, 2 Impasse Ronsard, 34340 Marseillan-Plage [tel/fax 06 15 49 09 90 / 04 67 21 90 10 ls; info@paradou.com; www.paradou.com]** Exit A9 junc 34 or 35 onto N113/N312 dir Agde & Sète. Fr Agde foll sp Sète to Marseillan-Plage. Site well sp on N112. Med, hdg pitch, pt shd; htd wc; chem disp; mv service pnt; baby facs; shwrs inc; el pnts (10A) €3.50; gas; lndtte; shop 1km; tradsmn; rest, bar 1km; snacks; playgrnd; dir access sand beach adj; 15% statics; dogs €1.50; phone; wifi; bus 1km; poss cr; CKE/CCI. "Gd area for cycling; ltd pitches avail for long o'fits; Gd clean facs, maybe stretched in ssn" ♦ ltd € 29.00   2013*

MARSEILLAN PLAGE *10F1* (S Coastal/Urban) *43.31365, 3.54779* **Camping Beauregard Plage, 250 Chemin de l'Airette, 34340 Marseillan-Plage [04 67 77 15 45; fax 04 67 01 21 78; reception@camping-beauregard-plage.com; www.camping-beauregard-plage.com]** On N112 Agde-Sète rd, turn S at rndabt to Marseillan-Plage onto D51 & foll camping sp thro town. Site immed on leaving town cent. Lge, hdg pitch, pt shd; wc; chem disp; mv service pnt; baby facs; shwrs inc; el pnts (6A) inc; lndtte; shop, rest & bar adj; rest-bar high ssn; playgrnd; sand beach adj; wifi; entmnt; TV rm; 5% statics; dogs €2 (allowed low ssn only); Eng spkn; adv bkg; poss cr; quiet; red low ssn. "Superb sand beach sheltered by dunes; some pitches soft & sandy; excel for beach holiday." ♦ 30 Mar-15 Oct. € 35.50   2013*

MARSEILLAN PLAGE *10F1* (500m SW Coastal) *43.30648, 3.53924* **Camping Europ 2000, 960 Ave des Campings, 34340 Marseillan-Plage [tel/fax 04 67 21 92 85; contact@ camping-europ2000.com; www.camping-europ2000.com]** Fr cent of Marseillan-Plage S on coast rd D51e, site on L. Med, hdg/mkd pitch, hdstg, pt shd; wc; chem disp; mv service pnt; shwrs inc; el pnts (10A) €3.50; gas; lndtte; shop & 500m; tradsmn; snacks; BBQ; playgrnd; sand beach adj; games area; 10% statics; dogs €2; phone; poss cr; Eng spkn; adv bkg; quiet; red low ssn CKE/CCI. "Easy access to beach; friendly, helpful owner; gd family-run site." ♦ 1 Apr-20 Oct. € 28.00   2009*

MARSEILLAN PLAGE *10F1* (500m SW Coastal) *43.31036, 3.54601* **Camping La Plage, 69 Chemin du Pairollet, 34340 Marseillan-Plage [04 67 21 92 54; fax 04 67 01 63 57; info@laplage-camping.net; www.laplage-camping.net]** On D612 fr Agde to Sète, turn R at rndabt dir Marseillan-Plage. Foll sp for site at 2nd rndabt. Site on L in 150m. Med, hdg pitch, pt shd; wc; chem disp; mv service pnt; shwrs inc; child/baby facs; el pnts (10A) inc; gas; lndtte (inc dryer); rest, snacks; bar; BBQ; playgrnd; dir access to sand beach adj; watersports; games area; entmnt; TV; 1% statics; dogs €4; phone; extra for beach front pitches; poss cr; Eng spkn; adv bkg; quiet; ccard acc, CKE/CCI. "Excel, popular, family-run site; superb beach; sm pitches; gd, friendly atmosphere." ♦ 15 Mar-6 Nov. € 34.00   2010*

MARSEILLAN PLAGE *10F1* (1km SW Coastal) *43.31275, 3.54638* **Camping La Créole, 74 Ave des Campings, 34340 Marseillan-Plage [04 67 21 92 69; fax 04 67 26 58 16; campinglacreole@wanadoo.fr; www.campinglacreole.com]** Fr Agde-Sète rd N112, turn S at rndabt onto D51 & foll sp thro town. Narr ent easily missed among lger sites. Med, hdg/mkd pitch, hdstg, pt shd; wc; chem disp; mv service pnt; baby facs; shwrs inc; el pnts (6A) €3.50; lndtte; shop; rest, snacks, bar adj; playgrnd; sand beach adj; tennis 1km; games area; entmnt; 10% statics; dogs €3; phone; adv bkg; min stay 7 nights Jul-Aug; quiet; red low ssn; CKE/CCI. "Vg, well-kept site; dir access to excel beach; naturist beach 600m." ♦ 1 Apr-15 Oct. € 34.50   2012*

MARSEILLAN PLAGE *10F1* (1km SW Coastal) *43.30586,
3.53788* **Camping Les Sirènes, 1078 Ave des Campings,
34340 Marseillan-Plage [tel/fax 04 67 21 92 83]** On N112
Agde-Sète rd, turn S onto D51 at rndabt, & foll sps in town.
Site at end of rd thro lge area of camp sites. V lge, hdg/mkd
pitch, hdstg, pt shd; wc; chem disp; shwrs inc; el pnts (10A)
inc; gas 300m; lndtte; shop 100m; tradsmn; playgrnd; pool
complex; waterslides; sand beach adj; watersports; tennis 1km;
cycle hire; horseriding; games area; games rm; entmnt; sat TV;
no statics; dogs €2.80; Eng spkn; quiet; red low ssn; CKE/CCI.
"Vg site in excel location; gd facs; seaside town nr with all facs;
excel beach." ♦ 15 May-15 Sep. € 40.00   2010*

"I need an on-site restaurant"

We do our best to make sure site
information is correct, but it is always best
to check any must-have facilities are still
available or will be open during your visit.

MARSEILLAN PLAGE *10F1* (1.5km SW Coastal) *43.31031,
3.54305* **Yelloh! Village Le Charlemagne, Ave des
Campings, 34340 Marseillan-Plage [04 67 21 92 49; fax
04 67 21 86 11; info@yellohvillage-mediterranees.com;
www.yellohvillage-mediterranees.com]** In Marseillan-Plage,
off N112 Sète-Agde rd, take D51e SW to site. Lge, hdg/mkd
pitch, shd; wc; chem disp; mv service pnt; baby facs; shwrs inc;
el pnts (6A) inc; lndtte; shop; rest, snacks; bar; playgrnd; 3 htd
pools; waterslide; sand beach 200m; games area; golf 5km;
internet; entmnt; 50% statics; dogs €4; phone; poss cr; Eng
spkn; adv bkg; red low ssn for 14+ days; quiet; ccard acc. "Site
also owns Nouvelle Floride opp on beach of similar standard;
lge pitches; lots of shops, rests nrby; many tour ops; poss
mosquitoes; excel." ♦ 15 Apr-1 Oct. € 44.00 (3 persons) 2008*

MARTEL *7C3* (5km SE Rural) *44.88538, 1.59929* **Camping
du Port, 46600 Creysse [05 65 32 20 82 or 05 65 32 27 59;
fax 05 65 38 78 21; contact@campingduport.com; www.
campingduport.com]** Exit A20 at Junc 55 foll D803 to Le
Pigeon, then take D15 to Saint Sozy, then D114 to Creysse
then foll signs to site Med, pt sl, pt shd by rv; wc (some
cont); shwrs inc; el pnts (6A) inc; lndtte; shops in Martel; rest
in Creysse; playgrnd; pool; canoe & cycle hire; dogs €1.50;
adv bkg; quiet. "Lovely grounds; gd access to rv; friendly;
v peaceful low ssn; ltd facs low ssn; Creysse beautiful vill."
1 May-20 Sep. € 26.40   2013*

MARTEL *7C3* (6km SW Rural) *44.87604, 1.57707* **FFCC
Camping La Plage, Rive Gauche de la Dordogne, 46200
Meyronne [05 65 32 23 26 or 06 32 02 82 82 (LS); contact@
camping-laplage.com; www.camping-laplage.com]**
W fr Souillac on D803 dir Martel; in 3km at Le Pigeon Bas
turn R onto D15 sp St Sozy; cont past St Sozy; in 1km cross
Rv Dordogne & site immed on R. Med, pt shd; wc; chem disp
(wc); baby facs; shwrs inc; el pnts (6A) €3; gas 500m; lndtte;
tradsmn; snacks; BBQ; playgrnd; pool; rv sw adj; canoeing;
horseriding; rock climbing; games area; internet; dogs €0.50;
poss cr; Eng spkn; adv bkg; some rd noise; ccard acc; CKE/CCI.
"Excel site by rv; Rocamadour 14km; caves of Padirc 18km." ♦
16 Jun-15 Sep. € 12.40   2011*

MARTEL *7C3* (500m NW Rural) *44.93852, 1.60805* **Camp
Municipal de la Callopie, Ave de Turenne, 46600
Martel [05 65 37 30 03 (Mairie); fax 05 65 37 37 27;
mairiedemartel@wanadoo.fr; www.tourisme-lot.com/fr]**
On NW o'skts of vill of Martel on D23, 100m fr rndabt on L,
ent opp Auberge des 7 Tours. Sm, shd; wc; shwrs inc; el pnts
(10A) €2; shops, rest, bar 200m; rv 5km; no statics; poss cr;
no adv bkg; rd noise. "Attractive, well-kept site in beautiful
medieval vill; busy high ssn; pleasant, helpful warden; gd, clean
san facs; warden calls pm or pay at Mairie; no twin-axles."
15 Apr-30 Sep. € 8.00   2012*

MARTRAGNY see Bayeux *3D1*

MARTRES DE VEYRE, LES see Clermont Ferrand *9B1*

⊞ MARTRES TOLOSANE *8F3* (2km E Rural) *43.19684,
1.06721* **Camp Municipal Le Plantaurel, Les Pesquès,
31220 Palaminy [05 61 97 03 71; fax 05 61 90 62 04]**
Exit A64 at junc 23 onto D6 to Cazères, cross rv bdge. Turn W
(R) on D62, foll rv for 1.5km. Site well sp, Lge, mkd pitch, shd;
htd wc; chem disp; mv service pnt; shwrs inc; el pnts (10A)
gas; lndtte; shop, rest 2km; snacks; playgrnd; entmnt; TV;
40% statics; phone; dir access to rv; dogs; adv bkg; red long
stay; CKE/CCI." (4 persons)   2008*

MARTRES TOLOSANE *8F3* (1.5km S Rural) *43.19060,
1.01840* **Camping Le Moulin, 31220 Martres-
Tolosane [05 61 98 86 40; fax 05 61 98 66 90; info@
domainelemoulin.com; www.domainelemoulin.com]**
Exit A64 junc 22 (fr N or S) & foll camping sps. Site sp adj Rv
Garonne. Med, hdg pitch, pt sl, pt shd; wc; chem disp; mv
service pnt; baby facs; shwrs inc; el pnts (6-10A) €4-6; gas;
lndtte; shops 1.5km; snacks; bar; BBQ; playgrnd; htd pool;
paddling pool; rv fishing adj; tennis; cycle hire; games area;
games rm; wifi; entmnt; TV; 20% statics; dogs €2.50; Eng
spkn; adv bkg rec high ssn; quiet; red long stay; red low ssn;
ccard acc; CKE/CCI. "Excel, well-maintained site; friendly
welcome; gd, modern san facs; water on all pitches; gd touring
base for Spain, Lourdes, etc." ♦ 23 Mar-30 Sep. € 22.90
SBS - D28   2012*

"Satellite navigation makes touring much easier"

Remember most sat navs don't know if
you're towing or in a larger vehicle – always
use yours alongside maps and site directions.

MARTRES TOLOSANE *8F3* (7km SW Rural) *43.13447,
0.93240* **Camp Municipal, Route de St Girons, 31360
St Martory [05 61 90 44 93 or 05 61 98 14 65; cccsm@
wanadoo.fr; www.petitespyrenees.com]** Leave A64 at junc
20. Turn N onto D117 twd St Martory. In 1km turn L (sp) soon
after Gendarmerie. Sm, hdg pitch, pt shd; htd wc (some cont);
chem disp (wc); shwrs inc; el pnts €2.50; dogs €1.50; quiet;
CKE/CCI. ♦ 15 Jun-15 Sep. € 9.90   2010*

FRANCE

MARVEJOLS 9D1 (1km NE Rural) 44.55077, 3.30440 Camping Village Le Coulagnet, Quartier de l'Empery, 48100 Marvejols [04 66 32 03 69] Exit A75 junc 38 onto D900 & N9. Foll E ring rd onto D999, cont over rv & foll sp to site; no R turn into site, cont 500m to Aire de Retournement, & turn L into site. Foll sp 'VVF', camping part of same complex. NB U-turn bef ent impossible long o'fits; nasty speed humps on app rd. Sm, hdg pitch, pt shd; wc (mainly cont); shwrs inc; el pnts (5A) inc (poss rev pol); lndtte (inc dryer); shop & 1km; BBQ (sep area); playgrnd; pool; rv adj; tennis; games area; games rm; TV rm; 50% statics; no dogs; phone; Eng spkn; adv bkg; quiet; ccard acc. "Well equiped site; san facs immac; sep area for tourers; interesting walled town; excel." ♦ 15 May-30 Aug. € 16.60   2010*

MARVILLE 5C1 (1km N Rural) 49.46294, 5.45859 Camp Syndicat Mixte de la Vallée de l'Othain, 55600 Marville [03 29 88 19 06 or 03 29 88 15 15; fax 03 29 88 14 60; marville.accueil@wanadoo.fr] Sp on D643 on app Marville fr both dirs. Med, hdg pitch, pt shd; wc (some cont); shwrs; el pnts (3A); lndtte; sm shop; snacks; rest; playgrnd; htd covrd pool adj; entmnt; 20% statics; quiet; CKE/CCI. "Easy access adj lake; gd NH." 1 Feb-30 Nov.   2012*

⊞ **MASEVAUX** 6F3 (N Urban) 47.77820, 6.99090 Camping Masevaux, 3 Rue du Stade, 68290 Masevaux [tel/fax 03 89 82 42 29; contact@camping-masevaux.com; www.camping-masevaux.com] Fr N83 Colmar-Belfort rd take N466 W to Masevaux; site sp. NB D14 fr Thann to Masevaux narr & steep - not suitable c'vans. Med, mkd pitch, pt shd; htd wc; chem disp; mv service pnt; baby facs; shwrs inc; el pnts (3-6A) €3.20-3.80; lndtte; shop 1km; tradsmn; snacks; bar; playgrnd; htd pool & sports complex adj; entmnt; internet; TV rm; 40% statics; dogs €0.50; no twin-axles; poss cr; Eng spkn; adv bkg; quiet; some rd noise; ccard acc; red long stay; CKE/CCI. "Pleasant walks; interesting town - annual staging of Passion Play; helpful, friendly owners; excel facs; gd cycle rtes; excel." ♦ € 10.40   2008*

MASSERET 7B3 (9km N Rural) 45.61142, 1.50110 Camping de Montréal, Rue du Petit Moulin, 87380 St Germain-les-Belles [05 55 71 86 20; fax 05 55 71 00 83; contact@campingdemontreal.com; www.campingdemontreal.com] S fr Limoges on A20; exit junc 42 onto D7B to St Germain-les-Belles; turn R onto D216; site on L in 500m. Site sp in vill. NB Care needed due narr rds. Med, hdg/mkd pitch, terr, pt shd; htd wc; chem disp; mv service pnt; shwrs inc; el pnts (10A) €3; lndtte (inc dryer); sm shop 1km; tradmn; rest, snacks, bar; BBQ; playgrnd; htd pool; lake sw adj; fishing; watersports; tennis; cycle hire 1km; wifi; entmnt; 12% statics; dogs €2.60; phone; poss cr; Eng spkn; adv bkg; quiet; ccard acc; red low ssn; CKE/CCI. "Peaceful site in attractive setting o'looking lake; excel san facs; conv A20; a gem of a site" ♦ 1 Apr-31 Oct. € 16.70 (CChq acc)   2013*

See advertisement

MASSERET 7B3 (5km E Rural) 45.53880, 1.57790 Camping Domaine des Forges (formerly Camping Plan l'Eau), Complexe Touristique Bourg, 19510 Lamongerie [05 55 73 44 57; fax 05 55 73 49 69; www.domaine-des-forges.fr] Exit A20 at junc 43 sp Masseret & foll sp Lamongerie. At rndabt turn R, site sp. Site ent bet 2 lge stone pillars. Med, sl, shd; wc; chem disp; shwrs (5A) €2.30 (poss long lead req some pitches); lndtte; sm shop; rest, snacks; playgrnd; lake beach & sw; fishing; tennis; golf nrby; fitness course thro woods & round lake; TV; poss cr; quiet. "Pleasant situation; clean facs; gd NH & longer." ♦ 1 Apr-30 Sep. € 10.30   2011*

MASSEUBE 8F3 (12km NE Rural) 43.50199, 0.68585 Camping Domaine Naturiste du Moulin de Faget (Naturist), Au Grange, 32450 Faget-Abbatial [05 62 65 49 09; fax 05 62 66 29 21; info@moulin-faget.com; www.moulin-faget.com] Fr Masseube D929 for 7 km; in Seissan R on D104 sp Faget-Abbatial; in 8.5km R at T-junc onto D40; site sp on L in 300m; at top of track after 500m. Sm, pt sl, unshd; wc; chem disp (wc); shwrs inc; el pnts (6A) €3.50; lndtte; tradsmn; rest; bar; lake adj; games area; cycle hire; 10% statics; no dogs; B & B avail all yr; Eng spkn; adv bkg; quiet; CKE/CCI. "Extremely quiet & secluded site in beautiful area; no play facs for children; friendly, helpful Dutch owners; modern san facs; gd walking, cycling; attractive vill nrby; excel." ♦ ltd 1 May-1 Oct. € 22.00   2009*

FRANCE

MASSEUBE *8F3* (400m E Rural) *43.42914, 0.58516* **Camping Berges du Gers, Route de Simorre, 32140 Masseube [05 62 66 01 75; camping.masseube@orange.fr; www. camping-masseube-lesbergesdugers.fr]** S fr Auch on D929 to Masseube; turn L onto D27 dir Simorre; site on L in 500m. Med, shd; wc; chem disp; shwrs inc; el pnts (6A) €3; gas 500m; lndtte; shop 500m; tradsmn; rest, snacks & bar 500m; BBQ; playgrnd; htd pool adj; access to rv; tennis; cycle hire; games area; games rm; entmnt; wifi; TV; 10% statics; dogs free; phone adj; Eng spkn; adv bkg; quiet; ccard acc; red low ssn; CKE/CCI. "Well-run site in pleasant setting; security barrier; vg." ♦ ltd 1 May 31 Oct. € 12.00   2011*

MASSEUBE *8F3* (2km E Rural) *43.42748, 0.61142* **Camping Aux Mêmes, 32149 Bellegarde [05 62 66 91 45; info@ camping-gascony.co.uk; www.gascogne-camping.fr]** Fr Masseube take D27 E dir Simorre & Bellegarde; in 2.5km turn L (having past sports stadium & driven up hill thro trees); site is 1st farm on R in 300m. Site sp. Sm, pt sl, unshd; wc; chem disp; shwrs inc; el pnts (6A) €3; lndtte (inc dryer); shop; snacks; bar; BBQ; playgrnd; pool; water sports, fishing, canoeing, windsufing & sailing nrby; tennis & golf nrby; cycle hire; games rm; wifi; TV; dogs; Eng spkn; adv bkg; quiet; excel." ♦ 1 Apr-15 Sep. € 18.00   2011*

MASSIAC *9C1* (7km N Rural) *45.31217, 3.17278* **Camp Municipal La Bessière, 43450 Blesle [04 71 76 25 82; mairie.de.blesle@wanadoo.fr; www.blesle.fr]** Fr Massiac take D909 N. In 5km at Babory turn L onto D8. In 1km turn L immed after x-ing rv bdge. Site sp. Sm, some hdg/mkd pitch, terr, pt shd; wc (some cont); chem disp (wc); mv service pnt; shwrs inc; el pnts (10A) €2.50; lndtte; BBQ; playgrnd; tennis; wifi; 30% statics; dogs €1; phone 200m; poss cr; quiet; red long stay; CKE/CCI. "Pleasant, clean site nr pretty vill; warm welcome, helpful warden; gd touring base; vg." ♦ ltd 1 Apr-2 Oct. € 8.30   2011*

MASSIAC *9C1* (800m SW Rural) *45.24703, 3.18765* **FFCC Camp Municipal de l'Allagnon, 17 Ave de Courcelles, 15500 Massiac [04 71 23 03 93 or 04 71 23 02 61; camping. allagnon15@orange.fr; www.paysdemassiac.com]** Exit A75 at Massiac onto N122 or N122e; cont on N122 dir Murat; site sp on L on rvside 800m along Ave de Courcelles (part of N122). Med, mkd pitch, shd; wc; mv service pnt; shwrs; el pnts (6A) €3; gas; lndtte; shops adj; playgrnd; pool adj; fishing; tennis; wifi; dogs €0.60; poss cr; Eng spkn; ccard acc; CKE/CCI. "Simple, popular site; helpful staff; conv A75; vg." ♦ 1 May-31 Oct. € 10.00   2011*

MASSIAC *9C1* (6km SW Rural) *45.23353, 3.13432* **Camp Municipal, Pré Mongeal, 15500 Molompize [04 71 73 62 90 or 04 71 73 60 06; fax 04 71 73 60 24; mairie.molompize@wanadoo.fr]** Fr N exit A75 junc 23 onto N122 dir Aurillac; site on L just bef Molompize. Or fr S exit A75 junc 24 onto N122e to Massiac; then join N122 dir Aurillac; then as bef. Med, pt shd; wc; chem disp (wc); shwrs inc; el pnts (10A); lndry rm; shops 500m; playgrnd; 6% statics; quiet; CKE/CCI. "Rvside site behind stadium; tennis courts; friendly warden; gd." ♦ ltd 15 Jun-15 Sep. € 6.95   2010*

MATEMALE *8G4* (1.7km SW Rural) *42.58209, 2.10563* **Camping Le Lac, Forêt de la Matte, 66210 Matemale [04 68 30 94 49; fax 04 68 04 35 16; www.camping-lac-matemale.com]** N on D118 fr Mont Louis; do not turn into Matemale, turn on D52 sp Les Angles; site on L in 500m. Sm, pt sl, pt shd; htd wc; mv service pnt; baby facs; shwrs; el pnts (3-6A) €2.60-4.20; lndtte; tradsmn; snacks; bar; BBQ; lake 200m; fishing; watersports; games area; games rm; dogs €1; open w/end & school hols rest of yr; quiet. "Friendly site amid pine trees." ♦ 1 Jun-30 Sep. € 15.00   2008*

MATHA *7B2* (5km S Rural) *45.83584, -0.30747* **Camping Le Relais de l'Etang, Route de Matha, Route de la Jarne Thors [05 46 58 26 81 or 05 46 58 75 36 (LS); paysmatha@ cc-matha.fr; www.paysdematha.com]** Fr Matha take D121 S twd Cognac. Site on L in 5km. Sm, hdg/mkd pitch, pt shd; wc (some cont); chem disp; shwrs inc; el pnts (10A) €2.60; lndtte; rest, snacks; bar; playgrnd; lake sw; dogs €1; adv bkg; quiet; CKE/CCI. "Gd for visiting Cognac." 15 May-30 Sep. € 5.80   2010*

MATHES, LES *7B1* (2.5km N Rural) *45.72333, -1.17451* **Camping La Palombière, 1551 Route de la Fouasse, 17570 Les Mathes [05 46 22 69 25; fax 05 46 22 44 58; camping. lapalombiere@wanadoo.fr; www.camping-lapalombiere. com]** Fr La Tremblade bypass foll sp Dirée on D268; site on R in 5km just past Luna Park. Med, pt shd; htd wc; chem disp; mv service pnt; baby facs; fam bthrm; shwrs inc; el pnts (6-10A) €4.50-5.; gas; lndtte (inc dryer); ice; shop; tradsmn; rest, snacks; bar; BBQ; playgrnd; htd pool; sand beach 5km; games area; wifi; 10% statics; dogs €3; phone; bus; Eng spkn; quiet; ccard not acc; red low ssn; CKE/CCI. "Spacious, tranquil site under oaks & pines; lge pitches; palatial san facs; superb beaches 5km (some naturist); excel, spacious site, helpful staff; immac maintained" ♦ 1 Apr-20 Oct. € 40.40   2013*

MATHES, LES *7B1* (3.5km N Rural) *45.72980, -1.17929* **Camping L'Orée du Bois, 225 Route de la Bouverie, La Fouasse, 17570 Les Mathes [05 46 22 42 43; fax 05 46 22 54 76; info@camping-oree-du-bois.fr; www. camping-oree-du-bois.fr]** Fr A10 to Saintes, then dir Royan. Fr Royan take D25 thro St Palais & La Palmyre twd Phare de la Coubre. Cont 4km past Phare & turn R on D268 to La Fouasse. Site on R in 4km. Lge, hdg/mkd pitch, hdstg, pt shd; wc (some cont); private san facs some pitches; chem disp; mv service pnt; baby facs; shwrs inc; el pnts (6A) inc; gas; lndtte (inc dryer); shop; rest, snacks; bar; BBQ; playgrnd; 3 htd pools; waterslide; sand beach 4km; tennis; cycle hire; golf 20km; games area; games rm; wifi; entmnt; sat TV rm; 50% statics; dogs €3.60; Eng spkn; adv bkg rec high ssn; quiet; ccard acc; red low ssn/ CKE/CCI. "Well-kept site in pine wood; local beaches ideal for sw & surfing; helpful staff; excel pool area; zoo in La Palmyre worth visit; min stay 7 days high ssn; excel." ♦ 28 May-10 Sep. € 38.00 (CChq acc)   2011*

MATHES, LES 7B1 (6km SW Coastal) 45.6974, -1.2286
**Camping Parc de la Côte Sauvage, Phare de la Coubre,
17570 La Palmyre [05 46 22 40 18 or 05 49 35 83 60;
contact@parc-cote-sauvage.com; www.parc-cote-
sauvage.com]** D25 fr Royan, thro La Palmyre, at rndabt foll sp
'Phare de la Coubre'. Turn L at junc sp as bef, turn L on R-hand
bend. Lge, mkd pitch, pt terr, pt shd; wc (some cont); chem disp;
mv service pnt; baby facs; shwrs inc; el pnts (6-10A) €5; gas;
Indtte; shop; rest/bar adj; snacks; playgrnd; pool complex; sand
beach 500m - can be v windy; tennis; cycle hire adj; boating;
surf school; entmnt; internet; TV; 25% statics; dogs €3 (not
acc Jul/Aug); poss v cr (NH area); Eng spkn; no adv bkg; ccard
acc; red low ssn; CKE/CCI. "Lge pitches." ♦ 1 May-15 Sep.
€ 34.00   2008*

MATHES, LES 7B1 (2km W Rural) 45.72826, -1.17593
**Camping La Pinède, La Palmyre, 17570 Les Mathes
[05 46 22 45 13; fax 05 46 22 50 21; contact@
campinglapinede.com; www.campinglapinede.com]**
Fr La Tremblade, take D141 twd Les Mathes. Turn W after
vill onto D141 E twd La Fouasse, foll sp. Site in 2km. Lge,
mkd pitch, pt shd; wc; chem disp; shwrs inc; el pnts (5A)
€6.90; Indtte; shop; rest, snacks; bar; BBQ; playgrnd; 2 pools
(1 htd, covrd); waterslides; sand beach 4km; tennis; cycle
hire; archery; games area; games rm; entmnt; mini-farm;
75% statics; dogs (sm only) €6.50; private san facs avail
for extra charge; adv bkg; quiet. "Dir access to rv; excel for
children." 1 May-20 Sep. € 39.00   2009*

See advertisement

MATHES, LES 7B1 (2km NW Rural) 45.73473, -1.17713
**Camping Atlantique Forêt, La Fouasse, 17570 Les
Mathes [05 46 22 40 46 or 05 46 36 82 77 (LS); www.
camping-atlantique-foret.com]** Fr La Tremblade by-pass,
foll sp Diree (D268). Drive thro vill & cont for 2km. Site on
L. Or fr La Palmyre on D141 twd Les Mathes; at rndabt take
dir La Fouasse. Last site on R. Med, pt shd; wc (a few cont);
chem disp; baby facs; shwrs inc; el pnts (6A) €4.50; gas; Indtte
(inc dryer); shop; tradsmn; rest, snacks, bar 500m; BBQ (gas
only); playgrnd; pool & tennis 300m; beach 4km; 2% statics;
dogs free; phone; poss cr; Eng spkn; adv bkg; ccard not acc;
quiet; CKE/CCI. "Pleasant, peaceful wooded site in beautiful
area; spacious & well-run; friendly, family-owned; gd san facs;
gd alt to nrby lge sites; excel for young children; cycle paths
thro forest; great place to stay; excel." ♦ ltd 15 Jun-15 Sep.
€ 21.00   2011*

⊞ MATHES, LES 7B1 (2km NW Coastal) 45.72482, -1.17465
**Camping Naturiste Le Petit Dauphin (Naturist), 1696
Route de la Fouasse, 17570 Les Mathes [05 46 06 38 23 or
06 76 37 57 65 (mob); lepetitdauphin2 @wanadoo.fr;
http://le-petit-dauphin.com]** Fr La Palmyre take D141E dir
Les Mathes; in 2.5km foll D141E to L sp La Fouasse (D141
goes strt on to Les Mathes); site sp on R in 2km. Med, pt shd;
wc; chem disp; mv service pnt; baby facs; fam bthrm; shwrs
inc; el pnts (10A) €3; gas; Indtte (inc dryer); ice; shops 1.5km;
rest, snacks; bar; BBQ; playgrnd; sand beach 5km; games
rm; internet; 5% statics; dogs €1.50; poss cr; Eng spkn; adv
bkg; quiet; red low ssn/long stay; CKE/CCI. "Family-run site;
welcoming, friendly & helpful; conv lge naturise beach & zoo at
La Palmyre; vg. ♦ ltd € 19.00   2009*

MATHES, LES *7B1* (2.5km NW Rural) *45.72098, -1.17165*
Camping La Clé des Champs, 1188 Route de la Fouasse, 17570 Les Mathes [05 46 22 40 53; fax 05 46 22 56 96; contact@la-cledeschamps.com; www.la-cledeschamps.com] S of La Tremblade, take D141 twd La Palmyre, site sp. Lge, mkd pitch, pt shd; htd wc (some cont); chem disp; baby facs; shwrs; el pnts (6-10A) inc; gas; lndtte; shop; rest, snacks; bar; BBQ; playgrnd; htd, covrd pool; paddling pool; sand beach 3.5km; gym, Jacuzzi & sauna; fishing & watersports 3km; cycle hire; games area; games rm; TV rm; entmnt; wifi; 30% statics; dogs €3.80; Eng spkn; adv bkg; ccard acc; quiet; red low ssn; CKE/CCI. "Well-equipped, busy site; many excel beaches in area; modern san facs; local oysters avail; Cognac region; Luna Park nrby." ♦ 30 Mar-15 Nov. € 40.00   2013*

See advertisement

MATHES, LES *7B1* (3km NW Rural) *45.73229, -1.17655*
Camping L'Estanquet, 2596 Route de la Fouasse, 17570 Les Mathes [05 46 22 47 32 or 05 46 93 93 51 (LS); fax 05 46 22 51 46; contact@campinglestanquet.com; www.campinglestanquet.com] Fr Royan take D25 to La Palmyre. Turn R in town cent onto D141 dir Les Mathes; cont on D141 passing racecourse on R; turn L bef Les Mathes along La Fouasse. Site in 2.5km on L. Lge, hdg pitch, pt shd; wc; chem disp; baby facs; shwrs inc; el pnts (10A) inc; gas; lndtte; shop; rest, snacks; bar; BBQ (gas only) playgrnd; pool; paddling pool; waterslide; sand beach 5km; fishing, windsurfing 5km; tennis; cycle hire; horseriding 1km; golf 9km; entmnt; games/TV rm; 85% statics; dogs €4; poss cr; adv bkg; quiet ♦ 1 May-30 Sep. € 26.90   2010*

MATIGNON see St Cast le Guildo *2E3*

MATOUR *9A2* (1km W Rural) *46.30475, 4.47858* Camp Municipal Le Paluet, Rue de la Piscine, 71520 Matour [03 85 59 70 92; lepaluet@matour.fr; www.matour.com] On W o'skts of Matour off Rte de la Clayette D987. Med, hdg/mkd pitch, pt shd; wc; chem disp; shwrs inc; el pnts (10A) inc; lndtte (inc dryer); shop 500m; bar; snacks; BBQ; playgrnd; pool high ssn; waterslide; lake fishing adj; tennis; games area; wifi; entmnt; TV; adv bkg; quiet; ccard acc; CKE/CCI. "Conv touring vineyards; highly rec; facs poss inadequate high ssn." ♦ 1 May-30 Sep. € 18.50   2012*

See advertisement on pages 32 & 33

MAUBEC see Cavaillon *10E2*

MAUBEUGE *3B4* (1km N Rural) *50.29545, 3.97696* Camp Municipal du Clair de Lune, 212 Route de Mons, 59600 Maubeuge [03 27 62 25 48; fax 03 27 60 25 94; camping@ville-maubeuge.fr; www.ville-maubeuge.fr] Fr Mons head S on N2 twd Maubeuge, site on L about 1.5km bef town cent, sp. Med, hdg/mkd pitch, some hdstg, pt sl, pt shd; htd wc; chem disp; baby facs; shwrs inc; el pnts (6A) inc (rev pol); lndry rm; shops 500m; hypmkt 1km; tradsmn; rest, snacks, bar 2km; BBQ; playgrnd; watersports 25km; cycle hire; games rm; internet; a few statics; dogs free; twin-axles acc (rec check in adv); phone adj; bus adj; adv bkg; some rd noise; ccard acc. "Attractive, wooded, well-kept site; busy but peaceful; spacious pitches - some asymmetric & pitching poss diff; friendly, helpful staff; excel, clean san facs; mkt Sat am; popular NH; excel; Very clean & tidy; gd value; Some rd noise" ♦ 1 Apr-30 Sep. € 19.15 SBS - P07   2013*

MAUBEUGE *3B4* (8km NE Rural) *50.34525, 4.02842* Camping Les Avallées, 19 Rue du Faubourg, 59600 Villers-Sire-Nicole [03 27 67 92 56; fax 03 27 67 45 18; loisirs-les-avallees@wanadoo.fr; www.loisirs-les-avallees.fr] N fr Maubeuge on N2; in 5km R onto D159 to Villers-Sire-Nicole. Site well sp. Lge, pt sl, terr, pt shd; wc; chem disp; el pnts (4A) €2; shwrs inc; shop (high ssn); rest, snacks; bar; BBQ; playgrnd; mainly statics; dogs; quiet. "Friendly owners; lake fishing; no twin-axles; vg." 1 Apr-14 Oct. € 7.00   2008*

MAUBOURGUET *8F2* (SW Urban) *43.46657, 0.03199* Camp Municipal de l'Echez, Rue Jean Clos Pucheu, 65700 Maubourguet [05 62 96 37 44 or 06 12 90 14 55 (mob); camping.maubourguet@yahoo.fr] On D935 (NW of Tarbes), sp in Maubourguet, on bank of Rv Echez. Sm, pt shd; wc; shwrs inc; mv service pnt; el pnts (10A); shops 200m; lndtte; playgrnd; TV; rv fishing 300m; quiet. "Pleasantly situated; pleasant country town." 1 Jun-15 Sep. € 11.00   2009*

MAULEON LICHARRE *8F1* (2km S Rural) *43.20795, -0.89695*
Camping Uhaitza Le Saison, Route de Libarrenx, 64130
Mauléon-Licharre [05 59 28 18 79; fax 05 59 28 06 23;
camping.uhaitza@wanadoo.fr; www.camping-uhaitza.com]
Fr Sauveterre take D936 twd Oloron. In 500m turn R onto D23
to Mauléon, then take D918 dir Tardets, site on R. Sm, hdg/
mkd pitch, pt sl, pt shd; wc; chem disp; mv service pnt; baby
facs; shwrs inc; el pnts (4-10A) €2.65-4.90; lndtte (inc dryer);
shops 1.5km; tradsmn; snacks; bar high ssn; BBQ; playgrnd;
pool 2km; rv fishing adj; tennis 2km; games rm; some
statics; dogs €2; adv bkg; quiet; CKE/CCI. "Lovely, quiet site
beside rv - steep access; friendly owners." ♦ 1 Mar-15 Nov.
€ 13.50   2010*

MAUPERTUS SUR MER see Cherbourg *1C4*

MAURIAC *7C4* (1km SW Rural) *45.21865, 2.31639*
Camping Le Val St Jean, Lac du Barrage d'Enchanet,
15200 Mauriac [04 71 67 31 13 or 06 80 14 59 45 (mob);
fax 04 71 68 17 34; valsaintejean@mauriac.fr; www.
tourismevalsaintjean.fr] Site adj lake; well sp. Med, hdg/mkd
pitch, terr, unshd; htd wc; chem disp; mv service pnt; shwrs
inc; el pnts (10A) €3.60; lndtte (inc dryer); shop; tradsmn; rest
1km; snacks; playgrnd; htd pool; paddling pool; waterslide;
sand beach & lake sw adj; fishing; golf adj; wifi; TV rm; some
statics; dogs €1.50; adv bkg; quiet; red low ssn; CKE/CCI.
"Excel, clean, tidy site; ltd facs low ssn; gd touring base." ♦
1 May-25 Sep. € 19.50 (CChq acc)   2010*

MAURIAC *7C4* (1.5km SW Rural) *45.21110, 2.32356* **Camp
Municipal La Roussilhe**, 15200 Mauriac [04 71 68 06 99]
Foll sp for Ally & Pleux on D681; downhill, past supmkt, sp
to R, 1st L. Med, pt shd; wc; 50% serviced pitches; shwrs; el
pnts (3A) €1.80; quiet. "Nice site adj football pitch; plenty of
shade." 7 Jun-7 Sep. € 6.00   2008*

MAUROUX see St Clar *8E3*

MAURS *7D4* (6km SE Rural) *44.68140, 2.26050* **FFCC**
Camping Le Moulin de Chaules, Route de Calvinet, 15600
St Constant [04 71 49 11 02; fax 04 71 49 13 63; camping@
moulin-de-chaules.com; www.moulin-de-chaules.com]
Fr N122 in Maurs, foll sp to St Constant on D663. Take by-pass
round St Constant & turn L to Calvinet, well sp fr Maurs.
Med, mkd pitch, terr, shd; wc; chem disp; baby facs; shwrs
inc; el pnts (4A) €3; lndtte (inc dryer); sm shop; tradsmn; rest;
snacks; bar; BBQ (gas); playgrnd; pool; games area; games rm;
wifi; some statics; no twin-axles; dogs €1.50; Eng spkn; adv
bkg; quiet; red low ssn/long stay; CKE/CCI. "Friendly Dutch
owner; excel facs; excel for young children; terr access steep
- care needed (tractor tow avail); gd." ♦ ltd 11 Apr-11 Oct.
€ 21.50   2009*

MAURS *7D4* (800m S Rural) *44.70522, 2.20586* **Camp
Municipal du Vert**, Route de Decazeville, 15600 Maurs
[04 71 49 04 15; fax 04 71 49 00 81; mairie@ville-maurs.fr]
Fr Maurs take D663 dir Decazeville. Site on L 400m after level
x-ing thro sports complex. Narr ent. Med, mkd pitch, shd; wc;
chem disp; baby facs; shwrs inc; el pnts (15A) inc; lndtte; shops
1km; playgrnd; pool; tennis; rv fishing; poss cr; adv bkg; quiet.
"V pleasant on side of rv; sports complex adj." ♦ 1 May-30 Sep.
€ 11.10   2008*

MAURY see St Paul de Fenouillet *8G4*

MAUSSANE LES ALPILLES see Mouriès *10E2*

MAUZE SUR LE MIGNON *7A2* (1km NW Rural) *46.20063,
-0.68186* **Camp Municipal Le Gué de La Rivière, Route
de St Hilaire-la-Palud**, 79210 Mauzé-sur-le-Mignon
[05 49 26 30 35 (Mairie); fax 05 49 26 71 13; mairie@ville-
mauze-mignon.fr; www.ville-mauze-mignon.fr] Site clearly
sp. Sm, hdg pitch, pt shd; wc; chem disp; mv service pnt; shwrs
inc; el pnts (10A) €3.25; lndtte; shop 1km; playgrnd; rv fishing;
quiet; adv bkg; Eng spkn; CKE/CCI. "Pleasant site; excel san
facs; warden calls am & pm." 1 Jun-6 Sep. € 6.90   2008*

MAYENNE *4E1* (1km N Rural) *48.31350, -0.61296*
Camp Municipal du Gué St Léonard, 818 Rue de
St Léonard, 53100 Mayenne [06 76 73 71 69; camping@
paysdemayenne.fr; www.paysdemayenne-tourisme.fr]
Fr N, sp to E of D23 & well sp fr cent of Mayenne on rvside.
Med, hdg/mkd pitch, pt shd; htd wc; chem disp; some serviced
pitches; shwrs inc; el pnts (10A) €2.20; lndtte; shop (high ssn)
& 1km; tradsman high ssn; snacks; rest 1km; BBQ; playgrnd;
htd pool high ssn inc; rv fishing adj; 8% statics; phone; extra
for twin-axles; adv bkg; some noise fr adj factory; red low ssn;
CKE/CCI. "Peaceful, well-kept site by rv; pleasant location adj
parkland walks; clean, dated facs; some pitches sm & access
poss diff; vg value." ♦ 15 Mar-30 Sep. € 18.30   2013*

MAYET see Ecommoy *4F1*

MAYRES *9D1* (500m S Rural) *44.66723, 4.08965* **Camping
La Chataigneraie, Hameau de Cautet**, 07330 Mayres [tel/
fax 04 75 87 20 40 or 04 75 87 20 97] Fr Aubenas on N102; L
after Mayres vill, over Ardèche bdge, up hill in 500m. Sm, mkd
pitch, terr, pt shd; wc (cont); shwrs inc; el pnts (3-6A) €2.50-4;
tradsmn; rv sw 2km; dogs €1; quiet; ccard acc. "Vg CL-type
site; secluded by tributary of Rv Ardèche; helpful owners."
♦ ltd Easter-1 Nov. € 13.00   2009*

MAZAMET *8F4* (1.5km E Urban) *43.49634, 2.39075* **FFCC**
Camp Municipal de la Lauze, Chemin de la Lauze, 81200
Mazamet [tel/fax 05 63 61 24 69; camping.mazamet@
imsnet.fr; www.ville-mazamet.com/camping]
Exit Mazamet dir St Pons on D612, site on R past rugby grnd.
Med, hdstg, pt sl, pt shd; wc (mainly cont); chem disp; mv
service pnt; baby facs; shwrs inc; el pnts (15A) €3.50; lndtte;
BBQ; htd pool adj; tennis; poss cr; adv bkg; some rd
noise; red long stay/CKE/CCI. "Well-kept site in 2 adj parts,
1 flat & other sl; office thro gateway - warden needed for
access; san facs excel; gd touring base 'Black Mountain'
region." ♦ 1 Jun-30 Sep. € 13.00   2009*

MAZAMET *8F4* (8km E Urban) *43.48061, 2.48664* **Camping
La Vallée du Thoré, La Lamberthe**, 81240 St Amans-Soult
[05 63 98 30 20; camping-valleethore@wanadoo.fr]
Fr Mazamet take D612 dir Béziers; site on L in 8km, clearly sp
in vill by nursery school. Sm, pt sl, pt shd; wc; chem disp; shwrs
inc; el pnts (6A) inc; gas; lndtte; tradsmn; shops, rest, snacks
& bar 500m; 30% statics; dogs free; Eng spkn; adv bkg; quiet;
CKE/CCI. "Lovely vill site close to rv; church bells stop at night;
vg." 1 May-30 Sep. € 13.20   2008*

MAZAN see Carpentras *10E2*

L'international de Jablines - www.camping-jablines.com - Tel: 0160260937

Base de loisirs de Jablines-Annet (77450)

MAZIERES see Chasseneuil sur Bonnieure *7B3*

MAZURES, LES see Rocroi *5C1*

MEAUDRE see Villard de Lans *9C3*

MEAULNE *7A4* (S Urban) *46.59667, 2.61352* **Camp Municipal Le Cheval Blanc, Route de Montluçon, 03360 Meaulne [04 70 06 91 13 or 04 70 06 95 34; fax 04 70 06 91 29; mairie.meaulne@wanadoo.fr; www. meaulne-ami.com]** Site off D2144 on bank Rv Aumance. Sm, pt shd; wc; chem disp (wc); shwrs inc; el pnts (12A) €2; lndtte; shop, rest, bar 300m; BBQ; playgrnd; rv fishing; canoeing; dogs; phone; quiet, some rd noise; CKE/CCI. "Pleasant, well-kept, basic site in beautiful rvside position; clean san facs; site yourself, warden calls 1300 & 1900 or put money in letterbox; poss flooding in high rainfall; excel NH." ♦ ltd 1 May-30 Sep. € 10.00   2009*

"That's changed – Should I let The Club know?"

If you find something on site that's different from the site entry, fill in a report and let us know. See www.caravanclub.co.uk/europereport.

MEAUX *3D3* (4km NE Rural) *49.00301, 2.94139* **Camping Village Parisien, Route des Otages, 77910 Varreddes [01 64 34 80 80; fax 01 60 22 89 84; direction@ villageparisien.com; www.villageparisien.com]** Fr Meaux foll sp on D405 dir Soissons then Varreddes, site sp on D121 dir Congis. Med, hdg/mkd pitch, pt shd; wc; chem disp; mv service pnt; baby facs; shwrs inc; el pnts (6A) €2; gas; lndtte (inc dryer); sm shop (high ssn); tradsmn; rest & snacks (high ssn); bar; BBQ; playgrnd; pool; paddling pool; waterslide; fishing; tennis; games area; cycle hire; golf 5km; games rm; wifi; entmnt; TV rm; 85% statics; dogs free; poss cr; Eng spkn; adv bkg; aircraft noise; ccard acc; red low ssn/long stay/CKE/CCI. "Conv Paris cent (drive to metro), Parc Astérix & Disneyland - tickets avail fr site; friendly, helpful staff; sm pitches; narr site rds; v busy, well-used site." 15 Mar-1 Nov. € 27.00   2009*

MEAUX *3D3* (10km SW Rural) *48.91333, 2.73416* **Camping L'International de Jablines, 77450 Jablines [01 60 26 09 37; fax 01 60 26 43 33; welcome@camping-jablines.com; www.camping-jablines.com]** Fr N on A1 then A104 exit Claye-Souilly. Fr E on A4 then A104 exit Meaux. Fr S on A6, A86, A4, A104 exit Meaux. Site well sp 'Base de Loisirs de Jablines'. Lge, mkd pitch, pt sl, pt shd; htd wc; chem disp; mv service pnt; baby facs; shwrs inc; el pnts (10A) inc; lndtte (inc dryer); shop; tradsmn; rest 500m; snacks; bar; BBQ; playgrnd; sand beach & lake sw 500m; fishing; sailing; windsurfing; tennis 500m; horseriding; cycle hire; internet; dogs €3; bus to Eurodisney; Eng spkn; adv bkg ess high ssn; quiet; red low ssn; ccard acc; CKE/CCI. "Clean, well-run, well-guarded site; vg pitches; pelasant staff; san facs poss tired high ssn; ideal for Disneyland (tickets for sale), Paris & Versaille." ♦ 31 Mar-29 Sep. € 28.00 (CChq acc)   2011*

See advertisement

⊞ MEAUX *3D3* (10km SW Urban) *48.87723, 2.78663* **Motor Caravan Park at Disneyland Paris, 77777 Marne-la-Vallée** Fr all dirs foll sp to Disneyland & foll sp to m'van (camping car) park. Easy to find. Lge, hdstg, unshd; htd wc; mv service pnt; shwrs inc; no el pnts; picnic area; rest etc in Disney Village; dogs; phone; bus, train adj; Eng spkn; quiet; ccard acc; m'vans only. Many other sites nr Disneyland cater for car/c'van o'fits. € 13.00   2009*

MEES, LES *10E3* (9km S Rural) *43.95377, 5.93304* **Camping Les Olivettes, Hameau-Les-Pourcelles, 04190 Les Mées [tel/fax 04 92 34 18 97; campingolivette@club-internet.fr; www.campinglesolivettes.com]** Exit A51 junc 20 (fr N) or 19 (fr S) & cross Rv Durance onto D4. Site bet Oraison & Les Mées. Turn onto D754 to Les Pourcelles & foll site sp. Sm, hdg/mkd pitch, pt sl, terr, pt shd; wc; chem disp; shwrs inc; el pnts (6A) €3.50; playgrnd; pool; 5% statics; dogs €1.50; Eng spkn; adv bkg; quiet. "Views over beautiful area; friendly owners; occasional out of ssn pitches avail; unrel opening; vg." ♦ ltd 15 Apr-15 Oct. € 15.00   2008*

MEGEVE *9B3* (2km SW Rural) *45.84120, 6.58887* **FFCC Camping Gai Séjour, 332 Route de Cassioz, 74120 Megève [tel/fax 04 50 21 22 58]** On D1212 Flumet-Megève rd, site on R 1km after Praz-sur-Arly, well sp. Med, mkd pitch, sl (blocks needed), pt shd; wc; chem disp; shwrs inc; el pnts (4A); lndry rm; shops, rest, bar 1km; dogs; Eng spkn; adv bkg; quiet; CKE/CCI. "Pleasant site with gd views, lge pitches; gd walks; 40km fr Mont Blanc; helpful owners." 20 May-15 Sep. € 10.90   2009*

MEHUN SUR YEVRE *4H3* (500m N Urban) *47.14797, 2.21725* **Camp Municipal, Ave Jean Châtelet, 18500 Mehun-sur-Yèvre [02 48 57 44 51 or 02 48 57 30 25 (Mairie); fax 02 48 57 34 16; www.ville-mehun-sur-yevre.fr/Le-camping]** Leave A71 junc 6 onto D2076 (N76) dir Bourges. App Mehun & turn L into site at 2nd traff lts. Ave Jean Châtelet is part of D2076. Sm, mkd pitch, pt shd; wc; chem disp; mv service pnt; shwrs inc; el pnts (6A) €2.80 (poss rev pol & long lead req some pitches); lndtte; shop, rest & bar 600m; supmkts 1km; playgrnd; pool & tennis adj; quiet with some rd noise; twin-axles extra; ccard not acc. "Excel NH conv for m'way; clean, modern san facs; water pnts poss long walk; gates locked 2200-0700 (high ssn); Facs open to elements; town rather run down, nice park." ♦ 8 May-30 Sep. € 16.65   2013*

MEHUN SUR YEVRE *4H3* (6km NE Rural) *47.09648, 2.18165* **Camp Municipal Pierre Sicard, 18120 Preuilly [02 48 57 12 04 or 02 48 51 30 08 (Mairie); fax 02 48 51 06 28; mairie.preuilly@wanadoo.fr]** S fr Vierzon on D27 sp Brinay & Quincy to Preuilly; take 2nd L to site in 500m; on R just past rv bdge. Med, hdg/mkd pitch, pt shd; wc; chem disp; shwrs inc; el pnts (5A) inc; lndtte; shop; snacks; bar; playgrnd; games area; tennis opp; a few statics; dogs €0.80; phone adj; adv bkg; quiet, but poss noise fr rest adj; CKE/CCI. "Gd touring base for wine rte; san facs old but clean; direct access to rv fishing & boating; fair." ♦ 1 May-30 Sep. € 9.80   2009*

MEJANNES LE CLAP see Barjac (Gard) *9D2*

MELE SUR SARTHE, LE *4E1* (500m SE Rural) *48.50831, 0.36298* **Camp Intercommunal La Prairie, La Bretèche, St Julien-Sarthe, 61170 Le Mêle-sur-Sarthe [02 33 27 18 74]** Turn off N12 onto D4; site sp in vill. Med, mkd pitch, pt shd; wc; chem disp; mv service pnt; shwrs; el pnts (6A) inc; lndtte; supmkt 300m; playgrnd; sand beach/lake 300m; sailing; tennis; adv bkg; CKE/CCI. "Part of excel sports complex; vg." 1 May-30 Sep. € 9.40   2009*

MELISEY *6F2* (2.5km N Rural) **Camping La Pierre, Route de Melay, 70270 Melisey [03 84 63 23 08 or 03 84 22 11 10; www.office-tourisme-melisey.fr]** Fr Lure on D486 to Melisey, L in vill onto D293 sp Melay. Site on L in 2.5km. Sm, hdg/mkd pitch, shd; wc; shwrs inc; el pnts (4A)€2.20; rest 2km; shop 2km; lndry rm; playgrnd; quiet; adv bkg. "V quiet, well-kept site; site yourself, warden calls; local c'van club organises reg social events and visitors are invited; gd site" ♦ 1 May-30 Sep. € 16.30   2013*

MELISEY *6F2* (500m E Rural) *47.75484, 6.58683* **Camping La Bergereine, 17bis Route des Vosges, 70270 Mélisey [tel/fax 06 23 36 87 16 (mob); isabelle.schweizer0704@ orange.fr]** Fr Lure (or by-pass) take D486 dir Le Thillot; site sp. Sm, pt shd; wc; chem disp; shwrs; el pnts inc; gas; leisure cent & pool 500m; fishing in adj rv; 25% statics; adv bkg; v quiet; CKE/ CCI. "Gd NH; simple farm site; attractive scenery." 1 Apr-30 Sep. € 8.00   2008*

MELISEY *6F2* (7km E Rural) *47.75525, 6.65273* **Camping La Broche, Le Voluet, 70270 Fresse [tel/fax 03 84 63 31 40; www.camping-broche.com]** Fr Lure head NE on D486 twd Melisey. Fr Mélisey stay on D486 twd Le Thillot, in 2.5km turn R onto D97 dir Plancher-les-Mines. In approx 5.5km site sp on R in Fresse. Sm, mkd pitch, pt sl, terr, pt shd; wc; chem disp; shwrs; el pnts (10A) €2.50; lndtte; ice; shop 200m; BBQ; playgrnd; lake sw & fishing adj; games area; games rm; some statics; dogs €1; phone; poss cr; adv bkg; quiet apart fr double-chiming church bells; CKE/CCI. "Secluded, relaxing site in attractive setting in regional park; friendly owner; conv Rte of 1000 lakes; great site." ♦ 1 Apr-15 Oct. € 9.00   2010*

⊞ **MELLE** *7A2* (8km S Rural) *46.15127, -0.12022* **Camping La Maison de Puits, 14 Rue de Beauchamp, 79110 Tillou [05 49 07 20 28; mark.hall@sfr.fr; www.hallmarkholidays. eu]** Fr Niort on D948. At Melle foll sp Angoulême, R turn (to ring rd & avoids Melle cent). At Total stn rndabt turn R onto D948 dir Chef-Boutonne. In 3.5km turn R onto D737 sp Chef-Boutonne. After approx 5km at x-rds of D111 & D737, strt over & take 2nd turn R in 1km (sm sp to Tillou) along narr rd sp Tillou. In 1.6km site on L. Sm, sl, unshd; wc; chem disp; shwr; el pnts (6A) €3; BBQ; splash pool; adv bkg; quiet. "CL-type site in meadow/orchard (6 vans only); quiet & peaceful; friendly, helpful British owners - help with house-hunting avail; ring ahead to book; interesting area" € 12.00   2013*

MELLE *7A2* (10km SW Rural) *46.14421, -0.21983* **Camp Municipal, Rue des Merlonges, 79170 Brioux-sur-Boutonne [05 49 07 50 46; fax 05 49 07 27 27]** On ent Brioux fr Melle on D150 turn R immed over bdge; site on R in 100m. Sm, pt shd; wc; shwrs inc; el pnts (6A) €1.80; lndry rm; shops 300m; playgrnd adj; quiet, some rd noise. "Pleasant rural setting; tidy, well-cared for site; ltd facs but clean; choose own pitch & pay at Mairie on dep if no warden; vg sh stay/NH." 1 Apr-31 Oct. € 5.40   2013*

MELLE *7A2* (6km NW Rural) *46.25877, -0.21463* **Camp Municipal La Boissière, Route de Chizé, 79370 Celles-sur-Belle [06 76 31 22 76 or 05 49 79 80 17 (Mairie); fax 05 49 32 95 10; mairie-cellessurbelle@wanadoo.fr; www. ville-celles-sur-belle.com]** Fr Melle or Niort on D948. Exit by-pass into Celles & in town foll sp to Sports Complex & camping. Sm, pt sl, pt shd; htd wc (some cont); shwrs inc; el pnts (6A); gas, shop 500m; BBQ; playgrnd; pool adj; rv 200m; lake 400m; tennis; 20% statics; dogs €0.85; adv bkg rec high ssn. "Warden calls am & pm; quiet apart fr football grnd adj; gd NH." ♦ 15 Apr-15 Oct.   2009*

MELUN *4E3* (3km S Rural) *48.52569, 2.66930* **Kawan Village La Belle Etoile, Quai Maréchal Joffre, 77000 Melun-La Rochette [01 64 39 48 12; fax 01 64 37 25 55; info@ campinglabelleetoile.com; www.campinglabelleetoile.com]** On ent La Rochette on D606 fr Fontainbleu pass Total stn on L; turn immed R into Ave de la Seine & foll site sp; site on L in 500m. Lge, hdg/mkd pitch, hdstg, pt shd; htd wc; chem disp; mv service pnt; shwrs; el pnts (6A) €3.50 (poss rev pol); gas; lndtte (inc dryer); shop 1km; rests in vill; snacks (high ssn); bar; BBQ; playgrnd; htd pool; paddling pool; rv fishing; games area; golf 8km; wifi; TV rm; 10% statics; phone; some statics; dogs €1.50; bus to stn - train to Paris; Eng spkn; adv bkg; some rlwy & rv noise, v little at night; ccard acc; red low ssn; CKE/CCI. "Pretty site; helpful owners; gd san facs; gates locked 2300; conv Paris, Fontainebleau & Disneyland (tickets fr recep); sports complex nrby; gd walking & cycling in forest along rv/canal; mkt Melun Wed; vd value; gd." ♦ 26 Mar-2 Oct. € 19.50 (CChq acc) 2011*

MENAT *7A4* (2km E Rural) *46.09579, 2.92899* **Camp Municipal des Tarteaux, 63560 Menat [04 73 85 52 47 or 04 73 85 50 29 (Mairie); fax 04 73 85 50 22; mairiemenat@ wanadoo.fr; www.ville-menat.com]** Heading SE fr St Eloy-les-Mines on D2144 foll sp Camping Pont de Menat. Exit D2144 at Menat opp Hôtel Pinal. Site alongside Rv Sioule. Med, terr, pt sl, shd; wc (cont); mv service pnt; shwrs incl; el pnts (16A) €2.70; lndtte; shop 2km; playgrnd; rv adj; fishing & boating 2km; wifi; adv bkg; quiet; CKE/CCI. "Beautiful site beside rv; basic san facs clean but in need of update (2011) - own san facs rec; Chateau Rocher ruins nrby; ok NH." 1 Apr-30 Sep. € 7.85 2013*

⊞ **MENDE** *9D1* (2km S Rural) *44.51409, 3.47363* **Camping Tivoli, Route des Gorges du Tarn, 48000 Mende [tel/fax 04 66 65 00 38; camping.tivoli0601@orange.fr; www. camping-tivoli.com]** Sp fr N88, turn R 300m downhill (narr but easy rd). Site adj Rv Lot. Med, pt shd; wc (some cont); chem disp; mv service pnt; shwrs incl; el pnts (6A) inc; lndtte; shop; hypmkt 1km; bar; playgrnd; pool; rv fishing; TV rm; some statics; dogs €1; quiet but rd noise; adv bkg. "Gd site nr town at back of indust est; v narr ent with little room to park." € 18.60 2009*

MENDE *9D1* (8km SW Rural) *44.50104, 3.40717* **Camping Le Clos des Peupliers, 48000 Barjac [04 66 47 01 16; leclosdespeupliers@wanadoo.fr]** Exit A75 junc 39 onto N88 dir Mende; turn off N88 N onto D42 sp Barjac; then turn almost immed turn R; rd goes thro sh narr but not diff tunnel (max height 3.4m). Site immed after tunnel, on S side of N88 adj Rv Lot. Med, mkd pitch, pt shd; wc; chem disp; shwrs incl; el pnts (6-10A) €2.50-3; lndtte; rest 300m; snacks; playgrnd; rv fishing adj; TV; dogs €1.30; quiet. "Pleasant rvside site; poss unkempt low ssn; helpful warden; basic, clean facs, ltd low ssn; gd walks." ♦ 1 May-15 Sep. € 9.00 2010*

MENESPLET see Montpon Ménestérol *7C2*

MENETRUX EN JOUX see Doucier *6H2*

MENIL see Château Gontier *4F1*

MENITRE, LA see Rosiers sur Loire, Les *4G1*

MENNETOU SUR CHER see Villefranche sur Cher *4G3*

MENOMBLET see Châtaigneraie, La *2H4*

MENS *9C3* (500m S Urban) *44.81493, 5.74860* **Camping du Pré Rolland, Rue de la Piscine, Place Richard-Wilm, 38710 Mens [04 76 34 65 80; fax 04 76 34 65 80; contact@ camping-prerolland.fr; www.camping-prerolland.fr]** Turn E fr N75 onto D526 sp Celles & Mens; site in 14km. Turn R at ent to town. Well sp. Med, hdg/mkd pitch, pt shd; wc; chem disp; mv service pnt; shwrs inc; el pnts (10A) €3; lndtte; snacks; sw nrby; entmnt; TV; 5% statics; dogs €1.50; phone; Eng spkn; adv bkg; quiet, but poss noise fr pool nr ent; red low ssn/long stay; CKE/CCI. "Beautiful area; mountain views; friendly owners; excel walking; painting courses high ssn; vg." ♦ ltd 1 May-30 Sep. € 14.50 2008*

> "I like to fill in the reports as I travel from site to site"
> You'll find report forms at the back of this guide, or you can fill them in online at www.caravaclub.co.uk/europereport.

⊞ **MERENS LES VALS** *8G4* (1km W Rural) *42.64633, 1.83083* **Camp Municipal Ville de Bau, Ville de Bau, 09110 Mérens-les-Vals [05 61 02 85 40 or 05 61 64 33 77; fax 05 61 64 03 83; camping.merens@wanadoo.fr; http:// merenslesvals.fr]** Fr Ax-les-Thermes on N20 sp Andorra past Mérens-les-Vals turn R nr start of dual c'way sp Camp Municipal. Site on R in 800m. Med, hdg pitch; htd wc (some cont); shwrs inc; el pnts (6-10A) €3.20-5.20 (poss rev pol); lndtte (inc dryer); shop; bar; BBQ; playgrnd; pool 8km; 20% statics; dogs €0.70; poss cr; quiet; ccard acc; CKE/CCI. "Excel site; gd clean san facs; gd walks fr site; conv Andorra, Tunnel de Puymorens." € 15.20 2012*

MERIBEL *9B3* (2km N Rural) *45.40779, 6.55883* **Camping Le Martagon, Le Raffort, Route de Méribel, 73550 Les Allues [04 79 00 56 29; fax 04 79 00 44 92; contact@ restaurant-martagon.com; www.restaurant-martagon. com]** Fr Moûtiers on D915 S to Brides-les-Bains then D90 S dir Méribel. Site on L at Le Raffort. Park in public car park & go to rest. Sm, hdstg, terr, unshd; htd wc; chem disp; mv service pnt; shwrs inc; el pnts (13A) €6; gas 200m; lndtte; shop 2km; tradsmn; rest; bar; no statics; dogs; adv bkg; rd noise; ccard acc. "Ski bus every 20 mins at site ent; skilift 100m; htd boot room; mountain-biking in summer." ♦ 1 Dec-30 Apr & 1 Jul-31 Aug. € 26.00 2011*

MERINCHAL *7B4* (S Urban) *45.91513, 2.48813* **Camp Municipal La Mothe, Château de Mérinchal, 23420 Mérinchal [05 55 67 25 56 (TO); fax 05 55 67 23 71; tourisme.merinchal@wanadoo.fr]** E fr Pontaumur on D941 twds Aubusson. R onto D27 to Mérinchal. Site in vill. Sm, pt sl, pt shd; wc; shwrs inc; el pnts €2; lndtte; shop, rest, bar nr; playgrnd; TV; fishing 500m; quiet. "Excel site in chateau grounds but poss clsd w/end if weddings etc in chateau - phone ahead to check." ♦ 1 Apr-30 Oct. € 8.50 2010*

FRANCE

MERS LES BAINS 3B2 (1.5km NE Rural) 50.07730, 1.41540
Camping Le Rompval, Lieudit Blengues, 154 Rue André Dumont, 80350 Mers-les-Bains [02 35 84 43 21 or 06 50 02 79 57 (mob); lerompval@baiedesommepleinair.com; www.campinglerompval.com] Fr Calais on A16, exit junc 23 at Abbeville onto A28. In 5km exit junc 2 onto D925 dir Friville-Escarbotin, Le Tréport. In approx 20km at rndabt junc with D19 foll sp Ault & at next rndabt take D940 twd Mers-les-Bains. Fr S on A28 exit junc 5 onto D1015 to Mers-les-Bains & foll sp Blengues & site. Med, hdg/mkd pitch, hdstg, unshd; htd wc; chem disp; mv service pnt; baby facs; fam bathrm; shwrs inc; el pnts (6-13A) €4-6.50; gas; lndtte (inc dryer); shop; supmkt 2km; tradsmn; snacks; bar; BBQ; playgrnd; htd, covrd pool; paddling pool; sand beach 2.5km; tennis 3km; cycle hire; games area; games/TV rm; library; wifi; entmnt; 25% statics; dogs €3; Eng spkn; adv bkg; quiet; ccard acc; red long stay/low ssn/CKE/CCI. "Vg site; gd facs." ♦ 29 Marr-11 Nov. € 21.50 (CChq acc) 2013*

See advertisement on page 276

MERVANS 6H1 (NE Rural) 46.80179, 5.19171 Camp Municipal du Plan d'Eau, Route de Pierre-de-Bresse, 71310 Mervans [03 85 76 16 63 (Mairie); fax 03 85 76 16 93; mairie-de-mervans@wanadoo.fr] E on N78 fr Chalon-sur-Saône. At Thurey fork L onto D204; at x-rds turn L onto D996 to Mervans. In vill take D313 dir Pierre-de-Bresse, site sp by lake. Sm, pt shd; wc (some cont); shwrs inc; el pnts (10A) inc; shop, rest adj; fishing nr; quiet; CKE/CCI. "Well-kept site, clean facs; lovely countryside; pleasant vill." ♦ 1 Jun-15 Sep. € 6.60 2008*

MERVENT see Fontenay le Comte 7A2

MERVILLE FRANCEVILLE PLAGE see Cabourg 3D1

MESCHERS SUR GIRONDE see Royan 7B1

MESLAND see Onzain 4G2

MESLAY DU MAINE 4F1 (2.5km NE Rural) 47.96409, -0.52979 Camp Municipal La Chesnaie, St Denis-du-Maine, 53170 Meslay-du-Maine [02 43 98 48 08 or 02 43 64 10 45 (Mairie); fax 02 43 98 75 52; camping.lachesnaie@wanadoo.fr; www.paysmeslaygrez.fr] Take D21 SE fr Laval to Meslay; turn L in cent of vill onto D152. Site on R in 2.5km. Med, hdg/mkd pitch, pt shd; wc (some cont); shwrs inc; el pnts (6A) €2.60 (poss long lead req); lndtte; shop & rest 2.5km; snacks; bar; playgrnd; lake adj; watersports, leisure cent adj; cycle hire; 10% statics; poss cr; adv bkg; ccard acc; CKE/CCI. "Excel clean & quiet site; san facs old but clean." ♦ Easter-30 Sep. € 9.40 2011*

MESNIL ST PERE 6F1 (1km NE Rural) 48.26329, 4.34633 Kawan Village Camping Lac d'Orient, Rue du Lac, 10140 Mesnil-St Père [03 25 40 61 85 or 03 85 72 27 21 (LS); fax 03 25 70 96 87 or 03 85 72 66 07 (LS); info@camping-lacdorient.com; www.camping-lacdorient.com] On D619 foll sps Lac de la Forêt d'Orient. Approx 10km fr Vendeuvre or 20km fr Troyes turn N on D43A, to Mesnil-St Père; site sp. Sp at ent to site: 'Camping Lac d'Orient' (with 'Kawan Village' in v sm lettering) Lge, pt sl, pt shd; wc (some cont); chem disp; mv service pnt; private san facs some pitches; baby facs; fam bthrm; shwrs inc; el pnts (10A) inc; lndtte (inc dryer); shop; tradsmn; rest 1km; snacks; bar; BBQ; playgrnd; 2 htd pools (1 covrd); paddling pool; jacuzzi; lake sw/shgl beach & watersports 500m; fishing; games area; tennis; games rm; wifi; entmnt; some statics; dogs €3; no c'vans/m'vans over 10m high ssn; phone; Eng spkn; adv bkg; quiet; ccard acc; red low ssn; CKE/CCI. "Peaceful site with mature trees; lge pitches; 1st class san facs; poss muddy when wet; conv Nigloland theme park & Champagne area; conv A26; Excel spacious site; excel cycle route; fantastic res over looking lake" ♦ 6 Apr-28 Sep. € 46.60 (CChq acc) SBS - J07 2013*

MESNOIS see Clairvaux les Lacs 6H2

MESSANGES 8E1 (2km S Coastal) 43.80070, -1.39220 Camping La Côte, Route de Vieux-Boucau, 40660 Messanges [05 58 48 94 94; fax 05 58 48 94 44; info@campinglacote.com; www.campinglacote.com] On D652 2km S of Messanges. Med, pt shd; wc; chem disp; mv service pnt; serviced pitches; shwrs inc; el pnts (6-10A) €3.90-4.90; lndtte; sm shop; supmkt 1km; tradsmn; snacks; playgrnd; pool complex; paddling pool; sand beach 1km; horseriding 300m; golf 2km; cycle hire; wifi; 5% statics; dogs €2.20; phone; adv bkg; Eng spkn; dogs poss early noise fr builders yard adj; red low ssn; CKE/CCI. "Peaceful, well-kept site adj pine woods; spacious pitches; easy access; helpful staff; clean san facs; vg pool; gd access to beaches; gd cycle tracks; excel." ♦ 1 Apr-30 Sep. € 20.50 2011*

MESSANGES 8E1 (2km SW Coastal) 43.79790, -1.40135 Airotel Camping Le Vieux Port, Plage Sud, 40660 Messanges [01 76 76 70 00; fax 05 58 48 01 69; contact@levieuxport.com; www.levieuxport.com] Fr S take D652 past Vieux-Boucau; site sp. Turn W at Super U rndabt. V lge, mkd pitch, hdstg, shd; wc; chem disp; mv service pnt; baby facs; fam bthrm; shwrs inc; el pnts (6-8A) €8.50; gas; lndtte (inc dryer); shop; supmkt 500m; tradsmn; rest, snacks; bar; BBQ; playgrnd; htd, pt cvrd pool + pool complex; paddling pool; waterslides; dir access to sand beach 400m; tennis; games area; cycle hire; horseriding; quadbikes; wifi; entmnt; TV; 10% statics; dogs €5.50; Eng spkn; adv bkg; poss cr; quiet; ccard acc; red low ssn/long stay; CKE/CCI. "V pleasant, clean site; superb, v lge pool complex; excel touring base." ♦ 2 Apr-25 Sep. € 48.50 (CChq acc) 2010*

MESSE see Couhé 7A2

METZ *5D2* (500m NW Urban) *49.12402, 6.16917* **Camp Municipal Metz-Plage, Allée de Metz-Plage, 57000 Metz** [03 87 68 26 48; fax 03 87 38 03 89; campingmetz@ mairie-metz.fr; www.mairie-metz.fr] Fr W exit A31 junc 33 Metz-Nord/Pontiffroy exit; cross rv brdges Pont Canal & Pont des Morts; then immed turn L into Allée de Metz-Plage; site in 200m (or after leaving A31 at junc 33, at rndabt turn R & foll sps). Fr E foll 'Autres Directions' over A31 & Rv Moselle, then as above. Lge, mkd pitch, hdstg, pt sl, pt shd; wc; chem disp; mv service pnt; baby facs; shwrs inc; el pnts (10A) inc (poss rev pol); lndtte; shop, snacks; playgrnd; pool adj; rv fishing adj; wifi; dogs €0.50; twin-axles & vehicles over 3,500 kg extra; poss cr; Eng spkn; adv bkg; traff noise fr rv bdge at far end; ccard acc;CKE/CCI. "Spacious, well-situated on rv with views; some gd sized pitches; helpful staff; poss long walk to san facs; rv unfenced; facs stretched if site full; early arr ess high ssn; vg." ♦ 22 Apr-3 Oct. € 18.50   2011*

MEURSAULT see Beaune *6H1*

MEYMAC *7B4* (500m NE Rural) *45.54075, 2.15533* **Camping Municipal La Garenne, Blvd de la Garenne, 19250 Meymac** [05 55 95 22 80; fax 05 55 95 66 12] Fr Meymac take D30 dir Sornac. Site ent on R appears to be via a car park, sp. Med, mkd pitch, terr, pt sl, pt shd; htd wc (some cont); shwrs inc; shops 1km; el pnts (10A) €2.75; lndtte; shop, rest, snacks, bar 500m; BBQ; playgrnd; some statics; dogs €0.70; quiet;CKE/CCI. "Lge pitches; site in wooded area; gd walking." ♦ 15 May-15 Sep. € 8.80   2010*

MEYRAS *9D2* (1km S Rural) *44.66846, 4.28329* **Camping Le Ventadour, Pont de Rolandy, 07380 Meyras** [tel/fax 04 75 94 18 15; info@leventadour.com; www. leventadour.com] Sp fr N102, on rvside, W of Pont-de-Labeaume. Med, pt shd; htd wc; shwrs inc; el pnts (6-10A) €3.20-4.20 (poss rev pol); lndtte; shop; supmkt 5km; tradsmn; snacks; bar; gas BBQ; playgrnd; fishing; wifi; some statics; dogs €2; Eng spkn; adv bkg; quiet; ccard acc. "Helpful owners; easy access; gd, clean facs; attractive site." 17 Apr-3 Oct. € 20.00   2010*

MEYRIEU LES ETANGS *9B2* (800m SE Rural) *45.50790, 5.20850* **Camping Base de Loisirs du Moulin, Commune du Pays St Jeannais, 38440 Meyrieu-les-Etangs** [04 74 59 30 34; fax 04 74 58 36 12; contact@camping-meyrieu.com; www.camping-meyrieu.com] Exit A43 at junc 8. Enter Bourgoin & foll sp for La Gare to pick up D522 SW twd St Jean-de-Bournay. Site next to lake 1km fr D522, sp. Med, mkd pitch, hdstg, terr, pt shd; wc; shwrs; el pnts (6-10A) €2.90-4.50; lndry rm; shop; rest; lake sw; pedalos; fishing; canoeing; archery; games rm; entmnt in ssn; TV; dogs €1.80; phone; adv bkg; quiet. "Views across lake; sm pitches; hdstg on all pitches for car; clean san facs & site; vg, nice site" ♦ 6 Apr-30 Sep. € 15.30   2013*

MEYRONNE see Martel *7C3*

MEYRUEIS *10E1* (3km N Rural) *44.19633, 3.45724* **FFCC Camping La Cascade, Salvinsac, 48150 Meyrueis** [04 66 45 45 45 or 06 85 84 07 15 (mob); fax 04 66 45 45 48; contact@camping-la-cascade.com; www. camping-la-cascade.com] N of Meyrueis on D996, on R. NB Do not app fr N - narr rd. Rec app fr Millau dir only. Sm, mkd pitch, pt sl, terr, pt shd; wc; chem disp; mv service pnt; baby facs; shwrs inc; el pnts (10A) €3; gas; lndtte; shop; tradsmn; BBQ; playgrnd; canoeing; fishing; horseriding; walking; 20% statics; dogs; poss cr; Eng spkn; adv bkg; ccard acc. "Friendly owners." ♦ 1 Apr-5 Nov. € 16.00   2010*

MEYRUEIS *10E1* (1km NE Rural) *44.18590, 3.43856* **Camping Le Pré de Charlet, Route de Florac, 48150 Meyrueis** [04 66 45 63 65; fax 04 66 45 63 24; lepredecharlet@gmail. com; www.camping-lepredecharlet.com] Exit Meyrueis on rd to Florac (D996). Site on R on bank of Rv Jonte. Med, mkd pitch, pt sl, terr, pt shd, pt sl; wc (some cont); chem disp; mv service pnt; baby facs; shwrs inc; el pnts (16A) inc; gas; lndtte; shop & 11km; tradsmn; bar; BBQ; playgrnd; pool 400m; rv fishing; phone; adv bkg; phone; quiet; ccard acc; red low ssn;CKE/CCI. "Friendly owner; excel walking area; not suitable lge o'fits; conv Les Gorges de la Jonte; excel." ♦ ltd 15 Apr-15 Oct. € 15.00   2010*

MEYRUEIS *10E1* (500m E Rural) *44.18075, 3.43540* **Camping Le Champ d'Ayres, Route de la Brèze, 48150 Meyrueis** [tel/fax 04 66 45 60 51; campinglechampdayres@ wanadoo.fr; www.campinglechampdayres.com] Fr W on D907 dir Gorges de la Jonte into Meyrueis. Foll sp Château d'Ayres & site. Med, hdg/mkd pitch, pt sl, pt shd; wc (some cont); chem disp; mv service pnt; baby facs; fam bthrm; shwrs inc; el pnts (6A) €3; lndtte; shop; tradsmn; snacks; bar; BBQ; playgrnd; htd pool; cycle hire; games area; games rm; wifi; 15% statics; dogs €1; phone; poss cr; Eng spkn; adv bkg; red low ssn; ccard acc;CKE/CCI. "Helpful owners; rec." ♦ 11 Apr-19 Sep. € 26.50   2012*

MEYRUEIS *10E1* (800m NW Rural) *44.18580, 3.41977* **Kawan Village Le Capelan, Route de Jonte, 48150 Meyrueis** [tel/fax 04 66 45 60 50; camping.le.capelan@wanadoo.fr; www.campingcapelan.com] Site sp on D996 on banks of Rv Jonte. Med, mkd pitch, shd; wc; chem disp; mv service pnt; baby facs; fam bthrm; shwrs inc; el pnts (4-10A) €3; gas; lndtte (inc dryer); shop; tradsmn; supmkt 500m; BBQ; rest 1km; snacks; bar; BBQ; playgrnd; htd pool; paddling pool; fishing; tennis 1km; games rm; games area; rockclimbing; wifi; entmnt; TV rm; 70% statics; Eng spkn; adv bkg; quiet; red low ssn; ccard acc;CKE/CCI. "Gd, scenic, rvside site; conv touring Gorges du Tarn & Cévennes National Park." ♦ 1 May-17 Sep. € 22.00 (CChq acc)   2010*

MEYSSAC *7C3* (2km NE Rural) *45.06150, 1.66402* **Intercommunal Moulin de Valane, Route de Collonges-la-Rouge, 19500 Meyssac** [05 55 25 41 59; fax 05 55 84 07 28; mairie@meyssac.fr; www.meyssac.fr] Well sp on D38 bet Meyssac & Collonges-la-Rouge. Med, mkd pitch, pt sl, pt shd; wc; chem disp; shwrs; el pnts (10A) €2.80; lndtte; shop; rest, snacks; bar; playgrnd; pool; tennis; many statics; adv bkg;CKE/CCI. "Within walking dist of attractive vill; quiet at night; vg san facs; rec." ♦ 1 May-30 Sep. € 13.00   2012*

MEYZIEU see Lyon *9B2*

FRANCE

MEZE *10F1* (1km N Coastal) *43.43019, 3.61070* **Kawan Village Beau Rivage, 113 Route Nationale, 34140 Mèze [04 67 43 81 48; fax 04 67 43 66 70; reception@camping-beaurivage.fr; www.camping-beaurivage.fr]** Fr Mèze cent foll D613 dir Montpellier, site on R 100m past rndabt on leaving town; well sp. Lge, mkd pitch, pt shd; wc; chem disp; mv service pnt; baby facs; shwrs inc; el pnts (3-6A) inc; lndtte; shop; supmkt 200m; rest, snacks; bar; BBQ; playgrnd; htd pool; paddling pool; sand beach 700m; fishing; sailing; tennis 900m; fitness rm; wifi; entmnt; TV rm; 50% statics; phone; dogs €6; poss cr; Eng spkn; adv bkg; quiet but rd noise; ccard acc; red low ssn;CKE/CCI. "Well equipped site; trees & narr access rds poss diff lge o'fits; vg modern san facs; lovely pool; pitches poss worn end of ssn; poor security - rear of site open to public car park; diff exit onto busy coast rd; conv Sète & Noilly Prat distillery; vg; excel site; close to town with gd market, marina and rest" ♦ 10 Apr-17 Sep. € 40.00   2013*

"We must tell The Club about that great site we found"

Get your site reports in by mid-August and we'll do our best to get your updates into the next edition of Caravan Europe.

MEZE *10F1* (2km N Rural) *43.44541, 3.61595* **Camp Municipal Loupian, Route de Mèze, 34140 Loupian [04 67 43 57 67 / 04 67 43 82 07 (ls); camping@loupian.fr; www.loupian.fr]** Fr Mèze tak D613 & turn L at 1st Loupian sp, then foll sp for site. Med, hdg/mkd pitch, pt shd; wc; chem disp; baby facs; shwrs; el pnts (6A) €2.50; lndtte; takeaway; snacks; bar; BBQ; playgrnd; sand beach 3km; tennis; entmnt; dogs €0.80; phone; poss cr; Eng spkn; adv bkg; quiet; red low ssn;CKE/CCI. "Pleasant site in popular area; plenty shade; friendly, helpful staff; vg san facs; gd beaches; excel fisherman's rest; gd rests at Mèze & Bouzigues; superb cycling on old rlwy rte fr site to Mèze (Voie Verte); rec; central to main attractions" ♦ ltd 8 Apr-16 Oct. € 13.50   2013*

MEZE *10F1* (5.5km NE Coastal) *43.45070, 3.66562* **Camping Lou Labech, Chemin du Stade, 34140 Bouzigues [04 67 78 30 38; fax 04 67 78 35 46; contact@lou-labech.fr; www.lou-labech.fr]** Exit A9 junc 33 onto D660/D613 S to Bouzigues; site sp. Part of Chemin du Stade borders sea. Sm, hdstg, terr, pt shd; wc; chem disp; baby facs; shwrs; el pnts (5A) £3; lndtte; tradsmn; rest 800m; bar; BBQ (charcoal sep area); playgrnd; wifi; TV; dogs free; poss cr; Eng spkn; quiet; red low ssn. "Delightful site; friendly, helpful staff; Bouzigues lovely vill." ♦ ltd Apr-Oct. € 21.00   2009*

MEZIERES EN BRENNE *4H2* (6km E Rural) *46.79817, 1.30595* **Camping Bellebouche, 36290 Mézières-en-Brenne [02 54 38 32 36; fax 02 54 38 32 96; v.v.n@orange.fr; www.village-vacances-bellebouche.com]** Sp on D925. Med, mkd pitch, pt sl, pt shd; wc (cont); chem disp (wc); baby facs; shwrs inc; el pnts €3.50; lndtte; shop 6km; rest high ssn; bar; BBQ (elec); playgrnd; lake sw adj; watersports; fishing; some statics; no dogs; phone; quiet; ccard acc;CKE/CCI. "In country park; gd walking, cycling, birdwatching; vg; san facs dated" 30 Apr-30 Sep. € 11.00   2013*

MEZIN *8E2* (4km NW Rural) *44.07281, 0.20774* **FLOWER Camping du Lac de Lislebonne, Le Bétous, 47170 Mézin-Réaup-Lisse [05 53 65 65 28; fax 05 53 65 34 05; domainelislebonne@free.fr or www.domainelislebonne. com or www.flowercampings.com]** Exit A62 junc 6 (Agen) dir Nérac on D656; cont on D656 to Mézin; then foll site sps. Sm, mkd pitch, pt shd; htd wc; shwrs inc; el pnts (12A) inc; gas; lndtte; shop; tradsmn; rest, snacks; bar; BBQ; playgrnd; lake sw & beach adj; cycle hire; games area; games rm; wifi; entmnt; TV; 45% statics; dogs €1.50; quiet; Eng spkn; adv bkg; ccard acc; red low ssn;CKE/CCI. "Vg touring base; gd walking; vg site." ♦ 24 Apr-30 Sep. € 18.50   2008*

See advertisement on pages 32 & 33

MEZOS *8E1* (1km SE Rural) *44.07980, -1.16090* **Le Village Tropical Sen Yan, 40170 Mézos [05 58 42 60 05; fax 05 58 42 64 56; reception@sen-yan.com; www.sen-yan. com]** Fr Bordeaux on N10 in 100km at Laharie turn W onto D38 dir Mimizan; in 12km turn L onto D63 to Mézos; turn L at mini-rndabt; site on L in approx 2km. Site 1.5km fr D63/ D38 junc NE of Mézos. Lge, hdg/mkd pitch, shd; wc (some cont); chem disp; baby facs; sauna; shwrs inc; el pnts (6A) inc; gas; lndtte (inc dryer); shop; rest, snacks; bar; BBQ (gas only); playgrnd; 2 pools (1 htd & covrd); paddling pool; waterslides; jacuzzi; sand beach 12km; rv adj; fishing; canoe hire 14m; watersports 15km; tennis; cycle hire; many sports & games; fitness cent; wifi; entmnt; games/TV (cab/sat) rm; 80% statics; dogs €5; no c'vans/m'vans over 8m; phone; Eng spkn; adv bkg; quiet; ccard acc; red low ssn;CKE/CCI. "Attractive, restful site; many plants, inc banana trees; modern, clean san facs; excel facs for families; mkt Mimizan Fri & Morcenx Wed." ♦ 1 Jun-9 Sep. € 47.00   2012*

MIANNAY see Abbeville *3B3*

MIGENNES see Joigny *4F4*

"I need an on-site restaurant"

We do our best to make sure site information is correct, but it is always best to check any must-have facilities are still available or will be open during your visit.

⊞ **MILLAS** *8G4* (3km W Rural) *42.69067, 2.65785* **FLOWER Camping La Garenne, 66170 Néfiach [04 68 57 15 76; fax 04 68 57 37 42; camping.lagarenne.nefiach@wanadoo.fr; www.camping-lagarenne.fr or www.flowercampings.com]** Fr Millas on R of D916, sp. Med, shd; htd wc (some cont); chem disp; baby facs; shwrs inc; el pnts (10A) €5; gas; lndtte; shop; snacks; bar; BBQ; playgrnd; pool high ssn; tennis 500m; games area; entmnt; wifi; 50% statics; dogs free; adv bkg rec high ssn; slight rd noise & poss noisy disco; red low ssn. "Friendly owners; gd facs" ♦ € 19.90   2011*

See advertisement on pages 32 & 33

FRANCE

MILLAU *10E1* (1km NE Urban) *44.10500, 3.08833* **Camping du Viaduc, Millau-Cureplat, 121 Ave du Millau-Plage, 12100 Millau [05 65 60 15 75; fax 05 65 61 36 51; info@ camping-du-viaduc.com; www.camping-du-viaduc.com]** Exit Millau on N991 (sp Nant) over Rv Tarn via Cureplat bdge. At rndabt take D187 dir Paulhe, 1st campsite on L. Lge, hdg/ mkd pitch, shd; htd wc; chem disp; some serviced pitches (extra charge); baby facs; shwrs inc; el pnts (6A) €4 (poss long lead req); gas; lndtte (inc dryer); shop high ssn; rest, snacks; bar; BBQ; playgrnd; htd pool; paddling pool; rv sw & private sand beach; wifi; entmnt; 20% statics; dogs €3; Eng spkn; some rd noise; ccard acc; red low ssn/long stay/CKE/CCI. "Peaceful, well-run site; helpful, welcoming staff; excel clean san facs; barrier clsd 2200-0700; many sports & activities in area; conv for gorges & viaduct tours; quiet low ssn; super site." ♦ 26 Apr-14Sep. € 45.50   2013*

MILLAU *10E1* (1km NE Urban) *44.11044, 3.08712* **Camping Larribal, Ave de Millau Plage, 12100 Millau [05 65 59 08 04; camping.larribal@wanadoo.fr; www. campinglarribal.com]** Exit Millau on D991 (sp Nant), cross rv & at rndabt take 3rd exit, site on L. Med, mkd pitch, shd; htd wc; chem disp; shwrs inc; el pnts (6A) €3; gas; lndtte; shop; tradsmn; playgrnd; rv sw adj; shgl beach; TV; 5% statics; dogs €1; phone; adv bkg; quiet but poss noise fr stadium across rv; red low ssn/long stay; CKE/CCI. "Peaceful, well-kept site on Rv Tarn; friendly, helpful staff; excel, clean san facs; lge o'fits poss diff access; high m'vans poss diff under trees; gd access to gorges; severe tree fluff in May; excel." ♦ 23 Apr-30 Sep. € 13.80   2011*

MILLAU *10E1* (1km NE Rural) *44.10640, 3.08800* **Camping Les Erables, Route de Millau-Plage, 12100 Millau [05 65 59 15 13; fax 05 65 59 06 59; camping-les-erables@ orange.fr; www.campingleserables.fr]** Exit Millau on D991 (sp Nant) over Rv Tarn bdge; take L at island sp to Millau-Plage & site on L immed after Camping du Viaduc & bef Camping Larribal. On ent Millau fr N or S foll sps 'Campings'. Med, hdg/ mkd pitch, shd; htd wc; chem disp; baby facs; shwrs inc; el pnts (10A) €3 (rev pol); lndtte (inc dryer); shop; snacks high ssn; bar; BBQ; playgrnd; rv sw, canoeing adj; wifi; entmnt; TV; dogs €1.20; phone; Eng spkn; adv bkg; some rd noise & fr nrby sites; ccard acc; red low ssn; CKE/CCI. "Peaceful, well-kept site on banks of Rv Tarn; lge shd pitches; friendly, helpful owners; excel modern san facs; some pitches poss diff lge o'fits; excel walking; beavers nrby; Millau Viaduct Vistor Centre a must; excel." ♦ 7 Apr-30 Sep. € 20.00   2012*

MILLAU *10E1* (2km NE Urban) *44.10240, 3.09100* **Camping Côte-Sud, Ave de l'Aigoual, 12100 Millau [tel/fax 05 65 61 18 83; camping-cotesud@orange.fr; www. campingcotesud.com]** Fr N exit A75 junc 45 to Millau. Turn L at 2nd traff island sp 'Camping'. Site on R over bdge in 200m. Fr S exit A75 junc 47 onto D809 & cross rv on by-pass, turn R at 1st traff island sp Nant on D991, cross bdge, site on R in 200m, sp. Site a S confluence of Rv Dourbie & Rv Tarn. Med, mkd pitch, pt sl, shd; wc; chem disp; shwrs inc; el pnts (5A) €3.50; gas; lndtte; shop; snacks; playgrnd; pool; rv sw adj; fishing, canoe hire & hang-gliding nrby; some statics; dogs €1.50; Eng spkn; adv bkg; red low ssn; CKE/CCI. "Excel site; gd san facs; pleasant, helpful owner; conv Tarn Gorges; lge mkt Fri." 1 Apr-30 Sep. € 20.50   2008*

MILLAU *10E1* (6km NE Rural) *44.15188, 3.09899* **Camping La Belle Etoile (formerly Camping d'Aguessac), Chemin des Prades, 12520 Aguessac [05 65 72 91 07 ou 06 72 23 10 56 (mob); fax 05 65 59 08 72; contact@camping-labelleetoile.fr; http:// camping-labelleetoile.fr]** Site on N907 in vill; ent on R v soon after level x-ing when app fr Millau. Alt approach fr J44.1 on A75 via D29, unmade rd fr A75 to Aguessa. Med, mkd pitch, pt shd; wc; chem disp; shwrs inc; el pnts (6A) inc; gas; lndtte; shops adj; bar; rv adj; fishing; canoeing; games area; sports grnd adj; wifi; entmnt; dogs €2; quiet; red long low ssn; CKE/CCI. "Nice, spacious, clean rvside site; gd position with mountain views; gd sized pitches; helpful & friendly staff; public footpath thro site along rv to picturesque vill; poss youth groups high ssn; excel touring base; V gd location" ♦ 15 May-20 Sep. € 16.00   2012*

MILLAU *10E1* (8.5km NE Rural) *44.16861, 3.11944* **Camping Les Cerisiers, Pailhas, 12520 Compeyre [05 65 59 87 96 or 05 65 59 10 35 (LS); contact@campinglescerisiers.com; www.campinglescerisiers.com]** Fr Millau N on D809 for 4km, then D907 to Pailhas; site at exit to vill on R. Med, mkd pitch, pt shd; wc; chem disp; shwrs inc; el pnts (6A) €3; lndry rm; shop; tradsmn; snacks; playgrnd; private beach on Rv Tarn; pool 3km; rock climbing; canoeing, mountain biking, paragliding & horseriding nrby; games rm; wifi; entmnt; 5% statics; dogs €1.50; phone; poss cr; Eng spkn; adv bkg; quiet; ccard acc; red low ssn; CKE/CCI. "Vg, clean site; helpful staff; birdwatching; Millau tourist train; conv Tarn gorges." ♦ ltd 1 May-15 Sep. € 15.00   2011*

MILLAU *10E1* (1km E Rural) *44.11552, 3.08692* **Camping Club Le Millau-Plage, Route de Millau-Plage, 12100 Millau [05 65 60 10 97; fax 05 65 60 16 88; info@ campingmillauplage.com; www.campingmillauplage.com]** Exit Millau on D991 (sp Nant) over Rv Tarn; at rndabt take final exit onto D187 sp Paulhe; site is 4th on L. Lge, mkd pitch, pt shd; wc; chem disp; shwrs inc; el pnts (5A) inc; gas; lndtte; shop; tradsmn; rest, snacks; bar; playgrnd; pool; multi-sports area; TV; play rm; 40% statics; dogs €3; poss cr; Eng spkn; adv bkg; quiet; ccard acc; red low ssn; CKE/CCI. "Magnificent scenery." ♦ 1 Apr-30 Sep. € 26.00   2008*

MILLAU *10E1* (1km E Urban) *44.10287, 3.08732* **Camping des Deux Rivières, 61 Ave de l'Aigoual, 12100 Millau [05 65 60 00 27 or 06 07 08 41 41 (mob); fax 05 65 60 76 78; camping.deux-rivieres@orange. fr / camp2rivieres@yahoo.fr; www.camping-des-deux-rivieres.fr]** Fr N on D911 foll sp for Montpellier down to rv. At rndabt by bdge turn L over bdge, site immed on L well sp. Fr S on D992 3rd bdge, sp camping. Sm, mkd pitch, shd; htd wc (50% cont); chem disp; shwrs inc; el pnts (8-10A) €3. (poss long lead req); gas; lndry rm; shops adj; tradsmn; snacks; playgrnd; fishing;dog €1.50; phone; poss cr; quiet; ccard not acc; red low ssn; CKE/CCI. "Basic site in gd situation by rv; friendly, helpful owners; gd san facs; gd base for touring gorges" 1 Apr-29 Oct. € 28.20   2013*

MILLAU *10E1* (1km E Rural) *44.10166, 3.09611* **Camping Les Rivages, Ave de l'Aigoual, 12100 Millau [05 65 61 01 07 or 06 10 75 65 94 (mob); fax 05 65 59 03 56; info@ campinglesrivages.com; www.campinglesrivages.com]** Fr Millau take D991 dir Nant (sp Gorges de la Dourbie & Campings). Cross Rv Tarn & cont on this rd, site is 500m after bdge on R. Lge, pt shd; htd wc (some cont); chem disp (wc); mv service pnt; serviced pitches (additional charge); baby facs; shwrs inc; el pnts (10A) inc (poss rev pol); lndtte (inc dryer); shop; supmkt 2km; tradsmn; rest, snacks; bar; BBQ (on legs only); playgrnd; 2 pools; spa; rv sw adj - shingle beaches; tennis & squash; fishing; canoeing nr; hang-gliding; games area; wifi; entmnt; games/TV rm; 10% statics; dogs €4; twin-axles acc (rec check in avd); phone; poss cr; Eng spkn; adv bkg; quiet; ccard acc over €30; red low ssn/long stay; CKE/ CCI. "Pleasant, busy, scenic site - esp rv/side pitches; helpful & friendly staff; gd san facs; vg rest/snack bar - home cooked & inexpenssive; gd security; views of Millau viaduct; easy access to town; mkt Wed & Fri." ♦ 15 Apr-30 Sep. € 34.00 SBS - D20   2011*

MILLAU *10E1* (2.5km E Rural) *44.10029, 3.11099* **FFCC Camping St Lambert, Ave de l'Aigoual, 12100 Millau [05 65 60 00 48; camping.saintlambert@orange.fr; www. campingsaintlambert.fr]** Fr N on either D809 or D11 foll dir D992 St Affrique/Albi. Turn L at rndabt over bdge onto D991 dir Nant. Site on R, sp. Fr S on D992 turn R at rndabt & dir as above. Med, mkd pitch, shd; wc (some cont); chem disp; mv service pnt; shwrs inc; el pnts (6A) €2.80; gas; lndtte; shop; bar; playgrnd; sm pool; sand/shgl beach & rv sw adj; wifi; 10% statics; dogs €1; poss cr; adv bkg; quiet; ccard acc; red low ssn; CKE/CCI. "Spacious site; gd low ssn; owners pleasant & helpful; twin-axles not acc." 1 May-30 Sep. € 15.50   2010*

MILLY LA FORET *4E3* (4km SE Rural) *48.39569, 2.50380* **Camping La Musardière, Route des Grandes Vallées, 91490 Milly-la-Forêt [01 64 98 91 91; fax 01 64 98 37 01; lamusardiere91@orange.fr]** Fr S exit A6 junc 14 onto D152 then D16 dir Milly; Rte des Grande Vallées is R turn 2km after Noisy-sur-Ecole (4km bef Milly). Look for 'Domain Regional' sps (not easy to read). Fr N exit A6 junc 13 onto D372 to Milly; exit Milly S on D16; Rte des Grandes Vallées turning to L in 1.5km. Site on L 1km along Rte des Grandes Vallées. Best app fr N. Lge, mkd pitch, hdstg, pt sl, pt shd; htd wc (some cont); chem disp; baby facs; fam bthrm; shwrs inc; el pnts (6A) inc; lndtte; shop 4km; tradsmn (w/end only low ssn); BBQ; playgrnd; htd pool/waterpark high ssn; paddling pool; cycle hire; 70% statics; dogs free; Eng spkn; adv bkg; ccard acc; red long stay; CKE/ CCI. "Wooded site; excel pools; helpful, friendly staff; gd walks in nrby forest." ♦ 15 Feb-15 Nov. € 22.20   2011*

MIMIZAN *7D1* (2km N Rural) *44.21997, -1.22968* **Camping du Lac, Ave de Woolsack, 40200 Mimizan [05 58 09 01 21; fax 05 58 09 43 06; lac@mimizan-camping.com; www. mimizan-camping.com]** Fr Mimizan N on D87, site on R. Lge, mkd pitch; pt shd; sandy; wc; chem disp; mv service pnt; baby facs; shwrs inc; el pnts (3A) inc; gas; lndtte; shop; (rest, snacks; bar; high ssn only); BBQ; playgrnd; sand beach 6km; lake adj - no sw; boating; fishing; entmnt; some statics; dogs €1.70; poss cr; adv bkg; quiet; red low ssn. "Nice site in lovely location; o'night area for m'vans; rec." ♦ ltd 27 Apr-20 Sep. € 20.15   2012*

MIMIZAN *7D1* (3km E Rural) *44.22296, -1.19445* **Camping Aurilandes, 1001 Promenade de l'Etang, 40200 Aureilhan [05 58 09 10 88 or 05 46 55 10 01; fax 05 46 55 10 00; www.village-center.com]** Fr N10 S of Bordeaux take D626 W fr Labouheyre twds Mimizan. Site 1km fr D626 by Lake Aureilhan. V lge, mkd pitch, pt shd; wc; mv service pnt; sauna; shwrs inc; el pnts (6-10A) inc; lndtte; shop; tradsmn; rest; playgrnd; htd pool complex; paddling pool; spa; sand beach 10km; dir access to lake; watersports; tennis; games rm; entmnt; statics; dogs €3; Eng spkn; adv bkg; ccard acc; quiet; ccard acc. ♦ 27 Apr - 09 Sep. € 44.00 (CChq acc)   2013*

"Satellite navigation makes touring much easier"

Remember most sat navs don't know if you're towing or in a larger vehicle – always use yours alongside maps and site directions.

MIMIZAN PLAGE *7D1* (700m E Coastal) *44.21629, -1.28584* **Camping de la Plage, Blvd d'Atlantique, 40200 Mimizan-Plage [05 58 09 00 32; fax 05 58 09 44 94; contact@ mimizan-camping.com; www.mimizan-camping.com]** Turn off N10 at Labouheyre on D626 to Mimizan (28km). Approx 5km after Mimizan turn R. Site in approx 500m. V lge, pt sl, shd; wc; mv service pnt; baby facs; shwrs; el pnts (10A) inc; lndtte (inc dryer); shop; BBQ; playgrnd; sand beach 850m; games area; wifi; entmnt; 20% statics; dogs €1.80; poss cr; no adv bkg; noisy. "Gd facs; town nrby. ♦ 2 Apr-26 Sep. € 20.50   2010*

MIMIZAN PLAGE *7D1* (3km E Coastal) *44.20420, -1.2908* **Club Marina-Landes, Rue Marina, 40202 Mimizan-Plage-Sud [05 58 09 12 66; fax 05 58 09 16 40; contact@ clubmarina.com; www.marinalandes.com]** Turn R off N10 at Labouheyre onto D626 to Mimizan (28km). Approx 5km fr Mimizan-Plage turn L at Camping Marina sp on dual c'way. Site sp on S bank of rv. V lge, hdg pitch, hdstg, pt shd; wc; chem disp; mv service pnt; baby facs; shwrs inc; el pnts (10A) €7; gas; lndtte; ice; shop; rest, snacks; bar; BBQ; playgrnd; 2 pools (1 htd, covrd); paddling pool; waterslide; sand beach 500m; tennis; horseriding; games area; cycle hire; games rm; fitness rm; golf 7km; wifi; entmnt; TV rm; some statics; dogs €5; poss cr; Eng spkn; adv bkg; ccard acc; quiet; red CKE/CCI. "Excursions to Dax, Biarritz & Bordeaux areas; excel leisure facs; vg." ♦ 1 May-12 Sep. € 42.00 (3 persons)   2010*

MIOS see Audenge *7D1*

MIRAMBEAU *7C2* (500m N Urban) *45.37822, -0.56874* **Camp Municipal Le Carrelet, 92 Ave de la République, 17150 Mirambeau [05 46 70 26 99]** Exit 37 fr A10 onto D730/D137 dir Mirambeau. Site opp Super U supmkt, behind tourist office. Sm, pt sl, pt shd; wc (cont); chem disp (wc); mv service pnt;; shwrs inc; el pnts (10A) €4 (poss rev pol); gas; lndtte; shops, rest adj; mostly statics; dogs €1.50; quiet. "Basic site; clean but tired facs; obliging warden; site yourself & warden calls evening; v muddy when wet; poss neglected low ssn; conv NH for A10." 1 Apr-31 Oct. € 11.00   2009*

MIRAMBEAU 7C2 (8km S Rural) 45.31430, -0.60290 **Camping Chez Gendron, 33820 St Palais [tel/fax 05 57 32 96 47; info@chezgendron.com; www. chezgendron.com]** N fr Blaye on N137; turn to St Palais, past church 1km; turn L twd St Ciers. Site sp R down narr lane. Or N fr Bordeaux on A10 exit juncs 37 or 38 onto N137 to St Palais & as above. Sm, mkd pitch, terr, pt sl, pt shd; htd wc; chem disp; shwrs; fam bthrm; el pnts (6A) inc; lndtte; shops 3km; tradsmn; rest, snacks; bar; BBQ; playgrnd; pool; paddling pool; games area; tennis 3km; games rm; wifi; TV; dogs free; phone; Eng spkn; adv bkg rec; quiet; red low ssn; CKE/CCI. "Peaceful & relaxed site in vineyards; lovely ambience; friendly, helpful Dutch owners; sep car park high ssn; superb san facs; ltd facs low ssn; pitches nr bar/recep poss noisy till late peak ssn; poss waterlogged after heavy rain; chem disp poor; excel Sun mkt."
♦ 1 Mar-31 Oct. € 18.00   2012*

⊞ **MIRAMBEAU** 7C2 (11km W Coastal) 45.38333, -0.72250 **Camping L'Estuaire, La Grange Godinet, 17150 St Thomas-de-Cônac [05 46 86 08 20; fax 05 46 86 09 18; info@lestuaire.com; www.lestuaire.com]** Exit A10 junc 37 Mirambeau onto D730 dir Royan. At St Ciers-du-Taillon foll sp St Thomas-de-Cônac, site sp. Lge, hdg/mkd pitch, unshd; htd wc; chem disp; mv service pnt; baby facs; shwrs inc; el pnts (5A) inc; lndtte (inc dryer); shop; tradsmn; rest, snacks; bar; BBQ; playgrnd; pool complex; padding pool; fishing; watersports nr; tennis; cycle hire; games area; gym; entmnt; TV rm; 60% statics; dogs €4; adv bkg; quiet. "Interesting area nr Gironde estuary; gd walking & cycling." ♦ € 20.00 (CChq acc)   2010*

⊞ **MIRAMONT DE GUYENNE** 7D2 (13km W Rural) 44.62918, 0.22126 **Camping Parc St Vincent, 47120 Lévignac-de-Guyenne [05 53 83 75 17 or 01425 275080 (UK); sara.batchelor777@orange.fr; www.psv47.com]** Fr Miramont take D668 to Allemans-du-Dropt, then D211. At junc D708 turn S to Lévignac, site sp. Fr Marmande N on D708 sp St Foy & Duras. Turn E at Lévignac church to further green site sp on D228. Sm, hdstg, pt shd; wc; chem disp; mv service pnt; shwrs inc; el pnts (5A) €2; gas; lndtte; shops 2.5km; tradsmn; rest, snacks; BBQ; playgrnd; pool; lake sw 6km; entmnt; TV rm; 90% statics; no dogs; phone; adv bkg; quiet; red low ssn; CKE/CCI. "Peaceful site; British owners make visitors welcome; gd NH or longer to/fr Spain." ♦ € 13.00   2010*

MIRAMONT DE GUYENNE 7D2 (6km NW Rural) **Camp Municipal Le Dropt, Rue du Pont, 47800 Allemans-du-Dropt [05 53 20 25 59 or 05 53 20 23 37 (Mairie); fax 05 53 20 68 91]** Fr D668 site well sp in vill. Sm, shd; wc (some cont); chem disp (wc); shwrs inc; el pnts (20A) €2; shop 400m; rest, snacks & bar 400m; playgrnd; canoeing, kayaking; quiet, but poss noise fr canoe/kayak pnt on site; CKE/CCI. "Attractive site on opp side of Rv Dropt to vill; friendly warden; ltd pitches for c'vans & lge o'fits due trees & o'hanging branches; basic but clean facs; excel." 1 Apr-15 Oct. € 7.00   2012*

MIRANDE 8F2 (1km NE Rural) 43.55235, 0.31371 **Camping Pouylebon (Devroome), Pouylebon, 32320 Montesquiou [05 62 66 72 10; campingpouylebon2@wanadoo.fr; http:// campingpouylebon.pagesperso-orange.fr]** Exit N21 NW at Mirande onto D159; in 10km, at Pouylebon, turn R onto D216; in 900m site on R, 600m down track. Sm, pt sl, pt shd; wc; chem disp; shwrs inc; el pnts (6A) €2.85; lndtte; ice; sm shop & 12km; snacks; bar; BBQ; playgrnd; pool; tennis, fishing & horseriding nr; games area; games rm; wifi; TV rm; dogs free; poss cr; Eng spkn; adv bkg; ccard not acc; red low ssn. "Rural retreat; charming, Dutch owners; meals on request; excel." 15 Apr-15 Oct. € 26.10   2013*

MIRANDE 8F2 (500m E Rural) 43.51432, 0.40990 **Camp Municipal L'Ile du Pont, Au Batardeau, 32300 Mirande [05 62 66 64 11; fax 05 62 66 69 86; info@camping-gers. com; www.camping-gers.com]** On N21 Auch-Tarbes, foll sp to site on island in Rv Grande Baise. Med, pt shd; htd wc (some cont); chem disp; mv service pnt; baby facs; shwrs inc; el pnts (6-10A) inc; lndtte (inc dryer); tradsmn; rest, snacks; bar; BBQ; playgrnd; pool; waterslides; canoeing; sailing; windsurfing; fishing; cycle hire; tennis; games rm; entmnt; 20% statics; dogs €1; adv bkg rec; quiet; red low ssn; ccard not acc; CKE/CCI. "Excel site; helpful staff." 15 May-15 Sep. € 17.60   2010*

MIRANDE 8F2 (10km NW Rural) 43.56500, 0.31972 **Camping Château Le Haget, Route de Mielan, 32320 Montesquiou [05 62 70 95 80; fax 05 62 70 94 83; info@ lehaget.com; www.lehaget.com]** SW fr Mirande on N21 for 9km. At Renault g'ge turn R onto D16, then immed R onto D34 sp Montesquiou. Site on L in 11km. Rec do not use D943 fr Auch. Med, hdg/mkd pitch, pt sl, pt shd; htd wc (some cont); chem disp; shwrs inc; el pnts (10A) €4; lndtte; rest, snacks; bar; playgrnd; pool; games area; games rm; 60% statics; dogs €3; Eng spkn; adv bkg; quiet; cc acc; CKE/CCI. "Wooded site full of wildlife & flowers; lge pitches, but poss access problems for lge o'fits; excel rest." 1 May-30 Sep. € 20.00 (3 persons)   2011*

MIREPOIX (ARIEGE) 8F4 (1km E Rural) 43.08871, 1.88585 **Camping Les Nysades, Route de Limoux, 09500 Mirepoix [05 61 60 28 63; fax 05 61 68 89 48; campinglesnysades@ orange.fr; www.camping-mirepoix-ariege.com]** E fr Pamiers on D119 to Mirepoix. Site well sp on D626. Med, hdg/mkd pitch, shd; wc; chem disp; shwrs; el pnts (6A) €3.50; shops 1km; pool; fishing 1km; tennis; some statics; dogs €2; quiet; red low ssn. "Lge pitches; gd san facs; interesting medieval town; mkt Mon; gd little site, walks along rv; Barrier open 07:00-23:00, if warden not on site he will collect fees later" ♦ 16 Apri-31 Oct. € 15.00   2012*

MITTLACH see Munster 6F3

CAMPING DE L'ÎLE DU BIDOUNET

Camping*** de l'Ile du Bidounet at Moissac welcomes you in a very beautiful park to enjoy a peaceful and natural holiday at the banks of the river Tarn. At 2 km of the historic town of Moissac, our park is ideally located to discover the South West and the Quercy. On site: swimming pool from April 15, fresh bread, hot showers, heated sanitary cabins in low season, washing machine, free WiFi zone.

St Benoît, 82200 Moissac (France)
Tel +33 (0)5 63 32 52 52
camping-bidounet@moissac.fr - www.camping-moissac.com

MODANE *9C4* (10km NE Rural) *45.22870, 6.78116* **Camp Municipal Val d'Ambin, Plan de l'Eglise, 73500 Bramans-le-Verney [04 79 05 03 05 or 06 16 51 90 91 (mob); fax 04 79 05 23 16; campingdambin@aol.com; www.camping-bramansvanoise.com]** 10km after Modane on D1006 twd Lanslebourg, take 2nd turning R twd vill of Bramans, & foll camping sp, site by church. App fr Lanslebourg, after 12km turn L at camping sp on D306 at end of vill. Med, unshd; htd wc; baby facs; shwrs; el pnts (12-16A) €3.70-5.20; lndtte (inc dryer); shops, rest, snacks, bar nr; BBQ: playgrnd; pool 10km; games area; entmnt; TV; some statics; dogs €1.60; no adv bkg; quiet. "Away-from-it-all site worth the climb; beautiful area; gd dog walk adj." 1 May-30 Oct. € 10.60   2010*

⊞ **MODANE** *9C4* (1km W Rural) *45.19437, 6.66413* **Camping Les Combes, Refuge de La Sapinière, Route de Bardonnèche, 73500 Modane [04 79 05 00 23 or 06 10 16 54 61 (mob); fax 04 79 05 00 23; camping-modane@wanadoo.fr; http://camping-modane.chez-alice.fr]** Exit A43 junc 30 onto D1006 thro Fourmeaux to o'skirts Modane; at Casino supmkt turn R onto D215; site in 500m on bend on hill (at junc with D216). Fr Fréjus tunnel site on L 1km bef Modane. Med, pt sl, pt shd; htd wc (some cont); chem disp; shwrs inc; el pts (6A) €3; lndtte; shop 1km; tradsmn; snacks; bar; playgrnd; pool 1km; tennis; winter sports; wifi; 10% statics; dogs €1.50; quiet. "Excel & conv NH for Fréjus tunnel; warm welcome; superb scenery; low ssn recep opens 1700 - site yourself." € 13.00   2011*

MOELAN SUR MER see Pont Aven *2F2*

MOIRANS EN MONTAGNE *9A3* (900m S Rural) *46.41980, 5.72381* **Camping Le Champ Renard, Ave de St Claude, 39260 Moirans-en-Montagne [03 84 42 34 98; fax 03 84 42 60 50; camping.champ.renard@wanadoo.fr; http://champ.renard.pagesperso-orange.fr/]** Fr St Claude foll Lons-Lyon rd (D436 to D470) to Moirans-en-Montagne (approx 25km by rd). Site opp sm indus est. Steep access rds. Med, mkd pitch, mainly sl, terr, pt shd; wc; shwrs inc; el pnts (6A) €2.60; shops 2km; tradsmn; snacks; bar; BBQ; playgrnd; pool; shgl beach & lake 6km; games area; dogs €1.20; adv bkg; some rd noise; CKE/CCI. "Friendly, helpful staff; 1 of better sites in area; attractive town & lake; pleasant sp walks." 15 Mar-15 Oct.   2008*

MOIRANS EN MONTAGNE *9A3* (5km NW Rural) *46.46833, 5.68864* **Camping Trélachaume, Lac de Vouglans, 39260 Maisod [tel/fax 03 84 42 03 26; www.trelachaume.com]** Fr St Claude take D436 NW past Moirans-en-Montagne; turn L onto D301 to Maisod; site well sp. Lge, mkd pitch, pt sl, pt shd; wc; chem disp; baby facs; shwrs inc; el pnts (5A) €2.70; lndtte; shop; tradsmn; rest, snacks; bar; BBQ; adventure playgrnd; paddling pool; lake sw/sand beach 800m; games rm; entmnt; 10% statics; dogs €1.50; phone; poss cr; Eng spkn; adv bkg; quiet; ccard acc; CKE/CCI. "Beautiful, uncrowded part of France; helpful owners; excel." ◆ 19 Apr-6 Sep. € 14.10   2008*

MOISSAC *8E3* (1.5km S Rural) *44.09664, 1.08878* **Camping De L'Ile du Bidounet, St Benoit, 82200 Moissac [tel/fax 05 63 32 52 52; info@camping-moissac.com; www.camping-moissac.com]** Exit A62 at junc 9 at Castelsarrasin onto N113 dir Moissac, site sp. Or fr N on N113 cross Rv Tarn, turn L at 1st rndabt & foll camp sp, site on L by rv. NB Height restriction 3.05m for tunnel at ent & tight turn lge o'fits. Med, hdg/mkd pitch, some hdstg, shd; wc (some cont); chem disp; mv service pnt; baby facs; shwrs; el pnts (6A) €3.10; gas 2km; lndtte; shop, rest & snacks 2km; tradsmn; bar; BBQ; playgrnd; pool (high ssn); fishing; watersports; boat & canoe hire; cycle hire; wifi; entmnt; 10% statics; dogs €1.50; phone; Eng spkn; adv bkg; quiet; ccard acc; red low ssn/long stay; CKE/CCI. "Excel rvside site in lovely area; extra for twin-axles; pitches tight lge o'fits; helpful staff; basic, clean san facs; conv lovely town & abbey; gd fishing; walking/cycling; vg cycle track by canal." ◆ 1 Apr-30 Sep. € 15.80   2012*

See advertisement

MOLIERES (DORDOGNE) see Lalinde *7C3*

MOLIERES (TARN ET GARONNE) *8E3* (1.5km E Rural) *44.18480, 1.38790* **Camping Domaine des Merlanes, 82220 Molières [05 63 67 64 05; fax 05 63 24 28 96; simone@domaine-de-merlanes.com; www.domaine-de-merlanes.com]** Fr N on N20, exit on D20 to Montpezat-de-Quercy & Molières; sp in vill. Sm, terr, pt shd; wc; chem disp; baby facs; shwrs; el pnts (6A) inc; tradsmn; rest; bar; playgrnd; htd pool; 10% statics; dogs €3; poss cr; Eng spkn; quiet; red low ssn; ccard acc; CKE/CCI. "Pleasant, Dutch owners; clean, well-kept site; excel children's facs; adv bkg ess high ssn; excel." 25 Apr-5 Sep. € 32.80   2009*

La Saint Martin
Camping & Caravan site ★★★★

2 swimming pools
1 heated indoor pool & Spa-Sauna
Chalets rental (2 to 6 persons)
Open from Easter to 1ˢᵗ November

DIRECT ACCESS TO THE BEACH

Tél. +33 (0)5 58 48 52 30 - MOLIETS PLAGE - Website: www.camping-saint-martin.fr

MOLIETS ET MAA *8E1* (2km W Coastal) *43.85166, -1.38375*
Camping Les Cigales, Ave de l'Océan, 40660 Moliets-Plage
[05 58 48 51 18; fax 05 58 48 53 27; reception@camping-
les-cigales.fr; www.camping-les-cigales.fr] In Moliets-et-
Maa, turn W for Moliets-Plage, site on R in vill. Lge, pt sl, shd;
wc; chem disp; mv service pnt; shwrs inc; el pnts (5A) €3.50;
lndtte; shop; tradsmn; rest, snacks; bar; BBQ; playgrnd; sand
beach 300m; games area; TV; many statics; dogs €2; adv bkg;
quiet; ccard acc; CKE/CCI. "Site in pine wood - sandy soil; narr
access tracks; excel beach & surfing; many shops, rests 100m."
1 Apr-30 Sep. € 25.00   2009*

MOLIETS ET MAA *8E1* (2km W Coastal) *43.85210, -1.38730*
Camping St Martin, Ave de l'Océan 40660 Moliets-Plage
[05 58 48 52 30; fax 05 58 48 50 73; contact@camping-
saint-martin.fr; www.camping-saint-martin.fr] On N10
exit for Léon, Moliets-et-Maa. At Moliets foll sp to Moliets-
Plage. Camp site after Les Cigales, by beach. V lge, hdg/mkd
pitch, pt sl, terr, pt shd; htd wc (some cont); chem disp; some
serviced pitches; baby facs; sauna; shwrs inc; el pnts (10A)
€5.30; gas; lndtte; shops; supmkt; rests; snacks; bar; playgrnd;
3 pools (1 htd, covrd); paddling pool; jacuzzi; dir access to sand
beach 300m; rv 250m; watersports; tennis; golf nr; games area;
cycle paths; entmnt; TV rm; dogs €5 (free low ssn); Eng spkn;
adv bkg rec high ssn (fee); quiet; ccard acc; red low ssn; CKE/
CCI. "Excel family site; vg san facs; gd for teenagers; gd cycling,
walking." 8 Apr-1 Nov. € 43.30   2011*

See advertisement

MOLOMPIZE see Massiac *9C1*

MOLSHEIM *6E3* (E Urban) *48.54124, 7.50003* **Camp**
Municipal de Molsheim, 6 Rue des Sports, 67120
Molsheim [03 88 49 82 45 or 03 88 49 58 58 (LS); fax
03 88 49 58 59; camping-molsheim@orange.fr; www.
mairie-molsheim.fr] On ent town fr Obernai on D1422 site
sp on R immed after x-ing sm rv bdge. Med, mkd pitch, pt shd;
wc; chem disp; mv service pnt; shwrs inc; el pnts (10A) €3;
lndtte; tradsmn; BBQ; pool adj; cycle hire; dogs €1.30; train
to Strasbourg 700m; poss cr; Eng spkn; adv bkg; quiet, but
poss rock concerts nrby Sat in summer; red low ssn; CKE/CCI.
"Pleasant site; san facs unisex low ssn. easy walk to town cent
& shops; Bugatti museum in town;" ◆ 8 Apr-16 Oct &
1 - 25 Dec. € 12.80   2011*

MONASTIER SUR GAZEILLE, LE *9C1* (1km SW Rural)
44.93662, 3.98453 **Camping Estela, Route du**
Moulin de Savin, 43150 Le Monastier-sur-Gazeille
[06 87 48 60 28 04 71 03 82 24 (mob); contact@
campingestela.com] Fr Le Puy-en-Velay E on D535; in 4km
fork R continuing on D535 to Le Monastier-sur-Gazeille; site
sp fr ent to vill. App only fr N end of vill. Site in bottom of
valley; gd power-weight ratio needed on departure. Sm, pt
shd; wc; shwrs; el pnts (3-10A) €3.20; lndtte; tradsmn; snack
bar; BBQ; playgrnd; rv sw; dog €2.50; wifi; quiet. "Lovely rvside
site in beautiful area; friendly staff; Le Monastier was start
of R. L. Stevenson's `Travels with a Donkey'." 1 Jun-30 Sep.
€ 18.20   2013*

MONBALEN *7D3* (Rural) **Ferme Equestre Crinière au**
Vent, Bouillon, 47340 Monbalen [05 53 95 18 61 or
06 70 68 79 92 (mob); www.criniereauvent.com] Site
15km N Agen & 13km S Villeneuve-sur-Lot. Fr Agen, take N21
N dir Villeneuve-sur-Lot. In approx 15km turn R onto D110 s
Laroque-Timbaut & foll 'Camping' sp. Fr Villeneuve-sur-Lot, take
N21 S dir Agen. In approx 10km turn L onto D110 sp Laroque-
Timbaut & foll 'Camping' sp. Sm, pt sl, shd; wc (some cont);
chem disp; shwrs inc; el pnts (10A) €2.20; lndry rm; tradsmn; bar
(soft drinks only); horseriding; no statics; dogs €1; little Eng spkn;
no ccard acc; CKE/CCI. "Owner v pleasant; horseriding for all
ages on site; vg." ◆ 15 Apr-30 Sep. € 8.20   2009*

MONCEAUX SUR DORDOGNE see Argentat *7C4*

MONDRAGON see Bollène *9D2*

MONESTIER DE CLERMONT *9C3* (700m SW Urban)
44.91515, 5.62809 **Camping Les Portes du Trièves,**
Chemin de Chambons, 38650 Monestier-de-Clermont
[04 76 34 01 24/ 04 76 34 06 20 (ls); fax 04 76 34 19 75;
camping.lesportesdutrieves@wanadoo.fr; www.
campingisere.com] Turn W off D1075. Sp in vill. 700m up
steep hill adj sw pool & school. Fr Grenoble take A51 to S
end of vill & foll sps to site. Sm, hdg/mkd pitch, hdstg, terr,
pt shd; htd wc; chem disp; mv service pnt; shwrs inc; el pnts
(6A) €2.70; lndtte (inc dryer); shop, rest, snacks & bar 800m;
playgrnd; htd pool 200m; tennis adj; lake 10km; games rm;
wifi; dogs free; bus 500m; quiet; Eng spkn; adv bkg; red long
stay; CKE/CCI. "Attractive, immac, well-run site; friendly,
helpful staff; clean san facs but sm; watersports at lake;
spectacular countryside; train to Grenoble; gd NH."
1 May-30 Sep. € 20.90   2013*

MONETIER LES BAINS, LE *9C3* (1km NW Rural) *44.98010, 6.49515* **Camp Municipal Les Deux Glaciers, 05220 Le Monêtier-les-Bains [04 92 46 10 08 or 06 83 03 70 72; fax 04 92 24 52 18; camping.monetier@orange.fr; www. monetier.com]** On D1091 12km NW of Briançon; pass thro Le Monêtier-les-Bains, in 1km site sp on L. Med, mkd pitch, hdstg, terr, shd; htd wc; chem disp; mv service pnt; baby facs; shwrs inc; el pnts (16A) €3.50; lndtte; tradsmn; shop, rest, snacks bar in vill 1km; playgrnd; dogs €1; phone 500m; bus 1km; adv bkg; red low ssn; CKE/CCI. "Excel, scenic site bef x-ing Montgenèvre pass; gd base for Ecrins National Park; easy access fr D1091; footpath to vill; vg." ♦ ltd Dec-Apr & Jun-Sep. € 14.00   2008*

MONFORT *8E3* (100m N Urban) *43.79628, 0.82315* **Camp Municipal de Monfort, 32120 Monfort [tel/fax 05 62 06 83 26 (Mairie); mairiemonfort@orange.fr]** SE fr Fleurance on D654 to Monfort, then foll sp to 'Centre Ville' & camping sp. Town has narr rds so foll sp & v narr app rd. Sm, hdg pitch, pt sl, pt shd; wc; chem disp (wc); shwrs inc, el pnts (5A) €1.50; shop, rest & bar 200m; BBQ; playgrnd; no twin-axles; dogs €0.50; quiet; ccard not acc; CKE/CCI. "Well-kept, scenic, CL-type site on ramparts of attractive Bastide vill; pitch yourself, warden calls am & pm; ltd pitches big enough for c'van; long walk to waste disposal; excel; pitches well prepd and solid" 1 May-15 Oct. € 9.50   2013*

MONISTROL D'ALLIER *9C1* (4km N Rural) *44.99148, 3.67781* **Camp Municipal Le Marchat, 43580 St Privat-d'Allier [04 71 57 22 13; fax 04 71 57 25 50; info@mairie-saintprivatdallier.fr; www.mairie-saintprivatdallier.fr]** Fr Le Puy-en-Velay W on D589. Turn R in cent of vill at petrol stn, site on R in 200m. Sm, hdg pitch, terr, shd; wc; chem disp; shwrs inc; el pnts (10A) €1.10; shops, bar in vill; playgrnd; quiet. "Beautifully-kept site; poss unkempt low ssn; not suitable lge o'fits." ♦ ltd 1 May-1 Nov. € 6.10   2009*

MONISTROL D'ALLIER *9C1* (S Rural) *44.96912, 3.64793* **Camp Municipal Le Vivier, 43580 Monistrol-d'Allier [04 71 57 24 14 or 04 71 57 21 21 (Mairie); fax 04 71 57 25 03; mairie-monistroldallier@wanadoo.fr; www.monistroldallier.com]** Fr Le Puy-en-Velay W on D589 to Monistrol-d'Allier. Turn L in vill immed after rlwy stn & cont down steep entry rd bef x-ing bdge. Site sp in town cent. Sm, mkd pitch, pt shd; wc; chem disp; shwrs inc; el pnts (5-10A) €2.60; shops, rest, snacks; bar 200m; BBQ; dogs; phone; train 500m; quiet; CKE/CCI. "Vg site steep valley." ♦ ltd 15 Apr-15 Sep. € 12.00   2008*

MONISTROL SUR LOIRE *9C1* (7km SE Rural) *45.21630, 4.21240* **Kawan Village Camping de Vaubarlet, 43600 Ste Sigolène [04 71 66 64 95; fax 04 71 66 11 98; camping@vaubarlet.com; www.vaubarlet.com]** Fr Monistrol take D44 SE twd Ste Sigolène & turn R into vill. In vill take D43 dir Grazac for 6km. Site by Rv Dunière, ent L bef bdge. Site well sp fr vill. Med, mkd pitch, pt shd; wc; chem disp; mv service pnt; shwrs inc; el pnts (6A) €3 (poss rev pol); lndtte (inc dryer); shop & 6km; tradsmn; rest, snacks; bar; BBQ; playgrnd; htd pool; paddling pool; rv sw adj; trout fishing; cycle hire; games area; wifi; entmnt; TV rm; 15% statics; phone; dogs €1; Eng spkn; adv bkg; quiet; red low ssn; ccard acc; CKE/CCI. "Friendly, helpful staff; well-run site; excel san facs; interesting museums nrby." ♦ 1 May-30 Sep. € 19.00 (CChq acc)   2010*

MONNERVILLE *4E3* (2km S Rural) *48.33256, 2.04702* **Camping Le Bois de la Justice, Méréville, 91930 Monnerville [01 64 95 05 34; fax 01 64 95 17 31; picquetfredo@orange.fr; http://campingboislajustice. pagesperso-orange.fr/]** Fr N20 S of Etampes, turn onto D18 at Monnerville, site well sp. Long narr app rd. Med, hdg/mkd pitch, pt sl, pt shd; htd wc; chem disp (wc); shwrs inc; el pnts (5A) €2.50; lndtte; snacks high ssn; bar; BBQ; cooking facs; playgrnd; htd pool high ssn; tennis; games area; TV rm; 50% statics; dogs €1; phone; Eng spkn; adv bkg; quiet; red low ssn; ccard acc. "Delightful woodland oasis in open countryside; beware caterpillars in spring (poisonous to dogs); friendly welcome; clean san facs; ideal for Chartres, Fontainebleau, Orléans, Paris or excel NH just off N20." ♦ 4 Feb-26 Nov. € 19.50   2012*

MONPAZIER *7D3* (3km SW Rural) *44.65875, 0.87925* **Camping Moulin de David, Route de Villeréal, 24540 Gaugeac-Monpazier [05 53 22 65 25 or 04 99 57 20 25; fax 05 53 23 99 76; contact@moulindedavid.com; www. moulindedavid.com]** Fr Monpazier, take D2 SW twd Villeréal, site sp on L after 3km. Narr app rds. Lge, hdg/mkd pitch, pt shd; htd wc; chem disp; mv service pnt; serviced pitches; baby facs; shwrs inc; el pnts (10A) inc gas; lndtte; shop; tradsmn; rest, snacks; bar; BBQ €8.; playgrnd; pool; paddling pool; lake sw & waterslide high ssn; fishing adj; tennis; games area; wifi; games/TV rm; cycle hire; archery; internet; entmnt; many statics; dogs €3; poss cr; Eng spkn; adv bkg; quiet; ccard acc; red low ssn; CKE/CCI. "Charming site nr lovely town; welcoming, helpful owners; excel facs, ltd low ssn; poss mosquitoes nr rv thro site; mkt Thu Monpazier; highly rec." ♦ 30 Mar-30 Sep. € 35.10   2013*

MONS LA TRIVALLE *10F1* **Camp Municipal de Tarassac, 34390 Mons-la-Trivalle [04 67 97 72 64; communemonslatrivalle@orange.fr]** Fr D908 turn S onto D14, sp Béziers; site off D14 on Rv Orb. Lge, mkd pitch, hdstg, pt sl, shd; wc (some portacabin); shwrs inc; el pnts; lndtte; tradsmn; rest, snacks; bar; shop; playgrnd; rv sw & fishing adj; playgrnd; dogs; phone; 10% statics; poss cr; quiet. "Fair sh stay; watersports cent adj; pitches bounded by boulders; beautiful area; Site a bit unkept; v natural envir; vg" € 14.50   2012*

MONSIREIGNE see Chantonnay *2H4*

MONT DORE, LE *7B4* (500m NW Urban) *45.57711, 2.80387* **Camp Municipal des Crouzets, 4 Ave des Crouzets, 63240 Le Mont-Dore [tel/fax 04 73 65 21 60 or 04 73 65 22 00 (Mairie); camping.crouzets@orange.fr; www.mairie-mont-dore.fr]** Take D130 fr Bourboule to Le Mont-Dore; site ent just on L after entering town. Poor sps. Lge, mkd pitch, hdstg, pt sl, unshd; htd wc; chem disp; mv service pnt adj; shwrs inc; el pnts (10A) €4.10 (poss rev pol); lndtte; tradsmn; shops & rests adj; BBQ; playgrnd; pool 4km; sports area; dogs €1.60; poss cr; Eng spkn; ccard acc; red low ssn. "Well-run site in town cent, but quiet; gd sized pitches; excel san facs; helpful warden; gd touring base; cable car to Puy de Sancy." ♦ 19 Dec-30 Sep. € 9.55   2010*

MONT DORE, LE

MONT DORE, LE 7B4 (1.5km NW Urban) 45.58685, 2.80098
Camp Municipal L'Esquiladou, Le Queureuilh, Route
des Cascades, 63240 Le Mont-Dore [04 73 65 23 74 or
04 73 65 20 00 (Mairie); fax 04 73 65 23 74; camping.
esquiladou@orange.fr; www.mairie-mont-dore.fr]
Fr Mont-Dore cent, take D996 dir La Bourboule (not D130).
Pass 'La Poste' on L & at rlwy stn app turn R, then L at T-junc
onto D996. In Queureuilh fork R at 'Route Cascades' sp, then
foll camping sp. Med, hdg/mkd pitch, hdstg, terr, pt shd;
htd wc; chem disp; mv service pnt; shwrs inc; el pnts (6-10A)
€2.80-4.10; gas; lndtte; shops 1km; tradsmn; BBQ; playgrnd;
pool; dogs €1.50; phone; adv bkg; ccard acc; red low ssn; CKE/
CCI. "V pleasant, well-run, quiet site; gd views; excel san facs;
gd mountain walks; poss itinerants; run down; like lge carpark,
but conv." ♦ ltd 26 Apr-18 Oct. € 9.85   2008*

MONT LOUIS 8G4 (3.5km N Rural) 42.51971, 2.09713
Camping Rural du Pla de Barrès, Route des Bouillouses,
66210 La Llagonne [04 68 04 26 04 or 04 68 04 21 97 (TO);
otmontlouis@wanadoo.fr; www.mont-louis.net/camping.
htm] Leave Mont-Louis N dir La Llagonne & Formiguères;
800m after rndabt (D118 junc with D618) turn L onto D60
& foll sp Lac des Bouillouses. Site sp on L at top of hill; cont
for 1km. Lge, pt shd; wc (cont); shwrs; el pnts (6A) €3.50;
playgrnd; paddling pool; rv sw adj; fishing; dogs €1; quiet; red
low ssn. "Most of site in pine forest; v busy high ssn; modern
san facs; ground poss rocky & boggy; poss mosquitoes;
beautiful area." ♦ 15 Jun-15 Sep. € 10.60   2010*

MONT LOUIS 8G4 (5km W Rural) 42.50636, 2.04671
Camping Huttopia Font-Romeu, Route de Mont-Louis,
66120 Font-Romeu [04 68 30 09 32; fax 04 68 04 56 39;
fontromeu@huttopia.com; www.huttopia.com]
W fr Mont-Louis on D618. Site on L bef Font-Romeu, opp
stadium. Fr Aix-les-Thermes or Puigcerdà turn E at Ur up
longish hill, thro town to site on R at o'skts. Lge, sl, pt shd; htd
wc; shwrs; el pnts (6-10A) €4.20-6.20; lndtte; shop; rest, bar
(w/ends); htd pool; paddling pool; tennis 500m; horserieing
1km; internet; entmnt; some statics; dogs €3.50; phone;
adv bkg; quiet. "Gd cent for mountain walks; site at 1800m
altitude." 19 Jun - 14 Sep. € 22.00 SBS - D29   2013*

MONT ST MICHEL, LE 2E4 (8km E Rural) 48.62820, -1.41450
Camping St Michel, Route du Mont-St Michel, 50220
Courtils [02 33 70 96 90; fax 02 33 70 99 09; infos@
campingsaintmichel.com; www.campingsaintmichel.
com] Fr E exit A84 junc 33 to N175. Take D43 coast rd
fr Pontaubault twds Le Mont-St Michel. Site in vill of Courtils
on L. Med, hdg/mkd pitch, some hdstg, pt sl, pt shd; htd wc;
chem disp; mv service pnt; baby facs; shwrs inc; el pnts (6A)
€3.50; gas; lndtte; shop; rest, snacks; bar; BBQ; playgrnd;
htd pool; sand beach 8km; cycle hire; games rm; internet;
entmnt; some statics; dogs €1; phone; bus adj; poss cr; Eng
spkn; adv bkg; quiet; ccard acc; red low ssn; CKE/CCI. "Excel,
flat site; helpful owner; excel modern san facs (unisex); cycle
paths adj; gd NH for St Malo." ♦ 5 Feb-14 Nov. € 19.50
(CChq acc)   2010*

MONT ST MICHEL, LE 2E4 (2km S Rural) 48.61476, -1.50887
Camping du Mont St Michel, 50150 Le Mont St Michel
[02 33 60 22 10; fax 02 33 60 20 02; stmichel@le-mont-
saint-michel.com; /www.ot-montsaintmichel.com]
Located at junc of D976 (Pontorson/Le Mont St Michel) with
D275, behind Hotel Vert. Lge, hdg/mkd pitch, pt shd; wc; chem
disp; mv service pnt; shwrs inc; baby facs; el pnts (5A) €2.80
(poss long lead req); gas; lndtte (inc dryer); lge supmkt & rest
adj; snacks; bar; playgrnd; sand beach 2km; fishing; cycle hire;
TV; dogs; phone; adv bkg; Eng spkn; ccard acc; red low ssn/
CKE/CCI. "Well-located, well-kept site; book in at hotel recep,
friendly & helpful; excel san facs; no provision to fill Aquaroll
etc; vg shady pitches behind hotel; poss noisy - lge m'van area
on opp side D275 quieter, closes end Sep; some pitches diff
due trees; poss muddy after heavy rain; gd walking & cycling;
beach at 2km reported unsafe for sw (quicksand)." ♦
5 Feb-12 Nov. € 15.10   2011*

MONT ST MICHEL, LE 2E4 (4km S Rural) 48.59622, -1.51244
Camping aux Pommiers, 28 Route du Mont-St Michel, 50170
Beauvoir [tel/fax 02 33 60 11 36; pommiers@aol.com;
www.camping-auxpommiers.com] N fr Pontorson foll D976
sp Le Mont St Michel. Site 5km on R on ent vill of Beauvoir.
Med, hdg/mkd pitch, pt shd; htd wc (some cont); chem
disp; mv service pnt; shwrs inc; el pnts (6A) €4.00; gas; lndtte;
shop; supmkt 4km; tradsmn; snacks; bar; BBQ; playgrnd; htd
pool; waterslide; sand/shgl beach 2km; tennis 900m; games
area; games rm; cycle hire; wifi; entmnt; TV; 30% statics; dogs
€1.20; Eng spkn; adv bkg; quiet; ccard acc; red low ssn/CKE/
CCI. "Busy site, rec arr early; friendly, helpful staff & owner;
tired clean facs; gd touring base; easy cycle ride to Mont
St Michel or pleasant walk." 30 Mar-11 Nov. € 24.80   2012*

MONTAGNAC 10F1 (500m E Rural) 43.48200, 3.48893 Camp
Municipal La Piboule, 9 Chemin de la Piboule, 34530
Montagnac [04 67 24 01 31] Exit A75 junc 59 Pézenas onto
D613 E to Montagnac. Site sp to E of Montagnac. Narr app rds
& parked cars unsuitable/v diff lge o'fits. Best app fr E on D5.
Med, hdg/mkd pitch, pt sl, pt shd; wc (cont); shwrs inc; el pnts
(10A) €3.20; lndry; shop, rest, snacks, bar 800m; playgrnd;
phone; CKE/CCI. "Clean san facs; short walk to pretty vill; diff
lge o'fits." 15 May-31 Oct. € 10.00   2009*

MONTAGNAC 10F1 (4km SE Rural) 43.45175, 3.51600
Camping Domaine St Martin-du-Pin, 34530 Montagnac
[04 67 24 00 37; fax 04 67 24 47 50; www.saint-martin-du-
pin.com] Exit A75 junc 59 onto D113 to Montagnac; 2km past
Montagnac turn R immed past picnic site at end of dual c'way,
site sp. Sm, hdg pitch, pt sl, pt shd; wc; chem disp; mv service
pnt; baby facs; shwrs inc; el pnts €3.50; lndtte; shop 4km;
tradsmn; BBQ; playgrnd; pool; games area; few statics; no
dogs; Eng spkn; adv bkg advised; quiet; CKE/CCI. "Delightful,
relaxing site; lge pitches, blocks req on most; clean facs; gd
touring base; beautiful views" ♦ 21 Mar-15 Oct. € 23.00
(CChq acc)   2013*

MONTAGNAC MONTPEZAT see Riez 10E3

MONTAGNY LES LANCHES see Annecy 9B3

FRANCE

MONT DORE, LE

394 ⊞Site open all year   Tell us about the sites you visit

MONTAIGU 2H4 (10km SE Rural) 46.93769, -1.21975
Camping L'Eden, La Raillière, 85600 La Boissière-de-Montaigu [02 51 41 62 32; fax 02 51 41 56 07; contact@domaine-eden.fr; www.domaine-eden.fr] Fr Montaigu S on D137, in 8km turn E on D62, thro Le Pont-Legé. Site sp on L off D62. Med, mkd pitch, shd; wc (some cont); shwrs inc; el pnts (10A) inc; gas; lndtte; shop & 4km; rest, snacks; bar; playgrnd; htd pool; tennis; entmnt; TV; 40% statics; dogs €2; poss cr; adv bkg; site poss open all year; red low ssn CKE/CCI. "Pleasant, quiet site in woodlands; clean facs; motor mover useful; excel." ♦ ltd 1 Mar-15 Nov. € 21.00   2009*

MONTALIEU VERCIEU 9B2 (1.5km NE Rural) 45.82756, 5.42052
Camp Municipal La Vallée Blue, 38390 Montalieu-Vercieu [04 74 88 63 67; fax 04 74 88 62 11; camping.valleebleue@wanadoo.fr; www.camping-valleebleue.com] S fr Ambérieu-en-Bugey on D1075; in 15km (nr Porcieu-Amblagnieu) site sp on L. Med, pt sl, pt shd; wc (some cont); chem disp; mv service pnt; shwrs; el pnts (6A) €3; gas; lndtte; sm shop; tradsmn; snacks; playgrnd; htd pool; aquapark; paddling pool; games area; dogs €1.90; phone; bus; ccard acc; red low ssn/long stay; CKE/CCI. "Immed access to Rv Rhône; conv NH fr D1075; vg." ♦ ltd 4 Apr-25 Oct. € 15.00   2009*

MONTARGIS 4F3 (2km NE Urban) 48.00821, 2.74965
Camp Municipal de la Forêt, 38 Ave Chautemps, 45200 Montargis [02 38 98 00 20] Heading N on N7 at town boundary take R fork sp with camping symbol. Med, mkd pitch, hdstg, shd; htd wc (some cont); shwrs inc; el pnts (5-10A) €2.90-5.80; shop 200m; playgrnd; pool adj; 50% statics; quiet. "Spacious pitches; facs dated but clean; poss muddy when wet; gate/recep closes 1900; no c'vans over 6m; conv for train to Paris; NH only." 1 Feb-30 Nov. € 9.50   2008*

MONTAUROUX see Fayence 10E4

MONTBARD 6G1 (1km W Urban) 47.6314, 4.33303
Camp Municipal Les Treilles, Rue Michel Servet, 21500 Montbard [03 80 92 69 50; fax 03 80 92 21 60; camping.montbard@wanadoo.fr; www.montbard.com] Lies off N side D980. Camping sp clearly indicated on all app including by-pass. Turn onto by-pass at traff lts at rndabt at junc of D905 & D980. Site nr pool. Med, hdg/mkd pitch, pt shd; wc; chem disp; shwrs inc; el pnts (16A) €4; lndry rm; shop 1km; supmkt 300m; tradsmn; BBQ; snacks; playgrnd; pool complex adj inc; cycle hire; rv sw 100m; dogs €1; phone; poss cr; quiet but rd/rlwy noise at far end; CKE/CCI. "Pleasant & well-kept site; gd pitches; lge, smart san facs; poss contract worker campers; quiet low ssn; interesting area; excel NH." ♦ 1 Mar-23 Oct. € 15.90   2011*

MONTBARREY 6H2 (1km SW Rural) 47.01230, 5.63161
FLOWER Camping Les Trois Ours, 28 Rue du Pont, 39380 Montbarrey [contact@camping-les3ours-jura.com; www.camping-les3ours-jura.com or www.flowercampings.com] Exit A39 junc onto D905 E; 1km after Mont-sur-Vaudrey on D472 turn L dir Montbarrey. Cross rv, site on L at rvside on edge of vill. Med, hdg/mkd pitch, shd; htd wc; chem disp; mv service pnt; baby facs; shwrs inc; el pnts (10A) inc; lndtte; shop 3km; rest, snacks; bar; BBQ; playgrnd; pool; games rm; wifi; TV; 10% statics; dogs; phone; bus; Eng spkn; adv bkg; quiet; ccard acc. "Improvements planned; vg walking/cycling fr site." ♦ 1 May-30 Sep. € 18.90   2010*

MONTBAZON 4G2 (300m N Rural) 47.29044, 0.71595
Camping de la Grange Rouge, 37250 Montbazon [02 47 26 06 43; fax 02 47 26 03 13; infos@camping-montbazon.com; www.camping-montbazon.com] On D910 thro Montbazon fr S to N, after x-ing bdge (part of D910) immed turn L to site. Clearly visible & clearly sp on W side of rd at N end of town. Med, mkd pitch, pt shd; wc (male cont); chem disp; shwrs inc; el pnts (10A) €4; lndtte; shops 300m; tradsmn; rest & bar adj; playgrnd; sm htd pool; fishing; tennis; TV rm; some statics; dogs €1.20; Eng spkn; adv bkg; quiet; ccard acc; red low ssn; CKE/CCI. "Lovely, rvside site in pretty town; helpful, friendly owner; basic facs dated but clean; conv Tours & a'routes." ♦ 2 Apr-29 Oct. € 15.50   2011*

MONTBAZON 4G2 (2km E Rural) 47.28924, 0.73436
Camping de la Plage, 37250 Veigné [02 47 26 23 00; fax 02 47 73 11 47; campingveigne@aol.com; www.touraine-vacance.com] Exit A10 junc 23 dir Montbazon onto D910. N of Montbazon after 'Les Gues' turn SE onto D50 to Veigné & site. Site in 2km on R at rvside. Med, mkd pitch, pt shd; htd wc; chem disp; mv service pnt; baby facs; shwrs, el pnts (10A) €4.50; gas 200m; lndtte; shop 200m; rest, snacks; BBQ; playgrnd; htd pool high ssn; canoeing; fishing; games area; entmnt; 13% statics; dogs €1.20; phone; Eng spkn; adv bkg; quiet, some rd/rwly noise; ccard acc; red low ssn/long stay; CKE/CCI. "Rvside site nr vill; gd san facs; gd for Loire chateaux & Tours; gd walking & cycling; site used as short cut by locals; poss clsd Oct, phone ahead." ♦ 1 Apr-31 Oct. € 13.10   2009*

MONTBERT 2H4 (500m SE Rural) 47.05133, -1.47930
Camping Le Relais des Garennes (Gendron), La Bauche Coiffée, 44140 Montbert [tel/fax 02 40 04 78 73; phgendron@wanadoo.fr; www.gites-de-france-44.fr/relais_garennes] Fr Nantes on N937 dir La Roche, at Geneston turn L dir Montbert & foll site sp. Or fr Nantes on N137 dir La Rochelle turn R at Aigrefeuille-sur-Maine for Montbert. Sm, mkd pitch, pt shd; htd wc; chem disp; baby facs; fam bthrm; shwrs inc; el pnts (10A) €2.50; lndry rm; htd pool 1km; tennis, sports facs nrby; sm lake; lake fishing adj; dogs; Eng spkn; adv bkg; quiet; CKE/CCI. "Peaceful, picturesque site; lge pitches; friendly owners; immac facs, but no individual wash rms; rabbits & hens on site; toys for children; many attractions nrby; pleasant walk to town; gd value; highly rec." ♦ 1 Jun-30 Sep. € 8.50   2010*

MONTBIZOT see Beaumont sur Sarthe 4F1

MONTBLANC see Béziers 10F1

⊞ **MONTBOUCHER** 7B4 (2km N Rural) **Camping La Chassagne (C J Camping), 23400 Montboucher** [05 55 64 22 87; cjcamping@aliceadsl.fr; www.cjcamping.com] W fr Bourganeuf on D951 for approx 5km, turn R at Elan g'ge sp Montboucher. Take 1st R sp Les Martys, go thro vill & up hill, turn L (sm house on L). Take next L & after La Chassagne vill sp foll 2 L-hand bends. Site on next R-hand bend. Sm, hdg, sl, pt shd; htd wc; chem disp; fam bthrm; shwrs inc; el pnts (10A) inc; lndtte; shops & rest 5km; fishing, tennis & golf 5km; dogs; adv bkg; quiet; CKE/CCI. "Well-kept CL-type site in beautiful area; friendly, helpful British owners; clean facs; levelling blocks req; excel touring base; adv bkg rec; mv service pnt in vill; excel." € 12.00   2010*

See advertisement on pages 32 & 33

FRANCE

MONTBRISON *9B1* (1.5km S Urban) *45.59133, 4.07806*
Camp Municipal Le Surizet, 31 Rue du Surizet, Moingt, 42600 Montbrison [04 77 58 08 30; fax 04 77 58 00 16] Fr St Etienne on D8, at rndabt junc with D204 turn L sp St Anthème & Ambert. Cross rlwy & turn R in 400m, site sp. Med, pt shd; wc; chem disp; mv service pnt; shwrs; el pnts (5-10A) inc; lndtte; shop 1km; BBQ sep area; playgrnd; pool; fishing; pool; tennis 2km; 60% statics; dogs €0.85; bus (every hr); quiet; adv bkg; CKE/CCI. "Pleasant, well-kept site; no twin-axles; vg value; highly rec NH or sh stay." 15 Apr-15 Oct. € 12.70   2009*

MONTBRISON *9B1* (2km W Rural) *45.59896, 4.04259*
Camping Le Bigi, Vinols, 42600 Bard [tel/fax 04 77 58 06 39; andre.drutel@orange.fr; www.camping-le-bigi.fr] Fr Montbrison cent take D113 twd Bard, site sp. Sm, hdg/mkd pitch, sl, terr, pt shd; wc; chem disp; mv service pnt; shwrs inc; el pnts (5A) inc; lndtte; tradsmn; playgrnd; htd pool; tennis; 60% statics; dogs €1.10; poss cr; CKE/CCI. "Helpful owner; well-run, delightful site in landscaped garden nr medieval town; no twin-axle c'vans." ♦ 31 May-15 Sep. € 14.50   2008*

"That's changed – Should I let The Club know?"

If you find something on site that's different from the site entry, fill in a report and let us know. See www.caravanclub.co.uk/europereport.

MONTBRON *7B3* (11km NE Rural) *45.74042, 0.58678* **Camping de l'Etang, Les Geloux, 16310 Le Lindois [05 45 65 02 67; fax 05 45 65 08 96; www.campingdeletang.com]** Fr S take D16 N fr Montbron, in 9km turn R onto D13, in 3km turn R onto D27. Site sp in vill opp lake. Sm, hdg/mkd pitch, pt sl, pt shd; htd wc; chem disp; baby facs; shwrs inc; el pnts (16A) €4.50; gas inc; lndtte; sm shop; rest, snacks; bar; sm library; playgrnd; lake sw & fishing; beach adj; dogs €1.50; phone; Eng spkn; adv bkg rec high ssn; ccard acc; quiet; CKE/CCI. "Loads of wildlife in attractive surroundings. Very pleasant & resful. There is a bar & gd quality restaurant on site. gd Value, rec" 1 Apr-1 Nov. € 17.50   2013*

MONTBRON *7B3* (6km SE Rural) *45.65972, 0.55805*
Camping Les Gorges du Chambon, Le Chambon, 16220 Eymouthiers [05 45 70 71 70; fax 05 45 70 80 02; info@gorgesduchambon.fr; www.gorgesduchambon.fr or www.les-castels.com] Fr N141 turn SE onto D6 at La Rochefoucauld; cont on D6 out of Montbron; after 5km turn L at La Tricherie onto D163; foll camp sp to site in approx 1.9km. NB Fr La Tricherie narr in places & some sharp bends. Med, mkd pitch, some hdstg, pt sl, pt shd; htd wc; chem disp; mv service pnt; baby facs; shwrs inc; el pnts (10A) inc; gas; lndtte (inc dryer); shop; tradsmn; rest, snacks; bar; BBQ (gas/charcoal only); playgrnd; pool; paddling pool; sand/shgl beach 15km; rv fishing; canoe hire; tennis; cycle hire; horseriding, golf nrby; games area; entmnt; internet; games/TV rm; 25% statics; no dogs; twin-axles; Eng spkn; adv bkg; quiet; ccard acc; red long stay/low ssn; CKE/CCI. "Beautiful, 'away from it all', scenic site in grounds of old farm; welcoming, helpful & friendly staff; lge pitches but some sl; excel san facs; superb rest; gd mkd walks; birdwatching & wildlife; poss motorbike rally on site end June; excel." ♦ 21 Apr-15 Sep. € 45.00 SBS - D11   2012*

See advertisement

MONTBRUN *7D4* (200m W Rural) *44.50612, 1.89667*
Camping Les Cournoulises, 46160 Montbrun [06 15 53 00 58 (mob); lescournoulises@sfr.fr; http://lescournoulises.perso.sfr.fr] Site just off D662, S side; 100m W of Montbrun. Sm, mkd pitch, pt shd; wc; chem disp (wc); shwrs inc; el pnts (6A) €3; lndtte; tradsmn; café; shops, rest, snacks & bar 6km; BBQ sep area (charcoal); playgrnd; direct acces to rv; canoe hire; fishing; paragliding; trekking; pool & tennis nrby; games area; dogs €0.50; Eng spkn; adv bkg; quiet; ccard not acc; red long stay; CKE/CCI. "Lge pitches; teepee & trapper tents on site (for hire)." ♦ ltd 1 Jun-30 Sep. € 10.80   2013*

MONTBRUN LES BAINS *10E3* (500m E Rural) *44.17621, 5.44767* **Camp Municipal Le Pré des Arbres, 26570 Montbrun-les-Bains [04 75 28 85 41 or 04 66 46 22 43 (LS); fax 04 75 28 81 16; camping@montbrunlesbains.com; www.montbrunlesbainsofficedutourisme.fr]** Site well sp in Montbrun. Sm, mkd pitch, terr, pt shd; wc; shwrs; el pnts (15A) €3.40; pool, tennis adj; some statics; dogs; quiet. "Gd, clean site; warden visits; walking dist to pleasant town & spa; thermal baths; interesting area." 15 Mar-15 Nov. € 10.20   2011*

MONTCABRIER *7D3* (2km NE Rural) *44.54865, 1.08229* **Camping Le Moulin de Laborde, 46700 Montcabrier [05 65 24 62 06; fax 05 65 36 51 33; moulindelaborde@ wanadoo.fr; www.moulindelaborde.com]** Fr Fumel take D673 NE & site 1km past Montcabrier on L. Med, hdg pitch, pt shd; wc; chem disp; baby facs; shwrs inc; el pnts (6A) €3; gas; lndtte; shop; tradsmn; rest, snacks; bar; playgrnd; pool; sm lake; games area; cycle hire; wifi; entmnt; TV rm; no dogs; phone; poss cr; Eng spkn; adv bkg; quiet, but some noise fr rd & local quarry; ccard not acc; red low ssn. "Pleasant, peaceful site; friendly owners; gd facs; gd rest; many attractions & activities nrby; vg." ♦ 22 Apr-8 Sep. € 23.70   2011*

MONTCLAR (ALPES DE HAUTE PROVENCE) *9D3* (2km N Rural) *44.40925, 6.34811* **Yelloh! Village Etoile des Neiges, St Jean, 04140 Montclar [04 92 35 01 29 or 04 92 35 07 08; fax 04 92 35 12 55; contact@etoile-des-neiges.com; www.etoile-des-neiges.com or www. yellohvillage.co.uk]** On D900 turn S at St Vincent-les-Forts twd Col St Jean & Digne, site sp at the Col. Med, terr, shd; htd wc; mv service pnt; sauna; steam rm; shwrs inc; el pnts (6A) inc; lndtte; supmkt 200m; tradsmn; rest; bar; snacks; playgrnd; htd, covrd pools; rv fishing; tennis; games area; entmnt; TV rm; dogs €3; adv bkg rec winter & summer; quiet. "Ski stn in winter; steep access rds to pitches poss diff; excel." ♦ 27 May-11 Sep & 17 Dec-26 Mar. € 31.00   2008*

See advertisement on inside front cover

MONTCLAR (AUDE) see Carcassonne *8F4*

MONTELIMAR *9D2* (12km N Rural) *44.63716, 4.77319* **Camping Floral, Derbières, 26740 La Coucourde [04 75 90 06 69; info@campingfloral.com; www. campingfloral.com]** Exit A7 at junc 17 Montélimar Nord, S on N7 for 4km. Site sp S of vill. Steep, rough app. NB Across rv fr power station cooling towers. NB If app fr Montélimar on N7, camp sp pt obscured. Sm, mkd pitch, hdstg, pt sl, pt shd; wc; mv service pnt; shwrs inc; el pnts (6A) €2; gas; lndtte; sm shop; rest, snacks; bar; playgrnd; pool; entmnt; dogs €1; Eng spkn; rd & some rlwy noise; red low ssn; CKE/CCI. "Friendly, welcoming owners; clean, tidy site; facs poss stretched high ssn; hdstg poss too sm lge o'fits; san facs poss unclean early ssn & site run down; many resident workers; NH only." € 13.00   2008*

MONTENDRE *7C2* (5km N Rural) *45.33156, -0.39526* **The Vines Camping, Chez Penaud, 17130 Coux [05 46 48 95 55 or 06 42 45 34 99 (mob); barry.playford@orange.fr; www.vinescoux.com]** Exit A10 at Mirambeau onto D730 dir Montendre; then D19 dir Jonzac; then D253 dir Coux; do not turn into Coux vill but cont on D253; cross rlwy & then over x-rds; turn L at sp Chez Penaud; foll sps. NB D253 is long & winding. Sm, some hdstg, unshd; htd wc; chem disp; shwrs inc; el pnts (6A) inc; gas 4km; lndtte; shops etc 4km; BBQ; lake fishing & golf nrby; dogs; Eng spkn; adv bkg; quiet; red long stay. "Beautiful, well-kept, CL-type site; lge pitches; friendly British Caravan Club owners; gd touring base; wine tasting; vg." € 14.00   2011*

⊞ **MONTENDRE** *7C2* (4km NW Rural) *45.30037, -0.43495* **Camping Twin Lakes, La Faiencérie, 17130 Souméras [tel/ fax 05 46 49 77 12 or 0114 2463800 (UK); twinlakesinfo@ hotmail.co.uk; www.twinlakesfrance.com]** Exit N10/ E606 at Montlieu-la-Garde onto D730 thro Montendre dir Mirambeau; go past Souméras vill on R, site sp on L. Or exit A10 junc 37; turn R onto D730; at rndabt turn R onto N137; in Mirambeau turn L onto D730; site on R in approx 14 km. Sm, hdg pitch, pt sl, pt shd; wc; chem disp (wc); fam bthrm; shwrs inc; el pnts (10-16A) €3; gas; shops 2.5km; tradsmn; snacks; bar; BBQ; playgrnd; htd pool; paddling pool; lake fishing; games rm; TV rm; 15% statics; dogs €1.50; Eng spkn; adv bkg; quiet; red long stay; clsd 15 Dec-5 Jan. "Vg British-owned site; meals arranged; gd touring base; vg." ♦ € 17.00   2008*

MONTERBLANC see Vannes *2F3*

MONTEREAU FAULT YONNE *4E3* (3km W Rural) *48.37472, 2.90382* **Camping La Grande Paroisse, La Noue Notre-Dame, 77130 La Grande-Paroisse [01 60 57 02 02; fax 01 60 74 28 93; tourisme.cc2f@cc-deuxfleuves.fr; www. cc-deuxfleuves.fr]** Exit A5 junc 17 onto D210 then D605 S to Montereau. In Montereau take D39 W & foll sp La Grand-Paroisse & site on rvside. Med, hdg/mkd pitch, hdstg, pt shd; wc; chem disp; mv service pnt; shwrs; el pnts (4-13A) €3-6; shop; supmkt 2km; rest 5km; bar 2km; BBQ; playgrnd; pool 5km; sand beach 8km; sw & fishing adj; sailing, windsurfing & watersports; sailing school; games area; entmnt; 60% statics; dogs; adv bkg; quiet. "Well-situated site; conv Fontainebleau; excel fishing, walking & sailing; vg." ♦ 16 Mar-31 Oct. € 10.00   2009*

MONTESQUIOU see Mirande *8F2*

"I like to fill in the reports as I travel from site to site"

You'll find report forms at the back of this guide, or you can fill them in online at www.caravaclub.co.uk/europereport.

MONTESTRUC SUR GERS *8E3* (2km NE Rural) *43.79257, 0.64291* **Camping en Saubis (Daguzan), Route de Céran, 32390 Montestruc-sur-Gers [05 62 62 26 12; contact@ chambresdhotesgers.com; www.chambresdhotesgers. com]** S fr Fleurance on N21; after Montestruc-sur-Gers (immed past level x-ing) turn L onto D240; then turn R onto D251 for 1.5km, take R fork. Farm ent on L in 500m with conifer drive, site on L 50m. Sm, shd; wc; chem disp (wc); shwrs inc; el pnts (6A) €2.50 (long cable poss req); shops 2km; BBQ; playgrnd; golf 4km; 2 statics; dogs; poss cr; quiet. "Gd CL-type site with gd facs; peaceful farm with pleasant walks; friendly farmer." 15 Apr-15 Oct. € 6.50   2010*

MONTEUX see Carpentras *10E2*

FRANCE

FRANCE

MONTFAUCON *7D3* (2km N Rural) *44.69197, 1.53480*
Kawan Village Domaine de la Faurie, 46240 Séniergues [05 65 21 14 36; fax 05 65 31 11 17; contact@camping-lafaurie.com; www.camping-lafaurie.com] Fr N20 turn E onto D2 sp Montfaucon, or fr A20 exit junc 56. In 5km site sp. Rd to site (off D2) is 500m long, single-track with passing places & steep but passable. Well sp fr A20. Med, mkd pitch, pt sl, pt shd; htd wc; chem disp; mv service pnt; baby facs; shwrs inc; el pnts (6-10A) €4.50-6.70; Indtte (inc dryer); shop; rest; playgrnd; htd pool; paddling pool; cycle hire; games area; wifi; TV rm; 30% statics; dogs €3; Eng spkn; adv bkg; quiet; ccard acc; red low ssn. "Superb, pretty site with great views; quiet & peaceful; lge pitches; excel facs & rest; gd touring base; poss intermittent elec supply some pitches (2010); many walks; conv A20." ♦ 9 Apr-30 Sep. € 22.90 (CChq acc)   2010*

See advertisement

"We must tell The Club about that great site we found"

Get your site reports in by mid-August and we'll do our best to get your updates into the next edition of Caravan Europe.

MONTFERRAND *8F4* (2km N Rural) *43.3902, 1.8277*
FFCC Domaine St Laurent, Les Touzets, 11320 Montferrand [04 68 60 15 80 or 06 76 60 58 42 (mob); campingsaintlaurent@orange.fr; www.campingdomainesaintlaurent.fr] S fr Toulouse on N113/D1113 past Villefranche-de-Lauragais. Turn L onto D43 for 4.2km; then R to St Laurent. Or fr A20 onto D218 bypassing Montferrand & cont directly to St Laurent; turn L at church. Site well sp. Sm, some hdg pitch, pt shd; wc; chem disp; sauna; shwrs inc; el pnts (6A) inc; Indtte; shop; rest, snacks; bar; playgrnd; pool; tennis; archery; cycle hire; games rm; entmnt; TV rm; some statics; dogs €2; Eng spkn; adv bkg; quiet; ccard not acc; red low ssn. "Attractive, peaceful, well-kept site; clean san facs; friendly owners; gd views; woodland walks." 1 Apr-30 Oct. € 22.00   2012*

MONTFERRAND *8F4* (6km SE Rural) *43.31451, 1.80246*
Camping Le Cathare, Château de la Barthe, 11410 Belflou [04 68 60 32 49; fax 04 68 60 37 90; info@auberge-lecathare.com; www.auberge-lecathare.com] Fr Villefranche-de-Lauragais on N113/D6113, foll D622 sp Toulouse/Carcassonne over rlwy, , canal, then immed L on D625 for 7km. Thro St Michel-de-Lanes then take D33 to Belflou; foll sp to Le Cathare. Sm, mkd pitch, pt shd; wc (some cont); chem disp; shwrs inc; el pnts (3-10A) €3-7.50; shops 12km; tradsmn; rest in ferme auberge; snacks, bar 4km; lake sw 3km; sand/shgl beach; some statics; dogs €1.20; v quiet; CKE/CCI. "Poss long walk to basic san facs - sh timer for lts & might prefer to use your own facs; Centre Nautique on lake; dramatic position overlooking lake" 15 Apr-1 Nov. € 18.20   2012*

MONTFERRAT see Abrets, Les *9B3*

MONTFRIN *10E2* (500m NW Urban) *43.87980, 4.58917*
Camping Belle Rive, Cours Antelme, 30490 Montfrin [tel/fax 04 66 57 20 79 or 06 20 89 57 04 (mob); fredbissiere@hotmail.fr; www.campingbellerive.fr] Fr Pont-du-Gard on D986 dir Beaucaire. Or on D2 SW fr Avignon. Well sp in vill; by rv & sw pool. Med, mkd pitch, pt shd; wc; chem disp; mv service pnt; shwrs inc; el pnts (10A) €3 (poss rev pol); Indtte; rest 500m; snacks; bar; BBQ; playgrnd; pool adj; rv fishing; canoeing; tennis nrby; games area; games rm; wifi; entmnt; TV; 20% statics; dogs €1; no twin-axles; Eng spkn; adv bkg; quiet; red low ssn; CKE/CCI. "Peaceful, informal site in woodland by Rv Gardon; spacious & uncrowded; welcoming owner; friendly & laid back; nr interesting vill with bullring; conv Avignon, Arles, Nimes; vg." ♦ ltd 1 May-15 Sep. € 15.50   2010*

MONTGAILLARD see Foix *8G3*

MONTGEARD see Villefranche de Lauragais *8F3*

MONTGENEVRE see Briançon *9C4*

MONTHERME see Charleville Mézières *5C1*

Just a stone's throw from the Lascaux caves, the cradle of prehistory, and 10 minutes from Sarlat and its historic chateaux, our camping village welcomes you for an unforgettable holiday in the shade of the truffle oaks.

Fancy getting away from it all, a spot of culture, sports, or relaxation, with a swimming pool, jacuzzi and water slide? Our camping village is the ideal destination for your holidays with family or friends.

Camping **Lascaux Vacances** - 24290 Saint Amand de Coly - Périgord
Tél. 00 33 (0) 553 508 157 - Fax 00 33 (0) 553 507 626
Email : mail@campinglascauxvacances.com
Site : www.campinglascauxvacances.com

yelloh!

MONTIGNAC *7C3* (7km E Rural) *45.05375, 1.23980* Yelloh! Village Lascaux Vacances, Route des Malénies, 24290 St Amand-de-Coly [05 53 50 81 57; fax 05 53 50 76 26; mail@campinglascauxvacances.com; www.camping lascauxvacances.com or www.yellohvillage.co.uk] Exit A89 junc 17 (Peyrignac) SE onto D6089 to Le Lardin-St Lazare. Join D62 S to Coly & then foll sp to Saint Amand-de-Coly. Site well sp. Med, hdg/mkd pitch, pt shd; wc; chem disp; mv service pnt; sauna; baby facs; shwrs; el pnts (10A) inc; lndtte; supmkt; rest, snacks; bar; BBQ; playgrnd; pool complex; paddling pool; waterslides; fishing nr; cycle hire nr; games area; games rm; wifi; entmnt; TV; 60% statics; dogs €4; phone; adv bkg; quiet; ccard acc; red long stay/low ssn. "Excel, peaceful, renovated site in superb location; warm welcome; lge pitches; excel touring base." ♦ 15 Apr-11 Sep. € 33.00   2011*

See advertisement above

"I need an on-site restaurant"

We do our best to make sure site information is correct, but it is always best to check any must-have facilities are still available or will be open during your visit.

MONTIGNAC *7C3* (6.5km SE Rural) *45.07211, 1.23431* Camping La Tournerie Ferme, La Tournerie, 24290 Aubas [05 53 51 04 16; la-tournerie@orange.fr; www. la-tournerie.com] Fr Montignac on D704 dir Sarlat-la-Canéda; in 5.5km turn L onto C1 sp St Amand-de-Coly; in 1.6km at x-rds turn L sp Malardel & Drouille; in 400m at Y-junc foll rd to R sp Manardel & La Genèbre; cont on this rd ignoring minor rds; in 1.6km at elongated junc take rd to R of post box; immed after passing Le Treuil farm on R turn R at x-rds La Tournerie. Site opp farm. Sm, terr, hdstg, terr, sl, unshd; htd wc; chem disp; shwrs inc; el pnts (6A) inc; lndtte; shop 6.5km; rest, bar 2.5km; BBQ; dogs; adv bkg ess. "Lovely, tranquil site; adults only; lge pitches with beautiful views; dogs; friendly, helpful British owners (CC members); excel san facs; twin-axles OK; request detailed directions or see website - sat nav not rec; excel touring base; excel site" ♦ ltd 1 Mar-30 Nov. € 23.00   2013*

MONTIGNAC *7C3* (500m S Urban) *45.05980, 1.15860* Camping Le Moulin du Bleufond, Ave Aristide Briand, 24290 Montignac [05 53 51 83 95; fax 05 53 51 19 92; info@bleufond.com; www.bleufond.com] S on D704, cross bdge in town & turn R immed of rv on D65; site sp in 500m nr stadium, adj Rv Vezere. Med, hdg pitch, pt shd; wc (some cont); shwrs inc; el pnts (10A) €3.50; shops 500m; rest, snacks; bar; BBQ; htd pool high ssn; paddling pool; tennis adj; fishing; wifi; entmnt; dogs €2; poss cr; quiet; ccard acc; red low ssn. "Pleasant site; pleasant, helpful owners; facs excel; poss diff lge o'fits due trees; conv Lascaux caves & town; gd walking area; Lovely site, we will return" 1 Apr-15 Oct. € 31.40   2012*

MONTIGNAC *7C3* (7km S Rural) *45.01765, 1.18811* FFCC Camping La Fage, 24290 La Chapelle-Aubareil [tel/fax 05 53 50 76 50 / 06 87 37 5 891 (Mob); contact@camping-lafage.com; www.camping-lafage.com] Fr Montignac take D704 twd Sarlat. In approx 7km take 2nd rd L & foll camp sp to site ent thro woods, 1km bef La Chapelle. Med, some hdstg, pt sl, pt shd; wc; mv service pnt; baby facs; shwrs inc; el pnts (10A); lndtte (inc dryer); shop; tradsmn; rest, snacks; bar; BBQ; playgrnd; htd pool; paddling pool; games area; wifi; entmnt; TV; 30% statics; dogs €1.80; adv bkg; red low ssn/ CKE/CCI. "Excel site; helpful owners; vg, clean san facs; red facs low ssn; gd rest at auberge in vill; conv Lascaux 2 & other pre-historic sites; gd walking." ♦ 1 May-30 Sep. € 23.60 (CChq acc)   2013*

MONTIGNAC *7C3* (8km SW Rural) *45.04107, 1.11915* Camping La Castillonderie, 24290 Thonac [05 53 50 76 79; fax 05 53 51 59 13; castillonderie@wanadoo.fr; www. castillonderie.nl] Take D706 dir Les Eyzies. At rndabt in Thonac turn R onto D65 sp Fanlac in 1km after x-rd take R, site is sp 1.5km. Narr app rd. Med, hdg/mkd pitch, hdstg, pt sl, pt shd; htd wc; chem disp; mv service pnt; baby facs; fam bthrm; shwrs inc; el pnts (10A) €4; gas 5km; lndtte (inc dryer); sm shop & 2km; tradsmn; rest, snacks; bar; BBQ; playgrnd; pool; paddling pool; canoeing 3km; wifi; entmnt; TV rm; 10% statics; dogs €0.50; phone; Eng spkn; adv bkg; quiet; ccard acc; red low ssn; CKE/CCI. "Peaceful, well-kept site; friendly, helpful Dutch owners;on site lake fishing; canoeing 3km; gd cent for historic visits & walks." ♦ 15 May-15 Sep. € 23.00   2013*

See advertisement on next page

FRANCE

MONTIGNAC 7C3 (9km SW Rural) 45.00178, 1.07155
Camping Le Paradis, La Reybeyrolle, 24290 St Léon-sur-
Vézère [05 53 50 72 64; fax 05 53 50 75 90; le-paradis@
perigord.com; www.le-paradis.com] On W bank of Rv
Vézère on D706 Montignac-Les Eyzies rd, 1km fr Le Moustier.
D706 poss rough rd. Med, hdg pitch, pt shd; htd wc; chem disp;
mv service pnt; baby facs; shwrs inc; el pnts (10A) €3.50; lndtte
(inc dryer); shop; tradsmn; rest, snacks; bar; BBQ; playgrnd; 2 htd
pools; paddling pool; beach adj; boat hire; rv sw & fishing; tennis;
cycle hire; games area; wifi; entmnt; TV rm; 25% statics; dogs
€2.50; phone; poss cr; Eng spkn; adv bkg; poss rd noise; ccard
acc; red low ssn/long stay; CKE/CCI. "Excel, high standard site
in gd location; friendly, conscientious Dutch owners; immac san
facs; gd pool, rest & takeaway; vg for families; tropical vegetation
around pitches - grounds like a garden; excel, espec low ssn." ♦
26 Mar-20 Oct. € 27.90 (CChq acc)   2012*

See advertisement below

MONTIGNAC CHARENTE see Angoulême 7B2

MONTIGNY EN MORVAN 4H4 (2km E Rural) 47.15627,
3.87476 Camp Municipal Plat du Lac, Bonin, 58120
Montigny-en-Morvan [03 86 84 75 76; fax 03 86 84 73 05;
montignyenmorvan@free] N fr Château-Chinon on D944.
At Montigny take D303 on R sp Barrage de Pannecière. Foll sp
Bonin & site. Access fr D303 narr & not rec lge o'fits. Med, pt
sl, shd; wc; chem disp; shwrs; el pnts (10A) inc (poss rev pol);
tradsmn; lake sw; fishing; CKE/CCI. "Pitches poss soft after
rain." 1 May-30 Sep. € 11.90   2009*

MONTIGNY LE ROI 6F2 (1km N Rural) 48.00084,
5.49637 Camping du Château, Rue Hubert Collot,
52140 Montigny-le-Roi [tel/fax 03 25 87 38 93;
campingmontigny52@wanadoo.fr; www.
campingduchateau.com] Fr A31 junc 8 for Montigny-le-Roi.
Site well sp in cent vill on D74. Med, terr, pt shd; htd wc;
chem disp; mv service pnt; baby facs; shwrs inc; el pnts (5A)
€3; lndry rm; shop; snacks; bar; BBQ; playgrnd; tennis; cycle
hire; entmnt. "Modern facs; steep ent; rests & shops in vill." ♦
15 Apr-15 Oct. € 12.00   2008*

MONTJEAN SUR LOIRE see Chalonnes sur Loire 2G4

MONTLIEU LA GARDE 7C2 (8km N Rural) 45.30233,
-0.23228 Camp Municipal Bellevue, 17210 Chevanceaux
[05 46 04 60 03 or 05 46 04 60 09 (Mairie)] N fr Montlieu on
N10 to Chevanceaux in 7km; site by church & primary school in
vill. Sm, mkd pitch, pt sl, pt shd; wc; chem disp; shwrs inc;
el pnts (6A) inc; shops, rest, bar in vill; snacks high ssn;
BBQ (gas, elec); playgrnd; pool adj; tennis; quiet; CKE/CCI.
"Peaceful, clean site in pleasant vill; lge pitches; warden visits
am; no security; easy walk to vill; walking/cycling along disused
rlwy; poss problems with local youths (2010); gd NH."
1 Apr-30 Oct. € 11.00   2010*

MONTLIEU LA GARDE *7C2* (1km NE Rural) *45.24849, -0.25097* **Camp Municipal des Lilas, Roch, 17210 Montlieu-la-Garde [05 46 04 44 12 (Mairie); fax 05 46 04 50 91; montlieulagarde@mairie17.com]** On L N10 sp Montlieu-la-Garde; take D730 into vill. Turn L at multiple sp on corner (diff to see) & in 1km turn R & foll site sp. Site along vill lane. Sm, pt sl, pt shd; wc; shwrs; el pnts inc; tradsmn; shop in vill; pool 1km; quiet, some rd noise. "Vg NH; clean san facs."
1 May-30 Sep. € 8.00   2010*

MONTLUCON *7A4* (12km NW Rural) *46.37795, 2.46695* Camp Municipal Le Moulin de Lyon, 03380 Huriel [06 11 75 05 63 or 04 70 28 60 08 (Mairie); fax 04 70 28 94 90; marie.huriel@wanadoo.fr; www.huriel. planet-allier.com] Exit A71 junc 10 & foll sp Domérat, then D916 to Huriel. Site well sp. Or fr N D943 turn SW at La Chapelaude to Huriel on D40, foll sp to site. Last km single track (but can pass on level grass) with steep incline to site ent. Site adj Rv Magieure. Med, hdg pitch, pt sl, pt shd; wc (some cont); chem disp; shwrs; el pnts (10A) €2.40 (poss rev pol); gas; lndry rm; shops, tradsmn; snacks, bar 1km; BBQ; playgrnd (on other side of rv); lake/rv fishing; tennis; TV; few statics; Eng spkn; quiet. "Peaceful, wooded site in lovely setting by lake; well-kept; friendly; site yourself, warden calls am & pm; no apparent security; uphill walk to vill (1km); lovely quiet site, clean facs" 15 Apr-15 Oct. € 5.90   2013*

MONTMARAULT *9A1* (5km N Rural) *46.36698, 2.95234* Camping La Ferme La Charvière, 03390 St Priest-en-Murat [04 70 07 38 24; fax 04 70 02 91 27; robert.engels@ wanadoo.fr; www.lacharviere.nl] Exit A71 junc 11 at Montmarault onto D68 dir Sazeret/Chappes. Site 4km beyond Sazeret, sp. Sm, pt shd; wc; shwrs inc; el pnts (10A) €3.50; lndtte; rest; playgrnd; pool; dogs €1; adv bkg; quiet; red low ssn; CKE/CCI. "Helpful Dutch owner; v ltd facs low ssn; san facs, stretched if busy; poss open in winter - phone to check; easy access to m'way." 1 Apr-31 Oct. € 16.00   2008*

MONTMARAULT *9A1* (4.5km NE Rural) *46.35995, 2.99213* Camping La Petite Valette, La Vallette, 03390 Sazeret [04 70 07 64 57 or 06 80 23 15 54 (mob); la.petite.valette@ wanadoo.fr; www.valette.nl] Leave A71 at junc 11 & take 3rd exit at 1st rndabt onto D46; after 400m turn L at next rndabt, site sp on L in 3km. Or N of Montmarault in vill of Sazeret site well sp. Narr rd fr vill to site poss diff lge o'fits. Easy to find. Med, hdg/mkd pitch, pt shd; htd wc; chem disp; baby facs; fam bthrm; shwrs inc; el pnts (6A) €2.95; gas; lndtte (inc dryer); tradsmn; rest (high ssn); snacks; bar; BBQ; playgrnd; htd pool; paddling pool; cycle hire; fishing; games area; dogs €2; Eng spkn; adv bkg; quiet; red low ssn. "Attractive, popular, well-run site; a bit isolated; Dutch family owners; spacious, clean san facs; gd rest; grassy pitches muddy when wet; pleasant walks; vg." ♦ 1 Apr-3 Oct. € 17.85   2011*

MONTMARAULT *9A1* (9km NE) *46.38107, 3.03926* **Camp Municipal, 03240 Deux-Chaises [04 70 47 12 33 or 04 70 47 12 74 (Mairie); fax 04 70 47 31 33; mairie-deux-chaises@pays-allier.com; www.auvergne-tourisme.info]** Exit A71 junc 11 onto N79 dir Moulins; in 8km turn off N79 to Deux-Chaises. Site in vill, well sp. Sm, hdg pitch, terr, pt sl, unshd; wc; shwrs; el pnts (16A) €2; shop; rest & bar 200m; playgrnd; tennis; lake fishing adj. "Well-kept site in beautiful setting; gd, basic facs; warden calls for fees pm; phone to check open bef arr, esp low ssn; vg rest nrby; gd NH."
1 Apr-30 Sep. € 10.50   2013*

MONTMAUR *9D3* (500m E Rural) *44.56866, 5.88326* Camping Mon Repos, Le Cadillon, 05400 Montmaur [04 92 58 03 14; campingmonrepos@gmail.com] Fr D994 Veynes-Gap, foll D937 N, turning R at bdge to keep on D937. Site sp. Sm, pt sl, shd; wc; chem disp; mv service pnt 6km; shwrs inc; el pnts (2-5A) €2-3; gas; lndtte; shop; tradsmn; snacks; playgrnd; pool 6km; entmnt; TV rm; 30% statics; dogs €1; quiet; Eng spkn; CKE/CCI. "Friendly, family-run site; excel walking." ♦ ltd 1 May-30 Sep. € 10.00   2009*

⊞ **MONTMAUR** *9D3* (7km SE Rural) *44.55003, 5.95114* **Camping au Blanc Manteau, Route de Céüse, 05400 Manteyer [02 97 57 82 56]** Take D994 fr Veynes twd Gap, past Montmaur; site sp fr vill of La Roche-des-Arnauds on D18 in 1km. Sm, mkd pitch, pt shd; htd wc (some cont); chem disp; baby facs; shwrs inc; el pnts (10A) €5.35; lndtte; shops 750m; snacks; bar; playgrnd; htd pool; tennis; adv bkg. "Gd sized pitches; some daytime rd noise; pleasant owner." ♦ 2010*

MONTMEDY *5C1* (500m NW Urban) *49.52126, 5.36090* Camp Municipal La Citadelle, Rue Vauban, 55600 Montmédy [03 29 80 10 40 (Mairie); fax 03 29 80 12 98; mairie.montmedy@wanadoo.fr; www.montmedy.fr] Fr D643 foll sp to Montmédy cent & foll site sp. Steep app. Sm, hdg pitch, pt sl, pt shd; wc; chem disp; shwrs inc; el pnts (5-10A) €2.80-3.97; lndry facs; shops 1km; tradsmn; playgrnd; dogs €1.90; phone; quiet; red long stay/low ssn; CKE/CCI. "Warden calls am & pm; facs clean, ltd low ssn; nr Montmedy Haut fortified town; 10A hook-up not avail high ssn; vg."
1 May-30 Sep. € 11.90   2010*

MONTMELIAN *9B3* (12km NE Rural) *45.55861, 6.16944* Camping Le Lac de Carouge, 73250 St Pierre-d'Albigny [tel/fax 04 79 28 58 16; campinglacdecarouge@orange.fr; www.campinglacdecarouge.fr] Exit A43 junc 23 dir St Pierre-D'Albigny; site ent on 2nd rndabt 3km bef vill. Med, hdg/mkd pitch, pt shd; wc; chem disp; baby facs; shwrs inc; el pnts (10A) €3; lndtte; shop 1km; tradsmn; rest; snacks & bar adj; playgrnd; rv sw adj; 20% statics; dogs €1.50; phone; Eng spkn; adv bkg; some rlwy noise; ccard acc; red low ssn; CKE/CCI. "By lake surrounded by mountains; v lge pitches; friendly owners; excel facs; vg." ♦ ltd 25 Apr-15 Sep. € 15.00   2008*

MONTMELIAN *9B3* (5km SE Rural) *45.47745, 6.04111* **FFCC Camping L'Escale, La Gare, 73800 Ste Hélène-du-Lac [04 79 84 04 11 or 06 20 40 32 22 (mob); campingescale@ wanadoo.fr; www.camping-savoie-escale.com]** Exit A43 junc 22 onto D923 dir Pontcharra & Les Mollettes; after x-ing A43 site on R. Med, hdg pitch, pt shd; wc; baby facs; shwrs inc; el pnts (6A) inc; gas; lndtte; rest, snacks; bar; BBQ; playgrnd; pool; wifi; 30% statics; dogs €1.50; poss cr; adv bkg; some rd & rlwy noise; CKE/CCI. "Gd san facs." 15 Feb-15 Oct. € 16.00   2010*

"There aren't many sites open at this time of year"

If you're travelling outside peak season remember to call ahead to check site opening dates – even if the entry says 'open all year'.

MONTMEYAN *10E3* (500m S Rural) *43.63830, 6.06080* **Camping Le Château de L'Eouvière, 83670 Montmeyan [tel/fax 04 94 80 75 54; contact@leouviere.com; www. leouviere.com]** Fr Montmeyan take D13 dir Fox-Amphoux; site 500m on R out of Montmeyan. Med, mkd pitch, terr, pt shd; wc; chem disp; baby facs; shwrs inc; el pnts (10A) €4 (poss rev pol); lndtte; tradsmn; rest, snacks; bar; BBQ (el only on pitch); playgrnd; pool; games rm; wifi; TV; no statics; dogs €1.50; Eng spkn; adv bkg; Eng spkn; quiet; red low ssn; no ccard acc. "Peaceful site in lovely area; friendly owners; diff access; steep slopes/uneven steps; poorly lit; adequate san facs." ♦ 1 May-31 Sep. € 27.00   2010*

MONTMIRAIL *3D4* (1km E Rural) *48.87299, 3.55147* **Camp Municipal Les Châtaigniers, Rue du Petit St Lazare, 51210 Montmirail [03 26 81 25 61; fax 03 26 81 14 27; mairie. montmirail@wanadoo.fr; www.montmirail.fr]** Site sp at junc of D933 & D373 at E o'skts of town. By sports stadium 150m twds town by Gendarmerie. med, mkd pitch, pt shd; wc (cont); own san rec; shwrs inc; el pnts (20A) €4; shops 500m; playgrnd; pool 500m; tennis; golf; ccard not acc; CKE/ CCI. "Peaceful, clean site approx 1 hr fr Paris; warm welcome, helpful warden; dated, clean san facs; call at warden's house L of ent for removal of barrier; barrier v nr main rd; fees collected pm (cash only); vg NH." 1 Apr- 31 Oct. € 9.50   2013*

MONTMORILLON *7A3* (500m E Urban) *46.42035, 0.87554* **Camp Municipal de l'Allochon, 31 Ave Fernand Tribot, 86500 Montmorillon [05 49 91 02 33 or 05 49 91 13 99 (Mairie); fax 05 49 91 58 26; camping@ ville-montmorillon.fr / montmorillon@cg86.fr; http:// en.tourisme-vienne.com]** On D54 to Le Dorat, approx 400m SE fr main rd bdge over rv at S of town. Site on L. Fr S v sharp RH turn into site. Med, mkd pitch, terr, pt shd; htd wc (some cont); mv service pnt; shwrs inc; el pnts (6-10A) €1.80-4.75; lndtte; shop 1km; rest, snacks, bar 500m; BBQ; playgrnd; htd, covrd pool adj; fishing; games area; wifi; TV; dogs; poss cr; adv bkg; some rd noise; CKE/CCI. "Delightful, peaceful, well-kept site; lge pitches; friendly, hard-working warden; gd touring base; vg value; v clean facs; relaxing; rec" ♦ 1 Mar-31 Oct. € 11.00   2013*

MONTOIRE SUR LE LOIR *4F2* (500m S Rural) *47.74750, 0.86351* **Camp Municipal Les Reclusages, Ave des Reclusages, 41800 Montoire-sur-le Loir [tel/fax 02 54 85 02 53; camping.reclusages@orange.fr; www. mairie-montoire.fr]** Foll site sp, out of town sq, over rv bdge & 1st L on blind corner at foot of old castle. Med, some mkd pitch, pt shd; wc (some cont); chem disp; mv service pnt; shwrs inc; el pnts (6-10A) €2.90-3; lndtte; shops 500m; bar; snacks; playgrnd; htd pool adj; playgrnd; canoeing; fishing; wifi; 5% statics; adv bkg; quiet; red low ssn. "Lovely location nr Rv Loir; peaceful, well-kept, secure site; some rvside pitches; friendly, helpful warden; excel clean san facs, ltd low ssn; gd cycling; conv troglodyte vills; excel." ♦ 7 May-17 Sep. € 12.00   2013*

MONTPELLIER *10F1* (8km N Rural) *43.65135, 3.89630* **Camping Le Plein Air des Chênes, Route de Castelnau, 34830 Clapiers [04 67 02 02 53; fax 04 67 59 42 19; contact@ pleinairdeschenes.net; www.pleinairdeschenes.net]** Exit A9 junc 28 onto N113/D65 twd Montpellier. Leave at junc with D21 sp Jacou & Teyran, site sp on L. NB Site ent/exit v narr & no place to stop when leaving. Med, mkd pitch, pt sl, terr, pt shd; wc (some cont); shwrs inc; private san facs some pitches (extra charge); el pnts (10A) inc; gas; lndtte; shops 800m; rest, snacks; bar; playgrnd; pool; paddling pool; waterslides; sand beach 16km; tennis; games area; horseriding; wifi; 60% statics; dogs €6; quiet; red long stay/low ssn. "Vg site; site rds tight for lge o'fits; pitches muddy in wet." ♦ 1 Mar-31 Dec. € 45.50   2011*

See advertisement on pages 88 & 89

MONTPELLIER *10F1* (6km SE Rural) *43.57611, 3.92583* **FFCC Camping Le Parc, Route de Mauguio, 34970 Lattes [04 67 65 85 67; fax 04 67 20 20 58; camping-le-parc@ wanadoo.fr; www.leparccamping.com]** Exit A9 junc 29 for airport onto D66. In about 4km turn R onto D172 sp Lattes & campings, cross over D21. Site ent in 200m on R. Med, hdg pitch, shd; wc; chem disp; shwrs inc; el pnts (10A) inc; gas; lndtte; sm shop; huge shopping cent 1km; tradsmn; snacks high ssn; playgrnd; pool; sand beach 4km; wifi; 15% statics; dogs €3; Eng spkn; adv bkg (dep); quiet; CKE/CCI. "Friendly, helpful owners; lge pitches but dusty; gd facs, excel pool & snack bar; conv Cévennes mountains & Mediterranean beaches; hiking & mountain biking; barrier locked 2200." ♦ 3 Apr-31 Oct. € 25.90   2009*

MONTPELLIER *10F1* (4km S Rural) *43.55426, 3.89353* **Camping L'Oasis Palavasienne, Route de Palavas, 34970 Lattes [04 67 15 11 61; fax 04 67 15 10 62; oasis.palavasienne@ wanadoo.fr; www.oasis-palavasienne.com]** Leave A9 at exit Montpellier Sud. Take D986 sp Palavas. About 1.5km after Lattes take slip rd sp Camping; turn under dual c'way. Site opp. Lge, hdg pitch, pt shd; wc; gym & sauna; shwrs inc; el pnts inc; lndtte; shop; rest, snacks; bar; playgrnd; htd pool; rv adj; sand beach, watersports 4km; cycle hire; horseriding 2km; entmnt; disco; TV; statics; dogs €4; free bus to beach; Eng spkn; adv bkg ess; some traff noise; CKE/CCI. "Bus to Palavas & Montpellier." 5 Apr-13 Sep. € 29.00   2008*

MONTPEZAT DE QUERCY see Caussade *8E3*

FRANCE

MONTPON MENESTEROL *7C2* (300m N Rural) *45.01280, 0.15828* **Camping La Cigaline, 1 Rue de la Paix, Route de Ribérac, 24700 Montpon-Ménestérol [05 53 80 22 16; cathyetdaniel@monespace.net]** Fr Montpon town cent traff lts take D730 N to Ménestérol. Site on L bef bdge beside Rv Isle. Med, hdg/mkd pitch, pt shd; wc; chem disp; shwrs inc; el pnts (10A) inc; gas 500m; lndtte; shop 100m; tradsmn; rest, snacks; bar; BBQ; playgrnd; lake sw 200m; boat hire; fishing; tennis 200m; cycle hire 500m; leisure park nrby; TV rm; 2% statics; dogs €1.50; Eng spkn; adv bkg (30% dep); quiet; ccard acc; red low ssn; CKE/CCI. "Gd touring base for St Emilion region; gd walking, cycling; vg." ♦ 1 Apr-30 Sep. € 14.00   2011*

MONTPON MENESTEROL *7C2* (10km SE Rural) *44.94153, 0.21260* **Camping Domaine de Chaudeau (Naturist), 24700 St Géraud-de-Corps [05 53 82 49 64; fax 05 53 81 18 94; chaudeau.naturiste@wanadoo.fr; www. domainedechaudeau.com]** Fr Montpon take D708 S; after 8km turn E on D33 for St Géraud-de-Corps; foll black & white sp Chaudeau. Fr St Foy-la-Grande take D708 N; after 11km on exit St Méard-de-Gurçon turn E & foll sp as above. Med, hdg/ mkd pitch, shd; wc; chem disp; shwrs inc; el pnts (5A) €3.90; lndtte; shop; snacks; bar; pool; lake sw; fishing; games area; entmnt; some statics; dogs €2.40; phone; quiet; ccard not acc; red low ssn. "Excel site; INF card req but holiday membership avail; v lge pitches." 1 Apr-30 Sep. € 19.00   2009*

MONTPON MENESTEROL *7C2* (4km S Rural) *44.96046, 0.16506* **Camping La Tuilière, 24700 St Rémy-sur-Lidoire [tel/fax 05 53 82 47 29 or 06 87 26 28 04 (mob); contact@ campinglatuiliere.com; www.campinglatuiliere.com]** On W side of D708 4km S of Montpon-Ménestérol. Med, hdg/ mkd pitch, shd; wc; chem disp; shwrs inc; el pnts (10A) €3.20; gas; lndtte; sm shop 3km; tradsmn; rest, snacks; bar; playgrnd; pool;lake adj; tennis; 20% statics; dogs €1.20; poss cr; Eng spkn; adv bkg; quiet; red long stay; ccard acc; CKE/CCI. "Excel rest." ♦ 1 May-16 Sep. € 12.40   2008*

"That's changed – Should I let The Club know?"

If you find something on site that's different from the site entry, fill in a report and let us know. See www.caravanclub.co.uk/europereport.

⊞ **MONTPON MENESTEROL** *7C2* (9km W Rural) *44.99857, 0.07228* **Camp'Gite Les Loges, 24700 Ménesplet [05 53 81 84 39; fax 05 53 81 62 74; aquabrite@hotmail.com; www.camp-gite.com]** Fr Montpon-Ménestérol W on D6089. After Ménesplet turn S onto D10 sp Minzac. Turn L after level x-ing, foll sp. Sm, pt hdg pitch, hdstg, pt shd; wc; chem disp; shwrs inc; el pnts (16A) €4; lndtte (inc dryer); shops 2.5km; rest; BBQ; playgrnd; games area; no statics; dogs €2; Eng spkn; adv bkg; quiet; CKE/CCI. "Excel, peaceful site in pleasant countryside; friendly, attentive staff." ♦ € 15.00   2009*

⊞ **MONTREJEAU** *8F3* (1.5km N Rural) *43.09234, 0.55457* **Camping Midi-Pyrénées, Chemin de Loubet, 31210 Montréjeau [05 61 95 86 79; fax 05 61 95 90 67; camping-midi-pyrenees@wanadoo.fr; www.campingmidipyrenees. com]** Exit A64 junc 17 onto A645; in 500m at rndabt turn R onto D817 dir Montréjeau; in 3km turn R onto D34; in 800m (having passed Carrefour Supmkt) do not turn R onto D34 sp Cugeron, but in 50m turn R onto D34D (diff turn off curve to lane behind cemetry); in 200m turn L into Chemin de Loubet; site on R in 300m. Site well sp. Med, hdstg, pt sl, some terr, pt shd; htd wc; mv service pnt; shwrs inc; el pnts (6A) €3.20; rest, snacks; bar; playgrnd; htd pool; rv & lake 2km; wifi; entmnt; 70% statics; dogs €1; extra for twin-axles; quiet; CKE/CCI. "Gd site; excel views Pyrenees; gd welcome; gd modern san facs; excel infinity pool" € 12.00   2011*

MONTREJEAU *8F3* (7km S Rural) *43.02864, 0.57852* **Camping Es Pibous, Chemin de St Just, 31510 St Bertrand-de-Comminges [05 61 94 98 20 or 05 61 88 31 42; fax 05 61 95 63 83; contact@es-pibous.fr; www.es-pibous.fr]** Turn S fr D817 onto D825 sp Bagnères-de-Luchon & Espagne. Foll past 'Super U' to lge rndabt & turn R sp St Bertrand-de-Comminges/Valcabrère then at 1st traff lts turn R & foll sp for St Bertrand & site. Or exit A64 junc 17 onto A645 sp Bagnères-de-Luchon to lge rndabt, then as above. Med, hdg/mkd pitch, pt shd; htd wc; chem disp; mv service pnt; baby facs; shwrs inc; el pnts (6A) €3.70; gas; lndtte; shop; rest, bar 300m; playgrnd; pool; fishing, tennis 3km; TV; 20% statics; dogs; poss cr; adv bkg; quiet; ccard acc; red low ssn. "Peaceful, friendly site; pitches among trees; clean dated san facs, ltd low ssn; lndtte is owner's washing machine, not always avail (2010); gd touring area nr mountains; picturesque town in walking dist." ♦ 1 Mar-30 Sep. € 12.00   2010*

MONTREJEAU *8F3* (8km S Rural) *43.02898, 0.60859* **Camp Municipal Bords de Garonne, Chemin du Camping, 65370 Loures-Barousse [05 62 99 29 29 or 05 62 99 21 28 (Mairie)]** Exit A64 junc 17 onto A645 by-passing Montréjeau. Or fr Montréjeau take D825 sp Luchon & 'Espagne'. In 5km cont onto D33. Site on R in 3km, visible fr rd. Med, shd; htd wc (some cont); chem disp (wc); mv service pnt; shwrs; el pnts (10A) inc; shop 500m; rest, bar 400m; shops 500m; 80% statics; adv bkg; some Eng spkn; quiet but some rd noise; CKE/CCI. "Pleasant site; touring pitches on rvside; friendly, helpful staff; clean san facs; barrier clsd 12 noon Sat until Mon am low ssn; ring/visit Hotel de Ville nrby for barrier code; easy walk to vill; ideal as NH to/fr Spain." ♦ 15 Feb-15 Nov. € 11.50   2011*

MONTREJEAU *8F3* (1km W Rural) *43.08624, 0.55414* **Camping Essi Les Hortensias, Route de Tarbes, 31210 Montréjeau [05 61 95 74 43]** Fr St Gaudens on D817, R at foot of steep hill, sp 'Tarbes Poids Lourds' to avoid Montréjeau cent. Site on L in 1km. On W outskirts of town, well sp on rd to Tarbes. Sm, pt shd; wc; chem disp; shwrs; el pnts (15A) inc; shops 1km; BBQ; pool 1km; playgrnd; some rd noise; ccard not acc; CKE/CCI. "Gd NH; no twin-axles." 1 Apr-31 Oct. € 11.50   2010*

MONTRESOR *4H2* (3km W Rural) *47.15782, 1.16026*
Camping Les Coteaux du Lac, 37460 Chemillé-sur-Indrois
[02 47 92 77 83; fax 02 47 92 72 95; lescoteauxdulac@
wanadoo.fr; www.lescoteauxdulac.com] Fr Loches on
D764; then D10 dir Montrésor; cont to Chemillé-sur-Indrois.
Med, pt sl; wc; chem disp; mv service pnt; baby facs; shwrs inc;
el pnts (6A) €3.90; lndtte (inc dryer); sm shop; rest, snacks; bar;
BBQ: playgrnd; htd pool; paddling pool; lake fishing & boating;
trekking in Val d'Indrois; games rm; wifi; entmnt; TV rm; dogs
€1.70; phone; Eng spkn; quiet. "Excel setting by lake; immac,
modern san facs; beautiful vill 600m; 3km along cycle track (old
rlwy)." ♦ 3 Mar-15 Oct. € 34.10   2013*

See advertisement on pages 32 & 33

⊞ **MONTREUIL** *3B3* (500m N Rural) *50.46853, 1.76280*
FFCC Camping La Fontaine des Clercs, 1 Rue de l'Eglise,
62170 Montreuil [tel/fax 03 21 06 07 28; desmarest.mi@
wanadoo.fr; www.campinglafontainedesclercs.fr] Fr N
or S turn SW off D901 at rndabt onto D349 to Montreuil; turn
R immed after rlwy x-ing (onto Rue des Préaux); in 120m turn
R; site in 100m on R; sp on Rv Canche. Or take 2nd R ALMOST
immed after (20m) rlwy-xing (onto Grande Ville Basse); in 50m
fork R (Rue de l'Eglise); site in 200m on R. NB Poss difff access
lge o'fits. Med, mkd pitch, hdstg, pt sl, terr, pt shd; htd wc;
chem disp; mv service pnt; shwrs inc; el pnts (10A) €4; shops
500m; tradsmn; BBQ; pool 1.5km; rv adj; fishing; games rm;
wifi; 60% statics; dogs €2; site clsd over New Year; adv bkg
rec high ssn; quiet; no ccard acc; red low ssn; CKE/CCI. "Busy,
basic site in beautiful spot; helpful owner; dated san facs (2010);
steep & narr site rd with tight turns to terr pitches, some sm;
not suitable lge o'fits; some generous pitches beside rv; vet in
Montreuil; attractive, historic town - uphill walk; conv NH Le
Touquet, beaches & ferry; San facs improving" € 14.70   2013*

"I like to fill in the reports as I travel from site to site"
You'll find report forms at the back of this guide, or you can fill them in online at www.caravaclub.co.uk/europereport.

⊞ **MONTREUIL BELLAY** *4H1* (4km E Rural) *47.15263,
-0.13599* FFCC Camping Le Thouet, Les Côteaux-du-
Chalet, route Bron 49260 Montreuil-Bellay [02 41 38 74 17
or 06 19 56 32 75 (mob); campinglethouet@alicepro.fr;
www.campinglethouet.com] Fr D347 N of Montreuil-Bellay
take dir 'Centre Ville'; turn L immed bef rv bdge & foll sp to Les
Côteaux-du-Chalet. Access via narr, rough rd for 1km. Med, pt
shd; wc; chem disp; shwrs inc; el pnts (10A) €3; gas; shop 4km;
tradsmn; bar; BBQ; playgrnd; pool; fishing; boating; dogs €2;
phone; 5% statics; adv bkg; quiet; ccard acc; red low ssn; CKE/
CCI. "Peaceful, spacious, British-owned site; lge area grass &
woods surrounded by vineyards; pitches in open grass field;
poss unkempt low ssn; gd walks; vill not easily accessed by foot;
unguarded rv bank poss not suitable children; v lge pitches" ♦
€ 26.00   2013*

MONTREUIL BELLAY *4H1* (1km W Urban) *47.13191, -0.15897*
Camping Les Nobis, Rue Georges Girouy, 49260 Montreuil-
Bellay [02 41 52 33 66; fax 02 41 38 72 88; contact@camping
lesnobis.com; www.campinglesnobis.com] Fr S on D938
turn L immed on ent town boundary & foll rd for 1km to site;
sp fr all dir. Fr N on D347 ignore 1st camping sp & cont on
D347 to 2nd rndabt & foll sp. Fr NW on D761 turn R onto D347
sp Thouars to next rndabt, foll site sp. Lge, hdg/mkd pitch, pt
shd; wc (some cont); chem disp; mv service pnt; shwrs inc; el
pnts (10A) €3 (poss long cable req, rev pol); gas; lndtte; shop;
tradsmn; rest, snacks; bar; playgrnd; htd pool; cycle hire; wifi;
TV rm; 50% statics; dogs; phone; poss cr; Eng spkn; adv bkg;
quiet; ccard acc; red long stay/low ssn; CKE/CCI. "Spacious site
between castle & rv; gd, modern san facs; local chateaux & town
worth exploring; 'aire de service' for m'vans adj; gd patissiere in
town" ♦ 30 Mar-5 Oct. € 22.50   2013*

"We must tell The Club about that great site we found"
Get your site reports in by mid-August and we'll do our best to get your updates into the next edition of Caravan Europe.

MONTREVEL EN BRESSE *9A2* (500m E Rural) *46.33911,
5.13615* Camping La Plaine Tonique, Base de Plein
Air, 01340 Montrevel-en-Bresse [04 74 30 80 52; fax
04 74 30 80 77; plaine.tonique@wanadoo.fr; www.
laplainetonique.com] Exit A40 junc 5 Bourg-en-Bresse N
onto D975; at Montrevel-en-Bresse turn E onto D28 dir Etrez
& Marboz; site sp on L in 400m. Or exit A6 junc 27 Tournus
S onto D975. V lge, hdg/mkd pitch, shd; wc; chem disp; mv
service pnt; baby facs; shwrs inc; el pnts (10A) inc; lndtte; shop;
rest, snacks; bar; BBQ; playgrnd; 3 htd, covrd pools; 2 paddling
pools; 2 waterslides; lake beach & sw adj; watersports; fishing;
tennis; cycle hire; games area; archery; mountain biking; entmnt;
TV; dogs €2.10; Eng spkn; adv bkg; quiet; ccard acc; red low
ssn. "Excel, busy, family site; superb leisure facs; vg clean
san facs; some pitches boggy after rain." ♦ 11 Apr-25 Sep.
€ 30.00   2012*

MONTRICHARD *4G2* (1km S Rural) *47.33384, 1.18766*
Camping Couleurs du Monde, 1 Rond Point de
Montparnasse, 41400 Faverolles-sur-Cher [02 54 32 06 08
or 06 74 79 56 29 (mob); fax 02 54 32 61 35; contact@
camping-couleurs-du-monde.com; www.camping-couleurs
-du-monde.com] E fr Tours on D796 thro Bléré; at Montrichard
turn S on D764 twd Faverolles-sur-Cher, site 200m fr junc, adj to
Carrefour supmkt - on L by 2nd rndabt. Med, mkd pitch, hdstg,
pt shd; wc; chem disp; mv service pnt; baby facs; sauna; shwrs
inc; el pnts (10A) €4 (rev pol); lndtte (inc dryer); supmkt adj; rest,
snacks; bar; BBQ; playgrnd; htd pool; paddling pool; waterslide
500m; beach & sw 600m; tennis 500m; cycle hire; games area;
games rm; beauty cent; wifi; entmnt; TV rm; dogs €2; Eng spkn;
adv bkg; quiet, but some rd noise; ccard acc; red low ssn/CKE/
CCI. "Site in gd location nr vineyards; gd sports activities; vg."
♦ ltd 31 Mar-29 Sep. € 21.00   2011*

MONTRICOUX 8E3 (500m W Rural) 44.07660, 1.61103 **FFCC Camping Le Clos Lalande, Route de Bioule, 82800 Montricoux [tel/fax 05 63 24 18 89; contact@camping-lecloslalande.com; www.camping-lecloslalande.com]** Fr A20 exit junc 59 to Caussade; fr Caussade take D964 to Montricoux, where site well sp. Med, hdg/mkd pitch, pt shd; wc; chem disp; mv service pnt; baby facs; shwrs inc; el pnts (6A) €3.60; lndtte; shop 1km; tradsmn; snacks; bar & 1km; BBQ; playgrnd; pool; rv & shgl beach 400m; fishing; watersports; tennis; cycle & canoe hire; games area; wifi; TV rm; 10% statics; dogs €2.50; phone; bus 400m; poss full; some Eng spkn; adv bkg (rec high ssn); CKE/CCI. "Peaceful, quiet, well-kept site by rv at mouth of Aveyron gorges; beautiful area, inc Bastide vills; great family site; friendly, helpful owners; mkt Weds; easy walk to town; highly rec." ◆ 26 Apr-19 Sep. € 17.40   2010*

MONTROLLET 7B3 (NE Rural) 45.98316, 0.89702 Camping Auberge La Marchadaine, Beaulieu, 16420 Montrollet [05 45 71 09 88 or 06 63 07 82 48 (mob); aubergedelamarchadaine@gmail.com; www.auberge-camping-16.com] N fr St Junien on D675, turn W onto D2 to Montrollet. Auberge sp in vill. Sm, pt shd; wc; chem disp (wc); shwr; el pnts (6A) inc; gas; shop 4km; tradsmn; rest; bar; playgrnd; fishing; internet; dogs free; phone; Eng spkn; adv bkg; quiet; CKE/CCI. "Delightful CL-type site o'looking lake; vg rest." € 9.50   2010*

"I need an on-site restaurant"

We do our best to make sure site information is correct, but it is always best to check any must-have facilities are still available or will be open during your visit.

MONTSALVY 7D4 (800m S Rural) 44.70029, 2.50674 **Camp Municipal de la Grangeotte, Route d'Entraygues, 15120 Montsalvy [04 71 49 26 00 or 04 71 49 20 10 (Mairie); fax 04 71 49 26 93; mairie-montsalvy@wanadoo.fr; www.montsalvy.fr]** On W of D920 behind sports complex. Sm, mkd pitch, pt sl, pt shd; wc; shwrs; el pnts (3-6A) €2.50-3.70; lndtte; shops in vill; rest, snacks; bar; playgrnd; htd pool adj (Jun-Aug); fishing 2km; games area; adv bkg; quiet but some rd noise. "Pleasant vill; entmnt; views fr some pitches; friendly warden." 1 Jun-15 Sep. € 12.10   2008*

MONTSAUCHE LES SETTONS 4G4 (4km SE Rural) **FFCC Camping de la Plage des Settons, Rive Gauche, Lac des Settons, 58230 Montsauche-les-Settons [03 86 84 51 99; fax 03 86 84 54 81; camping@settons-tourisme.com; www.settons-tourisme.com]** Fr Montsauche foll sp Château-Chinon. In 500m fork L to Les Settons. After 2km foll sp for Rive Gauche, after 1km L at bend for site. Med, hdg/mkd pitch, terr, pt shd; wc; chem disp; mv service pnt; shwrs inc; el pnts (4A) inc (long lead req); lndtte; shops 500m; tradsmn; BBQ; playgrnd; pool nrby; sand/shgl lake beach adj; fishing; pedalos; lake sw; cycle hire; dogs free; Eng spkn; poss noisy; ccard acc; CKE/CCI. "In cent of Parc du Morvan; direct access to Lac des Settons; access rd busy pm." ◆ ltd 15 Apr-15 Oct. € 19.90   2011*

MONTSAUCHE LES SETTONS 4G4 (5km SE Rural) 47.17114, 4.06037 Camping L'Hermitage de Chevigny, 58230 Mouxen-Morvan [03 86 84 50 97; www.mouxenmorvan.fr] Fr Montsauche take D520 S & after approx 5km turn L on D290; at T-junc in 3km turn L & in further 800m turn L into Chevigny & foll sp to L'Hermitage. App rds narr & twisting. Med, hdg/mkd pitch, pt shd; htd wc (mainly cont); chem disp; shwrs inc; el pnts (6A) €4.70; gas; lndtte (inc dryer); sm shop; tradsmn; snacks; bar; playgrnd; lake sw; watersports; fishing; games area; dogs €1.80; adv bkg; Eng spkn; quiet; ccard not acc; CKE/CCI. "Peaceful, secluded woodland site; clean facs; friendly, helpful owner; gd cycling & walking; less well-known part of France; excel." 15 Apr-30 Sep. € 15.60   2010*

"Satellite navigation makes touring much easier"

Remember most sat navs don't know if you're towing or in a larger vehicle – always use yours alongside maps and site directions.

MONTSAUCHE LES SETTONS 4G4 (6km SE Rural) 47.18175, 4.05293 **FFCC Camping Les Mésanges, Rive Gauche, 58230 Montsauche-les-Settons [tel/fax 03 86 84 55 77; campinglesmesanges@orange.fr]** Fr Montsauche take D193 to Les Settons, then D520 dir Chevigny. Foll sp to site on W side of lake. Med, mkd pitch, terr, pt sl, pt shd; wc (some cont); chem disp; mv service pnt; baby facs; shwrs inc; el pnts (16A) inc; gas; lndtte (inc dryer); shop; rest 1km; snacks; playgrnd; lake sw; fishing; games area; games rm; dogs €0.80; poss cr; Eng spkn; quiet; adv bkg; CKE/CCI. "Beautiful, lakeside site; well-maintained; gd for families - lge play areas; excel." ◆ 15 May-15 Sep. € 19.00   2010*

MONTSAUCHE LES SETTONS 4G4 (7km SE Rural) 47.18578, 4.07056 **Camping Plage du Midi, Lac des Settons Les Branlasses, 58230 Montsauche-les-Settons [03 86 84 51 97; fax 03 86 84 57 31; campplagedumidi@aol.com; www.settons-camping.com]** Fr Salieu take D977 bis to Montsauche, then D193 'Rive Droite' to Les Settons for 5km. Cont a further 3km & take R fork sp 'Les Branlasses' Centre du Sport. Site on L after 500m at lakeside. Med, mkd pitch, terr, pt shd; htd wc; chem disp; mv service pnt; baby facs; shwrs inc; el pnts (10A) €3.60; gas; lndtte (inc dryer); shop; tradsmn; rest 3km; snacks; bar; BBQ; playgrnd; htd, covrd pool; lake sw; sand beach adj; watersports; cycle hire; horseriding 2km; wifi; entmnt; dogs €1; phone; poss cr; Eng spkn; adv bkg; poss noisy; red low ssn; ccard acc; CKE/CCI. "Site in gd situation; muddy when wet." ◆ Easter-15 Oct. € 14.10 (CChq acc)   2010*

MONTSOREAU *4G1* (500m NE Rural) *47.21805, 0.05270* Kawan Village L'Isle Verte, Ave de la Loire, 49730 Montsoreau [02 41 51 76 60 or 02 41 67 37 81; fax 02 41 51 08 83; isleverte@cvtloisirs.fr; www.camping isleverte.com] At Saumur on S side of rv turn R immed bef bdge over Rv Loire; foll sp to Chinon & site. Fr N foll sp for Fontevraud & Chinon fr Rv Loire bdge; site on D947 in vill on banks of Loire opp 'Charcuterie' shop. Med, mkd pitch, pt shd; wc; chem disp; mv service pnt; baby facs; shwrs inc; el pnts (16A) €3.50 (poss long lead req); gas; lndtte (inc dryer); shops 200m; tradsmn; rest & in vill; snacks; bar; playgrnd; pool; paddling pool; rv fishing/watersports; tennis; car and cycle hire; games area; golf 13km; wifi; entmnt; TV rm: some statics; dogs €2; bus to Saumur; poss cr; Eng spkn; adv bkg rec high ssn; rd noise & poss disco noise; ccard acc; red low ssn; CKE/CCI. "Pleasant rvside site in beautiful situation; various sized/shaped pitches; adequate san facs; poss irreg cleaning low ssn; vg rest; barrier clsd 2200-0700; gd security; pleasant vill; gd" ♦ 1 Apr-30 Sep. € 23.00 (CChq acc)   2013*

See advertisement

MONTSURS *4F1* (500m N Rural) *48.13784, -0.55170* Camp Municipal de la Jouanne, Rue de la Jouanne, 53150 Montsûrs [02 43 01 00 31 (Mairie); fax 02 43 02 21 42; commune.montsurs@wanadoo.fr] Well sp fr town cent. Med, pt shd; wc; chem disp (wc); shwrs inc; el pnts (6A) inc; lndry rm; shop, rest, snacks, bar 500m; playgrnd; rv fishing adj; phone; adv bkg rec; quiet; no ccard acc; CKE/CCI. "Pretty, well-kept rvside site in pleasant situation; peaceful; conv many medieval vills; ask at house opp if barrier clsd; highly rec." 1 Jun-30 Sep. € 8.61   2008*

MOOSCH see Thann *6F3*

MORCENX *8E1* (2km S Rural) *44.00735, -0.89612* Camping à La Ferme Fortanier (Labadie), 1180 Route de Rion, 40110 Morcenx [05 58 07 82 59; mauricette.labadie@wanadoo. fr] Fr N10 turn E at junc 14 onto D38 dir Mont-de-Marsan. At Morcenx turn R on D27. Site on R 1km past Camping Le Clavé. Well sp. Sm, hdg/mkd pitch, shd; wc; chem disp (wc); shwrs inc; el pnts (6A) €2.50-3.50; gas; lndtte; shop, rest, bar 1km; BBQ; playgrnd; pool; lake 3km; 5% statics; dogs; phone 500m; adv bkg; quiet; CKE/CCI. "Friendly owners; well-kept, clean, tidy site; peaceful & relaxing." 1 Mar-30 Sep. € 10.00   2008*

MORCENX *8E1* (7km W Rural) *44.03529, -0.94612* Aire Naturelle La Réserve (Lemercier), 1870 Ave de l'Océan, 40110 Garrosse [05 58 04 38 12; dlemercier@club-internet.fr; www.camping-lareserve.com] Exit N10 junc 14 onto D38 dir Morcenx; foll camping sps for 5km; site on L. Sm, pt sl, shd; wc; chem disp (wc); shwrs inc; el pnts (6-10A) €4.50; playgrnd; sm pool; snacks; games area; 25% statics; dogs €1; some Eng spkn; quiet. "Site in pine trees; conv N10; friendly, helpful owners." ♦ 1 Apr-30 Sep. € 9.10   2010*

MOREE *4F2* (2.5km SW Urban) *47.88932, 1.20109*
Camping La Maladrerie, Rue du Plessis, 41160
Fréteval [02 54 82 62 75 or 06 88 69 21 92 (mob); fax
02 54 82 62 75; campingdelamaladrerie@orange.fr; www.
camping-de-la-maladrerie.fr] E fr Le Mans on D357 to
Fréteval; turn L in vill. Sp. Med, mkd pitch, pt shd; wc; chem
disp; mv service pnt; shwrs inc; el pnts (4-6A) €1.55-2.30; gas;
lndtte; shops 800m; bar; BBQ; playgrnd; pool; rv sw 200m;
lake fishing on site; 5% statics; Eng spkn; ccard acc; CKE/
CCI. "Delightful, well-kept, quiet site; friendly owner; some
facs in need of update (2011); poss ltd facs low ssn; site was
a medieval leper colony; highly rec." ♦ ltd 1 Apr-30 Oct.
€ 10.45   2013*

MOREE *4F2* (2km W Rural) *47.88885, 1.21101* **Camp**
Municipal, Route de l'Etang, 41160 Fréteval
[02 54 82 63 52 (Mairie); fax 02 54 82 07 15; fréteval.
mairie@wanadoo.fr] Site 100m fr D357 by Rv Loir in vill cent,
500m fr lake. Ent/exit thro concrete posts & fencing
- not for lge o'fits. Med, mkd pitch, pt shd; wc (some cont);
shwrs inc; el pnts inc; shops 500m; playgrnd; fishing; quiet, some
rd noise. "Lovely, location on Rv Loir; diff ent/exit, esp med/lge
o'fits; facs need update; conv beautiful town of Vendôme; site
run down (2009)." 1 Jun-31 Aug. € 7.50   2009*

MOREE *4F2* (500m NW Rural) *47.90643, 1.22755* **Camp**
Municipal La Varenne, Plan d'Eau de la Varenne,
41160 Morée [02 54 82 06 16 or 02 54 89 15 15; fax
02 54 89 15 10; mairie-de-moree@wanadoo.fr]
W fr Orléans on N157/D357 or N fr Vendôme on D910 &
foll sp in vill onto D19 to site. Sm, pt shd; htd wc; chem disp;
mv service pnt; shwrs inc; el pnts (8A) €3; gas, shops 400m;
snacks; bar; playgrnd; lake sw & beach adj; fishing; canoeing;
tennis 500m; golf 5km; wifi; adv bkg; red long stay; CKE/CCI.
"Lovely, lakeside site; ltd san facs stretched if site full; popular
with school parties high ssn; poss unrel opening dates."
1 May-30 Sep. € 11.50   2010*

MORESTEL *9B3* (8km S Urban) *45.63521, 5.57231* **Camping**
Les Epinettes, 6 Rue du Stade, 38630 Les Avenières [tel/
fax 04 74 33 92 92; infos@camping-les-avenieres.com]
S fr Morestel on D1075, turn onto D40 to Les Avenières, site
well sp. Med, hdg/mkd pitch, hdstg, pt shd; htd wc; chem disp;
mv service pnt; baby facs; shwrs inc; el pnts (10A); lndtte; shop;
tradsmn; rest, snacks; bar; BBQ; playgrnd; pool adj; rv sw 2km;
entmnt; TV rm; 35% statics; dogs; phone; adv bkg; noise fr adj
stadium; red low ssn; ccard acc; CKE/CCI. "Phone ahead low
ssn to check open." ♦ 1 May-30 Sep.   2008*

MORESTEL *9B3* (NW Urban) *45.67694, 5.46587* **Camp**
Municipal La Rivoirette, Rue François Perrin, 38510
Morestel [04 74 80 14 97; info@morestel.com; www.
morestel.com] Foll camping sps in town. Site by sports
complex on D517. (NB No Entry sps do not apply to campers).
Med, pt shd; wc; shwrs inc; el pnts (8A) €2.70; supmkt 1km;
pool & sports complex adj; dogs; quiet. "Sm, poss awkward
pitches; twin-axles extra charge; ent barrier operated by adj sw
pool staff; excel NH." 1 May-30 Sep. € 10.90   2010*

MORET SUR LOING *4E3* (2km NW Rural) *48.38333, 2.80194*
Camping Les Courtilles du Lido, Chemin du Passeur, 77250
Veneux-les-Sablons [01 60 70 46 05; fax 01 64 70 62 65;
lescourtilles-dulido@wanadoo.fr; www.les-courtilles-
du-lido.fr] Use app fr N6 sp Veneux-les-Sablons & foll sp. 1km
fr N6. Or fr Moret foll sp; long, tortuous rte; narr streets; 35m,
1-width tunnel. NB sp say 'Du Lido' only. Lge, mkd pitch, pt shd;
wc; chem disp; mv service pnt; shwrs inc; el pnts (10A) €3; gas;
lndtte; shops 1km; tradsmn; rest, snacks; bar; playgrnd; sm pool;
tennis; wifi; 75% statics; dogs €1.50; poss cr; Eng spkn; adv
bkg; rlwy noise at night; ccard acc; CKE/CCI. "Early arr rec; lge
pitches; clean facs but poss insufficient high ssn; friendly owners;
vg for children; lovely old town; conv Fontainebleau & train to
Paris; excel." 9 Apr-20 Sep. € 16.50   2011*

MOREZ *9A3* (3km N Rural) *46.54218, 6.01907* **Camp**
Municipal La Bucle, 15 Route Germain Paget, Les Pontets,
39400 Morbier [tel/fax 03 84 33 48 55; info.bucle@
wanadoo.fr] Fr N on N5 look for sps 10km after St Laurent.
Pass supmkt & lge car pk on R, take sharp L turn after L bend in
rd. Fr S turn R 50m past bdge. Med, some hdstg, pt sl, pt terr,
unshd; wc; shwrs inc; el pnts (10A) €2.30; lndtte; shops 1km;
pool; dogs €0.60; quiet; red low ssn; gd NH. "Lovely site &
town; site poss unkempt." 1 Jun-10 Sep. € 14.50   2009*

MOREZ *9A3* (9km S Rural) *46.48368, 5.94885* **Camping**
Le Baptaillard, 39400 Longchaumois [03 84 60 62 34;
camping-lebaptaillard@orange.fr; www.haut-jura.com]
Foll D69 S, site sp on R. Med, mkd pitch, pt sl, pt shd; htd wc;
chem disp; shwrs inc; el pnts (6A) €2.50; lndtte; shop; rest,
snacks, bar 3km; playgrnd; paddling pool; fishing 3km; tennis;
skiing; games rm; some statics; adv bkg ess winter; quiet.
"Beautiful CL-type site; views; lge pitches; friendly staff"
1 Jan-30 Sep, 1 Dec-31 Dec. € 30.45   2013*

MORLAIX *2E2* (6km NE Rural) *48.61583, -3.76822*
Camping Vert de Morlaix (Berric), Ferme de Kerroyal,
Bois de La Roche, 29610 Garlan [02 98 79 12 54 or
06 14 39 21 61 (mob); fax 02 98 63 24 47; nills.bretagne@
wanadoo.fr] Fr Morlaix take D786 dir Lannion, in 6km turn
R; farm on L in 1km. Foll blue & white camping sps. Clearly
sp fr D786. Sm, hdg pitch, pt shd; wc; chem disp forbidden
(2009); shwrs inc; el pnts €2; bar (in ssn); lndtte; playgrnd; htd
pool 5km; TV; dogs; quiet; ccard not acc. "Pleasant CL-type
site; goats, pony & duckpond; conv Roscoff & Marlaix; gd." ♦
Easter-31 Oct. € 10.00   2009*

MORLAIX *2E2* (11km E Rural) *48.60283, -3.73833*
Camping Aire Naturelle la Ferme de Croas Men (Cotty),
Garlan, 29610 Plouigneau [tel/fax 02 98 79 11 50;
fermecroasmen@free.fr; http://camping.croamen.
pagesperso-orange.fr/] Fr D712 rndabt W of Plouigneau
twd Morlaix (exit from N12) 2km R sp Garlan; thro Garlan site
1km on L, well sp. Sm, hdg pitch, pt shd; wc; 50% serviced
pitches; chem disp; baby facs; shwrs; el pnts (6A) €3.20;
playgrnd; horseriding 200m; farm museum; donkey/tractor
rides; some statics; dogs €1; Eng spkn (daughter); quiet; CKE/
CCI. "Lovely, well-kept CL-type farm site; excel facs; ideal for
children; produce avail inc cider & crêpes." ♦ 1 Apr-31 Oct.
€ 11.40   2010*

FRANCE

MORLAIX 2E2 (15km S Rural) 47.91293, -4.23981 **Aire Naturelle Les Bruyères, 29410 Le Cloître-St Thégonnec [02 98 79 71 76 or 01736 362512 (UK); www. caravancampingsites.co.uk/france/29/bruyeres.htm]** Fr Morlaix take D769 S twd Huelgoat/Carhaix & Le Cloître-St Thégonnec. At Le Plessis after 14.5km turn L for Le Cloître-St Thégonnec. When ent vill, take L fork at Musée des Loups, 1st L, 500m then R to camp. Sm, mkd pitch, pt sl, pt shd; wc; chem disp; shwrs inc; gas; lndry rm; shop 500m; rest; bar; BBQ; playgrnd; dogs €2; quiet; adv bkg; CKE/CCI. "Helpful British owners; NB no electricity/el pnts; water htd by gas; oil lamps in san block; camp fires; enjoy camping like it used to be; for stays outside of Jul/Sep tel to request." 1 Jul-15 Sep. € 16.00   2008*

MORMOIRON 10E2 (4km E Rural) 44.05713, 5.22798 **Camping Les Verguettes, Route de Carpentras, 84570 Villes-sur-Auzon [04 90 61 88 18; fax 04 90 61 97 87; info@ provence-camping.com; www.provence-camping.com]** E on D942 fr Carpentras dir Sault. Site at ent to Villes-sur-Auzon beyond wine cave. Or at Veulle-les-Roses turn E onto D68. Cont thro Sottenville-sur-Mer. Site on L in 2km. Lge, hdg/ mkd pitch, pt sl, pt shd; htd wc; chem disp; shwrs inc; el pnts (6A) inc; lndtte; shops 1km; rest; pool; paddling pool; tennis; games rm; fishing 300m; tennis; wifi; TV rm; dogs €2.60- 3.60; adv bkg rec all times; quiet; red low ssn. "Scenic location; gd walking & cycling; friendly, helpful owner; families with children sited nr pool, others at end of camp away fr noise; poss muddy when it rains; sm pitches not suitable lge o'fits; red facs low ssn; new toilet/shower block" ♦ 23 Mar - 30 Sep. € 24.50   2013*

MORNAS 10E2 (2km E Rural) 44.21540, 4.74530 **Camping Domaine Le Beauregard, Route d'Uchaux, 84550 Mornas [04 90 37 02 08; fax 04 90 37 07 23; beauregard@ franceloc.fr; www.camping-beauregard.com or www. campings-franceloc.fr]** Exit A7 at Bollène, then N7 twd Orange. On N end of Mornas turn L on D74 to Uchaux, site after 1.7km, sp. Lge, pt sl, shd; htd wc (some cont); chem disp; mv service pnt; shwrs inc; el pnts (6-10A) €3.30-4.40; gas; lndtte; shop; rest, snacks; bar; BBQ; playgrnd; 2 pools (1 htd, covrd); paddling pool; games rm; tennis; golf; horseriding; cycle hire; wifi; entmnt; dogs €4.15; 80% statics; adv bkg rec high ssn; quiet; Eng spkn; ccard acc; red CKE/CCI. "Open until 2230; phone ahead to check open low ssn; gd san facs; many derelict vans; poorly maintained & ltd facs low ssn" ♦ 3 Apr-26 Sep. € 28.00   2010*

MORNAY SUR ALLIER see St Pierre le Moûtier 4H4

⊞ **MORTAGNE SUR GIRONDE** 7B2 (1km SW Coastal) 45.47600, -0.79400 **Aire Communale Le Port, 17120 Mortagne-sur-Gironde [05 46 90 63 15; fax 05 46 90 61 25; mairie-mortagne@smic17.fr]** Fr Royan take D730 dir Mirambeau for approx 28km. Turn R in Boutenac-Touvent onto D6 to Mortagne, then foll sp Le Port & Aire de Camping-Car. M'vans only. Sm, unshd; chem disp; mv service pnt; shwrs €1; el pnts (10A) inc; shop 500m; rest, snacks, bar 600m; dogs; poss v cr; quiet. "Car/c'vans poss acc; shwrs & mv service pnt 800m fr site; fees collected 0900; all pitches have views; excel." € 6.00   2013*

MORTAIN 2E4 (8km S Rural) 48.57039, -0.94883 **Camping Les Taupinières, La Raisnais, 50140 Notre-Dame-du-Touchet [02 33 69 49 36 or 06 33 26 78 82 (mob); belinfrance@fsmail.net; www.lestaupinieres.com]** Fr Mortain S on D977 sp St Hilaire-du-Harcouët; shortly after rndabt take 2nd L at auberge to Notre-Dame-deTouchet. In vill turn L at post office, sp Le Teilleul D184, then 2nd R sp La Raisnais. Site at end of lane on R (haycart on front lawn). Sm, hdstg, pt sl, pt shd; wc; chem disp; shwrs inc; el pnts (10A) inc (poss long lead req); washing machine on request; NB no wc or shwrs Dec-Feb but water & el pnts all year; shop & rest 1km; htd pool 8km; DVD library; wifi; dogs; adv bkg; quiet. "Pleasant, tranquil, spacious CL-type site adj farm; lovely outlook; adults only; friendly, helpful British owners; well-kept, clean san facs; adv bkg rec; highly rec." 1 Mar-30 Nov. € 15.00   2011*

MORTAIN 2E4 (500m W Urban) 48.64808, -0.94350 **Camp Municipal Les Cascades, Place du Château, 50140 Mortain [02 33 79 30 30 (Mairie0; mairie.de.mortain@wanadoo.fr; www.ville-mortain.fr]** On D977 S fr Vire twd St Hilaire-du-Harcouët; site in cent of Mortain, sp to R. Sm, pt shd; wc; chem disp; mv service pnt; shwrs inc; el pnts (6A) inc; shop 200m; sm playgrnd; no statics; dogs; m'van parking area outside site; CKE/CCI. "Sm extra charge for twin-axles; gd san facs." ♦ Easter-30 Sep. € 10.00   2010*

MORTEAU 6H2 (S Urban) 47.05304, 6.59908 **Camping Le Cul de la Lune, Rue du Pont Rouge, 25500 Morteau [03 81 67 17 52 or 03 81 67 18 53; fax 03 81 67 62 34; otsi. morteau@wanadoo.fr; www.morteau.org]** Fr Besançon take N57 E then D461. In Morteau foll sps to Pontarlier then 'Toutes Directions'. Site on R over rlwy/rv bdge sp Montlebon (D48). Clearly sp thro'out town. Across rv bdge. Sm, pt shd; wc (some cont); shwrs inc; el pnts (10A) €3; shops 300m; tradsmn; rv sw, fishing & boating; cycling; dogs €1.50; poss v cr; adv bkg; noise fr rd & rlwy; red low ssn. "Beautiful location on rv bank; gd modern san facs; pt of site v wet after heavy rain; poss v cold at nights (altitude)." 1 Jun-10 Sep. € 15.00   2010*

MORZINE 9A3 (7km SW Rural) 46.15070, 6.64307 **Camping La Grange au Frêne, Les Cornuts, 74260 Les Gets [04 50 75 80 60 ou 04 50 75 80 55; fax 04 50 75 84 39; www.alpensport-hotel.com]** Fr Morzine go S on D902 to Les Gets. Site sp at end of vill. Sm, hdg/mkd pitch, terr, pt sl, pt shd; htd wc; 50% serviced pitches; baby facs; shwrs inc; el pnts (2-4A) €3-5; lndtte; shop 3km; tradsmn; rest, snacks & bar 3km; playgrnd; climbing; golf, tennis & adventure park nr; games rm;TV rm; dogs; phone; Eng spkn; adv bkg; quiet. "Excel site." ♦ 24 Jun-15 Sep. € 17.00   2010*

MORZINE 9A3 (3km NW Rural) 46.19510, 6.67715 **Camping-Caravaneige Les Marmottes, 74110 Essert-Romand [tel/ fax 04 50 75 74 44 or 06 12 95 00 48 (mob); contact@ campinglesmarmottes.com; www.campinglesmarmottes. com]** Exit A40 junc 18 or 19 onto D902 twd Morzine, then turn L onto D328 to Essert-Romand. Fr A40 take junc 18 to Morzine. Sm, hdstg, unshd; wc; chem disp; serviced pitches; baby facs; shwrs inc; el pnts (3-10A) €4.50-8; lndtte; shop 2km; tradsmn; playgrnd; lake sw 3km; TV; some statics; dogs €1; ski-bus; Eng spkn; adv bkg; quiet; red long stay; CKE/ CCI. "Specialises in winter c'vanning for skiers; tractor to tow to pitch in snow." ♦ 21 Jun-7 Sep & 22 Dec-13 Apr. € 16.50   2009*

FRANCE

MOSNAC 7B2 (Rural) 45.50557, -0.52304 **Camp Municipal Les Bords de la Seugne, 34 Rue de la Seugne, 17240 Mosnac [05 46 70 48 45; fax 05 46 70 49 13; mosnac@ mairie17.com]** Fr Pons S on N137 for 4.5km; L on D134 to Mosnac; foll sp to site behind church. Sm, mkd pitch, pt shd; htd wc; shwrs inc; el pnts (6A) inc; gas; 10% statics; dogs free; Eng spkn; adv bkg; no ccard acc; quiet; red long stay; CKE/CCI. "Charming, clean, neat site in sm hamlet; site yourself, warden calls; helpful staff; excel, spotless san facs; conv Saintes, Cognac & Royan." 15 Apr-15 Oct. € 10.44   2011*

MOSTUEJOULS see Peyreleau 10E1

MOTHE ACHARD, LA 2H4 (5km NW Rural) 46.64107, -1.71046 **Camping Château de la Forêt, Rue de la Forêt, 85150 St Julien-des-Landes [02 51 46 62 11; fax 02 51 46 60 87; camping@domainelaforet.com; www. domainelaforet.com]** Take D12 fr La Mothe-Achard to St Julien. Turn R onto D55 at x-rds & site sp on L. Med, hdg/ mkd pitch, pt shd; wc; all serviced pitches; shwrs inc; el pnts (6A) €4.20; gas; lndtte (inc dryer); shop & in vill; rest, snacks; bar; BBQ; playgrnd; 2 htd pools; games rm; sand beach 12km; lake fishing adj; cycle hire; tennis; wifi; entmnt; dogs €2.70; 60% statics; poss cr; adv bkg rec high ssn; quiet; red low ssn; CKE/CCI. "Part of private chateau estate, popular with British visitors; gd for families; excel facs; gates clsd 2200-0800." 15 May-15 Sep. € 29.00 (3 persons)   2010*

MOTHE ACHARD, LA 2H4 (5km NW Rural) 46.65285, -1.74759 **Camping La Guyonnière, 85150 St Julien-des-Landes [02 51 46 62 59; fax 02 51 46 62 89; info@ laguyonniere.com; www.laguyonniere.com]** Leave A83 junc 5 onto D160 W twd La Roche-sur-Yon. Foll ring rd N & cont on D160 twd Les Sables-d'Olonne. Leave dual c'way foll sp La Mothe-Achard, then take D12 thro St Julien-des-Landes twd La Chaize-Giraud. Site sp on R. Lge, hdg pitch, pt sl, pt shd; wc; chem disp; shwrs inc; el pnts (6A) €3.50 (long lead rec); gas; lndtte; shop; tradsmn; rest, snacks; bar; BBQ; playgrnd; 2 pools (1 htd, covrd); water park; waterslide; sand beach 10km; lake fishing, canoe hire, windsurfing 400m; cycle hire; internet; cab/sat TV rm; some statics; dogs €3; phone; Eng spkn; adv bkg; ccard acc; red low ssn. "V lge pitches; gd views; friendly owners; gd walking area." ♦
26 Apr-28 Sep. € 23.50 SBS - A12   2008*

See advertisement above

MOTHE ACHARD, LA 2H4 (6km NW Rural) 46.64469, -1.73346 **FLOWER Camping La Bretonnière, 85150 St Julien-des-Landes [02 51 46 62 44 or 06 14 18 26 42 (mob); fax 02 51 46 61 36; camp.la-bretonniere@wanadoo.fr; www. la-bretonniere.com or www.flowercampings.com]** Fr La Roche-sur-Yon take D160 to La Mothe-Achard, then D12 dir St Gilles-Croix-de-Vie. Site on R 2km after St Julien. Med, mkd pitch, pt sl, pt shd; wc (some cont); chem disp; mv service pnt; baby facs; shwrs inc; el pnts (6-12A) €2-4.50; lndtte; ice; shops 7km; tradsmn; bar 1km; BBQ; playgrnd; 2 pools, htd covrd; sand beach 12km; fishing; sailing & lake sw 2km; tennis; cycle hire; games area; games rm; wifi; entmnt; TV rm; 20% statics; dogs €2; Eng spkn; adv bkg; quiet; ccard acc; red low ssn; CKE/CCI. "Excel, friendly site adj dairy farm; lge pitches; 10 mins fr Bretignolles-sur-Mer sand dunes." ♦ ltd
1 Apr-15 Oct. € 26.00   2009*

See advertisement on pages 32 & 33

MOTHE ACHARD, LA 2H4 (7km NW Rural) 46.66280, -1.71380 **Camping La Garangeoire, 85150 St Julien-des-Landes [02 51 46 65 39; fax 02 51 46 69 85; info@ garangeoire.com; www.camping-la-garangeoire.com or www.les-castels.com]** Site sp fr La Mothe-Achard. At La Mothe-Achard take D12 for 5km to St Julien, D21 for 2km to site. Or fr Aizenay W on D6 turn L dir La Chapelle-Hermier. Site on L, well sp. Lge, hdg/mkd pitch, pt sl, shd; wc; chem disp; mv service pnt; some serviced pitch; baby facs; fam bthrm; shwrs inc; el pnts (16A) inc (poss rev pol); gas; lndtte (inc dryer); shop; rest, snacks; bar; BBQ (gas/el); playgrnd; htd pool complex; paddling pool; waterslide; lake fishing; sand beach 12km; horseriding; tennis; cycle hire; games area; games rm; wifi; entmnt; 50% statics (tour ops); dogs €4; twin-axles acc (rec check in adv); phone; poss cr; Eng spkn; adv bkg (ess Aug); ccard acc; red low ssn; CKE/CCI. "Busy, well-run site set in chateau parkland; some v lge pitches; pleasant helpful owners; excel, clean facs; gd for families & all ages; pitches quiet - entmnt well away fr pitches; super site; gd site in every way" ♦
7 Apr-24 Sep. € 37.00 SBS - A42   2012*

See advertisement on inside back cover

FRANCE

MOTTE TERNANT, LA *6G1* (S Rural) *47.32309, 4.33086* Camping Le Village, 21210 La Motte-Ternant [tel/fax 03 80 84 30 11; campinglevillagelamotte-t@orange.fr; www.campinglamotteternant.eu] Exit A6 junc 23 onto D980 to Précy-sous-Thil; then take D36 to Fontangy; turn R onto D26 to La Motte-Ternant. Fr Saulieu take D26 to La Motte-Ternant. Site in 10km. Site sp, but diff to see fr S (obscured by building). Sm, pt sl, shd; wc; chem disp (wc); shwrs inc; el pnts (16A) €3.50; tradsmn; shop & bar 800m; tradsmn; BBQ; dogs free; Eng spkn; adv bkg; quiet; ccard acc. "Delightful, friendly site with views; helpful Dutch owners; hot water poss extremely hot - children take care; gd." 1 Apr-15 Oct. € 12.00   2010*

> ## "There aren't many sites open at this time of year"
>
> If you're travelling outside peak season remember to call ahead to check site opening dates – even if the entry says 'open all year'.

MOUCHAMPS *2H4* (1km SE Rural) *46.77493, -1.05510* Camp Municipal Le Hameau du Petit Lay, Route de St Prouant, Chauvin, 85640 Mouchamps [tel/fax 02 51 66 25 72; wbm85640@mouchamps.com; www.lehameaudupetitlay.com] Fr Chantonnay to D137 NW; 1km past St Vincent-Sterlanges turn R sp Mouchamps; turn R onto D113 sp St Prouant & camping; site on L in 1 km. Sm, hdg/mkd pitch, pt shd; wc, chem disp; shwrs inc; el pnts €2.50; lndtte; shop, rest, snacks & bar 1km; playgrnd adj; htd pool adj; quiet, but traff noise am; CKE/CCI. "Barrier clsd 2200-7000; vg." ♦ 15 Jun-15 Sep. € 10.80   2010*

MOUCHARD *6H2* (4km NE Rural) *47.00358, 5.82366* Camping Les Radeliers, 1 Rue Edgar Faure, 39600 Port-Lesney [03 84 73 81 44; camp.portlesney@aliceadsl.fr; www.camping-les-radeliers.com] N fr Arbois on N83, cross junc with D472 & turn L in 1.5km sp Port-Lesney. Site sp. Med, mkd pitch, pt shd; wc; chem disp; shwrs inc; el pnts (13A) €4; lndtte; shop 300m; rest opp & 200m; snacks; bar 200m; playgrnd (for use by vill); sand/shgl beach & rv sw adj; canoeing; kayak hire; canyoning; 2% statics; dogs €1.70; bus & phone adj; poss cr; Eng spkn; adv bkg; quiet; twin-axles extra; red low ssn; CKE/CCI. "Tranquil site in delightful rvside setting; helpful staff; poss youth groups high ssn; gd walking & cycling; Salt Mine Museum in Salins-les-Bains worth visit; plenty riverside pitches" ♦ ltd 1 May-30 Sep. € 13.20   2013*

MOULIHERNE see Vernantes *4G1*

MOURIES *10E2* (2km E Rural) *43.68207, 4.91769* Camping à la Ferme Les Amandaies (Crouau), Mas de Bou Malek, 13890 Mouriès [04 90 47 50 59; fax 04 90 47 61 79] Fr Mouriès take D17 E sp Salon-de-Provence. Site sp on R 200m past D5 junc. Foll site sp to farm in 2km. Sm, pt shd; wc; shwrs inc; el pnts €2 (rec long lead) (poss rev pol); tradsmn; BBQ; dogs; quiet. "Simple CL-type site; a few lge pitches; friendly owners; dated, dimly-lit san facs; conv coast & Avignon; book in using intercom on LH wall at ent to shwr block." 15 Mar-10 Oct. € 13.00   2009*

MOURIES *10E2* (7km NW Urban) *43.72138, 4.80950* Camp Municipal Les Romarins, Route de St Rémy-de-Provence, 13520 Maussane-les-Alpilles [04 90 54 33 60; fax 04 90 54 41 22; camping-municipal-maussane@wanadoo.fr; www.maussane.com] Fr Mouriès N on D17, turn onto D5 on o'skts of vill dir St Rémy-de-Provence, turn immed L site on R adj municipal pool. Med, hdg pitch, pt shd; wc; chem disp; baby facs; shwrs inc; el pnts (4A) €3.50; gas 200m; lndtte; shops 200m; BBQ; playgrnd; pool adj inc; tennis free; cycle hire; internet; TV; dogs €2.50; buses in ssn; adv bkg rec; quiet, but some rd noise; red long stay; ccard acc; CKE/CCI. "Well-kept, well-run site in lovely area; on edge of vill; excel san facs; some pitches diff m'vans due low trees; gd security; excel." ♦ 15 Mar-15 Oct. € 19.50   2009*

MOUSSEAUX SUR SEINE see Bonnières sur Seine *3D2*

MOUSTERLIN see Fouesnant *2F2*

MOUSTIERS STE MARIE *10E3* (300m S Rural) *43.83963, 6.22150* Camping Le Vieux Colombier, Quartier St Michel, 04360 Moustiers-Ste Marie [tel/fax 04 92 74 61 89 or 04 92 74 61 82 (LS); Contact@lvcm.fr; http://camping.vieux.colombier.pagesperso-orange.fr/] Fr Moustiers go E on D952 dir Castellane. Site on R in 300m opp garage. NB Steep, winding access rd. Med, mkd pitch, sl, terr, pt shd; htd wc; 80% serviced pitches; chem disp; mv service pnt; baby facs; shwrs inc; el pnts (3-6A) €2.70-3.40 (rev pol); gas; lndtte; shop 600m; snacks; bar; BBQ; playgrnd; lake sw 5km; wifi; canoeing; windsurfing; dogs €2; Eng spkn; adv bkg ess high ssn; quiet; ccard acc; CKE/CCI. "Helpful staff; steep terrs, park at top & walk down; gd, clean san facs; steep uphill walk to lovely vill; conv Gorges du Verdon; gd walking; vg." ♦ ltd 1 Apr-30 Sep. € 14.00   2009*

> ## "That's changed – Should I let The Club know?"
>
> If you find something on site that's different from the site entry, fill in a report and let us know. See www.caravanclub.co.uk/europereport.

MOUSTIERS STE MARIE *10E3* (1km SW Rural) *43.84371, 6.21475* FFCC Camping St Jean, Route de Riez, 04360 Moustiers-Ste Marie [tel/fax 04 92 74 66 85; camping-saint-jean@wanadoo.fr; www.camping-saint-jean.com] On D952 opp Renault g'ge & petrol station. Med, some hdg pitch, pt sl, pt shd; htd wc (some cont); chem disp; mv service pnt; baby facs; shwrs inc; el pnts (6-10A) €3.60-4.70; gas; lndtte; sm shop & 700m; tradsmn; snacks; BBQ (elec/gas); playgrnd; fishing; sand beach, lake sw & boating 4km; climbing nr; cycle rtes; games area; games rm; wifi; TV; 10% statics; dogs €2.10; poss cr; Eng spkn; adv bkg; quiet; ccard acc; red low ssn; CKE/CCI. "Excel site in lovely location by rv; dated san facs (2010); some pitches diff lge o'fits; easy uphill walk to beautiful vill; conv Gorges du Verdon; gd value." ♦ ltd 1 Apr-16 Oct. € 16.50   2011*

MOUSTIERS STE MARIE *10E3* (500m W Rural) *43.84497, 6.21555* **Camping Manaysse, 04360 Moustiers-Ste Marie [04 92 74 66 71; fax 04 92 74 62 28; www.camping-manaysse.com]** Fr Riez take D952 E, pass g'ge on L & turn L at 1st rndabt for Moustiers; site on L off RH bend; strongly advised not to app Moustiers fr E (fr Castellane, D952 or fr Comps, D71) as these rds are diff for lge vehicles/c'vans - not for the faint-hearted. Med, mkd pitch, pt sl, pt shd; wc (some cont); chem disp; mv service pnt; shwrs inc; el pnts (6-10A) €2.50-3.50; shops 500mtrs; tradsmn; s'market 10m, playgrnd; dogs €0.50; adv bkg; quiet; CKE/CCI. "Welcoming, family-run site; super views; gd unisex san facs; cherry trees on site - avoid parking under during early Jun; steep walk into vill; lge o'fits do not attempt 1-way system thro vill, park & walk; gd." ♦ ltd 1 Apr-24 Oct. € 14.40 2012*

"I like to fill in the reports as I travel from site to site"

You'll find report forms at the back of this guide, or you can fill them in online at www.caravaclub.co.uk/europereport.

MOUTIERS *9B3* (3km N Rural) *45.50700, 6.49097* **Camping Eliana, 188 Rue des Pommiers, 73260 Aigueblanche [04 79 24 23 87 or 06 73 57 17 76; campingeliana@ hotmail.com; www.campingeliana.com]** Fr Albertville take N90 S & exit 38 for Aigueblanche. Foll sp in vill for 'Camping' on D97 dir La Léchère. Site on L 700m after supmkt; well sp. NB Final L turn from D97 is through a NO ENTRY sign. Sm, hdg/mkd pitch, terr, shd; htd wc; chem disp; mv service pnt; shwrs inc; el pnts (4-10A) €2-3.80; gas 1km; lndtte; shop 1km; tradsmn; rest, snacks; bar; BBQ; htd pool 500m; cycle hire; wifi; some statics; dogs €0.30; quiet; CKE/CCI. "Well-managed site in orchard; gd, clean facs; warden calls 1800; sm pitches poss diff lge o'fits." ♦ ltd 1 Apr-31 Oct. € 8.80 2010*

MOUTIERS *9B3* (4km S Rural) *45.45294, 6.56232* **Camping La Piat, Ave Greyffié de Bellecombe, 73570 Brides-les-Bains [04 79 55 22 74; fax 04 79 55 28 55; campinglapiat@ wanadoo.fr; www.camping-brideslesbains.com]** Fr Moûtiers on D915 to Brides-les-Bains into town cent. Turn R onto Ave Greyffié de Bellecombe & foll sp to site. Med, mkd pitch, some hdstg, pt sl, terr, pt shd; wc (some cont); chem disp; mv service pnt; baby facs; shwrs inc; el pnts (3-10A) €2.10-3.70; gas; lndtte; shops, rest, snacks & bar 500m; tradsmn; playgrnd; pool adj; 10% statics; dogs €0.90; phone adj; bus 500m; ski lift 500m; poss cr; Eng spkn; adv bkg; quiet but some rd noise; ccard acc; red low ssn; CKE/CCI. "Gd mountain base; Brides-les-Bains is thermal spa town specialising in obesity treatments; some pitches v muddy in wet weather." ♦ 10 Apr-16 Oct. € 10.80 2010*

MOUTIERS EN RETZ, LES see Pornic *2G3*

MOYAUX *3D1* (3km NE Rural) *49.20860, 0.39230* **Camping Château Le Colombier, Le Val Séry, 14590 Moyaux [02 31 63 63 08; fax 02 31 61 50 17; mail@camping-lecolombier.com; www.camping-lecolombier.com]** Fr Pont de Normandie on A29, at junc with A13 branch R sp Caen. At junc with A132 branch R & foll sp Lisieux, D579. Turn L onto D51 sp Blangy-le-Château. Immed on leaving Moyaux turn L onto D143 & foll sp to site on R in 3km. Lge, mkd pitch, pt shd; wc; chem disp; mv service pnt; baby facs; shwrs inc; el pnts (10A) inc (poss lead req); gas; lndtte (inc dryer); sm shop; tradsmn; rest, snacks; bar; BBQ; playgrnd; htd pool; tennis; cycle hire; excursions; horseriding nr; games area; wifi; entmnt; games/TV rm; some static tents/tour ops; dogs free; no c'vans/m'vans over 7m high ssn; phone; Eng spkn; adv bkg; quiet; ccard acc; red long stay/low ssn; CKE/CCI. "Beautiful, peaceful, spacious site in chateau grounds; ltd san facs low ssn; lge pool, but no shade, seats or sunshades around; vg for children; gd shop & crêperie; shgl paths poss diff some wheelchairs/pushchairs; if dep bef 0800 must move to car park overnight; mkt Sun." ♦ ltd 1 May-15 Sep. € 36.00 SBS - N04 2013*

MOYENNEVILLE see Abbeville *3B3*

MUIDES SUR LOIRE *4G2* (6km E Rural) *47.64803, 1.61165* **Camp Municipal du Cosson, Route de la Cordellerie, 41220 Crouy-sur-Cosson [02 54 87 08 81; fax 02 54 87 59 44; mairie-de-crouy-sur-cosson@wanadoo.fr]** Fr Muides-sur-Loire, take D103 E dir Crouy-sur-Cosson. In vill, turn R onto D33 dir Chambord. Site 200m fr village, well sp. Med, mkd pitch, pt shd; wc; shwrs inc; el pnts (6A) inc (poss rev pol); lndry rm; shops 500m; tradsmn; rest 300m; snacks; bar 300m; BBQ; playgrnd; rv fishing nr; few statics; dogs; phone; adv bkg; quiet; CKE/CCI. "Pleasant site; woodland setting; nr Rv Loire; poss long-stay workers." Easter-1 Nov. € 11.20 2010*

MUIDES SUR LOIRE *4G2* (500m S Rural) *47.66611, 1.52916* **Camping Le Château des Marais, 27 Rue de Chambord, 41500 Muides-sur-Loire [02 54 87 05 42; fax 02 54 87 05 43; chateau.des.marais@wanadoo.fr; www. chateau-des-marais.com]** Exit A10 at junc 16 sp Chambord & take D2152 sp Mer, Chambord, Blois. At Mer take D112 & cross Rv Loire; at Muides-sur-Loire x-rds cont strt on for 800m; then turn R at Camping sp; site on R in 800m. Lge, mkd pitch, pt sl, shd; htd wc; chem disp; mv service pnt; all serviced pitches; baby facs; sauna; shwrs inc; el pnts (6A) inc (poss rev pol); gas; lndtte (inc dryer); shop; rest, snacks; bar; BBQ; playgrnd; htd covrd pool complex; waterslides; paddling pool; jaccuzi; lake fishing; watersports nrby; cycle hire; tennis; games area; games rm; wifi; TV; 50% statics (tour ops); dogs €6; twin-axles acc (rec check in adv); Eng spkn; adv bkg; ccard acc; red low ssn; CKE/CCI. "busy lively site in wooded area in chateau grnds; gd sized pitches; excel, clean san facs; friendly staff; plenty of gd quality children's play equipmnt; sh walk to rv; conv Loire chateaux; plenty to do in area; mkt Sat Blois; pitches grass, can be a problem when wet" ♦ 12 May-15 Sep. € 57.60 SBS - L10 2013*

FRANCE

MUIDES SUR LOIRE *4G2* (W Rural) *47.67326, 1.52763* **Camp Municipal Belle Vue, Ave de la Loire, 41500 Muides-sur-Loire [02 54 87 01 56 or 02 54 87 50 08 (Mairie); fax 02 54 87 01 25; mairie.muides@wanadoo.fr; www.muides.fr]** Fr A10/E5/E60 exit junc 16 S onto D205. Turn R onto D2152 then D112 over rv. Site on S bank of rv on D112 W of bdge. Tight U-turn into site fr N. Med, mkd pitch, pt shd; wc; chem disp/mv service pnt; shwrs inc; el pnts (5A) €3.90 (poss long lead req),(poss rev pol); gas in vill; lndtte; shops 200m; rest, snacks adj; playgrnd; rv fishing adj; sw 4km; cycling; dogs €2; vehicle barrier; quiet; no ccard acc; CKE/CCI. "Neat, clean, basic, spacious site; ladies shwrs need upgade (2011); gd views over rv; some pitches by fast-flowing (unfenced) rv; little shade; excel cycling." ♦ 1 May-15 Sep. € 15.47   2013*

⊞ **MULHOUSE** *6F3* (4km NE Urban) *47.78267, 7.39453* **Camping Le Safary, 35 Rue de la Forêt-Noire, 68390 Sausheim [tel/fax 03 89 61 99 29 or 06 85 44 16 64 (mob); camping.safary@wanadoo.fr; www.campinglesafary.fr]** Exit A36/E54 junc 20 onto D201 N dir Battenheim & Baldersheim, site on E of D201, sp. Med, hdg/mkd pitch, pt shd; wc; chem disp; shwrs inc; el pnts (6-10A) €3-4; lndtte; shops 2km; snacks; bar; 60% statics; dogs €1; quiet; CKE/ CCI. "Barrier clsd 2200-0800; few facs for size of site, poss inadequate if site full; poss itinerants." € 13.00   2009*

MULHOUSE *6F3* (2km SW Rural) *47.73405, 7.3235* **Camping de l'Ill, 1 Rue de Pierre Coubertin, 68100 Mulhouse [03 89 06 20 66; fax 03 89 61 18 34; campingdelill@ wanadoo.fr; www.camping-de-lill.com]** Fr A36 take Mulhouse/Dornach exit & foll sp Brunstatt at 1st traff lts. At 2nd traff lts turn R, foll University/Brunstatt/Camping sps, site approx 2.5km on rvside. Lge, some mkd pitch, pt sl, pt shd; wc; chem disp; mv service pnt; baby facs; shwrs inc; el pnts (5A) €3.70; gas; supmkt & rest 1km; tradsmn; snacks; pool; internet; dogs €1.50; tram 500m; quiet but some rlwy noise; red low ssn/CKE/CCI. "Welcoming recep; cycle along rv to town cent; OK NH." 1 Apr-17 Oct. € 14.70   2009*

"We must tell The Club about that great site we found"

Get your site reports in by mid-August and we'll do our best to get your updates into the next edition of Caravan Europe.

⊞ **MULHOUSE** *6F3* (10km SW Rural) *47.72225, 7.22590* **FFCC Camping Parc La Chaumière, 62 Rue de Galfingue, 68990 Heimsbrunn [tel/fax 03 89 81 93 43 or 03 89 81 93 21; accueil@camping-lachaumiere.com; www.camping-lachaumiere.com]** Exit A36 junc 15; turn L over m'way; at rndabt exit on D166 sp Heimsbrunn; in vill turn R at rndabt; site end of houses on R. Med, hdg pitch, hdstg, pt sl, shd; htd wc; chem disp; mv service pnt; shwrs inc; el pnts (10A) €3 (poss rev pol); lndry rm; shop 1km; tradsmn; snacks; playgrnd; pool; 50% statics; dogs €1; quiet; ccard acc; CKE/CCI. "Sm pitches not suitable long o'fits; beautiful wine vills on La Route des Vins; museum of trains & cars in Mulhouse." € 10.50   2010*

MUNSTER *6F3* (800m E Rural) *48.03944, 7.14250* **Camping Le Parc de la Fecht, Route de Gunsbach, 68140 Munster [03 89 77 31 08 or 04 99 57 21 21; dirparcdelafecht@ village-center.com; www.village-center.com]** Clear site sp on all app to Munster & in town. Site on D10. Lge, hdg/ mkd pitch, pt shd; wc; chem disp; mv service pnt; sauna; shwrs inc; el pnts (6A) inc; lndtte (inc dryer); shops adj; rest, snacks; bar; BBQ; playgrnd; htd pool complex, paddling pool, waterslide adj; fishing; games rm; wifi; entmnt; TV; some statics; dogs €3; phone; Eng spkn; quiet; ccard acc; CKE/CCI. "Pleasant, wooded site; friendly & helpful staff; gd walking & cycling; o'night waiting area." ♦ 1 May-12 Sep. € 16.80 (CChq acc)   2010*

MUNSTER *6F3* (3km E Rural) *48.0453, 7.1798* **Camping Beau Rivage, 8 Rue des Champs, 68140 Gunsbach [tel/fax 03 89 77 44 62; beaurivagecamping@wanadoo.fr; www. beau-rivage-gunsbach.com]** Site on rv off D417 Colmar to Munster rd. Med, pt shd; htd wc; chem disp; shwrs inc; el pnts (3-6A) €2.20-3.20; gas; lndtte; shop (high ssn); supmkt 2.5km; snacks; bar; playgrnd; rv adj; fishing; sports area; 50% statics; dogs €0.70; adv bkg; quiet; CKE/CCI. "Excel for visiting Albert Schweitzer house & memorial." 1 Apr-20 Oct. € 10.00   2008*

MUNSTER *6F3* (4km E Rural) *48.05160, 7.20527* **Camping La Route Verte, 13 Rue de la Gare, 68230 Wihr-au-Val [03 89 71 10 10; info@camping-routeverte.com; www. camping-routeverte.com]** Take D417 out of Colmar twd Munster & turn R int Wihr-au-Val. Site on L 800m. Well sp. Med, mkd pitch, pt sl, shd; wc; chem disp; mv service pnt; shwrs inc; el pnts (4-6A) €2.80-3.95; lndtte; shops, rest, bar 50m; pool 4km; games rm; dogs €1.50; phone; poss cr; adv bkg; quiet; red long stay; CKE/CCI. "Delightful, popular, clean site amid vineyards; owner helpful & friendly; not suitable lge c'vans (6m max); excel san facs; highly rec." ♦ 25 Apr-30 Sep. € 9.25   2011*

MUNSTER *6F3* (2km SW Rural) *48.03105, 7.11350* **FFCC Camping Les Amis de la Nature, 4 Rue du Château, 68140 Luttenbach-près-Munster [03 89 77 38 60; fax 03 89 77 25 72; an-munster@wanadoo.fr; www.camping-an.fr]** Fr Munster take D10 sp Luttenbach; site sp. Lge, mkd pitch, pt shd; htd wc; chem disp; mv service pnt; baby facs; sauna; shwrs inc; el pnts (4-6A) €3.25-4.40/6.20; lndtte (inc dryer); shop; rest, snacks; bar; BBQ; playgrnd; htd pool; dir access to rv; tennis 1km; fishing; games area; games rm; wifi; entmnt; TV; 50% statics; dogs €1.50; poss cr; Eng spkn; quiet; ccard acc; quiet. "Lovely setting by stream; basic san facs, some grubby (2010); gd value." ♦ 6 Feb-30 Nov & 18 Dec-7 Jan. € 10.50   2010*

MUNSTER *6F3* (9km SW Rural) *47.98250, 7.01865* **Camp Municipal de Mittlach Langenwasen, 68380 Mittlach [03 89 77 63 77; fax 03 89 77 74 36; mairiemittlach@ wanadoo.fr; www.mittlach.fr]** Fr Munster on D10 to Metzeral then R onto D10. Site at end rd in 6km. Med, hdg/ mkd pitch, pt sl, pt shd; wc; chem disp; shwrs inc; el pnts (6-10A) €2.45-6: gas; lndtte (inc dryer); sm shop & 6km; tradsmn; playgrnd; 10% statics; dogs €0.80; Eng spkn; adv bkg; quiet; red low ssn; CKE/CCI. "Peaceful, wooded site at bottom of valley; helpful staff; san facs gd & clean; gd walking base; plenty of interest locally; excel." ♦ ltd 15 Apr-30 Sep. € 10.25   2010*

FRANCE

⊞ **MUR DE BRETAGNE** 2E3 (6km N Rural) 48.25568, -2.98801 **Camping Le Boterff d'en Haut, 22320 St Mayeux [02 96 24 00 65; info@leboterff.com; www. brittanyforholidays.com]** N fr Mur-de-Bretagne on D767 to St Mayeux. Turn R into vill & R after vill hall (Salle Municipal); to T-junc, turn R & site on L. App via 750m single-track lane. Car parking in rd outside. Sm, unshd; wc; chem disp; shwrs inc; el pnts (6A) inc; gas 8km; shops, snacks & bar 2km; rest 5km; BBQ; lake sw & watersports 8km; adv bkg; dogs €1 (2 max); quiet; ccard not acc; red low ssn/long stay. "Peaceful, remote CL-type site; gd san facs; gd touring cent; gd walks & cycling; when wet, cars parked off site; excel; (2013) Chgd owner, still British, very welcoming; superb CL type site; beautiful area" € 20.00   2013*

"I need an on-site restaurant"

We do our best to make sure site information is correct, but it is always best to check any must-have facilities are still available or will be open during your visit.

MUR DE BRETAGNE 2E3 (2km SW Rural) 48.19872, -3.01282 **Camping Le Point de Vue, 104 Rue du Lac, 22530 Mur-de-Bretagne [02 96 26 01 90; fax 02 96 28 59 44; camping-lepointdevue@orange.fr; www.camping-lepointdevue.fr]** Fr Mur-de-Bretagne take D18 & foll site sp; ent opp view point of Lake Guerlédan. Med, terr, pt sl, pt shd; wc (mainly cont); chem disp; shwrs inc; el pnts (10A) inc; lndry rm; shops, rest 1.5km; bar 50m; playgrnd; sand beach/lake 500m; dogs €1; poss cr; wifi; quiet; CKE/CCI. "Gd watersports; hot water may be ltd to a few hrs a day in low ssn; gd walking & cycling around lake." ♦ 15 Feb-15 Nov. € 15.10   2013*

MUR DE BRETAGNE 2E3 (4km NW Rural) 48.20950, -3.05150 **Camping Nautic International, Route de Beau Rivage, 22530 Caurel [02 96 28 57 94; fax 02 96 26 02 00; contact@ campingnautic.fr; www.campingnautic.fr]** Fr Loudéac on N164 into Caurel. Fork L 100m past church, site is 1st on L, beside Lac de Guerlédan. NB App fr Pontivy on D767 via Mur-de-Bretagne v steep in places & not rec when towing. Med, mkd pitch, terr, pt shd; wc (some cont); chem disp; mv service pnt; baby facs; sauna; shwrs inc; el pnts (10A) €4.90; lndtte (inc dryer); shop (high ssn); BBQ; playgrnd; htd pool; paddling pool; jacuzzi; lake fishing; watersports & horseriding nr; cycle hire; tennis; fitness rm; games/TV rm; sauna; dogs €2.50; adv bkg; no c'vans/m'vans over 8m; quiet; ccard acc; red low ssn; CKE/CCI. "Peaceful site in attractive countryside by lake; gd pitches, some poss diff lge o'fits; dated facs, poss stretched when site full; wonderful pool & lake." ♦ 15 May-25 Sep. € 24.00   2013*

MURAT 7C4 (10km NE Rural) 45.12926, 2.96745 **Camping La Prade, Route de Murat, 15150 Neussargues-Moissac [04 71 20 50 21; camping@neussargues-moissac.fr; www. neussargues-moissac.fr]** Site sp on N122. Sm, hdg/mkd pitch, terr, unshd; htd wc; chem disp; baby facs; shwrs inc; el pnts (10A) inc; lndtte; shop 700m; tradsmn; rest, snacks, bar 700m; playgrnd; 40% statics; dogs €0.60; phone; bus 700m; adv bkg; quiet; CKE/CCI. "Clean, modern facs; excel views." ♦ 15 Jun-15 Sep. € 9.25   2008*

MURAT 7C4 (1km SW Urban) 45.10303, 2.86599 **Camp Municipal de Stalapos, 8 Rue de Stade, 15300 Murat [04 71 20 01 83 or 04 71 20 03 80; fax 04 71 20 20 63; agyl@camping-murat.com; www.murat.fr]** Fr N122 site sp fr cent of Murat dir Aurillac (thro indus est), adj Rv Alagnon. Lge, some hdstg, pt sl, pt shd; wc (cont); chem disp; shwrs inc; el pnts (6-16A) €2.50-6.30; lndtte; shops 1km; playgrnd; rv fishing adj; dogs free; poss cr; no adv bkg; also winter ssn, phone ahead; quiet; red CKE/CCI. "Peaceful location; basic but clean san facs; warden lives on site; excel touring base; gd views medieval town." ♦ 1 May-30 Sep. € 7.20   2010*

MURAT 7C4 (5km SW Rural) 45.07781, 2.83047 **Aire Naturelle Municipal, 15300 Albepierre-Bredons [04 71 20 20 49]** SW fr Murat on D39 dir Prat-de-Bouc; site sp fr cent of Albepierre. Sm, pt shd; wc (some cont); chem disp (wc); shwrs inc; el pnts (10A) €2; shops, rest & bar 300m; dogs free; quiet; ccard not acc; CKE/CCI. "Excel, peaceful location; basic, clean facs; warden visits am & pm; vg walking amidst extinct volcanoes; gd." 15 Jun-15 Sep. € 6.80   2009*

MURAT 7C4 (6km W Rural) **Camp Municipal Le Vallognon, 15300 Laveissière [04 71 20 11 34; fax 04 71 20 20 48; campinglaveissiere@orange.fr]** Site sp fr N122 W from Murat Sp Aurilla, after 4km turn right onto D439 site on left after 300m. Med, pt shd; wc; shwrs inc; el pnts inc; lndtte; shops 300m; playgrnd; htd pool adj; quiet, some rd noise; CKE/ CCI. "Conv for Cantal Mountains; gd hill walking; gd site" ♦ 1 Jan-3 Apr, 1Jun-4 Sep, 20 Dec-31 Dec. € 14.60   2013*

MURE ARGENS, LA see St André les Alpes 10E3

MUROL 7B4 (1km S Rural) 45.56275, 2.93825 **Camping Sunêlia La Ribeyre, Route de Jassat, St Victor-la-Rivière, 63790 Murol [04 73 88 64 29; fax 04 73 88 68 41; info@ laribeyre.com; www.laribeyre.com]** Exit 6 fr A75 onto D978 S sp Champeix/St Nectaire, then D996 to Murol. In Murol take D5 S sp Besse-et-St Anastaise. In approx 500m take D618 twd Jassat & site in 500m on rvside. Sp fr Murol. Lge, mkd pitch, pt shd; wc (some cont); chem disp; serviced pitches; baby facs; shwrs inc; el pnts (6-10A) €6.45-11.40 (poss rev pol); lndtte (inc dryer); shop 1km; tradsmn; rest; bar; BBQ; playgrnd; pools (1 htd, covrd) & aqua park; paddling pool; waterslides; lake sw & sand beach adj; fishing; boat hire; tennis; horseriding; hiking; games area; games rm; wifi; entmnt; TV rm; 30% statics; dogs €2.80; Eng spkn; adv bkg; quiet; ccard acc; red low ssn; CKE/ CCI. "Beautiful setting by lake; spacious pitches, some by lake; gd san facs; excel sw complex; ideal touring base & family site; great walks fr site; activities for all ages; barrier operated 2300-0700; quiet low ssn; groups welcome low ssn; vg." ♦ 1 May-15 Sep. € 27.10   2011*

MUROL 7B4 (1km S Rural) 45.57400, 2.95735 **FFCC Camp Le Repos du Baladin, Groire, 63790 Murol [04 73 88 61 93; fax 04 73 88 66 41; reposbaladin@free.fr; www.camping-auvergne-france.com]** Fr D996 at Murol foll sp 'Groire' to E, site on R in 1.5km just after vill. Med, hdg/mkd pitch, pt sl, terr, shd; htd wc (some cont); chem disp; sauna; baby facs; shwrs inc; el pnts (5A) €4; lndtte (inc dryer); shop 1.5km; tradsmn; snacks; bar; playgrnd; htd pool; lake sw 5km; wifi; dogs €3; poss cr; poss noise high ssn; Eng spkn; CKE/CCI. "Lovely site with immac san facs; friendly, helpful owners; easy walk into town through fields" 27 Apr-7 Sep. € 33.70   2013*

MUROL *7B4* (2km W Rural) *45.56902, 2.93005* **Camping de la Plage, Lac Chambon, 63790 Murol [04 73 88 60 04; fax 04 73 88 80 08; lac.chambon@wanadoo.fr; http://lac-chambon-plage.fr]** Exit A75 junc 6 sp Champeix/St Nectaire; cont for 34km thro St Nectaire to Murol on D996; 1km past Murol turn L sp Lac Chambon/Centre Touristique; bear L past lge car park to site ent. Lge, hdg/mkd pitch, terr, pt shd; htd wc; chem disp; mv service pnt; shwrs inc; baby facs; el pnts (6A) €3.70; gas & 2km; lndtte; shop; rest, snacks & bar in hotel; playgrnd; lake sw & fishing adj; tennis; cycle hire; entmnt; TV; statics; dogs €1; phone; Eng spkn; adv bkg; quiet; ccard acc; CKE/CCI. "Vg site; facs stretched high ssn; gd birdwatching & walking." ♦ ltd 1 May-15 Sep. € 16.50   2010*

MUROL *7B4* (2km W Rural) *45.57516, 2.91428* **Camping Le Pré Bas, 63790 Chambon-sur-Lac [04 73 88 63 04; fax 04 73 88 65 93; prebas@campingauvergne.com; www.campingauvergne.com]** Take D996 W fr Murol twd Mont-Dore. Site 1.5km on L, twd lake. Lge, hdg/mkd pitch, pt sl, pt shd; wc; chem disp; mv service pnt; serviced pitches; baby facs; shwrs inc; el pnts (6A) €4.70; gas 1km; lndtte; ice/freezer; shop & 1km; tradsmn; snacks; bar (high ssn); BBQ; playgrnds; 2 pools (1 htd, covrd); waterslides; lake sw; games area; library; entmnt; TV rm; 40% statics; dogs €2.10; phone; poss cr; Eng spkn; adv bkg; quiet; red low ssn; CKE/CCI. "Excel family-run site by Lac Chambon; superb views; friendly, helpful staff; immac san facs; excel pool complex; rock pegs ess; access to sm pitches poss diff lge o'fits; excel walking area." ♦ 24 Apr-30 Sep. € 23.70   2012*

MUROL *7B4* (5km W Rural) *45.56979, 2.90185* **Camping Les Bombes (formerly Municipal), Chemin de Pétary, 63790 Chambon-sur-Lac [04 73 88 64 03 or 06 88 33 25 94 (mob); les-bombes-camping@orange.fr; www.camping-les-bombes.com]** Site is on D996. Nr exit fr vill Chambon. Well sp. Med, mkd pitch, pt shd; wc (some cont); chem disp; mv service pnt; shwrs; el pnts (6A) €4.50; lndtte; shops; tradsmn; rest 500m; snacks; bar; BBQ; playgrnd; pool; lake sw 1km; TV rm; 5% statics; dogs €2.20; phone; quiet; Eng spkn; adv bkg; red low ssn; CKE/CCI. "Beautiful area; gd, clean, well-maintained facs stretched in high ssn; lge pitches; friendly, helpful owners; excel." ♦ 15 May-30 Sep. € 23.80   2012*

MUY, LE *10F4* (1km E Rural) *43.46832, 6.59202* **RCN Camping Domaine de la Noguière, 1617 Route de Fréjus, 83490 Le Muy [04 94 45 13 78; fax 04 94 45 92 95; info@rcn-domaine delanoguiere.fr; www.rcn-domaine delanoguiere.fr]** Exit A8 junc 37 dir Roquebrune-sur-Argens & Puget-sur-Argens & take DN7 for 8km. Site on R. V lge, mkd pitch, some hdstg, pt shd; htd wc; baby facs; shwrs inc; el pnts (6A) inc; gas; lndtte (inc dryer); shop; tradsmn; rest, snacks; bar; BBQ; playgrnd; pool complex; waterslides; sand beach 15km; lake fishing 2km; tennis; games area; games rm; wifi; entmnt; TV; statics; dogs €6; adv bkg; quiet. ♦ 19 Mar-30 Oct. € 43.90 (CChq acc)   2011*

MUZILLAC *2G3* (12km N Rural) *47.66220, -2.46837* **Camp Municipal de l'Etang de Célac, Route de Damgan, 56230 Questembert [02 97 26 11 24 or 02 97 26 11 38 (LS); fax 02 97 26 54 15; accueil@mairie-questembert.fr; www.questembert.com]** Fr N on N166, at Bohal exit onto D5 to Questembert; in town turn R dir La Vraie-Croix; site in 1km on D1C, by lake. Camping sp in town. Med, mkd pitch, pt sl, pt shd; htd wc (some cont); chem disp; mv service pnt; shwrs inc; el pnts (12A) €2.90; lndry rm; supmkt 500m; rest nrby; playgrnd; fishing; games rm; TV rm; dogs €1.50; quiet; CKE/CCI. "Site in attractive location by lake; nice pitches; clean san facs; diff access lge o'fits as ent zig-zags around concrete flower tubs; no twin-axles; m'van aire de service at ent; mkt Mon sp fr vill; vg." ♦ 15 Jun-15 Sep. € 11.35   2011*

MUZILLAC *2F3* (2.5km NE Rural) *47.56236, -2.44719* **Camping de la Blanche Hermine, Le Petit Boissignan, 56190 Muzillac [02 97 45 67 03 or 06 76 81 95 79 (mob); fax 02 97 45 67 06; info@lablanchehermine.fr; www.lablanchehermine.fr]** Exit Muzillac on D20 E dir Redon; site on R in 2.5km. Clearly sp. Med, hdg/mkd pitch, pt sl, shd; wc; chem disp; shwrs inc; el pnts (10A) €3.40; lndtte; snacks; bar; playgrnd; htd pool; paddling pool; games area; entmnt; wifi; 70% statics; dogs €2.10; red low ssn; CKE/CCI. "Gd site." 1 Apr-15 Oct. € 15.10   2011*

MUZILLAC *2G3* (5km NE Rural) *47.61394, -2.50140* **Camping Le Moulin de Cadillac, Route de Berric, 56190 Noyal-Muzillac [02 97 67 03 47; fax 02 97 67 00 02; infos@moulin-cadillac.com; www.moulin-cadillac.com]** Fr N165 take D140 N to Noyal-Muzillac, turn R at x-rds, site well sp; care on LH hairpin at rd junc 100m fr site. Sh app rd but steep & sharp bends. Med, hdg pitch, terr, shd; wc; chem disp; mv service pnt; baby facs; shwrs inc; el pnts (10A) €3.20; gas; lndtte; shop; tradsmn; rest; bar; playgrnd; htd pool; waterslide; beach 15km; fishing lake; tennis; games area; golf 15km; TV rm; 30% statics; dogs €1.80; phone; adv bkg rec high ssn; quiet; "In wooded valley away fr cr coastal sites; relaxing site." ♦ 1 May-30 Sep. € 16.40   2008*

MUZILLAC *2G3* (7km NE Rural) *47.58261, -2.41582* **Camp Municipal Borgnehue, Le Borg-Nehué, 56190 Le Guerno [02 97 42 99 38 or 02 97 42 94 76 (Mairie); fax 02 97 42 84 36; mairie-leguerno@wanadoo.fr; www.camping-leguerno.com]** Exit N165 onto D139 dir Questembert. In 5km turn L onto D20 dir Muzillac then in 2km R onto D139A to Le Guerno. Just pass vill sp do not foll rd round to R into vill but take C104 strt for 100m, then foll camping sp. Site on R just after leaving Le Guerno. When turning R into site, keep to L. Sm, hdg pitch, pt shd; wc; chem disp (wc); mv service pnt; baby facs; shwrs inc; el pnts (6-10A) €2.14-3.25; lndtte; playgrnd; some statics; phone; adv bkg; quiet. "Warden high ssn only; book in at vill shop or Mairie (site clsd 1300-1600); pitches lge but poss diff lge o'fits - need to unhitch; gd site." 1 Apr-31 Oct. € 8.00   2010*

MUZILLAC *2G3* (8km SW Coastal) *47.51780, -2.55539*
Camping Ty Breiz, 15 Grande Rue, Kervoyal, 56750
Damgan [tel/fax 02 97 41 13 47; info@campingtybreiz.
com; www.campingtybreiz.com] Fr Muzillac on D153 dir
Damgan, turn S for Kervoyal; site on L opp sm church. Med,
hdg/mkd pitch, pt shd; wc; shwrs inc; el pnts (6-10A) €3-3.50;
lndtte; wifi; playgrnd; sand beach 300m; dogs €1.50; Eng spkn;
adv bkg rec high ssn; quiet; ccard acc; red low ssn; CKE/CCI.
"Pleasant, welcoming, family-run site; excel san facs; quiet low
ssn; cycle path to Damgan; mkt Wed; vg." ♦ 26 Apr-15 Oct.
€ 21.40   2012*

MUZILLAC *2G3* (4km W Coastal) *47.52552, -2.51231*
Camping Le Bédume, Bétahon-Plage, 56190 Ambon-
Plages [02 97 41 68 13; fax 02 97 41 56 79; cledelles.
ambon@free.fr; www.bedume.com] Fr N165 take D20 W
dir Ambon, foll to Bétahon, site sp. Lge, mkd pitch, pt shd; wc;
chem disp; baby facs; shwrs inc; el pnts (5A) €4; lndtte; shop;
tradsmn; snacks; bar; BBQ; playgrnd; htd pool; paddling pool;
waterslide; sand beach adj; games area; games rm; entmnt; TV
rm; 75% statics; dogs €2; Eng spkn; adv bkg req; quiet; ccard
acc; red low ssn. ♦ 1 Apr-30 Sep. € 35.00   2009*

NAGES see Lacaune *8E4*

NAJAC *8E4* (Rural) *44.22011, 1.96985* **Camping Le**
Païsserou, 12270 Najac [05 65 29 73 96; fax 05 65 29 72 29;
info@camping-massifcentral.com; www.camping-
massifcentral.com/Najac.htm] Take D922 fr Villefranche-
de-Rouergue. Turn R on D39 at La Fouillade to Najac. Site by
rv, sp in vill. Or fr A20 exit junc 59 onto D926. At Caylus take
D84 to Najac. All appr v steep. Med, hdg pitch, shd; wc; chem
disp; shwrs inc; el pnts €3; lndtte; shops & rest in vill; tradsmn;
snacks; bar; htd, covrd pool adj (free); tennis adj; some statics;
dogs €1.50; phone; poss cr; Eng spkn; adv bkg; quiet; red low
ssn; CKE/CCI. "Conv for Aveyron gorges; friendly owners; ltd
facs low ssn; lovely vill; unrel opening low ssn, phone ahead;
Site yourself if recep clsed, avail pitches listed" 30 Apr-1 Oct.
€ 23.10   2012*

NALLIERS see Luçon *7A1*

NAMPONT ST MARTIN *3B3* (2km NE Rural) *50.37039,*
1.77546 **Camping Auberge des Etangs, 91 Rue Vallée de**
l'Authie, 62870 Roussent [03 21 81 20 10; www.auberge-
des-etangs.fr] 11km S of Montreuil on D901, take D139E to
Roussent, site on R in vill. Med, mkd pitch, pt sl, pt shd; wc;
chem disp; shwrs inc; el pnts (6A) inc; gas; lndtte; shop; rest,
snacks; playgrnd; rv fishing 2km; entmnt; TV; mostly statics;
quiet but noise fr hotel (disco). "Ltd space for tourers; NH
only." 1 Apr-30 Nov. € 21.00   2010*

NAMPONT ST MARTIN *3B3* (3km W Rural) *50.33595,*
1.71230 **La Ferme des Aulnes, 1 Rue du Marais, Fresne-**
sur-Authie, 80120 Nampont-St Martin [03 22 29 22 69
or 06 22 41 86 54 (mob LS); fax 03 22 29 39 43; contact@
fermedesaulnes.com; www.fermedesaulnes.com]
D901 S fr Montreuil 13km thro Nampont-St Firmin to
Nampont-St Martin; turn R in vill onto D485; site in 3km; sp
fr D901. Med, some hdg pitch, pt sl, pt shd; htd wc; chem disp;
mv service pnt; baby facs; shwrs inc; el pnts (6-10A) €6-12;
lndtte (inc dryer); shop 5km; tradsmn, rest, snacks, bar high ssn;
BBQ (not elec); playgrnd; htd, covrd pool; sand beach 12km;
archery; golf 1km; games area; wifi; entmnt; TV & cinema
rm; mostly statics; dogs €4; poss cr; adv bkg; quiet; CKE/CCI.
"Attractive site nr Calais; some pitches sm, some v sl; friendly
staff; clsd 2200-0800" ♦ 4 Apr-1 Nov. € 21.00 (3 persons)
(CChq acc) SBS - P13   2013*

See advertisement

NANCAY *4G3* (500m NW Rural) *47.35215, 2.18522* **Camp**
Municipal des Pins, Route de Salbris, La Chaux, 18330
Nançay [02 48 51 81 80 or 02 48 51 81 35 (Mairie); fax
02 48 51 80 60; info@les-pins-camping.com; www.
les-pins-camping.com] Site on D944 fr Salbris twd Bourges
clearly sp on L immed bef ent Nançay. Med, mkd pitch, hdstg,
shd; htd wc; chem disp; shwrs inc; el pnts (6A) inc; gas; lndtte;
shops 1km; playgrnd; tennis; golf 2km; fishing; 50% statics;
no twin-axles; adv bkg; quiet; CKE/CCI. "Lovely spot in pine
woods; friendly recep; clean san facs; poor site lighting;
beautiful vill; gd walking." 20 Apr- 08 Sep. € 9.40   2013*

NANCY *6E2* (6km SW Rural) *48.65730, 6.14028* **Campéole Le Brabois, 2301 Ave Paul Muller, 54600 Villers-lès-Nancy [03 83 27 18 28; fax 03 83 40 06 43; brabois@campeole.com; www.camping-brabois.com or www.campeole.com]** Fr A33 exit junc 2b sp Brabois onto D974 dir Nancy; after 400m turn L at 2nd traff lts; at slip rd after 2nd further traff lts turn R on slip rd & site on R; site well sp. Lge, mkd pitch, pt shd; htd wc (some cont); chem disp; mv service pnt; shwrs inc; el pnts (5-15A) €4.10-5.25 (poss rev pol)(ask for pitch with 15A if required); gas; lndtte; shop; tradsmn; supmkt & petrol 2km; rest; snacks (high ssn); bar; BBQ; playgrnd; games area; TV; dogs €2.60; bus adj (tickets fr recep); poss cr; Eng spkn; adv bkg; quiet; ccard acc; red low ssn; CKE/CCI. "Popular, well-run site; mostly lge pitches, but some sm; helpful staff; gd, clean, all new san facs; no twin-axle c'vans over 5.50m (m'vans OK); interesting town; rec arr early; vg NH; excel; Ltd wifi coverage" ♦ 1 Apr-15 Oct. € 28.20 SBS - J03   2013*

See advertisement on pages 14 & 15

NANCY *6E2* (10km NW Rural) *48.74733, 6.05700* **Camping Les Boucles de la Moselle, Ave Eugène Lerebourg, 54460 Liverdun [03 83 24 43 78 or 06 03 27 69 71 (mob); fax 03 83 24 89 47; francis.iung@orange.fr]** Fr A31 exit junc 22 to Frouard. In Frouard bear L onto D90 to Liverdun; cross rv bdge (sp Liverdun); under rlwy bdge L at traff lts, thro town, fork L & foll sp to site by on rvside by sports area. Do not turn L at site exit when towing. Lge, pt shd; htd wc; baby facs; shwrs (0730-1000) inc; el pnts (6A) €3.20; lndtte; shop & 1.5km; rest, snacks; bar; playgrnd; pool; entmnt; some statics; dogs €1.20; quiet except rlwy noise; ccard not acc; CKE/CCI. "Lovely site & area; helpful staff; Nancy worth visit; new owners 2012" 1 May-30 Sep. € 11.10   2012*

"Satellite navigation makes touring much easier"

Remember most sat navs don't know if you're towing or in a larger vehicle – always use yours alongside maps and site directions.

NANS LES PINS *10F3* (1km N Rural) *43.37535, 5.78510* **Camping Village Club La Sainte Baume, Quartier Delvieux Sud, 83860 Nans-les-Pins [04 94 78 92 68; fax 04 94 78 67 37; ste-baume@wanadoo.fr; www.saintebaume.com]** Exit A8 junc 34 dir St Maximin onto D560. Cross N7 & at next lge junc turn R onto D560 then immed L onto D80. Site 600m after sp Nans-les-Pins, L at traff lts then up private rd to site. Lge, mkd pitch, pt sl, shd; wc; chem disp; mv service pnt; baby facs; shwrs; el pnts (6A) inc; gas; lndtte (inc dryer); shop; rest, snacks; bar; BBQ; playgrnd; 3 pools; waterslide; jacuzzi; sand beach 35km; cycle hire; games area; gym; horseriding; wifi; TV; 90% statics; dogs €5; adv bkg; ccard acc; red low ssn. "Friendly staff; modern san facs; some pitches diff access; ltd facs low ssn; path into pleasant vill; mkt Wed am; excel." ♦ 1 Apr-30 Sep. € 33.00 (CChq acc)   2010*

NANT *10E1* (2km N Rural) *44.03578, 3.29008* **Camping Le Roc Qui Parle, Les Cuns, 12230 Nant [tel/fax 05 65 62 22 05; contact@camping-roc-qui-parle-aveyron.fr; www.camping-roc-qui-parle-aveyron.fr]** Fr Millau take D991E to site passing Val de Cantobre. Fr La Cavalerie take D999E to Nant & at T-junc on o'skts of Nant turn N; Millau & Les Cuns approx 2km; site on R. NB Steep decent into site. Med, hdg/mkd pitch, pt sl, pt shd; wc; serviced pitches; chem disp; mv service pnt; shwrs inc; el pnts (10A) €3.30; lndtte; shop; BBQ; playgrnd; rv sw & fishing on site; wifi; dogs free; adv bkg; quiet; no ccard acc; CKE/CCI. "Excel, well-run site in magnificent surroundings; lge pitches with views; warm welcome, friendly & helpful; excel facs; rv walk; rec." ♦ ltd 1 Apr-30 Sep. € 25.20   2013*

NANT *10E1* (4km N Rural) *44.04550, 3.30170* **RCN Camping Le Val de Cantobre, Domaine de Vellas, 12230 Nant [05 65 58 43 00 or 06 80 44 40 63 (mob); fax 05 65 62 10 36; cantobre@rcn.fr; www.rcn-valdecantobre.fr]** Exit A75 junc 47 (La Cavalerie/Nant); foll sp D999 E dir La Cavalerie/Nant for 12 km. At Nant at T-junc turn L onto D999 sp Val de Cantobre. Site on R in 4km. NB Steep access rd, care req. Rec park in parking area at ent to site & walk down drive to recep. Lge, mkd pitch, hdstg, terr, pt shd; wc (some cont); chem disp; mv service pnt; baby facs; shwrs inc; el pnts (6A) inc; gas; lndtte (inc dryer); shop; rest, snacks; bar; BBQ; playgrnd; htd pool; paddling pool; waterslide; tennis; cycle hire; games area; games rm; wifi; entmnt; games/TV rm; some tour op statics & tents; dogs €7; no c'vans/m'vans over 7m high ssn; no twin-axles; poss cr; Eng spkn; adv bkg ess; quiet; ccard acc; red low ssn. "Busy, popular, Dutch-owned site; in gd position - views fr most pitches; helpful, welcoming staff; clean, modern san facs but long walk fr some pitches; steep site rds & many steps; mkt Tue (July/Aug only); excel." ♦ 6 Apr-29 Sep. € 45.65 (CChq acc)   2011*

See advertisement opposite

NANT *10E1* (7km E) *44.01117, 3.20457* **Camping La Dourbie, Route de Nant, 12230 Saint-Jean-du-Bruel, Aveyron [05 65 46 06 40; fax 05 65 46 06 50; info@camping-la-dourbie.com; www.camping-la-dourbie.com]** Fr A75 take exit 47, twrds La cavalerie, Nat, St-Eulalie-de-Cernon. At rndabt take 3rd exit onto D999, go thro next rndabt, turn R cont D999 to site Med, hdg pitch, pt shd; wc; shwrs; el pnts (6,10, 16A) €2.-€4; mv service pnt; chem disp; lndtte; rest; bar; BBQ; dogs - 1 per pitch, leashed; htd pool; spa; playgrnd; wifi; canoeing; bungee jumping; paragliding; "Excel site, such a lot to do and see" ♦ 12 Apr-29 Sept. € 19.00   2013*

NANT *10E1* (1km S Rural) *44.01698, 3.30125* **Camping Les Deux Vallées, 12230 Nant [05 65 62 26 89 or 05 65 62 10 40; fax 05 65 62 17 23; www.lesdeuxvallees.com]** Exit A75 junc 47 onto D999 for 14km to Nant; site sp. Med, mkd pitch, pt shd; wc (some cont); own san; chem disp; mv service pnt; some serviced pitches; shwrs inc; el pnts (6A) €2 (poss rev pol); lndtte; tradsmn; rest; snacks; bar; shop 1km; pool 500m; playgrnd; entmnt; rv fishing; TV; dogs €1; phone; quiet; adv bkg; CKE/CCI. "Peaceful, well-kept, scenic site; friendly; clean, modern san facs; 15 mins walk fr vill cent; gd walking; rec." ♦ 1 Apr-28 Oct. € 25.00   2012*

FRANCE

NANT *10E1* (2.5km S Rural) *44.01319, 3.32032* **Camping Castelnau (Gely), 12230 Nant [05 65 62 25 15; isaetdom@ aliceadsl.fr; www.campingcastelnau.free.fr]** Fr Nant take D999 E twds Le Vigan; site is sp on L in 2.5km. Last 200m rough rd. Sm, pt shd; wc; chem disp (wc); shwrs inc; el pnts (11A) €2.50 (poss long lead req); lndtte; shop, rest, snacks, bar 2.5km; playgrnd; pool 3km; sw & fishing nr; some statics; dogs free; poss cr; adv bkg; quiet; ccard not acc; CKE/CCI. "Spacious CL-type site; lovely location; clean facs; conv Roquefort." ♦ 1 Apr-31 Oct. € 8.00   2009*

NANT *10E1* (500m SW Rural) *44.02105, 3.29390* **Camping Les Vernèdes, Route St Martin-Le Bourg, 12230 Nant [05 65 62 15 19]** Site sp fr vill cent. Sm, shd; wc (some cont); chem disp; shwrs inc; el pnts (10A) inc (long lead req); gas 500m; lndtte; rest adj; BBQ; playgrnd; dogs; Eng spkn; adv bkg; quiet; CKE/CCI. "Orchard site set in beautiful location; pleasant stroll to Nant cent; gd trout rest adj; gd touring base; v helpful owners; excel and great site to stay on." 1 Mar-31 Oct. € 11.50   2011*

⊞ **NANTES** *2G4* (3km N Urban) *47.24261, -1.55703* **Nantes Camping, 21 Blvd de Petit Port, 44300 Nantes [02 40 74 47 94; fax 02 40 74 23 06; nantes-camping@nge-nantes.fr; www.nantes-camping.fr]** Fr ring rd exit junc 39 sp Porte de la Chapelle & foll sp Centre Ville, Camping Petit Port or University when ent o'skts of Nantes. Site ent opp Hippodrome & nr racecourse & university; well sp. Take care tram lines. Lge, hdg/mkd pitch, some hdstg, pt shd; htd wc; serviced pitches; chem disp; mv service pnt; baby facs; shwrs inc; el pnts (16A) €4.90; gas; lndtte (inc dryer); sm shop; tradsmn; rest, snacks; bar; BBQ (charcoal only); playgrnd; htd, covrd pool & waterslide adj inc; cycle hire; entmnt; wifi €1 ; TV; 30% statics; dogs €3; bus & tram to city cent adj; twin-axles acc (extra charge); o'night m'van area; poss cr; Eng spkn; adv bkg (groups); quiet; ccard acc; red low ssn/long stay; CKE/CCI. "Well kept and maintained; excel san facs; Tram stop next to site, easy access to Nantes centre; Sw pool across the road with discount; ACSI red low ssn." ♦ € 30.00 (CChq acc)   2013*

⊞ **NANTES** *2G4* (6km E Rural) *47.25416, -1.45361* **Camping Belle Rivière, Route des Perrières, 44980 Ste Luce-sur-Loire [tel/fax 02 40 25 85 81; belleriviere@wanadoo.fr; www.camping-belleriviere.com]** Fr 'Nantes Périphérique Est' take exit 43 (at Porte d'Anjou) onto A811; exit A811 junc 24 dir Thouaré-sur-Loire on D68; at double rndabt by car showroom turn S & foll sp over rlwy bdge; site sp. Fr E via D68, thro Thouaré dir Ste Luce; at double rndabt by car showroom, S over rlwy bdge twd rv; site sp. Med, hdg/mkd pitch, hdstg, pt shd; wc (50% cont); chem disp; shwrs inc; el pnts (3-10A) €2.70-3.90 (extra charge in winter); gas; lndry rm; shops 3km; tradsmn; rest, snacks; bar; BBQ; playgrnd; wifi; 50% statics; dogs €1.45; poss cr; Eng spkn; adv bkg; quiet; red low ssn/CKE/CCI. "Beautifully-kept site; helpful owners; gd clean san facs; rvside walks; conv Nantes Périphérique & city cent; gd touring base; excel." ♦ € 14.40   2011*

NANTIAT *7B3* (600m W Urban) *46.00471, 1.15300* **Camp Municipal Les Haches, Ave de la Gare, 87140 Nantiat [05 55 53 42 43 (Mairie); fax 05 55 53 56 28]** Turn E off N147 at x-rds in Chamboret onto D711, site 1km on L, sp fr N147. Sm, pt sl, pt shd; wc; chem disp; shwrs inc; el pnts; shops 1km; rest, bar 600m; playgrnd; fishing; rlwy noise; CKE/CCI. "Gd, clean site & facs; lovely setting o'looking lake; phone ahead as opening dates not reliable; height barrier 2.50m; conv 'Martyr Village' at Oradour-sur-Glane; gd sh stay/NH." 15 Jun-15 Sep.   2008*

NANTUA *9A3* (1km W Urban) *46.14999, 5.60017* **Camp Municipal Le Signal, 17 Ave du Camping, 01130 Nantua [04 74 75 02 09 or 06 71 76 36 17 (mob); campinglesignal01@ orange.fr; www.camping-nantua.fr]** E on D1084 fr Pont d'Ain, rd passes alongside Nantua lake on R. At end of lake bef ent town turn R & foll sps. Sm, hdg/mkd pitch, unshd; wc; mv service pnt; shwrs inc; el pnts (16A) €2.50; shops 200m; rest, snacks; playgrnd; lake sw 300m; sports cent nr; some statics; dogs free; poss cr; quiet. "Attractive, spacious, well-kept site in lovely setting; friendly staff; town & shops minutes away; conv for m'way." 01 Apr-30 Oct. € 15.40   2012*

⊞ **NAPOULE, LA** *10F4* (2km N Coastal) *43.53913, 6.94273* **Camping Les Cigales, 505 Ave de la Mer, Quartier d'Etang, 06210 Mandelieu-la-Napoule [04 93 49 23 53; fax 04 93 49 30 45; campingcigales@wanadoo.fr; www. lescigales.com]** Take Mandelieu exit junc 40 fr A8 & turn R twice in Mandelieu cent into Ave des Ecureuils, sp Campings. Pass under a'route & in 1km turn L at T-junc into Ave de la Mer. Site in 50m on L. Or on DN7 fr Fréjus turn R at rndabt with fountains app Mandelieu. Or fr coast rd turn inland at bdge over Rv La Siagne into Blvd de la Mer & site in 1km on R. Med, hdg/mkd pitch, hdstg, shd; htd wc; chem disp; mv service pnt; baby facs; shwrs inc; el pnts (6A) €5.50; Indtte; shop 1.5km; rest, snacks; bar; playgrnd; pool; sand beach 800m; solarium; dir access to rv; fishing, sailing & other waterports 800m; wifi; entmnt; 50% statics; dogs €1.50; bus adj; poss cr; Eng spkn; adv bkg; some noise fr rd, rlwy, aircraft; ccard acc; red low ssn/long stay. "Excel location; ltd facs low ssn; gd pool; conv local transport; excel." ◆ € 41.00   2010*

"There aren't many sites open at this time of year"

If you're travelling outside peak season remember to call ahead to check site opening dates – even if the entry says 'open all year'.

NAPOULE, LA *10F4* (2km N Urban) *43.53507, 6.94258* **Camping Les Pruniers, 18 Rue de la Pinéa, 06210 Mandelieu-la-Napoule [04 93 49 99 23; fax 04 93 49 37 45; contact@bungalow-camping.com; www.bungalow-camping.com]** Fr A8 exit junc 40 & turn R twice in Mandelieu cent into Blvd des Ecureuils sp 'Sofitel Royal Casino'. Pass under a'route & in 1km turn L at T-junc into Ave de la Mer. At rndabt bear R & next R sp Pierre-Vacances. Turn R in 50m, site at end of rd. On DN7 fr Fréjus, turn R at rndabt with fountains app Mandelieu. Fr coast rd take slip rd for Mandelieu. Sm, mkd pitch, hdstg; shd; wc; chem disp; mv service pnt; shwrs inc; el pnts (5-20A) €4; Indtte; shop (high ssn) & 1.2km; snacks, bar in vill; playgrnd; htd pool; paddling pool; sand beach 500m; sea & rv fishing; wifi; entmnt; 60% statics (sep area); dogs €1.50; no twin-axle c'vans & max length c'van 6m, m'van 7m; poss cr; Eng spkn; adv bkg; quiet; red low ssn; ccard acc; red low ssn; CKE/CCI. "Delightful, peaceful site on rv opp marina; dated, clean san facs; excel base for area; easy cycling to beach & Cannes." 1 Apr-15 Oct. € 37.00   2010*

NAPOULE, LA *10F4* (3km N Urban/Coastal) *43.5234, 6.9308* **Camping Coté Mer (Formaly Camping de la Ferme), Blvd du Bon Puits, 06210 Mandelieu-la-Napoule [04 93 49 94 19; fax 04 93 49 18 52; info@campingcotemer.fr; www.campingdelaferme.com]** Fr A8 exit junc 40 & turn L in Mandelieu cent sp Fréjus; 200m after rndabt with palm tree centre, fork R into Ave Maréchal Juin & strt into Blvd du Bon Puits. Avoid La Napoule vill when towing. Med, shd; wc; shwrs €0.50; el pnts (10A) inc; gas; Indtte; shops; rest, snacks; bar; sand beach 700m; some statics; dogs €4.; poss v cr; adv bkg; quiet; red low ssn. "Nice atmosphere; some pitches v sm; friendly, helpful staff; dated but clean facs; pleasant sm bar & rest." ◆ 25 Mar-1 Oct. € 36.00   2013*

⊞ **NAPOULE, LA** *10F4* (5km N Urban/Coastal) *43.52547, 6.93354* **Camping L'Argentière, 264 Blvd du Bon-Puits, 06210 Mandelieu-la-Napoule [tel/fax 04 93 49 95 04; www.campingdelargentiere.com]** Fr A8 turn L in Mandelieu cent (sp Fréjus). At rndabt with fountains take 2nd exit, at next rndabt take 2nd exit to L of BP stn, at next rndabt take 2nd exit, site on R in 150m. Avoid La Napoule vill when towing. Med, hdg/mkd pitch, hdstg, pt shd; wc; chem disp; mv service pnt; shwrs inc; el pnts (10A) €3.20; Indtte; shop; hypmkt 1km; rest, snacks; bar; sand beach 800m; fishing; entmnt; TV rm; 80% statics; dogs €3; bus; Eng spkn; adv bkg ess in ssn; poss cr; quiet; CKE/CCI. "Clean san facs; lovely local beaches, conv to town" € 31.00   2012*

NARBONNE *10F1* (10km N Rural) *43.26009, 2.95552* **Camp Municipal, Rue de la Cave Coopérative, 11590 Sallèles-d'Aude [04 68 46 68 46 (Mairie); fax 04 68 46 91 00; ot.sallelesdaude@wanadoo.fr; www.salleles-daude.com]** Fr A9/E15 exit junc 36 onto D64 N & in approx 4km turn L to join D11 W. Cont on this rd for approx 18km, then turn L onto D13 S to Ouveillan. In vill, turn R onto D418 SW to Sallèles-d'Aude. Site in vill. NB Nr Canal du Midi some narr app rds. Sm, hdg/mkd pitch, pt shd; wc; chem disp; el pnts €2.50; shops 1km; BBQ; no statics; dogs; adv bkg; quiet. "Clean site nr canal; 16 pitches; warden calls am; excel." 1 May-30 Sep. € 11.00   2008*

NARBONNE *10F1* (10.5km NE Rural) *43.23821, 3.11063* **Camp Municipal Les Sablous, Ave de Coursan, 11110 Salles-d'Aude [04 68 33 61 73 (Mairie); mairie-salles-daude@wanadoo.fr]** Fr Narbonne on D6009; at Coursan turn R onto D1118 sp Salles-d'Aude, site sp in 5km on W edge of vill. Med, mkd pitch, pt shd; wc (cont); chem disp (wc); shwrs inc; Indry rm; shop adj; BBQ; playgrnd; dogs free; quiet; CKE/CCI. "No twin-axle c'vans; site ent diff for lge o'fits; fair NH." 1 Jul-31 Aug.   2010*

NARBONNE *10F1* (6km S Rural) *43.13662, 3.02595* **Les Mimosas Village Camping, Chaussée de Mandirac, 11100 Narbonne [04 68 49 03 72; fax 04 68 49 39 45; info@lesmimosas.com; www.lesmimosas.co.uk]** Leave A9 junc 38 at Narbonne Sud & at rndabt foll sp La Nautique. Turn L opp ent to Camping La Nautique & foll sp Mandirac & site. Lge, hdg/mkd pitch, hdstg, pt shd; htd wc; chem disp; mv service pnt; baby facs; fam bthrm; sauna; some serviced pitches; shwrs inc; el pnts (6A) inc; gas; Indtte (inc dryer); shop; rest, snacks; bar; BBQ (gas/elec); playgrnds; lge htd pool complex; paddling pool; waterslides; jacuzzi; sand beach 6km; watersports; rv fishing adj; fishing lake 300m; tennis; cycle hire; horseriding adj; gym; cycle hire; games area; games rm; wifi; entmnt; TV rm; 6% statics; dogs €4; lge o'fits rec phone in adv high ssn; adv bkg; Eng spkn; quiet; ccard acc; red low ssn/long stay; CKE/CCI. "Attractive site with lge pitches; gd choice of pitches; friendly, helpful staff; vg san facs; poss ltd low ssn; excel pool complex; vg for children; excel touring base in historic area; gd birdwatching; cycle path to Narbonne." ◆ 25 Mar-1 Nov. € 41.00 SBS - C35   2011*

See advertisement opposite

FRANCE

NARBONNE *10F1* (4km SW Urban) *43.14702, 3.00424*
Camping La Nautique, Chemin de la Nautique,11100 Narbonne [04 68 90 48 19; fax 04 68 90 73 39; info@campinglanautique.com; www.campinglanautique.com] Exit junc 38 fr A9 at Narbonne Sud. After toll take last rndabt exit & foll sp La Nautique. Site on R 2.5km fr A9 exit. Lge, hdg/mkd pitch, some hdstg, pt shd; chem disp; mv service pnt; individ san facs (wc, shwr) on each pitch inc; el pnts (10A) inc; gas; lndtte; shop & 3km; tradsmn; rest, snacks & bar high ssn; BBQ (elec only); playgrnd; htd pool; waterslide; paddling pool; canoeing; windsurfing; sand beach 10km; tennis; entmnt; wifi; 30% statics; dogs €6; Eng spkn; adv bkg; quiet with some rd noise; ccard acc; red low ssn/long stay; CKE/CCI. "Excel, well-run site; helpful, friendly Dutch owners; excel, clean facs; caution - hot water v hot; some pitches lge but narr; steel pegs req; pitches sheltered but some muddy after heavy rain; excel rest; many sports activities avail; cycle trips; gd walks nrby; highly rec" ♦ 1 Mar-31 Oct. € 43.80 SBS - C07   2013*

"That's changed – Should I let The Club know?"

If you find something on site that's different from the site entry, fill in a report and let us know. See www.caravanclub.co.uk/europereport.

⊞ **NARBONNE** *10F1* (12km SW Rural) *43.16296, 2.89186*
Camping La Figurotta, Route de Narbonne, 11200 Bizanet [04 68 45 16 26 or 06 88 16 12 30 (mob); fax 04 68 48 98 22; info@figurotta.eu; www.figurotta.eu] Exit A9 at Narbonne Sud onto slip rd N9/D6113 twd Lézignan-Corbières; in 3km at new rndabt head L twd D613 & then D224 sp Bizanet & site. App fr W not rec due narr D rds. Sm, mkd pitch, hdstg, pt sl, pt terr, shd; htd wc; chem disp; shwrs free; el pnts (4-6A) €2.50-3.50 (poss long lead req); gas; lndtte; sm shop & 2km; tradsmn; rest, snacks; bar; playgrnd; sm pool; sand beach 20km; games area; 5% statics; dogs €3 (sm dogs only); phone; Eng spkn; adv bkg; rd noise; red long stay/low ssn/CKE/CCI. "Pleasant, simple, well-run, scenic site; friendly & helpful; gd pool; gusty & stony site - steel pegs req; excel drainage; gd NH en rte Spain; vg; dated facs but beautifully clean" ♦ ltd € 34.00   2013*

NARBONNE PLAGE *10F1* (8km NE Coastal) *43.20592, 3.21056* Camping La Grande Cosse (Naturist), St Pierre-sur-Mer, 11560 Fleury-d'Aude [04 68 33 61 87; fax 04 68 33 32 23; contact@grandecosse.com; www.grandecosse.com] Exit A9 junc 37 & foll sp Narbonne-Plage. Cont thro Narbonne-Plage to St Pierre-sur-Mer, pass municipal site & turn R twd L'Oustalet, site sp. Lge, hdg/mkd pitch, pt shd; wc; serviced pitches; chem disp; mv service pnt; shwrs inc; el pnts (8A) €4; gas; lndtte; shop; rest, snacks; bar high ssn; playgrnd; htd pool; sand beach 300m; tennis; games area; games rm; gym; entmnt; boat hire; fishing; TV rm; 20% statics; dogs €4; phone; poss cr Aug; Eng spkn; adv bkg; red long stay/low ssn; ACSI; ccard acc; INF card req. "Excel, well-run site; gd pitches; helpful, friendly staff; excel san facs; naturist walk to lovely beach thro lagoons & dunes (poss flooded early ssn); mosquitoes poss problem Jun-Sep; flood risk after heavy rain; gd mkt St Pierre-sur-Mer." ♦ 28 Mar-4 Oct. € 32.50 (CChq acc)   2012*

NASBINALS *9D1* (1km N Rural) *44.67016, 3.04036* Camp Municipal, Route de St Urcize, 48260 Nasbinals [02 46 32 51 87 or 04 66 32 50 17; mairie.nasbinals@laposte.net; www.mairie-nasbinals.info] Fr A75 exit 36 to Aumont-Aubrac, then W on D987 to Nasbinals. Turn R onto D12, site sp. Med, pt sl, pt shd; htd wc; chem disp; mv service pnt; shwrs inc; el pnts (16A) €3; shop, rest in vill; BBQ; dogs; quiet; red CKE/CCI."Lovely loc gd views, no shd, facs inadequate peak ssn" ♦ ltd 15 May-30 Sep. € 8.40   2012*

NAUCELLE *8E4* (1km S Rural) *44.18818, 2.34825* **FLOWER** Camping du Lac de Bonnefon (FFCC), L'Etang de Bonnefon, 12800 Naucelle [05 65 69 33 20; fax 05 65 69 33 20; camping-du-lac-de-bonnefon.com or www.flowercampings.com] N fr Carmaux turn L off N88 Albi-Rodez rd at Naucelle Gare onto D997, sp Naucelle Centre. Site sp in 2km. Med, mkd pitch, pt sl, pt shd; htd wc; chem disp; mv service pnt; shwrs inc; el pnts (6A) €4.20; lndtte; shop 1.5km; rest, snacks; bar, playgrnd; htd pool; wifi; TV; many statics; dogs €2.50; poss cr; quiet; red low ssn; CKE/CCI. "Pleasant, clean site adj lge fishing lake; gd san facs; conv Sauveterre-de-Rouergue." ♦ 1 Apr-15 Oct. € 19.70   2009*

See advertisement on pages 32 & 33

NAUSSANNES see Beaumont du Périgord *7D3*

NAVARRENX 8F1 (200m S Urban) 43.31988, -0.76143
Camping Beau Rivage, Allée des Marronniers, 64190
Navarrenx [05 59 66 10 00; beaucamping@free.fr; www.
beaucamping.com] Fr E exit A64 junc 9 at Artix onto D281
dir Mourenx, then Navarrenx. Fr N on D947 thro Orthez to
Navarrenx (D947 fr Orthez much improved). Site well sp bet
walled (Bastide) town & rv. Med, hdg/mkd pitch, some hdstg, pt
sl, terr, pt shd; htd wc; chem disp; mv service pnt; some serviced
pitches; baby facs; fam bthrm; shwrs inc; el pnts (8-10A) inc;
lndtte (inc dryer); shop, rest & bar 300m; snacks; BBQ; playgrnd;
pool; rv fishing; rafting; tennis; cycle hire in town; games rm;
wifi; 15% statics; dogs €1.50; no c'vans/m'vans over 9m high
ssn; phone; Eng spkn; adv bkg; quiet; ccard acc; red low ssn;
CKE/CCI. "Lovely, peaceful, well-run site; nr interesting walled
town; helpful, friendly, British owners; clean san facs; gd pool;
gd area for walking, cycling; conv local shops & rests; mkt Wed;
rec." ♦ 31 Mar-15 Oct. € 24.50 SBS - D26   2011*

NAY 8F2 (2km N Rural) 43.20027, -0.25722 **Camping Les
Ô Kiri, Ave du Lac, 64800 Baudreix [05 59 92 97 73; fax
05 59 13 93 77; les-okiri@wanadoo.fr; www.lesokiri.net]**
Exit A64 junc 10 onto Pau ring rd D317 S, then D938 dir Nay
& Lourdes. Exit sp Baudreix fr in 2km turn R at rndabt & foll
sp to lake & site. Med, hdg/mkd pitch, pt shd; htd wc; chem
disp; mv service pnt; shwrs inc; el pnts (6-10A) €4-5.50; lndtte
(inc dryer); shop; tradsmn; supmkt 4km; rest, snacks; bar; BBQ;
playgrnd; lake sw complex; waterslides; tennis; cycle hire; wifi;
50% statics; dogs €2; adv bkg; quiet; ccard acc. "Conv Biarritz
& N Spain." ♦ 1 Apr-30 Sep. € 18.00 (CChq acc)   2010*

NEANT SUR YVEL 2F3 (3.5km N Rural) 48.04382, -2.33063
Camping Koad-Ar-Roc'h (Naturist), Le Bois de la Roche,
56430 Néant-sur-Yvel [02 97 74 42 11; koad-ar-roc-h@
wanadoo.fr; www.koad-ar-roch.com] NE fr Ploërmel on
D766 for 12km; D134 W for 3km to vill of Le Bois-de-la-Roche
& site ent in vill on L. Med, pt sl, pt shd; wc; chem disp (wc);
mv service pnt in Mauron; shwrs inc; el pnts (6A) €3.50; shop;
tradsmn; rest, snacks; bar; BBQ; playgrnd; pool; lake sw & fishing;
games rm; TV; 10% statics; dogs €4; no twin axles; Eng spkn;
adv bkg; quiet; ccard acc; INF card. "Unsophisticated, tranquil site
in extensive grounds; friendly owners; lge pitches; gd walking &
cycling." ♦ ltd 15 May-15 Sep. € 23.00   2010*

NEBOUZAT 9B1 (1km W Rural) 45.72569, 2.89008
Camping Les Domes, Les Quatre Routes de Nébouzat,
63210 Nébouzat [04 73 87 14 06 or 04 73 93 21 02 (LS);
fax 04 73 87 18 81; camping-domes@wanadoo.fr;
www.les-domes.com] Exit 5 fr A75 onto D213 twd Col
de la Ventouse; turn L on D2089 sp Tulle. Do not ent vill of
Nébouzat but cont for 1km. Take L onto D216 sp Orcival then
immed L. Site on L in 100m. Med, mkd pitch, hdstg, pt shd;
wc (mainly cont); chem disp; baby facs; shwrs inc; el pnts
(10-15A) €6 (poss long lead req); gas; lndtte; shop; tradsmn;
snacks; playgrnd; htd covrd pool; boules areas; walking; sailing;
windsurfing; entmnt; TV rm; phone; dogs free; Eng spkn; adv
bkg; quiet; red CKE/CCI. "Immac site; warm welcome; friendly,
helpful staff; sm pitches; gd san facs; conv Vulcania."
4 Apr-15 Sep. € 15.50   2008*

NEMOURS 4F3 (5km S Urban) 48.24073, 2.70389 **FFCC**
Camping de Pierre Le Sault, Chemin des Grèves, 77167
Bagneaux-sur-Loing [01 64 29 24 44; camping.bagneaux-
sur-loing@orange.fr] Well sp bef town fr both dir off D607.
Med, hdg/mkd pitch, pt shd; wc; shwrs inc; el pnts (3-6A) €2-3.10;
gas 2km; lndtte; shop 2km; tradsmn; playgrnd; tennis; 30% statics;
poss cr; some Eng spkn; ent barrier clsd 2200-0700; no adv bkg;
some rd noise; red low ssn; no ccard acc; CKE/CCI. "Lovely site by
canal & rv; excel clean facs." ♦ 1 Apr-31 Oct. € 11.76   2012*

NERAC 8E2 (800m SW Rural) 44.09948, 0.31028
Aire Naturelle Les Contes d'Albret, 47600 Nérac
[05 53 65 18 73; fax 05 53 97 18 62; lescontesdalbret@
orange.fr; www.albret.com] Exit A62 junc 7 onto D931 to
Laplume. Then turn W onto D15 & D656 to Nérac. Cont on
D656 dir Mézin & foll site sp to end of rd in 3km. Sm, pt sl, pt
shd; htd wc; chem disp; baby facs; shwrs inc; el pnts (6A) €2;
farm shop, other shops in vill; rest; playgrnd; pool; kayaking;
Eng spkn; adv bkg; quiet. "Vg, peaceful, CL-type site; excel
views; glorious garden." 1 May-30 Sep. € 13.00   2010*

NERIS LES BAINS 7A4 (1km NW Urban) 46.28695, 2.65215
Le Camping du Lac (Formerly Municipal), Ave Marx
Dormoy, 03310 Néris-les-Bains [04 70 03 17 59 or
04 70 03 24 70 (recep); fax 04 70 03 79 99; campingdulac-
neris@orange.fr; www.ville-neris-les-bains.fr] Site on N
side of Néris off D2144. Turn W at rndabt by blue tourist office,
opp park, & foll sp round 1 way system to site in 500m. Med,
hdg/mkd pitch, hdstg, pt sl, terr, pt shd; wc (some cont); chem
disp; shwrs inc; el pnts (10A); gas; shops 1km; tradsmn; snacks;
bar; playgrnd; covrd pool 500m; some statics; dogs €1; quiet;
red long stay. "6 pitches for m'vans at ent to site; space to wait
on car park if barrier clsd; pleasant town; vg; gd facs, quiet
lower pitches, gd NH" 1 Apr-22 Oct. € 15.30   2013*

NESLES LA VALLEE see Beaumont sur Oise 3D3

NESMY see Roche sur Yon, La 2H4

NEUF BRISACH 6F3 (6km NE Rural) 48.02724, 7.57230
Camping de L'Ile du Rhin, 68600 Biesheim [03 89 72 57 95;
fax 03 89 72 14 21; info@campingiledurhin.com; www.
campingiledurhin.com] On D415 Colmar to Freiburg
(Germany). Site on island in Rv Rhine, on R after French Customs
point off D415. Lge, hdstg, pt shd; wc; shwrs inc; el pnts (4-10A)
inc; lndtte; shop; snacks; htd, covrd pool adj; rv fishing 100m;
tennis; 50% statics; poss cr; Eng spkn; ccard acc. "Excel facs;
gates clsd 2000-0700; poss flooding some pitches; gd touring
base; vg." ♦ 6 Apr-4 Oct. € 18.85 (CChq acc)   2009*

NEUF BRISACH 6F3 (1.2km E Urban) 48.01638,
7.53565 **Camp Municipal Vauban, Entrée Porte de
Bâle, 68600 Neuf-Brisach [tel/fax 03 89 72 54 25 or
03 89 72 51 68 (Mairie); contact@camping-vauban.fr;
www.camping-vauban.fr]** Fr D415 (Colmar-Freiburg) at E of
Neuf-Brisach turn NE on D1 bis (sp Neuf-Brisach & Camping
Vauban). At next junc turn L & immed R into site rd. Med, pt
shd; wc; mv service pnt; shwrs €1; el pnts (10A) €4; shops in
town; playgrnd; pool 3km; 40% statics; dogs €1; adv bkg;
quiet; red low ssn; CKE/CCI. "Gd, well-run stie; fascinating
ramparts around town; excel NH; Lge pitches; friendly helpful
staff; Gd site; most statics being removed; helpful staff"
1 Jan-2 Jan, 20 Mar-31 Dec. € 20.40   2013*

NEUF BRISACH 6F3 (6km SE Rural) 47.97988, 7.59639
**FFCC Camping L'Orée du Bois, 5 Rue du Bouleau, 68600
Geiswasser** [tel/fax 03 89 72 80 13; valerie.schappler@
wanadoo.fr; http://camping-oree-du-bois.pagesperso-
orange.fr/] Site in vill cent; street name on bungalow; ent
bet bungalow & vegetable garden - tight turn, watch out
bungalow gutters. Sm, hdg pitch, pt shd; htd wc; chem disp;
shwrs inc; el pnts (10A) €2.50; lndtte; BBQ; playgrnd; dogs
free; Eng spkn; adv bkg; quiet; CKE/CCI. "Gd touring base;
friendly owner; vg." ♦ ltd 1 Apr-30 Sep. € 6.60   2009*

NEUFCHATEAU 6E2 (10km N Rural) 48.44364, 5.67616 **Camp
Municipal, Chemin de Santilles, Rue Principale, 88630
Domrémy-la-Pucelle** [03 29 06 90 70; fax 03 29 94 33 77;
mairie.domremylapucelle@packsurfwifi.com;
www.tourisme-lorraine.fr] Take D164 fr Neufchâteau, site
in cent of Domrémy vill, clear sp by stadium, nr Rv Meuse.
Sm, pt shd; wc; shwrs €0.90; el pnts (16A) €2.80; shops, rest
& bar 1km N or 4km S; tennis; quiet. "Site yourself, warden
calls (not Sun); nr birthplace of Joan of Arc." 1 Jun-31 Aug.
€ 6.35   2011*

NEUFCHATEAU 6E2 (500m NW Urban) 48.35609, 5.68845
**Camp Municipal, Place Pitet, Rue de Moulinot, 88300
Neufchâteau** [03 29 94 19 03 or 03 29 94 08 77 (Commune);
fax 03 29 94 33 77; contact@neufchateau-tourisme.com;
www.neufchateau-tourisme.com] Clear sp on ent town next
to sports stadium. Sm, pt shd; wc; chem disp; shwrs inc; el pnts
(10A) inc; lndry rm; shops 500m; htd pool nr; poss v cr; some
rlwy noise. "Sm pitches; gd san facs; ltd low ssn; poss unkempt
& untidy low ssn; no twin-axles; NH or sh stay." ♦
15 May-30 Sep. € 15.80   2008*

NEUFCHATEL EN BRAY 3C2 (900m NW Urban) 49.73781,
1.42803 **Camping Sainte Claire, 13 Rue Sainte
Claire**, 76270 Neufchâtel-en-Bray [02 35 93 03 93 or
06 20 12 20 98 (mob); fancelot@wanadoo.fr; www.
camping-sainte-claire.com] Fr S exit A28 junc 9 onto D928
sp Neufchâtel; in 1km, at bottom hill, turn L into Rue de la
Grande Flandre, following Leclerk supmkt sp; cont past supmkt
for 400m to Rue Ste Claire. Or Fr N exit A28 junc 7 onto D928
dir Neufchâtel; in approx 5km turn R onto D1 for Dieppe & in
1km turn L at site sp. Med, hdg/mkd pitch, hdstg, pt sl, terr,
pt shd; wc (some cont); chem disp; mv service point; serviced
pitches; shwrs inc; el pnts (6-10A) €4-6; lndtte (inc dryer); sm
shop; supmkt 500m; tradsmn; bar/rest, snacks; bar; playgrnd;
cycle hire; fishing; wifi; 30% statics; dogs free low ssn; phone
adj; bus 1km; poss cr; some Eng spkn; adv bkg; quiet; ccard
acc; red long stay; CKE/CCI. "Beautiful, spacious, busy site by
rv; well-kept & well-run; lge, med & sm pitches; not all pitches
have 10A, poss 6A pitches better; friendly, helpful owner; excel
clean san facs - poss long walk low ssn; wet rm for disabled;
wheelchair access/easy walking; pleasant walk along cycle rte
(old rlwy line) to town; Sat mkt; conv Le Havre/Dieppe ferries
& A28; sep o'night area; some drive-thro pitches; gd value sh
or long stay; popular NH; excel; Nice site as always; building an
Aire for m'vans for 2013; Busy, efficient site" ♦ 1 Apr-24 Oct.
€ 21.40   2013*

NEUILLY SUR MARNE see Paris 3D3

NEUNG SUR BEUVRON 4G3 (500m NE Rural) 47.53893,
1.81488 **FFCC Camp Municipal de la Varenne, 34 Rue de
Veilleas, 41210 Neung-sur-Beuvron** [tel/fax 02 54 83 68 52
or 06 27 92 39 14 (mob); camping.lavarenne@wanadoo.fr;
www.neung-sur-beuvron.fr/camping] On A10 heading S
take Orléans Sud exit & join N20 S. At end of La Ferté-St Aubin
take D922 SW twd Romorantin-Lanthenay. In 20km R onto
D925 to Neung. Turn R at church pedestrian x-ing in cent of
vill ('stade' sp), R at fork (white, iron cross) & site on R in 1km.
Site by rvside. Fr A71 exit junc 3 onto D923; turn R onto D925
& as above. Sm, hdg/mkd pitch, pt sl; pt shd; wc; chem disp;
mv service pnt; shwrs inc; el pnts (6A) €3.10; gas; lndtte; shops
1km; tradsmn; rest, bar 500m; playgrnd; tennis; few statics;
dogs; poss cr (Aug); Eng spkn; adv bkg; v quiet; ccard acc.
"Friendly, helpful warden; gd, immac facs; lge pitches; barrier
clsd 2200-0800; vg cent for hiking, cycling, birdwatching;
mkt Sat; Immac facs; friendly & helpful warden; Barrier clsd
between 22h00 & 08h00" Easter-20 Oct. € 11.80   2013*

NEUSSARGUES MOISSAC see Murat 7C4

NEUVE LYRE, LA 3D2 (Urban) 48.90750, 0.74486 **Camp
Municipal La Salle, Rue de l'Union, 27330 La Neuve-
Lyre** [02 32 60 14 98 or 02 32 30 50 01 (Mairie); fax
02 32 30 22 37; mairie.la-neuve-lyre@wanadoo.fr] Fr NE
on D830 into vill turn R at church (sp not visible), fr S (Rugles)
foll sp. Well sp fr vill. Med, pt shd; wc (some cont) ltd; chem
disp (wc); mv service pnt; shwrs €0.75; el pnts (5A) inc (poss
long lead req); shops 500m; fishing; 40% statics; dogs; quiet;
CKE/CCI. "Delightful, peaceful, clean site; site yourself, warden
calls; excel sh stay/NH." ♦ 15 Mar-15 Oct. € 7.60   2010*

NEUVEGLISE 9C1 (5km S Rural) 44.89500, 3.00157 **Flower
Camping Le Belvédère, Le Pont-de-Lanau, 15260
Neuvéglise** [04 71 23 50 50; fax 04 71 23 58 93; contact@
campinglebelvedere.com; www.campinglebelvedere.com]
S on A75/E11 exit junc 28 at St Flour; take D921 S twd
Chaudes-Aigues. Turn R sp 'Villages de Vacances de Lanau' &
site - do not app site thro Neuvéglise. Steep access poss diff
lge o'fits. Med, terr, pt shd; wc; chem disp; mv service pnt;
baby facs; sauna; shwrs inc; el pnts (6A) inc; gas; lndtte (inc
dryer); shop; rest, snacks; bar; BBQ (gas/charcoal); playgrnd;
htd pool; paddling pool; fishing; canoeing, windsurfing &
tennis nrby; sailing 15km; fitness rm; horseriding 20km;
fitness rm; wifi; entmnt; games/TV rm; 25% statics; dogs
free; twin-axles acc (rec check in adv); adv bkg; quiet; ccard
acc; red low ssn/long stay; CKE/CCI. "Views over Rv Truyère;
friendly, peaceful, family-run site; steep terrs & tight pitches
poss diff; gd, clean san facs; mkt Neuvéglise Fri; excel site,
beautiful views" ♦ 30 Mar-29 Sep. € 39.00   2013*

See advertisement on pages 32 & 33

NEUVEGLISE 9C1 (300m SW Rural) 44.92406, 2.97936 **Camp
Municipal Fontbielle, 15260 Neuvéglise** [04 71 23 50 50]
S fr St Flour on D921 for approx 20km. Turn R to Neuvéglise &
foll sp thro town. Sm, terr, pt shd; wc (some cont); chem disp
(wc); mv service pnt in town; shwrs inc; el pnts (6A) €2; lndtte
(inc dryer); shop, rest, snacks, bar 300m; BBQ; playgrnd; htd
pool 5km; tennis 150m; some statics; dogs €1; bus 300m; adv
bkg; quiet; CKE/CCI. "Well-maintained & well-run site; clean san
facs; gd touring base." ♦ ltd 1 Jun-30 Sep. € 5.50   2010*

NEUVIC (CORREZE) *7C4* (4km N Rural) *45.38245, 2.22901*
**Camping Domaine de Mialaret, Route d'Egletons,
19160 Neuvic [05 55 46 02 50; fax 05 55 46 02 65; info@
lemialaret.com; www.lemialaret.com]** Fr N on A89 exit
23 twds St Angel then D171 to Neuvic or foll sp fr Neuvic
on D991. Med, some hdg pitch, pt sl, pt shd; htd wc; chem
disp; mv service pnt; baby facs; shwrs inc; el pnts (10A) €3-4;
Indtte; shop; tradsmn; rest in chateau fr May; snacks high ssn;
bar; playgrnd; pool; 2 carp fishing pools; watersports nrby;
mini-farm; mountain bike routes; walking tours; games rm;
wifi; entmnt; TV rm; 30% statics (sep area); dogs free; phone;
bus 4km; poss cr; quiet; adv bkg; Eng spkn; red long stay/
low ssn; CKE/CCI. "Excel site in grounds of chateau; charming
owner, friendly staff; facs ltd low ssn; blocks req most pitches;
children's mini-zoo & rare sheep breeds nrby." 1 May-30 Sep.
€ 25.00   2009*

NEUVIC (CORREZE) *7C4* (4km N Rural) *45.41034,
2.28469* **Camping Le Soustran, Pellachal, 19160 Neuvic
[05 55 95 03 71 or 06 47 94 89 34 (mob); info@lesoustran.
com; www.lesoustran.com]** N fr Neuvic on D982 dir Ussel
for 4km; site on L 300m after bdge. Ent steepish & rough.
Med, mkd pitch, terr, pt shd; wc; chem disp; shwrs inc; el pnts
(6A) €3; Indtte; snacks; bar; BBQ; playgrnd; lake sw 300m; TV
rm; dogs €1; Eng spkn; quiet; CKE/CCI. "No twin-axles." ♦ ltd
1 May-15 Sep. € 16.00   2010*

NEUVIC (CORREZE) *7C4* (5km NE Rural) **Camping à la Ferme
Chez Père Jules (Van Boshuysen), Prentegarde, 19160
Liginiac [tel/fax 05 55 95 84 49; rob_ykie@hotmail.com]**
Exit A89 junc 23 onto D979 dir Bort-les-Orgues; in 5km (just
after La Serre) turn R onto D982; in 10km turn L to Liginiac;
cont thro vill & then turn R uphill onto D20. Site sp to R in
1.5km. Sm, pt sl, pt shd; wc; chem disp; shwrs inc; el pnts (4A)
inc; Indtte; shop 1.5km; sm rest; bar; BBQ; playgrnd; pool; lake
sw 2km; 5% statics; dogs; Eng spkn; adv bkg; quiet; CKE/CCI.
"Beautiful CL-type site; helpful Dutch owners; rallies welcome;
mv service pnt in Liginiac; vg; Higly rec" 1 Apr-30 Sep.
€ 15.00   2012*

⊞ **NEUVIC (CORREZE)** *7C4* (7km NW Rural) *45.42721,
2.20419* **Camping Le Vianon, Les Plaines, 19160 Palisse
[05 55 95 87 22; fax 05 55 95 98 45; camping.vianon@
wanadoo.fr; www.levianon.com]** Fr Neuvic take D47 twd
Pallisse. Site well sp. Med, mkd pitch, pt sl, pt shd; htd wc;
chem disp; mv service pnt; baby facs; shwrs inc; el pnts (16A)
€3.50; Indtte; shops; tradsmn; rest, snacks; bar; BBQ; playgrnd;
pool; lake fishing; sports activities; tennis; entmnt; internet;
TV rm; 15% statics; dogs €2; poss cr; Eng spkn; adv bkg;
quiet; red 7+ days; CKE/CCI. "Woodland walks; friendly Dutch
owners; vg rest & bar; clean facs." ♦ ltd € 25.85   2009*

NEUVIC (DORDOGNE) *7C3* (800m N Rural) *45.10571,
0.46930* **Camping Le Plein Air Neuvicois, Ave de Planèze,
24190 Neuvic [05 53 81 50 77; fax 05 53 80 46 50;
camping.le.plein.air.neuvicois@cegetel.net; www.
campingneuvicdordogne.com]** On D6089, 26km SW
fr Périgueux. After 24km, turn R sp Neuvic. Site clearly sp thro
vill, by rv after bdge. Med, pt shd; htf wc; baby facs; shwrs
inc; el pnts (6-10A) €3-4; Indtte; shop; rests 800m;
snacks; bar; pool; fishing; tennis; games rm; some statics; dogs
€0.50; phone; adv bkg; quiet; red low ssn/long stay. "Beautiful
location; lge pitches; charming owners; clean modern san facs;
vg." 1 Jun-15 Sep. € 12.00   2010*

NEUVILLE SUR SARTHE see Mans, Le *4F1*

NEVACHE *9C3* (6km W Rural) *45.03399, 6.54543* **Camp
Municipal de Foncouverte, 05100 Névache [04 92 21 38 21
or 04 92 21 49 95; michel.goiran@orange.fr]** Fr Briançon
take N94 NE twd Italian border dir Turin, then L onto D994 sp
Névache. Rd is narr with passing places. Site is 2nd in vill. Med,
pt sl, pt shd; wc; chem disp; shwrs inc; Indry rm; shop; tradsmn; Eng
spkn; quiet. "Vg for walkers; diff lge o'fits; no c'vans or m'vans
allowed on rds W of Névache 0900-1800 in summer."
1 Jun-20 Sep. € 9.50   2009*

NEVERS *4H4* (500m S Rural) *46.98210, 3.16110* **FFCC
Camping de Nevers, Rue de la Jonction, 58000 Nevers
[06 84 98 69 79; info@campingnevers.com; www.
campingnevers.com]** Fr E exit A77 junc 37 & foll dir 'Centre
Ville'. Site on R immed bef bdge over Rv Loire. Fr W (Bourges)
on D976 foll sp 'Nevers Centre' onto D907. In approx 3km bef
bdge turn R, site on L. Med, mkd pitch, hdstg, terr, pt shd; htd
wc; chem disp; mv service pnt; baby facs; shwrs inc; el pnts
(6-10A) €3-4.75; Indtte (inc dryer); supmkt 2km; tradsmn;
rest 500m; snacks; bar; BBQ; playgrnd; sand beach 200m; rv
fishing; cycle hire; internet; TV; 3% statics; dogs €0.50; phone;
bus 20m; poss cr; Eng spkn; adv bkg; rd noise; ccard not acc;
red low ssn; CKE/CCI. "Pleasant, scenic site on bank of Rv
Loire; on 3 levels - ltd el pnts on lower; gd clean san facs, poss
stretched high ssn; cycle paths along Loire; no twin-axles; poss
noisy when events at Nevers Magny-Cours racing circuit; gd
site; nr town" ♦ 12 Apr-13 Oct. € 26.45   2013*

NEVERS *4H4* (7km NW Urban) *47.01222, 3.07822*
**FFCC Camping La Loire, 2 Rue de la Folie, 58600
Fourchambault [03 86 60 81 59 or 06 11 05 18 69 (mob);
fax 03 86 60 96 24; campingdelaloire@dbmail.com; www.
camping-de-laloire.fr.st]** Fr Nevers on D40 thro town, site on
L bef rv bdge. Med, pt shd; wc; chem disp; mv service pnt;
shwrs inc; el pnts (6-10A) €3-4.50; Indtte; shop 500m; rest
100m; snacks; bar; BBQ; rv adj; dogs €0.50; bus; red long stay/
CKE/CCI. "Friendly, helpful staff; san facs need update & poss
unclean." ♦ ltd 9 Apr-31 Oct. € 10.50   2010*

NEVEZ see Pont Aven *2F2*

NEXON *7B3* (1km SW Rural) *45.67104, 1.18059* **Camp
Municipal de l'Etang de la Lande, 87800 Nexon
[05 55 58 35 44 or 05 55 58 10 19 (Mairie); fax
05 55 58 33 50; campingdelalande.nexon@orange.fr;
www.nexon.fr]** S fr Limoges on D704, take D15 W twd
Nexon. Exit Nexon by D11 sp Ladignac-le-Long & Camping,
site 3km S at junc with D17. Med, mkd pitch, sl, pt shd; htd
wc; shwrs; el pnts (5-10A); Indtte; shop; bar; rest, supmkt 1km;
playgrnd; lake sw adj; cycle hire; entmnt; TV rm; Eng spkn;
quiet. "Excel base for Limoges; site open to adj leisure park."
1 Jun-30 Sep. € 10.00   2013*

NEYDENS see St Julien en Genevois *9A3*

NIEDERBRONN LES BAINS *5D3* (1.5km N Rural) *48.96221, 7.64522* **Camp Municipal du Heidenkopf, Route de la Lisière, 67110 Niederbronn-les-Bains [03 88 09 08 46; camping-niederbronn@laregie.fr; www.niederbronn-les-bains.fr]** Fr Niederbronn NW on D1062/D662 & foll sp rd R into forest fr mineral spring. NB Last 500m single track - poss diff lge o'fits. Med, pt sl, terr, pt shd; htd wc (some cont); chem disp; mv service pnt; baby facs; shwrs inc; el pnts (6A) €3.30; gas; lndtte; shops 3km; tradsmn; BBQ; playgrnd; pool, tennis 600m; dogs €1.40; adv bkg; quiet; red long stay/low ssn. "V peaceful site; warm welcome; forest walks; rec pay day bef dep." ♦ 1 Apr-31 Oct. € 14.10   2010*

NIEDERBRONN LES BAINS *5D3* (1.5km SW Rural) *48.92958, 7.60428* **Camping Oasis Oberbronn, 3 Rue de Frohret, 67110 Oberbronn [03 88 09 71 96; fax 03 88 09 97 87; oasis.oberbronn@laregie.fr; http:// campingalsaceoberbronn.jimdo.com]** Fr D1062 turn S on D28 away fr Niederbronn; thro Oberbronn, site sp. Lge, mkd pitch, pt sl, pt shd; wc; chem disp; mv service pnt; sauna; shwrs inc; el pnts (6A) €4.30; lndtte; shop & 1.5km; tradsmn; rest, snacks; bar; BBQ; playgrnd; htd, covrd pool high ssn; paddling pool; tennis; wellness centre; fitness rm; walking, cycling, horseriding rtes; golf, games rm; fishing 2km; 20% statics; dogs €2.65; clsd 1200-1300; poss cr; adv bkg rec high ssn; quiet; red long stay/low ssn; ccard acc; CKE/CCI. "Vg site with views; part of leisure complex; sl area for tourers; some san facs tired; site gravel paths not suitable wheelchair users." ♦ ltd 1 Apr-30 Sep. € 15.05   2011*

⊞ **NIMES** *10E2* (7km NE Urban) *43.88323, 4.48791* **Camping Les Cyprès, 5 Rue de la Bastide, 30320 Bezouce [04 66 75 24 30; fax 04 66 75 64 78; cdavidian@wanadoo.fr]** Sp on N86 Nîmes-Avignon rd. Site not well sp in Bezouce - sign high on wall. Narr site access. Sm, pt shd; wc; chem disp; shwrs; el pnts (4-6A) €3.70; shop, rest, bar in vill; sm pool; mostly statics; dogs; poss cr; adv bkg; rd noise & cockerels. "Facs rustic & basic but clean; friendly & helpful owners; conv Pont-du-Gard, Nîmes, Arles; not rec lge o'fits; closes early evening low ssn; NH only." € 12.20   2008*

⊞ **NIMES** *10E2* (4km S Rural) *43.78776, 4.35196* **Camp Municipal Domaine de la Bastide, route de Générac, 30900 Nîmes [04 66 62 05 82; fax 04 66 62 05 83; immocamp@wanadoo.fr; www.camping-nimes.com]** Fr A9 exit junc 25 onto A54 dir Arles; in 2km exit A54 junc 1 onto D42 sp St Gilles; in 1.5km (at 2nd rndabt) turn R onto D135; in 2.5km at rndabt turn R onto D13; site on L. Or N fr Montpellier on N113/D6113 to Nimes; at Périphique Sud turn S onto D13 sp Générac; site on R 500m after rndabt junc with D613. Site well sp fr town cent. Lge, hdg/mkd pitch, hdstg, shd; htd wc; chem disp; mv service pnt; baby facs; shwrs inc; el pnts (10A) inc; gas; lndtte; shop; tradsmn; hypmkt nr; rest, snacks; bar; playgrnd; games area; wifi; TV rm; 10% statics; dogs €2.70; phone; bus; Eng spkn; adv bkg; quiet - some rd noise; red low ssn; CKE/CCI. "Excel, well-run site; lge pitches; friendly, helpful recep; Nîmes 20 mins by bus fr site." ♦ ltd € 30.20   2013*

NIOZELLES see Brillane, La *10E3*

NOAILLES see Brive la Gaillarde *7C3*

NOGENT SUR SEINE *4E4* (500m NE Rural) *48.50365, 3.50889* **Camp Municipal, Rue Villiers-aux-Choux, 10400 Nogent-sur-Seine [tel/fax 03 25 39 76 67 or 03 25 39 42 00 (Mairie)]** Fr Troyes site sp fr D619 on app to town & fr S ring rd, Site on rvside. Med, mkd pitch, some hdstg, pt shd; htd wc; shwrs; mv service pnt; el pnts; shop 500m; rest 100m; playgrnd; htd pool adj; tennis; quiet. "Pleasant site; poss many long-stay residents; gd NH." 1 Apr-5 Oct.   2009*

NOIRETABLE *9B1* (1km S Rural) *45.80817, 3.76844* **Camp Municipal de la Roche, Route de la Roche, 42440 Noirétable [04 77 24 72 68; fax 04 77 24 92 20]** Leave A72/ E70 junc 4 sp Noirétable; thro toll & turn SW onto D53. Ignore narr tourist rte sp to W; cont downhill to T-junc & turn R onto D1089. Take next L & site on R in 750m. Sm, mkd pitch, hdstg, pt terr, pt sl, pt shd; htd wc (cont); shwrs €1.50; el pnts (10A) €2.80; supmkt 1km; snacks, bar nr; playgrnd, lake adj; ccard not acc. "Warden lives on site, but barrier poss locked low ssn; rec phone ahead." 1 Apr-1 Nov. € 7.00   2011*

NOIRMOUTIER EN L'ILE *2H3* (2km E Coastal) *46.99769, -2.22331* **Camp Municipal Le Clair Matin, Les Sableaux, 85330 Noirmoutier-en-l'Ile [02 51 39 05 56; fax 02 51 39 74 36]** Ent Noirmoutier on D948 & foll sp to Les Sableaux. Site well sp. Med, mkd pitch, terr, pt shd; wc; mv service pnt; shwrs; el pnts (10A) €3.60; lndtte; shop; rest 500m; bar 150m; playgrnd; pool 2.5km; sand beach adj; fishing; dogs €1.20; adv bkg; quiet; red low ssn. "Excel site; gd clean san facs; excel cycle paths & beach fishing; lovely town." ♦ Easter-30 Oct. € 17.10 (3 persons)   2010*

NOIRMOUTIER EN L'ILE *2H3* (2km E Coastal) *46.99697, -2.22057* **Camping Indigo Noirmoutier La Vendette, Bois de la Chaize, 23 Rue des Sableaux, 85330 Noirmoutier-en-l'Ile [02 51 39 06 24; fax 02 51 35 97 63; noirmoutier@ camping-indigo.com; www.camping-indigo.com]** Ent Noirmoutier on D948, strt on over bdge & foll sp for Bois-de-la-Chaize, then 'campings'. Lge, pt shd; wc (some cont); chem disp; mv service pnt; baby facs; shwrs inc; el pnts (10A) €4.80; lndtte (inc dryer); tradsmn; snacks; bar; playgrnd; sand beach adj; fishing; boat-launching; cycle hire; internet; some statics; dogs €4; phone; poss cr; adv bkg; quiet; red low ssn; CKE/CCI ess. "Peaceful site in pine forest nr salt water marshes; gd for children." 1 Apr-1 Oct. € 21.00   2010*

See advertisement on next page

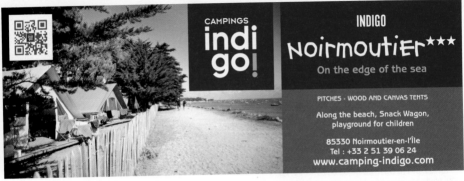

NOIRMOUTIER EN L'ILE *2H3* (10km SE Coastal) 46.94503, -2.18542 **Camping du Midi, 17 Rue du Camping, 85630 Barbâtre [02 51 39 63 74; fax 02 51 39 58 63; camping-du-midi@wanadoo.fr; www.camping-du-midi.com]** Cross to island by Passage du Gois D948 (low tide - 2.5 hrs per day) or bdge D38. Turn L after 2.5km off dual c'way to Barbâtre. Site sp N thro vill. V lge, pt sl, shd; wc; baby facs; shwrs; el pnts (10A) €6; gas; lndtte; shop 400m; rest, snacks; bar; BBQ (gas/elec); htd pool; paddling pool; sand beach adj; tennis; games area; entmnt; dogs €3.90; poss cr; no adv bkg; quiet; ccard acc; red low ssn. "Gd site; sandy but firm pitches; no longer municiapal & many changed planned (2011); food, wine and pool only avail high ssn" ♦ 1 Apr-20 Sep. € 26.90 (3 persons)   2011*

> "We must tell The Club about that great site we found"
>
> Get your site reports in by mid-August and we'll do our best to get your updates into the next edition of Caravan Europe.

NOIRMOUTIER EN L'ILE *2H3* (4km S) 46.96659, -2.22027 **Domaine Les Moulins, 54 Rue des Moulins, 85680 La Guérinière [0251 39 51 38; contact@camping-les-moulins.com; www.camping-les-moulins.com]** Cross to island on D38, sp to La Guérinière, imm turn L, site dir ahead. Lge, hdg, mkd, pt sl, pt shd pitch, htd WC, chem disp; mv service pnt, el pnts (10A) child/baby, facs, shwrs, lndtte, rest, bar, playgrnd, pool, beach, games area, games rm, wifi, 40%static, dogs, adv bkg, quiet, ccard acc, red low ssn, CKE/CCI, ACSI card acc. "Excel site, cycle hire 100m, shop adj" 1 Apri-30 Sept. € 47.60   2012*

NOIRMOUTIER EN L'ILE *2H3* (3.5km SW Coastal) 46.98609, -2.28790 **Camp Municipal La Bosse, 85740 L'Epine [02 51 39 01 07; campinglabosse@orange.fr]** Fr bdge take D38 to La Guérinière: turn W along D38 to L'Epine & foll camp sp to La Bosse. Lge, pt sl, unshd; wc; chem disp; shwrs inc; el pnts (5A) €2.50-3; lndtte; BBQ; playgrnd; sand beach, boat hire, sw & fishing 100m; entmnt; quiet; adv bkg. "Cheap & cheerful; many pitches sandy & v sl or uneven, others permanently occupied; poss windy; san facs adequate." ♦ 1 Apr-30 Sep. € 15.00   2009*

NOIRMOUTIER EN L'ILE *2H3* (8km W Coastal) 47.02409, -2.30374 **Camp Municipal La Pointe, L'Herbaudière, 85330 Noirmoutier-en-l'Ile [02 51 39 16 70; fax 02 51 39 74 15]** Fr bdge to island foll sp to Noirmoutier town, then to L'Herbaudière & port. At port turn L, 500m to site. Med, mkd pitch, unshd; wc; chem disp; mv service pnt; shwrs inc; el pnts (10A) €3.65 (long leads poss req); gas; lndtte; shop; rest, snacks & bar in town; playgrnd; beach adj; wifi; dogs €1.60; adv bkg; quiet; ccard acc; red low ssn; CKE/CCI. "Excel site in beautiful location; peaceful; sea views some pitches; poss windy (exposed to sea on 3 sides); helpful staff; clean, adequate facs; ground poss soft in some areas; gd cycle rtes on island; sh walk to fishing/pleasure harbour; rec." 18 Mar-15 Oct. € 16.50   2011*

NOLAY *6H1* (9km SW Rural) 46.87604, 4.55877 **Camp Municipal La Gabrelle, 39 La Varenne, 71490 Couches [03 85 45 59 49 or 03 85 98 19 20 (Mairie); fax 03 85 98 19 29; camping-la-gabrelle@orange.fr]** Exit A6 at junc 25 Chalon-sur-Saône Nord onto D978 sp Autun. In 26km at Couches, site NW of vill. Sm, hdg pitch, terr, pt shd; wc; shwrs inc; el pnts (6A) €2.80; lndtte; supmkt 5km; snacks; bar; playgrnd; lake adj; some daytime rd noise. "Attractive countryside nr wine area; gd facs; excel." ♦ 1 May-30 Sep. € 11.20   2010*

⊞ **NOLAY** *6H1* (1km NW Rural) 46.95084, 4.62266 **Camping La Bruyère, Rue du Moulin Larché, 21340 Nolay [tel/fax 03 80 21 87 59 or 06 88 16 06 18 (mob); http://www.nolay.com/fr/?/Logement/Les-campings]** Fr Beaune take D973 W dir Autun. In approx 20km, arr in vill of Nolay & cont on D973 thro vill. Site on L in 1km after vill, opp supmkt. Sm, hdg/mkd pitch, terr, pt shd; htd wc; chem disp; mv service pnt; shwrs inc; el pnts (10-12A) €3.60-4; lndtte; shop adj; supmkt, rest & bar 1km; BBQ; a few statics; phone adj; bus adj; Eng spkn; quiet; ccard acc; red low ssn; CKE/CCI. "Lovely, peaceful, well-kept site; friendly staff; gd, clean san facs, poss stretched if site busy; poss grape pickers in Sep; poss school & youth groups; attractive walk to bustling old town; gd touring base in wine area or NH." ♦ € 10.50   2013*

Dordogne
Périgord vert

Château Le Verdoyer ★★★★
Kawan Village Camping

www.verdoyer.fr

F 24470 Champs Romain
Tél. + 33 (0)5 53 56 94 64
Fax. + 33 (0)5 53 56 38 70
E mail : chateau@verdoyer.fr

Accomodations, restaurant, campsite ★★★★

NOLLEVAL *3D2* (200m N Rural) *49.49513, 1.48126* **Camp Municipal Le Clair-Ruissel, 9 Rue Marceau Fortin, 76780 Nolléval [tel/fax 02 35 90 83 26 or 02 35 90 83 47; mairie-nolleval@wanadoo.fr; www.normandie-tourisme.fr]** E fr Rouen on D31; in 29km at La Feuillie turn L onto D921 to Nolléval; at junc of D921 & D38 fork R onto D921; site on R in 200m. Site sp in vill. Sm, hdg/mkt pitch, pt shd; wc (some cont); chem disp (wc); shwrs inc; el pnts €3; shops, snacks & bar 500m; 50% statics; dogs; phone adj; quiet; adv bkg; CKE/CCI. "Vg site." 15 Mar-15 Oct. € 12.00   2011*

"I need an on-site restaurant"

We do our best to make sure site information is correct, but it is always best to check any must-have facilities are still available or will be open during your visit.

NONANCOURT *4E2* (4km E Urban) *48.76410, 1.23686* **Camp Municipal du Pré de l'Eglise, Rue Pré de l'Eglise, 28380 St Rémy-sur-Avre [02 37 48 93 87 or 02 37 62 52 00 (LS); fax 02 37 48 80 15; mairiesaintremy2@wanadoo.fr; www.ville-st-remy-sur-avre.fr]** Fr Dreux take N12 W to St Rémy; strt over 1st rndabt & at traff lts complex in 500m turn R & then immed R & foll site sp. Fr Evreux (W) on N12 to St Rémy; after x-ing rv bdge at traff lts complex strt ahead to rndabt (no L turn at traff lts), then immed R at end rv bdge as above. Site clearly sp in vill cent, sp 'Oscar' is for sports cent adj. NB Speed ramps on site app rd. Sm, hdg/mkd pitch (some grouped x 4), pt shd; wc; chem disp; fam bthrm; shwrs inc; el pnts (6A) €2.83 (poss rev pol); lndtte (inc dryer); tradsmn; rest 500m; playgrnd; tennis & trout fishing adj; TV; dogs; phone; poss cr; Eng spkn; adv bkg rec high ssn; factory adj poss noisy; ccard not acc; CKE/CCI. "Pleasant, popular, well-kept NH nr rv; welcoming warden; clean facs, some modern, ltd low ssn; no twin-axles (but negotiable); some pitches poss diff access; vill in walking dist; a gd find; Carrefour with fuel 1km; Excel site in middle of vill; warm welcome;" ♦ 1 Apr-30 Sep. € 15.65   2013*

NONETTE see Issoire *9B1*

NONTRON *7B3* (7km NE Rural) *45.56185, 0.71979* **Camping Manzac Ferme, Manzac, 24300 Augignac [05 53 56 31 34; info@manzac-ferme.com; www.manzac-ferme.com]** Fr Nontron take D675 N dir Rochechouart & after 7km on ent Augignac turn R sp Abjat-sur-Bandiat then immed R sp Manzac. Site on R 3.5km Sm, mkd pitch, pt hdstg, sl, pt shd; htd wc; chem disp; shwrs inc; el pnts (6A) inc; gas 6km; shops, rest, bar 5km; BBQ; rv fishing; dogs by arrangement; adv bkg; quiet. "Superb, peaceful, well-kept CL-type site; adults only; helpful British owners; excel san facs; phone ahead in winter; ideal for birdwatching & wildlife; highly rec." ♦ ltd Mar-Oct. € 24.00   2012*

NONTRON *7B3* (11km NE Rural) *45.55138, 0.79472* **Kawan Village Le Château Le Verdoyer, 24470 Champs-Romain [05 53 56 94 64; fax 05 53 56 38 70; chateau@verdoyer.fr; www.verdoyer.fr]** Fr Limoges on N21 twd Périgueux. At Châlus turn R sp Nontron (D6 bis-D85). After approx 18km turn L twd Champs Romain on D96 to site on L in 2km. Lge, terr, pt shd; wc; chem disp; mv service pnt; baby facs; shwrs inc; el pnts (10A) inc (poss rev pol); gas; lndtte (inc dryer); shop; rest, snacks; bar; B&B in chateau; BBQ (charcoal/gas); playgrnd; htd pool; paddling pool; waterslide; lake fishing & boating (sm boats); tennis; cycle hire; golf 25km; wifi; entmnt; games/TV rm; 20% statics; dogs €3; no c'vans/m'vans over 10m; phone; poss cr; Eng spkn; adv bkg; quiet; ccard acc; red low ssn; CKE/CCI. "Peaceful, Dutch-run site in grnds of chateau; lovely location; gd sized pitches, but terr; friendly staff; superb facs; poss steep access some pitches; grnd hard, but awnings poss; excel; highly rec." ♦ 20 Apr-30 Sep. € 42.00 (CChq acc) SBS - D21   2013*

See advertisement above

⊞ **NONTRON** *7B3* (1km S Urban) *45.51992, 0.65876*
**Camping de Nontron, St Martiel-de-Valette, 24300
Nontron [05 53 56 02 04 or 06 30 66 25 74 (mob);
camping-de-nontron@orange.fr; www.
campingdenontron.com]** Thro Nontron S twd Brantôme on
D675. Site on o'skts of town on L nr stadium. Sp. Med, hdg/
mkd pitch, pt shd; htd wc; mv service pnt; shwrs; el pnts (10A)
€3.50; gas; lndtte; shops adj; tradsmn; rest, snacks, bar 600m;
playgrnd; pool adj; paddling pool; games area; games rm;
entmnt; TV rm; statics; dogs €1; site clsd mid-Dec to early Jan;
poss cr; Eng spkn; quiet; CKE/CCI. "Pleasant owners; excel,
modern san facs; gd touring base." € 18.50   2012*

NORDAUSQUES see Ardres *3A3*

NORT SUR ERDRE *2G4* (1km S Rural) *47.42770, -1.49877*
**Camping Seasonova du Port Mulon - formaly
Municipal, Rue des Mares Noires, 44390 Nort-sur-Erdre
[02 36 81 00 01; fax 02 40 72 16 09; camping.nort-sur-
erdre@orange.fr; www.camping-portmulon.com]** Sp fr all
ents to town; foll 'Camping' & 'Hippodrome' sp. NB: C'vans
banned fr town cent, look for diversion sp. Med, shd; wc; chem
disp; shwrs inc; el pnts (6A) €2.40; lndtte (inc dryer); supmkt
1.5km; playgrnd; tennis; fishing; boating; dogs €0.90; adv
bkg; quiet; CKE/CCI. "Delightful, spacious, under-used site; gd
walking & cycling area, espec along Nantes canal & Rv Erdre;
Barrier perm locked, access when warden on site only"
1 May-1Nov. € 19.00   2013*

NOTRE DAME DE RIEZ *2H3* (1km NE Rural) *46.75523,
-1.89814* **Camping Domaine des Renardières, 13 Chemin
de Chêne Vert, 85270 Notre-Dame-de-Riez [02 51 55 14 17
or 06 20 98 37 46 (mob); fax 02 51 54 96 13; caroline.
raffin@free.fr; www.camping-renardieres.com]** On D38 to
Notre-Dame-de-Riez. Thro vill, over rv & 1st L over rlwy to site in
1km. Med, pt shd; wc; chem disp; baby facs; shwrs inc;
el pnts (6A) inc; gas; lndtte (inc dryer); tradsmn; rest, snacks; bar;
BBQ; playgrnd; htd pool; sand beach 5km; wifi; entmnt; TV rm;
20% statics; dogs €3; phone; Eng spkn; adv bkg; quiet; 15% red
low ssn; CKE/CCI. "Gd picturesque site; helpful owners; rec."
♦ ltd 1 Apr-2 Sep. € 20.00   2010*

NOTRE DAME DU TOUCHET see Mortain *2E4*

NOUAN LE FUZELIER *4G3* (S Urban) *47.53328, 2.03508*
**Camping La Grande Sologne, Rue des Peupliers,
41600 Nouan-le-Fuzelier [02 54 88 70 22; fax
02 54 88 41 74; info@campingrandesologne.com; www.
campingrandesologne.com]** On E side of D2020, at S end
of Nouan opp rlwy stn. Sp fr town cent & opp rlwy stn. NB Sat
nav not rec. Lge, mkd pitch, pt shd; wc (some cont); chem disp;
mv service pnt; baby facs; shwrs inc; el pnts (10A) €3 ; gas;
lndtte; shops 800m; tradsmn; rest, snacks; bar; playgrnd; htd
pool adj; tennis; games area; fishing; golf 15km; dogs €1; poss
cr; Eng spkn; adv bkg; quiet; red long stay/low ssn; CKE/CCI.
"Pretty site adj lake (no sw); some pitches boggy when wet;
facs poss stretched high ssn; ltd facs end of ssn & poss unclean;
public park at ent to site, but quiet; rec arr early; excel NH;
phone for entry low ssn; Wifi in bar area; excel site"
30 Mar-15 Oct. € 8.20   2013*

NOUVION EN THIERACHE, LE *3B4* (1.2km S Rural) *50.00538,
3.78292* **Camp Municipal du Lac de Condé, Promenade
Henri d'Orléans, Rue de Guise (Le Lac), 02170 Le
Nouvion-en-Thiérache [03 23 98 98 58; fax 03 23 98 94 90;
camping-lacdeconde@orange.fr; www.camping-
thierache.com]** Sp fr cent of Le Nouvion fr D1043 on D26, dir
Guise opp chateau. Med, hdg/mkd pitch, some hdstg, pt sl, pt
shd; wc; chem disp; shwrs inc; el pnts (4-8A) €3.20-3.90; lndtte
(inc dryer); shop 1km; tradsmn; rest, snacks, bar 1km; BBQ;
playgrnd; htd pool adj; tennis; canoe hire, horseriding nrby;
70% statics; dogs €0.80; phone; red long stay/CKE/CCI; ccard
acc. "Beautiful, spacious, lakeside site; busy even low ssn - rec
phone ahead; gd sized pitches; warm welcome, staff helpful;
gd san facs; gd for families; some pitches not suitable m'vans
due slope; muddy when wet; walk around lake; conv NH;
excel." ♦ 1 Apr-30 Sep. € 9.00   2013*

NOYERS *4G4* (200m S Rural) *47.69423, 3.99421* **Camp
Municipal, Promenade du Pré de l'Echelle, 89310 Noyers-
sur-Surein [03 86 82 83 72 (Mairie); fax 03 86 82 63 41;
mairie-de-noyers@wanadoo.fr]** Exit A6 at Nitry & turn R
onto D944. In 2km at N edge of Nitry, turn R onto D49 sp
Noyers. In 10km in Noyers, turn L onto D86 sp Centre Ville/
Camping. Immed after crossing rv & bef gate, turn L bet 2
obelisks. Site at end of track. Sm, mkd pitch, terr, shd; wc;
own san; chem disp; shwrs inc; el pnts €1.05; shop, rest,
snacks & bar 200m; BBQ; playgrnd; dogs; quiet, except church
bells. "Attractive, secluded site nr Rv Serein (6 pitches); ent
key fr Mairie on R after going thro town gate; ltd san facs."
€ 4.30   2008*

⊞ **NOYON** *3C3* (4km E Rural) **FFCC Camping L'Etang du
Moulin, 54 Rue du Moulin, 60400 Salency [03 44 09 99 81;
fax 03 44 43 06 78]** Take D1032 fr Noyon dir Chauny. On ent
Salency turn L & foll site sp. Site in 1km. Sm, pt sl, shd; htd
wc; chem disp; mv service pnt; shwrs €2; el pnts (10A) €1.60;
gas; shop, rest 4km; tradsmn; bar; BBQ; playgrnd; pool 3km;
fishing; tennis; 60% statics; dogs €1; quiet; CKE/CCI. "Site
unclean (Jan 2009)." ♦ € 14.30   2009*

NOYON *3C3* (8km S Rural) *49.50667, 3.01765* **FFCC
Camping Les Araucarias, 870 Rue du Général Leclerc,
60170 Carlepont [03 44 75 27 39; fax 03 44 38 12 51;
camping-les-araucarias@wanadoo.fr; www.camping-les-
araucarias.com]** Fr S, fr A1 exit junc 9 or 10 for Compiègne.
There take D130 sp Tracy-le-Val & Carlepont. Site on L 100m
fr Carlepont vill sp. Or fr N on D934 Noyon-Soissons rd take
D130 dir Carlepont & Tracy-le-Val. Site on R after vill on SW
twd Compiegne - not well sp. Sm, mkd pitch, pt sl, pt shd; htd
wc; chem disp; mv service pnt; baby facs; shwrs inc; el pnts
(6-10A) €3 (poss rev pol); gas; lndtte; shop, rest, bar 1km; BBQ;
playgrnd; mainly statics; dogs €1; poss cr; Eng spkn; adv bkg;
quiet; CKE/CCI. "Secluded site, previously an arboretum; close
Parc Astérix & La Mer-de-Sable (theme park); 85km Disneyland;
san facs poss scruffy low ssn; vg." ♦ ltd 21 Mar-21 Dec.
€ 10.00   2010*

NOZAY *2G4* (8km NW Rural) *47.59606, -1.71583*
Camp Municipal La Roche, 44170 Marsac-sur-Don
[02 40 87 54 77 (Mairie); fax 02 40 87 51 29; mairie.
marsacsurdon@wanadoo.fr] Fr N137 turn W onto D124
to Marsac-sur-Don. Fr vill take D125 W dir Guénouvry, site
sp. Sm, mkd pitch, pt sl, pt shd; htd wc; shwrs; el pnts €2.15;
rest, bar nrby; playgrnd; fishing; games area; walking circuit;
dogs €0.50; quiet; CKE/CCI. "Gd basic site." 1 May-30 Sep.
€ 5.10   2009*

NUITS ST GEORGES *6G1* (3km SW Urban) *47.10323, 4.94148*
Camping Le Moulin de Prissey, 21700 Premeaux-Prissey
[03 80 62 31 15; fax 03 80 61 37 29; www.cpg-moulin-
prissey.fr/] Exit Beaune on D974 twd Nuits-St Georges &
Dijon; app Premeaux-Prissey turn R soon after vill sp, under rlwy
bdge & foll site sp. Fr A31 exit at Nuits-St Georges & foll camp
sp for Saule-Guillaume, thro Premeaux-Prissey & foll site sp.
Sm, mkd pitch, pt sl, pt shd; wc (some cont); chem disp (wc);
mv service pnt; shwrs inc; el pnts (6A) inc; gas; lndtte; shops
3km; tradsmn; snacks; rest, bar 4km; BBQ; playgrnd; dogs
€0.90; poss cr; adv bkg; noisy rlwy adj; ccard not acc; CKE/CCI.
"Popular NH - arr early; sm pitches; access poss diff lge o'fits;
untidy & run down early ssn (2011); basic facs; gd cycling."
♦ ltd 1 Apr-15 Oct. € 18.20   2012*

NYONS *9D2* (1km NE Rural) *44.36523, 5.15365* **Camping**
Les Clos, Route de Gap, 26110 Nyons [04 75 26 29 90;
fax 04 75 26 49 44; info@campinglesclos.com; www.
campinglesclos.com] Fr rndabt in town cent take D94 sp Gap
& site on R in 1km. Med, hdg/mkd pitch, hdstg, pt shd; wc;
chem disp; shwrs inc; baby facs; el pnts (10A) inc; gas; lndtte;
shop; rest 1km; snacks; bar; BBQ (gas/elec only); playgrnd;
pool; shgl rv beach & fishing; entmnt (ltd); 20% statics;
dogs €2.20; phone; poss v cr; Eng spkn; adv bkg; ccard acc;
red low ssn; CKE/CCI. "Quiet, well-kept site in lovely area;
friendly, helpful staff; excel touring base." ♦ 1 Apr-30 Sep.
€ 22.00   2010*

NYONS *9D2* (12km NE Rural) *44.42569, 5.21904*
Camping de Trente Pas, 26110 St Ferréol-Trente-Pas
[04 75 27 70 69; contact@campingtrentepas.com; www.
campingtrentepas.com] Exit A7 junc 19 Bollène onto D994
& D94. L on D70 to St Ferréol-Trente-Pas. Site 100m fr vill on
banks of stream. Med, shd; wc; shwrs; el pnts (6A) €3.10;
lndry rm; sm shop & snacks high ssn; shop 2km; rest 200m;
bar; playgrnd; pool; games rm; tennis; cycle hire; horseriding
4km; entmnt; TV; 5% statics; dogs €2; quiet; red low ssn.
"Peaceful site nr rv; scenic area, views fr site; gd, clean san
facs; gd pool; on flood plain; excel value; rec." 1 May-31 Aug.
€ 14.80   2011*

NYONS *9D2* (12km NE Rural) *44.43507, 5.21248*
FFCC Camping Le Pilat, 26110 St Ferréol-Trente-Pas
[04 75 27 72 09; fax 04 75 27 72 34; info@campinglepilat.
com; www.campinglepilat.com] Fr D94 N or Nyons turn
N at La Bonté onto D70 to St Ferréol, site sp 1km N of vill.
Med, hdg pitch, shd; wc; chem disp; shwrs inc; el pnts (6A)
€4; lndtte; shop high ssn & 3km; tradsmn; snacks; playgrnd;
pool (solar heated); paddling pool; games area; outdoor gym;
entmnt; TV; 25% statics; dogs €1.50 high ssn; phone; poss cr;
Eng spkn; quiet; red low ssn; CKE/CCI. "Site among lavender
fields; pleasant, helpful owners; gd clean san facs; gd walking
& off-rd cycling; Thurs mkt Nyons; excel." ♦ 1 Apr-30 Sep.
€ 23.60   2012*

NYONS *9D2* (12km E Rural) *44.34319, 5.28357* **Camp**
Municipal Les Cigales, Allée des Platanes, 26110 Ste Jalle
[04 75 27 34 88 or 04 75 27 32 78 (mairie); mairie.
saintejalle@orange.fr] Fr Nyons take D94 dir Serres; in 10
km at Curnier turn R onto D64 to Ste-Jalle. In vill turn R onto
D108 dir Buis-les-Baronnies. Site on R in 300m. NB Dist by
rd fr Nyons is 20km. Sm, hdg pitch, pt shd; wc; chem disp;
shwrs inc; el pnts (10A) €2.20; lndtte; shop, rest, snacks, bar
200m; playgrnd; 15% statics; dogs; adv bkg; quiet. "Vg site in
attractive old vill." 1 May-30 Sep. € 7.40   2009*

"Satellite navigation makes touring much easier"

Remember most sat navs don't know if
you're towing or in a larger vehicle – always
use yours alongside maps and site directions.

⊞ **NYONS** *9D2* (6km SW Rural) *44.32830, 5.08380* **Camping**
Domaine Le Sagittaire, Le Pont de Mirabel, 26110
Vinsobres [04 75 27 00 00; fax 04 75 27 00 39; camping.
sagittaire@wanadoo.fr; www.le-sagittaire.com or www.
campings-franceloc.fr] Fr Nyons on D94, sp Orange, site on L
just after junc with D4, well sp. Lge, hdg pitch, pt shd; htd wc;
chem disp; shwrs inc; el pnts (6-10A) €4.70-5.70; gas; lndtte;
shop; tradsmn; rest, snacks, bar in ssn; playgrnd; htd, covrd pool;
waterslide; tennis; cycle hire; entmnt; TV; 25% statics; dogs €5;
poss cr; adv bkg; quiet but some rd noise on edge of site; ccard
acc; red long stay/low ssn; CKE/CCI. "Part of holiday complex in
attractive, uncommercialised area." € 31.00   2009*

NYONS *9D2* (7km SW Rural) *44.32942, 5.06605* **Camp**
Municipal Chez Antoinette, Champessier, 26110
Vinsobres [04 75 27 61 65 or 04 75 27 64 49 (Mairie); fax
04 75 27 59 20; camping-municipal@club-internet.fr]
Fr Nyons on D94 sp Orange. Turn R 500m after junc with D4
twd Vinsobres vill. Site 500m on L bef vill. Sm, mkd pitch, pt
shd; htd wc; chem disp; shwrs inc; el pnts (6A) €2.70; lndtte;
BBQ; playgrnd; adv bkg; quiet; ccard acc; CKE/CCI. "Peaceful,
v popular site; cramped san facs; steep unhill walk to vill; excel
touring area." ♦ Easter-31 Oct. € 8.20   2009*

NYONS *9D2* (4km NW Rural) *44.40829, 5.07993* **Camping**
Les Terrasses Provençales, Les Barroux, Novézan, 26110
Venterol [tel/fax 04 75 27 92 36; lesterrassesprovencales@
gmail.com; www.lesterrassesprovencales.com] Exit A7/E15
at junc 18 sp Nyons. Join D538 E twd Nyons. Site in Venterol,
sp bet Valréas & Nyons. Med, hdg/mkd pitch, hdstg, terr, pt
shd; wc; chem disp; baby facs; fam bthrm; shwrs inc; el pnts
(10A) €3.85 (poss rev pol); lndtte; shop; tradsmn; tradsmn; rest;
bar; BBQ; playgrnd; htd pool; cycle hire; games area; wifi; TV;
dogs €2; poss cr; some Eng spkn; quiet; ccard acc; CKE/CCI.
"Owner will tow c'van onto terr pitch; excel." ♦ 1 Apr-30 Sep.
€ 17.00 (CChq acc)   2010*

FRANCE

OBERNAI *6E3* (1km W Urban) *48.46460, 7.46750* **Camp Municipal Le Vallon de l'Ehn, 1 Rue de Berlin, 67210 Obernai [03 88 95 38 48; fax 03 88 48 31 47; camping@ obernai.fr; www.obernai.fr]** Fr N exit A35 junc 11 onto D426 sp Obernai. Foll D426 W around Obernai & foll site sp 'Camping VVF'. Fr S on A35 exit junc 12 sp Obernai. At 3rd rndabt turn L onto D426 Ottrott-Mont Ste Odile (look for sp Camping VVF). Do not tow into Obernai. Lge, mkd pitch, hdstg, pt sl, pt shd; htd wc; chem disp; mv service pnt; 75% serviced pitches; baby facs; shwrs inc; el pnts (16A) €4; gas 1km; lndtte (inc dryer); sm shop & 1km; tradsmn; BBQ; playgrnd; lge pool 200m; tennis, horseriding adj; wifi; dogs €1.10; phone; bus to Strasbourg & Obernai adj; train; poss cr; Eng spkn; adv bkg; quiet; ccard acc; 10% red CC members low ssn; red long stay/low ssn/CKE/CCI. "Attractive, well-kept, busy site on edge of picturesque town; sm pitches; welcoming, helpful staff; superb, clean facs; no entry after 19.30; rec arr early high ssn; c'vans, m'vans & tents all sep areas; excel bus/train links; ideal NH; highly rec; v well run site; lots of refurb 2013" ♦ 1 Jan-14 Jan, 11 Mar-31 Dec. € 23.50 *2013**

OCTON *10F1* (Rural) *43.66029, 3.32083* **Camping Le Village du Bosc (Naturist), Chemin de Ricazouls, 34800 Octon [04 67 96 07 37; fax 04 67 96 35 75; www.villagedubosc.net]** Exit 54 or 55 fr N9/A75 dir Octon onto D148, foll sp to Ricazouls/site. Med, terr, pt shd; wc; chem disp; shwrs; el pnts (10A)inc; rest, snacks; bar; shop; lndtte; playgrnd; htd pool; lake sw; watersports; 20% statics; dogs €3 (restricted area only); poss cr; adv bkg; red long stay; INF card. "Lovely, quiet site with wooded walks; friendly owners; clean facs; tight turns on terr access for lge o'fits; Octon vill pretty." ♦ ltd 27 Apr-30 Sep. € 29.20 *2013**

OCTON *10F1* (600m SE Rural) *43.65100, 3.30877* **Camping Le Mas des Carles, 34800 Octon [04 67 96 32 33]** Leave A75 at junc 54, foll sp for Octon, 100m after vill sp turn L & foll white site sp keeping L. Ent on L opp tel kiosk (sharp turn). Sm, some hdg/mkd pitch, pt sl, terr, pt shd; wc; chem disp; shwrs inc; el pnts (6-10A) inc; lndtte; lndry rm; shop 500m; rest adj; playgrnd; pool; boating/watersports in lake 800m; 30% statics; dogs; phone; poss cr; adv bkg; quiet; ccard not acc; CKE/CCI. "Pleasant site with views; helpful owner; facs a little tired (2006); take care low branches on pitches; Lac de Salagou with abandoned vill of Celles 1km." 1 Apr-10 Oct. € 21.40 *2012**

OFFRANVILLE see Dieppe *3C2*

OLARGUES *8F4* (N Rural) *43.55898, 2.91288* **Camp Municipal Le Baoüs, 34390 Olargues [04 67 97 71 50; otsi. olargues@wanadoo.fr; www.olargues.org]** Take D908 W fr Bédarieux, site immed bef ent Olargues. Site sp over sm bdge on L. At end of bdge turn R to site. Last 50m rough track & narr turn into site. Sm, pt shd; wc (cont); chem disp; shwrs inc; el pnts (6A); shop 300m; playgrnd; canoeing; cycle hire; internet; adv bkg Jul/Aug; quiet. "Helpful warden; hill climb to services block; site poss flooded by Rv Jaur in spring." 1 Jul-15 Sep. *2009**

OLLIERES SUR EYRIEUX, LES *9D2* (500m N Rural) *44.80730, 4.61500* **Kawan Village Le Mas de Champel, Route de La Voulte-sur-Rhône, 07360 Les Ollières-sur-Eyrieux [04 75 66 23 23; fax 04 75 66 23 16; info@masdechampel. com; www.masdechampel.com]** Fr D86 W on D120 at La Voulte-sur-Rhône or D21 at Beauchastel. Rds join at St Laurent-du-Pape. Cont on D120, turn R soon after D2 on ent Les Ollières bef descent into vill. Site sp. Med, terr, unshd; htd wc; chem disp; mv service pnt; shwrs inc; el pnts (10A) inc; lndtte (inc dryer); shops 1km; rest, snacks; bar; playgrnd; htd pool complex; paddling pool; fishing; canoeing; cycle hire; games area; guided walks; cycle hire; solarium; wifi; entmnt; TV; some statics; poss cr; adv bkg; quiet. "Pleasant site in lovely countryside." ♦ 16 Apr-30 Sep. € 24.00 *2009**

OLLIERES SUR EYRIEUX, LES *9D2* (2.5km S Rural) *44.78155, 4.61790* **Camping Le Chambourlas, Chambon de Bavas, 07360 Les Ollières-sur-Eyrieux [04 75 66 24 31; fax 04 75 66 21 22; info@chambourlas.com; www. chambourlas.com]** Fr Privas take D2 dir Le Cheylard; site on R in 14km at Les Ollières. D2 a v slow, twisty rd. Steep site ent. Med, mkd pitch, shd; wc; chem disp; baby facs; shwrs inc; el pnts (10A) inc; gas; lndtte; shop; rest, snacks; bar; BBQ; playgrnd; pool; paddling pool; lake sw & fishing; canoe hire; games area; wifi; TV rm; 10% statics; dogs €2.50; adv bkg; ccard acc. "Lovely site; lge pitches; warm welcome; gd walks fr site." ♦ Easter-30 Sep. € 31.50 *2009**

See advertisement on pages 32 & 33

OLLIERES SUR EYRIEUX, LES *9D2* (10km NW Rural) *44.82895, 4.52295* **L'Ardechois Camping, Le Chambon, 07190 Gluiras [04 75 66 61 87; fax 04 75 66 63 67; ardechois.camping@wanadoo.fr; www.ardechois-camping.fr]** Exit A7 junc 15 or 16 & cross rv onto D86. Turn W at Beauchastel onto D21/D120 dir Le Cheylard to St Sauveur-de-Montagut. In St Sauveur foll D102 St Pierreville & Mézilhac. Site approx 8km on bank Rv Glueyre on both sides D102 - steep access to pitches. Med, hdg/mkd pitch, terr, shd; htd wc; chem disp; mv service pnt; baby facs; shwrs inc; el pnts (6-10A) inc; gas; lndtte (inc dryer); shop & 8km; tradsmn; rest high ssn; snacks; bar; BBQ; playgrnd; htd pool; paddling pool; rv & sand beach adj; cycle hire; games area; wifi; entmnt; TV rm; 70% statics; dogs €4; Eng spkn; adv bkg ess in ssn; ccard acc; red low ssn/snr citizens; CKE/CCI. "Wonderful, friendly, family site in glorious countryside; helpful Dutch owners; excel rest; organised walks, picnics." ♦ 30 Apr-30 Sep. € 27.50 (CChq acc) *2009**

OLLIERGUES *9B1* (1.75km E Rural) *45.69008, 3.63289* **Camping Les Chelles, 63880 Olliergues [tel/fax 04 73 95 54 34; info@camping-les-chelles.com; www. camping-les-chelles.com]** Fr Olliergues take D37 N up hill dir Le Brugeron; then sharp L onto D87 dir La Chabasse; site sp. Med, hdg/mkd pitch, terr, shd; wc; chem disp; shwrs inc; el pnts (15A) €2.80; lndtte (inc dryer); shop 5km; rest, snacks; bar; playgrnd; pool; games area; games rm; wifi; TV; dogs €1; phone; Eng spkn; adv bkg; ccard acc. "Facs excel for families with young children; enthusiastic Dutch owners; gd walking; gd touring base; vg." ♦ ltd 1 Apr-31 Oct. € 13.00 *2009**

OLONNE SUR MER see Sables d'Olonne, Les *7A1*

OLONZAC *8F4* (6km N Rural) *43.3408, 2.7056* **Camping Le Mas de Lignières (Naturist), Montcélèbre, 34210 Cesseras-en-Minervois [tel/fax 04 68 91 24 86; lemas1@ wanadoo.fr; www.lemasdelignieres.com]** Fr Olonzac go N on D182 thro Cesseras & cont N dir Fauzan. Look for R turn to Montcélèbre - site on R behind lge, clsd brown gates (intercom) - not easy to find. Care needed thro Cesseras. Sm, hdg/mkd pitch, hdstg, pt sl, pt shd; wc (some cont); chem disp; baby facs; fam bthrm; shwrs inc; el pnts (6A) inc; gas; lndtte; sm shop & 2km; tradsmn; covrd pool; tennis; TV rm; 5% statics; dogs €1.50; phone; poss cr; adv bkg; red 10 days; quiet; ccard acc; INF card ess & avail at site. "Well-run, scenic site in remote location; lge pitches; fair san facs; nearest supmkt in La Redorte (10km); vg walks." ♦ ltd 26 Apr-30 Sep. € 25.50   2009*

OLONZAC *8F4* (9km E Rural) *43.28372, 2.82688* **FFCC Camping Les Auberges, 11120 Pouzols-Minervois [tel/ fax 04 68 46 26 50; vero.pradal@neuf.fr; www.camping-lesauberges.fr]** Fr D5 site 500m S of vill of Pouzols-Minervois. Sm, mkd pitch, pt shd; wc; chem disp (wc); shwrs inc; el pnts (5A) €3.50; gas adj; lndtte; shop adj; tradsmn; playgrnd; pool; 30% statics; dogs; poss cr; Eng spkn; adv bkg rec; quiet; CKE/CCI. "V popular site; friendly owners; sm Sat mkt at 'cave' opp." 15 Mar-15 Nov. € 16.00   2012*

OLORON STE MARIE *8F2* (2km W Urban) *43.17886, -0.62328* **Camping-Gîtes du Stade, Chemin de Lagravette, 64400 Oloron-Ste Marie [05 59 39 11 26 or 06 08 35 09 06 (mob); fax 05 59 36 12 01; camping-du-stade@wanadoo.fr; www.camping-du-stade.com]** Fr N on ring rd foll sp to Saragosse (Spain); at rndabt take 2nd exit onto D6 still sp Saragosse, site sp on R just after sports field. Fr S on D55 join ring rd & turn W at rndabt by McDonalds; sp. Med, hdg/mkd pitch, pt shd; wc; chem disp; shwrs inc; el pnts (6-10A) €4-6 (some rev pol); lndry rm; tradsmn; supmkt 1km; rest, snacks; BBQ; playgrnd; pool adj; rv fishing & sw 1km; tennis; cycle hire; wifi; entmnt; TV; dogs €1.20; adv bkg; quiet; twin-axles extra; red low ssn; CKE/CCI. "Well-kept site; lge pitches; helpful staff; clean facs but ltd low ssn & stretched high ssn; take care low tree; ground poss soft after rain; barrier clsd 1200-1500; excel base for Pyrenees; gd walking." ♦ 1 May-30 Sep. € 15.00   2011*

OMONVILLE LA ROGUE see Beaumont Hague *1C4*

ONESSE ET LAHARIE *8E1* (500m N Rural) *44.06344, -1.07257* **FFCC Camping Le Bienvenu, 259 Route de Mimizan, 40110 Onesse-et-Laharie [05 58 07 30 49 or 06 81 32 12 56 (mob); www.camping-onesse.fr]** On N10 Bordeaux-Bayonne rd, turn W onto D38 at Laharie. Site in 5km. Med, mkd pitch, pt shd; wc (some cont); chem disp; mv service pnt; shwrs inc; el pnts (10A) €4; lndtte; shop 100m; rest, bar adj; playgrnd; beach 20km; TV rm; some statics; dogs €1; adv bkg; quiet; red long stay; CKE/CCI. "Well-run, family site." 1 Mar-30 Sep. € 13.10   2008*

ONZAIN *4G2* (4km N Rural) *47.52620, 1.18718* **Camping Domaine de Dugny, 45 Route de Chambon-sur-Cisse, 41150 Onzain [02 54 20 70 66; fax 02 54 33 71 69; info@ dugny.fr; www.siblu.com/domainededugny]** Exit A10 junc 17 Blois onto D952 dir Tours. After 16km at rndabt at bdge to Chaumont, turn N dir Onzain. Take D45 N dir Chambon-sur-Cisse to Cabinette. Site sp on a minor rd to L, beside sm lake. Site well sp fr Onzain cent. Lge, hdg/mkd pitch, hdstg, pt sl pt shd; htd wc; chem disp; mv service pnt; serviced pitches; baby facs; fam bthrm; shwrs inc; el pnts (6-10A) inc; gas; lndtte; shop; tradsmn; rest, snacks; bar; BBQ; playgrnd; htd pool & paddling pool; waterslide; lake sw & 10km; fishing; cycle hire; games rm; games area; golf 8km; boat hire; entmnt; ultra-light flights; internet; TV rm; 90% statics; dogs €4.50; train 4km; Eng spkn; adv bkg; quiet; ccard acc; red low ssn; CKE/CCI. "Peaceful site; welcoming; clean san facs, but ltd low ssn; gd facs for children; poss diff in wet weather; chateaux close by - World Heritage site; gd NH." ♦ 9 Apr-1 Oct. € 45.00   2010*

ONZAIN *4G2* (1.5km SE Urban) *47.49081, 1.18847* **Camp Municipal, Rue de la Liberté, 41150 Onzain [02 54 20 85 15 or 02 54 51 20 40 (Mairie); fax 02 54 20 74 34; marie@ ville-onzain.fr; www.ville-onzain.fr]** Fr N of Chaumont-sur-Loire, at rndabt at junc D952 & D1 take D1 N twds Onzain then take 1st turn on R. Foll sp. Sm, hdg pitch, pt sl, pt shd; wc (some cont); chem disp; mv service pnt; shwrs inc; el pnts (10A) €2 (poss rev pol); gas; lndtte; shops, rest 500m; playgrnd; dogs €1.53; no twin-axle vans; gates locked 2000-0800; poss cr; rd & rlwy noise; ccard not acc; CKE/CCI. "Central for Loire chateaux; clsd 2200-0800." ♦ 1 May-15 Sep. € 7.80   2010*

OPIO see Grasse *10E4*

OPPEDE see Cavaillon *10E2*

FRANCE

ORANGE *10E2* (10km NE Rural) *44.16222, 4.93531* **Aire Naturelle Domaine des Favards, Route d'Orange, 84150 Violès [04 90 70 90 93; fax 04 90 70 97 28; favards@free.fr; www.favards.com]** Fr N exit A7 junc 19 Bollène. Foll D8 dir Carpentras & Violès. In Violès foll dir Orange & look for camp sp. Fr S exit A7 junc 22 sp Carpentras, take dir Avignon, then dir Vaison-la-Romaine to Violès. Avoid cent of Orange when towing. Sm, hdg/mkd pitch, unshd; htd wc (some cont); baby facs; shwrs inc; el pnts (6-10A) €3 (poss rev pol); lndry rm; tradsmn; snacks; bar; playgrnd; pool; dogs €1; poss cr; Eng spkn; adv bkg; quiet; no ccard acc; red low ssn; CKE/CCI. "Well-kept site; excel pitches - some v lge (extra charge); superb san facs, poss stretched; wine-tasting on site high ssn; gd touring base; poss dust clouds fr Mistral wind; pitches muddy when wet; gd." ♦ 1 May-30 Sep. € 15.00   2009*

ORANGE *10E2* (8km SE Urban) *44.11472, 4.90314* **Camp Municipal Les Peupliers, Ave Pierre-de-Coubertin, 84150 Jonquières [04 90 70 67 09; fax 04 90 70 59 01; www.jonquieres.fr]** Exit junc 22 fr A7 onto N7 S. In 2km turn L (E) onto D950. In 5km at rndabt turn L onto D977. In 200m turn L sp Jonquières, site on L in 2km, sp in vill. Site behind sports complex. Sp not obvious. Med, mkd pitch, pt shd; wc; chem disp; shwrs inc; el pnts (10A) inc; gas 500m; lndtte; wifi, shop, rest, snacks, bar 500m; playgrnd; pool; tennis adj; dogs €2.50; phone; poss cr; adv bkg; noise fr airfield (week days); ccard acc; CKE/CCI. "Excel, well-run, busy site; friendly & welcoming owners; vg, clean san facs; need care with high o'fits due trees; gates close 2200; Roman ruins nrby; popular long stay." 27 Apr-29 Sep. € 14.50   2013*

ORBEC *3D1* (500m N Urban) *49.02829, 0.40857* **Camp Municipal Les Capucins, Rue des Frères Bigot, 14290 Orbec [02 31 32 76 22; camping.sivom@orange.fr]** Exit A28 junc 15 to Orbec; on ent town foll site sp. If app fr D519 or D819 steep drag up to site & care req down to town. Sm, pt shd; wc; chem disp; shwrs inc; el pnts (10A) €2; shops 800m; playgrnd; dogs free; quiet. "Well-kept site; site yourself if office clsd; san facs old but clean; no twin-axles; access easy for lge o'fits; delightful countryside; excel." 25 May-8 Sep. € 7.00   2010*

ORBEY see Munster *6F3*

ORCET see Clermont Ferrand *9B1*

⊞ **ORCIVAL** *7B4* (6km NE Rural) *45.7067, 2.8593* **FFCC Camping La Haute Sioule, Route du Camping, 63210 St Bonnet-près-Orcival [04 73 65 83 32; fax 04 73 65 85 19; info@camping-auvergne.info; www.camping-auvergne.info]** Fr Clermont-Ferrand take N89 S then W twds La Bourboule for approx 20km. At junc with D216 turn L twds Orcival. Site in 4km. Foll site sp. Med, sl, pt shd; wc; mv service pnt; shwrs inc; el pnts (4-13A) €3-6.10; gas; lndtte; shops 250m; snacks; playgrnd; rv sw adj; golf; fishing adj; games rm; entmnt; 50% statics; dogs free; poss cr; Eng spkn; CKE/CCI. "Pleasant site; gd views; friendly owners; poss diff lge o'fits; many sheep & chickens on site (Jun 2011)." € 15.00   2010*

ORINCLES see Bagneres de Bigorre *8F2*

ORLEANS *4F3* (10km E Rural) *47.88830, 2.02744* **Camp Municipal Les Pâtures, 55 Chemin du Port, 45430 Chécy [02 38 91 13 27; camping@checy.fr; www.checy.fr]** Take D960 E twd Châteauneuf. In Chécy, foll site sp. Access thro town via narr streets. Sm, hdg pitch, pt shd; wc; chem disp; mv service pnt; shwrs €0.30/3 mins; el pnts (16A) €3.80; lndtte; shop 1km; BBQ; tennis; fishing; golf 5km; no statics; dogs €1; twin-axkes extra; Eng spkn; adv bkg; some noise fr adj site; CKE/CCI. "Vg, well-run site on Rv Loire; vg location; friendly, helpful warden; gd san facs; conv Orléans; poss open bef & after dates given; popular NH." ♦ 30 May-2 Oct. € 12.00   2011*

ORLEANS *4F3* (5km S Rural) *47.85603, 1.92555* **Camp Municipal d'Olivet, Rue du Pont-Bouchet, 45160 Olivet [02 38 63 53 94; fax 02 38 63 58 96; campingolivet@wanadoo.fr; www.camping-olivet.org]** To avoid height restriction, best app fr A71 exit junc 2 onto N271 dir Orléans-La Source. Cont on N271 until rd crosses N20 into Rue de Bourges. Pass commercial estate & hotel on L & turn L at traff lts into Rue de Châteauroux. Pass university (Parc Technologique), cross tramway & turn L at traff lts onto D14, Rue de la Source, then in 500m turn R (watch for pharmacy on L & green site sp) into Rue du Pont-Bouchet (narr rd). Site well sp on D14. NB Beware height restrictions on junc underpasses in Orléans cent. Med, hdg pitch, pt sl, pt shd; htd wc (some cont); chem disp; mv service pnt; shwrs inc; el pnts (16A) €3.10; lndtte; shop 500m; tradsmn; snacks; playgrnd; wifi; dogs €2.05; bus 400m; tram 2km (secure car park); poss cr; Eng spkn; adv bkg rec, confirm by tel bef 1800 (booking fee & dep); quiet - poss noisy at w/end; ccard not acc; red low ssn; CKE/CCI. "Well-run, busy site by Rv Loiret; friendly; excel clean san facs; guided tours of Orléans by site staff; gd walking; vineyards nr; vg." ♦ 6 Apr-12 Oct. € 17.90   2013*

> ## "There aren't many sites open at this time of year"
>
> If you're travelling outside peak season remember to call ahead to check site opening dates – even if the entry says 'open all year'.

ORLEANS *4F3* (10km SW Urban) *47.85539, 1.75352* **Camp Municipal Fontaine de Rabelais, Chemin de la Plage, 45130 St Ay [02 38 88 44 44 (Mairie); fax 02 38 88 82 14; maire@ville-saint-ay.fr; www.ville-saint-ay.fr]** Exit A10/E60 at junc 15 Meung-sur-Loire onto N152 dir Orléans, sp La Chapelle-St Mesmin; site sp on app to St Ay on N bank Rv Loire. Fr A71 exit junc 1 dir Blois & Beaugency onto N152. Lge, pt sl, pt shd; wc; chem disp; mv service pnt; shwrs inc; el pnts (6A) inc (poss rev pol); gas; shops 500m; tradsmn; rest 500m; BBQ; playgrnd; rv fishing & boating adj; dogs; phone; bus 500m; no twin-axles; Eng spkn; adv bkg; quiet but some rlwy noise; ccard not acc; red long stay; CKE/CCI. "Pleasant, clean, tidy site on Rv Loire; excel modern facs for sm site but poss stretched high ssn; rvside cycling/walking; conv Orléans & chateaux; poss early closure or late opening - rec call in adv to check; perfect NH" ♦ 15 Apr-31 Oct. € 14.20   2013*

ORLEANS 4F3 (3km W Urban) 47.89492, 1.86196
**Camp Municipal Gaston Marchand, Rue de la
Roche, 45140 St Jean-de-la-Ruelle [02 38 88 39 39 or
02 38 79 33 00 (Mairie); fax 02 38 79 33 62; sports@ville-
saintjeandelaruelle.fr; www.ville-saintjeandelaruelle.fr]**
App Orléans fr Blois on D2152/D152; 500m after passing
under A71, turn R into Rue de la Roche. Or app Orléans from
E on D2151/D215; 1km after passing Pont de l'Europe (still on
D2151/D215) turn L into Rue de la Roche. Site sp. Med, mkd
pitch, pt sl, pt shd; wc (some cont); chem disp; shwrs inc; el
pnts (6A) €2.60; gas; shops 2km; pool 1.5km; dogs €1.10; bus;
poss cr; adv bkg; some rd noise. "Well-kept site on bank of Rv
Loire; ltd san facs; gd value; conv Orléans; NH only."
1 Jul-31 Aug. € 9.80   2011*

"That's changed – Should I let The Club know?"

If you find something on site that's different from the site entry, fill in a report and let us know. See www.caravanclub.co.uk/europereport.

ORLEAT see Thiers 9B1

ORNANS 6G2 (1km E Rural) 47.10064, 6.16036 **Camping
La Roche d'Ully, Allée de la Tour de Peiltz, 25290 Ornans
[03 81 57 17 79; contact@larochedully.com; www.
camping-larochedully.com]** Fr Ornans foll blue sps to site
nr rvside. Med, mkd pitch, unshd; htd wc; chem disp; mv
service pnt; baby facs; sauna; shwrs; el pnts (10A) €4; lndtte
(inc dryer); shop; tradsmn; rest, snacks; bar; BBQ; playgrnd; 2
pools (1 htd, covrd); paddling pool; rv fishing; canoeing; cycle
hire; games area; wifi; 20% statics; dogs €3; adv bkg; quiet;
ccard acc; red low ssn. "Pleasant, family-run site in gd location;
Popular with students; some noise in ssn" ♦ 1 Apr-15 Oct.
€ 21.00 (CChq acc)   2012*

ORNANS 6G2 (6km SE Rural) 47.06366, 6.22277 **Camp
Municipal Le Pré Bailly, 25840 Vuillafans [03 81 60 91 52;
fax 03 81 60 95 68; mairie.vuillafans@wanadoo.fr; www.
vuillafans.fr]** Site sp fr D67 adj Rv Loue. Sm, mkd pitch, terr,
pt shd; htd wc; shwrs inc; el pnts (4-10A) €2-4.80; shop 300m;
rest, bar 200m; playgrnd; fishing; canoeing; phone adj; quiet.
"Simple site in pretty vill; gd walks; site yourself, warden calls."
15 Mar-30 Sep. € 8.90   2008*

ORNANS 6G2 (11km SE Rural) 47.04132, 6.26024
**Camp Municipal Le Champaloux, 25930 Lods
[03 81 60 11 (Mairie) or 06 72 54 51 41 (mob); fax
03 81 60 93 86; mairie.lods@wanadoo.fr; www.camping-
champaloux.fr]** Fr Ornans SE on D67. In Lods turn R across
Rv Loue. Site in 150m beside rv. Or N fr Pontarlier on N57/E23
to St Gorgon then W on D67 to Lods. Med, pt shd, hdstg; wc;
chem disp; mv service pnt; shwrs inc; el pnts (6A) €4; shop
1km; playgrnd; fishing; quiet. "Lovely, peaceful site by rv; on
disused rlwy stn in attractive area; site yourself, office opens
1830-2000; friendly, helpful warden; clean, adequate san facs;
dog shwr; vg rest 200m; woodland walks; excel."
15 Jun-30 Sep. € 12.40   2012*

ORNANS 6G2 (1km S Rural) 47.10070, 6.12795 **Camping
Domaine Le Chanet, 9 Chemin de Chanet, 25290 Ornans
[03 81 62 23 44; fax 03 81 62 13 97; contact@lechanet.com;
www.lechanet.com]** Fr Besançon take D67 25km to Ornans.
In Ornans at rndabt cont to town cent. Take 1st R, cross Rv
Loue then turn R. Foll sp to site in 1km. Look for R turn after
school. Med, hdg pitch, steep sl & terr, pt shd; htd wc; chem
disp; mv service pnt; baby facs; shwrs inc; el pnts (3-10A)
€3-3.50; lndtte; shop; tradsmn; snacks; bar; BBQ; sm playgrnd;
htd pool 500m; rv 1km; games area; many statics; dogs €1.50;
phone; poss cr; adv bkg; quiet; red low ssn. "Picturesque site;
sm pitches; facs poss stretched in ssn." ♦ 28 Mar-25 Oct.
€ 17.40   2009*

ORPIERRE 9D3 (500m E Rural) 44.31110, 5.69650 **Camping
Les Princes d'Orange, Flonsaine, 05700 Orpierre
[04 92 66 22 53; fax 04 92 66 31 08; campingorpierre@
wanadoo.fr; www.camping-orpierre.com]** N75 S fr Serres
for 11km to Eyguians. Turn R in Eyguians onto D30, 8km
to Orpierre, turn L in vill to site (sp). Med, mkd pitch, hdstg,
pt sl, terr, pt shd; wc; chem disp; mv service pnt; baby facs;
shwrs inc; el pnts (10A) €4.50; gas; lndtte; shop; snacks; bar;
playgrnd; htd pool; waterslide; tennis; games area; entmnt;
TV; fishing; some statics; dogs €1.60; adv bkg; red low ssn.
"Rock-climbing area; gd walking; beautiful, interesting vill." ♦
1 Apr-31 Oct. € 23.10 (CChq acc)   2010*

ORTHEZ 8F1 (1.5km SE Rural) 43.48793, -0.75882 **Camping
La Source, Blvd Charles de Gaulle, 64300 Orthez
[05 59 67 04 81; fax 05 59 67 02 38; info@camping-orthez.
com; www.camping-orthez.com]** Leave Orthez on D817 twd
Pau, turn L at sp Mont-de-Marsan & site on R in 300m. Sm, pt
sl, some hdstg, ltd shd; wc; mv service pnt; shwrs inc; chem
disp; el pnts (10A) €3.50; tradsmn; snacks; playgrnd; pool
2km; fishing; some statics; dogs €1.80; phone; wifi; v quiet;
red low ssn; CKE/CCI. "Peaceful, basic but well-maintained
site; friendly & helpful staff; gd, clean facs; some pitches
soft in wet weather; gd security; rec; gd NH" 1 Apr-31 Oct.
€ 12.00   2013*

OUILLY DU HOULEY see Lisieux 3D1

OUISTREHAM 3D1 (1km S Urban) 49.26909, -0.25498
**Camp Municipal Les Pommiers, Rue de la Haie Breton,
14150 Ouistreham [02 31 97 12 66; fax 02 31 97 12 66;
campinglespommiers14150@gmail.com; www.camping-
pommiers-ouistreham.fr]** Fr ferry terminal foll sp Caen on
D84 (Rue de l'Yser/Ave du Grand Large); in approx 1.5km site
sp at rndabt; take 3rd exit. Lge, hdg pitch, pt shd; htd wc; chem
disp; mv service pnt; shwrs inc; el pnts (10A) inc; gas; lndtte
(inc dryer); shop; supmkt 500m; tradsmn; playgrnd; pool 1km;
sand beach 1.8km; tennis; games area; 40% statics; dogs €0.90
poss cr; Eng spkn; no adv bkg; quiet, some rd noise; ccard acc;
CKE/CCI. "V conv for late or early ferry (5 mins to terminal); site
stays open for late Brittany ferry; busy high ssn; gd sized pitches;
sandy soil; gates open 0700-2300 (dep out of hrs, by request);
opens for late arr; staff pleasant & helpful; san facs clean but
basic, stretched high ssn; no twin-axles; nice walk/cycle along
canal to town; wonderful beaches; interesting area; mkt Thur;
conv NH & longer; excel; British twin axle caravans acc; Sep area
for NH; Gd for long stay; take away food and bread shop on
site" 15 Feb-15 Dec. € 18.70   2013*

⊞ **OUISTREHAM** *3D1* (6km S Rural) *49.23838, -0.25763*
**FFCC Camping des Capucines, rue de la Côte
Fleurie,14860** Ranville **[02 31 78 69 82; fax 02 31 78 16 94;
campingdescapucines.14@orange.fr; www.calvados-
tourisme.com]** App Caen fr E or W, take Blvd Péripherique
Nord, then exit 3a sp Ouistreham car ferry (D515). In approx
8.5km turn R onto D514 sp Cabourg, cross Pegasus Bdge &
foll sp Ranville across 2 rndabts; at x-rds in 500m turn L (at
sm campsite sp); site in 300m on L. Fr Ouistreham foll D514
dir Caborg to Pegasus Bdge, then as above. Med, hdg/mkd
pitch, terr, pt shd; htd wc; chem disp; mv service pnt; baby
facs; shwrs inc; el pnts (10A) inc (poss rev pol); gas; lndtte; sm
shop; supmkt 2km; rest, bar 1km; playgrnd; sand beach 3km;
60% statics; dogs €1.80; phone; bus 500m; poss cr; some Eng
spkn; adv bkg if arr late; quiet; ccard acc; red low ssn/CKE/
CCI. "Excel site in pleasant position; some pitches sm; helpful,
friendly owner; gd clean san facs; barrier open 0600-2400 but
if clsd low ssn use intercom at recep; conv ferries (if arr late
fr ferry, phone in adv for pitch number & barrier code & use
intercom at recep); take care o'hanging trees; conv Pegasus
Bdge, museum & war cemetery; vg, quiet well run site; conv for
ferry; hypermarket 3 miles" € 19.55   2013*

OUISTREHAM *3D1* (3km SW Urban) *49.24970,
-0.27190* **Camping Les Hautes Coutures, avenue de
la Côte de Nacre, 14970** Bénouville **[02 31 44 73 08
or 06 07 25 26 90 (mob LS); fax 02 31 95 30 80;
info@campinghautescoutures.com; www.
campinghautescoutures.com]** Leave Ouistreham ferry &
foll sp Caen & A13 over 2 rndabts. After 2nd rndabt join dual
c'way. Leave at 1st exit (D35) sp St Aubin d'Arquenay & ZA
de Bénouville. Turn R at end of slip rd, then L at T-junc; site in
200m uphill on R. Or fr Caen twd port on dual c'way, site has
own exit shortly after Pegasus Memorial Bdge exit; site clearly
visible on R of dual c'way. Lge, hdg pitch, pt sl & uneven,
pt shd; htd wc; chem disp; mv service pnt; baby facs; shwrs
inc; el pnts (10A) €5.50 (rev pol)(adaptors avail); lndtte (inc
dryer); hypmkt at Hérouville; tradsmn; rest, snacks; bar; BBQ;
playgrnd; htd, covrd pool; paddling pool; waterslide; jacuzzi;
beach 2km; fishing; horseriding & windsurfing 1km; golf 4km;
cycle hire; wifi; entmnt; games/TV rm; 30% statics; dogs €3;
no c'vans/m'vans over 12m high ssn; poss cr; Eng spkn; adv
bkg; ccard acc; red low ssn; CKE/CCI. "Busy, poss noisy holiday
complex o'verlooking Caen Canal; friendly staff; sm pitches;
access tight some pitches when busy; recep 0800-2000 high
ssn, but staff will open for late ferry arr if req in adv; ltd el pnts
(2009); cycle path to Caen; daily mkt in Ouistreham; conv NH;
access to pitches diff as high kerbs, some pitches on steep
slopes" ♦ 1 Apr-31 Oct. € 49.20 (CChq acc)   2013*

OUISTREHAM *3D1* (7km W Coastal) *49.2915, -0.3017*
**Camping des Hautes Sentes, Chemin des Hautes
Sentes, 14880** Hermanville **[02 31 96 39 12; fax
02 31 96 92 98; leshautessentes@yahoo.fr; www.
campingdeshautessentes.fr]** Well sp on D514 W
fr Ouistreham. Med, hdg/mkd pitch, pt shd; wc; chem
disp; shwrs inc; el pnts (6A) €2; lndtte; tradsmn; snacks;
bar; playgrnd; beach 700m; games area; entmnt; TV rm;
90% statics; dogs €1.52; bus 400m; Eng spkn; quiet. "Friendly,
pleasant site; clean facs; few tourist pitches." 1 Apr-30 Sep.
€ 16.70   2009*

⊞ **OUISTREHAM** *3D1* (12km NW Coastal) *49.31799, -0.35824*
**Camp Municipal La Capricieuse, 2 Rue Brummel, 14530
Luc-sur-Mer [02 31 97 34 43; fax 02 31 97 43 64; info@
campinglacapricieuse.com; www.campinglacapricieuse.
com]** Fr ferry terminal turn R at 3rd traff lts (D514) into Ave du
G. Leclerc. Cont to Luc-sur-Mer; 1st turn L after casino; site on
R in 300m. Ave Lecuyer is sp & Rue Brummel is off that rd. Lge,
hdg/mkd pitch, terr, pt shd; wc; mv service pnt; chem disp;
shwrs inc; el pnts (6-10A) €4.65-6.25; gas; lndtte; shop 300m;
tradsmn; playgrnd; sand beach adj; tennis; games rm; entmnt;
excursions; wifi; TV rm; dogs €2.50; Eng spkn; adv bkg by wk
only; quiet; ccard acc; red low ssn; CKE/CCI. "Excel location;
some lge pitches with easy access; clean, ltd facs low ssn; conv
beach & Luc-sur-Mer; conv WW2 beaches; excel site; conv for
ferries" ♦ 1 Apr-30 Sep. € 26.40   2013*

OUNANS *6H2* (1km N Rural) *47.00290, 5.66550* **Kawan
Village La Plage Blanche, 3 Rue de la Plage, 39380 Ounans
[03 84 37 69 63; fax 03 84 37 60 21; reservation@la-plage-
blanche.com; www.la-plage-blanche.com]** Exit A39 junc 6
sp Dole Centre. Foll N5 SE for 18km dir Pontarlier. After passing
Souvans, turn L on D472 sp Mont-sous-Vaudrey. Foll sp to
Ounans. Site well sp in vill. Lge, mkd pitch, hdstg, pt shd; wc;
chem disp; mv service pnt; shwrs inc; el pnts (6A) €4 (poss rev pol);
gas 1km; lndtte (inc dryer); shop 1km; supmkt 4km; tradsmn; rest,
snacks; bar; playgrnd; pool; paddling pool; shgl rv beach & sw
500m; trout & carp fishing lake; canoeing; cycle hire; horseriding;
wifi; entmnt; TV rm; 1% statics; dogs €2; Eng spkn; adv bkg rec
(bkg fee); quiet; red low ssn; ccard acc; CKE/CCI. "Superb rvside
pitches; friendly recep; excel san facs, recently updated (2013); gd
rest; excel" ♦ 1 Apr-30 Sep. € 24.00 SBS - J02   2013*

OURSEL MAISON see Crèvecoeur le Grand *3C3*

OUSSE see Pau *8F2*

OUST *8G3* (2km N Rural) *42.89343, 1.21381* **Camp
Municipal La Claire, Rue La Palere, 09140 Soueix-Rogalle
[05 61 66 84 88; campinglaclaire@orange.fr; http://haut-
couserans.ingenie.fr]** S fr St Girons on D618; in 13km, just
bef rndabt, turn R onto D32 (thro rock arch) to Soueix-Rogalle;
turn L at vill sq; site in 100m, just after x-ing rv bdge. NB Narr
ent, rec park in sq & walk down first. Sm, pt shd; htd wc (some
cont); shwrs inc; el pnts (10A) €3 (poss long lead req); lndtte;
shop 1.5km; rest 200m; playgrnd; paddling pool; fishing;
10% statics; dogs €1; phone; quiet; CKE/CCI. "Pleasant, well-
maintained, rvside site; lge pitches; basic san facs."
1 Mar-31 Oct. € 10.00   2011*

OUST *8G3* (9km SE Rural) *42.81105, 1.25558* **Camping Le
Montagnou, Route de Guzet, 09140 Le Trein-d'Ustou
[05 61 66 94 97; campinglemontagnou@wanadoo.fr;
www.lemontagnou.co.uk]** Fr St Girons S on D618 & D3 to
Oust. Fr Oust SE on D3 & D8 thro Seix & at Pont de la Taule
turn L onto D8 twd Le Trein-d'Ustou. Site on L just bef vill, sp.
Med, hdg pitch, pt shd; htd wc; chem disp; shwrs inc; el pnts
(6-10A) €3.50-5.50; lndry rm; mini shop, tradsmn & snacks
(Jul/Aug); rest nr; BBQ; playgrnd; fishing; rv sw 3km; tennis;
skiing 9km; wifi; 30% statics; dogs €1.50; phone; poss cr; adv
bkg; quiet; ccard acc; red low ssn; CKE/CCI. "Well-situated,
well-run rvside site; mountain views; gd sized pitches; friendly
British owners; gd walking; highly rec." ♦ 1 Mar-1 Dec.
€ 16.20   2010*

OUST *8G3* (S Rural) *42.87042, 1.21947* **Camping Les Quatre Saisons, Route d'Aulus-les-Bains, 09140 Oust [05 61 96 55 55; camping.ariege@gmail.com; www.camping4saisons.com]** Take D618 S fr St Girons; then D3 to Oust; on N o'skts of town turn L (sp Aulus) onto D32; in 1km site on R nr Rv Garbet. Med, hdg pitch, pt shd; htd wc; chem disp; shwrs inc; el pnts (5-10A) €2.80-5.60; lndtte; shop 200m; bar; playgrnd; pool; games area; TV; 25% statics; dogs €1.50; phone; Eng spkn; adv bkg rec; quiet; ccard acc; red low ssn; CKE/CCI. "In beautiful, unspoilt area; friendly site; footpath to vill; excel." 7 Mar-30 Sep. € 17.50   2012*

⊞ **OUST** *8G3* (2.5km S Rural) *42.87085, 1.20663* **Camping Le Haut Salat, La Campagne-d'en Bas, 09140 Seix [05 61 66 81 78 or 06 82 16 00 36; info@camping-haut-salat.com; www.camping-haut-salat.com]** Take D618 S fr St Girons, at Oust take D3 twds Seix. Site well sp just N of vill nr rv. Med, hdg/mkd pitch, pt shd; htd wc; baby facs; shwrs inc; el pnts (5-10A) €2 (long lead req); lndtte (inc dryer); shops 500m; bar; BBQ; htd pool; fishing; games area; games rm; wifi; entmnt; TV; 85% statics; dogs free; clsd 24 Dec-1 Jan; adv bkg; quiet; CKE/CCI. "Gd facs; gd walking area; pitches poss not open winter, phone ahead." € 16.50   2011*

OYE PLAGE see Calais *3A3*

OYONNAX *9A3* (8km E Rural) *46.25530, 5.55705* **Camping Les Gorges de l'Oignin, Rue du Lac, 01580 Matafelon-Granges [04 74 76 80 97; camping.lesgorgesdeloignin@wanadoo.fr; www.gorges-de-loignin.com]** Exit A404 junc 9 onto D979 dir Bourg-en-Bresse; in 700m turn R onto D18 to Matafelon-Granges; foll sp. NB Fr Oyonnax 22km by rd. Med, hdg/mkd pitch, hdstg, terr, pt shd; htd wc; chem disp; baby facs; excel hot shwrs inc; el pnts (10A) €3.40; lndtte; ltd shop or 3km; rest, snacks; bar; BBQ; playgrnd; 2 pools; paddling pool; lake sw adj; games area; wifi; TV rm; 10% statics; dogs €2.40; phone; Eng spkn; adv bkg; quiet; red low ssn; CKE/CCI.S'mkt 15km "Beautiful site on lake - boat launching; friendly, helpful staff; Jura National Park; Rv Ain gorges; excel." 15 Apr-25 Sep. € 20.80   2012*

PACAUDIERE, LA *9A1* (200m E Rural) *46.17512, 3.87639* **Camp Municipal Beausoleil, Route de Vivans, 42310 La Pacaudière [04 77 64 11 50 or 04 77 64 30 18 (Mairie); fax 04 77 64 14 40; lapacaudiere@wanadoo.fr; www.camping-rhonealpes.com]** NW on N7 Roanne to Lapalisse; turn R in La Pacaudière, D35; site well sp; fork R in 50m; site ent in 400m. Sm, hdg pitch, hdstg, sl, unshd; wc; chem disp; shwrs inc; el pnts (10A); gas; lndtte; shop; supmkt 500m; playgrnd; public pool high ssn; TV rm; quiet. "Pleasant NH in beautiful countryside; ltd facs low ssn; interesting area; Sat mkt." 1 May-30 Sep. € 13.50   2013*

PAIMBOEUF *2G3* (W Urban/Coastal) *47.28907, -2.03964* **Camp Municipal de l'Estuaire, Quai Eole, 44560 Paimboeuf [02 40 27 84 53 or 06 46 41 60 93 (mob); camping-lestuaire@orange.fr; www.campinglestuaire.fr]** Fr St Nazaire on D77; turn L at rndabt imm after town sp; site on L in 300m. Med, pt shd; htd wc; shwrs inc; el pnts (10A) €3.85 (poss rev pol & poss long lead req); lndtte; supmkt 3km; bar; crêperie rest adj; playgrnd; pool; rv adj; cycle hire; wifi; entmnt; dogs €1.25; adv bkg; red low ssn; CKE/CCI. "Poss itinerants." 4 Apr-30 Sep. € 11.50   2010*

PAIMPOL *1D3* (2.5km SE Coastal) *48.76966, -3.02209* **Camp Municipal Crukin, Rue de Crukin, Kérity, 22500 Paimpol [02 96 20 78 47 or 02 96 55 31 70 (Mairie); fax 02 96 20 75 00; contact@camping-paimpol.com; www.camping-paimpol.com]** On D786 fr St Brieuc/Paimpol, site sp in vill of Kérity 80m off main rd shortly bef abbey. Med, hdg pitch, pt shd; htd wc; chem disp; mv service pnt; baby facs; shwrs inc; el pnts (6A) €3.90 (poss rev pol); lndtte (inc dryer); shops 1km; tradsmn; playgrnd; shgl beach 250m; fishing; watersports; wifi; TV rm; 10% statics; dogs €2.10; bus 100m; poss cr; quiet; CKE/CCI. "Clean & tidy; sep m'van area; Beaufort Abbey nrby; excel sh stay/NH; plenty of space; facs ltd low ssn; walk to town along coast rd gd views" ♦ 1 Apr-4 Oct. € 16.55   2013*

PAIMPOL *1D3* (5km SE Coastal) *48.75993, -2.96233* **Camping Le Cap Horn, Route de Port-Lazo, 22470 Plouézec [02 96 20 64 28; fax 02 96 20 63 88; lecaphorn@hotmail.com; www.lecaphorn.com]** Site sp fr D786 at Plouézec dir Port-Lazo. Site 3km NE of Plouézec. Med, hdg/mkd pitch, pt sl, terr, pt shd; wc; chem disp; baby facs; shwrs inc; el pnts (6A) inc (poss rev pol); gas; lndtte; shop; rest 1km; snacks; bar; playgrnd; htd pool; paddling pool; direct access to shgl beach 500m; boating; games rm; entmnt; 20% statics; dogs €1; adv bkg; quiet; ccard acc; red C'Club members; red low ssn/long stay/CKE/CCI. "On 2 levels in valley & hillside; sea views; steep path to beach; gd facs; gd." ♦ 1 Apr-25 Sep. € 26.50   2011*

See advertisement on next page

PAIMPONT see Plélan le Grand *2F3*

PALAU DEL VIDRE see Elne *10G1*

⊞ **PALAVAS LES FLOTS** *10F1* (500m N Coastal) *43.53000, 3.92400* **Aire Communale/Camping-Car Halte, Base Fluviale Paul Riquer, 34250 Palavas-les-Flots [04 67 07 73 45 or 04 67 07 73 48; fax 04 67 50 61 04]** Fr Montpellier on D986 to Palavas. On ent town at 1st rndabt 'Europe' foll sp Base Fluviale & site sp. Med, mkd pitch, hdstg, pt shd; wc; chem disp; mv service pnt; shwrs inc; el pnts (16A) €2; lndtte; shop, rest, snacks, bar adj; sand beach 500m; phone; bus 200m; poss cr; some rd noise; ccard acc; CKE/CCI. "M'vans only; special elec cable req - obtain fr recep (dep); some pitches on marina quay; conv Montpellier, Camargue; 3 night max stay." € 10.00   2012*

PALAVAS LES FLOTS *10F1* (1km NE Coastal) *43.53346, 3.94820* **Camping Montpellier Plage, 95 Ave St Maurice, 34250 Palavas-les-Flots [04 67 68 00 91; fax 04 67 68 10 69; www.camping-montpellier-plage.com]** Site on D21ES on o'skts of vill twd Carnon. V Lge, pt mkd pitch, pt shd; wc (some cont); chem disp; shwrs inc; mv service pnt; el pnts (4A) inc; gas; lndtte; shops; tradsmn; rest, snacks; bar; BBQ; playgrnd; pool with spa facs; paddling pool; sand beach adj; games area; 50% statics; dogs; bus high ssn; poss cr; Eng spkn; adv bking; noisy; red low ssn; CKE/CCI. "Gd location; basic san facs, but lge pitches & friendliness of site outweigh this; gd security; poss somewhat unkempt; easy walk into Palavas - interesting sm port; flamingoes on adjoining lake; gd." ♦ 16 Apr-18 Sep. € 35.95   2011*

FRANCE

PALAVAS LES FLOTS *10F1* (2km E Urban/Coastal) *43.53867, 3.96076* **Camping Les Roquilles, 267b Ave St Maurice, 34250 Palavas-les-Flots [04 67 68 03 47; fax 04 67 68 54 98; roquilles@wanadoo.fr; www.camping-les-roquilles.fr]** Exit A9 junc 30 onto D986 dir Palavas. In Palavas foll sp Carnon-Plage on D62, site sp. V lge, mkd pitch, hdstg, pt shd; wc (mainly cont); chem disp; mv service pnt; serviced pitches; shwrs inc; el pnts (6A) €3.90; gas 100m; lndtte; rest, snacks; bar; playgrnd; 3 pools (1 htd); waterslide; sand beach 100m; entmnt; TV; 30% statics; no dogs; phone; bus; poss cr; Eng spkn; adv bkg; poss noisy high ssn; ccard acc; red low ssn/ long stay; CKE/CCI. "Excel pizza bar on site." 15 Apr-15 Sep. € 23.20   2008*

PALAVAS LES FLOTS *10F1* (1.5km SW Coastal) *43.51972, 3.90959* **Camping Palavas, Route de Maguelone, 34250 Palavas-Les-Flots [04 67 68 01 28 or 06 62 42 34 43 (mob); www.palavas-camping.fr]** Exit A9 junc 30 onto D986 dir Palavas-Les-Flots; cross bdge; turn R at rndabt, foll sp Maguelone; sit on L in 1km. Lge, hdg/mkd pitch, hdstg, pt shd; wc; chem disp; m'van water refill; baby facs; shwrs inc; el pnts (6A) inc; lndtte; supmkt; rest, snacks; bar; playgrnd; pool; paddling pool; spa pool; beach adj; games area; games rm; infant club; 30% statics; dogs €2.50; phone adj; bus 1.5km; poss cr; Eng spkn; w/e disco noise some pitches; red low ssn. "Great views; gd pool area; sep car park; vg." 16 Apr-15 Sep. € 38.00   2009*

PALINGES *9A2* (1km N Rural) *46.56118, 4.22516* **Camp Municipal du Lac, Le Fourneau, 71430 Palinges [03 85 88 14 49 or 06 06 88 14 49 (mob); camping. palinges@hotmail.fr]** N70 Montceau-les-Mines dir Paray, turn L onto D92 into Palinges cent (4km). By church turn L church onto D128. Site in 1km. Sm, hdg/mkd pitch, pt sl, pt shd; htd wc; chem disp; baby facs; shwrs inc; el pnts (10A) inc; lndtte; shop, rest 1km; snacks; bar; playgrnd; lake sw & fishing adj with beach; cycle hire; tennis; dogs €1.60; adv bkg; Eng spkn; quiet; no ccard acc; CKE/CCI. "Lge pitches; friendly & helpful owners; gd clean facs; poss a little unkempt; gd walking, cycling & lake sw; conv canal; highly rec." ♦ 1 Apr-30 Oct. € 18.50   2010*

PALME, LA see Sigean *10G1*

PALMYRE, LA see Mathes, Les *7B1*

PALUD SUR VERDON, LA *10E3* (1km E Rural) *43.78042, 6.34882* **Camp Municipal Le Grand Canyon, Route de Castellane, 04120 La Palud-sur-Verdon [tel/ fax 04 92 77 38 13 or 02 92 77 30 87 (Mairie); campinglapalud@wanadoo.fr]** W on D952 fr Castellane, site on L (S) of rd just bef vill La Palud (30km W of Castellane, max gradient 1-in-8). Or on D952 fr Moustiers-Ste-Marie site on R (S) after leaving vill La Palud (also with steep & narr sections). App fr Moustiers easier. Med, mkd pitch, pt sl, pt shd; wc (some cont); chem disp; mv service pnt; baby facs; shwrs inc; el pnts (10A €3.20 (poss rev pol); gas 800m; lndtte; shops, rest, snacks, bar 500m; dogs €0.50; phone; poss cr; quiet; ccard not acc. "Basic facs but well-kept; helpful staff; interesting area; conv Gorge du Verdon." ♦ ltd 15 Apr-30 Sep. € 9.70   2008*

PAMIERS *8F3* (800m N Rural) *43.12490, 1.60195* **Kawan Village L'Apamée, Route de St Girons, 09100 Pamiers [tel/ fax 05 61 60 06 89; campingapamee@orange.fr; http:// lapamee.com]** Fr N on D820 at traff lts turn R & cross narr bdge over Rv Ariège, Pont du Jeu-du-Mail, site sp. Med, mkd pitch, some hdstg, shd; htd wc; chem disp; mv service pnt; baby facs; shwrs inc; el pnts (10A) inc; lndtte (inc dryer); shop 800m; tradsmn; rest, snacks; bar; BBQ; playgrnd; htd pool; rv fishing; tennis 100m; games area; games rm; cycle hire; wifi; TV rm; 5% statics; dogs €2; phone; o'night area for m'vans; adv bkg; quiet but rd noise; red low ssn; CKE/CCI. "Clean, modern facs; helpful staff; poss unkempt & ltd facs early ssn; excel." ♦ 1 Apr-15 Nov. € 24.00 (CChq acc)   2010*

PAMPELONNE *8E4* (2km NE Rural) *44.12685, 2.25681* **Camping Thuriès, 81190 Pampelonne [05 63 76 44 01; fax 05 63 76 92 78; campthuries@wanadoo.fr]** N fr Carmaux on N88 turn L onto D78 sp Pampelonne. Site sp & 2km fr town over narr bdge; steep, winding rd. Or S fr Rodez on N88 turn R onto D17 sp Pampelonne. Site bef rv bdge on L. Sm, mkd pitch, shd; htd wc; chem disp; mv service pnt; shwrs inc; el pnts (6A) inc; lndtte; shop & 3km; tradsmn; rest, snacks 3km; dogs; phone; poss cr; Eng spkn; quiet; CKE/CCI. "Pleasant site; conv Albi & Rodez." 15 Jun-1 Sep. € 15.70   2009*

FRANCE

PARAY LE MONIAL 9A1 (1km NW Urban) 46.45750, 4.10472 **Camping de Mambré, Route du Gué-Léger, 71600 Paray-le-Monial [03 85 88 89 20; fax 03 85 88 87 81; camping. plm@gmail.com; www.campingdemambre.com]** Fr N79 Moulin to Mâcon; site at W end of town; just after level x-ing turn NE into Rte du Gué-Léger. Turn R into site after x-ing rv; well sp. Lge, hgd/mkd pitch, pt shd; wc; chem disp; shwrs inc; el pnts (10A) €3.40; lndtte; sm shop & 500m; snacks high ssn; bar; playgrnd; pool high ssn; dogs €2; quiet, but some rd noise; red low ssn; CKE/CCI. "Paray-le-Monial is pilgrimage cent; ltd facs & poorly maintained low ssn (2011); no designated fresh water pnts (2011); 15min walk to town along rv; excel cycling cent'; well maintained" 2 May-30 Sep. € 15.00 (CChq acc) 2012*

PARCEY see Dole 6H2

PARENTIS EN BORN 7D1 (2km W Rural) 44.34593, -1.10106 **FFCC Camp Municipal Pipiou, Route du Lac, 40160 Parentis-en-Born [05 58 78 57 25; fax 05 58 78 93 17; pipiou@parentis.com; www.parentis.com]** Site on D43 rd twds lake beach. In vill foll sp 'Lac'. After 2km where rest on R, turn R. Site is 150m on R. Lge, hdg/mkd pitch, pt shd; wc; chem disp; mv service pnt; 100% serviced pitches; baby facs; shwrs inc; el pnts (10A) €3.50 (poss rev pol); gas high ssn; lndtte; shop; rest, snacks; bar; playgrnd; lake sw & sand beach adj, fishing & watersports adj; entmnt; TV; 25% statics; dogs €1.30; phone; poss cr; adv bkg; quiet but pitches adj rd noisy; ccard acc; red low ssn/long stay/CKE/CCI. "Lovely lakeside location; phone to check open low ssn; some pitches tight; facs stretched high ssn; cycle tracks thro vill & woods; office not open w/ends low ssn or public hols when access/leaving site not poss; excel." 15 Feb-15 Nov. € 19.00 2009*

"I like to fill in the reports as I travel from site to site"

You'll find report forms at the back of this guide, or you can fill them in online at www.caravaclub.co.uk/europereport.

PARENTIS EN BORN 7D1 (NW Rural) 44.35233, -1.09039 **Camping L'Arbre d'Or, 75 Route du Lac, 40160 Landes [05 58 78 41 56; fax 05 58 78 49 62; contact@arbre-dor.com; www.arbre-dor.com]** Leave the Bordeaux m'way A63/N10 in Liposthey and drive towards Parentis (D43). The campsite is sp in Parentis Lge, mkd pitch shd or pt shd; wc; chem disp, child/baby facs, shwrs, el inc; lndtte inc dryer; rest, snacks, bar; BBQ; playgrnd; pool; sw 400m; games area; entmnt; wifi; dogs free; poss cr; Eng spkn; adv bkg acc; ccard acc; CKE/CCI; red low ssn; "Vg" € 27.60 1 Apr-31 Oct 2013*

PARENTIS EN BORN 7D1 (3km NW Rural) 44.35153, -1.10959 **Camping Calède, Quartier Lahitte, 40160 Parentis-en-Born [05 58 78 44 63; fax 05 58 78 40 13; contact@camping-calede.com; www.camping-calede.com]** Exit N10 junc 17 onto D43 to Parentis-en-Born; then take D652 dir Biscarrosse; site in 3km on L. Sp adj lake. Med, hdg pitch, pt shd; wc; chem disp; baby facs; shwrs inc; el pnts (5A) €3.25; gas; lndtte; shop 3km; tradsmn; snacks; bar; BBQ; playgrnd; lake sw & sand beach adj; sailing; fishing; dogs €0.50; phone; poss cr; Eng spkn; quiet; adv bkg; red low ss; CKE/CCI. "Peaceful site in remote location; well-kept pitches & san facs; friendly, helpful staff; site yourself if office clsd; rec." ♦ 1 May-30 Sep. € 17.00 2009*

"We must tell The Club about that great site we found"

Get your site reports in by mid-August and we'll do our best to get your updates into the next edition of Caravan Europe.

PARIS 3D3 (12km E Urban) 48.85385, 2.53794 **Camp Municipal La Haute Ile, Chemin de l'Ecluse, 93330 Neuilly-sur-Marne [01 43 08 21 21; fax 01 43 08 22 03; campingmunicipal.nsm@wandadoo.fr; www.tourisme93.com]** Fr Périphérique (Porte de Vincennes) foll N34 sp Vincennes. Shortly after passing Château de Vincennes on R, L at fork, sp Lagny. At next major x-rds sharp L (still N34) sp Chelles. Thro Neuilly-Plaisance to Neuilly-sur-Marne. In cent lge x-rds turn R sp N370 Marne-la-Vallée & A4 Paris. In 200m, bef rv bdge, foll Camp Municipal sp (no tent or c'van symbols on sp) turn L. Site at junc of rv & canal. Lge, mkd pitch, pt shd; wc (some cont); shwrs inc; el pnts (10A) inc (check rev pol); gas; lndtte adj; shop; rest adj; BBQ; playgrnd; rv fishing; 25% statics; dogs €2.85; bus/train 900m; poss cr; Eng spkn; adv bkg (rec high ssn); quiet. "Lovely location bet rv & canal (almost on an island); san facs inadequate & unclean when site full (2011); wooden posts on pitches poss diff manoeuvring lge o'fits; some sm pitches; poss unkempt (2011); soft after rain; gd base & transport for Paris; gd dog walks adj; gd NH." 1 Apr-30 Sep. € 23.00 2011*

⊞ **PARIS** 3D3 (15km SE Urban) 48.82963, 2.47720 **Camping Paris Est Le Tremblay, Blvd des Alliés, 94507 Champigny-sur-Marne [01 43 97 43 97; fax 01 48 89 07 94; champigny@campingparis.fr; www.campingchampigny.fr]** Rec rte for c'vans. Fr A4 (Paris-Reims) exit 5 sp Nogent/Champigny-sur-Marne. D45 dir Champigny to end of dual c'way at traff lts go R on N303 dir St Maur. Join N4 after 1km (traff lts) & take 2nd R (200m). Site sp. NB site also known as 'Camping de Champigny' or 'Camping International/IDF'. Med, hdg/mkd pitch, pt shd; htd wc (some cont); chem disp; mv service pnt; shwrs inc; el pnts (10A) inc; gas; lndtte (inc dryer); shop; rest, snacks; bar; games rm; internet; TV; playgrnd; 20% statics; dogs €2.60; adv bkg; some rd noise; red low ssn; ccard acc; CKE/CCI. "Vg site; easy parking nr metro or bus fr camp to rlwy stn direct to city & Disneyland; twin-axle c'vans book ahead or poss extra charge; take care to avoid grounding on kerb to pitches; clsd to cars 0200-0600." ♦ € 33.00 2011*

⊞ **PARIS** *3D3* (10km W Urban) *48.86843, 2.23471* **Camping Indigo Paris - Bois de Boulogne, 2 Allée du Bord de l'Eau, 75016 Paris [01 45 24 30 00; fax 01 42 24 42 95; paris@ camping-indigo.com; www.camping-indigo.com]** Site bet bdge of Puteaux & bdge of Suresnes. App fr A1: take Blvd Périphérique W to Bois de Boulogne exit at Porte Maillot; foll camp sp. App fr A6: Blvd Périphérique W to Porte Dauphine exit at Porte Maillot; foll camp sp. App fr Pont de Sèvres (A10, A11): on bdge take R lane & take 2nd rd R mkd Neuilly-sur-Seine; rd runs parallel to Seine; cont to site ent. App fr A13: after St Cloud Tunnel foll sp twd Paris; immed after x-ing Rv Seine, 1st R sp Bois de Boulogne; foll camp sps; traff lts at site ent. NB Sharp turn to site, poorly sp fr N - watch for lge 'Parking Borne de l'Eau 200m'. V lge, hdg/mkd pitch, hdstg, pt sl, pt shd; htd wc (some cont); chem disp; mv service pnt; baby facs; shwrs inc; el pnts (10A) inc; gas; lndtte; shop, rest & bar in ssn or 1km; pool 1km; TV; Metro Porte Maillot 4km; some statics; dogs €2; phone; bus to metro; extra €26 per night for twin-axles; poss cr; Eng spkn; adv bkg rec high ssn; rd noise; red low ssn; ccard acc; CKE/CCI. "Busy site in excel location; easy access A13; conv cent Paris; some v sm pitches; san facs poss unclean & stretched; walk over Suresne bdge for shops, food mkt, supmkt etc; some tour ops on site; gd security." € 37.90   2010*

See advertisement opposite

PARIS *3D3* (20km NW Urban) *48.94001, 2.14563* **Camping International Maisons Laffitte, Ile de la Commune, 1 Rue Johnson, 78600 Maisons-Laffitte [01 39 12 21 91; fax 01 39 12 70 50; info@campint.com; www.campint.com]** Easy access fr A13 sp Poissy; take D308 to Maisons-Laffitte; foll site sp bef town cent. Fr A15 take N184 S fr Poissy, foll sp St Germain; approx 6km after x-ing Rv Seine & approx 300m after x-ing lge steel bdge, take L lane ready for L turn onto D308 to Maison-Laffitte; foll camp sp. Or D301 to St Denis, then A86 exit Bezons, then dir Poissy, Noailles, Sartrouville & Maisons-Laffitte. NB Narr app rd diff due parked cars & high kerbs. Lge, hdg/mkd pitch, pt shd; htd wc; chem disp; mv service pnt; shwrs inc; el pnts (6A) €3.20 (poss rev pol); gas; lndtte; sm shop; tradsmn; hypmkt 5km; rest, snacks; bar; no BBQ; playgrnd; games area; TV rm; 50% statics; dogs €2.60; RER stn 1km; poss cr; Eng spkn; adv bkg; some noise fr rlwy & rv traff; ccard acc; red low ssn; CKE/CCI. "V busy, popular site on island in Rv Seine; ideal for visiting Paris (20 min by RER), Disneyland & Versailles; Mobilis ticket covers rlwy, metro & bus for day in Paris; friendly, helpful staff; poss ltd facs low ssn." ◆ 1 Apr-31 Oct. € 29.00   2011*

See advertisement on pages 88 & 89

PARRANQUET see Villeréal *7D3*

PARTHENAY *4H1* (8km SE Rural) *46.63294, -0.13428* **Camping La Ferme Naturiste de l'Oliverie (Naturist), 79200 Saurais [05 49 94 61 05 or 06 87 91 64 53 (mob); info@oliverie.com; www.oliverie.com]** Fr Parthenay take D59 SE dir Vasles. After 8km In La Chapelle-Bertrand turn L to Saurais then turn L onto D22 twd La Ferrière-en-Parthenay. After 2km turn L at site sp. Site on R. Sm, pt sl, pt shd; wc; chem disp (wc); shwrs inc; el pnts (10A) €3.25; tradsmn; snacks; bar; playgrnd; pool; 1 gite & B&B; Eng spkn; adv bkg; quiet. "Ltd el pnts (16 for 25 pitches); 45km Futuroscope; excel." ◆ 24 Apr-30 Sep. € 19.50 (CChq acc)   2010*

PARTHENAY *4H1* (1km SW Urban) *46.64160, -0.26740* **Camping Flower du Bois Vert, 14 Rue Boisseau, Le Tallud, 79200 Parthenay [05 49 64 78 43; fax 05 49 95 96 68; campingboisvert@orange.fr; www. camping-boisvert.com]** Site on D743 to Niort. Sp fr N & S. Fr S 1km bef town turn L at sp La Roche-sur-Yon immed after rv bdge turn R; site on R in 500m. Med, hdg/mkd pitch, some hdstg, pt sl, pt shd; htd wc (some cont); chem disp; mv service pnt; baby facs; shwrs inc; el pnts (6 or 10A) inc; lndtte (inc dryer); shops 1km; tradsmn; rest, snacks; bar; BBQ; playgrnd; htd pool complex; paddling pool; boating; fishing; tennis; cycle hire; games rm; wifi; entmnt; TV; 10% statics; phone; poss cr; adv bkg; noisy nr main rd & bar; ccard acc; red low ssn; CKE/CCI. "Rvside walk to town; m'van o'night area adj; Wed mkt; gd NH to Spain; conv Futuroscope; new facs, plenty hot water" ◆ 1Apr-30 Oct. € 37.50   2013*

See advertisement on pages 32 & 33

PARTHENAY *4H1* (9km W Urban) *46.62214, -0.35139* **Camp Municipal Les Peupliers, 79130 Azay-sur-Thouet [05 49 95 37 13 (Mairie); fax 05 49 95 36 14; mairie-azaysurthouet@cc-parthenay.fr; www.tourisme-gatine.com]** Fr Parthenay take D949 dir Secondigny to Azay-sur-Thouet; turn L onto D139 dir St Pardoux; site on L in 200m. Site adj stadium on rvside. Sm, mkd pitch, pt shd; wc; shwrs inc; el pnts (10A) €3; shop 250m; BBQ; playgrnd; quiet. "Pleasant, peaceful site; barrier open 0900; clean dated san facs, poss inadequate number high ssn (2009)." 15 Jun-30 Sep. € 9.90   2013*

⊞ **PARTHENAY** *4H1* (10km W Rural) *46.65738, -0.34816* **FFCC Camping La Chagnée (Baudoin), 79450 St Aubin le Cloud [05 49 95 31 44 or 06 71 10 09 66 (mob); gerard. baudoin3@wanadoo.fr; www.cc-parthenay.fr/la-chagnee]** Fr Parthenay on D949BIS dir Secondigny. Turn R in Azay-sur-Thouet onto D139 dir St Aubin, site on R in 2km, look for 'Gîte' sp. Sm, hdg pitch, terr, pt shd; wc; chem disp (wc); mv service pnt; shwrs; el pnts €3; lndtte; shops 1km; fishing; dogs; Eng spkn; quiet; "Charming, CL-type organic farm site o'looking lake; friendly, helpful owners; clean facs; open all yr providing use own san in winter; maps loaned for walking; excel; m'vans only during period Nov-March; Farmhouse meal avail weekly" ◆ € 10.70   2013*

PASSY see Sallanches *9A3*

PATORNAY see Clairvaux les Lacs *6H2*

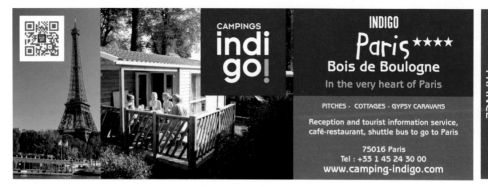

⊞ **PAU** *8F2* (5km E Rural) *43.28909, -0.26985* **FFCC Camping Les Sapins, Route de Tarbes, 64320 Ousse [05 59 81 79 03 or 05 59 81 74 21 (LS); lessapins64@orange.fr]** Site adj Hôtel des Sapins on S side of D817 (Pau-Tarbes rd). Sm, pt shd; wc; mv service pnt; shwrs inc; el pnts (4-6A) €2-3; shop adj; rest in hotel adj; fishing; poss cr; noisy; some rd noise. "Popular, pleasant NH; red facs low ssn; helpful owners; NH only." € 10.00   2009*

⊞ **PAU** *8F2* (6km W Rural) *43.32081, -0.45096* **Camping Le Terrier, Ave du Vert-Galant, 64230 Lescar [05 59 81 01 82; fax 05 59 81 26 83; contact@camping-terrier.com; www. camping-terrier.com]** Exit A64 junc 9.1 onto D817; in 3km, at rndabt junc with D509, turn L onto Blvd de L'Europe; in 1.5km at rndabt turn R onto Av du Vert Galant; site on R in 1km, 200m bef rv bdge. NB. If app on Av du Galant fr S, rec cont to next rndabt & app fr opp direction due tight, concealed ent. Med, hdg/mkd pitch; pt shd; htd wc; chem disp; mv service pnt; baby facs; shwrs inc; el pnts (3-10A) €2.80-6.10; gas; lndtte (inc dryer); shop 500m; tradsmn; hypmkt 2km; snacks & bar high ssn; playgrnd; htd pool high ssn; rv fishing adj; tennis; car wash; entmnt; wifi; 10% statics; dogs €1.60; bus 500m; poss cr; Eng spkn; adv bkg; quiet; ccard acc; red long stay; CKE/CCI. "Gd base for Pau & district; helpful new owners (2010); improved access (2011); vg clean san facs; excel food; no twin-axles; 2 golf courses nr; vg." ♦ ltd € 12.90   2011*

PAUILLAC *7C2* (1km S Rural) *45.18515, -0.74218* **FFCC Camp Municipal Les Gabarreys, Route de la Rivière, 33250 Pauillac [05 56 59 10 03 or 05 56 73 30 50; fax 05 56 73 30 68; camping.les.gabarreys@wanadoo.fr; www.pauillac-medoc.com]** On ent Pauillac on D206, turn R at rndabt, sp site. On app Quays, turn R bef 'Maison du Vin'. Site on L in 1km. Med, hdg/mkd pitch, hdstg, pt shd; wc; chem disp; mv service pnt; shwrs inc; el pnts (5-10A) €4-5.20; lndtte; shop 1km; tradsmn; BBQ; playgrnd; htd, covrd pool 1km; games rm; TV; 6% statics; dogs €2; Eng spkn; adv bkg; quiet; red low ssn; ccard acc; CKE/CCI. "Peaceful, well-kept, well-equipped site on estuary; nice clean san facs; conv wine chateaux; cycle rtes; mkt Sat; excel." ♦ 2 Apr-10 Oct. € 15.00   2011*

PAULHAGUET *9C1* (500m SE Rural) *45.19900, 3.52000* **Camping La Fridière, 6 Route d'Esfacy, 43230 Paulhaguet [04 71 76 65 54; campingpaulhaguet@wanadoo.fr; www. campingfr.nl]** On SE side of town on D4. Sm, hdg/mkd pitch, pt shd; htd wc; chem disp; mv service pnt; shwrs inc; el pnts (10-16A) €3.50; gas 500m; lndtte; shop, snacks 500m; tradsmn; bar; playgrnd; rv fishing; wifi; dogs €1; Eng spkn; quiet; CKE/CCI. "Useful NH; lge pitches; friendly Dutch owners; vg, clean san facs; vg facs for children; popular with young Dutch families; site unkempt end ssn (2010); mkt Mon; excel." ♦ 1 Apr-1 Oct. € 13.00   2010*

PAULHIAC see Biron *7D3*

PAUNAT see Bugue, Le *7C3*

⊞ **PAYRAC** *7D3* (1km N Rural) *44.80574, 1.47479* **Camping Panoramic, Route de Loupiac, 46350 Payrac-en-Quercy [05 65 37 98 45; fax 05 65 37 91 65; info@ campingpanoramic.com; www.campingpanoramic.com]** N fr Payrac on D820, turn L onto D147 sp Loupiac (200m after 'end of village' sp), site 300m on R. Sm, pt sl, hdstg, pt shd; htd wc; chem disp; baby facs; shwrs inc; el pnts (5A) €3 (poss rev pol); gas; lndtte; shop 1km; tradsmn; rest high ssn; snacks; bar; BBQ; playgrnd; pool 400m; rv sw 5km; canoe hire; cycle hire; wifi; entmnt; TV rm; 10% statics; phone; poss cr; Eng spkn; adv bkg; quiet; CKE/CCI. "Well-run, clean site; OK san facs - poss inadequate if site full; poss muddy in bad weather but hdstg avail; friendly, helpful Dutch owner; gd walking; excel winter NH." ♦ € 11.10   2013*

PAYRAC *7D3* (6km N Rural) *44.82182, 1.46801* **Camping Chez Francis (Gatignol), 46350 Loupiac [05 65 37 64 87; francis.gatignol@wanadoo.fr; http://chez.francis. pagesperso-orange.fr]** Fr N or S on D820, sp 'A la Ferme'. Sm, sl, pt shd; wc; chem disp (wc); shwrs inc; el pnts (4A) €2 (long lead poss req); lndtte; shops 2km; tradsmn; bar; playgrnd; pool; fishing; boating; tennis; golf 3km; TV; some statics; sm dogs; poss cr; Eng spkn; adv bkg; quiet. "Pleasant site; friendly owner; mkd ent for c'vans poss diff long o'fits - rec use ent for tents if gd power/weight ratio." 1 May-31 Oct. € 11.00 2010*

PAYRAC *7D3* (6km N Rural) *44.83527, 1.46008* **Camping Les Hirondelles, Al Pech, 46350 Loupiac [05 65 37 66 25; fax 05 65 37 66 65; camp.les-hirondelles@orange.fr; www.les-hirondelles.com]** Fr Souillac foll D820 for about 12km. Site on R bef dual c'way. Sm, hdg/mkd pitch, pt sl, shd; htd wc; chem disp; baby facs; shwrs inc; el pnts (6A) inc (poss rev pol); gas; lndtte (inc dryer); shop; tradsmn; rest, snacks; bar; playgrnd; htd pool; paddling pool; cycle hire; games area; wifi; entmnt; TV; 40% statics; dogs €2.50; phone; poss cr w/end; Eng spkn; adv bkg; quiet; CKE/CCI. "Vg friendly, helpful owners; clean site; gd views fr some pitches; excel." ♦ 1 Apr-15 Sep. € 23.20   2012*

PAYRAC *7D3* (500m S Rural) *44.78936, 1.47299* **FLOWER Camping Les Pins, 46350 Payrac-en-Quercy [05 65 37 96 32; fax 05 65 37 91 08; info@les-pins-camping.com; www.les-pins-camping.com or www.flowercampings.com]** Exit A20 junc 55 onto D804 dir Souillac; in 2.4km at next rndbt take 3rd exit onto D820; cont for 16km thro Payrac; site on R in 800m - tight R-hand turn. Med, hdg/mkd pitch, hdstg, terr, pt shd; wc; chem disp; mv service pnt; serviced pitches; shwrs inc; el pnts (10A) inc; gas 1km; lndtte; shop; rest, snacks; bar; BBQ; playgrnd; 2 htd pools; waterslide; paddling pool; tennis; wifi; entmnt; games/TV rm; many statics; dogs €3; no c'vans/m'vans over 7m high ssn; some rd & disco noise; adv bkg; Eng spkn; rd noise; ccard acc; red low ssn/long stay; CKE/CCI. "Lovely, well-kept site in interesting area; gd sized pitches; welcoming, friendly owners; clean san facs; vg pool; many pitches shaded with high firs; trees make access to some pitches diff; gd for young children; peaceful site low ssn; boggy in wet." ♦ 14 Apr-9 Sep. € 30.90 SBS - D25   2011*

See advertisement on pages 32 & 33

PAYRAC *7D3* (5km NW Rural) *44.80805, 1.41027* **Camping Les Grands Chênes (Naturist), Le Peyronnet, 46350 Lamothe-Fénelon [tel/fax 05 65 41 68 79; camping@les-grands-chenes.com; www.les-grands-chenes.com]** Fr N exit A20 junc 55 onto D820 dir Payrac; turn R onto minor rd to Lamothe-Fénelon; site on D12, sp in vill. Or fr N on D820 turn R in Payrac onto D36 (best route). Fr S exit junc 56 onto D801, then turn R onto D820 to Payrac. Access rds narr fr Payrac. Sm, mkd pitch, pt sl, pt shd; wc; chem disp; baby facs; shwrs inc; el pnts (6A) €3 (long lead poss req); lndtte; shop; tradsmn; rest 6km; snacks; bar; playgrnd; pool; games area; canoe hire, golf, horseriding nrby; 2% statics; dogs €1.50; poss cr; little Eng spkn; adv bkg; quiet; INF card req; red low ssn. "Charming, peaceful site in woodland; lovely location; attractive, unusual architecture on site; friendly staff; excel san facs; cycling rte on old rlwy; close to Rv Dordogne; excel." ♦ ltd 16 May-12 Sep. € 21.80   2009*

PEGOMAS see Cannes *10F4*

PEIGNEY see Langres *6F1*

PEILLAC *2F3* (1km N Rural) *47.72635, -2.21430* **Camp Municipal du Pont d'Oust, 56220 Peillac [02 99 91 39 33 or 02 99 91 26 76 (Mairie); fax 02 99 91 31 83; www.peillac.fr]** SW fr La Gacilly on D777; in 6km turn L onto D14 sp Les Fougerêts; cont thro Les Fougerêts, site on R in 1km opp canal. Or N fr Peillac on D14, folls sp Pont d'Oust; site on L. Med, pt shd; htd wc; shwrs inc; el pnts (10A) €2.75 (poss rev pol); lndtte; shops 1km; rest, bar 300m; BBQ; pool adj; quiet. "Nice, peaceful site by Rv Oust & canal; spacious pitches; helpful warden calls, site yourself; v flat, ideal for cycling; pretty vill; vg." 1 Jun-30 Sep. € 9.40   2011*

PEISEY NANCROIX see Bourg St Maurice *9B4*

PELUSSIN *9B2* (1km SE Rural) *45.41375, 4.69143* **Camping Bel'Epoque du Pilat, La Vialle, Route de Malleval, 42410 Pélussin [04 74 87 66 60; contact@camping-belepoque.fr; www.camping-belepoque.fr]** Exit A7 junc 10 at Ampuis onto D386/D1086 dir Serrières. In Chavanay turn R onto D7 to Pélussin, then take D79 S & foll site sp. Rec do not use satnav! Sm, hdg pitch, pt sl, pt shd; htd wc; chem disp; mv service pnt; baby facs; fam bthrm; shwrs inc; el pnts (6A) €3.50; gas; lndtte; shop 1.5km; tradsmn; rest, snacks; bar; BBQ; playgrnd; htd pool; paddling pool; tennis; games area; wifi; child entmnt; dogs €2.50; phone; train 10km; Eng spkn; adv bkg; quiet; ccard acc; CKE/CCI; "In nature reserve; excel touring base; vg walking; vg site." 1 Apr-30 Sep. € 22.00   2013*

PENESTIN *2G3* (1.5km N Coastal) *47.47687, -2.45204* **Camping Les Pins, Chemin du Val au Bois de la Lande, 56760 Pénestin [tel/fax 02 99 90 33 13; camping.lespins@wanadoo.fr; www.camping-despins.com]** Fr Roche-Bernard take D34 dir Pénestin, 2km bef town turn L sp Camping Les Pins. Site on R in 250m. Med, hdg/mkd pitch, pt sl, pt shd; htd wc; chem disp; mv service pnt; baby facs; shwrs inc; el pnts (10A) €3; gas; lndtte (inc dryer); shop & 2km; tradsmn; snacks; bar; BBQ; playgrnd; htd, covrd pool; outdoor pool with waterslides; paddling pool; waterslide; playgrnd; sand beach 3km; cycle hire; games area; games rm; wifi; entmnt; TV; 33% statics; dogs €1.20; phone; bus; poss cr; Eng spkn; adv bkg; quiet; red low ssn/long stay/CKE/CCI. "Sun mkt; excel." ♦ ltd 1 Apr-16 Oct. € 19.00   2011*

PENESTIN *2G3* (1.5km E Rural) *47.47890, -2.45390* **Camping Le Cénic, Route de la Roche-Bernard, 56760 Pénestin-sur-Mer [02 99 90 45 65; fax 02 99 90 45 05; info@lecenic.com; www.lecenic.com]** Fr La Roche-Bernard take N774 sp La Baule. In 1.5km turn R onto D34. At Pénestin turn L opp Intermarché & foll sp to site in 800m. Lge, mkd pitch, pt sl, pt shd; wc; chem disp; mv service pnt; shwrs inc; el pnts (4-6A) €4; lndtte; shop adj; snacks; bar; playgrnd; htd, covrd pool/aquatic park; paddling pool; waterslides; jacuzzi; beach 3km; lake fishing; tennis; games area; games rm; few statics; dogs €2.50; Eng spkn; adv bkg rec high ssn; poss noisy high ssn; red low ssn; CKE/CCI. "Vg site nr unspoilt coastline; lge pitches; pleasant staff; clean san facs; ltd number; take care when pitching due trees; vg Sun mkt." ♦ 3 Apr-16 Sep. € 27.00   2010*

PENESTIN *2G3* (2km S Rural) *47.47150, -2.46695* **Yelloh! Village Le Domaine d'Inly, Route de Couarne, 56760 Pénestin [02 99 90 35 09; fax 02 99 90 40 93; inly-info@ wanadoo.fr or info@yellohvillage-domaine-inlay.com; www.camping-inly.com, www.yellohvillage.com or www.yellohvillage-domaine-inlay.com]** Fr Vannes or Nantes on N165, exit junc 15 W onto D34 fr La Roche-Bernard to Pénestin, then onto D201, site sp on L. Lge, hdg/ mkd pitch, hdstg, pt shd; wc; chem disp; shwrs inc; el pnts (10A) inc; Indtte; shop; rest, snacks; bar; BBQ (charcoal); playgrnd; 2 pools (1 htd, covrd); paddling pool; waterslide; sand beach 1.8km; lake fishing; canoe hire; pony hire; cycle hire; tennis; games area; games rm; wifi; entmnt; TV rm; 75% statics; dogs €4; Eng spkn; adv bkg; ccard acc; red long stay/low ssn; CKE/CCI. "V pleasant, family site; excel." ♦ 6 Apr-22 Sep. € 40.00   2011*

See advertisement on inside front cover

PENESTIN *2G3* (3km S Coastal) *47.44527, -2.48416* **Camping Les Iles, La Pointe du Bile, 56760 Pénestin [02 99 90 30 24; fax 02 99 90 44 55; contact@camping-des-iles.fr; www. camping-des-iles.fr]** Fr La Roche Bernard take D34 to Pénestin; cont on D201 for 2.5km & foll site sp. Lge, hdg/mkd pitch, pt shd; wc; chem disp; mv service pnt; some serviced pitches; baby facs; shwrs inc; el pnts (10A) inc (poss rev pol); gas; Indtte (inc dryer); shop; tradsmn; rest, snacks; bar; BBQ (elec/charcoal); playgrnd; htd pool complex; paddling pool; waterslide; sand beach nrby; fishing adj; tennis; cycle hire; horseriding; wifi; entmnt; games/TV rm; some statics; dogs €4; no c'vans/m'vans over 7m high ssn; poss cr; Eng spkn; adv bkg; quiet but noisy nr rd; ccard acc; red low ssn; CKE/CCI. "Lovely site o'looking sea; direct access to shoreline; some pitches sm; helpful staff; clean modern unisex san facs; mkt Sun (also Wed in Jul/Aug); gd cycling, walking; vg." ♦ 6 Apr-30 Sep. € 41.00 (CChq acc) SBS - B06   2012*

PENNE SUR L'OUVEZE, LA see Buis les Baronnies *9D2*

PENVINS see Sarzeau *2G3*

⊞ **PERIERS** *1D4* (6km NE Rural) *49.21581, -1.35093* **Camping Le Clos Castel, 50500 Raids [02 33 17 23 61 or 07789 227484 (mob); leclosecastel@live.com; www. camping-france-normandy.com]** S fr Carentan on D791 to Raids; cont past vill on D791 for 300m; turn R to site, ent on R in 100m. Or N fr Periers on D791; turn L 300m bef Raids & then as bef. Site well sp. Sm, hdstg, unshd; wc; chem disp; shwrs inc; el pnts (6A) inc; shops 6km; tradsmn; bar; BBQ; dogs free; Eng spkn; adv bkg; ccard not acc. "New site (2011) also offering B&B accommotion; helpful British owners; conv D-day beaches; excel." € 15.00   2011*

PERIERS *1D4* (5km SE Rural) *49.16638, -1.34916* **FFCC Aire Naturelle Municipale Le Clos Vert, 50190 St Martin-d'Aubigny [02 33 46 57 03 or 02 33 07 73 92 (Mairie); fax 02 33 07 02 53; mairie-st-martin-daubigny@wanadoo.fr; www.gites-de-france-manche.com]** E fr Périers on D900 dir St Lô; in 4km turn R sp St Martin-d'Aubigny; site on L in 500m adj church. Sm, pt shd; wc; chem disp; shwrs inc; el pnts (6A) €2.50; Indry rm; shop 300m; rest & bar 500m; BBQ; playgrnd; fishing, tennis & golf 2km; quiet; CKE/CCI;"Charming, well-kept, useful site; facs basic but OK; easy 70km run to Cherbourg; no twin-axles; Basic quiet site in vill, bar & res within walking dist" ♦ 15 Apr-15 Oct. € 7.50   2013*

⊞ **PERIGUEUX** *7C3* (12km NE Rural) *45.21975, 0.86383* **Camping Le Bois du Coderc, Route des Gaunies, 24420 Antonne-et-Trigonant [05 53 05 99 83; fax 05 53 05 15 93; coderc-camping@wanadoo.fr; www.campinglecoderc.com]** NE fr Périgueux on N21 twd Limoges, thro Antonne approx 1km turn R at x-rds bet car park & Routiers café. Site in 500m. Sm, pt shd; wc; chem disp; baby facs; shwrs inc; el pnts (6-10A) €3-4; gas 5km; Indtte (inc dryer); ice; shop 4km; tradsmn; rest 1km; snacks; bar; BBQ; playgrnd; htd pool; rv sw & shgl beach adj; games area; games rm; wifi; TV; some statics; dogs €1; phone; Eng spkn; adv bkg; quiet; ccard acc; red low ssn/CKE/ CCI. "Secluded site; most pitches spacious; friendly, helpful owners; vg, clean san facs; rallies welcome; gd value, inc rest; highly rec." ♦ € 14.00   2011*

PERIGUEUX *7C3* (1.5km E Urban) *45.18693, 0.74132* **Camping de Barnabé, 80 Rue des Bains, 24750 Boulazac [05 53 53 41 45; fax 05 53 54 16 62; contact@barnabe-perigord.com; www.barnabe-perigord.com]** Exit A89 junc 15 onto D6021 to Périgueux; at rndabt by rv, cont strt on; at mini rndabt in 200m cont strt on; in 500m at T-junc turn R into Blvd du Petit Changé; in 500m turn L into Rue des Bains & site. Site will sp. Med, hdg/mkd pitch, pt shd; htd wc; chem disp; shwrs inc; el pnts (5-10A) €3.40-3.90; shops 500m; supmkt 1km; rest, snacks; bar; rv fishing; no statics; dogs €1.20; poss v cr; Eng spkn; adv bkg; quiet; red long stay/low ssn; ccard acc;"Pleasant rvside site in nice spot; sm pitches & cramped for lge o'fits; many pitches dark & v shady; san facs dated & poss unclean (2010); poss clsd low ssn - phone ahead; access to public using adj café; Périgueux delightful." 1 Apr-31 Oct. € 17.20   2013*

PERIGUEUX *7C3* (10km E Rural) *45.21306, 0.83780* **FFCC Camping au Fil de l'Eau, 6 Allée des Platanes, 24420 Antonne-et-Trigonant [05 53 06 17 88; fax 05 53 08 97 76; campingaufildeleau@wanadoo.fr; http://camping-aufildeleau.monsite-orange.fr/]** E fr Périgueux on N21 twd Limoges; sp on R at end of vill; camp 350m along rd to Escoire. Well sp. Sm, pt shd; wc; chem disp; shwrs inc; el pnts (5A) €3; Indtte; shops 1km; tradsmn; snacks; playgrnd; lake sw; canoe hire; fishing; cycle hire; some statics; adv bkg; quiet; CKE/CCI. "Pleasant site; gd base for area; helpful owners; clean facs; red facs low ssn; excel." ♦ 15 Jun-15 Sep. € 11.40   2008*

PERIGUEUX *7C3* (7km S Rural) *45.14900, 0.77880* **Camping Le Grand Dague, Route du Grand Dague, 24750 Atur [05 53 04 21 01; fax 05 53 04 22 01; info@legranddague.fr; www.legranddague.fr]** Fr cent Périgueux, take N21 & A89 twd Brive. Fork L onto D2 to Atur (main rd bears R). In Atur turn L after bar/tabac; foll site sp for 2.5km. Lge, pt sl, shd; htd wc; chem disp; baby facs; shwrs inc; el pnts (6A) inc; lndtte (inc dryer); ltd shop; tradsmn; rest, snacks; bar; BBQ; playgrnd; htd pool; paddling pool; cycle hire; games area; games rm; wifi; entmnt; TV rm; 70% statics; dogs €2; phone; Eng spkn; adv bkg; quiet; red low ssn; ccard acc; red low ssn; CKE/CCI. "Gd family site; friendly owners; site immac, even end of ssn; poss unkempt early ssn; lots to do; ltd touring pitches; excel." ♦ 20 Apr-26 Sep. € 29.00   2010*

PERNES LES FONTAINES see Carpentras *10E2*

PERONNE *3C3* (300m NE Urban) *49.93424, 2.94140* **Camp Municipal du Brochet, Rue Georges Clémenceau, 80200 Péronne [03 22 84 02 35; fax 03 22 73 31 01; peter.v.gent@orange.fr]** Fr N on D1017 turn R into town. L at lights & L immed after footbdge. 1st R & site on L. Well sp fr all dirs. Go to town cent then foll 'Intn'l Camping Site' sps. Sm, hdstg, pt sl, terr, pt shd; wc; chem disp; mv service pnt; shwrs €1.10; el pnts (16A) inc; lndtte; shops & rest 500m; playgrnd; bus 500m; dogs free; phone; poss cr; Eng spkn; adv bkg; quiet; CKE/CCI. "Pleasant, basic but clean site nr park & attractive town; grass pitches soft when wet; rec arr early high ssn; conv WW1 museum; vg." 1 Apr-1 Oct. € 14.70   2010*

PERONNE *3C3* (1km S Rural) *49.91805, 2.93227* **Camping du Port de Plaisance, Route de Paris, 80200 Péronne [03 22 84 19 31; fax 03 22 73 36 37; contact@camping-plaisance.com; www.camping-plaisance.com]** Exit A1/E15 junc 13.1 dir Peronne on D938 to D1017. Site on R o'looking canal. Well sp fr all dirs. Med, mkd pitch, pt shd; htd wc; chem disp; mv service pnt; shwrs inc; el pnts (6-10A) €4.30-7.95 (some rev pol & long lead poss req); lndtte; sm shop; tradsmn; supmkt nr; snacks high ssn; rest nr; bar; playgrnd; htd pool high ssn; jacuzzi; fishing; wifi; dogs €1.30; poss v cr; Eng spkn; poss some rd noise; red low ssn/long stay; ccard acc. "Pleasant, site; popular NH; helpful staf & owners; san facs adequate; gd play park & pool; gates locked 2200-0800 - when clsd, park outside; vg rest adj; rec visit to war museum in Péronne castle; popular with ralliers; no twin-axles; poss ltd security; facs need upgrading (2013); vg site, pleasant situation nr a canal; gd size pitches" ♦ 1 Mar-31 Oct. € 31.20 (3 persons)   2013*

PERONNE *3C3* (2km NW Rural) *49.94409, 2.90826* **Camping La Tortille, L'Orgibet, 80200 Cléry-sur-Somme [03 22 83 17 59 or 03 22 84 10 45 (LS); fax 03 22 83 04 14; jsg-bred@wanadoo.fr]** Exit A1/E15 junc 13.1 onto D938 to Cléry, dir Péronne. Site sp on rvside in 5km. Med, hdg pitch, hdstg, pt shd; wc; shwrs €1.20; el pnts (10A) €3.60; shop 4km; BBQ; playgrnd; rv fishing; games area; 80% statics; dogs €1.30; adv bkg; quiet; red long stay; CKE/CCI. "Peaceful site; sm pitches, poss bet statics; clean modern san facs; conv for A1 m'way" ♦ 1 Apr-31 Oct. € 14.80   2013*

PERPIGNAN *8G4* (4.5km NE Coastal) *42.73027, 2.92224* **Rouissillon Camping Catalan, Route de Bompas, 66000 Perpignan [04 68 63 16 92; camping.catalan@free.fr; http://camping-catalan.com]** Fr Perpignan N on D1, Bompas rd. Site on R bef rndabt. Med, shd; wc; serviced pitches; shwrs; el pnts (10A) €3.90; lndtte; shop 500m; rest, snacks; bar; pool; playgrnd; beach 10km; entmnt; TV; 60% statics; dogs €3; poss cr; adv bkg; CKE/CCI. "Pool deep, no shallow end." 15 Mar-31 Oct. € 19.30   2010*

PERPIGNAN *8G4* (6km S Rural) *42.63754, 2.89819* **Camping Les Rives du Lac, Chemin de la Serre, 66180 Villeneuve-de-la-Raho [04 68 55 83 51; fax 04 68 55 86 37; camping.villeneuveraho@wanadoo.fr]** Fr A9 exit Perpignan Sud, dir Porte d'Espagne. In 3km turn R onto N9 dir Le Boulou. In 1km after Auchan supmkt take slip rd to N91 dir Villeneuve-de-la-Raho. In 2km rd becomes D39, turn R to site, site on L in 1km. Beware ford on D39 in v wet weather (usually dry). Med, mkd pitch, pt sl, hdstg, pt shd; htd wc; chem disp; mv service pnt; shwrs inc; el pnts (6A) inc; lndtte; shop; supmkt 3km; rest, snacks; bar; BBQ (elec/gas); playgrnd; htd pool; lake sw, beach, fishing & watersports 1.5km; tennis 2km; some statics; dogs €1.60; phone; Eng spkn; adv bkg; poss noise fr adj picnic area w/ends; red low ssn; ccard acc; CKE/CCI. "Lakeside site with views; poor san facs & insufficient for site size; busy cycling/jogging path adj; conv trips to Spain; busy public beach nr." ♦ 15 Mar-15 Nov. € 17.50   2009*

PERROS GUIREC *1D2* (5km E Coastal) *48.81439, -3.38372*
Camp Municipal Le Palud, Port L'Epine, 22660 Trélévern
[02 96 91 73 11 or 02 96 23 71 91 (LS); fax 02 96 91 76 30;
campinglepalud.trelevern@orange.fr; www.trelevern.fr]
Fr Lannion on D788 to Perros-Guirec; at rndabt on sea front turn
R onto D6 dir Louannec & Trélévern; in 3km turn L to Trélévern.
Foll sps Port L'Epine & Camping Municipal. Med, mkd pitch,
unshd; wc; chem disp; baby facs; shwrs inc; el pnts (10A) inc;
gas 1km; lndtte; sm shop & 1km; tradsmn; rest, snacks; bar;
BBQ; playgrnd; beach adj; entmnt; internet; dogs €1.10; phone
adj; Eng spkn; adv bkg; quiet; ccard acc; red low ssn; CKE/CCI.
"Peaceful site with views; many pitches beside sea; rocks & sand
adj; excel." ♦ 4 Jun-12 Sep. € 20.55   2010*

PERROS GUIREC *1D2* (10km E Coastal/Rural) *48.81310,*
-3.38590 **RCN Port l'Epine, 10 Venelle de Pors-Garo,**
22660 Trélévern [02 96 23 71 94; fax 02 96 23 77 83;
portlepine@rcn.fr; www.rcn-campings.fr] N fr Guingamp
on D767 dir Lannion for approx 30km, then D788 dir Perros-
Guirec; at rndabt just outside Perros-Guirec turn R onto
D38 dir Trélévern. In Trélévern turn L at petrol stn & cont
twd beach, sp Port L'Epine & Cmp Municipal; site on L opp
Municipal site. NB Park on R at bottom of hill & walk to site
to collect check-in information. Med, hdg/mkd pitch, pt sl, pt
shd; wc; chem disp; serviced piches; shwrs inc; el pnts (16A)
inc (poss rev pol); gas; lndtte; shop; tradsmn; rest, snacks; bar;
BBQ; playgrnd; htd pool; paddling pool; dir access shgl beach;
cycle hire; games rm; wifi; entmnt; 30% statics; dogs €7; no
c'vans/m'vans over 6m high ssn; poss cr; Eng spkn; adv bkg;
quiet; ccard acc; red long stay/low ssn; CKE/CCI. "Pleasant,
family-run, friendly site; sea view & v lge pitches extra; narr
site rds; clean san facs, poss stretched high ssn; barrier clsd
2300-0700; vg for families with young children but not rec for
teenagers; mkt Perros-Guirec Fri." ♦ 6 Apr-29 Sep.
€ 45.65   2011*

See advertisement opposite

PERROS GUIREC *1D2* (1km SE Coastal) *48.79657, -3.42689*
Camp Municipal Ernest Renan, 22700 Louannec
[02 96 23 11 78; fax 02 96 23 35 42; mairie-louannec@
wanadoo.fr] 1km W of Louannec on D6. Lge, unshd; wc
(some cont); chem disp; mv service pnt; shwrs inc; el pnts (6A)
inc; gas; shop high ssn; rest; bar; playgrnd; htd pool; sand
beach adj; fishing & watersports adj; games rm; TV; dogs
€1.05; poss cr; adv bkg; Eng spkn; traff noise early am (minimal
away fr rd). "Well-kept site; pitches on seashore; clean san
facs; clsd 1200-1530, little parking space outside; highly rec."
♦ 1 Jun-30 Sep. € 16.55   2008*

PERROS GUIREC *1D2* (1km W Rural) *48.80617, -3.46541*
Camping La Claire Fontaine, Toul ar Lann, 22700
Perros-Guirec [02 96 23 03 55; fax 02 96 49 06 19; www.
camping-claire-fontaine.com] Fr Lannion N on D788 twd
Perros-Guirec. At 2nd rndabt W on D11, then N on D6, L fork
sp. Med, pt sl, pt shd; wc (some cont); chem disp; mv service
pnt; baby facs; shwrs inc; el pnts (4-6A) inc; lndtte; tradsmn;
shop; sand beach 800m; playgrnd; TV rm; some statics; dogs
€1; Eng spkn; adv bkg rec high ssn; quiet. "Helpful staff."
1 Jun-15 Sep. € 21.00   2008*

PERROS GUIREC *1D2* (3km NW Coastal) *48.82798, -3.47623*
Yelloh! Village Le Ranolien, Ploumanac'h, 22700
Perros-Guirec [02 96 91 65 65; fax 02 96 91 41 90; info@
yellohvillage-ranolien.com; www.leranolien.fr or www.
yellohvillage.co.uk] At Perros-Guirec harbour turn R at
Marina foll sp Trégastel. Up hill above coast into Perros Guirec
town. Cont strt thro traff lts & into La Clarté vill; strt at traff
lts & sharp R at Camping & Le Ranolien sp. Ent shortly on L.
Foll Trégastel sp all way. Lge, mkd pitch, pt sl, pt shd; htd wc;
mv service pnt; baby facs; shwrs inc; el pnts (16A) inc; lndtte;
shop; rest, snacks; bar; 2 pools (1 htd,covrd); waterslide; spa;
sand & rock beach; fishing; tennis; golf; horseriding; entmnt;
many tour op statics; dogs €4; poss cr; Eng spkn; adv bkg;
ccard acc. "Excel beaches; vg coastal walks nrby." ♦
9 Apr-18 Sep. € 40.00   2010*

See advertisement on inside front cover

PERTRE, LE *2F4* (1km W Rural) *48.03287, -1.03965* **Camp**
Municipal Le Chardonneret, Rue de Chardonneret,
35370 Le Pertre [02 99 96 99 27 or 06 79 50 41 77;
mairielepertre@wanadoo.fr; www.lepertre.fr] W fr Laval
on D57 turn S at La Gravelle onto D43 to Le Pertre. Or exit
A81 junc 5 S. Sm, hdg pitch, pt sl, pt shd; htd wc; shwrs; el pt
(16A) €1.80; lndry rm; BBQ; 20% statics; dogs; phone; quiet
but factory adj & church bells at night. "Warden calls am/pm;
o'night area for m'vans; basic shops in town; some run down
statics; gd NH." ♦ ltd   1 Jan-30 Sep. € 7.00   2009*

PERTUIS *10E3* (1.5km E Urban) *43.69014, 5.52489*
Camping Les Pinèdes du Luberon, Ave Pierre Augier,
Quartier St Sépulcre, 84120 Pertuis [04 90 79 10 98;
fax 04 90 09 03 99; pinedes-luberon@franceloc.fr;
www.campinglespinedes.com] Exit Pertuis on D973 twd
Manosque. After 1km fr cent of Pertuis turn R foll sp Camping
& Piscine. In 2km pass pool to site 100m on brow of hill. Lge,
hdg/mkd pitch, hdstg, terr, pt sl, pt shd; htd wc; chem disp;
mv service pnt; baby facs; shwrs inc; el pnts (6-10A) €4-8; gas;
lndry rm; shop & 2km; playgrnd; aquatic centre with 2 pools &
waterslide; trampolines; entmnt; 95% statics; dogs €5; phone;
quiet; red long stay; ccard acc (high ssn); red low ssn; CKE/
CCI. "Spacious, attractive, well-kept site; now privately owned
(2011) & few touring pitches; san facs need update (2011); mkt
high ssn; vg." ♦ 15 Mar-15 Oct. € 25.00   2011*

PERTUIS *10E3* (6km SW Rural) *43.64410, 5.45468* **Camping**
Messidor (Naturist), Route de St Canadet, 13610 Le
Puy-Ste Réparade [04 42 61 90 28; fax 04 42 50 07 08;
messidor@online.fr; www.messidor.fr] S fr Pertuis on
D956/D556 twds Aix-en-Provence; after 5km turn R onto
D561 twds Le Puy-Ste Réparade & Silvacane. At ent to vill take
sp Aix-en-Provence via St Canadet (D13). Cross canal & turn
immed 2nd R. Med, terr, pt sl, pt shd; wc; shwrs inc; el pnts
(4A) €3.20; lndtte; shop 3km; tradsmn; rest, snacks; bar; pool;
paddling pool; rv fishing & watersports; tennis; 50% statics;
dogs €2; Eng spkn; adv bkg; quiet; INF card req. "Gd facs &
pool; lovely views fr some pitches; sh walk to bus stop for Aix."
1 Apr-30 Sep. € 23.00 (CChq acc)   2009*

PESMES *6G2* (500m S Rural) *47.27612, 5.56451* **Camp Municipal La Colombière, Route de Dole, 70140 Pesmes [03 84 31 20 15; fax 03 84 31 20 54; campcolombiere@aol. com]** On D475 halfway bet Gray & Dole. S fr Pesmes immed on L after x-ing rv bdge. N fr Dole, site sp on R immed bef rest at rv bdge. Med, some hdg pitch, pt shd; wc; chem disp (wc); shwrs; el pnts (6-10A) €2.30-3.60; lndtte; shop 500m; rest adj; snacks; bar; cycle hire; dogs €1.20; phone; Eng spkn; adv bkg rec high ssn; some rd noise; no ccard acc. "Picturesque vill; helpful, friendly staff; gd san facs; vg; No twin axles" 1 May-31 Oct. € 12.60   2012*

PETIT PALAIS ET CORNEMPS see St Médard de Guizières *7C2*

PETITE PIERRE, LA *5D3* (2km S Rural) *48.84519, 7.31825* Camping Imsterfeld, Route Forestière, 67290 La Petite-Pierre [tel/fax 03 88 70 42 12; camping-imsterfeld@wanadoo.fr] Fr N61 turn E onto D13/D9 to La Petite-Pierre. Sm, hdg/mkd pitch, terr, pt shd; wc; chem disp (wc); shwrs €0.50; el pnts €2; tradsmn; BBQ; 75% statics; dogs; CKE/CCI. "Pleasant site with lake view (fenced); gd uphill walks to town." 1 May-30 Sep. € 10.50   2008*

PEUPLINGUES see Calais *3A3*

PEYNIER see Trets *10F3*

PEYRAT LE CHATEAU see Eymoutiers *7B4*

PEYREHORADE *8F1* (7km N Rural) *43.60318, -1.12970* Camping La Comtesse, Lieu-dit Claquin, 40300 Bélus [05 58 57 69 07; fax 05 58 57 62 50; campinglacomtesse@wanadoo.fr; www.campinglacomtesse.com] N fr Peyrehorade on D33; in 4km turn R sp Bélus; in 1.5km turn L; site on R in 1.5km, sp. Med, hdg/mkd pitch, pt shd; wc; chem disp; shwrs incl; el pnts (10A) €3.10; lndtte (inc dryer); shops, rests nrby; bar; BBQ; playgrnd; htd pool; games rm; entmnt; 50% statics; dogs €1.70; phone; adv bkg; red low ssn. "By pretty lake; friendly staff; ltd facs low ssn; vg." ♦ ltd 1 Apr-30 Sep. € 12.90   2009*

PEYRELEAU *10E1* (1km N Rural) *44.19126, 3.20470* **Camp Municipal de Brouillet, 48150 Le Rozier [05 65 62 63 98; fax 05 65 62 60 83; contact@campinglerozier.com; www. camping-lerozier.com]** Fr Millau take D809 N to Aguessac, onto D907; in Le Rozier, x bdge over Rv Tarn onto D996 & in 200m (opp church); take rd on R to site; sp. Lge, mkd pitch, pt shd; wc (some cont); chem disp (wc); baby facs; shwrs inc; el pnts (6A) €3.50; lndtte; shop 200m; playgrnd; htd pool; poss cr; adv bkg rec high ssn; quiet; red low ssn; CKE/CCI. "V pleasant, busy, spacious site adj rv; friendly recep; vg for m'vans; poss facs stretched & unclean; gd base for Tarn Gorges; gd area walking & birdwatching." ♦ ltd 1 Apr-20 Sep. € 15.70   2012*

PEYRELEAU *10E1* (1km N Rural) *44.19111, 3.20486* Camping Les Peupliers, 48150 Le Rozier [05 65 62 60 85 or 06 74 37 79 72 (mob); peupliers12@orange.fr; www. camping-lespeupliers.com] Fr Millau take D809 N to Aguessac, turn R onto D907 to Le Rozier. Cross bdge over Rv Tarn onto D996 & take rd on R to site; sp. Sm, mkd pitch, pt shd; wc; chem disp; shwrs inc; el pnts (6A) €2.50; lndry rm; shop, rest, bar 300m; tradsmn; snacks; BBQ; playgrnd; wifi; dogs free; bus 300m; Eng spkn; adv bkg rec high ssn; quiet; CKE/CCI. "Lovely, friendly, little site on Rv Jonte; gd base for walking etc." € 9.00   2009*

PEYRELEAU *10E1* (1km W Rural) *44.19470, 3.20210* Camping Saint Pal, Route des Gorges du Tarn, 12720 Mostuéjouls [tel/fax 05 65 62 64 46 or 05 65 58 79 82 (LS); saintpal@orange.fr; www.campingsaintpal.com] Exit A75 exit junc 44.1 onto D29 to Aguessac then L onto D907 to Mostuéjouls. Or fr Millau take D809 N to Aguessac, turn R onto D907 to Mostuéjouls. Site in 10km 500m fr Rozier bdge. Med, hdg/mkd pitch, shd; wc (some cont); chem disp; mv service pnt; baby facs; fam bthrm; shwrs; el pnts (6A) €3.20; gas; lndtte; shop & 1km; tradsmn; snacks; bar high ssn; BBQ; playgrnd; pool; rv sw & beach adj; games rm; organised walks; TV; 20% statics; dogs €2; phone; poss cr; Eng spkn; adv bkg; quiet; ccard acc; red low ssn/CKE/CCI. "Excel site & facs; gd walks, canoeing, fishing & birdwatching, beavers on rv bank opp; poss diff for lge o'fits." ♦ 1 May-30 Sep. € 27.50   2012*

PEYRELEAU *10E1* (1.2km NW Rural) *44.19810, 3.19442* FFCC Camping Les Bords du Tarn, 12720 Mostuéjouls [05 65 62 62 94; lesbordsdutarn@orange.fr; www. campinglesbordsdutarn.com] Exit A75 junc 44.1 onto D29 to Aguessac; turn L onto D907 dir Le Rozier & Peyreleau; site on R 1km bef Le Rozier. NB Do not use exit 44 fr A75 (as sat nav might instruct). Med, mkd pitch, pt sl, pt shd; wc; chem disp; baby facs; shwrs inc; el pnts (10A) €3.50; lndtte; sm shop & 1.2km; rest & 1.2km; snacks; bar; BBQ (charcoal/gas); playgrnd; htd pool; rv sw adj, pebble beach; canoe hire; climbing; paragliding; cycling; fishing; tennis; games rm; ltd wifi; entmnt; 10% statics; dogs €2; phone; poss cr; Eng spkn; adv bkg; quiet; ccard acc; red low ssn; CKE/CCI. "Site in beautiful area by rv; some v lge pitches; gd for rv sports; modern san facs; gd walking; conv Gorges du Tarn & Gorges de la Jonte; excel ." ♦ ltd 7 May-12 Sep. € 20.70   2010*

⊞ **PEYRIGNAC** *7C3* (1km W Rural) *45.16048, 1.18594* Camping La Garenne, La Brousse, 24210 Peyrignac [tel/fax 05 53 50 57 73; s.lagarenne@wanadoo.com; www. lagarennedordogne.com] E fr Périgueux on A89. At Peyrignac foll site sp. Narr, steep rd poss diff lge o'fits. Med, mkd pitch, pt sl, shd; htd wc; chem disp; mv service pnt; baby facs; shwrs inc; el pnts (6-10A) €4 (poss rev pol); gas; lndtte; shop; tradsmn; snacks; bar; playgrnd; sm pool; games area; 50% statics; dogs €1.50; poss cr; adv bkg; quiet; red low ssn; CKE/CCI. "Gd touring base; gd size pitches; clean san facs; v kind owners; vg site would rec." ♦ € 15.00   2011*

PEYRILLAC ET MILLAC see Souillac *7C3*

PEZENAS *10F1* (1km NE Urban) *43.46618, 3.42397*
Camping St Christol, Chemin de St Christol, 34120
Pézenas [04 67 98 09 00 or 06 11 39 59 17 (mob); fax
04 67 98 89 61; info@campingsaintchristol.com; www.
campingsaintchristol.com] Exit A75 junc 59 Pézenas N onto
N9 by-pass for town cent; turn R immed bef bdge; sp on R
in 200m. NB app rds narr. Med, hdg/mkd pitch, hdstg, shd;
wc (some cont); chem disp (wc); baby facs; shwrs inc; el pnts
(10A) €3.40; gas; lndtte; shop; tradsmn; rest, snacks; BBQ
area; playgrnd; pool; fishing; games rm; entmnt; TV; some
statics; dogs €1.70; poss cr; adv bkg rec Jul/Aug; quiet; ccard
acc; red low ssn; CKE/CCI. "Friendly, lively site; lge gravel
pitches but hard & dusty; poss diff to manoeuvre due trees;
san facs reasonable (2009); historic town." ♦ 15 Apr-15 Sep.
€ 18.00   2009*

"Satellite navigation makes touring much easier"

Remember most sat navs don't know if you're towing or in a larger vehicle – always use yours alongside maps and site directions.

PEZENAS *10F1* (6km S Rural) *43.38776, 3.42298* Camping
Le Pin Parasol, Le Causse, 34630 St Thibéry [tel/fax
04 67 77 84 29; camping-pin-parasol@wanadoo.fr; www.
campinglepinparasol.com] Fr A9 exit junc 34 onto D13 & foll
Pézenas sps; in 2.5km turn R to St Thibéry & site 150m on R.
Med, mkd pitch, pt shd; wc; mv service pnt; shwrs inc; el pnts
(10A) €5; supmkt 300m; tradsmn; rest, snacks; BBQ; playgrnd;
pool; paddling pool; sand beach 10km; tennis 1km; games rm;
rv sw 1km; fishing; entmnt; TV; 30% statics; dogs €4; sep car
park; poss cr; adv bkg; rd noise; ccard not acc; red low ssn;
CKE/CCI. "Vg site; vg san facs; lovely pool; gd value takeaway;
stone quarry & indus units nrby (not a problem); site poss dusty
low ssn; interesting vill." ♦ 1 Apr-30 Oct. € 19.00   2010*

PEZENAS *10F1* (500m SW Urban) *43.45419, 3.41573*
Campotel Municipal de Castelsec, Chemin de Castelsec,
34120 Pézenas [04 67 98 04 02; fax 04 67 98 35 40;
contact@camping-pezenas.com; www.camping-gites-
herault.com] Fr Béziers take N9 to Pézenas; foll Centre Ville
sps fr rndabt at edge of town onto Route de Béziers; in 600m
at next rndabt (at junc with D13) go strt over into Ave de
Verdun; in 400m take 1st L after McDonalds & pharmacy at
ent to Carrefour supmkt; foll Campotel sps; site on L in 300m.
Sm, mkd pitch, pt sl, pt terr, pt shd; wc; chem disp (wc); shwrs
inc; el pnts (10A) €2.90; lndtte; shops 500m; playgrnd; pool
1km; tennis adj; TV; 30% statics; dogs €1.40; adv bkg; quiet;
rd noise some pitches; red low ssn; CKE/CCI. "Great little site;
friendly staff; clean, dated san facs; some pitches unsuitable lge
o'fits; easy walk/cycle to interesting town; toy museum worth
visit; vg." ♦ 1 Apr-30 Oct. € 14.30   2011*

PEZULS see Bugue, Le *7C3*

PHALSBOURG *5D3* (2km N Rural) *48.78300, 7.25020*
FFCC Camping de Bouleaux (CC de F), 5 Rue des
Trois Journeaux, 57370 Vilsberg [03 87 24 18 72; fax
03 87 24 46 52; info@campinglesbouleaux.fr; www.
campinglesbouleaux.fr or www.campingclub.asso.fr]
Fr A4 exit junc 44 dir Phalsbourg. At x-rds turn L sp D661
Sarreguemines. Site on R in 2km. NB Site ent off steep descent
on D661. Lge o'fits take care leaving site & turning L - watch
rear overhangs. Lge, pt shd; wc; chem disp; mv service pnt;
baby facs; shwrs inc; el pnts (6A) inc; lndtte; shop; tradsmn;
BBQ; playgrnd; 15% statics; dogs €2; phone; bus 2km; Eng
spkn; adv bkg; quiet; red low ssn; CKE/CCI. "Peaceful, well-
kept site; welcoming, helpful Dutch owners; barrier clsd 1930;
gd facs; access to some pitches poss diff, some uneven; conv
m'way & NH to/fr Germany/Austria; gd NH" ♦ 1 Apr-31 Oct.
€ 23.50   2013*

PHALSBOURG *5D3* (6km SW Rural) *48.71922, 7.22643*
Camping du Plan Incliné, Hoffmuhl, 57820 Henridorff
[tel/fax 03 87 25 30 13 or 06 71 21 86 91 (mob);
campingplanincline@wanadoo.fr; www.camping
planincline.com] Exit A4 at junc 44. In Phalsbourg take D38
twds Lutzelbourg; turn R onto D98 dir Arzviller & foll sp to
Henridorff & site on R adj rv (narr ent). Med, some hdg/hdstp
pitches, pt shd; wc; chem disp; shwrs inc; el pnts (6A) €3; gas;
lndtte; shop 2km; tradsmn; rest, snacks; bar; playgrnd; pool
high ssn (spring water); rv sw, fishing & boating adj; entmnt;
60% statics; dogs €1; phone; Eng spkn; adv bkg; rlwy noise
& some rd & boat noise; red long stay; ccard not acc; CKE/
CCI. "In wooded valley; friendly, helpful owner; vg rest; grnd
soft when wet; cycle path to Strasbourg." ♦ 1 Apr-20 Oct.
€ 13.00   2008*

PICQUIGNY *3C3* (E Urban) *49.9445, 2.1458* Camp Municipal,
66 Rue du Marais, 80310 Picquigny [03 22 51 25 83
or 03 22 51 40 31 (Mairie); fax 03 22 51 30 98; http://
picquigny.free.fr] Site sp fr town cent. Med, unshd; wc; chem
disp; shwrs inc; el pnts (10A) inc; lndry rm; shop nr; playgrnd;
rv & fishing; mainly statics; dogs; quiet; occasional noise fr rlwy
line; adv bkg rec high ssn; "Pleasant site; modern san facs;
some shaded pitches bet statics; WW1 war cemetery nr town"
1 Apr-31 Oct. € 17.00   2013*

PIERRE BUFFIERE *7B3* (1.5km S Rural) *45.68937, 1.37101*
Camp Intercommunal Chabanas, 87260 Pierre-Buffière
[tel/fax 05 55 00 96 43] Approx 20km S of Limoges on A20,
take exit 40 onto D420 southbound; site on L in 500m. Foll sps
for 'Stade-Chabanas'. Med, hdg/mkd pitch (all grass gd size), pt
sl, pt shd; wc; chem disp (wc); shwrs inc; el pnts (10A) inc (poss
rev pol); lndtte; shop & snacks 2 km; playgrnd; fishing; dogs
€0.80; phone; adv bkg; quiet but some rlwy noise; red low ssn;
CKE/CCI. "Clean, quiet site; helpful staff; excel san facs; some
pitches diff for lge o'fits; no hanging; warden on site 1600-
2200, but gate poss locked all day low ssn (code issued); phone
ahead; conv Limoges; excel NH fr A20." ♦ 15 May-30 Sep.
€ 13.50   2012*

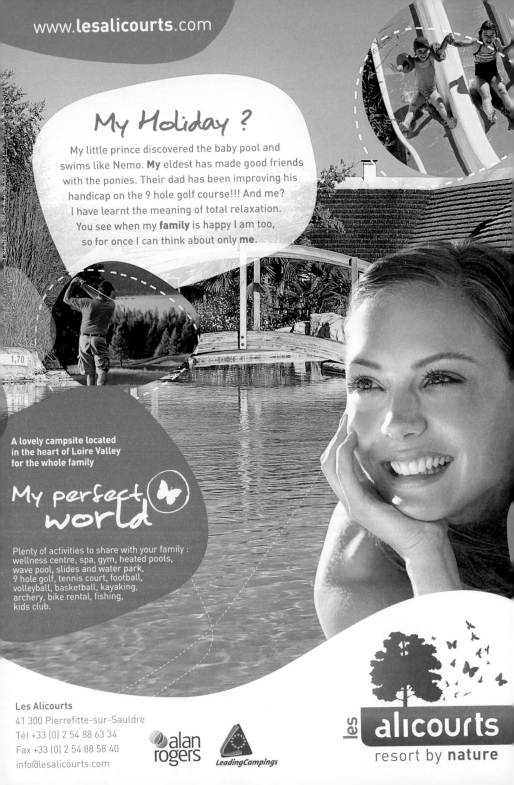

PIERREFITTE SUR SAULDRE *4G3* (6km NE Rural) *47.54444, 2.19138* **Les Alicourts Resort, Domaine des Alicourts, 41300 Pierrefitte-sur-Sauldre [02 54 88 63 34; fax 02 54 88 58 40; info@lesalicourts.com; www.lesalicourts.com]** Fr S of Lamotte-Beuvron, turn L on D923. After 14km turn R on D24E sp Pierrefitte. After 750m turn L, foll sp to site approx 750m on R. Med, pt shd; wc; mv service pnt; chem disp; baby facs; shwrs inc; el pnts (6A) inc; lndtte; shop; rest, snacks; bar; BBQ; playgrnd; 3 pools; waterslide; tennis; lake sw; kayak/pedalo hire; skating rink; cycle hire; fitness cent; games rm; entmnt; some statics; dogs €7; extra for lakeside pitches; poss cr (but roomy); Eng spkn; adv bkg; quiet; ccard acc; red low ssn; CKE/CCI. "Excel, peaceful site; gd, clean facs; v lge pitches." ♦ 29 Apr-6 Sep. € 52.00   2011*

See advertisement opposite

PIERREFONDS *3D3* (500m N Urban) *49.35427, 2.97564* **Camp Municipal de Batigny, 34 Rue de l'Armistice, 60350 Pierrefonds [03 44 42 80 83 / 09 71 20 42 08 (mob); fax 03 44 42 87 73; camping-de-pierrefonds@orange.fr]** Take D973 fr Compiegne; after 14km site on L adj sp for Pierrefonds at ent to vill. Med, hdg pitch, pt shd; htd wc; chem disp; mv service pnt; 90% serviced pitches; shwrs inc; el pnts (10A) €2.80 (poss rev pol); lndtte; shops 800m; rest in vill; dog €1; poss cr; adv bkg; rd noise; ccard not acc; red long stay; CKE/CCI; "Attractive, well-run, busy site; tight pitches for lge o'fits; clean san facs; poss unkempt low ssn; site yourself if recep clsd; cycle paths; nr Armistice train & museum" 6 Apr-30 Sep. € 13.00   2013*

PIERREFORT *7C4* (7km SW Rural) *44.85405, 2.77060* **FLOWER Camping La Source Aveyron, Presqu'ile de Laussac, 12600 Thérondels [05 65 66 27 10; fax 05 65 66 21 00; info@camping-la-source.com; www.camping-la-source.com or www.flowercampings.com]** Fr A75 at St Flour, take D921 to Les Ternes, then D990 thro Pierrefort. Approx 2km after Pierrefort, turn L onto D34. Go thro Paulhenc, site on L after approx 7km. Med, mkd pitch, terr, pt shd; wc; chem disp; mv service pnt; baby facs; shwrs inc; el pnts (6A) inc; gas; lndtte (inc dryer); shop; tradsmn; rest, snacks; bar; playgrnd; htd pool; paddling pool; waterslide; lake sw & beach adj; fishing; watersports; boat hire; tennis; games area; wifi; entmnt; TV; dogs €1.70; 35% statics; quiet; adv bkg rec high ssn; ccard acc; red low ssn/long stay; CKE/CCI. "Excel lakeside site; poss diff lge o'fits due lge trees." ♦ 27 May-9 Sep. € 28.50   2011*

⊞ **PIEUX, LES** *1C4* (6km S Rural) *49.48702, -1.79854* **Camp Municipal, 2 Route du Rozel, 50340 St Germain-le-Gaillard [02 33 52 55 64]** Take D650 fr Cherbourg. 3km beyond Les Pieux turn R sp Le Rozel. Site on R 100m. Sm, hdg pitch, some hdstg, unshd; htd wc; chem disp; shwrs inc; el pnts (15A) €2.60; ltd water stand pnts; lndry rm; shop; playgrnd; pool & sand beach 3km; 85% statics; adv bkg. "Modern, clean, well-kept san facs; rec arr early high ssn - ltd touring pitches; poss diff in wet." ♦ € 6.10   2008*

PIEUX, LES *1C4* (3km SW Coastal) *49.49444, -1.84194* **Kawan Village Le Grand Large, 11 Route de Grand Large, 50340 Les Pieux [02 33 52 40 75; fax 02 33 52 58 20; info@legrandlarge.com; www.legrandlarge.com]** Fr ferry at 1st rndabt take 1st exit sp Centre Ville. Closer to town cent foll old N13 sp Caen. In about 1.5km branch R onto D900 then L onto D650 sp Carteret. Foll this rd past Les Pieux, cont on D650 to sp Super U. Turn R & foll site sp onto D517, then D117 for 3km until reaching beach rd to site, on site on L in 2km. Lge, hdg/mkd pitch, pt shd; htd wc; chem disp; mv service pnt; baby facs; shwrs inc; el pnts (10A) €4.; gas; lndtte (inc dryer); shop; tradsmn; snacks high ssn; bar; BBQ; playgrnd; htd pool; paddling pool; sand beach adj; horseriding 4km; tennis; wifi; entmnt; games/TV rm; 40% statics; dogs free(1 per picth); c'vans/m'vans over 8m by request; phone; poss cr; Eng spkn; adv bkg; quiet; ccard acc; red low ssn/long stay; "Well-run site; rec for families; dir access to superb lge beach; friendly staff; clean modern san facs; barrier clsd 2100-0900; conv Cherbourg ferries but arr not rec after dark due sm country lanes; outside pitches avail for early dep for ferries; mkt Fri;" ♦ ltd 12 Apr-21 Sep. € 33.00 (CChq acc) SBS - N07   2013*

See advertisement below

PIEUX, LES *1C4* (4km SW Coastal) *49.48022, -1.84216* **Camping Le Ranch, 50340 Le Rozel [02 33 10 07 10; fax 02 33 10 07 11; contact@camping-leranch.com; www.camping-leranch.com]** S fr Cherbourg on D650 & turn R to Les Pieux, then take D117 to Le Rozel. Turn L thro Rozel, foll sps to site. Site is on R at end rd. Med, pt sl, unshd; wc; chem disp; baby facs; shwrs inc; el pnts(10A) €4.50;lndtte; shop; rest, snacks; bar; playgrnd; htd pool; waterslide; sand beach adj; fishing; watersports; games area; wifi; entmnt; mostly statics; dogs €3.20; quiet; red low ssn/long stay; CKE/CCI. 1 Apr-30 Sep. € 46.60   2013*

PINSAC see Souillac *7C3*

PIRIAC SUR MER *2G3* (3.5km E Coastal/Rural) *47.38705, -2.51021* **Camping Parc du Guibel, Route de Kerdrien, 44420 Piriac-sur-Mer [02 40 23 52 67; fax 02 40 15 50 24; camping@parcduguibel.com; www.parcduguibel.com]** Fr Guérande take D99 to La Turballe, D333 to St Sébastien. In St Sébastien turn R to Kerdrien over x-rds & site on R in approx 500m. Lge, mkd pitch, hdstg, pt sl, pt shd; wc (some cont); chem disp; mv service pnt; serviced pitches; shwrs inc; el pnts (3-10A) €2.90-4.30 (poss rev pol); gas; lndtte; shop; rest, snacks; bar; BBQ; playgrnd; htd pool high ssn; paddling pool; mini-waterslide; sand beach 1km; tennis; games area; cycle hire; entmnt; TV rm; 30% statics; dogs €2; phone; adv bkg; ccard acc; CKE/CCI. "Helpful owner; lovely, quiet location in woods; gd touring base.; Site split by rd; san facs need upgrade" ♦ 22 Mar-21 Sep. € 19.50   2012*

PIRIAC SUR MER *2G3* (1km S Rural) *47.37485, -2.53556* **Camping Armor-Héol, Route de Guérande, 44420 Piriac-sur-Mer [02 40 23 57 80; fax 02 40 23 59 42; armor-heol@ wanadoo.fr; www.camping-armor-heol.com]** Fr Guérande on D90 & D33, site sp. Lge, hdg/mkd pitch, pt shd; wc; chem disp; baby facs; shwrs inc; el pnts (5A) €4 (poss rev pol); gas; lndtte; shops 1km; rest, snacks; bar; BBQ; playgrnd; htd, covrd pool; waterslide; sand beach 700m; tennis; games area; games rm; fitness rm; 60% statics; dogs €4; adv bkg; quiet. "Attractive, well-maintained site; lge pitches." 3 Apr-19 Sep. € 32.00   2010*

PISSOS *7D1* (500m E Rural) *44.30831, -0.76987* **Camp Municipal l'Arriu, 40410 Pissos [05 58 08 90 38 or 05 58 04 41 40 (LS); fax 05 58 08 92 93; mairie.pissos@ wanadoo.fr; www.pissos.fr]** Fr N exit N10 junc 18 onto D834 to Pissos; at x-rds turn L onto D43 sp Sore; site on R in 500m, sp. Med, shd; wc; chem disp; shwrs inc; el pnts €2.10; ice; playgrnd; pool 500m; rv fishing 300m; quiet; red long stay. "Lge pitches; excel." 1 Jul-15 -Sep. € 11.50   2012*

⊞ **PITHIVIERS** *4F3* (8km S Rural) *48.10365, 2.24142* **Camping Le Clos des Tourterelles, Rue des Rendillons, 45300 Bouzonville-aux-Bois [02 38 33 01 00]** S fr Pithiviers on D921 twds Jargeau; enter Bouzonville; turn R immed bef cafe; site 500m on R; sp in vill. Med, pt shd; htd wc; chem disp; shwrs inc; el pnts (16A) inc; lndtte; shop 8km; playgrnd; 90% statics; adv bkg; quiet; CKE/CCI. "Ltd space for tourers - phone ahead rec; friendly, helpful owners; gd NH." ♦ € 11.00   2009*

⊞ **PLA, LE** *8G4* (750m S Rural) *42.71042, 2.07647* **Camp Municipal La Pradaille, Les Soulades, 09460 Le Pla [04 68 20 49 14 or 04 68 20 41 37 (Mairie); mairie.le-pla@ wanadoo.fr]** Fr Axat on D117 take D118 S dir Quérigut & foll sp Le Pla. Or fr Mont-Louis take D118/D16 N to Quérigut & cont to Le Pla. Site well sp just S of vill. Med, hdg/mkd pitch, pt sl, pt shd; htd wc; chem disp (wc); shwrs inc; el pnts (16A) €3.20; lndtte; tradsmn; shops etc 5km; BBQ; playgrnd; 30% statics; phone adj; adv bkg; quiet; red low ssn. "Excel walking & mountain biking; 8km winter skiing, 6km x-country skiing; excel." ♦ € 12.50   2008*

PLAINE SUR MER, LA see Pornic *2G3*

PLAISANCE (GERS) *8F2* (500m E Rural) *43.60805, 0.05370* **Camping de l'Arros, Allée de Ormeaux, 32160 Plaisance [05 62 69 30 28; infos@plaisance-evasion.com; www. plaisance-evasion.com]** N from Tarbes on D935, approx 25 km N of Maubourguet turn R onto D946 to Plaisance. Foll sp to site on o'skts of town. Sm, mkd pitch, some hdstg, pt sl, pt shd; wc (some cont); chem disp; baby facs; shwrs inc; el pnts (6A) inc; lndtte (inc dryer); shops 500m; tradsmn; rest, snacks; bar; BBQ (gas only); playgrnd; pool; cycle hire; games rm; wifi; entmnt; TV; 40% statics; dogs €2; phone; adv bkg ess high ssn; red low ssn; ccard acc; CKE/CCI. "Close to rv; canoes avail." ♦ ltd 1 Apr-30 Sep. € 22.20   2010*

PLANCOET *2E3* (Urban) *48.52035, -2.23213* **Camp Municipal Les Vergers, Rue du Verger, 22130 Plancoët [02 96 84 03 42 or 02 96 84 39 70 (Mairie); fax 02 96 84 19 49; mairie.plancoet@wanadoo.fr; www. mairie-plancoet.fr]** On D974 fr Dinan descend to bdge over rlwy lines & site well sp on L. Med, mkd pitch, pt shd; wc; chem disp; shwrs inc; el pnts (5A) inc; lndtte; shops 500m; sand beach 13km; rv fishing; cycle hire; TV; some statics; adv bkg rec high ssn; quiet; CKE/CCI. "Excel sand beach at Pen Guen; adj park & rv with canoeing; poss itinerants/mkt traders." 1 Jun-15 Sep. € 8.90   2010*

⊞ **PLELAN LE GRAND** *2F3* (7km SW Rural) *47.95950, -2.15260* **Camping du Château d'Aleth, Rue de l'Ecole, 56380 St Malo-de-Beignon [06 78 96 10 62 (mob); contact@camping-aleth.com; www.camping-aleth.com]** Fr N24 twds Rennes exit N onto D773 to St Malo-de-Beignon in 5km, site L by church. Sm, pt sl, pt shd; wc; chem disp; mv service pnt; shwrs inc; el pnts (10A) inc; lndtte; shop; snacks; BBQ; playgrnd; wifi; dogs free; quiet. "Pleasant, tranquil, well-kept site by lake; clean san facs; Themed cowboy & indian site" ♦ € 19.50   2013*

PLELAN LE GRAND *2F3* (8km NW Rural) *48.02403, -2.17282* **Camp Municipal Brocéliande, Rue du Chevalier Lancelot du Lac, 35380 Paimpont [02 99 07 89 16 or 02 99 07 81 18 (Mairie); fax 02 99 07 88 18; mairie. paimport@wanadoo.fr; www.camping-paimpont-broceliande.com]** Sp on N edge of Paimpont vill. On D773 dir St Méen-le-Grand/Concoret, 500m fr Paimpont. Med, hdg/mkd pitch, pt shd; wc; chem disp; shwrs inc; el pnts (5A) €3; gas 500m; lndtte; playgrnd; rv & lake sw & fishing adj; cycle hire; tennis; entmnt; internet; phone; bus in vill; quiet; red low ssn; CKE/CCI. "Pleasant, spacious, clean site; friendly; conv NH; no barrier; gd facs for children; sh walk to attractive vill; excel." ♦ 1 Apr-30 Sep. € 10.00   2009*

PLELO see Binic *2E3*

PLESTIN LES GREVES *2E2* (2km NE Coastal) *48.66805, -3.60060* **Camp Municipal St Efflam, Rue Lan-Carré, 22310 Plestin-les-Grèves [02 96 35 62 15; fax 02 96 35 09 75; campingmunicipalplestin@wanadoo.fr; www.camping-municipal-bretagne.com]** Fr Morlaix on D786 thro Plestin-les-Grèves; foll D786 sp St Efflam down hill to bay; site on R 850m along bay; sp. Lge, mkd pitch, pt sl, terr, pt shd; wc; chem disp; mv service pnt; shwrs inc; el pnts (7A) €2.50; gas; lndtte; tradsmn; rest; bar; BBQ; playgrnd; sand beach 150m; sw, fishing, boating adj; dogs €1.30; Eng spkn; adv bkg ess high ssn; ccard acc; red low ssn; CKE/CCI. "Excel; helpful recep." ♦ ltd 1 Apr-30 Sep. € 11.00   2009*

Send in your site reports by mid August 2014

PLESTIN LES GREVES *2E2* (4km NW Coastal) *48.68000, -3.65254* **Camp Municipal Les Pins, Route de Plestin, 29241 Locquirec [02 98 67 40 85 or 02 98 67 42 20 (Mairie); locquirec-mairie@wanadoo.fr]** At traff lts in Plestin take D42 N sp Locquirec. In 2km turn L onto D64 Rte de Plestin, cross bdge over estuary, site 2nd on R. Lge, mkd pitch, pt sl, pt shd; wc (some cont); shwrs; el pnts (10A); gas; lndtte; shops adj; tradsmn; playgrnd; sand beach adj; poss cr; quiet. "Superb location; overlooks lge sandy bay; san facs basic; low ssn poss unmanned after 1730 & el pnts locked; vg." 15 Jun-31 Aug. 2008*

"There aren't many sites open at this time of year"

If you're travelling outside peak season remember to call ahead to check site opening dates – even if the entry says 'open all year'.

PLEUBIAN see Tréguier *1D3*

PLEUMEUR BODOU see Trébeurden *1D2*

PLEUVILLE see Pressac *7A3*

PLEYBEN *2E2* (5km S Rural) *48.19316, -3.98160* **Camp Municipal de Pont-Coblant, 29190 Pleyben [02 98 73 31 22 or 02 98 26 68 11 (Mairie); fax 02 98 26 38 99; communedepleyben@wanadoo.fr]** On D785 Quimper rd. Turn L immed by phone box on ent Pont-Coblant. Med, mkd pitch, pt shd; wc; shwrs inc; el pnts (6-10A) €3.20; shop 4km; rest, bar adj; canoe & cycle hire; poss cr; quiet but some rd noise. "Beautiful site adj rv/canal; spacious pitches; dated facs, ltd low ssn; warden visits twice daily (or call at Mairie); poss unkempt low ssn." 15 Jun-15 Sep. € 9.20 2008*

PLOBANNALEC LESCONIL see Pont l'Abbé *2F2*

PLOEMEL see Auray *2F3*

PLOEMEUR see Lorient *2F2*

PLOERMEL *2F3* (2km N Rural) *47.94866, -2.42077* **Camping du Lac, Les Belles Rives, 56800 Taupont [tel/fax 02 97 74 01 22; contact@camping-du-lac-ploermel.com; www.camping-du-lac-ploermel.com]** Fr N24 foll D766e around Ploërmel or foll sp for Taupont (D8). Cent, take D8 twds Taupont & Lac-au-Duc 3km. Site clearly sp on R on edge of lake. Med, hdg/mkd pitch, pt shd; htd wc; mv service pnt; chem disp; shwrs inc; el pnts (5A) €3.50; gas; lndtte; shop; tradsmn; snacks; bar; BBQ; playgrnd; pool & waterslide nrby; sand beach & lake sw adj; watersports adj; cycle hire nrby; tennis; 10% statics; dogs €2.40; Eng spkn; adv bkg; quiet; ccard acc high ssn; red low ssn; CKE/CCI. "Pleasant site in lovely location; golf & horse riding 1km; friendly staff; vg" ♦ 1 Apr-30 Sep. € 13.50 2013*

⊞ **PLOERMEL** *2F3* (6km N Rural) *47.98425, -2.38191* **FFCC Camping Parc Merlin l'Enchanteur, 8 Rue du Pont, Vallée de l'Yvel, 56800 Loyat [02 97 93 05 52 or 02 97 73 89 45; fax 02 97 73 89 37; camelotpark@wanadoo.fr; www. campingmerlin.com]** Fr Ploërmel take D766 N sp St Malo. In 5km turn L to Loyat. Site on L on ent vill opp garage, adj sm lake. Med, hdg/mkd pitch, pt shd; htd wc; chem disp; mv service pnt; shwrs inc; el pnts (10-16A) €3.50-6 (poss rev pol); gas; lndtte; sm shop & other shops 600m; tradsmn high ssn; rest, bar 200m; BBQ; htd covrd pool; sand beach/lake sw with watersports 4km; fishing; tennis; games area; cycle hire; wifi €3.; 10% statics; dogs €2; phone 1km; adv bkg; quiet, but some rd noise; red long stay; ccard acc; red CKE/ CCI. "Lovely, peaceful site; spacious pitches; welcoming British owners; vg clean facs; gd indoor pool; poss soggy in winter; new 60km tarmac cycle trail adj; conv Château Josselin, Lizio & Brocéliande forest with legend of King Arthur; Pleasant site; Excel walking and cycling" ♦ € 21.00 (CChq acc) 2013*

PLOERMEL *2F3* (8km S Rural) *47.86354, -2.44612* **Camping Domaine du Roc, Rue Beaurivage, 56460 Le Roc-St André [02 97 74 91 07 or 06 48 07 68 05 (mob); contact@ domaine-du-roc.com; www.domaine-du-roc.com]** Fr N on N166 turn R onto D764/D4 to Le Roc-St André. Site in approx 3km at end of bdge over Nantes & Brest Canal. Med, hdg/ mkd pitch, pt shd; wc; baby facs; shwrs inc; el pnts (6A) €3.50; lndtte; shop adj; rest, snacks, bar in town; BBQ; playgrnd; htd, covrd pool; 50% statics; dogs €3; phone adj; poss cr; adv bkg; quiet; ccard acc; CKE/CCI. "Peaceful, well-situated site; gd touring base; excel cycle rtes adj canal." 1 Apr-31 Oct. € 15.00 2009*

PLOERMEL *2F3* (7km NW Rural) *47.96932, -2.47010* **Camping La Vallée du Ninian, Route du Lac, Le Rocher, 56800 Taupont [02 97 93 53 01; fax 02 97 93 57 27; infos@camping-ninian.com; www.camping-ninian.com]** Fr Ploërmel cent foll sp to Taupont or Lac au Duc; N on D8. Thro vill Taupont take L hand turn sp La Vallée du Ninian; site on L 1km fr Helléan. Sm, hdg pitch (lge), pt shd; wc; chem disp; shwrs inc; baby facs; el pnts (3-6A) €2-3.50; lndtte; shop; bar; playgrnd; htd pool; paddling pool; lake sw & watersports 4km; sand beach 4km; entmnt; dogs €1; quiet; adv bkg. "Farm produce; helpful owners; peaceful; gd facs for children; vg." ♦ 1 Apr-30 Sep. € 16.00 2009*

PLOMBIERES LES BAINS *6F2* (10km S Rural) *47.92460, 6.47545* **Camp Municipal Le Val d'Ajol, Rue des Oeuvres, 88340 Le Val d'Ajol [03 29 66 55 17; camping@valdajol.fr; www.valdajol.fr]** Fr N on N57 after Plombières-les-Bains turn onto D20 sp Le Val-d'Ajol. Site sps in vill. Sm, hdg pitch, pt shd; wc; chem disp; shwrs; el pnts (6A) €2.50; lndte; shop 1km; htd, covrd pool adj; wifi; TV; dogs; phone; adv bkg; quiet; CKE/CCI. "Excel site; excel, clean san facs; vg touring base." ♦ 15 Apr-30 Sep. € 13.00 2012*

PLOMBIERES LES BAINS 6F2 (2km W Rural) 47.96731, 6.44656 **Camping de l'Hermitage, 54 Rue du Boulot, 88370 Plombières-les-Bains [03 29 30 01 87; fax 03 29 30 04 01; contact@hermitage-camping.com; www. hermitage-camping.com]** Fr Plombières-les-Bains take D63 N dir Epinal; site sp. Med, hgd/mkd pitch, terr, pt shd; htd wc; chem disp; baby facs; fam bthrm; shwrs inc; gas; el pnts (4-10A) €3.20-5.30; lndtte; tradsmn; snacks; BBQ; playgrnd; pool; games area; games rm; TV; 10% statics; dogs €1.60; phone; no twin-axles; poss cr; Eng spkn; adv bkg; quiet; red low ssn/CKE/CCI. "Gd, unisex san facs; vg." 1 Apr-15 Oct. € 13.90   2011*

PLOMEUR see Pont l'Abbe 2F2

PLONEOUR LANVERN see Pont l'Abbé 2F2

PLONEVEZ PORZAY 2E2 (4km W Coastal) 48.14458, -4.26915 **Camping La Plage de Tréguer, Plage de Ste Anne-la-Palud, 29550 Plonévez-Porzay [02 99 92 53 52; fax 02 98 92 54 89; camping-treguer-plage@wanadoo.fr; www.camping-treguer-plage.com]** On D107 S fr Châteaulin. After 8km turn R to Ste Anne-la-Palud & foll sp. Lge, hgd/mkd pitch, hdstg, pt shd; wc (some cont); chem disp; mv service pnt; shwrs inc; el pnts (6A) €3.90; gas; lndtte; shop; tradsmn; snacks; bar; BBQ; playgrnd; sand beach adj; games area; games rm; entmnt; TV rm; some statics; dogs €2.20; Eng spkn; adv bkg; ccard acc; red low ssn; CKE/CCI. "Well-situated touring base; vg, friendly site; excel beach" ♦ 4 Apr-24 Sep. € 34.65 (CChq acc)   2013*

PLONEVEZ PORZAY 2E2 (4km W Coastal) 48.11042, -4.27983 **Camping Trezmalaouen, 20 Route de la Baie, 29550 Plonévez-Porzay [tel/fax 02 98 92 54 24; camping.trezmalaouen@wanadoo.fr; www.camping-trezmalaouen.com]** Fr Douarnenez take D107 N dir Plonévez-Porzay, site sp to L. Med, hgd/mkd pitch, some hdstg, pt shd; wc; chem disp; mv service pnt; baby facs; shwrs inc; el pnts; lndtte; BBQ; playgrnd; sand beach adj; tennis; games area; 75% statics; dogs €1.70; 2 accesible mobile homes; dogs €3; adv bkg; ccard acc; red long stay/low ssn/CKE/CCI. "Sea views; vg touring base." 1 Apr-15 Nov. € 18.00   2010*

PLOUAY 2F2 (4km NW Rural) 47.96415, -3.42297 **Camping Bois des Ecureuils, 29300 Guilligomarc'h [tel/fax 02 98 71 70 98 or 01202 881602 (UK); bois-des-ecureuils@aliceadsl.fr; www.bois-des-ecureuils.fr]** N fr Plouay on D769 dir Faouet, for 5km; turn L to Guilligomarc'h; site sp. Sm, mkd pitch, pt sl, shd; wc (some cont); chem disp; shwrs inc; el pnts (5A) €2.50; gas; lndtte; shop 3km; tradsmn; playgrnd; rv sw 3km; lake 6km; sand beach 25km; cycle hire; dogs €1; poss cr; Eng spkn; adv bkg; quiet; no ccard acc; CKE/CCI. "Friendly British owners; gd walking; excel peaceful site; lge pitches." ♦ ltd 2 Jun-2 Sep. € 11.00   2008*

PLOUEZEC see Paimpol 1D3

PLOUGASNOU 1D2 (1.5km SE Rural) 48.68548, -3.78530 **Camping Le Trégor, Route de Morlaix, Kerjean, 29630 Plougasnou [02 98 67 37 64; bookings@campingdutregor. com; www.campingdutregor.com]** At junc of D46 to Plougasnou. Site is on L just bef town sp. Sm, hdg/mkd pitch, pt shd; wc; chem disp (wc); shwrs inc; el pnts (6-10A) inc; gas; lndtte; shop 1km; BBQ; playgrnd; sand beach 1.2km; lake sw & watersports 3km; 10% statics; dogs €1; poss cr; adv bkg; quiet; no ccard acc; CKE/CCI. "Well-run site in beautiful area; British owners; dated but clean facs; ideal for walking, cycling & fishing; conv Roscoff ferries & Morlaix; phone if req NH after end Oct." Easter-31 Oct. € 15.00   2008*

PLOUGASNOU 1D2 (2km S Rural) 48.66472, -3.78062 **Camping Domaine de Mesqueau, 870 Route de Mesqueau, 29630 Plougasnou [02 98 67 37 45; fax 02 96 47 28 58; domaine-de-mesqueau@orange.fr; www.camping-bretagne-mer.com]** N fr Morlaix on D46 dir Primel-Trégastel, site sp 2km S of Plougasnou. Med, mkd pitch, pt shd; wc; chem disp; mv service pnt; baby facs; shwrs; el pnts (6A) inc; lndtte; shop 4km; tradsmn; rest, snacks; bar; BBQ; playgrnd; htd pool complex; sand beach 4km; lake fishing; tennis; games area; wifi; 30% statics; dogs €2; adv bkg; quiet. 1 May-25 Sep. € 20.00   2010*

See advertisement on pages 32 & 33

PLOUGASNOU 1D2 (3km NW Coastal/Urban) 48.71421, -3.81563 **Camp Municipal de la Mer, 29630 Primel-Trégastel [02 98 72 37 06 or 02 98 67 30 06; fax 02 98 67 82 79; primel-tregastel.camping.la-mer@wanadoo.fr]** Fr Morlaix take D46 to Plougastel on to Primel-Trégastel. Bear R in vill & 1st L opp cafe on R in 100 m. Med, unshd, wc; chem disp; mv service pnt; shwrs €1.80; el pnts (10A) inc; gas 1.5km; lndtte; shop, rest, bar 500m; tradsmn high ssn; playgrnd; sand beach 500m; dogs €1; phone; poss cr; no adv bkg; quiet; no ccard acc; CKE/CCI. "Fine coastal views; gd walking & cycling; ltd facs low ssn." ♦ ltd 1 Jun-30 Sep. € 17.00   2010*

PLOUGASTEL DAOULAS 2E2 (4.5km NE Coastal) 48.40134, -4.35419 **Camping Saint Jean, 29470 Plougastel-Daoulas [02 98 40 32 90; fax 02 98 04 23 11; info@campingsaintjean.com; www.campingsaintjean.com]** Fr Brest, take N165 E for approx 12km then leave m'way after Plougastel exit & foll sp. Site in 2km at end of rd by rv. Med, hdg pitch, some hdstg, pt sl, terr, pt shd; htd wc; chem disp; mv service pnt; baby facs; shwrs; el pnts (6A) €3 (poss rev pol); lndtte (inc dryer); shop; supmkt 2km; snacks; bar; BBQ; playgrnd; htd, covrd pool; paddling pool; waterslide; games area; wifi; entmnt; TV rm; some statics; dogs €2; poss cr; quiet; red low ssn. "Nice site by rv; steep in places; gd facs." ♦ 9 Apr-30 Sep. € 22.00 (CChq acc)   2011*

PLOUGONVELIN see Conquet, Le 2E1

PLOUGOULM see Roscoff 1D2

PLOUGRESCANT see Tréguier 1D3

PLOUGUENAST *2E3*   Pinábre Camping & Caravaning, Lingouet 22150 [02 96 26 80 04; www.campgite-brittany. com] Site is 50 miles fr St. Malo ferry port, bet Loudeac and Moncontour off the D768. Sm, pt sl, pt shd; wc; chem dis; fam bthrm; shwrs; el (16A) €3; Eng spkn; adv bkg; CKE/CCI; "Gd for walks & cycling; sm friendly site; excel facs; close to North & south coast; open plan, grassy site" Apr-Sep. € 12.00   2013*

PLOUGUERNEAU *2E2* (3km N Coastal) *48.63048, -4.52402* **Camping La Grève Blanche, St Michel, 29880 Plouguerneau [02 98 04 70 35 or 02 98 04 63 97 (LS); fax 02 98 04 63 97; lroudaut@free.fr; www. campinggreveblanche.com]** Fr Lannilis D13 to Plouguerneau, D32 sp La Grève, St Michel (look out for lorry rte sp). Avoid Plouguerneau vill when towing - tight RH bend. Med, pt sl, terr, unshd; wc; chem disp; mv service pnt; shwrs €1; el pnts (9A) €2.80; bar; shops 3km; playgrnd; sand beach; dogs €1.90; Eng spkn; adv bkg; red low ssn; CKE/CCI. "Excel location; sea views; helpful staff; facs clean & well-kept; low ssn recep open eves only; in fog lighthouse sounds all night otherwise quiet."
♦ ltd 16 Apr-10 Oct. € 11.60   2010*

PLOUGUERNEAU *2E2* (6km N Coastal) *48.63112, -4.44972* Camping du Vougot, Route de Prat-Leden, 29880 Plouguerneau [02 98 25 61 51; campingduvougot@ hotmail.fr; www.campingplageduvougot.com] Fr N12 at Landerneau exit N onto D770 to Lesneven, then D28/D32 to Plouguerneau. Fr Plouguerneau take D10 dir Guissény then turn W onto D52 dir Grève-du-Vougot, site sp. Med, hdg/mkd pitch, pt shd; wc; chem disp; mv service pnt; shwrs €0.50; el pnts (10A) €3.30; lndtte; shop 6km; tradsmn; snacks; playgrnd; sand beach 250m; watersports nr; wifi; entmnt; 30% statics; dogs €2.60; adv bkg; quiet; ccard acc; red long stay/low ssn; CKE/CCI. "Gd walking (GR34); interesting area; excel touring base." ♦
1 Apr-31 Oct. € 16.40   2011*

PLOUHA *2E3* (2km NE Coastal) *48.69022, -2.90930* **Camping Domaine de Keravel, La Trinité, 22580 Plouha [02 96 22 49 13; fax 02 96 22 47 13; keravel@wanadoo.fr; www.keravel.com or www.les-castels.com]** Fr St Brieux, take D786 twd Paimpol. In cent of Plouha at church & traff lts foll sp to Port Moguer. Med, pt sl, terr, hdg pitch, pt shd; wc; chem disp; shwrs inc; el pnts (10A) €3.80 (rev pol); gas; lndtte; shop; snacks; playgrnd; htd pool; paddling pool; beach 1km; tennis; fishing; entmnt; games rm; cycle hire; entmnt; TV rm; dogs €3; adv bkg; quiet; CKE/CCI. "Pleasant site; modern san facs; access pitches tight, site roads v narrow; sm pitches; helpful staff; lovely grounds." ♦ 26 Apr-27 Sep.
€ 24.10   2008*

See advertisement on inside back cover

PLOUHA *2E3* (5km NE Coastal) *48.71944, -2.95305* **Camping Le Varquez-sur-Mer, 5 Route de la Corniche, Bréhec-Plage, 22580 Plouha [02 96 22 34 43; fax 02 96 22 68 87; campinglevarquez@wanadoo.fr; www.camping-le-varquez.com]** Sp bet St Quay-Portrieux & Paimpol fr D786. Med, hdg/mkd pitch, hdstg, pt sl, pt shd; wc; chem disp; shwrs; el pnts (10A) €3.70; gas; lndtte; shop 4km; tradsmn; snacks; bar; BBQ; playgrnd; htd pool; paddling pool; sand beach 600m; entmnt; 30% statics; dogs €1.90; Eng spkn; quiet; ccard acc; CKE/CCI. "Lovely coast; peaceful, family-run site; adj walking rte G34." ♦ 4 Apr-4 Oct. € 19.20   2008*

PLOUHARNEL see Carnac *2G3*

PLOUHINEC *2F2* (1km SE Coastal) *47.66489, -3.22105* **Camping Le Moténo, Rue du Passage d'Etel, 56680 Plouhinec [02 97 36 76 63; fax 02 97 85 81 84; info@ camping-moteno.com; www.camping-le-moteno.com]** App Auray on D22, take 2nd turn L after Pont Lerois & foll sps. Lge, hdg/mkd pitch, pt shd; wc; chem disp; shwrs inc; el pnts (10A) inc; gas; lndtte; shop, rest, snacks; bar; playgrnd; htd, covrd pool; waterslide; jacuzzi; sand beach 800m; fishing & watersports 100m; cycle hire; games area; games rm; entmnt; TV; some statics; dogs €5; Eng spkn; adv bkg; quiet; red low ssn. "Pleasant site; gd base Carnac & Quiberon Peninsula."♦
3 Apr-11 Sep. € 32.00   2009*

PLOUHINEC *2F2* (5km S Coastal) **Camp Municipal de la Falaise, Rue de la Barre, 56410 Etel [02 97 55 33 79; fax 02 97 55 33 79; www.morbihan.com]** S fr L'Orient on D194/ D9/D781 dir Carnac; in 1.5km after x-ing rv brdge turn R onto D16 to Etel; foll sps for La Plage or Camping. Or N fr Carnac on D781; at Erdeven turn L onto D105 to Etel & then as bef. Med, mkd pitch, pt sl, pt shd; wc; mv service pnt; shwrs inc; el pnts inc; lndtte; shop 500m; tradsmn; playgrnd; sand beach; lake sw; boat trips; windsurfing; canoeing; phone; quiet; CKE/CCI.
1 Apr-18 Sep. € 16.50   2011*

PLOUVORN see Landivisiau *2E2*

PLOZEVET *2F2* (500m SW Rural) *47.98006, -4.43071* **Camping La Corniche, Route de la Corniche, 29710 Plozévet [02 98 91 33 94 or 02 98 91 32 93; fax 02 98 91 41 53; infos@campinglacorniche.com; www. campinglacorniche.com]** Fr N165 foll sp Audierne onto D784 to Plozévet & foll sps to site. Med, hdg pitch, pt shd; wc; chem disp; mv service pnt; baby facs; shwrs inc; el pnts (10A) €3.20 (poss rev pol); lndtte; shop; tradsmn; playgrnd; pool; beach 2km; wifi; 10% statics; dogs €2.20; red low ssn; CKE/CCI. "Clean site; lge pitches; vg pool; helpful owner; excel facs; gd cycling." ♦ 1 Apr-1 Oct. € 15.00 (CChq acc)   2010*

PLUMERGAT see Ste Anne d'Auray *2F3*

POET LAVAL, LE *9D2* (E Rural) *44.52961, 5.02227* **Camp Municipal Lorette, 26160 Le Poët-Laval [04 75 91 00 62 or 04 75 46 44 12 (Mairie); fax 04 75 46 46 45; camping. lorette@wanadoo.fr; www.campinglorette.fr]** Site 4km W of Dieulefit on D540. Med, mkd pitch, pt shd; wc; chem disp (wc); mv service pnt; shwrs inc; el pnts (6A) €2; lndtte; shop; tradsmn; rest 500m; snacks; playgrnd; pool; tennis; no statics; dogs €1.10; bus; phone; quiet; CKE/CCI. "Well-kept site with views; lge pitches; clean, modern facs; nr lavender fields (Jun/Jul); mkt in Dieulefit Fri; excel." ♦ 1 May-30 Sep.
€ 12.20   2013*

POET LAVAL, LE *9D2* (8km W Rural) *44.56423, 4.90788* Camping à la Ferme des Roures (Gontard), Route de St Gervais, Les Roures, 26160 La Bégude-de-Mazenc [04 75 46 21 80; gitesfrance@ferme-des-roures.com] Fr Montélimar E on D540 for 15km. Turn L onto D74 dir St Gervais. Foll sp for site. Sm, pt sl, shd; wc; chem disp; shwrs inc; el pnts (10A) €2.30 (poss rev pol); lndtte; gas & shop 4km; dogs €0.75; quiet; CKE/CCI. "Site in wood in pleasant area; friendly, helpful owners; clean facs." ♦ 1 May-15 Sep. € 8.50   2010*

POILLY LEZ GIEN see Gien *4G3*

POITIERS For sites convenient for Futuroscope, also see listings under Châtellerault and Jaunay Clan.

POITIERS *7A2* (10km N Rural) *46.65611, 0.30194* Camping du Futur, 9 Rue des Bois, 86170 Avanton [05 49 54 09 67; contact@camping-du-futur.com; www.camping-du-futur.com] Exit A10 junc 28. After toll take 1st exit at rndabt sp Avanton. Site well sp fr Avanton, but care needed thro Martigny & hotel complex. Med, hdg/mkd pitch, pt shd; wc; chem disp (wc); mv service pnt; shwrs inc; el pnts (6-10A) €3.50-3.80; lndtte; shop, rest & snacks 1km; tradsmn; bar; playgrnd; pool (high ssn); games area; games rm; wifi; TV; dogs €1.50; c'van storage; adv bkg; quiet; red low ssn; CKE/CCI. "Attractive, spacious site; well-kept & well-run; helpful British owners; vg clean san facs; ltd early ssn; 5 mins Futuroscope & A10; ideal NH or longer" ♦ 1 Apr-5 Nov. € 28.95   2013*

POITIERS *7A2* (4.5km S Rural) *46.54367, 0.33230* Camp Municipal de St Benoît, 2 Rue de Passe Lourdain, 86280 St Benoît [05 49 88 48 55; tourisme@ville-saint-benoit.fr; www.ville-saint-benoit.fr] Fr N or S turn W off D741 to St Benoît, site well sp. Med, mkd pitch, pt shd; wc; shwrs; el pnts (4A) €3; shops, rest, bar in vill; playgrnd; rv fishing & watersports adj; dogs €0.50; poss cr; adv bkg; rlwy noise adj; CKE/CCI. 1 Jun-6 Sep. € 12.20   2009*

POIX DE PICARDIE *3C3* (300m SW Rural) *49.77621, 1.97467* Camp Municipal Le Bois des Pêcheurs, Route de Forges-les-Eaux, 80290 Poix-de-Picardie [03 22 90 11 71 or 03 22 90 32 90 (Mairie); fax 03 22 90 32 91; camping@ville-poix-de-picardie.fr; www.ville-poix-de-picardie.fr] Fr town cent on D901 dir Beauvais, in 100m turn R onto D919 opp Citroën agent sp Camping; site on R in 500m. Fr Beauvais, turn L at bottom of steep hill opp Citroën agent; site in 500m on R. Med, hdg/mkd pitch, hdstg, pt shd; wc; chem disp; shwrs inc; el pnts (10A) €4 (poss long lead req); gas 300m; lndtte; shops, supmkt adj; rest, bar 500m; BBQ; playgrnd; htd, covrd pool 800m; rv & fishing adj; tennis 800m; games rm; cycle hire; wifi; TV; dogs €1.50; poss cr; Eng spkn; adv bkg; quiet; ccard not acc; red long stay; CKE/CCI. "Pleasant, peaceful, tidy site in delightful area; clean san facs; gd touring base; vg walking & cycling; train to Amiens; mkt Sun; rec." ♦ 1 Apr-30 Sep. € 14.00   2011*

POLIGNY *6H2* (1km SW Rural) *46.83455, 5.69840* Camp Communautaire de la Croix du Dan, 39800 Poligny [03 84 37 01 35; fax 03 84 73 77 59; cccgrimont@wanadoo.fr; www.ville-poligny.fr] Fr SW on N83 turn R at rndabt sp 'Centre'; site on R immed bef town sp Poligny. Fr N & NW take D905 into & thro town cent (no L turn on N83 S of Poligny), then foll sp Lons-Le Saunier. Site on L bef sportsgrnd - look for m'van sp. Do not overshoot ent, as diff to see. N5 fr E not rec as steep & hairpins. Med, mkd pitch, pt shd; wc (mainly cont); chem disp; shwrs inc; el pnts (10A) €6.40; lndtte; shops 1km; tradsmn; playgrnd; no statics; dogs; phone; poss cr; Eng spkn; quiet; CKE/CCI. "Excel, clean, tidy site; helpful warden; gates open 24hrs; twin-axles extra; pretty town." ♦ ltd 15 Jun-20 Sep. € 7.45   2009*

POMEYS see Chazelles sur Lyon *9B2*

POMMEROL see Rémuzat *9D2*

POMMEUSE *4E4* (1km SW Rural) *48.80860, 2.99300* Camping Le Chêne Gris, 24 Place de la Gare de Faremoutiers, 77515 Pommeuse [01 64 04 21 80; fax 01 64 20 05 89; info@lechenegris.com; www.lechenegris.com] Fr A4, take D634 SE dir Coulommiers, turn R onto D25 sp Pommeuse & Faremoutiers. Site on R after stn at Faremoutiers. Well sp. Lge, hdg pitch, hdstg, terr, pt shd; htd wc; chem disp; mv service pnt; baby facs; shwrs inc; el pnts (10A) inc; lndtte (inc dryer); shop; tradsmn; rest, snacks; bar; BBQ; playgrnd; 2 pools (1 htd, covrd); paddling pool; games rm; wifi; Tv rm; 80% statics; dogs €2.50; phone; Eng spkn; adv bkg; quiet; red low ssn; CKE/CCI. "Conv Paris, Disneyland & Parc Astérix; walking dist to trains - direct line to Paris; excel san facs; vg." ♦ 20 Apr-6 Nov. € 37.00 (CChq acc)   2008*

PONCIN see Pont d'Ain *9A2*

⊞ **PONS (CHARENTE MARITIME)** *7B2* (1km NE Rural) *45.59429, -0.53841* Camping Les Moulins de la Vergne, 9 Route de Colombiers, 17800 Pons [tel/fax 05 46 90 50 84 or 05 46 49 11 49; uffelen@wanadoo.fr; www.moulinsdelavergne.nl] Fr N on D137 take 1st exit Pons, turn L & foll yellow site sp. Fr S exit A10 junc 36 onto D732 & at 2nd rndabt take D137 N dir Saintes. In 4km turn R onto D125(E2) then R (S) onto D234, site sp on L. Fr town cent foll yellow sps in Pons - do not confuse with municipal site Le Paradis. NB c'vans not allowed thro Pons & should stay on by-pass. Med, mkd pitch, pt shd; htd wc; chem disp; shwrs inc; el pnts (10A) €3.50; lndtte; shops 1km; tradsmn; rest, snacks; bar; BBQ; playgrnd; pool; wifi; dogs €2; adv bkg; Eng spkn; rd noise; ccard acc; CKE/CCI. "Relaxed, friendly & helpful Dutch owners; clean san facs need update, ltd low ssn; excel rest; grass pitches soft in wet weather - park on site roads off ssn; no site lighting low ssn in touring area; site poss unkempt low ssn & poss mkt traders; conv touring base or NH nr A10 en rte Spain; rest closed Mon" ♦ € 25.30   2013*

CAMPING Risle-Seine ✱✱✱

Ideal as stopover point or full peaceful holidays
Adjoining lakes (80 ha) in the Risle Valley
Rental of wooden cottages on stilts
Panoramic view on the banks of the ponds

**0033 (0)2 32 42 46 65 - infos@camping-risle-seine.com
www.camping-risle-seine.com**

PONS (CHARENTE MARITIME) *7B2* (500m W Urban) 45.57791, -0.55552 **Camp Municipal Le Paradis, 1 Ave de Poitou, 17800 Pons [05 46 91 36 72; fax 05 46 96 14 15; campingmunicipalpons@voila.fr; www.pons-ville.org]** Well sp fr town o'skts. Med, mkd pitch, pt shd; wc; mv service pnt; shwrs inc; el pnts (6-10A) inc (poss rev pol); shops adj; tradsmn; pool, waterslide 100m; rv fishing 200m; TV; dogs €1.76. "Excel site in attractive grounds; helpful warden; interesting town; conv for Saintes, Cognac, Royan" ◆ 1 May-30 Sep. € 15.00   2013*

⊞ **PONS (CHARENTE MARITIME)** *7B2* (2km W Rural) 45.56976, -0.57906 **FFCC Camping Chardon, 13 Route des Bernards,Chardon 17800 Pons [50 46 95 01 25 or 06 18 19 39 10 (mob); camping.chardon@gmail.com; www.camping-chardon.com]** Fr N or S on A10, exit junc 36 onto D732 (take care as heavy, fast traff). Site sp on R in 1km. Narr ent to rd. Or fr N or S on N137 take D732 twd Gémozac, site on L 2km fr Pons. Site lies to S of D732, bet N137 & A10. Sm, hdg pitch, pt shd; wc; chem disp; serviced pitch; shwrs; el pnts (10A) €3; gas 2km; lndtte; shops 1km; tradsmn; rest; pizzeria; bar; playgrnd; pool 1km; 75% statics; dogs €1.50; adv bkg; quiet; no ccard acc. "Excel basic, rustic site; friendly owners; basic, open-air san facs; ltd low ssn; vg rest; conv Cognac, Saintes & Royan; low ssn phone ahead to check if open; conv NH A10 or N137;" ◆ ltd € 13.00   2013*

"That's changed – Should I let The Club know?"

If you find something on site that's different from the site entry, fill in a report and let us know. See www.caravanclub.co.uk/europereport

PONT AUDEMER *3D2* (8km W Rural) 49.31433, 0.40344 **Camping La Lorie (Lehaye), 5 La Lorie, 27210 Fort-Moville [02 32 57 15 49]** ` Sm, pt shd; wc; chem disp (wc); shwrs inc; el pnts (10A) inc; BBQ; rest, snacks, bar 2km; playgrnd; 10% statics; dogs; quiet; CKE/CCI. "CL-type site in attractive area; basic facs but clean; conv Le Havre, Honfleur; gd base" Easter-1 Nov. € 13.50   2012*

PONT AUDEMER *3D2* (2km NW Rural) 49.36660, 0.48739 **Camp Municipal Risle-Seine Les Etangs, 19 Route des Etangs, 27500 Toutainville [02 32 42 46 65; fax 02 32 42 24 17; camping@ville-pont-audemer.fr; www.ville-pont-audemer.fr]** Fr Le Havre on A131/E05 cross rv at Pont de Normandie (toll). Take D580 & at junc 3 branch R & take 2nd exit onto D22 sp Beuzeville. At edge of Fiquefleur take D180, then D675 dir Pont-Audemer. In Toutainville foll site sp, turn L just bef A13 underpass, then immed R. Site approx 2km on R. Med, hdg/mkd pitch, pt shd; wc; chem disp; mv service pnt; serviced pitches; shwrs inc; el pnts (5-10A) €3.95; lndtte (inc dryer); shop 1.5km; tradsmn; snacks; bar; BBQ; playgrnd; htd pool & tennis 1.5km; fishing; canoeing, watersports; cycle hire; games area; wifi; games/TV rm; dogs free; bus; Eng spkn; adv bkg; quiet; red long stay/low ssn; ccard acc. "Lovely, well-run site; helpful warden; barrier clsd 2200-0830 but flexible for ferry; many leisure activities; poss school groups at w/end; vg for dogs; 1hr Le Havre ferry; Fri mkt Pont-Audemer; conv NH; excel; Facs stretched low ssn" ◆ 15 Mar-15 Nov. € 22.00 SBS - N13   2013*

See advertisement

PONT AUTHOU see Brionne *3D2*

PONT AVEN *2F2* (10km N Rural) 47.92512, -3.68888 **Camping Les Genêts d'Or, KermerourPont Kereon 29380 Bannalec [tel/fax 02 98 39 54 35; info@holidaybrittany.com; www.holidaybrittany.com]** Fr Pont Aven/Bannalec exit on N165 N to Bannalec on D4; after rlwy x-ing turn R sp Quimperlé. In 1km turn R, sp le Trévoux; site on L 500m. Sm, hdg/mkd pitch, pt sl, pt shd; wc; chem disp; shwrs inc; el pnts (6A) €3.50; lndtte (inc dryer); shop 500m; supmkt 1km; rest, snacks; bar; BBQ (gas); playgrnd; pool 10km; sand beach 15km; games rm; cycle hire; some statics; dogs €1.50; Eng spkn; adv bkg; quiet, some non-intrusive rd/rlwy noise; ccard not acc; red long stay; CKE/CCI; ACSI acc. "Lovely, peaceful, well-kept site in orchard; lge pitches; welcoming, helpful British owners; immac san facs; Bannalec in walking dist; lovely area - excel touring base; highly rec; lovely hosts; easy walk into Bannalec" 1 Apr-30 Sep. € 23.95   2013*

FRANCE

PONT AVEN

PONT AVEN *2F2* (8km SE Coastal) *47.78799, -3.70064*
Camping de l'Ile Percée, Plage de Trénez, 29350 Moëlan-sur-Mer [02 98 71 16 25; camping-ilepercee-am@orange.fr; www.camping-ile-percee.fr] App thro Moëlan-sur-Mer, 6km SE of Pont-Aven or 6km SW of Quimperlé - watch for R turn after Moëlan. Take D116 sp to Kerfany. Keep strt at Kergroës, turn L after 500m sp L'Ile Percée. Med, pt sl, unshd; wc (some cont); baby facs; shwrs; el pnts (4-6A) €2.60-3.70; lndtte; snacks; bar; BBQ; playgrnd; sandy/rocky beach adj; sw, fishing & watersports adj; games area; entmnt; TV; some statics; dogs €1; phone; poss cr; adv bkg; v quiet. "Well-run site; sea views; ent narr & winding; sm pitches; manhandling ess; not suitable lge o'fits; san facs poss stretched high ssn." 1 Apr-19 Sep. € 17.50   2013*

PONT AVEN *2F2* (8km S Coastal) *47.79640, -3.77489*
Camping Les Chaumières, 24 Hameau de Kerascoët, 29920 Névez [02 98 06 73 06; info@camping-des-chaumieres.com; www.camping-des-chaumieres.com] S fr Pont-Aven thro Névez to Kerascoët. Med, hdg/mkd pitch, pt shd; wc; chem disp; mv service pnt; serviced pitches; shwrs inc; el pnts (4-10A) €3.40-4.30; gas 3km; lndtte (inc dryer); shop 3km; tradsmn high ssn; rest, snacks, bar adj; BBQ; playgrnd; sand beach 800m; dogs €1.50; Eng spkn; adv bkg ess; quiet; red low ssn; CKE/CCI. "Excel, well-organised site; facs poss stretched high ssn; gd play & games areas; sandy bay/beaches, cliff walks; San facs refurbished and upgraded; excel site; highly rec" ♦ 15 May-15 Sep. € 17.40   2013*

PONT AVEN *2F2* (10km S Coastal) *47.80492, -3.74510* **Camping Le St Nicolas, Port Manec'h, 29920 Névez [02 98 06 89 75; fax 02 98 06 74 61; info@campinglesaintnicolas.com; www.campinglesaintnicolas.com]** Take D783 W fr Pont-Aven for 2km, turn L onto D77 S thro Névez to Port Manech. Site well sp. Narr app to site. Lge, hdg/mkd pitch, pt sl, pt shd; wc (some cont); chem disp; shwrs inc; el pnts (6-10A) €3.70-4.70; gas; lndtte; tradsmn high ssn; rest, snacks, bar in vill; playgrnd; htd pool; paddling pool; sand beach 200m; watersports; games area; game rm; tennis, horseriding nrby; entmnt; TV rm; dogs €1.70; Eng spkn; adv bkg; quiet; ccard acc; red low ssn; CKE/CCI. "Pleasant, wooded site; friendly owners; sh walk to beach & cliff walks; gd touring base." ♦ 1 May-19 Sep. € 21.50   2010*

PONT AVEN *2F2* (3km SW Rural) *47.84500, -3.79000*
Domaine de Kerlann, Land Rosted, 29930 Pont Aven [02 98 06 01 77; fax 02 98 06 18 50; reservations@ledomainedekerlann.fr; www.siblu.fr/domainedekerlann] Fr Pont Aven foll sp twd Concarneau. After 1.5km, turn L onto D77 twd Névez. Site approx 1.5km on R. V lge, hdg/mkd pitch, hdstg, pt sl, pt shd; htd wc; chem disp; baby facs; shwrs inc; el pnts (8A) inc; gas; lndtte; shop; rest, snacks; bar; playgrnd; htd pools (1 covrd); waterslide; sand beach 3km; tennis; cycle hire; entmnt; child entmtn; TV rm; 85% statics; Eng spkn; adv bkg ess high ssn; ccard acc; red low ssn/low ssn; CKE/CCI. "Wooded site & areas poss muddy after rain; children's club all ssn; teenagers' club Jul/Aug; sports pitch; all facs open all ssn." ♦ ltd 4 Apr-21 Sep.   2009*

PONT AVEN *2F2* (5km SW Rural) *47.81749, -3.79959*
Camping Les Genêts, Route St Philibert, 29920 Névez [02 98 06 86 13 or 02 98 06 72 31; campinglesgenets@aol.com; www.campinglesgenets-nevez.com] Turn S off D783 onto D77 to Névez. At church in town, bear R & turn immed R to exit Névez with post office on R. Site on L, clearly sp. Med, hdg/mkd pitch, pt shd; wc (some cont); baby facs; shwrs inc; el pnts (3-6A) €2.40-5; gas 500m; lndtte; shops 500m; playgrnd; sand beach; 10% statics; dogs €1; some Eng spkn; adv bkg; quiet; CKE/CCI. "Excel beaches adj; vg." 15 Jun-15 Sep. € 14.90   2012*

PONT AVEN *2F2* (6km SW Coastal) *47.79906, -3.79033*
Camping Les Deux Fontaines, Raguenès, 29920 Névez [02 98 06 81 91; fax 02 98 06 71 80; info@les2fontaines.fr; www.les2fontaines.fr] Leave N165/E60 at Kérampaou foll sp D24 twds Pont Aven. In approx 4.5km turn R (S) foll sp Névez then Raguenès. Site 3km fr Névez. Lge, mkd pitch, pt shd; wc (some cont); shwrs inc; baby facs; el pnts (10A) €4.90; lndtte; shop; rest; bar; sand beach 800m; htd pool; tennis; 80% statics (tour ops); dogs €3.40; o'night facs for m'vans; adv bkg; red low ssn; 25 meter conn lead req'd; price inc waterpark acc & kids club "Busy high ssn; popular with British families;" ♦ ltd 27 Apr-7 Sep. € 32.90 (CChq acc)   2013*

PONT AVEN *2F2* (8km SW Coastal) *47.7946, -3.79816*
Camping de l'Océan, Impasse des Mouettes, Keroren, Raguenès, 29920 Névez [02 98 06 87 13; fax 02 98 06 78 26; campingocean@orange.fr; www.camping-ocean.fr] Leave N165 at Kérampaou; foll sp D24 dir Pont Aven; in 4.5km turn R onto D77; foll sp Névez then Raguenès; site 3km fr Névez. Med, hdg/mkd pitch, pt sl, pt shd; wc (some cont); serviced pitches; chem disp; baby facs; shwrs inc; el pnts (4-10A) €3.50-4.70; lndtte; shops 3km; tradsmn; rest, snacks & bar 2km; BBQ; sm playgrnd; htd covrd pool; sand beach 300m; sailing; fishing; games area; games rm; TV; 4% statics; dogs €1.50; phone; bus; poss cr; some Eng spkn; adv bkg rec high ssn; quiet; ccard acc; red low ssn; CKE/CCI. "Peaceful, well-run, family-owned site; dir access to beach; excel." ♦ ltd 15 May-15 Sep. € 20.60   2009*

PONT AVEN *2F2* (8km SW Coastal) *47.79597, -3.79877*
Camping du Vieux Verger - Ty Noul, Raguenès-Plage, 29920 Névez [02 98 06 86 08 or 02 98 06 83 17 (LS); fax 02 98 06 76 74; contact@campingduvieuxverger.com; www.campingduvieuxverger.com] Fr Pont-Aven take D783 dir Concarneau; in 2.5km L onto D77 to Névez; foll sp Raguenès-Plage; 1st site on R. Foll 'Vieux Verger' sps. Med, hdg/mkd pitch, pt shd; wc; chem disp (wc); shwrs inc; el pnts (4-10A) €3.20-4.20 (poss rev pol); shop (high ssn); rest 500m; playgrnd; sand beach 500m; statics in sep area; dogs free; phone; poss cr; quiet; red low ssn; CKE/CCI. "Well-run, well-kept site with pool & waterslides; highly rec low ssn." 16 Apr-25 Sep. € 15.50   2011*

PONT AVEN 2F2 (8km SW Coastal) 47.79330, -3.80110
Camping Raguénès-Plage, 19 Rue des Îles à Raguénès, 29920 Névez [02 98 06 80 69; fax 02 98 06 89 05; info@camping-le-raguenes-plage.com; www.camping-le-raguenes-plage.com] Fr Pont-Aven take D783 dir Trégunc; in 2.5km turn L for Névez, foll sps to Raguénès fr Névez. Or fr N165 take D24 at Kérampaou exit; in 3km turn R to Nizon; at church in vill turn R onto D77 to Névez; site on L 3km after Névez. Lge, mkd pitch, hdstg, pt shd; htd wc (some cont); mv service pnt; baby facs; sauna; shwrs inc; el pnts (6-15A) €4-6.90; gas; lndtte; shop; rest; snacks adj; bar; BBQ; playgrnd; htd, covrd pool; paddling pool; waterslide; direct access to sand beach adj; watersports school adj; tennis nr; games area; games rm; cycle hire; trampoline; games area; horseriding; wifi; entmnt; 20% statics (sep area); dogs €3.20; Eng spkn; adv bkg rec; quiet; red low ssn; ccard acc; CKE/CCI. "Pretty, wooded, family-run site; private path to beach; clean facs; 1st class site." ♦ 1 Apr-30 Sep. € 32.80 2011*

See advertisement

PONT CROIX see Audierne 2F1

PONT D'AIN 9A2 (800m E Urban) 46.04680, 5.34446
Camping de l'Oiselon, Rue E'mile Lebreüs, 01160 Pont-d'Ain [tel/fax 04 74 39 05 23; campingoiselon@free.fr] Fr A42 exit Pont-d'Ain foll D90 to vill. In vill cent turn R on D1075. Turn L immed after x-ing Rv L'Ain. Foll rd passing tennis club on L. Site on L, clearly sp. Lge, pt shd; wc; chem disp; baby facs; shwrs inc; el pnts (6-10A) €2.40-3.10 (poss rev pol); shops; rest, snacks'; BBQ; playgrnd; pool; rv sw & beach; fishing; canoeing; tennis adj; horseriding 5km; cycle hire; games area; entmnt; 30% statics; dogs free; poss cr; Eng spkn; adv bkg; quiet (poss some noise fr disco); CKE/CCI. "Gd, well-run site with easy access; helpful, friendly staff; gd clean san facs; site needs TLC (early ssn 2010); gd NH." ♦ 16 Mar-13 Oct. € 20.20 2012*

PONT DE L'ARCHE 3D2 (300m N Urban) 49.3060, 1.1546
Camp Municipal Eure et Seine, Quai Maréchal Foch, 27340 Pont-de-l'Arche [02 35 23 06 71 or 02 32 98 90 70 (Mairie); fax 02 32 98 90 89; campeure@orange.fr or campeure@pontdelarche.fr; www.pontdelarche.fr] Fr Rouen S on D6015 turn 1st L after x-ing rv bdge, drive downhill then L under bdge & strt on for 300m, site on R. Restricted width on app. Or exit A13 junc 20 onto D321 to Pont-de-l'Arche; turn L at War Memorial onto Place du Souvenir; in 300m to R at rv; site on L in 200m. Med, mkd pitch, pt shd; wc; chem disp; shwrs inc; el pnts (6-10A) €5.70-630; lndtte; shop 200m; rest; bar; playgrnd; rv fishing adj; wifi; 4% statics; dogs €1.15; phone; poss v cr; adv bking; rd noise; ccard acc; red long stay; CKE/CCI. "Pleasant, peaceful, clean rvside site in attractive medieval town; sm pitches; helpful warden; gd, modern san facs; recep 1000-1200 & 1600-2000; many shops clsd Wed pm; bus fr town to Rouen; popular NH & longer; Beautiful site nr Gothic church; excel" ♦ 1 Apr-30 Oct. € 16.15 2013*

"I like to fill in the reports as I travel from site to site"

You'll find report forms at the back of this guide, or you can fill them in online at www.caravaclub.co.uk/europereport.

⊞ **PONT DE L'ARCHE** 3D2 (10km S Rural) 49.22513, 1.22406
FFCC Camping Le St Pierre, 1 Rue du Château, 27430 St Pierre-du-Vauvray [tel/fax 02 32 61 01 55; eliane.darcissac@wanadoo.fr; www.lecampingdesaintpierre.com] Fr S exit A154 junc 3 or A13 junc 18 (Louviers) onto D6155 E until junc with D6015. Turn L & in 4km turn R to St Pierre. Fr N on D6015 after x-ing Rv Seine at Pont-de-l'Arche cont for approx 6km & turn L to St Pierre. Do not ent St Pierre fr E on D313 due low bdge under rlwy line. Med, hdg/mkd pitch, pt shd; wc; chem disp; shwrs inc; el pnts (6-10A) €2.80 (poss rev pol); lndry rm; shop 1km; BBQ; playgrnd; htd pool; 25% statics; dogs €1.20; site clsd 2 weeks at Xmas/New Year; Eng spkn; adv bkg rec; noise fr rlwy adj; CKE/CCI; "In grounds sm chateau; TGV rlwy line adj site; conv Giverny; friendly staff; ltd facs; NH; Site tired, expensive but OK for NH; not enough facs, scruffy and dirty" € 13.10 2013*

PONT DE SALARS *7D4* (1.5km N Rural) *44.29150, 2.72571* **Parc Camping du Lac, 12290 Pont-de-Salars [05 65 46 84 86; fax 05 65 46 60 39; camping.du.lac@ wanadoo.fr; www.camping-du-lac.fr.st]** Fr Rodez on D911 La Primaube-Millau rd, turn L bef ent Pont-de-Salars. Site sp. Lge, mkd pitch, pt sl, terr, pt shd; wc (some cont); chem disp; baby facs; shwrs inc; el pnts (3-6A) €2.50-3.50; gas; lndtte; shop & 1km; tradsmn; rest, snacks; bar; BBQ; playgrnd; pool; paddling pool; lake sw; sailing; fishing; entmnt; TV; 90% statics; no dogs; phone; poss cr; adv bkg; noisy nr entmnt area; ccard acc; red low ssn. "Beautiful situation; poor for c'vans, OK m'vans; diff lge o'fits; blocks req; site poss unclean end of ssn." ◆ ltd 1 Jun-30 Sep. € 17.00   2009*

PONT DE SALARS *7D4* (4km N Rural) *44.30471, 2.73526* **FLOWER Camping Les Terrasses du Lac, Route du Vibal, 12290 Pont-de-Salars [05 65 46 88 18 or 06 72 89 84 34 (mob); fax 05 65 46 85 38; campinglesterrasses@orange.fr; www.campinglesterrasses. com or www.flowercampings.com]** Fr Rodez S on N2088 to La Primaube. Turn L in La Primaube onto D911 for Pont-de-Salars. Turn L onto D523 by timberyard to Le Vibal & foll sp to site approx 4km fr vill cent. Or fr A75 exit junc 44.1 dir Pont-de-Salars, turn R onto D523 then as above. Lge, hdg pitch, terr, pt shd; wc; chem disp; mv service pnt; some serviced pitches; baby facs; shwrs inc; el pnts (6A) €4; gas; lndtte (inc dryer); shop; tradsmn; rest, snacks; bar; BBQ; playgrnd; htd pool; paddling pool; sand beach & lake sw adj; boating; fishing; games area; games rm; wifi; entmnt; TV; 30% statics; dogs €2; phone; Eng spkn; adv bkg; quiet; ccard acc; red low ssn/long stay; CKE/CCI. "Well laid-out site o'looking lake; gd touring base; vg." ◆ 1 Apr-30 Sep. € 23.50   2010*

See advertisement on pages 32 & 33

PONT DE SALARS *7D4* (7km SE Rural) *44.21420, 2.76660* **Camping Le Caussanel, Lac de Pareloup, 12290 Canet-de-Salars [05 65 46 85 19; fax 05 65 46 89 85; info@ lecaussanel.com; www.lecaussanel.com or www. les-castels.com]** Exit A75 junc 44.1 onto D911 dir Pont-de-Salars, then D993 Salles-Curan & D538 Canet-de-Salars, dir Lac de Pareloup. In 6km fork R to Le Caussanel: in 100m fork L to site. Fr N88 exit at La Primaube then D911 to Pont-de-Salars, then as above. Lge, mkd pitch, hdstg, pt sl, terr, pt shd; wc; mv service pnt; chem disp; baby facs; shwrs inc; el pnts (5A) inc; lndtte (inc dryer) shop or 10km; tradsmn; rest, snacks; bar; BBQ; playgrnd; htd pool; paddling pool; waterslide; fishing; windsurfing & sailing; lake fishing; tennis; boat & cycle hire; games rm; wifi; entmnt; 20% statics; dogs €3.90; Eng spkn; adv bkg; quiet; red low ssn; CKE/CCI. "Beautiful situation, views over lake; friendly owner; vg." ◆ 23 May-17 Sep. € 33.00 (CChq acc)   2009*

See advertisement on inside back cover

PONT DE SALARS *7D4* (8km S Rural) *44.21500, 2.77777* **Camping Soleil Levant, Lac de Pareloup, 12290 Canet-de-Salars [05 65 46 03 65; contact@camping-soleil-levant.com; www.camping-soleil-levant.com]** Exit A75 junc 44.1 onto D911 to Pont-de-Salars, then S on D993 dir Salles-Curan. Site in 8km bef bdge on L. Lge, mkd pitch, terr, pt sl, pt shd; htd wc (some cont); chem disp; baby facs; fam bthrm; shwrs inc; el pnts (6A) inc; gas; lndtte (inc dryer); shop 4km; tradsmn; snacks; bar; BBQ; playgrnd; lake sw & sand/shgl beach adj; fishing; watersports; tennis; games area; games rm; wifi; entmnt; TV rm; 10% statics; dogs €2; Eng spkn; adv bkg; quiet; ccard acc; red low ssn/CKE/CCI. "Lovely lakeside site; excel san facs." ◆ 1 May-30 Sep. € 25.00   2011*

PONT DE VAUX *9A2* (3.5km NE Rural) *46.44394, 4.98313* **Camping Les Ripettes, St Bénigne, 01190 Chavannes-sur-Reyssouze [03 85 30 66 58; info@camping-les-ripettes.com; www.camping-les-ripettes.pagesperso-orange.fr]** Take D2 fr Pont-de-Vaux sp St Trivier-des-Courtes for 3km. Immed after water tower on R turn L onto D58 sp Romenay, then immed L. Site well sp on L in 100m. Med, hdg/mkd pitch, pt sl, pt shd; htd wc; chem disp; mv service pnt; shwrs inc; el pnts (10A) €3.50; lndtte; shop & 3.5km; tradsmn; snacks; playgrnd; 2 pools; games area; wifi; 1 static; dogs €1.50; phone; Eng spkn; adv bkg rec high ssn; quiet, but some rd noise; ccard acc; red low ssn; CKE/CCI. "Lovely, popular site in beautiful location; spacious pitches; friendly, helpful owner; immac facs; gd pool area; gd touring base; hard to beat!" ◆ ltd 1 Apr-30 Sep. € 25.00   2013*

PONT DE VAUX *9A2* (5km W Rural) *46.44710, 4.89890* **Camping aux Rives du Soleil, 01190 Pont-de-Vaux [tel/ fax 03 85 30 33 65; info@rivesdusoleil.com; www. rivesdusoleil.com]** Leave D306 (N6) at Fleurville (bet Mâcon & Tournus) onto D933A dir Pont-de-Vaux. In 1km cross rv; site immed on R. Well sp. Lge, pt shd, wc; chem disp; mv service pnt; baby facs; shwrs inc; el pnts (6A) €3.50 (poss rev pol); gas; lndtte; shop; rest, snacks; bar; BBQ; playgrnd; pool; paddling pool; rv beach adj; fishing; boating; entmnt; TV; 15% statics; dogs €3.50; poss cr; Eng spkn; adv bkg; some rlwy noise; red long stay/low ssn. "Pleasant site adj rv & canal; Dutch owners; san facs need update; conv NH fr A6." 24 Apr-17 Oct. € 20.00   2010*

PONT DE VAUX *9A2* (15km W Rural) *46.47686, 4.80908* **Camp Municipal St Pierre, 71260 Lugny [03 85 33 20 25 or 03 85 33 21 96 (Mairie); fax 03 85 33 00 58]** W of A6/ N6; take C7 off D56 N out of Lugny; foll sp for Rest St Pierre; site adj & sp fr town. Diff app for lge o'fits. Sm, mkd pitch, pt shd; wc; shwrs inc; el pnts inc; lndry rm; shop 1.5km in Lugny; rest adj; v quiet; ccard not acc. "Simple site; lovely views of vineyards; warden calls am & pm; facs clean; gd local walks - steep fr town to site; gd rest adj." 1 May-30 Sep.   2010*

PONT D'OUILLY see Condé sur Noireau *3D1*

PONT DU CHATEAU *9B1* (3km SW) *45.77546, 3.24197*
**Camping Les Ombrages, Rue Pont du Château, 63111
Dallet [tel/fax 04 73 83 10 97; lesombrages@hotmail.com;
www.lesombrages.com]** E fr Clermont Ferrand on D769;
200m bef x-ing Rv Allier turn R onto D783/D769A; 50m after
x-ring rv turn L into Rue Pont du Château; site on L in 400m.
Sm, shd; wc; shwrs inc; el pnts (6A) €3.50; lndtte; shop; rest,
snacks; bar; playgrnd; 2 pools; paddling pool; rv sw adj; fishing;
canoeing; games rm; wifi; entmnt; TV; no dogs; quiet; red
low ssn. "Peaceful site; excel pitches by rv; gd for fishing &
canoeing." 12 May-15 Sep. € 17.50   2011*

PONT DU NAVOY see Doucier *6H2*

PONT EN ROYANS *9C2* (Rural) *45.06193, 5.33398*
**Camp Municipal Les Seraines, 38680 Pont-en-Royans
[04 76 36 06 30 or 04 76 36 03 09 (Mairie); fax
04 76 38 92 37; mairie.pont.en.royans@wanadoo.fr]**
App on D531 fr E or D518 fr St Marcellin fr N, site sp on ent
town. Sm, hdg pitch, hdstg, pt terr, pt shd; wc (mainly cont);
chem disp; mv service pnt; shwrs inc; el pnts (4A) €3; lndtte;
shops 500m; playgrnd; lake 8km; rv adj; tennis; entmnt; poss
cr; statics; dogs; quiet but some rd noise; CKE/CCI. "Site in 2
adj parts; helpful warden; rvside walk to town."
15 Apr-30 Sep. € 9.40   2010*

PONT EN ROYANS *9C2* (4km E Rural) *45.06439, 5.39426* **FFCC
Camping Le Gouffre de la Croix, 38680 Choranche [tel/fax
04 76 36 07 13; camping.gouffre.croix@wanadoo.fr;
www.camping-choranche.com]** App fr Pont-en-Royans only.
Site at far end of vill. Ent over narr bdge, OK with care. Sm,
mkd pitch, terr, pt shd; wc; chem disp; fam bthrm; shwrs inc;
el pnts (6A) €3.50; gas; lndtte; shop 4km; tradsmn; rest 500m;
snacks; bar; playgrnd; TV; 4% statics; dogs €2; phone; Eng
spkn; adv bkg; quiet; CKE/CCI. "Friendly site on trout rv; views
fr most pitches; excel walking area; excel." 25 Apr-16 Sep.
€ 16.00   2008*

PONT FARCY *1D4* (500m N Rural) *47.46810, 4.35709* **Camp
Municipal Pont-Farcy, Quai de la Vire, 14380 Pont-Farcy
[02 31 68 32 06 or 02 31 68 86 48; pontfarcy@free.fr;
www.pont-farcy.fr]** Leave A84 junc 39 onto D21 to Pont-
Farcy; site on L at ent to vill. Med, hdg/mkd pitch, terr, pt shd;
wc; chem disp; mv service pnt; shwrs inc; baby facs; el pnts
(10A) €2.50; shop, rest & bar 500m; playgrnd; rv fishing &
boating adj; tennis; cycle hire; 30% statics; dogs €1; phone;
adv bkg; quiet; CKE/CCI. "Barrier poss locked periods during
day but parking avail; helpful, friendly warden; clean facs;
mosquitoes at dusk" ♦ 1 May-15 Sep. € 10.00   2013*

PONT L'ABBE *2F2* (6km S Rural/Coastal) *47.79715, -4.22868*
**Camping des Dunes, 67 Rue Paul Langevin, 29740
Plobannalec-Lesconil [02 98 87 81 78; fax 02 98 82 27 05;
contact@camping-lesdunes.com; www.camping-
lesdunes-29.com]** Fr Pont l'Abbé, S on D102 for 5km to
Plobannelec; over x-rds; in 1km turn R, 100m after sports
field; green sp to site in 1km. Med, hdg/mkd pitch, pt shd; wc
(few cont); chem disp; mv service pnt; baby facs; shwrs inc; el
pnts (8A) €3.50; lndtte (inc dryer); shop & rests 1km; tradsmn;
snacks; bar; BBQ; playgrnd; sand beach 100m; games rm;
games area; dogs €2; poss cr high ssn; adv bkg; ccard acc; red
early ssn; CKE/CCI. "Helpful owner; nr fishing port; gd walking,
cycling & birdwatching; site gd for children." ♦ 3 Jun-9 Sep.
€ 20.80   2011*

PONT L'ABBE *2F2* (7km S Rural) *47.81241, -4.22147* **Yelloh!
Village L'Océan Breton, 29740 Plobannalec-Lesconil
[02 98 82 23 89; fax 02 98 82 26 49; info@yellohvillage-
manoir-de-kerlut.com; www.yellohvillage-
manoir-de-kerlut.com or www.yellohvillage.co.uk]** Fr Pont l'Abbé S on D102
to Plobannalec & head for Lesconil; site on L after supmkt.
Lge, hdg/mkd pitch, hdstg, pt shd; htd wc; serviced pitches;
mv service pnt; chem disp; sauna; shwrs inc; el pnts (5A) inc;
gas; lndtte; shop; tradsmn; rest, snacks; bar; playgrnd; htd,
covrd pool; waterslide; sand beach 2km; cycle hire; fitness rm;
tennis; games area; 80% statics; dogs €4; phone; Eng spkn;
adv bkg; quiet; ccard acc; red long stay/low ssn; CKE/CCI.
"Excel site for families; spacious pitches." ♦ 28 May-18 Sep.
€ 39.00   2011*

See advertisement on inside front cover

PONT L'ABBE *2F2* (5km SW Rural) *47.83264, -4.32630*
**Camping Caravaning Pointe de la Torche, 29120
Plomeur [02 98 58 62 82; fax 02 98 58 89 69; info@
campingdelatorche.fr; www.campingdelatorche.fr]**
Fr Quimper take D785 to Pont l'Abbé & on to Plomeur. After
Plomeur turn W twd La Pointe de la Torche & foll sps for 3km.
Lge, pt shd, mkd pitch; wc; chem disp; shwrs inc; baby facs;
el pnts (6A) €3.20; gas; lndtte; shop; rest; bar; sand beach
1.5km; pool; playgrnd; tennis; horseriding, fishing, golf, surfing
adj; 50% statics; dogs €2; Eng spkn; adv bkg; red low ssn. "V
quiet off ssn." 5 Apr-30 Sep. € 19.50   2008*

PONT L'ABBE *2F2* (3km W Rural) *47.86113, -4.26766* **Aire
Naturelle Keraluic, 29120 Plomeur [tel/fax 02 98 82 10 22;
camping@keraluic.fr; www.keraluic.fr]** Leave Quimper S
on D785 to o'skts Pont L'Abbe; turn R at 1st rndabt (junc with
D44); strt on at 2nd rndabt (junc with D2); in 1km turn R at 3rd
rndabt up narr rd sp St Jean-Trolimon; site on R in 1.5km. Site
2km NE of Plomeur & well sp. Sm, pt shd; wc; chem disp; baby
facs; shwrs inc; el pnts (6A) €2.90; gas; lndtte; sm shop or 3km;
tradsmn; BBQ; playgrnd; surfing 5km; games area; games rm;
internet; no dogs high ssn, £1.50 low ssn; no twin-axles; Eng
spkn; adv bkg (rec high ssn); quiet; ccard acc; red low ssn; CKE/
CCI. "Excel, well-kept, family-run site; friendly, helpful Dutch
owners; spacious pitches; gd leisure facs; ideal for children; gd
walking; gd surfing nrby; facs poss stretched high ssn, highly
rec low ssn." ♦ ltd 1 May-31 Oct. € 15.50   2010*

PONT L'ABBE *2F2* (5km NW Urban) *47.90602, -4.28339*
**Camp Municipal de Mariano, 29720 Plonéour-Lanvern
[02 98 87 74 80; fax 02 98 82 66 09; mairie@ploneour-
lanvern.fr; www.ploneour-lanvern.fr]** Fr Pont l'Abbé,
take D2 to Plonéour-Lanvern, site sp fr cent town; fr cent L of
church & strt to T-junc, turn R 2nd on L. Med, hdg pitch, pt
shd; wc; shwrs inc; el pnts (5A) €3; lndtte; shops 400m; pool
6km; playgrnd; sand beach 13km; tennis adj; dogs €1; adv bkg;
quiet. "Pleasant site; warden visits am & pm; gd touring base."
♦ 15 Jun-15 Sep. € 9.50   2009*

PONT L'ABBE *2F2* (10km NW Rural) *47.89462, -4.32863* **Camping Kerlaz, Route de la Mer, 29670 Tréguennec [tel/ fax 02 98 87 76 79; contact@kerlaz.com; www.kerlaz.com]** Fr Plonéour-Lanvern take D156 SW to Tréguennec. Med, hdg pitch, pt shd; wc; chem disp; mv service pnt; shwrs inc; el pnts (3-6A) €2.40-3.50; lndtte (inc dryer); shops 4km; snacks; BBQ; playgrnd; htd, covrd pool; sand beach 2km; cycle hire; 30% statics; dogs €1.30; Eng spkn; adv bkg; quiet; ccard acc; red low ssn. "Nice, friendly site." 1 Apr-30 Sep. € 15.30   2011*

PONT L'ABBE D'ARNOULT *7B1* (500m E Urban) *45.82592, -0.86568* **Camping Parc de la Garenne, 24 Ave Bernard Chambenoit, 17250 Pont-l'Abbé-d'Arnoult [05 46 97 01 46 or 06 09 43 20 11 (mob); info@lagarenne.net; www. lagarenne.net]** N fr Saintes on N137. In 18km turn L onto D18 to Pont-l'Abbé-d'Arnoult. In town turn L, foll camp sp to site adj sw pool. Med, shd; wc; chem disp; mv service pnt 150m; baby facs; shwrs inc; el pnts (6A) €4.20; gas; lndtte (inc dryer); shop, rest, snacks & bar 500m; snacks; BBQ (elec only); playgrnd; pool adj; tennis; games area; wifi; entmnt; TV rm; 10% statics; dogs €3; phone; Eng spkn; adv bkg; quiet; CKE/ CCI. "Well-run site; friendly; gd san facs; lack of maintenance early ssn (2011); gd." ♦ 1 May-15 Sep. € 21.00   2011*

PONT LES MOULINS see Baume les Dames *6G2*

PONT L'EVEQUE *3D1* (500m NW Urban) *49.28486, 0.17573* **Camping du Stade, Rue de Beaumont, 14130 Pont l'Evèque [02 31 64 15 03; www.campingdustade.fr]** Fr town cent take D675 W twd Caen, turn R at traff lts bef town o'skts to site in 300m. Site sp R in 300m on D118. Med, mkd pitch, pt shd; wc (some cont); chem disp; shwrs inc; el pnts (5A) €3 (poss rev pol); lndry rm; shops in town; tradsmn; playgrnd; beach 12km; rv fishing; tennis; 2% statics; quiet; ccard not acc; CKE/CCI. "Basic, clean site; friendly, helpful staff; dated san facs; no hedges - poss noisy high ssn; trees round site are starling roosts - don't site o'fit underneath! (2010); mkt Mon." ♦ ltd 1 Apr-31 Oct. € 11.00   2010*

PONT ST ESPRIT *9D2* (6km NW Rural) *44.30388, 4.58443* **Camping Le Pontet, 07700 St Martin-d'Ardèche [04 75 04 63 07 or 04 75 98 76 59; fax 04 75 98 76 59; contact@campinglepontet.com; www.campinglepontet. com]** N86 N of Pont-St Esprit; turn L onto D290 at sp Gorges de l'Ardèche & St Martin-d'Ardèche, site on R after 3km, lge sp. Med, mkd, pt shd; wc; chem disp; mv service pnt; shwrs inc; el pnts (6A) €3.60 (rev pol); gas; lndry rm; tradsmn; shop, rest high ssn; snacks; bar; playgrnd; pool; rv sw 1km; wifi; 5% statics; dogs €3; phone; Eng spkn; adv bkg; quiet (poss noisy w/end); ccard not acc; red low ssn; CKE/CCI. "Vg; helpful owners; peaceful out of ssn." ♦ 8 Apr-25 Sep. € 19.20   2011*

⊞ **PONT ST ESPRIT** *9D2* (7km NW Rural) *44.29808, 4.56535* **Camping Les Cigales, 30760 Aiguèze [04 66 82 18 52; fax 04 66 82 25 20; www.camping-cigales.fr]** N fr Pont-St Esprit on D6086 take D901 NW twd Barjac & D141 to St Martin-d'Ardèche. Site on L bef rv bdge. Avoid app fr St Martin-d'Ardèche over narr suspension bdge. Care at ent. Sm, mkd pitch, shd; wc; mv service pnt; shwrs inc; el pnts (4-10A) €3.13-5.88; gas; lndtte; shops, rest 500m; tradsmn; BBQ; htd pool; rv sw 500m; wifi; 25% statics; dogs €2; poss cr; adv bkg; rd noise; ccard not acc; CKE/CCI. "Helpful owner; easy walk to St Martin-d'Ardèche." € 17.76   2011*

PONT ST ESPRIT *9D2* (7.5km NW Urban) *44.30342, 4.56819* **Camp Municipal Le Village, Rue du Nord, 07700 St Martin-d'Ardèche [04 75 04 65 25; fax 04 75 98 71 38; denislaurent1@sfr.fr; www.ot-stmartin-ardeche.com]** N on D6086 fr Pont-St Esprit, turn L onto D290 at St Just. Foll D290 around St Martin-d'Ardèche, look out for site sp. Turn sharp R down under main rd & strt into site - take care if v high outfit. Med, mkd pitch, pt shd; wc; chem disp; shwrs inc; el pnts (4A) inc; lndtte; shop, rest, snacks, bar 200m; playgrnd; rv beach adj; fishing; tennis; adv bkg; quiet. "Nr lovely, quiet vill; popular site; san facs only adequate (2010); site poss unkempt low ssn." 28 Mar-28 Sep. € 13.00   2011*

PONT ST ESPRIT *9D2* (8km NW Rural) *44.30043, 4.57069* **Camping Indigo Le Moulin, 07700 St Martin-d'Ardèche [04 75 04 66 20; fax 04 75 04 60 12; moulin@camping-indigo.com; www.camping-indigo.com]** Exit A7 junc 19 to Bollène, then D994 to Pont-St Esprit & D6068/D86 to St Just. Turn L onto D290 to St Martin in 4km. Site on L on rvside. Med, pt sl, pt shd; htd wc; chem disp; mv service pnt; baby facs; shwrs inc; el pnts (10A) €4.90; lndtte (inc dryer); shop; rest 5km; snacks; bar; playgrnd; htd pool; paddling pool; rv sw & beach adj; fishing; canoe hire; tennis 500m; cycle hire; games area; internet; entmnt; TV rm; 5% statics; dogs €4; phone; Eng spkn; no adv bkg; ccard acc; quiet; red low ssn. "Friendly site; gd modern san facs; footpath to vill; rec." ♦ 22 Apr-1 Oct. € 245.00   2011*

PONT ST ESPRIT *9D2* (8km NW Rural) *44.28950, 4.58923* **Camping Le Peyrolais, Route de Barjac, 30760 St Julien-de-Peyrolas [04 66 82 14 94; fax 04 66 82 31 70; contact@ camping-lepeyrolais.com; www.camping-lepeyrolais.com]** N fr Pont-St. Esprit on D6086 turn L onto D901 sp Barjac. In 2.5km turn R at site sp, site in 500m up narr track on bank of Rv Ardèche. Med, mkd pitch, pt shd; wc; chem disp; mv waste; shwrs inc; el pnts (3-10A) €2.30-3.80; lndtte; shop & 3km; tradsmn; rest; bar; playgrnd; rv sw adj; fishing; kayaking; cycle & canoe hire; games area; hiking; horseriding; wifi; entmnt; TV rm; dogs €2; phone; poss cr; adv bkg; quiet; ccard acc; CKE/CCI. "Attractive, well-maintained site in beautiful location; clean facs; friendly owners; vg." ♦ 4 Apr-2 Oct. € 17.70   2009*

⊞ **PONT ST ESPRIT** *9D2* (8km NW Rural) *44.34423, 4.60434* **FFCC Camping Les Truffières, 201 Route de St Ramèze, 07700 St Marcel-d'Ardèche [04 75 04 68 35 or 06 82 01 28 30 (mob); soulier.valerie@wanadoo.fr]** S fr Bourg-St Andéol, turn W on D201; in vill foll sp to site located approx 3km W of vill. Med, mkd pitch, terr, pt shd; htd wc; mv service pnt; shwrs inc; el pnts (6A) €6.60 (poss rev pol); gas; lndtte; shops 3km; rest, snacks; bar; playgrnd; pool; entmnt; 70% statics; dogs €1.60; adv bkg; quiet; red low ssn; CKE/CCI. "Friendly owners; glorious views; gd san facs; conv NH nr A7." ♦ € 17.10   2009*

PONTAIX *9D2* (2km E Rural) *44.76585, 5.27270* **Aire Naturelle La Condamine (Archinard), 26150 Pontaix [04 75 21 08 19; fax 04 74 04 46 12; aurelie.goderiaux@ laposte.net]** W fr Die on D93; site on R just after D129. Fr E, 2km after Pontaix on L. Sm; wc; chem disp; shwrs inc; el pnts (10A) inc; lndry rm; shop 8km; BBQ; rv sw adj; dogs €1; adv bkg; quiet; CKE/CCI. "Excel CL-type site by Rv Drôme; helpful owner." ♦ 15 Apr-15 Oct. € 13.50   2011*

You can now fill in site reports online

⊞ **PONTARLIER** *6H2* (1km SE Rural) *46.90024, 6.37425*
FFCC Camping Le Larmont, Rue du Toulombief, 25300
Pontarlier [03 81 46 23 33; lelarmont.pontarlier@
wanadoo.fr; www.camping-pontarlier.fr] Leave N57 at
Pontarlier Gare & foll site sp. Site uphill, turning nr Nestlé
factory. Med, some hdstg, terr, unshd; htd wc; chem disp; mv
service pnt; shwrs inc; el pnts (10A) €4; gas; lndtte; sm shop;
Spar supmkt 1km; tradsmn; snacks; bar; playgrnd; pool 2km;
horseriding adj; skiing winter; wifi; 10-20% statics; dogs €1;
Eng spkn; adv bkg; red low ssn/CKE/CCI. "Friendly; easy access;
clean san facs; ltd pitches for awnings; site self out of office
hrs; well-behaved zebra on site; excel" ♦ ltd € 24.90 2013*

PONTARLIER *6H2* (12km S Rural) *46.81176, 6.30326*
Camp Municipal, 8 Rue du Port, 25160 St Point-
Lac [03 81 69 61 64 or 03 81 69 62 08 (Mairie); fax
03 81 69 65 74; camping-saintpointlac@wanadoo.fr;
www.camping-saintpointlac.com] Exit Pontarlier S on N57
dir Lausanne, turn R on D437 dir Malbuisson; in 6km turn R
onto D129 thro Les Grangettes to St Point-Lac. Site sp on L.
Med, mkd pitch, hdstg, pt shd; htd wc; chem disp; mv service
pnt; chem disp; shwrs inc; el pnts (16A) €4.50; lndtte (inc
dryer); shop; rest 300m; snacks; bar; BBQ; playgrnd; lake beach
adj; games area; entmnt; 5% statics; dogs €1.50; poss cr; Eng
spkn; adv bkg rec high ssn; quiet; ccard acc; red low ssn; CKE/
CCI. "Well-kept lakeside site in beautiful position; sm pitches;
no twin-axles; friendly staff; vg san facs; m'van o'night area
with facs opp; gd fishing, walking, birdwatching; excel." ♦
1 May-30 Sep. € 10.50 2010*

PONTAUBAULT *2E4* (Urban) *48.62983, -1.35205* **Camping
La Vallée de la Sélune, 7 Rue Maréchal Leclerc, 50220
Pontaubault** [tel/fax 02 33 60 39 00; campselune@
wanadoo.fr; www.camping-manche.com] Foll sp to
Pontaubault (well sp fr all dirs). In vill head twd Avranches. Turn
L immed bef bdge over Rv Sélune. In 100m turn L, site strt in
100m, well sp. Med, mkd pitch, pt sl, pt shd; wc; chem disp;
shwrs inc; el pnts (10A) inc; lndtte; shop; tradsmn; supmkt
6km; snacks, bar high ssn; playgrnd; pool 7km; sand beach
10km; tennis adj; fishing adj; horseriding, cycling & golf nrby;
wifi; 10% statics; dogs €1.30; poss cr; adv bkg rec; rd/rlwy
noise; ccard acc; red long stay/CKE/CCI. "Relaxing, clean,
tidy site; friendly British owner; vg, clean san facs; conv Mont
St Michel & Cherbourg ferries; gd NH; pleasant site; friendly
Yorkshire owner" ♦ 1 Apr-20 Oct. € 20.00 2013*

PONTAUBAULT *2E4* (4km E Rural) *48.61690, -1.29475*
Camp Municipal La Sélune, Rue de Boishue, 50220 Ducey
[02 33 48 46 49 or 02 33 48 50 52; fax 02 33 48 87 59;
ducey.tourisme@wanadoo.fr; www.ducey-tourisme.
com] Exit A84 junc 33 onto N176 E fr Pontaubault. In Ducey
turn R onto D178 twd St Aubin-de-Terregatte. Ent at sports
grnd in 200m. Sm, hdg pitch, pt sl, shd; wc; chem disp; shwrs
inc; el pnts (5A) €1.85 (poss rev pol; poss long lead req); gas;
lndtte; shop; rest, snacks, bar in vill; playgrnd; pool nr; sand
beach 25km; tennis adj; 10% statics; dogs €1.30; phone; bus;
poss cr; Eng spkn; adv bkg; quiet; CKE/CCI. "Well-maintained
site; warden calls am & pm; poss itinerants." ♦ 1 Apr-30 Sep.
€ 7.85 2011*

PONTAUBAULT *2E4* (6km SW Coastal) *48.56583, -1.47111*
Campéole Camping St Grégoire, Le Haut Bourg,
50170 Servon [02 33 60 26 03; fax 02 33 60 68 65;
saint-gregoire@campeole.com; www.camping-mont-
saint-michel.com or www.campeole.com] Foll N175
fr Pontaubault twd Pontorson. After 6km site sp on R twd
Servon vill. Med, hdg/mkd pitch, some hdstg, pt shd; wc;
chem disp; baby facs; shwrs; el pnts (6A) inc; lndtte (inc dryer);
sm shop; tradsmn; BBQ; playgrnd; pool; games rm; wifi; TV;
30% statics; dogs €2.60; adv bkg; quiet but some rd noise on
S side of site; ccard acc; red low ssn; CKE/CCI. "Conv ferries."
2 Apr-26 Sep. € 20.00 2010*

See advertisement on pages 14 & 15

PONTCHATEAU *2G3* (4km W Rural) *47.44106, -2.15981*
Kawan Village Le Château du Deffay, Ste Reine-de-
Bretagne, 44160 Pontchâteau [02 40 88 00 57; fax
02 40 01 66 55; info@camping-le-deffay.com; www.
camping-le-deffay.com] Leave N165 at junc 13 onto D33
twd Herbignac. Site on R approx 1.5km after Le Calvaire de la
Madeleine x-rds, 270m past Chateau ent. Site sp fr by-pass.
Lge, some hdg/mkd pitch, pt sl, pt terr, pt shd; wc; chem
disp; mv service pnt; baby facs; shwrs; el pnts (6-10A)
inc poss rev pol; lndtte (inc dryer); sm shop; rest, snacks;
bar; BBQ (charcoal/gas); playgrnd; htd, covrd pool; paddling
pool; lake fishing; tennis & free pedalos; cycle hire; golf
10km; wifi; entmnt; games/TV rm; 18% statics; dogs €1; Eng
spkn; adv bkg; ccard acc (not in rest); red low ssn; CKE/CCI.
"Excel site with trees in grnds of chateau by lake; friendly,
welcoming staff; gd clean san facs; some pitches lakeside &
not fenced; mkt Mon" ♦ 1 May-30 Sep. € 28.89 (CChq acc)
SBS - B25 2013*

PONTET, LE see Avignon *10E2*

PONTGIBAUD *7B4* (3km NE Rural) *45.84436, 2.87672*
Camping Bel-Air, 63230 St Ours [04 73 88 72 14; contact@
campingbelair.fr; www.campingbelair.fr] Exit A89 junc 26
onto D941 dir Pontgibaud; cont past Pontgibaud; in 1.5km turn
L onto D943; site in 1.3km on L. Site sp. Med, mkd pitch, pt sl,
shd; wc; chem disp; mv service pnt; baby facs; shwrs inc; el pnts
(6A) €3.30; gas; lndry rm; shop 1.5km; tradsmn; rest, snacks;
bar; BBQ; playgrnd; golf; games area; 5% statics; dogs €1; Eng
spkn; adv bkg; quiet, but some rd noise; CKE/CCI. "Peaceful,
basic site in beautiful area; helpful owner; clean facs, ltd low ssn;
conv Vulcania; excel." ♦ 1 May-27 Sep. € 17.60 2013*

PONTGIBAUD *7B4* (200m S Rural) *45.82978, 2.84517* **FFCC
Camp Municipal La Palle, Route de la Miouze, 63230
Pontgibaud** [04 73 88 96 99 or 04 73 88 70 42 (LS); fax
04 73 88 77 77; mairie.pontgibaud@wanadoo.fr; www.
ville-pontgiabud.fr] At W end of Pontgibaud turn S over
bdge on D986 & site in 500m on L, past site for La Palle
Chalets. Med, hdg/mkd pitch, hdstg, pt shd; htd wc (some
cont); chem disp; mv service pnt; shwrs inc; el pnts (10-16A)
inc; gas 400m; lndtte; shops 400m; tradsmn; rest; BBQ;
playgrnd; lake sw & beach 4km; games area; tennis, cycle hire
400m; entmnt; 5% statics; dogs; Eng spkn; adv bkg; rd & rlwy
noise; red long stay/low ssn; CKE/CCI. "Pleasant site nr sm
rv; helpful staff; gd touring base; pop concerts once a week
high ssn; conv Vulcania exhibition cent." ♦ 15 Apr-30 Sep.
€ 15.30 2010*

FRANCE

PONTOISE *3D3* (6km E Urban) **Camp Municipal Bellerive, Chemin de Bellerive, 95430 Auvers-sur-Oise [01 34 48 05 22; fax 01 30 36 70 30; www.auvers-sur-oise. com]** Exit N184 junc 7 sp Méry & Auvers-sur-Oise; in Méry foll sp to Auvers; immed on ent Auvers turn L sp Parking; foll rd (narr in places) to T-junc, turn L; foll Camping sp. Site 300m on L on rvside. Sm, shd; wc (some cont); chem disp (wc); shwrs inc; el pnts (6A) (poss rev pol); lndry rm; shop, rest, snacks & bar 1km; BBQ; adv bkg; quiet; CKE/CCI. "Easy access to Paris & Disneyland; sh walk to town where Van Gogh buried; gd." May-Oct. 2009*

PONTORSON *2E4* (400m NW Rural) *48.55805, -1.51444* **Kawan Village Haliotis, Chemin des Soupirs, 50170 Pontorson [02 33 68 11 59; fax 02 33 58 95 36; info@ camping-haliotis-mont-saint-michel.com; www.camping-haliotis-mont-saint-michel.com]** Exit A84 junc 33 onto N175 dir Pontorson; foll sp Centre Ville/Mont-St-Michel. Site well sp. Lge, hdg/mkd pitch, pt sl, pt shd; htd wc; chem disp; mv service pnt; baby facs; sauna; shwrs inc; el pnts (10-16A) inc (poss rev pol); gas; lndtte; shop; supmkt 400m; tradsmn; rest 400m; snacks; bar; BBQ; playgrnd; htd pool; paddling pool; spa; rv fishing; boating; tennis; cycle hire; games area; games rm; library; wifi; 25% statics; dogs €2; phone; bus 400m; poss cr; Eng spkn; adv bkg rec; quiet, poss noise till late w/ends; ccard acc; red low ssn; CKE/CCI. "Popular, well-kept, busy site; lge pitches; friendly, helpful owners; immac, unisex san facs; lovely pool & bar; rvside walk to town; cycle rte/bus to Mont St Michel; highly rec." ♦ ltd 15 Mar-11 Nov. € 33.35 (CChq acc) 2013*

PONTORSON *2E4* (7.5km NW Rural) *48.59415, -1.59855* **Camping Les Couesnons, Route de St Malo, 35610 Roz-sur-Couesnon [02 99 80 26 86; fax 02 99 80 31 04; contact@les-couesnons.com; www.lescouesnons.com]** Exit N175/N176 NW onto D797 dir St Malo on coastal rd; site sp 700m past Roz-sur-Couesnon on R. Med, hdg/mkd pitch, pt shd; htd wc; chem disp; baby facs; fam bthrm; shwrs inc; el pnts (6A) €3; lndtte; tradsmn; rest, snacks; bar; BBQ (charcoal & gas); playgrnd; games area; games rm; wifi; TV; 10% statics; dogs €2; Eng spkn; adv bkg; quiet; ccard acc; red low ssn/long stay; CKE/CCI. "Excel site; Mont St Michel 8km." ♦ 31 Mar-3 Nov. € 17.00 2010*

PONTRIEUX *2E3* (4km E Rural) **Camp Municipal du Bois d'Amour, 22260 Quemper-Guézennec [02 96 95 13 40 or 02 96 95 62 62; fax 02 96 95 36 07]** Exit N12 at Guincamp Est; D787 twds Pontrieux. At rndabt ent to Pontrieux, turn R & foll rd to indus est over level x-ing. Turn R along rv front, site in approx 200 yrds. Sm, hdg/mkd pitch, pt shd, mkd pitch; wc; shwrs; el pnts (16A) inc; lndtte; sm shop high ssn & 4km; tradsmn; playgrnd; fishing; 10% statics; ccard not acc; quiet; CKE/CCI. "Attractive site; some rvside pitches; clean, spacious san facs; pay at Marie in town low ssn; rv walks nrby; gd touring base." ♦ 15 Jun-15 Sep. € 13.00 2010*

⊞ **PONTRIEUX** *2E3* (500m W Rural) *48.69493, -3.16365* **Camping de Traou Mélédern (Moisan), Traou Mélédern, 22260 Pontrieux [02 96 95 69 27; campingpontrieux@ free.fr; http://campingpontrieux.free.fr]** N on D787 fr Guingamp; on ent town square turn sharp L sp Traou Mélédern, cross rv bdge & turn R alongside church. Site in 400m. Access poss diff for lge o'fits; steep exit on 1-way system. Med, hdg/mkd pitch, pt sl, pt shd; wc; chem disp; shwrs inc; el pnts (8A) €3; lndtte; shops, supmkt 1km; tradsmn; playgrnd; BBQ; dogs €1; phone; poss cr; Eng spkn; adv bkg; quiet but some daytime factory noise; CKE/CCI. "In orchard; excel touring base; friendly owner; steep junc nr site poss problem for lge o'fits; gd." ♦ € 11.00 2010*

PONTS DE CE, LES see Angers *4G1*

PORDIC see Binic *2E3*

PORGE, LE *7C1* (9km W Coastal) *44.89430, -1.20181* **Camping La Grigne, Ave de l'Océan, 33680 Le Porge [05 56 26 54 88; fax 05 56 26 52 07; campingduporge2@ wanadoo.fr; www.leporge.fr]** Fr Bordeaux ring rd take N215 twd Lacaneau. In 22km at Ste Hélène D5 to Saumos & onto Le Porge. Site on L of rd to Porge-Océan in approx 9km. V lge, mkd pitch, terr, pt sl, shd; wc; chem disp; shwrs inc; el pnts (10A) €5; gas; shop; lndtte; bar; snacks; playgrnd; beach 600m; tennis; games area; TV; dogs €1.90; poss cr; adv bkg; quiet. "Vg facs; great beach; excel cycle path network; red long stay/ low ssn." ♦ 1 Apr-30 Sep. € 22.00 2011*

PORNIC Caravans are prohibited in Pornic. If app fr E on D751 or fr SE on D213 remain on by-pass to N of Pornic & take D86 or D213 exit.

PORNIC *2G3* (700m N Urban) *47.12066, -2.10019* **Camping Bon Accueil, 8 Rue de St Père-en-Retz, 44210 Pornic [06 09 56 84 28 (mob); fax 02 40 82 87 45; bonaccueil44@ wanadoo.fr; www.camping-bon-accueil.fr]** Fr D213 exit Pornic cent N on D86. Site on L in 300m. Sm, hdg/mkd pitch, pt sl, pt shd; wc; chem disp; mv service pnt; baby facs; shwrs inc; el pnts (6A) inc; lndtte (inc dryer); shop 1km; rest, snacks; bar; BBQ; playgrnd; sm htd pool; sand beach 1.5km; entmnt; 50% statics; dogs €0.80; phone; bus adj; poss cr; Eng spkn; adv bkg; quiet; cc acc; CKE/CCI. "Nearest site to Pornic cent; friendly, welcoming owner; some pitches poss tight for lge o'fits; facs old but clean; gd/fair." ♦ 1 Apr-30 Sep. € 19.60 2009*

PORNIC *2G3* (10km N Urban) *47.20315, -2.03716* **Camping du Grand Fay, Rue du Grand Fay, 44320 St Père-en-Retz [02 40 21 72 89; fax 02 40 82 40 27; legrandfay@aol.com; www.camping-grandfay.com]** Fr Mairie in cent St Père-en-Retz take D78 E twds Frossay. After 500m turn R into Rue des Sports, after 200m turn L into Rue du Grand Fay. Site on L in 200m adj sports cent. Med, mkd pitch, pt sl, pt shd; wc (some cont); shwrs inc; el pnts (6A) €3.80; lndry rm; tradsmn; supmkt nrby; playgrnd; htd pool; beach 8km; lake fishing adj; games area; some statics; dogs €2; quiet; red low ssn; CKE/CCI. "Pleasant site nr sandy beaches." ♦ 1 Apr-15 Oct. € 16.00 2010*

FRANCE

PORNIC 2G3 (9km NE Rural) 47.14057, -2.20334 **Camping La Renaudière, 44770 La Plaine-sur-Mer [02 40 21 50 03; fax 02 40 21 09 41; info@campinglarenaudiere.cor; www.campinglarenaudiere.com]** S fr St Nazaire on D213 twd Pornic, turn onto D96 twd Préfailles. Fr Nantes D751 W to Pornic then D13, dir La Plaine-sur-Mer, then Rte de la Prée. Med, pt shd; wc; chem disp; baby facs; shwrs; el pnts (6-10A) €3.80; gas; lndtte; shop adj; rest, snacks; bar; BBQ; playgrnd; htd pool; beach & watersports 2km; entmnt; TV; some statics; dogs €2.50; adv bkg; CKE/CCI. ♦ 1 Apr-15 Sep. € 21.70   2008*

PORNIC 2G3 (2km E Rural) 47.11855, -2.06894 **Camping La Chênaie, 36 Rue du Patisseau, 44210 Pornic [02 40 82 07 31; fax 02 40 27 95 67; acceuil@ campinglachenaie.com; www.campinglachenaie.com]** Fr Nantes on D751 to Pornic, at 1st rndabt turn R. Fr St Nazaire on D213, foll sp Nantes & Le Clion-sur-Mer to avoid Pornic cent. Lge, hdg/mkd pitch, hdstg, pt sl, terr, pt shd; wc; chem disp; mv service pnt; baby facs; shwrs inc; el pnts (10A) €5; lndtte (inc dryer); shop; tradsmn; rest, snacks; bar; BBQ; playgrnd; 2 pools (1 htd, covrd); paddling pool; waterslide; sand beach 2.5km; horseriding; golf; cycle hire; wifi; entmnt; 35% statics; dogs €4; Eng spkn; adv bkg; quiet; ccard acc; red low ssn/long stay; CKE/CCI. "Lge pitches; friendly site; gd walking; gd touring base." ♦ 30 Apr-13 Sep. € 37.00   2011*

PORNIC 2G3 (4km E Rural) 47.11885, -2.07296 **Camping Le Patisseau, 29 Rue du Patisseau, 44210 Pornic [02 40 82 10 39; fax 02 40 82 22 81; contact@lepatisseau. com; www.lepatisseau.com]** Fr N or S on D213, take slip rd D751 Nantes. At rndabt take exit sp to Le Patisseau, foll sp. Med, hdg/mkd pitch, hdstg, pt sl, pt shd; htd wc; chem disp; mv service pnt; baby facs; fam bthrm; sauna; shwrs inc; el pnts (6A) inc; lndtte (inc dryer); shop; tradsmn; rest, snacks; bar; BBQ; playgrnd; 2 htd pools (1 htd, covrd); 2 htd paddling pools (1 covrd); 2 waterslides; sand beach 2.5km; jacuzzi; fitness rm; tennis 1km; cycle hire; games area; games rm; golf 2km; wifi; entmnt; TV; 35% statics; dogs €6; Eng spkn; adv bkg rec high ssn; quiet; ccard acc; red low ssn. "Excel, modern, family site; modern san facs block - lovely shwrs; 1hr walk on path fr back of site to Pornic." ♦ 7 Apr-12 Sep. € 42.00   2011*

See advertisement

PORNIC 2G3 (5km E Coastal) 47.09748, -2.0525 **Airotel Camping Village La Boutinardière, 23 Rue de la Plage, Le Clion-sur-Mer, 44210 Pornic [02 40 82 05 68; fax 02 40 82 49 01; info@laboutinardiere.com; www. camping-boutinardiere.com]** SW fr Nantes on D723; turn L on D751 twd Pornic. Foll dir La Bernerie-en-Retz & site sp. Lge, hdg pitch, pt sl, pt shd; wc; chem disp; mv service pnt; serviced pitches; baby facs; sauna; shwrs inc; el pnts (6-10A) €5-6 (poss rev pol); gas; lndtte; shop; supmkt; rest, snacks; bar; BBQ; playgrnd; 2 pools (1 htd, covrd); paddling pool; waterslide; jacuzzi; sand beach 200m; lake sw 3km; tennis; games rm; golf 5km; cycle hire; entmnt & activities; wifi; TV rm; 15% statics; dogs €5; bus nrby; poss cr; Eng spkn; adv bkg; quiet; red low ssn; ccard acc; red long stay/low ssn; CKE/CCI. "Excel family site; vg pool complex; v busy high ssn; Pornic interesting town." ♦ 3 Apr-27 Sep. € 37.00   2010*

PORNIC 2G3 (6km SE Rural/Coastal) 47.08450, -2.03650 **Camping Les Ecureuils, 24 Ave Gilbert Burlot, 44760 La Bernerie-en-Retz [02 40 82 76 95; fax 02 40 64 79 52; camping.les-ecureuils@wanadoo.fr; www.camping-les-ecureuils.com]** Fr Pornic take D13 S for 5km, then D66 for 1km; site sp. Lge, hdg pitch, pt sl, pt shd; wc; chem disp; baby facs; shwrs inc; el pnts (6-10A) €4; lndtte; shops 500m; snacks; bar; BBQ area; playgrnd; htd pool; paddling pool; waterslide; sand beach 350m; tennis; golf 5km; entmnt; children's club; 30% statics; dogs (up to 10kg only) €4; Eng spkn; adv bkg; quiet; ccard acc; red low ssn/CKE/CCI. "Excel." ♦ 10 Apr-19 Sep. € 30.00   2010*

PORNIC 2G3 (9km SE Coastal) 47.06383, -1.99732 **Camping Le Village de la Mer, 18 Rue de Prigny, 44760 Les Moutiers-en-Retz [02 40 64 65 90; fax 02 51 74 63 17; info@village-mer.fr; www.village-mer.fr]** Site sp on D97 dir Bourgneuf, site is 100m to SE of Les Moutiers-en-Retz. Lge, hdg/mkd pitch, pt shd; mv service pnt; chem disp; baby facs; shwrs inc; el pnts (8A) inc; gas; lndtte; shop adj; snacks; bar; BBQ; playgrnd; htd pool; waterpark; sand beach 400m; watersports; tennis; games rm; entmnt; internet; 50% statics; dogs €3; Eng spkn; adv bkg; red low ssn; ccard acc; CKE/CCI. "Quiet; ideal for families." ♦ 15 Jun-15 Sep. € 29.00   2008*

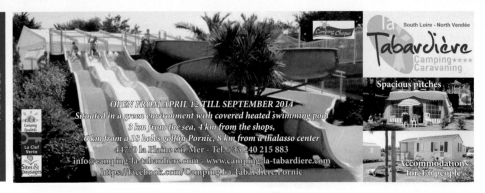

PORNIC 2G3 (2km W Coastal/Urban) 47.11866, -2.13023 **Camping du Golf, 40 Rue de la Renaissance, 44210 Pornic [02 40 82 46 17; fax 02 40 27 92 68; contact@campingdugolf.fr; www.campingdugolf.fr]** Fr Nantes, take D751 W dir Ste Marie. App Pornic, take D213 dir St Nazaire & foll sp Ste Marie & site; well sp. Med, mkd pitch, hdstg, pt shd; wc; chem disp; baby facs; fam bthrm; shwrs inc; el pnts (6-10A) €5-6; gas; lndtte; shop 500m; tradsmn; rest, snacks, bar high ssn; BBQ; playgrnd; htd pool; sand beach 800m; lake sw 200m; tennis; games rm; golf 1km; cycle hire; entmnt; TV; 90% statics; dogs €4; Eng spkn; adv bkg; quiet; red low ssn/long stay; ccard acc; CKE/CCI. "Conv coastal path; twin-axles not acc; ltd space for tourers." ♦ 1 May-30 Sep. € 20.00   2008*

See advertisement on page 334

PORNIC 2G3 (2km W Urban) 47.12219, -2.12780 **Camping Les Coeurés, 28 Rue des Coeurés, 44210 Ste Marie-sur-Mer [06 87 29 33 62 (mob); www.camping-pornic.com/les-coeures]** S fr St Nazaire on D213; turn R bef Pornic onto D286 to Ste Marie; turn R at rndabt onto D13, then 1st L. Site on L in 100m. Med, pt shd; wc (some cont); chem disp (wc); shwrs inc; el pnts (10A) €2.90; shop 300m; sand beach 3km; 10% statics; dogs €0.60; poss cr; quiet. "Excel site; san facs poss inadequate (early ssn 2010)." 1 May-30 Sep. € 11.70   2010*

PORNIC 2G3 (5km W Coastal) 47.11593, -2.15222 **Camping Domaine de la Madrague, Chemin de la Madrague, 44210 Ste Marie-sur-Mer [02 40 82 06 73; fax 02 51 74 11 93; madrague@franceloc.fr; www.madrague.net or www.campings-franceloc.fr]** Fr Pornic on D213 foll sp Ste Marie-sur-Mer. Foll D286 then R on D13. Turn L into Rue du Moulin Neuf, then R into Rue des Bougrenets. Cont on Rue Yves Ponceau, then Chemin de la Madrague to site. Lge, hdg/mkd pitch, pt sl, pt shd; htd wc; chem disp; mv service pnt; baby facs; fam bthrm; shwrs inc; el pnts (10A) €8; gas; lndtte; shop; tradsmn; rest, snacks; bar; playgrnd; htd pool; dir access to sand beach 500m; games area; wifi; entmnt; 80% statics; dogs €5; phone; bus; poss cr; adv bkg; quiet. "Clean, well-organised site; helpful staff; facs stretched high ssn; excel coastal path walks; gd for dog owners; sea views." ♦ 10 Apr-19 Sep. € 29.00   2009*

PORNIC 2G3 (5km W Rural) 47.14079, -2.15306 **FFCC Camping La Tabardière, 44770 La Plaine-sur-Mer [02 40 21 58 83; fax 02 40 21 02 68; info@camping-la-tabardiere.com; www.camping-la-tabardiere.com]** Take D13 NW out of Pornic sp Préfailles & La Plaine-sur-Mer. In about 5.5km turn R (nr water tower). Foll sps to site, about 1km fr main rd. NB C'vans not allowed in Pornic town cent, use by-pass. Lge, hdg/mkd pitch, hdstg, terr, pt shd; htd wc (some cont); chem disp; mv service pnt; baby facs; shwrs inc; el pnts (8A) €5; gas; lndtte (inc dryer); shop & 3km; tradsmn; snacks; bar; BBQ (gas/charcoal); playgrnd; 2 htd pools (1 covrd); paddling pool; waterslides; sand beach 3km; tennis; fishing 3km; horseriding 5km; multi-sport area; games rm; wifi; entmnt; TV rm; 40% statics; dogs €3.50; no c'vans/m'vans over 7.50m high ssn; Eng spkn; adv bkg; quiet; ccard acc; red low ssn; CKE/CCI. "Excel, peaceful site; vg facs for families; v clean unisex san facs; gates clsd 2230-0800." ♦ 7 Apr-23 Sep. € 36.10 (CChq acc) SBS - B31   2012*

See advertisement above

PORNIC 2G3 (8km W Coastal) 47.13261, -2.23138 **Camping Eléovic, Route de la Pointe St Gildas, 44770 Préfailles [02 40 21 61 60; fax 02 40 64 51 95; contact@camping-eleovic.com; www.camping-eleovic.com]** W fr Pornic on D13 to La Plaine-sur-Mer, turn S to Préfailles, cont twds Pointe-St Gildas 1km, L site sp. Med, hdg pitch, terr, pt shd; htd wc; chem disp; mv service pnt; serviced pitches; baby facs; shwrs inc; el pnts (6A) €4.90; lndtte; tradsmn; rest, snacks; bar; BBQ; htd, covrd pool; waterslide; playgrnd; sand beach adj; fishing; watersports; entmnt; TV; 20% statics; dogs €5; phone; Eng spkn; adv bkg; red low ssn/long stay/CKE/CCI; ccard acc. "Dir access to coast path; barrier clsd 2200-1000; vg." ♦ 3 Apr-26 Sep. € 31.10   2010*

PORNIC 2G3 (7km NW Coastal) 47.17614, -2.15462 **Camping Bel Essor, Rue de Tharon, 44730 St Michel-Chef-Chef [02 40 27 85 40 or 02 47 38 89 07 (LS); www.campingbelessor.com]** On D123 fr Pornic dir St Nazaire (Route Bleue) turn L sp Tharon-Plage. After 2nd rndabt take next turn R & keep R. Foll sps St Michel & site. Site on L after supmkt ent. Lge, mkd pitch, pt sl, pt shd; wc (some cont); chem disp (wc); shwrs inc; el pnts (6A) €4.20; lndtte; supmkt opp; tradsmn; snacks; bar; playgrnd; sand beach 400m; some statics; dogs €2; phone adj; poss cr in high ssn; Eng spkn; adv bkg; red low ssn; CKE/CCI. "Vg site; clean facs; helpful owners." ♦ 25 Apr-20 Sep. € 14.60   2009*

PORNIC *2G3* (8km NW Coastal) *47.17305, -2.15833* **Camping Clos Mer et Nature, 103 Rue Tharon, 44730 St Michel-Chef-Chef [02 40 27 85 71; fax 02 40 39 41 89; info@camping-clos-mer-nature.com; www.camping-clos-mer-nature.fr]** Take D213 fr Mindin. After 11km R on D77 sp St Michel-Chef-Chef 2nd R after cent of vill sp Tharon-Plage site on L after 1.5km. Lge, pt sl, pt shd; htd wc; mv service pnt; baby facs; shwrs inc; el pnts (6-10A) €3.50-4; lndtte; shop; supmkt 300m; snacks; playgrnd; pool; waterslide; sand beach 400m; fishing; sailing; windsurfing; tennis; cycle hire; games area; entmnt; some statics; dogs €3; o'night m'van area; adv bkg; quiet; red low ssn. "Lge pitches; vg, modern san facs; gd beaches." ♦ 1 Apr-17 Oct. € 20.00   2010*

PORNIC *2G3* (8km NW Coastal) *47.16007, -2.16274* **Camping Le Vieux Château, Ave du Vieux-Tharon, 44730 Tharon-Plage [02 40 27 83 47 or 06 23 46 06 60 (mob); camping.duvieuxchateau@wanadoo.fr; www.camping-duvieuxchateau.com]** Fr Pornic dir St Nazaire, turn W twd Tharon-Plage, site sp. Med, hdg/mkd pitch, terr, pt shd; wc; chem disp; shwrs inc; el pnts (6A) €4; lndtte; shop; tradsmn; snacks; bar; BBQ; playgrnd; htd pool; paddling pool; sand beach 500m; playgrnd; games rm; many statics; dogs €2; poss cr; Eng spkn; adv bkg; quiet; ccard acc; red long stay; CKE/CCI. ♦ 1 May-15 Sep. € 18.50   2009*

"We must tell The Club about that great site we found"

Get your site reports in by mid-August and we'll do our best to get your updates into the next edition of Caravan Europe.

PORNIC *2G3* (10km NW Coastal) *47.15076, -2.19481* **Camping Bernier, 56 Rue de la Cormorane, 44770 La Plaine-sur-Mer [02 40 21 04 31 or 06 63 82 39 91 (mob); fax 02 40 21 08 12; www.camping-lebernier.com]** S fr St Nazaire bdge on D213 twd Pornic, turn R, S of St Michel-Chef-Chef on D96. Cont to junc, turn R, cont to x-rd, turn L. In 500m on R. Or thro La Plaine-sur-Mer on D13, turn R on leaving vill past g'ge twd Port Giraud. Site on L in 1km. Med, some hdg pitch, pt shd; wc; chem disp; some serviced pitches; shwrs inc; el pnts (6A) €3.60; lndtte; shop 300m; snacks; playgrnd; htd pool; sand beach 600m; some statics; dogs €2.80; adv bkg; quiet; 40-50% red low ssn; 5% red CKE/CCI. "Excel family site site nr gd beaches." ♦ 1 May-30 Sep. € 19.10   2009*

PORNICHET *2G3* (2km E Urban/Coastal) *47.25280, -2.31910* **Camping du Bugeau, 33 Ave des Loriettes, 44380 Pornichet [02 40 61 02 02 or 02 40 61 15 44 (LS); fax 02 40 61 22 75; info@campingdubugeau.com; www.campingdubugeau.com]** W fr St Nazaire on D92 then L at rndabt at St Marguerite by car showrm; site sp 2nd L, site 500m on L. Med, hdg/mkd pitch, pt shd; htd wc; chem disp; mv service pnt; shwrs inc; el pnts (5A) €4.50; lndtte; shop & 500m; tradsmn; snacks; BBQ; playgrnd; htd, covrd pool; sand beach & watersports 500m; tennis 500m; cycle hire 1km; TV; 30% statics; dogs €1; Eng spkn; adv bkg; ccard acc; red low ssn. "Gd touring site." ♦ 10 Apr-26 Sep. € 25.70   2010*

PORNICHET *2G3* (4km E Rural) *47.26912, -2.29401* **Camping au Repos des Forges, 98 Route de la Villès-Blaise, 44380 Pornichet [02 40 61 18 84; fax 02 40 60 11 84; camping@campinglesforges.com; www.campinglesforges.com]** To N of D92 halfway bet St Nazaire & Pornichet. Accessible also fr N171; sp. Med, pt sl, pt shd; wc; chem disp; shwrs inc; el pnts (6-10A) €4-5; gas; lndtte; shop in ssn; snacks; playgrnd; htd pool; beach 3km; games area; games rm; TV rm; 70% statics; dogs €4; Eng spkn; adv bkg; quiet; CKE/CCI. "Friendly recep; barrier clsd 2300-0700; excel san facs." ♦ 1 Jul-31 Aug. € 22.00   2008*

PORT DES BARQUES see Rochefort *7B1*

PORT EN BESSIN HUPPAIN *3D1* (600m W Coastal) *49.34693, -0.77095* **Camping Port'land, Chemin du Sémaphore, 14520 Port-en-Bessin [02 31 51 07 06; fax 02 31 51 76 49; campingportland@wanadoo.fr; www.camping-portland.com]** Site sp fr D514 W of Port-en-Bessin. Lge, hdg/mkd pitch, hdstg, pt shd; htd wc; chem disp; mv service pnt; shwrs inc; el pnts (6-10A) €5; gas 1km; lndtte; shop; tradsmn; rest, snacks; bar; BBQ; playgrnd; htd, covrd pool; waterslide; paddling pool; sand beach 4km; tennis 800m; games area; games rm; wifi; entmnt; TV; 30% statics; dogs €3; Eng spkn; adv bkg; ccard acc; red long stay/low ssn; CKE/CCI. "Pleasant site; friendly, helpful staff; vg san facs; extra charge lger pitches; excel touring base for landing beaches etc." ♦ 1 Apr-2 Nov. € 35.00 SBS - N09   2013*

PORT LA NOUVELLE *10G1* (2km S Coastal) *42.99817, 3.04825* **Camping Côte Vermeille, Chemin des Vignes, 11210 Port-la-Nouvelle [04 68 48 05 80; fax 04 68 27 53 03; infos@camping-cote-vermeille.com; www.campings-franceloc.fr]** Fr N exit A9 junc 39 onto D6139 then D6009 twd La Palme. In 9km turn L onto D709, site in 6km. V lge, mkd pitch, pt shd; wc; chem disp; mv service pnt; el pnts (6A) €4; lndtte; shop; supmkt 3km; rest, snacks; bar; playgrnd; pool; paddling pool; waterslide; sand beach 200m; wifi; entmnt; TV; some statics; adv bkg; CKE/CCI. "Superb pool complex." ♦ 4 Apr-27 Sep. € 26.00   2009*

PORT LE GRAND see Abbeville *3B3*

PORT SUR SAONE *6F2* (800m S Rural) *47.68056, 6.03937* **Camp Municipal Parc de la Maladière, 70170 Port-sur-Saône [03 84 78 18 00 (Mairie); fax 03 84 78 18 09; serviceculturel@gmail.com; www.ville-port-sur-saone.fr]** Take D619 SE fr Langres or NW fr Vesoul. Site sp in vill bet rv & canal off D6 at municipal bathing area. Med, hdg pitch, pt shd; wc (mainly cont); own san facs; chem disp; shwrs inc; el pnts (6A) €3 (poss rev pol); lndtte; shops 800m; tradsmn high ssn; rest, bar adj; playgrnd; pool adj; fishing; tennis; adv bkg; ccard acc; quiet; CKE/CCI. "Peaceful site on island; rvside cycle path; gd walks; gd sh stay/NH" ♦ ltd 15 May-15 Sep. € 10.00   2013*

⊞ **PORT VENDRES** *10G1* (500m W Urban) *42.51775, 3.11314* **Aire Communale des Tamarins, Route de la Jetée, 66660 Port-Vendres [04 68 82 07 54]** Fr D914 at Port-Vendres at Banyuls side of town turn N on D86B sp Port de Commerce & Aire de Camping-Cars. Foll sp to site on R in 700m. Sm, hdstg, pt shd; chem disp; mv service pnt; wc (pt cont); own san; no el pnts (2009); gas 1km; shop 1km; rest 500m; snacks, bar 1km; playgrnd adj; shgl beach 100m; red low ssn. "NH, m'vans only; walking dist rlwy stn; poss cr even low ssn; a bit run down (Jun 2009)." € 8.40   2009*

PORTIRAGNES PLAGE *10F1* (Coastal) *43.28003, 3.36396* **Camping Les Sablons, Plage-Est, 34420 Portiragnes-Plage [04 67 90 90 55; fax 04 67 90 82 91; les.sablons@wanadoo.fr; www.les-sablons.com]** Fr A9 exit Béziers Est junc 35 onto N112. Then take D37 S to Portiragnes-Plage & foll sp. V lge, mkd pitch, shd; wc; chem disp; mv service pnt; baby facs; shwrs incl; el pnts (6A) incl; gas; lndtte; shop; rest, snacks; bar; BBQ; playgrnd; 2 htd pools; waterslide; sand beach 4km; diving; boating; fishing; tennis; games area; cycle hire; entmnt; 50% statics; dogs €4; phone; poss cr; Eng spkn; adv bkg; ccard acc; quiet. "Gd site on beach; modern san facs; nightly disco but quiet after midnight." ♦ ltd 1 Apr-30 Sep. € 46.00   2012*

See advertisement above

PORTIRAGNES PLAGE *10F1* (2km NE Coastal) *43.29138, 3.37333* **Camping Les Mimosas, Port Cassafières, 34420 Portiragnes-Plage [04 67 90 92 92; fax 04 67 90 85 39; info@mimosas.fr or les.mimosas.portiragnes@wanadoo.fr; www.mimosas.com]** Exit A9 junc 35 Béziers Est & take N112 sp Vias, Agde. After 3km at rndabt foll sp Portiragnes & cont along side of Canal du Midi. Cross canal, site sp. Lge, mkd pitch, hdstg, pt shd; wc; chem disp; mv service pnt; private san facs avail; baby facs; sauna; shwrs inc; el pnts (6-10A) €4; gas; lndtte (inc dryer); shop; supmkt; tradsmn; rest, snacks; bar; BBQ (gas); playgrnd; pools; paddling pool; waterslides; jacuzzi; sand beach 1km; cycle hire; games area; games rm; fitness rm; internet; entmnt; 50% statics; dogs €5.50; Eng spkn; adv bkg; quiet; ccard acc; red low ssn; CKE/CCI. "Excel touring base in interesting area; friendly welcome; superb water park; 4 star site; gd for families." ♦ 26 May-5 Sep. € 42.00   2011*

See advertisement opposite

POUANCE *2F4* (1.5km N Rural) *47.74850, -1.17841* **Camp Muncipal La Roche Martin, 23 Rue des Etangs, 49420 Pouancé [02 41 92 43 97 or 02 41 92 41 08 (Mairie); fax 02 41 92 62 30]** Take D6 (sp St Aignan) N fr town. After level x-ing turn L onto D72 (sp La Guerche-de-Bretagne). In 300m, site on L. Sm, mkd pitch, pt terr, pt sl; wc; mv service pnt; shwrs; el pnts (10A); gas; shops 1km; rest, bar 100m; playgrnd; direct access to lake; watersports; tennis; games area; tennis; poss cr; adv bkg. "Well-kept, friendly site o'looking lge lake; noise fr rd & sailing school." 1 Apr-30 Sep.   2012*

FRANCE

POUGUES LES EAUX *4H4* (1km N Urban) *47.08430, 3.09349*
Camp Municipal Les Chanternes, Ave du Paris, 58320 Pougues-les-Eaux [03 86 68 86 18 or 03 86 37 32 91; accueil@ot-pougueseseaux.fr; www.ot-pougueseseaux.fr] On E side of D907 in Pougues-les-Eaux at rear of open-air pool & thro same ent. Med, mkd pitch, pt shd; htd wc (some cont); mv service pnt; shwrs inc; el pnts; shops, rest & snacks in vill; pool adj; adv bkg; rd & rlwy noise; CKE/CCI. 1 Jun-30 Sep. 2009*

POUILLY SUR LOIRE *4G3* (1km N Rural) *47.28742, 2.94427*
Camp Municipal Le Malaga, Rue des Champs-sur-Loire, Les Loges, 58150 Pouilly-sur-Loire [tel/fax 03 86 39 14 54 or 03 86 58 74 38 (LS); www.ot-pouillysurloire.fr] Fr S exit A77 junc 26 onto D28a, turn L onto D59/D4289 W, bef rv bdge turn R, site in 1km on rv. Fr N on ent vill turn R at site sp into narr rd. Turn R along rv as above. Med, pt shd; wc; chem disp; shwrs inc; el pnts (10A) inc (poss long lead req & poss rev pol); lndry rm; shop & 1km; tradsmn; snacks; bar; BBQ; playgrnd; dogs €1; phone; no twin-axles or o'fits over 5m; poss cr; Eng spkn; quiet, but some rlwy noise & poss noisy w/end. "Beautifully kept site on banks of Loire; busy NH; spacious but uneven pitches; mixed reports san facs; poss youth groups; beautiful area; wine tasting nrby; poss mosquitoes; excel." ♦ 1 Jun-10 Sep. €11.60 2011*

POULDU, LE *2F2* (300m N Urban/Coastal) *47.76850, -3.54540* Camping Les Embruns, 2 Rue du Philosophe Alain, Clohars-Carnoët, 29360 Le Pouldu [02 98 39 91 07; fax 02 98 39 97 87; camping-les-embruns@wanadoo.fr; www.camping-les-embruns.com] Exit N165 dir Quimperlé Cent, onto D16 to Clohars-Carnoët. Cont on D16/D24/D1214 to Le Pouldu. Site on R on ent 1-way traff system. Site sp. Lge, hdg/mkd pitch, hdstg, terr, pt shd; htd wc; chem disp; mv service pnt; all serviced pitches; baby facs; fam bthrm; shwrs inc; el pnts (10A) inc; gas; lndtte (inc dryer); shop; tradsmn; rest, snacks; bar; BBQ; playgrnd; htd, covrd pool; paddling pool; sand beach 250m; watersports; tennis 200m; fishing; cycle hire; horseriding nr; children's farm; tennis; games area; games rm; wifi; TV rm; 40% statics; dogs €2.70; bus nrby; Eng spkn; adv bkg; quiet; ccard acc; red low ssn; CKE/CCI. "Excel family-run site in great location; luxury pitches extra charge; friendly, helpful owners; vg clean san facs; superb facs; gd walking along coastal paths; cycle rtes; great for dogs; town was home of Paul Gauguin; highly rec." ♦ 6 Apr-22 Sep. €31.50 2011*

See advertisement on next page

POULDU, LE *2F2* (2km N Rural) *47.78669, -3.55110*
Camping du Quinquis, 29360 Le Pouldu [02 98 39 92 40; fax 02 98 39 96 56; andrew.munro@clara.co.uk; www.campingquinquis.com] On D16 fr Quimperlé, 2km S of x-rds with D224. Or fr N165 exit Guidel junc 45; foll sps to Le Pouldu & zoo adj to site. Med, hdg pitch, pt sl, pt shd; wc; shwrs; el pnts (10A) inc; gas; lndtte; sm shop; snacks; bar; playgrnd; pool & paddling pool; sand beach 2km; tennis; cycle hire; games rm; entmnt; TV; 80% statics; dogs; phone; poss cr; quiet; red low ssn. "Vg, peaceful, British-owned site." ♦ 23 May-5 Sep. €21.00 2009*

POULDU, LE *2F2* (2.5km N Coastal) FFCC Camping de Croas An Ter, Quelvez, Le Pouldu, 29360 Clohars-Carnoët [02 98 39 94 19 or 06 24 88 68 20 (mob); campingcroasanter@orange.fr; www.campingcroasanter.com] On D49 fr Quimperlé to Le Pouldu. Site on L 3km after junc with D224. Med, pt sl, pt shd; wc; chem disp; mv service pnt; shwrs; el pnts (6A) €3.20; lndtte; shop & rest 1.5km; snacks & bar 200m; playgrnd; beach 1.5km; internet; dogs; bus 1.5km; Eng spkn; quiet; ccard acc; CKE/CCI. "Lge pitches; friendly owners; gd bathing & sailing; walks in wood & rv fr site; Tues mkt; vg." ♦ ltd 1 Jun-15 Sep. €11.80 2011*

POULDU, LE *2F2* (500m NE Rural) *47.77274, -3.54433*
Camping Keranquernat, 29360 Keranquernat [02 98 39 92 32; fax 02 98 39 99 84; camping.keranquernat@wanadoo.fr; www.camping-keranquernat.com] Fr Quimperlé D16 to Clohars-Carnoët, then D24 to Le Pouldu - twd port; turn R at x-rds nr Ar Men Résidence; site ent immed on R. Fr S on N165 exit junc 45 sp Guidel; in 1km turn W onto D162/D224, then foll sp Le Pouldu; site sp at town ent. Med, hdg/mkd pitch, pt shd; wc (some cont); chem disp; baby facs; shwrs; el pnts (3-5A) €3.50; lndtte; shops 300m; tradsmn; rest & bar nrby; BBQ; playgrnd; htd pool; paddling pool; sand beach 700m; fishing; sailing; tennis; cycle hire; games rm; TV; dogs €0.50; adv bkg; quiet; red low ssn; CKE/CCI. "Beautifully-kept, pretty site; welcoming owners; highly rec." 1 May-6 Sep. €16.50 2008*

POULDU, LE *2F2* (2km E Rural/Coastal) *47.77466, -3.50616*
Camping Les Jardins de Kergal, Route des Plages, 56520 Guidel [02 97 05 98 18; fax 02 97 32 88 27; jardins.kergal@wanadoo.fr; www.camping-lorient.com] Fr N165 Brest-Nantes take Guidel exit; thro Guidel & onto Guidel-Plages; camp sp in 1km. Lge, hdg/mkd pitch, hdstg, pt sl, pt shd; wc; chem disp; baby facs; shwrs inc; el pnts (10A) inc; lndtte; gas; shops 2km; tradsmn high ssn; rest, snacks, bar high ssn; BBQ; playgrnd; 2 pools (1 covrd); waterslide; sand beach 1.5km; tennis; entmnt; cycle hire; games area; games rm; wifi; TV; 75% statics; dogs €3; adv bkg; quiet but poss noisy youth groups high ssn; red low ssn; CKE/CCI. "Friendly, helpful, welcoming staff; well-run, peaceful site; conv beaches & touring" ♦ 29 Mar-30 Sep. € 41.00   2013*

POULE LES ECHARMEAUX *9A2* (1.5km W Rural) *46.15028, 4.45419* **Camp Municipal Les Echarmeaux, 69870 Poule-les-Echarmeaux [06 89 90 33 64 (mob) or 06 79 30 46 62; fax 04 74 03 68 71; www.poulelesecharmeaux.eu]** Turn E off D385 to Poule-Echarmeaux, site sp. Sm, hdg pitch, terr, pt shd; wc; shwrs inc; el pnts inc; shop 500m; playgrnd; adv bkg. "Beautifully situated site adj lake; nr Beaujolais wine area; excel sh stay; marked walks" 1 May-30 Sep. € 10.80   2013*

POULIGUEN, LE *2G3* (Urban/Coastal) *47.27130, -2.43012*
Camp Municipal du Clein, Ave de Kerdun, 44510 Le Pouliguen [02 40 42 43 99 or 02 40 15 08 08 (Mairie); fax 02 40 15 14 60; leclein@mairie-lepouliguen.fr] Fr La Baule (W end) take coast rd to Le Pouliguen & foll sps. Lge, pt shd; wc; shwrs; el pnts (6-10A) €3-3.50; playgrnd; sand beach, fishing, sailing 500m; windsurfing 1.50m; dogs €2; poss cr; red low ssn. Easter-15 Sep. € 12.00   2008*

POULIGUEN, LE *2G3* (SW Urban/Coastal) *47.27183, -2.44025* **Camp Municipal Les Mouettes, 45 Blvd de l'Atlantique, 44510 Le Pouliguen [tel/fax 02 40 42 43 98 or 06 37 09 21 66 (mob); lesmouettes@mairie-lepouliguen.fr]** Fr La Boule (W end) take coast rd to Le Pouliguen & foll sps to site on D45. Lge, mkd pitch, unshd; htd wc; baby facs; mv service pnt; shwrs; el pnts (6A) €3; lndtte; shop, supmkt 200m; rest, snacks; bar; playgrnd; beach 800m; fishing; sailing; cycle hire 200m; games area; entmnt; TV; dogs €2; no adv bkg. "Poss resident workers." 1 Apr-15 Oct. € 12.80   2008*

POULLAN SUR MER see Douarnenez *2E2*

POURVILLE SUR MER see Dieppe *3C2*

PRADEAUX, LES see Issoire *9B1*

⊞ **PRADES** *8G4* (500m N Urban) *42.62141, 2.42272* **Camp Municipal Plaine St Martin, Chemin du Gaz, 66500 Prades [04 68 96 29 83 or 06 86 38 54 17 (mob); prades.conflent@wanadoo.fr; www.leconflent.net/camping]** Site sp on ent town on N116 fr both dirs. (Or foll sp 'Piscine' - site 200m fr municipal sw pool). Med, hdg/mkd pitch, pt sl, shd; wc (some cont); chem disp; 50% serviced pitches; shwrs inc; el pnts (6-10A) €3.50; gas 500m; lndtte; shop, rest, snacks & bar 500m; playgrnd; htd, covrd pool nrby; fishing; 30% statics; dogs €1.45; phone; poss cr; adv bkg; quiet; ccard acc; CKE/CCI. "Pleasant site with many trees; lge pitches; facs old but clean; poss unkempt low ssn; excel touring base; music festival in Jul; mkt Tues; NH." € 11.50   2011*

PRADES *8G4* (10km NE Urban) *42.64269, 2.53367* **Camp Municipal Les Escoumes, Rue des Escoumes, 66320 Vinça [04 68 05 84 78 or 06 09 01 00 40 (mob); campinglesescoumes@orange.fr; www.ville-vinca.fr]** Fr Perpignan take N116 W twd Andorra. 10km E of Prades in vill of Vinça take 1st L foll camp sps to site (400m). Vinca 32km W of Perpignan. Med, mkd pitch, pt sl, pt shd; wc; chem disp; mv service pnt; shwrs inc; el pnts (6-10A) €3; gas; lndtte (inc dryer); shops 1km; supmkt at Prades; rest, bar in vill; private sand beach & lake sw; fishing; cycle hire; 20% statics; dogs €3.50; poss cr; Eng spkn; quiet. "Beautiful, quiet site; helpful staff." ♦ ltd 1 Apr-31 Oct. € 12.80   2011*

PRADES *8G4* (7km E Rural) *42.61722, 2.50111* **Camping Le Canigou, 66320 Espira-de-Conflent [04 68 05 85 40; fax 04 68 05 86 20; canigou@yahoo.com; www.canigou-espira.com]** On N116 Andorra-Perpignan, 2km after Marquixanes, R at sm site sp also sp 'Espira-de-Conflent'. Or, fr Perpignan on N116, turn L 7km bef Prades onto D25 & foll sp for 3.5km. Med, hdg/mkd pitch, pl sl, terr, shd; wc; chem disp; mv service pnt; shwrs; el pnts (6A) inc; lndtte; shop; tradsmn; rest, snacks; bar; playgrnd; rv pool; lake & watersports 5km; 5% statics; dogs €1.50; Eng spkn; adv bkg; quiet; red long stay/low ssn; ccard acc; CKE/CCI. "Beautiful rvside site; youth groups in summer; some noise; narr site rds not rec for lge o'fits." ♦ ltd 1 Feb-31 Oct. € 23.90   2009*

PRADES 8G4 (2km SW Rural) 42.60308, 2.39841 **Camping Bellevue, 18 Rue Bellevue, 66500 Ria-Sirach [tel/fax 04 68 96 48 96; camping.bellevue@free.fr; www.camping-bellevue-riasirach.com]** W on N116 fr Perpignan, thro Prades. In 1km at far edge of vill of Ria, turn L on D26A & foll sps to site. Access steep. Med, mkd pitch, pt sl, terr, shd; wc; baby facs; shwrs inc; el pnts (3-6A) €5.90-6.80; lndtte; shop 500m; bar; playgrnd; rv sw & fishing 500m; dogs €1; adv bkg; quiet; red CKE/CCI. "Peaceful with gd views." ♦ 1 Apr-30 Sep. € 10.00   2009*

PRADES 8G4 (5km W Rural) 42.58019, 2.35057 **Camping Mas de Lastourg, Serdinya, 66500 Villefranche-de-Conflent [04 68 05 35 25; maslastourg@aol.com; www.camping-lastourg.com]** W fr Prades on N116. Site on L of main rd 2km after Villefranche, turn L 100m after start of dual c'way. Med, hdg/mkd pitch, pt shd; wc; chem disp (wc); baby facs; shwrs inc; el pnts (6-10A) €4; lndtte; sm shop & 2km; tradsmn; rest, snacks; bar; BBQ; playgrnd; sm pool; a few statics; dogs €1; phone; poss cr; Eng spkn; adv bkg; quiet but some rd/rlwy noise; ccard acc; red low ssn; CKE/CCI. "Lovely site; helpful owners; easy access; gd pitches; conv 'Little Yellow Train'; phone ahead to check open low ssn; excel." ♦ 1 Apr-30 Sep. € 19.00   2011*

PRALOGNAN LA VANOISE 9B4 (500m S Rural) 45.37692, 6.72375 **Camp Municipal Le Chamois, Route de l'Isertan, 73710 Pralognan-la-Vanoise [04 79 08 71 54; fax 04 79 08 78 77; camping@pralognan.com; www.pralognan.com]** Fr Moûtiers take D915 to Pralognan. Pass under concrete bdge, turn SW & foll camping sp; keep L past recep of bigger Iseran site. Site on rvside. Lge, mkd pitch, terr, pt sl, unshd; htd wc (some cont); chem disp (wc); shwrs inc; el pnts (2-10A) €2.30-3.90; lndtte; shops 500m; htd pool 300m; rv fishing adj; dogs; poss cr; quiet. "Peaceful site in beautiful area; vg walks; friendly staff; cable car up mountain." 5 Jun-5 Sep.   2009*

PRALOGNAN LA VANOISE 9B4 (500m S Rural) 45.37667, 6.72236 **Camping Le Parc Isertan, Route de l'Isertan, 73710 Pralognan-la-Vanoise [04 79 08 75 24; fax 04 79 08 76 13; camping@camping-isertan.com; www.camping-isertan.com]** Fr Moûtiers, take D915 E to Pralognan. Pass under concrete bdge & foll camping sp. Site behind pool adj municipal site. Lge, hdstg, terr, pt shd; htd wc; chem disp; mv service pnt; baby facs; shwrs inc; el pnts (2-10A) €4-6.50; gas 500m; tradsmn; shop 500m; rest, snacks; bar; BBQ; playgrnd; drying rm & ski boot rm; htd, covrd pool & sports cent adj; horseriding 500m; some statics; dogs €1.50; phone; poss cr; Eng spkn; adv bkg; quiet; ccard acc; red low ssn/CKE/CCI. "Peaceful site with superb scenery; recep in hotel on site; vg walking; cable car in vill; cross country skiing at side of site; Free naveltte to ski lift; new spa facs (2012); excel site" ♦ 18 Dec-18 Apr & 21 May-24 Sep. € 23.90   2012*

PRATS DE CARLUX see Sarlat la Canéda 7C3

PRATS DE MOLLO LA PRESTE 8H4 (11km E Rural) 42.38892, 2.60620 **Camp Municipal Verte Rive, Chemin de l'Ile, 66260 St Laurent-de-Cerdans [04 68 39 54 64 or 04 68 39 50 04 (Mairie); fax 04 68 39 59 59; contact@ville-saint-laurent-de-cerdans.fr; www.ville-saint-laurent-de-cerdans.fr]** Fr Le Boulou, take D115 twd Prats-de-Mollo, turn L on D3 twd St Laurent. Site 4km fr Spanish border. Med, mkd pitch, pt sl, pt shd; htd wc; shwrs inc; el pnts (5A) €2.75; lndtte; shop 1.5km; BBQ; playgrnd; htd pool adj; some statics; poss cr; adv bkg; CKE/CCI. "Conv NH." ♦ 1 Jun-31 Oct. € 7.80   2010*

PRATS DE MOLLO LA PRESTE 8H4 (12km E Rural) 42.41200, 2.61800 **Camping Domaine Le Clols (Naturist), 66260 St Laurent-de-Cerdans [04 68 39 51 68; info@leclols.com; www.leclols.com]** Fr A9 at Le Boulou take D115 dir Prats-de-Mollo; 6km before Arles-sur-Tech take D3 on L sp St Laurent-de-Cerdans; at La Forge-del-Mitg turn sharp L sp Le Clols; site on R in 3km (narr, winding rd). Sm, pt sl, pt shd; wc (some cont); chem disp (wc); shwrs inc; el pnts (5-10A) €3-3.95; gas; lndtte; shop; snacks; playgrnd; pool; TV; some statics; dogs €2; adv bkg; quiet; red 10+ days; CKE/CCI. "Gd views; friendly British owners; gd walks fr site" ♦ ltd 1 May-30 Sep. € 24.00   2013*

"I need an on-site restaurant"

We do our best to make sure site information is correct, but it is always best to check any must-have facilities are still available or will be open during your visit.

PRE EN PAIL 4E1 (200m N Urban) 48.46094, -0.20140 **Camp Municipal Alain Gerbault, Rue des Troënes, 53140 Pré-en-Pail [02 43 03 04 28; camping.preenpail@wanadoo.fr]** Fr E on N12, turn R at major rndabt (sp D176 Domfront). Turn R twd sports cent & well sp fr there on N edge of vill. Sm, mkd pitch, pt shd; wc (some cont); chem disp; shwrs inc; el pnts (16A); shop 250m; rest, snacks; bar; playgrnd; htd pool adj; dogs €1.10; phone; CKE/CCI. "Pleasant wooded region; poss mkt traders on site; OK as touring base." 1 Apr-30 Sep.   2009*

PRECY SOUS THIL 6G1 (W Rural) 47.38721, 4.30645 **Camp Municipal du Parc de l'Hôtel de Ville, 17 Rue de l'Hôtel de Ville, 21390 Précy-sous-Thil [03 80 64 57 18 (Mairie); fax 03 80 64 43 37; precysousthil@orange.fr; www.cotedor-tourisme.com]** Exit A6 at junc 23 Bierre-lès-Semur exit onto D980 to Précy. Site sp in vill. Sm, pt sl, pt shd; wc; shwrs inc; el pnts (6A) inc; lndtte; shops 150m; rest & bar 300m; playgrnd; rv adj; tennis nr; horseriding; entmnt; TV; some statics; dogs €1.30; quiet. "In grnds of Town Hall; warden calls 1900-2100; mostly sl pitches; conv NH on way S" Easter-1 Nov. € 12.00   2013*

PREFAILLES see Pornic 2G3

PREIXAN see Carcassonne 8F4

PREMEAUX PRISSEY see Nuits St Georges *6G1*

PREMERY *4G4* (500m NW) *47.17804, 3.33692* **Camp Municipal Le Plan D'eau (Les Prés de la Ville), 58700 Prémery [03 86 37 99 42 or 03 86 68 12 40 (Mairie); fax 03 86 37 98 72; mairie-premery@wanadoo.fr; www. mairie-premery.fr]** N fr Nevers on D977 to Prémery; turn R after 2nd rndabt. Site sp on D977. Med, pt shd; wc (some cont); chem disp (wc); shwrs inc; el pnts (8-10A) €1-1.80; shops 500m; lake & rv adj with sand beach, sw, fishing & boating; tennis adj; adv bkg; quiet; 10% red 10+ days. "Lovely, well-run lakeside site in town park; excel facs; popular NH; nice walk to interesting town; poss market traders; excel value." ♦ 1 May-30 Sep. € 14.50   2013*

PREMIAN see St Pons de Thomières *8F4*

PRESILLY see St Julien en Genevois *9A3*

⊞ **PRESSAC** *7A3* (6km SW Rural) *46.09696, 0.48081* **Camping Rural des Marronniers, La Bussière, 16490 Pleuville [05 45 31 03 45; ssmpooleman1@aliceadsl.fr; www.conkertreefarmcampsite.bravehost.com]** S fr Poitiers on D741 to Pressac; turn R onto D34 to Pleuville then turn onto D30 dir Charroux, site on L in 1.5km - look for sp La Bussière. Sm, pt sl, pt shd; htd wc; chem disp; fam bathrm; shwrs inc; el pnts (10A) €2.50; gas; lndtte; shop 1km; rest 8km; snacks; bar 1km; BBQ; playgrnd; pool; games rm; dogs; adv bkg; quiet. "British-owned, CL-type farm site; open field - chickens & ducks roaming; gd touring base; excel." ♦ ltd € 8.00   2010*

PRESSIGNAC see Rochechouart *7B3*

PREUILLY see Mehun sur Yevre *4H3*

PREUILLY SUR CLAISE *4H2* (SW Urban) *46.85113, 0.92892* **Camp Municipal Bord de Claise, 37290 Preuilly-sur-Claise [02 47 94 50 04 (Mairie); fax 02 47 94 63 26]** Fr E on D725 descend hill into vill. At T-junc opp town hall turn R & in 30m take 2nd L sp Camping & Piscine - poss diff turn long o'fits due narr rd. Site adj pool in 300m. Sm, hdg pitch, pt shd; wc; chem disp (wc); shwrs inc; el pnts (6A) €3.20; lndtte; shop, rest, bar in vill; BBQ; playgrnd; htd pool adj; rv fishing adj; poss cr; quiet. "No twin-axles allowed." 1 May-15 Sep. € 7.50   2008*

PRIVAS *9D2* (8km NE Rural) *44.75721, 4.71298* **Camping L'Albanou, Quartier Pampelonne, 07000 St Julien-en-St Alban [04 75 66 00 97; camping.albanou@wanadoo.fr; www.camping-albanou.com]** Fr A7 exit junc 16 at Loriol dir Le Pouzin, go thro Le Pouzin on D104 dir Privas/Aubenas. Site in 6km on L just bef vill of St Julien-en-St Alban. Med, hdg/ mkd pitch, pt sl, pt shd; wc; chem disp; mv service pnt; baby facs; shwrs inc; el pnts (6A) €3.50; lndtte; shops 1km; tradsmn; snacks; playgrnd; pool; rv fishing adj; wifi; some statics; dogs €2; Eng spkn; adv bkg (poss not by phone); quiet; red low ssn; CKE/CCI. "Superb, well-run, clean site by rv; gd sized pitches; friendly, helpful owners; super pool; sh walk to sm town; rec arr bef 1500 high ssn; a great site." 22 Apr-30 Sep. € 20.00   2011*

PRIVAS *9D2* (3km E Rural) *44.73615, 4.62390* **Camping Le Moulin d'Onclaire, 07000 Coux [04 75 64 51 98; moulin@ onclaire.com; www.onclaire.com]** Fr Privas take D104 E twds Le Pouzin, sp Valence. Site on R after passing narr bdge to Coux. Sm, pt shd; wc; shwrs inc; el pnts (5A) €3; shop; snacks; rest & bar adj; BBQ; pool 3km; tennis; some statics; dogs €2; Eng spkn; adv bkg; CKE/CCI. "NH only." 1 Apr-6 Oct. € 13.00   2008*

PRIVAS *9D2* (1.5km S Urban) *44.72668, 4.59730* **Kawan Village Ardèche Camping, Blvd de Paste, Quartier Ouvèze, 07000 Privas [04 75 64 05 80; fax 04 75 64 59 68; jcray@wanadoo.fr; www.ardechecamping.fr]** Exit A7 junc 16 dir Privas. App Privas cross rv bdge & at rndabt take 2nd exit. Site ent opp supmkt, sp. Lge, mkd pitch, pt sl, pt shd; wc (mainly cont); chem disp; mv service pnt; baby facs; fam bthrm; shwrs inc; el pnts (10A) inc; lndtte; shops adj; supmkt 100m; rest, snacks; bar; BBQ; playgrnd; htd pool; paddling pool; rv fishing; tennis adj; wifi; entmnt; TV rm; 80% statics; dogs €3.30; Eng spkn; adv bkg; quiet, but some rd noise fr D2; ccard acc; red low ssn/long stay; CKE/CCI. "Very gd friendly site with English speaking owners. gd restaurant and shady pitches. Interesting area to visit." ♦ 15 Apr-28 Sep. € 31.00 (CChq acc)   2013*

PROISSANS see Sarlat la Canéda *7C3*

PRUNIERES see Chorges *9D3*

PUGET SUR ARGENS see Fréjus *10F4*

PUGET THENIERS *10E4* (2km NW Rural) *43.95801, 6.85980* **Camping L'Origan (Naturist), 2160 Route de Savé, 06260 Puget-Théniers [04 93 05 06 00; fax 04 93 05 09 34; origan@wanadoo.fr; www.origan-village.com]** On N202 fr Entrevaux (dir Nice) at Puget-Théniers, immed turn L at rlwy x-ing (sp), site approx 1km up track. Med, hdg/mkd pitch, hdstg, pt sl, terr, pt shd; htd wc; sauna; shwrs inc; el pnts (6A) €4; gas 2km; lndtte; shop; tradsmn; rest, snacks; bar; BBQ; playgrnd; htd pool; paddling pool; waterslide; fishing; tennis; archery; wifi; TV rm; 50% statics; dogs €2.50; phone; train to Nice; adv bkg; Eng spkn; ccard acc; red low ssn; INF card. "Sm pitches not suitable o'fits over 6m; hilly site but pitches level; facs run down early ssn (2009); interesting area." ♦ Easter-3 Oct. € 37.00   2009*

PUIMOISSON *10E3* (8km NE Rural) *43.89836, 6.18011* **Camping à la Ferme Vauvenières (Sauvaire), 04410 St Jurs [tel/fax 04 92 74 44 18; contact@ferme-de-vauvenieres.fr; www.ferme-de-vauvenieres.fr]** Fr Riez take D953 N to 1km beyond Puimoisson then fork R onto D108 sp St Jurs & site sp. Sm, pt shd; wc; chem disp; shwrs inc; el pnts (6A) €2.90; lndtte; shops 2km; BBQ; lake sw 2.5km; games area; dogs €0.75; Eng spkn; adv bkg; quiet; CKE/CCI. "Peaceful, basic site off beaten track; wonderful views; lavendar fields; friendly Dutch owner; clean san facs; poss stretched if site full; gd for mountain walking; D17 to Majastres v narr; gd Sunday mkt in Riez." 1 Apr-1 Oct. € 10.80   2010*

PUIVERT *8G4* (500m S Rural) *42.91596, 2.0441* **Camping de Puivert, Fontclaire, 11230 Puivert [04 68 20 00 58 or 06 22 45 15 74 (mob); fax 04 68 20 82 29; camping-de-puivert@orange.fr]** Take D117 W fr Quillan dir Lavelanet for 16km; at Puivert turn L onto D16; site in 500m by lake; well sp. Or E fr Foix on D117 for 45km; at Puivert turn R onto D16 & as bef. Med, hdg pitch, hdstg, terr, pt shd; wc; chem disp; mv service pnt; shwrs inc; el pnts (16A) €3; lndtte; shop & 500m; rests 500m; snacks; bar; BBQ sep area; lake sw & fishing adj; entmnt; internet; dogs; quiet; red low ssn. "Attractive area; lge pitches, some lakeside, some hill views; dated san facs but adequate & clean; museum in vill; chateau nrby; vg."
24 Apr-27 Sep. € 12.00   2011*

PUTANGES PONT ECREPIN *4E1* (1km W Rural) *48.76067, -0.24564* **Camp Municipal Le Val d'Orne, Le Friche, 61210 Putanges-Pont-Ecrepin [02 33 35 04 67 or 02 33 35 00 25 (Mairie); fax 02 33 35 49 50; mairie. putanges.61@wanadoo.fr; www.office-tourisme-putanges.com]** S fr Falaise on D909 to Putanges. Ent Putanges cross Rv L'Orne & ignore camping sp immed on L (Grand Rue). Go thro vill for approx 1km, turn L sp camping 200m. Site on R. Sm, hdg/mkd pitch, pt shd; wc; shwrs inc; el pnts (6-10A) €2.30-3.30; shops & rest 5 mins walk via rv bank; rv fishing; playgrnd; dogs €1.15; adv bkg; quiet. "Clean, well-run rvside site; site yourself, warden visits am & pm; ltd facs; gd."
1 Apr-30 Sep. € 7.50   2010*

PUY EN VELAY, LE *9C1* (500m N Urban) *45.05014, 3.88044* **Camping Bouthezard, Chemin de Bouthezard, Ave d'Aiguilhe, 43000 Le Puy-en-Velay [04 71 09 55 09 or 06 15 08 23 59 (mob); www.ot-lepuyenvelay.fr]** Fr Le Puy heading NW on N102 to city cent; look for sp Clermont & Vichy; turn R at traff lts in Place Carnot at sp for Valence; site on L on bank of rv. Site ent immed opp Chapel St Michel & 200m fr volcanic core. Med, some hdg pitches, pt shd; wc; chem disp; mv service pnt; shwrs inc; el pnts (6A) inc (rev pol); lndtte; sm shop; shop 200m & supmkt 500m; snacks; playgrnd adj; pool & tennis adj; games rm; dogs €0.85; poss cr; Eng spkn; adv bkg; noise of church bells (not night-time); ccard not acc; red low ssn; CKE/CCI. "Popular, well-kept site in gd location; busy - rec arr early; efficient staff; gd facs; gates clsd 2100-0700 low ssn; no twin-axles; may flood in v heavy rain; unrel opening dates - phone ahead low ssn; vg touring base on pilgrim rte to Spain." ♦ ltd 15 Mar-31 Oct. € 19.00   2012*

PUY EN VELAY, LE *9C1* (9km N Rural) *45.12473, 3.92177* **Camp Municipal Les Longes, Route des Rosières, 43800 Lavoûte-sur-Loire [04 71 08 18 79 or 04 71 08 50 13; mairie.lavoutesurloire@wanadoo.fr; www. lavoutesurloire.fr]** Fr Le Puy take N on D103 sp Lavoûte & Retournac. In Lavoûte turn R onto D7 bef rv bdge, site on L in 1km on rvside. Med, mkd pitch, pt shd; wc; mv service pnt; shwrs €1; el pnts (6A) €2.50; lndtte; shops 9km; bread 1km; tradsmn (high ssn); playgrnd; pool 1km; rv sw, fishing 50m; tennis; dogs €1.50; quiet. "Gd, friendly, scenic site; gd walking." ♦ 30 Apr-2 Oct. € 13.00   2011*

PUY EN VELAY, LE *9C1* (3km E Urban) *45.04431, 3.93030* **Camp Municipal d'Audinet, Ave des Sports, 43700 Brives-Charensac [tel/fax 04 71 09 10 18; camping.audinet@ wanadoo.fr; www.camping-audinet.fr]** Fr Le Puy foll green sp E twd Valence. Fr S on N88 foll sp twd Valence & on E side of town foll white sp. Lge, pt shd; wc (mostly cont); chem disp; mv service pnt; baby facs; shwrs inc; el pnts (6A) €3.30; lndtte; sm shop & shops 500m; supmkt 1.5km; rest, snacks; bar; BBQ; playgrnd; pool; rv & lake sw/fishing; internet; bus to town; quiet; red low ssn/long stay. "Spacious site on rvside; friendly, helpful staff; gd san facs, poss stretched high ssn; poss itinerants - but not a prob; no twin-axles; vg." ♦
30 Apr-20 Sep. € 12.50   2010*

PUY EN VELAY, LE *9C1* (9km E Rural) *45.06020, 3.95660* **Camping Le Moulin de Barette, Le Pont de Sumène, 43540 Blavozy [04 71 03 00 88; fax 04 71 03 00 51; hotel@ lemoulindebarette.com; www.lemoulindebarette.com]** Take N88 dir St Etienne. Exit after 7km at D156 Blavozy. At rndabt foll sp for Rosières & 1st L to Moulin-de-Barette. Med, mkd pitch, pt sl, pt shd; wc; chem disp; mv service pnt; shwrs inc; el pnts €4; rest; bar; playgrnd; TV rm; few statics; dogs €1; quiet; red long stay; ccard acc; CKE/CCI. "Part of hotel complex; dated san facs in need of refurb; gd rest; ltd el pnts; v quiet low ssn; site run down (2011); NH only." ♦ 20 Mar-30 Oct. € 14.70   2011*

PUY EN VELAY, LE *9C1* (7km S Rural) *44.99369, 3.90345* **Camping Comme au Soleil, Route du Plan d'Eau, 43700 Coubon [tel/fax 04 71 08 32 55; dumoulin-patrick@ club-internet.fr; www.camping-le-puy.fr]** S fr Puy-en-Velay on N88, turn E onto D38 to Coubon, site sp. Please do not use SatNav for final appr, cross bdge then foll sp to site. Sm, terr, pt shd; htd wc; chem disp; baby facs; shwrs inc; el pnts (10A) €3.50 (poss long lead req, poss rev pol); lndtte (inc dryer); ice; tradsmn; rest, snacks; bar; BBQ; playgrnd; pool; games area; cycle hire; 5% statics; dogs €1; bus1m; some Eng spkn; adv bkg; quiet; red low ssn; CKE/CCI. "Well-kept site; helpful owners; clean facs; vg rest; excel" ♦ 01 Feb - 31 Dec. € 11.80   2013*

PUY GUILLAUME *9B1* (1km W Rural) *45.96231, 3.46632* **Camping de la Dore, 86 Rue Joseph Claussat, 63290 Puy-Guillaume [04 73 94 78 51 or 06 70 14 56 10 (mob); contact@camping-auvergne-63.com; www.camping-auvergne-63.com]** N fr Thiers on D906 as far as Puy-Guillaume; at ent to town (lge sculpture on rndabt), turn L at rndabt onto D343 (which joins D63); then L again at next rndabt onto D63. Site on R by rv. Med, pt shd; wc (some cont); chem disp; some serviced pitches; shwrs inc; el pnts (6A) €3.65; lndtte; shops 1km; rest, snacks; bar; playgrnd; 3 pools; jacuzzi; rv fishing adj; dogs; phone adj; bus 11km adv bkg (rec high ssn); ccard acc; CKE/CCI. "Neat & tidy site in pleasant location; friendly staff; clean san facs; excel pool with bar; unrel opening/closing dates, rec phone ahead low ssn; excel." ♦ ltd 1 May-3 Sep. € 11.60   2011*

k W Rural) 44.49636, 1.08220
Club de Vacances Duravel, Route de Vire, 46700 Duravel
[05 65 24 65 06; fax 05 65 24 64 96; info@clubdevacances.eu;
www.clubdevacances.eu] Fr D811 Puy-l'Evêque to Fumel
rd at Duravel town cent, opp Mairie turn S onto D58 sp Vire-
sur-Lot. Site in 2.5km. Lge, hdg/mkd pitch, pt sl, pt shd; wc
(some cont); chem disp; mv service pnt; shwrs inc; el pnts (10A)
€4; gas; lndtte (inc dryer); shop; tradsmn; rest, snacks; bar;
playgrnd; 2 pools (1 htd); paddling pool; waterslide; beach nr;
tennis; games area; canoeing; fishing; cycle hire; wifi; entmnt;
12% statics; dogs; poss cr; Eng spkn; adv bkg; quiet; 10% red
low ssn; ccard acc; CKE/CCI. "Vg, lively site in lovely situation
by rv; friendly staff; excel facs; lovely pools; entmnt in Dutch; all
sps on site in Dutch - enquire at recep for info in Eng." ♦ ltd
24 Apr-30 Sep. € 26.50   2010*

PUYCELCI *8E3* (4km W Rural) *43.99254, 1.65140* **Centre
Naturiste Le Fiscalou (Naturist), 1 Route de Montclar,
81140 Puycelci [05 63 30 45 95; fax 05 62 30 32 88;
fiscalou@orange.fr; www.fiscalou.com]** Fr Bruniquel D964
S twd Castelnau. Take D1 sp Monclar-de-Quercy. Site on L
after 4km. Sm, pt sl, pt shd; wc; chem disp; shwrs inc; el pnts
(3A) €3.75 (poss long lead req); tradsmn; rest; bar; playgrnd;
pool; some statics; dogs €3.15; Eng spkn; adv bkg; quiet; red
long stay. "Pleasant, rustic site; excel touring base."
1 May-30 Sep. € 22.50   2008*

PUYSSEGURE *8E3* (200m N Rural) *43.75064, 1.06065*
**FFCC Camping Namasté, 31480 Puysségur [tel/fax
05 61 85 77 84; camping.namaste@free.fr; http://camping.
namaste.free.fr]** Fr Toulouse NW on N224/D1 sp Cadours;
at Puysségur in 30km foll Camping Namasté sp. (Puysségur is
1km NE of Cadours). Sm, pt shd; wc; baby facs; shwrs; sauna;
el pnts (4-10A) €3-5; lndtte; shop; rest, snacks; bar; BBQ;
playgrnd; pool; paddling pool; fishing; cycle hire; games area;
games rm; wifi; entmnt; some statics; dogs €1.50; quiet; red
low ssn. ♦ 1 May - 15 Oct. € 17.00 (CChq acc)   2012*

PYLA SUR MER *7D1* (7km S Coastal) *44.57243, -1.22030*
**Camping Le Petit Nice, Route de Biscarosse, 33115
Pyla-sur-Mer [05 56 22 74 03; fax 05 56 22 14 31; info@
petitnice.com; www.petitnice.com]** Fr Bordeaux on app
Arcachon foll sp for Dune-du-Pilat & 'campings'. At T-junc turn L;
foll 'plage' & camping sp on D218. Site on R. Lge, pt sl, shd; wc;
chem disp; mv service pnt; baby facs; shwrs inc; el pnts (5A) inc;
gas; lndtte; shop; rest, snacks; bar; playgrnd; htd pool; paddling
pool; sand beach adj; tennis; entmnt; TV rm; 50% statics; dogs
€5; poss cr; adv bkg; quiet but poss noisy disco; red low ssn/long
stay. "Open beach with steep wooden steps." 1 Apr-30 Sep.
€ 39.00   2008*

PYLA SUR MER *7D1* (7km S Coastal) *44.58517, -1.20868*
**Camping Village Centre La Forêt, Route de Biscarosse,
33115 Pyla-sur-Mer [05 56 22 73 28; fax 05 56 22 70 50;
contact@village-center.com; www.village-center.com]**
Fr Bordeaux app Arcachon on A660 by-pass rd; at La Teste-
de-Buch at rndabt foll sp for Dune du Pilat & 'campings'. At
T-junc in 4km turn L; foll 'plage' & camping sp on D218. Site
on R. Lge, hdg/mkd pitch, pt sl, shd; wc; chem disp; mv service
pnt; shwrs inc; el pnts (6A) inc; lndtte; shop; rest, snacks; bar;
BBQ; playgrnd; pool; sand beach 600m; solarium; tennis;
cycle hire; many statics (sep area); dogs €2; adv bkg; red low
ssn; ccard acc; CKE/CCI. "Forest setting at foot of sand dune;
well-organised; new san facs 2010; many facs; hang-gliding,
surfing, sailing, cycle rtes nrby." ♦ 4 Apr-20 Sep. € 34.80
(CChq acc)   2010*

PYLA SUR MER *7D1* (7km S Coastal/Rural) *44.57474,
-1.22217* **Yelloh! Village Panorama du Pyla, Route de
Biscarosse, 33115 Pyla-sur-Mer [05 56 22 10 44; fax
05 56 22 10 12; mail@camping-panorama.com; www.
camping-panorama.com or www.yellohvillage.co.uk]**
App Arcachon fr Bordeaux on A63/A660, at rndabt foll sp for
Dune-du-Pilat & 'campings'. Foll sp for 'plage' & 'campings'
on D218. Site on R next to Camping Le Petit Nice. Lge, mkd
pitch, pt sl, terr, pt shd; wc (some cont); chem disp; mv service
pnt; sauna; shwrs inc; el pnts (3-10A) inc; gas; rest, snacks;
bar; shop; playgrnd; htd pool; sand beach adj; tennis; TV;
entmnt; dogs €5; Eng spkn; adv bkg; quiet; red low ssn; CKE/
CCI. "Pleasant site on wooded dune; direct steep access to
excel beach; site rds v narr; ltd pitches for v lge o'fits; some
pitches sandy; gd facs; paragliding adj" ♦ 13 Apr-2 Oct.
€ 52.80   2013*

See advertisement on inside front cover

QUEAUX see Lussac les Châteaux *7A3*

QUEND PLAGE LES PINS see Fort Mahon Plage *3B2*

QUESTEMBERT see Muzillac *2G3*

QUETTEHOU *1C4* (2.5km E Urban/Coastal) *49.58520,
-1.26858* **Camping La Gallouette, Rue de la Gallouette,
50550 St Vaast-la-Hougue [02 33 54 20 57; fax
02 33 54 16 71; contact@camping-lagallouette.fr; www.
lagallouette.com]** E fr Quettehou on D1, site sp in St Vaast-
la-Hougue to S of town. Lge, hdg/mkd pitch, pt shd; wc;
chem disp; mv service pnt; baby facs; shwrs; el pnts (6-10A)
€3.80-4.60; gas; lndtte; shop; tradsmn; rest, snacks; bar; BBQ;
playgrnd; htd pool (solar heating); sand beach 300m; games
area; games rm; 10% statics; dogs €1.80; phone; poss cr; adv
bkg; quiet; red low ssn; CKE/CCI. "lovely friendly site; some
lge pitches; gd range of facs; sh walk to interesting town; excel
site" ♦ 1 Apr-30 Sep. € 37.05   2013*

PUY L'EVEQUE

PUY L'EVEQUE *7D3* (2.5km S Rural) *44.47780, 1.14214* **FFCC
Village-Camping Les Vignes, Le Méoure, Le Cayrou, 46700
Puy-l'Evèque [tel/fax 05 65 30 81 72; contact@camping-
lesvignes.fr; www.camping-lesvignes.fr]** App fr E on D911
dir Villeneuve-sur-Lot, just bef ent Puy-l'Evèque turn L, foll sp
for 3km. Site adj Rv Lot. Avoid town cent while towing. Med,
shd; wc; baby facs; shwrs; el pnts; (10A) €2.90; gas; lndtte;
shops 3km; tradsmn; snacks; bar; playgrnd; pool; tennis; games
area; fishing; cycle hire; entmnt high ssn; TV; dogs €1.50;
quiet; red over 55s/low ssn. "Lovely, peaceful site in beautiful
countryside; well-kept; warm welcome, friendly owners; gd san
facs." 1 Apr-30 Sep. € 18.00   2012*

PUY L'EVEQUE *7D3* (6km W Rural) *44.49636, 1.08220*

QUETTEHOU *1C4* (2km S Coastal) *49.57960, -1.30760*
**Camping Le Rivage, 75 Rue Ste Marie, 50630 Quettehou
[02 33 54 13 76; fax 02 33 43 10 42; camping.lerivage@
wanadoo.fr; www.camping-lerivage.fr]** Fr Quettehou on
D14, sp on L. Med, unshd; wc; shwrs inc; el pnts (6A) €4.30;
lndtte (inc dryer); shop; snacks; bar; BBQ; playgrnd; htd pool;
paddling pool; sand beach 400m; cycle hire; internet; entmnt;
50% statics; dogs €3; Eng spkn; adv bkg rec high ssn; quiet.
"Gd clean site." 1 Apr-30 Sep. € 19.50   2010*

QUIBERON *2G3* (1.5km N Coastal) *47.49978, -3.12021*
**Camping Do Mi Si La Mi, 31 Rue de la Vierge, St Julien-
Plage, 56170 Quiberon [02 97 50 22 52; fax 02 97 50 26 69;
camping@domisilami.com; www.domisilami.com]**
Take D768 down Quiberon Peninsular, 3km after St Pierre-
Quiberon & shortly after sp for rlwy level x-ing turn L into Rue
de la Vierge, site on R in 400m. Lge, hdg/mkd pitch, pt sl, pt
shd; wc (some cont); chem disp; mv service pnt; baby facs;
serviced pitches; shwrs inc; el pnts (3-10A) €2.80-4.30; gas;
lndtte (inc dryer); shop, snacks, bar adj; BBQ; playgrnd; sand/
shgl beach 100m; games area; cycle hire; sailing, horseriding,
tennis nr; wifi; 40% statics; dogs €2.40; poss cr; Eng spkn;
quiet; red low ssn; ccard acc; CKE/CCI. "Gd touring base; vg."
♦ 1 Apr-2 Nov. € 21.60   2011*

QUIBERON *2G3* (800m SE Urban) *47.47919, -3.10090*
**Camping Les Joncs du Roch, Rue de l'Aérodrome, 56170
Quiberon [tel/fax 02 97 50 24 37; www.campingquiberon.
com]** Foll sp to aerodrome. Site ent opp. Lge, pt shd; wc (some
cont); chem disp; shwrs inc; el pnts (10A) €4.20 (poss rev pol);
gas; shops 1km; sand beach 500m; some statics; dogs €2; poss
cr; quiet, but minimal aircraft noise. "Well-maintained, clean,
friendly, sheltered site; facs old but clean; easy access town/
beach; vg cycling." Easter-30 Sep. € 22.00   2010*

QUIBERON *2G3* (1.5km SE Coastal/Rural) *47.47641,
-3.10441* **Camping Le Bois d'Amour, Rue St Clément,
56170 Quiberon [02 97 50 13 52 or 04 42 20 47 25 (LS);
fax 02 97 50 42 67; info@homair.com; www.homair.com]**
Exit N165 at Auray onto D768. In Quiberon foll sp
'Thalassothérapie', site sp. Lge, hdg/mkd pitch, pt shd; wc;
mv service pnt; chem disp; baby facs; shwrs inc; el pnts (10A)
€5; gas; lndtte; shop; rest, snacks; bar; BBQ; playgrnd; htd
pool; beach 200m; games area; tennis; horseriding; cycle hire;
entmnt; dogs €5; adv bkg; quiet; Eng spkn; red low ssn; ccard
acc; CKE/CCI. ♦ 3 Apr-2 Oct. € 36.00   2012*

See advertisement on pages 32 & 33

QUIBERON *2G3* (1.5km SE Coastal) *47.47690, -3.09246*
**Camping Le Conguel, Blvd de la Teignouse, 56175
Quiberon [02 97 50 19 11; fax 02 97 30 46 66; info@
campingduconguel.com; www.campingduconguel.com]**
On D768 fr N, turn E at rlwy stn on ent Quiberon, foll sps for
Pointe du Conguel, site sp. Lge, mkd pitch, pt sl, unshd; wc;
baby facs; sauna; shwrs; el pnts €3.65; gas; lndtte; shop; rest,
snacks; bar; playgrnd; htd pool; paddling pool; waterslide; sand
beach adj; watersports; tennis; games area; games rm; fitness
rm; cycle hire; entmnt; internet; TV rm; adv bkg; quiet; red low
ssn. "Beautiful, varied coastline; excl family site." ♦
4 Apr-31 Oct. € 43.30   2009*

QUIBERON *2G3* (1km S Coastal) *47.47424, -3.10563* **Camp
Municipal Le Goviro, Blvd du Goviro, 56170 Quiberon
[02 97 50 13 54]** Fr D768 at Quiberon foll sp Port Maria &
'Centre Thalassothérapie'. Site 1km on L nr Sofitel hotel.
Lge, hdg/mkd pitch, terr, pt shd; wc (some cont); chem disp;
mv service pnt; shwrs; el pnts (13A) €3; gas; lndtte; rest
adj; playgrnd; sand beach, fishing & watersports adj; dogs
€1.65; poss cr; quiet. "Popular, well-run site in excel location;
lovely bay, gd sea views & coastal path; smallish pitches;
clean, adequate san facs, ltd low ssn." ♦ ltd 1 Apr-8 Oct.
€ 12.45   2010*

QUIBERVILLE PLAGE see Veules les Roses *3C2*

QUILLAN *8G4* (W Urban) *42.87358, 2.17565* **FFCC Camp
Municipal La Sapinette, 21 Ave René Delpech, 11500 Quillan
[04 68 20 13 52; fax 04 68 20 27 80; contact@camping-la-
sapinette.com; www.camping-la-sapinette.com]** Foll D118
fr Carcassonne to Quillan; turn R at 2nd traff lts in town cent;
site sp in town. Med, hdg/mkd pitch, some hdstg, sl, terr, pt
shd; htd wc; chem disp; mv service pnt; shwrs inc; el pnts (6A)
€3.10; lndtte; shops 400m; tradsmn; playgrnd; pool; leisure
cent 500m in town; wifi; TV; 25% statics in sep area; dogs
€1.60; poss cr; adv bkg; quiet; ccard acc; red low ssn/CKE/CCI.
"Gd touring base; sm pitches, some level; early arr rec; helpful
staff; gd san facs; excel pool; site poss tired end ssn; mkt Wed
& Sat; vet adj; highly rec." 1 Apr-30 Oct. € 19.20   2012*

"Satellite navigation makes touring much easier"

Remember most sat navs don't know if
you're towing or in a larger vehicle – always
use yours alongside maps and site directions.

QUILLAN *8G4* (8km NW Rural) *42.89296, 2.10464* **Camping
Le Fontaulié-Sud, 11500 Nébias [tel/fax 04 68 20 17 62;
www.fontauliesud.com]** In Quillan take D117 twd Foix. Turn
L at sp immed after leaving Nébias vill. Site in 1km. NB Steep
rd to site. Med, pt sl, pt shd; wc; chem disp; shwrs inc; el pnts
(4A) €2; lndtte; shop; snacks; bar; playgrnd; pool; paddling
pool; tennis, horseriding, watersports nr; TV rm; some statics;
dogs €1; adv bkg; quiet; CKE/CCI. "Beautiful scenery & many
mkd walks; owners friendly, helpful; ltd facs low ssn; gd
touring base." 1 May-15 Sep. € 16.00   2008*

QUIMPER *2F2* (9km SE Rural) *47.93811, -3.99959*
**Camping Vert de Creac'h-Lann (Hemidy), 202 Route
de Concarneau, 29170 St Evarzec [02 98 56 29 88 or
06 68 46 97 25 (mob); contact@campingvertcreachlann.
com; www.campingvertcreachlann.com]** S fr Quimper on
D783, 1.5km fr St Evarzec rndabt at brow of hill (easily missed).
Sm, hdg pitch, pt sl, pt shd; wc; chem disp; shwrs; el pnts (4-
13A) €3-3.50; lndtte; shop, rest, snacks & bar 3km; playgrnd;
sand beach 5km; 50% statics; dogs; poss cr; Eng spkn; adv
bkg; quiet; ccard not acc. "Lovely spacious site; lge pitches;
friendly, helpful owner; gd playgrnd; poss to stay after end Sep
by arrangement; lovely old town; gd touring base; daily mkt;
excel." 1 Jun-30 Sep. € 10.00   2011*

FRANCE

QUIMPER *2F2* (2km S Rural) *47.97685, -4.11060* **Camping L'Orangerie de Lanniron, Château de Lanniron, 29000 Quimper [02 98 90 62 02; fax 02 98 52 15 56; camping@lanniron.com; www.lanniron.com or www.les-castels.com]** Fr Rennes/Lorient: on N165 Rennes-Quimper, Quimper-Centre, Quimper-Sud exit, foll dir Pont l'Abbé on S bypass until exit sp Camping de Lanninon on R. At top of slip rd turn L & foll site sp, under bypass then 2nd R to site. Recep at Old Farm 500m before site. Lge, mkd pitch, pt shd; wc; chem disp; mv service pnt; some serviced pitches; baby facs; shwrs inc; el pnts (10A) inc; gas; lndtte (inc dryer); shop; supmkt adj; rest, snacks; bar; BBQ; playgrnd; htd pool; paddling pool; aquapark; rv fishing & beach; canoeing; 9-hole golf course on site; tennis; cycle hire; wifi; entmnt; games/TV rm; 25% statics; dogs €4.70; bus; poss cr; Eng spkn; adv bkg; ccard acc; red low ssn; CKE/CCI. "Excel, busy, family-run site in grnds of chateau by Rv Odet; well-spaced pitches; vg san facs; vg leisure facs." ♦ 12 May-15 Sep. € 45.00 SBS - B21 2011*

See advertisement on inside back cover

⊞ **QUIMPER** *2F2* (1km W Urban) *47.99198, -4.12536* **Camp Municipal Bois du Séminaire, Ave des Oiseaux, 29000 Quimper [tel/fax 02 98 55 61 09; camping-municipal@quimper.fr; www.mairie-quimper.fr]** Fr E on D765 to Quimper, bear L on 1-way system along rv. In 1km bear R over rv into Blvd de Boulguinan - D785. In 500m turn R onto Blvd de France (lge junc). In 1km bear R into Ave des Oiseaux, site on R in front of Auberge de Jeunesse. Med, hdg pitch, terr, pt shd; wc; chem disp (wc); shwrs inc; el pnts (5A) €3.30; lndry facs; shops, rest, snacks, bar 500m; BBQ; pool nr; sand beach 15km; 10% statics; phone; bus adj; poss cr; quiet; ccard acc; CKE/CCI. "Conv NH/sh stay." ♦ ltd 01 Jun-30 Sep. € 10.85 2013*

"There aren't many sites open at this time of year"

If you're travelling outside peak season remember to call ahead to check site opening dates – even if the entry says 'open all year'.

QUIMPER *2F2* (12km W Rural) *48.00126, -4.26925* **Camping La Rocaille, Kérandoaré, 29710 Plogastel-St Germain [02 98 54 58 13 or 06 72 34 73 13 (mob)]** Fr N165 exit Quimper Sud & foll sp dir Audierne onto D784; in 9km turn R at Kérandoaré; site sp in 200m. NB Avoid Quimper town cent. Sm, hdg/mkd pitch, terr, pt shd; wc (some cont); shwrs inc; el pnts (6A) inc; lndtte; shop 500m; tradsmn; beach 10km; Eng spkn; quiet. "Lovely touring area; friendly, helpful owner; vg san facs; poss diff m'vans if wet." 1 Jun-15 Sep. € 13.00 2009*

QUIMPERLE *2F2* (7km NE Rural) *47.90468, -3.47477* **Camping Le Ty-Nadan, Route d'Arzano, 29310 Locunolé [02 98 71 75 47; fax 02 98 71 77 31; info@tynadan-vacances.fr; www.tynadan-vacances.fr or www.les-castels.com]** To avoid Quimperlé cent exit N165 dir Quimperlé. As ent town turn R onto D22 dir Arzano. In 9km turn L at W end of Arzano (un-numbered rd) sp Locunolé & Camping Ty Nadan; site on L just after x-ing Rv Elle. Or fr Roscoff on D69 S join N165/E60 but take care at uneven level x-ing at Pen-ar-Hoat 11km after Sizun. Lge, hdg/mkd pitch, pt shd; htd wc; chem disp; mv service pnt; sauna; serviced pitches; baby facs; shwrs inc; el pnts (10A) inc (long lead poss req); gas; lndtte (inc dryer); shop; rest, snacks; bar; BBQ (gas/charcoal); playgrnd; htd pools (1 covrd); paddling pool; waterslides; spa; sand beach 18km; rv fishing, canoeing adj; tennis; cycle hire; horseriding; archery; games area; wifi; entmnt; sat TV/games rm; 40% statics; dogs €5.50; no c'vans/m'vans over 8.50m high ssn; Eng spkn; adv bkg; ccard acc; red low ssn/CKE/CCI. "Excel, peaceful site by rv; pitches poss narr for lge o'fits; friendly staff; barrier clsd 2300-0800; many activities; gd touring base." ♦ 31 Mar-2 Sep. € 46.00 (CChq acc) SBS - B20 2011*

See advertisement on inside back cover

QUIMPERLE *2F2* (1.5km SW Urban) *47.87250, -3.56952* **Camp Municipal de Kerbertrand, Rue du Camping, 29300 Quimperlé [02 98 39 31 30 or 02 98 96 04 32 (TO); fax 02 98 96 16 12; contact@quimperletourisme.com; www.quimperletourisme.com]** Exit N165 at Kervidanou junc SW of town. Foll sp 'Centre Ville' along Rue de Pont-Aven. In 1km turn L bef supmkt, sp v sm. Sm, hdg pitch, pt shd; wc; shwrs; el pnts €1.80; playgrnd; TV; dogs. "Delightful site; helpful warden." 1 Jun-15 Sep. € 10.29 2011*

QUINGEY *6H2* (200m E Urban) *47.10431, 5.88821* **Camp Municipal Les Promenades, Bord de la Loue, 25440 Quingey [03 81 63 74 01 or 03 81 63 63 25 (Mairie); fax 03 81 63 63 25; www.campingquingey.fr]** Site sp off N83 by-pass, then in Quingey. Thro vill, immed on L after bdge over Rv Loue. Sm, pt shd; wc; chem disp; shwrs inc; el pnts (6A) €3; lndtte; shop; snacks; rest; playgrnd; fishing, sailing, canoeing, tennis, cycle hire & archery adj; dogs €1; quiet but some daytime rd noise. "Run down, neglected (Sep 10)." ♦ 1 May-30 Sep. € 11.20 2010*

QUINGEY *6H2* (8.5km SW Rural) *47.04080, 5.81560* **FFCC Camp Municipal La Louve, Rue du Pont, 39600 Champagne-sur-Loue [tel/fax 03 84 37 69 12; camping.champagne@valdamau.com; http://camping_champagne.monsite-orange.fr/]** Fr Quingey on D17 sp Lombard & in approx 4km turn L sp Champagne-sur-Loue, Buffard (still D17). Site on L after bdge. Sm, shd; wc (some cont); mv service pnt; shwrs inc; el pnts (10A) €2.50; shops 2km; tradsmn; rest 1km; BBQ; playgrnd; fishing; dogs €1; adv bkg; quiet; CKE/CCI. "Well-kept, peaceful site in beautiful situation on rv; open plan - all grass, poss diff for m'vans if wet; used by groups canoeists; site yourself; office 0800-0900 & 1830-1930; vg." ♦ 1 Apr-30 Sep. € 7.00 2010*

QUINTIN *2E3* (NE Urban) *48.40128, -2.90672* **Camp Municipal du Lac, Chemin des Côtes, 22800 Quintin [02 96 74 92 54 or 02 96 74 84 01 (Mairie); fax 02 96 74 06 53; mairie@quintin.fr]** Fr N exit D790 at rndabt & foll sp 'Centre Ville'; at 2nd rndabt site sp; site on L 200m after 5th ped x-ing (narr rd, easy to miss). Fr S on D790 do not take slip rd (D7) but cont to rndabt - narr rds in town; then as above. Site N (100m) of town gardens & boating lake. Sm, pt sl, pt shd; wc (some cont); mv service pnt; shwrs; el pnts (6A) €2.80; BBQ; shops, rest, snacks, bar 500m; playgrnd; fishing; quiet, but poss noise fr sports complex adj. "Fair site; helpful wardn; poss insufficient of security (2011); interesting town." ♦ 15 Apr-30 Sep. € 8.52   2011*

"That's changed – Should I let The Club know?"

If you find something on site that's different from the site entry, fill in a report and let us know. See www.caravanclub.co.uk/europereport.

RABASTENS *8E3* (2km NW Rural) *43.83090, 1.69805* **Camp Municipal des Auzerals, Route de Grazac, 81800 Rabastens [05 63 33 70 36 or 06 23 81 85 69 (mob); fax 05 63 33 64 05; mairie.rabastens@libertysurf.fr]** Exit A68 junc 7 onto D12. In Rabastens town cent foll sp dir Grazac, site sp. Sm, hdg/mkd pitch, pt sl, terr, pt shd; wc (mainly cont); chem disp; shwrs inc; el pnts (10A) inc; lndtte; shop 2km; rest 2km; playgrnd; pool adj high ssn; quiet; adv bkg ess high ssn; CKE/CCI. "Attractive lakeside site; facs old but clean; office 0900-1200 & 1500-1900, otherwise height barrier in place; conv m'way NH; highly rec." 1 Apr-30 Sep. € 9.90   2010*

RAGUENES see Pont Aven *2F2*

RAIDS see Periers *1D4*

RAMATUELLE see St Tropez *10F4*

RAMBOUILLET *4E3* (3km SE Rural) *48.6252, 1.84495* **Camping Huttopia Rambouillet, Route du Château d'Eau, 78120 Rambouillet [01 30 41 07 34; fax 01 30 41 00 17; rambouillet@huttopia.com; www.huttopia.com]** Fr N exit D910 at 'Rambouillet Eveuses' & foll sp to site in 2.5km. Fr S exit at 'Rambouillet Centre' & foll sp to site back onto D910 (in opp dir), exit 'Rambouillet Eveuses' as above. Avoid Rambouillet town cent. Lge, hdg pitch, pt shd; htd wc (some cont); mv service pnt; chem disp; baby facs; shwrs inc; el pnts (6-10A) €4.60-6.80 (poss rev pol); lndtte; shop, tradsmn, rest, snacks; bar; BBQ (gas/elec); playgrnd; fishing adj; some statics; dogs €4; phone; sep car park; Eng spkn; adv bkg (rec high ssn); quiet; ccard acc; red low ssn; CKE/CCI. "Excel, busy, wooded site; conv Paris by train - parking at stn 3km; gd cycling rtes; interesting town." ♦ 3 Apr-5 Nov. € 25.20   2009*

RANG DU FLIERS see Berck *3B2*

RANVILLE see Ouistreham *3D1*

RAON L'ETAPE *6E3* (10km NE Rural) *48.45490, 6.94722* **Camping des Lacs, 88110 Celles-sur-Plaine [03 29 41 28 00; fax 03 29 41 18 69; camping@paysdeslacs.com; www. paysdeslacs.com/camping]** Fr Raon-l'Etape turn onto D392A to Celles-sur-Plaine, site sp. Med, hdg/mkd pitch, hdstg, pt sl, pt shd; htd wc (some cont); solarium; chem disp; shwrs inc; el pnts (4-10A) inc; lndtte; shop; tradsmn; snacks; bar; playgrnd; htd pool; sand beach & lake sw 400m; fishing; windsurfing; tennis; 10% statics; dogs €1.50; Eng spkn; adv bkg; quiet; ccard acc; red low ssn/long stay; CKE/CCI. "Poss unkempt & facs unclean low ssn, otherwise vg." ♦ 1 Apr-31 Oct. € 23.00   2010*

RAON L'ETAPE *6E3* (10km E Rural) *48.35281, 6.98903* **Camping des 7 Hameaux, 1 La Fontenelle, 88210 Ban-de-Sapt [03 29 58 95 75; camping7hameaux@wanadoo.fr; http://camping7hameaux.monsite-orange.fr/]** Fr St Dié NE on D49 to St Jean-d'Ormont (turn R after cathedral in St Dié). Then D32 sp 'Saales' to Ban-de-Sapt. Turn L onto D49 to La Fontenelle. Site on R 1km past sp to military cemetery. Or fr N59 take D424 sp Senones. In 3.3km in Moyenmoutiers turn R onto D37 sp Ban-de-Sapt. In 6.1km join D49. site on L in 1.3km. Sm, pt sl; wc; chem disp; shwrs €1; el pnts (6A) €2.50; rest, bar & shop 1km; tradsmn; pool 10km; quiet; adv bkg; ccard not acc; CKE/CCI. "Walks, cycle rtes; farm produce; friendly; vg." 1 Apr-31 Oct. € 8.00   2010*

RAON L'ETAPE *6E3* (5km SE Rural) *48.39474, 6.86232* **Camping Vosgina, 1 Rue la Cheville, 88420 Moyenmoutier [tel/fax 03 29 41 47 63; camping-vosgina@wanadoo.fr; www.vosges-camping.com]** On N59 St Dié-Lunéville rd, take exit mkd Senones, Moyenmoutier. At rndabt take rd twd St Blaise & foll camping sp. Site is on minor rd parallel with N59 bet Moyenmoutier & Raon. Med, hdg pitch, terr, shd; htd wc; shwrs inc; el pnts (4-10A) €2.20-5.50; gas; lndtte; sm shop & 3km; tradsmn; snacks; bar; 20% statics; dogs €1.50; Eng spkn; quiet but some rd noise; CKE/CCI. "Gd site for quiet holiday in a non-touristy area of Alsace; friendly recep; lovely countryside; many cycle/walking routes in area; barrier clsd 2200-0700." € 12.30   2008*

"I like to fill in the reports as I travel from site to site"

You'll find report forms at the back of this guide, or you can fill them in online at www.caravaclub.co.uk/europereport.

⊞ **RAON L'ETAPE** *6E3* (6km SE Rural) *48.36355, 6.83861* **Camping Beaulieu-sur-l'Eau, 41 Rue de Trieuche, 88480 Etival-Clairefontaine [tel/fax 03 29 41 53 51; camping-beaulieu-vosges@orange.fr; www.camping-beaulieu-vosges.com]** SE fr Baccarat on N59 turn R in vill of Etival-Clairefontaine on D424 sp Rambervillers & Epinal & foll sp for 3km. Ent on L. Med, mkd pitch, terr, pt shd; htd wc; mv service pnt; shwrs inc; el pnts (4-10A) €3.05-7.90; gas; shop; rest 400m; bar; playgrnd; rv sw & beach 400m; 10% statics; adv bkg rec high ssn; quiet; CKE/CCI. "Lovely, peaceful, clean site." € 10.50   2008*

RAUZAN *7D2* (200m N Rural) *44.78237, -0.12712* **Camping du Vieux Château, 33420 Rauzan [05 57 84 15 38; fax 05 57 84 18 34; contact@camping-levieuxchateau.com; www.camping-levieuxchateau.com]** Fr Libourne S on D670, site is on D123 about 1.5km fr D670, sp. Sm, mkd pitch, shd; wc; chem disp; baby facs; shwrs inc; el pnts (6A) €3.30 (poss rev pol); gas; lndtte; shop, tradsmn; rest 200m; snacks; sm bar & in 200m; playgrnd; pool; tennis; rv/lake 5km; cycle hire; horseriding; wine-tasting; entmnt; TV; 10% statics; dogs €2; poss cr; Eng spkn; adv bkg; quiet; red low ssn; ccard acc; CKE/CCI. "Lovely site but take care tree roots on pitches; helpful owners; basic san facs - ltd low ssn & poss not well-maintained, & poss stretched high ssn; access to some pitches diff when wet; conv vineyards." ♦ 29 Mar-11 Oct. € 24.50   2012*

RAVENOVILLE PLAGE see Ste Mere Eglise *1C4*

REALMONT *8E4* (2km SW Rural) *43.77092, 2.16336* **Camp Municipal La Batisse, Route Graulhet, 81120 Réalmont [05 63 55 50 41 or 05 63 45 50 68; fax 05 63 55 65 62; camping-realmont@wanadoo.fr; www.realmont.fr]** On D612 fr Albi heading S thro Réalmont. On exit Réalmont turn R on D631 where site sp. Site 1.5km on L on Rv Dadou. Sm, pt shd; wc; shwrs; el pnts (3A) inc; gas; shops, rest, snacks, bar 2km; playgrnd; rv adj; fishing; some statics; quiet. "Pleasant, peaceful, well-kept site; friendly warden; dated but clean san facs; nr Albi-Castres cycle rte; excel value; mkt Wed; gd" 1 Apr-30 Sep. € 11.50   2013*

RECOUBEAU JANSAC see Luc en Diois *9D3*

REGUINY *2F3* (1km S Urban) *47.96928, -2.74083* **Camp Municipal de l'Etang, Rue de la Piscine, 56500 Réguiny [02 97 38 66 11; fax 02 97 38 63 44; mairie.requiny@ wanadoo.fr; www.reguiny.com]** On D764 fr Pontivy to Ploërmel, turn R into D11 to Réguiny then foll sp. Med, pt shd; wc; chem disp; mv service pnt; baby facs; shwrs inc; el pnts (10A) €2.50; lndtte; shop 2km; rest, bar 1km; playgrnd; htd pool 500m; dogs €2; phone; Eng spkn; quiet; ccard acc; "Gd facs; gd touring base" 15 Jun-15 Sep. € 9.80   2013*

REGUSSE *10E3* (2.5km NW Rural) *43.66031, 6.15103* **Village-Camping Les Lacs du Verdon, Domaine de Roquelande, 83630 Régusse [04 94 70 17 95; fax 04 94 70 51 79; info@ homair.com; www.homair.com]** Fr W exit A8 junc 34 at St Maximin onto D560 Barjols, Tavernes, Montmeyan then D30 to Régusse. At rndabt in Régusse turn L twd St Jean & foll sp. Fr E exit A8 junc 36 Le Muy then Draguignan then D557 to Villecroze, Aups & Régusse. At rndabt turn R twd St Jean & foll sp. Lge, mkd pitch, pt shd; wc; chem disp; mv service pnt; shwrs inc; el pnts (6A) inc; gas; lndtte; shop; rest, snacks; bar; BBQ; playgrnd; pool; tennis; entmnt; internet; TV rm; 10% statics; dogs €5; poss cr; Eng spkn; adv bkg ess high ssn; quiet; ccard acc; CKE/CCI. "Beautiful area; mainly gravel pitches under pine trees; diff lge outfits without mover due to trees." ♦ 1 Apr-30 Sep. € 31.00   2010*

REHAUPAL see Tholy, Le *6F3*

REILLANNE *10E3* (2km W Rural) *43.86875, 5.63639* **Camping le Vallon des Oiseaux (Naturist), 04110 Reillanne [04 92 76 47 33; fax 04 92 76 44 64; info@levallon.com; www.levallon.com]** Fr Apt take D900 twd Céreste. Approx 2km after Céreste sharp turn L onto minor rd. Site sp. Med, pt sl, pt shd; wc; chem disp; shwrs inc; el pnts (4A) €3; lndtte; shop 2km; tradsmn; rest, snacks; bar; playgrnd; pool; TV rm; 5% statics; dogs €3; phone; poss cr; Eng spkn; adv bkg; quiet; red low ssn; INF card. "Friendly, helpful staff." ♦ 29 Mar-18 Oct. € 24.00   2008*

"We must tell The Club about that great site we found"

Get your site reports in by mid-August and we'll do our best to get your updates into the next edition of Caravan Europe.

REIMS *3D4* (16km SE Rural) *49.16687, 4.21416* **Camp Municipal, 8 Rue de Routoir, Courmelois, 51360 Val-de-Vesle [03 26 03 91 79; fax 03 26 03 91 79; valdevesle. mairie@wanadoo.fr; www.reims-tourism.com]** Fr Reims twd Châlons-en-Champagne on D944, turn L by camp sp on D326 to Val-de-Vesle, foll camp sp; look for tall grain silos by canal. NB do not turn L bef D326 due narr lane. Med, mkd pitch, shd; wc; chem disp; shwrs inc; el pnts (6-10A) €3 (long lead poss req); lndtte; shops 1km; tradsmn; BBQ; playgrnd; pool; rv fishing; dogs €1; poss v cr; adv bkg; some rlwy/rd noise (not a problem); ccard acc over €15; CKE/CCI. "Charming, well-kept, busy site amongst trees; popular NH; rec arrive early; informal pitching; friendly, helpful staff; new security gate, booking in req for code (2011); in sm vill (no shops); poss mosquito prob; cycle rte to Reims along canal; gd touring base" ♦ 1 Apr-15 Oct. € 9.50   2013*

REMIREMONT *6F2* (8km SE Rural) *47.94799, 6.63296* **Camping Le Pont de Maxonchamp, 3 Rue du Camping, 88360 Rupt-sur-Moselle [03 29 24 30 65 or 03 84 49 38 72; olivierleduc88@orange.fr; www.camping-vosges-88.com]** Fr Remiremont SE on N66/E51; site clearly sp to L; also visible 300m down lane. Sm, pt shd; wc; chem disp; shwrs €1; el pnts (10A) €3; shop 3km; playgrnd; rv sw adj; 20% statics; dogs €0.50; poss cr; quiet; CKE/CCI. "Attractive rvside site; if recep clsd site yourself; recep open eves; vg." ♦ 1 Apr-15 Oct. € 9.00   2011*

REMOULINS *10E2* (1.5km S Rural) *43.92655, 4.56445* **Camping Domaine de la Soubeyranne, Route de Beaucaire, 30210 Remoulins [04 66 37 03 21; fax 04 66 37 14 65; soubeyranne@franceloc.fr; www. soubeyranne.com or www.campings-franceloc.fr]** Exit A9 for Remoulins onto D986. On D6086 Remoulins to Nîmes rd turn L after x-ing bdge fr Remoulins. Site on L in 1km. Lge, mkd pitch, shd; wc; chem disp; baby facs; shwrs inc; el pnts (6A) €4.70; gas; lndtte; shop; rest, snacks; bar; BBQ; playgrnd; htd, covrd pool; paddling pool; fishing; tennis; TV rm; some statics; dogs €5; adv bkg; some rd & rlwy noise; CKE/CCI. "Gd site." 4 Apr-27 Sep. € 26.50   2009*

REMOULINS *10E2* (2km NW Rural) *43.94805, 4.54583*
**Camping La Sousta, Ave du Pont de Gard, 30210
Remoulins [04 66 37 12 80; fax 04 66 37 23 69; info@
lasousta.fr; www.lasousta.fr]** Fr A9 exit Remoulins, foll sp
for Nîmes, then sp 'Pont du Gard par Rive Droite' thro town.
Immed over rv bdge turn R sp 'Pont du Gard etc'; site on R
800m fr Pont du Gard. Lge, mkd pitch, hdstg, shd; wc; chem
disp; mv service pnt; baby facs; shwrs inc; el pnts (6A) €3; gas;
lndtte; shop; tradsmn; rest adj; snacks; bar; BBQ in sep area;
playgrnd; pool; tennis; rv sw adj; watersports; fishing; cycle
hire; wifi; entmnt; TV; 20% statics; dogs €2; poss cr; Eng spkn;
adv bkg; quiet; ccard acc; red low ssn; CKE/CCI. "Friendly,
helpful staff; poss diff lge o'fits due trees; excel touring
base; in walking dist Pont-du-Gard; vg." ♦ 1 Mar-31 Oct.
€ 23.90   2011*

REMOULINS *10E2* (4km NW Rural) *43.95594, 4.51588*
**Camping International Les Gorges du Gardon, Chemin
de la Barque Vieille, Route d'Uzès, 30210 Vers-Pont-
du-Gard [04 66 22 81 81; fax 04 66 22 90 12; camping.
international@wanadoo.fr; www.le-camping-
international.com]** Exit A9 junc 23 Remoulins & head NW
twd Uzès on D981. Pass turn for Pont-du-Gard & site on L in
1.5km. Or fr E on N100 turn N onto D6086 then D19A to Pont-
du-Gard (avoiding Remoulins cent). Lge, hdg/mkd pitch, pt shd;
wc; chem disp; mv service pnt; baby facs; shwrs inc; el pnts
(6A) inc; gas; lndtte; shop; tradsmn; rest, snacks; bar; playgrnd;
htd pool; rv sw & private beach adj; boating; fishing; tennis;
games area; games rm; entmnt; internet; TV rm; 10% statics;
dogs €2; no twin-axles or o'fits over 5m; Eng spkn; adv bkg;
quiet; ccard acc; red low ssn/long stay; CKE/CCI. "Beautiful
location; many sm pitches - some lge pitches to back of site;
friendly, cheerful owners; excel san facs, ltd low ssn; beavers in
rv; site poss subject to flooding & evacuation; superb; Conv for
the Pont du Gard, thoroughly rec staying several nights, unique
site" ♦ 15 Mar-30 Sep. € 23.20   2013*

REMOULINS *10E2* (7km NW Rural) *43.95788, 4.48716*
**Camping Le Barralet, 30210 Collias [04 66 22 84 52 or
06 11 56 01 21 (mob); fax 04 66 22 89 17; camping@
barralet.fr; www.camping-barralet.com]** W off A9 on D981
to Uzès; thro Remoulins; foll camp sp; turn S on D112 D3 to
Collias; sp in 4km on L past quarry on bend; turn L up narr rd &
site in 50m on R. Med, pt shd; wc; shwrs inc; el pnts €4 (adaptors
avail); lndtte; shop; rest, snacks; bar; pool; playgrnd; fishing &
canoe/kayak hire adj; tennis nr; games area; 30% statics; dogs €2;
phone; quiet; ccard acc; CKE/CCI. "Gd location; gd rvside walks
& cycling; sm pitches; poss lge youth groups use activity cent." ♦
1 Apr-20 Sep. € 19.00   2010*

REMUZAT *9D2* (9km NE Rural) *44.44598, 5.45913* **Aire
Naturelle de Pommerol (Morin), Quartier Lemoulin,
26470 Pommerol [04 75 27 25 63 or 04 75 98 26 25 (LS);
fax 04 75 27 25 63; camping.pommerol@wanadoo.fr]**
Fr Rémuzat, take D61 N dir La Motte-Chalancon. In vill, turn
R & cont on D61 for 6km dir La Charce, then turn R onto
D138 sp Montmorin/Pommerol. In 1km bear R onto D338 to
Pommerol. Site sp in 2km on R. Diff access for lge c'vans. Sm,
terr, pt shd; htd wc; chem disp; shwrs inc; el pnts €2 (long lead
req); lndtte; shop 9km; rest, snacks, bar, (high ssn only or 9km);
BBQ; playgrnd; htd pool 10km; lake sw, beach 12km; dogs €2;
Eng spkn; adv bkg; quiet; CKE/CCI. "Superb views; adv bkg ess
high ssn." 1 Apr-30 Oct. € 11.00   2009*

REMUZAT *9D2* (S Rural) *44.41036, 5.35272* **Camp
Municipal Les Aires, 26510 Rémuzat [04 75 27 81 43 or
04 75 25 85 78 (Mairie); camping.municipal@remuzat.fr;
www.remuzat.com]** Fr Rosans take D94 W for approx 10km;
then R onto D61 to Rémuzat; site on R at ent to vill, on rvside.
Sm, hdg/mkd pitch, pt shd; wc; chem disp; baby facs; shwrs
inc; el pnts (6-10A) €2.80-3.80; lndtte; shop nr; BBQ; dogs
€2.30; poss v cr if rallies; quiet; CKE/CCI. "Beautiful site, vill
& area; some sm pitches; helpful warden; san facs old but
clean; site poss clsd if weather bad; excel." ♦ May-30 Sep.
€ 9.50   2010*

REMUZAT *9D2* (10km W Rural) *44.41257, 5.26188*
**Camping La Vallée Bleue, La Plaine-du-Pont, 26510
Sahune [04 75 27 44 42 or 06 81 19 94 22 (mob); lavallee.
bleue0711@orange.fr; www.lavalleebleue.com]** On D94
well sp. Med, pt shd; wc; chem disp; shwrs; el pnts (6A) inc;
lndtte; shop 500m; tradsmn; rest, snacks; bar; playgrnd; pool;
5% statics; dogs €1.50; phone; poss cr; adv bkg; quiet; CKE/
CCI. "Golf & fishing nrby." ♦ 1 Apr-30 Sep. € 21.00   2008*

⊞ **RENNES** *2F4* (2km NE Urban) *48.13529, -1.64597*
**Camp Municipal des Gayeulles, Rue du Maurice Audin,
35700 Rennes [02 99 36 91 22; fax 02 23 20 06 34; info@
camping-rennes.com; www.camping-rennes.com]**
Exit Rennes ring rd N136 junc 14 dir Maurepas & Maison
Blanche, follow sp 'Les Gayeules' & site. Narr app to site. Med,
mkd pitch, hdstg, pt sl, pt shd; wc; chem disp; mv service pnt;
baby facs; some serviced pitches; shwrs; el pnts (10A) €3.50-4;
lndtte (inc dryer); shops 500m; tradsmn; snacks; office clsd
12.30-16.00; BBQ; playgrnd; pool adj; tennis, archery & mini-
golf nrby; internet; dogs €1; phone; bus; m'van o'night area;
Eng spkn; adv bkg; quiet; red low ssn/long stay; ccard acc; CKE/
CCI. "Lovely, well-kept, well-run site adj park; friendly, helpful
staff; lge pitches; slight sl for m'vans; 1st class facs; park adj;
reg bus to Rennes, a lovely city; sm m'van Aire de Service adj;
excel" ♦ € 17.00 (CChq acc)   2013*

RENNES LES BAINS *8G4* (S Rural) *42.91364, 2.31839*
**Camping La Bernède, 11190 Rennes-les-Bains
[04 68 69 86 49; fax 04 68 74 09 31; camping.
renneslesbains@wanadoo.fr; www.renneslesbains.org]**
S fr Carcassonne or N fr Quillan on D118, turn E at Couiza on
D613. In 5km turn R onto D14 to Rennes-les-Bains in 3km.
Drive thro vill, then turn L over bdge sp Sougraigne, then
immed L. Sm, mkd pitch, pt shd; wc; chem disp (wc); shwrs
inc; el pnts (5A) €2.55; lndtte; shop; tradsmn; rest in vill; bar;
playgrnd; rv adj; fishing; 10% statics; dogs €1.15; adv bkg;
quiet; CKE/CCI. "10 mins walk into town with thermal spa;
vg." ♦ 10 May-30 Sep. € 11.55   2008*

REOLE, LA *7D2* (S Urban) *44.57778, -0.03360* **Camp
Municipal La Rouergue, Bords de Garonne, 33190 La
Réole [05 56 61 13 55; fax 05 56 61 89 13; lareole@
entredeuxmers.com; www.entredeuxmers.com]** On N113
bet Bordeaux & Agen or exit A62 at junc 4. In La Réole foll sps
S on D9 to site on L immed after x-ing suspension bdge. Med,
pt shd; wc; shwrs inc; el pnts (3A) inc; gas; shop; tradsmn;
snacks; pool 500m; fishing, boating; dogs €2; some rd noise.
"Resident warden; 2m barrier clsd 1200-1500; Sat mkt on rv
bank." 15 May-15 Oct. € 14.00   2009*

RETHEL *5C1* (14km E Urban) *49.48234, 4.57589* **Camp Municipal Le Vallage, 38 Chemin de l'Assaut, 08130 Attigny [03 24 71 23 06 or 03 24 71 20 68; fax 03 24 71 94 00; mairie-d-attigny@wanadoo.fr]** E on D983 fr Rethel to Attigny; fr town cent take D987 twd Charleville; over rv bdge; 2nd turn on L; sp. Med, hdg/mkd pitch, hdstg, pt shd; wc; chem disp; shwrs inc; el pnts (10A) inc; lndry rm; shop 1km; tradsmn; pool & sports facs adj; playgrnd; fishing; tennis; 50% statics; dogs; phone; CKE/CCI. "Lovely quiet site; lge pitches; helpful staff; gd facs." 1 Apr-30 Sep. € 12.90   2010*

REVEL *8F4* (500m E Urban) *43.45454, 2.01515* **Camp Municipal Le Moulin du Roy, Tuilerie de Chazottes, off Ave de Sorèze, 31250 Revel [05 61 83 32 47 or 05 62 18 71 40 (Mairie); mairie@mairie-revel.fr; www. tourisme-revel.com]** Fr Revel ring rd take D1/D85 dir Sorèze, site sp. Med, hdg pitch, pt shd; mv service pnt; shwrs inc; el pnts €320; shop 500m; supmkt 1km; playgrnd; htd pool adj; lake sw & beach 2.5km; tennis adj; dogs €0.90; phone; bus; Eng spkn; daytime heavy traff noise; red CKE/CCI. "Pleasant, immac site; helpful staff; Sat mkt; vg." 2 Jun-7 Sep. € 10.20   2011*

REVEL *8F4* (5.5km E Urban) *43.45446, 2.06953* **Camping St Martin, Les Vigariés, 81540 Sorèze [05 63 50 20 19; fax 05 63 73 28 99; campingsaintmartin@gmail.com; www. campingsaintmartin.com]** Fr Revel take D85 sp Sorèze; site sp on N side of vill; turn L at traff lts; site on R in 100m. Sm, hdg/mkd pitch, some hdstg, pt shd; wc; chem disp; mv service pnt; shwrs inc; el pnts (10A) €3.60; lndtte; sm shop & rest 500m; snacks; bar; BBQ; playgrnd; pool; lake sw 3km; tennis; games rm; wifi; entmnt; TV; 20% statics; dogs €1.50; quiet; CKE/CCI. "Vg, well-kept site; friendly staff; excel san facs; fascinating medieval town; nr Bassin de St Ferréol; excel mkt in Revel; rec; poss noisy at w/end" ◆ 1 Apr-30 Sep. € 30.80   2013*

REVEL *8F4* (8km SE Rural) *43.40780, 2.08640* **Camping de la Rigole, 4 Route du Barrage, 81540 Les Cammazes [tel/ fax 05 63 73 28 99; campings.occitanie@orange.fr; http:// campingdlr.free.fr]** Fr Revel take D629 E to Les Cammazes. Thro vill 300m take 1st L. Site well sp, 1km fr vill. Med, mkd pitch, hdstg, terr, pt sl, terr, pt shd; wc; chem disp; shwrs inc; el pnts (4A) inc; lndtte; shop &1km; tradsmn; rest, snacks; bar; BBQ; playgrnd; pool; lake sw 5km; games area; TV rm; dogs €1; bus 3km; phone; poss cr; Eng spkn; adv bkg; v quiet; red low ssn; CKE/CCI. "Pretty, well laid-out, immac site; welcoming, helpful staff; help req to access some pitches; gd san facs; steep slopes on site; phone ahead to check open low ssn; excel." ◆ 15 Apr-1 Oct. € 18.50   2008*

REVEL *8F4* (4km S Rural) *43.43415, 2.01662* **Camping En Salvan, 31350 St Ferréol [05 61 83 55 95; lvt-en-salvan@ wanadoo.fr; www.camping-ensalvan.com]** Fr Revel head S on D629 up long hill. At lake at top turn R for 2km, site on R. Sm, mkd pitch, hdstg, shd; shwrs; mv service pnt; el pnts (3-10A) €2-3.90; lndtte; shop; BBQ; playgrnd; pool; paddling pool; games area; 20% statics; dogs €1; poss cr; quiet; red low ssn. "Pleasant site; sm pitches; tired end of ssn; poss school parties low ssn." 5 Apr-31 Oct. € 12.50   2008*

REVIGNY SUR ORNAIN *5D1* (250m S Urban) *48.82663, 4.98412* **Camp Municipal du Moulin des Gravières, Rue du Stade, 55800 Revigny-sur-Ornain [tel/fax 03 29 78 73 34 or 03 29 70 50 55 (Mairie); contact@ot-revigny-ornain.fr; www.gravieredumoulin.lezinnes.fr]** N fr Bar-le-Duc on D994 to Revigny-sur-Ornain; fr town cent take D995 twd Vitry-le-François. Site on R, sp. Sm, hdg/mkd pitch, pt shd; wc (some cont); chem disp; mv service pnt; baby facs; shwrs inc; el pnts (6A) €2.70; lndtte (inc dryer); supmkt 500m; snacks; playgrnd; tennis & cycle hire in town; TV rm; 3 statics; dogs; Eng spkn; adv bkg; v quiet; ccard not acc; CKE/CCI. "Pleasant, well-kept site; lge pitches; vg, modern facs; trout stream runs thro site; gd cycling along canal; mkt Wed adj; highly rec; excel site, beautifully kept" ◆ 29 Mar-7 Oct. € 12.80   2013*

REVIN *5C1* (N Rural) *49.94420, 4.63138* **Camp Municipal Les Bateaux, Quai Edgar Quinet, 08500 Revin [03 24 40 15 65 or 03 24 40 19 59 (LS); fax 03 24 40 21 98; camping.les. bateaux-revin@wanadoo.fr; www.ville-revin.fr]** Fr Fumay take D988 to Revin, or fr Charleville take D989/988 (23km) or take rte D1 E fr Rocroi. On ent Revin turn L after narr bdge (1-way) over Rv Meuse. Fr cent of Revin foll sp Montherme; at Total g'ge R fork, then turn L, 500m to site, sp. Med, hdg/mkd pitch, pt shd; htd wc; chem disp; baby facs; shwrs; el pnts (6A) inc (poss rev pol); lndtte; shop; supmkt 1km; tradsmn; playgrnd; rv fishing; paragliding nrby; games rm; TV rm; 5% statics; dogs €0.95; adv bkg; quiet; red low ssn; CKE/ CCI. "Peaceful, clean, rvside site; lge pitches; excel san facs; if office clsd site self & book in later; helpful warden; gd walks; excel." ◆ Easter-30 Oct. € 11.80   2010*

RHINAU *6E3* (500m NW Rural) *48.32123, 7.69788* **Camping Ferme des Tuileries, 1 Rue des Tuileries, 67230 Rhinau [03 88 74 60 45; fax 03 88 74 85 35; camping. fermetuileries@neuf.fr; www.fermedestuileries.com]** S on D468 at Boofzheim, turn L at sp Rhinau, D5. Site 2.4km after L turn. Ent Rhinau site 3rd turn R. Lge, mkd pitch, some hdstg; pt shd; wc; chem disp; mv service pnt; baby facs; shwrs inc; el pnts (2-6A) €1.40-3.20; gas; lndtte; shops 500m; tradsmn; rest & snacks (Jul/Aug); playgrnd; sm htd pool; lake sw; tennis; cycle hire; games area; entmnt; 50% statics; no dogs; poss cr; quiet. "Spacious site with excel facs; regimented; free ferry across Rv Rhine adj; vg." ◆ 1 Apr-30 Sep. € 9.90   2008*

RIBEAUVILLE *6E3* (2km E Urban) *48.19490, 7.33648* **Camp Municipal Pierre-de-Coubertin, Rue de Landau, 68150 Ribeauville [tel/fax 03 89 73 66 71; camping.ribeauville@ wanadoo.fr; www.camping-alsace.com]** Exit N83 junc 20 at Ribeauville onto D106 & foll rd to o'skts; at traff lts turn R & then immed R again. Site on R in 500m. Camp at sports grnd nr Lycée. Lge, mkd pitch, pt sl, pt shd; htd wc; chem disp; baby facs; shwrs inc; el pnts (16A) €3.50; gas; lndtte; sm shop; pool adj; wifi; dogs €1; poss cr; quiet; red low ssn;CKE/CCI. "Well-run site; friendly, helpful staff; park outside site bef checking in; clean san facs; resident storks; gd touring base; mkt Sat; highly rec; excel." ◆ 15 Apr-31 Oct. € 13.00   2011*

RIBEAUVILLE *6E3* (4.5km S Rural) *48.16200, 7.31691*
Camp Intercommunal, 1 Route du Vin, 68340 Riquewihr
[03 89 47 90 08; fax 03 89 49 05 63; camping.riquewihr@
wanadoo.fr; www.ribeauville-riquewihr.com]
Fr Strasbourg on N83/E25, take junc 21 (fr opp dir take junc
22) to Blebenheim/Riquewihr. D416 & D3 thro Blebenheim.
At T-junc turn R onto D1B, site on R at rndabt. Lge, hdg/
mkd pitch, some hdstg, pt sl, pt shd; htd wc; chem disp; mv
service pnt; baby facs; shwrs inc; el pnts (6A) €3.50 (poss rev
pol); gas; lndtte (inc dryer); shops 5km; tradsmn in ssn; snacks;
playgrnd; tennis; games area adj; dogs €1.20; poss cr; adv bkg;
noise fr main rd;wifi; ccard acc;CKE/CCI ess. "Rec arr early;
friendly staff; san facs clean; gd for sm children; lovely town;
m'van o'night area; office clsd 12.00-14.00" 28 Mar-31 Dec.
€ 20.90   2013*

RIBERAC *7C2* (500m N Rural) *45.25668, 0.34280* **Camp**
Municipal La Dronne, Route d'Angoulême, 24600 Ribérac
[05 53 90 50 08 or 05 53 90 03 10; fax 05 53 91 35 13;
ot.riberac@perigord.tm.fr] Site on L of main rd D709 immed
N of bdge over Rv Dronne on o'skts of Ribérac. Med, some hdg
pitches, pt shd; wc (some cont); shwrs inc; el pnts (10A) €2.50;
lndtte; supmkt 500m; tradsmn; snacks; playgrnd; pool 1km;
dogs €0.50; no twin-axles; quiet. "Vg, well-run site; pitches in
cent hdgd & shady; facs gd & clean but inadequate high ssn;
Fri mkt." ♦ 1 Jun-15 Sep. € 8.55   2010*

RIBES *9D2* (5km) *44.29545, 4.12436* **Camping Les Cruses,**
07260 Joyeuse [(33) (0)4 75 39 54 69; les-cruses@
wanadoo.fr; www.campinglescruses.com/] Sm mkd pitch,
shd, htd wc; chem disp; mv service pnt; child/baby facs; shwrs;
el pnts (10A); lndtte; tradsmn; rest, snacks, bar; BBQ; Eng spkn;
adv bkg; quiet; ccard acc; CKE/CCI. "Excel pool and jacuzzi. V
helpful and friendly owners. nr lively town and places to see"
1 Apr-30 Sept. € 29.00   2012*

RICHELIEU *4H1* (500m S Rural) *47.00774, 0.32078* **Camp**
Municipal, 6 Ave de Schaafheim, 37120 Richelieu
[02 47 58 15 02 / 02 47 58 10 13 (mob); commune-de-
richelieu@wanadoo.fr; www.tourisme-richelieu.fr]
Fr Loudun, take D61 to Richelieu, D749 twd Châtellerault; site
sp. Sm, hdg/mkd pitch, pt shd; wc; chem disp; shwrs inc; el pnts
(5-15A); lndtte; shop nr; playgrnd; pool 500m; fishing; tennis;
quiet; CKE/CCI. "Phone ahead to check site open low ssn; clean
site and facs; gd value" ♦ 15 May-15 Sep. € 10.20   2013*

RIEL LES EAUX *6F1* (1.8km W Rural) *47.97050, 4.64990*
Camp Municipal du Plan d'Eau, 21570 Riel-les-Eaux [tel/
fax 03 80 93 72 76; bar-camping-du-marais@wanadoo.fr]
NE fr Châtillon-sur-Seine on D965 twd Chaumont: after 6km
turn N onto D13 at Brion-sur-Ource; cont thro Belan-sur-Ource.
Site almost opp junc with D22 turning to Riel-les-Eaux; site well
sp. Sm, hdg pitch, pt shd; wc; chem disp; shwrs inc; el pnts (6A)
€3; tradsmn; snacks; bar; playgrnd; lake adj; fishing; Eng spkn;
quiet; CKE/CCI. "Conv Champagne area; excel." ♦
1 Apr-31 Oct. € 8.60   2009*

RIEZ *10E3* (5km N Rural) *43.86953, 6.13160* **Camp Municipal**
Les Lavandes, Chemin de Touires, 04410 Puimoisson
[04 92 74 71 49] N fr Riez on D953 to Puimoisson in 5km;
turn L onto D56; site in 1km on R. Med, mkd pitch, pt shd;
wc (cont) (own san rec); shwrs inc; shop, rest & snacks 1km;
dogs €1.50; quiet; ccard not acc;CKE/CCI. "Pleasant, clean site;
mountain views; ramp to gd basic facs; conv Gorges du Verdon
& Lac de Ste Croix - gd sw & beach; gd walking & cycling." ♦
1 Jun-30 Sep. € 9.40   2009*

RIEZ *10E3* (500m SE Urban) *43.81306, 6.09931* **Camping**
Rose de Provence, Rue Edouard Dauphin, 04500 Riez
[tel/fax 04 92 77 75 45; info@rose-de-provence.com;
www.rose-de-provence.com] Exit A51 junc 18 onto D82
to Gréoux-les-Bains then D952 to Riez. On reaching Riez strt
across rndabt, at T-junc turn L & immed R, site sp. Med, mkd
pitch, pt shd; wc; chem disp; shwrs inc; el pnts (6A) inc; lndtte;
rest, snacks, bar 500m; playgrnd; jacuzzi; lake sw 10km; tennis
adj; 5% statics; dogs €1.90; phone; adv bkg; no ccard; red
low ssn; CKE/CCI; "Beautiful, well-kept site; helpful, friendly
owners; gd san facs; nice vill; conv Verdon Gorge" ♦ ltd
3 Apr-3 Oct. € 17.70   2013*

RILLE *4G1* (4km W Rural) *47.45750, 0.21840* **Camping**
Huttopia Rillé, Base de Loisirs de Pincemaille, Lac de Rillé,
37340 Rillé [02 47 24 62 97; fax 02 47 24 63 61; rille@
huttopia.com; www.huttopia.com] Fr N or S D749 to Rillé,
foll sp to Lac de Pincemaille, site sp on S side of lake. Med,
shd; htd wc; chem disp; mv service pnt; baby facs; fam bthrm;
shwrs inc; el pnts (6-10A) €4.20-6.20; shop; rest, snacks; bar;
playgrnd; htd pool; lake sw & beach adj; fishing; watersports;
tennis; games rm; some statics; dogs €3.50; sep car park;
adv bkg. "Peaceful site; vg walking; excel." 24 Apr-5 Nov.
€ 24.00   2008*

RIOM *9B1* (5km NW Rural) *45.90614, 3.06041* **Camping de la**
Croze, St Hippolyte, 63140 Châtel-Guyon [04 73 86 08 27
or 06 87 14 43 62 (mob); fax 04 73 86 08 51; info@
campingcroze.com; www.campingcroze.com] Fr A71
exit junc 13; ring rd around Riom sp Châtel-Guyon to Mozac,
then D227. Site L bef ent St Hippolyte. Fr Volvic on D986 turn
L at rndabt after Leclerc supmkt & L again to D227. NB Not
rec to tow thro Riom. Lge, mkd pitch, pt sl, pt shd; htd wc;
chem disp; shwrs inc; el pnts (6-10A) €2.50; lndtte (inc dryer);
shops 2km; tradsmn; playgrnd; htd pool; wifi; 10% statics;
dogs €1.30; quiet; CKE/CCI. "Gd sightseeing area; mini-
bus to Châtel-Guyon (2km) high ssn; vg." 1 May-20 Oct.
€ 10.20   2010*

RIOM *9B1* (6km NW Rural) *45.91597, 3.07682* **Camping**
Clos de Balanède, Route de la Piscine, 63140 Châtel-
Guyon [04 73 86 02 47; fax 04 73 86 05 64; clos-balanede.
sarl-camping@wanadoo.fr; www.balanede.com] Fr Riom
take D227 to Châtelguyon, site on R on o'skts of town. Tight
turn into ent. Lge, pt sl, pt shd; wc; shwrs inc; el pnts (6-10A)
€3-3.50.; gas; lndtte; shop; rest, snacks; bar; playgrnd; 3 pools;
tennis; dogs €1.50; poss cr; Eng spkn; adv bkg; quiet; poss
open until 31 Dec; red low ssn/long stay. "Pleasant, well-run
site; san facs dated; some pitches steep & poss uneven; sh walk
to town; m'vans/campers not allowed up to Puy-de-Dôme -
must use bus provided; Conv for A71, gd NH; Gd quiet site;
conv for Clermont-Ferrand and Puy de Dôme" ♦
12 Apr-30 Sep. € 23.70   2013*

RIOM ES MONTAGNES 7C4 (10km SW Rural) 45.24821, 2.53650 **Camp Municipal Le Pioulat, 15400 Trizac** [04 71 78 64 20 or 04 71 78 60 37 (Mairie); fax 04 71 78 65 40; mairie.trizac@wanadoo.fr; www.chalets-decouverte.com] D678 W fr Riom-ès-Montagnes to Trizac. Site on R after leaving vill S twd Mauriac. Sm, hdg pitch, pt sl, pt shd; htd wc; chem disp; el pnts (5A) inc; gas, tradsmn, rest, bar, shops 1km; BBQ; lndtte; playgrnd; tennis nr; sand beach; lake sw; quiet; Eng spkn; adv bkg; phone; CKE/CCI. "Beautiful site, lovely scenery; friendly staff; clean facs; vg walking area; highly rec." ◆ 16 Jun-16 Sep. € 11.00   2010*

RIOZ 6G2 (E Rural) 47.42397, 6.07342 **Camp Municipal du Lac, Rue de la Faïencerie, 70190 Rioz** [03 84 91 91 59, 03 84 91 84 84 (Mairie) or 06 33 78 63 75 (mob); fax 03 84 91 90 45; mairiederioz@wanadoo.fr; www.rioz.fr] Site sp off D15. Med, some hdg pitch, some hdstg, pt shd; htd wc; baby facs; shwrs inc; el pnts (16A) €2.50; gas; shops 500m; rests in vill; playgrnd; pool adj; dogs €1.50; quiet, but some rd noise. "Site yourself, warden calls; some lge pitches; gd facs; footpath to vill shops." 1 Apr-30 Sep. € 10.40   2011*

"I need an on-site restaurant"

We do our best to make sure site information is correct, but it is always best to check any must-have facilities are still available or will be open during your visit.

RIOZ 6G2 (7km S Rural) 47.35873, 6.07855 **Camping L'Esplanade, Rue du Pont, 70190 Cromary** [03 84 91 82 00 or 03 84 91 85 84 (LS); benttom@hotmail.com; www.lesplanade.nl] Fr S on N57 take D14 E thro Devecey. At Vielley turn L onto D412. Site on L over rv. Fr N on N57 by-pass Rioz & take slip rd onto D15 sp Sorans. Turn L in vill, pass under N57 to They, then foll sp Cromary & site. Sm, hdg/mkd pitch, pt shd; wc (some cont); chem disp; shwrs inc; el pnts (4-8A) €2.10-3.10; lndtte; shop 3km; tradsmn; snacks; BBQ; playgrnd; rv sw adj; 40% statics; dogs €0.50; Eng spkn; adv bkg; quiet; ccard acc. "Well-kept site; welcoming Dutch owners; v muddy after heavy rain (no tractor help); many itinerants (Jul 08)." ◆ ltd 1 Apr-30 Nov. € 10.30   2008*

RIQUEWIHR see Ribeauville 6E3

RISCLE 8E2 (500m N Urban) 43.66324, -0.08180 **FFCC Camp Municipal Le Pont de l'Adour, Allée du Camping, 32400 Riscle** [05 67 36 00 08; fax 05 62 69 72 45; camping.dupontdeladour@wanadoo.fr; www.camping-adour.new.fr] On ent Riscle fr N on D935, site on L immed after x-ing Rv Adour. Med, hdg pitch, pt shd; wc (some cont); chem disp; mv service pnt; shwrs inc; el pnts (6A) inc; lndtte; shop; rest, snacks; pool adj; paddling pool; playgrnd; fishing; tennis; games area; entmnt; TV; dogs €1.50; quiet; red low ssn;CKE/CCI. "V quiet low ssn." ◆ 1 Apr-15 Oct. € 15.50   2010*

RIVIERE SAAS ET GOURBY see Dax 8E1

RIVIERE SUR TARN 10E1 (2km E Rural) 44.19100, 3.15675 **FLOWER Camping Le Peyrelade, Route des Gorges du Tarn, 12640 Rivière-sur-Tarn** [05 65 62 62 54; fax 05 65 62 65 61; campingpeyrelade@orange.fr; www.campingpeyrelade.com or www.flowercampings.com] Exit A75 junc 44.1 to Aguessac, then take D907 N thro Rivière-sur-Tarn to site in 2km. Fr Millau drive N on N9 to Aguessac, then onto D907 thro Rivière-sur-Tarn, & site sp on R. Lge, hdg/mkd pitch, terr, shd; wc; chem disp; mv service pnt; baby facs; shwrs inc; el pnts (6A) €4; gas; lndtte (inc dryer); shop; tradsmn; rest, snacks; bar; BBQ; cooking facs; playgrnd; htd pool; rv beach & sw adj; canoeing; games rm; cycle hire 100m; wifi; entmnt; TV; dogs €2; phone; bus; adv bkg; quiet; ccard acc; red low ssn;CKE/CCI. "Excel touring base in interesting area; rvside pitches extra charge." ◆ 16 May-12 Sep. € 27.00   2010*

See advertisement on pages 32 & 33

RIVIERE SUR TARN 10E1 (2.5km E Rural) 44.20083, 3.15944 **Camping du Moulin de la Galinière, Boyne, 12640 Rivière-sur-Tarn** [05 65 62 65 60 or 06 08 28 49 07 (mob); moulindelagaliniere@orange.fr; www.moulindelagaliniere.com] Exit A75 junc 44.1 La Gamasse onto D29 & foll sp Gorges du Tarn. Site ent bef Boyne vill, other side of bdge to Camping Le Pont, bef R turn. Site on bank Rv Tarn. Med, pt shd; wc; baby facs; shwrs inc; el pnts (6A) €3; lndtte; shops adj; tradsmn; rest, snacks; playgrnd; shgl beach; rv sw & fishing; wifi; TV; dogs €1; quiet. "Excel, clean facs, poss tired low ssn; pleasant owners." 1 Apr-30 Sep. € 14.00   2010*

RIVIERE SUR TARN 10E1 (2.5km E Rural) 44.20319, 3.15806 **FFCC Camping Le Pont, Boyne, 12640 Rivière-sur-Tarn** [05 65 62 61 12; nicolas.garlenq@orange.fr; www.campinglepont.com] Fr Millau head N on N9, R after 7km onto D907 sp Gorges du Tarn, site in 9km on R on ent to vill. Sm, pt shd; wc (some cont); chem disp; mv service pnt; shwrs inc; el pnts (8A) €2.50; lndtte; shops, rest adj; playgrnd; sw pool 2km; rv sw & fishing adj; dogs €1; quiet;CKE/CCI. "Gd base for Tarn gorges; canoeing & climbing nrby; facs dated but clean; helpful owner; excel." 1 Apr-30 Sep. € 14.00   2012*

RIVIERE SUR TARN 10E1 (250m SE Rural) 44.18680, 3.13650 **Camping Le Papillon, Les Canals, 12640 La Cresse** [tel/fax 05 65 59 08 42; info@campinglepapillon.com; www.campinglepapillon.com] Fr N on A75 exit junc 44.1 onto D29 to Aguessac; then turn L onto D547/D907; in 3km turn R sp La Cresse on D187. Site sp. Rivière-sur-Tarn on W bank of rv, site on E bank; Rivière-sur-Tarn 2km by rd. Rec app fr S. Sm, hdg/mkd pitch, terr, shd, pt shd; htd wc; chem disp; baby facs; fam bthrm; shwrs inc; el pnts (10A) €3; gas; lndtte; ice; tradsmn, rest, snacks; bar; BBQ (not charcoal); playgrnd; rv beach 150m; TV; 5% statics; dogs €2; Eng spkn; adv bkg; quiet; red long stay/low ssn;CKE/CCI. "Pleasant site, amazing views; new helpful Dutch owner (2009); excel facs; rec." 25 Apr-12 Sep. € 18.50   2009*

FRANCE

RIVIERE SUR TARN *10E1* (400m SW Rural) *44.18530, 3.13060* **Camping Les Peupliers, Rue de la Combe, 12640 Rivière-sur-Tarn [05 65 59 85 17; fax 05 65 61 09 03; lespeupliers12640@ orange.fr; www.campinglespeupliers.fr]** Heading N on N9 turn R dir Aguessac onto D907 twd Rivière-sur-Tarn. Site on R bef vill. Or fr A75 exit junc 44.1 sp Aguessac/Gorges du Tarn. In Aguessac, foll sp Rivière-sur-Tarn for 5km, site clearly sp. Med, hdg/mkd pitch, some hdstg, pt shd; wc (some cont); chem disp; mv service pnt; baby facs; fam bthrm; shwrs inc; el pt (6A) inc; gas; lndtte (inc dryer); shop 200m; tradsmn; rest; snacks, bar; BBQ; supmkt; playgrnd; htd pool; paddling pool; waterslide; rv sw & shgl beach adj; fishing; canoeing; watersports; horseriding; games area; wifi; entmnt; TV rm; tennis; some statics; dogs €3; phone; Eng spkn; adv bkg (rec high ssn); quiet; ccard acc; red low ssn;CKE/CCI. "Lovely rural site alongside the river Tarn. Friendly English speaking staff and owners. Beautiful scenery, kayaking avail. excel site for visiting the famous gorges" ♦ 1 Apr-30 Sep. € 35.00 (CChq acc)   2013*

> ## "Satellite navigation makes touring much easier"
> Remember most sat navs don't know if you're towing or in a larger vehicle – always use yours alongside maps and site directions.

ROANNE *9A1* (12km S Rural) *45.91576, 4.06108* **Camping De Mars, 56 route du Chateau de la Roche, 42123 Cordelle [04 77 64 94 42; campingdemars@yahoo.fr; www.camping-de-mars.com]** On D56 fr Roanne foll dir Lac Villarest; cross barrage & site 4.5km S of Cordelle well sp just off D56. Fr junc 70 on N7 to St Cyr-de-Favières. Foll sp to Château de la Roche on D17 & site on D56. Fr S take D56 immed after Balbigny; single track app, with restricted visibility. Or fr N82 exit for Neulise onto D26 to Jodard, then D56 twd Cordelle. Site on L in 11km. Med, pt sl, terr, pt shd, hdg pitch; wc; chem disp; serviced pitch; mv service pnt; shwrs; child/baby facs; el pnts (6A) inc; lndtte; shop; tradsmn; snacks; bar; playgrnd; pool; lake sw, fishing & watersports 500m; entmnt; 40% statics; Eng spkn; adv bkg rec high ssn; quiet; red long stay;CKE/CCI. "Peaceful; lovely views." ♦ ltd 01 Apr-15 Oct. € 22.00 (CChq acc)   2011*

See advertisement above

ROANNE *9A1* (5km SW Rural) *45.98830, 4.04531* **Camping L'Orée du Lac, Le Barrage, 42300 Villerest [tel/fax 04 77 69 60 88; camping@loreedulac.net; www. loreedulac.net]** Take D53 SW fr Roanne to Villerest; site sp in vill. Sm, mkd pitch, pt sl, pt shd; wc; chem disp (wc); shwrs inc; el pnts (6A) €3.70; shop 400m; rest, snacks; bar; playgrnd; pool; rv 300m; lake 100m; fishing; watersports; entmnt; wifi; TV; dogs €2.50; phone; Eng spkn; adv bkg rec high ssn; quiet; red low ssn;CKE/CCI. "Attractive site nr medieval vill; much of site diff lge/med o'fits; lower part of site diff when wet." 2 Apr-30 Sep. € 16.80   2012*

ROC ST ANDRE, LE see Ploërmel *2F3*

ROCAMADOUR *7D3* (1km E Rural) *44.80427, 1.62755* **FFCC Le Relais du Campeur, L'Hospitalet, 46500 Rocamadour [05 65 33 63 28; fax 05 65 10 68 21; lerelaiducampeur@ orange.fr; www.lerelaiducampeur.com]** Fr S exit D820 (Brive-la-Gaillarde to Cahors) at Payrac; R on D673, 21km to L'Hospitalet. Fr N exit D820 at Cressensac for D840 to Figeac & Rodez; turn R at D673; site at x-rds after 4km; site behind grocer's shop on L. Avoid app fr W thro Rocamadour (acute hairpin & rd 2.2m wide). Med, pt sl, pt shd; wc (some cont); chem disp; mv service pnt; baby facs; shwrs inc; el pnts (10A) €3; gas; lndtte (inc dryer); shop nrby; tradsmn; sm rest; BBQ; playgrnd; pool; cycling; wifi; dogs €2; Eng spkn; adv bkg; quiet; ccard acc; red low ssn. "Busy site, even low ssn; great location; friendly staff; vg san facs; excel." 1 Apr-31 Oct. € 15.00   2011*

ROCAMADOUR *7D3* (1km NW Rural) *44.81040, 1.61615* **FFCC Camping Ferme Branche, Route de Souillac, Les Campagnes, 46500 Rocamadour [05 65 33 63 37; campingfermebranche@ yahoo.fr; www.campingfermebranche.com]** Site on D247, 1km N of Rocamadour. Sm, pt shd; wc; (some cont); mv service pnt; shwrs inc; el pnts (6A) €2; lndtte; shop 1km; BBQ; playgrnd; dogs free; phone; quiet. "Lovely, open, spacious site; gd, clean facs; ltd el pnts; gd for dogs; nr chateau; facs stretched in ssn; friendly owner; great site for price" 1 Apr-15 Nov. € 10.60   2012*

FRANCE

ROCHE BERNARD, LA *2G3* (500m S Urban) *47.51946, -2.30517* Camp Municipal Le Patis, Chemin du Patis, 56130 La Roche-Bernard [02 99 90 60 13 or 02 99 90 60 51 (Mairie); fax 02 99 90 88 28; camping. lrb56@gmail.com; www.camping-larochebernard.com] Leave N165 junc 17 (fr N) junc 15 (fr S) & foll marina sp. NB Arr/exit OK on market day (Thurs) if avoid town cent. Med, mkd pitch, hdstg, pt shd; wc; chem disp; mv service pnt; shwrs inc; el pnts (6A) €4; lndtte; shops & snacks 500m; playgrnd; pool 1km; sand beach 18km; rv adj; sailing, boating at marina adj; dogs €2.30; m'van o'night area; poss cr; Eng spkn; adv bkg; quiet; ccard acc; red low ssn/long stay. "Excel clean site in lovely spot on rv bank; helpful staff; facs poss stretched high ssn; grass pitches poss soft - heavy o'fits phone ahead in wet weather; Thurs mkt; organic mkt Sat; ancient, pretty town up steep hill; gd walks; highly rec" ♦ 1 Apr-30 Sep. € 17.00   2013*

"There aren't many sites open at this time of year"

If you're travelling outside peak season remember to call ahead to check site opening dates – even if the entry says 'open all year'.

ROCHE CHALAIS, LA *7C2* (500m S Rural) *45.14892, -0.00245* Camp Municipal Les Gerbes, Rue de la Dronne, 24490 La Roche-Chalais [05 53 91 40 65 or 06 38 82 40 08 (mob); fax 05 53 90 32 01; campinggerbes@orange.fr; www. larochechalais.com] Fr S on D674 turn sharp L in vill at site sp. Site on R in 500m. Fr N take Coutras-Libourne rd thro vill; site sp on L beyond sm indus est. Med, mkd pitch, terr, pt shd; wc; shwrs inc; el pnts (5-10A) €2.60-3.60 (poss rev pol); lndtte; tradsmn; shops 500m; playgrnd; municipal pool inc; rv sw, fishing, boating & canoeing adj; leisure pk 5km; wifi; adv bkg; rlwy & factory noise; red long stay;CKE/CCI. "Pleasant, well-kept, well-run site nr rv; gd sized pitches, some rvside; gd clean san facs; rec pitch N side of site to avoid factory noise/smell; mkt Sat am; rec" ♦ 15 Apr-30 Sep. € 8.20   2013*

ROCHE DE GLUN, LA see Valence *9C2*

ROCHE POSAY, LA *4H2* (1.5km N Rural) *46.79951, 0.80933* Camping La Roche-Posay Vacances, Route de Lésigny. 86270 La Roche-Posay [05 49 86 21 23; info@ larocheposay-vacances.com; www.larocheposay-vacances.com] On A10 take exit 26 Châtellerault-Nord, La Roche-Posay; foll sp La Roche-Posay; foll the D725 to La Roche-Possay; at rndabt foll sp for 'Camping-Hippodrome'. Lge, hdg/mkd pitch, shd; htd wc; mv service pnt; shwrs inc; el pnts (16A) inc (check pol); gas; lndtte; shops 1km; rest, snacks; bar; BBQ (gas/elec); playgrnd; aquatic park; waterslides; htd, covrd pool; rv sw & fishing 1.5km; tennis; cycle hire; entmnt; 10% statics; dogs €1.50; poss cr; Eng spkn; adv bkg; quiet; red low ssn/long stay;CKE/CCI. "Excel, popular, well-maintained site; 1st class facs; barrier locks automatically 2300; parking avail outside; walk to town on busy rd with no pavement; spa town." ♦ 27 Apr-21 Sep. € 28.00   2011*

See advertisement

ROCHE POSAY, LA *4H2* (3km E Rural) *46.78274, 0.86942* Camp Municipal Les Bords de Creuse, Rue de Pont, 37290 Yzeures-sur-Creuse [tel/fax 02 47 94 48 32 or 02 47 94 55 01 (Mairie); www.yzeuressurcreuse.com] Fr Châtellerault take D725 E twds La Roche-Posay; after x-ing Rv Creuse, turn L onto D750 twds Yzeures-sur-Creuse; at traff lts in vill turn S onto D104; site on R in 200m at T-junc. Med, mkd pitch, pt sl, pt shd; wc; chem disp; shwrs inc; el pnts (6A) inc; lndtte; shop 500m BBQ; pool, rv sw, tennis adj; games rm; dogs; quiet; ♦ 15 Jun-31 Aug. € 15.40   2013*

ROCHE SUR YON, LA *2H4* (8km S Rural) *46.59340, -1.43839* Camping La Venise du Bocage, Le Chaillot, 85310 Nesmy [tel/fax 02 51 98 01 20; contact@la-venise-du-bocage.com; www.la-venise-du-bocage.com] Fr N take D747 dir La Tranche-sur-Mer. Take D36 twd Nesmy & site sp on R after 500m. Sm, mkd pitch, pt shd; wc (some cont); chem disp; baby facs; shwrs inc; el pnts (6-10A) €2.80-3.70; lndtte; ltd shop or 3km; rest & bar 3km; playgrnd; pool; tennis; horseriding, golf 3km; 25% statics; dogs €1.70; phone; poss cr; adv bkg; quiet; red low ssn. "Helpful, friendly owner; gd san facs; poss untidy end of ssn; poss barrier down & staff not avail to open for arr; NH only." ♦ 1 Apr-30 Sep. € 10.60   2009*

FRANCE

ROCHECHOUART *7B3* (1km S Rural) *45.81498, 0.82208* **Camping de la Météorite, Boischenu, 87600 Rochechouart [05 55 03 65 96; fax 05 55 05 97 62; campingdelameteorite@orange.fr; www. campingmeteorite.fr]** S fr Rochechouart on D675. Turn R onto D10 them immed L by lake into park. Site ent at far end of park by snack bar. Med, mkd pitch, pt sl, terr, shd; wc; chem disp; mv service pnt; shwrs inc; el pnts (10A) €3 (poss long lead req); gas; sm shop & 3km; tradsmn; rest adj; BBQ; playgrnd; htd pool; cycle hire; games area; games rm; entmnt; internet; TV; 10% statics; dogs free; phone; poss cr; Eng spkn; adv bkg; quiet; ccard acc; red low ssn. "Delightful, wooded site; renovated (2009); helpful owner; clean, modern san facs; gd pool (unfenced 2009); some v steep (10ft) terraces with no retaining walls (2009)." ♦ ltd Easter-30 Sep. € 18.00 (CChq acc)   2010*

⊞ **ROCHECHOUART** *7B3* (13km SW Rural) *45.73390, 0.68070* **Camping Chez Rambaud, 87440 Les Salles-Lavauguyon [05 55 00 08 90; fax 05 55 00 08 90; camping@chez-rambaud.com; www.chez-rambaud.com]** Fr Rochechouart on D675 then immed R onto D10 dir Videix & Verneuil, in 11km at Verneuil turn L to Les Salles-Lavauguyon. At Salles turn R at bottom of hill (leaving church on L) onto D34 sp Sauvagnac; in 300m turn L sp Chez Rambaud, site on L in 1km along narr rd. Sm, hdg/mkd pitch, some hdstg, sl, pt shd; htd wc; chem disp; shwrs inc; el pnts (10A) €3.50 (long lead poss req); lndtte; ice; shop, rest, bar 1.5km; supmkt 8km; BBQ; lake sw & sand beach 10km; horseriding & kayaking nrby; dogs €1.50; Eng spkn; adv bkg; quiet; no ccard acc;CKE/CCI. "Tranquil, CL-type site in National Park; views over wooded valley; enthusiastic, friendly & helpful British owners; excel, immac facs; levelling blocks poss req; some pitches inadequate for awnings; farm animals in pens on site; gd touring base; gd walking & cycling; easy walk to vill (1.5km); Richard The Lion Heart rte in vill; mkt in Rochechouart Sat; superb." ♦ ltd € 18.00   2012*

> ## "That's changed – Should I let The Club know?"
>
> If you find something on site that's different from the site entry, fill in a report and let us know. See www.caravanclub.co.uk/europereport.

ROCHEFORT *7B1* (1.5km N Coastal) *45.94986, -0.99499* **Camping Le Bateau, Rue des Pêcheurs d'Islande, 17300 Rochefort [05 46 99 41 00; fax 05 46 99 91 65; lebateau@ wanadoo.fr; www.campinglebateau.com]** Exit A837/ E602 at junc 31 & take D733 dir Rochefort. At 1st rndabt by McDonalds, take D733 dir Royan. At next rndabt 1st R onto Rue des Pêcheurs d'Islande. Site at end of rd on L. Med, hdg pitch, pt shd; wc; chem disp; shwrs inc; el pnts (8A) €4; lndtte; shop; tradsmn; rest, snacks; bar; playgrnd; pool; waterslide; watersports; fishing; tennis; games rm; entmnt; 25% statics; dogs €1.70; quiet; red low ssn;CKE/CCI. "Small pitches, a few o'look estuary; helpful staff; basic, clean san facs; poss scruffy low ssn - ducks & geese on site; no twin-axles; gd cycling, walking; mkt Tues & Sat." 1 Apr-1 Nov. € 14.50   2010*

ROCHEFORT *7B1* (500m S Urban) *45.93013, -0.95826* **Camping Municipal Le Rayonnement, 3, avenue de la Fosse aux Mâts [05 46 82 67 70; camping.municipal@ville-rochefort.fr; www.ville-rochefort.fr/decouvrir/camping]** Exit E602 at junc 31 & take D733 dir Rochefort. At rndabt by McDonalds, take D733 dir Royan. Cont on D733. At rndabt with plane take 3rd exit onto Bd Edouard Pouzat. At rndabt take 3rd exit onto Bd de la Résistance, at next rndabt take 1st exit & then turn L onto avenue de la Fosse aux Mâts. Site on L. Med,hdg pitch; hdstg, shd; wc; chem disp;mv service pnt; baby facs; shwrs inc; el pnts (15A) inc; lndtte; shop 100m; tradsmn; BBQ; playgrnd; games rm; cycle hire; entmnt; wifi;TV rm; 15% statics; dogs €1.05; phone; bus 100m; Eng spkn; adv bkg. "Bikes borrowed free of charge; rv Charente & its cycle path to the centre 800m away; v helpful staff; no c'vans over 6m; no twin-axles; san facs are renewed and v clean; Ecolabel campsite; vg." ♦ 27 Feb-03 Dec. € 14.10   2011*

ROCHEFORT *7B1* (8km W Coastal) *45.94828, -1.09592* **Camp Municipal de la Garenne, Ave de l'Ile-Madame, 17730 Port-des-Barques [05 46 84 80 66 or 06 08 57 08 75 (mob); fax 05 46 84 98 33; camping@ville-portdesbarques.fr; www.camping-municipal-portdesbarques.com]** Fr Rochefort S on D773, cross Rv Charente bdge & take 1st exit sp Soubise & Ile Madame. Cont strt thro Port-des-Barques, site on L opp causeway to Ile-Madame. Lge, mkd pitch, unshd; wc; chem disp; mv service pnt; baby facs; shwrs inc; el pnts (10A) inc; lndtte; shop 1km; rest 500m; snacks; bar 1km; playgrnd; htd pool; sand/shgl beach adj; wifi; 25% statics; dogs €1.26; phone; bus adj; poss cr; adv bkg; quiet; ccard acc; red low ssn/long stay;CKE/CCI. "Pleasant site; lge pitches; clean facs; Pitches a little scruffy, but level; Facs dated but clean" ♦ ltd 15 Mar-15 Oct. € 26.00   2013*

ROCHEFORT EN TERRE *2F3* (8km NE) *47.74455, -2.25997* **Camp Municipal de La Digue, Route 77 Le Guélin, 56200 St Martin sur Oust [02 99 91 55 76 or 02 99 91 49 45; fax 02 99 91 42 94; st-martin-oust@wanadoo.fr; www. tourismebretagne.com]** On D873 14km N of Redon at Gacilly, turn W onto D777 twd Rochefort-en-Terre; site sp in 10km in St Martin. Med, pt shd; wc; shwrs; el pnts (3-5A) €2.40; lndtte; shops adj; BBQ; playgrnd; rv fishing 50m; dogs €0.30; adv bkg; quiet; "Towpath walks to vill & shops; clean facs but ltd low ssn; well-maintained site; site yourself, warden calls am & eve; excel, refurbished facs (2013)" 1 May-30 Sep. € 8.00   2013*

ROCHEFORT EN TERRE *2F3* (600m S Rural) *47.69217, -2.34794* **Camping du Moulin Neuf, Chemin de Bogeais, Route de Limerzel, 56220 Rochefort-en-Terre [02 97 43 37 52; fax 02 97 43 35 45]** Fr Redon W on D775 twd Vannes, approx 23km turn R onto D774 sp Rochefort-en-Terre; immed after vill limit sp, turn sharp L up slope to ent. NB Do not drive thro vill. Med, hdg/mkd pitch, terr, pt sl, pt shd; mv service pnt; wc; chem disp; shwrs inc; el pnts ltd (10A) €4.50; lndtte; shops in vill; tradsmn; rest nr; BBQ; play area; htd pool high ssn; lake beach & sw 500m; some statics; dogs €3; poss cr; adv bkg; quiet; ccard acc;CKE/CCI. "Peaceful base for touring area; helpful owners; no vehicle movement or shwrs 2200-0700 (0800 low ssn), but wcs open; no twin-axles; excel." ♦ ltd 11 May-13 Sep. € 19.00   2011*

ROCHEFORT SUR NENON see Dole *6H2*

ROCHELLE, LA *7A1* (12km N Rural/Coastal) *46.25239, -1.11972* **Camp Municipal Les Misottes, 46 Rue de l'Océan, 17137 Esnandes [05 46 35 04 07 or 05 46 01 32 13 (Mairie); lesmisottes@yahoo.fr; www.campinglesmisottes. blogspot.com]** Fr N on D938 or N1327 turn W at Marans onto D105. In 7.5km turn S onto D9 then D202 to Esnandes. Enter vill, at x-rds strt, site on R in 200m. Fr La Rochelle D105 N to cent Esnandes, site sp. Med, mkd pitch, pt shd; wc (cont); shwrs inc; el pnts (10A) €2.85; lndtte; shops 500m; rest, bar 200m; snacks; playgrnd; pool; shgl beach 2km; canal fishing; 5% statics; dogs €1.60; poss cr; Eng spkn; adv bkg; quiet;CKE/ CCI. "Site on the edge of marshlands; poor san facs (2009); liable to flood; vg." 1 Apr-15 Oct. € 8.70   2009*

ROCHELLE, LA *7A1* (5km S Rural/Coastal) *46.11659, -1.11939* **Camping Les Sables, Chemin du Pontreau, 17440 Aytré [05 46 45 40 30; fax 05 46 27 89 02; camping_les_sables@ yahoo.fr; www.camping-les-sables.com]** Fr S (Rochefort) on D137, exit sp Aytré. At 2nd traff lts turn L & foll site sp. Lge, hdg pitch, pt shd; wc; chem disp; mv service pnt; baby facs; shwrs inc; el pnts (6A) €3; lndtte (inc dryer); shop; rest, snacks; bar; BBQ; playgrnd; 2 pools (1 htd, covrd); paddling pool; waterslide; cycle hire; games area; games rm; wifi; entmnt; 50% statics; dogs €1.50; phone; poss cr; Eng spkn; adv bkg; rlwy noise; ccard acc;CKE/CCI. "Vg." ♦ 1 May-31 Oct. € 26.00   2012*

ROCHELLE, LA *7A1* (8km S Coastal) *46.10409, -1.13093* **Camping Les Chirats-La Platère, Route de la Platère, 17690 Angoulins-sur-Mer [05 46 56 94 16; fax 05 46 56 65 95; contact@campingleschirats.fr; www. campingleschirats.fr]** Turn off N137 S of La Rochelle & go thro Angoulins-sur-Mer. Foll site sp fr vill N twd Aytré. After 300m turn L across rlwy at stn. Foll se 'plage' & site. Lge, hdg/ mkd pitch, hdstg, pt sl, pt shd; wc (some cont); chem disp; sauna; serviced pitches; shwrs inc; el pnts (6-10A) inc; gas; lndtte; shop & 2km; tradsmn; rest, snacks; bar; playgrnd; pools (1 htd, covrd); paddling pool; waterslide; jacuzzi; sand beach adj; fishing; fitness rm; games area; horseriding 1km; tennis 500m; TV rm; 10% statics; dogs €2.50; phone; poss cr; Eng spkn; adv bkg; quiet; ccard acc;CKE/CCI. "Gd facs; well-run site; aquarium worth a visit." ♦ Easter-30 Sep. € 26.90 2011*

See advertisement

ROCHELLE, LA *7A1* (500m SW Urban/Coastal) *46.15050, -1.15859* **Camp Municipal Le Soleil, Ave Michel Crépeau, 17000 La Rochelle [05 46 44 42 53 or 05 46 51 51 25 (Mairie)]** App La Rochelle on N11, prepare to take L turn sp Port des Minimes when 2 lge concrete water towers come into view. Foll Port des Minimes to rlwy stn (clock tower). Turn R for site over mini-rndabt then L, then L again onto Quai Georges Simenon. Turn L onto Rue Sénac de Meilan, then turn onto Ave Michel Crépeau, site on L, sp. Or fr S on N137 take D937 sp Port des Minimes & rest as above. Lge, mkd pitch, unshd, some hdstg; wc; chem disp; mv service pnt adj; shwrs inc; el pnts (6A) €3.65; shops 1km; tradsmn; BBQ area; beach 1km; some Eng spkn; adv bkg; some noise fr rd & port;CKE/CCI. "Walking dist cent La Rochelle & marina; sm pitches, facs basic; ltd space for tourers; free m'van o'night area opp site ent; daily mkt in town; site poss full by 1400 - rec arr early; NH only." 15 May-29 Sep. € 13.10   2009*

⊞ **ROCHELLE, LA** *7A1* (2km W Urban/Coastal) *46.16041, -1.18578* **Camp Municipal de Port Neuf, Blvd Aristide Rondeau, Port Neuf, 17000 La Rochelle [05 46 43 81 20; fax 05 46 00 25 23; camping-portneuf@orange.fr]** On ring rd fr N on N11 turn R onto N237 sp Ile-de-Ré, then turn S onto N537 sp La Pallice. In 1.2km turn L dir Port Neuf (Ave Jean Guiton), & in 800m turn R to site, sp. If app fr airport side take care to avoid Ile-de-Ré tollbooth. Lge, some hdstg, pt shd; htd wc (some cont); chem disp; baby facs; shwrs inc; el pnts (6A) €4 (poss rev pol); gas; lndttes nr; pool 2km; sand beach 1.5km; dogs €2.35; bus; poss cr; Eng spkn; some rd & aircraft noise; red low ssn;CKE/CCI. "Busy site in gd location; clean, well-maintained facs but ltd low ssn; phone ahead to check space high ssn or open low ssn, espec mid-winter; when office clsd some parking along rd adj football pitch; min stay 2 nights high ssn; poss itinerants; m'vans not allowed in old town; gd cycle path along seafront." € 17.00   2010*

ROCHELLE, LA *7A1* (3km NW Urban) *46.19190, -1.15853* **Camp Municipal Le Parc, Rue du Parc, 17140 Lagord [05 46 67 61 54 or 05 46 00 62 12 (Mairie); fax 05 46 00 62 01; contact@marie-lagord.fr; www.lagord.fr]** On N237 ring-rd N of La Rochelle, take D104 exit for Lagord. At rndabt in approx 800m turn L then 3rd L, site on L. Med, hdg/ mkd pitch, pt shd; wc; chem disp; shwrs inc; el pnts (10A) €3.60 (poss rev pol); lndtte; supmkt 2km; BBQ (gas only); playgrnd; beach 4km; few statics; dogs €1.10; bus; Eng spkn; adv bkg; quiet;CKE/CCI. "Gd facs & pitches; helpful staff; red facs low ssn; twin axles extra; conv Ile de Ré; cycle paths to La Rochelle & Ile de Ré; gd value; excel." ♦ 15 Jun-15 Sep. € 9.20   2011*

You can now fill in site reports online

FRANCE

ROCHELLE, LA 7A1 (5km NW Rural/Coastal) 46.19583, -1.1875
Camping au Petit Port de l'Houmeau, Rue des Sartières, 17137 L'Houmeau [05 46 50 90 82; fax 05 46 50 01 33; info@aupetitport.com; www.aupetitport.com] Exit N237 onto D104/D105 sp Lagord; at rndabt in 1km turn L onto D104; in 2.5km fork L onto D106 to L'Houmeau; at ent to town turn R into Rue des Sarthières sp Camping; site on R in 100m. Med, hdg/mkd pitch, hdstg, terr, shd; wc; chem disp; mv service pnt; baby facs; shwrs inc; el pnts (10A) €4.60 (poss rev pol); lndtte (inc dryer); tradsmn; shops & rest 400m; snacks; bar; BBQ (gas); playgrnd; shgl beach 1.5km; cycle hire; games rm; wifi; dogs €2; bus 400m; poss cr; Eng spkn; adv bkg rec; quiet; red low ssn; ccard acc;CKE/CCI. "Pleasant, friendly site; helpful owners; clean facs; no vehicle access 2230-0730; gd walking & cycling; conv Ile de Ré bdge; excel." ♦
1 Apr-30 Oct. € 30.15   2013*

ROCHETTE, LA (SAVOIE) 9B3 (2km S Rural) 45.44983, 6.10299 **Camp Municipal Le Lac St Clair, Chemin de la Plaine, 73110 Détrier [04 79 25 73 55 or 04 79 25 50 32 (Mairie); campinglarochette@orange.fr; www.la-rochette.com]** Exit A41 at Pontcharra junc 22; foll D925 NE sp La Rochette & Albertville. Take 1st sp turn to La Rochette on R. Pass supmkt & boating pool. Site 300m on R. Med, pt sl, pt shd; wc; chem disp; baby facs; shwrs inc; baby facs; el pnts (16A) €3.50; lndry rm; shop 500m; tradsmn; bar; BBQ; playgrnd; some statics; dogs €1.20; phone; poss cr; quiet. "Gd base for W Alps; easy access fr m'way; clean, modern san facs; peaceful site." ♦ ltd 1 May-30 Sep. € 13.30   2009*

⊞ **ROCROI** 5C1 (3km SE Rural) 49.89446, 4.53770 **Camping La Murée, 35 Rue Catherine-de-Clèves, 08230 Bourg-Fidèle [tel/fax 03 24 54 24 45; campingdelamuree@wanadoo.fr; www.campingdelamuree.com]** Site sp fr Rocroi on R. Sm, some hdstg, mkd pitch, pt sl, pt shd; htd wc; chem disp; baby facs; shwrs inc; el pnts (10A) €4; lndtte; shops 3km; rest; bar; tradsmn; BBQ; playgrnd; lake sw 4km; 60% statics; dogs €1.50; some Eng spkn; quiet; ccard acc; twin axle c'vans; adv bkg; CKE/CCI;. "Two fishing lakes on site; pleasant site; gd sh stay/NH; gd san facs, new management helpful & friendly; gd rest; scenic location" ♦ ltd
15 Jan-30 Nov. € 19.00   2013*

ROCROI 5C1 (8km SE Rural) 49.87200, 4.60446 **Camp Départemental du Lac des Vieilles Forges, 08500 Les Mazures [03 24 40 17 31; fax 03 24 41 72 38; cmpingvieillesforges@cg08.fr]** Fr Rocroi take D1 & D988 for Les Mazures/Renwez. Turn R D40 at sp Les Vieilles Forges. Site on R nr lakeside. Lge, mkd pitch, hdstg, pt sl, shd; htd wc; mv service pnt; shwrs inc; el pnts (6-10A) €2.50-4.30; lndtte; shop; tradsmn; snacks; playgrnd; shgl beach & lake sw; boating, fishing; tennis; cycle hire; entmnt high ssn; TV; 20% statics; dogs €1; poss cr; adv bkg; quiet. "Attractive walks; lake views fr some pitches; vg site." ♦ 16 Mar-4 Nov. € 13.00   2009*

RODEZ 7D4 (1km NE Urban) 44.35323, 2.58708 **Camp Municipal Layoule, 12000 Rodez [05 65 67 09 52; fax 05 65 67 11 43; contact@mairie-rodez.fr; www.mairie-rodez.fr]** Clearly sp in Rodez town cent & all app rds. Access at bottom steep hill thro residential area. Med, hdg/mkd pitch, hdstg, pt shd; wc (poss cont only low ssn); chem disp; mv service pnt; shwrs inc; el pnts (6A) inc; lndry rm; shop 1km; tradsmn; playgrnd; pool, golf, tennis nrby; no statics; no dogs; phone; quiet;CKE/CCI. "Site by lake & rv; gd sized pitches; helpful warden; clean facs; steep walk to historic town; gates clsd 2000-0700; 2 exits fr site, 1 uphill & poss v diff; interesting wild life; gd walks & cycling; excel NH." ♦
1 Jun-30 Sep. € 18.00 (3 persons)   2011*

ROESCHWOOG 5D3 (1km W Rural) 48.83215, 8.01916 **Camping du Staedly, 30 Rue de l'Etang, 67480 Roeschwoog [tel/fax 03 88 86 42 18; cc-uffried@cc-uffried.com]** Exit A35 junc 53 or 55 onto D468. Fr traff lts in cent of Roeschwoog go W sp Leutenheim into Rue de la Gare twd rlwy stn, cross rlwy & turn L immed to site. Med, mkd pitch, pt shd; htd wc; chem disp; shwrs inc; el pnts (6A) €3.10; lndtte; shop 2km; snacks; bar; lake sw; games area; TV; many statics; adv bkg; noisy Fri & Sat (bar). 1 Apr-31 Oct. € 9.00   2008*

ROGNY LES SEPT ECLUSES see Bleneau 4G3

ROHAN 2F3 (200m NW Rural) 48.07078, -2.75525 **Camp Municipal du Val d'Oust, Rue de St Gouvry, 56580 Rohan [02 97 51 57 58 or 02 97 51 50 33 (Mairie); fax 02 97 51 52 11; mairie.rohan@wanadoo.fr; www.morbihan.com]** Rue de St Gouvry runs NW fr Rohan parallel to D11, but other side of canal. Sm, mkd pitch, pt shd; wc; chem disp (wc); shwrs inc; el pnts €3.10; lndtte; shop, rest, snacks & bar 200m; BBQ; playgrnd; dogs €0.90; phone; adv bkg; CKE/CCI. "Pleasant site beside Nantes/Brest canal; gd cycling." ♦ 1 Jun-15 Sep. € 9.45   2011*

ROMAGNE SOUS MONTFAUCON see Dun sur Meuse 5C1

ROMANSWILLER see Wasselonne 6E3

ROMIEU, LA 8E2 (300m NE Rural) 43.98299, 0.50183 **Kawan Village Le Camp de Florence, 32480 La Romieu [05 62 28 15 58; fax 05 62 28 20 04; info@lecampdeflorence.com; www.lecampdeflorence.com]** Take D931 N fr Condom & turn R onto D41, where La Romieu sp next to radio mast. Go thro La Romieu & turn L at sp just bef leaving vill. Lge, hdg pitch, some hdstg, pt shd; wc; chem disp; mv service pnt; baby facs; shwrs inc; el pnts (10A) inc (poss rev pol); lndtte (inc dryer); shops in vill; tradsmn; rest in 16thC farmhouse; snacks; bar; BBQ; playgrnd; pool; paddling pool; waterslide; jacuzzi; leisure complex 500m; tennis; cycle hire; games area; archery; wifi; entmnt; TV/games rm; many statics; dogs €2.30; twin-axles acc (rec check in adv); Eng spkn; adv bkg ess; quiet; ccard acc; red low ssn; CKE/CCI. "Peaceful, Dutch-run site in pleasant location; gd sized pitches, most with views; welcoming, helpful staff; gd clean san facs; gd rest; poss muddy when wet; some noise fr disco, ask for pitch away fr bar; gd pool but take care sl ent; gd cycling; historic 11thC vill; mkt Wed Condom." ♦
1 Apr-10 Oct. € 37.50 SBS - D19   2013*

See advertisement on next page

FRANCE

Le Camp de Florence - 32480 La Romieu

Sun * Comfort * Nature * Water

The Gers - A region waiting to be discovered, an unspoilt landscape of rolling hills, sunflowers and historic fortified villages and castles. Peace, tranquillity, the home of Armagnac, Fois Gras and Magret de Canard. A 4* site with spacious pitches, panoramic views and luxury mobile homes for hire.

Tel: 0033 562 28 15 58
E-mail: info@lecampdeflorence.com - www.lecampdeflorence.com

⊞ **ROMILLY SUR SEINE** *4E4* (4km W Rural) *48.5259, 3.6646* Camping du Domaine de la Noue des Rois, Chemin des Brayes, 10100 St Hilaire-sous-Romilly [03 25 24 41 60; fax 03 25 24 34 18; contact@lanouedesrois.com; www. lanouedesrois.com] Site sp fr D619, on rvside. Lge, mkd pitch, pt shd; htd wc; mv service pnt; baby facs; shwrs; el pnts (16A) €3.50-5; gas; lndtte; shop; tradsmn; rest; bar; playgrnd; htd, covrd pool; paddling pool; waterslide; fishing; sailing; watersports; tennis; games area; entmnt; 90% statics; dogs (on lead) €3.50; Eng spkn; adv bkg; quiet; ccard acc; red long stay/low ssn; CKE/CCI. "Gd situation in wooded area; conv Paris & Disneyland; ltd pitches/facs for tourers." ♦ € 32.00   2012*

ROMORANTIN LANTHENAY *4G2* (500m E Urban) *47.35486, 1.75568* Camping de Tournefeuille, Rue de Long Eaton, 41200 Romorantin-Lanthenay [02 54 76 16 60; fax 02 54 76 00 34; camping.romo@wanadoo.fr; www. jmonnet-romorantin.com/camping/] Fr town cent on D724 to Salbis, foll sp thro several traff lts over bdge turn R into Rue de Long-Eaton, site sp. Med, pt shd; htd wc; shwrs inc; el pnts (10A) €3; gas; shop 500m; snacks; pool adj; playgrnd; fishing; cycle hire; wifi; dogs free; quiet; red low ssn. "Rv walk to town rec." 1 Apr-30 Sep. € 15.00 (3 persons)   2010*

RONCE LES BAINS see Tremblade, La *7B1*

RONDE, LA see Courçon *7A2*

ROQUE D'ANTHERON, LA see Cadenet *10E3*

ROQUE GAGEAC, LA see Sarlat la Canéda *7C3*

ROQUEBRUN *10F1* (300m SE Rural) *43.49775, 3.02834* Camping Campotel Le Nice de Roquebrun, Rue du Temps Libre, 34460 Roquebrun [04 67 89 61 99 or 04 67 89 79 97; fax 04 67 89 78 15; camping-campotel@wanadoo.fr; www.camping-lenice.com] N112 to St Chinian & take D20 dir Cessenon-sur-Orb, turn L onto D14 twd Roquebrun; site on L bef bdge over rv. Narr app rd. Sm, mkd pitch, some hdstg, pt sl, terr, pt shd; wc (some cont); chem disp; mv service pnt; shwrs inc; el pnts (6A) €2.50; lndtte; shops, rest, snacks, bar 1km; playgrnd; rv sw & shgl beach adj; rv sw, fishing, sailing, canoe hire adj; tennis; entmnt; 15% statics; dogs €1.30; phone; poss cr; adv bkg; quiet; ccard acc; CKE/CCI. "Excel cent for walking & cycling; beautiful scenery; ltd touring pitches; some gd, modern san facs; Not suitable for lge o'fits; need key for WC block; off clsd Sundays low ssn." 15 Mar-15 Nov. € 14.00   2012*

ROQUEBRUNE SUR ARGENS see Fréjus *10F4*

ROQUEFORT *8E2* (2.5km S Rural) *44.02093, -0.31032* Camp Municipal, Route de Pau, 40120 Sarbazan [05 58 45 64 93 (Mairie); fax 05 58 45 69 91] Fr Roquefort take D934 S twd Villeneuve-de-Marsan & Pau. In 2km camp sp on L in Sarbazan. Sm, mkd pitch, pt sl, shd; wc (some cont); shwrs inc; el pnts (5A) €1.60-2.40 (poss rev pol); lndtte; shops 2.5km; tradsmn; BBQ; playgrnd; tennis; dogs; quiet; red low ssn; CKE/CCI. "Peaceful, friendly; site yourself, warden calls am & pm; dated, clean san facs; some pitches soft after heavy rain; nr arena; highly rec." ♦ ltd 1 Apr-30 Oct. € 9.00   2009*

ROQUELAURE see Auch *8F3*

ROQUES see Toulouse *8F3*

ROQUETTE SUR SIAGNE, LA see Cannes *10F4*

ROSANS 9D3 (1.5km N Rural) 44.39547, 5.46094
**Camping Tamier Naturiste (Naturist), Route du Col
de Pomerol, Tamier 05150 Rosans [04 92 66 61 55 or
06 80 23 64 81 (mob); fax 04 92 87 47 24; tamier@
wanadoo.fr; www.naturisme-tamier.fr]** Off D94/D994
Serres to Nyons rd; turn N onto D25 at Rosans. Site sp in vill.
Med, mkd pitch, terr, pt shd; htd wc; chem disp; shwrs inc; el
pnts (6A) inc; lndtte; shop; tradsmn; rest, snacks; bar; playgrnd;
pool; games area; some statics; TV; adv bkg; quiet; ccard acc;
red low ssn. "Wonderful scenery; friendly owners; v steep
access rd; suggest park in upper car park nr ent bef going to
recep." 15 Apr-15 Oct. € 23.40   2009*

ROSANS 9D3 (4km W Rural) 44.38523, 5.42540 **Aire
Naturelle Le Gessy (Cagossi), 26510 Verclause [tel/fax
04 75 27 80 39 or 06 84 14 69 01 (mob); legessy@hotmail.
com; www.camping-legessy.com]** Site sp fr vill; 2km up
steep, narr, winding rd. Sm, hdstg, sl, terr, pt shd; wc; chem
disp (wc); shwrs inc; el pnts (6-10A) €3.50; supmkt & rest 2km;
snacks; bar; playgrnd; pool; 10% statics; dogs €2; Eng spkn;
adv bkg; quiet; CKE/CCI. "Spacious pitches; gd views; vg."
1 May-1 Oct. € 12.50   2010*

ROSCANVEL 2E1 (500m S Coastal) 48.30893, -4.55851
**Camp Municipal Le Kervian, Route du Camping, 29570
Roscanvel [02 98 27 43 23 or 02 98 27 48 51 (Mairie); fax
02 98 27 41 10; mairie@roscanvel.com]** Fr Crozon foll D355
dir Le Fret/Roscanvel. After Le Fret x-rds foll Municipal sp. Turn
L just bef Roscanvel. Sm, mkd pitch, terr, unshd; wc (some
cont); chem disp (wc); shwrs inc; el pnts (10A) €3.50; lndry
rm; shop & bar 1km; tradsmn; playgrnd; sand beach 800m;
horseriding nrby; some statics; dogs; phone adj; quiet; ccard
not acc; CKE/CCI. "Vg site; gd views; if office clsd go to Mairie
to check in." 15 Jun-15 Sep. € 7.50   2010*

ROSCOFF 1D2 (7km SW Coastal/Rural) 48.67142,
-4.05088 **Camp Municipal du Bois de la Palud, 29250
Plougoulm [02 98 29 81 82 or 02 98 29 90 76 (Mairie);
fax 02 98 29 90 76; mairie-de-plougoulm@wanadoo.fr]**
Fr D58 turn W on D10 sp Cléder/Plouescat; after 3km on ent
Plougoulm foll sp to site. Sm, hdg/mkd pitch, terr, pt shd; wc;
chem disp; shwrs inc; el pnts (8A) €3.50; lndry rm; shop 800m;
sand beach 1km; playgrnd; phone; some Eng spkn; adv bkg;
quiet; ccard acc; CKE/CCI. "Clean, tidy site in delightful area;
lovely views to sandy inlet; conv ferry; if arr late, site yourself;
warden calls am & pm; access all hrs with c'van; walk in first,
turning diff inside; also lower field with el pnts; sh walk to vill;
excel" ♦ ltd 15 Jun-5 Sep. € 14.50   2013*

ROSCOFF 1D2 (10km SW Coastal) 48.69033, -4.13879 **Camping
Village de Roguennic, 29233 Cléder [02 98 69 63 88;
fax 02 98 61 95 45; semcleder@wanadoo.fr; www.
campingvillageroguennic.com]** Fr D10 bet St Pol-de-Léon
& Lesneven, take coast rd at either Plouescat or Cléder, foll
Camping sp twd sea. Site sp. Lge, mkd pitch, pt sl, pt shd; wc;
mv service pnt; shwrs inc; el pnts (6A) €2.50; gas; lndtte; shop,
rest, snacks, bar (high ssn); playgrnd; htd pool (high ssn); sand
beach adj; tennis; games area; sailing school nr; entmnt; statics
sep area; dogs €1.10; phone; bus; adv bkg; quiet; ccard acc;
CKE/CCI. "Holiday vill, lovely early ssn; direct access to beach."
♦ 1 May-15 Sep. € 15.40   2010*

ROSCOFF 1D2 (3.5km W Coastal) 48.71411, -4.00866
**Camping aux Quatre Saisons, Perharidy, Le Ruguel, 29680
Roscoff [02 98 69 70 86; fax 02 98 61 15 74; camping.
roscoff@wanadoo.fr; www.camping-aux4saisons.com]**
Fr dock foll exit & camping sps; at rndbt exit N on D169 twd
cent ville; in 800m turn W dir Santec, foll camping sps, pass
travellers' site. Lge, hdg pitch, unshd; wc; chem disp; shwrs
inc; baby facs; el pnts (4-8A) €2.80-4.40; lndtte; shops 2km;
BBQ; playgrnd; sand beach; windsurfing; fishing; sailing; wifi;
entmnt; dogs €1; poss cr; adv bkg rec high ssn; quiet; red
low ssn. "Conv ferry; will open low ssn if bkd in adv; cheap &
cheerful." ♦ 1 Apr-9 Oct. € 11.80   2010*

"I need an on-site restaurant"

We do our best to make sure site
information is correct, but it is always best
to check any must-have facilities are still
available or will be open during your visit.

ROSIERES 9D2 (4km S Rural) 44.46423, 4.27278 **Camping
Arleblanc, 07260 Rosières [04 75 39 53 11; fax
04 75 39 93 98; info@arleblanc.com; www.arleblanc.com]**
S fr Aubenas on D104, turn L at Intermarché, site in 2.8km
down lane to site by Rv Baume. Lge, mkd pitch, shd; wc (some
cont); chem disp; shwrs inc; el pnts (10A) €3.75; gas; lndtte;
shop; tradsmn; rest; bar; playgrnd; pool; canoeing; tennis;
entmnt; TV rm; 40% statics; dogs free; poss cr; adv bkg; v
quiet; CKE/CCI. "Excel family-run site; lge pitches." ♦ ltd
15 Mar-31 Oct. € 23.00   2008*

ROSIERS SUR LOIRE, LES 4G1 (1km N Rural)
47.35908, -0.22500 **FLOWER Camping Val de Loire,
6 Rue Ste Baudruche, 49350 Les Rosiers-sur-Loire
[02 41 51 94 33; fax 02 41 51 89 13; contact@camping-
valdeloire.com; www.camping-valdeloire.com or www.
flowercampings.com]** Take D952 fr Saumur in dir Angers.
Site on D59 1km N of vill cent on L dir Beaufort-en-Vallée.
Med, hdg/mkd pitch, hdstg, pt shd; wc; chem disp; mv service
pnt; baby facs; 50% serviced pitch; shwrs inc; el pnts (10A)
€4.50; gas; lndtte; tradsmn; rest, snacks; bar; BBQ; playgrnd;
htd pool; paddling pool; lake sw 15km; waterslide; tennis;
games rm; internet; entmnt; TV rm; 15% statics; dogs €3; Eng
spkn; adv bkg; quiet; red long stay/low ssn; CKE/CCI. "Close
to Rv Loire; lge pitches; friendly, helpful staff; excel san facs;
gd touring base for chateaux region; excel." ♦ 1 Apr-30 Sep.
€ 36.50   2013*

See advertisement on pages 32 & 33

ROSIERS SUR LOIRE, LES 4G1 (6km NW Rural) 47.39231,
-0.27381 **Camping Port St Maur, 49250 La Ménitré
[02 41 45 60 80; fax 02 41 45 65 65; info@loiredelumiere.
com; www.loiredelumiere.com]** Exit Les Rosiers on D952
sp Angers. Site on L by rv. Med, mkd pitch, pt shd; wc; shwrs
inc; el pnts (5A) €2.30; lndtte; shops 1km; rest, snacks; bar;
playgrnd; games area; entmnt; boat trips on Loire; some statics;
dogs €1; some rd & rlwy noise. "Access to san facs by steps;
helpful warden." ♦ 1 May-15 Sep. € 7.60   2008*

FRANCE

ROSNAY *4H2* (500m N Rural) *46.70647, 1.21161* **Camp Municipal Les Millots, Route de St Michel-en-Brenne, 36300 Rosnay [02 54 37 80 17 (Mairie); fax 02 54 37 02 86; rosnay-mairie@wanadoo.fr]** NE on D27 fr Le Blanc to Rosnay; site sp 500m N of Rosnay on D44. Sm, some mkd pitch, pt shd; htd wc; chem disp; baby facs; shwrs inc; el pnts (6-10A) €2-3.50 (poss rev pol); lndtte; rest & shop 500m; BBQ; playgrnd; lake fishing; cycling; tennis; dogs; phone; poss cr; adv bkg; quiet; CKE/CCI. "lovely, tranquil, popular site; well-kept; excel modern san facs; warden collects fees twice daily; lakeside walks; excel walking, cycling, birdwatching & fishing; gd base for exploring Brenne National Park; vg value; excel" ♦ 16 Feb-15 Nov. € 8.50   2013*

⊞ **ROSTRENEN** *2E2* (2km S Rural) *48.23063, -3.29881* **Camping Fleur de Bretagne, Kerandouaron, 22110 Rostrenen [02 96 29 16 45 or 02 96 29 15 45; fax 02 96 29 16 45; info@fleurdebretagne.com; www. fleurdebretagne.com]** Fr Rostrenen town cent foll dir Champion supmkt & take next R turn sp D31 Silfiac. In approx 1km turn L, site sp. NB Rough, steep ent/exit. Med, mkd pitch, pt sl, terr, pt shd; wc; chem disp; mv service pnt; shwrs inc; el pnts (6A) €3 (poss rev pol); lndry rm; shop 2km; snacks; bar; BBQ; playgrnd; pool; fishing lake; watersports; horseriding nr; dogs €2; phone; Eng spkn; adv bkg; quiet; red low ssn; CKE/CCI. "Helpful British owners; san facs clean but need refurb (2010), ltd low ssn; wooded walks; poss muddy when wet; ltd opening Nov-Mar - phone ahead." ♦ € 16.00   2011*

⊞ **ROUEN** *3C2* (5km E Urban) *49.43154, 1.15387* **Camping L'Aubette, 23 Rue du Vert- Buisson, 76160 St Léger-du-Bourg-Denis [tel/fax 02 35 08 47 69; www.rouentourisme. com]** Fr Rouen E on N31 dir Darnétal & Beauvais; in 1km cont strt on onto D42/D138 dir St Léger-du-Bourg-Denis; in 400m turn L onto Rue du Vert Buisson; site on r in 800m just past stop sp. Site well sp as 'Camping' fr Rouen cent. Med, sl, terr, pt shd; wc (mainly cont); shwrs €1.60; el pnts (3-10A) €1.50-3; shops 400m; mainly statics; poss cr. "In attractive rv valley; conv city cent; v ltd touring pitches; v basic site, gd NH " € 9.50   2013*

ROUFFACH *6F3* (W Urban) *47.9557, 7.2964* **Camp Municipal, 4 Rue de la Piscine, 68250 Rouffach [03 89 49 78 13; fax 03 89 78 03 09; campingmunicipal. rouffach@orange.fr]** On D83 S fr Colmar bet Colmar & Cernay. Foll sp 'Sport, Loisirs, Piscine'. Sm, pt shd; htd wc; chem disp; mv service pnt; shwrs €1.50; el pnts (6A) €2.50; lndry rm; shop 500m; pool nr; quiet; CKE/CCI. "Clean site; pitch self, contact office when open; vg NH." 1 May-30 Sep. € 6.40   2009*

ROUFFIGNAC *7C3* (300m N Rural) *45.05473, 0.98708* **Camping Bleu Soleil, Domaine Touvent, 24580 Rouffignac-St-Cernin-de-Reilhac [05 53 05 48 30; infos@ camping-bleusoleil.com; www.camping-bleusoleil.com]** On D6 in Rouffignac, take D31 NE twd Thenon. Site clearly sp on R after 300m. Med, hdg/mkd pitch, pt sl, terr, pt shd; wc; chem disp; 75% serviced pitches; shwrs inc; el pnts (10A) €3.70; lndtte; shop; tradsmn; rest, snacks & bar high ssn; BBQ; playgrnd; htd pool; tennis; games rm; wifi; TV rm; 10% statics; dogs €2; phone; Eng spkn; adv bkg; quiet; red low ssn; ccard acc; CKE/CCI. "Relaxing site with views nr pretty vill;v. friendly, helpful owners; ltd facs low ssn; poss diff for lge o'fits; excel. " ♦ ltd 15 Apr-23 Sep. € 22.00   2011*

ROUFFIGNAC *7C3* (6km SW Rural) *45.07099, 0.97210* **Camping Le Coteau de l'Herm (Naturist), Route du Château de l'Herm, 24580 Rouffignac [05 53 46 67 77; fax 05 53 05 74 87; info@naturisme-dordogne.com; www. naturisme-dordogne.com]** Exit A89 junc 17 onto D6089 to Thenon; 1km past Thenon turn L onto D31 sp Rouffignac. In approx 10km turn R dir Prisse, site on L in 2km. Sm, mkd pitch, terr, pt sl, pt shd; htd wc; chem disp; shwrs inc; el pnts (4-10A) €3.50-4.50; gas; lndtte; shop; tradsmn; bar; snacks; BBQ; playgrnd; pool; cycle hire; dogs €3.75; Eng spkn; adv bkg; quiet; red long stay; CKE/CCI. "Excel site & facs; gd access; helpful Dutch owners; delightful location." ♦ 15 May-16 Sep. € 23.00   2008*

ROUSSET see Chorges *9D3*

ROUSSILLON *10E2* (2.5km SW Rural) *43.88973, 5.27596* **Camping L'Arc-en-Ciel, Route de Goult, 84220 Roussillon [04 90 05 73 96; campingarcenciel@wanadoo.fr]** Take D900 W out of Apt, then R on D201 sp Roussillon, then R on D4 for 1.5km, then L on D104 twd Roussillon. Take L fork twd Goult, site well sp 2.5km on L. No access for c'vans & m'vans in Roussillon vill. Med, mkd pitch, hdstg, pt sl, terr, pt shd; wc (some cont); chem disp; shwrs inc; el pnts (4A) €3.80; gas; lndry rm; sm shop & 2.5km (uphill); tradsmn; snacks; bar; playgrnd; pool; children's pool; games area; phone; adv bkg; quiet; CKE/CCI. "Tranquil woodland site; tight access some pitches; poss diff lge o'fits due trees; helpful staff; old san facs; beware rd humps & drainage channels on site access rds; some pitches poss diff lge o'fits; worth a detour; vg." ♦ 15 Mar-31 Oct. € 13.00   2010*

ROYAN *7B1* (6km NE Rural) *45.64796, -0.95847* FFCC **Camping Le Bois Roland, 82 Route de Royan, 17600 Médis [tel/fax 05 46 05 47 58; contact@le-bois-roland.com; www.le-bois-roland.com]** On N150 Saintes-Royan rd, site sp on R 100m beyond Médis vill sp. Med, pt shd; wc (some cont); chem disp; shwrs inc; el pnts (5-10A) €4.20-5.20; gas; lndtte (inc dryer); shop & 600m; tradsmn; snacks; bar; playgrnd; pool; paddling pool; sand beach 4km; entmnt; TV; dogs €2.80; phone; poss cr; adv bkg; Eng spkn; quiet; ccard acc; red low ssn; CKE/CCI. "Attractive, wooded site; friendly, family-run; facs poss stretched high ssn; waiting area avail; vg." ♦ 1 May-30 Sep. € 19.00   2010*

ROYAN *7B1* (5km E Rural) *45.62991, -0.94626* **Camping Le Clos Fleuri, 8 Impasse du Clos Fleuri, 17600 Médis [05 46 05 62 17; fax 05 46 06 75 61; clos-fleuri@wanadoo.fr; www.le-clos-fleuri.com]** On N150 Saintes-Royan rd turn S in Médis dir Semussac. Well sp. Med, hdg/mkd pitch, shd; wc (some cont); baby facs; fam bathrm; sauna; shwrs inc; el pnts (5-10A) €5-6.50; lndtte; shop in ssn & 2km; tradsmn; rest, snacks & bar in ssn; playgrnd; pool; paddling pool; sand beach 7km; games area; ltd entmnt; TV; 10% statics; dogs €3.50; phone; Eng spkn; adv bkg; quiet; ccard acc; red low ssn; CKE/CCI. "Lovely, peaceful, family-run site; san facs clean but dated; rec for young families; access poss diff lge o'fits; some pitches dark due o'hanging trees; excel, under-used site." ♦ 1 Jun-15 Sep. € 29.00   2010*

FRANCE

⊞ **ROYAN** *7B1* (1.7km SE Coastal) *45.61817, -1.00425* **Camping La Triloterie, 44 ter, Ave Aliénor d'Aquitaine, 17200 Royan** [05 46 05 26 91; fax 05 46 06 20 74; info@ campingroyan.com; www.campingroyan.com] Fr Royan PO, foll sp Bordeaux N730, on E of rd. Med, shd; htd wc; chem disp; mv service pnt; baby facs; shwrs inc; el pnts (4-12A) €4-6 (poss rev pol); shops 500m; BBQ; playgrnd; waterslide; sand beach 900m; wifi; entmnt; some statics; dogs €1.50; phone; poss cr/ noisy high ssn; some rd noise; red low ssn. "Excel site; conv for Royan town centre & St. George de Didonne." € 23.00   2011*

ROYAN *7B1* (5km SE Coastal) *45.58345, -0.98720* **Camping Bois-Soleil, 2 Ave de Suzac, 17110 St Georges-de-Didonne** [05 46 05 05 94; fax 05 46 06 27 43; camping. bois.soleil@wanadoo.fr; www.bois-soleil.com] Fr A10 exit junc 35 dir Saintes & Royan; on app Royan foll St Georges-de-Didonne sp onto bypass D25/D730/D25/D25E; go over 2 rndabts (with underpass between); at 3rd rndabt turn L sp Meschers-sur-Gironde; site on R in 500m. Site well sp. Lge, hdg/mkd pitch, hdstg, terr, pt shd; htd wc (some cont); chem disp; mv service pnt; baby facs; shwrs inc; el pnts (6A) inc (poss rev pol); gas; lndtte (inc dryer); shop; tradsmn; rest, snacks; bar; BBQ (gas); playgrnd; htd pool; paddling pool; dir access to sand beach adj; tennis; cycle hire; games area; wifi; entmnt; TV rm; 30% statics; dogs €3 (not acc end Jun-Aug inc); phone; poss cr; Eng spkn; adv bkg rec (ess Jul/ Aug); ccard acc; red low ssn; CKE/CCI. "Superb wooded site in vg location nr beach; popular & busy; generous pitches, some sandy; excel, clean san facs; vg shop & rest; many sandy beaches nrby." ♦ 2 Apr-9 Oct. € 42.00 (3 persons) (CChq acc)   2012*

See advertisement above

ROYAN *7B1* (6km SE Coastal) *45.59253, -0.98713* **Camping Idéal, Ave de Suzac, 17110 St Georges-de-Didonne** [05 46 05 29 04; fax 05 46 06 32 36; info@ideal-camping. com; www.ideal-camping.com] Fr Royan foll coast rd sp St Georges-de-Didonne. Site sp on D25 2km S of St Georges, opp Cmp Bois-Soleil. Lge, mkd pitch, shd; wc (some cont); chem disp; shwrs inc; el pnts (6-10A) €4.50-5.50; gas; lndtte; shop; tradsmn; rest, snacks; bar; playgrnd; htd pool; paddling pool; waterslide; jacuzzi; sand beach 200m; tennis 500m; cycle hire; horseriding 300m; games area; games rm; entmnt; some statics; no dogs; phone; poss noisy (bar); ccard acc; red low ssn; CKE/CCI. "Helpful staff." ♦ 7 May-5 Sep. € 27.80 (3 persons)   2010*

See advertisement below

ROYAN *7B1* (9km SE Rural) *45.59750, -0.90055* **Camping Bois De La Chasse, 17 Chemin de la Motte Ronde, 17120 Semussac** [0546223771; boisdelachasse@orange.fr; www.boisdelachasse.com] D730 fr Royan. Look for Tractor Monument at an island, turn next R sp Semussac into Rue de Didonne; after 500m turn L at sp D244 ARCES into Pl. de l'Eglise, then slight R into Rue du Lignou; turn L into Chemin de la Motte Ronde. Site is sp on L after 200m. Med, mkd pitch, pt shd; wc; chem disp; mv service pnt; shwrs inc; el pnts (6A) €5.10; gas; lndtte; sm shop; tradsmn; BBQ; playgrnd; 25% statics; dogs €1.80; phone; bus 500m; no twin-axles; Eng spkn; adv bkg; quiet; ccard acc; CKE/CCI. "Gd base for Royan/ Gironde; level pitches; local supmkt nrby; owner lives onsite; gd cycling; vg site." ♦ 01 Apr-31 Oct. € 19.78   2011*

ROYAN

ROYAN 7B1 (10km SE) 45.55713, -0.94655 Camping Soleil Levant, Allée de la Langée, 17132 Meschers-sur-Gironde [05 46 02 76 62; fax 05 46 02 50 56; info@camping-soleillevant.com; www.camping-soleillevant.com] Take D145 coast rd fr Royan to Talmont. At Meschers turn R foll camp sp twd port; sp. Med, pt shd; wc (some cont); chem disp; shwrs inc; el pnts (10A) €4.60; gas 1km; lndtte; snacks; bar; shop; playgrnd; sand beach 1.5km; free pool & paddling pool; watersports & horseriding adj; 20% statics; dogs €3; adv bkg; quiet; ccard acc; red low ssn; CKE/CCI. "Gd, busy site; sm pitches, some diff to get into; san facs poss unclean (2009); port & rest 300m; vill shop & daily mkt 500m; visits to Cognac & Bordeaux distilleries." 1 Apr-30 Sep. € 18.80   2010*

ROYAN 7B1 (2km NW Urban) 45.64470, -1.04160 Camping Le Royan, 10 Rue des Bleuets, 17200 Royan [05 46 39 09 06; fax 05 46 38 12 05; camping.le.royan@wanadoo.fr; www.le-royan.com] Take D25 by-pass fr Royan dir La Palmyre. Site sp. Lge, mkd pitch, hdstg, pt sl, pt shd; wc (some cont); chem disp; mv service pnt; baby facs; some serviced pitches; shwrs inc; el pnts (10A) inc; gas; lndtte (inc dryer); shop; rest, snacks; bar; BBQ; playgrnd; htd pool; paddling pool; waterslide; spa; sand beach 2.5km; lake sw 3km; solarium; games area; games rm; cycle hire; entmnt; TV; 55% statics; dogs €4; poss cr; adv bkg; rd noise; ccard acc; red low ssn/long stay/CKE/CCI. "Friendly, helpful owners; excel pool complex." 1 Apr-10 Oct. € 34.50 (3 persons)   2009*

ROYAN 7B1 (4km NW Urban/Coastal) 45.6309, -1.0498 Campéole Camping Clairefontaine, 6 Rue du Colonel Lachaud, Pontaillac, 17200 Royan [05 46 39 08 11; fax 05 46 38 13 79; clairefontaine@campeole.com; www.camping-clairefontaine.com or www.campeole.com] Foll Pontaillac sp fr Royan. Site sp in Clairefontaine (& Pontaillac). Lge, mkd pitch, pt shd; wc (some cont); chem disp; mv service pnt; fam bthrm; serviced pitches; shwrs inc; el pnts (10A) €4.10; gas; lndtte; tradsmn; shop; rest, snacks; bar; BBQ; playgrnd; 2 pools; sand beach 300m; tennis; casino 300m; wifi; TV rm; many statics; dogs €3; phone; Eng spkn; adv bkg (fee + dep req); quiet; ccard acc; red low ssn; CKE/CCI. "Lovely coastline; gd for family holiday; helpful owner; clean, unisex san facs; ltd touring pitches, some sm; gd security; site poss dusty; vg walking & cycling; coastal path Pontaillac to Royan." 2 Apr-26 Sep. € 27.60 (3 persons)   2010*

See advertisement on pages 14 & 15

ROYBON 9C2 (1km S Rural) 45.24639, 5.24806 Camping de Roybon, Route de St Antoine, 38940 Roybon [04 76 36 23 67; fax 04 76 36 33 02; info@campingroybon.com; www.campingroybon.com] Fr Roybon go S on D71 & foll sp. Med, mkd pitch, pt sl, pt shd; wc; chem disp; shwrs inc; el pnts (6A) €3.50; shops 1km; playgrnd; sw & watersports in lake adj; dogs €2.65; adv bkg; quiet; red low ssn. "V peaceful; gd, modern facs new; vg." 15 Apr-15 Oct. € 16.80   2009*

ROYERE DE VASSIVIERE 7B4 (6km S Rural) 45.79303, 1.90458 Camping La Presqu'île, Broussas, 23460 Royère-de-Vassivière [05 55 64 78 98; fax 05 55 64 76 78; presquile.camping@free.fr; http://presquile.camping@free.fr] Fr Royère-de-Vassivière S on D3 for 6km, turn R onto D34 dir Broussas, site 500m after Broussas. Med, hdg/mkd pitch, terr, shd; wc; chem disp; mv service pnt; shwrs inc; el pnts (10A) €3.10; lndtte (inc dryer); shop; tradsmn; rest, snacks, bar 500m; BBQ; playgrnd; lake sw & beach; fishing; games area; entmnt; 12% statics; dogs free; poss cr; Eng spkn; adv bkg; quiet; red low ssn; CKE/CCI. "Vg site; gd walking/cycling rtes around lake." 6 Jun-7 Sep. € 12.40   2010*

ROYERE DE VASSIVIERE 7B4 (6km SW Rural) 45.78869, 1.89855 Camping Les Terrasses du Lac, Vauveix, 23460 Royère-de-Vassivière [05 55 64 76 77; fax 05 55 64 76 78; lesterrasses.camping@free.fr; http://lesterrasses.camping.free.fr] Fr Eymoutiers take D43 for approx 10km then take D36 to Vauveix & foll sp. Med, hdg/mkd pitch, terr, pt shd; htd wc; chem disp; shwrs inc; el pnts (10A) €3.10 (poss rev pol); lndtte; rest, bar 300m; snacks 500m; sand beach, sw & watersports adj; horseriding; walking; cycling; TV rm; dogs free; phone 50m; quiet; CKE/CCI. "Helpful staff; lovely setting." 1 Apr-15 Oct. € 14.50   2010*

ROZ SUR COUESNON see Pontorson 2E4

ROZIER, LE see Peyreleau 10E1

RUE 3B2 (7km N Rural) 50.31367, 1.69472 Kawan Village Le Val d'Authie, 20 Route de Vercourt, 80120 Villers-sur-Authie [03 22 29 92 47; fax 03 22 29 92 20; camping@valdauthie.fr; www.valdauthie.fr] Best access via Rue or via D85/D485 fr D1001. Rd fr Vron to Villers-sur-Authie is narr single track across fields. Alt Exit 24 on A16 twrds Vron, foll sp Camping Vercourt thro town. Lge, hdg/mkd pitch, pt sl, pt shd; htd wc; chem disp; mv service pnt; sauna; steam rm; shwrs inc; baby facs; el pnts (6-10A) €5-8 (rev pol); gas; lndtte (inc dryer); shop; tradsmn; rest, snacks; bar; playgrnd; htd, covrd pool; paddling pool; sand beach 10km; tennis; games area; games rm; fitness rm; wifi; entmnt; TV rm; 60% statics; dogs €1.50; phone; poss cr; Eng spkn; adv bkg; quiet but poss noise fr chalets/statics; ccard acc; red low ssn; CKE/CCI. "Set in pleasant countryside; helpful, friendly owners; clean, unisex facs & spacious shwrs; sm sep area for tourers, but many touring pitches bet statics (2009); poss diff for lge o'fits; gd pool; v cr & noisy high ssn; excel." 1 Apr-9 Oct. € 25.00 (3 persons) (CChq acc)   2012*

RUE 3B2 (4km SE Rural) 50.25278, 1.71224 Camping de la Mottelette, Ferme de la Mottelette, 80120 Forest-Montiers [03 22 28 32 33 or 06 72 85 73 77 (mob); contact@la-mottelette.com; www.la-mottelette.com] Exit A16 junc 24 onto D32 dir Rue & L Crotoy; at rndabt junc with D235 cont on D32; site on L in 1.5km. Site sp on leaving A16. Sm, hdg/mkd pitch, unshd; wc; chem disp; baby facs; el pnts (6A) €4; lndtte (inc dryer); supmkt 4km; tradsmn; BBQ; playgrnd; games area; games rm; 20% statics; dogs €0.50; poss cr; Eng spkn; adv bkg; quiet; CKE/CCI. "Basic, clean site on working farm; welcoming, friendly owners; mkt Sat; conv A16; gd touring base or NH; vg." ltd 1 Apr-31 Oct. € 14.00 2011*

486 Site open all year   You can now fill in site reports online

⊞ **RUFFEC** 7A2 (5km NE Rural) 46.07505, 0.26055 **Camping Rural La Renardière, La Renardiere, 16700 Taizé-Aizie [05 45 30 15 81; larenardiere16700@orange.fr; www. la-renardiere.eu]** Fr N, leave Civray on D1/D8; in 8km pass x-rds (L turn sp Lizant, R turn sp Voulème); take next L turn (dir Le Gros Chêne) bef x-ing Rv Charente; foll sm rd up hill; site in 1km on R bef hamlet of Le Gros Chêne. Med, some hdg/mkd pitch, hdstg, pt shd; htd wc; chem disp; fam bthrm; shwrs inc; el pnts (10A) inc; lndtte; tradsmn; snacks & meals; BBQ; pool; lake sw & fishing 3km; cycle hire; games rm; wifi; dogs €1; adv bkg; quiet; ccard acc; red long stay; CKE/CCI. "CL-type site; friendly British owners; basic san facs low ssn; vg pool; excel; Very spacious with great views; gd for walking; v relaxing"
€ 17.50   2013*

RUFFEC 7A2 (3km SE Rural) 46.01500, 0.21304 **Camping Le Réjallant, Les Grands Champs, 16700 Condac [05 45 31 29 06 or 05 45 31 07 14; fax 05 45 31 34 76; cdc-ruffec-charente@wanadoo.fr]** Site sp fr N10 & fr town. App 1km fr turn-off. Med, hdg/mkd pitch, pt sl, shd; wc; chem disp (wc); shwrs inc; el pnts (10A) inc; lndtte; tradsmn; snacks; rest & bar 100m; sm playgrnd; rv sw, fishing 100m; dogs; Eng spkn; quiet; ccard not acc; CKE/CCI. "Some pitches v lge; clean facs - water poss v hot; shwrs ltd; gates open 0700-2100 high ssn; no entry/exit 1100-1600 low ssn; great for families." 15 May-15 Sep. € 13.00   2009*

⊞ **RUFFEC** 7A2 (10km W Rural) 46.00722, 0.09664 **Camping à la Ferme de Chassangne (Peloquin), Chassagne, 16240 Villefagnan [05 45 31 61 47; fax 05 45 29 55 87; contact@ campingdechassagne.fr; www.campingdechassagne.fr]** Exit N10 onto D740 W to Villefagnan. Site 1.8km SE of vill on D27. Sm, pt sl, pt shd; wc; chem disp (wc); shwrs; el pnts (10A) inc; lndtte; farm produce; shop, rest, snacks, bar 1.8km; playgrnd; pool; gites avail; dogs €1; poss cr; adv bkg; quiet. "Vg CL-type site; excel pool; gd cycle rtes." ♦ ltd € 12.50   2011*

RUFFIEUX 9B3 (500m W Rural) 45.84932, 5.83441 **Camping Le Saumont, 73310 Ruffieux [04 79 54 26 26; camping. saumont@wanadoo.fr; www.campingsaumont.com]** N fr Aix-les-Bains take D991 N to Ruffieux, sp just bef Ruffieux at junc with D904. Sm, hdg/mkd pitch, pt shd; wc; chem disp; serviced pitch; shwrs; el pnts (6A) inc; lndtte; shop 1.5km; snacks; bar; BBQ; playgrnd; 2 pools; lake & rv sw 2.5km; tennis; cycle hire; 10% statics; dogs €1.80; adv bkg; quiet; red low ssn. "Dusty rd thro site when hot & dry; muddy after rain." 1 May-26 Sep. € 20.00   2009*

RUFFIEUX 9B3 (4km W Rural) 45.85255, 5.79274 **Camping Le Colombier, Ile de Verbaou, 01350 Culoz [tel/fax 04 79 87 19 00; camping.colombier@free.fr; http:// camping.colombier.free.fr]** W fr Ruffieux or N fr Belley on D904, site sp off rndabt 1km E of Culoz. Med, hdg/mkd pitch, hdstg, pt shd; wc (some cont); chem disp; mv service pnt; baby facs; shwrs inc; el pnts (10A) €3; lndtte; shop 1km; tradsmn; rest, snacks; bar; playgrnd; lake sw adj; tennis; cycle hire; wifi; TV; some statics; dogs €1; phone; Eng spkn; adv bkg; quiet; ccard acc; red low ssn/CKE/CCI. "Gd touring base; conv Annecy." ♦ 23 Apr-26 Sep. € 16.50   2010*

RUMILLY 9B3 (4km N Rural) 45.90229, 5.92738 **Camping Les Charmilles, Route de Seyssel, 74150 Vallières [04 50 62 10 60; fax 04 50 62 19 45; lescharmilles. camping@wanadoo.fr; www.campinglescharmilles.com]** Exit A41 junc 15 at Alby onto D3 to Rumilly; 4km N of Rumilly in Vallières exit D910 on D14 sp Seyssel. Site on L in 500m. Med, mkd pitch, pt shd; wc; baby facs; shwrs inc; el pnts (6A) €3.50; gas; lndtte; shops 500m; tradmsn; rest, snacks; bar; BBQ; playgrnd; pool; paddling pool; games area; wifi; entmnt; TV; 25% statics; dogs €2; phone; adv bkg; quiet; red low ssn. "Gd, modern san facs; pleasant situation." ♦ 1 Apr-31 Oct. € 15.50   2010*

RUMILLY 9B3 (3.5km S Rural) 45.84083, 5.96277 **Camping Le Madrid, Route de St Félix, 74150 Rumilly [04 50 01 12 57; fax 04 50 01 29 49; contact@camping-le-madrid.com; www.camping-le-madrid.com]** S fr Rumilly on D910, take D3 left dir St Marcel for approx 600m & at 2nd rndabt turn R, site sp. Med, hdg/mkd pitch, some hdstg, pt shd; htd wc (some cont); chem disp; mv service pnt; baby facs; shwrs; el pnts (5-10A) €2.80-4.30; lndtte (inc dryer); shop 2km; tradsmn; rest, snacks; bar; BBQ; playgrnd; pool; paddling pool; fishing; cycle hire; games area; games rm; wifi; entmnt; 50% statics; dogs €2; adv bkg; quiet. ♦ 1 Apr-31 Oct. € 16.00 (CChq acc)   2010*

RUOMS 9D2 (2km N Rural) 44.47655, 4.35858 **Camping Les Coudoulets, Chemin de l'Ardèche, 07120 Pradons [04 75 93 94 95; fax 04 79 39 65 89; camping@coudoulets. com; www.coudoulets.com]** Site sp fr D579. Med, mkd pitch, shd; wc; chem disp; mv service pnt; baby facs; shwrs inc; el pnts (6A) €4; lndtte; shop 300m; rest, snacks; bar; playgrnd; htd pool; paddling pool; rv fishing nr; games area; 5% statics; dogs €2.50; Eng spkn; adv bkg; quiet. "Site o'looks Rv Ardèche; friendly, careful owners; excel pool." ♦ 18 Apr-19 Sep. € 25.00   2009*

> ## "Satellite navigation makes touring much easier"
> Remember most sat navs don't know if you're towing or in a larger vehicle – always use yours alongside maps and site directions.

RUOMS 9D2 (3km N Rural) 44.47375, 4.35325 **Camping du Pont des Champs des Souliers, Route de Chauzon, Chemin du Cirque de Gens, 07120 Pradons [04 75 93 93 98; campingdupont07@wanadoo.fr; www. campingdupontardeche.com]** S fr Aubenas on D104, on o'skts of town take D579 to Pradons. Thro vill, bef end vill sp turn R onto D308 opp Intermarché supmkt to Chauzon. Site 300m on L, site sp. Med, hdg/mkd pitch, pt shd; wc (some cont); chem disp; shwrs inc; el pnts (6-10A) €4.20 (poss rev pol); lndtte; shop 100m; rest 300m; snacks; bar; BBQ; playgrnd; htd pool; rv sw & sand beach adj; canoe hire; games area; wifi; TV; 15% statics; dogs €2.50; phone; bus; Eng spkn; adv bkg; quiet; red low ssn; CKE/CCI. "Friendly owners; lovely, rugged area; vg." ♦ 27 Mar-30 Sep. € 24.50   2010*

RUOMS *9D2* (3km S Rural) *44.42761, 4.33561* **Yelloh! Village La Plaine, 07120 Ruoms [04 75 39 65 83; fax 04 75 39 74 38; camping.la.plaine@wanadoo.fr; www. camping-la-plaine.com or www.yellohvillage.co.uk]** Exit Ruoms S on D579 dir Vallon-Pont-d'Arc; at junc in 2km turn S onto D111 dir St Ambroix. Site on L. Lge, hdg/ mkd pitch, pt shd; wc; baby facs; shwrs inc; el pnts (6A) inc; lndtte; shop; tradsmn; rest, snacks; bar; BBQ; playgrnd; pool; paddling pool; rv sw, fishing & private beach; games area; games rm; fitness rm; entmnt; some statics; dogs €7; red low ssn; CKE/CCI. 16 Apr-17 Sep. € 41.00   2010*

See advertisement on inside front cover

RUOMS *9D2* (4km SW) *44.43101, 4.32945* **Camping La Chapoulière, 07120 Ruoms [tel/fax 04 75 39 64 98 or 04 75 93 90 72; camping@lachapouliere.com; www. lachapouliere.com]** Exit Ruoms S on D579. At junc 2km S, foll D111 sp St Ambroix. Site 1.5km fr junc. Med, mkd pitch, pt sl, shd; wc; mv service pnt; baby facs; shwrs inc; el pnts (6A) €4; gas; lndtte; shop in ssn & 3km; rest, snacks; bar; pool; paddling pool; rv sw & fishing adj; canoeing; tennis 2km; games area; wifi; entmnt; TV; dogs €2.50; Eng spkn; adv bkg rec high ssn; quiet; red low ssn. "Beautiful pitches on rv bank; friendly; ltd facs low ssn; vg." ♦ Easter-30 Sep. € 27.00   2008*

RUOMS *9D2* (7km SW Rural) *44.41350, 4.27195* **Camping Sunêlia Le Ranc Davaine, 07120 St Alban-Auriolles [04 75 39 60 55; fax 04 75 39 38 50; camping.ranc. davaine@wanadoo.fr; www.camping-ranc-davaine.fr]** Leave A7/E15 at Montélimar/Aubenas exit, foll sp twd Aubenas on N102. Just past Villeneuve-de-Berg turn L onto D103, thro St Germain, then join D579 to Ruoms. S of Ruoms leave D579 sp Gorges de l'Ardèche & join D111 twd Grospierres. At Les Tessiers turn R onto D246, sp St Alban-Auriolles. After x-ing Rv Chassezac turn L twd Chandolas, in approx 800m turn left at site sp. Lge, shd; wc; chem disp; baby facs; sauna; steam rm; shwrs inc; el pnts (6-10A) inc; lndtte; shop; rest, snacks; bar; BBQ (el only); playgrnd; pool complex (inc 1 htd, covrd); waterslide; paddling pool; fishing; tennis; archery; fitness cent; wifi; entmnt; games/TV rm; 75% statics; dogs €4.90; adv bkg; quiet; ccard acc. "Helpful staff; conv Gorges de l'Ardèche; public rd divides site; excel pool complex & playgrnd; mkt Mon." ♦ 4 Apr-13 Sep. € 42.00   2008*

RUPT SUR MOSELLE see Remiremont *6F2*

RUSSEY, LE see Maîche *6G3*

RUYNES EN MARGERIDE *9C1* (4km E Rural) **Camping à la Ferme (Rolland), 15320 Clavières [04 71 23 45 50]** Fr St Flour, S on N9. After 7km turn L onto D4 thro Clavières & foll sps. Site in Chirol, foll Chirol sp. Sm, wc; shwrs inc; el pnts (long lead req); farm food avail; shops 2.5km; playgrnd; rv 2.5km; pool, tennis, golf, horseriding 10km; sailing, fishing 15km; quiet. "Isolated, with beautiful views, gd facs for a basic site; pay at old white house in Chirol." 1 Jun-30 Sep.   2009*

RUYNES EN MARGERIDE *9C1* (300m SW Rural) *44.99910, 3.21893* **Camp Municipal du Petit Bois, 15320 Ruynes-en-Margeride [tel/fax 04 71 23 42 26; contact@ revea-vacances.com; www.revea-vacances.fr/campings]** Fr St Flour SE on D909. After 7km turn L onto D4. Site in 7km, sp. Or exit junc 30 fr A75, turn R into vill & foll sp. Lge, pt sl, pt shd; htd wc (some cont); chem disp; mv service pnt; baby facs; shwrs inc; el pnts (6-10A) €3.50; gas; lndtte; shops, rest, bar 600m; BBQ; playgrnd; htd pool adj; TV rm; some log cabins; dogs €1.50; phone; Eng spkn; adv bkg; quiet; ccard acc; CKE/ CCI. "Attractive site with pine trees; gd views; few flat pitches; excel san facs; barrier clsd 1200-1500; gd cent for walking, horseriding & fishing; used as field work cent in term time; gd." ♦ 30 Apr-17 Sep. € 16.00 (CChq acc)   2011*

SABLE SUR SARTHE *4F1* (10km NE Rural) *47.86677, -0.20869* **Camp Municipal des Deux Rivières, 72430 Avoise [02 43 92 76 12; fax 02 43 95 62 48]** Fr Sablé take D309 twd Le Mans, after 10km thro vill of Parcé-sur-Sarthe, cont twds Le Mans & cross bdge over Rv Sarthe; sp for Avoise & camping sp on L. Site adj rv. Sm, hdg pitch, pt shd; wc; shwrs inc; el pnts inc (poss rev pol); gas; shops, rest, bar adj; playgrnd; BBQ; 10% statics; Eng spkn; adv bkg; quiet; CKE/CCI. "Vg, pleasant, clean site; off beaten track." 1 Jun-6 Sep. € 8.20   2009*

SABLE SUR SARTHE *4F1* (500m S Rural) *47.83101, -0.33177* **Camp Municipal de l'Hippodrome, Allée du Québec, 72300 Sable-sur-Sarthe [02 43 95 42 61; fax 02 43 92 74 82; camping@sablesursarthe.fr; www. tourisme.sablesursarthe.fr]** Sp in town (foll sm, white sp with c'van symbols or Hippodrome). Fr N on D306; at trff lts at junc with D309, go strt over & under rlwy brdg sp Centre Ville; foll camping sps. Med, hdg pitch, pt shd; wc; shwrs inc; el pnts (15A) €2.40; gas; BBQ; lndry rm; sm shop; tradsmn; snacks; playgrnd; pool; rv fishing; boat & cycle hire; canoeing; entmnt; TV rm; Eng spkn; quiet; ccard acc; red long stay/low ssn. "Excel site; gd, clean facs; helpful staff; some pitches by rv, some diff for lge fits." ♦ 2 Apr-16 Oct. € 15.00   2012*

SABLES D'OLONNE, LES *7A1* (4km N Rural) *46.54738, -1.80518* **Camping de Sauveterre, 3 Rue des Amis de la Nature, 85340 Olonne-sur-Mer [02 51 33 10 58; fax 02 51 21 33 97; info@campingsauveterre.com; www. campingsauveterre.com]** Fr Les Sables-d'Olonne take D32 N to Olonne-sur-Mer; then D80 twds St Gilles-Croix-de-Vie for 3.5km; after 2nd rndabt site is on L. Med, mkd pitch, pt shd; wc (some cont); chem disp; shwrs inc; el pnts (6A) inc; gas; lndtte; shop; rest, snacks; bar; playgrnd; htd pool; paddling pool; waterslide; sand beach 1.5km; many statics; dogs €2.10; poss cr; adv bkg rec high ssn; quiet; red low ssn; CKE/CCI. "Gd walking/cycling." 1 Apr-30 Sep. € 20.80   2008*

SABLES D'OLONNE, LES *7A1* (4km N Rural) *46.53320, -1.79379* **Camping Le Nid d'Eté, 2 Rue de la Vigne Verte, 85340 Olonne-sur-Mer [02 51 95 34 38; fax 02 51 95 34 64; info@leniddete.com; www.leniddete.com]** Fr Les Sables-d'Olonne take D32 N to Olonne-sur-Mer. L onto D80 twd St Gilles-Croix-de-Vie. Immed over rlwy bdge turn L, site on L. Med, pt hdg/mkd pitch, pt shd; wc; chem disp; baby facs; shwrs inc; el pnts (6A) €3.80; lndtte; shop & 2km; snacks; playgrnd; htd, covrd pool high ssn; beach 3km; entmnt; few statics; dogs €2.50; c'van winter storage; adv bkg; v quiet; red low ssn; CKE/CCI. "Pleasant site; excel." 4 Apr-26 Sep. € 23.80   2009*

FRANCE

SABLES D'OLONNE, LES 7A1 (5km N Coastal) 46.54613, -1.80591 **Camping La Loubine, 1 Route de la Mer, 85340 Olonne-sur-Mer [02 51 33 12 92; fax 02 51 33 12 71; info@ la-loubine.fr; www.la-loubine.fr]** Fr Les Sables-d'Olonne take D32 N to Olonne-sur-Mer then D80 dir St Gilles-Croix-de-Vie for 3.5km; turn L at junc to Plage-de-Sauveterre; ent to site immed on L after turn. Lge, hdg/mkd pitch, pt sl, pt shd; wc; chem disp; serviced pitches; shwrs inc; el pnts (5A) €3.65; gas; lndtte; shop; rest, snacks; bar; playgrnd; 2 htd pools (1 covrd); sand beach 1.8km; tennis; entmnt; TV; 50% statics; no dogs; poss cr; Eng spkn; adv bkg; noise fr rd & nightclub; ccard acc; CKE/CCI. "Site lit & guarded at night; lge car park for late arr; excel." ♦ 4 Apr-30 Sep. € 27.00   2009*

SABLES D'OLONNE, LES 7A1 (5km N Urban) 46.53166, -1.75843 **Camping Le Trianon, 95 Rue du Maréchal Joffre, 85340 Olonne-sur-Mer [02 51 23 61 61; fax 02 51 90 77 70; campingletrianon@wanadoo.fr; www.camping-le-trianon.com]** S on D160 La Roche-sur-Yon twd Les Sables-d'Olonne; at Pierre Levée turn R onto D80 sp Olonne-sur-Mer. Also sp fr D80 N. V lge, hdg/mkd pitch, pt shd, serviced pitches; htd wc; chem disp; shwrs inc; el pnts (6A) inc (extra for 10-16A); lndtte; shop; rest, snacks; bar; playgrnd; 2 pools (1 htd, covrd); waterslide; sand beach 5km; fishing & watersports 4km; tennis; golf; games area; entmnt; 40% statics; dogs €4.43; poss cr; adv bkg; quiet; red low ssn. "Pleasant situation; friendly, helpful staff; excel facs for families." ♦ 3 Apr-30 Oct. € 38.00   2011*

SABLES D'OLONNE, LES 7A1 (2km E Rural) 46.48098, -1.73146 **Camping Le Puits Rochais, 25 Rue de Bourdigal, 85100 Château-d'Olonne [02 51 21 09 69; fax 02 51 23 62 20; info@puitsrochais.com; www. puitsrochais.com]** Fr Les Sables-d'Olonne take D949 twd La Rochelle. Pass rndabt with lge hypermrkt 'Magasin Géant' & turn R at 1st traff lts at Mercedes g'age, then 1st L to site. Med, hdg/mkd pitch, pt shd; wc; chem disp; baby facs; shwrs inc; el pnts (6-10A) inc; lndtte; shop; supmkt 1km; rest, snacks; bar; BBQ (gas); playgrnd; htd pool; paddling pool; waterslide; sand beach 2km; tennis; cycle hire; games area; games rm; internet; entmnt; TV; 60% statics; dogs €3.30; phone; adv bkg; quiet; ccard acc; red low ssn/CKE/CCI. "Friendly, welcoming site; gd for families." ♦ 4 Apr-30 Sep. € 33.50   2011*

SABLES D'OLONNE, LES 7A1 (600m SE Urban/Coastal) 46.49171, -1.76536 **Chadotel Camping Les Roses, Rue des Roses, 85100 Les Sables-d'Olonne [02 51 95 10 42 or 02 51 33 05 05 (LS); fax 02 51 33 94 04; chadotel@ wanadoo.fr; www.chadotel.com]** Fr town cent foll dir Niort, turn down Blvd Ampère by Total petrol stn to Rue des Roses. Site opp take-away cafe & adj to hospital, lying bet D949 & sea front. Lge, hdg/mkd pitch, pt sl, pt shd; wc; chem disp; shwrs inc; el pnts (6A) inc (poss rev pol); gas 1.5km; lndtte; tradsmn; rest 500m; snacks (high ssn); bar; BBQ (gas); playgrnd; htd pool; waterslide; sand beach 500m; entmnt; cycle hire; games rm; wifi; TV rm; mostly statics; dogs €3.20; phone; poss cr; Eng spkn; adv bkg; ccard acc; red low ssn/long stay; CKE/CCI. "Conv for town & beach; close by harbour, shops, museums & salt marshes; san poss facs tired high ssn; shuttle buses; easy walk to beach and town cent; excel." ♦ 7 Apr-11 Nov. € 32.50   2011*

SABLES D'OLONNE, LES 7A1 (2km SE Urban) 46.47932, -1.74123 **Camping Les Fosses Rouges, La Pironnière, 8 Rue des Fosses Rouges, 85180 Château-d'Olonne [02 51 95 17 95; info@camping-lesfossesrouges.com; www.camping-lesfossesrouges.com]** Take D949 La Rochelle. At lge rndabt turn R, sp La Pironnière. Camp clearly sp on L in 1km. Lge, mkd pitch, shd; wc; shwrs inc; el pnts (10A) €3.60; gas; lndtte; shop & 500m; snacks; bar; playgrnd; htd pool; sand beach 1.5km; cycle hire; entmnt; internet; TV; 70% statics; dogs €1.60; poss cr; adv bkg; quiet; red low ssn. "Attractive site on o'skts fishing port; some pitches poss diff lge o'fits; gd pool." ♦ 8 Apr-30 Sep. € 19.00   2011*

SABLES D'OLONNE, LES 7A1 (4km SW Coastal) 46.51193, -1.81398 **Chadotel Camping La Dune des Sables, La Paracou, 85100 Les Sables-d'Olonne [02 51 32 31 21 or 02 51 33 05 05 (LS); fax 02 51 33 94 04; chadotel@ wanadoo.fr; www.chadotel.com]** Foll D160 to Les Sables-d'Olonne. Fr town foll sps to La Chaume & Les Dunes. Lge, mkd pitch, pt sl, unshd; wc; serviced pitches; shwrs inc; el pnts (6A) inc; gas; lndtte; shop; snacks; bar; BBQ (gas); playgrnd; pool; waterslide; sand beach 100m; tennis; cycle hire; games rm; entmnt; wifi; 75% statics; dogs €3; Eng spkn; adv bkg rec high ssn; red low ssn/long stay; CKE/CCI. "Great for family beach holiday; helpful warden." ♦ 7 Apr-22 Sep. € 32.50   2011*

SABLES D'OR LES PINS 2E3 (4km NE Coastal) 48.65158, -2.35647 **Camp Municipal Pont de l'Etang, Pléhérel-Plage, 22240 Fréhel [02 96 41 40 45 or 02 96 41 40 12 (Mairie); otfrehel@wanadoo.fr; www.frehelcamping.bzh.bz]** Best app fr D786 via D34 to Sables d'Or; then D34A to Pléhérel-Plage; just N of vill, sp. V lge, pt sl, pt shd; wc (some cont); chem disp; mv service pnt; shwrs inc; el pnts (6A) inc; lndry rm; mobile shops in high ssn; tradsmn; snacks; playgrnd; sand beach 200m; horseriding, tennis adj; v few statics; dogs €0.60; phone; poss cr; Eng spkn; poss noisy; CKE/CCI. "Lovely site amongst sand dunes; ideal for children; ltd facs low ssn." ♦ 1 Apr-30 Sep. € 13.00   2008*

SABLES D'OR LES PINS 3E2 (5.5km NE Coastal) 48.66418, -2.34260 **Camp Municipal Cap Fréhel/Les Grèves d'en Bas, 22240 Plévenon [02 96 41 43 34 or 02 96 29 60 51 (Mairie); mairie.plevenon.capfrehel@wanadoo.fr]** W fr St Malo on D168/D786; in 30km turn R onto D34 or D341 dir Cap Fréhel; site on R 2.5km bef Cap Fréhel. Med, pt hdg/mkd pitch, pt sl, pt shd; wc; chem disp; shwrs inc; el pnts (5A) €2.05; tradsmn; rest 2km; sand beach adj; 10% statics; dogs €0.75; quiet. "Access to coast path fr site; gd." Apr-Nov. € 9.75   2009*

SABLES D'OR LES PINS 2E3 (1.2km NW Coastal/Rural) 48.63230, -2.41229 **Camp Municipal Sables d'Or Les Pins (formerly La Saline), Rue du Lac, 22240 Plurien [02 96 72 17 40 or 02 96 72 17 23 (Mairie)]** Fr D786 turn N at Plurien onto D34 to Sables-d'Or. In 1km turn L & site on L after 200m. Med, pt sl, terr, pt shd; wc (some cont); chem disp; shwrs inc; el pnts (6A) €2.35; lndtte; shops 500m; playgrnd; sand beach 400m; dogs €0.50; phone; poss cr; Eng spkn; adv bkg; quiet; CKE/CCI. "Lovely, tranquile hillside site; some sea views; friendly, helpful warden; vg san facs; gates clsd 2200-0700; no pitching when office clsd, but lge car park opp; excel access to nature reserve & beautiful beaches." ♦ 1 Jun-15 Sep. € 10.05   2010*

SACQUENAY *6G1* (500m S Rural) *47.58924, 5.32178*
Aire Naturelle La Chênaie (Méot), 16 Rue du 19 Mars,
21260 Sacquenay [03 80 75 89 43 or 03 80 75 97 07;
fax 03 80 75 89 43; eric.meot@wanadoo.fr; http://
www.cotedor-tourisme.com/bourgogne/camping/aire-
naturelle-de-camping-de-la-chenaie] S on D974 turn L onto
D171A sp Occey & Sacquenay, site sp. Sm, pt sl, pt shd; wc;
shwrs inc; el pnts (6A); mv svp; lndtte; playgrnd; peaceful;
Eng spkn; adv bkg; quiet; red 10+ days; CKE/CCI; "Peaceful
site in orchard." 1 Apr-1 Oct. € 12.20   2013*

SAHUNE see Rémuzat *9D2*

SAILLANS *9D2* (8km E Rural) *44.69579, 5.30393* **Camp**
Municipal La Colombe, 26340 Aurel [04 75 21 76 29 or
04 75 21 71 88; fax 04 75 21 71 89; bern.pera@wanadoo.fr]
E of Saillans on D93, in vill of Vercheny turn S onto D357. Bef
vill of Aurel turn R by war memorial. Sm, mkd pitch, terr, shd;
wc (cont); shwrs inc; el pnts; lndtte; shops 4km; rest, snacks;
bar; playgrnd; pool; rv sw & fishing 5km; games area; some
statics; v quiet. "Peaceful, mountain site; beautiful views."
1 May-30 Sep.   2009*

SAILLANS *9D2* (500m W Rural) *44.69511, 5.18124* **Camping**
Les Chapelains, 26340 Saillans [04 75 21 55 47; camping@
chapelains.fr; www.chapelains.fr] Fr W on D93 turn onto
D493. Site well sp just bef Saillans vill boundary adj Rv Drôme.
Sm, hdg/mkd pitch, pt shd; wc; shwrs inc; el pnts (4-10A); gas;
lndtte; sm shop; rest; tradsmn; snacks; playgrnd; shgl beach;
games area; dogs; Eng spkn; adv bkg; quiet; ccard not acc;
CKE/CCI. "Attractive, well-run rvside site; some v sm pitches;
new san facs; friendly, helpful warden; rv walk to vill; rest open
low ssn." 15 Apr-15 Sep. € 21.00   2012*

SAILLY LE SEC see Albert *3B3*

ST AFFRIQUE *8E4* (1km E Urban) *43.95025, 2.89248* **Camp**
Municipal, Parc des Sports, La Capelle Basse, 12400
St Affrique [05 65 98 20 00; fax 05 65 49 02 29] Site on D99
Albi-Millau rd to St Affrique sp fr all dir in E end of town. Nr stn
& sports complex. Med, pt shd; wc (some cont); shwrs; el pnts
€2.75; shop 1km; rest, snacks & bar 1km; pool; rv fishing & sw;
tennis; adv bkg; quiet. "Gd clean facs, NH." 14 Jun-13 Sep.
€ 12.30   2012*

ST AGNAN *4G4* (Rural) *47.31812, 4.09520* **Camping du**
Lac, Le Château, 58230 St Agnan [03 86 78 73 70 or
01772 700531 (UK tel LS); fax 03 86 78 74 94; info@
campingburgundy.co.uk; www.campingburgundy.co.uk]
Exit A6 junc 22 onto D646 then D906 dir Saulieu; at La Roche-
en-Brenil turn R onto D226 to St Agnan. Site ent on R opp
junc. Fr Saulieu leave town S on D980 sp Autun; on o'skts turn
W onto D26B to Eschamps then D106 to St Agnan. Med, pt sl,
pt shd; wc (some cont); chem disp; shws inc; el pnts (6A) €3;
lndtte; shop; tradsmn; rest, snacks; bar; BBQ; playgrnd; lake sw
adj; kayak & pedalo hire nr; games rm; dogs €1.50; Eng spkn;
adv bkg; quiet; ccard acc; CKE/CCI. "Pretty, British-owned
site in grnds of chateau; v ltd facs low ssn." 15 Apr-15 Oct.
€ 12.95   2010*

ST AGREVE *9C2* (5km W Rural) *45.02423, 4.32760*
FFCC Camping La Prairie, Laillier, 07320 Mars [tel/fax
04 75 30 24 47; millardjf@camping-laprairie.com; www.
camping-laprairie.com] Fr St Agrève W on D120/D15, shortly
bef Mars site sp to R. Sm, hdgmkd pitch, pt shd; htd wc; chem
disp; mv service pnt; baby facs; shwrs inc; el pnts (6A) €3;
lndtte (inc dryer); shop, rest 5km; tradsmn; snacks; bar; BBQ;
playgrnd; fishing 800m; games area; entmnt; 10% statics; dogs
€0.50; phone; poss cr; adv bkg; quiet; CKE/CCI. "V attractive
area; gd walking, cycling; golf course nrby; vg." ♦
15 May-15 Sep. € 15.00   2010*

⊞ **ST AIGNAN SUR CHER** *4G2* (7km N Rural) *47.32361,*
1.36983 **FFCC Camping Domaine du Bien Vivre,**
13-15 Route du Petit Village, 41140 St Romain-
sur-Cher [02 54 71 73 74; fax 02 54 71 72 81;
domainedubienvivre@orange.fr; http://
domainedubienvivre.pagespro-orange.fr] Fr St Aignan-
sur-Cher N on D675; in 6km in St Romain-sur-Cher site sp to
L; foll sps for 3km. Sm, mkd pitch, pt sl, pt shd; wc; chem disp
(wc); shwrs inc; el pnts (6A) inc; shops & bar 3km; shops, rest &
snacks 6km; BBQ; playgrnd; dogs; Eng spkn; quiet; ccard acc;
CKE/CCI. "A vineyard site; helpful owner; ltd facs in winter;
sale of wines; conv Blois; gd." € 13.50   2010*

ST AIGNAN SUR CHER *4G2* (2km SE Rural) *47.26530,*
1.38875 **Camping Les Cochards, 1 Rue du Camping,**
Seigy, 41110 St Aignan-sur-Cher [02 54 75 15 59 or
06 72 09 45 24 (mob); fax 02 54 75 44 72; camping@
lesclochards.com; www.lescochards.com] On D17 heading
SE fr St Aignan twd Seigy on S bank of Rv Cher. Lge, mkd
pitch, pt shd; htd wc; chem disp; mv service pnt; baby facs;
shwrs inc; el pnts (5-10A) €3.80; lndtte (inc dryer); sm shop
& 3km; rest, snacks; bar; BBQ; playgrnd; pool; rv sw adj;
rv fishing; canoeing; games area; horseriding 3km; wifi;
entmnt; TV rm; 20% statics; dogs €1.40; phone; Eng spkn;
quiet; ccard acc; red low ssn; CKE/CCI. "Attractive, open site;
helpful owners; gd san facs; recep clsd 20.00; some pitches
waterlogged after rain; easy walk to attractive town; excel" ♦
1 May-30 Sep. € 31.95 (CChq acc)   2013*

ST AIGNAN SUR CHER *4G2* (4km NW Rural) *47.29411,*
1.33041 **Camp Municipal Le Port, 3 rue du Passeur, 41110**
Mareuil-sur-Cher [tel/fax 02 54 75 10 01; camping-leport@
orange.fr; www.camping-leport.fr] Fr St Aignan take D17
twd Tours (on S bank of Cher); site in 4km in vill of Mareuil-sur-
Cher behind church, thro new archway, on Rv Cher. By Mareuil
chateau. Or fr A85 sp. Sm, mkd pitch, pt shd; htd wc; chem
disp; shwrs inc; el pnts (16A) €5.50; ice/gas 50m; shop & baker
100m; supmkt adj; rest 4km; playgrnd; rv sw (shgl beach);
fishing; canoe hire; internet at supmkt; dogs €2; Eng spkn;
quiet, but some rd noise & poss events in chateau; no ccard
acc; CKE/CCI. "Beautiful, simple, rvside site; friendly staff; clean
san facs but ltd; opening/closing dates variable, phone ahead
to check; if office clsd enquire at supmkt adj (same owners); no
access 1300-1500; diff lge o'fits; no twin-axles; m'vans extra;
gd touring area" ♦ 15 Apr-30 Sep. € 28.60   2013*

ST ALBAN AURIOLLES see Ruoms *9D2*

ST ALBAN DE MONTBEL see Chambéry *9B3*

ST ALBAN SUR LIMAGNOLE see St Chély d'Apcher *9D1*

ST AMAND DE COLY see Montignac 7C3

ST AMAND EN PUISAYE 4G4 (500m NE Urban) 47.53294, 3.07333 **Camp Municipal La Vrille, Route de St Sauveur, 58310 St Amand-en-Puisaye [03 86 39 72 21 or 03 86 39 63 72 (Mairie); fax 03 86 39 64 97; saintam. mairie@wanadoo.fr; www.ot-puisaye-nivernaise.fr]** Fr N7 take D957 Neuvy-sur-Loire to St Amand, at rd junc in vill take D955 sp St Sauveur-en-Puisaye, site on R in 500m; clearly sp on all app to vill. Sm, mkd pitch, pt shd; wc (some cont); shwrs inc; el pnts €2.30; shop, rest, bar 500m; sailing & fishing in adj reservoir. "Vg simple site; gates clsd 2200-0700." 1 Jun-30 Sep. € 8.40   2008*

ST AMAND LES EAUX 3B4 (3.5km SE Rural) 50.43535, 3.46290 **FFCC Camping du Mont des Bruyères, 806 Rue Basly, 59230 St Amand-les-Eaux [tel/fax 03 27 48 56 87; info@campingmontdesbruyeres.com; www. campingmontdesbruyeres.com]** Exit A23 m'way at junc 5 or 6 onto ring rd D169, site sp. Fr N exit E42 junc 31 onto N52/N507 then D169. Avoid St Amand cent. Med, hdg/mkd pitch, pt sl, terr, shd; htd wc; mv service pnt; shwrs inc; el pnts (6A-10A) €4.20-6.30; lndtte; shop; tradsmn; bar; BBQ; playgrnd; wifi; pool 7km; 60% statics; dogs €1.50; adv bkg; quiet; red low ssn; CKE/CCI. "Attractive site on forest edge; most touring pitches under trees; access to some pitches diff due slopes; gd cycling; excel birdlife on site; fac gd & clean." 15 Mar-31 Oct. € 17.40 or €20.62 inc. 6A   2011*

ST AMAND LES EAUX 3B4 (7km NW Rural) 50.46313, 3.34428 **FFCC Camping La Gentilhommière, 905 Rue de Beaumetz, 59310 Saméon [tel/fax 03 20 61 54 03; campsameon@orange.fr; www.camping-lagentilhommiere.fr]** Fr A23 Paris-Lille, exit junc 3, sp St Amand, then L at rndabt foll sp Saméon. Site on R 300m. Med, hdg pitch, shd; htd wc; chem disp; shwrs inc; el pnts (3A) inc; gas; lndtte; shop 8km; tradsmn; snacks; bar; BBQ; playgrnd; fishing; 90% statics; dogs €0.80; poss cr; quiet; CKE/CCI. "Well-kept lovely site; 5 touring pitches only; charming owner; gd local rest; gd for Lille (park & ride fr a'route); 1km to train to Lille with Piscine Roubaix museum." ♦ 1 Apr-30 Oct. € 13.20   2011*

ST AMAND MONTROND 4H3 (3km SW Rural) 46.71808, 2.49159 **Camp Municipal La Roche, Rue de la Roche, 18200 St Amand-Montrond [tel/fax 02 48 96 09 36; camping-laroche@wanadoo.fr; www.st-amand-tourisme.com]** Exit A71/E11 junc 8 dir St Amand-Montrond on D300. Then foll sp to Montluçon on D2144 until rndabt on canal, turn R onto Quai Pluviôse/Rue de la Roche, site on R. Site sp on far side of town. Med, shd, pt sl; htd wc (some cont); shwrs inc; chem disp (wc); el pnts (5A) €2.90 (poss rev pol); lndtte (inc dryer); shops 900m; playgrnd; pool nr; rv fishing; tennis; wifi; entmnt; dogs; phone; quiet; CKE/CCI. "Popular NH, rec arr by 1700 high ssn; helpful warden; clean facs; tight for lge o'fits; rvside walk to pleasant town; gd." ♦ 1 Apr-30 Sep. € 10.40 2011*

ST AMAND MONTROND 4H3 (8km NW Rural) 46.77033, 2.42907 **FFCC Camping Les Platanes, 18200 Bruère-Allichamps [02 48 61 06 69 or 02 48 61 02 68 (Mairie); www.bruere-allichamps.fr]** Site on N edge of town on rvside. Sm, pt shd; wc; chem disp; shwrs €1; el pnts (10A) inc; shops 500m up the hill; tradsmn; snacks; playgrnd; rv fishing; quiet. "Lovely surroundings; san facs dated but clean; friendly staff; level walk to interesting vill; excel" 1 Apr-30 Sep. € 16.15   2013*

ST AMANT ROCHE SAVINE see Ambert 9B1

"There aren't many sites open at this time of year"

If you're travelling outside peak season remember to call ahead to check site opening dates – even if the entry says 'open all year'.

ST AMBROIX 9D2 (3km S Rural) 44.23748, 4.20163 **Camping Beau Rivage, Route de Uzès, Le Moulinet, 30500 St Ambroix [04 66 24 10 17; marc@camping-beau-rivage. fr; www.camping-beau-rivage.fr]** N on D904, after Les Mages in Sm. Camping sp on R. Foll sp approx 2-3km. Site off D37 twd Le Moulinet. Med, hdg/mkd pitch, pt sl, terr, pt sl, shd; wc (some cont); chem disp; shwrs inc; el pnts (6A) €3.50; gas; lndtte; shop 1km; tradsmn; rest, snacks 2km; bar 1km; playgrnd; pool; paddling pool; canoeing; wifi; no statics; dogs; poss cr; adv bkg; quiet; red low ssn; CKE/CCI. "Lovely location." ♦ ltd 1 May-1 Sep. € 20.00   2009*

ST AMBROIX 9D2 (200m W Rural) 44.26234, 4.19598 **Camping Le Clos, Place de l'Eglise, 30500 St Ambroix [04 66 24 10 08 or 06 07 54 57 66 (mob); fax 04 66 60 25 62; campingleclos@wanadoo.fr; www. camping-le-clos.fr]** Fr S on D904, in St Amboix turn L immed bef church. Site in 300m. Foll intn'l camping sp. Sm, mkd pitch, pt shd; wc; chem disp; shwrs inc; el pnts (3-10A) €2.70-5; lndtte; snacks; bar; playgrnd; pool; paddling pool; fishing; sailing; cycle hire; TV rm; 20% statics; dogs €2; adv bkg; quiet; red low ssn. "Well-kept san facs; access poss diff for lge o'fits." ♦ 1 Apr-31 Oct. € 17.50   2010*

ST AMBROIX 9D2 (12km NW Rural) 44.29104, 4.06840 **Camping des Drouilhedes, Peyremale-sur-Cèze, 30160 Bessèges [04 66 25 04 80; fax 04 66 25 10 95; info@ campingcevennes.com; www.camping-drouilhedes.com]** Leave D904 at St Ambroix onto D51 sp Bessèges. In Bessèges turn L over bdge sp Peyremale & in approx 1km turn R & foll camping sp. Med, hdg/mkd pitch, pt shd; wc (some cont); chem disp; baby facs; shwrs inc; el pnts (6A) €4.20; gas; lndtte; shop; tradsmn; rest, snacks; bar; BBQ (gas only); playgrnd; rv sw adj; tennis; games area; TV rm; 10% statics; dogs; phone; poss cr; Eng spkn; quiet; ccard acc; CKE/CCI. "Well-run, scenic site with excel facs; ideal for children; helpful Dutch owners." ♦ 1 Apr-30 Sep. € 21.85   2008*

STE ANASTASIE SUR ISSOLE see Brignoles 10F3

FRANCE

ST ANDIOL see Cavaillon *10E2*

ST ANDRE DE CUBZAC *7C2* (4km NW Rural) *45.00703, -0.47724* FFCC Camping Le Port Neuf, 1125 Route du Port Neuf, 33240 St André-de-Cubzac [tel/fax 05 57 43 16 44; camping.port.neuf@wanadoo.fr; http://camping.port. neuf.pagesperso-orange.fr] Fr A10 or N10 take exit sp St André. Well sp fr St André (narr rds) on D669. Sm, mkd/hdg pitch, hdstg, pt shd; htd wc; chem disp; mv service pnt; shwrs inc; el pnts (6A) €3 (poss long lead req); lndry rm; tradsmn; rest, snacks; bar; cycle hire; trout-fishing & boating in sm lake + rv 100m; horseriding nrby; pedalo hire; wifi; dogs €1; rlwy stn in vill to Bordeaux; quiet; Eng spkn; adv bkg; quiet; red/ CKE/CCI. "Lovely spot; friendly, helpful staff; san facs clean; terraine rather scruffy (2011);" vg" ♦ ltd 1 May-30 Sep. € 12.00   2013*

ST ANDRE DE LIDON see Cozes *8B1*

ST ANDRE DE SEIGNANX see Bayonne *8F1*

ST ANDRE DES EAUX see Baule, La *2G3*

⊞ **ST ANDRE LES ALPES** *10E3* (6km NE Rural) *44.00668, 6.55815* FFCC Camping L'Adrech, Route du Pont d'Allons, 04170 La Mure-Argens [04 92 89 17 81; contact@adrech. com; www.adrech.com] Fr E or W on N202 to St André-les-Alpes, turn N onto D955 dir Colmars, Site on R. Do not app fr N fr Barcelonette via Col d'Allos. Sm, mkd pitch, pt sl, pt shd; wc; chem disp (wc); shwrs inc; el pnts (3-6A) €3.50; snacks; bar; BBQ; watersports, lake sw nrby; wifi; 25% statics; dogs €1; Eng spkn; adv bkg; ccard acc; CKE/CCI. "Family-run site; helpful, friendly; gd touring base in interesting area." € 12.50   2008*

ST ANGEAU see Mansle *7B2*

STE ANNE D'AURAY *2F3* (6km N Rural) *47.72889, -2.95349* FFCC Aire Naturelle Nerhouit, 56400 Plumergat [02 97 57 70 62; nerhouit@tromp.net] Fr N165 turn N on D17 to Plumergat; site 3km W of Plumergat, sp. Sm, pt shd; wc; chem disp (wc); shwrs €0.50; el pnts (6A) inc (poss long lead req); lndtte; shop, rest, bar 3km; playgrnd; dogs; Eng spkn; adv bkg; quiet; CKE/CCI. "Pitches on lge grassy area; friendly Dutch owner; own cider avail; gd touring base." ♦ ltd 1 Jun-15 Sep. € 12.50   2009*

STE ANNE D'AURAY *2F3* (500m SW Rural) *47.69842, -2.96226* Camp Municipal du Motten, Allée des Pins, 56400 Ste Anne-d'Auray [02 97 57 60 27 or 02 97 57 63 91; fax 02 97 57 72 33; secretariat.general@sainte-anne-auray.com; www.sainte-anne-auray.com] Fr W on N165 take D17bis N to St Anne-d'Auray; then L onto D19 to town. This rte avoids Pluneret. Foll site sp. Med, mkd pitch, pt shd; wc; chem disp; shwrs inc; el pnts (10A) €3.20; lndtte; shops 1km; tradsmn; snacks; playgrnd; sand beach 20km; tennis; games area; TV; dogs; Eng spkn; adv bkg; poss cr; quiet; "Peaceful, well-kept site; best pitches immed R after ent; welcoming, helpful warden; gd clean san facs; excel touring base; conv Basilica Ste Anne d'Auray; excel" ♦ 15 Jun-15 Sep. € 17.40   2013*

ST ANTOINE D'AUBEROCHE see Thenon *7C3*

ST ANTOINE DE BREUILH see Ste Foy la Grande *7C2*

ST ANTONIN NOBLE VAL *8E4* (1.5km N Rural) *44.1595, 1.7564* FFCC Camp Municipal Le Ponget, Route de Caylus, 82140 St Antonin-Noble-Val [05 63 68 21 13 or 05 63 30 60 23 (Mairie); camping-leponget@wanadoo.fr] Fr Caylus take D19 S to St Antonin; site on R, well sp. Sm, hdg pitch, pt shd; htd wc; mv service pnt; shwrs inc; el pnts (3-6A) €2.50-3.70; gas; lndtte; shops, rest, snacks, bar 1km; playgrnd; sw 1km; dogs €1.20; phone; quiet; ccard not acc; CKE/CCI. "Well-kept site adj sports field; modern san facs; poss diff lge o'fits; gd walking; v gd friendly site, ex market Sundays, discount for 7 days." ♦ 2 May-30 Sep. € 11.70   2011*

ST ANTONIN NOBLE VAL *8E4* (6km N Rural) *44.19265, 1.69570* FFCC Camping Les Trois Cantons, Vivens, 82140 St Antonin-Noble-Val [05 63 31 98 57; fax 05 63 31 25 93; info@3cantons.fr; www.3cantons.fr] Fr Caussade take D926 dir Villefranche (do not take D5 or D19 sp St Antonin.) Site is on C5, sp. Fr St Antonin foll dir Caylus on D19. Just outside vill, after sm bdge where rd turns to R, turn L up hill. Foll this rd for 6km - narr rd. NB Hill steep & continuous. Med, mkd pitch, hdstg, pt sl, pt shd; htd wc (some cont); chem disp; mv service pnt; baby facs; shwrs inc; el pnts (6A) €4.75; gas; lndtte (inc dryer); shop; supmkt 8km; BBQ; playgrnd; htd, covrd pool; rv sw 8km; tennis; cycle hire; horseriding nr; canoeing; wifi; entmnt; TV rm; dogs €2; poss cr; Eng spkn; adv bkg; quiet; ccard acc; red low ssn; CKE/CCI. "Peaceful, clean, well-managed, family site in oak forest; unspoilt region; helpful Dutch owners; gravel pitches muddy in wet; gd." ♦ 16 Apr-30 Sep. € 22.00   2010*

ST ANTONIN NOBLE VAL *8E4* (1km E Rural) *44.15192, 1.77152* FLOWER Camping des Gorges de L'Aveyron, Marsac Bas, 82140 St Antonin-Noble-Val [05 63 30 69 76; fax 05 63 30 67 61; info@camping-gorges-aveyron. com; www.camping-gorges-aveyron.com or www. flowercampings.com] Fr Caussade on D926 dir Caylus for approx 5km; after Septfonds take D5 then D958 to St Antonin-Noble-Val; on ent to vill cont over rv & L thro tunnel onto D115 dir Fényerols & Cordes-sur-Ciel. Site in 1.5km on L. Med, hdg pitch, pt shd; wc; chem disp; mv service pnt; baby facs; shwrs inc; el pnts (6A) inc (poss rev pol); lndtte (inc dryer); shops; tradsmn; snacks; bar; playgrnd; pool; fishing rv adj; canoeing; cycle hire; wifi; 15% statics; dogs €2.50; poss cr; adv bkg; quiet; red long stay/low ssn; CKE/CCI. "Neat, tidy site; lge, shady pitches; friendly owners; gd san facs; gd walking & cycling." ♦ 17 Apr-26 Sep. € 21.90 (CChq acc)   2010*

See advertisement on pages 32 & 33

ST APOLLINAIRE see Chorges *9D3*

ST ARNOULT see Deauville *3D1*

FRANCE

ST ASTIER 7C3 (600m E Rural) 45.14735, 0.53308 **Flower Camping Le Pontet, Route de Montanceix, 24110 St Astier [05 53 54 14 22; fax 05 53 04 39 36; camping. lepontet@flowercampings.com; www.camping-dordogne-lepontet.com]** Take D6089 SW fr Périgueux; in 14km turn R sp St Astier; site on R on D41 on banks of Rv Isle. Med, mkd pitch, shd; wc; chem disp; shwrs inc; el pnts (6A) €2.55; gas; lndtte; shops 400m; snacks; BBQ; playgrnd; pool; paddling pool; sand beach adj; fishing; canoing; entmnt; statics; dogs; poss cr; adv bkg; v quiet; CKE/CCI. "Some areas soft in wet weather." 1 Apr-30 Sep. € 24.90   2012*

See advertisement on pages 32 & 33

ST AUBAN 10E4 (300m S Rural) 43.84509, 6.73452 **Camping La Pinatelle, 269 Chemin St Auban, 06850 St Auban [04 93 60 40 46; fax 04 93 60 42 45; contact@ camping-saintauban.com; www.camping-saintauban. com]** Fr D6085 take D2211, site well sp on R just bef vill. Sm, mkd pitch, hdstg, pt shd; wc; chem disp; mv service pnt; shwrs; el pnts (6A) inc; lndtte; supmkt 1km; tradsmn; rest, snacks; bar; playgrnd; sm pool; games area; 15% statics; dogs €1; phone; Eng spkn; adv bkg; quiet; CKE/CCI. "Family-run CL-type site in beautiful countryside; friendly, helpful owners; excel facs; gd walking, cycling." ♦ 14 Apr-16 Sep. € 16.00   2008*

ST AUBAN 10E4 (2km NW Rural) 43.86421, 6.73386 **Camping Le Haut Chandelalar (Naturist), 06850 Briançonnet [04 93 60 40 09; fax 04 93 60 49 64; info@ le-haut-chandelalar.com; www.le-haut-chandelalar.com]** Exit D6085 Gasse-Castellane rd onto D2211; site bet St Auban & Briançonnet. Or fr Nice on N202 dir Digne-les-Bains; at Puget-Théniers turn L onto D2211 dir St Auban; 1.5km after Briançonnet turn R at site sp; site on L in 900m. Med, mkd pitch, hdstg, pt sl, terr, pt shd; wc (some cont); chem disp (wc); baby facs; shwrs inc; el pnts (6A) inc; gas; lndtte; shop; tradsmn; rest, snacks; bar; BBQ; playgrnd; htd pool; entmnt; internet; TV rm; some statics; no dogs; phone; poss cr high ssn; adv bkg; Eng spkn; quiet; ccard acc; CKE/CCI. "Peaceful, secluded site with views; pleasant owners; some pitches poss diff access for lge o'fits - steep site rds with sharp bends & poss diff after heavy rain; gd touring base; gd walking; excel." ♦ ltd 1 May-30 Sep. € 25.20   2008*

ST AUBIN DE LUIGNE see Chalonnes sur Loire 2G4

ST AUBIN DU CORMIER 2E4 (E Urban) 48.25990, -1.39609 **Camp Municipal, Rue de l'Etang, 35140 St Aubin-du-Cormier [06 83 38 93 63 (mob) or 02 99 39 10 42 (Mairie); fax 02 99 39 23 25; mairie@ville-staubinducormier.fr]** NE fr Rennes on A84; in 20km exit junc 28 dir St Aubin-du-Cormier. Foll sp 'Centre Ville' then site sp. Poss diff for lge o'fits - narr app. Sm, pt sl, pt shd; wc; shwrs inc; el pnts (6-10A) inc; shops adj; supmkt 1km; lake fishing; 10% statics; dogs €0.65; poss cr; adv bkg; quiet; CKE/CCI. "Pleasant site adj lake; friendly; gd san facs; forest walks & around lake; pretty vill; vet 1km; excel; lovely site" 1 Apr-30 Sep. € 14.34   2013*

ST AUBIN SUR MER see Caen 3D1

ST AUGUSTIN (CHARENTE MARITIME) see St Palais sur Mer 7B1

ST AVERTIN see Tours 4G2

ST AVIT DE VIALARD see Bugue, Le 7C3

⊞ **ST AVOLD** 5D2 (1km N Urban) 49.10772, 6.70924 **FFCC Camping Le Felsberg, Centre International de Séjour, Rue en Verrerie, 57500 St Avold [03 87 92 75 05; fax 03 87 92 20 69; cis.stavold@wanadoo.fr]** Fr N on A4 exit junc 39 onto D633 to St Avold, stay in L hand lane at 2nd traff lts & turn L; pass under D603 for 2km & turn R. Site well sp in & around town; app up steep incline. Sm, hdg/mkd pitch, hdstg, pt sl, pt shd; wc; chem disp; mv service pnt; shwrs inc; el pnts (6-10A) €3-5; lndtte; tradsmn; hypmkt 1.5km; rest, bar high ssn; playgrnd; 50% statics; dogs €1; poss cr; adv bkg; ccard acc; red long stay; CKE/CCI. "German border 10km; sm pitches; gd facs; coal mine & archaeological park nrby worth visit; awkward, heavy duty security gate at site ent; conv NH nr m'way; gd." ♦ ltd € 14.00   2012*

"That's changed – Should I let The Club know?"

If you find something on site that's different from the site entry, fill in a report and let us know. See www.caravanclub.co.uk/europereport.

ST AYGULF 10F4 (500m N Coastal) 43.39151, 6.72648 **Camping de St Aygulf Plage, 270 Ave Salvarelli, 83370 St Aygulf Plage [04 94 17 62 49 or 06 12 44 36 52 (mob); fax 04 09 81 03 16; info@campingdesaintaygulf.fr; www. campingdesaintaygulf.fr]** Fr Roquebrunne on D7 at rndabt 100m after vill sp St Aygulf take 3rd exit leading to Rue Roger Martin du Gard. Keep turning L. Fr Fréjus on D559, rd bends R after bdge over beach access, turn R bef rd climbs to L. V lge, hdg/mkd pitch, shd; wc; chem disp; shwrs inc; el pnts (5A) €3.50; gas; lndtte; shop; rest, snacks; bar; playgrnd; dir access to sand beach adj; watersports & sports facs nr; fishing; games area; entmnt; statics; dogs €3; extra for twin-axles & v lge m'vans; adv bkg; ccard acc; red low ssn/long stay; CKE/CCI; "Gd." 24 Apr-25 Sep. € 34.00   2013*

ST AYGULF 10F4 (4km S Coastal) 43.40963, 6.72491 **Camping Le Plage d'Argens, 541 route Départementale 559 (RN 98), 83370 St Aygulf [04 94 51 14 97; fax 04 94 51 29 44; camping.lepontdargens@yahoo.fr; www. camping-caravaning-lepontdargens.com]** Well sp fr D559 bet Fréjus & St Aygulf, by Rv Argens. If app fr W pass site on R & return via next rndbt. Lge, mkd pitch, pt shd; htd wc; chem disp; mv service pnt; baby facs; shwrs; el pnts (6A) €2; gas; lndtte (inc dryer); shop; tradsmn; hypmkt 1km; rest, snacks; bar; playgrnd; htd pool; paddling pool; sand beach adj; cycle hire; wifi; TV rm; 5% statics; dogs €2.50; poss cr; Eng spkn; adv bkg; some rd noise; ccard acc; CKE/CCI. "Excel, well-run site by rv; sh walk to uncrowded beach (pt naturist); excel facs & pool; cycle track to St Aygulf & pt way to Fréjus." 1 Apr-20 Oct. € 30.00   2008*

See advertisement on next page

FRANCE

ST AYGULF *10F4* (2km W Rural) *43.40691, 6.70923*
Camping Les Lauriers Roses, Route de Roquebrune, 83370 St Aygulf [04 94 81 24 46; fax 04 94 81 79 63; lauriersroses-camping@orange.fr; www.info-lauriersroses.com] Exit A8 at junc 37 Puget-sur-Argens onto DN7 to Fréjus. At 1st rndabt after Fréjus town sp, turn R to St Aygulf at junc immed after rndabt. Pass under rlwy bdge & turn R onto D8. After bdge with traff lts foll rd up to junc & turn L onto D7, site in 1.5km on R. Med, mkd pitch, pt sl, terr, pt shd; wc; chem disp; baby facs; shwrs inc; el pnts (6-10A) €4-6; gas; lndtte; shop 500m; rest; bar; BBQ (gas only); playgrnd; htd pool & paddling pool; fitness area; sand beach 2km; games rm; entmnt; wifi; 10% statics; dogs €1.85; Eng spkn; adv bkg; quiet; ccard acc; CKE/CCI. "Excel, family-run, wooded site on hillside; diff acc some pitches for lge o'fits (max 8m) - owner assists with siting c'vans; no arr bet 1200-1500; mkt Tue & Fri." ♦ ltd 23 Apr-10 Oct. € 34.00   2011*

"I like to fill in the reports as I travel from site to site"

You'll find report forms at the back of this guide, or you can fill them in online at www.caravaclub.co.uk/europereport.

ST AYGULF *10F4* (2.5km W Coastal) *43.36566, 6.71264*
Camping Au Paradis des Campeurs, La Gaillarde-Plage, 83380 Les Issambres [04 94 96 93 55; fax 04 94 49 62 99; www.paradis-des-campeurs.com] Exit A8/E80 junc 37 at Puget-sur-Argens onto DN7 to by-pass Fréjus, then onto D559 twd Ste Maxime. Site on R 2km after passing thro St Aygulf, on LH bend bef hill. Or exit junc 36 onto D125 to Ste Maxime, then D559 dir Fréjus. Site on L after ent Les Issambres. Med, mkd pitch, hdstg, pt sl, terr, pt shd; htd wc; chem disp; mv service pnt; baby facs; fam bthrm; 30% serviced pitches (extra charge); shwrs inc; el pnts (6A) €4 (poss rev pol); gas 2km; lndtte; shop; tradsmn; rest; snacks; bar; BBQ; playgrnd; sand beach adj; cycle hire; golf 4km; games rm; internet; TV rm; dogs €3; poss cr; Eng spkn; quiet; ccard acc; red low ssn; CKE/CCI. "V popular low ssn; direct access via underpass to beach; excel san facs; superb views fr top level pitches - worth extra; gates shut at night & guarded; helpful owners; old rd to St Aygulf suitable for cycling; excel." ♦ 27 Mar-16 Oct. € 23.00 (3 persons)   2009*

ST AYGULF *10F4* (5km NW Rural) *43.41626, 6.70598*
Camping L'Etoile d'Argens, Chemin des Etangs, 83370 St Aygulf [04 94 81 01 41; fax 04 94 81 21 45; info@etoiledargens.com; www.etoiledargens.com] Exit A8 at junc 37 Puget-sur-Argens onto DN7 to Fréjus & D559 to St Aygulf, or fr DN7 take D7 to St Aygulf by-passing Fréjus & turn onto D8 to site. Lge, hdg/mkd pitch, shd; 25% serviced pitches; wc; chem disp; baby facs; shwrs inc; el pnts (10A) inc; gas; lndtte; shop; tradsmn; rest, snacks; bar; no BBQ; playgrnd; htd pool; sand beach 3km; rv fishing; tennis; archery; golf 1.5km; wifi; entmnt; 40% statics; dogs €5; poss cr; Eng spkn; adv bkg; quiet; ccard acc; red low ssn; CKE/CCI. "Friendly, helpful owners; gd facs, poss unclean low ssn; excel pool complex; ferry down rv to beach in ssn; vg." ♦ 1 Apr-30 Sep. € 52.00   2009*

See advertisement opposite

⊞ **ST BEAT** *8G3* (8km SE Rural) *42.87122, 0.73629*
Camp Municipal, 31440 Fos [05 61 79 35 94 or 05 61 79 41 61 (Mairie); mairie.fos@wanadoo.fr] S fr St Béat on N125 foll camping sp on site alongside Rv Garonne. Ring bell at recep to alert warden of arr. Sm, mkd pitch, unshd; htd wc; chem disp (wc); shwrs inc; el pnts (12A) inc; rest, bar 400m; playgrnd; tennis 300m; dogs; phone; CKE/CCI. "Basic facs; gd NH en route Spain; suitable sm o'fits only; have right money - warden never has change!" € 10.80   2008*

⊞ **ST BEAT** *8G3* (500m S Rural) *42.91030, 0.69098* Camp Municipal Clef de France, 31440 St Béat [05 61 94 35 39] On N125 at S exit to town, sp on L on rvside. Med, mkd pitch, pt shd; htd wc; shwrs inc; el pnts (5A) inc; shops, rest, bar 500m; playgrnd; pool 200m; fishing; boating; 95% statics; dogs; quiet. "Facs ltd low ssn; long walk to san facs; conv Spanish border; NH/sh stay only." 2009*

ST BENOIT DES ONDES See Cancale *2E4*

ST BERTRAND DE COMMINGES See Montréjeau *8F3*

FRANCE

ST BOIL *6H1* (1.5km S Rural) *46.64621, 4.69480* **Camping Moulin de Collonge, Route des Vins, 71940 St Boil [03 85 44 00 40 or 03 85 44 00 32; fax 03 85 44 00 40; millofcollonge@wanadoo.fr; www.moulindecollonge.com]** S on A6 take N80 at Chalon-Sud; W dir Le Creusot; 9km turn S on D981 thro Buxy to St Boil; sp on L thro vill. Sm, hdg/mkd pitch, pt shd; wc (few cont); baby facs; shwrs inc; el pnts (6A) €3.50 (poss no earth or rev pol); gas; lndtte; sm shop & 2km; tradsmn; rest, snacks; bar; BBQ; playgrnd; htd, covrd pool; lake fishing; cycle hire; wifi; entmnt; some statics; dogs; v cr high ssn; some Eng spkn; adv bkg; quiet; ccard acc; red low ssn; CKE/CCI. "Busy but quiet site; clean, dated san facs; uneven pitches & some sm - poss muddy when wet; gd cycling." ♦ 1 Apr-29 Sep. € 19.00   2009*

ST BONNET DE JOUX *9A2* (E Rural) **Camp Municipal, Route de Cluny, 71220 St Bonnet-de-Joux [03 85 24 73 87 (Mairie); st.bonnet.de.joux.mairie@ wanadoo.fr]** Site sp fr vill cent - also sp for tennis. Sm, hdg pitch, pt shd; wc (some cont); chem disp (wc); shwrs inc; shop, rest, bar in vill; BBQ; playgrnd; tennis adj; quiet. "Simple, ungated site in sm vill, beside sm lake; facs clean but ltd" 1 Jun-. € 9.00   2010*

ST BONNET PRES ORCIVAL see Orcival *7B4*

ST BONNET TRONCAIS see Cérilly *4H3*

⊞ **ST BREVIN LES PINS** *2G3* (N Coastal) *47.26553, -2.16918* **FFCC Camping de Mindin, 32-40 Ave du Bois, 44250 St Brévin-les-Pins [02 40 27 46 41; fax 02 40 39 20 53; info@ camping-de-mindin.com; www.camping-de-mindin.com]** On beach rd at N end of St Brevin. Med, shd; htd wc; chem disp; mv service pnt; baby facs; shwrs inc; el pnts (16A) €5.05; lndtte (inc dryer); shop; rest, snacks; bar; playgrnd; htd pool; paddling pool; sand beach adj; mainly statics; dogs €2.35; poss cr; adv bkg; ccard acc; red low ssn; CKE/CCI. "Sm, sandy pitches; gd san facs." € 15.70   2008*

⊞ **ST BREVIN LES PINS** *2G3* (1km S Coastal) *47.23800, -2.17030* **Camping La Courance, 100-110 Ave Maréchal Foch, 44250 St Brévin-les-Pins [02 40 27 22 91; fax 02 40 27 24 59; info@campinglacourance.fr; www. campinglacourance.fr]** Take Ave Foch fr cent of St Brevin, site on R, clearly sp. Lge, pt sl, shd; htd wc; baby facs; shwrs inc; el pnts (5A) €5.40 (poss long lead req); gas; lndtte; shops 1km; rest, snacks; bar; beach adj; 90% statics; dogs €2.50; quiet; red low ssn. "Well-maintained; steep, poss slippery paths." € 17.20   2009*

⊞ **ST BREVIN LES PINS** *2G3* (2km S Coastal) *47.21375, -2.15409* **Camping Les Rochelets, Chemin des Grandes Rivières, 44250 St Brévin-les-Pins [tel/fax 02 40 27 40 25; info@rochelets.com; www.rochelets.com]** Fr N or S on D213 exit sp Les Rochelets, site sp. Lge, hdg/mkd pitch, pt shd; wc (some cont); shwrs; el pnts (6-10A) €4.60-5.90; lndtte; tradsmn; rest, snacks; bar; playgrnd; htd pool; beach 100m; cycle hire; games area; games rm; wifi; entmnt; 30% statics; dogs €3.40; adv bkg; quiet; ccard acc; red low ssn. "Gd site for families; lots of entmnt & activities in high ssn; great location." € 21.50   2012*

ST BREVIN LES PINS *2G3* (2.4km S Coastal) *47.23514, -2.16739* **Camping Sunêlia Le Fief, 57 Chemin du Fief, 44250 St Brévin-les-Pins [02 40 27 23 86; fax 02 40 64 46 19; camping@lefief.com; www.lefief.com]** Fr Nantes dir St Nazaire. After St Nazaire bdge S on D213. Pass Leclerc & exit sp St Brévin-l'Océan/La Courance. At rndabt foll sp Le Fief. Lge, mkd pitch, hdstg, pt shd; wc; chem disp; mv service pnt; baby facs; sauna; shwrs inc; el pnts (6A) €6; gas; lndtte (inc dryer); shop; tradsmn; rest, snacks; bar; BBQ (gas/charcoal); playgrnd; 2 pools (1 htd, covrd); paddling pool; waterslide; jacuzzi; sand beach 800m; waterpark & waterslide etc adj; tennis; games area; games rm; wellness cent; fitness rm; cycle hire nr; gym; wifi; entmnt; TV rm; 30% statics; dogs €11; Eng spkn; adv bkg; quiet; ccard acc; red low ssn/long stay/CKE/CCI. "Excel for families; vg leisure facs." ♦ 7 Apr-30 Sep. € 41.00   2011*

See advertisement on next page

FRANCE

SAINT BREVIN LES PINS ~ CÔTE DE JADE ~ SOUTH BRITTANY ~ FRANCE

CAMPING, RENTAL & SPA

GROCERY - BAR - RESTAURANT - TAKE AWAY
CHILDREN'S PLAYGROUND
TENNIS - MULTISPORTS TERRAIN
INDOOR, HEATED SWIMMING POOL
10 ENTERTAINERS IN SEASON

FULL AND HALF PENSION

LE SPA

Aqua relaxation area, jets, waterfalls, pebble walk river, body treatments and facials, sauna, steam room, gym, Cinq Mondes® treatments, Power Plate® and LPG®

57, chemin du Fief
44250 SAINT BREVIN LES PINS
tel. : 0033 2 40 27 23 86
fax : 0033 2 40 64 46 19

www.lefief.com

camping le fief

ST BREVIN LES PINS *2G3* (5km S Coastal) *47.20441, -2.15773* Camping Les Pierres Couchées, Ave des Pierres Couchées, L'Ermitage, 44250 St Brévin-les-Pins [02 40 27 85 64; fax 02 40 64 97 03; www.siblu.com/lespierrescouchees] Sp fr D213 in St Brévin-l'Ermitage. Lge, mkd pitch, terr, pt shd; htd wc (some cont); baby facs; shwrs inc; el pnts (10A); lndtte; shop & 3km; tradsmn; rest, snacks; bar; BBQ; playgrnd; htd pool; paddling pool; waterslide; sand beach 300m; tennis; games area; games rm; fitness rm; cycle hire; horseriding 300m; golf 12km; entmnt; TV; 75% statics; dogs; Eng spkn; adv bkg; quiet; ccard acc; red low ssn; CKE/CCI. "Vg facs for families; friendly, helpful staff." ◆ 4 Apr-26 Sep. € 28.00   2009*

ST BRIAC SUR MER *2E3* (Urban/Coastal) *48.62765, -2.13056* FFCC Camping Emeraude, 7 Chemin de la Souris, 35800 St Briac-sur-Mer [tel/fax 02 99 88 34 55; campingemeraude@wanadoo.fr; www.camping-emeraude.com] SW fr Dinard to St Lunaire on N786, after passing Dinard golf course, site is sp to L. Lge, hdg/ pitch, pt shd; wc; chem disp; mv service pnt; baby facs; shwrs inc; el pnts (6A) €3.80; gas; lndtte (inc dryer); sm shop & 200m; tradsmn; snacks; bar; playgrnd; htd pool; paddling pool; water park; beach 700m & sand beach 1.5km; cycle hire; games area; games rm; wifi; entmnt; 40% statics; dogs €2.50; poss cr; adv bkg; red low ssn. "Excel, well-run site, quiet low ssn." ◆ 3 Apr-19 Sep. € 25.80   2010*

ST BRIAC SUR MER *2E3* (500m S Coastal) *48.61493, -2.12779* Camping Le Pont Laurin, Route de la Vallée Gatorge, 35800 St Briac-sur-Mer [02 99 88 34 64; fax 02 99 16 38 19; lepontlaurin@ouest-camping.com; www.ouest-camping. com] Fr St Briac, 500m S on D3. Lge, hdg/mkd pitch, some hdstg, pt shd; wc; chem disp; mv service pnt; baby facs; shwrs inc; el pnts (10A) €3 (poss rev pol); lndtte (inc dryer); shop & 500m; tradsmn; snacks; playgrnd; sand beach 1km; sailing; canoe hire nr; tennis nr; games area; sports cent adj; wifi; 4% statics; dogs €1.50; twin-axles not acc; Eng spkn; adv bkg; quiet; ccard acc; CKE/CCI. "Peaceful site; welcoming, helpful staff; clean, modern san facs; excel beaches; gd walking; interesting town; highly rec" ◆ 1 Apr-30 Sep. € 26.30 2013*

ST BRIAC SUR MER *2E3* (500m SW Coastal) *48.60422, -2.15616* Camp Municipal des Mielles, Rue Jules Jeunet, 22770 Lancieux [02 96 86 22 98 or 02 96 86 22 19; fax 02 96 86 28 20; campinglesmielles@orange.fr; www. mairie-lancieux.fr] Fr S on D786 at 500m past windmill turn L into Rue du Fredy. Site on R in 300m, sp. Lge, mkd pitch, unshd; wc (some cont); chem disp; shwrs inc; el pnts (6A) €3.20; lndtte; shop 500m; playgrnd; sand beach 400m; watersports 150m; tennis; wifi; entmnt; 2% statics; dogs €1.70; poss cr; CKE/CCI. "Well-managed, popular site; gd security in ssn; excel facs; hot water ltd low ssn." ◆ 1 Apr-30 Sep. € 10.50   2009*

ST BRICE SUR VIENNE see St Junien *7B3*

ST BRIEUC *2E3* (5km E Coastal) *48.53311, -2.67193* FFCC Camping Bellevue Mer, Pointe de Guettes, 22120 Hillion [02 96 32 20 39 or 02 96 31 25 05 (HS); fax 02 96 32 20 39; contact@bellevuemer.com; www.bellevuemer.com] Fr St Brieuc twds Dinan on N12 turn N at exit St René onto D712 to Hillion, then rd to Lermot. Site well sp. Narr, winding app rd. Med, unshd; wc; chem disp; mv service pnt; shwrs €0.15; el pnts (6A) 3 (poss rev pol); lndtte; shops 1.5km; tradsmn; bar; playgrnd; wifi; dogs €0.50; quiet; red low ssn. "Sea views fr most pitches; well-maintained site; welcoming, friendly owners; facs basic; narr site rds poss diff lge o'fits; vg." 28 Apr-16 Sep. € 19.20   2011*

ST BRIEUC *2E3* (2km S Rural) *48.50066, -2.75938* Camping des Vallées, Blvd Paul-Doumer, 22000 St Brieuc [tel/fax 02 96 94 05 05; campingdesvallees@wanadoo.fr; www. mairie-saint-brieuc.fr] Fr N12 take exit sp D700 Trégueux, Pleufragan & foll sp 'Des Vallées'. Site nr Parc de Brézillet Med, hdg pitch, some hdstg, pt shd; wc (some cont); chem disp; mv service pnt; baby facs; shwrs inc; el pnts (10A) €4; lndtte; shop; snacks; bar; playgrnd; htd pool; waterslide adj; sand beach 3km; 25% statics; dogs €2.40; adv bkg; CKE/CCI. "High kerbs to pitches." ◆ Easter-30 Oct. € 15.20 2008*

See advertisement on pages 32 & 33

STE CECILE

FRANCE

ST CALAIS *4F2* (500m N Urban) *47.92691, 0.74413*
Camp Municipal du Lac, Rue du Lac, 72120 St Calais
[02 43 35 04 81/ 02 43 63 15 15 (Town hall); camping.
stcalais@orange.fr] E fr Le Mans on D357 to St Calais; after
sharp (90 degree) L/H bend away fr town cent take L/H lane for
next junc in 100m; do not foll D357 bend to R but go strt ahead
on D429; in 200m turn R onto sm rd sp 'Conflans/Plan d'Eau'.
Site on R after football ground. Fr N exit A11 junc 5 onto D1 to
St Calais; turn R onto D357 dir Le Mans; in 200m turn R onto
D429 N; in 400 turn R into sm rd sp 'Conflans/Plan d'Eau to
site; Leave D357 at R angle bend by Champion supmkt; site in
100m. Site by lake on N edge of town, well sp fr cent. Ent easy
to miss. Med, hdg/mkd pitch, pt shd; wc; chem disp; mv service
pnt; shwrs inc; el pnts (6A) inc; lndry rm; shops 500m; tradsmn;
supmkt nrby; snacks & bar adj; BBQ; playgrnd; pool adj; lake sw
adj; some statics; dogs; poss cr; adv bkg; quiet; no ccard acc;
CKE/CCI; "Delightful, well-kept site; friendly, helpful warden;
spacious pitches, espec nr lake; easy rvside walk to town; gd
touring base" ♦ 1 Apr-15 Oct. € 17.15 02 43 35 15 13 2013*

ST CAST LE GUILDO *2E3* (Coastal) *48.62732, -2.25403*
**Camping Les Mielles, Blvd de la Vieux Ville, 22380 St Cast-
le-Guildo [02 96 41 87 60; info@campings-vert-bleu.com;
www.campings-vert-bleu.com]** Fr D786 at Matignon turn
onto D13 into St Cast. Cross over staggered x-rds foll site sp
down long gentle hill. R at next x-rds & site on R in 200m.
Lge, unshd, wc (mainly cont); chem disp; baby facs; shwrs
inc; el pnts (3-10A) €4.45-6.20; lndtte; shop; snacks; bar;
playgrnd; htd pool; sand beach 350m; entmnt; 95% statics;
dogs €2.40; poss cr; poss noisy; red low ssn. "Plenty of facs for
teenagers; gd san facs; ltd space for tourers." 15 Mar-2 Jan.
€ 19.95 2009*

ST CAST LE GUILDO *2E3* (500m N Coastal) *48.64198, -2.25601*
**Camping La Crique, Plage de la Mare, 22380 St Cast-Le-
Guildo [02 96 41 89 19; fax 02 96 81 04 77; info@campings-
vert-bleu.com; www.campings-vert-bleu.com]** On ent town
foll site sp. Med, mkd pitch, unshd; wc; chem disp; shwrs inc;
el pnts (6A) €4.60; lndtte; snacks; bar; playgrnd; beach 200m;
some statics (sep area); dogs €2.50; poss cr; adv bkg; quiet;
CKE/CCI. "Site on top of low cliff with path to beach; vg."
15 Mar-15 Sep. € 16.10 2010*

ST CAST LE GUILDO *2E3* (500m N Coastal) *48.63690,
-2.26900* **Camping Le Châtelet, Rue des Nouettes, 22380
St Cast-le-Guildo [02 96 41 96 33; fax 02 96 41 97 99;
info@lechatelet.com; www.lechatelet.com]** Site sp fr all dir
& in St Cast-le-Guildo but best rte: fr D786 at Matignon take
D13 into St Cast-le-Guildo, turn L after Intermarché supmkt
on R; foll sm site sp. Or app on D19 fr St Jaguel. Care needed
down ramp to main site. (NB Avoid Matignon cent Wed due
to mkt.) Lge, hdg/mkd pitch, pt sl, terr, pt shd; wc; chem disp;
mv service pnt; baby facs; shwrs inc; el pnts (8A) inc (50m cable
req); gas; lndtte (inc dryer); shop; snacks; bar; BBQ (charcoal/
elec); playgrnd; htd covrd pool; paddling pool; dir access sand
beach 300m (via steep steps); fishing; cycle hire 500m; games
rm; golf 2km; wifi; entmnt; TV; 10% statics (tour ops); dogs
€4; no c'vans/m'vans over 7m high ssn, otherwise by req; adv
bkg; ccard acc; red low ssn. "Site o'looks coast; extra for sea
view pitches; some pitches round fishing pond; gd for families
with young children; helpful staff; modern unisex san facs;
gates clsd 2230-0700; access to some pitches diff lge o'fits;
steep climb to beaches; mkt Mon." ♦ 23 Apr-14 Sep. € 40.82
SBS - B11 2011*

ST CAST LE GUILDO *2E3* (3.5km S Rural) *48.58441,
-2.25691* **Camping Le Château de Galinée, Rue de
Galinée, 22380 St Cast-le-Guildo [02 96 41 10 56; fax
02 96 41 03 72; contact@chateaudegalinee.com; www.
chateaudegalinee.com or www.les-castels.com]**
W fr St Malo on D168 thro Ploubalay. At La Ville-es-Comte
branch onto D786 & go thro Notre Dame-du-Guildo. Approx
2km after Notre Dame-du-Guildo turn 3rd L into Rue de
Galinée & foll sp to site. Do not go into St Cast. Lge, hdg/
mkd pitch, pt shd; htd wc; chem disp; mv service pnt; baby
facs; fam bthrm; sauna; shwrs inc; el pnts (10A) inc; lndtte
(inc dryer); shop; rest, snacks; bar; BBQ; playgrnd; htd pool
complex inc covrd pool; waterslide; paddling pool; sand beach
4km; fishing pond; tennis; games area; horseriding 6km; golf
3km; wifi; entmnt; games/TV rm; 30% statics; dogs €4; Eng
spkn; adv bkg; quiet; ccard acc; red low ssn/long stay/CKE/
CCI. "Peaceful, family site in lovely area; spacious, well laid-
out pitches; helpful staff; modern, clean san facs; pitches poss
muddy after rain; excel rest; mkt Fri & Mon." ♦
12 May-8 Sep. € 38.30 (CChq acc) SBS - B27 2011*

See advertisement on inside back cover

ST CAST LE GUILDO *2E3* (6km SW Rural) *48.59111, -2.29578*
**Camping Le Vallon aux Merlettes, Route de Lamballe,
22550 Matignon [02 96 41 11 61 or 06 70 31 03 22 (mob);
giblanchet@orange.fr; www.camping-matignon.com]**
Fr E & W take D786 to Matignon; 500m fr town cent turn SW
on D13 twds Lamballe. Med, pt sl, pt shd; wc (cont); chem
disp; mv service pnt; shwrs inc; el pnts (8A) €3.10; gas; lndtte;
shop; snacks; playgrnd; pool 4km; tennis; sand beach 6km;
some statics; dogs €0.75; adv bkg rec; quiet; ccard not acc;
CKE/CCI. "Lovely site on playing fields outside attractive town;
vg clean facs." ♦ Easter-30 Oct. € 12.70 2009*

> "We must tell The Club about
> that great site we found"
> Get your site reports in by mid-August
> and we'll do our best to get your updates
> into the next edition of Caravan Europe.

ST CAST LE GUILDO *2E3* (2km NW Coastal) *48.63268,
-2.27847* **Camping de la Fontaine, La Ville Norme, 22380
St Cast-le-Guildo [02 96 41 95 64 or 06 78 22 42 24 (mob);
camping.la-fontaine@orange.fr]** Exit D786 at Matignon
onto D13. Site well sp fr all dir. Take rd to beach of La Fresnaye
(500m). Med, terr; unshd; wc; chem disp; mv service pnt;
shwrs inc; el pnts (10A) €2.80-3.50 (poss long lead req); gas;
lndtte; shop 3km; rest 1.5km; playgrnd; sand/shgl beach 500m;
90% statics; phone; poss cr; Eng spkn; adv bkg (rec Jul/Aug);
quiet; CKE/CCI. "Sea views; clean modern san facs; coastal
path & sm coves; spectacular sunsets; gd." ♦ ltd
1 Apr-30 Sep. € 12.60 2008*

STE CATHERINE DE FIERBOIS see Ste Maure de Touraine
4H2

STE CECILE see Chantonnay *2H4*

Site report forms at back of guide   *Last year of report **497***

ST CERE

ST CERE *7C4* (SE Rural) *44.85792, 1.89761* **Camping Le Soulhol, Quai Salesses, 46400 St Céré [tel/fax 05 65 38 12 37; info@campinglesoulhol.com; www.campinglesoulhol.com]** Fr S on D940 twds St Céré turn onto D48 (Leyme); in 300m turn L (sp not easily seen); site in 200m. Site sp fr all dirs to St Céré. Lge, pt shd; wc; chem disp; mv service pnt; baby facs; shwrs; el pnts (10A) €3.60 (dated electrics); gas; lndtte; sm shop, tradsmn (high ssn); shops, rests in town 1km; snacks; pool; tennis; cycles hire (1 hr free); Eng library; internet; entmnt; TV rm; 10% statics; dogs €2; phone; quiet; red low ssn; ccard not acc; red low ssn/long stay; CKE/CCI. "Excel, spacious site; lge pitches; friendly, helpful staff; gd clean san facs; far end of site bet 2 rvs v quiet; poss flooding after heavy rain; mkt alt Weds." ♦ 1 May-20 Sep. € 15.50   2011*

ST CHELY D'APCHER *9D1* (8km E Rural) *44.77506, 3.37203* **FFCC Camping Le Galier, Route de St Chély, 48120 St Alban-sur-Limagnole [04 66 31 58 80; fax 04 66 31 41 83; accueil@campinglegalier.fr; www.campinglegalier.fr]** Exit A75 junc 34 onto D806, then E on D987 for 3km. Site 1.5km SW of St Alban on rvside. Sm, mkd pitch, pt sl; htd wc (some cont); chem disp; shwrs inc; el pnts (6A) €3.70; lndtte; shop 1.5km; snacks; bar; BBQ; playgrnd; pool; paddling pool; games rm; tennis 800m; wifi; some statics; dogs €1.60; poss cr; Eng spk; adv bkg; quiet; red low ssn/CKE/CCI. "Lovely setting by rv; friendly owners; clean san facs - stretched high ssn, ltd low ssn; gd walking, fishing; vg NH." ♦ 1 Mar-15 Oct. € 14.50 (3 persons)   2010*

⊞ **ST CHERON** *4E3* (3km SE Rural) *48.54435, 2.13840* **Camping Héliomonde (Naturist), La Petite Beauce, 91530 St Chéron [01 64 56 61 37; fax 01 64 56 51 30; helio@heliomonde.fr; www.heliomonde.fr]** N20 S to Arpajon; then D116 to St Chéron. Site bet Arpajon & Dourdan. Sp in town. Med, shd; htd wc (most cont); chem disp; mv service pnt; sauna; baby facs; shwrs inc; el pnts (10A) €3.80; lndtte (inc dryer); shop; supmkt 3km; rest, snacks; bar; BBQ; playgrnd; htd pool; paddling pool; tennis; games area; fitness rm; wifi; entmnt; TV; mainly statics; dogs €3; train (Paris) 2km; sep car park; adv bkg; quiet; red low ssn. "Open site; vg facs but ground condition left a lot to be desired (2011); gd rest; conv Versailles, Paris; gd." ♦ € 25.00 (CChq acc)   2011*

ST CHERON *4E3* (3.5km SE Rural) *48.54341, 2.13791* **Camping Le Parc des Roches, La Petite Beauce, 91530 St Chéron [01 64 56 65 50; fax 01 64 56 54 50; info@camping-parcdesroches.com; www.camping-parcdesroches.com]** N20 S to Arpajon; then D116 to St Chéron. Site bet Arpajon & Dourdan. Sp in town. Lge, hdg/mkd pitch, hdstg, pt shd; htd wc; chem disp; mv service pnt; baby facs; shwrs inc; el pnts (10A) €2-4; gas 200m; lndtte (inc dryer); shop 3km; tradsmn; rest, snacks; bar; BBQ; playgrnd; htd pool; paddling pool; tennis; solarium; games area; games rm; wifi; 70% statics; dogs; train 3km; Eng spkn; adv bkg; quiet but poss noisy high ssn; ccard acc; red low ssn; CKE/CCI. "Pleasant, wooded site; helpful, friendly owner; gd san facs; o'night pitches lge & nr ent; gd walking; Great site; V conv for train to Paris" ♦ 1 Mar-15 Dec. € 27.00   2011*

ST CHINIAN *10F1* (1km W) *43.42199, 2.93361* **Camp Municipal Les Terrasses, Route de St Pons, 34360 St Chinian [04 67 38 28 28 (Mairie); fax 04 67 38 28 29; mairie@saintchinian.fr]** On main Béziers-St Pons rd, D612, heading W on o'skts of St Chinian. Site on L. Med, terr, unshd; wc; shwrs inc; el pnts €2.15; shops 1km; poss cr; quiet. "Attractive site with gd views; sm pitches; diff access some pitches." 7 Jul-31 Aug. € 7.50   2009*

ST CHRISTOPHE *7A3* (2.5km NE Rural) *46.01467, 0.87679* **Camping En Campagne, Essubras, 16420 St Christophe [05 45 31 67 57; info@encampagne.com; www.encampagne.com]** Fr D82 St Christophe foll site sp for 2.5km. Sm, hdg pitch, pt shd; htd wc; chem disp; mv service pnt; baby facs; shwrs inc; el pnts (6-10A); inc; lndtte; rest; bar; playgrnd; htd pool; games area; dogs; Eng spkn; adv bkg; quiet. "Vg." 1 Apr-1 Oct. € 18.35   2010*

ST CIRQ LAPOIE *7D3* (2km N Rural) *44.46926, 1.68135* **Camping La Plage, Porte Roques, 46330 St Cirq-Lapopie [05 65 30 29 51; fax 05 65 30 23 33; camping-laplage@wanadoo.fr; www.campingplage.com]** Exit Cahors on D653, in Vers take D662 sp Cajarc. In 20km turn R at Tour-de-Faure over narr bdge, sp St Cirq-Lapopie, site 100m on R beside Rv Lot. Med, mkd pitch, shd; wc; baby facs; shwrs inc; el pnts (6-16A) €4-5; lndtte; shop; rest, snacks; bar; BBQ; playgrnd; pool; canoeing; watersports; wifi; entmnt; 5% statics; dogs €2; Eng spkn; adv bkg; quiet; red low ssn; CKE/CCI. "Pleasant, clean & tidy rvside site; v shady; low ssn site yourself, pay later; friendly, helpful owner; gd walking; excel." ♦ 1 Apr-15 Oct. € 18.80   2012*

ST CIRQ LAPOIE *7D3* (2.5km S Rural) *44.44871, 1.67468* **FFCC Camping La Truffière, Route de Concots, 46330 St Cirq-Lapopie [05 65 30 20 22; fax 05 65 30 20 27; contact@camping-truffiere.com; www.camping-truffiere.com]** Take D911, Cahors to Villefranche rd; in 20km turn N onto D42 at Concots dir St Cirq for 8km - site clearly sp. NB Do not app fr St Cirq-Lapopie. Med, pt sl, terr, shd; htd wc; chem disp; mv service pnt; baby facs; shwrs inc; el pnts (6A) €4; lndtte (inc dryer); ltd shop & 4km; rest, snacks; bar; playgrnd; htd pool; paddling pool; fishing 3km; cycle hire; entmnt; TV; dogs €1.50; phone; Eng spkn; adv bkg; quiet; ccard acc; red low ssn; CKE/CCI. "Well-kept site in gd location; friendly owners; excel facs, ltd low ssn; most pitches in forest clearings; lovely pool; gd." ♦ 22 Apr-15 Sep. € 20.00 (CChq acc)   2013*

ST CIRQ LAPOIE *7D3* (7km W Rural) *44.46991, 1.58701* **Camp Municipal, 46330 St Géry [05 65 31 40 08 (Mairie); fax 05 65 31 45 65; mairiestgery@wanadoo.fr]** Fr St Cirq foll N side Rv Lot on D662. Thro St Géry & after rlwy x-ing turn R bef petrol stn. Sp. Sm, pt sl, shd; wc (cont); el pnts (10A) €2.50 (poss long lead req); shop 2km; rv & fishing adj; quiet. "Clean facs; warden calls eve." 15 Jun-15 Sep. € 7.50   2010*

ST CLAR *8E3* (4km NE Rural) *43.89797, 0.81114* **Camping Les Roches (Naturist), Le Nèri, 32380 Mauroux [tel/fax 05 62 66 30 18; campinglesroches@wanadoo.fr; www. campinglesroches.net]** Fr Fleurance take D953 to St Clar then D167 for 3km to site on L. Well sp on D167. Sm, hdg pitch, pt sl, pt shd; wc; chem disp; mv service pnt; sauna; shwrs; el pnts (6A) €4; lndtte; shops; tradsmn; rest, snacks; bar; pool; lake fishing; entmnt; TV rm; some statics; dogs €1.80; phone; Eng spkn; adv bkg; quiet; red low ssn/long stay; INF card. "Beautiful site in remote location; pleasant, helpful owners; gd sized pitches; gd walking; excel." ♦ ltd 1 May-15 Sep. € 18.50   2009*

⊞ **ST CLAR** *8E3* (8km E Rural) *43.89075, 0.82837* **FFCC Centre Naturiste de Devèze (Naturist), 32380 Gaudonville [05 62 66 43 86; fax 05 62 66 42 02; herve@deveze.eu; www.deveze.eu]** Fr Fleurance to St Clar on D953; then take D40 sp Valence; in 700m take D13 sp Mauroux; in 700m take D167 to site in 4km on L. Lge, hdg pitch, pt sl, terr, pt shd; wc; chem disp; mv service pnt; 80% serviced pitches; shwrs inc; el pnts (5A) €4; gas; lndtte; shop; tradsmn; rest, snacks high ssn; bar; playgrnd; pool; lge lake; fishing; tennis; cycle hire; entmnt; TV rm; 15% statics; dogs €1.80; phone; site clsd 1 Jan-14 Feb; Eng spkn; adv bkg; quiet; ccard acc; red low ssn; INF card req. "Lovely site; highly rec." ♦ € 19.20   2008*

ST CLAUDE *9A3* (2km SE Rural) *46.37153, 5.87171* **Camp Municipal du Martinet, 12 le Martinet, 39200 St Claude [tel/fax 03 84 45 00 40 or 03 84 41 42 62 (LS); contact@ camping-saint-claude.fr; www.camping-saint-claude.fr]** On ent town foll 1-way, under bdge mkd 4.1m high, then take R turn 'Centre Ville' lane to next traff lts. Turn R then immed L sp Genève, turn R 300m after Fiat g'ge onto D290, site on R. Med, pt shd; wc (cont); chem disp; shwrs inc; el pnts (5A) €2.30; gas; lndtte; shops 1km; rest; htd pool adj; tennis; fishing; poss cr; adv bkg; quiet; red low ssn; CKE/CCI; "Warden calls am & pm only low ssn; ltd facs low ssn; excel walking; v attractive town; poss funfair on site in Jun - no prob; gd." 1 Apr-30 Sep. € 20.40   2013*

See advertisement on pages 32 & 33

ST COLOMBAN DES VILLARDS *9C3* (700m SW Rural) *45.29015, 6.22091* **Camping La Perrière, Route du Col du Glandon, 73130 St Colomban-des-Villards [04 79 59 16 07; fax 04 79 59 15 17; saint-colomban@franceloc.fr; www. campings-franceloc.fr]** Exit A43 junc 26 onto D927. Site at end of vill. Access rd narr & winding in places - not rec long o'fits. Sm, mkd pitch, hdstg, terr, pt shd; htd wc; mv service pnt; shwrs inc; el pnts €4; lndtte; shop 200m; BBQ; playgrnd; games area; phone; quiet. "Excel." ♦ 15 Jun-15 Sep. € 15.00   2009*

ST COULOMB see St Malo *2E4*

ST CREPIN ET CARLUCET see Sarlat la Canéda *7C3*

STE CROIX EN PLAINE see Colmar *6F3*

ST CYBRANET see Sarlat la Canéda *7C3*

ST CYPRIEN (DORDOGNE) *7C3* (1km S Rural) *44.85547, 1.03788* **Camping du Garrit, Le Garrit, 24220 St Cyprien [05 53 29 20 56; pbecheau@aol.com; www. campingdugarritendordogneperigord.com]** Fr W on D703 turn R bef town sp; cross rlwy & bear R; then sharp R at rv. Sp on D703 fr St Cyprien as 'Le Garrit'. Med, hdg/mkd pitch, pt shd; wc; chem disp; baby facs; shwrs inc; el pnts (6A) €3; lndtte; shop; BBQ; playgrnd; pool; canoeing; sailing; boat hire; fishing; dogs €1; phone; Eng spkn; adv bkg; rd & rlwy noise some pitches; CKE/CCI. "Lovely, rvside site; lge pitches; excel san facs; gd touring base for prehistoric caves; NH or sh stay." 1 May-15 Sep. € 15.00   2009*

ST CYPRIEN PLAGE *10G1* (3km S Coastal) *42.59939, 3.03761* **Camping Cala Gogo, Ave Armand Lanoux, Les Capellans, 66750 St Cyprien-Plage [04 68 21 07 12; fax 04 68 21 02 19; camping.calagogo@wanadoo.fr; www. campmed.com]** Exit A9 at Perpignan Nord onto D617 to Canet-Plage, then D81; site sp bet St Cyprien-Plage & Argelès-Plage dir Les Capellans. V lge, hdg/mkd pitch, pt shd; htd wc (some cont); chem disp; mv service pnt; baby facs; shwrs inc; el pnts (6A) €3.40; lndtte; supmkt; rest, snacks; bar; playgrnd; 2 pools; paddling pool; sand beach adj; tennis; games area; entmnt; TV rm; 30% statics; dogs €3.70; Eng spkn; adv bkg; red low ssn; ccard acc; CKE/CCI. "Excel site; gd pitches; lovely beach; suitable for partially-sighted." ♦ 10 May-20 Sep. € 29.80   2008*

ST CYPRIEN PLAGE *10G1* (1.5km SW Urban/Coastal) *42.61851, 3.01582* **Chadotel Camping Le Roussillon, Chemin de la Mer, 66750 St Cyprien [04 68 21 06 45 or 02 51 33 05 05 (LS); fax 02 51 33 94 04; chadotel@ wanadoo.fr; www.chadotel.com]** Exit A9 junc 42 Perpignan Sud onto D914 to Elne, D40 to St Cyprien. Site sp. Lge, hdg/ mkd pitch, unshd; htd wc; baby facs; shwrs inc; el pnts (6A) inc; gas; lndtte; shop; snacks; bar; BBQ (gas); playgrnd; htd pool; waterslide; sand beach 1km; cycle hire; games rm; TV rm; entmnt; bus to beach; dogs €3; Eng spkn; adv bkg; red long stay/low ssn; ccard acc. "Vg family site; gd touring base." ♦ 7 Apr-22 Sep. € 32.50   2011*

ST CYPRIEN PLAGE *10G1* (3km W Rural) *42.62360, 3.00094* **Camp Municipal Bosc d'en Roug, 66750 St Cyprien [04 68 21 07 95; fax 04 68 21 55 43; www.camping-saint-cyprien.com]** Exit A9 junc 42 & foll sp Argelès-sur-Mer on D914. Turn off onto D40 dir Elne & foll sp St Cyprien. Site sp. V lge, mkd pitch, pt shd; wc; chem disp (wc only0; mv waste; shwrs inc; (10A) inc; gas; lndtte; shop; rest, snacks; bar; playgrnd; htd pool; sand beach 3km; entmnt; 50% statics; dogs €2; phone; poss cr; Eng spkn; adv bkg; quiet; red low ssn. "Gd shady site in pleasant location on edge well-kept vill; helpful, friendly staff; gd rest & entmnt; no twin-axles." ♦ 9 Apr-17 Sep. € 25.00   2011*

ST CYPRIEN SUR DOURDOU see Conques *7D4*

ST CYR (VIENNE) see Jaunay Clan *4H1*

ST CYR SUR MER (VAR) see Bandol *10F3*

ST DENIS DU PAYRE see Luçon *7A1*

ST DONAT SUR L'HERBASSE 9C2 (6km N Rural) 45.14631, 5.02140 **FFCC Camping Les Falquets, Route de Margès, 26260 Charmes-sur-l'Herbasse [04 75 45 75 57 or 04 75 45 27 44 (LS); fax 04 75 45 66 17; info@lesfalquets. com; www.lesfalquets.com]** Exit A7 junc 13 onto D532 dir Romans-sur-Isère; at Chanos-Curson turn N onto D67 to Charmes (via St Donat-sur-l'Herbasse), then D121 dir Margès. Site sp in vill on rvside. Med, shd; wc (some cont); chem disp; shwrs inc; el pnts (6-10A) €2.80-3.50; Indtte; shop 3km; bar; playgrnd; lake sw, waterslide, windsurfing & tennis 3km; 25% statics; dogs free; phone; Eng spkn; adv bkg rec high ssn; quiet; red low ssn; CKE/ CCI. "Pleasant, well-kept site; old facs but clean; helpful warden; sh walk to vill; gd." ♦ 1 May-31 Aug. € 13.00   2009*

ST DONAT SUR L'HERBASSE 9C2 (500m S Rural) 45.11916, 4.99290 **Camping Domaine Les Ulèzes, Route de Romans, 26260 St Donat-sur-l'Herbasse [tel/fax 04 75 47 83 20; contact@domaine-des-ulezes.com; www.domaine-des-ulezes.com]** Exit A7 junc 13 onto D532 dir Romans-sur-Isère. In 5km turn N onto D67 thro St Donat. Site on edge of vill off D53 dir Peyrins, well sp. Med, hdg/mkd pitch, pt shd; wc; chem disp; mv service pnt; shwrs inc; el pnts (6-10A) €3.50-4.50; gas 1km; Indtte; ice; shop; tradsmn; rest, snacks; bar; BBQ (gas/elec); playgrnd; htd pool; games area; games rm; wifi; entmnt; TV; 10% statics; dogs €2; no twin-axles; Eng spkn; adv bkg; quiet; ccard acc; red low ssn; CKE/CCI. "Lovely rvside site; gd size pitches; welcoming, friendly owners; canal-side walk to town; gd touring base; vg." ♦ 1 Apr-31 Oct. € 18.50   2011*

ST ELOY LES MINES 7A4 (S Rural) 46.15144, 2.83321 **Camp Municipal La Poule d'Eau, Rue de la Poule d'Eau, 63700 St Eloy-les-Mines [04 73 85 45 47; fax 04 73 85 07 75; selm.maire@wanadoo.fr; www.sainteloylesmines.com]** On D2144 fr S turn W at 1st rndabt at St Eloy-les-Mines (Vieille Ville) onto D110; site 200m clearly sp. Fr Montluçon/ Montaigut, last rndabt; site by 2 lakes. Med, mkd pitch, pt sl, shd; wc; shwrs; el pnts (6A) inc; shop adj; tradsmn; playgrnd; lake sw, fishing & watersports adj; entmnt; adv bkg; quiet. "Barrier clsd 1200-1600; gd location; warden v proud of his site; excel sh stay/NH." 1 Jun-30 Sep. € 8.48   2008*

ST EMILION 7C2 (3km N Rural) 44.91695, -0.14160 **Camping Yelloh Saint Emilion - Domaine de la Barbanne, 2 lieu dit Les Combes, 33330 St Emilion [05 57 24 75 80; fax 05 57 24 69 68; info@camping-saint-emilion.com; www. camping-saint-emilion.com]** NB Trailer c'vans not permitted in cent of St Emilion. Fr A10 exit junc 39a sp Libourne onto D670. In Libourne turn E on D243 twd St Emilion. On o'skts of St Emilion turn L onto D122 dir Lussac & Montagne; site on R by lake in 3km. Or fr S, foll site sp off D670 to Libourne, nr Les Bigaroux. NB D122 S of St Emilion unsuitable for c'vans. Lge, hdg/mkd pitch, hdstg, shd; wc (some cont); chem disp; mv service pnt; baby facs; shwrs inc; el pnts (10A) inc; gas; Indtte (inc dryer); sm shop; tradsmn; rest, snacks;bar; BBQ (gas); playgrnd; htd pool; paddling pool; waterslide; fishing; canoes & pedalos avail; watersports nr; horseriding 8km; tennis; mountain bike circuit; cycle hire; wifi; entmnt; games/TV rm; 25% statics; dogs €4; no c'vans/m'vans over 10m; phone; poss cr; Eng spkn; adv bkg; quiet; ccard acc; red low ssn; CKE/ CCI. "Lovely, peaceful, well-run lakeside site; owners friendly & helpful; gd sized pitches; suitable lge o'fits; clean, modern san facs; free shuttle bus service to St Emilion; gd cycle rtes; excel." ♦ 26 Apr-29 Sep. € 53.10 SBS - D08   2013*

See advertisement on inside front cover

⊞ **ST EMILION** 7C2 (4km SE Rural) 44.85138, -0.10683 **Aire St Emilion Domaine du Château Gerbaud, 33000 St Pey-d'Armens [06 03 27 00 32 (mob); fax 05 57 47 10 53; contact@chateau-gerbaud.com; www.chateau-gerbaud. com]** Fr Libourne SE on D670/D936 dir Castillon-la-Bataille. In St Pey-d'Armens at bar/tabac foll sp Château Gerbaud vineyard. Parking & service pnt for m'vans for max 48 hours. "Friendly, Eng-speaking owners."   2010*

STE ENGRACE 8F1 (5km NW Rural) 43.01600, -0.85786 **FFCC Camping Ibarra, Quartier Les Casernes, 64560 Ste Engrâce [05 59 28 73 59; maryse@ibarra-chantina.com; www. ibarra-chantina.com]** D918 S fr Tardets-Sorholus; in 2km turn R onto D26; in 6km to L onto D113 sp Ste Engrâce; site on R in 5km. Site clearly sp just bef La Caserne. NB not suitable car+c'van. Sm, mkd pitch, pt shd; wc (some cont); chem disp; shwrs inc; el pnts (5A) €1.80; Indry rm; tradsmn; snacks 500m; bar; BBQ (sep area); playgrnd; 8% statics; dogs; quiet; CKE/CCI. "Pleasant site on rv bank; scenic views; spectacular Kakuetta gorges nrby; vg; narrow rd through gorge for several Kms before site" ♦ ltd 1 Apr-30 Sep. € 11.50   2013*

STE ENIMIE 9D1 (6km E Rural) 44.33777, 3.47583 **Camping Del Ron, 48320 Blajoux [tel/fax 04 66 48 54 71; camping. delron@orange.fr; www.campingdelron.com]** E fr Ste Enimie on D907b dir Ispagnac, site on R by Rv Tarn after Prades. Med, hdg shd, terr, pt shd; wc; shwrs inc; el pnts €3.80; Indtte; shop 300m; rest, snacks; bar; BBQ; playgrnd; htd pool; games area; rv sw & beach adj; fishing; canoe hire; wifi; 10% statics; dogs €0.60; adv bkg; quiet. "In Tarn Gorge with magnificent views; peaceful, espec low ssn; friendly owners; vg." ♦ 1 May-30 Sep. € 17.00   2009*

STE ENIMIE 9D1 (1.5km SW Rural) 44.35378, 3.40155 **Camp Couderc, Route de Millau, 48210 Ste Enimie [04 66 48 50 53; fax 04 66 48 58 59; campingcouderc@ orange.fr; www.campingcouderc.fr]** Leave Ste Eminie on D907B in dir Millau, site on L bank of Rv Tarn. Med, mkd pitch, pt sl, terr, pt shd; wc; chem disp; mv service pnt; baby facs; shwrs inc; el pnts (6A) €3; gas; shop; snacks; bar; playgrnd; pool; canoeing; dogs free; Eng spkn; quiet; red low ssn; CKE/ CCI. "Rd along gorge narr & twisting; busy, friendly, lovely site; gd modern facs." ♦ 1 Apr-30 Sep. € 18.00   2009*

SAINTES 7B2 (500m N Urban) 45.75511, -0.62871 **Camp Municipal au Fil de l'Eau, 6 Rue de Courbiac, 17100 Saintes [05 46 93 08 00 or 06 75 24 91 96 (mob); fax 05 46 93 61 88; campingaufildeleau@sfr.fr; www. camping-saintes-17.com]** Well sp as 'Camping Municipal' fr rndbts on by-pass N & S on D150 & D137 (thro indus area), adj rv. If app fr W on D128 (N side of Saintes), turn R at rndabt onto Rue de l'Abbatoir; in 800m turn L into Rue de Courbiac; site on R in 200m. NB 1st Mon in month street mkt & many rds clsd. Lge, pt shd; wc; chem disp; shwrs inc; el pnts (10A) €3.60; Indtte; shop; supmkt 1.5km; snacks; rest high ssn; bar; BBQ; playgrnd; sm pool; rv sw, fishing & boating adj; wifi; dogs €1.60; train 2km; Eng spkn; adv bkg; ccard acc; red low ssn/ long stay; CKE/CCI. "Excel site; vg san facs; excel rest; ground poss boggy when wet; gd touring base; mkt Wed & Sat; easy walk to attractive Roman town; huge open site, efficent recep" ♦ 20 Apr-15 Oct. € 22.65   2013*

ST ETIENNE DE BAIGORRY *8F1* (500m N Rural) *43.18370, -1.33569* **Camp Municipal L'Irouleguy, Borciriette, 64430 St Etienne-de-Baïgorry [05 59 37 43 96 or 05 59 37 40 80 (Mairie); fax 05 59 37 48 20; comstetiennebaigorry@wanadoo.fr]** W on D15 fr St Jean-Pied-de-Port to St Etienne-de-Baigorry; site on R 300m bef junc with D948; ent next to wine co-operative. Fr N on D948, on ent St Etienne-de-Baïgorry turn L onto D15; site in 300m on L. NB Don't be put off by entry down track L of winery - can't see site fr rd. Med, shd; wc; chem disp; shwrs inc; el pnts (6A) €2.70; lndtte; gas, shop 100m; htd pool adj; tennis adj; troutfishing; birdwatching; poss cr; adv bkg; quiet. "Scenic site by rv; lge pitches; plenty hot water; gd hill walking cent; out of ssn call at Mairie to open site for NH; Gd modern san facs" ◆ 1 May-30 Nov. € 9.23   2013*

ST ETIENNE DE FONTBELLON see Aubenas *9D2*

⊞ **ST ETIENNE DE MONTLUC** *2G4* (200m N Rural) *47.28002, -1.77967* **Camp Municipal de la Coletterie, Rue de Tivoli, 44360 St Etienne-de-Montluc [02 40 86 97 44 or 02 40 86 80 26 (Mairie); campinglacoletterie@st-etienne-montluc.net; www.st-etienne-montluc.net]** Well sp fr N165 (E60) in both dirs. Sm, hdg/mkd pitch, pt sl, pt shd; htd wc; chem disp; shwrs inc; baby facs; el pnts (15A) €3.80; lndtte (inc dryer); shop, rest, bar 500m; playgrnd; fishing; games area; dogs €1.20; phone; adv bkg; quiet; CKE/CCI. "vg; check open before travelling" ◆ € 10.30   2013*

ST ETIENNE DE VILLEREAL see Villeréal *7D3*

ST ETIENNE DU BOIS (VENDEE) see Legé *2H4*

STE EULALIE EN BORN *7D1* (W Rural) *44.30607, -1.17867* **Camp Municipal du Lac, 1590 Route du Lac, 40200 Ste Eulalie-en-Born [05 58 09 70 10 or 05 58 09 73 48 (Mairie); fax 05 58 09 76 89; contact@lecampingdulac.com; www.lecampingdulac.com]** N fr Mimizan on D87/D652. Pass Ste Eulalie & turn W at water tower, site sp. Med, mkd pitch, pt shd; wc; chem disp; mv service pnt; baby facs; shwrs inc; el pnts (10A) €3.90; gas; lndtte; snacks; bar; pool; lake sw & beach adj; boat hire; games area; some statics; dogs €2.10; phone; poss cr; Eng spkn; adv bkg; quiet; ccard acc; CKE/CCI. "On Lake Biscarrosse; vg for familes; do not confuse with site of similar name on Lac Aureilhan, 2km N of Mimizan." 1 Apr-30 Oct. € 17.50   2009*

ST EUSTACHE see Annecy *9B3*

ST EVARZEC see Quimper *2F2*

ST EVROULT NOTRE DAME DU BOIS see Aigle, L' *4E2*

ST FELIX DE REILLAC see Douze, La *7C3*

ST FERREOL TRENTE PAS see Nyons *9D2*

ST FLORENT SUR CHER *4H3* (7km SE Rural) *46.93663, 2.27071* **Camp Intercommunal, 6 Rue de l'Abreuvoir, 18400 Lunery [02 48 68 07 38 or 02 48 23 22 08; fax 02 48 55 26 78; fercher@fr-oleane.com]** Fr N151 turn S onto D27 at St Florent-sur-Cher, cont for 7km, site in vill cent of Lunery. Sm, hdg/mkd pitch, pt shd; wc; chem disp; mv service pnt; shwrs inc; el pnts (6A) €3.50 (poss rev pol); shop, rest in vill; playgrnd; fishing; tennis nr; no statics; bus 200m, train in vill; phone 100m; Eng spkn; red long stay; CKE/CCI. "Charming, peaceful, rvside site; quiet even high ssn; gd clean san facs; liable to flood low ssn - phone ahead to check open; gd." ◆ 15 Apr-15 Sep. € 15.00   2009*

ST FLORENTIN *4F4* (1km S Rural) *47.99252, 3.73450* **Camping L'Armançon, 89600 St Florentin [tel/fax 03 86 35 08 03 13 or 03 86 35 11 86 (mob); ot.saint-florentin@wanadoo.fr]** N fr Auxerre on N77 site on R app rv bdge S of town. Fr N pass traff islands, exit town up slope, x-ing canal & rv. Site immed on S side of rv bdge - turn R immed at end of bdg then under bdg to site. Site well sp fr all dirs. Med, hdg pitch, pt sl, pt shd; wc (cont); chem disp; shwrs inc; el pnts (10A) inc (poss long lead req); gas; lndtte; shop; café/bar; snacks; playgrnd; fishing; dogs €0.20; poss cr; some rd noise at night. "Well-kept site; excel, lge pitches; friendly manager; dated but clean san facs; diff, steep exit to main rd; gd nh" ◆ltd 2 Apr-11 Oct. € 12.60   2013*

ST FLOUR *9C1* (2km N Rural) *45.05120, 3.10778* **Camping International La Roche Murat, N9 15100 St Flour [04 71 60 43 63; fax 04 71 60 02 10; courrier@camping-saint-flour.com; www.camping-saint-flour.com]** Fr N or S on A75 exit junc 28; sp off rndabt on St Flour side of m'way. Site ent visible 150m fr rndabt. Med, hdg/mkd pitch, terr, pt shd; htd wc; chem disp; mv service pnt; shwrs inc; el pnts (10A) inc; gas; lndry rm; shops 4km; tradsmn; playgrnd; pool 2km; dogs; Eng spkn; adv bkg; quiet, v little rd noise; ccard not acc; CKE/CCI. "Busy site with gd views; sunny & secluded pitches; helpful warden; gd, clean facs; some pitches sm; when pitches waterlogged use site rds; old town high on hill worth visit; excel touring cent & conv NH fr A75; vg; v clean facs" ◆ 1 Apr-1 Nov. € 18.60   2013*

ST FLOUR *9C1* (SW Urban) *45.03313, 3.08306* **Camp Municipal Les Orgues, 19 Ave Dr Maillet, 15100 St Flour [04 71 60 44 01]** On A75 to St Flour, foll sps for 'ville haute'; at x-rds in town cent turn L (dir Aurillac). Ent in 250m, narr & steep on L bet houses, site sp opp poss obscured by parked cars. NB Site ent is on busy main rd & has 2m high barrier. If c'van over 2m, stop at barrier (c'van sticking out into rd), walk down to office & ask warden to unlock barrier - poss v dangerous. Med, mkd pitch, pt sl, pt shd; wc; shwrs inc; el pnts (6A) inc; shops, rest; bar 1km; playgrnd; covrd pool 1km; tennis; quiet; poss cr; CKE/CCI. "Friendly recep; gd pitches; gd NH." ◆ 1 Jun-1 Sep. € 11.85   2008*

ST FORT SUR GIRONDE *7B2* (4km SW Rural) *45.43278, -0.75185* **Camping Port Maubert, 8 Rue de Chassillac, 17240 St Fort-sur-Gironde [05 46 04 78 86; fax 05 46 04 16 79; bourdieu.jean-luc@wanadoo.fr; www. campingportmaubert.com]** Exit A10 junc 37 onto D730 dir Royan. Foll sp Port Maubert & site. Sm, hdg/mkd pitch, shd; wc (some cont); chem disp; mv service pnt; shwrs inc; el pnts (10A) €3.50; gas; lndtte; shop 4km; tradsmn; bar; BBQ; playgrnd; pool; sand beach 25km; cycle hire; games rm; TV; some statics; dogs €2; Eng spkn; adv bkg; quiet; ccard acc; red long stay/ CKE/CCI. "Pleasant, well-run site; low ssn ltd facs, OK NH." 6 Mar-31Dec. € 12.40   2010*

STE FOY LA GRANDE *7C2* (1.5km NE Rural) *44.84426, 0.22468* **Camping de la Bastide, Allée du Camping, 2 Les Tuileries, Pineuilh, 33220 Ste Foy-la-Grande [tel/fax 05 57 46 13 84; contact@camping-bastide.com; www. camping-bastide.com]** Fr W go thro town & turn off at D130 to site, well sp on Rv Dordogne. Med, mkd pitch, pt shd; wc; chem disp; mv service pnt; baby facs; shwrs inc; el pnts (10A) €3 (poss rev pol); lndtte; shops, snacks & bar 500m, playgrnd; pool; jacuzzi; fishing, canoeing; games rm; wifi; 10% statics; dogs €2; phone; poss cr; Eng spkn; adv bkg; v quiet; ccard acc; red low ssn; CKE/CCI. "Pretty, well-cared for site; sm pitches; helpful British owners; immac, modern san facs; high kerb stones onto pitches - poss diff lge o'fits; no twin-axles; mkt Sat; excel." ♦ 1 Apr-30 Oct. € 23.00   2013*

STE FOY LA GRANDE *7C2* (6km W Rural) *44.82954, 0.12290* **FLOWER Camping La Rivière Fleurie, 180 Rue Théophile, 24230 St Antoine-de-Breuilh [tel/fax 05 53 24 82 80; info@ la-riviere-fleurie.com; www.la-riviere-fleurie.com or www.flowercampings.com]** Turn S off D936 at W end of St Antoine-de-Breuilh; site 2.7km fr main rd in vill of St Aulaye adj Rv Dordogne. Well sp. Med, mkd pitch, pt shd; wc; chem disp; baby facs; shwrs inc; el pnts (10A) inc; gas; lndtte (inc dryer); shops 4km; hypmkt 5km; tradsmn; rest; bar; BBQ; playgrnd; htd pool; paddling pool; games rm; rv sw adj; tennis; horseriding; golf; canoeing & fishing nrby; wifi; entmnt; TV rm; 10% statics; dogs €2; phone; Eng spkn; adv bkg; quiet; red low ssn/long stay; CKE/CCI. "Peaceful, well-maintained site; spacious pitches; welcoming, helpful owners; excel san facs; church bells during day; vg cycling; mkt Sat in Ste Foy; highly rec." ♦ 10 Apr-16 Sep. € 26.90 (CChq acc)   2013*

STE FOY L'ARGENTIERE *9B2* (7km SE Rural) *45.65185, 4.56315* **Camp Municipal Les Verpillières, Les Plaines, 69850 St Martin-en-Haut [04 78 48 62 16; saintmartinenhaut@9business.fr; http://saintmartin. decideur.net]** Fr Craponne on W o'skts of Lyon SW on D311 to cent of St Martin-en-Haut; then take D122 S; site on L approx 200m fr x-rds. Site sp. Fr St Foy take D489 SE to Duerne, D34 to St Martin-en-Haut, then as above. This app not for lge o'fits, two 7-12% climbs out of St Foy & hairpins after Duerne. Med, mkd pitch, pt sl, shd; htd wc; shwrs; el pnts (10A) inc; lndtte; shops 500m; snacks; bar; playgrnd; tennis 300m; entmnt; 75% statics; poss cr; adv bkg; quiet. "Lovely wooded site with red squirrels; busy at w/end." 1 Apr-31 Oct. € 11.60   2011*

ST FRAIMBAULT see Domfront *4E1*

ST GALMIER *9B2* (2km E Rural) *45.59266, 4.33528* **Campéole Camping Val de Coise, Route de la Thiéry, 42330 St Galmier [04 77 54 14 82; fax 04 77 54 02 45; val-de-coise@campeole.com; www.camping-valdecoise.com or www.campeole.com]** Fr St Etienne take D1082 N. In 7km turn R onto D12 sp St Galmier; after x-ing rv bdge on outskirts of vill turn R & foll Camping sp for 2km. Or fr N on D1082 look for sp to St Galmier about 1.5km S of Montrond-les-Bains & turn L onto D6 to St Galmier. On D12 in St Galmier at floral rndabt with fountain if app fr N go L & fr S go R, uphill & foll site sp. Site approx 1.5km fr rndabt. Med, mkd pitch, hdstg, pt sl, pt shd; wc; chem disp; baby facs; shwrs inc; el pnts (16A) €4.10; gas; lndtte; sm shop & 2km; tradsmn; rest & snacks 2km; BBQ; playgrnd; htd pool; paddling pool; fishing; tennis 2km; cycle hire; games area; games rm; wifi; entmnt; TV rm; 20% statics; dogs €2.60; phone; Eng spkn; adv bkg; v quiet; ccard acc; red low ssn; CKE/CCI. "Pleasant rvside site; helpful staff; facs poss stretched high ssn; highly rec." ♦ 15 Apr-16 Oct. € 15.00   2011*

See advertisement on pages 14 & 15

ST GAUDENS *8F3* (1km W Rural) *43.11000, 0.70839* **Camp Municipal Belvédère des Pyrénées, Rue des Chanteurs du Comminges, 31800 St Gaudens [05 62 00 16 03; www. st-gaudens.com]** Foll camping sp fr St Gaudens town cent on D817 dir Tarbes. Site ent at top of hill on N side. Last rd sp is 'Belvédère'. Med, pt shd; htd wc; mv service pnt; shwrs inc; el pnts (4-13A) €3.50-6.00; gas; rest nrby; playgrnd; dogs €1.50; no adv bkg; some rd noise; ccard not acc. "Pleasant site; facs clean; gates clsd 1200-1500 & 2300-0700." 1 Jun-30 Sep. € 15.00   2013*

ST GAULTIER *4H2* (S Rural) *46.63235, 1.42145* **Camp Municipal L'Illon, Rue de Limage, 36800 St Gaultier [02 54 47 11 22 or 02 54 01 66 00 (Mairie); fax 02 54 01 66 09; st-gaultier.mairie@wanadoo.fr; www. mairie-saintgaultier.fr]** Site well sp in town. V narr thro town - best app fr W. NB App down short, steep hill with sharp R turn into site ent. Med, mkd pitch, pt sl, pt shd; wc (some cont); shwrs inc; el pnts inc; gas; shops 500m; playgrnd; rv & fishing 50m; quiet. "Lovely, peaceful setting nr rv; pitch yourself, warden calls; site ent poss too narr for twin-axles/ lge o'fits; gd cycle path on old rlwy track nrby." Easter-30 Sep. € 8.50   2010*

ST GAULTIER *4H2* (1km W Rural) *46.63406, 1.40863* **Camping L'Oasis du Berry, Rue de la Pierre Plate, 36800 St Gaultier [02 54 47 17 04; www.campoasisduberry.com]** Appr fr W (fr Le Blanc) on D951; turn R at sp St Gaultier, then foll sp L'Oasis du Berry. Well sp in vill. Med, hdg/mkd pitch, terr, pt shd; wc; chem disp; shwrs inc; el pnts (4-10A) €2.50-3.50; lndtte (inc dryer); shop; tradsmn; rest, snacks; takeaway; bar; BBQ; playgrnd; htd pool; games area; wifi; 30% statics; dogs €1.40; Eng spkn; adv bkg; quiet; CKE/CCI. "Pleasant site in wooded surroundings; nice clean san facs; gd pool; gd walks nrby; nr Voie Verte track; nr Brenne Regional Park; excel." 1 Apr-6 Nov. € 19.00   2011*

FRANCE

ST GENIEZ D'OLT 9D1 (750m NE Rural) 44.46861, 2.98166 **Campéole Camping La Boissière, Route de la Cascade, 12130 St Geniez-d'Olt [05 65 70 40 43; fax 05 65 47 56 39; boissiere@campeole.com; www. camping-aveyron.info or www.campeole.com]** Exit A75 junc 40 onto D998 dir St Laurent-d'Olt. Then foll sp St Geniez-d'Olt via D988/D45/D202/D45 to St Martin-de-Lenne. At T-junc turn R & foll site sp. Lge, hdg/mkd pitch, hdstg, pt sl, pt shd; htd wc; chem disp; baby facs; shwrs inc; el pnts (6A) €4.10; lndtte (inc dryer); shop; supmkt nr; tradsmn; rest; snacks; bar; BBQ; playgrnd; htd pool; paddling pool; tennis adj; fishing & canoeing nrby; games area; games rm; wifi; entmnt; 40% statics; dogs €2.80; phone; Eng spkn; adv bkg; quiet; ccard acc; red low ssn/CKE/CCI. "Lovely, tranquil site in Lot Valley; gd pool; sh walk into lovely town; gd cycling." ♦ 17 Apr-19 Sep. € 17.90   2010*

See advertisement on pages 14 & 15

ST GENIEZ D'OLT 9D1 (500m W Rural) 44.46210, 2.96240 **Kawan Village Marmotel, La Salle, 12130 St Geniez-d'Olt [05 65 70 46 51; info@marmotel.com; www.marmotel.com]** Exit A75 at junc 41 onto D37 dir Campagnac. Then onto D202, D45 & D988. Site situated on W of vill by Rv Lot on D19. Lge, hdg pitch, pt shd; wc; chem disp; mv service pnt; some pitches with individual san facs; baby facs; sauna; shwrs inc; el pnts (10A) inc; gas; lndtte (inc dryer); shop 500m; tradsmn; rest; snacks; bar; BBQ; playgrnd; htd pool; paddling pool; waterslide; lake fishing; tennis; games area; cycle hire; wifi; entmnt; TV rm; some statics; dogs €2; Eng spkn; adv bkg; quiet; red low ssn; ccard acc; CKE/CCI. "Highly rec; some pitches poss tight lge o'fits; poss muddy when wet; gd pool & rest." ♦ 1 May-24 Sep. € 31.00   2011*

ST GENIS LAVAL see Lyon 9B2

ST GENIX SUR GUIERS 9B3 (300 mtrs SE) 45.58878, 5.64252 **Les Bords du Guiers, Route de Pont Beauvoisin, 73240 Saint Genix sur Guiers [04 76 31 71 40; info@ lesbordsduguiers.com; www.lesbordsduguiers.com/]** On reaching vill on D1516 foll sp Le-Pont-de-Beauvoisin, site 300 mtrs on R. Med, hdg, mkd, pt shd pitch; WC; chem disp; mv service pnt; shwrs; el pnts (8-10A); trdsmn; BBQ; pool; games area; games rm; wifi; dogs; twin axle acc; quiet; Eng spkn; red low ssn; supmkt 6km; "Excel, quiet site; cycle hire; v helpful owners; gd base for site seeing or star watching." 30 Apr-25 Sept. € 21.00   2012*

ST GEORGES DE DIDONNE see Royan 7B1

ST GEORGES DE LEVEJAC see Vignes, Les 9D1

ST GEORGES DU VIEVRE 3D2 (2km E Rural) **Camping à la Ferme La Brettonnière (Séjourne), 27450 St Grégoire-du-Vièvre [02 32 42 82 67]** At traff lts on D130 in Pont Authou turn W onto D137 twd St Georges-du-Vièvre; after 7km turn L, sp Camping Rural; site in 1km. NB Steep rdway down & narr terrs poss unsuitable for c'vans. Sm, mkd pitch, terr, shd; wc; chem disp; shwrs inc; el pnts €4.20; shop 1km; playgrnd; pool 4km; adv bkg; quiet; CKE/CCI. "CL-type farm site; vg." Mar-Oct. € 15.30   2010*

ST GEORGES DU VIEVRE 3D2 (200m W Rural) 49.24248, 0.58040 **Camp Municipal du Vièvre, Route de Noards, 27450 St Georges-du-Vièvre [02 32 42 76 79 or 02 32 56 34 29 (LS); fax 02 32 57 52 90; camping.stgeorgesduvievre@wanadoo.fr; www. saintgeorgesduvievre.org]** Fr traff lts on D130 in Pont Authou turn W onto D137 to St Georges-du-Vièvre; in town sq at tourist info turn L uphill sp camping; site 200m on L. If app fr S on N138 at Bernay take D834 sp Le Havre to Lieurey. Turn R onto D137 to St Georges, then turn R at camping sp by sw pool. Sm, hdg pitch, pt shd; htd wc; chem disp; serviced pitches; shwrs inc; el pnts (5A) inc; gas 200m; lndtte; shops 200m; BBQ; playgrnd; pool (high ssn); tennis 50m; cycle hire; wifi at TO; dogs; Eng spkn; adv bkg (rec high ssn); quiet; CKE/CCI. "Peaceful; gd facs & pitches; well-run site; interesting area; gd cycling; vg." ♦ 1 Apr-30 Sep. € 13.30   2010*

ST GEORGES SUR LAYON see Doué la Fontaine 4G1

"I need an on-site restaurant"

We do our best to make sure site information is correct, but it is always best to check any must-have facilities are still available or will be open during your visit.

ST GEOURS DE MAREMNE 8E1 (500m W Rural) 43.68981, -1.23376 **Camping Les Platanes, 3 Route de Lecoume, 40230 St Geours-de-Maremne [05 58 57 45 35; fax 05 58 57 37 85; info@platanes.com; www.platanes.com]** Fr N10 take junc sp St Geours-de-Maremne. Site sp fr town cent. Med, pt sl, pt shd; htd wc; chem disp; shwrs inc; el pnts (6A) €4.70; gas; lndtte; shop nr; tradsmn; rest, snacks; bar; BBQ; playgrnd; pool (high ssn); sand beach 8km; tennis; games area; games rm; wifi; TV; 50% statics; dogs €1.50; phone; poss cr; adv bkg; quiet; ccard acc; red low ssn/long stay; CKE/CCI. "Friendly British owners; useful NH on N10." 1 Mar-15 Nov. € 27.50   2012*

ST GERAUD DE CORPS see Montpon Ménestérol 7C2

ST GERMAIN see Aubenas 9D2

ST GERMAIN DU BEL AIR see Gourdon 7D3

ST GERMAIN DU BOIS 6H1 (500m S Rural) 46.74661, 5.24613 **Camp Municipal de l'Etang Titard, Route de Louhans, 71330 St Germain-du-Bois [03 85 72 06 15 or 03 85 72 01 47; fax 03 85 72 03 38; mairie-71330-saint-germain-du-bois@wanadoo.fr]** Fr Chalon-sur Saône E on N78, exit at Thurey onto D24 to St Germain. Site sp on D13 adj lake. Sm, mkd pitch, terr, pt shd; wc; chem disp; mv service pnt; shwrs inc; el pnts (6A); lndtte; dogs; rest 300m; BBQ; playgrnd; htd, covrd pool in sports grnd adj; fishing; dogs; adv bkg; quiet; CKE/CCI. "Lge pitches; friendly warden; no sw in lake; pleasant town; gd cycling area." ♦ 1 May-15 Sep. € 7.60   2009*

ST GERMAIN LES BELLES

ST GERMAIN LES BELLES see Masseret 7B3

ST GERMAIN L'HERM 9B1 (500m W Rural) 45.45663,
3.54823 **Camping St Eloy, Route de la Chaise-Dieu, 63630
St Germain-l'Herm [04 73 72 05 13 or 04 73 34 75 53 (LS));
fax 04 73 34 70 94; sogeval@wanadoo.fr]** Take D906 S
fr Ambert to Arlanc, turn R onto D300 (D999A) to St Germain,
site sp on app to vill. Med, mkd pitch, pt sl, terr, pt shd; wc
(some cont); chem disp; mv service pnt; el pnts (8A) €3; lndry
rm; shop 500m; tradsmn; rest 500m; BBQ; playgrnd; pool;
10% statics; dogs €1.50; phone; adv bkg; quiet. "Pleasant
views; cycle & walking tracks fr vill; vg." ♦ ltd 15 Jun-30 Sep.
€ 12.00   2008*

ST GERVAIS D'AUVERGNE 7A4 (500m N Rural)
46.03706, 2.81733 **Camp Municipal L'Etang Philippe,
63390 St Gervais-d'Auvergne [tel/fax 04 73 85 74 84;
campingstgervais@wanadoo.fr; www.camping-loisir.com]**
Fr N144 3km S of St Eloy-les-Mines, take D987 S to St Gervais.
Site on R just bef town. Lge, hdg pitch, pt shd; wc; chem disp;
mv service pnt; shwrs inc; el pnts (10A) inc; lndtte; shop 500m;
tradsmn (Jul/Aug); playgrnd; lake sw & beach adj; cycle hire;
tennis; archery; entmnt; some statics; dogs €0.50; Eng spkn;
adv bkg; quiet; CKE/CCI. "Popular, well-maintained site; clean
facs; poss untidy low ssn & ltd facs; vg." ♦ Easter-30 Sep.
€ 10.00   2010*

ST GERVAIS D'AUVERGNE 7A4 (8km E Rural) 46.02741,
2.89894 **Camp Municipal Les Prés Dimanches,
63390 Châteauneuf-les-Bains [04 73 86 41 50 or
04 73 86 67 65 (LS); fax 04 73 86 41 71; mairie-chat-les-
bains@wanadoo.fr]** Fr Montaigut take N144 S twd Riom
& Clermont-Ferrand. In 9km at La Boule S onto D987 to
St Gervais. Take D227 E to Chateauneuf-les-Bains. In 7km L
onto D109. Site thro vill on R. Sm, hdg/mkd pitch; htd
wc; shwrs inc; el pnts (6A) inc; lndtte; shop 250m; rest adj;
playgrnd; fishing, tennis, canoeing nrby; spa baths 500m;
quiet; adv bkg; excel; CKE/CCI. "Lovely, well-kept site; helpful
warden. gd walks" ♦ ltd 30 Apr-15 Oct. € 13.00   2012*

ST GERVAIS LES BAINS 9B4 (10km SE Rural) 45.80275,
6.72207 **Camping Le Pontet, 2485 Route de Notre-
Dame-de-la-Gorge, 74170 Les Contamines-Montjoie
[04 50 47 04 04; fax 04 50 47 18 10; welcome@
campinglepontet.fr; www.campinglepontet.fr]**
Fr St Gervais take D902 to Les Contamines-Montjoie (sp);
go thro vill & foll sp to Notre Dame-de-la-Gorge; site in 2km
on L, clearly sp. Lge, mkd pitch, hdstg, pt shd; htd wc; chem
disp; baby facs; shwrs inc; el pnts (2-10A) €3-9.90; lndtte;
shops 2km; tradsmn; rest, snacks; playgrnd; fishing; lake adj;
leisure/sports park adj; tennis; horseriding; skilift 200m; dogs
free; phone; Eng spkn; adv bkg; quiet; ccard acc. "Mkd alpine
walks." ♦ 1 May-26 Sep & 1 Dec-30 Apr. € 15.00   2009*

ST GERVAIS LES BAINS 9B4 (2km S Rural) 45.87333,
6.72000 **Camping Les Dômes de Miage, 197 Route des
Contamines, 74170 St Gervais-les-Bains [04 50 93 45 96;
info@camping-mont-blanc.com; www.camping-mont-
blanc.com]** Exit A40 junc 21; fr N thro St Gervais, at sm
rndabt in cent foll sp Les Contamines onto D902, site 2km on
L. Med, mkd pitch, pt shd; htd wc (some cont); chem disp; mv
service pnt; baby facs; shwrs inc; el pnts (6A) €3.50 (poss rev
pol); gas; lndtte (inc dryer); shop; tradsmn; supmkt 7km; rest,
bar adj; snacks; BBQ; playgrnd; htd pool, tennis 800m; fishing
1km; cycle hire 800m; games area; wifi; TV rm; lux chalet to
rent; dogs €2 (free low ssn); bus adj; train 5.5km; Eng spkn;
adv bkg (bkg fee); quiet; ccard acc; red low ssn; CKE/CCI;
"Superb, well-kept, family-owned site in beautiful location;
welcoming, helpful & friendly; immac san facs; conv Tramway
du Mont Blanc excursions; mkt Thurs; excel" ♦ 1 May-9 Sep.
€ 24.80   2013*

See advertisement

ST GERY see St Cirq Lapopie 7D3

ST GILDAS DE RHUYS see Sarzeau 2G3

ST GILLES *10E2* (300m SW Urban) *43.67569, 4.42946*
**Camping de la Chicanette, Rue de la Chicanette, 30800
St Gilles [04 66 87 28 32; fax 04 66 87 49 85; camping.
la.chicanette@libertysurf.fr; www.campinglachicanette.fr]**
Site on D6572 W fr Arles, sp in cent of town, behind Auberge
de la Chicanette. Narr app rd, tight turn to ent. Med, hdg
pitch, pt shd; wc; chem disp; shwrs inc; el pnts (6A) €3 (rev
pol); lndtte; shop adj; snacks; bar; playgrnd; pool; entmnt;
20% statics; dogs €2; poss cr; quiet; red low ssn; CKE/CCI.
"Useful site; sm pitches; facs poss stretched high ssn; site poss
unkempt low ssn; interesting old town; bus to Nîmes; mkt
Sun." 1 Apr-30 Oct. € 20.00   2011*

ST GILLES CROIX DE VIE *2H3* (3km NE Rural) *46.71217,
-1.90613* **Camping Aire Naturelle Le Petit Beauregard, Rue
du Petit Beauregard, 85800 Le Fenouiller [02 51 55 07 98]**
N fr Les Sables d'Olonne take D38 twd St Gilles Croix-de-Vie.
Turn R onto D754 sp Le Fenouiller for 3km. Turn R; site well
sp in 500m. Sm, mkd pitch, pt shd; wc; chem disp; shwrs
inc; el pnts (6A) €3; lndtte; shop 1km; tradsmn; rest nr; BBQ;
playgrnd; pool; sand beach 3km; few statics; dogs; quiet; Eng
spkn; adv bkg; CKE/CCI. "Friendly, helpful owner; excel, clean
san facs; gd beaches nrby; St Gilles busy & cr." ♦
1 Apr-30 Sep. € 13.50   2009*

ST GILLES CROIX DE VIE *2H3* (3km NE Rural) *46.71201,
-1.91457* **Camping Le Chatelier, Chemin des Etrivières,
Route de Nantes, 85800 Le Fenouiller [tel/fax
02 28 10 50 75; www.domainelechatelier.fr]** Fr St Gilles-
Croix-de-Vie D754 NE, sp to Le Fenouiller, site on L. Med, mkd
pitch, pt shd; wc; chem disp; shwrs inc; baby facs; el pnts (6A)
(rec long lead); gas; lndtte (inc dryer); tradsmn; shops 2km;
snacks; bar; BBQ; playgrnd; htd pool high ssn; sand beach 3km;
games area; wifi; entmnt adj; TV rm; 50% statics; dogs; quiet.
"Friendly owners." ♦ Easter-15 Oct.   2010*

ST GILLES CROIX DE VIE *2H3* (5km E Rural) *46.69480,
-1.85310* **Camping Europa, Le Bois Givrand, 85800 Givrand
[02 51 55 32 68; contact@europacamp.com; www.
europacamp.com]** App site fr 'Leclerc' rndabt at St Gilles-
Croix-de-Vie, take D6 exit dir Coëx & Aizenay; at 1st & 2nd
rndabts go straight on; at 3rd rndabt take 1st exit; site on right
in 150m, opp boat builders. Lge, mkd pitch, pt shd; wc (mainly
cont); chem disp; serviced pitches; baby facs; shwrs inc; el pnts
(10A) inc; gas; lndtte; shop 3km; rest, snacks & bar high ssn;
BBQ; playgrnd; pool complex; waterslide; whirlpool; covrd
pool; paddling pool; sand beach 5km; rv fishing, boat hire
adj; fishing, watersports, cycle hire & horseriding 5km; golf nr;
tennis; wifi; entmnt; games/TV rm; 60% statics; dogs €2.70;
no c'vans/m'vans over 10m; adv bkg; ccard acc; red low ssn.
"Pleasant site; busy high ssn, quiet low ssn; facs poss stretched
high ssn; vg." ♦ ltd 1 Apr-31 Oct. € 30.60   2011*

ST GILLES CROIX DE VIE *2H3* (8km E Rural) *46.69665,
-1.83395* **Camping Le Pont Rouge, Ave Georges
Clémenceau, 85220 St Révérend [tel/fax 02 51 54 68 50;
camping.pontrouge@wanadoo.fr; www.camping-
lepontrouge.com]** W fr Aizenay on D6 rd for St Gilles-Croix-
de-Vie, turn R just past water tower into St Révérend. Foll sp
to site. Med, hdg pitch, pt sl, pt shd; htd wc; chem disp; mv
service pnt; baby facs; shwrs inc; el pnts (6A) €4 (poss long lead
req); lndtte; shop 1km; tradsmn; rest 3km; snacks; playgrnd;
htd pool; sand beach 8km; golf course with rest 3km; games
area; entmnt; TV; 50% statics; dogs €3; poss cr; Eng spkn; adv
bkg; quiet; red low ssn; CKE/CCI. "Attractive, secluded site; run
by enthusiastic young couple; clean modern san facs; plenty
hot water; working windmill (with tours) 1km; vg." ♦
1 Apr-30 Sep. € 19.00   2011*

ST GILLES CROIX DE VIE *2H3* (3km SE Coastal) *46.66748,
-1.90213* **Camping du Jaunay, 102 Route des Sables,
85800 Givrand [02 51 55 14 77; buro@campingduejaunay.
com; www.campingduejaunay.com]** S fr St Gilles-Croix-
de-Vie on D38 or B38b; site on R 200m after 2nd rndabt (1st
rndabt joins D38 with D38b, 2nd rndabt 400m further on).
Sm, mkd pitch, pt shd; htd wc; chem disp; shwrs inc; el pnts
(6A) €3; lndtte; shop or 3km; tradsmn; rest, snacks; bar; BBQ;
playgrnd; htd pool; canoe hire; fishing; sand beach 1.2km; TV;
30% statics; dogs €1.60; phone; adv bkg; red low ssn; CKE/
CCI. "Vg site; lge pitches; friendly, helpful owner; vg cycle
paths adj." Apr-Sep. € 14.00   2009*

ST GILLES CROIX DE VIE *2H3* (4km SE Rural) **Camping à la
Ferme Petit Bois, 85800 Givrand [06 21 55 26 89 (mob)]**
W fr Aizenay on D6 for 20km; turn L at rndabt sp Givrand;
site on L in 1km. Sm, hdg/mkd pitch, shd; htd wc; chem disp;
shwrs inc; el pnts (6A) €3; lndtte; shop 2km; BBQ; sand beach
4km; dogs free; poss cr; Eng spkn; quiet; CKE/CCI. "Well-kept
site; lge pitches; friendly owner; site yourself, owners calls eves;
many cycle tracks; gd access to coast; excel."
1 May-30 Sep. € 15.00 (3 persons)   2009*

ST GILLES CROIX DE VIE *2H3* (4km SE Coastal) *46.67095,
-1.90874* **Camping Les Cyprès, 41 Rue du Pont du
Jaunay, 85800 St Gilles-Croix-de-Vie [02 51 55 38 98; fax
02 51 54 98 94; contact@campinglescypres.com; www.
campinglescypres.com]** Site on S end of St Gilles-Croix-
de-Vie off D38, after rndabt sp Le Jaunay turn sharp L - hard
to spot. Lge, hdg pitch, shd; wc; chem disp, mv service pnt;
shwrs inc; el pnts (10A) €3; gas; lndtte; shop, tradsmn; rest,
snacks; bar; playgrnd; htd, covrd pool & jacuzzi; sand beach
600m; 12% statics; dogs €3.30; rv 100m; Eng spkn; adv
bkg €7.62 fee; quiet; ccard acc; red long stay/low ssn; CKE/
CCI. "Excel for family hols; family-run site; red facs low ssn;
footpath along rv to town cent." ♦ 9 Apr-17 Sep.
€ 23.00   2011*

See advertisement on next page

ST GILLES CROIX DE VIE *2H3* (4km SE Urban/Coastal) *46.67113, -1.90356* **Chadotel Le Domaine de Beaulieu, Rue du Parc, Route des Sables-d'Olonne, 85800 Givrand [02 51 55 59 46 or 02 51 33 05 05 (LS); chadotel@ wanadoo.fr; www.chadotel.com]** S on D38 fr St Gilles Croix-de-Vie, site sp on L. Lge, hdg/mkd pitch, pt shd; wc; serviced pitches; baby facs; shwrs inc; el pnts (6A) inc (poss long lead req); gas; lndtte; shop; snacks; bar; BBQ (gas); playgrnd; 2 pools; waterslide; sand beach 1km; tennis; golf 5km; entmnt; wifi; TV; dogs €3.20; adv bkg; quiet; red long stay/low ssn; ccard acc; CKE/CCI. "Gd site for families; red facs low ssn; low trees poss diff; gd." ♦ 7 Apr-22 Sep. € 30.00   2011*

ST GILLES CROIX DE VIE *2H3* (2km S Coastal) *46.67819, -1.91561* **Chadotel Camping Le Bahamas Beach, 168 Route des Sables, 85800 St Gilles-Croix-de-Vie [02 51 54 69 16 or 02 51 33 05 05 (LS); fax 02 51 33 94 04; chadotel@ wanadoo.fr; www.chadotel.com]** S fr St Gilles-Croix-de-Vie on Rte des Sables (D38), sp. Lge, hdg/mkd pitch, unshd; wc; chem disp (wc); shwrs inc; el pnts (6A) €4.70; gas; lndtte; sm shop (high ssn) & 3km; tradsmn; rest, snacks & bar (high ssn); BBQ (gas); playgrnd; htd covrd pool; waterslide; sand beach 800m; watersports; excursions; cycle hire; games area; games rm; entmnt; wifi; TV rm; many statics; dogs €3; phone; poss cr; Eng spkn; adv bkg; quiet; red long stay/low ssn; ccard acc; CKE/CCI. "Gd for children; superb pool; san facs ltd low ssn; facs far fr some pitches; excel cycle rtes along coast." ♦ ltd 7 Apr-2 Sep. € 31.00   2011*

ST GIRONS *8G3* (3km N Rural) *43.00731, 1.18409* **Camping Audinac Les Bains, 09200 Montjoie-en-Couserans [tel/ fax 05 61 66 44 50; accueil@audinac.com; www.audinac. com]** E fr St Girons take D117 twd Foix; after 2km uphill turn L onto D627; foll sp. Med, terr, pt shd; htd wc; chem disp (wc); mv service pnt; shwrs inc; el pnts (10A) €3.50; gas; lndtte (inc dryer); shops 5km; tradsmn; rest in ssn; playgrnd; pool high ssn; statics; dogs €1; no twin-axle; Eng spkn; adv bkg ess; quiet; ccard acc; red low ssn; CKE/CCI. "Spacious, attractive, well-kept site; facs ltd low ssn." ♦ 1 May-30 Sep. € 16.00   2010*

⊞ **ST GIRONS** *8G3* (2km SE Rural) *42.97400, 1.16582* **FFCC Camping Parc de Palétès, Route de Lacourt, 09200 St Girons [05 61 66 06 79 or 06 07 02 40 24 (mob); fax 05 61 66 76 86; contacts@parcdepaletes.com; www. parcdepaletes.com]** Fr S loop of D117 in St Girons at rndabt take D3 dir Lacourt (D3 runs parallel to D618 on E of rv & starts as Ave des Evadés de France); site sp on L in 1.5km. Note: D618 runs on W side of rv - cannot cross it bef Lacourt. Sm, pt sl, pt shd; wc; chem disp; mv service pnt; shwrs inc; el pnts (10A) €4; gas; lndry rm; shop; tradsmn; rest, snacks; bar; BBQ; playgrnd; pool; wifi; dogs €1.50; bus; phone; poss cr; Eng spkn; adv bkg; quiet; red low ssn; m'vans all year, c'vans 1 Jun-30 Sep; CKE/ CCI. "Gd site." ♦ € 17.00   2009*

ST GIRONS PLAGE *8E1* (Coastal) *43.95440, -1.35672* **Campéole Camping Les Tourterelles, 40560 St Girons-Plage [05 58 47 93 12; tourterelles@campeole.com; www. camping-tourterelles.com or www.campeole.com]** Exit N10 at Castets & take D42 W to St Girons, then to St Girons-Plage. Lge, pt sl, shd; wc; shwrs inc; el pnts (6A) €3.90; lndtte; shops 1km; BBQ; playgrnd; sand beach 200m; games area; games rm; entmnt; dogs €1; poss cr; quiet; red low ssn. "Site in pine trees; footpath to dunes & beach." 15 Mar-15 Oct. € 20.20   2012*

See advertisement on pages 14 & 15

ST GIRONS PLAGE *8E1* (Coastal) *43.95105, -1.35276* **Camping Eurosol, Route de la Plage, 40560 St Girons-Plage [05 58 47 90 14 or 05 58 56 54 90; fax 05 58 47 76 74; contact@camping-eurosol.com; www. camping-eurosol.com]** Turn W off D652 at St Girons on D42. Site on L in 4km. Lge, pt sl, pt shd; wc; chem disp; baby facs; serviced pitches; shwrs inc; el pnts (6-10A) inc; gas; lndtte; shop; rest, snacks; playgrnd; 2 pools; paddling pool; sand beach 700m; tennis; games area; games rm; horseriding adj; cycle hire; entmnt; TV rm; some statics; dogs €2.50; poss cr; red low ssn; quiet. "Pitches poss tight for long vans." ♦ 10 May-13 Sep. € 45.00 (4 persons)   2008*

See advertisement opposite

FRANCE

STE HERMINE *2H4* (11km NE Rural) *46.59555, -0.97247* **FFCC Camping Le Colombier (Naturist), 85210 St Martin-Lars [02 51 27 83 84; fax 02 51 27 87 29; lecolombier.nat@ wanadoo.fr; www.lecolombier-naturisme.com]** Fr junc 7 of A83 take D137 N; 3km past Ste Hermine turn R onto D52 to Le Poteau; turn L onto D10 to St Martin-Lars; 150m past St Martin-Lars turn R sp Le Colombier. Site ent on L in 200m. Lge, hdg/mkd pitch, pt sl, pt shd; wc; chem disp; shwrs inc; sauna; jaccuzi; el pnts (16A) €4.10; gas; lndtte; shops 6km; tradsmn, rest, snacks; bar; playgrnd; pool; wifi; 50% statics to let; dogs €3.80; poss cr; Eng spkn; adv bkg; quiet; ccard acc; red low ssn. "Well-run site; diff areas diff character; lge pitches; friendly Dutch owners; san facs clean but tired (2010); gd walking in site grnds & local area; conv Mervent National Park; excel; gd facs" ♦ ltd 1 Apr-1 Oct. € 26.50   2012*

ST HILAIRE DE LUSIGNAN see Agen *8E3*

"There aren't many sites open at this time of year"

If you're travelling outside peak season remember to call ahead to check site opening dates – even if the entry says 'open all year'.

ST HILAIRE DE RIEZ *2H3* (4km N Rural) *46.76333* **Camping La Puerta del Sol, 7 Chemin des Hommeaux, 85270 St Hilaire-de-Riez [02 51 49 10 10; fax 02 51 49 84 84; info@campinglapuertadelsol.com; www. campinglapuertadelsol.com]** N on D38 fr Les Sables-d'Olonne; exit onto D69 sp Soullans, Challans, Le Pissot. At next rndabt take 3rd exit & foll lge sp to site. Site on R in 1.5km. Lge, hdg/mkd pitch, pt sl, pt shd; wc; chem disp; serviced pitches; baby facs; sauna; jaccuzi; shwrs inc; el pnts (10A) inc (poss rev pol); lndtte (inc dryer); shop; rest, snacks; bar; BBQ (gas/ elec); playgrnd; htd pool; paddling pool; waterslide; sand beach 4.5km; watersports 5km; fishing 2km; tennis; horseriding; golf; cycle hire; games area; wifi; entmnt; games/TV rm; 50% statics; dogs €4; no c'vans/m'vans over 10m high ssn; Eng spkn; adv bkg; quiet; ccard acc; red low ssn; CKE/CCI. "Vg site; med sized pitches, some diff lge o'fits due odd shape; clean san facs; gd for families; Lovely pools and playgrnd" ♦ 1 Apr-30 Sep. € 33.00   2012*

ST HILAIRE DE RIEZ *2H3* (1km E Coastal) *46.74458, -2.00423* **Camping La Ningle, 66 Chemin des Roselières, 85270 St Hilaire-de-Riez [02 51 54 07 11; fax 02 51 54 99 39; campingdelaningle@wanadoo.fr; www.campinglaningle. com]** Fr St Hilaire, take rd sp Sion-sur-l'Océan. At traff lts/ rndabt, foll sp 'Autres Campings' until site sp is seen. Med, hdg/mkd pitch, pt shd; wc; chem disp; serviced pitches; shwrs inc; el pnts (10A) inc; gas; lndtte; shop; tradsmn; bar; playgrnd; pool; sand beach 1.5km; tennis; fitness rm; poss cr; adv bkg; dogs €2; Eng spkn; red low ssn; CKE/CCI. "Highly rec; friendly, helpful staff; gd sized pitches; well-maintained; excel." ♦ ltd 20 May-10 Sep. € 31.90   2009*

ST HILAIRE DE RIEZ *2H3* (5km NW Coastal) *46.73970, -1.98410* **Camping La Parée Préneau, 23 Ave de la Parée Préneau, 85270 St Hilaire-de-Riez [02 51 54 33 84; fax 02 51 55 29 57; contact@campinglapareepreneau.com; www.campinglapareepreneau.com]** Fr N on D38 foll sp Sion-sur-l'Océan & St Hilaire-de-Riez cent. At next rndabt take 1st exit (petrol stn on R) & foll sp La Parée Préneau; site on L in 2km. Or fr S on D38, go thro St Gilles-Croix-de-Vie & pass St Hilaire-de-Riez; at rndabt turn L sp Sion-sur-l'Océan & St Hilaire-de-Riez cent, then as above. Lge, hdg pitch, pt sl, shd; wc (some cont); baby facs; shwrs inc; jaccuzi; el pnts (6A) inc; lndtte (inc dryer); supmkt nrby; tradsmn; bar; BBQ (charcoal/ gas); playgrnd; 2 htd pools (1 covrd); paddling pool; jacuzzi; sand beach 1km; fishing 1km; windsurfing 5km; games area; wifi; entmnt; TV/games rm; dogs €3; no c'vans/m'vans over 7m high ssn; Eng spkn; adv bkg; ccard acc; red low ssn; CKE/CCI. "Simple, relaxed site; family-run; some pitches poss tight lge o'fits; unisex san facs, mixed reports; v quiet low ssn; mkt Thu & Sun; gd." ♦ 7 May-9 Sep. € 27.00   2011*

ST HILAIRE DU HARCOUET *2E4* (1km W Urban) *48.58105, -1.09771* **FFCC Camp Municipal de la Sélune, 50600 St Hilaire-du-Harcouët [02 33 49 43 74 or 02 33 49 70 06; fax 02 33 49 59 40; info@st-hilaire.fr; www.st-hilaire.fr]** Sp on N side of N176 twd Mont St Michel/St Malo/Dinan, on W side of town; well sp. Med, hdg pitch, pt sl, pt shd; wc; chem disp; shwrs inc; el pnts (16A) €1.95; lndry rm; shops 1km; snacks 500m; playgrnd; pool 300m; wifi; dogs €0.70; red long stay/CKE/CCI. "Peaceful, beautifully maintained site; easy access; helpful, pleasant warden; superb san facs; gate locked 2200-0730; excel." 23 Apr-16 Sep. € 7.70   2011*

ST HILAIRE LA FORET *7A1* (4km SW Rural) *46.44836, -1.52860* **Camping Les Batardières, Rue des Bartardières, 85440 St Hilaire-la-Forêt [02 51 33 33 85]** Fr Sables d'Olonne take D949 twd Avrillé. 7km after Talmont-St-Hilaire fork R on D70 to St Hilaire-la-Forêt. In 3km turn R on ent vill. Site 70m on L. Med, hdg pitch, pt shd; wc; chem disp; serviced pitches; shwrs inc; el pnts (6A) €3.50; lndtte; shop adj; playgrnd; sand beach 5km; free tennis; cycling; no statics; dogs €1.50; adv bkg; quiet; CKE/CCI. "Excel; spacious pitches; clean facs; excel for families; rec." 9 April -22 Sept. € 20.00   2012*

ST HILAIRE LA FORET *7A1* (1km NW Rural) *46.44846, -1.52643* **Camping La Grand' Métairie, 8 Rue de la Vineuse-en-Plaine, 85440 St Hilaire-la-Forêt [02 51 33 32 38; fax 02 51 33 25 69; info@camping-grandmetairie.com; www.la-grand-metairie.com]** Fr D949 turn S onto D70, sp St Hilaire-la-Forêt, or fr Avrillé take D19. Site at ent to vill. Lge, hdg/mkd pitch, pt shd; wc; chem disp; serviced pitches; sauna; baby facs; shwrs inc; el pnts (10A) inc (poss rev pol); gas; lndtte (inc dryer); shop; tradsmn; rest, snacks; bar; BBQ; playgrnd; 2 htd pools (1 covrd); paddling pool; sand beach 3km; tennis; jacuzzi; fitness rm; games rm; games area; cycle hire; golf 15km; wifi; entmnt; TV; 80% statics; dogs €4; phone; poss cr; Eng spkn; adv bkg; quiet; ccard acc; red long stay/low ssn/CKE/CCI. "Gd base for beaches, La Rochelle & Ile de Ré; friendly, helpful owners; cycle rtes fr site; excel." ♦ 2 Apr-24 Sep. € 29.00   2011*

ST HILAIRE LA PALUD *7A2* (5km NW Rural) *46.28386, -0.74344* **Flower Camping Le Lidon, Le Lidon, 79210 St Hilaire-la-Palud [05 49 35 33 64; fax 05 49 35 32 63; info@le-lidon.com; www.le-lidon.com]** Exit A10 junc 33 onto E601 then N248 & N11 S. At Epannes foll D1 N to Sansais, then D3 to St Hilaire-la-Palud. Foll sp Canal du Mignon & site. NB Access to site over narr angled bdge, extreme care needed - v diff lge o'fits. Med, hdg/mkd pitch, pt shd; wc; chem disp; mv service pnt; baby facs; fam bthrm; shwrs inc; el pnts (10A) inc; gas 4km; lndtte; ice; shop; tradsmn; rest, snacks; bar; BBQ; playgrnd; htd pool; paddling pool; rv fishing; canoe hire; cycle hire; wifi; entmnt; 5% statics; dogs €2.50; some Eng spkn; adv bkg; quiet; ccard acc; red low ssn; CKE/CCI. "Secluded site in Marais Poitevin Regional Park (marsh land); gd sized pitches; excel clean san facs; gd walking, cycling, birdwatching; vg." ♦ 9 Apr-29 Sep. € 26.00 (CChq acc)   2011*

See advertisement on pages 32 & 33

ST HILAIRE ST FLORENT see Saumur *4G1*

ST HONORE LES BAINS *4H4* (W Urban) *46.90413, 3.83919* **Camp Municipal Plateau du Guet, 13 Rue Eugène Collin, 58360 St Honoré-les-Bains [03 86 30 76 00 or 03 86 30 74 87 (Mairie); fax 03 86 30 73 33; mairie-de-st-honore-les-bains@wanadoo.fr; www.st-honore-les-bains.com]** On D985 fr Luzy to St Honoré-les-Bains. In cent vill turn L on D106 twd Vandenesse. Site on L in 150m. Or N fr Château-Chinon 27km. Then D985 to St Honoré. Med, mkd pitch, pt hdstg, pt terr, pt shd; htd wc; mv service pnt; shwrs inc; el pnts (10A) €2.90; lndtte; shop, rest, snacks, bar 300m; playgrnd; htd pool 300m; ady bkg; quiet; CKE/CCI. "Gd, modern san facs; pleasant, conv site town, gd walking ." ♦ 1 Apr-26 Oct. € 8.60   2012*

ST HONORE LES BAINS *4H4* (1km W Rural) *46.90680, 3.82843* **Camping & Gîtes Les Bains, 15 Ave Jean Mermoz, 58360 St Honoré-les-Bains [03 86 30 73 44; fax 03 86 30 61 88; camping-les-bains@wanadoo.fr; www.campinglesbains.com]** Fr St Honoré-les-Bains foll site sp as 'Village des Bains' fr town cent on D106 twd Vandenesse. Med, hdg/mkd pitch, some hdstg, pt sl, shd; wc (some cont); chem disp; mv service pnt; baby facs; shwrs inc; el pnts (6A) €3.50; gas; lndtte (inc dryer); shop 1km; rest, snacks; bar; BBQ; playgrnd; pool; paddling pool; waterslide; fishing; tennis; horseriding 300m; cycle hire; wifi; entmnt; games/TV rm; dogs €1.50; Eng spkn; adv bkg; quiet low ssn; ccard acc; CKE/CCI. "Helpful staff; poor maintenance & san facs need refurb; gd walking; sm pitches & poss waterlogged after rain; mkt Thu." ♦ 1 Apr-31 Oct. € 16.00   2011*

ST JACQUES DES BLATS *7C4* (Rural) *45.05181, 2.71377* **Camp Municipal Les Blats, Route de la Gare, 15800 St Jacques-des-Blats [04 71 47 06 00 or 04 71 47 05 90 (Mairie); fax 04 71 47 07 09; i-tourisme-st-jacques@wanadoo.fr]** Sp fr N122, 3km SW of Lioran Tunnel in vill of St Jacques-des-Blats; 300m fr N122 down steep app rd; sp in vill adj rv. Sm, hdg pitch, pt shd; htd wc; chem disp; shwrs; el pnts (10A); lndtte; shops 200m; rest 200m; bar; BBQ; playgrnd; TV; 30% statics; quiet; CKE/CCI. "Gd walking trails fr site; lift to summit Plomb du Cantal." 1 May-30 Sep. € 9.00   2009*

ST JANS CAPPEL see Bailleul *3A3*

ST JEAN D'ANGELY *7B2* (500m W Rural) *45.94868, -0.53645* **Camping Val de Boutonne, 56 Quai de Bernouet, 17400 St Jean-d'Angély [05 46 32 26 16; fax 05 46 32 29 54; info@valba.net; www.campingcharentemaritime17.com]** Exit A10 at junc 34; head SE on D939; turn R at 1st rndabt into town. Site sp. Med, mkd pitch, shd; wc (some cont); chem disp; mv service pnt; shwrs inc; el pnts (6A) €3.55; lndtte; sm shop; tradsmn; rest, snacks, bar 200m; playgrnd; aquatic cent 500m; wifi; TV rm; 10% statics; dogs €1.20; phone adj; Eng spkn; adv bkg; quiet; ccard acc; red long stay; CKE/CCI; "Pleasant, friendly, well-kept site by Rv Boutonne; helpful owners; gd san facs, outdated; poss open in Oct - phone ahead; vg" ♦ 1 Apr-30 Sep. € 22.35   2013*

ST JEAN DE CEYRARGUES see Alès *10E1*

ST JEAN DE COUZ see Echelles, Les *9B3*

ST JEAN DE LOSNE *6H1* (800m E Rural) *47.10232, 5.27521* **Camp Municipal Les Herlequins, 21170 St Jean-de-Losne [03 80 39 22 26; fax 03 80 29 05 48; www.saintjeandelosne.com]** Site sp on ent town fr N on D968. Access fr town on Quai National & Rue du Port-Bernard on N bank of Rv Saône. Med, hdg/mkd pitch, hdstg, pt shd; wc (some cont); shwrs; el pnts (10A); shop 1km; rest, snacks; bar; BBQ; playgrnd; sand beach; poss cr; adv bkg; quiet. 1 May-30 Sep.   2008*

ST JEAN DE LUZ *8F1* (3km N Coastal) *43.40549, -1.64222*
**Camping Bord de Mer, 71 chemin d'Erromardie, 64500
St Jean-de-Luz** [tel/fax 05 59 26 24 61; bord-de-mer64@
orange.fr] Exit A63 junc 3 onto D810 dir St Jean-de-Luz. In
1km cross rlwy & immed turn sharp R sp Erromardie. Site on
sharp turn L bef beach. Ent by plastic chain fence bef ent to
prom, but easy to miss. App poss diff lge o'fits due hairpin
turn - drive on to car park where may be poss to turn. Med,
hdg pitch, pt sl; terr; wc (mainly cont); chem disp; mv service
pnt; shwrs inc; el pnts (10A) €3,50; lndy rm; tradsmn; snacks;
bar; BBQ; sand beach adj; dogs; quiet; red low ssn. "Nice site
in excel position; owner connects el pnts; cliff walk to town;
NH en route Spain; San facs refurbished" ♦ ltd 1 Apr-31 Oct.
€ 41.00   2013*

ST JEAN DE LUZ *8F1* (3km N Urban/Coastal) *43.40777,
-1.63777* **Chadotel Camping International Erromardie,
Ave de la Source, 64500 St Jean-de-Luz** [05 59 26 07 74
or 02 51 33 05 05 (LS); fax 05 59 51 12 11; camping-
international@wanadoo.fr or info@chadotel.com; www.
erromardie.com or www.chadotel.com] Fr A63 exit junc
3 sp St Jean-de-Luz. At traff lts at end of slip rd turn L onto
D810 sp St Jean; in 1km cross rlwy & immed turn sharp R sp
Erromardie, site on R in 1km opp beach. Lge, hdg/mkd pitch, pt
sl, shd; wc; chem disp (wc); shwrs inc; el pnts (5A) inc; lndtte;
shop; rest, snacks; bar; BBQ (charcoal); playgrnd; pool; sand/
shgl beach adj; fishing 2km; watersports 3km; golf, entmnt;
wifi; TV rm; many statics; dogs €3.20; c'vans over 7m not acc
high ssn; adv bkg; quiet; ccard acc; red long stay. "Facs &
office poss clsd after 1800 low ssn; poss poor security; twin-
axle c'vans acc;mkd Tue & Fri." 7 Apr-11 Nov. € 32.50 2011*

ST JEAN DE LUZ *8F1* (2km NE Coastal) *43.40563,
-1.64216* **Camping de la Ferme Erromardie, 40 Chemin
d'Erromardie, 64500 St Jean-de-Luz** [05 59 26 34 26; fax
05 59 51 26 02; contact@camping-erromardie.com; www.
camping-erromardie.com] Exit A63 junc 3 onto D810 sp
St Jean-de-Luz. After 1km x rlwy and turn immed sharp R sp
Erromardie. Site ent on R in 3km just bef rest/bar. Lge, hdg/
mkd pitch, shd; wc; chem disp; mv service pnt; baby facs;
shwrs inc; el pnts (6-16A) €3.80-4.30; gas; lndtte; tradsmn;
rest, snacks; bar; playgrnd; sand beach adj; many statics; dogs
€1.50; poss cr; Eng spkn; adv bkg; red low ssn; CKE/CCI.
"Well-run site; cheerful, helpful staff; gd san facs; ltd water
pnts in 2nd field; lovely, sandy beaches; coastal walk into
St Jean-de-Luz; Basque museum nrby; site in 3 sections, large
o'fits should ask for pitch on touring field; popular site; excel
modern san facs" ♦ 15 Mar-30 Sep. € 36.30   2013*

ST JEAN DE LUZ *8F1* (3km NE Coastal) *43.41339, -1.61710*
Camping Itsas-Mendi, Acotz, 64500 St Jean-de-Luz
[05 59 26 56 50; fax 05 59 26 54 44; itsas@wanadoo.fr;
www.itsas-mendi.com] Exit A63 junc 3 sp St Jean-de-Luz;
take D810 dir Biarritz; in 3km turn L sp Acotz Plage & Camping;
site well sp. Lge, hdg pitch, pt sl, terr; shd; htd wc; chem disp;
mv service pnt; sauna; shwrs inc; fam bthrm; el pnts (10A) inc;
lndtte (inc dryer); shop; rest, snacks; bar; BBQ; playgrnd; htd
pools; paddling pool; waterslides & aquatic area; tennis; games
area; beach 500m; wifi; TV rm; dogs €2.20; phone; poss cr; Eng
spkn; quiet but rlwy adj; red low ssn; CKE/CCI. "Friendly staff;
excel." ♦ 3 Apr-13 Oct. € 40.00 (CChq acc)   2012*

ST JEAN DE LUZ *8F1* (4km N Rural) *43.41527, -1.61666*
**Camping Atlantica, Quartier Acotz, 64500 St Jean-
de-Luz** [05 59 47 72 44; fax 05 59 54 72 27; info@
campingatlantica.com; www.campingatlantica.com]
Exit A63 at junc 3 sp St Jean-de-Luz-Nord. Take D810 twd
Biarritz & at top of hill foll sp Acotz Plage; site well sp. Lge,
mkd pitch, pt sl, pt shd; wc; mv service pnt; shwrs inc; baby
facs; el pnts (6A) €4.70; lndtte; shop; rest, snacks; bar;
playgrnd; pool; paddling pool; beach 500m; entmnt; games/TV
rm; 35% statics; dogs €2.50; bus; poss cr; Eng spkn; adv bkg;
some rd & rlwy noise; ccard acc; red low ssn; CKE/CCI. "Vg
pool; gd san facs; various pitch sizes; not suitable v lge o'fits
due narr site rds; excel." ♦ 1 Apr-30 Sep. € 29.50   2010*

ST JEAN DE LUZ *8F1* (4km NE Coastal) *43.41674, -1.62274*
**Camping Duna-Munguy, 881 Chemin Duhartia, Quartier
Acotz, 64500 St Jean-de-Luz** [05 59 47 70 70; fax
05 59 47 78 82; camping-duna-munguy@wanadoo.fr;
www.camping-dunamunguy.com] Exit A63 at junc 3
St Jean-de-Luz Nord. Take D810 twd Biarritz, turn L at 2nd rise
then R at T-junc & down hill under rlwy bdge sp Acotz Plages.
Site well sp. NB Steep downhill app. Sm, mkd pitch, hdstg, pt
shd; htd wc; chem disp; shwrs inc; jacuzzi; el pnts (10A) €4
(poss rev pol); lndtte; playgrnd; sm pool; sandy beach 300m;
golf 5km; wifi; TV; 80% statics; dogs €4; phone; bus 1km (at
top of hill); poss cr; Eng spkn; adv bkg; quiet but rlwy noise;
ccard not acc; CKE/CCI. "Steep app poss diff long o'fits; sm
pitches - poss liable to flood; gd san facs with smart shwrs;
helpful owner; no sea views but sheltered in storms; gd coastal
walks; rec." ♦ ltd 15 Feb-15 Nov. € 26.00   2009*

ST JEAN DE LUZ *8F1* (4km NE Coastal) *43.41861, -1.62320*
**Camping Merko Lacarra, 820 Route des Plages, Plage
d'Acotz, 64500 St Jean-de-Luz** [05 59 26 56 76; fax
05 59 54 73 81; contact@merkolacarra.com; www.
merkolacarra.com] Exit A63 at junc 3 St Jean-de-Luz Nord.
Take D810 twd Biarritz, turn L at 2nd rise then R at T-junc &
down hill under rlwy bdge sp Acotz Plages, site on L. NB steep
downhill app. Med, pt sl, pt shd; wc; chem disp; shwrs; el
pnts (16A) £4; lndtte; shop; café/bar; sand beach over rd; wifi;
15% statics; dogs €1.50; m'van o'night sep area; Eng spkn;
quiet; ccard acc; red low ssn; CKE/CCI. "Well-kept, busy site;
some pitches awkward due trees/bushes; poss cr high ssn; lovely
walking/cycling; gd." ♦ 27 Mar-16 Oct. € 27.00   2010*

ST JEAN DE LUZ *8F1* (5km NE Coastal) *43.41791, -1.62397*
**Camping Les Tamaris Plage, Quartier Acotz, 64500
St Jean-de-Luz** [05 59 26 55 90; fax 05 59 47 70 15;
contact@tamaris-plage.com; www.tamaris-plage.com]
Fr A63 take St Jean-de-Luz Nord exit. Turn R sp Guéthary. After
1km turn L sp Acotz, Campings-Plages. Then foll sps to Tamaris
Plage. Med, hdg/mkd pitch, pt sl, pt shd; wc (some cont); chem
disp; mv service pnt; baby facs; shwrs inc; el pnts (7A) €3; gas;
lndtte; shop; rest, snacks, bar 1.5km; BBQ; playgrnd; beach
adj; games rm; games area; entmnt; TV rm; 50% statics; dogs
€5; phone; poss cr; poss noisy; Eng spkn; red low ssn; CKE/
CCI. "Luxurious facs block has fountain & flowers; excel." ♦
21 Mar-5 Nov. € 24.00   2008*

ST JEAN DE LUZ *8F1* (5km NE Coastal) *43.41640, -1.62482* Camping-Plage Soubelet, Quartier Acotz, 64500 St Jean-de-Luz [05 59 26 51 60; www.soubelet-plage.com] Fr St Jean take D810 twd Biarritz. Bef Guéthary turn L to Acotz/ Plages. Turn R down hill, under rlwy bdge & turn L. Site on R in 300m. Lge, mkd pitch, hdstg, pt shd; htd wc; chem disp; baby facs; shwrs inc; el pnts (15A) €4; lndtte; shop; snacks; playgrnd; sand beach adj; 5% statics; dogs free; poss cr; Eng spkn; quiet. "Gd sea views; poss ltd san facs low ssn & stretched high ssn, conv Bidart for rests, shops etc." ♦ 1 Apr-15 Oct. € 22.50   2008*

"That's changed – Should I let The Club know?"

If you find something on site that's different from the site entry, fill in a report and let us know. See www.caravanclub.co.uk/europereport.

⊞ **ST JEAN DE LUZ** *8F1* (6km SE Rural) *43.34591, -1.61724* Camping Chourio, Luberriaga, 64310 Ascain [05 59 54 06 31 or 05 59 54 04 32; www.tourisme-aquitaine.fr] Fr St Jean-de-Luz take D918 sp Ascain. In 6km turn R at traff lts, in 250m over rv bdge & turn L at mini-rndabt. Site sp in town. Med, pt shd; wc; chem disp; mv service pnt; shwrs inc; el pnts (6A) €2.80; tradsmn; rest, snacks, bar 1km; phone; poss cr; quiet; CKE/CCI; "Friendly, family-owned, relaxed site in lovely countryside; conv Spanish border; Tues & Sat mkt St Jean-de-Luz; vg; v helpful owners" 20 Mar-15 Nov. € 14.00   2013*

ST JEAN DE LUZ *8F1* (10km SE Rural) *43.35748, -1.57465* Camping d'Ibarron, 64310 St Pée-sur-Nivelle [05 59 54 10 43; fax 05 59 54 51 95; camping.dibarron@wanadoo.fr; www.camping-ibarron.com] Fr St Jean take D918 twd St Pée, site 2km bef St Pée on R of rd. Lge, shd; wc (mainly cont); chem disp; mv service pnt; shwrs inc; el pnts (6A) €3.95; gas 3km; lndtte; shop, tradsmn, snacks high ssn; supmkt adj; playgrnd; pool; sand beach 10km; wifi; TV/games rm; 5% statics; dogs €1.60; phone; Eng spkn; adv bkg; quiet, a little traff noise; red low ssn; CKE/CCI. "Well-kept site in scenic location; spacious pitches; welcoming, helpful owner; gd san facs; on main rd & no footpath to vill; walk along rv into vill; mkt Sat; excel." ♦ 1 May-30 Sep. € 19.80   2011*

ST JEAN DE LUZ *8F1* (10km SE Rural) *43.36288, -1.56638* Camping Goyetchea, Route d'Ahetze, 64310 St Pée-sur-Nivelle [05 59 54 19 59; info@camping-goyetchea.com; www.camping-goyetchea.com] Fr St Jean-de-Luz take D918 twd St Pée-sur-Nivelle. Turn L at Hotel Bonnet at Ibarron D855. Site on R in 800m. Med, pt shd; wc (some cont); chem disp; baby facs; shwrs inc; el pnts (6A) €3.80; gas; lndtte; shop; supmkt 800m; tradsmn; rest, snacks; bar; BBQ; playgrnd; pool; paddling pool; sand beach 10km; lake sw 4km; games area; wifi; entmnt; TV rm; 10% statics; dogs €1.50; adv bkg; quiet; ccard acc; red low ssn; CKE/CCI. "Excel site in lovely area; friendly, helpful owners; vg." ♦ 5 Jun-18 Sep. € 20.60 2010*

⊞ **ST JEAN DE LUZ** *8F1* (3km SW Rural) *43.37064, -1.68629* Camping Larrouleta, 210 Route de Socoa, 64122 Urrugne [05 59 47 37 84; fax 05 59 47 42 54; info@larrouleta.com; www.larrouleta.com] Exit A63 junc 2 St Jean-de-Luz Sud. Pass under D810 & take 1st L sp Urrugne. Loop back up to N10 & turn R, site sp in 500m. Or fr S on D810, 2km beyond Urrugne vill (by-pass vill), turn L into minor rd, site 50m on R. Lge, hdg/mkd pitch, hdstg, pt shd; htd wc; chem disp; baby facs; shwrs inc; el pnts (10A) inc (poss rev pol); gas; lndtte; shop; hypmkt 1.5km; tradsmn; rest (Jul/Aug); snacks; bar; playgrnd; htd, covrd pool; lake sw, fishing & boating; sand beach 3km; tennis; games; wifi; entmnt; no statics (2010); dogs €2; phone; bus 200m; poss cr; some Eng spkn; adv bkg ess high ssn; ccard acc; red low ssn; CKE/CCI; "Pleasant, well-kept, well-run family site nr lake; excel san facs (unisex low ssn) & pool; friendly & helpful (ask for dir on dep to avoid dangerous bend); some pitches unrel in wet but can park on site rds/hdstg; poss ltd facs low ssn; conv A63, Biarritz & en rte Spain; excel; Conv m'way & hypermarket/fuel" ♦ ltd € 32.50   2013*

ST JEAN DE LUZ *8F1* (4km SW Coastal) *43.39320, -1.69310* Camping Juantcho, Route de la Corniche, Socoa, 64122 Urrugne [tel/fax 05 59 47 11 97; camping.juantcho@orange.fr; www.camping-juantcho.com] Leave A63 at junc 2. Keep to L lane & immed after passing toll booth take exit to Socoa, site on R on cliff top rd - busy & steep. Lge, hdg/mkd pitch, terr, pt shd; wc; chem disp; shwrs inc; el pnts (5A) €4.20; lndtte; shop & snacks in ssn; playgrnd; beach 500m; fishing, watersports; entmnt 500m; some statics; dogs €2.50; poss cr; quiet; red low ssn/long stay; CKE/CCI. "Pleasant site; beautiful beach; helpful, friendly staff; ltd facs low ssn; can get v windy at top of site; ferry fr Socoa to St Jean high ssn." 1 May-30 Sep. € 18.30   2010*

ST JEAN DE LUZ *8F1* (7km SW Rural) *43.33277, -1.68527* Camping Sunêlia du Col d'Ibardin, Route d'Ascain, 64122 Urrugne [05 59 54 31 21; fax 05 59 54 62 28; info@col-ibardin.com; www.col-ibardin.com] Exit A63 junc 2, ignore slip rd to R 50m, turn L & in 100m turn R onto D810 S. In 2km at rndabt foll sp Col d'Ibardin, Ascain; after 4km site on R immed past minor rd to Col d'Ibardin. Med, hdg/mkd pitch, some hdstg, pt sl, pt terr, pt shd; 5% serviced pitch; wc; chem disp; baby facs; shwrs inc; el pnts (5-10A) €5.50-6.50 (poss rev pol); gas; lndtte (inc dryer); shop; tradsmn; supmkt 5km; rest, snacks & bar in ssn; BBQ; playgrnd; htd pool; paddling pool; sand beach 6km; tennis; games area; games rm; wifi; entmnt; TV; 5% statics; dogs €2.80; phone; Eng spkn; adv bkg; quiet; ccard acc; red low ssn/long stay; CKE/CCI. "Lovely, well-run site in woodland; fair sized pitches; helpful, friendly owner; gd san facs; pleasant bar/rest; mountain rlwy nr; gd touring base for Pyrenees & N Spain; excel." ♦ 1 Apr-30 Sep. € 32.00   2011*

See advertisement opposite

FRANCE

ST JEAN DE MAURIENNE *9C3* (Urban) *45.27034, 6.35023* Camp Municipal des Grands Cols, 422 Ave du Mont-Cenis, 73300 St Jean-de-Maurienne [tel/fax 04 79 64 28 02 or 06 64 09 77 48 (mob); info@campingdesgrandscols. com; www.campingdesgrandscols.com] Site sp fr D1006 in St Jean-de-Maurienne; site behind shops 100m fr town cent behind trees/parking. Med, hdg/mkd pitch, hdstg, pt sl, pt shd; wc; chem disp; mv service pnt; 20% serviced pitches; shwrs inc; el pnts (16A) €3; lndtte; supmkt 1km; tradsmn; snacks; bar; playgrnd; pool 1.5km; lake 3km; games rm; TV; dogs €1; Eng spkn; helpful staff; clean san facs; interesting town; excel for serious cycling; gd NH for Fréjus tunnel; excel." 8 May-24 Sep. € 16.00   2010*

ST JEAN DE MONTS *2H3* (2km N Coastal) *46.80666, -2.09970* Camping La Davière Plage, Route de Notre-Dame, 85160 St Jean-de-Monts [tel/fax 02 51 58 27 99; info@daviereplage.com; www.daviereplage.com] Site on L off D38 Rte de Notre Dame fr St Jean & 2km W of Notre-Dame. Well sp. Med, hdg/mkd pitch, pt shd; wc; chem disp; shwrs; el pnts (10A) €3.90; gas; lndry rm; shops adj; tradsmn; rest, snacks; bar; playgrnd; sand beach, watersports 700m; sports area; entmnt; TV rm; dogs €3.35; red low ssn; CKE/CCI. "Gd family site close to amenities; mkd cycle & walking trails; o'night area for m'vans." 1 May-30 Sep. € 19.95   2010*

ST JEAN DE MONTS *2H3* (SE Urban/Coastal) *46.78029, -2.05629* Campéole Camping Les Sirènes, Ave des Demoiselles, 85160 St Jean-de-Monts [02 51 58 01 31; fax 02 51 59 03 67; sirenes@campeole.com; www. vendee-camping.info or www.campeole.com] Site in town cent; ent town on D753 fr Challans, turn R at junc, then 1st L at church. Take 2nd L (Ave des Demoiselles). Site on L. V lge, pt sl, shd; wc (some cont); chem disp; shwrs inc; el pnts (10A) €4.10; gas; lndtte; sm shop adj or 2km; rest, snacks; bar; playgrnd; pool; sand beach 500m; fishing, watersports 500m; cycle hire; games area; entmnt; dogs €2.50; adv bkg ess high ssn; quiet; red low ssn. "Vg site; sm unmarked pitches." ♦ 2 Apr-12 Sep. € 22.50   2010*

See advertisement on pages 14 & 15

ST JEAN DE MONTS *2H3* (2km SE Urban) *46.78841, -2.03008* Camping Le Bois Masson, 149 Rue des Sables, 85167 St Jean-de-Monts [02 51 58 62 62 or 05 56 07 90 17; fax 02 51 58 29 97; boismasson@siblu.fr; www.siblu.com/leboismasson] Fr Challans pass thro Le Perrier to St Jean-de-Monts. At 1st rndabt take last exit dir Les Sables-d'Olonne. Foll Les Sables at next rndabts & at 4th rndabt turn R, site on R shortly after Camping Le Bois Dormant. V lge, hdg/mkd pitch, pt shd; htd wc; chem disp; baby facs; shwrs inc; el pnts (6A) inc; gas; lndtte; shop; rest, snacks; bar; BBQ (gas); playgrnd; 2 htd pools (1 covrd); waterslide; sand beach 2.5km; fishing, windsurfing, watersports nrby; entmnt; internet; TV; 4% statics; no dogs; Eng spkn; adv bkg; quiet; 20% red low ssn. "Excel, busy, popular, family site; narr access rds; mkt Sat." ♦ 4 Apr-20 Sep.   2009*

"I like to fill in the reports as I travel from site to site"

You'll find report forms at the back of this guide, or you can fill them in online at www.caravaclub.co.uk/europereport.

ST JEAN DE MONTS *2H3* (3km SE Coastal) *46.78160, -2.01810* Camping Zagarella, Route des Sables, Le Puy Blanc, 85160 St Jean-de-Monts [02 51 58 19 82; fax 02 51 59 35 28; zagarella@zagarella.fr; www.zagarella.fr or www.campings-franceloc.fr] On D38, S fr St Jean-de-Monts. Med, hdg/mkd pitch, pt shd; wc; chem disp; baby facs; shwrs inc; el pns (16A) inc; gas; lndtte (inc dryer); shop; tradsmn; rest, snacks; bar; playgrnd; htd pool; tennis; cycle hire; fitness rm; aqua gym; games rm; entmnt; children's club Jul/Aug; wifi; TV; 50% statics; dogs €3; phone; poss cr; Eng spkn; adv bkg; red low ssn; CKE/CCI. "Vg, clean site; gd pool." ♦ ltd 24 Apr-25 Sep. € 32.00   2010*

FRANCE

ST JEAN DE MONTS *2H3* (6km SE Coastal) *46.75638, -2.00749* **Camping La Yole, Chemin des Bosses, Orouët, 85160 St Jean-de-Monts** [02 51 58 67 17; fax 02 51 59 05 35; contact@la-yole.com; www.la-yole.com] Take D38 S fr St Jean-de-Monts dir Les Sable d'Olonne & Orouet. At Orouet turn R at L'Oasis rest dir Mouette; in 1.5km turn L at campsite sp; site on L. Situated bet D38 & coast, 1km fr Plage des Mouettes. On arr, park in carpark on R bef registering. Lge, hdg/mkd pitch, pt shd; wc; chem disp; serviced pitch; baby facs; jacuzzi; shwrs inc; el pnts (10A) inc; lndtte (inc dryer); shop; tradsmn; rest, snacks; bar; BBQ area (gas only); playgrnd; 2 pools (1 htd covrd); paddling pool; waterslide; jacuzzi; sand beach 2km; tennis; fishing; horseriding 3km; watersports 6km; wifi; entmnt; games/TV rm; many statics (tour ops); sm dogs €7; no c'vans/m'vans over 8m; poss cr; Eng spkn; adv bkg ess; ccard acc; red low ssn; CKE/CCI. "Busy, well-run site; san facs clean, not spacious; excel cycle paths; mkt Wed & Sat; vg." ♦ 2 Apr-26 Sep. € 34.00 (CChq acc) SBS - A23 2012*

See advertisement above

ST JEAN DE MONTS *2H3* (1km W Coastal) *46.79931, -2.07378* **Camping Le Bois Joly, 46 Route de Notre Dame-de-Monts, 85165 St Jean-de-Monts** [02 51 59 11 63; fax 02 51 69 11 06; contact@camping-leboisjoly.com; www.camping-leboisjoly.com] N on D38 circular around St Jean-de-Monts; at rndabt past junc with D51 turn R dir Notre Dame-de-Monts, site on R in 300m. Lge, hdg/mkd pitch, pt shd; wc; chem disp; baby facs; sauna; shwrs inc; el pnts (6A) inc rev pol; lndtte; shops 1km; rest, snacks, bar high ssn; playgrnd; 2 pools (1 htd, covrd); waterslide; sand beach 1km; games area; wifi; entmnt; TV rm; 25% statics; dogs €3; phone; poss cr; Eng spkn; adv bkg; ccard acc; red low ssn; ACSI; CKE/CCI. "Ideal for families; gd san facs; lge pitches; coastal & inland cycleways nrby; excel." ♦ 13 Apr-29 Sep. € 34.00 2012*

See advertisement below

ST JEAN DE MONTS *2H3* (1km NW Rural) *46.80083, -2.08013* **Camping La Buzelière, 79 Rue de Notre Dame, 85169 St Jean-de-Monts** [02 51 58 64 80; fax 02 28 11 03 61; buzeliere@aol.com; www.buzeliere.com] Take D38 fr St Jean-de-Monts to Notre Dame-de-Monts. Site on L. Med, hdg/mkd pitch, pt sl, pt shd; wc; chem disp; serviced pitch; baby facs; fam bthrm; shwrs inc; el pnts (10A) inc; gas; lndtte; shop 1km; tradsmn; snacks; bar; BBQ; playgrnd; htd pool; sand beach 1km; games area; games rm; TV; 20% statics; dogs €2.50; phone adj; Eng spkn; adv bkg; quiet; ccard acc; red low ssn; CKE/CCI. "Many sports inc golf nr; clean san facs; red facs low ssn; excel." ♦ 1 May-30 Sep. € 29.70 2012*

Send in your site reports by mid August 2014

ST JEAN DE MONTS *2H3* (3km NW Coastal) *46.80389, -2.09452* **Camping Le Fief, 168 Rue de Moulin Cassé, 85160 St Jean-de-Monts [02 51 58 63 77]** Fr St Jean on D38 NW, after 3km take L to le Fief-Haut / Route du Fief, then L again, sp immed on L. Rue de Moulin Cassé runs parallel to D38, nearer coast. Sm, pt shd; wc (cont); shwrs inc; el pnts (6A) €2.50; lndtte; shop & 3km; tradsmn; sand beach 2km; some statics; poss cr; adv bkg (rec high ssn); quiet; red low ssn. "Helpful owners; gd value for area; gd." ♦ May-Sep. € 13.00   2008*

ST JEAN DE MONTS *2H3* (3.5km NW Urban/Coastal) *46.80825, -2.10461* **Camping Les Amiaux, 223 Rue de Notre-Dame-de-Monts, 85160 St Jean-de-Monts [02 51 58 22 22; fax 02 51 58 26 09; accueil@amiaux.fr; www.amiaux.fr]** Site on D38 mid-way bet St Jean-de-Monts & Notre-Dame-de-Monts. V lge, hdg/mkd pitch, pt shd; htd wc; chem disp; serviced pitches; baby facs; shwrs inc; el pnts (10A) inc; gas; lndtte; sm shop; rest, snacks; bar; BBQ (gas & elec); playgrnd; htd, covrd pool; waterslides; sand beach 700m; tennis; cycle hire; horseriding 2km; golf 4km; games area; games rm; wifi; entmnt; TV rm; 50% statics; dogs €2.50; Eng spkn; adv bkg; ccard acc; red low ssn; CKE/CCI. "Excel, family site; gd facs; conv Puy du Fou theme park; rec long stay." ♦ 3 May-30 Sep. € 26.50   2009*

ST JEAN DE MONTS *2H3* (6km NW Coastal) *46.81831, -2.13006* **Camping La Forêt, 190 Chemin de la Rive, 85160 St Jean-de-Monts [02 51 58 84 63; camping-la-foret@wanadoo.fr; www.hpa-laforet.com]** Fr St Jean-de-Monts, take D38 twd Notre-Dame-de-Monts for 6km, over rndabt then turn L (last turning bef Notre-Dame-de-Monts) sp Pont d'Yeu, then immed L, site on L in 200m, on parallel rd to main rd. Med, hdg/mkd pitch, pt shd; wc; chem disp; shwrs inc; el pnts (6A) €3.80; gas; lndtte; shop; tradsmn; snacks; pool; playgrnd; htd pool; sand beach 500m; horseriding nrby; TV; 30% statics; dogs €2.50; phone; poss cr; Eng spkn; adv bkg; quiet; Eng spkn; BBQ; CKE/CCI. "Friendly, helpful owners; clean san facs; not suitable twin-axles; some pitches diff c'vans; excel." ♦ ltd 2 May-20 Sep. € 27.00   2009*

ST JEAN DE MUZOLS see Tournon sur Rhône *9C2*

ST JEAN DU GARD *10E1* (1.3km N Rural) *44.11346, 3.89208* **Camping Les Sources, Route du Mialet, 30270 St Jean-du-Gard [04 66 85 38 03; fax 04 66 85 16 09; camping-des-sources@wanadoo.fr; www.camping-des-sources.fr]** Fr Alès take D907 twd Anduze & St Jean-du-Gard. At St Jean turn R at traff lts on D983 (dir Florac), then R on D160 & foll camp sp. NB: Do not enter town cent when towing - narr rds. Med, hdg pitch, terr, shd; htd wc (some cont); chem disp; shwrs inc; el pnts (6A) inc; gas; shop; tradsmn; snacks; bar; playgrnd; pool; dogs €2.50; Eng spkn; adv bkg ess Jul/Aug; quiet. "Lovely, well laid-out site; pitches sm, not rec for lge o'fits; friendly, helpful family owners; modern san facs, ltd low ssn; conv National Park of Cévennes." ♦ 1 Apr-30 Sep. € 24.00   2010*

ST JEAN DU GARD *10E1* (2km W Rural) *44.11241, 3.86023* **Camping à la Ferme le Petit Baigneur (Rossel), Les Deux Chemins, 30270 St Jean-du-Gard [04 66 85 32 05; fax 04 66 85 35 47; http://le-petit-baigneur.pagesperso-orange.fr/]** Site on S side of D907 at W end of St Jean-du-Gard by-pass & 250m beyond D907/260 junc. If app fr W go past site ent & make U turn at layby opp D907/260 junc - due acute angle of site ent. Sm, pt shd; wc; chem disp (wc); shwrs inc; el pnts (6A) €1.50; lndtte; shop 1.5km; tradsmn; rest, snacks, bar 1.5km; BBQ; playgrnd; rv & shgl beach adj; fishing; TV; no statics; dogs; phone; some rd noise; red low ssn; CKE/CCI. "Family-run, simple, pleasant site by rv; san facs dated but clean; tourist steam train 1.5km; mkt Tues." ♦ Easter-15 Sep. € 11.85   2008*

ST JEAN DU GARD *10E1* (3km W) *44.11250, 3.85320* **Camping Mas de La Cam, Route de St André-de-Valborgne, 30270 St Jean-du-Gard [04 66 85 12 02; fax 04 66 75 32 07; camping@masdelacam.fr]** On S side of D 907, 1.1km W of W end of town by-pass, W of sp Camping les Baigneurs on non-Corniche rd to Florac. NB: Due to acute angle of slip rd off D907, if app fr W on D907 must go 500m past slip rd & make U-turn at layby opp D907-D9 junc. Slip rd sh but v narr; turn L after x-ing rv, L twd tennis court. Med, hdg/mkd pitch, pt sl, shd; wc; shwrs; el pnts (6A) €4.50; lndtte; rest, snacks; shops 1.3km; playgrnd; TV rm; entmnt; pool; tennis; cycle hire; quiet; red low ssn. "excel site; friendly owners." Easter-30 Sep. € 16.00   2013*

See advertisement

ST JEAN EN ROYANS *9C2* (6km NE Rural) *45.05917, 5.25353* **FFCC Camp Municipal, 26190 St Nazaire-en-Royans [04 75 48 41 18 or 04 75 48 40 63 (Mairie); contact@saint-nazaire-en-royans.com]** Exit A49 onto D1532 to St Nazaire-en-Royans, site is on E edge of vill on D76, 700m fr cent, well sp. Med, hdg pitch, pt sl, pt shd; wc (some cont); chem disp; shwrs inc; el pnts (6A) €3.80; lndtte; shops & rest 700m; playgrnd; dogs €1.22; no ccard acc; quiet; CKE/CCI. "Clean san facs; helpful warden; gate clsd 2200-0700; conv mountains of Vercors; aquaduct on Rv Isère worth seeing; excel." ♦ 1 May-30 Sep. € 9.00   2011*

ST JEAN EN ROYANS *9C2* (500m SW Urban) *45.01132, 5.28609* **Camp Municipal, Ave de Provence, 26190 St Jean-en-Royans [04 75 47 74 60]** Exit A49 junc 8 onto D1532 to St Nazaire-en-Royans. Shortly after passing under high rlwy arch in St Nazaire turn R on D76 to St Jean-en-Royans. Site at S end of St Jean; sp (different site fr Camp Municipal St Nazaire). Med, hdg pitch, pt shd; wc; chem disp; mv service pnt; shwrs inc; some el pnts (10A) €2; lndtte; shops 500m; playgrnd; rv fishing 50m; some statics; dogs €1; daytime factory noise. "Pleasant, relaxing, under-used site in semi-parkland; dated, clean san facs; lge pitches; no twin-axle vans; rec use drinking water fr san facs, not fr old water pumps; gd walking." 1 May-30 Sep. € 8.60   2008*

ST JEAN FROIDMENTEL see Cloyes sur le Loir *4F2*

ST JEAN PIED DE PORT *8F1* (3km E Rural) *43.17763, -1.21317* **Aire Naturelle La Paix des Champs (Jasses), Ferme Asoritzia, Route de Jaxu, 64220 St Jean-le-Vieux [05 59 37 02 63]** E fr St Jean-Pied-de-Port on D933. In 2km turn L onto D22 sp Jaxu, site on R in 1km. Sm, pt shd, wc; chem disp (wc); shwrs inc; el pnts (10A) inc; lndry facs; supmkt 1km; playgrnd; pool 2km; trout-fishing; dogs €0.50; quiet; CKE/CCI. "Lovely, peaceful site with mountain views; san facs OK but basic, stretched high ssn; poss run down low ssn; interesting town on pilgrim rte to Spain." ♦ ltd 15 Apr-30 Sep. € 12.50   2010*

ST JEAN PIED DE PORT *8F1* (200m S Urban) *43.16126, -1.23662* **Camp Municipal de Plaza Berri, Ave de Fronton, 64220 St Jean-Pied-de-Port [05 59 37 11 19 or 05 59 37 00 92; fax 05 59 37 99 78; mairie.stjeanpieddeport@wanadoo.fr; www.saintjeanpieddeport-paysbasque-tourisme.com]** Fr N on D933 thro town & cross rv. In 50m bear L at sm rndabt, site in 200m, sp. Enquire at Hôtel de Ville (Town Hall) off ssn. Narr app rds. Med, some mkd pitch; pt sl, pt shd; wc; chem disp; mv service pnt; shwrs inc; el pnts (5A) €2.50 (poss rev pol); shops 400m; pool 500m; quiet; CKE/CCI. "Nice site; busy, rec arr early high ssn; dogs; friendly warden; if recep unmanned, site yourself & report later; san facs need refurb (2011); gd walks & scenery; used by walkers on pilgrim rte; pelota court adj; mkt Mon; gd NH; Lovely site" ♦ 23 Apr-1 Nov. € 13.00   2012*

ST JEAN PIED DE PORT *8F1* (1.5km W Rural) *43.17304, -1.25416* **Europ Camping, 64220 Ascarat [05 59 37 12 78; fax 05 59 37 29 82; europcamping64@orange.fr; www.europ-camping.com]** Site on D918 bet Uhart-Cize & Ascarat. Well sp. Med, hdg/mkd pitch, pt shd; wc; chem disp; mv service pnt; sauna; shwrs inc; el pnts (6A) €4 (poss rev pol); lndtte; shop 2km; tradsmn; rest, snacks; bar; playgrnd; pool; paddling pool; games area; games rm; 30% statics; dogs €2.50; adv bkg; quiet; ccard acc; red low ssn; CKE/CCI. "Beautiful location; helpful staff; ltd facs low ssn; only basic food in bar/rest; ground v soft when wet; vg." ♦ 1 Apr-30 Sep. € 23.50   2011*

ST JEAN PIED DE PORT *8F1* (3km W Rural) *43.17745, -1.25970* **Camping Narbaïtz Vacances Pyrénées Basques, Route de Bayonne, 64220 Ascarat [05 59 37 10 13 or 05 59 37 09 22 (LS); fax 05 59 37 21 42; camping-narbaitz@wanadoo.fr; www.camping-narbaitz.com]** Site on L of D918 St Jean to Bayonne 3km fr St Jean, sp. Med, hdg/mkd pitch, pt sl, pt shd; htd wc (some cont); chem disp; mv service pnt; baby facs; shwrs inc; el pnts (6-10A) €4.50-5.50 (poss rev pol); lndtte (inc dryer); shop, snacks & bar in ssn; tradsmn; playgrnd; htd pool; trout-fishing; canoeing; kayaking; cycling; internet; entmnt; 5% statics; dogs free; phone; poss cr; Eng spkn; adv bkg; quiet; ccard acc high ssn; red low ssn; CKE/CCI. "Attractive, clean, family-run site; lovely views; helpful owners; vg facs; rec m'vans use top of site when wet; nr Spanish border (cheaper petrol); excel." ♦ 3 Apr-18 Sep. € 24.00   2010*

ST JORIOZ see Annecy *9B3*

ST JORY DE CHALAIS see Thiviers *7C3*

ST JOUAN DES GUERETS see St Malo *2E4*

ST JULIEN DE LAMPON see Sarlat la Canéda *7C3*

ST JULIEN DE PEYROLAS see Pont St Esprit *9D2*

ST JULIEN DES LANDES see Mothe Achard, La *2H4*

ST JULIEN EN BEAUCHENE *9D3* (7km N Rural) *44.66440, 5.70742* **Camping Le Champ La Chèvre, 26620 Lus-La-Croix-Haute [04 92 58 50 14; fax 04 92 58 55 92; info@campingchamplachevre.com; www.campingchamplachevre.com]** Turn E off D1075 thru Lus vill, site SE of vill nr sw pool on D505. Med, mkd pitch, pt sl, terr, pt shd; wc; chem disp; shwrs €1; el pnts (6A) €4.05; gas; lndtte; shops 300m; snacks; playgrnd; htd pool adj; fishing; some statics; dogs €2.65; poss cr; adv bkg; quiet; ccard acc; CKE/CCI. "Mountain views; helpful staff; excel pool; many waymkd walks; vg." ♦ ltd 27 Apr-30 Sep. € 16.40 (CChq acc)   2009*

ST JULIEN EN BORN 8E1 (2km W Rural) 44.07107, -1.24557
Aire Naturelle Piou de Pelle, 1312 Route du Sable-Blanc, 40170 St Julien-en-Born [05 58 42 88 87; jacques.vigneres@orange.fr; http://vigneres.monsite-orange.fr] Fr St Julien-en-Born cent take D652 N dir Bias; in 900m take 2nd turning to L after bdge over rv into Route du Stade; site on R in 1.5km. Sm, pt shd; wc; chem disp; shwrs inc; el pnts €3; shops 2km; BBQ; playgrnd; sand beach 5km; dogs; phone; adv bkg. "Quiet site; beautiful beaches nrby; friendly owners; vg." 1 May-30 Sep. € 10.50   2010*

ST JULIEN EN GENEVOIS 9A3 (5km SE Rural) 46.12015, 6.10565 Kawan Village La Colombière, 166 Chemin Neuf-Chef-Lieu, 74160 Neydens [04 50 35 13 14; fax 04 50 35 13 40; la.colombiere@wanadoo.fr; www.camping-la-colombiere.com] Exit A40 junc 13 onto D1201 dir Cruseilles; in 1.75km turn L to Neydens; turn R at church; site on R in 200m. Site sp. NB: Do not go into St Julien-en-Genevois when towing. Med, hdg/mkd pitch, hdstg, pt sl, pt shd; htd wc; chem disp; mv service pnt; baby facs; shwrs inc; el pnts (6-10A) inc, extra for 15A; gas; lndtte (inc dryer); sm shop & 500m; farm produce; rest, snacks; bar; BBQ; playgrnd; 2 pools (1 sm htd, covrd); paddling pool; lake fishing 1km; cycle hire; wifi; entmnt; games/TV rm; 10% statics; dogs €2.50; no c'vans/m'vans over 10m high ssn; park & ride bus; poss cr; Eng spkn; adv bkg; quiet, but some rd & aircraft noise; ccard acc; red low ssn; CKE/CCI. "Family-owned site; friendly, helpful staff; boggy after heavy rain; conv Geneva - guided tours high ssn; open for m'vans all year; gd NH; excel" ♦ 2 Apr-12 Nov. € 29.00 SBS - M08   2013*

ST JULIEN EN GENEVOIS 9A3 (6km S Rural) 46.09921, 6.08357 Camping Le Terroir, 184 Chemin de Cluijoie, 74160 Présilly [04 50 04 42 07; fax 04 50 04 55 53; camping.le.terroir@wanadoo.fr; www.camping-le-terroir.fr] Fr St Julien-en-Genevois S on D1201 for 5km. At traff lts after rndabt junc with D18, turn R twd Présilly, Route de Viry. Site on L past vill on D18. Sm, mkd pitch, pt shd; htd wc; chem disp; shwrs inc; el pnts (5-10A) €3-3.50; lndtte; tradsmn; rest 5km; snacks, bar 2km; BBQ; playgrnd; htd pool 6km; TV rm; some statics; dogs; poss cr; Eng spkn; adv bkg; quiet; CKE/CCI. "Gd touring base." 1 May-15 Sep. € 10.50   2008*

ST JULIEN EN ST ALBAN see Privas 9D2

ST JUNIEN 7B3 (1km N Urban) 45.89616, 0.89979 Camp Municipal de la Glane, Allée des Pommiers, Ave Corot, 87200 St Junien [05 55 02 34 86 or 06 74 09 85 88 (mob); fax 05 55 02 34 88; camping@saint-junien.fr; www.mairie-saint-junien.fr] Fr Limoges take D941/N141 W to St Junien. Or 9km NE Rochechouart on D675. Site in town, well sp adj stadium & pool. Med, hdg pitch, pt sl, pt shd; wc; chem disp; mv service pnt; baby facs; shwrs inc; el pnts (10A) €3.47; lndtte; BBQ; playgrnd; htd pool 300m; rv fishing 200m; 6% statics; dogs; phone; adv bkg; quiet; CKE/CCI. "Modern san facs; many sloping pitches, some boggy after rain; vg." ♦ ltd 15 May-15 Sep. € 7.04   2010*

ST JUNIEN 7B3 (4km E Rural) 45.88078, 0.96539 FFCC Camp Municipal de Chambery, 87200 St Brice-sur-Vienne [05 55 02 18 13; fax 05 55 02 93 36; mairiest-brice@wanadoo.fr; www.tourismelimousin.com] Fr St Junien take D32 E sp St Brice & St Victurnien; on leaving St Brice on D32 turn L & foll sp; site on L in 500m, on E edge of vill. Or app on D32 fr E, turn R onto C2 bef St Brice-sur-Vienne town sign, sp 'Campings & Gite Rural'. Sm, hdg/mkd pitch, hdstg, pt sl, pt shd; htd wc; chem disp; mv service pnt; serviced pitches; shwrs inc; el pnts (10A) €3.40; lndtte; shop in vill; playgrnd; rv nr; dogs; adv bkg; CKE/CCI; "Peaceful, clean site in park; spacious pitches o'look lake & countryside; site yourself, office open 1hr am & pm; barrier clsd 2200-0700; conv Oradour-sur-Glane; excel" ♦ 1 May-15 Sep. € 6.20   2013*

ST JURS see Puimoisson 10E3

ST JUST (CANTAL) 9C1 (Urban) 44.88997, 3.21028 FFCC Camp Municipal, 15320 St Just [04 71 73 72 57, 04 71 73 70 48 or 06 31 47 05 15 (mob); fax 04 71 73 71 44; info@saintjust.com; www.saintjust.com] Exit junc 31 fr A75, foll sp St Chély-d'Apcher D909; turn W onto D448 twds St Just (approx 6km); sp with gd access. Med, mkd pitch, pt sl, terr, pt shd; htd wc; chem disp; mv service pnt; shwrs inc; el pnts (10A) €2.20; lndtte; shop; snacks; bar; pool high ssn; fishing; tennis; cycle hire; dogs; phone; some Eng spkn; v quiet; ccard acc; red low ssn/long stay. "Vg site; friendly, helpful warden; ltd facs low ssn; excel tennis & pool; gd touring base; area for m'vans." Easter-30 Sep. € 9.80   2011*

ST JUST EN CHEVALET 9B1 (1km NW Rural) 45.91459, 3.84026 Camp Municipal Le Verdillé, 42430 St Just-en-Chevalet [tel/fax 04 77 65 17 82 or 04 77 65 00 62 (Mairie); campingleverdille@sfr.fr] Exit A72 at junc 4, join D53 NE twd St Just-en-Chevalet. Foll sp in town to camping/piscine. Due to steep gradients avoid D1 when towing. Med, hdg pitch, pt sl, pt shd; wc (mainly cont); chem disp; mv service pnt; shwrs inc; el pnts (16A) €3; lndtte; shops & supmkt 500m; rest 500m; snacks, bar adj; htd pool & tennis adj; 10% statics; dogs €1.70; phone; Eng spkn; adv bkg; quiet; CKE/CCI. "Friendly owners." 1 May-30 Sep. € 18.90   2013*

ST JUST LUZAC see Marennes 7B1

ST JUSTIN 8E2 (2km NW Rural) 44.00166, -0.23502 Camping Le Pin, Route de Roquefort, 40240 St Justin [tel/fax 05 58 44 88 91; campinglepin@wanadoo.fr; www.campinglepin.com] Fr St Justin on D933, take D626 twd Roquefort. Site on L in 2km, well sp fr town. Sm, shd; wc; shwrs inc; el pnts (6A) €3; lndtte; shop & 2km; rest, snacks; bar; playgrnd; pool; rv fishing 2km; cycle hire; horseriding; games area; entmnt; TV; some statics; dogs €1.50; poss cr; adv bkg; quiet; red low ssn/snr citizens; CKE/CCI. "Pleasant, spacious site; facs old but clean & poss stretched when site full; beautiful vill." ♦ 1 Apr-30 Sep. € 18.00   2009*

ST LAGER BRESSAC see St Vincent de Barrès 9D2

ST LAMBERT DU LATTAY *4G1* (Urban) **FFCC Camp Municipal La Coudraye, Rue de la Coudraye, 49190 St Lambert-du-Lattay [02 41 78 44 26 or 02 41 78 49 31; miche.rip@wanadoo.fr; www.saintlambertdulattay.fr]** Fr Angers on D160 thro vill cent dir Chemillé. Site sp on L adj wine museum in 200m. Poor sp f N. Sm, hdg pitch, pt sl, pt shd; wc (some cont); chem disp; mv service pnt; shwrs inc; el pnts (10A) €2.65-4.70; gas; lndtte; playgrnd; rv 500m; fishing 50m; entmnt; dogs €0.80; adv bkg. "Lovely, quiet site; wine museums worth visiting; site yourself, warden calls am & pm; gd walking; fair NH." ♦ 1 Apr-31 Oct. € 7.80   2010*

ST LARY SOULAN *8G2* (Rural) *42.81538, 0.32329* **Camp Municipal La Lanne, 65170 St Lary-Soulan [05 62 39 41 58 or 05 62 40 87 85 (LS); fax 05 62 40 01 40; camping@saintlary-vacances.com; www.saintlary-vacances.com]** On Bielsa-Aragnouet rd, sp on on ent vill. Site in side street E of main rd & ent not sp. Look for ent with tall trees at each side. Med, mkd pitch, pt sl, shd; htd wc; chem disp; shwrs inc; el pnts (2-10A) €3-7; gas; lndtte; shop 250m; rest, snacks, bar 400m; playgrnd; htd pool adj; TV rm; adv bkg; quiet; red low ssn. "Vg san facs." ♦ 30 Nov-30 Sep. € 15.00   2008*

⊞ **ST LARY SOULAN** *8G2* (2km N Rural) *42.8400, 0.33983* **Camping Le Rioumajou, 65170 Bourisp [05 62 39 48 32 or 06 07 99 30 09 (mob); info@camping-le-rioumajou.com; www.camping-le-rioumajou.com]** On W side of D929 2km N of St Lary-Soulon & 500m N of Bourisp. Lge, hdg/mkd pitch, hdstg, shd; wc; chem disp; shwrs inc; el pnts (10A) €6; gas; lndtte; shop; tradsmn; rest, snacks, bar; htd pool; playgrnd; tennis; entmnt; TV rm; phone; dogs €1.50; poss cr; Eng spkn; adv bkg; quiet; CKE/CCI. "Conv Bielsa tunnel; St Lary-Soulan attractive; gd walking & watersports." € 17.30   2008*

ST LAURENT DE CERDANS see Prats de Mollo la Preste *8H4*

ST LAURENT DU PAPE see Voulte sur Rhône, La *9D2*

ST LAURENT DU VAR see Cagnes sur Mer *10E4*

ST LAURENT DU VERDON *10E3* (2km W Rural) *43.71066, 6.05789* **Domaine Naturiste d'Enriou (Naturist), 04500 St Laurent-du-Verdon [04 92 74 41 02; fax 04 92 74 01 20; domaine.enriou@voila.fr; www.domainedenriou.com]** Fr Riez foll D11 S, site on D311 to St Laurent-du-Verdon & sp fr D11/D311 junc immed N of Quinson. Med, shd; wc; chem disp; shwrs inc; el pnts (3-6A) €3.60-4; gas; shops; rest, snacks; playgrnd; 2 pools; sw lake 500m; canoes; archery; fishing; entmnt; TV; few statics; dogs €3.80; adv bkg; v quiet; INF card req. "Vg, friendly, peaceful site; lovely spot; conv Gorges du Verdon." 15 May-30 Sep. € 26.50   2009*

ST LAURENT EN BEAUMONT see Salle en Beaumont, La *9C3*

ST LAURENT EN GRANDVAUX *6H2* (500m SE Rural) *46.57645, 5.96214* **Camp Municipal Le Champs de Mars, 8 Rue du Camping, 39150 St Laurent-en-Grandvaux [03 84 60 19 30 or 06 03 61 06 61; fax 03 84 60 19 72; champmars.camping@wanadoo.fr / champmars.camping@orange.fr; www.st-laurent39.fr]** E thro St Laurent on N5 twd Morez, site on R, sp `Caravaneige' at ent. Med, mkd pitch, hdstg, pt sl, pt shd; htd wc; chem disp; mv service pnt; shwrs inc; some serviced pitches; el pnts (4-10A) €3.60-5-90; lndtte; shops & supmkt in vill; playgrnd; TV rm; 20% statics; dogs; phone; adv bkg; quiet; red low ssn; CKE/CCI. "Gd site; peaceful low ssn; gd NH; friendly staff" ♦ 15 Dec-31 Oct. € 26.25   2013*

ST LAURENT MEDOC *7C1* (2km N Rural) *45.17479, -0.83994* **Camping Le Paradis, 8 Rue Fournon, 33112 St Laurent-Médoc [tel/fax 05 56 59 42 15 or 06 27 73 50 00 (mob); leparadismedoc@orange.fr; www.leparadismedoc.com]** On W side of D1215 at Ballac. Med, hdg/mkd pitch, pt shd; wc; chem disp; mv service pnt; baby facs; shwrs inc; el pnts (10A) €4; lndtte; tradsmn; snacks; bar; playgrnd; pool; paddling pool; games area; wifi; entmnt; TV; some statics; dogs €1.60; adv bkg; quiet. "Excel site; helpful staff." 3 Apr-24 Oct. € 14.30   2010*

ST LAURENT NOUAN see Beaugency *4F2*

ST LAURENT SUR SEVRE *2H4* (5km S Rural) *46.92452, -0.87406* **Camp Municipal La Vallée de Poupet, 85590 St Malô-du-Bois [02 51 92 31 45; fax 02 51 92 38 65; camping@valleedepoupet.com; www.valleedepoupet.com]** Fr N on N149 turn S onto D752 at La Trique. At St Malô-du-Bois (4km) foll sp for 4.5km. Fr S fr Mauléon on N149 turn L onto D11 twd Mallièvre; after Mallièvre turn R onto D752. After 2.5km turn R & foll sp. Steep app to site. Med, mkd pitch, pt shd; wc; chem disp; mv service pnt; baby facs; shwrs inc; el pnts (6A) €2.80; lndtte; shops 2km; tradsmn; rest; bar 500m; playgrnd; htd, covrd pool; fishing; entmnt; 10% statics; dogs €1.50; phone adj; Eng spkn; adv bkg; quiet; CKE/CCI. "Excel rvside site." ♦ 15 May-15 Sep. € 18.00   2010*

ST LAURENT SUR SEVRE *2H4* (1km W Rural) *46.95790, -0.90290* **Camping Le Rouge Gorge, Route de la Verrie, 85290 St Laurent-sur-Sèvre [02 51 67 86 39; campinglerougegorge@wanadoo.fr; www.camping-lerougegorge-vendee.com]** Fr Cholet on N160 dir La Roche-sur-Yon; at Mortagne-sur-Sèvre take N149 to St Laurent-sur-Sèvre. In St Laurent foll sp La Verrie on D111. Site on R at top of hill. Or take 762 S fr Cholet to St Laurent. Site sp in town. Med, hdg/mkd pitch, pt sl, pt shd; htd wc; chem disp; mv service pnt; baby facs; shwrs inc; el pnts (4-13A) €2.95-4.10; lndtte (inc dryer); shop; snacks; bar; playgrnd; pool; paddling pool; rv & lake fishing 800m; games area; golf 15km; wifi; 30% statics; dogs €2; adv bkg; quiet; red low ssn; CKE/CCI. "Peaceful family site; woodland walks & mountain biking; attractive sm town; close to Puy du Fou Theme Park" ♦ 15 Mar-30 Sep. € 27.35   2013*

ST LEGER DE FOUGERET see Château-Chinon *4H4*

ST LEGER DU BOURG DENIS see Rouen *3C2*

You can now fill in site reports online

ST LEGER LES MALEZES 9D3 (300m E Rural) 44.64551, 6.20436 **Camping La Pause, Route du Barry, 05260 St Léger-les-Mélèzes [04 92 50 44 92; fax 04 92 50 77 59; info@camping-la-pause.fr; www.camping-la-pause.com]** Fr N85 Route Napoléon turn E onto D14 St Laurent-du Cros. At La Plaine take D113 to St Léger, site sp. Med, pt shd; htd wc; baby facs; chem disp; mv service pnt; shwrs inc; el pnts (2-10A) €2-10; gas; lndtte (inc dryer); shop 100m; rest, snacks; bar; BBQ; playgrnd; htd pool; tennis; horseriding; games area; games rm; wintersports; entmnt; 60% statics; dogs €1.50; adv bkg; quiet. € 13.00   2010*

ST LEGER SOUS BEUVRAY 4H4 (1km N Rural) 46.93157, 4.10088 **Camping De La Boutière, 71990 St Léger-sous-Beuvray [06 80 40 81 28 / 03 85 82 48 86 (ls); camping@ la-boutiere.com; www.la-boutiere.com]** Take N81 SW fr Autun dir Bourbon-Lancy & in approx 10km, turn R onto D61 to St Léger. Site sp in vill. Sm, mkd pitch, pt sl, pt shd; wc; chem disp; shwrs inc; el pnts (6-10A) €3.70; shops 1km; 5% statics; dogs €2.70; phone; wifi; twin-axle c'vans €80; poss cr; quiet; red low ssn; CKE/CCI; "Pleasant, well-kept, Dutch-owned site; gd, modern san facs; vg." 1 Apr-31 Aug. € 16.00   2013*

ST LEON SUR VEZERE see Montignac 7C3

ST LEONARD DE NOBLAT 7B3 (12km N Rural) 45.94311, 1.51459 **Camp Municipal du Pont du Dognon, 87240 St Laurent-les-Eglises [05 55 56 57 25; fax 05 55 56 55 17; mairie-st-laurent-les-eglises@wanadoo.fr]** Take D941 fr St Léonard-de-Noblat; after 1.5km turn L (N) on D19 thro Le Châtenet-en-Dognon. Site in approx 4km, bef St Laurent-les-Eglises. Med, mkd pitch, terr, pt shd; htd wc; shwrs inc; el pnts (5A) €2.62; gas; lndtte; shop & 3km; rest, snacks; BBQ; pool; shgl beach; canoeing; tennis; cycle hire; entmnt; dogs €0.90; adv bkg; quiet. "Vg site." 15 Apr-15 Oct. € 11.25   2009*

ST LEONARD DE NOBLAT 7B3 (2km S Rural) 45.82300, 1.49200 **Camping de Beaufort, 87400 St Léonard-de-Noblat [05 55 56 02 79; info@campingdebeaufort.com; www.campingdebeaufort.com]** Leave A20 S-bound at junc 34 dir St Léonard, onto D941. In 18km on ent St Léonard, 300m after x-ing Rv Vienne, fork R (sp). Site on R in 2km. Med, hdg pitch, pt sl, pt shd; htd wc; chem disp (wc); shwrs inc; el pnts (15A) €3-4; lndtte; shop & 4km; tradsmn; bar; playgrnd; fishing; dogs €1.50; phone; poss cr; adv bkg; ccard acc; CKE/ CCI. ♦ Easter-30 Sep. € 13.00   2012*

ST LEONARD DES BOIS 4E1 (Rural) 48.35353, -0.07669 **Camp Municipal Les Alpes Mancelles, Le Bourg, 72130 St Léonard-des-Bois [02 43 33 81 79; fax 02 43 34 49 02; campalpesmancelles@free.fr; www.ot-alpes-mancelles. com]** SW of Alençon on D1/D121 to Gesvres; turn L onto D149 to St Léonard-des-Bois; site sp on Rv Sarthe. Or easy access fr Fresnay-sur-Sarthe N on D15/D112. Med, mkd pitch, pt sl, pt shd; wc; shwrs inc; el pnts (6A) inc (poss rev pol); lndtte; shop, snacks & bar nrby; playgrnd; rv watersports; dogs €0.50; phone; CKE/CCI. "Pretty, well-run, basic site by rv; gd san facs; well-marked walks; gd touring base; interesting vill." 1 Apr-30 Sep. € 11.40   2009*

ST LEU D'ESSERENT see Chantilly 3D3

ST LOUIS 6G3 (2km N Rural) 47.59428, 7.58930 **Camping au Petit Port, 10 Allée des Marronniers, 68330 Huningue [tel/fax 03 89 69 05 25 03 89 70 01 71; contact@ campinghuningue.fr; www.campinghuningue.fr]** S fr Mulhouse on A35, exit onto D105 & foll sps to Huningue; after level x-ing site sp on rvside. Sm, shd; wc; mv service pnt; shwrs inc; el pnts (6A) €2; shop 1km; rest, bar 500m; htd pool 2km; 50% statics; dogs; bus to Basle; poss cr; quiet. "Excel NH on banks of Rv Rhine; helpful staff; clean facs; poss diff access lge o'fits." ♦ 15 Apr-15 Oct. € 10.40   2010*

ST LUNAIRE see Dinard 2E3

ST MAIXENT L'ECOLE 7A2 (SW Urban) 46.40836, -0.21856 **Camp Municipal du Panier Fleuri, Rue Paul Drévin, 79400 St Maixent-l'Ecole [05 49 05 53 21; fax 05 49 76 50 90]** Take D611 twd Niort, at 2nd set of traff lts nr top of hill out of town turn L. Foll camping sps into ent. Med, mkd pitch, pt sl, pt shd; wc (some cont); mv service pnt; shwrs inc; el pnts (10A); tradsmn; rest, snacks, bar 1km; playgrnd; htd pool adj; tennis; dogs; quiet; ccard not acc. "Warden on site am & eve, if office locked go to house nr wc block; ltd/basic facs low ssn; interesting town; NH en rte Spain."   2010*

ST MALO 2E4 (500m Urban/Coastal) 48.63558, -2.02731 **Camp Municipal Cité d'Alet, Allée Gaston Buy, Saint-Servan 35400 St Malo [02 99 81 60 91 or 02 99 40 71 11 (LS); fax 02 99 40 71 37; camping@ville-saint-malo.fr; www.ville-saint-malo.fr/campings]** Fr ferry terminal go twd St Malo, site sp at rndabt immed past docks. Fr all other dir foll sp for port/ferry, then site sp. Site off Place St Pierre, St Servan-sur-Mer. App thro old part of city poss diff for lge o'fits. Lge, mkd pitch, pt sl, pt shd; wc; chem disp; mv service pnt; shwrs inc; el pnts (10A) inc (poss rev pol & long elec cable poss req); lndtte; shops, tradsmn, rest, snacks 500m; bar; playgrnd; sand beach 500m; dogs €2.35; bus; phone; poss v cr; Eng spkn; adv bkg; quiet; ccard acc; CKE/CCI. "Well-run, scenic site; staff helpful & friendly; sm pitches, access to some diff lge o'fits; san facs basic but OK (poss v slippery); WW2 museum adj; noise fr harbour when foggy; mkt Fri; Parts of site steep, lovely walks, cliff top views of Dinard & St Malo, walk to St Malo worth while" ♦ ltd 26 Apr-21 May, 1 Jul-25 Sep. € 14.40   2013*

ST MALO 2E4 (2km NE Coastal) 48.68173, -1.97748 **Camp Municipal Le Nicet, Ave de la Varde, Rothéneuf, 35400 St Malo [02 99 40 26 32; fax 02 99 21 92 62; camping@ ville-saint-malo.fr; www.ville-saint-malo.fr/campings/]** Fr St Malo take coast (busy & narr) rd Ave JF Kennedy twd Cancale; pass Camping Nielles on L bef district of Rotheneuf; turn L at camping sp just after sm g'ge on L; turn L at T-junc; site in view. Med, mkd pitch, pt sl, pt terr, unshd; wc; chem disp, shwrs inc; el pnts (5-10A) inc (rev pol); lndtte; shops 800m; tradsmn; playgrnd; sand beach adj; dogs €2.30; poss cr & noisy high ssn; Eng spkn; adv bkg; ccard acc; CKE/CCI. "Clean, well-run site on cliff top; can be exposed if pitched nr edge with sea view; secluded beach via steep steps; some pitches sm." ♦ 1 Jul-1 Sep. € 17.50   2009*

FRANCE

ST MALO 2E4 (8km NE Coastal) 48.69000, -1.94200
**Camping des Chevrets, La Guimorais, 35350 St Coulomb
[02 99 89 01 90; fax 02 99 89 01 16; campingdeschevrets@
wanadoo.fr; www.campingdeschevrets.fr]** St Malo to
Cancale coast rd D201; La Guimorais on L 3km E of Rothéneuf,
strt thro vill; fairly narr app. V lge, hdg/mkd pitch, pt sl, pt shd;
wc; chem disp; mv service pnt; baby facs; shwrs inc; el pnts
(6A) €3.35 (poss rev pol); gas; lndtte; shop; rest, snacks; bar;
BBQ; playgrnd; sand beach adj; games area; cycle hire; internet;
entmnt; 50% statics; dogs; poss cr; Eng spkn; adv bkg; quiet;
ccard acc; red low ssn/long stay; CKE/CCI. "Vg location with 2
bays; vg site." ♦ 6 Apr-1 Nov. € 21.95   2009*

ST MALO 2E4 (1km E Coastal) 48.66737, -1.98486
**Camp Municipal Les Nielles, 47 Ave du Président
Kennedy, Paramé, 35400 St Malo [02 99 40 26 35; fax
02 99 21 92 62; camping@ville-saint-malo.fr; www.
ville-saint-malo.fr/campings/]** Fr cent of St Malo (avoiding
old walled town) E on D201 parallel & adj to coast; few site
sp & poss not easy to find. Med, mkd pitch, unshd; wc (some
cont); shwrs inc; el pnts (10A) inc; shop 900m; rest, bar 500m;
playgrnd; sand beach adj; fishing; dogs €2.40; poss cr; some rd
noise. "Excel for beach & ferry; pitches nr beach v exposed if
weather bad." ♦ 1 Jul-31 Aug. € 17.25   2009*

⊞ **ST MALO** 2E4 (5km S Urban) 48.65762, -1.95932
**Camping De La Fontaine, 40 Rue de la Fontaine
aux Pèlerins, 35400 St Malo [02 99 81 62 62; fax
02 99 81 68 95; contact@campinglafontaine.com; www.
campinglafontaine.com]** N fr Rennes on D137 turn R onto
D301 sp Cancale. Turn R onto D155 sp Mont-St Michel, site in
L in 100m. Med, hdg/mkd pitch, pt shd; htd wc; chem disp; mv
service pnt; baby facs; fam bthrm; shwrs; el pnts (10A) €3.80
(poss rev pol); gas; lndtte; shop & 250m; tradsmn; rest, snacks;
bar; BBQ; htd pool; sand beach 5km; cycle hire; games area;
bouncy castle; table tennis; wifi; entmnt; 80% statics; dogs €3;
phone; poss cr; quiet; ccard acc; red low ssn; CKE/CCI. "Gd
touring base; conv ferry" € 23.30   2013*

ST MALO 2E4 (5km SE Rural) 48.60916, -1.98663 **Camping
Le P'tit Bois, La Chalandouze, 35430 St Jouan-des-Guérets
[02 99 21 14 30; fax 02 99 81 74 14; camping.ptitbois@
wanadoo.fr; www.ptitbois.com]** Fr St Malo take D137
dir Rennes; after o'skts of St Malo turn R twd St Jouan-des-
Guérets, site sp. Lge, hdg/mkd pitch, pt shd; wc; chem disp; mv
service pnt; baby facs; shwrs inc; el pnts (10A) inc; gas; lndtte
(inc dryer); shop; rest, snacks; bar; BBQ (gas/elec); playgrnd;
2 htd pools; (1 covrd); waterslides; paddling pool; jacuzzi;
turkish bath; sand beach 2km; tidal rv fishing, watersports
2km; tennis; cycle hire; wifi; entmnt; games/TV rm; 50% tour
ops/statics; dogs €4-6; lge c'vans/m'vans by request; adv bkg;
ccard acc; min 3 persons high ssn; red low ssn/CKE/CCI. "Well-
kept, well-run site; busy even low ssn; friendly, helpful staff; gd
clean san facs, one block unisex; some narr site rds poss diff lge
o'fits; conv Le Mont-St Michel & ferries; excel" ♦
6 Apr-15 Sep. € 58.60 (3 persons) SBS - B03   2013*

ST MALO 2E4 (3km S Rural) 48.61469, -1.98663
**Camping Domaine de la Ville Huchet, Rue de la
Passagère, Quelmer, 34500 St Malo [02 99 81 11 83;
fax 02 99 81 51 89; info@lavillehuchet.com; www.
lavillehuchet.com]** Fr ferry port, foll sps for D137 dir Rennes;
site sp fr 'Madeleine' rndabt on leaving St Malo. Or fr S on
D137 take D301 sp St Malo centre. Take 1st exit at next
2 rndabts (thro indus est) & cont on this rd (sharp R-hand
bend), then under bdge, site on R. New rndabts poss under
construction on this rte in 2010/11. Lge, hdg/mkd pitch, pt
sl, pt shd; wc; chem disp; mv service pnt; baby facs; shwrs
inc; el pnts (6A) inc; lndtte (inc dryer); shop; rest, snacks; bar;
BBQ (charcoal/gas, sep area); playgrnd; 2 htd pools (1 covrd
pool planned for 2011); paddling pool; water park; sand
beach 4km; cycle hire; games area; games rm; wifi; entmnt;
TV; 40% statics; dogs €3.50; no c'vans/m'vans over 7.50m
except by request; poss cr; Eng spkn; adv bkg; quiet, but some
rd noise; red low ssn. "Spacious site in grnds of sm chateau;
helpful owner; modern san facs; lge pitches avail; some
pitches v shady; conv ferries & Mont St Michel." ♦
6 Apr-23 Sep. € 34.60 SBS - B32   2011*

See advertisement

ST MALO DU BOIS see St Laurent sur Sèvre 2H4

ST MARCEL D'ARDECHE see Pont St Esprit 9D2

ST MARCELLIN *9C2* (7km E Rural) *45.12122, 5.33775*
Camping Château de Beauvoir, 38160 Beauvoir-en-Royans
[04 76 64 01 79; fax 04 76 38 49 60; chateaudebeauvoir@
wanadoo.fr] On D1092 Romans to Grenoble, turn into narr
uphill rd D518 to vill; L into site, sp. Care needed on app rd
& ent gate narr. Sm, shd; htd wc; shwrs inc; el pnts (10A) €2;
lndtte; shop 6km; bar; rest 2km; 10% statics; dogs; adv bkg
rec; quiet; "Vg site on château lawn; gd walking."
1 Apr-31 Oct. € 11.60   2013*

⊞ **STE MARIE AUX MINES** *6E3* (1km E Urban) *48.23520,
7.16995* FFCC Camping Les Reflets du Val d'Argent,
20 Rue d'Untergrombach, 68160 Ste Marie-aux-Mines
[03 89 58 64 83; fax 03 89 58 64 31; reflets@calixo.net;
www.les-reflets.com] Fr Sélestat N59 into Ste Marie. Go thro
vill to traff lts & turn L. 1km to site; sp. Med, hdg/mkd pitch, pt
sl, pt shd; htd wc; chem disp; mv service pnt; shwrs inc; el pnts
(5-15A) €3.30-9.90; lndtte; shop & 1km; tradsmn; rest, snacks;
bar; BBQ; playgrnd; pool; games rm; TV; 5% statics; dogs
€3.50; phone; adv bkg; quiet; red low ssn; CKE/CCI. "Pleasant
site but facs run down & need refurb; winter skiing 5km." ♦
€ 17.20   2008*

STE MARIE DU MONT *1D4* (6km NE Coastal) *49.41935,
-1.18118* Camping Utah Beach, La Madeleine, 50480
Ste Marie-du-Mont [02 33 71 53 69; fax 02 33 71 07 11;
contact@camping-utahbeach.com; www.camping-
utahbeach.com] 50km S of Cherbourg on N13 turn L onto
D913 to Ste Marie-du-Mont. Foll D913 to coast & sp to Utah
Beach Memorial - approx 4km. Site on beach rd D421. Med,
hdg/mkd pitch, pt sl, pt shd; wc; chem disp; mv service pnt;
shwrs inc; el pnts (6A) inc; gas; lndtte; shop; tradsmn; snacks;
bar; playgrnd; htd pool; sand beach 50m; water/beach sports;
tennis; games rm; archery; internet; entmnt; excursions;
55% statics; dogs €2.90; phone; quiet; adv bkg; red low
ssn; ccard acc; red low ssn; red CKE/CCI. "Well-kept site; gd
touring base; site of US landing in 1944; gd birdwatching."
1 Apr-20 Sep. € 24.30   2008*

See advertisement on pages 32 & 33

STE MARIE DU MONT *1D4* (3km SE Coastal) *49.36564,
-1.17721* Camping La Baie des Veys, Le Grand
Vey, 50480 Ste Marie-du-Mont [02 33 71 56 90 or
06 09 82 61 82 (mob); jerome.etasse@orange.fr; www.
campinglabaiedesveys.com] N of Carentan exit N13 onto
D913 thro Ste Marie-du-Mont. At lge calvary 2km after vill,
turn R onto D115 sp Le Grand Vey. Turn R at sea edge, site on
R in 100m. Med, hdg/mkd pitch, pt shd; wc; chem disp (wc);
shwrs inc; el pnts (6A) €3; lndtte; shop & 6km; snacks; bar;
BBQ; htd pool; cycle hire; wifi; 10% statics; dogs free; Eng
spkn; adv bkg; quiet. "Site beside salt flats; helpful, friendly
owners; gd birdwatching, fishing; conv Utah Beach, D-Day
museums etc." ♦ ltd 1 May-15 Sep. € 16.00   2010*

STES MARIES DE LA MER *10F2* (700m E Coastal) *43.45633,
4.43576* Camping La Brise, Rue Marcel Carrière, 13460 Les
Stes Maries-de-la-Mer [04 90 97 84 67; fax 04 90 97 72 01;
info@camping-labrise.fr; www.camping-labrise.fr] Sp on
o'skts on all rds. Take N570 fr Arles or D58 fr Aigues-Mortes.
V lge, unshd; htd wc (mainly cont); mv service pnt; shwrs inc;
el pnts (16A) €4.90; lndtte (inc dryer); sm shop & 500m; rest
500m; snacks; BBQ; 2 htd pools; paddling pool; beach adj;
fishing; fitness area; wifi; entmnt; TV rm; some statics; dogs
€5.20; site clsd mid-Nov to mid-Dec; red low ssn. "Gd facs;
v cr Aug; poss mosquitoes; gd security; beach improved with
breakwaters; m'vans can use free municipal car park with facs;
recep open fr 0900-1700 but clsed 1200-1400; vg winter Nov;
pitches poorly mrkd, dirty & dusty." ♦ 1 Jan-11 Nov, 16 Dec-
31 Dec. € 22.80 (CChq acc)   2013*

ST MARTIAL DE NABIRAT see Gourdon *7D3*

ST MARTIAL ENTRAYGUES see Argentat *7C4*

ST MARTIN D'ARDECHE see Pont St Esprit *9D2*

ST MARTIN DE CRAU *10F2* (W Urban) *43.63750, 4.80570*
Camping La Crau, 4 Ave de St Roch, 13310 St Martin-
de-Crau [04 90 47 17 09; fax 04 90 47 09 92; contact@
campingdelacrau.com; www.campingdelacrau.com] Fr W
take D453 sp St Martin-de-Crau. L at 1st traff lts. Fr E take
D453 thro town & R at traff lts by Hotel. Site behind Hôtel de
la Crau, 50m up side rd running N off D453 on D83b. Fr N (St
Rémy) on D27 turn R in town & as bef. Med, hdg/mkd pitch,
shd; wc (some cont); chem disp; mv service pnt; shwrs inc;
el pnts (6A) inc; lndtte; shop & 300m; tradsmn; rest, snacks;
bar; playgrnd; pool (high ssn); TV rm; dogs €2; Eng spkn; adv
bkg; poss noise fr local airfield; red long stay/low ssn; ccard
acc (Visa); CKE/CCI. "Site run by adj hotel; poss itinerants; facs
dated (plans for upgrading); special private pitch extra; noisy
nr pool; under-staffed low ssn; gd birdwatching; mkt Fri." ♦
Apr-Oct. € 22.00   2008*

ST MARTIN DE LONDRES *10E1* (2km E Rural) *43.79180,
3.73911* FFCC Camping Le Pic St-Loup, 34380 St Martin-de-
Londres [04 67 55 00 53; fax 04 67 55 00 04; depelchinp@
aol.com] Fr Ganges take D986 S. In St Martin turn L onto
D122, site sp. Med, some hdg/mkd pitch, pt sl, pt shd; wc;
chem disp; shwrs inc; el pnts (6A) inc; gas; lndtte; shop; rest,
snacks; bar; playgrnd; htd covrd pool; 10% statics; poss cr; adv
bkg; quiet but some rd noise; ccard not acc; red long stay; CKE/
CCI. "Friendly, helpful owner; some pitches sm for van, awning
& car; lger pitches on lower terr; dated san facs; excel pool;
lower field muddy when wet." 1 Apr-30 Sep. € 20.00   2009*

ST MARTIN DE SEIGNANX see Bayonne *8F1*

ST MARTIN DE VALAMAS 9C2 (500m N Rural) 44.94249, 4.36779 Camp Municipal La Teyre, 07310 St Martin-de-Valamas [04 75 30 47 16] At N end of vill across single-track bdge. Well sp. Sm, mkd pitch, pt shd; wc (cont); chem disp (wc); shwrs inc; el pnts (6A) inc; lndry rm; playgrnd; games area; quiet. "Lge pitches; vg." ♦ ltd 1 May-30 Sep. € 12.00   2009*

ST MARTIN DES BESACES 1D4 (W Rural) 49.00923, -0.85738 Camping Le Puits, La Groudière, 14350 St Martin-des-Besaces Calvados [tel/fax 02 31 67 80 02; enquiries@lepuits.com; www.lepuits.com] Fr Caen SW on A84 dir Rennes, Villers-Bocage & exit junc 41 to St Martin-des-Besaces. At traff lts in vill turn R & foll site sp, site on L at end of vill in 500m. Fr Cherbourg foll sp St Lô onto m'way. After Torini-sur-Vire at junc with A84 foll sp Caen & exit junc 41, then as above. Sm, hdg/mkd pitch, pt sl, pt shd; wc; chem disp; mv service pnt; shwrs inc; el pnts (6A) €5 (poss rev pol); gas; lndtte; shop 500m; tradsmn; rest 500m; snacks; bar; BBQ; sm playgrnd; pool 10km; sand beach 35km; lake adj; fishing; cycling; equestrian trails; entmnt; no statics; dogs €1.50; adv bkg; quiet, but some rd noise; red low ssn; ccard acc; CKE/CCI. "Pleasant CL-type orchard site; welcoming, helpful Irish owners; no arr bef 1400; lge pitches with garden; 'super' pitches extra cost; san facs v basic & inadequate if site full - little privacy; B&B in farmhouse; suitable for rallies up to 30 vans; c'van storage; war museum in vill; conv Caen ferries; excel" ♦ 1 Mar-31 Oct. € 29.00   2013*

"I need an on-site restaurant"

We do our best to make sure site information is correct, but it is always best to check any must-have facilities are still available or will be open during your visit.

ST MARTIN EN CAMPAGNE 3B2 (3km N Coastal) 49.96631, 1.20469 Camping Domaine Les Goélands, Rue des Grèbes, 76370 St Martin-en-Campagne [02 35 83 82 90; fax 02 35 83 21 79; domainelesgoelands@orange.fr; www.lesdomaines.org] Fr Dieppe foll D925 twd Le Tréport & Abbeville. Turn L at rndabt on D113 twd St Martin-en-Campagne. Cont thro vill to St Martin-Plage (approx 3km) & foll 'Camping' sp to site on L. Lge, hdg/mkd pitch, hdstg, pt sl, terr, pt shd; htd wc; 100% serviced pitches; chem disp; baby facs; shwrs inc; el pnts (16A) inc (poss rev pol); gas; lndtte; shop 1km; tradsmn; snacks (& in vill), bar high ssn; BBQ; playgrnd; htd pool & waterslide 1km; sand/shgl beach 500m; fishing; tennis; cycle hire; golf 20km; horseriding, archery 15km; TV; 40% statics; dogs €2; Eng spkn; adv bkg; quiet; ccard acc; red CKE/CCI. "Gd touring area; ltd recep hrs low ssn; no late arr area; poss resident workers low ssn; mkt Dieppe Sat; vg site." ♦ 1 Mar-8 Nov. € 25.50   2010*

ST MARTIN EN HAUT see Ste Foy l'Argentiere 9B2

ST MARTIN EN VERCORS see Chapelle en Vercors, La 9C3

ST MARTIN LARS see Ste Hermine 2H4

⊞ **ST MARTIN SUR LA CHAMBRE** 9B3 (2km N Rural) 45.36883, 6.31458 Camping Le Petit Nice, Notre Dame-de-Cruet, 73130 St Martin-sur-la-Chambre [tel/fax 04 79 56 37 72 or 06 76 29 19 39 (mob); campinglepetitnice@yahoo.fr; www.camping-petitnice.com] Fr N on A43 exit junc 26 & foll sp to cent of La Chambre, thro town to rndabt & turn R into Rue Notre Dame-du-Cruet. Foll site sp & in 2km turn R thro housing, site on L in 200m. Sm, terr, pt shd; htd wc; chem disp; shwrs inc; el pnts (3-10A) €3; lndtte; shop & 2km; rest, snacks; bar; playgrnd; pool; wifi; 80% statics; dogs €1; poss cr; Eng spkn; adv bkg; quiet; CKE/CCI. "By stream with mountain views; clean, modern san facs." ♦ € 13.00   2009*

ST MARTIN SUR OUST see Rochefort en Terre 2F3

ST MATHIEU 7B3 (3km E Rural) 45.71413, 0.78835 Camp Municipal du Lac, Les Champs, 87440 St Mathieu [05 55 00 34 30 (Mairie); fax 05 55 48 80 62] On D699 heading E in dir of Limoges 1.8km fr vill turn on L (N). Sp fr vill cent. Med, hdg/mkd pitch, terr, pt shd; wc; baby facs; shwrs €3.50; el pnts €3; lndtte; shops 3km; rest adj; playgrnd; lake sw & beach; windsurfing; pedalos; dog €3.50; quiet. "Attractive, well-kept site; pleasant situation on lakeside; lge pitches; site yourself, warden calls; beautiful lake with lots of activities." 1 May-30 Sep. € 18.00   2013*

ST MATHIEU 7B3 (9.5km SW Rural) 45.67752, 0.63937 Camp Municipal St Martial, Le Cros de l'Ouvrage, 24360 Busserolles [tel/fax 05 53 60 53 04; mairie.busserolles@wanadoo.fr; www.campingbusserolles.com] Fr S on D675 turn W onto D90 to Busserolles. Fr N turn off at St Mathieu onto D699 & then S onto D88. Site sp in Busserolles. Sm, hdg/mkd pitch, pt sl, pt shd; wc; chem disp (wc); shwrs inc; el pnts inc; lndtte; shop 10km; BBQ; playgrnd; lake sw adj; games area; dogs €1; adv bkg; quiet; CKE/CCI. "Peaceful site in sm vill; vg." 15 Jun-15 Sep. € 11.00   2008*

STE MAURE DE TOURAINE 4H2 (6km NE Rural) 47.14831, 0.65453 Camping Le Parc de Fierbois, 37800 Ste Catherine-de-Fierbois [02 47 65 43 35; fax 02 47 65 53 75; contact@fierbois.com; www.fierbois.com or www.les-castels.com] S on D910 fr Tours, thro Montbazon & cont twd Ste Maure & Châtellerault. About 16km outside Montbazon nr vill of Ste Catherine look for site sp. Turn L off main rd & foll sp to site. Or exit A10 junc 25 onto D760E, then D910 N sp Tours; in 6.5 km turn R to Ste Catherine-de-Fierbois; site on L 1.5km past vill. Lge, hdg/mkd pitch, pt shd; wc; chem disp; mv service pnt; baby facs; shwrs inc; el pnts (10A) €5; lndtte (inc dryer); shop; rest, snacks; bar; BBQ; playgrnd; 2 htd pools (1 covrd); waterslide; paddling pool; sand/shgl beach at lake; boating; fishing; tennis; cycle hire; games area; games rm; wifi; entmnt; TV; statics; dogs free; twin-axles acc (rec check in adv); poss cr; Eng spkn; adv bkg; ccard acc; red low ssn; CKE/CCI. "Excel, well-kept family site; helpful staff; gd touring base; peaceful low ssn; rec." ♦ 23 Apr-7 Sep. € 44.00 SBS - L20   2011*

See advertisement on inside back cover

Tell us about the sites you visit

STE MAURE DE TOURAINE *4H2* (1.5km SE Rural) *47.10483, 0.62574* **Camp Municipal Marans, Rue de Toizelet, 37800 Ste Maure-de-Touraine [02 47 65 44 93; www.tourisme-saintemauredetouraine.fr]** Fr A10 take Ste Maure exit junc 25 & foll D760 twd Loches. At 4th rndabt turn L & then immed R. Site on R in 500m. Site sp fr m'way. Med, mkd pitch, pt shd; wc; chem disp; mv service pnt; shwrs inc; el pnts (10A) €3.20 (poss long cables req); supmkt 500m; shops, rest, bar 1km; BBQ; playgrnd; pool 1.5km; fishing; tennis; roller blade court; dogs €1.42; phone; Eng spkn; adv bkg; quiet. "Well-kept, basic site; cheerful staff; gd, clean facs - poss stretched when busy; if office clsd site yourself; barrier down 2200-0700; late arr area outside barrier; no twin-axles; poss itinerants in sep area; vg." ♦ 10 Apr-30 Sep. € 7.80   2011*

⊞ **STE MAURE DE TOURAINE** *4H2* (1.5km S Rural) *47.10861, 0.61440* **Aire de Service Camping-Cars Bois de Chaudron, 37800 Ste Maure-de-Touraine [02 47 34 06 04]** Fr S on D910 dir Tours, as ent town, site on R adj junc at traff lts; sm sp on dual-c'way. Sm; wc; mv service pnt; shwrs; el pnts €2 (on only some pitches); lndtte; wifi; m'vans only. "New Aire de Service (2009); warden calls; conv N/S journeys." € 5.00   2009*

> ## "Satellite navigation makes touring much easier"
> Remember most sat navs don't know if you're towing or in a larger vehicle – always use yours alongside maps and site directions.

STE MAURE DE TOURAINE *4H2* (6km W Rural) *47.10705, 0.51016* **Camping du Château de la Rolandière, 37220 Trogues [tel/fax 02 47 58 53 71; contact@larolandiere.com; www.larolandiere.com]** Exit A10 junc 25 onto D760 dir Chinon & L'Ile-Bouchard. Site sp on S side of rd in 5.5km. Sm, hdg/mkd pitch, pt sl, pt shd; wc; chem disp; baby facs; shwrs inc; el pnts (10A) €4.40 (poss long lead req); gas 6km; lndtte (inc dryer); shop 4km; supmkt 9km; tradsmn; snacks; bar; BBQ; playgrnd; htd pool; paddling pool; rv & sand beach 4km; games area; games rm; wifi; TV rm; dogs €3; Eng spkn; adv bkg; quiet; red low ssn; CKE/CCI. "Beautiful, well-maintained, family-run site in chateau grnds; friendly, helpful owners; gd clean san facs; excel for young families; gd dog walking; conv Loire chateaux." ♦ Apr-30 Sep. € 24.50   2011*

ST MAURICE D'ARDECHE see Aubenas *9D2*

ST MAURICE DE LIGNON *9C1* (1km E Rural) *45.22299, 4.15156* **FFCC Camping du Sabot, 813 Route du Stade, 43200 St Maurice-de-Lignon [04 71 65 32 68; campingdusabot@aol.com; www.campingdusabot.fr]** Take N88 N fr Yssingeaux or S fr St Etienne. Site well sp in St Maurice. Med, mkd pitch, pt terr, pt shd; htd wc (some cont); chem disp; mv service pnt; shwrs; el pnts (6A) €3.60; lndtte; shops; rest, snacks 250m: BBQ; playgrnd; games area; wifi; 70% statics; dogs €1; phone 500m; poss cr; Eng spkn; adv bkg; quiet. "Warm welcome; helpful owner; blocks poss req; v busy w/ends; ltd touring pitches; conv touring base; mkd walks fr site." 15 Apr-15 Oct. € 11.00   2010*

ST MAURICE L'EXILE (1.4km N) *45.40240* **Camping La Colombière, 20 Rue Mata, La Colombier, 38550 Saint-Maurice l'Exile [(033) 474 862 567; contact@camping-lacolombiere.com; www.ww.camping-lacolombiere.com]** Fr N7 turn off at exit St Maurice-l'Exile, foll sp to vill. Take exit rd sp Vienne (toll Free) via RN7 exit to vill and foll sp to site Sm,hdg pitch, pt shd; wc (cont); mv service pnt; child baby facs; fam bthrm; shws; lndry rm; el pnts 9A; dogs; playgrnd; pool (htd); games area; entmnt; wifi; waterslide; tennis; quiet; Eng spkn; ccard acc; "Lovely warm welcome, heated indoor pool, wifi"♦ 1 Apr-31-Oct. € 18.50   2012*

⊞ **ST MAURICE SUR MOSELLE** *6F3* (4.5km NE Urban) *47.88888, 6.85758* **Kawan Village Domaine de Champé, 14 Rue des Champs Navés, 88540 Bussang [03 29 61 61 51; fax 03 29 61 56 90; info@domaine-de-champe.com; www.domaine-de-champe.com]** Fr N66/E512 in Bussang, site from town sq. Opp Avia filling stn. Med, hdg/mkd pitch, pt sl, pt terr, pt shd; htd wc (some cont); chem disp; mv service pnt; baby facs; sauna; shwrs; el pnts (6-10A) €5-6; lndtte (inc dryer); shop 500m; tradmsn; rest, snacks; bar; BBQ; playgrnd; htd pool; paddling pool; waterslide; rv 1km; tennis; cycle hire; fitness rm; games area; games rm; wifi; entmnt; TV; 10% statics; dogs €3; phone; bus 1km; poss cr; Eng spkn; quiet; adv bkg; ccard acc; red low ssn; CKE/CCI. "Excel site behind hospital grnds; lovely views; welcoming, helpful owners; dated but clean unisex san facs; vg rest; excel walks, cycle path." ♦ ltd € 25.00 (CChq acc)   2012*

ST MAURICE SUR MOSELLE *6F3* (10km E Rural) *47.88170, 6.94435* **Camp Municipal Bénélux-Bâle, Rue de la Scierie, 68121 Urbès [03 89 82 78 76 or 03 89 82 60 91 (Mairie); fax 03 89 82 16 61; mairie.urbes@wanadoo.fr; www.urbes.fr.st]** Site off N66 on N side of rd at foot of hill rising W out of Urbès. At foot of Col de Bessang. Lge, hgd/mkd pitch, pt shd; wc; chem disp; shwrs; el pnts (4-10A); lndtte; bar; playgrnd; rv & lake sw & fishing adj; dogs; 60% statics; adv bkg rec high ssn; quiet; CKE/CCI. "Gd sh stay/NH; beautiful area." 1 Apr-31 Oct.   2008*

ST MAURICE SUR MOSELLE *6F3* (W Rural) *47.8555, 6.8117* **Camping Les Deux Ballons, 17 Rue du Stade, 88560 St Maurice-sur-Moselle [03 29 25 17 14; stan@camping-deux-ballons.fr; www.camping-deux-ballons.fr]** On N66 on E side of rd in vill, site on L before petrol stn. Clearly sp. Lge, mkd pitch, pt sl, pt shd; wc; chem disp; mv service pnt; baby facs; shwrs inc; el pnts (4-15A) €4.15-5.20; gas; lndtte; shop 500m; snacks; bar; pool; waterslide; tennis; games rm; internet; TV rm; dogs €3.20; phone; poss cr; Eng spkn; adv bkg; quiet; red low ssn; ccard not acc; CKE/CCI. "Some pitches sm; excel site; cycle path fr site." ♦ 17 Apr-27 Sep. € 20.30   2008*

STE MAXIME *10F4* (2.5km N Rural) *43.32536, 6.62213* **Camping La Beaumette, Route du Plan de la Tour, 83120 Ste Maxime [04 94 96 10 92 or 04 94 96 14 35 (LS); fax 04 94 96 35 38; camping@labeaumette.com; www.labeaumette.com]** Leave Ste Maxime on D25 dir Le Muy, site on L. Med, shd; wc (own san rec); chem disp; shwrs inc; el pnts (6A) €5; lndry rm; shop 500m; pool; beach 1km; dogs; 50% statics; dogs €1; phone; quiet; adv bkg; CKE/CCI. "Vg site; open to end Oct if gd weather but liable to flood in severe weather." ♦ ltd 1 Apr-30 Sep. € 21.00 (CChq acc)   2008*

FRANCE

STE MAXIME *10F4* (5km NE Coastal) *43.33028, 6.66800* **Camping Les Cigalons, La Nartelle, 83120 Ste Maxime [04 94 96 05 51; fax 04 94 96 79 62; contact@ campingcigalon.fr; www.campingcigalon.fr]** Site on D559 E of Ste Maxime, go thro La Nartelle & turn L into lane immed after seafood rest. Site on L after 25m. Med, mkd pitch, pt sl, shd; wc; chem disp; shwrs; el pnts (10A) €4; lndtte; sm shop; rest, snacks, bar adj; paddling pool; sand beach adj; wifi; some statics; dogs €2.50; poss cr; adv bkg; v quiet. "Site in gd position; friendly owners; dated san facs; sm v hard compacted earth pitches; car parking poss diff." ♦ 4 Apr-17 Oct. € 26.00   2010*

ST MAXIMIN LA STE BAUME *10F3* (3km S Rural) *43.42848, 5.86498* **Camping Caravaning Le Provençal, Route de Mazaugues, 83470 St Maximin-la-Ste Baume [04 94 78 16 97; fax 04 94 78 00 22; camping.provencal@ wanadoo.fr; www.camping-le-provencal.com]** Exit St Maximin on N560 S twd Marseilles. After 1km turn L onto D64. Site on R after 2km. Lge, mkd pitch, pt sl, shd; wc; mv service pnt; shwrs inc; el pnts (6-10A) €3.40-4.40; gas; lndtte; shop & bar; rest high ssn; snacks; bar; playgrnd; pool; TV; some statics; adv bkg; CKE/CCI. "gd NH" 1 Apr-30 Sep. € 16.10   2012*

ST MAYEUX see Mur de Bretagne *2E3*

ST MEDARD DE GUIZIERES *7C2* (500m N Rural) *45.01989, -0.05876* **Camp Municipal Le Gua, Terrain du Guâ, 33230 St Médard-de-Guizières [tel/fax 05 57 69 82 37]** On N89 bet Libourne & Montpon-Ménestérol; in St Médard foll sp 'Base de Loisirs'; site adj sw pool. Med, mkd pitch, shd; wc (some cont); chem disp (wc); shwrs inc; el pnts €2.60; shop, rest, snacks, bar 500m; playgrnd; pool adj; rv fishing adj; dogs; quiet. "Conv Bordeaux, St Emillion & vineyards; vg." ♦ ltd 15 Jun-15 Sep. € 7.00   2009*

⊞ **ST MEDARD DE GUIZIERES** *7C2* (4km S Rural) *44.99694, -0.06330* **FLOWER Camping Le Pressoir, Queyrai, 33570 Petit-Palais-et-Cornemps [05 57 69 73 25; fax 05 57 69 77 36; contact@campinglepressoir.com; www. campinglepressoir.com or www.flowercampings.com]** Leave A89/E70 junc 11 onto D1089 E to St Médard-de-Guizières; then take D21 S & foll site sp 'Le Pressoir' (site bef Petit-Palais). Fr Castillon-la-Bataille on D936 Bergerac-Bordeaux rd take D17/D21 sp St Médard & foll site sp. Take care on access & exit. Med, hdg/mkd pitch, pt sl, pt shd; htd wc; chem disp; shwrs inc; el pnts (10A) inc; gas; lndtte; shop; tradsmn; rest, snacks; bar; BBQ; playgrnd; htd pool; cycle hire; games area; wifi; entmnt; TV rm; 30% statics; dogs €1.90; Eng spkn; adv bkg; quiet; ccard acc; red low ssn; CKE/CCI. "Close to vineyards; basic san facs; gd rest; 90% static tents and chalets not much space for tourers. Facs excel but busy; lovely area for cycling" ♦ € 26.50   2012*

See advertisement on pages 32 & 33

STE MENEHOULD *5D1* (1km E Rural) *49.08937, 4.90969* **Camp Municipal de la Grelette, Chemin de l'Alleval, 51800 Ste Menéhould [06 73 91 98 83 (mob) or 03 26 60 80 21 (Mairie); fax 03 26 60 62 54; mairie@ ste-menehould.fr; www.ste-menehould.fr]** Exit A4 junc 29 to Ste Menéhould; foll sp 'Centre Ville' thro town to Mairie & central sq on D3; then foll sp 'Piscine' & 'Camping' on D3; cont uphill with rlwy on R; turn R over narr rlwy bdge, then L to site in 200m. Sm, pt sl, pt shd; wc; shwrs inc; chem disp; el pnts (4A) €3.40; lndtte nryby; tradsmn; supmkt 500m; rest, snacks, bar 1km; pool adj; dogs €1.05; poss cr; adv bkg; Eng spkn; no ccard acc; CKE/CCI. "Delightful site; helpful warden; recep 08.00-10.00 & 18.00-20.00, access to o'fits over 2m poss restricted at other times, confirm dep with warden; vg, clean san facs; interesting old town." 1 May-30 Sep. € 6.50   2011*

STE MERE EGLISE *1C4* (9.5km NE Coastal) *49.46650, -1.23540* **Kawan Village Le Cormoran, 2 Rue du Cormoran, 50480 Ravenoville-Plage [02 33 41 33 94; fax 02 33 95 16 08; lecormoran@wanadoo.fr; www. lecormoran.com]** NE on D15 fr Ste Mère-Eglise to Ravenoville, turn L onto D14 then R back onto D15 to Ravenoville Plage. Turn R on D421, Rte d'Utah Beach, site on R in 1km. Or fr N13 sp C2 Fresville & ent Ste Mère-Eglise, then take D15. Lge, hdg/mkd pitch, some hdstg, unshd; wc; chem disp; mv service pnt; baby facs; sauna; shwrs inc; el pnts (6A) inc; gas; lndtte (inc dryer); shop; tradsmn; snacks; bar; BBQ (charcoal/ gas); playgrnd; 2 htd pools (1 covrd); paddling pool; jacuzzi; sand beach adj (across main rd); tennis; cycle hire; horseriding; games area; archery; wifi; entmnt; TV/games rm; 60% statics; dogs €3; twin-axles acc (rec check in adv); poss cr; Eng spkn; adv bkg; quiet; ccard acc; red low ssn; CKE/CCI. "Popular, family-run site; lge pitches; warm welcome, helpful recep; well-kept san facs, poss tired end of ssn; poss v windy; vg children's facs; special pitches for early dep for ferry; m'van o'night area; excel." ♦ 5 Apr-28 Sep. € 33.00 (CChq acc) SBS - N12   2011*

STE MERE EGLISE *1C4* (500m E Urban) *49.41006, -1.31078* **Camp Municipal, 6 Rue due 505eme Airborne, 50480 Ste Mère-Eglise [02 33 41 35 22; fax 02 33 41 79 15; mairie-sme@wanadoo.fr; www.sainte-mere-eglise.info]** Fr Cherbourg S on N13 to cent of Ste Mère-Eglise (avoiding by-pass); at vill sq turn L on D17 to site, next adj sports grnd. Med, some hdstg, pt sl, pt shd, wc (some cont); chem disp (wc); shwrs inc; el pnts (12A) €4 (poss rev pol); gas 500m; lndtte; shop & bar 500m; rest, snacks, BBQ; playgrnd; sand beach 10km; tennis; cycle hire; 5% statics; games rm; dogs €1.50; phone; poss cr; little Eng spkn; adv bkg; CKE/CCI. "Nice, basic site; clean facs; friendly warden; if warden absent site yourself & pay later; conv ferries & D-Day beaches etc; gates open 6am for early dep; rec." ♦ 15 Mar-1 Oct. € 23.00   2011*

ST MICHEL CHEF CHEF see Pornic *2G3*

ST MICHEL DE DEZE see Collet-de-Dèze, Le *9D1*

You can now fill in site reports online

⊞ **ST MICHEL DE MAURIENNE** *9C3* (500m SE Rural) *45.21276, 6.47858* **FFCC Camping Le Marintan, 1 Rue de la Provalière, 73140 St Michel-de-Maurienne [04 79 59 17 36; contact@gite-lemarintan.com; http://gite-lemarintan.com/camping]** Fr D1006 foll sp in town to 'Centre Touristique' & 'Maison Retraite'. Rue de la Provalière is a L turn fr D1006 immed bef rlwy bdge. Sm, hdg pitch, unshd; htd wc; chem disp; shwrs inc; el pnts inc; lndtte (inc dryer); shops in town; rest; bar; pool; some statics; dogs €1; quiet. "Gd touring base, but no character; conv forskiing at Val Thorens via gondola lift at Orelle." € 11.95 2013*

> ## "There aren't many sites open at this time of year"
>
> If you're travelling outside peak season remember to call ahead to check site opening dates – even if the entry says 'open all year'.

ST MICHEL EN GREVE *2E2* (1km NE Coastal) *48.69277, -3.55694* **Camping Les Capucines, Voie Romaine, Kervourdon, 22300 Trédez-Locquémeau [02 96 35 72 28; fax 02 96 35 78 98; les.capucines@wanadoo.fr; www.lescapucines.fr]** Fr Lannion on D786 SW twd St Michel-en-Grève, sp Morlaix; in approx 700m, after steep descent & 'Landebouch' sp, turn R & R again in 100m at x-rds. Fr Roscoff take D58 to join N12 at junc 17; NE of Morlaix at next junc turn onto D786 twd Lannion; site down narr app rd on L on leaving St Michel-en-Grève (slow down at town exit sp), then R at x-rds. Med, hdg/mkd pitch, pt sl, pt shd; wc; chem disp; mv service pnt; all serviced pitches; baby facs; shwrs inc; el pnts (10A) inc; gas; lndtte (inc dryer); shop & 1km; tradsmn; snacks; bar; BBQ (charcoal/gas); playgrnd; htd, covrd pool; paddling pool; sand beach 1km; watersports 1km; cycle hire; games rm; games area; wifi; games/TV rm; 15% statics; dogs €2; phone; no c'vans/m'vans over 9.50m high ssn; Eng spkn; adv bkg; quiet; ccard acc; red low ssn/long stay; CKE/CCI. "Excel, peaceful, well-kept site; gd sized pitches; helpful owners; clean san facs; gd pool; gd touring base; mkt Lannion Thu." ♦ 2 Apr-23 Sep. € 27.00 SBS - B13 2011*

See advertisement

ST MICHEL ESCALUS see Léon *8E1*

ST MIHIEL *5D2* (1km NW Rural) *48.90209, 5.53978* **Camping Base de Plein Air, 1Chemin du Gué Rappeau, 55300 St Mihiel [03 29 89 11 70 / 06 75 10 18 94 (mob); fax 03 29 89 07 18; base.de.plein.air@wanadoo.fr; www.tourisme-lorraine.fr]** Site on W bank of rv. Sp app St Mihiel. Fr town cent take rd sp Bar-le-Duc (D901) 1st R after rv bdge. Med, mkd pitch, pt shd; htd wc (mainly cont); chem disp; mv service pnt; shwrs inc; el pnts (10A) €2.60; lndtte; shops, rest, bar 1km; tradsmn; playgrnd; htd pool 1km; canoeing & sailing; games area; TV; 10% statics; bus 1km; adv bkg; quiet; CKE/CCI; "Site developed as youth cent; facs clean but tired; pleasant scenery; lge pitches; very friendly" 1 Apr-1 Nov. € 9.00 2013*

STE NATHALENE see Sarlat la Canéda *7C3*

ST NAZAIRE EN ROYANS see St Jean en Royans *9C2*

ST NAZAIRE LE DESERT *9D2* (200m E Rural) *44.56952, 5.27750* **Camp Municipal, 26340 St Nazaire-le-Désert [04 75 26 42 99 or 04 75 27 52 31 (LS); info@camping-stnazaire.com; www.camping-stnazaire.com]** Well sp in St Nazaire-le-Désert. Med, mkd pitch, terr, shd; wc (own san rec); chem disp (wc); shwrs inc; el pnts €3; shops nrby; rest, snacks; bar; BBQ; playgrnd; htd pool; games rm; wifi; entmnt; dogs; phone; no twin-axles; poss cr; Eng spkn; adv bkg rec high ssn. "Busy, friendly site in beautiful location; v lge o'fits poss diff to pitch; gd." 1 May-30 Sep. € 10.00 2009*

ST NECTAIRE *9B1* (1km SE Rural) *45.57971, 3.00173* **Camping Le Viginet, chemin du Manoir, 63710 St Nectaire [04 73 88 53 80 or 08 25 80 14 40; fax 04 73 88 41 93; info@camping-viginet.com; www.camping-viginet.com]** Exit A75/E11 junc 14 onto D996 dir Mont-Doré. In E side of St Nectaire (opp Ford g'ge) turn sharp L up v steep hill; rd widens after 100m; site on R after bends. Car park at site ent. Med, hdg/mkd pitch, pt sl, pt shd; wc; chem disp; mv service pnt; baby facs; shwrs inc; el pnts (10A) €4; gas; lndry rm; shops, rest & bar 1.5km; snacks; playgrnd; pool; dogs €2;Eng spkn; poss cr; adv bkg; quiet; ccard not acc; CKE/CCI. "Nice pitches; gd views; gd sm pool; gd walking in hills around site" ♦ ltd 1 Apr-30 Sep. € 29.90 2013*

ST NECTAIRE 9B1 (500m S Rural) 45.57556, 3.00169 **Camping La Clé des Champs, Les Sauces, Route des Granges, 63710 St Nectaire [04 73 88 52 33; campingcledechamps@free.fr; www. campingcledeschamps.com]** S bound exit A75 at junc 6 to join D978 sp Champeix; N bound exit junc 14 to join D996 sp Champeix/St Nectaire. In St Nectaire turn L at VW/Audi g'ge on L (site sp); site 300m on L. Med, hdg/mkd pitch, pt sl, pt shd; wc (some cont); chem disp; mv service pnt; shwrs inc; el pnts (2-6A) €2.10-3.50 (poss rev pol); gas; lndtte; shops 1km; playgrnd; pool; wifi; some statics; dogs €2; poss cr; adv bkg; poss noisy high ssn; red low ssn; CKE/CCI. "Well-kept, clean site; spectacular scenery; helpful owner; vg san facs." ♦ 9 Apr-1 Oct. € 18.00   2011*

ST NECTAIRE 9B1 (1km S Rural) 45.57541, 2.99942 **Camping La Vallée Verte, Route des Granges, 63710 St Nectaire [04 73 88 52 68; lavalleeverte@neuf.fr; www.valleeverte. com]** Fr A75 exit junc 6 onto D978 & D996 to St Nectaire. On ent o'skts St Nectaire turn L immed at site sp, site in 300m. Med, pt shd; htd wc; chem disp; mv service pnt; fam bthrm; shwrs inc; el pnts (5-8A) €3-3.50; lndtte (inc dryer); shop; tradsmn; snacks; bar; playgrnd; lake sw 5km; 20% statics; dogs €1.50; phone; Eng spkn; adv bkg; quiet; red low ssn; CKE/CCI. "Vg, friendly, well-maintained, family-run site." ♦ 15 Apr-18 Sep. € 15.00   2011*

ST NIC 2E2 (1.5km SW Coastal) 48.19373, 4.30157 **Camping Domaine de Ker-Ys, Pentrez-Plage, 29550 St Nic [02 98 26 53 95; fax 02 98 26 52 48; info@homair.com; www.ker-ys.com]** Turn W off D887 onto D108 & into St Nic, & foll sp Pentrez-Plage & site. Lge, pt shd; wc; chem disp; baby facs; shwrs inc; el pnts (10A) inc; gas; lndtte (inc dryer); shop; snacks; BBQ; bar; htd pool complex; paddling pool; waterslide; sand beach adj; watersports; tennis; games area; wifi; entmnt; TV rm; some statics; dogs €2.50; adv bkg; ccard acc; red low ssn. "Gd family site in lovely location; vg beach; friendly, helpful staff." ♦ 1 Apr-15 Sep. € 28.00   2010*

ST NICOLAS DU PELEM 2E3 (1.5km SW Rural) 48.30983, -3.17923 **Camp Municipal de la Piscine, Croas-Cussuliou, Rue de Rostrenen, 22480 St Nicolas-du-Pélem [02 96 29 51 27; fax 02 96 29 59 73]** Fr Rostrenen, take D790 NE twd Corlay. In 11km, turn L sp St Nicolas-du-Pélem. Site in 500m on R, opp pool. Med, pt shd; wc (some cont); chem disp (wc); shwrs inc; el pnts (10A) inc; gas; shops 1.5km; htd pool opp; dogs; quiet; CKE/CCI. "Clean, well-kept site; choose own pitch, warden will call; excel touring base." ♦ ltd 15 Jun-15 Sep. € 10.00   2012*

ST NIZIER LE DESERT 9A2 (E Rural) 46.05447, 5.15911 **Camp Municipal La Niziere, 01320 St Nizier-le-Désert [04 74 30 35 16 or 06 74 33 13 48 (mob); fax 04 74 30 32 78; laniziere@cc-chalamont.com]** Fr Bourg-en-Bresse take D1083 SW for 4km, L onto D22 dir Dompierre-sur-Veyle (13km). Turn R onto D90 at Les Brires at camping sp, site in 2km on R by lakeside. Med, mkd pitch, shd; wc (mostly cont); mv service pnt; shwrs inc; el pnts (6A) €2; lndry rm; shop 500m; playgrnd; fishing; tennis; 75% statics; quiet. "Unspoilt, peaceful site; off beaten track; access poss diff for c'vans; gd cycling." 15 Apr-31 Aug. € 10.00   2008*

ST OMER 3A3 (8km NE Rural) 50.80152, 2.33924 **Camping La Chaumière, 529 Langhemast Straete, 59285 Buysscheure [03 28 43 03 57; camping.lachaumiere@ wanadoo.fr; www.campinglachaumiere.com]** Take D928 fr St Omer (see NOTE) twd Bergues & Watten & foll sp St Momelin. Stay on rd until Lederzeele & turn R onto D26 twds Cassel. After approx 2km turn R just bef rlwy bdge sp Buysscheure & site. Turn L after church, R, then site on L 500m. Single-track rd after church. NOTE on D928 fr St Omer height limit 3m; use adj level x-ing sp rte for vehicles over 3m. NB app fr Cassel diff, especially for wide or long o'fits; also rd thro Cassel cobbled & poss more diff to find. Sm, hdg/mkd pitch, hdstg; pt sl, unshd; wc; chem disp; mv service pnt; baby facs; shwrs inc; el pnts (6A) inc; lndry rm; shop 1km; rest, snacks; bar; BBQ; playgrnd; htd pool; paddling pool; fishing lake; cycle hire; archery; entmnt; wifi; TV; dogs €1; Eng spkn; adv bkg; quiet, but poss some rlwy noise; ccard not acc; red low ssn; CKE/CCI. "Lovely, well-kept site; friendly, family-run; conv ferries - but poss no exit bef 0800; gd sized pitches - some may req o'fit manhandling due hedges; gd san facs, ltd in number, stretched when site full; no arr bef 12 noon; close to WW1/WW2 sites; local vet; excel; Friendly well kept site, gd bar and food" ♦ 1 Apr-30 Sep. € 22.00   2013*

ST OMER 3A3 (10km E Rural) 50.73490, 2.37463 **FFCC Camping Le Bloem Straete, 1 Rue Bloemstraete, 59173 Renescure [03 28 49 85 65 / 06 80 21 28 46 (ls); lebloemstraete@yahoo.fr; www.lebloemstraete.fr]** E fr St Omer on D642 thro Renescure dir Hazebrouck; turn L (site sp) onto D406 Rue André Coo on bend on leaving Renescure; over level x-ing; site on L thro gates. Sm, hdg pitch, hdstg, pt shd; htd wc; chem disp (wc); shwrs inc; el pnts (2-6A) €2.50 (poss rev pol); lndtte; shop, rest, snack & bar 1km; playgrnd; tennis; games rm; wifi; 70% statics; dogs; poss cr; Eng spkn; quiet; adv bkg; CKE/CCI. "Conv Calais ferry & tourist sites; manoeuvring poss diff due high kerbs; m'van area; poss lack of maintenance early ssn (2011); Very helpful owners, site clean and tidy; Worth finding!; Excel facs; easy access to ports" ♦ ltd 15 Apr-15 Oct. € 16.00   2013*

ST OMER 3A3 (3km SE Urban) 50.74612, 2.30566 **Camp Municipal Beauséjour, Rue Michelet, 62510 Arques [tel/fax 03 21 88 53 66; camping-arques@wanadoo.fr; www. ville-arques.fr]** Fr junc 4 of A26 foll sp Arques to town cent. Foll sp Hazebrouck. After x-ring canal site sp 'Camping ***' on L. NB Drive 25m bef correct turning to site. Site signs small and easily missed. Med, hdg/mkd pitch, pt sh; wc; chem disp; mv service pnt; baby facs; shwrs inc; el pnts (6A) €3 (poss rev pol); lndtte; shops, rest, snack & bar 1.5km; BBQ playgrnd; lake fishing; 80% statics; dogs; phone, wifi; Eng spkn; adv bkg; some noise fr rlwy & mill across lake; ccard acc; CKE/CCI. "Neat, tidy site; well-run; lge pitches but tight access; friendly, helpful warden; excel, clean facs; m'van o'night area adj (no el pnts); site boggy when wet; gd cycling along canal; lakes & nature park nrby; conv Cristal d'Arques; canal lift & preserved rlwy in town; Calais & Dunkerque 50 mins drive; useful NH; vg." ♦ 1 Apr-31 Oct. € 18.00   2013*

ST OMER 3A3 (5km NW Rural) 50.78310, 2.18790
**Camping Le Frémont, 62910 Serques [03 21 39 86 55;
campinglefremont@aol.com]** Fr D943 Calais-St Omer, site on
L 1.5km SE of Moulle past Tilques exit just over brow of hill on
D943 - don't overshoot. Med, sl, terr, pt shd; wc; chem disp;
shwrs €1.35; el pnts (10A) inc; lndtte; shop; rest, snacks 2km;
bar; pool 5km; golf 4km; 90% statics; adv bkg; some noise.
"Basic site (6 pitches); conv Calais ferry; gd san facs; gd NH."
♦ 1 Apr-15 Oct. € 16.30   2008*

ST OMER 3A3 (10km NW Rural) 50.81890, 2.17870 **Kawan
Village Château du Gandspette, 133 Rue du Gandspette,
62910 Eperlecques [03 21 93 43 93 or 03 21 12 89 08 (LS);
fax 03 21 95 74 98; contact@chateau-gandspette.com;
www.chateau-gandspette.com]** Fr Calais SE on A26/E15 exit
junc 2 onto D943 foll sp Nordausques-St Omer. 1.5km after
Nordausques turn L onto D221 twd Eperlecques; site 5km on
L. Do not ent Eperlecques. (Larger o'fts should cont on D943
fr Nordausques to Tilques; at rndabt foll sp for Dunkerque
(D300) then D221 dir Eperlecques, site on R. Med, hdg/mkd
pitch, some hdstg, pt sl, pt shd; wc; chem disp; mv service pnt;
baby facs; shwrs inc; el pnts (6A) inc (some rev pol); gas; lndtte
(inc dryer); supmkt 800m; tradsmn; rest (high ssn); snacks;
bar; BBQ (charcoal/gas); playgrnd; 2 pools (1 htd); fishing
3km; horseriding & golf 5km; tennis; cycle hire; wifi; entmnt;
games/TV rm; 15% statics; dogs €1; no c'vans/m'vans over
8m; phone; poss cr; Eng spkn; adv bkg; quiet; ccard acc; red
low ssn; CKE/CCI. "Beautiful, well-kept, busy site; spacious,
mainly sl pitches; charming, helpful owners; superb, clean san
facs; vg pool & playgrnd; excel rest; site poss muddy in wet;
conv NH for ferries - early dep catered for; poss poor security;
gd for dogs; rec visit WW2 'Le Blockhaus' nr site; conv A26;
highly rec; conv for ferry to Dover" ♦ 29 Mar-30 Sep. € 38.00
(CChq acc) SBS - P08   2013*

ST PABU 2E1 (2km NW Coastal) 48.57643, -4.62854
**Camping L'Aber Benoît, 89 Rue de Corn ar Gazel,
29830 St Pabu [02 98 89 76 25; info@camping-aber-
benoit.com; www.camping-aber-benoit.com]**
E fr Ploudalmézeau on D28; in 5km L to St Pabu. Site sp in
vill. Med, hdg pitch, pt shd; wc; chem disp; mv service pnt;
baby facs; shwrs inc; el pnts (6A) €3; lndtte; shop, rest (high
ssn); snacks; BBQ; playgrnd; beach 100m; wifi; entmnt; TV rm;
10% statics; dogs €1; poss cr; CKE/CCI. "Facs stretched high
ssn; vg." ♦ Easter-30 Sep. € 11.90   2013*

ST PAIR SUR MER see Granville 1D4

ST PALAIS (GIRONDE) see Mirambeau 7C2

ST PALAIS SUR MER 7B1 (1km N Rural/Coastal) 45.65163,
-1.10898 **Camping Le Logis, 22 Rue des Palombes, 17420
St Palais-sur-Mer [05 46 23 20 23 or 05 46 22 38 22;
fax 05 46 23 10 61 or 05 46 23 65 10; reservations@
yukadivillages.com; www.yukadivillages.com]** On rd N out
of Royan, after vill of St Palais-sur-Mer, site sp on R after petrol
stn. V lge, pt sl, terr, shd; htd wc (some cont); chem disp; baby
facs; shwrs inc; el pnts (6A) inc; lndtte (inc dryer); shop & 2km;
tradsmn; snacks; bar; BBQ; playgrnd; pool; paddling pool;
waterslide; aquapark; shgl beach 1km; tennis; games area; wifi;
entmnt; TV; 35% statics; dogs; poss cr; Eng spkn; adv bkg;
ccard acc; red low ssn. "La Palmyre zoo nr; excel water park."
17 May-7 Sep. € 38.50   2010*

ST PALAIS SUR MER 7B1 (7km N Rural) 45.67550,
-1.09670 **Camping Le Logis du Breuil, 17570 St Augustin
[05 46 23 23 45; fax 05 46 23 23 43 33; info@logis-du-breuil.
com; www.logis-du-breuil.com]** N150 to Royan, then D25
dir St Palais-sur-Mer. Strt on at 1st rndabt & 2nd rndabt; at
next rndabt take 2nd exit dir St Palais-sur-Mer. At next traff
lts turn R dir St Augustin onto D145; site on L. NB Sat nav can
direct thro diff & narr alternative rte. Lge, mkd pitch, pt shd, pt
sl; wc (some cont); chem disp; mv service pnt; baby facs; shwrs
inc; el pnts (6A) inc (50m cable poss req); gas; lndtte (inc dryer);
shop; supmkt; rest, snacks; bar; BBQ (gas/elec); playgrnd; pool;
paddling pool; sand beach 5km; fishing 1km; tennis; cycle
hire; horseriding 400m; golf 3km; excursions; games area;
games rm; wifi; entmnt; games/TV rm; 10% statics; dogs €3;
no c'vans over 12m; phone; poss cr; Eng spkn; adv bkg; ccard
acc; red low ssn; CKE/CCI. "Nice peaceful site; lge pitches in
wooded area; gd alt to cr beach sites; friendly owner; san facs
clean; gd for young families; excel." ♦
12 May-30 Sep. € 27.50 SBS - A04   2011*

ST PALAIS SUR MER 7B1 (8km N Rural) 45.68888, -1.11034
**Camping Les Vignes, 3 Rue des Ardilliers, 17570
St Augustin [tel/fax 05 46 23 23 51; campinglesvignes17@
alicepro.fr; www.campinglesvignes17.com]** On app Royan
on D733, after x-ing D14 turn R sp St Palais (by-pass Royan
cent). At rndabt on D25 foll sp St Augustin. Site on R. Med,
mkd pitch, pt shd; wc (some cont); shwrs; el pnts (5-10A)
€3.90-4.70; gas; lndtte; shop; tradsmn; rest, snacks; bar;
playgrnd; pool, paddling pool 200m; waterslides; cycle hire;
wifi; entmnt; 70% statics; dogs €1.50; phone; adv bkg; red
long stay/low ssn; CKE/CCI. "Remote, peaceful, welcoming
site; basic facs, ltd low ssn; immac pools." ♦ Easter-1 Nov.
€ 15.70   2009*

ST PALAIS SUR MER 7B1 (500m NE Coastal) 45.64245,
-1.07677 **Camping de Bernezac, 2 Ave de Bernezac, 17420
St Palais-sur-Mer [05 46 39 00 71; fax 05 46 38 14 46;
acccf-ber@wanadoo.fr; www.acccf.com]** Foll sp off Royan-
St Palais coast rd. Med, pt shd; wc; chem disp; mv service pnt;
50% serviced pitches; baby facs; shwrs inc; el pnts (6A) €3.70
(poss rev pol); lndtte; shop 800m; rest, snacks; BBQ; playgrnd;
beach adj; lake fishing 1km; entmnt; TV; 30% statics; dogs €1;
Eng spkn; adv bkg; quiet. "Helpful, friendly staff."
15 Mar-15 Oct. € 20.80   2009*

ST PALAIS SUR MER 7B1 (1.5km E Rural/Coastal)
45.64656, -1.07300 **Camping Les Ormeaux, 44 Ave de
Bernezac, 17420 St Palais-sur-Mer [05 46 39 02 07; fax
05 46 38 56 66; campingormeaux@aliceadsl.fr; www.
camping-ormeaux.com]** Foll sp fr D25 Royan-St Palais rd.
Rec app ent fr R. Ent & camp rds narr. Lge, pt shd; wc; baby
facs; shwrs inc; el pnts (6A) €7.50; gas; lndtte; shop; snacks;
bar; playgrnd; htd pool; sand beach 800m; entmnt; TV;
98% statics; dogs €4; quiet; red low ssn. "Ltd touring area &
access diff for lge o'fits or m'vans - tents or sm m'vans only."
♦ 1 Apr-31 Oct. € 27.00 (3 persons)   2009*

FRANCE

ST PALAIS SUR MER *7B1* (2km E Coastal) *45.64396, -1.06325* Camping Le Val Vert, 108 Ave Frédéric Garnier, 17640 Vaux-sur-Mer [05 46 38 25 51; fax 05 46 38 06 15; camping-val-vert@wanadoo.fr; www.val-vert.com] Fr Saintes on N150 dir Royan; join D25 dir St Palais-sur-Mer; turn L at rndabt sp Vaux-sur-Mer & Centre Hospitaliers; at traff lts ahead; at 2nd rndabt take 3rd exit & then turn immed R. Site on R in 500m. Med, hdg pitch; wc; chem disp; mv service pnt; baby facs; shwrs inc; el pnts (6A) €5.50 or (10A) €6.00; gas; lndtte; shop; rest, snacks; gas/elec BBQ; playgrnd; htd pool; paddling pool; sand beach 900m; watersports; fishing; cycle hire; tennis 400m; horseriding & golf 5km; games area; games rm; some wifi; entmnt; dogs €3.40; no c'vans/m'vans over 6.50m high ssn; adv bkg; ccard acc; red low ssn; "Well-kept, family-run site; gd sized pitches; unisex san facs; no twin-axles; a stream runs alongside site; sh walk to pleasant vill; daily mkt in Royan; excel" ♦ ltd 6 Apr-30 Sep. € 31.30 (3 persons) (CChq acc) SBS - A25   2013*

ST PALAIS SUR MER *7B1* (2km SE Coastal/Urban) *45.64272, -1.07183* Camping Nauzan-Plage, 39 Ave de Nauzan-Plage, 17640 Vaux-sur-Mer [05 46 38 29 13; fax 05 46 38 18 43; info@campinglenauzanplage.com; www.campinglenauzanplage.com] Take either coast rd or inland rd fr Royan to Vaux-sur-Mer; site not well sp. Lge, mkd pitch, pt shd; wc; chem disp; baby facs; shwrs inc; el pnts (10A) €5.50; gas; lndtte; shop; supmkt 1km; rest, snacks; bar; playgrnd; sm pool; sand beach 450m; tennis 200m; games/TV rm; 10% statics (sep area) dogs €5; adv bkg (rec Jul/Aug); quiet; red low ssn/long stay; CKE/CCI. "Gd site; helpful staff; gd cycling rtes." ♦ 1 Apr-30 Sep. € 32.00 (3 persons)   2010*

ST PALAIS SUR MER *7B1* (3km NW Coastal) *45.6500, -1.1193* Camping La Côte de Beauté, 157 Ave de la Grande Côte, 17420 St Palais-sur-Mer [05 46 23 20 59; fax 05 46 23 37 32; campingcotedebeaute@wanadoo.fr; www.camping-cote-de-beaute.com] Fr St Palais-sur-Mer foll sp to La Tremblade & Ronce-les-Bains. Site on D25, 50m fr beach, look for twin flagpoles of Camping Le Puits de l'Auture & lge neon sp on R; site in 50m. Med, hdg pitch, shd; htd wc; baby facs; shwrs inc; el pnts (6A) €4.20; lndtte; supmkt adj; tradsmn; rest, snacks; bar; playgrnd; sand beach 200m across rd; tennis, cycle hire adj; golf 2km; some statics; dogs €3; adv bkg; quiet; red low ssn. "Clean, tidy site; friendly staff; steep descent to beach opp - better beach 600m twd La Tremblade; cycle track to St Palais & Pontaillac." 1 May-30 Sep. € 25.80 (3 persons)   2010*

ST PALAIS SUR MER *7B1* (3km NW Coastal) *45.6482, -1.1108* Camping La Grande Côte, 167 Ave de la Grande Côte, 17420 St Palais-sur-Mer [tel/fax 05 46 23 20 18; info@campinglagrandecote.com; www.campinglagrandecote.com] Fr Royan, take D25 thro St Palais, site on R where rd runs close to sea. Look for flags. Med, mkd pitch, pt shd; htd wc; baby facs; shwrs inc; el pnts (6A) €4.20; gas; lndtte; rest adj; bar; BBQ; sand beach 200m; dogs €3; bus; quiet; CKE/CCI. "Helpful staff; excel site." ♦ 1 May-12 Sep. € 23.60   2009*

ST PALAIS SUR MER *7B1* (3km NW Coastal) *45.64930, -1.11785* Camping Le Puits de l'Auture, La Grande Côte, 17420 St Palais-sur-Mer [05 46 23 20 31; fax 05 46 23 26 38; campingpuitsdelauture@voila.fr; www.camping-puitsdelauture.com] Fr Royan take D25 onto new rd past St Palais foll sp for La Palmyre. At 1-way section turn back L sp La Grande Côte & site is 800m; rd runs close to sea, flags at ent. Lge, pt shd; htd wc; serviced pitches; baby facs; shwrs inc; el pnts (10A) inc; gas; lndtte; shop; snacks; bar; playgrnd; htd pool; sand beach opp & 500m; fishing; games area; internet; 25% statics; no dogs; poss cr; Eng spkn; adv bkg rec; quiet; red low ssn; ccard acc; CKE/CCI. "Well-maintained, well laid-out, excel site; san facs stretched high ssn & 'tired'; poss cr but carefully controlled; friendly, helpful staff." ♦ 1 May-30 Sep. € 31.00 (3 persons)   2008*

ST PANTALEON *7D3* (4km NE Rural) *44.36760, 1.30634* Camping des Arcades, Moulin de St Martiel, 46800 St Pantaléon [05 65 22 92 27 or 06 80 43 19 82 (mob); fax 05 65 31 98 89; info@des-arcades.com; www.des-arcades.com] Fr N20 3km S of Cahors take D653 sp Montcuq, after 17km site in hamlet of St Martial on L. Med, mkd pitch, pt sl, pt shd; wc; chem disp; shwrs inc; el pnts (6A) €4; lndtte; sm shop; tradsmn; rest, snacks; bar; BBQ; playgrnd; htd pool; paddling pool; lake sw & fishing adj; wifi; 5% statics; dogs €1.50; Eng spkn; adv bkg; quiet; red low ssn; ccard acc; CKE/CCI. "Vg Dutch-owned site with restored 13thC windmill; sm lake; clean facs." ♦ 23 Apr-30 Sep. € 20.00   2012*

ST PARDOUX *9A1* (4km SW Rural) *46.03752, 2.95436* Camping Elan, Route de Villemorie, 63440 Blot-l'Eglise [04 73 97 51 70 or 06 10 21 40 58 (mob); fr@camping-elan.com; www.camping-elan.com] Fr N on N144 take D16 to Blot, fr S take D50, foll site sp. Sm, hdg/mkd pitch, pt shd; wc; chem disp (wc); shwrs inc; el pnts (5-10A) €2.50-4.50; gas 200m; lndry rm; shop 200m; rest, snacks; bar; playgrnd; tennis; games area; TV; dogs €1; no twin-axles; Eng spkn; adv bkg; quiet; red low ssn/long stay/CKE/CCI. "In beautiful area; lge pitches; friendly Dutch owners; clean but basic san facs; site open low ssn by arrangement; gd touring base; conv Vulcania; gd." 1 Apr-30 Sep. € 12.50   2009*

ST PARTHEM see Decazeville *7D4*

ST PAUL DE FENOUILLET *8G4* (7km E Rural) *42.80811, 2.6058* Camping Le Maurynate, La Caunette Basse, 66460 Maury [04 68 67 11 01; lemaurynate@orange.fr; www.lemaurynate.fr] W fr St-Paul-de-Fenouillet on D117 to Maury in 6km; cont past Maury on D117; site on L in 1km, just bef level x-ing. Sm, hdg/mkd pitch, pt shd; htd wc; chem disp; mv service pnt; baby facs; shwrs inc; el pnts (10A) €3.50; lndtte; sm shop; BBQ; playgrnd; dogs €2.00; Eng spkn; adv bkg; quiet; some rd noise; CKE/CCI. "Vg site; prehistoric history region." 1 Apr-31 Aug. € 24.70   2013*

ST PAUL DE FENOUILLET *8G4* (7km E Rural) *42.80782, 2.60579* Camping Le Maurynate (Formerly Municipal Les Oliviers), 66460 Maury [04 68 67 11 01; fax 04 68 59 08 74; lemaurynate@orange.fr; http://www.lemaurynate.fr] Heading W on D117. Site immed after level x-ing on R 500m bef Maury. Sm, mkd pitch, shd; wc (cont); shwrs inc; el pnts; shop, rest, bar 1km; playgrnd; CKE/CCI. "Some rd noise fr level x-ing; immac san facs" 1 Apr-30 Aug. € 16.50   2012*

⊞ **ST PAUL DE FENOUILLET** 8G4 (S Rural) 42.80762, 2.50235 **Camping de l'Agly, Ave 16 Août 1944, 66220 St Paul-de-Fenouillet [04 68 59 09 09; fax 04 68 59 11 04; contact@camping-agly.com; www.camping-agly.com]** Heading W on D117; turn L at traff lts in St Paul; site on R in 200m, well sp. Sm, hdg/mkd pitch, pt sl, pt shd; wc; chem disp; shwrs inc; el pnts (16A) €4.20; gas & supmkt 500m; pool 1km; rv sw 500m; quiet; red low ssn; site clsd Jan; CKE/CCI. "Vg site; friendly warden; mountain scenery; gd climbing & cycling; conv for Château's Payrepertuse & Quéribus" ♦ € 15.35   2012*

ST PAUL DE VARAX see Bourg en Bresse 9A2

ST PAUL DE VEZELIN 9B1 (3.5km N Rural) 45.91159, 4.06615 **Camping d'Arpheuilles, Lac de Villerest, 42590 St-Paul-de-Vézelin [04 77 63 43 43; arpheuilles@wanadoo.fr; www.camping-arpheuilles.com]** Take D53 fr Roanne 10km. Turn L onto D8 twd St German-Laval. Turn L at Dancé onto D112 to St-Paul-de-Vézelin. Turn L on ent to vill. Or fr A72 exit junc 5 onto D8, then D26. V diff single track fr vill (3km) - v steep in places. Med, mkd pitch, pt sl, pt shd; wc (some cont); chem disp; mv service pnt; shwrs inc; el pnts (5-6A) €3; gas; lndtte; shop; tradsmn; rest, snacks; bar; BBQ; playgrnd; pool; paddling pool; lake sw & sand beach adj; TV; few statics; dogs free; phone; Eng spkn; adv bkg; 20% red 3+ days; quiet. "Beautiful location; helpful owner; well-managed with gd facs; various sports facs." 1 May-10 Sep. € 19.50   2010*

ST PAUL EN FORET see Fayence 10E4

ST PAULIEN 9C1 (2.5km SW Rural) 45.12041, 3.79357 **Camping de la Rochelambert, 43350 St Paulien [04 71 00 54 02; fax 04 71 00 54 32; infos@camping-rochelambert.com; www.camping-rochelambert.com]** Fr St Paulien take D13; turn L onto D25 sp La Rochelambert; site on L in 1.5km. Med, mkd pitch, terr, pt shd; wc (some cont); chem disp; mv service pnt; shwrs inc; el pnts (10A) €3.10; lndtte; shop 3km; tradsmn; snacks; bar; BBQ; playgrnd; pools; paddling pool; tennis; 15% statics; dogs €1.50; phone; poss cr; Eng spkn; adv bkg; quiet; red low ssn; CKE/CCI. "Gd touring base; gd walking & fishing; app poss diff lge/long o'fits; gd." ♦ ltd 1 Apr-30 Sep. € 16.60   2011*

ST PEE SUR NIVELLE see St Jean de Luz 8F1

⊞ **ST PEREUSE** 4H4 (1km SE Rural) 47.05720, 3.81580 **Camping Le Manoir de Bezolle, 58110 St Péreuse-en-Morvan [03 86 84 42 55; fax 03 86 84 43 77; info@ camping-bezolle.com; www.camping-bezolle.com]** 9km W of Château-Chinon on D978 Autun-Nevers. Site sp at junc with D11 to St Péreuse on N side of D978. Med, pt sl, pt terr, pt shd; wc htd; chem disp; mv service pnt; baby facs; shwrs inc; el pnts (10A) inc (long lead poss req & avail on loan); lndtte; vg shop; rest, snacks; bar; BBQ (charcoal/gas/elec); playgrnd; 2 pools; paddling pool; lakeside walks; fishing; wifi; entmnt; dogs €2; no c'vans/m'vans over 8m; quiet; ccard acc; red low ssn; CKE/CCI. "Peaceful, well-kept site; most pitches shaded; gd views fr upper pitches; some steep site rds; friendly, helpful Eng owners; modern, well-kept san facs; gd pool; gd food in rest; rest, shop, bar & pools clsd low ssn; gd touring base Morvan National Park & Burgundy; excel walks adj to site; excel." ♦ € 32.00 (CChq acc) SBS - L19   2011*

ST PHILBERT DE GRAND LIEU 2H4 (400m N Rural) 47.04202, -1.64021 **Camping La Boulogne, Ave de Nantes, 44310 St Philbert-de-Grand-Lieu [32 40 78 88 79; fax 32 40 78 76 50; accueil@camping-la-boulogne.com; www. camping-la-boulogne.com]** Fr Nantes on A83 exit junc 1 or 2 onto D178 - D117 dir St Philbert; turn L onto D65 (Ave de Nantes) to St Philbert; site on R in 500m adj rv & sp. Or fr Machecoul take bypass to St Philbert & then D65 as narr rds thro town. Med, hdg/mkd pitch, pt shd; wc; chem disp; baby facs; shwrs inc; el pnts (6A) inc; lndtte; shops & supmkt 500m; tradsmn; bar; BBQ; playgrnd; htd, covrd pool 200m; lake adj; fishing; games area; wifi; entmnt; 10% statics; dogs €1; phone; bus adj; no twin-axles; Eng spkn; adv bkg; quiet; red low ssn; CKE/CCI. "Well-kept, secure site; new enthusiastic, helpful owners (2010); gd." ♦ 1 Apr-31 Oct. € 13.50   2011*

ST PIERRE D'ALBIGNY see Montmelian 9B3

ST PIERRE D'ARGENCON see Aspres sur Buëch 9D3

ST PIERRE DE CHARTREUSE 9C3 (2km S Rural) 45.32570, 5.79700 **Camping de Martinière, Route du Col de Porte, 38380 St Pierre-de-Chartreuse [04 76 88 60 36; fax 04 76 88 69 10; camping-de-martiniere@orange.fr; www. campingdemartiniere.com]** Site is situated on D520B thro Gorge-du-Guiers-Mort after St Pierre-de-Chartreuse. Med, mkd pitch, pt shd; htd wc; chem disp; mv service pnt; baby facs; shwrs inc; el pnts (2-10A) €2-7.20; gas; lndtte (inc dryer); shop; tradsmn; rest, snacks; bar; BBQ; playgrnd; pool; paddling pool; rv fishing 500m; 15% statics; dogs €1.50; phone; poss cr; Eng spkn; adv bkg; ess high ssn; quiet; red low ssn; ccard acc; red low ssn; CKE/CCI. "Excel site; lge pitches; friendly owner; excel mountain/hill walking, cycling; Grand Chartreuse Monastery 4km; vg; Route to site and area demanding, gd car/c'van ratio advised; beautiful site in lovely setting" 1 May-11 Sep. € 9.10   2013*

ST PIERRE DU VAUVRAY see Pont de l'Arche 3D2

ST PIERRE LAFEUILLE see Cahors 7D3

ST PIERRE LE MOUTIER 4H4 (8km NW Rural) 46.81730, 3.02746 **Camp Municipal La Bruyère, 18600 Mornay-sur-Allier [02 48 74 57 01 or 02 48 74 56 07 (Mairie); www. mornaysurallier.fr]** Fr W on D2076 turn R onto D45 & foll sp. Site just bef x-ing Rv Allier. Sm, pt shd; wc; shwrs inc; el pnts (12A); shop 500m; bar 200m; quiet. "Tidy site with clean facs, run by volunteers; pitch self & warden collects fees; excel NH." 15 May-15 Sep.   2009*

ST PIERRE QUIBERON 2G3 (1.5km SE Coastal) 47.50400, -3.12028 **Camp Municipal du Petit Rohu, Rue des Men-Du, 56510 St Pierre-Quiberon [02 97 50 27 85 or 02 97 30 92 00 (Mairie)]** On D768 dir Quiberon, 1km past exit for St Pierre-Quiberon turn L at camp sp. Turn R in 200m & L after 250m at T-junc sp Le Petit Rohu. Site on R in 50m on beach. Well sp. Med, mkd pitch, pt sl, unshd; wc; shwrs; mv service pnt; el pnts (10A) inc; gas; lndtte; sm shop & bar nrby; snacks adj; playgrnd; sand beach adj; boating; fishing; sports area; some statics; dogs; poss cr; quiet. "Well-kept site in excel location on beach front; excel facs; gd cycling; gd footpath to Quiberon & Port-Haliguen." ♦ 3 Apr-3 Oct. € 14.00   2009*

FRANCE

ST PIERRE QUIBERON *2G3* (3km SE Coastal) *47.53981, -3.13417* **Camp Municipal de Kerhostin, Allée du Camping, 56510 St Pierre-Quiberon [02 97 30 95 25 or 02 97 30 92 00 (Mairie); fax 02 97 30 87 20; mairie.saintpierrequiberon@wanadoo.fr; www. saintpierrequiberon.fr]** Off D768 turn SE onto Rue des Goélettes by rlwy x-ing (no thro rd sp), turn L at 1st sm island, turn L at end, site 300m on R. Med, mkd pitch, pt shd; wc; shwrs inc; el pnts (6A) inc; lndtte; shops adj; rest, snacks, bar 500m; playgrnd; pool 2km; sand beach 200m; dogs; poss cr; no adv bkg; red low ssn. 28 Apr-11 Sep. € 15.50   2010*

ST PIERRE QUIBERON *2G3* (1.5km NW Coastal) *47.53400, -3.14000* **FLOWER Camping Relais de l'Océan, 16 Ave de Groix, Kerhostin, 56510 St Pierre-Quiberon [02 97 30 91 29; fax 02 97 30 80 18; info@relaisdelocean.com; www. relaisdelocean.com or www.flowercampings.com]** S on D768 fr Carnac at traff lts in Kerhostin turn R into Rue de Sombreuil then Ave de Groix, site sp. Lge, hdg/mkd pitch, pt shd; wc; chem disp; baby facs; shwrs inc; el pnts (12A) inc; gas; lndtte; shop 1km; tradsmn; rest, snacks; bar; BBQ; playgrnd; sand beach adj; games area; games rm; cycle hire; golf 15km; entmnt; TV; 20% statics; dogs €3; Eng spkn; adv bkg; quiet; ccard acc; red low ssn/CKE/CCI. "Pleasant site; gd sized pitches; gd amenities; gd for families; popular with surfers; vg." ♦ 1 Apr-30 Sep. € 22.90   2010*

See advertisement on pages 32 & 33

"That's changed – Should I let The Club know?"

If you find something on site that's different from the site entry, fill in a report and let us know. See www.caravanclub.co.uk/europereport.

ST POINT see Cluny *9A2*

ST POINT LAC see Pontarlier *6H2*

ST POL DE LEON *1D2* (2km E Coastal) *48.69103, -3.9673* **Camping Ar Kleguer, Plage de Ste Anne, 29250 St Pol-de-Léon [02 98 69 18 81; fax 02 98 29 12 84; info@camping-ar-kleguer.com; www.camping-ar-kleguer.com]** In St Pol-de-Léon foll Centre Ville sp. At cathedral sq (2 towers) with cathedral on L descend hill & in 150m, bef church with tall belfry, turn L foll Plage & camping sp. On reaching sea turn L (N); site at end, well sp. NB Narr, busy rds in town. Med, mkd pitch, terr, pt sl, pt shd; wc (some cont); chem disp; mv service pnt; baby facs; shwrs inc; el pnts (10A) €4.20 (long lead poss req); lndtte; shops 500m; tradsmn; snacks; bar; htd pool; paddling pool; waterslide; beach adj; tennis; games rm; 40% statics; dogs €2.80; poss cr; adv bkg; poss noisy; CKE/CCI. "Well-kept, attractive site; modern facs; gd views; conv Roscoff ferry." 1 Apr-30 Sep. € 18.70   2009*

ST POL DE LEON *1D2* (2km E Coastal) *48.69355, -3.96930* **Camping de Trologot, Grève du Man, 29250 St Pol-de-Léon [02 98 69 06 26 or 06 62 16 39 30 (mob); fax 02 98 29 18 30; camping-trologot@wanadoo.fr; www. camping-trologot.com]** From the port of Roscoff take D58 go briefly on the D769 then back on to the D58 foll the sp to Morlaix over six rndabts (approx 4miles/6.5km). Just after passing under a rlwy bdge, take the exit for the D769 (sp St Pol de Léon, Kerlaudy, Penzé) then turn L. Stay on the D769 for 1.8 km, just past the graveyard turn R at the rndabt and go strt over the next rndabt (sp Campings/Plage) at the end of the road turn L and the turning for the site will be on L after 1km and is sp. Do not use SatNav. Fr the E on the N12 take the exit for the D19 (sp Morlaix St pol de Leon) at the rndabt take the 2nd exit cont twds St-Pol-de Leon on the D58. Take the exit to the D769 (SP St-Pol-de-Leon) then foll above directions from the graveyard. Med, hdg/mkd pitch, unshd; wc (some cont); chem disp; mv service pnt; baby facs; shwrs inc; el pnts (10A) €3.65; lndtte (inc dryer); sm shop & 600m; tradsmn; snacks; bar; BBQ (gas/charcoal only); playgrnd; htd pool; paddling pool; sm sand beach adj; wifi; entmnt; games/TV rm; 20% statics; dogs €2.05; no c'vans/m'vans over 7m high ssn; poss cr; adv bkg; quiet; ccard acc; red long stay/low ssn/CKE/CCI. "Lovely, well-kept site; ideal NH for Roscoff ferry; gd sized pitches; helpful owners; clean, modern san facs; gd for family beach holiday; peaceful area, many walks nrby; beautiful town; highly rec" ♦ 1 May-30 Sep. € 18.50 (CChq acc) SBS - B29   2013*

ST POL DE LEON *1D2* (5km SE Coastal) *48.65805, -3.92805* **Yelloh! Village Les Mouettes, La Grande Grève, 29660 Carantec [02 98 67 02 46; fax 02 98 78 31 46; camping@les-mouettes.com; www.les-mouettes.com or www. yellohvillage.co.uk]** Fr Morlaix take D58 N sp Roscoff; at lge rndabt turn R sp Carantec on D173; turn L at 1st rndabt; strt on at 2nd & 3rd rndabt past Casino supmkt; turn L next rndabt; site on L. Or fr Roscoff take D58 sp Mortaix, then D173 to Carantec; foll sp town cent, then site. Lge, mkd pitch, pt shd; wc; chem disp; mv service pnt; baby facs; shwrs inc; sauna/jaccuzi; el pnts (10A) inc (poss rev pol); gas; lndtte (inc dryer); shop; snacks; 2 bars; BBQ (charcoal only); playgrnd; htd pool complex (1 covrd); waterslide; paddling pool; sand/shgl beach 1km; fishing; golf 1.5km; tennis; cycle hire; games area; wifi; entmnt; games/TV rm; 50% statics; dogs €5; no c'vans/m'vans over 8m; poss cr; Eng spkn; adv bkg; noise fr boatyard; ccard acc; red low ssn; CKE/CCI. "Attractive site with sea views; clean, modern san facs; impressive pool complex; plenty to do on site; mkt Thu." ♦ 6 Apr-9 Sep. € 46.00 SBS - B14   2011*

See advertisement on inside front cover

ST POL DE LEON *1D2* (7km SE Rural) *48.64912, -3.92126* **Camping Les Hortensias (Jacq), Kermen, 29660 Carantec [02 98 67 08 63; contact@leshortensias.fr; www. leshortensias.fr]** Fr Roscoff on D58 dir Morlaix. Turn L after approx 10km onto D173, then turn R at 1st rndabt, site in 200m. site sp. Sm, mkd pitch, unshd; wc; chem disp; mv service pnt; shwrs inc; el pnts (6A) €3; gas 3km; lndtte (inc dryer); shop 3km; playgrnd; htd, covrd pool 6km; beach 2.5km; dogs €0.80; adv bkg; quiet; CKE/CCI. "Conv Roscoff ferry; views of bay; friendly staff; poss unkempt low ssn; organic produce in shop; gd touring base; no gates allows early departure; excel NH" ♦ 1 May-30 Sep. € 12.56   2013*

You can now fill in site reports online

FRANCE

ST POL DE LEON *1D2* (6km S Urban) *48.63476, -3.92962*
**Camp Municipal de Kerilis, Menez Izella, 29670
Henvic [02 98 62 82 10 or 02 98 62 81 11 (Mairie); fax
02 98 62 81 56; commune-henvic@wanadoo.fr]** Exit D58
(St Pol-de-Léon to Morlaix rd) at Henvic; foll sp. Site 800m after
exit main rd, behind football stadium. NB 2m height barrier
open 0830-1230 & 1300-2000, so unsuitable late arrivals/
early departures. Med, pt shd; wc; shwrs inc; el pnts €2.10
(poss long lead req); lndry rm; supmkt nr; playgrnd; sand
beach 8km; quiet; CKE/CCI. "Pleasant, simple, well-run site;
helpful warden; access only poss bef 12.30 or bet 1630 &
1900 (2011), or phone Mairie in office hours." 1 Jul-31 Aug.
€ 9.45   2009*

ST POL DE LEON *1D2* (6km W Coastal) *48.68622,
-4.07682* **Camping Ar Roc'h, Moguériec, 29250 Sibiril
[02 98 29 97 14]** S fr Roscoff on D58 for approx 6km, then
take D10 W & in 4km turn N to Moguériec. Site sp just bef ent
Moguériec. Sm, hdg/mkd pitch, unshd; wc; chem disp; shwrs
€1; el pnts (2-4A) €2.80; lndry rm; BBQ; sand beach 500m;
no statics; dogs €1; quiet; CKE/CCI. "Well-kept, pretty site;
old facs but well-maintained; gd views across estuary fr some
pitches; vg." 15 Jun-15 Sep. € 14.00   2010*

⊞ **ST POL DE LEON** *1D2* (7km W Coastal) *48.68972, -4.08396*
**Camp du Theven, Moguériec, 29250 Sibiril [02 98 29 96 86;
fax 02 98 61 23 30; roudaut.theven.29@wanadoo.fr; http://
camping.theven.29.pagesperso-orange.fr/]** Fr Roscoff ferry
on D58, at junc with D10 take Sibiril/Cléder turn. In Sibiril pass
church & turn R past water tower, foll sp Port de Moguériec,
site sp. Sm, hdg/mkd pitch, terr, pt shd; wc; shwrs €1; el pnts
(4-6A) €3.80; lndtte; shop; supmkt 5km; snacks; bar; BBQ;
playgrnd; sand/rocky beach adj; fishing; boat hire; entmnt;
90% statics; dogs €1; Eng spkn; adv bkg; quiet; CKE/CCI.
"Friendly, helpful owner; liable to close for 10 day periods low
ssn - phone ahead to check open; san facs ltd & need refurb
(2010)." € 11.40   2010*

ST PONS DE THOMIERES *8F4* (4km N Rural) *43.51223,
2.75289* **Aire Naturelle La Borio de Roque, Route de la
Salvetat, 34220 St Pons-de-Thomières [04 67 97 10 97;
fax 04 67 97 21 61; info@borioderoque.com; www.
borioderoque.com]** On D907, R at sp, foll track for 1.2km
to site. Sm, hdg pitch, terr, shd; wc; chem disp; shwrs inc; el
pnts (10A) €3; lndtte; tradsmn; bar; playgrnd; pool; Eng spkn;
some statics; dogs €2; adv bkg rec high ssn; CKE/CCI. "Excel,
welcoming, clean, secluded site; diff access lge/underpowered
o'fits down single, dirt track - no turning/passing." ♦
15 May-15 Sep. € 20.25   2008*

ST PONS DE THOMIERES *8F4* (8km NE Rural) *43.52181,
2.83027* **Camp Municipal Les Terrasses du Jaur, Chemin
de Notre Dame, 34390 Prémian [04 67 97 27 85 or
04 67 97 06 40 (Mairie); mairie-de-premian@orange.fr;
http://camping-premian.fr]** Go E on D908 fr St Pons-de-
Thomières twd Olargues for 8km. Imposs to turn R down rv
to site, cont on D908, turn round & app fr E, turn L into site.
Sm, hdg pitch, pt sl, terr, pt shd; wc; chem disp; shwrs inc;
el pnts (10A) €1.80; lndtte; shop; BBQ; fishing 100m; quiet;
30% statics; adv bkg; CKE/CCI. "Gd, scenic site; clean san facs;
poss pitching all year with ltd facs; cycle path nr; town rather
run down." 26 May-15 Oct. € 8.50   2009*

ST PONS DE THOMIERES *8F4* (2km E Rural) *43.49055,
2.78527* **Camping Village Les Cerisiers du Jaur, Les
Marbrières-du-Jaur, Route de Bédarieux, 34220 St Pons-
de-Thomières [04 67 95 30 33; fax 04 67 28 09 96; info@
cerisierdujaur.com; www.cerisierdujaur.com]** Fr Castres
on D612 to St Pons; go thro town cent under rlwy bdge; turn L
onto D908 sp Olargues. Site on R in 500m. Med, hdg/mkd pitch,
terr, pt shd; wc; chem disp; mv service pnt; baby facs; shwrs inc;
el pnts (10A) €4; lndtte; ltd shop; tradsmn; rest 1km; snacks;
BBQ; playgrnd; pool; cycle hire; games area; wifi; dogs €1.50;
phone; poss cr; Eng spkn; quiet; ccard acc; red low ssn; CKE/
CCI. "Excel site nr Rv Jaur; welcoming, friendly, helpful owner;
vg san facs; cycle route fr site; an oasis!; hot water not very hot;
expensive in l/s" ♦ 29 Mar-26 Oct. € 24.00   2013*

ST PONS DE THOMIERES *8F4* (11km W Rural) *43.47776,
2.65768* **Camp Municipal de Cabanes, Route de
St Pons, 81270 Labastide-Rouairoux [05 63 98 49 74 or
05 63 98 07 58; tourisme@labastide-rouairoux.com; www.
labastide-rouairoux.com]** E fr Labastide-Rouairoux twd
St Pons on D612. Site adj D612 immed after leaving Labastide
vill. Sm, hdg/mkd pitch, terr, pt shd; wc; chem disp; shwrs; el
pnts inc; shop 1km; tradsmn; adv bkg; some rd noise; CKE/
CCI. "Lovely site; poss diff lge o'fits due to terr." 15 Jun-15 Sep.
€ 11.00   2009*

"I like to fill in the reports
as I travel from site to site"
You'll find report forms at the back of
this guide, or you can fill them in online
at www.caravaclub.co.uk/europereport.

ST POURCAIN SUR SIOULE *9A1* (SE Urban) *46.30643,
3.29207* **Camp Municipal de l'Ile de la Ronde, Quai de
la Ronde, 03500 St Pourçain-sur-Sioule [04 70 45 45 43
or 06 60 94 75 20 (mob); camping.iledelaronde@live.
fr / contact@campingiledelaronde.fr; www.ville-saint-
pourcain-sur-sioule.com]** On D2009, 31km S of Moulins; in
St Pourçain-sur-Sioule town cent turn R immed bef rv bdge; site
ent on L in 100m. NB Sp in town easily missed. Med, hdg pitch,
pt shd; wc; chem disp; mv service pnt; shwrs; el pnts (6A) inc;
lndtte; shops adj; playgrnd; pool 1km; dogs; adv bkg; quiet;
CKE/CCI. "Well-run, busy site in pretty town; extra charge for
lger pitches; barrier clsd 2000-0800; gd rest nr; mkt Sat; great
value; excel; recep and barrier clsd 12h00-14h00" ♦
1 Apr-1 Oct. € 14.80   2013*

ST PRIVAT *7C4* (400m N Rural) *45.14382, 2.09938* **Camping
du Chanaux, Rue du Queyrel, 19220 St Privat [tel/
fax 05 55 28 28 77 (Mairie); francois-michel.perrier@
wanadoo.fr; www.saint-privat-19.fr/camping]** Fr Argentat
on D980 for 17km dir Pleaux & Mauriac, rd steep & winding
in parts. Sm; wc; chem disp; mv service pnt; el pnts (10A) €3;
shops, rests in vill; sm lake adj; some statics. 1 May-31 Oct.
€ 6.20   2009*

ST PRIVAT D'ALLIER see Monistrol d'Allier *9C1*

FRANCE

ST QUAY PORTRIEUX *2E3* (600m NW Coastal) *48.66269, -2.84550* **Camping Bellevue, 68 Blvd du Littoral, 22410 St Quay-Portrieux** [02 96 70 41 84; fax 02 96 70 55 46; campingbellevue22@orange.fr; www.campingbellevue.net] Foll D786 thro St Quay-Portrieux twd Paimpol; turn R at traff lts sp St Quay-Portrieux; foll site sp; site in 2.5km. Lge, hdg/mkd pitch, hdstg, pt sl, terr, pt shd; wc (some cont); chem disp; mv service pnt; baby facs; shwrs inc; el pnts (6A) €3; gas; lndtte (inc dryer); shop; tradsmn; snacks; BBQ; playgrnd; htd pool; paddling pool; sand beach adj & 600m; games area; golf 3km; wifi; TV rm; 8% statics; dogs free; Eng spkn; adv bkg; quiet; ccard acc; red low ssn; CKE/CCI. "Beautiful position with sea views; direct access to sm cove; friendly staff; gd, clean facs; vg." ♦ 28 Apr-16 Sep. € 19.20   2011*

See advertisement above

ST QUENTIN *3C4* (E Urban) *49.85536, 3.31033* **Camp Municipal, 91 Blvd Jean Bouin, 02100 St Quentin** [03 23 06 94 05 / 03 23 06 94 21; auberge.camping@ville-saint-quentin.fr; www.campingmunicipaldesaint-quentin] Fr all app rds foll sp Centre Ville/Auberge de Jeunesse (c'van on sign). Poss diff to find - foll canal rd. Sp 'Terrain de Camping'. Press intercom at barrier for ent. Poorly sp - easy to drive past. Sm, mkd pitch, hdstg, pt shd; htd wc (most cont); chem disp; shwrs inc; el pnts (6A) €4.10; supmkt 1km; pool adj; dogs free; bus adj; quiet; ccard acc; CKE/CCI. "Lovely little site by canal; usefully placed; secure; easy access to lge, gritty pitches; helpful warden; clean modern san facs; gates clsd 2200-0700; pleasant canal walk adj; poss itinerants; vg" ♦ 1 Jun-30 Sep. € 13.10   2013*

ST QUENTIN *3C4* (10km SW Urban) *49.78222, 3.21333* Camping Le Vivier aux Carpes, 10 Rue Charles Voyeux, 02790 Seraucourt-le-Grand [03 23 60 50 10; fax 03 23 60 51 69; contact@camping-picardie.com; www.camping-picardie.com] Fr A26 take exit 11 St Quentin/Soissons; S 4km on D1 dir Tergnier/Soissons. Fork R onto D8 to Essigny-le-Grand & in vill foll camping sp W to Seraucourt. Fr St Quentin, S 10km on D930 to Roupy, E on D32 5km to Seraucourt-le-Grand. Site N of Seraucourt on D321. Narr ent fr rd unsuitable lge o'fits. Med, hdg/mkd pitch, some hdstg, pt shd; wc; chem disp; mv service pnt; baby facs; shwrs inc; el pnts (10A) inc (poss rev pol); gas; lndtte; shop & supmkt 200m; tradsmn; snacks; BBQ; playgrnd; pool nr; angling; golf, tennis, horseriding adj; games rm; wifi; 30% statics; dogs €1; c'van storage; Eng spkn; adv bkg; quiet; CKE/CCI. "Delightful, well-run site; busy, even low ssn - rec arr early; ltd hdstg; peaceful low ssn; gd, lge pitches; narr site rds; friendly, helpful staff; gd, clean san facs; pitches by lake poss boggy when wet; poss flooding; marked footpaths round lakes; vg angling; mosquito probs; Disneyland 90 mins; conv Channel ports; warn staff night bef if v early dep; excel; lovely site but busy; facs stretched but clean" ♦ 1 Mar-31 Oct. € 28.50 SBS - P14   2013*

Send in your site reports by mid August 2014

FRANCE

ST QUENTIN EN TOURMONT *3B2* (500m S Rural) *50.26895, 1.60263* **Camping Le Champ Neuf, 8 Rue du Champ Neuf, 80120 St Quentin-en-Tourmont [03 22 25 07 94; fax 03 22 25 09 87; campinglechampneuf@orange.fr; www. camping-lechampneuf.com]** Exit D1001 or A16 onto D32 to Rue, take D940 around Rue & foll sp St Quentin-en-Tourmont, Parc Ornithologique & Domaine du Marquenterre to site. Site sp fr D204. Lge, hdg/mkd pitch, pt shd; htd wc; chem disp; mv service pnt; baby facs; shwrs inc; el pnts (5-10A) inc; lndtte (inc dryer); shop; tradsmn; snacks; bar; BBQ; playgrnd; htd, covrd pool complex; paddling pool; beach 2km; games area; cycle hire; horseriding 500m; wifi; entmnt high ssn; many statics; dogs €1; phone; adv bkg; quiet; ccard acc. "Excel Ornithological Park nrby; well-kept, pleasant site; friendly, helpful owner; gd cycle paths." ♦ 1 Apr-1 Nov. € 30.00   2011*

See advertisement opposite

ST QUENTIN EN TOURMONT *3B2* (1km S Rural) *50.26978, 1.59855* **Camping des Crocs, 2 Chemin des Garennes, 80120 St Quentin-en-Tourmont [03 22 25 73 33; fax 03 22 25 75 17; contact@campingdescrocs.com; www. campingdescrocs.com]** Exit D1001 or A16 onto D32 to Rue. When W of Rue turn off onto D4 heading W. In 2km turn R onto D204 & foll sp Le Bout des Crocs, then Parc Ornithologique. Site on R. Med, hdg/mkd pitch, unshd; wc; chem disp; baby facs; shwrs €1; el pnts (6A) €3; lndtte; tradsmn; playgrnd; TV rm; 80% statics; dogs €0.50; CKE/CCI. "V quiet site; nr Marquenterre bird reserve; immac facs, but poss long walk; cycle tracks to beach & inland; mosquitoes poss problem; vg." 1 Apr-1 Nov. € 14.00   2009*

ST QUENTIN LA POTERIE see Uzès *10E2*

ST RAMBERT D'ALBON *9C2* (Urban) *45.29992, 4.80722* **Camping des Claires, 26140 St Rambert-d'Albon [tel/fax 04 75 31 01 87; info@camping-des-claires.com; www. camping-des-claires.com]** Fr A7 exit junc 12 dir Chanas, turn S onto N7. In 1km turn R to St Rambert, turn R at rndabt by rlwy stn, under rlwy bdge & foll site sp. Med, pt sl, shd; wc; chem disp (wc); baby facs; shwrs inc; el pnts (6-10A) €4-8; gas; lndtte; tradsmn; rest, snacks; bar in vill; BBQ; playgrnd; pool; sports area; entmnt; 50% statics; dogs €1.40; phone adj; Eng spkn; some rlwy noise; CKE/CCI. "Pleasant site; friendly staff; old but clean san facs; excel NH." 1 Apr-15 Oct. € 15.40   2010*

ST RAMBERT D'ALBON *9C2* (8km NE Rural) *45.32400, 4.90510* **Camping Le Temps Libre, Quartier Font Rozier, 38150 Bougé-Chambalud [04 74 84 04 09; fax 04 74 84 15 71; info@temps-libre.fr; www.temps-libre.fr or www.campings-franceloc.fr]** Fr A7 take exit junc 12 Chanas onto D519, dir Grenoble for 8km. Or fr N7 take exit D519 E sp Grenoble. Site sp at 1st rndabt & well sp in vill. Med, hdg/mkd pitch, hdstg, pt sl, terr, pt shd; wc; chem disp; serviced pitches; shwrs inc; el pnts (9A) €5.70 lndtte; shop in ssn & supmkt 10km; tradsmn; rest high ssn; snacks; bar high ssn; playgrnd; 3 htd pools with chutes (1 covrd); tennis; fishing; pedal boats; wifi; 50% statics; dogs €4.50; Eng spkn; adv bkg; poss noisy; red low ssn; ccard acc; CKE/CCI. "Useful NH S of Lyon; ltd facs low ssn; busy w/end; excel pools; poss flooding in heavy rain; excel." ♦ 29 Mar-27 Sep. € 22.50   2008*

ST RAPHAEL See also sites listed under Agay.

ST RAPHAEL *10F4* (4.5km N Rural) *43.44611, 6.80610* **Douce Quiétude, 3435 Blvd Jacques Baudino, 83700 St Raphaël [04 94 44 30 00; fax 04 94 44 30 30; info@ douce-quietude.com; www.douce-quietude.com or www.les-castels.com]** Exit A8 at junc 38 onto D37 then D100 sp Agay. Foll sp Valescure-Boulouris, site sp. NB c'vans not permitted on St Raphaël seafront. Lge, hdg/mkd pitch, hdstg, pt sl, pt shd; wc; chem disp; baby facs; serviced pitches; shwrs; el pnts (10A) inc; gas; lndtte (inc dryer); shop; tradsmn; rest; takeway; bar; BBQ (gas only); playgrnd; 2 pools (1 htd); waterslide; paddling pool; waterslide; sand beach 5km; cycle hire; gym; games area; games rm; wifi; entmnt; TV; many tour ops statics; dogs €5; phone; bus; poss v cr; Eng spkn; adv bkg; noise fr entmnt high ssn; ccard acc; red low ssn; CKE/CCI. "Lge pitches; excel facs; noisy disco nightly high ssn; sm touring pitches mostly amongst statics; vg." ♦ 30 Apr-8 Oct. € 54.00 (3 persons) (CChq acc)   2011*

See advertisement below

ST REMEZE see Vallon Pont d'Arc *9D2*

ST REMY DE PROVENCE *10E2* (500m E Urban) *43.78836, 4.84093* **Camping Pégomas, Ave Jean Moulin, 13210 St Rémy-de-Provence [tel/fax 04 90 92 01 21; contact@ campingpegomas.com; www.campingpegomas.com]** On D99 fr W dir Cavaillon, ignore R fork to St Rémy 'Centre Ville' (& sat nav!). Pass twin stone sculptures on rndabt, at 2nd rndabt turn into Ave Jean Moulin , site on R in 400m - v sharp turn into site. Fr E Exit A7 junc 25 on D99 W dir St Rémy. Ignore sp 'Centre Ville', pass under aquaduct & across rndabt. At next rndabt turn L into Ave Jean Moulin, then as above. Do not attempt to tow thro town. Med, hdg/mkd pitch, shd; htd wc (mainly cont); chem disp; mv service pnt; baby facs; shwrs inc; el pnts (6A) €3.50 (poss rev pol & long lead req); gas; lndtte; shop 300m; tradsmn; snacks; bar; playgrnd; pool & paddling pool high ssn; entmnt; TV; dogs €1.70; phone; poss cr; Eng spkn; adv bkg; quiet; ccard acc; red low ssn/long stay; CKE/CCI. "Well-run, busy site; clean san facs; lge o'fits poss diff some sm pitches; gd pool; gd touring base; recep clsd 2000 hrs, lge lay-by outside; mkt Wed am; excel for walking" 16 Mar-26 Oct. € 46.60   2013*

ST REMY DE PROVENCE *10E2* (1km NW Rural) *43.7967, 4.82378* **Camping Monplaisir, Chemin Monplaisir, 13210 St Rémy-de-Provence [04 90 92 22 70; fax 04 90 92 18 57; reception@camping-monplaisir.fr; www.camping-monplaisir.fr]** Exit D99 at St Rémy onto D5 going NW dir Maillane, in 110m turn L & foll sp in 500m. Avoid going thro town. Med, hdg pitch, hdstg, shd; htd wc; chem disp; mv service pnt; baby facs; fam bthrm; shwrs inc; el pnts (10A) €3.90; gas; lndtte; shop; supmkt 500m; tradsmn; snacks; bar high ssn; BBQ (gas/elec); playgrnd; pool; paddling pool; cycle hire; wifi; entmnt; dogs €2; phone; bus 1km; Eng spkn; adv bkg; quiet; ccard acc; red long stay/low ssn; CKE/CCI. "Immac, well-run site; mostly gd sized pitches; clean, modern san facs; gd touring base; highly rec; site clsd last Saturday in Oct; excel site" ♦ 11 Mar-19 Oct. € 28.80   2013*

See advertisement

ST REMY SOUS BARBUISE see Arcis sur Aube *4E4*

ST RENAN *2E1* (2km NW Urban) *48.43899, -4.62959* **Camp Municipal Lokournan, Route de Brêles, 29290 St Renan [02 98 84 37 67 or 02 98 84 20 08 (Mairie); fax 02 98 32 43 20]** On D27 fr St Renan dir Lanildut, site sp in 2km. Sm, hdg pitch, pt sl, pt shd; wc; chem disp; shwrs inc; el pnts €3.10; shop 1km; no statics; dogs; adv bkg; CKE/CCI. "Vg." ♦ ltd 1 Jun-15 Sep. € 9.00   2010*

ST REVEREND see St Gilles Croix de Vie *2H3*

ST ROMAIN DE JALIONAS see Cremieu *9B2*

ST ROMAIN SUR CHER see St Aignan sur Cher *4G2*

ST ROME DE DOLAN see Severac le château *9D1*

⊞ **ST ROME DE TARN** *8E4* (300m N Rural) *44.05302, 2.89978* **Camping de la Cascade des Naisses, Route du Pont, 12490 St Rome-de-Tarn [05 65 62 56 59; fax 05 65 62 58 62; contact@camping-cascade-aveyron. com; www.camping-cascade-aveyron.com]** Fr Millau take D992 to St Georges-de-Luzençon, turn R onto D73 & foll sp to St Rome. In St Rome turn R along Ave du Pont-du-Tarn, site sp. Diff, steep app for sm/underpowered car+c'van o'fits. Med, hdg/mkd pitch, hdstg, terr, pt shd; htd wc; own san; chem disp; mv service pnt; baby facs; shwrs inc; el pnts (6A) inc; lndtte (inc dryer); shop; rest; bar; playgrnd; pool; paddling pool; rv fishing, boating; tennis; cycle hire; wifi; entmnt; 40% statics; dogs €6; Eng spkn; adv bkg; quiet; red low ssn; CKE/CCI. "Lovely rvside pitches; pleasant vill; friendly, helpful staff; each level has a wc but steep walk to shwr block; owners will site vans; conv Millau viaduct; excel tranquil, scenic site." ♦ € 27.40   2010*

ST ROME DE TARN *8E4* (10km W Rural) *44.05131, 2.82865* **FFCC Camping La Tioule, 12400 St Victor-et-Melvieu [05 65 62 51 93; carriere.nic@wanadoo.fr; http:// campinglatioule.pagesperso-orange.fr/]** Fr Millau or St Affrique on D999 at Lauras take D23 sp Tiergues, then D250/D50 sp St Victor-et-Melvieu. Other app not rec due narr, winding rds. Sm, mkd pitch, pt sl, terr, pt shd; wc; chem disp; mv service pnt; shwrs inc; el pnts (16A) €2.80; lndtte; tradsmn; BBQ; playgrnd; pool; dogs; adv bkg; quiet; CKE/CCI. "Beautiful area; vg site." 1 Jul-31 Aug. € 12.00   2008*

ST SATURNIN (PUY DE DOME) *9B1* (Rural) *45.68442, 3.06163* Domaine La Serre de Portelas (Naturist), 63450 St Saturnin [04 73 39 35 25 or 04 73 91 21 31 (LS); fax 04 73 39 35 76; ffn-laserre@ifrance.com; www.ffn-laserre.com] On A75 S fr Clermont-Ferrand exit junc 5 onto D213 W-bound sp Tallende. In 4km turn N on D96 sp Chadrat. Site on L about 3.5km after Chadrat. Turn acute L at end of tel posts. Or take N89 S fr Clermont-Ferrand twd Theix, turn S onto D96 & foll rd to site, sp. Sm, pt sl, pt shd; wc; chem disp; shwrs inc; el pnts (6A) €3.20; gas; lndtte; sm shop & 6km; tradsmn; snacks; BBQ; playgrnd; pool; paddling pool; tennis; games area; wifi; 35% statics; dogs; phone; quiet; red low ssn/long stay; INF card req. "Lovely site with views; friendly owners; gd facs; gd base Auvergne; excel." 15 Jun-15 Sep. € 15.00   2008*

ST SATURNIN (PUY DE DOME) *9B1* (9km W Rural) *45.66977, 3.00054* Camping La Clairière, Rouillas-Bas, 63970 Aydat [tel/fax 04 73 79 31 15; info@campinglaclairiere.com; www.campinglaclairiere.com] S fr Clermont-Ferrand exit A75 junc 5 onto D213 W & foll sp Lac d'Aydat. At x-rds at end Rouillas-Bas turn L, site 100m on L. Sm, hdg pitch, terr, pt shd; htd wc; chem disp; shwrs inc; el pnts (10A) €3.50 (poss rev pol); lndtte; shop 600m; rest 250m; snacks high ssn; playgrnd; wifi; 10% statics; dogs €1; Eng spkn; adv bkg rec high ssn; quiet; red low ssn. "V pleasant site; friendly, helpful owner; clean facs poss stretched when site full; excel walking." 15 Apr-30 Sep. € 13.00   2009*

ST SAUVEUR EN PUISAYE *4G4* (2km N Rural) *47.63076, 3.19231* FFCC Camping Parc des Joumiers, Route de Mézilles, 89520 St Sauveur-en-Puisaye [03 86 45 66 28; fax 03 86 45 60 27; campingmoteljoumiers@wanadoo.fr; www.camping-motel-joumiers.com] Fr A6 S, exit at sp Joigny-Toucy onto D955 thro Aillant-sur-Tholon to Toucy, then cont to St Sauveur. Or N fr St Sauveur on D7 sp Mézilles, site on R in 1.5km. Site well sp at main x-rds in town. Med, hdg/mkd pitch, pt shd; htd wc; chem disp; shwrs inc; el pnts (5-10A) €2.80-3.80; gas; lndtte; tradsmn; rest, snacks; bar; BBQ; playgrnd; htd pool; lake sw & beach adj; fishing; games area; cycle hire; wifi; some statics; dogs €1.80; phone; poss cr; no adv bkg; quiet; ccard acc; 5% red long stay/CKE/CCI. "Helpful staff; lge pitches with lake views." ♦ ltd 16 Mar-16 Oct. € 16.30   2010*

ST SAUVEUR LE VICOMTE see Haye du Puits, La *1D4*

ST SAVIN *7A3* (1km N Rural) *46.56892, 0.86772* Camp Municipal Moulin de la Gassotte, 10 Rue de la Gassotte, 86310 St Savin-sur-Gartempe [05 49 48 18 02; fax 05 49 48 28 56; saint.savin@ag86.fr; www.saintsavin.com] E fr Chauvigny on D951 to St Savin; fr St Savin N on D11; well sp. Fr S on D5 cross rv; meet D951, turn R & site on R. Fr S on D11 use 'poids lourds' (heavy vehicles) rec rte to meet D951. Sm, pt shd; wc; chem disp; mv service pnt; shwrs inc; el pnts (12A) €2.70; lndry rm; shop, rests & bars 500m; tradsmn; playgrnd; rv fishing adj; TV; quiet; CKE/CCI. "Beautiful, peaceful site by rv; helpful warden; san facs old but clean; sh walk to vill; murals in Abbey restored by UNESCO." ♦ 14 May-15 Sep. € 6.80   2011*

ST SAVINIEN *7B2* (1km S Rural) *45.87789, -0.68441* Camping L'Ile aux Loisirs (La Grenouillette), 17350 St Savinien [05 46 90 35 11; fax 05 46 91 65 06; contact@ileauxloisirs.com; www.ileauxloisirs.com] Fr St Jean-d'Angély take D18 to St Savinien. Site on S side of town; cross rv bdge in vill; site on L after 300m. Med, pt shd; wc; shwrs inc; el pnts (6A) €4.50; (rev pol); lndtte; shop; bar; snacks; playgrnd; pool adj; tennis & mini-golf nrby; entmnt; dogs €1; adv bkg; quiet, some rd noise; red low ssn; ccard acc. "Pleasant, well-run site; attractive town." 1 Apr-22 Sep. € 16.10   2009*

ST SAVINIEN *7B2* (5km SW Rural) *45.85243, -0.70660* Camping du Petit Bonheur, 14 Rue du Port, 17350 Crazannes [05 46 74 44 25 or 06 75 04 40 91 (mob); contact@dupetit-bonheur.com; www.dupetit-bonheur.com] Fr St Savinien take D18 for 700m, turn L onto D119 sp Crazannes. Site on L on ent vill. Med, mkd pitch, pt sl, pt shd; wc (some cont); chem disp; facs; shwrs inc; el pnts (6A) €4.30; gas; lndtte; shops 300m; tradsmn; BBQ (gas/elec); playgrnd; htd pool; rv sw, fishing 100m; internet; 5% statics; dogs €1; adv bkg; quiet; red low ssn; CKE/CCI. "Peaceful, CL-type site nr Rv Charente; new san facs planned for 2011; gd cycling." 1 Mar-31 Oct. € 15.50   2010*

ST SEBASTIEN *7A3* (1km SW Rural) *46.38871, 1.52249* Camp Municipal La Garenne, Route de la Garenne, 23160 St Sébastien [05 55 63 50 39; fax 05 55 63 44 62] Exit A20 junc 20 & foll sp dir La Souterraine on D5. In 4km turn L to St Sébastien. On ent vill turn R, R again, site on L just after equestrian cent. Sm, mkd pitch, pt sl, terr, pt shd; wc; shwrs inc; el pnts €2.90; shop, rest 500m; dogs; quiet. "Gd NH nr A20; gd touring base." 15 Apr-15 Oct. € 4.00   2010*

ST SEINE L'ABBAYE *6G1* (N Rural) *47.44073, 4.79236* Camp Municipal, Rue de la Foire aux Vaches, 21440 St Seine-l'Abbaye [03 80 35 00 09 or 03 80 35 01 64 (Mairie)] On D971 in vill of St Seine-l'Abbaye, turn N onto D16. Turn R uphill, sp camping & turn R thro gateway in stone wall. Narr streets in vill. Or fr N on D974, avoiding Dijon, turn R onto D959 at Til-Châtel, then D901 Moloy/Lamargelle. Turn L in Lamargelle onto D16 St Seine-l'Abbaye. Turn L uphill at edge of vill & as above (avoids narr streets). Sm, pt sl, hdstg, pt unshd; wc (cont); chem disp; shwrs inc; el pnts (10A) €2.50 (rev pol); shops 500m; pool 4km; rv 500m; dogs; v quiet; CKE/CCI. "Pleasantly situated site; basic but immac san facs; fees collected fr 1900 hrs; lovely vill; conv Dijon or as NH; excel." 1 May-30 Sep. € 8.40   2011*

ST SEURIN DE PRATS see Ste Foy la Grande *7C2*

ST SEVER *8E2* (1km N Urban) *43.76570, -0.56312* FFCC Camping Les Rives de l'Adour, Ave René Crabos, 40500 St Sever [05 58 76 04 60; camping.deladour@orange.fr; www.camping-lesrivesdeladour.com] S on D933 fr Mont-de-Marsan, cross D924 then bdge over Rv Adour. Look immed for access rd on L bef rlwy x-ing & steep climb up to St Sever. Site sp adj Parc des Sports. Med, hdg/mkd pitch, shd; htd wc; mv service pnt; shwrs inc; el pnts (13A) €2.50; sm shop & 1km; lndtte (inc dryer); playgrnd; pool nrby inc; tennis; sailing; fishing; cycle hire; games rm; wifi; TV; dogs €1.50; quiet; red low ssn/long stay. "Gd san facs; gd." 1 Apr-31 Oct. € 12.50   2009*

STE SEVERE SUR INDRE 7A4 (200m N Urban) 46.48843,
2.06902 **Camp Municipal, Route de l'Auvergne, 36160
Ste Sévère-sur-Indre [02 54 30 50 28 (Mairie); fax
02 54 30 63 39]** On D917 fr La Châtre, site on R 200m after
g'ge on L. Sm, pt shd; wc (some cont); mv service pnt; shwrs
inc; el pnts (10A) €1.70; gas, shop, rest, bar 500m; playgrnd
adj; fishing; dogs; quiet. "Tiny site in pleasant vill; gd facs;
associations with Jacques Tati & Georges Sand; vg NH."
Easter-1 Nov. € 6.80   2008*

STE SEVERE SUR INDRE 7A4 (6km SE Rural) 46.47194,
2.14660 **Camping Pérassay, Le Bourg, 36160 Pérassay
[02 54 30 63 25; camping@the-french-connection.net;
www.the-french-connection.net]** Fr Ste Sévère take D917
S & after approx 6km turn L onto D71 sp Pérassay. Site on L
in cent of vill opp tabac. Sm, pt sl, pt shd; wc; chem disp (wc);
shwrs inc; el pnts (16A) €2.50; lndtte; BBQ; lake sw 10km; 1
static; dogs €2.50; adv bkg; quiet; red low ssn. "Lovely CL-type
site in quiet location; friendly British owner; vg san facs; vg." ♦
1 Apr-31 Oct. € 15.00   2009*

STE SIGOLENE see Monistrol sur Loire 9C1

ST SORNIN see Marennes 7B1

ST SOZY see Souillac 7C3

ST SULPICE LES FEUILLES 7A3 (5km NW Rural) 46.33187,
1.31137 **Camping du Lac de Mondon, Mondon, 87160
Cromac [05 55 76 83 99 or 05 55 76 93 34; camping-
mondon@orange.fr; www.campingdemondon.com]**
Exit A20 junc 22 onto D912 to St Sulpice-les-Feuilles; cont on
D912 for 3km until junc with D2; foll sp to Cromac on D105,
site sp. Med, hgd/mkd pitch, hdstg, pt sl, pt shd; htd wc; chem
disp; mv service pnt; baby facs; shwrs inc; el pnts (10A) €3.20;
lndtte (inc dryer); sm shop & shop 6km; tradsmn; rest, snacks;
bar; BBQ (gas); playgrnd; htd pool; paddling pool; waterslide;
tennis; games area; games rm; wifi; entmnt; dogs €1; Eng
spkn; adv bkg; quiet; red low ssn/long stay; CKE/CCI. "Gd
cycling; gd touring base; vg." ♦ 17 Apr-3 Oct. € 13.00 2010*

ST SYLVESTRE SUR LOT see Villeneuve sur Lot 7D3

⊞ ST SYMPHORIEN 7D2 (1km S Rural) 44.41831,
-0.49232 **FFCC Camping La Hure, Route de Sore,
33113 St Symphorien [tel/fax 05 56 25 79 54 or
06 86 77 09 27 (mob); campingdelahure@wanadoo.fr]**
S thro Langon on app to . Foll sp Villandraut, St Symphorien.
Sp fr vill 1km S on D220, opp Intermarché. Med, shd; htd
wc; chem disp; mv service pnt; shwrs inc; el pnts (5A) €2.50;
lndtte; shops; rest, snacks; playgrnd; pool adj; tennis; rv fishing;
many statics; dogs €1.30; adv bkg; red low ssn. "Helpful staff;
basic facs; site in pinewoods; gd cycling, walks, beaches."
€ 9.10   2009*

ST THEOFFREY 9C3 (E Rural) 44.99990, 5.77920 **FFCC
Camping Ser-Sirant, Petichet, 38119 St Théoffrey
[04 76 83 91 97; fax 04 76 30 83 69; campingsersirant@
wanadoo.fr; www.euro-campsite.com]** N fr La Mure on
N85 dir Grenoble. At traff lts in Petichet turn E, site on lakeside
in 500m. Med, mkd pitch, pt terr, pt shd; wc; chem disp; mv
service pnt; shwrs inc; el pnts (6-10A) €3-4.50; lndtte; shop
8km; tradsmn; rest 1km; snacks; sm playgrnd; lake sw & beach
adj; watersports; dogs €1.50; phone; bus 1km; Eng spkn; adv
bkg; quiet; CKE/CCI. "Gd site with views; most pitches req
blocks; helpful owners; excel walking & cycling; highly rec."
1 May-Oct. € 16.90   2010*

ST THIBERY see Pézenas 10F1

ST TROPEZ 10F4 (6km SE Rural) 43.21804, 6.57830
**Camping Moulin de Verdagne, Route du Brost, 83580
Gassin [04 94 79 78 21; fax 04 94 54 22 65; info@
moulindeverdagne.com; www.moulindeverdagne.com]**
Foll N559 N fr Cavalaire for 6km. Take 1st R after town traff
lts in La Croix-Valmer, site sp on R. Site in 2km, surrounded by
vineyards. Rough app rd/track. Med, mkd pitch, terr, pt shd;
wc (some cont); chem disp; shwrs inc; el pnts (6A) €4; lndtte;
shop 4km; tradsmn; rest, snacks; bar; playgrnd; pool; sand
beach 5km; dogs €3; 60% statics; phone; poss cr; Eng spkn;
quiet; ccard acc; red low ssn/long stay. "Vg site; friendly recep;
tight bends & narr pitches poss diff long o'fits; pool 2m deep."
1 Apr-31 Oct. € 23.90   2011*

ST TROPEZ 10F4 (7km S Rural) 43.24092, 6.57404 **Parc
Saint James Gassin, Parc Montana, Route de Bourrian,
83580 Gassin [04 94 55 20 20; fax 04 94 56 34 77;
gassin@camping-parcsaintjames.com; www.camping-
parcsaintjames.com]** Exit A8 at junc 36 St Tropez; after
Port-Grimaud foll sp Cavalaire-sur-Mer S on D559 where clearly
sp. V lge, hdg/mkd pitch, hdstg, terr, pt shd; htd wc; shwrs inc;
el pnts (6A) inc; lndtte; shop; rest, snacks; bar; BBQ; playgrnd;
htd pool; paddling pool; spa/jacuzzi; beach 4km; tennis; games
area; games rm; entmnt (child & adult); internet; golf 12km;
50% statics; dogs €5; phone; Eng spkn; adv bkg ess high
ssn; quiet but some rd noise; ccard acc; red long stay/low ssn.
"Conv St Tropez; scenic drives; vg site in a great location." ♦
9 Jan-18 Nov. € 40.00   2011*

Welcome to the Gulf of St-Tropez, in the middle of a 20ha forest of pines and cork oaks ; 1,5 km from the beach of Pampelonne. Relax aera : Jacuzzi, hammam, sauna, fitness.

Heated water park 4000 m². Rental of bungalows and mobile homes

www.tournels.com

Route de Camarat F-83350 Ramatuelle • Tel : 00 33 (0) 4 94 55 90 90 • Fax : 00 3 (0) 4 94 55 90 99

ST TROPEZ *10F4* (7km S Coastal) *43.23198, 6.65924*
Riviera Villages Kon-Tiki, Plage de Pampelonne, 83350
Ramatuelle [04 94 55 96 96; fax 04 94 55 96 95; kontiki@
riviera-villages.com; www.riviera-villages.com] Foll
Ramatuelle on D93 sp fr St Tropez; site sp on L. V lge, mkd
pitch, pt sl, pt shd; wc; chem disp; baby facs; shwrs inc; el pnts
(6A) inc; gas; lndtte; shop; rest, snacks; bar; playgrnd; sand
beach adj; watersports; tennis; archery; entmnt; TV; mainly
statics; dogs; poss cr; adv bkg ess high ssn; quiet; red low ssn;
ccard acc; CKE/CCI. "Touring area sm & poss a bit unkempt
end of ssn; some sm pitches; coastal walks; conv St Tropez &
hill vills." 1 Apr-31 Oct. € 40.00   2009*

ST TROPEZ *10F4* (8km S Rural) *43.20596, 6.65083*
Yelloh! Village Les Tournels, Route de Camarat, 83350
Ramatuelle [04 94 55 90 90; fax 04 94 55 90 99; info@
tournels.com; www.tournels.com or www.yellohvillage.
co.uk] Exit A8 at Le Muy dir St Maxime, St Tropez. Take D61 dir
Ramatuelle then foll sp 'Le Plages' & Camarat lighthouse. V lge,
mkd pitch, terr, shd; htd wc (some cont); chem disp; mv service
pnt; some serviced pitches; sauna; shwrs inc; el pnts (5A) inc;
gas; lndtte; shops; rest, snacks; bar; playgrnd; htd pool; paddling
pool; sand beach 1.5km; (shuttle bus high ssn); tennis; games
area; fitness rm; cycle hire; wifi; entmnt; TV; 90% statics; dogs
€4; Eng spkn; adv bkg; quiet; ccard acc; red low ssn; CKE/CCI.
"Peaceful site on wooded hillside; well-kept & well-run; lower
pitches full long term winter o'fits; lovely views upper terr levels
but access via steep, narr rd - poss diff long o'fits, mechanical
help avail." 1 Apr-6 Nov. € 59.00   2011*

See advertisement

ST VAAST LA HOUGUE see Quettehou *1C4*

⊞ **ST VALERY EN CAUX** *3C2* (1.5km SW Coastal) *49.85853,
0.70450* **Camp Municipal d'Etennemare, 21 Rue du
Hameau Etennemare, 76460 St Valery-en-Caux [tel/fax
02 35 97 15 79; servicetourisme@ville-saint-valery-en-
caux.fr]** Fr Dieppe on D925 foll camping sp on ent town.
Med, mkd pitch, pt sl, pt shd; htd wc; chem disp; baby facs;
shwrs inc; el pnts (6A) inc; lndtte; shop; tradsmn; rest 800m;
playgrnd; htd pool & tennis in town; shgl beach; adv bkg;
quiet; ccard acc; CKE/CCI. "Site poss clsd low ssn - phone to
check; clean, tidy site." ♦ € 14.45   2010*

⊞ **ST VALERY EN CAUX** *3C2* (W Coastal) *49.86839, 0.71154*
Aire Communale, Quai d'Aval, Plage Ouest, 76460
St Valery-en-Caux [02 35 97 00 22 or 02 35 97 00 63 (TO);
servicetourisme@ville-saint-valeryen-caux.fr]** Sp fr cent of
St Valery-en-Caux along rv/seafront to harbour. Sm, chem disp;
mv service pnt; water fill €4; lndtte, shops, rests nr; phone; free
parking for 48 hrs. M'vans only. "M'vans only; rec arr early;
low ssn free except Fri, Sat & Sun." € 4.00   2012*

ST VALERY SUR SOMME *3B2* (2km S Rural) *50.15333, 1.63583* **Camping Le Domaine du Château de Drancourt, 80230 Estréboeuf [03 22 26 93 45; fax 03 22 26 85 87; chateau.drancourt@wanadoo.fr; www.chateau-drancourt.com or www.les-castels.com]** Exit A28/E402 junc 1 at Abbeville onto D40 twd Noyelles-sur-Mer. At rndabt with D940 turn L sp St Valery-sur-Somme. At next rndabt go strt over dir Le Tréport, then at next rndabt at junc with D48 take last exit (sp Estréboeuf), turn immed L & foll sps to site. NB.1-way system at recep area. Lge, some hdg/mkd pitch, pt sl, pt shd; wc; chem disp; mv service pnt; baby facs; shwrs inc; el pnts (10A) inc (poss rev pol); gas; lndtte; shop; rest, snacks; bar; BBQ; playgrnd; 2 htd pools (1 covrd); paddling pool; fishing adj; golf driving range; watersports 2km; sand beach 8km; horseriding 12km; tennis; games hall; cycle hire; entmnt; 80% statics; dogs €4.50; poss cr & noisy; Eng spkn; adv bkg; ccard acc; red low ssn; CKE/CCI. "Conv, busy, popular NH in grnds of chateau; friendly staff; facs poss stretched when site full; red facs low ssn; bird sanctuary in estuary nrby; gd" ♦ 30 Mar-15 Sep. € 48.50   2013*

See advertisement on inside back cover

ST VALERY SUR SOMME *3B2* (1km SW Urban/Coastal) *50.18331, 1.61786* **Camping Le Walric, Route d'Eu, 80230 St Valery-sur-Somme [03 22 26 81 97; fax 03 22 60 77 26; info@campinglewalric.com; www.campinglewalric.com]** Ringrd round St Valery D940 dir Le Tréport. Cont to 3rd rndabt (1st rndabt Carrefour supmkt on L) 3km & take 1st exit (R) sp St Valery & Cap Hornu D3. Site on R in 2km at ent to town sp. Lge, hdg/mkd pitch, some hdstg, pt shd; wc; chem disp; mv service pnt; baby facs; shwrs inc; el pnts (6A) inc; gas; lndtte (inc dryer); shop; tradsmn; bar; BBQ; playgrnd; htd pool; paddling pool; beaches nr; fishing; boat & cycle hire; tennis; games area; games rm; wifi; entmnt high ssn; 70% statics; dogs €3; phone; Eng spkn; adv bkg; quiet; ccard acc; red low ssn/long stay; CKE/CCI. "Well-kept, well-run, busy site in excel location; clean dated san facs; cycle rtes, canal track; steam train; delightful medieval town; mkt Sun; excel" ♦ 1 Apr-1 Nov. € 40.00 (3 persons)   2013*

"We must tell The Club about that great site we found"

Get your site reports in by mid-August and we'll do our best to get your updates into the next edition of Caravan Europe.

ST VALERY SUR SOMME *3B2* (3km SW Rural) *50.17632, 1.58969* **Camping de la Baie, Routhiaville, 80230 Pendé [03 22 60 72 72; Contact@campingdelabaie.eu; www.campingdelabaie.net]** Just off D940 twd Tréport, well sp. Sm, hdg pitch; wc (some cont); chem disp; shwrs inc; el pnts (6A) €4; lndtte; shop 2km; tradsmn; playgrnd; 95% statics; adv bkg; quiet; red low ssn; CKE/CCI. "Well-run, clean, tidy site & san facs; friendly, helpful owners; low trees in places need care; cycle rte to St Valery; adequate NH." 27 Mar-16 Oct. € 15.50   2013*

ST VALERY SUR SOMME *3B2* (1km W Urban) *50.18447, 1.62263* **Camping de la Croix l'Abbé, Place de la Croix l'Abbé, 80230 St Valery-sur-Somme [03 22 60 81 46; w.a.georges@wanadoo.fr]** Ringrd round St Valery D940 dir Le Tréport. Cont to 2nd rndabt (1st rndabt Champion supmkt on L) 3km & take exit sp St Valery & Cap Hornu D3. Site 250m beyond Camping Le Walric. Lge, hdg/mkd pitch, pt sl, unshd; wc (some cont); chem disp; shwrs inc; el pnts (10A) inc; shop 1km; tradsmn; rest, snacks; bar; playgrnd; htd, covrd pool; sand/shgl beach 1km TV rm; 85% statics; bus adj; poss cr; Eng spkn; quiet. "San facs need update; gd location for walk to town; sh stay/NH only." 1 Apr-30 Nov. € 20.00   2009*

ST VALLIER *9C2* (400m N Rural) *45.18767, 4.81225* **Camp Municipal Les Iles de Silon, 26240 St Vallier [04 75 23 22 17 or 04 73 23 07 66; camping.saintvallier@orange.fr; www.saintvallier.com/campings]** On N7 just N of town, clearly sp in both dirs on rvside. Med, hdg sm pitch size restriced, pt shd; wc; chem disp; shwrs inc; el pnts (10A) €2.30 (poss long cable req); lndtte; shop & 500m; snacks; BBQ; playgrnd; pool 1km; watersports; tennis adj; some statics; dogs €2.30; Eng spkn; adv bkg; quiet but some rlwy noise; ccard acc; CKE/CCI. "Attractive, gd quality site; views over rv; lge pitches; friendly warden; gd immac san facs; rec arr bef 1600 high ssn; cycle path along Rhône; gd value; Cycle/walking track adj; excel well managed site; v gd facs and staff" ♦ ltd 15 Mar-15 Nov. € 7.40   2013*

"I need an on-site restaurant"

We do our best to make sure site information is correct, but it is always best to check any must-have facilities are still available or will be open during your visit.

ST VALLIER *9C2* (5km W Rural) *45.17917, 4.73960* **Camping L'Oasis, Le Petit Chaléat, 07370 Eclassan [04 75 34 56 23; fax 04 75 34 47 94; info@oasisardeche.com; www.oasisardeche.com]** Leave N7 at St Vallier, cross Rhône to Sarras. Then across D86 onto D6 sp St Jeure-d'Ay, in 7km turn R foll sp to site. App rd twisting & narr, many sharp bends & no passing places. Sm, hdg/mkd pitch, terr, pt shd, 80% serviced pitch; wc; chem disp; shwrs inc; el pnts (3-6A) €3.40-3.90; gas; lndtte; shop; tradsmn; rest, snacks; bar; playgrnd; pool; rv adj; archery; golf 10km; 20% statics; dogs €2.50; Eng spkn; adv bkg; quiet; ccard not acc; CKE/CCI. "Lovely setting by rv; tractor tow to pitch; not rec NH due diff app." 23 Apr-15 Sep. € 20.00   2010*

ST VALLIER DE THIEY see Grasse *10E4*

ST VARENT *4H1* (2km S Rural) *46.89741, -0.24147* **Camp Municipal La Grande Versenne, 79330 St Varent [05 49 67 62 11 (Mairie); fax 05 49 67 67 87; villestvarent@wanadoo.fr]** Site sp on D938 at Bouillé-St Varent. Sm, hdg pitch, pt shd; wc; baby facs; shwrs inc; el pnts (10A) €2.50; supmkt nr; playgrnd; rv nrby; no statics; dogs €0.50; adv bkg; quiet. "Friendly staff; gd NH." ♦ 1 Apr-31 Oct. € 9.50 2012*

ST VICTOR ET MELVIEU see St Rome de Tarn *8E4*

FRANCE

ST VINCENT DE BARRES 9D2 (5km N Rural) 44.69272, 4.71634 **FFCC Camp Municipal Les Civelles d'Ozon, 07210 St Lager-Bressac [04 75 65 01 86; fax 04 75 65 13 02; tour-a@ wanadoo.fr; www.camping-ardeche-lescivelles.com]** S fr Privas on D2 dir Montélemar; site well sp on L. S fr Valence on N86; turn R onto D22; site sp to L, narr rd - or cont to rndabt, turn L onto D2 to Montélimar & as above. Sm, hdg/mkd pitch, pt sl, pt shd; serviced pitches; wc; chem disp; shwrs inc; el pnts (10A) inc (poss rev pol); lndtte; shops 3km; playgrnd; pools & paddling pool adj inc (Jul/Aug); tennis; games rm; dogs €2.50; adv bkg; quiet; red low ssn; CKE/CCI. "Helpful warden; rec arr early espec at w/e; popular NH; excel." ♦ ltd 1 Apr-30 Sep. € 17.00   2008*

ST VINCENT DE BARRES 9D2 (1km SW Rural) 44.65659, 4.69330 **Camping Le Rieutord, 07210 St Vincent-de-Barrès [04 75 65 07 73; moncamping@wanadoo.fr; www. ardeche-sud-camping.com]** Fr N exit A7 junc 16 Loriol onto D104 & foll sp Le Pouzin then Chomérac (do not foll 1st sp St Vincent-de-Barrès - narr rd). At rndabt foll D2 dir Le Teil-Montélimar for 6km. When arr at St Vincent (vill on L), turn R & foll site sp for 1.5km. Fr S exit junc 18 Montélimar Sud, foll sps Montélimar then Privas. Cross Rv Rhône, go thro Rochemaure sp Privas. At Meysse turn L after bdge dir Privas. Foll D2 for 4.5km then turn L dir St Bauzile to site in 3km. Med, hdg pitch, pt sl, pt shd; htd wc; shwrs inc; el pnts (16A) €3; lndtte; shop; snacks; bar; cooking facs; playgrnd; pool; paddling pool; waterslide; tennis; games area; games statics; €2; no c'vans over 6m or twin-axles; Eng spkn; adv bkg; quiet CKE/CCI. "Tranquil site in beautiful setting nr old walled town; pleasant owners; gd touring base." 4 Apr-31 Oct. € 15.00   2010*

ST VINCENT DE COSSE see Sarlat la Canéda 7C3

ST VINCENT DE PAUL see Dax 8E1

ST VINCENT LES FORTS 9D4 (1km N Rural) 44.45682, 6.36529 **Campéole Camping Le Lac, Le Fein, 04340 St Vincent-les-Forts [04 92 85 51 57; fax 04 92 85 57 63; lac@campeole.com; www.camping-montagne.com or www.campeole.com]** W fr Barcelonnette on D900/D900b, past St Vincent-les-Forts dir Le Lautaret. Turn R onto D7 & foll narr steep winding rd to end, site sp o'looking lake. Lge, mkd pitch, terr, sl, pt shd; wc; chem disp; mv service pnt; baby facs; shwrs inc; el pnts (6A) €4.10; lndtte (inc dryer); shop; tradsmn; rest, snacks; bar; BBQ; playgrnd; pool; paddling pool; lake sw & beach 500m; fishing; watersports; tennis; horseriding; games area; games rm; wifi; child entmnt; 30% statics; dogs €3.50; phone; Eng spkn; adv bkg; quiet; ccard acc; red low ssn; CKE/CCI. "Simple site in superb scenic location; many leisure activities; vg walking in area; vg." ♦ 20 May-25 Sep. € 25.00   2012*

See advertisement on pages 14 & 15

ST VINCENT SUR JARD see Jard sur Mer 7A1

ST YORRE 9A1 (500m SW Rural) 46.06056, 3.46014 **Camping Les Gravières, Rue de la Gravière, 03270 St Yorre [04 70 59 21 00 or 06 27 35 14 26 (mob); fax 04 70 59 20 09; camping-st-yorre@orange.fr; www. camping-vichy.com]** Fr A71 exit junc 12 sp Gannat. At Bellerive turn R onto D131 sp Hauterive. L over bdge to St Yorre. Foll camping sp. C'vans banned fr St Yorre town cent. Med, hdg pitch, pt shd; wc (some cont); chem disp; baby facs; shwrs inc; el pnts (4-10A) inc; dry rm; shops 1km; tradsmn; snacks; BBQ; playgrnd; pool & sports cent adj; fishing; games area; dogs; phone adj; adv bkg; quiet; CKE/CCI. "Gd touring base." ♦ 1 May-30 Sep. € 14.70   2008*

> ## "Satellite navigation makes touring much easier"
>
> Remember most sat navs don't know if you're towing or in a larger vehicle – always use yours alongside maps and site directions.

ST YRIEIX LA PERCHE 7B3 (1.7km N Rural) 45.52793, 1.20021 **Camping Plan d'Eau d'Arfeuille, 87500 St Yrieix-la-Perche [05 55 75 08 75; fax 05 55 75 26 08; camping@ saint-yrieix.fr]** Site well sp on L on D704 fr St Yrieix-la-Perche N dir Limoges. Fr other dirs look for sp 'Porcelaine Village' - site in same rd. Med, hdg pitch, terr, pt shd; htd wc; chem disp; mv service pnt; baby facs; shwrs; el pnts (10A) inc; lndtte (inc dryer); rest; bar; playgrnd; pool; waterslide; lake sw & beach adj; fishing; canoeing; games area; entmnt; adv bkg; quiet. "Pleasant situation; friendly staff." 15 Apr-15 Sep. € 12.40   2010*

⊞ **ST YRIEIX LA PERCHE** 7B3 (8km W Rural) 45.55460, 1.11867 **FFCC Camping Les Vigères, Le Chalard [05 55 09 37 22; fax 05 55 09 93 39; infovigeres@aol.com; www.lesvigeres.com]** Take N20 to Limoges then N704 to St Yrieix. In St Yrieix turn W on D901 to Châlus. 1st vill is Le Chalard & site is 1km after vill. Sm, hdg/mkd pitch, pt shd; wc; chem disp; shwrs inc; el pnts (3-10A) €3-4; lndtte; shops 2km; BBQ; playgrnd; pool; lake sw & sand beach adj; fishing; library; adv bkg; v quiet; 10% red low ssn; CKE/CCI. "Vg, peaceful site; welcoming British owners; clean san facs; ltd low ssn (htd extension planned 2010); poss unkempt low ssn; historic area; rec." ♦ € 14.50   2009*

ST YRIEIX LA PERCHE 7B3 (12km NW Rural) 45.59175, 1.11131 **Camp Municipal de Bel Air, 87500 Ladignac-le-Long [05 55 09 39 82 or 05 55 09 30 02 (Mairie); fax 05 55 09 39 80; camping-ladignac@wanadoo.fr; www. ladignac.com]** Exit Limoges S on N21 to Châlus. Turn E on D901 sp St Yrieix to Ladignac. Turn N to lakes at sp. Site on R. Med, pt shd, hdg pitch; wc; chem disp; mv service pnt; shwrs inc; el pnts (6A) €3.70; lndtte; shop & 1km; tradsmn; playgrnd; lake sw 500m; games/TV rm; 10% statics; dogs €1.10; phone; no twin-axles; Eng spkn; adv bkg; quiet; red low ssn; CKE/CCI. "Beautiful lakeside site; spacious pitches; clean san facs; barrier with card operation - early ssn apply to Mairie in vill sq for card; cycling; walking; excel." 1 Jun-30 Sep. € 11.50   2011*

ST YRIEIX SUR CHARANTE see Angouleme 7B2

SALBRIS *4G3* (500m NE Urban) *47.43006, 2.05427*
Camping de Sologne, 8 Allée de la Sauldre, Route
de Pierrefitte, 41300 Salbris [02 54 97 06 38; fax
02 54 97 33 13; campingdesologne@wanadoo.fr; www.
campingdesologne.fr] Exit A71 junc 4; take D724 bypass,
then take D2020 N (do not take D724 into town); turn E onto
D55 (Route de Pierrefitte); Impasse de la Sauldre leading to
Allée de la Sauldre is 2nd turning on R in 200m (narr & easy to
miss). Med, hdg/mkd pitch, pt shd; wc; chem disp; baby facs;
shwrs inc; el pnts (10A) inc (some rev pol); gas; lndtte; shop
200m; hypmkt 1km; rest, snacks; bar high ssn; playgrnd; lake
adj; fishing; boat hire; karting 6km; wifi; TV rm; 25% statics;
dogs €1; phone; poss cr; Eng spkn; adv bkg; some noise
fr rlwy, rd & motor circuit; ccard acc; red low ssn; CKE/CCI.
"Excel, well-kept site in pleasant lakeside location; friendly,
helpful owners; gd san facs poss stretched if site busy & ltd low
ssn; poss scruffy early ssn (2009); gd rest; gd dog walks adj;
conv NH for m'way; beautiful site by lake, easy access to town"
♦ 1 Apr-30 Sep. € 26.50   2013*

SALERNES *10F3* (4km E Rural) *43.55360, 6.29781* **Camping
Club Le Ruou, Les Esparrus, 83690 Villecroze-les-Grottes
[04 94 70 67 70; fax 04 94 70 64 65; info@leruou.com;
www.leruou.com]** Fr Draguignan take D557 thro Flayosc,
then D560 dir Salernes. Site sp on L. Med, mkd pitch, terr,
shd; htd wc; chem disp; mv service pnt; baby facs; el pnts
(6-10A) €4.20-6; gas; lndtte (inc dryer); shop; rest, snacks; bar;
BBQ: playgrnd; htd pool; paddling pool; waterslide; fishing;
games area; archery; wifi; entmnt; games/TV rm; adv bkg;
35% statics; dogs €3.20; adv bkg; quiet. ♦ 1 Apr-31 Oct.
€ 28.00   2011*

SALERNES *10F3* (W Rural) *43.56606, 6.22561* **Camp
Municipal Les Arnauds, 83690 Salernes [04 94 67 51 95;
fax 04 94 70 75 57; lesarnauds@ville-salernes.fr; www.
village-vacances-lesarnauds.com]** W fr Draguignan on
D557 thro Salernes; site sp on L on W o'skts of town; to avoid
town cent turn R at rndabt on E o'skts sp Villecroze; take 1st
L at next 2 rndabts & foll site sp. Med, hdg/mkd pitch, pt shd;
wc; chem disp; baby facs; shwrs; el pnts (10A) inc; lndtte (inc
dryer); bar; playgrnd; rv sw adj; tennis; wifi; dogs €2; Eng spkn;
adv bkg; quiet; ccard acc; red low ssn; CKE/CCI. "Excel, rvside
site & san facs; warm welcome; gd night lighting; some sm
pitches poss diff lge o'fits; no twin-axles; no entry 1200-1500;
take torch into shwrs, lights on sh time switch." ♦
2 May-30 Sep. € 10.55   2010*

SALERNES *10F3* (5km NW Rural) *43.57302, 6.18816*
Camping Le Relais de la Bresque, Chemin de la
Piscine, 83690 Sillans-la-Cascade [04 94 04 64 89; fax
04 94 77 19 54; info@lerelaisdelabresque.com; www.
lerelaisdelabresque.com]** Fr W on D560 to Sillans-la-Cascade
& take D22 N to site, 1.5km on R. Med, shd, mkd pitch; htd
wc; chem disp; shwrs inc; el pnts (5-10A) €3-5; lndtte; ltd shop;
tradsmn; rest, snacks; bar; playgrnd; pool; rv 1.5km; cycle hire;
horseriding; archery; fitness course; games area; games rm;
wifi; entmnt; TV; 65% statics; dogs €2; Eng spkn; quiet; adv
bkg rec; red low ssn. "Well-run, clean site; lovely walk to vill;
unrel opening dates - phone ahead low ssn." 1 Apr-27 Oct.
€ 20.00   2008*

SALERS *7C4* (800m NE Rural) *45.14756, 2.49857* **Camp
Municipal Le Mouriol, Route de Puy-Mary, 15410
Salers [04 71 40 73 09 or 04 71 40 72 33 (Mairie); fax
04 71 40 76 28; www.salers.fr]** Take D922 SE fr Mauriac dir
Aurillac; turn onto D680 E dir Salers; site 1km NE of Salers on
D680 dir Puy Mary, opp Hôtel Le Gerfaut; sp fr all dir. Med,
hdg/mkd pitch, sl, pt shd; wc (some cont); chem disp; shwrs
inc; el pnts (16A) €4.60 (long lead poss req); lndtte; shops,
rest, snacks & bar 1km; BBQ; playgrnd; tennis; hill-walking;
WIFI; dogs; bus 1km; phone; poss cr; no adv bkg; quiet; 10%
red 10 days; CKE/CCI. "Generous pitches; san facs gd but
stretched if site full; peaceful low ssn; excel cycling & walking;
beautiful medieval vill; vg; well kept" ♦ 1 Apr-30 Oct.
€ 11.90   2012*

SALERS *7C4* (800m W Rural) *45.13304, 2.48762*
Camping à la Ferme (Fruquière), Apcher, 15140 Salers
[04 71 40 72 26] D922 S fr Mauriac for 17km; L on D680 sp
Salers; in lane on R sp Apcher - immed after passing Salers
town sp. Sm, pt shd; wc (some cont), chem disp (wc); shwrs
inc; el pnts (10A) €2.30; shop 300m; dogs; poss cr; quiet; CKE/
CCI. "Sm farm site; welcoming, friendly owner; excel clean san
facs, plenty hot water; beautiful countryside; gd."
1 May-30 Sep. € 8.20   2011*

SALERS *7C4* (7km W Rural) *45.11625, 2.42343* **Camp
Municipal Les Moulin du Teinturier, 9 Rue de
Montjoly,15140 St Martin-Valmeroux [04 71 69 43 12 or
04 71 69 20 32 (Mairie); fax 04 71 69 24 52; mairie.saint-
martin-valmeroux@wanadoo.fr]** Fr Mauriac S on D922;
sp on D37 E; 500m on L on Rv Maronne. Med, hdg pitch, pt
shd; wc; serviced pitch; shwrs; el pnts (6A) €2.70; lndtte; shop;
rest; BBQ; playgrnd; rv fishing; walking; tennis, horseriding &
pool adj; TV; quiet. "Site on Rv Maronne; gd walking; ideal
exploring Auvergne."♦ 15 Jun-15 Sep. € 10.20   2008*

SALIES DE BEARN *8F1* (2km NW Urban) *43.47639, -0.9382*
Camp Municipal de Mosquéros, Ave Al Cartéro, 64270 Salies-
de-Béarn [05 59 38 12 94; mairie-salies@wanadoo.fr] Leave
A64 at exit 7 onto D430 S sp Salies de Béarn. After 500m take
D330 on R sp 'Casino' & turn R onto D17 at rndabt. Site sp
in town, on D17 Bayonne rd NW of town. Site next to 'Base
Plein Aire des Mosquéros'. NB Avoid town - narr streets & diff
when busy. Med, hdg/mkd pitch, pt sl, terr, pt shd; wc; chem
disp; shwrs inc; el pnts inc (10A) inc; lndtte; shops 2km; rest,
snacks, bar 1km; pool, sports facs adj; fishing 1km; golf 2km;
horseriding 3km; TV; quiet; "Excel site; excel serviced pitches;
helpful warden; old but clean san facs; levelling blocks req
some pitches; poss diff lge o'fits; barrier clsd 2200-0700; mkt
Thu." ♦ 15 Mar-15 Oct. € 14.30   2009*

SALIES DU SALAT *8F3* (2km S Rural) *43.07621, 0.94683*
Complex Touristique de la Justale, Chemin de St Jean, 31260
Mane [05 61 90 68 18; fax 05 61 97 40 18; contact@village-
vacances-mane.fr; www.village-vacances-mane.fr]** Fr A64
exit 20 onto D117, turn R in vill at sp 'Village de Vacances'. Site
on R in approx 500m. Sm, pt shd; wc; chem disp; mv service
pnt; shwrs inc; el pnts (6A) €3.60 (poss rev pol); lndtte; shops
500m; playgrnd; pool; fishing; tennis; horseriding; internet; TV
rm; dogs €1.20; phone' adv bkg. "Lovely, peaceful site; lge
pitches; helpful staff; excel facs; sinage poss diff to follow"
1 Apr-31 Oct. € 11.80   2013*

SALIGNAC EYVIGNES see Sarlat la Canéda *7C3*

FRANCE

SALINS LES BAINS 6H2 (500m N Rural) 46.94650, 5.87896
Camp Municipal, 39110 Salins-les-Bains [03 84 37 92 70;
campingsalins.kanak.fr; www.salinscamping.com]
SE fr Besançon on N83. At Mouchard take D472 E to Salins.
Turn L at rndabt at N of Salins, well sp nr old stn. If app fr E take
2nd exit fr rndabt (blind app). Sm, pt shd; wc; shwrs inc; el pnts
(10A) €3.10; lndry rm; supmkt 500m; playgrnd; htd pool adj;
10% statics; adv bkg; quiet but some rd noise at 1 end & primary
school at other; "Well-run site; clean, modern san facs; excel
touring base N Jura; not often visited by British; far end of site
quieter; gd NH; Barrier locked 10:00-07:00" ♦ 31 Mar-1 Oct.
€ 13.40   2013*

SALLANCHES 9A3 (2km SE Rural) 45.92470, 6.65528
Camping Miroir du Mont Blanc, 1213 Chemin de
Mont-Blanc-Plage, 74700 Sallanches [04 50 58 14 28 or
04 50 58 12 04 (LS); fax 04 50 93 95 23; beatrice.brosse2@
wanadoo.fr] Fr Geneva on D1205 into Sallanches. Take 1st L
after 2nd set of traff lts (by post office) sp 'Hôpital'. Foll rd thro
traff lits & over rndabt when rd turns sharp R & runs alongside
m'way. In 2km site ent on R beside rndabt. Or exit A41 junc
21 or 22 dir Lac de Passy, site sp. Med, mkd pitch, shd; wc;
shwrs inc; el pnts (6A) €2.50; gas 2km; lndry rm; shops 2km;
tradsmn; rest, snacks; bar; playgrnd; pool & paddling pool
200m; waterslide; lake sw & sand/shgl beach adj; tennis;
fishing; sailing; windsurfing 50m; entmnt; adv bkg rec; rd
noise; red low ssn. "Situated bet m'way & rlwy."
15 May-15 Sep. € 13.00   2009*

SALLANCHES 9A3 (2km SE Rural) 45.92723, 6.64710
Camping Mont Blanc Village L'Ecureuil, 490 Route
des Follieux, 74700 Sallanches [04 50 58 43 67; fax
04 50 58 44 61; contact@camping-ecureuil.com; www.
camping-ecureuil.com] App fr Chamonix on D1205, turn
R opp Ford g'ge ent Sallanches; strt on thro traff lts, over
sleeping policemen, under rlwy bdge & fork R at Braconne
rest; strt at next junc to site in 200m. Med, hdg; wc; chem disp;
mv service pnt; shwrs inc; el pnts (10A) €2.50; gas; lndtte (inc
dryer); shops 1km; tradsmn; rest (not every day); bar; playgrnd;
pool nr; lake sw & sand/shgl beach; games area; games rm;
TV; some statics; dogs €1; poss cr; quiet; ccard acc; red low
ssn; CKE/CCI. "Gd, clean, spacious site; mountain views; well
drained after rain; excel." Easter-15 Oct. € 15.60   2009*

SALLANCHES 9A3 (4km SE Rural) 45.92388, 6.65042
Camping Village Center Les Iles, Lac de Passy 245
Chemin de la Cavettaz, 74190 Passy [04 50 58 45 36 or
04 99 57 21 21; www.passy-mont-blanc.com or www.
village-center.com] E fr Geneva on A40, exit junc 21 onto
D339 dir Passy; in 400m turn L onto D39 dir Sallanches; at
rndabt in 1.5km turn L onto D199 dir Domancy; immed after
rlwy x-ing in 500m turn R into Chemin de Mont Blanc Plage;
site at end of rd in 1km. Or E fr Sallanches on D1205 dir
Chamonix; in 3km turn L (1st into filter to turn L) onto D199;
in 1km turn L immed bef level x-ing; site at end of rd. Lge, hdg/
mkd pitch, pt shd; wc (some cont); baby facs; shwrs inc; el pnts
(8A) inc; lndtte; shop & 3km; snacks; playgrnd; htd pool; shgl
lake beach & sw adj; fishing; entmnt; statics; dogs €3; phone;
Eng spkn; adv bkg; quiet; ccard acc high ssn; red low ssn; CKE/
CCI; "Mountain views; conv Chamonix; vg site" ♦
6 Apr-29 Sep. € 26.40 (CChq acc)   2013*

SALLE EN BEAUMONT, LA 9C3 (4km SE Rural) 44.87593,
5.83710 Camping Belvédère de l'Obiou, Les Egats, 38350
St Laurent-en-Beaumont [tel/fax 04 76 30 40 80; info@
camping-obiou.com; www.camping-obiou.com] Clearly
sp on D1085. Sm, pt sl, pt terr, pt shd; htd wc; chem disp;
mv service pnt; baby facs; shwrs; el pnts (4-10A) €3-6 (poss
rev pol); lndtte (inc dryer); shop 7km; tradsmn; rest, snacks;
playgrnd; htd, covrd pool; games rm; wifi; TV; 5% statics; dogs
€2; poss cr; Eng spkn; rd noise; red long stay/low ssn; CKE/CCI;
"Superb, immac, family-run site; excel facs; helpful owners;
excel rest & pool; picturesque & interesting area; gd local
walks" ♦ 15 Apr-15 Oct. € 30.20 (CChq acc)   2013*

SALLE EN BEAUMONT, LA 9C3 (1.5km W Rural) 44.85573,
5.84503 Camping Le Champ Long, Chemin de Bas-
Beaumont, 38350 La Salle-en-Beaumont [04 76 30 41 81;
fax 04 76 30 47 21; champlong38@orange.fr; www.
camping-champlong.com] S fr Grenoble on N85 for approx
12km, turn R by primary school on ent La Salle-en-Beaumont.
Well sp fr main rd. Med, hdg/mkd pitch, hdstg, terr, shd; wc;
chem disp; mv service pnt; baby facs; shwrs inc; el pnts (10A)
€3.50; lndtte (inc dryer); tradsmn; rest, snacks; bar; BBQ;
playgrnd; pool; paddling pool; games area; games rm; wifi;
entmnt; TV; 30% statics; dogs €2.30; Eng spkn; adv bkg; quiet;
CKE/CCI. "Gd site for families; gd touring base - many sports/
leisure activities nrby; friendly, helpful owners will assist with
tractor if req; views fr some pitches; lge o'fits rec to pitch nr
recep; excel." ♦ ltd 1 Apr-15 Oct. € 16.00   2010*

SALLELES D'AUDE see Narbonne 10F1

SALLES (GIRONDE) 7D1 (500m SW Rural) 44.54475,
-0.87506 FFCC Camping Parc du Val de l'Eyre, 8 Route du
Minoy, 33770 Salles [05 56 88 47 03; fax 05 56 88 47 27;
levaldeleyre2@wanadoo.fr; www.camping-
parcduvaldeleyre.com] Exit junc 21 fr A63, foll dir to Salles
on D3. On edge of Salles turn L on D108 at x-rds. Ent to site on
L after rv opp Super U supmkt building. Lge, pt shd; wc; chem
disp; mv service pnt; baby facs; shwrs inc; el pnts (10A) €4 (poss
rev pol); gas; lndtte; shops adj; supmkt nr; rest, snacks; bar;
BBQ; playgrnd; htd pool; lake & rv sw; fishing; canoeing; tennis
500km; games area; horseriding 8km; entmnt; 80% statics;
dogs €4; quiet but entmnt poss noisy; ccard acc; red low
ssn. "Attractive site; gd san facs but poss stretched when
site busy; ltd facs low ssn; gd NH only." ♦ 27 Mar-13 Nov.
€ 28.00   2011*

⊞ **SALLES (GIRONDE)** 7D1 (4km SW Rural) 44.52039,
-0.89631 Camping Le Bilos, 37 Route de Bilos, 33770 Salles
[05 56 88 36 53; fax 05 56 88 45 14; lebilos@aol.com;
www.lebilos] Exit A63 junc 21; foll sp Salles on D3; turn
L onto D108/D108E3 sp Lugos; pass Carrefour supmkt on R;
in 2km bear R & site on R in 2km. Med, pt shd; htd wc; chem
disp; shwrs inc; el pnts (3-6A) €2.20-3.50; gas; lndtte; shop;
supmkt 2.5km; BBQ sep area; playgrnd; 80% statics; dogs;
adv bkg; quiet; "Pleasant, peaceful site in pine forest; sm, well-
drained pitches, ltd space for tourers, friendly owners, old but
clean san facs, ltd low ssn, cycle lane thro forest, vg NH en rte
Spain; Friendly welcome" € 16.10   2013*

SALLES CURAN (3km N) 44.20167, 2.77705 **Camping Beau Rivage, Route des Vernhes, 12410 Salles-Curan [05 65 46 33 32; fax 05 65 46 33 96; camping-beau-rivage@orange.fr; www.beau-rivage.fr]** Fr Rodez D911 turn S onto the D993 sp Salles Curan.Foll rd for approx 7km; turn R after lake bdge to site on R in approx 1.5km. Med, pt shd; wc; chem disp; shwrs inc; el pnts (6A) inc; lndtte; shop; rest; playgrnd; pool; shgl beach & lake; fishing; watersports nrby; horseriding nrby; games rm; TV; quiet; dogs €3.90; adv bkg;"Excel site on lake location, lovely area, gd walks & lots of activities nrby" Jun-Sep. € 34.90   2013*

SALLES CURAN 8E4 (2km NW Rural) 44.18933, 2.76693 **Camping Les Genêts, Lac de Pareloup, 12410 Salles-Curan [05 65 46 35 34; fax 05 65 78 00 72; contact@camping-les-genets.fr; www.camping-les-genets.fr]** Fr D911 Rodez-Millau rd take D993 S for approx 9km, then R onto D577, site sp on R by lake. Lge, pt sl, shd; wc; mv service pnt; baby facs; fam bthrm; shwrs; el pnts (6A) inc; lndtte (inc dryer); shop; rest, snacks; pizzeria; bar; htd pool; paddling pool; lake sw & beach; sailing; fishing; cycle hire; games area; wifi; entmnt; 40% statics; dogs €4; adv bkg; red long stay/low ssn. "Beautiful area; ltd facs low ssn." ♦ 17 May-14 Sep. € 34.00 (CChq acc) SBS - D07   2013*

SALLES D'AUDE see Narbonne 10F1

SALLES LAVAUGUYON, LES see Rochechouart 7B3

SALLES SUR VERDON, LES 10E3 (N Rural) 43.78129, 6.21298 Camp Municipal Les Ruisses, 83630 Les Salles-sur-Verdon [04 98 10 28 15; fax 04 98 10 28 16; lesruissescamping@orange.fr; www.sallessurverdon.com] Fr Moustiers foll D957, site on L just bef Les Salles. Lge, mkd pitch, pt shd; wc (some cont); baby facs; shwrs inc; el pnts (6A) €3.20; lndtte; shop, snacks, bar high ssn; playgrnd; shgl beach & lake nr; fishing; dogs €1.15; no adv bkg; quiet; ccard acc; CKE/CCI. "Pleasant site; ltd facs low ssn but gd hot shwrs & clean facs." ♦ 15 Feb-15 Nov. € 11.05   2009*

SALLES SUR VERDON, LES 10E3 (2km E Rural) 43.77574, 6.24561 **FFCC Camping L'Aigle, Quartier St Pierre, 83630 Aiguines [tel/fax 04 94 84 23 75; contact@camping-aigle.fr; www.camping-aigle.fr]** Fr D957 fr Les Salles or Moustiers turn onto D19 & cont for approx 7km. Site sp 1km beyond vill. Rd steep, winding & with hairpins & vill narr for lge o'fits. Med, sl, terr, pt shd; wc; mv service pnt; baby facs; shwrs inc; el pnts (6A) inc; lndtte; rest, snacks; BBQ; playgrnd; ent barrier; dogs €3; phone; Eng spkn; quiet; ccard acc; red low ssn; CKE/CCI. "Lake views; clean, modern facs; steep, twisting access to terr pitches poss diff lge o'fits; highly rec." ♦ 24 Aug-19 Sep. € 29.00   2010*

SALLES SUR VERDON, LES 10E3 (3km E Rural) 43.79653, 6.24315 **Camp Municipal Le Galetas, Quartier Vernis, 83630 Aiguines [tel/fax 04 94 70 20 48; campinglegaletas@aol.com; www.aiguines.com/galetas.html]** Fr S foll D957 twd Moustiers-Ste Marie then take D71 to Aguines & foll sp. Lge, pt shd; wc; chem disp; mv service pnt; shwrs; el pnts (6A) €2.50; lndtte; shop; snacks; bar; lake sw; watersports some statics; dogs €1; quiet. "Views of lake." 1 Apr-15 Oct. € 14.60   2008*

SALLES SUR VERDON, LES 10E3 (500m W Rural) 43.77552, 6.20719 **Camping La Source, Lac de Sainte Croix, Quartier Margaridon, 83630 Les Salles-sur-Verdon [04 94 70 20 40; fax 04 94 70 20 74; contact@camping-la-source.eu; www.camping-la-source.eu]** Fr Moustiers on D957, foll sp Camping Les Pins (adj) via rd round vill. Med, hdg/mkd pitch, hdstg, pt terr, pt shd; wc (some cont); chem disp; child/baby facs; serviced pitches; shwrs inc; el pnts (10A) €3.80 (poss rev pol); gas; lndtte; shop, rest, snacks, bar 500m; BBQ; playgrnd; dir access to lake; lake sw & shgl beach adj; watersports; canoe hire; TV rm; dogs €2.20; phone; Eng spkn; adv bkg; quiet; ccard acc; red low ssn; CKE/CCI. "Excel facs; superb situation; well-run site conv Gorges du Verdon; friendly, helpful owners; gates clsd 2200-0700; some sm pitches - manhandling poss req; highly rec." ♦ 15 Apr-10 Oct. € 17.40   2010*

SALLES SUR VERDON, LES 10E3 (500m W Rural) 43.77628, 6.2090 **FFCC Camping Les Pins, Lac de Sainte Croix, 83630 Les Salles-sur-Verdon [04 98 10 23 80; fax 04 94 84 23 27; campinglespins83@orange.fr; www.campinglespins.com]** Fr Moustiers on D957 to Les Salles-sur-Verdon. Site clearly sp in vill on lakeside, via track round vill. Med, hdg/mkd pitch, hdstg, terr, pt shd; wc; chem disp; mv service pnt; serviced pitches; baby facs; shwrs inc; el pnts (6A) inc; gas; lndtte; shop 200m; tradsmn; bar; playgrnd; shgl beach & lake sw 200m; fishing; canoe hire; watersports; wifi; dogs €1.95; Eng spkn; adv bkg; quiet; ccard acc; red low ssn/long stay/CKE/CCI. "Lovely views; excel, friendly site; busy high ssn, facs poss stretched; gd touring base." ♦ 1 Apr-16 Oct. € 22.90   2011*

SALON DE PROVENCE 10E2 (12km NE Rural) 43.72125, 5.20495 **FFCC Camping Durance Luberon, Domaine du Vergon, 13370 Mallemort [04 90 59 13 36; fax 04 90 57 46 62; duranceluberon@orange.fr; www.campingduranceluberon.com]** Exit A7 junc 26 onto D7n dir Aix-en-Provence. In 11km turn L at rndabt onto D561 dir Charleval (passing Pont-Royal golf course). In 1km turn L dir Mallemort, site on R in 1km, sp. Med, hdg/mkd pitch, pt shd; htd wc; chem disp; mv service pnt; shwrs inc; el pnts inc (6-10A) €3.80-4.50; gas; lndtte; sm shop & 3km; tradsmn; rest adj; snacks; bar; BBQ; playgrnd; htd pool; paddling pool; rv fishing 1km; tennis; cycle hire; horseriding adj; wifi; 5% statics; dogs €2; phone; Eng spkn; adv bkg; quiet; red low ssn; ccard not acc; CKE/CCI. "Gd site with lge pitches; friendly owners; clean, modern san facs; gd touring base; excel" ♦ 1 Apr-30 Sept. € 22.00   2013*

SALON DE PROVENCE 10E2 (5km NW Rural) 43.67820, 5.06480 **Camping Nostradamus, Route d'Eyguières, 13300 Salon-de-Provence [04 90 56 08 36; fax 04 90 56 65 05; gilles.nostra@gmail.fr; www.camping-nostradamus.com]** Exit A54/E80 junc 13 onto D569 N sp Eyguières. After approx 1.5km turn R opp airfield onto D72d, site on R in approx 4km just bef T-junc. Or fr N exit A7 junc 26 dir Salon-de-Provence. Turn R onto D17 for 5km dir Eyguières, then L onto D72, site on L. Med, hdg/mkd pitch, pt shd; wc; chem disp; mv service pnt; baby facs; shwrs inc; el pnts (4-6A) €2.95-5.15; gas; lndtte (with dryer); shop 3km; tradsmn; rest, snacks; bar; BBQ; playgrnd; pool; paddling pool; games area; wifi; entmnt; TV; 15% statics; dogs €3; phone; Eng spkn; adv bkg (bkg fee); quiet; ccard acc; red low ssn; CKE/CCI. "Pleasant site; busy high ssn; welcoming owner with vg sense of humour!; poss diff access lge o'fits; dusty when dry; gd walking." ♦ 1 Mar-30 Nov. € 21.60 (CChq acc)   2011*

SALORNAY SUR GUYE see Cluny *9A2*

⊞ **SALSES LE CHATEAU** *10G1* (1km N Rural) *42.84420,
2.92778* **FFCC Camp International du Roussillon, 66600
Salses-le-Château [04 68 38 60 72; fax 04 68 52 75 46;
camping-roussillon@orange.fr; www.camping-roussillon.
com]** Fr N on A9 exit junc 40 on D6009/D900 dir Perpignan;
site on R, N of town. Fr S exit A9 junc 41. Site has hotel, rest &
camping. Med, hdg pitch, hdstg, pt shd; wc; chem disp; shwrs
inc; el pnts (5-6A) €3 (poss rev pol); gas; lndtte; shops 2km;
tradsmn; rest, snacks; pizza adj low ssn; bar; BBQ (no elec);
playgrnd; pool; 40% statics; dogs €3; phone; Eng spkn; adv
bkg; some rd & rlwy noise; red long stay; ccard acc; CKE/CCI.
"Helpful, friendly owners; red facs low ssn & poss unkempt
pitches; gd access for lge m'vans; mosquitoes; popular NH."
♦ ltd € 22.00   2009*

SALVETAT SUR AGOUT, LA *8F4* (4km N Rural) *43.62739,
2.67919* **Camping Goudal, Route de Lacaune, La Gâche,
34330 La Salvetat-sur-Agout [04 67 97 60 44; fax
04 67 97 62 68; info@goudal.com; www.goudal.com]**
Fr St Pons-de-Thomières take D907 N dir Lacaune. Go thro
La Salvetat, site sp. Med, mkd pitch, pt sl, terr, pt shd; wc;
chem disp; mv service pnt; baby facs; shwrs inc; el pnts (4-6A)
€4; gas; lndtte; shop; rest high ssn; BBQ; playgrnd; entmnt;
some statics; dogs €2; poss cr; Eng spkn; adv bkg; quiet; CKE/
CCI. "Friendly Dutch owners; spacious site in woodland; vg."
1 May-30 Sep. € 17.35   2009*

SALVETAT SUR AGOUT, LA *8F4* (10km E Rural) *43.60653,
2.77940* **Camping Le Pioch, 34330 Fraisse-sur-Agout
[04 67 97 61 72; NICO-OUDHOF@wanadoo.fr; www.
lepioch.nl/fr/]** Fr Salvetat take D14 E twd Fraisse-sur-Agout.
In 6km look for sp on L (2km bef Fraise). Med, pt sl, pt shd; wc; shwrs inc;
el pnts (6A) €2.50; gas; lndtte; shop; tradsmn; rest, snacks;
bar; BBQ; playgrnd; dogs €1.50; Eng spkn; adv bkg; quiet;
CKE/CCI. "Excel walking area; views fr site." 1 May-30 Sep.
€ 12.50   2009*

"There aren't many sites open at this time of year"

If you're travelling outside peak season
remember to call ahead to check site opening
dates – even if the entry says 'open all year'.

SAMOENS *9A3* (5km SE Rural) *46.07392, 6.83768*
**Camp Municipal Le Pelly, 74740 Sixt-Fer-à-Cheval
[04 50 34 12 17; fax 04 50 89 51 02; camping@
sixtferacheval.net; www.sixtferacheval.com/camping/]**
Take D907 NE fr Sixt. Site sp on R after 6km bef bdge over Rv
Giffre. Med, pt sl, pt shd; wc; chem disp; baby facs; shwrs inc;
el pnts (10A) inc; lndtte; tradsmn; snacks; bar; BBQ; playgrnd;
horseriding 500m; dogs €1.55; phone; quiet. "Gd walking;
alpine flowers & wildlife; helpful wardens." 1 Jun-13 Sep.
€ 12.10   2009*

⊞ **SAMOENS** *9A3* (750m S Rural) *46.07731, 6.71851*
**Camping Caravaneige Le Giffre, La Glière, 74340 Samoëns
[04 50 34 41 92; fax 04 50 34 98 84; camping.samoens@
wanadoo.fr; www.camping-samoens.com]** Leave A40 at
junc 15 sp Fillinges/St Jeoire. Foll D907 thro Taninges E for
11km, sp Samoëns. At W town boundary turn R immed after
wooden arch over rd, foll sp to Parc des Loisirs. Site on R after
sw pool & park. Lge, mkd pitch, pt shd; htd wc (few cont);
chem disp; mv service pnt; baby facs; private san facs avail;
shwrs inc; el pnts (6-10A) €3.20-4.75; lndtte (inc dryer); shops
750m; tradsmn, rest, snacks adj; BBQ; playgrnd; htd pool adj;
fishing lake adj; tennis; cycle hire; htd ski storage/drying rm;
Samoëns ski gondola 150m; wifi; TV rm; 5% statics; dogs €2;
phone; poss cr; adv bkg ess high ssn; quiet; ccard acc; red CKE/
CCI. "Friendly staff; some facs ltd low ssn; on arr, park on
rdside bef checking in; excel winter site." ♦ € 18.50   2011*

⊞ **SAMOENS** *9A3* (5km W Rural) *46.08944, 6.67874*
**Camp Municipal Lac et Montagne, 74440 Verchaix [tel/
fax 04 50 90 10 12; www.verchaix.com]** Fr Taninges take
D907 sp Samoëns for 6km, site to R of main rd in Verchaix.
Med, shd; shwrs; el pnts (10A) €4.10; lndtte (inc dryer); shops
nr; rest, bar adj; playgrnd; rv & lake adj; tennis; some statics;
dogs €1.40; phone; adv bkg; quiet. "Gd touring base." ♦
€ 8.50   2009*

SAMOREAU see Fontainebleau *4E3*

SAMPZON see Vallon Pont d'Arc *9D2*

SANARY SUR MER *10F3* (4km NE Urban) *43.13147, 5.81483*
**Campasun Mas de Pierredon, 652 Chemin Raoul Coletta,
83110 Sanary-sur-Mer [04 94 74 25 02; fax 04 94 74 61 42;
pierredon@campasun.com; www.campasun-pierredon.fr]**
Take D11 fr Sanary, cross m'way & 1st L. Site on R in approx
1km. Med, shd; htd wc; chem disp; mv service pnt; shwrs inc;
el pnts (10A) inc; lndtte; shop; supmkt 800m; rest, snacks; bar;
playgrnd; htd pool; paddling pool; waterslides; beach 3km;
tennis; wifi; entmnt; TV; dogs €4; poss cr; adv bkg rec; rd
noise; red low ssn; red CKE/CCI; "Gd family site" ♦
19 Apr-30 Sep. € 47.00   2013*

⊞ **SANARY SUR MER** *10F3* (2km SE Urban) *43.11271,
5.82915* **Camping Les Playes, 419 Rue Grand, 83140 Six-
Fours-les-Plages [04 94 25 57 57, 06 08 25 97 32 (mob)
or 06 72 09 62 79 (mob); fax 04 94 07 19 90; camplayes@
wanadoo.fr; www.camplayes.com]** Fr Six-Fours-les-Plages
foll sp 'Camping Les Playes'. Site situated bet D11 & D63. Med,
mkd pitch, hdstg, pt sl, terr, shd; htd wc; chem disp; shwrs inc;
el pnts (10A) €4.50; lndtte; shops 300m; tradsmn; rest, snacks;
bar; htd pool; beach 1.5km; wifi; dogs €4; bus 300m; poss
cr; adv bkg; quiet; ccard acc; red low ssn; CKE/CCI. "Site on
hillside on edge of wood; friendly recep; ltd space for tourers;
rec phone ahead; poss diff lge o'fits; gd." € 30.00   2011*

SANARY SUR MER *10F3* (1.5km W Coastal) *43.12400, 5.78695* **Campasun Parc Mogador, 167 Chemin de Beaucours, 83110 Sanary-sur-Mer [04 94 74 53 16; fax 04 94 74 10 58; mogador@campasun.eu; www.campasun-mogador.eu]** Fr A50 exit junc 12 dir Bandol. Camping sp on R bef Sanary (for 2 sites). Lge, pt shd; htd wc; mv service pnt; baby facs; shwrs inc; el pnts (10A) inc; gas; lndtte (inc dryer); ltd shop; rest, snacks; bar; playgrnd; htd pool; paddling pool; shgl beach 800m; fishing, watersports 1km; games area; wifi; entmnt; TV; 40% statics; dogs €2.40 (not acc Jul/Aug); bus nrby; adv bkg rec; quiet; red low ssn. "Busy site; gd sized pitches; excel, modern san facs; narr site rds & overgrowing trees poss diff lge o'fits; poss muddy after heavy rain; attractive port." ◆ 14 Mar-6 Nov. € 40.30   2011*

SANCERRE *4G3* (4km N Rural) *47.34215, 2.86571* **Flower Camping Les Portes de Sancerre, Quai de Loire, 18300 St Satur [02 48 72 10 88; camping.sancerre@flowercampings.com; www.camping-cher-sancerre.com]** Fr Sancerre on D955 thro cent St Satur & St Thibault. Turn L immed bef Loire bdge. Site on R in 100m. Med, hdg pitch, shd; wc; chem disp; mv service pnt; shwrs inc; el pnts (10A) inc (long lead poss req); lndtte (inc dryer); shop 500m; tradsmn; rest 500m; playgrnd; pool adj; rv sw via slipway; canoe hire adj; tennis; cycle hire; games area; entmnt; TV rm; 50% statics; dogs €2; poss cr; some Eng spkn; adv bkg; quiet, but poss noise fr public rv slipway & watersports; CKE/CCI. "Nice site; some pitches sm, some with rv view; friendly & helpful staff; gd clean san facs, rec own in peak ssn; rvside walks; gd touring cent; vg." ◆ 1 Apr-29 Sep. € 17.50   2012*

See advertisement on pages 32 & 33

SANCHEY see Epinal *6F2*

SANDUN see Guérande *2G3*

"That's changed – Should I let The Club know?"

If you find something on site that's different from the site entry, fill in a report and let us know. See www.caravanclub.co.uk/europereport.

SANGUINET *7D1* (3km N Rural) *44.49915, -1.07911* **Camping Lou Broustaricq, 2315 Route de Langeot, 40460 Sanguinet [05 58 82 74 82; fax 05 58 82 10 74; loubrousta@wanadoo.fr; www.lou-broustaricq.com]** Take Arcachon exit off Bordeax-Bayonne m'way. After 5km twd S on D3 & D216 to Sanguinet. Site sp in town off Bordeaux rd. V lge, mkd pitch, pt shd; htd wc (some cont); chem disp; shwrs inc; el pnts (10A) inc; lndtte (inc dryer); shop; rest, snacks, bar high ssn; BBQ; playgrnd; pool; waterslide; lake sw & sand beach 500m; watersports; sailing school; tennis; games area; cycle hire; entmnt; golf nr; wifi; TV rm; 60% statics; no dogs; Eng spkn; adv bkg; quiet; red low ssn; ccard acc; CKE/CCI. "In lovely wooded area; gd cycle tracks; gd for children; vg; touring pitches sep from statics; nice pool; gd cycling; nr army base, some aircraft noise" ◆ 1 Apr-30 Sep. € 51.00   2013*

SANGUINET *7D1* (1.5km S Rural) *44.48372, -1.09449* **Campéole Camping Le Lac Sanguinet, 526 Rue de Pinton, 40460 Sanguinet [05 58 82 70 80; fax 05 58 82 14 24; lac-sanguinet@campeole.com; www.campeole.com]** Foll Le Lac sp at rndabt in Sanguinet, turn L on lakeside, site on L in 600m. Lge, mkd pitch, pt shd; wc; mv service pnt; shwrs inc; el pnts (6-10A) €4.10; lndtte; shops 500m; tradsmn; snacks; bar; BBQ (not charcoal); playgrnd; htd pool; paddling pool; sand beach, lake sw & sailing nrby; watersports; games area; games rm; cycle hire; wifi; entmnt; some statics; dogs €3.10; extra €26 for twin-axles; poss cr; quiet; red low ssn; CKE/CCI. "Spacious site in pine woods; cycle path around lake; san facs poss run down low ssn; friendly, helpful staff." 30 Apr-19 Sep. € 26.50   2009*

See advertisement on pages 14 & 15

SANGUINET *7D1* (2km SW Rural) *44.48402, -1.09098* **Camping Les Grands Pins, Ave de Losa, Route du Lac, 40460 Sanguinet [05 58 78 61 74; fax 05 58 78 69 15; info@campinglesgrandspins.com; www.campinglesgrandspins.com]** Foll Le Lac sp at rndabt in Sanguinet. Turn L at lakeside. Site on L in 450m opposite yacht club. Lge, hdg pitch, shd; wc; chem disp; (wc); shwrs inc; child/baby facs; el pnts (3-10A) inc; lndtte; rest, snacks; bar; playgrnd; pool; sand beach & lake sw adj; boating; windsurfing; fishing, canoeing; tennis; cycle hire; TV; 50% statics; dogs €2; poss cr; Eng spkn; adv bkg; poss noisy; red low ssn; CKE/CCI. "Clean site; rest & bar poss clsd low ssn; parking for m'vans adj." ◆ 1 Apr-31 Oct. € 37.00   2008*

SARLAT LA CANEDA *7C3* (12km N Rural) *44.97450, 1.18832* **Camping Les Tailladis, 24200 Marcillac-St Quentin [05 53 59 10 95; fax 05 53 29 47 56; info@tailladis.com; www.tailladis.com]** N fr Sarlat on D704 dir Montignac. After 7km turn L & foll sp to site. NB Access along fairly narr lane. Med, hdg pitch, pt sl, terr, pt shd; wc; chem disp; mv service pnt; shwrs inc; el pnts (10A) €3.80; gas; lndtte; shop; rest, snacks & bar (Apr-Oct); pool; lake sw; fishing; canoeing; 6% statics; dogs €2; phone; poss cr; Eng spkn; adv bkg; ccard acc; red low ssn. "Excel site; friendly & helpful Dutch owners; immac san facs, ltd early ssn; vg food in rest; c'van storage." ◆ 1 Mar-30 Nov. € 22.00   2011*

SARLAT LA CANEDA *7C3* (6km NE Rural) *44.93666, 1.23318* **Camping Le Val d'Ussel, 24200 Proissans [05 53 59 28 73; fax 05 53 29 38 25; www.homair.com]** Fr Sarlat, take D704 N & foll sps to Proissans. Fr Périgueux, take N89 to Thenon, D67 to Chambon, D704 to sps to Proissans. Fr Brive, N89 twd Périgueux, D60 S. Med, pt sl, pt shd; wc; chem disp; shwrs inc; baby facs; el pnts (6-10A); gas; lndtte; tradsmn; rest, snacks; bar; BBQ; playgrnd; 2 htd pools; lake adj; fishing; shgl beach 15km; tennis; games area; cycle hire; entmnt; TV; many statics; dogs; adv bkg; quiet; red low ssn. 27 Apr-7 Sep.   2008*

SARLAT LA CANEDA *7C3* (6km NE Rural) *44.90404, 1.28210* Camping Les Grottes de Roffy, 24200 Ste Nathalène [05 53 59 15 61; fax 05 53 31 09 11; contact@roffy.fr; www.roffy.fr] Fr N end of Sarlat take D47 NE for Ste Nathalène. Site on R 1km bef vill. Or fr A20 exit junc 55 onto ND804/D703 dir Carlux. Turn R onto D61B then D47 to Ste Nathalène, site thro vill on L. Lge, hdg/mkd pitch, terr, pt shd; htd wc; chem disp; baby facs; shwrs inc; el pnts (6A) €3; gas; lndtte; shop; tradsmn; rest, snacks; bar; BBQ; playgrnd; 4 pools inc paddling pool; canoeing; tennis; games area; games rm; cycle hire; entmnt; 40% statics (inc tour ops); dogs €2.10; extra for 'comfort' pitches; Eng spkn; adv bkg (ess Jul/Aug); CKE/CCI. "Excel rest & shop; helpful staff; lovely site." ♦ 17 Apr-19 Sep. € 25.30   2009*

SARLAT LA CANEDA *7C3* (7km NE Rural) *44.91825, 1.27870* Camping Domaine des Mathévies, Les Mathévies, 24200 Ste Nathalène [05 53 59 20 86 or 06 14 10 95 86 (mob); mathevies@mac.com; www.mathevies.com] Exit A20 junc 55 Souillac & foll sp Roufillac. At Roufillac, foll sp to Carlux & cont to Ste Nathalène, site sp N of Ste Nathèlene. Sm, hdg/mkd pitch, pt shd; wc; chem disp; mv service pnt; shwrs; el pnts (10A) €4; snacks; bar; playgrnd; pool; paddling pool; tennis; games area; wifi; sat TV; some statics; dogs €1.50; adv bkg; quiet. "Gd, British-owned site; lge pitches, most with views." ♦ Easter-30 Sep. € 21.50 SBS - D04   2010*

SARLAT LA CANEDA *7C3* (8km NE Rural) *44.90030, 1.29700* Camping La Châtaigneraie, 24370 Prats-de-Carlux [05 53 59 03 61 or 05 53 30 29 03 (LS); fax 05 53 29 86 16; lachataigneraie@orange.fr; www.lachataigneraie24.com] Fr Sarlat take D704 E twd Souillac, after 3km turn L onto D704A/D703. At Roufillac turn L opp rv bdge onto D61 sp Carlux. In Carlux fork L onto D47B & in 4km turn L at site sp, site on R in 500m. Med, hdg/mkd pitch, terr, pt shd; wc; chem disp; baby facs; shwrs inc; jaccuzi; el pnts (10A) inc (poss rev pol); gas; lndtte; shop; rest, snacks; sm bar; BBQ (elec/charcoal); playgrnd; htd pool; paddling pool; waterslide; fishing; tennis; games area; cycle circuit; wifi; entmnt; games/TV rm; dogs €2.30; no c'vans/m'vans over 7m (inc towbar) high ssn; poss cr; quiet; ccard acc; red low ssn. "Excel site; friendly, helpful owners; vg clean san facs; vg pool area; some pitches diff due position of trees; mkt Sarlat Wed & Sat am." ♦ 21 Apr-16 Sep. € 32.50   2011*

SARLAT LA CANEDA *7C3* (9km NE Rural) *44.90803, 1.29212* Camping La Palombière, 24200 Ste Nathalène [05 53 59 42 34; fax 05 53 28 45 40; la.palombiere@ wanadoo.fr; www.lapalombiere.fr] Take D47 fr Sarlat to Ste Nathalène, thro vill, past Mill Rest, fork L on o'skts by cemetary. Site sp on R in 300m - sharp R turn & access poss diff. Med, terr, shd; wc; chem disp; baby facs; shwrs inc; el pnts (10A) inc; lndtte; shop; rest, snacks; bar; BBQ; htd pools; waterslide; tennis; gym; games rm; games area; entmnt; TV; 70% statics (tour ops); dogs €2; Eng spkn; adv bkg; quiet; 10% red low ssn. "Lovely, well-run site; friendly owners; immac san facs; vg rest with views; poss diff for lge o'fits due trees, narr site rds & pitch sizes; highly rec." ♦ 30 Apr-13 Sep. € 25.70   2009*

SARLAT LA CANEDA *7C3* (10km NE Rural) *44.95778, 1.27280* Camping Les Péneyrals, Le Poujol, 24590 St Crépin-et-Carlucet [05 53 28 85 71; fax 05 53 28 80 99; camping.peneyrals@wanadoo.fr; www.peneyrals.com] Fr Sarlat N on D704; D60 E dir Salignac-Eyvignes to Le Poujol; S to St Crépin. Site sp. Lge, hdg pitch, pt sl, terr, pt shd; htd wc; chem disp; mv service pnt; all serviced pitch; baby facs; shwrs inc; el pnts (5-10A) €3.40-3.90; lndtte; shop; rest, snacks; bar; playgrnd; 4 pools (1 htd, covrd); paddling pool; waterslide; fishing; tennis; games area; entmnt; 50% statics; dogs €2.40; phone adj; Eng spkn; adv bkg; quiet; red low ssn; ccard acc; red low ssn. "Friendly owners; superb family & touring site." ♦ 11 May-12 Sep. € 29.20   2010*

SARLAT LA CANEDA *7C3* (12km NE Rural) *44.96347, 1.32817* FLOWER Camping Le Temps de Vivre, Route de Carlux, 24590 Salignac-Eyvignes [tel/fax 05 53 28 93 21; contact@temps-de-vivre.com; www.temps-de-vivre.com or www.flowercampings.com] Fr Sarlat N on D704, bear R onto D60 to Salignac-Eyvigues. Fr Salignac take D61 S dir Carlux, site sp in 1.5km on R. Sm, hdg/mkd pitch, terr, pt shd; wc; chem disp; mv service pnt; baby facs; fam bthrm; shwrs inc; el pnts (10A) €4; gas; lndtte; shop; tradsmn; BBQ; supmkt 2km; rest & bar (high ssn); snacks; pool; playgrnd; games area; golf; tennis; fishing; dogs €2; 40% statics; poss cr; quiet; phone; adv bkg (fee); Eng spkn; ccard acc; CKE/CCI. "Lovely, well-kept site; gd sized pitches; friendly, helpful owners; lge o'fits poss diff access some pitches; rec." ♦ 23 Apr-24 Sep. € 21.50   2011*

See advertisement on pages 32 & 33

SARLAT LA CANEDA *7C3* (1km E Rural) *44.89328, 1.22756* Camping Indigo Sarlat Les Périères, Route de la Croix d'Allon, 24200 Sarlat-la-Canéda [05 53 59 05 84; fax 05 53 28 57 51; sarlat@camping-indigo.com; www. camping-indigo.com] Site on R of D47 to Proissans & Ste Nathalène. NB steep access rds. Med, mkd pitch, terr, shd; wc; mv service pnt; sauna; baby facs; shwrs inc; el pnts (6A) €3.90; gas; lndry rm; shop; tradsmn; bar; BBQ (gas/charcoal); playgrnd; 2 pools (1 htd covrd); games rm; tennis; some statics; dogs; poss cr; Eng spkn; adv bkg; quiet; ccard acc; red low ssn. "Lovely site; friendly, helpful staff; san facs clean too few; excel pool complex; steep site rds; access poss diff med & lge o'fits; excel." ♦ ltd Easter-30 Sep. € 27.50   2010*

See advertisement on next page

SARLAT LA CANEDA *7C3* (10km E Rural) *44.8674, 1.3578* Camping Les Ombrages, Rouffillac, 24370 Carlux [09 53 53 25 55; fax 05 53 28 62 18; ombragesperigord@ free.fr; www.ombrages.fr] 12km W thro Souillac on D703. Turn L at x-rds in Rouffillac & immed turn L bef rv bdge into site. Med, some mkd pitch, pt shd; wc; chem disp; shwrs inc; el pnts (6A) €2.70; gas 1km; lndtte; shop 1km; tradsmn (high ssn); rest 500m; snacks; bar; BBQ; playgrnd; pool adj; rv sw adj; fishing; tennis; games area; cycle & canoe hire; internet; TV rm; 2% statics; dogs €2; phone; poss cr; Eng spkn; adv bkg; quiet but some rd noise; ccard acc; red low ssn; CKE/CCI. "Pleasant, well-kept, rvside site; enthusiastic new owners live on site; pitching poss diff due trees; san facs (open air) poss stretched high ssn; cycle track; vg; Lovely peaceful site; lots of entertainment" 15 Apr-15 Oct. € 13.10   2012*

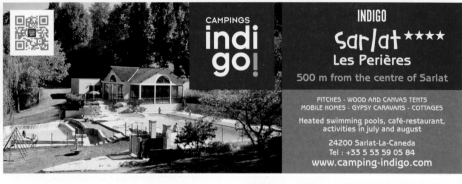

SARLAT LA CANEDA *7C3* (12km E Rural) *44.86345,
1.37350* **Camping Le Mondou, Le Colombier, 24370
St Julien-de-Lampon [tel/fax 05 53 29 70 37; lemondou@
camping-dordogne.info; www.camping-dordogne.info]**
Fr Sarlat-la-Canéda take D704/D703 E; cross rv at Rouffillac,
ent St Julien-de-Lampon & turn L at x-rds; site sp on R in 2km.
Med, hdg/mkd pitch, pl, pt shd; wc; chem disp; mv service
pnt; baby facs; shwrs inc; el pnts (6A) €3.50; gas 700m; lndtte;
shop 2km; tradsmn; rest, snacks; bar; BBQ; playgrnd; pool &
paddling pool; rv sw, fishing & waterports 300m; games rm;
games area; cycle hire; wifi; 10% statics; dogs €1; phone; poss
cr; Eng spkn; adv bkg; quiet; red low ssn. "Beautiful views;
friendly, helpful owners; sm, uneven pitches; gd cycle paths."
♦ 1 May-15 Oct. € 21.00   2012*

SARLAT LA CANEDA *7C3* (5km SE Rural) *44.85480, 1.23760*
**Camping Les Acacias, Route de Cahors, 24200 Sarlat-la-
Canéda [05 53 31 08 50; fax 05 53 59 29 30; camping-
acacias@wanadoo.fr; www.acacias.fr]** Foll sp La Canéda vill
& site fr D704 S fr Sarlat. NB Last few metres of app v narr rd.
Med, hdg/mkd pitch, pt sl, shd; wc; chem disp; mv service pnt;
baby facs; shwrs inc; el pnts (6-10A) €3.50-4.50; gas; lndtte;
supmkt 3km; tradsmn; rest, snacks; bar; playgrnd; 2 pools;
games area; wifi; entmnt; some statics; dogs €1.50; phone;
bus; adv bkg; quiet; ccard acc; red low ssn/CKE/CCI. "Clean,
modern san facs; helpful, enthusiastic owners; ideal touring
base; mkt Wed & Sat." 1 Apr-30 Sep. € 16.50   2010*

SARLAT LA CANEDA *7C3* (8km SE Rural) **Camping Le Plein
Air des Bories, 24200 Carsac-Aillac [tel/fax 05 53 28 15 67;
camping.lesbories@wanadoo.fr]** Take D704 SE fr Sarlat sp
Gourdon; diff RH turn to site after Carsac vill. Easier access
on D703 fr Vitrac. Med, pt sl, shd; wc (male cont); baby
facs; shwrs; el pnts (3-6A) inc; gas; lndtte; sm shop & 1.5km;
tradsmn; snacks; bar; htd pool; rv sw, canoe hire, boating &
fishing; tennis 700m; dogs €1.30; poss cr; Eng spkn; quiet;
CKE/CCI. "Clean, shady rvside site; friendly owners." ♦
1 Jun-15 Sep. € 18.00   2012*

SARLAT LA CANEDA *7C3* (8km SE Rural) *44.86340, 1.29727*
**Camping Les Chênes Verts, Route de Sarlat, 24370
Calviac-en-Périgord [05 53 59 21 07; fax 05 53 31 05 51;
chenes-verts@wanadoo.fr; www.chenes-verts.com]**
S fr Châteauroux on A20 leave at Souillac exit. Join D703
heading W twd Sarlat; branch R onto D704a soon after
Calviac-en-Périgord, site on R in 2km. Or take D704/704A SE
fr Sarlat. Site in 8km on L; clearly sp & flags at ent. Med, hdg/
mkd pitch, pt sl, pt shd; wc; chem disp; mv service pnt; baby
facs; shwrs inc; el pnts (6A) inc (25m cable rec); gas; lndtte;
sm shop; tradsmn; rest, snacks; bar; BBQ (gas/charcoal only);
playgrnd; 2 pools (1 htd, covrd); paddling pool; canoeing; cycle
hire; golf 7km; games area; games rm; entmnt; TV; 70 statics
(sep area); no dogs; Eng spkn; adv bkg; quiet but some noise
fr bar; red long stay; ccard acc; CKE/CCI. "Pleasant, peaceful
site; gd sized pitches but sandy, so muddy when wet; new
owners updating facs; excel pool; mkt Sat Sarlat." ♦
1 Apr-30 Sep. € 30.30   2008*

SARLAT LA CANEDA *7C3* (10km SE Rural) *44.8289, 1.2667*
**Camping Le Rocher de la Cave, 24200 Carsac-Aillac
[05 53 28 14 26; fax 05 53 28 27 10; rocher.de.la.cave@
wanadoo.fr; www.rocherdelacave.com]** Fr Sarlat-la-Canéda
take D704 S twd Carsac-Aillac & turn L bef vill. Follow sp.
Med, hdg/mkd pitch, pt shd; wc; shwrs inc; el pnts (10A) €3;
gas; lndtte; shop; tradsmn; rest, snacks; bar; playgrnd; pool;
paddling pool; canoe hire; tennis 500m; games area; entmnt;
5% statics; dogs; phone; quiet; red low ssn. "Rvside site; gd."
♦ ltd 1 May-15 Sep. € 16.80   2008*

SARLAT LA CANEDA *7C3* (10km SE Rural) *44.81536, 1.29245*
**Camping Les Granges, 24250 Groléjac [05 53 28 11 15;
fax 05 53 28 57 13; contact@lesgranges-fr.com; www.
lesgranges-fr.com]** Fr Sarlat take D704 SE, sp Gourdon.
Site sp nr cent of Groléjac on R. Care on acute corner after
rlwy bdge. Med, hdg, terr, pt shd; wc; chem disp; baby facs;
serviced pitches; shwrs inc; el pnts (6A) €3.65; gas; lndtte (inc
dryer); shop; rest, snacks; bar; playgrnd; htd pool; paddling
pool; waterslide; rv & lake fishing 1km; cycle hire; games rm;
wifi; entmnt; TV; 40% statics; dogs €3; poss cr; Eng spkn; adv
bkg; ccard acc; red low ssn; CKE/CCI. "Historical & beautiful
area; vg site & facs." ♦ 23 Apr-11 Sep. € 24.60   2010*

FRANCE

SARLAT LA CANEDA *7C3* (13km SE Rural) *44.80227, 1.29448* Camping du Lac de Groléjac, Plan d'Eau, 24250 Groléjac [05 53 59 48 70; fax 05 53 29 39 74; contact@camping-dulac-dordogne.com; www.camping-dulac-dordogne.com] On D704 SE fr Sarlat twd Goudon, Groléjac in 11km. In vill cent, foll sp 'Plan d'Eau'; pass thro vill & turn R in front of Le Marais Rest, in 100m turn L dir Nabirat. Site on L in 500m. Med, hdg pitch, pt shd; wc; chem disp; baby facs; shwrs; el pnts (10A) €3; gas; lndtte; sm shop; sm rest, snacks; bar; playgrnd; sand beach & lake sw; fishing; watersports; cycle hire; wifi; dogs €1.50; Eng spkn; adv bkg; quiet; ccard acc; CKE/CCI. "Popular site on man-made lake with artificial sand beach; excel." ♦ 15 Apr-15 Oct. € 11.50   2009*

SARLAT LA CANEDA *7C3* (6km S Rural) *44.82375, 1.25080* Camping La Bouysse de Caudon, 24200 Vitrac [05 53 28 33 05; fax 05 53 30 38 52; info@labouysse.com; www.labouysse.com] S fr Sarlat on D46 dir Vitrac. At Vitrac 'port' bef bdge turn L onto D703 sp Carsac. In 2km turn R & foll site sp, site on L. Well sp. Med, hdg/mkd pitch, pt shd; wc; chem disp; baby facs; shwrs inc; el pnts (10A) €4.30; gas; lndtte; shop; tradsmn; rest, snacks; bar; BBQ; playgrnd; pool; rv sw & shgl beach; fishing; canoe hire; tennis; games area; internet; entmnt; 8% statics; dogs €2; phone; poss cr; Eng spkn; adv bkg (dep); quiet; ccard acc; red low ssn; CKE/CCI. "Beautiful family-run site on Rv Dordogne; helpful owner; plenty gd clean san facs; gd access rv beach; muddy when wet; many Bastides in area; excel." ♦ 2 Apr-25 Sep. € 20.00   2011*

See advertisement below

SARLAT LA CANEDA *7C3* (8km S Rural) *44.82525, 1.25360* Camping Domaine de Soleil-Plage, Caudon-par-Montfort, 24200 Vitrac [05 53 28 33 33; fax 05 53 28 30 24; info@soleilplage.fr; www.soleilplage.fr] On D46, 6km S of Sarlat twd Vitrac, turn L onto D703 to Château Montfort, R to site dir Caudon, sp. Site beyond Camping La Bouysse on rvside, 2km E of Vitrac. If coming fr Souillac on D703; when app Montfort rd v narr with overhanging rock faces. Narr access rds on site. Lge, hdg pitch, pt shd; htd wc; chem disp; mv service pnt; baby facs; serviced pitches; shwrs inc; el pnts (16A) inc (poss rev pol); gas; lndtte (inc dryer); shop; rest, snacks; bar; BBQ; playgrnd; htd pool; paddling pool; waterslide; rv sand beach adj; fishing; canoeing; tennis; cycle hire; golf 1km; horseriding 5km; games rm; wifi; entmnt; TV; 45% statics; dogs €3.50; no c'vans/m'vans over 7m Jun-Aug; phone; Eng spkn; adv bkg ess Jul/Aug; quiet; ccard acc; red low ssn/groups; CKE/CCI. "Lovely site in beautiful location; friendly, welcoming owner; variety of pitches - extra for serviced/rvside (shady); san facs clean; superb aquatic complex; poss muddy when wet; highly rec." ♦ 6 Apr-30 Sep. € 36.50 (CChq acc) SBS - D15   2013*

See advertisement above

Caudon 24200 VITRAC - France
info labouysse.com - www.labouysse.com

Site owned by French family. English spoken.

Along the river Dordogne near the well known Caudon rock, direct access to beach area where you can swim or go canoeing. Beautiful site near Montfort château, Sarlat (6km.) and many other Dordogne sights.
Green pitches, with trees and hedges giving some shade.
Lovely swimming pool. A wide range of accommodations available (country cottages, mobile homes, gîtes and pitches).
On the site: grocery's, bar and snack bar (open from 15th June until 31st August) – washing machine, dryer and iron - WiFi

Site report forms at back of guide   *Last year of report*   **545**

SARLAT LA CANEDA *7C3* (9km S Rural) *44.81628, 1.21508*
Camping Beau Rivage, Gaillardou, 24250 La Roque-Gageac [05 53 28 32 05; fax 05 53 29 63 56; camping.beau.rivage@wanadoo.fr; www.beaurivagedordogne.com]
On S side of D703, 1km W of Vitrac adj Rv Dordogne. Lge, mkd pitch, pt shd; htd wc (some cont); chem disp; baby facs; shwrs inc; el pnts (6A) €3.50; gas; lndtte; shop; rest 200m; snacks; bar; playgrnd; htd pool; rv beach; canoeing; tennis; games area; cycle hire; horseriding; archery; golf 2km; wifi; entmnt; TV; some statics; dogs €3; phone; poss cr; Eng spkn; adv bkg rec high ssn; quiet; red low ssn; "Gd touring base" ♦
4 Apr-20 Sep. € 23.65   2013*

SARLAT LA CANEDA *7C3* (9km S Rural) *44.82442, 1.16939*
Camping La Plage, 83 Près La Roque-Gageac, 24220 Vézac [06 85 23 22 16; campinglaplage24@orange.fr; www.camping-laplage.fr] On banks of Rv Dordogne, 500m W of La Roque-Gageac on D703. Med, mkd pitch, shd; wc; chem disp (wc); shwrs inc; el pnts (3A) €2.40; gas; sm shop 1km; BBQ; playgrnd; pool; shgl beach & rv sw; fishing; canoeing; some statics; poss cr; adv bkg; quiet; red CKE/CCI. "Attractive site; excel pitches; kind, helpful owers; basic san facs but clean; ltd facs low ssn; highly rec. ccard not acc; New (2012) immac san facs" 1 Apr-30 Sep. € 20.00   2012*

SARLAT LA CANEDA *7C3* (9km S Rural) *44.78648, 1.20930*
Camping Le Pech de Caumont, 24250 Cénac-et-St-Julien [05 53 28 21 63 or 05 53 28 30 67; fax 05 53 29 99 73; jmilhac@pech-de-caumont.com; www.pech-de-caumont.com] D46 fr Sarlat to Cénac, cross rv & cont on D46 thro Cénac; site ent on L 500m past End of Vill sp. Do not go thro Domme. Med, hdg/mkd pitch, pt sl, terr, pt shd; wc; chem disp; shwrs inc; el pnts (6A) €3.10; lndtte; shops 1km; snacks & sm bar (400 high ssn); BBQ; playgrnd; pool; rv sw 2km; TV rm; 20% statics; dogs; phone; poss cr; Eng spkn; adv bkg; quiet; ccard acc; red low ssn; CKE/CCI. "Views fr most pitches; modern, clean san facs; helpful owners; popular, tidy, family-run site; excel." 15 Jun-15 Sept. € 15.45   2012*

SARLAT LA CANEDA *7C3* (10km S Rural) *44.80436, 1.20589*
Camp Municipal, Le Port de Domme, 24250 Cénac-et-St Julien [05 53 28 31 91 or 05 53 31 41 31 (Mairie)]
D46 fr Sarlat to Vitrac then Cénac; cross rv & site on L on ent Cénac. Med, mkd pitch, pt shd; wc; chem disp; shwrs inc; el pnts (6A) inc (poss long lead req); lndtte; shop, rest, snacks, bar 200m; playgrnd; rv sw, boating & fishing adj; games area; dogs; phone; adv bkg; quiet; no ccard acc. "Pleasant site in excel rvside location; clean facs but dated & ltd low ssn; ground rather rough & poss flooded after rain; site opens earlier if demand; vg NH."
1 Jun-15 Sep. € 13.60   2009*

SARLAT LA CANEDA *7C3* (10km S Rural) *44.81521, 1.22362* Camping La Rivière de Domme, 24250 Domme [05 53 28 33 46; fax 05 53 29 56 04; contact@camping-riviere-domme.com; www.camping-riviere-domme.com]
Fr Sarlat take D46 to Vitrac. Cross rv bdge on D46E. In 1km at T-junc turn R on D50 & in 1km turn R at sp into site. Sm, pt shd; wc; chem disp; shwrs inc; el pnts (10A) €2.50 (poss rev pol); lndtte; shops 4km; playgrnd; pool; games area; few statics; Eng spkn; adv bkg; quiet; red low ssn. "Generous pitches; pleasant owner; modern san facs; many walks fr site." ♦ 4 Apr-3 Oct. € 10.80   2009*

SARLAT LA CANEDA *7C3* (10km S) *44.82527, 1.24222*
Camping La Sagne, Lieu dit Lassagne, 24200 Vitrac [05 53 28 18 36; info@camping-la-sagne.com; www.camping-la-sagne.com] On A20 exit 55 (Souillac) & head towards Sarlat; take D703 in dir Montfort; turn L & foll sp to site. Med, mkd pitch; wc; chem disp; el pnts (16A) inc; shop; bar; playgrnd; pool; paddling pool; jacuzzi; rv fishing; wifi; dogs €3; Eng spkn; quiet; ccard acc. "Superb location in the Dordogne; undergoing major refurb for the 2012 ssn." 6 Apr-30 Sep.
€ 30.00   2011*

See advertisement below

Camping le Perpetuum ★★★

**La Rivière
24250 Domme**

Welcome to Le Perpetuum with Fabienne and David

Located on the riverbank, only 8 kilometres from Sarlat and near to the fascinating sites of Domme, La Roque-Gageac, Beynac, les Milandes, etcetera.

You will be seduced by the green and quiet surroundings. Familial and convivial reception. Campsite of 4 hectares offering 120 level touring pitches on grass. Motorcaravan service point.

Organized entertainment during the summer period (dance evenings, karaoke, canoe trips, boules competitions, morning activities for children...). On site snack bar, grocery and daily fresh bread. Heated swimming pool.

Mobile homes and caravans for rent, very attractive low season rates (off -30% up to -40%).

For more information, please call 00 33 5 53 28 35 18 or send us an email. www.campingleperpetuum.com. So see you soon!

SARLAT LA CANEDA 7C3 (10km S Rural) 44.82181, 1.22587 Camping Le Bosquet, La Rivière, 24250 Domme [05 53 28 37 39; fax 05 53 29 41 95; info@lebousquet.com; www.lebosquet.com] Fr Sarlat take D46 S to Vitrac cross rv on D46E. Sp at junc, site 500m on R. Sm, hdg/mkd pitch, pt shd, wc; chem disp; shwrs inc; el pnts (6A) €2.50 (long lead poss req); gas; lndtte; sm shop; tradsmn; snacks; pool; rv sw & fishing 500m; wifi; 50% statics; dogs €2; Eng spkn; adv bkg; quiet; CKE/CCI. "Friendly, helpful owners; excel clean facs but poss stretched high ssn; gd shd but sm pitches." ♦ 1 Apr-26 Sep. € 12.50   2009*

SARLAT LA CANEDA 7C3 (10km S Rural) 44.81725, 1.21944 Camping Le Perpetuum, 24250 Domme [05 53 28 35 18; fax 05 53 29 63 64; leperpetuum.domme@wanadoo.fr; www.campingleperpetuum.com] Fr Sarlat take D46 to Vitrac; cross rv bdge to D46E; in 1km turn R onto D50, R again in 1km at site sp. Med, hdg/mkd pitch, hdstg, pt shd; wc; chem disp; mv service pnt; baby facs; shwrs inc; el pnts (10A) €3.50; lndtte; sm shop (farm produce); supmkt 3km; tradsmn; snacks; bar; BBQ; playgrnd; pool; rv sw & beach adj (Rv Dordogne); canoeing; games area; entmnt; TV rm statics; dogs €2; poss cr; some Eng spkn; adv bkg; quiet; ccard acc; red low ssn/CKE/CCI. "Site fronts rv; busy high ssn; relaxed, friendly atmosphere; gd sized pitches; cheerful, helpful owners; gd san facs; gd pool; gd local dog walks; late arr area at ent." ♦ 1 May-6 Oct. € 20.80   2013*

See advertisement above

SARLAT LA CANEDA 7C3 (12km S Rural) 44.79175, 1.16266 Camping Bel Ombrage, 24250 St Cybranet [05 53 28 34 14; fax 05 53 59 64 64; belombrage@wanadoo.fr; www.belombrage.com] Fr Sarlat take D46 sp Bergerac, rd then conts as D57; after 8km turn L at Vézac sp Castelnaund. After 1.6km at T-junction turn L onto D703 & in 180m turn R onto D57. Cont thro Castelnaund on D57; site on L in 3km. Lge, hdg pitch, shd; wc; chem disp; baby facs; shwrs inc; el pnts (10A) inc; gas 800m; lndtte (inc dryer); tradsmn; shop 800m; rest, snacks & bar 100m; BBQ; playgrnd; pool; paddling pool; rv sw & beach; fishing; tennis 800m; cycle hire; horseriding 2km; games area; wifi; games/TV rm; library; dogs free; no c'vans/m'vans over 8m high ssn; adv bkg; quiet; ccard acc; red long stay; CKE/CCI. "Attractive, well-run site by rv; popular with British; lge pitches; modern san facs; peaceful early ssn; ideal base for Dordogne; mkt Thu; excel." ♦ 1 Jun-5 Sep. € 22.70 SBS - D01   2012*

SARLAT LA CANEDA 7C3 (4km SW Rural) 44.86500, 1.18750 Camping Domaine de Loisirs Le Montant, Negrelat, Route de Bergerac, 24200 Sarlat-la-Canéda [05 53 59 18 50; fax 05 53 59 37 73; contact@camping-sarlat.com; www.camping-sarlat.com] Leave Sarlat on D57 dir Bergerac. Turn R opp school 'Pré de Cordy', site in 2.3km, sp. Med, hdg/mkd pitch, hdstg, terr, pt shd; htd wc; chem disp; mv service pnt; baby facs; fam bthrm; shwrs inc; el pnts (6-10A) €3.60; lndtte; shop 3km; tradsmn; rest, snacks; bar; BBQ; playgrnd; htd, covrd pool; waterslide; paddling pool; jacuzzi; games area; games rm; golf nr; wifi; entmnt; TV rm; 1% statics; dogs €1; Eng spkn; adv bkg rec high ssn; quiet; ccard acc; red low ssn; CKE/CCI. "Vg, pleasant site; many sports activities & excursions." ♦ 1 May-20 Sep. € 22.50   2008*

"We must tell The Club about that great site we found"

Get your site reports in by mid-August and we'll do our best to get your updates into the next edition of Caravan Europe.

SARLAT LA CANEDA 7C3 (8km SW Rural) 44.83560, 1.15873 Camping Les Deux Vallées, La Gare, 24220 Vézac [05 53 29 53 55; fax 05 53 31 09 81; contact@campingles2vallees.com; www.campingles2vallees.com] Exit A20 junc 55 onto D804 dir Sarlat-la-Caneda; cont onto D703/D704A/D704 to Sarlat; then take D57 SW to Vézac; immed after sp for vill take 1st R to site. Or fr E leave D703 onto D57; 250m after junc with D49 turn L & foll sp to site. Med, hdg/mkd pitch, hdstg, pt shd; htd wc; chem disp; baby facs; shwrs inc; el pnts (6-10A) €4.10; gas; lndtte (inc dryer); ice; shop; tradsmn; rest, snacks; bar; BBQ; 2 playgrnds; 3 pools; rv 500m, shgl beach; cycle hire; games area; games rm; entmnt July/Aug; TV; 6% statics; dogs €2; poss cr; Eng spkn; adv bkg ess Jul/Aug; quiet but rlwy adj; ccard acc; red low ssn/long stay; CKE/CCI; "Excel site; helpful, friendly Dutch owners; ltd san facs low ssn; poss muddy when wet; gd local walks" ♦ 17 Feb-12 Nov. € 41.10   2013*

See advertisement on next page

SARLAT LA CANEDA

Camping Les Deux Vallées***

GPS: 44.8356/1.15873 (lat./long.)

A quiet site with excellent views of Beynac Castle and 30 min
free WiFi per day on your pitch.
Only 8km from Sarlat and 400m from the Dordogne River.
Open mid Feb – mid Nov.

Special offer 18% reduction in low season 2014
(for touring pitches all inclusive, presentation of this guidebook required)

La Gare • 24220 Vézac • Dordogne • France • tel. +33 5 53 29 53 55
e-mail: contact@campingles2vallees.com • web: www.campingles2vallees.com

SARLAT LA CANEDA *7C3* (9km SW Rural) *44.82585, 1.15322* Camping La Cabane, 24220 Vézac [05 53 29 52 28; fax 05 53 59 09 15; contact@lacabanedordogne.com; www. lacabanedordogne.com] Fr Sarlat-La-Canéda take D57 thro Vézac. On leaving Vézac turn L immed bef rlwy bdge, site sp on R on bank of Rv Dordogne. Lge, hdg/mkd pitch, pt shd; wc; shwrs inc; el pnts (6-10A) €2;60-3.20; gas; lndtte; shop high ssn; rest & snacks 3km; BBQ; playgrnd; htd covrd pool; rv sw & shgl beach adj; TV rm; internet; some statics; dogs €1; phone; poss cr; Eng spkn; adv bkg; quiet; ccard acc; red low ssn; CKE/ CCI. "Well-shaded, rvside site; lge pitches; clean facs; friendly, helpful family owners; rvside walk to Beynac Château; gd." ♦ ltd 1 Apr-30 Sep. € 12.20   2010*

SARLAT LA CANEDA *7C3* (10km SW Rural) *44.83819, 1.14846* Camping Le Capeyrou, 24220 Beynac-et-Cazenac [05 53 29 54 95; fax 05 53 28 36 27; lecapeyrou@ wanadoo.fr; www.campinglecapeyrou.com] Fr W on D703 on R (opp sm supmkt & baker) immed past vill of Beynac. Or fr N on D57 fr Sarlat; in vill immed on L on rv. Med, hdg pitch, some hdstg, pt shd; wc; chem disp; mv service pnt; baby facs; shwrs inc; el pnts (6-10A) €3.50-4.20; lndtte; shop & rest adj; snacks; bar; playgrnd; pool; wifi; dogs €2: poss cr; Eng spkn; adv bkg; some rd & rlwy noise; ccard acc; red low ssn. "View of chateau most pitches; helpful, friendly owners; clean san facs; excel lge pool; rvside walk to attractive vill; excel NH." ♦ Apr-30 Sep. € 27.80   2012*

SARLAT LA CANEDA *7C3* (10km SW Rural) *44.80519, 1.15852* Camping-Caravaning Maisonneuve, Vallée de Céou, 24250 Castelnaud-la-Chapelle [05 53 29 51 29; fax 05 53 30 27 06; contact@campingmaisonneuve.com; www.campingmaisonneuve.com] Take D57 SW fr Sarlat sp Beynac. Cross Rv Dordogne at Castelnaud; site sp 500m on L out of Castelnaud on D57 twd Daglan. Foll narr rd across bdge (or alt ent - cont on D57 for 2km, sp on L for c'vans). Med, hdg/ mkd pitch, some hdstg, pt shd; htd wc (some cont); chem disp; mv service pnt; child/baby facs; fam bthrm; shwrs inc; el pnts (6- 10A) €4-4.90; gas; lndtte; shop, rest, snacks & bar high ssn; BBQ; playgrnd; pool; paddling pool; rv & shgl beach; fishing; tennis 2km; cycle hire; games rm; wifi; entmnt; TV rm; 10% statics; dogs €2; Eng spkn; adv bkg ess high ssn; quiet; ccard acc; red low ssn/CKE/ CCI. "Vg, spacious site; helpful owners; modern, clean facs; gd walking, cycling." ♦ 27 Mar- 2 Nov. € 20.40   2011*

See advertisement opposite

SARLAT LA CANEDA *7C3* (12km SW Rural) *44.83760, 1.11296* Camping Le Tiradou, Chemin du Grand- Fosse, 24220 St Vincent-de-Cosse [05 53 30 30 73; fax 05 53 31 16 24; contact@camping-le-tiradou.com; www. camping-le-tiradou.com] Take D703 fr La Roque-Gageac thro Beynac & onto St Vincent; site is 2km fr Beynac on R. Med, hdg/mkd pitch, shd; wc; chem disp (wc); shwrs inc; el pnts (6A) inc; lndtte (inc dryer); shop; tradsmn; snacks; bar; BBQ; playgrnd; pool; paddling pool; rv fishing, boating, watersports & beach adj; cycle hire; wifi; TV; some statics; dogs €1.80; phone; Eng spkn; adv bkg; quiet; ccard acc. "Gd touring base along Rv Dordogne." ♦ 5 Apr-25 Oct. € 22.60   2008*

"I need an on-site restaurant"

We do our best to make sure site information is correct, but it is always best to check any must-have facilities are still available or will be open during your visit.

SARLAT LA CANEDA *7C3* (18km SW Rural) *44.83610, 1.06230* Domaine Le Cro Magnon, La Raisse, 24220 Allas-les-Mines [05 53 29 13 70; fax 05 53 29 15 79; contact@domaine-cro- magnon.com; www.domaine-cro-magnon.com] Fr Sarlat two Bergerac/Le Buisson on D57/D703 turn L after St Cyprien & rv x-ing onto D48 sp site & Berbiguières. Approx 1.5km after Berbiguières turn L at site sp. Do not foll any earlier sp to site as rds impassable to c'vans & m'vans. App steep, narr & twisting but gd surface. NB App via Berbiguières only. Med, pt shd; wc; chem disp; mv service pnt; baby facs; sauna; jaccuzi; shwrs inc; el pnts (6A) inc; gas; lndtte (inc dryer); shop; rest, snacks; BBQ (gas/elec); playgrnd; 2 pools (1 htd covrd); waterslides; paddling pool; rv fishing 800m; horseriding nrby; tennis; cycle hire; games area; sm gym; wifi; entmnt; games/ TV rm; dogs €3.60; no c'vans/m'vans over 10m; adv bkg; quiet; ccard acc; red low ssn. "Lge pitches, many in shady, woodland setting; gd, clean san facs." ♦ 16 Jun-15 Sep. € 30.40 SBS - D24   2011*

SARLAT LA CANEDA *7C3* (9km W Rural) *44.90805, 1.11527*
Camping Le Moulin du Roch, Le Roch, Route des Eyzies, 24200 Sarlat-la-Canéda [05 53 59 20 27; moulin.du.roch@wanadoo.fr; www.moulin-du-roch.com or www.les-castels.com] Fr A20 take exit 55 at Souillac dir Sarlat. At rndabt in Sarlat (just under rlwy viaduct) take 1st exit & foll sp thro Sarlat dir Périgueux. As come to end of Sarlat turn L onto D6 dir Les Eyzies (becomes D47 in 2km). Site on L in approx 9 km on D47. Fr N on D704 to Sarlat, turn R at hypmkt, then as above. Lge, hdg/mkd pitch, terr, pt shd; htd wc; chem disp; mv service pnt; baby facs; some serviced pitches; shwrs inc; el pnts (6A) inc; gas; lndtte (inc dryer); shop; rest, snacks; bar; BBQ (gas/charcoal only); playgrnd; htd pool; paddling pool with mini waterslide; fishing lake; tennis; canoeing & horseriding nrby; wifi; entmnt; games/TV rm; 45% statics; no dogs; twin-axles; Eng spkn; adv bkg rec Jun-Aug; quiet; ccard acc; red low ssn/long stay; CKE/CCI. "Well-run, family owned site; lge pitches; clean facs but poss long, steep walk;some noise from adj rd; gd rest & pool; m'vans poss not acc after prolonged heavy rain due soft ground; mkt Sat." ♦ 28 Apr-16 Sep. € 36.00 (CChq acc) SBS - D02   2013*

See advertisement on insode back cover

SARLAT LA CANEDA *7C3* (9km W Rural) *44.89382, 1.11322* **Camping Les Charmes, Malartigue-Haut, 24200 St André-d'Allas [05 53 31 02 89 or 06 74 22 45 70 (mob); fax 05 53 31 06 32; les.charmes@wanadoo.fr; www.campinglescharmesdordogne.com]** Fr Sarlat dir St Cyprien on D25; site on R 200m bef rd forks with D35 to Le Bugue; 8km along narr rd; poss hard to find. Med, hdg/mkd pitch, pt sl, pt shd; wc; chem disp; baby facs; shwrs inc; el pnts (6A) €3.40; lndtte (inc dryer); shop; tradsmn; rest, snacks; bar; BBQ; playgrnd; 2 pools (1 htd, covrd); paddling pool; waterslide; bicycle & canoe hire; tennis; games area; games rm; wifi; entmnt; TV; 10% statics; dogs €1.50; phone; Eng spkn; adv bkg; quiet; ccard acc; red low ssn; CKE/CCI. "Friendly & helpful; sep car park; excel." ♦ ltd 1 Apr-30 Sep. € 17.80   2010*

SARLAT LA CANEDA *7C3* (4km NW) *44.90929, 1.18738* **FFCC Camping Le Rivaux, Route de Périgueux, 24200 Sarlat-la-Canéda [05 53 59 04 41]** Fr Sarlat take D47 sp Les Eyzies & Périgueux; after approx 2km, take D6. Site on R after approx 300m. Med, hdg/mkd pitch, pt sl, pt shd; wc; chem disp; shwrs inc; el pnts (2-6A) €1.50-2.80; gas; lndry rm; shops 3km; tradsmn high ssn; BBQ; playgrnd; pool 4km; games rm; dogs; phone; quiet; adv bkg rec high ssn; CKE/CCI. "Spacious pitches; gd touring base; vg." ♦ ltd 1 Apr-30 Sep. € 11.00   2009*

SARZEAU *2G3* (7km SE Coastal) *47.50551, -2.68308* **Camping Manoir de Ker An Poul, 1 Route de la Grée, Penvins, 56370 Sarzeau [02 97 67 33 30; fax 02 97 67 44 83; manoirdekeranpoul@wanadoo.fr; www.manoirdekeranpoul.com]** Fr E exit N165 1km E of Muzillac, sp Sarzeau D20 & cont approx 20km to junc of D20 & D199, S on D199 sp Penvins. Fr W, 6km E of Vannes, exit N165 onto N780 sp Sarzeau, in 9.5km S onto D199 sp Penvins. Lge, hdg pitch, pt sl, pt shd; wc (some cont); chem disp; baby facs; shwrs inc; el pnts (6-10A) €4; lndtte (inc dryer); shop; rest adj; snacks; bar; BBQ; playgrnd; htd pool; sand beach 700m; tennis; games area; cycle hire; wifi; entmnt; TV rm; 30% statics; dogs €4; poss cr; Eng spkn; adv bkg; quiet; red low ssn; CKE/CCI. "Spacious pitches; warm welcome; lovely situation in grnds of chateau." ♦ 3 Apr-25 Sep. € 25.00 2010*

See advertisement on inside back cover

SARZEAU *2G3* (2.5km S Coastal) *47.50720, -2.76083* **Camping La Ferme de Lann Hoëdic, Rue Jean de la Fontaine, Route de Roaliguen, 56370 Sarzeau [02 97 48 01 73; contact@camping-lannhoedic.fr; www.camping-lannhoedic.fr]** Fr Vannes on N165 turn onto D780 dir Sarzeau. Do not ent Sarzeau, but at Super U rndabt foll sp Le Roaliguen. After 1.5km turn L to Lann Hoëdic. Med, mkd pitch, pt shd; htd wc; chem disp; mv service pnt; baby facs; fam bthrm; shwrs inc; el pnts (10A) €3.20; gas; lndtte (inc dryer); shop 800m; tradsmn; rest 2km; snacks; bar 1km; playgrnd; sand beach 800m; cycle hire; wifi; 10% statics; dogs €2; phone; Eng spkn; adv bkg; quiet; red low ssn; CKE/CCI. "Peaceful, well-managed, family-run site; warm welcome; excel, clean facs; beautiful coastline - beaches & dunes; highly rec." ♦ 1 Apr-31 Oct. € 17.80 (CChq acc)   2011*

This family site is situated in the Dordogne Valley. Spacious, shady touring pitches along the river, Canadian tents and Cottages. Facilities are around the traditional farm. Swimming, diving, fishing and canoeing in the Céou river. Excellent location to explore the stunning Périgord region. Three recent sanitary blocks - one heated. Facilities for babies & disabled. Laundry. 6/10A electricity. WiFi. Shop. Restaurant. Bar. Swimming and paddling pools. Minigolf. Play areas. TV. Games. Dance evenings. Sport tournaments. From A20 take exit 55 on the D703 towards Sarlat and Beynac. Follow signs for D57 (Castelnaud la Chapelle).

★★★
Camping Maisonneuve
www.campingmaisonneuve.com
Castelnaud-la-Chapelle | Dordogne | Aquitaine
contact@campingmaisonneuve.com
T : +33(0)5 53 29 51 29

SARZEAU *2G3* (4km S Coastal/Rural) *47.50589, -2.77139* Camping An Trest, Route de la Plage de Roaliguen, 56370 Sarzeau [02 97 41 79 60; fax 02 97 41 36 21; letreste@campingletreste.com; www.an-trest.com] Fr E on D780 turn L at 1st rndabt nr Super U supmkt sp Le Roaliguen, site sp on L. NB ignore R turn to Sarzeau after sp Port Navalo. Lge, hdg/mkd pitch, pt sl, pt shd; wc (some cont); chem disp; baby facs; shwrs inc; el pnts (10A) €4.20; gas; lndtte (inc dryer); supmkt 2km; tradsmn; snacks; bar in ssn; BBQ; playgrnd; htd pool & paddling pool; waterslide; sand beach 800m; tennis; horseriding, golf 3km; wifi; TV rm; 5% statics; dogs €2.50; phone; Eng spkn; adv bkg; quiet; 20% red low ssn; ccard acc; CKE/CCI. "Pleasant, well-run site; gd touring base; helpful owners." ♦ Easter-26 Sep. € 23.50   2010*

SARZEAU *2G3* (2km SW Rural) *47.52255, -2.79713* **Lodge Club Presqu'île de Rhuys (formerly Le Bohat), Route d'Arzon Lower Bohat, 56370 Sarzeau [02 97 41 78 68; fax 02 97 41 71 97; info@lodgeclub.fr; http://www.lodgeclub.fr/]** Fr Vannes on N165, exit onto D780 to Sarzeau. Do not turn off this main rd to Sarzeau (town not suitable for m'vans or c'vans) but cont twd Arzon; 1km after 2nd rndabt turn L for Le Bohat & Spernec, then take 1st R. Fr S on N165 take D20 at Muzillac, thro Surzur & cont to join D780 to Sarzeau. Then as above. Lge, hdg/mkd pitch, pt shd; wc; chem disp; mv service pnt; baby facs; shwrs inc; el pnts (10A) inc; gas; lndtte; shop; tradsmn; rest, snacks; bar; BBQ (gas/charcoal); playgrnd; 2 htd pools (1 covrd); paddling pool; waterslide; sand beach, watersports 4km; fishing; cycle hire; golf 6km; pony rides; horseriding 2km; wifi; entmnt; games/TV rm; 4% statics; dogs €3.70; phone; poss cr; Eng spkn; adv bkg; quiet; ccard acc; red low ssn; CKE/CCI. "Busy, well-kept, Dutch-owned site; lge pitches; excel, helpful staff; clean san facs; excel pools; gd for families; cycle tracks; gd touring base; mkt Thu; vg." ♦ 28 Apr-21 Sep. € 34.30 SBS - B07   2012*

SARZEAU *2G3* (3km SW Rural) *47.50941, -2.80747* Camping à la Ferme L'Abri-Côtier (Rio), 56730 Route de Sarzeau, 56730 St Gildas-de-Rhuys [02 97 45 27 42 or 06 11 97 31 76 (mob); contact@abri-cotier.com; www.abri-cotier.com] Fr Sarzeau take D198 sp St Gildas-de-Rhuys. Site in 3km. Med, hdg/mkd pitch, pt shd; wc; chem disp; mv service pnt; baby facs; fam bthrm; shwrs inc; el pnts (10A) €3 (poss long lead req); gas; lndtte; shop, rest & bar 2km; tradsmn; snacks; BBQ (charcoal/gas); beach 2.5km; games area; wifi; TV; dogs €1; bus 100m; Eng pkn; adv bkg; v quiet; ccard acc. "Well-run, clean, reliable site; lge pitches; friendly staff; cannot fault!" ♦ 1 Apr-30 Sep. € 15.00   2011*

SARZEAU *2G3* (5km SW Coastal) *47.48976, -2.80075* Camping Saint Jacques, 1 Rue Pratel Vihan, 56370 Sarzeau [02 97 41 79 29; fax 02 97 48 04 45; info@camping-stjacques.com; www.camping-stjacques.com] Fr Sarzeau on D780, at 2nd rndabt foll dir St Jacques, site sp. Lge, mkd pitch, pt shd; wc (come cont); chem disp; baby facs; shwrs inc; el pnts (4-6A) €2.55; gas; lndtte; shop; snacks; bar; BBQ; playgrnd; sand beach adj; tennis; fishing; sailing school; cycle hire; entmnt; 10% statics; dogs €1; Eng spkn; adv bkg; quiet; red low ssn; ccard acc; CKE/CCI. "Poss untidy site; many long-stay c'vans; excel beach & dunes; gd sea sw; NH only." ♦ 1 Apr-30 Sep. € 13.55   2009*

SARZEAU *2G3* (6km W Coastal) *47.52865, -2.84772* Camping du Menhir, La Saline, 56730 St Gildas-de-Rhuys [02 97 45 22 88; contact@camping-bretagnesud.com; www.camping-bretagnesud.com] Take D780 Vannes-Port Navalo rd; 6km after Sarzeau turn L sp La Saline & Camping Menhir. Lge, mkd pitch, pt shd; wc; baby facs; shwrs inc; el pnts (6-10A) €4-5; gas; lndtte (inc dryer); sm shop high ssn or 3km; tradsmn; rest, snacks; bar; playgrnd; htd pool; waterslides; paddling pool; sand beach 1km; tennis; games area; games rm; dogs €3; adv bkg; quiet; red low ssn. "Lge pitches; gd san facs; excel." ♦ 26 May-6 Sep. € 29.50 2009*

SAUCHY LESTREE see Marquion *3B4*

SAUGNACQ ET MURET *7D1* (4km W Rural) *44.40946, -0.82623* Camping Le Muretois, 40410 Saugnacq-et-Muret [tel/fax 05 58 09 62 14] Exit A63/N10 junc 18 at Le Muret, site within 500m of N10 at junc with D20, sp. Nr Hotel Le Caravaniers. Sm, mkd pitch, pt shd; wc (own san rec); chem disp (wc); shwrs; el pnts (10A) (some rev pol); lndtte; shop 500m; rest 100m; snacks; bar; playgrnd; rv fishing 3km; tennis; cycle hire; dogs; phone; poss cr; adv bkg rec high ssn; quiet; CKE/CCI. "Friendly, basic site; gd NH; take care el pnts; unrel opening dates - phone ahead to check!" 1 Apr-30 Sep. € 10.00   2008*

"Satellite navigation makes touring much easier"

Remember most sat navs don't know if you're towing or in a larger vehicle – always use yours alongside maps and site directions.

SAUGUES *9C1* (500m W Rural) *44.9586, 3.5417* Camp Municipal de la Seuge, Ave du Gévaudan, 43170 Saugues [04 71 77 80 62 or 06 65 15 04 32; fax 04 71 77 66 40; camping@mairie-saugues.com; www.mairie-saugues.com] 500m W fr Saugues on D589 twd Paulhac, turn R into Ave de Gévaudan. Site on L in 100m. Well sp. Med, mkd pitch, pt shd; htd wc; chem disp; mv service pnt; baby facs; shwrs inc; el pnts (10A) €2.50; lndtte; shop; snacks; bar; playgrnd; BBQ; fishing; boating; canoeing; games area; adv bkg; ccard not acc; CKE/CCI. "Gd cent for gorges of Allier & Le Puy-en-Velay; barriers clsd at night; lge grass pitches." 15 Apr-15 Oct. € 10.60   2008*

SAUJON *7B1* (1.5km N Rural) *45.68646, -0.94000* Aire Naturelle Le Logis de la Lande (Renouleau), Route de l'Ilatte, 17600 Saujon [05 46 02 84 31 or 06 77 38 62 98 (mob); christianerenouleau@wanadoo.fr; http://camping-lalande.monsite-orange.fr/] Fr N150 Saujon by-pass turn onto D1 dir Le Gua. At end slip rd turn L & at rndabt foll sp L'Ilatte. Site in 500m on R immed after R bend. Avoid Saujon cent. Sm, pt sl, pt shd; wc; chem disp; shwrs; el pnts (6A) €4; lndry rm; shop, rest, snacks & bar 2km; playgrnd; beach 12km; dogs €2 poss cr; v quiet. "Pleasant, well-kept, CL-type site; san facs clean but ltd in number; inland fr crowded coast, not full peak ssn; excel." Apr-Oct. € 11.80   2010*

SAUJON *7B1* (2km N Rural) *45.68326, -0.93741* **FFCC Camping du Lac du Saujon, Aire de la Lande, Voie des Tourterelles, 17600 Saujon [05 46 06 82 99; fax 05 46 06 83 66; info@campingdulac.net; www. campingdulac.net]** Fr N150 Saujon by-pass turn onto D1 dir Le Gua. Foll sp to site. Med, mkd pitch, pt shd; wc; chem disp; mv service pnt; shwrs inc; el pnts (5-10A) €4-6; lndtte (inc dryer); shop; rest, snacks; bar; BBQ; playgrnd; htd, covrd pool adj; fishing; tennis; cycle hire; jogging course, horseriding nr; wifi; entmnt; 33% statics; dogs €3.50; phone; poss cr; Eng spkn; adv bkg; red low ssn; CKE/CCI. "Excel site." ♦ 1 Apr-30 Oct. € 17.50   2010*

See advertisement on pages 32 & 33

SAULCE, LA *9D3* (2km E Rural) *44.42559, 6.02944* **Camping Le Lac, Route Napoléon, 05110 Curbans [04 92 54 23 10; fax 04 92 54 23 11; info@au-camping-du-lac.com; www. au-camping-du-lac.com]** S fr Gap on N85 twd Sisteron for 16km; R to La Saulce over ; in vill turn L onto D19 & over canal. Turn L again. Site 1km on L. Med, pt shd; wc; chem disp; shwrs inc; el pnts (6A) €3; lndtte; shop 2km; tradsmn; rest; bar; playgrnd; pool; paddling pool; fishing; 10% statics; dogs €2; poss cr; Eng spkn; adv bkg; quiet; CKE/CCI. "Enthusiastic family owners; lge pitches." ♦ 1 Apr-10 Oct. € 19.00   2008*

SAULIAC SUR CELE see Cabrerets *7D3*

SAULIEU *6G1* (1km N Rural) *47.28936, 4.22401* **Camping Le Perron/Camping de Saulieu, Route de Paris, 21210 Saulieu [03 80 64 16 19; camping.salieu@wanadoo.fr; www. aquadis-loisirs.com]** On D906 on L of rd on ent fr N. Sp. Lge, hdg/mkd pitch, pt sl, pt shd; htd wc; chem disp; mv service pnt; shwrs inc; el pnts (10A) €3.90; gas; lndtte; sm shop; tradsmn; rest in ssn; bar; playgrnd; pool; paddling pool; lake fishing; tennis; wifi; dogs €1.50; adv bkg; quiet, but poss rd noise some pitches; red low ssn; CKE/CCI. "Nr town but rural feel; quiet at far end of site, away fr pool & playgrnd; no twin-axles; many rests in town; gd walking area; gd" ♦ ltd 2 Apr-4 Nov. € 15.30 (CChq acc)   2013*

SAULT *10E3* (2km NE Rural) *44.10165, 5.42260* **Camp Municipal du Defends, Route de St Trinit, 84390 Sault [04 90 64 07 18 or 04 90 64 02 30 (Mairie); campingsault@ wanadoo.fr]** NE fr Sault on D950 dir St Trinit; site on R in 2km. Med, some mkd pitch, shd; wc; chem disp; shwrs inc; el pnts (6A) €3.70 (poss long lead req); gas 1km; supmkt 1km; BBQ; playgrnd; 10% statics; dogs; phone adj; poss cr; Eng spkn; CKE/CCI. "Site in woodland; conv Mont Ventoux & Gorges de la Nesque; gd cycling; gd." 7 Apr-30 Sep. € 12.70   2011*

SAUMUR See also sites listed under Bourgueil, Coutures, Doué-la-Fontaine, Montsoreau, Les Rosiers-sur-Loire and Vernantes.

SAUMUR *4G1* (1km N Urban) *47.25990, -0.06440* **Flower Camping de L'Ile d'Offard, Rue de Verden, 49400 Saumur [02 41 40 30 00; fax 02 41 67 37 81; iledoffard@ flowercampings.com; www.flowercampings.com]** Exit A85 junc 3 onto N347; ent town past rlwy stn & cross Rv Loire bdge; turn L immed over bdge & foll sp Chinon alongside rv. At rndabt turn L & take 1st L to site; foll sp. Site on island facing Saumur castle. Lge, hdg/mkd pitch, hdstg, pt sl, pt shd; htd wc; chem disp; mv service pnt; baby facs; shwrs inc; el pnts (10A) €4 (poss rev pol); gas; lndtte (inc dryer); shops in ssn; tradsmn; rest; snacks, bar; playgrnd; htd pool; paddling pool; jacuzzi; rv sw & fishing, boating adj; tennis; cycle hire; games area; wifi; entmnt; 20% tour ops statics; dogs €1.50; poss cr; Eng spkn; adv bkg (non-refundable bkg fee); some rlwy noise; ccard acc; red low ssn/ CKE/CCI. "Pleasant, busy, well-run site; ideal for children; hdstg pitches in winter; helpful staff; clean, unisex san facs, some need refurb & poss ltd low ssn; most pitches lge but some v sm pitches bet statics - lge o'fits check in advance; gd bar & rest; site recently became private - hedges & trees etc need attention (2011); can be muddy when wet; gd cycle rtes; some rlwy noise; nice riverside and bridge walk to town" ♦ ltd 2 Mar-16 Nov. € 26.00   2013*

See advertisement on pages 32 & 33

SAUMUR *4G1* (7km NE Rural) *47.29937, -0.01218* **Camping Le Pô Doré, 49650 Allonnes [tel/fax 02 41 38 78 80 or 06 09 26 31 28 (mob); camping.du.po.dore@wanadoo.fr; www.camping-lepodore.com]** NE fr Saumur on N347 & turn R onto D10. Site 3km W of Allonnes on R. Med, hdg/mkd pitch, some hdstg; pt shd; wc; chem disp; mv service pnt; shwrs inc; el pnts (6-10A) €3-4 (poss rev pol); lndtte; tradsmn; rest, snacks; bar; playgrnd; htd pool; cycle hire; entmnt; 25% statics; dogs €1.50; phone; poss cr; some Eng spkn; some rlwy noise; ccard acc; red low ssn; CKE/CCI. "Gd, clean & tidy site; helpful staff; dirty, sandy soil; conv wine rtes, caves, museums & a'route; conv NH/sh stay." ♦ 12 Mar-15 Nov. € 19.00 2011*

SAUMUR *4G1* (6km E Rural) *47.24755, -0.00033* **Camping Domaine de la Brèche, 5 Impasse de la Brèche, 49730 Varennes-sur-Loire [02 41 51 22 92; fax 02 41 51 27 24; mail@etang-breche.com; www.domainedelabreche.com or www.les-castels.com]** Exit Saumur on N152 twd Tours & site sp fr either dir. Site on N side of rd (6km W of Varennes) app fr lge lay-by giving easy ent. Lge, hdg pitch, pt shd; wc; chem disp; mv service pnt; 20% serviced pitch; baby facs; shwrs inc; el pnts (10A) €3.50; gas; lndtte; shop; tradsmn; rest, snacks; bar; playgrnd; 2 htd pools (no shorts); waterslide; cycle hire; tennis; games rms; entmnt; internet; TV rm; 30% statics; dogs; phone; Eng spkn; adv bkg (ess Jul/Aug); quiet but rd noise in some areas; ccard acc; red low ssn; CKE/CCI. "Spacious site & pitches; well-organised; excel facs; auto barrier clsd 2300-0700; helpful staff; excel." ♦ 30 Apr-15 Sep. € 33.00   2009*

See advertisement on inside back cover

SAUMUR

SAUMUR *4G1* (5km NW Rural) *47.29440, -0.14120* **Camping de Chantepie, Route de Chantepie, 49400 St Hilaire-St Florent [02 41 67 95 34; fax 02 41 67 95 85; info@campingchantepie.com; www.campingchantepie.com]** Fr Saumer take D751 on S bank of Rv Loire sp Gennes. Turn L 3km N of St Hilaire-St-Florent just bef lge sp for a supmkt & bef mushroom museum. Site sp. Or fr N after x-ing rv on N347, take turn sp St Hilaire-St-Florent & join D751 for Gennes; site is 3km N of St Hilaire-St Florent, well sp fr D751. NB Easy to miss turning. Lge, hdg/mkd pitch, pt shd; htd wc; chem disp; mv service pnt; baby facs; shwrs inc; el pnts (10A) inc (poss rev pol); gas; lndtte; shop; tradsmn; snacks; bar/café; BBQ; playgrnd; 2 pools (1 htd, covrd); paddling pool; rv beach 200m; fishing; tennis & golf 2km; horseriding, boating 5km; cycle hire; games rm; wifi; entmnt; games/TV rm; 10% statics; dogs €4; no c'vans/m'vans over 10m; Eng spkn; adv bkg; quiet; ccard acc; red low ssn; CKE/CCI. "Excel site nr rv; well-spaced, lge pitches, some with rv views; access to some pitches diff lge o'fits; friendly, helpful staff; excel san facs, conv Loire cycle rte; mkt Sat Saumur" ♦ 28 Apr-15 Sep. € 39.00 (CChq acc) SBS - L06 2013*

> ## "There aren't many sites open at this time of year"
>
> If you're travelling outside peak season remember to call ahead to check site opening dates – even if the entry says 'open all year'.

SAUMUR *4G1* (8km NW Rural) *47.30982, -0.14492* **Camping La Croix Rouge, Rue de la Croix Rouge, 49160 St Martin-de-la-Place [02 41 38 09 02 or 06 32 17 14 61 (mob); campinglacroixrouge@laposte.net; www.campinglacroixrouge.com]** Exit A85 junc 3 sp Saumur. Take slip rd immed bef bdge then L sp 'Angers Touristique'. Site on L at vill sp. Fr Saumur take D347 N across rv then turn L onto D952 dir Angers. At St Martin-de-la-Place foll sp for site. Med, mkd pitch, pt shd; wc; chem disp; mv service pnt; shwrs; el pnts (6-10A) €3.-4.; lndtte; shop 600m; sm rest, bar 200m; playgrnd; rv sw, sailing adj; dogs €1.50; bus 150m; Eng spkn; adv bkg; quiet; ccard/chq not acc; red low ssn/CKE/CCI. "Beautiful, tranquil site on Rv Loire; friendly, helpful owners; 26 steps to clean spacious san facs; disabled facs at grnd level; 2m high security fence by rv; barrier clsd 2200-0700; no twin-axles; conv Saumur; excel; very pleasant site" ♦ ltd 14 Apr-30 Sep. € 12.50 2013*

SAUSHEIM see Mulhouse *6F3*

SAUVETERRE DE BEARN *8F1* (S Rural) *43.39518, -0.94416* **Camping du Gave, Ave de la Gare, 64390 Sauveterre-de-Béarn [05 59 38 53 30; fax 05 59 36 19 88; camping-du-gave@wanadoo.fr]** Site on D933 on S side of town. Ent immed off rndabt at end of rv bdge. Med, mkd pitch, shd; wc (some cont); chem disp (wc); shwrs; el pnts (6A) inc; lndtte; shop & 200m; tradsmn; rest 1km; snacks; bar; playgrnd; rv sw adj; canoeing; 10% statics; dogs; poss cr; adv bkg; quiet. "Facs poss stretched in ssn; friendly management; footpath to medieval town." ♦ 1 Apr-30 Sep. € 12.80 2008*

SAUVETERRE DE GUYENNE *7D2* (8km NW Rural) *44.72564, -0.15066* **Camping Château Guiton (Naturist), 33760 Frontenac [05 56 23 52 79; fax 05 56 23 99 40; accueil@chateau-guiton.com; www.chateau-guiton.com]** N of Sauveterre-de-Guyenne turn W onto D123 sp Frontenac. Turn L just bef vill sp Château Guiton. Sm, mkd pitch, pt sl, pt shd; wc; chem disp; sauna; shwrs; el pnts (6-10A) €3.50; lndtte; shop; tradsmn; rest & bar 4km; playgrnd; pool; gym; TV rm; dogs €2; phone; Eng spkn; adv bkg; quiet; ccard acc; red low ssn; INF card req. "Pt-wooded site in cent wine region; friendly owner; gd cycling; conv Bordeaux; gd." 15 May-30 Sep. € 23.50 2009*

SAUVETERRE LA LEMANCE see Villefranche du Périgord *7D3*

SAUVIAN see Valras Plage *10F1*

SAUXILLANGES *9B1* (500m SW Rural) *45.54578, 3.36451* **FFCC Camping Les Prairies, Chemin des Prairies, 63490 Sauxillanges [04 73 96 80 22 or 06 50 51 95 75; contact@camping-lesprairies.fr; www.camping-lesprairies.fr]** Exit A75/E11 junc 13 to D996, E twd Sauxillanges. Turn R 100m after Gendarmerie in vill. Sp. Med, mkd pitch, shd; wc (some cont); chem disp; some serviced pitches; shwrs inc; el pnts (6A) inc (poss rev pol); lndtte; shop; BBQ; playgrnd; pool adj (Jul/Aug); paddling pool; fishing adj; tennis; 5% statics; dogs €2; Eng spkn; adv bkg ess high ssn; quiet; ccard acc. "Charming, interesting town; excel." ♦ 15 Jun-15 Sep. € 16.50 2010*

SAVENAY *2G3* (2km E Rural) *47.35651, -1.92136* **Camp Municipal du Lac de Savenay, Route du Lac, 44260 Savenay [tel/fax 02 40 58 31 76]** Site well sp in Savenay. Med, mkd pitch, terr, pt shd; htd wc; shwrs inc; el pnts (10A) €2.07; gas adj; lndtte; tradsmn; snacks; sm playgrnd; pool adj; fishing;dog €1.20 quiet; "Vg, clean site in attractive lakeside park; lge pitches" ♦ 1 May-30 Sep. € 16.34 2013*

SAVERNE *6E3* (1.3km SW Urban) *48.73148, 7.35561* **FFCC Camping de Saverne, Rue du Père Libermann, 67700 Saverne [tel/fax 03 88 91 35 65; info@campingsaverne.com; www.campingsaverne.com]** Take Saverne exit fr A4, junc 45. Site well sp nr town cent. Med, hdg/mkd pitch, hdstg, pt sl, terr, pt shd; htd wc; chem disp; mv service pnt; shwrs inc; el pnts (6-10A) €3.10-5.70 (poss rev pol); lndry rm; supmkt 1.5km; playgrnd; pool 1km; 20% statics; dogs €1.60; poss cr; adv bkg; quiet; ccard acc; red low ssn/CKE/CCI. "Pleasant, busy, well-run site; pitches mostly terr; warm welcome, friendly staff; excel san facs; long steep walk back fr town; m'van aire de service nr ent; trains to Strasbourg fr town; poss itinerants; gd." ♦ 1 Apr-30 Sep. € 12.40 2011*

SAVERNE *6E3* (5km SW Rural) *48.69172, 7.32958* **Camping au Paradis Perdu, 31 Rue de Hirschberg, St Gall, 67440 Thal-Marmoutier [03 88 70 60 59]** Fr Saverne, use minor rds rather than by-pass; foll sp Thal-Marmoutier then foll camp sps to St Gall & site; access thro archway - poss tight for lge vans. Sm, pt sl, pt shd; wc; chem disp; shwrs; el pnts (3-6A); shops 3km; rest, snacks; bar; playgrnd; dogs €1.20; adv bkg; quiet. "Pleasant setting in orchard; facs basic but gd." 1 Apr-15 Oct. € 12.80 2009*

FRANCE

SAVERNE 6E3 (13km SW) **Camping du Rocher, 57850 Dabo [tel/fax 03 87 07 47 51; ot-dabo@claranet.fr; www. ot-dabo.fr]** Fr Saverne take D132 to Lutzelbourg, then D98 to Haselbourg & D45 to Dabo. Go thro vill; site sp on R in 2km. Sm, mkd pitch, pt shd; wc; shwrs €1.50; el pnts (6-10A) €2-3.30; shop 2km; playgrnd; cycling; fishing; quiet; "Site yourself, warden calls; fair sh stay/nh" ♦ ltd Easter-1 Nov. € 11.00   2013*

SAVIGNY EN VERON 4G1 (500m W Rural) 47.20059, 0.13932 **FFCC Camping La Fritillaire, Rue Basse, 37420 Savigny-en-Véron [02 47 58 03 79; fax 02 47 58 03 81; www.aquadis-loisirs.com]** Fr Montsoreau on D751 or D7 on S bank of Rv Loire, foll sp to Savigny-en-Véron & site. Med, mkd pitch, pt shd; htd wc; chem disp; mv service pnt; baby facs; shwrs inc; el pnts (10A) inc (poss rev pol); lndtte; rest, snacks & bar 500m; BBQ; playgrnd; htd, covrd pool 4km; games area (under-7s); tennis; cycle hire; horseriding; some statics; dogs €1; adv bkg; quiet; red low ssn; CKE/CCI. "Excel, peaceful site; friendly owners; gd clean facs, ltd low ssn; gd touring base Loire chateaux; vg cycle rtes; poss workers staying on site (2009)" ♦ 29 Mar - 20 Oct. € 13.00   2013*

SAVINES LE LAC 9D3 (2km SW Rural) 44.51812, 6.38445 **Camp Municipal Les Eygoires, Route de Barcelonnette, 05160 Savines-le-Lac [04 92 44 20 48 or 04 92 44 20 03 (Mairie); fax 04 92 44 39 71; camping.municipal.savinelelac@orange. fr; www.savines-le-lac.fr]** Take N94 to Savines. Site on D954 on N side of rd. Lge, mkd pitch, terr, pt shd; wc (some cont); baby facs; shwrs; el pnts (5A) €3.40; lndtte; shop; snacks; bar; playgrnd; lake sw & shgl beach; sailing; some statics; dogs €1.70; adv bkg; quiet. 10 May-13 Sep. € 14.85   2010*

SCAER 2F2 (200m E Rural) 48.02765, -3.69628 **Camp Municipal de Kérisole, Rue Pasteur, 29390 Scaër [02 98 57 60 91 or 02 98 59 42 10 (LS); fax 02 98 57 66 89; mairie.scaer@altica.com; www.ville-scaer.fr]** Fr N165 take D70 to Rosporden, then N on D782, site well sp in Scaër. Thro town foll sp to site. Med, pt sl, pt shd; wc; chem disp; mv service pnt; baby facs; shwrs; el pnts (10A) €2.65; lndtte (inc dryer); shop, rest, snacks & bar 300m; playgrnd; pool 700m; fishing; 5% statics; dogs; Eng spkn; adv bkg; quiet; CKE/CCI. "Site at ent to forest, forest walk adj; excel san facs; isolated at night, gate locked 2200; warden visits 2hrs am, 2hrs pm; vill poorly served with rests/bars; fair." ♦ 15 Jun-31 Aug. € 9.90   2011*

SECONDIGNY 4H1 (500m S Rural) 46.60486, -0.41599 **Camp Municipal du Moulin des Effres, 79130 Secondigny [05 49 95 61 97; fax 05 49 63 55 48; contact@ campingmoulindeseffres.fr; www.campings-poitou-charentes.com]** D949 to Secondigny, S onto D748. Site sp on L in 800m on lakeside. Med, mkd pitch, pt sl, pt shd; wc; chem disp; shwrs inc; el pnts (6-10A) inc; lndtte (inc dryer); shops 500m; tradsmn; rest 400m; snacks; pool; paddling pool; lake fishing adj; tennis; wifi; entmnt; TV; 10% statics; dogs; phone; poss cr; quiet; ccard acc; red low ssn; CKE/CCI. "In pleasant surroundings nr attractive vill; poss itinerants." 1 Apr-31 Oct. € 19.50   2011*

SEDAN 5C1 (11km SE Rural) 49.66265, 5.04718 **Camp Municipal du Lac, Route de Mouzon, 08140 Douzy [03 24 26 31 19 or 03 24 26 31 48 (Mairie); fax 03 24 26 84 01; aubergedulac@free.fr; www.camping-douzy.com]** On N43 fr Sedan-Metz to Douzy. Turn R (S) at traff lts in Douzy & site in 500m on L. Clearly sp. Med, few hdstg, pt shd; few hdstg; wc; 60% serviced pitch; shwrs inc; el pnts (6A) €3 (poss rev pol); gas 1km; lndtte; shops 1km; tradsmn; rest adj; snacks; bar; playgrnd; shgl beach & lake sw adj; waterslides; tennis; dogs €1.50; poss cr; Eng spkn; adv bkg; some rd & light aircraft noise; red long stay; CKE/CCI. "Helpful staff; pitches mostly uneven; gd san facs; gd rest adj." ♦ 15 Apr-1 Oct. € 11.00   2011*

SEDAN 5C1 (1km W Urban) 49.69868, 4.93848 **Camp Municipal La Prairie, Prairie de Torcy, Blvd Fabert, 08200 Sedan [03 24 27 13 05 or 03 24 27 73 42; fax 03 24 22 14 78; christophe.lagnier@mairie-sedan.fr]** Fr A34(A203) exit junc 4 dir Sedan cent. Cont strt thro town & over rlwy bdge; in 500m cont over viaduct, site visible on R, turn R at next traff lts at end of viaduct, site 100m on R. Easy to find. Med, pt shd; no hdstg; wc (some cont); chem disp; mv service pnt; shwrs inc; el pnts (10A) €3.15; lndtte; shop 300m; rest, snacks & bar 500m; BBQ; sm playgrnd; pool 500m; dogs €1; no twin-axles; phone; poss cr; adv bkg; some traff noise; no ccard acc; red long stay; CKE/CCI. "Pleasant, peaceful site in lovely spot by rv; haphazard parking; rough/uneven ground; friendly, helpful staff; san facs dated but clean; poss muddy when wet; pleasant walk to interesting town; mkt traders for fair mid-Sep; gd value; highly rec; local Patisserie comes to site" ♦ 1 Apr-30 Sep. € 6.00   2013*

SEES 4E1 (S Urban) 48.59875, 0.17103 **Camp Municipal Le Clos Normand, Ave du 8 mai 1945, 61500 Sées [02 33 28 87 37 or 02 33 28 74 79 (LS); fax 02 33 28 18 13; tourisme@sees.fr; www.ville-sees.fr]** C'vans & lge m'vans best app fr S - twd rndabt at S end of by-pass (rec use this rndabt as other rtes diff & narr). Well sp. Narr ent. Sm, hdg pitch, pt shd; wc; chem disp; mv service pnt; shwrs inc; el pnts (4A) €2.50; gas; lndtte; supmkt opp; snacks & bar 100m; rest 500m; playgrnd; pool 2km; fishing; 10% statics; no twin axles; dogs €1.25; some Eng spkn; adv bkg; slight rd noise; CKE/CCI. "Spacious, well-cared for pitches; helpful, friendly warden; gd san facs, poss stretched if site full; excel mv service pnt; gates clsd 2100 (2000 low ssn)" ♦ 1 May-30 Sep. € 16.95   2013*

SEGRE 2F4 (7km NW Rural) 47.71003, -0.95165 **Camping Parc de St Blaise, 49520 Noyant-la-Gravoyère [02 41 61 93 09; campingstblaise@orange.fr; www. campingsaintblaise.fr]** Fr Segré take D775 dir Pouancé to Noyant, site/park sp in vill on R. Sm, hdg pitch, terr, pt shd; wc; chem disp; shwrs inc; el pnts (6A) inc; shop & 1km; tradsmn; rest; bar; playgrnd; lake sw adj; aquatic park; fishing; horseriding; entmnt; dogs; phone; CKE/CCI. "Clean, well-maintained site in leisure park; gd views; slate mine worth visit." ♦ 15 Jun-30 Sept. € 17.00   2012*

SEIGNOSSE see Hossegor 8E1

FRANCE

SEILHAC *7C4* (4km SW Rural) *45.35018, 1.64642* **Camp Municipal du Pilard, La Barthe, 19700 Lagraulière [05 55 73 71 04; fax 05 55 73 25 28; mairie.lagrauliere@ wanadoo.fr; www.lagrauliere.correze.net]** Exit A20 junc 46 onto D34 to Lagraulière, site sp. NB Lge o'fits rec take D44 & D167E fr Seilhac. Sm, mkd pitch, pt shd; wc; chem disp (wc); shwrs inc; el pnts (3-6A) €3 (poss rev pol); gas 2km, shop 700m; rest, snacks & bar 1km; BBQ; playgrnd; htd pool adj; tennis; dogs €1; phone adj; Eng spkn; quiet; CKE/CCI. "Quiet, clean site nr pleasant vill; warden calls." ♦ ltd 15 Jun-15 Sep. € 9.00   2011*

SEILHAC *7C4* (2.5km NW Rural) *45.37750, 1.70227* **Camp Municipal Le Lac de Bournazel, 19700 Seilhac [05 55 27 05 65; fax 04 73 93 71 00]** Fr Seilhac W on D1120 for 1.5km turn R at rndabt for 1km, clearly sp. Lge, mkd pitch, terr, pt shd; wc; chem disp; mv service pnt; baby facs; shwrs inc; el pnts (6-10A) €3.05; lndtte; shop in ssn; rest, bar; snacks 100m; BBQ; playgrnd; lakeside beach & sw adj; 25% statics; dogs €1.10; Eng spkn; adv bkg; CKE/CCI. "Clean site with public access; lge pitches." 1 Apr-30 Sep. € 13.85   2009*

SELESTAT *6E3* (4km N Rural) *48.29144, 7.48236* **Camping à la Ferme St Paul (Loos), 67600 Ebersheim [03 88 85 71 80; fax 03 88 85 71 05; fermest.paul@orange.fr]** Exit Sélestat on N83 to N & site on R in approx 4km, sp. Sm, pt shd; wc; chem disp; mv service pnt; shwrs €1; el pnts €2; gas 1km; lndtte; shops 1km; snacks; rest & bar Sat eve; playgrnd; horseriding, tennis 1km; dogs €1; adv bkg; quiet; CKE/CCI. "CL-type site; friendly owner." 1 Apr-30 Oct. € 7.00   2009*

SELESTAT *6E3* (5km N Rural) **Camping Rural (Weiss), 17 Rue du Buhl, 67600 Ebersheim [03 88 85 72 97; elizabeth. trau@wanadoo.fr]** Fr S or N on N83 in vill of Ebersheim foll green Camping Rural sps. Sm, pt shd; wc; shwrs inc; el pnts inc; shop 500m; cooking facs; quiet; adv bkg; ccard not acc; CKE/CCI. "Gd touring base; friendly, helpful warden." ♦ 15 Jun-15 Sep. € 10.00   2010*

SELESTAT *6E3* (6km N Rural) *48.32600, 7.42510* **Camping de l'Ours, Route d'Ebersheim, 67650 Dambach-la-Ville [06 50 92 00 26; camping-de-l-ours@orange.fr; www. pays-de-barr.com]** Exit A35 at junc 16 for D1422 dir Obernai. After approx 2km take D210 for Dambach-la-Ville & foll sp. Med, mkd pitch, pt shd; wc; chem disp; shwrs inc; el pnts (5A) €2.50; lndtte; shop, rest, snacks, bar 1km; BBQ; playgrnd; sports area; tennis adj; dogs €1.90; quiet; lake 15km; pool 7km; library 1km; cinema 7km; . "Attractive medieval town; spacious site, large pitches." ♦ Easter-1 Nov. € 11.70   2013*

SELESTAT *6E3* (S Urban) *48.25470, 7.44781* **Camp Municipal Les Cigognes, Rue de la 1ère D.F.L, 67600 Sélestat [03 88 92 03 98 or 03 88 58 87 20; fax 03 88 92 88 63; camping-selestat@orange.fr; www.selestat-tourisme.com]** Site sp D1083 & D424. Fr S town cent turn E off D1083 & foll sps to site adj schools & playing fields. Med, mkd pitch, pt shd; wc; mv service pnt; chem disp; shwrs inc; el pnts (5-16A) inc; gas; lndtte; shops; rest, snacks, bar 500m; playgrnd; pool 300m; rv & lake nrby; entmnt; dogs €1; train to Strasbourg nrby; poss cr; Eng spkn; adv bkg rec high ssn; quiet but some noise fr local football area; CKE/CCI. "Well-run site; helpful staff; clean san facs; easy walk to old town; mkt Sat; rec" ♦ 15 Apr-30 Sep. € 17.30 (3 persons)   2013*

SELESTAT *6E3* (12km W Rural) *48.27287, 7.29052* **Camping du Haut-Koenigsbourg, Rue de la Vancelle, 68660 Lièpvre [03 89 58 43 20; fax 03 89 58 98 29; camping.haut-koenigsbourg@wanadoo.fr; www.liepvre.fr/camping]** Fr Sélestat W on N59 twd Lièpvre vill then R at factory car park & foll site sps. Fr Ste Marie-aux-Mines on N59 turn L at rndabt after tunnel. Med, mkd pitch, pt sl, pt shd; htd wc; mv service pnt; shwrs inc; el pnts (4-8A) €3-4.20; lndtte; shop 1km; tradsmn; bar; BBQ; playgrnd; TV rm; 10% statics; dogs €2; poss cr; quiet; CKE/CCI. "V well maintained site; gd location; would rec. gd walks and cycling lovely site" ♦ 15 Mar-15 Oct. € 12.40   2012*

SELESTAT *6E3* (5km NW Rural) *48.28915, 7.41787* **Aire Naturelle (Palmer), 11 Rue Faviers, 67759 Scherwiller [03 88 92 94 57; fax 03 88 82 05 39; campingpalmer@ yahoo.fr; www.campingpalmer.fr]** Fr N foll N83 to Ebersheim then D81 to Scherwiller. Site sp off D35 at N end vill. Sm, pt shd; wc; chem disp; shwrs €2.40; el pnts (6A) €2.80; gas 1km; tradsmn; shop, rest, snacks & bar 1km; BBQ; playgrnd; pool 5km; dogs €1; Eng spkn; quiet; ccard acc; CKE/CCI. "Friendly site on wine route; facs basic; easy walk to vill; easy access to Rhine/Germany; vg." 15 May-15 Sep. € 9.80   2011*

SELLES SUR CHER *4G2* (300m E Rural) *47.27666, 1.55935* **Camp Municipal Les Châtaigniers, Blvd Kléber Lousteau, 41130 Selles-sur-Cher [02 54 97 67 26; camping.les. chataigniers@orange.fr; http://campingleschataigniers.e-monsite.com]** N fr Valençay on D965 dir Blois to Selles-sur-Cher; site on R, 250m after rndabt junc with D51. Med, mkd pitch, pt shd; wc; chem disp; mv service pnt (outside gate); shwrs inc; el pnts €3.50; tradsmn; shop, rest & bar 500m; BBQ; playgrnd; pool 1km; canoeing; no rv sw; 4% statics; dogs free; no twin-axles; adv bkg; quiet; CKE/CCI. "Well-kept, spacious site by Rv Cher; lge pitches; walks by rv; attractive sm town; gd." ♦ 15 Apr-24 Sep. € 7.00   2011*

SELONGEY *6G1* (500m SW Rural) *47.58248, 5.18408* **Camp Municipal Les Courvelles, Rue Henri Jevain, 21260 Selongey [03 80 75 52 38 or 03 80 75 70 74 (Mairie); fax 03 80 75 56 65; info@solongey.com; www.selongey.com]** Exit A31 junc 5 N of Dijon onto D974 N for 3km to Orville: turn W in Orville sp Selongey & site; site in approx 2km. Sm, some hdstg, unshd; wc; chem disp; shwrs inc; el pnts (6A) €2; shop 1km; tennis; quiet; CKE/CCI. "Well-kept, friendly site; warden calls am & eve; rec arr bef 1600 & site yourself if req hdstg; no twin-axles; poss itinerants; conv m'way/NH; excel." ♦ 1 May-30 Sep. € 10.00   2011*

SELTZ *5D4* (1km S Rural) *48.88269, 8.10001* **Camping Die Grüne Les Peupliers, 67470 Seltz [03 88 86 52 37; peupliers@ville-seltz.fr]** Fr Seltz on D468, turn L in 1km at sp. Lge, pt shd; wc; chem disp; mv service pnt; shwrs; el pnts (6A) €3; rest; bar; playgrnd; lake fishing & boating adj; 85% statics; dogs €1.50; ccard acc; CKE/CCI. "Sm pitches." ♦ 1 Apr-30 Sep. € 17.70   2008*

SEMUR EN AUXOIS *6G1* (3.5km S Rural) *47.46812, 4.35589*
FFCC Camping Lac de Pont, 16 Rue du Lac, 21140 Pont-et-Massène [03 80 97 01 26 or 03 80 97 01 26 (LS); contact@camping-lacdepont.fr; www.campinglacdepont.fr]
Exit A6 junc 23 twd Semur-en-Auxois on D980; after sh dist turn R sp 'Lac de Pont' D103. Med, some hdg pitch, pt sl, pt shd; wc; chem disp; mv service pnt; baby facs; shwrs inc; el pnts (6A) €3.50; gas; lndtte; shop; tradsmn; rest 500m; snacks; bar; BBQ; playgrnd; lake sw, sand beach adj; diving platform; watersports on lake; tennis; games rm; cycle hire; 30% statics; dogs €2; phone; poss cr; Eng spkn; quiet; ccard acc; CKE/CCI. "Warm welcome, helpful owners; generous pitches, some shady; san facs dated; vg for teenagers - games/meeting rm; 'Petit Train' goes round site & into Semur; cycle rte/walks adj; gd touring base; nr A6 m'way; walled, medieval town; superb" 30 Apr-3 Oct. € 16.20   2013*

SENERGUES see Conques *7D4*

SENNECEY LE GRAND *6H1* (6km E Rural) *46.65480, 4.94461*
Château de L'Epervière, Rue du Château, 71240 Gigny-sur-Saône [03 85 94 16 90; fax 03 85 94 16 97; info@domaine-eperviere.com; www.domaine-eperviere.com]
Fr N exit A6 junc 26 (Chalon Sud) onto N6 dir Mâcon & Tournus; at Sennecey-le-Grand turn E onto D18 sp Gigny-sur-Saône; site sp 1km S of Gigny-sur-Saône. Or fr S exit A6 junc 27 (Tournus) onto N6 N to Sennecey-le-Grand, then as above. NB Diff to find signs fr main rd. Lge, hdg/mkd pitch, hdstg, pt shd; htd wc; chem disp; mv service pnt; baby facs; jacuzzi/sauna; shwrs inc; el pnts (6A) inc; gas; lndtte (inc dryer); sm shop; tradsmn; rest, snacks; pizzeria; bar high ssn; BBQ; playgrnd; 2 pools (1 htd, covrd); paddling pool; lake & rv nr; fishing; tennis 400m; cycle hire; wifi; entmnt; games/TV rm; tour op statics & chalets; dogs €3; no c'vans/m'vans over 18m high ssn; poss v cr; Eng spkn; adv bkg; quiet; ccard acc; red low ssn; CKE/CCI. "Superb, spacious, well-run site in grounds of chateau nr sm lake; lovely, lge pitches; warm welcome, pleasant staff; excel san facs; gd pools & rest; vg for families; wine tasting; interesting wild life; boggy when wet; conv NH fr a'route; fantastic site; level pitches; great facs" ◆ 1 Apr-30 Sep. € 49.40 SBS - L12   2013*

See advertisement on inside back cover

SENNECEY LE GRAND *6H1* (5km NW Rural) *46.67160, 4.83301* Camping La Héronnière, Les Lacs de Laives, 71240 Laives [tel/fax 03 85 44 98 85; camping.laives@wanadoo.fr; www.camping-laheronniere.com] Exit A6 junc 26 (fr N) or junc 27 (fr S) onto N6. Turn W at Sennecey-le-Grand to Laives. Foll sp 'Lacs de Laives'. Sp on D18. Med, hdg/mkd pitch, some hdstg, pt shd; wc; chem disp; shwrs inc; el pnts (6A) €4.80; lndtte; shop; rest 300m; snacks; playgrnd; sm htd pool; lake sw & beach nrby; fishing; windsurfing; watersports; cycle hire; dogs €1.60; Eng spkn; adv bkg; quiet, but some rd noise fr A6; CKE/CCI. "Lovely, level, lakeside site; excel, busy NH; may fill up after 1500; gd shwrs; rest at lakeside (high ssn); popular with bikers; vg; Pretty site, laid back helpful staff, gd nh, romantic res by lakeside 3 mins walk; excel facs; clean modern san facs" ◆ 29 Mar-13 Oct. € 35.90   2013*

SENONCHES *4E2* (500m S Rural) *48.55569, 1.03851* Camping Huttopia Senonches, Ave de Badouleaux, 28250 Senonches [04 37 64 22 35 or 02 37 37 81 40 (reservations); fax 04 72 85 08 02; senonches@huttopia.com; www.huttopia.com] Fr Senonches cent take D155 dir Etang de Badouleaux, site sp. Med, pt shd; htd wc; baby facs; shwrs; el pnts (6-10A) €4.60-6.80; rest, snacks; bar; playgrnd; pool; tennis adj; cycle hire; games area; entmnt; internet; TV rm; some statics; dogs €4; adv bkg; quiet. ◆ 3 Jul-5 Nov. € 18.00   2009*

SENS *4F4* (1km S Urban) *48.18312, 3.28803* Camp Municipal Entre Deux Vannes, Ave de Senigallia, 89100 Sens [03 86 65 64 71 or 03 86 65 37 42 (LS); fax 03 86 95 39 41; http://ville-sens.fr] Fr NW on D606 to Sens; site bet on E side of D606; foll sp. Med, mkd pitch, pt shd; wc (some cont); chem disp (wc); mv service pnt; baby facs; shwrs inc; el pnts (16A) inc; lndtte; shop; tradsmn high ssn; rest nrby; playgrnd; adv bkg rec; some noise fr rd & commercial premises nrby during day; ccard acc; CKE/CCI. "Excel site; opp rv & superb park area; friendly, helpful warden; san facs old but clean; gate locked 2200; easy walk to town." 15 May-15 Sep. € 13.50   2011*

SEPPOIS LE BAS see Altkirch *6F3*

⊞ **SEPTEMES LES VALLONS** *10F3* (1km NE Urban) *43.40688, 5.36185* Camping Le Verdière, 4 Chemin de la Haute Bédoule, 13240 Septèmes-les-Vallons [04 91 65 59 98 or 06 28 19 20 25 (mob); fax 04 91 65 59 98; camping.laverdiere@wanadoo.fr; www.camping-la-verdiere.com] Exit A51 junc 1 onto D543 dir Septèmes-les-Vallons; at 5-pnt rndabt in 1km take 2nd exit; at next rndabt in 800m turn R under m'way; immed turn R again (on other side m'way) into Chemin de la Haute Bédoule; site on L in 800m. NB Take care using sat nav, can take to m'way running alongside site but no turning for 1km in either dir. Sm, pt shd; wc; el pnts (6A) €2.50; shops nrby; supmkt 1km; bar; pool; internet; 40% statics; dogs €3; 70% statics; bus & train 1km; Eng spkn; rd noise; red low ssn. "Touring pitches shady; gd san facs; OK." € 21.50   2011*

SERAUCOURT LE GRAND see St Quentin *3C4*

SERENT *2F3* (500m NE Rural) *47.82479, -2.50182* Camp Municipal du Pont Salmon, Rue Général de Gaulle, 56460 Sérent [02 97 75 91 98 or 06 61 09 49 56; mairie.serent@fr.oleane.com; www.serent.fr] S fr Ploërmel on N166 take D10 W 5km to Sérent. At E end of vill turn R twd Le Pont Salmon, site on R. Med, hdg pitch, pt sl, pt shd; htd wc (male all cont); chem disp; mv service pnt; shwrs inc; el pnts (10A) €2.35 (poss rev pol); lndtte (inc dryer); shops 300m; BBQ; playgrnd; htd pool; 5% statics; adv bkg; quiet. "Excel, well-kept site; gd san facs; Resistance Museum at St Marcel-Malestroit." ◆ ltd 1 Jun-31 Aug. € 7.95   2009*

SERGE SUR BRAY *4F2* (500m SW Rural) *47.92268, 0.84921* Camp Municipal, Ave de la Gare, 41170 Sargé-sur-Bray [02 54 72 73 17 (Mairie)] E fr Le Mans on D357, turn L onto D921 to Sargé-sur-Bray, site sp. Sm, shd; wc; chem disp (wc); shwrs inc; el pnts (10A) €1; lndtte; shop, rest, snacks, bar 1km; BBQ; rv sw 100m; some statics; dogs; quiet; ccard acc; CKE/CCI. "Helpful warden; gd local shops; gd birdwatching; vg." ◆ 1 Apr-30 Sep. € 9.90   2010*

SERIGNAC 7D3 (5km W Rural) 44.43103, 1.06902 **Camping Le Clos Barrat (Naturist), 46700 Sérignac [05 65 31 97 93; fax 05 65 31 91 17; contact@leclosbarrat.com; www. leclosbarrat.fr]** Fr Fumel by-pass turn S on D139 to Montayral, rd cont but becomes D4. Site sp bet Mauroux & St Matré. Med, pt shd, mkd pitch; wc; chem disp; shwrs inc; el pnts (6A) inc; gas; lndtte; shop; tradsmn; rest; snacks; playgrnd; pool; paddling pool; wifi; entmnt; TV; some statics; dogs €1.60; quiet; ccard acc. "Nr Rv Lot; INF card req - can be bought on site; helpful staff; excel." 1 May-25 Sep. € 23.00   2010*

SERIGNAC PEBOUDOU see Cancon 7D3

SERIGNAN PLAGE 10F1 (300m W Coastal) 43.26741, 3.33473 **Yelloh! Village Aloha, 34410 Sérignan-Plage [04 67 39 71 30; fax 04 67 32 58 15; www.yellohvillage-aloha.com or www.yellohvillage.co.uk]** Exit A9 at Béziers Est; take D64 then D37E to Sérignan-Plage; turn R at Centre Commercial. Lge, hdg/mkd pitch, shd; htd wc; chem disp; mv service pnt; baby facs; shwrs inc; el pnts (10A) inc; gas; lndtte (inc dryer); shop; rest, snacks; bar; BBQ; playgrnd; 3 htd pools; 2 waterslides; sand beach adj; watersports; tennis; games area; games rm; wifi; entmnt; TV; 50% statics; dogs €3; phone; bus adj; Eng spkn; adv bkg; quiet; ccard acc; red low ssn; CKE/CCI. "Gd family site; gd." ♦ ltd 23 Apr-10 Sep. € 43.00   2008*

See advertisement on inside front cover

SERIGNAN PLAGE 10F1 (500m W Coastal) 43.26715, 3.33051 **Camping Village Domaine de Beauséjour, La Maïre, 34410 Sérignan-Plage [04 67 39 50 93; fax 04 67 32 01 96; info@camping-beausejour.com; www.camping-beausejour.com]** Fr A9/E15, exit Béziers Est junc 35 onto D64 S. In 4km turn L onto D37E to Sérignan-Plage. Site on R just bef shops. Lge, hdg/mkd pitch, pt shd; wc; chem disp; mv service pnt; shwrs inc; el pnts (10A) inc; gas; lndtte (inc dryer); shop; tradsmn; hypmkt nr; rest, snacks; bar; BBQ; playgrnd; htd pool; paddling pool; waterslide; sand beach adj; games rm; entmnt; TV; 50% statics; dogs €3.50; poss cr; Eng spkn; adv bkg; quiet; ccard acc; red long stay/low ssn; CKE/CCI. "Vg site; excel beach; excel facs; weekly mkts in vill." ♦ 1 Apr-30 Sep. € 42.00   2010*

SERIGNAN PLAGE 10F1 (1km W Coastal) 43.26398, 3.3210 **Yelloh! Village Le Sérignan Plage, Les Orpelières, 34410 Sérignan-Plage [04 67 32 35 33; fax 04 67 32 26 36; info@leserignanplage.com; www.leserignanplage.com or www.yellohvillage.co.uk]** Exit A9 junc 35. After toll turn L at traff lts onto N112 & at 1st rndabt strt on to D64. In 5km turn L onto D37E Sérignan-Plage, turn R on narr 1-way rd to site. Adj to Camping Sérignan-Plage (Naturist site). V lge, hdg/mkd pitch, pt shd; wc (some cont); chem disp; mv service pnt; baby facs; shwrs inc; el pnts (5A) inc; gas; lndtte (inc dryer); shop; hypmkt 6km; rest, snacks; bar; BBQ; playgrnd; 2 pools (1 htd, covrd); paddling pool; Club Nautique - sw, sailing & water-ski tuition on private beach; tennis; horseriding; wifi; entmnt; TV; many statics; dogs €4; use of naturist private beach & facs adj; poss v cr; Eng spkn; adv bkg; poss noisy; red low ssn; no ccard acc; CKE/CCI. "Busy, even low ssn: excel pool; some tourers amongst statics & sm sep touring area." 21 Apr-2 Oct. € 48.00   2010*

See advertisement on inside front cover

SERIGNAN PLAGE 10F1 (1.5km W Coastal) 43.26154, 3.32131 **Camping Le Clos de Ferrand (Naturist), 33 Ave de Beziers, 34410 Sérignan-Plage [04 67 32 14 30; fax 04 67 32 15 59; centrenaturiste.closferrand@wanadoo.fr; www.leclosferrand-centrenaturiste.fr]** Exit A9 junc 35 onto D64 dir Valras-Plage. At Sérignan town turn L on D37E to Sérignan-Plage 5km, site sp. Med, hdg/mkd pitch, pt shd; wc; chem disp; shwrs inc; el pnts (2-6A) €4-5; lndtte; shop; snacks; rest; bar; playgrnd; TV rm; beach adj; rv 1km; fishing; boat hire; no dogs; adv bkg; quiet; ccard not acc; INF card req; CKE/CCI. "Direct access to beach; gd sized pitches." ♦ ltd 10 May-20 Sep. € 38.00 (CChq acc)   2008*

SERIGNAN PLAGE 10F1 (1.6km W Coastal) 43.26308, 3.31976 **Camping Le Sérignan-Plage Nature (Naturist), Les Orpelière, 34410 Sérignan-Plage [04 67 32 09 61; fax 04 67 32 26 36; info@leserignannature.com; www. leserignannature.com]** Exit A9 junc 36 Beziers Est onto D64. At Sérignan town turn L on D37E to Sérignan-Plage. After 4km turn R on single-lane dual c'way. At T-junc turn L & immed L again in 50m to site. Lge, mkd pitch, pt shd; wc (some cont); chem disp; mv service pnt; baby facs; shwrs inc; el pnts (5A) inc (poss rev pol); gas; lndtte (with dryer); shop; rest, snacks; bar; BBQ; playgrnd; pool complex; sand beach; golf 15km; beauty cent; cycle hire; wifi; TV rm; 75% statics; dogs €4; poss cr; Eng spkn; adv bkg rec; quiet, but some noise fr disco (quiet by 2330); red long stay/low ssn; CKE/CCI. "Lovely, clean site & facs; helpful staff; Cmp Le Sérignan Plage (non-naturist) adj with use of same private beach & facs; pool also shared - for naturists' use 1000-1200 only; cycle rtes adj; excel." 21 Apr-2 Oct. € 47.10 (CChq acc)   2010*

SERIGNAN PLAGE 10F1 (5km W Rural) 43.26965, 3.28631 **FFCC Camping Le Paradis, Route de Valras-Plage, 34410 Sérignan [tel/fax 04 67 32 24 03; http://camping-leparadis.com]** Exit A9 junc 35 Béziers Est onto D64 dir Valras-Plage. Site on L on rndabt at S end of Sérignan by-pass, 1.5km S of Sérignan. Med, mkd pitch, pt shd; wc; chem disp; shwrs; el pnts (6A) inc; gas; lndtte; shop; supmkt opp; rest, snacks & bar high ssn; snacks; playgrnd; pool (high ssn); sand beach 2km; no dogs; poss cr; Eng spkn; adv bkg rec; quiet except for twice weekly disco (high ssn only) to 0030 & some rd noise; red low ssn/CKE/CCI. "Excel, well-kept, family-run site; immac san facs; nr gd beaches; vg value low ssn; el pnts poss no earth" ♦ 1 Apr-30 Sep. € 30.00   2012*

SERRIERES 9C2 (3km W Rural) 45.30872, 4.74622 **Camping Le Bas Larin, 88 Route de Larin Le Bas, 07340 Félines [tel/fax 04 75 34 87 93 or 06 80 05 13 89 (mob); camping. baslarin@wanadoo.fr; www.camping-bas-larin.com]** Exit A7 junc 12 Chanas or fr N7, exit at Serrières onto D1082; cross canal & rv; cont over rndabt at winding hill, camp on L nr hill top. Sp fr N7 & D1082, but easily missed - foll sp Safari de Peaugres. Med, terr, shd; wc; chem disp; baby facs; shwrs inc; el pnts (4-10A) €2.50-3.50; lndtte; shops 2km; rest adj; playgrnd; pool; paddling pool; games area; games rm; wifi; entmnt; some statics; dogs free; Eng spkn; some rd noise; CKE/CCI. "Friendly, family-run site; beautiful views; helpful staff; easy access pitches; popular with Dutch; excel." ♦ 1 Apr-30 Sep. € 17.00   2011*

SERVON see Pontaubault 2E4

FRANCE

SETE *10F1* (11km SW Coastal) *43.34194, 3.58440* **Camping Le Castellas, Cours Gambetta, 34200 Sète [04 67 51 63 00; fax 04 67 51 63 01; www.le-castellas.com www.village-center.com]** On D612/N112 bet Agde and Sète. Foll sp for 'Plages-Agde'. Lge, hdg pitch, pt shd; wc; chem disp; shwrs inc; el pnts (6A) inc; gas; lndtte; shop; rest, snacks; bar; playgrnd; 2 htd pools; sand beach 150m (across busy rd); tennis; games area; cycle hire; entmnt; dogs €3; poss cr; Eng spkn; adv bkg; rd & rlwy noise; red low ssn/long stay; CKE/CCI. "Bull-fighting in ssn; superb beach; twin-axles welcome" ♦ 06 Apr -29 Sep. € 59.10 (CChq acc)   2013*

SEVERAC LE CHATEAU *9D1* (1km SE Urban) *44.31841, 3.06412* **FFCC Camping Les Calquières (formerly Municipal), Ave Jean Moulin, 12150 Sévérac-le-Château [05 65 47 64 82; contact@camping-calquieres.com; www. camping-calquieres.com]** Exit A75 onto A75 Sévérac & Rodez; foll 'Camping' sps to avoid narr town rds. Med, hdg pitch, pt shd; wc (some cont); 50% serviced pitches; shwrs inc; el pnts (6A) €3.40; (poss long lead & rev pol); lndry rm; shop 250m; tradsmn; rest, snacks; bar; playgrnd; htd, covrd pool; games area; fishing; tennis; wifi; some statics; dogs €1.50; adv bkg; quiet, but poss noise fr sports facs adj; red long stay/low ssn; CKE/CCI. "Lovely, spacious site with gd views; lge pitches; friendly owners; vg clean san facs; if office clsd site self; gd touring base; conv A75; busy NH, espec w/end." ♦ 1 Apr-15 Oct. € 30.60   2012*

SEVERAC LE CHATEAU *9D1* (15km SE Rural) *44.27302, 3.21538* **Camp Municipal, 48500 St Rome-de-Dolan [tel/fax 04 66 44 03 81 or 04 66 48 83 59; mairie-stromededolan@ wanadoo.fr; www.saint-rome-de-dolan.com]** Exit A75 junc 42 to Sévérac, then take D995 fr Séverac-le-Château then E thro Le Massegros to St Rome-de-Dolan. Site on R at ent to vill, sp. NB Rec not to use GPS. Sm, pt sl, pt terr, pt shd; wc; chem disp; shwrs inc; el pnts (6A) €2.20; lndtte; shop 5km; tradsmn; rest, snacks, bar 5km; BBQ; playgrnd; rv sw 5km; dogs €0.80; phone 50m; Eng spkn; adv bkg; quiet; CKE/CCI. "Simple, well-kept, well-run site in beautiful location nr Gorges du Tarn; fantastic views some pitches; friendly, helpful warden; clean san facs; some pitches sm & need mover; bird watching, inc vultures; walking; highly rec." ♦ 1 May-30 Sep. € 12.00   2011*

SEVRIER see Annecy *9B3*

SEYNE *9D3* (800m S Rural) *44.34270, 6.35896* **Camping Les Prairies, Haute Gréyère, 04140 Seyne-les-Alpes [04 92 35 10 21; fax 04 92 35 26 96; info@ campinglesprairies.com; www.campinglesprairies.com]** Fr Digne-les-Bains, take D900 N to Seyne. Turn L on ent Seyne onto D7, site sp beside Rv La Blanche. Med, mkd pitch, pt shd; htd wc; chem disp; mv service pnt; baby facs; shwrs inc; el pnts (10A) €3.50; gas; lndtte; shop 800m; tradsmn; rest 800m; snacks; bar; BBQ; playgrnd; htd pool; tennis 300m; horseriding 500m; dogs €2; phone; Eng spkn; adv bkg; quiet; ccard acc; red low ssn; CKE/CCI. "Immac, tidy, peaceful site." 18 Apr-12 Sep. € 19.00   2009*

SEYSSEL *9B3* (400m N Urban) *45.96324, 5.83574* **Camping Le Nant Matraz, 15 Route de Genève, 74910 Seyssel [tel/ fax 04 50 59 03 68]** On L of D992 sp Frangy. Lge supmkt opp. Med, mkd pitch, pt shd; wc (some cont); chem disp; mv service pnt; shwrs inc; el pnts (6A) inc; lndtte; shop adj; snacks; bar; BBQ; playgrnd; pool in town; boat hire; rv fishing; games rm; some statics; dogs; Eng spkn; adv bkg; rd/rlwy noise; ccard acc. "On banks of Rv Rhône." 1 Apr-30 Sep. € 15.00   2010*

"That's changed – Should I let The Club know?"

If you find something on site that's different from the site entry, fill in a report and let us know. See www.caravanclub.co.uk/europereport.

SEZANNE *4E4* (500m NW Rural) *48.72115, 3.70247* **Camp Municipal, Route de Launat, 51120 Sézanne [tel/fax 03 26 80 57 00/ 03 26 80 57 00 (mob); campingdesezanne@wanadoo.fr]** W'bound on N4 Sézanne by-pass onto D373 & foll site sp. Fr E turn R at 1st junc on Sézanne bypass & foll sps 'Camping & Piscine'. Avoid town cent. Med, mainly sl, pt shd; serviced pitches; wc (some cont); shwrs inc; shop, el pnts (10A) inc; shop 500m; rest in town 1km; sm playgrnd; pool adj; waterslide; wifi; dogs €1.05; no ccard acc; CKE/CCI. "Nice, well-kept site, v busy high ssn; generous pitches, some v sl; helpful manager; excel, immac san facs; levelling blocks req some pitches; request gate opening/ closing at back bungalow of 2 opp site; nice vill; vg; well run site; excel value" ♦ 1 Apr-30 Sep. € 14.15   2013*

SIBIRIL see St Pol de Léon *1D2*

⊞ **SIGEAN** *10G1* (5km N Rural) *43.06633, 2.94100* **Camping La Grange Neuve, 17 La Grange Neuve Nord, 11130 Sigean [tel/fax 04 68 48 58 70; info@camping-sigean.com; www.camping-sigean.com]** Exit junc 39 fr A9; pass over A9 (fr N) then 1st R sp La Réserve Africaine. Do not go into Sigean. Med, hdg/mkd pitch, hdstg, pt sl, terr, pt shd; wc; chem disp; mv service pnt; shwrs inc; el pnts (6A) €4; lndtte; shop; rest; snacks; bar; playgrnd; pool; waterslide; sand beach 5km; wifi; TV rm; 5% statics; dogs €3; poss cr; adv bkg; quiet but some rd noise; red low ssn; CKE/CCI. "Easy access; gd san facs; excel pool; ltd facs low ssn; phone ahead to check open low ssn; gd NH." ♦ € 18.00   2011*

SIGEAN *10G1* (8km SE Rural) *42.95800, 2.99586* **Camping Le Clapotis (Naturist), 11480 La Palme [04 68 48 15 40; info@leclapotis.com; www.leclapotis.com]** On D6009 S fr Narbonne turn L 8km S of Sigean. After 350m turn R at camping sp. Site in 150m. Final app rd narr but negotiable for lge vans. Lge, mkd pitch, pt shd; wc (cont); shwrs inc; el pnts (4A) €4; gas; rest & bar in ssn; pool; sm lake beach; tennis; games area; internet; many statics; dogs €2; poss cr; Eng spkn; adv bkg; quiet; red low ssn; Naturists INF card req; ccard acc; red low ssn. "Pleasant, basic, friendly site; sm pitches; helpful owners; san facs dated but clean; gd pool; poss strong winds - gd windsurfing; La Palme vill 15 mins walk." 15 Mar-15 Oct. € 22.00   2009*

FRANCE

SIGNY L'ABBAYE 5C1 (N Urban) 49.70123, 4.41971
Camp Municipal de l'Abbaye, 08460 Signy-l'Abbaye
[03 24 52 87 73; mairie-signy-l.abbaye@wanadoo.fr]
Take D985 N twd Belgium fr Rethel to Signy-l'Abbaye. Foll sp
fr town cent to Stade & Camping. Site by sports stadium. Sm,
some hdg/hdstg pitch, pt sl, pt shd; htd wc; chem disp; shwrs
inc; el pnts (10A) €2.90 (poss rev pol); lndry rm; shops, rest
500m; playgrnd; sports cent adj; rv fishing adj; dogs €0.60;
little Eng spkn; adv bkg; v quiet; CKE/CCI. "Lovely site in gd
location; friendly warden; san facs excel (shared with public
fr sports cent); strong awning pegs req on gravel hdg pitches,
or can park on open grassed area." ♦ ltd 1 May-30 Sep.
€ 6.40   2009*

SIGOULES 7D2 (1.5km N Rural) 44.77135, 0.41076 **Camp
Municipal La Gardonnette, Les Coteaux de Sigoulès,
24240 Pomport-Sigoulès [tel/fax 05 53 58 81 94;
campingdelagardonnette@wanadoo.fr]** S fr Bergerac take
D933 S. After 6km at top of hill turn R by La Grappe d'Or Rest
onto D17 sp Pomport/Sigoulès. Thro Pomport, site at bottom
of hill on R by lake. Med, mkd pitch, pt sl, shd; wc; chem disp;
shwrs inc; el pnts (6A); lndtte; shop, snacks, bar 1km; playgrnd;
lake sw adj; fishing; canoeing; tennis; games area; entmnt; TV;
25% statics; dogs; phone; Eng spkn; adv bkg; ccard acc; CKE/
CCI. "Barrier ent; facs clean but well worn & in need of refurb;
gd security." 1 Apr-30 Sep.   2009*

"I like to fill in the reports
as I travel from site to site"
You'll find report forms at the back of
this guide, or you can fill them in online
at www.caravaclub.co.uk/europereport.

SILLE LE GUILLAUME 4F1 (3km N Rural) 48.20352, -0.12774
**Camping Indigo Les Mollières, Sillé-Plage, 72140 Sillé-
le-Guillaume [02 43 20 16 12; molieres@camping-indigo.
com; www.camping-indigo.com]** Fr Sillé-le-Guillaume take
D5 N, D203 to site. Med, shd; htd wc; chem disp; mv service
pnt; shwrs inc; el pnts (13A) inc; lndtte (inc dryer); shop;
tradsmn; supmkt 2km; snacks; playgrnd; htd pool; padding
pool; lake sw; fishing; watersports; cycle hire; games area;
internet; some statics; dogs; quiet; ccard acc. "Site in pine
forest." ♦ 1 Jun-11 Sep. € 13.30   2009*

SILLE LE GUILLAUME 4F1 (3km N Rural) 48.20928,
-0.13444 **FFCC Camping La Forêt, Sillé-Plage, 72140
Sillé-le-Guillaume [02 43 20 11 04; fax 02 43 20 84 82;
campingsilleplage@wanadoo.fr / info@campingsilleplage.
com; www.campingsilleplage.com]** Exit Sillé on D304 sp
Mayenne. After 2km at x-rds turn R; across next x-rds & turn
L at next x-rds; sp Sillé-Plage; site on R in 500m, visible. Sp
fr other dir. Med, pt shd; wc; mv service pnt; shwrs inc; el pnts
(10A) €4.10; gas; shop; tradsmn; playgrnd; tennis; boating; lake
sw; fishing; 40% statics; dogs €1.15; poss cr; rd noise; CKE/
CCI. "Pleasant lakeside & forest scenery (some pitches amongst
trees); highly rec." 31 Mar-31 Oct. € 17.80   2013*

SILLE LE GUILLAUME 4F1 (2km NW Rural) 48.18943,
-0.14130 **Camping Les Tournesols, Route de Mayenne,
Le Grez, 72140 Sillé-le-Guillaume [02 43 20 12 69 or
06 98 04 74 29 (mob); campinglestournesols@orange.fr;
www.campinglestournesols.com]** Exit Sillé on D304/D35
sp Mayenne; in 2km at x-rds turn R; site in 150m on L, easily
visible & sp. Med, hdg/mkd pitch, pt sl, pt shd; htd wc; chem
disp; mv service pnt; shwrs inc; el pnts (6A) inc (poss long
lead req); lndtte (inc dryer); shop; tradsmn; snacks; bar; BBQ
(gas); playgrnd; rv/lake sw & canoeing 2km; fishing 1km;
cycle hire; entmnt; internet; mini golf; bouncy castle; football;
babmington; volley ball; jeux de boules; TV; wifi; 20% statics;
dogs €2 Rabies cert req'd; no twin-axles; Eng spkn; adv
bkg; quiet; ccard acc; red long stay; CKE/CCI. "Beautiful
site; friendly, helpful Dutch owners; pleasant town; conv Le
Mans; gd; welcoming owner" ♦ 1 May-30 Sep. € 24.00
(CChq acc)   2013*

SILLE LE PHILIPPE 4F1 (2km SW Rural) 48.10880, 0.33730
**Camping Le Château de Chanteloup, Parc de l'Epau Sarl,
72460 Sillé-le-Philippe [02 43 27 51 07 or 02 43 89 66 47; fax
02 43 89 05 05; chanteloup.souffront@wanadoo.fr; www.
chateau-de-chanteloup.com or www.les-castels.com]** Leave
A11/E50 at junc 7 Sp Le Mans Z1 Nord. After toll turn L onto
N338. Foll this & turn L onto D313 sp Coulaines, Mamers &
Ballon. Take D301 (at lge supmkt) & in approx 13km site is sp
just after ent to Sillé-le-Philippe. Avoid cent Sillé-le-Philippe.
Med, some mkd pitch, pt sl, pt shd; wc; chem disp; baby facs;
shwrs inc; el pnts (10A) €4. (poss rev pol); gas; lndtte (inc
dryer); ltd shop & 2km; tradsmn; rest high ssn; snacks; bar;
BBQ; playgrnd; pool; paddling pool; lake fishing; horseriding
& golf 10km; games area; wifi; entmnt; games/TV rm; dogs
free; twin-axles & lge o'fits by request; sep o'night area with
elec & water; poss v cr; Eng spkn; adv bkg; higher charge
during Le Mans events; quiet; ccard acc; red low ssn; CKE/CCI.
"Lovely, tranquil, spacious site in chateau grnds; pleasant,
helpful staff; dated, clean san facs - poss far fr pitches; some
pitches in wooded areas poss tight lge o'fits; gd rest; gd for
Le Mans; rec; no facs to drain waste water from m'van" ♦
1 Jun-3 Aug. € 47.60 SBS - L13   2013*

See advertisement on inside back cover

SINGLES 7B4 (900m SE Rural) 45.54310, 2.54278 **Camping
Le Moulin de Serre, 63690 Singles [04 73 21 16 06; fax
04 73 21 12 56; moulin-de-serre@wanadoo.fr; www.
moulindeserre.com]** N fr Bort-les-Orgues on D922; in 14km
at Les Quatre-Vents turn L onto D25; at Larodde turn R onto
D73. Site well sp fr D922. NB Diff access for v lge o'fits due
bends on app rds. Med, hdg/mkd pitch, pt shd; htd wc; chem
disp; mv service pnt; shwrs inc; el pnts (5-10A) €3.70-4.70;
lndtte (inc dryer); shop; tradsmn; snacks; bar; BBQ (sep areas);
playgrnd; pool; fishing & canoeing on lake nrby; games area;
TV; 40% statics; dogs €1.80; phone; adv bkg; ccard acc; red
low ssn; CKE/CCI. "Lovely site; friendly staff; vg." ♦
12 Apr-14 Sep. € 17.85   2008*

SIREUIL see Angouleme 7B2

SISTERON *10E3* (2.5km N Rural) *44.21467, 5.93643* **Camp Municipal Les Prés Hauts, 44 Chemin des Prés Hauts, 04200 Sisteron [tel/fax 04 92 61 00 37 or 04 92 61 19 69; contact@ camping-sisteron.com; www.camping-sisteron.com]** On W of D951. Lge, hdg pitch, pt sl, pt shd; wc; chem disp; serviced pitches; shwrs inc; el pnts (10A) €4 (poss rev pol); lndtte; shop & 1.5km; playgrnd; pool; tennis; fishing; entmnt; dogs €2; Eng spkn; quiet; ccard acc; red low ssn; CKE/CCI. "Lovely, well-kept, busy site; excel location, gd views; lge pitches & gd for m'vans; helpful, friendly warden; site yourself low ssn; vg facs, ltd low ssn; interesting old town, gd mkt; conv a'route; vg; Ent Barrier clsd at 20.00; Stunning pool; huge pitches; gd facs; friendly helpful staff; handy for m'way" ♦ 1 Apr - 30 Sep. € 30.70   2013*

SIVRY SUR MEUSE see Dun sur Meuse *5C1*

SIX FOURS LES PLAGES see Sanary Sur Mer *10F3*

SIXT SUR AFF see Gacilly, La *2F3*

SIZUN *2E2* (Rural) *48.40038, -4.07635* **Camp Municipal du Gollen, 29450 Sizun [02 98 24 11 43 or 02 98 68 80 13 (Mairie); fax 02 98 68 86 56; mairie.sizun@ wanadoo.fr; www.mairie-sizun.fr]** Fr Roscoff take D788 SW onto D69 to Landivisiau, D30 & D764 to Sizun. In Sizun take D18 at rndabt. At end of by-pass, at next rndabt, take 3rd exit. Site adj pool. Sm, pt shd; wc (some cont); shwrs inc; el pnts (10A) 2.50 (poss rev pol); lndry rm; shops 500m; playgrnd; htd pool adj high ssn; phone; no twin-axles; poss cr; no adv bkg; quiet; ccard not acc; CKE/CCI. "Lovely litte site; simple & restful by rv in nature park; friendly recep; site yourself if warden not avail; vg." 16 Apr-30 Sep. € 10.50   2011*

SOISSONS *3D4* (1km N Urban) *49.39295, 3.32701* **Camp Municipal du Mail, 14 Ave du Mail, 02200 Soissons [03 23 74 52 69; fax 03 23 75 05 21; campingdumail@ gmail.com; www.tourisme-soissons.fr]** Fr N on D1; foll town cent sp to 1st rndabt; turn R, cross rv & immed R into Ave du Mail. Foll sp 'Camping Piscine'. Site well sp beside sw pool. Rd humps & tight ent on last 500m of access rd. (Poss to avoid tight ent by going 150m to rndabt & returning). Or fr S on D1, turn R sp Centre Ville along Ave de Château-Thiery; at 3rd rndabt turn R into Rue du Général Leclerc to Place de la Republique; cont strt over into Blvd Gambette for 500m, then turn L into Ave de l'Aisne, leading into Ave du Petit Mail; then as above. Med, hdg/mkd pitch, hdstg, pt shd; htd wc; chem disp; mv service pnt; shwrs inc; el pnts (6A) inc (poss rev pol); lndtte (inc dryer); shop; rest, snacks; bar 1km; BBQ; playgrnd; pool adj; cycle hire; wifi; 5% statics; dogs €1; phone; poss cr; quiet; ccard acc; clsd 1 Jan & 25 Dec; CKE/CCI. "Pleasant, well-run site in interesting area; gd sized pitches, some nr rv; poss muddy, park on site rds in winter; m'van pitches all hdstg; helpful, friendly staff; gd clean, modern unisex san facs; rvside walks/cycling; gate clsd 2200-0700; lge mkt Wed & Sat; vg winter NH; Conv for town" ♦ € 17.75 2 Jan-24 Dec, 26 Dec-31 Dec   2013*

SOLLIES PONT *10F3* (1.5km SE Rural) *43.18519, 6.06324* **Camping à la Ferme Le Petit Réal (Cambray), Le Cros de Castel, 1095 Chemin de Sauvebonne, 8310 Solliès-Pont [04 94 28 94 80; mireille.cambray@wanadoo.fr; http:// cambray.pagesperso-orange.fr]** Exit A57 junc 8 onto D97 dir Solliès-Pont; in 500m turn L at 2nd rndabt onto D58; cont thro Solliès-Pont on D58 dir Le Crau & Hyères; site on L in 2km. Sm, hdg/mkd pitch, pt shd; wc; chem disp (septic tank friendly chemicals only); shwrs inc; el pnts (2-3A) €1.90-2.40; farm fruit & veg shop nrby; table tennis; quiet. "Quiet site bet orchards with mountain view; clean modern san facs; chem disp at mv service pnt at Casino supmkt in 2km; conv A57; vg." ♦ ltd 1 Apr-30 Sep. € 10.60   2011*

SOMMIERES *10E1* (2km SE Rural) *43.77550, 4.09280* **Camping Domaine de Massereau, 1990 Route d'Aubais, 30250 Sommières [04 66 53 11 20 or 06 03 31 27 21 (mob); fax 04 11 71 50 20; info@ massereau.fr; www.massereau.fr, www.massereau. co.uk or www.les-castels.com]** Exit A9 junc 26 at Gallargues, foll sp Sommières; site sp on D12. NB Danger of grounding at ent fr D12. Use this route 24/7 - 03/08 (due to festival in Sommières). Otherwise exit A9 junc 27 onto D34 to Sommières, foll sps to "Centre Historique" dir Aubias; cross bdge (sharp turn) & turn R onto D12; site on L in 3km. Med, hdg/mkd pitch; pt sl, pt shd; wc (some cont); chem disp; mv service pnt; baby facs; serviced pitch; sauna; jaccuzi; shwrs inc; el pnts (16A) inc; gas; lndtte; shop; tradsmn; rest, snacks; bar; BBQ (gas); playgrnd; pool; waterslide; paddling pool; rv sw 500m; horseriding & canoeing nrby; tennis; cycle hire; running track; trampoline; games area; games rm; wifi; entmnt; TV; 50% statics; dogs €3.90; no c'vans/m'vans over 7m high ssn; phone; poss cr; Eng spkn; adv bkg; quiet; ccard acc; red low ssn; CKE/CCI. "Lovely, tranquil, well-run site adj vineyard; lge pitches, some uneven; pleasant staff; modern san facs; narr site rds; sl/uneven pitches & trees diff lge o'fits; tight ents, diff without mover; excel." ♦ 1 Apr-10 Nov. € 39.40 SBS - C33   2011*

See advertisement on next page

SOMMIERES *10E1* (3km SE Rural) *43.76120, 4.11961* **Camping Les Chênes, Les Teullières Basses, 30250 Junas [04 66 80 99 07 or 06 03 29 36 32 (mob); fax 04 66 51 33 23; chenes@wanadoo.fr; www.camping-les-chenes.com]** Fr Sommières take D12 S (sp Gallargues) 3km to junc with D140 L (N) for 1km. Site on R 300m up side rd. Sp. Med, pt sl, shd; wc (cont); chem disp; shwrs inc; el pnts (3-10A) €3-4.20 (long lead poss req); lndtte; shops 1km; playgrnd; pool; beach & rv sw 2km; games area; wifi; some statics; dogs €3; phone; sep car park; adv bkg; quiet; red low ssn; CKE/CCI. "Gd shade; gd san facs; friendly, helpful staff; vg." 5 Apr-12 Oct. € 12.20   2008*

FRANCE

★★★★★ domaine de

Massereau

prenons le temps de vivre...

100
1914 · 2014

www.massereau.com

Between the Cevennes and the Mediterranean, and surrounded by vineyards.

A tranquil family campsite.

Chalets, cottages, mobile homes and high quality camping pitches.

Heated swimming pool and leisure pool with water slides.

Restaurant, snack bar, pizzeria, bar, food store.

Restaurant, snack bar, pizzeria, bar, food store, tennis, sauna, turkish bath, jacuzzi, cycle hire.

Open from 12/04 to 01/11

Rental accommodation (low season) : 7 nights reserved = 1 free night

Camping pitches (low season) : 7=6 / 14=11 / 21=14

1990 Route d'Aubais, 30 250
Sommières
camping@massereau.com
04 66 53 11 20

SOMMIERES *10E1* (4km SE) **Camping L'Olivier, 112 Route de Congénies Junas, 30250 Sommieres [04 66 80 39 52 or 04 66 80 98 05; www.campinglolivier.fr]** Fr Nîmes, take D40 twd Sommieres. At Congenies take D140 L to Junas, site sp in vill. Sm, pt sl, pt shd; wc; chem disp; shwrs inc; shops 500m; el pnts (6A) €5, poss inc on certain pitches; snack; pool; ; games area; fishing; tennis; dog €3; ping pong; mini golf; tennis; trampoline; wifi; quiet; adv bkg; "Entmnt thurs eve; excel home made pizzas; v friendly, helpful owners" 29 Mar-19 Oct. € 15.80   2013*

SOMMIERES *10E1* (500m NW Urban) *43.78672, 4.08702* **Camp Municipal Le Garanel, 110 Rue Eugène Rouché, 30250 Sommières [tel/fax 04 66 80 33 49; campingmunicipal.sommieres@wanadoo.fr; www.sommieres.fr]** Fr S on A9 exit junc 27 N & foll D34 then take D610 twd Sommières. By-pass town on D610, over rv bdge; turn R for D40, Rue Condamine. After L turn for Nîmes pull out to make sharp R turn sp 'Camping Arena' (easy to miss this R turn). At T-junc turn R, site thro car park. Fr N on D610 turn L at 4th junc sp 'Ville Vieille' & site adj rv. Site sp fr D610 fr N. NB Narr streets nr site. Sm, hdg/mkd pitch, pt shd; htd wc (some cont); chem disp; mv service pnt; shwrs inc; el pnts (10A) inc; lndtte; shops, rest, snacks 300m; tradsmn; bar 200m; BBQ; pool; beach 25km; tennis adj; dogs €2; bus 500m; twin-axle restrictions; poss cr; Eng spkn; adv bkg; quiet but noise fr vill car park; CKE/CCI. "Well-kept site in great location nr medieval town cent; some open views; friendly, helpful warden; well-kept, dated facs; nice sm pool; poss some workers' statics low ssn; rv walks; Voie Verte cycle rte; interesting town & area; site subject to flooding at any time; mkt Sat." 1 Apr-30 Sep. € 14.95   2013*

SONZAY *4G1* (500m W Rural) *47.52620, 0.45070* **Kawan Village L'Arada Parc, 88 Rue de la Baratière, 37360 Sonzay [02 47 24 72 69; fax 02 47 24 72 70; info@laradaparc.com; www.laradaparc.com]** Exit A28 junc 27 to Neuillé-Pont-Pierre; then D766 & D6 to Sonzay; turn R in town cent. Site on R on o'skirts immed past new houses; sp. Med, hdg/mkd pitch, pt sl, pt shd; wc; chem disp; mv service pnt; 20% serviced pitches; baby facs; shwrs inc; el pnts (10A) €4.10 (poss rev pol); gas; lndtte (inc dryer); shop; tradsmn; rest, snacks; bar; BBQ; playgrnd; 2 pools (1 htd, covrd); paddling pool; spa; lake sw 9km; rv fishing 500m; gym; cycle hire; games area; wifi; entmnt; TV rm; 15% statics; dogs €2; phone; bus to Tours; Eng spkn; adv bkg; quiet; ccard acc; red long stay/low ssn; CKE/CCI. "Peaceful, well-kept site; friendly, helpful owners & staff; clean, modern facs; gd views; vg rest; poss diff for lge o'fits when site full/cr; barrier clsd 2300-0800; many walks, inc in attractive orchards; 60km fr Le Mans circuit; rec." ♦ 26 Mar-1 Nov. € 30.80 (CChq acc)   2012*

SOREDE see Argelès sur Mer *10G1*

⊞ **SORGUES** *10E2* (1km NE Urban) *44.02083, 4.89166* **Camping La Montagne, 944 Chemin de la Montagne, 84700 Sorgues [04 90 83 36 66; fax 04 90 39 82 94; contact@campinglamontagne.com; www.campinglamontagne.com]** Exit A7 at Avignon Nord junc 23 twd Carpentras on D942, then N on D6 to Sorgues; site sp fr a'route but foll 'Zone Industrielle' sps. App via steep ramp. Med, shd; wc; shwrs inc; el pnts (15A) €4.50; lndtte; shop; rest, snacks; bar; playgrnd; pool; internet; entmnt; TV; 10% statics; dogs €2.50; adv bkg; quiet but m'way noise. "Ltd facs low ssn." € 18.50   2008*

See advertisement on pages 32 & 33

Send in your site reports by mid August 2014

FRANCE

SOSPEL *10E4* (4km NW Rural) *43.89702, 7.41685* **Camping Domaine Ste Madeleine, Route de Moulinet, 06380 Sospel [04 93 04 10 48; fax 04 93 04 18 37; camp@ camping-sainte-madeleine.com; www.camping-sainte-madeleine.com]** Take D2566 fr Sospel NW to Turini & site 4km on L; sp fr town. Rd to site fr Menton steep with many hairpins. Med, mkd pitch, pt sl, pt terr, shd; wc; chem disp; mv service pnt; shwrs €0.50; el pnts (10A) €2.90; lndtte; pool; beach 20km; rv 3km; dogs €1.50; Eng spkn; adv bkg rec high ssn; quiet; 10% red low ssn; CKE/CCI. "Friendly, busy site; gd facs; gd pool but has no shallow end; stunning scenery." 31 Marr-29 Sep. € 21.00   2011*

SOUBES see Lodève *10E1*

SOUBREBOST see Bourganeuf *7B4*

SOUILLAC *7C3* (5km SE Rural) *44.85503, 1.52257* **Camp Municipal Beauregard, 46200 Pinsac [05 65 37 85 83 or 05 65 37 06 02]** S on D820 thro Souillac, turn L on o'skts onto D43 immed bef Rv Dordogne. Site in 5km. Sm, pt shd; wc; shwrs inc; el pnts (5A) €2.90; lndry rm; shop 1km; rest & bar 100m; snacks; fishing; dogs €0.70; Eng spkn; quiet. "Useful rvside NH/sh stay espec low ssn; warden calls pm; basic facs." 1 Jun-30 Sep. € 9.00   2008*

SOUILLAC *7C3* (7km SE Rural) *44.87716, 1.57361* **Camping Les Borgnes, 46200 St Sozy [tel/fax 05 65 32 21 48; info@ campinglesborgnes.fr; www.campinglesborgnes.fr]** Exit A20 junc 55; foll sp Martel on D803; in 5km turn R onto D15 to St Sozy; site just bef rv bdge. Med, pt shd; wc (some cont); chem disp; mv service pnt; shwrs inc; el pnts €3; gas; lndtte; shop nr; tradsmn; rest, snacks; bar;supmkt 2km, rest 2km; BBQ; playgrnd; pool; paddling pool; rv sw adj; canoe hire; 60% statics; dogs €1; phone; Eng spkn; adv bkg; quiet, some rd noise; ccard acc; red CKE/CCI. " helpful British owners, working hard to improve site (2008); gd" ♦ltd 1 May-30 Sep. € 12.00   2013*

> ## "Satellite navigation makes touring much easier"
> Remember most sat navs don't know if you're towing or in a larger vehicle – always use yours alongside maps and site directions.

SOUILLAC *7C3* (1km S Rural) *44.88197, 1.48253* **Camp Municipal du Pont de Lanzac, 46200 Lanzac [05 65 37 02 58; fax 05 65 37 02 31; mairie.lanzac@ wanadoo.fr; www.lanzac.fr]** S on D820 thro Souillac; immed after x-ing Rv Dordogne site visible on R of D820. Sm, shd; wc (mainly cont); chem disp; shwrs inc; el pnts (6A) €3; gas; shops 1km; rest, snacks; playgrnd; rv sw; fishing; canoe hire; TV; some statics; dogs; adv bkg; CKE/CCI. "Gd site in lovely location; free-style pitching; helpful warden; clean, basic san facs; easy stroll into Souillac along rv; poss itinerants; unrel opening dates - phone ahead; gd NH." ♦ July-Aug. € 10.50   2011*

SOUILLAC *7C3* (5km S Rural) *44.86602, 1.49715* **Camping Verte Rive, 46200 Pinsac [05 65 37 85 96 or 06 65 37 85 96 (mob); fax 05 65 32 67 69; camping-laverterive@orange.fr; www.location-dordogne-chalet.com]** Fr Souillac S on D820. Turn L immed bef Dordogne rv bdge on D43 to Pinsac. Site on R in 2km on rvside. Med, hdg/mkd pitch, shd; wc (some cont); chem disp; baby facs; shwrs inc; el pnts (10A) €4.; gas; lndtte; shop & 1km; rest, snacks; bar; playgrnd; pool; canoeing; games rm; 20% statics; dogs €2; poss cr; Eng spkn; adv bkg ess high ssn; quiet; ccard acc; red low ssn; CKE/ CCI. "Pleasant, peaceful, wooded site on Rv Dordogne; gd san facs; poss mosquitoes by rv; gd pool; excel" ♦ 1 Apr-15 Sep. € 31.10   2013*

⊞ **SOUILLAC** *7C3* (300m SW Urban) *44.89150, 1.47654* **Aire Communale, Rue de la Pomme, 46200 Souillac [05 65 32 71 00]** Take D820 to Souillac cent then D804/D703 dir Sarlat. In 200m turn L, site ent on R at Parking Baillot. Sm, hdstg, unshd; chem disp; wc; water & el pnts €2; shop, rest 300m; free parking for m'vans only. "Rec arr early; ltd hdstg."   2010*

SOUILLAC *7C3* (5km SW Rural) *44.87340, 1.43389* **Camp Municipal La Borgne, 24370 Cazoulès [05 53 29 81 64 or 05 53 31 45 25 (Mairie); fax 05 53 31 45 26; sitecazoules@ orange.fr or campingcazoules@orange.fr; www.cazoules. pagesperso-orange.fr]** Fr Souillac, take D804/D703 twd Sarlat. In 4km in vill of Cazoulès turn L & foll site sps. Site on R just bef rv bdge & adj Rv Dordogne. Lge, pt shd; wc; baby facs; shwrs inc; el pnts (10A) €3; lndtte; sm shop; supmkt 4km; BBQ; playgrnd; pool; paddling pool; canoe trips; boat hire; fishing; tennis adj; 15% statics; dogs €1; quiet; "Poss mosquito problem; helpful staff" ♦ 15 Jun-15 Sep. € 15.00   2013*

SOUILLAC *7C3* (1km W Urban) *44.88895, 1.47418* **FLOWER Camping Les Ondines, Ave de Sarlat, 46200 Souillac [05 65 37 86 44 or 06 33 54 32 00; fax 05 65 32 61 15; info@camping-lesondines.com; www.camping-lesondines.com or www.flowercampings.com]** Turn W off D820 in cent Souillac onto D804/D703 sp Sarlat. In 200m turn L at sp into narr rd. Ent 400m on R adj rv. Lge, mkd pitch, pt sl, pt shd; wc; chem disp; shwrs inc; el pnts (5A) inc; lndtte; shop; rest 1km; BBQ; playgrnd; htd pool & aquatic park nrby; tennis; fishing; canoeing; horseriding; entmnt; some statics; dogs €2; phone; Eng spkn; quiet; red low ssn; CKE/ CCI. "Gd touring base nr rv; helpful staff; clean facs; conv NH Rocamadour & caves; easy access fr D820; vg." ♦ 2 Apr-29 Sep. € 17.90   2011*

See advertisement on pages 32 & 33

SOUILLAC *7C3* (6km W Rural) *44.88577, 1.40678* **Camping La Périgourdine (Levet), Le Bourg, 24370 Peyrillac-et-Millac [05 53 29 72 12 or 06 07 22 15 07 (mob); francoislevet@aol.com; www.campinglaperigourdine.fr]** Fr cent of Souillac, W on D804 then D703 to Peyrillac-et-Millac; in vill turn L at sp to site. Drive past farmhouse, ent 75m on R, narr app rd. Sm, pt shd; htd wc; shwrs inc; el pnts (16A) €3; lndtte; tradsmn; shop, rest, bar etc 5km; BBQ; playgrnd; pool; games area; rv; dogs €2; adv bkg; quiet; no ccard acc; CKE/CCI. "CL-type site; friendly, helpful owners; ltd facs low ssn; not suitable lge o'fits as access narr, sloping & sharp bend; gd cycle rtes." € 13.50   2010*

FRANCE

SOUILLAC 7C3 (7km NW Rural) 44.93599, 1.43743 **Camping La Draille, La Draille, 46200 Souillac [05 65 32 65 01; fax 05 65 37 06 20; la.draille@wanadoo.fr; www.ladraille. com]** Leave Souillac on D15 sp Salignac-Evvigues; at Bourzolles in 6km take D165; site sp in 500m on L. Med, hdg pitch, pt sl, pt shd; wc; chem disp; baby facs; shwrs inc; el pnts (4A) €4.; lndtte; shop; rest, snacks; bar; BBQ; pool; 25% statics; dogs €3; phone; poss cr; Eng spkn; adv bkg; quiet; ccard acc; CKE/CCI. "Lovely location; friendly; gd walks; highly rec" ♦ 27 Apr- 5 Oct. € 26.00   2013*

SOUILLAC 7C3 (8km NW Rural) 44.94510, 1.44140 **Domaine de la Paille Basse, 46200 Souillac [05 65 37 85 48; fax 05 65 37 09 58; info@lapaillebasse. com; www.lapaillebasse.com or www.les-castels.com]** Exit Souillac by D15 sp Salignac, turn onto D165 at Bourzolles foll sp to site in 3km. NB Narr app, few passing places. Lge, hdg pitch, terr, pt shd; wc; chem disp; mv service pnt; shwrs inc; el pnts (3-10A) €4-6; gas; lndtte (inc dryer); shop; rest, snacks; bar; BBQ; playgrnd; pool; paddling pool; waterslide; tennis; cycle hire; games area; golf 5km; organised outdoor activities; wifi; entmnt; TV/cinema rm; dogs €4; adv bkg; quiet; ccard acc; red low ssn. "Excel site in remote location; friendly, helpful staff; clean facs; some shwrs unisex; restored medieval vill." ♦ 15 May-15 Sep. € 24.80 (CChq acc) SBS - D06   2009*

See advertisement on inside back cover

SOULAC SUR MER 7B1 (1km S Coastal) 45.50136, -1.13185 **Camping Le Palace, 65 Blvd Marsan-de-Montbrun, Forêt Sud, 33780 Soulac-sur-Mer [05 56 09 80 22; fax 05 56 09 84 23; info@camping-palace.com; www. camping-palace.com]** Fr ferry at Le Verdon-sur-Mer S on D1215, site sp. Or fr S on D101. V lge, hdg/mkd pitch, shd; wc; mv service pnt; baby facs; shwrs inc; el pnts; lndtte; shop; rest, snacks; bar; BBQ; playgrnd; htd, covrd pool; paddling pool; waterslide; sand beach 400m; cycle hire; internet; entmnt; 65% statics; dogs €3; adv bkg; quiet. "Ideal for family beach holiday." 1 May-27 Sep. € 25.00   2008*

SOULAC SUR MER 7B1 (2km S Rural) 45.48568, -1.11909 **Camping Club de Soulac Le Lilhan, 8 Allée Michel Montaigne, 33780 Soulac-sur-Mer [tel/fax 05 56 09 78 78; contact@lelilhan.com; www.camping-club-soulac.com]** Fr S on D1215 dir Le Verdon, turn W dir Lilhan & L'Amélie-sur-Mer, site sp. Lge, hdg/mkd pitch, pt shd; htd wc; chem disp; mv service pnt; sauna; shwrs; el pnts (10A) inc; lndtte (inc dryer); shop; supmkt 3m; rest, snacks; bar; playgrnd; pool; sand beach 2km; tennis; wifi; entmnt; some statics; dogs €2.95; adv bkg; quiet. ♦ 1 Apr-30 Sep. € 25.00   2009*

SOULAC SUR MER 7B1 (13km S Coastal) 45.43357, -1.14519 **Camp Municipal du Gurp, 51 Route de l'Océan, 33590 Grayan-et-L'Hôpital [05 56 09 44 53 or 05 56 09 43 01 (Mairie); fax 05 56 09 54 73; mairie.grayan@ orange.fr; www.grayan.fr]** Take D101 fr Soulac. Turn R after 5km sp Grayan & R at x-rds. Site clearly sp. V lge, mkd pitch, hdstg, shd; wc; chem disp; baby facs; shwrs inc; el pnts (4-10A) €2.88; lndtte; shop; rest, snacks; bar; playgrnd; sand beach adj; tennis; games area; games rm; entmnt; wifi; TV; dogs €1.50; poss cr; quiet. "In pine forest; gd, vast beaches; mv service pnt outsite site (fee payable)." 1 Jun-15 Sep. € 17.40   2011*

SOULAC SUR MER 7B1 (13km S Coastal) 45.41600, -0.12930 **Centre Naturiste Euronat (Naturist), 33590 Grayan-l'Hôpital [05 56 09 33 33; fax 05 56 09 30 27; info@ euronat.fr; www.euronat.fr]** Fr Soulac, take D101 twd Montalivet, turn W at camp sp onto rd leading direct to site. Fr Bordeaux, take D1215 sp Le Verdon-sur-Mer. Approx 8km after Lesparre-Médoc turn L onto D102. In Venday-Montalivet bear R onto D101. In 7.5km turn L sp Euronat. V lge, mkd pitch, hdstg, shd; htd wc (some htd); chem disp; mv service pnt; all serviced pitches; baby facs; shwrs inc; el pnts (10A) inc; gas; lndtte (inc dryer); shop; rest, snacks; bar; BBQ; playgrnd; 3 htd pools (1 covrd); paddling pool; thalassotherapy & beauty treatment cent; sand beach adj; tennis; horseriding; cinema; archery; cycle hire; golf driving range; wifi; entmnt; TV; 30% statics; dogs €3; phone; Eng spkn; adv bkg; quiet; red low ssn; INF card req. "Expensive, but well worth it; lge pitches; excel" ♦ 1 Apr-1 Nov. € 50.40 (CChq acc)   2013*

SOULAC SUR MER 7B1 (1.5km SW Coastal) 45.49958, -1.13899 **Camping Les Sables d'Argent, Blvd de l'Amélie, 33780 Soulac-sur-Mer [05 56 09 82 87; fax 05 56 09 94 82; sables@lelilhan.com; www.sables-d-argent.com]** Drive S fr Soulac twd L'Amélie-sur-Mer. Clearly sp on R. Med, mkd pitch, pt sl, pt shd; wc; shwrs inc; el pnts (10A) inc (poss long lead req); lndtte; shop; rest, snacks; bar; private sand beach adj; fishing; tennis; internet; entmnt; TV; 60% statics; dogs €2.95; poss cr; red low ssn. "Nice area, but major erosion of coast so no access to beach (2009); poss diff lge o'fits; old san facs (2009); Soulac sm, lively mkt town." 1 Apr-30 Sep. € 24.95   2009*

SOULAC SUR MER 7B1 (3km SW Coastal) 45.48068, -1.14538 **Camping L'Océan, 62 Allée de la Négade, L'Amélie, 33780 Soulac-sur-Mer [05 56 09 76 10; fax 05 56 09 74 75; camping.ocean@wanadoo.fr; http:// camping.ocean.pagesperso-orange.fr/]** Fr S on D1215 fr Soulac-sur-Mer; turn L onto D102 to Vendays-Montalivet; then turn R onto D101 Soulac-sur-Mer; in 14km turn L onto D101E2 sp L'Amélie-sur-Mer; in 2km at sp Camping L'Océan turn L into Allée de la Négade. Site on R. Lge, mkd pitch, pt shd; wc; chem disp; shwrs inc; el pnts (10A) €4; lndtte; shop; rest 500m; snacks; bar; BBQ (charcoal, sep area); playgrnd; sand beach 600m; cycle hire; tennis; games area; games rm; internet; TV; dogs €2.50; adv bkg; ccard not acc; red low ssn; CKE/CCI. "Sandy pitches; several cycle tracks; vg." ♦ ltd 1 Jun-15 Sep. € 22.40   2010*

SOULAINES DHUYS 6E1 (500m N Rural) 48.37661, 4.73829 **Camping La Croix Badeau, 6 Rue Croix Badeau, 10200 Soulaines-Dhuys [03 25 27 05 43 or 03 26 82 35 31 (LS); responsable@croix-badeau.com; www.croix-badeau.com]** 500m N of junc D960 & D384, behind lge church of Soulaines-Dhuys, well sp. Sm, hdg/mkd pitch, hdstg, pt shd; wc (some cont); chem disp; shwrs inc; el pnts (4A) €2.50; lndtte; shop 500m; playgrnd; tennis; rv 300m; dogs €1; phone; Eng spkn; quiet; CKE/CCI. "Excel, clean site in interesting vill" 1 Apr-15 Oct. € 13.90   2012*

FRANCE

SOULLANS *2H3* (500m NE Urban) *46.79840, -1.89647* **Camp Municipal Le Moulin Neuf, Rue St Christophe, 85300 Soullans [02 51 68 00 24 (Mairie); fax 02 51 68 88 66; camping-soullans@wanadoo.fr]** Fr Challans ring rd take D69 sp Soullans. Site sp on L just bef town cent. Med, hdg/mkd pitch, pt shd; wc (some cont); shwrs inc; el pnts (4A) inc; gas 500m; lndtte; shop 500m; playgrnd; beach 12km; tennis; phone adj; poss cr; adv bkg; quiet; CKE/CCI. "Simple site; lovely walks & cycling; no twin-axles; vg." 15 Jun-15 Sep. € 10.00   2011*

SOURAIDE see Cambo les Bains *8F1*

SOURSAC *7C4* (1km NE Rural) *45.28066, 2.20999* **Camp Municipal de la Plage, Centre Touristique du Pont Aubert, 19550 Soursac [05 55 27 55 43 or 05 55 27 52 61 (Mairie); fax 05 55 27 63 31; vvpontaubert@correze.net; www. vvpontaubert.correze.net]** Fr Mauriac take D678 to Chalvignac. Bear R onto D105 at 3km (12% descent) to cross Barrage de l'Aigle & 2km 12% ascent on D105E/D16, winding rd. In further 3km pass junc to Latronche, 1st R to site. Med, mkd pitch, terr, pt sl, shd; wc; mv service pnt; baby facs; shwrs inc; el pnts (6A) €2.50; lndtte; shop 1km; rest, snacks; bar; playgrnd; lake sw & waterslide nrby; fishing; archery; cycle hire; games area; entmnt; TV; some statics; dogs €1.50; adv bkg; quiet; "Attractive site by lake; well worth detour; gd, clean san facs; excel." ♦ 15 Jun-15 Sep. € 15.00   2008*

SOUSTONS *8E1* (6km NE Rural) *43.79193, -1.29455* **Camping Le Tuc, 155 Rue Henri Goalard, 40140 Azur [05 58 48 22 52 or 06 77 60 22 75 (mob); fax 05 58 48 33 53; campingletuc@wanadoo.fr; www.campingletuc.com]** Exit N10 junc 11 at Magescq onto D150 dir Azur; site on R 1km SE fr Azur. Site sp fr Azur. Med, hdg pitch, pt shd; wc; chem disp; shwrs inc; el pnts (6-10A) €3.20; gas; lndtte; shop, tradsmn (high ssn); BBQ; playgrnd; pool; paddling pool; lake watersports & fishing 2km; tennis; games area; games rm; wifi; TV rm; 50% statics; dogs €2; phone; poss cr; adv bkg; quiet; red low ssn; CKE/CCI. "Woodland walks; excel." ♦ 1 Apr-15 Sep. € 15.40   2010*

SOUSTONS *8E1* (6km NE Rural) *43.78694, -1.30861* **Camping Village La Paillotte, 40140 Azur [05 58 48 12 12; fax 05 58 48 10 73; paillotte@franceloc.fr; www.paillotte. com or www.campings-franceloc.fr]** Exit N10 junc 11; cont thro Magescq & after a short distance, turn L onto D150 to Azur. Turn L by church, after 1.5km site sp on L. Lge, mkd pitch, pt shd; wc (some cont); chem disp; mv service pnt; baby facs; shwrs inc; el pnts (10A) inc; lndtte (inc dryer); shop; rest, snacks; bar; BBQ (gas/elec); playgrnd; htd, covrd pool; paddling pool; waterslide; lake sw & sand beach adj; dinghy sailing; windsurfing; fishing; cycle hire; tennis; horseriding 7km; wifi; entmnt; games/TV rm; statics (tour ops); no dogs; no c'vans/m'vans over 7m high ssn; bus; site bkg; ccard acc; red low ssn; CKE/CCI. "Lakeside site with stream thro; facs ltd low ssn; mkt Soustons Mon." ♦ ltd 28 May-25 Sep. € 39.00   2010*

SOUSTONS *8E1* (6.5km NE Rural) *43.78430, -1.30473* **Camping Azu'Rivage, 720 Route des Campings, 40140 Azur [tel/fax 05 58 48 30 72; info@campingazurivage.com; www.campingazurivage.com]** Exit m'way A10 at exit Magescq & take D150 W for 8km to Azur, site sp fr church adj La Paillotte. Med, pt shd; wc; baby facs; shwrs inc; el pnts (10A) €7.40; lndtte; sm shop & 6km; rest, snacks; playgrnd; pool; paddling pool; sand beach & lake sw; tennis; boating; watersports; entmnt; TV rm; dogs €2; poss cr; adv bkg; ccard acc; red long stay; red low ssn. "Delightful forest setting adj lake; v busy high ssn; san facs poss stretched high ssn; rec." ♦ 15 May-30 Sep. € 15.00   2010*

⊞ **SOUTERRAINE, LA** *7A3* (2km NE Rural) *46.24368, 1.50606* **Camping Suisse Océan, Etang-du-Cheix, 23300 La Souterraine [05 55 63 33 32 or 05 55 63 59 71; fax 05 55 63 21 82]** Fr N145/E62 take D72 sp La Souterraine. Strt over 1st rndabt, at 2nd rndabt turn R, then L to L'Etang de Cheix. Fr N exit A20 junc 22 onto D912 sp La Souterraine; at T-junc turn L & foll outer rd D912b; at rndabt turn L to Etang-du-Cheix; in 50m turn L to site. Sp fr D912b. Sm, hdg/mkd pitch, hdstg, pt sl, terr, pt shd; htd wc (some cont); chem disp; mv service pnt; shwrs inc; el pnts (10A) €3.50; lndtte; sm shop & 2km; tradsmn; rest, snacks; bar; playgrnd; sand lake beach, fishing, sailing adj; diving (summer); tennis; 10% statics; dogs €1.20; poss cr; Eng spkn; adv bkg; quiet but night noise fr factory nrby; CKE/CCI. "Superb location by lake; lge pitches; sl rds on site could ground lge o'fits - walk site bef pitching; san facs in Portacabin; ltd facs low ssn inc el pnts & inadequate when site full; pleasant sm town; mkt Thur & Sat; site fair." ♦ € 15.30   2012*

SOUTERRAINE, LA *7A3* (6km E Rural) *46.24534, 1.59083* **Camp Municipal Etang de la Cazine, 23300 Noth [tel/fax 05 55 63 31 17; mairiedenoth@wanadoo.fr]** Exit A20 junc 23 onto N145 dir Guéret; turn L on D49 sp Noth. Site opp lake. Sm,pt shd;mkd pitch, pt sl; wc, chem disp; mv service pnt; shwrs inc; el pnts (16A) €3; ltd snacks; bar; playgrnd; dog €1.50; lake fishing & sw adj; quiet; CKE/CCI. "Gd touring base; gd; San facs portacabins; excel NH and short stay; rural location" 31 Mar-7 Nov. € 16.00   2013*

SOUTERRAINE, LA *7A3* (10km S Rural) *46.15129, 1.51059* **Camp Municipal, 23290 St Pierre-de-Fursac [05 55 63 65 69 or 05 55 63 61 28 (Mairie); fax 05 55 63 68 20; www. communes-fursac.fr]** Exit A20 at junc 23.1 onto D1 S twd St Pierre-de-Fursac. Site on L at ent to vill dir 'Stade'. Sm, mkd pitch, pt sl, pt shd; wc; shwrs inc; el pnts (6A) €2 (poss rev pol); shop 500m; playgrnd; phone; quiet. "Pleasant, well-kept site o'looking vill; san facs basic but clean; fine NH; gd" ♦ ltd 15 Jun-15 Sep. € 8.00   2013*

STELLA PLAGE see Touquet Paris Plage, Le *6B2*

⊞ **STENAY** *5C1* (250m W Urban) *49.49083, 5.18333* **Port de Plaisance - Motor Caravan Parking Area, Rue du Port, 55700 Stenay [03 29 80 64 22 or 03 29 74 87 54; fax 03 29 80 62 59; otsistenayaccueil@orange.fr]** Off D947 fr town cent. Foll sp to rv port. NB M'vans only. Sm, hdstg; mv service pnt; shwrs inc; el pnts (6A) inc; shop 600m; rest 300m; quiet. "Adj to rv; excel san facs; NH only." ♦ ltd € 8.00   2013*

FRANCE

⊞ **STRASBOURG** 6E3 (3km W Urban) 48.57525, 7.71730
**FFCC Camping La Montagne Verte, 2 Rue Robert Forrer,
67200 Strasbourg [03 88 30 25 46; fax 03 88 27 10 15;
aquadis1@wanadoo.fr / contact@aquadis-loisirs.com;
www.aquadis-loisirs.com]** Fr A35 about 2km S of Strasbourg
exit junc 4 for Montagne-Verte. Foll camp sp, 1st R to site
on R in approx 1km. Sp off D1004 & D392 to W of city, 1km
fr town side of Boulevard de Lyon. Fr town cent foll sp for St Dié/
Colmar as camp sp intermittent. NB Fr S on D392 height limit
3.3m on app rd to site. NB Use of sat nav rec. Lge, pitch, pt shd;
wc; chem disp; baby facs; shwrs inc; el pnts (6A) inc (poss rev
pol); gas; lndtte (inc dryer); shop 200m; rest 250m; tradsmn;
bar; BBQ; playgrnd; pool; tennis; games area; wifi; few statics;
dogs €1.90; bus/tram to city; Eng spkn; ccard acc; red CKE/CCI.
"Well-kept site adj rv; san facs need update; pitches v soft after
rain; easy access to city inc superb network of cycle tracks &
paths; excel for visiting Strasbourg; gd dog walks; gd; road and
rail noise at night; Office clsd 12.30-15.00" € 26.55   2013*

SUEVRES see Blois 4G2

⊞ **SULLY SUR LOIRE** 4F3 (500m NW Rural) 47.77180,
2.36200 **Camping Le Jardin de Sully, 1Route
Orleans, 45600 Pope-sur-Loire [02 38 67 10 84 or
07 81 11 47 65 (mob); lejardindesully@gmail.com; www.
camping-lejardindesully.fr]** Fr N on D948 to Sully then turn
R at rndabt immed bef x-ing bdge over Rv Loire onto D60 in
St Père-sur-Loire, dir Châteauneuf-sur-Loire. Sp to site in 200m.
Fr S thro Sully on D948, cross Rv Loire & turn L at rndabt onto
D60. Well sp fr town. Med, hdg/mkd pitch, hdstg, pt shd; htd
wc (some cont); chem disp; mv service pnt; baby facs; serviced
pitches; shwrs inc; el pnts (10A) inc (poss rev pol); gas; lndtte;
shop; tradsmn; snacks; pizzeria; bar; BBQ; playgrnd; htd, covrd
pool 500m; sand beach adj; tennis; cycle hire; games rm; cycle
hire; wifi; entmnt; sat TV; 18% statics; dogs €2; phone; bus;
some Eng spkn; adv bkg rec; quiet; ccard acc; red low ssn/CKE/
CCI. "Pleasant, well-kept, well laid-out site on rvside adj nature
reserve; gd, well-kept san facs; pleasant walk along rv to town;
long distance footpath (grande randonnée) along Loire passes
site; gd dog walks; gd cycling; gd winter site & NH en rte S;
recep might be clsd low ssn, need to phone for barrier code
ent; fairy-tale chateau in Sully; gd loc; san facs inadequate;
new owner keen to bring the standards up" ♦ 1 Apr-11 Nov.
€ 27.00   2013*

SURGERES 7A2 (500m S Urban) 46.10180, -0.75376
**Camping La Gères, 10 Rue de la Gères, 17700
Surgères [05 46 07 79 97 or 06 64 03 89 32 (mob); fax
05 46 27 16 78; contact@campingdelageres.com; www.
campingdelageres.com]** Site sp in Surgères, on banks of Rv
Gères, & fr Surgères by-pass. Sm, mkd pitch, pt shd; wc (cont);
mv service pnt; shwrs; el pnts (6A) €3.50; lndtte (inc dryer);
shop 300m; rest, snacks & bar 800m; pool & tennis 800m;
dogs €1.50; phone; poss cr; ccard acc; CKE/CCI. "Adj to park;
m'vans extra charge; poss itinerants; NH only." 1 Apr-30 Sep.
€ 16.50   2009*

SURIS 7B3 (1km N Rural) 45.85925, 0.63739 **Camping
La Blanchie, 16270 Suris [tel/fax 05 45 89 33 19 or
06 12 15 66 03 (mob); lablanchie@wanadoo.fr; www.
lablanchie.co.uk]** Fr N141 halfway bet Angoulême & Limoges
take D52 S at La Péruse to Suris; in 3km turn E up a narr lane
to site. Sm, some hdstg, pt sl, pt shd; wc; chem disp; shwrs
inc; el pnts (10A) €4; lndtte (inc dryer); playgrnd; pool; lake/rv
sw & sand beach 2.5km; tennis, golf, Futuroscope nrby; wifi;
some statics; dogs €0.50; c'van storage; adv bkg; quiet; red
long stay; CKE/CCI. "Welcoming, friendly British owners; clean
site in lovely area; ltd facs; gd touring base" ♦ 1 Apr-30 Sep.
€ 20.40   2013*

⊞ **SURTAINVILLE** 1C4 (1km W Coastal) 49.46447, -1.82919
**Camp Municipal Les Mielles, 80 Route des Laguettes,
50270 Surtainville [tel/fax 02 33 04 31 04; camping.
lesmielles@wanadoo.fr; www.surtainville.com]**
S fr Cherbourg on D650, take D66 W thro Surtainville, site on
R. Med, pt sl, unshd; htd wc (male cont); chem disp; shwrs
inc; el pnts (4A) €2.50; lndtte; playgrnd; sand beach 100m;
30% statics; dogs €1; adv bkg; quiet; CKE/CCI. "Excel beach."
♦ ltd € 8.70   2009*

SUZE LA ROUSSE see Bollène 9D2

TADEN see Dinan 2E3

⊞ **TAIN L'HERMITAGE** 9C2 (5km NE Rural) 45.10715,
4.89105 **Camping Chante-Merle, 26600 Chantemerle-
les-Blés [04 75 07 49 73; fax 04 75 07 45 15;
campingchantemerle@wanadoo.fr; www.campingchante-
merle.fr/]** Exit A7 at Tain-l'Hermitage. After exit toll turn L
twd town, next turn R (D109) to Chantemerle; site sp. Cont for
5km, site on L. Sm, hdg/mkd pitch, pt shd; htd wc; chem disp;
serviced pitches; baby facs; shwrs inc; el pnts (10A) €4.50; lndtte;
shops 300m; tradsmn; rest & snacks high ssn; bar; playgrnd;
pool; tennis 500m; wifi; 10% statics; dogs €2; site clsd Jan; adv
bkg ess; quiet but some rd noise; CKE/CCI. "Helpful manager;
popular site; excel facs." ♦ € 23.10   2012*

TAIN L'HERMITAGE 9C2 (500m SE Urban) 45.06727, 4.84880
**Camp Municipal Les Lucs, 24 Ave du Président Roosevelt,
26600 Tain-l'Hermitage [tel/fax 04 75 08 32 82 or
04 75 08 30 32; camping.tainlhermitage@wanadoo.fr;
www.campingleslucs.fr]** Fr N or S exit A7 junc 13 dir Tain-
l'Hermitage onto N7. Cont N twd town cent; at fuel station
on R & Netto supmkt sp prepare to turn L in 80m; ent to site
in 35m. Fr N on N7 prepare to turn R after fuel station on R.
Site alongside Rv Rhône via gates (locked o/night). Well sp adj
sw pool/petrol stn. Med, hdg/mkd pitch, some hdstg, pt shd;
wc (some cont); chem disp; mv service pnt; shwrs inc; el pnts
(6A) inc (poss rev pol); lndtte; shops, snacks adj; playgrnd;
pool complex adj inc; dogs €1.40; phone; no twin-axles; Eng
spkn; some rd/rlwy noise; red low ssn; ccard not acc; CKE/CCI.
"Pretty, well-kept, well-run site by Rhône; lovely views; secure
site; friendly staff; excel, clean san facs; excel pool complex; no
twin-axles, no c'vans over 5.50m & no m'vans over 6m (poss
high ssn only); rvside walk to town; Valrhona chocolate factory
shop nrby; mkt Sat; gd touring base; popular NH; highly rec."
♦ ltd 15 Mar-15 Oct. € 22.30   2013*

TALLARD see Gap 9D3

FRANCE

⊞ **TANINGES** *9A3* (1km S Rural) *46.09899, 6.58806* **Camp Municipal des Thézières, Les Vernays-sous-la-Ville, 74440 Taninges [04 50 34 25 59; fax 04 50 34 39 78; camping. taninges@wanadoo.fr; www.taninges.com]** Take D902 N fr Cluses; site 1km S of Taninges on L - just after 'Taninges' sp on ent town boundary; sp Camping-Caravaneige. Lge, pt shd; htd wc (some cont); chem disp; mv service pnt; shwrs inc; el pnts (6-10A) €2.50-4; lndtte (inc dryer); ltd shop; tradsmn; shops, rest, snacks, bar 1km; BBQ; playgrnd; pool at Samoens 11km; tennis; wifi; TV rm; dogs €1.30; phone; poss cr; Eng spkn; quiet; ccard acc; CKE/CCI. "Splendid site with magnificent views; peaceful & well-kept; lge pitches; friendly, helpful staff; excel facs; conv for N Haute Savoie & Switzerland to Lake Geneva; excel." ♦ € 22.60   2012*

"There aren't many sites open at this time of year"

If you're travelling outside peak season remember to call ahead to check site opening dates – even if the entry says 'open all year'.

⊞ **TARADEAU** *10F3* (3km S Rural) *43.44116, 6.42766* **Camping La Vallée de Taradeau, Chemin La Musardière, 83460 Taradeau [tel/fax 04 94 73 09 14; campingdetaradeau@hotmail.com; www. campingdetaradeau.com]** Exit A8 junc 13 & take DN7 to Vidauban. Opp Mairie take D48 dir Lorgues then D73 N twd Taradeau for 1.5km. Site sp - rough app rd - on rvside. Med, mkd pitch, shd; htd wc; mv service pnt; shwrs inc; el pnts (2-10A) €2.50-6.50; lndtte; rest, snacks; bar; playgrnd; pool; caneoing; games area; games rm; wifi; entmnt; some statics; dogs €3; adv bkg; quiet; CKE/CCI. "Pleasantly situated site; friendly, helpful staff; vg pool." € 22.00   2011*

TARASCON *10E2* (6km N Rural) *43.85503, 4.62556* **Camping Lou Vincen, 30300 Vallabrègues [04 66 59 21 29; fax 04 66 59 07 41; contact@campinglouvincen.com; www. campinglouvincen.com]** N fr Tarascon on D81A, then D183A. Med, hdg/mkd pitch, hdstg, shd; htd wc (some cont); chem disp; mv service pnt; shwrs inc; el pnts (6A) €3.40; gas; lndtte; shop, rest, snacks, bar 100m; playgrnd; pool; tennis; fishing; horseriding 3km; TV; dogs €1.30; adv bkg; quiet but noise fr skateboarders opp; ccard acc; red long stay/ low ssn/CKE/CCI. "Pitches poss sm for lge o'fits; ltd facs low ssn; attractive vill; gd base for Camargue." 1 Apr-30 Oct. € 15.80   2008*

⊞ **TARASCON** *10E2* (5km SE Urban) *43.78638, 4.71789* **Camp Municipal du Grès, 33 Ave du Docteur Barbarin, 13150 St Etienne-du-Grès [04 90 49 00 03 or 06 11 42 45 68; campingmunicipaldugres@wanadoo.fr; www.campingalpilles.com]** Fr Arles take N570 dir Avignon D99 E dir St Rémy. Site sp on o'skts of St Etienne. Sm, hdg pitch, pt shd; wc (some cont); chem disp; mv service pnt; san fans; el pnts (16A) €4 ; shop 1km; wifi; no statics; dogs €1; quiet; CKE/CCI. "Gd, peaceful site; friendly staff; gd san facs, recently updated" € 13.00   2013*

TARASCON *10E2* (5km SE Rural) *43.76744, 4.69331* **Camping St Gabriel, Route de Fontvieille, 13150 Tarascon [04 90 91 19 83; contact@campingsaintgabriel.com; www. campingsaintgabriel.com]** Take D970 fr Tarascon, at rndabt take D33 sp Fontvieille, site sp 100m on R. Med, hdg pitch, shd; htd wc; chem disp; mv service pnt; shwrs inc; el pnts (6A) €3.30; gas; lndtte; shop; rest adj; snacks; bar; playgrnd; htd pool; rv fishing; games rm; wifi; TV; 30% statics; dogs €2; bus 3km; site clsd mid-Feb & Xmas/New Year; adv bkg; quiet but some rd noise; CKE/CCI. "Well-kept, charming site; excel base for Camargue & Arles; modern san facs; sm pitches poss not suitable lge o'fits; gd." ♦ 1 Mar-30 Nov. € 17.00 (CChq acc)   2010*

TARASCON SUR ARIEGE *8G3* (4km N Rural) *42.87910, 1.62829* **Camping du Lac, 1 Promenade du Camping, 09400 Mercus-Garrabet [tel/fax 05 61 05 90 61 or 06 86 07 24 18 (mob); info@campinglac.com; www. campinglac.com]** N20 S fr Foix, after 10km exit Mercus over N20 sp, cross rlwy line. At T-junc turn R thro Mercus, site R over level x-ing. Tight bend into site off long, narr ent drive. Med, hdg/mkd pitch, terr, shd; wc (some cont); chem disp; baby facs; shwrs inc; el pnts (6-10A) €3.40-4.90; lndtte; shop; tradsmn; supmkt 4km; rest, bar 1km; BBQ; htd pool; rv & lake sw, fishing & watersports adj; games rm; 20% statics; dogs €2; phone; some Eng spkn; adv bkg (fee); some rd & rlwy noise; red long stay; CKE/CCI. "Clean facs; friendly owners; diff ent for long c'vans; sm pitches; 60km Andorra; a real find!." ♦ ltd 11 Apr-19 Sep. € 23.00   2008*

TARASCON SUR ARIEGE *8G3* (600m SE Rural) *42.83981, 1.61215* **Kawan Village Le Pré-Lombard, Route d'Ussat, 09400 Tarascon-sur-Ariège [05 61 05 61 94; fax 05 61 05 78 93; leprelombard@wanadoo.fr; www. prelombard.com]** Travelling S twd Andorra join N20 to Tarascon. Approx 17km S of Foix after 3 rndabts & x-ing a bdge, at 4th rndabt turn L, after rlwy on D618 foll site sp. This rte avoids cent of Tarascon. Lge, hdg/mkd pitch, pt shd; htd wc; chem disp; mv service pnt; shwrs inc; el pnts (10A) inc; gas; lndtte (inc dryer); shop; rest, snacks; bar; BBQ; playgrnd; htd pool; paddling pool; kayaking, rv fishing & sw adj; canyoning & climbing nrby; tennis; cycle hire; archery; wifi; entmnt; games/TV rm; 50% statics; dogs €4; no c'vans/m'vans over 6m; Eng spkn; adv bkg rec high ssn; ccard acc; red low ssn; CKE/CCI. "Busy, well-run, family site in lovely location by rv; spacious pitches; helpful owner; gd san facs, poss stretched high ssn; plenty for teenagers to do; gd base for exploring area; excel winter NH en rte to Spain; poss rallies low ssn; excel" ♦ 15 Mar-15 Oct. € 36.00   2013*

TARASCON SUR ARIEGE *8G3* (3km SW Rural) *42.81311, 1.58908* **Camping Les Grottes, Dumaines de la Hille, 09400 Alliat [05 61 05 88 21; fax 05 61 03 89 91; info@ campingdesgrottes.com; www.campingdesgrottes.com]** S fr Foix on N20 dir Andorra, turn R onto D8 just past Tarascon-sur-Ariège sp Niaux/Vicdessos. Site on R in 2km. Med, hdg/mkd pitch, hdstg, pt shd; wc (some cont); chem disp; mv service pnt; shwrs inc; el pnts (6-10A) €2; lndtte (inc dryer); shop; rest nrby; snacks; bar; playgrnd; htd pool; paddling pool; waterslide; games area; entmnt; TV; 20% statics; dogs €2; phone; adv bkg; quiet. "Lovely, peaceful site in valley; ideal NH for Andorra or long stay; prehistoric cave paintings nr; excel." 1 Mar-1 Nov. € 25.00 (CChq acc)   2010*

⊞ **TARASCON SUR ARIEGE** *8G3* (1.5km NW Rural) *42.85606, 1.58861* **Camping Le Sédour, Florac, 09400 Surba [05 61 05 87 28; fax 05 61 01 49 33; info@ campinglesedour.com; www.campinglesedour.com]** Fr rndbt 1km N of Tarascon take 1st R sp Massat. Turn R in 100m, site on L in Surba vill. Med, hdg/mkd pitch, pt sl, pt shd; wc; chem disp; some serviced pitches; shwrs inc; el pnts (10A) inc; lndtte (inc dryer); supmkt 1km; tradsmn; rest, bar 300m; playgrnd; 60% statics; dogs €2; poss cr; some Eng spkn; adv bkg; quiet; red long stay; CKE/CCI. "Friendly, helpful owners; gd facs; poss diff access lge o'fits; conv for Ariège valleys & prehistoric park; mountain views." ♦ € 20.00   2009*

TARDETS SORHOLUS *8F1* (1km S Rural) *43.11143, -0.86362* **Camping du Pont d'Abense, 64470 Tardets-Sorholus [tel/ fax 05 59 28 58 76 or 06 78 73 53 59 (mob); camping. abense@wanadoo.fr; www.camping-pontabense.com]** Take D918 S to Tardets, turn R to cross bdge onto D57. Site sp on R. Tardets cent narr. Med, shd; wc; chem disp; shwrs inc; el pnts (3A) €3.20; lndry rm; shop, rest, snacks & bar 500m; tradsmn; rv & beach nrby; fishing; some statics; dogs €2; quiet; adv bkg; red low ssn; CKE/CCI. "Informal pitching; facs old & poss unclean; gd birdwatching; Lovely, quaint site; v clean; nr gorges" Easter-Mid Nov. € 14.70   2012*

TAUPONT see Ploërmel *2F3*

TAUTAVEL see Estagel *8G4*

TEICH, LE *7D1* (1.5km W Rural) *44.63980, -1.04272* **Camping Ker Helen, Ave de la Côte d'Argent, 33470 Le Teich [05 56 66 03 79; fax 05 56 66 51 59; camping.kerhelen@ wanadoo.fr; www.kerhelen.com]** Fr A63 take A660 dir Arcachon & exit junc 2 onto D3 then D650 thru Le Teich. Site sp on L. Med, hdg pitch, pt shd; htd wc; chem disp; mv service pnt; baby facs; shwrs inc; el pnts (10A) €3.70; lndtte (inc dryer); rest, snacks; bar; no BBQ; playgrnd; pool; canoeing; horseriding; wifi; entmnt; TV; 75% statics; adv bkg; some rd noise; CKE/CCI. "Less cr than coastal sites in Arcachon region; bird reserve nrby; v gd." ♦ 16 Apr-16 Oct. € 23.00   2011*

TELGRUC SUR MER *2E2* (1km S Coastal) *48.22386, -4.37223* **Camping Le Panoramic, 130 Route de la Plage, 29560 Telgruc-sur-Mer [02 98 27 78 41; fax 02 98 27 36 10; info@camping-panoramic.com; www.camping-panoramic.com]** Fr D887 Crozon-Châteaulin rd, turn W on D208 twd Trez-Bellec Plage, site sp on R in approx 1.5km. Med, hdg/mkd pitch, terr, pt shd, wc (some cont); chem disp; mv service pnt; baby facs; shwrs inc, el pnts (6-10A) €3.50-4.50; lndtte (inc dryer); shop & rest ltd opening time; snacks; bar; BBQ; playgrnd; htd, covrd pool; paddling pool; jacuzzi; sand beach 700m; tennis; cycle hire; games rm; wifi; TV rm; some statics; dogs €2; adv bkg; quiet; ccard acc; red low ssn; CKE/CCI. "Vg, well-run, welcoming site; access to pitches poss diff due trees & narr site rds; rec; some facs tired need updating" ♦ 1 May-15 Sep. € 26.50   2012*

See advertisement

TELGRUC SUR MER *2E2* (2.5km S Coastal) *48.21003, -4.36881* **Camping Pen-Bellec, Trez Bellec, 29560 Telgruc-sur-Mer [02 98 27 31 87 or 02 98 27 76 55; camping. penbellec@orange.fr; www.camping-telgruc.fr]** Fr D887 turn S onto D208 for Telgruc-sur-Mer. In Telgruc take rd mkd 'Plage Trez Bellec' & cont to far end where rd rises & turns inland. Sm, mkd pitch, unshd; wc; mv service pnt; shwrs €1.50; el pnts (3A) €3; shop 3km; tradsmn; rest 3km; playgrnd; sand beach adj; watersports adj; cycle hire; games area; dogs €1.50; poss cr; Eng spkn; adv bkg; poss noisy. "Excel location by beach with views; well-kept; friendly, helpful owners; san facs adequate; exposed in bad weather; gd cliff walking; gd touring base; highly rec." Jun-Sep. € 11.50   2011*

TELGRUC SUR MER *2E2* (1.5km SW Coastal) *48.22553, -4.37103* **Camping L'Armorique, 112 Rue de la Plage, 29560 Telgruc-sur-Mer [02 98 27 77 33; fax 02 98 27 38 38; contact@campingarmorique.com; www. campingarmorique.com]** Fr D887 Châteaulin to Crozon; turn S on D208 at sea end of Telgruc-sur-Mer. NB Steep hairpins on site access rds poss diff long/low powered o'fits. Med, hdg/mkd pitch, terr, pt shd; wc; chem disp; mv service pnt; baby facs; shwrs inc; el pnts (10A) €3.50; shop; lndtte (inc dryer); tradsmn; snacks; takeaway; bar; playgrnd; htd pool; waterslide pool; paddling pool; sand beach 700m; deep-sea diving, climbing & horseriding nrby; games area; games rm; entmnt; wifi; TV; 20% statics; dogs €2.50; adv bkg; quiet; ccard acc; red low ssn; CKE/CCI. "Pleasant, peaceful, well-wooded site; run by enthusiastic couple; clean san facs; lge playgrnd; walking & cycling rtes nrby; vg." ♦ ltd 2 Apr-30 Sep. € 19.00 (CChq acc)   2011*

TELGRUC SUR MER 2E2 (1km W Coastal) 48.22696, -4.36844 Camping Les Mimosas, Kergreis, 106 Rue de la Plage, 29560 Telgruc-sur-Mer [tel/fax 02 98 27 76 06; campingmimosa@ wanadoo.fr; www.campingmimosa.com] Fr D887 Crozon-Châteaulin rd turn SW onto D208 into Telgruc. Fr town sq foll sp Trez-Bellec-Plage. In 900m, after exiting town, turn L & L, site clearly sp. Med, hdg/mkd pitch, terr, pt shd; wc; chem disp; shwrs inc; el pnts (10A) €1.80; lndtte; shop 600m; sand beach 1km; playgrnd; tennis; dogs €0.80; poss cr; adv bkg rec high ssn; quiet; CKE/CCI. "Gd." 1 Apr-30 Sep. € 10.20   2009*

TENDE 10E4 (9km S Rural) 44.00746, 7.55448 **Camp Municipal, Quartier Barnabin, 06540 Fontan** [04 93 04 55 86] Site is on D6204 200m N of Fontan on rvside. Sm, pt sl, pt shd; wc (some cont); shwrs inc; el pnts; lndtte; shop, rest, snacks, bar 200m; playgrnd; dogs; phone; adv bkg; some rd noise; CKE/CCI. "Pleasant site nr scenic vill of Saorge; site yourself if recep shut (ltd open hrs)." 15 Jun-15 Sep.   2009*

TERRASSON LAVILLEDIEU 7C3 (4km W Rural) 45.12041, 1.26199 **Camping La Salvinie, Bouillac-Sud, 24120 Terrasson-Lavilledieu** [05 53 50 06 11 or 06 03 61 55 72; camping.lasalvinie@orange.fr; www.camping-salvinie.com] Exit A89 junc 18 onto D6089 dir Terrasson-Lavilledieu. Cross Rv Vézère & turn immed L, site in 4km sp. Med, hdg/mkd pitch, shd; wc; chem disp; mv service pnt; shwrs; el pnts (6A) €2.60; gas; lndtte; shop & 4km; tradsmn; ice; supmkt 3km; rest, snacks; bar; BBQ; playgrnd; pool; games area; games rm; wifi; 10% statics; dogs €1; no twin-axles; poss cr; Eng spkn; adv bkg; quiet; ccard acc. "Excel, scenic site; friendly owners; Terrasson interesting town; mkt Thurs." 1 Apr-31 Oct. € 11.10   2009*

TEUILLAC 7C2 (Rural) 45.09163, -0.54808 **Camp Municipal, Le Bourg, 33710 Teuillac** [05 57 64 34 55; accueil@mairie-teuillac.com; www.teuillac.a3w.fr] Fr D137 turn onto D134 at Le Poteau twd Teuillac, site in 2km adj Mairie. Sm, pt shd; wc; baby facs; shwrs; el pnts €3; snacks; pool; fishing nr; quiet. "Pleasant, peaceful site surrounded by grape vines; conv Bordeaux; vg, useful NH." May- Sep. € 7.00   2011*

THANN 6F3 (7km NW Rural) 47.85071, 7.03058 **FFCC Camping La Mine d'Argent, Rue des Mines, 68690 Moosch** [03 89 82 30 66 or 03 89 60 34 74; fax 03 89 42 15 12; moosch@camping-la-mine-argent.com; www.camping-la-mine-argent.com] Turn L off N66 Thann-Thillot rd in cent of Moosch opp church; foll sps for 1.5km, ent on R, narr app. Med, mkd pitch, pt sl, pt terr, pt shd; wc; chem disp; mv service pnt; shwrs inc; el pnts (6-10A) €3.00-5.60; gas; lndtte; tradsmn; shops 1.5km; playgrnd; 10% statics; dogs €0.60; phone; adv bkg; quiet; ccard acc; red low ssn/CKE/CCI. "Well-kept site in wooded valley; busy w/end; helpful staff; excel walking; highly rec" 5 Apr-15 Oct. € 18.95   2013*

THARON PLAGE see Pornic 2G3

THENON 7C3 (3km SE Rural) 45.11883, 1.09119 Camping Le Verdoyant, Route de Montignac, 24210 Thenon [05 53 05 20 78; fax 05 67 34 05 00; contact@ campingleverdoyant.fr; www.campingleverdoyant.fr] Sp fr A89, take D67 fr Thenon to Montignac. Site on R in 4km. Med, mkd pitch, pt sl, terr, pt shd; wc; chem disp (wc); shwrs inc; el pnts (10A) €3.15; shops 2km; tradsmn; snacks; bar; gas; lndtte; playgrnd; pool; lake fishing; wifi; dogs €1.60; adv bkg; quiet; 20% statics; dogs €1.75; Eng spkn; quiet; red low ssn; CKE/CCI. "Beautiful setting away fr tourist bustle; friendly owners; excel base for area." 1 Apr-30 Sep. € 14.10   2011*

THENON 7C3 (10km W Rural) 45.13165, 0.92867 **Camping de la Pélonie, La Bourgie, 24330 St Antoine-d'Auberoche** [05 53 07 55 78; fax 05 53 03 74 27; www.lapelonie.com] Fr Périgueux on A89 twd Brive; 5km past St Pierre-de-Chignac, site sp on L; turn L at picnic area - go under rlwy bdge; site ent on L. Med, mkd pitch, pt shd; wc; chem disp; shwrs inc; el pnts (10A) €3.80 (poss req long cable); lndtte; gas; shop; tradsmn; rest, snacks; bar; playgrnd; htd pool; paddling pool; wifi; TV; 20% statics; dogs €2; phone; poss cr; Eng spkn; adv bkg; quiet; ccard acc; red low ssn; CKE/CCI. "Delightful site; pleasant, welcoming owners; gd, clean facs; excel facs for children; some pitches diff lge o'fits; gd touring base." 11 Apr-17 Oct. € 17.50   2011*

THERONDELS see Pierrefort 7C4

"That's changed – Should I let The Club know?"

If you find something on site that's different from the site entry, fill in a report and let us know. See www.caravanclub.co.uk/europereport.

THIEMBRONNE 3A3 (500m NW Rural) 50.62114, 2.05424 Camping Les Pommiers, 1 Route des Desvres, 62560 Thiembronne [tel/fax 03 21 39 50 19; campinglespommiers@ orange.fr; www.camping-pommiers.com] SW fr St Omer for 25km on D928 to Fauquembergues. NW on D158 for 4km past water tower. Site sp. Med, mkd pitch, sl, shd; wc; chem disp; shwrs €0.30; el pnts (6A) €2.60; lndtte (inc dryer); shop 1km; snacks; playgrnd; pool; games area; entmnt; TV; 75% statics; poss cr; adv bkg; quiet. 15 Mar-15 Oct. € 14.40   2009*

THIERS 9B1 (7km NE Rural) 45.89874, 3.59888 **Camping Les Chanterelles, Chapon 63550 St Rémy-sur-Durolle** [04 73 93 60 00; fax 04 73 94 31 71; contact@revea-vacances.com; www.revea-vacances.fr] On A72/E70 W dir Clermont-Ferrand, exit at junc 3 sp Thiers. Foll sp twd Thiers on N89 into L Monnerie. Fr vill, take D20 & foll sp St Rémy. In St Rémy, foll 'Camping' sp. Do not app thro Thiers as narr rds v diff for lge o'fits. Med, terr, pt shd; htd wc; chem disp; mv service pnt; shwrs inc; el pnts (10A) €3.50; gas; lndtte (inc dryer); shop; tradsmn; BBQ; playgrnd; htd pool; paddling pool; waterslide; lake sw 600m; windsurfing; tennis 600m; TV rm; some statics; dogs €1.50; adv bkg; quiet; ccard acc; CKE/CCI. "Vg site in beautiful situation with views; modern, clean facs; some noise at w/end fr statics; excel" 30 Apr-15 Sep. € 25.70 (CChq acc)   2013*

FRANCE

THIERS *9B1* (8km W Rural) *45.86845, 3.47616* **Camp Municipal Pont Astier, 63190 Orléat [tel/fax 04 73 53 64 40; mairie.orleat@orleat.com]** On A72 take exit 2 onto D906 S for 2.5km. Turn R on N89 for Clermont-Ferrand. Turn R at Pont-de-Dore onto D224. Site 3km on R. Med, hdg pitch, pt sl, pt shd; wc (some cont); chem disp; shwrs inc; el pnts (10A) €4; lndtte; shop 3km; tradsmn; snacks; bar; BBQ; playgrnd; pool; fishing; tennis; dogs €0.90; Eng spkn; adv bkg; red low ssn; CKE/CCI. "By Rv Dore; lge pitches, but some damp; poss mosquito prob; site ent poss diff; unrel opening dates." ♦ 1 May-30 Sep. € 12.00   2009*

THIERS *9B1* (4km NW Rural) *45.87168, 3.48538* **Camping Base de Loisirs Iloa, Courty, 63300 Thiers [04 73 80 92 35 or 04 73 80 88 80 (LS); fax 04 73 80 88 81; http://ville-thiers.fr]** Exit A72 junc 2 for Thiers; at rndabt turn L sp Vichy but take D44 sp Dorat; pass under m'way, site beyond Courty on L sp Les Rives-de-Thiers. Sm, mkd pitch, pt shd; wc (some cont); chem disp; mv service pnt; some serviced pitches; shwrs inc; el pnts (6A) €2.20; gas 5km; lndtte; supmkt 5km; tradsmn; playgrnd; pool & sports adj; lake fishing; tennis; entmnt; TV rm; dogs; CKE/CCI. "Well-maintained; vg, clean san facs; friendly warden; quiet low ssn; vg NH." ♦ ltd 9 May-7 Sep. € 12.25 (3 persons)   2011*

THIEZAC see Vic sur Cère *7C4*

⊞ **THILLOT, LE** *6F3* (1km NW Rural) *47.88893, 6.75683* **Camp Municipal du Clos de Chaume, 36 Rue de la Chaume, 88160 Le Thillot [03 29 25 10 30; fax 03 29 25 25 87; campingmunicipal@ville-lethillot88.fr; www.ville-lethillot88.fr]** Site sp on N o'skts of town N on N66, on R behind sports cent. Med, pt sl, pt shd; htd wc; shwrs inc; el pnts (6A) €1.80; gas; lndtte; shops 1km; playgrnd & tennis adj; few statics; adv bkg; quiet. "Attractive, well-maintained site; friendly staff; vg san facs; excel touring base." € 6.10   2012*

THILLOT, LE *6F3* (2.5km NW Rural) *47.89322, 67.3803* **Camping Le Clos Martin, 5 Rue du Clos-Martin, 88160 Ramonchamp [03 29 25 05 38]** At Ramonchamp on N66 (travelling E) turn R & foll sp. Sm, pt shd; wc; chem disp; shwrs €1.30; el pnts (6A) €2 (poss rev pol); lndtte; shops, rest 200m; BBQ; playgrnd; rv fishing; dogs €0.50; phone; quiet; CKE/CCI. "Pleasant site; helpful owners; gd walking & cycling." 1 Apr-15 Sep. € 7.30   2008*

THIONVILLE *5C2* (500m NE Urban) *49.36127, 6.17534* **Camp Municipal, 6 Rue du Parc, 57100 Thionville [03 82 53 83 75; fax 03 82 53 91 27; camping.municipal@ mairie-thionville.fr]** Exit A31 at sp Thionville Cent; foll sp 'Centre Ville'; foll site sp dir Manom. Sm, mkd pitch, some hdstg, pt shd; wc; chem disp; mv service pnt; shwrs inc; el pnts (3-10A) €2.40-4.65; shop 250m; rest snacks; bar 250m; playgrnd; pool 1km; boating; fishing; dogs €1.20; poss cr; Eng spkn; adv bkg; quiet; red long stay; CKE/CCI. "Well-kept site; some rvside pitches; friendly warden; gd san facs; rec arr early high ssn; 5 min walk thro lovely adj park to town; vg." ♦ 1 May-30 Sep. € 14.40   2013*

THIVIERS *7C3* (10km N Rural) *45.49950, 0.90690* **Camping Maisonneuve, 1 Chemin de Maisonneuve, 24800 St Jory-de-Chalais [tel/fax 05 53 55 10 63; camping.maisonneuve@ wanadoo.fr; www.camping-maisonneuve.com]** N fr Thiviers on N21 for 6km; turn L on D98 thro Chaleix; site on L bef ent St Jory. Other rtes v narr. Sm, hdg/mkd pitch, hdstg, pt sl, pt shd; wc (some cont); chem disp; mv service pnt; sauna; shwrs inc; el pnts (10A) €3.50; lndtte (inc dryer); shop 500m; rest, snacks; bar; playgrnd; pool; fishing lake; games rm; internet; TV; 10% statics; dogs €1; Eng spkn; adv bkg; quiet; red low ssn/long stay/CKE/CCI. "Pretty site in attractive countryside; lge pitches, some v shaded; helpful, welcoming owners; excel." ♦ 1 Apr-31 Oct. € 20.50   2010*

THIVIERS *7C3* (10km N Rural) *45.50255, 0.91447* **Camping Moulin du Touroulet, Moulin du Tourelet, 24800 Chaleix [tel/fax 05 53 55 23 59; touroulet@hotmail.com; www. camping-touroulet.com]** Fr Limoges on N21 S twd Périgueux, thro vill of La Coquille, in about 4.5km turn R onto D98 twd St Jory-de-Chalais & Chaleix. In 4km turn L to vill & site 1km further on. Take care narr bdge & site ent. Sm, pt sl, some hdstg, pt shd; pt htd wc; chem disp; shwrs inc; el pnts (8A) €3; lndry rm; shop 1.5km; tradsmn; rest; bar; BBQ; pool; fishing; games rm; entmnt; internet; dogs €0.50; adv bkg; quiet; CKE/ CCI. "Beautiful site in tranquil rvside setting; spacious & well-kept; welcoming, helpful British owners; fishing avail on site owner's lake in tranquil setting; basic, ltd san facs; stretched high ssn; excel bar/rest; hdstg pitches sl & uneven; Xmas package; excel." 1 Mar-31 Dec. € 18.00   2012*

⊞ **THIVIERS** *7C3* (7km NE Rural) *45.47390, 0.93808* **Camping La Petite Lande, Lieu-dite La Petitie Lande, 24800 St Jory-de-Chalais [09 61 36 00 57 or 06 98 23 86 60 (mob); fax 05 53 62 42 89; info@la-petite-lande.com; www.la-petite-lande.com]** N fr Thiviers on D21; in 6km turn L onto unclassified rd sp 'La Petite Lande' campsite; foll sps to site in 500m. Sm, unshd; htd wc; chem disp; shwrs inc; el pnts (6A) €3.50; lndtte; shops 6km; rest & bar 3km; BBQ; sm playgrnd; pool (above grnd); dogs €1; Eng spkn; quiet; ccard acc; red low ssn. "Relaxing, CL-type site; new site (2011); helpful Dutch owners; v gd, clean facs plans to expand" ♦ ltd € 10.00   2012*

⊞ **THIVIERS** *7C3* (2km E Rural) *45.41299, 0.93209* **Camping Le Repaire, Ave de Verdun, 24800 Thiviers [tel/fax 05 53 52 69 75; camping.le.repaire@gmail.com; www. camping-thiviers-perigord.com]** N21 to Thiviers; at rndabt take D707 E dir Lanouaille; site in 1.5km on R. Med, hdg/mkd pitch, pt sl, terr, pt shd; htd wc; chem disp; mv service pnt; shwrs inc; el pnts (12A) €3; lndtte; shop 2km; snacks; BBQ; playgrnd; covrd pool; lake fishing; entmnt; games rm; TV rm; 5% statics; dogs €1.60; phone; no twin-axles; poss cr; Eng spkn; adv bkg; quiet; red low ssn; CKE/CCI. "Lovely site - one of best in area; friendly owners; clean san facs; some pitches unrel in wet weather; excel." ♦ ltd € 14.00   2009*

THOISSEY *9A2* (1km SW Rural) *46.16512, 4.79257* **Camping Hortus - La Route des Vins, Ave du Port, 01140 Thoissey [04 74 04 02 97; info@camping-hortus.com; www. camping-hortus.com]** S on D306 turn L onto D9 thro Dracé. Turn sharp R immed after x-ing Rv Saône, site sp. Lge, mkd pitch, pt shd; htd wc; mv service pnt; shwrs inc; el pnts (10A) inc; lndtte; shop; rest, snacks; bar; BBQ; playgrnd; htd pool; paddling pool; Rv beach & sw adj; fishing; watersports; tennis; games rm; games area; wifi; entmnt; TV; 2% statics; dogs €2; phone; poss cr; Eng spkn; adv bkg; quiet; ccard acc; CKE/CCI. "Vg touring base for vineyards; lge pitches; vg, modern san facs." ♦ 23 Apr-30 Sep. € 20.00   2011*

THOLY, LE *6F3* (6km N Rural) *48.12005, 6.73181* **Camping Le Barba, 45 Le Village, 88640 Rehaupal [03 29 66 35 57; barba@campingdubarba.com; www.campingdubarba.com]** Fr Gérardmer on D417 after 8km site sp on R 2km bef Le Tholy. Foll sp to Rehaupal, site on R on ent to vill. Sm, mkd pitch, pt shd; wc; chem disp; shwrs inc; el pnts (3-10A) €2.80-5.50; gas; lndtte; shop adj; tradsmn; rest; some statics; dogs €1; Eng spkn; quiet. "Friendly owner; scenic site; vg walking." 1 May-26 Sep. € 8.40   2010*

"I like to fill in the reports as I travel from site to site"

You'll find report forms at the back of this guide, or you can fill them in online at www.caravaclub.co.uk/europereport.

THOLY, LE *6F3* (1.3km NW Rural) *48.08897, 6.72869* **Camping de Noirrupt, 15 Chemin de L'Etang, 88530 Le Tholy [03 29 61 81 27; fax 03 29 61 83 05; info@ jpvacances.com; www.jpvacances.com]** Fr Gérardmer, take D417 W, turn R in Le Tholy up hill onto D11. Site on L on secondary rd to Epinal & sp. Med, terr, pt shd; wc (some cont); chem disp; baby facs; sauna; shwrs inc; el pnts (2-6A) €3-5; gas; lndtte; shops 1km; snacks; bar; BBQ; htd pool; tennis; entmnt; TV rm; some statics; dogs €1.50; poss cr; some rd noise; red long stay. "Pleasant, well laid-out site in lovely area; sm pitches; vg." 15 Apr-15 Oct. € 20.30   2009*

THONAC see Montignac *7C3*

THONNANCE LES MOULINS *6E1* (2km W Rural) *48.40630, 5.27110* **Camping La Forge de Ste Marie, 52230 Thonnance-les-Moulins [03 25 94 42 00; fax 03 25 94 41 43; info@laforgedesaintemarie.com; www. laforgedesaintemarie.com or www.les-castels.com]** Fr N67 exit sp Joinville-Est, foll D60 NE sp Vaucouleurs. In 500m turn R onto D427 sp Poissons & Neufchâteau. Site on R in 11km. NB Swing wide at turn into site fr main c'way, not fr what appears to be a run in. Site ent narr. Lge, hdg/mkd pitch, pt sl, pt terr,pt shd; wc; chem disp; mv service pnt; serviced pitches; baby facs; shwrs inc; el pnts (6A) inc; gas; lndtte (inc dryer); shop; tradsmn; rest, snacks; bar; BBQ; htd, covrd pool; paddling pool; sm lake on site; boating; freshwater fishing; cycle hire; games area; wifi; entmnt; games/TV rm; 25% statics; dogs €2; no c'vans/m'vans over 8m; phone; Eng spkn; adv bkg; ccard acc; red low ssn; CKE/CCI. "Vg, well-kept, busy site; friendly, helpful owners; access poss diff to some terr pitches/sharp bends on site rds; muddy after rain; vg rest; mkt Fri; lovely spacious, well run site, beautiful area; swing wide at ent" ♦ 20 Apr- 06 Sep. € 36.00 (CChq acc) SBS - J04   2013*

See advertisement on inside back cover

THONON LES BAINS *9A3* (3km NE Rural) *46.39944, 6.50416* **Camping Le Saint Disdille, 117 Ave de St Disdille, 74200 Thonon-Les-Bains [04 50 71 14 11; fax 04 50 71 93 67; camping@disdille.com; www.disdille.com]** Exit A41/A40 junc 14 Annemasse onto D1005 & foll sp Thonon twd Evian. At Vongy rndabt foll sp St Disdille & site. Site 200m fr Lake Geneva. V lge, mkd pitch, shd; wc; baby facs; shwrs; el pnts (6-10A) €4; gas; lndtte (inc dryer); shop; tradsmn; rest, snacks; bar; BBQ; playgrnd; lake sw & beach 200m; fishing; watersports; tennis; cycle hire; games area; games rm; wifi; entmnt; 30% statics; dogs €3; adv bkg ess; quiet; ccard acc; red low ssn; CKE/CCI. "Well-situated; well-equipped site; gd touring base for very nice area". ♦ 1 Apr-30 Sep. € 35.40   2013*

See advertisement below

THONON LES BAINS *9A3* (10km W Rural) *46.35638, 6.35250* **Campéole Camping La Pinède, 74140 Excenevex [04 50 72 85 05 or 04 50 72 81 27 (Mairie); fax 04 50 72 93 00; pinede@campeole.com; www.camping-lac-leman.info or www.campeole.com]** On D1005 to Geneva, 10km fr Thonon, turn R at Camping sp. V lge, htd/mkd pitch, shd; htd wc; child facs; shwrs inc; chem disp; mv service pnt; child facs; el pnts (10A) €4.10; gas; lndtte; shop; rest, snacks; bar; BBQ; playgrnd; sports area; tennis; lake sw, fishing, watersports & sand beach adj; horseriding 1km; entmnt; internet; TV; 75% statics; dogs €3.50; poss cr; adv bkg; quiet; red low ssn. "excel lakeside site; friendly & efficient staff" 2 Apr-10 Sep. € 24.20   2013*

See advertisement on pages 14 & 15

THOR, LE see Isle sur la Sorgue, L' *10E2*

THORE LA ROCHETTE see Vendôme *4F2*

THORENS GLIERES *9A3* (2km N Rural) *46.01642, 6.24394* **Camping Nantizel, 135 Route de Nantizel, 74570 Thorens-Glières [04 50 22 43 42]** Fr A410 exit 19. Take D1203 twd Annecy. In 10km after S-bend take D5 E to Thorens-Glières & foll camping sp to site. Sm, pt sl, pt shd; wc; own san rec; chem disp; shwrs inc; el pnts (3A) €2.30; shops 4km; playgrnd; dogs €1.30; v quiet. "Scenic CL-type site on alpine farm; highly rec." 15 Jun-15 Sep. € 12.00   2008*

THORENS GLIERES *9A3* (3km SE Rural) *45.98416, 6.27153* **Camping Rural Les Combes d'Usillon, 461 Chemin des Combes d'Usillon, 74570 Thorens-Glières [04 50 22 81 10; campingville@aol.com]** Fr Thorens-Glières take D5 S twd Aviernoz. In 1km turn L twd La Louvatière. Site sp Camping Rural in 2km on rvside. Sm, pt shd; shwrs inc; el pnts €1.85; lndtte; shop 2.5km; rest; dogs; v quiet. "Quiet, scenic site 'away-from-it-all'; site yourself; pleasant owner; drinking water fr owner's house; gd walking." 15 May-15 Sep. € 10.00   2008*

THORENS GLIERES *9A3* (3km NW Rural) *46.00200, 6.19190* **Aire Naturelle Le Moulin Dollay, 206 Rue du Moulin Dollay, 74570 Groisy [tel/fax 04 50 68 00 31; moulin.dollay@orange.fr; www.moulin.dollay@orange.fr]** Fr Annecy take D1203 N. At Champion supmkt fork L to Groisy. Thro Groisy & over rv bdge, turn R sp La Roche-sur-Foron, site on L. Sm, mkd pitch, pt shd; htd wc; chem disp; mv service pnt; baby facs; fam bthrm; shwrs inc; el pnts (6A) €3; gas 1km; lndtte (inc dryer); shops 1km; tradsmn; snacks; BBQ; bar 5km; playgrnd; rv sw adj; TV rm; no dogs; train 500m; phone; o'night m'van area; adv bkg; quiet; red long stay. "Excel site with immac san facs; friendly owner." ♦ 1 May-15 Sep. € 16.00   2008*

THOUARCE *4G1* (500m SW Rural) *47.26524, -0.50747* **Camp Municipal de l'Ecluse, 18 Ave des Trois Ponts, 49380 Thouarcé [02 41 54 14 36 (Mairie); fax 02 41 54 09 11; mairie.thouarce@wanadoo.fr; www.thouarce.fr]** Exit A87 junc 24 onto D160/D55 dir Beaulieu-sur-Layon & Thouarcé. Site sp adj Rv Layon. Sm, pt shd; wc (cont for men); shwrs inc; el pnts €1.70; gas; shops 500m; supmkt 1km; playgrnd; htd, covrd pool, tennis nr; fishing; extra charge (€30+) for twin-axles; no adv bkg; quiet; CKE/CCI. 15 Apr-15 Sep. € 6.80   2009*

THURY HARCOURT *3D1* (500m NE Rural) *48.98930, -0.46966* **FFCC Camping Vallée du Traspy, Rue du Pont Benoît, 14220 Thury-Harcourt [02 31 79 61 80 or 02 31 52 53 54; fax 02 31 84 76 19]** App fr N on D562 fr Caen, take L fork into town after pool complex. In 100m turn L at Hôtel de la Poste, 1st L to site, clearly sp adj Rv Orne. Med, mkd pitch; terr, pt shd; wc (some cont); chem disp; mv service pnt; shwrs inc; el pnts (4A) inc; gas; lndtte; shop 1km; tradsmn; snacks; bar; BBQ; playgrnd; htd pool nr; rv adj & lake nrby; fishing; canoeing; entmnt; 20% statics; dogs €2.90; phone; poss cr; Eng spkn; adv bkg rec high ssn; quiet; CKE/CCI. "Friendly owners; well-maintained pitches; san facs need update; o'night area for m'vans; gd walking." ♦ 1 Apr-30 Sep. € 18.40   2011*

TIL CHATEL *6G1* (2km E Rural) *47.53042, 5.18700* **Camping Les Sapins, 21120 Til-Châtel [03 80 95 16 68; http://www.restaurantlessapins.eresto.net]** Leave A31 junc 5 onto D974 dir Til-Châtel. Site on R in 500m adj Rest Les Sapins. Sm, pt sl, pt shd, serviced pitch; wc (some cont); shwrs inc; el pnts (10A) inc; shops 2km; rest, snacks; bar; poss v cr; Eng spkn; adv bkg; minimal rd noise; CKE/CCI. "Clean site; basic san facs; no twin-axles; conv NH fr a'route" 1 Apr-30 Sep. € 17.00   2013*

TIL CHATEL *6G1* (5km W Urban) *47.52204, 5.10918* **Camp Municipal des Capucins, Rue des Capucins, 21120 Is-sur-Tille [03 80 95 02 08; fax 03 80 95 08 33; www.is-sur-tille.com]** Leave A31 at junc 5 S onto D974 dir Til-Châtel; turn R onto D959 to Is-sur-Tille. Site on L at sports grnd, well sp. Sm, shd; wc (cont); chem disp; shwrs inc; el pnts (3A) inc; lndry rm; shops, rest, bar 1km; tradsmn; pool adj; poss cr; quiet. "Delightful, floral vill; site yourself; warden calls am & pm; facs old but clean; poss itinerants; poss security probs - NH only." 1 Jun-30 Sep. € 10.05   2010*

TINTENIAC *2E4* (500m N Rural) *48.33111, -1.83315* **Camp Municipal du Pont L'Abbesse, Rue du 8 Mai 1945, 35190 Tinténiac [02 99 68 09 91 or 02 99 68 02 15 (Mairie); fax 02 99 68 05 44]** Fr D137 turn E onto D20 to Tinténiac; go strt thro vill to canal; sp just bef canal bdge; turn L. Site behind Brit Hôtel La Guinguette, on Canal d'Ille et Rance. Sm, hdg/mkd pitch, pt sl, pt shd; htd wc; shwrs; el pnts inc; shops, rest, snacks & bar adj; playgrnd; fishing; few statics; quiet; CKE/CCI. "Delightful, busy site; gd san facs; lovely walks/cycling along canal" ♦ 1 Mar-31 Oct. € 10.00   2013*

TINTENIAC *2E4* (2km S Rural) *48.31058, -1.82027* **Camping Les Peupliers, Manoir de la Besnelais, 35190 Tinténiac [02 99 45 49 75; fax 02 99 45 52 98; camping.les.peupliers@wanadoo.fr; www.les-peupliers-camping.fr]** On D137 Rennes to St Malo rd; after Hédé foll rd to Tinténiac about 2km; site on main rd on R, sp. Med, hdg/mkd pitch, pt sl, pt shd; wc (some cont); chem disp; mv service pnt; shwrs inc; el pnts (6A) €2.90 (poss rev pol); lndtte; shops 2km; tradsmn high ssn; rest, snacks; bar; playgrnd; htd pool; lake fishing; tennis; games area; internet; TV rm; 30% statics; dogs €1.60; phone; adv bkg; red low ssn; CKE/CCI. "Pleasant, quiet, well-kept site; gd pool & park; on pilgrim rte to Spain." ♦ ltd 1 Apr-30 Sep. € 18.20   2010*

TONNERRE *4F4* (1.5km NE Urban) *47.86003, 3.98429* **Camp Municipal de la Cascade, Ave Aristide Briand, 89700 Tonnerre [03 86 55 15 44 or 03 86 55 22 55 (Mairie); fax 03 86 55 30 64; ot.tonnerre@wanadoo.fr; www.tonnerre.fr]** Best app via D905 (E by-pass); turn at rndabt twd town cent L after x-ing 1st rv bdge. Or fr D444 strt over rndabt in town cent, over canal bdge & site on L. On banks of Rv Armançon & nr Canal de l'Yonne, 100m fr junc D905 & D944. Med, pt shd; htd wc; chem disp; mv service pnt; baby facs; shwrs inc; el pnts (6A) inc; lndtte (inc dryer); shop; tradsmn; bar; playgrnd; htd pool 1km; rv sw adj; fishing; entmnt; TV rm; 10% statics; Eng spkn; adv bkg; noise fr nrby rlwy; ccard acc; CKE/CCI. "Pleasant, spacious, shady site in arboretum; friendly warden; lge pitches; excel clean san facs; often damp underfoot; site poss untidy early ssn (2011); no twin-axles; interesting town; gd cycling/walking along canal; conv site; excel." ♦ 1 Apr-15 Oct. € 14.90 (CChq acc) 2012*

⊞ **TORCY** *3D3* (3km N Urban) *48.85921, 2.65057* **Camping Le Parc de la Colline, Route de Lagny, 77200 Torcy [01 60 05 42 32; fax 01 64 80 05 17; info@camping-de-la-colline.com; www.camping-de-la-colline.com]** Exit A104 junc 10 W onto D10 sp Torcy/Noisiel. Site on L in 1km. Lge, hdg/mkd pitch, terr, pt shd; htd wc (some cont); chem disp; mv service pnt; shwrs inc; el pnts (6A) €3.70; lndtte (inc dryer); shop; hypmkt 3km; playgrnd; htd pool; waterslide; lake beach & sw 1km; tennis; wifi; TV rm; some statics; dogs €4.90; poss cr; Eng spkn; adv bkg; ccard acc; CKE/CCI. "Conv Disneyland, Parc Astérix, Paris; conv RER by site minibus; helpful staff; steep app to pitches but tow avail." ♦ € 26.80 2010*

TORIGNI SUR VIRE *1D4* (1km S Rural) *49.02833, -0.97194* **Camping Le Lac des Charmilles, Route de Vire, 50160 Torigni-sur-Vire [02 33 56 91 74; fax 02 33 55 91 13; contact@camping-lacdescharmilles.com; www.camping-lacdescharmilles.com]** Exit A84 junc 40 onto N174 dir Torigni-sur-Vire/St Lô; site on R in 4km. Opp municipal stadium. Med, hdg/mkd pitch, hdstg, pt sl, pt shd; htd wc; chem disp; mv service pnt; baby facs; fam bthrm; shwrs inc; el pnts (16A) inc (long lead poss req); lndtte (inc dryer); shop; tradsmn; rest, snacks; bar; BBQ; playgrnd; htd pool; lake sw adj; cycle hire; games area; games rm; wifi; TV; 30% statics; dogs €1.50; phone; poss cr; Eng spkn; adv bkg; quiet; ccard acc; red low ssn; CKE/CCI. "Lovely, well-kept, well-laid out site; clean, modern san facs; interesting town; excel; excel shopping in the town within walking dist" ♦ 23 Mar-30 Sep. € 34.40 (CChq acc) 2013*

TORREILLES PLAGE *10G1* (Coastal) *42.76750, 3.02972* **Camping Sunêlia Les Tropiques, Blvd de la Méditerranée, 66440 Torreilles-Plage [04 68 28 05 09; fax 04 68 28 48 90; contact@campinglestropiques.com; www.campinglestropiques.com]** Exit A9 junc 41 onto D83 E dir Le Barcarès, then D81 dir Canet-Plage. At 1st rndabt turn L onto D11 sp Torreilles-Plage, site sp. Lge, hdg/mkd pitch, shd; wc; chem disp; mv service pnt; baby facs; shwrs inc; el pnts (6A) inc; gas; lndtte; shops; rest, snacks; bar; 2 playgrnds; 2 pools; paddling pool; waterslide; sand beach 400m; tennis; cycle hire; games area; gym; internet; entmnt; TV rm; 80% statics; dogs €4; poss cr; Eng spkn; ccard acc; red low ssn/long stay/CKE/CCI. "Vg family site; excel leisure & san facs." ♦ 9 Apr-1 Oct. € 48.50 2011*

TORREILLES PLAGE *10G1* (Coastal) *42.76556, 3.02710* Chadotel Camping Le Trivoly, Blvd des Plages, 66440 Torreilles-Plage [04 68 28 20 28 or 02 51 33 05 05 (LS); fax 04 68 28 16 48; chadotel@wanadoo.fr; www.chadotel.com] Torreilles-Plage is sp fr D81, site in vill cent. Lge, hdg/mkd pitch, pt shd; wc; serviced pitches; shwrs inc; el pnts (6A) inc; gas; lndtte; shop; snacks; bar; playgrnd; htd pool; waterslide; sand beach 800m; tennis; cycle hire; watersports; games rm; wifi; TV rm; entmnt; dogs €3.20; Eng spkn; adv bkg; quiet; ccard acc; red long stay. "Gd walking in Pyrenees; vg." ♦ 7 Apr-22 Sep. € 32.50 2011*

TORREILLES PLAGE *10G1* (N Coastal) *42.76760, 3.02820* **Camping Le Calypso, Blvd de la Plage, 66440 Torreilles-Plage [04 68 28 09 47; fax 04 68 28 24 76; info@camping-calypso.com; www.camping-calypso.com]** Take D617 fr Perpignan sp Canet-Plage & D81 to St Laurent. 1.7km prior to St Laurent on R hand side of rd. 2nd site on L on way to beach. Lge, mkd pitch, shd; wc; chem disp; baby facs; shwrs; private san facs avail; el pnts (6A) inc; gas; lndtte; supmkt; rest, snacks; bar; playgrnd; htd pool complex; sand beach 300m; games area; games rm; cycle hire; wifi; entmnt; TV; 40% statics; dogs €4; poss cr; adv bkg rec high ssn; quiet; ccard acc. "Trips to vineyards; many activities; superb pool complex." ♦ 1 Apr-30 Sep. € 37.00 2009*

"We must tell The Club about that great site we found"

Get your site reports in by mid-August and we'll do our best to get your updates into the next edition of Caravan Europe.

TORREILLES PLAGE *10G1* (8km N Coastal) *42.76503, 3.02841* **Camping La Palmeraie, Blvd de la Plage, 66440 Torreilles-Plage [04 68 28 20 64; fax 04 68 59 67 41; info@camping-la-palmeraie.com; www.camping-la-palmeraie.com]** Exit A9/E15 junc 41 at Perpignan Nord onto D83 twd Le Barcarès for 10km. At int'chge turn R at junc 9 onto D81 dir Canet-Plage, cont for 3km to lge rndabt & turn L sp Torreilles-Plage, site on R. Lge, hdg/mkd pitch, shd; wc; chem disp; shwrs inc; el pnts (5-10A) €4-7; gas; lndtte; shop; rest, snacks; bar; BBQ (gas only); playgrnd; pool; sand beach 600m; tennis; horseriding nr; games area; games rm; entmnt; TV rm; some statics; dogs €5; Eng spkn; adv bkg; quiet; red low ssn; ccard acc; CKE/CCI. "Attractive site; friendly, helpful staff." ♦ 11 Apr-26 Sep. € 28.00 2008*

TORTEQUESNE see Douai *3B4*

TOUCY *4F4* (300m S Urban) *47.73159, 3.29677* **Camping des Quatre Merlettes, Rue du Pâtis, 89130 Toucy [03 86 44 13 84; fax 03 86 44 28 42; campingdetoucy@wanadoo.fr]** On D3, 25km SW of Auxerre to Toucy. After rv x-ing take 1st L sp 'Base de Loisirs'. Site on S bank of Rv Quanne. Med, pt shd; wc; mv service pnt; shwrs inc; el pnts (3A) €3.10; shops 500m; htd pool; fishing; some statics; dogs; poss cr; adv bkg; quiet. "Pleasant vill; pleasant, helpful warden; no twin-axles; mkt Sat." 1 Apr-15 Oct. € 7.50 2010*

TOUL *6E2* (7km E Rural) *48.65281, 5.99260* **Camping de Villey-le-Sec, 34 Rue de la Gare, 54840 Villey-le-Sec [tel/ fax 03 83 63 64 28; info@campingvilleylesec.com; www. campingvilleylesec.com]** Exit Toul E on D909 or exit A31 junc 15 onto D400 (W, in dir Hôpital Jeanne d'Arc); at rndabt turn L onto D909 to Villey-le-Sec; in vill site S by Rv Moselle, sp. V steep app rd. Med, hdg/mkd pitch, hdstg, pt shd; wc; chem disp; mv service pnt; baby facs; shwrs inc; el pnts (6-10A) €3.70-4.50; gas; lndtte; shop; hypmkt nr; rest, snacks; bar; BBQ; playgrnd; games area; dogs €1.80; phone; Eng spkn; no adv bkg; quiet; ccard acc; red long stay/low ssn. "Peaceful, well-kept site on rvside; lovely location; lge pitches; friendly; vg san facs, poss stretched; cycle paths; popular NH, ess arr bef 1800 high ssn." ♦ 1 Apr-30 Sep. € 26.30   2013*

TOULON SUR ARROUX *4H4* (500m W Urban) *46.69419, 4.13233* **Camp Municipal Le Val d'Arroux, Route d'Uxeau, 71320 Toulon-sur-Arroux [03 85 79 51 22 or 03 85 79 42 55 (Mairie); fax 03 85 79 62 17]** Fr Toulon-sur-Arroux NW on D985 over rv bdge; rturn L in 100m, site sp. Med, pt shd; wc; chem disp; mv service pnt; shwrs inc; el pnts (6A) €3.25; lndtte; shops 500m; playgrnd; rv sw adj; 30% statics; dogs; quiet but some rd noise. "Rvside site; boules park adj; beautiful Buddhist temple 6km; gd" ♦ 16 Apr-15 Oct. € 9.55   2013*

⊞ **TOULOUSE** *8F3* (5km N Urban) *43.65569, 1.41585* **Camping Toulouse Le Rupé, 21 Chemin du Pont de Rupé, 31000 Toulouse [05 61 70 07 35; fax 05 61 70 93 17; campinglerupe31@wanadoo.fr; www.camping-toulouse. com]** N fr Toulouse on D820, sp. Poss tricky app fr N for long vans, suggest cont past Pont de Rupé traff lts to next rndabt & double back to turn. Fr S on ring rd exit junc 33A (after junc 12), turn immed R & foll sp. Lge, hdg/mkd pitch, hdstg, pt shd; htd wc (some cont); chem disp; mv service pnt; baby facs; shwrs inc; el pnts (6A) €4; lndtte (inc dryer); shop; tradsmn; rest, snacks; bar; playgrnd; lake fishing; games rm; wifi; TV; 50% statics; dogs €1.50; phone; bus; poss cr (esp public hols); Eng spkn; no adv bkg; ccard acc; CKE/CCI "If site clsd 1200-1500, park in layby just bef site & use speakerphone; gd clean san facs; rock pegs poss req; itinerant camp opp but no probs, site security excel; conv Airbus factory tours; space theme park 10km; NH only as expensive." € 36.20   2011*

TOUQUES see Deauville *3D1*

TOUQUET PARIS PLAGE, LE *3B2* (1km S Coastal) *50.51091, 1.58867* **Camping Caravaning Municipal Stoneham, Ave François Godin, 62520 Le Touquet-Paris-Plage [03 21 05 16 55; fax 03 21 05 06 48; caravaning. stoneham@letouquet.com; www.letouquet.com]** Fr Etaples on D939; stay in L-hand lane at traff lts dir airport & cont strt on (Ave du Général de Gaulle); L at traff lts sp Golf (Ave du Golf); foll rd to rndabt; turn R onto Ave François Godin (site sp); at next rndabt site on R. Or cont another 500m along Ave du Général de Gaulle to x-rds; turn L into Ave Louis Quetelart; in 500m at T-junc turn L into Ave François Godin; site on L in 200m. Lge, hdg pitch, pt shd; wc; shwrs inc; el pnts (6A) inc (poss rev pol); lndtte; shops 1km; tradsmn; playgrnd; htd pool 2km; sand beach 1km; 95% statics; dogs €2; poss cr even low ssn; adv bkg exc; CKE/CCI. "Pleasant site; conv for town; helpful staff; excel facs; recep closes 1800 (low ssn 2010); m'van 'aires' nr harbour & equestrian cent; mkt Sat." 2 Feb-15 Nov. € 26.60   2011*

TOUQUET PARIS PLAGE, LE *3B2* (5km S Coastal) *50.47238, 1.57717* **Camp Municipal de la Mer, Cours des Champs Elysées, 62780 Stella-Plage [03 21 84 60 60; fax 03 21 09 58 36; info@campingdelamer.com; www. campingdelamer.com]** S fr Etaples on D940, in 4km turn R dir Stella-Plage; at lge rndabt by sea front turn L to site; at end of rd. Lge, unshd; wc; el pnts (10A) €5; lndtte; shops etc nrby; direct access to beach 200m; tennis nrby; aqualand, golf & horseriding in Le Touquet; some statics; dogs €0.90; quiet. "Interesting, sandy site sheltered by dunes; busy high ssn; san facs clean; v busy site, poss noisy" ♦ 14 Jun-9 Sep. € 16.60   2013*

TOUQUET PARIS PLAGE, LE *3B2* (6km S Coastal) *50.47343, 1.59178* **Camping La Forêt, 149 Blvd de Berck, 62780 Stella-Plage [03 21 94 75 01; info@laforetstella.fr; www. laforetstella.fr]** Exit A16 junc 26 onto D393 to Etaples; turn L onto D940 dir Berck; foll sp Stella-Plage. Blvd de Berck is turning S off D144 W to Stella-Plage. Med, hdg/mkd pitch, unshd; wc; baby facs; shwrs; el pnts €5; gas; lndtte (inc dryer); shop; tradsmn; playgrnd; fishing nrby; sandy beach 2km; tennis 900m; sailing; wind surfing; games area; games rm; entmnt; wifi; 80% statics; dogs €2.50; phone; bus adj; poss cr; Eng spkn; adv bkg; quiet; red low ssn. "Gd site; tourist attractions nrby." 1 Apr-30 Sep. € 22.00   2011*

TOUQUIN *4E4* (2.5km W Rural) *48.73305, 3.04697* **Camping Les Etangs Fleuris, Route de la Couture, 77131 Touquin [01 64 04 16 36; fax 01 64 04 12 28; contact@ etangs-fleuris.com; www.etangsfleuris.com or www. paris-camping.com]** On D231 fr Provins, turn R to Touquin. Turn sharp R in vill & foll sp to site on R in approx 2km. Or fr Coulommiers, take D402 SW twd Mauperthuis, after Mauperthuis L twd Touquin. Foll sp in vill. NB Beware two unmarked speed bumps on entering vill. Med, hdg/mkd pitch, hdstg, pt shd; htd wc; chem disp; mv service pnt; shwrs inc; el pnts (10A) inc; gas; lndtte (inc dryer); sm shop on site & 2.5km; tradsmn; snacks; bar; BBQ; playgrnd; htd pool; paddling pool; fishing; games area; games rm; wifi; entmnt; TV rm; 20% statics (inc tour ops); dogs €1.50; phone; adv bkg; quiet; ccard acc; red CKE/CCI; "Peaceful site; no twin-axle c'vans high ssn; conv Paris & Disneyland" 30 Mar-15 Sep. € 20.00   2013*

TOUR DU MEIX, LA see Clairvaux les Lacs *6H2*

TOUR DU PARC, LE see Sarzeau *2G3*

TOURNAN EN BRIE *4E3* (1km S Rural) *48.73317, 2.76069* **Caravaning Fredland, Parc de Combreux, 77220 Tournan-en-Brie [01 64 07 96 44; fax 01 64 42 00 61; fred. chauvineau@wanadoo.fr]** Foll N4 E fr Paris. 15km beyond junc with N104 turn R onto D10 sp Liverdy. Site immed on R on lakeside Med, mkd pitch, pt sl, pt shd; wc; chem disp; shwrs inc; el pnts (6A) inc; lndtte; rest, snacks; bar; BBQ; playgrnd; htd pool; fishing; games area; 75% statics; poss cr; Eng spkn; adv bkg; quiet. "Conv for Paris; 10 min walk to stn; dated san facs; pleasant site." 1 Mar-31 Oct. € 24.00   2008*

TOURNEHEM SUR LA HEM see Ardres *3A3*

FRANCE

TOURNIERES *1D4* (500m S Rural) *49.23017, -0.93256* **Camping Le Picard, 14330 Tournières [02 31 22 82 44; fax 02 31 51 70 28; paulpalmer@orange.fr; www. normandycampsite.com]** Fr Bayeux foll D5/D15 W to Tournières, 5km past Le Molay-Littry. Fr N13 Cherbourg-Bayeux, E of Carentan turn S onto N174 then E on D15 to Tournières. Site sp opp Tournières church. Sm, hdg pitch, pt shd; htd wc; chem disp; serviced pitches; shwrs inc; el pnts (10A) €4.30; shop 5km; tradsmn; rest, snacks; bar; playgrnd; htd pool; boating; fishing; wifi; some statics; no dogs; phone; adv bkg; quiet; ccard acc; CKE/CCI. "Delightful, British-owned site; conv Normandy beaches, Bayeux, Cherbourg ferry; helpful owners bake croissants & will do laundry; san facs need refurb/ update; c'van storage; clean well maintained site; staff very helpful & friendly; nice fishing pool with Carp; home cooked food avail; themed evenings inc food" ♦ 31 Apr-1 Nov. € 21.00 2013*

⊞ **TOURNON SUR RHONE** *9C2* (500m N Rural) *45.07000, 4.83000* **FFCC Camping de Tournon HPA, Quai Farconnet, 1 Promenade Roche-de-France, 07300 Tournon-sur-Rhône [tel/fax 04 75 08 05 28; camping@camping-tournon.com; www.camping-tournon.fr]** Fr Tain l'Hermitage cross Rhône, turn R onto D86; in approx 1km R at end of car park; turn L after 50m, site on R on Rv Rhône. Or fr N on D86, sp on L by car park. Med, shd; htd wc (some cont); chem disp; mv service pnt; shwrs inc; el pnts (6-10A) €4-6.50; gas; lndtte; shop, rest, snacks & bar nr; playgrnd; pool 1km; canoeing; internet; some statics; dogs €2; phone; mv'van o'night area; c'van storage avail; poss cr; Eng spkn; adv bkg rec; ccard not acc high ssn; red long stay/low ssn; CKE/CCI. "Pleasant, well-kept site in wooded location; rvside pitches; friendly owners; clean, dated san facs (unisex low ssn); some sm pitches & narr site rds poss diff lge o'fits; gd security; footbge to Tain-l'Hermitage; fr mid-Jun rock concerts poss held nrby at w/end; gd" ♦ € 16.00 2013*

TOURNON SUR RHONE *9C2* (6km N Rural) *45.12116, 4.80023* **FFCC Camping L'Iserand, Rue Royal, 07610 Vion [04 75 08 01 73; fax 04 75 08 55 82; iserand@tele2.fr; www.iserandcampingardeche.com]** Take D86 N fr Tournon, site 1km N of Vion on L. Med, hdg/mkd pitch, sl, terr, pt shd; htd wc (some cont); chem disp; mv service pnt; baby facs; shwrs inc; el pnts (10A) €3; gas; lndtte; site & 1km; tradsmn; rest 1km; snacks; bar; BBQ; playgrnd; pool; beach; cycle hire; canoeing 1km; entmnt; TV rm; 20% statics; dogs €3; bus 1km; phone; poss cr; adv bkg; Eng spkn; rd & rlwy noise; red low ssn; CKE/CCI. "Excel site; friendly owner lives on site - will take low ssn visitors." 7 Apr-30 Sep. € 16.00 (CChq acc) 2009*

TOURNON SUR RHONE *9C2* (2.5km W Rural) *45.06591, 4.79446* **Camping Les Acacias, 190 Route de Lamastre, 07300 Tournon-sur-Rhône [tel/fax 04 75 08 83 90; info@ acacias-camping.com; www.acacias-camping.com]** Fr D86 Tournon turn W onto D532 dir Lamastre, site on R in approx 2km. Med, pt shd; wc (some cont); chem disp; shwrs; el pnts (6A) €3.30; gas; lndtte; rest; shop 2km; playgrnd; pool; dogs €2.20; poss cr; Eng spkn; rd noise; adv bkg; red low ssn; CKE/CCI. "Nr steam rlwy; gd pitches; some noise fr sawmill; vg, friendly site." ♦ 1 Apr-30 Sep. € 15.96 2008*

TOURNON SUR RHONE *9C2* (3km W Rural) *45.06650, 4.78830* **FFCC Camping Le Manoir, 222 Route de Lamastre, 07300 Tournon-sur-Rhône [04 75 08 02 50 or 06 70 00 06 13 (mob); fax 04 75 08 57 10; info@lemanoir-ardeche.com; www.lemanoir-ardeche.com]** Leave Tournon on D532 just bef x-ing rv, dir Lamastre. Site on R after 3km (4th site). Med, mkd pitch, pt shd; wc (50% cont); chem disp; mv service pnt; shwrs inc; el pnts (10A) €3.60; lndtte; shop 2.5km; tradsmn; snacks; bar; BBQ; playgrnd; pool; rv adj; TV rm; entmnt; 70% statics; dogs €2.50; phone; poss cr; adv bkg; quiet but some rd noise; ccard acc; red CKE/CCI. "Pleasant, family-run, rvside site; friendly, hard-working staff; gd facs; gd walking, vineyard tours; narr access to pitches poss diff lge o'fits; vg." ♦ 1 Apr-30 Sep. € 18.50 2010*

TOURNON SUR RHONE *9C2* (4km W Rural) *45.06786, 4.78516* **Camping Le Castelet, 113 Route du Grand Pont, 07300 St Jean-de-Muzols [04 75 08 09 48; fax 04 75 08 49 60; courrier@camping-lecastelet.com; www. camping-lecastelet.com]** Exit Tournon on D86 N; in 500m turn L on D532 twd Lamastre; in 4km turn R on D532 over bdge & turn immed R into site. Med, mkd pitch, some hdstg, terr, pt shd; wc (some cont); chem disp; baby facs; shwrs inc; el pnts (10A) €4.50; gas; lndtte; shop on site & supmkt 4km; tradsmn; bar; BBQ; playgrnd; pool; paddling pool; fishing; games rm; wifi; entmnt; TV; dogs €2; adv bkg; quiet, but some rd noise; red low ssn; ccard not acc. "Lovely, family-run site in beautiful setting; excel facs" 1 Apr-13 Sep. € 5.20 2013*

TOURNUS *9A2* (1km N Urban) *46.57244, 4.90854* **Camping de Tournus, 14 Rue des Canes, 71700 Tournus [tel/fax 03 85 51 16 58; reception@camping-tournus.com; www. camping-tournus.com]** Fr N6 at N of town E opp rlwy stn & rest 'Le Terminus;' foll site sp. Med, some mkd pitch, hdstg, pt sl, pt shd; wc (some cont); chem disp; mv service pnt; shwrs inc; el pnts (10A) €4.70 (long lead poss req)(poss rev pol); gas; lndtte (inc dryer); tradsmn; snacks; bar; BBQ; playgrnd; htd pools adj; rv fishing 100m; wifi; TV; dogs €2.60; Eng spkn; quiet but rd & rlwy noise some pitches; red low ssn; CKE/CCI. "Peaceful, rvside site in nice position; popular NH, conv A6 - rec arr early; helpful staff; clean facs poss stretched high ssn & ltd low ssn; poss extra charge twin-axles; rv walk into town; gd cycling nrby; abbey worth visit; vg; well kept site; helpful staff" ♦ 1 Apr-30 Sep. € 34.40 (CChq acc) 2013*

TOURNUS *9A2* (9km S Rural) *46.48768, 4.91286* **FFCC Camping International d'Uchizy - Le National 6, 71700 Uchizy [tel/fax 03 85 40 53 90; camping.uchizylen6@ wanadoo.fr; www.camping-lenational6.com]** Exit A6 junc 27 & foll N6 S; sp on L, turn L over rwly bdge on lane to site on L. Adj Rv Saône. Med, shd; wc; shwrs inc; el pnts (6A) €3.90; gas; shop; snacks; playgrnd; pool; fishing; boat hire; dogs €1; poss cr; adv bkg; m'way & train noise; red low ssn. "Attractive, well-maintained site; gd, modern san facs; pitches soft & muddy in rain: arr early for rvside pitch." 1 Apr-30 Sep. € 15.20 2011*

TOURNUS 9A2 (10km W Rural) 46.59182, 4.77746
**Aire Naturelle de Camping à la Ferme de Malo
(Goujon), Champlieu, 71240 Etrigny [03 85 92 21 47 or
03 85 92 23 40; fax 03 85 92 22 13; fam@aubergemalo.
com; www.aubergemalo.com]** S on N6 to Tournus; after
rwly stn turn R onto D14; after passing under rlwy DO NOT
fork L to foll D14 - cont strt onto D215 dir St Gengoux-le-
National. In 8km, in Nogent, turn R at lge stone drinking
trough onto D159; at 2nd x-rds turn L onto D459 (sp
Champlieu); at 1st x-rds turn L into Champlieu; site on L 500m
after vill, bef rv. Sm, pt shd; wc (cont); chem disp (wc); shwrs
inc; el pnts (6-10A) €3 (long lead poss req); lndtte; tradsmn;
rest 1km; playgrnd; tennis 3km; horseriding; dogs; adv bkg
ess high ssn; quiet; no ccard acc; CKE/CCI. "Pitch yourself,
owner calls 1800; san facs poss stretched high ssn; additional
pitches & pool opp main site; adj to Rv Grison." 1 May-1 Nov.
€ 9.80   2010*

⊞ **TOURS** 4G2 (6km E Rural) 47.40226, 0.77845 **Camping
Les Acacias, Rue Berthe Morisot, 37700 La Ville-aux-Dames
[02 47 44 08 16 or 02 62 19 18 08 (LS); fax 02 47 46 26 65;
camplvad@orange.fr; www.camplvad.com]** Fr Tours take
D751 E sp Amboise; after 6km at rndabt where La Ville-aux-
Dames sp to R, go strt on for 200m, then turn R, site sp. Med,
shd; htd wc; chem disp; mv service pnt; serviced pitch; shwrs;
el pnts (10A) €4.50; gas; lndtte; sm shop; supmkt 1km; rest
nrby; playgrnd; pool 500m; tennis 600m; fitness trail, mountain
bike circuit, fishing 100m; wifi; 30% statics; dogs €2; bus
nr; playgrnd; adv bkg; rd & rlwy noise; CKE/CCI. "Well-kept,
well-run site; excel san facs, ltd low ssn; conv town cent; many
long-term residents; gd site; conv NH" ♦ € 23.50   2013*

TOURS 4G2 (8km E Rural) 47.39273, 0.81085 **Camping Les
Peupliers, 37270 Montlouis-sur-Loire [02 47 50 81 90 or
03 86 37 95 83; aquadis1@wanadoo.fr; www.aquadis-
loisirs.com]** On D751, 2km W of vill of Montlouis. Fr N foll
sp to Vouvray (keep on N side of Rv Loire to avoid Tours) &
cross rv by bdge to Montlouis. Sp at last minute. NB App fr E
a 'Q-turn' to get into site. Lge, hdg pitch, pt shd; htd wc;
chem disp; mv service pnt; baby facs; shwrs inc; el pnts (6A)
€2; lndtte; shop 2km; tradsmn; playgrnd; tennis; 12% statics;
dogs €1.90; Eng spkn; adv bkg; some rd & rlwy noise;
ccard acc; CKE/CCI. "Clean, tidy site; poss clsd mid-Oct; lge
pitches; mkt Sun in Amboise; vg." ♦ 1 Apr-31 Oct. € 15.50
(CChq acc)   2012*

TOURS 4G2 (5km SE Urban) 47.37070, 0.72305 **Camping Les
Rives du Cher, 61 Rue de Rochepinard, 37550 St Avertin
[02 47 27 87 47; fax 02 47 25 82 89; contact@camping-
lesrivesducher.com; www.camping-lesrivesducher.com]**
Fr Tours, take D976 S of rv sp Bléré/Vierzon into St Avertin vill.
Take next L at traff lts over 1st of 2 bdges. Site on R in 450m,
not well sp. Med, hdg/mkd pitch, some hdstg, pt shd; wc
(some cont); chem disp; mv service pnt; shwrs inc; el pnts (10A)
€4.20 (poss rev pol); lndtte; shops 400m; rest, snacks & bar
adj; playgrnd; htd pool adj; tennis; fishing; wifi; dogs €1.20;
bus nr by; phone; Eng spkn; adv bkg; quiet; ccard acc; red long
stay; CKE/CCI. "Clean & tidy site but needs updating; some lge
pitches; friendly owner; some resident workers; frequent bus to
Tours" ♦ 1 Apr-15 Oct. € 19.20   2013*

TOURS 4G2 (8km SW Urban) 47.35530, 0.63401 **Camping
La Mignardière, 22 Ave des Aubépines, 37510 Ballan-Miré
[02 47 73 31 00; fax 02 47 73 31 01; info@mignardiere.com;
www.mignardiere.com]** Fr A10 exit junc 24 onto N585 &
D37 by-pass. At exit for Joué-lès-Tours foll sp Ballan-Miré onto
D751. Turn R at 1st set traff lts & foll site sp to W of lake. Lge,
hdg/mkd pitch, hdstg, pt shd; htd wc; chem disp; mv service
pnt; 10% serviced pitch; baby facs; shwrs inc; el pnts (6-10A)
€3.50; lndtte (inc dryer); sm shop; tradsmn; snacks; bar 200m;
BBQ; playgrnd; htd, covrd pool; windsurfing & fishing 1km;
tennis; cycle hire; squash; wifi; entmnt; TV rm; dogs; phone;
Eng spkn; adv bkg; quiet, but some rd/rlwy noise; red low ssn;
CKE/CCI. "Conv Loire valley & chateaux; friendly, helpful staff;
unisex facs low ssn; gd cycle paths; vg site; rec. " ♦
1 Apr-23 Sep. € 22.00   2009*

TOURS 4G2 (8km W Rural) 47.38950, 0.59616 **Camping
L'Islette, 23 Rue de Vallières, 37230 Fondettes
[02 47 42 26 42; www.camping-de-lislette.ruedesloisirs.com]**
Foll D952 W fr Tours twd Saumur. In approx 6km turn R at traff
lts onto D276 at Port-de-Vallières. Site on L in approx 2km.
Sm, hdg pitch, pt shd; wc (some cont); mv service pnt; shwrs
inc; el pnts (10A) €2.50; shop 2km; playgrnd; pool 4km; dogs;
bus; poss cr; adv bkg; quiet; CKE/CCI. "Pleasant site; helpful
owners; facs poss stretched if site full; poss boggy when wet;
conv for Langeais & Luynes chateaux" ♦ ltd 1 Apr-31 Oct.
€ 9.40   2013*

TOURS 4G2 (10km W Rural) 47.38110, 0.55830 **Camping
Club Les Granges, Le Bourg, 37230 Luynes [02 47 55 79 05
or 01 76 61 65 94; fax 02 47 40 92 43; reception@
campinglesgranges.fr; www.campinglesgranges.fr]**
W fr Tours on D952 dir Saumur; in 9km turn R at Le Port-de-
Luynes dir Luynes, site on R in 500m. Med, hdg/mkd pitch, pt
shd; htd wc; mv service pnt; baby facs; shwrs inc; el pnts (10A)
€3.70; lndtte; shops; tradsmn; snacks; bar; BBQ; playgrnd;
pool; fishing 500m; tennis 700m; games area; games rm;
wifi; TV; some statics; dogs €2.50; adv bkg; quiet; ccard acc.
"Pleasant site; gd touring base Loire valley." ♦ 2 May-27 Sep.
€ 20.00   2009*

TOURS 4G2 (10km W Rural) 47.35054, 0.54964 **Camping
de la Confluence, Route de Bray, 37510 Savonnières
[02 47 50 00 25; fax 02 47 50 15 71; camping.
confluence37@orange.fr; http://camping-confluence.
savonnieres.fr]** Fr Tours take D7 on S of Rv Cher. Site on R on
ent Savonnières on rvside. Med, hdg/mkd pitch, hdstg, pt shd; wc
(some cont); chem disp; mv service pnt; baby facs; shwrs; el pnts
(10A) €3.60; lndtte; shops 500m; tradsmn; rest 100m; bar adj;
BBQ; playgrnd; canoe hire; tennis adj; dogs €1.20; phone; bus
200m; Eng spkn; adv bkg; quiet; red low ssn; CKE/CCI. "Well-kept
site with rv views; friendly, efficient staff; modern unisex san facs;
some pitches narr & awnings diff; lovely vill with basic facs; gd
touring base; gd birdwatching, cycling; highly rec. " ♦
22 Apr-1 Oct. € 16.80   2012*

TOURY *4F3* (SW Urban) *48.19361, 1.93260* **Camp Municipal, Rue de Boissay, 28310 Toury [02 37 90 50 60 (Mairie); fax 02 37 90 58 61; mairie-toury@wanadoo.fr; www. ville-toury.fr]** Fr Orléans take N20 N. Site well sp. Sm, pt shd; wc; chem disp (wc); shwrs inc; el pnts (6A) €3; gas 1km; shop 800m; rest 200m; bar 100m; BBQ; playgrnd; no statics; dogs; poss cr' rd & rlwy noise. "NH only; warden calls; poss itinerants low ssn & unclean san facs; high ssn rec arrive bef 1600 to ensure pitch." 15 Apr-15 Oct. € 7.00   2010*

TOUSSAINT see Fécamp *3C1*

TOUTAINVILLE see Pont Audemer *3D2*

TOUZAC see Fumel *7D3*

TRANCHE SUR MER, LA *7A1* (300m N Urban/Coastal) *46.34563, -1.44296* **Camp Municipal Le Vieux Moulin, Ave Maurice Samson, 85360 La Tranche-sur-Mer [tel/fax 02 51 28 93 48; campinglevieuxmoulin@latranchesurmer.fr; www.latranchesurmer.org]** On ent town foll sp for Gendarmerie, sp adj supmkt. Lge, mkd pitch, pt shd, pt sl, pt shd; wc; chem disp; baby facs; shwrs inc; el pnts (6A) inc; lndry rm; shop 400m; sand beach 350m; 50% statics; dogs €2.60; poss cr; adv bkg (dep); quiet; CKE/CCI. "Ltd touring pitches - some sm; town cent & beach 5 mins walk." 14 Mar-11 Oct. € 20.00   2009*

TRANCHE SUR MER, LA *7A1* (2km NE Coastal) *46.39206, -1.40199* **Camping Le Clos Cottet, Route de la Tranche-sur-Mer, 85750 Angles [02 51 28 90 72; fax 02 51 28 90 50; contact@camping-clos-cottet.com; www. camping-clos-cottet.com]** Fr N on D747 twd La Tranche-sur-Mer, site is on R sp after passing Angles, lge, hdg/mkd pitch, some hdstg, pt shd; htd wc (some cont); chem disp; mv service pnt; serviced pitch; baby facs; shwrs inc; el pnts (5A) €4; gas; lndtte (inc dryer); shop; tradsmn; rest, snacks; bar; BBQ; playgrnd; 2 pools (1 htd, covrd); paddling pool; waterslide; jacuzzi; sand beach 4km (free bus high ssn); lake fishing; games area; games rm; fitness rm; wifi; entmnt; 60% statics; dogs €3; Eng spkn; adv bkg; quiet; red low ssn/CKE/CCI. "Excel family site; vg facs; helpful, friendly staff." ♦ 7 Apr-22 Sep. € 25.00   2011*

See advertisement on pages 32 & 33

TRANCHE SUR MER, LA *7A1* (2.6km NE Rural) *46.36286, -1.41936* **Camping Les Blancs Chênes, Route de la Roche-sur-Yon, 85360 La Tranche-sur-Mer [02 51 30 41 70 or 02 51 27 37 80 (res); fax 02 51 28 84 09; info@camping-vagues.oceanes.com; www.camping-vagues-oceanes.com]** Site sp on rd D747. Lge, mkd pitch, pt shd; mv service pnt; wc; baby facs; shwrs inc; el pnts (6A) inc; gas; lndtte; shop; tradsmn; rest, snacks; bar; BBQ; playgrnd; htd, covrd pool; paddling pool; waterslide; sand beach 1.8km; tennis; games area; games rm; entmnt; statics; dogs; shuttle bus to beach; quiet; Eng spkn; adv bkg; ccard acc; red low ssn; CKE/CCI. "Superb pool complex." ♦ Easter-11 Sep. € 28.00   2010*

TRANCHE SUR MER, LA *7A1* (3km NE Rural) *46.37250, -1.41528* **Camping Les Almadies, La Charrière des Bandes, Route de la Roche-sur-Yonne, 85360 La Tranche-sur-Mer [02 51 30 36 94; fax 02 51 30 37 04; info@lesalmadies. com; www.lesalmadies.com]** S fr La Roche-sur-Yonne on D747, site sp. Lge, mkd pitch, pt shd; wc; chem disp; baby facs; shwrs; el pnts (10A) €3.65; lndtte; shop; rest, snacks; bar; BBQ; htd pool; paddling pool; waterslides; sand beach 3km; bus to beach high ssn; cycle hire; games area; entmnt; internet; TV; dogs; adv bkg; quiet; red low ssn. "Pleasant site; vg facs for children; helpful, friendly staff." 4 Apr-27 Sep. € 25.30 (CChq acc)   2008*

TRANCHE SUR MER, LA *7A1* (500m E Coastal) *46.34611, -1.43225* **Camping La Baie d'Aunis, 10 Rue de Pertuis-Breton, 85360 La Tranche-sur-Mer [02 51 27 47 36; fax 02 51 27 44 54; info@camping-baiedaunis.com; www. camping-baiedaunis.com]** Fr La Roche-sur-Yon on D747 to La Tranche-sur-Mer; at 1st rndabt turn R, at 2nd rndabt (by Super U) turn L, at 3rd rndabt turn R - (all sp Centre Ville); ahead at min-rndabt & site on L in 100m. Med, hdg/mkd pitch, hdstg, pt shd; htd wc; chem disp; mv service pnt; baby facs; shwrs inc; el pnts (10A) inc; gas; lndtte; shop 600m; tradsmn; rest, snacks; bar; BBQ; playgrnd; htd pool; sand beach adj; sailing; sea-fishing; watersports; tennis 500m; cycle hire adj; games rm; entmnt; TV; 10% statics; dogs (not Jul/Aug) €2.30; Eng spkn; adv bkg (ess Jul/Aug); quiet; ccard acc; red low ssn; CKE/CCI. "Vg, friendly site; helpful staff; excel san facs; excel rest; poss diff ent for lge o'fits; gd beaches, lovely area;" ♦ 26 Apr-15 Sep. € 35.10   2013*

See advertisement below

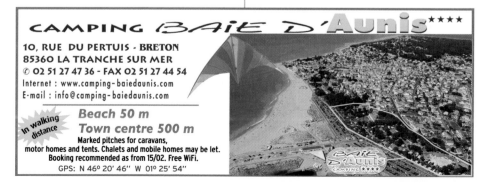

TRANCHE SUR MER, LA 7A1 (3km E Coastal) 46.34810, -1.38730 **Camping du Jard, 123 Blvd du Lattre de Tassigny, 85360 La Tranche-sur-Mer [02 51 27 43 79; fax 02 51 27 42 92; info@campingdujard.fr; www. campingdujard.fr]** Foll D747 S fr La Roche-sur-Yon twd La Tranche; at rndabt on outskirts of La Tranche turn L onto D46 sp La Faute-sur-Mer; cont for approx 5km. At rndabt turn R sp La Faute-sur-Mer 'par la côte'; then R at next rndabt onto D46 sp La Tranche-sur-Mer 'par la côte' & La Grière-Plage (ignore all previous La Grière sps); site on R in 1km. Rough app rd. Lge, hdg/mkd pitch, pt shd; wc; chem disp; serviced pitch; baby facs; sauna; shwrs inc; el pnts (10A) inc; lndtte (inc dryer); shop; rest, snacks; bar; BBQ (charcoal/gas); playgrnd; 2 pools (1 htd, covrd); paddling pool; waterslide; sand beach 700m; tennis; games area; fitness cent; cycle hire; horseriding 10km; golf 20km; wifi; entmnt; games/TV rm; 75% statics (tour ops); no dogs; no c'vans over 8m high ssn; Eng spkn; adv bkg; rd noise; ccard acc; red low ssn/CKE/CCI. "Lovely, well-run, clean & tidy site; busy high ssn; gd sized pitches, some sm; gd, well-kept san facs; gd pool; superb beach across busy coastal rd; easy parking at other beaches; poss flooding in wet weather; mkt Tue & Sat." ♦ 15 May-12 Sep. € 36.00   SBS - A03   2011*

TREBES see Carcassonne 8F4

TREBEURDEN 1D2 (4km N Coastal) 48.79078, -3.55787 **Camping L'Espérance, Penvern, 22560 Trébeurden [02 96 91 95 05; fax 02 96 91 98 12; accueil@camping-esperance.com; www.camping-esperance.com]** Fr Lannion on D65 to Trébeurden, then D788 sp Trégastel, site in 5km. Med, hdg/mkd pitch, pt shd; wc (some cont); chem disp; mv service pnt; baby facs; shwrs inc; el pnts (5-10A) €2.80-3.50; gas; lndtte; shop 2km; playgrnd; sand beach adj; golf adj; TV; 10% statics; dogs €1.50; bus; Eng spkn; adv bkg; quiet; ccard not acc; CKE/CCI. "Pleasant site; some pitches sm; nr GR34 long dist walking rte." ♦ 1 Apr-30 Sep. € 16.80   2010*

TREBEURDEN 1D2 (3.5km NW Coastal) 48.79905, -3.58386 **Camp Municipal Le Dourlin, L'Île Grande, 22560 Pleumeur-Bodou [02 96 91 92 41 or 02 96 23 91 17 (Mairie); infos. tourisme@pleumeur-bodou.com; www.pleumeur-bodou. com]** Off D788 N fr Trébeurden. Foll minor rd thro vill to site on coast. Well sp. Med, mkd pitch, unshd; wc; chem disp; mv service pnt; shwrs inc; el pnts (6A) €2.35; lndtte; shops 500m; supmkt nrby; rest, snacks; bar; BBQ; playgrnd; sand/shgl beach adj; sailing; fishing; games area; wifi; dogs €0.60; phone; bus; poss cr; Eng spkn; quiet; CKE/CCI. "Popular site in excel location - fine sea views; excel facs; gd walking, cycling; ornithological cent nr; 8km circular coast rd round peninsula; gd." ♦ 30 Apr-27 Sep. € 8.75   2010*

TREDION 2F3 (1.3km S Rural) 47.78295, -2.59060 **Camp Municipal l'Etang aux Biches, Route d'Elven, 56350 Trédion [02 97 67 14 06; fax 02 97 67 13 41]** E fr Vannes on N166 for 15km to Elven; in town foll sps N on D1 for Trédion. Site on L in 5km. Sm, hdg/mkd pitch, pt sl, pt shd; wc; shwrs €1.10; el pnts (3A) €1.90; shop 1.5km; tradsmn; playgrnd; quiet. "Peaceful; inland fr v busy coast." ♦ 1 Jul-31 Aug. € 5.40   2010*

TREGASTEL 1D2 (1.5km N Coastal) 48.82549, -3.49135 **Tourony Camping, 105 Rue de Poul-Palud, 22730 Trégastel [02 96 23 86 61; fax 02 96 15 97 84; contact@ camping-tourony.com; www.camping-tourony.com]** On D788 fr Trébeurden dir Perros Guirec, site on R immed after exit Trégastel town sp & immed bef bdge over Traouieros inlet, opp Port de Ploumanac'h. Med, hdg/mkd pitch, pt shd; wc (some cont); chem disp; mv service pnt; baby facs; shwrs inc; el pnts (6A) €3; gas; lndtte; shop 400m; tradsmn; snacks; bar; BBQ; playgrnd; sand beach adj; lake fishing; tennis; cycle hire; games area; golf, horseriding nrby; entmnt; TV; 15% statics; dogs €1.50; Eng spkn; adv bkg; quiet; ccard acc; red long stay/low ssn; CKE/CCI. "Pleasant site in gd location; friendly, helpful staff; gd touring base Granit Rose coast." ♦ 4 Apr-25 Sep. € 17.40   2009*

TREGASTEL 1D2 (3km W Coastal/Rural) 48.80995, -3.54140 **Camping du Port, 3 Chemin des Douaniers, 22560 Landrellec [02 96 23 87 79 or 06 73 78 32 64 (mob); renseignements@camping-du-port-22.com; www. camping-du-port-22.com]** Turn off D788 to Landrellec & foll rd thro vill past shop for 100m, take care tight turn L. Site in 500m. Med, hdg/mkd pitch, pt sl, pt shd; htd wc; chem disp; mv service pnt; serviced pitches; baby facs; shwrs inc; el pnts (10-15A) €3.20-3.50; gas; lndtte (inc dryer); shop; tradsmn; rest, snacks; bar; BBQ; playgrnd; pool 2km; direct access to sandy/rocky beach; fishing, boating, waterskiing; cycle hire; games rm; wifi; entmnt; TV rm; 25% statics; dogs €2.50; Eng spkn; adv bkg; quiet; ccard acc; red low ssn; CKE/CCI. "Immac, family-owned site; beautiful location; direct access beach; beach front pitches extra charge but narr; coastal path runs thro site; lots of lovely beaches nrby; telecoms museum worth visit; excel." ♦ 3 Apr-3 Oct. € 17.00   2011*

See advertisement opposite

TREGUENNEC see Pont l'Abbé 2F2

TREGUIER 1D3 (8km N Coastal) 48.84877, -3.21065 **Camp Municipal de Beg Vilin, 22820 Plougrescant [02 96 92 56 15 or 02 96 92 51 18 (Mairie); fax 02 96 92 59 26; mairie.plougrescant@wanadoo.fr; www. plougrescant.fr]** Take D8 N out of Tréguier to Plougrescant. At St Gonéry/Plougrescant turn R foll sp. Site 1.5km NE of Plougrescant. Med, pt shd; wc; shwrs inc; el pnts €3.60; lndtte (inc dryer); shops 2km; tradsmn; sand/rock beach adj; some statics; dogs free; phone; quiet. "Quiet, peaceful site low ssn; busy, cr site high ssn; rocky beach, some sand; gd." ♦ 12 Jun-12 Sep. € 10.35   2010*

TREGUIER 1D3 (10km N Coastal) 48.85810, -3.22013 **FFCC Camping Le Varlen, 4 Pors-Hir, 22820 Plougrescant [02 96 92 52 15; fax 02 96 92 50 34; info@levarlen.com; www.levarlen.com]** Take D8 N out of Tréguier to Plougrescant. Go past old chapel then immed bef church turn R sp Pors-Hir to site in 1km on R. Sm, mkd pitch, pt sl, pt shd; wc; mv service pnt; baby facs; shwrs inc; el pnts (6-10A) €3.50-3.90 (poss rev pol); lndtte; shop; tradsmn; bar; playgrnd; sports area; shgl beach 300m; 90% statics; dogs €1.50; adv bkg; quiet; ccard acc; red low ssn. "Friendly, helpful owners; some pitches sm & poss diff lge o'fits/m'vans; coastal walks." 1 Mar-15 Nov. € 14.70   2013*

TREGUIER *1D3* (9km NE Coastal) *48.85537, -3.13231*
**Camping Port La Chaîne, 22610 Pleubian [02 96 22 92 38;
fax 02 96 22 87 92; info@portlachaine.com; www.
portlachaine.com]** Fr Paimpol take old D786 W & pick up
new D786 over estuary & thro Lézardrieux. After 3km at
rndabt turn R (N) onto D33 thro Pleumeur-Gautier to Pleubian;
then D20 twds Larmor-Pleubian; turn L after 2km twd coast
& foll site sp. Lge, mkd pitch, pt sl, pt shd; wc (some cont);
chem disp; serviced pitch; baby facs; shwrs inc; el pnts (16A)
inc; gas; Indtte (inc dryer); tradsmn; rest, snacks; bar; BBQ
(charcoal/gas); playgrnd; htd pool; paddling pool; shgl beach
adj; watersports nr; sea-fishing; open air gym; cycle hire in
vill; wifi; entmnt; games/TV rm; 30% statics; dogs €2.90; no
c'vans/m'vans over 7m high ssn; poss cr; Eng spkn; adv bkg
ess; quiet; ccard acc; red low ssn. "Lovely, peaceful site; excel
views fr some pitches; helpful owners; gd clean san facs." ◆
9 Apr-22 Sep. € 26.60   2011*

TREGUNC *2F2* (3km S Coastal) *47.81065, -3.85091* **Camping
des Etangs de Trévignon, Kerlin, 29910 Trégunc [tel/fax
02 98 50 00 41; camp.etangdetrevignon@wanadoo.fr;
www.camping-etangs.com]** Exit N165/E60 at Kérampaou.
S on D122 to Trégunc, then cont S on D1 to Trévignon. Site
in 3km. Foll sp. Lge, hdg/mkd pitch, pt shd; wc (some cont);
chem disp; baby facs; shwrs inc; el pnts (5A) €3.20; gas; Indtte;
shop 2km; tradsmn; rest 3km; snacks; bar; BBQ; playgrnd;
htd, covrd pool high ssn; waterslide; sand beach 800m; cycle
hire; TV rm; 5% statics; dogs €1.80; phone; Eng spkn; adv
bkg; quiet; red low ssn/long stay; ccard acc; red CKE/CCI. "In
nature reserve with bird sanctuary nr; excel." ◆ 1 Jun-15 Sep.
€ 20.50   2009*

TREGUNC *2F2* (5.5km S Coastal) *47.80705, -3.83863* **Camping
La Pommeraie, St Philibert, 29910 Trégunc [02 98 50 02 73;
fax 02 98 50 07 91; info@campingdelapommeraie.
com; www.campingdelapommeraie.com]** Fr D783 bet
Concarneau & Pont-Aven, turn S in Trégunc onto D1 twd
Pointe de Trévignon. In 5.5km look for site sp. Turn L to
St Philibert & Névez. Ent immed on L. Lge, hdg/mkd pitch, pt
shd; wc (some cont); chem disp; shwrs inc; mv service pnt;
some serviced pitches; el pnts (10A) €2; gas; Indtte; shop on
site & 250m; rest, snacks; bar; playgrnd; htd pool; paddling
pool; sand beach 1km; boating; fishing; games rm; cycle hire;
entmnt; TV; 60% statics; dogs €3.50; Eng spkn; adv bkg;
quiet; ccard acc; red low ssn; CKE/CCI. "Pleasant site in apple
orchard; warm welcome." ◆ 1 May-26 Sep. € 29.00   2009*

TREGUNC *2F2* (3.5km SW Coastal) *47.83384, -3.89173*
**Camping La Plage Loc'h Ven, Plage de Pendruc, 29910
Trégunc [02 98 50 26 20; fax 02 98 50 27 63; contact@
lochven.com; www.lochven.com]** Fr N165 exit at
Kérampaou sp Trégunc. At rndbt W of Trégunc foll Loc'h Ven
sp thro Lambell, site on coast. Med, hdg/mkd pitch, pt sl, pt
shd; htd wc; chem disp; baby facs; shwrs inc; el pnts (4-10A)
€3-4.60; gas; Indtte; shop 4km; tradsmn; rest, snacks, bar 4km;
playgrnd; sand/shgl beach adj; games area; TV; 40% statics;
dogs free; poss cr; Eng spkn; adv bkg; quiet. "Easy walk to
beach, rock pools & coastal footpath; helpful owners."
28 Apr-20 Sep. € 15.00   2008*

TREIGNAC *7B4* (4.5km N Rural) *45.56023, 1.81369*
**Camping La Plage, Lac des Barriousses, 19260 Treignac
[05 55 98 08 54; fax 05 55 98 16 47; camping.laplage@
flowercampings.com; www.laplagecamping.com]**
On D940 opp Lac des Barriousses. Med, mkd pitch, pt sl, terr,
shd; htd wc; chem disp; mv service pnt; shwrs inc; el pnts (6A)
€2.80; Indtte; sm shop on site & 4.5km; rest 500m; snacks;
lake sw, boating, fishing adj; 5% statics; dogs €1.20; poss cr;
adv bkg; quiet; CKE/CCI. "Beautiful area & outlook; friendly;
facs unclean low ssn." ◆ 30 Mar-29 Sep. € 22.70   2013*

See advertisement on pages 32 & 33

TREIGNAC *7B4* (10km SE Rural) *45.50262, 1.86911* **Camping
Le Fayard (Naturist), Cors, 19260 Veix [05 55 94 00 20 or
0031 113301245 (N'lands); veen514@zonnet.nl; www.
le-fayard.com]** Fr Treignac take D16 dir Lestards. 1km after
Lestards take D32 S & in 2km turn R dir Cors, site sp. Sm, mkd
pitch, pt sl, pt shd; wc; chem disp; baby facs; fam bthrm; shwrs
inc; el pts (6A) €3.50; Indtte; shop 7km; tradsmn; rest 10km;
bar; playgrnd; htd pool; games area; dogs €2; adv bkg; quiet;
CKE/CCI. "Friendly Dutch owners; relaxing site in National Park
of Limousin." ◆ 1 May-19 Sep. € 16.20   2012*

FRANCE

TREIGNAC *7B4* (10km NW Rural) *45.57956, 1.70852*
Camp Municipal Le Merle/Badinage, 19370 Chamberet
[05 55 98 30 12 (Mairie); fax 05 55 98 79 34; mairie.
chamberet@wanadoo.fr; www.chamberet-correze.net]
S fr Eymoutiers on D30 or N fr Treignac on D16. In Chamberet
foll sp Camping Badinage, opp lake take rd up past some
houses, site 250m at end. Sm, mkd pitch, hdstg, pt sl, terr,
shd; wc; chem disp (wc); mv service pnt at stadium; shwrs
inc; el pnts (6A) €1.50; gas 1km; lndtte (inc dryers); shop, rest
& bar 1km; BBQ; playgrnd; pool & lake sw 250m; cycle hire;
dogs; quiet; CKE/CCI. "Peaceful site; pay at Camping du Bois
Combet opp (tel 05 55 98 96 83); vg." ♦ ltd 15 Jun-15 Sep.
€ 9.90   2009*

TREIN D'USTOU, LE see Oust *8G3*

TRELEVERN see Perros Guirec *1D2*

TREMBLADE, LA *7B1* (3km W Rural) *45.75849, -1.17420*
Camping Le Pacha, Rue Bouffard, 17390 La Tremblade
[05 46 36 14 44 or 06 16 38 45 46] Sp from D25 bypass
around La Tremblade. Med, shd; wc; shwrs inc; el pnts (10A);
tradsmn; snacks; bar; playgrnd; pool; beach 5km; entmnt; TV;
some statics; dogs; quiet. "Peaceful site amongst pine trees;
san facs old, could be cleaner (2009); Viaduct de la Seudre
3km." Easter-15 Oct. € 22.00   2009*

TREMOLAT see Bugue, Le *7C3*

TREPORT, LE *3B2* (1km N Urban) *50.05805, 1.38860* **Camp**
Municipal Les Boucaniers, Rue Pierre Mendès-France,
76470 Le Tréport [02 35 86 35 47; fax 02 27 28 04 10;
camping@ville-le-treport.fr; www.ville-le-treport.fr] Fr Eu
take minor rd sp to Le Tréport under low bdge. On ent o'skts
of Le Tréport, turn R at traff lts, camp ent 100m on R. Site nr
stadium. Lge, hdstg, pt shd; htd wc; shwrs inc; el pnts (6A)
€4.60; lndtte; shop; rest, snacks; bar; playgrnd; sand beach
2km; games rm; entmnt; TV; 10% statics; dogs €1.60; quiet;
red facs low ssn. "Busy, well-kept, well-run site; some lge
pitches; gd, clean san facs; gd sep m'van area; lots to see in Le
Tréport; m'van Aire de Service adj; gd value; excel" ♦
28 Mar-30 Sep. € 14.55   2013*

TREPORT, LE *3B2* (1km S Coastal) *50.05311, 1.36623* **Camp**
International du Golf, 102 Route de Dieppe, 76470 Le
Tréport [02 27 28 01 50; fax 02 27 28 01 51; evergreen2@
wanadoo.fr] Fr Dieppe, take D925 NE twd Le Tréport for 20km
bef taking D940 sp Floques/Le Tréport. Site on L at top of hill
on o'skts of Le Tréport. Foll sp. Lge, mkd pitch, shd; wc; chem
disp; mv service pnt; 30% serviced pitches; shwrs inc; el pnts
(5A) €4.60; shop 1km; rest, snacks, bar 500m; playgrnd; shgl
beach 600m; fishing; sailing; windsurfing; 10% statics; dogs
€3; poss cr; adv bkg; quiet; red low ssn; ccard acc; CKE/CCI.
"Site neglected (2009); san facs need update; more suitable
tents only; fairly steep hill down fr site to town." 1 Apr-20 Sep.
€ 15.00   2009*

TREPT *9B2* (2.5km E Rural) *45.68701, 5.35190* **Camping Le**
Domaine des Trois Lacs Du Soleil, La Plaine de Serrières,
38460 Trept [04 74 92 92 06; fax 04 74 92 93 35; info@
les3lacsdusoleil.com; www.camping-les3lacsdusoleil.com]
Exit A432 at junc 3 or 3 & head twd Crémieu then Morestel.
Trept bet these 2 towns on D517, site sp by lakes. Lge, pt
shd; wc; chem disp; baby facs; shwrs inc; el pnts (6A) inc;
lndtte (inc dryer); shop; tradsmn; rest, snacks; bar; BBQ (gas);
playgrnd; pool complex; paddling pool; waterslides; lake sw
& beach adj; fishing; tennis; archery; fitness rm; games area;
horseriding 2km; wifi; entmnt; TV rm; 5% statics; dogs €2.50;
phone; adv bkg; Eng spkn; quiet; ccard acc; red low ssn. "Gd
family site; gd, modern san facs." ♦ 1 May-13 Sep.
€ 32.50   2011*

See advertisement

⊞ **TRETS** *10F3* (4km SW Rural) *43.44178, 5.62847* **Camping**
Le Devançon, Chemin de Pourachon, 13790 Peynier
[04 42 53 10 06; fax 04 42 53 04 79; infos@ledevancon.com;
www.ledevancon.com] Leave A8 at Canet or Pas-de-Trets or
leave D6 at Trets & take D908 to Peynier. In vill cont on D908
sp Marseille. Site on R at end vill after g'ge. Med, mkd pitch, all
hdstg, pt sl, shd; htd wc; chem disp; mv service pnt; shwrs inc;
el pnts (3-10A) €3-5; gas; lndtte; shop; tradsmn; snacks; rest &
bar (high ssn) BBQ; playgrnd; pool; paddling pool; sand beach
30km; tennis; entmnt; TV rm; 50% statics; dogs €1; some Eng
spkn; adv bkg; quiet; ccard acc; red long stay/CKE/CCI. "Excel
facs & site; helpful owner; poss diff manoeuvring onto pitches
for lge o'fits; few water points; ltd facs low ssn; gd touring
area." ♦ € 19.00   2010*

TREVIERES *1D4* (Rural) *49.31308, -0.90578* **Camp Municipal Sous Les Pommiers, Rue du Pont de la Barre, 14710 Trévières [02 31 22 57 52 or 02 31 92 89 24; fax 02 31 22 19 49; mairie@ville-trevieres.fr]** Turn S off N13 onto D30 sp Trévières. Site on R on ent to vill. Med, hdg/mkd pitch, pt shd; wc (cont); chem disp; mv service pnt; shwrs inc; el pnts (10A) €3; lndtte; shops 500m; rest; playgrnd; sand beach 10km; rv fishing adj; poss cr; adv bkg rec high ssn; quiet; CKE/CCI. "Delightful site in apple orchard; lge pitches; vg san facs; conv D-Day beaches." ♦ 1 Apr-30 Sep. € 10.60   2011*

TREVIERES *1D4* (3km NE Rural) *49.32530, -0.86480* **Camping La Roseraie d'Omaha, Rue de l'Eglise, 14710 Surrain [tel/fax 02 31 21 17 71; camping-laroseraie@orange.fr; www.camping-laroseraie.com]** Take N13 fr Bayeux twds Cherbourg. In approx 12km take D208 sp Surrain. Site sp in vill. Med, mkd pitch, pt sl, pt shd; wc; el pnts (6A) €4.60; lndtte; shop; snacks; playgrnd; htd pool; tennis; entmnt; 50% statics; dogs €2.50; Eng spkn; adv bkg; quiet. "Friendly recep; touring pitches bet statics; access rds restricted; conv Bayeux & D-Day Museums." ♦ 1 Apr-20 Sep. € 17.30   2009*

"I need an on-site restaurant"

We do our best to make sure site information is correct, but it is always best to check any must-have facilities are still available or will be open during your visit.

TREVOUX see Villefranche sur Saône *9B2*

TRIE SUR BAISE *8F2* (2.5km NE Rural) *43.34400, 0.36970* **Camping Fontrailles, Le Quartier Lanorbe, 65220 Fontrailles [05 62 35 62 52; detm.paddon@orange.fr; www.fontraillescamping.com]** Fr N on N21 leave Mirande & turn L (S) at end of town sp Trie-sur-Baïse onto D939; after St Michel look out for silos on R after 7km, site sp. Fr S at Miélan turn onto D3/D17 sp Trie-sur-Baïse to Fontrailles. Sm, pt sl, pt shd; wc; chem disp (wc); shwrs inc; el pnts (9A) €2.50; shop, rest, snacks & bar 3km; BBQ; playgrnd; pool; tennis; fishing; wifi; dogs; Eng spkn; adv bkg; quiet; red long stay; CKE/CCI. "Delightful, well-kept CL-type site in orchard; friendly, helpful British owners; excel pool & tennis nrby; gd walking; conv Lourdes, Pyrenees & Spain; mkt Trie-sur-Baïse Tues; Excel site; beautiful views" 1 Jul-30 Sep. € 17.00   2012*

TRINITE SUR MER, LA see Carnac *2G3*

TRIZAC see Riom ès Montagnes *7C4*

TROCHE see Uzerche *7B3*

TROGUES see Ste Maure de Touraine *4H2*

TROYES *4E4* (2km NE Urban) *48.31150, 4.09630* **Camp Municipal de Troyes, 7 Rue Roger Salengro, 10150 Pont-Ste Marie [tel/fax 03 25 81 02 64; info@troyescamping. net; www.troyescamping.net]** Fr N exit A26 junc 22 onto D677. site on R opp stadium & adj Esso g'ge, just pass junc with D960. Fr S exit A26 junc 23 for Pont-Ste-Mairie. Pont-Ste-Marie & site 'municipal' well sp fr all dirs & in town. NB Queues form onto rd outside site, use Esso g'ge to turn if queue too long. Med, some hdg/mkd pitch, some hdstg, pt shd; htd wc; chem disp; mv service pnt; shwrs inc; el pnts (10A) (long lead poss req); gas; lndtte (inc dryer); sm shop; tradsmn; supmkt nrby; rest nrby; snacks; takeaway; BBQ; playgrnd; htd pool; cycle hire; games area; games rm; wifi; TV; dogs €1.15; bus opp; poss cr; Eng spkn; adv bkg; ccard acc; red low ssn/long stay; CKE/CCI. "Busy, popular, transit site in parkland - rec arr early; vg pool; some lge pitches; some pitches soft when wet; diff access some pitches; twin-axles acc at recep's discretion; red facs low ssn; Troyes Cathedral, museums & old quarter worth visit; Lac d'Orient & Lac du Temple nrby; conv NH; Gd res by the river bridge 3 min walk from site ent; conv for m'way; pleasant friendly site; clean facs; excel snacks/rest; Stay 7 nights pay for 6" ♦ 1 Apr-15 Oct. € 29.00   2013*

TROYES *4E4* (16km E Rural) *48.28998, 4.28279* **Camping La Fromentelle, Ferme Fromentelle, 10220 Dosches [03 25 41 52 67; fax 03 25 40 78 38; www.tourisme-champagne-ardenne.com]** Exit A26 junc 23 onto D619 dir Bar-sur-Aube. In 8.5km turn L onto D1 sp Géraudot (take care bends). Site on L in 5km. Sm, mkd pitch, pt sl, pt shd; wc; chem disp; mv service pnt; shwrs inc; el pnts (6A) €3 (long lead poss req)(poss rev pol); BBQ; playgrnd; sand beach 5km; lake sw 5km; games area; dogs €1.50; adv bkg; quiet; CKE/ CCI. "Beautiful farm/CL-type site in old orchard; well-kept & well-run; warm welcome, charming owner; clean san facs; gd for birdwatching, sailing, watersports on lakes; excel cycle tracks; nr nature reserve, lakes & forest; conv A26; Facs very clean; Excel spacious pitches; gd facs" ♦ 30 Apr-15 Oct. € 15.00   2013*

TROYES *4E4* (10km SE Rural) *48.20106, 4.16620* **Le Base de Loisirs au Plan D'Eau 'Les Terres Rouges', 10390 Clérey [03 25 46 04 45; fax 03 25 46 05 86; terres-rouges@ wanadoo.fr; www.les-terres-rouges.fr]** Exit A5 junc 21 onto D671 S dir Bar-sur-Seine & Dijon; site on R in 3.5km. Or SE fr Troyes on D671 dir Bar-sur-Seine, foll sp Clérey; then as bef. Site well sp. App over gravel track thro gravel quarry area. Sm, hdstg, pt shd; wc (1 cont); chem disp; shwrs €1; el pnts (5-10A) €3.20 (poss rev pol); shops 4km; tradsmn; rest, snacks; bar; playgrnd; lake sw; tennis; lakes for fishing, waterskiing, boating; 10% statics; dogs; phone; wifi €3 per day; adv bkg; quiet; no ccard acc; CKE/CCI. "Gd, basic NH; clean, v basic san facs; friendly, helpful owners; gate opens 0600; conv fr a'route to Calais" ♦ Easter-30 Sep. € 14.50   2013*

TUFFE *4F1* (1km N Urban) *48.11866, 0.51148* **FFCC Camping du Lac, Route de Prévelles, 72160 Tuffé [02 43 93 88 34; fax 02 43 93 43 54; camping.tuffe@wanadoo.fr; www. camping.tuffe.fr]** Site on D33, sp. Med, hdg/mkd pitch, pt shd; htd wc; chem disp; mv service pnt; baby facs; fam bthrm; shwrs inc; el pnts (6A) €2.50; lndtte; snacks; bar; BBQ; playgrnd; fishing; TV; wifi; lake sw adj; 10% statics; dogs €2; Eng spkn; adv bkg; CKE/CCI. "Well-kept, pretty lakeside site; adj tourist train; clean san facs; friendly staff" ♦ 30 Mar-30 Sep. € 24.70   2013*

FRANCE

TULETTE *9D2* (2.2km S Rural) *44.26485, 4.93180* **Camping Les Rives de L'Aygues, 142 chemin des rives de l'Eygues, 26790 Tulette [tel/fax 04 75 98 37 50; camping.aygues@ wanadoo.fr; www.lesrivesdelaygues.com]** Exit D94 at Tulette onto D193 S; site in 2.2km on L. Site sp. Med, hdg/mkd pitch, hdstg, shd; wc; chem disp; shwrs inc; el pnts (6A) €4.20; gas; tradsmn; snacks; bar; playgrnd; htd pool; direct access to rv; games area; internet; 5% statics; dogs €2.50; phone; Eng spkn; adv bkg; quiet; ccard acc; red low ssn; CKE/CCI. "Lovely, peaceful, family-run site in woodland by Rv Aygue; gd san facs; gd pool; vineyards & lavendar fields nr; excel" ♦ ltd 1 May-25 Sep. € 35.20   2013*

TULLE *7C4* (3km NE Rural) *45.28330, 1.78673* **Camp Municipal Bourbacoup, Ave du Lieutenant-Colonel Faro, 19000 Tulle [05 55 26 75 97; fax 05 55 21 73 62]** Fr Tulle, take D1120 NW dir Limoges. Turn R onto D23 & foll site sp. Med, mkd pitch, pt shd; wc (some cont); shwrs inc; el pnts inc; supmkt 3km; rest, bar 1km; pool 1km; rv adj; dogs; quiet. "Pretty site beside stream; easy cycle ride to town; dated but clean san facs." ♦ 1 Jul-31 Aug. € 11.30   2010*

TULLE *7C4* (4km SE Rural) *45.24992, 1.78948* **Camping Le Pré du Moulin, 19150 Laguenne [tel/fax 05 55 26 21 96; camping@lepredumoulin.com; www.lepredumoulin.com]** Exit Tulle on D1120 twd Aurillac, pass ATAC commercial cent on R, cross bdge & 1st L to camp site. Last 1km on unmade rd, but not diff. Sm, pt sl, pt shd; wc; chem disp; shwrs inc; el pnts (6A) €2.50; gas; lndtte; shops 2km; tradsmn; snacks; pool; rv fishing adj; cycle hire; €1.50; adv bkg rec high ssn; quiet; red low ssn; CKE/CCI. "Attractive, peaceful, well-kept British-owned site; steep climb to adequate san facs" 1 Apr-1 Oct. € 16.00   2010*

TURBALLE, LA see Guérande *2G3*

TURCKHEIM see Colmar *6F3*

TURSAC see Eyzies de Tayac, Les *7C3*

UCHIZY see Tournus *9A2*

UGINE *9B3* (7km NW Rural) *45.76141, 6.33702* **Camping Champ Tillet, 28 Rue Chenevier, 74210 Marlens [04 50 44 33 74; fax 04 50 66 23 44; duchamptillet@ wanadoo.fr; www.champtillet.com]** D1508 S fr Annecy after leaving Lake. Take by-pass past Faverges dir Ugine. After rndabt, site on R at junc bef Marlens, sp. Med, hdg pitch, pt shd; htd wc (some cont); chem disp (wc); baby facs; shwrs inc; el pnts (10A) €4. (poss rev pol); lndtte (inc dryer); shops adj; tradsmn; supmkts 3km; rest, snacks; playgrnd; pool; paddling pool; rv fishing 500m; cycle hire; wifi; some statics; dogs €1; some rd noise - adj extensive cycle track; red low ssn; ccard acc; CKE/CCI. "Gd walks; lovely views; barrier clsd 2300-0700; helpful staff; shops 4km" ♦ 1 Apr-30 Sep. € 39.10   2013*

URBES see St Maurice sur Moselle *6F3*

URCAY *4H3* (6km NE Rural) *46.6430, 2.6620* **Camping Champ de la Chapelle, St Bonnet-Tronçais, 03360 Braize [04 70 06 15 45; info@champdelachapelle; www. champdelachapelle.com]** Fr D2144 take D978A for Tronçais. 1.5km on L fr Rond-de-Montaloyer. Site sp. Med, mkd pitch, pt sl, pt shd; wc; chem disp; shwrs; el pnts (10A) €3.50; lndtte; shop; tradsmn; rest 5km; snacks; bar; playgrnd; pool; lake & rv sw 5km; games area; some statics; dogs €1; Eng spkn; adv bkg; ccard acc; red low ssn/CKE/CCI. "Excel walking & flora/ fauna in ancient oak forest; some lge pitches; peaceful site." 2 Apr-31 Oct. € 14.50   2010*

URRUGNE see St Jean de Luz *8F1*

⊞ **URT** *8F1* (E Rural) *43.49353, -1.27960* **Camping Ferme Mimizan, 64240 Urt [tel/fax 05 59 56 21 51; contact@ lafermedemimizan.fr; www.lafermedemimizan.fr]** E fr Bayonne on A64/E80, exit junc 4 sp Urt; in vill turn sharp R at PO & foll sps; site on R in 1km. Fr N on D12 cross Rv Adour by metal bdge & turn L immed past church, site on R in 1.5km. Med, pt shd; wc; shwrs inc; el pnts (10A) €3.50; playgrnd; pool; paddling pool; wifi; some statics; adv bkg; poss noise fr static residents; red low ssn; CKE/CCI. "V peaceful out of ssn; friendly owners; gd walking & cycling; conv coast & Pyrenees; gd NH." € 19.50   2009*

URT *8F1* (500m S Rural) *43.49165, -1.29677* **Camping Etche Zahar, Allée des Mesplès, 64240 Urt [05 59 56 27 36; fax 05 59 56 29 62; info@etche-zahar.fr; www.etche-zahar.fr]** Exit A64 at junc 4 dir Urt. Fr N on N10 exit junc 9 at St Geours-de-Maremme onto D12 S to Urt, site sp. Fr town cent head W, L at rndabt, L again to site. Sm, hdg pitch, pt sl, pt shd; wc; chem disp; baby facs; shwrs inc; el pnts (10A) €3.50; lndtte (inc dryer); shop 500m; tradsmn; snacks; bar; BBQ; rest 500m; playgrnd; pool; paddling pool; fishing; games area; cycle hire; wifi; entmnt; 25% statics; dogs €2.20 (not acc Aug); phone; Eng spkn; adv bkg; quiet; CKE/CCI. "Peaceful site; welcoming, pleasant owners; gd walking & cycling." ♦ 1 Mar-15 Nov. € 21.30   2010*

USTOU see Oust *8G3*

⊞ **UZER** *9D2* (4km SW Rural) *44.49964, 4.30621* **FLOWER Camping St Amand, 07110 Laurac-en-Vivrais [04 75 36 84 45; st-amand@wanadoo.fr; www. campingsaintamand.com or www.flowercampings.com]** S fr Aubenas on D104 to Uzer; cont past vill; turn L 400m after junc with D4. Med, pt shd; wc (some cont); chem disp; shwrs; baby facs; el pnts (6A) inc; lndtte; tradsmn; rest, snacks; BBQ (gas); playgrnd; pool; paddling pool; games area; entmnt; 30% statics; dogs €1.50; Eng spkn; adv bkg; quiet; ccard acc; red low ssn; CKE/CCI. "Vg touring base; gd walking; peaceful, family site." 3 Apr-25 Sep. € 17.90   2008*

See advertisement on pages 32 & 33

UZERCHE *7B3* (200m SE Rural) *45.42148, 1.56592* **Camp Municipal La Minoterie, Route de la Minoterie, 19140 Uzerche [tel/fax 05 55 73 12 75; nicolas@uzerche.fr; http://camping.uzerche.fr]** Fr N exit A20 at junc 44 for Uzerche on D920; proceed thro tunnel & cross town bdge. Site clearly sp on ent to town on rvside. Steep app rd & sharp bend. NB Narr app rd used by lorries fr nrby quarry. Site well sp. NB Steep exit. Sm, mkd pitch, pt sl, shd; wc; chem disp; shwrs inc; el pnts (10A) €2.90; lndtte; shops 200m; tradsmn; BBQ; playgrnd; fishing; kayak hire; white water sports cent; rock-climbing; tennis; games rm; TV rm; Eng spkn; quiet; CKE/CCI. "Lovely pitches on river's edge; helpful warden; clean san facs; not suitable lge m'vans; sh walk along rv to beautiful old vill; gd local walks; poss risk of flooding; v quiet end of ssn; conv NH; excel." 1 May-2 Oct. € 13.30   2012*

UZERCHE *7B3* (9km SW Rural) *45.36861, 1.53849* **Camp Municipal du Lac du Pontcharal, 19140 Vigeois [05 55 98 90 86 or 05 55 98 91 93 (Mairie); fax 05 55 98 99 79; mairievigeois@wanadoo.fr; www.vigeois.com]** Fr A20 exit 45 onto D3 to Vegeois then D7. Site is 2.5km SE of Vigeois. Med, pt sl, shd; wc; chem disp; shwrs inc; el pnts (15A) €3.50 (poss rev pol); gas; lndtte; shop; rest, snacks; bar; playgrnd; lake sw & beach; fishing; watersports; games area; tennis 2km; entmnt; TV; dogs €0.90; adv bkg; quiet. "Delightful, well-kept site in picturesque setting; excel san facs." ♦ 1 Jun-15 Sep. € 10.70   2012*

UZERCHE *7B3* (9km SW Rural) *45.40833, 1.47898* **FFCC Camping à la Ferme Domaine Vert (Broeks), Les Magnes, 19230 Troche [tel/fax 05 55 73 59 89; www. ledomainevert.nl]** Exit A20 junc 45 onto D3 to Vigeois, 2km after Vigeois turn R onto D50 sp Lubersac. After 5km (ignore sp to Troche) foll site sp to R. NB Narr, twisty rds, not suitable lge o'fits. Sm, pt sl, pt shd; shwrs; lndry rm; el pnts €2.50 (poss rev pol); meals avail; fishing 4km; canoeing nr, lake sw; wifi; dogs €1.50; Eng spkn; quiet; red CKE/CCI. "Popular, peaceful, well-kept farm site; many pitches v sl; welcoming, friendly Dutch owners; adv bkg ess high ssn; lovely lake; vg." 1 Apr-1 Oct. € 17.00   2010*

"Satellite navigation makes touring much easier"

Remember most sat navs don't know if you're towing or in a larger vehicle – always use yours alongside maps and site directions.

UZERCHE *7B3* (12km SW Rural) *45.34632, 1.51493* **Aire Naturelle du Bois Coutal (Veysseix), Perpezac-le-Noir, 19410 Vigeois [05 55 73 71 93; fax 05 55 73 27 66; boiscoutal@wanadoo.fr]** Exit A20/E09 S fr Uzerche at junc 46 onto D920 N & foll sp Perpezac-le-Noir. Go thro Perpezac on D156 N dir Vigeois & foll site sp. Site in 4km. Sm, sl, pt shd; wc; chem disp; shwrs inc; el pnts inc (6A) €2.50; lndtte; shop, rest, snacks, bar 3km; playgrnd; pool; games rm; entmnt; few statics; dogs; poss cr; Eng spkn; adv bkg; v quiet. "Friendly, helpful owner; clean facs; gd NH." 15 Apt-15 Oct. € 9.00   2009*

UZES *10E2* (800m N Rural) *44.02231, 4.42087* **Camping La Paillotte, Quartier de Grézac, 30700 Uzès [04 66 22 38 55; fax 04 66 22 26 66; campinglapaillotte@orange.fr; www. lapailloteuzes.monsite-orange.fr]** Exit A9 junc 23 sp Remoulins. Fr Remoulins take D981 to Uzès. Aim for town cent 1-way ring rd. Site sp clearly. Narr rds for 800m passing cemetery. Med, hdg/mkd pitch, terr, shd; wc; shwrs inc; el pnts (10A) inc; gas; lndtte; shop; tradsmn; rest high ssn; snacks; bar; playgrnd; pool; paddling pool; cycle hire; games area; games rm; entmnt; some statics; adv bkg; quiet; CKE/CCI. "Facs clean but water temperature poss variable; Nice rest" 20 Mar-30 Sep. € 35.00   2013*

UZES *10E2* (2km E Rural) *44.03202, 4.45557* **Camping Le Moulin Neuf, 30700 St Quentin-la-Poterie [04 66 22 17 21; fax 04 66 22 91 82; lemoulinneuf@yahoo.fr; www.le-moulin-neuf.fr]** North fr Uzès on D982; after 3km turn L onto D5; in 1.5km fork R, keeping on D5; in 200m turn R onto D405 (Chemin du Moulin Neuf); site on L in 500m. Med, mkd pitch, pt shd; wc; chem disp; mv service pnt; shwrs inc; el pnts (5A) €3.50; lndtte; shop on site & 2km; snacks; bar; playgrnd; htd pool; fishing; tennis; cycle hire; horseriding; 10% statics; dogs €1.50; o'night m'van area; poss cr; v quiet. "Site off beaten track; busy high ssn, rec phone in adv; conv touring base; barrier clsd 2230-0700; poss mosquito problem; Uzès a lovely town." 1 Apr-25 Sep. € 19.50   2011*

UZES *10E2* (3km SW Rural) *43.99843, 4.38424* **Camping Le Mas de Rey, Route d'Anduze, 30700 Arpaillargues [tel/ fax 04 66 22 18 27; info@campingmasderey.com; www. campingmasderey.com]** Sp fr Uzès. Exit by D982 sp Anduze. After 2.5km cross narr bdge, turn L in 100m on site app rd. Med, hdg/mkd pitch, hdstg, pt sl, shd; wc; chem disp; fam bthrm; shwrs inc; el pnts (10A) €4 (rev pol); lndtte; shop on site & 3km; tradsmn; rest, snacks; bar; BBQ; playgrnd; pool; TV rm; dogs €2; phone; poss cr; Eng spkn; adv bkg; quiet; red low ssn/ snr citizens; CKE/CCI. "Clean, comfortable, busy site; helpful Dutch owners; some v lge pitches; gd for sm children; excel cycling; Uzès interesting." ♦ 1 Apr-15 Oct. € 21.00   2010*

VACQUEYRAS see Carpentras *10E2*

VADENCOURT see Guise *3C4*

VAISON LA ROMAINE *9D2* (500m NE Urban) *44.24518, 5.07886* **Camping du Théâtre Romain, Chemin du Brusquet, 84110 Vaison-la-Romaine [04 90 28 78 66; fax 04 90 28 78 76; info@camping-theatre.com; www. camping-theatre.com]** Fr town cent foll sp for Théâtre Romain & site. Ent to Chemin du Busquet on rndabt at Théâtre Romain. Or site sp off Orange-Nyons rd thro town (do not ent town cent). Med, hdg/mkd pitch, pt shd; htd wc (some cont); chem disp; mv service pnt; serviced pitches; baby facs; shwrs inc; el pnts (5-10A) €3-4.50; gas 500m; lndtte (inc dryer); shop 500m; tradsmn; bar; BBQ; playgrnd; pool; games rm; wifi; some statics; dogs €2; Eng spkn; adv bkg ess high ssn (bkg fee); quiet; ccard acc; red low ssn; CKE/CCI. "Excel, well-kept site; busy low ssn due long stay residents, rec book in adv; mainly gd sized pitches but some sm; most pitches suitable m'vans; clean, unisex san facs; attractive town; mkt Tues; highly rec; excel as usual; old Roman town centre, 10 mins walk from campsite" ♦ 15 Mar-5 Nov. € 37.50   2013*

VAISON LA ROMAINE 9D2 (4km NE Rural) 44.26240, 5.12950 Camping L'Ayguette, 84110 Faucon [04 90 46 40 35 or 06 18 47 33 42 (mob); fax 04 90 46 46 17; info@ayguette. com; www.ayguette.com] Exit Vaison NE on D938, R on D71, thro St Romain-en-Viennois. Then R onto D86 sp Faucon. Site on R, well sp. Med, mkd pitch, terr, shd; htd wc; chem disp; baby facs; shwrs inc; el pnts (10A) €2.50 (poss long lead req); lndtte; shop, supmkt 4km; tradsmn; snacks; bar; BBQ; playgrnd; htd pool; wifi; dogs €1.80; adv bkg; quiet; ccard acc; red low ssn/long stay; CKE/CCI. "Excel, well-run site; lge pitches in forest setting; friendly, helpful owners; excel mod facs inc hairdryers & children's shwrs; tractor tow avail."
1 Apr-30 Sep. € 22.00   2009*

VAISON LA ROMAINE 9D2 (4km NE Rural) 44.26806, 5.10651 Camping Le Soleil de Provence, Route de Nyons, Quartier Trameiller, 84110 St Romain-en-Viennois [04 90 46 46 00; fax 04 90 46 40 37; info@camping-soleil-de-provence.fr; www.camping-soleil-de-provence.fr] Leave A7 at junc 19 Bollène onto D94 dir Nyons. After Tullette turn R onto D20 & then D975 to Vaison-la-Romaine; fr Vaison take D938 sp Nyons; in 4km R & in 150m L to site; well sp. Lge, terr, hdg/mkd pitch, pt shd; htd wc; chem disp; some serviced pitches; shwrs inc; el pnts (10A) €4; gas; lndtte; shop; tradsmn; rest high ssn; snacks; bar; playgrnd; pool; paddling pool; wifi; entmnt; dogs: poss cr; adv bkg; quiet, but weekly disco eves; ccard not acc; red low ssn; CKE/CCI. "Popular, scenic, family-run site; gd pools; lovely town; poss strong Mistral winds Sep; mkt Tues; excel." ♦ 15 Mar-31 Oct. € 23.00   2009*

⊞ **VAISON LA ROMAINE** 9D2 (800m SE Rural) 44.23440, 5.08955 FFCC Camping Club International Carpe Diem, Route de St Marcellin, 84110 Vaison-la-Romaine [04 90 36 02 02; fax 04 90 36 36 90; contact@camping-carpe-diem.com; www.camping-carpe-diem.com or www.campings-franceloc.fr] S on A7 exit Orange; foll sp to Vaison; at Vaison on Nyons rd (D938) turn S at rndabt by supmkt dir Carpentras. In 1km turn L at junc to St Marcellin, site immed on L. Lge, hdg/mkd pitch, terr, pt shd; wc (some cont); chem disp; mv service pnt; shwrs inc; el pnts (6-10A) €4.70-5.70; gas; lndtte; shop on site & 800m; tradsmn; pizzeria, snacks, bar high ssn; playgrnd; 2 pools; paddling pool; waterslide; intrnt; internet; TV rm; 10% statics; dogs €5; site clsd 21 Dec-16 Jan; poss cr; Eng spkn; adv bkg; red low ssn; ccard acc; CKE/CCI. "Lively site; helpful staff; poss dust from nrby quarry; poss muddy pitches; gd san facs; gd cent for Provence" ♦ € 31.00   2013*

VAISON LA ROMAINE 9D2 (6km SE Rural) 44.23728, 5.14959 Camping Les Trois Rivières, Quarter des Jonches, 84340 Entrechaux [04 90 46 01 72; fax 04 90 46 00 75; doc@camping-3rivieres.com; www.camping-les3rivieres. com] Take D938 fr Vaison twd Malaucène for 3.5km. Turn E onto D54 to Entrechaux; site well sp at rndabts at both ends of vill. Narr app rd. Med, pt sl, shd; wc (mostly cont); shwrs; el pnts (3-10A) €2.50-4.50; gas; lndtte; shop 2km; rest, snacks; bar; playgrnd; rv shgl beach, sw & fishing; horseriding; games rm; some statics; wifi; entmnt; TV; some statics; dogs €2; poss cr; quiet; adv bkg; red low ssn. "Tranquil site in Les Gorges du Toulourenc; access diff lge o'fits most pitches; 3km fr Entrechaux; nice walks." 1 Apr-30 Sep. € 14.50   2010*

VAISON LA ROMAINE 9D2 (5km NW Rural) 44.26446, 5.05242 Camping Domaine de La Cambuse, Route de Villedieu, 84110 Vaison-la-Romaine [04 90 36 14 53 or 06 32 18 15 54 (mob); dom.lacambuse@wanadoo.fr; www.domainelacambuse.com] Fr Vaison-la-Romaine N on D51 sp Villedieu. After 4km fork R onto D94 sp Villedieu. Site on R after 300m. Sm, terr, pt shd; wc (some cont); chem disp; shwrs inc; el pnts (6A) €3; gas 4km; tradsmn; snacks, bar in ssn; pool; paddling pool; 5% statics; dogs €1.52; phone; poss cr; quiet; CKE/CCI. "Site in vineyard on hillside; friendly, helpful owners." 1 May-15 Oct. € 11.00   2011*

VAL ANDRE, LE 2E3 (3km S Coastal) 48.58944, -2.55083 Campéole Camping Les Monts Colleux, 26 Rue Jean Le Brun, 22370 Pléneuf-Val-André [02 96 72 95 10; fax 02 96 63 10 49; monts-colleux@campeole.com; www. camping-montscolleux.com or www.campeole.com] Site 800m off D786 & off D78, sp fr Pléneuf town cent. Rec app only fr Pléneuf centre; at traff lts turn twards Les Plages, then site sp - adj municipal pool. Med, hdg/mkd pitch, hdstg, pt sl, pt shd; htd wc; chem disp; mv service pnt; shwrs inc; el pnts (6-10A) €4.10 (poss rev pol); lndtte (inc dryer); shops, rest nr; tradsmn; bar; BBQ; playgrnd; covrd pool adj; sand/shgl beach 300m; tennis; games area; golf 1km; wifi; entmnt; TV rm; 40% statics; dogs €2.60; phone; Eng spkn; adv bkg; quiet; ccard ac; red low ssn/CKE/CCI. "Pleasant combination of gd beach, port & vill with mkt; san facs basic but clean." ♦ 1 Apr-30 Sep. € 17.90   2009*

See advertisement on pages 14 & 15

VAL D'AJOL, LE see Plombières les Bains 6F2

VAL DE VESLE see Reims 3D4

VAL D'ISERE 9B4 (1km E Rural). 45.44622, 6.99218 Camping Les Richardes, Le Laisinant, 73150 Val-d'Isère [tel/fax 04 79 06 26 60; campinglesrichardes@free.fr; http:// campinglesrichardes.free.fr] Leave Val d'Isère going E twds Col de l'Iseran on D902, site on R 1.5km bef Le Fornet vill. Med, pt sl, unshd; wc; shwrs €1; el pnts (3-6A) €1.90-3.80; pool 1.5km; dogs €0.50; quiet; CKE/CCI. "Peaceful site; delightful owner." 15 Jun-15 Sep. € 9.96   2009*

VALENCAY 4H2 (1km W Urban) 47.15656, 1.55202 Camp Municipal Les Chênes, Route de Loches, 36600 Valençay [tel/fax 02 54 00 03 92 or 02 54 00 32 32] App town fr E on D960 or N/S on D956, foll sp for D960 Luçay-le-Mâle. Ignore 1st sp for camping (Veuil); D960 is next L in town. Foll sp for pool & camping. Site adj pool mkd by flags. Sm, hdg/mkd pitch, pt shd; wc; chem disp; shwrs inc; el pnts (6A) €3.20 (poss rev pol); lndtte; shop; tradsmn; BBQ; playgrnd; htd pool adj (high ssn); tennis adj; fishing; TV rm; dogs; adv bkg; quiet; red long stay; CKE/CCI. "Excel, well-kept site in parkland with lake; lge pitches; gd, clean facs; poss muddy after heavy rain; gate clsd 2200-0700; sh walk to impressive chateau; day's drive to Calais or Le Havre ferries." ♦ ltd 1 May-30 Sep.
€ 11.94   2010*

VALENCE 9C2 (7.5km N Rural) 44.99723, 4.89383 **Camping Le Soleil Fruité, Les Pêches, 26300 Chateauneuf-sur-Isère [04 75 84 19 70; fax 04 75 78 05 85; contact@lesoleilfruite. com; www.lesoleilfruite.com]** Exit A7 junc 14 Valence Nord onto D67 sp Chateauneuf-sur-Isère, site sp to W of village. Med, hdg/mkd pitch, pt shd; wc; baby facs; chem disp; mv service pnt; shwrs inc; el pnts (6A) €4; lndtte (inc dryer); shop 8km; tradsmn; rest, snacks, bar; BBQ; playgrnd; pool; paddling pool; wifi; entmnt; TV; 15% statics; dogs €2 (not acc high ssn); no twin-axles; phone; poss cr; Eng spkn; adv bkg; quiet; ccard acc; red low ssn; CKE/CCI. "Vg, family-run site; lge pitches; friendly owner; clean, modern san facs; rest/takeaway open early Jun (2011); ltd water pnts; cycle friendly." ♦ 26 Apr-15 Sep. € 24.60   2011*

VALENCE 9C2 (12km SE Rural) 44.91560, 5.06520 **Camping Sunêlia Le Grand Lierne, 26120 Chabeuil [04 75 59 83 14; fax 04 75 59 87 95; grand-lierne@franceloc.fr; www. grandlierne.com or www.campings-franceloc.fr]** Fr A7 S take Valence Sud exit dir Grenoble. After 8km take D68 on R twd Chabeuil. Turn L at rndabt on o'skts of vill & foll site sp on by-pass; do not go into vill. On arr, park in lay-by at end of app rd & walk to recep to book in. Or app off D125 NE of Chabeuil. Lge, some mkd pitch, hdstg, shd; wc; chem disp; baby facs; shwrs inc; el pnts (6-10A) €4-8; gas; lndtte; shop; rest, snacks; bar; BBQ (gas/elec); playgrnd; htd pool; whirlpool; waterslide; paddling pool; archery; golf 3km; games area; wifi; entmnt; games/TV rm; 80% statics; dogs €5 (no dogs Jul/Aug): no c'vans/m'vans over 7m high ssn; poss cr; Eng spkn; adv bkg rec; poss noisy high ssn; ccard acc; red low ssn; CKE/CCI. "Site in oak forest; friendly staff; clean san facs; gd facs & all-round entmnt; some sm pitches, poss diff lge o'fits; no twin-axles; gd for families; mkt Chabeuil Tue, mkt Valence Thur; gd but regimented!" ♦ 22 Apr-18 Sep. € 31.00   2010*

⊞ **VALENCE** 9C2 (3km S Urban) 44.91871, 4.87561 **Camp Municipal de l'Epervière, Chemin de l'Epervière, 26000 Valence [04 75 42 32 00; fax 04 75 56 20 67; eperviere26@ orange.fr; www.valence-espaces-evenements.com]** Exit A7 at Valence Sud & turn N onto N7, site well sp fr N7. When app fr S on N7 turn L at traff lts 500m after Géant supmkt. Fr N on N7 look for R turn 2km S of Valence. Lge, hdstg, pt shd; htd wc; mv service pnt; shwrs inc; el pnts (10A) €4.90 (poss rev pol); lndtte; supmkt 500m; rest adj; rest, snacks; bar; playgrnd; htd pool; fishing in Rv Rhône; watersports cent adj; games area; TV; 30% statics; site clsd mid-Dec to mid-Jan; poss cr; Eng spkn; no adv bkg; rd noise; ccard acc; red low ssn; CKE/CCI. "Generous pitches in wooded area; clean, dated san facs; office opp side of rd behind other buildings & up steps; pool in hotel complex; poss unkempt low ssn; poss itinerants; excel; v clean, bright, airy san facs; recep now at ent" ♦ ltd 17 Jan-16 Dec. € 17.50   2013*

VALENCE 9C2 (9km NW Rural) 45.00726, 4.84862 **Camp Municipal Les Vernes, 26600 La Roche-de-Glun [04 75 84 54 11 or 04 75 84 60 52 (Mairie); mairie.rdg@ wanadoo.fr; www.ladrometourisme.com]** Turn W off N7 at Pont-d'Isère. On ent La Roche-de-Glun foll camping sp. Sm, hdg/mkd pitch, shd; wc (some cont); serviced pitches; chem disp; shwrs inc; el pnts (10A) €1.40; lndtte; shop 500m; BBQ; htd pool adj in ssn inc; sports cent adj; 50% statics; phone; poss cr; adv bkg; quiet; no ccard acc; red low ssn; CKE/CCI. "Pleasant site; friendly resident warden; gd, clean san facs; vg municipal pool adj; barrier clsd 2200-0700; vg value; vg NH." ♦ 1 May-30 Sep. € 13.90   2011*

VALENCE D'AGEN 8E3 (1km S Rural) 44.09663, 0.88986 **Camp Municipal Val de Garonne, Route des Charretiers, 82400 Valence-d'Agen [05 63 39 61 67; tourisme. valencedagen@wanadoo.fr]** Exit town on D953 sp Auch, turn R after x-ing rv 1st L. Site sp behind pool on R. Sm, pt shd; wc (cont); shwrs; el pnts inc; shops 1km; rest, snacks adj; playgrnd; games area; poss cr; quiet. "Height barrier to car park opened by warden; no external water pnts for m'vans." 1 Jul-31 Aug. € 10.00   2008*

VALENSOLE 10E3 **Domaine du Petit Arlane (Naturist), Route de Riez, 04210 Valensole [04 92 74 82 70; fax 04 92 74 99 35; contact@domainepetitarlane.fr; www. domainepetitarlane.fr]** Leave A51 junction 18 to Valensole 15km, from Valensole take D6 signed Riez, site on left 5km. (Very bendy roads) Med, mkd pitch, some hdstg, pt sl, some terr; chem disp; mv service pnt; shwrs; el pnts (6- 15A) €3.90-8; gas 5km; lndtte (inc dryer); tradsmn; rest; snacks; bar; BBQ; playgrnd; pool; games area; internet; wifi; tv rm; dogs leashed €3.30; twin axles; Eng spkn; adv bkg; ccard acc; 10% statics; inf card advised; "beautiful site, many pitches face lakes; gd local walks from local villages; bkg ess" ♦Ltd € 25.20   2013*

VALLABREGUES see Tarascon 10E2

VALLIERES see Rumilly 9B3

VALLOIRE 9C3 (500m N Rural) 45.17000, 6.42960 **Camp Caravaneige Municipal Ste Thècle, Route des Villards, 73450 Valloire [04 79 83 30 11; fax 04 79 83 35 13; camping-caravaneige@valloire.net; www.valloire.net]** Exit A43 junc 29 onto D306 to St Michel-de-Maurienne, then onto D902 to Valloire. At vill mkt turn R over rv to site. Climb fr valley 15% gradient max. Med, mkd pitch, some hdstg, unshd; htd wc (cont); chem disp; mv service pnt; baby facs; fam bthrm; shwrs inc; el pnts (13A) €3.60; lndtte (inc dryer); shop 300m; rest 500m; bar 200m; playgrnd; pool; paddling pool; waterslide; fishing; tennis; fitness rm; wifi; TV rm; dogs free; phone 100m; bus; Eng spkn; adv bkg; quiet; red long stay; ccard acc. "Superb mountain scenery for walking & cycling; excel." ♦ ltd 12 Dec-23 Apr & 1 Jun-30 Sep. € 18.00   2010*

VALLON EN SULLY 7A4 (500m S Rural) 46.53019, 2.61447 **Camp Municipal Les Soupirs, Allée des Soupirs, 03190 Vallon-en-Sully [04 70 06 50 96 or 04 70 06 50 10 (LS); fax 04 70 06 51 18; mairie.vallonensully@wanadoo.fr; www. vallonensully.com]** N fr Montluçon on N144; in 23km at traff lts where D11 crosses N144 turn L & foll camping sp for Vallon-en-Sully. After bdge over Rv Cher turn L in 50m. Site in 100m. If N or S on A71 exit at junc 9 Vallon-en-Sully; turn N on N144; in 3km at traff lts turn L. Med, pt shd; wc (cont); chem disp (wc); shwrs; el pnts (6-20A) €2-4; shops 500m; rest, snacks, bar adj; TV rm; dogs; bus 500m; adv bkg; quiet. "Peaceful, spacious site on banks of rv & canal; immac san facs; lge pitches; risk of flooding in wet; gd cycling along canal; gd NH; vg." 13 Jun-12 Sep. € 6.00   2009*

VALLON PONT D'ARC *9D2* (9km E Rural) *44.39146,
4.51057* **Camping Carrefour de l'Ardèche, Route de
Bourg-St Andéol, Quartier Gourdaud, 07700 St Remèze
[04 75 04 15 75; fax 04 75 04 35 05; carrefourardeche@
yahoo.fr; www.ardechecamping.net]** D4 E fr Vallon-Pont-
d'Arc. Site on L on bend 500m after St Remèze vill. Med, mkd
pitch, pt shd; wc; chem disp; baby facs; shwrs inc; el pnts (6A)
€3.50; gas; lndtte; shop; snacks; bar; playgrnd; pool; cycle hire;
canoeing; fishing 5km; entmnt; TV; dogs €2.50; adv bkg; quiet;
ccard acc. "Surrounded by vineyards; vg." ♦ 15 Apr-30 Sep.
€ 20.00   2009*

VALLON PONT D'ARC *9D2* (1km SE Rural) *44.39783, 4.40005*
**Camping Le Provençal, Route des Gorges, 07150 Vallon-
Pont-d'Arc [04 75 88 00 48; fax 04 75 88 02 00; contact@
camping-le-provencal.fr; www.camping-le-provencal.fr]**
Fr Aubenas take D579 thro Vallon-Pont-d'Arc to S. Turn L on
D290 N of rv; site on R in 500m (middle of 3 sites). Fr Alès,
N on D904/D104. At St Ambroix turn R onto D51 then D579
to Vallon-Pont-d'Arc. Lge, pt shd; htd wc; shwrs inc; el pnts
(8A) €3.90; gas; lndtte; shop; rest, snacks; bar; playgrnd;
htd pool; canoeing; fishing; sailing; tennis; internet; some
statics; dogs €4; poss cr; Eng spkn; adv bkg; quiet; ccard acc.
"Friendly, helpful staff; site at NW end of spectacular Gorges
de l'Ardèche." ♦ Easter-20 Sep. € 29.50   2008*

VALLON PONT D'ARC *9D2* (1km SE Rural) *44.39777, 4.39861*
**Camping Nature Park L'Ardéchois, Route des Gorges de
l'Ardèche, 07150 Vallon-Pont-d'Arc [04 75 88 06 63; fax
04 75 37 14 97; ardecamp@bigfoot.com; www.ardechois-
camping.com or www.les-castels.com]** Fr Vallon take D290
Rte des Gorges & site on R betd rd & rv. Lge, hdg/mkd pitch,
hdstg, pt sl, shd; htd wc; chem disp; mv service pnt; baby facs;
fam bthrm; serviced pitch (extra charge); private bthrm avail
(by reservation); shwrs inc; el pnts (6-10A) inc; gas; lndtte (inc
dryer); shop; tradsmn; rest, snacks; bar; BBQ; playgrnd; htd
pool; paddling pool; tennis; canoeing; games area; cycle hire;
internet; entmnt; TV rm; dogs €7.70; Eng spkn; adv bkg; quiet;
ccard acc; red low ssn; CKE/CCI. "Spectacular scenery; excel
rvside site; helpful staff; price depends on size of pitch; gd san
facs; 5 star site." ♦ 15 Apr-30 Sep. € 49.00   2011*

VALLON PONT D'ARC *9D2* (1.5km SE Rural) *44.39467,
4.39909* **Mondial Camping, Route des Gorges, 07150
Vallon-Pont-d'Arc [04 75 88 00 44; fax 04 75 37 13 73;
reserv-info@mondial-camping.com; www.mondial-
camping.com]** Fr N exit A7 Montélimar Nord junc 17 onto N7
then N102 dir Le Teil, Villeneuve-de-Berg. Turn S onto D103/
D579 dir Voguë, Ruoms then Vallon-Pont-d'Arc. Take D290,
Rte des Gorges de l'Ardèche to site in 1.5km. Fr S exit A7 junc
19 at Bollène, dir Bourg-St Andéol, then D4 to St Remèze &
Vallon-Pont-d'Arc. App to Vallon fr E thro Gorges de l'Ardeche
not rec. Lge, hdg/mkd pitch, shd; htd wc; chem disp; mv
service pnt; serviced pitches (extra charge); baby facs; shwrs
inc; el pnts (6-10A) inc; gas; lndtte (inc dryer); shop; rest,
snacks; bar; playgrnd; htd pool; paddling pool; waterslides &
aqua park; canoeing; tennis adj; games rm; entmnt; internet;
TV; some statics; dogs €4.50; phone; poss cr; Eng spkn; adv
bkg; quiet; ccard acc; red low ssn/snr citizens; CKE/CCI. "Dir
access to rv, Ardèche gorges & canoe facs; gd touring base;
excel site." ♦ 1 Apr-30 Sep. € 42.00   2011*

VALLON PONT D'ARC *9D2* (3km SE Rural) *44.39333,
4.39465* **Camping Le Clapas, La Vernède, 07150 Salavas
[04 75 37 14 76; contact@camping-le-clapas.com; www.
camping-le-clapas.com]** D579 S fr Vallon-Pont-d'Arc to
Salavas; 250m after Salavas turn L. Well sp. Med, mkd pitch,
pt sl, shd; wc; chem disp; mv service pnt; shwrs inc; el pnts
(10A) €3; lndtte; shop on site & 2km; rest 2km; snacks; bar;
BBQ (gas/elec); playgrnd; direct access to private rv beach;
rv sw; fishing; canoeing; rafting; canyoning; games area;
games rm; wifi; entmnt; TV rm; dogs €2; poss cr; Eng spkn;
adv bkg; quiet; ccard acc; red low ssn; CKE/CCI. "Beautiful,
well-kept site by Rv Ardèche; friendly, helpful staff; poss diff
lge o'fits; conv Ardèche Gorges; excel." ♦ ltd 23 Apr-20 Sep.
€ 20.00   2010*

VALLON PONT D'ARC *9D2* (800m W Rural) *44.40509,
4.37827* **Camping La Roubine, Route de Ruoms, 07150
Vallon-Pont-d'Arc [tel/fax 04 75 88 04 56; roubine.
ardeche@wanadoo.fr; www.camping-roubine.com]**
Site on W side of Vallon-Pont-d'Arc off D579, well sp by
rvside. Med, hdg/mkd pitch, pt shd; htd wc; chem disp; mv
service pnt; baby facs; shwrs inc; el pnts (10A) €4.50; gas;
lndtte (inc dryer); shop; rest, snacks; bar; playgrnd; htd pool;
sm waterslide; rv & sand beach adj; fishing; canoeing; tennis;
cycle hire; games area; wifi; entmnt; TV rm; 20% statics; dogs
€4; Eng spkn; adv bkg; quiet; ccard acc. "Excel, well-run site in
lovely area; excel rest; guided walks high ssn." ♦
23 Apr-9 Sep. € 47.00   2011*

VALLON PONT D'ARC *9D2* (2km W Rural) *44.4086, 4.3542*
**Camping La Plage Fleurie, Les Mazes, 07150 Vallon-
Pont-d'Arc [04 75 88 01 15; fax 04 75 88 11 31; info@
laplagefleurie.com; www.laplagefleurie.com]** Site on main
'Route Touristique' of Ardèche: D579, 4.5km SE of Ruoms turn R
at sp La Plage Fleurie in 1.5km. Fr N sp easily missed; no sp fr S.
Lge, mkd pitch, pt sl, terr, shd; wc; baby facs; shwrs inc; chem
disp; el pnts (10A) €4.20; gas; lndtte; shop on site & 1.5km;
tradsmn; snacks; rest; bar; BBQ; playgrnd; pool; sand beach &
rv; canoe hire; fishing; sailing; entmnt; TV rm; 10% statics; dogs
€4; Eng spkn; adv bkg rec high ssn; quiet; red low ssn; CKE/CCI.
"Conv Gorges de l'Ardèche; gd position on rvside; excel san
facs." ♦ 24 Apr-13 Sep. € 29.90   2008*

VALLON PONT D'ARC *9D2* (2km W Rural) *44.41251, 4.35018*
**Camping L'Arc en Ciel, Route de Ruoms, Les Mazes, 07150
Vallon-Pont-d'Arc [04 75 88 04 65; fax 04 75 37 16 99;
info@arcenciel-camping.com; www.arcenciel-camping.
com]** Fr Ruoms take D579 dir Vallon. After 4km bear R for Les
Mazes. Pass thro vill & in about 1.7km bear L at camp sp. Lge,
pt sl, pt shd; wc; baby facs; shwrs; el pnts (10A) €4; lndtte;
shop; rest, snacks; bar; playgrnd; pool; paddling pool; shgl
beach & rv; fishing; canoeing; tennis, horseriding nr; games rm;
wifi; entmnt; some statics; dogs €3.50; poss cr; adv bkg; quiet;
ccard acc; red low ssn. "Pleasant site on rv bank; excel." ♦
3 Apr-1 Oct. € 31.00   2010*

VALLON PONT D'ARC 9D2 (2km W Rural) 44.40645, 4.36448 Camping Le Beau Rivage, Les Mazes, 07150 Vallon-Pont-d'Arc [tel/fax 04 75 88 03 54; campingbeaurivage@ wanadoo.fr; www.beaurivage-camping.com] Take D579 W fr Vallon. After approx 1km bear L for Les Mazes at rndabt. After 800m turn L down side rd for site. Med, mkd pitch, terr, shd; wc (some cont); chem disp; baby facs; shwrs; el pnts (6A) €3.90; gas; lndry rm; shop on site & 2km; tradsmn; rest 2km; bar; BBQ; playgrnd; htd pool; fishing; sailing; canoe hire; entmnt; TV rm; 5% statics; dogs €2; phone; poss cr; Eng spkn; ccard acc; red low ssn; CKE/CCI. "Vg quality, clean, family site; dir access to rv; friendly owners; poss diff access some pitches for lge o'fits due trees; excel." 1 May-13 Sep. € 24.00   2009*

VALLON PONT D'ARC 9D2 (3km W Rural) 44.42332, 4.31565 Camping Le Chassezac, Route d'Alès, 07120 Sampzon [04 75 39 60 71 or 06 81 96 68 76 (mob); fax 04 75 39 76 35; info@campinglechassezac.com; www. campinglechassezac.com] Fr Aubenas S on D579. Approx 2.5km past Ruoms at rndabt, turn R onto D111. Foll sp 2km to site on R. Med, mkd pitch, pt shd; wc (some cont); chem disp; mv service pnt; baby facs; shwrs inc; el pnts (6A) €3.90; lndtte; shop; rest, snacks; bar; BBQ (gas only); playgrnd; pool; rv adj; fishing; cycle & canoe hire; horseriding; TV; 15% statics; dogs €2; phone; o'night m'van area; poss cr; Eng spkn; adv bkg; quiet; CKE/CCI. "Friendly, helpful staff; vg." ♦ ltd 1 Apr-30 Sep. € 20.50 (CChq acc)   2008*

VALLON PONT D'ARC 9D2 (5km NW Rural) 44.42900, 4.35515 FLOWER Camping Le Riviera, 07120 Sampzon [04 75 39 67 57; fax 04 75 93 95 57; leriviera@wanadoo.fr; www.campingleriviera.com or www.flowercampings.com] Fr Ruoms take D579 E twd Vallon-Pont-d'Arc. After 2km turn R over narr bdge twd Sampzon on D161. Site immed on L. Lge, mkd pitch, pt shd; wc; chem disp; mv service pnt; shwrs inc; el pnts (10A) inc; gas; lndtte; shop 100m; rest, snacks; bar; BBQ; playgrnd; pool; paddling pool; rv & shgl beach adj; tennis; games rm; cycle hire; horseriding; entmnt; TV rm; some statics; dogs €4; poss cr; some rd noise; red low ssn. "Attractive pools." 1 Apr-30 Sep. € 40.00   2009*

See advertisement on pages 32 & 33

VALLON PONT D'ARC 9D2 (5km NW Rural) 44.42958, 4.35528 Yelloh! Village Soleil Vivarais, 07120 Sampzon [04 75 39 67 56 or 04 66 73 97 39; fax 04 75 39 64 69; info@soleil-vivarais.com; www.soleil-vivarais.com or www.yellohvillage.co.uk] Fr Ruoms take D579 E twd Vallon-Pont-d'Arc. After 2km turn R over narr bdge twd Sampzon on D161. Site immed on R. Lge, hdg/mkd pitch, shd; wc; chem disp; mv service pnt; baby facs; shwrs inc; el pnts (10A) inc; gas; lndtte; shop; rest, snacks; bar; playgrnd; pool; shgl beach & rv 500m; canoe hire; tennis; games rm; entmnt Jul/Aug; TV; 50% statics; dogs €3; poss cr; Eng spkn; adv bkg; quiet; ccard acc. "Interesting area; busy site in gd location; sm pitches poss diff lge o'fits; gd entmnt." ♦ 15 Apr-11 Sep. € 42.00   2008*

See advertisement on inside front cover

VALLORCINE 9A4 (1km SE Rural) 46.0242, 6.92370 Camping des Montets, Le Buet, 74660 Vallorcine [04 50 54 60 45 or 04 50 54 24 13 (LS); fax 04 50 54 01 34; camping.des. montets@wanadoo.fr; http://camping-montets.com] N fr Chamonix on D1506 via Col de Montets; Le Buet 2km S of Vallorcine; site sp nr Le Buet stn. Fr Martigny (Switzerland) cross border via Col de la Forclaz; then D1506 to Vallorcine; cont to Le Buet in 1km. Med, hdg/mkd pitch, pt shd; wc (some cont); chem disp (wc); shwrs inc; el pnts (3-6A) €2-3; lndtte; shops 1km; sm rest; tradsmn; snacks; tennis adj; no statics; dogs; train 500m; Eng spkn; quiet; red long stay; CKE/CCI. "Site with spectacular views; friendly owners; ltd flat pitches for c'vans/m'vans (others for tents in field), rec phone ahead; clean san facs; excel walking direct fr site; free train pass to Chamonix; vg." ♦ ltd 1 Jun-15 Sep. € 16.00   2011*

VALLOUISE see Argentière La Bessée, L' 9C3

VALOGNES 1C4 (1km N Urban) 49.51154, -1.47534 Camp Municipal Le Bocage, Rue Neuve, 50700 Valognes [02 33 95 82 03 or 06 10 84 59 33 (mob); environement@ mairie-valognes.fr; www.mairie-valognes.fr] Off N13 Cherbourg to Carentan take 1st exit to Valonges, turn L just past Champion at Lidl sp; site sp bef & in town. Fr Carentan dir, take 3rd R after 4th set traff lts. Sm, hdg/mkd pitch, hdstg, pt shd; wc; chem disp (wc); shwrs inc; el pnts (10A) €3.55 (poss rev pol); gas; supmkt 100m; rest, snacks, bar nr; dogs €0.66; poss cr; quiet; ccard not acc; CKE/CCI. "Super little site; clean san facs; friendly staff; conv Cherbourg ferries (17km) & town; poss itinerants; warden calls 1900-2000, site self if office clsd; gates clsd 2200-0600; ideal NH; Excel as always" ♦ 1 Apr-15 Oct. € 14.60   2012*

VALRAS PLAGE 10F1 (500m N Urban/Coastal) 43.25416, 3.28861 Camping Le Levant, Ave Charles Cauquil, 34350 Valras-Plage [04 67 32 04 45; camping.dulevant@free.fr; www.campingdulevant.com] Exit A9 junc 35 onto D64 twd Valras-Plage. At rndabt junc with D19, turn L into Ave Charles Cauquil, site sp. Med, hdg mkd pitch, pt shd; htd wc; chem disp; mv service pnt; baby facs; shwrs inc; el pnts (10A) inc; lndtte; ltd shop; tradsmn; snacks; bar; BBQ; playgrnd; htd pool; paddling pool; sand beach 800m; games area; games rm; wifi; 40% statics; dogs €4; Eng spkn; adv bkg; quiet; red low ssn; CKE/CCI. "Well-cared for, family-run site; friendly & helpul; gd san facs; vg early ssn; excel." 16 Apr-18 Sep. € 35.00   2011*

VALRAS PLAGE 10F1 (1km N Coastal) 43.25670, 3.28480 Camping Les Sables du Midi (formerly L'Occitanie), Chemin de Querelles, 34350 Valras-Plage [04 67 32 33 86; www.siblu.fr/lessablesdumidi] Fr A9/E15 exit junc 35 at Béziers Est & join D64 sp Valras-Plage. Site is immed on L after rndabt at ent to Valras-Plage Est. Lge, hdg/mkd pitch, hdstg, pt sl, shd; htd wc; chem disp; mv service pnt; baby facs; shwrs inc; el pnts (5A) inc (poss rev pol); lndtte; shop 1km; tradsmn; rest, snacks; bar; BBQ (gas/charcoal only); playgrnd; pool; paddling pool; waterslide; sand beach 1km; sailing; fishing; games area; wifi; entmnt; games/TV rm; 75% statics; no dogs; c'van/m'van max 7m Jul/Aug; poss cr; Eng spkn; adv bkg; ccard acc; red low ssn/long stay; CKE/CCI. "Lively town; mkt Mon & Fri am." ♦ 1 Jun-11 Sep. € 48.00   2009*

VALRAS PLAGE *10F1* (3km SW Coastal) *43.23750, 3.26166* Camping Domaine de la Yole, 34350 Valras-Plage [04 67 37 33 87; fax 04 67 37 44 89; info@campinglayole. com; www.campinglayole.com] Leave A9/E15 at Béziers-Ouest junc 36; foll D64 twd coast dir Valras-Plage, then Valras-Plage-Ouest & site sp. V lge, hdg/mkd pitch, hdstg, shd; wc (some cont); chem disp; mv service pnt; baby facs; shwrs inc; el pnts (5A) inc; gas; lndtte (inc dryer); supmkt; rest, snacks; bar; BBQ (charcoal/gas); playgrnd; 2 pools; paddling pool; waterslide; sand beach 400m; tennis; cycle hire; horseriding 3km; games area; games rm; wifi; entmnt; TV; tour ops statics; dogs €4.50 (not on beach); poss cr; Eng spkn; adv bkg; quiet but some rd noise; ccard acc; red low ssn; CKE/CCI. "Excel site; v busy high ssn; some gd sized pitches - book ahead high ssn; gd for all age groups; mkt Mon & Fri." ♦ 23 Apr-17 Sep. € 49.50 SBS - C03   2010*

VALRAS PLAGE *10F1* (3km SW Coastal) *43.23101, 3.25330* Camping Les Vagues, Chemin des Montilles, 34350 Vendres-Plage [04 67 37 33 12; fax 04 67 37 50 36; contact@lesvagues.net; www.sandaya.fr] Exit A9 junc 36 onto D64 to Valras-Plage then Vendres-Plage. Site sp. Lge, pt shd; wc; baby facs; shwrs inc; el pnts (10A) inc; lndtte (inc dryer); shop; rest, snacks; bar; playgrnd; htd pool complex inc wave machine; paddling pool; waterslides; jacuzzi; sand beach 400m; games area; horseriding 5km; wifi; entmnt; TV rm; 75% statics; dogs €7; adv bkg; red low ssn. "Recep helpful; clean san facs; excel." ♦ 1 Apr-30 Sep. € 51.00   2010*

See advertisement on pages 88 & 89

VALRAS PLAGE *10F1* (5km NW Rural) *43.29273, 3.26710* Camping La Gabinelle, 7 Rue de la Grille, 34410 Sauvian [04 67 39 50 87 or 04 67 32 30 79; info@lagabinelle.com; www.lagabinelle.com] Exit A9 at Béziers Ouest, turn R twd beaches sp S to Sauvian on D19. Site 500m on L thro town. Med, pt shd; wc; chem disp; shwrs inc; el pnts (5A) €3; lndtte; shops, rest, snacks adj; bar; playgrnd; pool; sand beach 5km; fishing 1km; canoeing 2km; tennis; games area; games rm; entmnt; TV; dogs €3.50; adv bkg; quiet, but poss noise fr bar; red low ssn/long stay. "Friendly; suitable lge m'vans; low ssn ltd san facs & poss unkempt; sh walk to delightful old vill." ♦ 12 Apr-12 Sep. € 19.00   2009*

VALREAS *9D2* (1km N Rural) *44.39264, 4.99245* Camping La Coronne, Route de Pègue, 84600 Valréas [04 90 35 03 78; fax 04 90 35 26 73; la.coronne@wanadoo.fr; www. campings-vaucluse.com] Fr Nyons take D538 W to Valréas. Exit town on D10 rd to Taulignan, immed after x-ing bdge over Rv Coronne turn R into D196 sp Le Pègue. Site on R in 100m on rvside. Sp app fr E but easy to miss; app fr W; well sp in Valréas. Med, hdg/mkd pitch, pt shd; wc (some cont); chem disp; mv service pnt; shwrs inc; el pnts (6A) inc; gas; lndtte; shop; tradsmn; rest, snacks; bar; BBQ; playgrnd; pool; paddling pool; fishing; wifi; entmnt; TV; dogs €4; phone; poss cr; Eng spkn; adv bkg; quiet; ccard acc; red low ssn; CKE/CCI. "Sm pitches; excel pool; facs need refurb & poss unclean; site clsd 2200-0700." ♦ ltd 1 Apr-31 Oct. € 22.00   2011*

VALREAS *9D2* (7km NE Rural) Camp Municipal La Rochecourbière, Ave du Grillon, 26230 Grignan [04 75 46 50 06; mairie.grignan@wanadoo.fr; www. ville-grignan.fr] Sp at E end of D541 bypass of Grignan; Ave du Grillon runs NE off D541; site in 100m. Do not go into town. Sm, hdg/mkd pitch, pt sl, pt shd; wc (some cont); chem disp (wc); shwrs inc; el pnts inc; dogs; quiet. "Unspoilt, simple site outside ramparts of historic town; clean, modern san facs; if office clsd site self or contact Mairie; gd." ♦ 1 Jul-31 Aug. € 13.00   2010*

VALREAS *9D2* (8km W Rural) *44.41131, 4.89112* Camping Les Truffières, 1100 Chemin de Bellevue-d'Air, Nachony, 26230 Grignan [tel/fax 04 75 46 93 62; info@lestruffieres. com; www.lestruffieres.com] Fr A7 take D133 E twds Grignan. On W o'skts of vill turn S on D71. In 1km turn L at sp. Site is 200m on R. Fr Nyons take D538 W to Grignan. Sm, mkd pitch, shd; wc; chem disp; mv service pnt; shwrs inc; el pnts (10A) €4.20; gas; lndtte; shop 1km; tradsmn, rest, snacks high ssn; bar; communal BBQ only; playgrnd; pool; fishing; 5% statics; no dogs; Eng spkn; adv bkg; quiet; red low ssn; CKE/CCI. "Excel, well-wooded site by lavendar fields; pleasant owners; immac san facs; gd pool; some pitches diff access; site poss dusty; 20 min stroll to town" ♦ 20 Apr-30 Sep. € 31.50   2013*

VANDENESSE EN AUXOIS *6G1* (3km NE Rural) *47.23661, 4.62880* Camping Le Lac de Panthier, 21320 Vandenesse-en-Auxois [03 80 49 21 94; fax 03 80 49 25 80; info@lac-de-panthier.com; www.lac-de-panthier.com] Exit A6 junc 24 (A38) at Pouilly-en-Auxois; foll D16/D18 to Vandenesse; turn L on D977bis, cross canal bdge & cont strt for 3km to site on L. Fr SW (Autun) on D981 approx 12km after Arnay-le-Duc turn R onto D994 sp Châteauneuf. At x-rds cont onto D977bis then as above. Lge, hdg/mkd pitch, pt sl, terr, pt shd; wc; chem disp (wc); sauna; baby facs; shwrs inc; el pnts (6A) inc (some rev pol); lndtte (inc dryer); shop on site & 6km; rest, snacks; bar; BBQ; playgrnd; 2 pools (1 htd, covrd); paddling pool; waterslide; sand beach 50m; fishing; cycle hire; wifi; entmnt; sat TV; dogs €3; adv bkg ess; Oct open Fri, Sat & Sun; CKE/CCI. "Lovely area; views fr higher pitches; well-run site operating with Les Voiliers adj; lge pitches, most sl & blocks req; facs poss stretched high ssn; gd cycling & walks round lake; popular NH; vg." ♦ 9 Apr-8 Oct. € 28.00   2011*

VANDIERES see Dormans *3D4*

⊞ **VANNES** *2F3* (5km N Rural) *47.73035, -2.72795* Camping du Haras, 5 Kersimon-Vannes/Meucon, 56250 Monterblanc [02 97 44 66 06 or 06 71 00 05 59 (mob); fax 02 97 44 49 41; contact@campingvannes.com; www. campingvannes.com] App fr N165 turn L onto D767 sp Airport. Go N for 7km & turn R onto D778 for 1km & turn R again. After 1km approx, turn L onto Airport Perimeter Rd, site sp on W side. App fr N on D767, join D778 & as above. Med, hdg/mkd pitch, hdstg, pt shd; htd wc; chem disp; mv service pnt; fam bthrm; shwrs inc; el pnts (4-16A) €3-8; gas; lndtte (inc dryer); sm shop; tradsmn; snacks; bar; BBQ; playgrnd (covrd); htd pools (covrd); paddling pool; waterslides; sauna; wellness cent; sand beach 12km; lake sw 3km; fishing; tennis; horseriding 300m; trampoline; cycle hire; outdoor fitness; games rm; wifi €2; 30% statics; dogs €4; Ltd facs low ssn; NH; Eng spkn; adv bkg; quiet with minimal airplane noise in the day; ccard acc; red long stay/long ssn/CKE/CCI. "Lovely site; ltd space for tourers; rec" ♦ € 36.00   2013*

FRANCE

VANNES *2F3* (3km S Rural) *47.62754, -2.74117* **FFCC Camping Moulin de Cantizac, 2 Rue des Orchidées, 56860 Séné [tel/fax 02 97 66 90 26; info@camping-vannes.com; www.camping-vannes.com]** S fr Vannes on D199 twds Séné. Site on L at rndabt beside rv. Med, hdg pitch, pt sl, pt shd; wc (some cont); chem disp; baby facs; shwrs inc; el pnts (10A) €3.90; gas; lndtte (inc dryer); tradsmn; sm shop; snacks; playgrnd; htd pool; sand beach 4km; boating; games area; games rm; wifi; 10% statics; dogs €2.30; quiet; red low ssn. "Superb cent for birdwatching." 1 May-15 Oct. € 21.90 2010*

VANNES *2F3* (3km SW Coastal) *47.63365, -2.78008* **FFCC Camp Municipal de Conleau, 188 Ave Maréchal Juin, 56000 Vannes [02 97 63 13 88; fax 02 97 40 38 82; camping@mairie-vannes.fr; www.mairie-vannes.fr]** Exit N165 at Vannes Ouest junc; Conleau sp on R. Site twd end of rd on R. If on N165 fr Auray take 1st exit sp Vannes & at 2nd rndabt R (sp) to avoid town cent. C'vans not allowed thro town cent. Lge, mkd pitch, pt sl, pt shd; wc; chem disp; mv service pnt; shwrs; el pnts (6A) €3.50 (some rev pol); lndtte; tradsmn; playgrnd; sea water pool nr; sand beach 300m; entmnt; TV; dogs €1.50; bus adj; adv bkg; quiet; ccard acc. "Most pitches sl; sep area for m'vans by rd - little shd & poss long walk to san facs." ♦ 1 Apr-30 Sep. € 17.30 2008*

See advertisement on pages 32 & 33

VANNES *2F3* (5km SW Coastal) *47.62190, -2.80056* **Camping de Penboch, 9 Chemin de Penboch, 56610 Arradon [02 97 44 71 29; fax 02 97 44 79 10; camping.penboch@ wanadoo.fr; www.camping-penboch.fr]** Exit Brest-Nantes N165 Vannes by-pass at junc with D127 sp Ploeren & Arradon. Foll sp Arradon. Site well sp. Lge, hdg/mkd pitch, pt shd; wc (some cont); chem disp; mv service pnt; baby facs; shwrs inc; el pnts (10A) inc (poss rev pol); lndtte (inc dryer); sm shop on site & 2km; tradsmn; sm shop; snacks; bar; BBQ; playgrnd; 2 htd pools (1 covrd); paddling pools; waterslide; sand beach 200m; cycle hire 2km; games area; games rm; wifi; TV rm; some statics; dogs €3.50; no c'vans/m'vans over 7m high ssn; Eng spkn; adv bkg rec high ssn; quiet; ccard acc; red low ssn; CKE/CCI. "Excel site; gd clean san facs; some pitches sm; steel pegs req; o'flow area with facs; plenty for youngsters; 20 mins walk to Arradon; gd coast walks." ♦ 6 Apr-28 Sept. € 58.50 SBS - B33 2012*

VANNES *2F3* (6km SW Coastal) *47.62108, -2.84025* **Camping de l'Allée, 56610 Arradon [02 97 44 01 98; fax 02 97 44 73 74; www.camping-allee.com]** Fr Vannes take D101 & D101A to Arradon. Take by-pass & take 1st exit at rndabt & foll sp. Site to SW of Arradon. Fr Auray on D101 turn R on C203 immed after Moustoir. Med, some hdg/mkd pitch, pt sl, pt shd; wc; chem disp; baby facs; shwrs inc; el pnts (10A) €4.60 (poss long leads req); gas; lndtte; sm shop on site & 2km; tradsmn; snacks; playgrnd; htd pool; shgl beach 600m; games/TV rm; 5% statics; dogs €2; Eng spkn; adv bkg; quiet; red low ssn; CKE/CCI. "Delightful, family-run site partly in orchard; site yourself if office clsd; immac modern san facs; gd walks; gd touring base; highly rec" ♦ 1 Apr-30 Sep. € 19.15 2013*

VANS, LES *9D1* (3.5km NW Rural) *44.41613, 4.09229* **Camping Le Mas du Serre, 07140 Gravières [04 75 37 33 84; camping-le-mas-du-serre@wanadoo.fr; www.campinglemasduserre.com]** NW fr Les Vans on D901 dir Villefort; in 2km turn R onto D113 dir Gravières; in 1.5km turn R bef bdge. NB Awkward turn downhill. Foll site sp. Recep in cent of site. Med, pt sl, pt terr, hdstg, shd; wc (some cont); chem disp (wc); shwrs inc; el pnts (6A) €3 (long lead poss req); supmkt 4km; snacks; bar; pool; paddling pool; boating on rv nrby; canyoning & caves nrby; games area; entmnt; 10% statics; dogs €1.50; adv bkg; quiet; red low ssn. "Beautiful scenery; san facs clean but ltd; gd walking." 1 Apr-1 Oct. € 18.50 2009*

> ## "There aren't many sites open at this time of year"
>
> If you're travelling outside peak season remember to call ahead to check site opening dates – even if the entry says 'open all year'.

VANS, LES *9D1* (5km NW Rural) *44.43722, 4.08028* **Camping Les Gorges de Chassezac, Champ d'Eynes, 07140 Malarcesur-la-Thines [04 75 39 45 12; campinggorgeschassezac@ wanadoo.fr; www.campinggorgeschassezac.com]** Fr Les Vans cent, dir Gravière, approx 5km thro Gravière cont, site on L. Med, mkd pitch, pt sl, terr, shd; wc (many cont); chem disp; shwrs; el pnts (6A) €3; gas; lndtte; shop; tradsmn; snacks; bar; playgrnd; rv adj; TV; dogs €1; entmnt; poss cr; Eng spkn; adv bkg; quiet; CKE/CCI. "Peaceful site." ♦ ltd 1 May-31 Aug. € 14.00 2010*

VARADES see Ancenis *2G4*

VARCES ALLIERES ET RISSET see Grenoble *9C3*

VARENNES EN ARGONNE *5D1* (N Rural) *49.22935, 5.03424* **Camp Municipal Le Pâquis, Rue St Jean, 55270 Varennesen-Argonne [03 29 80 71 01 (Mairie); fax 03 29 80 71 43; mairievarennesenargonne@wanadoo.fr]** On D946 Vouziers/Clermont-en-Argonne rd; sp by bdge in vill, on banks of Rv Aire, 200m N of bdge. NB Ignore sp by bdge to Camping Lac Vert (not nr). Med, pt shd; wc; shwrs inc; el pnts (3-6A) €2.90; lndtte; shops adj; BBQ; playgrnd; rv fishing; dog €0.40; quiet. "Pleasant site with gd facs; gd (hilly) cycle ride taking in US WWI cemetary." 24 Apr-1 Oct. € 7.90 2009*

VARENNES SUR LOIRE see Saumur *4G1*

⊞ **VARILHES** *8G3* (Urban) *43.04714, 1.63096* **FFCC Camp Municipal du Parc du Château, Ave de 8 Mai 1945, 09120 Varilhes [05 61 67 42 84 or 05 61 60 55 54 (TO); campingdevarilhes@orange.fr; www.campingdevarilhes. com]** Exit N20/E9 at sp Varilhes. Turn N in town on D624. Site 250m on L (sp) just bef leisure cent adj Rv Ariège. Med, mkd pitch, terr, pt shd; htd wc; mv service pnt; baby facs; shwrs inc; el pnts (5-10A) €5.90-6.40; lndtte; shops adj & 200m; tradsmn; rest 200m; snacks; bar 300m; playgrnd; pool adj; rv fishing adj; games area; wifi; 20% statics; dogs; adv bkg; quiet. ♦ € 18.00 2012*

FRANCE

⊞ **VARILHES** *8G3* (3km NW Rural) *43.06258, 1.62101*
FFCC Camping Les Mijeannes, Route de Ferriès, 09120
Rieux-de-Pelleport [05 61 60 82 23; fax 05 61 67 74 80;
lesmijeannes@wanadoo.fr; www.campinglesmijeannes.
com] Exit N20 sp Varilhes; on app Varilhes cent join 1-way
system; 1st R at Hôtel de Ville; over rv bdge; foll camp sps; site
2km on R. Med, hdg pitch, pt shd; htd wc; mv service pnt;
chem disp; shwrs inc; el pnts (10A) €4.60; tradsmn; bar; BBQ;
playgrnd; pool; volley; badminton; fishing; kids club; entmnt;
games area; TV; dogs €1.10; some Eng spkn; adv bkg; quiet;
red low ssn; CKE/CCI; ACSI; "Peaceful site by rv - on island
formed by rv; helpful owner; gd size pitches; excel san facs;
weekly theme nights high ssn; excel." € 20.00   2013*

VARREDDES see Meaux *3D3*

VARZY *4G4* (1km N Rural) *47.37242, 3.38311* **Camp
Municipal du Moulin Naudin, 58210 Varzy [03 86 29 43 12;
fax 03 86 29 72 73]** Fr N151 in Varzy, turn N onto D5, site sp.
Sm, pt shd; some hdg pitch; wc; shwrs inc; el pnts (6A) inc;
tradsmn; shops 1.5km; fishing; tennis nrby; quiet. "Quiet site
on edge of town; gd NH." 30 Apr-1 Oct. € 12.00   2011*

VATAN *4H3* (8km N Rural) *47.13479, 1.85121* **Camp
Municipal St Phalier, 2 Chemin Trompe-Souris, 18310
Graçay [02 48 51 24 14 or 02 48 51 42 07 (Mairie); fax
02 48 51 25 92; camping-gracay@wanadoo.fr; www.
camping.gracay.info]** Leave A20 at junc 9 & take D83 to
Graçay. On o'skts of vill turn L & immed turn L foll sp to
Cent Omnisport & site. Sm, pt shd; wc (some cont); chem
disp; shwrs €1.02; el pnts (10A) €2.69; rest, bar & shop 1km;
tradsmn; playgrnd & pool adj; fishing; dogs €1.02; phone; Eng
spkn; quiet; CKE/CCI. "Lovely, peaceful, well-kept site by sm
unfenced lake & park; plenty of space lge o'fits - site yourself;
excel clean san facs; poss itinerants, but no problem; vill in
walking dist; gd NH fr A20." 1 Apr-15 Sep. € 10.40   2013*

VATAN *4H3* (1km S Rural) *47.06540, 1.80043* **Camping Le
Moulin de la Ronde (Naturist), Route de la Ronde, 36150
Vatan [02 54 49 83 28; www.moulindelaronde.com]**
Fr town cent take D136 S twds A20; at supmkt turn R; site on L
500m; sp. Sm, hdg/mkt pitch, pt shd; htd wc; chem disp; shwrs
inc; el pnts (10A) €2.50 (long lead poss req); gas 1km; supmkt
400m; tradsmn; snacks; bar; BBQ; playgrnd; pool; games
area; games rm; dogs €1.60; adv bkg; quiet; red low ssn/
long stay; INF card req. "Pleasant, simple site; helpful owners;
dated & modern san facs; mkt Wed; gd NH." 1 Apr-30 Sep.
€ 16.50   2011*

VATAN *4H3* (500m W Urban) *47.07131, 1.80573* **Camp
Municipal de la Ruelle au Loup, Rue du Collège, 36150
Vatan [02 54 49 91 37 or 02 54 49 76 31 (Mairie); fax
02 54 49 93 72; camping-mairie1@wanadoo.fr; www.vatan-
en-berry.com]** Exit A20 junc 10 onto D922 to town cent. Take
D2 dir Guilly & foll site sp - 2nd on L (easily missed). Med, hdg/
mkd pitch, pt shd; wc; mv service pnt; shwrs inc; el pnts (10A)
€3 (rev pol); lndtte; shops, rests 200m; playgrnd; pool adj; adv
bkg; quiet; ccard not acc; CKE/CCI. "Pleasant, well-kept site
in park; spacious pitches; basic but clean san facs; twin-axles
extra; site yourself; warden calls pm; easy access fr a'route;
conv Loire chateaux." ♦ 15 Apr-15 Sep. € 15.00   2011*

VAUVERT *10E2* (5km SE Rural) *43.65440, 4.29610* **FLOWER
Camping Le Mas de Mourgues, Gallician, 30600 Vauvert
[tel/fax 04 66 73 30 88; info@masdemourgues.com;
www.masdemourgues.com or www.flowercampings.
com]** Exit A9 junc 26 onto D6313/D6572. Site on L at x-rds
with D779 sp to Gallician & Stes Marie-de-la-Mer. Med, mkd
pitch, pt shd; wc; chem disp; mv service pnt; shwrs inc; el pnts
(6A) inc; lndtte; shop; snacks; BBQ; pool; games area; internet;
15% statics; dogs €3; phone; Eng spkn; adv bkg; rd & farming
noise; ccard acc; red low ssn; CKE/CCI. "Enthusiastic, helpful
British owners; some diff, long narr pitches; ground stony;
clean facs but poss stretched high ssn; excel pool; excel
cycling; gd; vg site" ♦ 15 Mar-31 Oct. € 30.90   2013*

See advertisement on pages 32 & 33

VAUX SUR MER see St Palais sur Mer *7B1*

VAYRAC *7C4* (3.5km S Rural) *44.93462, 1.67981* **FFCC
Camping Les Granges, Les Granges-de-Mezel, 46110
Vayrac [05 65 32 46 58; fax 05 65 32 57 94; info@les-
granges.com; www.les-granges.com]** App Vayrac on D803;
turn S at square in town sp "Campings"; site in 3.5km on
banks of Rv Dordogne. Sp in Vayrac. Alt rte fr D803 in St Denis-
les-Martel on D80 S - shorter on narr rds; site sp. Lge, pt shd;
wc; shwrs inc; el pnts (10A) €4; gas; lndtte; shop; rest, snacks;
bar; playgrnd; pool; paddling pool; fishing; canoeing; cycling;
games area; entmnt; TV; dogs €1.60; adv bkg; quiet; red low
ssn. "Vg children's amenities; facs fair; poss mosquitoes."
8 May-20 Sep. € 20.20   2012*

VEDENE see Avignon *10E2*

VEIGNE see Montbazon *4G2*

VEIX see Treignac *7B4*

VELLES see Châteauroux *4H2*

VENAREY LES LAUMES *6G1* (600m W Urban) *47.54448,
4.45043* **Camp Municipal Alésia, Rue du Docteur Roux,
21150 Venarey-les-Laumes [tel/fax 03 80 96 07 76 or
03 80 96 01 59 (Mairie); camping@ville-venareyleslaumes.fr;
www.venareyleslaumes.fr]** SE fr Montbard on D905, site
well sp fr Venarey on D954. Med, hdg/mkd pitch, hdstg, pt
shd, some hdstg; htd wc; shwrs inc; el pnts (16A) €3; lndtte
(inc dryer); shops 1km; tradsmn; BBQ; playgrnd; sand beach
& lake sw; cycle hire; TV rm; some statics; dogs €1; phone;
poss cr; Eng spkn; adv bkg; red low stay; ccard acc; CKE/CCI.
"Well-kept site in scenic area; lge pitches; pleasant wardens;
gd, clean san facs; barrier clsd 2200-0700; cycle tracks to Canal
de Bourgogne" ♦ 1 Apr-15 Oct. € 12.00   2013*

Nature, Tranquillity and Relaxation… between the sea and the mountains, in the heart of the Côte d'Azur, an ideal base to discover the coast and the rear country.

FRANCE

VENCE *10E4* (3km W Rural) *43.7117, 7.0905* **Camping Domaine La Bergerie, 1330 Chemin de la Sine, 06140 Vence [04 93 58 09 36; fax 04 93 59 80 44; info@ camping-domainedelabergerie.com; www.camping-domainedelabergerie.com]** Fr A8 exit junc 47 & foll sp Vence thro Cagnes-sur-Mer. Take detour to W around Vence foll sp Grasse/Tourrettes-sur-Loup. At rndabt beyond viaduct take last exit, foll site sp S thro La Sine town; long, narr rd to site, up driveway on R. Lge, mkd pitch, hdstg, pt sl, shd; wc; chem disp; mv service pnt; baby facs; shwrs inc; el pnts (5A); gas; lndtte; shop on site & 5km; tradsmn; rest, snacks; bar; BBQ (gas only); playgrnd; pool; paddling pool; lake fishing; tennis; games area; dogs; poss cr; Eng spkn; adv bkg; quiet; ccard acc; red long stay/low ssn; CKE/CCI. "Shady site; helpful staff; clean san facs; no twin-axles or c'vans over 5m; gd dog walks; Vence lovely & excel touring base" ♦ 25 Mar-15 Oct. € 26.00 (CChq acc) 2013*

See advertisement

VENCE *10E4* (6km W Rural) *43.69958, 7.00785* **Camping Les Rives du Loup, Route de la Colle, 06140 Tourrettes-sur-Loup [04 93 24 15 65; fax 04 93 24 53 70; info@ rivesduloup.com; www.rivesduloup.com]** Exit A8 junc 47 at Cagnes-sur-Mer. Foll sp La Colle-sur-Loup, then Bar-sur-Loup (D6). Site in Gorges-du-Loup valley, 3km bef Pont-du-Loup. Sm, pt shd; wc; baby facs; shwrs inc; el pnts (5A) €3.50 (poss rev pol); lndtte; shop; rest, snacks; bar; playgrnd; pool; fishing; tennis; guided walks; horseriding 5km; wifi; 60% statics; dogs €3.50; adv bkg; quiet. "Many activities avail; beautiful location; cramped pitches" 1 Apr-30 Sep. € 29.50 2013*

VENDAYS MONTALIVET *7C1* **Camping Village Vacances Les Acacias, Route de St-Vivien, 33590 Vensac [05 56 09 58 81; fax 05 56 09 50 67; contact@les-acacias-du-medoc.fr; www.les-acacias-du-medoc.fr]** Via Bordeaux exit 8 on the A10 dir Le Verdon/Pointe de Grave. Lge, mkd pitch, pt shd; wc; chem disp; baby facs; shwrs inc; el pnts (6A) inc; gas; lndtte; shop; market (once a wk); rest; bar; BBQ; playgrnd; pool (solar htd); paddling pool; cycle hire; wifi; dogs €3.50; adv bkg. "Set in woodlands; friendly staff - welcome drink on Sun; v gd site." ♦ 01 Apr-30 Sep. € 24.50 2011*

VENDAYS MONTALIVET *7C1* (6km NE Rural) *45.39875, -1.04828* **Camp Municipal du Vieux Moulin, 15 Route du Moulin, 33590 Vensac [tel/fax 05 56 09 45 98 or 06 64 64 13 12 (mob); campingduevieuxmoulin@vensac-medoc.com; www.campingduvieuxmoulin.fr]** Turn off D1215 to Vensac. Foll sp to windmill (moulin à vent), which is adj site. Site is 500m to W of Vensac. Med, pt shd, mkd pitch; wc; chem disp; shwrs inc; el pnts (3A) €3; lndtte (inc dryer); shop; rest, snacks; bar; BBQ (charcoal, sep area); playgrnd; pool; sand beach 8km; surfing, sand yachting & horseriding 8km; games area; games rm; wifi; entmnt; TV; 65% statics; dogs €1.50; adv bkg; quiet; ccard acc; CKE/CCI. "Excel ambiance; ltd facs low ssn; tourers in sep field; now municipal site - many changes planned (2010)." ♦ ltd 17 Mar-31 Oct. € 14.60 2010*

VENDAYS MONTALIVET *7C1* (1km S Rural) *45.35285, -1.05985* **Camping Les Peupliers, 17 Route de Sarnac, 33930 Vendays-Montalivet [tel/fax 05 56 41 70 44; lespeupliers33@hotmail.com; www.camping-montalivet-lespeupliers.com]** NW fr Lesparre-Médoc on D1215 for 9km. Then W on D102 to Vendays-Montalivet. In town cent foll D101 twd Hourtin. Turn L in 100m (sp), site on L in 200m. Med, mkd pitch, shd; wc; chem disp; baby facs; shwrs inc; el pnts (4-6A) €2.80-3.50; gas; lndtte; shop 400m; tradsmn; snacks; BBQ; playgrnd; pool; sand beach 10km; entmnt; fitness rm; TV rm; cycle hire; 10% statics; dogs €2; phone; Eng spkn; adv bkg; quiet; red long stay/low ssn; ccard acc; CKE/CCI. "Friendly owners; excel san facs; poss ltd el pnts high ssn; excel cycle paths adj; conv Médoc vineyards." ♦ 1 May-30 Sep. € 15.00 2008*

VENDAYS MONTALIVET *7C1* (3km W Rural) *45.36698, -1.09885* **Camping Le Mérin, 7 Route de Mérin, 33930 Vendays-Montalivet [tel/fax 05 56 41 78 64; www.campinglemerin.com]** NW fr Lesparre-Médoc on D1215 for 9km; then W on D102 to Vendays-Montalivet. Cont on D102 twds Montalivet-les-Bains. Site on L in 3km. Lge, hdg pitch, pt shd; wc; shwrs; el pnts (6-10A) €2.80-3.30; lndtte; shop 3km; tradsmn in ssn; BBQ; playgrnd; sand beach 4km; fishing; cycle hire; games area; entmnt; 5% statics; dogs €1; adv bkg; CKE/CCI. "Working farm; basic facs; gd." 1 Apr-31 Oct. € 11.50 2010*

VENDAYS MONTALIVET *7C1* (6km W Coastal) *45.37040, -1.14442* **Camp Municipal de Montalivet, Ave de l'Europe, 33930 Vendays-Montalivet [05 56 09 33 45; fax 05 56 09 33 12; campingmunicipal-vendays@wanadoo.fr]** Take D101 fr Soulac to Vendays, D102 to Montalivet-les-Bains. Site sp bef ent to Montalivet. Turn L at petrol stn, site 500m on L. V lge, mkd pitch, shd; wc; chem disp; mv service pnt; shwrs inc; el pnts inc; lndtte; shop; rest, snacks; bar; playgrnd; paddling pool; beach 700m; dogs €1.87; quiet; adv bkg. "Site in pine forest; gd mkt 1km; naturist beaches N & S of Montalivet." ♦ 1 May-30 Sep. € 14.70 (CChq acc) 2010*

⊞ **VENDAYS MONTALIVET** *7C1* (6km W Coastal) *45.36325, -1.14496* **Camping CHM Montalivet (Naturist), 46 Ave de l'Europe, 33340 Vendays-Montalivet [05 56 73 26 81 or 05 56 73 73 73; fax 05 56 09 32 15; infos@chm-montalivet. com; www.chm-montalivet.com]** D101 fr Soulac to Vendays-Montalivet; D102 to Montalivet-les-Bains; site bef ent to vill; turn L at petrol stn; site 1km on R. V lge, mkd pitch, pt sl, pt shd; wc; chem disp; mv service pnt; shwrs inc; el pnts (6A) inc; gas; lndtte (inc dryer); 2 supmkts; rests; snacks; bar; playgrnd; htd pool; sand beach adj; games area; games rm; cycle hire; wifi; entmnt; wifi; TV rm; 50% statics; dogs €6.90; phone; poss cr; Eng spkn; adv bkg; quiet; red long stay/low ssn; ccard acc; INF card. "Vast, peaceful site in pine forest; superb lge naturist beach adj; excel facs for children of all ages; vg." ♦ ltd € 40.00 2011*

⊞ **VENDOIRE** *7B2* (3km W Rural) *45.40860, 0.28079* **Camping du Petit Lion, 24320 Vendoire [05 53 91 00 74; info@lepetitlion.co.uk; www.lepetitlion.co.uk]** S fr Angoulême on D939 or D674, take D5 to Villebois-Lavalette, then D17 to Gurat. Then take D102 to Vendoire, site sp. Sm, hdg pitch, some hdstg, pt shd; htd wc; shwrs inc; el pnts (10A) €3; lndtte; sm shop on site & 7km; rest, snacks; bar; playgrnd; pool; paddling pool; lake fishing; tennis; internet; 10% statics; dogs €2; rally fields; British owners; adv bkg; quiet; CKE/CCI. ♦ ltd € 11.00 2010*

"That's changed – Should I let The Club know?"

If you find something on site that's different from the site entry, fill in a report and let us know. See www.caravanclub.co.uk/europereport

VENDOME *4F2* (500m E Urban) *47.79122, 1.07586* **Camping au Coeur du Vendôme, Rue Geoffroy-Martel, 41100 Vendôme [02 54 77 00 27; www.aucoeurdevendome.com]** Fr N10 by-pass foll sp for town cent; in town foll sp Camping; site adj to pool 500m. Lge, mkd pitch, pt shd; wc; chem disp; baby facs; shwrs inc; el pnts (6A) €3.20; lndry rm; shops, rest & bar 500m; BBQ; playgrnd adj; htd pool adj; rv fishing adj; games area adj; 5% statics in sep area; dogs €1.80; phone; some Eng spkn; quiet but some rd noise; ccard not acc; red long stay; CKE/CCI. "Pleasant rvside setting; new ownership (2011) & improvements in hand; clean san facs - a trek fr outer pitches; sports cent, pool & theatre adj; recep 0900-2100; barrier clsd 2200-0630; vg." ♦ 15 May-15 Sep. € 15.00 (CChq acc) 2011*

VENDOME *4F2* (8km W Rural) *47.80206, 0.95835* **Camp Municipal de la Bonne Aventure, Route de Cunaille, 41100 Thoré-la-Rochette [02 54 72 00 59; fax 02 54 89 41 01; camping@cpvendome.com]** Fr Vendôme take D917 twd Montoire. After 6km turn R onto D82 for Thoré; thro vill & cont to vill exit sign, foll site sp. NB: there are 2 rds to Montoire - foll sp to vill. Med, pt shd; wc; chem disp; shwrs; el pnts (5A) €2.70 (long lead poss req); lndtte; shop 2km; tradsmn; snacks; fishing & watersports adj; playgrnd; tennis; entmnt; games area; dogs €1; Eng spkn; adv bkg; CKE/ CCI. "Peaceful, pretty site by Rv Loir; well-kept facs; helpful warden; gd." 6 Jun-1 Sep. € 10.00 2010*

VENOSC see Bourg d'Oisans, Le *9C3*

VENSAC see Vendays Montalivet *7C1*

VERCHAIX see Samoëns *9A3*

VERDON SUR MER, LE *7B1* (Rural/Coastal) *45.54068, -1.09335* **Camping Le Royannais, 88 Route de Soulac, 33123 Le Verdon-sur-Mer [05 56 09 61 12; fax 05 56 73 70 67; camping.le.royannais@wanadoo.fr; www. royannais.com]** Fr Bordeaux on D1215 dir Le Verdon-sur-Mer (Royan); on o'skts of Verdon, 100m beyond sp 'Royan Ahead, Verdon Right' turn R dir Verdon (by large buoy); site on L in 200m. Med, mkd pitch, hdstg, pt shd; htd wc; chem disp; baby facs; serviced pitches; shwrs inc; el pnts (4-6A) €4.70-5.80; gas; lndtte; shop; snacks; bar; BBQ; playgrnd; pool complex; waterslide; beach 400m; cycle hire; 40% statics; dogs €2.80; phone; bus; Eng spkn; adv bkg; quiet; red long stay; CKE/CCI. "Charming wooded site; gd shwrs; ferry to Royan 30 mins." ♦ 1 Apr-15 Oct. € 19.00 2008*

VERDUN *5D1* (1km SW Urban) *49.15428, 5.36598* **Camping Les Breuils, 8 Allée des Breuils, 55100 Verdun [03 29 86 15 31; fax 03 29 86 75 76; contact@camping-lesbreuils.com; www.camping-lesbreuils.com]** Fr W (Paris) on A4/E50, exit junc 30 onto D1916/D603/D330; cont over rndabt junc with D34 onto D330; at next rndabt in 100m turn R into Allée des Breuils. Or fr E (Metz) exit junc 31 onto D964/D330; cont on D330 past junc with D34A; at rndabt in 150m turn L into Allée des Breuils. Site sp nr Citadel. Avoid Verdun town cent due to 1-way streets. Allée des Breuils runs parallel to D34 on E side of rwly. Site well sp fr D603 & all other directions. Steepish ent. Lge, hdg/mkd pitch, some hdstg, pt sl, pt shd; wc; chem disp; mv service pnt; baby facs; shwrs inc; el pnts (6A) €4.40 (poss some rev pol); gas; lndtte; sm shop on site & 3km; tradsmn, rest, snacks & bar (high ssn); playgrnd; pool; waterslide; cycle hire; fishing; sports cent; wifi; dogs €1.90; phone; poss cr; Eng spkn; adv bkg rec high ssn; little rlwy noise; ccard acc; red low ssn/long stay; CKE/ CCI. "Pleasant, clean, well-kept, busy site; grass pitches beside lge pond, some lge; poss long walk to water taps; some site rds tight for lge o'fits; gd pool; poss lge youth groups Sept; interesting historial town; cycle rtes around WWI battlefields; easy walk to Citadel with WWI museum; excel; gd rest; friendly staff; san block a little tired, poss stretched if site full, otherwise vg" ♦ ltd 1 Apr-30 Sep. € 29.00 2013*

VERDUN *5D1* (6km NW Rural) *49.20998, 5.36567* **FFCC Camp Municipal sous Le Moulin, 55100 Charny-sur-Meuse [03 29 84 28 35 or 03 29 86 67 06 (LS); fax 03 29 84 67 99; mairie.charny.sur.meuse@wanadoo.fr; www.charny-sur-meuse.fr]** N fr Verdun on D964; turn L onto D115 to Charny-sur-Meuse; site sp. Med, pt sl, pt shd; wc (all cont) (own san rec); mv service pnt; shwrs inc; el pnts (6A) €2.50; fishing; dogs €1; CKE/CCI. "CL-type site; open pitches round lake; facs adequate; useful touring base; conv WWI sites; gd." 1 May-30 Sep. € 7.00   2011*

VERDUN SUR GARONNE *8E3* (300m NE Rural) *43.85789, 1.24124* **FFCC Camping Le Grand Gravier, Chemin des Allées, 82600 Verdun-sur-Garonne [05 63 64 32 44 or 05 63 26 30 64 (LS); camping@garonne-gascogne.com; www.garonne-gascogne.com]** Exit A20/E09 at junc 68 onto A72 & exit junc 10 onto D820 S to Grisolles. At rndabt turn R onto D813 NW for 3km, then L at rndabt onto D6 W sp Verdun-sur-Garonne. Cross rv bdge; site sharp R in 200m. Med, hdg pitch, pt shd; wc (mainly cont); mv service pnt; shwrs inc; el pnts (6A) €2.80; shop 1km; BBQ; playgrnd; rv fishing; tennis; games rm; 30% statics; dogs €1; adv bkg; quiet; red long stay; CKE/CCI. "Pleasant, interesting site; next to fast flowing rv, poss floods in wet weather; gd facs." 22 May-5 Sep. € 9.40   2010*

VERDUN SUR LE DOUBS *6H1* (500m W Rural) *46.90259, 5.01777* **Camp Municipal La Plage, Quai du Doubs Prolongé, 71350 Verdun-sur-le-Doubs [03 85 91 55 50 or 03 85 91 52 52; fax 03 85 91 90 91; mairie. verdunsurledoubs@wanadoo.fr; www.tourisme-verdun-en-bourgogne.com]** SE on D970 fr Beaune to Verdun-sur-le-Doubs & foll sp in town. Or on D973 or N73 twd Chalon fr Seurre, turn R onto D115 to Verdun; site on bank of Rv Saône. Lge, mkd pitch, pt sl, shd; wc (some cont); chem disp; shwrs inc; el pnts (10A) €2.10; shops 500m; rest, snacks & bar 500m; BBQ; playgrnd; htd pool adj; waterslide; fishing; tennis; wifi; dog €1; phone; quiet. "Lovely rvside location; lge pitches; helpful warden; interesting sm town; confluence of 3 rivers: La Saône, Le Doubs & La Dheune; fishermen's paradise; excel." May-Sep. € 9.20   2011*

VERMENTON *4G4* (500m W Rural) *47.65897, 3.73087* **Camp Municipal Les Coullemières, route de Coullemières, 89270 Vermenton [03 86 81 53 02; fax 03 86 81 63 95; contact@camping-vermenton.com; www.camping-vermenton.com]** Lies W of D606 - turn off D606 into Rue Pasteur (tight turn & narr rd), strt on at x-rds into Ave de la Gare. Turn R at stn, L over level x-ing. Well sp in vill adj to rv but sps low down & easy to miss. Med, hdg/mkd pitch, pt shd; htd wc (some cont); chem disp; shwrs inc; el pnts (6A) €3; lndtte; shop 500m; rest 200m; playgrnd; tennis; fishing, boating; cycle hire; TV rm; 5% statics; dogs €1; bus; adv bkg rec high ssn; quiet; ccard acc. "Peaceful, well-run rvside site; gd facs; absolutely immac; weight limit on access rds & pitches; no twin-axles; gd walks & cycling; conv Chablis vineyards; beautiful town with 12thC church; Excel site; staff helpful" ♦ 1 Apr-30 Sep. € 17.90   2013*

VERMENTON *4G4* (2km W Rural) *47.66199, 3.70493* **Camp Municipal Le Moulin Jacquot, Route de Bazarnes, 89460 Accolay [tel/fax 03 86 81 56 48 or 03 86 81 56 87 (Mairie); mairie.accolay@wanadoo.fr]** N fr Vermenton on N6 dir Auxerre; in 2km turn L onto D39 sp Accolay. Cross bdge, turn R thro vill; site on R at 200m adj Canal du Nivernais. Sm, mkd pitch, shd; wc; chem disp; mv service pnt; shwrs inc; el pnts (6A) €2.20; lndtte; shops, rest 300m; bar 200m; playgrnd; adv bkg; quiet; ccard not acc; red long stay; CKE/CCI. "Site yourself; grassy pitches poss boggy; pleasant sm vill; caves 11km; gd, flat cyling along canal." ♦ ltd 1 Apr-1 Oct. € 8.20   2009*

VERNANTES *4G1* (2km E Rural) *47.38996, 0.06797* **Camping Intercommunal de la Grande Pâture, Route de Vernoil, 49390 Vernantes [02 41 51 45 39; contact@camping-grande-pature.com; www.camping-grande-pature.com]** Fr Saumur on N147. Take D767 to Vernantes then D58 dir Vernoil. Site sp. Sm, pt shd; wc; mv service pnt; shwrs inc; el pnts (10A) €1.80; shop 200m; rest; BBQ; playgrnd; tennis; fishing adj; some statics; adv bkg; quiet; CKE/CCI. 15 Jun-30 Sep. € 8.00   2009*

VERNANTES *4G1* (4km E Rural) *47.38310, 0.10036* **Camping La Sirotière, La Sablonnière, 49390 Vernoil-le-Fourrier [02 41 67 29 32; ann.bullock@orange.fr]** Fr Vernantes foll sp Vernoil & Super U; at rndabt (Super U on L) strt over & at end vill (at Barthelemy sp on L) turn R sp La Sablonnière. Foll rd up hill & turn R 300m after 2nd x-rds sp, & foll long drive to site. If coming fr Noyant (N) on D767 do not use satnav after Noyant, but foll dirs above. Fr A85 exit junc 2 onto D53 to St Philbert & Vernantes, then as above. Sm, pt sl, pt shd; htd wc; chem disp; shwrs inc; el pnts (10A) inc; lndtte; shop on site & bar 1km; rest 2km; cycle hire; dogs by request; Eng spkn; adv bkg; quiet; no ccard acc. "Peaceful CL-type site; British owners; adults only; site yourself if no reply at bell; vg." 1 Mar-31 Dec. € 13.00   2009*

VERNANTES *4G1* (4km NW Rural) *47.43700, 0.00600* **Camping La Fortinerie, La Fortinerie, 49390 Mouliherne [02 41 67 59 76; north.john.a@gmail.com; www. lafortinerie.com]** Fr Vernantes take D58 dir Mouliherne; opp Château Loroux (Plaissance) turn L; at x-rds turn R, site over 1.5km on L. Sm, pt shd; wc; chem disp; mv service pnt; shwrs inc; el pnts (16A) €5 (poss rev pol); ice; shop 4km; rest & bar 3km; BBQ; no statics; dogs free (by arrangement); B&B avail; adv bkg; quiet. "Peaceful CL-type site; only sound is crickets! Lge pitches; helpful, friendly British owners; beautiful chateau town; conv Loire valley & vineyards; excel." ♦ ltd 1 May-30 Sep. € 10.00   2011*

⊞ **VERNANTES** *4G1* (9km NW Rural) *47.4304, 0.0397* **Camping Le Chant d'Oiseau, 49390 Mouliherne [02 41 67 09 78; info@loire-gites.com; www.loire-gites.com]** Fr Saumur take D767 twd Noyant. Turn L in Vernantes then R onto D58 twd Mouliherne. Foll this rd to gatehouse of Chateau du Louroux then 1st R opp 'Plaisance' farm. Foll rd for 1km. Site on R. Fr Mouliherne on D58 for 3km, turn L at x-rds with wooden cross. Fork R in 700m, site on L. NB App by bumpy forest road. Sm, pt sl, pt shd; wc; chem disp; shwrs inc; el pnts (6A) €5; BBQ; pool; cycle hire; wifi; some statics; dogs (low ssn only); Eng spkn; quiet. "Wonderful CL-type site; helpful, friendly British owners; gd facs but poss unkempt & not suitable winter stay; gd birdwatching." ♦ ltd € 18.50 2008*

VERNET see Auterive *8F3*

VERNET LES BAINS *8G4* (1km N Rural) *42.55506, 2.37756*
Camping L'Eau Vive, Chemin de St Saturnin, 66820 Vernet-les-Bains [04 68 05 54 14; fax 04 68 05 78 14; contact@
leauvive-camping.com; www.leauvive-camping.com]
On app to town cent on D116 turn R over rv & site 1st R
1km at end of rd. Med, mkd pitch, terr, pt shd; wc; chem
disp; serviced pitch; mv service pnt; shwrs inc; el pnts (6-10A)
€3-4.50; lndtte; shop 1km; tradsmn; rest, snacks; bar; BBQ;
playgrnd; pool; waterslide; tennis 500m; games area; TV rm;
40% statics; dogs €2; Eng spkn; quiet; red low ssn. "Beautiful
area; friendly owners; gd walking; site rec." ♦ 29 Apr-30 Sep.
€ 22.00   2010*

VERNET LES BAINS *8G4* (2km N Rural) *42.56598, 2.38864*
Camping Las Closes, Route de Fillois, 66820 Corneilla-de-Conflent [04 68 05 66 48 or 06 81 85 14 46 (mob); www.
las-closes.fr] Exit N116 at Villefranche-de-Conflent onto D116
dir Vernet-Les-Bains; in 2km turn L into Corneilla-de-Conflent.
Foll sp, site approx 1km. Med, mkd pitch, pt sl, terr, pt shd; wc
(some cont); chem disp; shwrs inc; el pnts (10A) €3.20; lndtte;
shop 500m; playgrnd; pool; wifi; dogs free; phone; adv bkg;
CKE/CCI. "Beautiful views; helpful owners; interesting area." ♦
1 Apr-30 Oct. € 11.80   2010*

VERNET LES BAINS *8G4* (2km NE Rural) *42.56567, 2.41984*
Camping Les Sauterelles, Col de Millères, 66820 Fillols
[tel/fax 04 68 05 63 72] Fr Perpignan take N116 to Prades,
then D27 S. Foll sps to Chalet des Cortalets. Suitable for sm
o'fits. Med, pt sl, pt shd; wc (cont); mv service pnt; shwrs;
el pnts (5A) €3; shop; snacks; bar; BBQ; playgrnd; pool; no
dogs; phone; adv bkg; quiet. "Attractive site; friendly owners;
mountain walking, caves, vineyards; historical locations; gd
views." ♦ 1 Jun-30 Sep. € 11.00   2008*

VERNET LES BAINS *8G4* (3km NW Rural) *42.56255, 2.36050*
Camping Le Rotja, Ave de la Rotja, 66820 Fuilla [tel/
fax 04 68 96 52 75; info@camping-lerotja.com; www.
camping-lerotja.com] Take N116 fr Prades dir Mont-Louis,
500m after Villefranche-de-Conflens turn L onto D6 sp Fuilla;
in 3km just bef church, turn R at sp to site. D6 narr but passing
places. Sm, mkd pitch, pt sl, terr, pt shd; htd wc; chem disp;
baby facs; shwrs inc; el pnts (10A) €3.25; gas; lndtte; shop
2km; rest 100m; snacks; BBQ (gas); playgrnd; pool; rv adj;
10% statics; dogs €2; phone; Eng spkn; adv bkg; quiet; ccard
acc; red long stay; CKE/CCI. "Peaceful site; views of Mount
Canigou; friendly Dutch owners; gd hiking." ♦ 1 Apr-31 Oct.
€ 20.25   2010*

VERNET, LE *9D3* (800m N Rural) *44.28170, 6.39080* Camping
Lou Passavous, Route de Roussimat, 04140 Le Vernet
[04 92 35 14 67; fax 04 92 35 09 35; loupassavous@
orange.fr; www.loupassavous.com] Fr N on A51 exit junc
21 Volonne onto N85 sp Digne. Fr Digne N on D900 to Le
Vernet; site on R. Fr S exit A51 junc 20 Les Mées onto D4,
then N85 E to Digne, then as above. Sm, pt sl, pt shd; htd wc;
chem disp; baby facs; shwrs inc; el pnts (10A) €3.75; lndtte;
shop; tradsmn; rest, snacks; bar; playgrnd; pool; fishing; games
area; wifi; entmnt; TV; some statics; dogs €1.50; poss cr; Eng
spkn; adv bkg; quiet; ccard acc; CKE/CCI. "Scenic location;
gd, clean facs; Dutch owners; gd walking." ♦ 15 Apr-1 Oct.
€ 18.50   2009*

VERNEUIL SUR SEINE *3D3* (1.5km N Rural) *48.99567,
1.95681* Camping-Caravaning 3* du Val de Seine, Chemin
du Rouillard, 78480 Verneuil-sur-Seine [01 39 71 88 34
or 01 39 28 16 20; fax 01 39 71 18 60; vds78@orange.fr;
www.vds78.com] Exit A13 junc 8 & foll sp to Verneuil; site
sp twd rvside. Med, mkd pitch, hdstg, pt shd; htd wc; shwrs
inc; chem disp; mv service pnt; el pnts (6A) €4.25; lndtte; shop
on site & 1km; rest, snacks; BBQ; playgrnd; lake sw & beach
600m; fishing; watersports; horseriding; games area; some
statics; dogs €2; Paris 20 mins by train; Eng spkn; quiet; ccard
acc; red low ssn. "V pleasant site adj Rv Seine; friendly, helpful
staff; gd facs & activities; site and area run down." ♦
15 Apr-30 Sep. € 17.50   2012*

VERNIOZ see Auberives sur Varèze *9B2*

"I like to fill in the reports as I travel from site to site"

You'll find report forms at the back of this guide, or you can fill them in online at www.caravaclub.co.uk/europereport.

VERNON *3D2* (2km W Rural) *49.09625, 1.43851* Camping
Les Fosses Rouges, Chemin de Réanville, 27950 St Marcel
[02 32 51 59 86 / 06 22 42 19 11 l/s; camping@cape27.fr;
www.cape-tourisme.fr] Exit A13/E5 junc 16 dir Vernon onto
D181; in 2km at rndabt turn L onto D64e dir St Marcel; in 2km
at 5-exit rndabt take 1st R onto Chemin de Réanville (D64)
& foll camping sp. At 1st major bend to R, cont strt ahead,
site on L in 50m. Med, mkd pitch, pt sl, pt shd; htd wc; chem
disp; shwrs inc; el pnts (6-10A) €3.20-4.20; gas; shops 600m
steep hill; BBQ; playgrnd; pool 4km; some statics; dogs €0.50;
adv bkg; quiet; no ccard acc; CKE/CCI. "Well-kept, well-run
scenic site; friendly, helpful owner; gd clean san facs; parking
for m'vans at St Marcel - cont past site over rndabt for 900m,
turn sharp L past hotel on R & parking on R; lovely little vill;
conv Giverny, but access diff lge o'fits; Gd size pitches" ♦ ltd
1 Mar-31 Oct. € 10.20   2013*

VERS *7D3* (Rural) *44.48442, 1.55380* Camp Municipal
de l'Arquette, 46090 Vers [05 65 31 42 59 (Mairie) or
06 33 65 06 23 (mob); mairie-vers@wanadoo.fr; www.
commune-de-vers.net] Fr Cahors foll D653 on N side Rv Lot
to Vers; in vill turn R over bdge onto D662 sp St Cirq-Lapopie;
turn R in 100m, foll site sp. Use this rte to avoid low bdge
2.9m. Med, mkd pitch, shd; wc; chem disp; mv service pnt;
shwrs inc; el pnts (10A) €4 (rev pol); lndry rm; shop & rest
200m; playgrnd adj; dogs €1.50; phone; poss cr; Eng spkn; adv
bkg; ccard not acc; CKE/CCI. "Attractive rvside site; friendly
staff; excel san facs; gd walks; poss flood risk; poss noisy youth
groups w/ends; conv Pech-Merle cave paintings."
1 May-30 Sep. € 12.00   2009*

VERS PONT DU GARD see Remoulins *10E2*

VERSAILLES *4E3* (3km E Urban) *48.79455, 2.16038* **Camping Huttopia Versailles, 31 Rue Berthelot, Porchefontaine, 78000 Versailles [01 39 51 23 61; fax 01 39 53 68 29; versailles@huttopia.com; www.huttopia.com]** Foll sp to Château de Versailles; fr main ent take Ave de Paris dir Porchefontaine & turn R immed after twin gate lodges; sp. Narr access rd due parked cars & sharp bends. No sp rec use SatNav. Lge, mkd pitch, pt sl, terr, pt shd; htd wc; chem disp; mv service pnt; baby facs; shwrs inc; el pnts inc (6-10A) €4.60-6.80; gas; lndtte; shop 500m; tradsmn; rest, snacks; bar; BBQ; playgrnd; htd pool; games area; cycle hire; TV rm; 20% statics; dogs €4; low ssn/long stay; CKE/CCI. "Wooded site; sm, sl, uneven pitches poss diff lge o'fits; friendly, helpful staff; excel, clean san facs, stretched high ssn; conv Paris trains & Versailles Château." ♦ 3 Apr-4 Nov. € 45.00   2012*

VERT EN DROUAIS see Dreux *4E2*

VERTEILLAC *7C2* (600m NE Urban) *45.35064, 0.37010* **Camp Municipal Le Pontis Sud-Est, 24320 Verteillac [05 53 90 37 74; fax 05 53 90 77 13; j-c.rouvel@wanadoo.fr; www.camping-le-pontis.com]** N fr Ribérac on D708 dir Angoulême; leaving Verteillac turn R at 'Camping' sp, then L at gendarmerie, then 1st R. Site adj stadiium. Sm, hdg pitch, sl, unshd; wc, chem disp (wc); mv service pnt; shwrs inc; el pnts (6A) €1.90; lndry rm; shop, rest, snacks, bar nrby; BBQ; pool 500m; wifi; 70% statics; dogs €0.50; quiet; CKE/CCI. "Easy access to pitches; m'van pitches sm; facs modern but ltd & in need of maintenance (2009); ltd el pnts; attractive vill; Ribérac mkt Fri." ♦ 4 Apr-15 Nov. € 8.10   2009*

VERVINS *3C4* (7km N Rural) *49.90676, 3.91977* **FFCC Camping du Val d'Oise, 3 Rue du Mont d'Origny, 02580 Etréaupont [03 23 97 48 04; www.evasion-aisne.com]** Site to E of Etréaupont off N2, Mons-Reims rd. Site adj football pitch on banks of Rv Oise. Well sp fr main rd. Sm, hdg/mkd pitch, pt shd; wc (some cont); shwrs inc; el pnts (6A) €3.30 (poss rev pol); shops 500m; tradsmn; playgrnd; tennis; sports field adj; rv & fishing adj; dogs €0.30; quiet. "Pretty, tidy site; warm welcome; v clean san facs; site self if recep clsd; no twin-axles; conv rte to Zeebrugge ferry (approx 200km); gd walking & cycling; gd" 1 Apr-31 Oct. € 19.25   2013*

⊞ **VESOUL** *6G2* (1.5km W Rural) *47.63026, 6.12858* **Camping International du Lac, Ave des Rives du Lac, 70000 Vesoul [03 84 76 22 86; camping_dulac@yahoo.fr; www.camping-vesoul.com]** 2km fr D619, sp fr W end of by-pass, pass indus est to lge lake on W o'skts. Ent opp Peugeot/Citroën factory on lakeside. Lge, mkd pitch, pt shd; htd wc; mv service pnt; baby facs; shwrs inc; el pnts (6A) €3; gas; lndtte; shops 2km; rest; bar; playgrnd; pool, paddling pool, waterslides 300m; fishing; tennis; games area; some statics; dogs €2; site clsd mid-Dec to early Jan; adv bkg; ccard acc; red CKE/CCI. "Super site screened fr indus est by trees; gd size pitches but poss soft after rain; excel aqua park nr; gd cycle rtes; V gd" ♦ 1 Mar-4 Dec. € 17.95   2012*

VEULES LES ROSES *3C2* (3.5km E Rural) *49.88351, 0.85188* **Camp Municipal Le Mesnil, Route de Sotteville, 76740 St Aubin-sur-Mer [tel/fax 02 35 83 02 83; lemesnil76@orange.fr; www.campinglemesnil.com/]** On D68 2km W of St Aubin-sur-Mer. Med, hdg pitch, terr, unshd; mv service pnt; 30% statics; htd wc; shwrs inc; el pnts (10A) €3.70 (pos rev pol); lndtte; shop; tradsmn; playgrnd; sand beach 1.5km; wifi; ccard acc; CKE/CCI. ♦ 1 Apr-31 Oct. € 22.75   2012*

VEULES LES ROSES *3C2* (6km E Rural) *49.86083, 0.89079* **Camping Les Garennes de la Mer, 12 Route de Luneray, 76740 Le Bourg-Dun [02 35 83 10 44; camping_lesgarennesdelamer@hotmail.fr; www.lesgarennes.fr]** Fr Veules-les-Roses, take D925 twd Dieppe. Site sp in Le Bourg-Dun - 1km SE. Sm, mkd pitch, pt sl, pt shd; wc; shwrs inc; el pnts (16A) €4; gas; lndtte; shops 250m; supmkt 5km; tradsmn; shgl beach 3km, dog €1; 60% statics; Eng spkn; poss cr; adv bkg; quiet; ccard acc; CKE/CCI. "Well-kept site; vg san facs." ♦ ltd 1 Apr-15 Oct. € 26.30   2013*

VEULES LES ROSES *3C2* (10km E Coastal) *49.90558, 0.92787* **Camp Municipal de la Plage, 123 Rue de la Saâne, 76860 Quiberville-Plage [02 35 83 01 04 or 02 35 04 21 33 (Mairie); fax 02 35 85 10 25; campingplage3@wanadoo.fr]** Fr Dieppe on D75, site sp in Quiberville-Plage on D127. Lge, hdg/mkd pitch, unshd; wc; mv service pnt; shwrs; el pnts (6-10A) €4.10-4.80; lndtte; rest in vill; playgrnd; beach adj; tennis adj; games area; dogs €1.40; phone; adv bkg; quiet. "Conv Dieppe ferry; pleasant site." ♦ 1 Apr-31 Oct. € 19.30   2009*

VEULES LES ROSES *3C2* (300m S Coastal/Rural) *49.87586, 0.80314* **Camping Les Mouettes, 7 Ave Jean Moulin, 76980 Veules-les-Roses [02 35 97 61 98; fax 02 35 97 33 44; camping.les.mouettes0509@orange.fr]** On ent vill fr Dieppe on D925, turn R onto D68, site in 500m up hill (14%). Lge, hdg/mkd pitch, pt shd; htd wc; chem disp; mv service pnt; baby facs; shwrs inc; el pnts (6A) €4.70; gas; lndtte (inc dryer); sm shop; tradsmn; supmkt 8km; snacks; bar; BBQ; playgrnd; htd, covrd pool; paddling pool; shgl beach 800m; fitness rm; games area; games rm; wifi; entmnt; TV; 10% statics; dogs €2.00; adv bkg; Eng spkn; quiet; ccard acc; red long stay/low ssn/CKE/CCI. "Pleasant area; peaceful, well-kept site; vg." ♦ 1 Apr-4 Nov. € 20.80   2011*

VEURDRE, LE see St Pierre le Moûtier *4H4*

VEYNES *9D3* (2km SW Rural) *44.51889, 5.79880* **FFCC Camping Les Rives du Lac, Les Iscles, 05400 Veynes [04 92 57 20 90; contact@camping-lac.com; www.camping-lac.com]** Off D994. Sp on lakeside. Med, mkd pitch, hdstg, pt sl, pt shd; wc; chem disp; mv service pnt; baby facs; shwrs; el pnts (10A) €3.50; lndtte; snacks; bar; BBQ; playgrnd; cvred pool; paddling pool; lake sw & beach adj with games in high ssn; watersports; mountain biking; climbing; open air cinema twice weekly; wifi; dogs €2.50; bus 500m; phone; adv bkg; quiet, occasional rlwy noise; ccard acc; red low ssn; CKE/CCI. "Attractive, well-run site on shore of sm lake; welcoming staff; san facs excel; something for all ages" 1 May-30 Sep. € 23.00   2013*

VEZAC see Sarlat la Canéda *7C3*

VEZELAY *4G4* (3km N Rural) *47.48280, 3.75904* **Camp Municipal Le Pâtis, Route de Givry, 89450 Asquins [03 86 33 30 80; mairie.asquins@wanadoo.fr]** Fr Vézelay take D951 N to Asquins, & turn R to site on rvside - tight turn. Site sp. Sm, pt shd; htd wc; chem disp (wc); baby facs; shwrs inc; el pnts €3; shop 500m; BBQ; playgrnd; dogs; poss cr; quiet; CKE/CCI. 1 Jun-30 Sep. € 8.00   2008*

VEZELAY *4G4* (2km SE Rural) *47.45879, 3.77150* **Camp Municipal, 89450 St Père [03 86 33 36 58 or 03 86 33 26 62 (Mairie); fax 03 86 33 34 56; mairie-saint-pere@wanadoo.fr; www.saint-pere.fr]** Fr Vézelay take D957, turn onto D36 to St Père. Site sp. Med, pt shd; wc (cont); shwrs inc; el pnts (10A) €2.20 (poss rev pol); shops 500m; playgrnd; rv adj; fishing; canoeing; tennis; some statics; poss cr; quiet. "Pleasant site; conv Morvan National Park; warden comes am & pm; basic san facs need update; gd walking area." 1 Apr-30 Sep. € 6.60   2010*

VEZELAY *4G4* (600m S Rural) *47.45675, 3.78768* **FFCC Camping de Vézelay L'Ermitage, 1 Route de l'Étang, 89450 Vézelay [tel/fax 03 86 33 24 18; www.vezelaytourisme.com]** Foll sp fr cent of Vézelay to 'Camping Vézelay' & Youth Hostel. Sm, pt sl, pt shd; wc; chem disp; mv service pnt; some serviced pitches; shwrs inc; el pnts (4-6A) €2.50 (rev pol); shops 500m; tradsmn (high ssn); poss cr; Eng spkn; quiet; no ccard acc; CKE/CCI. "Pleasant, peaceful, scenic site; welcoming; gd, clean facs; some pitches diff lge o'fits & blocks req; recep eve only - site self & sign in when open; some pitches muddy after heavy rain; Vézelay the starting point of one of the pilgrim rtes - superb abbey; excel." 1 Apr-31 Oct. € 8.50   2010*

VIAS *10F1* (3km S Coastal) *43.29055, 3.39863* **Camping Californie Plage, 34450 Vias-Plage [04 67 21 64 69; fax 04 67 21 54 62; californie-plage@wanadoo.fr; www.californie-plage.fr]** W fr Agde on D612 to Vias; turn S in town & foll sps 'Mer' over canal bdge & sp to site. Lge, mkd pitch, shd; wc; chem disp; shwrs inc; el pnts (5-10A) €1.50-3.50; gas; lndtte; supmkt; rest, snacks; bar; playgrnd; htd/covrd pool; paddling pool; waterslide; sand beach adj; cycle hire; internet; entmnt; TV rm; 10% statics; dogs €4.60; Eng spkn; adv bkg; ccard acc; CKE/CCI. ♦ 1 Apr-30 Oct. € 33.00   2008*

VIAS *10F1* (3km S Coastal) *43.29800, 3.41750* **Camping Les Salisses, Route de la Mer, 34450 Vias-Plage [04 67 21 64 07; fax 04 67 21 76 51; info@salisses.com; www.salisses.com]** Turn S off D612 (Agde-Béziers rd) in Vias & foll sp to Vias-Plage. Cross Canal du Midi bdge & site on R. Lge, mkd pitch, pt shd; wc; chem disp; sauna; steam rm; baby facs; shwrs inc; el pnts (6A) inc; gas; lndtte (inc dryer); shop; rest, snacks; bar; BBQ; playgrnd; 3 pools (1 htd, covrd); waterslide; sand beach 1km; tennis; cycle hire; games area;; wifi; entmnt; TV rm; 80% statics; dogs €3.50; quiet; ccard acc. "Vg family hols; interesting town & mkt in Agde; sm pitches" ♦ 16 Apr-17 Sep. € 42.00 (CChq acc)   2012*

VIAS *10F1* (3km S Coastal) *43.29083, 3.41783* **Yelloh! Village Le Club Farret, Farinette-Plage, 34450 Vias-Plage [04 67 21 64 45; fax 04 67 21 70 49; farret@wanadoo.fr; www.camping-farret.com or www.yellohvillage.co.uk]** Fr A9, exit Agde junc 34. Foll sp Vias-Plage on D137. Sp fr cent of Vias-Plage on L, immed after Gendarmerie. V lge, mkd pitch, pt shd; wc; chem disp; mv service pnt; baby facs; shwrs inc; el pnts (6A) inc; gas; lndtte; shop; rest, snacks; bar; playgrnd; htd pool; sand beach adj; watersports; tennis; cycle hire; fitness rm; games area; games rm; entmnt; TV; some statics; dogs €4; Eng spkn; adv bkg; quiet; ccard acc; red low ssn; CKE/CCI. "Excel facs, entmnt; excursions; gd security." ♦ 29 Mar-29 Sep. € 52.00   2011*

See advertisement on inside front cover

VIAS *10F1* (5km SW Coastal) *43.29708, 3.42072* **Camping La Carabasse, Route de Farinette, 34450 Vias-Plage [04 67 21 64 01; fax 04 67 21 76 87; lacarabasse@siblu.fr; www.lacarabasse.fr]** Fr S on A9 exit 34 & take 1st exit onto N312 sp Vias & Agde. After 8km take RH lane twd Béziers on D612. Branch R to Vias-Plage & at rndabt foll sp for Vias-Plage on D137. Site 1km on L. V lge, hdg/mkd pitch, pt shd; htd wc; chem disp; baby facs; shwrs inc; some pitches with indiv san facs; el pnts (6A) inc (poss rev pol); gas; lndtte; shop; rest, snacks; bar; BBQ; playgrnd; 2 htd pools; waterslide; sand beach 800m; tennis; watersports; golf 10km; entmnt; TV; 80% statics; no dogs; Eng spkn; adv bkg ess; quiet but poss noisy high ssn; red low ssn; CKE/CCI. "Vg local produce inc wines; organised activities; pitches poss tight med/lge o'fits due trees; many excel facs - vg for young families." ♦ 4 Apr-19 Sep.   2009*

VIAS *10F1* (5km SW Coastal) *43.29093, 3.40383* **Camping Les Flots Bleus, Côte Ouest, 34450 Vias-Plage [04 67 21 64 80; fax 04 67 01 78 12; campinglesflotsbleus@wanadoo.fr; www.camping-flotsbleus.com]** Fr D612 at Vias, take D137 sp Vias-Plage. After x-ing Canal du Midi turn R sp Côte Ouest, site sp. Lge, some hdg/mkd pitch, hdstg, pt shd; wc (some cont); chem disp; mv service pnt; baby facs; shwrs inc; el pnts (6A) inc; lndtte; shop; tradsmn; rest, snacks; bar; playgrnd; htd pool complex; waterslide; sand beach adj; games area; cycle hire; entmnt; 50% statics; dogs €3.50; adv bkg; quiet; red low ssn; CKE/CCI. "Facs clean but poss stretched high ssn; gd." 7 Apr-16 Sep. € 32.00   2009*

VIAS *10F1* (3km W Rural) *43.31222, 3.36320* **Camping Sunêlia Le Domaine de la Dragonnière, 34450 Vias [04 67 01 03 10; fax 04 67 21 73 39; contact@dragonniere.com; www.dragonniere.com]** Exit A9 junc 35 onto D64 twd Valras-Plage, then D612 dir Agde & Vias. Site on R bef Vias. Or exit junc 34 onto D612A. At Vias turn R onto D612 sp Béziers, site on L. NB Take care high speed humps at sh intervals. V lge, hdg/mkd pitch, pt shd; wc; chem disp; mv service pnt; sauna; shwrs inc; el pnts (6A) inc; gas; lndtte (inc dryer); shop; tradsmn; rest, snacks; bar; BBQ; playgrnd; htd pool complex; paddling pool; sand beach 3km (free shuttle high ssn); tennis; games area; cycle hire; wifi; entmnt; TV rm; 80% statics; dogs €5; phone; poss cr; Eng spkn; adv bkg; traff & aircraft noise; ccard acc; red low ssn; CKE/CCI. "Vg site in botanical reserve; excel for children & teenagers high ssn; Canal du Midi nrby; opp Béziers airport; site poss flooded after heavy rain." ♦ 9 Apr-18 Sep. € 50.20 (3 persons)   2010*

VIC SUR CERE *7C4* (500m E Rural) *44.98136, 2.62930*
Camp Municipal du Carladez, Ave des Tilleuls, 15800 Vic-sur-Cère [04 71 47 51 04 or 04 71 47 51 75 (Mairie); fax 04 71 47 50 59; vic-sur-cere@wanadoo.fr; www. vicsurcere.com] Fr Aurillac on N122 site sp on ent Vic-sur-Cère on R. Lge, pt shd; wc (some cont); shwrs inc; el pnts (6A) €2.50; supmkt 100m; pool 500m; playgrnd, tennis & mini-golf nrby; rv fishing; poss cr; adv bkg; quiet. "Gate clsd 2000; office clsd Sun; no pitching without booking in; plenty of rm high ssn; helpful warden; clean facs." ◆ 1 Apr-30 Sep. € 6.90   2011*

VIC SUR CERE *7C4* (1.5km SE Rural) *44.97142, 2.63319* **Camping La Pommeraie, 15800 Vic-sur-Cère [04 71 47 54 18; fax 04 71 49 63 30; pommeraie@ wanadoo.fr; www.camping-la-pommeraie.com]** Fr Vic-sur-Cère take D54 twd Pierrefort & Chaudes-Aigues, initially sp Salvanhac. Foll yellow site sp over rv, under rlwy bdge. Foll D154 up steep, narr, winding hill for 1.5km. Foll camp sp R into narr lane. Med, terr, pt shd; wc (some cont); baby facs; serviced pitches; shwrs inc; el pnts (6A) €4.20; lndtte; shop high ssn; rest, snacks; bar; no BBQ; playgrnd; pool; paddling pool; fishing; tennis; wifi; entmnt; TV rm; many statics; dogs €2.50; poss cr; adv bkg rec; red low ssn; ccard acc. "Peaceful, scenic site; best pitches at top but steep access; not suitable elderly or infirm; gd san facs; mkt Tue, Fri." ◆ 1 Jun-10 Sep. € 26.00   2011*

VICHY *9A1* (2km SE Urban) *46.10756, 3.43670* **FFCC Camping La Croix St Martin, Allée du Camping, 99 Ave des Graviers, 03200 Abrest [04 70 32 67 74 or 06 10 94 70 90 (mob); camping-vichy@orange.fr; www. camping-vichy.com]** Exit D906 at Abrest onto D426 N (Ave des Graviers); in 900m turn L into Allée du Camping. Site sp fr D906, both N & S of Abrest. Med, hdg/mkd pitch, shd; wc; chem disp; baby facs; mv service pnt; shwrs inc; el pnts (10A) €3.50; dogs €1; lndtte (inc dryer); tradsmn; snacks; bar; BBQ hire; conv store; playgrnd; htd pool; games area; entmnt; wifi; phone; 15% statics; phone; Eng spkn; adv bkg; quiet; ccard acc; red low ssn; CKE/CCI. "Gd cycling along river allier through Vichy." ◆ 10 Apr-10 Oct. € 16.10   2013*

VICHY *9A1* (1.5km S Rural) *46.11555, 3.43006* **Camping Beau Rivage, Rue Claude Decloître, 03700 Bellerive-sur-Allier [04 70 32 26 85; fax 04 70 32 03 94; camping-beaurivage@ wanadoo.fr; www.camping-beaurivage.com]** Fr Vichy cross rv bdge over Rv Allier onto D1093, turn L at rndabt foll sp Campings, sp to Beau Rivage. Site on L on rv bank, past Cmp Les Acacias. Med, shd; wc; chem disp; mv service pnt; baby facs; shwrs inc; el pnts (10A) €3.10; gas; lndtte (inc dryer); shop; supmkt 1km; tradsmn; snacks; BBQ; playgrnd; 2 htd, covrd pools; waterslide; fishing; canoeing; cycle hire; games area; tennis 2km; archery; wifi; entmnt; TV rm; 50% statics; dogs €1; poss cr; quiet; red low ssn. "Lovely rvside site, but no rv sw allowed; Lge o'fits have diff pitching; easy cycle ride to lovely city" ◆ 1 Apr-15 Oct. € 31.05 (CChq acc)   2013*

VICHY *9A1* (1km SW Rural) *46.11648, 3.42560* **Camping Les Acacias, Rue Claude Decloître, 03700 Bellerive-sur-Allier [04 70 32 36 22; fax 04 70 32 88 52; camping-acacias03@ orange.fr; www.camping-acacias.com]** Cross bdge to Bellerive fr Vichy & foll Hauterive sp onto D1093. Strt over at 1st rndabt & turn L at 2nd rndabt onto D131 dir Hauterive. At 3rd rndabt turn L at sp 'piscine'. Foll sm camping sps along rv side. Or fr S leave D906 at St Yorre & cross Rv Allier, then foll sp to Bellerive. Site sp at rndabt on app to Bellerive adj Rv Allier. On final app, at sp showing site in either dir, keep L & foll site sp along rv bank to recep. NB Many other sites in area, foll sp carefully. Med, hdg/mkd pitch, shd; wc; chem disp; baby facs; shwrs inc; el pnts (10A) €3.40; gas; shops 1km; snacks; BBQ; playgrnd; pool; fishing; boating; TV; 20% statics; dogs €1; adv bkg; ccard acc; red low ssn; CKE/CCI. "Well-run site; helpful owner; gd san facs; free Vichy Célestins water at spring in lovely town." 1 Apr-10 Oct. € 16.90   2011*

VICHY *9A1* (5km SW Rural) *46.07961, 3.38213* **FLOWER Camping La Roseraie, 1093 Route de Randan, 03700 Brugheas [04 70 32 43 33; fax 04 70 32 26 23; camping. laroseraie@wanadoo.fr; www.campinglaroseraie.com or www.flowercampings.com]** Fr Vichy on D1093, foll sp to Brugheas. Site well sp. Med, hdg/mkd pitch, some hdstg, pt shd; wc; chem disp; baby facs; shwrs inc; el pnts (6A) inc; gas; lndtte; shop on site & 3km; tradsmn; rest; snacks, bar high ssn; BBQ; playgrnd; htd pool; paddling pool; waterslide; mini-area; games area; games rm; wifi; entmnt; TV rm; 10% statics; dogs free; adv bkg; quiet; ccard acc; red long stay; CKE/CCI. "Lovely pool." ◆ 15 Mar-15 Nov. € 19.50   2010*

See advertisement on pages 32 & 33

VIELLE ST GIRONS see Léon *8E1*

⊞ **VIELMUR SUR AGOUT** *8F4* (S Rural) *43.62094, 2.09293* **FFCC Camping Le Pessac, 14 Quartier du Pessac, 81570 Vielmur-sur-Agout [tel/fax 05 63 74 30 24; info@camping-lepessac.com; www.camping-lepessac.com]** W on D112 fr Castres, after 13km turn L D92 S. 200m after level x-ing turn L, site in 100m, sp. Med, mkd pitch, pt shd; wc; mv service pnt; baby facs; shwrs; el pnts (6A) €3.30; lndtte; shop; bar; playgrnd; pool; paddling pool; fishing; tennis nr; wifi; entmnt; 20% statics; dogs €1; red low ssn; CKE/CCI. "Clean site; helpful, pleasant staff." € 10.70   2008*

VIERZON *4G3* (2.5km SW Urban) *47.20937, 2.08079* **Camp Municipal de Bellon, Route de Bellon, 18100 Vierzon [02 48 75 49 10 / 02 48 53 06 14 (ls); fax 02 48 71 40 94; campingmunicipal-vierzon@wanadoo.fr / ot-vierzon@wanadoo.fr; www.officedetourismedevierzon.com]** Fr N on A71 take A20 dir Châteauroux, leave at junc 7 onto D2020 & then D27 dir Bourges; pass Intermarché supmkt on L, after next traff lts turn L into Route de Bellon; site in 1km on R, sp. NB Do not go into town cent. Med, hdg/mkd pitch, pt sl, pt shd; wc; chem disp; mv service pnt; shwrs inc; el pnts (6A) €3 (some rev pol); gas; lndry rm; shops 1km; rest, snacks; bar; BBQ (gas/elec); playgrnd; fishing; boat hire; internet; no statics; dogs; phone; poss cr; Eng spkn; adv bkg; quiet but some rlwy noise; no ccard acc; CKE/CCI. "Attractive, well-kept site by rv; gd sized pitches but some poss diff to negotiate; gd san facs, poss tired high ssn; nice little rest o'looking rv; gates clsd 2300-0700; warden on site 1700-2200; poss itinerants; ideal NH; gd site; friendly recep" ♦ 1 May-30 Sep. € 13.10   2013*

⊞ **VIERZON** *4G3* (5km NW Rural) *47.24590, 1.99000* **Aire Communale, Place de la Mairie, 18100 Méry-sur-Cher [02 48 75 38 18]** Fr Vierzon on D2076 dir Tours. Site clearly sp on L on ent Méry-sur-Cher. Sm, mkd pitch, hdstg, ltd shd; wc; chem disp; mv service pnt; el pnts inc; shop 100m; dogs; phone; bus; rd noise; m'vans only - max 48 hrs. "Well-maintained site; pay at machine on ent (credit cards only); excel NH." € 5.00   2011*

VIEUX BOUCAU LES BAINS *8E1* (800m N Coastal) *43.79309, -1.40607* **Camp Municipal Les Sablères, Bldv du Marensin, 40480 Vieux-Boucau-les-Bains [05 58 48 12 29 or 05 58 48 13 22; fax 05 58 48 20 70; camping-lessablères@wanadoo.fr; www.les-sablères.com]** Foll sps fr cent of vill twd beach, site sp fr D652. V lge, mkd pitch, pt sl, shd; wc (some cont); chem disp; mv service pnt; baby facs; shwrs inc; el pnts (8A) €3.90; lndtte; shops, rest & snack 1km; BBQ; playgrnd; sand/surf beach 300m; lake sw nrby; games area; 20% statics; dogs €1.80; phone; poss cr; Eng spkn; adv bkg; quiet; red low ssn; CKE/CCI. "Site by lge sand dune; vg." ♦ ltd 1 Apr-15 Oct. € 18.30   2010*

VIGAN, LE (GARD) *10E1* (2km E Rural) *43.99141, 3.63760* **Camping Le Val de l'Arre, Route du Pont de la Croix, 30120 Le Vigan [04 67 81 02 77 or 06 82 31 79 72 (mob); fax 04 67 81 71 23; valdelarre@wanadoo.fr; www.valdelarre.com]** E fr Le Vigan on D999. Turn R at 1st rndabt over bdge. Turn L immed after bdge; site in 400m, well sp. Height limit 3.5m. Med, mkd pitch, pt sl, pt shd; wc (some cont); chem disp; shwrs inc; el pnts inc (10A) €3.50 (poss rev pol); gas & 2km; lndtte; tradsmn; shop on site & 2km; rest, snacks; playgrnd; htd pool; fishing 4km; entmnt; games rm; TV; dogs €2; phone; Eng spkn; adv bkg; some rd noise; ccard acc; red low ssn; CKE/CCI. "Peaceful, well-run rvside site; friendly, helpful owners; gd touring base; rec for nature lovers." ♦ 1 Apr-30 Sep. € 18.00   2011*

VIGAN, LE (GARD) *10E1* (7km S Rural) *43.92896, 3.59061* **Camp Municipal, 30120 Montdardier [04 67 81 52 16 or 04 67 81 52 46 (Mairie); fax 04 67 81 53 22]** Fr D999 in Le Vigan turn S onto D48 dir Aveze to Montdardier in 5km; site on W of D48. Site sp (sm brown) in Mondardier. NB D48 narr & steep with hairpins - not rec lge o'fits. Sm, pt sl, pt shd; htd wc; shwrs; el pnts (6A) €1-1.50; shop 300m; playgrnd; dogs; poss cr; quiet; adv bkg. "Warden calls." 1 May-31 Oct. € 9.70   2009*

VIGAN, LE (LOT) see Gourdon *7D3*

VIGEOIS see Uzerche *7B3*

VIGNEAUX, LES see Argentiere la Bessee, L' *9C3*

VIGNES, LES *9D1* (4.5km N Rural) *44.36207, 3.23135* **Aire Naturelle de Camping à la Ferme (Bonnal), Le Bouquet, 48500 St Georges-de-Lévéjac [04 66 48 81 82; campingbonnal@orange.fr; www.cardoule.com/lebouquet]** Exit A75 junc 42 onto D955 to Le Massegros; turn L onto D32 sp La Canourgue; at next x-rds turn L to Le Bouquet. Site sp at x-rds. Sm, pt sl, pt shd; wc; chem disp (wc); shwrs inc; el pnts (10A); wifi; dogs; phone; adv bkg; quiet. "Site is lge field on a farm; v peaceful, nr Gorge du Tarn; all basic facs; owners helpful." ♦ 1 May-30 Sep.   2009*

⊞ **VIHIERS** *4G1* (10km SE Rural) *47.07419, -0.41104* **Camping Le Serpolin, St Pierre-à-Champ, 49560 Cléré-sur-Layon [02 41 52 43 08; fax 02 41 52 39 18; info@loirecamping.com; www.loirecamping.com]** Take D748 S fr Vihiers by-pass sp Argenton Château. In 2km turn L at sp Cléré-sur-Layon onto D54. Cont thro vill to 1st mkd x-rd, turn R, site last house along this lane. Sm, some hdstg, pt shd; htd wc; chem disp; shwrs inc; el pnts (6A) €4; lndtte; BBQ; playgrnd; pool; fishing; cycle hire; wifi; dogs free; Eng spkn; adv bkg rec; quiet; red low ssn; CKE/CCI. "Peaceful, CL-type site; clean san facs; helpful British owners; rallies by arrangement; conv chateaux; Futuroscope; vg." € 13.00   2008*

VILLARD DE LANS *9C3* (800m N Rural) *45.07750, 5.55620* **Camping Caravaneige L'Oursière, 38250 Villard-de-Lans [04 76 95 14 77; fax 04 76 95 58 11; oursiere@franceloc.fr; www.camping-oursiere.fr]** Site clearly visible on app to town fr D531 Gorges d'Engins rd (13km SW Grenoble). App fr W on D531 not rec for c'vans & m'vans due o'hangs. Lge, terr, unshd; htd wc (some cont); chem disp; mv service pnt; baby facs; shwrs inc; el pnts (10A) €4-6; gas; lndtte; shops, snacks; rest; BBQ; playgrnd; pool & waterspark 800m; drying rm; wifi; 20% statics; dogs €5; poss cr; Eng spkn; adv bkg; quiet; ccard acc; red low ssn; CKE/CCI. "Excel all winter sports; under new ownership (2011); friendly owners; san facs need upgrade (2010)" ♦ 21 May-25 Sep & 11 Dec-7 May. € 18.50   2013*

⊞ **VILLARD DE LANS** *9C3* (10km N Rural) *45.12951, 5.53215* **Camping Caravaneige Les Buissonnets, 38112 Méaudre [04 76 95 21 04; fax 04 76 95 26 14; camping-les-buissonnets@wanadoo.fr; www.camping-les-buissonnets.com]** Fr Grenoble take D1532 to Sassenage then D531 to Lans-en-Vercors. Turn R at rndabt onto D106, site sp at ent to vill of Méaudre off D106. Approx 30km SW of Grenoble by rd & 18km as crow flies. Med, sl, unshd; htd wc; chem disp; mv service pnt; shwrs inc; el pnts (6-10A) €4-6; lndtte; shops 500m; snacks; rest 500m; pool 300m; playgrnd; games area; bus to ski slopes; clsd 1 Dec-10 Nov; Eng spkn; quiet; higher price in winter. "Gd skiing cent; conv touring Vercours; levellers ess; highly rec." ♦ € 14.50   2010*

VILLARDONNEL see Carcassonne *8F4*

VILLARS COLMARS see Colmars *9D4*

VILLARS LES DOMBES *9A2* (200m S Urban) *45.99763, 5.03163* **Camping Indigo Parc des Oiseaux, 164 Ave des Nations, 01330 Villars-les-Dombes [04 74 98 00 21 or 04 92 75 27 94; parc-des-oiseaux@camping-indigo.com; www.camping-indigo.com]** N fr Lyon on N83, site in town cent on R by sw pool. Lge, some hdstg, pt shd; wc; mv service pnt; shwrs inc; el pnts (10A) €4.50; lndtte (inc dryer); shop1km; tradsmn; rest, snacks; bar; BBQ gas; playgrnd; htd pool adj inc; paddling pool; rv fishing adj; tennis; cycle hire; games area; entmnt; 60% statics; dogs €3. "Excel site; lge pitches; modern san facs; gd security; bird park 10 mins walk; popular NH" ♦ 29 Mar - 2 Nov. € 20.40 (CChq acc)   2013*

VILLECROZE LES GROTTES see Salernes *10F3*

VILLEDIEU LES POELES *1D4* (500m S Urban) *48.83638, -1.21694* **Camping Les Chevaliers, 2 Impasse Pré de la Rose, 50800 Villedieu-les-Poêles [02 33 61 02 44; fax 02 33 49 49 93; contact@camping-deschevaliers.com; www.camping-deschevaliers.com]** Exit A84 junc 38 onto D999 twd Villedieu, then R onto D975 & R onto D924 to avoid town cent. Foll sp fr car park on R after x-ing rv. Med, hdg/mkd pitch, hdstg, pt shd; htd wc; chem disp; mv service pnt; shwrs inc; baby facs; el pnts (6A) inc poss rev pol; lndtte (inc dryer); shop 500m; supmkt 2km; rest, snacks; bar; BBQ; playgrnd; htd pool; rv fishing; boating; tennis; games rm; wifi; entmnt; TV; dogs €1.50; phone; poss cr; Eng spkn; adv bkg; quiet; red low ssn; CKE/CCI. "Peaceful site; lge pitches but kerbs poss diff lger o'fits; gd, modern san facs; interesting historic town; avoid arr Tue am due mkt; conv A84 & Cherbourg ferry; vg; exceptional facs all new; well worth a visit to town; excel site; rest extended 2011; staff very helpful" ♦ ltd 23 Mar-30 Sep. € 34.40   2013*

VILLEFAGNAN see Ruffec *7A2*

VILLEFORT (LOZERE) *9D1* (3.4km N Rural) *44.46133, 3.92736* **Camping du Lac, Morangiès, 48800 Pourcharesses [04 66 46 81 27 or 06 84 12 11 18 (mob); fax 04 66 69 77 49; contact@camping-lac-cevennes.com; www.camping-lac-cevennes.com]** Well sp on D906 nr Villefort dir Pourcharesses. Steep access rd. Med, hdg/mkd pitch, terr, pt shd; wc; chem disp (wc); baby facs; shwrs inc; el pnts €1.50; lndtte; tradsmn; playgrnd; pool; lake sw; some statics; dogs €1.50; poss cr; Eng spkn; adv bkg, ess high ssn. "Diff access to terr (with view) for lge o'fits, but worth effort; excel." 1 May-30 Sep. € 12.50   2009*

"I need an on-site restaurant"

We do our best to make sure site information is correct, but it is always best to check any must-have facilities are still available or will be open during your visit.

VILLEFORT (LOZERE) *9D1* (600m S Rural) *44.43536, 3.93323* **Camp Municipal Les Sédariès, Ave des Cévennes, 48800 Villefort [04 66 46 84 33; fax 04 66 46 89 66; http:// sedaries.villefort-cevennes.com/]** On D906 heading S fr Villefort twd Alès. Sm, terr, pt shd; wc; chem disp (wc); shwrs inc; el pnts (6A) €2; lndtte; shops, rest, bar in town; BBQ; lake sw, fishing 2km; dogs €1; phone; poss cr; quiet; CKE/CCI. "Attractive, scenic site; bureau clsd 1000-1830." 1 Jun-30 Sep. € 9.00   2009*

VILLEFRANCHE DE CONFLENT see Prades *8G4*

⊞ **VILLEFRANCHE DE LAURAGAIS** *8F3* (8km SW Rural) *43.35498, 1.64862* **Camping Le Lac de la Thésauque, Nailloux, 31560 Montgeard [05 61 81 34 67; fax 05 61 81 00 12; camping.thesauque@laposte.net; www.camping-thesauque.com]** Fr S exit A61 at Villefrance-de-Lauragais junc 20 onto D622, foll sp Auterive then Lac after Gardouch vill, site sp. Fr N turn off A61 at 1st junc after tolls S of Toulouse onto A66 (sp Foix). Leave A66 at junc 1 & foll sp Nailloux. Turn L on ent vill onto D662 & in 2km turn R onto D25 & immed R to site, sp. Med, mkd pitch, hdstg, terr, pt shd; htd wc; chem disp; shwrs inc; el pnts (10A) inc; lndtte; shop; rest, snacks; bar; BBQ; playgrnd; pool; fishing; boating; tennis; wifi; 70% statics; dogs; poss cr; ccard acc; red low ssn; CKE/CCI. "Scenic, peaceful location; conv NH for A61; helpful owners; ltd facs low ssn; gd security; steep app to sm terr pitches poss diff lge o'fits." ♦ € 23.10   2012*

VILLEFRANCHE DE ROUERGUE *7D4* (9km SE Rural) *44.26695, 2.11575* **Camping Le Muret, 12200 St Salvadou [05 65 81 80 69 or 05 65 29 84 87; info@lemuret.com; www.lemuret.com]** Fr Villefranche on D911 twd Millau, R on D905A sp camping & foll camping sp 7km. Sm, hdg/mkd pitch, shd; wc; shwrs inc; el pnts (16A) €4.50; gas & ice at farm; lndtte; shops 9km; tradsmn; rest, snacks; bar; lake adj; fishing; dogs €2; phone; adv bkg; v quiet; red long stay; CKE/CCI. "Lovely setting; gd sized pitches; san facs need refurb (owners aware)." ♦ 5 Apr-22 Oct. € 26.00   2012*

VILLEFRANCHE DE ROUERGUE *7D4* (1km SW Urban) *44.34207, 2.02731* **FFCC Camping du Rouergue, 35 Ave de Fondies, Le Teulel, 12200 Villefranche-de-Rouergue [tel/ fax 05 65 45 16 24; campingrouergue@wanadoo.fr; www. campingdurouergue.com]** Best app fr N on D922, then D47 dir Monteils & Najac; avoid 1-way system in town; ent thro sports stadium. Site well sp. Med, hdg/mkd pitch, hdstg, shd; wc (some cont); chem disp; mv service pnt; baby facs; serviced pitches; shwrs inc; el pnts (16A) €3.50; lndtte; shop; tradsmn; rest, snacks; bar; playgrnd; pool; sports stadium adj; tennis 1km; wifi; entmnt; TV rm; 15% statics; dogs €1; bus high ssn; extra for twin-axles; Eng spkn; adv bkg (30% dep); quiet; ccard acc; red low ssn/long stay/CKE/CCI. "Well-kept, peaceful site; easy access; lge pitches; pleasant, friendly owner; excel clean san facs; pool v sm; gd security; easy walk/cycle to town; m'van services outside site; rec; very hot water, gd supply" ♦ 13 Apr-30 Sep. € 21.60   2013*

VILLEFRANCHE DE ROUERGUE *7D4* (10km W Rural) *44.38404, 1.88802* **Camping Le Moulin de Bannac, 12200 Martiel [05 65 29 44 52; fax 05 65 29 43 84; info@ camping-lac-aveyron.com; www.bannaclelac.com]** On rd D911 to S bet Martiel & Limogne. Med, hdg/mkd pitch, pt sl, pt shd; wc; chem disp; mv service pnt; shwrs inc; el pnts (16A) inc; gas; lndtte; shop 1km; rest, snacks; bar; BBQ; playgrnd; pool; fishing; entmnt; internet; 6% statics; dogs €1.50; adv bgk; quiet; Eng spkn; CKE/CCI. "Wooded setting & lake." ♦ 1 Apr-30 Sep. € 13.00   2008*

VILLEFRANCHE DU PERIGORD *7D3* (1km E Urban) *44.62757, 1.08159* **FFCC Camping La Bastide, Route de Cahors, 24550 Villefranche-du-Périgord [05 53 28 94 57; fax 05 53 29 47 95; campinglabastide@wanadoo.fr; www. camping-la-bastide.com]** On N660 fr Villefranche-du-Périgord dir Cahors; site past Post Office on R nr top of hill on town o'skts. Med, hdg/mkd pitch, terr, pt shd; wc; chem disp; mv service pnt; baby facs; shwrs inc; el pnts (6-10A) €3-4; lndtte; shops 300m; rest, snacks; bar; playgrnd; pool; tennis 300m; fishing; entmnt; 25% statics; dogs €1; poss cr; adv bkg; quiet; red low ssn; CKE/CCI. ACSI; wifi; "Steep, terr site but easy access, can be soft in wet weather; charming owners; excel touring base; vg; V nice town within walking dist" ♦ ltd 3 Apr-16 Oct. € 22.00   2012*

VILLEFRANCHE DU PERIGORD *7D3* (6km SW Rural) *44.59025, 1.04799* **Moulin du Périé Camping - Caravaning, 47500 Sauveterre-la-Lémance [05 53 40 67 26; fax 05 53 40 62 46; moulinduperie@wanadoo.fr; www.camping-moulin-perie. com or www.flowercampings.com]** Fr N fr Villefranche-du-Périgord take D710 S dir Fumel. At Sauveterre-la-Lémance turn L at traff lts, cross level x-ing & in 400m turn L sp Loubejac & site; site on R in 4km. Tight ent bet tall hedges 2.6m apart for 30m. Fr E fr Cahors on D660 & turn L onto D46 sp Loubejac. Cont thro Loubejac & turn L at T-junc, foll sp Sauveterre. Site on R in 4km. Med, pt sl, pt shd; wc; chem disp; mv service pnt; baby facs; shwrs inc; el pnts (10A) inc (poss rev pol); gas; lndtte (inc dryer); shop; rest, snacks; bar; BBQ; playgrnd; pool; paddling pool; sm lake & beach; trout fishing; tennis 3km; cycle hire; archery; entmnt; games/TV rm; 25% statics; dogs €4.60; poss cr; Eng spkn; adv bkg rec; quiet; ccard acc; red low ssn; CKE/CCI. "Beautiful, well-run site in grnds of old mill; welcoming, friendly family owners; clean, dated san facs; vg rest; site rds narr, not suitable v lge o'fits; gd touring base; excel." ♦ 14 May-17 Sep. € 32.10 (CChq acc)   2011*

VILLEFRANCHE DU QUEYRAN see Casteljaloux *7D2*

VILLEFRANCHE SUR CHER *4G3* (9km SE Rural) *47.26917, 1.86265* **FFCC Camp Municipal Val Rose, Rue du Val Rose, 41320 Mennetou-sur-Cher [02 54 98 11 02 or 02 54 98 01 19 (Mairie)]** Site sp fr D976/D2076 fr Villefranche (sm white sp); site on R in SW side of vill of Mennetou. To avoid narr bdge in town fr N76 onto A20, just outside town, turn imm R, site sp after L turn. Sm, pt shd; htd wc; chem disp; shwrs inc; el pnts (6A) €2; lndtte; snacks & shops adj; rest in town; playgrnd; htd pool adj; rv adj; dogs €0.20; adv bkg; quiet. "Delightful, well-kept site; friendly, helpful warden; excel, spotless san facs; excel lndtte; pretty, walled town 5 mins walk along canal; mkt Thurs; vg value; gem of a site" ♦ 13 May-5 Sep. € 6.50   2012*

VILLEFRANCHE SUR SAONE *9B2* (10km E Rural) *45.99104, 4.81802* **FFCC Camp Municipal le Bois de la Dame, 521 Chemin du Bois de la Dame, 01480 Ars-sur-Formans [04 74 00 77 23 or 04 74 00 71 84 (Mairie); fax 04 74 08 10 62; mairie.ars-sur-formans@wanadoo.fr]** Exit A6 junc 31.1 or 31.2 onto D131/D44 E dir Villars-les-Dombes. Site 500m W of Ars-sur-Formans on lake, sp. Med, mkd pitch, pt sl, terr, pt shd; wc (cont); chem disp; shwrs inc; el pnts (6A) €3.10; lndtte; playgrnd; fishing lake; 60% statics; dogs €1.50; poss cr; adv bkg rec high ssn; CKE/CCI. "Average site, but pretty & interesting vill; ltd facs low ssn; no twin-axles; higher pitches have unguarded precipices." ♦ 1 Apr-30 Sep. € 12.20   2011*

VILLEFRANCHE SUR SAONE *9B2* (3km SE Rural) *45.97243, 4.75237* **Camp Municipal La Plage Plan D'Eau, 2788 Route de Riottier, 69400 Villefranche-sur-Saône [04 74 65 33 48; fax 04 74 60 68 18; campingvillefranche@voila.fr; www. villefranche.net]** Exit A6 junc 31.2 Villefranche. Fr N turn R at rndabt, cross over a'route & str over next rndabt; cont to site on R bef Rv Saône. Or fr S turn R at rndabt & cont to site as above. Look for sp on rndabt. Med, shd; wc (some cont); chem disp; mv service pnt; shwrs inc; el pnts (6A) €4; gas; lndry rm; shop 1km; tradsmn; snacks in ssn; bar; lake sw adj; fishing; wifi; 10% statics; adv bkg; quiet; ccard acc; CKE/CCI. "Busy site in gd position; easy access & nr m'way but quiet; a bit run down & san facs not v clean; gd walking; NH only." ♦ 1 May-30 Sep. € 15.60   2011*

VILLEFRANCHE SUR SAONE *9B2* (6km SE Rural) *45.93978, 4.76811* **Camp Municipal La Petite Saône, Rue Robert Baltié, 01600 Trévoux [tel/fax 04 74 00 14 16 or 04 74 08 73 73 (Mairie); mairie.trevoux@wanadoo.fr; http://ladombes.free.fr/Camping/Trevoux.htm]** Fr Villefranche take D306 S to Anse. Turn L onto D39/D6 for Trévoux, site sp in town, on bank of Rv Saône. Lge, pt shd; wc (mainly cont); shwrs; el pnts (6A) inc; shops 1km; playgrnd; rv fishing & sw adj; entmnt; 75% statics; dogs; adv bkg high ssn; quiet; m'van o'night area at ent; red/CKE/CCI. "Spacious rvside site nr vill; helpful staff; clean facs; well maintained; access poss diff lge o'fits due statics; gd cycling rtes nrby; Trévoux interesting history." ♦ 1 Apr-30 Sep. € 10.00   2012*

VILLEFRANCHE SUR SAONE 9B2 (5km S Rural) 45.94050, 4.72680 **Camping Les Portes du Beaujolais, 495 Ave Jean Vacher, 69480 Anse [04 74 67 12 87; fax 04 74 09 90 97; campingbeaujolais@wanadoo.fr; www.camping-beaujolais.com]** Exit A6 junc 31.2 at Villefranche & foll D306 S to Anse (foll sp Champion supmkt). Site well sp off D39, on banks of Rvs Saône & L'Azergues. Lge, hdg/mkd pitch, hdstg, pt shd; htd wc (some cont); chem disp; mv service pnt; shwrs inc; el pnts (10A) €5.50; lndtte; shop; supmkt 700m; snacks; bar; playgrnd; pool; paddling pool; lake sw; cycle hire; wifi; TV rm; 20% statics; dogs €2; phone; Eng spkn; adv bkg; rd noise fr A6 nrby & some rwly noise; red low ssn; CKE/CCI. "Pleasant, friendly site; pitches poss tired end of ssn; some pitches sm, uneven & diff lge o'fits; ltd facs low ssn & poss stretched high ssn; shwrs sometimes cold (2011); pool poss overcrowded; poss muddy when wet; lge field avail at rear but no shade; rvside walk; Anse 10 min walk - bus to Lyons; narr gauge rlwy adj; lge o'night area; conv NH" ♦ 1 Mar-31 Oct. € 37.50   2013*

VILLEFRANCHE SUR SAONE 9B2 (8km NW Rural) 46.04751, 4.66041 **Camping Domaine de la Maison Germain, Route de Salles, Impasse de Charpenay, 69460 Blaceret [04 74 67 56 36; patrick.bossan@wanadoo.fr; www.bossan.tk]** Exit A6 junc 31.1 onto D43 dir Arnas; cont to Blaceret then turn L onto D20; in 500m turn R into lane; recep on R, but site strt on. Sp 'Camping à la Ferme'. Sm, hdg pitch, pt shd; wc; shwrs inc; el pnts (10A) inc; rest; Eng spkn; adv bkg; quiet. "Charming, CL-type site on sm vineyard in heart of Beaujolais region; only 6 pitches, rec phone in adv; san facs clsd in cold weather but site open; site poss open 15 Mar-15 Nov, depending on weather (2011); conv NH." 1 Apr-31 Oct. € 16.00   2011*

VILLENEUVE DE BERG 9D2 (2km N Rural) 44.57251, 4.51041 **Camping Domaine Le Pommier, 07170 Villeneuve-de-Berg [04 75 94 82 81; fax 04 75 94 83 90; info@campingpommier.com; www.campinglepommier.com]** Site off rndabt at E end of by-pass to Villeneuve-de-Berg on N102. If app fr Aubenas do not go thro town. Steep incline, poss req tractor. Lge, mkd pitch, hdstg, terr, pt sl, pt shd; htd wc; chem disp; mv service pnt; baby facs; fam bthrm; shwrs inc; el pnts (6A) €4; lndtte; supmkt; rest, snacks; bar; BBQ (gas); playgrnd; htd pools; waterslides; paddling pool; tennis; games area; games rm; cycle hire; wifi; entmnt; sound-proofed disco high ssn; TV rm; 30% statics; dogs €4; Eng spkn; adv bkg; quiet; ccard acc; red low ssn/long stay; CKE/CCI. "Vg Dutch-owned site; superb pool complex; excel san facs." ♦ 30 Apr-17 Sep. € 30.50   2010*

VILLENEUVE DE BERG 9D2 (5km E Rural) 44.58722, 4.52565 **FFCC Camping Les Arches, Le Cluzel, Route de Mirabel, 07580 St Jean-le-Centenier [04 75 36 75 45; info@camping-les-arches.com; www.camping-les-arches.com]** Situated midway bet Aubenas & Montélimar. Fr W leave N102 just bef St Jean-le-Centenier onto D458 dir Mirabel, site in 500m nr rlwy arches. Med, hdg/mkd pitch, terr, pt shd; htd wc; chem disp; mv service pnt; baby facs; shwrs inc; el pnts (10A) €3.90; lndtte; shop 5km; tradsmn; rest, snacks; bar; BBQ; playgrnd; rv sw & fishing; canoeing; entmnt; some statics; dogs €1.80; bus adj; poss cr; Eng spkn; quiet; ccard acc. "V pleasant site in 2 sections divided by sm rv; simple & immac; peaceful location; helpful owner." ♦ 24 Apr-20 Sep. € 20.00   2010*

VILLENEUVE DE LA RAHO see Perpignan 8G4

VILLENEUVE LES GENETS see Bléneau 4G3

VILLENEUVE LOUBET see Cagnes sur Mer 10E4

⊞ **VILLENEUVE SUR LOT** 7D3 (7km E Rural) 44.39590, 0.78664 **Camping Le Sablon, 47140 St Sylvestre-sur-Lot [05 53 41 37 74; campinglesablon@wanadoo.fr]** Fr Villeneuve E on D911 sp Cahors; in 5km, site on R immed on ent St Sylvestre. Sm, hdg/mkd pitch, shd; htd wc; mv service pnt; playgrnd; pools & paddling pool; waterslide; fishing adj; 25% statics; dogs €1.50; quiet. "Pleasant, family-owned site; gd facs but run down low ssn; muddy when wet - no hdstg; poss itinerants." € 10.00   2009*

VILLENEUVE SUR LOT 7D3 (8km E Urban) 44.39576, 0.80491 **Camping Les Berges du Lot, Place de la Mairie, 47140 St Sylvestre-sur-Lot [05 53 41 22 23 or 05 53 41 24 58 (Mairie)]** Exit Villeneuve-sur-Lot on D911 sp Cahors. Site in cent of St Sylvestre-sur-Lot. Foll Camping sp to rear of La Mairie (Town Hall) & supmkt; site accessed via car park to R of main rd. Sm, mkd pitch, pt shd; wc; chem disp; shwrs inc; el pnts (16A) €3.30 (poss long lead req); shops & supmkt adj; rest, bar 1km; sm pool; boating; fishing; birdwatching; Eng spkn; quiet. "Popular, comfortable, scenic site; clean facs; helpful staff; adv bkg rec high ssn; many long term residents, inc British; mkt Wed & Sun am, when access diff; rec" ♦ 15 May-30 Sep. € 11.50   2013*

VILLENEUVE SUR LOT 7D3 (1.5km S Urban) 44.39446, 0.71504 **Camping Municipal du Rooy, Rue de Rooy, 47300 Villeneuve-sur-Lot [05 53 70 24 18 or 05 53 36 17 30; tourisme.villeneuve-sur-lot@wanadoo.fr]** Site sp to E of N21. Med, mkd pitch, pt sl, terr, pt shd; wc (some cont); chem disp; shwrs inc; el pnts (6-10A) €1.50-2.30; lndtte; shops 2km; tradsmn; BBQ; pool nrby; rv 5m; 15% statics; dogs €0.30; phone; poss cr; no ccard acc; quiet, but rlwy noise; CKE/CCI. "Gd, friendly site; helpful warden; some pitches poss flooded in bad weather (keep to L of site); san facs old but clean; conv NH or visit old city." 15 Apr-30 Sep. € 8.10   2009*

VILLEREAL 7D3 (2km N Rural) 44.65723, 0.72820 **Camping Château de Fonrives, 47210 Rives, Villeréal [05 53 36 63 38; fax 05 53 36 09 98; contact@campingchateaufonrives.com; www. campingchateaufonrives.com]** Fr Bergerac take N21 S for 8km, turn L onto D14 thro Issigeac; site is just outside vill of Rives in grounds of chateau. Med, pt sl, pt shd; wc; baby facs; shwrs inc; el pnts (6A) inc; gas; lndtte; shop; rest; bar; BBQ; playgrnd; 2 pool (1 htd, covrd); waterslide; lake sw; fishing; golf; cycle hire; games rm; entmnt; some statics; dogs €5; Eng spkn; adv bkg; quiet but some noise fr weekly disco; ccard acc; CKE/CCI. "Spacious site; gd, lge pool; van poss manhandled on some shady pitches; easier access pitches without shade; friendly owners; B&B avail; interesting town; mkt Sat; huge pitches nr pool/bar; poss noisy" ♦ 13 Apr-28 Sep. € 47.00   2013*

VILLEREAL 7D3 (7km NE Rural) 44.65331, 0.80953 **Camping Le Moulin de Mandassagne, 47210 Parranquet [tel/fax 05 53 36 04 02; isabelle.pimouguet@orange.fr; www. haut-agenais-perigord.com]** Fr D104/D2 bet Villeréal & Monzaipon turn N sp Parranquet, site sp. Sm, mkd pitch, pt shd; wc; chem disp; shwrs inc; el pnts (6A) inc; gas; lndry rm; shop adj; snacks; playgrnd; pool; fishing; tennis; entmnt; TV; poss cr; Eng spkn; adv bkg; v quiet. "Lovely countryside; friendly owners." ♦ 1 Apr-1 Oct. € 15.00   2008*

VILLEREAL 7D3 (10km SE Rural) 44.61426, 0.81889 **Camping Fontaine du Roc, Les Moulaties, 47210 Dévillac [05 53 36 08 16; fax 05 53 61 60 23; fontaine.du.roc@ wanadoo.fr; www.fontaineduroc.com]** Fr Villeréal take D255 sp Dévillac, just beyond Dévillac at x-rds turn L & L again sp Estrade; site on L in 500m. Med, hdg/mkd pitch, hdstg, pt shd; wc; chem disp; shwrs inc; el pnts (5-10A) €3.50-4.50 gas; lndtte; shop 7km; tradsmn; rest, snacks; bar; BBQ; playgrnd; pool; paddling pool; fishing 500m; cycle hire; games rm; wifi; TV; 2% statics; dogs €3.50; phone; Eng spkn; adv bkg; quiet; red low ssn/long stay; no ccard acc; CKE/CCI. "Peaceful, well-cared for site; helpful owner; lge pitches." 1 Apr-30 Sep. € 19.00   2010*

VILLEROUGE LA CREMADE see Lezignan Corbieres 8F4

VILLERS LES NANCY see Nancy 6E2

VILLERS SIRE NICOLE see Maubeuge 3B4

VILLERS SUR AUTHIE see Rue 3B2

VILLES SUR AUZON see Mormoiron 10E2

⊞ **VILLEVAUDE** 3D3 (2km E Rural) 48.91258, 2.67025 **Camping Le Parc de Paris, Rue Adèle Claret, Montjay-la-Tour, 77410 Villevaudé [01 60 26 20 79; fax 01 60 27 02 75; info@campingleparc.fr; www. campingleparc.fr]** Fr N, A1 twds Paris, then A104 to Marne-la-Vallée, exit at junc 6B (Paris Bobigny), then D105 to Villevaudé, then to Montjay & site sp. Fr S exit A104 at junc 8 to Meaux & Villevaudé. Lge, hdg/mkd pitch, pt sl, pt shd; htd wc; serviced pitches; chem disp; mv service pnt; baby facs; shwrs inc; el pnts (10A) €5; lndtte (inc dryers); shop 5km; tradsmn; rest high ssn; snacks; bar; playgrnd; lake sw & sand beach 5km; tennis 200m; games area; games rm; wifi; entmnt; TV rm; 50% statics; dogs €6; phone; Eng spkn; adv bkg; ccard acc; red low ssn; CKE/CCI. "Conv Disneyland, Paris, Parc Astérix (Disney tickets fr recep); gd san facs; twin-axles acc if adv bkg; drive to local station (10mins) & park free; shuttle service to Disneyland; gd sh stay; san facs tired, pitches sm and uneven" ♦ € 28.00   2013*

VILLIERS CHARLEMAGNE see Chateau Gontier 4F1

VILLIERS LE MORHIER see Maintenon 4E2

⊞ **VILLIERS SUR ORGE** 4E3 (600m SE Urban) 48.65527, 2.30409 **Camping Le Beau Village, 1 Voie des Prés, 91700 Villiers-sur-Orge [01 60 16 17 86; le-beau-village@ wanadoo.fr; www.beau-village.com]** Rec app fr N20, exit sp La Ville-du-Bois & Carrefour. Take rd for Villiers-sur-Orge & turn R at traff lts with sm Renault g'ge. Site sp 200m on L. Care needed on app due to narr rds. Med, hdg pitch, pt shd; htd wc; chem disp; mv service pnt; shwrs inc; el pnts (10A) inc (poss rev pol); gas; lndtte; shops 700m; tradsmn; bar; playgrnd; kayaking; games rm; wifi; dogs €2; phone; train 700m; recep clsd w/ends Dec to Feb; poss cr; quiet; red low ssn. "Pleasant, well-run site; conv Paris; ltd space for lge o'fits." € 18.00   2009*

VIMOUTIERS 3D1 (700m N Urban) 48.93236, 0.19646 **Camp Municipal La Campière, Ave Dr Dentu, 61120 Vimoutiers [02 33 39 18 86 (Mairie); fax 02 33 36 51 43; campingmunicipalvimoutiers@wanadoo.fr; www. vimoutiers.fr]** App Vimoutiers fr N on on D579/D979/D916, site on R 300m after passing junc with D16; turn R at flag poles (200m after Avia petrol station). Or appr fr Gacé on D979 turn L at flag poles (on D916 just bef junc with D16). Site nr stadium & not well sp. Sm, hdg pitch, pt shd; wc; chem disp; shwrs inc; el pnts (6A) €2.40; lndry rm; shop 200m; rest, snacks 800m; playgrnd adj; pool & sports facs 2km; rv fishing, sw & boating 2km; tennis; cycle hire; 10% statics; dogs €1.50; poss cr; adv bkg; noise fr nrby factory; red low ssn; CKE/CCI. "Excel, well-maintained, pretty site at cent of Camembert cheese industry; helpful, friendly warden; vg, clean san facs; unrel opening dates - phone ahead low ssn; attractive town." ♦ 1 Apr-31 Oct. € 9.00   2011*

VINCELLES see Auxerre 4F4

VINSOBRES see Nyons 9D2

VIOLES see Orange 10E2

VION see Tournon sur Rhône 9C2

⊞ **VIRIEU LE GRAND** *9B3* (5km NE Rural) *45.87483, 5.68428*
**Camping Le Vaugrais, Chemin de Vaugrais, 01510
Artemare [04 79 87 37 34; fax 04 79 87 37 46; contact@
camping-le-vaugrais.fr; www.camping-le-vaugrais.fr]**
N fr Belley on D1504 then D904 to Artemare; sp in vill. Well sp
fr D904 on rvside. Sm, pt shd, hdg pitch; wc (some cont); chem
disp (wc); baby facs; shwrs inc; el pnts (5A) €3.50; lndtte; shop
500m; tradsmn; snacks; bar; BBQ; playgrnd; pool; fishing; wifi;
1% statics; dogs €1; Eng spkn; adv bkg; quiet; red low ssn;
CKE/CCI. "Charming site in gd location; some lge pitches with
views; friendly owners; clean san facs, poss inadequate high
ssn; nice pool; Artemare within walking dist; gd food at hotel
in town; excel." ♦ ltd € 18.00 SBS - M12   2011*

VIRIEU LE GRAND *9B3* (2.5km S Rural) *45.82954, 5.64432*
**Camping Le Lac, 01510 Virieu-le-Grand [tel/fax
04 79 87 82 02 or 06 80 33 43 06 (mob); campingvirieu@
orange.fr; www.campingvirieu.com]** Fr S on D904 site sp
on R. Uneven app. Med, hdg pitch, terr, pt shd; wc; mv service
pnt; shwrs inc; el pnts (6A) €3; tradsmn; shops 4km; snacks;
BBQ; playgrnd; lake beach, sw & fishing; cycle hire; wifi; some
statics; dogs €3.10; some rd & rlwy noise. "Clean, pleasant,
scenic, lakeside site; clean facs; helpful owner." 7 Apr-28 Sep.
€ 14.60   2008*

VISAN see Valréas *9D2*

VITRAC see Sarlat la Canéda *7C3*

VITRE *2F4* (N Rural) *48.23090, -1.18087* **Camp Municipal
du Lac, 35210 Châtillon-en-Vendelais [02 99 76 06 32 or
02 99 76 06 22 (Mairie); fax 02 99 76 12 39]** Take D178
fr Vitré fr Fougères. In 11km branch L onto D108, sp Châtillon-
en-Vendelais. Foll sp thro vill & turn R after level x-ing &
bef bdge; site in 1km. Med, pt sl, pt shd; wc; shwrs inc; el pnts
(6A) €3.10 (poss rev pol); lndtte; shop & 1km; playgrnd; tennis;
lake adj; fishing; 10% statics; quiet; CKE/CCI. "Pleasant site;
clean san facs; warden on site 0900-1000 only; levelling blocks
req most pitches; quiet low ssn; gd walks; nature reserve (birds)
nr." 15 May-30 Sep. € 11.50   2012*

VITRE *2F4* (2km SE Urban) *48.10889, -1.19823* **Camp
Municipal Ste Etienne, Route d'Argentré-du-Plessis, 35500
Vitré [02 99 75 25 28 or 02 99 74 43 53; fax 02 99 74 04 12;
www.ot-vitre.fr]** Exit A11 at junc 5 onto D857 twd Vitré.
Take Vitré ring rd twd Rennes; 500m fr ring rd S on D88 twd
Argentré-du-Plessis & foll camp sp. Sm, hdg pitch, pt sl, shd;
wc (some cont); chem disp (wc); mv service pnt; shwrs inc;
el pnts (10A) inc; shop 1km; supmkt 800m; sports complex
adj; 25% statics; dogs; quiet but some rd & military aircraft
noise; ccard not acc; CKE/CCI. "Peaceful site; gd size pitches
but access to some poss diff; pitch yourself, warden calls am
& eves - friendly & helpful; facs dated but clean; no security;
poss unkempt low ssn; poss itinerants." 1 Apr-31 Oct.
€ 9.90   2008*

VITRY LE FRANCOIS *6E1* (4km SE Rural) *48.69673, 4.63039*
**Aire Naturelle Camping Nature (Scherschell), 13 Rue de
l'Evangile, 51300 Luxémont-et-Villotte [03 26 72 61 14 or
06 83 42 83 53 (mob); eric.scherschell@wanadoo.fr; www.
camping-nature.net]** Fr Châlons sp on N44, site sp at E end
of Vitry-le-François by-pass (N4); foll sp to R, then foll 3km
to site. Fr S take exit for Vitry-le-François & pass lorry park; in
approx 1km, turn L at rndabt; foll sp to Luxémont-et-Villotte;
site in vill on R. Sm, some hdstg, pt sl, shd; wc; chem disp;
mv service pnt; shwrs inc; el pnts (6A) inc (poss rev pol & long
lead req); gas 2km; shop 6km; tradsmn; BBQ; playgrnd; lake
sw 500m; fishing; dogs €1; poss cr; Eng spkn; adv bkg; quiet;
no ccard acc; CKE/CCI. "Delightful, CL-type site; well-kept
& immac; helpful, friendly owners; gd, clean unisex san facs;
no twin-axles; nr canal & cycle paths; excel." 1 May-15 Oct.
€ 14.60   2012*

VITRY LE FRANCOIS *6E1* (2km W Urban) *48.73020,
4.58114* **Camp Municipal La Peupleraie, 6 Esplanade de
Tauberbischofsheim, Quai des Fontaines, 51300 Vitry-
le-François [03 26 74 20 47 or 03 26 74 20 47 (Mairie);
fax 03 26 41 22 88; camping@vitry-le-francois.net; www.
vitry-le-francois.net]** Fr N on N44 turn R onto N4 at island
with lge stone triumphal arch (sp Paris) & cont on dual c'way
for 300m; then immed after sharp L bend turn R thro lge
parking area. Med, hdg pitch, pt shd; wc; shwrs inc; el pnts
(5A) inc; gas; shops adj; rest, snacks, bar 500m; dogs €1.55;
quiet, but some rd noise. "Delightful site; tight ent poss diff
lge o'fits, no twin-axles; lge pitches; san facs dated & poss tired
end of ssn (2011); interesting town in walking dist; vg NH."
1 May-15 Oct. € 13.10   2011*

VITTEAUX *6G1* (1km W Rural) *47.40134, 4.52951* **Camp
Municipal La Gare, 21350 Vitteaux [03 80 49 60 87 or
03 80 49 61 25 (Mairie)]** Sp fr vill nr Hippodrome. Sm, hdg
pitch, shd; wc; chem disp (wc); shwrs inc; el pnts (6A) €2.50;
lndry rm; rest, snacks & bar 1km; BBQ; playgrnd; htd covrd
pool nr; dogs €1; quiet. "Part of sports complex; warden calls
am & pm; pick your spot; no security barrier." ♦ 1 Apr-15 Sep.
€ 8.00   2008*

VITTEFLEUR see Cany Barville *3C2*

VITTEL *6F2* (1km NE Urban) *48.20762, 5.95531* **Camping
de Vittel, 270 Rue Claude Bassot, 88800 Vittel
[03 29 08 02 71; aquadis1@wanadoo.fr; www.aquadis-
loisirs.com]** Fr Chaumont/Dijon at traff lts take Epinal road
into Place Gen de Gaulle; turn L over bdge & foll sp. Fr Epinal
turn R over bdge at Place Gen de Gaulle & foll sp. Med, hdg/
mkd pitch, hdstg, pt shd; htd wc (mainly cont); chem disp;
shwrs inc; el pnts (6A) inc; lndtte; shop 1km; tradsmn; pool.
Tennis 2km; dogs €3.10; poss cr; Eng spkn; adv bkg; quiet;
CKE/CCI. "Interesting town; on Tour de France rte; walking
& cycling rtes; san facs unclean." 3 Apr-17 Oct. € 16.20
(CChq acc)   2010*

VIVIER SUR MER, LE see Dol de Bretagne *2E4*

VIVONNE *7A2* (500m E Rural) *46.42511, 0.26409*
Camp Municipal, Chemin de Prairie, 86370 Vivonne
[05 49 43 25 95 or 05 49 43 41 05 (Mairie); fax
05 49 43 34 87; vivonne@cg86.fr] Exit N10 where it by-passes Vivonne & ent town. Site in municipal park to E of town. Med, pt shd; wc; shwrs €2; el pnts (6A) €2.35; lndtte; playgrnd; noise fr rlwy, quieter w/end. "Welcoming, helpful resident warden; clean facs; sh walk to town cent; worth a visit; as gd as ever." ♦ May-Sep. € 7.80   2010*

"Satellite navigation makes touring much easier"

Remember most sat navs don't know if you're towing or in a larger vehicle – always use yours alongside maps and site directions.

VIVONNE *7A2* (5km E Rural) *46.42640, 0.33154* **Club Soleil de Poitiers, Domain Bois de la Pardière (Naturist), Route d'Aslonnes, 86370 Château-Larcher [05 49 43 56 02; la-pardiere@laposte.net; http://assoc.wanadoo.fr/club. soleil.poitiers]** Exit N10 at Vivonne onto D742 to Château-Larcher; turn L onto D88; site on R in 1.2km. Sm, mkd pitch, pt shd; wc; chem disp; shwrs; el pnts €3.40; lndry rm; shops 2km; BBQ; pool; games rm; dogs free; Eng spkn; adv bkg; quiet. "Simple site; friendly welcome; gd clean san facs; gd touring base or NH; excel." 26 Jun-30 Sep. € 13.70   2011*

VIZILLE *9C3* (500m N Urban) *45.08660, 5.76814* **FFCC
Camping Le Bois de Cornage, Chemin du Camping, 38220 Vizille [tel/fax 04 76 68 12 39; campingvizille@wanadoo. fr; www.campingvizille.com]** Site sp just off Rte Napoléon, N85 & Rte de Briançon D1091. Site on N outskirts of town. Well sp. Med, hdg/mkd pitch, pt sl, terr, shd; wc; chem disp; mv service pnt; baby facs; shwrs inc; el pnts (10-16A) €4.50-5.50 (long lead poss req); gas 500m; lndtte; shops 200m; supmkt 500m; tradsmn; rest, snacks; bar; playgrnd; htd pool; gd cycling & climbing nrby; 10% statics; dogs €0.80; no vans over 5m acc; bus; poss v cr; Eng spkn; adv bkg rec high ssn; quiet; red long stay/low ssn; CKE/CCI. "Helpful owner; excel clean facs; mkd walks nrby; poss mosquitoes; frequent buses to Grenoble & Bourg-d'Oisans; vg" 24 Apr-10 Oct. € 15.90   2013*

VIZILLE *9C3* (7km S Rural) *45.02055, 5.77522* **Camp Municipal Napoléon, 38220 Laffrey [04 76 13 36 74; contact@mairie-laffrey.com; www.mairie-laffrey.com]** Exit Grenoble on D1085. S thro Vizille to Laffrey. Steep climb on narr rd. Site 200m S of vill at top of steep hill on Rte Napoléon. Site sp fr town. Med, mkd pitch, pt sl, pt shd; wc; shwrs inc; el pnts (6A) €3.50; lndtte; shop in ssn; snacks; lake sw & watersports; dogs €1.50; some rd noise. "Gd sized pitches." 15 Jun-15 Sep. € 11.50   2009*

VOGUE see Aubenas *9D2*

VOLONNE see Château Arnoux *10E3*

VOLSTROFF *5D2* (1.5km SE Rural) *49.29772, 6.26989* **FFCC
Camp du Centre de Loisirs et Culture de Volstroff, Route de Luttange, 57940 Volstroff [03 82 56 93 40; fax 03 82 50 39 90; campingvol@aol.com; www.campingvol.com]** Exit A31 junc 37.2 E onto D918; in 5km at end vill of Stuckange turn R sp Volstroff, Luttange. Go thro Volstroff, site in R in 3km. Med, hdg/mkd pitch, hdstg, pt sl, shd; wc (some cont); chem disp; mv service pnt; baby facs; shwrs inc; el pnts (8A) €2.30; gas; lndtte (inc dryer); shop; rest, snacks; bar; playgrnd; pool; lake sw adj; waterslide; watersports; horseriding; tennis; cycle hire; wifi; entmnt; dogs; phone; Eng spkn; adv bkg; poss cr; ccard acc; red low ssn; CKE/CCI. "Lovely lake adj site; many facs for children; excel." ♦ 11 Apr-25 Oct. € 18.00 (4 persons)   2009*

VOLVIC *9B1* (E Urban) *45.87213, 3.04381* **Camp Municipal Pierre et Sources, Rue de Chancelas, 63530 Volvic [04 73 33 50 16; fax 04 73 33 54 98; camping@ville-volvic.fr; www.ville-volvic.fr]** Exit Riom on D986: foll sp for Pontgibaud & Volvic. Site sp to R on app to town. Sm, shd; htd wc; chem disp; mv service pnt (open all year); shwrs inc; el pnts (12A) €3.50; lndtte; sm shop; tradsmn; some statics; dogs €1.50; Eng spkn; adv bkg; quiet; red low ssn. "Pleasant site with lovely views; welcoming & helpful; excel, cleans san facs; access some pitches poss diff, particularly for lge o'fits; conv Volvic factory tour. 1 May-30 Sep. € 15.00   2011*

VONNAS *9A2* (300m NW Rural) *46.22152, 4.98805* **Camp Municipal Le Renom, 240 Ave des Sports, 01540 Vonnas [tel/fax 04 74 50 02 75; campingvonnas@wanadoo.fr; www.vonnas.com]** Fr Bourg-en-Bresse take D1079 W sp Mâcon. In 15km take D26 or D47 S to Vonnas; turn R in town cent (ignore sp on o'skts of town) & site on R in 300m by leisure cent. Med, hdg/mkd pitch, pt shd; wc; chem disp; baby facs; shwrs inc; el pnts (10A) €4.15; lndtte; shop 300m; BBQ; htd pool, tennis adj; rv fishing; 30% statics; dogs €1; quiet. "Warm welcome; interesting town; mkt Thurs; gd site, but expensive" ♦ ltd 30 Mar-29 Sep. € 19.45 (CChq acc)   2013*

VOREY *9C1* (4km NE Rural) *45.20305, 3.94464* **Camping Domaine du Pra de Mars, Le Chambon de Vorey, 43800 Vorey-sur-Arzon [tel/fax 04 71 03 40 86; leprademars@ wanadoo.fr; www.leprademars.com]** On D103 dir Retournac. Med, hdg/mkd pitch, pt sl, pt shd; htd wc (some cont); chem disp; some serviced pitches; mv service pnt; baby facs; fam bthrm; shwrs inc; el pnts (5A) €3; lndtte; rest, snacks; bar; BBQ; htd pool; dogs €1.50; bus; phone; Eng spkn; adv bkg; quiet; ccard acc; CKE/CCI. "Beautiful rvside setting; welcoming owners; facs clean but need update (2009); vg." 3 Apr-27 Sep. € 13.50   2009*

VOREY *9C1* (300m SW Rural) *45.18576, 3.90679* **Camping Les Moulettes, Chemin de Félines, 43800 Vorey-sur-Arzon [04 71 03 70 48 or 04 71 03 79 49; fax 04 71 03 72 06; contact@camping-les-moulettes.fr; www.camping-les-moulettes.fr]** Fr Le Puy take D103 sp Vorey. Site sp in vill; L in main sq. Sm, hdg pitch, pt shd; wc; shwrs inc; el pnts (10A) €3.20; lndtte; shops in vill; rest, snacks; bar; playgrnd; pool; paddling pool; waterslide; fishing adj; games area; some statics; dogs €1.50; Eng spkn; adv bkg; quiet; red low ssn. "Peaceful site by rv; gd sized pitched, many on rv bank; friendly owners." ♦ May-Sep. € 16.50   2011*

VOUECOURT *6E1* (Rural) *48.26774, 5.13671* **Camp Municipal Rives de Marne, Rue de Verdun 52320 Vouécourt [03 25 01 39 58 or 03 25 02 44 46 (Mairie); fax 03 25 02 44 46; camping-vouecourt@wanadoo.fr]** N fr Chaumont on N67; sp to site in 17km; thro vill by Rv Marne; site on L bef main rv bdge, almost opp Mairie; well sp. Sm, mkd pitch; pt shd; wc (some cont); chem disp; shwr; el pnts (10A) €2.20 (poss rev pol); gas; shop 5km; rest 1km; tradsmn; playgrnd; fishing; adv bkg; CKE/CCI. "Lovely, peaceful, rvside site; gd sized pitches; friendly warden calls pm; clean, dated san facs; rv poss floods in winter; forest walks & cycling; popular NH; excel." 1 May-30 Sep. € 13.80   2013*

VOUILLE *4H1* (Urban) *46.63968, 0.16488* **Camp Municipal, Chemin de la Piscine; 86190 Vouillé [05 49 51 90 10 (after 1800) or 05 49 54 20 30 (Mairie); fax 05 49 51 14 47; vouille@cg86.fr; www.tourisme-vienne.com]** Fr Parthenay take N149 twds Vouillé; go thro Vouillé & turn R onto D43 by Super U. At bottom of hill turn R twds town cent; site sp behind Cheval Blanc rest nr rvside. Sm, mkd pitch, shd; wc; chem disp (wc); shwrs inc; el pnts (3A); lndry rm; shop; supmkt 1km; rest 500m; bar; playgrnd adj; fishing; dogs; quiet. "Site yourself; useful NH; ideal Futuroscope." ♦ 1 May-30 Aug. € 10.00   2011*

VOUILLE LES MARAIS see Marans *7A1*

VOULTE SUR RHONE, LA *9D2* (4km N Rural) *44.82663, 4.76171* **Camping La Garenne, Quartier La Garenne, 07800 St Laurent-du-Pape [tel/fax 04 75 62 24 62; info@ lagarenne.org; www.lagarenne.org]** Well sp fr La Voulte. Fr Valence S on D86 La Voulte, approx 15km turn W onto D120; 300m after St Laurent-du-Pape cent, turn R bef PO. Med, pt terr, pt shd; wc; chem disp; shwrs inc; el pnts (6A) inc (poss rev pol); gas; lndtte; shop; rest, snacks; bar; playgrnd; pool; cycle hire; wifi; entmnt; dogs €2.50; poss v cr; Eng spkn; adv bkg; quiet; red low ssn/long stay; CKE/CCI. "Popular site; friendly, helpful Dutch owners; views fr terr pitches; gd clean san facs; sh walk to vill; vg" ♦ 1 Mar-1 Nov. € 33.50   2013*

"There aren't many sites open at this time of year"

If you're travelling outside peak season remember to call ahead to check site opening dates – even if the entry says 'open all year'.

VOULTE SUR RHONE, LA *9D2* (4km NE Rural) *44.82004, 4.81960* **Camp Municipal Les Voiliers, 07800 Beauchastel [04 75 62 24 04; fax 04 75 62 42 32; camping.lesvoiliers@ orange.fr; www.camping-les-voiliers.fr]** S fr Valence on D86; in 15km at junc with D86E (nr Beauchastel), cont on D86 for 800m; turn L across Rhône in front of hydro station; site in 400m. Site sp fr N & S on D86 & in Beauchastel. Med, terr, shd; htd wc (most cont); snacks; shwrs inc; el pnts (5A) €3; lndtte; shops 500m; snacks; bar; BBQ; playgrnd; pool; paddling pool; horseriding; canoeing; rv sw; tennis; games area; entmnt; 15% statics; dogs €2.50; poss cr; quiet; red low ssn. "Friendly; gd san facs; NH only." 1 Apr-31 Oct. € 18.00   2011*

⊞ **VRAIGNES EN VERMANDOIS** *3C4* (Rural) *49.88777, 3.06488* **Camping des Hortensias, 22 Rue Basse, 80240 Vraignes-en-Vermandois [03 22 85 64 68; accueil@ campinghortensias.com; www.campinghortensias.com]** Fr N on A1/E15 take exit 13 onto D1029 sp St Quentin; strt rd 16km until rndabt, take D15 (Vraignes) exit; site sp 1st on R in vill. Or fr S & A26, take junc 10 onto D1029 sp Péronne; after 15km at rndabt take D15 as bef. Sm, hdg pitch, hdstg, pt shd; htd wc; chem disp; shwrs €1.20; el pnts (4-8A) €2.50-4.50 (poss long lead req); lndtte; shop 2km; tradsmn; snacks & bar 1.5km; BBQ; a few statics; dogs €1.30; quiet; red long stay; CKE/CCI. "Lovely farm site; sm pitches, poss muddy when wet; helpful, friendly owners; vg, clean san facs; conv for Somme battlefields & m'way; excel" € 12.50   2013*

VUILLAFANS see Ornans *6G2*

WACQUINGHEN see Marquise *3A3*

WASSELONNE *6E3* (1km W Urban) *48.63739, 7.43209* **FFCC Camp Municipal, Rue des Sapins, 67310 Wasselonne [tel/ fax 03 88 87 00 08; camping-wasselonne@wanadoo.fr; www.suisse-alsace.com]** Fr D1004 take D244 to site. Med, mkd pitch, terr, pt shd; wc; mv service pnt; shwrs inc; el pnts (5-10A) €2.30-3.70; gas; lndtte; shop; rest, snacks; bar; playgrnd; htd, covrd pool high ssn; 30% statics; dogs €0.60; quiet; CKE/CCI. "Pleasant town; facs OK; cycle rte to Strasbourg; gd NH." 15 Apr-15 Oct. € 11.70   2010*

WASSELONNE *6E3* (5km NW Urban) *48.64487, 7.39953* **Camp Municipal, La Vosgesia, 67310 Romanswiller [tel/ fax 03 88 87 45 54]** Fr Saverne take D1004 twd Strasbourg. 1km N of Wasselonne turn R onto D260 & cont twd town cent, turn R onto D224 sp Romanswiller & 'Camping Piscine'. Turn L into 'Centre des Loisirs'. Sm, hdg pitch, pt shd; wc; chem disp; all serviced pitches; shwrs inc; el pnts (10A) inc; lndry rm; shops 2km; rest, snacks; BBQ; playgrnd; htd pool 5km; games area; cycle hire; 90% statics; dogs; poss cr; some Eng spkn; poss noisy; CKE/CCI. "Well-kept, scenic site; pleasant town." 1 May-30 Sep. € 12.00   2010*

WATTEN *3A3* (200m W Urban) *50.83353, 2.21005* **Camping Le Val Joly (Le Val Joli), Rue de Aa, 59143 Watten [tel/fax 03 21 88 23 26 or 03 21 88 24 75; www.campings-nord.com]** NW fr St Omer on D943; N of Tilques turn N onto D300; in 5km at rndabt turn R onto D207 sp Watten; at T-junc turn L onto D213; cross rv brdg & turn L in 500m at camping sp. Med, mkd pitch, pt shd; wc; chem disp; shwrs €2; el pnts (10A) €2.20-3.10; lndtte; shops adj; supmkt nr; tradmn; playgrnd; fishing & cycling along rv/canal; 90% statics; dogs; adv bkg; quiet but some rd & rlwy noise; ccard not acc. "Spacious, attractive, well-kept site; conv NH for ferries; welcoming, friendly, helpful owner; basic, clean san facs; secure gates, locked 2200-0700, but off rd parking; no site lighting (2010); few touring pitches - arr early or phone ahead high ssn; access to rv walk; glass works at Arques; vet nr; vg." 1 Apr-31 Oct. € 10.65   2013*

WATTWILLER see Cernay *6F3*

WIMEREUX *3A2* (1km S Coastal) *50.76131, 1.60769* **Camp Municipal L'Olympic, 49 Rue de la Libération, 62930 Wimereux [03 21 32 45 63; fax 03 21 83 68 94; camping. wimereux@orange.fr; www.ville-wimereux.fr]** A16 exit 32 & foll sp Wimereux Sud to vill; turn R at rndabt to site. Or N fr Boulogne on D940, at vill sp Wimereux & rndabt, turn R. Med, hdg/mkd pitch, pt sl, unshd; wc; chem disp; baby facs; shwrs inc; el pnts (6A) €4; BBQ; lndry rm; shop adj; tradsmn; rest; playgrnd; pool 4km; beach 800m; sailing; fishing; mainly statics; dogs €2; Eng spkn; some noise fr rds & rlwy; ccard acc; CKE/CCI. "Conv Boulogne; basic facs, stretched high ssn & poss irreg cleaning low ssn (2010); hot water runs out early; poss waterlogging after rain; gd vet in attractive seaside town; poor security, take care thieves at night (2009); useful NH only" 18 Mar-20 Oct. € 23.00   2013*

⊞ **WIMEREUX** *3A2* (1.5km S Coastal) *50.75277, 1.60722* **Caravaning L'Eté Indien, Hameau de Honvault, 62930 Wimereux [03 21 30 23 50; fax 03 21 30 17 14; ete.indien@ wanadoo.fr; www.eteindien-wimereux.com]** Fr Calais on A16 exit junc 32 sp Wimereux Sud. Thro Terlincthun R after x-ing rlwy, site in 700m on R - narr, v rough rd. Med, pt sl, terr, unshd; wc; chem disp; mv service pnt; serviced pitches; baby facs; shwrs inc; el pnts (10A) inc; gas; lndtte (inc dryer); shop; snacks; bar; BBQ (gas); playgrnd; htd pool; paddling pool; sandy beach 1.5km; games area; games rm; wifi; entmnt; 90% statics; dogs €3; phone; poss cr; Eng spkn; adv bkg; some rlwy noise; red low ssn/long stay. "Conv A16, Calais ferries; rec low ssn phone to check site open; ltd touring pitches & poss steep; muddy & unpleasant in winter; rlwy runs along one side of site; NH only if desperate!; New sw pool and MV area; gd clean facs (2012)" ♦ € 21.00   2012*

WINGEN SUR MODER *5D3* (W Rural) *48.91565, 7.36934* **Camp Municipal/Aire Naturelle, Rue de Zittersheim, 67290 Wingen-sur-Moder [03 88 89 71 27 (Mairie); fax 03 88 89 86 99; mairie@wingen-moder.com; www. wingen-moder.com]** W fr Haguenau on D919 to W end Wingen-sur-Moder. Site sp by rlwy arch. Sm, mkd pitch, terr, pt shd; wc; chem disp; shwrs inc; el pnts (13A) inc; shop 500m; rest nr; Eng spkn; adv bkg; quiet; CKE/CCI. "Excel, peaceful site but adj sports field poss used by youth groups/motorbikers high ssn; clean facs; warden calls am & pm; gd walking/cycling." 1 May-30 Sep. € 11.40   2009*

WISSANT *3A2* (6km NE Coastal/Rural) *50.91853, 1.71039* **Camping Côte d'Opale Le Blanc Nez, 18 Rue de la Mer, 62179 Escalles [tel/fax 03 21 85 27 38; camping.blancnez@ laposte.net; http://camping.blancnez.free.fr]** Fr A16 take junc 40 to Cap Blanc-Nez. Site situated on W edge of Escalles on D940 twd sea. Med, mkd pitch, pt sl, pt shd; wc; chem disp; mv service pnt; shwrs €1; el pnts (4A) inc (long lead poss req, pos rev pol); gas; lndry rm; shop; tradsmn; rest, snacks; bar; playgrnd; sand/shgl beach 1km; wifi; 25% statics; dogs €1.50; phone; bus 100m; poss cr; adv bkg; quiet; ccard acc; CKE/CCI. "Nice site in need of refurb; busy; clean, dated san facs; ltd hot shwrs/hot water, espec low ssn; diff access for lge o'fits due parked cars; sm pitches; elec linked to pitch number - no choice; gd location & walking; gd NH." 15 Mar-15 Nov. € 19.00   2012*

WISSANT *3A2* (6km NE Coastal) *50.91226, 1.72054* **Camping Les Erables, 17 Rue du Château d'Eau, 62179 Escalles [03 21 85 25 36; boutroy.les-erables@wanadoo.fr; www. camping-les-erables.fr/]** Fr A16 take exit 40 onto D243 thro Peuplingues. Site sp to L on ent Escalles (on sharp R bend). Steep ent. Don't be put off by No Entry signs - 1-way system for c'vans on app rd. Sm, mkd pitch, hdstg, terr, unshd; htd wc; chem disp; mv service pnt; shws €1.20; private san facs extra; el pnts (6-10A) €3.50-€4.50; lndtte (inc dryer); shop 2km; tradsmn; rest & snacks 500m; BBQ; sand beach 2km; dogs; phone; poss cr/noisy at w/end; Eng spkn; adv bkg; CKE/CCI. "Lovely, well-kept open site with great views; family owned; spacious pitches but poss haphazard pitching; welcoming staff; immac, modern facs; gates open 0800-2200; 2 pitches for disabled visitors with san facs; coast walks; sh walk to vill; conv tunnel & ferries; Gd site with view of Channel; Excel grass pitch site; friendly helpful owners" ♦ 1 Apr-11 Nov. € 23.40   2013*

"That's changed – Should I let The Club know?"

If you find something on site that's different from the site entry, fill in a report and let us know. See www.caravanclub.co.uk/europereport.

WISSANT *3A2* (4km E Rural) *50.88290, 1.70938* **Camping La Vallée, 901 Rue Principale, 62179 Hervelinghen [03 21 36 73 96 or 03 21 85 15 43; www. campingdelavallee.net]** Fr Calais exit A16 onto D244 & foll sp St Inglevert. Site on L at end Hervelinghen vill. Med, hdg/ mkd pitch, pt shd; htd wc; chem disp; shwrs €1; el pnts (6A) €3.60 (poss rev pol); lndry rm; rest, snacks; bar; BBQ; playgrnd; sand/shgl beach 3km; games area; wifi; 75% statics; dogs €1; Eng spkn; no adv bkg - phone to check availability; quiet; CKE/ CCI. "Family-run site; clean san facs; conv Calais, Cité Europe; gd walking in area" ♦ ltd 1 Apr-31 Oct. € 14.50   2013*

XONRUPT LONGEMER see Gérardmer *6F3*

YCHOUX *7D1* (10km E Rural) *44.33060, -0.97975* **Camp Municipal du Lac des Forges, 40160 Ychoux [05 58 82 35 57 or 05 58 82 36 01 (Mairie); fax 05 58 82 35 46]** Fr Bordeaux take N10 S & turn onto D43 at Liposthey W twd Parentis-en-Born. Site in 8km on R, past vill of Ychoux. Sm, pt sl, pt shd; wc; chem disp; mv service pnt; shwrs; el pnts (5-10A) €3.50 (rev pol); lndtte; shops 1km; rest; bar; playgrnd; TV rm; lake adj; fishing; sailing; dogs €1.50; quiet. "Levelling blocks poss req; pitches nr rd poss noisy." 15 Jun-10 Sep. € 14.00   2013*

YPORT *3C1* (800m Coastal) **Camp Municipal La Chenaie, Rue Henri-Simon, 76111 Yport [02 35 27 33 56]** Take D940 fr Fécamp SW, D211 to Yport to site. Med, pt shd; wc; shwrs; shops 500m; el pnts (4A); shgl beach 1km; many statics; poss cr; quiet. "Conv Le Havre."   2012*

See advertisement on pages 32 & 33

YPORT *3C1* (300m SW Coastal/Rural) *49.73746, 0.30959*
**Camping Le Rivage, Rue Hottières, 76111 Yport [tel/fax
02 35 27 33 78; contact@camping-lerivage.com; http://
www.camping-lerivage.com/]** Fr D940 bet Etretat & Fécamp
take D11 2km NE of Les Loges, meeting up with D211 & head
twd Yport. Site on D211. Or foll sp fr Yport. Med, pt sl, some
hdstg, terr, unshd; wc; chem disp; shwrs; el pnts (6A) inc
(poss long lead req); lndry rm; shops 1km; snacks; bar; BBQ;
shgl beach 300m; games rm; TV rm; phone; adv bkg; quiet.
"Well-situated, o'looking sea; steep descent to beach; san facs
inadequate high ssn & long walk fr most pitches; rec stop at
top of site & walk to recep bef pitching, as turning poss diff lge
o'fits." 25 Mar-30 Sep. € 17.50   2012*

YSSINGEAUX *9C1* (300m SE Urban) *45.13251, 4.12522*
**Camp Municipal de Choumouroux, 43200 Yssingeaux
[04 71 65 53 44 or 04 71 59 01 13 (Mairie); fax
04 71 65 19 35]** N88 Le Puy to St Etienne on R bef Yssingeaux;
ent next to school, opp petrol stn. Sm, pt shd; wc (cont);
chem disp; mv service pnt; shwrs inc; el pnts (10A) inc; shops
500m; playgrnd; fishing; dogs €1.20; quiet. "Gd location
amongst extinct volcanoes; well-maintained." 1 May-30 Sep.
€ 10.20   2008*

YVOIRE see Douvaine *9A3*

YYVRE L'EVEQUE see Mans, Le *4F1*

CORSICA

AJACCIO *10H2* (3km NW Coastal) *41.93725, 8.72851*
**Camping Les Mimosas, Route d'Alata, 20000 Ajaccio
[04 95 20 99 85; fax 04 95 10 01 77; campingmimosas@
wanadoo.fr; www.camping-lesmimosas.com]** Foll N194
round N of Ajaccio & then directions to Super U; 1st R off
rndabt immed after Super U; after rndabt site in 1km up narr
rd. Med, hdg/mkd pitch, hdstg, pt sl, shd; wc; chem disp; mv
service pnt; serviced pitches; shwrs inc; el pnts (5-10A) €2.80;
gas 1km; lndtte (inc dryer); sm shop & 1km; tradsmn; rest,
snacks; bar; playgrnd; shgl beach 1km; wifi; 5% statics; no
dogs; phone; adv bkg; quiet; 10% red low ssn/CKE/CCI. "Conv
Ajaccio; gd rest on site." ♦ ltd 1 Apr-18 Oct. € 17.60 2008*

⊞ **ALERIA** *10H2* (7km N Coastal) *42.16155, 9.55265*
**Camping-Village Riva-Bella (Part Naturist), 20270 Aléria
[04 95 38 81 10; fax 04 95 38 91 29; rivabella.corsica@
gmail.com; www.rivabella-corsica.com]** Fr Bastia S on N198
for 60km, site sp to L. Poor rd access (2011). Med, pt shd; wc;
mv service pnt; steam rm; sauna; shwrs; el pnts €4.30; lndtte;
shop; tradsmn; rest, snacks; bar; playgrnd; sand beach adj;
fishing; watersports; tennis; cycle hire; games area; fitness rm;
spa treatments; wifi; entmnt; TV rm; 10% statics; dogs €3.50;
naturist site 15 May-20 Sep, non-naturist rest of year - but
always sm end beach avail for naturists; adv bkg; quiet; red low
ssn/long stay; INF card. "Site untidy early ssn (2011); poss insect
problem." ♦ € 36.00   2011*

ALGAJOLA *10G2* (800m E Coastal) *42.60844, 8.87409*
**Camping de la Plage en Balagne, 20220 Algajola [tel/fax
04 95 60 71 76 or 06 09262638 (mob); campingalgajola@
wanadoo.fr; www.camping-de-la-plage-en-balagne.com]**
Site 6km W fr L'lle-Rousse on N197 dir Algajola. On R opp
Hotel Pascal Paoli bef Algajola. Med, pt shd; htd wc (some
cont); chem disp; mv service pnt; shwrs inc; el pnts (6A) €4;
lndtte; shop; rest, snacks; bar; playgrnd; sand beach adj; games
area; gym; entmnt; some statics; dogs €1.50; tram; poss cr; adv
bkg; quiet; ccard acc. "Poss very busy high ssn; san facs v tired
early ssn (2011); rest, snacks & bar on beach - poss clsd low
ssn; tram to l'lle-Rousse & Calvi fr site gd for touring inland;
gd." 15 Mar-15 Nov. € 22.70   2011*

BASTIA *10G2* (5km N Coastal) **Camping Les Orangers,
Licciola, 20200 Miomo [06 12 53 73 33; fax 04 95 33 23 65;
www.camping-lesorangers.com/]** Foll main coast rd D80 N
4km fr ferry. Site well sp on L of rd. Sm, shd; wc; shwrs; el pnts;
shop; tradsmn; rest, snacks; bar; sandy/shgl beach adj; TV; quiet;
CKE/CCI. "Poss run down low ssn; friendly owners; vg rest; site
ent tight for lge o'fits; no m'vans (2011); poss unrel opening
dates." 1 Apr-30 Sep.   2012*

BASTIA *10G2* (11km S Coastal) *42.62922, 9.46835* **Camping
San Damiano, Lido de la Marana, 20620 Biguglia
[04 95 33 68 02; fax 04 95 30 84 10; san.damiano@
wanadoo.fr; www.campingsandamiano.com]** S fr Bastia on
N193 for 4km. Turn SE onto Lagoon Rd (sp Lido de Marana).
Site on L in 7km. Lge, pt shd; wc; chem disp; baby facs; shwrs
inc; el pnts (6A) €3.40; lndtte; shop; rest; playgrnd; pool; sandy
beach adj; cycle path; games area; games rm; dogs €0.90; Eng
spkn; ccard acc; red long stay'/low ssn; CKE/CCI. "San facs
basic but clean." ♦ 1 Apr-31 Oct. € 22.00   2013*

BIGUGLIA see Bastia *10G2*

BONIFACIO *10H2* (15km N Coastal) *41.47326, 9.26318*
**Camping Rondinara, Suartone, 20169 Bonifacio
[04 95 70 43 15; fax 04 95 70 56 79; reception@rondinara.fr;
www.rondinara.fr]** Fr Bonifacio take N198 dir Porte-Vecchio
for 10km, then turn R onto D158 dir Suartone (lge camp sp
at turning). Site in 5km. NB D158 single track, many bends &
hills. Med, pt sl, shd; wc; mv service pnt; shwrs inc; el pnts
(6A) €3.60; lndtte; shop; rest, snacks; bar; BBQ; playgrnd; pool;
sand beach 400m; watersports; games area; games rm; some
statics; dogs €2.60; poss cr; Eng spkn; no adv bkg; quiet; red
low ssn; ccard acc; CKE/CCI. "Excel rest; idyllic location by
bay." 15 May-30 Sep. € 31.90   2013*

BONIFACIO *10H2* (4km NE Rural) *41.39986, 9.20141*
**Camping Pian del Fosse, Route de Sant' Amanza, 20169
Bonifacio [tel/fax 04 95 73 16 34; camping@piandelfosse.
com; www.piandelfosse.com]** Leave Bonifacio on D58 dir
Sant' Amanza, site on L in 4km. Sm, hdg/mkd pitch, terr, shd;
wc; chem disp; mv service pnt; baby facs; shwrs inc; el pnts
(4A) €3.80; lndtte; shop; tradsmn; snacks; BBQ; playgrnd; sand/
shgl beach 3km; 20% statics; dogs €2.50; poss cr; Eng spkn;
quiet; red snr citizens/long stay. "Pitches poss diff lge m'vans
due o'hanging trees,vg; ccard acc" ♦ ltd Easter-15 Oct.
€ 41.50   2013*

FRANCE - CORSICA

BONIFACIO *10H2* (4km NE Rural) *41.41842, 9.17898*
Pertamina Village U Farniente, Route de Porto Vecchio,
20169 Bonifacio [04 95 73 05 47; fax 04 95 73 11 42;
pertamina@wanadoo.fr; www.camping-pertamina.com]
Fr Bonifacio take RN198 N, site on R in 4km. Med, hdg/mkd
pitch, pt sl, pt shd; wc (some cont); chem disp; mv service pnt;
baby facs; shwrs inc; el pnts (6A) inc; gas; lndtte (inc dryer);
shop; rest, snacks; bar; playgrnd; htd pool; paddling pool;
waterslide; beach 3km; tennis; cycle hire; fitness rm; wifi;
entmnt; TV rm; 50% statics; dogs; poss cr; adv bkg; ccard acc;
CKE/CCI. "Access to pitches diff; excel." ♦ 1 Apr-15 Oct.
€ 33.00 (CChq acc)   2009*

CALVI *10G2* (1.8km SE Coastal) *42.55228, 8.76423* Camping
Paduella, Route de Bastia, 20260 Calvi [04 95 65 06 16 or
04 95 65 13 20; fax 04 95 31 43 99; camping.paduella@
wanadoo.fr; www.campingpaduella.com] On N197 fr Calvi;
on R 200m after rndabt by Casino supmkt. Med, mkd pitch, pt
sl, terr, pt shd; wc chem disp; baby facs; shwrs inc; el pnts (6A)
€3.65; lndtte; shop/supmkt; snacks; bar; playgrnd; sand beach
300m; 25% statics; dogs; poss cr; Eng spkn; quiet; CKE/CCI.
"Poss best site in Calvi; immac san facs but slippery when wet,
especially ramp; vg." ♦ 15 May-15 Oct. € 21.00   2013*

CALVI *10G2* (4km SE Coastal) *42.55403, 8.78879* Camping
La Dolce Vita, Ponte Bambino, Route de Bastia, 20260
Calvi [04 95 65 05 99; fax 04 95 65 31 25; www.dolce-vita.
org] N197 twd L'Ile Rousse. Site on L, by rest, immed after
x-ing rv bdge. Adj Bastia-Calvi. Lge, shd; wc; baby facs; shwrs
inc; el pnts (10A) €4; gas; lndtte; shop; rest, snacks; bar;
playgrnd; sand beach 150m; TV rm; dir access to rv; fishing;
sailing windsurfing; poss cr; quiet, but some aircraft & rlwy
noise. 1 May-30 Sep. € 24.70   2008*

CALVI *1G2* (13 SW Urban) *42.46451, 8.68012* La Morsetta
Camping, Route Calvi-Porta, 20260 Calvi [04 95 65 25 28;
fax 04 95 65 25 29; info@lamorsetta.net; www.
lamorsetta.net] Drive via the D81 from Calvi to Galeria.
Then about 12 km via the D81b coastal rd dir Calvi. Take the
direct route D81b from Calvi, 20 km. Med, pt shd; wc; shwrs;
el pnts €3.20; rest; bar; wifi; dog €1.70 ♦ 1 May-15 Oct.
€ 46.60   2013*

CALVI *10G2* (1.6km SW Coastal) *42.55290, 8.76870*
Camping La Pinède, Route de la Pinède, 20260 Calvi
[04 95 65 17 80; fax 04 95 65 19 60; info@camping-calvi.
com; www.camping-calvi.com] S fr L'Ile-Rousse on N197;
well sp ent Calvi; 1st ent on R to Rte de la Pinède, 2nd ent 1km
after 1st. Lge, shd; wc; chem disp; mv service pnt; shwrs; el pnts
(6A) €3.50; lndtte; shop; supmkt nrby; rest, snacks; bar; playgrnd;
pool; beach 250m; tennis; games area; dogs €2; train to Calvi &
Ile-Rousse 250m; ccard acc. "Too much shd; clean facs; superb
beach." 1 Apr-31 Oct. € 27.50 (CChq acc)   2008*

CARGESE *10H2* (4km N Coastal) *42.1625, 8.59791* Camping
Le Torraccia, Bagghiuccia, 20130 Cargèse [tel/fax
04 95 26 42 39; contact@camping-torraccia.com; www.
camping-torraccia.com] N fr Cargèse twd Porto on D81 for
3km. Site on L. Med, terr, pt shd; wc; baby facs; shwrs inc;
ltd el pnts (6A) €3.10; lndtte; shop; rest 4km; snacks; bar;
playgrnd; pool; sand beach 1km; games area; internet; no adv
bkg; red low ssn. "Nearest site to Porto without diff traffic
conditions." 21 Apr-30 Sep. € 20.10   2013*

CERVIONE *10G2* (7km NE Coastal) *42.36326, 9.52978*
Camping Merendella, Moriani-Plage, 20230 San Nicolao
[04 95 38 53 47; fax 04 95 38 44 01; merendella@orange.fr;
www.merendella.com] Site 44km S of Bastia at Moriani-
Plage; foll N193 & N198 fr Bastia to Moriani Plage, on E (beach
side) of N198, 700m after supmkt. Med, hdg/mkd pitch, shd;
wc; chem disp; mv service pnt; shwrs inc; el pnts (5A) €5.10;
lndtte; shop & supmkt 1km; rest, snacks; bar; playgrnd; htd,
covrd pool; dir access to beach adj; tennis 500m; games area;
games rm; TV rm; no dogs Jul/Aug; adv bkg; quiet; ccard acc;
CKE/CCI. "Idyllic beachside pitches; friendly, helpful, efficient
staff; easy access; excel." ♦ 1 Apr-31 Oct. € 26.00   2010*

CERVIONE *10G2* (6km SE Coastal) *42.32155, 9.54546*
Camping Calamar, Prunete, 20221 Cervione
[04 95 38 03 54 or 04 95 34 08 44 (LS); fax 04 95 31 17 09;
contact@campingcalamar.eu; www.campingcalamar.eu]
On N198 S fr Prunete for 6km. Turn L at x-rds, site in 500m
beside beach, sp. Sm, pt shd; wc; shwrs inc; el pnts €2.50;
lndtte; shop 500m; tradsmn; snacks; bar; BBQ; sand beach adj;
sailing; watersports; games area; dogs free; Eng spkn; adv bkg;
quiet; red low ssn. "Friendly owner; pleasant site with trees &
shrubs; excel." 1 Apr- 19 Oct. € 19.20   2013*

CORBARA see Ile Rousse L' *10G2*

CORTE *10G2* (500m S Rural) *42.30109, 9.15098* FFCC
Camping Le Restonica, Quartier Porette, Faubourg
St Antoine, 20250 Corte [tel/fax 04 95 46 11 59; vero.
camp@worldonline.fr] Fr N193 Ajaccio to Corte, twd cent
of town. Pass petrol stn on R then sharp turn R before x-ing
bdge (acute angle). Site on R in 200m opp Chapelle St Antoine.
Sharp turn down hill to ent. Med; wc; shwrs inc; el pnts €3.50;
gas; shops 200m; rest; sports complex 150m; adv bkg; quiet.
"Beautiful old town; gd walking & horseriding." 1 May-15 Oct.
€ 17.00   2008*

GHISONACCIA *10H2* (4km E Coastal) *41.99850, 9.44220*
Camping Arinella Bianca, Route de la Mer, Bruschetto,
20240 Ghisonaccia [04 95 56 04 78; fax 04 95 56 12 54;
arinella@arinellabianca.com; www.arinellabianca.com]
S fr Bastia on N193/N198 approx 70km to Ghisonaccia. At
Ghisonaccia foll sp opp pharmacy to beach (plage) & Rte de la
Mer. In 3km turn R at rndabt & site well sp. NB When towing
keep to main, coastal rds. Lge, hdg/mkd pitch, shd; wc (some
cont); chem disp; mv service pnt; baby facs; shwrs inc; el pnts
(6A) €5.50 (poss rev pol); gas; lndtte (inc dryer); shop; tradsmn;
rest, snacks; bar; BBQ; playgrnd; htd pool; paddling pool; sand
beach adj; fishing; watersports; tennis; horseriding adj; cycle
hire; games area; games rm; wifi; entmnt; TV rm; 45% statics;
dogs €6; Eng spkn; adv bkg; red low ssn; ccard acc; CKE/CCI.
"Clean, well-run site; attractive lake in cent; trees make access
to pitches diff; helpful owner & staff." ♦ 16 Apr-30 Sep.
€ 38.00   2009*

GHISONACCIA *10H2* (4km E Coastal) *41.9998, 9.44731*
**Camping Marina d'Erba Rossa, Route de la Mer, 20240
Ghisonaccia [04 95 56 25 14 or 04 95 56 21 18; fax
04 95 56 27 23; info@marina-erbarossa.com; www.
marina-erbarossa.com]** Drive into town on N198. Site sp
down D144 (easy to miss). Take D144 E to coast & site on R
after 5km. Lge, hdg/mkd pitch, shd; wc; chem disp; shwrs;
el pnts (5-6A) inc (long lead rec); lndtte; shop; rest; pizzeria;
snacks; playgrnd; pool; private sand beach; watersports; tennis;
cycle hire; horseriding; entmnt; some statics; dogs €4; adv bkg;
quiet. ♦ 5 Apr-25 Oct. € 37.20   2008*

ILE ROUSSE, L' *10G2* (7km SE Rural) *42.62706, 9.01081*
**Camping Le Clos des Chênes, Route de Belgodère,
20226 Lozari [04 95 60 15 13 or 04 95 60 41 27 (LS);
fax 04 95 60 21 16; cdc.lozari@wanadoo.fr; www.
closdeschenes.fr]** E on fr L'Ile Rousse on N197 E twd Bastia.
After 7km turn S at Lozari onto N197 sp Belgodère; site on
R after 1.5km. Lge, sl, pt shd; wc; chem disp; baby facs;
shwrs inc; el pnts (4-10A) €3.80-6.05 (long cable req); gas;
lndtte; shop; tradsmn; rest; bar; pizzeria; BBQ; playgrnd; pool;
paddling pool; waterslide; sand beach 1.5km; tennis; games
rm; 10% statics; dogs €3.50; poss cr; some Eng spkn; adv bkg;
red low ssn; ccard acc; CKE/CCI. "Tranquil site; most pitches
haphazard amongst oaks, some with views; ltd facs low ssn; gd
touring cent; daily mkt." ♦ 1 May-30 Sep. € 26.45   2008*

LECCI *10H2* (8km S Rural) *41.67200, 9.30152* **Camping
Mulinacciu, 20137 Lecci [04 95 71 47 48; fax
04 95 71 54 82; infos@campingmulinacciu@.com; www.
camping-mulinacciu.com]** N fr Porto-Vecchio on N198 for
approx 10km. Cross double bdge over Rv Oso & turn L onto
unmade rd opp D668 dir San Cipriano. Site sp down this rd.
Med, some hdstg, pt shd; wc; baby facs; shwrs inc; el pnts (5A)
€3.50; lndtte; shop; tradsmn; rest; snacks; bar; playgrnd; pool;
paddling pool; waterslide; sand beach 7km; fishing; tennis;
games area; games rm; wifi; entmnt; TV; some statics; dogs
€2; phone; Eng spkn; quiet. "Access to rv; friendly owners."
15 Jun-15 Sep. € 22.00   2010*

LOZARI see Ile Rousse, L' *10G2*

OLMETO *10H2* (3km S Coastal) *41.69803, 8.89667* **Camping
Vigna Maggiore, 20113 Olmeto-Plage [04 95 76 02 07;
fax 04 95 74 62 02; contact@vignamaggiore.com; www.
vignamaggiore.com]** Site is approx 5km N of Propriano at
junc N196 & D157 Med, terr, pt shd; wc; chem disp; mv waste;
shwrs inc; el pnts €3.60; lndtte; rest; bar; playgrnd; pool; sand
beach 1km; games area; some statics; poss cr; no adv bkg;
CKE/CCI. 1 Apr-30 Sep. € 20.90   2009*

OLMETO *10H2* (5km SW Coastal) *41.69563, 8.88866*
**Camping Village Esplanade, Tour de la Calanca, 20113
Olmeto-Plage [04 95 76 05 03; fax 04 95 76 16 22;
campingesplanade@orange.fr; www.campingesplanade.
com]** S fr Olmeto on N196 twd Propriano; turn R onto D157;
site in 1km. Med, mkd pitch, pt sl, terr, shd; wc; shwrs inc;
el pnts (6-10A) €3; lndtte; shop; rest, snacks; bar; playgrnd;
pool; paddling pool; games rm; some statics;
dogs free; sep car park; Eng spkn; adv bkg; quiet; ccard
acc. "Pleasant, shady site in gd location." 1 Apr-15 Oct.
€ 22.70   2008*

PIANOTTOLI CALDARELLO *10H2* (3.5km SE Coastal)
41.47272, 9.04327 **Camping Kevano Plage, Route du
bord de mer 20131 Pianottoli-Caldarello [04 95 71 83 22;
fax 04 95 71 83 83; campingkevano@gmail.com; www.
campingkevano.com]** Turn off N196 in Pianottoli at x-rds
onto D122 for 1km. Turn R in Caldarello, site on L in 2km.
Med, mkd pitch, pt sl, terr, pt shd; wc; chem disp; mv service
pnt; shwrs inc; el pnts (4-6A) €2.50; lndtte; shop; tradsmn;
pizzeria, rest, snacks; bar; playgrnd; sand beach 400m; entmnt;
TV; some statics; dogs €1; phone; poss cr; Eng spkn; adv bkg
rec high ssn; quiet; ccard acc; CKE/CCI. "Beautiful, family-run
site in macchia amongst huge boulders; san facs tired but
clean; no dogs on beach Jul/Aug" ♦ ltd 27 Apr-30 Sep.
€ 42.00   2013*

PIETRACORBARA *10G2* (4km SE Coastal) *42.83908,
9.4736* **Camping La Pietra, Marine de Pietracorbara,
20233 Pietracorbara [04 95 35 27 49; fax 04 95 35 28 57;
lapietra@wanadoo.fr; www.la-pietra.com]** Fr Bastia on
D80 N. In 20km ent vill & turn L onto D232. Site on R in 1km at
marina beach. Well sp. Med, hdg/mkd pitch, shd; htd wc; mv
service pnt; baby facs; shwrs inc; el pnts (20A) €3.50; lndtte;
shop; tradsmn; rest on beach; bar; BBQ; playgrnd; pool; sand
beach 600m; lake fishing; tennis; wifi; TV; dogs €2.50; bus nr;
Eng spkn; red low ssn; ccard acc; CKE/CCI. "Generous pitches;
helpful owners; excel facs; beautiful pool; gd rest." ♦ 20 Mar-
4 Nov. € 28.70 (CChq acc)   2011*

PORTO *10G2* (1km E Rural) *42.26275, 8.71020* **Camping
Sole e Vista, Rue d'Ota, 20150 Porto [04 95 26 15 71; fax
04 95 26 10 79; campingsporto@voila.fr; www.camping-
sole-e-vista.com]** On D81 Ajaccio-Calvi rd, turn E onto D124.
Ent thro Spar supmkt car park in Porto. NB rd fr Calvi diff for
c'vans. Lge, mkd pitch, terr, pt sl, shd; wc; chem disp; mv
service pnt; shwrs inc; el pnts (16A) €3.50; gas; lndtte; shop
adj; tradmsn; snacks; bar; BBQ; playgrnd; shgl beach 1.5km;
internet; TV rm; some statics; dogs; poss cr; Eng spkn; adv bkg;
quiet; red CKE/CCI. "Vg; modern san facs." 1 Apr-15 Oct.
€ 22.50   2010*

PORTO *10G2* (1.5km E Coastal) *42.26211, 8.71011*
**Camping Les Oliviers, 20150 Porto [04 95 26 14 49; fax
04 95 26 12 49; lesoliviersporto@wanadoo.fr; www.
campinglesoliviers.com]** On D81 fr Porto on R bank of Rv
Porto nr Pont de Porto. Site nr rv a sh distance downhill fr Cmp
Sole e Vista. Check for access, poss ltd space for c'vans. Lge,
terr, shd; wc; baby facs; shwrs; el pnts (5A) inc; lndry rm; shop
high ssn; tradsmn; snacks; bar; BBQ; playgrnd; beach 1km; rv
sw adj; sailing & windsurfing 1km; tennis; cycle hire; archery;
entmnt; TV; no dogs high ssn; quiet; ccard acc. "Gd, clean,
modern facs; ent to site upper levels v steep." 1 Apr-10 Nov.
€ 27.50   2008*

PORTO POLLO *10H2* (500m E Coastal) *41.71126, 8.80485*
**Camping Alfonsi-U-Casselo, 20140 Serra-di-Ferro
[04 95 74 01 80; fax 04 95 74 07 67]** Turn W onto D157 off
N196 Propriano-Olmeto rd sp Porto-Pollo. After narr rv bdge
turn L on D757. Site in 4km on L bef Porto-Pollo vill. Med,
mkd pitch, pt shd; wc; mv service pnt; shwrs; el pnts (10A) €3;
lndtte; shop 800m; supmkt in vill; rest high ssn; snacks; bar;
sand beach adj; no dogs; poss cr; no adv bkg; poss noisy; ccard
acc; CKE/CCI. "Pleasant site in gd situation." ♦ 1 Jun-30 Oct.
€ 22.60   2009*

PORTO VECCHIO *10H2* (5km N Rural/Coastal) *41.63275, 9.29288* **Camping La Vetta, Ste Trinité, 20137 Porto-Vecchio [04 95 70 09 86; fax 04 95 70 43 21; info@ campinglavetta.com; www.campinglavetta.com]** On L (W) of N198 N of Ste Trinité. Sp in advance fr N & S. Med, pt sl, shd; wc; shwrs inc; el pnts (10A) €3; gas; lndtte; shop 800m; supmkt 3km; rest, snacks; playgrnd; games area; pool; sand beach 3km; Eng spkn; quiet but some rd noise; ccard acc. "Excel bay for snorkelling, sw & windsurfing." 1 Jun-1 Oct. € 21.50   2008*

PORTO VECCHIO *10H2* (5km NE Coastal) *41.62273, 9.2997* **Camping Les Ilots d'Or, Ste Trinité, Route de Marina di Fiori, 20137 Porto-Vecchio [04 95 70 01 30 or 04 95 36 91 75; fax 04 95 70 01 30; info@ campinglesilotsdor.com; www.campinglesilotsdor.com]** Turn E off N198 5km N of Porto-Vecchio at Ste Trinité twd San Ciprianu. In 1km fork R, site in 300m on left Med, pt sl, pt terr, shd; wc (cont); shwrs inc; el pnts (6A) €3.50; gas; lndtte; shop; rest, snacks; bar; sand beach adj; poss cr; quiet. "Well-organised site; helpful family owners; many vg beaches in easy reach." 2 May- 30 Sep. € 22.00   2013*

PORTO VECCHIO *10H2* (2km S Rural) *41.57084, 9.27609* **Camping U-Stabiacciu, Route de Palombaggia, 20137 Porto-Vecchio [04 95 70 37 17; fax 04 95 70 62 59; stabiacciu@wanadoo.fr; www.stabiacciu.com]** Foll ring-rd N198 to S Porto-Vecchio, take 1st L sp Palombaggia. Site in 50m. Ramps at site ent. Med, shd; wc (some cont); mv service pnt; shwrs inc; el pnts (5A) €3 (long lead poss req); lndtte; shop in ssn; tradsmn; rest, snacks; bar; BBQ; playgrnd; jacuzzis; sand beach 4km; 3% statics; dogs; phone; Eng spkn; rd noise; ccard acc; CKE/CCI. "Excel beaches; sh stay only." 1 Apr-14 Oct. € 19.10   2009*

PORTO VECCHIO *10H2* (8km W Coastal) *41.59336, 9.35718* **Camping Club La Chiappa (Naturist), 20137 Porto-Vecchio [04 95 70 00 31; fax 04 95 70 07 70; chiappa@wanadoo.fr; www.chiappa.com]** On N198 fr Bastia heading S thro Porto-Vecchio. 2km S turn L to Pointe de la Chiappa & foll camp sp. Lge, pt shd; wc; chem disp; shwrs; el pnts inc; lndtte; sauna; shop; rest; bar; playgrnd; pool; watersports; private sand beach adj; tennis; horseriding; entmnt; TV rm; 10% statics; dogs €6; adv bkg; quiet; red low ssn. "Superb site in lovely setting in naturist reserve; excel beach; vg facs; gd rest." 14 May-8 Oct. € 37.00   2011*

SAGONE *10H2* (2km N Rural) *42.13030, 8.70550* **Sagone Camping, Route de Vico, 20118 Sagone [04 95 28 04 15; sagone.camping@wanadoo.fr; www.camping-sagone. com]** Fr Sagone dir Cargèse then D70 dir Vico, site sp. Lge, mkd pitch, pt shd; wc; chem disp; mv service pnt; baby facs; shwrs inc; el pnts €4.50; lndtte (inc dryer); shop; rest, snacks; bar; BBQ; playgrnd; pool; beach 2km; tennis 100m; cycle hire; horseriding 1km; entmnt; TV rm; 10% statics; dogs €2.30; adv bkg; quiet. ♦ 1 May-30 Sep. € 25.70 (CChq acc)   2011*

ST FLORENT *10G2* (1km SW Coastal) *42.67394, 9.29205* **Camping U Pezzo, Route de la Roya, 20217 St Florent [tel/ fax 04 95 37 01 65; contact@upezzo.com; www.upezzo. com]** Exit St Florent for L'Ile-Rousse on D81 then N199 Route de la Plage. After 2km sharp R immed after x-ing bdge. Med, terr, pt shd; wc; mv service pnt; baby facs; shwrs inc; el pnts (10A) €4; lndtte; shop; rest, snacks; bar; sand beach adj; fishing; sailing; windsurfing; waterslide; horseriding; mini-farm for children; dogs €3.50; adv bkg; quiet; red low ssn; CKE/CCI. "Pleasant site" 01 Apr-15 Oct. € 19.00   2013*

SERRA DI FERRO see Porto Pollo *10H2*

VENACO *10G2* (3km E Rural) *42.22388, 9.19364* **Camping La Ferme de Peridundellu, 20231 Venaco [tel/fax 04 95 47 09 89 / 06 12 95 51 65 (mob); campingvenaco@ wanadoo.fr; http://campingvenaco.monsite-orange.fr]** S on N200 fr Corte for 15km; R on D143; at bdge keep R towards Venaco; site on L in 1.5km on bend. Sm, pt sl, pt shd; htd wc; chem disp (wc); shwrs inc; el pnts (6-10A) €5.; lndtte; shop 2km; tradsmn; rest adj; snacks & bar 2km; quiet; CKE/ CCI. "CL-type site; beautifully situated; gd walking country; friendly owner; highly rec" Apr-Sep. € 17.20   2013*

ILE DE RE

ARS EN RE *7A1* (400m S Coastal) *46.20395, -1.52014* **FFCC Camping du Soleil, 57 Route de la Grange, 17590 Ars-en-Ré [05 46 29 40 62; fax 05 46 29 41 74; contact@ campdusoleil.com; www.campdusoleil.com]** On ent Ars-en-Ré on D735, pass Citroën g'ge & in 700m take 3rd L dir Plage de la Grange. Site sp. Med, hdg/mkd pitch, shd; wc; chem disp; mv service pnt; baby facs; fam bthrm; shwrs inc; el pnts (4-10A) €3.70-4.90; lndtte; shop; rest, snacks; bar; BBQ (gas/elec); playgrnd; htd pool; paddling pool; sand beach 400m; tennis; games area; cycle hire; wifi; TV rm; 35% statics; dogs €3.20; phone; adv bkg; red low ssn; CKE/CCI. "Pleasant, pretty site with pines & bamboo; helpful, friendly staff; gd pool; gd cycling & walking." ♦ 15 Mar-15 Nov. € 34.00 (3 persons)   2011*

ARS EN RE *7A1* (300m NW Coastal) *46.21130, -1.53017* **Airotel Camping Le Cormoran, Route de Radia, 17590 Ars-en-Ré [05 46 29 46 04; fax 05 46 29 29 36; info@ cormoran.com; www.cormoran.com]** Fr La Rochelle take D735 onto Ile-de-Ré, site sp fr Ars-en-Ré. Med, hdg/mkd pitch, hdstg, pt shd; wc; chem disp; mv service pnt; baby facs; sauna; shwrs inc; el pnts (10A) €5; lndtte; shop 800m; tradsmn; rest, snacks; bar; playgrnd; htd pool; beach 500m; tennis; cycle hire; games area; games rm; golf 10km; entmnt; some statics; dogs €5.50; Eng spkn; adv bkg; quiet; ccard acc; red low ssn; CKE/CCI. "Delightful vill; vg site." ♦ 1 Apr-30 Sep. € 40.00 (3 persons)   2012*

See advertisement opposite

COUARDE SUR MER, LA *7A1* (4km SE Coastal) *46.17733, -1.38629* **Campéole Camping Les Amis de la Plage, Ave Pas des Boeufs, 17580 Le Bois-Plage-en-Ré [tel/fax 05 46 09 24 01; contact@les-amis-de-la-plage.com; www.les-amis-de-la-plage.com or www.campeole.com]** Fr toll bdge fr La Rochelle foll D201 to Le Bois-Plage-en-Ré; on ent vill take 1st L sp 'Plage-des-Boeufs' & 'Municipal'. Site on R at end of rd. Lge, pt sl, pt shd; wc; chem disp (wc); mv service pnt; baby facs; shwrs inc; el pnts (10A) €4.10; lndtte; shops & mkt 1km; tradsmn; rest & snacks adj; BBQ; playgrnd; sand beach adj; pool adj; 5% statics; dogs €2; phone; bus 1km; poss cr; Eng spkn; quiet; ccard acc; red low ssn; CKE/CCI. "Friendly, easy-going site; pitches on sand/soil/dry grass; vg." 2 Apr-30 Sep. € 19.00 (3 persons)   2010*

See advertisement on pages 14 & 15

COUARDE SUR MER, LA *7A1* (4km SE Coastal) *46.17850, -1.38320* **Camping Les Varennes, Raise Maritaise, 17580 Le Bois-Plage-en-Ré [05 46 09 15 43; fax 05 46 09 47 27; les-varennes@wanadoo.fr; www.les-varennes]** Fr toll bdge at La Rochelle, foll D201 to Gros-Jonc (1km bef Le Bois-Plage-en-Ré cent); turn L at rndabt; after 350m turn R; site on R in 500m. Med, mkd pitch, shd; htd wc (some cont); chem disp; mv service pnt; baby facs; shws inc; el pnts (10A) €5.30; lndtte; shop & rest 1km; snacks; bar; BBQ (sep area); playgrnd; htd, covrd pool; sand beach 300m; cycle hire; wifi; TV; 70% statics; dogs €6; poss cr; Eng spkn; adv bkg; quiet; ccard acc; red low ssn/long stay; CKE/CCI. "Excel, site; many cycle tracks; vg." ♦ 1 Apr-30 Sep. € 38.00 (3 persons)   2008*

COUARDE SUR MER, LA *7A1* (4km SE Coastal) *46.17405, -1.37865* **Sunêlia Parc Club Interlude, 8 Route de Gros Jonc, 17580 Le Bois-Plage-en-Ré [05 46 09 18 22; fax 05 46 09 23 38; infos@interlude.fr; www.interlude.fr]** Fr toll bdge at La Rochelle foll D201 to Gros-Jonc. Turn L at rndabt at site sp. Site 400m on L. Lge, hdg/mkd pitch, hdstg, pt shd; htd wc; chem disp; mv service pnt; baby facs; fam bthrm; sauna; some serviced pitches; shwrs inc; el pnts (10A) inc; gas; lndtte (inc dryer); shop; rest, snacks; bar; BBQ; playgrnd; 2 pools (1 htd, covrd); sand beach; watersports; jacuzzi; solarium; tennis nr; games area; boat & cycle hire; fitness rm; wifi; TV rm; 45% statics; dogs €8; poss cr; Eng spkn; o'night area for m'vans; adv bkg ess; quiet; red low ssn. "Excel, well-run, relaxing site; busy but not noisy; vg facs; some sm, sandy pitches - extra for lger; gd rest; nrby beaches excel; excel lge clean well run site; walk to great beach; gd atmosphere, entmnt and shop" ♦ 13 Apr-22 Sep. € 67.20   2013*

COUARDE SUR MER, LA *7A1* (5km SE Coastal) *46.16793, -1.36351* **Camping Antioche, Route de Ste Marie, 17580 Le Bois-Plage-en-Ré [05 46 09 23 86; fax 05 46 09 43 34; camping.antioche@wanadoo.fr]** Fr toll bdge fr La Rochelle, at 1st rndabt take D201 sp Le Bois-Plage. In about 9km, site on L. Med, hdg/mkd pitch (sandy), pt sl, pt shd; wc; chem disp; mv service pnt; shwrs inc; el pnts (6A) inc; lndtte; shop & 3km; playgrnd; snacks; bar; BBQ; cooking facs; sand beach adj; entmnt; some statics; dogs €6; phone; poss cr; Eng spkn; adv bkg; ccard acc; red low ssn/long stay/CKE/CCI. "Lovely site with gd sized pitches; direct access to beach & cycle path; friendly staff; clean facs." ♦ 4 Apr-19 Sep. € 37.00 (3 persons) 2009*

COUARDE SUR MER, LA *7A1* (500m W Urban/Coastal) *46.19348, -1.43427* **Camp Municipal Le Remondeau, 12 Route Petite Noue, 17670 La Couarde-sur-Mer [05 46 29 84 27; campingleremondeau@wanadoo.fr]** Fr toll bdge foll D735 to rndabt on W side of La Couarde-sur-Mer & take D201. Foll sp to site. Lge, pt sl, pt shd; htd wc; chem disp; mv service pnt; baby facs; shwrs inc; el pnts (10A) €3.70; lndtte (inc dryer); tradsmn; BBQ; playgrnd; sand beach adj; wifi; few statics; dogs; Eng spkn; no adv bkg; quiet; red long stay; CKE/CCI. "Vg site." ♦ ltd Easter-30 Oct. € 19.00   2010*

COUARDE SUR MER, LA *7A1* (2.5km W Coastal) *46.20296, -1.45505* **Camping Le Bois Henri IV, Route d'Ars, 17670 La Couarde-sur-Mer [tel/fax 05 46 29 87 01; campingduboishenri4@aliceadsl.fr; www.campingduboishenri4.17-flash.com]** On D735 W fr La Couarde-sur-Mer, site ent bet 2 pedestrian x-ings - easy to miss. Med, hdg/mkd pitch, pt shd; wc; chem disp; mv service pnt; baby facs; shwrs inc; chem disp (wc); el pnts (5A) €4; lndtte (inc dryer); shop; BBQ (gas/elec); playgrnd; sand beach 200m; cycle hire; wifi; TV rm; 30% statics; dogs €2; poss cr; Eng spkn; adv bkg; quiet; red low ssn; CKE/CCI. "Busy site; long, sandy beaches; friendly owner; clean, dated san facs; birdwatching in salt marshes; 100km of flat cycling pathways; vg." ♦ ltd 1 Apr-30 Sep. € 22.00   2011*

COUARDE SUR MER, LA *7A1* (800m NW Coastal) *46.20408, -1.46740* Camping de l'Océan, 50 Route d'Ars, 17670 La Couarde-sur-Mer [05 46 29 87 70; fax 05 46 29 92 13; info@campingocean.com; www.campingocean.com] Fr La Rochelle take D735 over bdge to Ile de Ré. Past St Martin-de-Re & La Couarde twd Ars-en-Ré. Site on R, 2.5km after La Couarde. Lge, hdg/mkd pitch, shd; htd wc; chem disp; mv service pnt; baby facs; fam bthrm; shwrs inc; el pnts (10A) €5.50; lndtte (inc dryer); shop, rest, snacks; bar; no BBQ; playgrnd; 2 pools (1 htd); paddling pool; sand beach adj; watersports; tennis; games area; cycle hire; horseriding 1.5km; golf 6km; wifi; entmnt; 40% statics; dogs €5; phone; poss cr; Eng spkn; adv bkg; rd noisy; ccard acc; red low ssn; CKE/CCI. "Popular site in superb location; some sm pitches with diff access; site rds & ent to pitches narr; gd, clean san facs; friendly staff; twin-axles not rec; recep clsd 1230-1400, if clsd, park in yard facing recep; gd walking & cycling; excel; Toll fee to island €27.50" ♦ 16 Apr-18 Sep. € 49.00 (3 persons)   2012*

COUARDE SUR MER, LA *7A1* (2km NW Coastal) *46.20473, -1.44470* Camping La Tour des Prises, Route d'Ars D735, 17670 La Couarde-sur-Mer [05 46 29 84 82; fax 05 46 29 88 99; camping@lesprises.com; www.lesprises.com] Fr toll bdge foll D735 or D201 to La Couarde, then Rte d'Ars for 1.8km to R turn; site sp & 200m on R. Med, hdg/mkd pitch, pt shd; htd wc (some cont); chem disp; mv service pnt; baby facs; shwrs inc; el pnts (16A) €5.50; lndtte; shop; tradsmn; snacks; playgrnd; htd, covrd pool; beach 600m; sailing school; games rm; cycle hire; wifi; 30% statics; dogs €4.; Eng spkn; adv bkg; quiet; ccard acc; red low ssn; CKE/CCI. "Excel, well-managed, clean site; lge indiv pitches, mixed sizes; helpful owner & staff; excel pool; many cycle/walking tracks; beach 10 mins walk; ideal for families; large o'fits drive cautiously, no one way" ♦ 2 Apr-30 Sep. € 47.20 (3 persons)   2013*

ST CLEMENT DES BALEINES *7A1* (S Coastal) *46.22567, -1.54424* FFCC Camping La Côte Sauvage, 336 Rue de la Forêt, 17590 St Clément-Des-Baleines [05 46 29 46 63; fax 04 73 77 05 06; contact@lesbalconsverts.com; www.lesbalconsverts.com] Fr cent of vill, foll sp to site at edge of forest. Lge, mkd pitch, pt sl, pt shd; wc; chem disp; mv service pnt; baby facs; shws inc; el pnts (10A) €4 (poss long lead req); shop 300m; tradsmn; snacks; shgl beach adj; cycle routes adj; sw; wifi; dogs €3; phone; Eng spkn; quiet; red low ssn; CKE/CCI; "Gd location; some pitches uneven; gd modern san facs; poss unrel opening dates; gd" ♦ 6 Apr-29 Sep. € 29.00 (CChq acc)   2013*

STE MARIE DE RE *7A1* (Coastal) *46.14504, -1.31509* Camp Municipal La Côte Sauvage, La Basse Benée 17740 Ste Marie-de-Ré [05 46 30 21 74 or 05 46 30 21 24 (LS); fax 05 46 30 15 64; camping.stemarie @ orange.fr; www.mairie-sainte-marie-de-re.fr] Site sp fr main rd. V narr rds thro town. Med, mkd pitch, pt shd; wc; chem disp; mv service pnt; shwrs inc; el pnts (16A) €3.50; shop; supmkt 2km; snacks; bar; playgrnd; sand beach adj; fishing; quiet; ccard acc; red low ssn; CKE/CCI; "Excel location but poss windy; helpful owners; gd value snack bar; free parking for m'vans adj; highly rec" 1 Apr - 19 Oct. € 15.00   2013*

⊞ **STE MARIE DE RE** *7A1* (3km NW) *46.16083, -1.35222* Camping Les Grenettes, Route De L'Ermitage, 17740 Ste Marie De Re [05 46 30 22 47; fax 05 46 30 24 64; contact@hotel-les-grenettes.com; www.campinglesgrenettes.com] Foll sp for D201 'Itinéraire Sud' after toll bdge in the dir of Le Bois-de-Plage; after approx 2km turn L. Med, mkd pitches, pt shd; wc; chem disp; mv service pnt; baby facs; shwrs inc; el pnts (6A) €4.50; gas; shop; rest; BBQ; playgrnd; pool; water slide; paddling pool; sea 200m; fishing; tennis; cycle hire; entmnt; wifi; TV; statics; dogs €4; Eng spkn; adv bkg; ccard acc. "V nice site close to sea; v gd rest." € 32.00   2011*

ST MARTIN DE RE *7A1* (4km E Coastal/Urban) *46.18194, -1.33110* Flower Camping de Bel Air, Route de la Noué, 17630 La Flotte-en-Ré [05 46 09 63 10; camping.bel-air@flowercampings.com; www.bel-air-camping.com] Fr toll bdge take D735 to La Flotte. Turn R at rndabt to town into Route de la Noué, site sp.. Lge, hdg/mkd pitch, pt shd; wc (some cont); chem disp; mv service pnt; shwrs inc; el pnts (6A) €3.84; lndtte; rest, snacks; bar; playgrnd; beach 800m; tennis; games rm; entmnt; wifi; phone; adv bkg; quiet. "Walk to shops, harbour, beach etc; gd; friendly staff" ♦ 30 Mar-3 Nov. € 29.00   2013*

See advertisement on pages 32 & 33

ST MARTIN DE RE *7A1* (2km SE Coastal) *46.18370, -1.30820* FFCC Camping Les Peupliers, 17630 La Flotte-en-Ré [05 46 09 62 35; fax 05 46 09 59 76; contact@lespeupliers.com; www.les-peupliers.com] Site sp fr D735, Route du Fort-la-Prée, main rd on Ile-de-Ré. Lge, hdg/mkd pitch, pt shd, wc; chem disp; mv service pnt; shwrs inc; el pnts (5A) inc; lndtte; shop; supmkt 900m; tradsmn; rest, snacks; bar; BBQ (gas only); playgrnd; htd pool; paddling pool; sand beach 800m; games area; wifi; entmnt; TV rm; 80% statics; dogs €5; phone; Eng spkn; adv bkg rec; quiet; ccard acc; CKE/CCI. "Sea views; some pitches sm; ltd touring ptiches; poss cr low ssn; gd sports facs." ♦ 30 Apr-24 Sep. € 35.00 (3 persons)   2010*

ST MARTIN DE RE *7A1* (5km SE Rural) *46.18740, -1.34390* Camping La Grainetière, Route St Martin, 17630 La Flotte-en-Ré [05 46 09 68 86; fax 05 46 09 53 13; la-grainetiere@orange.fr; www.la-grainetiere.com] 10km W fr toll bdge, site sp on La Flotte ring rd. Med, pt shd; wc; chem disp; mv service pnt; baby facs; shwrs inc; el pnts (10A) €4.50; gas; lndtte; shop; tradsmn; playgrnd; htd pool; sand beach 3km; cycle hire; wifi; TV rm; 70% statics; dogs €4.50; poss cr; Eng spkn; adv bkg; rd noise; red low ssn; CKE/CCI; "Beautiful, clean, wooded site; haphazard pitching; helpful owners; gd san facs; gd pool; daily mkt; vg" ♦ 2 Apr- 30 Sep. € 23.00   2013*

See advertisement opposite

ST MARTIN DE RE *7A1* (800m S Urban) *46.19913, -1.36682* **Camp Municipal Les Remparts, Rue Les Remparts, 17410 St Martin-de-Ré [05 46 09 21 96; fax 05 46 09 94 18; camping.stmartindere@wanadoo.fr; www.saint-martin-de-re.fr]** Foll D735 fr toll bdge to St Martin; sp in town fr both ends. Med, hdg/mkd pitch, pt sl, pt shd; wc; chem disp; mv service pnt; shwrs inc; el pnts (10A) €3.70; lndtte; shop; snacks; BBQ; playgrnd; pool 3km; sand beach 1.3km; dogs €2; Eng spkn; adv bkg; quiet; ccard acc; red low ssn; CKE/CCI. "Busy site in brilliant location; san facs dated but clean; gd basic rest; poss children's groups mid-ssn; some pitches boggy when wet; gd cycling; site poss unkempt end ssn; vg mkt; beautiful situation on outskirts of a lovely town, gd size pitches" ♦ 12 Mar-18 Nov. € 23.00 (3 persons)   2013*

ILE D'OLERON

BREE LES BAINS, LA (N) *46.02027, -1.35762* **Camping Antioche d'Oléron, 17840 La Brée-les-Bains [05 46 47 92 00; fax 05 46 47 82 22; info@camping-antiochedoleron.com; www.camping-antiochedoleron. com]** Go over bdge on D26 onto D734; turn R after St Georges onto D273E1 dir La Brees-les-Baines; turn L at T junction; campsite sp. Med, mkd pitch; wc; chem disp; mv service pnt; serviced pitches; shwrs inc; el pnts (10A) €5.50; rest; bar; playgrnd; pool; jacuzzi; paddling pool; cycle hire (high ssn); games rm; wifi; Eng spkn. "Gd site; entmnt in summer months; v gd pool." 2 Apr-24 Sep. € 31.80   2011*

See advertisement below

BREE LES BAINS, LA *7A1* (500m NW Coastal) *46.01861, -1.35446* **Camp Municipal Le Planginot, Allée du Gai Séjour, 17840 La Brée-les-bains [05 46 47 82 18; fax 05 46 75 90 74; camping.planginot@orange.fr; www. leplanginot.com]** N fr St Pierre d'Oléron on D734, turn R for La Brée on D273, site sp (if sp diff to see - foll 'plage' sp). Lge, mkd pitch, pt shd; htd wc; chem disp; mv service pnt; shwrs inc ltd hot water; el pnts (10A) €3.60; lndtte; snacks; rest in high ssn; playgrnd; beach adj; dogs €2; Eng spkn; adv bkg; quiet; red low ssn; 15% statics; "Well-kept site in quiet location; friendly, helpful staff; immac san facs; gd cycling; daily mkt nrby; excel value low ssn; excel." ♦ 15 Mar-15 Oct. € 13.20   2012*

BREE LES BAINS, LA *7A1* (3km NW Coastal) *46.03855, -1.37521* **Camp Municipal, 10 Blvd d'Antioche, 17650 St Denis-d'Oléron [05 46 47 85 62; camping-municipal-st-denis-doleron@wanadoo.fr; www.st-denis-oleron.com]** Clear sp fr D734 in St Denis-d'Oléron town cent. 300m fr port. Lge, mkd pitch, pt sl, pt shd; htd wc; chem disp; mv service pnt; shwrs inc; el pnts (6A) €3.95; gas; lndtte; shop; rest nrby; snacks; playgrnd; sand beach adj; fishing; tennis; dogs €2.55; phone; poss cr; Eng spkn; quiet; CKE/CCI. "Some sea views; gd facs; some pitches v soft; ideal for beach holiday with children; gd." 15 Mar-30 Sep. € 13.40 (3 persons)   2010*

Route des Huîtres
17480 Le Chateau d'Oleron
Tel: 0033 (0)5 46 47 62 37
Fax: 0033 (0)5 46 47 71 70

www.camping-labrande.com 29°C from 05/04 to 11/11

CHATEAU D'OLERON, LE *7B1* (Urban/Coastal) *45.88970, -1.20028* Camping Les Remparts, Blvd Philippe-Daste, 17480 Le Château-d'Oléron [05 46 47 61 93; fax 05 46 47 73 65; camping@les-remparts.com; www.les-remparts.com] Fr cent Le Château-d'Oléron take D734 dir Dolus d'Oléron rd. After x-ing ramparts/moat turn R at next rndabt, site on R Lge, pt sl, pt shd; wc (mainly cont); mv service pnt; shwrs inc; el pnts (5A) €3.90; lndtte; shop nrby; tradsmn; rest, snacks, bar nrby; playgrnd; sand beach adj; some statics; dogs €2; phone; quiet; red low ssn/long stay. "Pleasant site for NH/sh stay." 1 Mar-30 Nov. € 17.50 (3 persons)   2009*

CHATEAU D'OLERON, LE *7B1* (1km W Coastal) *45.88207, -1.20648* Camping Airotel Domaine d'Oléron, Domaine de Montravail, 17480 Le Château-d'Oléron [05 46 47 61 82; fax 05 46 47 79 67; info@camping-airotel-oleron.com; www.camping-airotel-oleron.com] Clearly sp fr D734 after x-ing bdge. Not well sp fr N of island. Ent to site thro stables & horseriding cent. Med, mkd pitch, pt shd; wc; shwrs inc; el pnts (8-10A) €3.90 (poss rev pol); gas; lndtte; shop & 500m; snacks; bar; BBQ; playgrnd; htd pool; sand beach 1km; fishing; tennis; equestrian centre; games area; cycle hire; some statics; dogs €3; poss cr; Eng spkn; adv bkg; quiet; red low ssn/CKE/CCI. "Gd site but poss unkempt early ssn; sparse water points; easy walk to town." ♦ 1 Apr-31 Oct. € 22.50   2010*

See advertisement below

CHATEAU D'OLERON, LE *7B1* (2.5km NW Coastal) *45.90415, -1.21525* Camping La Brande, Route des Huîtres, 17480 Le Château-d'Oléron [05 46 47 62 37; fax 05 46 47 71 70; info@camping-labrande.com; www.camping-labrande.com or www.campings-oleron.com] Cross bdge on D26, turn R & go thro Le Château-d'Oléron. Foll Rte des Huîtres to La Gaconnière to site. Lge, shd; wc; mv service pnt; baby facs; sauna; steam room; shwrs inc; el pnts (6-10A) €4-6; gas; lndtte (inc dryer); shop; tradsmn; rest in ssn; snacks; bar; BBQ; playgrnd; 3 pools (1 htd, covrd); waterslide; sand beach 300m; tennis; cycle hire; games area; golf 6km; wifi; entmnt; TV rm; 60% statics; dogs €3; sep car park; Eng spkn; adv bkg; ccard acc; red low ssn; CKE/CCI. "Pleasant owners; pitches at far end adj oyster farm - some noise fr pumps & poss mosquitoes; 10 min cycle ride into town; v gd; crowded even in Sep" ♦ 31 Mar-11 Nov. € 39.00   2013*

See advertisement above

"I like to fill in the reports as I travel from site to site"

You'll find report forms at the back of this guide, or you can fill them in online at www.caravaclub.co.uk/europereport.

heated swimming pool 28°C

pitch, rental of mobile homes, bungalows, chalets, and gypsy caravan

Riding farm

Isle of Oléron - Charente Maritime - www.camping-airotel-oleron.com - phone 00 33 5 46 47 61 82 - fax. 00 33 5 46 47 79 67

FRANCE - ÎLE D'OLERON

ST DENIS D'OLERON see Brée les Bains, La *7A1*

ST GEORGES D'OLERON *7A1* (5km E Coastal) *45.98738, -1.29347* **Camping La Gautrelle (CC de F), Plage des Saumonards, 17190 St Georges-d'Oléron [05 46 47 21 57; fax 05 46 75 10 74; lagautrelle.ccdf@wanadoo.fr; www.campingclub.asso.fr]** Fr viaduct, take D734 to St Pierre. At 3rd traff lts, turn R to Sauzelle, thro vill & L for St Georges & immed to R sp CCDF La Gautrelle. Site at end of lane in approx 1.5km & adj to beach. Lge, mkd pitch, shd; wc; shwrs inc; el pnts (6A) inc (long cable req); shops adj; sand beach; fishing; some statics; dogs €2.32; adv bkg; quiet; CKE/CCI. "Splendid beaches; forest walks, fishing; ltd el pnts." ♦ 1 Apr-30 Sep. € 19.85   2009*

"We must tell The Club about that great site we found"

Get your site reports in by mid-August and we'll do our best to get your updates into the next edition of Caravan Europe.

ST GEORGES D'OLERON *7A1* (6km E Coastal) *45.96820, -1.24483* **Camping Signol, Ave des Albatros, Boyardville, 17190 St Georges-d'Oléron [05 46 47 01 22; fax 05 46 47 23 46; contact@signol.com; www.signol.com]** Cross bdge onto Ile d'Oléron & cont on main rd twd St Pierre-d'Oléron. Turn R at Dolus-d'Oléron for Boyardville & foll sp in vill. Lge, hdg/mkd pitch, pt sl, pt shd; wc (most cont)(own san facs rec); mv service pnt; chem disp; baby facs; shwrs inc; el pnts (6A) €4.60; gas; lndtte; shops adj; tradsmn; bar; playgrnd; htd pool; paddling pool; sand beach 800m; many statics; no dogs Jul/Aug, low ssn €4; Eng spkn; adv bkg; red low ssn. "Fine site but san facs poor & inadequate for size of site & stretched peak ssn; size & quality of pitches variable, poss far fr san facs; poss flooding in wet weather." ♦ 1 May-30 Sep. € 29.80 (CChq acc)   2008*

See advertisement above

ST GEORGES D'OLERON *7A1* (800m SE Rural) *45.97310, -1.32020* **Chadotel Camping Le Domaine d'Oléron, La Jousselinière, 17190 St Georges-d'Oléron [05 46 76 54 97 or 02 51 33 05 05 (LS); fax 02 51 33 94 04; info@chadotel.com; www.chadotel.com]** After x-ing Viaduct (bridge) onto island foll sp dir St Pierre d'Oléron & St Georges-d'Oléron on D734; turn R on rndabt immed see Leclerc supmkt on R; at next rndabt turn L sp 'Le Bois Fleury'; pass airfield 'Bois 'Fleury' on R; take next R & then immed L. Site on L in 500m. Lge, mkd pitch, terr, pt shd; wc; chem disp; mv service pnt; baby facs; shwrs inc; el pnts (6A) inc; gas; lndtte (inc dryers); shop; snacks; bar; BBQ (gas only) sep area; playgrnd; pool; waterslide; paddling pool; sand beach 3km; cycle hire; games area; wifi; entmnt; games/TV rm; 40% statics; dogs €3.20; no c'vans/m'vans over 8m high ssn; Eng spkn; adv bkg ess high ssn; poss noise fr nrby sites w/end high ssn; ccard acc; red long stay/low ssn; CKE/CCI. "Popular, well-organised, clean site; friendly, helpful staff; lovely pool; cycle paths; excel." ♦ 7 Apr-22 Sep. € 31.00 SBS - A41   2011*

ST GEORGES D'OLERON *7A1* (4km SW Coastal) *45.95386, -1.37932* **Camping Les Gros Joncs, Les Sables Vigniers, 17190 St Georges-d'Oléron [05 46 76 52 29; camping.gros.joncs@wanadoo.fr; www.les-gros-joncs.fr]** Fr Ile d'Oléron toll bdge, by-passing Le Château-d'Oléron, NW on D734 to St Pierre-d'Oléron & St Georges-d'Oléron. At Chéray, foll sps to site. V lge, pt shd; wc; shwrs; el pnts (10A) €3; lndtte; shop; rest, snacks; bar; playgrnd; htd pool; paddling pool; jacuzzi; rocky beach 200m; sand beach 1km; games area; TV; some statics; dogs €3; adv bkg; quiet. "Excel pool; great location; clean facs; rec." ♦ 23 Mar-23 Oct. € 43.10 (3 persons)   2011*

See advertisement on next page

ST GEORGES D'OLERON *7A1* (3km W Coastal) *45.94756, -1.37386* **Camping Le Suroit, L'Ileau de la Grande Côte, 17190 St Georges-d'Oléron [05 46 47 07 25 or 06 80 10 93 18 (mob); fax 05 46 75 04 24; camping@lesuroit.fr; www.camping-lesuroit.com]** Fr Domino cent foll sp for beach, turn L for L'Ileau. Strt at x-rds. Fork L for La Cotinière, site on R in 150m. Lge, mkd pitch, shd; htd wc; baby facs; shwrs inc; el pnts (10A) €4; gas; lndtte; shop; rest, snacks; bar; BBQ; playgrnd; htd, covrd pool; sand beach adj; tennis; games area; cycle hire; entmnt; TV; some statics; dogs €4; adv bkg; quiet; red low ssn. "Excel, well-organised site." ♦ 4 Apr-3 Oct. € 25.00   2009*

FRANCE - ILE D'OLERON

Les Sables Vignier - Route Côtière entre Domino et la Cotinière - 17190 Saint-Georges d'Oléron
Tél.: 05 46 76 52 29 - www.camping-les-gros-joncs.com

ST GEORGES D'OLERON *7A1* (3km W Coastal) *45.96119, -1.37032* **Camping Les Grosses Pierres, Les Sables Vigniers, 17190 St Georges-d'Oléron [02 51 27 37 80; fax 05 46 76 54 85; info@vagues-oceanes.com; www.camping-vagues-oceanes.com]** Site sp fr D734. Lge, mkd pitch, some hdstg, terr, pt shd; wc; chem disp; shwrs inc; el pnts (10A) inc; gas; lndtte (inc dryer); shop; rest, snacks; bar; BBQ; playgrnd; 2 pools (1 htd, covrd); paddling pool; waterslide; sand beach 900m; games rm; wifi; entmnt; 95% statics; dogs; phone; Eng spkn; adv bkg; ccard acc; CKE/CCI. 3 Apr-18 Sep. € 34.65   2010*

"I need an on-site restaurant"
We do our best to make sure site information is correct, but it is always best to check any must-have facilities are still available or will be open during your visit.

ST PIERRE D'OLERON *7B1* (3km W Coastal) *45.90164, -1.30266* **Camping La Perroche Leitner, 18 Rue de Renclos de la Perroche, 17310 St Pierre-d'Oléron [05 46 75 37 33; fax 05 49 85 12 57; camping-la-perroche-leitner@ wanadoo.fr]** Site about 10km fr bdge on W coast of Ile d'Oléron. Fr bdge foll sp to Grande Village/Vert-Bois/La Remigeasse & La Perroche. Well sp. Med, hdg/mkd pitch, hdstg, terr, pt shd; wc (some cont); chem disp; mv service pnt; shwrs inc; el pnts (10A) inc; gas; lndtte; shop; tradsmn; BBQ; playgrnd; direct access sand beach 200m; games area; dogs €2.80; Eng spkn; quiet; ccard acc; red low ssn. "Superb site; site staff connect/disconnect el pnts." ♦ 1 Apr-15 Sep. € 28.70   2010*

ST PIERRE D'OLERON *7B1* (3.5km W Coastal) *45.92394, -1.34273* **FFCC Camp Municipal La Fauche Prère, Ave des Pins, La Cotinière, 17310 St Pierre d'Oléron [05 46 47 10 53; fax 05 46 75 23 44; camping@saint-pierre-oleron.com; www.saint-pierre-oleron.com]** Fr bdge foll D734 N to St Pierre-d'Oléron. Turn L onto D274 for La Cotinière, site bef vill on L, sp. Med, mkd pitch, pt sl, shd; wc; chem disp (wc); mv service pnt; baby facs; shwrs €0.80; el pnts (12A) €4; lndtte; shop; playgrnd; sand beach adj; dogs €2; poss cr; CKE/CCI. "Direct access to beach; most pitches sandy; gd." 1 Apr-30 Sep. € 18.00 (3 persons)   2010*

ST TROJAN LES BAINS *7B1* (1.5km SW Coastal) *45.83159, -1.21389* **Camp Municipal Les Martinets, 11 Ave des Bris, 17370 St Trojan-les-Bains [05 46 76 02 39; fax 05 46 76 42 95; lesmartinets@wanadoo.fr; http://lesmartinets.monsite-orange.fr/]** Fr D26 cont on toll bdge rd then L onto D126 to St Trojan-les-Bains. Foll sp for 'Campings' & 'Plage' then sp for Gatseau-Plage. Lge, mkd pitch, pt sl, terr, pt shd; wc (few cont); chem disp; mv service pnt; shwrs inc; el pnts (6A) €3.40 (poss long lead req); gas 500m; lndtte; shops 300m; tradsmn; snacks high ssn; playgrnd; sand beach 1km; cycle hire; 5% statics; dogs €1.40; phone; Eng spkn; adv bkg; ccard acc; red low ssn; CKE/CCI. "Some sm pitches & some on sand; fair; poss new owners 2011 & site redevelopment." ♦ ltd 15 Jan-15 Nov. € 12.50   2008*

"Satellite navigation makes touring much easier"
Remember most sat navs don't know if you're towing or in a larger vehicle – always use yours alongside maps and site directions.

ST TROJAN LES BAINS *7B1* (1.5km SW Rural) *45.82947, -1.21632* **Camping La Combinette, 36 Ave des Bris, 17370 St Trojan-les-Bains [05 46 76 00 47; fax 05 46 76 16 96; la-combinette@wanadoo.fr; www.combinette-oleron. com]** Fr toll bdge stay on D26 for 1km, L onto D275 & L onto D126 to St Trojan-les-Bains. Strt ahead at rndabt with figure sculpture, then R at next rndabt sp Campings. In 1km turn L at rd fork, site on R in 1km. Lge, shd; wc; baby facs; shwrs inc; el pnts (5-10A) €3-3.90; gas; lndtte; shop; rest, snacks; playgrnd; pool; beach; 2km; sauna; spa; gym; games area; cycle hire; wifi; entmnt; dogs €2.20; poss cr; quiet. "Gd touring base; some super pitches; friendly owners; facs poss stretched high ssn; poss flooding in heavy rain; vg." ♦ 1 Apr-31 Oct. € 24.70   2010*

SITES IN ANDORRA

⊞ **ANDORRA LA VELLA (ANDORRA)** *8G3* (7km NE Urban) *42.53333, 1.57527* **Camping Internacional, Ctra de Vila s/n, AD200 Encamp [tel/fax 831 609; info@ campinginternacional.com; www.campinginternacional. com]** On rd thro Encamp turn at traff lts & motor museum. Med, mkd pitch, pl sl, pt shd; wc; chem disp; mv service pnt; shwrs inc; el pnts (6A) €4.20; lndtte; shop; supmkt 100m; tradsmn; snacks; bar; htd pool; TV rm; 40% statics; dogs; phone; bus; skilift 12km; adv bkg; poss v cr; Eng spkn; quiet; CKE/CCI. "Sm pitches; gd rests nr; friendly, family-run."
€ 20.80   2008*

⊞ **ANDORRA LA VELLA (ANDORRA)** *8G3* (600m S Urban) *42.50166, 1.51527* **Camping Valira, Ave de Salou, AD500 Andorra-la-Vella [tel/fax 722 384; campvalira@andorra. ad; www.campvalira.com]** Site on E site of main rd S fr Andorra-la-Vella; behind sports stadium; clearly sp. Lge, mkd pitch, hdstg, terr, pt shd; htd wc; chem disp; mv service pnt; shwrs inc; el pnts (3-10A) €3.50-6 (no earth); gas; lndtte; shop; rest, snacks; bar; playgrnd; htd covrd pool; paddling pool; wifi; dogs €2.10; Eng spkn; adv bkg; quiet, but some rd noise; red low ssn; CKE/CCI. "Conv NH for shopping; 25mins walk to main shops; excel immac facs; vg rest; beware of sudden storms blowing up." ◆ € 24.70   2012*

AVIGNON *10E2* (1km NW Urban) *43.95670, 4.80222* **Camping du Pont d'Avignon, 10 Chemin de la Barthelasse, 84000 Avignon [tel 04 90 80 63 50; fax 03 86 37 79 20; camping.lepontdavignon@orange.fr; www.camping-avignon.com]** Exit A7 junc 23 Avignon Nord dir Avignon Centre (D225) then Villeneuve-les-Avignon. Go round wall & under Pont d'Avignon; then cross rv dir Villeneuve, lle de la Barthelasse. Turn R onto lle de la Barthelasse. Lge, hdg/mkd pitch, mostly shd; wc; chem disp; mv service pnt; baby facs; shwrs inc; el pnts (6-10A); gas; lndtte; shop; rest, snacks; bar; BBQ; cooking facs; playgrnd; pool; paddling pool; tennis; games area; games rm; wifi; entmnt; TV; dogs €2.70; phone; car wash; poss cr; Eng spkn; adv bkg ess high ssn; quiet but some rd, rlwy & rv barge noise; ccard acc; red low ssn/long stay; CKE/CCI. "Superb, well-run, busy site; welcoming staff; clean, dated facs; ltd number; lovely pool; gd sized pitches but most with high kerbs; poss flooded low ssn; extra for c'vans over 5.50m; Avignon festival Jul/Aug; best site for Avignon - 20 mins walk or free ferry; rec arr early even low ssn" ◆ 1 Apr-31 Oct. € 34.90   2013*

⊞ **CANILLO (ANDORRA)** *8G3* (Urban) *42.56740, 1.60235* **Camping Pla, Ctra General s/n, AD100 Canillo [tel 851 333; fax 851 280; campingpla@cyberandorra.com; www. campingpla.cyberandorra.com]** App Canillo fr S, pass Tarrado petrol stn on R; take 1st exit at 1st rndabt opp lge hotel, over bdge & turn L to site. Med, mkd pitch, pt shd; htd wc; chem disp; baby facs; shwrs inc; el pnts (5-10A) €3; gas; lndtte; rest, snacks in town; bar; playgrnd; htd, covrd pool & sports facs in town; skilift 100m; 75% statics; dogs; bus adj; Eng spkn; adv bkg; ccard not acc. "Excel location for skiing but poss unkempt/untidy low ssn." € 14.00   2011*

MASSANA, LA (ANDORRA) *8G3* (2km N Rural) *42.56601, 1.52448* **Camping Borda d'Ansalonga, Ctra General del Serrat, AD400 Ordino [tel 850 374; fax 735 400; campingansalonga@andorra.ad; www. campingansalonga.com]** Fr Andorra-la-Vella foll sp La Massana & Ordino. Turn L twd El Serrat, site on R, well sp. Lge, pt shd; htd wc; chem disp; baby facs; shwrs inc; el pnts (10A) €5.60; gas; lndtte; shop; tradsmn; rest; bar; BBQ; playgrnd; pool; games rm; winter statics for skiers; dogs; phone; Eng spkn; quiet; CKE/CCI. "Statics moved to storage area in summer; quieter than sites on main thro rte." 17 Oct-25 Apr & 15 Jun-15 Sep. € 23.85   2011*

⊞ **MASSANA, LA (ANDORRA)** *8G3* (2km NW Rural) *42.55361, 1.48916* **Camping Xixerella, Ctra de Pal, AD400 Erts [tel 836 613; fax 839 113; c-xixerella@ campingxixerella.com; www.campingxixerella.com]** Fr Andorra la Vella take rd for La Massana; fr there foll sps for Xixerella & vill of Pal. Site on L. Med, terr, pt shd; htd wc; chem disp; shwrs; el pnts (5A) €5.90 (poss no earth); lndtte (inc dryer); shop; rest; bar; playgrnd; pool; crazy golf; wifi; entmnt; some statics; dogs €4.20; phone; site clsd Oct; Eng spkn; adv bkg; quiet; ccard acc; red long stay; CKE/CCI. "Lovely site, lovely setting; clean, modern facs; helpful staff; not all pitches level; no drying rm for ski gear; gd mountain walks; long walk to dispose of rubbish; site poss untidy/unkempt low ssn)." ◆ € 25.20   2010*

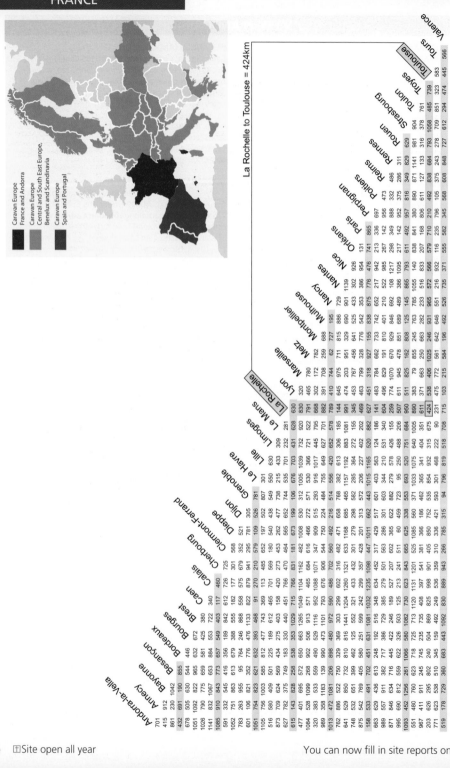

Caravan Europe
France and Andorra

Caravan Europe
Central and South East Europe,
Benelux and Scandinavia

Caravan Europe
Spain and Portugal

La Rochelle to Toulouse = 424km

You can now fill in site reports online

REGIONS AND DEPARTMENTS OF FRANCE

ALSACE
67 Bas-Rhin
68 Haut-Rhin

AQUITAINE
24 Dordogne
33 Gironde
40 Landes
47 Lot-et-Garonne
64 Pyrénées-Atlantiques

AUVERGNE
03 Allier
15 Cantal
43 Haute-Loire
63 Puy-de-Dôme

BOURGOGNE
21 Côte-d'Or
58 Nièvre
71 Saône-et-Loire
89 Yonne

BRETAGNE
22 Côtes-d'Armor
29 Finistère
35 Ille-et-Vilaine
56 Morbihan

CENTRE
18 Cher
28 Eure-et-Loir
36 Indre
37 Indre-et-Loire
41 Loir-et-Cher
45 Loiret

CHAMPAGNE-ARDENNE
08 Ardennes
10 Aube
51 Marne
52 Haute-Marne

CORSE
02A Corse-du-Sud
02B Haute-Corse

FRANCHE-COMTE
25 Doubs
39 Jura
70 Haute-Saône
90 Territoire-de-Belfort

LANGUEDOC-ROUSSILLON
11 Aude
30 Gard
34 Hérault
48 Lozère
66 Pyrénées-Orientales

LIMOUSIN
19 Corrèze
23 Creuse
87 Haute-Vienne

LORRAINE
54 Meurthe-et-Moselle
55 Meuse
57 Moselle
88 Vosges

MIDI-PYRENEES
09 Ariège
12 Aveyron
31 Haute-Garonne
32 Gers
46 Lot
65 Hautes-Pyrénées
81 Tarn
82 Tarn-et-Garonne

NORD/PAS-DE-CALAIS
59 Nord
62 Pas-de-Calais

NORMANDIE
14 Calvados
27 Eure
50 Manche
61 Orne
76 Seine-Maritime

PARIS-ILE DE FRANCE
75 Paris
77 Seine-et-Marne
78 Yvelines
91 Essonne
92 Haut-de-Seine
93 Seine-St-Denis
94 Val-de-Marne
95 Val-d'Oise

PAYS DE LA LOIRE
44 Loire-Atlantique
49 Maine-et-Loire
53 Mayenne
72 Sarthe
85 Vendée

PICARDIE
02 Aisne
60 Oise
80 Somme

POITOU-CHARENTES
16 Charente
17 Charente-Maritime
79 Deux-Sèvres
86 Vienne

PROVENCE-COTE D'AZUR
04 Alpes-de-Haute-Provence
05 Hautes-Alpes
06 Alpes-Maritimes
13 Bouches-du-Rhône
83 Var
84 Vaucluse

RHONE-ALPS
01 Ain
07 Ardèche
26 Drôme
38 Isère
42 Loire
69 Rhône
73 Savoie
74 Haute-Savoie

The first two digits of a French postcode correspond
to the number of the department in which that town or village is situated

Source : French Government Tourist Office

UNITED KINGDOM

ENGLISH CHANNEL

Southampton
Portsmouth
Bournemouth
Poole
Weymouth
Exeter
Torquay
Plymouth
Falmouth

Santander
Bilbao
Santander
Rosslare
Cork
Rosslare

GUERNSEY
St Peter Port
JERSEY
St Helier

Barfleur
Quettehou
CHERBOURG
Les Pieux
Valognes
Beaumont-Hague
St-Vaast
Barneville
Carteret
La Haye-du-Puits
Ste-Mère-Église
Grandcamp-Maisy
Ste Marie-du-Mont
Carentan
Lessay
Périers
N13
D2
Trévières
Isigny-sur-Mer
Tournières
N174
Agon-Coutainville
Coutances
D972
D2
Annville
Hambye
Brehal
Granville
Villedieu-les-Poêles
D971
Balleroy
Torigni-sur-Vire
St Martin des-Besaces
Pont-Farcy
D999
D524

Perros-Guirec
Trégastel
Tréguier
Paimpol
Trébeurden
Lannion D788
Plougasnou
Roscoff
St-Pol-de-Léon
Brignogan-Plages

A B C D
1 2 3 4

Map I

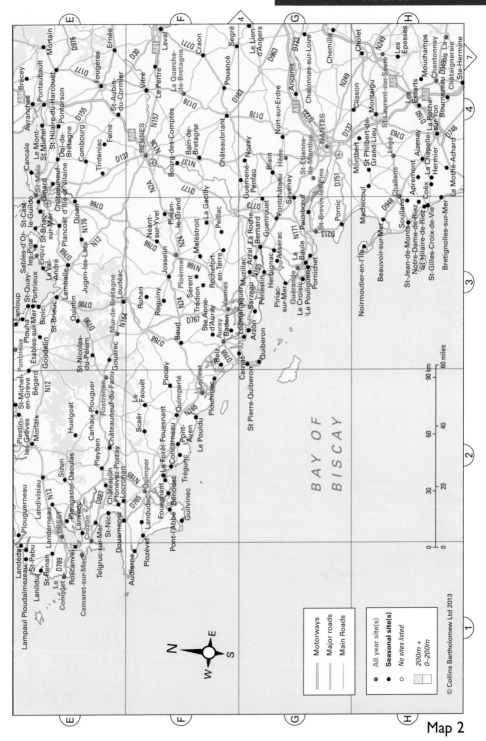

7

E

F

4

G

H

7

4

3

2

1

Mortain
Brécey
D976
Pontaubault
St-Hilaire-du-Harcouët
Avranches
Le Mont-St-Michel
St-Hilaire-du-Harcouët
Pontorson
Fougères
Ernée
Laval
Segré
Le Lion d'Angers
Craon
Pouancé
Chemillé
Cholet
N249
Les Epesses
Mouchamps
Chantonnay
Ste-Hermine
D771
La Guerche-de-Bretagne
Vitré
Le Pertre
D30
D777
St-Aubin-du-Cormier
La Guerche-de-Bretagne
D178
Châteaubriant
Nort-sur-Erdre
Ancenis
Chalonnes-sur-Loire
D723
D963
Clisson
Montaigu
St-Laurent-sur-Sèvre
Les Essarts
La Roche-sur-Yon
D948bis
Châtaigneraie
Cancale
St-Malo
Dinard
Dol-de-Bretagne
Combourg
D155
Feins
Tinteniac
Bourg-des-Comptes
D137
RENNES
N137
N157
N12
N24
D175
Bain-de-Bretagne
N171
D137
NANTES
Montbert
St-Philbert-de-Grand-Lieu
Legé
Aizenay
La Chapelle-Hermier
Apremont
Coëx
La Mothe-Achard
D746
St-Cast-le-Guildo
Plancoët d'Ille-et-Vilaine
Châteauneuf
St-Brieuc
Erquy
Le Val-André
Lamballe
Jugon-les-Lacs
Dinan
D766
N176
D792
Loudéac
Mur-de-Bretagne
N164
Néant-sur-Yvel
Plélan-le-Grand
La Gacilly
Malestroit
Peillac
Guémené-Penfao
Blain
Héric
St-Étienne-de-Montluc
Savenay
Pontchâteau
D773
La Roche-Bernard
Arzal
Muzillac
Guérande
La Baule
Le Croisic
St-Brevin-les-Pins
Pornic
D213
St-Philbert-de-Grand-Lieu
Machecoul
Beauvoir-sur-Mer
St-Jean-de-Monts
Notre-Dame-de-Riez
St-Hilaire-de-Riez
St-Gilles-Croix-de-Vie
Bretignolles-sur-Mer
D948
Soullans
Challans
Lanloup
St-Quay-Portrieux
Binic
Quintin
Rohan
Josselin
Ploërmel
Sérent
Trédion
Rochefort-en-Terre
Questembert
Sérzeau
Péaule
Guenrouet
Assérac
Herbignac
Piriac-sur-Mer
Le Pouliguen
Le Croisic
Le Pouliguen
Pornichet
Paimbœuf
Pontrieux
Plouha
Étables-sur-Mer
Bégard
Goudelin
St-Nicolas-du-Pélem
Gouarec
Reguiny
Baud
Ste-Anne-d'Auray
Auray
Baden
Vannes
Locminé
Arzon
Quiberon
Belz
D768
D767
N24
N165
D780
St-Michel-en-Grève
Plestin-les-Grèves
Morlaix
Huelgoat
Carhaix-Plouguer
Rostrenen
Châteauneuf-du-Faou
Le Faouët
Scaër
Le Pouldu
Plouay
Quimperlé
Lorient
Ploemeur
Carnac
St-Pierre-Quiberon
N12
D700
D790
N164
Landéda
Ploudalmézeau
Plouguerneau
Landivisiau
Landerneau
Sizun
Pleyben
Plougastel-Daoulas
BREST
Crozon
Camaret-sur-Mer
Telgruc-sur-Mer
St-Nic
Locronan
Pont-Croix
Audierne
Plozévet
Landudec
Guilvinec
Plonévez-Porzay
Châteaulin
Douarnenez
Quimper
Pont-l'Abbé
Bénodet
Fouesnant
La Forêt-Fouesnant
Concarneau
Trégunc
Pont-Aven
Le Pouldu
N165
N785
N12
D765
D787
Lampaul
Lanildut
St-Pabu
St-Renan
Le Conquet
Roscanvel
D789

N

W — E

S

BAY OF
BISCAY

Motorways
Major roads
Main Roads

All year site(s)
Seasonal site(s)
No sites listed
200m +
0-200m

90 km   60 miles
0   0

© Collins Bartholomew Ltd 2013

Map 2

FRANCE

Map 3

Map 4

FRANCE

Map 5

© Collins Bartholomew Ltd 2013

All year site(s)
Seasonal site(s)
No sites listed
200m +
0–200m

N E S W

90 km
60 miles
60
40
30
20

GERMANY

Frankfurt am Main
Mannheim
Karlsruhe
Stuttgart
Saarbrücken
Köln

Seltz
Roeschwoog D263
Niederbronn-les-Bains
Dambach D862
Baerenthal
Wingen-sur-Moder
Haguenau D1063
D1061
La Petite-Pierre
Phalsbourg
D662
Keskastel D656
St-Avold N33
D910
D603
D955
D954
Thionville
Volstroff
Buttoncourt
METZ
Jarny
D14
D1
Corny-sur-Moselle
Briey
D643
Heudicourt-sous-les-Côtes
Mandres-aux-Quatre-Tours
N52
St-Mihiel
D618
Verdun
D903
D964
Varennes-en-Argonne
D603
Givry-en-Argonne
D1916
Revigny-sur-Ornain
Grandpré
D982
Ste-Menéhould
Châlons-en-Champagne
D977
N44
D931
D3
D980

LUXEMBOURG

NETHERLANDS
Aachen
Maastricht
Liège
Namur
BELGIUM
Charleroi
BRUXELLES

Givet
D8051
Revin
Charleville-Mézières
D988
Rocroi N51
Signy-l'Abbaye
Rethel
N43
Sedan
D8043
Montmédy
Marville
D947
Dun-sur-Meuse
Stenay
N58
Le Chesne
Buzancy
D947
D987

© Collins Bartholomew Ltd 2013

Motorways
Major roads
Main Roads

SWITZERLAND

Zürich

Biel

BERN

Basel

St-Louis

MULHOUSE

STRASBOURG

NANCY

DIJON

BESANÇON

Freiburg im Breisgau

Neuf-Brisach
Colmar
Rouffach
Munster
Cernay
Thann
Altkirch
Seppois-le-Bas
Delle
Mandeure
Maîche
Belfort

Saverne
Herning
Wasselonne
Molsheim
Obernai
Rhinau
Sélestat
Ribeauvillé
Ste-Marie-aux-Mines
Kaysersberg

Blâmont
Baccarat
Raon-l'Étape
St-Dié
Corcieux
Gérardmer
Le Tholy
La Bresse
Le Thillot
Masevaux

Lunéville
Bayon
Charmes
Bruyères
Épinal
Granges-sur-Vologne
Remiremont
Plombières-les-Bains
Mélisey
Lure
Vesoul

Toul
Neufchâteau
Bulgnéville
Vittel
Contrexéville
Clefmont
Montigny-le-Roi
Fontenoy-le-Château
Bourbonne-les-Bains
Luxeuil-les-Bains
Port-sur-Saône
Bonnal
Rioz
L'Isle-sur-le-Doubs
Baume-les-Dames
Morteau
Levier
Salins-les-Bains
Arbois
Poligny
Champagnole
Pontarlier
Malbuisson
Vallorbe
St-Laurént-en-Grandvaux

Bar-le-Duc
Ligny-en-Barrois
Thonnance-les-Moulins
Froncles-Buxières
Andelot-Blancheville
Chaumont
Langres
Auberive
Sacquenay
Til-Châtel
Gray
Pesmes
Auxonne
Dole
Ounans
Mouchard
Lons-le-Saunier
Doucier
Bonlieu
Clairvaux-les-Lacs

Vitry-le-François
Éclaron-Braucourt-Ste-Livière
Braucourt
Joinville
Soulaines-Dhuys
Brienne-le-Château
Géraudot
Mesnil-St Père
Vouécourt
Riel-les-Eaux
Marcenay
Châtillon-sur-Seine
Laignes
Arc-en-Barrois
Montbard
Venarey-les-Laumes
Semur-en-Auxois
Précy-sous-Thil
La Motte-Ternant
Saulieu
Vandenesse-en-Auxois
Lucenay-l'Évêque
Épinac
Autun
Arnay-le-Duc
Bligny-sur-Ouche
Nolay
Chagny
Chalon-sur-Saône
St-Boil
Selongey
St-Seine-l'Abbaye
Nuits-St-Georges
Beaune
St-Jean-de-Losne
Quingey
Ornans
Montbarrey
Marnay
Verdun-sur-le-Doubs
Mervans
St-Germain-du-Bois
Sennecey-le-Grand
Louhans

A26
N4
N135
N67
N4
N57
D955
N333
N59
D614
D611
D674
D964
D958
D614
D384
D619
D619
A5
D671
D960
D65
D74
D417
D619
A31
D974
D67
D965
D67
D10
A36
A31
A6
A31
A38
D906
D971
D905
D973
N6
N80
N73
N6
N83
N57
A36
N57
N5
A39
A40
D1083
D78
N78
D673
D72
N83
D461
D437
D437
D893
D83
N19
D64
D165
D429
D164
D166
D420
D166
D415
N66
D417
N66
M415
D39
D83
D419
N19
D1004
D1004
A35
A35
D1083
D1004

Map 6

Meaulne · Hérisson · Montluçon · Lapeyrouse · Menat · Pontgibaud · Orcival · Murol · Le Mont-Dore · La Bourboule · Riom-ès-Montagnes · Allanche · Murat · Vic-sur-Cère · Pierrefort · Laguiole · Estaing · Espalion · Laissac · Pont-de-Salars · Rodez

Avrillé · Le Givre · Longeville-sur-Mer · La Tranche-sur-Mer · Vallon-en-Sully · Châteaumeillant · Néris-les-Bains · Évaux-les-Bains · St-Éloy-les-Mines · Boussac · Chénérailles · Mérinchal · Singles · Bort-les-Orgues · Neuvic · Salers · Mauriac · St-Privat · Aurillac · Vic-sur-Cère · Montsalvy · Conques · Decazeville · Villefranche-de-Rouergue · Marcillac-Vallon

Les Sables-d'Olonne · St-Hilaire-la-Forêt · Jard-sur-Mer · St-Martin-de-Ré · Argenton-sur-Creuse · La Châtre · Ste-Sévère-sur-Indre · Gouzon · Guéret · Aubusson · Felletin · Royère-de-Vassivière · Herment · Meymac · Soursac · Clergoux · Marcillac-la-Croisille · Argentat · Beaulieu-sur-Dordogne · Bretenoux · St-Céré · Lacapelle-Viescamp · Maurs · Figeac · Montbrun · Cajarc

ÎLE DE RÉ · St-Clément-des-Baleines · Ars-en-Ré · La Couarde-sur-Mer · Ste-Marie-de-Ré · St-Savin · Montmorillon · Châtillac · Lussac-les-Châteaux · Crozant · Dun-le-Palestel · Fleurat · La Souterraine · St-Sébastien · St-Sulpice-les-Feuilles · Bessines-sur-Gartempe · Bourganeuf · Treignac · Tulle · Correze · Egletons · Sélihac · Vayrac · Martel · Souillac · Carennac · Gramat · Rocamadour · Brengues · Limogne-en-Quercy

LA ROCHELLE · Châtelaillon-Plage · La Brée-les-Bains · St-Georges-d'Oléron · St-Pierre-d'Oléron · ÎLE D'OLÉRON · Le Château-d'Oléron · St-Trojan-les-Bains · Chauvigny · L'Isle-Jourdain · Le Dorat · Bellac · Nantiat · St-Christophe · Montrollet · Confolens · St-Léonard-de-Noblat · LIMOGES · Ambazac · Bonnac-la-Côte · Eymoutiers · Bugeat · Uzerche · Donzenac · Brive-la-Gaillarde · Terrasson-Lavilledieu · Montignac · Sarlat-la-Canéda · Gourdon · Payrac · Cazals · St-Cirq-Lapopie · Puy-l'Évêque · Castelfranc · St-Pantaléon · Cahors

POITIERS · Vivonne · Dienné · Pressac · D951 · Compreignac · Cognac · Suris · Rochechouart · St-Junien · Pierre-Buffière · Chalus · Thiviers · Brantôme · Les Eyzies-de-Tayac · Le Bugue · Belvès · Monpazier · Villeréal · Monbalen · Beauville

Vivonne · Couhé · Civray · Ruffec · Mansle · Angoulême · La Rochefoucauld · Montbron · Nontron · St-Mathieu · Châlus · St-Yrieix-la-Perche · Nexon · Afxe-sur-Vienne · Masseret · Magnac-Bourg · Lubersac · Pompadour · Hautefort · Périgueux · Neuvic · Douzac · Rouffignac · Douville · Lalinde · Bergerac · Lamonzie · Villeneuve-sur-Lot · Fumel · Monsempron · Villeréal · Cancon · Aiguillon

Marans · Coulon · St-Maixent-l'École · Lusignan · Melle · Chef-Boutonne · Aubeterre-sur-Dronne · Ribérac · Verteillac · Mareuil · Vendoire · La Roche-Chalais · Montpon-Ménestérol · Coutras · St-Médard-de-Guizières · Ste-Foy-la-Grande · Duras · Miramont-de-Guyenne · Castillonnès · Villeneuve-sur-Lot · Damazan · Aiguillon

Coulonges-sur-l'Autize · Fontenay-le-Comte · Maillezais · Courçon · St-Hilaire-la-Palud · Mauzé-sur-le-Mignon · Algrefeuille-d'Aunis · Surgères · Dampierre-sur-Boutonne · St-Jean-d'Angély · Matha · Cognac · Jonzac · Montlieu-la-Garde · Bedenac · Bayas · St-André-de-Cubzac · St-Émilion · Castillon-la-Bataille · La Réole · Sauveterre-de-Guyenne · Casteljaloux

Luçon · L'Aiguillon-sur-Mer · Rochefort · Pont-l'Abbé-d'Arnoult · St-Savinien · Le Douhet · Saintes · Pons · Gémozac · Mirambeau · Blaye · Teuillac · Bourg · St-Ciers-sur-Gironde · Blanquefort · BORDEAUX · Cadillac · Rauzan · Targon · St-Symphorien · Saugnacq-et-Muret · St-Médard-de-Guizières

Maremmes · Breuillet · Les Mathes · St-Palais-sur-Mer · Royan · Cozes · Mortagne-sur-Gironde · St-Fort-sur-Gironde · Archiac · Beignes-Ste-Radegonde · Mosnac · Vendays-Montalivet · Montendre · Pauillac · Lesparre-Médoc · St-Laurent-Médoc · Hourtin · Carcans · Lacanau-Océan · Le Porge · Andernos-les-Bains · Arès · Le Teich · Audenge · La Teste-de-Buch · Salles · Ychoux · Pissos

ÎLE D'OLÉRON · Le Verdon-sur-Mer · Soulac-sur-Mer · Andernos-les-Bains · Pyla-sur-Mer · Arcachon · Biscarrosse · Parentis-en-Born · Sanguinet · Gastes · Ste-Eulalie-en-Born · Mimizan-Plage · Mimizan

Bay of Biscay

A · B · C · D · 1 · 2 · 3 · 4

Map 7

Map 8

© Collins Bartholomew Ltd 2013

All year site(s)
Seasonal site(s)
No sites listed
200m +
0–200m

Motorways
Major roads
Main Roads

SPAIN

ANDORRA

90 km   60   30   0
60 miles   40   20   0

SWITZERLAND

ITALY

Torino
Pinerolo
Cuneo
Isola
Entraunes

Martigny
Vallorcine
Châtel
Évian-les-Bains
Thonon-les-Bains
Douvaine
Chamonix-Mont-Blanc
St-Gervais-les-Bains
Aosta
Morzine
Taninges
Samoëns
Cluses
Sallanches
Flumet
Megève
Beaufort
Bourg-St-Maurice
Bellentre
Val-d'Isère
Pralognan-la-Vanoise
Moûtiers
Méribel
La Chambre
St-Martin sur-
Albertville
Ugine
Faverges
Châtelard
Lescheraines
Allevard
Lanslebourg-Mont-Cenis
Modane
St-Michel-de-Maurienne
Valloire
St-Jean-de-Maurienne
La Grave
Le Monêtier-les-Bains
Briançon
Guillestre
St-Léger-les-Mélèzes
Embrun
Montclar
Seyne
Le Vernet
Barcelonnette
Colmars
Aiguilles

Divonne-les-Bains
St-Claude
Gex
Genève
St-Julien-
Bonneville
Thorens-Glières
Frangy
ANNECY
La Clusaz
Doussard
La Rochette
Chambéry
Montmélian
St-Pierre-de-Chartreuse
St-Colomban-des-Villards
Le Bourg-d'Oisans
Vizille
St-Théoffrey
L'Argentière-la-Bessée
Chorges
Savines-le-Lac
Montmaur
Gap
Veynes
Aspres-sur-Buëch
Orpierre

Morez
St-Paul
Dortan
Chézery-Forens
Annemasse
Bons-en-Genevois
Oyonnax
Nantua
Seyssel
Rumilly
Ruffieux
Aix-les-Bains
Les Échelles
Voiron
GRENOBLE
Autrans
Villard-de-Lans
Monestier-de-Clermont
Entraigues
Mens
Lalley
La Salle-en-Beaumont
Châtillon-en-Diois
St-Julien-en-Beauchêne
Luc-en-Diois
Rosans

Moirans-en-Montagne
Hauteville-Lompnes
Virieu-le-Grand
Belley
Morestel
St-Genix-sur-Guiers
Les Abrets
Meyrieu-les-Étangs
Crémieu
Auberives-sur-Varèze
St-Rambert-d'Albon
Roybon
Cognin-les-Gorges
La Chapelle-en-Vercors
Die
Pontaix
Saillans
Crest
Châtillon-sur-Chalaronne
Trept
St-Marcellin
Beaurepaire
Barbières
Buis-les-Baronnies
Vaison-la-Romaine

Pont-d'Ain
Montluel
Villars-les-Dombes
Condrieu
Givors
Pélussin
Sérrières
Annonay
St-Vallier
Tain-l'Hermitage
Tournon-sur-Rhône
VALENCE
La Voulte-sur-Rhône
Marsanne
Cléon-d'Andran
Le Poët-Laval
Dieulefit
Nyons
Rémuzat

Cuiseaux
Montrevel-en-Bresse
Chavannes-sur-Suran
Bourg-en-Bresse
LYON
Ste-Foy-l'Argentière
St-Galmier
St-Donat-sur-l'Herbasse
St-Agrève
Lamastre
Albussière
Baix
Montélimar
Viviers
Larnas
Valréas
Bollène
Andéol-Bourg-St-
Pont-St-Esprit

Tournus
Cormatin
Mantenay-Montlin
Pont-de-Vaux
Mâcon
Vonnas
Thoissey
Châtillon-sur-Chalaronne
Villefranche-sur-Saône
Feurs
Chazelles-sur-Lyon
ST ÉTIENNE
Bourg-Argental
Monistrol-sur-Loire
St-Didier-
Le Cheylard
Privas
St-Vincent-de-Barrès
Meysse
Ruoms
Barjac
Tulette

Marcigny
St-Bonnet-de-Joux
Cluny
Charolles
La Clayette
Matour
Fleurie
Poule-les-Écharmeaux
Ollières
Balbigny
Vorey
Yssingeaux
St-Martin-de-Valamas
St-Eyriers
Darbrès
Aubenas
Villeneuve-de-Berg
Uzer
Balazuc
Vallon-Pont-d'Arc
St-Ambroix

Paray-le-Monial
St-Paul-de-Vézelin
Roanne
Thiers
Pont-du-Château
Noirétable
Courpière
Arlanc
La Chaise-Dieu
Allègre
St-Paulien
Langeac
Le Puy-en-Velay
Monistrol-d'Allier
St-Cirgues
Langogne
Mayres
Les Vans
Labastide
Villefort
Le Collet-de-Dèze
Ste-Énimie
La Malène
Les Vignes

Digoin
Le Donjon
St-Sichon
Puy-Guillaume
CLERMONT-FERRAND
Aydat
Issoire
St-Germain-l'Herm
Paulhaguet
Brioude
Ruynes-en-Margeride
Saugues
Le Bac-d'Issarlès
Darbres
Laubert
Mende
Chanac
La Canourgue
Séverac-le-Château
St-Geniez-d'Olt

Bourbon-l'Archambault
St-Pourçain-sur-Sioule
Montmarault
St-Pardoux
Gannat
Riom
Volvic
St-Nectaire
St-Saturnin
Sauxillanges
Ambert
Montrison
Massiac
St-Flour
Faverolles
Chaudes-Aigues
Neuvéglise
St-Chély-d'Apcher
Marvejols
Nasbinals
St-Just

Dompierre-sur-Besbre
Lapalisse
La Pacaudière
Châtel-Montagne
Vichy
St-Yorre
Châtel-de-Neuvre

Map 9

FRANCE

MEDITERRANEAN SEA

CORSICA

MONACO
NICE

MONTPELLIER
MARSEILLE
TOULON

SPAIN

Motorways
Major roads
Main Roads

All year site(s)
Seasonal site(s)
No sites listed
200m +
0–200m

© Collins Bartholomew Ltd 2013

Map 10

Motorhome Insurance... talk to an expert

GUARANTEED SAVING
TO BEAT YOUR RENEWAL PREMIUM BY AT LEAST £25*

Protect your motorhome with over 25 years of expert know-how

Club Motorhome specialist cover includes:

- **New for old cover** up to 24 months from new – no mileage limit
- **Personal effects cover** includes equipment and baggage, with a £500 individual limit, which includes portable TVs, DVD players, radios, etc. up to a total value of £3,500
- **Full policy cover when touring Europe** for up to 270 days
- **Cover for all Club-organised events** – not always covered by other policies

> **"** I'm delighted with the service, the premium is very competitive and the online quote system was so easy **"**
>
> *Sara Reynolds, Member, Cheshire*

Get peace of mind, get your quote today

0800 028 4809
www.caravanclub.co.uk/motorhomeinsure

THE CARAVAN CLUB

Caravan Europe Site Report Form

If campsite is already listed, complete only those sections of the form where changes apply
or alternatively use the Abbreviated Site Report form on the following pages.

Sites not reported on for 5 years may be deleted from the guide

Year of guide used	20.........	Is site listed?	Listed on page no.	Unlisted	Date of visit	......../......../.........

A – CAMPSITE NAME AND LOCATION

Country		Name of town/village site listed under *(see Sites Location Maps)*				
Distance & direction from centre of town site is listed under *(in a straight line)*		...................km	eg N, NE, S, SW	Urban	Rural	Coastal
Site open all year?	Y / N	Period site is open *(if not all year)*	................./................. to	................./.................		
Site name					Naturist site	Y / N
Site address						
Telephone			Fax			
E-mail			Website			

B – CAMPSITE CHARGES

Charge for outfit + 2 adults in local currency	PRICE		EL PNTS inc in this price?	Y / N	Amps ....

C – DIRECTIONS

Brief, specific directions to site (in km) *To convert miles to kilometres multiply by 8 and divide by 5 or use Conversion Table in guide*	
GPS	Latitude...(eg 12.34567) Longitude...(eg 1.23456 or -1.23456)

D – CAMPSITE DESCRIPTION

SITE size ie number of pitches	Small Max 50	SM	Medium 51-150	MED	Large 151-500	LGE	Very large 500+	V LGE	Unchanged
PITCH size	*eg small, medium, large, very large, various*								Unchanged
Pitch features if **NOT** open-plan/grassy		Hedged	HDG PITCH	Marked or numbered	MKD PITCH	Hardstanding or gravel	HDSTG		Unchanged
If site is **NOT** level, is it		Part sloping	PT SL	Sloping	SL	Terraced	TERR		Unchanged
Is site shaded?		Shaded	SHD	Part shaded	PT SHD	Unshaded	UNSHD		Unchanged

E – CAMPSITE FACILITIES

WC	Heated	HTD WC	Continental	CONT	Own San recommended	OWN SAN REC
Chemical disposal point		CHEM DISP		Dedicated point		WC only
Motorhome waste discharge and water refill point				MV SERVICE PNT		
Child / baby facilities (bathroom)		CHILD / BABY FACS		Family bathroom		FAM BTHRM
Hot shower(s)		SHWR(S)		Inc in site fee?	Y / N	Price...................(if not inc)
ELECTRIC HOOK UP *if not included in price above*		EL PNTS		Price..		Amps...
Supplies of bottled gas		GAS		On site	Y / N	Or in .... Kms
Launderette / Washing Machine		LNDTTE	Inc dryer Y / N			LNDRY RM *(if no washing machine)*

You can also complete forms online: www.caravanclub.co.uk/europereport

CUT ALONG DOTTED LINE

F – FOOD & DRINK

Shop(s) / supermarket	SHOP(S) / SUPMKT	On site		or		.... kms	
Bread / milk delivered	TRADSMN						
Restaurant / cafeteria	REST	On site		or		.... kms	
Snack bar / take-away	SNACKS	On site		or		.... kms	
Bar	BAR	On site		or		.... kms	
Barbecue allowed	BBQ	Charcoal		Gas		Elec	Sep area
Cooking facilities	COOKING FACS						

G – LEISURE FACILITIES

Playground	PLAYGRND						
Swimming pool	POOL	On site		or ....km		Heated	Covered
Beach	BEACH	Adj		or ....km		Sand	Shingle
Alternative swimming *(lake)*	SW	Adj		or ....km		Sand	Shingle
Games /sports area / Games room	GAMES AREA	GAMES ROOM					
Entertainment in high season	ENTMNT						
Internet use by visitors	INTERNET	Wifi Internet		WIFI			
Television room	TV RM	Satellite / Cable to pitches		TV CAB / SAT			

H – OTHER INFORMATION

% Static caravans / mobile homes / chalets / cottages / fixed tents on site					..............% STATICS
Dogs allowed	DOGS	Y / N	Price per night .... *(if allowed)*		
Phone	PHONE	On site	Adj		
Bus / tram / train	BUS / TRAM / TRAIN	Adj	or .... km		
Twin axles caravans allowed?	TWIN AXLES Y / N	Possibly crowded in high season		POSS CR	
English spoken	ENG SPKN				
Advance bookings accepted	ADV BKG	Y / N			
Noise levels on site in season	NOISY	QUIET	If noisy, why?		
Credit card accepted	CCARD ACC	Reduction low season		RED LOW SSN	
Camping Key Europe or Camping Card International accepted in lieu of passport	CKE/CCI	INF card required *(If naturist site)*		Y / N	
Facilities for disabled	Full wheelchair facilities	♦	Limited disabled facilities	♦ ltd	

I – ADDITIONAL REMARKS AND/OR ITEMS OF INTEREST

Tourist attractions, unusual features or other facilities, eg waterslide, tennis, cycle hire, watersports, horseriding, separate car park, walking distance to shops etc	YOUR OPINION OF THE SITE:
	EXCEL
	VERY GOOD
	GOOD
	FAIR POOR
	NIGHT HALT ONLY
Your comments & opinions may be used in future editions of the guide, if you do not wish them to be used please tick	

J – MEMBER DETAILS

ARE YOU A:	Caravanner		Motorhomer		Trailer-tenter?
NAME:			MEMBERSHIP NO:		
			POST CODE:		
DO YOU NEED MORE BLANK SITE REPORT FORMS?		YES		NO	

Please use a separate form for each campsite and do not send receipts. Owing to the large number of site reports received, it is not possible to enter into correspondence. Please return completed form to:

The Editor, Caravan Europe, The Caravan Club
FREEPOST, PO Box 386, (RRZG-SXKK-UCUJ)
East Grinstead RH19 1FH
(Please use this address only when mailing from within the UK)

Caravan Europe Site Report Form

If campsite is already listed, complete only those sections of the form where changes apply
or alternatively use the Abbreviated Site Report form on the following pages.

Sites not reported on for 5 years may be deleted from the guide

Year of guide used	20.........	Is site listed?	Listed on page no.	Unlisted	Date of visit ..../........./.........

A – CAMPSITE NAME AND LOCATION

Country		Name of town/village site listed under *(see Sites Location Maps)*			
Distance & direction from centre of town site is listed under *(in a straight line)* ....km		eg N, NE, S, SW	Urban	Rural	Coastal
Site open all year?	Y / N	Period site is open *(if not all year)* ..../.................. to ..../..................			
Site name				Naturist site	Y / N
Site address					
Telephone		Fax			
E-mail		Website			

B – CAMPSITE CHARGES

Charge for outfit + 2 adults in local currency	PRICE		EL PNTS inc in this price?	Y / N	Amps ....

C – DIRECTIONS

Brief, specific directions to site (in km) *To convert miles to kilometres multiply by 8 and divide by 5 or use Conversion Table in guide*	
GPS	Latitude..(eg 12.34567) Longitude...(eg 1.23456 or -1.23456)

D – CAMPSITE DESCRIPTION

SITE size ie number of pitches	Small Max 50	SM	Medium 51-150	MED	Large 151-500	LGE	Very large 500+	V LGE	Unchanged
PITCH size	*eg small, medium, large, very large, various*								Unchanged
Pitch features if NOT open-plan/grassy		Hedged	HDG PITCH	Marked or numbered	MKD PITCH	Hardstanding or gravel	HDSTG		Unchanged
If site is NOT level, is it		Part sloping	PT SL	Sloping	SL	Terraced	TERR		Unchanged
Is site shaded?		Shaded	SHD	Part shaded	PT SHD	Unshaded	UNSHD		Unchanged

E – CAMPSITE FACILITIES

WC	Heated	HTD WC	Continental	CONT	Own San recommended	OWN SAN REC
Chemical disposal point		CHEM DISP		Dedicated point		WC only
Motorhome waste discharge and water refill point		MV SERVICE PNT				
Child / baby facilities (bathroom)		CHILD / BABY FACS		Family bathroom		FAM BTHRM
Hot shower(s)		SHWR(S)		Inc in site fee?	Y / N	Price...................*(if not inc)*
ELECTRIC HOOK UP *if not included in price above*		EL PNTS		Price..		Amps..
Supplies of bottled gas		GAS		On site	Y / N	Or in .... Kms
Launderette / Washing Machine	LNDTTE		Inc dryer Y / N		LNDRY RM *(if no washing machine)*	

You can also complete forms online: www.caravanclub.co.uk/europereport

CUT ALONG DOTTED LINE

F – FOOD & DRINK

Shop(s) / supermarket	SHOP(S) / SUPMKT	On site		or		.... kms
Bread / milk delivered	TRADSMN					
Restaurant / cafeteria	REST	On site		or		.... kms
Snack bar / take-away	SNACKS	On site		or		.... kms
Bar	BAR	On site		or		.... kms
Barbecue allowed	BBQ	Charcoal		Gas	Elec	Sep area
Cooking facilities	COOKING FACS					

G – LEISURE FACILITIES

Playground	PLAYGRND					
Swimming pool	POOL	On site		or ....km	Heated	Covered
Beach	BEACH	Adj		or ....km	Sand	Shingle
Alternative swimming *(lake)*	SW	Adj		or ....km	Sand	Shingle
Games /sports area / Games room	GAMES AREA	GAMES ROOM				
Entertainment in high season	ENTMNT					
Internet use by visitors	INTERNET	Wifi Internet		WIFI		
Television room	TV RM	Satellite / Cable to pitches		TV CAB / SAT		

H – OTHER INFORMATION

% Static caravans / mobile homes / chalets / cottages / fixed tents on site				...............% STATICS
Dogs allowed	DOGS	Y / N	Price per night .... *(if allowed)*	
Phone	PHONE	On site	Adj	
Bus / tram / train	BUS / TRAM / TRAIN	Adj	or .... km	
Twin axles caravans allowed?	TWIN AXLES Y / N	Possibly crowded in high season		POSS CR
English spoken	ENG SPKN			
Advance bookings accepted	ADV BKG	Y / N		
Noise levels on site in season	NOISY	QUIET	If noisy, why?	
Credit card accepted	CCARD ACC	Reduction low season		RED LOW SSN
Camping Key Europe or Camping Card International accepted in lieu of passport	CKE/CCI	INF card required *(If naturist site)*		Y / N
Facilities for disabled	Full wheelchair facilities	♦	Limited disabled facilities	♦ ltd

I – ADDITIONAL REMARKS AND/OR ITEMS OF INTEREST

Tourist attractions, unusual features or other facilities, eg waterslide, tennis, cycle hire, watersports, horseriding, separate car park, walking distance to shops etc	YOUR OPINION OF THE SITE:
	EXCEL
	VERY GOOD
	GOOD
	FAIR POOR
	NIGHT HALT ONLY

Your comments & opinions may be used in future editions of the guide, if you do not wish them to be used please tick ....

J – MEMBER DETAILS

ARE YOU A:	Caravanner		Motorhomer		Trailer-tenter?	
NAME:			MEMBERSHIP NO:			
			POST CODE:			
DO YOU NEED MORE BLANK SITE REPORT FORMS?			YES		NO	

Please use a separate form for each campsite and do not send receipts. Owing to the large number of site reports received, it is not possible to enter into correspondence. Please return completed form to:

The Editor, Caravan Europe, The Caravan Club
FREEPOST, PO Box 386, (RRZG-SXKK-UCUJ)
East Grinstead RH19 1FH
(Please use this address only when mailing from within the UK)

Caravan Europe Site Report Form

If campsite is already listed, complete only those sections of the form where changes apply
or alternatively use the Abbreviated Site Report form on the following pages.

Sites not reported on for 5 years may be deleted from the guide

Year of guide used	20.........	Is site listed?	Listed on page no.	Unlisted	Date of visit	......./......./.........

A – CAMPSITE NAME AND LOCATION

Country		Name of town/village site listed under *(see Sites Location Maps)*				
Distance & direction from centre of town site is listed under *(in a straight line)* ....km			eg N, NE, S, SW	Urban	Rural	Coastal
Site open all year?	Y / N	Period site is open *(if not all year)*	................./................. to ..../.................			
Site name					Naturist site	Y / N
Site address						
Telephone		Fax				
E-mail		Website				

B – CAMPSITE CHARGES

Charge for outfit + 2 adults in local currency	PRICE		EL PNTS inc in this price?	Y / N	Amps ....

C – DIRECTIONS

Brief, specific directions to site (in km) *To convert miles to kilometres multiply by 8 and divide by 5 or use Conversion Table in guide*	
GPS	Latitude....................................*(eg 12.34567)* Longitude....................................*(eg 1.23456 or -1.23456)*

D – CAMPSITE DESCRIPTION

SITE size ie number of pitches	Small Max 50	SM	Medium 51-150	MED	Large 151-500	LGE	Very large 500+	V LGE	Unchanged
PITCH size	*eg small, medium, large, very large, various*								Unchanged
Pitch features if NOT open-plan/grassy	Hedged	HDG PITCH	Marked or numbered	MKD PITCH	Hardstanding or gravel	HDSTG			Unchanged
If site is NOT level, is it	Part sloping	PT SL	Sloping	SL	Terraced	TERR			Unchanged
Is site shaded?	Shaded	SHD	Part shaded	PT SHD	Unshaded	UNSHD			Unchanged

E – CAMPSITE FACILITIES

WC	Heated	HTD WC	Continental	CONT	Own San recommended	OWN SAN REC	
Chemical disposal point		CHEM DISP		Dedicated point		WC only	
Motorhome waste discharge and water refill point				MV SERVICE PNT			
Child / baby facilities (bathroom)		CHILD / BABY FACS		Family bathroom		FAM BTHRM	
Hot shower(s)		SHWR(S)		Inc in site fee?	Y / N	Price....................*(if not inc)*	
ELECTRIC HOOK UP *if not included in price above*		EL PNTS		Price........................		Amps........................	
Supplies of bottled gas		GAS		On site	Y / N	Or in .... Kms	
Launderette / Washing Machine	LNDTTE		Inc dryer Y / N		LNDRY RM *(if no washing machine)*		

You can also complete forms online: www.caravanclub.co.uk/europereport

F – FOOD & DRINK

Shop(s) / supermarket	SHOP(S) / SUPMKT	On site		or		.... kms
Bread / milk delivered	TRADSMN					
Restaurant / cafeteria	REST	On site		or		.... kms
Snack bar / take-away	SNACKS	On site		or		.... kms
Bar	BAR	On site		or		.... kms
Barbecue allowed	BBQ	Charcoal	Gas	Elec		Sep area
Cooking facilities	COOKING FACS					

G – LEISURE FACILITIES

Playground	PLAYGRND					
Swimming pool	POOL	On site		or ....km	Heated	Covered
Beach	BEACH	Adj		or ....km	Sand	Shingle
Alternative swimming *(lake)*	SW	Adj		or ....km	Sand	Shingle
Games /sports area / Games room	GAMES AREA	GAMES ROOM				
Entertainment in high season	ENTMNT					
Internet use by visitors	INTERNET	Wifi Internet		WIFI		
Television room	TV RM	Satellite / Cable to pitches		TV CAB / SAT		

H – OTHER INFORMATION

% Static caravans / mobile homes / chalets / cottages / fixed tents on site				.............% STATICS	
Dogs allowed	DOGS	Y / N	Price per night .... *(if allowed)*		
Phone	PHONE	On site	Adj		
Bus / tram / train	BUS / TRAM / TRAIN	Adj	or .... km		
Twin axles caravans allowed?	TWIN AXLES Y / N	Possibly crowded in high season		POSS CR	
English spoken	ENG SPKN				
Advance bookings accepted	ADV BKG	Y / N			
Noise levels on site in season	NOISY	QUIET	If noisy, why?		
Credit card accepted	CCARD ACC	Reduction low season		RED LOW SSN	
Camping Key Europe or Camping Card International accepted in lieu of passport	CKE/CCI	INF card required *(If naturist site)*		Y / N	
Facilities for disabled	Full wheelchair facilities	♦	Limited disabled facilities		♦ ltd

I – ADDITIONAL REMARKS AND/OR ITEMS OF INTEREST

Tourist attractions, unusual features or other facilities, eg waterslide, tennis, cycle hire, watersports, horseriding, separate car park, walking distance to shops etc	YOUR OPINION OF THE SITE:
	EXCEL
	VERY GOOD
	GOOD
	FAIR / POOR
	NIGHT HALT ONLY

Your comments & opinions may be used in future editions of the guide, if you do not wish them to be used please tick ....

J – MEMBER DETAILS

ARE YOU A:	Caravanner		Motorhomer		Trailer-tenter?
NAME:			MEMBERSHIP NO:		
			POST CODE:		
DO YOU NEED MORE BLANK SITE REPORT FORMS?			YES		NO

Please use a separate form for each campsite and do not send receipts. Owing to the large number of site reports received, it is not possible to enter into correspondence. Please return completed form to:

The Editor, Caravan Europe, The Caravan Club
FREEPOST, PO Box 386, (RRZG-SXKK-UCUJ)
East Grinstead RH19 1FH
(Please use this address only when mailing from within the UK)

Caravan Europe Site Report Form

If campsite is already listed, complete only those sections of the form where changes apply
or alternatively use the Abbreviated Site Report form on the following pages.

Sites not reported on for 5 years may be deleted from the guide

Year of guide used	20.........	Is site listed?	Listed on page no.	Unlisted	Date of visit ..../........./.........

A – CAMPSITE NAME AND LOCATION

Country		Name of town/village site listed under (see Sites Location Maps)			
Distance & direction from centre of town site is listed under (in a straight line)	..................km	eg N, NE, S, SW	Urban	Rural	Coastal
Site open all year?	Y / N	Period site is open (if not all year)	................./................. to ..../.................		
Site name				Naturist site	Y / N
Site address					
Telephone		Fax			
E-mail		Website			

B – CAMPSITE CHARGES

Charge for outfit + 2 adults in local currency	PRICE		EL PNTS inc in this price?	Y / N	Amps ....

C – DIRECTIONS

Brief, specific directions to site (in km) *To convert miles to kilometres multiply by 8 and divide by 5 or use Conversion Table in guide*	
GPS	Latitude.......................................(eg 12.34567) Longitude.......................................(eg 1.23456 or -1.23456)

D – CAMPSITE DESCRIPTION

SITE size ie number of pitches	Small Max 50	SM	Medium 51-150	MED	Large 151-500	LGE	Very large 500+	V LGE	Unchanged
PITCH size	eg small, medium, large, very large, various								Unchanged
Pitch features if NOT open-plan/grassy	Hedged		HDG PITCH	Marked or numbered		MKD PITCH	Hardstanding or gravel	HDSTG	Unchanged
If site is NOT level, is it	Part sloping		PT SL	Sloping		SL	Terraced	TERR	Unchanged
Is site shaded?	Shaded		SHD	Part shaded		PT SHD	Unshaded	UNSHD	Unchanged

E – CAMPSITE FACILITIES

WC		Heated	HTD WC	Continental	CONT	Own San recommended		OWN SAN REC
Chemical disposal point			CHEM DISP		Dedicated point		WC only	
Motorhome waste discharge and water refill point				MV SERVICE PNT				
Child / baby facilities (bathroom)			CHILD / BABY FACS		Family bathroom		FAM BTHRM	
Hot shower(s)			SHWR(S)		Inc in site fee?	Y / N	Price...................(if not inc)	
ELECTRIC HOOK UP if not included in price above			EL PNTS		Price.........................		Amps........................	
Supplies of bottled gas			GAS		On site	Y / N	Or in .... Kms	
Launderette / Washing Machine			LNDTTE		Inc dryer Y / N		LNDRY RM (if no washing machine)	

You can also complete forms online: www.caravanclub.co.uk/europereport

CUT ALONG DOTTED LINE

F – FOOD & DRINK

Shop(s) / supermarket	SHOP(S) / SUPMKT	On site		or		.... kms	
Bread / milk delivered	TRADSMN						
Restaurant / cafeteria	REST	On site		or		.... kms	
Snack bar / take-away	SNACKS	On site		or		.... kms	
Bar	BAR	On site		or		.... kms	
Barbecue allowed	BBQ	Charcoal		Gas		Elec	Sep area
Cooking facilities	COOKING FACS						

G – LEISURE FACILITIES

Playground	PLAYGRND						
Swimming pool	POOL	On site		or ....km		Heated	Covered
Beach	BEACH	Adj		or ....km		Sand	Shingle
Alternative swimming *(lake)*	SW	Adj		or ....km		Sand	Shingle
Games /sports area / Games room	GAMES AREA	GAMES ROOM					
Entertainment in high season	ENTMNT						
Internet use by visitors	INTERNET	Wifi Internet		WIFI			
Television room	TV RM	Satellite / Cable to pitches		TV CAB / SAT			

H – OTHER INFORMATION

% Static caravans / mobile homes / chalets / cottages / fixed tents on site				............% STATICS
Dogs allowed	DOGS	Y / N	Price per night .... *(if allowed)*	
Phone	PHONE	On site	Adj	
Bus / tram / train	BUS / TRAM / TRAIN	Adj	or .... km	
Twin axles caravans allowed?	TWIN AXLES Y / N	Possibly crowded in high season		POSS CR
English spoken	ENG SPKN			
Advance bookings accepted	ADV BKG	Y / N		
Noise levels on site in season	NOISY	QUIET	If noisy, why?	
Credit card accepted	CCARD ACC	Reduction low season		RED LOW SSN
Camping Key Europe or Camping Card International accepted in lieu of passport	CKE/CCI	INF card required *(If naturist site)*		Y / N
Facilities for disabled	Full wheelchair facilities	♦	Limited disabled facilities	♦ ltd

I – ADDITIONAL REMARKS AND/OR ITEMS OF INTEREST

Tourist attractions, unusual features or other facilities, eg waterslide, tennis, cycle hire, watersports, horseriding, separate car park, walking distance to shops etc	YOUR OPINION OF THE SITE:
	EXCEL
	VERY GOOD
	GOOD
	FAIR | POOR
	NIGHT HALT ONLY
Your comments & opinions may be used in future editions of the guide, if you do not wish them to be used please tick	

J – MEMBER DETAILS

ARE YOU A:	Caravanner		Motorhomer		Trailer-tenter?	
NAME:			MEMBERSHIP NO:		
			POST CODE:		
DO YOU NEED MORE BLANK SITE REPORT FORMS?		YES		NO	

Please use a separate form for each campsite and do not send receipts. Owing to the large number of site reports received, it is not possible to enter into correspondence. Please return completed form to:

The Editor, Caravan Europe, The Caravan Club
FREEPOST, PO Box 386, (RRZG-SXKK-UCUJ)
East Grinstead RH19 1FH
(Please use this address only when mailing from within the UK)

Caravan Europe Site Report Form

If campsite is already listed, complete only those sections of the form where changes apply
or alternatively use the Abbreviated Site Report form on the following pages.

Sites not reported on for 5 years may be deleted from the guide

Year of guide used	20.........	Is site listed?	Listed on page no.	Unlisted	Date of visit	......./......./.........

A – CAMPSITE NAME AND LOCATION

Country		Name of town/village site listed under *(see Sites Location Maps)*			
Distance & direction from centre of town site is listed under *(in a straight line)*	....................km	eg N, NE, S, SW	Urban	Rural	Coastal
Site open all year?	Y / N	Period site is open *(if not all year)*	................/................. to ..../.................		
Site name				Naturist site	Y / N
Site address					
Telephone		Fax			
E-mail		Website			

B – CAMPSITE CHARGES

Charge for outfit + 2 adults in local currency	PRICE		EL PNTS inc in this price?	Y / N	Amps ....

C – DIRECTIONS

Brief, specific directions to site (in km) *To convert miles to kilometres multiply by 8 and divide by 5 or use Conversion Table in guide*	
GPS	Latitude...*(eg 12.34567)* Longitude...*(eg 1.23456 or -1.23456)*

D – CAMPSITE DESCRIPTION

SITE size ie number of pitches	Small Max 50	SM	Medium 51-150	MED	Large 151-500	LGE	Very large 500+	V LGE	Unchanged
PITCH size	*eg small, medium, large, very large, various*								Unchanged
Pitch features if **NOT** open-plan/grassy	Hedged	HDG PITCH	Marked or numbered	MKD PITCH	Hardstanding or gravel	HDSTG			Unchanged
If site is **NOT** level, is it	Part sloping	PT SL	Sloping	SL	Terraced	TERR			Unchanged
Is site shaded?	Shaded	SHD	Part shaded	PT SHD	Unshaded	UNSHD			Unchanged

E – CAMPSITE FACILITIES

WC	Heated	HTD WC	Continental	CONT	Own San recommended	OWN SAN REC
Chemical disposal point		CHEM DISP		Dedicated point		WC only
Motorhome waste discharge and water refill point				MV SERVICE PNT		
Child / baby facilities (bathroom)		CHILD / BABY FACS		Family bathroom		FAM BTHRM
Hot shower(s)		SHWR(S)		Inc in site fee?	Y / N	Price...................*(if not inc)*
ELECTRIC HOOK UP *if not included in price above*		EL PNTS		Price..		Amps..
Supplies of bottled gas		GAS		On site	Y / N	Or in .... Kms
Launderette / Washing Machine	LNDTTE		Inc dryer Y / N		LNDRY RM *(if no washing machine)*	

You can also complete forms online: www.caravanclub.co.uk/europereport

F – FOOD & DRINK

Shop(s) / supermarket	SHOP(S) / SUPMKT	On site		or		.... kms
Bread / milk delivered	TRADSMN					
Restaurant / cafeteria	REST	On site		or		.... kms
Snack bar / take-away	SNACKS	On site		or		.... kms
Bar	BAR	On site		or		.... kms
Barbecue allowed	BBQ	Charcoal		Gas	Elec	Sep area
Cooking facilities	COOKING FACS					

G – LEISURE FACILITIES

Playground	PLAYGRND						
Swimming pool	POOL	On site		or ....km	Heated	Covered	
Beach	BEACH	Adj		or ....km	Sand	Shingle	
Alternative swimming *(lake)*	SW	Adj		or ....km	Sand	Shingle	
Games /sports area / Games room	GAMES AREA	GAMES ROOM					
Entertainment in high season	ENTMNT						
Internet use by visitors	INTERNET	Wifi Internet		WIFI			
Television room	TV RM	Satellite / Cable to pitches		TV CAB / SAT			

H – OTHER INFORMATION

% Static caravans / mobile homes / chalets / cottages / fixed tents on site					................% STATICS
Dogs allowed	DOGS	Y / N	Price per night .... *(if allowed)*		
Phone	PHONE	On site	Adj		
Bus / tram / train	BUS / TRAM / TRAIN	Adj	or .... km		
Twin axles caravans allowed?	TWIN AXLES Y / N	Possibly crowded in high season		POSS CR	
English spoken	ENG SPKN				
Advance bookings accepted	ADV BKG	Y / N			
Noise levels on site in season	NOISY	QUIET	If noisy, why?		
Credit card accepted	CCARD ACC	Reduction low season		RED LOW SSN	
Camping Key Europe or Camping Card International accepted in lieu of passport	CKE/CCI	INF card required *(If naturist site)*		Y / N	
Facilities for disabled	Full wheelchair facilities	♦	Limited disabled facilities	♦ ltd	

I – ADDITIONAL REMARKS AND/OR ITEMS OF INTEREST

Tourist attractions, unusual features or other facilities, eg waterslide, tennis, cycle hire, watersports, horseriding, separate car park, walking distance to shops etc	YOUR OPINION OF THE SITE:	
	EXCEL	
	VERY GOOD	
	GOOD	
	FAIR	POOR
	NIGHT HALT ONLY	
Your comments & opinions may be used in future editions of the guide, if you do not wish them to be used please tick		

J – MEMBER DETAILS

ARE YOU A:	Caravanner		Motorhomer		Trailer-tenter?	
NAME:			MEMBERSHIP NO:			
			POST CODE:			
DO YOU NEED MORE BLANK SITE REPORT FORMS?		YES			NO	

Please use a separate form for each campsite and do not send receipts. Owing to the large number of site reports received, it is not possible to enter into correspondence. Please return completed form to:

The Editor, Caravan Europe, The Caravan Club
FREEPOST, PO Box 386, (RRZG-SXKK-UCUJ)
East Grinstead RH19 1FH
(Please use this address only when mailing from within the UK)

Caravan Europe Site Report Form

If campsite is already listed, complete only those sections of the form where changes apply
or alternatively use the Abbreviated Site Report form on the following pages.

Sites not reported on for 5 years may be deleted from the guide

Year of guide used	20.........	Is site listed?	Listed on page no.	Unlisted	Date of visit	......./......./.........

A – CAMPSITE NAME AND LOCATION

Country		Name of town/village site listed under *(see Sites Location Maps)*			
Distance & direction from centre of town site is listed under *(in a straight line)*		...................km	eg N, NE, S, SW	Urban	Rural	Coastal

Site open all year?	Y / N	Period site is open *(if not all year)*	................./................. to ..../.................

Site name			Naturist site	Y / N
Site address				

Telephone		Fax	
E-mail		Website	

B – CAMPSITE CHARGES

Charge for outfit + 2 adults in local currency	PRICE		EL PNTS inc in this price?	Y / N	Amps ....

C – DIRECTIONS

Brief, specific directions to site (in km) *To convert miles to kilometres multiply by 8 and divide by 5 or use Conversion Table in guide*	
GPS	Latitude...*(eg 12.34567)* Longitude...*(eg 1.23456 or -1.23456)*

D – CAMPSITE DESCRIPTION

SITE size ie number of pitches	Small Max 50	SM	Medium 51-150	MED	Large 151-500	LGE	Very large 500+	V LGE	Unchanged

PITCH size	eg small, medium, large, very large, various								Unchanged

Pitch features if **NOT** open-plan/grassy	Hedged	HDG PITCH	Marked or numbered	MKD PITCH	Hardstanding or gravel	HDSTG	Unchanged

If site is **NOT** level, is it	Part sloping	PT SL	Sloping	SL	Terraced	TERR	Unchanged

Is site shaded?	Shaded	SHD	Part shaded	PT SHD	Unshaded	UNSHD	Unchanged

E – CAMPSITE FACILITIES

WC		Heated	HTD WC	Continental	CONT	Own San recommended		OWN SAN REC	
Chemical disposal point		CHEM DISP		Dedicated point			WC only		
Motorhome waste discharge and water refill point				MV SERVICE PNT					
Child / baby facilities (bathroom)		CHILD / BABY FACS		Family bathroom			FAM BTHRM		
Hot shower(s)		SHWR(S)		Inc in site fee?	Y / N	Price...................*(if not inc)*			
ELECTRIC HOOK UP *if not included in price above*		EL PNTS		Price.......................................		Amps...			
Supplies of bottled gas		GAS		On site	Y / N	Or in .... Kms			
Launderette / Washing Machine	LNDTTE		Inc dryer Y / N		LNDRY RM *(if no washing machine)*				

You can also complete forms online: www.caravanclub.co.uk/europereport

CUT ALONG DOTTED LINE

F – FOOD & DRINK

Shop(s) / supermarket	SHOP(S) / SUPMKT	On site		or	.... kms
Bread / milk delivered	TRADSMN				
Restaurant / cafeteria	REST	On site		or	.... kms
Snack bar / take-away	SNACKS	On site		or	.... kms
Bar	BAR	On site		or	.... kms
Barbecue allowed	BBQ	Charcoal	Gas	Elec	Sep area
Cooking facilities	COOKING FACS				

G – LEISURE FACILITIES

Playground	PLAYGRND					
Swimming pool	POOL	On site		or ....km	Heated	Covered
Beach	BEACH	Adj		or ....km	Sand	Shingle
Alternative swimming (lake)	SW	Adj		or ....km	Sand	Shingle
Games /sports area / Games room	GAMES AREA	GAMES ROOM				
Entertainment in high season	ENTMNT					
Internet use by visitors	INTERNET	Wifi Internet		WIFI		
Television room	TV RM	Satellite / Cable to pitches		TV CAB / SAT		

H – OTHER INFORMATION

% Static caravans / mobile homes / chalets / cottages / fixed tents on site				...............% STATICS
Dogs allowed	DOGS	Y / N	Price per night .... (if allowed)	
Phone	PHONE	On site	Adj	
Bus / tram / train	BUS / TRAM / TRAIN	Adj	or .... km	
Twin axles caravans allowed?	TWIN AXLES Y / N	Possibly crowded in high season		POSS CR
English spoken	ENG SPKN			
Advance bookings accepted	ADV BKG	Y / N		
Noise levels on site in season	NOISY	QUIET	If noisy, why?	
Credit card accepted	CCARD ACC	Reduction low season		RED LOW SSN
Camping Key Europe or Camping Card International accepted in lieu of passport	CKE/CCI	INF card required (If naturist site)		Y / N
Facilities for disabled	Full wheelchair facilities	♦	Limited disabled facilities	♦ ltd

I – ADDITIONAL REMARKS AND/OR ITEMS OF INTEREST

Tourist attractions, unusual features or other facilities, eg waterslide, tennis, cycle hire, watersports, horseriding, separate car park, walking distance to shops etc	YOUR OPINION OF THE SITE:
	EXCEL
	VERY GOOD
	GOOD
	FAIR POOR
	NIGHT HALT ONLY
Your comments & opinions may be used in future editions of the guide, if you do not wish them to be used please tick	

J – MEMBER DETAILS

ARE YOU A:	Caravanner		Motorhomer		Trailer-tenter?
NAME:			MEMBERSHIP NO:		
			POST CODE:		
DO YOU NEED MORE BLANK SITE REPORT FORMS?		YES		NO	

Please use a separate form for each campsite and do not send receipts. Owing to the large number of site reports received, it is not possible to enter into correspondence. Please return completed form to:

The Editor, Caravan Europe, The Caravan Club
FREEPOST, PO Box 386, (RRZG-SXKK-UCUJ)
East Grinstead RH19 1FH
(Please use this address only when mailing from within the UK)

Caravan Europe
Abbreviated Site Report Form

Use this abbreviated Site Report Form if you have visited a number of sites and there are no changes (or only small changes) to their entries in the guide. If reporting on a new site, or reporting several changes, please use the full version of the report form. **If advising prices,** these should be for an outfit, and 2 adults for one night's stay. **Please indicate high or low season prices and whether electricity is included.**

Remember, if you don't tell us about sites you have visited, they may eventually be deleted from the guide.

Year of guide used	20.........	Page No.	....	Name of town/village site listed under	
Site Name				Date of visit	...... /...... /......
GPS	Latitude..(eg 12.34567) Longitude..(eg 1.23456 or -1.23456)				

Site is in: Andorra / Austria / Belgium / Croatia / Czech Republic / Denmark / Finland / France / Germany / Greece / Hungary / Italy / Luxembourg / Netherlands / Norway / Poland / Portugal / Slovakia / Slovenia / Spain / Sweden / Switzerland

Comments:

Charge for outfit + 2 adults in local currency	High Season	Low Season	Elec inc in price?		Y / N	............amps
			Price of elec (if not inc)			............amps

Year of guide used	20.........	Page No.	....	Name of town/village site listed under	
Site Name				Date of visit	...... /...... /......
GPS	Latitude..(eg 12.34567) Longitude..(eg 1.23456 or -1.23456)				

Site is in: Andorra / Austria / Belgium / Croatia / Czech Republic / Denmark / Finland / France / Germany / Greece / Hungary / Italy / Luxembourg / Netherlands / Norway / Poland / Portugal / Slovakia / Slovenia / Spain / Sweden / Switzerland

Comments:

Charge for outfit + 2 adults in local currency	High Season	Low Season	Elec inc in price?		Y / N	............amps
			Price of elec (if not inc)			............amps

Year of guide used	20.........	Page No.	....	Name of town/village site listed under	
Site Name				Date of visit	...... /...... /......
GPS	Latitude..(eg 12.34567) Longitude..(eg 1.23456 or -1.23456)				

Site is in: Andorra / Austria / Belgium / Croatia / Czech Republic / Denmark / Finland / France / Germany / Greece / Hungary / Italy / Luxembourg / Netherlands / Norway / Poland / Portugal / Slovakia / Slovenia / Spain / Sweden / Switzerland

Comments:

Charge for car, caravan & 2 adults in local currency	High Season	Low Season	Elec inc in price?		Y / N	............amps
			Price of elec (if not inc)			............amps

Please fill in your details and send to the address on the reverse of this form.
You can also complete forms online: www.caravanclub.co.uk/europereport

CUT ALONG DOTTED LINE

Year of guide used	20.........	Page No.	....	Name of town/village site listed under	
Site Name				Date of visit	.... /....... /........
GPS	Latitude..(eg 12.34567) Longitude...(eg 1.23456 or -1.23456)				

Site is in: Andorra / Austria / Belgium / Croatia / Czech Republic / Denmark / Finland / France / Germany / Greece / Hungary / Italy / Luxembourg / Netherlands / Norway / Poland / Portugal / Slovakia / Slovenia / Spain / Sweden / Switzerland

Comments:

Charge for outfit + 2 adults in local currency	High Season	Low Season	Elec inc in price?	Y / N	............amps
			Price of elec (if not inc)		............amps

Year of guide used	20.........	Page No.	....	Name of town/village site listed under	
Site Name				Date of visit	.... /....... /........
GPS	Latitude..(eg 12.34567) Longitude...(eg 1.23456 or -1.23456)				

Site is in: Andorra / Austria / Belgium / Croatia / Czech Republic / Denmark / Finland / France / Germany / Greece / Hungary / Italy / Luxembourg / Netherlands / Norway / Poland / Portugal / Slovakia / Slovenia / Spain / Sweden / Switzerland

Comments:

Charge for outfit + 2 adults in local currency	High Season	Low Season	Elec inc in price?	Y / N	............amps
			Price of elec (if not inc)		............amps

Year of guide used	20.........	Page No.	....	Name of town/village site listed under	
Site Name				Date of visit	.... /....... /........
GPS	Latitude..(eg 12.34567) Longitude...(eg 1.23456 or -1.23456)				

Site is in: Andorra / Austria / Belgium / Croatia / Czech Republic / Denmark / Finland / France / Germany / Greece / Hungary / Italy / Luxembourg / Netherlands / Norway / Poland / Portugal / Slovakia / Slovenia / Spain / Sweden / Switzerland

Comments:

Charge for outfit + 2 adults in local currency	High Season	Low Season	Elec inc in price?	Y / N	............amps
			Price of elec (if not inc)		............amps

Your comments & opinions may be used in future editions of the guide, if you do not wish them to be used please tick ....

Name ....

Membership No. ....

Post Code ....

Are you a Caravanner / Motorhomer / Trailer-Tenter?

Do you need more blank Site Report forms?   YES / NO

Please return completed forms to:
The Editor, Caravan Europe
The Caravan Club
FREEPOST
PO Box 386 (RRZG-SXKK-UCUJ)
East Grinstead
RH19 1FH
(Please use this address only when mailing from within the UK)

You can also complete forms online: www.caravanclub.co.uk/europereport

Caravan Europe
Abbreviated Site Report Form

Use this abbreviated Site Report Form if you have visited a number of sites and there are no changes (or only small changes) to their entries in the guide. If reporting on a new site, or reporting several changes, please use the full version of the report form. **If advising prices,** these should be for an outfit, and 2 adults for one night's stay. **Please indicate high or low season prices and whether electricity is included.**

Remember, if you don't tell us about sites you have visited, they may eventually be deleted from the guide.

Year of guide used	20.........	Page No.	....	Name of town/village site listed under	
Site Name				Date of visit	.... /....... /........
GPS	Latitude...(eg 12.34567) Longitude...(eg 1.23456 or -1.23456)				

Site is in: Andorra / Austria / Belgium / Croatia / Czech Republic / Denmark / Finland / France / Germany / Greece / Hungary / Italy / Luxembourg / Netherlands / Norway / Poland / Portugal / Slovakia / Slovenia / Spain / Sweden / Switzerland

Comments:

Charge for outfit + 2 adults in local currency	High Season	Low Season	Elec inc in price?	Y / N	.............amps
			Price of elec (if not inc)		.............amps

Year of guide used	20.........	Page No.	....	Name of town/village site listed under	
Site Name				Date of visit	.... /....... /........
GPS	Latitude...(eg 12.34567) Longitude...(eg 1.23456 or -1.23456)				

Site is in: Andorra / Austria / Belgium / Croatia / Czech Republic / Denmark / Finland / France / Germany / Greece / Hungary / Italy / Luxembourg / Netherlands / Norway / Poland / Portugal / Slovakia / Slovenia / Spain / Sweden / Switzerland

Comments:

Charge for outfit + 2 adults in local currency	High Season	Low Season	Elec inc in price?	Y / N	.............amps
			Price of elec (if not inc)		.............amps

Year of guide used	20.........	Page No.	....	Name of town/village site listed under	
Site Name				Date of visit	.... /....... /........
GPS	Latitude...(eg 12.34567) Longitude...(eg 1.23456 or -1.23456)				

Site is in: Andorra / Austria / Belgium / Croatia / Czech Republic / Denmark / Finland / France / Germany / Greece / Hungary / Italy / Luxembourg / Netherlands / Norway / Poland / Portugal / Slovakia / Slovenia / Spain / Sweden / Switzerland

Comments:

Charge for car, caravan & 2 adults in local currency	High Season	Low Season	Elec inc in price?	Y / N	.............amps
			Price of elec (if not inc)		.............amps

Please fill in your details and send to the address on the reverse of this form.
You can also complete forms online: www.caravanclub.co.uk/europereport

CUT ALONG DOTTED LINE

Year of guide used	20.........	Page No.	....	Name of town/village site listed under			
Site Name					Date of visit	.... /....... /........	
GPS	Latitude..(eg 12.34567) Longitude..(eg 1.23456 or -1.23456)						

Site is in: Andorra / Austria / Belgium / Croatia / Czech Republic / Denmark / Finland / France / Germany / Greece / Hungary / Italy / Luxembourg / Netherlands / Norway / Poland / Portugal / Slovakia / Slovenia / Spain / Sweden / Switzerland

Comments:

Charge for outfit + 2 adults in local currency	High Season	Low Season	Elec inc in price?	Y / N	............amps
			Price of elec (if not inc)		............amps

Year of guide used	20.........	Page No.	....	Name of town/village site listed under			
Site Name					Date of visit	.... /....... /........	
GPS	Latitude..(eg 12.34567) Longitude..(eg 1.23456 or -1.23456)						

Site is in: Andorra / Austria / Belgium / Croatia / Czech Republic / Denmark / Finland / France / Germany / Greece / Hungary / Italy / Luxembourg / Netherlands / Norway / Poland / Portugal / Slovakia / Slovenia / Spain / Sweden / Switzerland

Comments:

Charge for outfit + 2 adults in local currency	High Season	Low Season	Elec inc in price?	Y / N	............amps
			Price of elec (if not inc)		............amps

Year of guide used	20.........	Page No.	....	Name of town/village site listed under			
Site Name					Date of visit	.... /....... /........	
GPS	Latitude..(eg 12.34567) Longitude..(eg 1.23456 or -1.23456)						

Site is in: Andorra / Austria / Belgium / Croatia / Czech Republic / Denmark / Finland / France / Germany / Greece / Hungary / Italy / Luxembourg / Netherlands / Norway / Poland / Portugal / Slovakia / Slovenia / Spain / Sweden / Switzerland

Comments:

Charge for outfit + 2 adults in local currency	High Season	Low Season	Elec inc in price?	Y / N	............amps
			Price of elec (if not inc)		............amps

Your comments & opinions may be used in future editions of the guide, if you do not wish them to be used please tick ....

Name ....

Membership No. ....

Post Code ....

Are you a Caravanner / Motorhomer / Trailer-Tenter?

Do you need more blank Site Report forms?   YES / NO

Please return completed forms to:
The Editor, Caravan Europe
The Caravan Club
FREEPOST
PO Box 386 (RRZG-SXKK-UCUJ)
East Grinstead
RH19 1FH
(Please use this address only when mailing from within the UK)

You can also complete forms online: www.caravanclub.co.uk/europereport

Caravan Europe
Abbreviated Site Report Form

Use this abbreviated Site Report Form if you have visited a number of sites and there are no changes (or only small changes) to their entries in the guide. If reporting on a new site, or reporting several changes, please use the full version of the report form. **If advising prices,** these should be for an outfit, and 2 adults for one night's stay. **Please indicate high or low season prices and whether electricity is included.**

Remember, if you don't tell us about sites you have visited, they may eventually be deleted from the guide.

Year of guide used	20.........	Page No.	....	Name of town/village site listed under	
Site Name				Date of visit	.... /....... /.......
GPS	Latitude...(eg 12.34567) Longitude...(eg 1.23456 or -1.23456)				

Site is in: Andorra / Austria / Belgium / Croatia / Czech Republic / Denmark / Finland / France / Germany / Greece / Hungary / Italy / Luxembourg / Netherlands / Norway / Poland / Portugal / Slovakia / Slovenia / Spain / Sweden / Switzerland

Comments:

Charge for outfit + 2 adults in local currency	High Season	Low Season	Elec inc in price?	Y / N	.............amps
			Price of elec (if not inc)		.............amps

Year of guide used	20.........	Page No.	....	Name of town/village site listed under	
Site Name				Date of visit	.... /....... /.......
GPS	Latitude...(eg 12.34567) Longitude...(eg 1.23456 or -1.23456)				

Site is in: Andorra / Austria / Belgium / Croatia / Czech Republic / Denmark / Finland / France / Germany / Greece / Hungary / Italy / Luxembourg / Netherlands / Norway / Poland / Portugal / Slovakia / Slovenia / Spain / Sweden / Switzerland

Comments:

Charge for outfit + 2 adults in local currency	High Season	Low Season	Elec inc in price?	Y / N	.............amps
			Price of elec (if not inc)		.............amps

Year of guide used	20.........	Page No.	....	Name of town/village site listed under	
Site Name				Date of visit	.... /....... /.......
GPS	Latitude...(eg 12.34567) Longitude...(eg 1.23456 or -1.23456)				

Site is in: Andorra / Austria / Belgium / Croatia / Czech Republic / Denmark / Finland / France / Germany / Greece / Hungary / Italy / Luxembourg / Netherlands / Norway / Poland / Portugal / Slovakia / Slovenia / Spain / Sweden / Switzerland

Comments:

Charge for car, caravan & 2 adults in local currency	High Season	Low Season	Elec inc in price?	Y / N	.............amps
			Price of elec (if not inc)		.............amps

Please fill in your details and send to the address on the reverse of this form.
You can also complete forms online: www.caravanclub.co.uk/europereport

CUT ALONG DOTTED LINE

Year of guide used	20..........	Page No.	....	Name of town/village site listed under	

Site Name					Date of visit	.... /....... /........

GPS   Latitude...*(eg 12.34567)* Longitude..*(eg 1.23456 or -1.23456)*

Site is in: Andorra / Austria / Belgium / Croatia / Czech Republic / Denmark / Finland / France / Germany / Greece / Hungary / Italy / Luxembourg / Netherlands / Norway / Poland / Portugal / Slovakia / Slovenia / Spain / Sweden / Switzerland

Comments:

Charge for outfit + 2 adults in local currency	High Season	Low Season	Elec inc in price?	Y / N	............amps
			Price of elec (if not inc)		............amps

Year of guide used	20..........	Page No.	....	Name of town/village site listed under	

Site Name					Date of visit	.... /....... /........

GPS   Latitude...*(eg 12.34567)* Longitude..*(eg 1.23456 or -1.23456)*

Site is in: Andorra / Austria / Belgium / Croatia / Czech Republic / Denmark / Finland / France / Germany / Greece / Hungary / Italy / Luxembourg / Netherlands / Norway / Poland / Portugal / Slovakia / Slovenia / Spain / Sweden / Switzerland

Comments:

Charge for outfit + 2 adults in local currency	High Season	Low Season	Elec inc in price?	Y / N	............amps
			Price of elec (if not inc)		............amps

Year of guide used	20..........	Page No.	....	Name of town/village site listed under	

Site Name					Date of visit	.... /....... /........

GPS   Latitude...*(eg 12.34567)* Longitude..*(eg 1.23456 or -1.23456)*

Site is in: Andorra / Austria / Belgium / Croatia / Czech Republic / Denmark / Finland / France / Germany / Greece / Hungary / Italy / Luxembourg / Netherlands / Norway / Poland / Portugal / Slovakia / Slovenia / Spain / Sweden / Switzerland

Comments:

Charge for outfit + 2 adults in local currency	High Season	Low Season	Elec inc in price?	Y / N	............amps
			Price of elec (if not inc)		............amps

Your comments & opinions may be used in future editions of the guide, if you do not wish them to be used please tick ....

Name ....

Membership No. ....

Post Code ....

Are you a Caravanner / Motorhomer / Trailer-Tenter?

Do you need more blank Site Report forms?   YES / NO

Please return completed forms to:
The Editor, Caravan Europe
The Caravan Club
FREEPOST
PO Box 386 (RRZG-SXKK-UCUJ)
East Grinstead
RH19 1FH
(Please use this address only when mailing from within the UK)

You can also complete forms online: www.caravanclub.co.uk/europereport

Caravan Europe
Abbreviated Site Report Form

Use this abbreviated Site Report Form if you have visited a number of sites and there are no changes (or only small changes) to their entries in the guide. If reporting on a new site, or reporting several changes, please use the full version of the report form. **If advising prices,** these should be for an outfit, and 2 adults for one night's stay. **Please indicate high or low season prices and whether electricity is included.**

Remember, if you don't tell us about sites you have visited, they may eventually be deleted from the guide.

Year of guide used	20.........	Page No.	....	Name of town/village site listed under	
Site Name				Date of visit	.... /....... /........
GPS	Latitude...(eg 12.34567) Longitude...(eg 1.23456 or -1.23456)				

Site is in: Andorra / Austria / Belgium / Croatia / Czech Republic / Denmark / Finland / France / Germany / Greece / Hungary / Italy / Luxembourg / Netherlands / Norway / Poland / Portugal / Slovakia / Slovenia / Spain / Sweden / Switzerland

Comments:

Charge for outfit + 2 adults in local currency	High Season	Low Season	Elec inc in price?	Y / N	.............amps
			Price of elec (if not inc)		.............amps

Year of guide used	20.........	Page No.	....	Name of town/village site listed under	
Site Name				Date of visit	.... /....... /........
GPS	Latitude...(eg 12.34567) Longitude...(eg 1.23456 or -1.23456)				

Site is in: Andorra / Austria / Belgium / Croatia / Czech Republic / Denmark / Finland / France / Germany / Greece / Hungary / Italy / Luxembourg / Netherlands / Norway / Poland / Portugal / Slovakia / Slovenia / Spain / Sweden / Switzerland

Comments:

Charge for outfit + 2 adults in local currency	High Season	Low Season	Elec inc in price?	Y / N	.............amps
			Price of elec (if not inc)		.............amps

Year of guide used	20.........	Page No.	....	Name of town/village site listed under	
Site Name				Date of visit	.... /....... /........
GPS	Latitude...(eg 12.34567) Longitude...(eg 1.23456 or -1.23456)				

Site is in: Andorra / Austria / Belgium / Croatia / Czech Republic / Denmark / Finland / France / Germany / Greece / Hungary / Italy / Luxembourg / Netherlands / Norway / Poland / Portugal / Slovakia / Slovenia / Spain / Sweden / Switzerland

Comments:

Charge for car, caravan & 2 adults in local currency	High Season	Low Season	Elec inc in price?	Y / N	.............amps
			Price of elec (if not inc)		.............amps

Please fill in your details and send to the address on the reverse of this form.
You can also complete forms online: www.caravanclub.co.uk/europereport

CUT ALONG DOTTED LINE

Year of guide used	20.........	Page No.	....	Name of town/village site listed under	
Site Name				Date of visit	.... /....... /........

GPS	Latitude...(eg 12.34567) Longitude..(eg 1.23456 or -1.23456)

Site is in: Andorra / Austria / Belgium / Croatia / Czech Republic / Denmark / Finland / France / Germany / Greece / Hungary / Italy / Luxembourg / Netherlands / Norway / Poland / Portugal / Slovakia / Slovenia / Spain / Sweden / Switzerland

Comments:

Charge for outfit + 2 adults in local currency	High Season	Low Season	Elec inc in price?	Y / N	.............amps
			Price of elec (if not inc)		.............amps

Year of guide used	20.........	Page No.	....	Name of town/village site listed under	
Site Name				Date of visit	.... /....... /........

GPS	Latitude...(eg 12.34567) Longitude..(eg 1.23456 or -1.23456)

Site is in: Andorra / Austria / Belgium / Croatia / Czech Republic / Denmark / Finland / France / Germany / Greece / Hungary / Italy / Luxembourg / Netherlands / Norway / Poland / Portugal / Slovakia / Slovenia / Spain / Sweden / Switzerland

Comments:

Charge for outfit + 2 adults in local currency	High Season	Low Season	Elec inc in price?	Y / N	.............amps
			Price of elec (if not inc)		.............amps

Year of guide used	20.........	Page No.	....	Name of town/village site listed under	
Site Name				Date of visit	.... /....... /........

GPS	Latitude...(eg 12.34567) Longitude..(eg 1.23456 or -1.23456)

Site is in: Andorra / Austria / Belgium / Croatia / Czech Republic / Denmark / Finland / France / Germany / Greece / Hungary / Italy / Luxembourg / Netherlands / Norway / Poland / Portugal / Slovakia / Slovenia / Spain / Sweden / Switzerland

Comments:

Charge for outfit + 2 adults in local currency	High Season	Low Season	Elec inc in price?	Y / N	.............amps
			Price of elec (if not inc)		.............amps

Your comments & opinions may be used in future editions of the guide, if you do not wish them to be used please tick ....

Name ....

Membership No. ....

Post Code ....

Are you a Caravanner / Motorhomer / Trailer-Tenter?

Do you need more blank Site Report forms?   YES / NO

Please return completed forms to:
The Editor, Caravan Europe
The Caravan Club
FREEPOST
PO Box 386 (RRZG-SXKK-UCUJ)
East Grinstead
RH19 1FH
(Please use this address only when mailing from within the UK)

You can also complete forms online: www.caravanclub.co.uk/europereport

Mountain Passes and Tunnels

Passes/Tunnel Report Form

Name of Pass/Tunnel ....

To/From ....

Date Travelled...

Comments (eg gradients, traffic, road surface, width of road, hairpins, scenery)

....

....

....

Year of Guide used:..

ARE YOU A Caravanner	Motorhomer	Trailer-tenter?

==

Passes/Tunnel Report Form

Name of Pass/Tunnel ....

To/From ....

Date Travelled...

Comments (eg gradients, traffic, road surface, width of road, hairpins, scenery)

....

....

Year of Guide used:..

ARE YOU A: Caravanner	Motorhomer	Trailer-tenter?

CUT ALONG DOTTED LINE

Mountain Passes and Tunnels

Passes/Tunnel Report Form

Name of Pass/Tunnel ....

To/From ....

Date Travelled...

Comments (eg gradients, traffic, road surface, width of road, hairpins, scenery)

....

....

....

Year of Guide used:..

ARE YOU A Caravanner	Motorhomer	Trailer-tenter?

===

Passes/Tunnel Report Form

Name of Pass/Tunnel ....

To/From ....

Date Travelled...

Comments (eg gradients, traffic, road surface, width of road, hairpins, scenery)

....

....

Year of Guide used:..

ARE YOU A: Caravanner	Motorhomer	Trailer-tenter?